CORNUCOPIA

A SOURCE BOOK OF EDIBLE PLANTS

by

Stephen Facciola

KAMPONG PUBLICATIONS
Vista, 1990

Library of Congress Catalog Card Number: 90-92097

ISBN 0-9628087-0-9

First printing, November 1990
Second printing, May 1992
Printed in the United States of America

10 9 8 7 6 5 4 3 2

Kampong Publications
1870 Sunrise Drive
Vista, CA 92084

Preface

In your hands is one of the most remarkable efforts to come out of the struggle to preserve the genetic diversity of our planet. It is not a dry policy statement preaching of far-away places and unlikely schemes, nor is it an impenetrable tract full of untraceable Latin names and fascinating but useless details. Rather Steve Facciola has put together an easy-to-understand, easy-to-use compendium of the diversity of food plants available today to consumer, gardener, and scientist. It includes thousands of cultivars of hundreds of crop species, as well as many mushrooms and microorganisms. It can serve as both a reference for information on plants, and a guide to actually finding, growing, and using them. As far as I know, it is unique.

No one can say exactly how many plant species there are, but scientists seem to constantly raise their estimates. Yet of the several hundred thousand that are known, at least 20,000 have usefully edible parts, such as seeds, tubers, fruits or leaves. Although humans have tasted them all at one time or another, only three or four thousand have ever been used on a regular basis.

Over tens of thousands of years, these few plants have been mankind's bulwark against starvation. Moreover, during the past 5,000 years or so certain specimens of certain species have been slowly molded to fit human requirements...they have become "domesticated". During the last two centuries, a burst of breeding and crop development has yielded thousands of selected cultivars, collectively suited to meet almost any climate, soil type, or disease or pest threat. This seemingly vast cornucopia of food resources represents one of the best of all human efforts, and is our greatest treasure - more valuable than all the industrial development that has grown in parallel with it.

Indeed, the contribution crop-developers have made to history is seldom if ever mentioned in history books, and yet their effects have been more profound (and much more beneficial in most cases) than all the politics and politicians that now fill the pages of those books. It has recently been pointed out, for example, that development of the potato in Europe probably made possible the Industrial Revolution because it provided the Europeans with food security for the first time, and that in turn allowed millions to leave the land to work in the factories.

Nonetheless, with all mankind's efforts to develop crops, the selection of target species has been very narrow. Fewer then 150 species have been brought into what most people would consider substantial "agriculture". And far fewer than that have been raised to a point where they approach their potential. Most of the world's food is being produced from a mere twenty or so, grossly overworked, species. Indeed, the preponderance of human food comes from only four: wheat, rice, corn, and potatoes. It is a dangerously small larder for feeding a whole planet.

Thus, although our modern food supply is one of the most remarkable of human achievements and new technologies promise even greater harvests in the future, there exist thousands of wondrous resources of which we have taken little advantage. Yet ironically, just as we realize the importance of this underexploited heritage, it is being threatened. In the last twenty years, for example, hundreds of varieties of plants have been lost - not only from the rainforests but also from our gardens.

All this is why Steve Facciola's effort is so important. It is a guide not only to your grandparents' favorite garden veggies, but to exotic delights now scarecly known even to botanists. In total, his book records the more than 3,000 species available in the U.S. and abroad. For over a hundred crops, detailed varietal descriptions of culture and taste are given. The sources listed are not only for seeds, but also for different types of nursery stock, for specialty produce and food products and for unusual items such as mushroom spawn and starter cultures.

This book should appeal to anyone interested in our plant heritage, in what to grow next summer, or in what to do with that strange fruit in the market. For everyone from browser to botanist, the utility of this effort is obvious.

Noel Vietmeyer

Introduction

There are approximately fifteen thousand species of plants recorded in the literature as having been used as food by man. One hundred fifty or more of these have been cultivated on a commercial scale and innumerable cultivars of the more important crops have been developed. Yet today, most of the world is fed by approximately twenty crops including wheat, rice, maize, millet, sorghum, potato, sweet potato, cassava, peas, beans, peanuts, coconuts and bananas. And of the estimated eight thousand cultivars of apples that have been described, only a handful are available in supermarkets.

Our knowledge of the remaining edible plants represents thousands of years of trial and error by our ancestors and should be more greatly utilized. Many of these plants have desirable traits or properties that have not been exploited and may have some yet to be discovered. In addition, only a small percentage of cultivars is being grown commercially compared to a generation or two ago. While some newer cultivars provide valuable traits such as resistance to pests and diseases, many older traditional cultivars also have great merit and should be preserved and made more available. Breeding is overly focused on developing strains of industry standards, such as Red Delicious apples, rather than creating truly unique cultivars like Butterblossom squash or Saturn peach.

In recent years, however, an increased awareness has created expanded markets for new and unusual foods, heirloom cultivars, and foods grown without the use of chemical fertilizers and toxic pesticides and herbicides. More of these are becoming available all the time. The purpose of this book is to provide a guide to those having the most current interest and potential future value. As much diversity as possible is included without being redundant. Species were selected to provide a broad range of the more than fifty different usage categories including edible fruits, seeds, leaves, roots, stems, flavorings, flowers, oils, beverages, tea and coffee substitutes and sugars and sugar substitutes. Cultivar selection has focused on traditional and well-adapted favorites, family heirlooms, gourmet and specialty market items, and the most promising of the newest releases. Sources for both seeds and nursery stock are provided as well as specialty produce and specialty food products.

Approximately three thousand species have been selected including the higher plants in addition to organisms once classified as plants but now treated in separate kingdoms. These include algae, fungi and bacteria.

Over one hundred and ten major crops have been chosen for detailed cultivar listings representing the most popular fruits, vegetables, nuts, herbs, grains and mushrooms. Also included are fruit and nut tree rootstocks, salad mixes, sprouting seeds and starter cultures.

Taxonomic nomenclature of families, genera and species follows that of Tanaka and Kunkel, the most recent works on edible plants of the world, as much as possible. Some older names that are used in the trade are retained. Others that have been maintained in the trade for an unreasonable time are rejected. Classification of cultivars is modified after Lewis and Hortus Third.

Cornucopia is intended to be an authoritative reference book as well as a useful tool. It has been written for gardeners, small-scale and alternative farmers, researchers dealing with new food crops, cooks, economic botanists, genetic preservations, natural foods enthusiasts, nutritionists, those in the specialty and gourmet foods business, and colleges and universities. References have been selected to provide a balance between technical and popular works.

The book is divided into three primary sections: Botanical listings, Cultivar listings and Sources. The Botanical listings are presented alphabetically by plant family, genus and species. Following the genus and species is the vernacular name or names, a default code for the type of plant material or product offered, a description of how the plant is used, distribution, annotated bibliographical citations, and sources. In some instances the source code is followed by codes for the type of plant material or product offered that override the default code. The type of plant material or product coded for listing includes plants, seeds, sets, dwarf and espalier stock, scionwood, seedlings and fresh produce or food products. When the source code is followed by a {PR} code, fresh produce is being offered. When the source code is followed by {PR} and is also underlined, the plant has more than one usage and an explanation is needed or a food product is being offered. In these instances refer to *Sells the following product/s:* under the companies listing in the Sources chapter. Annotated bibliographical citations direct the reader to more information on culture, propagation, nutrition, preparation, and where to find culinary information and recipes for that species or cultivar. Botanical synonyms, represented by the symbol →, are placed alphabetically within each family.

The most important and popular crops have been selected for the Cultivar listings. Subheadings and endnotes are freely used where appropriate to group cultivars into horticultural classes. This facilitates the finding of unique types without having to read through long lists. Under each subheading, cultivars are presented alphabetically. Following the cultivar name are synonyms (if any), relative days to maturity, a description of the most important features, origin, annotated bibliographical citations, and sources. Descriptions were taken from reliable sources whenever possible, at other times catalogs were used. Cultivars of other species are listed in the Botanical listings.

Included in the Sources chapter are the names, addresses and telephone numbers of the more than 1350 firms and institutions whose catalogs have been surveyed, including approximately 1050 from the United States and Canada, 150 from overseas, and 150 non-commercial sources (botanical gardens, arboreta, research stations, etc.). Descriptions of each companies offerings are given followed by information on catalog price, retail or wholesale status, currencies accepted, overseas shipments, minimum order, and whether they print an English language catalog. Each company has a unique code that is used to indicate what products they list. Retail company codes are presented in normal text, wholesale companies in italics, and non-commercial sources in bolded text. Some institutions have requested their complete addresses not be listed, to emphasize they do not want requests from the general public.

Every effort has been made to find commercial sources. Only when none could be found were sources such as botanical gardens and research stations used. Many rare and valuable species are apparently only available from such sources. It should be noted however that many of these institutions have limited facilities or budgets and cannot respond to the general public. Primarily material is exchanged with other institutions on a reciprocal basis. Private individuals who have a sufficiently large collection may also make arrangements for trade.

Many of the best cultivars are similarly unavailable through the trade. Organizations such as the California Rare Fruit Growers, North American Fruit Explorers, Rare Fruit Council International, International Ribes Association, Seed Savers Exchange and the Grain Exchange are invaluable sources of such material and welcome new members. They do not sell seeds or plants however. It is best to write them and ask for a membership application and then follow their normal procedures of exchange. They are also good sources for material that is no longer available from the trade. A small number of such listings that were offered during the compilation of this book but dropped before publication have been retained for historical interest. These are indicated by "Dropped by" followed by the code for the company that last offered them. When the code cannot be found in the Sources chapter, the company is out of business, no longer mail orders, or requested not to be listed.

Acknowledgements

I would like to thank the following friends and colleagues for their assistance in the writing of this book: Library staff - New York Botanical Garden, Library staff - Brooklyn Botanic Garden, Patrick J. Worley, Gilbert A. Voss of Quail Botanical Gardens, Alison Voss, H. Ron Hurov of Hurov's Tropical Seeds, Debbie Peterson of The Pits, Jim Bauml of the Los Angeles State and County Arboretum, Dennis Sharmahd, Steve Disparti, Dr. Kim Hummer and Joseph Postman of the National Clonal Germplasm Repository, Nancy Breuninger, Elizabeth Schneider, Wayne Carlson of Maskal Forages, Beth Petlack of Frieda's Finest Produce Specialties, Claude Sweet, Harry Stillman, Wayne Armstrong, Barbara Burch, William Blackmon of Louisiana State University, Nicholas Yensen of NyPa Inc., Peggy Wagoner of the Rodale Research Center, Paul Thomson - co-founder of the California Rare Fruit Growers, Vincent Rizzo, John Battaglino, Dan Milbocker of Hampton Roads Agricultural Experiment Station, Dr. Chuck Walker of Kansas State University, Dr. K.M. El-Zik of Texas A & M University, C.T. Kennedy - historian for the California Rare Fruit Growers, Doug Richardson of Richardson's Seaside Banana Garden, Kent Whealy of the Seed Savers Exchange, Michael Linder of the Sproutletter, Paul Zmoda, Steve Meyerowitz of the Sprout House, Tom Hickmann of Cal West Seeds, Judy Felix, Susan Hamilton of Plant it Hawaii, Martin Price of ECHO, Andy Mariani of Mariani Orchards, R. Gardner of the North Carolina Botanical Garden, Jan Blüm of Seeds Blüm, Craig and Sue Dremann of Redwood City Seed Co., Arris Sigle of Cheyenne Gap Amaranth, Roy Danforth and Paul Noren of the Imeloko Agroforestry Project, J. Konopka of the International Board for Plant Genetic Resources, Randy Permpoon, Chris Olano of the Miami Coconut Seed Orchard. Allan Corrin of Corrin Produce Inc., Fred Stoker of Fred's Plant Farm, Jim Gilbert of Northwoods Nursery, Professor Roger D. Way of Cornell University, Jennifer Quigley of the Arnold Arboretum, Ken Turkington, Steven Spangler of Exotica Rare Fruit Nursery, Bill Nelson and Tom del Hotal of Pacific Tree Farms, Michael McConkey of Edible Landscaping, Alex Eppler, Mark Dafforn of the National Academy of Sciences, Dr. Arthur O. Tucker of Delaware State University, Julia F. Morton of the Morton Collectanea, David Silber, Nick Cockshutt, Cyrus and Louise Hyde of Well-Sweep Herb Farm, Tom Cooper of Rancho Nuez Nursery, Julie Molony, Bob Hornback, Gunther Kunkel, Mark Futterman, Dr. Robert Bond, Dr. Frank Ballard, Michael Collins of the University of Kentucky, Betty Stechmeyer of Gem Cultures, Phil Restenberg of Lupin Triticale Enterprises, Tom Gallenberg of Wolf River Valley Seeds, Hugh Holborn of Datil Do-it Hot Sauce, Chris Rollins of Preston B. Bird and Mary Heinlein Fruit and Spice Park, Campbell G. Davidson of the Morden Research Station, Stephen Brayer of Tripple Brook Farm, Dr. Robert Stebbins and Dr. Porter Lombard of Oregon State University, J. Stewart Nagle, Fred Janson of Pomona Book Exchange, Gerald Reed of Universal Foods Corporation, Steven McKay of the International Ribes Association, William F. Whitman - co-founder of the Rare Fruit Council International, Wendy Krupnick of Shepherd's Garden Seeds, Dr. S.J. Sheen of the University of Kentucky, and Beverly Berkley of Fowler Nurseries.

Contents

BOTANICAL LISTINGS

ALPHABETICAL LISTING OF PLANT FAMILIES

ACANTHACEAE

Beloperone californica - *Chuparosa* {PL} The red flowers, which resemble cucumber in flavor, may be eaten raw or cooked. Diegueño Indians are known to have sucked the flower for its nectar, as desert hikers do today. Southwestern North America, Mexico. CLARKE, KIRK; G60, *J0*

Rungia klossii - *Moku, Tani, Kenkaba, Aimbe* {S} Leaves and stems are eaten raw in salads, cooked as a potherb, or used as a flavoring. They contain iron, vitamin C, and Beta-carotene. The biennial herb is harvested three to four months after planting and continues bearing for up to two years. Papua New Guinea. HACKETT [Cu], MAY, R.; **X14**

ACERACEAE

Acer caudatum - *Ra-li-shing* {PL} The leaf is used as a tea substitute. Tibet, Nepal. TANAKA; B96, N84{S}

Acer circinatum - *Vine maple* {PL} Sap is made into sugar and maple syrup. Pacific Coast of North America. GIBBONS 1979; A2{S}, A80M, C34, D95, E15{S}, E87, H23M{S}, I47{S}, J26, *J75M*, K38{S}, K47T{S}, K63G{S}, *M51M*, N0, etc.

Acer distylum - *Hitotsuba-kaede* {S} Sugar and maple syrup are manufactured from the sap. Japan. TANAKA; *P63*

Acer ginnala - *Amur maple* {PL} Young leaves are used as a tea substitute. Japan, China. TANAKA; B96, C9M{S}, *C33*, D45, E87, F70, G16, G41, H49, I28, J47, *J75M*, K38{S}, K63G{S}, M76, etc.

Acer grandidentatum - *Big-tooth maple* {PL} The sap is boiled down to produce maple syrup. Western North America. KIRK; B94{S}, G43M, *G89M*, I53, O93{S}

Acer macrophyllum - *Oregon maple, Big-leaved maple* {S} The sweet sap can be used for maple syrup and sugar manufacture. Yellow flower-clusters are sweet with nectar and may be eaten right from the tree. Pacific Coast of North America. DOMICO, GIBBONS 1979; A80M{PL}, B92{PL}, B94, *C73*{PL}, D96, E15, G59M, G60{PL}, I49M{PL}, *J75M*{PL}, K38, K47T, K63G, *M51M*{PL}, N0{PL}, O93, etc.

Acer negundo* → *Negundo aceroides

Acer nigrum - *Black maple, Black sugar-maple* {S} The sap is used for maple sugar and maple syrup. Closely related to A. saccharum and one of the principal producers of commercial maple syrup. Eastern North America. MEDSGER; *G21M*{PL}, K47T, K63G, *K89*, *K89*{PL}, N84

Acer pensylvanicum - *Striped maple, Moosewood* {S} Although a small tree it is an abundant producer of very sweet sap which yields more sugar per gallon than larger maples. It is said to have a better flavor than other maples. Eastern North America. GIBBONS 1966a; D95{PL}, *F38*, G43M{PL}, *H8*{PL}, K47T, K63G, *K89*{PL}, N7T{PL}, *N71M*, N84, P49, *R28*

Acer pseudoplatanus - *Sycamore maple, Plane-tree maple* {S} In Europe a wine is made from the sap which also yields maple syrup. Children in England suck the wings of the growing keys to obtain the sweet exudation that accumulates on them. Eurasia. HEDRICK 1919; B9M{PL}, D62, *G30*{PL}, *G66*, *G89M*{PL}, K38, K47T, K63G, *N71M*, N93M, O93, P5, P49, *R28*, R78, etc.

Acer rubrum - *Red maple, Swamp maple* {PL} The French Canadians make sugar from the sap which is called *plaine*. Good maple syrup is also produced from this tree although the yield is comparatively small. Eastern North America. FERNALD, HEDRICK 1919; A79M{S}, C9M{S}, D45, D95, E33M, *G21M*, H49, I4, J16, J70{S}, K38{S}, K63G{S}, M76, N0, N7T, etc.

Acer saccharinum - *Silver maple, River maple, White maple* {PL} The sap is considered by some to be sweeter and whiter than that of the sugar maple. It is boiled down to make sugar and syrup. Eastern North America. FERNALD, MEDSGER; A82, *B99M*, C9M{S}, *F51*, *G66*{S}, H49, I4, I9M, *I61*{S}, J70{S}, K38{S}, L27M, N0, N25M

Acer saccharophorum* → *Acer saccharum

Acer saccharum - *Sugar maple* {PL} Leading producer of maple syrup and sugar. Maple butter or honey and maple cream are different forms of maple sugar. The Indians cooked the dewinged seeds in butter and milk. The sap can be used in place of water to brew herbal teas made from sassafras and spicebush. Maple wax or *sugar-on-snow* is a delicious, chewy product made by boiling the sap beyond the syrup point until it reaches the consistency of molasses, then pouring it on fresh snow. Eastern North America. FERNALD, GIBBONS 1962 [Re], NEARING [Cu, Re], ROOT 1980a, THOMPSON, B. [Cu, Re]; A82, C9M{S}, *D32*, D45, D95, G41, *G66*{S}, I4, J70{S}, K38{S}, K63G{S}, L27M, M76, N7T

CULTIVARS

High Sugar: The sugar content of sugar-maple sap usually varies between 2 and 3%. The high yield strains produce sap with double the sugar content or around 4%. As a result, one half the fuel is needed in the syrup manufacturing process which requires 40 gallons of sap to make one gallon of syrup. LOGSDON 1981; C97M

Acer saccharum ssp. nigrum* → *Acer nigrum

Acer spicatum - *Mountain maple* {S} The sweet sap can be used to make maple syrup. Eastern North America. GIBBONS 1979; *F38*, G43M{PL}, K63G, N84, O93

Negundo aceroides - *Box-elder, Ash-leaved maple* {S} Highly valued as a producer of maple syrup and sugar. Groves have been planted in

Illinois and other areas. The sugar from the sap of this tree is said to be whiter than that produced by other maples. North America. FERNALD, HEDRICK 1919; *B99M*{PL}, *C73*{PL}, G60{PL}, *G66*{PL}, K38, K47T, K63G, *M69M*{PL}, *N71M*, N93M, O53M, O93, P5, Q40, R78, etc.

ACTINIDIACEAE

Actinidia arguta - *Hardy kiwi, Tara vine, Bower berry* {PL} The small, emerald green fruits are eaten out of hand, dried, or made into jam, jellies and wine. They are considered to be sweeter than the common kiwi fruit. The vine is rich in sap, which is drinkable. Eastern Asia, cultivated. TANAKA, THOMSON 1988 [Cu]; A14, B9M, B32, B96, D62{S}, D95, G96, H4, H53M{SC}, I39, L99M, M77, *N71M*{S}, P38{S}, R78{S}, etc. (for cultivars see Kiwi, page 366)

Actinidia arguta var. cordifolia - {SC} The smooth green fruits are the size of a grape, have sweet flesh, and are eaten out of hand. China. KUNKEL, THOMSON 1988; H53M (also see Kiwi, page 366)

CULTIVARS

1563-51: Red pétiole on leaf. Originally from the Arnold Arboretum in Massachusetts. H53M

Female: Female form from New Zealand. Each leaf has a heart-shaped base. The fruit has a good flavor. H53M

Actinidia callosa - *Mei-soh-khan* {SC} The ripe fruits are acid and may be eaten raw or dried for use in pastries. China, Japan. KUNKEL, TANAKA.

CULTIVARS

Female: Fruit egg-shaped to oblong, green tinged with red, spotted. Flowers white or creamy yellow, fragrant. Leaves oval to oblong, with a short point. H53M

Actinidia chinensis* → *Actinidia deliciosa

Actinidia cordifolia* → *Actinidia arguta var. cordifolia

Actinidia coriacea - *Chinese egg-gooseberry* {SC} The small, egg-shaped fruits are eaten. They have brownish skin with white dots and are very juicy. China. SIMMONS 1972; **U8**

Actinidia deliciosa - *Kiwi fruit, Chinese gooseberry, Yang-t'ao* {S} Fuzzy, subacid fruits are rich in vitamin C and may be eaten raw or cooked. When firm-ripe they are tart-sweet and used in salad dressings or other dishes where tartness is desired. When soft-ripe they are sweeter and are eaten out of hand, or used in fruit salads, ice cream, pies, cakes and other desserts. *Pavlova* cake, consisting of kiwis, meringue and whipped cream, is the national dessert of New Zealand. China, cultivated. BEUTEL [Re], MORTON 1987a, SALE [Cu], SCHNEIDER [Cul, Re], THOMSON 1988 [Cu, Pro]; A79M, B32{PL}, C9M, C56M{PL}, D81{PO}, D81M{PO}, E87{PL}, F80, G96{PL}, H4, K47T, L97{PL}, N84, O53M, P38, etc. (for cultivars see Kiwi, page 366)

Actinidia x fairchildii (A. arguta x A. chinensis) - {SC} Artificial hybrid. Ripe fruits are eaten. First made by David Fairchild between a male kiwi and a female hardy kiwi. The resulting hybrids have characteristics intermediate between the two parent species. KUNKEL, TANAKA; H53M

CULTIVARS

799-78: Has the characteristics of A. arguta but the leaves are larger and longer. H53M

Actinidia kolomikta - *Hardy kiwi, Arctic beauty kiwi, Kishmish, Manchurian gooseberry* {PL} The fruit is eaten fresh, dried, or preserved in salt. Young leaves are parboiled and eaten in soups, cooked and seasoned and used as a potherb, or preserved in salt. China, Japan, cultivated. TANAKA, THOMSON 1988 [Cu]; A91, B74, B75, C34, E63, E87, H4, H53M{SC}, H65, J61M, M75, M77, *N71M*{S}, N84{S}, P38{S}, etc. (for cultivars see Kiwi, page 366)

Actinidia melanandra - *Red kiwi* {SC} The fruit is one inch long, egg-shaped, reddish in color, and can be eaten out of hand. A good pollinator for A. arguta var. cordifolia. Eastern Asia. THOMSON 1988; H53M (also see Kiwi, page 366)

CULTIVARS

1064-79: Fruit ovoid, glabrous, smooth; about 1 inch long and 1 inch across; brown with a white patina. Self-fertile. Lance shaped leaves with a white underside. H53M

Actinidia polygama - *Silver vine, Matatabi* {PL} Young leaves are eaten raw with vinegared miso, or roasted and mixed with tea. Ripe fruits are smooth-skinned, bright orange in color, and are eaten raw, made into a liqueur, or dried for later use. Unripe fruits are pickled in salt. Eastern Asia. TANAKA, THOMSON 1988; H53M{SC}, I49M, P49{S}

CULTIVARS {SC}

418-77: Sel-fertile. Large green leaves. Very vigorous grower. H53M

Female: Fruits are elongated and the color of a persimmon; flavor fair. Variegated. H53M

Male: Leaves rounded or tapered to their bristly, hairy stalks, variegated silvery-white and sometimes yellowish. Flowers creamy white, very fragrant. H53M

Actinidia purpurea - *Purple Chinese gooseberry* {SC} Ripe fruits are sweet, purple in color and are eaten out of hand. China. TANAKA; H53M

CULTIVARS

713-78: Fruit purple, pleasantly flavored, similar to A. arguta. Female. H53M

Saurauia nepaulensis - *Goginá* {S} The yellowish fruits, the size of a cherry, are consumed with sugar by the natives of Kampuchea and Viet Nam. Also used to adulterate honey. Himalayan region, Southeast Asia. UPHOF, WATT; **Z25M**

ADIANTACEAE

Adiantum capillus-veneris - *Maidenhair fern* {PL} In the Arran Islands the fronds are dried and used as a tea substitute. The flavoring *capillaire* was once popular in England. The fern was simmered in water for several hours, and the liquid was then made into a thick syrup with sugar and orange water. Capillaire was then mixed with fruit juice and water to form soft drinks. Northern temperate region. HEDRICK 1919, MABEY; D95, G60, J48, L55, L91M{S}, M42, N37M, O53M{S}

AGAVACEAE

Agave americana - *Century plant, Maguey* {S} *Aguamiel*, the sap from the flowering stem is sweet and can be drunk. It is also fermented into the alcoholic beverage *pulque*, which upon distillation produces the spirit *mescal*. Kickapoo Indians bake the tender, asparagus-like flower stalks on hot stones. The resulting product is called *quiote*. The bulbous leaf base is sweet and is eaten after roasting. Central America. HEDRICK 1919, LATORRE 1977b, STEINKRAUS; A69, B85{PL}, D1M{PL}, *E53M*, H4{PL}, H52{PL}, I28{PL}, K47T, O53M, O93, P5, Q46, S44

Agave asperrima - {S} The juice is used for sweetening. Southwestern North America. KUNKEL; F85, S44

Agave atrovirens - *Maguey manso* {S} *Pulque* and *mescal* are produced from the sap. The flower stalk is roasted and eaten. Southwestern North America to Mexico. TANAKA; C27M, S44, T25M

Agave deserti - *Desert agave* {PL} Flowers and flower buds are eaten. Young flower stalks are baked in earth ovens until they form a sweet, starchy cake called *mescal* said to taste like bananas and pineapple. The leaf bases are similarly prepared. *Pulque* is made from the sap. Nectar from the flowers was consumed directly by the Indians. Southwestern North America. CLARKE [Re], TANAKA, TATE; A69{S}, B85, D1M, F85, I98M{S}, L50, S44{S}

Agave parryi - *Century plant* {S} Young flower stalks are roasted and eaten. Nectar from the flowering stalk can be made into a sweet syrup. Southwestern North America. MCGREGOR, MEDSGER; A69, C27M, D1M{PL}, F31M{PL}, F85, H4{PL}, H52, H52{PL}, I28{PL}, I33, N84, Q41, S44, T25M

Agave quiotifera* → *Agave salmiana

Agave salmiana - *Maguey ceniso* {S} Occasionally used for manufacturing *pulque*. Flower stalks are cut for *quiote*, which is sold in the streets and is chewed by the natives like sugar cane. Southwestern North America. UPHOF; **U26**

Agave shawii - *Shaw's agave* {PL} The sweet nectar from the base of the flowers can be used directly. An endangered species. California. CLARKE, TANAKA; B85, F31M, F85{S}

Agave sisalana - *Sisal hemp* {S} The heart of the new shoots is eaten in Java. An alcoholic beverage can be distilled from the sap of the flower stalk. Mexico, cultivated elsewhere. TANAKA; I33, Q41

Agave tequilana - *Mezcal, Chino azul* {S} Cultivated from Jalisco to Sinaloa, for the production of the alcoholic beverages *mezcal* and *tequila*, which are distilled from the roasted bases of the plants. Mexico. UPHOF; S44

Agave utahensis - *Utah aloe* {S} The centers of the plants consisting of the buds, short stalks, and leaf bases are placed in stone lined pits and baked until they form a sweet cake. They can be dried for future use or soaked in water to produce a flavorful beverage. Roots and flower stalks are also edible. Western North America. GIBBONS 1973, HARRINGTON, H.; F31M{PL}, F89M{PL}, G18{PL}, H52, H52{PL}, I33, K49T, N84, Q41

Dasylirion longissimum - {S} Used in the preparation of a distilled liquor. Mexico. TANAKA; A0M{PL}, A69, C27M, H52, I28{PL}, I33, K77M{PL}, N51{PL}, N84, O53M, Q38, Q41, S44

Dasylirion texanum - *Texas sotol* {PL} Central part of the bud containing a sugary pulp, was roasted in mescal pits and used as food by the Indians. It was also made into a beverage, *sotol*. Texas. UPHOF; *A19*, H4

Dasylirion wheeleri - *Wheeler sotol* {S} Central bud was roasted in mescal pits and consumed by the Indians. *Sotol* was also made from this plant. Southwestern North America. UPHOF; A0M{PL}, A69, C27M, C98, D1M{PL}, *E53M*, F31M{PL}, I28{PL}, I33, I47, I99, K47T, L13, N37M{PL}, N51{PL}, O93, S44, etc.

Hesperoyucca whipplei - *Chaparral yucca* {S} Stalks are eaten raw or roasted in a pit. Flowers are boiled and eaten. Seeds are ground into flour. Southwestern North America. TANAKA; A0M{PL}, C9M, F31M{PL}, F80, G60{PL}, *H71*, *I62*{PL}, I98M, *N43*{PL}, N84, O53M, O93, *P17M*, *P63*, S44, etc.

Polianthes tuberosa - *Tuberose* {PL} In Java the flowers are eaten by the Chinese in vegetable soup. They are added to the substrate in the manufacture of *kecap*, an Indonesian soy sauce. Also the source of tuberosa-flower water. Cultivated. MACNICOL [Re], STEINKRAUS, TANAKA; D24, E47M, H33, I91, J27, L29, M31, M37M, M45M, M61, M77

Samuela carnerosana - *Palma barreta* {S} The young flower clusters are eaten boiled or roasted. Mexico. TATE, UPHOF; A69, F85, S44

Yucca aloifolia - *Spanish bayonet, Spanish dagger* {S} Crisp flower petals are eaten raw in salads. Flowers are dipped in egg batter and fried. After peeling, the flower stalk is boiled and eaten. Florida, Caribbean. MORTON 1977; C9M, F80, F85, H4{PL}, I28{PL}, I33, *I62*{PL}, *J25*{PL}, K38, *L5M*, O53M, P5, *Q15G*, *Q32*, S44, etc.

Yucca arborescens* → *Yucca brevifolia

Yucca baccata - *Banana yucca, Dátil* {S} Fleshy fruits are sweet and can be used in pies. The pulp is scraped out and dried for later use or boiled down to a paste, molded into cakes and then dried. They are later eaten as sweetmeats. Flowers and tender flower stalks are also eaten. Southwestern North America. CLARKE, GIBBONS 1966a, HARRINGTON, H., TATE; C9M, E61{PL}, *G66*, H52, I33, I47, J25M, J25M{PL}, K38, K47T, N37M{PL}, O53M, O93, *P17M*, S44, etc.

Yucca brevifolia - *Joshua tree* {S} The flower clusters, before the buds open, can be parboiled in salt water to remove the bitterness, drained, and cooked again and served like cauliflower. Opened buds, which are rich in sugar, are roasted and eaten as candy. Roots are eaten raw, boiled, or roasted. Seeds are also edible. Southwestern North America. TANAKA, TATE; A69, C9M, C27M, C98, F80, G60{PL}, *G66*, I33, I98M, L13, O53M, O93, *P17M*, S44, T25M, etc.

Yucca carnerosana* → *Samuela carnerosana

Yucca elata - *Soap-tree yucca* {S} The flowers are eaten raw or in preserves. Fruits are edible raw or cooked. An extract of the roots is used to produce foam in beverages. Southwestern North America. KUNKEL, MACNICOL, UPHOF; A69, C9M, C27M, C98, D1M{PL}, F79M, *I23*{PL}, I33, J25M, J25M{PL}, O53M, *P63*, Q41, S44, T25M, etc.

Yucca elephantipes - *Spanish dagger, Izote* {S} After removing the bitter anthers and ovaries, the flowers are dipped in egg batter and fried. Rich in vitamin C and niacin, they are also added to salads, soups, and stews. The tender stem tips stripped of their leaves, called *cogollo de izote*, are eaten in El Salvador. Central America. UPHOF, WILLIAMS, L.; C9M, *E53M*, I57{PL}, N84, *P17M*, *P63*, *Q32*, Q41, S95

Yucca filamentosa - *Adam's needle, Eve's thread* {PL} Large, fleshy fruits are eaten. Flowers make a tasty and attractive addition to salads. Southwestern North America. GIBBONS 1979, HEDRICK 1919; A79M{S}, B32, C9M{S}, C32, E30, E33M, F89, G25M{S}, *G66*{S}, H4, H49, H63, I33{S}, K63, O53M{S}, etc.

Yucca glauca - *Soapweed yucca* {PL} Immature fruits are peeled, boiled, and served with butter and seasonings. The young flower stalk is cooked and the whitish inner portion eaten. Flowers and flower buds are eaten raw in salads or cooked as a potherb. North America. GIBBONS 1966a, HARRINGTON, H., KINDSCHER; B32, C9, C9M{S}, C13M{S}, *F51*, H49, I33{S}, I47{S}, I63M, I77M, J78, L13{S}, M35M, N37M, O53M{S}, etc.

Yucca mohavensis* → *Yucca schidigera

Yucca schidigera - *Spanish dagger, Wild date* {S} Young stems are chopped and cooked or baked like a sweet potato. Fruits and flowers are eaten raw or in jellies. Southwestern North America. TANAKA; F85, G60{PL}, I33, I98M, N84, Q41, S44

Yucca whipplei* → *Hesperoyucca whipplei

AIZOACEAE

Glottiphyllum linguiforme - {PL} Roots are used in the Transvaal for making a *kaffir beer* the fermenting action being due to the presence of a yeast and two molds. South Africa. FOX, F.; B85, G91M

Khadia acutipetala - {S} The roots are used by the natives of Transvaal for the preparation of *khadi*, a fermented liquor. South Africa. FOX, F., TATE; H52, N84

Sesuvium portulacastrum - *Sea purslane, Gelang pasir* {PL} Seacoast plant with succulent, salty leaves that are eaten raw or cooked. They are also pickled like samphire. The leaves should be well rinsed in water to remove some of the salty taste. Good source of vitamin C. Pantropic, Southern United States. FERNALD, GIBBONS 1979, HEDRICK 1919, OCHSE, WATT; *F73, J25*

Trianthema pentandra → *Zaleya pentandra*

Trianthema portulacastrum - *Ulisman, Toston* {S} Succulent, fleshy leaves are eaten. The have a delightfully salty flavor, and are delicious in a salad dressed with apple cider vinegar. Tropical seacoasts. GIBBONS 1973, NIETHAMMER, WATT; F85, N84

Zaleya pentandra - *Horse purslane* {S} The ash from the plant is used as a salt substitute. Tropical Asia, Tropical Africa. UPHOF, WATT; **Z77M**

ALISMATACEAE

Alisma plantago → *Alisma plantago-aquatica*

Alisma plantago-aquatica - *Water plantain, Mad-dog weed* {S} The bulb-like bases are eaten after being dried to rid them of their acrid properties. Northern temperate region. FERNALD, GIBBONS 1979; B28{PL}, B51, C64M, C64M{PL}, D62, F80, H30{PL}, I99, M15{PL}, M73{PL}, N11{PL}, *N71M*, N84, O53M, *Q24*, S7M, etc.

Sagittaria latifolia - *Arrowhead, Duck potato, Wapatoo* {PL} Tubers are eaten boiled, creamed, fried and roasted, having a flavor similar to potatoes. It is best to peel the tubers after cooking them. The Indians sliced the boiled tubers and strung them on strings (like dried apples) to dry for winter use. North America. ANGIER [Re], CLARKE [Re], FERNALD, GIBBONS 1962 [Re]; D58, D62{S}, *F73*, G26, G47M, G85, H82, J7M, *J25*, J41M, K25, K85M, M72, M73M, N3M, N11, etc.

Sagittaria rigida - *Sessile-fruited arrowhead* {PL} The tubers are eaten, tasting like potatoes. Eastern North America. CROWHURST 1972 [Re], PETERSON, L.; D58, G26, G47M, N11

Sagittaria sagittifolia - *Arrowhead, Water archer* {PL} The tuber is eaten, boiled and seasoned. Young leaves and petioles are also edible. Eurasia. TANAKA; J7, K34, M15, M73, N84{S}, O53M{S}, *Q24*{S}, S7M{S}

Sagittaria sinensis - *Chinese arrowhead, Chee koo, Kuwai* {PL} Starchy tubers are chopped and cooked with pork or sliced and fried like potato chips. The protein content of 4 to 7% is high for a root crop. Young shoots are also eaten. Commonly found in Chinatown markets and used in Chinese and Japanese cuisines. China, Japan. COST 1988, DAHLEN [Pre, Cul], HARRINGTON, G. [Cu, Cul], HERKLOTS [Cu]; H82, I90M, K34, M39

ALLIACEAE

Allium akaka - *Valik, Wolag* {PL} Young plants are considered a delicacy and are sold in the bazaars of Teheran. They are used as an addition to rice in pilafs. Iran, Temperate Asia. HEDRICK 1919; R52

Allium ampeloprasum - *Levant garlic, Perennial sweet leek, Yorktown onion* {PL} Cultivated for its very large bulbs which are eaten raw or used as a condiment. Mediterranean region, Asia Minor, cultivated. FERNALD, KUNKEL, VILMORIN, ZEVEN; B61M, B61M{S}, L86{S}, M77M

CULTIVARS

Alsea Valley Elephant: An elephant garlic that sets seed. Large bulb. Roots quickly. Lavender blossoms. **U33**

Creole Elephant: Small to medium size bulbs have a strong flavor for an elephant garlic. Bulbs can be stored for up to two years. Low maintenance crop; can be left in the ground from year to year. **U33**

Elephant: (Elephant Garlic) Very large bulbs can weigh over a pound. Preferred by some to regular garlic because of its milder flavor and ease of peeling. Mild enough to be eaten raw in salads. Also excellent baked, broiled, steamed, or boiled and served as a side dish. HALPIN [Cu], HAWKES [Cul]; A26{PR}, B73M, C11, C82, C96{PR}, D2M, F11, F19M, G16, G19M, H87M, *J63*, K13{PR}, K22, L7M, L97M{PR}, M46, etc.

Perlzwiebel: Multiplying cultivar that produces a cluster of solid (not layered) spherical white bulbs, much used for pickles in Holland and Germany. Does not produce seed. Originally from the Institute of Genetics, Gatersleben, Germany. **U33**

Allium ampeloprasum var. babingtonii - *British leek, Welsh leek* {PL} Bulbs are gathered and eaten in Western Ireland and Southwest England. Thought to be a relic of former cultivation. A very showy perennial with round, deep-purple flower heads. Grows to a height of 3 feet. British Isles. ZEVEN; M82

Allium ampeloprasum Porrum Group - *Leek* {PL} Leaves and long white stalk are eaten steamed, boiled, or braised much like asparagus. Stalk can be sliced thinly and added to salads. Also used to give a mild onion flavor to other foods. Widely used in gourmet French cuisine, especially *vichyssoise*. HALPIN, HEDRICK 1919, MORTON 1976; A1M, C3, C3{S}, C16{S}, D62{S}, E97{S}, F35M, G68, K63, L57, M82 (for cultivars see Leek, page 369)

Allium aschersonianum - *Ga'abal* {S} The raw bulb is eaten by bedouins. Israel. BAILEY, C.; **W59M**

Allium bakeri → *Allium chinense*

Allium canadense - *Canada onion, Wild garlic, Meadow leek* {S} The whole plant is gathered before the flowers appear and used like *scallions*. Top-setting bulbils make a fine onion-flavored pickle. The bulb is pure white, crisp, mild and of pleasant flavor. Forms a cluster of large bulbs under cultivation. North America. DORE, FERNALD, GIBBONS 1962 [Re], HEDRICK 1919, KINDSCHER; D62, J39M, J39M{PL}, J42{PL}, J43

Allium cepa - *Onion* Bulbs are eaten raw, cooked, dried, pickled, or to flavor other foods. Leaves can be used as *scallions*. Sprouted seeds are eaten. The outer scales produce a dye which is used to color easter eggs. Cultivated. HEDRICK 1919, TANAKA, UPHOF; (for cultivars see Onion, page 400, also see Sprouting Seeds, page 485)

Allium cepa Aggregatum Group - *Potato onion, Multiplier onion, Shallot* Unlike other onions these divide underground to form a cluster of bulbs. Some of the best gourmet onions are in this group. In Thailand, red shallots are fermented into *hom-dong*. STEINKRAUS, VILMORIN [Cu]; (for cultivars see Onion, page 400)

Allium cepa 'Perutile' - *Ever-ready onion, Everlasting onion* {PL} Hardy perennial onion forming clumps of leaves about a foot high. The leaves are finer in texture and milder than those of the Welsh onion, but are grown and used in the same manner. HERKLOTS, LARKCOM 1984; P92, R53M

Allium cernuum - *Nodding onion, Lady's leek* {PL} The strong-flavored bulbs are eaten raw, boiled, and pickled. Also used to flavor other foods. North America. GESSERT, GIBBONS 1962 [Re], HARRINGTON, H.; B33M, C9, C73M, E15{S}, F1M{S}, G47M{S}, G89, H37M, I37M, J40, J42, J42{S}, J43{S}, J91, L13{S}, etc.

Allium chinense - *Rakkyo* {PL} The bulbs, which have an excellent crisp texture and a strong onion-like but distinctive odor, are eaten raw or cooked. In China and Japan, they are often pickled in vinegar with either sugar, honey or soy sauce added. They can also be preserved in salt, sake lees or sweet sake. Sold in the United States in bottles or cans as *pickled scallions* or *rakkyo-zuke*. China, cultivated. HERKLOTS, MANN [Cu, Pro], TANAKA, UPHOF, YASHIRODA; G20M{PR}, N49M{PR}, *S70*

Allium drummondii - *Cebolla del monte, Wild onion* {S} Used as a condiment by the Kickapoo Indians. Bulbs are eaten as a vegetable. North America, Mexico. KINDSCHER, LATORRE 1977b; D62

Allium fistulosum - *Welsh onion, Ciboule, Japanese bunching onion, Negi, Chang fa* {S} The leaves are one of the principal sources of *scallions*. Mostly used as a condiment for other foods. Widely used in Chinese and Japanese cuisine. Cultivated. HALPIN, HARRINGTON, G., HERKLOTS, LARKCOM 1984; C82, C85M, D29{PL}, E5M{PL}, F1M, G64, G68, G84{PL}, H3M{PL}, I91, M53{PL}, M82{PL}, N45{PL}, O53M, S55, etc. (for cultivars see Onion, page 400)

Allium geyeri - *Geyer onion* {PL} The bulbs are eaten by the Navajo Indians. Western North America. HARRINGTON, H., TANAKA; L13{S}, O57

Allium kurrat - *Kurrat-nabati, Salad leek* {S} This is believed to be the leek of ancient Egypt, the leaves having been found in Egyptian tombs. It is still cultivated there today, and also in Arabia and the Middle East. Closely related to the common leek, and used in a similar manner. Southwest Asia. DARBY, GESSERT, ZEVEN; **U33**

Allium ledebourianum - *Asatsuki, Siu yuk* {S} The leaves are eaten raw, in soups, sautéed, or used as a garnish for chilled tofu. Bulbs are pickled in brine, vinegar, or syrup. The flavor resembles wild onion and chives, with a hint of garlic. China, Japan. HERKLOTS, SHURTLEFF 1975, TANAKA; **U63, V19, V34, V73, V73M, W5, W59M, X39, Y29, Z24, Z98**

Allium longicuspis - *Top-setting wild garlic* {PL} Bulbs are eaten, resembling rocambole. They have a good garlic flavor. Perennial plant is believed to be the wild parent of garlic. Central Asia. ZEVEN; **U33, U63, V50, Z24**

Allium obliquum - *Twistedleaf garlic* {S} Cultivated since ancient times in Siberia for the bulbs which are used as a substitute for garlic. Eurasia. HEDRICK 1919; F1M, K47T, N84

Allium odoratum → Allium tuberosum

Allium odorum - *Fragrant-flowered garlic, Chinese chives* {S} Leaves are eaten raw or used to flavor other foods. Suitable for edible landscaping, having white flowers with a red stripe down the center of each petal. Central Asia. COST 1988, GESSERT, KUNKEL; C61M, D62, E7M, F1M, F80, I22{PL}, M77M{PL}, N84, O53M, Q40{PL}

Allium oleraceum - *Wild garlic* {S} The young leaves are used in Sweden to flavor stews and soups or fried with other herbs. Europe. HEDRICK 1919; D62, N84, S7M

Allium x proliferum (A. cepa x A. fistulosum) - *Egyptian onion, Topset onion, Tree onion, Walking onion* {PL} Strong flavored bulbils are used as a flavoring or are added to cucumber pickles. The green leaf tips are used like chives; white lower stalks are chopped raw into salads; young thinned stalks are used as *scallions*, and the fat, hollow leaves can be slit and stuffed with cottage cheese. Cultivated. HALPIN [Cu], LARKCOM 1984, VILMORIN [Cu]; C3, C11, C44, C67M, D29, E5M, E61, F31T, G68, H3M, K13, K22, K85, L7M, N45, etc. (for cultivars see Onion, page 400)

Allium ramosum → Allium odorum

Allium rubellum - *Himalayan onion* {S} In India, the hill people eat the bulbs raw or cooked. The leaves are dried and preserved as a condiment. Eurasia. HEDRICK 1919, WATT; **V73M**

Allium sativum - *Garlic* {PL} Bulbs are roasted, baked, boiled, sautéed, broiled or used as a flavoring for other foods. The mild-flavored young leaves are considered a delicacy, and are used in salads, soups, egg-dishes, etc. Flowering stalks, sometimes called *garlic chives*, are also used for flavoring and are occasionally sold in bunches in oriental stores. The seeds and sprouted seeds are also eaten. Can be grown in indoor windowsill gardens. Does not produce bulbils. Cultivated. COST 1988, HARRIS [Re], MORTON 1976, TANAKA; A56, C81M, C85M, D11M, D65, D82, G19M, G68, G71, H3M, H33, H42, H54, J20, J33, M82, etc. (for cultivars see Garlic, page 335, also see Sprouting Seeds, page 485)

Allium sativum Ophioscorodon Group - *Top-setting garlic, Rocambole, Spanish garlic, Serpent garlic, Ophio garlic* {PL} Both the bulbs and bulbils are used to flavor food, providing a mild garlic flavor. The flower stalk coils then straightens, later producing a cluster of pea-sized bulbils at the top of the stalk. Young chive-like leaves are preferred by some for their delicate flavor. HAWKES, KRAFT, LARKCOM 1984 [Cu], MORTON 1976, VILMORIN [Cu]; A49D, C43M, C43M{S}, E5M, E7M, E48, G68, G84, H3M, J63, J82, K13, K22, K49M, K85, M82, etc. (for cultivars see Garlic, page 335)

Allium schoenoprasum - *Chives* {PL} The mildly pungent leaves are used for flavoring soups, sauces, eggs, butter, cream cheese, etc. Flowers are eaten in egg, cheese and fish dishes, or used as a garnish. Cultivated. LATHROP, LEGGATT [Re], MORTON 1976, TANAKA; C3, C3{S}, C82, C82{S}, F21, F31T, G84, H40, H46{S}, K22, K66{S}, K85, N19M

CULTIVARS

Blush: A light mauve flowered cultivar which blushes with a deep pink flower center. Same usage as common chives. R53M

Dwarf: Compact, low growing form of chives that only reaches a height of 3 to 6 inches. Attractive, pink blossoms. Excellent for a border edging. C9, M82

Extra Fine Leaved: A special strain with a very fine leaf which is much in demand by growers for bunching. S55{S}

Forescate: Good flavor for culinary use. The clumps of attractive foliage and clear, bright rose-red flower heads also make it an outstanding ornamental. C9, I39, J37M, M77

Fruhlau: (F_1) Earlier and more productive than the standard type. Fewer plants can be cut more frequently. Grows to 9 inches high. L91M{S}

Grolau: (Windowsill Chives) Bred in Switzerland for greenhouse forcing. Can be grown on a windowsill, and because of its thick, dark green foliage will not yellow or become leggy. Produces best when kept continuously cut. Good strong flavor. C53{S}, I39{S}, N81{S}

Pink: A good culinary type with pink blossoms. R53M

Allium schoenoprasum var. foliosum → Allium ledebourianum

Allium schoenoprasum var. sibiricum - *Siberian chives, Giant chives* {PL} The leaves and bulbs are pickled, used as a condiment or eaten in dumplings. Has a stronger garlic flavor than common chives. Temperate Asia, North America. TANAKA; C61M{S}, P92, R53M

Allium scorodoprasum - *Sand leek, Giant garlic* {S} Bulbs are used for flavoring. It is still cultivated in some parts of the U.S.S.R. Eurasia. KUNKEL, ZEVEN; **U63, V50, V73, V73M, V89, W92, X8, Z24, Z98**

Allium senescens - *Broadleaf chives, Sekka-yama-negi* {PL} Bulbs, leaves, and young shoots are used as food. Eurasia. TANAKA; B97, C9, C61M, C61M{S}, E30, F1M{S}, F35M, F57M, H46{S}, J37M, J91, *L22*, M77M, M82, N84{S}, etc.

Allium sibiricum → *Allium schoenoprasum var. sibiricum*

Allium sphaerocephalum - *Round-headed garlic, Ballhead onion* {S} Bulbs are eaten by the people near Lake Baikal, Siberia. Dried leaves are used as food in India. Eurasia. HEDRICK 1919, TANAKA, WATT; C73M{PL}, D62, E33{PL}, I78{PL}, I91{PL}, *N71M*, N84, O53M, *P95M*{PL}, *Q24*, S7M

Allium splendens - *Chishima-rakkyo* {PL} Small bulbs are eaten boiled or pickled in a mixture of sake, vinegar, and soy. Japan. UPHOF; C9, M77M

Allium stellatum - *Prairie onion* {S} The bulbs are eaten. North America. PETERSON, L., TANAKA; D62, G47M, H70M, H70M{PL}, J39M, J39M{PL}, J41M, J41M{PL}, J42, J42{PL}, K47T

Allium thunbergii - *Yama-rakkyo* {S} Young plants and leaves are eaten raw, in soups, as a potherb, oil-roasted or preserved in salt. Bulbs are pickled in brine, vinegar, and syrup. Eastern Asia. TANAKA; **Y27M**

Allium tricoccum - *Ramps, Wood leek* {S} Unfolding leaves and bulbs have a mild, sweet flavor and resemble leeks. They can be chopped fine and added to salads, fried, boiled and served with cream sauce, used in leek soups or canned for winter use. North America. ANGIER [Re], DOUTT, FERNALD, GIBBONS 1962 [Re], MEDSGER, SCHNEIDER [Cul, Re]; B51, D75T{PL}, E33M{PL}, G64, H61M, I44{PL}, I87{PL}, J7, J82, K47T, K63{PL}, N7T{PL}, N9M, N9M{PL}, *Q24*, etc.

Allium triquetrum - *Three-cornered leek* {S} The flat leaves have a milder and more delicate flavor than the onion. They are eaten in Algeria. Mediterranean region. FAIRCHILD 1930; C73M{PL}, N84, O53M, *P95M*{PL}, Q76{PL}, R77M

Allium tuberosum - *Garlic chives, Chinese chives, Chinese leek, Nira, Gow choy* {PL} Mild garlic-flavored leaves are used in cooking, especially miso soup. Oil from the seeds is used as food. The blanched leaves, called *gau wong, chive shoots* or *yellow chives*, are a delicacy eaten with pork or poultry or stirred into noodle dishes at the last minute. Flowers, flower stems, and seedheads are all edible. Cultivated. ALTSCHUL, COST 1988 [Cul], DAHLEN [Pre, Cul], GESSERT, HERKLOTS, LARKCOM 1984 [Cu]; C3, C3{S}, C82, C82{S}, E5M{PR}, G84, H40, H46{S}, K22, K22{S}, K66{S}, K85, L59, L59{S}, M53, N19M, etc.

CULTIVARS {S}

Broad Leaved: Long, thick white stems with large, broad dark-green leaves of excellent flavor. Used in Chinese cooking and stir-frying with eggs and meat. Very vigorous plant; height 13 to 15 inches; can be cut several times. Good for blanching culture. *K16M, L79G, Q39, S63M*

Flowering: (Chinese Leek Flower, Gow Choy Fah, Tenderpole) A cultivar selected for the edible flower buds and long, flower stalks. Unusual leek-like flavor, stronger than Chinese chive leaves. Excellent fried, pickled, and in soups. Widely grown in south China and Southeast Asia. COST 1988 [Cul], DAHLEN [Pre, Cul]; B1M, D55, I77, L59, *L79G, S70*

Green Belt: Specially selected for its dark green color, large and broad leaves, and disease resistance. Vigorous plant produces numerous tillers in a short period and is tolerant to winter temperature and summer heat. Ideal for year-round growing. Soft, pleasant flavored leaves; excellent for seasoning and kimchee making. F85, *L79G, Q3*

Hanzhong: Produces numerous green leaves with broad, thick blades; tender texture, with little fiber content. Very hardy; can survive a light frost and emerge early in the spring. Also suitable for growing under plastic cover in spring. *O54*

Mauve: Has the same excellent garlic flavor as regular garlic chives, but features attractive mauve flowers. J82

New Belt: Thick, green leaves, 10 millimeters in width. Slightly more vigorous than the standard cultivar. Prolific and resistant to disease. Both stalks and buds are eaten. May be harvested at any stage for use raw in salads. Very important vegetable for Chinese dishes. Q34, *S70*

Vietnamese: Giant garlic chives from Viet Nam. Young flower stalks are stir-fried, steamed, or boiled. C82, C82{PL}

Allium unifolium - *One-leaf onion* {PL} Bulbs and young shoots are fried and eaten. Western North America. TANAKA; F1M{S}, M77M, N84{S}, O57, *P95M*

Allium ursinum - *Ramsons, Bear's garlic* {S} Finely chopped leaves are used in cooking. They have an overpowering garlic odor which dissipates on cooking. The small green bulbils are used as a caper substitute. Eurasia. LAUNERT, MABEY, MICHAEL [Re]; C73M{PL}, I22{PL}, M77{PL}, *N71M*, N84, O48, O53M, *P95M*{PL}, *Q24*, R53M, S7M, S55

Allium validum - *Swamp onion* {S} Although the bulbs are somewhat fibrous they are very acceptable as a flavoring ingredient for soups and stews. Western North America. CLARKE, MEDSGER; **V73M, Z25M**

Allium victorialis - *Longroot onion* {S} Bulbs and brittle stems are eaten. Eurasia. KUNKEL, TANAKA; D62, N84, *P95M*{PL}, *Q24*, Q40{PL}, S7M

Allium vineale - *Crow garlic, Field garlic* {S} Tender young tops can be chopped finely and used in salads. Bulbs are sometimes used but they have a very strong flavor and odor. Eurasia, naturalized in North America. ANGIER, FERNALD, GIBBONS 1962, MEDSGER; D58, D62, K47T, N84, O48

Allium wallichii - *Jimbur* {S} Leaves are used as a condiment. Himalayan region. ALTSCHUL; D62, N84, Q40{PL}, S7M

Brodiaea douglasii - {S} Corms are edible raw, but are at their best when roasted slowly in hot ashes for up to an hour, after which they become rather sweet. The young seedpods may be used as a potherb. Western North America. KIRK; I47, J93T, O53M

Brodiaea pulchella - *Blue dicks* {S} The corms are eaten raw, fried, boiled and roasted. Flowers are eaten in salads. Western North America. CLARKE; B11T{PL}, F79M, J25M, K49T, L13

Dichelostemma pulchella → *Brodiaea pulchella*

Tulbaghia alliacea - *Wild garlic, Isikhwa* {S} Leaves and stems are cooked and eaten like spinach or are chopped fine, seasoned with salt and used as a relish. The flowers are regarded as a delicacy by Zulu women. Bulbs are cooked with meat. Southern Africa. FOX, F.; N84

Tulbaghia violacea - *Society garlic* {PL} Flat leaves have a mild, garlic flavor and are used as a flavoring in soups and salads. The attractive pink flowers are produced year round in warm climates, and can be used as a garnish, eaten in salads, or used to flavor other foods. South Africa. FOX, F., LATHROP; B11T, D62{S}, E47M, E48, E61, *F53M*, F93G, G96, H51M, J27, L29, L56, L86, M53, N84{S}, O35G, Q40, etc.

CULTIVARS

Silver Lace: (Variegated, Tricolor) Dwarf, clumping plant with attractive grass-like leaves of deep green, margined with pink and white. Makes a fine container plant. More ornamental than the common type. B11T, B92, C9, D29, E48, G20, H3M, L29, L86, M82

ALTINGIACEAE

Liquidamber orientalis - {S} Source of a gummy resin, called *Asian styrax*, used to flavor tobacco, chewing gum, baked goods, and candy. Asia Minor. MORTON 1976, TANAKA; **Z25M**

Liquidamber styraciflua - *Sweet gum* {S} Produces a gummy resin that is chewed to sweeten the breath and clean the teeth, and also to flavor tobacco. It is called *storax*, or *American styrax*. Does not produce much resin in the Northern states. Eastern North America to Central America. MORTON 1976; A82{PL}, C9M, E47, E47{PL}, F70{PL}, H4{PL}, *H71*, I28{PL}, J47{PL}, K38, K63G, *L5M*, N93M, *Q32*

AMARANTHACEAE

Achyranthes aspera - *Prickly chaff flower, Apamarga, Latjira* {S} Young leaves and the leafy tops of the stems are eaten as *lalab* (side-dish) and as *bayam* or *bayem* (spinach) in *sayor* (soup). Used as a salt substitute in Chad. The seeds boiled in milk, *chach*, or whey are regarded as a good tonic in India. Old World Tropics. BHANDARI, CRIBB, DALZIEL, OCHSE, UPHOF; F85, N84

Alternanthera amoena* → *Alternanthera ficoidea

Alternanthera ficoidea - *Bayam mèrah, Bayam bang* {PL} The young leaves are eaten raw with rice, boiled as a potherb, or eaten with *sambal*, a hot-pepper mixture. Southeast Asia. OCHSE; G96, I90M

Alternanthera sessilis - *Bayam kremah, Chuk-tsit-tsoi* {S} Leaves are eaten in salads, soups, curries, with fish or rice, and steamed as a potherb. Flowers are eaten in China. Tropics. ALTSCHUL, TANAKA, UPHOF; F85, I90M{PL}, N84

Alternanthera versicolor - *Pink cress* {S} Pink-red serrated leaves make an attractive addition to salads. They are mild flavored and can be boiled and used as a potherb, mixed with stronger flavored greens. Southern Asia. KUNKEL; E49, I90M{PL}

Amaranthus atropurpureus - *Lal-nati* {S} Leaves are boiled and used as a potherb. Southern Asia. WATT; N84

Amaranthus caudatus - *Inca wheat, Kiwicha, Pendant amaranth* {S} Mild flavored greens are boiled and used as a potherb, or cooked in soups and stews. They can be harvested as thinnings from amaranth grain fields. Seeds are popped, ground into flour for baking, cooked into a porridge, or mixed with crude sugar to make a confection called *boroco*. Cultivated. COLE [Re], KAUFFMAN [Cu], NATIONAL RESEARCH COUNCIL 1984, SAUER, WILLIAMS, L.; A16, D62, F80, F85, I99, J20, K49T, L86, N84, O53M, O89

Amaranthus cruentus - *Mexican grain amaranth* {S} Leaves are steamed and used as a spinach substitute. Sprouted seeds are eaten in salads and natural-foods cuisine. In Guatemala, the seeds are used for *tortillas* or parched and popped, then made into a confection called *niguas*. Flowers are used to color ceremonial maize bread. Cultivated. COLE [Re], KAUFFMAN [Cu], NATIONAL RESEARCH COUNCIL 1984, SAUER; C25M{PR}, D26M{PR}, I16{PR}, I20{PR}, I51M, I51M{PR}, J25M, L9M, O53M, S55 (for cultivars see Amaranth, page 228)

Amaranthus dubius - *Khada sag, Bayam bhaji* {S} The leaves of this species are considered very palatable. They are eaten as a potherb in India, West Africa, the Caribbean, and Indonesia. One of the best cultivars is Claroen, particularly popular in Benin and Suriname. Seeds are also eaten. Tropics. CHAUHAN, NATIONAL RESEARCH COUNCIL 1984; S55

Amaranthus edulis* → *Amaranthus mantegazzianus

Amaranthus gangeticus* → *Amaranthus tricolor

Amaranthus gracilis* → *Amaranthus viridis

Amaranthus graecizans - *Prostrate amaranth* {S} Young, tender leaves and stems have a bland, mild flavor. They are steamed and used as a potherb with purslane, mustard, and other greens with a more pronounced flavor. Seeds are eaten raw, parched, or ground into flour or meal. North America. HARRINGTON, H., KINDSCHER, KIRK; N84, O53M

Amaranthus hybridus - *Rough pigweed, Spleen amaranth* {S} Leaves and young seedlings are eaten in salads, soups, and stews. Seeds are eaten or ground into flour. Has the potential, through crossbreeding, of imparting early maturity to the white-seeded grain amaranths. North America, widespread. MORTON 1977, NATIONAL RESEARCH COUNCIL 1984; D62 (for cultivars see Amaranth, page 228)

Amaranthus hypochondriacus - *Mercado grain amaranth, Guegui, Bledo, Ramdana, Rajgira* {S} The seeds are eaten toasted, made into *tortillas* and *chappaties*, rolled into balls, or powdered and drunk as *atole*. Popped grain is soaked in milk and sugar, or mixed with honey to form cakes called *laddoos* in India and *alegrias* in Mexico. Young leaves are used like spinach. Sprouted seeds are used in salads. Cultivated. COLE [Re], HALPIN [Cul, Nu], JONES, M. [Re], KAUFFMAN [Cu], NATIONAL RESEARCH COUNCIL 1984, NIETHAMMER [Re], SAUER; C43M, E59Z, F24, J73, J82, K20, K49T, L9M, N42{PL} (for cultivars see Amaranth, page 228, also see Sprouting Seeds, page 485)

Amaranthus lividus - *Purple amaranth, Vleeta, Horsetooth amaranth* {S} Cultivated in the gardens of the ancient Greeks and Romans for the purple-red leaves, eaten as a potherb. Ground seeds are made into cakes and porridge. Eurasia. KUNKEL, NATIONAL RESEARCH COUNCIL 1984, WATT; K49M, N84

CULTIVARS

Bonfire: 60 days. Bright red at all stages of growth. Rapid grower, high yielding and tasty. Downy mildew resistant. Good for frying and Oriental dishes. O39M

Fire Chief: 60 days. Stems and leaves are a deep crimson color. Height before flowering is 8 to 10 feet. Very nice for frying and cooking. O39M

Harvest Express: 60 days. Vigorous, uniform growth; light green, tasty leaves good for frying and Oriental dishes. Good for both kitchen garden and open field growing. Downy mildew resistant. O39M

Amaranthus mangostanus* → *Amaranthus tricolor

Amaranthus mantegazzianus - *Quinoa de Castilla* {S} Seeds are used as a grain crop. Cultivated in Argentina but becoming rare. Andean South America. COLE, COONS, TANAKA, ZEVEN; N84, O53M

CULTIVARS

Bolivia 153: Black-seeded cultivar suitable for milling into flour. Mostly uniform red plants, 2 to 4 feet tall, characterized by one very thick floral spike. Medium to long season. L79M

Amaranthus oleraceus* → *Amaranthus lividus

Amaranthus paniculatus - *Reuzen amaranth* {S} Leaves are a good substitute for spinach. Starchy seeds are ground into flour and used in baking. Cultivated. TANAKA.

CULTIVARS

Oeschberg: Very productive plant; height 3 feet; produces up to one half pound of nutritious seed on a square yard. C61M, G84{PL}, J73, N84, S91M

Amaranthus patulus* → *Amaranthus retroflexus

Amaranthus quitensis - *Sangorache, Ataco* {S} Occasionally cultivated for its stout, intensely red inflorescences which are a source of dye used for coloring *chicha* and ceremonial maize dishes. The leaves are eaten as a potherb. Seeds are ground into flour. Andean South America. KUNKEL, SAUER, ZEVEN; **Z98**

Amaranthus retroflexus - *Redroot amaranth, Wild beet, Pigweed* {S} Leaves and stems, while still young and tender, are eaten alone as a potherb or mixed with stronger flavored greens such as cress, dandelion and chicory. Amaranth meal is greatly improved by roasting the seeds before grinding. It is then mixed with cornmeal and used as *pinole* to make bread, cakes, and gruel. Seeds are occasionally sprouted and eaten. North America. ANGIER [Re], CLARKE [Re], GIBBONS 1962 [Re], HARRINGTON, H.; D58, D62, N84

Amaranthus spinosus - *Prickly amaranth, Spiny calalu, Careless weed* {S} The young leaves and tender stems, before the spines form, are used as a spinach. Older ones are highly esteemed after the spines have been removed. Pantropical. BURKILL, OCHSE, WATT, WILLIAMS, L.; D62, F85, N84

Amaranthus tricolor - *Chinese spinach, Hinn choy, Bayam, Calalu, Sag* {S} Leaves are eaten raw, boiled, steamed, stir-fried, or used in soups, stews, curries, frittatas, omelettes, pastas, sauces, etc. The crisp interior of large stems makes a tasty cooked vegetable. An excellent hot weather substitute for spinach. Cultivated. BURKILL, COLE [Re], HALPIN [Cul, Nu], HARRINGTON, G. [Cul], HERKLOTS, NIETHAMMER [Re], OCHSE, VILMORIN [Cu]; A2, A79M, D62, E24, E59, E83T, F85, G67M, H49, I39, J73, J82, L86{PL}, N84, O89, S55, etc. (for cultivars see Amaranth, page 228)

Amaranthus viridis - *Green amaranth, Green calalu, Bayam hèdjo* {S} Leaves are used as a spinach substitute. Leafy stems and flower clusters are similarly used. Tropics. BURKILL, CRIBB, OCHSE, TANAKA; F85, N84, P9

Amaranthus x sp. (A. cruentus x A. powellii) - *Hopi red-dye amaranth, Komo* {S} A form selected for its bright red pigmentation. A water extract of the flower clusters is used to color the pink maize wafer bread (*piki*) used in Hopi ceremonial dances. Seeds are also edible. Cultivated. SAUER; A2, E59Z, F42, I16, I77, I99, K49T, L79M

Celosia argentea - *Quailgrass, Soko* {S} Leaves, tender stems, and young inflorescences are steamed and eaten as a potherb, or finely cut and used in soups. In Africa there are both green and red types. An edible oil is extracted from the seeds. The protein extracted from the leaves, known as *sokotein*, is used as a food supplement. Tropics. DALZIEL, MARTIN 1975, OCHSE, OOMEN, PIRIE, VAN EPENHUIJSEN [Cu]; D33, F85, N84

Celosia trigyna - *Silver spinach, Ajefowo* {S} Young and tender leafy shoots are finely cut up and used in soups and sauces. Tropical Africa. DALZIEL, FOX, F., VAN EPENHUIJSEN [Cu]; N84

Iresine herbstii - *Blood leaf, Beef steak* {PL} Leaves are squeezed in water to obtain a red dye used for coloring agar-agar jellies. New Guinea, cultivated. BURKILL, TANAKA; E48, G96, H51M, M33G

AMARYLLIDACEAE

Narcissus jonquilla - *Jonquil* {PL} The flowers are eaten in salads, candied, or made into desserts. Cultivated. CROWHURST 1973 [Re], MACNICOL; C73M, D62{S}, E11, H37M, N84{S}, R52

AMBROSIACEAE

Ambrosia artemisiifolia - *Ragweed* {S} Achenes contain 19% oil, having slightly better drying properties than soybean oil. They have been suggested for edible purposes, as the oil is relatively free from linolenic acid. Sometimes called *oil of ragweed*. North America. UPHOF; D58, D62, N84

Ambrosia maritima - {S} Leaves are eaten in soups as a condiment. Also used for flavoring liqueurs. Africa, Mediterranean region. DALZIEL, UPHOF; **W92**

ANACARDIACEAE

Anacardium giganteum - *Cajú do matto* {S} Fleshy receptacles are eaten green, cooked and roasted, or made into alcoholic beverages. Northern South America. TANAKA; **X88M**

Anacardium occidentale - *Cashew* {S} Kidney-shaped kernels are the cashew nuts of commerce. After preparation, they are eaten raw, roasted or made into cashew butter. They also give flavor to *Madeira* wine. The fleshy receptacle, the *cashew apple*, is eaten fresh, dried or made into chutney, vinegar, pickles, a carbonated beverage *cashola*, a brandy *fenni*, and a gin-like liquor *koniagi*. Cultivated. GARNER [Pro], JOHNS [Cul], MORTON 1987a, POPENOE, W. 1920 [Cu], ROSENGARTEN, UPHOF; A79M, B62, E29{PL}, F85, J22{PL}, J51M{PR}, N84, O93, P5, P38, Q12, Q18, *Q93*{PL}

Bouea gandaria* → *Bouea macrophylla

Bouea macrophylla - *Maprang, Gandaria, Kundang* {PL} The young leaves are eaten raw with *sambal ontjom*. Fruits with a sweetish sour flavor are peeled and eaten raw. Others have an acid flavor and are used as a substitute for sour lime and tamarind. Unripe fruits are used in making *rujak* and *asinan* (desserts). Malaysia. BURKILL, MORTON 1987a, OCHSE, RIFAI; E29

CULTIVARS {SC}

Wan: (Sweet) Small, plum-sized, orange fruit. Much sought after because of its fine flavor. When fully ripe, the entire fruit including the skin but not the seeds is eaten. Originated near Bangkok, Thailand. Introduced into Florida in 1967, by William F. Whitman. MORTON 1987a, WHITMAN; **T73M**

Buchanania lanzan - *Almondette tree, Chironji, Charoli* {S} The seeds, which have an excellent flavor somewhat reminiscent of pistachio nuts, are eaten raw and roasted, or used in the preparation of sweetmeats. The fruit has a pleasant, sweetish, subacid flavor. Also the source of a light yellow, wholesome oil that has a pleasant aroma and may be used as a substitute for almond or olive oil. Commonly found at Indian stores in North America. Also popular in England, where the seeds are known as *almondettes*. Tropical Asia. JAFFREY [Re], MACNICOL [Re], MENNINGER, ROSENGARTEN, UPHOF; F74{PR}, Q46

Choerospondias axillaris* → *Spondias axillaris

Dracontomelon dao - *Yun meen, Jên-mien-tzu* {S} The small, sourish-sweet fruits are cooked with soy sauce and eaten with rice, or used for flavoring curries. In Canton, they are commonly served with minced pork. Leaves are also edible. Philippines. BURKILL, DAHLEN [Re], MARTIN 1975, PONGPANGAN, TANAKA; N84

Harpephyllum caffrum - *Kaffir plum* {S} Tart, juicy, red fruits are sometimes eaten raw, but are more often made into a delicious jelly. South Africa, cultivated. KUNKEL, TANAKA; A79M, C9M, E29, E29{PL}, E29{PR}, *E53M*, *G66*, *I61*, O53M, P5, P38, *Q32*, R33M, R60, S91M, etc.

Lannea coromandelica → *Lannea grandis*

Lannea grandis - *Wodier wood, Kayoo djaran* {S} Trunk is the source of a gum, *jingan gum*, much used in confectionery. Young leaves and shoots are eaten uncooked, steamed as *lalab* (spinach) with rice, and mixed in *sayor* (soup). Powdered bark is used as a flavoring for roast fowl. Southeast Asia. BURKILL, OCHSE, UPHOF; F85, N84, Q46

Mangifera caesia - *Bindjai* {S} Young fruits are sliced and eaten raw with ketjap or sambal. In Sumatra, the pulp is salted and preserved in bottles stoppered with ashes, then used as an admixture to small fishes wrapped in leaves. The leaves are eaten raw or used as a condiment. Fresh or dried seeds are grated, mixed with spices and dried fish, and eaten as a side-dish with rice. Malaya. MORTON 1987a, OCHSE, TANAKA; N84, P38

Mangifera foetida - *Horse mango* {S} Before being eaten, the peeled young fruits, which have a strong turpentine-like flavor, are pickled, preserved in syrup, or used for chutneys and curries. They are sometimes consumed with a sambal sauce. Ripe fruits of sweet types are eaten fresh. Southern Asia, cultivated. BURKILL, MORTON 1987a, OCHSE, RIFAI, TANAKA, WATT; N84, P38

Mangifera indica - *Mango* {S} Fruit is eaten fresh, in curries, made into chutney, jams, pickles, wine, vinegar, etc. Seeds are used in the preparation of *dodol* or pudding; a starch and an edible fat are also extracted from them. Dried unripe fruits, *amchoor*, are used in Indian cuisine. Flowers and young leaves are also edible. Cultivated. GARNER [Pro], JAFFREY [Cul], KUNKEL, MORTON 1987a [Cu], OCHSE, POPENOE, W. 1920 [Cu], SCHNEIDER [Cul, Re], TANAKA; A88T{PR}, C56M, E29, E29{PL}, E29{PR}, F74{PR}, J83T{PR}, L54{PR}, N84, P38, Q12, Q46; (for cultivars see Mango, page 383)

Mangifera odorata - *Kuweni mango, Kuini* {S} The ripe fruits are sour-sweet, with a strong turpentine-like aroma, and are eaten fresh or prepared as syrup, jam and sweets. Unripe fruits are pickled, used in curries, or eaten with vinegar. Malaysia, Indonesia. BROWN, BURKILL, MORTON 1987a, RIFAI, TANAKA; **T73M**

Pleiogynium solandri - *Burdekin plum* {S} The large, ribbed seeds have a pleasant flavor and are eaten. Fruits are used in jams and jellies. They develope their best flavor when allowed to soften and ripen for several days after they are harvested. Australia. CRIBB, MOWRY [Pro], UPHOF; N84, O84, P38, R15M, R33M

Pleiogynium timorense → *Pleiogynium solandri*

Rhus aromatica - *Fragrant sumac* {PL} The acid red fruits are made into *Indian lemonade*. Kiowa indians ate the berries mixed with corn meal, beaten with sugar or boiled into a tea. North America to Mexico. KINDSCHER, MEDSGER; B9M, C9M{S}, *C47*, D95, *F51*, *H90*{S}, I53, K38{S}, K47T{S}, K63G{S}, *K89*, *K89*{S}, *M69M*, M92, O93{S}, etc.

Rhus chinensis - *Sumac, Tibri* {PL} The fruit is eaten. Also used as a salt substitute and a vegetable rennet in the preparation of curds. China, Himalayan region. TANAKA; F85

Rhus copallina - *Shining sumac, Winged sumac* {PL} Fruits are used to make *Indian lemonade*. North America. ANGIER, FERNALD, HEDRICK 1919, MEDSGER, UPHOF; B9M, *B52*, E33M, E87, *F51*, H49, I11M, I11M{S}, I19, K38{S}, K63G{S}, *K89*, *M69M*, M77M, O53M{S}, O93{S}, etc.

Rhus coriaria - *Sicilian sumac, Elm-leaved sumac, Tartak* {S} Crushed fruits, along with Origanum syriacum, are the principal ingredients of *zatar*, a popular spice mixture used in Middle Eastern cuisine. In Syria a valued drink is prepared by soaking the berries in milk. Immature fruits are used as a caper substitute. Middle East, Mediterranean region. HEDRICK 1919, MORTON 1976; J66M{PR}, L50M{PR}, N84

Rhus glabra - *Smooth sumac, Scarlet sumac* {PL} A refreshing pink lemonade-like beverage is prepared by bruising the fruit in water, thus freeing the malic acid, straining the resulting liquid through cloth, and then adding sugar. The peeled young shoots and the peeled roots can be eaten raw. North America. FERNALD, GIBBONS 1962 [Re], KINDSCHER, MEDSGER, TURNER 1979 [Re]; *B52*{S}, C9M{S}, C81M, D95, *F51*, H4, I4, I11M, I11M{S}, I15{S}, I19, I47{S}, J26, M35M, O53M{S}, etc.

Rhus integrifolia - *Lemonade berry* {S} Fruits are crushed in water to make a cooling beverage. Boiling should be avoided as this releases tannic acids. The Indians dried the berries for winter use when they made a kind of hot pink lemonade. Southwestern North America. CLARKE, HEDRICK 1919, MEDSGER; B94, C9M, F85, *H71*, I47, *I61*, I98M, K15, K47T, N84, O53M

Rhus javanica - *Nurude, Mu-yen* {S} A salt derived from the fruit is used to flavor foods and to coagulate *tofu*. Indonesia. TANAKA; **V19**

Rhus ovata - *Sugar bush* {S} The pulp of the fruit is sucked for the pleasingly tart juice that forms on its surface. A sweetish white sap exudes from the fruit and is used as an acid flavoring or a sugar substitute. Leaves are boiled to make tea. Southwestern North America. CLARKE, MEDSGER, UPHOF; B94, C9M, F79M, G59M, G60{PL}, *H71*, *I61*, I98M, K15, K47T, *K48*, L13, N84, *P63*

Rhus trilobata - *Lemonade sumac, Squaw berry* {PL} Fruits are eaten fresh, dried, mixed with corn meal, or made into jam, lemon pie, or sumac ade. Southwestern North America. CLARKE [Re], KIRK, UPHOF; D95, E61, F80{S}, G60, *G66*{S}, H4, *I23*, I47{S}, I99{S}, J25M, J25M{S}, J26, K38{S}, *K89*{S}, M35M, etc.

Rhus typhina - *Staghorn sumac, Vinegar tree* {PL} Very sour fruits are used in pies and soaked in water to make *Indian lemonade*. Eastern North America. FERNALD, KUNKEL, MEDSGER; A80M, B9M, C9M{S}, D45, E15{S}, E33M, *F51*, I4, I11M, *I62*, I99{S}, *J75M*, K38{S}, M35M, *M69M*, O53M{S}, etc.

Schinus molle - *California peppertree* {S} Dried, roasted berries are used as a pepper substitute. Oil distilled from the fruit is used as a spice in baked goods and candy. The fruits are brewed into wine. They are also pulverized and used in cooling drinks called *horchatas* or *atoles* in Central America. South America, cultivated. MORTON 1976, TANAKA, WILLIAMS, L.; C9M, C98, F80, *G66*, I28{PL}, *I61*, I99, *J86*{PL}, K38, N93M, O53M, O84, P5, *P17M*, *Q32*, S92, etc.

Schinus terebinthifolius - *Brazilian pepper, Pink peppercorns, Red peppercorns* {S} The peppery seeds, imported from Réunion, are sold in expensive specialty markets and are used as a spice in Cajun and Nouvelle cuisines. However, they are known to cause rashes, vomiting, and diarreah in some sensitive individuals. South America, cultivated. VON WELANETZ; A79M, C9M, C43M{PL}, C94M{PR}, C98, F37T{PL}, F85, *G66*, *I61*, I99, *J86*{PL}, K52{PR}, O53M, O93, P5, *P17M*, *Q15G*, *Q32*, etc.

Sclerocarya birrea - *Dineygama* {S} Sugary fruits, the size of a plum, are eaten or made into an alcoholic cider. Milky kernels are eaten like peanuts. Tropical Africa. HEDRICK 1919, TANAKA, UPHOF; N84

Sclerocarya birrea ssp. caffra → Sclerocarya caffra

Sclerocarya caffra - *Marula* {S} The tart, juicy fruit is eaten or made into jelly. An alcoholic cider is brewed from its juice, which is also boiled down to a thick black syrup used by the natives to sweeten their Guinea-corn gruel. Seed kernels, tasting like walnuts or peanuts, are eaten with *mealie meal*, or ground into flour. They contain 4 times the vitamin C of oranges. *Sakoa oil*, extracted from the kernel, contains 28% protein and is used in cooking. Southern Africa. FOX, F., MENNINGER, TANAKA, VAN WYK; *G66*, N84, O53M, O93, P5, P38, R47, S29

Spondias axillaris - *Hsuan-tso* {S} Fruit is edible. Bark is chewed like betel nut. China. TANAKA, VON REIS; **Y76**

Spondias cytherea → Spondias dulcis

Spondias dulcis - *Ambarella, Vi apple, Tahiti mombin* {S} The ripe fruits are eaten fresh, dried, cooked in coconut milk, put in syrup with agar-agar, or made into jams, drinks, wine, and marmalade. Unripe fruits are made into jelly, pickles and relishes or used as a sour flavoring for sauces, soups and stews. Young leaves are pleasantly acid and are consumed raw, steamed with salted fish and rice, or used as a seasoning. Cultivated. KENNARD [Pro], MORTON 1987a, POPENOE, W. 1920 [Cu, Pro], RICHARDSON [Re], STURROCK, TANAKA; E29, E29{PL}, E29{PR}, F85, N84, P38

Spondias lutea → Spondias mombin

Spondias mangifera - *Malayan mombin, Amra, Buah amara, Klontjing* {S} Young leaves and fruits are used in Indonesian cuisine to add a sour, lemony flavor to curry and other dishes. Fruits are also pickled in oil, salt and chilis or preserved in sugar. Panicles are eaten raw or cooked as a vegetable. Tropical Asia. BURKILL, MORTON 1987a, OCHSE, TANAKA, WATT; N84, P38, P38{SC}, Q46

Spondias mombin - *Yellow mombin, Hog plum, Ciruela tronadora* {S} The fleshy fruits are pleasantly acid and are eaten fresh or stewed with sugar, and are also made into cider-like drinks, ice cream, jams and jellies. Huastec Indians use them to flavor *aguardiente*. In Amazonas, they are used to produce a wine sold as *vinho de taperiba*. Unripe fruits are pickled and eaten like olives. Young leaves are cooked as greens. The bark is added to sugarcane juice when making *pulque*. Tropical America. ALCORN, JOHNS [Cul], KENNARD, MORTON 1987a, POPENOE, W. 1920 [Cu, Pro], STURROCK; F85, N84

Spondias pinnata → Spondias mangifera

Spondias purpurea - *Red mombin, Spanish plum, Ciruela* {S} Spicy, subacid fruits are consumed fresh, stewed with raw sugar, or are boiled and dried for future use. Also made into jams, jellies and beverages. Unripe fruits are pickled in vinegar or made into a tart, green sauce. The sour leaves and shoots, containing 5.5% protein, are eaten raw or cooked. Tropical America. DUKE, KENNARD, MORTON 1987a, POPENOE, W. 1920 [Cu, Pro], STURROCK, WILLIAMS, L.; E29{PL}, F85, N84, P38{SC}

Spondias tuberosa - *Imbú* {S} The greenish yellow, thick-skinned fruit has soft, melting, almost liquid flesh with a pleasant, subacid flavor suggestive of a sweet orange. It is eaten fresh or made into ice cream, jams, jellies and drinks. In northern Brazil, a famous custard-like dessert called *imbúzada* is prepared by adding the juice of the fruit to boiled sweet milk. Brazil. HEDRICK 1919, KENNARD, MORTON 1987a, POPENOE, W. 1920, UPHOF; **T73M**

ANGIOPTERIDACEAE

Angiopteris lygodiifolia - *Ryûbintai, Tree fern* {S} Stem piths are rich in starch, eaten by the natives. Produces an aromatic oil used to perfume coconut oil. Japan, Polynesia. HEDRICK 1919, TANAKA, UPHOF; **V19**

ANNONACEAE

Annona x atemoya (A. cherimola x A. squamosa) - *Atemoya* {S} A garden hybrid of the cherimoya and the sugar apple grown in the tropics for its sweetish fruit, which is usually eaten chilled. Has some of the qualities of the cherimoya, but is mostly grown in warmer climates where the cherimoya does not succeed. GARNER, MORTON 1987a [Cu], MOWRY, SCHNEIDER [Nu, Re], STURROCK; *B59*{PR}, I83M{PL}, N84, P5, P38

CULTIVARS {GR}

African Pride: (Kaller) Large fruit, up to 20 ounces; skin dull green, smooth to medium rough; flesh rubbery in texture, free of discoloration and bitterness next to the skin, flavor good; seeds few. Tree dwarfish, comes into production early; a biannual bearer in Florida, the first crop in September and October, the second in March and April. Originated in Israel; introduced commercially in Australia. BROOKS 1972, MORTON 1987a; *B58M*, F68, L6, Q93

Bradley: Small to medium-sized fruit, symmetrical round in shape, of excellent flavor. Tree a heavy producer. Good for back yard growers. Originated in Florida. **T73M{SC}**

Geffner: Medium-sized fruit with rubbery flesh and fair flavor. Tree a heavy producer. F68, L6

Page: Medium-size fruit, tends to split on the tree. Sets good crops without hand pollination. Originated on the property of Morrison Page in the Redlands, Florida. One of the first named selections of atemoya. MORTON 1987a; F68, L6

Pink's Mammoth: (Mammoth, Pink's Prolific) Very large, irregular-shaped fruit, up to 5 pounds; quality good though the flesh immediately below the rind is usually brownish and bitter. Large open tree, takes several years to come into production. Originated in Queensland, Australia. MORTON 1987a; Q93

Priestly: Medium-sized fruit with few seeds and an excellent flavor; susceptible to splitting if left on the tree too long. F68

Annona cherimola - *Cherimoya* {S} The delicious fruits, tasting like a cross between a pineapple and a banana, are best eaten out of hand. Or they can be used in ice cream, custards, cakes, pies, sherbets and other desserts or turned into soft drinks and alcoholic beverages. Andean South America, cultivated. GARNER [Pro], JOHNS [Cul], MORTON 1987a [Cu], POPENOE, W. 1920 [Cu], SCHNEIDER [Nu, Re], SIMMONS 1972; A44M{PR}, C56M{PL}, D57{PL}, E13G{PR}, E29, E29{PL}, I49M{PL}, I99, J83T{PR}, O93, P5, P38, *Q32*, Q41, *Q49M*{PL}, etc. (for cultivars see Cherimoya, page 290)

Annona cinerea - *Anon morado, Riñon* {S} The violet-tinted fruits, resembling a large sugar apple, have an unusually sweet flavor. Sold in the markets of Colombia. Southern Caribbean region. HEDRICK 1919, PEREZ-ARBELAEZ, UPHOF; **Y2**

Annona diversifolia - *Ilama* {S} The sweet fruits are eaten fresh, being one of the best for the tropical lowlands. Pale-green fruited types have very sweet white flesh. Pink-fruited kinds have a rose-pink tinged flesh that is more acidic like that of the cherimoya. Central America. KENNARD, MORTON 1987a, MOWRY, POPENOE, W. 1920 [Cu], SIMMONS 1972; F85, N84, P38

CULTIVARS {SC}

Imery: Large, pink-fleshed type. Not as flavorful as some of the white-fleshed strains introduced to the United States from Guatemala. Introduced into Florida from El Salvador. MORTON 1987a; **T73M**

Annona glabra - *Pond apple, Alligator apple* {S} The fruit is eaten raw, though not of good quality. Some types have fair flavor that can be improved by boiling. Also made into jelly and wine. Valued as a rootstock for other Annona species in wet soils. Florida, Tropical America. MORTON 1977, MORTON 1987a, POPENOE, W. 1920; E29, E29{PL}, E29{PR}, F85, *J25*{PL}, *L5M*, N84, P38

Annona lutescens - *Anona amarilla* {S} Cultivated as a fruit tree in Alta Verapaz, Guatemala. The flesh of the fruit is pale yellow. Central America. WILLIAMS, L.; **Y2**

Annona mannii → Anonidium mannii

Annona montana - *Mountain soursop, Guanábana cimarrona, Araticú grande* {PL} Fruits are juicy, refreshingly subacid, peculiarly aromatic and of a fair flavor similar to the soursop. Can be grown at slightly higher elevations, with cooler temperatures, than the soursop. West Indies. KENNARD, MORTON 1987a, POPENOE, W. 1920; E29, F85{S}, J36

Annona muricata - *Soursop, Guanábana* {PL} Ripe fruits are juicy, refreshingly acid and are eaten raw. Also used in ice cream, sherbets, custards, and mixed with wine or brandy. A popular Cuban beverage *champola de guanábana* is made from the strained pulp and milk. Young leafy, shoots are steamed and eaten. Unripe fruits are roasted, fried or boiled or used in soups. Leaves are brewed into *corossol tea*. Cultivated. GARNER [Pro], HEDRICK 1919, MORTON 1987a [Cu], OCHSE, POPENOE, W. 1920 [Cu], RICHARDSON [Re], STURROCK; A79M{S}, D57, E29, E29{PR}, E29{S}, F68, F85{S}, I83M, J22, N84{S}, P38{S}, *Q93*

CULTIVARS {GR}

Cuban Fiberless: Medium to large, oblong fruit, 8 to 15 inches long; thin yellow-green skin, covered with short spines which become shorter and separate as the fruit ripens; juicy, white flesh with a subacid to sweet flavor, fiberless; numerous dark brown seeds. Tree small, upright, vigorous. J22, *Q93*

Whitman Fiberless: Large fruit of good flavor, completely fiberless. Can be eaten with a spoon like ice cream, spitting out the small seeds. Tree bears regularly. Second generation seedling selection of Cuban Fiberless, which seldom fruits in Florida. WHITMAN; **U27T{SC}**

Annona purpurea - *Soncoya* {S} The fruit is round, brownish-gray in color, with soft bright-orange flesh of a pleasant aromatic flavor suggesting that of the northern pawpaw (Asimina triloba). It is usually eaten fresh or strained for juice and drunk as a beverage. Central America, cultivated. MORTON 1987a, POPENOE, W. 1920, STURROCK, UPHOF, WILLIAMS, L.; **T73M, Z72**

Annona reticulata - *Bullock's heart, Custard apple* {S} The sweetish fruits vary considerably in quality. Some are eaten fresh, but most often they are used in preserves, drinks, ice cream, custards, ices, milk shakes, and other desserts. Cultivated. GARNER [Pro], MORTON 1987a [Cu], POPENOE, W. 1920 [Cu], STURROCK; A79M, E29, E29{PL}, E29{PR}, F68{PL}, F85, N84, O93, Q46

CULTIVARS

Fiji Sweet: An improved sweet-fleshed cultivar collected in Fiji. F85

Annona scleroderma - *Posh-té* {S} The delicious, aromatic fruit is eaten out of hand. It is much richer than the soursop, with a suggestion of the flavor of the white sapote (Casimiroa edulis). Central America. POPENOE, W. 1920; P38

Annona senegalensis - *Wild custard apple, Abo, Amamense* {S} The round, deep orange fruit has a pineapple-like aroma and the flavor of apricots. It is considered one of the best fruits of Tropical Africa. Unopened flower buds are eaten in soup and are also used to flavor other foods. Leaves are edible, containing 8.2% protein when dried. West Tropical Africa. DALZIEL, FOX, F., KUNKEL, MORTON 1987a; F85, N84, P38{CF}

Annona squamosa - *Sugar apple, Sweetsop, Custard apple* {S} Sweet, creamy fruits are highly regarded as a dessert fruit in the Tropics. Mostly eaten fresh, but sometimes made into sherbets, ice cream, jellies, preserves, or a fermented cider. Cultivated. GARNER [Pro], MORTON 1987a [Cu], POPENOE, W. 1920, TANAKA; A79M, *B59*{PR}, D57{PL}, E29, E29{PL}, E29{PR}, F68{PL}, F85, N84, P5, *P17M*, Q12, Q18, *Q25*, Q46, etc.

CULTIVARS {PL}

Red: Roundish fruit, 2 to 3 inches in diameter; skin pale green blushed with pink, small protuberances evenly distributed; soft, light pink flesh with a sweet melting flavor, numerous brown seeds scattered throughout; ripens in early spring. Small tree with long, pointed, pale green leaves. Brought into Hawaii from Queensland, Australia. J22

Seedless: Completely seedless fruit, slightly malformed; less appealing in flavor than seeded types. Splits badly during hot, humid summer weather; resists splitting in the cooler, drier winter months. MORTON 1987a, WHITMAN; **T73M{SC}**

Ubol: A cultivar with a relatively hard skin covering that prevents the fruit from splitting. Introduced into Florida from Thailand, by William F. Whitman. WHITMAN; **T73M{SC}**

Anonidium mannii - *Junglesop* {S} The very large elongated fruits, weighing between ten and fifteen pounds, are eaten out of hand. The soft, yellow flesh varies from sweet and delicious to somewhat sour, depending on the cultivar and the maturity of the fruit when picked. Tropical Africa. UPHOF; **X44**

Artabotrys uncinatus - *Climbing ylang ylang* {S} Flowers are used to scent tea. Southeast Asia. TANAKA; F85, Q46

Asimina grandiflora - *Florida pawpaw* {PL} Fruits are said to be eaten. Can be hybridized with A. triloba. Southeastern North America. DARROW, TANAKA; N37M

Asimina obovata → Asimina grandiflora

Asimina parviflora - *Dwarf pawpaw* {PL} The fruits are edible but not pleasant. Hybridizes with A. triloba. Southeastern North America. DARROW; N37M, N51

Asimina triloba - *Pawpaw, Michigan banana, False banana* {PL} Soft, creamy fruits have the flavor of banana custard and are delicious eaten out of hand. They can also be used for making preserves, pies, ice cream, cookies, cakes, and other sweet desserts. North America. ANGIER [Re], DARROW, FERNALD, GIBBONS 1962 [Re], LOGSDON 1981, SIMMONS 1972, THOMSON 1974 [Cu, Pro]; A80M, A82, B73M, C91, C91{S}, D37, F16, F57M, H4, H53{S}, I11M, I49M, I60, I74, J33, K38{S}, K63G{S}, N15, N37M, N84{S}, etc.

CULTIVARS {GR}

Davis: Small to medium, kidney-shaped fruit, up to 4 3/4 inches long; weight 4 ounces or more; skin green when ripe; flesh yellow, sweet, flavor good, seeds large; ripens the first week in October in Michigan. Keeps well in cold storage. Originated in Bellevue, Michigan by Corwin Davis. Introduced in 1961. BROOKS 1972; B74{PL}, B99, C91, K16{PL}, K67

Mary Foos Johnson: Good sized fruit with smooth, flavorful flesh and relatively few seeds. Originated in Mollala, Oregon by Jim Gilbert of Northwoods Nursery. I49M

Mitchell: Very tasty, large fruit on a handsome tree with large leaves. H4

Overleese: Large, oval to round fruits, weight up to 6 ounces; flesh firm, flavor very good; ripens the first week in October in Michigan. Tree very vigorous; productive, bears fruit in clusters of 3 to 5. Introduced in 1974. B99, C91, H4, K67

Rebecca's Gold: Blunt, kidney-shaped fruit, weight 3 1/2 to 6 ounces; skin smooth and somewhat tender, green with slight bloom, turns yellowish when ripe; flesh chrome-yellow, melting, sweet and aromatic; seed unusually large, mostly 8 per fruit. Tree vigorous, upright, free of suckering; self-fruitful, bears 4 to 5 fruit per stem. Originated in Bellevue, Michigan by Corwin Davis. K67

Sunflower: Fruit large, about 8 to 12 ounces, borne in clusters of up to 5; skin has a yellowish cast when ripe; flesh butter-colored, flavor excellent; seeds few, often only 6 to 8; ripens the first week in October in Michigan. Tree wide rather than pyramidal; blooms and ripens its fruit slightly later than most cultivars; self-fertile; hardy in southern Michigan. Originated near Chaute, Kansas. B74, C91, I49M, K67

Sweet Alice: Large fruit with good flavor, borne in large clusters without hand-pollination. Originated in Mentor, Ohio by Homer L. Jacobs of the Holden Arboretum. G75{CF}, K67

Taylor: (Taylor #1) Small to medium-sized fruit; skin green when ripe; flesh yellow, sweet, flavor slightly better than Davis; ripens the first week in October. Tree fairly productive, bears fruit in clusters of up to 7. Discovered by Dr. Lee Taylor of Michigan State University. Introduced in 1974. C91

Taytwo: (Taylor #2) Large fruit, weighing up to 10 ounces; skin light green in color when ripe; flesh yellow, of excellent flavor; ripens from the 10th of October onward in southern Michigan. Tree a rather shy bearer. Discovered by Dr. Lee Taylor of Michigan State University. Introduced in 1974. C91

Zimmerman: One of the superior selections collected by the late George A. Zimmerman of Piketown, Pennsylvania during the first half of the 20th century. E62{PL}

Cananga odorata - *Ylang-ylang* {S} Fragrant flowers are used to scent coconut oil. The essential oil distilled from the flowers is used as a flavoring in candies, icings, baked goods, soft drinks, and chewing gum. Southeast Asia. MORTON 1976, UPHOF; A79M, F85, J36{PL}, N84

Friesodielsia obovata - *Monkey fingers* {S} The scarlet fruits have a sweetly acid and mildly peppery flavor when eaten raw. They can be cooked as a rich red acid jelly or fermented into a pleasant wine. Southern Africa. FOX, F.; F85

Monanthotaxis caffra - *Dwaba berry* {S} The slightly acidulous fruits are eaten fresh. Southern Africa. FOX, F.; Z77M

Monodora myristica - *Calabash nutmeg, Jamaica nutmeg* {S} Spicy seeds, resembling true nutmeg in flavor, are commonly sold in African markets. They are used to flavor soups and other foods. Tropical Africa. BURKILL, DALZIEL, MORTON 1976, UPHOF; F85, N84

Monodora tenuifolia - *Striped calabash-nutmeg* {S} The aromatic seeds are widely used locally for seasoning soups and other foods. Fruits are also eaten. West Tropical Africa. DALZIEL, IRVINE 1960, MORTON 1976; N84

Rollinia deliciosa - *Biribá, Countess' fruit, Amazon custard-apple* {PL} The yellow fruits have a juicy, melting flesh of a very pleasing flavor, reminiscent of lemon meringue pie. Mostly eaten fresh, but can be used for pies, ice cream and cakes or made into wine. One of the most promising fruits of the expanding rare fruit market in Australia. Brazil, cultivated. MORTON 1987a, POPENOE, W. 1920, UPHOF; F68, J22, N84{S}, P38{S}, *Q93*

Rollinia mucosa - *Wild cachiman, Wild sweetsop* {S} Yellow fruits have a white, mucilaginous, sweet pulp. Eaten fresh or in desserts. Tropical America. KENNARD, MARTIN 1987, UPHOF; N84, P38

Stelechocarpus burakol - *Keppel apple* {S} Round fruits, born on the trunks of the tree, are juicy, sweet, and fragrant. It is claimed that after eating these fragrant fruits, one's whole body is permeated with the smell of roses. Malaysia. FAIRCHILD 1930, RIFAI; T73M

Uvaria chamae - *Bush banana* {S} The fruit is edible, having a flavor somewhat resembling that of bananas. Tropical Africa. DALZIEL; N84

Xylopia aethiopica - *Ethiopian pepper, Spice tree* {S} Seeds and fruits are the source of an aromatic peppery spice once commonly exported to Europe. Now used locally to flavor coffee, palm wine and various dishes. Sold in markets of Senegal and other parts of Africa. Tropical Africa, cultivated. HEDRICK 1919, MORTON 1976, UPHOF; F85, N84

Xylopia frutescens - *Malagueto chico* {S} The fruits have an acrid, aromatic taste and are used as a substitute for pepper. It is said that the flesh of wild pigeons feeding on them permanently takes on their flavor. Brazil, Guiana. HEDRICK 1919, LOVELOCK, TANAKA; P28

APIACEAE (*UMBELLIFERAE*)

Aciphylla squarrosa - {S} Roots are said to be very good tasting. New Zealand. KUNKEL; N84, S43M

Aegopodium podagraria - *Gout weed, Ashweed, Ground elder, Herb Gerard* {S} Young leaves and stems, having an unusual tangy flavor, are eaten raw in salads, cooked as greens, or made into fritters. Consumed by the country people of Northwest Germany during spring, in *grüne suppe* (green soup). Eurasia, naturalized in North America. HEDRICK 1919, LARKCOM 1984, LAUNERT, MABEY, MICHAEL [Re], UPHOF; B9M{PL}, B47{PL}, D11T{PL}, D62, E61, K2{PL}, N84, O48

Ammi majus - *Bishop's weed, Queen Anne's lace* {S} The seeds are used as a condiment. Eurasia. KUNKEL; B44, C13M, C43M, C43M{PL}, C61M, D26, E7M, E73M, F24, F44, F80, H80, J82, J88, K66, O53M, *Q25*, Q34, *Q52*, etc.

Ammi visnaga - *Toothpick, Bishop weed* {S} Leaves are chewed for their pleasant aromatic flavor. Eurasia. TANAKA; I99

Anethum graveolens - *Dill* {PL} The young leaves, known as *dill weed* or *baby dill*, are used as a seasoning for salads, soups, eggs, vegetables, sour cream, cream cheese, gravlax, vinegars, and sauces. Seeds and flowers add flavor to pickles, gravies, stews, mustards and breads. Dill oil is used by the food industry in pickles, condiments, meat products, chewing gum, and candy. Sprouted seeds are eaten in breads, soups, and salad dressings. Both leaves and seeds can be brewed into tea, that made from the latter having a milder flavor. Eurasia, cultivated. GESSERT, GRIEVE, HEDRICK 1919, LATHROP [Cu], LEGGATT, MARCIN, MORTON 1976, ROOT 1980b; B75{S}, C13M{S}, D29, F21, G84, H3M, H40, I39{S}, I91{S}, J66, K22{S}, *M35*, N19M (also see Sprouting Seeds, page 485)

CULTIVARS {S}

Aroma: Dark-green, leafy plants produce much more green matter before forming seed. Has a particularly fine fragrance and flavor. Excellent for *dill weed*, used either fresh or dried. Vigorous, bushy plants are heavy yielding and late blooming. Tetraploid. J82, K22, L89

Bouquet: 65 days. Leaves deep blue-green; stems slender; large, fairly compact head. Plant is relatively bushy, 30 to 40 inches, slightly earlier than Mammoth. Once the leaves turn yellow, they remain yellow for a long time before turning brown. The best cultivar to grow for the production of seeds. GESSERT; *A75*, *B39M*{PL}, B75M, C13M, C44, D26, D29{PL}, D82, E99, F24, F82, G68, H46, *H61*, K66, K73, L97, M49, etc.

Dukat: Leaves blue-green; flavor very good, mellow and sweetly aromatic, never bitter or overly pungent. Plant vigorous; an abundant producer of leaves; holds longer at the leaf stage than other dills. *A1*, A13, C13M, C53, C81M, E5T, E81M, I77, J7, K66, *R23*, R53M, S27, S55

Dura: Early outdoor type. Fine, light-colored foliage. High yielding. Produces numerous, small flower clusters ideal for use in pickling. Originated in Sweden. P69, S27

Long Island Mammoth: (Mammoth) 70 days. Leaves greenish, comparatively few in number. Plant 24 to 36 inches tall, vigorous, runs to seed very readily. Produces large productive heads which make unusual decoration. Grown primarily for the seeds. A2, *A74*{PL}, *A75*, B78, C44, D26, F12, F24, G16, G64, G71, *H61*, H66, L7M, S55, etc.

Sari: An improved form which is more aromatic than other types. L91M

Tetra: High quality tetraploid dill developed especially for its lush green foliage. Grows bushier and more vigorously than standard dill. Slow to bolt. Excellent for *dill weed*. Has double the normal number of chromosomes resulting in greater vigor and increased yields of foliage and seed. A87M, E81M, I39, Q34

Vierling: A German cultivar specially selected to produce extra large flat-topped clusters of tiny yellow, green and white flowers for cutting, either fresh or dried. The fragrant, very fine feathery leaves are an attractive bluish-green. Very productive plant; height 2 1/2 feet. C13M, C61M, E81M, *O1*, O53M, *Q52*

Anethum graveolens 'Sowa' - *Indian dill, Satapashpi* {S} The fresh leaves are eaten with steamed rice or used for flavoring soups. Although pungent and bitter, the seeds are more popular than common dill and are an essential ingredient in curry powder. In Indonesia, they are used in pastries and drinks. Plants are taller than common dill, attaining a height of 2 to 4 feet. GESSERT, MORTON 1976, TANAKA; C43M, C82, F85, J67M, J82, K22, O48, S59M

Anethum sowa → *Anethum graveolens*

Angelica archangelica - *Angelica* {PL} The leafstalks are blanched and eaten like celery or combined with rhubarb in pies, sauces, and jams. Aromatic, licorice-flavored leaves are eaten in salads or cooked with fish or poultry. Candied flower stems and leafstalks are used in pastries, cakes, and confectionery. The seeds and roots are the source of an essential oil that flavors ice cream, candy, baked goods, puddings, cordials, *Benedictine*, *Chartreuse*, *vermouth*, gins, etc. Dried leaves are used in the preparation of hop bitters. Leaves, seeds, and roots are brewed into tea. Eurasia, cultivated. GRIEVE [Pre, Re], LATHROP, MARCIN, MORTON 1976, TANAKA, UPHOF, VILMORIN [Cu]; C3, C13M{S}, C67M, C81M, D29, E5M{PR}, E61, F31T, F35M, G84, H3M, H46{S}, I89M{PR}, J66M{PR}, K22, N19M, N45, etc.

Angelica atropurpurea - *Purple angelica, Masterwort* {S} Tender new stems and leafstalks are peeled and eaten in salads or blanched and used like asparagus. When boiled in two waters, they form a vegetable that strongly resembles stewed celery. The young leaves can be added to fish dishes, soups and stews. Roots, leafstalks and stems are candied. North America. CROWHURST 1972 [Re], FERNALD, MORTON 1976; C64M, F85, G47M, J39M

Angelica gigas - *Oni-no-dake, Korean angelica* {S} The young leaves are pickled, boiled or fried and eaten. Eastern Asia. TANAKA; C13M, C81M{PL}

Angelica sylvestris - *Woodland angelica, Wild angelica, Ground ash* {S} Young stems and leaves are boiled and eaten as a vegetable. The chopped leaves are a good addition to stewed fruits, especially rhubarb. Stems and leafstalks are used in candies and sweetmeats. Eurasia. MABEY [Pre, Re], TANAKA; D62, *N71M*, N84, O48, O53M, Q34

Angelica ursina - *Ezonyû* {S} Young leaves and stems are eaten raw or dried and stored for later use. Eastern Asia. TANAKA; **U71M, V34, Y43M**

Anthriscus cerefolium - *Chervil, French parsley, Cerfeuil* {PL} The leaves, when young, impart a warm, aromatic flavor to soups, stews, stuffings, egg dishes, potato salads, sauces, dressings, and tossed salads. They constitute the basis of the herbal mixture known by the French name of *fines herbes*. As a garnish they are added to meats and fish. The flowers are also used as a seasoning. Roots are consumed. Eurasia, cultivated. DE SOUNIN [Cul], HEDRICK 1919, KRAFT, LATHROP [Cu], LEGGATT [Re], MORTON 1976, VILMORIN; C3, C3{S}, C9, C81M{S}, E5M{PR}, E7M{S}, F21, F31T, F35M, G84, H3M, H46{S}, K66{S}, *M35*, *N40*{PR}, etc.

CULTIVARS {S}

Brussels Winter: An improved European selection. Leaves are dark green, lacy, with a pleasant anise flavor. Plant is vigorous, slow to bolt, becomes much larger, and is more resistant to both heat and cold than older types. C53, D68, G6, I39, I77, Q34, *R11M*

Crespo: An improved form of a very old European strain. Very finely curled, moss-like foliage. One of the slowest to run to seed. P59M

Curled: (Curly, Cerfeuil Frisé) The leaves are crisped or curled, very ornamental, and are better for garnishing; the aroma and flavor are the same as common chervil. It is more easily cultivated, earlier, of more vigorous growth, less hardy, and more productive. BURR [Cu], VILMORIN; B75, C13M, C81M, E99, F24, G93M, H3M, I91, J73, K22, K71, M46, M82, M95

Lettuce Leaf: An improved form with very large leaves. K2

Vertissimo: Hardy type with dark green leaves. Very slow in running to seed. Grows back quickly after having been cut. Sown in the summer for a winter harvest. P59M

Anthriscus sylvestris - *Woodland chervil, Beaked parsley, Cow parsley* {S} Young leaves are sometimes eaten as a potherb or dried and stored for future use. Small quantities can be used for seasoning soups, salads, omelettes, casseroles, baked potatoes, and bean dishes. The roots are edible and are recommended for improvement by selection and breeding. Eurasia. MABEY, VILMORIN; D62, F80, K47T, *N71M*, N84

Apium graveolens - *Celery* Leafstalks are blanched and eaten raw in salads, fried, braised, steamed, stuffed with cream cheese, or added to soups, stews, stuffings, and casseroles. Leaves can be chopped and added to tossed green salads. Celery seed, seed extract, and oil are used for flavoring sauces, soups, omelettes, beverages, pickles, celery salt, bakery products, etc. Eurasia, cultivated. CARCIONE [Re], FELL 1982b, LARKCOM 1984, MORTON 1976, ROOT 1980b [Cul], UPHOF, VILMORIN [Cu]; (for cultivars see Celery, page 289)

Apium graveolens Rapaceum Group - *Celeriac, Celery root, Turnip-rooted celery, Knob celery* Roots are sliced or grated and eaten raw in salads, braised, puréed, marinated, baked, mashed, cooked as a vegetable, or used in soups, stews, fritters, and stuffings. Fermented celeriac root juice, sold under the brand names *Biotta* and *Eden*, is popular with those following a natural foods diet. Leaves can be used for flavoring soups and stews. Often succeeds in areas not suited for celery culture. DE SOUNIN [Cul], HALPIN [Cu], HAWKES [Re], HEDRICK 1919, HUNTER 1973a, KRAFT, ORGAN, SCHNEIDER [Pre, Re], UPHOF, VILMORIN [Cu]; (for cultivars see Celeriac, page 288)

Apium graveolens Secalinum Group - *Leaf celery, Soup celery, Cutting celery, Céleri a couper* {S} A group of cultivars that have been little improved by cultivation, and closely resemble the wild celery. Generally, they produce an abundance of erect-growing leaves. The stalks are hollow, rather thin, tender, and brittle. They send up great numbers of suckers, and are grown for their strongly aromatic leaves, which are cut like parsley and used for flavoring soups and stews. After being cut they produce new leaves. LARKCOM 1984, VILMORIN, ZEVEN; C67M{PL}, C85M, E5T, F24, G64, H46, I77, J82, K49M, O48, P83M, R53M, S55

CULTIVARS

Afina: Large, clumping, upright plant that produces numerous shoots; leafstalks hollow and tender. Very aromatic, dark-green foliage, excellent for flavoring soups. Regrows quickly after having been cut. P59M

Amsterdam Fine: Attractive 12 to 18 inch plant with crisp, dark green, somewhat serrated foliage that looks like a very shiny, flat-leaved parsley. Fresh or dried, they add a rich, mellow flavor to foods. Very easy to dry and does not lose its flavor in storage. Ready for picking when stalk celery is high in price. *E91G*, K66, N84

French Dinant: Sends out a multitude of narrow thin stalks. Has a much fuller flavor than common stalk celery and is excellent for seasoning soups, stews, salads, and dressings. Resistant to light frosts. Can be dried and stored for winter use. A2, I39, L91M

Golden Medium Early: (Chinese Golden Medium Early, Golden Leaved) Yellowish-green leaves with long, crisp hollow stalks. Smaller and more delicate than Western cultivars. Has a very pleasant aroma, and a more subtle combination of flavors than Western types. D55, L59, *L79G*

Heung Kunn: (Chinese Celery, Kintsai) The plant has a branching rather than a bunching habit, which makes it easier to harvest individual leafstalks as needed. These are thin, hollow, have a strong flavor, and should de picked when young as older ones lose their crisp tenderness. Both the leaves and stalks are used in stir-fried dishes, or used as a garnish in bowls of soup. COST 1988 [Cul], DAHLEN [Pre, Cul], KRAFT [Cu, Cul]; A2, A79M, E59, H49, M46, N84, S55, *S63M*

Par-Cel: Attractive plant with tender, dark-green leaves that resemble parsley; height approximately 18 inches. Rich, warm aromatic flavor. European heritage cultivar from the seed bank at Gatersleben, Germany. Traditionally boiled, eaten raw, or used specifically for soup flavoring. L91M

Smallage: 90 days. Plants are tall, to 2 feet, with slender, yellowish green stalks and leaves. The leaves are smaller and more flavorful than those of regular celery, and are used for seasoning soups and stews. Both the leaves and stalks are blanched for use by planting densely. E49, F80, K2, L86, *P39*

Zwolsche Krul: An old Dutch heritage cultivar with extra dark green leaves and a height of 2 1/2 to 3 feet. Bred for the production of leaves not leafstalks. Quite hardy, hardier than common stalk celery. Excellent in soups and stews, and for drying. C53, D11M, J20

Arracacia xanthorhiza - *Peruvian carrot, Apio, Arracacha* {PL} The starchy tubers are eaten boiled, steamed, fried, added to soups and stews, or made into fritters and *chicha*. In flavor, they are faintly reminiscent of parsnips or celery with a hint of sweetness, and the texture is like that of potato or cassava. Also the source of a starch used in foods. Blanched young shoots can be eaten in salads or cooked as a vegetable. Andean South America, cultivated. DUKE, HERKLOTS, HODGE 1954 [Cu, Pro], NATIONAL RESEARCH COUNCIL 1975a, NATIONAL RESEARCH COUNCIL 1989, ORTIZ 1979; **U71M, U93M**

Athamanta cervariaefolia → *Athamanta sicula*

Athamanta cretensis - *Candy carrot* {S} Seeds are used for flavoring liqueurs. Mediterranean region. HEDRICK 1919; D62, N84, *Q24*, S7M

Athamanta sicula - *Spignel* {S} The root is said to be eaten. Mediterranean region. HEDRICK 1919; **W59M, X47, Y99**

Bunium bulbocastanum - *Earth chestnut, Tuberous-rooted caraway* {S} Starchy tubers are eaten raw in salads or boiled and served as a vegetable. Leaves are used like parsley. The flowers and seeds are employed as condiments. Eurasia. KUNKEL, LOVELOCK, TANAKA, UPHOF; F80, I99

Bupleurum rotundifolium - *Thorowax* {S} Leaves are eaten in salads or cooked as a potherb. Also said to be used as a spice. Eurasia. HEDRICK 1919, TANAKA; C61M, N84, O48

Carum bulbocastanum → *Bunium bulbocastanum*

Carum carvi - *Caraway* {PL} Seeds are widely used for flavoring breads, sauerkraut, sausages, *Kümmel* cheese, cookies, cakes, brandy *schnapps*, and a liqueur, also called *kümmel*. They are often sugar-coated and eaten as a confection. The young leaves form a good salad while older ones may be boiled and served like spinach or added to soups and stews. Roots are boiled and eaten or chopped and used in soups. Seeds are crushed and brewed into a tea. The seed oil is used commercially in ice cream, candy, pickles, soft drinks, etc. Eurasia, cultivated. GRIEVE, HEDRICK 1919, KRAFT, MARCIN, MORTON 1976, ROOT 1980b [Cul], UNDSET, UPHOF, VILMORIN [Cu]; B75{S}, C3{S}, C11{S}, C13M{S}, C43M, F21, F31T, F35M, G84, H46{S}, K22{S}, *M35*, N19M, N45

Carum copticum → *Trachyspermum ammi*

Carum segetum → *Ridolfia segetum*

Chaerophyllum bulbosum - *Turnip-rooted chervil, Tuberous chervil, Cerfeuil tubéreux* {S} The roots are eaten boiled, steamed, puréed, or used as a garnish for game. Their flesh is aromatic, floury, and sweet, with a peculiar aromatic flavor. The flavor is excellent and unlike that of any other vegetable. Do not peel the roots or the flavor will be ruined. For a change, the cooked roots can be sliced and fried in butter and served garnished with parsley. Eurasia. BROUK, ORGAN [Pre], ROHDE, VILMORIN [Cu]; N84

CULTIVARS

Altan: Stocky, cream-colored roots with a delicious flavor. Will keep in storage for 2 to 3 months. P59M

Chaerophyllum bulbosum ssp. prescottii - *Siberian chervil-turnip, Prescott chervil* {S} The roots are cooked and eaten. They are longer and larger than the common tuberous-rooted chervil, but their flavor is coarser and more like that of the parsnip. Siberia. VILMORIN; **W5, X33, Z88**

Chaerophyllum prescottii → *Chaerophyllum bulbosum ssp. prescottii*

Conopodium denudatum → *Conopodium majus*

Conopodium majus - *Pig nut* {S} The small, tuberous roots are peeled and eaten raw in salads, boiled, roasted, or used in broths and soups. They are said to taste like a cross between raw chestnuts and fresh hazelnuts, with a hot after-taste of radish. Northern Europe. HEDRICK 1919, MABEY, MICHAEL [Re]; F80, N84, O48

Coriandrum sativum - *Coriander, Cilantro, Chinese parsley, Yuen sai, Dhania* {S} Young, aromatic leaves are pickled, stir-fried, used as a garnish, or eaten in soups, fish dishes, guacamole, and salads. Seeds are widely used to season curries, breads, puddings, sausages, cakes, liqueurs, gin essences, and spicy sauces. Confectioners form little pink and white comfits from them. They are often dry roasted to bring out their full flavor and aroma. In Southeast Asia, they are chewed with betel nut. The roots are used extensively in Thai cooking. Mediterranean region, cultivated. CRAWFORD [Pre, Re], GRIEVE, HALPIN, HARRINGTON, G. [Cu, Cul], HERKLOTS, KENNEDY, D. [Cul], KRAFT [Re], SHURTLEFF 1979, TANAKA, UPHOF; *B39M*{PL}, E59, E99, F21{PL}, F71M, G84, H40{PL}, H46, K22, L59, L79M, L90G{PR}, *M35*{PL}, N19M{PL}

CULTIVARS

Bengal Giant: Leaves and seeds are used in Mexican and Oriental cooking. Height of plant 3 1/2 feet. Flowers, much like Queen Anne's lace, are useful for cutting, both fresh and for the glossy green seed heads. I91, N84

Indian: 40 days. Annual type with oblong-shaped seeds. Seeds are sweeter and have a fuller flavor; used in curries or eaten like candy when sugar coated. Crushed leaves are more aromatic and superior in flavor to commercial coriander. Most highly esteemed cultivar in India. J73

Kasturi Sweet Scented: An improved form with very aromatic foliage. O39M

Large Leaved: 35 days. A relatively slow flowering type which produces large quantities of young leaves for vegetable use. D55

Moroccan: One of the best cultivars for the production of seeds. Quick to bolt and with minimal leaf production. N84, S55

Santo: (Slow Bolt, Long Standing, Leafy) A new strain that produces lush vegetative growth through several cuttings and is relatively non-bolting. Although it is slow to bolt to seed, it is best to make succession plantings every few weeks to ensure a continuous harvest. Height 18 inches. Most productive in cool weather. *C28*, D92{PL}, I39, I99, J73, K66, L59, L89, M46, N52

Crithmum maritimum - *Samphire, Rock samphire, Sea fennel* {PL} The salty, slightly spicy leaves are pickled in vinegar, added to salads, or used like capers for flavoring other foods. In Italy and Greece, the leaves are washed, cut into small pieces, and mixed with olive oil and lemon juice to prepare an agreeable salad dressing. Mediterranean region. BIANCHINI, FRANKE [Nu], GRIEVE, HAWKES, MICHAEL [Pre, Re], UPHOF, VILMORIN [Cu]; E5M, E48, E61, G96, H51M, K22, L56, M82

Cryptotaenia canadensis - *Honewort, Wild chervil* {S} Young leaves, stems, and flowers are boiled and eaten as a potherb, chopped and added to salads, or used in green soups. The roots can be scrubbed and boiled in salted water for 20 minutes and served with butter and a sprinkling of parsley, or with a cream sauce. The seeds can be used as a flavoring for cookies, cakes, and breads. Stems are candied in sugar. North America. CROWHURST 1972, FERNALD, GIBBONS 1979; K47T

Cryptotaenia japonica - *Mitsuba, Japanese parsley, Japanese honewort, Trefoil* {S} The leaves and blanched leafstalks are eaten raw in salads and sandwiches, boiled, fried, added to soups, or used in egg dishes, tempura, and as a garnish. Often dressed with ground sesame seeds or soy sauce. Roots can be blanched for five minutes, then sautéed in sesame oil, or they can be boiled together with diced parsnips. Seeds are utilized as a seasoning. Japan, cultivated. COST 1988 [Cul], HARRINGTON, G. [Cu, Cul], LARKCOM 1984, MORTON 1976, SHURTLEFF 1975, TANAKA, YASHIRODA; C13M, C43M{PL}, E49, E59, E61{PL}, G20M{PR}, G33, G68, G84{PL}, J73, K22, K22{PL}, L59, M46, O53M, etc.

CULTIVARS

Masumori: 30 days. A favorite cultivar in Japan. D55

Cuminum cyminum - *Cumin* {S} Aromatic seeds are widely used for flavoring soups, pickles, breads, cakes, cookies, *Leyden* and *Kuminost* cheeses, curry powders, chutneys, chili sauce, cordials, etc. Occasionally they are candied. The ground spice is a standard ingredient of commercial curry powder. Cumin seed oil is used in condiments, sausages, meat sauces, etc. Especially popular in Spanish, Mexican, and Indian cuisines. Eurasia, cultivated. DE SOUNIN, LATHROP [Cu], MORTON 1976, PAINTER [Cul, Re], ROOT 1980b [Cul], USDA; A2, C11, C13M, *E91G*, F24, F80, I39, I91, K22, L91M, M46, M82, S55

CULTIVARS {PR}

Black: (Siyah Zeera, Shah Zeera) An expensive spice occasionally sold in Indian stores. The seeds are darker, finer, and more complex in flavor than ordinary cumin. Sometimes confused with Nigella sativa. JAFFREY; A88T, F74

Daucus carota - *Wild carrot, Queen Anne's lace* {S} Roots are sometimes cooked and eaten as a vegetable or added to soups and stews. The aromatic seeds are used for flavoring stews, soups, fish chowders, and savory sauces. Dried and roasted roots are ground and utilized as a substitute for coffee. Flower clusters can be French-fried into a carrot-flavored gourmet treat. Northern temperate region. CROWHURST 1972, FERNALD, GIBBONS 1979, HARRINGTON, H.; C11, C13M, C43M, C82, D11T{PL}, F24, F33, I11M, I19, I19{PL}, I37M{PL}, I94{PL}, J53, M47M, N9M{PL}, etc.

Daucus carota Sativus Group - *Carrot* The sweet roots are widely used raw in salads, boiled, steamed, fried, pickled, made into jam and wine, or used in soups, stews, casseroles, etc. Pigment from the juice of the orange-red cultivars is sometimes used for coloring butter. An alcoholic tincture of the seeds is used in French liqueurs. Carrot seed oil is used as a flavoring. Carrot root juice, both raw and fermented, is a very popular beverage with natural foods enthusiasts. It is sometimes made into a syrup used for sweetening. The leaves are sometimes eaten. Flour, made from dried roots, may be used to flavor and thicken soups, dips, sauces, breads, pancakes, muffins, puddings, and custards. Pectic acid can be extracted from the root and solidified into a wholesome, appetizing jelly. FELL 1982b, GRIEVE [Cu, Re], LARKCOM 1984, MARTIN 1975, MILIUS [Re], TANAKA, UPHOF, VILMORIN [Cu]; (for cultivars see Carrot, page 283)

Daucus pusillus - *American carrot, Rattlesnake weed* {S} Roots were consumed by the Navajo and Nez Percé Indians. The Navajo of northern Arizona are reported to still use the plant, eating the roots raw or cooked. Western North America. KIRK, YANOVSKY; I98M

Echinophora spinosa - *Prickly samphire, Sea parsnip* {S} The roots are edible, having the flavor of parsnips. The young leaves are said to make excellent pickles. Mediterranean region. HEDRICK 1919; **Y10**

Eryngium campestre - *Snakeroot* {S} Young shoots are used as a substitute for asparagus. Candied roots are occasionally eaten in France and England. They are also cooked and used as a vegetable. Europe. TANAKA, UPHOF; *N71M*, N84, *Q24*, S7M

Eryngium foetidum - *Culantro, Recao de monte, False coriander* {PL} Young leaves are sometimes eaten raw or steamed and served with rice. They have a strong coriander-like aroma, and are more commonly used as a garnish for fish and for flavoring soups and curries. Roots are used as a condiment in soups and meat dishes to which they impart a very agreeable flavor. The seeds are also said to be used. In West Indian markets of New York and other large cities, a seasoning mixture called *sofrito* is widely sold. Its three main ingredients are culantro, cilantro, and *ajicitos* (small chilis, usually mild bonnet peppers, Capsicum chinense). Tropical America, cultivated. ALTSCHUL, CHANTILES [Re], DUKE, MORTON 1976, OCHSE, UPHOF, WILLIAMS, L.; C43M, F80{S}, M82

Eryngium maritimum - *Sea holly, Sea eryngo* {S} The young, tender, flowering shoots, when blanched, may be boiled and eaten like asparagus. When boiled or roasted, the roots are said to resemble chestnuts or parsnips in taste. The candied roots were known as *eringoes*, to which Shakespeare refers in The Merry Wives of Windsor. They were a vital ingredient of the Elizabethan dish, *marrow-bone pie*. European coasts, Asia Minor. GENDERS 1977, GRIEVE, HEDRICK 1919, MABEY; B61M, D62, H3M{PL}, J67M, M82{PL}, N84, O53M, P92{PL}, S55

Ferula assa-foetida - *Asafoetida, Food-of-the-gods* {S} The roots are the source of a gum resin used as a flavoring in lentil soup, curried fish, vegetarian dishes, sauces, drinks, pickles, cakes, etc. It is a standard ingredient of Worcestershire sauce and is widely employed in spice blends and condiments. Also popular in natural foods cuisine as a substitute for garlic. Young shoots are consumed as a cooked green vegetable. The cabbage-like folded heads are eaten raw as a delicacy. Roots are roasted and eaten. Southwest Asia, cultivated. GRIEVE, HEDRICK 1919, JAFFREY, MORTON 1976, UPHOF, VON WELANETZ; A2, A88T{PR}, C43M, C43M{PL}, E7M, F74{PR}, I99{PL}, M82{PL}, N84

Ferula communis - *Giant anise fennel* {S} Leaves are edible. North Africa. MARTIN 1975; C43M, C43M{PL}, I99, N84

Ferula foetida - *Higra* {S} Leaves are used as greens. Source of a resin having the same use as that from F. assa-foetida. Southern Asia. TANAKA, UPHOF, WATT; **W3M**

Foeniculum vulgare - *Fennel, Wild fennel, Bitter fennel, Sweet fennel* {PL} The anise-flavored leaves are used as a garnish or as a seasoning for soups, salads, sauces, and fish. Aromatic seeds, whole or ground, are used in stuffings, sausages, breads, cookies, cakes, cheese, confectionery, liqueurs, etc. Fennel oil is also employed for flavoring. The stems and flower heads are used as vegetables. Dried stalks form the basis of the famous Provencal red mullet dish, *rouget flambé au fenouil*. Sprouted seeds are added to salads. A tea can be made by steeping the seeds or leaves in hot water. Roots are edible. Southern Europe, cultivated. BAILEY, C., CLARKE [Re], GRIEVE, MABEY, MARCIN, MICHAEL [Re], MORTON 1976, ROOT 1980b [Cul], VILMORIN [Cu]; B61M{S}, C13M{S}, D29, E99{S}, F31T, F35M, G68{S}, G84, H46{S}, I91{S}, *M35*, N19M (also see Sprouting Seeds, page 485)

CULTIVARS

Bronze: (Red, Copper, Rubrum) The foliage, especially the new growth, is an attractive brownish-purple in color. Clusters of flat-topped ocher flowers. It is a vigorous grower, and can be used very effectively in a border. Good for culinary use. C11{S}, C13M{S}, C43M, C43M{S}, C53{S}, C67M, D29, E99{S}, F24{S}, G84, H40, K22, *M35*, N19M

Greek: Produces extremely large amounts of foliage and seed for culinary use. H40

Foeniculum vulgare Azoricum Group - *Florence fennel, Finocchio* {S} The blanched leafstalks are eaten raw in salads, steamed, sautéed, braised, puréed, fried, baked, or used in antipasto, soups, chowders, and pasta dishes. Fresh leaves can be used in salads or to give a slight anise flavor to foods. Dried or fresh, they are used in salad dressings. The seeds, which appear in the second year, may be used for flavoring cookies and candies. GRIEVE, HALPIN [Cu, Cul], KRAFT [Re], LARKCOM 1984, SCHNEIDER [Pre, Re], VILMORIN; C13M, C43M{PL}, D29{PL}, F21, F44, G68, G84{PL}, G93M, H40, J20, J66{PL}, L7M, L89, M46

CULTIVARS

Argenta: Forms a bulb quickly, yet is very resistant to bolting. Quality very good. Similar to Zefa Fino but the knobs are more closely packed. Considerably earlier than Zefa Tardo. *R11M*

Autumn Giant: Medium late cultivar which should be sown in July. Medium tall, erect plants produce very large, pure-white heads or knobs of thick, fleshy but very tender texture. *E53M*

Cantino: A very reliable cultivar for spring sowing. Very resistant to bolting and produces fine quality bulbs. S55

Cristal: A selected strain recommended for areas with a short spring and hot summers. Plant in June and July for a fall harvest. Produces a medium-sized, roundish, brilliant pure-white bulb with full, crisp stalks. Q11M

Mammoth: Slow bolting, forms a large, thick bulb before running to seed. Best sown as a fall crop. Pleasant anise-like flavor, delicious cooked or eaten raw in salads. F13

Perfection: Developed in Europe for cool, northern climates. Matures quickly, is easier to grow, and is fairly resistant to bolting. Produces a round, medium sized bulb that is fleshy, tender, and crisp. Delicate aniseed flavor. L91M, P83M, S55

Romy: Large, globular bulbs, the shape preferred by Italian fennel aficionados; crisp delicate flesh with a refined sweet flavor. Produces more usable flesh because it lacks the tough, fibrous wrapper leaves that the more long-standing cultivars may develop. An extremely early maturing Italian heirloom. Suitable for an early spring or fall harvested crop. K66

Sicilian: (Carosella) The plant is used while in the state of running to bloom; the stems fresh and tender, are broken and served up raw, still enclosed in the expanded leaf-stalks. The flavor is quite similar to finocchio, recalling tarragon or chervil. Bulbs can be used in place of finocchio. HALPIN, KRAFT [Re], VILMORIN; C92, I99, K49M

Sirio: An Italian bred cultivar which produces large, white, solid bulbs on compact plants. Very sweet flavor and quite aromatic. Quick maturing and best sown in July for use in autumn. N81, S45M, S61

White Mountain: Medium early cultivar. Best if sown February in a greenhouse for transplanting, or direct sown March through July. Short, erect plants produce very large, snow-white bulbs in late summer. *E53M*

Zefa Fino: (Fino) Slow bolting, can be sown in late spring or early summer with success, whereas other cultivars go to seed before forming a bulb. Vigorous plant, 12 to 18 inches tall; forms a large, tender, very sweet bulb. Recently introduced, and one of Europe's top varieties, bred at the Swiss Federal Research Station. LARKCOM 1984; D68, E24, G6, I39, I77, I99, J7, K49T, K66, N81, Q34, *R11M*, S27, *S75M*

Zefa Tardo: (Wadenswil) Produces thicker bulbs than Zefa Fino with heavy sheaths. Tall foliage. Recommended sowing is late spring to early summer, although late summer to early autumn plantings can be made in mild winter climates. N81, Q34, *R11M*, S27, *S75M*

Glehnia littoralis - *Corkwing, Hama-bôfû* {S} The young leaves and leafstalks are used for their agreeable flavor and fragrance. They are pickled and are often served with sliced raw fish and vinegared dishes. One of the seven herbs that flavor *toso*, sweet Japanese sake. Said to taste like a cross between angelica and tarragon. Grows in strong sun on coastal sand dunes. Eastern Asia. COOK, LOVELOCK, UPHOF, YASHIRODA; **V19**

Heracleum cordatum → *Heracleum sphondylium ssp. montanum*

Heracleum lanatum - *Cow parsnip* {S} The young leafstalks are eaten raw or cooked as greens. Chopped leaves may be added to salads. Peeled stalks can be eaten raw, but are best when cooked. Dried base of the plant and ashes from the burned leaves are used as a substitute for salt. The cooked root is said to have the flavor of rutabaga. Dried seeds are used as a seasoning for soups, stews, and potato salad. Northeast Asia, North America. CROWHURST 1972, FERNALD, GIBBONS 1979, HALL [Pre, Re], HARRINGTON, H., KIRK, UPHOF; C11, C13M, F80, F85, H61M, I98M, I99, J39M, K47T, N7, N45

Heracleum maximum* → *Heracleum lanatum

Heracleum persicum - {S} The seeds are used as a condiment in pickles. Southwest Asia. UPHOF; **X36, Z24**

Heracleum pubescens - *Downy cow-parsnip* {S} The young shoots are filled with a sweet, aromatic juice and are eaten raw by the natives of the Caucasus. Southern Europe, Asia Minor. HEDRICK 1919; **Y89M**

Heracleum sphondylium - *European cow-parsnip, Hogweed* {S} The young shoots and leaves may be boiled and eaten as a green vegetable, and when just sprouting from the ground resemble asparagus in flavor. From the boiled leaves and fruits an alcoholic beverage, called *bartsch*, is prepared. Employed in France to flavor liqueurs. A sweet substance resembling sugar is said to form upon the dried leafstalks, which is eaten as a great delicacy. The peduncles before flowering can be eaten as a vegetable or added to soups. Eurasia. FERNALD, HEDRICK 1919, LAUNERT, UPHOF; F80, F85, K47T, *N71M*, N84, S7M

Heracleum sphondylium ssp. montanum - *Cow parsnip* {S} The root is black, sweet scented, and is used like angelica by the Sicilians. Europe. HEDRICK 1919; I31, N84

Laser trilobum - *Gladich, Baltracan* {S} Stems are eaten. Seeds are used as a condiment. The water in which the leaves are boiled is drunk as wine and is very refreshing. Eurasia. HEDRICK 1919; D62

Laserpitium latifolium - *Laserwort, White gentian* {S} The Romans used the root with cumin in seasoning preserved artichokes. A decoction of the seeds is used in beer. Eurasia. HEDRICK 1919, UPHOF; D62, N84, S7M

Laserpitium siler - {S} Roots and seeds are used by mountain people as a condiment. Seeds are used in Austria for the preparation of a liqueur. Europe. UPHOF; N84, S7M

Leptotaenia dissecta* → *Lomatium dissectum

Levisticum officinale - *Lovage* {PL} The leafstalks and stem bases are blanched and eaten like celery or candied. Young leaves can be chopped and added to salads, soups, omelettes, stews, and seafood dishes. Seeds, either whole or ground, are used for flavoring soups, breads, cookies, confectionery, and French liqueurs. They are sometimes pickled like capers. The flowers are eaten. Roots are the source of *oil of lovage*, used for flavoring. An aromatic tea is made from the dried leaves or grated roots. Roots may be chopped and preserved in honey. Eurasia, cultivated. GRIEVE, HEDRICK 1919, LATHROP, LEGGATT [Re], MORTON 1976, UPHOF, VILMORIN [Cu]; C3, C3{S}, C13M{S}, D29, F21, F31T, G84, H46{S}, I77M, J66, K22, K85, N19M, N45

Ligusticum monnieri - *Giêng sàng, Xà-sàng* {S} Occasionally cultivated in North Vietnam where the herb is used as a condiment. Temperate Asia. UPHOF; F85

Ligusticum scoticum - *Scotch lovage* {S} The young shoots and leafstalks are blanched and used as a celery substitute in tossed green salads or as a flavoring for soups and stews. Young shoots and roots are occasionally candied like angelica. The green stem is peeled and eaten. Roots are chewed. Northern temperate region. ANGIER [Re], FERNALD, GIBBONS 1964 [Re], GRIEVE, HEDRICK 1919, UPHOF; R53M, R53M{PL}

Lomatium californicum - *Wild celery-parsley* {S} Both the large, aromatic roots and flavorful tops were eaten by the Indians. An endangered species. Western North America. I99

Lomatium dissectum - *Fern-leaved biscuit-root* {S} Roots are dried and cooked. Western North America. YANOVSKY; A2, I99

Lomatium macrocarpum - *Large-fruited biscuit-root* {S} The roots are eaten raw, or dried and ground into flour and made into cakes. Tea may be prepared from the leaves, stems and flowers. The tiny seeds are nutritious raw or roasted, and can be dried and ground into flour. North America. HART, KIRK, YANOVSKY; E15

Lomatium nudicaule - *Cow parsley, Smyrnium* {S} The leaves and stems are eaten as a vegetable or used like celery in soups. An infusion of the leaves, stems, and flowers is utilized as a beverage. Roots are sometimes cooked and eaten. In the young plant the vitamin C is remarkably high, one cup providing more than the adult Recommended Dietary Allowance. Western North America. HEDRICK 1919, HILTY [Nu, Pre], YANOVSKY; A2, E15, G82M{PL}, I99

Lomatium utriculatum - *Desert gold, Pomo celery* {S} Young leaves and shoots are eaten as greens. North America. YANOVSKY; A2, E15, K47T

Meum athamanticum - *Spignel, Meu, Baldmoney* {S} The crushed fresh herb can be rubbed on to pork or lamb before cooking. As a condiment it adds a subtle, sweetish-aromatic flavor to soups, stews, and vegetable dishes. The roots are collected and consumed as a parsnip-like vegetable by the Highlanders of Scotland. Europe. GRIEVE, LAUNERT, MABEY, UPHOF; K47T, N84, O48, *Q24*, S7M

Myrrhis odorata - *Sweet cicely* {PL} The sweet, anise-like leaves can be eaten raw in salads, added to soups and stews, used as a garnish for fish dishes, or brewed into tea. Because of its sweet flavor, it is cooked with fruits such as plums and rhubarb to reduce the amount of sugar needed. Roots are boiled and served with oil and vinegar or candied. The fresh seeds are chewed or chopped and mixed with salads to give them an aromatic flavor. Seeds are used for flavoring brandy and *Chartreuse*. Alpine Europe, cultivated. FELL 1982b, GRIEVE, HEDRICK 1919, LAUNERT, MARCIN, MORTON 1976, PAINTER [Cul, Re], UPHOF, VILMORIN [Cu]; C3, C9, C11{S}, C13M{S}, C67M, E7M{S}, E15{S}, G84, G96, K22, K53{S}, N45, O53M{S}

Oenanthe javanica - *Water dropwort, Seri* {PL} Young leaves and stems are eaten raw, steamed, boiled with fish and meat, or chopped fine and used as a seasoning in soups, sukiyaki, and chicken dishes. The slender white roots grow about one foot long in the water, and the prettiest of these are highly esteemed for cooking. In Japan, seri and six other herbs are customarily boiled in rice gruel on January 7th. Seeds are said to be edible. Southeast Asia. ALTSCHUL, HAWKES [Cul], HERKLOTS, OCHSE, TANAKA, YASHIRODA; M82

CULTIVARS {S}

Su Zhou: Medium early cultivar with few fibers and excellent taste. *O54*

Oenanthe pimpinelloides - *Meadow parsley* {S} The roots have been esteemed as food in certain areas. They are said to be starchy, with a flavor somewhat like a filbert. Europe. GRIEVE, HEDRICK 1919; F85, N84

Oenanthe sarmentosa - *Pacific water dropwort, Water parsley* {S} The black tubers have sweet, snow-white, farinaceous flesh that was esteemed by the Indians. Has a cream-like taste when boiled, with a slight parsley flavor. Western North America. HEDRICK 1919, MEDSGER, YANOVSKY; F85

Oenanthe stolonifera* → *Oenanthe javanica

Osmorhiza aristata - *Yabu-ninjin* {S} Young leafstalks are eaten boiled and seasoned, put into soups, or cooked with soy sauce. Roots are eaten raw. The young plant is also cooked and eaten. Southern Asia, Eastern Asia. TANAKA; **V19, X33**

Osmorhiza claytonii - *Anise sweet-cicely* {S} The roots and stems are sometimes eaten as vegetables. Aromatic roots and unripe seeds are used as anise-like flavorings. North America. PETERSON, L., YANOVSKY; B61M, H61M, I31, J39M, J39M{PL}, J42

Osmorhiza longistylis - *Anise-root, Smooth sweet-cicely, Sweet myrrh* {PL} Roots have the spicy taste of anise and are chewed, made into a tea, or used as a flavoring. Anise-flavored leaves and green seeds may be added to salads. Dry seeds are used in cakes, candies and liqueurs. North America. MEDSGER, PETERSON, L., TANAKA; J48

Osmorhiza occidentalis - *Western sweet-cicely* {S} The roots have a sweet licorice or anise flavor and may be dried, ground into a powder and used as a flavoring for cookies and other foods. Dried seeds are used as a seasoning, fl or nibbled raw when they are still fleshy. Western North America. HARRINGTON, H., KIRK; *E66M*

Pastinaca sativa - *Parsnip, Wild parsnip* {S} Roots are eaten raw, boiled, steamed, sautéed, mashed, puréed, baked, or used in soups, stews, sauces, cakes, pies, and puddings. They are also made into marmalade, syrup, beer, and wine. Young leaves and shoots are added to soups or mixed with other greens and eaten as a cooked vegetable. The seeds make a fine condiment, being similar in taste to dill. Eurasia, cultivated. CARCIONE, FELL 1982b, GRIEVE [Re], HAWKES [Re], LAUNERT, MABEY, TANAKA, VILMORIN [Cu]; D58, D62, J82, L86, *N71M*, N84, O48, O53M (for cultivars see Parsnip, page 412)

Perideridia sp. - *Yampa, Squawroot, Ipo, False caraway* {S} The fleshy roots have a pleasant, sweet, nutty flavor and are eaten raw, boiled, baked or preserved for winter use. Occasionally they are dried, ground into flour, and baked in cakes. The seeds are used as a caraway-like seasoning, or parched and eaten in porridge. Western North America. HALL [Re], HARRINGTON, H. [Re], HEDRICK 1919, KIRK, MEDSGER, YANOVSKY; F42

Petroselinum crispum - *Wild parsley, Sheep's parsley* {S} Leaves are used as a garnish or added to soups. The herb can be fried in hot butter and served as a vegetable with fish. Eurasia. LAUNERT, MABEY; L91M, *N71M*, O48

Petroselinum crispum Hortense Group - *Parsley* Leaves are widely used as a garnish or for seasoning soups, stews, salads, dressings, omelettes, *tabouli*, stuffings, etc. Parsley oil, derived from the leaves and seeds, is used by the food industry in sauces, pickles, meats, bakery products, and soups. The stems are dried and powdered and used as a food coloring. Fresh or dried leaves can be brewed into a pleasant tasting tea. GRIEVE, MARCIN, MORTON 1976, ROOT 1980b [Cul], UPHOF, VILMORIN [Cu]; (for cultivars see Parsley, page 410)

Petroselinum crispum Radicosum Group - *Hamburg parsley, Turnip-rooted parsley, Parsnip-rooted parsley, German parsley* {S} The thick, fleshy, parsnip-like roots are thinly sliced or grated, and eaten raw in salads. They are also a popular ingredient in soups and stews or can be roasted, mashed, and fried, or made into chips the way potatoes are. The flavor is delicious and somewhat reminiscent of a combination of celery and parsley, but with a nuttier flavor. Young leaves are such a popular soup and stew ingredient, they are known as *soup greens*. HALPIN [Cu, Cul], KRAFT [Re], ORGAN [Pre, Re], RODALE [Cu], SCHNEIDER [Cul, Re], VILMORIN; A16, C13M, C85M, F24, *F72*, G16, G71, G84{PL}, *H61*, J7, K73, L7M, L79, M13M, *N40*{PR}, etc. (for cultivars see Parsley, page 410)

Petroselinum sativum* → *Petroselinum crispum

Peucedanum nudicaule* → *Lomatium nudicaule

Peucedanum ostruthium - *Masterwort, Hog-fennel* {S} The leaves are boiled and eaten as a potherb. Aromatic roots are used in the preparation of gin, Swiss cheese, and certain herb-cheeses. Europe. HEDRICK 1919, LOVELOCK, TANAKA, UPHOF; F37T{PL}, J82, K47T, N84, *Q24*, S7M

Peucedanum palustre - *Marsh hog's-fennel* {S} In some Slavic countries, the roots are used as a substitute for ginger. Europe. GRIEVE, HEDRICK 1919, LOVELOCK, UPHOF; **V73**, **V73M**, **V84**

Phellopterus littoralis* → *Glehnia littoralis

Pimpinella anisum - *Anise* {S} Aromatic seeds are used as a seasoning in cakes, cookies, breads, cheese, *anisette* liqueur, *anise milk*, confectionery, beverages, wine, icings, etc. The fresh leaves can be chopped and used in salads, soups, stews, vegetable dishes, and sauces. Source of a distilled oil that flavors licorice candy, chewing gum, ice cream, and pickles. Both leaves and seeds are brewed into a sweet, licorice-like tea. Cultivated. GRIEVE, LATHROP [Cu, Cul], MARCIN, MORTON 1976, ROOT 1980b [Cul], UPHOF, VILMORIN; B75, C3, C11, C13M, C81M, D29{PL}, G84, H3M, H3M{PL}, H25, H46, K22, *M35*, N19M{PL}

Pimpinella major - *Greater burnet-saxifrage, White saxifrage* {S} Roots are the source of an essential oil used to flavor candy and liqueurs. Eurasia. MORTON 1976; F35M{PL}, K47T, N84, O48

Pimpinella saxifraga - *Burnet saxifrage* {S} Young leaves and shoots have the flavor of cucumber and can be eaten in salads or used in cooling drinks. They have been tied in bundles and hung in casks of beer, ale, and wine to improve the flavor. The flower heads were formerly made into wine. Seeds are coated with sugar and eaten as a confection. An essential oil from the root is used for flavoring candy and liqueurs. Eurasia. GRIEVE, MORTON 1976, ROOT 1980b [Cu, Cul]; C11, C43M, C43M{PL}, I99, J82, K47T, M53{PL}, M77M{PL}, *N71M*, N84, O48

Ridolfia segetum - {S} An aromatic herb that can be used as a condiment. Mediterranean region. HEDRICK 1919; **U63**, **V73M**, **W59M**

Selinum monnieri* → *Ligusticum monnieri

Silaum silaus - *Pepper saxifrage, Meadow saxifrage* {S} Sometimes cooked as an acid potherb. Europe. HEDRICK 1919; *N71M*, N84, O48

Silaus flavescens* → *Silaum silaus

Siler trilobum* → *Laser trilobum

Sison amomum - *Bastard stone-parsley* {S} The aromatic leaves and seeds can be used as a condiment. Roots are edible, and are said to have the taste of celery. Eurasia. HEDRICK 1919, UPHOF; N84, O48

Sium cicutaefolium - *Water parsnip* {S} Roots have an agreeable nutty flavor and are consumed as food by some Indian tribes in the United States and Canada. The aromatic leaves were eaten by the Klamath Indians as a relish. Eastern North America. FERNALD, UPHOF; G47M

Sium sisarum - *Skirret* {PL} The sweet, floury white roots are eaten raw in salads, boiled, stewed, braised, baked, batter-fried, creamed, or used in soups, stews, pies, and curries. They are delicious when mashed with potatoes, served with a cheese sauce, or dressed in a vinegar marinade and served alone as a salad. Sometimes used as a substitute for coffee. Eurasia, cultivated. HALPIN [Cu, Cul], ORGAN, UPHOF, VILMORIN [Cu]; A2{S}, D62{S}, F80{S}, G84, G96, H51M, I39, K2{S}, K22, K49M, K85, L56, M82, N45, O53M{S}, R47{S}, R53M, R53M{S}, etc.

Sium suave* → *Sium cicutaefolium

Smyrnium olusatrum - *Alexanders, Black lovage* {S} Young shoots and leafstalks are blanched and eaten like celery in salads, soups, sauces, and stews. The thicker stems may be used as a cooked vegetable, and the flowerbuds as a salad. Leafy seedlings can be used as a parsley substitute. The roots are boiled and served with oil and vinegar or used in soups. They are said to be more tender if kept all winter in a cool place. Spicy seeds are used as a pepper substitute. Was cultivated for several centuries, until recent times when it was gradually replaced by celery. Eurasia. HEDRICK 1919, LARKCOM 1984, LOVELOCK, MABEY, MACNICOL [Re], MICHAEL [Pre, Re], PAINTER [Cul, Re], UPHOF, VILMORIN [Cu]; D62, F37T{PL}, F80, I99, J82, N19M{PL}, N84, O48, O53M, P83M, S55

Smyrnium perfoliatum - *Perfoliate alexanders* {S} The blanched leafstalks are eaten raw in salads or used as a potherb. It is considered superior to S. olusatrum, as it not only blanches better, but is more crisp and tender, and not so harsh flavored. Southern Europe. BURR, HEDRICK 1919; N84, O53M

Tordylium apulum - *Roman pimpernel, Small hartwort* {S} Young plants are eaten as a vegetable in some parts of Greece. In Italy, they are used as a condiment. Eurasia. LOVELOCK, UPHOF; **X47, Y18, Y99, Z19**

Trachymene glaucifolia - *Native carrot* {S} The root is reported to be edible, either raw or cooked. Australia. CRIBB; N84

Trachyspermum ammi - *Ajowan, Ajwain, Ammi* {S} The aromatic, pungent seeds are widely used for seasoning curries, vegetable dishes, fritters, cookies, and breads. Their flavor is said to be a combination of anise and oregano with a hint of black pepper. They are also considered a good preservative for canned foods. Ajowan oil, sweeter than oil of thyme, is extracted form both the plant and seeds and used for flavoring. Southern Asia, cultivated. JAFFREY, MACMILLAN, MORTON 1976, UPHOF; A88T{PR}, F74{PR}, J73

Zizia aurea - *Golden alexanders* {S} The golden flower clusters, with the main stem removed, are a welcome addition to a tossed green salad. They also make a delicious cooked vegetable, somewhat in the manner of broccoli. Eastern North America. CROWHURST 1973 [Re]; B51, G47M, H61M, J4, J39M, J39M{PL}, J41M, J41M{PL}, J42, J42{PL}

APOCYNACEAE

Carissa arduina* → *Carissa bispinosa

Carissa bispinosa - *Amatungula, Num-num* {S} The small red fruits, the size of a cherry, have few seeds and are eaten fresh. Southern Africa. FOX, F., MOWRY, POPENOE, W. 1920; **Y2, Z77M**

Carissa carandas - *Karanda, Christ's thorn* {S} Fruits are eaten raw or cooked. When ripe they are eaten fresh as a dessert, or made into wine, drinks, syrups, preserves, tarts, and an acid jelly used with meat and fish. Unripe fruits are pickled. Tropical Asia, cultivated. KENNARD, MORTON 1987a, STURROCK [Pre], WATT; F85, N84, P38, Q12, Q46

Carissa edulis - *Arabian num-num* {S} The milky red pulp of the fruit is sweet and pleasant and is eaten fresh or made into jelly, preserves and vinegar. Pieces of the root are used as a condiment to disguise fish odor or as bitters macerated in rum or gin. Tropical Africa. DALZIEL, FOX, F.; N84

Carissa grandiflora* → *Carissa macrocarpa

Carissa macrocarpa - *Natal plum, Amatungula* {S} The ripe, bright red fruits are eaten out of hand, made into jellies, syrups, pickles, tarts and pies, or stewed into a sauce that very much resembles cranberry sauce. South Africa, cultivated. CREASY 1982 [Re], MORTON 1987a, POPENOE, W. 1920 [Cu], RICHARDSON [Pre, Re], THOMSON 1976; A79M, B62, C9M, F68{PL}, G96{PL}, H49{PL}, H51M{PL}, I57{PL}, K38, *L5M*, N84, O89, P5, P38, R41, etc.

CULTIVARS {GR}

Fancy: Large, nearly round fruit with a pointed end; skin dark red; flesh whitish, flavor very good, seeds few. Bush ornamental, grows 6 feet tall; self-fertile, bears fruit all year along the California coast; flowers fragrant. Makes a uniform hedge. *B41*, C56M, E48, *F53M*

Carissa spinarum - *Karaunda* {S} The fruits are eaten in tarts. Tropical Asia. TANAKA, WATT; F85

Fernaldia pandurata - *Loroco* {S} Flowers are cooked as greens, folded into egg batter, or added to a kind of *tortilla*. Central America. TANAKA, WILLIAMS, L.; **X94**

Hancornia speciosa - *Mangabeira, Mangaba* {S} The pleasant, subacid fruits, yellow streaked with red, are eaten fresh or made into juice, preserves, sherbet and wine. Much esteemed as a marmalade in some parts of Brazil. Brazil. HEDRICK 1919, MARTIN 1987, TANAKA, UPHOF; **T73M**

Plumeria acutifolia* → *Plumeria rubra f. acutifolia

Plumeria rubra - *Frangipani* {S} Flowers are eaten in sweetmeats. Tropical America, cultivated. BURKILL, KUNKEL; A79M, B84{PL}, C56M{PL}, F31M{PL}, F85, G18, G96{PL}, I57{PL}, I83M{PL}, J27, J27{PL}, N84, O53M, Q46, S44, etc.

Plumeria rubra f. acutifolia - *Pagoda tree, Chi-tan-hua* {S} Dried flowers are used as a substitute for tea. Tropical America, cultivated. BURKILL, TANAKA; G91M{PL}, M19, N84, O53M, Q46

Vallaris heynei - *Chama nat* {S} In Thailand, both the leaves and flowers are eaten. Southeast Asia. BURKILL; **Z25M**

Voacanga thouarsii - *Wild frangipani* {S} Fleshy pulp of the fruit is eaten. Wood ashes are used as a substitute for salt in the Sudan. Tropical Africa, Madagascar. FOX, F., KUNKEL; N84

Willughbeia angustifolia - *Kubal madu* {S} The round, bright orange fruit is eaten. Its flesh, which surrounds the large flat seeds, has a sweet, tangy flavor reminiscent of orange sherbet. Borneo. O19, O19{PL}

APONOGETONACEAE

Aponogeton distachyus - *Cape asparagus, Water onion, Water hawthorne* {PL} Flowering spikes are eaten pickled, or as a substitute for asparagus and spinach. The starchy roasted roots are also eaten. Southern Africa. FOX, F., HEDRICK 1919; H30, H82, I90M, K25, M15, M39

AQUIFOLIACEAE

Ilex cassine - *Cassine* {PL} Dried, roasted leaves are used as a tea substitute. Should be used in moderation. Can cause dizziness and have a laxative effect. North America. FERNALD, HEDRICK 1919, MEDSGER, MORTON 1977; *E66*, F85{S}, H4, *I17M*, *J25*, K18, *L5M*{S}, N37M

Ilex glabra - *Inkberry, Gallberry, Appalachian tea* {PL} Dried leaves, after roasting, make a good substitute for yaupon tea. Contains caffeine. Eastern North America. FERNALD, GIBBONS 1979; B9M, H4, *H8*, *J25*, K38{S}, *L5M*{S}, M75, N37M, N84{S}, P49{S}, R78{S}

Ilex latifolia - *Tara-yô, Holly tea* {PL} The leaves are used as a tea substitute, and the seeds as a substitute for coffee. Japan, China. KUNKEL, TANAKA; H4, *H8*, N37M, *P63*{S}, P86

Ilex opaca - *American holly* {PL} Roasted leaves were the most popular tea substitute during the Civil War. Being free of caffeine, they lack the stimulating properties of maté and yaupon. North America. FERNALD, GIBBONS 1966b; E33M, E47, F80{S}, G23, *G28*, H4, H49, I47{S}, K18, K38{S}, K47T{S}, K63G{S}, *K77*, M76, O93{S}, *P63*{S}, etc.

Ilex paraguariensis - *Yerba maté, Paraguay tea, Jesuit tea* {S} Dried, crushed leaves are used as a stimulating beverage, containing about 1% caffeine. It has a light green color, a pleasant aroma and a slightly bitter flavor. The most popular beverage in South America, preferred over coffee and tea. Usually graded into Maté grosso, Maté fino, and Maté entrefino. Andean South America, cultivated. BROUK, SCHERY, UPHOF; C43M{PL}, C56M{PL}, E48{PL}, G25M, G96{PL}, H4{PL}, H49, I39{PR}, I59G{PL}, J82, J82{PL}, N84, O93, P38, R47, S55, etc.

Ilex verticillata - *Winterberry, Black alder* {PL} Leaves are dried slowly in a warm attic, crumbled, and then used as a substitute for Oriental tea. Does not contain caffeine. Eastern North America. FERNALD, GIBBONS 1979; B9M, B32, *C47*, D95, E97, G89, H4, I47{S}, K38{S}, *K89*, L12, *M69M*, M76, N7T, O53M{S}, etc.

Ilex vomitoria - *Yaupon, Cassena, Dahoon, Carolina tea* {PL} A mildly stimulating beverage, containing caffeine, is prepared from the leaves. They are roasted slowly in an oven, powdered, and steeped in first cold then boiling water. Also used to flavor ice cream and soft drinks. Southeastern North America. FERNALD, GIBBONS 1979, SCHERY; *A19*, *E66*, H4, *I17M*, I77M, K18, K38{S}, K47T{S}, K63G{S}, N37M, N84{S}

ARACEAE

Acorus calamus - *Calamus, Sweet flag, Myrtle sedge* {PL} Rootstocks are candied, chewed, used as a ginger substitute, and to sweeten the breath. Calamus oil is used to flavor liqueurs, cordials, bitters, ice cream, soft drinks, and vinegar. Inner portion of young shoots makes a very palatable salad. Temperate Asia, cultivated. FERNALD, GIBBONS 1962 [Re], MORTON 1976, UPHOF; C43M, C64M, C64M{S}, D75T, E33M, G47M{S}, G85, G96, H4, J73, K22, L56, M15, M73, N3M, N11, etc.

Acorus gramineus - *Grass-leaved sweet flag, Sekishô* {PL} Rhizomes are peeled, finely chopped, steeped in several waters, and then eaten fried or oil-roasted. They are said to have a stronger and more pleasing taste than sweet flag, and can be used as a flavoring. Japan. HEDRICK 1919, TANAKA; B28, D43, *E66*, E83Z, F70, G96, H4, H30, H79M, I28, *I62*, K85M, M15, N3M

Amorphophallus campanulatus - *Whitespot giant arum, Telinga potato, Indo-konnyaku* {S} Corms, leaves, and petioles can be eaten after proper preparation. The corms are then boiled with tamarind leaves, made into pickles, and cooked in syrup. Tropical Asia. BURKILL, HERKLOTS, OCHSE, TANAKA; F85, M31{PL}, N84

Amorphophallus paeoniifolius → *Amorphophallus campanulatus*

Amorphophallus rivieri - *Devil's tongue* {PL} The large brown tubers are peeled, cooked, and pounded to extract their starch, which is solidified with dissolved limestone into an edible gel called *konnyaku* or *yam cake*. Used in Japanese cuisine, and valued for its ability to cleanse the digestive tract without being a laxative. Konnyaku noodles, known as *shirataki*, are widely used in sukiyaki. Southeast Asia, cultivated. SHURTLEFF 1975 [Re], SHURTLEFF 1976 [Re], TANAKA; A79M, D62, E47M, G20M{PR}, N49M{PR}, N84

Amorphophallus variabilis - *Kembang bangké* {S} After proper preparation, tubers and young shoots may be eaten. From the tubers, an edible gel (*konnyaku*) is manufactured. Southeast Asia. BURKILL, OCHSE, TANAKA; F85

Arisaema triphyllum - *Jack-in-the-pulpit, Indian turnip* {PL} Fleshy roots are cut into very thin slices and allowed to dry for several months, after which they can be eaten like potato chips, crumbled to make a cereal, or ground into cocoa-flavored flour for baking cakes, cookies, rolls, muffins, and pancakes. Eastern North America. ANGIER, FERNALD [Pre], GIBBONS 1966b [Pre, Re]; B33M, B77, C43M, C49, C56, D75T, E33M, *G28*, I11M, I44, K33M, K63, M77M, N8, N9M, N9M{S}, etc.

Calla palustris - *Wild calla, Water arum, Water dragons* {PL} In Scandinavia the roots are dried, macerated, boiled, and made into a kind of bread, *missen bread*. Northern temperate region. FERNALD [Pre]; B28, C49, C64M, D62, D62{S}, D75T, H30, I44, I87, J7, M15, M73M, N84{S}, *Q24*{S}, S7M{S}, etc.

Colocasia esculenta - *Taro, Coco-yam* {PL} Tubers are eaten boiled, fried, steamed, in soups, stews, puddings, pounded into dumplings, or employed as a starch. In Hawaii, they are sliced and fried into taro chips and fermented into a pasty mass called *poi*. Young leaves and leaf stalks are eaten as a vegetable, called *luau*, especially after forcing when they taste like mushrooms. Leaf stalks are also used for thickening soups. Spadices were baked with fish or pork, as a delicacy. Cultivated. BOND, DEGENER, GREENWELL, HAWKES [Re], MAY, R. [Nu, Re], SCHNEIDER [Cul, Re], TANAKA; *B59*{PR}, C56M, E31M, E47M, E70M{PR}, F21M{PR}, G20M{PR}, G85, H4, H82, I28, I90M, K34, K85M, M73M, N3M, *N40*{PR}, etc.

CULTIVARS

Akado: Corm purple; flesh white with yellowish fibers. Leaf stalks greenish-bronze, shading into dark reddish-purple at base and apex. Medium-tall, stiffly erect, stocky plant; grown primarily under upland culture; produces more than 20 cormels. Matures within 10 months. Cormels are good baked or steamed. The vivid leaf stalks, and sprouts from small cormels grown in darkness make excellent greens. Probably a native of Japan. WHITNEY; **T54**

Apuwai: Corm cream-colored; flesh white with indistinct, yellowish fibers. Short, moderately spreading, very stocky plant; essentially a wetland taro. Matures within 6 to 9 months. Leaves are highly prized for *luau*; corms are very good baked or steamed. Also makes good poi of a very light, silver color, soft in consistency, and easy to pound and prepare. Native Hawaiian cultivar. WHITNEY; **T54**

Bun-Long: (Chinese) Corm cream-colored; flesh white with conspicuous purple fibers. Has a crispy texture when baked or boiled. Used commercially for taro chips. Tall, well spreading, stocky plant; grown under both wetland and dryland culture. Matures within 9 to 12 months. Young leaves are desirable for *luau* because of their large size, tenderness and comparative non-acridity. Introduced into Hawaii from China. WHITNEY; **T54**

Eleele Naioea: Corm dark reddish-purple; flesh lilac-purple with conspicuous darker purple fibers. Medium-tall, well spreading plant; petioles blackish; grown under upland culture. Matures within 8 to 12 months. Produces red poi that is highly prized. Native Hawaiian cultivar. One of the so-called *royal black taros* of the early Hawaiians. WHITNEY; **T54**

Kai Kea: Corm light pink; flesh white, tinged with pink, especially at the apex. Medium-tall, well spreading plant; primarily grown under wetland culture. Matures within 8 to 12 months. Makes a translucent amber poi of excellent quality that was highly esteemed by the Hawaiian chiefs. Native Hawaiian cultivar. WHITNEY; **T54**

Kakakura-Ula: Corm cream-colored to white; flesh white with yellowish fibers. Good baked or steamed. Medium-tall to tall, moderately spreading plant; grown under upland culture; reproduces by rhizomes. Leaf stalk striped light and dark green, overlaid with brilliant reddish-purple, white at base. Matures within 9 to 12 months. One of the most beautiful of all taros. Introduced into Hawaii from the South Seas. WHITNEY; **T54**

<u>**Lehua Maoli:**</u> Corm dark pinkish-lilac; flesh light purplish-lilac with darker purple fibers. Medium-tall, well spreading, slender plant; grown under both wetland and upland culture. Matures within 8 to 12 months. The primary cultivar used for *Lehua red poi*, which often commands a premium in price. A favorite native Hawaiian cultivar. WHITNEY; **T54**

<u>**Lehua Palaii:**</u> Corm light pink; flesh lilac-purple with darker purple fibers. Short to medium-tall, stiffly erect, slender plant; grown principally under upland culture; quite hardy and a good yielder. Matures within 12 to 18 months. Makes red poi of excellent quality. Native Hawaiian cultivar. One of the royal taros, formerly grown for and eaten only by the chiefs. WHITNEY; **T54**

<u>**Mana Eleele:**</u> Corm dark purple; flesh white tinged with lilac near the apex, with yellowish fibers. Medium-tall, erect plant; grown almost exclusively under upland culture. Matures within 9 to 12 months. Mainly used as a table taro, either baked or steamed. Said to be the most drought-resistant of the Hawaiian taros. WHITNEY; **T54**

<u>**Mana Keokeo:**</u> Corms large; skin white, light lilac-pink to purple at the leaf scars; flesh chalky white with yellowish fibers. Excellent baked or steamed. Also a favorite for *kulolo*, a Hawaiian pudding prepared from grated raw taro and coconut milk, steamed underground. Medium-tall, erect plant; grown almost exclusively under upland culture; yields well even under adverse conditions. Matures within 7 to 12 months. WHITNEY; **T54**

<u>**Mana Uliuli:**</u> Corm cream-colored, dark purple along leaf-scar rings; flesh yellow with light yellow fibers; tough and rubbery when cooked. Makes good poi of distinctly yellow color. Medium-tall, erect, moderately stocky plant; grown primarily under upland culture; branches prolifically. Matures within 9 to 12 months. Introduced into Hawaii from the South Seas. WHITNEY; **T54**

<u>**Mana Ulu:**</u> Corm yellow; flesh yellow with light yellow fibers. Excellent cooked, having a somewhat dry, mealy, flaky texture and an orange-yellow color that is much more attractive than that of most other cultivars. Medium-tall, slender, erect plant; does well under both upland and wetland culture. Matures within 7 to 12 months. Native Hawaiian cultivar. WHITNEY; **T54**

<u>**Ohe:**</u> Corm light pink; flesh white with a light pinkish tinge, especially near the apex, and yellowish fibers. Medium-tall, well spreading, stocky plant; grown primarily under upland culture; especially well adapted to elevations above 1,500 feet. Matures within 12 to 16 months. Makes gray poi of excellent quality. Native Hawaiian cultivar. WHITNEY; **T54**

<u>**Piialii:**</u> Corm brilliant reddish-purple; flesh lilac-purple with darker purple fibers. Short, erect, stocky plant; grown primarily under wetland conditions. Matures within 8 to 12 months. Makes a red poi that is highly prized for flavor and quality. One of the oldest cultivars grown in Hawaii, known in the early days as one of the royal taros. WHITNEY; **T54**

<u>**Piko Kea:**</u> Corm pale pink; flesh white with pinkish apex and yellowish fibers; fairly firm in texture, will absorb more water in the preparation of poi than most cultivars. Makes light bluish-gray poi of very good quality. Medium-tall, erect, moderately stocky plant; grown almost exclusively in wetland patches; widely adapted. Matures within 15 to 18 months. Native Hawaiian cultivar. WHITNEY; **T54**

<u>**Tsurunoko:**</u> (Araimo) Corm white; flesh white with yellowish fibers. Short, spreading, moderately spreading plant; grown almost exclusively under upland culture; produces as many as 40 cormels. Often matures within 6 months. Cormels are eaten baked or steamed. Sprouts from cormels grown in darkness are also eaten. Most important Japanese cultivar in Hawaii. Valued primarily for its excellent keeping qualities. WHITNEY; **T54**

Cyrtosperma chamissonis - *Te babai, Giant swamp taro* {PL} Large tubers are eaten boiled. They are also mashed into a dough, which is kneaded and then left to ferment before being recooked in an earth oven. Pacific Islands. MASSAL, TANAKA; **T67M, Z5**

Monstera deliciosa - *Ceriman* {S} Juicy, subacid fruits have an excellent aroma and taste, combining the flavors of banana and pineapple. They are eaten out of hand or used in ices, sherbets, and soft drinks. Even ripening of the fruit may be encouraged by wrapping the whole in paper, placing it in a refrigerator for 24 hours, and then leaving it at room temperature until soft. Central America, cultivated. JOHNS, KENNARD, RICHARDSON [Re], SCHNEIDER, STURROCK; *B59*{PR}, C9M, C56M{PL}, D57{PL}, E29{PL}, E29{PR}, *E53M*, F68{PL}, O53M, O93, P5, *P17M*, *Q32*, S91M

Peltandra virginica - *Arrow arum, Tuckahoe* {PL} Seeds are slightly sweetish, suggesting in taste parched Indian corn. A bread can be made from them, tasting like corncake with a strong flavor of cocoa. Eastern North America. FERNALD; *F73*, G85, H30, H61M{S}, J7M, *J25*, K85M, M15, M77M, N3M

Philodendron bipinnatifidum - *Banana de Macaco* {S} The red fruits are edible and much esteemed in some parts of southern Brazil. Pulp is used for making a jelly. Brazil. UPHOF; C9M, *E53M*, F85, N84, O53M, O93, P5, *P17M*, *Q25*, *Q32*, S45M

Philodendron selloum - *Arborescent philodendron* {S} Fruits are used in compotes. Brazil, cultivated. UPHOF; *B41*{PL}, C9M, C56M{PL}, *E53M*, F85, *H71*, I57{PL}, *L5M*, N84, O93, P5, *P17M*, *Q25*, S91M

Spathiphyllum phryniifolium - *Busnay, Huisnay* {S} The tender young inflorescences are used in soups or fried in egg batter. They have also been eaten raw with no ill effects. Leaves and young shoots are edible, containing 6.5% protein. Central America. DUKE, MARTIN 1975, WILLIAMS, L.; N84

Xanthosoma atrovirens - *Yautia amarilla, Tannia* {PL} Young leaves, rich in protein and minerals, are cooked and eaten. The corms form one of the staple starchy foods of Dominica. Tropical America. HERKLOTS, TANAKA; M73M

Xanthosoma brasiliense - *Tahitian taro, Tanier spinach, Belembe* {PL} Leaves, stems, and tender upper portion of the petioles are used as potherbs. They can contain few oxalate crystals and are preferred over other species of Xanthosoma and Colocasia in the popular West Indian stew called *calalu*. Tropical America, cultivated. MARTIN 1975, MASSAL, OOMEN [Re]; **T73M, Z72**

Xanthosoma maffafa - *Mafaffa* {PL} Corms are pounded and made into *fufu*, a starchy food. Northern South America. DALZIEL; Z37

Xanthosoma sagittifolium - *Yautia, Malanga blanca, Indian kale* {PL} Corms are peeled and then eaten boiled, baked, puréed, in soups and stews, made into chips, pancakes, fritters, etc. Young leaves and petioles are cooked and eaten like spinach. Tropical America, cultivated. HAWKES [Re], SCHNEIDER [Pre, Re], TANAKA; *B59*{PR}, E31M, L29, *N40*{PR}

Xanthosoma violaceum - *Violet-stemmed taro, Primrose malanga, Woo chai* {PL} Young leaves and petioles are chopped and eaten as a spinach. Cormels are peeled and used in stews, custards, and pancakes. Tropical America. BURKILL, HARRINGTON, G. [Cu, Cul], OCHSE; H4, M73M

ARALIACEAE

Acanthopanax divaricatus - *Ô-ukogi* {S} Leaves are parboiled and dried for use as a winter vegetable. Also used for seasoning sake wine. Dried leaves are a tea substitute. China, Japan. TANAKA; **T41M**

Acanthopanax sessiliflorus - *Manshû-ukogi* {S} Young leaves are boiled as a vegetable, older ones are used as a tea substitute. The bark makes wine much fancied by the Chinese. China. TANAKA; *G66*, M35M{PL}, N84, S36M

Acanthopanax sieboldianus - *Ukogi, Wu-chia* {S} Young leaves are boiled and eaten, having a delicious, somewhat fragrant flavor. Also used as a tea substitute. A liquor is brewed from the plant. China, Japan. TANAKA; D95{PL}, J7{PL}, M92{PL}, N36{PL}, P49, *P63*, R78

Aralia cordata - *Udo, Japanese asparagus, Tu-huo* {S} Blanched shoots are crisp and tender with a unique lemon-like flavor. When used in salads, they are peeled, cut into shavings, and soaked in ice water for an hour before serving with French dressing. To prepare as asparagus or for soup, boil in several changes of water first. A favorite of David Fairchild, the famous plant explorer. Japan. FAIRCHILD 1945, FERNALD, HAWKES [Cul], SHURTLEFF 1975, UPHOF; **T41M, U4, V19, V34, V73M, X33, X39, Y27M, Z98**

Aralia hispida - *Bristly sarsaparilla* {PL} Roots are used for tea and *root beer*. North America. PETERSON, L.; N9M, N9M{S}

Aralia nudicaulis - *Wild sarsaparilla* {S} The rootstock is often used as an ingredient in *root beer*. Also used as a refreshing herbal tea. North America. FERNALD, MARCIN; A2, M16{PL}

Aralia racemosa - *American spikenard, Life-of-man, Pettymorrel* {PL} The roots are pleasantly aromatic and are one of the popular ingredients of *root beer*, imparting a licorice flavor. Menomoni Indians prepared a dish of the roots mixed with wild onion, wild gooseberry, and sugar. Berries are made into jelly. North America. FERNALD; B28, B51{S}, E33M, I31{S}, N84{S}, R53M

Aralia spinosa - *Hercules' club, Devil's walking stick, Angelica tree* {PL} Young unfolding leaves, before the prickles form, are gathered and used as a potherb. They are chopped finely, flavored with vinegar, and served with rice. North America. FERNALD, GIBBONS 1979; *B68, F5*, F85{S}, H4, *I17M*, K63G{S}, M92, N37M, N84{S}, P5{S}

Panax ginseng → ***Panax pseudoginseng***

Panax japonica - *Tochiba-ninjin* {S} Roots are used in tea and liqueurs. Eastern Asia. TANAKA; **V19**

Panax pseudoginseng - *Asiatic ginseng, San-ch'i* {S} Roots are chewed, used in liqueurs, or made into a tea. Eastern Asia. TANAKA; F85

Panax quinquefolius - *American ginseng* {PL} Aromatic roots are candied and used as a masticatory. Leaves and roots are brewed into tea. North America. GIBBONS 1966b, MARCIN; A36, A36{S}, A83M, A83M{S}, C39M{S}, C43M, E33M, E71M, F37T, F78, F78{S}, F78{PR}, G68{S}, G84, K22, N7T{PL}, N8, etc.

Panax schinseng → ***Panax pseudoginseng***

Panax trifolius - *Dwarf ginseng* {PL} Bulb-like roots when boiled in salted water, become very palatable, either as a hot vegetable or eaten cold like salted nuts. North America. FERNALD; A51M

Trevesia palmata - *Bhotala, Snowflake bush* {S} Flower buds are eaten cooked. Himalayan region. TANAKA; A79M, C9M, C56M{PL}, F85, G96{PL}, N84, O53M, O93, *Q25, Q32*

ARAUCARIACEAE

Araucaria angustifolia - *Paraná pine, Brazilian pine* {S} The nutritious seeds are eaten. Flavor of the kernel is mealy and somewhat sweet, resembling the taste of sweet potatoes. Gum of trees also consumed. Brazil, Argentina. KUNKEL, MENNINGER; C56M{PL}, F85, I83M{PL}, K63G, N84, O93, S29, S95

Araucaria araucana - *Monkey puzzle, Chile pine* {PL} Starchy seeds, called *piñones*, are eaten fresh, boiled, roasted, or made into an alcoholic beverage. Chile, Argentina. HEDRICK 1919, UPHOF; B74, B94{S}, C56M, D95, E87, H4, I83M, J61M, L91M{S}, N0, *N71M*{S}, O53M{S}, O93{S}, P49{S}, *R28*{S}, R78{S}, etc.

Araucaria bidwillii - *Bunya bunya* {S} The kernel of the seed is starchy and delicious, having the texture of a waxy boiled potato, with a flavor of chestnuts. They are eaten raw, boiled, roasted, or ground into flour. Germinated seeds produce an underground *earth nut*, which has a coconut-like flavor. Australia. CRIBB, MENNINGER; *A19*{PL}, A79M, C9M, C56M{PL}, H4{PL}, I28{PL}, *I61*, I83M{PL}, O84, P5, P38, *Q25, Q32*, Q46, *Q52*{PL}, R33M, etc.

ARECACEAE (*PALMAE*)

Acanthorrhiza aculeata → *Cryosophila nana*

Acrocomia intumescens - *Macauba* {S} Base of new fronds is eaten as *palm-cabbage*. The seeds are the source of a cooking oil. Brazil. KUNKEL; **X88M**

Acrocomia mexicana - *Palmito de coyol* {S} The tender leaf base is eaten raw, boiled, roasted, or pickled. Fruits are eaten or made into an oil similar to coconut oil, called *oil of coyol*. Sweet sap from the trunk is fermented into a palm wine, *vino de coyol*. Seed kernels are edible. Central America. MENNINGER, TANAKA, UPHOF, WILLIAMS, L.; **X94**

Acrocomia sclerocarpa - *Gru gru nut, Palmeira mucajá* {S} Young leaves are eaten as a vegetable. The sweet kernel is eaten or manufactured into a cooking oil. Pulp of the fruit is edible, having the flavor of apricot. Tropical America. HEDRICK 1919, TANAKA; **X88M**

Acrocomia totai - *Totai, Mbocaya palm* {PL} The seed kernel oil, when refined, is suitable for edible purposes. An important source of cooking oil in Bolivia and Paraguay. South America. MENNINGER, UPHOF; C56M, E71

Aiphanes caryotifolia - *Chascara, Mararay* {PL} Oily seeds are eaten or used in jams and confiture. Colombia to Brazil. DUKE, KUNKEL; D43, E29, E29{S}, E71, I85M

Areca catechu - *Betel nut, Pan* {S} Thin slices of the seed kernel are made into a quid, smeared with slaked lime, wrapped in a fresh leaf of Piper betle, and chewed as a stimulating masticatory. It causes the lips, tongue, and teeth to become red, and if used frequently, black. Young leaves are eaten as a vegetable. Skin of the fruit is edible. Southeast Asia, cultivated. ALTSCHUL, MENNINGER, ROSENGARTEN; B7, D43{PL}, E71{PL}, F85, J22{PL}, N84, O93, P5, P38, Q12, *Q25*, Q46, *Q52*{PL}, R33M, S54M, etc.

Areca sapida → ***Rhopalostylis sapida***

Arenga ambong - *Ambung* {PL} The heart of the stem produces a *sago* starch. Buds are edible. Philippines. BROWN, W., TANAKA; C56M, D43, E71, I85M{S}, N84{S}, R33M{S}

Arenga engleri - *Formosan sugar palm* {S} Young leaves and buds are eaten. Pith of stems yields a starch. Sap from the inflorescence is made into sugar. Taiwan. TANAKA, WESTER; C56M{PL}, D43{PL}, E71{PL}, F85, I28{PL}, N84, P5, R33M

Arenga pinnata - *Sugar palm, Gomuti palm* {S} Pith of stems furnishes a starch used in pastries or *tjèndol*, a kind of syrup. Sap from the inflorescence is sweet and can be drunk fresh, boiled down to a sugar, fermented into *tuwak*, distilled into *arrak*, or made into vinegar. Buds are cooked as a vegetable or pickled. Young seeds are made into preserves. Malaysia. HESSELTINE, MACMILLAN, OCHSE, UPHOF; E71{PL}, F85, I85M, N84, P5, R33M, S54M

Arenga tremula* → *Arenga ambong

Arenga wightii - *Dadsel* {S} Palm wine, or *toddy*, is brewed from the sap. India. WATT; F85

Astrocaryum tucuma - *Palmeira tucumá, Tucum* {S} Both fruits and kernels are the source of an oil, *tucuma oil*, similar to coconut oil. The yellow fruit pulp has a flavor similar to apricot and is fermented into *tucuma wine*. South America. BROUK, CAVALCANTE, TANAKA, UPHOF; P28

Attalea cohune* → *Orbignya cohune

Attalea funifera - *Coquilla nut* {S} The fruits are eaten. Seed kernels a source of oil used in the manufacture of margarine. Brazil. KUNKEL, TANAKA; **X88M**

Bactris gasipaes* → *Guilielma gasipaes

Bactris maraja - *Marajah palm* {S} The pulp of the fruit has a pleasant, acid flavor and is eaten or brewed into a wine. Brazil. HEDRICK 1919, TANAKA; **X88M**

Borassus aethiopum - *Black rhum palm* {S} The terminal bud or *palm-cabbage* is eaten raw in salads, or cooked as a vegetable. The fresh sap is a refreshing drink and yields one of the best palm wines. Germinated seeds are used as a tasty vegetable. Fruits are also eaten. Eastern Africa. FOX, F., TANAKA; F85, I99, N84

Borassus flabellifer - *Palmyra palm* {S} Sweet sap from the inflorescence is drunk as a beverage. It also produces palm wine, a sugar called *gur* or *jaggery*, molasses, candy, and vinegar. Young fruits are pickled. Pulp of mature fruits is eaten or made into *punatoo*. Immature jelly-like seeds are eaten or canned for export. Sprouted seedlings are peeled and eaten raw, sun-dried or cooked. They also yield a starch made into gruel with rice, herbs, chilis, and fish. Terminal bud is eaten. Salt is prepared from the leaves. Tropical Asia. MENNINGER, MORTON 1988, UPHOF; E71{PL}, I85M{PL}, Q46, S54M

Brahea armata* → *Erythea armata

Brahea dulcis - *Palma dulce* {PL} The fruits, called *michire* or *miche*, are sweet and edible. Mexico. UPHOF; C56M

Brahea edulis* → *Erythea edulis

Butia capitata - *Jelly palm, Pindo palm* {S} Orange fruits are sweet, aromatic, with somewhat the flavor of apricots. They can be eaten fresh or made into jellies, jams, cakes, pies, etc. Sometimes found in specialty markets. Brazil, cultivated. RICHARDSON [Re], TANAKA; A79M, C9M, C56M{PL}, D43{PL}, D57{PL}, E29, E29{PL}, E29{PR}, E71{PL}, H4, H4{PL}, *I61*, I83M{PL}, *L5M*, O53M, R33M, etc.

Butia yatay - {S} Terminal buds are eaten as a vegetable. Fruits are used for making brandy. Kernels are also edible. Argentina to Paraguay. TANAKA, UPHOF; C56M{PL}, I28{PL}, I85M{PL}, N84, O53M, O93, P5, *P17M*, *Q25*, *Q32*

Calyptronoma dulcis - {S} Flowers are used for making candy. Cuba. KUNKEL; F85

Caryota cumingii - *Fish-tail palm* {S} Pith of stems are a source of *sago* starch. Buds are also edible. Philippines. BROWN, W., TANAKA; E71{PL}, F85, I85M{PL}, N84, R33M

Caryota mitis - *Smaller fish-tail palm* {S} Slightly bitter buds are cooked and eaten with rice. Stems are a source of starch. Seeds are edible after removing the poisonous fruit wall. Southern Asia, cultivated. BURKILL, MENNINGER, TANAKA; A79M, C9M, D43{PL}, E29, E29{PL}, *E53M*, E71{PL}, I28{PL}, I85M, I85M{PL}, *K48*, O93, P5, *Q32*, Q41, R33M, S54M, etc.

Caryota rumphiana - *Suwarnkung* {S} Terminal bud or *palm-cabbage* is eaten as a steamed vegetable with rice, in soups, or fried with coconut milk and spices. The stems are a source of *sago* starch. Indonesia. OCHSE, TANAKA; E71{PL}, F85, I85M{PL}, N84, R33M

Caryota urens - *Toddy palm, Fish-tail palm* {S} Very young unfolding leaves are used as a vegetable. Juice of the trunk is made into sugar and an alcoholic beverage. Stems are a source of a starch. Southern Asia, cultivated. BURKILL, UPHOF; *A19*{PL}, C9M, C56M{PL}, D43{PL}, E71{PL}, I28{PL}, I85M{PL}, *K48*, N43M{PL}, O93, P5, Q12, Q18, *Q32*, Q46, R33M, etc.

Chamaedorea costaricana - *Pacaya* {S} Young inflorescences are eaten raw in salads, dipped in egg batter and fried, boiled, or used in soups. Costa Rica. WILLIAMS, L.; C56M{PL}, D43{PL}, F85, I28{PL}, I85M{PL}, *K46*{PL}, N84, O93, *P17M*, *Q25*, Q41, R33M

Chamaedorea elegans* → *Collinia elegans

Chamaedorea graminifolia - *Pacaya* {PL} Unopened flower clusters are eaten in salads, folded into egg batter and fried, or used as a boiled vegetable. Central America. TANAKA, UPHOF, WILLIAMS, L.; F85{S}, I85M

Chamaedorea tepejilote - *Pacaya* {PL} The young inflorescences are taken from the spadices and eaten raw, boiled, or fried in egg batter. Probably the best of the Chamaedoreas for this purpose. Mexico. HEDRICK 1919, WILLIAMS, L.; C56M, D43, E71, F85{S}, I28, N84{S}, P5{S}, *Q25*{S}, Q41{S}, *Q52*

Chamaerops excelsa* → *Trachycarpus fortunei

Chamaerops humilis - *Palmetto, Dwarf fan-palm* {S} The young shoots or suckers from the bottom of the plant, called *cafaglioni*, are eaten in Italy. Very young leaf buds are eaten as a vegetable. Dried fruits are also edible. Mediterranean region, cultivated. HEDRICK 1919, UPHOF; A79M, C9M, C56M{PL}, D43{PL}, E71{PL}, H4{PL}, *I61*, K38, L91M, N37M{PL}, N93M, O53M, P5, R33M.

Coccothrinax dulcis* → *Calyptronoma dulcis

Cocos coronata* → *Syagrus coronata

Cocos nucifera - *Coco-palm, Coconut* {S} Inflorescences are eaten as a vegetable; also the source of sugar, vinegar, and palm wine. Pulp of seeds is eaten raw, shredded, in desserts, or made into coconut oil, coconut milk (*santan*), coconut butter (*santan kanil*), *macaroons*, *ghee*, etc. The immature fruit or *water coconut* has jelly-like pulp that is considered a delicacy. Terminal bud is eaten raw. The Nawasi cultivar has an edible husk. Coconut sport or *makapuno* is a delicacy that comes from a strain in which the coconut water is replaced with a thick curd. Another delicacy is the *coconut apple*, a spongy mass that forms inside a germinating seed at the expensive of the water and albumen. Scorched roots are a coffee substitute. Sprouted seeds are eaten like celery. Pith of stems is made into bread, or pickled. *Ontjom*, *tempeh bongrek*, *nata de coco* and *dageh kelapa* are fermented products made from coconut. Cultivated. DUKE, FAIRCHILD 1930, MACMILLAN, OCHSE, ROSENGARTEN, SHURTLEFF 1979, STEINKRAUS, TANAKA, UPHOF; *B59*{PR}, E71{PL}, F85, N84, *P17M*, Q41, Q46, S54M, S54M{PL}

CULTIVARS {PL}

Cross Breed: Starts bearing after 4 to 5 years. Disease resistant. Heavy producer, up to 250 nuts annually when mature. Color green. R0

Golden Malayan Dwarf: (Golden Coconut) Small, atrractive, golden-yellow nut. Dwarf, heavy yielding tree, much shorter than the typical coconut. Has a life expectancy half to one third that of common tall forms. Over 90% resistant to lethal yellowing disease. Introduced into Florida from the Malay Archipelago by an expedition sponsored by W.J. Matheson. **T72M{S}**

Green Malayan Dwarf: Small, solid green nut. Dwarf, heavy yielding tree, half to one third the size of common tall forms; bears when about 4 or 5 years old with only 2 or 3 feet of bare trunk exposed. Full production of about 100 nuts per tree is reached in the ninth or tenth year. Tolerant to lethal yellowing disease. I85M, J99{S}

Hybrid Supreme: Starts bearing after 3 years. Very heavy producer, 300 to 350 nuts annually when mature. Color golden-yellow, red and green. R0

King: Distinct cultivar, said to have originated in Sri Lanka. Bears a yellow, ovoid fruit, called *tambili* in the immature stage when it is distinguished by its clear, sweet juice which furnishes a pleasant refreshing drink. Also esteemed for culinary purposes. Susceptible to lethal yellowing disease. MACMILLAN; **T72M{S}**

Laccadive Dwarf: Starts bearing after 2 1/2 to 3 years. Yields 250 nuts annually when mature. Color green and yellow. Excellent for tender, sweet coconut water. R0

Makapuno: Very distinct and desirable type whose interior is filled with soft, sweet, jelly-like flesh that can be eaten with a spoon. Originated in the Philippines where it is popular for making a delicious, delicate ice cream. There, Makapuno fruits sell locally for four times the amount of ordinary coconuts. **T72M{S}**

Maypan: Large green nut, sometimes variegated with brownish or yellowish tints depending on the seed parents. Tree intermediate in size between the two parents; bears approximately 100 nuts beginning about the 5th year. Highly resistant to lethal yellowing disease. Malayan Dwarf x Panama Tall. Developed in Jamaica. I85M

Panama Tall: (San Blas) Notable for its unusually high yield of coconut milk. Tall tree, about 50% resistant to lethal yellowing disease. Widely grown in Jamaica. Originated on the Pacific coast of Panama; presumably introduced there from the Philippines. **T72M{S}**

Red Malayan Dwarf: Small, attractive, solid red nuts; tend to remain on the tree and not fall to the ground when ripe as the nuts produced by tall cultivars do. Dwarf, heavy yielding tree; comes into bearing much sooner than other types, when only 2 or 3 feet high. Tolerant to lethal yellowing disease. **T72M{S}**

Collinia elegans - *Neanthe bella palm, Parlour palm* {S} The young, unexpanded flower spikes are eaten like asparagus. Fruits are used as food by the Chinantecs, Zapotecs, and other Indian tribes. Central America, cultivated. HEDRICK 1919, UPHOF; A79M, C9M, C56M{PL}, D43{PL}, E29, E29{PL}, *E53M*, F85, I28{PL}, I57{PL}, *L5M*, L29{PL}, L91M, P5, *Q32*, R33M, etc.

Copernicia cerifera → *Copernicia prunifera*

Copernicia prunifera - *Carnauba* {S} The trunk is the source of a *sago* starch and an edible gum. Roots are used as a substitute for *sarsaparilla*. The young inflorescences are consumed. Seeds are used as a coffee substitute. Tropical South America. GENDERS 1977, KUNKEL, TANAKA; A79M, E71{PL}, F85, I85M{PL}, N84

Corozo oleifera - *American oil palm, Noli palm, Dendê do pará* {S} Pulp of the fruit yields a reddish oil, similar to red palm oil, called *oil of corozo*, used for culinary purposes. The kernels contain a white oil that, when refined, is utilized for making margarine. Can be crossed with Elaeis guineensis, producing hybrids of low or medium stature. South America, cultivated. CAVALCANTE, DUKE, TANAKA, UPHOF, ZEVEN; F85

Corypha elata - *Buri palm, Gabang* {S} Terminal buds are eaten raw, cooked with rice or made into pickles. Pith of stems is a source of *sago*. The sap yields a fermented drink (*tuba*), palm sugar, and vinegar. Kernels of young seeds are eaten or made into a sweetmeat. Southern Asia. BURKILL, MACMILLAN, OCHSE, TANAKA; E71{PL}, F85, I85M, N84, R33M, S54M

Cryosophila nana - {S} Pulp of the fruit is eaten. It has abundant juice of a penetrating, sweet flavor that is well suited for making palm wine. Mexico. HEDRICK 1919; **Z25M**

Diplothemium maritimum - *Coast palm, Coco da praia* {S} The fruit is eaten, being an ovate or obovate drupe with greenish-yellow, fibrous, acid-sweet flesh. Reportedly superior to the fruits of Butia if eaten at the dead ripe stage. Brazil. HEDRICK 1919; **X88M**

Elaeis guineensis - *African oil palm* {PL} The fleshy pulp of the fruit produces *red palm oil* used in West African cuisine, especially red palm oil stew. Seed kernels are the source of *palm kernel oil*, used as an industrial oil in the manufacture of margarine, shortenings, etc. The kernels are also eaten raw, roasted, or cooked with cinnamon and sugar. Cultivated. HEDRICK 1919, MENNINGER, TANAKA, UPHOF; E71, F85{S}, I85M, J36, N84{S}, *Q52*, R33M{S}, S54M{S}

Elaeis melanococca → *Corozo oleifera*

Erythea armata - *Mexican blue palm* {S} The fruit is edible. Mexico. TANAKA; A79M, C9M, C56M{PL}, D43{PL}, E71{PL}, H4{PL}, *H71*, I28{PL}, *I61*, I85M, I98M, *J86*{PL}, *K48*, N84, O53M, Q41, R33M, etc.

Erythea edulis - *Guadalupe fan palm* {S} Sweet pulp of fruit is eaten. Young leaf-buds from the heart of the tree are used as a vegetable. Caribbean region. UPHOF; C9M, C56M{PL}, D43{PL}, E71{PL}, *H71*, I28{PL}, *I61*, I83M{PL}, I98M, *K46*{PL}, *K48*, L29{PL}, N84, O93, Q41, S95, etc.

Euterpe edulis - *Assaí palm, Para palm* {S} The long, terminal bud is one of the sources of *hearts of palm*. A tropical delicacy, they are eaten raw in salads, sautéed in butter, or pickled like artichoke hearts. Fruits are used to make a beverage. Tropical South America. HEDRICK 1919, NATIONAL RESEARCH COUNCIL 1975a, TANAKA; E71{PL}, I85M, N84, O93, P5, *P17M*, *Q25*, *Q52*{PL}, Q41, R33M

Euterpe oleracea - *Cabbage palm, Acaí* {S} The pulp of the fruit is added to water to make a violet-colored beverage or juice. It is then consumed with tapioca and sugar, cassava meal and grilled fish or dried shrimp, as a porridge cooked with cassava meal, or as an ice cream or popsickle flavoring. The terminal leaf-bud is eaten as *hearts of palm*, said to resemble artichoke. Tropical America, cultivated. CAVALCANTE, HEDRICK 1919, TANAKA; E71{PL}, F85, P5

Guilielma gasipaes - *Pejibaye, Peach palm* {PL} The fruits, high in protein, are eaten roasted or boiled with salt, or made into sweet *chichas*. Dried fruits are ground to a flour that is mixed with eggs and vegetables to make *tortillas*. Seeds are the source of an edible oil, called *oil of macanilla*. Kernels are eaten or made into a meal used to flavor milk drinks. A salt substitute is obtained by cooking the spadix. The young flowers may be chopped and added to omelettes. A valuable source of *hearts of palm* because it produces multiple shoots. Tropical America, cultivated. ALMEYDA 1980 [Cu, Pro], DUKE, MENNINGER, MORTON 1987a [Cu], NATIONAL

RESEARCH COUNCIL 1975a, UPHOF; E71{PL}, F85, I85M{PL}, J36{PL}, N84, R33M

Heterospathe elata - *Sagisi* {S} Terminal buds are used as a vegetable. The seeds are chewed with betel nuts. Philippines. BROWN, W., BURKILL, UPHOF; E71{PL}, F85, N84, R33M

Hyphaene coriacea - *Gingerbread palm* {S} The pulp of the fruit is eaten. Also the source of a palm wine. Eastern Africa. FOX, F., UPHOF; E71{PL}, R33M

Hyphaene natalensis - *South African doum palm, Lala palm* {S} The sap furnishes a palm wine that is said to taste like ginger beer when ripe. Bushmen relish the milk from the seed which has the flavor and color of coconut milk. The shoots of the germinated seeds are eaten as a vegetable. Southern Africa. FOX, F.; N84, R33M

Hyphaene thebaica - *Egyptian doum palm, Gingerbread palm* {S} Terminal buds are used as cabbage. The thin, dry rind of the fruit is made into molasses, cakes, and sweetmeats. Unripe kernels are edible. The germinated seedlings just below the ground are used as a vegetable. Northern Africa. MENNINGER, UPHOF; E71{PL}, F85, N84

Iriartea ventricosa - *Palmeira paxiuba barriguda* {S} Heart of the shoots is eaten as *palm-cabbage*. The flowers yield an ash used as a substitute for common salt. Guiana-Brazil. KUNKEL, TANAKA; I85M{PL}, N84

Jessenia bataua - *Pataudá palm, Seje* {S} The fruits yield an excellent light greenish-yellow oil which is almost identical with olive oil. It is used in cooking or as a coloring for chocolates. A nutritious milk-like beverage is made by mixing the juice of the pulp with manioc meal. Northern South America. BALICK [Nu], CAVALCANTE, KUNKEL, UPHOF; N84, R33M

Jessenia polycarpa - *Seje, Ibe* {PL} The violet-colored fruit, about the size of a pigeon's egg, has a thin, oily flesh that is sweet and edible. Its pulp yields a yellow oil, called *manteca negra*, that closely resembles olive oil and is sold in markets of Colombia. The milky residue forms a nutritious beverage known as *vucuta*. Northern South America. DUKE, HEDRICK 1919, NATIONAL RESEARCH COUNCIL 1975a, PEREZ-ARBELAEZ, UPHOF; I85M

Jubaea chilensis - *Chilean wine palm, Coco de Chile, Honey palm* {S} The sap from the trunk is fermented into palm wine, or boiled down to a syrup called *miel de palma* or *palm honey*. Fruits are candied. Edible kernels are called *cokernuts, pygmy coconuts*, or *coquitos* and have been introduced into the specialty foods market. They have a nutty taste raw and are also used in sweetmeats. Chile, cultivated. HEDRICK 1919, MENNINGER, UPHOF; C9M, C56M{PL}, D43{PL}, D57{PL}, E71{PL}, I28{PL}, *I61*, I83M{PL}, N40{PR}, N84, N93M, O93, P5, P38, S95, etc.

Jubaea spectabilis* → *Jubaea chilensis

Livistona saribus - *Tro* {PL} Fruits are eaten after maceration in vinegar or a salt solution. Terminal buds are used as cabbage. Tropical Asia. BURKILL, UPHOF; C56M, E71, N84{S}

Lodoicea callipyge* → *Lodoicea maldivica

Lodoicea maldivica - *Coco-de-mer, Double coconut* {S} The immature seed contains a delicately-textured, translucent, jelly-like substance that is sweet and melting and much appreciated as a dessert delicacy, often served with a dressing of liqueur. Terminal shoots are eaten and are often preserved in vinegar. Seychelles. HEDRICK 1919, LIONNET, MENNINGER; N84

Mauritia flexuosa - *Buriti palm, Wine palm, Miriti* {S} A juice prepared from the fruit pulp is consumed with sugar and cassava meal, or made into a sweet *doce de buriti*. The pulp also yields an edible oil. An edible starch is derived from the pith of the trunk. Potable sap from the inflorescence is drunk or made into palm wine or sugar. Tropical South America. CAVALCANTE, HEDRICK 1919; E71{PL}, N84, R33M

Mauritia martiana - *Caraná* {S} A juice is prepared from the pulp of the fruit which has, to some people, a better flavor than that of miriti. It is consumed with cassava meal and sugar. Brazil. CAVALCANTE; **X88M**

Mauritia vinifera* → *Mauritia flexuosa

Metroxylon rumphii - *Spiny sago palm* {S} The trunk yields *sago*, an important starch used in porridge, cakes, puddings, soups, breads and pastries. Much is exported from Malaysia and Indonesia. In the Kai and Tanimbar Islands, the pith is roasted and eaten. Malaysia, Pacific Islands, cultivated. BURKILL, MASSAL, MAY, R. [Re], UPHOF; S54M

Metroxylon sagu - *Sago palm* {S} The heart of the trunk is steamed, roasted, added to stews, or preserved. Also the source of a *sago* starch, resembling tapioca and used in much the same way. Ripe fruits, though astringent, are eaten as a delicacy by the native people. Terminal buds are steamed and eaten as a side-dish with rice, added to stews, or pickled. Southern Asia, cultivated. MACMILLAN, OCHSE, TANAKA; N84

Nannorrhops ritchieana - *Mazani palm* {PL} Young leaves, inflorescences, and fruits are eaten. Arabia to India. TANAKA, WATT; C56M, E71

Oenocarpus bacaba - *Bacaba oil-palm* {S} The fruit yields a colorless, sweet oil used to adulterate olive oil. Fruits are also used to prepare a cocoa-like drink. Guiana, Brazil. ALTSCHUL, HEDRICK 1919; **X88M**

Oenocarpus distichus - *Bacaba de azeite* {S} The pulp of the fruit contains 25% of a clear, yellow oil that can substitute perfectly for olive oil. *Bacaba branca*, a milky drink, and *bacaba vernelha*, a yellow-red beverage used pure or with sugar and cassava meal, are both produced from the fruit. These beverages are sometimes fermented into vinegar. Guiana, Brazil. CAVALCANTE, TANAKA, UPHOF; **X88M**

Oenocarpus multicaulis - *Palmeira bacaba-y, Becabinha* {S} Juice made from the fruit pulp is used as an oily beverage. The seeds are edible. Terminal buds are used as cabbage. Also the source of an edible oil. Peru, Brazil. CAVALCANTE, KUNKEL, TANAKA; N84, R33M

Oncosperma filamentosum - *Anibong, Nibong, Gendiwung* {S} The heart, or cabbage, is delicately white with a very sweet, nutty flavor. It can be used raw in salads, and when boiled it resembles asparagus or kale. Flowers are used to flavor rice. Malaysia. BURKILL, HEDRICK 1919, TANAKA; F85

Orbignya cohune - *Cohune palm* {S} Seed kernels are the source of an oil used in cooking or the manufacture of margarine. Fruits are made into sweetmeats. Sap is used for winemaking. Central America. DUKE, MENNINGER, UPHOF; A79M, E71{PL}, F85, N84

Orbignya martiana - *Babassú* {S} A cooking oil is extracted from the kernels. They are also eaten as a snack or made into a nut milk. Watery endosperm, *água de côco*, is consumed as a beverage. Sap from the stem produces a palm wine. The palm heart or *palmito* is used as food. Ashes from burned stems are used as a salt substitute. Babassú flour is mixed with milk and sugar to produce a chocolate-like drink. Brazil. MAY, P., NATIONAL RESEARCH COUNCIL 1975a; **X88M**

Phoenix canariensis - *Canary Islands date palm* {S} Source of a sap used like *palm honey*, or syrup. The fruit is also edible. Canary

Islands, cultivated. KUNKEL, TANAKA; C9M, C56M{PL}, D43{PL}, E71{PL}, F85, H4{PL}, *I61*, I85M{PL}, K38, *L5M*, L91M, N84, O53M, P5, *Q32*, R33M, etc.

Phoenix dactylifera - *Date palm* {S} The ripe fruits are eaten out of hand, in breads, cakes, pastry, confectionery, etc. Traditionally they are stuffed with butter or nuts, baked, boiled with onions in milk, fried with eggs, made into date syrup, or used as a coffee substitute. The male inflorescence is eaten as a delicacy. Unripe fruit is pickled. Seeds are sometimes eaten. Also the source of *hearts of palm, toddy, arrak*, and an edible manna. Cultivated. DONKIN, NIXON [Cu], POPENOE, P., POPENOE, W. 1920; A79M, C9M, C56M{PL}, D57{PL}, E29, E29{PL}, E71{PL}, I28{PL}, J82, K38, O53M, *P17M*, Q12, *Q32*, Q46, R33M, S95, etc. (for cultivars see Date, page 323)

Phoenix paludosa - *Bengal date palm* {S} Fruits are eaten in curries. The pith is edible. Southern Asia. BURKILL, TANAKA; D43{PL}, F85, G25M, R33M, S54M

Phoenix pusilla - *Inchu* {S} The edible fruit is sweet and mealy, tasting like chestnuts. Also used to make palm sugar and an alcoholic beverage. Southern Asia. BURKILL, TANAKA, WATT; I85M{PL}, R33M

Phoenix reclinata - *Senegal date* {S} The sap is fermented into a palm wine. Seeds are used as a coffee substitute. The terminal bud is used as a vegetable. Ripe fruits are sweet and tasty and are eaten raw. Tropical Africa, cultivated. FOX, F., HEDRICK 1919, TANAKA; C9M, C56M{PL}, D43{PL}, E29, E29{PL}, E71{PL}, I28{PL}, I85M{PL}, *K46*{PL}, *L5M*, O53M, O93, P5, *P17M*, *Q32*, Q41, R33M, S95, etc.

Phoenix sylvestris - *Wild date palm* {PL} Sap from the stem can be drunk as a beverage. It is also boiled down to a palm sugar, *jaggery*, or fermented into palm wine and distilled into *arrak*. The fruit is sometimes eaten. Southern Asia. MACMILLAN, TANAKA, UPHOF; C56M, E71, F85{S}, I28, P5{S}, Q41{S}

Pseudophoenix vinifera - {S} The saccharine juice obtained from the stem is fermented into a drink. West Indies. TANAKA; F85

Ptychosperma elegans - *Cabbage palm* {S} Unexpanded leaves are eaten as a vegetable. Australia. TANAKA; D43{PL}, E29, E29{PL}, E71{PL}, F85, I85M, I85M{PL}, *J25*{PL}, *L5M*, N84, P5, *Q25*, *Q32*, *Q52*{PL}, R33M, etc.

Raphia farinifera - *Madagascar raffia palm* {S} The stem is the source of a sweet beverage, *harafa*. Also the source of a starch. Fruits and seed kernels are eaten. Boiled fruit pulp yields a yellow fat, *Raphia butter*, of good taste when fresh. Africa, Madagascar. HEDRICK 1919, MENNINGER, UPHOF; I85M{PL}, N84, O93

Raphia hookeri - *Ivory Coast raffia palm, Giant raffia palm* {S} The abundant sap of the young inflorescence yields an excellent palm wine, known as *mimbo* or *doka*. Stems are the source of a starch. Central buds are eaten as *palm-cabbage*. Tropical Africa, cultivated. HEDRICK 1919, KUNKEL, STEINKRAUS, UPHOF; F85, N84

Raphia ruffia* → *Raphia farinifera

Raphia vinifera - *Wine raffia palm, Bamboo palm* {S} Sap from the flower stalks is brewed into a palm wine. It is also boiled down into a palm sugar. Fruit is edible, but somewhat bitter. Tropics. TANAKA; N84

Rhopalostylis sapida - *Nika palm, Nikau palm* {S} Young inflorescences are eaten. The terminal bud, or blanched heart is juicy, succulent, with an agreeably nutty flavor even when raw. New Zealand. COLENSO, HEDRICK 1919; C9M, C56M{PL}, D43{PL}, E71{PL}, I28{PL}, I83M{PL}, I85M, *K46*{PL}, N84, O93, P5, *Q25*, *Q49M*{PL}, *Q52*{PL}, R33M, S44, etc.

Roystonea elata - *Florida royal palm* {PL} The edible fruits fall to the ground when ripe. Terminal bud is used for cabbage. Southeastern North America. MORTON 1977; D43, E29, E29{S}, E71, I85M, *J25*, N84{S}, R33M{S}

Roystonea oleracea - *Cabbage palm* {S} The terminal bud, of a white color and delicate flavor, is boiled as a vegetable or made into pickles. Pith of the stem yields a starch. West Indies. HEDRICK 1919; D43{PL}, F85, *N79M*, N84, O93, P5, *Q25*, R33M

Sabal etonia - *Scrub palmetto, Scrub cabbage* {PL} Terminal bud, or cabbage, is used as a vegetable. The fruits are also eaten. Southeastern North America. MORTON 1977; D43, E29, E29{S}, E71, I85M, N37M, N84{S}, R33M{S}

Sabal minor - *Dwarf palmetto* {S} The pith of the stem is edible. Southern North America. HEDRICK 1919; C56M{PL}, D43{PL}, E71{PL}, F80, F85, H4, H4{PL}, I28{PL}, K18{PL}, N37M{PL}, N93M, O53M, O93, P5, *Q25*, *Q32*, Q41, R33M, etc.

Sabal palmetto - *Cabbage palmetto, Swamp cabbage* {PL} The pulp of the fruit is very sweet and prune-like in flavor. It is eaten raw, made into syrup, or dried and made into bread. Terminal bud is a delicacy raw or cooked. The pith of the upper trunk is chewed for the sweetish juice, made into a pumpkin-like pie, or boiled with raisins and syrup as a pudding. Ashes serve as a salt substitute. Southeastern North America. HAWKES [Re], MORTON 1977; A79M{S}, C9M{S}, C56M, D43, E29, E29{S}, E71, H4, I28, *J25*, K18, K47T{S}, *L5M*{S}, N37M, P5{S}, *Q32*{S}, R33M{S}, etc.

Sabal texana - *Texas palmetto, Palma huíchira* {S} The fruit is eaten. Formerly, the heart was dried and pounded into a meal. Southwestern North America. LATORRE 1977b; B83M, D43{PL}, F85, N37M{PL}, N51{PL}, O93, P5, *Q25*, *Q32*, R33M

Salacca conferta - *Salak hutan, Asam payo* {S} The intensely acid pulp of the fruit is used to season curries, or it is boiled and made into a sweetmeat. Malaysia. BURKILL, HEDRICK 1919, TANAKA; S54M

Salacca edulis - *Salak* {S} Considered one of the finest palm fruits for eating out of hand. The yellow-white pulp is slightly crisp with a delicious blend of acids and sugars. Also eaten cooked with spices, pickled, or preserved in salt water and sugar. Seeds are edible. Indonesia, cultivated. HEDRICK 1919, MENNINGER, UPHOF; **T73M**

CULTIVARS

Gondak: On the island of Bali, where the best salak grow, this is one of the two leading cultivars. Self-pollinating, can produce fruit on single trees, without the aid of a pollinator. WHITMAN; **U27T**

Nangka: One of the two best cultivars grown in Bali. Bears fruit without the aid of pollen from another tree, whereas salak originating outside of Bali produce both male and female trees. WHITMAN; **U27T**

Scheelea butyracea - *Wine palm, Palma real* {PL} The terminal buds are cooked and eaten as a vegetable. Sap from the trunk yields a good palm wine or *toddy*. Seeds are eaten and are also the source of an edible oil. In Panama, they are mashed and mixed with roasted green plantain, forming a dish called *sango*. Tropical South America. DUKE, PEREZ-ARBELAEZ, TANAKA; E71

Scheelea macrocarpa - *Coroba* {S} Seeds are edible, though the kernels are extremely hard. Also the source of an edible oil. South America. MENNINGER, UPHOF; **X88M**

Scheelea preussii - *Corozo* {S} The terminal bud is eaten, either raw or cooked. Oil from the seed is said to be edible. Central America. UPHOF, WILLIAMS, L.; **X94**

Serenoa repens - *Saw palmetto* {PL} Fruits are edible. Florida pioneers once made a carbonated soft drink from the juice of the berries and called it *Metto*. Produces several delicious palm hearts the size of a walnut. All but one can be harvested without killing the tree. Seeds are edible. Southeastern North America. GIBBONS 1979, MORTON 1977, UPHOF; C56M, D43, E29, E29{S}, E71, F85{S}, I28, *J25*, *L5M*{S}, N37M, N84{S}, P5{S}, R33M{S}

Syagrus comosa - *Jeriva, Baba de boi* {PL} An edible oil is extracted from the nut. Brazil. TANAKA; I85M

Syagrus coronata - *Licuri palm, Nicuri, Ouricuru palm* {PL} Pulp of the fruit is consumed by the natives. Kernels are the source of an oil used in the manufacture of margarine. The pith of the stem is used to make bread. Brazil. HEDRICK 1919, UPHOF; E71, F85{S}, I28

Trachycarpus fortunei - *Chinese windmill palm* {S} The young inflorescence is eaten in much the same way as bamboo sprouts. Fresh flowers and the terminal bud are also apparently consumed. China, cultivated. ESSIG, HEDRICK 1919, TANAKA; A79M, C9M, C56M{PL}, D43{PL}, E71{PL}, H4, H4{PL}, *H71*, I85M{PL}, K38, L91M, N37M{PL}, O53M, P5, R33M, etc.

Washingtonia filifera - *California fan palm* {S} The berry-like, black fruits have a thin, sweet pulp that tastes somewhat like dates or butterscotch. They are eaten fresh, dried, or made into jellies and drinks. Seeds are ground into meal for making bread or porridge. Terminal bud is eaten roasted. Southwestern North America. CLARKE, KIRK, MEDSGER, UPHOF; C9M, C27M, C56M{PL}, D43{PL}, E71{PL}, G60{PL}, I33, *I61*, K38, L91M, N93M, O53M, R33M, S4

Zalacca conferta* → *Salacca conferta

ARISTOLOCHIACEAE

Asarum canadense - *American wild ginger* {PL} Flowers and rootstocks have a fragrance and taste suggestive of ginger and can be used as a flavoring. Candied wild ginger is prepared by boiling in sugar water until a syrup forms. The roots are then rolled in granulated sugar, while the syrup can be used on ice cream and other desserts, or mixed with water to form a beverage that is a digestive aid. Eastern North America. ANGIER, FERNALD, GIBBONS 1962, HALL [Pre, Re]; B0, B33M, C9, C43M, C49, C73M, D75T, E33M, *F51*, G89, L46, N7T, N9M, N9M{S}

Asarum caudatum - *Long-tailed wild ginger* {PL} Rootstocks can be used as a ginger substitute. Leaves are brewed into a tea. Western North America. KIRK, UPHOF; B92, D62{S}, E63M, E87, G37M, G60, I39, J26, *J75M*, K79, L26, O53M{S}

ASCLEPIADACEAE

Asclepias incarnata - *Swamp milkweed* {PL} Unopened flower buds were made into soup with deer broth, added to cornmeal mush, and dried and stored for winter use, by the Menominee Indians. Young fruits are boiled and eaten. North America. YANOVSKY; B51{S}, E7M{S}, G47M{S}, G89, H61M{S}, H63, I11M, I19, J40, J42, J42{S}, J43{S}, J48, K53{S}, N9M, N9M{S}, etc.

Asclepias speciosa - *Showy milkweed* {S} Young shoots are boiled and eaten like asparagus. Tender tops of older plants are steamed as a potherb. The gum was used for chewing. Flower buds young fruits, roots, and raw flowers are also used. North America. CLARKE, FERNALD, HARRINGTON, H.; F80, G60{PL}, I99, N84

Asclepias syriaca - *Common milkweed* {S} In the spring the new shoots, while still young and tender, are cooked and eaten like asparagus. The leaves before they become tough are steamed like spinach. Unopened flower clusters are a broccoli substitute. If picked at the proper moment the young pods resemble okra when cooked. Sprouted seeds are eaten. North America. FERNALD, GIBBONS 1962 [Pre, Re], HARRINGTON, H., KINDSCHER; C43M, D58, D62, F24, F80, H61M, J40, K47T, K49M, K53, L86, N9M, N9M{PL}, N84, O53M, etc.

Asclepias tuberosa - *Butterfly-weed, Pleurisy root* {S} Tender shoots can be eaten cooked like asparagus. The Sioux Indians prepared a crude sugar from the flowers, but this technology seems to have been lost. Some authors report that the tubers are edible, others say they are poisonous. Leaves and inflorescences are also eaten. North America. FERNALD, HARRINGTON, H., HEDRICK 1919, MEDSGER, UPHOF, YANOVSKY; B51, C9{PL}, C9M, C32{PL}, D26, E33M{PL}, G47M, G84{PL}, G89, I77M{PL}, J40, J40{PL}, K53, N9M, N9M{PL}, O53M, etc.

Ceropegia bulbosa - *Khapparkadu* {PL} Succulent leaves and stems are acidic and are eaten stewed in curries. Tuberous roots are eaten after the bitterness is removed by boiling. India. TANAKA, TATE, WATT; M33G

Fockea angustifolia - *Water root, Khoa, Kghoa* {PL} The swollen rootstocks have whitish, watery flesh with a nutty flavor and are eaten raw when young or used for making jam and preserves. Southern Africa. FOX, F., TATE; H52

Fockea edulis - *Kambro* {PL} The large tubers have been used to make a *konfyt*, as an alternative to watermelon. Southern Africa. FOX, F.; A0M, B84, B85, E48, F31M, G18, G94, H52, K77M, L50, *N43*

Leptadenia hastata - *Idar* {S} Leaves are eaten in soups or used for making sauces. The flowers and tender shoots are eaten like spinach. West Tropical Africa. DALZIEL, HEDRICK 1919, UPHOF; N84

Leptadenia lancifolia* → *Leptadenia hastata

Pergularia daemia - *Leshwe* {S} The leaves, stalks and flowers are cooked and eaten as potherbs. India. FOX, F., TANAKA; N84

Telosma cordata - *Yeh-lai-hsiang, Bunga siam* {PL} In Thailand, both the flowers and leaves are eaten. The fleshy roots are made into a sweetmeat by the Chinese in Java. Tropical Asia. BURKILL, TANAKA, UPHOF; E75, F85{S}

ASPARAGACEAE

Asparagus acutifolius - {S} The young shoots have a uniquely bitter, aromatic flavor. They are excellent in omelets or seasoned with oil and lemon juice. Preferred by some gourmets because of its stronger flavor. Mediterranean region. BIANCHINI, HEXAMER; N84

Asparagus aphyllus - {S} Young shoots are eaten in Greece. Mediterranean region. HEDRICK 1919; **W59M, Z25M**

Asparagus cochinchinensis - *Tenmondô* {S} Tuberous roots are eaten after preserving in sugar. Fruits also said to be edible. Southeast Asia. ALTSCHUL, TANAKA; F85

Asparagus officinalis - *Asparagus* {S} Young shoot tips are eaten boiled, steamed, sautéed, stir-fried, etc. Lower part of shoot can be used in soups. Blanched or white asparagus is preferred by some for its more delicate flavor. Seeds are used as a coffee substitute. Cultivated. HEDRICK 1919, UPHOF; D62, N84, S7M (for cultivars see Asparagus, page 254)

Asparagus sarmentosus - {S} Fleshy roots are eaten in Sri Lanka. In China they are candied. Southern Asia. HEDRICK 1919; *E53M*, *L5M*, N84, O93, *P17M*, *Q25*, *Q32*

ASPIDIACEAE

Dryopteris fragrans - *Serlik* {S} The leaves are made into a tea. Central Asia, North America. TANAKA; **Z25M**

ASPLENIACEAE

Asplenium bulbiferum - *Pikopiko* {S} Roots and young uncurled shoots are used as food. New Zealand. KUNKEL, NATUSCH; N84

Asplenium nidus - *O-tani-watari* {S} Leaves are parboiled and eaten. Ash from burned leaves is used as a substitute for salt. Tropics. CROFT, KUNKEL, TANAKA; *E53M*, H20{PL}, I28{PL}, M42{PL}, N84, O33, P5, *P17M*, *Q25*

ASTERACEAE (*COMPOSITAE*)

Achillea atrata - *Achillea noire* {S} Used in the same way as musk yarrow in the preparation of *iva liqueurs*. Europe. UPHOF; N84, *Q24*, S7M

Achillea decolorans - *Garden mace* {PL} The aromatic leaves are used as a substitute for tea. Also used as a flavoring for soups and stews, potato salad, etc. Europe. F35M, G96, J82, M82, N84{S}, P92, R53M

Achillea erb-rotta ssp. moschata - *Musk yarrow* {S} Source of a liqueur, called *esprit d'iva*, *iva liqueur*, or *iva wine*, produced in Italy. In Switzerland, *iva bitter* is produced. Europe. TANAKA, UPHOF; K47T, N84, S7M

Achillea ligustica - *Milfoil* {S} In England, the herb forms one of the main ingredients of an old-fashioned cordial, called *lovage*, along with the garden lovage (Levisticum officinale), and tansy (Tanacetum vulgare). Europe. GRIEVE; N84

Achillea millefolium - *Yarrow, White yarrow* {S} Young leaves are occasionally eaten in salads, cooked as a vegetable, or added to soups and sauces. In Germany, they add a characteristic flavor to *gründonnerstag suppe*. The leaves and flowers are brewed into an aromatic tea. In parts of Sweden, the herb is employed as a substitute for hops in the preparation of beer. An essential oil, derived from the flowering tops, is used commercially for flavoring soft drinks and alcoholic beverages. Northern temperate region, cultivated. GRIEVE, HEDRICK 1919, LOVELOCK, MARCIN, MICHAEL [Re], MORTON 1976, PAINTER [Cul, Re], UPHOF; C3, C67M{PL}, G59M{PL}, G68, G84{PL}, H40{PL}, H46, H80, I11M, I11M{PL}, I19, I19{PL}, K22{PL}, K53, N11M, etc.

CULTIVARS {PL}

Pink: (Rosea) Very aromatic foliage. Brilliant clusters of deep-pink flowers. Also good in dried arrangements, although the flowers lose their shape. C11{S}, C13M{S}, C43M, C67M, D11T, D92, F21, F31T, G68{S}, I22, I39, K22, K85, N19M, N84{S}, etc.

Achillea moschata → ***Achillea erb-rotta ssp. moschata***

Achillea nana - {S} Used in the preparation of *iva liqueurs*. Europe. UPHOF; K47T, N84, *Q24*, S7M

Ageratum conyzoides - *Meie parari* {S} The fragrant flowers and foliage are used for scenting coconut oil in southeastern Polynesia. Tropics. BROWN, F.; N84

Anacyclus pyrethrum - *Pellitory of Spain* {S} Source of an essential oil used in liqueurs. Roots are sometimes used for chewing. Mediterranean region. UPHOF, ZEVEN; R53M, R53M{PL}

Anthemis cotula - *May-weed, Dog fennel, Mansanilla* {S} An aromatic herb used for flavoring in Peru. Also used for making an herbal tea similar to chamomile. Northern temperate region. ALTSCHUL; D58, D62, K47T, N84

Anthemis nobilis → ***Chamaemelum nobile***

Arctium lappa - *Great burdock, Wild gobô* {S} Roots are sliced, boiled, and eaten as a vegetable. The peeled leaf-stalks and tender, young leaves are boiled and served like spinach or asparagus. Leaf-stalks are also parboiled and used as a substitute for cardoon. The pith of the flower-stalk can be eaten raw in tossed salads, boiled as a potherb, or made into a confection. Seeds can be sprouted and eaten like bean sprouts. Eurasia, naturalized in North America. ANGIER, FERNALD, GIBBONS 1962 [Re], GRIEVE, LARKCOM 1984, MACNICOL; A2, C11, C13M, D29, D29{PL}, D40G, D62, F24, K20, K47T, L86, *N71M*, N84, O48, O53M, S55, etc.

Arctium lappa 'Esculenta' - *Gobô, Japanese burdock* {S} Very young roots can be peeled and used in salads like radishes. Older roots are stir-fried, sautéed, roasted, added to soups and stews, or cooked with tofu, miso, yuba, etc. In Japan, both the stems and roots are pickled. Before use, the roots are shredded or cut into thin strips, and soaked in water to remove any strong flavors. HALPIN [Cu, Cul], HARRINGTON, G. [Cul], HERKLOTS, SCHNEIDER [Cul, Re], SHURTLEFF 1975 [Pre, Re]; A2, C82, E56{PR}, E59, E66T{PR}, G33, G44M{PR}, H67M{PR}, I99, J83T{PR}, K49M, N84

CULTIVARS

Ami: Straight, cylindrical roots; 24 to 28 inches long; white skin; good tightness in neck. Excellent uniformity. Good flavor and crispness; slow in turning spongy inside. Reddish colored petioles. Good winter hardiness. For fresh market and processing. Q88

Sakigake: 120 days. Rapid-growing, solid roots are flavorful, smooth, and white in color. Matures earlier than other cultivars and becomes 2 feet long or more and 3/4 to 1 inch in diameter without becoming pithy. A leading cultivar in Japanese markets. E49, E83T

Takinogawa Long: 150 days. Long, smooth, slender root; 30 to 36 inches in length, about 1 inch in diameter; flesh is light-yellow, with very little fiber. Largest diameter is attained when grown in deep soils. Petioles are reddish colored. Mild, bittersweet flavor. The most popular cultivar grown in Japan. C43M{PL}, D55, E49, E59Z, G6, I39, J20, J73, J82, K49T, L59, N84, S55, S61, *S63M*, etc.

Tokiwa: Large roots, 1 to 1 1/2 inches in diameter and 3 or more feet in length. Very light yellow flesh. Should be planted early in spring through mid-summer. E83T

Watanabe Early: 120 days. A very rapid grower, producing long, slender roots about 30 inches long with fine-textured flesh of good flavor. Very popular in Japan. M46, O53M, *S63M*

Arctium minus - *Burdock, Beggar's buttons* {S} The young leaves and leaf-stalks are eaten as potherbs. Young flower stalk is peeled and eaten raw, used as a salad, or cooked as asparagus. Peeled and sliced roots can be eaten with sesame seeds and soy sauce. Roasted and ground roots are used as a coffee substitute. Eurasia, naturalized in North America. HARRINGTON, H., MABEY, MEDSGER, MICHAEL [Pre, Re]; A2, D58, F85, I99, K47T, N84, O48

Arctotheca calendulaceum - {S} Said to be used in cooking. The pollen is much appreciated. Southern Africa. KUNKEL; F85, N84, R41, R77M

Artemisia abrotanum - *Old man, Southernwood* {PL} The young, bitter shoots and leaves are sometimes employed as an ingredient of beer. In Italy, they are used to flavor cakes and confections. Also brewed into a tea. Eurasia. HEDRICK 1919, MICHAEL [Pre, Re], MORTON 1976, PAINTER, UPHOF; C9, C43M, C67M, C81M, D29, D62{S}, E61, F21, G84, H3M, I39, J66, K85, M82, N19M, etc.

Artemisia absinthium - *Wormwood* {PL} The herb has been used in the preparation of a liqueur, *absinthe*, now banned in many countries. Also employed for flavoring other alcoholic beverages including *vermouth* and *muse verte*. At one time it was a common substitute for hops in beermaking. The flowering tops are used in continental Europe to counteract the greasiness of goose and duck dishes. Eurasia, cultivated. CORNELL, GIBBONS 1962, GRIEVE, MABEY, MORTON 1976, UPHOF; C3, C11{S}, C13M{S}, C67M, D29, D62{S}, F21, F24{S}, F31T, G84, H40, I77M, K22, N19M, N42, etc.

Artemisia afra - *African wormwood* {PL} The herb is used in some parts of Africa in the same way that A. absinthium is used. Southern Africa. UPHOF; C43M, C81M, G84, K22, K85, M82, N42, N84{S}, R41{S}, R77M{S}

Artemisia annua - *Sweet wormwood, Sweet Annie* {PL} In China, the plant is used as a medium for growing Aspergillus employed in brewing wine. Eurasia, cultivated. TANAKA; C3, C13M{S}, C43M, C43M{S}, C67M, D40G{S}, E7M{S}, F21, F35M, G84, K22, L7M{S}, *M35*, M53, N19M, N42, etc.

Artemisia asiatica - *Nishi-yomogi* {PL} In Japan, the leaves are pounded with steamed glutinous-rice to give it flavor and color. The resulting cake or dumpling is known as *yomogi-mochi*. The young leaves are eaten with barley. Eastern Asia. ALTSCHUL, TANAKA; C43M

Artemisia dracunculus - *Russian tarragon, Wild tarragon* {S} The oily seeds were eaten by the Indians of Utah and Nevada. Leaves were baked between hot stones and consumed with salt water. The leaves are also eaten in salads or used as an inferior substitute for French tarragon. North America. LARKCOM 1984, LATHROP, MASEFIELD, YANOVSKY; B1M, B13, C11, C43M{PL}, C82{PL}, C85M, *E91G*, G51, G64, G93M, G96{PL}, I67M, I77, J20, S55, etc.

Artemisia dracunculus 'Sativa' - *French tarragon* {PL} The young, licorice-flavored tips and leaves are added to salads, vinegar, pickles, sauces, etc. Fresh or dried leaves are essential ingredients of *béarnaise*, *tartare*, and *béchamel* sauces and tarragon mustard. The young shoots are cooked and eaten as a potherb. In the Near East, cooked or raw, they are served as an appetizer. Eurasia, cultivated. DE SOUNIN, GRIEVE, HEDRICK 1919, ROOT 1980a, ROOT 1980b [Cul], VILMORIN; C3, C9, C43M, C67M, C82, F21, F31T, G84, H40, J82, K22, *M35*, N19M

CULTIVARS

Epicure: A new fragrant cultivar. G55, I39

Artemisia frigida - *Fringed wormwood* {PL} Leaves are used by the Hopi Indians for flavoring sweet-corn. North America, Northern Asia. KIRK, LATHROP, UPHOF; A49D, C40, C43M, D29, D62{S}, F35M, G55, *G66*, G84, I47{S}, J25M, J25M{S}, L57, L86, M82, N19M, etc.

Artemisia genipi - *Spiked wormwood* {S} The herb is used in the preparation of *eau d'absinthe*. Europe. HEDRICK 1919; L91M, N84, *Q24*, S7M

Artemisia glacialis - *Genépi des glaciers* {S} The herb is used for flavoring *vermouth* and liqueurs. Europe. UPHOF; D62, K47T, N84, O53M, *Q24*, S7M

Artemisia indica → Artemisia asiatica

Artemisia judaica - *Semen contra, Graines à vers* {S} Used as a condiment and for flavoring liqueurs. Mediterranean region, Southwest Asia. TANAKA, UPHOF; F85

Artemisia lactiflora → Artemisia vulgaris

Artemisia laxa → Artemisia umbelliforme

Artemisia ludoviciana - *Louisiana wormwood, White prairie-sage, Cudweed, Estafiate* {PL} Leaves and flower-heads are used as a seasoning, or made into tea. Leaves are also used as a garnish for wild game and pork dishes. Chopped leaves can be added to sauces and gravies. Seeds are also eaten. North America. CROWHURST 1973, HUTSON [Cul], YANOVSKY; C67M, *E66M*, F31T, F93G, G84, *G89M*, *I23*, I47{S}, J25M, J25M{S}, J41M, J41M{S}, J43{S}, M82, N19M, etc.

Artemisia maritima - *Sea wormwood, Wormseed* {S} The herb is used for flavoring. Eurasia. UPHOF; N84, R53M{PL}, S55

Artemisia mutellina → Artemisia umbelliforme

Artemisia pontica - *Roman wormwood, Petite absinthe* {PL} Used for flavoring aperitifs and cordials, and also for the preparation of *Pontic vermouth*. Southern Europe. BROUK, GRIEVE, MORTON 1976; C3, C9, C67M, C81M, D29, E5M, G84, H3M, J82, K22, K85, *M35*, M82, N19M, N45, etc.

Artemisia princeps - *Japanese mugwort, Yomogi* {S} The leaves and young seedlings are eaten in salads and soups, after the bitterness has been removed. After being boiled briefly, the leaves are pounded into glutinous-rice dumplings (*mochi*). They impart a delightful color, aroma, and flavor. Mugwort mochi is widely available at natural foods stores in North America. Japan. TANAKA, YASHIRODA; E56{PR}, **V19**

Artemisia spicata → Artemisia genipi

Artemisia stelleriana - *Beach wormwood, Old woman, Shiro-yomogi* {PL} Leaves are used for flavoring rice dumplings. Northern temperate region. TANAKA; B9M, B28, B92, C9, C13M{S}, C43M, E30, I63M, J24, J37M, K22, K79, K85, *L22*, L56, L57, *L95*, M82, O48, etc.

Artemisia umbelliforme - *Alpine wormwood* {S} The herb is used for the preparation of a tea and liqueur, often with the addition of absinthe. Southern Europe. UPHOF; D62{PL}, G82M{PL}, K47T, K79{PL}, N84, O53M, S7M

Artemisia vulgaris - *Mugwort* {PL} Young shoots and leaves are an indispensable condiment for fat poultry such as geese and ducks, as well as fat pork, mutton, and eel. In Japan, they are boiled and eaten as a potherb, or used to give flavor and color to festival rice-cakes, *mochi* and *dango*. Dried leaves and flowering tops are added to country beer, or steeped into tea. Northern temperate region. FERNALD, GRIEVE, LAUNERT, MARCIN, MORTON 1976, ROOT 1980b [Cul], UPHOF; C3, C11{S}, C13M{S}, C43M, C67M, C81M, D29, D40G{S}, E61, F21, F24{S}, F31T, G84, H3M, H25{S}, N45, N84{S}, etc.

CULTIVARS

White: (Yomogi-Na, Junn Jiu Choi, White Wormwood, Ghostplant) Tall, showy plant with pale-green, trifoliate leaves and distinctive 8 to 10 inch long, reddish-purple leaf stalks. Height 3 to 5 feet. Produces spikes of creamy flowers in late summer. Has a strong, rather resinous or "floral" taste similar to chrysanthemum leaves. Used in soups or fried as a side dish. DAHLEN [Cul, Re]; C43M, E5M, G84, K22, K85, M82, N84{S}

Balsamita major - *Costmary, Bible-leaf, Alecost* {PL} Young, tender leaves are chopped and used sparingly in salads. They are also used as a seasoning for ale and beer, sauces, stuffings, soups, poultry, and stews. Whole leaves can be laid in cake pans to flavor cakes while baking. Flower petals are used for conserves. The dried leaves are often brewed into tea. Southwest Asia, cultivated. GRIEVE, LARKCOM 1984, LATHROP, MACNICOL, MORTON 1976; C3, C9, C11{S}, C67M, D29, E61, F31T, F35M, G84, J66, K22, N19M, N45

Balsamorhiza hookeri - *Hooker's balsam-root* {S} The roots are eaten raw or cooked. Seeds are also consumed. Western North

America. HEDRICK 1919, MEDSGER, YANOVSKY; G82M{PL}, O53M

Balsamorhiza sagittata - *Arrowleaf balsam-root, Oregon sunflower* {S} Young shoots and leaves are eaten raw in salads or boiled as a potherb. The seeds are roasted and ground into flour for breadmaking. Roots are eaten raw, cooked, or roasted and used as a coffee substitute. Flathead Indians baked them in a fire pit, like camass, for at least three days. The young, immature flower-stalk can be peeled, and the tender inner portion eaten raw, like celery. Western North America. HART, HEDRICK 1919, KIRK, KUNKEL, YANOVSKY; A2, E15, *E66M*, F44, F85, I47, K47T, K62, L91M, N84, O53M, *Q24*, S7M

Bellis perennis - *English daisy* {S} Flower petals of the cultivated forms, and the whole flowers of the wild plant are eaten in salads. Flower buds can be eaten in sandwiches, soups, and salads. Preserved in vinegar, they serve as a substitute for capers. The leaves are occasionally used as a potherb. Eurasia, cultivated. HEDRICK 1919, LARKCOM 1984, LAUNERT, LEGGATT [Re], MACNICOL [Re]; A16, A53M, C11, D62, *E91G*, F24, F80, G84{PL}, J82, K22{PL}, K53, K85{PL}, M82{PL}, N45{PL}, *N71M*, etc.

Berlandiera lyrata - *Chocolate flower* {S} Flowers are used for seasoning foods. Western North America. YANOVSKY; *I23*{PL}, I37M{PL}, J25M, J25M{PL}, K49T, L13, L91M, N84

Bidens pilosa - *Spanish needles, Beggar's ticks* {S} The young shoots and leaves are eaten raw or steamed, added to soups and stews, or dried and stored for future use. Also used as a substitute for tea. In the Philippines, the plant is used in the preparation of a rice wine, called *tafei* or *sinitsit*. Cosmopolitan. CRIBB, FOX, F., MARTIN 1975, UPHOF, VAN EPENHUIJSEN; D62, F80, N84

Bidens tripartita - *Water agrimony, Ta-ukogi* {S} Young leaves are boiled and eaten. Tropics. TANAKA; D62, I99, N84, O53M

Cacalia atriplicifolia - *Pale Indian-plantain* {S} Young leaves are eaten as a potherb. North America. KUNKEL; G47M, J39M, J39M{PL}, J43

Cacalia farfaraefolia - *Tamabuki* {S} The young plants are boiled and put into soup, eaten with soy sauce, or seasoned with miso or ground walnut. Japan. TANAKA; **V19**

Calendula arvensis - *Kinsen-ka, Souci des Champs* {S} Young shoots and leaves are boiled and eaten. The flower-heads are pickled. In the Sinai and Negev desert areas, the Bedouins use the leaves as a condiment for clarified butter (*samin*). Mediterranean region, Southwest Asia. BAILEY, C., KUNKEL, TANAKA; **V73, V83M, V84, V89, W59M, W92, X36, X39, Y17M, Z98**

Calendula officinalis - *Pot marigold* {S} Fresh flower petals are chopped and sprinkled on tossed salads. When dried, they have a more concentrated flavor, and are used for seasoning soups, puddings, cakes and cookies, and for coloring butter and cheese. Both flowers and petals can be used for tea, the flower-petal tea being less bitter. Pot marigold is sometimes employed as an adulterant of saffron. Southern Europe, cultivated. BRYAN [Cu, Cul], GRIEVE, HEDRICK 1919, LARKCOM 1984, LEGGATT [Re], MACNICOL [Re], MORTON 1976; C9M, C13M, C67M{PL}, D29{PL}, F24, F33, G84{PL}, H3M{PL}, K22, K53, M82{PL}, N19M{PL}, N45{PL}, *N71M*

CULTIVARS

<u>Hen and Chickens:</u> An unusual form in which the normal orange double flower is surrounded by smaller secondary flowers arranged in sun and planet form, having stalks emerging from just beneath the petals of the central parent bloom. Suitable for culinary use. Q34

<u>Kablouna Gold:</u> (Kablouna Yellow) A very distinct and unique form of calendula, especially recommended for culinary use. Plants are 18 to 20 inches tall; free flowering. Blooms are about 2 inches across. Flowers form a crested center, reminiscent of a miniature honeycomb, concealing the eye. In some the center extends 2/3 of the way to the tips of the single petals. B97{PL}, C61M, F80, G87, I99, J20, K49T, K66, L91M, Q34

<u>Kablouna Mix:</u> Mixture of gold, orange, and lemon, some with radiant dark centers. Can be cut from early summer to frost. Does well in cool summer areas. C53, L91M, O53M

<u>Kablouna Orange:</u> Similar to Kablouna Yellow, but with deep orange flowers. Has a neat crested center not showing the eye. Excellent for culinary use and cut flower arrangements. Blooms well in cool weather when many other flowers have not started or have finished flowering. C61M, D68, J20, Q34

Carduus eriophorus* → *Cirsium eriophorum

Carduus nutans - *Musk thistle* {S} The pith of the flowering stem is said to be delicious when boiled for a brief time in salted water and dressed. The dried flowers are used in some countries as a rennet to curdle milk. Eurasia. FERNALD; D58, *N71M*, N84, O48

Carlina acanthifolia - *Acanthus-leaved thistle* {S} The receptacle of the flowers may be used like that of an artichoke. Mediterranean region. HEDRICK 1919; D62, L91M, N84, O53M, *Q24*, S7M

Carlina acaulis - *Dwarf carline-thistle, Silver thistle* {S} Flower receptacles are boiled and eaten like artichokes in some mountainous regions of Europe. In the Alps they are known as *chardousse*, in the Cévennes as *cardavelle*, and to the Germans they are *wild artichokes*. Europe. LOVELOCK, TANAKA; C13M, D62, E61{PL}, *E91G*, K47T, K98, L91M, *N71M*, N84, O53M, S7M

Carlina vulgaris - *Carline thistle* {S} The receptacle of the flowers can be eaten in the same manner as an artichoke. Eurasia. HEDRICK 1919; *N71M*, N84, O48, O53M, *Q24*, S7M

Carthamus lanatus - {S} Said to be the source of an edible oil. Mediterranean region, Southwest Asia. TANAKA; **U63, V73, V83M, V89, W59M, X39, Y10, Y17M, Y89M, Z98**

Carthamus tinctorius - *Safflower, Mexican saffron* {S} Dried flowers are the source of a red and a yellow dye used for coloring butter, liqueurs, and confectionery. In the food industry it serves as an adulterant of saffron. The seeds are fried and eaten in chutney, or used as a substitute for rennet in coagulating milk. Also the source of an edible oil widely utilized in salads, cooking, margarine, etc. Leaves can be eaten as a potherb or seasoned with soy sauce. Eurasia, cultivated. GRIEVE, ROOT 1980b [Cul], TANAKA, UPHOF; C3, C11, C13M, C43M, E7M, E61, F24, F37T, G51, G68, G84, J73, K22, M46, N84, etc.

Centaurea cyanus - *Cornflower, Bachelor's button* {S} The flowers are eaten as a vegetable, used as a garnish and are added to beer. They also yield a blue dye used for coloring sugar and gelatine. Mediterranean region. LEGGATT, MACNICOL; A2, C9M, D26, E73M, F24, F44, H80, I15M, I94, I94{PL}, J53, J88, M47M, N11M, O53M, etc.

Centaurea nigra - *Lesser knapweed, Hardhead* {S} Flower petals have been used in salads. Europe, naturalized in North America. MABEY; D62, *N71M*, N84, O48, O53M, P83M, *Q24*, S55

Chamaemelum nobile - *Roman chamomile, English chamomile* {PL} Fresh or dried flowers are made into a pleasant-tasting tea. In Spain, they flavor *manzanilla sherry*. The whole herb is used in making herb beers. The small sprigs, gathered at the proper time, can be used to lend a subtle flavor to cream sauces, butter, honey, and sour cream. Eurasia, cultivated. BRYAN [Cul, Re], GRIEVE [Cu], MACNICOL, MARCIN, MORTON 1976, PAINTER, UPHOF; C3, C13M{S},

C67M, C82, C82{S}, D29, F21, F31T, G84, J66, J73{S}, J82, *M35*, N19M, N45, etc.

CULTIVARS

Lawn: Low growing, dense mat with strong, sweet odor; 2 inches high. Produces many flowers, which can be used for tea. This is the English lawn chamomile so long used for benches and flagstone filler. The flowers must be removed to make a successful lawn. E5M, K22, K85, P83M{S}

Treneague: More compact and tight growing than Lawn chamomile; 1 to 2 inches high. Very sweet, apple-scented foliage. Does not produce flowers, so requires no cutting for a successful lawn. Withstands quite acid soil. Probably originated as a sport from the Buckingham Palace lawns in 1932. A49D, C9, C43M, D29, E61, F35M, K85, L56, M82, R53M, S55

Chamomilla aurea - *German chamomile, Hungarian chamomile* {PL} The dried flower-heads are brewed into an aromatic tea. Also used for flavoring fine liqueurs of the French type, such as *Benedictine* and *D.O.M.*. Source of an essential oil utilized by the food industry for enhancing fruit flavors in ice cream, candy, baked goods, and chewing gum. Mediterranean region. MORTON 1976, UPHOF; C3, C13M{S}, C67M, D29, D29{S}, F21, G84, H25{S}, J20{S}, J66, J82{S}, K22{S}, N19M

Chrysanthemum balsamita* → *Balsamita major

Chrysanthemum coronarium - *Garland chrysanthemum, Shun-giku, Chop suey greens* {S} The aromatic leaves and tender stems are parboiled and seasoned with soy sauce, miso, or ground sesame seeds. They are also eaten raw in salads, stir-fried, made into fritters, or used as a seasoning for soups and suki-yaki. In Japan, a fragrant pickle, *kikumi*, is made with fresh chrysanthemum petals. The flowers can also be blanched briefly and added to salads, or prepared as tempura. Eurasia, cultivated. COST 1988 [Cul, Re], HALPIN, HARRINGTON, G. [Cu, Cul], HERKLOTS, KRAFT [Re], LARKCOM 1980, MACNICOL [Re], PAINTER [Re], TANAKA; A79M, B49, C9M, C43M{PL}, C53, C82, C85M, E24, E59, F33, F44, G6, G33, L89, M46, O53M, etc.

CULTIVARS

Aonami: Vigorous plant yields profuse branches in the fall; yields are about 1 1/2 times higher than common cultivars. Rich aromatic flavor. Good adaptability to greenhouse culture. Tolerant to cold; easy to grow under low temperature conditions. *Q28*

Flavon: Medium-sized, attractive green leaves with a pleasant flavor. Excellent in salads or cooked with fish. Very easy to grow; can be grown year round; slightly spreading growth habit. *Q3*

Hua Ye: 30-60 days. Early Chinese cultivar. Tender stem, about 11 3/4 inches long; blades green in color, ellipse shaped; delicate fragrance. Widely adapted. Resistant to disease. Quick growing; suitable for growing outdoors or in protected fields. *O54*

Large Leaved: (Round Leaved) 35 days. Large, oblong leaves, dark-green in color; thick and very smooth. Very popular for stir-frying or for adding to soups; rich aromatic flavor. Plant in early spring or fall. D55, E49, K49M, L59, *L79G*, *S63M*, *S70*

Maiko: Dark-green, aromatic leaves. Used for *ohi-tashi* and *yosenabe*, and as a potherb to be boiled with meat. Can be harvested 50 days after sowing, or when about 8 inches tall in temperate areas. Very vigorous grower; prolific producer of lateral shoots; prefers cool weather conditions. Best sown between summer and early fall. *S63M*

Narrow Leaved: Narrow-leaved cultivar with bi-color flowers. I99

Ohba: Large, thick, very uniform leaves; soft texture; good flavor and aroma. Early maturing. Adapted to various usage. *Q28*

Sanae: Selected as an early strain that branches well when topped. Medium-sized, lobed, very tender leaves with a unique aroma. High yielding. Excellent development of branches. Easy to grow. *Q28*

Small Leaved: (Serrate Leaved) 35 days. Similar to Large Leaved, but the leaves are smaller and deeply serrated, and the flavor is slightly milder. D55, E49, K49M, L59, *L79G*, *S63M*, *S70*

Chrysanthemum indicum - *Mother chrysanthemum* {PL} Flower-heads are pickled in vinegar. Young leaves are eaten fried or boiled. Also used as a tea. The seeds are edible. Eastern Asia. ALTSCHUL, TANAKA; N37M

Chrysanthemum leucanthemum* → *Leucanthemum vulgare

Chrysanthemum x morifolium - *Ryôri-giku, Edible chrysanthemum* {PL} The flower-heads are boiled and served as a salad with fish or tofu, and seasoned with vinegar or soy sauce. They are also prepared as tempura, pickled, dried, or added to soups. The aromatic leaves are used in fritters or made into a tea. Flowers or flower petals can also be brewed into a tangy, aromatic tea. For a sweeter tea, the petals only are used. Eastern Asia, cultivated. CLARKE [Re], GESSERT, LEGGATT [Re], MARCIN, TANAKA, YASHIRODA [Pre, Re]; C9, N84{S}

Chrysanthemum parthenium* → *Tanacetum parthenium

Chrysanthemum segetum - *Corn marigold, Tung-hao* {S} Young shoots are consumed as a vegetable in some parts of Asia, especially in China. Eurasia. UPHOF; D62, E33, F24, F80, *N71M*, N84, O48, O53M, P83M, S45M, S55

Cicerbita alpina - *Mountain sow-thistle* {S} The bitter stem is peeled and eaten raw by the Laplanders. Europe. HEDRICK 1919; **V73M, Z88**

Cichorium endivia - *Endive, Escarole* Leaves are eaten raw in salads, boiled, steamed, sautéed, braised, or cooked in soups and stews. The mature plants are sometimes blanched before harvesting to reduce the bitter flavor. In Java, they are pickled in brine. Eurasia, cultivated. CARCIONE [Re], LARKCOM 1984, VILMORIN [Cu]; (for cultivars see Endive, page 326)

Cichorium intybus - *Chicory* {S} The somewhat bitter leaves are eaten raw in salads, boiled, steamed, braised, or used in soups and stews. Some types are grown for their blanched shoots, others for their roots, which are eaten as a vegetable or used as a substitute for coffee. The attractive blue flowers can be used in salads, fresh or pickled. Eurasia, cultivated. FERNALD, GIBBONS 1962 [Re], HALPIN [Cu, Cul], HARRINGTON, H., LARKCOM 1984, MACNICOL [Re], UPHOF, VILMORIN [Cu]; C9M, C13M, E7M, E73M, F59, G47M, G84{PL}, H61M, H80, I15M, I94, I94{PL}, K62, M47M, N11M, etc. (for cultivars see Chicory, page 299)

Cirsium arvense - *Canada thistle* {S} The young shoots and flower stalks are boiled and eaten as a vegetable. Roots can be eaten raw or cooked. The herb has been used to coagulate milk. Northern temperate region. LAUNERT, UPHOF; D58, *N71M*, N84

Cirsium eriophorum - *Woolly-headed thistle* {S} Young leaves and shoots are eaten as a salad. The young stalks, peeled and soaked in water to remove the bitterness, are said to be excellent, either boiled or baked in pies in the same manner as rhubarb. The pulpy receptacles are eaten like those of the artichoke. Eurasia. GRIEVE, HEDRICK 1919; F85, N84, O48, *Q24*

Cirsium lanceolatum* → *Cirsium vulgare

Cirsium oleraceum - *Meadow cabbage* {S} Very young succulent parts of the plant are cooked and used as a vegetable in some regions of Russia and Siberia. The swollen root-stock, gathered before the plant flowered, was formerly used as a table vegetable. Eurasia. HEDRICK 1919, UPHOF, VILMORIN; *N71M*

Cirsium palustre - *Marsh thistle* {S} The young shoots and peeled flower-stalks are eaten raw in salads, or boiled and served as a vegetable. Eurasia. FERNALD, GRIEVE, HEDRICK 1919, LARKCOM 1984; N84, O48

Cirsium tanakae - *Nohara-azami* {S} Young leaves are eaten in soups, fried, or oil-roasted. Roots are scraped into pieces, steeped in water and preserved in miso. The flower heads are fried or used in salads. Eastern Asia. TANAKA; **V19**

Cirsium vulgare - *Common thistle, Bull thistle, Bur thistle* {S} Young flower-stalks and roots are boiled and eaten as a vegetable. The young leaves can be soaked overnight in salted water and then cooked and eaten. Receptacles are cooked and served like artichokes. The dried flowers are used as a substitute for rennet in curdling milk for cheesemaking. Roasted seeds are occasionally eaten. Eurasia, naturalized in North America. CLARKE [Re], FERNALD, HARRINGTON, H.; N84

Cnicus benedictus - *Blessed thistle* {S} The herb is used for flavoring. In Germany, it forms an ingredient of *kölner klosterpillen*. Mediterranean region. TANAKA, UPHOF; A2, C13M, C43M, C43M{PL}, E81M, F24, F80, G84{PL}, H3M{PL}, I99, J82, M82{PL}, N45{PL}, N84, O53M, S55, etc.

Cnicus eriophorus → ***Cirsium eriophorum***

Cnicus oleraceus → ***Cirsium oleraceum***

Cnicus palustris → ***Cirsium palustre***

Conyza canadensis - *Canada fleabane, Horseweed, Hime-mukashi-yomogi* {S} In Japan, the young leaves and seedlings are eaten boiled, cooked with rice, or dried for future use. Source of an essential oil used commercially for flavoring candy, condiments, and soft drinks. North America. ALTSCHUL, FOX, F., MORTON 1976, TANAKA; D58, F85, J43, K47T, *N71M*, N84, O48

Coreopsis cardaminifolia - {S} A decoction of the herb was used as a beverage by the Zuñi Indians. North America. UPHOF, YANOVSKY; **V73**

Cosmos caudatus - *Margarita* {S} In Indonesia, the young leaves and tops are eaten raw, cooked, added to stews, or mixed with grated coconut and oriental radish. The leaves are also mixed with rice to prepare yeast. Tropical America. BURKILL, OCHSE; F85

Crassocephalum crepidioides - *Ebolo* {S} Young leaves and shoots are used as a potherb. Tropical Africa. DALZIEL, TANAKA, VAN EPENHUIJSEN; F85

Cynara cardunculus - *Cardoon* {S} The blanched leaf-stalks are eaten boiled, batter-fried, braised, sautéed, pickled, or used in soups and stews. In Italy, raw strips are dipped into olive oil or *bagna cauda*, a hot anchovy and garlic dip. The root is thick, fleshy, tender, and of an agreeable flavor. It can be cooked like carrots or parsnips. The young leaves and stalks were eaten as a salad in ancient Rome. Flower receptacles can be eaten like artichokes. In Portugal, dried flowers are used as a substitute for rennet in making *Serra* cheese. Cultivated. BIANCHINI, HALPIN [Cu, Cul], HEDRICK 1919, KOSIKOWSKI, KRAFT [Re], MACNICOL [Re], SCHNEIDER [Pre, Re], VILMORIN [Cu]; C11, C43M{PL}, C82, C85M, D29{PL}, E59T{PL}, E61, E61{PL}, F35M{PL}, G68, G84{PL}, J20, J73, M46, *N40*{PR}, P83M, etc.

CULTIVARS

Champion: An improved type from Canada with large, tender stalks. G64

Gigante d'Ingegnoli: Large, very tender stalks, completely free of spines. Somewhat resistant to dry growing conditions. Q11M

Gigante di Romagna: Very large, tender stalks. Harvested in December. Decorative as well as useful. S55

Large Smooth: Select strain, much improved over the old artichoke-leaved type. Smooth, thick, heavy stalks. Grows to 6 feet tall. Requires rich soil. C44, C92

Plein Blanc Inerme: Large, smooth, solid white stalks. Grows 3 to 4 feet high with an equal diameter. An excellent home garden type from France. J7

Suffolk: Tall vigorous plant, height 5 feet. Large, tender stalks. Harvested in December. Attractive in both the vegetable and flower garden. C81M

Tenderheart: 120-150 days. Plants grow 3 to 4 feet tall with deeply cut leaves, multiple side-branches, and a heavy flower-head with purple bristles. Blanched stalks of the inner leaves are tender and are used as a winter vegetable. 90 days from transplants. G51, G93M

Cynara humilis - *Wild artichoke, Coque* {S} In Morocco, the dried flowers are employed as a rennet in coagulating *raipe*, a type of sweetened junket. The flower receptacles are used in the preparation of a popular *tagine* (stew). Mediterranean region. WOLFERT [Pre, Re]; **Z19**

Cynara scolymus - *Artichoke* {S} The fleshy receptacles (sometimes called crowns), and the floral bracts are eaten raw, boiled, steamed, baked, fried, stuffed, marinated, etc. Small, or *baby artichokes*, that form on the lateral shoots are pickled, preserved in oil, or used in soups, stews, and omelettes. When marinated, they are sold as *artichoke hearts*. In Italy, the dried receptacles are utilized in soups. The tender, inner portion of the flower stalk has a sweet, nutty flavor and is eaten raw or cooked. Flowers are used as a substitute for rennet. The young leaf-stalks, which were once known as *artichoke chard*, are blanched and eaten like cardoon. Also used in the preparation of an alcoholic beverage, *cyna*. Cultivated. BIANCHINI, BRYAN [Cul, Re], BURR, CARCIONE, GRIEVE [Re], HACKETT, VILMORIN [Cu]; D76, D76{PL}, E5M{PL}, E97{PL}, F35M{PL}, G68, I99, K85{PL}, L97

CULTIVARS

French Green Globe: An improved Green Globe type with thick scales. Also used for dried flower arrangements. C85M

Grande Beurre: 210 days. Large, flattened, spineless heads. Very consistent in size. Fleshy and delicious. Grows 6 to 8 feet tall. Developed to bear in its first year. Particularly well suited for growing as an annual. **U33**

Green Globe: Large heads, nearly round, and with a dusky, purplish tint; thick, highly flavored scales. Receptacles are very fleshy, more so than in most cultivars. Plants grow 4 to 6 feet high, 6 to 8 feet wide. Mature plants may yield 12 to 20 buds each. The standard cultivar, valued for its ability to produce uniform plants from seed. A87M, C44, C92, D11M, E4{PL}, E38, E49, E67G{PL}, E67G{PR}, F11{PL}, G71, J7, L89, L97{PL}, M13M, N39, etc.

Green Globe Improved: 180 days. Much improved strain. Large, globe-shaped heads; deep-green throughout, no purple tint; 2 to 4 inches in diameter. Consistently heavy-bearing plants, 4 1/2 to 5 feet tall; the number of sharp spines greatly reduced making it easy to harvest. Like Green Globe, produces heads the first year from seed. C92, F82, I67M, I91, I91{PL}, J20, K71, *L59G*, L91M, M46, Q34

Purple: This cultivar is quite similar to Green Globe. Grows 4 feet tall and produces flower-heads with purple bracts. E49

Purple Sicilian: Produces the small, deep purple artichokes the French and Italians eat "cru" or raw, when very young and tender. Also good steamed. Heat tolerant, but not cold resistant; mulch if temperatures drop below freezing, or over-winter in large tubs. I77, K49M

Texas Hill: Low-chill artichoke. Adapted to Southwest conditions of high heat and alkalinity and warm winter temperatures. Heads variable in size; first buds large, later ones more numerous but smaller; 14 to 28 per plant. Produces about 30% purple bracts. Grows 4 feet tall by 4 feet wide. Developed by Duane Palmer from USDA germplasm. A87M, *I85*

Violetto di Chioggia: (Violetto) Produces a flavorful and attractive purple head, decorative enough for the flower border. More elongated than the Green Globe type. Some heads will be green from this seed, so select the best before planting out. These selected plants can then be propagated by division. I77, J20, P83M, S55

Violetto di Romagna: (Purple Romanesco) Produces large, globe-shaped, greenish violet heads that are spineless. B8, Q34

Dahlia pinnata - *Garden dahlia* {S} The tubers are eaten as a vegetable in some parts of Mexico. Flower petals can be eaten in salads. A sweet extract of the tuber, marketed as *Dacopa*, is used as a beverage or flavoring. It is mixed with hot or cold water or milk, or sprinkled on ice cream. Its naturally sweet, mellow taste is said to combine the characteristic flavors of coffee, tea, and chocolate. Central America, cultivated. HEDRICK 1919, UPHOF; D62, L69{PL}, L69{PR}, N84

Emilia coccinea - *Tassel flower* {S} Leaves are eaten raw in salads, or cooked as a potherb. Tropical Africa. DALZIEL, TANAKA; N84, P9

Emilia sagittata → Emilia coccinea

Emilia sonchifolia - *Floras paint brush, Yieh-hsia-hung* {S} The young, not yet flowering plant is eaten in salads, soups, or steamed and consumed as a side dish with rice. Frequently sold in the native markets of Java. Tropics, weedy. CRIBB, OCHSE, TANAKA; N84

Erechtites valerianifolia - *Brazilian fireweed* {S} In Indonesia, the flowering tops are eaten raw, or steamed and served with rice. Tropical America. BURKILL, CRIBB, OCHSE; **Y10**

Erigeron canadensis → Conyza canadensis

Farfugium japonicum → Ligularia kaempferi

Galactites tomentosa - {S} Young leaves and shoots are cooked with oil and salt. The tender flower-stem is also eaten. Mediterranean region. HEDRICK 1919; **W92, Z88**

Galinsoga parviflora - *Quickweed, Gallant soldier, Guascas* {S} The leaves, stems, and flowering shoots are cooked and eaten as a potherb, or added to soups and stews. In Colombia, the herb is sold in jars, dried and ground into a green powder. It is used there to flavor soups and stews, especially those made with chicken. The fresh juice can be drunk mixed with tomato or other vegetable juices. South America, naturalized in North America. CRIBB, FERNALD, GIBBONS 1979, HARRINGTON, H., LAUNERT, ORTIZ 1979; F85

Grindelia squarrosa - *Resinweed, Gum plant* {S} The fresh or dried leaves are used to make an aromatic, slightly bitter but pleasing tea. A sticky, resinous sap that covers the leaves can be used as a chewing gum substitute. Western North America. KINDSCHER, KIRK; H61M

Guizotia abyssinica - *Niger seed, Ramtil* {S} The seeds are eaten fried, used as a condiment, or mixed with honey and flour and made into sweet cakes. Also the source of an edible oil used in cooking, as a substitute for *ghee*, or an adulterant of sesame oil. In Ethiopian cooking, it is used in place of *niter kibbeh*, a clarified, spiced butter. Sold as *thistle seed* for feeding birds in the United States. Tropical Africa. BIANCHINI, UPHOF, VON WELANETZ, WATT; A25, D3, D62, F12, F19M, F85, G26, K27M, M13M, M75

Gynura crepidioides → Crassocephalum crepidioides

Gynura procumbens → Gynura sarmentosa

Gynura sarmentosa - *Bâu dât, Rau hung lui* {S} The leaves are used as a condiment. Tropical Asia. BURKILL, UPHOF; **Y10**

Helianthus annuus - *Sunflower* The seeds are eaten raw, boiled, roasted, salted, or made into sunflower butter and *tempeh*. Also the source of an edible oil used in salads, cooking, margarine, etc. Young seedlings, called *sunflower lettuce*, are popular with natural foods enthusiasts. The flower receptacles can be steamed and served like artichokes. Ground seeds are sometimes added to soups. Germinated seeds are blended with water and fermented into *seed yogurt* or *seed cheese*. The young petioles are eaten grilled and seasoned with oil and salt. Roasted hulls of seeds are used as a substitute for coffee. North America, cultivated. BIANCHINI, HEDRICK 1919, HEISER 1976, HUGHES [Re], KULVINSKAS, MACNICOL [Re], ROSENGARTEN, SHURTLEFF 1979, UPHOF, WILSON, G; (for cultivars see Sunflower, page 508, also see Sprouting Seeds, page 485)

Helianthus annuus ssp. lenticularis - *Wild sunflower* {S} Parched seeds are ground into meal and used in breads, cakes, and rich soups. The roasted shells, after the starch has been removed, or the roasted seeds are used in preparing a coffee-like beverage. An edible oil can be extracted from the pounded seeds. North America. ANGIER, FERNALD, GIBBONS 1962, HARRINGTON, H., KINDSCHER, MEDSGER, TURNER 1979 [Pre, Re]; A2, D58, E73M, F44, F59, H80, I15M, I47, J25M, M47M, *N71M*

Helianthus giganteus - *Giant sunflower* {S} The seeds were ground into flour, mixed with corn meal and used for making bread by the Choctaw Indians. North America. UPHOF; J41M, J41M{PL}, J43, N37M{PL}, N84

Helianthus x laetiflorus (H. rigidus x H. tuberosus) - *Showy sunflower* {S} Natural hybrid. The edible tubers are said to have a flavor indistinguishable from that of the Jerusalem artichoke. North America. GIBBONS 1979, MEDSGER; D11T{PL}, G47M, J39M, J39M{PL}, J41M, J41M{PL}, J42{PL}, J43, *Q24*

Helianthus maximilianii - *Maximilian's sunflower* {S} The tubers may be eaten raw, roasted, or boiled. North America. KIRK, YANOVSKY; D62, H70M, I11M, I11M{PL}, I47, I53{PL}, J25M, J25M{PL}, J41M{PL}, K49M, K49Z, L41, L66{PL}, *M25*, *Q24*, etc.

CULTIVARS

Prairie Gold: Perennial sunflower with Jerusalem artichoke-like tubers which are edible but not very productive. The Land Institute in Salina, Kansas is investigating their oil-seed potential as part of a non-tillage permaculture system. K62

Helianthus tuberosus - *Jerusalem artichoke, Sunchoke, Topinambour* {PL} Tubers are eaten raw in salads, steamed, fried, baked, pickled, pureéd, or used in soups, casseroles, and pies. Commercially, they are used in the preparation of *artichoke spaghetti*. Roasted tubers are used as a substitute for coffee. Sometimes marketed as Sunchoke, although this name was originally given to the hybrid between the Jerusalem artichoke and the common sunflower, which has been investigated as a possible sugar crop. North America, cultivated. ANGIER, FERNALD, GIBBONS 1962, HALPIN [Cu, Cul], HEISER 1976, HERKLOTS, KINDSCHER, SCHNEIDER [Pre, Re], VILMORIN

[Cu]; A57M{PR}, B73M, C43M, C44, C82, D11M, D65, E24, E70M{PR}, F11, G16, G69M, G71, G89, H42, H61M{S}, H83, etc.

CULTIVARS

Dave's Shrine: Long, slender tuber with an unusually high dry matter ratio. More starchy and "salty" tasting whereas others are crisp and sweet. **U33**

Dwarf Sunray: Relatively dwarf, bushy plants; height 5 to 7 feet. Unique in that it flowers freely and can therefore be used as a dual purpose plant in the flower border. Tubers are so crisp and tender that no peeling of the outer skin is necessary. L91M

French Mammoth White: (White Mammoth) Large, knobby, white-skinned tuber; difficult to clean; matures late; does not store well. Tall, vigorous plant; height 8 to 10 feet; heavy yielding. Standard knobby type cultivar. I99, K49M

Fuseau: 95 days. Large, tapered, sweet potato-like tubers; 4 to 5 inches long, 1 to 1 1/2 inches in diameter; skin tan-colored, very smooth and entirely free of the knobs that characterize the common types and makes cleaning difficult. Matures early, about a week later than Stampede. Height 7 to 9 feet. Tubers are very elongated even in sandy soil. An old French cultivar. A32, A91, I99, K49M

Golden Nugget: Long, thin tubers; shaped somewhat like an elongated radish or carrot; 3 to 3 1/2 inches long, 1/2 to 1 inch in diameter; skin very smooth, free of knobs, dark reddish-orange in color. Excellent for pickling. Non-aggressive growth habit. Produces heavy crops of consistently small tubers. Matures within a week of Stampede. A32, K49M

Large Tuber: An improved type selected for large tuber size. B75, L59

Long Red: Large, tapered, sweet potato-like tubers; similar to Fuseau. Glossy, red-colored skin. K49M

Magenta Purple: Large, brilliantly colored tubers. I99

Maine Giant: An old Maine cultivar that has been compared to most of the others available and provides superior performance. J20

Purple: Produces large crops of purple tubers. C82

Red: Elongated, red-skinned tubers with a nutty flavor. Bushy plants that grow 4 to 8 feet tall with small, sunflower-like blossoms. F35M, G68, M82

Silver Skinned: Grows 7 to 9 feet tall. Each plant will yield about 4 1/2 pounds of silver-skinned tubers. L91M

Smooth Garnet: (Garnet) Long, medium-sized, ruby-red tubers; smooth and free of knobs. A32, K49M

Stampede: 90 days. A special high-yielding, extra-early strain. Flowers in July and matures more than a month before common cultivars. White-skinned tubers are large, often weighing over 1/2 pound each. Relatively dwarf; height about 6 feet. Winter hardy in severe cold. Developed by Indians in northern Ontario who selected plants for earliness and tuber size. G6

Helichrysum angustifolium* → *Helichrysum italicum

Helichrysum italicum - *Curry plant* {PL} The finely chopped or minced leaves may be used to flavor omelettes, scrambled eggs which are not cooked for long, or stuffed eggs. Flower-heads are used for tea. Also the source of an essential oil and extract, which are used to enhance fruit flavors in candy, ice cream, baked goods, soft drinks, and chewing gum. Southern Europe. MORTON 1976, PAINTER [Re]; C9, C43M, C67M, F21, F31T, F35M, G84, G96, H40, I63M, J66, J82, K22, *M35*

Helichrysum petiolatum - *Licorice plant, Silver licorice* {PL} The roots have a distinct licorice-like flavor and can be used for culinary purposes. Cultivated. E48, E61, F15M, F21, F35M, G96, H4, H40, H51M, H79M, J82, M15T, M82, N84{S}

Helichrysum serpyllifolium - *Hottentot tea* {S} Leaves are used as a substitute for tea. Southern Africa. FOX, F., MORTON 1976; **Z25M**

Hypochoeris maculata - *Spotted hawkweed* {S} Young leaves are occasionally eaten in salads, or boiled in broths. Eurasia. TANAKA; O48

Hypochoeris radicata - *Spotted cat's-ear* {S} The young leaves can be eaten raw in salads, boiled and served like spinach, or briefly wilted in hot bacon grease or peanut oil. Europe. CRIBB, FOX, F., GIBBONS 1979, MABEY; D62, *N71M*, N84

Inula crithmoides - *Golden samphire* {S} Young leaves are occasionally eaten as a potherb. The fleshy leaves and young shoots were formerly pickled in vinegar, and added to salads as a relish. They were often used as an adulterant of true samphire, Crithmum maritimum. Europe. BURR [Cu], GRIEVE; **V84, W92, Y10**

Inula helenium - *Elecampane, Horse-heal, Elf dock* {PL} The root is made into candy, sweetmeats, and syrup. Also used for flavoring puddings, fish sauces, beer, cordials, *vermouth*, and French and Swiss *absinthe*. The young, bitter leaves were used as a potherb by the ancient Romans. Eurasia, cultivated. FERNALD, GIBBONS 1966b [Re], GRIEVE [Cu], MORTON 1976, UPHOF; C9, C11{S}, C13M{S}, C43M, C67M, C81M, D29, E61, E61{S}, F24{S}, F35M, G84, N45, *N71M*{S}, O53M{S}, etc.

Lactuca alpina* → *Cicerbita alpina

Lactuca indica - *Indian lettuce, Indian salad* {S} The leaves are eaten raw in salads, steamed, or added to soups. In Indonesia, they are used for wrapping and frying fish, especially eels. Asia, cultivated. HERKLOTS, OCHSE; D33

Lactuca perennis - *Perennial lettuce* {S} Young or blanched leaves are used as salads in some parts of southern Europe. They are also occasionally eaten boiled like spinach or endive. Europe. BURR, UPHOF, VILMORIN; F80, N84, O53M, S7M

Lactuca saligna* → *Lactuca indica

Lactuca sativa - *Lettuce* The leaves are widely eaten raw, especially in tossed salads and sandwiches. Also boiled as a potherb, pickled, braised, sautéed, fried, puréed, or used in soups and stews. Larger leaves can be used as natural cups for seafood or fruit salads. In the Middle East, the bulghur wheat salad *tabouli* is wrapped in lettuce leaves and eaten out-of-hand. Sprouted seeds can be used in salads and sandwiches. Cultivated. CARCIONE, FELL 1982b, HERKLOTS, LARKCOM 1984 [Cul, Re], OCHSE, ROOT 1980a, VILMORIN [Cu]; (for cultivars see Lettuce, page 372)

Lactuca sativa Angustana Group - *Celtuce, Asparagus lettuce, Chinese lettuce* {S} Young leaves are eaten raw in salads, cooked, preserved, or served with miso. The thick, tender stem is crisp and juicy, with a flavor variously described as being like that of lettuce, celery, artichoke, asparagus, squash, or chard. It is peeled, sliced, and eaten raw, braised, sautéed, pickled, stir-fried or cooked in soups. DAHLEN [Pre, Cul], FELL 1982b, KRAFT [Re], HALPIN [Cu, Cul], HERKLOTS, TANAKA, VILMORIN; A16, B49, B75, C85M, D11M, D55, *F72*, I39, J7, K49M, K71, L42, L79, L91M, O53M, etc.

CULTIVARS

Narrow Leaf: Very long, narrow leaves; 2 inches wide, 12 inches or more long. The pointed leaves have a very decorative, drooping habit. Originated in southern China. E83T

Red: (Grüne Rübe) A form of asparagus lettuce with reddish stems and bronzy leaves. Grown and used in the same way as the common form. VILMORIN; **Z98**

Round-Leaved: Slightly crumpled leaves, more or less the shape of Romaine lettuce leaves; somewhat darker green than Narrow Leaf. Similar growth habit. Originated in Taiwan. E83T

Lactuca scariola → Lactuca serriola

Lactuca serriola - *Prickly lettuce, Wild lettuce, Compass plant* {S} The young, tender leaves make a very good salad, cut in pieces with a little chopped onion and served with French dressing. As a potherb, it needs very little cooking and is excellent when served with a hot dressing of melted butter and vinegar. Seeds are the source of Egyptian *lettuce seed oil*, a semi-drying, pleasant-flavored oil used in foods. Eurasia, naturalized in North America. GIBBONS 1966b, MEDSGER, UPHOF; D58, D62, L86, *N71M*, N84, O48

Lapsana communis - *Nipplewort* {S} The young leaves are eaten raw in salads and sandwiches, cooked like spinach, or added to omelettes, soups, and casseroles. They are said to have a bitter, or radish-like taste. Eurasia. HEDRICK 1919, LAUNERT [Re]; D62, *N71M*, N84, O48

Leontodon hispidus - *Rough hawkbit* {S} Young leaves are eaten in salads. Roasted roots have been recommended as a substitute for coffee. Eurasia. MABEY, UPHOF; *N71M*, N84, O48, O53M

Leucanthemum vulgare - *Oxe-eye daisy* {S} The young leaves are finely chopped and eaten in salads, sandwiches, omelettes, or added to soups. Pungent in flavor, they should be used sparingly or mixed with other salad plants. The flower-heads can be used in the same way as dandelion for home winemaking. Eurasia, naturalized in North America. FERNALD, GIBBONS 1979, LAUNERT; C9M, D11T{PL}, E33M{PL}, E73M, F44, F66, G47M, H61M, I19, I19{PL}, J53, J82, M47M, N9M, N9M{PL}, N11M, etc.

Ligularia kaempferi - *Silveredge, Tsuwabuki, Japanese silver leaf, Wild butterbur* {S} Petioles are boiled in water to remove the harsh flavor, skinned of their outer bark, and used to add flavor to salads and other dishes, or otherwise served like those of Petasites japonicus. Japan. SHURTLEFF 1975, TANAKA, YASHIRODA; F85

Ligularia tussilaginea → Ligularia kaempferi

Madia sativa - *Chile tarweed* {S} Seeds are eaten raw, roasted, dried, or used for *pinole*. The crushed seeds are a good addition to soups. Also the source of a sweet, edible oil, called *madia oil*, used as a substitute for olive oil. Western North America, South America, cultivated. GIBBONS 1979, HEDRICK 1919, KIRK, MEDSGER, TANAKA; I99, N84

Matricaria chamomilla → Chamomilla aurea

Matricaria matricarioides - *Pineapple-weed* {S} The fresh or dried flowers make a pale golden, pineapple-scented tea when steeped in hot water. Western North America. GIBBONS 1979, NORTON, PETERSON, L.; C11, E7M, N84, O48

Matricaria recutica → Chamomilla aurea

Mycelis muralis - *Wall lettuce* {S} Leaves are eaten in salads. Eurasia. MABEY; D62

Onopordon acanthium - *Scotch thistle, Cotton thistle* {S} The fairly large flower receptacles can be cooked and eaten like those of the artichoke. Tender young shoots are peeled, boiled, and served like cardoon or burdock. An oil expressed from the seeds has been used for culinary purposes. Floral parts are used as an adulterant of saffron. Mediterranean region. FERNALD, GRIEVE, HEDRICK 1919, LAUNERT, UPHOF; C13M, C43M, C43M{PL}, D62, H79M{PL}, I99, K47T, L91M, M82{PL}, *N71M*, N84, O48, O53M, *Q24*, S7M, S55, etc.

Onopordon illyricum - *Illyrian cotton-thistle* {S} Flower-heads are eaten like those of artichoke. Europe. LOVELOCK; **W59M, W92, Y10, Y18**

Pectis papposa - *Fetid marigold, Chinchweed* {S} Flowers are used by Indians of New Mexico for seasoning meat. Southwestern North America. KIRK, UPHOF, YANOVSKY; K49T

Petasites frigidus - *Sweet coltsfoot* {S} The young leaves are mixed with other greens and used as a potherb by the Eskimos in Alaska. Young stalks and flower heads are cooked and eaten. Roots are roasted and eaten. Western North America. HELLER, KUNKEL, UPHOF; **T41M, W5**

Petasites frigidus var. palmatus → Petasites palmatus

Petasites japonicus - *Fuki, Sweet coltsfoot, Butterbur* {PL} The leafstalks are boiled and seasoned with salt or soy sauce, pickled and used in winter soups, or preserved in miso and sake lees. The flowerbuds have a slightly bitter yet agreeable flavor and are prized as a vegetable and condiment in Japan. They are eaten while still green with miso or boiled down in soy sauce. Eastern Asia, cultivated. SHURTLEFF 1975, SHURTLEFF 1976 [Re], TANAKA, UPHOF, YASHIRODA [Cu, Cul]; F35M, J37M

Petasites japonicus var. giganteus - *Akita-buki, Giant sweet coltsfoot* {PL} Leafstalks are parboiled and seasoned with soy sauce or candied. They are occasionally canned. The flower buds are eaten as a vegetable or used as a condiment. Similar to P. japonicus, but with much larger leafstalks. Eastern Asia, cultivated. TANAKA; B77, E61, H3M, K22, K85

Petasites palmatus - *Palmate butterbur, Sweet coltsfoot* {S} The young flower-stalks, before the flowerbuds appear, can be boiled until tender and seasoned with salt and butter. The flowerbuds are also cooked and eaten. Leafstalks are peeled and eaten raw. Ash of the plants is used as a substitute for salt. North America. FERNALD, GIBBONS 1979, TANAKA, YANOVSKY; A2, I99

Picridium vulgare → Reichardia picroides

Pluchea indica - *Indian sage, Lontas* {S} Young leaves, shoots and inflorescences are eaten raw in tossed green salads, steamed and served as a side-dish with rice, added to soups, or mixed with hot pepper sauce. Also used as a condiment. Tropical Asia, Australia. MARTIN 1975, OCHSE; F85

Polymnia sonchifolia - *Yacon, Llacon, Strawberry jicama, Bolivian sunroot* {PL} The sweet, juicy tubers, when properly grown, can be eaten out-of-hand like a fruit. Otherwise they can be sliced and added to tossed salads, or shredded and mixed with other sweet roots such as carrots and sweet potatoes in cold salads. The tubers are sweeter after they have been cured in the sun, although some of their crisp texture may be lost. In the Andes, the grated pulp is squeezed through a cloth to yield a sweet, refreshing drink. The juice is also concentrated to form dark-brown blocks of sugar called *chancaca*. Leaves are said to be edible. Andean South America, cultivated. HERKLOTS, KUNKEL, NATIONAL RESEARCH COUNCIL 1989, UPHOF; I99, *Q49M*

Pulicaria odora - {S} Cultivated in Yemen for its pleasant odor and edible leaves. Mediterranean region, Southwest Asia. HEDRICK 1919; **W59M**

Ratibida columnaris* → *Ratibida columnifera

Ratibida columnifera - *Coneflower, Mexican hat* {S} The leaves and flower-heads may be brewed into a pleasant tea. Western North America. KIRK, YANOVSKY; D62, E73M, F59, F59{PL}, G47M, H80, I11, I47, I53{PL}, J25M, J41M, J41M{PL}, J88, K62, L91M, N11M, etc.

Reichardia picroides - *French scorzonera* {S} The leaves have a pleasant, agreeable flavor, and while young and tender, are mixed in salads. Roots are also eaten. Macaronesia, Mediterranean region. BURR [Cu], HEDRICK 1919, VILMORIN; **W59M, Y10, Z98**

Santolina chamaecyparissus - *Lavender cotton, Grey santolina* {PL} The aromatic leaves can be used for flavoring broths, sauces, meats, fish, grain dishes, etc. Southern Europe, cultivated. BRYAN [Cu, Re]; C11{S}, C13M{S}, C43M, C67M, F21, G84, H40, K22, K53{S}, *M35*, N19M, O53M{S}

Saussurea lappa - *Costus, Kuth* {S} Aromatic roots are occasionally used as a spice. They have a characteristic penetrating odor reminiscent of violet, orris and vetiver. Himalayan region. ATAL, KUNKEL; **V84**

Scolymus grandiflorus - {S} The stalks are eaten raw or boiled. Mediterranean region. HEDRICK 1919; **Y10**

Scolymus hispanicus - *Spanish salsify, Spanish oyster-plant, Golden thistle* {S} The fleshy roots are eaten boiled, mashed, baked, or used as a substitute for coffee. Young leaf-stalks are blanched and consumed in salads. Flowers are used to adulterate saffron. Mediterranean region. BURR, HAWKES, HEDRICK 1919, KUNKEL, ORGAN [Cu, Cul], TANAKA, VILMORIN; **U4, W92, Y10, Y89M, Z98**

Scolymus maculatus - *Spotted golden thistle* {S} Young leaves are eaten as a spinach. The roots are boiled and eaten. Mediterranean region. HEDRICK 1919, KUNKEL; **W92**

Scorzonera hispanica - *Black salsify, Mock oyster, Coconut root* {S} The long, blackish roots are eaten boiled, steamed, baked, batter-fried, or cooked in soups and stews. Young, tender shoots, known as *chards*, can be added to tossed salads. The flower buds, whether raw or cooked and cooled, can be eaten as a salad. The yellow flower petals have their own distinct flavor and may be sprinkled on a salad. Also used in the French dish *omelette aux fleurs de salsifis*. Roasted roots are used as a coffee substitute. Mediterranean region. FELL 1982b, HALPIN [Cu, Cul], KRAFT [Re], MACNICOL [Re], SCHNEIDER [Pre, Re], UPHOF, VILMORIN; C92, D11M, D62, E81M, E97, G64, I39, I99, J7, J82, K49M, L91M, *N40*{PR}, O48, O53M, R47, S55, etc.

CULTIVARS

Duplex: Very long, cylindrical roots, 8 to 10 inches in length; blunt ended; deep black skin; creamy white flesh with a delicious flavor; quality excellent. High yielding. Should be planted early in rich, deeply worked soil. C85M, P59M, S27

Flandria: 80 days. A new cultivar introduced by a distinguished European breeder. Very uniform, cylindrical roots, about 12 inches long; tapered to a point; smooth, dark black skin; tender white flesh. The flavor is nut-like, mild, and somewhat reminiscent of coconut. Very productive. Somewhat susceptible to bolting. J20, P59M

Giant Black Russian: (Geante Noire de Russie) Very long, thin, smooth black roots with large shoulders characterize this European market growers selection. Roots are longer than white salsify, to 15 inches or more. Deep, loose soil is required for best production. G68, S45M, S61

Gigantia: 120 days. A select European strain. Roots are long and cylindrical and relatively stout. The flavor is rich, and the texture smooth and firm. Delicious raw. G6, K49T

Maxima: Roots are 11 to 13 inches long, cylindrical with a blunt end. Production capacity is very good. Has performed very well in Dutch Official Cultivar Testing. *A75*

Omega: An improved type with very long, slender, black roots and a short top. More productive and of better quality than standard sorts. Despite the great length of the root, it is easy to dig up. *R11M*

Sigesbeckia orientalis - *Amia* {S} The fragrant flowers and foliage are used for scenting coconut oil. Southeastern Polynesia. BROWN, F.; **V50, V84, V89, Y10, Y17M**

Silphium laciniatum - *Rosinweed, Compass plant* {S} The resinous exudation that forms on the upper parts of the flower-stalk has been used as a chewing gum. North America. FERNALD, MEDSGER; G47M, G89, H63{PL}, H70M, H70M{PL}, J39M, J39M{PL}, J40, J40{PL}, J41M, J41M{PL}, J42, J42{PL}, J43, K47T, N37M{PL}, etc.

Silybum marianum - *Milk thistle* {S} Young leaves are trimmed of prickles and eaten raw or boiled. The stems can be peeled, chopped, and used in salads, or soaked in water to remove the bitterness and then stewed like rhubarb. Young flower receptacles are boiled and served like those of artichoke. Seeds are roasted and used as a coffee substitute. The roots are also edible, either raw or cooked. Mediterranean region. CLARKE, GRIEVE, LARKCOM 1984, MABEY, UPHOF; C13M, C43M, C43M{PL}, E48{PL}, F24, F80, I99, K2, K22{PL}, K47T, L91M, M15T{PL}, M82{PL}, *N71M*, O53M, S55, etc.

Solidago canadensis - *Canada goldenrod* {S} Seeds were eaten by Indians of several tribes. The leaves can be used for tea. North America. MARCIN, UPHOF; A2, B51, D11T{PL}, E33M{PL}, F85, K47T, *N71M*, N84, O48, S7M

Solidago graminifolia - *Fragrant goldenrod* {S} Fresh or dried leaves are used as a substitute for tea. North America. C64M, J39M{PL}, J42, J42{PL}, K47T, N84

Solidago missouriensis - *Missouri goldenrod* {S} Young leaves are eaten in salads or cooked as a potherb. The dried leaves and the dried, fully expanded flowers make good tea. North America. KIRK, YANOVSKY; J43

Solidago odora - *Sweet goldenrod, Mountain tea* {PL} The dried leaves and dried, fully expanded flowers are used for brewing an aromatic anise-flavored tea. North America. FERNALD, GIBBONS 1962, MARCIN, MEDSGER; B51{S}, C11{S}, C13M{S}, D29, D92, F80{S}, H61M{S}, I11M, I11M{S}, I19, I37M, K22, M77M, M82, N84{S}, etc.

Solidago suaveolens* → *Solidago odora

Solidago virgaurea - *European goldenrod* {S} Leaves are used as a substitute for tea. Eurasia. MARCIN, UPHOF; F35M{PL}, K47T, *N71M*, N84, *Q24*, S7M, S55

Sonchus arvensis - *Field sow-thistle* {S} The young shoots and leaves are eaten in salads, added to curries, or cooked like spinach and served with rice. Roots are used as a substitute for coffee. In Indonesia, an improved type is grown for its leaves. Eurasia. CROWHURST 1972, HARRINGTON, H., LAUNERT, OCHSE, TANAKA; N84

Sonchus asper - *Prickly sow-thistle, Puha tiotio* {S} The tender leaves and flowering tops may be used raw in salads or cooked and served like spinach. The stems should be bruised and the bitter, milky juice washed out before eating or cooking. Eurasia. CRIBB, KIRK, OCHSE, PAINTER [Pre, Cul]; N84, O48

Sonchus oleraceus - *Common sow-thistle* {S} Young leaves are employed as an ingredient of salads, boiled like spinach, or cooked in soups, soufflés, frittatas, and porridges. The young stalks are peeled of their outer skin and boiled and served like asparagus. The roots are also used as food. New Zealand Maoris chewed the milky sap as gum. Eurasia. CLARKE [Re], COLENSO, CRIBB, FOX, F., FULLER [Re], GRIEVE, MEDSGER, MICHAEL [Re]; *N71M*, N84

Spilanthes acmella - *Toothache plant, Alphabet plant, Australian cress* {S} The young leaves and shoot tips, either raw or steamed, are eaten as a side-dish with rice. Tropics. OCHSE, TANAKA; A2, C13M, F85, I99, J82

Spilanthes acmella 'Oleracea' - *Pará cress, Brazil cress* {S} The leaves, when mixed with salads, impart to them a pungent flavor, and have the effect of stimulating the action of the salivary glands. Also used as a potherb. Milder in flavor and with larger purple leaves than toothache plant. OCHSE, TANAKA, VILMORIN; I99, K49T

Spilanthes oleracea → ***Spilanthes acmella***

Stevia rebaudiana - *Sweet-herb of Paraguay, Sugar leaf* {PL} Leaves contain stevioside, a substance three hundred times sweeter than sucrose. In South America, the dried leaves are ground for use as a sweetener or soaked in water and the liquid employed in making preserves. The leaves are sometimes chewed by those wishing to reduce their intake of sugar. Herbal tea manufacturers utilize the powdered herb as a sugar substitute. Paraguay, Brazil. INGLETT, MORTON 1976; A52M{PR}, B7{PR}, F85{S}, G96, I59G, I59G{PR}, M82

Synedrella nodiflora - *Babadotan lalaki* {S} Young leaves are steamed and used by the Javanese as *lalab*, a side-dish of the rice table. Tropics. UPHOF; N84

Tagetes erecta - *Aztec marigold* {S} The dried flowers are the source of a yellow dye occasionally used for coloring butter and cheese. Also used as an adulterant of saffron. The flowers of some cultivars can be eaten. Central America. MORTON 1976, TANAKA; D62, I59G, I99, K49T, O53M

CULTIVARS

Yellow Climax: The petals of the mild-flavored flowers can be used as colorful garnishes. B75, G79, L42

Tagetes filifolia - *Irish lace marigold* {S} The plants are used for flavoring. Cultivated. KUNKEL; C13M, C44, C81M{PL}, K22{PL}, O53M, T1M

Tagetes lucida - *Mexican tarragon, Sweet marigold, Sweet mace, Pericón* {PL} The leaves are used as a substitute for tarragon in seasoning soups, sauces, vinegars, herbal butters, etc. Dried leaves and flowering tops are brewed into a pleasant anise-flavored tea. Mexico. HEDRICK 1919, HUTSON [Re], MORTON 1976, VILMORIN; C13M{S}, C67M, D92, E5M, E61, F35M, F93G, G96, H40, I16{S}, I16{PR}, I59G{S}, J73{S}, J82{S}, K22, K49T{S}, etc.

CULTIVARS {S}

Huichol: Leaves slightly more narrow than the type, turn reddish under certain conditions. Traditional clone used by the Huichol Indians of San Andres Cohamiata, Jalisco, Mexico. Collected at an elevation of 5,000 to 6,000 feet. **U26**

Tagetes minuta - *Muster John-Henry, Mexican marigold* {S} The dried leaves are used as an aromatic seasoning for soups, broths, meats, and vegetables. Source of an essential oil used commercially in ice cream, candy, baked goods, gelatin desserts, and soft drinks. South America. FERNALD, MORTON 1976; C43M{PL}, D29{PL}, E5M{PL}, H3M, H3M{PL}, I99, J82, K22, K49T, N84, O48, O53M, P1G, R47, S55, etc.

Tagetes patula - *French marigold* {S} Leaves are used as a condiment in Africa. The dried flowers serve as an adulterant of saffron or as coloring for butter and cheese. Flowers are said to be used in refreshing drinks. Central America. KUNKEL, MORTON 1976; D62, K22, K49T, N84, O53M, S55

Tagetes tenuifolia - *Lemon marigold* {S} The flowers of some cultivars have a pleasant citrus-like flavor and can be used sparingly as a garnish, in salads and sandwiches, or added to desserts and wines. Central America. C13M, F35M{PL}, K22, O53M

CULTIVARS

Lemon Gem: Floriferous, single, forget-me-not type flowers with a bright lemon-yellow color. Both leaves and flowers have a lemon-like aroma and flavor. Excellent in hot pudding sauces. Very early, compact, ball-shaped plant with fine, lacy foliage. A13, B75, B97{PL}, C53, D11M, D68, E81M, E89M, *E91G*, H3M{PL}, I39, I77, J82, K49M, K66, L79, L91M, T1M, etc.

Lulu: Plants are mound-shaped, 8 inches tall, covered with small, lemon-yellow single blooms. Foliage is fern-like. Excellent for rockeries. *E91G*, I77, K49M, L42

Tangerine Gem: Dime size, golden orange single flowers make unique cut flowers for small arrangements. Both the petals and leaves have a tangerine-like fragrance and flavor. Compact, dome-shaped plants have lacy, fern-like foliage. Excellent for borders. E33, E81M, *E91G*, H3M{PL}, I77, J82, K49M, K66, L42, Q34, S55, T1M

Tanacetum parthenium - *Feverfew* {PL} Dried flowers are used as tea, or in wine and certain pastries. Eurasia, cultivated. UPHOF; C11{S}, C13M{S}, C43M, C67M, F21, G84, H46{S}, J82, J82{S}, K22, N19M, N45, N84{S}, O53M{S}

CULTIVARS

Golden: (Yellow) Same as the species, but with a yellow tint to the leaves. A1M, A49D, C11{S}, C13M{S}, C43M, C43M{S}, E81M{S}, F35M, G84, H51M, J66, J82, *L22*, L56, R53M{S}, etc.

Tanacetum vulgare - *Tansy, Bitter buttons* {PL} The young, aromatic leaves are finely chopped and used in salads, puddings, cakes, fritters, fish-dishes, etc. Tansy-cheese is made by steeping the herb and pouring the extract into the milk before the curds are made. The juice extracted from the leaves was used to flavor omelettes known as *tansies*. Flowers have a unique flavor and are eaten or used for garnishing. The leaves and flowering tops are brewed into a bitter, somewhat lemon-flavored tea. Eurasia, cultivated. FERNALD, GRIEVE, LEGGATT [Re], MABEY, MACNICOL [Re], MARCIN, MICHAEL [Re], ROOT 1980b; C3, C3{S}, C13M{S}, C67M, F21, F31T, G84, H40, H46{S}, K22, *M35*, N19M, N45

CULTIVARS

Fernleaf: (Curled, Crispum) More decorative than the common form with deeper green, more delicate foliage and larger orange-yellow flowers. Compact, lacy, fern-like leaves. Good as an ornamental garnish. Lower growing, height 2 to 2 1/2 feet. Will spread slowly to fill any allotted space. Doesn't flower as frequently. B28, C9, C11{S}, C13M{S}, C43M, D29, F35M, G96, K2, K2{S}, K22, *L22*, L86, M82, N19M, etc.

Taraxacum albidum - *Shirobana-tanpopo* {S} Young plants, young leaves, flowers, and roots are eaten after being parboiled. The whole plant is dried and used as a substitute for tea. Japan. TANAKA; K47T, N84

Taraxacum officinale - *Dandelion, Pissenlit, Radicchiello* {S} Young leaves are eaten in salads, boiled, steamed, sautéed, fried, braised, etc. The roots are eaten raw, or cooked and served like salsify. The blanched leaf-stalks, or crown, can be eaten raw or as a cooked vegetable. Dandelion wine is made from the flowers. The unopened flower-buds, while still inside the crown, are eaten in pancakes, omelettes, and fritters. Roasted roots are ground and used as a substitute for coffee. The flowers are used as an ingredient in the Arabic cake called *yublo*. Both the leaves and roots are brewed into tea. Sprouted seeds can be eaten. Northern temperate region, cultivated. GIBBONS 1962, HALPIN [Cu, Cul], HARRINGTON, H., LEGGATT [Re], MACNICOL [Re], MARCIN, MICHAEL [Re], UPHOF, VILMORIN [Cu]; A2, C82, C82{PL}, C92, E70M{PR}, F24, I99, K22, *N71M*, N84

CULTIVARS

Amélioré à Coeur Plein: A very distinct cultivar, surpassing the wild plant not so much in the size as in the very great number of the leaves, which form a regular tuft or clump, instead of a plain rosette. It yields a very abundant crop without taking up much ground, and blanches very easily and, indeed, almost naturally. VILMORIN; C53, F33, P59M, S55, S95M

Broad Leaved: (Thick-Leaved, Cabbage-Leaved) 95 days. Large, broad, dark-green leaves; more deeply lobed along the axis of the leaf than those of the wild dandelion; thick and tender. Easily blanched plants are semi-erect, forming a rosette of leaves. In rich soil, each plant spreads 18 to 24 inches across. Doesn't go to seed as quickly as the French types. B75, C85M, E38, F35M{PL}, G51, G57M, G71, I39, J7, J82, L42, L86, M13M, O53M, R47, etc.

Mauser's Trieb: This is a special cultivar that has been bred to be forced like Barbe de Capucin chicory. Should be grown as an annual and forced in the same manner. C53

Vert de Montmagny: (Vert de Montmagny Amélioré) Large, long, dark green leaves; well lobed and denticulated; may be blanched or not. Vigorous and productive plants. Best sown in early spring or fall. G68, K66, S95M

Tarchonanthus camphoratus - *Camphor bush, Hottentot tobacco* {S} The camphor-flavored leaves are chewed. Also a substitute for tea. South Africa. KUNKEL, UPHOF; F85, N84

Thelesperma ambiguus* → *Thelesperma filifolia

Thelesperma filifolia - *Showy Navajo tea* {S} Leaves and flowers are used as a substitute for tea. Western North America. J25M

Thelesperma gracile - *Navajo tea, Cota, Greenthread* {S} The leaves and dried flowers are used as a substitute for tea. The color of the tea is greenish-yellow to dark yellow-red, and when properly made it is delicious with just a hint of mint in its aftertaste. Flower buds can also be eaten. Western North America. GIBBONS 1979, HARRINGTON, H., HUGHES, KIRK; J25M

Thelesperma megapotamicum* → *Thelesperma gracile

Tragopogon dubius - *Goat's beard* {S} The young stems, when a few inches high, and the bases of the lower leaves are used as potherbs. Young roots are eaten raw or cooked. Northern temperate region. FERNALD, HARRINGTON, H., KIRK; D58, K47T

Tragopogon majus* → *Tragopogon dubius

Tragopogon porrifolius - *Salsify, Oyster plant, Vegetable oyster* {S} Roots are eaten raw in salads, boiled, baked, sautéed in butter, added to soups, or grated and made into cakes. The young shoots (*chards*), flower buds, and flowers may be eaten in salads, either raw or cooked and cooled. Flowers are also pickled. Young flower-stalks are cooked and dressed like asparagus. Sprouted seeds can be used in salads and sandwiches. The milky latex from the roots was used as chewing gum by British Columbia Indians. Mediterranean region, cultivated. GRIEVE [Re], HALPIN [Cu, Cul], HAWKES [Re], HEDRICK 1919, LARKCOM 1984, UPHOF, VILMORIN [Cu]; A2, B49, D62, E38, E59, K49M, *N40*{PR}, N84, O48

CULTIVARS

Improved Mammoth Sandwich Island: 120 days. Smooth roots with sweet, tender, snow-white flesh. Has a mild, pleasing flavor said to resemble that of oysters. Stores well. E97

Mammoth Long Island: An improved Mammoth Sandwich Island type. C44

Mammoth Sandwich Island: 120 days. Long white roots grow 8 inches long or more, measure 1 to 1 1/2 inches across at the shoulder, slightly tapering and uniform; creamy white flesh. May be left in the ground over winter for early spring use. Requires a long season but is easy to grow. Introduced before 1894. A16, A25, B75M, C85M, D11M, F19M, G16, G64, G71, *H61*, J7, M13M, M46, N39, O53M, etc.

White French: White carrot-shaped root that makes delicious soup, resembling oysters in flavor. Easy to grow; can be left in the ground all winter and late into spring. L97

Tragopogon pratensis - *Goat's beard* {S} The flowering stems, including the buds, are cooked and served like asparagus. Young leaves, shoots, and diced roots can be used in salads. The fully developed taproot is blanched, peeled, and cooked and eaten like salsify. The whole herb may be cooked in soups and stews. Eurasia, naturalized in North America. FERNALD, LAUNERT [Re]; D62, H61M, *N71M*, N84, O48, S7M, S55

Tussilago farfara - *Coltsfoot* {PL} The young leaves, flower buds, and young flowers can be eaten in salads, soups, or as a potherb. Fresh or dried leaves and flowers are used for preparing an aromatic tea. The slender rootstock is candied in sugar syrup. A delicious country wine is made from the flowers. Ash from the leaves is used as a salt substitute. Northern temperate region. CROWHURST 1972 [Re], FERNALD, GIBBONS 1966b, GRIEVE, HALL [Pre, Re], LAUNERT [Re], MACNICOL [Re], MARCIN, MICHAEL [Pre, Re]; A2{S}, C43M, C67M, E61, F35M, G96, H3M, I22, J82, K47T{S}, M16, M53, M82, N9M, *N71M*{S}, etc.

Vernonia anthelmintica - *Kinka-oil ironweed* {S} Said to be used as a spice. Southern Asia. KUNKEL; F85

Wedelia biflora - {S} The leaves are stuffed with grated coconut, rolled, and then either steamed or boiled. In the New Hebrides, the leaves are used for wrapping fish, to which they impart flavor. A tea is made from the leaves and roots. Polynesia. ALTSCHUL, BROWN, W., MASSAL; **Y10**

ATHEROSPERMATACEAE

Atherosperma moschatum - *Tasmanian sassafras* {S} The bark, either fresh or dried, is made into a pleasant tasting tea. Australia, Tasmania. CRIBB; N84, O53M, S65M

Laurelia aromatica* → *Laurelia serrata

Laurelia sempervirens - *Chilean laurel* {S} Bark and leaves are used as a spice. Chile. KUNKEL; **Z25M**

Laurelia serrata - *Peruvian nutmeg* {S} Fruits and leaves are used as a spice in some parts of Peru. Chile, Argentina. HEDRICK 1919, KUNKEL, UPHOF; **Z25M**

ATHYRIACEAE

Diplazium esculentum - *Kuware-shida, Pakó* {PL} Very young leaves are eaten raw in salads, or steamed and eaten with rice. Tropical Asia. BROWN, W., BURKILL, OCHSE; M42, N84{S}

AVERRHOACEAE

Averrhoa bilimbi - *Bilimbi, Cucumber tree* {S} Very acid fruits are pickled like cucumbers, candied, preserved in syrup, eaten as a relish with meat or fish, or used in curries, marmalade, chutneys, jams, jellies, and lemonade-like drinks. Flowers are made into conserves. Southeast Asia, cultivated. GARNER [Pro], HEDRICK 1919, MORTON 1987a, POPENOE, W. 1920, STURROCK, UPHOF; F85, N84, S97M{PL}

Averrhoa carambola - *Carambola, Starfruit* {S} Juicy fruits of the sweet type can be eaten out of hand, dried, sliced into fruit and vegetable salads, or used in ices, sherbets, drinks, Bavarian creams, mousses and other desserts. Sour types or slightly underripe fruits are pickled, cooked with fish and poultry or made into relish and jelly. The acid flowers are eaten in salads or made into conserves. Leaves have been eaten as a substitute for sorrel. Cultivated. GARNER [Pro], HEDRICK 1919, MORTON 1987a, POPENOE, W. 1920 [Cu], RICHARDSON [Re], SCHNEIDER [Re]; A79M, *B59*{PR}, E29, E29{PL}, E29{PR}, F85, *L33M*{PR}, L54{PR}, L97G{PR}, *N40*{PR}, N84, O53M, O93, P38, *Q32*, Q46, S54M{PL}, etc.

CULTIVARS {GR}

Arkin: Uniform fruit, 4 to 5 inches long, with small wings; bright yellow to yellow-orange skin and flesh; very sweet, juicy, firm flesh with few seeds; keeps and ships very well. Tree partially self-fruitful; bears heavily from October to December in Hawaii, earlier in Florida, from December to March in California. The leading commercial cultivar. F68, I83M, J22, L6, *Q93*

Fwang Tung: Fruit 5 to 8 inches long, with long wings; pale yellow skin and flesh; very sweet and juicy, firm flesh with few seeds; ripe when wing edges are still green. Beautiful starry shape when cut in slices. Bears heavily from October to January in Hawaii. F68, J22, *Q93*, S97M

Golden Star: Large, deeply winged fruit; skin bright golden yellow, very waxy; flesh juicy, crisp, mildly subacid to sweet in flavor, contains no fibers; high in carbohydrates and vitamins A and C, good for fruit and vegetable salads. Tree bears well and regularly without cross-pollination. Originated in Homestead, Florida. Introduced in 1965. BROOKS 1972, MORTON 1987a; I83M{CF}, J36

Hoku: Fruit 5 to 6 inches long; bright yellow skin and flesh; juicy, firm flesh with a sweet, rich flavor, few seeds. Attractive star-like shape when cut in slices. Bears heavily from September to January. Selected by the University of Hawaii. J22

Kajang: Fruit 4 to 5 inches long; bright yellow skin and flesh; sweet, juicy, firm flesh with few seeds. Beautiful star shape when cut in slices. Bears heavily from October to December in Hawaii. J22

Maha: Roundish fruit with light yellowish-white skin; white flesh; low acid content; sweet and crunchy. Originated in Hawaii. D57, J36, *Q93*, S97M

Sri Kembangan: (Kembangan) Elongated pointed fruit, 5 to 6 inches in length; bright yellow-orange skin and flesh; juicy, sweet, firm flesh with few seeds, flavor rich and sweet; dessert quality excellent. Bears heavily from September to January in Hawaii. Originated in Thailand. D57, J22, *Q93*

Wheeler: Medium to large, elongated fruit; orange skin and flesh; mildly sweet flavor. Tree a very heavy bearer. D57

BALANITACEAE

Balanites aegyptiaca - *Desert date, Soapberry tree* {S} The fruits are eaten fresh, dried, or made into an alcoholic beverage. Seed kernels are eaten raw or dried, added to soups, or made into a kind of bread. Also the source of an edible oil, *zachun oil*. Leaves and flowers are used as vegetables. Drier Africa to Southwest Asia. MENNINGER, UPHOF, ZEVEN; F85, N84, Q46

Balanites maughamii* → *Balanites wilsoniana

Balanites wilsoniana - *Torchwood, Mkonga* {S} Fruits are sometimes eaten. Seeds are the source of a clear oil, similar to olive oil. Tropical Africa. FOX, F., MENNINGER, UPHOF; N84

BALSAMINACEAE

Impatiens biflora* → *Impatiens capensis

Impatiens capensis - *Jewelweed, Spotted touch-me-not* {S} The succulent stems, while still young and tender, can be cut up and cooked like green beans or served with cream sauce in the manner of asparagus. North America. GIBBONS 1966b, MEDSGER; C64M, D62, F85, N9M

Impatiens glandulifera - *Jewelweed* {S} Raw seeds, having the taste of nuts, are eaten or pressed for their edible oil. The leaves are used as a vegetable. India, cultivated. KUNKEL, TANAKA, WATT; D62, F35M{PL}, F80, L91M, N84

Impatiens pallida - *Pale jewelweed* {S} The crisp young shoots, after five minutes of simmering in boiling water, are excellent when added to sukiyaki, chow mein, and other Oriental dishes. When eaten as a vegetable on their own, they should be cooked in one or two changes of water and then served with butter or vinegar. North America. CROWHURST 1972, GIBBONS 1979; N9M

BAMBUSACEAE

Arundinaria gigantea - *Southern cane, Large cane* {PL} Seeds are eaten as a cereal or ground into a flour. The young sprouts are used like bamboo shoots. North America. FERNALD, HEDRICK 1919, MEDSGER, PETERSON, L.; A79, D43, M16, M33M

Bambusa arundinacea - *Spiny bamboo, Thorny bamboo* {S} Young sprouts are edible. They should be cooked in two changes of water to remove the bitterness. In Thailand, a fermented vegetable product, *naw-mai-dong*, is prepared from the shoots. The sugary sap is made into a popular drink. Seeds are also edible. Tropical Asia, cultivated. STEINKRAUS, TANAKA, YOUNG 1954, YOUNG 1961; K47T, L59M{PL}, N84, O53M, Q12, Q18, Q46, *R28*

Bambusa bambos* → *Bambusa arundinacea

Bambusa beecheyana* → *Sinocalamus beecheyana

Bambusa multiplex* → *Leleba multiplex

Bambusa oldhamii* → *Leleba oldhamii

Bambusa tulda - *Peka, Talda bans* {PL} Tender shoots are eaten as a vegetable or made into pickles. Southern Asia. HEDRICK 1919, WATT; D43

Bambusa vulgaris* → *Leleba vulgaris

Dendrocalamus asper - *Buloh betong, Deling petung* {PL} Very young shoots, before they emerge from the soil, are tender and sweet. They are cooked and eaten as a vegetable, pickled in vinegar, preserved in salt, or cut into strips and used as a substitute for macaroni in soups. India, cultivated. BURKILL, OCHSE; D43

Dendrocalamus latiflorus* → *Sinocalamus latiflorus

Dendrocalamus strictus - *Male bamboo, Báns* {S} The young shoots are cooked as a vegetable. Seeds are also eaten. Source of an edible manna that can be used for cooking or making sweetmeats. India, cultivated. DONKIN, WATT; A79{PL}, D43{PL}, L59M{PL}, O53M, Q12, Q18, *Q32*, Q46

Leleba multiplex - *Hedge bamboo, Pring tjendani, Hôrai-chiku* {PL} Young shoots, though bitter, can be eaten if they are harvested before they emerge from the soil, and then parboiled in water. Tropical Asia. OCHSE, TANAKA; A78, A79, D43, E17M, I45M

Leleba oldhamii - *Lü-chu, Ryoku-chiku* {PL} The young sprouts can be used as *bamboo shoots*. China. TANAKA; A78, A79, C56M, D43, I28, L29, L59M, M5M

Leleba vulgaris - *Common bamboo, Daisan-chiku* {PL} Very young shoots, while still tender, are cooked and eaten with rice, added to soups, or made into pickles. Southern Asia, cultivated. BURKILL, OCHSE, TANAKA; C56M, D43

Oxytenanthera abyssinica - *Savannah bamboo, Woody bamboo-grass* {S} The young shoots are sometimes consumed. Grains are cooked and eaten like rice. Sap from the stems can be drunk immediately or stored and fermented into wine. The wine can be mixed with other drinks like lager beer. Cultivated in the highland areas of Tanzania. Eastern Africa. IRVINE 1960, KUNKEL, MARTIN 1975, MGENI, VON REIS; N84

Oxytenanthera braunii* → *Oxytenanthera abyssinica

Phyllostachys arcana - *Half-black bamboo* {PL} Said to have good edible shoots. China. D43, I45M, J68

Phyllostachys aurea - *Golden bamboo, Fishpole bamboo, Hotei-chiku* {PL} Fresh shoots are eaten as a vegetable. They have very little bitterness even when eaten raw. Seeds are also edible. China, cultivated. KUNKEL, YOUNG 1954, YOUNG 1961; A79, *B41*, B93M, C56M, D43, E17M, *F53M*, H4, I28, I45M, I83M, J68, L59M, M5M, M33M, etc.

Phyllostachys aureosulcata - *Yellow-groove bamboo* {PL} Young sprouts make good *bamboo shoots* as they are relatively free of bitterness or acridity, even when eaten raw. China. YOUNG 1954, YOUNG 1961; A35, A79, B28, C34, D43, E17M, H49, I45M, J68, L59M, *L95*, M16, M33M

Phyllostachys bambusoides - *Ma-dake, Timber bamboo* {PL} The large shoots are somewhat acrid, and should be prepared for eating by boiling in a considerable amount of water or by boiling in several changes of water. China, cultivated. YOUNG 1954, YOUNG 1961; A78, A79, B93M, C34, D43, E17M, H4, I45M, J61M, J68, L59M, M5M, M16

Phyllostachys congesta* → *Phyllostachys purpurata

Phyllostachys dulcis - *Sweetshoot bamboo, Pah koh poo chi* {PL} The new shoots which emerge in early spring are free of acridity, and are excellent for eating purposes. One of the most highly esteemed bamboos in China, where it is called *vegetable bamboo*. Used in salads, soups, stews and stir-fried dishes, or it is canned, salted, and pickled. China, cultivated. HALPIN, HERKLOTS, YOUNG 1954, YOUNG 1961; A78, A79, D43, I45M, J61M, J68

Phyllostachys elegans - *Flowered bamboo* {PL} Reported to have tasty, early spring time shoots. China. A79, D43

Phyllostachys flexuosa - *Zig-zag bamboo* {PL} Shoots are edible, appearing in midspring. They are slightly acrid in the raw state, and should be boiled first before using in salads, etc. China. UPHOF, YOUNG 1954; A35, A78, A79, D43, I45M, J68, L59M, M5M, M33M

Phyllostachys heterocycla f. pubescens* → *Phyllostachys pubescens

Phyllostachys makinoi - *Kei-chiku, Kwei-chu* {PL} Young sprouts are used for food. China. TANAKA; D43, L59M

Phyllostachys nidularia - {PL} Highly prized for their shoots, not only because they are among the earliest to appear in spring, but because of their delicate food qualities. The cooked shoots have somewhat the flavor of hominy corn. China. YOUNG 1954; A79, D43, L59M

Phyllostachys nigra - *Black bamboo, Kuro-chiku* {PL} The new shoots are somewhat acrid and can be prepared for eating by first boiling in a change of water. The water being changed after the first eight to ten minutes. When so prepared they have a distinctive taste and aroma. China, cultivated. UPHOF, YOUNG 1954; A78, A79, C56M, D43, H4, I28, I45M, I83M, J61M, J68, L29, L59M, M5M, M16, M33M, N37M, etc.

Phyllostachys nigra f. boryana - *Unmon-chiku, Bory bamboo* {PL} Young sprouts are used as *bamboo shoots*. Prepared in a similar manner to P. nigra. China, cultivated. TANAKA, YOUNG 1954, YOUNG 1961; A78, A79, D43, I45M, J68, L59M

Phyllostachys nigra f. henonis - *Henon bamboo, Ha-chiku* {PL} The young shoots are eaten, having the characteristic flavor and aroma of P. nigra. China, cultivated. TANAKA, YOUNG 1961; A78, A79, D43, H4, I45M, J68, L59M, M5M

Phyllostachys nuda - {PL} Edible *bamboo shoots* are of excellent quality and only slightly acrid when eaten raw. Boiling in water for only a short time would make them suitable for salads. China. HERKLOTS, YOUNG 1954; A35, A79, D37, D43, I45M, I49M, J61M

Phyllostachys pubescens - *Moso bamboo, Chiang-nan-chu, Mao tsoh* {PL} Young sprouts are noticeably acrid raw but are fragrant when cooking. When prepared by a change of water in cooking they are extensively eaten, either cooked alone or with other foods, stir-fried, pickled, or canned and exported. Tender *winter shoots* or *dung sun*, harvested as early as December, are of excellent flavor and esteemed as a delicacy. China, cultivated. HERKLOTS, TANAKA, YOUNG 1961; A35, A78, A79, C27G{PR}, D43, L59M, M5M, N84{S}

Phyllostachys purpurata - {PL} Young shoots are slightly bitter when raw and are used as a cooked vegetable after boiling in a change of water. China. YOUNG 1954; A78, A79, D43, I45M, J61M, J68, L59M

Phyllostachys rubromarginata - *Red-margined bamboo* {PL} The tender, young shoots have a small degree of bitterness or acridity, and after boiling in water they are eaten in salads, stir-fried dishes, etc. China. YOUNG 1954; A78, A79, D43, I45M, J68, L59M, M16

Phyllostachys viridi-glauscens - {PL} Young sprouts are virtually free of acridity or bite and are eaten as a cooked vegetable, pickled, put in soups, salted, etc. China. YOUNG 1954, YOUNG 1961; A78, D43, I45M

Phyllostachys viridis - *Green sulphur* {PL} The young shoots are almost entirely free of acridity and could be sliced finely and used raw in salads. They are more commonly boiled first and then used cold in salads, stir-fried, braised, added to stews, etc. China. YOUNG 1954, YOUNG 1961; A79, D43, I45M, L59M, M16

CULTIVARS

Robert Young: The culms emerge a light pea green, then upon exposure to the sun turn a striking yellow with an occasional green stripe. It may taste even better than the species. A79, D43, H4, J68, L59M

Phyllostachys vivax - *Giant timber bamboo* {PL} The new shoots are free of acridity or bite when raw. Species with this quality would appear to be more nutritious since less of the vitamins and minerals are dissipated in the cooking water. China. YOUNG 1954, YOUNG 1961; A79, D43, I45M

Sasa kurilensis - *Chishima-zasa* {PL} Sprouts are edible, either cooked, canned, or preserved. It is said that they are so popular in Japan that a license is required to collect them. Seeds are also edible. Japan, Korea. TANAKA; A78, A79, D43, I45M, L59M, M16

Semiarundinaria fastuosa - *Narihira bamboo, Narihira-dake* {PL} New shoots that appear in spring are practically free of bitterness or bite. Although small they are of good quality when cooked. Japan. UPHOF, YOUNG 1954, YOUNG 1961; A78, A79, D43, E17M, H4, I45M, J68, L59M, M5M, M33M, N51

Sinocalamus beecheyanus - *Beechy bamboo* {PL} An important source of commercial *bamboo shoots* in southern China. The ground around the base of the clump should be mounded with soil well before the shoots appear. In this way all light that would cause the shoots to develop an intense bitterness is excluded. China, cultivated. YOUNG 1954, YOUNG 1961; D43

Sinocalamus latiflorus - *Big jute bamboo, Machiku, Ma-chu* {PL} Widely grown in Canton for its excellent edible shoots which are robust, relatively solid, and unusually free of any unpleasant taste when raw. Shredded and dried they are used in Chinese-style snacks in Japan. China, Southern Asia. HERKLOTS, TANAKA, YOUNG 1961; M5M

BARRINGTONIACEAE

Barringtonia butonica - *Bonnet D'Eveque* {S} The oily seeds and fruits are eaten green as vegetables. Pacific Islands. HEDRICK 1919; **X88M**

BASELLACEAE

Anredera cordifolia - *Madeira vine* {PL} The succulent, slightly mucilaginous leaves may be eaten raw in salads or used as a potherb. Tubers are boiled and eaten like potatoes. Central America, South America. TANAKA, UPHOF; E48, E83T, G18, K77M, M31, M61, S91M

Basella alba - *Ceylon spinach, Malabar spinach, Poi sag, Saan choi* {S} The succulent leaves and stem tips are an excellent hot weather substitute for spinach. They can be eaten raw in salads, boiled, steamed, stir-fried, or added to soups, stews, tofu-dishes, and curries. An infusion of the leaves is used as a tea. The purplish sap from the fruits is used for coloring agar-agar, pastries, and sweets. A little lemon juice added to the dye enhances the color. Tropics, cultivated. DAHLEN [Cul, Re], HALPIN [Cu, Cul], HAWKES [Re], HEDRICK 1919, HERKLOTS, MARTIN 1975, OCHSE, UPHOF, VILMORIN [Cu], WINTERS [Nu]; B49, D11M, E49, E59, I39, J20, J34, K49M, L91M, N84, P1G, P38, Q34, R47, S59M, S93M, etc.

CULTIVARS

Eclipse: 55-60 days. Very early, small, compact plant. Leaves thick, medium to deep green. Can be planted very close together. Suitable for home gardens and for frame culture. Yields very well under warm humid conditions. O39M

Red: (Red Stemmed, Rubra) Leaves, stems, and flowers are tinged with red. Ornamental in appearance, however, best used in salads as it loses much of the pigment when cooked and becomes unattractive. D62, E49, F85, I77, I91, N84, O93, P38, *S70*

Basella rubra* → *Basella alba

Boussingaultia baselloides* → *Anredera cordifolia

Ullucus tuberosus - *Ulloco, Melloco* {PL} Tubers may be boiled and served with vinegar. When boiled and fried they taste like potatoes. In the cold altiplano areas of the Andes they are frozen and then dried, the resulting product being called *chuño*, a name first used for dried potatoes but now used for any desiccated vegetable. The *chuño* prepared from these tubers is called *lingli*. Leaves are eaten in salads or as a potherb. Andean South America, cultivated. DUKE, HERKLOTS, HODGE 1951, NATIONAL RESEARCH COUNCIL 1989, VILMORIN [Cu]; **W77M, Z98**

BATIDACEAE

Batis maritima - *American saltwort, Jamaica samphire* {PL} The salty, succulent leaves are sometimes eaten in salads. They are also cooked or used for pickles. Makes a salty purée after boiling and straining to remove "strings". American coasts. HEDRICK 1919, MORTON 1977, TANAKA; *F73*, F85{S}

BERBERIDACEAE

Berberis aquifolium* → *Mahonia aquifolium

Berberis aristata - *Indian barberry, Nepal barberry* {S} Flower buds are used in sauces. Dried fruits, known as *zirishk turash*, are used as a substitute for raisins in desserts. Himalayan region. HEDRICK 1919, KUNKEL, WATT; N51{PL}, N84, O46, P49, *P63*, Q12, Q40

Berberis asiatica - *Himalayan barberry, Raisin barberry* {S} The large, purplish fruits are dried and used like raisins in desserts. They are said to make the best *Indian raisins*. Himalayan region. HEDRICK 1919, HENDRICKSON, SIMMONS 1972; N84, O46, O53M, *P63*, Q40

Berberis buxifolia - *Magellan barberry, Calafate* {PL} When ripe, the large, black, pleasantly-flavored fruits may be eaten out of hand. In England, both green and ripe fruits are used like gooseberries in making pies, tarts, and preserves. Southern Chile and Argentina. HEDRICK 1919, SIMMONS 1972, UPHOF, VALENZUELA; P86

Berberis darwinii - *Darwin barberry* {S} The dark-purple fruits are eaten or made into preserves. Chile, Patagonia. HEDRICK 1919, HENDRICKSON; D95{PL}, K47T, *N71M*, N84, O53M, P49, *P63*, P86{PL}, *R28*, R78

Berberis haematocarpa* → *Mahonia haematocarpa

Berberis lycium - *Indian barberry* {S} Fruits are eaten raw or made into preserves. The young shoots and leaves are consumed as a vegetable. An infusion of the leaves is used as a substitute for tea. Himalayan region. HEDRICK 1919; N84, O53M, *P63*, Q40

Berberis nervosa* → *Mahonia nervosa

Berberis repens* → *Mahonia repens

Berberis trifoliolata* → *Mahonia trifoliolata

Berberis vulgaris - *European barberry* {S} Berries are eaten raw, candied, preserved in syrup, made into jellies, sauces, pies, tarts and cakes, or pickled in vinegar and used as a substitute for capers. In some countries the juice is used like that of lemons in the preparation of cooling drinks, and for flavoring ices, sherbets, and punches. *Confiture d'épine vinette*, a celebrated French jam, is made from a seedless form. The leaves are eaten as an acid nibble or used to season meat. Dried young leaves and branch-tips make an excellent refreshing tea. Eurasia, cultivated. FERNALD, GRIEVE [Re], HEDRICK 1919, JOHNS [Cul], LAUNERT, SIMMONS 1972 [Cu], UPHOF; *N71M*, N84, N93M, O53M, P49, R78, S7M

Mahonia aquifolium - *Oregon hollygrape, Holly barberry* {PL} The acid fruits are used in pies, jellies, jams, beverages, and confectionery. When fermented, the juice makes a palatable and wholesome wine. The bright yellow flowers are eaten or used to make a lemonade-like drink. North America, cultivated. DOMICO, FREITUS [Re], HEDRICK 1919, MEDSGER; A2{S}, *B60*, C9, C9M{S}, D95, G60, K38{S}, K63G{S}, *L49*, M76, M77, N84{S}, O53M{S}, *P63*{S}

Mahonia haematocarpa - *Red hollygrape, Mexican barberry, Algerita* {S} The bright blood red berries are pleasantly acid in flavor and are primarily used for making jellies. Southwestern North America. HARRINGTON, H., MEDSGER; J25M

Mahonia nervosa - *Oregon grape* {S} Ripe fruits are too acid to eat raw, but stewed with sugar or other fruits, or made into jams, jellies, and pies, they are very good. They can also be used to enhance the flavor of bland fruits or prepared like lemonade to make a refreshing drink. Young, tender leaves are simmered in a small amount of water and eaten as a snack. Western North America. SIMMONS 1972 [Cu], TURNER 1979 [Pre, Re]; A2, C9M, D95{PL}, E15, G82M{PL}, I47, *J75M*, K38, K63G, N84, O53M, *P63*

Mahonia repens - *Creeping barberry, Creeping Oregon grape* {PL} The tart fruits are eaten raw, roasted, pickled in vinegar, or made into jellies, jams, wines, and a lemonade-like beverage. A distinctive jelly can be made by using half apple juice to half barberry juice. Western North America. HARRINGTON, H., HART, UPHOF; A2{S}, B44M, C9, C9M{S}, *C33*, D95, I15{S}, I63M, J25M{S}, J26, K38{S}, L13{S}, M35M, *M51M*, O53M{S}, etc.

Mahonia swaseyi - *Texas mahonia, Agrito, Wild currant, Chaparral berry* {PL} The fruits are yellowish-orange, up to a half inch in diameter, and pleasantly acid. They can be used in concentrated juices and blends, sauces, tarts and pies, or made into wine, relish, pickles, pies, jams, jellies, candies, and "raisins". Roasted seeds are used as a substitute for coffee. Recommended for improvement by selection and breeding. Southwestern North America. DURAND 1972; N51

Mahonia trifoliolata - *Agrito, Laredo mahonia, Mexican barberry* {S} The bright red fruit has a subtle, tart flavor which is quite pleasant and is eaten raw or used in jellies, preserves, cakes and tarts. Southwestern North America. LATORRE 1977a [Re], LATORRE 1977b, UPHOF; B83M, B94, H4{PL}, N37M{PL}

BETULACEAE

Betula alleghaniensis - *Yellow birch* {S} The sweet sap makes a pleasant drink or it can be boiled down to a syrup. Dried leaves are used as a substitute for tea. Twigs and leaves, having the flavor of wintergreen, can be used as condiments. North America. FERNALD, MEDSGER; D95{PL}, *G66*, K38, K47T, K63G, *N71M*, N84, O53M, O93, *P17M*, P49, *P63*, *Q32*, R78

Betula lenta - *Sweet birch, Black birch, Cherry birch* {S} Dried leaves and the reddish bark from the larger roots are used in brewing a delightful tea. The sweet sap is drunk as a beverage, boiled down to sugar and syrup, or fermented into *birch beer*, wine and vinegar. An essential oil, distilled from the twigs and bark, is sometimes used as a wintergreen flavoring. Inner bark has been used for food. Eastern North America. ANGIER, FERNALD, GIBBONS 1962, LOGSDON 1981, MARCIN, MEDSGER; *B68*{PL}, *G66*, K38{PL}, K47T, K63G, M16{PL}, N7T{PL}, *N71M*, N84, P49, *P63*

Betula lutea* → *Betula alleghaniensis

Betula nigra - *Red birch, River birch* {PL} The sap from the trunk is said to make a pleasant drink, and when boiled down, to furnish sugar. It can also be fermented into *birch beer*. North America. FERNALD, TANAKA; *B52*, C9M{S}, *C33*, D45, D95, *F51*, G23, H49, I77M, K18, K38{S}, K47T{S}, M76, *N71M*{S}, *Q32*{S}, etc.

Betula papyrifera - *Paper birch, Canoe birch, White birch* {PL} Very young leaves, shoots, and catkins may be eaten in salads, or stir-fried dishes. The sap is prized as a pleasant, sweet drink, and by boiling it can be reduced to syrup, or finally, sugar. It is also sometimes used in making *birch beer* and vinegar. A tea is made from the young leaves. North America, cultivated. BRYAN [Cul, Re], FERNALD, MEDSGER; A2{S}, C9M{S}, *C33*, D45, G41, H49, I4, I15{S}, J16, J47, *J75M*, K38{S}, L91M{S}, M77, N0, etc.

Betula populifolia - *Gray birch* {S} The sap is consumed as a sweet beverage or fermented into beer and vinegar. Inner bark, ground into flour, is used as an emergency breadstuff. Eastern North America. FERNALD, TANAKA; B96{PL}, C9M, D62, D95{PL}, E47{PL}, *G66*, K38, K47T, K63G, N84, O93, *P63*, *Q32*

BIGNONIACEAE

Catalpa ovata - *Ki-sasage, Azusa* {S} Flowers and young pods are eaten. China, cultivated. TANAKA; B96{PL}, E7M, F80, *G89M*{PL}, K47T, K63G, N84, O93, P49, *R28*, R78, S95

Crescentia alata - *Mexican calabash, Morrito* {S} The ripe seeds, when ground, are mixed with raw rice, roasted pumpkin seeds, lemon peel, sugar, water, and ice and made into a non-alcoholic beverage called *horchata*. They also yield a bland, relatively stable edible oil. Fruits are sometimes eaten or made into a drink. Tropical America. MENNINGER, TANAKA, WILLIAMS, L.; N84

Crescentia cujete - *Calabash tree, Calabazo, Jicara-nut, Morro* {S} Young fruits are pickled like walnuts. The seeds have been much used in Curacao to make syrup or a popular confection called *carabobo*. For syrup, the seeds are pounded fine, mixed with sugar and a little water and boiled. Roasted seeds are mixed with roasted wheat to form a flavorful, aromatic coffee substitute marketed as *cafe du grain*. In Africa, the leaves are cooked in soups with those of Adansonia. Tropical America. DUKE, HEDRICK 1919, MENNINGER, UPHOF; A79M, E56{PR}, F85, F93M{PR}, N84

Dolichandrone rheedii - *Thakut* {S} The young fruits and flowers are eaten as a vegetable by the Burmese. Burma, Andaman Islands. TANAKA; **Z25M**

Dolichandrone stipulata - {S} Flowers are eaten by the Burmese and are brought to local markets. Burma. HEDRICK 1919; **Y2**

Kigelia africana - *Sausage tree* {S} In Kenya, the fruits are used in the preparation of *muratina*, a sweet-sour, effervescent beverage made from sugar cane juice. It is consumed as a refreshing beverage in place of Western-style beers, especially at festivals and social gatherings. Roasted seeds are eaten as a famine food. Tropical Africa. FOX, F., HEDRICK 1919, STEINKRAUS; A79M, B62, C56M{PL}, F85, I83M{PL}, *N79M*, N84, O53M, O93, P5, Q12, Q18, Q46, R41, S29, etc.

Kigelia pinnata* → *Kigelia africana

Oroxylum indicum - *Sward fruit tree, Indian trumpet-flower* {S} The young leaves and flowers are eaten uncooked as a side-dish with rice. This is usually prepared by mixing them with various spices, including chilis, fish paste, red onions, candle nut, lemon grass, and ginger. Young fruits are cut into pieces, boiled, and eaten with rice. The large seeds are said to be edible. Southeast Asia. MENNINGER; A79M, F85, N84, Q46

Parmentiera aculeata - *Food candle tree, Guachilote* {S} When ripe, the yellow, banana-shaped fruits are quite sweet and may be eaten raw, cooked, roasted, or made into pickles, preserves and sweetmeats. In flavor, the raw fruit is said to resemble sugar cane. Central America. KENNARD, UPHOF, WILLIAMS, L.; F85, N84

Parmentiera alata* → *Crescentia alata

Parmentiera cerifera - *Candle tree* {PL} Cultivated in the West Indies and other tropical regions for its edible fruits. Mexico. ZEVEN; **T71**

Parmentiera edulis* → *Parmentiera aculeata

Spathodea campanulata - *African tulip tree* {S} The flower buds contain a sweet, watery liquid that is considered tonic. Winged seeds are said to be edible. Tropical Africa, cultivated. DALZIEL, DUKE,

IRVINE 1960; A79M, C56M{PL}, F85, I83M{PL}, L29{PL}, M20, O84, P5, *P17M*, *Q32*, Q46, *R28*, R33M, S92

Tabebuia pallida - *Pink tabebuia* {S} Leaves are used to make a tea. West Indies. ALTSCHUL; C9M, *L5M*, N84, P5, *Q25*

BISCHOFIACEAE

Bischofia javanica - *Toog, Nhôi, Akagi* {S} Seeds and fruits are eaten. Young leaves are used as a condiment. Tropical Asia. TANAKA; F85, *I61*, I83M{PL}, *K46*{PL}, N84, P5

BIXACEAE

Bixa orellana - *Anatto, Lipstick plant* {S} The seeds, called *achiote* or *roucou*, are briefly steeped in hot oil or lard which is then strained, cooled, and used as coloring and flavoring for meat, poultry, fish, and vegetable dishes. In Yucatan, the whole seed is ground with various spices into a paste, giving a more pronounced flavor. The seed coat is the source of a yellow pigment widely used in the food industry for coloring cheese, butter, and margarine. Tropical America, cultivated. DUKE, MENNINGER, ORTIZ 1979, UPHOF, WILLIAMS, L.; A79M, C3M{PR}, C81M, F80, F85, G25M, *G66*, I99, M19, N84, O42, O46, O53M, P5, *P17M*, P38, Q46, R33M, etc.

BLECHNACEAE

Stenochlaena palustris - *Paku miding, Pakis bang* {PL} Young leaves and shoots, wine-red in color, are eaten either raw or steamed with rice and are said to resemble amaranth. A soup can also be made from them, the water of which, is likewise red. Tropical Asia. BROWN, W., BURKILL, OCHSE, UPHOF; E48, N84{S}

BOMBACACEAE

Adansonia digitata - *Baobob, Monkey bread, Cream of tartar tree, Ethiopian sour gourd* {S} Acid pulp of the fruit is eaten, made into drinks, and used as a flavoring or to curdle milk. Young leaves are eaten as a potherb or made into *kuka*, a powder used to thicken soups and stews. Seeds are eaten mixed with millet meal, used as a coffee substitute, or made into *lalu*, a powder used as flavoring or a baking powder substitute. *Reniala oil* or *fony oil*, derived from the seeds, is edible. Tender roots are eaten. Shoots of germinating seeds are edible. Tropical Africa. DALZIEL, DUKE, FOX, F., MENNINGER, UPHOF, VON WELANETZ; A79M, B62, C27M, I33, I83M{PL}, K77M{PL}, L91M, N43M{PL}, O53M, O93, P5, P38, R41, R77M, S44, S92, etc.

Adansonia gregorii - *Australian bottle tree* {S} Seeds are eaten raw or roasted. Pulp of fruit is somewhat acid, also eaten. Australia. KUNKEL, UPHOF; B62, C27M, *N79M*, N84, O33, P5, *P17M*, P38, *Q32*, Q41, R15M, R33M, S44, S92, T7, etc.

Bombax buonopozense - *Red-flowered silk cotton tree* {S} The fleshy, rather mucilaginous calyces are consumed in soups or used in sauces, as a substitute for roselle (Hibiscus sabdariffa). Young leaves, often dried, are eaten as a potherb. Tropical Africa. DALZIEL, UPHOF; F85, N84

***Bombax ceiba* → Ceiba pentandra**

Bombax ellipticum - *Mokok* {PL} Seeds of the white-flowered form are eaten as a snack food. Mexico. ALCORN; L50

***Bombax glabra* → Pachira aquatica**

***Bombax malabaricum* → Salmalia malabarica**

Bombax munguba - *Munguba* {S} The seed contains 20-25% of a clear yellow oil which is edible. Tropical America. TANAKA; **X88M**

Ceiba acuminata - {S} Unripe fruits are eaten. Central America. KUNKEL; K77M{PL}, L13

Ceiba aesculifolia - *Ceibillo* {S} Young fruits and ripe seeds are eaten after cooking or roasting, in some parts of Yucatan. Mexico. UPHOF, WILLIAMS, L.; **Z25M**

Ceiba pentandra - *Kapok tree, Silk cotton tree* {S} Tender leaves, buds, and fruits are mucilaginous and are eaten like okra. Seeds are roasted and ground, eaten in soups, or used as a flavoring. Presscakes from the seeds can be used for making *tempeh*. They also yield a pleasant tasting cooking oil. Flower petals are eaten. In Indonesia, the sprouted seeds are eaten raw, cooked, added to soups, or made into *sambal goreng* (coconut-milk sauce). Wood ashes are used as a salt substitute. Tropics, cultivated. BURKILL, DUKE, HEDRICK 1919, MENNINGER, OCHSE, SHURTLEFF 1979, WATT; A79M, C27M, C56M{PL}, F85, N84, P5, Q12, Q18, Q46, S44

Durio dulcis - *Lahong, Tutong* {S} When ripe the fruit is an attractive dark purplish-red and has a bright yellow, very sweet aril with an extremely offensive odor. It is soft, creamy and caramel-like with a delicious flavor reminiscent of pineapple cream without the acidity. The sweetest and most ill-smelling of all Durio species. Borneo. SOEGENG-REKSODIHARDJO; O19, O19{PL}

Durio graveolens - *Tabelak, Durian mah* {S} The orange-yellow fruit is very distinct from that of the common durian, and has a fleshy, dark red aril, without odor and with a very sweet flavor. It is much preferred by the natives for relish and is usually made into *sajur*, soup prepared from fresh water fish. Indonesia. ALTSCHUL, SOEGENG-REKSODIHARDJO; Z12

Durio kutejensis - *Lai* {S} Ripe fruits are eaten fresh. They are yellow in color and have soft, short spines. The thick-textured, yellowish orange flesh has a distinctive flavor, drier and firmer than Isu, sweet but less sweet and less strongly flavored than durian. They have a slight aroma when fully ripe. Indonesia, cultivated. RIFAI, SOEGENG-REKSODIHARDJO; O19, O19{PL}

Durio zibethinus - *Durian* {S} Ripe fruits have a foul odor, but a delicious flavor, much described. Usually eaten out of hand, but also made into candy, preserves, ice cream and paste. Unripe fruits are cooked with coconut milk and spices. Fermented fruits are eaten as *tempoyak*. Fresh seeds are roasted and eaten or cut in slices and fried. Dried up seeds are boiled as a delicacy. Smoke from burned fruit peels give flavor to fish dishes. Flower petals and young leaves and shoots are also edible. Southeast Asia, cultivated. BURKILL, GARNER [Pro], MORTON 1987a [Cu], OCHSE, POPENOE, W. 1920 [Cu], STEINKRAUS, WATT; F85, J22{PL}, N84, O19, O19{PL}, O93, P38, R59

Durio sp. - *Isu* {S} Small, round durian-like fruits, about 5 inches in diameter; yellow shells, covered with sharp spines, easy to open; yellow flesh surrounding 1 to 3 seeds in each of 5 locules; little aroma. The flesh is thicker textured than durian, somewhat like peanut butter. Flavor rich, similar to durian but less sweet and with a slight tangy aftertaste. Highly ornamental tree with large, glossy green leaves, a rich golden color on the undersides. Borneo. O19, O19{PL}

***Eriodendron aesculifolium* → Ceiba aesculifolia**

Pachira aquatica - *Malabar chestnut, Guinea chestnut, Provision tree, Saba nut* {PL} Seeds are eaten raw, tasting like peanuts. Roasted or fried in oil they have the flavor of chestnuts, and can be ground into a flour for bread baking. Young leaves and flowers are used as a vegetable. Brazil, Guiana, cultivated. DUKE, HEDRICK 1919, MENNINGER; A79M, E29, F85{S}, G20, I83M, K77M, L6, M7M, N43M, N84{S}, O93{S}, P38{S}

Pachira insignis - *Mamorana grande* {S} Kernels of the nuts are edible after being roasted. Young leaves and flowers are eaten.

Tropical America. HEDRICK 1919, MENNINGER, TANAKA; F85, N84, P38

Pachira macrocarpa* → *Pachira aquatica

Patinoa almirajo - *Almirajo* {S} The fleshy aril which completely covers the seeds is edible and considered a delicacy by the natives. Cultivated by the Indians of the Chocó region of Colombia. Tropical South America. DUKE, SOEGENG-REKSODIHARDJO; **U27T**

Quararibea cordata - *Chupa-chupa, South American sapote* {S} The fibrous, yellow-orange pulp of the fruit is sweet and can be eaten out of hand. The flavor is reminiscent of a very sweet pumpkin, with overtones of mango and apricot. Types with very little fiber may be utilized for juice. Colombia to Peru. HACKETT, HODGE 1960, MORTON 1987a, POPENOE, W. 1924; **T73M, W78M, X79**

Salmalia malabarica - *Red silk-cotton tree, Semal, Pan-ya* {S} Flowers and flower buds are eaten as a vegetable. Fleshy calyces of the large red flowers are used in curries. Ripe seeds are roasted and eaten, or used as a source of cooking oil in place of cotton-seed oil. Tropical Asia, cultivated. BURKILL, HAWKES, MACMILLAN, WATT, TANAKA; A79M, B62, C27M, F80, F85, *N79M*, O93, *P17M*, P38, Q12, Q18, *Q32*, Q46

BORAGINACEAE

Anchusa azurea - *Anchusa* {S} The bright, gentian-blue flowers are an excellent addition to a tossed salad, particularly when mixed with rose petals. They are also used as an attractive garnish. Europe. LARKCOM 1984, LEGGATT [Re]; J53, N84

Anchusa capensis - *Cape forget-me-not* {S} The vivid blue flowers are prized as an addition to salads, including seafood, fruit, potato, vegetable and tossed green salads. Also used in cold drinks, pasta, puddings, custards, icings, and hot or cold soups. Leaves are also eaten. South Africa, cultivated. KUNKEL; A53M, F85, N84

Anchusa officinalis - *Alkanet, Bugloss* {S} Young leaves and shoots are boiled or steamed and eaten like spinach, especially in the south of France and parts of Germany. The flowers are eaten as a vegetable or used as a garnish. Europe. HEDRICK 1919, LAUNERT, LEGGATT [Re]; A2, C43M, C43M{PL}, E61{PL}, E81M, F80, G84{PL}, H3M{PL}, J82, K22, *N71M*, N84, O48, S55

Borago officinalis - *Borage* {PL} Fresh leaves, tasting of cucumbers, are added to salads, eaten as a potherb, or used in the preparation of cooling drinks. The blue flowers are eaten in salads, preserved, candied, made into syrup, or used as garnishes. Dried stems are used for flavoring beverages, among which *negus* and *claret cup*. Flower corollas can be used to color vinegar blue. Both leaves and flowers are brewed into tea. Mediterranean region, cultivated. DE SOUNIN [Cul], HALPIN, LAUNERT, MACNICOL [Re], MARCIN, MICHAEL [Pre, Re], UPHOF; C3{S}, C13M{S}, C67M, D29, F21, G84, H40{S}, H46{S}, J66, K22{S}, *M35*, N19M, N45

Buglossoides arvense - *Corn gromwell* {S} Young leaves are used as a boiled vegetable. Eurasia. TANAKA; **V84, Y10**

Cynoglossum officinale - *Hound's tongue* {S} Young leaves are used in some areas of Switzerland as a salad and vegetable. Eurasia. UPHOF; D62, F80, *N71M*, N84, O48, O53M, P83M, *Q24*, R53M, S7M, S55

Heliotropium curassavicum - *Seaside heliotrope, Nena* {S} Leaves are eaten in salads or boiled as a potherb. Dried leaves are brewed into a tea. Ashes of the plant are used as a substitute for salt. Tropical America. DUKE, KUNKEL, TANAKA, WILLIAMS, L.; **W59M, Y10, Y29M**

Lithospermum officinale - *Gromwell* {S} Leaves are used as a substitute for tea, called *Bohemian tea* or *Croatian tea*. Eurasia. UPHOF; E61{PL}, F80, N84, O48, O53M, R53M, R53M{PL}, S7M

Mertensia maritima - *Sea bugloss, Oyster plant* {PL} The fleshy leaves, whose taste has given it the name oyster plant, are eaten both raw and cooked. Rhizomes are consumed as food by the Eskimos of Alaska. Northern temperate region. LOVELOCK, MABEY, UPHOF; R53M

Pentaglottis sempervirens - *Evergreen alkanet* {S} The azure blue flowers can be used in salads. Europe. LARKCOM 1980; N84

Pulmonaria officinalis - *Lungwort, Jerusalem cowslip* {PL} Young basal leaves can be used for salads, boiled as potherbs, or added to soups, stews, and vegetable dishes. Europe. LAUNERT, MABEY; K85, M82, P92, R53M

Pulmonaria saccharata - *Jerusalem sage* {PL} Said to be used as a spice. Southern Europe. TANAKA; G55, M92

Symphytum officinale - *Comfrey* {PL} Young leaves are chopped and added to salads, cooked as a potherb, or used in soups, sautés, pastas, and au gratin dishes. A Teutonic fritter called *schwarzwurz* is made from leaves stuffed with cheese, dipped in egg batter, and then fried. Mature leaves were used to flavor cakes and a sauce base known as *panada*. Blanched stalks are used like asparagus. Peeled roots are cut up and used in vegetable soups. Dried leaves and roots are used for tea. The roasted roots are mixed with those of chicory and dandelion and used as a coffee substitute. Eurasia, cultivated. GRIEVE, HALPIN [Cu, Cul], HEDRICK 1919, MABEY [Re], MARCIN, MICHAEL [Pre, Re], MORTON 1976; C39M, C67M, C82, D29, D65, E71M, F21, F31T, G84, G96, I42, I42{PR}, J25M{S}, J66, J73, K22, N45, *N71M*{S}, etc.

Symphytum peregrinum* → *Symphytum x uplandicum

Symphytum tuberosum - *Tuberous comfrey* {PL} The roots, when roasted until brown and brittle, then ground, make a very good substitute for coffee, with a smoothness that is not even found in real coffee. Europe, naturalized in North America. GIBBONS 1979; *P95M*, R53M

Symphytum x uplandicum - *Russian comfrey* {PL} A natural hybrid. Young leaves are boiled or steamed and served like spinach, or used in soups, soufflés, and au gratin dishes. Health food enthusiasts liquidize the leaves and consume them as *green drink*. Dried leaves are used for tea, the best flavor coming from those that have been dried quickly. They can also be ground to a green flour that can be used in gravies, soups, and stews. Caucasus Mountains, cultivated. HILLS, L. [Nu, Re], ZEVEN; C11, C60M, D62{S}, D76, F37T, I39, I91{S}, *M35*, N84{S}, O48{S}, S55{S}

CULTIVARS

Bocking 4: Leaves broad, round tipped, very large, recovering rapidly after cutting. Stems strong, solid, wings small. Flower color is Bishops Violet 34/3 when fully open. Recommended for use in liquidized *green drink*. HILLS, L.; J82

Bocking 14: (Webster's) Leaves pointed, slightly serrated at the edges. Flower stems slender, frequent, entirely wingless. Flowers are Imperial Purple 33/3 fading to Lilac Purple 031/3. Considered too bitter for use in *green drink*. HILLS, L.; J82, L86, P83M, S55

Trichodesma zeylanicum - {S} Leaves are cooked and eaten as a side-dish with groundnuts or added to beer to ensure proper fermentation. The seeds yield an edible oil. Tropical Asia, Tropical Africa. FOX, F., MARTIN 1975, MENNINGER, QUIN; N84, O53M, R15M, S92, T7

BRASSICACEAE (*CRUCIFERAE*)

Alliaria officinalis* → *Sisymbrium officinale

Alliaria petiolata - *Garlic mustard, Hedge garlic* {S} The garlic-flavored leaves can be finely chopped and added to tossed salads, cooked as a potherb, or eaten with bread and butter. In England, they are mixed with mint leaves and made into a sauce to serve with salt-fish, lamb, or mutton dishes. Eurasia. GRIEVE, HEDRICK 1919, LAUNERT, MABEY, MICHAEL [Re], UPHOF; D62, F80, J67M, *N71M*, N84, O48, O53M, P83M, S55

Arabis alpina - *Alpine cress, Mountain rock-cress* {S} The young leaves and flowers are an agreeable substitute for cress. They can be eaten raw, cooked, or mixed with other greens as a flavoring. North America. FERNALD, GIBBONS 1979; B97M{PL}, C85M, D26, D62, E5T, E89M, F80, J20, N84, O48, *Q24*, S7M, S55

Arabis caucasica - *Rock-cress, Barbeen, Shahat* {PL} In Iran, Iraq and the Gulf States of Arabia, the fresh leaves are commonly used as a garnish in salads like watercress. In Iran they are also used as a potherb. Southwest Asia, cultivated. MALLOS [Re]; B97M, C9, C40, D11T, D62, F35M, H98, L66, L91M{S}, N84{S}

Armoracia lapathifolia* → *Armoracia rusticana

Armoracia rusticana - *Horseradish* {PL} The fresh roots are used for flavoring meats, vegetables, pickles, etc. They are also processed into sauce, powder, and vinegar. In Japan, the powdered root is used to adulterate true *wasabi* powder. Young leaves have a pleasant flavor and can be added to salads or cooked as a potherb. Sprouted seeds are eaten in salads. Roots can be brought indoors in the winter and forced into producing white, tender, sweet leaves. In Germany, sliced roots are cooked like parsnips. Eurasia, naturalized in North America. FERNALD, GIBBONS 1966b, HALPIN [Cu, Cul], LARKCOM 1984, MABEY, SCHNEIDER [Cul, Re], TANAKA, UPHOF, VILMORIN [Cu]; A94M{PR}, C43M, D65, E5M, F1, F11, F31T, G23, G71, H42, J83, K22, L97

CULTIVARS

Big Top: A newly selected strain that is vigorous, widely adapted, and resistant to foliage disease, rust and bacteria spot. Plant in the early spring in a rich soil that maintains good moisture. Plant with the flat end up. I50

Bohemian: (Bohemian Giant) Hardy, easy to grow cultivar. Produces large, white roots of superior quality that make a gourmet sauce. Grate and mix with mayonnaise. Has a pleasantly pungent flavor. Plant in moist, well-drained soil and full sun. B73M, C11, C82, E97, G16

Hybrid: An outstanding, hybrid horseradish with superior disease resistance, smoother roots, and bigger yields. Pungent roots add flavor to meats and relishes. Dig roots during cool weather of spring and fall. E97

Maliner Kren: Vigorous grower, producing large white roots. Earlier, larger, whiter than the standard type. True Bohemian horseradish, the standard cultivar for condiment use. Originally from Germany. B75, C85M, D11M, I39, K71, N39

New Bohemian: (Kiester's New Bohemian) Improved Maliner Kren or Bohemian type, known for its vigorous growth and large-size roots. Makes a strong quick growth and produces a heavy crop, particularly on land which has been well prepared. The small sets or roots are planted in the spring to furnish large, straight, smooth roots for use the following season. C63, *C84*, G44

Newcastle Ivory: An improved form with pure white flesh. Selected by Fowler Nurseries. E4

Barbarea praecox* → *Barbarea verna

Barbarea verna - *Upland cress, American cress, Belle-Isle cress* {S} The young leaves have a pleasant flavor similar to water-cress and are eaten in salads as a garnish or flavoring. They are also used in cress soup. In hot weather the plant runs to seed very rapidly, the flavor then becoming very hot. Seeds are used as a source of oil. Sprouted seeds can be eaten in salads. Europe, cultivated. FERNALD, HALPIN, KRAFT, LARKCOM 1984, UPHOF, VILMORIN; A2, C44, C92, E38, F24, *F72*, F82, G51, G71, J73, K22, K71, L91M, M46, N84, etc.

Barbarea vulgaris - *Winter cress, Yellow rocket* {S} Young leaves and shoots, while still tender, may be chopped fine and added to tossed green salads. Somewhat older leaves make a good potherb if cooked in two or more waters, the first removing some of the bitter flavor. The undeveloped flower clusters are gathered and used like broccoli. During mid-winter warm spells, the plant has the ability to grow vigorously and produce greens. Northern temperate region. ANGIER, FERNALD, GIBBONS 1962, MEDSGER; D58, F24, I39, *N71M*, N84, O48

CULTIVARS

Variegata: A variegated form. N84

Brassica adpressa* → *Hirschfeldia incana

Brassica alba* → *Sinapis alba

Brassica alboglabra* → *Brassica oleracea

Brassica arvensis* → *Sinapis arvensis

Brassica balearica - {S} Said to be used as a vegetable. Balearic Islands. TANAKA; **Z25M**

Brassica campestris* → *Brassica rapa

Brassica carinata - *Abyssinian cabbage, Abyssinian mustard, African cabbage, Karate* {S} Tender leaves and young stems, up to twelve inches high, can be eaten raw in salads. Older leaves and stems are cooked and served like collards or mustard. The inflorescence may be used as a broccoli-like vegetable. Seeds are the source of an edible oil. East Africa, cultivated. LARKCOM 1984 [Cu], OOMEN, ZEVEN; D33, N84, O48

CULTIVARS

TexSel: (Tamu TexSel, Tel-Tex) The plants in the early growth stages develop a rosette of leaves from a very short stem. At full height the plants are 3 to 5 feet. The foliage is green to light glaucous, mostly glabrous. Similar in growth characteristics to mustard and collards. Immature plants are excellent as a green leafy vegetable. The flavor is somewhat milder than collards without the pungency of mustard greens. Developed at Texas A&M University. ANONYMOUS 1972; E83T, F80, J34, L89G

Brassica cretica - {S} The young shoots are used as a vegetable in Greece. Eastern Mediterranean. HEDRICK 1919; **U71M, X8**

Brassica fimbriata* → *Brassica napus

Brassica hirta* → *Sinapis alba

Brassica japonica* → *Brassica rapa

Brassica juncea - *Indian mustard, Gai choi, Mustard greens, Karashi-na* {S} Leaves are eaten raw, pickled, as a potherb, stir-fried, boiled, or added to soups and stews. Pickled leaves are known as *sajur asin* and *hum choy*. The seeds are very pungent and are often used whole to season meats and other foods. They yield an edible oil widely used for pickling in Bengali and Kashmiri cooking. Powdered seeds are the source of *brown mustard*, a prepared mustard that is stronger than that produced from other species. The roots of some forms are eaten. Sprouted seeds can be used in salads. Protein extracted from the leaves mixes well with banana pulp and is well adapted as a pie filling. Cultivated. HALPIN [Cu, Cul], HAWKES [Re], HERKLOTS, HESSELTINE, JAFFREY, MORTON 1976, OCHSE, PIRIE,

SCHNEIDER [Cul, Re], STEINKRAUS, TANAKA; A79M, C82, E59, H49, L59, R47 (for cultivars see Mustard, page 395)

Brassica kaber → ***Sinapis arvensis***

Brassica napiformis → ***Brassica juncea***

Brassica napobrassica → ***Brassica napus***

Brassica napus - *Rape, Colza* {S} The seeds are pressed for their oil which is used as a salad or cooking oil. They are also used to adulterate mustard seed. *Rapeseed oil* is widely produced in Canada, while *colza oil* is common in India and China. Leaves are eaten in salads or as a potherb. Inflorescences can be used like broccoli. Sprouted seeds are eaten in salads. Cultivated. BIANCHINI, SCHERY, TANAKA, UPHOF; A25, D58, G26, *I59M*, I93M, I99M, J99G, L63M, N84, O48

CULTIVARS

Canola: Rapeseed is high in erucic acid and glucosinolates, which have anti-nutritional properties. In 1974, Canadian plant breeders produced a "double low" cultivar of rapeseed that was low in both erucic acid and glucosinolates, and by 1981 a second "double low" cultivar was produced from B. rapa. In 1979, the name Canola was adopted for all the new "double low" cultivars. Canola oil is used as a salad and cooking oil and in products such as mayonnaise, margarine, and shortening. DE PETERS; E56{PR}, E70M{PR}, G6, M63M{PR}

Dwarf Essex: (Broad Leaf Essex) Rapid growing dual-purpose crop; will thrive in almost any soil. Used extensively in some areas for early greens. Can also be used instead of *mustard and cress* as an indoor seedling crop, and as a sprouting seed. Sown outside it makes a good cut-and-come-again crop. A56, D47M, E38, *E53*, G27M, G71, H54, *H64T*, H66, J34, K71, L14, M49, M95M, N11, S55, etc.

Rangi: Resistant to aphids and club root rot. A good oil seed and often used as a green manure. Prefers a cool growing season, moderate rainfall, and a sunny, dry harvesting period. Needs protection from strong winds to prevent seed pods shattering. D47M

Rape Salad: (Salad Rape) In England, when boxes of seedlings are sold as *mustard and cress* they are often neither, but are in fact Rape Salad. This is much milder than mustard or cress and is more like cabbage in taste. It is an excellent salad vegetable. Rape Salad runs to seed much more slowly than mustard or cress, hence it can be used over a longer period. LARKCOM 1984 [Cu]; B49, F19M, J73, O48, O53M, S55

Brassica napus Napobrassica Group - *Rutabaga, Swede, Swedish turnip* {S} The turnip-like roots are eaten boiled, steamed, baked, fried, mashed, etc. In Sweden, small rutabagas are brushed with oil and baked until tender. The lid is then cut off, a wedge of cheese inserted, the lid replaced, and the whole is served hot. Rutabagas are hardier than turnips and take from four to six weeks longer to mature. Flesh color is usually yellow and the texture is richer than a turnip. The leaves can be used as a potherb. BURR, FELL 1982b, HEDRICK 1919, RODALE [Cu], VILMORIN [Cu]; O48 (for cultivars see Rutabaga, page 478)

Brassica napus Pabularia Group - *Curled kitchen kale* {S} The leaves and plant tops are eaten as a vegetable. In comparison with common kale, the plant is generally taller and more spreading, with less frilled, grayish-green leaves. In the southern United States, it is planted as animal fodder as well but many prefer its flavor to other kales. Plants are extremely cold-hardy. HALPIN, TANAKA.

CULTIVARS

Blue Siberian: Vigorous, very spreading plant. Large, coarse leaves; plain at the center with cut and frilled edges of a deep bluish-green color. Grows 12 to 16 inches tall with a spread of 24 to 36 inches. Very hardy. K49M

Dwarf Siberian: (German Sprouts) 60-70 days. A vigorous, sprawling plant, growing 12 to 15 inches high and bearing large, coarse, blue-green leaves with frilled edges. Very cold hardy. *A1*, A69M, B71, B75, C92, F44, *G1M*, G51, G57M, G64, G67M, H94, K27M

Hanover Salad: 30 days. An extra early, fast-growing cultivar with large, smooth leaves. When used fresh, it has a strong but good flavor; mild when steamed. Harvest leaves when small and tender. Best for early spring salads before other cultivars mature. G57M, L7M

Premier: (Early Hanover) 68 days. Produces thick, deep-green, serrated leaves with slightly frilled margins; more serrated than Smooth Long Standing. Main stems of over-wintered plants remain short while developing many growing points. Substantially higher yielding than most other cultivars when seeded in fall for a spring harvest. Also excellent for early spring planting. *A1*, *C28*, D47M, F19M, *G1M*, G93M, L89, M95M

Siberian: (Siberian Kale, Siberian Curled) 60-70 days. Vigorous, fast-growing plant; grows 12 to 18 inches tall; leafy and sprawling with large, blue-green leaves with frilly edges. Can withstand frost, which actually improves the texture and flavor. The leading cultivar in the southern part of the United States. Will stand the entire winter in much of the South. Widely used as cooked greens or chopped for use in sandwiches and salads. A2, A16, *A75*, C44, D82, D87, F42, H66, *I59M*, I99, K71, L14, L89, M46, M95M, N84, etc.

Siberian Improved: (Improved Dwarf Siberian) 65 days. Hardy, spreading plant with broad, thick, grayish-green plume-like leaves that are plain at the center and slightly frilled at the edges. Stands cold especially well. Grows 12 to 16 inches tall with a spread of 24 to 36 inches. A27M, A87M, *C28*, *D12*, F12, *G83M*, J34, *L59G*, L97, N16, N39

Smooth Long Standing: (Slow Seeding, Long Seasons, Late Hanover, Hanover Long Standing) 32-75 days. Slow-growing, large-leaved cultivar that stands well. Can also be used raw or as a steamed vegetable before other cultivars mature. Fresh flavor is strong with a trace of hotness; milder when steamed. Smooth, blue-green leaves. Grows 12 to 14 inches tall. Produces over a long harvest season. A2, *G1M*, *H61*

Spring: (Smooth, Early Hanover Salad) 35 days. Large, round, smooth, thick leaves; dark green in color; mild, sweet flavor. Very fast-growing and hardy. Grows 10 to 12 inches tall. Produces an abundance of foliage in a short time. Usually sown in early spring but can be overwintered. A2, F80, *G1M*, J73, M95M

Brassica narinosa → ***Brassica rapa***

Brassica nigra - *Black mustard* {S} The pungent seeds are used whole to season pickles, sausages, and sauerkraut. When ground, they form mustard powder or dry mustard, a common ingredient of curry powders in the Near East. Mixed with vinegar and spices they constitute the commercially prepared mustard used as a relish on frankfurters, etc. The tender leaves can be chopped finely and added to tossed green salads, or cooked as a potherb. Young flower clusters are prepared like broccoli. Sprouted seeds are eaten. Eurasia, naturalized in North America. GIBBONS 1962, GRIEVE [Cu], HARRINGTON, H., MABEY [Re], MORTON 1976, UPHOF, VILMORIN; C11, C13M, C69M{SP}, C81M, D58, D62, F35M{PL}, F80, *F91*{SP}, G91{SP}, J73, K20, *L14M*{SP}, L24{SP}, M46, M46{SP}, etc. (also see Sprouting Seeds, page 485)

Brassica nipposinica → ***Brassica rapa***

Brassica oleracea - *Wild cabbage* {S} Although slightly bitter raw, the leaves are quite acceptable to eat after being cooked in two or more changes of water. Atlantic coast of Europe, Mediterranean region. MABEY, MICHAEL; N84

Brassica oleracea Acephala Group - *Kale, Collard, Flowering kale, Flowering cabbage* The leaves are eaten boiled, steamed, sautéed, used as a garnish, or added to soups and stews. Unopened flower clusters, sometimes called *broccolini*, can be used like broccoli and have a flavor reminiscent of a cross between broccoli and asparagus. In Ireland, kale or cabbage are traditionally served in a dish called *colcannon*, which is made with potatoes, leeks, and milk or cream. Collards are popular in the southern United States and are commonly cooked with hamhocks, fatback bacon, and other types of pork. HALPIN [Cul, Re], KRAFT [Re], SCHNEIDER [Cul, Re], VILMORIN [Cu]; (for cultivars see Kale, page 353 and Collard, page 303, also see Sprouting Seeds, page 485)

Brassica oleracea Alboglabra Group - *Chinese broccoli, Chinese kale, Gai-lohn, Kai-laan, Fat-shan* {S} The leaves, flower stalks, and young inflorescences are steamed, stir-fried, cooked with oyster sauce, or used in sukiyaki. The florets can be cut from the stalk, dipped in tempura batter, and deep-fried. Stems that have been briefly cooked are marinated in a spicy dressing and served as a kind of pickle. HARRINGTON, G. [Cu, Cul], HERKLOTS [Cu], KRAFT [Re], TANAKA; A79M, C82, E49, E59, E83T, H49, K22, *N40*{PR}, N84, R47

CULTIVARS

Full White: A heat-tolerant cultivar that has short internodes and thick leaves. Good for salads or frying when stalks are harvested with flower buds. *Q39*

Green Lance: (F_1) 45 days. Highly heat-resistant, vigorous and rapid growing with thicker stems than open pollinated types. Ready for use about 10 days earlier. After the main stem is cut, it branches freely for extended harvest. *A1*, C85M, D11M, E59, *G13M*, I39, J7, J82, *K16M*, L91M, M29, M46, O53M, P83M, Q34, S55, T1M, etc.

Large Leaf: 40-50 days. Large, roundish leaves, light green in color; longer and much broader than other types. Crisp and flavorful, good for all culinary purposes. Grows in hot or cold weather. *O53*

White Flowered: 60-70 days. Large, smooth, bright-green, pointed leaves; tender, crisp, fleshy stems. Very hardy and will tolerate heat but bolts readily. Quick growing. Suitable for growing in spring and summer. D55, F42, F85, G93M, J73, L42, L59, *L79G*, *S70*

Yellow Flowered: 60-70 days. Leaves are light-green. Plants are dwarf with yellow flowers. Very hardy and will tolerate heat, but may bolt in cold weather. G67M, L59, *L79G*

Brassica oleracea Botrytis Group - *Cauliflower, Perennial broccoli* The immature flower heads are eaten raw in salads, boiled, steamed, braised, fried, used in soups and casseroles, prepared as tempura, etc. Young leaves can be used for greens. The flower stalk and the midveins of the larger leaves make first-rate eating, though they are usually neglected, except in counties which like cauliflower soup. Sprouted seeds are eaten. CARCIONE, LARKCOM 1984, ROOT 1980a, TANAKA, VILMORIN [Cu]; (for cultivars see Cauliflower, page 286)

Brassica oleracea Capitata Group - *Cabbage, Savoy cabbage, Red cabbage* The leaves are eaten raw in salads and *cole slaw*, steamed, boiled, pickled, fermented into *sauerkraut*, etc. Fermented sauerkraut juice, sold under the brand names *Biotta* and *Eden*, is popular with natural foods enthusiasts. In Yugoslavia, whole heads of cabbage are fermented like sauerkraut. Called *kiseo kupus*, it is used in *sarma* (stuffed sour cabbage rolls with smoked spareribs). Stems can be eaten boiled or pickled after having been peeled. The sprouted seeds are very good eating. CARCIONE, CHANTILES, HUNTER 1973a, LARKCOM 1984, PEDERSON, STEINKRAUS, TANAKA, VILMORIN [Cu]; (for cultivars see Cabbage, page 279, also see Sprouting Seeds, page 485)

Brassica oleracea Gemmifera Group - *Brussels sprouts* The small, cabbage-like heads are eaten raw in salads, boiled, steamed, sautéed in butter, served with cream sauce, or used in soups. They are especially good cooked and eaten in a cold salad with chestnuts and apples. As the sprouts mature the lower leaves are removed to facilitate harvesting of the sprouts. These thick, collard-like leaves can be finely chopped, steamed, and served with butter and lemon juice. CARCIONE [Pre], RICHMOND, S. [Re], SCOTT, TANAKA, VILMORIN [Cu]; (for cultivars see Brussels Sprouts, page 276)

Brassica oleracea Gongylodes Group - *Kohlrabi* The swollen, fleshy, turnip-like stem is eaten raw in salads or marinades, steamed, boiled, braised, stuffed, or served with Hollandaise or other sauces. Kohlrabi is at its best when young and tender before it becomes necessary to peel it, as much of the flavor lies just below the skin. The young leaves, especially those of the Prague cultivars, can be used as potherbs. CARCIONE, HALPIN [Cul], KRAFT [Re], ORGAN [Re], SCHNEIDER [Cul, Re], TANAKA, VILMORIN [Cu]; (for cultivars see Kohlrabi, page 369)

Brassica oleracea Italica Group - *Sprouting broccoli, Purple cauliflower, Cape broccoli* The immature flower heads and tender parts of the stems are eaten raw in salads, steamed, boiled, sautéed, prepared as tempura, marinated, served au gratin or with a cream sauce, etc. In preparing broccoli for the table, it is best to quarter the stem lengthwise so it cooks more rapidly and insures that the delicate buds are not overcooked. Leaves are also eaten. CARCIONE [Pre], VILMORIN [Cu]; (for cultivars see Broccoli, page 274)

Brassica oleracea Tronchuda Group - *Portuguese cabbage, Couve tronchuda, Galician cabbage, Braganza, Sea-kale cabbage* {S} The midribs of the outer leaves are thick, white, and fleshy. When cooked, they somewhat resemble sea-kale in texture and flavor. In Portugal, the large, flat, tender leaves are shredded with a special implement and used in the preparation of the national soup *caldo verde*. The heart, or middle of the plant, is peculiarly delicate and agreeably flavored, without any of the coarseness so often found in Brassicaceous crops. It can be cut into pieces, boiled, and then braised. ANDERSON, J. [Re], BURR [Cu], ORGAN [Re], VILMORIN; C44, E83T, G68, O53M

CULTIVARS

De Valhascos: Tender and delicate. J73

Gloria de Portugal: Large, wide leaves with very tender midribs and stem. J73

Manteiga: (Penca de Chaves) Known as "Butter cabbage" in Portugal. J73

Pencuda da Povoa: Known as "Village Heading" in Portugal. J73

Pencuda Espanhola: Known as "Spanish Heading" in Portugal. J73

Portuguesa: Early-type which is known as "Cabbage of Six Weeks" in Portugal. J73

Brassica oleracea 'Dalmeny' - *Dalmeny sprouts, Cabbage sprouts* {S} Artificial hybrid. Cabbage x brussels sprouts. A new "old" vegetable, the result of a cross between the common heading cabbage and brussels sprouts. The stem is a foot or more in height, and is not only thickly set with sprouts or small cabbages, like brussels sprouts, but terminates in a cabbage of medium size. BURR, FELL 1982b.

CULTIVARS

Fisher's: Golden Acre cabbage x an unspecified brussels sprouts. Most of the plants will make good solid heads like cabbage; some produce heads along the stem like brussels sprouts. Developed by Fisher's Garden Store, Belgrade, Montana. D82

Ormavon: (F_1) 117 days. Produces a head of cabbage on top and sprouts up and down the stem. A practical, space saving, dual-purpose vegetable. The crisp, tasty, and tender cabbage tops can be harvested without affecting the sprouts which mature to a fine quality and hold in excellent condition for several months. Developed by the British National Vegetable Research Station. L91M

Brassica parachinensis → *Brassica rapa*

Brassica perviridis → *Brassica rapa*

Brassica rapa - *Field mustard, Wild turnip* {S} Leaves are eaten boiled, oil-roasted, pickled, or added to soups. The finely chopped, very young leaves can be added to a tossed green salad. Immature flower clusters are cooked and served like broccoli. The seeds can be ground into a powder and used as a seasoning. Eurasia. CROWHURST 1972, TANAKA; N84

CULTIVARS

Hon Tsai Tai: (Flowering Purple Pak Choy) 45 days. Vigorous, cool-weather plant grown for its attractive flowering stalks. Leaves are dark green, deeply lobed and have purple-red veins. Under ideal conditions each plant will produce up to 40 deep purple-red stalks, which should be harvested as the bright yellow flowers begin to open. Cut above the leaves to ensure continuous production. A2, D55, E59, E83T, I77, J20, L59, M46, O53M, P83M, S55, S61

Tarahumara Espinaca: Plants grow to 6 feet tall. Young leaves can be used in green salads. Also tasty fried. Cultivated by the Tarahumara Indians of Mexico. Introduced there by the Spanish. Dropped by I16

Tarahumara Mostasa: (Mocoasali) Leaves are mild in flavor and can be added to green salads when young. The seeds are ground and added to *pinole*. Wild in the fields of the Tarahumara Indians. Old World introduction. I16

Variegated: Similar to the species, except the leaves are variegated white and green. C7M

Brassica rapa Chinensis Group - *Bok choy, Pak-choi, Chinese white cabbage, Tsoi sum, Yow choy* {S} The leaves, tender leafstalks, and in some cultivars the flowering stems, are eaten raw in salads, stir-fried, steamed, or pickled. Some cultivars also yield an edible oil. Bok choy leaves are widely used in wonton and other similar Chinese broths. In China, bok choy is sometimes dried and stored for several weeks before use. The product is called *bok choy kan*. When pickled in salt, the leaves rapidly lose fifty percent of their vitamin B but the content can be increased nearly fourfold if the leaves are pickled in a paste of salt and rice bran. Rice bran pickles are called *nuka-miso-zuke* in Japan. HALPIN [Cu, Cul], HARRINGTON, G., HERKLOTS, KRAFT [Re], LARKCOM 1984, OCHSE, SCHNEIDER [Pre, Re], SHURTLEFF 1975; A79M, A87M, C27G{PR}, C82, C85M, D11M, E24, F82, G93M, J34, L59, L89, L97, M95, N39, etc. (for cultivars see Bok Choy, page 273)

Brassica rapa Japonica Group - *Potherb mustard, Japanese mustard* {S} Leaves are used as a potherb, pickled, or added to soups. The flavor is pleasant and mild compared to mustard. HERKLOTS, TANAKA.

CULTIVARS

Green Spray: (F_1) Light green, entire, flavorsome leaves. Suitable for harvesting either in the young stage or when mature. Used for boiling, pickling or *ohi-tashi*. Very vigorous, high-yielding plant with good cold tolerance; early maturing. Good for both fall and winter harvests. *S63M*

Kyoto: Vigorous growing plant produces numerous slender, white stalks. Narrow, dark-green leaves, deeply cut and fringed at the edges; non pungent. Highly resistant to cold. Grows extensively during the winter season. *S70*

Mibu-Na: Long, smooth-edged, relatively flat leaves, more rounded than Mizu-Na; 12 inches long, only 1 to 1 1/2 inches wide; narrow, greenish petioles. Excellent for pickling. Sown late summer to fall, often being overwintered for an early spring crop. Spring planted crops produce edible flower stalks. Makes a superior cut-and-come-again vegetable. E83T

Mizu-Na: (Kyô-Na, Thousand Veined Mustard) 65 days. Leaves are deeply divided into many linear or filiform thread-like lobes, giving it an attractive feathery appearance. Narrow, white petioles. While Mibu-Na is chiefly pickled, this cultivar is seldom pickled but is more often used in sukiyaki-like Japanese dishes. Also good in salads. GESSERT, HARRINGTON, G. [Cu, Cul], HERKLOTS, LARKCOM 1984, TANAKA, ZEVEN; C53, E24, E83T, F42, F44, G6, G33, I77, J73, K22, K66, L59, L89, O53M

Tokyo Beau: (F_1) 70 days. Vigorous, uniform grower with broad shiny leaves, deep green in color. Mild, fresh, mustard-like flavor. Similar to Tokyo Belle, but grows larger, up to 4 1/2 pounds. Cold hardy and bolt resistant. Has ornamental value as an edging plant in home gardens from autumn to winter. *K16M*, Q34

Tokyo Belle: (F_1) 60 days. Large, vigorous plant, much improved over open-pollinated types. The stalks are thicker, wider, and whiter; the leaves are broader, glossy dark-green with sharp cut lobes. Has a sweeter, milder flavor. Cold tolerant, can be fall planted and harvested even in snow. Also very ornamental. I77, *K16M*, L42, L89, S27

Brassica rapa Pekinensis Group - *Chinese cabbage, Celery cabbage, Pe-tsai, Wong bok, Napa, Siew choy* {S} Leaves are eaten raw in salads and slaws, stir-fried, steamed, marinated, braised, or added to soups. Pickled it is known as *tsukemono*. In Korea, it is fermented into a spicy, sauerkraut-like vegetable called *kimchi*. *Kimchi* is a general term, more specific names being used depending on the substrate, processing methods, seasons, and localities. *Tongbaechu-kimchi* and *bossam-kimchi* are based on Chinese cabbage. Sprouted seeds are eaten in salads and sandwiches. HALPIN, HARRINGTON, G. [Cu, Cul], HERKLOTS [Cu], JAFFREY, LARKCOM 1984, SCHNEIDER [Pre, Re], STEINKRAUS, TANAKA; A79M, C82, D11M, E38, F19M, F82, F92, G93M, H49, L59, M95 (for cultivars see Chinese Cabbage, page 302, also see Sprouting Seeds, page 485)

Brassica rapa Perviridis Group - *Mustard spinach, Komatsu-na* {S} Leaves are eaten raw in salads, cooked as a potherb, stir-fried, pickled, or used in soups. In eastern Honshu, they are used in the preparation of a New Year's ceremonial rice-cake soup, *zôni*. Young seedlings are also used as a vegetable. The thick, tuberous root of some forms is pickled and eaten. HALPIN [Cu], HERKLOTS, LARKCOM 1984, TANAKA, UPHOF.

CULTIVARS

Kuromaru: (F_1) Upright plant with oval, glossy dark-green leaves. Tight petiole resists damage during harvest. Can be harvested in about 20 days from a summer sowing, 50 days in autumn. Productive all year round. High tolerance to heat and cold, turnip mosaic virus, and black rot. *Q28*

Okiyo: (F_1) Dark green color. Useful for soup, pickling, stir-frying. Vigorous, quick-growing plant. All season type, suitable for continuous sowing from spring to late fall; can be harvested 30 days after sowing during the summer. *S63M*

Savanna: (F_1) 30 days. Uniform, early maturing Tendergreen type. Vigorous, upright plant with large, round, thick, glossy dark-green leaves. Mild flavor. Develops fewer yellow leaves as crop matures. Faster growing and slower bolting than open pollinated types. Shows good tolerance to heat, cold and drought. Fast recovery after harvest. Introduced in 1979 by T. Sakata Co. *C28*, D11M, F13, F19M, G71, I91, J7, *K16M*, M46, Q34, T1M

Tendergreen: 30-50 days. Spreading; medium-green, broad, smooth, thick leaves have a very mild, bland flavor with hardly a hint of mustard-like hotness. Grows to about 18 inches tall in fertile soil and should be thinned to at least 8 inches apart. Bolts about May 1st from a February planting in western Washington. A25, B35M, C44, E49, F19M, F82, G33, G67M, H66, J73, K73, L59, M95, N16

Tendergreen II: (F_1) 50 days. Very vigorous plant; heavy producer of large, thick, glossy dark-green leaves. Continues to produce over a long period. Slower bolting than open pollinated types. Shows less tendency toward yellowing of leaves. Used as cooked greens or raw in salads. Introduced in 1979 by Abbott and Cobb. *A1*, *F72*, H94, J34, M29

Tokyo: 30 days. Very popular Japanese cultivar of fine quality. D55

Brassica rapa Rapifera Group - *Turnip, Fodder turnip, Stubble turnip* {S} Roots are eaten raw, pickled, braised, puréed, or used in soups, stews, casseroles, etc. They can be harvested when the size of a seedling radish and used in salads. A bread is sometimes made from turnips. First they are peeled, boiled, and the juice is pressed out. When dry, wheat flour is added, the mixture is kneaded, fermented briefly, made into loaves, and then baked. The leaves are used as a potherb. Sprouted seeds are eaten in salads and sandwiches. CARCIONE, EVELYN, VILMORIN [Cu]; B13, D47M, *E53*, O48 (for cultivars see Turnip, page 525, also see Sprouting Seeds, page 485)

Brassica rapa Ruvo Group - *Broccoli raab, Turnip broccoli, Rapini, Sparachetti, Cima di rapa* {S} The flowering stems and leaves have a pleasant bitter flavor and are eaten boiled, steamed, braised, sautéed, or served with pasta, potatoes, Italian sausage, etc. A very popular vegetable with Italians, who traditionally prepare it with garlic and olive oil. Young, tender leaves are sometimes eaten in salads. HALPIN [Cu, Cul], KRAFT [Re], SCHNEIDER [Pre, Re], UPHOF; G67M, I39, I84, J7, J20, J84, N39, *N40*{PR}

CULTIVARS

Broccoletto: An Italian "seedling" crop. Each plant produces a single, sweet broccoli-like head. Can be broadcast or sown in rows, thinning to a minimum of 4 inches. Harvest whole plants as soon as buds show, usually when 9 to 12 inches tall. Sow in succession from early spring to fall. An ideal catch crop. J7, P83M, S55

Centoventina: (120 Days, 120 Giorni) Sown in autumn for harvesting during the winter in mild climates. One of the latest of all cultivars, maturing in about 120 days. B8, Q11M

Early Pugliese: 60 days. For spring sowing. Runs to seed quickly. Small flower heads and turnip-like leaves. Cut young flower heads for steamed, spicy greens. C44

Fall Raab: (Late Rappone, Salad Rappone) 90 days. Grows 18 to 22 inches tall. Tasty strap-shaped leaves, medium to dark-green in color; long standing. Winter hardy; seeded in late fall for an early spring harvest. Greens similar to turnip tops. In mild winter areas, produces multiple small florets when the weather turns colder. *A1*, *C28*, C44, F82, G57M, G71

Novantina: 90 days. Produces numerous shoots that are eaten during the winter in the same manner as asparagus. Usually sown from July to October in Italy. Matures relatively late, in about 90 days. Q11M

Quarantina: 40 days. Usually harvested at about 12 inches tall, when all the blossoms have opened, and eaten boiled or pan-fried. Matures very early, in about 40 days. B8, Q11M

Sessantina: 60 days. Not as early as Quarantina, but more voluminous. Quality excellent. Usually sown from July to October in Italy. Rapid growing, matures in about 60 days. K66, Q11M

Spring Raab: 60 days. Extra early fine-flavored spring raab. Plants grow quickly without developing a center head. Grows to 12 inches with numerous, tender side shoots. Seeded in early spring; harvested before weather becomes hot; bolts quickly. Can also be used for an early fall harvest. Not winter hardy. A13, A87M, B75, C53, C92, D11M, G57M, G64, G71, I67M, J7, K73, L42, M13M, M29, etc.

Brassica rapa Sarson Group - *Sarson, Toria* {S} Source of *Indian colza oil*, used in pickles, preserves, curries and other culinary preparations. Also grown as a vegetable crop in the hills and plains of northwestern India, the young leaves and flowering stalks being used as greens. In some areas sarson *sag* is relished when eaten with maize *chappaties*, butter, and buttermilk. ANONYMOUS 1950, CHAUHAN, VAUGHAN, WATT, ZEVEN.

CULTIVARS

Brown Sarson: (Kali Sarson) Flower clusters, hairy leaves and seed oil are used for culinary purposes. Highly self-sterile. Resembles Toria more than it does Yellow Sarson. Matures slightly later than Toria. Has a slightly lower oil content than Yellow Sarson. Grown in the Punjab area of India. ANONYMOUS 1950, CHAUHAN, TANAKA, WATT; **U76, Y81**

Toria: (Indian Rape) The smooth leaves and seed oil are used for culinary purposes. Highly self-sterile. Very sensitive to drought during pod formation. Sown in September and harvested in January, making it the earliest maturing Indian oleiferous brassica. An important oil-seed crop in the Punjab area of India. ANONYMOUS 1950, TANAKA, WATT; **U76, Y81**

Yellow Sarson: (Indian Colza) Source of a seed oil much used in the diet of the Hindus. The tender leaves and shoots are relished as a potherb. Self-sterile. Matures somewhat later than Toria. Also more drought resistant, but more susceptible to insects and diseases. An important oil-seed crop in parts of India. ANONYMOUS 1950, CHAUHAN, TANAKA, WATT; **U76, Y81**

Brassica rapa 'Tyfon' - *Tyfon, Holland greens* {S} 40 days. A cross between Chinese cabbage and stubble turnip. Highly nutritious, productive, fast growing crop; can be grown in all parts of the country. Extremely winter-hardy and bolt resistant. If harvested by cutting back, several cuttings can be made at 30 to 40 day intervals. Best cut when young and tender. Mild-flavored, can be used in salads or as a cooked vegetable. *A1*, D47M, E97, G27M, *G50*, I39, J34, L89, M46

Brassica rapa 'Yukosai' - *Yukosai* {S} A hybrid of komatsu-na and pak-choi. Bright dark-green leaves with long dark-green leafstalks. Grows more vigorously than other leafy cultivars from a summer planting. Plant grows 8 to 12 inches tall 25 to 30 days after sowing. Shows stronger heat tolerance and moderate tolerance to turnip mosaic virus. Good for all season cropping. *Q28*

Brassica sinapistrum* → *Sinapis arvensis

Brassica tournefortii - *Wild turnip-rape, Punjab rai* {S} Leaves and young shoots are eaten. Seeds are the source of an edible oil. Eastern Mediterranean, Southwest Asia. KUNKEL, TANAKA, ZEVEN; **W59M, Y81, Z7M**

Brassica x sp. (B. oleracea x B. rapa) - {S} Artificial hybrids. Cabbage x various forms of B. rapa. The leaves are eaten fresh in salads, stir-fried or pickled.

CULTIVARS

Hakuran: A hybrid between common cabbage and Chinese cabbage. Intermediate in shape between the two parents. The head resembles a large, loose Napa type Chinese cabbage, contains 50 to 60 leaves and weighs 2 1/4 to 4 1/2 pounds. Leaves are crisp, juicy, tasty and have less fiber. Moderate yield and disease resistance. Matures later than Chinese cabbage and has greater heat tolerance; more suited to tropical and sub-tropical areas. NISHI; *Q28*

Senposai: 35 days. A hybrid between common cabbage and komatsu-na produced by embryo culture. Thick, green leaves; tender and soft like komatsu-na, moderately sweet like cabbage. Heat resistant; grows vigorously all year round, even in summer. Very rapid-growing. High in vitamins and minerals. Developed by Kirin Brewery Co., Ltd in cooperation with Tokita Seed Co., Ltd. B75, *S70*

Brassica 'Colbaga' - *Colbaga* {S} Very large roots, purple above ground, white below the soil; flesh white, firm like a rutabaga. Flavor unique, delicate, combines the flavors of Chinese cabbage, rutabaga and cabbage. Can be used both cooked or raw in cole slaw or other salads. Grow and store like a rutabaga. Will keep all winter. Developed by Professor E.M. Meader at the University of New Hampshire.

CULTIVARS

Fisher's Improved: An improved cultivar developed by Fisher's Garden Store, Belgrade, Montana. D82

Brassica 'Narovit' - *Narovit* {S} 45 days. A cross between Chinese cabbage, kale, and turnips. A sweet, high-yielding, quick growing green. Although turnip-like, the plant is grown for greens only. Highly nutritious. A sweet, mild addition to salads and stir-fried dishes, or it can be boiled. M46

Bunias erucago - *Corn rocket* {S} The young, tender leaves are used in refreshing spring soups or as a side dish. They have a characteristic, aromatic flavor that goes well with white Spanish beans (Dutch case knife beans) in dishes such as *ris e barland* soup from Lombardy. Mediterranean region, Southwest Asia. BIANCHINI; **V73M, V83M, W92, Y10, Y17M, Z98**

Bunias orientalis - *Turkish rocket* {S} Young leaves and shoots are eaten raw in salads or boiled as a potherb, especially in some parts of Russia and Poland. Eurasia. HEDRICK 1919, UPHOF, VILMORIN [Cu]; F80

Cakile edentula - *American sea-rocket* {S} The succulent, young leaves, stems, and unripe capsules are eaten raw in salads, having the flavor of horseradish. Older leaves and flower buds can be combined with milder flavored greens and used as a potherb. The roots are occasionally dried, ground, mixed with flour and used for making bread. Northern temperate region. FERNALD, GIBBONS 1964, MEDSGER; F85, I99

Cakile maritima - *Sea rocket* {S} Young leaves and stems, flower buds, and unripe pods are eaten raw in salads and sandwiches, or mixed with milder greens for use as potherbs or seasonings. The roots are pounded, mixed with flour, and eaten during times of scarcity. European coasts, North Africa. BIANCHINI, CLARKE, HEDRICK 1919; N84, S92

Camelina sativa - *Gold of pleasure, False flax, Siberian oil-seed* {S} The seeds yield an oil which is used for culinary purposes. Eurasia. HEDRICK 1919, VAUGHAN [Nu]; **U4, V50, V83M, V89, W92, X8, X39, X63, Y10, Y17M, Z19, Z98**

Capsella bursa-pastoris - *Shepherd's purse, Chinese cress, Water chestnut vegetable* {S} The young leaves and stems are cooked and eaten like spinach. They are said to have a cabbage-like flavor when blanched and served as a salad. At one time cultivated and brought to the markets of Philadelphia. Seedpods can be used as a peppery seasoning for soups and stews. Fresh or dried roots are used as a ginger substitute or candied in syrup. The seeds are sometimes gathered and ground into meal. In Japan, the plant was one of the essential ingredients in the ceremonial rice and barley gruel eaten on January 7th. Eurasia, cultivated. BURR [Cu], FERNALD, HARRINGTON, H., HERKLOTS, LARKCOM 1984, LAUNERT [Re], MEDSGER, TANAKA; A2, C11, C82, D58, D62, F24, F37T{PL}, I99, J73, J82, K20, L86, *N71M*, O48, Q34, R47, etc.

Cardamine amara - *Large bitter-cress* {S} Young leaves can be eaten alone as a salad, or used like rocket and watercress to enhance the flavor of other salads with its aromatic, piquant taste. Eurasia. BIANCHINI, HEDRICK 1919, UPHOF; **Y10**

Cardamine diphylla → ***Dentaria diphylla***

Cardamine flexuosa - *Wavy bitter-cress* {S} Young leaves and roots are eaten raw with vinegar and soy sauce, or cooked and used as a potherb. Europe. TANAKA; **Y10, Y17M**

Cardamine hirsuta - *Hairy bitter cress, Lamb's cress* {S} The young leaves and flowers are eaten raw in salads, used as a garnish, or cooked and served like spinach. Eurasia. CRIBB, HEDRICK 1919, LARKCOM 1984; N84, O48

Cardamine oligosperma - *Bitter cress, Spring cress* {S} Leaves are eaten as a vegetable. Western North America. I99

Cardamine pratensis - *Cuckoo flower, Lady's smock* {S} The young leaves, shoots, and flower buds have a pungent, cress-like flavor and can be added to fresh green salads, sandwich spreads, sauces, or served alone with an oil and vinegar dressing. Northern temperate region. CROWHURST 1972, LARKCOM 1984, LAUNERT [Re], MICHAEL, VILMORIN; *N71M*, N84, O48, P83M, S55

Cardaria draba - *Hoary cress* {S} Young leaves and shoots are eaten in salads or as a potherb. The pungent seeds are used as a seasoning. Eurasia. HEDRICK 1919, UPHOF; D58, N84, O48

Carrichtera annua - *Iglayglih* {S} Young leaves and stems are eaten raw. Canary Islands to Southwest Asia. BAILEY, C.; **V73M, Y18**

Cochlearia anglica - *English scurvy-grass* {S} The young leaves and flower-heads are eaten raw in salads and sandwiches. Europe. MICHAEL [Pre, Re]; N84

Cochlearia danica - *Danish scurvy-grass* {S} Young leaves are eaten raw in tossed green salads. As a cultivated plant, it is considered superior to C. officinalis. Northern temperate region. LARKCOM 1980, MICHAEL; **V87, Y10, Z25M**

Cochlearia officinalis - *Scurvy grass, Spoonwort* {S} The succulent, slightly salty leaves and flower-heads are added to tossed green salads, soups, sauces, or used as a filling for bread and butter sandwiches and stuffed vegetables. Once taken on long sea voyages on account of its high vitamin C content. Circumpolar. BURR [Cu], HEDRICK 1919, LAUNERT, PAINTER [Re], ROOT 1980b, VILMORIN; C85M, D62, J82, *N71M*, N81, N84, O48, O53M

Conringia orientalis - {S} Seeds are the source of a light-yellow oil used for cooking purposes. Europe. UPHOF; **V73M, V89, W3M, W5, X8, Y17M, Z24, Z98**

Crambe cordifolia - *Tartar sea-kale* {PL} Young leaves are eaten as a potherb. The root is also reported to be edible. Southwest Asia to Central Asia. HEDRICK 1919, WATT, ZEVEN; B28, C2, E7M{S}, F39M, G55, G82M, L91M{S}, N84{S}, O35G, O53M{S}, P86, *Q24*{S}

Crambe maritima - *Sea-kale* {S} The blanched leafstalks are eaten raw in salads, boiled, baked, braised, or otherwise prepared as asparagus. When properly cooked, they retain their firmness and have a very agreeable flavor, somewhat like that of hazelnuts, with a very slight bitterness. The leaves can be boiled until soft, minced, seasoned with garlic and served as spinach. Plants can be forced indoors for winter use. Eurasia. HALPIN [Cul], HAWKES [Cul], KRAFT [Re], LARKCOM 1984, LAUNERT, MABEY, VILMORIN [Cu]; D11T{PL}, E30{PL}, J24{PL}, K49M, *L22*{PL}, L90M, N84, O48, O53M, *Q24*, R53M{PL}

CULTIVARS

Lily White: Young leaves are totally devoid of the purple tinge that develops on those of the common type when they are exposed to the light, becoming green under similar conditions. In other respects they are identical. VILMORIN; B49, L91M, O53M, P83M, S55

Crambe orientalis - {S} The very thick roots are used as a substitute for horseradish. Young flower-stalks can be prepared in the same manner as broccoli. Eurasia. HEDRICK 1919; **U71M, V73M, Z24**

Crambe tatarica - *Tartar bread plant* {S} Young, blanched leaf-stalks are eaten raw or cooked, like those of C. maritima. The root is thick, fleshy, and sweet and is eaten raw as a salad, as well as cooked and seasoned with oil, vinegar, and salt. Eurasia. HEDRICK 1919, TANAKA, UPHOF; **U71M, V50, V73M, W3M, X10, X39, Y89M, Z24**

Dentaria diphylla - *Two-leaved toothwort, Pepper-root, Crinkleroot* {PL} The crisp, white rootstock is a popular nibble, having the flavor of cress or horseradish. It can be added to green salads and sandwiches, eaten as a radish-like relish with salt, or grated and prepared like horseradish. Eastern North America. FERNALD, GIBBONS 1979, MEDSGER; A51M, C49, D75T, E63M, I44, J48, M77M, N9M, N9M{S}

Dentaria laciniata - *Cut-leaved toothwort* {PL} The crisp roots have a pungent, peppery taste and are chopped and added to salads, or used in the preparation of spicy relishes and sauces. They are very good eaten in sandwiches with luncheon meats, whose salt helps bring out their flavor. North America. ANGIER [Re], CROWHURST 1972, GIBBONS 1966b; I44, J48, N9M, N9M{S}

Descurainia pinnata - *Tansy mustard* {S} Leaves, when boiled or roasted between hot stones, were eaten by Indians of several tribes. The seeds were mixed with cornmeal, added to soups, or boiled to a mush and consumed with salt. In Mexico, they are made into refreshing drinks with lime juice, claret and syrup. Pods make an interesting mustard-flavored nibble. North America. CLARKE, GIBBONS 1979, KIRK, MEDSGER, UPHOF; D58

Descurainia sophia - *Tansy mustard, Flixweed* {S} The pungent seeds are sometimes made into mustard. Young leaves are used as a potherb. Sprouted seeds are eaten in salads and sandwiches. American Indians baked the leaves in firepits and used the ground seeds as *pinole* in breads, gruels, and soups. Eurasia, naturalized in North America. HARRINGTON, H., KAVENA [Re], TANAKA, UPHOF; D62, F85, I99

Diplotaxis muralis - *Wall rocket* {S} The young leaves have a piquant flavor, somewhat resembling arugula but with a sharp aftertaste. Finely chopped, they can be used sparingly in salads or as a flavoring for cooked dishes. The perennial plant is resistant to heat, and would make a good warm weather substitute for arugula in suitable climates. Mediterranean region. BIANCHINI; **V73M, W35, X8, Y17M, Y89M**

Eruca sativa - *Rocket-salad, Arugula, Roquette, Rucola* {S} Young leaves have a distinct, spicy flavor and are eaten raw in salads, or sautéed with garlic and olive oil. One of the popular ingredients of *mesclun* and *misticanze*, salad mixtures of baby and bitter lettuces and mild herbs. Older leaves that have become too hot to be eaten alone can be puréed and added to soups and sauces. The flowers are used as a garnish and are available at some specialty markets. Seeds are used as a substitute for mustard, and also yield an edible oil called *jamba oil*. Eurasia, cultivated. HALPIN [Cu, Cul], KRAFT [Re], LARKCOM 1984, SCHNEIDER [Cul, Re], UPHOF, VILMORIN [Cu]; A16, A97{PL}, C3, C44, E5M{PR}, E99, F15M{PL}, F24, F93G{PL}, G6, G68, G82, I91, J73, J85T{PR}, K22, K66, M46, etc.

CULTIVARS

Rocket Improved: A spicy, improved cultivar of Arugula. Less prone to bolting to seed than the standard type. Continuous sowings and cutting will provide for a constant supply and keep foliage tender. Does best in cool weather. Q34

Eutrema wasabi - *Wasabi, Japanese horseradish* {S} The fleshy rhizomes are grated and prepared into an attractive fresh green paste which is the essential condiment for Japanese raw sliced fish (*sashimi*). Considered to have a distinct flavor and pungency that is superior to common horseradish. Leaves, flowers, leafstalks, and freshly sliced rhizomes are soaked in salt water and then mixed with sake lees to make a popular pickle called *wasabi-zuke*. Eastern Asia, cultivated. COST 1988 [Cul], HAWKES [Re], HODGE 1974 [Cu], SHURTLEFF 1975 [Re], TANAKA, YASHIRODA [Cul]; E66T{PR}, *K74*{PR}, *S70*

Farsetia clypeata → Fibigia clypeata

Fibigia clypeata - *Paper pumpkinseeds* {S} The young leaves are eaten in salads like cress. Eastern Mediterranean. HEDRICK 1919; C61M, D62, E81M, F80, I63M{PL}, N84, *O1*, O53M, *Q24*, *Q52*, S7M

Hesperis matronalis - *Dame's rocket, Damask, Scented rocket* {S} In many countries, especially in Germany, the young leaves, before flowering, are gathered and eaten like cress in salads. Seeds are the source of an oil, called *honesty oil, huile de Julienne*, or *rotreps oel*. The sprouted seeds can be eaten. Eurasia. GRIEVE, UPHOF; B44, B97M{PL}, C3, C3{PL}, C9M, D26, E89M, E99, F24, G47M, H63{PL}, K53, N11M, N19M{PL}, O53M, etc.

Hirschfeldia incana - *Greek mustard* {S} Young plants are consumed with oil and lemon juice in some parts of Greece. Southern Eurasia. UPHOF; D62

Iberis amara - *Rocket candytuft* {S} Seeds are occasionally used as a source of mustard. Eurasia. UPHOF; C61M, D62, E7M, F24, F85, N84, O48, O53M, S7M

Lepidium campestre - *Bastard cress, Pepperwort* {S} Finely chopped leaves and young shoots can be used to give a watercress-like taste to salads, omelettes, soups, and sauces. The pungent, unripe seedpods can be added to hot soups and stews. Northern temperate region. LAUNERT [Re], PETERSON, L.; D62, K47T, N84

Lepidium draba → Cardaria draba

Lepidium latifolium - *Dittander* {S} The peppery leaves are used in salads, sauces, and as a potherb. Seeds are used as a condiment. The hot, pungent root resembles horseradish, for which it may be used as a substitute. Was once cultivated in England and by the ancient Greeks. Northern temperate region. MABEY, UPHOF; N84, O48

Lepidium meyenii - *Maca* {PL} The sweet, pleasant flavored roots resemble a small pear in both size and shape. The fresh roots are sometimes baked in underground pits. After being dried, they are cooked in water or milk to form a sweet, aromatic porridge called *mazamorra*. Maca roots are also placed in sugar cane rum (*aguardiente*), to which they impart a special aroma and flavor. Leaves are also edible. Andean South America. HERKLOTS, LEON, NATIONAL RESEARCH COUNCIL 1989; **Z15M**

Lepidium sativum - *Cress, Garden cress* {S} Young leaves are eaten in salads, sandwiches, soups, omelettes, with sliced hard-boiled eggs, etc. Commonly grown in combination with mustard as a cut-and-come-again seedling crop called *mustard and cress*. The fresh or dried seed pods can be used as a pungent seasoning. In Ethiopia, the seeds are grown for their edible oil, while in the United States they are utilized as a sprouting seed. Roots are occasionally used as a condiment. Cultivated. BIANCHINI, DUKE, HALPIN, LARKCOM 1984, UPHOF, VILMORIN [Cu]; C13M, E7M, E33, E99, F24, F33, H46, I99, J73, L7M, L14, L57, *N71M*, N84 (also see Sprouting Seeds, page 485)

CULTIVARS

Armada: New type of broad-leaved cress. Has a stronger stem and grows faster. The leaves are darker and oak-leaf shaped. K50

Broad Leaved: (Mega Cress, Broad Leaved French) 10-40 days. The leaves are oval in shape, about 2 inches long, and about 1 inch broad; the blade of the leaf is entire, without any divisions, merely notched somewhat on the edges. The stalks are slender and somewhat irregular in outline. Less desirable as a salad plant but good for use in soups. BURR, VILMORIN; C53, E5T, F24, L91M, M13M

Curled: (Peppergrass, Curly Cress, Early Curled) 10-30 days. In this cultivar the divisions of the leaves are finer and more numerous than in the common kind; they are also curled and more or less frilled on the edges like some types of parsley, which gives the foliage a very ornamental appearance. Used in salads and as a garnish. BURR, VILMORIN; A16, C13M, D11M, D82, E24, F1, F13, F24, F44, F92, G6, J25M, K66, M13M, M49, S61, etc.

Extra Curled: (Triple Curled) 10-30 days. The blade of the leaf is divided into a few lobes, which are almost entire, the edges only being cut into a kind of fringe. The divisions are very fine, numerous, and curled in such a manner as to cause the plant to resemble a tuft of green moss. Leaf-stalks are comparatively short, which gives the plant a dense and compact appearance. VILMORIN; C85M, J7, L91M

Greek: A fast growing salad crop that can be broadcast in succession and cut when young. A completely new addition to the mixed salad. Delicious peppery taste. Discovered in Greece. P83M, S55

Groka: Large, oval, entire leaves; attain a dark-green color at an early age. Very vigorous and quick growing. The strong, sturdy plant is trouble free and easy to grow. Maintains its attractive appearance well. P59M, *R11M*

Moss Curled: 10 days. Fine cut leaves resemble parsley; dwarf and compact in growth. Tastes like water cress. Ready just 10 days from seeding; sow every 2 weeks year round. Can be grown indoors in pots to provide winter greens. G16, Q34

Reform: 50 days. A vigorous broad-leaf cultivar. Leaves are sword shaped, 3 to 5 inches long. Tangy, peppery-sweet cress flavor. Will grow and thrive in ordinary garden soil. Seed can be freely broadcast in the bed or row and seedlings don't need thinning. Grows very quickly; sow every month from early spring until hot weather and again all fall. Recently introduced from Holland. K66

Lepidium virginicum - *Wild pepper-grass, Virginia cress* {S} The mustard-flavored leaves or young shoots are chopped and mixed in salads, used as a garnish, or cooked as greens. Unripe pods, pleasantly pungent in flavor, are chopped, mixed with vinegar and served as a condiment with soups and stews. North America. CROWHURST 1972, GIBBONS 1979, MEDSGER, MORTON 1976; D58, D62, F85

Lobularia maritima - *Sweet alyssum* {S} Leaves, young stems, and flowers can be used as a flavoring herb in salads or other dishes where pungency is desired. Cultivated. BOCEK, NYERGES; E7M, E59Z, *E66M*, F24, F35M{PL}, F80, F95, K15, K49M, K53, K62, N11M, N84, O53M

Lunaria annua - *Penny flower, Honesty, Money plant* {S} The roots, when gathered before the flowers form, can be eaten raw in salads. Pungent seeds are used as a substitute for mustard. Europe. HEDRICK 1919, UPHOF; A53M, B77M, C13M, C43M{PL}, C81M, C82, E7M, F24, F33, G84{PL}, K53, L59, *M65M*{PL}, N19M{PL}, N42{PL}, N45{PL}, etc.

Lunaria biennis* → *Lunaria annua

Matthiola incana - *Stock* {S} The highly fragrant flowers are eaten as a vegetable or used as a garnish, especially with sweet desserts. Pods are also edible. Mediterranean region, cultivated. LEGGATT [Re], TANAKA; B75, F85, G71, K66, L89

Megacarpaea polyandra - {S} The plant is eaten as a vegetable. Roots are used as a condiment. Himalayan region. CHITTENDEN; N84

Nasturtium officinale - *Water cress* {S} Leaves and shoots are employed as an attractive garnish, eaten in salads, or used in soups, canapes, omelettes, etc. Blended with butter it makes a tangy spread for sandwiches. Seeds are occasionally made into mustard. The seeds can also be sprouted like alfalfa or grown as a seedling crop. Eurasia, cultivated. CARCIONE, FERNALD, FOX, F., GIBBONS 1962 [Re], HALPIN [Cu, Cul], HARRINGTON, G., LARKCOM 1984, VILMORIN [Cu]; A25, A53M, C3, C53, E99, G6, G84{PL}, J73, K25{PL}, K66, L59, M13M, M39{PL}, M72{PL}, N11, etc.

CULTIVARS

Improved Broad-Leaved: (Large Improved, Broad Leaf) 50 days. An improved cultivar with large, broad, oval leaves and a mildly pungent flavor. Home gardeners should have a very moist, shady spot, as it is usually grown along river banks. Harvest in cool temperatures. Perennial. F1, F13, J7, K49M, L42, L97

Radicula nasturtium-aquaticum* → *Nasturtium officinale

Radicula palustris* → *Rorippa islandica

Raphanus caudatus* → *Raphanus sativus

Raphanus landra* → *Raphanus raphanistrum ssp. landra

Raphanus maritimus* → *Raphanus raphanistrum ssp. maritimus

Raphanus raphanistrum - *White charlock, Wild radish* {S} Young leaves and shoots are minced and added to salads or cooked as a potherb. The seeds are very pungent and are said to form an excellent substitute for mustard. Sprouted seeds make a very tasty addition to a salad. Eurasia, naturalized in North America. BIANCHINI, HEDRICK 1919, LAUNERT; D58, O48

Raphanus raphanistrum ssp. landra - *Landra, Italian radish* {S} The radical leaves are prepared with oil and eaten as a salad. Mediterranean region. HEDRICK 1919; **W59M, Z98**

Raphanus raphanistrum ssp. maritimus - *Sea radish, Spanish radish* {S} Leaves and roots are eaten as a potherb. The succulent roots can be used as a substitute for horseradish. Mediterranean region. HEDRICK 1919; **Y89M, Z98**

Raphanus sativus - *Radish, European radish, Fodder radish* {S} The hot, spicy roots are eaten raw in salads, as an appetizer, pickled, used for garnishing, etc. Leaves may be boiled as greens or used as a cress. Young flower clusters are eaten as a cooked vegetable. The tender pods of some forms are served with beer in Germany. Seeds are the source of an edible oil. The sprouted seeds are widely used in the food industry for spicy sprout mixtures. Cultivated. HEDRICK 1919, LARKCOM 1984, TANAKA, UPHOF, VILMORIN [Cu]; O48 (for cultivars see Radish, page 461, also see Sprouting Seeds, page 485)

Raphanus sativus Caudatus Group - *Rat-tail radish, Mougri, Singri, Serpentine bean, Monkey-tail radish* {S} The long, slender seedpods can grow to two feet or more in length, and have an attractive purple tint. In India, where they are primarily grown the pods are eaten in salads, boiled, pickled, or cooked with ghee or in curries. It is best to harvest them when still tender and free of fibers, usually at ten or twelve inches. BURKILL, TANAKA, VILMORIN [Cu], WATT; C82, E83T, I99, S93M

CULTIVARS

Long Purple: An improved type with long purple pods. R0

Raphanus sativus Longipinnatus Group - *Daikon, Lobak, Lo bok, Oriental radish* {S} The roots are grated and eaten raw, marinated, stir-fried, pickled, etc. Pickled roots are known as *takuan* or *takuwan*. Young leaves and flower clusters are stir-fried, boiled, added to soups, or pickled. The young seedlings may be cooked like spinach. In Korea, *chonggak-kimchi*, *yeolmu-kimchi*, and *dongchimi* are some of the forms of *kimchi* prepared with oriental radishes. The peppery seeds can be added to tossed salads. Both the roots and leaves are dried and stored for later use. Pods are also eaten. HALPIN, HARRINGTON, G. [Cu, Cul], HERKLOTS [Cu], HESSELTINE, KRAFT, SCHNEIDER [Cul, Re], SHURTLEFF 1975 [Re], STEINKRAUS, TANAKA; E56{PR}, E59, E66T{PR}, F24, F85, G20M{PR}, H67M{PR}, H91{PR}, L86 (for cultivars see Radish, page 461, also see Sprouting Seeds, page 485)

Rorippa indica - *Inu-garashi* {S} Young stems and leaves are eaten. Southern Asia. TANAKA; F85

Rorippa islandica - *Yellow marsh-cress* {S} The young leaves and stems make a good substitute for watercress. Young seedlings are also eaten. Europe, naturalized in North America. CRIBB, MEDSGER, TANAKA; D62, N84

Sinapis alba - *White mustard, Yellow mustard* {S} In England, the young seedlings are commonly grown together with those of cress for use in salads and sandwiches. They are usually harvested when two or three inches high. Milder in flavor than those of black mustard, the seeds are preferred for making lighter mustards, such as American frankfurter mustards. The leaves of mature plants can be used as a potherb. Eurasia, cultivated. BROUK, GRIEVE, HARRINGTON, H., HERKLOTS [Cu], LARKCOM 1984, MORTON 1976, VILMORIN; C13M, C53, C85M, D62, E81M, F15M{PL}, H46, I99, J82, K20, L91M{SP}, M82{PL}, O48, O53M, Q34, S55, S59M, etc. (also see Mustard, page 395 and Sprouting Seeds, page 485)

CULTIVARS

Fine White: For growing as *mustard and cress*, i.e. as a companion for plain or Moss Curled cress in containers all year round. They should be sown 3 days after cress to mature concurrently. Tops are usually cut close to the soil surface with scissors. If grown outdoors, it makes an excellent cut-and-come-again crop. S55

Sinapis arvensis - *Charlock, Field mustard, Agricultural mustard* {S} Seeds are widely used as a condiment in Southern Russia, where they are sold in markets. Young, finely chopped leaves lend a piquant flavor to salads, cottage cheese, patés, omelettes, and sandwiches. Larger leaves can be used as a potherb. The flower buds are prepared and served like broccoli. Flowers are used as a vegetable or garnish. Sprouted seeds can be used in salads and sandwiches. Eurasia, naturalized in North America. CROWHURST 1972, GRIEVE, HEDRICK 1919, LAUNERT, UPHOF; B49, D58, *N71M*, N84, O48, P83M

Sisymbrium alliaria* → *Alliaria petiolata

Sisymbrium altissimum - *Tumble mustard* {S} The leaves and shoots, when young and tender, are eaten raw in salads or cooked as a potherb. Seeds were ground into a meal and used for making gruel and flavoring soup. Northern temperate region. HARRINGTON, H.; D58, N84

Sisymbrium canescens* → *Descurainia pinnata

Sisymbrium crassifolium - {S} The stems and leaves, when boiled and eaten, are said to taste like cabbage. Spain. TANAKA; Z19

Sisymbrium irio - {S} Young leaves, stems, and flowers are eaten raw in salads. Mediterranean region. BAILEY, C.; F85

Sisymbrium officinale - *Hedge mustard, Tumble-mustard* {S} The young leaves and shoots are added to tossed salads, used in sauces, soups, and omelettes, or prepared as a potherb. The seeds can be parched and ground into a nutritious flour for making gruel or seasoning soups. Eurasia, naturalized in North America. FERNALD, HARRINGTON, H., HEDRICK 1919, KIRK, LAUNERT, NIETHAMMER [Re]; D62, *N71M*, N84, O48

Sisymbrium sophia* → *Descurainia sophia

Sophia pinnata* → *Descurainia pinnata

Stanleya pinnata* → *Stanleya pinnatifida

Stanleya pinnatifida - *Prince's plume, Indian cabbage* {S} The tender stems and leaves have a cabbage-like taste and may be prepared in the same manner. They can be quite bitter at first, but boiling in several waters removes the astringency. Seeds are sometimes parched, ground, and made into mush. Western North America. KINDSCHER, KIRK, YANOVSKY; G60{PL}, I63M{PL}, I98M, J93T, L13

Thlaspi arvense - *Penny cress, Treacle mustard* {S} Young leaves and shoots are eaten raw in salads or sandwiches, used in soups, omelettes, and sauces, or cooked as a potherb. The flavor is somewhat like mustard, with a hint of onion. The seeds are used as a mustard-like condiment. Sprouted seeds are occasionally eaten. Eurasia, naturalized in North America. FERNALD, HARRINGTON, H., LARKCOM 1984, LAUNERT; D58, D62, F80, F85, N63M, *N71M*, N84, O48

Wasabia japonica* → *Eutrema wasabi

BROMELIACEAE

Aechmea bracteata - *Izchu, Ixchu* {S} The berries are said to be edible. Mexico to Colombia. WILLIAMS, L.; F85, N84

Aechmea magdalenae - *Pingwing, Pita* {PL} Acid fruits are eaten raw or cooked. They are said to be better when made into beverages. Central America, Tropical South America. DUKE, WILLIAMS, L.; N84{S}, P38

Ananas bracteatus - *Piña de playon* {S} Occasionally cultivated for its sweet fruits. Paraguay. DUKE, ZEVEN; N84

Ananas comosus - *Pineapple* {PL} Ripe fruits are eaten raw, preserved, cooked with ham, candied, used in pies, puddings, ice cream, and sherbets, or made into jams, juice, vinegar, wine, etc. Unripe fruits are eaten raw with hot pepper sauce. Terminal buds are eaten raw, cooked as a vegetable, or put in soups. Flower-spikes are peeled, sliced, and used as a steamed vegetable or added to stews. Young shoots, called *hijos de piña*, are eaten in salads. In the Philippines, the juice is fermented into a sweet, gelatinous dessert, called *nata de piña*. The rind of the fruit is made into *chicha de piña*. Tropical America, cultivated. COLLINS [Cu], DUKE, JOHNS [Cul], MORTON 1987a [Cu, Pro], OCHSE, STEINKRAUS, UPHOF; C56M, M49M, N84{S}, P38

CULTIVARS

Hawaiian King: A lush deep-green, smooth leaved cultivar grown commercially in Hawaii. Plants grow 2 to 3 feet tall at maturity and are covered with large violet blooms on dense spiked heads from January to March. Harvest season is May through September. G17

Honey Gold: One of the largest pineapples, often reaching 15 pounds in weight. Has a large base and a narrow crown. Flesh yellow, juicy, moderately acidic, very aromatic, rich in flavor. Plant grows 3 feet tall with a spread of 3 feet. Originated in Hawaii. D57{OR}

Natal Queen: Medium-sized, conical fruit, weight 1 1/2 to 2 pounds; skin deep yellow, with deep eyes; flesh juicy, crisp, aromatic, of fine, delicate flavor with a small, tender core. Dwarf, compact plant, produces numerous shoots and no slips. Sport of the old Queen cultivar originating in South Africa. COLLINS, MORTON 1987a; **T73M**

Red Spanish: Medium-sized, more or less round fruit, weight 3 to 6 pounds; skin orange-red, with deep eyes; flesh pale-yellow, fibrous, large-cored, aromatic and flavorful. Breaks off easily and cleanly at the base in harvesting; stands handling and shipping well. Highly resistant to fruit rot; subject to gummosis. The most popular cultivar in the West Indies, Venezuela and Mexico. MORTON 1987a; **T73M**

Smooth Cayenne: (Sweet Spineless) Large, cylindrical fruit; weight 4 to 10 pounds; rind orange, eyes shallow; flesh yellow, low in fiber, juicy and rich; flavor excellent, mildly acid. Highly prized for canning. Plant nearly free of spines except for the needle at the leaftip. Selected and cultivated by the Indians of Venezuela; introduced from Cayenne, French Guyana in 1820. MORTON 1987a; E31M, N84{S}

Sugarloaf: (White Sugarloaf) Fruit more or less conical, sometimes round, not colorful; weight averages 1 1/2 to 3 pounds. Flesh white to yellow, very sweet, juicy. Leaves of the plants and crowns pull out easily. Too tender for shipping. MORTON 1987a; D57, I83M

Variegated: An attractive plant with green and yellow striped leaves. When approaching maturity it turns cherry pink at the base of all its fronds. It soon sends up short stalks topped by pale white fruit with flaming red tops. Both the skin and flesh of the ripe fruit is albino white and sweet as honey. E29, G17, N84{S}

Bromelia karatas → *Karatas plumieri*

Bromelia pinguin - *Pinguin, Piñuela* {S} When ripe, the pulp of the fruit is acid but makes an excellent refreshing drink. It is also used to make vinegar. The fried inflorescence is eaten in El Salvador. Shoots at the base of the plant are eaten raw or cooked. Sold in local markets. Caribbean region. DUKE, KENNARD, UPHOF, WILLIAMS, L.; N84, P38

Karatas plumieri - *Piñuela* {S} The fruits, raw or cooked, are used in making refreshing beverages called *atol de piñuela* or *atol de piña*. Tender, blanched leaf bases of young shoots are eaten as a cooked vegetable or used in soups, stews, and egg dishes. Young inflorescences are cooked and eaten or used with eggs. Central America. WILLIAMS, L.; N84, P38

Puya caerulea - {S} Very young shoots are eaten in salads. Chile. KUNKEL; Q41

Puya chilensis - {S} Very young shoots are eaten in salads. Chile. KUNKEL; N84, Q38, Q38{PL}

BUDDLEIACEAE

Buddleia asiatica - *Winter lilac, Sau dau chuot, Glentud ulangan* {PL} The root, dried and powdered is used in the preparation of a fermented liquor. Tropical Asia. ALTSCHUL, TANAKA; G20, G96, H4, M82, N84{S}, O93{S}

Buddleia salviifolia - *Sagewood* {PL} Fresh or dried leaves are used as a substitute for tea. Southern Africa. FOX, F.; O35G

BURSERACEAE

Boswellia serrata - *Frankincense, Indian olibanum tree* {S} The flowers and seeds are eaten. Also the source of an edible gum. Southern Asia. MENNINGER, TANAKA, WATT; Q46

Bursera simaruba - *West Indian birch, Gumbo-limbo* {PL} Leaves are used as a substitute for tea. West Indies. TANAKA; D87G

Canarium album - *White Chinese olive, Ch'ing-kuo* {S} The fruits, when pickled in salt or preserved in honey, are highly esteemed as a condiment or as a side dish. Also used in wines and liqueurs. Seed kernels are also eaten. Readily available in Chinatown markets. Southeast Asia, cultivated. CHANG, W., PORTERFIELD, TANAKA; **U71M**

Canarium asperum - *Mayagyat* {S} Fruits are eaten. Seeds are roasted and used as a substitute for coffee. Philippines. VON REIS; F85

Canarium commune - *Java almond, Kenari* {S} The seeds have a rich, pleasant flavor and are eaten in pastries or with rice. In Celebes, they are made into bread. An edible oil is extracted from them. Also used as a condiment. Indonesia, cultivated. HEDRICK 1919, KUNKEL, MENNINGER, TANAKA; F85, N84

Canarium edule → *Dacryodes edulis*

Canarium indicum → *Canarium commune*

Canarium odontophyllum - *Borneo olive, Dabai, Sibu olive* {S} The blue-black fruits can be eaten raw or used in the same manner as olives. For fresh eating, they are prepared by soaking in hot water for ten minutes until they soften, then eaten with soy sauce or salt with a meal or as a savory snack. The flavor is unique and the texture thick and oily, like a good avocado. Indonesia, Malaysia. ALTSCHUL, TANAKA; O19, O19{PL}

Canarium ovatum - *Pili nut* {S} When roasted, the sweet nuts have a delicious flavor and are served like almonds, or used in confections, preserves, ice cream, and nut milks. In some areas they are used to adulterate chocolate. The oil obtained from the nuts is sweet, and suitable for culinary purposes. Pulp of the fruit is boiled and eaten or pressed for its edible oil. Philippines. MENNINGER, ROSENGARTEN, UPHOF; A79M, F85, J22{PL}, R59

Canarium schweinfurthii - *Papo canary tree, Incense tree* {S} The greenish, oily fruits are eaten in many parts of Africa. They are best softened in warm water before eating. The seed contains an oil which is a possible substitute for *shea butter*. In Angola the fruit is used as a condiment. Tropical Africa. DALZIEL, MENNINGER; N84

Commiphora myrrha - *Myrrh* {PL} Source of a fragrant, pungent gum-resin used commercially to flavor soft drinks, soups, candy and chewing gum. Southwest Asia. KUNKEL, MORTON 1976; F35M

Dacryodes edulis - *Bush butter tree, Safu, Eben tree* {S} The dark purple fruit is eaten raw, roasted, boiled or with curries. When placed in hot water it softens and swells, and all the flesh then slides easily off the seed. It is usually salted and tastes like a warmed ripe avocado, with a slight sour flavor. Has a seven percent protein content, which is very high for a fruit. Tropical Africa. DALZIEL, HEDRICK 1919, UPHOF; **X44**

Dacryodes rostrata - *Kambayau* {S} The oblong, smooth-skinned, black or bluish-black fruits are eaten. They have oily, yellowish-purple flesh that is sweet and creamy. Similar to the Borneo olive. Malaysia, Indonesia. ALTSCHUL; O19, O19{PL}

CABOMBACEAE

Brasenia schreberi - *Water shield, Junsai* {PL} Young, curled leaf tips, which are coated with a thick transparent mucilage, are eaten as a salad with vinegar, sake and soy sauce, dressed with vinegared bean cake, pickled, or added to soups as a thickener. Considered a great delicacy in Japan. Often bottled and sold in Japanese markets. The starchy, tuberous roots may be peeled, boiled and eaten, dried and stored, or ground into flour. Widespread. FERNALD, GIBBONS 1979, HEDRICK 1919, KIRK, SHURTLEFF 1975, TANAKA, UPHOF, YASHIRODA [Cul]; H30

CACTACEAE

Acanthocereus pentagonus → *Acanthocereus tetragonus*

Acanthocereus tetragonus - *Barbed-wire cactus, Pitahaya* {PL} The fruit is scarlet, glossy, round or oblong, about two inches long. Flesh is juicy, red, with numerous small, black seeds. When ripe, the fruit may be eaten raw. Tender stems are cooked and eaten. Central America, Florida Keys. ALCORN, MORTON 1977; B85, C99, F31M, Q41{S}

Ariocarpus fissuratus - *Living rock* {S} Juice of the plant is used in the preparation of *tesguino*, a slurry-like, alcoholic beverage prepared by fermentation of germinated maize or maize stalk juice. An important beverage of the Tarahumares, Huicholes, Tepehuanos, and other Indian people of Northwestern Mexico. Southwestern North America. STEINKRAUS; A69, B84{PL}, C27M, C99{PL}, D1M{PL}, F31M{PL}, G18, H52, H52{PL}, I33, K47M, L91M, N84, Q38, S44, T25M, etc.

Carnegiea gigantea - *Saguaro, Giant cactus* {S} The sweet fruits are eaten raw, cooked, dried, preserved, or made into jam, syrup, refreshing drinks, or a ceremonial wine called *nawait*. Seeds are ground into flour, used in *atole* and *pinole*, soups, sweetmeats, or made into a buttery paste used on tortillas. Also the source of an edible oil. Southwestern North America. CROSSWHITE [Pre, Re], KIRK, NIETHAMMER [Re], UPHOF; A0M, A69, A79M, B85{PL}, C27M, C99{PL}, D1M{PL}, F31M{PL}, F80, G18{PL}, H52, I16, I33, K47M, L13, N7M, O53M, T25M, etc.

Cereus dasyacanthus → *Echinocereus dasyacanthus*

Cereus engelmannii → *Echinocereus engelmannii*

Cereus hexagonus - *Ciergé pascal* {S} Fruits are pale red, thick-rinded, and have white or pinkish pulp and black seeds. They may be eaten out of hand and parts of the stems can be used as a vegetable. Caribbean region. BRITTON 1937, KUNKEL, ZEVEN; F85, H52{PL}, I33

Cereus jamacaru - *Jamacaru* {S} The large, bright red fruit has white, edible pulp and is usually eaten out of hand. Stems are sometimes used as a vegetable. Brazil. BRITTON 1937, CORREA; B85{PL}, *E53M*, I33, N84, Q41, S44, T25M

Cereus pernambucensis - *Jumbeba* {S} Fruits are narrowly oblong, purplish red, and when mature they split on one side exposing the white, edible pulp and black seeds. Brazil to Paraguay. BRITTON 1937, TANAKA; B85{PL}, F85, I33, Q41

Cereus peruvianus - *Pitahaya* {S} The fruits are pinkish-red, with a white pulp that is juicy, sweet, somewhat aromatic, and much appreciated. David Fairchild recommended freezing thin slices of the fruit after they had been sprinkled with sugar and lime juice. The peel of the fruit can be candied. Young stems are sometimes eaten. Commonly cultivated as an ornamental in California, Florida, and Hawaii. Cultivated. KUNKEL, MORTON 1987a, TATE [Re]; *A19*{PL}, A48M{PL}, A69, *B41*{PL}, B85{PL}, C27M, C99{PL}, D1M{PL}, *E53M*, F31M{PL}, *F53M*{PL}, I33, I59G, K47M, N84, P38, T25M, etc.

Cereus variabilis → *Cereus pernambucensis*

Cereus weberi → *Pachycereus weberi*

Cleistocactus baumanii - *Pitahayacita* {PL} The fruits are edible. Bolivia-Uruguay. ALTSCHUL; A0M, B85, *E53M*{S}, F31M, H52, H52{S}, I33, N84{S}, Q41{S}, S44{S}

Cleistocactus smaragdiflorus - *Sitiquira* {S} Fruits are eaten. Bolivia-Argentina. ALTSCHUL; B85{PL}, F31M{PL}, H52, I33, N69, N84, Q41, T25M

Coryphantha arizonica → *Coryphantha vivipera var. arizonica*

Coryphantha vivipera var. arizonica - *Sour cactus* {S} The pleasantly sour fruits were gathered by the Navajo Indians, dried in the sun, and used like dried currants. Southwestern North America. TATE; C27M, F89M, I33, Q38, Q41, S44

Cylindropuntia fulgida - {PL} Juicy fruits are eaten raw, or made into jellies or refreshing beverages. Southwestern North America. TANAKA; C27M{S}, F31M, H52

Cylindropuntia imbricata - *Cholla, Walking-stick cactus* {S} Unopened flower buds are boiled or steamed and then added to stews, tossed salads or potato salads. When dried they are less mucilaginous. The fruit is eaten raw or cooked in New Mexico and Arizona. Southwestern North America. NIETHAMMER [Pre, Re], YANOVSKY; B88{PL}, C27M, C99{PL}, D1M{PL}, F31M{PL}, F85, F89M, H52, H52{PL}, H60, I33, N84, S44, T25M

Echinocactus grandis - {S} The candied pulp of the stems, called *acitrón* or *cubiertos de biznaga*, is eaten as a sweet, or used to flavor meat hash or desserts. Mexico. LATORRE 1977a [Pre, Re], VON WELANETZ; C27M, H52, I33, N84, Q38, Q41, S44

Echinocactus horizonthalonius - *Manca caballo* {S} The fruits are sliced, candied, and sold as confections. Pulp of the stems is used in making sweetmeats. Southwestern North America. TATE, UPHOF; A69, C27M, C99{PL}, D1M{PL}, F31M{PL}, H52, I33, N84, Q38, Q41, S44

Echinocactus ingens - {S} The pulp of the stems is used in sweetmeats. Fleshy parts are eaten in salads. Mexico. BRITTON 1937, KUNKEL; A69, C27M, D1M{PL}, *E53M*, F31M{PL}, G18{PL}, I33, K47M, N84, Q38, Q41, S44, T25M

Echinocactus viridescens → *Ferocactus viridescens*

Echinocactus wislizenii → *Ferocactus wislizenii*

Echinocereus conglomeratus - *Alicoche, Pitahaya de Agosto* {S} The somewhat acid fruits are eaten. Mexico. BRITTON 1937, UPHOF; A69, I33, K47M, Q38, Q41, S44

Echinocereus dasyacanthus - *Chihuahua* {S} The fruit is small, greenish-purple, rich in sugar, and when fully ripe is delicious to eat, much like a gooseberry. Southwestern North America. HEDRICK 1919, YANOVSKY; A69, C27M, C99{PL}, D1M{PL}, F31M{PL}, H52, I33, K47M, N69, N84, Q38, Q41, S44

Echinocereus engelmannii - *Indian strawberry* {S} Fruits are eaten fresh, served with cream and sugar, or cooked into conserves, jams, and sauces. They are said to have a delicious strawberry-like flavor. Southwestern North America. HEDRICK 1919, TANAKA, TATE; A69{PL}, B84{PL}, B85{PL}, C27M, F31M{PL}, H52, I33, N84, Q38, Q41, S44, T25M

Echinocereus enneacanthus - *Strawberry cactus* {S} Fruits are eaten fresh or preserved. The flavor of the fruit is so much like strawberries that preserves made from them cannot be distinguished from strawberry jam. Southwestern North America. BRITTON 1937, TATE; A69, B84{PL}, B85{PL}, C27M, C99{PL}, F31M{PL}, H52, I33, N69, N84, Q41, S44, T25M

Echinocereus stramineus - *Mexican strawberry* {S} The red fruits have a pleasant strawberry-like flavor and are usually eaten raw. Southwestern North America. YANOVSKY; A69, B84{PL}, C27M, C99{PL}, D1M{PL}, F31M{PL}, H52, H52{PL}, I33, N69, N84, Q38, Q41, S44, T25M, etc.

Echinocereus triglochidiatus - *Red hedgehog-cactus* {S} Bright red fruits are eaten fresh or made into preserves. The fruit pulp is sliced and baked like squash, or made into a sweet pickle by baking it in sugar. Southwestern North America. UPHOF; A0M{PL}, C27M, C99{PL}, H52, H52{PL}, I33, J25M, N69, N84, Q38, Q41, S44, T25M

Escontria chiotilla - *Chiotilla* {S} Purple, fleshy fruits are eaten fresh. Sold in the market at Tehuacán under the name of *geotilla* and *tuna*. The dried fruit is said to have the flavor of gooseberries. Mexico. BRITTON 1937; H52, N84, Q41, S44, T25M

Espostoa lanata - *Cotton ball, Peruvian old man* {PL} Sweet, juicy fruits are white with pinkish scales and are eaten raw. They are called *soroco* in Southern Ecuador. Ecuador, Peru. BRITTON 1937; A0M, B84, B85, C99, *E53M*{S}, F31M, G18, H52, I33{S}, K63M, O53M{S}, Q38, Q38{S}, Q41{S}, S44{S}, T25M{S}, etc.

Eulychnia acida - *Copao* {S} Fleshy, somewhat acid fruits are edible. Chile. VALENZUELA; Q38, Q41, T25M

Ferocactus acanthodes - *Barrel cactus* {S} The fruit is eaten raw, dried, or made into a syrup which is then fermented into an alcoholic beverage. A potable sap is obtained by scooping out the pulp from the stem and squeezing out the juice. Pulp of the stems is also used to make cactus candy. Seeds are ground and made into a meal-cake. Flower buds are cooked and eaten. Southwestern North America. CLARKE, KIRK, TANAKA, TATE [Re]; A0M{PL}, A69, C27M, C99, D1M{PL}, F31M{PL}, F79M, F80, F85, I33, K47M, N84, Q41, S44

Ferocactus hamatacanthus* → *Hamatocactus hamatacanthus

Ferocactus viridescens - *Coast barrel cactus* {S} Reddish fruits are pleasantly acid, somewhat resembling the taste of a gooseberry and are usually eaten fresh. Flower buds are eaten cooked. Southwestern North America. HEDRICK 1919, TATE; B84{PL}, F31M{PL}, F85, H52, I33, N84, S44

Ferocactus wislizenii - *Arizona barrel cactus, Bisnaga* {S} The pulp of the stems is watery, slightly acid and is used to quench the thirst. Pieces of it, soaked in syrup or sugar and dried, resemble candied citron in taste and texture. Seeds are parched, ground and used for bread and gruel. Flower buds and fruits are edible. Southwestern North America. HEDRICK 1919, NIETHAMMER [Re], TATE; A0M{PL}, A48M{PL}, A69, C27M, C99{PL}, D1M{PL}, F31M{PL}, G18{PL}, H52, H52{PL}, I33, K47M, N84, Q41, S44, T25M, etc.

Hamatocactus hamatacanthus - *Turk's head, Lemon cactus* {S} In some parts of Mexico, the fruits are used as a substitute for lemons in giving an acid flavor to drinks, pies, or cakes. The fruit is dried and eaten as a sweetmeat. Unopened flower buds are delicious soaked in water overnight and boiled or fried. They taste like artichokes. Southwestern North America. TATE, UPHOF; A69, B84{PL}, C27M, D1M{PL}, G18, H52, I33, K47M, K63M{PL}, N84, Q38, Q38{PL}, Q41, S44, T25M, etc.

Harrisia aboriginum - *Shellmound apple-cactus* {S} Yellow fruits are eaten raw. Southeastern North America. MORTON 1977; I33

Harrisia eriophora var. fragrans* → *Harrisia fragrans

Harrisia fragrans - *Fragrant apple-cactus* {S} The dull red fruits are eaten raw. Southeastern North America. MORTON 1977; H52, I33, N84, S44

Harrisia gracilis var. aboriginum* → *Harrisia aboriginum

Harrisia gracilis var. simpsonii* → *Harrisia simpsonii

Harrisia simpsonii - *Apple cactus* {S} Fruits are dull red or yellowish, juicy, and are eaten raw. Southeastern North America. MORTON 1977; I33

Hylocereus ocamponis - *Pitahaya roja* {PL} The skin as well as the sweet pulp of the fruit are a wine-red color. Usually eaten out of hand. Also grown as an ornamental hedge plant. Central America to Colombia. MORTON 1987a, PEREZ-ARBELAEZ, ZEVEN; F31M, P38

Hylocereus polyrhizus - *Pitahaya* {S} Red, thick-skinned fruit has pulp that is white or sometimes pinkish, and a sweet and pleasant flavor. It is used in making *refrescos*, or eaten out of hand. Panama to Colombia. POPENOE, W. 1924; **Y10**

Hylocereus undatus - *Night-blooming cereus, Strawberry pear, Pitahaya* {PL} Sweet, juicy fruits are eaten out of hand, in cooling drinks, sherbets, preserves, etc. A syrup made of the whole fruit is used to color pastries and candy. The unopened flower buds are cooked and eaten. Also grown as an ornamental for its fragrant night-blooming flowers. Hand pollination is recommended for good fruit production. Cultivated. MORTON 1987a, POPENOE, W. 1924, TATE [Re]; F31M, F85{S}, G18, G94, P38, Q41{S}

Lemaireocereus chichipe - *Chichipe* {S} The edible fruit is red both within and without, and is sold in the Mexican markets. Like many other Mexican cactus fruits, it has a name different from that of the plant; it is called *chichituna*. Mexico. BRITTON 1937; A0M{PL}, A69, H52, N84, Q38, S44, T25M

Lemaireocereus queretaroensis - *Pitahaya* {S} When fully ripe the edible fruit is deep red. The flesh is dark red to purple and has a sweet delicious flavor. Mexico. POPENOE, W. 1924; A69, N84

Lemaireocereus schottii* → *Lophocereus schottii

Lemaireocereus stellatus* → *Stenocereus stellatus

Lemaireocereus thurberi* → *Marshallocereus thurberi

Lemaireocereus weberi* → *Pachycereus weberi

Lophocereus schottii - *Senita* {S} The small red fruits are eaten fresh. Southwestern North America. FELGER, UPHOF; A69, A79M, B85{PL}, C27M, F31M{PL}, F85, G18{PL}, H52{PL}, I33, K47M, N84, Q38, Q41

Machaerocereus gummosus - *Pitahaya agria, Creeping devil* {S} The fruit is much relished for its sweet but tart flavor. It may be eaten fresh, dried, or made into unsweetened jams. Mexico. FELGER, TATE [Re], UPHOF; C99{PL}, H52, N84, Q41, S44

Mammillaria mammillaris* → *Mammillaria simplex

Mammillaria meiacantha - *Viejito* {S} The oblong, scarlet fruits are very good to eat. Southwestern North America. HEDRICK 1919; A0M{PL}, C99{PL}, H52, H52{PL}, I33, N84, Q38, Q41, S44

Mammillaria simplex - {S} Fruits are edible. The plant is said to yield a milky juice that is sweet and wholesome. Northern South America. HEDRICK 1919; B84{PL}, B85{PL}, C27M, F31M{PL}, H52, H52{PL}, K63M{PL}, N69, N84, Q38, Q41, S44, T25M

Marshallocereus thurberi - *Organ-pipe cactus, Pitahaya dulce* {S} The fruits are large, sweet, and delicious. They are eaten fresh skin and all, dried, or made into wines and syrups. They are sometimes combined with prickly pears to make a candy called *dulce pitahaya*, or made into a jam that is served as a topping for the Mexican custard *flan*. Seeds are dried and powdered into meal. The petals are also eaten. Southwestern North America. FELGER, TATE, YANOVSKY; A69, A79M, B84{PL}, B85{PL}, C27M, C99{PL}, D1M{PL}, *E53M*, F31M{PL}, G18{PL}, I33, N84, Q38, Q41, S44, T25M, etc.

Melocactus communis - *Melon cactus* {S} The small fruits are eaten. The juice of the plant is used to quench thirst. Central America,

Caribbean region. BRITTON 1937, HEDRICK 1919, TANAKA; F85, Q41

Melocactus ruestii - *Barba de viejo* {S} The fruit is sweet and edible. Central America. WILLIAMS, L.; S44, T25M

Myrtillocactus geometrizans - *Garambullo* {S} Small, bluish-purple fruits are eaten fresh as a dessert, resembling blueberries in flavor. The dried fruits are similar to raisins in appearance and are used in much the same way. The flowers are often eaten raw in salads or cooked with eggs. Central America. BRITTON 1937, HEGYI; A0M{PL}, A69, B85{PL}, C27M, *E53M*, F31M{PL}, F85, G18{PL}, I33, K47M, N84, Q38, Q41, S44, T25M, etc.

Neocardenasia herzogiana - {S} The fruit is eaten. Said to be the finest tasting cactus fruit, with a flavor of pineapple and strawberry. Peru. WINTER; A69, B85{PL}, H52, I33, K63M{PL}, N84, Q38, Q38{PL}, Q41, S44, T25M

Opuntia basilaris - *Beavertail cactus* {PL} Unripe fruits are boiled or baked to the consistency of applesauce. Ripe fruits are eaten raw, dried, or made into syrup or jam. The syrup can be used to flavor candy, sauces, ice cream, and other dishes calling for fruit. Young pads are sliced and substituted for green beans in stews and other dishes. Flowers and flower buds are cooked and eaten. Southwestern North America. CLARKE [Re], YANOVSKY; B85, B88, C27M{S}, C99, F31M, F89M, G18, H52, H60, I98M{S}, N69{S}, S44{S}, T25M{S}

Opuntia compressa → ***Opuntia vulgaris***

Opuntia dillenii - *Dillen prickly-pear* {S} Fruits are insipid but very juicy, and are eaten raw or made into syrup or jelly. Young joints are cut into pieces and boiled, or dried in the sun for future use. Florida, Caribbean region. MORTON 1977; F85, H52, Q41, Q46

Opuntia ficus-indica - *Prickly pear, Indian fig, Tuna* {PL} Sweet, juicy fruits are very refreshing, the best ones being much like watermelons. They are very good chilled and eaten out of hand, the seeds simply swallowed. Also used in ices, jams, tarts, cakes, drinks, etc. Young pads, called *nopalitos*, are boiled and used like snap beans in salads, soups, omelettes, or pickles. In Japan they are made into *narazyke, saboran*, and *saboten glacé*. Cultivated. HALPIN [Cul], POPENOE, W. 1920, SCHNEIDER [Cul, Re], SIMMONS 1972 [Cu], TATE [Re]; B85, C27M{S}, C89{PR}, C99, F31M, K47M{S}, *N40*{PR}, N69{S}, O53M{S}, Q41

CULTIVARS

Burbank's Spineless: (Spineless, Thornless) Some have sweet fruit, others can be used for their pads which do not require despining. Many cultivars of spineless, or nearly spineless cactus were developed by Luther Burbank. Unfortunately, most of those named and released have been lost and the generic name Burbank's Spineless has become widely used. D33{SC}, G17, G18, I74

Green: Seeds from a commercial cultivar that is occasionally sold in specialty stores. I33{S}

Malta: Fruit large, 4 inches long and 2 inches thick; skin yellow, turning light red when fully ripe; flesh salmon with crimson shadings, sweet but not of best quality. Bears abundantly. Very few, short, weak, hair-like spines; bristles wholly absent. Introduced in 1907 by Luther Burbank. Original material collected by David Fairchild. HOWARD; N45M{SC}

Quillota: Large, attractive fruit; skin thin, easily peeled, yellow blushed with crimson; flesh pale-greenish, almost white; ripens from September to April. Unlike other Opuntias, it drops all its fruit when ripe, thus saving the trouble of picking. Introduced in 1911 by Luther Burbank. HOWARD; N45M{SC}

Florida White: (White Fruit) Strong growing plant, nearly free of spines and bristles. Excellent quality fruit. Introduced by John Rock of San Jose, California, early in the 1870's. HOWARD; N45M{SC}

Opuntia fulgida → ***Cylindropuntia fulgida***

Opuntia humifusa - *Devil's tongue, Western prickly-pear* {PL} The fruit has purplish pulp that is somewhat acid or sweetish. It is eaten raw, roasted, stewed, or dried for later use. Young joints are roasted and eaten. North America. HEDRICK 1919, MEDSGER; B88, C27M{S}, C99, E30, E61, F89M, H61M{S}, I33{S}, I37M, K47T{S}, *L22*, M16, M77M, N9M, N9M{S}, T25M{S}, etc.

Opuntia imbricata → ***Cylindropuntia imbricata***

Opuntia leucotricha - *Duraznillo* {PL} Aromatic, white or red fruits are eaten raw or made into a fermented beverage, *colonche*. The custom of making this beverage is said to be more than two thousand years old. Mexico. STEINKRAUS, UPHOF; F31M, Q41{S}

Opuntia lindheimeri var. linguiformis → ***Opuntia linguiformis***

Opuntia linguiformis - *Cow's tongue, Lengua de vaca* {S} Fruits are used in making syrup or jelly. Southwestern North America. TATE [Re]; A69, B85{PL}, C27M, D1M{PL}, F31M{PL}, G18{PL}, H52{PL}, I33, K47M, Q41, S44, T25M

Opuntia megacantha - *Mission tuna, Nopal* {S} Widely cultivated for the fruits from which some of the best edible tunas are derived. They are eaten raw or made into various products. *Queso de tuna* is composed of the dried fruits pressed into large, thick cakes. *Miel de tuna* is a syrup prepared from the fruits. *Melcoacha* is a thick paste made from the boiled juice. *Colonche* is boiled and fermented juice. *Nochote* is fermented tuna juice, *pulque*, and water. Tender, young joints are used as a vegetable. Cultivated. LATORRE 1977a, TATE [Re], UPHOF; F85, Q41, S44

Opuntia phaeacantha - *Bastard fig* {PL} Juicy fruits are eaten raw, dried, pickled, made into jelly, or baked with sugar, butter, cinnamon, and lemon juice. The seeds are dried, parched, and ground into a meal for use in gruel and cakes. Young stems are boiled or roasted and then used like green beans with scrambled eggs. North America. HARRINGTON, H., TATE [Re]; A51M, A69{S}, B88, C27M{S}, C99, D1M, F31M, F80{S}, F89M, H52, H52{S}, H60, I33{S}, K47T{S}, M16, Q41{S}, S7M{S}, S44{S}, etc.

Opuntia polyacantha - *Many-spined opuntia* {S} Fruits are eaten raw, or dried for future use. The dried fruits can be mixed into stews or used to thicken soups. Young joints are boiled and fried. Western North America. HART; B88{PL}, C27M, C99{PL}, F31M{PL}, F89M{PL}, H52, H52{PL}, H60{PL}, I33, K47M, N84, Q41, S44, T25M

Opuntia pottsii - *Prickly pear* {S} The Hopi Indians take the stems, spines and all, boil them and squeeze out the juice, and mix it with cornmeal used in making *tortillas*. It acts as the white of an egg does in making the meal more cohesive. Southwestern North America. TATE; H52, N84

Opuntia rafinesquii → ***Opuntia humifusa***

Opuntia robusta - *Dinner plate* {S} Fruits are eaten raw, puréed, or made into jellies, jams, pies, gelatin desserts, sherbets, syrups, or *colonche*. Young joints are boiled and used as a vegetable. Mexico. STEINKRAUS, TATE [Re]; B85{PL}, F85, H52, H52{PL}, N84, Q41

Opuntia streptacantha - *Tuna cardona* {S} Fruits are eaten raw, used in the preparation of sweetmeats, or made into *colonche*, a sweet alcoholic beverage. Young pads are used as a vegetable. Mexico. KUNKEL, STEINKRAUS, TATE; F85, Q41

Opuntia tenuispina - *Prickly pear* {S} The fruits are said to make the best cactus wine. The juice is allowed to stand until the wine thickens and sours to taste. It is then bottled and capped. This makes a delicious, cooling summer drink. Southwestern North America. TATE; N69

Opuntia tomentosa - *Tree pear* {PL} Fruits are eaten raw, or are used to make jams and jellies that have a flavor rather like that of guava jelly. A succulent cactus chutney is made by mixing the fruit with raisins, apples, onions, lemon peel, dates, sugar, vinegar, and spices. Mexico, cultivated. CRIBB, TATE [Re]; F31M, Q41{S}

Opuntia tuna - *Tuna, Nopal, Panini* {S} The sweet, juicy fruits are delicious to eat out of hand. Also used in ices, jams, jellies, cakes, muffins, ice cream, sauces, compotes, wine, or to color beverages and confectionery. Half-ripe fruits, when dried, have the flavor of dried green apples. Tender pads are boiled and then used as a substitute for string beans in soups, stews, omelettes, fritters, souffles, casseroles, stuffings, etc. Jamaica, cultivated. GIBBONS 1967 [Re], TANAKA, TATE [Re]; F85, G18{PL}, O93, Q41

Opuntia vulgaris - *Eastern prickly-pear* {PL} Fruits are eaten raw, stewed, or dried for later use. Unripe fruits and tender, young joints can be added to soups and stews and will impart an okra-like mucilaginous quality. Cultivated, naturalized in North America. GIBBONS 1964, MEDSGER; B61M, B61M{S}, B85, B88, C99, F31M, F80{S}, H60, I74, M16, Q41{S}

Oreocereus hendriksenianus - *Chica-chica* {S} The fruit is edible. Chile. ALDUNATE; A69, B84{PL}, C27M{PL}, H52{PL}, I33, Q38, Q38{PL}, Q41, S44

Pachycereus pecten-aboriginum - *Cardón hecho hecho* {S} Seeds are ground into a meal that is made into cakes, eaten by Indians and Mexicans. Mexico. UPHOF; A69, C27M, F80, I33, N84, Q38, Q41, S44, T25M

Pachycereus pringlei - *Cardón* {S} The ripe fruits are eaten raw or made into a refreshing drink. Pulp of ripe and unripe fruits are mixed together, mashed and kneaded and the juice poured off, and the resulting sticky mixture is made into cakes and dried. Toasted seeds are ground into an oily paste, formed into balls, and eaten with salt. It tastes something like sesame butter, only better. The flowers are eaten fresh. Mexico. FELGER, TATE; A0M{PL}, A69, B84{PL}, B85{PL}, *E53M*, F31M{PL}, G18{PL}, I33, L91M, N84, Q38, Q41, S44, T25M

Pachycereus weberi - *Cardón, Candebobe* {S} The spiny fruits are edible. Mexico. BRITTON 1937; A69, F31M{PL}, N84, Q38, Q41, T25M

Peniocereus greggii - *Deerhorn cactus* {S} Bright scarlet, fleshy fruits are eaten raw, cooked, or made into jam. The tubers are parboiled, dipped in batter, and made into fritters. In Louisiana, they are roasted in ashes in a fireplace. They can also be cut into small strips, soaked in cold water for thirty minutes, drained and dried, and then deep fried. Southwestern North America. HEDRICK 1919, KUNKEL, TATE [Re]; C27M, D1M{PL}, F85, H52, I33, N84, Q41, S44, T25M

Pereskia aculeata - *Barbados gooseberry, Lemon vine, Blade apple* {PL} Fruits are juicy, somewhat acid, occasionally eaten raw but usually stewed or made into jam and preserves. The succulent leaves and young shoots can be used as a substitute for purslane in salads, marinades and cooked dishes. Tropical America, cultivated. MORTON 1987a, OCHSE, TATE, UPHOF; E48, F31M, G18, H4, P38

Pereskiopsis aquosa - *Tuna de agua, Tasajillo* {S} Yellowish-green, pear-shaped fruits are used in making cooling drinks and for preserves. Mexico. BRITTON 1937; **X98**

Polaskia chichipe → *Lemaireocereus chichipe*

Rathbunia alamosensis - *Sina, Boa constrictor* {S} Small, bitter fruits are sometimes eaten fresh. Mexico. FELGER; A69, C27M, C99{PL}, F31M{PL}, N84, Q41, S44, T25M

Rhipsalis cassutha - *Mistletoe cactus* {PL} The edible fruits are produced in great numbers. They are soft, juicy and sweet, like small grapes. Cultivated. HEGYI; A90, F31M, F85{S}, G18, N69{S}

Stenocereus stellatus - *Joconostle* {S} The spiny, red fruit is edible. It is said to make the most delicious of all cactus jams. In Mexico, it is used as the filling for small turnovers which are served hot with local goat cheese. Mexico. TANAKA, TATE; H52, I33, N84, Q38, Q41, S44, T25M

Trichocereus chiloensis - *Cardón de candelabro, Quisco* {S} Fruits are eaten raw or processed into a brandy and a syrup. Chile-Argentina. UPHOF, VALENZUELA; I33, Q38, Q41

Trichocereus spachianus - *Torch cactus* {S} Fruits are eaten raw or used in ice cream and sherbets. The new tender shoots, peeled and diced, may be added to a vegetable salad or boiled and served with butter. Argentina. KUNKEL, TATE; A69, B85{PL}, C27M, *E53M*, F31M{PL}, G18{PL}, I33, N69, N84, Q38, Q41, S44, T25M

CAESALPINIACEAE

Bauhinia carronii - {S} The white flowers secrete a considerable quantity of nectar. Australian aborigines sucked this nectar directly from the flower or washed it out with water. Australia. CRIBB, DONKIN; *Q25*, R33M

Bauhinia esculenta → *Tylosema esculentum*

Bauhinia hookeri - {S} Flowers produce a considerable quantity of nectar. This can be sucked directly from the flower, or washed out with water and used as a beverage or for sweetening. Australia. CRIBB; N84, P5, *P17M*, *Q25*, Q46, R33M

Bauhinia malabarica - *Amli, Bentjuluk, Alibangbang* {S} The young leaves are sour and are eaten raw as a side-dish with rice, or as a flavoring for meats and fish. Young shoots are used as a vegetable. Tropical Asia. OCHSE, TANAKA, UPHOF; F85, Q12, Q46

Bauhinia purpurea - *Camel's foot tree, Deva kanchan* {S} Flowers and flower buds are cooked and eaten as a potherb, used in curries, or pickled. Leaves are also edible. Tropical Asia. MARTIN 1975, TANAKA; C9M, C56M{PL}, F80, F85, *J25*{PL}, K38, *L5M*, L91M, N84, P5, Q12, *Q15G*, Q18, *Q32*, R33M, etc.

Bauhinia racemosa - *Kachnál, Burmese silk orchid* {S} Leaves are pickled. Seeds are also edible. Southeast Asia. KUNKEL, WATT; F85, N84, O93, P5, *P17M*, Q12, Q18, *Q32*, Q41, Q46, *R28*

Bauhinia retusa - *Semla* {S} A clear gum, resembling *gum arabic*, is collected by making cuts in the bark and used in sweetmeat manufacture. Himalayan region. TANAKA; N84, P5, *P17M*, Q12, Q18, *Q32*, Q41, Q46

Bauhinia tomentosa - *St. Thomas tree, Kupu-kupu* {S} Young, sour leaves are eaten as a vegetable with rice, added to soups, or used as a flavoring for other foods. Seeds are eaten. Tropical Asia. HEDRICK 1919, OCHSE; C56M{PL}, F85, *H71*, N84, P5, Q46, R33M

Bauhinia variegata - *Mountain ebony, Kanchanar, Kurol* {S} Young leaves, young pods, and flowers are eaten as a vegetable. Flower buds are pickled. The seeds are also much appreciated. Tropical Asia. HEDRICK 1919, KUNKEL, TANAKA; C56M{PL}, F85, *G66*, I83M{PL}, M19, M20, N84, O84, O93, P5, *P17M*, Q12, Q18, Q46, *R28*, R41, R60, etc.

Caesalpinia gilliesii - *Bird of paradise tree* {S} Flower stamens are used to adulterate saffron. Brazil to Argentina, cultivated. CORREA; A79M, B62, C9M, C56M{PL}, F79M, F80, I33, K38, L13, N37M{PL}, N84, O53M, P5, *P17M*, R33M, etc.

Caesalpinia pulcherrima - *Peacock flower, Pride of Barbados* {S} Young seeds, having a sweetish flavor, are eaten fresh or cooked. Flowers are cooked and eaten. Tropics, cultivated. PONGPANGAN, TANAKA; A79M, B62, C9M, C27M, C56M{PL}, F79M, F80, I33, *L5M*, L13, L91M, M19, N84, O53M, P5, etc.

Cassia auriculata - *Tanner's senna, Ranawara, Matara tea* {S} Young leaves, pods and flowers are occasionally eaten. Dried flowers are use as a coffee substitute, while the dried leaves are used as tea. Tropical Asia. MACMILLAN, WATT; F85, N84, O53M, P5, *P17M*, Q12, Q46

Cassia bicapsularis - *Wild currant, Cafe de pobre* {S} The pulp of the fruit is sweet and edible with somewhat the flavor of tamarind. Toasted seeds are used as a coffee substitute. Tropical America. DUKE, WILLIAMS, L.; C56M{PL}, F85, *H71*, *K48*, N37M, *N79M*, N84, O93, *P17M*, *Q32*

Cassia fistula - *Golden shower* {S} Flowers are edible. Leaves and fruits are also eaten, however they act as a mild laxative. Southern Asia, cultivated. DUKE; C9M, E7M, F80, I99, *L5M*, M19, M20, O84, P5, *P17M*, Q12, Q18, *Q32*, R33M, S92, etc.

Cassia floribunda - *Smooth senna, Tajumas* {S} The steamed young shoots and leaves are eaten as a potherb or cooked in soups and stews. Unripe seeds are cooked or roasted and eaten as a side-dish with rice. Seeds are used as a coffee substitute in some parts of Guatemala. Tropical America, cultivated. OCHSE, UPHOF; F80, F85, N84, O93, P5, *P17M*, Q12, *Q25*, R33M

Cassia laevigata* → *Cassia floribunda

Cassia leschenaultiana - *Lauki, Tuan-ie-ch'ien-ming* {S} Leaves and stems are used as a substitute for tea. Eastern Asia. TANAKA; F85

Cassia mimosoides - *Tea senna* {S} Young branches and leaves are used as a substitute for tea. Tropics. TANAKA; F85, N84

Cassia obtusifolia - *Sicklepod, Ebisu-gusa* {S} Leaves are used as a vegetable. In the Sudan, they are fermented into a high protein (20%) meat substitute called *kawal*. A pale yellowish juice that accumulates during the fermentation process is skimmed off and made into a stew with okra, beef jerky, and salt. Seeds are used as a tea substitute. Tropics. DIRAR, TANAKA; D58, F85, N84

Cassia occidentalis - *Coffee senna* {S} Young leaves, unripe pods, and flowers are eaten as a steamed vegetable. A coffee substitute, *Magdad coffee* or *Florida coffee*, is prepared from the roasted seeds. Tropics, naturalized in Southern North America. DUKE, FERNALD, MEDSGER, OCHSE; F85, *N79M*, N84, P5, *P17M*

Cassia siamea - *Cassod tree* {S} Flowers are eaten in curries. Indonesia, cultivated. BURKILL, TANAKA; B62, C9M, F85, *N79M*, N84, O84, O93, P5, *P17M*, Q12, Q18, *Q25*, *Q32*, Q46, R33M, S29, etc.

Cassia tomentosa - *Alcaparro* {S} Tender pods, leaves, and flowers are eaten as a vegetable. Buds are used as a caper substitute. Tropics. DUKE, MACMILLAN; C9M, D62, F85, N84, O93, S95

Cassia tora - *Sickle pod, Sickle senna, Coffee weed* {S} Young leaves and shoots are steamed as a potherb or cooked and eaten with rice. They contain about 6% protein. The seeds, roasted or cooked in the pod, are eaten as a side-dish at the rice table. Roasted seeds are used as a coffee substitute. Tropics. DUKE, OCHSE; G47, F85, N84, Q12

Ceratonia siliqua - *Carob, St. John's bread, Locust bean* {S} Pods are sweet, rich in sugars and protein, somewhat fibrous. They are sometimes eaten as a sweetmeat, but are usually made into a molasses called *pasteli*, alcoholic beverages, or ground into powder. Carob powder is used as a chocolate substitute in drinks, cakes, candies and baked goods. *Locust bean gum* or *tragasol*, extracted from the seeds, is used to thicken sauces, pickles, salad dressings and ice cream. Roasted seeds are used as a coffee substitute. Cultivated. COIT, GOULART [Nu, Re], HEDRICK 1919, MORTON 1987a, UPHOF; A79M, B62, C9M, D95{PL}, E29, E29{PL}, E29{PR}, <u>I89M</u>{PR}, K38, K63G, <u>L67</u>{PR}, N84, N93M, O53M, S92, etc.

CULTIVARS {GR}

<u>Casuda:</u> Medium-long, flat fruit, 5 to 7 inches in length and about 1 inch wide; of a dark brown color; sugar content about 50%, protein about 5%, quality very good; not susceptible to worms. Tree a good bearer. In California best adapted to foothill areas, but also does very well in the desert. Originated in Valencia, Spain. THOMSON 1971; **U26**{SC}

<u>Santa Fe:</u> Large, slightly curved fruit, up to 7 inches long; skin thin, light brown; good sugar content, 47.6%, flavor very good; usually harvested during September and the first 10 days of October; immune to worms. Tree spreading, precocious; self fertile, bears heavy crops annually; does especially well in coastal foothills. Originated in Santa Fe Springs, California. Introduced in 1922. BROOKS 1972, MORTON 1987a; L6

<u>Sfax:</u> Very large, thick fruit; sugar content about 51%; ripens very early, September 10 to 30 at Vista; milling quality good. Excellent for eating out of hand as it is soft, very sweet and tasty. Tree vigorous, spreading; yields heavily in alternate years. In southern California best suited to foothills some distance from the coast. Originated in Tunis, Tunisia. Introduced into the U.S. in 1959 by Dr. J. Elliot Coit, Vista, California. BROOKS 1972, THOMSON 1971; **U26**{SC}

<u>Tylliria:</u> Large fruit, 6 to 9 inches long; sugar content averages 47.4%, protein 5.81%, good flavor; excellent quality for milling; ripens late, in October. Tree comes into bearing late, with no commercial yields before 10 years from budding. In California best adapted to foothills near the coast. Good commercial cultivar; widely grown for export on Cyprus where it originated in ancient times. BROOKS 1972; **U26**{SC}

Cercidium floridum - *Palo verde* {S} Immature seeds and pods are eaten as a vegetable, having a pleasant taste similar to peas and beans. Dry seeds are ground and made into breads, cakes, and beverages. Leaves are eaten as greens. Southwestern North America. CLARKE, FELKER, KUNKEL, UPHOF; B94, C9M, C27M, C98, *E66M*, *F53M*{PL}, F79M, F80, G60{PL}, *H71*, I33, *J0*, *J86*{PL}, K15, N37M{PL}, O93, etc.

Cercidium microphyllum - *Small-leaved palo verde* {S} The seeds are eaten fresh or ground and mixed with mesquite meal. Southwestern North America. CLARKE, KIRK, YANOVSKY; B94, C9M, C27M, C98, *E66M*, F79M, F80, F85, *H71*, I33, I98M, *J0*, N84, O93

Cercidium torreyanum* → *Cercidium floridum

Cercis canadensis - *Red bud* {PL} Acid flowers are eaten raw in salads. Unopened buds are pickled in vinegar and used as a caper substitute. Buds, flowers, and young pods are good sautéed in butter or made into fritters. High in vitamin C. North America. FERNALD, GIBBONS 1979, ZENNIE [Nu]; A50, B9M, C9, C9M{S}, D95, E87, G23, H4, I4, I77M, K38{S}, K63G{S}, M77, N84{S}

Cercis occidentalis - *California redbud* {S} Roasted pods and seeds are eaten. Flowers are used in salads. Buds are pickled like capers. Western North America. KIRK, YANOVSKY; A2, C9M, D95{PL},

E63{PL}, F80, G59M, G60{PL}, H4{PL}, *I61*, *I62*{PL}, I83M{PL}, I99, K38, K47T, L2{PL}, L13, etc.

Cercis siliquastrum - *Judas tree* {S} The flowers have a pleasant acid taste and are eaten raw in salads or dipped in batter and made into fritters. Flower buds are pickled in vinegar and used as a condiment. Mediterranean region. HEDRICK 1919, MACNICOL; B96{PL}, C9M, D95{PL}, E87{PL}, F80, H4{PL}, K38, K47T, K63G, *N71M*, N93M, O53M, O93, P5, *Q32*, etc.

Cynometra cauliflora - *Nam-nam* {S} The fleshy, subacid fruit has a pleasant flavor suggesting an unripe apple and is eaten fresh, stewed or preserved. Fried with batter, it is said to make a good fritter. Young fruits are pickled, eaten with sambal, or prepared with fish. Tropical Asia. HEDRICK 1919, MACMILLAN, TANAKA; **T73M**

Daniellia oliveri - *African copaida balsam* {S} Young leaves are used as a condiment. Tropical Africa. DALZIEL; F85, N84

Dialium guineense - *Velvet tamarind* {S} The aril surrounding the seeds has an agreeably acid flavor and is commonly eaten. When dry, it is chewed or macerated in cold water to form an acid beverage. West Tropical Africa. DALZIEL, HEDRICK 1919, MACMILLAN; F85, N84, P28

Dialium sp. - *Keranji ayer* {S} Small fruits, about 3/4 of an inch long; thin, brittle shells, dull velvety-black in color, easily opened; soft, burnt-orange flesh that separates easily from the seed. The flavor of the raisin-like flesh, which keeps for months, is tangy but not too tart. Although slow growing, it may fruit quickly. Borneo. O19, O19{PL}

Gleditsia triacanthos - *Honey locust, Sweet locust* {S} Seed pods are cooked and eaten while still small and tender. The sweet pulp is eaten as a nibble, made into sugar, and fermented into a beer. Young seeds taste like raw peas. North America, cultivated. FERNALD, GIBBONS 1979, LOGSDON 1981; B61M, C9M, F85, G67{PL}, K38, K63G, L91M, N84, N93M, O53M, O89, P49

CULTIVARS {GR}

Ashworth: Very sweet pulp with a melon-like flavor. Tree extremely hardy, thornless. K16

Gymnocladus dioicus - *Kentucky coffee tree* {S} The fully ripe seeds may be roasted, ground, and used as a coffee substitute. Thorough roasting, at least three hours at 300° F., is necessary to destroy the poisonous hydrocyanic acid in the ripe seeds. Eastern North America. GIBBONS 1979; A79M, *B52*{PL}, B61M, D45{PL}, D95{PL}, E7M, *F51*{PL}, G41{PL}, K38, K63G, M35M{PL}, N37M{PL}, N84, N93M, O53M, etc.

Hymenaea courbaril - *West Indian locust, Courbaril, Guapinol* {S} The whitish pulp around the seeds is sweet and is eaten. Also mixed with water to make an *atole*, or fermented into an alcoholic beverage. The protein content is high for a fruit. Tropical America. HEDRICK 1919, TANAKA, UPHOF, WILLIAMS, L.; F85, N84

Parkinsonia microphyllum* → *Cercidium microphyllum

Poinciana gilliesii* → *Caesalpinia gilliesii

Poinciana pulcherrima* → *Caesalpinia pulcherrima

Saraca bijuga - *Sok nam, Ashok* {S} The aromatic flowers, having a sourish flavor, are eaten locally as a potherb. Fruits are chewed instead of Areca nuts. Leaves are also edible. Southeast Asia. BURKILL, PONGPANGAN, TANAKA; N84, Q12, Q46

Saraca indica* → *Saraca bijuga

Schotia capitata - {S} Nectar of the flowers is sucked. Southern Africa. PALMER; F85

Schotia latifolia - *Forest boerboom* {S} The young green pods are roasted and eaten. Seeds are also edible. Southern Africa. FOX, F.; C9M, N84, P5

Tamarindus indica - *Tamarind* {S} The acid fruit pulp is used in drinks, preserves, curries, jellies, syrups, sauces and chutneys. Compressed blocks of pulp are sold as *wet tamarind* in ethnic stores. Leaves are eaten in soups, salads, and curries. Young pods are eaten mixed with spices or fish or added whole to soups and stews. Seeds are roasted and eaten, used as a coffee substitute, and also yield an edible oil, gum, and starch. The bark of the tree is chewed as a delicacy. Flowers are eaten raw in salads or cooked. The seedlings, when about a foot high are used as a vegetable. Cultivated. COST 1988 [Cul, Re], CRAWFORD [Re], DUKE, MORTON 1987a, OCHSE, POPENOE, W. 1920 [Cu, Nu], RICHARDSON [Re], TANAKA; A79M, *B59*{PR}, E29, E29{PL}, E29{PR}, F68{PL}, F80, I83M{PL}, *L5M*, L90G{PR}, P5, *P17M*, *Q32*, R47, S29, etc.

Tylosema esculentum - *Marama bean, Gemsbok bean* {S} After roasting, the seeds have a delicious nutty flavor that tastes like coffee beans or roasted cashews. They have a protein content comparable to soybeans, and an oil content that approaches that of the peanut. The edible oil is similar to almond oil in consistency and taste. Sweet tubers can be baked, boiled, or roasted. Southern Africa. FOX, F., MENNINGER, NATIONAL RESEARCH COUNCIL 1979; N84, *P17M*, Q41

CALYCANTHACEAE

Calycanthus floridus - *Carolina allspice, Sweet shrub* {PL} The aromatic bark is sometimes used as a spice. Eastern North America. HEDRICK 1919; A50, A93M, B96, C9, C9M{S}, C13M{S}, E33M, *F51*, G23, *G28*, H4, I11M, *L49*, *N71M*{S}, O53M{S}, etc.

Calycanthus occidentalis - *California allspice* {PL} Said to be used as a spice. Southwestern North America. TANAKA; B92, B94{S}, *C73*, G59M, G60, H4, *P63*{S}, S7M{S}

Calycanthus praecox* → *Chimonanthus praecox

Chimonanthus praecox - *Wintersweet, Kara-ume* {S} Flowers are eaten with oil and salt. The flower petals are used to flavor and scent tea. Korea-China, cultivated. REHDER, TANAKA; D95{PL}, E7M, E63{PL}, E87{PL}, H4{PL}, K38, K47T, K63G, N37M{PL}, *N71M*, N93M, O53M, O93, P5, R78, etc.

CAMELLIACEAE

Camellia japonica - *Garden camellia* {S} The dried flowers are eaten as a vegetable or used in the preparation of *mochi*. Seeds are the source of an oil, called *tsubaki oil*, used for culinary purposes. Leaves form a tea substitute. Eastern Asia, cultivated. BROUK, MACNICOL, TANAKA, ZEVEN; B32{PL}, B96, B96{PL}, H4{PL}, K38, L59{PL}, *N71M*, N84, N93M, O53M, *P39*, P49, S91M

Camellia kissi - *Kissi* {PL} Leaves are used locally as a tea. Fruits are said to be edible. Subtropical Asia. ALTSCHUL, TANAKA, WATT; I52, I52{SC}

Camellia reticulata - *Tô-tsubaki* {PL} Source of a seed oil that is used for culinary purposes. China. TANAKA; *N73*

Camellia sasanqua - *Sazanka, Sasanqua tea* {S} Seeds are the source of *tea seed oil*. When refined it is suitable for use in foods. In Japan, the leaves are mixed with tea to give it a pleasant aroma. Japan-China, cultivated. HEDRICK 1919, TANAKA, UPHOF, ZEVEN; B32{PL}, B96, B96{PL}, G96{PL}, H4{PL}, K38, N84, O93, *P39*, S95

Camellia sinensis - *Tea plant, Cha* {S} Cured leaves are the source of common tea. *Leppet* or *leptet tea* consists of green tea-leaves pressed and preserved, and afterwards prepared as a vegetable by mixing with garlic, salt, oil, and other ingredients. Green tea powder is used in Japanese confectionery. *Tea cider* or *tea fungus* is an effervescent, sub-acid, fermented beverage made from tea leaf extracts. In Tibet, salt and butter are added to boiled brick tea, and the mixture is churned until it resembles cocoa. The flowers are made into tempura using the edible seed oil. Fruits are eaten. Subtropical Asia, cultivated. ALTSCHUL, CREASY 1982 [Cu, Pre], MACMILLAN, MITCHELL [Cu], SCHERY, STEINKRAUS, TANAKA, VON REIS, WILKES; A79M, A93M{PL}, B74{PL}, G64, H4{PL}, J22{PL}, N37M{PL}, *N71M*, N84, O48, O93, P5, *P17M*, *P39*, P86{PL}, Q46, *R28*, S95, etc.

CULTIVARS {GR}

Large Leaf: Similar to Small Leaf, but with larger foliage and flowers. B96

Small Leaf: An excellent shrub for the landscape that has small white flowers in the autumn. B96, B96{S}

Thea sinensis → *Camellia sinensis*

CAMPANULACEAE

Campanula punctata - *Hotaru-bukuro* {S} Flowers and leaves are used as potherbs. Eastern Asia. KUNKEL, TANAKA; D62, J37M{PL}, K47T, N84, *Q24*, S7M

Campanula rapunculoides - *Rover bellflower, Creeping bellflower* {S} The fleshy roots are somewhat sweet and are a pleasant addition to tossed green salads. They are also good when boiled for twenty minutes and served with butter or a cream sauce. Eurasia, naturalized in North America. CROWHURST 1972, FERNALD, GIBBONS 1979, HARRINGTON, H.; D62, E15, F80, G82M{PL}, J48{PL}, K47T, N9M, N9M{PL}, *N71M*, N84, O48, O53M, *Q24*, S7M

Campanula rapunculus - *Rampion* {S} Tender young leaves can be added to tossed salads or cooked as a potherb. The white, fleshy roots, when young, are agreeable sliced and eaten like radishes in salads, while the older roots are boiled, roasted, or fried like turnips. The young shoots may be blanched like asparagus and prepared in the same manner. Eurasia, cultivated. GRIEVE, LAUNERT, ORGAN, PAINTER, VILMORIN [Cu]; G82M{PL}, K47T, M82{PL}, *N71M*, N84, O48, O53M, *Q24*

Canarina campanulata → *Canarina canariensis*

Canarina canariensis - {S} Fruits are eaten out of hand or made into preserves. Roots and young shoots are also said to be edible. Canary Islands. HEDRICK 1919, KUNKEL; **Z25M**

Phyteuma orbiculare - *Round-headed rampion* {S} The leaves and fleshy roots are occasionally consumed in salads and as a cooked vegetable, like the true rampion. Europe. UPHOF; I63M{PL}, J67M, K47T, N84, O48, *Q24*, S7M

Phyteuma spicatum - *Spiked rampion* {S} The thick, fleshy roots can be eaten in salads or as a boiled vegetable. Europe. HEDRICK 1919; F80, K47T, *N71M*, N84, O53M, *Q24*, S7M

CANELLACEAE

Canella alba → *Canella winterana*

Canella winterana - *Canella, White cinnamon, Cinnamon bark* {PL} The aromatic leaves and the bitter, very pungent bark are used as condiments in the West Indies. Dried bark is exported to spice merchants and utilized in seasoning mixtures. Florida, West Indies. GRIEVE, MORTON 1976, UPHOF; D87G, *J25*

CANNABIDACEAE

Cannabis sativa - *Hemp* {S} Seeds are parched and eaten as a condiment, or made into cakes and fried. In Japan, they are called *asanomi*, and are used in *ganmo* (deep-fried tofu burgers). The seed oil may be used for culinary purposes. Central Asia, cultivated. FERNALD, HARRINGTON, H., HEDRICK 1919, KIRK, SHURTLEFF 1975; *N71M*

Humulus lupulus - *Hops* {S} A bitter substance found in the glandular hairs of the female cones is used in beer to give it flavor and aroma, and to prevent decomposition by bacteria. They are also used in herb beers. Young shoots are eaten in salads or used as a substitute for asparagus. In France and Belgium, the cooked shoots are known as *jet de houblon*. The flavor is unique and to many tastes delicious. Leaves and cones are brewed into tea. Fleshy rhizomes are sometimes eaten. For the production of shoots, young root cuttings are grown in clumps or small hillocks. Northern temperate region, cultivated. BIANCHINI [Cul], CREASY 1982, FERNALD, GRIEVE [Cu, Re], KUNKEL, MARCIN, ORGAN [Cu, Re], UPHOF; B7, C13M, C82{PL}, D29{PL}, D62, D76{PL}, G68, G84{PL}, H65{PL}, I59G, J20, L7M, N84, O53M

CULTIVARS {PL}

Brewer's Gold: High quality hop with a pungent aroma and high alpha acid content. Similar to Bullion but the cone tends to be smaller, and matures a week to ten days later; exhibits the same lack of stability in storage. Perennial vine requires strong trellis and ample water. Mildew-resistant, high yielding. Hops ripen August to September. ROMANKO; E68, F11, G93M, *M81M*

Bullion: A rich, aromatic hop with high bittering compounds and resins. Unusual taste and aroma. Very vigorous, produces 1,800 to 2,400 pounds per acre. In Oregon, it is harvested after Fuggle, usually during the first week in September. The oil content increases as the harvest is delayed. Lacks storage stability unless kept at temperatures below 32° F. Used mostly as a bittering hop in strong English-style bitter ales and stouts. ROMANKO; A99

Cascade: A Fuggle hybrid developed at Oregon State University. The cones are buttery to the rub and the aroma is at once fragrantly aromatic and powerful. In Oregon, it matures after Fuggle and before Bullion. It is a poor keeper and requires cold storage immediately after baling. Resistant to downy mildew. Excellent for giving both flavor and aroma to American light lagers. ROMANKO; A91, A99, E12, E12{PR}, E68, I39, I39{PR}, *M81M*

Early Cluster: An excellent hop with a consistently high brewing value. Has a relatively unrefined aroma and is usually blended with other hops that are more aromatic. Produces hops in small to medium clusters. Averages 8 to 9 bales of cones per acre. Resistant to verticillium wilt; susceptible to downy mildew. The dominant hop cultivar in the United States. Originated in Oregon around 1908 as a mutation of English Clusters. ROMANKO; A91

Fuggle: Has an aroma which is fairly pronounced and somewhat spicy but not pungent. Usually used in dark beers and stouts. Vine reaches 20 feet in length. The most mildew resistant cultivar grown in the Northwest. It is early maturing and low yielding. Considered to be a cool weather hop. Baled hop has fair keeping qualities. The best cultivar for the home brew enthusiast. ROMANKO; A99, E68, *M81M*, R53M

Golden: (Yellow, Aureus) An ornamental hop that grows 15 feet tall and has attractive, bright yellow-golden climbing foliage. E81M{S}, K47T{S}, N84{S}, P86, P92, *Q24*{S}, R53M

Hallertauer: (Hallertauer Mittelfrueh) An excellent hop with a mellow, spicy aroma and flavor. Excellent for dry hopping, but a poor bittering hop. Good for light and dark lagers. Produces 700 to 900 pounds per acre. Susceptible to mite infestations. Grown commercially in the Kootenai Valley of Idaho. The traditional German aroma hop. Full German names translates as "Midseason Hop of the Hallertau District". ROMANKO; A99, E12, E12{PR}, I99

Hersbrucker: A German hop similar to Hallertauer. E12

Nugget: A good yielding, high alpha bittering hop. E12

Tettnang: (Tettnanger, Deutscher Fruehhopfen) Has an exceptionally mild aroma that seems to enhance grain aromas. Medium bitterness. Excellent for finishing lagers. Matures a few days earlier than Hallertauer. Produces about a thousand pounds of dried hops per acre. Used by some of America's major brewers. Originated in the Tettnang district of Germany. ROMANKO; A91, A99, E12, E12{PR}

Willamette: Excellent all-purpose hop. An improved Fuggle hybrid. Disease resistant. Traditional English ale type. Low in bitterness with a spicy, noble aroma. Often used as a finishing hop in ales and stout. A99, E12, E12{PR}, I39, I39{PR}

Wye Challenger: A red-stemmed, free flowering cultivar that is resistant to mildew. Vine reaches 20 feet in length. R53M

Humulus lupulus var. cordifolius - *Karahana-sô* {S} Young leaves and roots are edible. The fruit is used to make wine. Female cones are used as a substitute for hops. Eastern Asia. TANAKA; **V19**

CANNACEAE

Canna achiras - *Canna* {S} The rhizomes are eaten. Also one of the sources of the West Indian arrowroot known as *tous le mois*. Chile, Argentina. HEDRICK 1919; **W59M**

Canna coccinea - *Indian shot* {PL} The fleshy rhizomes are the source of a starch known as *tous le mois*. Tropical America, cultivated. HEDRICK 1919; C56M

Canna edulis - *Achira, Edible canna* {S} Starchy rhizomes are sometimes boiled and eaten. In Peru, they are baked for up to twelve hours after which they become a white, translucent, fibrous and somewhat mucilaginous mass with a sweetish taste. Even after baking the large, glistening starch kernels can be seen with the naked eye. At Cuzco, the baked rhizomes are sold at the festival of Corpus Christi. Young shoots can be eaten as a green vegetable. Immature seeds are cooked in *bocoles* (fat tortillas). Also the source of an *arrowroot* which is made into cakes in Colombia. Tropical America, cultivated. ALCORN, GADE 1966, HERKLOTS, MACMILLAN, NATIONAL RESEARCH COUNCIL 1989, OCHSE, UPHOF; D33, D62, I99{PL}, N84, P1G{PL}, P38

Canna flaccida - *Golden canna* {PL} Rhizomes are said to yield an *arrowroot*. North America. FERNALD, TANAKA; *F73*, F85{S}, *J25*, K85M, *L5M*{S}, N37M, N84{S}

CAPPARIDACEAE

Boscia albitrunca - *Shepherd's tree* {S} Flower buds are pickled and used as a caper substitute. The roasted and ground roots are used as a substitute for coffee. Fruits are crushed in fresh milk to make a tasty dish. Seeds are edible. Roots are also the source of meal and a syrup. Southern Africa. FOX, F., UPHOF; *G66*, N84, O53M, O93, P5

Capparis aphylla* → *Capparis decidua

Capparis decidua - *Sodad, Kureel* {S} In India, the flower bud is eaten as a potherb or pickled. Both the ripe and unripe fruit are prepared into a bitter-tasting pickle. The unripe fruit is also cooked and eaten. Children enjoy sucking the floral nectar. The roots, when burned, yield a vegetable salt. North Africa. BHANDARI, HEDRICK 1919, TANAKA; Q46

Capparis mitchellii - *Native pomegranate* {S} The fruit is eaten by the natives. Australia. UPHOF; N84, R15M

Capparis ovata - *Caper berry* {S} The flower buds can be pickled and used like capers. Mediterranean region to Southwest Asia. KUNKEL; **Z19**

Capparis sepiaria - *Indian capers* {S} Flower buds are pickled and used as a substitute for capers. Southern Africa to Asia. TANAKA; N84, Q46

Capparis spinosa - *Caper, Alcapparra* {PL} Flower buds are pickled and used to flavor sauces, butters, salads, stuffings, hors d'oeuvres, fish, meat, cheese, etc. The young fruits and the tender branch tips are also pickled; these are sometimes found in specialty stores. Young sprouts are eaten like asparagus. Mediterranean region, cultivated. BIANCHINI, CREASY 1982, HEDRICK 1919, PAINTER [Re], VILMORIN [Cu]; C13M{S}, C56M, D29, E5M, E59T, F37T, I77{S}, I83M, I91{S}, J66M{PR}, K2{S}, K85, O53M{S}, O89{S}, T7{S}, etc.

CULTIVARS {S}

Spineless: (Senza Spine) A cultivar that is free of spines. The flower buds and immature fruits are pickled in vinegar or brine and used as a condiment. Q11M

Crateva nurvala* → *Crateva religiosa

Crateva religiosa - *Garlic pear* {S} Young shoots and leaves are eaten as a spinach substitute. The fruit is occasionally eaten, usually roasted. In Burma, the flowers are pickled and eaten for their digestive action. The seeds are also consumed. Tropical Africa, Tropical Asia. HEDRICK 1919, MENNINGER, TANAKA, UPHOF; F85, N84, Q46

Crateva tapia - *Garlic pear, Tapia, Zapotilla amarillo* {S} The edible fruit has a mealy pulp like that of a pear, is sweetish, and has an odor like garlic. Tropical America. HEDRICK 1919; P28

CAPRIFOLIACEAE

Lonicera caerulea - *Yonomi* {S} Fruits are eaten raw or in preserves. Temperate Asia. TANAKA; N84, O53M

Lonicera caerulea var. edulis - *Edible honeysuckle, Sweetberry honeysuckle, Blueberried honeysuckle* {PL} Milder in flavor than the fruits of other honeysuckles, they can be eaten raw but mostly they are used to make jams, jellies and refreshing drinks. Temperate Asia, cultivated. DARROW, TANAKA; A65, B47, G1T, G54, K64, K81, L27M{CF}, M35M, N24M, N26, N36

Lonicera henryi - *Hosoba-suikazura* {PL} The stems, leaves, and flowers are all edible. China. TANAKA; D95

Lonicera japonica - *Japanese honeysuckle, Suikazura* {S} Leaves, buds, and flowers are made into a tea. The flowers are sucked for their sweet nectar, used as a vegetable or made into syrup and puddings. Parboiled young leaves are used as a vegetable. China, Japan, naturalized in North America. CROWHURST 1973 [Re], LEGGATT [Re], TANAKA; F85, *G66*, K38, L59{PL}, N84, O93, P5, P49, *P63*, R78

Viburnum alnifolium - *Hobblebush, Moosewood* {PL} Ripe fruits are sweet and palatable, tasting like raisins or dates. However, the stone is large and the edible pulp is thin. North America. FERNALD, GIBBONS 1979, SIMMONS 1972; E33M, K63G{S}, N7T, *P63*{S}, P86

Viburnum cassinoides - *Withe-rod, Nannyberry, Appalachian tea, False Paraguay tea* {PL} The scant pulp of the fruit is sweet and well flavored, hanging on the tree into the winter. A bright amber tea with a pleasant taste can be prepared from the dried leaves. They are first steamed over boiling water, rolled between the fingers, allowed to stand overnight, and then dried in an oven. Eastern North America. GIBBONS 1966b; B47, B61M{S}, E33M, K47T{S}, K63G{S}, M92, N24M, N84{S}

Viburnum cotinifolium - *Smoketree viburnum* {S} The ripe, sweetish fruits are eaten. Himalayan region. HEDRICK 1919, WATT; F80, K47T, N84, O46, *P63*, Q12, Q40

Viburnum edule - *Squashberry, Mooseberry* {S} Fully ripe fruits are mildly acid, pleasant tasting, and can be eaten raw. They are also used for *squash*, juice, sauces, jams, and jellies. The Indians dried or preserved them for winter use. North America. FERNALD, GIBBONS 1966b, HARRINGTON, H. [Re], HELLER; G82M{PL}, I47, *J75M*

Viburnum lentago - *Wild raisin, Sweet viburnum, Sheepberry* {PL} The bluish-black fruits are edible. They are variable in size and quality, the best being half an inch long, pulpy, very sweet, somewhat juicy, and pleasant to the taste. North America. GIBBONS 1966b, MEDSGER, SIMMONS 1972; B15M, *C47*, D45, G41, G67, *H45M*, I15{S}, K38{S}, K47T{S}, K64, *K89*{S}, L27M, *L49*, M35M, *M69M*, etc.

Viburnum nudum - *Smooth withe-rod, Possum haw* {PL} The fruits are apple-shaped, compressed, about a quarter inch long, deep blue in color, of a sweetish taste and may be eaten raw. Eastern North America. HEDRICK 1919; A93M, B61M{S}, H4, *I17M*, I19, N37M

Viburnum odoratissimum - *Tse-woh-shue* {PL} The reddish-purple to black fruits are edible. China. VON REIS; H4, *J25*, N84{S}

Viburnum opulus - *Guelder-rose, European cranberry-bush* {S} Bright red fruits are sour and are used as a substitute for the cranberry in making jelly, preserves, sauce, and wine. In Norway and Sweden they are eaten with honey and flour. Northern temperate region, cultivated. HEDRICK 1919, SIMMONS 1972; *B52*{PL}, C9M, *C47*{PL}, D62, F80, J32{PL}, K38, K47T, K63G, L91M, *M69M*{PL}, N84, N93M, O53M, *Q32*, R53M{PL}, etc.

Viburnum opulus 'Xanthocarpum' - *Yellow guelder-rose, Golden European cranberry* {PL} The yellow fruits, becoming transclucent gold in the fall, are recommended for wine making. Makes an excellent color accent when grown with red-fruited forms. Cultivated. SIMMONS 1972; K63G{S}, N36, P86

Viburnum pauciflorum* → *Viburnum edule

Viburnum prunifolium - *Black haw, Stagbush* {PL} Bluish-black fruits are variable as to size, sweetness, and amount of pulp. At their best they are good to eat out of hand, otherwise they are used for jams, jellies, sauces, drinks, etc. North America. GIBBONS 1966b, MEDSGER; B9M, C9, *C47*, D95, F80{S}, *G66*, K38{S}, K47T{S}, K67, *K89*, *K89*{S}, L12, M77, N7T, O93{S}, etc.

Viburnum rufidulum - *Southern blackhaw, Rusty blackhaw* {PL} Fruits are said to be eaten or nibbled. North America. KUNKEL; D30, I37M, I53, K18, K63G{S}, K67

Viburnum setigerum - *Tea viburnum* {S} Leaves are used as a tea substitute. China. UPHOF; *B15*{PL}, E47{PL}, F85, *H8*{PL}, K22{PL}, K38, K47T, K63G, M92{PL}, N84, O93, *P63*

Viburnum theiferum* → *Viburnum setigerum

Viburnum trilobum - *High-bush cranberry, American cranberry-bush, Pembina* {PL} The red fruits make an excellent substitute for cranberries. They can be used to make sauce, juice, jams, jellies, and wine. A good source of vitamin C. North America. DARROW, GIBBONS 1966b, SIMMONS 1972, TURNER 1979; A15M{PR}, A91, *C47*, C63, D45, D65, D69, D76, G26, G41, G89, M35M, N9M, N9M{S}, N26, etc.

CULTIVARS {GR}

Phillips: Selected for fruit in which the bitterness has disappeared, making it excellent for jelly. Much superior to Wentworth. Introduced by Professor E.M. Meader of New Hampshire. F43M

Wentworth: An outstanding early cultivar selected and named by the United States Bureau of Plant Industry after analyses of acid and pectin content were made, and jelly tests were undertaken. Abundant, large red fruits with excellent flavor. Good for making preserves. DARROW; *A74*, B9M, C11M, E87, F43M, *G4*, *G30*, *H8*, J7, *K31*, K63G{S}, N24M, N36

CARICACEAE

Carica candamarcensis* → *Carica pubescens

Carica chrysopetala* → *Carica x heilbornii

Carica goudotiana - *Papayuelo* {S} Fruits are pale yellow tinged with magenta, and can be eaten raw. The flesh has the taste of a mildly acid apple, with the pulp around the seeds being milder and more pleasant. Natives eat the pulp with sugar as a dessert. Colombia. BADILLO, NATIONAL RESEARCH COUNCIL 1989, VON REIS; N84, P38

Carica x heilbornii (C. pubescens x C. stipulata) - *Mountain papaya* {GR} Natural and artificial hybrids. The fruits are eaten raw or cooked. Usually produces parthenocarpic fruit. Andean South America. BADILLO.

CULTIVARS

Babaco: Fruits are bright-yellow, commonly 12 inches in length, 5-angled, with hollowed sides. The juicy flesh is distinctly fragrant and somewhat acid in flavor. The large cavity in the center contains a white cottony substance that is usually sweeter than the outside flesh. Eaten out of hand skin and all, stewed, added to salads, or made into *dulces*, preserves, cakes, puddings, and sauces. A small amount of sugar sprinkled over the fruit greatly improves the flavor. Sometimes available in specialty markets. BADILLO, ENDT [Pre, Re], NATIONAL RESEARCH COUNCIL 1989, POPENOE, W. 1924, UPHOF; C56M, G20, *G49*, I83M, I89, L6, *N40*{PR}, N84, *O97*, P38, *Q49M*

Lemon Creme: Medium-sized, cylindrical fruit; skin lemon yellow; flesh firm, refreshing, mildly sweet with a slight lemon-like flavor and aroma. Vigorous, compact plant, produces abundant crops; mostly self-fertile. Seedling cross of Toronchi. Originated in New Zealand. J23{OR}

Toronchi: Fruits are yellow, 4 to 6 inches long, very fragrant. The higher level of the papain enzyme in the Toronchi makes it less desirable as a fresh fruit. The best way to eat this one fresh is to blend it together with a banana as this seems to counteract the enzyme. To deactivate the enzyme altogether, boiling is the only way. It is useful in making sauces, jams, pie fillings, and pickles. ENDT [Pre, Re]; C56M, N84{S}, O93{S}, P38{S}, *Q49M*

Carica monoica - *Orange papaya, Peladera* {S} Small to very small fruits that have a high level of papain. Most can only be eaten in a cooked form, when they are said to resemble stewed apricots. The flesh is somewhat tough and is excellent for dried or candied fruit, and also freezes well. Used for hybridizing with other mountain papayas. Andean South America. BADILLO, ENDT [Pre, Re], NATIONAL RESEARCH COUNCIL 1989; N84, O93, *Q49M*{PL}

Carica papaya - *Papaya* {S} Ripe fruits are eaten out of hand, preserved, dried, candied, added to salads, or made into pies, jams, ice cream, juice, jellies, sherbets, etc. Unripe green fruits are boiled, pickled, added to mixed vegetable soups or used as an extender in soy *tempeh*. In Mexico, they are cooked in cane juice during raw sugar manufacture. The peppery seeds are used as a spice, especially in salad dressings. Leaves, inflorescences, and flowers are steamed and eaten with rice, or added to soups and stews. In Indonesia, the flowers are candied. Young stems are cooked and eaten. The pith of older ones is eaten raw. Tropical America, cultivated. ALCORN, GARNER [Pro], HAWKES [Re], MAY, R. [Nu, Re], MORTON 1987a, OCHSE, POPENOE, W. 1920 [Cu], RICHARDSON [Re], SCHNEIDER [Cul, Re], SHURTLEFF 1979, STURROCK, TANAKA, UPHOF; A79M, B59{PR}, B62, C9M, F68{PL}, F85, I28{PL}, J82, M20, N84, O53M, O93, P5, *P17M*, Q12, Q41, etc. (for cultivars see Papaya, page 410)

Carica parviflora - *Papaya de monte, Coral* {PL} The small, edible fruits are orange-colored, nearly red when ripe, and are said to have the fragrance and flavor of Spondias. Ecuador, Peru. BADILLO; *Q49M*

Carica pentagona → *Carica x heilbornii*

Carica pubescens - *Mountain papaya, Chihualcan* {S} The small, fragrant fruits are usually too acid for eating out of hand. They can be stewed, preserved, candied, or used in cakes, sauces, chutneys, cocktails, etc. When cooked, the fruit holds its shape and the juice remains clear. South America, cultivated. BADILLO, ENDT [Pre, Re], MACMILLAN, NATIONAL RESEARCH COUNCIL 1989, POPENOE, W. 1920, SIMMONS 1972, UPHOF; C56M{PL}, I28{PL}, I83M{PL}, N84, O89, O93, *Q49M*{PL}, R47

Carica quercifolia - *Higuera del monte* {S} The date-sized fruits, said to have a quite agreeable flavor, are eaten candied or made into preserves. Tropical South America. BADILLO, POPENOE, W. 1920, UPHOF, WILDER; F85, N84, O93

Carica stipulata - *Chamburro, Siglalón* {PL} The seedy fruits have a high papain content and are best eaten cooked and peeled. They are excellent for jams and sauces, and are also made into fruit drinks, normally in blends with other juices. Small, firm fruits can be frozen fresh. Tropical South America. BADILLO, ENDT [Pre, Re], NATIONAL RESEARCH COUNCIL 1989; O93{S}, *Q49M*

Jacaratia dodecaphylla → *Jacaratia spinosa*

Jacaratia mexicana - *Papaya orejona* {S} Fruits are eaten cooked, as a salad, or made into sweetmeats. Central America. BADILLO, UPHOF, WILLIAMS, L.; **X98**

Jacaratia spinosa - *Mamão, Mamao bravo* {S} The sweet fruit is eaten fresh, preserved in syrup, or prepared into compotes and sweetmeats. Brazil. BADILLO, TANAKA; P28

Pileus mexicanus → *Jacaratia mexicana*

CARYOCARACEAE

Caryocar nuciferum - *Souari nut, Butternut* {S} Large white kernels, having a rich, delicious, almond-like flavor, are eaten raw, roasted or cooked in salt water. They also yield an edible oil that is excellent for preparing meat, fish, and bakery products. The oily, yellow pulp of the fruit may be cooked and eaten as a vegetable. Brazil, Guiana. HEDRICK 1919, MACMILLAN, MENNINGER, ROSENGARTEN, UPHOF; **X79**

Caryocar villosum - *Pequiá, Arbre à beurre* {S} The fruit pulp is eaten, having a faint smell of rancid butter. Also the source of an edible oil. Seeds are edible. Guiana, Brazil. BURKILL, NATIONAL RESEARCH COUNCIL 1975a, PRANCE, SCHERY, VON REIS; **X88M**

CARYOPHYLLACEAE

Agrostemma githago - *Corn cockle* {S} Young leaves have been used as a vegetable with vinegar and bacon for emergency food during times of want. Eurasia. UPHOF; D62, F85, *N71M*, N84, O48, O53M, O89, P83M, Q34, S45M, S55

Arenaria peploides → *Honkenya peploides*

Dianthus barbatus - *Sweet William* {S} The flowers have a mild flavor and are used as a garnish for vegetable and fruit salads, cakes and other desserts, soups, cold drinks, icings and deviled eggs. Cultivated. A53M, F85, N84

Dianthus caryophyllus - *Clove pink, Carnation* {S} Flower petals smell strongly of cloves and are candied, used as a garnish in salads, for flavoring fruits, fruit salads, ice cream and vinegars, or as a substitute for roses in the making of syrup. The flowers can also be infused in wine or pickled in vinegar and mashed into a sauce for lamb. They should be removed from their calyx and have the bitter white bottom of the petals snipped off. Cultivated. GESSERT, MACNICOL [Cul, Re], MORTON 1976, PAINTER [Re]; A1M{PL}, C13M, C81M, C81M{PL}, E7M, E89M, F35M{PL}, I77, J82{PL}, M82{PL}, N45{PL}, N84, S7M

Dianthus plumarius - *Cottage pink* {S} Flower petals are made into butters, cordials, syrups, sauces, vinegars, etc. Cultivated. CLARKE [Re], GESSERT; B97M{PL}, D11T{PL}, D62, D92{PL}, E7M, E81M, F24, F35M{PL}, H79M{PL}, I77, K53, K66, L86, L91M, O53M, etc.

Dianthus superbus - *Fringed pink, Nadeshiko* {S} Leaves, stems, and tops are boiled and steeped in water, then eaten as a potherb, fried, oil-roasted, etc. Young plants are also eaten. Children suck the flower for its sweet nectar. Eastern Asia, cultivated. TANAKA; C40{PL}, E7M, H79M{PL}, K47T, K53, L66{PL}, L91M, N63M, *N71M*, N84, O53M, *Q24*, S7M

Honkenya peploides - *Seabeach sandwort, Sea chickweed* {S} Young leaves and stems are eaten raw as a salad or relish, or boiled and used as a potherb. The succulent stems can be made into pickles which are said to have a pleasant pungent taste. In Iceland, the plant is steeped in sour whey and allowed to ferment. The resulting liquor is said to taste like olive oil and is used as a beverage. Northern temperate region. FERNALD, HEDRICK 1919, HELLER, UPHOF; D62, O48

Paronychia argentea - *Thé Arabe, Algerian tea* {S} An infusion of the flowers is used as a tea. Mediterranean region. HUTCHINSON, UPHOF; I63M{PL}, K47T, N84

Paronychia capitata - *Thé Arabe, Algerian tea* {S} Flowers are used as a substitute for tea. Mediterranean region. HUTCHINSON; **Z25M**

Paronychia jamesii - *James whitkow-wort* {PL} The herb is used by the Kiowa Indians for the preparation of a tea. Western North America. UPHOF; I63M

Petrorhagia prolifera - *Little leaf tunic flowers* {S} Flowers are sometimes used as a tea. Mediterranean region. UPHOF; B9M{PL}, D62, N84, *Q24*, S7M

Silene acaulis - *Moss campion* {S} It has been reported that boiled parts of the plant with butter are consumed as a vegetable among the Icelanders. Arctic and Alpine regions. FERNALD, KIRK, UPHOF; C40{PL}, D11T{PL}, D62, H98{PL}, J37M{PL}, J93T, K47T, K79{PL}, L13, L66{PL}, L91M, N7, N84, O48, O53M, *Q24*, S7M, etc.

Silene cucubalis → *Silene vulgaris*

Silene vulgaris - *Bladder campion* {S} The young shoots when about two inches long are a palatable cooked green, having a flavor suggestive of green peas, but with a slight bitter taste. Blanching the new shoots as they emerge from the ground will reduce bitterness. A purée made from the boiled shoots is said to be nearly equal to the best purée of spinach. The leaves can be chopped and added to salads or used in soups, stews, and sauces. Eurasia, naturalized in North America. CROWHURST 1972, FERNALD, GIBBONS 1979, HEDRICK 1919, LAUNERT; D62, E63M{PL}, F80, H61M, J67M, *N71M*, N84, O48, O53M, *Q24*, S7M, S55

Stellaria media - *Chickweed* {S} The tender, juicy leaves and stems are added to tossed green salads and sandwiches, or they can be boiled and eaten like spinach. Natural foods enthusiasts liquify chickweed, along with other assorted greens, to make what they call *green drink*. Indians used the tiny seeds for bread or to thicken soup. Young seedlings can be cut with scissors and left to regrow. Flowering tops are used as a vegetable or garnish. Northern temperate region. CLARKE [Re], CRIBB, FERNALD, GIBBONS 1966b, HARRINGTON, H., LARKCOM 1984, LEGGATT [Re], MABEY, MICHAEL [Re]; A2, F24, F80, F85, K20, L86, *N71M*, N84, O48, P1G, R47

Tunica prolifera* → *Petrorhagia prolifera

Vaccaria pyramidata - *Cockle* {S} Said to be used as a condiment. Eurasia. KUNKEL; C61M

CECROPIACEAE

Cecropia palmata - *Trumpet tree, Snakewood tree* {S} The ripe fruits have the consistency and somewhat the flavor of figs. They are eaten fresh or used as a filling for cakes. Young buds are eaten as potherbs. West Indies, Northern South America. KUNKEL, MOWRY, RICHARDSON [Re]; N84

Cecropia peltata - *Indian snakewood, Trumpet tree* {S} Young buds are eaten as a potherb. Tropical America. HEDRICK 1919; F85, N84, P38

Myrianthus arboreus - *Monkeyfruit* {S} The large, yellow fruit has numerous four or five-sided sections that release a flavorful juice when bitten into. The juice can be either sweet or sour, depending on the tree. Young shoots and leaves are eaten in soups. Tropical Africa. DALZIEL, TANAKA; N84

Pourouma cecropiaefolia - *Amazon grape, Uvilla* {S} Fruits are purple, grape-like, up to an inch and a half in diameter, with a large pit and a sweet, juicy white pulp. They are consumed out of hand and are also made into wine. A relatively fast grower, it begins to fruit in three years. The tree is recommended for testing as a home-garden crop throughout the humid tropics. Western Amazon. MORTON 1987a, NATIONAL RESEARCH COUNCIL 1975a; **T73M**

CELASTRACEAE

Cassine aethiopica - *Cape cherry* {S} The sweet, cherry-like fruits are eaten. Tropical Africa. FOX, F., HEDRICK 1919, TANAKA; F85

Cassine schlechteri* → *Cassine aethiopica

Catha edulis - *Khat, Arabian tea, Abyssinian tea* {S} Dried leaves are occasionally used in the preparation of a tea, much esteemed in Arabia and adjacent territories. More commonly, the fresh leaves and tender shoots are chewed to produce a stimulating effect not unlike amphetamines or several cups of strong black coffee. In Ethiopia, the leaves form an ingredient of *tej*, a honey wine or *mead*. Drier Africa to Arabia. FOX, F., HEDRICK 1919, MACMILLAN, SCHERY, UPHOF, VARISCO; A79M, B7, C13M, C43M{PL}, F85, G96{PL}, L29{PL}, M82{PL}, N84, P38

Celastrus paniculatus - *Shrubby bittersweet, Memory improver* {S} Young flowers are used as a vegetable. India. KUNKEL; F85, N84

Elaeodendron orientale - *Olive wood, Let-pet-ben* {S} Leaves are used by the natives as a substitute for tea. Tropical Asia. HEDRICK 1919; F85

Elaeodendron sphaerophyllum* → *Cassine aethiopica

Euonymus europeus - *Spindle tree* {S} Fruits and seeds are the source of a yellow dye used for coloring butter. Also reported to be the source of an edible manna. Eurasia. DONKIN, UPHOF; C9{PL}, G41{PL}, *G66*, *G89M*{PL}, J7{PL}, K38, K47T, L91M, *N71M*, N93M, O53M, O93, P49, *R28*, R78, etc.

Euonymus japonicus - *Japanese spindle tree, Masaki* {S} Young leaves are eaten. Older ones are powdered and used for coloring other foods. Japan, cultivated. HEDRICK 1919, TANAKA; *B41*{PL}, *F53M*{PL}, F85, *I62*{PL}, N84, N93M, P49, *P63*, P86{PL}, Q40, *R28*, R78

Maytenus boaria - *Mayten tree* {S} The seeds are the source of a cooking oil. Chile, Argentina. CORREA; C9M, C56M{PL}, *H71*, *I61*, *I62*{PL}, I83M{PL}, *K46*{PL}, N84, O93, P86{PL}

CELTIDACEAE

Celtis australis - *European hackberry, Lotus berry* {S} The small, insipidly sweet, cherry-like fruits are eaten raw or made into wine. Sometimes sold in markets of the Balkans. Said to have been the lotus fruit of the ancient Lotophagi or Lotus eaters. Mediterranean region. DARBY, HEDRICK 1919, SIMMONS 1972, UPHOF, WATT; C9M, F80, *H71*, *I62*{PL}, *I68*{PL}, K47T, N37M{PL}, N93M, O53M, O93, P5, P49, Q40, Q46, R78, etc.

Celtis laevigata - *Southern hackberry* {PL} The orange-red fruits, although sweet and edible, are generally small with very little pulp. North America. HENDRICKSON, MEDSGER, SIMMONS 1972; F85{S}, I53, *J25*, *L5M*

Celtis mississippiensis* → *Celtis laevigata

Celtis occidentalis - *Hackberry, Sugarberry* {PL} The small, cherry-like fruits are very sweet and pleasant to the taste. They are eaten out of hand or can be used to make jellies and jams. The Indians ate the pounded fruits with parched corn and fat, or used them as a flavoring for meat. North America. FREITUS [Re], GIBBONS 1979, HENDRICKSON, MEDSGER, YANOVSKY; B9M, C9M{S}, *C33*, D45, D95, *F51*, G41, *G66*{S}, H49, I9M, I47{S}, K38{S}, *M69M*, *N71M*{S}, N93M{S}, O53M{S}, etc.

Celtis pallida* → *Celtis spinosa

Celtis reticulata - *Western hackberry, Palo blanco* {S} The sweet, fleshy berries are eaten raw, made into jelly and cakes or used as a seasoning for meat. Western North America. KINDSCHER, MEDSGER, YANOVSKY; B83M, B94, D95{PL}, F85, G60{PL}, I47, K47T, N84

Celtis sinensis - *Chinese hackberry* {S} Leaves are eaten boiled, or used as a substitute for tea. Ripe fruits are also eaten. Eastern Asia. TANAKA; C9M, F85, *H71*, *I61*, *I62*{PL}, *L47*{PL}, N84, O53M, O93, P49, *R28*, R78

Celtis spinosa - *Spiny hackberry, Granjeno* {S} The small, sweetish fruits are eaten raw, or may be ground, seed and all, into flour. A hot tea is made from the bark. Papago Indians still consider the fruit a good food source. Southwestern North America. KIRK, LATORRE 1977b; B83M, N51{PL}

Celtis tournefortii - *Tawax* {S} The small fruits are eaten. Western Asia. TANAKA; N84, *P63*

CEPHALOTAXACEAE

Cephalotaxus drupacea → Cephalotaxus harringtonia

Cephalotaxus harringtonia - *Japanese plum-yew, Inu-gaya* {S} The female plant bears a fleshy fruit that is thick, juicy, and remarkably sweet, with a faint suggestion of the pine in its flavor. Eastern Asia. HEDRICK 1919; D95{PL}, K38, K47T, N37M{PL}, N51{PL}, N84, N93M, O53M, O93, P49, *P63*, *R28*, R78

CHENOPODIACEAE

Ambrosinia mexicana → Chenopodium botrys

Atriplex canescens - *Fourwing saltbush, Chamisa* {S} The seeds may be ground into a meal, mixed with water, and drunk as a refreshing beverage, or mixed with some other meal and used as flour. The leaves and young shoots have a distinct salty taste and can be used as greens. When burned the green herb yields culinary ashes high in mineral content, which are used by Hopi cooks to enhance the color in blue corn products. Southwestern North America. KAVENA [Pre, Re], KIRK, UPHOF; C9M, *E53*, F12, F79M, G60{PL}, *G66*, I47, J25M, J25M{PL}, J26{PL}, N37M{PL}, N84, O53M, P5, *R28*, R33M, etc.

Atriplex confertifolia - *Shadscale* {S} Seeds are ground into a meal that is used for bread and mush. Water in which the leaves are boiled is used for corn pudding. Southwestern North America. YANOVSKY; C4, C98, *E53*, *E66M*, I47, K15, K47T, K62, *N79M*, N84, O93

Atriplex halimus - *Sea orache, Sea purslane* {S} Young leaves and tips of branches are eaten raw in salads or used in soups, casseroles, pastas, quiches, and vegetable dishes. Also the source of an edible manna. Mediterranean region, Southwest Asia. BRACKETT [Re], DONKIN, KUNKEL; *N79M*, N84, O93, P5, *P17M*, *P63*, P86{PL}, *Q15G*, Q76{PL}, *R28*, S92, S95

Atriplex hastata - *Hastate orache* {S} The leaves are used as a spinach substitute. They are somewhat bland and are best mixed with stronger flavored greens, such as Portulaca, Lepidium, or Alliaria. Their natural salt content blends well with a little lemon juice. Seeds can be ground into a flour. Northern temperate region. CLARKE, LAUNERT; **U4, V87, Y17M**

Atriplex hortensis - *Orach, Mountain spinach, Butter leaves* {S} Young leaves are used as a warm weather spinach substitute. Traditionally, they are mixed with sorrel leaves to modify the acidity of the latter. Also used in soups, stews, pastas, quiches, and crepes. Seeds are used in soups and muffins. Eurasia, cultivated. HALPIN, HEDRICK 1919, KRAFT [Re], KUNKEL, VILMORIN [Cu]; A2, C13M, C53, E24, F24, F35M{PL}, I39, I77, I99, J20, J82, K49M, K66, L86, O48, etc.

CULTIVARS

Chakwat: An improved cultivar from northern India with dark green leaves. Both the leaves and plant size are slightly smaller than Yellow orach. E83T

Magenta Purple: Very attractive deep-purple orach with excellent flavor. Grows 2 to 3 feet tall. K49T

Red: (Purple, Rubra) Both stems and leaves are a dark-red color, giving the whole plant an attractive appearance. Popular as a garnish in the restaurant trade. Usually turns green when cooked, it is claimed that some clones retain their color. A2, C11, C13M, C53, E7M, E24, F35M{PL}, F80, G92, I77, I99, J20, K17M, K49M, M82{PL}, O48, S55, etc.

Yellow: (Golden, White, Blonde, Belle Dame) Leaves are very pale green, almost yellow. The most widely grown cultivar in France, considered to be the sweetest and most tender type for use as a boiled or steamed vegetable. C53, E24, E83T, F80, K66, O48, P59M, S55

Atriplex patula - *Halberd-leaved saltbush, Spearscale* {S} Young plants, or tender growing tips of older plants, are very good eaten raw in salads or cooked and served like spinach. Zuni Indians mix the ground seeds with black Indian corn to make round meal-balls which are steamed on a rack over boiling water. Northern temperate region. FERNALD, GIBBONS 1979, HARRINGTON, H.; D58, G47M{PL}, *N71M*, N84, O48

Atriplex patula ssp. hastata → Atriplex hastata

Atriplex semibaccata - *Australian saltbush* {S} The red berries are eaten as tasty snacks or they are added to salads. The flavor is said to be reminiscent of tomatoes. Australia, naturalized in North America. CLARKE; C9M, *E66M*, F79M, *H64T*, *J0*, K15, *N79M*, N84, O93, P5, *P17M*, R15M, R33M

Axyris amaranthoides - *Inu-hôkigi* {S} Young plants and young leaves are eaten as potherbs. China. TANAKA; **V89, Y10, Y17M, Z24**

Beta vulgaris ssp. maritima - *Wild sea beet, Sea spinach* {S} Young, tender leaves are eaten in salads. Older ones are boiled or steamed and used as a spinach substitute. The flavor is considered to be superior to the cultivated beets and chards. Mediterranean region, Atlantic Coast of Europe. MABEY, MICHAEL [Re]; N84, O48

Beta vulgaris Cicla Group - *Swiss chard, Spinach beet, Seakale beet, Indian spinach* Leaves are used as a hot weather substitute for spinach. Leaf stalks of chard are usually cut from the leaf and cooked separately as an asparagus substitute. One popular way is to braise them and serve with buttered breadcrumbs. Some cultivars of chard have edible roots. BRYAN [Cu, Re], FELL 1982b, SCHNEIDER [Cul, Re]; (for cultivars see Swiss Chard, page 510)

Beta vulgaris Crassa Group - *Beet, Sugar beet, Mangel wurzel* {S} Young leaves can be used in salads, either raw or lightly cooked. Older leaves are sometimes used as a spinach substitute. Roots are eaten cooked, pickled, made into *borscht*, or grated and used raw in salads. Cooked roots are also added to salads when cold. Fermented beet root juice is sold under the brand names *Biotta* and *Eden*. Sugar beets are a source of sugar, syrup and molasses. CARCIONE [Pre], HUNTER 1973a, LARKCOM 1984; K49M, O48 (for cultivars see Beet, page 262)

Chenopodium album - *Lamb's quarters, White goosefoot, Fat hen* {S} Leaves and young stem tips, while still tender, make a very acceptable spinach substitute. They are particularly good when mixed with dock greens (Rumex spp.). Seeds are ground into a flour used in breads, pancakes, muffins, and biscuits. Young inflorescences are cooked and eaten. Sprouted seeds are edible. Eurasia, naturalized in North America. FERNALD, GIBBONS 1962, GIBBONS 1979, MICHAEL [Re]; A1M, A2, C11, C13M, C43M, D58, F80, F85, I99, J82, K22, K47T, *N71M*, N84, O48, etc.

CULTIVARS

Magenta: A distinct strain developed by Oak and Stone of Covelo, California which supplies the San Francisco restaurant trade. Leaves are an attractive, fluorescent magenta. Considered by the developers to be one of the best tasting of all potherbs. B49

Chenopodium album ssp. amaranticolor - *Anserine amarante* {S} Leaves are used as a spinach substitute. An attractive foliage plant suitable for edible landscaping. Has brilliant color when young - upper leaves are violet-red, the stem is striped red, and flowers are produced in long red panicles. Eurasia. TANAKA; N84

Chenopodium amaranticolor → Chenopodium album ssp. amaranticolor

Chenopodium ambrosioides - *Epasote, Mexican tea* {S} The herb is used to flavor corn, black beans, mushrooms, fish, soups, stews, chili sauces, shellfish, and freshwater snails. An infusion of the leaves is used as a tea substitute. Tender leaves are sometimes used as a potherb. Cooking the leaves with beans is said to reduce flatulence. Mexico, naturalized in North America. DUKE, HUTSON [Re], LATORRE 1977a [Re], MORTON 1976, PAINTER, WILLIAMS, L.; C11, C13M, C43M, D29{PL}, D87, E5M{PR}, F24, G84{PL}, H40{PL}, I16{PR}, J25M, J73, K22{PL}, L67, L67{PR}, etc.

Chenopodium berlandieri - *Southern huauzontle, Bledo extranjero* {S} Leaves are fried in butter with onion and used like spinach. Young leaves and tender shoots are sometimes used in salads. Seeds are the source of a meal used for bread or gruel. Southwestern North America. HARRINGTON, H., HUGHES [Re], KINDSCHER, TANAKA; I99

Chenopodium bonus-henricus - *Good King Henry, Mercury, Allgood* {S} The young leaves are eaten as a potherb, either alone or mixed with other greens like cabbage, chard, or spinach. Young shoots are cut under the ground like asparagus, peeled, and used as a substitute for that vegetable, called *Lincolnshire asparagus*. Tender flower clusters are eaten, considered by some to be the best part. Eurasia, cultivated. HALPIN [Cul], HEDRICK 1919, ORGAN, PAINTER [Re], VILMORIN [Cu]; B49, C11, C13M, C67M{PL}, C81M{PL}, D62, E61{PL}, F24, F35M{PL}, I39, K22, K22{PL}, *N71M*, N84, O53M, etc.

Chenopodium botrys - *Jerusalem oak, Feather geranium, Ambrosia* {S} Leaves are sometimes used as a potherb. Also used as a tea substitute. Northern temperate region. FERNALD, TANAKA; A2, C13M, C16, C43M, C81M, C81M{PL}, D29{PL}, E81M, F37T{PL}, G84, H3M, I99, J20, K85{PL}, M15T{PL}, M82{PL}, O53M, etc.

CULTIVARS

Green Magic: 31 days. Vigorous plant with oak-leaf shaped leaves; taller than the type. Relatively strong scented. Delicious, nutty flavor. Developed in The Netherlands. E24, N84

Chenopodium capitatum - *Strawberry blite, Strawberry spinach, Beetberry* {S} The young leaves and tender shoots are used raw in salads or cooked like spinach. Succulent fruits may be added to a tossed salad, or eaten boiled and seasoned. They can also be used as a red dye for other foods. Northern temperate region. FERNALD, GIBBONS 1979, HARRINGTON, H., HELLER; A76, E83T, F80, K49M, M82, M82{PL}

Chenopodium ficifolium - *Ko-akaza* {S} Young plants and flower buds are eaten in soups, vegetable dishes, fried, oil-roasted, or parboiled and used as a potherb. Older leaves are similarly used. Roasted seeds are used like sesame to flavor other foods. Eurasia. TANAKA; N84

Chenopodium foliosum* → *Chenopodium capitatum

Chenopodium giganteum - *Tree spinach* {S} The leaves are used as a potherb. Eurasia. KUNKEL; N84

CULTIVARS

Magentaspreen: (Magentaspreen Lamb's Quarters) Vigorous plant, to 5 feet tall; large leaves, new growth is a brilliant magenta color. Sow spring into early summer. Tastiest eaten young, raw or cooked as spinach. C43M, F42, I99, K49T

Chenopodium glaucum - *Glaucous goosefoot* {S} Young leaves and tender stem tips are used as a spinach substitute. Eurasia. FOX, F., TANAKA; D62

Chenopodium murale - *Australian spinach, Sowbane, Salt greens* {S} Leaves are eaten as a potherb or used in the preparation of sauces. Parched and ground seeds are consumed. Eurasia. CRIBB, FOX, F., WATT, YANOVSKY; I16

Chenopodium nuttaliae - *Huauzontle* {S} Flower clusters are steamed like broccoli, or mixed with cheese, dipped in egg batter, and fried. They are a menu item at some of the finer Mexican restaurants. Young leaves are used as a mild flavored spinach substitute. Seeds are eaten or ground into a flour. Southwestern North America to Central America. NATIONAL RESEARCH COUNCIL 1975a, WILSON, H.; J73

Chenopodium pallidicaule - *Cañihua, Kaniwa* {S} The small seed is toasted and ground into a nutty-tasting flour that is mixed with sugar and milk and eaten as a breakfast cereal. Cañihua flour or *cañihuaco* is also made into small cookies (*quispiño*), is used with wheat flour in breads, cakes and puddings, and is made into a hot beverage similar to hot chocolate. Andean South America, cultivated. GADE 1970, NATIONAL RESEARCH COUNCIL 1989, SIMMONDS 1965; D33, I99

Chenopodium quinoa - *Quinoa, Petty rice* {S} The nutritious seeds are used in soups, stews, breads, biscuits, cakes, cereals and pasta, or made into *tempeh* and *chicha*. Young leaves can be used like spinach. Sprouted seeds are eaten in salads. An alkaline ash from the burned stems is chewed with coca leaf. Andean South America, cultivated. NATIONAL RESEARCH COUNCIL 1989, SIMMONDS 1965, STEINKRAUS, WOOD, R. [Pre, Re]; D62, E31{PR}, F86M{PR}, G92, H91{PR}, I43T{PR}, J25M, J56{PR}, J82, K49M, M63M{PR}, N84, Q34 (for cultivars see Quinoa, page 460, also see Sprouting Seeds, page 485)

Chenopodium rubrum - *Red goosefoot* {S} Young leaves may be eaten raw, boiled as a potherb, or used in soups and stews. Seeds are ground into a flour. Eurasia. MICHAEL [Re], YANOVSKY; D62, K47T, N84

Chenopodium urbicum - *Upright goosefoot, City goosefoot* {S} Young leaves are used as a spinach substitute. Northern temperate region. MEDSGER; N84

Enchylaena tomentosa - *Barrier saltbush, Ruby saltbush* {S} Young leaves can be used as a green vegetable. Red berry-like fruits are sweet and succulent. Australia. CRIBB; N84, O53M, T7

Halimione portulacoides - *Sea purslane* {S} Leaves are eaten raw in salads or cooked as a potherb. They are thick and succulent, and have a good crunchy texture and natural saltiness. Mediterranean region, Eurasia. KUNKEL, LARKCOM 1984, MABEY, MICHAEL [Pre, Re]; **Y10**

Spinacia oleracea - *Spinach, Epinard, Hôren-sô* Leaves are eaten raw in salads, steamed, sautéed, puréed, used in soups, pastas, omelettes, soufflés, chiches, etc. Sprouted seeds are used in salads. Eurasia, cultivated. HEDRICK 1919, VILMORIN; (for cultivars see Spinach, page 483)

Suaeda maritima - *Sea blite* {S} Leaves and tender growing tips are eaten as a cooked vegetable after some of the saltiness has been removed. Or the salty leaves can be added to other foods to season them. Young shoots are pickled in vinegar and eaten alone or used as a relish. Widespread. CRIBB [Pre], GIBBONS 1964 [Pre, Cul], GIBBONS 1979; D62

CHLORANTHACEAE

Chloranthus brachystachys* → *Sarcandra glabra

Hedyosmum mexicanum - *Té azteco, Vara blanca* {S} Mature fruits are whitish, succulent, sweet and edible. A substitute for tea can be made by placing two or three leaves in a cup of hot water. Leaves are used to flavor contraband liquor in Colombia. Tropical America. DUKE, WILLIAMS, L.; **X94**

Sarcandra glabra - *Tea scent, Senryô* {S} Seeds are dried, roasted and used as a substitute for sesame seeds. Leaves are used for scenting tea. Indomalaya, cultivated. MARTIN 1975, TANAKA; F85

CHRYSOBALANACEAE

Chrysobalanus icaco - *Coco plum, Icaco plum* {S} Fruits are eaten raw, stewed with sugar, dried like prunes, or made into jams and jelly. In Cuba, the wild fruit is gathered and made into a sweet preserve, which is served in Havana restaurants as a *sobremesa* or dessert. Seed kernels are roasted and eaten. In preserving the fruits, they are pierced right through the seed which permits the syrup to penetrate, and after separation from the shell, the nut-like kernel is eaten with the fruits. Tropical America, cultivated. HEDRICK 1919, JOHNS [Cul], MENNINGER, MORTON 1977, POPENOE, W. 1920, STURROCK; D87G{PL}, E29, E29{PL}, E29{PR}, *J25*{PL}, *L5M*, N84, P38

CULTIVARS

__Butt:__ Largest of all coco plums. Grown for its large seeds. Quality of fruit only fair. Introduced into Florida from Costa Rica. WHITMAN; **T73M**

Couepia polyandra - *Olosapo, Zapote bolo, Zapotillo amarillo* {PL} The fruit is two to three inches long with juicy, yellow pulp, sweet and quite good but fibrous. Not popular enough to be sold at local markets. Central America. UPHOF, WILLIAMS, L.; E29

Licania platypus - *Sansapote, Monkey apple* {S} The fruit has deep yellow fibrous flesh that is sweet and juicy, and an odor that is similar to pumpkin pie. Often sold in markets but not universally appreciated since it is thought to be unwholesome. Tropical America. MORTON 1987a, TANAKA, UPHOF, WILLIAMS, L.; **T73M**

Parinari capensis - *Dwarf mobolo, Sand apple* {S} The sweet outer flesh of the fruit, although somewhat dry and astringent, is eaten. It has a strong characteristic flavor, and is buried in the sand for some time before it is considered fit to eat. It can also be dried and eaten as a soft cake. In Botswana, it is used for making beer. Juice of the fruit can be drunk fresh or boiled to the consistency of a liquid porridge or gruel. Crushed kernels are eaten as a relish with meat. Southern Africa. FOX, F.; N84

CISTACEAE

Cistus albidus - {S} Leaves are used among the Arabs of Algeria as a tea. Dried leaves are often used to adulterate marjoram. Mediterranean region. BROUK, UPHOF; N37M{PL}, N84, O93, *P63*, Q76{PL}, S7M, S95

Cistus creticus - *Cretan labdanum* {PL} Said to be used as a condiment. Eastern Mediterranean region. KUNKEL; Q76

Cistus ladanifer - *Labdanum, Spanish manna* {S} Source of a fragrant, balsam-like resin that is sometimes eaten. In the food industry, it is employed for flavoring baked goods, soft drinks, ice cream, candy, and chewing gum. The seeds are ground into flour and used for making cakes and breads. Also yields a sweet manna. Mediterranean region. DONKIN, HEDRICK 1919, KUNKEL, MORTON 1976; B92{PL}, C11, *F53M*{PL}, F80, *G66*, *H71*, I39, *I62*{PL}, I99, *J0*, K15, L91M, M82{PL}, O93, *Q32*, etc.

Cistus salviifolius - *Rock rose* {S} Dried leaves are used as an adulterant of marjoram. Mediterranean region. BROUK; B92{PL}, F80, *H71*, K15, K47T, N37M{PL}, N93M, O53M, O93, P5, *P17M*, *P63*, *Q15G*, *Q32*, S7M, etc.

Cistus villosus - *Shaggy rock-rose* {S} The plant is used in Greece as a substitute for tea. Also said to be used as a condiment. Mediterranean region. HEDRICK 1919, KUNKEL; C9M, E7M, *H71*, *I61*, K15, K47T, N84, O93, *P17M*, *Q15G*

CLEOMACEAE

Cleome gynandra → *Gynandropsis gynandra*

Cleome icosandra → *Cleome viscosa*

Cleome integrifolia - *Rocky Mountain beeplant* {S} Young shoots, leaves, and flowers are boiled and eaten as potherbs. Plants were gathered by the Tewa Indians of New Mexico and after removing the alkaline taste, were eaten with cornmeal porridge. The seeds were sometimes ground into a meal for gruel or bread. Seedpods can be boiled and eaten. North America. GIBBONS 1979, HARRINGTON, H., KINDSCHER, UPHOF, YANOVSKY; F59, F80, J25M, J93T, L13, L91M

Cleome monophylla - *Rusperbossie, Sekalerothane* {S} Leaves are boiled or steamed and used as a substitute for spinach. Young shoots and flowers are similarly used. The pungent seeds are used as a substitute for mustard. Tropical Africa, Southern Asia. FOX, F., QUIN, VON REIS; N84

Cleome serrulata → *Cleome integrifolia*

Cleome viscosa - *Spider flower* {S} Young shoots and leaves, having a sharp, mustard-like flavor, are eaten boiled with chilis and salt. The pungent seeds are used as a substitute for mustard in curries. Pods are made into pickles. The juice is used as a condiment. Tropics. BURKILL, HEDRICK 1919, TANAKA, UPHOF, WATT; F80, F85, N84, O53M, R15M, T7

Gynandropsis gynandra - *Cat's whiskers, Spiderherb, Mamang* {S} Leaves are eaten as a potherb, added to soups and stews, or used to flavor sauces. The pungent seeds are used as a substitute for mustard. They also yield an edible oil. In Thailand, the leaves are mixed with salt and sugar and fermented into a pickle-like product, called *pak-sian-dong*. Flowers are also eaten. Tropics, Subtropics. FOX, F., HEDRICK 1919, OCHSE, STEINKRAUS, UPHOF; F85, J73, N84

Gynandropsis pentaphylla → *Gynandropsis gynandra*

Isomeris arborea - *Bladderpod* {S} Green pods are eaten cooked by the Cahuilla Indians. Southwestern North America. UPHOF, YANOVSKY; B94, D95{PL}, F85, G59M, G60{PL}, I98M, K15, N84

CLUSIACEAE (*GUTTIFERAE*)

Calophyllum inophyllum - *Alexandrian laurel, Kamani* {S} Ripe fruits and seeds are edible. Unripe fruits are pickled. Oil from the seeds is used to scent coconut oil. Tropics. ALTSCHUL, GIBBONS 1967, TANAKA; F85, P5, Q46

Garcinia benthami - *Bentham mangosteen, Bunag* {S} Small, obpyriform fruits that are eaten out of hand, having acid white pulp of an agreeable flavor. Malaysia. UPHOF; F85

Garcinia cochinchinensis - *Búa nhà* {S} The fruit is the size of a plum, reddish-yellow, with a juicy, pleasantly acid pulp. Cut in slices, it is eaten raw or used as a flavoring in place of vinegar. The leaves are used as a condiment in fish dishes. Indochina. HEDRICK 1919, TANAKA; **X88M**

Garcinia dulcis - *Sweet garcinia, Taklang-anak, Moendoe* {S} Despite the specific epithet, the fruits are usually sour. They can be eaten fresh, but are mostly used in preserves, jams, drinks, candied, or dried. Indonesia to the Philippines. RIFAI, TANAKA; F85{OR}

Garcinia hombroniana - *Bruas, Mangis hutan* {S} Fruits are eaten raw or in preserves, being of fine quality. The juicy, melting white pulp has a subacid flavor reminiscent of the peach. Has been recommended for improvement by selection and hybridization with other species. Malaysia. BURKILL, TANAKA, UPHOF; O19, O19{PL}

Garcinia livingstonei - *Imbé, African mangosteen* {PL} Ripe fruit is the size of a small plum, orange-red, with a thin layer of sweet, acidulous flesh of very pleasant taste. The highly colored pulp is used in the preparation of a purplish, claret-like wine. Tropical Africa, cultivated. KENNARD, MOWRY, UPHOF; E29, E29{PR}, E29{S}, F68, J36, N84{S}

Garcinia mangostana - *Mangosteen* {S} One of the best tasting tropical fruits, often called the "queen of fruits". The white pulp is aromatic, juicy, with a texture so soft it almost melts in the mouth, and a sweet, delicate flavor. Usually eaten out of hand, but also made into desserts or cooked with rice or syrup. Seeds are occasionally eaten after boiling or roasting. Indonesia, cultivated. ALMEYDA 1976a [Cu, Pro], GARNER [Pro], MORTON 1987a, POPENOE, W. 1920 [Cu], UPHOF; F85, J22{PL}, N84, O93, P38, *Q93*{PL}, R59

Garcinia morella - *Indian gamboge tree, Tamal* {S} The small, yellow fruit is eaten, being esteemed as a dessert fruit. Seeds yield a yellow fat used in cooking and confectionery, and also as a substitute for *ghee*. Source of *gamboge*, a gum-resin sometimes used in food. Indochina. HEDRICK 1919, TANAKA, UPHOF, WATT; F85

Garcinia pictorius - *Cochin gorka* {S} The yellow, juicy fruits have a pleasantly acid flavor and can be eaten raw. Also used for jams and preserves. Southeast Asia. MACMILLAN, TANAKA; E29, E29{PL}, E29{PR}, F85, N84, P38

Garcinia prainiana - *Cherapu* {S} The roundish fruit is smooth, yellow in color, and has an acid edible pericarp and a subacid pulp. It is eaten like the mangosteen. Malaysia. TANAKA, UPHOF; **W54**

Garcinia venulosa - *Gatásan* {S} The fruit is oblate, about 2 inches in diameter, smooth, greenish in color and has agreeably acid pulp. In the Philippines, it is usually eaten with fish. Southeast Asia, Philippines. BROWN, W., TANAKA; F85

Garcinia xanthochymus → *Garcinia pictorius*

Garcinia sp. - *Kundong, Cherry mangosteen* {S} Small, mangosteen-like fruit, 1 to 1 1/2 inches long; flesh white, melting, subacid, with a good juicy flavor that is thirst-quenching and refreshing. Small, slow-growing tree, outgrows mangosteen during the second year of its growth. Borneo. O19, O19{PL}

Mammea africana - *African mammee apple* {S} Seeds are consumed as food in some parts of Africa. The fruit is also edible. Tropical Africa. DALZIEL, UPHOF; N84

Mammea americana - *Mammee apple, Mamey de Santo Domingo, Abricó do Pará* {PL} The ripe fruit is eaten out of hand, with wine, with sugar and cream, or made into sauces, pies, tarts and jams. Preserves made from the pulp taste remarkably like apricot preserves. Mature green fruits are high in pectin and make an excellent jelly when combined with high-acid fruits that are low in pectin, like the pineapple. From the fragrant white flowers a liqueur is distilled, which is known as *eau de créole*, or *crême de créole*. In Brazil, fermented *toddy* is made from the sap of the tree. Caribbean region, cultivated. JOHNS [Cul], MORTON 1987a, POPENOE, W. 1920, STURROCK; F85{S}, J36, S97M

Mesua ferrea - *Ironwood, Nag champa, Indian rose chestnut* {S} Young leaves, having a sourish, astringent flavor, can be eaten raw. If well cooked, the oily seeds are edible. The fruit is reddish and wrinkled when ripe. It resembles a chestnut in size, shape, and taste. Tropical Asia. HEDRICK 1919, PONGPANGAN, TANAKA, ZEVEN; F85, N84, P5, Q12, Q18

Ochrocarpus africana → *Mammea africana*

Pentadesma butyracea - *Owala oil tree, Butter tree* {S} Seeds are the source of a pale yellow edible fat, known as *Sierra Leone butter*, used for cooking and in the manufacture of margarine. When young they are edible, but become sour or bitter when old and are then occasionally used as a substitute for cola nuts. West Tropical Africa. BURKILL, DALZIEL, IRVINE 1960, UPHOF; N84

Rheedia acuminata - *Madroño* {PL} The fruits have a translucent whitish pulp that is juicy, slightly aromatic, and pleasantly subacid. They can be eaten out of hand or used in jams, preserves and drinks. Tropical America. KENNARD, MORTON 1987a, POPENOE, W. 1924, UPHOF; E29, E29{PR}, E29{S}

Rheedia brasiliensis - *Bacuparí* {S} The aril-like, translucent white pulp of the fruits is subacid, with an excellent flavor suggesting that of the mangosteen. They are highly prized eaten out of hand, or especially when made into a *doce* or jam. Brazil. MORTON 1987a, POPENOE, W. 1920; **T73M, X88M**

Rheedia longifolia - *Charichuelo* {S} The yellow fruit is eaten fresh or used for preserves. Peru. VON REIS; **X88M**

Rheedia macrophylla - *Bacury-pary, Bacuripari* {PL} A medium sized fruit with firm yellow rind and soft, white subacid flesh that is agreeable eaten fresh or made into jam. Panama to Brazil. MORTON 1987a, POPENOE, W. 1920, UPHOF; E29, E29{PR}, E29{S}

Rheedia madruno → *Rheedia acuminata*

COCHLOSPERMACEAE

Cochlospermum religiosum - *Silk cotton tree* {S} The oil-cakes from the pressed seeds may be eaten. Source of an insoluble gum used as a substitute for tragacanth in ice-cream making. Tropical Asia. BURKILL, TANAKA, UPHOF; F85, N84

COMBRETACEAE

Anogeissus latifolia - *Ghatti tree* {S} Source of *ghatti gum* or *India gum*, an exudation of the stem that is used in sweetmeats. Also used in the food industry as an emulsifier. Southern Asia. BROUK, SCHERY, UPHOF; F85, Q46

Anogeissus leiocarpus - *Savannah tree* {S} Source of an insoluble gum, eaten in Kordofan. Roots are made into chewsticks. Tropical Africa. UPHOF; F85, N84

Combretum grandiflorum - {S} Flowers are sucked for their sweet nectar. West Tropical Africa. DALZIEL; N84

Combretum paniculatum - {S} Flowers are sucked by children. Leaves are used as a substitute for spinach. Tropical Africa. DALZIEL, KUNKEL; **Y78, Z25M**

Combretum platypterum - {S} The flowers are sucked for their sweet nectar. Leaves are eaten in soups. Tropical Africa. DALZIEL; N84

Terminalia arjuna → *Terminalia glabra*

Terminalia bellarica - *Belleric* {S} Fruits are dark red, somewhat like a small plum, with a pleasant, subacid flavor. They are called in commerce *baleric myrobalans* and are used for making preserves. The kernels are also edible but are said to have a narcotic effect. Southern Asia to the Philippines. BURKILL, TANAKA, UPHOF, WATT; F85, N84, Q12, Q18, Q46

Terminalia catappa - *Tropical almond, Indian almond, False kamani* {S} Seed kernels are eaten out of hand or roasted, having the flavor of almonds. They may be chopped and added to cookie or bread mixes, or stirred into icings, dessert fillings, candies, soups, or stews. The sun-dried kernels yield 38-54% of a bland, yellow, semi-drying oil which is edible and not as likely to become rancid as true almond oil. It is used in cooking. The fruits have a tender skin and a thin layer of edible, subacid, juicy flesh. Tropical Asia, cultivated. DUKE, GIBBONS 1967, KENNARD, MENNINGER, MORTON

1985 [Nu], ROSENGARTEN; A79M, F85, N84, P5, *P17M*, Q12, Q46

Terminalia ferdinandiana - *Billy goat plum, Manmohpan* {S} The fruit, which looks and tastes like an English gooseberry, is one of the world's richest known sources of natural ascorbic acid. Samples of the fruit were found to contain between 2,300 and 3,150 milligrams of ascorbic acid per 100 grams of edible fruit. Aborigines have eaten the fruit for years, but it was not until 1981 that scientists from Sydney University discovered its unusual properties. Australia. BRAND; N84, P38, R15M, S92

Terminalia glabra - *Arjoon sadura* {S} In India, a decoction of the bark with milk is used as a beverage. Seeds are also edible. Tropical Asia. HEDRICK 1919, KUNKEL, WATT; F85, N84, Q12, Q18, Q46

Terminalia kaernbachii - *Okari nut* {S} Seed kernels, having an excellent mild, almond-like flavor, are eaten raw, roasted or baked. The flavor is improved by light roasting, with salt. Also the source of a vegetable butter. New Guinea, cultivated. ALTSCHUL, MASSAL [Nu], MENNINGER, UPHOF; F85, N84

Terminalia tomentosa - *Saj, Laurel* {S} The astringent juice from the bark is employed in the manufacture of palm sugar. Ashes of the bark are used as a substitute for lime in betel-nut chewing. Southern Asia. TANAKA, UPHOF, WATT; N84, Q12, Q18

COMMELINACEAE

Commelina communis - *Day-flower* {PL} Young leaves, shoots, and flowers are cooked as a potherb, and served with butter, salt and miso, or rice. They can also be chopped fine and added to salads. Japan-China, naturalized in North America. ALTSCHUL, FERNALD, GIBBONS 1979, MEDSGER, PETERSON, L., TANAKA; N9M, N9M{S}

Tradescantia virginiana - *Spiderwort* {PL} Very young shoots and leaves are eaten in tossed salads, parboiled and fried, or chopped fine they can be added to potato salad. Also good as a potherb served with butter or an oil and vinegar dressing, or added to soups and stews. The flowers make an attractive edible garnish, and can also be candied. North America. CROWHURST 1972 [Re], FERNALD, KINDSCHER, PETERSON, L., UPHOF; A1M, B28, B97M, C81M, E33M, F35M, H3M, I37M, J7, J91, L55, M16, N7T, O53M{S}

CONVOLVULACEAE

Calonyction aculeatum* → *Calonyction album

Calonyction album - *Moonflower* {S} Young leaves and fleshy calyces are steamed and eaten as a vegetable, or used in curries, soups, stews, etc. They may be used either fresh or dried. In India, the young seeds are also eaten. North America, cultivated. BURKILL, MACMILLAN, MACNICOL, MARTIN 1975, MORTON 1977, OCHSE, WATT; B62, C13M, C44, E7M, F24, F80, H54, L91M, N39, N84, O53M, O89, S91M

Ipomoea alba* → *Calonyction album

Ipomoea aquatica - *Water spinach, Kangkong, Ong choy, Engtsai* {S} Young leaves and stems are eaten boiled, steamed, stir-fried, or added to soups, stews, curries and sambals. Young stems are used as an ingredient in pickles. The protein content of the leaves is high making this one of the best green-leaved foods. Cultural methods emphasize the production of young, succulent tips. These can be eaten raw in salads. The roots are occasionally cooked and eaten. Tropics, cultivated. COST 1988, DAHLEN [Pre, Re], HEDRICK 1919, HERKLOTS [Cu, Re], MACMILLAN, MARTIN 1975, OCHSE, UPHOF; B75, E83T, F85, G67M, J20, J82, N84, Q34, R47, *S63M*, *S70*

CULTIVARS

Green Stem: (Gonn Ong Choi) Large leaves, narrower than those of Light Green Stem; smaller stems, approximately 1/2 inch in diameter. Both the stems and leaves are medium-green in color. High yields and quality. Grows during the entire season. DAHLEN; L59

Light Green Stem: (Seui Ong Choy) Large leaves, larger and more pointed than those of Green Stem; the stem is relatively thick and lighter green in color. Harvest by picking young shoots to promote new growth. Very popular in Taiwan and Vietnam. DAHLEN; D55

Ipomoea batatas - *Sweet potato* {S} Tubers are eaten raw, boiled, steamed, baked, fried, mashed, batter-fried as tempura, dried for later use, or fermented into the alcoholic beverages *awamori* and *chicha*. They can also be used in pies, cakes, breads, puddings, cookies, etc. In Japan, they are used for *imo miso*. Chopped and dried tubers are boiled with rice or ground into flour which is mixed with wheat flour and made into cake or bread. Also the source of a starch, called *Brazilian arrowroot*. The leaves and tips of actively growing shoots are used as a substitute for spinach. Tropical America, cultivated. CARCIONE, FELL 1982b, HALPIN [Cu, Cul], HERKLOTS [Cu], HESSELTINE, OCHSE, SHURTLEFF 1976, STEINKRAUS, TANAKA, UPHOF, VILMORIN; N84 (for cultivars see Sweet potato, page 509)

Ipomoea digitata - *Spanish woodbine, Khoai xiêm* {S} The oblong tubers have a slightly sweet taste, and are eaten like sweet potatoes. Leaves are also eaten. Tropics. HEDRICK 1919, MARTIN 1975, TANAKA; F85, N84, Q38, S44

Ipomoea tuberosa* → *Ipomoea digitata

Ipomoea turpethum* → *Operculina turpethum

Operculina turpethum - *Indian jalap, Turpeth* {S} The soft, sweet stem is sucked or chewed. Fleshy, unripe fruits are eaten raw or boiled like peas. Leaves are also edible. Tropical Asia, Australia. CRIBB, HEDRICK 1919, MARTIN 1975; F85

CORNACEAE

Cornus canadensis - *Bunchberry, Dwarf cornel* {PL} The rather dry fruits can be added to breakfast cereals, or used in jellies, fruit sauces, pies, and puddings. Bunchberries are said to be an excellent ingredient for steamed plum puddings. Northern temperate region. CROWHURST 1972, FERNALD, GIBBONS 1979, HALL [Re], KIRK, MEDSGER, TURNER 1979 [Re]; A2{S}, C49, D75T, D95, E15{S}, G37M, I15{S}, I44, J26, J53{S}, *J75M*, J78, K63G{S}, K75M, M77, N8, N84{S}, etc.

Cornus capitata - *Thammal, Thanboi* {S} The fruit is sweetish, mingled with a slight bitter taste, and is eaten or made into preserves in India. Himalayan region. HEDRICK 1919, WATT; D95{PL}, E63{PL}, H4{PL}, K38, M90{PL}, N0{PL}, N84, O93, *P17M*, P38, *P63*, Q40

Cornus kousa - *Yamabôshi* {PL} The oblate red fruits, called *yang-mei*, are very juicy and of a fair flavor. Consumed in some parts of China. Young leaves are eaten by mountain people in Japan. Japan-China. TANAKA, WILSON, E.; B32, C92{S}, E47, E47{S}, *F51*, *G66*{S}, J16, J47, K38{S}, K63G{S}, L2, N0, N84{S}, O93{S}

Cornus mas - *Cornelian cherry* {PL} The pleasant-tasting fruits are eaten raw, dried, preserved in syrup, or made into tarts, preserves, sauces, sweetmeats and marmalades. In England, they were at one time commonly kept in brine and used like olives. Also the source of an alcoholic beverage, known in France as *vin de cornoulle*. In Norway, the flowers are used for flavoring distilled spirits. Seeds were ground and used as a coffee substitute. Eurasia, cultivated. BIANCHINI, BRYAN [Cul, Re], HEDRICK 1919, HENDRICKSON, JOHNS, SIMMONS 1972 [Cu], UPHOF; B32, D37, D95, E47{S},

E87, *G30*, *G66*{S}, I77M, J47, K38{S}, K63G{S}, M77, N0, N84{S}, O53M{S}, etc.

CULTIVARS {GR}

Bulgarian: Large, pear-shaped fruit; skin deep scarlet to violet; flesh lighter scarlet, high in sugar, of excellent flavor; stone small. High in vitamin C. Tree very productive. Originated in Bulgaria. Introduced into the United States by Alexander I. Eppler. D47{OR}

Cream: An improved cream-colored cultivar from eastern Europe. Creamy skin; lighter cream flesh. Excellent quality. Introduced into the United States by Alexander I. Eppler. D47{OR}

Golden Glory: Improved ornamental strain with more abundant star-like yellow flowers in early spring. Edible red fruits in July. Grows as a large, upright multi-stemmed shrub (20-25 feet), or can be pruned to tree-like form. C9, F57M, *K31*

Romanian: Large, spherical fruit; skin bright red; flesh lighter red, high in sugar, very delicately flavored; quality excellent. Tree highly productive. Originated in Romania. Introduced into the United States by Alexander I. Eppler. D47{OR}

Russian Giant: Very large, barrel-shaped fruit; skin deep scarlet; flesh lighter scarlet, high in sugar, of excellent flavor; stone small. Tree high yielding. Originated in the U.S.S.R. Introduced into the United States by Alexander I. Eppler. D47

Yellow: An improved yellow cultivar from eastern Europe. Yellow skin; lighter yellow flesh. Excellent quality. Introduced into the United States by Alexander I. Eppler. D47{OR}

Dendrobenthamia capitata → *Cornus capitata*

Dendrobenthamia japonica → *Cornus kousa*

Macrocarpium mas → *Cornus mas*

CORYLACEAE

Corylus americana - *American hazelnut, Wild filbert* {PL} The thick-shelled nuts have small, sweet kernels that are eaten raw or used in soups, breads, cookies, cakes and candies. Indians of the prairie regions preferred them in the milk stage when they are softer and sweeter. North America. FERNALD, GIBBONS 1979, KINDSCHER, MEDSGER, TURNER 1979 [Pre, Re]; A91, B15M, *B52*, C11M, D45, D72, F19M, G23, G45M, *G66*, H4, I4, J33, K38{S}, M76, N7T, etc.

CULTIVARS {SC}

Winkler: Prolific bearer of large nuts. Winter hardy to at least 30^0 below zero. Highly resistant to eastern filbert blight. Widely used as a parent in breeding with C. avellana. Introduced by Snyder Bros., Center Point, Iowa, in 1918. E62, E62{PR}, E62{S}, I25M, I25M{S}

Corylus avellana - *Filbert, Hazelnut, Cobnut* {S} The nut is eaten raw, as *noces* in oil, or roasted and used in breads, cakes, candies, cookies, pies, cereals and nut milks. Also the source of a clear, yellow, edible oil used in salad dressings, sauces, cookies, etc. Eurasia, cultivated. MABEY, MENNINGER, ROSENGARTEN, UPHOF, VON WELANETZ; C38{PL}, E32M{PL}, G23{PL}, G45M{PL}, *G66*, *G66*{PL}, G72{PL}, I15, K38, K63G, N0{PL}, *N71M*, N93M, O53M, O93, R78, etc. (for cultivars see Filbert, page 334)

Corylus avellana f. fusco-rubra - *Red filbert, Red-leaf filbert, Purple-leaved filbert* {GR} Nuts are edible, having a reddish or deep purple husk. Cultivated. REHDER.

CULTIVARS

Fortin: Superior to other red leaf filberts in that it maintains its red foliage throughout the summer. Catkins and nut husks are also red. Produces an abundance of small flavorful nuts. Pollinated by Butler and Ennis. Selected by Michael Dolan of Burnt Ridge Nursery. B74, J61M

Rote Zeller: Ornamental tree with small, oval-shaped, tasty nuts. Long reddish-purple catkins appear in winter and early spring, red leaves in spring, and reddish husks and nuts in summer. Leaves later turn bronze, except for the tips of new growth. Light producer. *F91Z*, I49M

Corylus californica → *Corylus cornuta var. californica*

Corylus chinensis - *Chinese tree hazel, Chên* {PL} The nuts are edible. A large upright tree that does not produce suckers. Drought resistant. Eastern Asia. TANAKA; E91M

Corylus colurna - *Turkish tree hazel, Constantinople nut* {PL} Nuts are edible. The tree is upright, non-suckering, and very drought resistant. Useful in hybridizing with C. avellana. Eurasia. JAYNES, ZEVEN; A91, B74, E62, E62{PR}, E87, G41, *G66*, *G66*{S}, H49, J61M, K38{S}, K47T{S}, K63G{S}, N0, *N71M*{S}, Q40{S}, etc.

Corylus colurna var. chinensis → *Corylus chinensis*

Corylus colurna var. jacquemontii - *Indian tree hazel* {PL} The nuts are edible. An upright growing tree that does not produce suckers. Himalayan region. TANAKA; A91

Corylus x colurnoides (C. avellana x C. colurna) - *Trazel* {PL} Artificial hybrid. The edible nut can be eaten raw or used in breads, cakes, puddings, nut milks, etc. Combines the non-suckering, winter-hardy, vigorous growth of the tree hazel with the free falling, early bearing, large nut size of the filbert. TANAKA; A91, B74, E97, J61M

CULTIVARS {GR}

Chinoka: Attractive, medium to large nut with a mild flavor; free falling; matures early. Tree bears heavy crops annually; a good producer of catkins, making it a good pollinator. E91M, E91M{OR}, E91M{PL}

Fingerlakes: Large, elongated nut of excellent quality. Vigorous, shapely tree; precocious and productive; very hardy. Resistant to aphids and bud mites. Requires a pollinator. Introduced by Miller Nurseries. H65

Gellatly Mix: A mixture of seedlings of the best named trazels, mostly Gellatly selections, including Chinoka, Eastoka, Faroka, Laroka, Erioka, Zeroka, and Morrisoka. A91{PL}

Laroka: Long nut of good size and very good flavor; shell thin; generally free falling. Excellent landscape value; vigorous growth; large, dark green leaves to 6 inches in diameter. E62, E62{PR}, E62{S}, E62{SC}, E91M, E91M{OR}, I60{PL}

Corylus cornuta - *Beaked hazelnut* {PL} The nuts can be eaten raw, dried for later use, or ground into a flour or meal. The meal can be mixed with sugar, water, and candied orange peel and then used to fill turnovers, pies, etc. North America. GIBBONS 1979, HARRINGTON, H., MEDSGER; A91, B74, *G66*, I15{S}, *J75M*, N84{S}

Corylus cornuta var. californica - *California hazel* {PL} The nuts are eaten fresh or preserved for winter use by several Indian tribes, among which the Cowlitz, Squaxin, and Snohomish. Western North America. UPHOF; B92, B94{S}

Corylus ferox - *Himalayan hazelnut* {S} The small, thick-shelled nuts are edible, tasting like the common filbert. Himalayan region. HEDRICK 1919; U7M

Corylus heterophylla - *Siberian filbert* {S} Nuts are hard-shelled, of a relatively good flavor, and are eaten raw. Leaves are variegated, with a deep carmine, heart-shaped spot at the center. Eastern Asia. TANAKA, ZEVEN; E91M{PL}, F85, *G66*, *G66*{PL}, S36M

Corylus jacquemontii → *Corylus colurna var. jacquemontii*

Corylus maxima - *Lambert's filbert, Giant filbert* {PL} The large, edible nuts are eaten raw or used in nut milks, nut butters, cakes, pies, breads, etc. Nuts of this species where once called filberts and those of C. avellana, hazelnuts or *cobnuts*, but the distinctions have been obscured by breeding and selection. Mediterranean region, cultivated. MASEFIELD; A91, *G66*{S} (for cultivars see Filbert, page 334)

Corylus rostrata → *Corylus cornuta*

Corylus sieboldiana - *Japanese hazelnut, Tsuno-hashibami* {S} Nuts are eaten or used as a source of an edible oil. Eastern Asia. TANAKA; N84

Corylus tibetica - *Tibetan tree filbert* {S} The nuts are edible. A non-suckering upright grower, whose eventual height is the smallest of the tree hazels. Himalayan region. TANAKA; **T41M**

Corylus x vilmorinii (C. chinensis x C. avellana) - *Chinese trazel* {PL} Artificial hybrid. Nuts are eaten. The Chinese tree hazel parent contributes a characteristic rounded nut with a slightly thinner shell than the Turkish trazel. REHDER; A91

Corylus x sp. (C. avellana x C. americana) - *Hazelbert, Mildred filbert* {PL} Artificial hybrid. The nuts are edible. Combines the cold hardiness and resistance to eastern filbert blight of the American hazelnut, with the desirable nut qualities of the European filbert. JAYNES; A91, E97

CULTIVARS

George Slate: Mixed seedlings of hybrids made by George Slate at Geneva, New York, using C. americana 'Rush' as one of the parents. They were never named due to poor yield, shy catkin production, and susceptibility to big bud mite. JAYNES; E62, E62{S}

Graham: Nut is large, of good quality. Tree is resistant to Eastern filbert blight; an annual bearer. Originated in Ithaca, New York. Winkler x Longfellow. BROOKS 1972; E62, E62{PR}, E62{S}, E62{SC}

Potomac: Rush x Du Chilly, introduced in 1951. Nut averages 185-195 per pound, yields 50% kernels, resembles Barcelona. Tree is vigorous, productive, suited to areas where the European filbert cannot be grown due to lack of hardiness. BROOKS 1972; B99

Reed: Rush x Bolwyller, introduced in 1951. Nut averages 180-190 per pound, yielding 48% kernels, resembles Red Aveline. Tree is vigorous, productive, suited to areas where the European species cannot be successfully grown due to lack of hardiness. BROOKS 1972; Dropped by B99

Skinner: Originated by Fred Ashworth, St. Lawrence Nurseries, Heuvelton, New York. Nut large, a little wider than long; kernel plump, flavor good; resembles Barcelona; ripens Sept. 24 in Heuvelton. Tree is very hardy, tolerant of blight. Dropmore x Italian Red seedling. BROOKS 1972; L27M

Corylus x sp. (C. avellana x C. cornuta) - *Filazel* {PL} Artificial hybrid. Nuts are edible. The hybrids are intended to combine the hardiness of the beaked hazel with the nut quality of the European filbert. Many of the hybrids have the Peace River strain of C. cornuta as the pistillate parent. JAYNES; H49, J61M, L33

CULTIVARS

Big Red: Nut large, about the size of a Barcelona, kernel well-filled; moderately thick shell. Early ripening. Tree has a multi-stem, suckering habit of growth. Of interest to short season growers for home use, breeding material, or local markets. A91

Gellatly 502: Medium-sized nuts with good quality and excellent flavor; very good kernel filling. Hardy, productive tree; produces vigorous seedlings. Peace River x European. E91M, E91M{OR}

Gellatly Mix: A mixture of seedlings from the best quality, early ripening Gellatly selections including Myoka, Petoka, and Manoka. A91

Gellatly's Earliest: Selected from thousands of seedlings of Gellatly hybrids for early ripening qualities. Recommended for short season areas into Zone 4. A91

Goldner: Ornamental tree; reaches approximately 8 feet in height; can produce for 10 years or more; blight susceptible, especially where American hazel blight is prevalent. Gellatly strain. K16{S}

Grimo 188P: A seedling selection resulting from a cross of the Myoka and Petoka cultivars. E91M, E91M{GR}

Grimo 190A: A seedling selection resulting from a cross of the Myoka and Petoka cultivars. E91M{GR}

Manoka: Produces a high percentage of vigorous seedlings that are among the earliest and hardiest of the filazels. Suitable for Zones 5 to 7. E91M

Myoka: Nut is well filled, with a prominent fuzzy skin on the kernel; thick shell. Ripens very early, making it suitable for short season areas. E91M

Peace River Cross: Seedlings of the original Peace River hybrids made by J.U. Gellatly. Likely back-crossed to C. avellana. Of interest to breeders and growers in short season areas as it produces large nuts early in the season. A91

Petoka: Moderately thin shell; good flavored kernel with a thin pellicle. Produces a high percentage of vigorous seedlings. E91M{OR}

COSTACEAE

Costus afer - *Ginger lily* {S} Said to be used as a spice. Tropical Africa. DALZIEL, TANAKA; N84

Costus speciosus - *Wild ginger, Tebu, Setawar* {S} Tender shoots are boiled or steamed and eaten as a vegetable. Fruits and rhizomes are occasionally eaten. Tropical Asia. BURKILL, HEDRICK 1919, MACMILLAN, TANAKA, WATT; A79M, F27M{PL}, F80, F85, J27{PL}, L62M{PL}, N34M{PL}, N84, O53M, O93, P5

CRASSULACEAE

Dudleya edulis - *Mission lettuce* {PL} The fleshy leaves are eaten raw. Stems are slightly sweet and are refreshing to chew, though often leaving a chalky aftertaste. These plants were considered a delicacy by the Cahuilla Indians. Southwestern North America. CLARKE; G60

Rhodiola rhodantha → *Sedum rhodanthum*

Rhodiola rosea - *Roseroot* {S} Young, succulent leaves and shoots are eaten raw in salads, steamed and served like spinach, pickled, or preserved in oil. The stems can be cooked and eaten like asparagus. Roots are boiled, seasoned with butter, and served with meat or fish. Northern temperate region. ANGIER, FERNALD, GIBBONS 1979, HELLER, UPHOF; C40{PL}, H52, H98{PL}, N63M, N84, O53M, *Q24*, S7M, S44

Sedum acre - *Wall pepper, Biting stonecrop* {S} The leaves are dried and ground for a spicy seasoning. Eurasia, naturalized in North America. A29{PL}, D62, H4{PL}, H51M{PL}, I63M{PL}, J7, J20, K11M{PL}, K47T, L26{PL}, L91M, M16{PL}, *N71M*, O53M, *Q24*, etc.

Sedum anacampseros - *Evergreen orpine* {PL} The plant is eaten as a vegetable in soups. Europe. HEDRICK 1919; A0M, A29, G55, G82M, H52{S}, I22, K11M, K47T{S}, L26, N84{S}, O53M{S}, *Q24*{S}, S7M{S}

Sedum reflexum - *Jenny stonecrop* {PL} Young leaves and shoots are eaten raw in salads by the Dutch. The slightly astringent sour taste of this plant makes it a useful addition to a tossed green salad. It can also be used as a potherb or added to soups. One of the ingredients of Alexander von Humboldt's favorite soup. Eurasia. LARKCOM 1984, LAUNERT [Re], ROOT 1980b, UPHOF; A0M, A29, D62, H4, I22, J7{S}, J37M, K11M, K47T{S}, L26, M16, *M65M*, *N71M*{S}, N84{S}, O53M{S}, *Q24*{S}, etc.

Sedum rhodanthum - *Queen's crown* {S} The young shoots can be cut into small pieces and mixed with lettuce for a salad. Young leaves are very acceptable eaten raw or boiled as a potherb. North America. HARRINGTON, H.; J93T, L13

Sedum roseum* → *Rhodiola rosea

Sedum telephium - *Orpine, Live forever* {S} The leaves have sometimes been used as a salad. Eurasia. GRIEVE; D62, K47T, N9M, N9M{PL}, *N71M*, N84, O48

CUCURBITACEAE

Acanthosicyos horridus - *Naras, Narra melon* {S} The fruits have a pleasant, sweet-acid flavor and are eaten fresh or preserved. Seeds, called *butter pits*, are eaten roasted or boiled or stored for later use. The kernel has a soft consistency like butter. They also yield an edible oil. Pulp of the fruit is used to separate casein from milk after being heated. Southern Africa. FOX, F., MENNINGER, UPHOF; C27M

Acanthosicyos naudinianus - *Herero cucumber* {S} Fruits are eaten boiled, roasted, or made into pickles. When fresh they are a thirst quencher. Also used as a rennet for curdling milk. The seeds contain 35% protein and are roasted and ground into flour or used in confectionery. Southwest Africa. FOX, F., MENNINGER; N84, R41

Benincasa cerifera* → *Benincasa hispida

Benincasa hispida - *Wax gourd, Winter melon, White gourd, Ash pumpkin, Doan gwa, Tong qua, Petha* {S} Mature fruits are eaten raw, stir-fried, braised, stuffed, pickled in miso, added to curries, or made into sweet pickles, preserves, and sweetmeats. In the Chinese dish *tung kwa chung* or *winter melon pond*, the pulp and seeds are scooped out, the cavity is filled with soup ingredients, and the gourd is steamed for 2 1/2 hours. Young leaves, flower-buds, and immature fruits are steamed and eaten or added to stews. Seeds are eaten fried or roasted. Tropical Asia, cultivated. BURKILL, COST 1988 [Cul], DAHLEN [Pre, Cul], HARRINGTON, G. [Cu, Cul], HAWKES [Re], HERKLOTS [Cu, Re], KRAFT, OCHSE, SHURTLEFF 1976, VILMORIN; A79M, B75, C27G{PR}, C82, E59, G67M, G93M, H49, I39, J82, L9M, O39M, R0, R47, S59M, etc.

CULTIVARS

Large Round: 90 days. Fruits are round in shape, 20 inches in diameter; skin is light green covered with a white bloom when mature. Fine, white flesh. K49M, L59

Long White: 90 days. Extra long cylindrical fruits, weighing about 20 pounds. D55

Small: Small fruits, weighing about 5 pounds. Fine, white flesh. Good for home gardens and for making *wax gourd pond*. L59

Super Soup: Very long fruit; 39 inches in length, 8 inches in diameter; weight 55 to 65 pounds; smooth green rind, without bloom; thick flesh. Suitable for fresh market and processing. Very vigorous, short-day plant. The longest wax gourd in Taiwan. *Q39*

White Warrior: An improved Indian cultivar that is sown from May to July. S93M

Benincasa hispida 'Chieh-Qwa' - *Fuzzy gourd, Hairy melon, Mao qua, Mao gwa, Chieh-kwa, Small white gourd* {S} Young fruits are cooked and eaten like zucchini in soups, breads, casseroles, stir-fried dishes, etc. Their size and shape are ideal for stuffing, just large enough so that each half makes a single portion. To prepare, the fuzzy coat is removed and the green skin peeled. CHANG, W. [Re], DAHLEN [Cul, Re], HARRINGTON, G. [Cu, Cul], HERKLOTS, TANAKA; A79M, C82, D55, E59, E83T, F80, G67M, G93M, H49, K49M, L42, L59, *N40*{PR}, N84

CULTIVARS

Round: A form with fruit that is roundish or oval in form instead of the typical narrow, cylindrical shape. Best harvested young, when about 12 to 16 ounces in weight. COST 1988 [Cul]; E59

Citrullus colocynthis - *Colocynth* {S} The fruits, after being boiled repeatedly to remove the bitter principles, are pickled or made into preserves. Seeds are roasted and eaten or ground into flour and used in the preparation of *chappaties*. They also yield an edible oil. Northern Africa, Southern Europe. BHANDARI, HEDRICK 1919, KUNKEL, TANAKA, WATT; F80, F85, N84

Citrullus lanatus - *Watermelon* {S} Ripe fruits are cooled and eaten raw, in fruit salads, or made into wine. Watermelon juice is a popular item in natural foods stores. A syrup can also be prepared from the juice. Unripe fruits are eaten in soups or pickled in sake lees. In China, the roasted seeds are widely eaten and the fruit pulp is made into jam. Seeds are also ground into flour for breads and cakes, added to soups and stews, or pressed for their edible oil. Tropical Africa, cultivated. BHANDARI, CHANG, W., HEDRICK 1919, JOHNS [Cul], MENNINGER, OCHSE, ROSENGARTEN, TANAKA, UPHOF, VILMORIN [Cu]; C27G{PR}, F85, N84, O93 (for cultivars see Watermelon, page 530)

Citrullus lanatus ssp. colocynthoides - *Wild watermelon, Tsama, Egusi-ibara* {S} Seeds are dried, stripped of their coats, ground, and used to enrich and thicken broths, stews, and egusi soup. Fermented seeds are employed as a seasoning for soup or pottage. Roasted seeds, along with peanuts and chilis, are ground into a delicious oily paste called *ose-oji*, eaten with kola nuts, eggplants, or spread on bread. They also yield an edible oil used in salads and cooking. Leaves are cooked and eaten as potherbs. Tropical Africa. FOX, F., OKOLI 1984, VAN EPENHUIJSEN, ZEVEN; D33

Citrullus lanatus Citroides Group - *Citron melon, Preserving melon* {S} The rind of the fruit is pickled, crystallized, or made into jams, jellies, sweetmeats, and preserves. Fruit pulp is inedible. BURR, CARCIONE [Re], HAWKES [Re], JOHNS [Cul], TANAKA; C81M, D65, E38, F24, G68, N50{PR}

CULTIVARS

Black Seeded: Wild Chinese type. Produces fruit up to 50 pounds in weight. I99

Green Seeded: (Colorado Preserving Melon) 100 days. This is quite distinct from the ordinary preserving melon, the seeds being of light green color. Flesh very firm and solid, with few seeds. Very productive, one vine producing up to 25 fruits. Makes beautiful, clear, nearly transparent preserves. BURPEE; A69M, D27, I64

Pink Seeded: Produces fruit up to 10 pounds in weight. I99

Red Seeded: 100 days. Round, light green fruit, marbled and striped with darker shades of green; flesh white with red marks, solid, seedy; seeds red. Will keep until December. Makes excellent transparent preserves. A69M, B13, D11M, D27, E49, I39, I67M, J7, K20, K49M, K71, M13M, T1M

Citrullus vulgaris* → *Citrullus lanatus

Citrullus vulgaris* var. *fistulosus* → *Praecitrullus fistulosus

Coccinia cordifolia* → *Coccinia grandis

Coccinia grandis - *Ivy gourd, Scarlet gourd, Tindora* {S} The young leaves and long slender tops of the stems are cooked and eaten as a potherb, in soups, or as a side dish with rice. Young and tender green fruits are eaten raw in salads, boiled, fried or added to curries. The ripe, scarlet fruit is fleshy and sweet and is eaten raw, or it is occasionally candied. Sometimes available at ethnic and specialty food markets. Tropical Asia, cultivated. HERKLOTS, OCHSE, RAMACHANDRAN [Nu], TANAKA; *B59*{PR}, F74{PR}, F85, N84

Colocynthis vulgaris* → *Citrullus colocynthis

Cucumis africanus - *Horned cucumber, Jelly melon* {S} Young leaves are eaten as a potherb. The bitter fruit is occasionally eaten. Southern Africa. FOX, F., MARTIN 1975; **U14, X77M**

Cucumis anguria - *West Indian gherkin, Bur cucumber* {S} Young, prickly fruits are peeled and eaten raw, boiled and served with hot pepper sauce, added to soups or made into pickles. The flesh is white, firm, and of a very agreeable cucumber flavor, without the slightest bitterness. In the process of pickling, the spongy flesh absorbs a large quantity of vinegar. Young leaves are said to be edible. Tropics, cultivated. BURR, HAWKES [Cul], HERKLOTS, KUNKEL, UPHOF, VILMORIN [Cu]; B73M, B75, D11M, E97, F42M{PR}, *F60*, G27M, G64, G67M, I39, I99, J34, J73, K71, L97, etc.

Cucumis dipsaceus - *Teasel gourd, Arabian cucumber, Ekaleruk* {S} Seeds are cooked and eaten. Leaves and fruits are also edible. Tropical Africa. KUNKEL, MARTIN 1975, MORGAN; F85

Cucumis melo - *Melon* {S} Fruits are eaten out of hand, dried, candied, or made into preserves. Italians traditionally serve melon with *proscuitto* (cured ham) as an appetizer. Surplus melons are sometimes converted into molasses and sugar. Seeds are eaten as a snack or blended with fruit juice to form a refreshing drink. Also the source of an edible oil. Cultivated. CARCIONE, HEDRICK 1919, MENNINGER, RODALE [Cu], TANAKA, VILMORIN [Cu]; F85 (for cultivars see Melon, page 385)

Cucumis melo ssp. agrestis - *Wild melon* {S} The bitter fruit pulp is edible, and the seeds are collected and eaten. Tropical Africa, naturalized in Southwestern North America. TANAKA, UPHOF, ZEVEN; **Y75, Z98**

Cucumis melo Chito Group - *Vine peach, Mango melon, Vegetable orange, Lemon cucumber* {S} The fruit is the size of an orange or a lemon, yellow or greenish yellow when ripe, with a thin, leathery skin. It is peeled and eaten out of hand, added to fruits salads, or more commonly made into pies, preserves, and marmalades. Unripe fruits are pickled whole. FISHER, TANAKA, UPHOF; B73M, D11M, E3, *F60*, I39, K71

Cucumis melo Conomon Group - *Pickling melon, Tea melon, Tsa gwa* {S} Fruits are eaten raw, preserved, or stuffed with minced meats and then cooked. They are also chopped fine and used to season steamed meat or fish, salads and soups. Both immature and mature fruits are made into sweet or sour pickles, or pickled in shiro-miso. Those pickled in sake lees, called *nara-zuke*, form one of the most expensive and popular pickles sold in Japan. CHANG, W. [Re], HARRINGTON, G. [Cu, Cul], HAWKES [Re], HERKLOTS [Re], SHURTLEFF 1975, TANAKA, UPHOF, VON WELANETZ; G20M{PR}, L59

CULTIVARS

Ao-Uri: (Viridis, Green Melon) 73 days. Medium-sized fruit, 10 to 12 inches long, 4 to 4 1/2 inches in diameter; rind smooth, bright deep-green with distinct slender white stripes; flesh white, thick. Excellent for pickles as well as for cooking. G33, *P39*

Kuromon: 85 days. Oblong fruit, tapered towards the ends, 12 inches long and about 4 inches in diameter; skin dark green with light green stripes, very smooth; thinner flesh than Numame Early. Good for cooking or pickling, especially good for stuffing. Vigorous, disease resistant plants. E83T

Numame Early: Cylindrical fruit, 8 to 12 inches long and 2 to 3 inches in diameter. Light green skin turns almost white when fully ripe. Very thick, juicy, crisp flesh with a relatively small seed cavity. Excellent for pickling. Popular in cool northern areas of Japan. E83T, *S63M*

Shima-Uri: (Variegata, Striped Melon) Rich green fruits with pale green stripes, about 6 inches long. Good for home gardens and pickling. *S70*

Shiro-Uri: (Albus, White Melon) 50 days. Long-oval fruit, somewhat club-shaped; 8 inches long, 3 inches at the widest section at full maturity; very light green rind, turns white on maturing. Medium-thick, crisp flesh. Can be harvested when young for the early market. G33, *P39*

Silver Charm: (F_1) 68 days. Slender, straight fruit; 10 inches long, 2 to 2 1/2 inches in diameter; light green skin with few shallow ribs; thin, tender flesh. For salads, pickling and cooking. Vigorous, prolific vine; mosaic and downy mildew resistant. Also tolerant to wet, hot and humid weather conditions. *Q39*

Tokyo Early White: Medium fruits, about 10 inches long. Much earlier in maturity than Tokyo Large White. Very good for fresh market and pickling. *S70*

Tokyo Large White: Large fruit, about 12 inches long; light green, turning almost white when fully ripe. Good for pickling. Very prolific. *S70*

Cucumis melo Dudaim Group - *Queen Anne's pocket melon, Pomegranate melon, Plum granny* {S} Small fruits, having a very fragrant, musky aroma, are occasionally used for preserves. Primarily used as a fragrance material. HEDRICK 1919, UPHOF, VILMORIN; A21, E7M, H53, I39, L7M

Cucumis melo Flexuosus Group - *Serpent melon, Snake melon, Kakri* {S} The fruits, tasting like cucumber, are often crooknecked or coiled. They are refreshing when eaten raw in hot weather. Or they may be added to salads with salt and vinegar, preserved, cooked in curries, or pickled. Seeds are eaten or used in confectionery. CHAUHAN, TANAKA, UPHOF, VILMORIN.

CULTIVARS

Cooking Queen: Very large fruits, 3 to 5 feet long. Ideally suited for cooking purposes. S93M

Long Green: Fruits are 1 to 1 1/2 feet long, finely ribbed, with very tender flesh. Normally eaten in the same manner as cucumber. Sown from November to April in India. S59M

Lucknow Linen: Long, slender fruit with sweet, juicy flesh. Grown during the hot, dry season in India. *S36*, S93M

Mekty White Trailing: 70 days. Slightly curved fruit, 30 inches long and 3 1/2 inches in diameter; skin creamy white, spineless. Recommended for home gardens and fresh market. Also a good item for specialty and ethnic markets. Monoecious, indeterminate vine. *L59G*

Cucumis melo Flexuosus Group 'Armenian' - *Armenian cucumber, Yard long cucumber* {S} Fruits are eaten raw or cooked. They are long, ribbed, pale green in color, sometimes coiled in shape, and are easily digested even by those who cannot digest standard cucumbers. The flesh remains crisp and hard even when the fruit becomes soft or flexible. Vines should be trellised if straight fruit is desired. CARCIONE, CREASY 1982; B73M, D11M, G33, G51, G64, G67M, *G83M*, H95, *I62*{PL}, J34, J73, K71, M13M, M95, N16, O89, etc.

CULTIVARS

The Duke: Improved type with bitter-free, crunchy fruits that never get pithy or hollow-hearted. Their texture is juicy and crisp, and the skins do not need peeling. Best harvested at about 12 inches. When cut crosswise, the ridged exteriors form neatly scalloped slices. K66

Cucumis melo Momordica Group - *Phoot, Kachra, Snap melon* {S} Fruits are small, smooth, oval or cylindrical, with mealy, somewhat insipid or slightly sour flesh. When young and tender, they are eaten raw or cooked as a vegetable. Ripe fruits are used as a dessert. CHAUHAN, WATT; S93M

Cucumis metuliferus - *African horned cucumber, Kiwano, Jelly melon* {S} The distinctive fruit is yellowish-orange when ripe and studded with numerous spiny protuberances. The flesh is bright green, translucent, slightly mucilaginous, with a more or less bland flavor. Sold in specialty markets in the United States, where it is promoted as having a banana-lime flavor and is used in fruit cups, cocktails, sundaes, parfaits, and drinks. In Africa, the fruits are not considered desirable and are eaten in times of scarcity. Leaves are sometimes cooked and eaten. Used as a rootstock and a source of resistance to diseases for C. sativus. Tropical Africa. FOX, F., TANAKA, ZEVEN; E7M, E13G{PR}, F80, I99, K49M, *N40*{PR}, N84, O53M, O89, O93, P5, *Q32*, Q34, R47, S91M, etc.

Cucumis prophetarum - *Globe cucumber* {S} Unripe fruits are pickled like the common cucumber. Ripe fruits are bitter, but are sometimes boiled and eaten. The leaves are edible. Tropical Africa to Arabia. BURR, MARTIN 1975, VILMORIN; **X77M, Y14M**

Cucumis sativus - *Cucumber* The fruits are eaten raw, in salads, sautéed, marinated, added to stews, stuffed with minced meat, oil-roasted, served with sour cream or yogurt, or pickled. *Kimchi* made from cucumbers is known as *oisobaegi* and *oiji*. In Japan, they are pickled in rice bran. Seed kernels are eaten raw or roasted. They yield an oil, *huile de concombre*, resembling olive oil, used in salads and French cooking. Young leaves and stems are eaten as a potherb. In Indonesia, the steamed leaves are pounded together with rhizomes of galanga, wrapped in banana leaves and roasted. Southern Asia, cultivated. FELL 1982b, HARRINGTON, G. [Cul], LARKCOM 1984, OCHSE, STEINKRAUS, TANAKA, UPHOF, VILMORIN [Cu]; (for cultivars see Cucumber, page 316)

Cucurbita argyrosperma → ***Cucurbita mixta***

Cucurbita ficifolia - *Chilacoyote, Malabar gourd, Fig-leaved gourd* {S} Young fruits can be cut and used like a cucumber. Ripe fruits are sometimes boiled and eaten or made into an alcoholic drink. A confection is made from the flesh by boiling it with crude sugar. Seeds are roasted and eaten like peanuts. Central America. BROUK, HERKLOTS, LOVELOCK, NATIONAL RESEARCH COUNCIL 1989, TANAKA, WILLIAMS, L.; F80, K49M, P1G, R47

Cucurbita foetidissima - *Buffalo gourd, Calabazilla* {S} The seeds, containing 30-35% protein and up to 34% oil, are roasted and eaten, ground into a meal for gruel, or pressed for their edible oil. Roots are the source of a starch used as a sweetener or stabilizer, and for making puddings similar to tapioca. Young fruits, although bitter, are sometimes eaten or dried for future use. Flowers are said to be edible after preparation. Southwestern North America. DE VEAUX, KINDSCHER, KIRK, NATIONAL RESEARCH COUNCIL 1975a, NIETHAMMER [Re]; D33, D58, E7M, I98M, J25M, R47

Cucurbita maxima - *Calabaza, Winter squash* Fruits are eaten baked, boiled, fried, steamed, mashed, used in pies, breads, cakes, and confectionery, or processed into starch. Seeds are eaten raw, roasted, or ground to a meal. Young stems, leaves, and flowers are cooked and eaten. Leaves contain 5% protein. Southern America, cultivated. DUKE, HERKLOTS, TANAKA, VILMORIN [Cu]; (for cultivars see Squash, page 488)

Cucurbita melanosperma → ***Cucurbita ficifolia***

Cucurbita mixta - *Cushaw, Winter squash* Fruits are eaten boiled, baked, fried and mashed, or made into pies, breads, cakes, candies, etc. They are generally stringy, watery, and less rich in flavor than those of C. maxima, C. moschata, and C. pepo. Widely grown in Mexico for the large, tasty seeds, which are eaten raw, fried, roasted, or ground and used in sauces. In Mexico, the flowers are fried, sometimes with cotton-seed. Central America. ALCORN, BROUK, HERKLOTS, SCHERY, VILMORIN; (for cultivars see Squash, page 488)

Cucurbita moschata - *Kabocha, Winter squash* {S} Fruits are eaten raw, boiled, fried, baked, mashed, steamed, stuffed, or used in pies, puddings, soups, breads, cakes, etc. They are sometimes dried, ground into flour and made into bread. Young fruits can be pickled. Flowers, leaves, and young stems are eaten as potherbs or added to soups and stews. The oily seeds are eaten raw, or roasted in salt. Central America, cultivated. DUKE, FELL 1982b, HERKLOTS, MORTON 1977, OCHSE, TANAKA, VILMORIN; O93 (for cultivars see Squash, page 488)

Cucurbita pepo - *Summer squash, Pumpkin* Young fruits are eaten steamed, boiled, fried, stuffed, etc. Mature fruits are baked, mashed, puréed, or used in pies, soups, stews, cakes, breads, custards, and pancakes. Seeds are eaten raw, parched, roasted, ground into meal, or pressed for their edible oil. Roasted seeds are known as *pepitas*. *Pepitorio* is a confection, resembling popcorn balls, made of the seeds combined with a heavy syrup. Leaves, young shoots, and tendrils are eaten as a potherb or stir-fried. Flowers and flower buds are eaten boiled, stuffed, added to sandwiches, made into fritters, or dried for later use. Sprouted seeds are used in salads. Central America, cultivated. FELL 1982b, HARRINGTON, G. [Cul], HERKLOTS, LEGGATT [Re], MACNICOL [Re], ROSENGARTEN, SAWYER, TANAKA, UPHOF, VILMORIN [Cu], WILLIAMS, L., WILSON, G.; (for cultivars see Pumpkin, page 458, and Squash, page 488)

Cucurbita x sp. (C. digitata x C. palmata) - *Desert coyote gourd* {S} Narrow-leaf hybrid of the most desert hardy, Arizona wild gourds. Prolific producer of ornamental fruit and edible seed. Southwestern North America. I16

Cucurbita x sp. (C. palmeri x C. mixta) - *Chichicoyota* {S} Wild gourd interbred with Sonoran squash. Seeds are eaten. Southwestern North America. I16

Cyclanthera pedata - *Achoccha, Korila, Pepino de rellenar* {S} Young fruits, having the taste of cucumbers, are eaten raw or made into pickles. Mature fruits are cooked with oil and vinegar, added to stews, or stuffed with ground meat or other fillings and baked. Leaves and tender shoots are eaten. Tropical America. DUKE, HERKLOTS, NATIONAL RESEARCH COUNCIL 1989, UPHOF, WILLIAMS, L.; D62, I59G, I99, N84

Cyclanthera tonduzii - *Caiba* {S} The young fruits and the tender new growths are eaten by the country people of Costa Rica. Central America. WILLIAMS, L.; F85

Fevillea cordifolia - *Sequa, Antidote vine* {S} The seeds yield an edible, pleasant tasting oil with an odor somewhat reminiscent of peanut oil. On a weight per fruit basis, the seed oil content of Fevillea is apparently higher than in any other dicotyledon and among the highest ever recorded for any plant. Recommended as a commercial oil crop for tropical rain forests. Tropical America. GENTRY; **U71M**

Gynostemma pentaphyllum - *Amacha-zuru* {S} Leaves and stems are cooked and eaten. The leaves have a sweet taste and are used as tea. Eastern Asia. TANAKA; F85

Hodgsonia capniocarpa → ***Hodgsonia macrocarpa***

Hodgsonia macrocarpa - *Hodgsonia seed, Lard seed, Akar kapajang* {S} Seed kernels are eaten after roasting or baking. They are often crushed and cooked together with fish, meat or vegetables. Also the source of an oil used for culinary purposes. The yellow fruits are also edible. Indomalaya, cultivated. MENNINGER, TANAKA, UPHOF, ZEVEN; F85

Lagenaria leucantha → *Lagenaria siceraria*

Lagenaria longissima → *Lagenaria siceraria*

Lagenaria siceraria - *Bottle gourd, Calabash, Lauki* {S} Young fruits are eaten boiled, steamed, fried, pickled, added to soups and curries, or made into fritters. They vary in quality, but the carefully selected cultivars of India and China are choice vegetables, as good as summer squashes of the Temperate Zone. Leaves and young shoots are used as potherbs. In West Africa, the seeds are sometimes used in melon soups. A vegetable curd similar to soybean *tofu* can be made from the seeds. They also yield an oil used in cooking. Paleotropics, cultivated. CHAUHAN, DAHLEN [Cul, Re], DALZIEL, FOX, F., HERKLOTS, MARTIN 1979 [Cu, Nu]; *B59*{PR}, F85, O53M

CULTIVARS

<u>Calcutta Giant Round:</u> Grown during the monsoon season in India. S93M

<u>Early Green Long:</u> Fruits about 1 1/2 feet long and 3 1/2 inches in diameter, with the stem end somewhat narrower than the blossom end. L59, *L79G*

<u>Extra Long:</u> 90 days. Fruit 30 inches long by 3 inches in diameter, sometimes to 3 feet; flesh thick and tender, delicious. Very popular in southern Asia. D55

<u>Guada:</u> Selected by New Guineans for its edible immature fruits which are eaten as are zucchinis. Continues to thrive in hot wet conditions and is pest resistant. An extremely vigorous climber useful for shading heat sensitive plants. R47

<u>Large Long:</u> Fruits about 3 feet long and 8 inches in diameter, weighing about 20 pounds. For vegetable use, they should be picked when young. L59, *L79G*

<u>Long White Prolific:</u> Bears a heavy crop of fruits 16 to 20 inches in length and 3 to 4 inches in diameter, but when fully matured the fruits will attain 30 inches in length. An all-season strain. S59M

<u>Medium Long:</u> 90 days. Fruit yellowish green, 15 inches long by 4 inches in diameter; flesh firm, white. Used for cooking and soup when they are young. Can be grown on the ground like a pumpkin or along a trellis. Very popular in Taiwan. D55

<u>Pusa Summer Prolific Long:</u> Large fruits, 1 1/2 to 2 feet long and of very good quality. Best picked when young and tender. An improved cultivar that is a prolific bearer. Suitable for growing in spring and summer. E83T, R0, R50, S59M

<u>Rainy Queen:</u> Long, slim, attractive fruits; 3 1/2 to 5 feet long. S93M

<u>Singapuri Giant Long:</u> Used for frame culture in Bangladesh. O39M

<u>Summer King:</u> Fruits uniform yellowish green, narrow at the stem end, 1 1/2 to 2 feet long; flesh firm, white. An old, popular bush cultivar for commercial use and home gardens. O39M

<u>Verma Wonder:</u> New, prolific summer cultivar that produces fruits on very small plants. S93M

Lagenaria siceraria 'Clavata' - *Yûgao* {S} *Kampyo*, the dried, ribbon-like, peeled pulp of the fruit, when seasoned with soy sauce, forms one of the essential ingredients of *sushi*, and the Buddhist ceremonial dishes *gomoku-meshi* and *shôjin-ryôri*. Also called *dried gourd shavings*, they are reconstituted in lightly salted water for 20 to 30 minutes before use. Used for tying foods into rolls, little packages, or bundles, they are simmered until soft and transparent and can be eaten with the rolled food. SHURTLEFF 1975, TANAKA; <u>G20M</u>{PR}, <u>N49M</u>{PR}, *S63M*

Lagenaria siceraria 'Longissima' - *Cucuzzi, Cucuzzi caravasi, Italian edible gourd, New Guinea bean, New Guinea butter vine* {S} Fruits are thin, up to 4 feet long or more, and have a flavor and texture said to be like cooked green beans. Normally harvested when 6 to 25 inches long, under ideal growing conditions they can remain tender up to 5 1/2 pounds. They are eaten steamed, sautéed, stuffed and baked, or coated with an egg-flour batter and fried in hot oil. For straight, blemish-free fruits, grow on a trellis. DARK; B73M, C44, C92, E49, *F60*, F80, G51, G93M, *H61*, I39, J83M, K49M, K71, L59, N16, O89, etc.

Lagenaria vulgaris → *Lagenaria siceraria*

Luffa acutangula - *Angled luffa, Cee gwa, Chinese okra, Jhinga* {S} Young fruits are eaten raw in salads, boiled, steamed, stuffed, stir-fried, coated with batter and fried, pickled, cooked with coconut milk, or added to soups, stews, and curries. In China and Japan, they are sliced and dried before being cooked in broths. Young leaves may be eaten in salads or cooked as greens. Flowers and flower buds are dipped in batter and sautéed. Mature seeds are roasted, salted, and eaten as a snack. Tropical Asia, cultivated. COST 1988 [Cul, Re], HALPIN [Cu, Cul], HARRINGTON, G. [Cu, Cul], HERKLOTS [Cu], KRAFT [Re], OCHSE, TANAKA; A79M, B75, C81M, C82, D55, E59, F80, G93M, H49, J20, K49M, L7M, L42, L59, S91M, etc.

CULTIVARS

<u>Ping-Ann:</u> (F_1) Long, slender green fruit with 10 angular ridges; ready for harvest when 13 to 14 inches long and 1 1/2 to 2 inches in diameter. Used as a summer squash after the peel is removed. Early, prolific vine; highly tolerant to heat and wet weather. *Q39*

<u>Pusa Nasdar:</u> Light-green, medium size fruit. Mid early plant; flowers in 60 days in summer crop only; bears 15-20 fruits. Recommended for sowing in spring and also during the rainy season. Also used for frame culture. N91, O39M, R0, S59M

<u>Striped Long Arro:</u> Slim fruits have ridges running length-wise. Very productive. S93M

<u>Twelve Leaves:</u> Usually used for field culture in India and Bangladesh. N91, O39M

Luffa aegyptiaca → *Luffa cylindrica*

Luffa cylindrica - *Smooth luffa, Vine okra, Dishcloth gourd, Dhundhul* {S} Young fruits are eaten raw in salads like cucumbers, sliced and dried for later use, pickled, or used in soups, stews, and curries. The stem tops, young leaves, flower-buds, and flowers are steamed and served with rice. Seeds are roasted with salt and eaten as a delicacy. Also the source of a cooking oil and a product similar to *tofu*. Tropical Asia, cultivated. HERKLOTS, MARTIN 1979,

OCHSE, TANAKA; A21, B62, C9M, C13M, C43M{PL}, C82, D55, E49, G16, G84{PL}, J73, L9M, M46, O53M, R47, etc.

CULTIVARS

Long Green: Cylindrical fruits of excellent quality. Very heavy bearing over a long period of time. R0, S93M

Satputia: Also known as "bunch sponge gourd", since it produces up to 7 fruits at one node. R0

Seven Star: (F_1) Short, cylindrical, light green fruit; 7 inches long, 2 1/2 to 3 inches in diameter; weight 17 1/2 ounces. High quality fruit with very good texture. Vigorous, prolific, early plant; not sensitive to day-length for fruit setting. Especially recommended for long day planting. *Q39*

Smooth Short: 90 days. Round, short cylindrical type. Young fruits are harvested for vegetable use when about 6 inches long. L59

Verma's Fortune: Fruits are usually 1 1/2 to 2 feet long, and are borne on dwarf vines. They retain their edible quality up till their full maturity. S93M

Luffa operculata - *Wild luffa* {S} Young fruits are said to be eaten in soups and stews. Tropical America. BRUCHER; F80, I16

Momordica balsamina - *Balsam apple* {S} The fruits are pickled, or after prolonged soaking are cooked or added to soups. Young leaves and tendrils are used as potherbs. Seeds are eaten. Tropics, cultivated. DALZIEL, FOX, F., HEDRICK 1919, WATT; F85, K49M, N84

Momordica charantia - *Bitter melon, Balsam pear, Bitter gourd, Foo gwa, Karela* {S} Unripe fruits are eaten boiled, stuffed, fried, pickled, or used in soups, stews, chop suey, and stir-fried dishes. In classic Chinese cuisine, they are prepared with fermented black soybeans. To prepare the fruit, cut in half lengthwise, scoop out seeds and fiber, and parboil or soak in salt to reduce bitterness. Leaves and young shoots are boiled and eaten as a vegetable or added to curries. Tropics, cultivated. CREASY 1982, HARRINGTON, G. [Cu, Cul], HERKLOTS [Cu, Re], KRAFT [Re], OCHSE, TANAKA; A79M, B75, C82, C92, D62, E49, E59, F80, G33, G93M, H49, I39, J7, J82, K49M, L42, *N40*{PR}, etc.

CULTIVARS

Bengal Pride: (Market More) Very smooth dark-green fruits, 8 to 10 inches long. Very few spines and of excellent quality. Very vigorous plant; produces many short side branches which allows for a high yield over a long period. Suitable for dry as well as rainy seasons. Average yield 10 to 12 pounds per plant. O39M

Coimbatore Long: (Coimbatore Long White) Fruits are greenish-white, pale cream in color when ripe, 5 to 8 inches long. Prolific bearer. Most popular cultivar of South India. Usually grown during the rainy season. R0, R50, S59M, S93M

Hong Kong: 80 days. Short, slightly tapered fruit, about 5 inches long. Dark green skin. Rich bitter flavor. Plant is susceptible to wind damage; needs to be grown with supports. D55, L59

Madrasi Giant: An improved Indian cultivar with extra long fruits. O39M

Monsoon Matchless: Rainy season trailing cultivar, with fruits about 18 inches long. S93M

Moonshine: (F_2) Attractive, ivory-white fruits; 6 inches long, up to 1 pound each. Needs a long growing season. Does well trellised in a cold frame. A second generation hybrid. I99

Prodigy: Oblong-shaped fruit, about 8 inches long and 2 1/4 inches in diameter. Distinctive white skin and flesh. Refreshing slight bitterness. Good for stir-frying; also very tasty in salads. Vigorous, heat-tolerant plant. Suitable for open field growing. *S63M*

Taiwan Large: (Large) 80 days. Dark green fruit, 10 inches long by 3 inches in diameter, with a tapering end. A high yielder for planting in spring or summer. D55, L59

The Longest: Pointed, oval shaped fruits, 12 to 18 inches long and 1 1/2 inches broad, having an agreeable bitter taste. Can be sown for either a spring or summer crop. S59M

Uchhe: (Small Bitter Gourd) Very small fruit, 3 to 4 inches long. Prolific plant. Sown from February to July in India. N91, O39M, S59M

Verma's Monarch: Large, thick, bitter-sweet fruits, 9 to 12 inches in length. S93M

Momordica cochinchinensis - *Spiny bitter melon, Bhat karela, Fak kao* {S} Young, immature fruits are boiled and eaten as a vegetable or cooked in curries. Leaves are also consumed. Tropical Asia, cultivated. BROWN, W., BURKILL, HERKLOTS, MARTIN 1975, UPHOF; F85

Momordica grosvenorii* → *Thladiantha grosvenorii

Praecitrullus fistulosus - *Tinda, Squash melon, Dilpasand* {S} The young fruits are cooked and eaten as a vegetable, either alone or with lentils, dal, gram, etc. They can also be pickled, candied, or made into preserves. The fruit is at its best for cooking when it can be easily cut with a knife and the seeds have not hardened. It is the most popular vegetable during summer in North India. Cultivated. CHAUHAN, TANAKA, WATT, ZEVEN; F74{PR}, R50

CULTIVARS

L.S. 48: A high yielding cultivar from India. S59M

Market Pride: An improved Indian cultivar. R0

Round White: Globular, whitish fruits produced in great abundance. Sown from February to July in India. S93M

Summer Prolific Long: Fruits are best harvested when immature. They should be tender and somewhat hairy. Sown from February to April or during June and July in India. S59M

Sechium edule - *Chayote, Vegetable pear, Mirliton, Christophine, Chocho* {PL} Fruits are eaten raw, pickled, sautéed, baked, steamed, stuffed, or made into fritters, sauces, tarts, pies, puddings, sweet-meats, etc. The mature, protruding seeds, which might be called *vegetable scallops*, are the best part. Briefly sautéed in butter they have a delicious nutty flavor. When deep-fried, they taste remarkably like french-fried potatoes. Young shoots, leaves, and tendrils are eaten like asparagus. The roots, known as *chinchayote* or *chinta*, are eaten boiled, baked, fried, or candied in syrup. Also the source of a starch. Tropical America, cultivated. FELL 1982b, HALPIN [Cu, Cul], HAWKES [Re], HERKLOTS [Cu], OCHSE, SCHNEIDER [Re], SHURTLEFF 1979, TANAKA, WILLIAMS, L.; A44M{PR}, *B59*{PR}, C82, D35, L9M, M1M{PR}, *N40*{PR}

Sicana odorifera - *Casa banana, Melocotôn, Musk cucumber, Zucchini melon* {S} The ripe fruits, having a pleasant aromatic flavor, are sliced thinly and eaten raw, or made into jams and preserves. In Nicaragua, they are used to flavor a refreshing drink known as *cojombro*. Unripe fruits are cooked as a vegetable or added to soups and stews. Tropical America. DUKE, HAWKES, KENNARD, MACMILLAN, MORTON 1987a [Cu], NATIONAL RESEARCH COUNCIL 1989, UPHOF, WILLIAMS, L.; **T73M, U33, X94**

Sicyos angulata - *Bur cucumber, Star cucumber* {S} The leaves and fruits are said to be edible. North America. HEDRICK 1919, TANAKA; D58

Telfairia occidentalis - *Fluted gourd, Fluted pumpkin* {S} The seeds, having a pleasant almond-like flavor, are eaten roasted, boiled, or ground and used in egusi soup. When thoroughly dried they are powdered and used to thicken soups. They also yield a cooking oil. Young shoots and leaves are eaten as a potherb, added to soups and stews, or cooked with yam and palm oil. Tropical Africa. HERKLOTS, MARTIN 1975 [Cu], OKOLI 1983 [Cu], OOMEN, TANAKA, VAN EPENHUIJSEN; **X82**

Thladiantha grosvenorii - *Lo han kuo* {S} The pulp of the fruit is intensely sweet, owing to the presence of a glycoside, and may have economic potential as the source of a non-calorific sweetener. Eastern Asia. JEFFREY; F85

Trichosanthes anguina* → *Trichosanthes cucumerina

Trichosanthes cucumerina - *Snake gourd, Padval, Chichinda, Chichinga, Snake tomato* {S} The young fruits are peeled, sliced or cut into pieces, and boiled and eaten like green beans, or used in curries, sambals, and stews. The bright red pulp around the mature seeds is extracted and used in cooking, like tomatoes. Leaves and young shoots are eaten. It is the usual practice to tie a small stone to the tip of a developing fruit to ensure that it grows straight. Tropical Asia. HEDRICK 1919, HERKLOTS [Cu, Re], MACMILLAN, MARTIN 1975, OKOLI 1984, VAN EPENHUIJSEN; D33, E49, F85, H53, J82, K71, N84, N91, R15M, *S36*, S59M, *S70*

CULTIVARS

Extra Long: (Extra Long Special) Very long, narrow fruits, 3 to 4 feet in length. May also be picked while quite young. R0, R50

Keragage: An improved cultivar from Bangladesh. O39M

Long White: Handsome, innocuous serpent-shaped fruits. Sown from April to July in India. S93M

Trichosanthes cucumeroides - *Japanese snake gourd, Karasu-uri* {S} Immature fruits are preserved in salt or miso. Tubers are the source of a starch. Japan, China. TANAKA; O53M

Trichosanthes kirilowii - *Chôsen-karasu-uri* {S} Fruits are eaten. Young budlings are boiled and eaten as a vegetable. Roots are the source of a starch. Eastern Asia. TANAKA; F85

Trichosanthes kirilowii var. japonica - *Ki-karasu-uri* {S} Fruits are preserved in salt or made into gruel. Seeds are the source of an edible oil. The starch obtained from the roots is mixed with rice or wheat flour and made into rice crackers, dumplings, or noodles. Japan. TANAKA; **V19**

CUPRESSACEAE

Juniperus communis - *Juniper* {S} The aromatic fruits are used as a pepper substitute and for flavoring sauerkraut, stuffings, and patés. In Sweden, they are made into a conserve. Roasted berries are used as a substitute for coffee. The dried berries and the oil distilled from them are utilized commercially to flavor gin, liqueurs, cordials, meat products, etc. In France, a kind of beer called *genevrette* is made from fermented juniperberries and barley. Tea made from the berries has a spicy, gin-like flavor. Eurasia, cultivated. BRYAN [Cu, Cul], GRIEVE, HEDRICK 1919, HENDRICKSON, MARCIN, MICHAEL [Pre, Re], MORTON 1976, PAINTER [Re], UPHOF; B94, E47, F80, *G89M*{PL}, *J75M*{PL}, K38, M35M{PL}, N93M, O53M, O93, P5, *Q32*, Q40, *R28*, R53M, etc.

Juniperus deppeana* → *Juniperus pachyphlaea

Juniperus horizontalis - *Creeping juniper* {PL} Fruits are roasted and used in the preparation of a coffee-like beverage. Young branch tips are used as a substitute for tea. North America. TURNER 1978; B9M, B94{S}, *I62*, *J75M*, M92

Juniperus osteosperma* → *Juniperus utahensis

Juniperus pachyphlaea - *Alligator juniper, Sweet-fruited juniper* {S} The fruits are eaten raw, roasted, or dried, ground into meal, and prepared as mush or cakes. They are purplish, globose, half an inch in diameter and have a sweetish, palatable pulp. Southwestern North America. HEDRICK 1919, KIRK, YANOVSKY; *A19*{PL}, B94, F80, J25M, K38, K47T, N84, O53M, O93, S95

Juniperus rigida - *Nezu, Needle juniper* {S} Berries are edible, having been eaten by the Ainus. Also used as a spice. Eastern Asia. TANAKA; F85, K22{PL}, N37M{PL}, N84, O53M, P49, *P63*, *Q32*, *R28*, R78

Juniperus scopulorum - *Rocky Mountain juniper, Colorado red-cedar* {S} Fruits are eaten raw, boiled, or roasted. They can be used to flavor meat, imparting a taste somewhat like sage. The fruits and the young shoots have been used to make a kind of tea. Dried fruits are ground into a meal for mush and cakes, or roasted and made into a substitute for coffee. Western North America. HARRINGTON, H., TURNER 1978; B94, D95{PL}, E15, E47, *G66*, *G66*{PL}, I15, I47, J25M, J25M{PL}, J26{PL}, *J75M*{PL}, K38, K47T, L75, etc.

Juniperus utahensis - *Utah juniper* {S} Fresh and ground fruits were consumed by the Indians. Often put into cakes. Southwestern North America. UPHOF; B94, E15, N84, O93, *P63*

Juniperus virginiana - *Eastern red cedar* {S} Young branchlets and fruits are used for making a beverage. Eastern North America. KUNKEL; C9M, C11M{PL}, D95{PL}, E47, *G9M*{PL}, *G28*{PL}, *G66*{PL}, J16{PL}, K38, K47T, K63G, *M69M*{PL}, N84, N93M, O53M, *Q32*, etc.

Sabina virginiana* → *Juniperus virginiana

Thuja occidentalis - *American arbor-vitae, Northern white cedar* {PL} The Ojibwe Indians made a pleasantly sweet soup from the pith of the young shoots. Leafy branchlets are sometimes brewed into an aromatic tea. North America. FERNALD, GIBBONS 1966b, HEDRICK 1919; C9M{S}, *C33*, E47, *G9M*, H49, I4, J16, J47, J70{S}, K38{S}, K47T{S}, *K75*{S}, *N71M*{S}, N93M{S}

CYCADACEAE

Cycas revoluta - *Japanese sago-palm, Sotetsu* {S} Seeds are eaten fresh or roasted. Dried and ground to a powder, they are mixed with brown rice and fermented into *date miso* or *sotetsu miso*. After the removal of a toxic principle, the heart of the trunk is sliced and eaten baked or powdered. It also yields a starch from which dumplings are made. These are eaten together with sugar and sweet potato. An intoxicating drink is also made from it. Japan, cultivated. BURKILL, SHURTLEFF 1976, TANAKA, UPHOF; A79M, C9M, C78{PL}, D43{PL}, G91M{PL}, H4{PL}, H20{PL}, I85M{PL}, *L5M*, L29{PL}, N84, O53M, P5, *P39*, R33M, etc.

CYCLANTHACEAE

Carludovica palmata - *Panama hat plant, Hat palm* {S} Young leaves and shoot tips, called *nacumas*, are eaten in salads. They are said to have the flavor of asparagus. The inner portions of the lower leafstalks and the berries are edible. Rhizomes are used as a salad and potherb in various parts of Latin America. The young inflorescences are also consumed. Tropical America. DUKE, KUNKEL; *E53M*, F85, N84, O93, *Q52*{PL}

CYPERACEAE

Cyperus esculentus - *Chufa, Earth almond, Tiger nut, Nut-sedge* {PL} The tuberous roots are eaten raw, boiled, roasted, candied, cooked and added to soups, or used in confectionery, cookies, puddings, ice cream, sherbets, etc. They have an agreeable, slightly sweet, nut-like flavor. Ancient Egyptians cooked them in barley juice to add a sweet taste, then ate them as dessert nuts. In Valencia, Spain, a refreshing beverage called *horchata de chufas* is prepared by mixing the ground tubers with water, cinnamon, sugar, vanilla, and ice. In Ghana, *atadwe milk* is made from the ground tubers, water, wheat flour, and sugar. Roasted tubers are a coffee substitute. Chufa oil is considered to be a superior table oil that compares favorably with olive oil. The base of the plant can be used in salads. Pantropic, cultivated. ANGIER [Re], CLARKE, FERNALD, GIBBONS 1966b [Re], HARRINGTON, H., HERKLOTS, ROSENGARTEN, VILMORIN [Cu]; C64M, D58, D76, E50, F12, F80, G26, G92, I99, J29, K47T, L9M, N11, N84, O35G, O53M, etc.

Cyperus flabelliformis - {S} A solution of the ash from the burned leaves is used as a salt substitute in cooking other leafy vegetables. Tropical Africa. FOX, F.; O53M

Cyperus haspan - *Dwarf papyrus* {PL} Salt is prepared from the ash of the plant. Made on a small scale by some tribes in Eastern Africa. Pantropic. UPHOF, WATT; G85, H30, H82, I90M, K34, K85M, M72, M73, M73M, N3M, N84{S}

Cyperus longus - *Galingale* {PL} Tubers are used as a spice in soups, pies, and sweets. Galingale was one of the favorite spices of the medieval kitchen. It was an ingredient of *pokerounce*, a sort of medieval cinnamon toast. Europe. MABEY [Re]; H30, M73M, N84{S}, *Q24*{S}

Cyperus rotundus - *Coco grass, Nut-grass* {S} The nut-like tubers are eaten raw, boiled, or roasted. When freshly dug, the flavor is very strong, resembling Vicks VapoRub. If tubers are allowed to dry, they become milder. Tropics, Subtropics, naturalized in North America. CRIBB, FERNALD, MEDSGER, MORTON 1977; **V84M**

Eleocharis dulcis - *Chinese water chestnut, Matai* {PL} The sweet, crisp corms are eaten raw, cooked, stir-fried, or dried for later use. Widely used in Chinese dishes, especially chop suey. A flour or starch made from the dried, powdered corms, is used to thicken sauces, and to give a crispy coating to foods that are deep-fried. The plant is used for making salt in Zimbabwe. Tropical Asia, cultivated. ALTSCHUL, CHANG, W. [Re], CREASY 1982, GESSERT, HARRINGTON, G. [Cu, Cul], HEDRICK 1919, HERKLOTS, ROSENGARTEN, SCHNEIDER [Cul, Re], VON WELANETZ; C27G{PR}, G85, H30, H82, I74, K25, K85M, M15, M39, M72, M73M, N3M, *N40*{PR}

Eleocharis tuberosa* → *Eleocharis dulcis

Scirpus acutus* → *Scirpus lacustris

Scirpus californicus - *Totora, California bulrush* {PL} The rhizomes and the peeled, lower twelve inches of the stem are baked and eaten, or dried for later use. North and South America. HEISER 1978; *J25*, K85M

Scirpus lacustris - *Great bulrush, Tule* {S} Young shoots are eaten raw or cooked. The pollen can be collected and mixed with meal for making bread, mush, or pancakes. Seeds are ground into a meal and used in the same manner as the pollen. The rootstocks are eaten raw or cooked, and can be made into syrup and flour. Buds at the ends of the rhizomes are crisp, sweet, and excellent eaten raw. Widespread. GIBBONS 1979, HARRINGTON, H., KIRK; B28{PL}, D58, G47M, H30{PL}, H82{PL}, K47T, N3M{PL}, N11{PL}, *N71M*, N84, O53M, *Q24*

Scirpus lacustris var. creber* → *Scirpus validus

Scirpus paludosus - *Alkali bulrush, Nutgrass* {S} Rhizomes were consumed raw or made into a flour for bread. Also the pollen was mixed with bread by several Indian tribes. North America. FERNALD, UPHOF; D58, N11

Scirpus validus - *Tall bulrush, Great American bulrush* {PL} Young shoots and roots are eaten cooked or preserved in rice bran. The tender base of the stem is eaten raw in salads. Pollen is used in soups and breads. The bruised young roots, boiled in water, furnish a sweet syrup. Seeds are edible. North America. FERNALD, MEDSGER, TANAKA; C64M, C64M{S}, *F73*, G26, H30, *J25*, J39M

DAVIDSONIACEAE

Davidsonia pruriens - *Davidson's plum, Ooray* {S} The plum-like fruit, bluish-black when ripe, has soft, juicy purple flesh with relatively small seeds. Although very acid, when stewed with sugar or made into jam or jelly, it is very enjoyable with a distinctive sharp flavor. Considered one of the best native fruits of Australia. Australia. CRIBB, MACMILLAN; *Q25*

DILLENIACEAE

Dillenia indica - *Elephant apple, Chalta* {S} Fruits are aromatic, juicy, acid, and are usually used in curries, preserves, drinks, or fermented into vinegar. The fleshy calyx has an agreeable acid taste and is eaten raw or cooked, put in curries, or made into jellies, drinks, and sherbets. Southern Asia. HEDRICK 1919, MACMILLAN, TANAKA; *A19*{PL}, A79M, E29{PL}, F85, N84, O93, P5, Q12, Q18, Q46

Dillenia philippensis - *Katmón* {PL} Fruits are smooth, green, somewhat flattened and sour in flavor. They are used in jellies, preserves, refreshing drinks, curries, eaten with salt or used to flavor other foods. Philippines. BROWN, W., TANAKA, UPHOF; E29, F85{S}

DIOSCOREACEAE

Dioscorea alata - *White yam, Air potato, Greater Asiatic yam* {PL} The tuber is eaten boiled, roasted, baked, mashed, fried, made into chips, french fries, flours, or used as a thickener in soups. Bulbils, or aerial tubers, are cooked and eaten in the same manner as the tubers. Pacific Islands, cultivated. HAWKES [Re], HERKLOTS [Cu], MARTIN 1976b [Cu, Nu], OCHSE, SCHNEIDER [Cul, Re], TANAKA; N84{S}, P38

CULTIVARS

Florido: Compact tubers, produced singly or in pairs; surface nearly free of roots; quality and flavor very good. Early sprouting, early maturity. High yields. Susceptible to leaf-spot disease and nematodes; intermediate resistance to anthracnose. Originated in Puerto Rico by Franklin W. Martin. **U1**

Forastero: Somewhat irregular tubers, produced singly or in multiples; surface smooth and almost free of roots. Superior cooking and processing qualities. Irregular sprouting, vigorous growth. Excellent yields. Susceptible to leaf-spot disease. Originated in Puerto Rico by Franklin W. Martin. **U1**

Gemelos: Compact, cylindrical, perfectly shaped tubers; produced in multiples; surface smooth, nearly free of roots. Quality very high. Early sprouting, usually gives excellent yields. Originated in Mayaguez, Puerto Rico by Franklin W. Martin. **U1**

Dioscorea batatas* → *Dioscorea opposita

Dioscorea bulbifera - *Air potato, Potato yam* {PL} Underground tubers are sometimes eaten. Bulbils are more commonly consumed having an agreeable taste. They are eaten boiled, baked, mashed, fried, etc. Produces large numbers of bulbils over long periods of time, making it especially suited to the home garden. Inflorescences are apparently eaten. Tropics, cultivated. HEDRICK 1919, MARTIN 1974 [Cu, Nu], ROOT 1980a, TANAKA; D92, F85{S}, N84{S}, P38, R47

Dioscorea cayenensis - *Yellow yam, Guinea yam, Attoto yam* {S} The tubers have a rough outer skin, the flesh is pale yellow and when cooked is palatable, mealy and dry. Eaten boiled, mashed, roasted, fried, baked, put in soups and stews, made into fritters, etc. A tea is made from the leaves. Tropics, cultivated. ALTSCHUL, HERKLOTS, TANAKA; **U1**

Dioscorea esculenta - *Lesser Asiatic yam, Goa yam, Fancy yam* {S} Tubers are eaten after being cooked or roasted. The taste is sweet and pleasant, with somewhat the flavor of sweet potatoes or chestnuts. They can be used in soups, stews, mashed and fried as cakes, boiled, baked, etc. Tropics, cultivated. OCHSE, TANAKA, UPHOF; **X62**

CULTIVARS {PL}

Doli: Good-sized tuber cluster, produces both normal tubers and one oversize tuber. Tubers larger than normal, white-fleshed. Yields only fair. **U1**

Muni: Good-sized tuber cluster, tends to produce another tuber on the same head. Tubers have good size and shape, white flesh. Good yields. **U1**

Dioscorea japonica - *Jinenjo, Glutinous yam, Yama-no-imo* {PL} Tubers are eaten boiled or baked. Grated, they are called *tororo-imo* and are eaten with vinegar, added to soups, mixed with eggs and served as a topping for noodle and rice dishes, or used as a binding agent for other foods, such as the flour in *soba*. Vine tips are eaten steamed or stir-fried. Bulbils are edible. Eastern Asia. SHURTLEFF 1975 [Re], SHURTLEFF 1976 [Re], TANAKA, VON WELANETZ; E66T{PR}, H91{PR}, *K74*{PR}, *Q28*

Dioscorea macrostachya - *Panil book* {PL} Leaves and shoots are used in stews. Tubers are cooked and eaten. Mexico. ALCORN, KUNKEL; F31M, K77M, N43M, N84{S}

Dioscorea opposita - *Cinnamon vine, Chinese yam, Naga-imo* {PL} The tubers resemble D. japonica and are used similarly, but have little binding strength. They are eaten boiled, baked, fried, mashed, grated and added to soups, or mixed with vinegar. A starch derived from the tubers is called *Guiana arrowroot*. Hardy as far North as Canada. Eastern Asia, cultivated. FELL 1982b, FERNALD, TANAKA, UPHOF, VILMORIN [Cu]; E7M, F80, G20M{PR}, I74, I99, J82, K49M

Dioscorea oppositifolia - *East Indian yam, Kavalakodi* {S} Both the tubers and aerial tubers are edible. Young flowering spikes are also eaten. India. TANAKA, WATT; F85

Dioscorea trifida - *Cush cush yam* {PL} The flesh of the edible tubers varies from white to purple. They may be baked whole or peeled and cut into pieces for boiling. The cooked flesh is smooth in texture, attractive, and of an unusual rich flavor that is readily appreciated and sufficiently moist in the mouth. Caribbean region, cultivated. HERKLOTS, MARTIN 1978b [Cu, Nu]; **Z72**

DIPTEROCARPACEAE

Shorea robusta - *Sal tree* {S} Seeds are the source of *sal butter*, used in cooking like ghee and as a substitute for *cocoa butter* in chocolate manufacture. The fruits are occasionally eaten. Southern Asia. BURKILL, TANAKA, UPHOF, WATT; N84, Q46

DRACAENACEAE

Cordyline australis - *Ti-kouka, Cabbage tree, Whanake* {S} Young leaves and shoots are eaten raw or roasted. The roots are sometimes eaten or brewed into an intoxicating drink. New Zealand. COLENSO, FULLER [Re], TANAKA; C9M, C56M{PL}, C92, F85, I28{PL}, *I61*, L91M, N84, O53M, P5, *P17M*, *Q32*, R33M, S43M, S92, etc.

Cordyline fruticosa - *Ti, La'i, Andong* {S} The root is high in sugar and when baked it has a flavor not unlike that of molasses candy. This confection can be eaten or used to sweeten puddings and other foods. Roasted roots are fermented in water and then distilled into an alcoholic beverage, *okolehao*. Young leaves are eaten as a potherb. Tropical Asia, Oceania. DEGENER, GIBBONS 1967, HEDRICK 1919, OCHSE; A79M, C56M{PL}, *E53M*, F85, G25M, H49{PL}, I33, M20{PL}, N84, O93, *Q25*, *Q32*, R33M

Cordyline terminalis → *Cordyline fruticosa*

Dracaena angustifolia - *Semar, Sudji* {S} Very young leaves are cooked and eaten as a side-dish with rice. More often they are pounded and mixed with water to yield a juice that is used for giving green color to an Indian pastry made of glutinous rice. Roasted fruits are eaten in the Andaman and Nicobar Islands. Tropical Asia. BHARGAVA, BURKILL, OCHSE; F85

Pleomele angustifolia → *Dracaena angustifolia*

Sansevieria gracilis - {PL} The flowers are edible. Southern Africa. KUNKEL; E48, K77M, N43M

DROSERACEAE

Drosera rotundifolia - *Roundleaf sundew* {S} The juice is used to curdle milk. The curds and whey that are produced are apparently consumed directly. In Italy a liquor called *rossoli* is distilled from its juices. Northern temperate region. FERNALD, HEDRICK 1919; C8{PL}, D62, I31, J8, N84, O42, S7M, S44

EBENACEAE

Diospyros digyna - *Black sapote, Chocolate pudding fruit* {PL} The fruit pulp is soft, rich, dark chocolate brown in color and somewhat sweet. It is best eaten mashed with a little orange, lemon, or lime juice and then chilled before serving. Also used in preserves, pies, ice cream, cakes, and other desserts, or fermented into a brandy-like beverage. Central America, cultivated. MORTON 1987a, MOWRY, POPENOE, W. 1920 [Cu, Pro], RICHARDSON [Pre, Re]; *B59*{PR}, D57, E29, E29{PR}, E29{S}, I83M, J22, L6, N84{S}, P38{S}, *Q93*

Diospyros discolor - *Mabolo, Velvet apple, Butter fruit* {S} Fruits are eaten fresh as dessert or in salads, and are fried in butter as a vegetable. They are apple shaped, with a velvety, reddish-brown skin. The flesh of ripe fruits is white or cream colored, mealy, aromatic, and somewhat sweet. In the Philippines, the unripe fruit is preferred, being crisp like an apple but juicier and sweeter. Tropical Asia. JOHNS [Cul], KENNARD, MORTON 1987a, POPENOE, W. 1920, STURROCK, TANAKA; F85, R59

Diospyros ebenaster → *Diospyros digyna*

Diospyros kaki - *Japanese persimmon, Kaki* {S} Fruits are eaten fresh or dried. Used in pies, puddings, cakes, breads, cookies, ice cream, and many other desserts. Non-astringent varieties can be sliced and tossed into a green salad. Leaves are used to improve the flavor of pickled radishes. The peel can be powdered and used as a sweetener. Roasted seeds have served as a coffee substitute. Asia, cultivated. GRIFFITH [Pre, Re], MORTON 1987a, POPENOE, W. 1920 [Cu, Pro], SCHNEIDER [Cul, Re], TANAKA; B96, D62, *G66*, H4, H4{PL}, I99, K38, K47T, *N71M*, O53M, P5, *P17M*, P38, *P39*, *Q32*, etc. (for cultivars see Persimmon, page 443)

Diospyros lotus - *Date plum* {S} The fruits are the size of a cherry, yellow in color, changing to blue-black when ripe. They are eaten fresh, dried, or over-ripe (bletted), like the medlar. Dried fruits are sweet, with somewhat the flavor of dates. Also used as a rootstock for D. kaki. Asia, cultivated. HEDRICK 1919, UPHOF; F80, *G66*, I99, K38, K47T, K63G, N0{PL}, *N71M*, N84, N93M, O53M, O93, *P17M*, P38, *P39*, R78, etc.

Diospyros mespiliformis - *Rhodesian ebony, Jackal berry* {S} Pulp of the fruit is very sweet and is eaten raw, made into preserves, dried for future use or fermented into an alcoholic beverage. The Hausas use it for making a soft toffee, called *ma'di*. Tropical Africa. FOX, F., TANAKA, UPHOF; F85, N84, P38

Diospyros oleifera - *Yu-tsu* {S} The fruit is edible after the astringency has been removed or when it is over-ripe (bletted). China. TANAKA; **Y76**

Diospyros texana - *Black persimmon, Texas persimmon, Sapote prieto* {S} Small fruits are black when ripe, with a soft, very sweet flesh that stains the tongue black. They can be eaten fresh or dried. Southwestern North America. HEDRICK 1919, MEDSGER, RILEY 1976; *A19*{PL}, B83M, B94, D95{PL}, I53{PL}, N37M{PL}, P38, *P63*

Diospyros virginiana - *American persimmon* {PL} Fruits are eaten raw or dried, in cakes, breads, pies, puddings, tarts, jams and pancakes or fermented into beer, wine and vinegar. Molasses can be made from the pulp. A tea made from the leaves tastes like sassafras and is high in vitamin C. Roasted seeds are used as a coffee substitute. North America, cultivated. FERNALD, GIBBONS 1962, GRIFFITH; A80M, A82, *B52*, B94{S}, C9M{S}, D95, E87, *G66*{S}, H4, I53, K38{S}, K63G{S}, L99M, N84{S}, O53M{S}, etc. (for cultivars see Persimmon, page 443)

Diospyros whyteana - *Bladder nut* {S} Fruits are edible. The seeds are used as a coffee substitute. Southern Africa. FOX, F., KUNKEL; F85, N84, O53M, R41, R77M

Euclea crispa - *Blue guarri* {S} The leaves are edible. Fruits are also eaten. Southern Africa. FOX, F., KUNKEL; **Y78**

EHRETIACEAE

Bourreria ovata - *Oval-leaf strongbark* {PL} Ripe fruits are edible although not very palatable. In the Bahamas, a tea is made from the bark. Southeastern North America. ALTSCHUL, MORTON 1977; D87G

Cordia abyssinica* → *Cordia myxa

Cordia alliodora - *Laurel negro* {S} The fruits are used as food by a number of Indian tribes. According to Kunkel, the bark is used as a condiment. Tropical America. KUNKEL, UPHOF; N84

Cordia boissieri - *Wild olive, Nacahuita* {PL} Fruits are probably eaten or used to manufacture molasses. Southwestern North America. ALTSCHUL; B83M{S}, H4, I83M

Cordia dichotoma - *Clammy cherry, Thanapet* {S} The sticky, mucilaginous fruit is eaten. Unripe fruits are salted and made into paste or cakes. Flowers, leaves and seeds are also eaten. Southeast Asia. ALTSCHUL, CRIBB, MARTIN 1975, MENNINGER, TANAKA; F85, P5, Q12, Q18, Q46

Cordia myxa - *Sebestan, Sapistan plum, Assyrian plum* {S} Ripe fruits have a sticky, mucilaginous pulp that is mixed with honey to make a sweetmeat called *alewa*, or to sweeten gruels and porridges. Unripe ones are eaten as a vegetable or pickled. The kernel is eaten, tasting somewhat like a filbert. Flowers and leaves are used as vegetables. Tropics, cultivated. DALZIEL, HEDRICK 1919, MARTIN 1975, MENNINGER, TANAKA; N84, P5

Cordia sebestena - *Geiger tree* {S} Ripe fruit is eaten raw, boiled, or pickled. It is somewhat fibrous and not particularly sweet. Tropical America, cultivated. MORTON 1977, TANAKA; F85, *J25*{PL}, N84, O93, P5

Ehretia acuminata - *Koda tree, Púna* {S} Fruits are the size of a pea, red-orange in color, and insipidly sweet. They are eaten raw when ripe. The unripe fruits are pickled. China, Himalayan region. HEDRICK 1919, WATT; Q46

Ehretia anacua - *Anaqua, Anacua* {PL} The fruits are eaten. Southwestern North America. LATORRE 1977b; *A19*, B83M{S}, N37M

Ehretia buxifolia* → *Ehretia microphylla

Ehretia microphylla - *Philippine tea, Pala* {S} Leaves are used as a substitute for tea in parts of the Philippines. The fruit is also edible. Tropical Asia. TANAKA, UPHOF; F85

ELAEAGNACEAE

Elaeagnus angustifolia - *Russian olive, Oleaster* {PL} Yellow fruits are dry, mealy, and somewhat sweet. They are eaten fresh, or made into jellies, sherbets, wine, etc. Mediterranean region to Southwest Asia, cultivated. HEDRICK 1919, SIMMONS 1972; B73M, C9, C9M{S}, *C33*, D45, D95, G41, H4, I4, I15{S}, J16, K38{S}, L99M, N25M, O53M{S}, etc.

Elaeagnus angustifolia var. orientalis - *Trebizond date* {PL} The fruit is similar to the above, but of better quality. Once commonly sold in the markets of Iran and Turkey, but now rare. The flowers are also more fragrant and contain much nectar. Western Asia. SIMMONS 1972, TANAKA.

CULTIVARS

King Red: Grows to 30 feet tall with ornamental, silvery foliage and red fruits that are produced in autumn. Hardy to Zone 4. A new introduction from the New Mexico experiment station. The seeds originally came from Afghanistan. F43M

Elaeagnus argentea* → *Elaeagnus commutata

Elaeagnus commutata - *Silverberry, Gin'yô-gumi* {S} The dry, mealy fruits may be eaten raw or cooked. They are good when used in soup and make an excellent jelly. Alaskan Indians fry them in moose fat. North America. FERNALD, HELLER, KIRK; D95{PL}, E7M, E87{PL}, *G66*{PL}, I47, I63M{PL}, *J75M*{PL}, K38, K63G, M35M{PL}, *N71M*, N84, N93M, O53M, *P63*, *R28*, etc.

Elaeagnus latifolia - *Bastard oleaster, Wild olive* {S} When ripe the olive-shaped fruit is pale red or cherry colored and is acid or somewhat astringent. Cooked and sweetened with sugar, it makes a very agreeable compote. Also used in cakes and tarts. Tropical Asia. HEDRICK 1919, TANAKA; P38

Elaeagnus multiflora - *Gumi, Natsu-gumi, Longipe bush, Mu-pan-hsia, Cherry elaeagnus* {S} Ripe fruits are reddish-orange, juicy, pleasantly acid and are sometimes eaten out of hand. Usually made into pies, tarts, jellies, sauces, wine, etc. China, Japan. BRYAN [Cu, Re], SIMMONS 1972 [Cu]; C56M{PL}, F43M{PL}, H4, H4{PL}, I83M{PL}, K47T, K67{PL}, *N71M*, O53M, O93, P49, *P63*, *R28*, R78, S95, etc.

CULTIVARS {GR}

Red Cherry: A choice shrub with fragrant flowers and tasty red fruits. H4

Variegated: Variegated leaves, fragrant flowers, and edible red fruit. H4

Elaeagnus orientalis* → *Elaeagnus angustifolia var. orientalis

Elaeagnus parvifolia* → *Elaeagnus umbellata var. parvifolia

Elaeagnus philippensis - *Lingaro* {PL} The fruits are pink to pale red, juicy, tart-sweet, and pleasant to eat out of hand when fully ripe. Also used to make a highly-colored jelly. Philippines. MOWRY,

STURROCK; C56M, E29, E29{PR}, E29{S}, I83M, N84{S}, P38{S}

Elaeagnus pungens - *Nawashiro-gumi* {S} Fruits are edible. Usually manufactured into jam, soft drinks, liqueurs, etc. Japan. TANAKA; C9M, F85, H4{PL}, K47T, N84, P38, *P63*

Elaeagnus umbellata - *Autumn olive, Aki-gumi* {PL} The ripe fruits are bright red when ripe, juicy, pleasantly acid, and good to eat out of hand. They are also used dried, or made into jams, sauces, preserves, and pies. China, Japan, cultivated. TANAKA; A91, B9M, C11M, *C33*, *F51*, *G9M*, *G66*{S}, H4, I4, I47{S}, J16, J26, K63G{S}, O53M{S}, Q46{S}, etc.

CULTIVARS {GR}

Hidden Springs: A selection made by Hidden Springs Nursery for better flavor and larger fruit. Grows to 15 feet, with ornamental silvery foliage and fragrant yellow flowers much loved by bees. Hardy to Zone 4. F43M

Jazbo: Selected for its sweet, tasty fruit that is the color of a pomegranate. Fruits are ripe when they drop in your hand; if there is still a tannic flavor, set out for a few days in the kitchen. They can be eaten out of hand or used on cereal, in sweetbreads, or in pancakes. J61M

Elaeagnus umbellata var. parvifolia - *Bammerwa* {S} The fruit is eaten raw, pickled, or put in curries. India. TANAKA, WATT; O46

Hippophae rhamnoides - *Sea buckthorn, Tsarap* {S} Acid fruits are very high in vitamins C and A. They are eaten with milk and cheese, or made into sauces, marmalade, and jelly. The juice can be preserved in honey and used as an addition to fruit preserves, as a sweetener for herbal teas, or as a basis for liqueurs. Common in European health food stores. Eurasia. HEDRICK 1919, LAUNERT [Nu], SIMMONS 1972 [Cu]; B94, F43M{PL}, *G66*, *G66*{PL}, K38, K47T, K64{PL}, L91M, M35M{PL}, M77{PL}, *N71M*, N93M, O53M, Q46, R53M, etc.

CULTIVARS {SC}

East German: An East German selection that originally came from the U.S.S.R. F43M{GR}

Novostj Altaja: (Altai News) Medium-sized fruit of high quality, mean weight .51 grams; carotenoid content 6.8 mg. per 100 grams, ascorbic acid content 53 mg. per 100 grams. Tree very productive, averaging 15.2 tons per hectare; relatively free of spines. The most wilt-resistant cultivar developed to date. **Y29**

Vitaminnaja: Medium-sized fruit of good quality, mean weight .48 grams, more acidic than Novostj Altaja; carotenoid content 9.5 mg. per 100 grams, ascorbic acid content 90 mg. per 100 grams. Tree moderately productive, somewhat susceptible to wilt. Developed in the Altai region of the U.S.S.R. **Y29**

Hippophae salicifolia - *Sea buckthorn* {S} The ripe fruits are used to make jelly or syrup. Himalayan region. TANAKA, WATT; F80, N84, O46, Q40

Shepherdia argentea - *Silver buffalo-berry, Nebraska currant* {PL} The fresh fruits are tart but pleasant and are eaten raw, cooked or dried for winter use. Also used to make jelly, sauce, pies, preserves, soups and drinks. North America. GIBBONS 1979, HARRINGTON, H. [Re], KINDSCHER, TURNER 1979 [Nu, Re]; *C33*, D45, D65, D95, F43M, G60, H49, I47{S}, J25M{S}, J73{S}, K38{S}, K64, *K89*, L27M, M35M, O53M{S}, etc.

CULTIVARS {GR}

Sakakaweja: An improved selection with better flavor and larger fruits. Separate male and female plants; should be planted with several other trees to assure pollination. F43M

Shepherdia canadensis - *Russet buffalo-berry* {S} The bitter fruits are eaten dried, smoked or pressed into cakes. Also made into jelly and a lemonade-like drink. An Indian confection, *Indian ice cream*, is made by beating the berries in water until a foam is formed, then adding sugar. Small amounts of saponin in the fruits cause the foaming action. North America. FERNALD, HARRINGTON, H., HELLER, TURNER 1979 [Nu, Re], UPHOF; A91{PL}, *G66*, I15, I47, I99, J26{PL}, *J75M*{PL}, K49T, M35M{PL}

ELAEOCARPACEAE

Elaeocarpus bancroftii - *Johnstone River almond, Kuranda nut, Kuranda quandong* {S} The kernel of the very thick and hard nut is eaten raw. Its flavor has been variously described as comparable to that of a coconut, inferior to that of the commercial almond, as delicate as a filbert, or just plain delicious. Australia. CRIBB, MENNINGER; N84, P38

Elaeocarpus grandis - *Blue quandong, Silver quandong* {S} Thin layer of fruit pulp is eaten, either out of hand, or by squashing the flesh and mixing it with water to make a paste which is then eaten raw. Australia, Fiji. ALTSCHUL, CRIBB; F85, P5, *Q25*, *Q32*, R33M

Elaeocarpus serratus - *Ceylon olive, Wild olive, Veralu* {S} Fleshy, subacid fruits can be eaten raw. They are also used in drinks and curries, or they are pickled in the manner of olives. Southern Asia. MACMILLAN, TANAKA, UPHOF; F85

Muntingia calabura - *Strawberry tree, Panama berry, Jamaica cherry, Capulín* {S} The fruits, about half an inch in diameter, have a sweet, juicy flesh that is very good to eat out of hand. They are also used in jams, tarts, pies, or added to cold cereal like blueberries. There are both red and yellow fruited forms. Fruits have a high vitamin C content. An infusion of the leaves is used as a tea. Tropics, cultivated. HEDRICK 1919, KENNARD, MORTON 1987a, STURROCK [Nu]; F68{PL}, F85, N84

EMPETRACEAE

Empetrum atropurpureum - *Purple crowberry* {S} Fruits are watery, with a mildly medicinal flavor that is improved by freezing. They are usually eaten cooked with the addition of sugar and an acid fruit, such as the cranberry. In puddings they make a good substitute for currants. Also fermented into an alcoholic drink. Eastern North America. FERNALD, GIBBONS 1979; **Z25M**

Empetrum hermaphroditium→Empetrum nigrum ssp. hermaphroditium

Empetrum nigrum - *Crowberry, Curlewberry* {S} Watery fruits are used in drinks, puddings, pies, jellies, ice cream, or made into wine. The Eskimos dry or freeze them for winter use. They thaw the frozen berries and mash them together with seal oil or whale blubber to produce a kind of pudding. In Iceland they are made into a beverage with sour milk. The twigs are brewed into a tea. Northern temperate region. HELLER, SIMMONS 1972 [Cu], TURNER 1979 [Re], UPHOF; K47T, N84, O53M, S7M, S69

Empetrum nigrum ssp. hermaphroditium - *Mountain crowberry* {PL} Fruits are edible, being similar to E. nigrum, except the flowers are bisexual. Therefore, only one tree is needed for fruit production. Northern temperate region. SIMMONS 1972; K79

Empetrum nigrum ssp. japonicum - *Gankô-ran* {S} The fruit is sweet and is eaten raw or processed into jam and syrup. Japan. TANAKA; N63M

Empetrum rubrum - *South American crowberry* {PL} Fruits are eaten in Antarctic regions. Supposed to have tonic properties. Chile, Patagonia, Falkland Islands. UPHOF; K79

EPACRIDACEAE

Styphelia triflora - {S} The fruits have a sweetish flesh around a large seed. They are edible. Australia. CRIBB, UPHOF; R15M

EPHEDRACEAE

Ephedra nevadensis - *Mormon tea, Squaw tea, Nevada jointfir* {S} A pleasant tea is prepared by steeping the green or dried twigs in boiling water until they turn an amber or pink color. The seeds are roasted and ground into flour to make a bitter bread or mush. Western North America. CLARKE, GIBBONS 1979; A49G, C43M{PL}, D95{PL}, E61{PL}, *E66M*, F79M, I47, J25M, J25M{PL}, J82, K15, K47T, N84

Ephedra torreyana - *Joint fir, Brigham Young tea, Mexican tea* {PL} An excellent tea can be made by boiling the stems for a few minutes and allowing the brew to steep. Southwestern North America. GIBBONS 1973, HARRINGTON, H.; I63M

Ephedra viridis - *Green ephedra, Mormon tea* {S} The twigs are broken into small pieces and brewed into a tea. In some parts of Utah, Nevada and Arizona, they add sugar, lemon juice or strawberry jam. Roasting the twigs before brewing the tea is said to improve its flavor. Seeds are roasted and eaten or ground into a meal or flour. Western North America. HARRINGTON, H., KIRK; A2, C11, C43M, C43M{PL}, D95{PL}, *E66M*, G84{PL}, *I23*{PL}, I47, I63M{PL}, K47T

ERICACEAE

Agapetes saligna - {S} The leaves are used as a substitute for tea in Sikkim. India. HEDRICK 1919; F85

Agapetes variegata - *Dieng-jalanut* {S} Flowers are cooked and eaten with rice. India. ALTSCHUL; **Z25M**

Andromeda glaucophylla - *Bog rosemary* {PL} The leaves are used to brew a delicious, aromatic tea. Boiling or steeping is said to extract a harmful toxin, andromedotoxin. A safer method would be to place the leaves in a jar of water and set it in direct sunlight to make "sun tea". North America. FERNALD; B9M, C40, D62{S}, E87, *I62*, J7, *J75M*, K47T{S}, K79, L91M{S}, M92, N84{S}

Andromeda polifolia → *Andromeda glaucophylla*

Arbutus andrachne - *Strawberry tree* {S} The fruits are eaten. Eastern Mediterranean region. HEDRICK 1919; K47T, O67, *P63*, P86{PL}

Arbutus canariensis - *Canary madrona* {S} The fruits are made into a sweetmeat. Canary Islands. HEDRICK 1919; **Z25M**

Arbutus menziesii - *Pacific madrone* {S} The attractive fruits may be eaten raw, boiled or steamed. After boiling they can be dried and stored for future use. Western North America. HEDRICK 1919, KIRK; A2, B94, *C73*{PL}, E15, E87{PL}, F80, G60{PL}, I98M, *J75M*{PL}, N84, *P63*

Arbutus unedo - *Strawberry tree, Killarney strawberry* {S} The sweet, somewhat mealy fruits are eaten raw, preserved, used in sherbets and *aguardiente*, or made into syrup, wine, brandy, liqueurs or a cider-like beverage. Mediterranean region. ANDERSON, J., BIANCHINI, HEDRICK 1919, SIMMONS 1972 [Cu], UPHOF; A79M, C9M, C56M{PL}, H4{PL}, *I61*, *I62*{PL}, I99, J61M{PL}, K63G, L91M, N84, N93M, O53M, P5, *Q32*, etc.

CULTIVARS {GR}

Elfin King: Round, bright red fruits, to 1 inch in diameter; sweet flavor. Slow growing, ornamental plant; very compact, to 3 feet tall; comes into bearing early, sets fruit freely. Ideal for container culture. I83M, *O97*

Arctostaphylos columbiana - *Columbia manzanita* {S} Fruits are eaten fresh, cooked, or made into jelly or a cider-like beverage. It is best to harvest the fruit when slightly underripe, as fully mature pulp becomes mealy. Northwestern North America. ALDERMAN 1975; A2, B94

Arctostaphylos glauca - *Great-berried manzanita* {S} Fresh fruits are eaten raw or made into jelly and a beverage that resembles cider in flavor. Dried ones are ground into flour. Southwestern North America. CLARKE [Re], YANOVSKY; B94, F85, G60{PL}, K47T

Arctostaphylos patula - *Greenleaf manzanita* {S} The ripe fruits are pleasantly acid, the taste being similar to that of green apples. They are used for making jelly and cider. Western North America. MEDSGER; B94, D95{PL}, F85, I47, I63M{PL}, K47T, N84

Arctostaphylos stanfordiana - *Stanford's manzanita, Myacoma manzanita* {S} The yellowish-brown fruits, when dry, are said to be more flavorful than those of other manzanitas. California. B94, F80

Arctostaphylos uva-ursi - *Bearberry, Kinnikinik* {PL} Fruits are bland and mealy and are usually eaten cooked, preserved, or made into jellies, jams, marmalades, sauces and pastes. The dried leaves are used as tea in some parts of Russia, called *Kutai tea* or *Caucasian tea*. Northern temperate region. FERNALD, FREITUS [Re], GIBBONS 1966b, HARRINGTON, H., UPHOF; A50, *C33*, D95, E15{S}, I15{S}, *I62*, I47{S}, I63M, J25M{S}, J26, J78, K63G{S}, K75M, N84{S}, O53M{S}, etc.

Azalea indica - *Satsuki* {PL} Leaves, flowers, and galls are edible. Japan. TANAKA; B9M, E81, K38{S}, M90, N1M, N84{S}, N93M{S}, R78{S}

Azalea kaempferi - *Yama-tsutsuji* {PL} The leaves are boiled and eaten. Flowers are eaten raw or cooked. Japan. TANAKA; B96, D62{S}, D95, E81, K38{S}, M92, N1M, O93{S}

Azalea nudiflora - *Pinxter flower, Honeysuckle azalea* {PL} An irregular growth, called *May apple*, that forms on the twigs is crisp, juicy, and refreshing. It is eaten as a thirst quencher, sliced and mixed into tossed salads, or pickled in spiced vinegar. North America. GIBBONS 1979, MEDSGER; A34M, B9M, B61M{S}, *B68*, D46, E47, *G28*, K38{S}, L55, M90, N84{S}

Azalea oldhamii - *Kinmô-tsutsuji* {PL} Flower petals are sometimes eaten. Taiwan. TANAKA; I52, L2, M8, N37M, N51

Azalea periclymenoides → *Azalea nudiflora*

Calluna vulgaris - *Heather* {S} The dried flower heads make a good tea, and it is said that Robert Burns drank a *Moorland tea* of heather mixed with dried leaves of bilberry, blackberry, speedwell, thyme, and wild strawberry. A kind of *mead* was once brewed from the flowers. The young shoots have been used instead of hops to flavor beer. Northern temperate region. HEDRICK 1919, MABEY, MACNICOL [Re], MICHAEL [Pre, Re]; B9M{PL}, C13M, D46{PL}, D62, F22{PL}, F80, *G66*, K22{PL}, K38, L91M, *N71M*, O48, O53M, O93, *Q24*, S55, etc.

Chamaedaphne calyculata - *Leather-leaf, Bog-rosemary* {S} An aromatic tea-like beverage can be brewed from the leaves. Boiling or steeping is said to extract a harmful toxin, andromedotoxin. An alternative would be to place the leaves in a jar of water and set it in direct sunlight to make "sun tea". Northern temperate region. FERNALD; D62, K47T, N84

CULTIVARS {GR}

Nana: Dwarf, compact form with white heath-like flowers on arching stems in early spring. Good for shady areas. C76

Chiogenes hispidula - *Creeping snowberry, Birchberry, Moxie-plum* {S} The white fruits are refreshing, pleasantly acid, with a delicate flavor of wintergreen. They are eaten raw with cream and sugar, or made into delicious preserves. A tea made from the leaves has a mild flavor of wintergreen. North America. FERNALD, MEDSGER, SIMMONS 1972 [Cu]; D62, K47T

Epigaea repens - *Trailing arbutus, Mayflower* {PL} The fragrant flowers are spicy and slightly acid and may be eaten raw as a nibble or added to salads. Eastern North America. FERNALD, GIBBONS 1979, PETERSON, L.; A25M, B0, C49, C73M, D62, D75T, E33M, G82M, I31{S}, I44, J78, K22, *K41*, K85, N7T, N45, etc.

Erica cerinthoides - {S} The flowers are sucked for their abundant, sweet nectar. South Africa. KUNKEL; K81M, N84, R77M

Gaultheria adenothrix - *Aka-mono* {S} Berries are eaten or brewed into wine. Eastern Asia. TANAKA; **V19**

Gaultheria antipoda - *Snowberry, Koropuku* {S} The small white fruits are eaten, being of good flavor. New Zealand. COLENSO, UPHOF; D62, K47T, N84, O93, S43M

Gaultheria fragrantissima - *Indian wintergreen* {S} Fruits are eaten. Leaves are used as a substitute for tea. Southern Asia. BURKILL, TANAKA; **Z25M**

Gaultheria hispida - *Snowberry, Waxberry* {S} The white or pale pink fruits are edible but somewhat bitter. Tasmania. CRIBB; D62, K47T, N84, O53M, R33M, S65M

Gaultheria hispidula* → *Chiogenes hispidula

Gaultheria humifusa* → *Gaultheria myrsinites

Gaultheria miqueliana - *Miquel berry, Shiratama-no-ki* {S} Fruits are white or pink, and are eaten preserved in sugar. Eastern Asia. SIMMONS 1972, TANAKA; D62, E63{PL}, E87{PL}, K47T, N84

Gaultheria myrsinites - *Western wintergreen* {S} The small red fruits are eaten raw, cooked, or preserved, or used in jams and pies. Young, tender leaves are especially suited for use as greens. Both the fruits and leaves have the flavor of wintergreen. Fresh or dried leaves are used as tea. Western North America. HARRINGTON, H., KIRK; J93T, K79{PL}

Gaultheria ovatifolia - *Mountain checkerberry, Oregon wintergreen* {PL} Fruits are red, very spicy, and are eaten raw or cooked. Western North America. GESSERT, KIRK, SIMMONS 1972; K75M

Gaultheria procumbens - *Wintergreen, Checkerberry, Tea-berry* {PL} The spicy fruits are eaten raw, used in pies, or made into jam, jelly, and syrup. Leaves are made into a very agreeable tea, called *mountain tea*. Stronger tea, candy, and wine are made from the fermented bright-red leaves. Source of oil of wintergreen, used to flavor birch beer, candy, and chewing gum. Very young leaves make a pleasant nibble. Eastern North America. GIBBONS 1966b [Pre, Re], MARCIN, MORTON 1976, UPHOF; A51M, C9, C13M{S}, C73M, C81M, D75T, E33M, F16, F57M, I44, *J75M*, L2, N7T, N19M, N84{S}, etc.

Gaultheria shallon - *Salal* {S} Sweet, juicy fruits are eaten raw, cooked, dried, preserved, or used in pies, jellies, jams, syrups, pancakes, drinks, or made into wine. Northwest Indians used them to sweeten other fruits, or ate them with oil, fish eggs or salmon. Dried fruits can be used like raisins in cookies and fruit cakes. Western North America. CLARKE [Re], CREASY 1982 [Cu], TURNER 1979 [Re]; A2, C11, D62, D95{PL}, E15, G59M, G60{PL}, I47, J61M{PL}, *J75M*{PL}, K38, K47T, K63G, *Q24*

Gaylussacia baccata - *Black huckleberry* {S} The deliciously spicy, sweet fruits are eaten raw, dried, preserved, cooked with sugar, used in pies, jams, puddings, tarts and preserves, or made into wine. Eastern North America. FERNALD, GIBBONS 1979, HENDRICKSON [Re]; K47T

Gaylussacia brachycera - *Box huckleberry* {PL} The blue fruits are edible but not highly regarded. Eastern North America. HENDRICKSON; A51M, D46

Gaylussacia dumosa - *Dwarf huckleberry* {PL} Fruits are black, juicy, deliciously spicy and are eaten raw, used as a pie filling, or added to pancakes and muffins. Eastern North America. CROWHURST 1972, FERNALD; H4, N37M

Gaylussacia frondosa - *Dangleberry, Blue tangle* {S} The dark-blue berries are juicy and sweet, and can be eaten raw or used in puddings, fruit salads, jellies, and fruit sauces. Eastern North America. CROWHURST 1972 [Re], FERNALD, HEDRICK 1919, MEDSGER; **T41M, U7M**

Gaylussacia ursina - *Bear huckleberry* {S} Fruits are eaten raw or cooked. Eastern North America. TANAKA; **Z25M**

Ledum glandulosum - *Glandular Labrador tea* {PL} An aromatic tea can be brewed from the fresh or dried leaves. Dried leaves are sometimes mixed with other non-aromatic teas, such as goldthread or comfrey. The fresh leaves can also be chewed. Western North America. GIBBONS 1979; D95, N84{S}

Ledum groenlandicum - *Labrador tea* {S} The spicy leaves make a very palatable and refreshing tea. When lemon is added they can be used as an iced tea. The leaves were once added to beer to make it heady. Eastern North America. ANGIER, HEDRICK 1919, MARCIN, MEDSGER; C76{PL}, D62, E61{PL}, I31, *J75M*{PL}, L91M, N84

Ledum palustre - *Crystal tea ledum, Wild rosemary, Bog-tea* {S} Aromatic leaves are used as a substitute for tea. Considered by some to make a better tea than L. groenlandicum. Northern regions. FERNALD, HELLER; C76{PL}, K47T, N84, R53M{PL}

Ledum palustre var. diversipilosum - *Iso-tsutsuji* {PL} Young stems, leaves, and flower buds are dried and used as a tea substitute. Eastern Asia. TANAKA; K79, N63M{S}

Menziesia ferruginea - *False huckleberry, Pacific menziesia* {S} The berries are eaten fresh or dried by the Quileute Indians of Western Washington. Western North America. UPHOF; L91M

Oxycoccus erythrocarpus* → *Vaccinium erythrocarpum

Oxycoccus macrocarpus* → *Vaccinium macrocarpon

Oxycoccus palustris* → *Vaccinium oxycoccus

Rhododendron arboreum - *Tree rhododendron, Buráns* {S} Tender leaves are eaten as a cooked vegetable. The flowers have a sweet, sour taste, and are said to make a good subacid jelly. Large quantities may cause intoxication. Himalayan region. HEDRICK 1919, MACNICOL [Re], TANAKA, WATT; C20{PL}, E81{PL}, E87{PL}, F80, K38, K47T, L2{PL}, M90{PL}, N1M{PL}, N93M, O53M, P49, Q40, Q46, *R28*, R78, etc.

Rhododendron indicum* → *Azalea indica

Rhododendron kaempferi* → *Azalea kaempferi

Rhododendron lapponicum - *Lapland rosebay* {S} Leaves and flower tops are used as a substitute for tea. Northern temperate region. HEDRICK 1919; **V52, Z25M, Z84, Z88**

Rhododendron oldhamii → Azalea oldhamii

Satyria warczewiczii - *Muela* {S} The juicy and acidulous fruits are good to eat. Jellies and confections may be made from them. Costa Rica. DUKE, WILLIAMS, L.; Z25M

Vaccinium angustifolium - *Low sweet blueberry* {PL} The fruits are eaten raw, cooked, dried, in jellies, puddings, pies, cakes, soups, etc. They are smaller than V. corymbosum or V. ashei, but are very sweet, with a slight honey flavor. Ripens about one month sooner than the highbush blueberry. Grown commercially in cold, northern areas like Maine and is largely used for canning. Eastern North America, cultivated. FERNALD, HENDRICKSON [Cu, Pro], MEDSGER, SIMMONS 1972; A38M{PR}, A91, B9M, B26, *B68*, C9, D75T, F16, *H8*, M92

CULTIVARS {GR}

Pütte: A true lowbush type. Plants mature at 8 to 14 inches tall and yield large berries in dense clusters. Has survived -40^0 F. in central Sweden. Developed at the Swedish University of Agricultural Science, Balsgård, Sweden. Patented. L27M{CF}

Vaccinium angustifolium var. laevifolium → Vaccinium lamarckii

Vaccinium arboreum - *Farkleberry, Tree huckleberry, Sparkleberry* {PL} Fruits are dry and insipid. They are occasionally eaten. Reported to be an excellent rootstock for rabbiteye blueberries. North America. BLOUNT, TANAKA; H4, K18, N37M

Vaccinium arctostaphylos - *Caucasian whortleberry, Chernika kavkazk* {S} The edible fruits are small, purplish, and round to pear-shaped. Leaves are used as a substitute for tea. Eastern Mediterranean region. DURAND 1979, REHDER, TANAKA; K47T, N84, P86{PL}

Vaccinium ashei - *Rabbiteye blueberry* {S} Fruits are eaten raw, cooked, dried, or used in muffins, jams, nut breads, pies, pancakes, etc. The plants are low-chill, heat and drought resistant, and are recommended for southern and Gulf Coast states. Southeastern North America. HENDRICKSON; H4{PL}, N84, P38 (for cultivars see Blueberry, page 269)

Vaccinium atrococcum - *Black highbush blueberry* {S} The large, blue-black fruits are sweet, juicy, and very flavorful. They are eaten out of hand, with cream and sugar, or used in jellies, tarts, and wines. North America. CROWHURST 1972, SIMMONS 1972; T41M, U7M

Vaccinium bracteatum - *Shashanbo* {S} Fruits are eaten or brewed into wine. Eastern Asia. TANAKA; F85

Vaccinium caesariense - *New Jersey blueberry* {S} When ripe, the dark-blue fruits are eaten raw or used in jams, jellies, pies, dumplings, etc. North America. CROWHURST 1972 [Re], TANAKA; U7M

Vaccinium calycinum - *Ohelo kaulaau, High-bush ohelo* {S} Small quantities of the bitter fruits are added to the true ohelo berry before cooking to impart a special flavor to them. Hawaii. DEGENER; F85

Vaccinium canadense → Vaccinium myrtilloides

Vaccinium cereum - *Ohelo berry* {S} Fruits are pale yellow to dark red in color and are eaten raw, or cooked in the form of pies and sauces. Pacific Islands. DEGENER; F85

Vaccinium corymbosum - *Highbush blueberry* {S} The large, sweet fruits are widely grown and marketed. They may be eaten fresh, dried, preserved in water or syrup, used in compotes, pastries, pies, muffins, pancakes, cereals, jellies, jams, fritters, puddings, etc. Dried fruits are used like raisins or currants in many recipes or added to soups and stews. North America. ANGIER, GIBBONS 1962 [Re], HENDRICKSON [Cu, Pro], UPHOF; B9M{PL}, *B68*{PL}, K38, M92{PL}, N84, O93, P49, *R28* (for cultivars see Blueberry, page 269)

Vaccinium corymbosum var. pallidum - *Blue Ridge blueberry* {PL} The sweet fruits are eaten raw. Said to be superior to all other blueberries. Berries are borne in dense clusters at the end of the previous year's wood, making them easy to pick. Eastern North America. BRITTON 1913, HENDRICKSON; E33M

Vaccinium crassifolium - *Creeping blueberry* {PL} The fruits are eaten. Southeastern North America. TANAKA; D95

CULTIVARS {GR}

Wells Delight: Fruit edible; black to purplish-black; has a slight aromatic flavor; ripens in late July to September. Plant grows only 5 to 8 inches tall, has a trailing effect as it forms a nearly solid evergreen carpet. Evergreen leaves are reminiscent of Japanese holly. Recommended as an ornamental, low maintenance ground cover. D46, D95, E63, E87, F16, H98, J61M, N37M

Vaccinium darrowi - *Darrow blueberry* {GR} Fruits are eaten. Hybridizes with V. ashei. Eastern North America. TANAKA, ZEVEN.

CULTIVARS

Jonblue: Small, blue-black fruit; very sweet, having a distinct blueberry flavor. Plant grows only 2 to 3 feet tall, will spread 4 to 5 feet, making a very large spreading bush. Foliage bluish, attractive, evergreen in the South. Flowers pink, ornamental. Recommended for dry, sandy, upland soil. Northernmost hardiness unknown. N37M

Vaccinium deliciosum - *Alpine blueberry, Rainier bilberry* {PL} When fully ripe, the fruits are sugary sweet with a delightful aroma and a full, rich flavor. They are best eaten out of hand. Rare in cultivation. Western North America. ABRAMS, EIGHME; P86

Vaccinium erythrocarpum - *Southern cranberry, Mountain cranberry, Dingleberry* {S} The transparent, scarlet berries are excellent in flavor, second only to the lingonberry. They are eaten raw or used in jellies. Recommended for improvement by cultivation. Eastern North America. HEDRICK 1919, HENDRICKSON, SIMMONS 1972, UPHOF; K47T

Vaccinium floribundum - *Mortiño, Colombian blueberry* {PL} The fruits are round, glaucous blue, juicy, subacid, and pleasant to the taste. They are eaten raw, made into preserves, and used in a special dish with molasses, spices and other chopped fruits on All Souls' Day. Sold in the local markets of Ecuador and Colombia. Andean South America. NATIONAL RESEARCH COUNCIL 1989, POPENOE, W. 1924, UPHOF; P86

Vaccinium lamarckii - *Early sweet blueberry* {PL} The fruits are eaten. Considered to be the best of the lowbush type blueberries. Eastern North America. TANAKA; M16

Vaccinium macrocarpon - *Cranberry* {PL} The fruits are too acid to be eaten raw. However, they are widely used in sauces, refreshing drinks, jellies, syrups, pies, muffins, puddings, ice cream, sherbet, cookies, tarts, etc. A teaspoon of salt, added to the cooking berries, is said to take the place of half the sugar ordinarily used in recipes. Northern temperate region. ANGIER, FERNALD, GIBBONS 1962 [Re], MEDSGER, SIMMONS 1972 [Cu], TURNER 1979 [Re]; A38M{PR}, A51M, K47T{S}, L27M, M16

CULTIVARS {GR}

Early Black: Small fruit, when ripe almost black; flesh firm, good for keeping, shipping, and the table; ripens very early, colors well in storage when picked green. Vines comparatively slender, producing uprights rather than runners. Originated about 1825 with Captain Cyrus Cahoon, a Cape Cod cranberry-grower. DANA; S30, S81M

Hamilton: Outstanding miniature plant, 4 inches x 5 inches; non-vining, very slowly forms a cushion covered in spring with pink flowers followed by red fruits. Originally from the Arnold Arboretum. C76, D46, J78, K79

Langlois: Commercial cultivar selected for its drooping flowers and very large red fruit. Grows 10 inches high by 18 inches wide. K79

McFarlin: Berries large, red becoming dark red when ripe; flesh tender, extra fine in flavor; ripens in midseason, variable in keeping and shipping quality. Vines coarse, leaves medium green, rather large. One of the few cranberries grown in both the East and West. Originated with T.H. McFarlin, South Carver, Mass., about 1874. DANA; U7M{SC}

Pilgrim: Prolific x McFarlin. Fruit large; skin purplish-red with yellow undercover; ripens late, keeping quality good. Bush a prolific bearer, greater than Early Black or Howes; resistant to feeding by the leafhopper that spreads false blossom virus. Originated in Whitesbog, New Jersey by the USDA. Introduced in 1961. BROOKS 1972; S30

Smack: Produces large, well-flavored fruit that makes excellent jelly, jams and pies. Introduced by Windmill Point Farm and Nursery. N24M

Wilcox: Howes x Searles. Medium-sized fruit; skin deep red; ripens very early, keeping quality fair. Vine vigorous, very productive, somewhat resistant to false blossom disease. Originated in Beltsville, Maryland by the USDA. Released in 1950. BROOKS 1972; U7M{SC}

Vaccinium maderense* → *Vaccinium padifolium

Vaccinium membranaceum - *Mountain huckleberry, Big whortleberry* {S} The edible fruits are black or maroon in color, borne singly or in pairs, and are among the largest and best flavored of all wild blueberries. The plant is extremely drought resistant. North America. CLARKE, HELLER, HENDRICKSON; A2, C11T{PR}, C12{PR}, D95{PL}, *G66*, I15, I47, J26{PL}

Vaccinium myrsinites - *Florida evergreen blueberry* {PL} Fruits are blue or blackish, and are eaten raw or in compotes and pies. Southern North America. MORTON 1977, UPHOF; N37M, P86

Vaccinium myrtilloides - *Canada blueberry, Sour-top blueberry* {S} The fruits, blue with a heavy bloom, are more acid than is usual for a blueberry and have an agreeable piquancy. They are eaten fresh or used in pies, cakes, preserves, etc. Leaves are used for tea. North America. FERNALD, KUNKEL, SIMMONS 1972; *J75M*{PL}, K47T, N84

Vaccinium myrtillus - *Whortleberry, Bilberry, European blueberry* {S} Fruits are eaten raw, with milk or cream, or used in pancakes, tarts, jellies, preserves, compotes, confectionery, as a side dish for game or meat, etc. They are also brewed into wine or used to color other wines. The leaves are used as a substitute for tea. Eurasia. BIANCHINI, MABEY, MICHAEL [Re], SIMMONS 1972 [Cu], TANAKA; D62, F80, K47T, K63G, L91M, N84, N93M, O48, O53M, P49, P86{PL}, *R28*, S95

Vaccinium ovalifolium - *Black huckleberry, Kuro-usugo* {S} Fruits are light-blue, sweet, borne singly rather than in clusters, and are eaten raw, dried, or cooked. Western North America, Eastern Asia. HELLER, TANAKA, TURNER 1979; D62, N63M

Vaccinium ovatum - *California blueberry, Evergreen huckleberry* {S} When ripe, the berries are black and somewhat sweet. They are eaten fresh, cooked, or dried. Because of their strong flavor they are better for cooking in pies and other dishes than for eating out of hand. Western North America. CLARKE, HENDRICKSON; A2, A80M{PL}, E15, F80, G59M, I49M{PL}, J61M{PL}, *J75M*{PL}, N84

CULTIVARS {GR}

Mareen's Select: A seedling selection by Mareen Kruckeberg of MsK Nursery, Seattle, Washington. The glowing red new growth is the outstanding feature, as showy as flowers and lasting for months. Excellent for acid bed or shrub border. K79

Vaccinium oxycoccus - *Small cranberry* {PL} The acid fruits are used for jellies, sauces, refreshing drinks, pies, and preserves. While smaller than V. macrocarpon, the flavor is said to be superior. Northern temperate region. FERNALD, HEDRICK 1919, MEDSGER, SIMMONS 1972; D62{S}, D95, E87, J78, K47T{S}, O53M{S}, P86

Vaccinium padifolium - *Madeiran whortleberry* {S} The berries are black, juicy, gratefully acid, and edible. Madeira. HEDRICK 1919; K47T, K79{PL}, N84

Vaccinium pallidum* → *Vaccinium corymbosum var. pallidum

Vaccinium palustre* → *Vaccinium oxycoccus

Vaccinium parvifolium - *Red whortleberry, Red huckleberry* {S} Bright red, sour fruits are eaten raw, dried for later use, or used in tarts, jams, jellies, and pies. They make an attractive red jelly, and a light jam that is excellent on waffles or French toast. Western North America. CLARKE, EIGHME, HEDRICK 1919, HELLER; A2, A80M{PL}, E15, F80, *G66*, J61M{PL}, *J75M*{PL}, K47T

Vaccinium pennsylvanicum* → *Vaccinium angustifolium

Vaccinium praestans - *Kamchatka bilberry, Cherry blueberry, Iwa-tsutsuji* {S} The large, red fruits are eaten. They are said to have a delicious flavor. Northeast Asia. DURAND 1979, HEDRICK 1919; N84, O53M, P86{PL}

Vaccinium reticulatum* → *Vaccinium cereum

Vaccinium reticulo-verosum - *New Guinea blueberry* {S} Small, blue-black fruits are edible. The tree is ornamental with large, turgid, thick leaves, and flowers heavily scented of cloves. New Guinea. DURAND 1978; Z25M

Vaccinium scoparium - *Grouseberry, Whortleberry* {PL} Fruits are eaten raw with cream and sugar, cooked into a sauce, made into pies, jams, and jellies, or added to muffins, breads, and pancakes. Dried fruits are used to flavor other foods or to thicken soups. Fresh or dried leaves can be used to make a kind of tea. Western North America. HARRINGTON, H. [Re]; D95

Vaccinium sempervirens - *Rayner's blueberry* {GR} The fruits are edible. Southeastern North America.

CULTIVARS

Bloodstone: Fruit edible; black to purplish-black; has a slight aromatic flavor; ripens in late July to September. Evergreen plant, 5 to 8 inches high, indefinitely broad; has a trailing effect as it spreads. Makes a very good, low maintenance ground cover. Not recommended for areas with excessive soil moisture, high temperatures, and high humidity. F16, N37M

Vaccinium stamineum - *Deerberry, Squaw huckleberry* {S} The fruit is eaten raw, although the quality varies greatly from shrub to shrub. When cooked and served cold they are considered delicious, suggesting a combination of gooseberry and cranberry sauce, with the slight bitter taste of grapefruit marmalade. Jelly made from the fruit has a novel greenish-amber color. Eastern North America. CROWHURST 1972, FERNALD, GIBBONS 1979, MEDSGER; K63G, N7T{PL}, N84

Vaccinium uliginosum - *Bog bilberry* {S} The black, juicy fruits are eaten raw, preserved, made into jam, or fermented into an alcoholic beverage. In France, they are said to be used for coloring wine. Northern temperate region. HEDRICK 1919, HELLER, TANAKA; K47T, K63G, N63M, N84

Vaccinium vacillans - *Late low blueberry* {S} The berries are very sweet and may be eaten raw or used in pies, puddings, and muffins. Considered to be one of the best blueberries. Eastern North America. CROWHURST 1972, FERNALD, MEDSGER; **T41M, U7M, Z25M**

Vaccinium vitis-idaea - *Cowberry, Lingonberry, Mountain cranberry* {PL} The acid fruits are regarded by many as the best of the cranberries. They are made into sweet cranberry-like sauces and served with Swedish pancakes, omelettes, and puddings. In Finland, they are used to make a popular sweet fruit soup called *mehukeitto*. They also make excellent tarts, jellies, and preserves. In Scandinavian countries, the berries are placed in barrels filled with cold water, and sold on world markets. Leaves are used as a substitute for tea. Northern temperate region. FERNALD, HEDRICK 1919, MEDSGER, SIMMONS 1972 [Cu], TURNER 1979 [Re], VON WELANETZ; A15M{PR}, A57M{PR}, B9M, D95, E63M, F35M, F80{S}, H49, J61M, *J75M*, J78, K47T{S}, K79, N37, O53M{S}, *Q24*{S}, R53M{S}, etc.

CULTIVARS {GR}

Ernte Krone: Open-pollinated seed of the improved cultivar Ernte Krone, intended as breeding material. NCGR; **U7M{S}**

Koralle: Similar to large-fruited forms but fruits are larger than normal, a darker red, and hold on the plant all winter if not picked and eaten. Much in demand by those who want fruit production for various lingonberry products. Seedling selection originating at the Warsaw Agricultural University. E87

Masovia: Large-fruited seedling selection that originated at the Warsaw Agricultural University. NCGR; **U7M{SC}**

Sussi: The first lingonberry to be bred for size and quantity of fruit per plant. Plants are small (4 to 8 feet) and need diligent hand-weeding, mulching, attention to pH, and adequate but not excessive watering until established. Developed at the Swedish University of Agricultural Science, Balsgård, Sweden. Patented. L27M{CF}

EUPHORBIACEAE

Aleurites moluccana - *Candle nut, Kukui* {S} Roasted seeds are eaten in small quantities, as larger amounts can be laxative. In Hawaii, they are made into a condiment called *inimona*, by pounding them into a paste that is mixed with salt and chilis. Also used to flavor and thicken Indonesian and Malayan curries. An edible oil is extracted from the roasted seeds and the presscake that remains is fermented into *dageh moonchang*. The powdered seeds are used as an adjuvant in the manufacture of palm sugar. Southeast Asia, cultivated. DEGENER, GIBBONS 1967, OCHSE, SHURTLEFF 1979, SOLOMON; A45{PR}, A79M, C94{PR}, F85, N84, O93, P5, P38, *Q25*, Q46

Baccaurea angulata - *Red angled-tampoi, Ajong* {S} The bright red fruit is eaten. Borneo.

CULTIVARS

Sweet: A recently discovered sweet cultivar of a species previously thought to produce only sour fruit. Small, attractive fruit, about 1 1/2 inches long; sweet, juicy and refreshing, with just the slightest tartness. Tree small; produces fruit in large bunches; highly ornamental; dioecious; strictly tropical in its requirements. O19, O19{PL}

Baccaurea dulcis - *Chupa, Rambai, Kapundung* {S} The small, round, yellow fruits are eaten fresh. They have pleasant, melting white flesh that is normally sweet, sometimes acid. Sold in local markets. Southeast Asia. HEDRICK 1919, MORTON 1987a, RIFAI; **T73M**

Baccaurea motleyana - *Rambai, Rambeh* {PL} The small, oval, brownish-yellow fruits are sweet to acid and are eaten fresh, stewed or preserved. An alcohol beverage is prepared from the juice. Has good potential for increased cultivation. Malaysia, cultivated. MACMILLAN, MORTON 1987a, RIFAI, TANAKA; O19, O19{S}, S54M

Bridelia cathartica - *Munohya-menda* {S} The small, round, dark-red to almost black fruits are eaten raw. In Rhodesia, the Tonga chew the leaves, then drink water, the leaves causing the water to acquire a sweet taste. Southern Africa. FOX, F., VON REIS; N84

Chrozophora plicata - *Giradol* {S} Petals, fruits, and sap are the source of a red and blue dye, *tournesol*, used for coloring liqueurs, wine, pastries, and Dutch cheeses. Northern Africa. UPHOF; F85, N84

Cicca acida - *Otaheite gooseberry, Star gooseberry* {S} Fruits are usually too sour to eat raw. When cooked they become bright red and make excellent jams, preserves, and pies. They are also pickled, made into vinegar, or used as a tamarind substitute to give a sour flavor to other foods. They may be of value as a natural red coloring agent in preserves made from mixed fruits. The young leaves are cooked as greens in India and Indonesia. Tropics, cultivated. ALTSCHUL, KENNARD, MORTON 1987a, OCHSE, TANAKA; F85, N84, P38, S54M{PL}

Cnidoscolus chayamansa - *Chaya, Tree spinach* {PL} Young, tender leaves and stem tips are cut into small pieces and used as a potherb. They are also used in soups, stews, and *atoles*, or mixed with onion and egg to make a delightful *tortilla*. Contains hydrocyanic acid and should not be eaten raw. When properly cooked the leaves are high in protein, calcium, iron, and vitamins A and C. Central America. MARTIN 1978c [Cu, Nu], NATIONAL RESEARCH COUNCIL 1975a, WILLIAMS, L.; D33

Croton reflexifolius - *Copalchí, Hoja amarga, Sasafrás* {S} The aromatic fruits, leaves, or bark are sometimes used to flavor the local rum in El Salvador. Central America. WILLIAMS, L.; **X94**

Emblica officinalis - *Emblic, Myrobalan, Amla* {S} Acid fruits have a very high vitamin C content. They are eaten raw with salt, sugar, or chilis. Also used in jellies, preserves, pickles, tarts, sweetmeats, relishes, or as a sour flavoring. Dried fruit chips are seasoned with caraway seeds, salt, and yogurt and eaten after fasting. Unripe seeds and leaves are edible. Tropical Asia, cultivated. MARTIN 1975, MENNINGER, MORTON 1960 [Cu, Nu], MORTON 1987a; F85, N84, P5, P38, Q12, Q18

Euphorbia helioscopia - *Tôdai-gusa* {S} Young stems are edible when cooked or oil roasted. Young leaves are used as a tea substitute. Northern temperate region. TANAKA; F85, N84

Euphorbia tetragona - {S} Flowers are rich in nectar which is sometimes used in confectionery. South Africa. PALMER; I33

Leichhardtia australis - *Doubah* {S} The fruits were roasted and eaten by the Aborigines. Flowers, leaves and roots are also edible. Australia. CRIBB, O'CONNELL; N84

Macaranga grandifolia - *Samac* {S} Leaves, bark, and fruit are added to sugar cane juice that is fermented into *basi*, a traditional alcoholic beverage of the Ilocanos on Luzon. Philippines. STEINKRAUS; F85

Macaranga tanarius - *Samac* {S} The dried leaves, bark and fruit are used like those of M. grandifolia in the preparation of *basi*. Tropical Asia. STEINKRAUS, UPHOF; F85

Manihot esculenta - *Cassava, Yuca, Manioc, Mandioca* {PL} Young leaves are boiled like spinach or added to stews. Roots are eaten boiled, fried, baked, made into flour, *farina*, sweetmeats, breads, syrup, pastries, *fufu*, chips, and *arrowroot*. The refined starch from the tubers, known as *tapioca pearls*, is used in soups, puddings, and dumplings. In powdered form it is called *tapioca flour*, and is employed as a thickening agent for sauces. Juices from the root are boiled to make the condiment *cassareep*, or fermented into *chicha*, *kaschiri*, and other alcoholic beverages. Other fermented products are *gari*, *tapé*, *ontjom*, *uji* and *tempeh*. Tropical South America, cultivated. HAWKES [Re], HEDRICK 1919, MARTIN 1975, MAY, R. [Nu, Re], OCHSE, SCHERY, SCHNEIDER [Cul, Re], STEINKRAUS, TANAKA, UPHOF; *B59*{PR}, C27M{S}, E29, F85{S}, H4, I28, J66M{PR}, L90G{PR}, *N40*{PR}, N84{S}

Manihot glaziovii - *Maniçoba, Mandioca brava, Ceara rubber* {S} Tubers are sometimes eaten. Otherwise they are a source of starch. The oily seeds are also eaten. Brazil. TANAKA; F85

Phyllanthus acidus* → *Cicca acida

Phyllanthus emblica* → *Emblica officinalis

Phyllanthus nobilis - *Barudo* {S} The fruit is green, acid, said to be eaten when immature. Mexico. VON REIS; **X94**

Ricinodendron africanum* → *Ricinodendron heudelotii

Ricinodendron heudelotii - *Manketti nut, Essang nut* {S} The dried kernels are ground and used in stews or eaten as a relish. They also yield an edible oil, sometimes called *essang oil*. Tropical Africa. DALZIEL, MENNINGER, UPHOF; N84

Ricinodendron rautanenii - *Mongongo nut, Manketti nut* {S} Pulp of the fruit is eaten raw or cooked, and is also dried and ground for use in porridge. When eaten fresh it resembles a date, though not as sweet. After boiling, it turns maroon and tastes like apple sauce. The nutritious and tasty kernels are eaten raw or roasted. Roasted kernels taste like roasted cashew nuts but after prolonged roasting have the flavor of "fine old cheese". Also the source of *manketti nut oil*, used for cooking. Tropical Africa. FOX, F., UPHOF; N84

Sapium sebiferum - *Chinese tallow tree, Petroleum tree* {S} Outer covering of the seed produces a fat said to be used as a substitute for lard or cacao butter. Eastern Asia. TANAKA; A80M{PL}, C56M{PL}, F80, F85, *G66*, H4, H4{PL}, *I62*{PL}, K38, *L5M*, L90{PL}, N37M{PL}, O53M, P5, *P17M*, Q12, *Q32*, Q46, etc.

Sauropus androgynus - *Rau n'got, Sweet leaf bush, Katook, Chekkurmanis* {S} The tender tips, young leaves, flowers, and immature fruits are steamed and eaten as a potherb or put in soup. Leaves are used to give a green color to pastry, fermented glutinous rice, and the alcoholic beverage *brem bali*. Ripe fruits can be made into sweetmeats. Southern Asia. HACKETT, MARTIN 1975, OCHSE, OOMEN, STEINKRAUS; F85, O19, O19{PL}

Tetracarpidium conophorum - *Owusa nut* {S} Leaves, young shoots and fruits are eaten with rice in Sierra Leone. The seeds are eaten raw or roasted, and are often served with corn on the cob. They also yield and edible oil, called *n'ghat oil*. West Tropical Africa. DALZIEL, MENNINGER, TANAKA; **X44**

EURYALACEAE

Euryale ferox - *Gorgon, Foxnut* {S} The soft, pulpy, glutinous fruit is highly esteemed in China as a cooling tonic food. Fresh or dried seeds are eaten and are also a source of starch. Very young stalks and rhizomes are edible. Frequently cultivated in India and China. The seeds are available in Chinatown markets. China to Southeast Asia. HEDRICK 1919, MENNINGER, TANAKA, UPHOF; *O54*

FABACEAE

Abrus pulchellus - *Malay licorice* {S} Roots are used as a substitute for licorice in Malaysia. Old World Tropics. UPHOF; F85

Aeschynomene indica - *Kusa-nemu* {S} Leaves are eaten fresh, parboiled and added to soups, cooked as a potherb, stir-fried, etc. The whole plant is dried in the shade, finely chopped, roasted and used as a tea substitute. Old World Tropics. TANAKA; F85, N84

Amorpha canescens - *Leadplant, Wild tea* {S} An infusion of the dried leaves makes a yellow, pleasant tasting tea. Western North America. KINDSCHER, YANOVSKY; *B29M*, G47M, H63{PL}, I47, J40, J40{PL}, J41M, J41M{PL}, J42, J42{PL}, J43, K47T, K62, L91M, M77M{PL}, etc.

Amorpha fruticosa - *Indigo bush, False indigo, Itachi-hagi* {S} The fruit is crushed and used as a condiment. Western North America, Japan. TANAKA; B94, B96{PL}, C11, C13M, D62, I11M{PL}, I37M{PL}, I98M, J25M, *K89*{PL}, *M69M*{PL}, N24M{PL}, N37M{PL}, N93M, O53M, etc.

Amphicarpaea bracteata* → *Amphicarpaea monoica

Amphicarpaea monoica - *Hog peanut, Ground peanut* {S} The subterranean, peanut-like seeds are sweet and delicious eaten raw, having more the flavor of shelled garden beans than peanuts. They can be boiled and served with butter or cream, or used in soups and stews. Seeds produced by the above ground pods can be boiled and eaten. Formerly cultivated for its seeds in the southern United States. North America. CROWHURST 1972, FERNALD, GIBBONS 1979, KINDSCHER, MEDSGER; F85

Apios americana - *Groundnut, Potato bean, Indian potato* {PL} The sweet, starchy tubers are eaten raw, boiled, fried, roasted, or otherwise prepared like potatoes. They can be added to soups, stews, and casseroles, or mashed and used in breads. Menomini Indians made a preserve by boiling the tubers in maple syrup. Groundnuts contain seventeen percent crude protein, more than three times that of potatoes. The seeds are sometimes used like peas or beans. North America. ANGIER, BLACKMON 1986a [Cu, Re], FERNALD, KINDSCHER, MEDSGER, NATIONAL RESEARCH COUNCIL 1979, VILMORIN; B61M{S}, C49, C73M, D75T, E47M, I44, M16

CULTIVARS

LA85 Series: William Blackmon of Louisiana State University has been doing research into developing this plant as a commercial crop. He is close to releasing named cultivars that will do well in certain areas of the country, especially the Southeast. LA85-034 has been a very consistent producer under different growing conditions and is being considered for release for use in home gardens. This material is currently available to researchers. BLACKMON 1986b; **T63T**

Apios tuberosa* → *Apios americana

Arachis hypogaea - *Peanut, Groundnut* {S} Seeds are eaten raw, boiled, steamed, roasted, salted, in confectionery, made into peanut butter, ground into flour for breads, etc. Source of peanut oil, used in salads, margarine, and preferred over all others for stir-fry cooking. Used for the universally popular groundnut soup in Africa. In Asia, peanuts are used as a substrate for *miso*, *ontjom*, *dageh*, *tempeh*, and other fermented foods. Once used as an adulterant of coffee, called *Austrian coffee*. Young shoots, leaves, and unripe pods are eaten as potherbs. Sprouted seeds are consumed. South America, cultivated. HALPIN [Cu, Cul], HERKLOTS, OCHSE, ROSENGARTEN [Re], SHURTLEFF 1979, STEINKRAUS, TANAKA, UPHOF, WILSON, E.G. [Re]; L59, N84, O53M (for cultivars see Peanut, page 425, also see Sprouting Seeds, page 485)

Aspalathus contaminatus* → *Aspalathus linearis

Aspalathus linearis - *Rooibos tea, Red tea* {PR} Source of a low tannin, caffeine-free tea with a very agreeable aroma and a pleasant, nonastringent taste. Can be drunk hot or cold (sweetened or not), diluted with milk, flavored with cinnamon or other spices, or used as an excellent base for punch. Has a high protein and vitamin C content. A portion will yield twice as much full-flavored brew as the same amount of ordinary tea. Usually marketed as *Kaffree tea* in the United

States. South Africa. CHENEY [Cu], FOX, MORTON 1983 [Nu, Pre]; A52M, C95

Astragalus boeticus - *Swedish coffee* {S} Cultivated in certain parts of Europe for its seeds, which are roasted, ground, and used as a substitute for coffee. Mediterranean region. HEDRICK 1919, ZEVEN; **U63, W59M**

Astragalus caryocarpus → *Astragalus crassicarpus*

Astragalus crassicarpus - *Groundplum milk-vetch, Buffalo pea* {PL} The thick, fleshy, unripe pods, which resemble green plums, are eaten raw or cooked. When cooked, they are usually prepared and served whole in the same manner as the edible-podded sugar pea or Chinese snow pea. Sometimes the pods are cooked and spiced for pickles. North America. KINDSCHER, MEDSGER; J41M, J41M{S}

Astragalus glycyphyllos - *Milk vetch* {S} The herb is occasionally used for tea. Eurasia. UPHOF; *N71M*, N84, O53M, *Q24*, S7M

Astragalus gummifer - *Tragacanth* {S} Source of a *gum tragacanth*, much appreciated for use in salad dressings, syrup, sauces, confectionery, etc. Eurasia. KUNKEL, UPHOF; **V89, Z24**

Cajanus cajan - *Pigeon pea* {S} Very young seeds are cooked and eaten like green peas, especially in rice dishes. Dried seeds are used in soups and curries, or fermented into *dhokla* and *tempeh kacang iris*. Unripe pods are also eaten in curries. The leaves and young shoots, having a protein content of about nine percent, are cooked as a potherb. In Indonesia, the germinated seeds are eaten when about one inch long. Split dried pigeon peas are available as *toovar*, *toor* or *arhar* dal in Indian markets. Known as *gandules* in Latin America, the canned fresh peas can be found in the specialty sections of some supermarkets. Southern Asia, cultivated. CHANTILES [Re], DUKE, HAWKES [Re], HERKLOTS, JAFFREY, MARTIN 1975, OCHSE, SHURTLEFF 1979, STEINKRAUS, VON WELANETZ; A52M{PR}, A79M, A88T{PR}, D33, F74{PR}, F85, L9M, N84, O93, P1G, P38, Q12, *Q25*, Q46, R47, etc.

CULTIVARS

2-B: Bushy plant that only grows to 3 feet tall, or about half the size of other types. D33

Black: Black-seeded cultivar that has performed well in Florida and in other areas where it has been distributed by ECHO. D33

Short Day: Early maturing strain that is day length independent and does well under short day conditions. D33

Cajanus indicus → *Cajanus cajan*

Canavalia ensiformis - *Jack bean, Chickasaw lima* {S} The immature pods, before the seeds inside them have swelled, are eaten raw, preserved in salt, or boiled and served like snap-beans. Ripe seeds are used as a substitute for coffee. Unripe seeds can be eaten boiled, roasted with salt, or peeled and used like fava beans. In Indonesia, the seeds are fermented into *tempeh kara bedog*. The young leaves are prepared like spinach. Fresh unripe seeds are considered poisonous. West Indies, cultivated. HAWKES [Re], HERKLOTS, NATIONAL RESEARCH COUNCIL 1979 [Nu, Pre], SHURTLEFF 1979, TANAKA, UPHOF; A79M, D33, E83T, F85, Q12, Q46, *S70*

Canavalia gladiata - *Sword bean* {S} Unripe pods are boiled and served as a green vegetable like string beans. The full-grown but still green seeds are cooked and eaten. Dry, fully mature seeds are edible after extensive boiling and peeling of the seed coat. They can also be detoxified by fermentation to *tempeh*. In Japan, the young pods are sliced and pickled in soy sauce with radishes, eggplants, and lotus, and the seeds are boiled and mashed with sugar. The leaves are used as a potherb. Tropical Asia, cultivated. HERKLOTS [Cu], NATIONAL RESEARCH COUNCIL 1979 [Nu, Pre], TANAKA; D33, N84, R47, *S70*, S93M

Canavalia maritima - *Mackenzie bean* {S} In Malaysia, the flowers are eaten as a flavoring. The young pods are eaten when young. Young seeds are said to make a good *pease porridge*. Paleotropics. BURKILL; *F73*{PL}, F80, F85, I59G, *N79M*, N84, O93, *P17M*, *Q25*, *Q32*, R15M, S92, T7

Canavalia rosea → *Canavalia maritima*

Caragana ambigua - *Shinalak* {S} Fruits and flowers are eaten raw or cooked. Central Asia. HEDRICK 1919, TANAKA; **Z25M**

Caragana arborescens - *Siberian pea tree* {PL} Young, green pods are eaten as a vegetable in some parts of Siberia. The mature seeds, containing up to thirty six percent protein, can be used in recipes calling for dried beans or peas. Bland in flavor, they are best cooked in spicy dishes like chili. Siberia, cultivated. HEDRICK 1919, PETERSON, T., UPHOF; *C33*, E15{S}, E47{S}, G67, I47{S}, I77M, J26, J61M, L63M{S}, M35M, *M69M*, N0, N25M, N93M{S}, O53M{S}, etc.

Cicer arietinum - *Chick pea, Garbanzo* {S} Fresh or dried seeds are consumed in soups, stews, sweetmeats, *falafel*, etc. Also fermented into *dhokla* and *tempeh*. Parched seeds are eaten as a snack, or they can be ground and used as a coffee substitute. Roasted roots are also a coffee substitute. Widely utilized in India, where it is called *Bengal gram*, and when split, *chana dal*. Chick-pea flour or *besan* is used in batters, sauces, soups, sweetmeats, fritters, pancakes, and dumplings. Crisp, chick-pea flour noodles, called *sev*, are a popular snack food in India. A strong, acid dew forms on the plant overnight which is gathered and made into vinegar or cooling drinks. Young leaves, shoots and pods are used as potherbs. Sprouted seeds are eaten. Eurasia, cultivated. DUKE [Nu], HEDRICK 1919, HERKLOTS, JAFFREY [Re], SHURTLEFF 1979, STEINKRAUS, UPHOF, VILMORIN [Cu], VON WELANETZ; A88T{PR}, B75, D11M, E97, F85, G71, H19M{PR}, L50M{PR}, L79M, L99{PR}, M46, *N71M* (also see Sprouting Seeds, page 485)

CULTIVARS

Ayelet: A very productive mid-early cultivar, resistant to ascochyta. Sown in January and February in Israel. The plant is erect. Kernels are medium sized, dark colored and mainly used for home consumption. Yields are 15% higher than in other cultivars. *P75M*

Black Seeded: Small seeds, one or two per pod. Plants produce numerous pods. Should be planted close together to form a lush canopy of blue-green foliage. Likes hot weather and is drought tolerant. Originated in Ethiopia. A2

Brown Seeded: Small-seeded "deshi" type of Indian origin, better suited to home gardens than the large commercial types. Developed and recommended for use in the interior Northwest and other short-season, dry areas. Not appropriate for coastal fog belts. A2

Green Seeded: Best choice for sprouting. Green inside as well. For cultural recommendations, see Brown Seeded. A2

Kabuli Black: 95 days. Very hardy and vigorous cultivar originating in Kabul, Afghanistan and released by Washington State University. Medium-sized, solid black seed; two seeds per pod. Somewhat tolerant of cold soils. Drought resistant. Has grown to maturity easily in the Bitterroot Mountains of Montana. E24, E59Z, F74{PR}, I99, K17M, K49T, L79M

Mayo Winter: Plump, beige seeds. Dry farmed on a Sonora, Mexico ejido (communal farm). Adapted to the low, hot desert where it is planted with the winter rains. An introduced staple. I16

Tarahumara: Small, dark-brown seeds, smaller than Mayo Winter. Prolific, very drought and insect resistant plant. Fall crop from the bottom of Copper Canyon, Mexico where it is dry farmed. Adapted to growing at different elevations, from sea level to 10,000 feet. I16, K49T

Whitey: Late cultivar with large white kernels. Sown in February and March in Israel. The plant is tall. Used for consumption of the whole kernels, of which the skin peels off after a relatively short period of cooking. Recommended for seeding in higher rainfall areas, or with supplementary irrigation on fertile soils. *P75M*

Cicer songaricum - {S} The young shoots can be pickled or used as a potherb. Seeds are eaten both raw and cooked. A vinegar is made from an acid dew that forms on the leaves. Southern Asia. TANAKA, WATT; **Z98**

Clitoria ternatea - *Butterfly pea, Kordofan pea* {S} Flowers are used to give a blue tinge to rice cakes and boiled rice. The young pods are consumed like string beans. Leaves are also used to dye food or are eaten as a potherb. Tropics, cultivated. BURKILL, HEDRICK 1919, MARTIN 1975, TANAKA, ZEVEN; A79M, B62, *E53M*, E83T, F80, J27{PL}, O53M, O89, O93, P5, *P17M*, Q12, *Q25*, *Q32*, S91M, etc.

Cordeauxia edulis - *Yeheb, Ye-eb, Jeheb* {S} The nutritious seeds, the size of a small macadamia nut or large filbert, have a smooth consistency and a delicious, chestnut-like flavor. They can be eaten raw or cooked. An infusion of the leaves is used as a substitute for tea. An endangered species adapted to hot, dry regions of uncertain rainfall. Begins to bear prolifically when only 3 to 4 feet high. Somalia. MACMILLAN, NATIONAL RESEARCH COUNCIL 1979 [Nu], UPHOF; **Z69M**

Crotalaria glauca - {S} Leaves, flowers, and pods are eaten as potherbs. Tropical Africa. HEDRICK 1919; **Y78**

Crotalaria longirostrata - *Chipilín, Chapile* {S} The young shoots are steamed and served whole, the leaves and flowers having been stripped off and eaten separately for their pronounced snap-bean-like flavor. The leaves can be ground with garlic and brushed on bread or added sparingly to white sauce. When added to tamales that are made with butter instead of oil, the flavor combination is said to be unforgettable. Central America, cultivated. UPHOF, WILLIAMS, L.; F80, F85

Crotalaria ochroleuca - *Sun hemp* {S} The flowers and leaves are eaten. Tropical Africa. KUNKEL; D33

Cyamopsis psoralioides → ***Cyamopsis tetragonolobus***

Cyamopsis tetragonolobus - *Guar, Cluster bean* {S} The unripe pods are eaten in curries, fried in oil, salted, or dried for later use. The protein-rich seeds are also eaten. Source of guar gum, used by food manufacturers as a stabilizer and thickener in ice creams, bakery goods, and salad dressings. Sprouted seeds are occasionally eaten. Young pods are available at Indian markets in New York and other large cities. Tropical Asia. HERKLOTS, MACMILLAN, NATIONAL RESEARCH COUNCIL 1975a, TANAKA; A79M, D33, F80, I99M, N84, Q46, *S36*

CULTIVARS

Barasati: 90-120 days. Bushy annual grows 2 to 6 feet tall. Trifoliate leaves. Long racemes of purple flowers followed by 1 1/4 to 2 inch pods in clusters all up the stem. A cultivar much grown in India for the young pods, which are highly esteemed as a pleasant and delicate vegetable. Dropped by F80

Deshi Small: An improved from with short, blocky pods. Low seed to pod ratio. Sown from April to May and from July to August in India. Adapted to hot, dry conditions. R0

Long Podded: 60 days. Climbing, branching type plant, grows to 3 feet. Adaptable to a wide range of climatic conditions. Matures early. R50

New Spring: 45 days. One of the best cultivars for table use. The extra long, 10 to 11 inch pods are produced in 2 or 3 flushes. S93M

Pusa Navbahar: 40 days. Single-stemmed, high yielding plant, bears at every node. Smooth, glossy green pods, 6 inches long. Can be grown during both spring and rainy seasons. R0, R50, S59M

Surati Makhani Long: An improved type from India with long, smooth pods. Low seed to pod ratio. Sown from July to August in India. R0

Cyclopia subternata - *Caspa tea* {S} Leaves are the source of the commercial Caspa tea. South Africa. UPHOF; N84, R41, R77M

Cytisus scoparius → ***Sarothamnus scoparius***

Dalea candida → ***Petalostemon candidum***

Dalea sp. - *Toronjil* {S} The highly aromatic herb is used to prepare a tea resembling lemon grass or lemon verbena, but with a more subtle and complex flavor. Annual plant with short racemes of small blue-purple flowers and lacy, delicate pinnate foliage. Low, sprawling trailer when grown in poor, compacted soil, as by paths. Grows to four feet in good soil. Mexico. F80

Daviesia latifolia - *Hop bitter-pea* {S} Leaves have been used as a substitute for hops. Australia. CRIBB; *N79M*, N84

Desmanthus brachylobus - *Illinois bundleflower* {S} The protein rich seeds are edible but without much flavor. Being evaluated by the Land Institute of Salina, Kansas as an edible legume for growing with perennial grains in a non-tillage permaculture system. North America. *B29M*, F12, F80, G47M, J39M, J39M{PL}, J40{PL}, K62, L41, *M25*, M77M{PL}, N84

Desmanthus illinoensis → ***Desmanthus brachylobus***

Diphysa robinioides - *Cuachipil, Guachipilín* {S} The yellow flowers become mucilaginous when steamed, and are often added to beans or are eaten with tortillas. Central America. F80, F85

Dolichos biflorus → ***Macrotyloma uniflorum***

Dolichos lablab → ***Lablab purpureus***

Dolichos lablab var. lignosus → ***Dolichos lignosus***

Dolichos lignosus - *Australian pea, Ballar* {S} The tender seeds are eaten fried, or cooked and salted like green peas. Pods are eaten at all stages of development. The dried seeds are consumed as a split pulse. Southern Asia. TANAKA; N84, S92

Dolichos malosanus - *Baput, Igikindye* {S} The flowers and fruits are consumed as vegetables by the natives. Central Africa. UPHOF; N84

Ervilia sativa → ***Vicia ervilia***

Ervum monanthos → ***Vicia monantha***

Erythrina americana - *Flor de colorín, Tzompantle* {PL} In Mexico, the petals and young inflorescences are fried and eaten, especially in tamales at Easter time. Tender leaves are used for greens. Central America. ALCORN, KUNKEL; C43M, F80{S}, F85{S}, I83M

Erythrina berteroana - *Coral-bean, Pito* {S} Flowers and immature inflorescences are eaten as a vegetable with meat, in stews, and in egg dishes. Tender shoots and leaves are eaten raw, or more commonly, cooked in stews with other foods. Tropical America. MARTIN 1975, TANAKA, WILLIAMS, L.; **X94**

Erythrina edulis - *Basul, Balú, Chachafruto* {S} The extremely large, succulent seeds have a pleasant, slightly sweet flavor and are usually boiled and eaten like lima beans with corn, cassava, bread or potatoes. They are sometimes mashed with cheese and are also fried. Contains about twenty percent protein. Northern South America. NATIONAL RESEARCH COUNCIL 1989, PEREZ-ARBELAEZ; **T73M**

Erythrina glauca - *Ahuijote* {S} The flowers are folded into batter, cooked and eaten. Central America. WILLIAMS, L.; **X94**

Erythrina herbacea - *Eastern coral-bean, Cherokee bean* {PL} The flowers make an acceptable vegetable when boiled. Young leaves are occasionally cooked and eaten. Southeastern North America. MORTON 1977; B61M, B83M{S}, C36, C56M, F85{S}, H4, *I17M*, *J25*, K18, N37M, N51, P5{S}

Erythrina rubrinervia - *Galitto, Pito* {S} Flowers and flower buds are eaten like string beans in El Salvador and Guatemala. Young leaves are used in soup. Central America. ALTSCHUL, UPHOF; F85

Faba vulgaris - *Fava bean, Broad bean* {S} The unripe seeds, when small and tender, can be eaten raw as an hors d'oeuvre. Older ones are steamed, sautéed, puréed, or eaten with pasta or rice. Dried seeds are boiled, ground into flour, or pickled in salt. In China and Indonesia, they are fermented into *soy sauce* and *tempeh kacang babi*, respectively. Sprouted seeds are cooked and eaten. Young pods are cooked as a vegetable or added to soups and stews. Popped seeds are salted and eaten as a snack, or roasted like peanuts. In Mexico, a purée of the cooked seeds is folded into tortilla dough used for making thick, cake-like *tortillas*. Leaves are eaten as a potherb. Cultivated. COST 1988 [Cul], HALPIN [Cu, Cul], HARRINGTON, G., HERKLOTS, KRAFT [Re], MARTIN 1975, SCHNEIDER [Pre, Re], STEINKRAUS, TANAKA, VILMORIN [Cu]; A25, D76, E97, G51, J25M, K71, M46, O48 (for cultivars see Fava Bean, page 328)

Flemingia vestita - *Soh-phlong* {S} The soft, fleshy, tuberous root is eaten raw, being somewhat sweet and juicy and having an agreeable, nut-like flavor. Rich in iron and phosphorous, and contains more than three times the protein of cassava. Also employed as a source of starch. Cultivated as a minor food crop in the Khasi and Jaintia hills of Assam. India. NATIONAL RESEARCH COUNCIL 1979, SINGH, H., TANAKA, WATT; **Y81**

Galega officinalis - *Goat's rue* {PL} Young leaves are eaten like spinach. The herb is used as a substitute for rennet in making cheese. Eurasia. GRIEVE, HEDRICK 1919; C43M, D95, E61, E61{S}, F24{S}, G84, H3M, J37M, K22, K85, *L22*, L66, N45, *N71M*{S}, O53M{S}, etc.

Genista tinctoria - *Dyer's greenwood, Dyer's broom* {S} The flower buds are pickled and used in sauces as a substitute for capers. Seeds have been suggested as a possible substitute for coffee. Eurasia. GRIEVE, HEDRICK 1919; C11, C43M{PL}, C81M{PL}, D95{PL}, E61{PL}, G84{PL}, J82, J82{PL}, K22, K38, *N71M*, O53M, P49

Geoffroea decorticans → *Gourliea decorticans*

Gliricidia sepium - *Madre de cacao* {S} The flowers are cooked as potherbs or folded into an egg batter and fried. Tropical America. WILLIAMS, L.; A79M, F80, F85, N84, P5, *P17M*, Q12, *Q32*, Q46, S7G

Glycine max - *Soybean, Soyabean* {S} Unripe seeds are boiled or steamed and eaten like green lima beans or peas. The protein-rich dried seeds are boiled, baked or pressure-cooked, and used in soups, stews and casseroles. Also the source of an oil used in salads and cooking. Toasted seeds are eaten as a peanut-like snack. Strongly roasted ones are ground into an excellent coffee substitute. Soy flour is used in making noodles, pasta, and confectionery. *Kinako*, a tan or beige flour made from whole roasted soybeans that has a nutty flavor and fragrance, is used in many of Japan's most popular confections. Soybean sprouts may be eaten raw, or added to omelettes, soufflés and stir-fried dishes. In Indonesia, the young leaves are eaten, raw or steamed, and served with rice. Made into numerous fermented and unfermented products, including *soymilk*, *tofu*, *okara*, *yuba*, *shoyu* (soy sauce), *tamari*, *kecap*, *miso*, *tempeh*, *natto*, *hama-natto* and *sufu*. Eastern Asia, cultivated. HALPIN [Cu, Cul], HARRINGTON, G., HERKLOTS [Cu], OCHSE, PIPER [Cu, Re], SHURTLEFF 1975 [Re], SHURTLEFF 1976, SHURTLEFF 1979, STEINKRAUS, TANAKA, WOLF [Pre, Re]; C94{PR}, D58, G20M{PR}, N49M{PR} (for cultivars see Soybean, page 482, also see Sprouting Seeds, page 485)

Glycine tabacina - {S} The taproot is reported to have the flavor of licorice, and to have been chewed by the Aborigines. Australia. CRIBB; N84, R15M

Glycyrrhiza echinata - *Wild licorice* {S} Roots are a source of Russian and German licorice. Southern Eurasia. HEDRICK 1919; D62, F80

Glycyrrhiza glabra - *Licorice, Italian licorice, Spanish licorice* {PL} The sweet roots are used for chewing. Also the source of licorice powder and extract, widely employed in candy, baked goods, ice cream, soft drinks, etc. It is used by brewers to give thickness and blackness to porter and stout. The leaves, called *nakhalsa*, are used as a substitute for tea in Mongolia. A tea made from the powdered rootstock is consumed directly, or added to other herbal teas to sweeten them naturally. Grain coffees can be flavored with the extract. The roots contain glycyrrhizin, which is fifty times sweeter than sucrose. Mediterranean region, cultivated. GRIEVE [Cu], HEDRICK 1919, MARCIN, MORTON 1976, RITTER [Re], TANAKA; A1M, C43M, D29, D62{S}, F21, F37T, G84, G96, H3M, K85, L86, M82

CULTIVARS

Pontefract: A hardier but tougher cultivar than Poznan. Introduced into Great Britain by Dominican monks. R53M

Poznan: A cultivar of Polish origin with a high sugar content. R53M

Russian: (Persian, Kanzô) The sweet extract obtained from the roots is used to flavor soy sauce, tobacco, foods, and drinks. Refined glycyrrhizin is used as a sweetener. TANAKA, UPHOF; A2{S}

Glycyrrhiza glandulifera → *Glycyrrhiza glabra*

Glycyrrhiza lepidota - *American licorice* {S} The long, sweet, fleshy roots are chewed, added to other foods for flavoring, or dried and brewed into tea. American Indians roasted them in embers, and they were then said to taste like sweet potatoes. The young, tender shoots can be eaten raw. Roots contain six percent glycyrrhizin. North America. FERNALD, HART, KINDSCHER, KIRK, MEDSGER, UPHOF; J39M{PL}, J41M, J41M{PL}, N84

Glycyrrhiza missouriensis - *Wild licorice* {S} The sweet roots can be used as a substitute for commercial licorice. North America. F80

Glycyrrhiza uralensis - *Chinese licorice, Kan-ts'ao* {S} Roots are used as a sweetener for foods and tobacco. Eastern Asia. TANAKA; **W5**, **X33**

Gourliea chilensis → *Gourliea decorticans*

Gourliea decorticans - *Chanal, Chañar* {S} The fleshy, subacid fruits are usually eaten when sweet and over-ripe, as a "honey" or *arrope*. They are also used in the preparation of an alcoholic beverage called *aloja de chañar*. Leaves are cooked and eaten. An important food in the Chaco region of Chile. Temperate South America. HEDRICK 1919, TANAKA, UPHOF, VALENZUELA; *J0*

Hardenbergia violacea - *Purple coral-pea, False sarsaparilla* {S} A slightly sweet, pleasant-flavored beverage can be prepared by boiling the leaves in water. At one time the roots were also reportedly used for this purpose. Australia. CRIBB; C56M{PL}, E48{PL}, G96{PL}, I28{PL}, L91M, M7M{PL}, *N79M*, N84, O33, P5, *Q32*, R15M, R33M, S92, T7, etc.

Hedysarum alpinum* → *Hedysarum boreale

Hedysarum boreale - *Licorice-root, Sweet root* {S} The young, tender roots are eaten, having a somewhat sweet, carrot or licorice-like flavor. They can be sliced and eaten raw, boiled, baked or added to soups. North America. FERNALD, GIBBONS 1979, HELLER, MEDSGER, UPHOF; A76, *E66M*, K49T

Hedysarum mackenzii - *Licorice-root, Sweetbroom* {S} The long, flexible roots have a sweet, licorice-like flavor and are much eaten in the spring but become woody and lose their juiciness and crispness as the season advances. Western North America. FERNALD, HEDRICK 1919, KIRK, UPHOF; A76

Hedysarum occidentale - *Sweetvetch, Licorice root* {S} The roots have a sweet, licorice-like taste and can be eaten raw or cooked. Western North America. KIRK; **Z25M**

Indigofera dosua - {S} Flowers are said to be eaten as a potherb in India. Southern Asia. WATT; N93M

Indigofera pseudo-tinctoria - *Koma-tsunagi* {S} The leaves and flowers are boiled and eaten. Eastern Asia. TANAKA; N84

Indigofera pulchella - *Sakena* {S} Flowers are occasionally eaten as a vegetable. Southern Asia. TANAKA, WATT; F85, Q46

Indigofera tinctoria - *Indigo* {PL} Leaves are the source of a deep blue dye sometimes used to counteract the slightly yellow color of icing sugar. Southern Asia, cultivated. BROUK; C43M, C81M, D62{S}, F15M, F85{S}, F93G, G84, J82{S}, N84{S}, Q12{S}

Inocarpus edulis - *Polynesian chestnut, Tahitian chestnut* {S} Seeds are eaten raw, boiled, roasted or baked, having somewhat the flavor of chestnuts. Although quite palatable, they are reputed to be somewhat indigestible, even when cooked. Grated seeds are used for making flat cakes, breads and puddings. In the Marquesas, a purée of the cooked seeds is flavored with coconut cream. Malaysia, Pacific Islands, cultivated. MASSAL, MENNINGER, ROSENGARTEN, TANAKA, UPHOF; F85

Kennedya prostrata - *Running postman* {S} The leaves are used as a substitute for tea. Australia. CRIBB; F80, *N79M*, N84, O33, O53M, O93, P5, *Q32*, R15M, R33M, S91M, S92, T7

Lablab purpureus - *Bonavista bean, Hyacinth bean* {S} Young, tender pods and immature seeds are boiled and used as a curry vegetable. The fresh or dried leaves are eaten like spinach. Flowers are eaten raw, steamed, or added to soups and stews. Dried seeds can be cooked and eaten as a vegetable, prepared as *tofu*, or fermented into *tempeh kara kara* and *dosa*. Slit seeds are known as *vall dal* in India. The sprouted seeds are comparable to soybean or mung bean sprouts. The large, starchy root is edible. Tropics, cultivated. FERNALD, HAWKES [Re], HEDRICK 1919, HERKLOTS [Cu], MACMILLAN, NATIONAL RESEARCH COUNCIL 1979 [Nu], OCHSE, SHURTLEFF 1979, STEINKRAUS; B75, C92, E7M, E59, F74{PR}, F80, F85, I91, K22, L90M, L91M, M13M, O93, P1G, R47, *S70*, S91M, etc.

CULTIVARS

Highworth: The pods are non-shattering, mature at the same time, and grow above the foliage at the top of the stems so that harvesting them is easy. Quick maturing, and yields well in widely different environments. Developed in Queensland, Australia. NATIONAL RESEARCH COUNCIL 1979; N84, *P17M*, *R59G*

Purple: 75 days. Ornamental plant with purple pods and purple flowers. Seeds are black. Pods retain their purple color if sautéed quickly. **U33**

Pusa Extra Early: An improved form that matures very early. O39M

Valor: Long, tender white pods produced in abundance. Matures in 1 1/2 to 2 months. R50

Walpapdee: Produces flat, light green pods in clusters. R50

Lathyrus davidii - *Itachi-sasage* {S} The young plants, including stems, pods, and inflorescences, are parboiled and then eaten as a potherb, fried, roasted, or used as ingredients of soups and other cooked dishes. Leaves and stems may also be cooked and eaten separately. Eastern Asia. TANAKA; **U87, Z98**

Lathyrus japonicus ssp. maritimus - *Beach pea* {S} Young seedpods, when less than an inch long, can be stir-fried like Chinese snow pea pods. Immature seeds are eaten raw, boiled and served like green peas, or used in soups. The ripe, dried seeds are powdered and made into dumplings, or roasted and used as a substitute for coffee. Seeds may be sprouted and used like garden peas. Northern temperate region. BRACKETT [Re], FERNALD, GIBBONS 1964, KIRK, TANAKA, UPHOF; A2, A76, E15, F80, F85, H61M, O53M

Lathyrus maritimus* → *Lathyrus japonicus ssp. maritimus

Lathyrus sativus - *Chickling vetch, Grass-pea, Wedge-pea, Doukhobor pea* {S} The unripe seeds are eaten like green peas. When ripe and dried, they may be used to make pea-soup. The flour from the dried seeds is occasionally mixed with that of wheat or rye, and made into bread. In India, the seeds are parched and boiled, and made into *chappaties*, paste-balls, and curries. Unripe pods and leaves are also boiled and eaten. A disease called lathyrism occasionally occurs in people whose diet consists of thirty to fifty percent chickling vetch. Southern Eurasia, cultivated. BROUK, BURKILL, BURR, HEDRICK 1919, LOVELOCK, TANAKA, VILMORIN, WATT; F80, I99, N84, O48, O53M

Lathyrus tuberosus - *Earth chestnut, Tuberous vetch, Dutch mice* {S} In Europe, the plants are sometimes cultivated for their tubers, which have an agreeable, pleasant taste, much resembling that of the sweet chestnut. They can be eaten either boiled or roasted. Eurasia. BURR, FERNALD, HEDRICK 1919, VILMORIN; E7M, E83T, *N71M*, N84, O48

Lens culinaris - *Lentil* {S} The seeds are parched and eaten, or boiled and used in soups, stews, casseroles, curries, purées, stuffings, etc. Lentil flour, derived from yellow lentils, can be mixed with cereal flour and used in making breads. The young pods are eaten fresh or cooked like string beans. Sprouted seeds are widely eaten in salads, vegetable dishes, soups, etc. Southwest Asia, cultivated. BROUK, HEDRICK 1919, MACMILLAN, UPHOF, VILMORIN [Cu]; N84, O53M (also see Sprouting Seeds, page 485)

CULTIVARS

Chilean: Plants are short in height with attractive fern-like leaves. Can be grown in the winter in areas where winter vegetables can be grown. G47

HarLen: An extremely hardy lentil which has survived temperatures of -10° F. Attractive, profusely flowering plants; mostly tan-colored seeds. A very rare cultivar of ancient Grecian heritage. Performs very well in gardens. G47{CF}

Red: (Egyptian, Masoor) {PR} Seeds the size and form of those of the common lentil but with a dark skin and of a salmon color inside. Flowers light red. Season of maturity the same as the common lentil. Hulled, split seeds, called *masoor dal*, are used in Indian and Middle

Eastern cuisines. Turns yellowish when cooked. BURR, HEDRICK 1919; A52M, A88T, C8M, E31, F74 (also see Sprouting Seeds, page 485)

Verte du Puy: (Puy Green, Lentille Verte) Distinct type with small seeds, only about 1/4 inch in diameter, but very thick; pale-green in color, spotted and marbled with dark green. Holds its shape when cooked. Considered a great delicacy and used primarily as a salad, dressed with vinaigrette, to be part of a tray of *hors d'oeuvres varis*. Grown in the departments of Haute-Loire and Cantal, France. VILMORIN, VON WELANETZ; C94M{PR}, J66M{PR}, **Y75**

Lens esculenta* → *Lens culinaris

Lespedeza bicolor - *Yama-hagi* {S} Young leaves, stems, and flowers are eaten boiled or fried. The leaves can also be used as a substitute for tea. Seeds are occasionally boiled and eaten with rice. Eastern Asia. KUNKEL, TANAKA; *B52*{PL}, D95{PL}, F12, F80, G26, H49{PL}, J16{PL}, K38, *M25*, *M69M*{PL}, N11, N51{PL}, *N71M*, O53M, *P39*, etc.

Lotus tetragonolobus* → *Tetragonolobus purpureus

Lupinus albus - *White lupin, Lupini, Turmos* {S} The seeds, after soaking for about three hours in water to free them of their bitter taste, are cooked and eaten or used in soups. They are sold in some European countries, especially during village festivals. The toasted seeds are eaten as a snack, much like peanuts, salted almonds, or roasted pumpkin seeds. De-bittered and salted seeds are served in bars and cafés as an appetizer. In Turkey, the ground seeds are mixed with breadflour. The peduncles are pickled. Roasted seeds are used as a substitute for coffee. Mediterranean region. BIANCHINI, GLADSTONES, GRIEVE, KUNKEL, UPHOF; F85, L50M{PR}, N81, N84, O48

Lupinus albus Saccharatus Group - *Sweet lupin, Snowbean* {S} The seeds are relatively free of bitter tasting alkaloids and can be used without any preparation. Sweet lupin flour is used in the preparation of *lupin pasta*, a recently introduced commercial product. Immature pods can be sliced and eaten like snap beans. In 1928-29, the German breeder R. von Sengbusch was the first to succeed in finding low alkaloid or "sweet" lupin plants out of many thousands being tested. Later breeding produced cultivars that combined sweetness with early maturity and more rapid growth. GLADSTONES; D33, F80, F86G{PR}, I99M, K49T, M63M{PR}, P1G, R47 (also see Sprouting Seeds, page 485)

CULTIVARS

Kiev: (Kievskij) Edible, sweet type developed in the Ukraine. Nutritious seeds are high in digestible protein (40%). Hardy annual to 3 feet tall. Also an excellent nitrogen fixing green manure crop. I99, *P17M*

Primorsky: 110 days. Low alkaloid seeds (less than .03%), 1,560 per pound; average protein content 37.5%. Oil content 9% to 13%. Short plants; average height 28 to 31 inches. Blooms early, 54 days from planting. H7M, N32

Strain 21: 114 days. Low alkaloid seeds, 1,436 per pound; contain no trypsin inhibitors. Crude fiber approximately 12% to 15%. Short plants; average height 30 to 33 inches. Blooms early, 56 days from planting. H7M, N32

Ultra: 110 days. Low alkaloid seeds, 1,440 per pound; average protein content 34.3%. Short plants; height 30 to 32 inches. Blooms early, 57 days from planting. The cultivar most commonly used for sweet lupin pasta. Originated in Germany by Schultz and Velsen. Introduced in 1950. H7M, N32

Lupinus angustifolius - *Blue lupin, Narrow-leaved lupin* {S} The seeds, of low alkaloid cultivars, are used in the preparation of *tempeh*. Mediterranean region, cultivated. SHURTLEFF 1979, STEINKRAUS; F80, N81, N84, O48, P49, R47, S7M

CULTIVARS

Uniwhite: Low alkaloid type with a permeable seed coat. White seeds and flowers. Reduced pod-shattering. One of the leading cultivars in western Australia. Developed there by J.S. Gladstones. Introduced in 1967. GLADSTONES; *J0*

Lupinus luteus - *Yellow lupin* {S} Roasted seeds have been used as a substitute for coffee for centuries. They are also ground into flour. The fresh seeds contain lupinotoxin, a poison, that is removed by a special process. Low alkaloid strains were developed prior to 1930 by von Sengbusch. Mediterranean region, cultivated. GLADSTONES, KUNKEL, MALLOS, TANAKA, UPHOF; F80, *J0*, K15, K47T, L91M, N81, N84, O48, O53M

Lupinus mutabilis - *Tarwi, Andean lupin, Pearl lupin, Chocho* {S} The seeds are soaked in water for several days to leach out bitter alkaloids, and are then boiled and eaten. In some countries, they are salted and served as a popular snack. Tarwi seed has a protein content of up to fifty percent, which is among the highest of any legume seed. The seeds also yield a light colored oil suitable for culinary use. Andean South America. NATIONAL RESEARCH COUNCIL 1979, NATIONAL RESEARCH COUNCIL 1989; D33

Lupinus perennis - *Wild lupin* {S} The seeds are eaten like peas after proper preparation. North America. FERNALD, HEDRICK 1919, MEDSGER; E7M, F59, G47M, H63{PL}, H80, J39M, J39M{PL}, J40, J40{PL}, J41M, J41M{PL}, J43, J53, K62, M77M{PL}, N11M, etc.

Macroptilium lathyroides - *Phasemy bean, Mungong liago* {S} Seeds are sometimes eaten as a substitute for mung beans. Tropical America. BROWN, W., TANAKA; **Y17M, Z98**

Macrotyloma uniflorum - *Madras gram, Horse gram* {S} Seeds are parched, and then boiled, fried, or used in curries. Also the source of an edible oil, and flour that is processed into sweetmeats. The fleshy root was roasted and eaten by the Aborigines of Australia. Tropical Africa, Tropical Asia. CRIBB, HEDRICK 1919, SCHERY, TANAKA, WATT; D33, F80, F85, N84, O93, *P17M*, Q46

Medicago hispida* → *Medicago polymorpha

Medicago laciniata - *Handagug-hadhari* {S} The herb is used as a condiment for tea, or is mixed with boiled water and sugar to form a beverage. Macaronesia to Southwest Asia. BAILEY, C.; **U63, V89, Z98**

Medicago lupulina - *Black medic, Hop clover* {S} The herb is used as a potherb. Seeds may be parched and eaten, or ground into flour. Eurasia, naturalized in North America. KIRK, TANAKA; D58, D62, E24, F24, K47T, *N71M*, N81, N84, O48, O53M, S55

Medicago orbicularis* → *Medicago polymorpha

Medicago polymorpha - *Toothed bur-clover* {S} Young leaves, stems, and flowers are eaten raw in salads, cooked as a potherb, stir-fried, or used in soups. Also dried or preserved. Widespread. TANAKA; F85, *P75M*

Medicago sativa - *Alfalfa, Lucerne* {S} Sprouted seeds are widely eaten in salads, sandwiches, omelettes, breads, soups, stews, etc. The vitamin rich leaves may be dried and sprinkled on cereal or added to soups and stews. Fresh or dried leaves and flower-heads are blended with red clover and spearmint or peppermint, and brewed into tea. In China, the young branch tops are lightly cooked and added to meat dishes. The young leaves are added to salads. Seeds can be ground into meal for making mush or bread. Eurasia, cultivated. CLARKE [Re], CROWHURST 1972, HERKLOTS, KULVINSKAS, LARKCOM 1984 [Cu], MARCIN; B49, C9M, D62, E38, F24, F85,

H64T, J82, L86, N84, O48, O53M, S55 (also see Sprouting Seeds, page 485)

CULTIVARS

Buffalo: Recommended for the Central Plains, where long, dry periods are common. Grows early in the spring and recovers quickly after cutting. High yielding. One of the first cultivars bred for resistance to bacterial wilt. Susceptible to pea aphid. Introduced in 1942. HANSON; A56, *H64T*, K62, K71

CUF 101: A non-hardy, non-dormant cultivar grown from southern New Mexico to the Central Valley of California. Resistant to pea aphid, spotted alfalfa aphid and blue alfalfa aphid. One of the principal cultivars used for the production of alfalfa seeds for sprouting. Introduced in 1977. HANSON; *B90*, *J64*, N84, *P67*

Iroquois: A very winter hardy North American alfalfa. The most dependable cultivar for the far North. Resistant to bacterial wilt. Seed in spring and late summer, 15 to 20 pounds per acre. Requires good drainage and sweet soil (pH at least 6.5) with adequate potash and phosphorous. Introduced in 1966. HANSON; B13, G6, *G50*, I93M

Kansas: (Kansas Common) Extremely hardy; also wilt and drought resistant. Successfully grown in all climates. Makes a good hay and pasture crop, also excellent for improving the soil. Use 15 to 25 pounds per acre for drilled sowing, 25 to 30 pounds for broadcast sowing. A superior strain during the early periods of alfalfa development. H54, K71

Moapa 69: An intermediate-dormant cultivar selected from the widely grown Moapa. Resistant to spotted alfalfa aphid. Widely used in California for producing alfalfa seeds for sprouting. In sprout production it has been shown to have higher yields but a lower protein percentage. HANSON; *B90*, *J64*

Nitro: An annual, nonwinter-dormant alfalfa. It is superior to regular perennial alfalfas for nitrogen fixing because it does not enter dormancy and continues to fix nitrogen until it is killed by frost. In tests Nitro provided 124 pounds of nitrogen per acre versus 95 pounds for dormant types. The seeding rate is 8 to 15 pounds per acre. Discovered by University of Minnesota researchers. Introduced in 1986. HANSON; J20

Ranger: The hardiest, most prolific, and economical type of alfalfa to plant in the northern Great Plains and New England. Semi-dormant type. Sow 15 to 20 pounds per acre in well-drained, thoroughly prepared and limed soil. One of the first cultivars bred for resistance to bacterial wilt. In sprout production, it has lower fresh-weight yields and higher protein percentage. Introduced in 1942. HANSON; A25, C4, D47M, *E53*, *H64T*, I47, *J64*

Vernal: A hardy, heavy-yielding cultivar with high winter hardiness. Resistant to the deadly bacterial wilt. Will withstand early and frequent cuttings. Good for both hay and pasture. Introduced in 1953. Was the leading cultivar for nearly 25 years. Being replaced by newer cultivars that have higher levels of multiple-pest resistance and increased yield potential. HANSON; A56, B13, *B90*, D47M, *E53*, *G50*, H49, *H64T*, I47, I93M, J44, *J64*, K71, M95M, N32, etc.

Melilotus alba - *White sweet-clover* {S} The fresh, young leaves are eaten in tossed green salads. They can also be cooked and served as a potherb, or added to soups and stews. Flowers are used as a vanilla-like flavoring. The pea-like seeds can be used as a seasoning for bean and split-pea soups. Eurasia. CROWHURST 1972, KUNKEL; D58, *E53*, F85, H49, I47, I99, I99M, J44, K47T, *N71M*, N84, O48, O53M

Melilotus altissima - *Sweet-clover* {S} The herb is used like that of Trigonella caerulea for flavoring green cheese in Switzerland. Young shoots are consumed as a vegetable. Eurasia. UPHOF; N84, O53M

Melilotus macrorhhiza* → *Melilotus altissima

Melilotus officinalis - *Yellow sweet-clover* {S} The herb is used in Switzerland for flavoring *Schabzieger* or *Sapsago* cheese. The crushed, dried leaves can be used as a substitute for vanilla in flavoring puddings, cookies, and pastries. Young shoots are eaten like asparagus. Roots are consumed as food among the Kalmuks. Eurasia, cultivated. CROWHURST 1972, GRIEVE, KUNKEL, MACNICOL [Re], ROOT 1980b, UPHOF; A56, B13, C85M, D58, *E53*, F44, H49, I47, I99M, J44, J97M, K5M, K71, *N71M*, O53M, S55, etc.

Moghania vestita* → *Flemingia vestita

Mucuna pruriens - *Velvet bean, Cowitch, Cowhage, Benguk* {S} Young pods are cooked and eaten like string beans. The seeds are utilized in *miso* manufacture. In Indonesia, they are fermented into *tempeh benguk*, *tapeh* and *dageh benguk*. The young leaves are steamed or boiled and eaten with rice. Tropical Asia, cultivated. HEDRICK 1919, OCHSE, SHURTLEFF 1979, STEINKRAUS, TANAKA; F85, N84, Q12

Myroxylon balsamum - *Balsam of Tolu* {S} The trunk is the source of an aromatic, slightly bitter resin that yields an extract used for flavoring chewing gum, baked goods, candy, ice cream and soft drinks. Tropical South America. MORTON 1976; P5

Myroxylon balsamum var. pereirae - *Balsam of Peru* {S} Source of a hot, spicy, bitter resin used as a flavoring in chewing gum, baked goods, candy and other foods. In Guatemala, the seeds are added to *aguardiente*, just as a bitter almond may be put into a bottle of *tequila* in Mexico. Central America. MORTON 1976; F85

Myroxylon pereirae* → *Myroxylon balsamum var. pereirae

Olneya tesota - *Desert ironwood* {S} The seeds are parched or roasted and eaten for their peanut-like flavor. They may be used in place of navy or pinto beans in chowders and casseroles. They are also ground into flour by the Cahuilla Indians and used in gruels and cakes. Southwestern North America. CLARKE [Re], HEDRICK 1919, KIRK; C27M, C98, F79M, F80, F85, I33, *J86*{PL}, S44

Ononis arvensis* → *Ononis spinosa

Ononis repens* → *Ononis spinosa

Ononis spinosa - *Rest-harrow, Wild licorice* {S} Young, tender shoots are eaten as a potherb, or pickled and used as a sauce with meat in salads. The roots are chewed for their licorice-like flavor. Mediterranean region. GRIEVE, HEDRICK 1919, MABEY; D62, E61{PL}, *N71M*, N84, O48, *Q24*, S7M, S55

Pachyrhizus erosus - *Jicama, Yam bean, Mexican water chestnut, Potato bean, Saa got* {S} The crisp, juicy, sweet tubers are eaten raw, stir-fried, boiled, roasted, braised, or used in soups. They are often sliced thin and sprinkled with salt, chili pepper, and lemon juice. Their crunchy texture is retained even after cooking, which makes them a popular substitute for water chestnuts in Chinese cooking. Also the source of a starch used in custards and puddings. Tropical America, cultivated. HALPIN [Cu, Cul], HERKLOTS, NATIONAL RESEARCH COUNCIL 1979 [Cu], SCHNEIDER [Pre, Re], TANAKA; A79M, D33, E29, E29{PL}, E29{PR}, E59, F19M, F24, G51, G93M, I33, J73, L9M, *N40*{PR}, O53M, etc.

Pachyrhizus tuberosus* → *Pachyrhizus erosus

Petalostemon candidum - *White prairie-clover* {S} A tea-like beverage can be made from the dried leaves. The roots are eaten raw or chewed for their pleasant, sweet flavor. Western North America. KINDSCHER, UPHOF, YANOVSKY; G47M, H63{PL}, I31, J39M, J39M{PL}, J40{PL}, J41M, J41M{PL}, J42, J42{PL}, J43, K47T, N84

Petalostemon purpureum - *Purple prairie-clover* {S} The dried leaves are used as a substitute for tea. Roots were used for chewing by Indians of the Missouri River region. Western North America. UPHOF, YANOVSKY; D26, D82, F95, G47M, J25M, J40{PL}, J41M, J41M{PL}, J42, J42{PL}, J43, K47T, K62, L41, N11M, etc.

Phaseolus aconitifolius → *Vigna aconitifolia*

Phaseolus acutifolius - *Tepary bean* {S} The dried seeds are eaten boiled or baked. When well cooked, teparies are light and mealy and have a rich bean-like aroma. In northern Mexico, teparies are popular as a base for soups and stews. They are also parched and ground into meal that can be added to boiling water for *instant beans*. The plant can produce large quantities of nutritious seeds in climates too arid for other beans. Southwestern North America. HERKLOTS, KAVENA [Re], MEDSGER, NATIONAL RESEARCH COUNCIL 1979, NIETHAMMER [Nu, Re]; C76M, D33, I16{PR} (for cultivars see Tepary Bean, page 511)

Phaseolus acutifolius var. tenuifolius - *Wild tepary, Willow-leaf tepary* {S} Seeds are cooked and eaten. The wild tepary is a vine, sometimes up to three meters high, that often climbs up desert shrubs. In comparison, domesticated types are either semi-vining or bushy, self-standing plants that can be grown as a field crop or in small gardens. Southwestern North America. KIRK, NATIONAL RESEARCH COUNCIL 1979; I16

Phaseolus adenanthus - *Dau ma* {S} Cultivated in some areas for the tuberous roots, which are cooked and eaten. Seeds are also edible. Tropics. DALZIEL, HEDRICK 1919, WATT; F85

Phaseolus angularis → *Vigna angularis*

Phaseolus calcaratus → *Vigna umbellata*

Phaseolus caracalla → *Vigna caracalla*

Phaseolus coccineus - *Runner bean* {S} The young, tender pods are eaten boiled, steamed, sautéed, baked, etc. They are usually French-cut in lengthwise strips before cooking. Immature seeds are used as shelled beans. Ripe, dried seeds can be used like dried kidney or lima beans. The flowers have a bean-like flavor, and are eaten in salads. Young leaves are used as a potherb. The starchy, tuberous root is sometimes eaten. Central America, cultivated. BRENNAN, BRYAN [Cul, Re], FELL 1982b, HALPIN [Cu, Cul], HERKLOTS, KUNKEL, MARTIN 1975, NATIONAL RESEARCH COUNCIL 1979, VILMORIN [Cu]; (for cultivars see Runner bean, page 477)

Phaseolus lathyroides → *Macroptilium lathyroides*

Phaseolus limensis → *Phaseolus lunatus*

Phaseolus lunatus - *Lima bean, Sieva bean, Madagascar bean* The shelled beans are boiled and used in soups, stews, *succotash*, etc. Dried seeds are eaten in soups and stews or fermented into *tempeh kara*. The sprouted seeds are used as a vegetable in Chinese dishes. Young pods are steamed and eaten as a side dish with rice, or added to soups and stews. The leaves are also steamed and eaten, though they are often bitter. Tropical America, cultivated. DUKE [Nu], HERKLOTS, OCHSE, RODALE [Cu], SHURTLEFF 1979, VILMORIN; (for cultivars see Lima Bean, page 378, also see Sprouting Seeds, page 485)

Phaseolus metcalfei - *Metcalfe bean, Wild cocolmeca* {S} The pea-sized seeds are cooked and eaten. Young pods are also used for food. In parts of Mexico, the roots are used as a catalyst in the preparation of *tesguino*, an alcoholic beverage. Southwestern North America. HEDRICK 1919, KIRK, KUNKEL, MEDSGER, STEINKRAUS; I16

Phaseolus polystachyos - *Wild bean* {S} Fresh or dried seeds are cooked and eaten like the common kidney bean. North America. FERNALD, MEDSGER, YANOVSKY; **U63, Y17M**

Phaseolus retusus → *Phaseolus metcalfei*

Phaseolus vulgaris - *Kidney bean, French bean, Common bean* {S} Young pods are eaten raw in salads, boiled, steamed, sautéed, marinated, pickled, etc. The immature seeds are boiled or steamed and served as a vegetable, or used in *succotash*, stews, etc. Dried seeds are boiled, baked, puréed, used in soups, dips, casseroles, salads and chili or fermented into *tempeh*. Young leaves are used as a potherb. Sprouted seeds of Red Kidney and Pinto beans are commonly eaten. Cultivated. HERKLOTS, OCHSE, SHURTLEFF 1979, VILMORIN [Cu], WITHEE [Pre, Re]; (for cultivars see Kidney Bean, page 355, also see Sprouting Seeds, page 485)

Phaseolus vulgaris ssp. mexicana - *Wild common bean* {S} Small, shiny bean with varied markings. Pole type. Still eaten by isolated Tarahumares. Mexico. I16

Pisum elatius → *Pisum sativum ssp. elatius*

Pisum sativum - *Pea* Unripe seeds are eaten raw, boiled, steamed, sautéed, etc. Dried seeds are used in soups and stews, puréed, ground into flour, or fermented into *dhokla*, *tempeh* and *dosa*. Roasted seeds are used as a substitute for coffee. The immature pods of some cultivars are eaten raw or used in stir-fried dishes. The young leaves and shoots are used as a potherb. Sprouted seeds are eaten in salads, vegetable dishes, soups, etc. Cultivated. CARCIONE, HERKLOTS, STEINKRAUS, UPHOF, VILMORIN [Cu]; (for cultivars see Pea, page 413, also see Sprouting Seeds, page 485)

Pisum sativum ssp. elatius - *Pea of the oasis, Maquis pea, Hammez* {S} Seeds are eaten when dried or are made into flour. Mediterranean region. Often cultivated in the oasis of the Sahara. North Africa, Southwest Asia. UPHOF, ZEVEN; **Y75, Z23M, Z98**

Platymiscium pinnatum - *Quira macawood, Cachimbo, Cristobal* {S} Roasting corn meal in the leaves of this tree is reputed to impart an agreeable flavor. Tropical South America. DUKE; F85

Pongamia pinnata - *Robinier, Kuro-yona* {S} The fruit is eaten. Tropical Asia. BURKILL, TANAKA, WATT; F85, *J25*{PL}, *L5M*, *N79M*, N84, O84, P5, *P17M*, Q12, Q18, *Q25*, Q46

Psophocarpus palustris - *Niamadi soso* {S} Young pods and rhizomes are consumed as vegetables in some parts of Africa. The leaves are also edible. Tropical Africa. DALZIEL, MARTIN 1975, UPHOF; Q12

Psophocarpus tetragonolobus - *Winged bean, Goa bean* {S} The immature pods can be eaten raw or cooked, having the taste of snap beans. Young leaves and shoots are used as potherbs. Unripe seeds can be used in soups. The protein-rich dried seeds are roasted and eaten like peanuts, used as a coffee substitute, or fermented into *tempeh*. Also the source of an edible oil. The slightly sweet, tuberous roots contain twenty percent protein or more, which is much higher that contained in other roots and tubers such as cassava. They are eaten raw, or cooked like potatoes. Flowers and flower buds can be eaten in salads, steamed, or batter-fried like tempura. The light blue flowers are also used for coloring foods. Crisp hypertrophies, formed by a parasitic mold, are consumed as a delicacy by the Sundanese in Indonesia. They are known as *djaät kèkèd*. Tropical Asia, cultivated. HERKLOTS [Cu], NATIONAL RESEARCH COUNCIL 1975b, OCHSE, SCHNEIDER [Cul, Re], SHURTLEFF 1979 [Cul, Re], UPHOF; A79M, *B59*{PR}, F85, G25M, N84, P38, Q12, R47, S59M, *S70*, S91M

CULTIVARS

Bogor: Long-podded type, often reaching 8 inches in length. Although larger than other strains, the pods retain their tenderness. Originated in Indonesia. D33

Chimbu: Grown for the long pods which stay tender to a large size. They also have an attractive crimson-red color. D33

Day Neutral: Most cultivars will not produce blossoms until days are quite short. These special day-neutral cultivars will produce regardless of day length and so can potentially be grown considerably north of their usual limit in southern Florida. The seed should be scarified first for good germination. D33

Square: Selected for its potential as a commercial cultivar due to the unique shape of the pod which makes it better suited to packing in containers. D33

Thai: 50 days. An improved type from Thailand. Very vigorous vine, easy to grow. Prefers relatively cool weather. E59

Psoralea esculenta - *Prairie turnip, Indian breadroot* {PL} The starchy, glutinous root is eaten raw, boiled, baked, fried, roasted, or dried and stored for future use. Dried roots can be ground into flour and used for seasoning other food, thickening soups, and making bread and puddings. The raw root is said to have a sweetish, turnip-like taste. Has been recommended for improvement by breeding and selection. North America. ANGIER [Re], FERNALD, HARRINGTON, H., KINDSCHER, MEDSGER, NATIONAL RESEARCH COUNCIL 1979; J40

Psoralea glandulosa - *Jesuit's tea, Culen* {S} Leaves are used as a substitute for tea. In Valparaiso, Chile a delicious carbonated beverage is made from the boiled leaves. Andean South America. ALTSCHUL, HEDRICK 1919, MACMILLAN; F85

Psoralea lutea* → *Psoralea glandulosa

Pterocarpus indicus - *Rosewood, Narra, Padauk* {S} The young leaves and fragrant flowers are eaten. Tropical Asia. BURKILL, TANAKA; A79M, F85, N84

Pterocarpus marsupium - *Gun-kino tree* {S} Flowers and seeds are eaten. Also used in the preparation of some European wines. Southern Asia. MENNINGER, TANAKA; F85, N84, P5, Q46

Pueraria lobata - *Kuzu, Kudzu* {S} The roots are occasionally steamed or boiled, and served with soy sauce, miso, or salt. Also the source of an excellent starch used as a crispy coating for deep-fried foods, or for thickening sauces or soups. It is also made into noodles, or like agar or gelatin serves as a jelling agent for salads, confections, and desserts. The tender, young leaves and shoots are eaten raw, boiled, sautéed, fried, or pickled. Fresh picked shoots are said to taste like a cross between a bean and a pea. The flowers are cooked and eaten or made into pickles. Eastern Asia, cultivated. DAHLEN [Pre, Cul], FERNALD, HERKLOTS [Cu], SHURTLEFF 1977 [Pre, Re], TANAKA; C92, E56{PR}, E66T{PR}, F80, *G28*{PL}, J33{PL}, K38, *K74*{PR}, L86, N84, O93, *P39*

Pueraria phaseoloides - *Tropical kuzu, Kuzu-ingen* {S} The tuberous root can be eaten. Tropical Asia. BURKILL, TANAKA; A79M, F85, N84, *P17M*, Q12, *R59G*

Pueraria thunbergiana* → *Pueraria lobata

Robinia neomexicana - *New Mexico locust* {S} Flowers are eaten raw. Southwestern North America. YANOVSKY; B94, *E66M*, *G89M*{PL}, J25M, K63G, L13, *P63*

Robinia pseudacacia - *Black locust* {PL} The flowers are dipped in egg batter and fried, added to pancake batter, or made into a pleasant drink. Young, tender pods are sometimes boiled and eaten. The slightly acid, oily seeds may be boiled and used like peas or beans. North America, cultivated. CROWHURST 1972, FERNALD, GIBBONS 1979, MEDSGER; C9M{S}, *D32*, D45, D95, E84, G41, H4, I4, J16, J26, K63G{S}, N25M, N93M{S}, O53M{S}

Sarothamnus scoparius - *Scotch broom* {S} Flower buds are added to salads, made into wine, or pickled in vinegar and used like capers. The tender green tops have been used like hops to give a bitter flavor to beer. Roasted seeds are used as a substitute for coffee. Eurasia, cultivated. GRIEVE [Cu], HEDRICK 1919, MABEY [Re], MACNICOL [Cul, Re], UPHOF; B61M, C11, C13M, C43M{PL}, C81M{PL}, E33M{PL}, E81M, I99, K38, K63G, L91M, *M69M*{PL}, M82{PL}, N93M

Sesbania aegyptiaca* → *Sesbania sesban

Sesbania bispinosa - *Agati* {S} Seedpods are used as a substitute for peas. Flowers are also edible. Tropical Africa, Tropical Asia. BURKILL, TANAKA; F85, N84

Sesbania grandiflora - *Agati, Vegetable hummingbird* {S} The flowers are eaten raw in salads, boiled, fried, or used in curries, soups, and stews. They are rich in sugar and iron and are said to taste like mushrooms. Before eating, the center part of the flower is removed to reduce bitterness. The long, narrow pods are eaten as a vegetable dish, much like string beans. In Indonesia, the protein-rich seeds are fermented into *tempeh turi*. Young leaves and shoots are eaten in salads, stews, or as a potherb. Tropics, cultivated. HEDRICK 1919, HERKLOTS, MACNICOL [Re], MARTIN 1975, NATIONAL RESEARCH COUNCIL 1979 [Nu], OCHSE, SHURTLEFF 1979; A79M, E49, E83T, F80, F85, *N79M*, N84, O33, P5, *P17M*, Q12, *Q32*, Q46, R47, R50, etc.

CULTIVARS

Coccinea: A form with attractive scarlet flowers. Collected in India. F85

Sesbania pachycarpa* → *Sesbania sesban

Sesbania sesban - *Egyptian sesban* {S} The flowers, leaves, and immature fruits are cooked and eaten. In tropical Africa, the seeds are used to make a fermented flavoring paste called *soumbara*. Old World Tropics. DALZIEL, MARTIN 1975, TANAKA; E49, F85, N84, O93, P5, *P17M*, Q12, Q46, R50, S29, S93M

Sophora davidii - *Pai-tz'u-hua* {S} The flowers are eaten. China. ALTSCHUL, TANAKA; N84

Sophora japonica - *Japanese pagoda tree, Enju, Wai-shue* {S} Young leaves and flowers are cooked and eaten or used as a substitute for tea. The seeds are the source of a starch. Eastern Asia. ALTSCHUL, TANAKA; A79M, A80M{PL}, B62, C9M, D95{PL}, E7M, E47, H4{PL}, I77M{PL}, I83M{PL}, K38, L91M, *N79M*, N84, O53M, etc.

Sphenostylis stenocarpa - *African yam bean* {S} The protein-rich seeds are eaten as a vegetable, either alone, in soups, or with yams, maize or rice. In Nigeria, the hard seeds are soaked in water overnight before being ground for use in the local dish *muke*. The spindle-shaped tubers are also rich in protein. Their white flesh is eaten raw, or cooked like potato, which it resembles in taste. Leaves are also edible. Tropical Africa. MARTIN 1975, NATIONAL RESEARCH COUNCIL 1979, VAN EPENHUIJSEN; U37M

Tephrosia purpurea - *Purple tephrosia* {S} Roots are used in Africa for flavoring milk. The seeds are used as a substitute for coffee. Tropics. BURKILL, DALZIEL, UPHOF; F85, N84

Tetragonolobus purpureus - *Asparagus pea, Winged pea, Bin dow* {S} The young, tender pods can be eaten raw in salads, sautéed in butter, stir-fried, or added to soups and stews. Their flavor is said to be like asparagus. It is best to harvest the pods before they reach one inch in length, for they quickly become tough. Seeds are eaten like peas. Roasted seeds are used in the preparation of a coffee-like beverage. Mediterranean region, cultivated. FELL 1982b, HAR-

RINGTON, G. [Cul], KUNKEL, LARKCOM 1984, ORGAN [Cu], VILMORIN; D62, E83T, L91M, N84, O48, P83M, Q34, S55

Trifolium agrarium - *Yellow clover* {SP} Sprouted seeds are eaten in salads and sandwiches. The dried flower-heads are used as a substitute for tea. The sprouted seeds are grown on a commercial scale in parts of the United States. Eurasia, cultivated. PETERSON, L.; C69M, *F91* (also see Sprouting Seeds, page 485)

Trifolium hybridum - *Alsike clover* {S} Dried flower-heads make a delicate and healthful tea when mixed with other teas. The leaves and flower-heads can be eaten boiled, or after soaking for several hours in salty water. Dried flower-heads and seeds can be ground into a nutritious flour. Eurasia, cultivated. PETERSON, L.; A25, A56, B13, B49, D58, E38, *E53*, G71, H54, I93M, I99M, J44, J97M, K62, K71, N32, etc.

Trifolium incarnatum - *Crimson clover* {S} The sprouted seeds can be eaten in salads, sandwiches, soups, etc. Dried flower-heads are used as a substitute for tea. Seeds can be ground into flour. Mediterranean region, cultivated. PETERSON, L.; B49, *C14*{SP}, D58, F11, G9, G93M, H54, H80, I47, I99, I99M, K71, L24{SP}, L89, N11M, N84, O53M, etc. (also see Sprouting Seeds, page 485)

Trifolium ornithopodioides - *English fenugreek* {S} The dried leaves are coumarin-scented and have been suggested as a substitute for fenugreek. England. MABEY; **U63**

Trifolium pratense - *Red clover* {SP} Leaves and flower-heads are dried, powdered and sprinkled on boiled rice. Fresh, young leaves and flower-heads can be eaten in salads and sandwiches, boiled, cooked in soy sauce, or added to soups. Sprouted seeds are preferred by some over alfalfa sprouts for their crisper texture and more robust flavor. Fresh or dried flowers are brewed into a delicate, sweet tea. Eurasia, cultivated. LEGGATT [Re], MACNICOL [Cul, Re], MARCIN, MEDSGER, MICHAEL [Pre, Re], TANAKA; B49{S}, *B90*, C69M, C85M{S}, F37T, F44{S}, *F91*, F97M, G82, G91, H49{S}, I47{S}, I58, J44{S}, J97M{S}, K20, etc. (also see Sprouting Seeds, page 485)

Trifolium repens - *White clover* {S} Leaves are eaten in salads or as a potherb. The dried flower-heads are used as a substitute for tea. They are also ground, along with the seeds, into a powder that is sprinkled on other foods. Flowers are eaten in sandwiches or made into syrup. Eurasia, cultivated. FERNALD, HEDRICK 1919, MICHAEL [Pre, Re]; B49, F24, G26, H54, I93M, J97M, N84, O53M, S55

CULTIVARS

White Dutch: Low-growing, creeping, perennial clover with small white flower-heads and small leaves. Used primarily for lawns but also in pasture mixtures, as a green manure, or for hay. Also used for undersowing in vegetable beds as a living mulch. Must be watered in the summer. Sow 4 to 10 pounds per acre. A25, A56, B49, C85M, D65, *E53*, F11, G6, G71, G93M, H33, H49, I47, I99M, K27M, M13M, etc.

Trigonella arabica - *Nafal* {S} In the Sinai and Negev desert areas, the Bedouins use the leaves as a condiment for clarified butter (*samin*). Saharo-Arabian region. BAILEY, C.; **U63**

Trigonella caerulea - *Sweet trefoil, Curd herb* {S} The dried, powdered leaves and flowers are used in Switzerland for flavoring and coloring *Schabzieger* or *Sapsago* cheese. In some parts of Tyrol it flavors *brotwürze* bread. Also used as a condiment in soups and potato dishes. A decoction of the herb is used as an aromatic tea, or for flavoring China tea. Young seedlings are eaten with oil and salt. Mediterranean region to Southwest Asia. HEDRICK 1919, MACNICOL, TANAKA, UPHOF, USDA; D62

Trigonella corniculata - *Lukaika, Piring* {S} The young leaves and stem tips are eaten as a potherb. Mediterranean region to Southwest Asia. TANAKA, WATT; **U63, Z98**

CULTIVARS

Kasuri: (Kasuri Methi) An excellent soft-core cultivar of methi used as a *sag* or a potherb. Several cuttings can be taken from a single crop. Slower growing than common methi or fenugreek, and remains in a rosette condition during most of its vegetative growth period. Produces bright, orange-yellow flowers. Grown in cooler northwestern parts of India from September through the winter months. A88T{PR}, E83T, S59M, S93M

Trigonella foenum-graecum - *Fenugreek, Methi* {S} The aromatic leaves are a popular potherb in India. They can also be used sparingly in salads. In the Near East, the germinated seeds are added to a lamb stew traditionally flavored with honey. The ground seeds are used to give a maple flavor to confectionery, and are one of the principal ingredients of curry powder. Roasted seeds are used as a substitute for coffee. Sprouted seeds can be braised in olive oil with parboiled cardoon stalks. Seeds and leaves may be brewed into a pleasant tea. The essential oil is employed as a flavoring for imitation maple syrup, vanilla compositions, rum, butterscotch, licorice, pickles and cheese seasoning. Mediterranean region to Southwest Asia. ATAL, GRIEVE, HEDRICK 1919, KRAFT, LARKCOM 1984 [Cu], MALLOS [Re], MARCIN, ROOT 1980b [Cul]; C11, C13M, C81M, C85M, E7M, F24, G57M, G68, G87, I99M, J73, K22 (also see Sprouting Seeds, page 485)

Ulex europaeus - *Gorse* {S} Flower buds are pickled in vinegar and eaten in salads. The leaf-buds are used as a substitute for tea. The flowers can be made into wine. Europe, North Africa. EVELYN, GRIEVE, MACNICOL [Cul, Re], MICHAEL [Pre, Re]; C43M{PL}, F80, *G66*, K38, L91M, *N71M*, N93M, O48, O53M, P49, Q46, *R28*, R78, S95

Vicia cracca - *Cow vetch* {S} Young stems and leaves are eaten as a potherb. Leaves are also used as a substitute for tea. The seeds are eaten boiled or roasted. Eurasia. HEDRICK 1919, ZEVEN; N63M, *N71M*, N84, O53M, S55

Vicia ervilia - *Ervil, Bitter vetch* {S} The seeds are occasionally eaten in soups. Mediterranean region. HEDRICK 1919, UPHOF; **V83M, Y75, Z19, Z98**

***Vicia faba* → Faba vulgaris**

Vicia grandiflora var. kitaibeliana - *Bigflower vetch* {S} The leaves of some cultivars can be eaten as a green vegetable. Eastern Asia.

CULTIVARS

Woodford: Makes a good salad plant. The leaves are as mild as a raw lettuce leaf, without the grassy flavor of raw clover and the bitter taste associated with most edible but non-salad plant leaves. Primarily used as a winter-annual pasture plant for feeding livestock and as a green manure. Developed at the University of Kentucky. LOGSDON 1980; **U53T**

Vicia monantha - *Auvergne lentil, Bard vetch, One-flowered tare* {S} The thick, floury, lentil-like seeds are eaten boiled or in soups. Mediterranean region. BAILEY, C., BURR, UPHOF, VILMORIN; **Z23M, Z98**

Vicia narbonensis - *French vetch, Narbonne vetch* {S} The seeds are eaten. Mediterranean region. HEDRICK 1919; **W59M, Y17M, Z98**

Vicia sativa - *Common vetch, Winter tare, Lentil of Canada* {S} Fresh or dried seeds are eaten in soups. Dried seeds are also ground into flour, mixed with that of corn, rye, or wheat, and made into bread. Young leaves and shoots are eaten. Also used as a substitute for tea. Eurasia, cultivated. BURR, HEDRICK 1919, TANAKA; D58, H61M, N81, N84, O48, O53M, P83M, S55

Vicia tetrasperma - *Smooth tare, Kasuma-gusa* {S} Young leaves and shoots are cooked and eaten as a vegetable. Also used as a coffee substitute. Eurasia. TANAKA; N84, O48

Vicia sp. - *Sprouting vetch* The sprouted seeds are eaten in salads and sandwiches, being similar to lentil sprouts. (for sources see Sprouting Seeds, page 485)

Vigna aconitifolia - *Moth bean* {S} In India, the protein-rich seeds are used as a pulse, either whole or split. The split beans, or dal, are boiled, parched, fried in oil or used in the preparation of a salted snack called *bhujia*, which looks like broken macaroni. They are also substituted for Bengal gram in the preparation of *dhokla*, a fermented cake made from rice and dal. Young, tender pods are eaten as a vegetable. Tropical Asia. HERKLOTS, KUNKEL, NATIONAL RESEARCH COUNCIL 1979, STEINKRAUS, WATT; F74{PR}, F80, F85, K49T

Vigna angularis - *Azuki bean, Adzuki bean, Aduki bean, Chinese red bean* {S} The seeds are candied, or boiled and served with rice or other cereals. They can be popped like corn or used as a coffee substitute. Also made into *sweet bean paste* or *an*, which is used as a filling in *mochi*, steamed buns, and other Japanese cakes and confections. The young, tender pods can be eaten like snap beans. Seeds to be used for sprouting are sold as Chinese Red Bean in the United States. Eastern Asia, cultivated. HARRINGTON, G. [Cu, Cul], HAWKES [Re], KRAFT, SACKS, SHURTLEFF 1975, SHURTLEFF 1977 [Re], TANAKA; E59Z, F80, H66, H91{PR}, J73, L7M, L59, M46, M63M{PR} (also see Sprouting Seeds, page 485)

CULTIVARS

Express: 118 days. Small beans, about 2/3 the size of Navy beans. Shiny and dark red, the edible quality is unique. Express was developed by Johnny's Selected Seeds, and is a genuine Japanese type. It is one of the earliest maturing adzuki beans. Vigorous, upright plants. G6

Late Tamba: Large, dark-red seeds of very high quality. Dwarf type plant. Very popular in Japan. *S63M*

Minoka: Later maturing cultivar, with less yield than Tarkara but more than Express in northern California. Small, light-red beans; stands more heat and drought than other dry beans. U33

Tarkara: Early-maturing adzuki with good yields of small, dark-red beans. U33

Vigna caracalla - *Snail vine, Corkscrew flower* {S} In Mexico, the Warihios employ the large root as a riser in making their fermented drink, *batari*. Paleotropics. ALTSCHUL; C9M, *F53M*{PL}, F85, G96{PL}, L29{PL}, L91M, N84, O93, S91M

Vigna catjang → *Vigna unguiculata ssp. cylindrica*

Vigna cylindrica → *Vigna unguiculata ssp. cylindrica*

Vigna luteola - *Kuanga* {S} The roots are eaten. Seeds are also edible. Tropics. FOX, F.; Y17M

Vigna mungo - *Black gram, Urid, Urd* {S} Seeds are boiled and eaten, ground into meal for bread, or made into spiced balls. They are the chief constituent of the wafer biscuits known in India as *papar* or *papadum*. Also an essential ingredient of *idli* and *dosa*, acid-leavened fermented cakes made from rice and dal. The leaves are edible. Tropical Asia, cultivated. JAFFREY [Re], MACMILLAN, MARTIN 1975, STEINKRAUS, WATT, ZEVEN; A88T{PR}, C94{PR}, F74{PR}, I99, K49T

Vigna radiata - *Mung bean, Golden gram* {S} The seeds, either whole or as dal, are boiled and eaten, added to soups and stews or fermented into *idli, ontjom hitam* and *tempeh kacang hijau*. Sprouted seeds are widely eaten in salads, stir-fried dishes, soups, etc. The ground seeds are used in place of, or to adulterate adzuki-bean meal. Immature seeds are boiled, purèed, and served as a dip. Young pods are eaten like Chinese snow peas. Young leaves are steamed and eaten. The seeds are the source of a starch, *hunkwe*, used in the manufacture of *cellophane noodles* or *fun see*. Tropics, cultivated. HARRINGTON, G. [Cu, Cul], HERKLOTS, OCHSE, SHURTLEFF 1979, STEINKRAUS, TANAKA; *A75*, C27G{PR}, C85M, J7, J34, L59 (also see Sprouting Seeds, page 485)

CULTIVARS

Berken: (Berken's Jumbo) Small, round, olive-green beans; pods 3 inches long, with up to 12 seeds per pod. Somewhat twining plant, averages 24 inches tall. Produces sprouts in 3 to 5 days, dry shell beans in 90 days. May be sprouted indoors or grown outdoors for a seed crop. Standard, widely adapted cultivar. B75, D11M, G71, L7M, M95M

Min Guang No. 1: 87 days. One thousand-kernel weight, 58 to 65 grams. Protein content 23.5%; rich in minerals and B vitamins. Tolerant to poor soil and drought; not tolerant to waterlogging. Used for medicinal purposes, food and beverages or sprouts. *O54*

TexSprout: Large, shiny green seeds; shatter-resistant pods, 12 or more seeds per pod. Upright bush produces an abundance of pods. Seeds germinate rapidly to produce sprouts superior in both sprout size and sprout yield. Moderate resistance to powdery mildew, pod borer, aphids, and drought stress. Generally earlier maturing and higher yielding than Berken or Lincoln cultivars. Used as a dry bean or for sprouts. L89G

Ying Ge: 90 days. Medium late cultivar, most suitable for producing sprouts. One thousand-kernel weight, 47.5 to 50 grams. Protein content 23.96%; rich in vitamins and minerals. Plant height about 2 feet; tolerant to drought and poor soil. *O54*

Zhong Lu No. 1: 67 days. Medium early cultivar with dark green seeds. Concentrated pod set high on the plant; matures evenly; pods do not split. Resistant to lodging, leaf blight and powdery mildew. *O54*

Vigna sesquipedalis → *Vigna unguiculata ssp. sesquipedalis*

Vigna sinensis → *Vigna unguiculata*

Vigna umbellata - *Rice bean, Red bean* {S} The young leaves and pods are steamed and eaten as a side-dish with rice. Dried seeds are boiled and served with rice, or used in soups and stews. Sprouted seeds are eaten. Tropical Asia, cultivated. HERKLOTS, NATIONAL RESEARCH COUNCIL 1979, OCHSE; D33, F85, P1G, R47

Vigna unguiculata - *Cowpea, Southern pea, Protopea, Lobia* {S} Immature seeds are steamed, boiled, sautéed, stir-fried, etc. The dried seeds are used in soups, stews, *hoppin' John*, purées, ground into flour or fermented into *dosa* and *tempeh kacang merah*. Roasted seeds are used as a substitute for coffee. In tropical Africa, large-leaved forms are cooked and eaten like spinach. They are use in Indonesia for the preparation of *oorab*, a dish consisting of steamed young leaves mixed with grated coconut and chili paste. Young pods can be eaten like French beans. Sprouted seeds are eaten. Tropics, cultivated. BRENNAN [Re], FELL 1982b, HALPIN [Cu, Cul], HERKLOTS [Cu], OCHSE, SHURTLEFF 1979, TANAKA, VAN EPENHUIJSEN; F85, I99M, N84, *P67* (for cultivars see Cowpea, page 314, also see Sprouting Seeds, page 485)

Vigna unguiculata ssp. cylindrica - *Catjang* {S} Young pods are eaten as a vegetable. Seeds are also consumed. Tropics, cultivated. TANAKA, WATT; F12, F85, *M25*, Q46

Vigna unguiculata ssp. sesquipedalis - *Asparagus bean, Yard long bean, Dow gauk* {S} The immature pods, which may grow to twenty four inches, are eaten raw, steamed, stir-fried, or sautéed. They are best if harvested when young and tender. The raw pods are sweet, crisp, and have a delicious mushroom-like flavor. Young leaves and stems can be boiled or steamed, and served like spinach. Seeds are eaten boiled with rice, or mashed. The sprouted seeds are also consumed. Cultivated. FELL 1982b, HALPIN, HARRINGTON, G. [Cu, Cul], HERKLOTS, KRAFT [Re], TANAKA; A79M, B73M, C82, D11M, E49, G33, G51, G71, J73, J83M, K49T, L9M, M1M{PR}, N16, *N40*{PR}, etc.

CULTIVARS

Black-Seeded: 70 days. Long, round, thick deep-green pod; 12 to 15 inches long, 1/4 inch in diameter. Seeds are blackish when mature. Good garden or market cultivar. *A75*, B35M, D55, L7M, L59

Black Striped-Seeded: 60 days. A newly developed cultivar, producing high quality beans. D55, *L79G*

Charlotte: An earlier maturing type which produces longer pods, 16 to 24 inches, while still remaining tender; deep green color. Heat and drought tolerant; climbs well. Small, black seeds. Good quality for home or market use. *A75*

Dwarf: Light green pods, 8 1/2 to 10 1/4 inches long; should be picked daily; early maturing at 11 weeks. Prolific plant, likes lots of heat and water if drainage is sufficient; tolerates shade. Unusual in that it will not climb. P1G

Extra Long Black-Seeded: Pods are longer and more slender than the red-seeded type; will grow 2 to 2 1/4 feet long under optimum conditions, but are usually harvested at 15 to 18 inches when the pods are more tender. Deep green color; fine quality for snap bean use. Seeds are small and black. *S63M*

Extra Long Red-Seeded: A leading market cultivar that will grow pods two feet long under optimum conditions, but is usually harvested at 12 to 16 inches when the pods are more tender. Heat and drought tolerant. Seed brownish-red. G93M, *S63M*

Green Pod Kaohsiung: Long, slender, round green pods; 17 1/4 to 18 inches long; tender, sweet and delicious, of fine quality for snap bean use. Rampant, very prolific vine; tolerant of heat and wet weather. *Q39*

Orient Wonder: (Oriental Wonder) 70 days. Specially selected Japanese strain. Rich green pods, long and slender, 15 to 18 inches in length; tender and fleshy, of excellent eating quality. Seeds are slow to develop so pods stay smooth. Sets better in cool or drier weather than similar cultivars. C85M, *G13M*, G27M, *K16M*, L79, L97

Purple-Podded: 80-90 days. Pods are purple, 18 inches long, medium-thick. Vines are vigorous, productive, ornamental in foliage and fruit. When ready for harvest, the pods are easy to pick as their bright purple color stands out among the green foliage. They are unique in retaining their pigmentation even after being cooked. K49M, L7M

Red-Seeded: 75 days. Light-green pods, slightly smaller in diameter than Black-Seeded. Seeds maroon-brown with darker brown streaks. Good garden cultivar. *A75*, D55, L7M, L59

Two-Tone: 88 days. Thick, green pods with bicolored white and reddish-brown seeds. Pods develop slight strings if left to grow much beyond the harvest stage. Has longer vines and is more productive than other cultivars, but requires a longer growing season. L7M

Vigna vexillata - *Wild mung* {S} The tubers have a soft, easily peeled skin and creamy, edible, tasty flesh. They can be eaten raw, boiled, or roasted, like sweet potato or cassava. Particularly rich in protein, tubers analyzed in India having shown a fifteen per cent protein content. Old World Tropics. FOX, F., NATIONAL RESEARCH COUNCIL 1979; D33, N84

Voandzeia subterranea - *Bambara groundnut, Congo goober* {S} Seeds are eaten fresh, boiled, roasted and ground to a meal, and popped like maize. The meal is mixed with oil and condiments, fried, and made into cakes or balls known as *bakuru* in Nigeria. Young pods are eaten in stews. Roasted seeds are a coffee substitute. The leaves are also edible. Tropical Africa, cultivated. DALZIEL, FOX, F., HERKLOTS [Cu], MACMILLAN, MARTIN 1975, MENNINGER, NATIONAL RESEARCH COUNCIL 1979 [Nu], OCHSE; F85, N84, P38

Wisteria floribunda - *Japanese wisteria, Fuji* {S} Young leaves and flowers are boiled and eaten. The seeds are eaten roasted. Japan. TANAKA; D62, D95{PL}, H4{PL}, H61M, I49M{PL}, K38, N13{PL}, *N71M*, O93, P5, *P17M*, *P39*, P49, *Q32*, S95, etc.

Wisteria frutescens - *American wisteria* {S} The fresh flowers are eaten in tossed green salads. They are said to be excellent when dipped in batter and fried in oil as fritters. North America. FERNALD, PETERSON, L.; H4{PL}, K38, K63G, N37M{PL}, N84, P5, *P63*

Wisteria sinensis - *Chinese wisteria* {PL} Flowers are folded into egg-batter and made into fritters, used for preserves or brewed into wine. Seeds are also edible. China, cultivated. MACNICOL [Re], TANAKA; C9, C9M{S}, C32, C36, D95, E7M{S}, *F51*, G23, *G28*, H4, *I61*{S}, I83M, K38{S}, L91M{S}, O53M{S}, etc.

FAGACEAE

Castanea alnifolia - *Downy chinquapin, Trailing chinquapin* {PL} The edible nuts are small, but larger than C. pumila, and of excellent quality. Burs have few prickles. Grows into a clumping bush by means of underground stems. Southeastern North America. MEDSGER, SMITH, A.; N37M

Castanea crenata - *Japanese chestnut, Kuri* {S} Nuts are eaten raw, cooked like potatoes, roasted, boiled with rice, seasoned with sugar, etc. Individual trees are variable in regards to size of nut, resistance to blight, and astringency of the kernel. Boiling in salted water removes the astringency. Some cultivars have the largest nuts of any species. Japan. JAYNES, SMITH, A., TANAKA; **V19, Y27M** (for cultivars see Chestnut, page 297)

Castanea dentata - *American chestnut* {PL} Nuts are small, but the sweetest of any species. They are eaten raw, roasted, puréed, added to stuffings or breads, etc. The Indians used the roasted nuts as a coffee substitute, and also made a chocolate substitute from the kernels. Eastern North America. FERNALD, MEDSGER; A33, A91, B94{S}, C11M, D45, D72, D72{S}, E84, *G66*, I25M{S}, J61M, *K89*, M76, N25M

CULTIVARS {GR}

Essex: Ontario selection from the wild that shows resistance to blight. Small nut with very good flavor; good kernel filling. Hardy and productive. E91M{OR}, N24M

Kelly: Has exhibited the most blight resistance, and is the most consistent bearer of any tested at Niagara-on-the-Lake, Ontario. Small to medium nut with very good flavor. Vigorous, upright, healthy tree. Originated in Pennsylvania. E91M, E91M{OR}

Oakville: A typical pure American selection from Oakville, Ontario, Canada. E91M{OR}

Watertown #3: Small nut with very good flavor; very good kernel filling. Hardy and productive. New York selection from the wild. E91M{OR}

Wexford: From Wexford County in northern Michigan where blight is not a problem. Useful for isolated blight free areas in the Midwest. I60{PL}

Castanea henryi - *Henry chestnut* {S} Nuts are eaten, and are said to have excellent eating quality. China. UPHOF; **Y76**

Castanea mollissima - *Chinese chestnut* {PL} Nuts are eaten raw, roasted, boiled, puréed, etc. The skin, or pellicle, of the kernel is easily peeled. Unlike other nuts, chestnuts are high in carbohydrates and low in fats and oils. Trees are resistant, though not immune, to the chestnut blight. China. CREASY 1982, DAHLEN [Pre, Re], JAYNES, MENNINGER; *D32*, E47, F19M, *F51*, G23, G41, H4, I15{S}, J16, K63G{S}, L97, N15, N25M, N84{S} (for cultivars see Chestnut, page 297)

Castanea nana → *Castanea alnifolia*

Castanea x neglecta (C. dentata x C. pumila) - *Chinknut* {GR} Apparently a natural hybrid between the American chestnut and Chinquapin. The nuts are eaten. North America. KUNKEL.

CULTIVARS

Rush: An improved selection. K67

Castanea ozarkensis - *Ozark chinquapin* {S} The small, tasty nut is eaten. North America. JAYNES; **T41M**

Castanea pumila - *Chinquapin, Allegheny chinkapin* {PL} Nuts are small, about half the size of C. dentata, and have a very sweet and nutty flavor. They are eaten raw or roasted. Trees are usually dwarf and are prolific producers of nuts. Sometimes sold in southern markets. North America. JAYNES, MEDSGER; D37, E33M, H4, K47T{S}, K67, M76

CULTIVARS {GR}

#1: Bears abundant crops of sweet, medium sized nuts. G75

#2: Bears abundant crops of sweet, medium sized nuts. G75

Jayne: Hybrid. Matures at an early age and is very vigorous. Nuts ripen the last week in August, bearing one to three nuts per bur. M76

Castanea sativa - *Italian chestnut, Spanish chestnut* {S} Nuts are eaten raw, roasted, boiled, puréed, or dried. Also used in desserts, stuffings, patés, *polenta*, confectionery (*marrons glacés*), brandy, etc. Made into a flour, *farine de châtaigne*, that is used in breads, fritters (*castagnacci*), puddings, or for thickening soups. Also a coffee substitute. Sugar is extracted from the nuts. Cultivated. BIANCHINI, FERNALD, HEDRICK 1919, ROSENGARTEN [Re], TANAKA, UPHOF; A80M{PL}, E84{PL}, H19M{PR}, I49M{PL}, I89M{PR}, I99, J66M{PR}, K63G, L99{PR}, *N71M*, N84, N93M, P5, P49, *Q32*, Q46, R78, S95, etc. (for cultivars see Chestnut, page 297)

Castanea seguinii - *Chinese chinquapin, Seguin chestnut* {PL} Nuts are small, but unlike the chinquapins, there are three nuts per bur. They are of good flavor and are eaten in some parts of China. Valuable in breeding because of its dwarf stature and heavy bearing at a young age. China. JAYNES, UPHOF; B96

Castanea x sp. (C. crenata x C. mollissima) - *Korean chestnut* {PL} Artificial hybrid. Japanese chestnut x Chinese chestnut. Nuts are edible. By nature of their origin the trees are quite hardy. JAYNES.

CULTIVARS

Meader New Hampshire #4: Blight resistant Korean seedlings that survive in New Hampshire. Trees grow to 30 feet tall and produce 1/2 bushel of clean good quality nuts each. Selected by Professor E.M. Meader. A91

Castanea x sp. (C. crenata x C. sativa) - {PL} Artificial hybrid. Japanese chestnut x Italian chestnut. The nuts are eaten.

CULTIVARS

Greenmantle: Produces heavy crops of the largest size nut. Quality is excellent, typical of C. sativa, while the great size of its nuts derives from the C. crenata in its background. Leaf characteristics are those of C. crenata. Membrane somewhat convoluted. E84

Castanea x sp. (C. mollissima x C. dentata) - *American hybrid chestnut* Artificial hybrid. Chinese chestnut x American chestnut. Nuts are eaten. The hybrids combine the sweet nut quality of C. dentata, with the larger nut size and blight resistance of C. mollissima. JAYNES; C11M, D72, D76, E97, H65, K67 (for cultivars see Chestnut, page 297)

Castanea x sp. (C. mollissima x C. sativa) - {PL} Artificial hybrid. Chinese chestnut x Italian chestnut. Nuts are eaten.

CULTIVARS

Greenmantle: Produces good-sized nuts in quantity that are sweeter than the typical Italian chestnuts. Their most significant quality is the ease with which the membrane can be peeled off. E84

Simpson: Broad, spreading tree, hardier and much more vigorous as a seedling than Chinese chestnut. Larger nut size than Chinese chestnut. Originated in New York. B99, E62, E62{PR}, E62{S}, E62{SC}, I60

Castanopsis chrysophylla → *Chrysolepis chrysophylla*

Castanopsis cuspidata - *Japanese chinquapin, Tsubura-jii* {PL} The cotyledon of the nut is eaten either boiled or roasted. China to Japan. KUNKEL, TANAKA; H4, N37M, *P39*{S}

Castanopsis indica - *Hinguri, Dieng-ka-sut* {S} Seeds are eaten. The fruit is also reported to be edible. Southern Asia. ALTSCHUL, TANAKA, WATT; F85

Castanopsis sempervirens → *Chrysolepis sempervirens*

Chrysolepis chrysophylla - *Golden chinquapin, Giant chinquapin* {S} Nuts are less than half an inch long and have a hard shell. The kernel is very sweet and is much appreciated. Attractive evergreen foliage makes it a good ornamental. Western North America. MEDSGER, SMITH, A.; A2, A80M{PL}, B94, D95{PL}, F85

Chrysolepis sempervirens - *Bush chinquapin, Sierra chinquapin* {PL} The nuts, which resemble filberts, are sweet and can be eaten raw or roasted. Evergreen shrub is a good candidate for edible landscaping. Grows better at lower elevations than C. chrysophylla. Western North America. CLARKE, KIRK, MEDSGER, SMITH, A.; B74, B94{S}, D95

Fagus americana → *Fagus grandifolia*

Fagus grandifolia - *American beech* {PL} Nuts are small but very sweet and nutritious. They are eaten raw, roasted, or made into flour. Also the source of an edible oil. Young expanding leaves may be cooked as a potherb. Germinating seeds are tender, crisp, sweet, and nutty, and are very good raw or cooked. Roasted seeds are a substitute for coffee. North America. ANGIER [Re], FERNALD, GIBBONS 1979, MEDSGER, ROSENGARTEN; A82, B9M, *F38*{S}, H49, I9M, J33, K18, K28, K38{S}, K63G{S}, *K89*, *M69M*, M77, N7T, N37M, N84{S}, etc.

Fagus orientalis - *Oriental beech* {S} Seeds are the source of an edible oil. Southwest Asia. TANAKA; *G66*, K63G, O93, S36M

Fagus sylvatica - *European beech* {S} Nuts are eaten raw, or roasted and salted. An oil extracted from the nuts is said to be equal in delicacy to olive oil. It is used in salads, for frying, or made into *beechnut butter*. Young leaves are eaten in salads or used to make a potent liqueur, beech leaf *noyau*. Eurasia, cultivated. FERNALD, MABEY [Re], MICHAEL [Re]; B9M{PL}, *B60*{PL}, C9M,

D95{PL}, *G66*{PL}, H49{PL}, K38, K47T, K63G, *K89*{PL}, L91M, *M51M*{PL}, *N71M*, N84, N93M, O53M, etc.

Lithocarpus densiflora - *Tanbark oak* {PL} Evergreen tree of California and Oregon. California Indians ate the acorns, leaching them in hot water to remove the tannins, and then drying and grinding them for baking. Western North America. KROCHMAL; A80M, B94{S}, C9M{S}, D95, G60

Lithocarpus edulis - *Mateba-shii* {PL} Acorns are eaten raw or roasted. Japan. TANAKA; H4, N37M, *P39*{S}

Pasania edulis* → *Lithocarpus edulis

Quercus aegilops* → *Quercus macrolepis

Quercus agrifolia - *Coast live oak, California live oak* {S} Acorns were leached in water until the astringency was removed, and then ground into meal for use in breads and soup. California. CLARKE; B94, C9M, *C73*{PL}, D95{PL}, F85, G59M, G60{PL}, *H71*, *I61*, *I62*{PL}, I83M{PL}, K47T, *L47*{PL}, N84

Quercus alba - *White oak* {PL} Acorns are eaten after leaching. It is said that those with red or pink splotches on the shell are the sweetest. They can be baked slowly in a low oven, mixing in butter and salt, until the acorns no longer taste raw. When cooled they make a tasty, salted nut, something like a cross between sunflower seeds and popcorn. North America. LOGSDON 1981, MEDSGER, TURNER 1979; A80M, A91, *B52*, C11M, D45, *F51*, H4, H49, I4, I60, K18, K47T{S}, *M69M*, M76, N25M, etc.

CULTIVARS

Lint: An old cultivar released by the Tennessee Valley Authority. Selected for its very heavy production of acorns. I60

Quercus x bebbiana (Q. alba x Q. macrocarpa) - {PL} Artificial hybrid. White oak x burr oak. Acorns are edible.

CULTIVARS

Oikos: A vigorous, fast growing selection often reaching five feet in two years. Acorns are sweet and can be eaten out of hand. Seedlings appear to be similar to burr oak in habit. I60

Quercus bicolor - *Swamp white oak* {PL} Acorns are quite large, and unlike those of other oaks, are attached to long stems. After leaching, they are roasted and ground into a meal, which are molded into cakes or loaves or mixed with other food. North America. MEDSGER; A80M, B9M, B53, C11M, D45, D95, *F51*, *G66*{S}, *G89M*, I60, K63G{S}, *K89*, *M69M*, N37M, N84{S}, P5{S}, *P63*{S}, etc.

Quercus borealis* → *Quercus rubra

Quercus cerris - *Italian oak, European turkey oak* {S} Acorns are ground into flour and made into bread. A manna-like substance, *gaze*, is collected from the branches, and boiled down to a syrup. The syrup can be used for sweetening food or mixed with flour to form a sweetmeat, *gazenjubeen*. Eurasia. DONKIN, HEDRICK 1919, UPHOF; D95{PL}, G41{PL}, I60{PL}, K63G, N37M{PL}, *N71M*, *N73*{PL}, N84, N93M, P5, P49, *R28*, R78, S95

Quercus garryana - *Oregon white oak* {PL} The acorns have a high tannin content and should be leached before using. They can then be roasted and ground to a flour for use in cakes, breads, and muffins. Also a good thickener for soups and sauces. Western North America. TURNER 1979; A2{S}, A80M, B94{S}, *C73*, D95, E15{S}, J26, *J75M*, N0

Quercus graeca* → *Quercus macrolepis

Quercus ilex - *Holm oak, Holly oak* {S} Acorns are mixed with clay and made into a kind of cake or bread, something like a delicate soft chocolate or black nougat. It is eaten with lard, milk, cheese, or honey. Also the source of an edible oil. Mediterranean region to Southwest Asia. KUNKEL, USAI; C9M, H49{PL}, *H71*, *I61*, *I62*{PL}, K63G, *N71M*, N84, N93M, O93, P5, P49, Q40, *R28*, R78, S95, etc.

Quercus lobata - *Valley oak, California white oak* {S} Acorns are ground to a meal or flour and used in breads, muffins, cookies, pancakes, etc. Some types are almost entirely free of tannin. Western North America. CLARKE, MEDSGER; A80M, B92{PL}, B94, C9M, *C73*{PL}, D95{PL}, G59M, G60{PL}, *H71*, *I61*, *I62*{PL}, K63G, *L47*{PL}, N84, P5, etc.

Quercus macrocarpa - *Burr oak, Mossy-cup oak* {PL} The acorns of this species are among the most palatable of all. They are used in breads, muffins, griddle cakes, soups, dumplings, etc. In the leaching process, gelatine can be used to remove the bitterness without extracting the sugar. North America. FERNALD, JAYNES; A80M, C9M{S}, C11M, D45, D69, *F51*, G67, I4, I53, I60, *J75M*, K63G{S}, *M69M*, N25M, *P63*{S}, etc.

CULTIVARS {GR}

Ashworth: Precocious producer of small to medium, high quality acorns containing little tannic acid. Biennial bearing. Original tree was discovered by Fred Ashworth while delivering milk by horse and wagon. He stopped along the way, and having little to eat decided to try some of the acorns from a nearby tree, which turned out to be good and sweet. Reselected over a 25 year period. LOGSDON 1981; I60, L27M, N24M

Krieder: A vigorous seedling selection from the Midwest noted for its very large acorns and fast growth. I60

Sweet Idaho: Found in northern Idaho from two isolated cross-pollinating trees. Eaten dry or still fresh, they are not just non-bitter but actually sweet. Best used ground in cakes and breads. A91

Quercus macrolepis - *Valonia oak* {PL} The acorns have no bitter principle and are eaten raw or boiled. Also the source of an edible manna. Eurasia. DONKIN, TANAKA; D95, *N73*

Quercus michauxii* → *Quercus prinus

Quercus muehlenbergii - *Yellow chestnut oak* {PL} Acorns are quite sweet and are rather pleasant eating. They are good roasted in an oven with butter and salt, or dipped in clarified sugar. North America. GIBBONS 1962, JAYNES, MEDSGER; C11M, I60, K18, K63G{S}, *K89*, N51

Quercus palustris - *Pin oak* {PL} Acorns are sometimes eaten. North America. KUNKEL; A91, C9M{S}, C11M, *C33*, D45, *F51*, G41, H49, I4, I60, J16, J47, K38{S}, K47T{S}, M76, P5{S}, etc.

Quercus prinus - *Rock chestnut oak, Basket oak* {PL} The acorns are large and bitter. After leaching, they are eaten roasted, boiled, or used in breads, cakes, muffins, etc. Eastern North America. HEDRICK 1919, JAYNES, MEDSGER; A80M, G41, H4, *I17M*, K18, K63G{S}, N37M, N84{S}

Quercus robur - *English oak, Truffle oak* {PL} Acorns are eaten or ground into flour. They are used as a substitute for coffee, called *eichel kaffee*. Also the source of a manna, *diarbekei*, used instead of butter in cooking. Eurasia, cultivated. HEDRICK 1919, MABEY [Pre], UPHOF; A80M, A91, *C47*, E47{S}, G41, I4, I60, K38{S}, K63G{S}, *K89*, N37M, N84{S}, P5{S}

Quercus rubra - *Red oak* {PL} The bitter acorns are edible after proper leaching. North America. KUNKEL; A80M, C9M{S}, C11M, *C47*{S}, D45{S}, D95{S}, G41, I4, I9M, *I62*, J47, K63G{S}, *M69M*, N0, N25M, N84{S}, etc.

Quercus suber - *Cork oak* {S} Acorns are eaten, especially after roasting. Mediterranean region, cultivated. CLARKE, HEDRICK

1919; A80M{PL}, C9M, D95{PL}, *H71*, *I61*, *I62*{PL}, I83M{PL}, J61M{PL}, K47T, *L47*{PL}, N37M{PL}, *N71M*, N93M, P5, P49, etc.

FLACOURTIACEAE

Carpotroche brasiliensis - *Canudo de pito* {S} The whitish pulp of the fruit is sweet to subacid and is eaten. Tropical South America. PEREZ-ARBELAEZ; P28

Dovyalis abyssinica - *Abyssinian gooseberry* {S} A small, globose fruit with thin, tender skin and juicy, melting flesh with an aroma and flavor faintly suggestive of apricot. More desirable for eating out of hand than the Ceylon gooseberry. When ripe it makes a very agreeable jelly and fruit punch. Eastern Africa. KENNARD, MORTON 1987a, STURROCK, UPHOF; **T73M**

Dovyalis caffra - *Kei apple, Umkokolo* {S} Fruits are yellow-orange, juicy, aromatic, and pleasantly acid when fully ripe. Sometimes eaten out of hand, but mostly used in jams, jellies, marmalades, compotes and pickles. The fruit pulp is high in pectin and small amounts can be added to fruits that do not jell well. Southern Africa, cultivated. FOX, F., KENNARD, MORTON 1987a, POPENOE, W. 1920 [Cu, Pro], UPHOF; C56M{PL}, *G66*, I83M{PL}, N84, O53M, P5, *P17M*, P38, R41, R77M, S29

Dovyalis hebecarpa - *Ceylon gooseberry, Ketembilla* {S} Fruits are maroon-purple, velvety, somewhat juicy, and usually acid in flavor. Some types are sweeter and are said to taste like gooseberries. Otherwise used in jams, jellies, preserves, and to flavor meat and fish. Tropical Asia, cultivated. KENNARD, MORTON 1987a, POPENOE, W. 1920 [Cu], RICHARDSON [Re], STURROCK, UPHOF; F85, N84, P38

Dovyalis longispina - {S} The fruit is bright red flecked with white and is said to be edible and pleasantly flavored. Southeast Africa. FOX, F.; **Z77M**

Dovyalis x sp. (D. abyssinica x D. hebecarpa) - *Florida gooseberry, Tropical apricot, Apricot velvet berry* {S} Artificial hybrid. The fruits are brownish-orange, somewhat fuzzy, with a juicy, melting, orange-yellow flesh of a very agreeable acid apricot flavor when fully ripe. Good eaten out of hand, or made into jams, preserves, syrups, soft drinks and pies. MORTON 1987a, STURROCK; F68{PL}, N84, P38

CULTIVARS {GR}

Prodigal: An improved form with excellent flavor. Tree very productive. Selected in Florida. E29

Flacourtia cataphracta - *Runealma plum, Paniala* {S} The fruit is round, about the size of a cherry, and a russet-purple color when ripe. The flesh is firm, dark red when ripe, with a pleasant, mildly acid flavor. Sometimes eaten out of hand, otherwise it makes excellent jams, jellies and preserves. Acid young shoots are eaten in Indonesia. Tropical Asia. MACMILLAN, MORTON 1987a, MOWRY, STURROCK, UPHOF; F85, P5, *Q25*, Q46

Flacourtia indica - *Governor's plum, Ramontchi* {S} Fruits resemble crabapples or small plums in shape and are deep red to purple in color. The soft juicy pulp is, at its best, sweet and agreeable and can be eaten out of hand. Otherwise used in jellies, jams, preserves and pies. Tropical Asia, cultivated. MORTON 1987a, MOWRY, POPENOE, W. 1920 [Cu], RICHARDSON [Pre, Re], STURROCK; E29, E29{PL}, E29{PR}, F68{PL}, F85, N84, P38, Q46

Flacourtia inermis - *Lovi-lovi, Plum of Martinique* {S} The reddish-purple fruits are the size of a small cherry. They are usually too acid to eat out of hand, though sometimes the fruits are sweet. Mostly used for jelly, syrup, pies, tarts, preserves and pickles. Tropics. HEDRICK 1919, KENNARD, MORTON 1987a, RIFAI, TANAKA, UPHOF; E29{PL}, F85, N84

Flacourtia jangomas* → *Flacourtia cataphracta

Flacourtia ramontchi* → *Flacourtia indica

Flacourtia rukam - *Rukam, Indian prune* {S} Ripe fruits are purple, juicy, subacid, and can be eaten out of hand, especially after rolling them between the palms to reduce astringency. Also used to make jellies, jams and preserves. In Indonesia, they are cooked with tamarind, chilis, palm sugar, shallots, and fish sauce. The beautifully red young shoots are eaten raw in salads. Tropical Asia. KENNARD, MORTON 1987a, MOWRY, OCHSE, STURROCK; E29{PL}, F85, N84

Oncoba spinosa - *Oncob, Snuffbox tree* {S} The mealy fruits are edible, having somewhat the flavor of pomegranates or green apples. Seeds are the source of an edible oil. Tropical Africa. FOX, F., TANAKA; N84, O53M

Pangium edule - *Pangi, Pakem, Kepayang* {S} Seeds are eaten after the poisonous hydrocyanic acids have been removed. Unripe ones are used for preparing *sayor lodeh*, a spicy Indonesian side-dish. Ripe ones are fermented in pits, after which they become chocolate-brown, greasy and slippery and are known as *keluwak* or *kloowak*. *Keluwak* has a distinctive, slightly bitter flavor and serves for the preparation of stews, soups and condiments. Another fermentation produces *dageh peechong*, which is similar to *keluwak* but is sweeter and more slippery in texture. Also the source of a good cooking oil. Southeast Asia. BURKILL, OCHSE, SHURTLEFF 1979 [Cul, Re], TANAKA; A45{PR}, C94{PR}, N84

FLAGELLARIACEAE

Flagellaria indica - *Supplejack* {S} Young leafy shoots are boiled and eaten as a potherb. The fruits are also edible. In the Andaman and Nicobar Islands the sweet stems are chewed like sugar cane. Islands of Pacific and Indian Oceans. BHARGAVA, CRIBB; F85

FOUQUIERIACEAE

Fouquieria splendens - *Ocotillo, Coach whip* {S} Bright red flowers are soaked in an equal amount of water overnight and used as a beverage. This may be mixed with other fruit juices or consumed as is. The capsules and flowers can be eaten raw or cooked. Southwestern North America. CLARKE, KIRK; A0M{PL}, A69, B94, C98, C99{PL}, D1M{PL}, F85, I33, K47M, K49T, K77M{PL}, L13, N43M{PL}, N84, O53M, O93, Q41, S44, T25M, etc.

FUMARIACEAE

Fumaria officinalis - *Fumitory* {S} The herb, including the flowers, is added to sour milk, a few sprays to every pint. When the milk has soured thickly, the fumitory is shaken free of the curd and discarded. It gives a tangy taste to the milk and also acts as a preservative, preventing the rancid taste that often spoils soured milk. Both fresh and dried leaves may be used. Eurasia, cultivated. BAIRACLI-LEVY; J82, *N71M*, N84, O48, O53M, R53M

GENTIANACEAE

Canscora diffusa - *Chang-bato* {S} The herb is used as a tea substitute. Tropics. UPHOF; F85

Gentiana cruciata - *Cross gentian* {S} Roots are sometimes used in the manufacture of *gentian bitters*. Eurasia. BROUK, UPHOF; D11T{PL}, D62, F80, I22{PL}, K47T, N84, O53M, *Q24*, S7M

Gentiana lutea - *Yellow gentian* {S} The roots are used in the preparation of bitter liqueurs, called *gentian bitters*, *gentian brandy*, *enzian schnapps*, or *edelenzian*. Most of the enzian drinks are only flavored with gentian and their alcohol is derived from other sources. They are consumed as appetizers or taken with heavy or fatty meals to aid digestion. Eurasia. BROUK, LAUNERT, UPHOF; D62, E59T{PL}, E61{PL}, F80, I63M{PL}, J82, K47T, L66{PL}, L91M, *N71M*, O48, O53M, *Q24*, R53M, S55, etc.

Gentiana pannonica - {S} Roots are sometimes used in the manufacture of *gentian bitters*. Europe. BROUK, UPHOF; N84

Gentiana punctata - *Spotted gentian* {S} Roots are sometimes used in the manufacture of *gentian bitters*. Europe. BROUK, UPHOF; D62, G82M{PL}, O53M, *Q24*

Gentiana purpurea - *Purple gentian* {S} Roots are sometimes used in the manufacture of *gentian bitters*. Europe. BROUK, UPHOF; D62, K47T, K53, N84, O53M, *Q24*, S7M

GERANIACEAE

Erodium cicutarium - *Red-stemmed filaree, Alfilerea, Stork's-bill* {S} The young leaves are eaten raw or used as a potherb. They are added to salads, sauces, omelettes, sandwiches, or soups. May be used in recipes that call for the leaves of beet, plantain, sow thistle or amaranth. Eurasia, naturalized in North America. CLARKE [Re], FERNALD, HARRINGTON, H., LAUNERT [Re]; D62, F79M, K15, *N71M*, N84

Erodium moschatum - *Musk-clover, White-stem filaree* {S} Leaves are used raw in salads, or cooked as a potherb. Eurasia, naturalized in North America. YANOVSKY; D62, K47T

Geranium incanum - *Bergtee* {S} The leaves are used as a tea substitute. Southern Africa. FOX, F.; K81M, N84, R41

Geranium thunbergii - *Gen-no-shôko, Chuisoni-phul* {S} Young leaves are edible. Older leaves, when the plant is at its peak of growth, are dried and used as a tea substitute. Himalayan region to Eastern Asia. TANAKA, YASHIRODA; D62, N84, O53M

Geranium viscosissimum - *Sticky geranium* {S} The flowers are edible. They can be added to salads or used to decorate hors d'oeuvres. Western North America. *E66M*, F44, I63M{PL}, K98, L13, N84, S7M

Pelargonium crispum - *Lemon geranium* {PL} Crushed leaves are used to flavor soups, poultry, fish, sauces, fruit dishes, and vinegar. Cake pans can be lined with the leaves and the batter will be infused with their essence. The flavor of jellies may be enhanced by adding leaves to the jar when the hot jelly is poured in. Southern Africa, cultivated. CLARKE, MORTON 1976; C81M, D29, F21, G84, N84{S}, R77M{S}

CULTIVARS

Lemon Crispum: (Fingerbowl Geranium) Small, crinkled leaves with a strong lemon fragrance. Pink blooms; upright growth habit. Good for cooking and potpourri. The geranium traditionally put in finger bowls. C3, C9, C53M, C89M, E5M, G84, G96, H3M, H51M, J66, K22, K57M, K85, M33G, M82, etc.

Limoneum: Small, fan-shaped leaves with an extra strong lemon scent. Upright growth habit; attractive rose-pink flowers. C43M, C53M, F15M, F93G, H40, H51M, K57M, K85, L57, M82

Orange: (Citronella, Prince of Orange) Exceptional viola-like blooms of lavender with maroon spots. Low, bushy plant. Leaves have an orange or citronella fragrance. C3, C9, C53M, C89M, E5M, F21, G84, G96, H51M, J82, K22, K85, L56, L57, M53, M82, etc.

Prince Rupert: Small ruffled leaves, larger than Lemon Crispum; very strong citrus scent. Rose-pink blooms; strong, upright grower. Good pot plant. C3, C9, C53M, C67M, F31T, G52, G96, H40, H51M, J66, J82, K22, K57M, M53, N19M, etc.

Pelargonium exstipulatum - *Pennyroyal geranium* {S} Leaves can be used to flavor jellies, cakes, and desserts. Southern Africa. MORTON 1976; N84, R77M

Pelargonium fragrans - *Nutmeg geranium* {PL} The leaves are used to flavor jellies, cakes, puddings, stuffings, punches, teas, vinegars, and potato salad. Cultivated. LATHROP, MCKILLIGAN, MORTON 1976; C3, C53M, C67M, D29, F21, F31T, G52, G96, H40, H51M, K22, K57M, M33G, *M35*, M53, N19M, etc.

CULTIVARS

Variegated: Strongly marked with snow white or creamy yellow, giving the leaves a blizzard effect; same nutmeg aroma. C9, C53M, C81M, D29, F15M, G96, H51M, J66, K85, L57, M82

Pelargonium graveolens - *Rose geranium* {PL} Leaves and flowers can be used to lend flavor and fragrance to juice, wine, desserts, soups, sugar, vinegar, jellies, sauces, custards, and canned and baked fruits. Flowers are also eaten in salads. Leaves are brewed into a tea. South Africa. BRYAN [Cu, Re], GESSERT, LARKCOM 1984, LEGGATT [Re], MARCIN, MORTON 1976; A49D, C3, D29, E5M{PR}, F31T, F35M, F93G, H3M, H40, J82, K2, K85, L86, M15T, O53M{S}, R77M{S}

CULTIVARS

Attar of Roses: Compact mound of light green, trilobed leaves, less finely cut than typical graveolens; musky rose scent. Very attractive pink or lavender flowers. Useful in potpourri. C53M, C67M, C81M, C89M, G84, G96, H3M, H40, H51M, J66, K22, K57M, K85, M33G, *M35*, M53

Dr. Livingston: (Skeleton Leaf Rose) Strong lemon and rose scent. Vigorous growth; light green, deeply cut foliage. Flowers are rose colored spotted with red. C3, C9, C53M, C67M, F21, F31T, G52, G96, H40, H51M, K22, K57M, M33G, *M35*, M53

Grey Lady Plymouth: (Silver Leaf Rose) Silver-grey leaves with a narrow white edge, strongly rose-scented. Vigorous plant; pink flowers. Variegated form of Old Fashioned Rose. C9, C53M, C67M, C81M, C89M, E59T, F37T, G96, H40, H51M, K22, K57M, K85, *M35*, M53, etc.

Old Fashioned Rose: Very hardy, vigorous, tall, bushy plant; deeply cut grey-green leaves; extremely fragrant, the odor resembling Rosa rugosa. Rose colored flowers produced in umbels. Ancestor of many scented geraniums. C53M, C81M, C89M, E5M, F37T, G52, G84, J66, J82, K22, K57M, K85, L56, *M35*, M82, N19M, etc.

Rober's Lemon Rose: Irregularly lobed, grey-green, oak-like leaves with a strong lemon-rose scent. Tall, compact plant; small orchid-like flowers. C3, C9, C53M, C67M, F31T, G52, G84, G96, H40, H51M, K22, K57M, *M35*, M53, N19M

True Rose: Old fashioned rose fragrance; deeply cut foliage; lavender blooms. The favorite for potpourri. C9, F37T, G96, J66, K22

Pelargonium limoneum* → *Pelargonium crispum

Pelargonium melissinum - *Lemon balm geranium* {PL} The strongly scented leaves can be used to flavor cakes, jellies, vinegar, drinks, butter, salad dressings, cookies, tarts, etc. Cultivated. MCKILLIGAN [Re]; A49D, C53M, C81M, C89M, E5M, F15M, G84, G96, H3M, H40, H51M, K22, K57M, K85, L56, L57, M82, etc.

Pelargonium nervosum - *Lime geranium* {PL} Leaves and flowers are used to flavor cakes, jellies, puddings, drinks, vinegar, wine and soups. Cultivated. GESSERT, LATHROP; C3, C9, C53M, D29, F21, F31T, G52, G96, H40, H51M, J66, K22, K57M, M53, N19M, etc.

Pelargonium odoratissimum - *Apple geranium* {PL} The apple-scented leaves are used to flavor jellies and desserts. Also used in syrups, sauces, salads, rolls, punch, as a substitute for paprika, etc. Tropical Africa, cultivated. MCKILLIGAN, MORTON 1976; C3, C9, C53M, C67M, C89M, F21, F31T, G84, G96, H40, H51M, K22, K57M, K57M{S}, M33G, N19M, O53M{S}, R77M{S}, etc.

Pelargonium tomentosum - *Peppermint geranium* {PL} The leaves and flowers have a strong mint scent and can be used for flavoring cakes, puddings, pies, cookies, tarts, teas, and other desserts. South Africa. GESSERT, MORTON 1976; C7M, C9, C53M, D29, F21, F31T, G96, H3M, H40, K22, K57M, M33G, N19M, O53M{S}, R77M{S}, etc.

CULTIVARS

Bode's: Large green, deeply cut, velvety leaves with a refreshing mint-like scent. White flowers. Similar to regular peppermint geranium but with a stronger scent. E5M, M53, N19M

Pungent: Deeply cut, skeleton-like, velvety grey leaves with a strong peppermint scent. Large, upright plant, rarely blooms. Excellent in peppermint tea or for potpourri. C9, C53M, C67M, C81M, E5M, G52, G84, G96, H40, H51M, K22, K57M, K85, *M35*, M82, etc.

Pelargonium torento - *Ginger geranium* {PL} The ginger-scented leaves are used to flavor, cakes, jellies, drinks, desserts, etc. They can also be eaten in sandwiches. Cultivated. MCKILLIGAN; C9, C53M, D29, F21, F31T, G84, G96, H51M, J66, K22, K57M, K85, *M35*, M53, N19M, etc.

Pelargonium 'Chocolate Mint' - *Chocolate mint geranium* {PL} Velvety leaves with a dark brown center. Strong mint aroma. Showy, pink blooms. Trailing growth habit makes it suitable for hanging baskets. Leaves are used for flavoring. C9, C53M, C67M, C81M, D29, F31T, G84, G96, H40, H51M, J66, K22, K57M, M33G, M53, etc.

GINKGOACEAE

Ginkgo biloba - *Maidenhair tree, Ichô, Ya-chiao-tzu* {PL} Fresh seeds, called *ginkgo nuts*, *ginnan*, or *pai-kua*, are harvested in the fall, roasted, and eaten as a seasonal delicacy. Canned or dried seeds are boiled and used in soups, stews, stir-fried dishes, tempura, with deep-fried tofu, etc. Also the source of an edible oil. Cultivated. CHANG, W. [Re], COST 1988 [Cul, Re], HEDRICK 1919, MENNINGER, ROSENGARTEN, SHURTLEFF 1975; C9M{S}, C27G{PR}, D45, E47, E47{S}, *F51*, F70, G41, H4, I4, *I61*{S}, L70, L99M, M75, O53M{S}, etc.

GNETACEAE

Gnetum gnemon - *Meninjau, Melinjo, Bagu* {S} The kernels, after cooking and drying, are pounded into cakes which are fried in coconut oil and eaten with rice, palm sugar, tea, etc. Fruits and inflorescences are used in soups. Young leaves are steamed and used as a potherb. Peels of ripe fruits are dried and used in soups or fried in oil. The sap from the stem is drinkable. Tropical Asia. MAY, R. [Nu, Re], MENNINGER, OCHSE, SHURTLEFF 1979, TANAKA; N84

GROSSULARIACEAE

Grossularia cynosbasti → ***Ribes cynosbasti***

Ribes americanum - *American black currant* {PL} The fruits have a distinct, musky flavor and are only palatable when cooked. They can be used in jellies and pies. Eastern North America. HEDRICK 1919, MEDSGER; N37M

Ribes aureum - *Golden currant* {PL} The fruits are large and flavorful. They are used in jellies, sauces, and pies. Indian tribes mixed the dried berries with dried buffalo meat and tallow to form *pemmican*. Western North America. HARRINGTON, H. [Re], HEDRICK 1919, MEDSGER; A91, C58, D95, E87, G54, *G66*, *G66*{S}, I15{S}, I47{S}, I99{S}, J25M{S}, J26, K47T{S}, M35M, *N71M*{S}, O53M{S}, etc.

CULTIVARS {GR}

Gwen's: A superior selection from the wild. Long, bluish-black fruits follow aromatic yellow flowers. Productive, hardy, and drought resistant. A91

Idaho: Large, tear-drop shaped, blue-black fruits with very good flavor. Excellent for jelly, wine, jams and pies. Fragrant yellow flowers. Especially easy to harvest. A91

Large Fruited: An improved type with large fruit. M35M

Oregon Orange: An orange-fruited selection. U33

Ribes bracteosum - *Stink currant* {S} Fruits are eaten fresh, or are boiled with salmon roe, dried, and stored for winter use. Western North America. HELLER, KUNKEL, UPHOF; U7M

Ribes cereum - *Wax currant, Squaw currant* {PL} Fruits are eaten fresh or dried. Also used in *pemmican*, jellies, jams, sauces, and pies. The young leaves are sometimes eaten. Flowers are also edible. Western North America. CLARKE [Re], HARRINGTON, H.; D95, *G89M*, I47{S}

Ribes cynosbasti - *American wild gooseberry, Prickly gooseberry* {S} The fruits are pleasantly subacid when ripe and are good for quenching thirst. They also make excellent pies, jellies, and preserves. North America. MEDSGER, UPHOF; N37M

Ribes divaricatum - *Coast gooseberry* {PL} Fruits are sweet and juicy and are eaten fresh or dried. Considered to be one of the finest flavored native gooseberries. Young leaves and unripe fruits are used to make a sauce. Western North America, cultivated. HEDRICK 1919, TURNER 1979.

CULTIVARS

Worcesterberry: At one time thought to be a hybrid of R. grossularia and R. nigrum, and was sold as such by a nurseryman in Worcester. Berries are born in trusses like currants. They change from green to purplish black when ripe. Can be used liked cooked gooseberries or black currants. Said to be immune to mildew. MASEFIELD, SIMMONS 1972 [Cu], TURNER 1979; D47

Ribes grossularia - *European gooseberry* {S} Fruits are eaten raw, puréed, pickled, in jam, jelly, pies, tarts, ice cream, puddings, relishes, syrups, gooseberry fool, or made into wine. In France, where it is called *groseille à maquereau*, its use is limited almost entirely to a sauce made for mackerel and other oily fish. Eurasia, cultivated. HENDRICKSON, JOHNS [Cul], MABEY [Re], SCHNEIDER [Cul, Re]; N84, O53M (for cultivars see Gooseberry, page 336)

Ribes hirtellum - *American gooseberry, Hairy gooseberry* The pleasant tasting fruits are eaten raw, cooked or dried. Also used in jams, jellies, preserves, pies, tarts, and other desserts. North America, cultivated. FERNALD, TURNER 1979 [Re]; (for cultivars see Gooseberry, page 336)

Ribes hudsonianum - *Hudson Bay currant* {S} Fruits are used in jams, jellies, preserves and syrups. The Indians of Canada ate them with oil, fish eggs, meat, or other fruits. North America. HELLER, TURNER 1979 [Re]; D62

Ribes lacustre - *Prickly currant, Swamp black currant* {S} The berries are very juicy and tart, have a foul odor when crushed, but when eaten by the handful the odor is inoffensive and when cooked they make a good sauce. North America. FERNALD, HELLER; U7M

Ribes missouriensis - *Missouri gooseberry* {S} The fruit has a rich, subacid, vinous flavor, which is very agreeable. Somewhat too acid to be eaten raw but when ripe makes delicious tarts. North America. HEDRICK 1919; **T41M** (for cultivars see Gooseberry, page 336)

Ribes nigrum - *Black currant* {S} Fruits are used in jellies, pies, tarts, puddings, drinks, etc. Also used in the preparation of a liqueur, *cassis*. Dried leaves are use as a tea substitute. Leaves are eaten in soups. Flower buds are used in ice cream and liqueurs. Eurasia, cultivated. HEDRICK 1919, MACNICOL, UNDSET, UPHOF; A91{PL}, *G66*, *G66*{PL}, K47T, *N40*{PR}, N84, P49 (for cultivars see Currant, page 321)

Ribes odoratum - *Buffalo currant, Missouri currant, Clove currant* {PL} The sweet, ripe fruits are eaten raw, cooked, dried or made into jams, jellies, pies, juice and syrup. Leaves are cooked with meat or dried and used for tea. North America. KINDSCHER, MEDSGER, UPHOF; *A74*, A91, B47, C9, D37, E59Z, F67, J29, *K31*, N24M, N26, N84{S}

CULTIVARS {GR}

Crandall: (Crandleberry, Pruterberry, Pewterberry) Fruit medium to large, produced in clusters; skin smooth, very thick, tough; skin color bluish-black; flavor tart-sweet; high in pectin; ripens late, period of ripening unusually long. Bush is upright, often 8 feet in height; very vigorous; with dark green leaves and fragrant, yellow blossoms. Succeeds in regions having hot summers. Originated by R.W. Crandall, Newton, Kansas. Introduced in 1888. HEDRICK 1925; D47, H16, I49M, I74, J61M, *M81M*, N0

Ribes petraeum - *Rock red currant* {S} Fruits are eaten raw or in tarts, jams, jellies, and preserves. One of the species from which red currant cultivars are derived. Eurasia, cultivated. BROUK, MASEFIELD, TANAKA; N84 (for cultivars see Currant, page 321)

Ribes sativum - *Red currant, White currant* {S} Fruits are eaten fresh, in compotes, jams, jellies, sauces, puddings, pies, syrups, drinks, or made into wine. They have a high vitamin C content. *Confiture de Bar-le-Duc* is a preserve made from sugar syrup and whole red or white currants whose seeds are meticulously removed by a goose feather. Eurasia, cultivated. HENDRICKSON, JOHNS, SCHNEIDER [Cul, Re], UPHOF, VON WELANETZ; C94M{PR}, K47T, *N40*{PR} (for cultivars see Currant, page 321)

Ribes triste - *American red currant, Drooping currant* {S} Red berries are similar to the garden red currant. They are sometimes eaten raw, but are mostly used in pies, cakes, and preserves. North America. FERNALD, HELLER, KUNKEL, MEDSGER; **U7M**, **Z25M**

Ribes ussuriense - *Karafuto-kuro-suguri* {S} The fruit is edible. Northeast Asia. TANAKA; **U7M** (for cultivars see Currant, page 321)

Ribes x sp. (R. grossularia x R. nigrum) - *Jostaberry, Yostaberry* {PL} Artificial hybrid. The fruits, high in vitamin C, are eaten fresh or made into jam, juice, preserves, syrups and cordials. They combine the refreshing acidity of the gooseberry with the distinct aroma of the black currant. Far more vigorous than all existing cultivars of either of its parents. Leaves and shoots are fully resistant to all diseases causing leaf drop and mildew. KENNEDY, C.; A91, B75, C15M, D37, D47, D76, E33, E97, G87, H42, I36, I43, I49M, J7, J61M, L99M, N0, N24M, etc.

CULTIVARS {GR}

Jostagranda: (Jogranda) Large, round fruit, more than 1 inch in diameter; skin deep purple; quality excellent. Ripens at the end of the raspberry season; will stay on the bush at full maturity for a week or longer; has a long shelf life. Bush very productive, more so than the type; spineless. Cross-pollinates with Jostina. Developed in Germany by Rudolph Bauer. D47, *P68M*

Jostaki: Large, roundish fruit, about 1 inch in diameter; dark purple to black skin; excellent quality; resembles Jostagranda. Tree very productive and hardy, spineless. Developed in Germany by Rudolph Bauer. D47{OR}

Jostina: Large, round fruit, about 3/4 inch in diameter; larger than the type; skin deep purple; quality excellent. Tree very productive, more so than the type; spineless; very winter hardy. Cross-pollinates with Jostagranda. Resistant to white pine blister rust, powdery mildew and currant bud mite. Developed in Germany by Rudolph Bauer. D47, *P68M*

Swiss Red: A unique type from the Wadenswil station in Switzerland that has dull red rather than dark-purple to black fruit. Very vigorous, upright plant; free of thorns; relatively productive. D37, D47

GUNNERACEAE

Gunnera chilensis* → *Gunnera tinctoria

Gunnera tinctoria - *Panke* {PL} The young leaf stalks are peeled and eaten raw or cooked as a vegetable. They have a subacid flavor. Chile, Argentina. HEDRICK 1919, KUNKEL; C56M, E63, H30, I28, K47T{S}, L2, N84{S}

HALORAGIDACEAE

Myriophyllum brasiliense - *Cavallinho d'agua, Parrot's feather* {PL} Young shoot tips are used as a vegetable. South America. CORREA; M73M

HELICONIACEAE

Heliconia bihai* → *Heliconia caribaea

Heliconia caribaea - *False plantain* {PL} Young shoots are consumed as a vegetable. The rhizomes are a source of starch. Seeds are also edible. Tropics. HEDRICK 1919, KUNKEL; A79M, F27M, F85{S}, N84{S}

HELLEBORACEAE

Aquilegia buergeriana - *Yama-odamaki* {S} The sweet flowers are eaten or sucked for their nectar. Leaves are also edible. Eastern Asia. TANAKA; D62, H79M{PL}, N63M

Caltha leptosepala - *Western marsh-marigold* {S} Young leaves, before the flowers emerge, are used raw in salads or boiled and eaten with a cream sauce. The flower buds can be added to salads or pickled and used as a substitute for capers. Western North America. HARRINGTON, H.; A76, D62, E15, J93T{CF}

Caltha palustris - *Marsh marigold, American cowslip* {PL} Young leaves are eaten like spinach, especially after having been boiled in two or more changes of water and cooked in a cream sauce. Flower buds are pickled in vinegar and used as a substitute for capers. The attractive golden flowers make an excellent wine. Roots are also edible. Northern temperate region. CROWHURST 1972 [Re], FERNALD, GIBBONS 1966b, MACNICOL [Re], MEDSGER, TANAKA, UPHOF; B33M, B77, C9, D62{S}, D75T, E33M, H82, I44, J78, K34, *L22*, L46, M73M, N9M, N9M{S}, O53M{S}, etc.

Caltha palustris var. barthei - *Ezo-ryûkin-ka* {S} The petiole is boiled as a potherb and seasoned, added to soups, or cooked with a thick sweet sauce to make *tsukudani*. Boiled flowers are eaten with miso. Roots are dried and put into dumplings. Eastern Asia. TANAKA; D62

Nigella arvensis - *Black bread weed* {S} The seeds are used for flavoring breads and other foods. Eurasia. HEDRICK 1919; **V73M**, **V83M**, **V84**, **W92**, **X8**, **Y17M**, **Y89M**, **Z24**, **Z98**

Nigella damascena - *Love-in-a-mist* {S} Seeds are used as a condiment. Mediterranean region, cultivated. HEDRICK 1919; B77M, C13M, C16, E7M, E24, E61, E81M, E99, F24, G84{PL}, I39, J82, L86, M82{PL}, O53M, S55, etc.

Nigella orientalis - *Yellow fennel-flower* {S} Seeds are sometimes used to adulterate pepper. Eurasia. MOLDENKE; N84

Nigella sativa - *Black cumin, Black caraway, Fennel flower* {S} The aromatic seeds, *kalongi* or *siyah daneh*, are sprinkled on rolls, breads and cakes, or used as a flavoring in curries, pickles, preserved lemons, Armenian string cheese (*Tel-banir*), *Haloumi* cheese and vegetable dishes. One of the ingredients of *panchphoran*, an Indian spice mixture. Eurasia, cultivated. DER HAROUTUNIAN, HEDRICK 1919, JAFFREY, MALLOS, VILMORIN [Cu], VON WELANETZ; A88T{PR}, C13M, E7M, F42, F74{PR}, F80, F85, J66M{PR}, *N71M*, N84, O53M, Q34

HELWINGIACEAE

Helwingea japonica - *Hana-ikada* {S} Young leaves are cooked with rice or boiled as a potherb. Young flowers and young shoots are also eaten. Japan, China. TANAKA, UPHOF; **T41M**

HERNANDIACEAE

Hernandia moerenhoutiana - *Pipi, Huni* {S} Used for scenting coconut oil. Cook Islands. ALTSCHUL; F85

HIPPOCRATEACEAE

Hippocratea comosa - *Amandier des bois, Fava de arara* {S} The edible seeds are oily and sweet. Tropical America. HEDRICK 1919; **X88M**

HYDRANGEACEAE

Hydrangea anomala - *Climbing hydrangea, Tsuru-ajisai* {PL} The leaves are crushed and eaten fresh with miso, tasting like cucumber. Boiled leaf decoction was used to make a kind of syrup. The sap is sweet and drinkable. Eastern Asia. TANAKA; *B15*, B28, C9, C32, D46, D95, E63, E87, H4, K38{S}, K47T{S}, M77, M98, N37, O53M{S}, R78{S}, etc.

Hydrangea aspera - *Tu-chang-shan* {PL} The leaves are used as a tea substitute. Southern Asia. TANAKA; E87, H4, N84{S}

Hydrangea macrophylla - *Garden hydrangea, Ama-cha* {PL} Young leaves when dried and rubbed between one's hands become very sweet and are used to make a tea called *sweet tea* or *tea of heaven*, used in Buddhist ceremonies. The leaves contain phellodulcin, which may be used as a sugar substitute. Asia, cultivated. HEDRICK 1919, TANAKA, UPHOF, YASHIRODA; B75, H4, *I62*, I77M, N84{S}

Hydrangea petiolaris → *Hydrangea anomala*

HYDROCOTYLACEAE

Centella asiatica - *Gotu-kola, Indian pennywort* {PL} The leaves are eaten raw in tossed salads, steamed and served with rice, or cooked in vegetable soups and stews. In Thailand the juice of the leaves is used as a refreshing drink. A tea made from the leaves, called *long-life tea*, was regularly consumed by Professor Li Chung Yon, who reputedly lived 265 years and married 24 times. Warmer regions of the Old World. BOND, DUKE, OCHSE; C43M, D29, E5M, F37T, F85{S}, G84, H3M, H40, H51M, I59G, J82, K22, K85, M82

Hydrocotyle asiatica → *Centella asiatica*

Hydrocotyle sibthorpioides - *Water pennywort, Chidome-gusa* {PL} The whole plant, which has somewhat the odor of parsley, is eaten raw, steamed as a potherb, or cooked with chilis and other spices. Paleotropics, naturalized in North America. OCHSE, UPHOF; E48

Hydrocotyle vulgaris - *Pennywort* {PL} Leaves have a strong carroty taste and are eaten boiled. Europe. CRIBB; K25, M72

HYDROPHYLLACEAE

Eriodictyon californicum - *Yerba santa* {PL} An aromatic, sweet tea is made from the fresh or dried leaves. The fresh leaves are chewed for their refreshing taste and to relieve thirst. An extract of the leaves is used to flavor baked goods, candy, ice cream and soft drinks. Western North America. CLARKE, GIBBONS 1979, KIRK, MORTON 1976; G60

Hydrophyllum canadense - *John's cabbage, Shawanese salad* {S} The young leaves and tender stem tips are sometimes eaten raw, but mostly they are cooked as a delicate potherb. North America. FERNALD; **T41M, V73, Z24**

Hydrophyllum virginianum - *Virginia waterleaf, Indian salad, Shawnee salad* {PL} When young and tender the leaves make a tasty addition to a tossed salad. They are also good boiled or steamed as a spinach substitute. North America. FERNALD, HEDRICK 1919, MEDSGER; G89, J39M, J42, K47T{S}

HYPERICACEAE

Hypericum perforatum - *St. John's wort* {PL} The herb and fruit are sometimes used as a tea. Flowers can be used for making *mead*. Eurasia. CROWHURST 1973 [Re], UPHOF; C43M, C81M, D29, D62{S}, E5M, F21, G84, H3M, K85, M82, N9M, N9M{S}, N45, *N71M*{S}, N84{S}, etc.

HYPOLEPIDACEAE

Pteridium aquilinum - *Bracken, Pasture brake, Eagle fern, Warabi* {PL} Young *croziers*, or uncoiled fronds, are boiled until tender, dressed with butter or cream sauce, and served on toast. Uncooked stalks are preferred by some for their mucilaginous qualities. A starch, derived from the roots, is made into dumplings which are eaten with sugar and soy flour as a delicacy. Rhizomes have been used as a hops substitute. Cosmopolitan. ANGIER [Re], FERNALD, HEDRICK 1919, MEDSGER, TANAKA; A80M, D62, D75T, E33M, I44, N7T, N9M

ILLICIACEAE

Illicium floridanum - *Florida anise* {PL} Said to be used as a spice. Southeastern North America. TANAKA; B96, D95, H4, K18, M77, N37M

Illicium verum - *Star anise* {S} The unripe fruit is chewed after meals to aid digestion and sweeten the breath. Dried fruits are used to flavor curries, pickles, cookies, cakes, tea, coffee, and sweetmeats. The distilled oil is used in candy, ice cream, soft drinks, and liqueurs. Southern Asia. CHANG, W. [Re], HEDRICK 1919, MORTON 1976, ROOT 1980b, TANAKA; F85, *G66*, N84

IRIDACEAE

Crocosmia aurea - {PL} Flowers are the source of a yellow dye that is used as a substitute for saffron. Tropical Africa. UPHOF; J37M, N84{S}

Crocus sativus - *Saffron* {PL} Flower styles are used to flavor and color sauces, creams, biscuits, preserves, liqueurs, soups, curries, rice dishes, cakes, puddings, sweetmeats, eggs, butter and cheese. Also used as a tea substitute. Roots are eaten roasted. Eurasia, cultivated. HEDRICK 1919, KUNKEL, MACNICOL, MORTON 1976, PAINTER [Re], ROOT 1980b, WOLFERT [Pre]; C81M, D62, E11,

F37T, H3M, H37M, I39, I91, I99M, J82, K2, K33M, M77, M98, O57, Q40, R52, etc.

CULTIVARS

Cashmirianus: Large size, high quality bulbs from Kashmir. Fragrant, violet-blue flowers in autumn. Rich orange stigmas which form commercial saffron. Yields about 24 pounds per acre. Q40

Crocus serotinus - {PL} Flowers are used as a saffron substitute in coloring food. Southern Europe. TANAKA; O57, *P95M*

Gladiolus cruentus - {S} The flowers are eaten raw in salads or used as a boiled vegetable. Southern Africa. FOX, F.; **Z25M**

Gladiolus dalenii - *Khahla-ea-kholo* {S} The anthers are removed and the flowers are eaten raw as a salad or used as a potherb. Children suck the flowers for their copious quantities of nectar. Southern and Eastern Africa. FOX, F.; N84, R77M

Gladiolus ecklonii - {S} The flowers can be eaten raw or used as a potherb. Southern Africa. FOX, F.; **Z25M**

Iris x germanica - *German iris* {S} Rhizomes are dried and used as a flavoring or sometimes they are chewed. Eurasia. MORTON 1976, UPHOF; K53

Iris x germanica 'Florentina' - *Florentine iris, Fleur-de-lis, Orris root* {PL} The dried rhizomes produce an essential oil, *orris oil*, used to flavor soft drinks, candy, and chewing gum, and to enhance fruit flavors in food manufacturing. Also chewed to sweeten the breath. MORTON 1976, TANAKA, WOLFERT; C56, C67M, C81M, D29, E5M, G84, H51M, I37M, J66, K22, K85, L56, M53, M82, N19M, Q40, etc.

Iris missouriensis - *Rocky Mountain iris* {S} Seeds are used as a substitute for coffee. North America. KUNKEL; A2, C40{PL}, C98, *E66M*, F44, G60{PL}, *H64T*, I47, I63M{PL}, J25M, K15, K47T, L13, L75, *Q24*, etc.

Iris pallida - *Sweet iris* {PL} *Orris oil*, derived from the dried rhizomes, is used to flavor soft drinks, candy, and chewing gum, and to enhance fruit flavors in food manufacturing. Europe. MORTON 1976; C56, N84{S}, Q40

Iris setosa - *Hiôgi-ayame* {PL} Parched seeds are ground and used as a coffee substitute. Rhizomes are eaten or used as a source of starch. Northern temperate region. HEDRICK 1919, TANAKA, UPHOF; A76{S}, B44M, B77, C56, E63M, F67, I47{S}, J37M, J48, M77M, N84{S}

Moraea edulis* → *Moraea fugax

Moraea fugax - *Uintjie* {S} The bulbous roots are eaten roasted, boiled, or stewed with milk. They are said to taste much like potatoes or boiled chestnuts. Southern Africa. FOX, F., HEDRICK 1919; B11T{PL}, N84, R77M, R93, R93{PL}

Romulea bulbocodium - {S} Bulbous roots are said to be eaten by shepherds. Northern Africa. FAIRCHILD 1930; B11T{PL}, N84, O53M, R52{PL}

Tigridia pavonia - *Common tigerflower* {S} Roasted starchy corms have been used as food by Mazatecs and other Indian tribes in Mexico since pre-hispanic times. The eyes from the corms, when they begin to sprout, are probably eaten. Central America, cultivated. UPHOF, WILLIAMS, L.; C27M, D62, F85, J7{PL}, M7M{PL}, N84, R77M

Tritonia crocata - *Greater African ixia* {S} The flowers are used to adulterate saffron. Southern Africa. KUNKEL; B11T{PL}, C27M, N84, R77M, R93, R93{PL}, S44

IXONANTHACEAE

Irvingia gabonensis - *Dika nut, Wild mango, Mopae* {S} The seeds are used in soups and as a seasoner for various native dishes. When ground and heated they form the principal ingredient of the paste known as *dika bread* or *Gabon chocolate*, a staple food. They also yield *dika butter*, which is comparable to cocoa-butter and is used as an adulterant of chocolate. Tropical Africa. DALZIEL, MENNINGER, TANAKA; F85, N84

Irvingia smithii - *Denge* {S} The seeds are rich in fat, and although smaller than those of other Irvingia species they are reportedly the best tasting. Tropical Africa. DALZIEL; **X44**

Klainedoxa gabonensis - *Sopei nut* {S} Seeds are eaten fresh, roasted or crushed into a paste. The paste is rich and oily and is mixed with other foods as a gravy or relish. Tropical Africa. DALZIEL, UPHOF; N84

JUGLANDACEAE

Carya x brownii (C. cordiformis x C. illinoensis) - *Pleas nut* {PL} Hybrid. Pecan x bitter nut. The seeds are edible. Generally considered bitter. The claim by some that the name pleas refers to the pleasing flavor of the kernels is erroneous. Seldom productive north of St. Louis, Missouri. Introduced in 1916 by E. Pleas of Collinsville, Oklahoma. JAYNES, KELSEY, KRÜSSMANN, ROOT 1980a; G75, I40{OR}, I60

Carya carolinae-septentrionalis - *Carolina hickory nut, Southern shagbark* {S} The large, sweet seeds are eaten. Southeastern North America. KROCHMAL, TANAKA; **T41M**

Carya cathayensis* → *Juglans cathayensis

Carya cordiformis - *Bitternut, Swamp hickory* {S} The bitter, astringent seeds are sometimes eaten. Natural hybrids between the bitternut and other hickory species are valued for their ornamental qualities. North America. JAYNES; K18{PL}, K63G, *K89*, *R28*

Carya floridana - *Scrub hickory, Florida hickory* {PL} Seeds are edible. Southeastern North America. TANAKA; *J25*, N37M

Carya glabra - *Pignut* {PL} The edible seeds vary considerably in quality, some being bitter and astringent, others are sweet and pleasant tasting. Eastern North America. GIBBONS 1979, JAYNES, MEDSGER; I60, *J25*, K18, K63G{S}, *K89*, *K89*{S}, N25M, P49{S}, R78{S}

Carya illinoensis - *Pecan, Black hickory* {PL} Seeds are eaten raw, salted, in pies, candies, cakes, cookies, breads, ice cream, etc. *Hickory milk*, prepared from the seeds, was used to thicken soups, season corn cakes and hominy, or was fermented into an alcoholic beverage. Also the source of an edible oil. The leaves are said to be used as a tea. North America, cultivated. FERNALD, HEDRICK 1919, KUNKEL, MENNINGER, ROSENGARTEN [Re], UPHOF; A38M{PR}, A91, C11M, D45, D72, D72{S}, G23, G72, I9M, I25M{S}, J33, K38{S}, K47T{S}, *M69M*, N15, N25M, etc. (for cultivars see Pecan, page 432 and Rootstocks, page 470)

Carya laciniosa - *Shellbark hickory, King nut* {PL} The edible seeds are sweet and of very fine flavor. They can be eaten raw or used in cakes, pies, etc. Their cracking quality is poor in comparison to the shagbark hickory. The sap is sweet, and when boiled down makes a syrup or sugar as delicious as that of the maple. North America, cultivated. FERNALD, JAYNES, MEDSGER; A82, A91, *B52*, C11M, D45, D72, D72{S}, D76, *F51*, G23, H49, I25M{S}, K38{S}, *K89*{S}, *M69M*, N25M, N37M, etc. (for cultivars see Hickory, page 352)

Carya x laneyi (C. ovata x C. cordiformis) - {GR} Probably a natural hybrid. Shagbark hickory x bitternut. Nuts are edible. Generally faster growing, bears at a younger age, and matures nuts earlier than shagbark but lacks the high quality kernel. JAYNES, KUNKEL.

CULTIVARS

De Acer: Nut large; shell thin; flavor like that of shagbark hickory, pleasant; of best quality of any crosses with this parentage. Tree bears very well. Originated in Urbana, Iowa by Linn County Nurseries, Center Point, Iowa. Introduced in 1950. BROOKS 1972; E41M{SC}

Roof: Produces a large nut. Potential material for use as an interstem for grafting on C. cordiformis. Originated in Iowa. I40

Carya myristiciformis - *Nutmeg hickory* {PL} The seeds are edible. North America. KROCHMAL, TANAKA; A80M, N37M, N51

Carya x nussbaumeri (C. illinoensis x C. laciniosa) - *Hican* {PR} Natural and artificial hybrids. Pecan x shellbark hickory. Seeds are edible. The hybrids exhibit many of the desirable traits of the parent species, but are generally unproductive. JAYNES; M31M (for cultivars see Hican, page 351)

Carya ovata - *Shagbark hickory* {PL} Seeds are sweet and delicious. They are eaten raw, roasted, in pies, cakes, breads, cookies, candies, etc. From them the Indians prepared a kind of oily *hickory milk*, or *powcohicora*, which was used like butter on bread, sweet potatoes and vegetables. They also ground the seeds into meal or flour and used it to thicken broths and soups. North America. FERNALD, GIBBONS 1962 [Re], ROSENGARTEN, TURNER 1979 [Re]; A38M{PR}, A91, *B52*, B74, C9M{S}, C11M, D45, D72, D72{S}, D95, *F51*, G16, H49, I4, I25M{S}, K38{S}, L27M, *M69M*, N0, N25M, etc. (for cultivars see Hickory, page 352)

Carya pecan* → *Carya illinoensis

Carya tomentosa - *Mockernut, White-heart hickory* {S} Seeds are sweet and edible, but the shell is very thick and hard and the kernel is so difficult to extract the squirrels even leave them to accumulate under the trees. Eastern North America. GIBBONS 1979, HEDRICK 1919, JAYNES; *G66*, K18{PL}, K63G, *K89*

Carya x sp. (C. illinoensis x C. ovata) - *Hican* {PR} Natural and artificial hybrids. Pecan x shagbark hickory. The seeds are edible. JAYNES; M31M (for cultivars see Hican, page 351)

Juglans ailantifolia - *Japanese walnut, Siebold walnut, Oni-gurumi* {S} Seeds are eaten raw, cooked, or used in confectionery. Young buds and fruit stalks are boiled and eaten. Recommended as an ornamental by some because of its tropical appearance and long clusters of seeds. Japan, cultivated. JAYNES, TANAKA; D95{PL}, *G66*, K38, K47T, K63G, N24M{PL}, N84, P49, *P63*, R78

Juglans ailantifolia var. cordiformis - *Heartnut, Hime-gurumi* {PL} The seeds are eaten raw, used in cooking, or made into candies, pies, cakes, etc. The flavor is mild and pleasant, resembling that of the butternut. Also the source of an edible oil. Similar to Japanese walnut, but with a more pronounced heart shape. Japan, cultivated. JAYNES, ROSENGARTEN, TANAKA; C58, D72, H65, I15{S}, I25M{S}, I49M, K38{S}, K63G{S}, L33, L99M, M31M, N25M, N84{S}, *P39*{S} (for cultivars see Heartnut, page 351)

Juglans x bixbyi (J. cinerea x J. ailantifolia var. cordiformis) - *Buartnut, Bixby walnut, Butterjap* {PL} Artificial hybrid. The seeds are edible. Combines the aromatic kernel flavor and superior climatic adaptability of the butternut, with the higher yield, better appearance, and crackability of the heartnut. JAYNES, ROSENGARTEN; C58, D76, *G66*, H49, I49M, I60

CULTIVARS

Barney: Nut large; resembles a butternut but with a smoother shell; ripens earlier than most walnuts. Kernel of good quality, but difficult to remove from shell. Tree very hardy; grows rapidly; productive. Originated in Westbank, British Columbia, Canada by J.U. Gellatly. Introduced in 1938. BROOKS 1972; A91

Butterheart: Heart-shaped nut, cracks out in half or whole kernels. Kernels sweet and rich, with no trace of bitterness. Tree very winter hardy, ornamental, bears early. Requires a pollinator. Introduced by Miller Nurseries. H65

Cobles #1: Large nut. Tree slow to come into bearing, ornamental. Originated in Pennsylvania. K16{S}

Corsan: Full, round nut much like Fioka. Vigorous, productive tree. Named by J.U. Gellatly. Originated as a seedling from the Toronto suburban planting of the late George H. Corsan, at Echo Valley. A91, E91M{OR}

Fioka: Produces 55 nuts per pound, up to 24% kernel; shell hard, cracking quality good. Has the flavor of the butternut. Tree vigorous; bears annually; extremely hardy; grafts well to black walnut rootstock. Originated by J.U. Gellatly. Introduced in the early 1930's. BROOKS 1972; A91, E91M{OR}, K16

Hancock: Very large, spreading tree. Nut somewhat bland. Originated in Massachusetts. K16

Mitchell: Nut intermediate between parents; shell spiny, cracks easily; flavor resembles a butternut. Tree slightly protogynous, but probably self-fruitful most years. Originated in Scotland, Ontario, Canada by Claude Mitchell. Introduced in 1930. Won first prize in 1932 in a Michigan nut contest. BROOKS 1972; B99, E41M{SC}, E91M, E91M{GR}, I40, K16{S}, N24M

Pierce: Extremely hardy, grows where heartnuts are not hardy. Very vigorous, one seedling at five years of age was 20 feet tall and producing a heavy crop. Nuts grow in clusters of 10 to 15 and have good cracking qualities. K16{OR}, L27M, N24M

Wallick: Favored by Ken Dooley for its flavor and for use in Christmas candy. Originated in Indiana. K16{OR}

Juglans californica - *California walnut, Southern California black walnut* {S} Sweet, thick-shelled seeds are eaten raw, used in pies, cakes, cookies, etc. Said to have a better flavor than the Eastern black walnut. Sometimes used as a rootstock for Persian walnuts. California. CLARKE, KIRK, MEDSGER, WICKSON; B94, I83M{PL}

Juglans cathayensis - *Chinese walnut, Cathay walnut* {S} Seeds are eaten roasted with salt, or made into confections and sweetmeats. A considerable amount are processed into an edible oil. China. MENNINGER, UPHOF; *G66*, M35M{PL}, N84, *R28*

Juglans cinerea - *Butternut, White walnut* {PL} The oily, sweet-tasting nuts are eaten raw, or used in cakes, cookies, breads, muffins, candies, etc. The sweet sap can be boiled down to syrup and sugar or added to maple sap. Unripe fruits are pickled in vinegar, sugar, and spices. Seeds yield an oil is used in cooking. Eastern North America, cultivated. ANGIER [Re], FERNALD, GIBBONS 1962, MEDSGER, ROSENGARTEN; A38M{PR}, A82, *B52*, B74, C11M, D72, D72{S}, E15{S}, F19M, G23, G67, H65, I4, I15{S}, N25M, etc. (for cultivars see Butternut, page 277)

Juglans hindsii - *Hinds walnut, Northern California black walnut* {PL} The small, thick-shelled seeds are good to eat raw. Commonly used as a rootstock for Persian walnuts. California. JAYNES, KIRK; *B71M*, B93M, B94{S}, *C54*, *C73*, *D18*, G59M{S}, G60, K47T{S} (for cultivars see Rootstocks, page 470)

Juglans honorei* → *Juglans neotropica

Juglans x intermedia (J. nigra x J. regia) - *Intermediate walnut* {GR} Artificial hybrids. Black walnut x Persian walnut. Nuts are eaten. BEAN, REHDER.

CULTIVARS

Hill #2: An improved strain. Like many other hybrids resulting from this cross the trees are somewhat lacking in fertility. K16

Kwik Krop: (Stark Kwik Krop) Precocious bearer, often bears 2 to 3 years after planting. Nut shell thin, cracks easily; kernel plump, mild-flavored, light in color, high percentage of nut; matures early; resembles black walnut. Tree hardy, large and vigorous, moderately productive. Originated in Roswell, New Mexico by Louis B. Boellner. Introduced in 1956. BROOKS 1972; L33

Juglans major - *Arizona walnut, Arizona black walnut* {S} Small seeds are sometimes eaten. Also used as a rootstock. Southwestern North America. JAYNES, KIRK, YANOVSKY; B94

Juglans mandschurica - *Manchurian walnut, Siberian walnut* {S} Seeds are eaten raw or roasted. Also the source of an edible oil. Kernels are well filled, but they are difficult to extract. Recommended for severe cold climates. Sometimes used as a cold-hardy rootstock. Eastern Asia. JAYNES, TANAKA; A80M{PL}, *G66*, H85{PL}, I15, K47T, M31M{PL}, M35M{PL}, N25M{PL}, N84, *P39*, P49

Juglans microcarpa - *Texas walnut, Texas black walnut, Nogalillo* {S} The small, thick-shelled seeds are sometimes eaten. Also used as a rootstock. Southwestern North America. JAYNES, LATORRE 1977b; A80M{PL}, B94, *G66*, I25M, K47T, P86{PL}

Juglans neotropica - *Andean walnut, Nogal, Ecuadorian black walnut* {PL} The nuts have a very thick, bony shell and a kernel of rich and pleasant flavor. They are mixed with sugar and milk to make a sweetmeat, called *nogada de Ibarra*, that is sold at local markets in Ecuador. Trees are nearly evergreen and have a low chilling requirement. Ecuador, Colombia. NATIONAL RESEARCH COUNCIL 1989, POPENOE, W. 1924, TANAKA, UPHOF; D57{OR}, *Q49M*

Juglans nigra - *Eastern black walnut* {PL} Nuts have a rich, distinctive, delicious flavor and are widely used in pastries, confectionery, ice cream, cakes, pies, nut-breads, cookies, puddings, and muffins. The oil extracted from the nut is used as a seasoning in bread, pumpkin, squash, and other foods. Unripe fruits are pickled. Yields sweet sap that can be made into syrup or sugar. North America. FERNALD, GIBBONS 1962 [Re], ROSENGARTEN, TURNER 1979 [Re]; A38M{PR}, A52M{PR}, A82, *B52*, B74, C11M, C11M{S}, D72, D72{S}, E47, G23, H4, H65, H69T{PR}, I4, I15{S}, N15, N25M, etc. (for cultivars see Black Walnut, page 265)

Juglans regia - *Persian walnut, English walnut* {S} Nuts are eaten raw, in baked goods, candies, ice cream, sauces, soups, nut milks, etc. Unripe fruits are pickled in vinegar, added to jams, preserved in syrup, or made into brandy. Finely ground shells are used in the stuffing of *agnolotti* pasta. Leaves are used as a tea. Walnut meal is used as a thickening agent for savory and sweet dishes. Also the source of an edible oil used in salads or cooking. Eurasia, cultivated. COST 1988 [Cul], MALLOS [Re], MENNINGER, ROOT 1980a, ROSENGARTEN, UPHOF; A82{PL}, C9M, D81{PO}, D81M{PO}, G41{PL}, G45M{PL}, I25M, K38, K63G, N84, N93M, O53M (for cultivars see Walnut, page 528, and Rootstocks, page 470)

Juglans regia 'Carpathian' - *Carpathian walnut, Hardy walnut* {PL} The nuts are eaten in the same manner as Persian walnuts. They are recommended for colder areas of northeastern United States and Canada. Introduced from the Carpathian mountains of Poland by Reverend Paul C. Crath. JAYNES; A80M, *B52*, B75, D76, E82, E82{S}, F19M, F93, G23, H49, K38{S}, L33, *L47*, *M69M*, M76, etc. (for cultivars see Walnut, page 528)

Juglans sieboldiana* → *Juglans ailantifolia

LAMIACEAE (*LABIATAE*)

Acinos alpinus - *Alpine basil thyme* {PL} The herb is used for flavoring. Europe. MORTON 1976; K22, K47T{S}, M92

Acinos arvensis - *Basil thyme, Acinos* {S} In old English cookery, the flowering tops were used to season jugged hare. The herb is said to impart an appealing flavor to the flesh of animals that eat it. Similar to thyme in odor and flavor but milder and more pleasant. Eurasia. MORTON 1976; F35M{PL}, N84, O48, P92{PL}, S55

Agastache anethiodora* → *Agastache foeniculum

Agastache cana - *Hoary balm of Gilead, Mosquito plant, Wild hyssop* {PL} A very fragrant herb that is useful for putting in a *claret cup*. Southwestern North America. HEDRICK 1919; J25M{S}, K22, K85

Agastache foeniculum - *Anise hyssop, Licorice mint* {PL} The anise-flavored leaves are used for making a pleasant tea. Fresh or dried leaves are added to fruit salads and drinks as seasoning. The flowers also have an anise or licorice flavor and can be used in a similar manner. North America. CROWHURST 1972, LATHROP, MEDSGER, MORTON 1976; C11{S}, C13M{S}, C43M, C61M, C67M, E7M{S}, F21, F31T, G84, G96, K22, L56, *M35*, N19M, etc.

CULTIVARS

Texas American: (Texas American Pennyroyal) Similar to anise hyssop but with an anise-pennyroyal fragrance. Height 2 feet. K85

Agastache mexicana - *Mexican giant hyssop* {PL} The highly aromatic young leaves are used for flavoring and for tea. Mexico. MORTON 1976; C43M, D11T, G82M, K22, K85, P9{S}, *Q24*{S}, Q76

Agastache neomexicana - {S} Leaves are used for flavoring and as a substitute for tea. Southwestern North America. MORTON 1976, YANOVSKY; **W20**

Agastache rugosa - *Korean mint* {PL} The fresh or dried leaves, anise-like in odor and flavor, are used for seasoning meats and dressings and are steeped for tea. Young shoots and leaves are boiled and eaten. Eastern Asia. MORTON 1976, TANAKA; A2{S}, C13M{S}, C67M, C81M, D62{S}, F80{S}, H3M, H46{S}, J66, J82, K22, K85, M77M, N19M, N45, O48{S}, etc.

Agastache urticifolia - *Giant hyssop, Sawtooth mountain-mint* {S} Seeds are eaten raw or cooked. The dried flowers and leaves can be used to make an herbal tea. Western North America. KIRK, YANOVSKY; F44, I47, I98M, J93T

Amaracus dictamnus* → *Origanum dictamnus

Blephilia ciliata - *Downy wood-mint* {S} The mildly aromatic leaves can be prepared as tea like those of the true mints. North America. PETERSON, L.; E61{PL}, J39M, J43

Blephilia hirsuta - *Cherokee mint, Hairy wood-mint* {PL} Fresh or dried leaves are used as a substitute for tea. North America. PETERSON, L.; F43, K22, K85

Calamintha acinos* → *Acinos arvensis

Calamintha grandiflora - *Mint savory, Showy savory, Showy calamint* {PL} The leaves have a pleasant mint-like fragrance and flavor and can be used as a seasoning or for tea. Southern Europe. C11{S}, C43M, D29, E59T, E61, F31T, G96, H51M, K22, K85, L56, M82, N84{S}, *Q24*{S}, S7M{S}, etc.

Calamintha nepeta - *Lesser calamint* {PL} The herb can be used for flavoring. It has a stronger pennyroyal-like fragrance and a more pungent taste than calamint. Eurasia. MORTON 1976; E61, G84, K22, K85, M82, N84{S}, O48{S}, S55{S}

Calamintha officinalis* → *Calamintha sylvatica

Calamintha sylvatica - *Calamint* {S} An herb with a strong aromatic fragrance and a pleasantly pungent flavor. It is used in the preparation of zucchini and other "Roman style" vegetables, and has also been employed for flavoring roasts and stews. In Roman kitchens it was credited with removing the fetid odor and "gamey" taste of meat that had begun to spoil. The flavor is said to resemble a cross between mint and marjoram. Flowers are used for conserves. Eurasia. BIANCHINI, MABEY, MACNICOL, MORTON 1976; F15M{PL}, F35M{PL}, F80, H3M{PL}, I91, I99, M82{PL}, N84, O48, S7M

Calamintha sp. - *Niebita* {PL} An Old World culinary herb, originally from Italy. Indispensable for bean and mushroom dishes. Hardy perennial, height 2 feet, does best in full sun. Showy, pale lavender flowers. C43M

Cedronella cana* → *Agastache cana

Cedronella canariensis - *Balm of Gilead* {PL} Leaves are used in the preparation of a tea, called *thé de Canaries*. Macaronesia. UPHOF; C43M, C81M, D29, F35M, F37T, F43, G84, G96, H51M, I99{S}, K22, K85, L56, M82, N42, S55{S}, etc.

Cedronella triphylla* → *Cedronella canariensis

Clinopodium vulgare - *Wild basil, Field basil* {S} Fresh or dried leaves are used for flavoring tomato sauce, omelettes, egg sandwiches, fish chowders, broiled fish, rice dishes, etc. The fresh leaves can be made into tea. Europe, naturalized in North America. CROWHURST 1972, MABEY, MICHAEL [Pre, Re], PETERSON, L.; D62, J82, M82{PL}, *N71M*, N84, O48

Coleus amboinicus* → *Plectranthus amboinicus

Coleus aromaticus* → *Plectranthus amboinicus

Coleus blumei - *Sayabana, Jacob's coat* {S} Tubers are eaten. The leaves are eaten with bread and butter, or bruised and put into country beer. Southeast Asia. BURKILL, DUKE; F85, O53M

Coleus dazo - *Daju, Rizuka* {S} The starchy roots are washed by hand to remove the skin, then boiled and served. In flavor they are similar to an Irish potato. They can also be pickled. Tropical Africa. DALZIEL, TANAKA; **X44**

Coleus dysentericus* → *Solenostemon rotundifolius

Coleus parviflorus - *Country potato, African potato* {PL} The subterranean tubers are consumed like potatoes, either raw, baked, steamed, added to soups and stews, or mashed and fried as croquettes. Powdered tubers are sometimes used as a substitute for potatoes for the preparation of minced-meat balls. Southern Asia. MACMILLAN, OCHSE, TANAKA; **Y81**

Coleus rotundifolius* → *Solenostemon rotundifolius

Coleus tuberosus* → *Coleus parviflorus

Conradina verticillata - *Cumberland rosemary, Mountain rosemary* {PL} The leaves have a strong, pleasant scent reminiscent of rosemary and are occasionally used as a substitute in cooking. An endangered species. Eastern North America. A93M, B28, C76, D46, G96, I11M, J66, K22, K85, L55, N37M

Coridothymus capitatus* → *Thymus capitatus

Cunila origanoides - *Maryland dittany, Stone mint* {PL} The leaves have a pleasant, mint-like flavor and can be made into a refreshing tea. Both fresh and dried leaves are used. North America. CROWHURST 1972, MORTON 1976, PETERSON, L.; C43M, C67M, D62{S}, E5M, E61, H51M, H61M{S}, M82

Dracocephalum moldavica - *Moldavian balm, Moldavian dragon's-head* {S} The lemon-scented leaves can be used for tea. Young shoots are edible. Eurasia. VON REIS; D62, E7M, F80, N84, O53M, S55

Elsholtzia ciliata - *Naginata-kôju, Hsiang-ju, Kinh giói* {PL} Young plants are eaten raw in salads when finely cut, boiled as a potherb, or used as an aromatic condiment for vegetable dishes. Eastern Asia. BOND [Cul], TANAKA; D62{S}, K22, K85

Elsholtzia cristata* → *Elsholtzia ciliata

Galeobdolon luteum* → *Lamiastrum galeobdolon

Glechoma hederacea - *Ground ivy, Alehoof, Gill-over-the-ground* {PL} Fresh or dried leaves are used for making an herbal tea. The young shoots and leaves are eaten like spinach or cooked in vegetable soups, to which they lend a special flavor. The Saxons added the herb to their beer to clarify it and improve its flavor and keeping qualities. Eurasia, naturalized in North America. CROWHURST 1972, GIBBONS 1966b, GRIEVE, LAUNERT, MABEY, MICHAEL [Re], MORTON 1976; A1M, C43M, D62{S}, E33M, F35M, *G89M*, N45, *N71M*{S}, N84{S}, O48{S}, *Q24*{S}, R53M

Hedeoma drummondii - *New Mexican pennyroyal, Toronjil, Poleo* {PL} An infusion of the flowering tops is used as a hot beverage. Also employed as a peppermint-like flavoring. Southwestern North America. ALTSCHUL, LATORRE 1977b, YANOVSKY; C43M

Hedeoma pulegioides - *American pennyroyal, Squaw mint* {PL} The leaves have a very strong mint-like aroma and taste and can be brewed into a refreshing tea, or used as a culinary flavoring. Source of an essential oil used in the food industry for flavoring beverages, ice cream, candy, and baked goods. North America. CROWHURST 1972, GIBBONS 1979, MORTON 1976, PETERSON, L.; A1M, A2{S}, B51{S}, C13M{S}, C43M{S}, F37T, F35M, G84, I11M, I11M{S}, K2, K22, M82, N45

Hoslundia opposita - *Mshwee* {S} The small, orange to red fruit, composed of an elongated, succulent calyx, has soft, very sweet pulp and is eaten fresh. Has been recommended for improvement. Leaves are also eaten. Tropical Africa. DALZIEL, FOX, F., MARTIN 1975, TANAKA, VON REIS; N84

Hyptis pectinata - *Comb hyptis* {S} In Nigeria, the leaf is sometimes used as a seasoning in soup. The plant is used by the Sakalava of Madagascar for making rum. Tropical America. DALZIEL, UPHOF; **W35, Y2**

Hyptis suaveolens - *Konivari, Bush tea plant, Sangura* {S} The tips of the shoots are added to food as a flavoring. A porridge or a refreshing beverage can be made by soaking the mucilaginous seeds in water. The aromatic leaves are used for preparing a mint-flavored tea substitute. Tropical America. ALTSCHUL, DUKE, MORTON 1976, TANAKA, WILLIAMS, L.; F80, F85, I16, R47

Hyssopus officinalis - *Hyssop* {PL} The leaves and the tops of the young shoots are used for seasoning soups, salads, sauces, pickles, custards, meats, etc. Source of an essential oil employed as a flavoring for bitters and alcoholic beverages, especially liqueurs like *Chartreuse*. Flowers are added to salads or made into syrup. The dried herb can be brewed into tea. Mediterranean region, cultivated. GRIEVE, MACNICOL, MARCIN, MICHAEL [Re], MORTON 1976, ROOT 1980b [Cul], UPHOF; C9, C13M{S}, C67M, F21, F31T, G84, H40, H46{S}, J66, K22, L63M{S}, *M35*{S}, N19M, N84{S}

CULTIVARS

Pink: (Rose, Rosea) Very similar to common hyssop, but with attractive flowers that are pale pink in color. Grows approximately 18 inches tall. C11{S}, D29, E5M, E61, F35M, M15T, M82, M92, N84{S}, O48{S}, R53M{S}, S55{S}

Sissinghurst: Selected form with many terminal spires of light pink flowers. Larger leaves and more erect habit than common hyssop. C9, K22

Koellia virginiana → *Pycnanthemum virginianum*

Lallemantia iberica - *Balingu shahri* {S} Leaves are used as a potherb in Iran. The seeds are the source of an edible oil, called *lallemantia oil*. Southwest Asia. UPHOF; D62

Lamiastrum galeobdolon - *Yellow archangel* {S} The young shoots and leaves are eaten boiled or sautéed in butter. Southern Eurasia. MABEY; N84, O48, S7M

CULTIVARS {PL}

Variegated: Deep green foliage brushed with striking silver variegation; bright yellow flowers in spring; height 6 inches. Excellent rapid growing ground cover or rock wall plant, in partial sun and shade. *A74*, D95, E30, I22, J37M, K22, K85, *L22*, M92

Lamium album - *White dead-nettle* {S} The young leaves and stem tips are boiled and eaten as potherbs or added to omelettes. Also cooked with eel and sorrel in the French dish *anguille au vert a la flamande*. The flowers are candied. Eurasia. GRIEVE, HEDRICK 1919, MICHAEL [Re], UPHOF; N84, O48

Lamium amplexicaule - *Henbit* {S} Young leaves and flowering tips are eaten in salads, boiled as a potherb, cooked in rice gruel, or used in dumplings. Eurasia, naturalized in North America. FERNALD, KIRK, TANAKA; **V50, W59M, Y10, Y89M**

Lamium purpureum - *Archangel red dead-nettle* {S} The young leaves are used as a potherb. Young flowering tips are boiled or candied. Eurasia. HEDRICK 1919, KUNKEL, MABEY; *N71M*, N84, O48

Lavandula angustifolia - *English lavender* {PL} Leaves, petals, and flowering tips are added to salads, dressings, soups, stews, vinegar, honey, jellies, wine, and soft drinks. The fragrant flowers can be candied or used as a garnish for fruit cups. Fresh or dried flowers are brewed into tea. Source of an essential oil utilized as a flavoring by the food manufacturing industry. Mediterranean region, cultivated. BRYAN [Cul], GRIEVE [Cu], LARKCOM 1984, LEGGATT [Re], MACNICOL [Re], MARCIN, MORTON 1976, PAINTER [Re], ROOT 1980b; C13M{S}, C43M, C67M, D29, E61, F21, F24{S}, F35M, G84, H40, K22, *M35*, N19M, N45, N84{S}, etc.

CULTIVARS

Gray Lady: Compact plant, to 18 inches tall, robust and rapid growing. Grayer foliage than the species. Dark-violet colored flowers. Introduced by J.J. Grullemans of Wayside Gardens, Mentor, Ohio, before 1967. A49D, C43M, E5M, M82

Hidcote: Slow, compact grower, to 2 1/2 feet tall. Attractive shiny green foliage and rich, dark aster-violet flowers. Raised by Major Lawrence Johnston, Hidcote Manor, Gloucestershire, England, before 1950. C3, C11{S}, C13M{S}, C81M, E59T, F37T, F88, G84, J66, K22, K85, *M65M*, M82, N19M

Jean Davis: (Rosea) Forms small, compact tidy mounds, to 18 inches tall. Attractive, light-rose colored flowers. Excellent for borders and knot gardens. A49D, B77, C43M, C81M, D29, E5M, E59T, J66, K22, K85, *L22*, L56, L57, *M65M*, M82, N19M, etc.

Munstead: Dwarf, compact growth, 18 to 24 inches tall. Dark aster-violet flowers. Blooms several weeks earlier than other cultivars. Raised by Gertrude Jekyll, Munstead Wood, Surrey, England. Introduced in 1916. A97, C11{S}, C13M{S}, C43M, C67M, F21, F24{S}, F37T, G84, J66, K22, *M35*, *M65M*, N19M, N45, etc.

Sharon Roberts: Hardy to 0° F.; has withstood temperatures of -10° F. Flowers are deepest lavender, intensely fragrant. Blooms twice each season, in June and again in September. I39

Lavandula x intermedia (L. angustifolia x L. latifolia) - *Lavandin* {PL} Natural and artificial hybrids. English lavender x spike lavender. The essential oil is used for flavoring. Hybrids of this cross are more vigorous growing, easier to grow, and yield more oil than their parents and are replacing them as an industrial source of essential oil. MORTON 1976.

CULTIVARS

Delphinensis: (Lavender of Dauphine) Growing wild in France and Switzerland, this cultivar is collected for its oil. Larger and more robust growing, the flower spikes are longer and heavier. A49D, C13M{S}, M82

Grappenhall: Large growing cultivar, to 3 feet tall. Slightly larger leaves than the type. Long spikes of richly colored, pale mauve flowers excellent for cutting and bunching. Introduced by Messrs. Clibran of Altricham, England, about 1902. P86, P92

Grosso: (Fat Spike) Vigorous hybrid with large, intensely fragrant gray leaves, twice the size of English lavenders. Excellent for landscaping purposes, a mature 5 year old plant forming an even mound about 16 inches high and 3 feet across with virtually no pruning. Disease resistant. Hardy to below 0° F. Holds its foliage well through the winter. Grown commercially in France for its oil. Named after the French lavender specialist Pierre Grosso. C2, C91T, M82, P92

Lavandula latifolia - *Spike lavender, Sweet lavender* {PL} Flowers are the source of an essential oil sometimes used for flavoring salads and jellies. Mediterranean region. TANAKA; A97, C3, C11{S}, C13M{S}, E5M, E59T, E61, E81M{S}, F24{S}, J66, J82, K22, K85, M82, *Q24*{S}, etc.

Lavandula officinalis → *Lavandula angustifolia*

Leonotis nepetaefolia - *Giant lion's ear, Zungzu* {S} Flowers are eaten in Tanzania. Eastern Africa. VON REIS; F80, F85, G96{PL}, I39, I99, K22{PL}, K85{PL}, N84, R41, R77M

Leonurus cardiaca - *Motherwort* {S} The flowering tops are used as a flavoring for beers, ales, and stout. Fresh or dried flowers can also be added to soups, particularly lentil or split-pea soup, and can be brewed into a tea. Eurasia. CROWHURST 1973, MACNICOL [Re]; C11, C13M, C43M{PL}, D58, E5M{PL}, E61{PL}, F21{PL}, F24, F35M{PL}, G84{PL}, H46, I99, L63M, N45{PL}, O53M, etc.

Leonurus sibiricus - *Chivirico, Siberian motherwort* {S} Young plants and plant tops are eaten. In China, the roots are cooked with pork. Eastern Asia, cultivated. ALTSCHUL, BURKILL, TANAKA; F85, I59G, I99, K49T

Lycopus uniflorus - *Bugleweed* {S} The crisp, white tubers are eaten raw in salads, boiled, pickled, or added to soups and stews. Boiled a short time in salted water, they are said to be an agreeable vegetable, much suggesting the *crosnes* of European markets. North America. CROWHURST 1972, FERNALD, PETERSON, L.; **U4**

Majorana heracleoticum → *Origanum vulgare ssp. hirtum*

Majorana hortensis → *Origanum majorana*

Majorana onites → *Origanum onites*

Majorana syriaca → *Origanum syriacum*

Marrubium vulgare - *Horehound* {PL} The bitter, pungent leaves are candied, made into syrup and herb beer, or used as a flavoring for liqueurs. The crushed leaves can also be added to honey, and eaten off the spoon. Fresh or dried leaves are brewed into tea. Mediterranean region, naturalized in North America. CLARKE, GIBBONS 1966b, GRIEVE, MARCIN, MORTON 1976, PAINTER

[Re], UPHOF; C3{S}, C13M{S}, C67M, F21, F31T, F35M, G84, H40, H46{S}, J66, K22, *M35*, N19M, N45

Melissa officinalis - *Balm, Lemon balm* {PL} The leaves have a pleasant lemon fragrance and are used for flavoring salads, soups, egg dishes, butter, tarragon vinegar, *claret cups*, sauces, etc. Also liqueurs such as *Chartreuse* and *Benedictine*. Fresh or dried leaves can be used to make a very refreshing tea. Eurasia, cultivated. GRIEVE, MARCIN, MICHAEL [Re], MORTON 1976, ROOT 1980b [Cul], TANAKA; C3, C3{S}, C9, C13M{S}, C67M, E5M{PR}, F21, F31T, G84, H40, H46{S}, K22, *M35*, N19M

CULTIVARS

All Gold: (Gold Leaf, Golden) The richly scented, pubescent leaves keep their bright chartreuse-yellow coloration throughout the season, unlike the fading Variegated cultivar. This property is fully developed when the plant is grown in partial shade. Grows 18 inches tall and 18 inches wide. C2, C43M, H79M, P92

Lime: (Lime Balm) Grown and used the same as lemon balm, but has a distinct lime-like scent. Height 3 feet. Hardy in zones 4 to 9. A1M, B97, C11{S}, C13M{S}, F37T, H3M, H40, J66, N42

Variegated: (Aurea) The new spring growth has attractive yellow variegations. These fade during flowering and summer heat, but provide color at a time of year when little else is available. After flowering, cut back to promote the growth of additional variegated leaves. LATHROP; A1M, A49D, C9, C43M, C67M, C81M, E5M, E61, F35M, J66, K22, K85, *L22*, L56, M82, etc.

Melittis melissophyllum - *Bastard balm* {S} A coumarin-scented herb occasionally used for making a *Maiwein* or *Maibowle* type beverage. Europe. UPHOF; N84, *Q24*

Mentha aquatica - *Water mint* {PL} The herb has a strong, distinctive, peppermint-like fragrance and flavor and is used as a seasoning for peas, potatoes, egg and cheese dishes, and for meat hash in Southeast Asia. In South Africa, it is used as a substitute for tea. Eurasia. GIBBONS 1966b, LATHROP, MABEY, MORTON 1976; A1M, B28, C43M, C67M, E59T, H30, I90M, L56, N3M, N42, N84{S}, O48{S}, O53M{S}, S7M{S}, S55{S}, etc.

CULTIVARS

Variegated: Attractive, green and white variegated foliage. Aromatic lilac-pink flowers. Height 6 inches. H30

Mentha aquatica var. crispa - *Curled mint, Crisp-leaved mint, Balm mint* {PL} An herb with a resinous, pineapple-like odor that is used for flavoring jellies, sauces, dressings, punch, and liqueurs. The fresh or dried leaves make a pleasant tea. Eurasia, naturalized in North America. MORTON 1976, PETERSON, L.; *B39M*, C67M, E59T, F31T, F35M, G57M{S}, G96, H3M, H4, H46{S}, H49, H51M, K22, K85, *M35*, M53, etc.

Mentha aquatica 'Citrata' - *Bergamot mint* {PL} The leaves yield a citrus-scented essential oil similar to true bergamot oil. After being refined it can be used in food flavoring and forms an ingredient of *Chartreuse*. GRIEVE, MORTON 1976; A1M, C67M, E5M, F15M, L57, M82

CULTIVARS

Eau de Cologne: (Eau de Cologne Mint, Perfume Mint) Dark-green, roundish leaves. Sweet, aromatic fragrance suggestive of old fashioned toilet water. Grows to 18 inches tall. Use in tea blends, cold drinks, and salads. LEGGATT [Re]; A1M, C67M, C81M, E5M, F35M, H3M, H40, I39, J66, K22, M53, M82, N42

Lemon Bergamot: (Lemon Mint) Light-green, crinkly leaves with a refreshing lemon and mint flavor and fragrance. Good for tea and in fish dishes. Small, pinkish, edible flowers. Grows to 20 inches tall. A1M, C67M, K22, K85, P92

Lime: (Lime Mint) Similar to orange mint, but with a slightly different lime-like scent and flavor. Attractive plant with round dark green leaves, dark purple runners and light purple flowers. Height 12 to 18 inches. Very good for tea and jellies. Can also be used for oils and potpourri. A1M, C43M, C67M, E61, F35M, F37T, F43, F93G, H3M, H51M, I11M, J66, J82, K22, K85, M53, M82, N42, etc.

Orange Bergamot: (Orange Mint) Broad, smooth, dark-green leaves edged with purple. Purple flowers bloom from mid to late summer. Green, branching stems tinged with red, reach 2 feet in height. Very strong citrus-like scent and taste. Makes a very good tea. C9, C67M, F21, F31T, F35M, F93G, G84, H40, J66, K22, *M35*, M53, N19M, N42, N45, etc.

Mentha arvensis - *Field mint, Corn mint, Wild mint* {PL} American Indians used the leaves for flavoring corn meal mush or for baking fish. Their strong odor and flavor makes them especially suited for adding to chutneys. The fresh or dried leaves can be made into tea. Also the source of an essential oil used in candies and beverages. Northern temperate region. CLARKE, KIRK, MABEY [Re], TANAKA; M16, N9M, N9M{S}

Mentha arvensis ssp. haplocalyx - *Húng gioi* {PL} Used for scenting tea. Has an unusual sweet scent, reminiscent of sweet heliotrope. Southeast Asia. TANAKA; K22, K85, M82

Mentha arvensis var. villosa - *American wild mint* {S} The fragrant, pleasant-tasting leaves are used as a seasoning. The Indians of Maine roasted them over a fire and ate them as a relish with salt. An infusion of the leaves is used as a beverage. North America. HEDRICK 1919, MEDSGER, YANOVSKY; G47M

Mentha arvensis f. piperascens - *Japanese mint, Japanese field mint, Hakka* {PL} The flowers are used for scenting tea. Source of *Japanese mint oil* or *Japanese peppermint oil*, used in confectionery, cakes, and beverages. The leaves and shoots are eaten cooked or preserved. Has a strong peppermint or spearmint-like fragrance. Japan. MORTON 1976, SCHERY, TANAKA, YASHIRODA; C43M, F43, K22, K85, M82

Mentha canadensis → *Mentha arvensis*

Mentha x cardiaca → *Mentha x gentilis*

Mentha cervina - *Hart's pennyroyal* {PL} Leaves have a strong pennyroyal fragrance and can be used for tea. Europe. C43M, K22, K85, M82{CF}

Mentha citrata → *Mentha aquatica*

Mentha x cordifolia (M. spicata x M. x villosa) - *Heart-leaved mint* Natural and artificial hybrids. Applemint x spearmint. The leaves are used for flavoring. One type is grown commercially outdoors in southern England. MORTON 1976; (for cultivars see Mint, page 390)

Mentha crispa → *Mentha aquatica var. crispa*

Mentha x gentilis (M. arvensis x M. spicata) - *American applemint, Red mint* {PL} Natural hybrid. Field mint x spearmint. The leaves are occasionally used for flavoring, having a refreshing odor and taste. In the United States, this plant is the principal source of *oil of spearmint*, used mainly in chewing gum. Naturalized in North America. MORTON 1976, UPHOF.

CULTIVARS

Austrian: (Austrian Mint) Delightful flavor reminiscent of spearmint. Essential seasoning for the ravioli-like Austrian dish, *topfen nudeln* stuffed with mashed potatoes and cottage cheese. J82, M82

Ginger: (Ginger mint) Leaves light-green to grayish, slightly variegated with gold, pointed. Distinctive, brisk, fruity, mint-like flavor with a hint of ginger. Makes a nice tea. Grow in sun or partial shade. Ornamental novelty; grows 1 to 2 feet tall. A1M, A49D,

C81M, E59T, E61, F35M, F37T, F43, H3M, J82, K2, K22, K85, M53, M82, N19M, etc.

Golden: (Golden Mint) Low, spreading plant to 1 foot tall. Smooth, green leaves variegated with yellow streaks. Stays bright golden throughout the summer. Pale purple flowers; appealing fruity flavor. A49D, K85

Scotch: (Scotch Mint, Variegated Scotch Mint) Erect growing plant, 1 to 1 1/2 feet tall; numerous short branches. Broad, spearmint-like foliage, variegated a vivid gold and green. Sweet smelling, mild, spearmint-like aroma and flavor. E61, I39, M15T

Mentha haplocalyx → *Mentha arvensis ssp. haplocalyx*

Mentha longifolia - *Horse-mint* {S} The fresh herb is used as a seasoning in Indian chutneys. In Afghanistan, it is sprinkled on mast (curds). Leaves are candied or used as a substitute for tea. The dried leaves and flowering tops are the source of a peppermint-like essential oil employed for flavoring candy. Eurasia. ALTSCHUL, MORTON 1976, TANAKA, WATT; A1M{PL}, K47T, L56{PL}, M82{PL}, N84, O53M, *Q24*, R41, R77M, S7M

CULTIVARS {PL}

Capensis: (Cape Spearmint) Unusual long, narrow, grey-green leaves and a soft, spearmint flavor and aroma. Height 2 feet. Can be used for tea. C43M, N42, N84{S}, S44{S}

Silver: (Silver Mint) Ornamental, slender, silver-grey leaves; grows 1 to 2 feet tall. Strong, refreshing spearmint odor and flavor. Good for tea or culinary use. Also attractive in dried arrangements. Hardy in Zones 4 to 9. A49D, B97, C43M, C67M, D29, E5M, E61, H3M, H40, J82, K22, K85, L56, *M35*, M82, N42, etc.

Mentha x niliaca → *Mentha x villosa*

Mentha x piperita (M. aquatica x M. spicata) - *Peppermint* {PL} Natural hybrid. Water mint x spearmint. The aromatic leaves are widely used in sauces, jellies, jams, fruit salads, drinks, etc. In the Middle East, they are finely chopped and added to tossed salads as generous portions. The fresh or dried leaves make a refreshing tea that can be consumed hot or cold. Source of an essential oil utilized by the food industry in flavoring ice cream, candy, chewing gum, and alcoholic drinks, including *Benedictine* and *crème de menthe*. GIBBONS 1966b [Re], GRIEVE [Cu], MARCIN, MORTON 1976, ROOT 1980b [Cul], UPHOF; C9, C67M, F21, F31T, G84, H40, H46{S}, J66, K22, *L22*, M16, *M35*, N19M (for cultivars see Mint, page 390)

Mentha pulegium - *European pennyroyal, English pennyroyal* {PL} The leaves have a strong, pungent, menthol-like fragrance and taste and are used as a seasoning for stuffings, meat sauces, stews, and game. In England, a famous stuffing was once made of pennyroyal, pepper, and honey. The dried leaves give a subtle flavor to stewed prunes, apricots, or mixed dried fruit. Fresh or dried leaves and stem tips can be used for preparing an aromatic tea. Europe, cultivated. GRIEVE [Cu], MABEY, MARCIN, MICHAEL [Re], MORTON 1976; C9, C11{S}, C13M{S}, C67M, D92, E99{S}, F21, F31T, G84, H40, *M35*, M53, N19M, N42, N84{S}, O53M{S}, etc.

CULTIVARS

Dwarf: Has a menthol-like aroma similar to regular English pennyroyal but is much lower in growth. Only grows to a height of 1 or 2 inches and is more compact. C43M, M82

Mentha requienii - *Corsican mint, Spanish mint, Crème de menthe* {PL} The entire plant has a very strong crème-de-menthe fragrance and taste. As a flavoring, it is used mainly in liqueurs. Also widely grown as an ornamental ground cover in mixed herb plantings and rock gardens. Mediterranean region. GESSERT, LATHROP, MORTON 1976; C9, C43M, C67M, E48, F21, F31T, G55, G84, G96, H4, J66, K22, M33G, M53, N19M, etc.

Mentha rotundifolia → *Mentha suaveolens*

Mentha spicata - *Spearmint, Green mint, Lamb mint* {PL} Leaves and flowers are used as a flavoring or garnish in salads, sauces, soups, fruit drinks, vegetable dishes, desserts, dressings, etc. Fresh or dried leaves are brewed into a refreshing tea that can be used hot or cold. Source of an essential oil that flavors ice cream, candy, soft drinks, etc. Eurasia, cultivated. BRYAN [Cul, Re], GRIEVE [Cu], LEGGATT [Re], MARCIN, MORTON 1976, ROOT 1980b [Cul], TANAKA, UPHOF; C67M, F31T, H40, H46{S}, J66, K22, *L22*, M16, *M35*, N19M, N45 (for cultivars see Mint, page 390)

Mentha suaveolens - *Pineapple mint* {PL} Young leaves can be used for flavoring, as a garnish, or brewed into tea. The plant is low-growing, 10 to 12 inches high with small, white-blotched leaves. The foliage has a distinct pineapple-like fragrance and flavor when young, becoming more mint-like with age. Cultivated. GESSERT, LATHROP, MORTON 1976; C3, C9, C67M, E59T, E61, F21, F31T, G84, G96, J66, K22, N19M, N42

Mentha sylvestris → *Mentha longifolia*

Mentha x verticillata (M. aquatica x M. arvensis) - *Whorled mint* {S} Probably a natural hybrid. Water mint x field mint. The leaves are used for flavoring. MABEY; U7M, Y10

Mentha x villosa 'Alopecuroides' - *Applemint, Round-leaved mint* {PL} The leaves have a delicate apple and spearmint-like aroma and taste and are used fresh for garnishing or flavoring. Considered by connoisseurs to be superior to spearmint for all culinary purposes but especially as a tea herb. Europe, cultivated. GESSERT, LATHROP, LEGGATT [Re], MORTON 1976; C3, C67M, F21, F31T, G84, G96, H40, J66, K22, M16, *M35*, M53, N19M, N45

CULTIVARS

Bowles': (Bowles' Mint) A larger form of applemint with similar uses. Rust free. Originally from E.A. Bowles garden. R53M

Egyptian: (Egyptian Mint) The leaves have a strong, spearmint-like fragrance and taste and can be used in teas, iced drinks, fruit cocktails, and fish dishes. Ornamental plant with striking pale-lavender flowers, height 3 feet, very hardy. A1M, C43M, D29, E61, F31T, F43, H3M, K22, K85, L57, M33G, M53, M82, N42

Woolly: (Woolly Mint) The fragrant leaves are highly esteemed in England for home use, especially in mint sauce. MORTON 1976; A1M, C9, E5M, H51M

Mentha x villosa-nervata (M. longifolia x M. spicata) - *English mint, English spearmint* {PL} Hybrid. Horse-mint x spearmint. A popular mint in England where it is grown in greenhouses for the fresh market trade. Lush, lustrous green leaves with a strong spearmint flavor. Delicious in mint sauce. MORTON 1976; A1M, D29, E5M, F35M, F37T, H3M, H40, I11M, J82, K22, K81, K85, L86, M53

Micromeria bromeii - *St. John's mint* {PL} Native ground cover, growing to three inches in moist areas. Strong mint-like flavor. Apparently used as a culinary and tea herb. Florida. H40

Micromeria chamissonis → *Satureja douglasii*

Micromeria juliana - *Savory* {S} The herb is used for flavoring. Mediterranean region. HEDRICK 1919; K47T

Micromeria obovata → *Satureja viminea*

Micromeria viminea → *Satureja viminea*

Micromeria sp. - *Emperor's mint* {S} Found thriving amidst the ruins of Emperor Hadrian's remarkable summer villa near Rome. Has a bold, mint-like fragrance and flavor. J82

Micromeria sp. - *Roman mint* {PL} Found growing wild near Rome where it is widely used in cooking. Mint-like odor and flavor, reminiscent of both Menthol spearmint and pennyroyal. J82

Monarda austromontana - *Mexican bergamot, Mt. Pima oregano* {PL} Leaves are used as a seasoning in Mexico, especially for meat dishes. Also brewed into a tea. Can be used like commercial oregano but has a different and more subtle flavor. Mexico. ALTSCHUL, HUTSON, MORTON 1976; I16{PR}, I16{S}, K22

Monarda citriodora - *Lemon bee-balm, Lemon bergamot, Lemon mint* {S} The lemon-scented leaves can be used for flavoring or brewed into tea. Hopi Indians boiled the leaves with hares and other wild game. Southwestern North America. GESSERT, YANOVSKY; A49D{PL}, C13M, C43M, C43M{PL}, D26, E59T{PL}, E61, E73M, F24, F31T{PL}, F59, I11, I91, J25M, N11M, etc.

Monarda clinopodia - *White basil-balm* {PL} Fresh or dried leaves and flower-heads are brewed into tea. Said to be excellent when mixed with other teas. North America. PETERSON, L.; L55, M16, M77M, N9M, N9M{S}

Monarda didyma - *Oswego tea, Bee balm* {PL} The fresh or dried leaves and flower-heads are used for making an excellent aromatic tea. Young tips are used as a garnish for fruit salads and cool drinks and for flavoring cheese, stuffings, tossed salads, and apple jelly. The fresh flowers can be tossed on a mixed green salad. Dried leaves add flavor to *Earl Grey* tea. Leaves are eaten boiled with meat, by the Tewa Indians. North America. LARKCOM 1984, LEGGATT [Re], MACNICOL [Re], MARCIN, MEDSGER, MICHAEL [Re], MORTON 1976, PAINTER [Re], ROOT 1980b [Cul], UPHOF; *B39M*, B97M, C13M{S}, C67M, E99{S}, G59M{S}, G84, G96, H40, I11M, K22, K53{S}, L65M, N9M, N9M{S}, etc.

CULTIVARS {S}

Lavender: (Lavender Bergamot) Citrus and oregano scented leaves and flowers that make a very pleasant and soothing tea. Grows to 4 feet tall. K49T

Monarda fistulosa - *Wild bergamot, Horsemint* {PL} The entire plant above ground may be used as a potherb, cooked with other foods as a seasoning, or dried for future use. Fresh or dried leaves are brewed into a refreshing, aromatic tea. The flowers make an attractive edible garnish in a salad. North America. GIBBONS 1979, KINDSCHER, KIRK, MORTON 1976, UPHOF; B33M, B51{S}, C2, C13M{S}, C43M, C43M{S}, F88, G47M{S}, G89, G89{S}, H46{S}, H63, I11M, J39M, J42, J43{S}, etc.

Monarda fistulosa var. menthaefolia - *Oregano de la sierra* {S} The aromatic leaves have traditionally been used as a seasoning for cabrito, wild game and meat. The unique oregano-like flavor is favored by Southwestern chefs, especially for flavoring semi-soft ricotta cheese. Southwestern North America. HUTSON, KAVENA [Re]; H3M{PL}, J25M, J25M{PL}, L13, N29{PR}

Monarda menthaefolia → ***Monarda fistulosa var. menthaefolia***

Monarda pectinata → ***Monarda citriodora***

Monarda punctata - *Horsemint, Spotted monarda* {S} Leaves are brewed into an aromatic tea. North America. PETERSON, L.; C13M, C43M{PL}, D40G, E59T{PL}, E61{PL}, F80, G47M, H46, I11M{PL}, I19{PL}, I91, J39M, J40, L55{PL}, M77M{PL}, *Q24*, etc.

Monardella odoratissima - *Mountain pennyroyal, Coyote mint* {PL} Fresh or dried, the aromatic leaves and flower-heads are steeped into a clear, refreshing, mint-like tea. Western North America. CLARKE; G96, J93T{S}, M77M, *Q24*{S}

Monardella villosa - *Coyote mint* {PL} The leaves and flower heads, fresh or dried, are steeped (not boiled) in water to form a clear tea. It has a sweet, spicy aroma and a slightly bitter, mint-like flavor. Southwestern North America. CLARKE, MORTON 1976; B92, G60

Nepeta cataria - *Catnip, Catmint* {PL} The leaves can be candied, or brewed into an aromatic, mint-like tea. In France, the leaves and young shoots are used for seasoning sauces, soups, and stews. Eurasia, cultivated. GIBBONS 1966b, GRIEVE, MACNICOL, MARCIN, MORTON 1976, VILMORIN; C3, C13M{S}, C67M, E61, F21, F31T, G84, H40, H46{S}, K22, K53{S}, *M35*, N19M

CULTIVARS

Lemon: (Citriodora) Leaves have a pleasant, lemon-like aroma and flavor which makes it more appealing to humans and somewhat less so to cats. Lower growing than common catnip. Makes a refreshing tea. C11{S}, C13M{S}, C43M, C43M{S}, C67M, E5M, E61, G84, I91{S}, J66, K22, K85, M82, etc.

Purple-Flowered: Identical to common catnip in every respect except for the color of the flowers. C43M, C43M{S}

Nepeta hederacea → ***Glechoma hederacea***

Ocimum americanum → ***Ocimum canum***

Ocimum basilicum - *Sweet basil* {S} Young leaves and flowering tops, both fresh and dried, are used for seasoning tomato sauce, vinegar, soups, salads, omelettes, etc. Also the principal ingredient of *pesto* sauce. Flowers are also used as a garnish. In the Near East, the seeds are eaten alone or added to bread dough and other foods as a flavoring. They become mucilaginous when soaked in water and are made into a refreshing beverage, called *cherbet tokhum* in Mediterranean countries. Source of an essential oil used in catsups, mustards, sauces and vinegars. Old World Tropics and Subtropics. HAMPSTEAD [Cu, Re], LEGGATT [Re], MORTON 1976, ROOT 1980b [Cul], UPHOF; B75, C13M, C43M, C81M, E61, F21{PL}, F24, F31T{PL}, G84{PL}, J20, *M35*{PL}, M53{PL}, N19M{PL} (for cultivars see Basil, page 261)

Ocimum canum - *Hoary basil, Hairy basil, Meng luk* {S} Young leaves are eaten steamed, as a side-dish with rice, or added to curries. Also used as a flavoring in sauces, salads, soups, poultry stuffings, meat dishes, etc. The seeds, when soaked in water, swell into a gelatinous mass which is mixed with coconut milk and sugar to form a sweet, cooling beverage. Old World Tropics and Subtropics. FOX, F., MORTON 1976, OCHSE, SHURTLEFF 1979 [Re], TANAKA; F85, S55 (for cultivars see Basil, page 261)

Ocimum gratissimum - *East Indian basil, Tree basil, Clove basil* {PL} The leaves are eaten as a potherb, or cooked with other foods as a flavoring. Seeds are sometimes eaten in India. Tropics. BURKILL, MORTON 1976, WATT; C13M{S}, C43M, E5M, E81M{S}, F85{S}, G84, J82, J82{S}, M82, N19M, N84{S}

Ocimum gratissimum var. viride - *Tea bush, Green basil* {PL} The leaves have the flavor of lemon thyme and are used in salads and as a seasoning for soups, meats, and poultry stuffing. Also brewed into tea, which is drunk as a beverage with milk and sugar. Tropical Africa. DALZIEL, FOX, F., MORTON 1976; C43M

Ocimum kilimandscharicum - *Camphor basil* {PL} The leaves have a very distinctive camphor-like fragrance and are occasionally brewed into tea. East Africa. B75{S}, C13M{S}, C43M, C43M{S}, E5M, F15M, F85{S}, G84, J20{S}, J82, M53, M82, N42, Q12{S} (for cultivars see Basil, page 261)

Ocimum micranthum - *Peruvian basil* {PL} The herbage is used in the preparation of soups and stews to which it imparts a characteristic flavor. Tropical America. WILLIAMS, L.; C43M, C43M{S}, E5M, G84, K22{S}, M53

Ocimum sanctum - *Holy basil, Sacred basil, Tulsi, Pagoda basil* {PL} Fresh leaves are eaten raw in salads, cooked as a potherb, or used as a flavoring for fruit dishes, sweet yeast breads, jellies and preserves. They are sweetly spicy with a sharp, pronounced clove scent and pungency. Also brewed into a refreshing tea. The mucilaginous seeds are made into a sweet, cooling beverage. Tropical Asia, cultivated. BURKILL, COOK, CRIBB, HAMPSTEAD, HERKLOTS, MORTON 1976; C11{S}, C13M{S}, C43M, C67M, D29, D87{S}, E7M{S}, G84, H3M, K22{S}, *M35*, M53, M82, N19M, N42, etc.

CULTIVARS

Purple: (Purple Tulsi, Krishna Tulsi) The whole plant has a reddish-purple tint and a clove-like aroma and taste, much sweeter than common tulsi. Development of full purple coloration requires strong sunlight and hot temperatures. The seeds are non-mucilaginous. DARRAH; C43M, C43M{S}, G84, M82

Ocimum viride → *Ocimum gratissimum var. viride*

Origanum dictamnus - *Dittany of Crete, Hop marjoram* {PL} The aromatic foliage is used for flavoring salads and vermouth. In Saxon kitchens it was an ingredient of a sauce to be used with fish. Combined with parsley, garlic, thyme, salt and pepper, it added a pleasant, aromatic flavor. The flowering tops are dried and brewed into tea. Mediterranean region. GESSERT, JONES, D., LATHROP, MORTON 1976; C9, C43M, C67M, C81M, D29, E5M, E61, F31T, G96, H51M, J82, K22, K85, M53, N19M, etc.

Origanum heracleoticum → *Origanum vulgare ssp. hirtum*

Origanum majorana - *Sweet marjoram, Knotted marjoram* {PL} Leaves, flowers, and tender stems are used for flavoring syrups, stews, dressings, liqueurs, sauces, soups, sausages, stuffings, geese, etc. The aromatic seeds flavor candy, beverages, condiments, and meat products. Fresh or dried leaves are brewed into a sweet, mellow tea with a flavor that resembles a blend of thyme, rosemary, and sage. Eurasia, cultivated. LEGGATT [Re], MACNICOL [Re], MARCIN, MORTON 1976, TANAKA, UPHOF; C9, C13M{S}, C43M, C43M{S}, C67M, F21, F31T, G84, H40, H46{S}, J66, K22, K22{S}, K66{S}, *M35*, N19M, N42, etc.

CULTIVARS

Golden: (Golden Marjoram, Creeping Gold Marjoram, Aurea) Crinkled, yellow to white leaves. Grows to 6 inches tall. Makes an attractive, golden-green ground cover; also a good potted plant. A49D, C43M, C67M, D29, E61, F35M, H3M, H40, H51M, J78, L56, L86, M82

Variegated: Attractive plant with fragrant leaves, variegated with cream and green. Height 8 inches. G15

Origanum x majoricum (O. majorana x O. vulgare) - *Hardy marjoram, Culinary oregano, Cooking oregano, Italian oregano* {PL} Natural hybrid. Sweet marjoram x oregano. Has the appearance and flavor of marjoram, but some of the hardiness of the oregano. Hardy to Zone 6. Released by the United States Department of Agriculture. Grows 18 to 24 inches tall. Does not set seed. Excellent flavor for culinary use. C9, D29, J66, M82

Origanum maru → *Origanum syriacum*

Origanum onites - *Pot marjoram, Cretan oregano, Turkish oregano, Rigani* {PL} The herb has a strong thyme-like aroma and flavor. Fresh or dried, it is used in salads or for flavoring, especially in heavy meats and meat dishes. It can also be brewed into a tea. Eurasia. DE SOUNIN, LATHROP, MORTON 1976; C9, C43M, E5M, F31T, F43, G84, H40, J82, K22, K85, *L22*, L57, M82, N19M, O53M{S}, *Q24*{S}, etc.

Origanum pulchellum - *Showy oregano* {PL} The herb is used for flavoring pizza and other Italian dishes. Mediterranean region. C2, C9, C43M, C43M{S}, D29, E5M, F15M, G55, G96, J37M, K22, K85, M82, N19M, N42, etc.

Origanum syriacum - *Za'tar, Syrian oregano, Bible hyssop* {PL} Leaves and flowering tops are used as a seasoning, having a flavor reminiscent of a blend of thyme, marjoram, and oregano. In the Middle East, the dried herb is mixed with sumac to form the spice blend known as *zatar* which is used, along with olive oil, as a topping for breads. Bedouins grind the dried leaves, add salt, and eat the dry mixture on bread. Eastern Mediterranean region. BAILEY, C., FLEISHER, WOLFERT; A3{PR}, E5M, J66, J82, K22, K85, L50M{PR}

CULTIVARS

Aegypticum: An improved form. M82

Origanum tytthantum - *Kirghiz oregano, Russian oregano* {PL} The herb has an excellent flavor and can be used for culinary purposes. Central Asia. K22, K85, M82

Origanum vulgare - *Wild marjoram, Common oregano* {PL} Fresh leaves and tender shoots are cooked as greens in India. The fresh or dried leaves are used for seasoning soups, stews, casseroles, sauces, olives, stuffings, and egg dishes. Also brewed into an herbal tea. The flowering tops are sometimes put into beer and ale to flavor and preserve it. Eurasia. GRIEVE, HEDRICK 1919, MABEY [Re], MARCIN, MICHAEL, MORTON 1976; C43M, C81M, E61, F21, F24{S}, F31T, F35M, G84, H3M, H51M, *M35*, M53, N19M, N42, N45, etc.

CULTIVARS

Dark: (Dark Oregano) More upright growth than common oregano, to 2 feet tall. Larger, darker leaves. Excellent for seasoning. E5M, K22, K85

Dwarf: (Dwarf Oregano, Compactum Nanum) Grows 2 to 4 inches high, 24 inches across. Produces a dense mat of dark-green foliage that turns purple in winter, and short purplish flower-spikes in summer. A fine ground cover for sunny areas; excellent for rockeries. Strong, spicy flavor. The dried foliage is a flavorful seasoning. Does well on a cool windowsill during the winter. C9, K22, K79, K85, M82, N42

Golden: (Golden Oregano, Golden Creeping Oregano) Compact, creeping habit, to 6 inches high. Attractive golden colored foliage. Good ground cover for rock gardens and edges of flower beds. Mild, thyme-like oregano flavor used in Mediterranean cooking. C9, C43M, C67M, C81M, D92, E5M, F43, H3M, J66, J82, K22, L56, *M35*, M53, M82, N19M, N42, etc.

Jim Perry's: Small-leaved, deep green, sweet oregano with excellent flavor. Selected from numerous seedlings by Jim Perry of Starkville, Mississippi. D92

Seedless: (Seedless Oregano) Leaves resemble sweet marjoram; the flowers resemble a combination of sweet marjoram flowers and oregano flowers. An excellent culinary herb, as strong and distinct as Greek oregano but sweeter and less biting. Hardy to 10° F. Brought to the United States from Goeta, Italy in 1917. Likely a natural hybrid between oregano and marjoram. C43M, I99

Silver: (Silver Oregano) Ornamental silver leaves. Mild oregano flavor. Can be used in cooking. Tender perennial; height 12 inches. Does best when grown in full sun. F93G

Variegated: (Variegated Oregano) Attractively speckled and streaked with golden variegation that contrasts prominently against the deep green background. Mildly flavored. Prostrate habit, height 8 inches. Excellent for edging or in the rock garden. C9, N42

White: (White Oregano, Viride) Culinary type with excellent flavor. Height 1 to 2 feet. A1M, C11{S}

White Anniversary: Bright green leaves, broadly margined in white. Spring growth in a white ground hugging mat, changing to a pale cream by fall. Height 8 inches. Flowers inconspicuous. I39

Origanum vulgare ssp. gracile → *Origanum tytthantum*

Origanum vulgare ssp. hirtum - *Winter marjoram, Winter sweet marjoram* {PL} The herb is used for flavoring salads, soups, broths and stuffings. Fresh or dried leaves are steeped for tea. Mediterranean region. HEDRICK 1919, UPHOF; N42, N84{S}

CULTIVARS

Greek: (Greek Oregano) Bright green leaves; white flowers. Grows 1 1/2 to 2 feet tall. Strong, aromatic, spicy flavor. Excellent culinary oregano, a standard in pasta and tomato sauces. If you go to the store and buy a jar of "oregano", this is probably the kind you'll be receiving. C9, C11{S}, C13M{S}, C67M, E5M{PR}, G84, H40, H51M, J85T{PR}, K22, K66{S}, *M35*, M53, N19M, N42, etc.

Italian: (Italian Oregano) Somewhat narrow leaves. Aromatic, strong, resinous flavor. Used in spaghetti sauce and pizza. More bushy and upright than Greek oregano; height 12 inches. C67M, C81M, E5M, E5M{PR}, F35M, F43, F52, F93G, H40, *M35*, N45

Sicilian: (Sicilian Oregano) White flowering oregano with a heady, sweet pungent aroma. Height 18 inches. Excellent for culinary purposes. Edible flowers. I39

Perilla crispa → *Perilla frutescens*

Perilla frutescens - *Shiso, Beefsteak plant, Tia to* {PL} Leaves are salted and used as a condiment for tofu and as a garnish for tempura. The young seedlings are eaten raw with *sashimi* (raw fish). Immature flower-clusters serve as a garnish for soups and chilled tofu, while older ones are fried. The seeds are preserved in salt or used as a spice in pickles, tempura, and miso. Source of an essential oil used to flavor candy and sauces. The seed oil is occasionally used for culinary purposes. Eastern Asia, cultivated. HAWKES [Re], MORTON 1976, SHURTLEFF 1975, SHURTLEFF 1976 [Re], TANAKA, YASHIRODA; C67M, C81M, D29, E66T{PR}, F24{S}, F85{S}, G20M{PR}, G84, *K74*{PR}, K85, L57

CULTIVARS {S}

Aromatic Flatleaf: Large, fragrant leaves. Makes a fine tea herb. I99

Curled: (Curly) Darker purple leaves than Aka Shiso, with ruffled edges. Slightly smaller than other cultivars but preferred by some for its superior flavor. Mild peppermint-like aroma. C13M, I99

Green: (Ao Shiso) Bright green leaves with a cinnamon-like scent and a taste reminiscent of ginger. The leaves are milder in flavor than Aka Shiso and are preferred for fresh use in salads and as a garnish. SHURTLEFF 1975, YASHIRODA; A2, A49G, A79M, D55, E59, F37T{PL}, F80, G33, H49, I39, K49M, L59, M46, N84, S55, etc.

Green Cumin: A rare and unique type whose leaves have the aroma of cumin. Excellent for culinary use, both fresh and dried. I99

Lemon: Similar to Curled perilla, but with green leaves and a more lemon-like taste. C13M

Red: (Aka Shiso, Purple, Crispy) Reddish-purple leaves with a strong aroma and flavor. Used for giving a purplish-red color and unique flavor to pickled *ume* plums, ginger root, and the tubers of Chinese artichoke. Also pickled in salt and used as a wrapping for *mochi* in confections. SHURTLEFF 1975, TANAKA, YASHIRODA; A79M, C13M, C43M{PL}, D55, E59, F33, F37T{PL}, G6, G33, H49, I99, J20, L7M, L59, M46, etc.

Perilla nankinensis → *Perilla frutescens*

Perovskia atriplicifolia - *Russian sage* {PL} The small, lavender flowers are sweet and can be eaten in salads or used as a garnish. Himalayan region. TANAKA; B92, C9, E30, F31T, F57M, G96, H63, I37M, J37M, *L22*, *L95*, M77, N19M

Phlomis lychnitis - *Lamwick plant* {S} The herb is sometimes used to adulterate sage, Salvia officinalis. Southwestern Europe. UPHOF; N84, S7M

Phlomis tuberosa - *Bodmon sok* {S} Roots are eaten cooked by the Kalmucks. Eurasia. HEDRICK 1919; E7M, N84

Plectranthus amboinicus - *Cuban oregano, Country borage, Spanish thyme, Five seasons herb* {PL} The fresh leaves have an oregano-like aroma and are cooked with fish or goat's flesh in order to disguise their strong smell. They are also used as a potherb, added to chili paste, or mixed with minced young fruits to form a side-dish for rice. In India, they are added to wine and beer. Also steeped for tea. Tropics, cultivated. HERKLOTS, MORTON 1976, OCHSE, PAINTER; C43M, D29, E5M, G96, H3M, H51M, J82, L56, M82, N42

CULTIVARS

Variegated: Thick, succulent, very pungent leaves; 2 to 4 inches long. Medium green in color, variegated with white around the edges. Leaves are chopped for use in Puerto Rican and Spanish dishes. C43M, G96, M82

Plectranthus madagascariensis - {S} The nutritious tubers are eaten. Madagascar. TANAKA; E48, N84, R41

Plectranthus tuberosus → *Coleus parviflorus*

Pogostemon cablin - *Patchouli, Patchouly* {PL} Fresh leaves are sometimes used as a seasoning. The dried, cured leaves yield an essential oil that flavors chewing gum, baked goods, and candy. Tropical Asia. MORTON 1976, TANAKA; C43M, D29, E5M, E48, F35M, F37T, F93G, G84, H51M, K22, K85, L56, M53, M82, N42, etc.

Pogostemon heyneanus - *Java patchouli, Smooth patchouli* {PL} The dried herb is used in the preparation of a country spirit. Southern Asia. TANAKA; D29, G96, I59G, K22, K85, M82, N19M

Poliomintha incana - *Rosemary mint* {PR} Fresh leaves and flowers are eaten off the stem with beans, added to scrambled eggs, boiled, or dipped in salt. The dried herb is used as a flavoring agent. A favorite of the Hopis. Southwestern North America. KIRK, YANOVSKY; N29

Poliomintha longiflora - *Mexican oregano* {PL} The aromatic leaves have a strong oregano-like flavor reminiscent of Lippia graveolens. Used as a condiment by the Kickapoo Indians and also a popular oregano in Southwestern cuisine. Mexico. HUTSON [Cul], LATORRE 1977b; F93G, G96, K22, M82

Prunella vulgaris - *Self-heal, All-heal* {PL} A refreshing beverage can be made by soaking the leaves, either freshly chopped or dried and powdered, in cold water. Young shoots and leaves are eaten raw in salads, cooked with other greens as a potherb, or added to soups and stews. Eurasia, naturalized in North America. KIRK, LAUNERT, YANOVSKY; A2{S}, C11{S}, C13M{S}, C43M, C81M, D62{S}, E81M{S}, F37T, F80{S}, I19, K22, K47T{S}, K85, N9M, N45, *N71M*{S}, etc.

Pycnanthemum incanum - *Hoary mountain-mint* {PL} Fresh or dried leaves are brewed into an aromatic, mint-like tea. North America. GIBBONS 1979, PETERSON, L.; F57M, I11M, I11M{S}, K22, M77M

Pycnanthemum muticum - *Short-toothed mountain mint* {PL} The leaves have a pleasant mint-like aroma and flavor and can be used for preparing a refreshing tea. North America. GIBBONS 1979, PETERSON, L.; H51M, K22, M82, N19M

Pycnanthemum pilosum - *Hairy mountain-mint* {PL} Fresh or dried leaves are used for tea, having a delicious mint-like flavor. North America. PETERSON, L.; D62{S}, E61, G84, H46{S}, J66, J82, J82{S}, K22, M82, N42, N45, N84{S}, S55{S}

Pycnanthemum virginianum - *Virginia mountain-mint* {PL} Chippewa Indians used the flowers and buds for seasoning meat and broth. The fresh or dried leaves are steeped into a refreshing mint-like tea. Eastern North America. YANOVSKY; C13M{S}, C81M, E61, F15M, G47M{S}, G89, G89{S}, J41M, J41M{S}, J42, J42{S}, J43{S}, K22, K47T{S}, K85, L56, etc.

Rosmarinus officinalis - *Rosemary* {PL} Young shoots and leaves are used as a seasoning for stuffings, soups, sausages, vermouth, sauces, fish, lamb, etc. The flowers have a somewhat milder flavor and are also utilized as a flavoring. They can be candied, preserved, or added to jellies, honey, vinegar, and wine. Fresh or dried leaves and flowers make a good tea, especially when combined with tansy. Mediterranean region. BRYAN [Cu, Re], DE SOUNIN, GRIEVE [Cu], LEGGATT [Re], MACNICOL [Re], MARCIN, MICHAEL [Re], MORTON 1976; C13M{S}, C67M, C91T, D29, F21, F31T, G84, G96, H40, H46{S}, J66, *M35*, N42, N45

CULTIVARS

Arp: Thick, dull gray-green leaves, spread apart on the stems. Semi-upright growth; height 5 feet. Light-blue flowers; dull fragrance. Hardy to -10^0 F., making it the hardiest cultivar known at the present. Selected in 1972 from a plant growing in Arp, Texas, by Mrs. Madalene Hill. C9, C43M, C81M, C91T, E5M, E59T, F37T, G96, H51M, J66, K22, M53, M82, N19M, N42, etc.

Blue Spire: (Blue Spears) The new branches are spear-like and upright, arching and twisting downward with age. An interesting beginning for bonsai and topiary. It has a fine flavor, also. Origin unknown. C81M, F52, H40, K22, K85, L56, M82

Gorizia: Long broad leaves, double the size of common plants, extend from thick, rigidly upright stems. The new growth is creamy; the more mature part of the stem is a reddish brown. Medium-blue flowers in spring and sometimes in late summer. The aroma of the leaves is mild with just a hint of ginger. From Gorizia, a city on the Italian-Yugoslav border. C43M, C91T, M53, M82

Joyce De Baggio: (Golden Rain) Medium-sized, pointed leaves, variegated with gold edge and green center. Compact, bushy habit; self-branching. Strong, sharp fragrance and flavor similar to the species, which is considered best for culinary use. Dark-blue flowers, very sparse. Attractive landscape specimen, appearing bright gold from a distance. C43M, C81M, C91T, G96, M82, N42

Trailing: (Creeping, Prostratus) Medium-green, short, narrow leaves; white, arching stems. Height 3 feet; grows rapidly, self-layers. Mild flavor. Excellent ground cover or hanging potted plant. C9, C43M, C67M, C81M, E5M, E61, F21, F31T, F35M, G96, H40, H51M, J66, K22, K85, M82, etc.

Tuscan Blue: Tall, vigorous, upright growth, moderate branching even with pinching; height 6 feet. Short, wide, light medium-green leaves, thickly clustered on the stems. The large leaves are ideal for drying in quantity. A1M, C9, C43M, C81M, D29, E5M, E59T, E61, F35M, J66, K22, K85, L29, L56, M82, etc.

Salvia apiana - *White sage* {S} Seeds are sold as a natural food to be soaked in water overnight and drunk in water, fruit juice or eaten with cereal. Leaves can be used in cooking. Western North America. WHISTLER; G59M, G60{PL}, G84{PL}, I98M, I99, *J0*, K15, L67{PR}, L86, M15T{PL}, N84

Salvia ballotaeflora - *Majorano mexicano* {S} An infusion of the flowering tops is used as an aromatic tea. Southwestern North America. VON REIS, YANOVSKY; B83M

Salvia calycina* → *Salvia pomifera

Salvia carduacea - *Thistle sage* {S} Roasted seeds are ground into flour. Also made into a cooling beverage by the Indians of California. Southwestern North America. UPHOF; I98M, N84

Salvia chinensis* → *Salvia japonica

Salvia clevelandii - *Cleveland's sage, Blue sage* {PL} The leaves have a pleasant fragrance and flavor and are a good substitute for common sage in cooking. Western North America. LATHROP; C9, C9M{S}, C43M, C81M, D29, E5M, G59M{S}, G60, G84, G96, H51M, K22, K85, N19M, O53M{S}, etc.

CULTIVARS

Aromas: An improved selection that is very fragrant. B92

Salvia columbariae - *Golden chia* {S} Seeds were parched, ground into *pinole*, and made into dark-colored cakes and loaves. The Indians also mixed it with corn meal when making mush or with ground wheat for gruel. A refreshing beverage is made by soaking the seeds in water and adding sugar and lemon, lime, or orange juice. The leaves are occasionally used as a sage-like seasoning. Sprouted seeds are eaten in salads and sandwiches. Western North America. ANGIER, CLARKE [Re], KIRK, MEDSGER, YANOVSKY; A2, A49G, F85, G59M, I16, I98M, *J0*, J25M, K47T, L13, L86, L91M, N29{PR}, N84

Salvia elegans* → *Salvia rutilans

Salvia fruticosa - *Greek sage* {PL} Leaves are used as a spice or as an adulterant of common sage, S. officinalis. Although somewhat inferior in quality, it is easier to grow indoors. Eastern Mediterranean region. KUNKEL; C82, F43, J82, K22, K85, N42

Salvia glutinosa - *Hardy sage, Yellow sage, Jupiter's distaff* {S} In Holland, the aromatic leaves are used to give flavor to country wines. Eastern Mediterranean region. GRIEVE; C13M, D11T{PL}, D62, E61{PL}, F80, L56{PL}, N51{PL}, N84, O53M, *Q24*, Q40, S7M

Salvia grandiflora - *Balsamic sage* {S} In England, the tea made from this sage was once preferred to that of all others. Also used as a condiment. Eastern Mediterranean region to Southwest Asia. GRIEVE, TANAKA; N84

Salvia hispanica - *Mexican chia* {S} When soaked in water, the seeds form a gelatinous mass which is flavored with fruit juices and consumed as a cooling drink. The gelled seeds can also be prepared as a gruel or pudding. Sprouted seeds are eaten in salads, sandwiches, soups, stews, etc. Due to their mucilaginous properties, they are sprouted on clay or other porous materials, and clay animals or *chia pets* are sold commercially for this purpose. The seeds are ground into meal and made into breads, biscuits, muffins, and cakes. Central America, cultivated. ALTSCHUL; C43M, C43M{PL}, D62, E5T, F71M, J25M, K20, N84, P92{PL}, R47 (also see Sprouting Seeds, page 485)

Salvia horminum* → *Salvia viridis

Salvia indica - {S} Cultivated in India for its leaves, which are added to country beer to which they impart a fresh, pleasant aroma and taste. Tropical Asia. HEDRICK 1919; Z25M

Salvia japonica - *Aki-no-tamura-sô* {S} Children suck the flower. Eastern Asia. TANAKA; C13M, E61{PL}, F85

Salvia lanigera - *Nu'aymih* {S} The plant serves as a condiment for tea. Mediterranean region. BAILEY, C.; U71M

Salvia lavandulifolia - *Spanish sage, Lavender sage* {PL} Source of an essential oil used commercially to flavor ice cream, candy, baked goods, chewing gum, soft drinks, and alcoholic beverages. Also used as an adulterant of common sage. Southwestern Europe. MORTON 1976; B28, E5M, K85, M82, N84{S}

Salvia mellifera - *Black sage* {S} The aromatic leaves can be brewed into a tea. Early settlers in California used them to season sausage, poultry, and meat stuffings. Western North America. CLARKE; C43M{PL}, D62, E61{PL}, G60{PL}, I98M, *J0*, K15, M82{PL}, N84

Salvia moorcroftiana - *Moorcroft's salvia* {S} The peeled stalks are occasionally eaten. Himalayan region. WATT; C43M, C43M{PL}, F80, G84{PL}, N51{PL}, N84, O46, O53M, Q40

Salvia multicaulis - *Bardagawsh* {S} Bedouins of the Sinai and Negev use the plants as a condiment for tea or prepared as a beverage with boiled water and sugar. Eastern Mediterranean region to Southwest Asia. BAILEY, C.; **Z25M**

Salvia officinalis - *Common sage, Broadleaf sage* {PL} The herb is widely utilized as a seasoning for meats, fowl, stuffings, cheese, soups, stews, sausages, sauces, sage-milk, etc. Young leaves and flowers are eaten raw, boiled, pickled, or in bread and butter sandwiches. Fresh or dried leaves are steeped into an aromatic tea. The flowers can be sprinkled on salads to add color and fragrance. Sage extract and oil are used commercially to flavor ice cream, candy, baked goods, etc. Mediterranean region, cultivated. BRYAN [Cul, Re], GRIEVE, HEDRICK 1919, LARKCOM 1984, LEGGATT [Re], MACNICOL [Re], MARCIN, MICHAEL [Re], MORTON 1976, TANAKA, UPHOF; C13M{S}, C67M, F21, F31T, G84, H40, H46{S}, J66, K22, K66{S}, *M35*, M53, N19M, N84{S}

CULTIVARS

Berggarten: The largest-leaved culinary sage. Grows to 18 inches tall. Originally from the Royal Gardens in Hanover, Germany. K22

Dwarf: (Dwarf Sage, Nana) Small leaves. Compact, low-growing habit; height 12 inches, spreads to 2 feet across. Bright-blue flowers. Makes a good border, rock garden, or container plant. C9, C43M, C67M, C81M, D29, E5M, G96, H51M, I39, K22, K85, *M35*, M82, N42

Golden: (Golden Sage, Aurea) Leaves brilliantly colored chartreuse-yellow with a few dark-green areas around the veins. Compact, dense growth habit, height 18 inches. Attractive border plant. Hardy to 10^0 F. Also a good culinary herb. C67M, E5M, E61, F35M, G84, G96, H51M, I39, J66, J82, K22, K85, *M35*, M53, N42, etc.

Holt's Mammoth: (Mammoth Sage, Giant) Very large, rounded leaves borne well above the soil, keeping them clean. Strong flavor; quality very good. Vigorous growth, to 3 feet tall and 3 feet in diameter. Heavy producer. Excellent for culinary use and good for drying in quantity. Rarely flowers and never runs to seed. Introduced prior to 1888. BURPEE; C43M, D29, F35M, G15, I39, J66, K22, K85, M82

Purple: (Purple Sage, Purpurea) Aromatic, deep red-purple, strap-like foliage; retains its color throughout the growing season. Compact, bushy growth habit, height 18 inches. Ornamental but also has a good flavor and can be used like common sage in cooking. C9, C43M, C67M, D29, E5M, E61, F31T, G84, H40, H51M, J66, J82, K22, K85, *M35*, N19M, etc.

Town of Bath: Similar to garden sage and with the same uses; however, has the added attraction of lovely pale pink flowers. Adapted to full sun or partial shade. Hardy in Zones 4 to 9. N42

Tricolor: (Tricolor Sage, Variegated Sage) Leaves are brightly variegated in cream, purple-red, and pink. Grows to 2 feet tall. Hardy to 10^0 F. Very ornamental but also has the flavor of common sage and can used as a culinary seasoning. C9, C67M, D29, E61, F31T, G84, G96, H51M, J66, J82, K22, K85, *M35*, M53, N19M, etc.

Salvia polystachya* → *Salvia apiana

Salvia pomifera - *Apple sage* {PL} *Sage apples*, semi-transparent galls caused by the sting of an insect are collected from the branches and made into a kind of sweetmeat or conserve, which is regarded by the Greeks as a great delicacy. The leaves have a strong odor and flavor resembling lavender and common sage and are used as an adulterant of the latter. An infusion of the herb is used as a tea in some parts of Greece. Eastern Mediterranean region. GRIEVE, MORTON 1976, UPHOF; M82

Salvia pratensis - *Meadow sage, Meadow clary* {S} The pungent, bitter-flavored herb was formerly used for flavoring beer and wine. It also serves as an adulterant of the common sage. Europe. KUNKEL, MORTON 1976; C11, C13M, D11T{PL}, D95{PL}, E61{PL}, H46, I99, L66{PL}, L91M, M15T{PL}, M82{PL}, *N71M*, N84, O53M, Q40, S7M, etc.

Salvia reflexa - *White chia, Lanceleaf sage* {S} Seeds are used in the preparation of a cooling drink. North America, Mexico. ALTSCHUL; N84

Salvia rutilans - *Pineapple sage* {PL} The herb has a distinct pineapple-like fragrance and flavor and is added to fruit salads, desserts, and cold drinks. Fresh or dried leaves can be used as a mild-flavored substitute for common sage in cooking. An infusion of the leaves is used as a substitute for tea. Cultivated. GESSERT, LATHROP, MORTON 1976; C3, C9, C67M, F21, F31T, F43, G84, G96, H40, I77M, J66, K22, *M35*, N19M, N42, N45, etc.

CULTIVARS

Dwarf: (Gracilis) Small, compact form of pineapple sage. Good for flower borders and also makes a very good potted plant. Bright-red flowers. Tender to hard frosts. M33G

Honeydew: (Honeydew Melon Sage) Oval leaves with a strong aroma of honeydew melons. Intense deep-red flowers. Similar to pineapple sage in growth habit and usage. Height 30 inches. C43M, F37T, K22, K85, M15T, N42

Pink: (Rosea) Similar to pineapple sage but with pink flowers instead of red. L29

Salvia sclarea - *Clary sage, Garden clary* {PL} Young, tender leaves are dipped in cream, fried and eaten with sugar-and-orange sauce, or dipped in egg batter and fried as fritters. Finely chopped leaves are cooked in soups and omelettes. They are added to *Rhine* wine to impart a muscatel taste, and also flavor *vermouth*, beer, ale and liqueurs. The ornamental flowers have a pleasant taste and can be sprinkled on a tossed salad. Eurasia. GRIEVE [Cu], HEDRICK 1919, LARKCOM 1984, LATHROP, MACNICOL [Re], MORTON 1976, PAINTER [Re], UPHOF; C9, C11{S}, C13M{S}, C67M, D29, F21, F24{S}, G84, G96, H51M, K22, N19M, N42, N45, N84{S}, O53M{S}, etc.

CULTIVARS {S}

Turkestanica: (Turkish Clary, Vatican Clary) Similar to clary sage in appearance and usage except for the pinkish stems, larger white flowers that are tinged with pink, and the light bracts, often almost white. Blooms over an extended period during the summer. C43M, C43M{PL}, J24{PL}, O53M, Q34

Salvia tiliaefolia - *Lindenleaf sage, Tarahumara chia* {S} Seeds are sold in the markets of Mexico for making a drink, which is sometimes mixed with barley water. They are roasted, ground and added to water, forming a gel. Central America. UPHOF; C43M{PL}, I16, I99, K49T, N84

Salvia triloba - *Greek sage* {PL} The strongly aromatic leaves are used for tea. Dried leaves are mixed with those of the common sage as an adulterant. Mediterranean region. KUNKEL, MORTON 1976; E5M, F37T, M82, P92

Salvia verbenaca - *Vervain sage, Wild English clary* {PL} Young leaves are eaten fried, candied, or cooked in omelettes. The flowers are used for flavoring salads. Macaronesia to Southwest Asia. KUNKEL; D62{S}, E61, K22, K85, N84{S}

Salvia viridis - *Joseph sage, Bluebeard sage, Annual clary, English clary, Painted sage* {PL} In England, the leaves were once added to salads, soups, and cooked greens. The seeds are eaten fried with honey and are also used as a condiment. Source of an essential oil used for flavoring certain wines and beers. Mediterranean region to Southwest Asia. GESSERT, GRIEVE, HEDRICK 1919, MORTON 1976, UPHOF; A49D, C13M, C43M, C53{S}, D29, E5T{S}, E81M{S}, F35M, G84, H3M, I39{S}, J82{S}, M15T, M82, P83M{S}, S55{S}, etc.

Satureja calamintha* → *Calamintha sylvatica

Satureja douglasii - *Yerba buena, Oregon tea* {PL} The dried leaves steeped in water make a palatable tea. American Indians rolled the leafy stems into a ball and dried them for later use. Western North America. KIRK, MEDSGER, MORTON 1976; C43M, D95, E5M, E61, F35M, G60, G84, G96, H40, H51M, L86, M15T, M53, M82

Satureja hortensis - *Summer savory* {S} Fresh leaves and shoots are used as a garnish in salads, and are rubbed on meat before cooking. Dried leaves and flowering tops are widely used for flavoring bean dishes, soups, stews, stuffings, cakes, puddings, and sausages. The leaves can be harvested before the plant blooms and brewed into a tea with a tangy, marjoram-like flavor. Eurasia, cultivated. GRIEVE [Cu], HEDRICK 1919, MARCIN, MORTON 1976, ROOT 1980b [Cul]; C3, C81M, C81M{PL}, D29, F21{PL}, F35M{PL}, G84{PL}, G93M, H46, I91, J20, J66{PL}, K22, K66, N19M{PL}, etc.

Satureja montana - *Winter savory* {PL} Leaves and flowering tops are used for seasoning soups, salads, sauces, fish, stuffings, egg dishes, poultry, meats, vegetables, etc. Has a stronger, sharper flavor than summer savory. Fresh or dried leaves are steeped for tea. Mediterranean region. GRIEVE, LATHROP, MARCIN, MICHAEL [Re], MORTON 1976, ROOT 1980b [Cul]; C3, C13M{S}, C67M, F21, F31T, G84, H46{S}, I77M, J66, K22, *M35*, N19M, N45

CULTIVARS

Creeping: (Dwarf, Trailing, Nana, Repanda) Prostrate form making a mound of twisted branches; minute bright-green leaves; white flowers. Height 3 to 4 inches. Attractive in rock gardens and hanging baskets. Strong flavor similar to winter savory. Same usage as other savories. A49D, C9, C81M, E5M, E61, H40, I39, J66, J78, J82, K22, K85, L56, L57, M82, N19M, etc.

Purple: (Purpurea) An attractive, compact form of savory; height 9 inches. Small, green leaves with a similar but sweeter flavor and aroma than the common winter savory. Showy heads of bright purple flowers in late summer. P92

Satureja thymbra - *Thryba, Barrel sweetener, Za'atar rumi, Roman hyssop* {PL} The leaves are used as a seasoning for brine-cured olives, grilled meat, meat ragouts, and vegetables. A strong infusion of the herb is used in the fall to clean wine-barrels in preparation for the new vintage. In Crete, thryba is principally used as tea for pleasure and refreshment. It is said to be one of the best-tasting of all the herbal teas. Eastern Mediterranean region. GRIEVE, WHALLON; E5M, K22, K85, M82

Satureja viminea - *Costa Rican mint bush, Jamaican mint bush, Shrubby savory* {PL} The small, bright-green leaves have a strong pennyroyal-like fragrance and flavor and can be used for tea or seasoning. Shrub-like perennial. West Indies. BURR, HEDRICK 1919; C43M, E61, F35M, G96, J82, K22, K85

Satureja vulgaris* → *Clinopodium vulgare

Scutellaria baicalensis - *Soksokeun-phul* {S} Young leaves are eaten as a boiled vegetable, while the whole plant is dried and used as a substitute for tea. Central Asia. TANAKA; N84, O35G{PL}, *Q24*, R87{PL}

Sideritis theezans - *Mountain tea, Tsai, Tsailopita* {PR} Leaves and flowering tops are used as an aromatic tea. Sold in local markets and at ethnic stores in New York and other large cities. Greece. UPHOF; A7M

Solenostemon rotundifolius - *Hausa potato, Fra-fra potato* {PL} The tubers are eaten like potatoes, either cooked or raw. Leaves are also edible. Tropical Africa, cultivated. DALZIEL, FOX, F., HERKLOTS, MARTIN 1975; **W90**, **X44**{S}

Stachys affinis* → *Stachys sieboldii

Stachys officinalis - *Betony, Bishop's wort* {PL} An infusion of the leaves and flowering tops makes a refreshing, aromatic beverage. Europe. MACNICOL, MARCIN, MICHAEL [Re], MORTON 1976, PAINTER; C13M{S}, C43M, C67M, C81M, D29, F24{S}, G84, H51M, I99{S}, J82, K85, M82, *N71M*{S}, N84{S}

Stachys palustris - *Marsh woundwort* {S} The crisp, white tubers are eaten raw, roasted, boiled, or dried and made into bread. Young shoots are cooked and eaten like asparagus. Northern temperate region. FERNALD, GRIEVE, HEDRICK 1919, KIRK; J41M, J41M{PL}, *N71M*, N84, O48

Stachys sieboldii - *Chinese artichoke, Crosnes, Chorogi* {PL} The crisp, white tubers have a nutty, artichoke-like flavor and are eaten raw, fried, roasted, steamed, boiled, or pickled. In Japan, they are pickled like *ume* plums in a mixture of salt and red beefsteak leaves (Perilla). Tubers quickly discolor when exposed to the air, and are said to lose their flavor when peeled. Eastern Asia, cultivated. HAWKES [Re], HEDRICK 1919, HERKLOTS [Cu], LARKCOM 1984 [Re], ORGAN [Cul], TANAKA, UPHOF, YASHIRODA; C43M, C82, E83T, E97, I99, K49M, L91M, R53M

Teucrium massiliense - *Cha tô dât* {S} Used as a substitute for tea. Indochina. TANAKA; D62

Teucrium polium - *Ja'adah* {S} The plant is mixed with boiled water and sugar to form a refreshing beverage. Also used as a spice. Mediterranean region, Southwest Asia. BAILEY, C., KUNKEL; D11T{PL}, D62, I63M{PL}, N84, *Q24*, S7M

Teucrium scorodonia - *Wood germander, Sage-leaved germander* {PL} A strong of infusion of the bitter leaves and flowers, called *ambroise*, is used in France and the Channel Islands as a substitute for hops in flavoring ale. Europe. GRIEVE, HEDRICK 1919, MORTON 1976; C11{S}, C43M, D11T, D29, D95, E61, F35M, F80{S}, H51M, M82, N42, *N71M*{S}, O53M{S}, *Q24*{S}, R53M{S}, S55{S}, etc.

Thymbra spicata - *Za'atar hommar, Donkey hyssop* {PL} Occasionally used as a condiment. The flavor of its essential oils is similar to those of Origanum syriacum, Thymus capitatus, and Satureja thymbra. Eastern Mediterranean region. FLEISHER; G96, M82{CF}

Thymus azoricus* → *Thymus caespititius

Thymus broussonetii - *Pine-scented thyme* {PL} Used as a spice. North Africa. KUNKEL; G96, K85, M82

Thymus caespititius - *Azores thyme, Cretan thyme* {PL} The fresh leaves have a tangerine-like scent and are used for flavoring custards.

They are also used as a substitute for lemon thyme, or in combination with it. Macaronesia, Mediterranean region. MORTON 1976; C43M, E5M, G96, J24, K22, K63, K79, K85, M82, N19M, N42, N84{S}, R53M

CULTIVARS

Celery: (Celery Thyme) Low, compact grower that forms small mounds of growth. Narrow, very small, light green leaves that have a celery-like aroma. Light pink flowers. Half hardy. A49D, F15M

Thymus capitatus - *Conehead thyme, Za'atar farsi, Persian hyssop* {PL} Sometimes used as a condiment. Also the source of an essential oil, called *Spanish origanum oil*, employed in the food industry for flavoring baked goods, condiments, meats, beverages, ice cream, and candy. Mediterranean region. FLEISHER, MORTON 1976, UPHOF; C43M, K22, K85, M82, N19M

Thymus x citriodorus (T. pulegioides x T. vulgaris) - *Lemon thyme* The strongly lemon-scented leaves are used as a seasoning for salads, soups, sauces, fish, poultry, cheese, desserts, beverages, etc. An infusion of the leaves makes a very refreshing tea. GESSERT, MORTON 1976, VILMORIN; (for cultivars see Thyme, page 512)

Thymus herba-barona - *Caraway thyme* {PL} The herb has a fragrance reminiscent of caraway seeds and is an excellent seasoning for soups, vegetables, poultry, etc. It was once used to rub the baron of beef, before it was roasted, and came to be called *herbe baronne*. Mediterranean region. GESSERT, GRIEVE, LATHROP; C3, C81M, D29, E5M, E61, F21, F31T, G96, H40, H51M, J66, J82, K22, *M35*, M53, N19M, etc.

CULTIVARS

Nutmeg: (Nutmeg Thyme) Very low, creeping growth habit; height 4 inches. A rapid grower. Blooms a week later than caraway thyme with deeper pink flowers in late summer. Pronounced fragrance somewhat reminiscent of nutmeg. Same culinary use as caraway time. Excellent for paths between stepping stones. A49D, C43M, C67M, C81M, E5M, F37T, G84, H3M, J66, J82, K22, K85, L56, M82, N42, etc.

Thymus mastichina - *Mastic thyme, Spanish marjoram* {PL} Leaves are used for seasoning. Also the source of a distilled oil, called *oil of wild marjoram*, used extensively for flavoring meat sauces and soups. Mediterranean region. GRIEVE, MORTON 1976, UPHOF; C43M, D62{S}, E61, K47T{S}, M82, N84{S}

Thymus pannonicus - *Marschall thyme* {PL} Sometimes used as a condiment. Europe. A1M, A49D, C43M, F31T, K22, K85, M82, N84{S}

Thymus praecox ssp. arcticus - *Mother-of-thyme, Wild thyme, Creeping thyme, Serpolet* {PL} The herb is employed as a seasoning for salads, sauces, stews, seafood dishes, vinegar, stuffings, pickles, etc. In Iceland, it is used to give an agreeable flavor to sour milk. In Switzerland, it is rubbed over goat's milk cream cheese, called *banon*, to which it imparts flavor. Dried flowers are steeped for tea. Also the source of an essential oil that flavors *Benedictine*. Eurasia. FOX, H., GIBBONS 1979, HEDRICK 1919, MORTON 1976; B97M, C3, C13M{S}, C43M, C67M, E59T, F37T, G84, H46{S}, K22, M53, N19M, N84{S}, O53M{S}

CULTIVARS

Britannicus: Forms a fuzzy, grey-green mat; height 8 inches. Has an appealing scent of lemon and thyme. Very hardy. Good for teas and culinary use. Also good as a ground cover and for grey gardens. A49D, E5M, E61, F43, K22, K85, M82

Red-Flowered: (Creeping Red, Coccineus) Forms dark-green mats of foliage; height 1 to 2 inches. Flowers profusely in early summer, with star-like scarlet flowers. Blooms later than mother-of-thyme. Withstands heat well. A49D, D29, E5M, F31T, I39, J66, K22, K85, M82, N19M

Thymus pulegioides - *Wild thyme, Creeping thyme* {PL} The leaves of some cultivars can be used for flavoring. Europe. C43M, K47T{S}, M82, N84{S} (for cultivars see Thyme, page 512)

Thymus quinquecostatum - *Ibuki-jakô-sô* {PL} Source of an essential oil used for flavoring. Central to Eastern Asia. TANAKA; C43M

Thymus serpyllum* → *Thymus praecox ssp. arcticus

Thymus vulgaris - *Thyme* Leaves and flowering tops, both fresh and dried, are widely used for flavoring stuffings, soups, cheese, vinegar, gravies, sausages, etc. In Spain, they are added to the brine in which olives are pickled. The fresh or dried leaves can be brewed into a pungent, spicy tea. Young shoots are used as a garnish. Mediterranean region, cultivated. BRYAN [Cul, Re], GRIEVE [Cu], LEGGATT [Re], MACNICOL [Re], MARCIN, MORTON 1976, ROOT 1980b [Cul]; (for cultivars see Thyme, page 512)

Thymus zygis - *Sauce thyme* {PL} Leaves are used as a condiment. Southwestern Europe. BROUK, GRIEVE; F31T, K47T{S}

LARDIZABALACEAE

Akebia quinata - *Akebi* {PL} The somewhat sweet fruits are eaten raw with lemon juice or puréed and made into a cream or a drink. Soft young shoots are used in salads or for salt pickling. The bitter skin of the fruit is fried and eaten. Leaves are used as a tea substitute. Japan, cultivated. FERNALD, HEDRICK 1919, JOHNS, KAJIURA, SIMMONS 1972 [Cu], TANAKA; C9, C36, D62{S}, E63, E87, F80{S}, H4, J61M, M16, M77, *N71M*{S}, N93M{S}, O53M{S}, *P39*{S}, R78{S}, etc.

Akebia trifoliata - *Mitsuba-akebi* {S} Pulp of the fruit is white, fleshy, somewhat sweet, and is eaten out of hand or made into refreshments. Valued for the novel sausage-like shape and deep purple color. The dried, young leaves are used for tea. Japan. KAJIURA, SIMMONS 1972 [Cu], TANAKA, UPHOF; B96{PL}, F85, K47T, N84, O93, *P39*, P49, *R28*, R78

Decaisnea fargesii* → *Holboellia fargesii

Holboellia coriacea - *Sausage vine* {PL} The fruit is purple, about 2 inches long and 1 inch wide. The pulp is white with jet black seeds. It is edible but the taste is generally considered to be insipid. China. SIMMONS 1972, TANAKA; D95, E87, P86

Holboellia fargesii - *Wu-yüeh-kua-t'êng* {S} The fruits are edible. They are of interest for their startling metallic-blue color. China. TANAKA; D95{PL}, E87{PL}, K63G, L91M, *N71M*, *N73*{PL}, N84, O53M, P49

Holboellia latifolia - *Dombyem* {S} Fruits are purple, sausage-shaped, with many black seeds contained in the white pulp. The taste is rather insipid, however in the Himalayas it is considered very palatable. Usually eaten out of hand but with experimentation other suitable ways of using it may be found. Himalayan region. HEDRICK 1919, SIMMONS 1972 [Cu]; F85, N84, Q40

Lardizabala biternata - *Aquiboquil, Zabala fruit* {S} The fruits are somewhat sweet and are much appreciated in Chile where they are collected and sold in the local markets. Considered a novelty because of the sausage-like, deep purple fruits. Chile. Peru. HEDRICK 1919, SIMMONS 1972 [Cu]; **Z25M**

Stauntonia hexaphylla - *Japanese stauntonia, Mube* {PL} The purple, walnut-shaped fruits have white pulp with a sweet, honey-like flavor. They are eaten out of hand or made into refreshments. Highly esteemed in Japan. China to Japan. KAJIURA, SIMMONS 1972 [Cu], UPHOF; N37M, *P63*{S}, P86

LAURACEAE

Beilschmiedia anay - *Anay* {S} Small, pear-shaped fruits that are eaten out of hand. They have yellow flesh that is high in oil and has a rich flavor. Central America, Northern South America. DUKE, WILLIAMS, L.; F85

Benzoin aestivale* → *Lindera benzoin

Cinnamomum aromaticum - *Cassia, Chinese cinnamon* {S} The bark, and an essential oil derived therefrom, are used to flavor curries, confectionery, beverages, baked goods, chewing gum, and condiments. Immature fruits, or *cassia buds*, are used for flavoring breads, cakes, chocolate and pickles. China. COST 1988 [Cul], KUNKEL, MORTON 1976, UPHOF; N84

Cinnamomum burmannii - *Batavia cinnamon, Indonesian cassia* {S} The dried bark, taken from the trunk, is the source of an important spice much used in the Netherlands. Cultivated in Java and Sumatra. Indonesia. MORTON 1976, UPHOF; F85

Cinnamomum cassia* → *Cinnamomum aromaticum

Cinnamomum iners - *Wild cinnamon* {S} The aromatic bark and leaves are used for seasoning, especially in curries. An essential oil, distilled from the leaves, is used to flavor candy and sweetmeats. Tropical Asia. MORTON 1976, TANAKA; F85

Cinnamomum japonicum - *Yabu-nikkei, Shan-kuei* {PL} The bark is used as a substitute for cinnamon and cassia in flavoring foods. Fruits are collected and used as a substitute for cacao beans. Seed oil may be used in food. Eastern Asia. TANAKA; B96

Cinnamomum loureiri - *Saigon cassia* {S} The bark is rich in essential oil, has a sweet, pungent flavor, and is much esteemed in China and Japan. Considered superior to Ceylon cinnamon for seasoning cinnamon toast, apple pie, and other foods. Unripe fruits are dried and sold as *cassia buds*. Southeast Asia. HEDRICK 1919, MORTON 1976, UPHOF; **Z25M**

Cinnamomum obtusifolium - *Annam cinnamon* {S} Aromatic leaves are used in curries. The bark of the stem and the leaves is used as a spice. Southern Asia. BURKILL, TANAKA, WATT; **Z25M**

Cinnamomum tamala - *Indian cassia, Tejpat* {S} Aromatic leaves are dried and used as a flavoring in Indian cooking. In Kashmir, they serve as a substitute for *paan* (betel leaves). The bark, known as *Indian cassia lignea* is commonly used to adulterate Ceylon cinnamon. India. ATAL, HEDRICK 1919, MORTON 1976; **Z25M**

Cinnamomum zeylanicum - *Cinnamon, Ceylon cinnamon* {PL} The bark is commonly used to flavor curries, baked goods, apple butter, puddings, beverages, etc. Essential oils from the bark and leaves are similarly used. Southern Asia, cultivated. MORTON 1976, UPHOF; A79M{S}, C56M, F68, F85{S}, G96, I83M, J22, M82, N84{S}, P38{S}

Laurus azorica - *Azores bay* {S} The leaves are used as a condiment. Macaronesia. KUNKEL; N84

Laurus nobilis - *Sweet bay, Laurel* {PL} Leaves are widely used to flavor soups, stews, stuffings, tomato sauces, gravies, poultry, etc. The dried fruits and the leaf oil are also used for flavoring. Berries are distilled to make a liqueur called *fioravanti*. Dried leaves are brewed into an herbal tea. Mediterranean region, cultivated. BIANCHINI, BRYAN [Cu, Re], MARCIN, MORTON 1976; C3, C9M{S}, C67M, G84, H4, *I61*{S}, I77M, I83M, K22, K63G{S}, K67, N19M, *N40*{PR}, O53M{S}

Lindera benzoin - *Spice bush, Wild allspice* {PL} Young leaves, twigs, and fruits contain an aromatic oil and make a very fragrant tea. The twigs are best gathered when in flower as the nectar adds considerably to the flavor. Dried and powdered fruits can be used as a substitute for allspice. The new bark is pleasant to chew. Eastern North America. FERNALD, GIBBONS 1979, HALL [Pre, Re]; B9M, *B68*, *F5*, *G28*, H4, H49, H70M, I99{S}, K63G{S}, *M69M*, M92, N7T, N9M, N9M{S}, N37M, etc.

Lindera glauca - *Yama-kôbashi, Shan-hu-shu* {S} The fruits are used as a substitute for pepper. Powdered leaves are mixed into noodles and dumplings. Eastern Asia. TANAKA; F85, K47T

Lindera obtusiloba - *Dankôbai, Shui-luo-po* {PL} Young buds and leaves are used as a tea substitute, called *jaku-zetsu-cha*. Young leaves are fried and served as a Buddhist ceremonial dish. Eastern Asia. TANAKA; E63, E87, N37M

Litsea cubeba - *Mountain pepper, May-chang* {S} Scented young fruits are used as a substitute for cubeb pepper in flavoring goat's meat and fish. The fragrant flowers are eaten or used to flavor tea. Roots are cooked with pork. All parts of the plant have a pleasant lemon-like aroma. Tropical Asia. ALTSCHUL, MORTON 1976, UPHOF; **U71M, Y76**

Litsea garciae - *Engkala, Pepe babae* {S} The fruit is eaten raw or cooked. It has thin, bright pink edible skin and creamy white flesh that is similar to avocado, but softer and with a more delicate flavor. Before eating, it is rolled or bruised briefly, as one would a lemon or pomegranate. Indonesia, Philippines. VON REIS; O19, O19{PL}

Litsea thunbergii - *Tabu-no-ki* {PL} Dried leaves are ground into a flour, mixed with wheat flour to make cakes and used as a substitute for rice cakes. The fruit is made into a steamed dumpling called *saji-mochi*. Eastern Asia. TANAKA; F85{S}, H4, N51

Machilus thunbergii* → *Litsea thunbergii

Ocotea pretiosa - *Canela sassafras* {S} The bark is used as a substitute for cinnamon. Brazil. HEDRICK 1919; P28

Persea americana - *Avocado* {S} Buttery fruits are much eaten in salads, soups, *guacamole*, sandwiches, spreads, ice cream, with tortillas, seasoned with salt, pepper, sugar and lime juice, made into wine, etc. The flesh is the source of avocado oil, a mild, pleasant tasting oil used in salad dressings. A tea made from the leaves is commonly sweetened with sugar cane juice. Toasted leaves are used to season stews and bean dishes. Tiny, unpollinated fruits are marketed as *cocktail avocadoes*. Central America, cultivated. DUKE, GIBBONS 1967, MORTON 1987a [Cu], POPENOE, W. 1920 [Cu, Pro], RICHARDSON [Re], THOMSON 1983 [Cu, Pro], UPHOF, VON WELANETZ; F85, *N40*{PR}, P38 (for cultivars see Avocado, page 255 and Rootstocks, page 470)

Persea borbonia - *Red bay, Tisswood* {PL} Fresh or dried leaves are used to flavor soup, especially crab gumbo, stews, meats, stuffings, poultry, and other Creole dishes. The flavor and quality are comparable to Laurus nobilis. Also made into a tea. Southern North America. MEDSGER [Pre], MORTON 1977, UPHOF; B96, H4, H4{S}, *I17M*, I37M, K18, K67, N37M, N51, O67{S}

Persea schiedeana - *Coyó avocado, Cojou, Chucte, Chinini* {S} The fruits are eaten in salads. Quality is variable from seedling trees. The best fruits are quite large, the brownish pulp free from fibers or nearly so, and the flavor a very appealing combination of avocado and coconut. Central America. MORTON 1987a, SIMMONS 1972, WILLIAMS, L.; (for cultivars see Rootstocks, page 470)

Persea thunbergii* → *Litsea thunbergii

Sassafras albidum - *Sassafras* {PL} The roots are added to maple sap and brewed into a pleasant tea. Strong tea can be made into jelly. Young leaves are used in salads or dried and powdered to form *filet powder*, used in Creole cooking for thickening soups, stews, chowders, and gravies. A condiment is prepared by boiling the dried root bark with sugar and water until it forms a thick paste. Young buds are eaten. North America. ANGIER, FERNALD, GIBBONS 1962, HEDRICK 1919; A82, B9M, *B52*, C17M{PR}, C81M, D76, H4, H49, J66M{PR}, K2, K47T{S}, K63G{S}, *K89*{S}, *M69M*, M77M, N37M, etc.

Sassafras variifolium* → *Sassafras albidum

Umbellularia californica - *California bay, California laurel, California nutmeg* {PL} The leaves are used for flavoring soups, stews, and meat dishes. They are packaged commercially in San Francisco and sold as a sweet bay substitute. The flavor is much stronger. Nuts are parched and eaten or ground into flour for bread. Bark of the root is sometimes used as a coffee substitute. Western North America. CLARKE, CREASY 1982, KIRK, YANOVSKY; A80M, B74, C9M{S}, *C73*, D95, E15{S}, E87, F35M{PR}, G59M{S}, G60, I49M, *I61*{S}, I83M, I99{S}, J61M, L67{PR}, N0, O53M{S}, etc.

LECYTHIDACEAE

Bertholletia excelsa - *Brazil nut, Pará nut* {S} Seeds are eaten raw, roasted, salted or used in ice cream, baked goods and confections. The kernels are the source of an oil, Brazil nut oil, suitable for culinary purposes. Venezuela-Brazil. MENNINGER, ROSENGARTEN [Re], UPHOF; **U41, W11**

Grias cauliflora - *Anchovy pear* {S} The fruits are pear-shaped, russet-brown, and are eaten raw, or when unripe are pickled like the mango, which they resemble in taste. Caribbean region. HEDRICK 1919, MACMILLAN; **X88M**

Gustavia speciosa - *Chupo* {S} Fruits are edible. It is said that eating the fruits causes the body to turn yellow. Northern South America. HEDRICK 1919; **X88M**

Gustavia superba - *Chupo, Membrillo* {S} Eaten raw or cooked, the pulp of the fruit is also used like grease to cook rice. Panama. DUKE; N84

Lecythis pisonis - *Sapucai nut* {S} The oily seeds are similar to the Brazil nut in size and shape. They are eaten raw and are considered quite delicious. When fresh they are soft, not crisp like the cashew nut. Brazil. ALTSCHUL, MENNINGER; P28

LEMNACEAE

Lemna minor - *Lesser duckweed* {PL} Occasionally used as a vegetable. Widespread. MARTIN 1975; C7M, E13, H30, H82, K34, K85M, M15, M39, M73M

Spirodela polyrhiza - *Big duck's meat* {PL} Sometimes used as food. Widespread. KUNKEL; D58, G47M{S}, N11

Wolffia arrhiza - *Khai-nam, Mijinko-uki-kusa* {S} A floating, aquatic plant that is cultivated and used as a vegetable in Burma, Laos, and Thailand. The taste is excellent, a little like sweet cabbage. Recommended for mass culture because of its rapid multiplication and high nutrient content. Contains 20% protein, 44% carbohydrate, 5% fat, vitamins C, A, B_6, B_2, and nicotinic acid. One of the smallest flowering plants on earth. Widespread. HILLS, C. 1978, NATIONAL RESEARCH COUNCIL 1976, ZEVEN; **V73, W59M**

LENTIBULARIACEAE

Pinguicula vulgaris - *Butterwort* {S} A cultured milk is reportedly prepared by pouring milk over a strainer on which fresh leaves of butterwort have been laid. The milk is left for a day or two until it sours. It becomes solid like yogurt and is most delicious. A small portion can be saved to inoculate another batch of milk. Northern temperate region. FERNALD; L91M, N84, O42, S7M

LEONTICACEAE

Bongardia chrysogonum - *Chrysogomum* {PL} The roots are roasted or boiled and used as food in Iran. Leaves are eaten in the same manner as sorrel. Southwestern Asia. HEDRICK 1919; R52

LEPTOSPERMACEAE

Astartea fascicularis - {S} The leaves are used as a tea substitute. Australia. TANAKA; M7M{PL}, *N79M*, N84, *P17M*, *Q32*, R15M, S92, T7

Backhousia citriodora - *Sweet verbena tree, Native myrtle* {S} A lemon-like essential oil, extracted from the leaves, can be used for flavoring. Australia. TANAKA; N84, *Q25*

Baeckea virgata - *Twiggy heath myrtle* {S} Leaves are used as a tea substitute. It produces a pleasant drink with a good aroma similar to that of Leptospermum. Australia. CRIBB; F85, *N79M*, N84, O33, O84, O93, P5, *P17M*, *Q25*, *Q32*, R15M, S92

Eucalyptus bridgesiana* → *Eucalyptus stuartiana

Eucalyptus cinerea - *Silver-dollar eucalyptus, Argyle apple* {S} The plant is the source of a kind of edible manna. Australia. DONKIN; B62, C9M, C13M, C43M{PL}, C81M{PL}, D95{PL}, F80, G84{PL}, H4{PL}, *I61*, I91, K85{PL}, M82{PL}, O33, O53M, R33M, etc.

Eucalyptus citriodora - *Lemon-scented gum* {S} Produces a sweet, manna-like substance that is scraped off the leaves and eaten. Australia. DONKIN; C9M, C13M, C43M{PL}, C81M{PL}, E61{PL}, F80, *G66*, G84{PL}, *I61*, K85{PL}, L91M, M82{PL}, O53M, O84, R33M, etc.

Eucalyptus dumosa - *Congoo mallee, Water mallee* {S} Produces a sweet, manna-like substance called eucalyptus manna or *lerp*, prepared into a delicious drink. The bark of young roots is baked and eaten. It is said to be rather sweet, resembling the taste of malt. Australia. CRIBB, DONKIN, UPHOF; *N79M*, N84, P5, *P17M*, *Q25*, *Q32*, R15M

Eucalyptus eximia - *Yellow bloodwood* {S} The plant produces a sweet, manna-like substance. Australia. DONKIN; F85, *N79M*, N84, P5, *P17M*, *Q25*, *Q32*, R15M, S92

Eucalyptus foecunda - *Narrow-leaved red mallee* {S} Said to be the source of an edible manna. Australia. DONKIN; *N79M*, N84, P5, *Q25*, R15M, S92, T7

Eucalyptus globulus - *Blue gum* {S} An essential oil, distilled from the fresh or dried leaves, is used to flavor candies, baked goods, ice cream, and liqueurs. Australia. MORTON 1976, TANAKA; C9M, C13M, C43M{PL}, D29{PL}, F80, *G66*, G84{PL}, *I61*, K38, K85{PL}, M82{PL}, N84, O53M, Q12, S92, etc.

Eucalyptus gomphocephala - *Tuart gum* {S} The plant produces an edible mann-like substance. Australia. DONKIN; C9M, *G66*, N84, O33, P5, *P17M*, *Q15G*, *Q25*, *Q32*, R15M, R33M, S92, S95, T7, etc.

Eucalyptus gummifera - *Red bloodwood* {S} The flowers produce copious amounts of nectar which the natives sucked directly, or mixed with water to make a sweet drink called *bool*. Australia. CRIBB; *N79M*, N84, P5, *P17M*, *Q25*, *Q32*, R15M

Eucalyptus gunnii - *Cider gum, Cider tree* {S} A sugary sap that exudes from the trunk can be drunk directly or left to ferment into a sort of hard cider. Also the source of an edible manna. Australia. CRIBB, DONKIN, TANAKA; C9M, D95{PL}, E7M, E87{PL}, H4{PL}, L91M, N37M{PL}, *N79M*, N84, O53M, P5, R15M, R33M

Eucalyptus intermedia - *Pink bloodwood* {S} The copious nectar produced by the flowers can be sucked, or mixed with water to form a sweet drink. Australia. CRIBB; *N79M*, N84, O84, *P17M*, *Q25*, R15M

Eucalyptus leucoxylon - *Yellow gum* {S} Source of an essential oil used to flavor certain candies, baked goods and ice cream. Australia. MORTON 1976, ZEVEN; C9M, F80, *H71*, L91M, *N79M*, N84, O33, P5, *P17M*, *Q15G*, *Q25*, *Q32*, R15M, S92

Eucalyptus maculata - *Spotted gum* {S} The plant is the source of a sweet, mann-like substance called eucalyptus manna or *lerp*. Australia. DONKIN; C9M, F93G{PL}, *G66*, *H71*, *K46*{PL}, *K48*, O33, O84, O93, P5, *Q32*, Q46, R15M, R33M, S92, S95, etc.

Eucalyptus mannifera - *Manna gum* {S} An exudation that forms on the leaves and twigs, called manna or *lerp* is used as food. Whitish, sugary deposits left on the leaf surface by evaporation of this exudate are generally termed manna. The exudate is produced by insects feeding on the leaves and in some cases contains a considerable concentration of sugar extracted from the plant. Australia. CRIBB, DONKIN; B94, *N79M*, N84, O53M, O93, P5, *P17M*, *Q25*, *Q32*, R15M

Eucalyptus pachyphylla - *Red-bud mallee, Intjiynya* {S} The nectar from the flowers can be sipped directly, or mixed with water to make a sweet beverage. Australia. O'CONNELL; *N79M*, N84, O33, O93, P5, *P17M*, Q46, R15M, S92, T7

Eucalyptus papuana - *Ghost gum, Ulimpa* {S} A type of honey dew or manna is collected from under the bark and eaten. Australia. O'CONNELL; C56M{PL}, *H71*, *N79M*, N84, O84, O93, P5, *P17M*, *Q25*, *Q32*, Q41, R15M, R33M, S92

Eucalyptus polybractea - *Blue mallee* {S} The essential oil derived from the leaves is used as a flavoring in certain candies, baked goods, and ice cream. Australia. MORTON 1976; *N79M*, N84, O93, P5, R15M

Eucalyptus pulverulenta - *Silver-leaved mountain gum* {S} A sweet, manna-like substance that forms on the leaves and twigs is collected and eaten. It sometimes falls in such large amounts that a tree appears to be raining. Australia. CRIBB, DONKIN; B94, C9M, C56M{PL}, D95{PL}, *E53M*, *H71*, *I61*, *I62*{PL}, *K48*, O53M, O93, P5, *P17M*, *Q25*, *Q32*, R15M, R33M, S92, etc.

Eucalyptus radiata - *White-top peppermint* {S} Said to be the source of a nutritious, saccharine substance called eucalyptus manna or *lerp*. Australia. DONKIN; C9M, *G66*, J82, *N79M*, N84, O53M, O93, P5, *P17M*, *Q25*, *Q32*, R15M, S55, S92, S95, etc.

Eucalyptus resinifera - *Kino eucalyptus, Red mahogany* {S} The sap is the source of a saccharine drink. Also produces an edible manna. Australia. DONKIN, KUNKEL; C9M, *G66*, N84, O84, P5, *P17M*, *Q25*, *Q32*, Q46, R15M, *R28*, R33M, S29, S92, S95, etc.

Eucalyptus rubida - *Candlebark gum* {S} Source of an edible manna-like substance. It is said that one tree can produce up to twenty pounds. Australia. CRIBB, DONKIN; B94, *N79M*, N84, O53M, O93, P5, *P17M*, *Q25*, *Q32*, Q41, R15M, R33M, S65M, S92, S95, etc.

Eucalyptus smithii - *Gully gum* {S} One of the principal producers of Eucalyptus oil, an essential oil distilled from the fresh or dried leaves. It is highly aromatic, pungent, bitterish, and is used to flavor certain candies, baked goods, and ice cream. Australia. MORTON 1976; C9M, *G66*, *N79M*, N84, O93, P5, *P17M*, *Q25*, *Q32*

Eucalyptus stuartiana - *Apple eucalyptus* {S} Produces an edible manna-like substance. Australia. DONKIN; E81M, F15M{PL}, F93G{PL}, J82, N84, O93, P5, *P17M*, *Q25*, *Q32*, Q41, R15M, R33M, S92, S95, etc.

Eucalyptus tereticornis - *Forest red gum* {S} Said to produce a nutritious, saccharine substance that falls from the leaves like manna. Australia. DONKIN; C9M, *H71*, O84, O93, P5, *P17M*, Q12, *Q15G*, *Q25*, *Q32*, Q46, R15M, R33M, S7G, S29, S92, etc.

Eucalyptus terminalis - *Kutcha bloodwood* {S} An edible manna, procured from the leaves and young branches is eaten by the natives of northern Queensland. Australia. CRIBB, DONKIN, HEDRICK 1919; N84, *P17M*, *Q25*, Q46, R15M

Eucalyptus viminalis - *Ribbon eucalyptus, Manna gum* {S} Produces a white, manna-like exudate of a very pleasant, sweet taste, much esteemed by the Aborigines of Australia. They collected it after it fell to the ground or scraped it from the leaves. Heavily covered leaves were pounded and baked. Australia. CRIBB, DONKIN, UPHOF; C9M, D95{PL}, D96, F80, *G66*, *H71*, *I61*, O53M, O93, P5, *P17M*, R15M, R33M, S7G, S65M, S92, etc.

Kunzea pomifera - *Muntries, Native apple* {PL} The fleshy capsules are gathered by the natives of sandy desert areas and used for making jams, preserves and tarts. Australia. CRIBB, TANAKA; D95

Leptospermum coriaceum - {S} The flowers produce copious nectar that can be sucked directly, or added to water to make a sweet beverage. Australia. DONKIN; *N79M*, N84, *Q25*, R15M, S92

Leptospermum ericoides - *Kanuka* {S} Young tips can be used to prepare a refreshing tea-like beverage. New Zealand. NATUSCH; N84

Leptospermum flavescens - *Yellow tea-tree, Tantoon tea-tree* {S} Leaves are used as a tea substitute. Australia. CRIBB, UPHOF; F85, *N79M*, N84, O84, O93, P5, *P17M*, *Q25*, *Q32*, R15M, R33M, S95

Leptospermum laevigatum - *Coast tea-tree* {S} The dried leaves are used for making tea. Australia. ZEVEN; C9M, C13M, C56M{PL}, F85, *H71*, *I61*, I83M{PL}, O33, O84, O93, P5, *P17M*, *Q32*, R15M, R33M, S65M, S92, etc.

Leptospermum liversidgei - {S} The leaves can be used as a tea substitute. Australia. BEAN; *N79M*, N84, O93, P5, *Q25*, *Q32*

Leptospermum petersonii - *Lemon tea-tree* {S} Leaves are used to brew a strongly aromatic tea. A few leaves added to the pot when making Chinese tea produces a refreshing variation. Australia. CRIBB; F85, N84, O33, O84, *P17M*, R15M, R33M

Leptospermum pubescens - *Kayo umur panjang* {S} The leaves are used as a tea substitute. Australia and Tasmania. HEDRICK 1919, TANAKA; N84, P5, *P17M*, R15M

Leptospermum scoparium - *Manuka, Broom tea-tree* {S} Fresh, pungent leaves are used to produce an aromatic, very agreeable tea substitute. Manna is reported to form on the leaves. Australia and New Zealand. CRIBB, DONKIN, HEDRICK 1919, UPHOF; C56M{PL}, F15M{PL}, F85, M82{PL}, *N79M*, N84, O93, P5, *P17M*, *Q25*, *Q32*, R33M, S43M, S65M

Melaleuca genistifolia - {S} Said to be used as a tea substitute. Australia. ENGLER; O93, *Q32*

Melaleuca leucadendron - *Cajuput-oil tree, Paper-bark tree* {S} The fruits and leaves are used for tea. Also the source of an essential oil that flavors candy and beverages. Australia. ATAL, KUNKEL, TANAKA; *H71*, *I61*, *I68*{PL}, N84, O33, O84, O93, P5, *P17M*, *Q25*, *Q32*, R15M, R33M, S92, T7, etc.

LILIACEAE

Aloe arborescens - {S} The flowers are sucked for their sweet nectar. Southern Africa. KUNKEL; C56M{PL}, F31M{PL}, G18{PL}, I28{PL}, N84, O93, Q38, Q41, *Q52*

Aloe barbadensis - *Aloe vera* {PL} The gel of the leaves is sometimes used as an ingredient of commercial jellies. Seeds are also eaten. Cultivated. TANAKA; C43M, C67M, D29, E61, F35M, G18, G84, G96, H40, I57, J66, K22, K85, *L33M*{PR}, N19M, etc.

Aloe candelabrum - {PL} The sweet nectar produced by the flowers is consumed directly. Southern Africa. FOX, F.; A0M, G91M, O93{S}

Aloe chabaudii - {PL} Flowers are eaten as a vegetable. Tropical Africa. KUNKEL; E48, H52, N84{S}, O93{S}

Aloe ferox - *Cape aloe* {S} Flowers are sucked for their sweet nectar. Leaves are soaked and cooked as a vegetable or preserved in syrup flavored with ginger, lemon juice, and the very young shoots of fig trees. South Africa. FOX, F., TATE [Re]; C56M{PL}, *E53M*, F31M{PL}, F80, G84{PL}, G91M{PL}, I28{PL}, J82, N84, O53M, O93, Q38, Q41, *Q52*, S44, T25M, etc.

Aloe greatheadii - {S} The flowers are used as food. Tropical Africa. KUNKEL; H52{PL}, N84, S44

Aloe littoralis - {S} Flowers are used as a spinach-like potherb. The juicy leaves are said to be tasty both raw or boiled. Southwest Africa. FOX, F.; H52{PL}, N84

Aloe macrocarpa - {S} The flowers are eaten as a vegetable, or cooked and used for seasoning meat and starchy foods. Tropical Africa. REYNOLDS, G.; **Z25M**

Aloe marlothii - *Mountain aloe* {S} The flowers are sucked for their sweet nectar. Southern Africa. FOX, F.; A0M{PL}, B84{PL}, C27M, C56M{PL}, F31M{PL}, F85, G91M{PL}, H52, H52{PL}, N84, P5, Q38, Q41, S44

Aloe vera → ***Aloe barbadensis***

Aloe zebrina - {PL} Flowers and flower buds are eaten. In Angola, the flowers are boiled, pressed, and made into cakes. The sweet nectar of the flowers is consumed. The juicy leaves are used as a masticatory. Southern Africa. FOX, F., REYNOLDS, G.; H52, N84{S}

Asphodeline lutea - *Asphodel, Jacob's rod* {S} The ancient Greeks and Romans roasted the roots like potatoes and ate them with salt and oil, or mashed them with figs. Mediterranean region. HEDRICK 1919; D11T{PL}, K47T, L91M, N84, O53M, *Q24*, Q40, *Q52*, R87{PL}, S7M

Calochortus gunnisonii - *Gunnison mariposa* {S} Fresh bulbs are eaten raw with salt and taste like a raw potato. When fried or baked they have a crisp nut-like texture and a pleasing flavor. Dried, they are pounded into a flour for making porridge or mush. Flower buds are eaten raw in salads. The seeds are ground and eaten. Western North America. HARRINGTON, H., KINDSCHER, UPHOF; L13

Calochortus nuttallii - *Nuttall's mariposa-lily, Sego lily* {S} The bulbs are excellent eaten raw, boiled or fried. Their flavor is greatly improved by steaming them in fire pits, or by roasting them over a smoky fire. Flowers and flower buds make a tasty addition to a tossed salad. The whole plant can be used as a potherb. Seeds are ground into meal. Western North America. CLARKE, GIBBONS 1979 [Pre], KIRK, MEDSGER; A2, I47, J25M, N7

Camassia esculenta → ***Camassia leichtlinii***

Camassia leichtlinii - *Leichtlin's camass, Wild hyacinth* {S} The bulbs are eaten raw, boiled, baked in pits, fried, used in pies, or dried for future use. They were boiled down to a molasses which was used on festival occasions by various Indian tribes. North America. CLARKE, HEDRICK 1919, KINDSCHER; A2, B0{PL}, D62, E33M{PL}, G47M, I99M{PL}, K47T, K81M{PL}, L91M, O53M, O57{PL}, O93, *Q24*, S7M

Camassia quamash - *Quamash, Blue camass* {S} Bulbs are eaten raw, boiled, baked, fried, or used in camass pie. The Indian method of steaming and roasting in pits produces brown or blackish bulbs that are rich in sugar content. They were sometimes boiled down to a syrup, or pounded into cakes which could be sun-dried for future use. Western North America. GIBBONS 1979, HARRINGTON, H., HART, MEDSGER; A2, D62, E15, E33{PL}, F44, F80, G60{PL}, H37M{PL}, I47, I99, *J75M*{PL}, K47T, L89, O53M, *Q24*, etc.

Camassia scilloides → ***Camassia leichtlinii***

Chlorogalum pomeridianum - *Soap plant, Amole, Wild potato* {S} The bulb is roasted, then peeled and eaten, or peeled first, and then boiled and eaten. Young shoots are slowly baked or steamed to provide nourishing greens. Tender, young leaves may be eaten raw. Southwestern North America. KIRK, MEDSGER; D33, F80, G59M, I98M, I99

Clintonia borealis - *Corn-lily, Cow-tongue* {PL} Very young, unrolling leaves are extensively used as a potherb by country people in parts of Maine. They also make a palatable salad, with a slightly sweetish, cucumber-like flavor. North America. FERNALD, GIBBONS 1979; C49, D75T, E33M, E63M, F85{S}, I31{S}, I44, I87, K47T{S}, N84{S}, O93{S}

Convallaria keiskei - *Suzuran, Kimikage-sô, Pi-pi-chui* {S} Flowers and flower buds are preserved in salt, or mixed with tea leaf and drunk. The whole plant is cooked as a potherb or put in miso soup. Asia. TANAKA; N84

Convallaria majalis - *Lily-of-the-valley* {PL} In some parts of Germany, a wine is prepared from the flowers, mixed with raisins. Eurasia, cultivated. GRIEVE; C49, C73M, C81M, F57M, G55, H33, I44, I91, L56, *L95*, M16, M37M, *M65M*, M98, N7T, etc.

Erythronium albidum - *White trout-lily* {PL} The young leaves are crisp, tender, mild, and tasty eaten raw. Flower stalks, flower buds, and the white, bell-shaped flowers can be eaten raw or cooked. Boiled bulbs are considered to be delicious. North America. GIBBONS 1979; B0, E33M, E63M, G37M, H63, J78, L46, N8, O57

Erythronium americanum - *Yellow adder's-tongue, Trout-lily* {PL} Bulbs are eaten raw, boiled, or roasted. They have a crisp, chewy, very pleasant taste. Flower stalks, flower buds, and flowers are edible raw or cooked. Leaves may be eaten raw in salads. North America. FERNALD, GIBBONS 1979, HARRINGTON, H.; A34M, B0, B77, C49, D75T, E33M, E63M, G47M{S}, H49, I44, M37M, N7T, N8, N9M, N9M{S}, N45, etc.

Erythronium dens-canis - *Dog's-tooth violet* {S} Roots are eaten, often with reindeer's or cow's milk in Mongolia and Siberia. Also the source of a starch used in vermicelli and cakes. Leaves are eaten boiled. Eurasia. HEDRICK 1919, UPHOF; D62, E33{PL}, K47T, L91M, N84, O53M, O57{PL}, *P95M*{PL}, *Q24*{PL}, R52{PL}, S7M

Erythronium dens-canis var. japonica → ***Erythronium japonicum***

Erythronium japonicum - *Katakuri* {PL} The bulbs are the source of a starch, *katakuri-ko*, used in dumplings, confectionery, fritters, to thicken soup, or in dietetic food. Preferred over other starches for use in sauces which must thicken but not jell upon cooling. Japan, Korea. SHURTLEFF 1975, TANAKA; M77M, N84{S}, O57, R52

Erythronium oreganum - {S} Bulbs are eaten raw, boiled, roasted, or are dried and stored for later use. Western North America. KUNKEL; *J75M*{PL}, K47T, L91M, N84

Fritillaria camtschatcensis - *Rice-of-the-earth, Kamchatka lily, Chocolate lily* {PL} Bulbs are eaten raw, boiled, roasted, or are dried for winter use. In Kamchatka, the natives make puddings by mixing them with the berries of Empetrum nigrum. Also the source of a flour or starch used for bread, or put in soups. Northern temperate region. HEDRICK 1919, HELLER, LOVELOCK, TANAKA, TURNER 1979, UPHOF; A76{S}, D62{S}, F85{S}, K79, L13{S}, M77M, N63M{S}, O57, *P95M*, R52

Fritillaria verticillata - *Baimo* {PL} Young plants, petals, and flower buds are parboiled and used in soups, seasoned potherbs, or cooked with soy sauce. The bulbs are eaten fried or candied. China, cultivated. TANAKA; C73M, N84{S}, O57, *P95M*, R52

Hemerocallis dumortieri - *Narrow dwarf day-lily, Hime-kanzô* {S} Flower buds may be fried when fresh, or dried and used in soups or chopped with tea. Young shoots are also edible. Eastern Asia. TANAKA; D62, F1M{PL}, N63M

Hemerocallis flava → *Hemerocallis lilio-asphodelus*

Hemerocallis fulva - *Tawny day-lily, Shina-kanzô* {PL} Young shoots are eaten steamed, boiled, or sautéed in oil or butter. Flower buds are used in salads, boiled, pickled, or stir-fried. Flowers are dipped in batter and fried tempura style, or added to omelettes. Dried flowers, called *golden needles*, *gum-tsoy*, or *gum-jum*, are used in soups and stews. Bulbs are boiled and creamed, baked, eaten raw, mashed, or made into fritters. Eurasia, naturalized in North America. CHANG, W. [Re], GIBBONS 1962, HALPIN [Cul], HARRINGTON, H. [Cu, Pre], TANAKA, VON WELANETZ; A91, B0, B73M, B77, C27G{PR}, D62, D65, E33M, F35M, *G28*, I44, I78, I87, M16, *M65M*, M77M, N7T, etc.

Hemerocallis fulva 'Kwanso' - *Double tawny day-lily, Yabu-kanzô* {PL} A starch is extracted from the bulb. Young leaves, shoots, and flowers are used as vegetables. TANAKA; *L95*, M92, N84{S}

Hemerocallis lilio-asphodelus - *Yellow day-lily, Lemon lily, Wasure-gusa* {PL} Flowers and flower buds may be dipped in a batter of egg, milk, flour, and seasoning and browned like fritters in oil or butter. The fleshy roots, boiled in salted water, taste like a blend of sweet corn and salsify. Dried flowers give flavor to soups, stir-fries, and noodle dishes. Young shoots are eaten raw, or cooked like asparagus. China, cultivated. FERNALD, GESSERT; B77, D24, D62{S}, F1M, F85{S}, J91, M16, M77M, M98, N84{S}, *Q24*{S}

Hemerocallis middendorffii - *Ezo-zentei-ka* {PL} Young leaves and flowers are eaten. Eastern Asia. TANAKA; B28, B77, D62{S}, F1M, *L95*, M8, M77M, *Q24*{S}

Hemerocallis middendorffii var. esculenta - *Nikkô-kisuge, Edible day-lily* {PL} Young leaves are eaten boiled. The flowers are fancied by mountain people, who eat them with vinegared sauce. Japan. TANAKA; M77M, N63M{S}

Hemerocallis minor - *Grassleaf day-lily, Hosoba-kisuge* {S} Young leaves and shoots are boiled and eaten. The flowers are eaten as a relish with meat, or dried and used in soups and stir-fries. The bulbs may be baked, steamed, roasted, or stir-fried. Japan, China. GESSERT, HEDRICK 1919, TANAKA; D62, F1M, F1M{PL}, M77M{PL}, N84

Leopoldia comosa - *Grape hyacinth, Cippolini, Volvi* {S} The bulbs are eaten boiled with vinegar, pickled, or added to omelettes. Cooked bulbs, preserved in oil, are used in antipasto or as a relish. Their slightly bitter flavor is appreciated by certain ethnic groups, especially Greeks and Italians, who believe they are diuretic and help stimulate the appetite. Preserved bulbs are common in ethnic markets of larger cities in North America. Fresh bulbs are less frequently available. Mediterranean region. BIANCHINI, UPHOF; C73M{PL}, H19M{PR}, K47T, K81M{PL}, L99{PR}, N84, O53M, S7M

Lilium amabile - *Friendly lily, Koma-yuri* {PL} Young plants, flower buds, and bulbs are cooked and eaten as vegetables. Korea. TANAKA; G37M

Lilium auratum - *Goldband lily, Yama-yuri* {PL} The mucilaginous bulb is eaten boiled, sweetened, powdered and used in dumplings, or used in a Japanese dish with eggs. Japan, cultivated. ALTSCHUL, HEDRICK 1919, TANAKA; G37M, K18, K33M, L91M{S}, M77, N84{S}

Lilium auratum var. platyphyllum - *Saku-yuri* {PL} The bulb is eaten boiled, sweetened, with egg dishes, etc. Japan. TANAKA; A70, C9, E33, J77M, M98

Lilium brownii - *Hong Kong lily, Pai-ho, Paak-hop, Bok-hop* {PR} The bulbs are eaten baked, or grated, when they may be added to soup to thicken it. Fresh bulbs contain protein, starch, and a small amount of cane sugar which gives them a pleasant taste. The starch is extracted and sold as *pai-ho-fen* or *lily-root flour*. Dried white flower petals, called *one hundred unities*, are used to flavor soups and red-cooked dishes. According to Altschul, the fruits are edible. Bulbs are sometimes found in San Francisco's Chinatown. China. ALTSCHUL, CHANG, W. [Re], HERKLOTS, PORTERFIELD, UPHOF, VON WELANETZ; C27G, L90G

Lilium lancifolium - *Tiger lily, Chia-peh-ho, Oni-yuri* {PL} Bulbs are eaten boiled, pickled, or employed as a source of starch. When properly cooked they are highly esteemed and somewhat resemble the parsnip in flavor. The flowers, both fresh and dried, are eaten in soups, salads, omelettes, and rice dishes. China-Japan, cultivated. BRYAN [Cu, Re], HAWKES [Re], HERKLOTS, LEGGATT [Re], MACNICOL, PORTERFIELD [Nu], TANAKA; D24, E5M, G82M, J7, K18, K33M, K47T{S}, M77, M92, N63M, N84{S}

Lilium longiflorum - *White trumpet-lily, Regal lily, Teppô-yuri* {PL} Mild, slightly sweet bulbs are peeled, parboiled, and used as a delicacy in *chawan-mushi* and *ganmo* treasure balls. A starch is extracted from the bulb. Stems, leaves, and flowers are also edible. China-Japan, cultivated. SHURTLEFF 1975, TANAKA; *I17M*, J77M, N84{S}, Q40

Lilium sargentiae - *Sargent lily* {S} Flowers are consumed in some parts of China. China. UPHOF; D62

Lilium superbum - *American turkscap-lily* {PL} Fleshy bulbs are cooked and eaten or are used for thickening soup. Eastern North America. HEDRICK 1919, MEDSGER, PETERSON, L.; A34M, A70, C49, D62, E33M, E63M, H49, I31{S}, J40, J41M, J41M{S}, J77M, K18, K47T{S}, M77, N7T, etc.

Lilium tigrinum → *Lilium lancifolium*

Muscari botryoides - *Italian grape-hyacinth* {PL} The flowers and flower buds can be pickled in vinegar. Mediterranean region, naturalized in North America. CROWHURST 1973 [Re], MACNICOL; C73M, E11, E15{S}, E33, F67, H37M, K33M, K81M, M98, N84{S}, *P95M*

Muscari comosum → *Leopoldia comosa*

Muscari neglectum - *Musk hyacinth, Nutmeg hyacinth* {S} The flowers, when sprinkled over puréed rhubarb, add a wonderful scented flavor. Bulbs are also eaten. Mediterranean region. HEDRICK 1919, LEGGATT [Re]; N84, O53M

Muscari racemosum → *Muscari neglectum*

Nothoscordum fragrans → *Nothoscordum inodorum*

Nothoscordum inodorum - *False garlic* {S} The plant has been used like garlic to season smoked sausage. South America. HEDRICK 1919; F85, N84, O53M, S7M

Ornithogalum pyrenaicum - *Prussian asparagus, Bath asparagus, French asparagus* {S} Young, unexpanded inflorescence is cooked and served as an asparagus-like vegetable. Still collected and sold around Bristol and Bath, England. Western Europe. GRIEVE, LOVELOCK, MABEY; D62, E48{PL}, G96{PL}, H51M{PL}, N84, O48, O53M, S7M

Ornithogalum umbellatum - *Star-of-Bethlehem* {PL} Flowers have been eaten baked in bread. The bulbs are sometimes eaten, however some authors report that they are poisonous to grazing animals. Eurasia, naturalized in North America. FERNALD, HEDRICK 1919; C73M, E33, E33M, E47M, *F51*, *G28*, H37M, I78, K33M, M98, N84{S}, O48{S}, O53M{S}, R53M, S7M{S}, etc.

Phormium tenax - *New Zealand flax* {S} The flowers produce a honey-like nectar that is very wholesome eating. A long hollow grass-stalk or straw can be used to suck the pure nectar from the calyx. New Zealand. COLENSO, NATUSCH; C9M, C56M{PL}, E61{PL}, H4, *H71*, *I61*, *I62*{PL}, L29{PL}, O53M, O93, P5, *Q32*, R78, S43M, S91M, etc.

Polygonatum biflorum - *Small Solomon's-seal* {PL} The young, tender shoots make an excellent vegetable when boiled and served like asparagus. Rhizomes can be sliced crosswise and fried in bacon fat, or boiled in alkaline water, washed and peeled, and then reboiled. Also the source of a starch. Eastern North America. GIBBONS 1979, HEDRICK 1919, MEDSGER; B33M, B77, C9, C49, D75T, E33M, I22, I44, J43{S}, K18, M37M, N7T, N8, N9M, N9M{S}, etc.

Polygonatum multiflorum* → *Polygonatum biflorum

Smilacina racemosa - *False Solomon's-seal, Treacle berry* {PL} Young shoots are eaten like asparagus. The juicy fruits are bitter-sweet, suggesting bitter molasses. They can be eaten raw, cooked, or made into jellies and sauces. Caution is recommended, as they can be cathartic. Cooking them removes much of the purgative element. Rootstocks are soaked in lye, parboiled, and eaten like potatoes or pickled. North America. FERNALD, FREITUS [Re], HEDRICK 1919, KIRK; B33M, B51{S}, B77, C9, C49, D75T, E33M, G89, I44, J39M, M77M, N9M, N9M{S}, O53M{S}

Streptopus amplexifolius - *Clasping-leaved twisted-stalk, Liver berry, Wild cucumber* {S} The juicy, cucumber-flavored berries may be eaten raw, or cooked in soups and stews. Reported to be slightly cathartic in some localities only. Young shoots are eaten raw in salads or cooked like asparagus. They also have a cucumber-like flavor. Roots are sometimes used in salads for their cucumber flavor. North America. ANGIER [Re], GIBBONS 1979, HELLER, KIRK, NORTON; I47, L13, N84, O53M, S7M

Streptopus roseus - *Rose mandarin, Scootberry* {PL} Young leaves and shoots are added to salads to impart a cucumber flavor. Fruits are also edible, but are cathartic if eaten in large quantities. North America. HENDRICKSON, PETERSON, L.; E63M, N7T, N9M, N9M{S}

Uvularia sessilifolia - *Bellwort, Wild oats* {PL} Young shoots, while still tender enough to be broken off with the fingernail, are cooked and served like asparagus. Rootstocks are said to be cooked or used in diet drinks. Eastern North America. FERNALD, GIBBONS 1979; A34M, B33M, C49, D75T, E33M, E63M, I44, M16, N8

Veltheimia bracteata - *Winter red-hot-poker* {PL} The flowers are eaten like spinach. Southern and Eastern Africa. HEDRICK 1919, KUNKEL; B11T, H37M, K81M, N84{S}, R93{S}

LIMNOCHARITACEAE

Limnocharis flava - *Yellow velvetleaf, Berek* {PL} The young leaves with their succulent petioles, the flower stalks, and the young inflorescences are steamed like endive or spinach, put in soups, or mixed with other vegetables and grated coconut. Tropics. OCHSE, OOMEN; M15

LINACEAE

Linum lewisii - *Prairie flax, Rocky Mountain flax* {S} The seeds are cooked and eaten, both for their high nutritive value and for the agreeable flavor which they add to other foods. North America. KINDSCHER, MEDSGER; E73M, F44, G47M, G59M, H80, I15M, I94, I94{PL}, J25M, J25M{PL}, J53, J88, L89, M47M, N7M, N11M, N29M, etc.

Linum perenne - *Wild flax, Blue flax* {S} Roasted seeds are dried, ground, and eaten. They have a high oil content and can also be used to flavor other foods. Due to their cyanide content they should not be eaten raw, but are safe after cooking. North America. KIRK; B97M{PL}, C11, C13M, C67M{PL}, C92, E5T, E89M, F24, F57M{PL}, G82M{PL}, J48{PL}, J82, K53, *L95*{PL}, O53M, etc.

Linum perenne ssp. lewisii* → *Linum lewisii

Linum usitatissimum - *Flax, Linseed* {S} Seeds are eaten in breads and cereals, sprouted and used in salads, or brewed into an herbal tea. Also the source of an edible oil. Roasted seeds are used as a coffee substitute. Unripe fruits are used in chutneys. Eurasia, cultivated. LOGSDON 1977 [Cu], MARCIN, RITTER, SCHERY, TANAKA; C3{PL}, C13M, E24, F24, F80, H3M{PL}, J73, J82, K22{PL}, L86, L91M, N45{PL}, *N71M*, N84, O53M, etc. (also see Sprouting Seeds, page 485)

CULTIVARS

Foster: Golden-yellow seeds with a mild flavor. Used for oil and culinary purposes. A sesame seed substitute. **T76, U33**

LYTHRACEAE

Lagerstroemia parviflora - *Crape myrtle, Bákli* {S} The gum is said to be sweet and edible. India. WATT; F85

MAGNOLIACEAE

Magnolia coco - *Yeh-hê-hua* {PL} Flowers are used to scent tea-leaf. Indonesia. TANAKA; H4

Magnolia denudata - *Yulan, Haku-mokuren* {S} The flower-buds, after the calyx has been removed, are pickled and used for flavoring rice. China. HEDRICK 1919; E63{PL}, E87{PL}, H4, H4{PL}, K38, K47T, N84, O93, P49, *P63*, *R28*, R78

Magnolia grandiflora - *Bull bay* {S} The flowers are pickled in some parts of England, and are considered exquisite in flavor. Also said to be used as a spice and condiment. Eastern North America, cultivated. HEDRICK 1919, LEGGATT, TANAKA; A79M, B32{PL}, C9{PL}, C9M, D95{PL}, E63{PL}, H4, H4{PL}, H49{PL}, *I61*, K38, *L5M*, N93M, O53M, *R28*, etc.

Magnolia hypoleuca - *Hô-no-ki* {S} Young leaves and flower-buds are boiled and eaten as a vegetable. Older leaves are powdered and sprinkled on food as a flavoring. Whole dried leaves are placed on a charcoal brazier or barbecue, filled with miso, leeks, daikon, and shii-take, and broiled. The delightful aroma of the leaves permeates the miso mixture, called *hoba miso*, which is then served with rice or rice patties. Eastern Asia. SHURTLEFF 1976 [Re], TANAKA; N51{PL}, N84, P49, R78

Magnolia kobus - *Kobushi, Hsin-i* {S} Flowers and flower-buds are boiled and eaten. The leaves are eaten or used as a substitute for tea. Older ones are powdered and sprinkled on food as a flavoring. Japan. TANAKA; D95{PL}, H4, H4{PL}, *H8*{PL}, K38, K47T, K63G, N0{PL}, *N71M*, N84, O53M, O93, *P39*, P49, *R28*, R78, etc.

Magnolia virginiana - *Sweet bay, Laurel magnolia* {PL} Leaves are used to give flavor to roasts and gravies. Also used to brew an herbal tea. North America. MARCIN, MEDSGER; B9M, B32, C9, D95, E63, *E66*, E87, H4, H4{S}, J47, K18, K47T{S}, M77, N37M, N51, etc.

Magnolia yulan → *Magnolia denudata*

Michelia alba - *Yü-lan, Ginkô-boku* {PL} Flowers are used for scenting tea. China. TANAKA; C56M, I83M

Michelia champaca - *Champaca* {S} The aromatic, bitter bark is sometimes used to adulterate cinnamon. Fruits are said to be edible. Tropical Asia. HEDRICK 1919, TANAKA; A79M, C56M{PL}, F85, I83M{PL}, N84, O53M, O93, P5, P38, Q12, Q18, Q46

Michelia figo - *Banana shrub* {PL} Leaves are used for scenting tea. China. TANAKA; B96, C56M, E63, E87, G96, H4, I83M, L29, *O97*

Talauma ovata - *Talauma tea* {S} Leaves are used for making an herbal tea. Tannin is present along with coumarin. Brazil. BURKILL, MARTIN 1975, TANAKA; **X88M**

MALPIGHIACEAE

Bunchosia argentea - *Ciruela del monte* {PL} The fruits are about the size of a quail egg, reddish-orange in color, not very juicy, but with concentrated sugars much like a dried fig or an American persimmon. They are usually eaten out of hand. Venezuela. CLIFT; E29, E29{PR}, E29{S}

Bunchosia armeniaca - *Ciruela verde* {PL} Round, light green to orange fruits have cream-colored, very sweet, rather cloying pulp that is eaten out of hand or made into preserves. Northern South America. MARTIN 1987, POPENOE, W. 1924; E29, E29{PR}, E29{S}, F68

Byrsonima crassifolia - *Nance, Golden spoon* {S} The yellow, cherry-sized fruits are eaten raw, cooked as a dessert, used in jams, soups, carbonated beverages, stuffings for meats, or fermented into an alcohol beverage, *chicha*. The *chicha* is often frozen on a stick or distilled into a rum-like liquor called *crema de nance*. An edible fat is extracted from the fruits with boiling water. Mexico to Paraguay, cultivated. DUKE, KENNARD, MORTON 1987a, WILLIAMS, L.; F85, N84, P38

Byrsonima spicata - *Maricao* {S} Fruits are edible. The juicy pulp is too acid for eating out of hand but can be used to make jelly or jam. Tropical America. KENNARD; N84, P38

Malpighia coccigera - *Singapore holly* {PL} The fruits are eaten fresh or used in tarts, jellies, and marmalades. West Indies, cultivated. KUNKEL, TANAKA; F85{S}, G20, G96, H51M

Malpighia glabra → *Malpighia punicifolia*

Malpighia punicifolia - *Acerola, Barbados cherry, West Indian cherry* {PL} Bright-red, somewhat acid fruits are eaten raw, stewed, or made into juice, sauces, syrups, jellies, jams, wines, or purées. The sauce or purée can be used as a topping for cakes, puddings, ice cream, or sliced bananas. Fresh juice is used in gelatin desserts, fruit punches, or sherbets. The vitamin C content of the fruits is very high and they have been used in the preparation of vitamin tablets and other nutritional supplements. Caribbean region. GARNER [Pro], KENNARD, MORTON 1987a [Cu], MOSCOSO, RICHARDSON [Pre, Re]; *A19*, C56M, D57, E29, E29{PR}, E29{S}, F68, F85{S}, G96, I59G, N84{S}, P38, Q46{S}

CULTIVARS {GR}

Dwarf: A low-growing cultivar, to about 2 feet tall. Does well in a hanging basket. Can take colder weather than others, to 22^0 F. E31M

Florida Sweet: Fruit large, 1 1/4 inches in diameter; skin thick; flesh very juicy, flavor apple-like, semi-sweet; vitamin C content high (1500 to 2000 mg per 100 mg juice). Tree erect, with open-type growth and outstanding yields. Originated in Homestead, Florida by the Florida Sub-Tropical Experiment Station. BROOKS 1972, MORTON 1987a; J36

Manoa Sweet: Orange-red fruit of the sweet type. Tree upright, spreading, very productive. Originated in Honolulu, Hawaii by Henry Y. Nakasone, University of Hawaii. Introduced in 1963. BROOKS 1972; G20, I83M

Malpighia urens - *Cow-itch cherry, Grosse cérise* {S} The edible fruits are reddish, juicy, and refreshing. West Indies. UPHOF; **Z25M**

MALVACEAE

Abelmoschus esculentus - *Okra, Gumbo, Lady's finger* {S} Young fruits are eaten steamed, boiled, pickled, sautéed, deep fried, and braised. Fresh or dried, they are used to thicken soups, stews, and sauces. Seeds are eaten boiled, pickled, ground into meal for bread, made into *tofu* or *tempeh*, or used as a coffee substitute. Also the source of an edible oil. The leaves, flower buds, flowers, and calyces can be cooked as greens. Leaves are dried, crushed into a powder, and stored for future use. Tropical Asia, cultivated. HALPIN [Cu, Cul], HEDRICK 1919, MARTIN 1982 [Nu], SCHNEIDER [Pre, Re], SHURTLEFF 1979; O93 (for cultivars see Okra, page 399)

Abelmoschus ficulneus - *Inland roselle* {S} Stems and roots are roasted. The seeds are often used in sweetmeats, and are employed in Arabia for scenting coffee. Widespread. KUNKEL, TANAKA, WATT; **Y81**

Abelmoschus manihot - *Sunset hibiscus* {S} Young leaves may be eaten raw, steamed, boiled, or added to soups. On account of their sweet taste and mucilaginous quality they are often eaten with papaya leaves in order to remove the bitter taste of the latter. Flower buds are also eaten. Eastern Asia, cultivated. MAY, R. [Nu, Re], OCHSE, TANAKA; D62, F85, H79M{PL}, N37M{PL}, N84, P5

Abelmoschus moschatus - *Musk mallow, Ambrette* {S} Young leaves and shoots are eaten in soups. The leaves are also used to clarify sugar. Unripe pods, called *musk okra*, are eaten as a cooked vegetable. Seeds are used as a flavoring for liqueurs or to scent coffee. Source of an essential oil used to flavor baked goods, ice cream, candy, and soft drinks. Roots are edible. Southern Asia, cultivated. CRIBB, MORTON 1976, TANAKA; F85, M82{PL}, Q12

Abutilon asiaticum → *Abutilon guineense*

Abutilon guineense - *Country mallow, Indian mallow* {S} The flowers can be eaten raw. Leaves are eaten like marsh mallow. The edible seeds are rich in protein and fat. Also the source of an edible oil, comparable to soya and cotton-seed oil. Old World Tropics. HEDRICK 1919, TANAKA, UPHOF; F85, N84

Abutilon indicum → *Abutilon guineense*

Abutilon megapotamicum - *Brazilian mallow* {PL} The flowers are eaten as a vegetable. Brazil. LOVELOCK; C56M, G96, H4, N37M, N84{S}, P86

Alcea rosea - *Hollyhock* {S} Young leaves are used in Egyptian cookery. Flower petals and cooked flower buds are eaten in salads. Petals are also used to brew a refreshing tea. The roots yield a nutritious starch. Cultivated. GESSERT, HEDRICK 1919, LARKCOM 1984, LEGGATT, MACNICOL [Re], MARCIN; E5M{PL}, E7M, E24, F24, F35M{PL}, G59M, H46, I99, J82, K22{PL}, K49M, K66, N19M{PL}, O53M, O89, etc.

Alcea rosea 'Nigra' - *Black hollyhock* {S} The purplish-black petals are used as a natural coloring for wines and herbal teas. When added to teas it imparts an attractive, deep rose-purple color. GRIEVE, ZEVEN; A49D, C9{PL}, F80, G82M{PL}, J82, K22{PL}, L90M, N84, O53M, *Q24*, Q34, S55

Althaea officinalis - *Marsh mallow* {PL} Roots are boiled, sliced, and fried with onions. A decoction of the root may be used as a substitute for egg whites in meringue or chiffon pies. Also made into a tea or mixed with sugar, arabic gum, and egg whites to form a confection. Leaves are eaten as a potherb. Flowers are used for tea and were the base of a famous confection, *paté de gimauve*. Europe, cultivated. GIBBONS 1966b [Pre, Re], HEDRICK 1919, MACNICOL [Re], UPHOF; C11{S}, C43M, C81M, E5T{S}, E61, E61{S}, F24{S}, G84, H3M, I39{S}, J73{S}, K85, N45, O53M{S}

Althaea rosea* → *Alcea rosea

Azanza garckeana - *Rhodesian tree hibiscus, Snot apple* {S} The sweet, mucilaginous pulp of the fruit is eaten, usually before it is quite ripe. Dried fruits are used for jellies. Southern Tropical Africa. FOX, F., KUNKEL; N84

Callirhoe involucrata - *Purple poppy-mallow* {PL} The sweet, starchy root, having somewhat the flavor of a sweet potato, is cooked and eaten. The mucilaginous leaves have a pleasant flavor and are good for thickening soup. North America. HEDRICK 1919, KINDSCHER; F95{S}, *G89M*, I11{S}, I31{S}, J25M, J25M{S}, J78, J91, L91M{S}, N37M

Gossypium arboreum - *Tree cotton* {S} The seeds contain a large amount of oil, used as a substitute for olive oil. Leaves are also edible. Paleotropics, cultivated. MARTIN 1975, TANAKA; D62

Gossypium barbadense - *Sea-island cotton* {S} Seed oil is used in salads, canned foods, or manufactured into margarine. The seeds are also ground into a flour used in bakery products. Leaves are probably edible. Tropical South America, cultivated. KUNKEL, TANAKA; F85, N84

Gossypium herbaceum - *Short-staple American cotton* {S} Seeds are the source of *cotton-seed oil*, used as a salad or cooking oil, in margarine, vegetable shortenings, and canned fish. Presscakes from the seeds can be used for making *tempeh*. The seeds are eaten roasted or used as a coffee substitute. The leaves are eaten. Cultivated. HEDRICK 1919, MARTIN 1975, SHURTLEFF 1979, TANAKA, UPHOF; *E53M*, E81M, F85, J82, L86, N84, O53M, O93, Q41, *Q52*{PL}

Gossypium hirsutum - *Upland cotton* {S} The seed oil is used as a salad oil or in the manufacture of margarine. Seeds are used as food after the toxic substance gossypol has been removed, or in the case of glandless cultivars they are consumed without this preparation. Immature fruits are also edible. North America, cultivated. ALCORN, TANAKA; D58, D87G{PL}, F85, N84, *Q52*{PL}

CULTIVARS

Hopi Short-Stapled: Rare, prehistoric cultivar with attractive flowers. Productive. Selected over the centuries for northeastern Arizona's extreme conditions. Ceremonial use. Grows well in low or high desert areas. I16

Gossypium hirsutum Nonglanduliferous Group - *Glandless cotton* {S} Cotton that is free of the pigment glands that contain the toxic substance gossypol. The high protein (40%) kernels have a nutty flavor when roasted and can be eaten out of hand, boiled and used like rice in casseroles or soups, milled into flour for baking, or ground into a spread similar to peanut butter called *cotton-nut butter*. A coagulated cotton-seed protein curd, called *Tamucurd*, has also been developed and can be used as a cream cheese substitute or a link-sausage type meat substitute product. BLANKENSHIP [Nu], LUSAS [Nu].

CULTIVARS

Tamcot GCNH: A glandless, multi-adversity resistant cultivar developed at the Texas Agricultural Experiment Station. Produces high quality seed for processing into end products. Yields and earliness of Tamcot GCNH are equal to that of glandular cultivars under many conditions. ANONYMOUS 1988; L89G{OR}

Hibiscus abelmoschus* → *Abelmoschus moschatus

Hibiscus acetosella - *False roselle, Asam susur, Som kop* {S} Young leaves and shoots are eaten raw, steamed, or in soups and stews. They may be cooked with other foods to give them a sour, sorrel-like flavor. Tropical Africa. FOX, F., MARTIN 1975, MORTON 1987a, OCHSE; D33, D62, E48{PL}, F80, F85, K47T, N84, O53M, S91M

Hibiscus bifurcatus - *Vinagreira, Flor de paisto* {S} The slightly acid leaves are cooked and eaten as a vegetable in some parts of Brazil. In Guatemala, the mucilaginous sap is said to have been used to clarify sugar syrup. Tropical America. UPHOF, WILLIAMS, L.; **X94**

Hibiscus cannabinus - *Kenaf, Hemp-leaved hibiscus* {S} Young leaves are used as a potherb, put in soups, or added to a mixture called *kwa'do*, made of Parkia pulp and condiments. Seeds, which yield an edible oil, are eaten roasted or made into a type of cake. Flowers are edible. Tropical Asia, cultivated. BURKILL, FOX, F., TANAKA; N84

Hibiscus diversifolius - *Cape hibiscus* {S} Young leaf blades are used as a cooked vegetable. The flowers are eaten with groundnuts. Tropical Africa. CRIBB, FOX, F.; F85, N84, O53M, R41, S44, T7

Hibiscus eetveldianus* → *Hibiscus acetosella

Hibiscus ficulneus* → *Abelmoschus ficulneus

Hibiscus furcatus - *Rubinstein spinach, Napiritta* {S} Young, tender leaves are eaten as a vegetable. Southern Asia. MACMILLAN; F85

Hibiscus manihot* → *Abelmoschus manihot

Hibiscus rosa-sinensis - *Chinese hibiscus* {PL} Flowers are eaten raw, steamed, made into a kind of pickle, or used for coloring foods, including preserved fruits, toddy, sliced pineapple, agar-agar jellies, and cooked vegetables. The young leaves are sometimes used as a spinach substitute. Eastern Asia, cultivated. HEDRICK 1919, LEGGATT [Re], TANAKA; G96, H4, J27, N84{S}

Hibiscus sabdariffa - *Roselle, Jamaica, Florida cranberry, Indian sorrel* {S} The fleshy calyx is used in salads, jellies, cranberry-like sauces, soups, chutneys, pickles, tarts, puddings, syrups, wine, *Red Zinger* tea, *nata* (sweet gel), or roasted and made into a coffee substitute. It is made into a refreshing beverage by boiling, sweetening with sugar cane, and flavoring with ginger. Acid leaves are eaten in salads and curries. Seeds are roasted and ground into flour, then used in oily soups and sauces. Tropical Asia, cultivated. DUKE, HEDRICK 1919, MACNICOL [Re], MENNINGER, MORTON 1987a [Cu], RICHARDSON [Re], TANAKA; A87M, B62, C95{PR}, E49, G84{PL}, I99, K49T, L9M, N84, O53M, O93, P5, S55, S59M, S91M, etc.

CULTIVARS

Nigerian: Calyxes are only slightly red, but are larger than the type. D33

Ruby Red: A superior selection with pink flowers and the calyx much deeper ruby-red than the type. F80

Hibiscus schizopetalus - *Fringed hibiscus, Fûrin-bussôge* {PL} The flowers are edible. East Tropical Africa. TANAKA; E48, G20, G96, J27, N84{S}, O93{S}

Hibiscus surattensis - *Mankin-aoi* {S} Acid leaves are eaten raw in salads, cooked as a potherb, put in curries, or used to flavor meat and fish. The twigs are also used as greens. Tropical Asia and Africa. BROWN, W., BURKILL, TANAKA, UPHOF; F85

Hibiscus syriacus - *Rose of Sharon* {S} Leaves are eaten or used as a tea substitute. Flowers are edible. Eastern Asia, cultivated. HEDRICK 1919, TANAKA; A34M{PL}, B9M{PL}, B67{PL}, C9{PL}, F80, G23{PL}, H4, H4{PL}, H49{PL}, K38, K63G, O53M, O93, P5, Q40, etc.

Hibiscus tiliaceus - *Hau, Mahoe, Cotton tree* {S} The flowers can be eaten as a potherb or dipped in batter and fried. Leaves are eaten, fermented into a sauce, used as a substrate for the *tempeh* starter culture, or boiled in salted water to form a beverage called *Onge tea*. Tropics, cultivated. BHARGAVA, BURKILL, CRIBB, DUKE, MORTON 1977, SHURTLEFF 1979; A79M, D87G{PL}, F85, *L5M*, M20{PL}, N84, O93, P5, *Q25*, *Q32*, R33M

Kydia calycina - *Baranga* {S} A mucilaginous material obtained from the stems is used for clarifying sugar. Southern Asia. TANAKA, WATT; Q46

Malva crispa* → *Malva verticillata

Malva neglecta - *Common mallow, Dwarf mallow* {S} Tender shoots are eaten as a salad. Leaves are steamed or boiled like spinach, or added to soups. Immature fruits, called *cheeses* or *biscuits*, are eaten raw in salads, pickled, boiled, fried, or added to tomato or chicken soup. A decoction of the roots may be used as an egg white substitute in making meringue pies. Dried leaves are made into a tea. Eurasia, naturalized in North America. GIBBONS 1966b, HARRINGTON, H., HEDRICK 1919, KIRK, NIETHAMMER; *N71M*

Malva parviflora - *Cheese weed* {S} Leaves are eaten raw or as a potherb. Young fruits are eaten raw in salads, or cooked into many different dishes much like peas. The ground fruits, with a few leaves for color, can be used for a creamed vegetable soup that resembles pea soup. Eurasia, naturalized in North America. CLARKE [Re], TANAKA; **V89**, **Y10**, **Z98**

Malva rotundifolia* → *Malva neglecta

Malva sylvestris - *Blue mallow, High mallow* {S} Mucilaginous leaves are eaten as a spinach, put in soups to give them a good, smooth texture, or used as a tea substitute. The flowers are used as a vegetable or garnish. Unripe fruits, called *cheeses*, are eaten as a nibble. Eurasia, naturalized in North America. HEDRICK 1919, LEGGATT [Re], MABEY, MICHAEL, UPHOF; C11, E61{PL}, E83T, F15M{PL}, F85, J82, K2, L90M, *N71M*, N84, O48, O53M, P83M, *Q24*, S7M, S55, etc.

Malva verticillata - *Whorled mallow* {S} The young, mucilaginous leaves and shoots are eaten boiled, roasted, or added to soups. One of the earliest domesticated plants of China. About 500 AD, it was an important vegetable with cultivars like purple and white-stemmed, large and small-leaved. China, naturalized in North America. TANAKA, ZEVEN; **Y17M**, **Z19**, **Z24**, **Z98**

Malva verticillata 'Crispa' - *Curled mallow, Castillian mallow* {S} Leaves are eaten boiled, fried, roasted and dressed with soybean oil, or dried and eaten with soy sauce. They are very elegantly curled and crisped at the edges and are sometimes used for garnishing desserts and other dishes. TANAKA, UPHOF, VILMORIN [Cu]; E7M, E24, E83T, F35M{PL}, F42, F85, I39, I99, J20, J67M, K49T, K63{PL}, N84, O53M, Q34, S55, etc.

Modiola caroliniana - *Mauve, Cheeses* {S} Cajuns make a refreshing drink by soaking a handful of leaves in a quart of water for two or more hours. Many drink it every day. North America. F80, K47T, N84

Sida rhombifolia - *Teaweed, Broomjue sida* {S} The leaves are used as a tea substitute in some parts of the Canary Islands and Mexico. As a leafy vegetable they contain about 7.4% protein. Tropics. DUKE, MARTIN 1975, UPHOF; D62, F85

Sidalcea neomexicana - *Prairie mallow* {S} The leaves can be eaten cooked as greens. Western North America. KIRK; L13

Thespesia populnea - *Portia tree, Seaside mahoe, Milo* {S} Young leaves are eaten raw, boiled, or put in soups. Flowers and flower buds may be eaten raw, cooked, or dipped in batter and fried. The fruits are eaten preserved. Tropics. BURKILL, DUKE, KUNKEL, MORTON 1977, TANAKA; D62, D87G{PL}, F85, *L5M*, N84, O93, P5, *P17M*, Q12, Q46

Urena lobata - *Pink-flowered burr* {S} Seeds are used in soups or porridge for the sake of their mucilaginous qualities. The young leaves are eaten as a vegetable or dried and used as an adulterant of patchouli leaves. Tropics. CRIBB, DALZIEL, MARTIN 1975, TANAKA; F85, N84

MARANTACEAE

Calathea allouia - *Lerén, Sweet corn-root, Topi-tambo* {PL} When cooked, the crisp tubers are very agreeable, with a flavor like sweet corn. They are boiled and eaten with a flavored sauce or used as a side-dish. Their unique texture makes them a gourmet item that could compete with popular hors d'oeuvres. Young flower clusters are cooked and eaten. The leaves are used for wrapping tamales and other foods, to which they impart flavor. West Indies. DUKE, HAWKES [Cul], HERKLOTS, MARTIN 1976a [Cu, Pre], WILLIAMS, L.; **U1**, **X79**

Maranta arundinacea - *Arrowroot, West Indian arrowroot* {S} Tubers are eaten raw, roasted, grated into a course meal, or made into *arrowroot powder*. The highly digestible starch is used in pastries, biscuits, and is preferred to flour in thickening soups, sauces, and gravies. Unlike flour it does not add a mealy taste. Tropics, cultivated. BROUK, HERKLOTS, UPHOF; <u>A52M</u>{PR}, <u>H91</u>{PR}, N84

Phrynium capitatum - *Lá deaong* {S} In China, the leaves are wrapped around articles of food prior to boiling to impart color and an agreeable flavor. They are also added to the liquid in the manufacture of vinegar. Southeast Asia. HEDRICK 1919, TANAKA; F85

Phrynium placentarium* → *Phrynium capitatum

Thalia geniculata - *Swamp lily, Aurmá-rana* {PL} Young leaves are edible. The rhizomes are baked and eaten or made into a kind of *arrowroot* South America. TANAKA; F85{S}, G85, *J25*, K85M

Thaumatococcus daniellii - *Sweet prayer-plant, Katemfe* {S} The seeds, when chewed, are very sweet and for an hour or so thereafter cause sour foods eaten or drunk to taste very sweet. They are also used for sweetening bread, fruits, palm wine and tea. Tropical Africa. BURKILL, DALZIEL, INGLETT; F85, G25M, H49, N84

MARTYNIACEAE

Ibicella lutea - *Yellow unicorn-plant* {S} The plant produces an abundance of fruits which are pickled or made into sweetmeats. Brazil, Argentina. BRETTING, HALPIN, VILMORIN; **V73**, **V83M**, **W59M**, **X35M**, **X89**

Martynia fragrans* → *Proboscidea louisianica ssp. fragrans

Martynia lutea* → *Ibicella lutea

Martynia proboscidea* → *Proboscidea louisianica

Proboscidea jussieui* → *Proboscidea louisianica

Proboscidea louisianica - *Devil's claw, Unicorn plant* {S} Young fruits, while still tender enough to be pierced with a fork, can be sliced and added to soups as a thickening. Or they can be parboiled and eaten as a vegetable or pickled in vinegar. The seeds, high in protein, are consumed raw or cooked and also yield an edible oil. North America. GIBBONS 1979, HALPIN [Cu], HARRINGTON, H. [Re], KINDSCHER, KIRK, VILMORIN; A49G, C43M, C43M{PL}, C61M, C81M, E7M, E81M, I99, K47T, K71, L91M, O53M

Proboscidea louisianica ssp. fragrans - *Chihuahuan devil's-claw, Cuernitos* {S} The half-ripe seed-pods are cooked and eaten as a vegetable. Soft, immature seeds are eaten raw, roasted, or ground into a paste. The Tarahumara of Mexico boil and eat the fresh leaves as a potherb with beans. Southwestern North America. BRETTING, HEDRICK 1919; F85, I99

Proboscidea parviflora - *Uña de gato, Devil's claw* {S} Young seeds are eaten fresh for their milky or coconut-like taste. Mature seeds are oily and are being investigated as a source of an edible oil. Southwestern North America. BRETTING; F85

CULTIVARS

Paiute: White-seeded domesticate from the Shivwits Paiute Reservation in Southwest Utah. Adapted to the high semi-desert where it is planted in June. I16

Pima Black-Seeded: Short, multi-clawed cultivar. Discovered by the Pima Indians. Should be planted during the summer rainy season in low desert areas. I16

Tohono O'odham White-Seeded: The seeds can be eaten like sunflower seeds, or pressed for their oil. Beautiful purple flowers followed by 15 inch claws. The black claws are split and woven to produce the black designs on Pima and Papago Indian baskets in Arizona. I16, J25M, J73

MELASTOMATACEAE

Clidemia hirta - *Pixirica* {S} The edible fruit is slightly sweet and very refreshing. Tropical America. KUNKEL, TANAKA; F85

Conostegia xalapensis - *Capirote* {S} Fruits are purple when mature, juicy, have a fair to good flavor, and are eaten out of hand. Sold in the markets of Central America. Tropical America. UPHOF, WILLIAMS, L.; **Y2**

Rhexia virginica - *Meadow beauty, Deer grass* {PL} The leaves have a sweetish and slightly acid flavor and make a pleasant salad, or they can be boiled and served with lemon or vinegar. Tubers can be chopped and added to salads, or eaten as a pleasant nut-like nibble. Eastern North America. CROWHURST 1972, FERNALD, GIBBONS 1979, MEDSGER, PETERSON, L.; A51M, I31{S}, L55, N84{S}

MELIACEAE

Aglaia odorata - *Chinese perfume-plant, Mock lime, Juran* {PL} The fragrant, bright yellow flowers are dried and used for scenting tea. Said to be the most exquisitely scented of all flowers, like vanilla but with spicy undertones. Tender leaves are eaten as a vegetable. Southern China. GENDERS 1977, HEDRICK 1919, MORTON 1976; G96, L59

Azadirachta indica - *Neem tree* {S} Leaves and flowers, having a bitter flavor, are sometimes eaten as potherbs. In Laos, the young leaves are eaten with water-buffalo meat salad. Southern Asia. BURKILL, IRVINE 1960, PONGPANGAN, SING; A79M, F85, I83M{PL}, K22{PL}, N84, P5, P17M, P38, Q12, *Q32*, Q46, S29

Cedrela sinensis* → *Toona sinensis

Lansium domesticum - *Langsat, Lanzone* {S} Fruits are juicy, aromatic, subacid, and are considered one of the best fruits of the Malay region. They are eaten out of hand, candied, preserved in syrup, or made into wine. Southeast Asia. ALMEYDA 1977 [Cu], GARNER [Pro], MORTON 1987a, POPENOE, W. 1920; N84, O19, O19{PL}, O93, R59, S54M

CULTIVARS {GR}

Conception: Large, cream-yellow fruit, 1 1/2 inches in diameter; sweet pulp of excellent quality. Tree a heavy producer, bears fruit in clusters like grapes. Named after the Conception Mountains in the Philippines. Introduced into Florida in the 1950's by William F. Whitman. WHITMAN; **U27T{SC}**

Duku: (Doekoe) Fruit round, from 1 to 2 inches in diameter, with a thicker, darker-colored skin more leathery than that of the langsat. Produced in clusters of two to five fruits. Tree robust, symmetrical; crown wide; foliage dense. S54M

Melia azadirachta* → *Azadirachta indica

Owenia acidula - *Emu apple* {S} The edible fruits are round, red, hard-fleshed, with deep red pulp that is intensely acid. It could possibly be used for drinks, juices, or jellies. One recommendation is that the fruit be buried for several days before eating. Australia. CRIBB, SIMMONS 1972 [Cu]; N84, P5, *Q25*, R15M, S92

Owenia reticulata - *Desert walnut* {S} Seed kernels have a pleasant taste, but so much force is needed to extract them from their hard shells, that only fragments are obtained for eating. Australia. MENNINGER; N84, R15M, S92

Sandoricum indicum* → *Sandoricum koetjape

Sandoricum koetjape - *Santol, Kechapi* {S} The whitish, translucent, subacid pulp of the fruit is eaten fresh, with spices, dried, candied, cooked with fish, canned in syrup, used in jams, jellies, and marmalades, or fermented into an alcoholic beverage. Canned fruits and marmalade can be found in some Oriental markets. Tropical Asia, cultivated. MORTON 1987a, POPENOE, W. 1924, TANAKA; F85, N84, R59

CULTIVARS {SC}

Bangkok: Large, golden to yellow-brown fruit of excellent quality. Originated in Thailand. Introduced into Florida by William F. Whitman as the Manila cultivar. WHITMAN; **U27T**

Manila: An improved type selected in the Philippines. P38

Toona sinensis - *Chanchin* {S} Young leaves are boiled and eaten with rice, cooked with soy sauce, or used as a tea substitute. In Northern China, the young buds are blanched in nurseries and eaten as a vegetable. The fruits are also edible. China. ALTSCHUL, TANAKA; E87{PL}, *G66*, K38, N84, O53M, P86{PL}, Q46

MELIANTHACEAE

Melianthus major - *Honey flower* {S} The honey-like nectar of the flowers is collected and eaten. South Africa. HEDRICK 1919, SCHERY; C9M, C56M{PL}, L91M, N84, O93, *P63*, P86{PL}, R41, R77M

Melianthus minor - *Dwarf honey-flower* {S} Flowers are very rich in nectar which is collected and eaten. South Africa. TANAKA; N84, O53M, O93

MENISPERMACEAE

Dioscoreophyllum cumminsii - *Serendipity berry, Ito-igbin* {S} The intensely sweet, mucilaginous pulp of the fruit is considered the sweetest known naturally occurring substance (up to 3,000 times sweeter than sucrose). Has been recommended as a non-carbohydrate sugar substitute. Fruits keep for several weeks at room temperature. The small, yam-like tubers are eaten in southern Nigeria. Tropical Africa. HOLLOWAY [Pro], INGLETT; F85, N84

Sphenocentrum jollyanum - {S} The roots are acid and bitter when first eaten, but are reported to create a sweet sensation when non-sweet foods are eaten thereafter. Fruits are also eaten, having a mango-like flavor. West Tropical Africa. DALZIEL, INGLETT, IRVINE 1960, UPHOF; N84

Stephania hernandifolia - *Loi tiên, Lá moi, Kua tom luet* {S} A kind of jelly is prepared from the squeezed leaves. Southeast Asia. TANAKA; F85

Tiliacora triandra - *Yanang, Tao yanang, Akar kunyit-kunyit* {PR} The leaves are puréed and employed for dissipating bitterness in the preparation of spicy young bamboo shoots, eaten with rice in Thailand. Also used in soups. Available in oriental markets - fresh, fresh-frozen or canned. Indochina, Malaya. PONGPANGAN; L90G

MENYANTHACEAE

Menyanthes trifoliata - *Buckbean, Bogbean* {PL} The bitter leaves have been used as a substitute for hops in brewing beer. Roots are employed for making *missen bread* (famine bread), or used as a masticatory. Northern temperate region. FERNALD, HEDRICK 1919, HELLER; H30, J7, M15, N84{S}, O53M{S}, P92, S7M{S}

Nymphoides cristata → *Nymphoides indica*

Nymphoides indica - *Water snowflake, Yin-lien-hua, Gagabuta* {PL} Young leaves, stems, flower buds, and fruits are eaten boiled or used in curries. Old World Tropics. BURKILL, TANAKA; G85, I90M, K25, K85M, M73M, N3M

Nymphoides peltata - *Floating heart, Asaza* {PL} The young leaves and flower buds are used as potherbs. Eurasia. TANAKA; B28, G85, H4, H30, H82, I90M, J7, K25, M15, M72, N3M

MESEMBRYANTHEMACEAE

Carpobrotus aequilaterus - *Pig's face, Sea fig* {S} The leaves are baked and eaten. Juicy fruits are sometimes eaten, and are said to remotely suggest the flavor of strawberry. American and Australian coasts. HEDRICK 1919, UPHOF, WICKSON; N84, S44, S92

Carpobrotus deliciosus - *Sweet Hottentot-fig* {PL} Succulent fruits are eaten fresh, as a garnish for fruit salads, dried and eaten like candy, or made into jams and preserves. South Africa. TATE; H52

Carpobrotus edulis - *Hottentot fig* {S} The mucilaginous, sweetly acid fruits are eaten raw, dried, cooked, pickled, or made into chutneys and preserves. Succulent leaves are used in salads, or as a substitute for the pickled cucumber. South Africa, cultivated. CLARKE, FOX, F., HEDRICK 1919, JOHNS, KIRK, SIMMONS 1972 [Cu]; F31M{PL}, H52{PL}, *J0*, N84, O93, Q41, S44

Conicosia pugioniformis - {S} The leaves make a good substitute for spinach. South Africa. HEDRICK 1919; C27M, I33, N84, R77M

Disphyma australe - *Pig's face* {PL} In Australia, the leaves are pickled. Australia and New Zealand. TANAKA; H52, S44{S}

Mesembryanthemum aequilaterale → *Carpobrotus aequilaterus*

Mesembryanthemum crystallinum - *Ice plant* {S} The acid, succulent, somewhat salty leaves are eaten raw in salads, boiled as a potherb, made into pickles like cucumbers, or used as a garnish. Macaronesia, Mediterranean region, cultivated. CLARKE [Re], HEDRICK 1919, LARKCOM 1984 [Re], VILMORIN [Cu]; C92, D62, E83T, F85, H52, I33, I99, N84, O48, P83M, Q41, S55

Mesembryanthemum edule → *Carpobrotus edulis*

Mesembryanthemum pugioniforme → *Conicosia pugioniformis*

Mesembryanthemum stellatum → *Trichodiadema stellatum*

Mestoklema tuberosum - {S} The roots contain a ferment used for brewing beer and a yeast substitute for bread making. South Africa. FOX, F.; G91M{PL}, H52, L50{PL}, N84, Q41

Trichodiadema stellatum - *Kieriemoor* {S} In some parts of South Africa the plant is used for making beer. Also used as a yeast substitute for making bread. Southern Africa. UPHOF; B85{PL}, F31M{PL}, G91M{PL}, H52, H52{PL}, I33, N84, S44, T25M

MIMOSACEAE

Acacia aneura - *Mulga acacia* {S} The seeds are ground, cooked, and eaten by the Aborigines of Australia. The bark exudes an edible gum. A sweet, red *lerp* that forms on the leaves and branches is eaten. A large succulent gall produced by the tree, known as *mulga apple*, is said to quench the thirst. Australia. CRIBB, O'CONNELL, UPHOF; C9M, F80, F85, *H71*, *J0*, O84, O93, P5, *P17M*, *Q25*, *Q32*, Q46, R15M, R33M, S92, T7, etc.

Acacia arabica → *Acacia nilotica*

Acacia catechu - *Cutch tree* {S} *Cutch*, *katha*, or *khar*, a gum obtained by boiling chips of heartwood, is an indispensable ingredient of *paan*, or betel-leaf chew material. Southern Asia. BURKILL, TANAKA, WATT; A79M, F80, F85, N84, Q12, Q18, Q46

Acacia concinna - *Soap pod* {S} The acid leaves are eaten or use as a substitute for tamarinds in chutneys. In Laos, they are used in soups and for marinating fish before drying them. Fruits are roasted and eaten, or used as a sour flavoring for meat dishes. Flowers are used as a vegetable. India. ALTSCHUL, HEDRICK 1919, SING, VON REIS, WATT; F85, Q46

Acacia farnesiana - *Cassie, Sweet acacia* {S} Leaves may be used as a substitute for tamarind in flavoring chutneys. Sprouted seeds are reportedly consumed. The pods are roasted and eaten. Tropical America, cultivated. CRIBB, HEDRICK 1919, TANAKA; B62, B83M, E7M, F80, H4, I83M{PL}, *L5M*, L91M, N93M, P5, *Q32*, Q46, R15M, R33M, S44, etc.

Acacia giraffae - *Camel-thorn* {S} The trunks are the source of an edible gum, called *Cape gum*. Seeds are used as a substitute for coffee. Southwest Africa. KUNKEL, TANAKA; C9M, *G66*, N84, O53M

Acacia greggii - *Texas mimosa, Catclaw-acacia, Cat's paw* {S} Pods are eaten raw, boiled, or pounded into a coarse meal and make into porridge or cakes. The dried seeds are said to make a good bean-substitute when added to ham dishes. They have a high protein and oil content. Southwestern North America. CLARKE [Re], KIRK, YANOVSKY; B83M, B94, C9M, C27M, C98, *E66M*, F79M, F80, G60{PL}, I98M, K15, N84, Q46

Acacia horrida → *Acacia karroo*

Acacia karroo - *Doornboom* {S} The stems produce a good, edible gum, called *Cape gum*. Seeds are used as a substitute for coffee. Southern Africa. FOX, F., UPHOF; C9M, C56M{PL}, F80, *G66*, *J0*, N84, O53M, O93, *Q15G*, R41, R77M

Acacia leucophloea - *Ruteera gum, Safed* {S} Young pods are used as a vegetable. Seeds are ground and mixed with flour. The ground bark is used to flavor a spirit brewed from sugar cane and palm juice. Southern Asia. HEDRICK 1919, TANAKA, WATT; N84, Q46

Acacia myrtifolia - {S} The leaves have been used as a substitute for hops in beer making. Australia. CRIBB; *J0, N79M,* N84, O93, P5, *P17M, Q32,* R15M, *R28,* S65M, S92, S95, T7

Acacia nilotica - *Egyptian mimosa, Egyptian thorn* {S} Source of *Babul gum* or *gum arabic*, eaten mixed with sesame seeds, fried in ghee, or used in the preparation of candied flowers and other sweetmeats. Seeds are roasted and used as a condiment, or mixed with dates and fermented into an alcoholic beverage. Tender young pods and leaves are used as vegetables. The flowers are made into fritters. Tropical Africa to Southwest Asia. HEDRICK 1919, MACNICOL, MARTIN 1975, TANAKA, UPHOF, WOLFERT [Cul]; F85, *N71M,* N84, *P17M,* Q12, Q18, Q46, *R28,* R33M, S95

Acacia oshanessii - {S} The flowers are very pleasant to eat. They can be mixed in a light batter, and fried to make small fritters which go very well served with sugar and whipped cream. Australia. CRIBB; *Q25*

Acacia pendula - *Weeping myall* {S} The tree exudes a large quantity of superior, transparent gum. Australia. TANAKA; C9M, C56M{PL}, F80, I83M{PL}, *K48, N79M,* N84, O93, P5, *P17M, Q15G, Q25, Q32,* R15M, R33M, S92, S95, etc.

Acacia podalyriaefolia - *Queensland silver-wattle* {S} Flowers may be mixed in a light batter and fried to make small fritters which go very well served with sugar and whipped cream. Australia. CRIBB; A79M, C9M, C56M{PL}, E7M, F80, *H71, I61,* N84, O33, O53M, O84, P5, R15M, R33M, S92, etc.

Acacia pycnantha - *Golden wattle* {S} Said to produce an edible gum. Australia. TANAKA; *J0, N79M,* N84, O89, O93, P5, *P17M, Q25, Q32,* R15M, R33M, S92, S95

Acacia senegal - *Gum acacia, Gombier blanc* {S} Source of a resin gum called *gum arabic* or *kordofan*, used in sweetmeats, jellies and other confections. North Africa to India. SCHERY, UPHOF; A79M, Q46

Acacia spectabilis - *Mudgee wattle* {S} The flowers are stripped from their stems and eaten. More distinctive in flavor than A. oshanessii and A. podalyriaefolia. They can be steeped in liqueur brandy and sugar, coated with batter and deep-fried. Australia. CRIBB; F85, *N79M,* N84, O84, O93, P5, *P17M, Q25, Q32,* R15M, R33M, S92, S95

Acacia suaveolens - *Sweet-scented wattle* {S} Aromatic leaves are used as a tea substitute. Australia. HEDRICK 1919; F80, *N79M,* N84, O93, P5, *P17M, Q25, Q32,* R15M, R33M, S92, S95

Acacia tortilis - *Israeli babool, Umbrella thorn* {S} The tree is said to produce the best of *gum arabic* or *gomme rouge*. Drier Tropical Africa, Arabia. HEDRICK 1919, UPHOF; *G66, N79M,* N84, *P17M,* Q12, *Q15G,* Q18, Q41, Q46, *R28,* R41, R77M, S29, S92, S95, etc.

Adenanthera pavonina - *Red sandalwood, Coral pea* {S} Seeds are eaten raw, or roasted and shelled and eaten with rice, tasting like soy beans. The husked kernels contain 25% of their weight of oil, with a protein content of 39%. Young leaves are cooked and used as a vegetable. Tropical Asia, cultivated. MENNINGER, PONGPANGAN; A79M, F80, F85, N84, P5, *P17M,* Q12, Q18, *Q25, Q32,* Q46, S29

Albizia julibrissin - *Mimosa* {S} Young leaves are used as a potherb. Dried ones are used as a tea substitute. Flowers are eaten as a vegetable or crystallized. Cultivated. HEDRICK 1919, KUNKEL, MACNICOL; C9M, C27M, C36{PL}, D95{PL}, E87{PL}, I33, I83M{PL}, K38, *L5M, M69M*{PL}, N37M{PL}, N84, O53M, S92

Albizia montana - {S} The pods are sometimes used as a condiment. Malaysia-Indonesia. HEDRICK 1919, KUNKEL; F85

Albizia odoratissima - *Fragrant albizia* {S} Bark is used in the manufacture of a fermented sugar-cane wine, called *basi*, consumed in the Philippines. Tropical Asia. BROWN, W., STEINKRAUS, UPHOF; F85, Q12, Q18, Q46

Inga cinnamomea - *Ingá-assú* {S} The fruit is large, edible and sweet. Perhaps this refers to the pulp surrounding the seeds. Brazil. TANAKA; **X88M**

Inga dulcis* → *Pithecellobium dulce

Inga edulis - *Ice-cream bean, Ingá-cipó, Guavo-bejúco* {PL} Fruits contain several large seeds surrounded by white, translucent, jelly-like pulp of a sweet, perfumed taste, much liked by Ecuadorians of all classes. Tropical America, cultivated. POPENOE, W. 1924; *Q49M*

Inga feuillei - *Pacay, Guamá* {S} The white, sugar-rich, frothy pulp of the fruit is widely eaten as a snack in Peru and Ecuador, where it has been esteemed since the time of the Incas. Andean South America, cultivated. NATIONAL RESEARCH COUNCIL 1989, UPHOF; **T49M**

Inga laurina - *Guamá, Sackysac inga, Cuajiniquil* {S} The sweet, white, slightly aromatic aril that surrounds the seeds is eaten out of hand. Seeds are edible, having somewhat the flavor of almonds. Tropical America. ALTSCHUL, KENNARD, PEREZ-ARBELAEZ; **X94, Y2**

Inga marginata - *Ingá mirim, Pacai de los rios* {S} Pods contain a sweet, white, edible pulp that surrounds the black seeds, which are also eaten. Bolivia-Brazil. ALTSCHUL, KUNKEL, PEREZ-ARBELAEZ; **X88M**

Inga micheliana - *Cushín* {S} The leaves are used in Cobán to wrap tamales, to which they impart a purple color. Central America. WILLIAMS, L.; **X94**

Inga paterno - *Paterno, Ice-cream bean* {S} Sweet, white pulp around the seeds is eaten raw and is much appreciated. The immature seeds are blanched, salted, and used in salads or desserts. Central America. TANAKA, WILLIAMS, L.; E29{PL}, F85, N84, P38

Inga preussii - *Guajiniquil* {S} Deep green pods are occasionally consumed as a vegetable, after prolonged boiling. The soft, velvety, succulent aril is eaten raw. Central America. TANAKA; F85

Inga spectabilis - *Guavo real, Guavo de Castilla* {S} Sometimes cultivated for the pods which contain a sweet, white, juicy aril surrounding the black seeds. Central America, cultivated. HEDRICK 1919, PEREZ-ARBELAEZ; N84, P38

Inga sp. - *Ice-cream bean* {PL} The white fruit pulp, or aril, is sweet, juicy, aromatic, somewhat like cotton candy, and is usually eaten out of hand. I83M, L6, P38{S}

Leucaena esculenta - *Guaje* {S} The immature, green seeds are stripped from the pods and eaten as a side-dish with salt, or used in soups and salads, with tortillas, etc. They have a unique garlic-like flavor, much appreciated by some. Pods turn red and open easily when the seeds are ready to eat. Leaves are edible. Mexico. HEDRICK 1919, MARTIN 1975; C56M{PL}, F80

Leucaena glauca* → *Leucaena latisiliqua

Leucaena latisiliqua - *Ipil-ipil, Jumbie bean, Lead tree* {S} Young leaves, pods, and flower buds are eaten raw, steamed, in soups, with rice, or mixed with chilis and other spices. Unripe seeds are mixed with grated coconut and fish or meat, wrapped in banana leaves, and cooked. Mature but not dry seeds are eaten raw or cooked, as a delicacy. Dried seeds are used as a coffee substitute, or fermented into *tempeh lamtoro* and *dageh lamtoro*. Tropics, cultivated. CRIBB, MORTON 1976, OCHSE, SHURTLEFF 1979, TANAKA; A79M, F80, F85, I83M{PL}, *K48*, L13, N84, O93, P5, Q12, *Q15G*, *Q25*, *Q32*, Q46, R33M, R50, S29, etc.

CULTIVARS

Low-Mimosene: The leaves of most clones contain mimosene, an unusual amino acid, which can be harmful if eaten in large quantities. Low-mimosene cultivars can be eaten with some caution. NATIONAL RESEARCH COUNCIL 1979; D33, R47

Leucaena leucocephala* → *Leucaena latisiliqua

Mimosa pudica - *Sensitive plant* {S} The delicately fragrant flowers can be crystallized or used for the preparation of distilled flower water. Tropics, cultivated. CROWHURST 1973; B62, C85M, C89M{PL}, C92, D27, E38, F92, G25M, G57M, I64, I67M, J20, L59, M13M, *Q32*, etc.

Neptunia oleracea - *Water mimosa, Rau nhút, Pak kachet* {S} The spongy, floating leaves and stems are crisp and juicy and are eaten in salads or used as a potherb. Young seedpods are also cooked and eaten. Grown in tanks in Thailand and Vietnam and sold in markets. Tropics. HEDRICK 1919, NATIONAL RESEARCH COUNCIL 1976, TANAKA, UPHOF; N84

Parkia africana* → *Parkia biglobosa

Parkia biglandulosa - {S} Seeds are eaten roasted, used as a flavoring for other foods, or made into a sort of coffee. They can also be fermented into a strongly scented, cheese-like substance that is used as a seasoning. Seedlings are also consumed. Malaysia. KUNKEL, MENNINGER; A79M, F85, P38, Q12, Q46

Parkia biglobosa - *Monkey cutlass, Nutta* {S} Pods have a sweetish farinaceous pulp that can be eaten fresh or made into sweetmeats and drinks. The seeds are fermented into an odoriferous paste, called *kinda* or *netetou*, which is preserved and used as a food or seasoner. A coffee substitute, called *café du Sudan*, is prepared from the parched seeds. West Tropical Africa. DALZIEL, MENNINGER, TANAKA, UPHOF; P38

Parkia filicoidea - *West African locust bean* {S} Seeds are boiled and fermented into *dawadawa*, a strong smelling, blackish cheese-like paste used as food and seasoning. Its odor is destroyed by frying or roasting. The dry, soft pulp of the fruit is ground to a yellow meal. Powdered seeds are used for flavoring soup and rice dishes, or mixed with water to form a refreshing gruel. West Tropical Africa. DALZIEL, HESSELTINE, MENNINGER, TANAKA; N84, P38

Parkia javanica - *Kedawung, Kedaung* {S} Young seeds are roasted and eaten as a side-dish, or added to fish and meat-dishes. Pods are used as a condiment. Indonesia-Philippines. KUNKEL, OCHSE; F85, N84, O93, P38, Q12, Q18, Q46

Parkia roxburghii* → *Parkia javanica

Parkia speciosa - *Nitta tree, Peteh* {S} Seeds are eaten raw, boiled, roasted, or added to soups, having a bitter, rather strong flavor. Dried seeds are peeled and fried in oil. The light yellow, pear-shaped receptacles of the inflorescences are cut into slices and eaten raw. Young leaves are consumed raw. Pods are used as a garlic-like flavoring. Malaysia, Indonesia. BURKILL, OCHSE, SHURTLEFF 1979, TANAKA, UPHOF; A45{PR}, C94{PR}, F85{OR}

Pithecellobium dulce - *Manila tamarind, Madras thorn, Guamachil* {S} The sweet, pulpy aril surrounding the seeds is eaten out of hand, boiled, or made into a refreshing beverage. Tropical America, cultivated. BURKILL, TANAKA, UPHOF; F85, *N79M*, N84, O93, P5, *P17M*, P38, Q12, Q18, *Q32*, Q46, R50, S59M, S93M

Pithecellobium flexicaule - *Texas ebony* {S} Seeds are toasted and eaten. Young pods are consumed as a cooked vegetable. The thick seedcoat is used as a substitute for coffee. Southwestern North America. UPHOF; B83M, C27M, F80, F85, N51{PL}

Pithecellobium lobatum - *Jengkol, Ngapi-nut* {S} Seeds are eaten raw, boiled, salted, or cooked with coconut milk or oil. Young leaves, flowers, and fruits are eaten. A delicacy, called *emping*, is made by pounding the cotyledons one by one into the shape of cakes which are then sun dried. The emping is fried in coconut oil, sprinkled with salt, and eaten at the rice table. Seeds are the source of a starch. Southeast Asia, cultivated. MENNINGER, OCHSE, TANAKA, UPHOF; P38

Prosopis chilensis - *Kiawe, Algaroba, Mesquite* {S} The pods contain a sweet, pulpy, nutritious material. They are ground whole and made into bread, cakes, mush, and porridge. Also used for a sweet drink, *atole*, or fermented into a beer. Seeds are also edible. South America, naturalized in North America. KUNKEL, YANOVSKY; C9M, C98, F85, *H71*, *J86*{PL}, N84

Prosopis glandulosa - *Honeypod, Honey mesquite* {PL} The green pods, containing a sweet pulp, are cooked and eaten as a delicacy. Dried pods are ground into a meal used in breads, cakes, etc. Also the source of a gum resembling gum arabic. Southwestern North America. MEDSGER, TANAKA; B83M{S}, G60, I53

Prosopis juliflora - *Mesquite* {S} Pods are eaten raw, roasted, chewed, or ground into a meal. Ground meal is mixed with water to form a refreshing beverage, which is drunk immediately, made into pudding, or allowed to ferment into a sort of beer. Ripe seeds may be soaked overnight and baked with molasses and salt pork, like kidney beans. The sweet flowers are eaten raw, roasted, or made into tea. Trunks exude a sweet gum used in candy making. Drier Tropical America. CLARKE [Re], GIBBONS 1979, HARRINGTON, H., HEDRICK 1919, NABHAN 1984a, NIETHAMMER [Nu, Re], UPHOF; A69, A79M, C9M, F79M, F80, I98M, *J0*{PL}, N84, O93, Q12, Q18, Q46, R50, S29, S95, etc.

Prosopis pubescens - *Screw bean, Tornillo* {S} Pods are eaten raw, roasted, ground into a meal for cakes, made into an alcoholic beverage, or boiled down to an excellent sweet syrup or molasses. Southwestern North America. KIRK, MEDSGER, UPHOF; B94, C98, F79M, F80, G60{PL}, I33

Prosopis spicigera - *Jhand* {S} The mealy, sweetish pulp that surrounds the seeds of unripe pods is eaten raw, dried and preserved, or boiled with vegetables, salt, and butter. Mature pods are eaten as a fruit. Young leaves and a gum obtained from young plants are also edible. Southern Asia. BHANDARI, HEDRICK 1919; F85, N84, S95

Tetrapleura tetraptera - *Arida* {S} The fruit, rich in sugar, is used in soups, sauces, and other foods after it is ground or roasted. The pulp is soaked in palm wine to strengthen or flavor it. Tropical Africa. DALZIEL, TANAKA; F85, N84

MOLLUGINACEAE

Glinus lotoides - *Ganduibud* {S} Tender young leaves and stems are consumed as a vegetable. Tropics. UPHOF, WATT; N84

Mollugo verticillata - *Carpet weed, Indian chickweed* {S} The entire plant can be cooked and eaten as a potherb, or added to vegetable soups during the last minutes of cooking. Tropical America, naturalized in North America. CROWHURST 1972, FERNALD, KIRK; D58

MONIMIACEAE

Peumus boldus - *Boldo* {S} The sweet, aromatic, fruits are eaten. Leaves and bark are used as condiments. Chile. KUNKEL, TANAKA; N84

MORACEAE

Artocarpus altilis - *Breadfruit, Fruta de pan* {PL} The unripe fruit is eaten as a starchy vegetable either boiled, baked, roasted, fried, steamed, mashed, creamed, puréed, or turned into soups, puddings, cakes, and pies. Ripe fruits are somewhat sweet, and are occasionally eaten raw or fermented into a cheese-like food *popoi*, resembling Hawaiian *poi*. Dried fruits are made into flour. The male inflorescence is eaten as a vegetable or used in the preparation of a sweetmeat. Southeast Asia, cultivated. DEGENER, DUKE, GIBBONS 1967, HAWKES [Re], MASSAL, MAY, R. [Nu, Re], MORTON 1987a [Cu], POPENOE, W. 1920 [Cu, Pro], ROSENGARTEN, SCHNEIDER [Pre, Re]; *B59*{PR}, **T73M, X94, Z63**

CULTIVARS {SC}

Puero: Large, spherical or elongated fruit; rind yellow-green with small brown spots, very rough, spiny, thin; pulp light yellow, smooth, of excellent flavor. Cooks quickly. Highly esteemed Tahitian cultivar, considered one of the very best. MORTON 1987a; **U27T**

Artocarpus altilis 'Seminifera' - *Seeded breadfruit, Breadnut* {S} The nutritious seeds, called *pan de pepita*, are boiled, fried or roasted and have a flavor somewhat reminiscent of chestnuts. They are commonly peeled before being eaten. Occasionally found in Spanish markets of New York and other large North American cities. Cultivated. BENNETT [Nu], KENNARD, MASSAL, MENNINGER, POPENOE, W. 1920, ROSENGARTEN; F85, N84

Artocarpus anisophyllus - *Entawak* {S} The oblong, spiny, golden-brown fruit is usually eaten out of hand. It has delicious, bright-orange flesh, firmer in texture and less sweet than that of A. sericicarpus. Borneo. O19, O19{PL}

Artocarpus champeden → ***Artocarpus integer***

Artocarpus chaplasha - *Chaplash* {S} Seeds are parboiled, fermented and then baked and eaten. Southeast Asia. BURKILL, TANAKA; Q46

Artocarpus communis → ***Artocarpus altilis***

Artocarpus gomezianus - *Tapang* {S} Small fruits with deep crimson flesh that are too sour to be eaten raw but can be used for making jams and jellies. Unripe fruits are pickled and eaten with rice. Malaysia. BURKILL, TANAKA; F85

Artocarpus heterophyllus - *Jackfruit* {S} The ripe, malodorous fruits are eaten raw, fried in curries, preserved in syrup, dried, cooked in milk, or made into an alcoholic beverage. Very young fruits and leaf-shoots are eaten in soups and stews. Seeds are boiled, fried, ground into flour and made into biscuits, or roasted like chestnuts. The young male inflorescences are eaten mixed with chilis, fish paste, sugar, salt, etc. Rind of the fruit yields a fair jelly. Southern Asia, cultivated. DUKE, MORTON 1987a [Cu], OCHSE, POPENOE, W. 1920 [Cu, Pro], RICHARDSON [Pre, Re], STEINKRAUS; E29{PL}, E29{PR}, F68{PL}, F85, I83M{PL}, *N40*{PR}, N84, P38, Q12, Q46, *Q93*{PL}

CULTIVARS {PL}

NS #1: Medium to large fruit of unsurpassed quality. An excellent cultivar widely grown in Southeast Asia. Originated in Malaysia. Introduced into Florida by William F. Whitman and Dr. Robert McNaughton. WHITMAN; **T73M**{SC}

Orange-Fleshed: Selected from thick-fleshed, best quality fruit. O19, O19{S}

Artocarpus hypargyraeus - *Kwai-muk* {S} When ripe, the pulp of the fruit is orange-red to red, and has an agreeable, subacid to acid flavor. It is eaten out of hand, or may be preserved in syrup or dried. Southern China. MORTON 1987a; **T73M, Y2**

Artocarpus integer - *Champedak* {S} The pulp of the ripe fruits is golden-yellow, rather slimy, strongly odoriferous, almost like that of the durian. It is eaten fresh, fried together with flour, or mixed into *dodol*, a kind of pudding. Unripe fruits are used as a cooked vegetable or may be added to soups. The ripe seeds are roasted and eaten as a delicacy. Leaves are also edible. Southeast Asia. MARTIN 1975, MORTON 1987a, OCHSE, RIFAI; F85

CULTIVARS {GR}

Orange-Fleshed: Relatively small, cylindrical fruit, about 14 inches long and 7 inches in diameter; thick, pinkish-orange flesh, very rich, sweet, and juicy, and of a creamy texture. Has a richer flavor, with less fiber and acidity than jackfruit. Grows in a frost free tropical or sub-tropical climate. One of the best of the several types of Champedak. O19, O19{S}

Artocarpus integrifolia → ***Artocarpus heterophyllus***

Artocarpus lakoocha - *Lakoocha, Monkey jack* {S} Fruits have a pleasant, sub-acid flavor, and are occasionally eaten raw but are mostly used in curries or chutneys. The male inflorescence, acid and astringent, is pickled. The flat, broad seeds are edible. Bark is chewed as a substitute for betel nut. Southern Asia. HEDRICK 1919, KUNKEL, MACMILLAN, MORTON 1987a, UPHOF; F85, N84, P38, Q12, Q46

Artocarpus odoratissimus - *Marang* {S} The ripe fruits are fleshy, aromatic, sweet and juicy, similar to the jackfruit but of much better quality. Usually eaten as a dessert fruit. Unripe fruits are eaten as a boiled vegetable. Seeds are roasted and eaten. Rind of the fruit is said to be edible. Philippines to Indonesia. KUNKEL, POPENOE, W. 1920, TANAKA, UPHOF; O19, O19{PL}, R59

Artocarpus polyphema → ***Artocarpus integer***

Artocarpus sericicarpus - *Pedalai* {S} A round, bright orange fruit, similar to the jackfruit inside but has a superior flavor, firmer flesh and less aroma. The sweet creamy flesh is easy to eat, with the segments clinging to the core when the skin is removed. Borneo, Philippines. ALTSCHUL; O19, O19{PL}

Artocarpus sp. - *Utu* {S} The fruit resembles a small, golden-brown jackfruit. Cream-colored flesh is "eat-all", with no waste. The flavor is neither sweet nor sour, but tangy and very pleasing, reminiscent of yogurt. Can be used in the same manner as breadfruit. The large, hard-shelled seeds can be roasted and eaten. Borneo. O19, O19{PL}

Brosimum alicastrum - *Ramón breadnut, Mayan breadnut* {S} Seeds are eaten raw, boiled and mashed like potatoes, made into juice and marmalades, or roasted, when they develope a nutty, cacao-like flavor. Ground seeds are made into a *masa* to mix with corn for making *tortillas*, added to milk and sugar to make a nutritious and tasty milk shake, mixed with honey, or steeped in boiling water to make a coffee-like beverage. The latex from the trunk is mixed with chicle or drunk like cow's milk. Central America. NATIONAL RESEARCH COUNCIL 1975a, PETERS [Nu], ROSENGARTEN; E29, E29{PL}, F85

Broussonetia kazinoki - *Kozo* {PL} Young leaves are eaten as a vegetable. Fruits and flowers are also edible. Japan. TANAKA; N37M

Chlorophora excelsa - *Iroko fustic tree* {S} The fruit is edible. Its juice is used as a condiment. Young leaves are also eaten. Tropical Africa. MARTIN 1975, TANAKA; N84

Cudrania tricuspidata - *Chinese che, Cudrang, Silkworm thorn* {PL} The fruits are similar to a mulberry and turn a dull maroon color when mature. While still firm they are relatively tasteless. When soft ripe, like a persimmon, they are sub-acid to sweet and may be quite delicious. Eastern Asia. DARROW, HENDRICKSON, UPHOF; B96, D37, D95, M31M, M31M{SC}, N37M, N84{S}

CULTIVARS

Female: Large, flavorful fruit; ripens in late summer to fall. Small, thorny tree; bears heavy crops annually. Requires a male tree for fruit production. K67

Male: Small, thorny tree. Used primarily as a pollinator for female trees. Occasionally produces a few small fruits. K67

Ficus auriculata - *Roxburg fig, Timla* {S} Fruits are eaten raw, in curries, or made into jam. When pollinated with a small stick dipped in olive oil, they are said to grow to four inches in diameter. Tropical Asia. BURKILL, FAIRCHILD 1930, HEDRICK 1919, KUNKEL; C56M{PL}, I83M{PL}, N84, O93, P38{SC}, Q41, S91M

Ficus awkeotsang* → *Ficus pumila var. awkeotsang

Ficus capensis - *Cape fig, Brown cluster-fig* {S} The fruits are sweet and are usually eaten out of hand or made into jam. Young aerial shoots are eaten as a vegetable. Bark is chewed with cola nuts for the alleviation of thirst. Tropical Africa. DALZIEL, FOX, F., KUNKEL; N84, O53M, O93, R41

Ficus carica - *Fig* {PL} Fruits are eaten raw, dried, preserved, brewed into wine and brandy, dried and ground into a coffee substitute, candied, processed into jams, paste, syrup, stuffed with walnuts or almonds and small pieces of citron, used in cookies, bread, brownies, pastries, pies, etc. The latex is used to coagulate milk for making cheese and junket. Cultivated. BIANCHINI, BRYAN [Cu, Re], MORTON 1987a, UPHOF; A50, C56M, *G66*{S}, G96, I57, K2, N84{S} (for cultivars see Fig, page 331)

Ficus glomerata* → *Ficus racemosa

Ficus hirta - *Dieng-soh-rompian, Boowah kontol monjèt* {S} Very young top-shoots are eaten raw, as a side-dish with rice. The ripe, yellow or red fruits have a sweet taste and are relished by the natives, especially children. Tropical Asia. OCHSE; F85

Ficus pseudopalma - *Philippine fig* {S} The young leaves are delicious eaten raw in salads or cooked as a potherb. Fruits are also edible. Philippines. KUNKEL, MARTIN 1975; **T73M**

Ficus pumila - *Creeping fig, Mu-lien, Hsüeh-li* {PL} In China, the fruit is picked ripe and placed in a porous bag to squeeze the juice out. This juice is then cooked and cooled into a gelatinous jelly, called *pai-liang-fên*, which is cubed, mixed with water, syrup and flavorings and consumed as a refreshing beverage. Available canned as *grass jelly* or *ai-yü jelly* in ethnic stores. Eastern Asia. TANAKA, VON WELANETZ; C89M, *F53M*, G96, H4, H51M, L29, L90G{PR}, N84{S}

Ficus pumila var. awkeotsang - *Chinese jello-vine, Ai-yü-tzu* {S} The fruit is sometimes eaten out of hand, but usually it is processed into an edible jelly or drink, in much the same manner as the species. Eastern Asia. TANAKA; F85, G25M, H49, N84, O42

Ficus racemosa - *Cluster fig, Gúlar* {S} Ripe fruits are eaten fresh, dried and ground into flour and taken with sugar and milk, or used for preparing a cold jelly. The powder from roasted fruits forms a valuable breakfast food. Unripe fruits are pickled or used in soups. Young shoots are eaten raw or cooked. Tropical Asia to Australia. CRIBB, HEDRICK 1919, OCHSE, TANAKA; F85, N84, P5, Q12, Q41

Ficus roxburghii* → *Ficus auriculata

Ficus rumphii - *Pilkhan, Gaiaswat* {S} Fruits are edible. Young leaves are also eaten. Malaysia. BURKILL, TANAKA, WATT; F85

Ficus sycomorus - *Sycamore fig, Pharaoh's fig* {S} The sweet, aromatic fruits have been eaten since the days of the ancient Egyptians. Gashing of the immature fruits is an ancient technique that hastens their ripening. The latex is used as a vegetable rennet. Northern Africa to Southwest Asia. GALIL, HEDRICK 1919, MOLDENKE, UPHOF; N84

Morus alba - *White mulberry* {S} Fruits are eaten raw, in pies, tarts, jellies, drinks, or brewed into a wine. Dried fruits are a delicious snack, or they can be used like dried figs or raisins in puddings, cookies, and muffins. Young shoots are sometimes eaten with rice and condiments, put in stews, or used as a substitute for tea. Also the source of an edible manna. China, cultivated. DONKIN, GIBBONS 1962 [Re], SIMMONS 1972 [Cu], TANAKA; A79M, C9M, G41, I47, *I61*, K38, *K46*{PL}, K47T, M16{PL}, N0{PL}, N84, N93M, O53M, Q12, Q46, etc. (for cultivars see Mulberry, page 391)

Morus alba var. indica - *Indian mulberry, Ainu mulberry* {S} In Bombay, the dark red fruits are sold in the bazaars for making compotes and tarts. The leaves are also edible. Tropical Asia. HEDRICK 1919, MACMILLAN, TANAKA; Q12

Morus alba var. stylosa - *Kuwa* {S} Fruits are eaten raw, made into jam, or brewed into a wine. The leaves are sometimes eaten or used as a tea substitute. Eastern Asia. TANAKA; **T41M, V19, Y27M**

Morus australis - *Korean mulberry* {S} The sweet, juicy, dark red fruit is eaten raw or brewed into a wine. Eastern Asia. HENDRICKSON, TANAKA; F85, N84

Morus bombycis* → *Morus alba var. stylosa

Morus indica* → *Morus alba var. indica

Morus laevigata - *Himalayan mulberry, Tút* {S} The long, cylindrical, sweetish fruit is eaten raw and is also excellent when stewed with sugar. Southern Asia. HEDRICK 1919, TANAKA; Q46

Morus nigra - *Black mulberry, Persian mulberry* {S} The fruits are eaten raw, dried, in jams, compotes, puddings, pies, sauces, or mixed with honey or mead to form refreshing drinks. Dried fruits can be ground into a flour. Asia Minor, cultivated. BRYAN [Cu, Re], HACKETT, JOHNS [Cul]; C9M, D77M{PL}, D95{PL}, F11{PL}, G23{PL}, G41{PL}, H4{PL}, H53, I49M{PL}, K38, K47T, N84, N93M, O53M, P49, etc. (for cultivars see Mulberry, page 391)

Morus rubra - *Red mulberry* {PL} Ripe fruits are eaten fresh with cream and sugar, or made into pies, jams, jellies, marmalades, juices, muffins, fruit-cakes, etc. Dried fruits are ground and mixed with almond and other nuts to form a delicious confection. Young shoots and unfolding leaves are eaten raw or boiled and served with butter and salt. North America. ANGIER, FERNALD, GIBBONS 1962 [Re], MEDSGER, TURNER 1979 [Re]; A34M, H4, K38{S}, M16, N84{S}, P49{S} (for cultivars see Mulberry, page 391)

Streblus asper - *Dieng-soh-khydang, Khorua* {S} The yellow, aromatic fruit is eaten. Juice from the stem is used to curdle milk. Tropical Asia. MACMILLAN, TANAKA; Q46

Treculia africana - *African breadfruit* {S} Seeds are boiled or roasted, peeled, and eaten as a dessert nut, or fried in oil. They are also ground to a meal, cooked, and used in soups or nut milks. An edible oil is sometimes extracted from them. Tropical Africa. DALZIEL, MENNINGER, TANAKA; N84

MORINGACEAE

Moringa oleifera - *Horseradish tree* {S} The long, bean-like pods are used in soups and curries or made into pickles. Young, mustard-flavored leaves, twigs, and flowers are eaten raw in salads, cooked as potherbs, or put in soups and curries. Immature seeds are eaten like peas. Mature seeds, when roasted or fried, are said to resemble peanuts. They also yield *ben oil*, used in salads and cooking. The pungent root is used as a substitute for horseradish. Young, tender seedlings make an excellent cooked green vegetable. Leaves contain 7-10% protein. Tropical Asia, cultivated. DUKE, HAWKES [Re], HEDRICK 1919, MARTIN 1975, MENNINGER, MORTON 1976, OCHSE; A79M, C27M, D33, D57{PL}, E83T, F85, I59G, I99, N84, O93, P5, Q12, Q46

CULTIVARS

Hybrid: An improved hybrid type developed in India. R50

Moringa ovalifolia - *Phantom tree* {PL} Highly prized in Africa for its horseradish-like root, and its edible leaves and fruits. Southern Africa. FOX, F.; A0M, C27M{S}, I33{S}, K77M, L50, O93{S}

Moringa pterygosperma → *Moringa oleifera*

MUSACEAE

Ensete edule → *Ensete ventricosum*

Ensete ventricosum - *Abyssinian banana* {S} The chopped and grated pulp of the corms and leaf sheaths is fermented and used as a flour in making *kocho* bread. One hundred percent kocho flour or a mixture of kocho and other cereal flours may be used. Kocho is usually eaten with cheese, kale, ground meat, chickpea or bean sauce, and seasoned with spiced butter. The endosperm of the seeds is consumed as food. Tropical Africa. SIMMONDS 1966, STEINKRAUS, UPHOF; A79M, C9M, C27M, C56M{PL}, *E53M*, *F53M*{PL}, *H71*, I28{PL}, I57{PL}, L91M, N84, O53M, O93, P5, *Q32*, etc.

Musa basjoo - *Bashô* {PL} The nectar of the flowers is sweet and drinkable. Japan, cultivated. TANAKA; C56M, H4

Musa ensete → *Ensete ventricosum*

Musa x paradisiaca - *Banana, Plantain* {S} Unripe fruits are steamed, boiled, dried, baked, fried, made into flour, or parched and used as a coffee substitute. Ripe fruits are eaten out of hand, or used in ice cream, bread, muffins, cream pies, sweetmeats, etc. Ashes of the plant may be used as a salt substitute. Male flower-heads are eaten in curries or cooked with coconut milk. Individual flowers are prepared separately in curries or with palm oil. Inner parts of the stem are eaten boiled or made into flour and starch. The pulp is fermented into vinegar, beers and wines. The nectar of the flowers is consumed. Cultivated. DUKE, MORTON 1987a, OCHSE, REYNOLDS, P., SIMMONDS 1966, STEINKRAUS, UPHOF; F80, L54{PR}, L62M{PL}, N84, O53M, O93, *P17M*, *Q32*, S95 (for cultivars see Banana, page 258)

Musa sapientum → *Musa x paradisiaca*

Musa troglodytarum - *Fe'i banana* Origin unknown, possibly a natural hybrid. Very ripe fruits are eaten raw, or more commonly they are baked or boiled. The yellow flesh discolors the urine of those who eat it. In New Caledonia, bunches are buried in mud to hasten the ripening process. Polynesia, cultivated. MASSAL, SIMMONDS 1966; (for sources see Banana, page 258)

Musa ventricosa → *Ensete ventricosum*

MYOPORACEAE

Myoporum deserti - *Turkey bush* {S} The sweet, yellow fruits are eaten. Australia. CRIBB; N84, R15M

MYRICACEAE

Comptonia asplenifolia → *Comptonia peregrina*

Comptonia peregrina - *Sweet fern* {PL} The aromatic leaves, both fresh and dried, are made into a palatable tea. Menomini Indians of Wisconsin used them as a seasoning. Young fruits are eaten as a pleasant nibble. Eastern North America. ANGIER [Pre], FERNALD, GIBBONS 1979, MEDSGER, UPHOF; B9M, D30, D95, E33M, *H8*, M92, P86

Myrica cerifera - *Wax-myrtle, Southern bayberry* {PL} Aromatic leaves and berries make an attractive and agreeable substitute for bay leaves in flavoring soups, stews, roasted meats, and seafood. The leaves are also brewed into a robust tea. Fruits are eaten fresh, preserved, or fermented into wine. North America. FERNALD, GIBBONS 1979, TANAKA; C13M{S}, C43M, *E66*, *F73*, H4, H49, I47{S}, I77M, *J25*, K18, K47T{S}, K85, *L5M*{S}, N37M, N84{S}, etc.

Myrica faya - *Candleberry, Firetree* {S} Fruits are eaten raw or made into preserves. Macaronesia. HEDRICK 1919; D62

Myrica gale - *Sweet gale, Bog myrtle* {S} Aromatic fruits and leaves are used to flavor broth, soups, stews, and meats. Dried leaves make a delicate and palatable tea. The herb is sometimes put in beer and ale to add flavor and increase foaming. Northern temperate region. FERNALD, HEDRICK 1919, MABEY [Re], MICHAEL [Re], MORTON 1976, UPHOF; N84, S55

Myrica nagi → *Myrica rubra*

Myrica pensylvanica - *Northern bayberry* {PL} Dried leaves are used to season crab-boil, stock, broth, soup, stew, or chowder. The leaves, which impart a delicate aroma and subtle flavor are removed before serving. Eastern North America. GIBBONS 1964; B9M, C9, C13M{S}, *C47*, C81M, D95, E87, *G30*, H49, H49{S}, K22, K38{S}, K85, M77, N84{S}, O53M{S}, etc.

Myrica rubra - *Chinese bayberry, Yang-mei, Kàiphal* {S} The agreeable, subacid, deep red fruits are eaten fresh, cooked, preserved, or made into a refreshing drink or a kind of liqueur. Seed kernels are also said to be edible. Recommended for improvement by selection and breeding. Eastern Asia. HEDRICK 1919, TANAKA, UPHOF; F80, N84, Q40

MYRISTICACEAE

Horsfieldia irya - *Warun* {S} The fruits are eaten by the native peoples. Also used as a condiment. Tropical Asia. KUNKEL, VON REIS; N84

Myristica fragrans - *Nutmeg* {S} Seeds are the source of nutmeg, used to flavor custards, eggnog, sauces, cakes, puddings, and pies. *Mace*, the dried aril, seasons soups, sauces, fruit salads, cakes, pickles, and baked goods. Powdered mace, sprinkled on cooked cabbage, masks the sulfide odor. The flesh of the fruit is cut into slices and eaten as a delicacy with *sambal* (hot-pepper sauce), pickled, candied, preserved, or made into a nutmeg-flavored jam. Indonesia, cultivated. KENNARD, MENNINGER, MORTON 1976, OCHSE, ROOT 1980b, UPHOF; F85, L55G{PR}, N84

Virola surinamensis - *Ucuuba-branca* {S} The seeds are the source of an edible fat. Tropical America. ALTSCHUL; **X88M**

MYRSINACEAE

Ardisia boissieri - {S} Flowers and fruits are cooked with fish to add flavor. The leaves are eaten. Philippines. BROWN, W., MARTIN 1975, UPHOF; F85

Ardisia escallonioides - *Marbleberry* {PL} The acid fruits are eaten raw. Tropical America. MORTON 1977, WILLIAMS, L.; D87G, *J25*

Ardisia squamulosa* → *Ardisia boissieri

Embelia ribes - *Memory Improver, Areuj kathembang* {S} Young leaves and branchlets are eaten raw as a side-dish with rice, usually mixed with other greens. The sour leaves are used as a substitute for tamarind in soups and vegetable dishes. Ripe fruits have a sour-sweet flavor and are eaten as a delicacy. Both the leaves and fruits are used to prepare a sweet, refreshing drink. Dried fruits are used as an adulterant of black pepper. Young stems are chewed as a delicacy. India to Indonesia. OCHSE, UPHOF; F85

Embelia robusta - *Cottam* {S} The fruits are eaten or used to adulterate black pepper. Southern Asia. KUNKEL, TANAKA; F85

Embelia tsjerium-cottam* → *Embelia robusta

Myrsine africana - *African boxwood* {S} Fruits are eaten or used as an adulterant of black pepper. Tropical Africa. KUNKEL, TANAKA; E48{PL}, *E53M*, *G66*, G96{PL}, *I62*{PL}, *L47*{PL}, N37M{PL}, N84, O53M, O93, P5, Q46, R41, R77M

MYRTACEAE

Acca sellowiana* → *Feijoa sellowiana

Acmena smithii* → *Eugenia smithii

Amyrsia foliosa - *Arrayan* {S} The small purple fruit is usually eaten out of hand. It has juicy, whitish pulp with a flavor that is mildly subacid and pleasant, somewhat suggestive of that of the grape. Leaves are used for flavoring jellies. Ecuador. PEREZ-ARBELAEZ, POPENOE, W. 1924; **V73**

Austromyrtus dulcis - {S} Small, pale lilac or almost white fruits that can be eaten out of hand. They have very soft skin, small seeds, and soft pulp with a sweet, mildly aromatic flavor. Considered one of the best native fruits of Australia. Australia. CRIBB; F85

Eugenia aggregata - *Cherry of the Rio Grande* {PL} When ripe, the fruits are reddish-purple, juicy, firm in texture, and pleasantly subacid. They are very good eaten out of hand or can be used for jams and jellies. In addition to producing desirable fruit, the tree is quite ornamental and deserves to be more widely grown. Brazil. DRYSDALE, MARTIN 1987, MAXWELL, RODALE; C56M, D57, F68, I83M, N84{S}, P38{S}

Eugenia apiculata* → *Myrceugenella apiculata

Eugenia aromatica* → *Syzygium aromaticum

Eugenia axillaris - *White stopper* {PL} Ripe fruits are black, sweet, juicy, and can be eaten raw. Florida, West Indies. MORTON 1977; D87G

Eugenia brasiliensis* → *Eugenia dombeyi

Eugenia cabelludo - *Cabelludo* {S} The fruits resemble large gooseberries in appearance. When fully ripe they are yellow, nearly one inch in diameter, downy externally, and with flesh that is juicy, subacid, and pleasant in flavor. Also has value as an ornamental plant. Brazil. POPENOE, W. 1920, TANAKA; **X88M**

Eugenia carissoides - *Cedar Bay cherry* {S} The edible fruits are red, pear-shaped, aromatic, and have a pleasant tart flavor. Australia. N84, P38, *Q93*{PL}

Eugenia cumini* → *Syzygium cumini

Eugenia dombeyi - *Grumichama, Brazil cherry* {PL} Fruits are deep crimson, the size of a cherry, with soft, melting flesh of a mild subacid flavor reminiscent of a Bing cherry. They are excellent to eat out of hand or may be used in jams, jellies and pies. Brazil, cultivated. GARNER [Pro], KENNARD, MORTON 1987a, POPENOE, W. 1920 [Cu], RICHARDSON [Re], STURROCK; D57, E29, E29{S}, F68, F85{S}, I83M, J22, N84{S}, P38{S}, *Q93*

Eugenia edulis* → *Phyllocalyx edulis

Eugenia foliosa* → *Amyrsia foliosa

Eugenia jambos* → *Syzygium jambos

Eugenia klotzschiana - *Pera do campo* {S} The pear-shaped, golden yellow fruits are used for jellies. They have soft, juicy, acid flesh, and are highly aromatic in odor and flavor. Occasionally cultivated. Brazil. POPENOE, W. 1920, UPHOF; **T73M**

Eugenia leuhmanni* → *Syzygium leuhmanni

Eugenia luschnathiana* → *Phyllocalyx luschnathianus

Eugenia malaccensis* → *Syzygium malaccense

Eugenia moorei* → *Syzygium moorei

Eugenia myrtifolia* → *Syzygium paniculatum

Eugenia pitanga* → *Stenocalyx pitanga

Eugenia polycephala* → *Syzygium polycephalum

Eugenia selloi* → *Phyllocalyx edulis

Eugenia smithii - *Lilly pilly* {S} The fruits are sometimes eaten although they are not highly regarded. Grown mostly for its decorative and adaptive qualities. It has been suggested that this species could be hybridized with other species that have better fruit. Australia. CRIBB, JOHNS; C9M, C56M{PL}, F85, *N79M*, N84, O53M, O93, P5, *P17M*, *Q25*, *Q32*, R33M

CULTIVARS

Purple: A form that bears purple fruit. N84, P5

Eugenia stipitata - *Guaba brasiliensis, Pichi, Araca-boi* {S} The yellow fruits are eaten, being among the largest of the genus, often 2 1/2 to 3 1/2 inches wide - up to 4 3/4 inches when cultivated. Fruit pulp is pale yellow, soft and delicate, sour, very aromatic, and has excellent juicing characteristics. Also makes an excellent dessert when mixed with whipped cream or frozen dessert toppings. Loses flavor when cooked and is best quick-boiled for jam. Amazonian region. HOWELL, MORTON 1987a; **U27T**

Eugenia uniflora - *Surinam cherry, Brazilian cherry, Pitanga da praia* {S} Ripe fruits are ribbed, crimson to purplish-black in color, and have juicy, aromatic, sub-acid flesh that is considered the best of the Eugenias. They are delicious eaten out of hand or can be made into jams, jellies, pies, compote, sherbet, drinks, and syrup. Unripe fruits are used in relishes and chutneys. Red colored fruits make a light red wine while the black fruits lose their color on fermenting and make a clear white wine. The aromatic leaves are used as a substitute for tea. Tropical America, cultivated. GARNER [Pro], MORTON 1987a, POPENOE, W. 1920 [Cu, Pro], RICHARDSON, RILEY 1971, STURROCK, UPHOF; A79M, C56M{PL}, D57{PL}, E29, E29{PL}, E29{PR}, F85, G96{PL}, *L5M*, N84, P5, P38, *Q25*

CULTIVARS {GR}

Black: Large, black fruit, 1 inch or more in diameter. Delicious, nectarine-like flavor. A lighter producer, with fewer crops per year than California cultivars. Originated in Florida. L6

Chamba: Large, plump, rounded fruits; 1 inch or more in diameter; skin bright orange-red; flesh very juicy, not tart but sweet with a distinct, refreshing flavor. Small, bushy tree. Originated in Kona, Hawaii. D57{OR}

Lolita: (Westree 317) Small black fruit, averages 1 inch in diameter; flesh moderately sweet, flavor excellent. Recommended for fresh eating, jams, salads, jellies and ice cream flavoring. Tree usually bears two crops, one in January and another in June. Originated in Carlsbad, California by Nelson E. Westree. Introduced in 1957. BROOKS 1972; I83M, L6

Lorver: Large fruit, 1 inch or more in diameter. Tree larger than Lolita and other California cultivars, can reach the size of a small tree. Produces fewer crops per year. Originated in Florida. L6

Nacha: (Westree 194) Large fruit, up to 1 1/2 inches in diameter; skin brilliant red, attractive; flesh firm but tender, juicy, sprightly subacid, sugar content moderate. Tree vigorous and productive, usually bears in June and January. Originated in Carlsbad, California by Nelson E. Westree. I83M

Vermillion: Large fruit, 1 inch or more in diameter. Delicious, nectarine-like flavor. Vigorous shrub, under good conditions can reach the size of a small tree. Originated in Florida. L6

Westree 369: Medium-sized, red fruit with good flavor. Tree extremely heavy bearing; precocious, bears as early as 3 years of age; produces well in dry weather. Will bear continuously under optimal conditions. Originated in Carlsbad, California by Nelson E. Westree. Introduced in 1971. I83M, L6

Eugenia uvalha - *Uvalha* {S} A small, yellow or orange, thin-skinned fruit that is used principally for making refreshing drinks. The flesh is soft, juicy and acid, with an intense and agreeable aroma. Brazil. POPENOE, W. 1920; N84, P38, S97M{PL}

Feijoa sellowiana - *Feijoa, Pineapple guava* {PL} Ripe fruits have the flavor of pineapple and strawberry and a delightful, penetrating aroma that can scent a room. They are best eaten out of hand but can also be used in pies, cakes, puddings, jams, jellies, ice cream, mousses, etc. The flower petals are very sweet and spicy and can be nibbled or added to fruit salads. They should be harvested after they have begun to soften. Brazil, cultivated. CLARKE, MORTON 1987a [Cu], POPENOE, W. 1920 [Cu, Pro], SCHNEIDER [Cul, Re]; B74, C9M{S}, C56M, D11M{S}, E13G{PR}, F16, H4, *I61*{S}, I76M{PR}, K38{S}, L29, L91M{S}, M16, N37M, *N40*{PR}, O53M{S}, etc. (for cultivars see Feijoa, page 330)

Luma apiculata → *Myrceugenella apiculata*

Marlierea edulis - *Cambucá verdadeiro* {S} The fruits are eaten raw or made into preserves. Brazil. CORREA; **X88M**

Mitranthes sartoriana - *Pichiché, Arrayan* {S} Often cultivated for its juicy fruits that are said to have a rich, spicy, subacid flavor. They are eaten fresh or after having been dried. Also the source of a refreshing beverage. Mexico. UPHOF; N84, P38

Myrceugenella apiculata - *Luma* {PL} Ripe fruits are deep purple to black and have soft, translucent white flesh. The flavor is aromatic, mildly sweet, somewhat like eucalyptus, the better fruits being much like Ugni molinae. Texture may vary from succulent and juicy to nearly dry. They are eaten out of hand. Chile, Argentina. HEDRICK 1919, RILEY 1982, SIMMONS 1972; N84{S}, P86

Myrciaria cauliflora → *Plinia cauliflora*

Myrciaria floribunda - *Rumberry, Guava berry* {S} The dark red to black fruits are used as the basis of a strong wine and a liqueur that were formerly exported from St. Thomas to Denmark. They have sweet, aromatic pulp and are also eaten fresh or made into jams and tarts. West Indies, Tropical South America. MORTON 1987a, UPHOF; **T73M**

Myrciaria glomerata - *Yellow jaboticaba* {S} The small, yellow fruits have sweet pulp and are eaten out of hand. Brazil. E29{PL}, E29{PR}, N84, P38

Myrciaria jaboticaba → *Plinia jaboticaba*

Myrciaria paraensis - *Camu-camu* {PL} The fruits are maroon or purple-black when ripe, soft and juicy, and either acid or sweet in flavor. Half-ripe fruits contain high levels of ascorbic acid and the juice is frozen or bottled and exported to the United States for the production of vitamin C tablets for the natural foods market. Brazil. MORTON 1987a; E29, E29{PR}

Myrciaria vexator - *Blue grape* {PL} The small purple fruits have a thin, sweet flesh and are eaten raw. Tropical America. E29, E29{PR}

Myrtus apiculata → *Myrceugenella apiculata*

Myrtus communis - *Myrtle* {PL} Dried fruits and flower buds are used for flavoring meats, poultry, sauces, liqueurs, and syrups. The sprigs were formerly added to wine to increase its potency. An essential oil, distilled from the leaves and twigs, is used as a condiment, especially when mixed with other spices. In Italy, the flower buds are eaten. Mediterranean region, cultivated. MORTON 1976, ROOT 1980b, SIMMONS 1972 [Cu], TANAKA; C3, C9M{S}, C13M{S}, C67M, D29, G96, I57, K22, K47T{S}, K85, L91M{S}, M82, N84{S}, O53M{S}

CULTIVARS {GR}

Triloba: (Sacred Myrtle) A form with three leaves at every joint instead of two. Esteemed by Jews for use in religious ceremonies and for decorating at the Feast of Tabernacles. SIMMONS 1972; D29, E48, M82

Myrtus foliosa → *Amyrsia foliosa*

Myrtus molinae → *Ugni molinae*

Myrtus mucronata → *Ugni molinae*

Myrtus ugni → *Ugni molinae*

Phyllocalyx edulis - *Pitanga tuba* {S} Fruits are ribbed, aromatic, acid, and suitable for jam. Brazil. UPHOF; **X88M**

Phyllocalyx luschnathianus - *Pitomba, Uvalha do campo* {PL} When ripe, the fruits are bright orange-yellow, thin-skinned, and have soft, melting, juicy flesh with a highly aromatic, slightly acid flavor. They are good eaten fresh and are said to make an excellent jelly. In Brazil, they are also used in preserves and carbonated beverages. Brazil. GARNER [Pro], MORTON 1987a, POPENOE, W. 1920, STURROCK; F68, *Q93*

Pimenta acris → *Pimenta racemosa*

Pimenta dioica - *Allspice* {PL} Dried fruits, with the aroma and flavor of nutmeg, cloves, and cinnamon, are used to flavor pickles, sauces, ketchup, sausages, soups, ice cream, etc. Mexican Indians used them for flavoring chocolate. The leaves may be used as a condiment or steeped into tea. An essential oil, obtained from the leaves, seasons meat products, baked goods, candy, and chewing gum. Tropical America, cultivated. ALCORN, GRIEVE, MORTON 1976, ROOT 1980b [Cul], TANAKA, UPHOF; A79M{S}, C56M, D57, F68, F85{S}, I83M, N84{S}, O93{S}

Pimenta racemosa - *West Indian bay, Bay-rum tree* {S} The bark and fruits are used as condiments. In the Caribbean, they are used in *blaff*, fresh caught fish plunged into broth. In the food industry, the leaf oil, oleoresin, and extract are used to flavor soups, meats, and condiments. Caribbean region, cultivated. MACMILLAN, MORTON 1976, TANAKA, VON WELANETZ; **T70, W59M**

Plinia cauliflora - *Jaboticaba* {PL} The thick-skinned fruits are purplish, grape-like, and have translucent, juicy pulp and a pleasant vinous flavor. They are primarily eaten out of hand but are also made into juice, jellies, jams, wine, and syrups. In taste and appearance they are remarkably similar to some cultivars of the muscadine grape. Tropical South America, cultivated. GARNER [Pro], MORTON 1987a [Cu], POPENOE, W. 1920, RICHARDSON [Re], STURROCK; A79M{S}, *B59*{PR}, C56M, D57, E29, E29{PL}, E29{PR}, F68, F85{S}, I83M, J22, N84{S}, O93{S}, P38{S}, *Q93*, etc.

CULTIVARS {SC}

<u>Paulista:</u> Large to very large fruit; skin thick and leathery; flesh juicy, subacid to sweet, quality very good; ripens relatively late; resistant to rust. Tree strong growing, highly productive though it bears a single crop. Introduced into California in 1904. MORTON 1987a; **T49M**

Plinia jaboticaba - *Jaboticaba de Sao Paulo* {S} A highly esteemed fruit in Brazil where it is eaten fresh, or used in jellies, wines and cordials. Closely related to P. cauliflora, it often furnishes many of the fruits sold as jaboticabas in the markets of Rio de Janeiro. Brazil. GARNER [Pro], POPENOE, W. 1920, UPHOF; N84, P38

Pseudanamomis umbellifera - *Monos plum* {PL} Small yellow fruits with juicy, sweet pulp that is eaten out of hand. Puerto Rico. KUNKEL; J36

Psidium araca* → *Psidium guineense

Psidium cattleianum* → *Psidium littorale

Psidium friedrichsthalianum - *Costa Rican guava, Cás* {S} The sulphur-yellow fruits have soft, white flesh that is highly acid and lacks the musky aroma and flavor that characterizes some of the other guavas. Flavor of the shell is somewhat like the pear and is excellent for making pies. The white pulp is used to make jams, jellies, and lemonade-like drinks. Pectin content of the fruits is high and they make a good firm jelly, even when ripe. Central America, cultivated. GARNER [Pro], MORTON 1987a, POPENOE, W. 1920, SIMMONS 1972, STURROCK, WILLIAMS, L.; E29, E29{PL}, E29{PR}, F85, J36{PL}, N84, P38

Psidium guajava - *Guava, Lemon guava* {S} Aromatic fruits are eaten raw, stewed, baked, dried, sliced with cream, or made into jellies, preserves, pies, shortcakes, drinks, chutneys, etc. A thick jam, called *goiabada* or *guava cheese*, is of commercial value in Brazil, Florida and Cuba. *Cascos de guayaba*, the stewed fruitshells, are a much esteemed dessert in the West Indies. Roots are said to be used in soups. The seeds are the source of an edible oil. Tropical America, cultivated. DUKE, GARNER [Pro], MENNINGER, MORTON 1987a [Cu], POPENOE, W. 1920 [Cu, Pro], RICHARDSON [Re], SCHNEIDER [Cul, Re], STURROCK, UPHOF; A44M{PR}, A79M, *B59*{PR}, C56M{PL}, E29, E29{PL}, E29{PR}, *L5M*, L6{PL}, L29{PL}, <u>L54</u>{PR}, P5, *P17M*, P38, Q46, R47, etc. (for cultivars see Guava, page 350)

Psidium guineense - *Brazilian guava, Aracá, Guisaro* {S} The small, greenish-yellow fruits are subacid to acid in flavor and lack the strong musky aroma of P. guajava. Ripe fruits are said to have a slight strawberry flavor and to make a distinctive, light pink jelly that is superior to that made from other guavas. Otherwise the fruits can be baked, stewed, or made into paste. Has been crossed with the common guava to produce dwarf, hardy, heavy-bearing hybrids. Tropical South America, cultivated. GARNER [Pro], MORTON 1987a, POPENOE, W. 1920, STURROCK, WILLIAMS, L.; F85, N84, P38

Psidium littorale - *Yellow strawberry guava, Chinese strawberry guava* {PL} The sulphur-yellow fruits are larger, sweeter, and more delicate in flavor than the red strawberry guava. Many people prefer them for eating out of hand and they are also excellent for blending with high-acid fruits of low pectin content for jelly making. Tropical South America, cultivated. POPENOE, W. 1920, STURROCK, UPHOF; C9M{S}, C56M, D57, E29, E29{PR}, E29{S}, F68, F85{S}, *G49*, *H71*{S}, I49M, *I61*{S}, I83M, L6, N84{S}, P38{S}, etc.

Psidium littorale var. longipes - *Red strawberry guava, Cattley guava* {S} Ripe fruits are subacid, aromatic, with somewhat the flavor of strawberries, and are eaten fresh or made into jellies, custards, ices, jams, sauces, shortcakes, wines, and refreshing drinks. The flavor is more pronounced than that of the yellow strawberry guava but lacks the muskiness of the common guava. Tropical South America, cultivated. CLARKE, GIBBONS 1967 [Re], MORTON 1987a, POPENOE, W. 1920, STURROCK, UPHOF; C9M, D11M, D57, E29, E29{PL}, E29{PR}, F68{PL}, *G49*{PL}, *I61*, I83M{PL}, L6{PL}, M20, O53M, O89, P38, *Q49M*{PL}, etc.

CULTIVARS {SC}

<u>John Riley:</u> Large, round fruit, 1 1/2 inches in diameter; skin dark red, pebbled; flesh cherry red, flavor excellent; seeds small, innocuous, numerous; ripens over an exceptionally long period, June to January. Tree bushy, slow growing; very hardy, no damage noted at repeated exposures of 26^0 F. Originated in Los Altos, California by Gary Meltzer. **T49M**

Psidium microphyllum - *Puerto Rican guava, Guayaba agria* {S} The small, yellow, aromatic fruits are relatively tart and are mostly used for making jelly, especially in Puerto Rico. West Indies. KENNARD, UPHOF; **U27T**

Psidium molle* → *Psidium guineense

Psidium pyriferum* → *Psidium guajava

Psidium sartorianum* → *Mitranthes sartoriana

Psidium sp. - *Criollo guava* {S} A heavy bearing, small-fruited guava. Excellent flavor, good for drying, and makes rich flavored conserves. Gives a high yield of jelly as it contains much pectin. A small tree thriving with almost no care. Often fruits in one year from seed and foot-tall seedlings have fruited so it should be a good container plant. Mexico. **F80**

Rhodomyrtus tomentosa - *Downy rose-myrtle, Ceylon hill-cherry, Hill gooseberry* {S} The small, purple fruits may be eaten out of hand and are said to make excellent pies. In India and Ceylon they are made into a jelly, which in flavor somewhat resembles apple-jelly, and a jam called *theonti*. Also valuable as an ornamental shrub with rose-pink flowers that turn purple as they age. Southeast Asia, cultivated. MACMILLAN, MAXWELL, POPENOE, W. 1920, STURROCK, UPHOF; F85, N84, P5, P38, *Q25*, *Q93*{PL}, R47

Stenocalyx pitanga - *Pitanga* {S} The refreshingly acid fruits are eaten. Brazil, Uruguay. HEDRICK 1919; **W59M, Z63**

Syzygium aqueum - *Water apple, Watery rose apple* {PL} Fruits are mildly fragrant, sometimes crisp and juicy, and usually of sweetish but faint flavor. They are eaten raw to quench the thirst, or made into a syrup. Superior types are sometimes sliced raw into salads. Tropical Asia, cultivated. BROWN, W., GARNER [Pro], MORTON 1987a, UPHOF, WESTER; N84{S}, *Q93*

Syzygium aromaticum - *Clove* {S} Flower buds are dried and used to season ham, sausages, baked apples, mincemeat, pies, preserves, pickles, etc. Also the source of an oil and extract important in the food industry for flavoring beverages, gelatine desserts, chewing gum, bakery products, ice cream, candies, and sauces. The fruit pulp is eaten. Dried flowers are chewed. Indonesia, cultivated. BURKILL,

DE SOUNIN [Cul], KUNKEL, MACNICOL [Re], MORTON 1976, TANAKA; F85, J22{PL}, N84

Syzygium coolminianum - *Blue lilly pilly* {S} The rounded, purple-blue fruits are eaten and are said to be among the best of the Australian Eugenias. They contain a single, small seed which often rattles in the central cavity when the fruit is ripe. They are eaten raw or made into jelly. Australia. CRIBB, JOHNS; *N79M*, *Q25*

Syzygium cordatum - *Water berry* {S} The purple-black, pleasantly acid fruits are eaten raw, made into a refreshing drink, or fermented into an alcoholic beverage. Southern Africa. FOX, F., SIMMONS 1972; N84

Syzygium cumini - *Java plum, Jambolan, Duhat* {S} Fruits are purple, olive-shaped, somewhat astringent, and may be eaten raw or made into jam, sherbet, jelly, juice, tarts, puddings, preserves, liquors, and a mild-flavored vinegar. The astringency is sometimes removed before cooking by soaking in salt water. In the Philippines, the powdered bark is used in the preparation of *basi*, a wine made from sugar cane juice. Tropical Asia, cultivated. GARNER [Pro], KENNARD, MORTON 1987a [Cu], POPENOE, W. 1920, RICHARDSON [Re], STEINKRAUS; D57{PL}, F85, I83M{PL}, *L5M*, N84, P38, Q46, R59

Syzygium guineense - *Water pear, Water berry* {S} Very ripe fruits, red to purple-black in color, are palatable and are eaten fresh or used for making beverages and vinegar. Tropical Africa. DALZIEL, FOX, F., UPHOF; N84

Syzygium jambos - *Rose apple* {PL} Ripe fruits are crisp, sweet, somewhat juicy, with a delicate rose-water fragrance. They can be eaten out of hand, stewed, candied, stuffed with rice and baked, preserved in syrup, used in marmalades, jellies, confectionery, and sauces, or fermented into wine. When cooked with custards or puddings they impart a rose flavor. The flowers are candied. Tropical Asia, cultivated. GARNER [Pro], HEDRICK 1919, MACNICOL, MORTON 1987a, POPENOE, W. 1920, RICHARDSON [Re], STURROCK, UPHOF; C56M, D57, E29, E29{PR}, E29{S}, F68, F85{S}, G96, I83M, L29, N84{S}, P38{S}, *Q25*{S}, Q46{S}, *Q93*, S54M, etc.

Syzygium leuhmanni - *Cherry alder* {S} The red, pear-shaped fruits are often borne in great quantities, and are eaten out of hand or used to make jelly. Also recommended for its highly decorative young foliage which has bright pink tints. Australia. CRIBB, JOHNS; *N79M*, N84, P5, P38, *Q25*, *Q32*, R33M

Syzygium malaccense - *Mountain apple, Malay apple* {PL} Ripe fruits are crisp and juicy, with a mild, refreshing, subacid flavor. They are often stewed with cloves or combined with other fruits in pies, tarts, custards, salads, cocktails, and fruit punch. When baked, the petals of hibiscus flowers are employed to impart a pink or deep red color. The flowers are preserved in syrup or eaten in salads. Young leaves and shoots, while still red, are eaten raw with rice. Tropical Asia, cultivated. GARNER [Pro], HEDRICK 1919, JOHNS [Cul], KENNARD, MORTON 1987a [Cu], OCHSE, POPENOE, W. 1920, RICHARDSON [Re]; D57, E29, E29{PR}, E29{S}, F85{S}, J36, N84, *Q93*

CULTIVARS {SC}

Kingston: One of the largest of all malay apples, having produced fruit up to 6 inches long and weighing over a pound. Good quality. Introduced into Florida from Jamaica, by William F. Whitman. Now widely grown in the tropics. WHITMAN; **T73M**

Rookman: Fruit very sweet, with a texture like that of a peach. Originated in Trinidad where it is grown commercially and sold in the markets. Introduced into Florida by Al Will. **U27T**

Syzygium moorei - *Robby, Durobby* {S} The large, rounded fruit is cream-colored and can be eaten raw or used to make jelly. Australia. CRIBB; *Q25*

Syzygium paniculatum - *Australian bush-cherry* {S} The juicy, aromatic, rose-purple fruits are often eaten out of hand to quench the thirst or made into jellies. Widely planted in California as an ornamental hedge. Australia. CLARKE [Re], UPHOF; *B41*{PL}, C9M, F85, *H71*, *I61*, I99, N84, O93, P5, *P17M*, P38, *Q25*, *Q32*, Q41, R33M, etc.

Syzygium polyanthum - *Indonesian bay, Daun salam, Laurel leaf* {PR} Dried leaves are used as an aromatic flavoring for sauces, soups, rice, tempeh, cookies, and vegetable dishes. The blackened leaves are simmered with the dish, then removed before serving. They can also be ground to a powder for use in marinades or in the making of Indonesian cookies. Ripe fruits are also edible. Available at Indonesian, oriental and specialty stores. Southeast Asia, cultivated. BURKILL, OCHSE, SHURTLEFF 1979 [Re], VON WELANETZ; A45, C94

Syzygium polycephalum - *Gowok, Kupa* {S} The violet-colored young leaves and shoots are eaten raw with rice. Ripe fruits have an agreeable sour flavor and are eaten out of hand or made into jelly. Has been recommended for improvement by scientific breeding. Indonesia. GARNER [Pro], OCHSE, UPHOF; **U27T**

Syzygium samarangense - *Samarang rose apple, Wax jambu, Java apple* {S} The fruits are pear-shaped, waxy, with flesh that is spongy, dry to juicy, subacid, and very bland in flavor. In Malaya, they are eaten raw with salt, cooked as a sauce, or stewed with true apples. Tropical Asia. GARNER [Pro], MORTON 1987a; E29, E29{PL}, E29{PR}, N84, P38{SC}

CULTIVARS {GR}

Pink: Colorful pink fruit, smaller than Srinark. Eating quality only fair. Grown mostly for its decorative appearance. WHITMAN; F68

Srinark: (Copper Colored) Large, white-fleshed fruit, usually with a single seed. Pulp crisp in texture; flavor somewhat bland. Grown on a limited commercial scale in Florida, where it is thought to be the best flavored wax jambu. Introduced into Florida from Thailand, by William F. Whitman. WHITMAN; F68

Syzygium tomentosum → ***Eugenia cabelludo***

Ugni molinae - *Chilean guava, Temo* {PL} The small, reddish-purple, aromatic fruits are pleasantly flavored and are very good eaten out of hand, added to cereals like blueberries, or made into jams, jellies, and refreshing drinks. Seeds are used as a substitute for coffee. The leaves are used for tea. Chile. GARNER [Pro], HEDRICK 1919, NATIONAL RESEARCH COUNCIL 1989, SIMMONS 1972 [Cu]; C56M, *F53M*, F70, K2

NAUCLEACEAE

Mitragyna parvifolia - *Káem* {S} The fruit is eaten raw or cooked. Northern India. TANAKA; F85

Mitragyna stipulosa - *African linden* {S} Fruits are reported to be sweet-tasting. West Tropical Africa. INGLETT; N84

Nauclea esculenta → ***Nauclea latifolia***

Nauclea latifolia - *Negro peach, Pin-cushion fruit* {PL} The sweet, juicy, reddish pulp of the fruit is eaten, and is said to resemble the strawberry in flavor and texture. Flower-heads are eaten as a vegetable. Tropical Africa. HEDRICK 1919, MACMILLAN, UPHOF; J36, N84{S}

Nauclea orientalis - *Negro peach, Gempol* {S} Young leaves and tender tips are steamed and eaten with rice. The fruit is consumed in Africa. Southeast Asia. OCHSE, TANAKA; F85, N84, *Q25*, R15M

Sarcocephalus orientalis → *Nauclea orientalis*

Sarcocephalus xanthoxylon - *Ndea* {S} The fruit is the size of a peach, with flesh-colored skin, and small black seeds arranged in a circular pattern like those of the kiwi. The edible pulp has somewhat the flavor of a mushy apple. Tropical Africa. **X44**

NELUMBONACEAE

Nelumbium speciosum → *Nelumbo nucifera*

Nelumbo lutea - *Water chinquapin, American water-lotus* {PL} Starchy rhizomes, when baked, are said to resemble sweet potatoes. Half-ripe seeds are delicious raw or cooked, having somewhat the flavor of chestnuts. Mature seeds are eaten parched, baked, boiled, or ground and used for bread or thickening soups. Young leaf-stalks and unrolling leaves are eaten as a potherb. North America. FERNALD, KINDSCHER, MEDSGER, TURNER 1979 [Pre, Re]; D58{S}, E7M{S}, *F73*, G26{S}, G47M{S}, G85, H30, I90M, J7M, *J25*, K34, K85M, M15, M73M, N3M, N11{S}, etc.

Nelumbo nucifera - *Pink lotus, Chinese lotus, Lin ngau* {PL} Rhizomes are eaten boiled, pickled, stir-fried, in tempura, or preserved in sugar. Also the source of a starch, *nagau fan*. Seeds are eaten raw, roasted, boiled, pickled, candied, popped like popcorn, or used as a coffee substitute. Young leaves can be used raw in salads or tossed with sesame oil. Petals may be floated in soups or used as a garnish. Stamens are used for flavoring tea. Tropical Asia to Australia. CHANG, W. [Re], COST 1988 [Cul], CREASY 1982, HARRINGTON, G. [Cu, Cul], HEDRICK 1919, HERKLOTS, MACNICOL, ROSENGARTEN, SHURTLEFF 1975 [Re], TANAKA, UPHOF, VON WELANETZ [Pre]; A79M{S}, E56{PR}, E66T{PR}, G20M{PR}, G85, H82, H91{PR}, J7, K25, K34, *K74*{PR}, K85M, L91M{S}, M15, M73M, *N40*{PR}, O93{S}, P38{S}, S7M{S}, etc.

CULTIVARS {S}

Man He: 110 days. Medium cultivar. Mainly eaten cooked; after cooking it is glutinous and fragrant; can also be eaten raw. Sow late April for a harvest in late August. Rootstocks have a large number of branches, should not be grow too closely. *O54*

Zao Hua: 90-95 days. A high-quality and extremely early cultivar. Fresh, sweet, crisp and tender; good for eating raw. Sow early to late-April for a harvest at the end of July. Easy to harvest, the rootstocks being distributed in the upper layer of soil. Tolerant to fertile soil. Closer spacing gives higher yields. *O54*

Nelumbo pentapetala → *Nelumbo lutea*

NYCTAGINACEAE

Abronia latifolia - *Yellow sand verbena* {S} The long stout roots are eaten by the Chinook Indians. Western North America. MEDSGER, YANOVSKY; I99, L13

Mirabilis expansa - *Mauka, Miso* {PL} Sun-dried tubers are boiled or fried, and eaten as a vegetable. Traditionally, they are chopped, boiled, and mixed with honey or syrup, toasted grain, tomatoes, and fish. The cooking water makes an especially flavorful drink. Their 7% protein content is an appreciable amount for a root crop. Leaves are eaten in salads. Grows well in cold, harsh climates. Andean South America. NATIONAL RESEARCH COUNCIL 1989, TANAKA; **W83M**

Mirabilis jalapa - *Four-o'clock, Marvel of Peru* {S} A crimson dye, obtained by steeping the flowers in water, is used to color cakes and jellies. The seeds are used to adulterate black pepper. Leaves are occasionally eaten. South America, cultivated. TANAKA, UPHOF; A16, A56, B77M, C44, E7M, E73M, F24, F92, G57M, H54, I99, J20, K53, O53M, O89, etc.

NYMPHAEACEAE

Castalia tuberosa → *Nymphaea tuberosa*

Nuphar advena - *Common spatterdock* {PL} Rootstocks are sometimes eaten raw, roasted, or boiled with meat. Seeds can be ground into a flour or meal and used to thicken soups. Eastern North America. HEDRICK 1919, UPHOF; D58, G26, G47M, H30, N11

Nuphar luteum - *Yellow water-lily* {S} Rootstocks are boiled and eaten as a vegetable. Also a source of starch. Seed kernels are parched and eaten with salt and cream or ground into flour for bread making. When parched, they swell considerably but do not crack like popcorn. A refreshing drink is made from the flowers. Leaf stalks are edible. Europe, North America. FERNALD, HEDRICK 1919, MACNICOL; *F73*{PL}, *J25*{PL}, N84, P38, *Q24*, S7M

Nymphaea advena → *Nuphar advena*

Nymphaea caerulea - *Blue lotus of Egypt, Blue water lily* {PL} Seed kernels are ground into flour or boiled whole. The starchy tubers are eaten boiled or roasted like potatoes. Flowers are used as a vegetable. Tropical Africa. FOX, F., TANAKA; P38

Nymphaea lotus - *Egyptian lotus, White lotus* {S} Seeds are pickled, put into curries, roasted in heated sand, or ground and mixed with flour to make cakes. Unripe fruits are eaten raw in salads. The flower-stems are eaten raw or cooked. Tubers are consumed raw or roasted. Tropical Africa, Tropical Asia. HEDRICK 1919, PONGPANGAN, TANAKA; F85

Nymphaea lutea → *Nuphar luteum*

Nymphaea odorata - *Fragrant water-lily* {PL} Flowerbuds are pickled or eaten as a cooked vegetable. The leaves are used in soups and stews. Tubers are also edible. North America. FERNALD, KUNKEL, TANAKA; C36, C64M, D62, *F73*, G85, H30, I44, J7M, *J25*, K34

Nymphaea stellata - *Blue lotus of India* {S} Rhizomes are sometimes eaten raw or roasted. Seeds are parched and eaten. The flowers are also edible. Tropical Africa, Tropical Asia, cultivated. HEDRICK 1919, TANAKA, UPHOF; F85

Nymphaea tuberosa - *Tuberous water-lily, White water lily* {PL} Seeds are rich in starch, oil and protein, and can be fried like popcorn or parched and the winnowed kernels ground into flour or creamed like corn. The bitter tubers are occasionally eaten. North America. FERNALD, GIBBONS 1979, PETERSON, L.; D58, G26, G47M, N11

NYPACEAE

Nypa fruticans - *Nipa palm* {S} Inflorescences are cooked in nipa syrup to produce an energy-giving sweetmeat. Sap is made into sugar, vinegar, or an alcoholic beverage, called *tuba, soom, tuwak*, or *toddy*. Unripe seeds are eaten raw, preserved in syrup, or used in making sweetmeats. In Malaysia they flavor a commercial ice cream, *Attap Chi*, and enter local ice confections. In the Philippines, nipa vinegar is used to prepare chicken *adobo* and *pacsiw*. Tropical Asia, Australia. HACKETT, HAMILTON, HEDRICK 1919, MENNINGER, STEINKRAUS, UPHOF; N84, R33M, S54M

NYSSACEAE

Nyssa aquatica - *Water tupelo, Water gum* {S} Fruits are sometimes eaten raw, but mostly they are made into preserves. North America. FERNALD, MEDSGER; D95{PL}, H4{PL}, K38, K63G, N37M{PL}, N84, O93, P5, *P17M*, *P63*, *R28*

Nyssa ogeche - *Ogeeche lime, Sour tupelo, Ogeeche plum* {PL} The large red fruits have an agreeably acid flavor and make very good preserves or refreshing lemonade-like drinks. Eastern North America. FERNALD; *I17M*, K18, K63G{S}, N84{S}

Nyssa sylvatica - *Tupelo, Black gum* {PL} The bluish fruits have a thin, sharply acid pulp that is pleasant to roll in the mouth as a masticatory. Also used in preserves. North America. FERNALD, MEDSGER; *B52*, C9, C9M{S}, D95, H4, H49, I77M, J16, J47, K38{S}, *M69M*, M76, N0, N7T, O53M{S}, etc.

OLACACEAE

Anacolosa luzoniensis - *Galo* {S} Thin-shelled nuts are eaten, said to have the flavor of a mixture of sweet corn and chestnut. They have good quality and may be eaten raw or cooked. Contains 3.9 to 11.1% protein, 1.8 to 8% fat, and 33.4 to 39.5% carbohydrates. Young fruits are delicious when boiled, while the pulp of mature fruits is also edible cooked. Philippines. CORONEL, MENNINGER, UPHOF; **X62**

Scorodocarpus borneensis - *Woodland onion* {S} The leaves are used for seasoning, as a substitute for onion or garlic. Seeds are boiled and eaten by natives in Malaya. Fruits are also edible. Malaysia, Indonesia. BURKILL, MENNINGER; F85

Ximenia americana - *Wild olive, Tallow-wood, Seaside plum, False sandalwood* {PL} The fruits, resembling yellow plums, have an acid-sweet, aromatic, almond-like flavor, and are eaten raw, pickled, preserved, or made into beer. Flower petals are eaten in soups. Seeds are the source of a non-drying oil, used in India as a substitute for *ghee*. Young leaves are used as a potherb. Roasted kernels are edible, but may be purgative if eaten in quantity. Tropics, Subtropics. HEDRICK 1919, KUNKEL, MENNINGER, MORTON 1977, ROSENGARTEN [Nu], UPHOF; D87G, J36, N84{S}, Q46{S}

Ximenia caffra - *Sour plum, Monkey plum* {S} The flesh, just under the skin, is refreshingly tart and is eaten raw. Both over-ripe and dried fruits are said to resemble prunes. Juice of the pulp is boiled and mixed with sorghum meal to make a tasty sour porridge. Seeds are eaten and also yield an edible oil. Southern Africa. FOX, F.; N84

OLEACEAE

Chionanthus virginicus - *Fringe-tree, Old man's beard* {PL} The fruits are said to be pickled like olives. Eastern North America. KUNKEL; A50, C9, C9M{S}, D95, E63, H4, H49, I77M, K38{S}, K47T{S}, K63G{S}, M77, N37M, N51, O53M{S}, etc.

Forestiera neo-mexicana - *Wild olive* {PL} Although small, it has been suggested that the fruits may be used like the true olive. Southwestern North America. TANAKA; *A19*, D95, G60, *G89M*, *I23*, J25M, J25M{S}, *R28*{S}

Fraxinus angustifolia - *Narrow-leaf ash* {S} In Morocco, the fruits are used as a condiment. Mediterranean region. UPHOF; F85, *N73*{PL}, N84, P5, *P17M*

Fraxinus excelsior - *European ash* {S} Very young winged fruits, or keys, are pickled in vinegar and used as a condiment for other foods. The leaves are sometimes used as an adulterant for tea. Also the source of an edible manna. Europe. DONKIN, HEDRICK 1919, MABEY, MICHAEL [Cul, Re]; G41{PL}, *G66*, K38, K47T, K63G, *N71M*, N93M, O53M, O93, P5, *P17M*, P49, *P63*, *Q32*, R78, S95, etc.

Fraxinus ornus - *Manna ash, Flowering ash* {S} The stems are the source of a sweet, nutritious exudate, or manna that is occasionally eaten. Eurasia. DONKIN, HEDRICK 1919, UPHOF; *A19*{PL}, A80M{PL}, D95{PL}, *G66*, I77M{PL}, K38, K47T, N0{PL}, *N71M*, N93M, O53M, O93, P49, *Q32*, R78, etc.

Fraxinus oxyphylla* → *Fraxinus angustifolia

Jasminum grandiflorum* → *Jasminum officinale

Jasminum humile - *Raggul cha* {S} The leaves are used as a condiment. In India, a tea is made from the leaves and bark. Eastern Africa. KUNKEL, VON REIS; C13M, F80, F85, H4, N84, O46, O53M, Q40, Q46

Jasminum odoratissimum - *Madeira jasmine* {PL} Flowers are used for flavoring or scenting tea. Madeira. TANAKA; G96, H4, H51M, L29, N37M

Jasminum officinale - *Poet's jasmine* {S} The fragrant flowers are eaten, or used to flavor or scent tea. They are the source of an essential oil that imparts a bittersweet, floral tone to baked goods, ice cream, candy, chewing gum, and *maraschino cherries*. Taiwan. LEGGATT [Re], MACNICOL [Re], MARCIN, MORTON 1976; C13M, E7M, F15M{PL}, F80, H51M{PL}, H79M{PL}, M82{PL}, N37M{PL}, O46, O53M, O93, *Q32*, Q40, Q46, S91M, etc.

Jasminum officinale 'Grandiflorum' - *Catalonian jasmine, Tea jasmine, Spanish jasmine* {PL} Dried flowers are used to scent Chinese tea leaf. TANAKA; E48, G96, H4, L29

Jasminum paniculatum - *Jasmine, Sieu-hing-hwa* {S} Flowers are used with those of J. sambac for scenting tea, in the proportion of 10 pounds of the former to 30 pounds of the latter, 40 pounds of the mixture being required for 100 pounds of tea. China. GRIEVE, HEDRICK 1919; F85

Jasminum sambac - *Arabian jasmine, Pikake, Sambac-mo-le-hwa* {PL} The dried flowers are used to scent tea leaf, especially Chinese-style *jasmine tea*. Also the source of an essential oil that is employed as a flavoring. Southern Asia. GRIEVE, MORTON 1976, TANAKA, ZEVEN; E48, G20, G96, H4, H51M, J27, L29, L59, M33G

Noronhia emarginata - *Madagascar olive, Noronha* {S} The small, olive-like fruit is eaten, and is said to have somewhat the flavor of a fresh lychee. Madagascar. MACMILLAN, UPHOF; F85, *L5M*

Olea africana - *Wild olive, Golden-leaved olive* {S} The fruit is used as a substitute for olives. Leaves are used as a condiment. Also a substitute for tea. Tropical Africa. FOX, F., KUNKEL; F80, F85, *G66*, *N79M*, N84, O53M, P5, *Q25*, *Q32*, R33M

Olea europaea - *Olive* {S} Fruits are usually pickled or cured with water, brine, oil, salt or lye. Those dried in the sun and eaten without curing are called *fachouïlles*. Cured fruits are eaten as a relish, stuffed with pimentos or almonds, or used in breads, hors d'oeuvres, soups, salads, *tapenades*, etc. *Olives schiacciate* are olives picked green, crushed, cured in oil, and used as a salad. Olive oil is used in salads and cooking and because of its distinct flavor is considered a condiment. Popcorn topped with olive oil and nutritional yeast is a popular snack with advocates of natural foods cuisine. The tree is the source of an edible manna. Mediterranean region, cultivated. BIANCHINI, DONKIN, KLEIN, UPHOF; A79M, C9M, C56M{PL}, F80, G96{PL}, H49, *J86*{PL}, K38, L91M, M82{PL}, N93M, O53M, O93, P5, *P17M*, *Q32*, etc.

CULTIVARS {GR}

Ascolano: Very large, ellipsoidal fruit; skin color very light even when perfectly ripe; pit very small. Contains very little bitterness and requires only moderate lye treatment. Excellent for pickles, but needs proper aeration during pickling to develop acceptable color. Tree a heavy bearer, widely adapted. Also known as the "white olive of Ascoli". **U8{SC}**

Barouni: Large fruit, almost as large as Sevillano. Trees spreading and easy to harvest. Withstands extremely high temperatures. The variety usually shipped to the East Coast for makers of home-cured olives. Originally from Tunisia. S59

El Greco: Selected for its heavy and reliable cropping and good oil content. One of the earliest bearing olives, producing good sized, small stoned fruit. Originated in New Zealand. *O97*, R77

Gordal: Medium to large, plump fruit; ripens early; resembles Sevillano. A popular pickling olive in Spain, producer of most of the world's table olives. One of the principal cultivars grown on the plain around Seville in Andalucia which has the perfect climate and soil for the mass production of olives. Q24M

Haas: Fruit is larger than Manzanillo with a smaller pit. Oil content moderate. Easy to cure, being excellent for canning and brining. Tree is a heavy, early bearer; bears bi-annually. Specially selected from Manzanillo parents. Dropped by I99M

Little Ollie: Bushy, multi-stemmed shrub, only 4 to 6 feet tall when mature. Dark green leaves. Produces medium-sized fruit of average quality. Makes an excellent border plant. D95, I83M

Manzanillo: Large, rounded-oval fruit; skin brilliant purple, changing to deep blue-black when mature, resists bruising. Ripens early, several weeks earlier than Mission. The pulp parts readily with its bitterness and is exceedingly rich when pickled. Excellent for oil and pickles. Tree spreading, vigorous, a prolific bearer. Introduced to California from Spain. WICKSON; B93M, G17, I83M, K39M{PR}, *L47*, *Q93*, S59

Mission: Medium-sized, oval fruit; skin deep purple changing to jet-black when ripe; flesh very bitter but firm, freestone; ripens rather late. Good for pickling and oil, especially ripe pickles. Average oil content. Most widely used for cold-pressed olive oil in California. Tree vigorous, heavy-bearing. More cold resistant than other cultivars. Grown at the old missions in California. *D23M*, K39M{PR}, S59

Picholine: Small, elongated fruit; skin light green, changing to wine red, then to red-black when ripe; pulp fleshy, firm-textured. Tree vigorous, medium-sized, bears heavy crops regularly. Cured olives have a delicate, subtle, lightly salty, nut-like flavor. Usually salt-brine cured. Widely grown in certain parts of Provence, France where it used for *olives farcies* (variously stuffed olives). Popular in gourmet and specialty markets. K52{PR}, O71M, R77

Pyramidalis: Self-shaping olive suitable for a large conservatory. Also grown outdoors in the South or South West of England, along a very warm wall. R77

Redding Picholine: Very small, perfectly oval fruit; skin dark purple or blue-black when ripe; ripens early, several weeks earlier than Mission. Loses its bitterness quickly during pickling, the resulting pickles being of sweet and of very pleasant flavor. Also produces oil of good quality. Tree small, makes a good rootstock on which to graft improved cultivars. WICKSON; U8{SC}

Rubra: Medium-small, ovate fruit; skin jet black when ripe; ripens 3 to 4 weeks earlier than Mission. Best suited for oil, but is also used for pickling. Tree large; precocious, often producing fruit the second year; an exceptionally prolific bearer. Very hardy and reliable even in dry situations. Originated in France. WICKSON; U8{SC}

Sevillano: Very large fruit, bluish-black when ripe; stone large, clinging; ripens early. Little oil content, only useful in pickling. Used for making Sicilian style salt-brine cured olives and the largest *Queen olives* of Spain; also the leading canning cultivar. Tree a strong grower and regular bearer; requires deep, rich, well-drained soil; will not stand much cold. KLEIN, WICKSON; K39M{PR}, *Q93*, S59

Verdale: Medium to large, almost round fruit; skin very green till nearly ripe, then vinous red, finally deep black, somewhat dull; pulp fleshy, dry; stone very large; ripens early. Flavor and texture when pickled very good. Primarily used for green olives. Tree dwarf, lacking in vigor; a regular, moderately heavy bearer. *Q93*, S59

Osmanthus americana - *American olive, Yen-kuei* {PL} Fragrant flowers are used to flavor or scent tea leaf. The fruit is macerated in brine and eaten like the true olive. North America. TANAKA; *G66*{S}, H4, K18, K47T{S}, N37M, N84{S}

Osmanthus fragrans - *Fragrant olive, Kwei-hua* {PL} The unripe fruits are preserved in brine like olives. Very fragrant flowers are used by the Chinese to impart a pleasant aroma to tea, wine and sweets such as lotus seed soup, pastries, and steamed pears. Available in oriental stores preserved in sweetened brine or as a sugary paste called *cassia blossom jam*. Eastern Asia. COST 1988 [Cul], TANAKA, UPHOF; G96, H4, *I62*, J27, L29, L59, M82, N37M, N84{S}, *Q32*{S}

Syringa microphylla - *Little-leaf lilac, Sung-lo-cha* {PL} Flowers are used as a substitute for tea. China. ALTSCHUL; A50

Syringa vulgaris - *Lilac* {PL} Flowers are eaten raw or folded in batter and made into fritters. They can be crystallized by dipping in beaten egg white and then rolling in granulated sugar. Europe. MACNICOL; A91, C9M{S}, *C33*, *C47*, D69, *F51*, F80{S}, *G9M*, G41, *H45M*, K38{S}, K47T{S}, K63G{S}, M76, N93M{S}, etc.

ONAGRACEAE

Chamaenerion angustifolium - *Fireweed* {S} The leaves are eaten raw, boiled, or used as a tea in some parts of Russia, known as *Kaporie tea* or *Kapor tea*. Vigorous new shoots are used as a substitute for asparagus. Young flower stalks may be added to salads. The sweet pith of the large stalks is chewed, used to flavor and thicken soups and stews, or made into ale and vinegar. Eurasia, naturalized in North America. FERNALD, GRIEVE, HARRINGTON, H., HEDRICK 1919, UPHOF; A2, A76, C82, D62, E15, F44, F80, I47, J25M, J40, J40{PL}, K47T, M77M{PL}, N9M, N9M{PL}, S7M, etc.

Chamaenerion latifolium - *Dwarf fireweed, River beauty* {S} The succulent new shoots and tender, fleshy young leaves are cooked and eaten. Leaves are used as a tea substitute. Preferred by some over common fireweed. Northern temperate region. FERNALD, GIBBONS 1979, HARRINGTON, H., HELLER, KUNKEL, PETERSON, L.; A76, I47

Epilobium angustifolium → *Chamaenerion angustifolium*

Epilobium hirsutum - *Great hairy willow-herb* {S} The leaves are used as a substitute for tea, known as *Kaporie tea*. In South Africa, they are sucked for their salty taste. Eurasia. FOX, F., GRIEVE; D62, *N71M*, N84

Epilobium latifolium → *Chamaenerion latifolium*

Fuchsia arborescens - *Pipilito, Flor de verano* {PL} The berries are sweet and edible. Central America. VON REIS, WILLIAMS, L.; E21M, F85{S}, L29

Fuchsia boliviana - {PL} The fruits have a sweetish taste and are eaten by the natives. Bolivia. ALTSCHUL; L29, N84{S}

Fuchsia cordifolia - *Melocotón* {PL} The large fruits are eaten or used to quench the thirst. Guatemala. WILLIAMS, L.; E21M, N84{S}

Fuchsia excorticata - *Konini, Kotukutuku* {S} The purple-black, sub-acid, perfumed fruits are eaten raw, or may be used in pies, tarts, cakes, desserts, and dessert sauces. They have a unique flavor, and like rose hips, should be combined with potato flour or corn starch to temper the slight astringency. New Zealand. BRYAN [Cu, Re], COLENSO, SIMMONS 1972; N84, S43M

Jussiaea suffruticosa* → *Ludwigia suffruticosa

Ludwigia scabra* → *Ludwigia suffruticosa

Ludwigia suffruticosa - {S} According to Tanaka, either the peel of the stem or the leaf is used as a substitute or tea. Kunkel says it is probably used as a spice. Southern Asia. KUNKEL, TANAKA; F85, N84

Oenothera biennis - *Evening primrose, German rampion* {S} The roots are sweet, somewhat resembling salsify or parsnips. They are scraped, sliced, and then eaten boiled, fried, scalloped, au gratin, or added to soups and stews. Young shoots are sometimes added to salads, but more commonly they are used as a potherb. The sweet flowers can be used as a salad or pickle garnish. Young pods are steamed and eaten. Northern temperate region. ANGIER [Pre, Re], FERNALD, GIBBONS 1979, HALL [Re], HITCHCOCK, VILMORIN [Cu]; B44, C13M, C81M{PL}, C92, E99, F24, G84{PL}, H61M, I39, J43, K53, N9M, N9M{PL}, O53M, R53M, etc.

Oenothera hookeri - *Hooker's evening-primrose* {S} The young, blanched leaves and shoots can be used in salads or boiled as a potherb. Roots are boiled and cooked like parsnips. The young, pod-like fruits can be cooked and eaten. Western North America. HARRINGTON, H., KIRK; A2, *E66M*, E73M, F44, F59, F59{PL}, F80, G60, G60{PL}, I47, K15, K47T, L75, N11M, O53M, etc.

ONOCLEACEAE

Matteuccia pensylvanica - *Ostrich fern* {PL} The thick, succulent, unrolled fronds, called *fiddleheads* or *croziers*, are salted and boiled, and served on toast with oil, butter, cream, or a cream sauce. Or they may be cut into small pieces, mixed with bread crumbs, milk, and eggs, and baked into a superior escalloped dish. They are available fresh in specialty markets or as canned and frozen products. The crowns can be forced for winter use. Rootstocks are eaten boiled or roasted. Northern temperate region. FERNALD, GIBBONS 1964 [Pre, Re], SCHNEIDER [Cul, Re], VON ADERKAS; B33M, B77, C9, C11T{PR}, C49, D61, D75T, E33M, E63M, I44, J42, *J75M*, L91M{S}, M98, N9M, N9M{S}, *N40*{PR}, O53M{S}, etc.

Matteuccia struthiopteris* → *Matteuccia pensylvanica

Onoclea sensibilis - *Sensitive fern* {PL} The young *fiddleheads* are sometimes used as a vegetable. Rootstocks have also been used as food. North America, Northeast Asia. MEDSGER, YANOVSKY; B33M, C36, C49, D75T, E33M, E63M, *F51*, I22, I44, J48, L91M{S}, M98, N7T, N9M, N9M{S}, etc.

Pteretis nodulosa* → *Matteuccia pensylvanica

ORCHIDACEAE

Aplectrum hyemale - *Puttyroot, Adam and Eve* {PL} The corms may be boiled for twenty minutes and served with butter. Eastern North America. PETERSON, L.; B61M{S}, D62, E33M, K47T{S}, N7T, N84{S}

Dactylorhiza maculata - *Adder's grass, Hen's kames* {S} *Salep* is made from the tubers. Eurasia. LOVELOCK, TANAKA; D62

Dendrobium salaccense - *Cooking orchid* {S} The leaves are added to rice that is being cooked, imparting a strong, pleasant flavor and aroma to the dish. Tropical Asia. BURKILL, UPHOF; **Z25M**

Epidendrum cochleatum - *Tree orchis* {PL} The pseudobulbs are used to provide an edible mucilage like that of okra. Tropical America. LOVELOCK; F75M, I57, N43M, N84{S}

Leptotes bicolor - {PL} The fruit is used in some parts of Brazil for flavoring food, especially ice cream. It has a coumarin-like odor and is sweeter than vanilla but less penetrating. Brazil, Paraguay. HEDRICK 1919, UPHOF; C30, F75M, F94, H20, N84

Orchis maculata* → *Dactylorhiza maculata

Orchis mascula - *Male orchis* {S} The dried root is sometimes cooked and eaten. Also a source of *salep*, *bassorine* or *sahlab*, a fine white to yellowish-white powder used as food. It is usually mixed with milk, honey, and spices to form a beverage. In India, it is used in sweetmeats and chocolates. A sweet porridge, *racahout*, is made from acorn flour, cocoa, sugar, and *salep*. Eurasia. HEDRICK 1919, MABEY, UPHOF, WATT; L50M{PR}, N84

Orchis militaris - *Soldier orchid* {S} Tubers are cooked and eaten. They yield the starchy, mucilaginous substance known as *salep*, obtained by macerating the pulp in water. Also used for sweetmeats. Temperate Eurasia. HEDRICK 1919, KUNKEL; N84

Orchis morio - *Gandergoose, Green-winged orchis* {S} The dried root is cooked and eaten. Also furnishes a *salep* of commerce. Salep is very nutritive and demulcent. It is boiled with milk and water and flavored with sugar and wine, cloves, cinnamon, and ginger. Eurasia. GRIEVE, HEDRICK 1919; N84

Tetramicra bicolor* → *Leptotes bicolor

Vanilla fragrans* → *Vanilla planifolia

Vanilla planifolia - *Vanilla* {PL} Principle source of vanilla pods or *vanilla beans*, used for flavoring ice cream, confectionery, chocolate, syrups, cakes, puddings, baked goods, soft drinks, yogurt, liqueurs, etc. Tropical America, cultivated. MORTON 1976, TANAKA, UPHOF; C43M, F69, F75M, G53M, G96, I57, N84{S}

Vanilla pompona - *West Indian vanilla* {PL} The short, thick pods, called *vanillon* or *vanilloes*, are used as a substitute for true vanilla in flavoring foods. Caribbean region. MACMILLAN, MORTON 1976; E48, H20

Vanilla tahitensis - *Tahitian vanilla* {PR} Pods are used for flavoring foods. Thought by some to be more delicate, more fragrant and moister than the common vanilla. Grown commercially in Tahiti and Hawaii. Polynesia, cultivated. MORTON 1976; F33, J66M

OROBANCHACEAE

Aeginetia indica - {S} A leafless, parasitic herb that grows on the roots of various grasses. It is prepared with sugar and nutmeg and eaten as an antiscorbutic. India. HEDRICK 1919; **U87, V84M, Y17M**

Orobanche cernua - *Tarthuth* {S} The roots are roasted and eaten. Mediterranean region to Southwest Asia. BAILEY, C.; **W59M**

OSMUNDACEAE

Osmunda cinnamomea - *Cinnamon fern, Zenmai* {PL} The young, unexpanded fronds, or *buckhorns*, are eaten as a nibble or cooked in soups. In Japan, they are prepared by simmering with deep-fried tofu in dashi (soup stock) and shoyu (soy sauce). Eastern North America. FERNALD, SHURTLEFF 1975, YANOVSKY; B33M, C9, C36, C49, D75T, E33M, *F51*, H63, I4, I22, I44, I77M, J37M, M77, N9M, etc.

Osmunda claytoniana - *Interrupted fern* {PL} Young fronds are eaten. The center of the clump below ground level is the source of a small edible pith called *fern butter*. Northern temperate region. FREY, TANAKA; B33M, B77, C9, C49, E33M, E63M, H33, H63, I22, N7T, N8, N9M

OXALIDACEAE

Biophytum sensitivum - *Surelle sensitive, Chua me la me* {PL} The leaves are eaten in Indochina. Southeast Asia. TANAKA; D62{S}, G96

Oxalis acetosella - *Sour-grass* {S} The sour leaves are high in oxalic acid, but small amounts may be used like sorrel in salads, soups, and sauces, or chewed for their mildly tonic and refreshing qualities. Northern temperate region. FERNALD, MABEY, MICHAEL [Re], VILMORIN [Cu]; N84, O48

Oxalis corniculata - *Procumbent yellow wood-sorrel* {S} Leaves are eaten raw in salads, cooked as a potherb with milder flavored greens, or used to give a sour flavor to other foods. The fruits are chewed as a refreshing nibble. Cosmopolitan. OCHSE; N84

Oxalis deppei - *Deppe's wood-sorrel* {PL} Young leaves are used like sorrel in salads and soups. The flowers are excellent in a salad, alone or mixed with corn salad. Fleshy roots are eaten boiled. Mexico, cultivated. HEDRICK 1919, VILMORIN [Cu]; G96, H51M, J7, J37M

Oxalis oregana - *Redwood sorrel* {PL} The leaves and stalks may be eaten raw in salads, or a mass of them is allowed to ferment slightly to make a tasty dessert. A sort of rhubarb pie is made from the sour leaf stalks. Western North America. KIRK; B92, D95, E63M, G37M, G60, I22, L26, N84{S}

Oxalis stricta - *Yellow wood-sorrel* {S} Leaves are consumed raw, cooked as a green vegetable, or chewed to quench the thirst. The seed pods, called *little bananas*, are edible. Flowers and roots are also eaten. North America. KINDSCHER, UPHOF, YANOVSKY; D58, K47T, N84

Oxalis tuberosa - *Oca* {PL} When dried in the sun the edible tubers become wrinkled, dry, floury, and sweet, and the calcium oxalate content is reduced. They are then eaten raw, boiled in soups and stews, or candied like sweet potatoes. Further drying produces *cavi*, which is eaten with honey or sugar cane as a dessert, and *chuña de oca*, a desiccated product that gives a distinctive flavor to stews. The leaves are edible. Andean South America. HERKLOTS, HODGE 1951, MARTIN 1975, NATIONAL RESEARCH COUNCIL 1989, ORGAN; *Q49M*

Oxalis violacea - *Violet wood-sorrel* {PL} The acid, salty leaves are eaten raw in sandwiches and salads or cooked as a potherb. Flowers make an attractive and tasty garnish for salads. Flower stalks and roots are also eaten. North America. KINDSCHER, MORTON 1976, YANOVSKY; I11M

PAEONIACEAE

Paeonia albiflora* → *Paeonia lactiflora

Paeonia lactiflora - *Chinese peony, Shao-yao* {S} Roots are boiled and eaten by the nomads of Northern Asia, who also powder the seeds to mix with their tea. Central to Eastern Asia. HEDRICK 1919; N84

Paeonia officinalis - *Peony, Common peony* {S} In Europe, the hot seeds were once ground into a spice and used to flavor ale or accompanying food. The flowers are eaten as a vegetable or used to scent tea. Eurasia. LOVELOCK, MACNICOL [Re], UPHOF; B77{PL}, C9{PL}, D62, L91M, N84, O53M, S7M

Paeonia suffruticosa - *Tree peony, Botan, Mu-tan* {S} Fallen flower petals are parboiled and sweetened for a teatime delicacy or cooked in various dishes. China. TANAKA; B9M{PL}, C9{PL}, D62, K38, *M65M*{PL}, N84, P49, *P63*, *R28*, R78

PANDACEAE

Panda oleosa - *Kana* {S} The oily seeds have a nutty flavor and are occasionally eaten. In Gabon and Cameroon, the oil or crushed seeds are used as a condiment or sauce. West Tropical Africa. DALZIEL, MENNINGER; N84

PANDANACEAE

Freycinetia banksii - *Kie-kie* {PL} The large, fleshy, thick white floral bracts are sugary and are eaten raw or made into jelly. Ripe fruits are also eaten. New Zealand. COLENSO, FULLER, HEDRICK 1919; G96

Pandanus amaryllifolius - *Pandan wangi, Daun pandan* {PR} The fragrant young leaves are cooked and eaten or used as a condiment. Fresh or dried, they add flavor, a distinctive musky odor and natural green color to tofu, jellies, doughs, curries, syrups, sauces, coconut rice, and the Indonesian and Malaysian sweets *chendol* and *nyonya kuey*. They are widely used in Sinhalese yellow rice and Indonesian *nasi kunyit* (glutinous yellow rice), being added to the cooking oil with other spices before the rice and liquid are added to the pot. Southeast Asia. COST 1988 [Cul], SHURTLEFF 1979, STONE, UPHOF, VON WELANETZ; A45, C94

Pandanus fascicularis - *Kewda, Padang* {S} Male spadices, popularly called flowers, are used for imparting flavor to betel nut. They also yield *kewda water* or *kewra water*, which is employed as a flavoring for syrups, soft drinks, Sinhalese curries, and an Indian rice dish called *biriani*. India. ATAL, DUTTA, VON WELANETZ; A88T{PR}, F74{PR}, Q46

Pandanus latifolius* → *Pandanus amaryllifolius

Pandanus odoratissimus* → *Pandanus tectorius

Pandanus odorus* → *Pandanus amaryllifolius

Pandanus tectorius - *Nicobar breadfruit* {S} Fleshy pulp of the fruit may be eaten raw, cooked, or made into flour, paste and thin, flat cakes. The flour is mixed with palm syrup or diluted with water to form a popular drink. Tender, white bases of the young leaves are eaten raw or cooked. The terminal bud is consumed like palm cabbage. Aerial roots are cooked and eaten or processed into a beverage. Seeds are consumed after careful preparation. Flowers and pollen are also edible. Inflorescence bracts are used for scenting coconut oil. Malaysia to Polynesia. ALTSCHUL, DEGENER, DUKE, HEDRICK 1919, MASSAL, TANAKA, UPHOF; F85, N84

PAPAVERACEAE

Glaucium flavum - *Horned poppy* {S} Seeds are the source of a clear yellow oil used in food. Mediterranean region. HEDRICK 1919, UPHOF; F85, L91M, *N71M*, N84, O48, O53M, *Q24*, R41, S7M, S55

Meconopsis nepalensis - *Himalayan poppy, Satin poppy* {S} An edible oil is extracted from the seeds. Himalayan region. TANAKA; K47T, L91M, N84, S3M

Papaver orientale - *Oriental poppy* {S} Said to be used as a condiment. Unripe capsules, though very acrid and hot in taste, are reportedly eaten as a delicacy. Turkey to Iran. HEDRICK 1919, TANAKA; B97M{PL}, C9{PL}, D62, F24, F35M{PL}, H63{PL}, J53, J73, K53, L86, *M65M*{PL}, N84, S55

Papaver rhoeas - *Corn poppy, Shirley poppy, Flanders poppy* {S} Young leaves are cooked and seasoned like spinach, or used as a flavoring in soups and salads. A syrup prepared from the scarlet flower petals has been employed as an ingredient in soups and gruels. They also yield a red pigment used for coloring, especially wine. The seeds are used in cakes, breads, and rolls or pressed for their oil, an excellent substitute for olive oil. Eurasia, cultivated. BIANCHINI, GESSERT [Cu], GRIEVE, HEDRICK 1919, LARKCOM 1984,

MABEY, MACNICOL [Re], UPHOF; A2, D26, D62, E7M, E33, F66, G59M, H80, I47, J53, J82, J88, M47M, N11M, O53M, etc.

Papaver somniferum - *Breadseed poppy, Opium poppy* {S} Young seedlings are eaten as a vegetable. Seeds are widely used in breads, cakes, rolls, milky soups, rice dishes, stews, curries, salad dressings and sweetmeats, or pressed for their oil. When crushed and sweetened, they are used as a filling for crêpes, strudels, pastries, etc. *Poppyseed oil* is used like olive oil in French cooking, where it is known as *olivette*. Mediterranean region to Asia Minor. BURR [Cu], HEDRICK 1919, MORTON 1976, PAINTER [Cul, Re], UPHOF, VON WELANETZ; A2, E7M, E99, I99, L79, L90M, N84, O48, R53M, S7M, S55

CULTIVARS

Hungarian Blue-Seeded: Capsules large; seeds grayish-blue, numerous. Flowers large, lavender, tulip-like. This is the cultivar commonly grown for its seeds which are used in baking and oil extraction. E59Z, F35M{PL}, O53M

Hutterite: Plants 2 to 3 feet tall, prolific. Capsule ovate. Flowers large, crinkled, pale white with a lavender-banded throat. Best appearance when massed. Used for breads and cakes. J25M, K49Z

White Persian: Seeds white, smaller and milder in flavor than the blue-seeded cultivars. White-seeded forms are preferred in India, Japan and some Scandinavian countries for use in breads, cakes and cookies. A88T{PR}, J73

PASSIFLORACEAE

Passiflora adenopoda - *Grenadilla de monte* {S} The orange colored pulp of the fruit is sweet and edible. Central America, Colombia. VON REIS; **Y17M**

Passiflora alata - *Maracujá grande* {S} Large, yellow fruits with an agreeable flavor, much appreciated for making drinks. Peru, Brazil. UPHOF; N84, O93, P5, P38

CULTIVARS {GR}

Ruby Glow: Very large flowers, 5 to 6 inches long; deep crimson petals and blue and white striped filaments with an intense sweet fragrance. Tropical looking, 6 inch, glossy green leaves are not bothered by caterpillars. Produces a delicious grapefruit-sized, yellow fruit when cross pollinated. G20, J23, L29

Passiflora ambigua - *Granadilla de monte* {S} The large, edible fruits are at first sweet, becoming sour after sucking for a while. Mexico to Panama. VON REIS, WILLIAMS, L.; **X94**

Passiflora antioquiensis - *Banana passionfruit* {S} Yellow, ellipsoid fruits have an aromatic pulp that is eaten out of hand, or used to prepare refreshing drinks. Similar to P. mollissima, but the fruit is juicier and of better eating quality, and the flowers are bright red. Colombia-Ecuador. NATIONAL RESEARCH COUNCIL 1989, UPHOF; L91M, N84, O93, *O97*{PL}, P38, *Q49M*{PL}

Passiflora caerulea - *Blue crown passion-flower* {S} Ripe fruits are eaten raw or made into a refreshing drink. Unripe fruits are boiled and eaten. The flowers can be made into syrup. Brazil-Argentina, cultivated. CROWHURST 1973, KUNKEL, SIMMONS 1972, TANAKA; B62{PL}, C56M{PL}, C85M, C92, D11M, D27, E89M, G20{PL}, G25M, H51M{PL}, J23{PL}, J27{PL}, J61M{PL}, L29{PL}, *Q32*, S91M, S92, etc.

Passiflora coccinea - *Scarlet passionfruit* {PL} The fruit is yellow-mottled and striped, edible. Mostly grown for the showy red and white flowers. Northeastern South America. MARTIN 1970, TANAKA; C56M, G96, H4, I57, N84{S}, O93{S}, P5{S}, *Q25*{S}

Passiflora edulis - *Purple passionfruit, Purple granadilla* {PL} When ripe, the aromatic fruits are allowed to wrinkle and develope sweetness, and are then eaten raw, juiced, made into syrup, or used in sauces, custard, cakes, sherbet, pies, fruit soups, candies, ice cream, etc. A soft drink called *passaia*, and a wine sold as *parchita seco* are made from passionfruit. The seeds yield an edible oil. South America, cultivated. MORTON 1987a, POPENOE, W. 1920 [Cu, Pro], SCHNEIDER [Re]; A79M{S}, *B59*{PR}, C9M{S}, C56M, E13G{PR}, E29, E29{PR}, F21M{PR}, F80{S}, G96, H51M, I49M, J61M, K38{S}, L6, L91M{S}, O53M{S}, etc.

CULTIVARS {GR}

Alice: Selected by Clive Simms Nursery from numerous seedling plants. Free flowering; self-fertile; with excellent flavored sweet fruit. S30

Black Knight: Fragrant, dark purple-black fruit, the size and shape of a large egg; flavor excellent. Vigorous, compact vine; self-fertile, very fruitful. Fragrant white and purple flowers. Handsome glossy foliage. Excellent for containers. G20, I83M, J23, L29

Crackerjack: A selected, heavy bearing, large-fruited form with purple-black, rounded fruits, much larger than normal for this species and full of flavorsome, juicy pulp. An espalier trained plant in a 12 inch pot can produce up to 50 fruits in a season. Fruits from early autumn through to winter. *O97*, R77

Edgehill: Similar to Black Knight, but more vigorous, larger growing, and with larger purple fruit. One of the best outdoor cultivars for Southern California. Originated in Vista, California. G20

Frederick: Large, nearly oval fruit; greenish-purple with a reddish cast; slightly tart flavor. Good for eating out-of-hand, excellent for juicing. Extremely vigorous, self-fruitful vine; very productive; more compact than P. edulis f. flavicarpa. Kahuna x Brazilian Golden. Originated in Lincoln Acres, California by Patrick Worley. I83M, J23

Kahuna: Very large, medium purple fruit; sweet, subacid flavor. Good for juicing. Vigorous, productive vine; self-fertile. Produces over a long season, beginning in mid-summer in southern California. Large, attractive foliage. J23

Lacey: A hybrid of the purple and the yellow forms (P. edulis x P. edulis f. flavicarpa). *Q93*

Paul Ecke: (Ecke Select) Medium-sized purple fruit of very good quality. Suitable for juicing and eating out-of-hand. Compact, very productive vine. Originated in Encinitas, California. I83M

Purple Giant: Very large fruit, dark purple when mature. P5{S}, *P17M*{S}, S92{S}

Rainbow Sweet: Small, round fruit, 2 inches long; an attractive mango-red color; pulp whitish, juicy, sweet, rich and delicious; small, black edible seeds. Vigorous, fast-growing vine. J22

Red Giant: A, large red-fruited cultivar that originated in Australia. P5{S}

Red Riveira: Large, round to elliptical fruit; weight 3 to 6 ounces; skin reddish-purple; flesh bright orange with orange juice in cavities, flavor tart-sweet. Natural hybrid between P. edulis and P. edulis f. flavicarpa. Originated in Kona, Hawaii by Confessor Riveira. D57{OR}

Red Rover: Medium to large, roundish fruit; rind an attractive, clear red color; sweet, notably rich flavor with tart overtones. Good for eating out-of-hand or juicing. Vine very vigorous and productive; compact; self-fertile. Kahuna x Brazilian Golden. Originated in Lincoln Acres, California by Patrick Worley. I83M, J23

Sunnypash: Giant black passionfruit grafted to P. caerulea to promote a stronger vine. Produces heavier crops on a wider range of soil types. S59

Passiflora edulis f. flavicarpa - *Yellow passionfruit, Maracujá peroba* {S} Origin unknown, may be a mutation of the purple passionfruit. The fruit is generally larger and the vines are much more vigorous and productive. The pulp and juice are more acid, and there is a higher percentage of juice to pulp than in the purple form. Grown in somewhat warmer climates. AKAMINE; D57{PL}, N84, O53M, O93, P5, *P17M*, P38, *Q25*, *Q32*, Q41, S92

CULTIVARS {GR}

Brazilian Golden: Large, golden-yellow fruits, larger than standard forms. Flavor somewhat tart. Extremely vigorous vine; requires cross-pollination. Extra large, fragrant flowers, white with a dark center; blooms during mid-summer. Produces one large crop beginning in late August or early September. I83M, J23

Golden Giant: (Yellow Giant) A large yellow-fruited cultivar that originated in Australia. P5{S}, R47{S}

Passiflora herbertiana - *Australian passionfruit* {S} The oval fruits are said to have a pleasant flavor. Australia. HEDRICK 1919; N84, O53M, R15M, R33M

Passiflora incarnata - *Maypop, Apricot vine* {PL} Ripe fruits are eaten out of hand, or made into jellies, jams, wines, sherbets, and refreshing drinks. The leaves are said to be delicious as a cooked green or eaten raw in a salad. Flowers are eaten as a vegetable or made into syrup. Southeastern North America. FERNALD, GIBBONS 1979 [Re], MACNICOL [Re], MEDSGER, SIMMONS 1972 [Cu], SMITH, J.; F80{S}, G84, I11M{S}, I19, I19{S}, I37M, I49M, I74, K20{S}, L55, L99M, M16, M77M, N84{S}

Passiflora laurifolia - *Water lemon, Jamaica honeysuckle, Belle-apple, Sweet cup* {S} The orange-yellow fruits have a fragrant, juicy, agreeably subacid pulp that is eaten fresh or processed into a refreshing beverage. One way of enjoying it is to make a hole in one end of the fruit and suck out the pulp and seeds. Tropical America, naturalized in Hawaii. MORTON 1987a; E29, E29{PL}, E29{PR}, F85, N84

Passiflora ligularis - *Sweet granadilla, Poka* {S} Considered by many to be the best of the passifloras. The orange-yellow fruits contain a soft, translucent, perfumed pulp of very agreeable taste. They are cut in half and eaten with a spoon, or the strained juice can be used for making cooling drinks and sherbets. Tropical America, naturalized in Hawaii. MORTON 1987a, POPENOE, W. 1920; D57{PL}, G20{PL}, L91M, N84, O93, *O97*{PL}, P5, P38

Passiflora maliformis - *Chulupa, Sweet calabash* {S} Sweet, juicy, aromatic fruits are said to have a grape-like flavor. The seedy pulp is eaten out of hand, made into cold drinks, or scooped from the shell and served with wine and sugar. Tropical America, cultivated. MARTIN 1970, MORTON 1987a, NATIONAL RESEARCH COUNCIL 1989; E29, E29{PL}, E29{PR}, N84, P5, P38

Passiflora manicata - {PL} The smallish, green fruits have orange pulp with few seeds and an agreeable, piquant flavor. They can be eaten out of hand or mixed with milk to make a pleasant beverage. South America. MARTIN 1970; C56M, J23

Passiflora mixta - *Curuba de indio* {PL} Green to greenish yellow fruits have a pleasant, aromatic flavor similar to those of P. manicata and may be used in a similar manor. Central America to Bolivia. MARTIN 1970, PEREZ-ARBELAEZ; J23

Passiflora mollissima - *Banana passionfruit, Tacso, Curuba de Castilla* {S} The yellow, oblong, aromatic fruits are eaten out of hand, used in ice creams, cocktails, fruit salads, jellies, pies, puddings, sauces and sherbets, or made into a liqueur, *crema de curuba*. The juice is highly prized and is also fermented into wine. Andean South America. MORTON 1987a, NATIONAL RESEARCH COUNCIL 1989, UPHOF; A79M, C56M{PL}, F80, J23{PL}, L91M, N84, O53M, O89, P5, *P17M*, P38, R47, S44, S91M, S92, etc.

Passiflora platyloba - *Montesa granadilla, Granadilla ácida* {PL} The acid fruits are used in making ices and refreshing drinks. Central America. KUNKEL, WILLIAMS, L.; G96

Passiflora quadrangularis - *Giant granadilla* {S} Unripe fruits are steamed or boiled and eaten in soups, or cut into pieces, breaded, and cooked in butter with pepper and nutmeg. The bland, melon-like pulp of the ripe fruit, with the inner skin removed, is eaten raw, candied, canned in syrup, used in fruit salads, pies, jellies, cold drinks, sauces, wine, or served with sugar and shaved ice. Roots of old vines are baked or roasted and eaten like yams. Tropical America, cultivated. DUKE, MORTON 1987a, OCHSE, UPHOF; A79M{PL}, E29, E29{PL}, E48{PL}, G20{PL}, G96{PL}, J22{PL}, L91M, N84, O53M, O93, P5, *P17M*, P38, *Q32*, Q41, etc.

Passiflora rubra - *Pomme de liane zombie* {S} Fruits are eaten or added to *chicha*. Said to contain a narcotic. Tropical America. TANAKA, VON REIS; **V84**

Passiflora seemannii - *Guate-guate* {S} Fruits are eaten raw or mixed with milk to make a *fresco*. Panama-Colombia. DUKE; N84, O93, P5

Passiflora serrato-digitata - *Tagua-tagua* {PL} The yellow, globose, brittle fruit has sweet, white pulp said to have the flavor of guava. Tropical America. MARTIN 1970; J23

Passiflora suberosa - *Corky-stemmed passionflower* {PL} Small bluish-black fruits are sometimes eaten raw by children. Tropical South America. CRIBB, MORTON 1977; F85{S}, G96

Passiflora tripartita - *Tacso* {S} Fruits are oblong, deep yellow when ripe, often blushed with red on one side. The pulp is deep orange colored, juicy, of pungent subacid flavor. They are eaten out of hand or used to prepare refreshing drinks and ice creams. Ecuador. POPENOE, W. 1924; **Z25M**

Passiflora van-volxemii → ***Passiflora antioquiensis***

Passiflora vitifolia - *Grape-leaved passionfruit* {PL} Yellowish fruits with a thin, parchment-like shell. White pulp, very fragrant, with a sweet to subacid flavor. Used as a dessert or for making refreshing beverages. Central America to Peru. MARTIN 1970; E29, G96

CULTIVARS {GR}

Scarlet Flame: Large, 5 to 7 inch, bright red-scarlet flowers that cover the plant. If cross pollinated, an egg-shaped fruit is produced that is ornamental, with white spots and stripes on a watermelon green ground color. It is tart and fragrant with the taste of strawberries, and as with P. edulis, it should be allowed to become wrinkled before eating. G20, J23, J27

Passiflora warmingii - *Maracujá mirim* {S} The ovoid fruits have a white, pleasant flavored pulp that is preserved in syrup. Colombia-Brazil. UPHOF; **X47**

Tacsonia mollissima → *Passiflora mollissima*

PEDALIACEAE

Ceratotheca sesamoides - *False sesame* {S} Leaves are consumed as a vegetable or added to soups for their mucilaginous properties. Seeds are eaten like those of sesame, and are also put in soups with the leaves. They also yield an edible oil. Often sold in markets. Tropical Africa. TANAKA, UPHOF, ZEVEN; N84

Pedalium murex - *Burra gookeroo* {S} Leaves are eaten as a vegetable. The leafy stems have been used to thicken buttermilk. Tropical Africa, Tropical Asia. HEDRICK 1919, UPHOF, WATT; F85, N84

Sesamum alatum - *Gazelle's sesame, Tacoutta* {S} The seeds are ground into flour, used in soups, or pressed for their edible oil. Leaves are used as a vegetable. Tropical Africa. DALZIEL, KUNKEL, TANAKA, ZEVEN; **U71M, Z77M**

Sesamum indicum - *Sesame* {S} Seeds are eaten dry, toasted, sprinkled on breads, cakes, and cookies, fermented into *tempeh*, or used for *halwa* and other confections. They yield an oil, sometimes called *bene oil*, used in salads, margarine, and shortenings, or roasted and employed as a flavoring. *Gomashio* is a seasoning made of the roasted, ground seeds mixed with salt. Crushed seeds, hulled or unhulled, form sesame paste, sesame butter, and *tahini*. Sprouted seeds are eaten in salads. Leaves are eaten raw in salads, as a potherb, or in beverages and soups. Sesame seed presscake is made into confections or fermented into *dageh*. In the Sudan, a filtrate of the ashes from burnt stalks is added to stews. Tropical Africa, cultivated. BEDIGIAN, HARRINGTON, H. [Cu, Cul], OCHSE, PAINTER [Re], ROSENGARTEN, SHURTLEFF 1975, SHURTLEFF 1979, TANAKA; C9{PL}, C11, C13M, E7M, E59, F24, G47, G68, J73, K22, O53M (also see Sprouting Seeds, page 485)

CULTIVARS

__90 Day:__ Seed from the Organic Seed Program at the University of California, Davis. I99

__Black Seeded:__ Plants tall and lanky, branching, susceptible to lodging and shattering. Seeds are jet black, not as bitter as tan types, popular in oriental cooking. Often toasted and ground to a powder, mixed with sugar, and used for coating certain Chinese sweets. COST 1988 [Cul]; E66T{PR}, F85, H91{PR}, *K74*{PR}

__Black Thai:__ 120 days. Very tasty black seeds, esteemed in oriental cooking. Drought tolerant plant, 5 to 6 feet tall, with much candelabra-like tillering. Landrace from Thailand. K49T

__Brown Turkey:__ 115 days. Dark brown seeds. Drought tolerant plant, 5 to 6 feet tall. Harvest when 5 to 10% of seed capsules are beginning to open. Landrace from Turkey. K49T

__Tan Anatolia:__ 118 days. Light-colored seeds similar to commercial sesame. Drought tolerant plant, 5 to 6 feet tall. Landrace from the central plateau of Asia Minor. K49T

__White Seeded:__ Selected for its very light seeds. Plants are quite tall and not especially early. **T76**

Sesamum orientale → *Sesamum indicum*

Sesamum radiatum - *Black beniseed, Ekuku* {S} Young leaves and shoots are finely cut, cooked and eaten with cereals or added to soups. They have a mucilaginous texture and unpleasant smell. Seeds are eaten and also yield an edible oil. Tropical Africa, cultivated. DALZIEL, VAN EPENHUIJSEN, ZEVEN; N84

PENAEACEAE

Penaea mucronata - {S} Source of a tragacanth-like gum composed of yellowish-red, roundish, small grains, having a liquorice taste. Southern Africa. UPHOF; N84, R41, R77M

PEPEROMIACEAE

Peperomia acuminata - *Culantro de montana* {PL} Leaves are used as a seasoning, either dried or boiled. Tropical America. VON REIS; E48

Peperomia maculosa - *Cilantro peperomia* {S} The coriander-flavored leaves are used for seasoning beans and meats. Sold in local markets. Tropical America. ALCORN; E48, N84, O53M, O93, *Q32*

Peperomia pellucida - *Greenhouse tea plant, Suna-kôsho* {S} A small, weedy plant with succulent leaves and shoots that can be eaten in salads or used as a potherb. In the West Indies, the leaves are also brewed into tea. Tropical America. MARTIN 1975, ZEVEN; N84

PERIPLOCACEAE

Hemidesmus indicus - *Indian sarsaparilla* {S} Roots are the source of a syrup used as a flavoring agent in foods, instead of true *sarsaparilla* (Smilax spp.). Southern Asia. TANAKA; F85, N84

Mondia whytei - {S} The root is aromatic and is said to have a vanilla-like flavor. It is used by Zulus to make a beverage similar to ginger beer. Leaves are also edible. Southern Africa. FOX, F., MARTIN 1975; **Y78**

Tacazzea apiculata - {S} The small, yellow-green flowers, sometimes tinged with purple, are quite decorative and are considered edible. Tropical Africa. IRVINE 1960; N84

PHILESIACEAE

Lapageria rosea - *Chilean bellflower, Copihue* {S} The fruits are yellow, the size of an egg, and have sweet, white, juicy pulp that is eaten fresh or processed. National flower of Chile. Chile, cultivated. HEDRICK 1919, VALENZUELA; L91M, O53M, P86{PL}, R77{PL}

PHYTELEPHASIACEAE

Phytelephas macrocarpa - *Ivory nut palm* {S} Young shoots are eaten as a vegetable. Fruits are consumed when young or used as a coffee substitute. The sweet liquid of the unripe seed has been used to quench the thirst. Tropical America, cultivated. HEDRICK 1919, KUNKEL, MENNINGER; N84

PHYTOLACCACEAE

Phytolacca acinosa - *Indian pokeberry* {S} The leaves are boiled and eaten like spinach or used in curries. Young shoots are used as a substitute for asparagus. Tropical Asia. BURKILL, HEDRICK 1919, TANAKA, WATT; F80, F85, N84, O53M, Q40

Phytolacca acinosa var. esculenta - *Yama-gobo* {S} Young leaves are cooked and eaten like spinach, oil-roasted, or put in soups. Roots are also edible. Tropical Asia. BROWN, W., BURR, TANAKA; S44

Phytolacca americana - *Pokeweed, Pokeberry, Poke salad* {S} Unfolding leaves are cooked and served like spinach. Young shoots are excellent when prepared like asparagus, or they can be made into pickles. The tender, clear, inner portion may be rolled in white corn meal and fried. They are sometimes blanched before using, and also forced in dark cellars for winter use. Ripe berries are used for coloring wine, frostings, and candies. Seeds and roots are poisonous. North America. ANGIER [Re], BURR [Cu], FERNALD, GIBBONS 1962 [Pre, Re], MEDSGER, MORTON 1977, UPHOF; C11, C13M, D58, E61{PL}, F37T{PL}, F80, G68, I99, J82, K47T, K49M, N9M, N9M{PL}, S55

CULTIVARS

__White Stem:__ Parent plant has white stems and the berries yield a golden-peach dye instead of purple. It is not known if it comes true from seed. F80

Phytolacca decandra → *Phytolacca americana*

Phytolacca dioica - *Bella sombra* {S} Young leaves and shoots are cooked and eaten as vegetables. Fruits are made into jellies and jams or used to give red color to wines. Argentina, cultivated. FOX, F., TANAKA; C9M, F80, *G66*, I33, L50{PL}, N84, O53M, O93, P5, Q41, S44, S95

Phytolacca esculenta → *Phytolacca acinosa var. esculenta*

Phytolacca rivinoides - *Venezuela pokeberry* {S} Cooked leaves and shoots are eaten as a vegetable. Leaves are boiled and used for tea. Tropical America. ALTSCHUL, UPHOF, WILLIAMS, L.; F85

PINACEAE

Abies amabilis - *Amabilis fir* {S} Young branch tips are used as a substitute for tea. Northwestern North America. TURNER 1978; A2, *B60*{PL}, B94, *C33*{PL}, D95{PL}, *J75M*{PL}, K38, K47T, K63G, *K75*, *N71M*, N84, *R28*, R78

Abies balsamea - *Balsam fir* {S} The aromatic, resinous pitch that exudes from the trunk, called *Canada balsam* or *spruce gum*, is molded into short sticks and used for chewing. It yields an oleoresin used to flavor candy, baked goods, ice cream and beverages. Inner bark can be ground into flour and used as an emergency food. Tips of twigs are used for tea. Eastern North America. MEDSGER, MORTON 1976, PETERSON, L., TURNER 1978; *B60*{PL}, B94, *C33*{PL}, D45{PL}, *G9M*{PL}, H49{PL}, I4{PL}, J70, K38, K63G, *K75*, N84, O53M, O93, R78, etc.

Abies excelsior - *Great silver fir* {S} Young shoots are used as a tea substitute. The inner bark, or cambium, is used as an emergency food. Northwestern North America. TURNER 1978, YANOVSKY; A2, *B60*{PL}, C9M, *C33*{PL}, D95{PL}, E47, I15, I47, I99, J26{PL}, K38, *K75*, L91M, *M51M*, O53M, etc.

Abies grandis → *Abies excelsior*

Abies lasiocarpa - *Subalpine fir* {S} The branch tips are used as a substitute for tea. Western North America. TURNER 1978; B94, C9M, *C33*{PL}, D95{PL}, *G66*, I15, I47, J26{PL}, *J75M*{PL}, K38, K63G, *K75*, L75, N84, O53M, *R28*, R78, etc.

Larix occidentalis - *Western larch* {S} *Larch gum*, exuded from the trunk and branches, is sometimes used for chewing. In the food industry it has become a substitute for gum arabic and serves as a thickener, stabilizer, emulsifier, and binder. The sap is made into a sweet syrup. Also the source of an edible manna. Western North America. BROUK, DONKIN, HART, YANOVSKY; A2, B94, *G66*, I15, I47, J26{PL}, *J75M*{PL}, K38, K63G, M35M{PL}, N84, O53M, P49

Picea abies - *Norway spruce* {PL} The leafy branch or young shoot is used in the preparation of *spruce beer*. Eurasia. HEDRICK 1919; *B99M*, C11M, *D32*, D45, *G9M*, H49, I4, J16, J47, J70{S}, K38{S}, K47T{S}, K63G{S}, *M51M*, O53M{S}, etc.

Picea excelsa → *Picea abies*

Picea glauca - *White spruce* {PL} *Spruce oil*, distilled from the leaves and twigs, is used in the food industry to flavor chewing gum, ice cream, soft drinks, and candy. Young cones are eaten roasted, fried, or pickled. The inner bark is used as an emergency food. The trunk yields a gum used for chewing. North America. FERNALD, KUNKEL, MORTON 1976; *B99M*, C11M, *D32*, D45, *G9M*, H49, I4, J16, J70{S}, *J75M*, K38{S}, K63G{S}, *K75*{S}, O53M{S}, *Q32*{S}, etc.

Picea mariana - *Black spruce* {S} The young twigs are boiled with honey, molasses, or maple sap and fermented with yeast to produce the famous beverage *spruce beer*. A resinous exudation, *spruce gum*, is collected from the branches and used as a masticatory. Also a source of *spruce oil*, used commercially for flavoring. North America. GIBBONS 1962 [Re], MORTON 1976, UPHOF; B94, *F38*, *G66*, *J75M*{PL}, K38, K63G, *N71M*, N84, P49, *P63*, R78

Pinus armandii - *Chinese white pine, Yu-sung* {PL} The seeds are eaten and are esteemed as a great delicacy. China. TANAKA; A51M, B94{S}, D95, F85{S}, G43M, I83M, N84{S}, *P63*{S}

Pinus ayacahuite - *Mexican white pine* {S} The Tepehuan of Chihuahua eat the seeds in the western Sierra Madre. Mexico. LANNER; B94, E6{PL}, F85, G43M{PL}, I28{PL}, *P63*, S7G, S95

Pinus cembra - *Swiss stone pine* {S} Seeds are eaten in certain pastries and dairy foods. They also yield an edible oil. Eurasia. HEDRICK 1919, JAYNES, UPHOF; C9M, D37{PL}, E6{PL}, E47, E87{PL}, F80, J47{PL}, K22{PL}, K38, K47T, M35M{PL}, N0{PL}, *N71M*, N93M, *P17M*, *Q32*, etc.

Pinus cembroides - *Mexican pinyon* {S} The oily seed kernels are eaten raw, roasted, ground into flour for baking into cakes, or made into a nut butter. Of all the piñons, they are richest in protein and the lowest in starch. Southwestern America. JAYNES, LANNER, MENNINGER; B94, *F38*, I83M{PL}, N51{PL}, O93, P38, *P63*

Pinus cembroides var. edulis → *Pinus edulis*

Pinus cembroides var. maximartinezii → *Pinus maximartinezii*

Pinus cembroides var. monophylla → *Pinus monophylla*

Pinus cembroides var. parryana → *Pinus x quadrifolia*

Pinus coulteri - *Coulter's pine, Big-cone pine* {S} The large seeds are eaten in California. Southwestern North America. MENNINGER, UPHOF; B94, C9M, D95{PL}, D96, G60{PL}, *G66*, I83M{PL}, K38, K47T, K63G, *N71M*, N93M, O93, P5, *Q32*, etc.

Pinus densiflora - *Japanese red pine* {S} Seeds are eaten. The male strobili, inner bark, young fruits, and leaves have all been recorded as being edible. Japan, Korea. TANAKA; A80M{PL}, B9M{PL}, C9M, D95{PL}, E47, F80, *G66*, I77M{PL}, K38, K47T, N0{PL}, *N71M*, O53M, *P39*, *Q32*, etc.

Pinus edulis - *Colorado piñon, Rocky Mountain nut pine* {S} The oily, protein-rich seeds are eaten raw or roasted, or used in breads, cookies, confectionery, nut butters, ice cream, sauces, stuffings, pilafs, etc. Or they can be ground into a meal and used in gruels, soups, and puddings, or mixed with cornmeal or sunflower seed meal. The needles are brewed into a tea. Soft centers of green cones, when roasted, form a syrupy food. The sweet cambium is cut into thin strips and cooked like spaghetti. Southwestern North America. ANGIER [Re], HARRINGTON, H., LANNER [Nu, Re], MEDSGER; C9M, C11G{PR}, D95{PL}, E47, F43M{PL}, G43M{PL}, H49{PL}, I15, I25M, I83M{PL}, J25M, J26{PL}, J70, K38, L75, *P17M*, etc.

Pinus excelsa → *Pinus wallichiana*

Pinus gerardiana - *Chilgoza pine* {S} The seeds are eaten raw or roasted as a dessert in the same way as pistachio nuts. They are greatly appreciated in areas of the world where they grow, and are gathered and sold in native markets. Large quantities are imported into India from Afghanistan. Himalayan region. MENNINGER; B94, D95{PL}, I83M{PL}, K63G, *N79M*, N84, O46, O53M, *P17M*, *P63*, Q12, Q18, Q40, Q46

Pinus griffithii → *Pinus wallichiana*

Pinus jeffreyi - *Jeffrey pine* {S} The large seeds are eaten. Western North America. MENNINGER; B9M{PL}, B94, C9M, *C73*{PL}, D95{PL}, D96, E4{PL}, E47, G43M{PL}, G60{PL}, *G66*, *I62*{PL}, K38, *K75*, N93M, etc.

Pinus koraiensis - *Korean nut pine, Chinese nut pine* {S} Seeds are eaten raw or roasted, used as an ingredient of candies, glutinous rice desserts, congee, fancy kimchi, a kind of steak tartare, or fried as a garnish for savory dishes. Large quantities are exported by China. Eastern Asia. COST 1988 [Cul, Re], ROSENGARTEN; B9M{PL}, B96{PL}, C9M, D95{PL}, E7M, E47, E87{PL}, E91M{GR}, F43M{GR}, F80, I25M, K38, M75{PL}, M92{PL}, *N71M*, *P39*, etc.

CULTIVARS {GR}

Gibbs: Original tree in St. Paul d'Abbortsford, Quebec is over 100 years old and considered the oldest Korean pine nut in North America. L27M{PL}, N24M, N24M{PL}

Grimo: An improved selection from Ontario, Canada. N24M

Morgan: Improved type with large seeds. N24M

Pinus lambertiana - *Sugar pine* {S} When cut into or wounded, the heartwood exudes a sap that forms lumps of a sugary substance that is sometimes used for sweetening food. When used in quantity it is cathartic. The seeds have a sweet kernel that is eaten raw, roasted, or pounded into cakes. Pacific Coast of North America. DONKIN, HEDRICK 1919, MEDSGER; A2, B94, C9M, *C73*{PL}, D95{PL}, D96, E4{PL}, *G66*, I99, K38, K47T, *K75*, *N71M*, O53M, P5, etc.

Pinus maximartinezii - *Martinez piñon* {S} The edible seeds are very large, up to an inch long and as tasty as those of other species of piñon pine. Sold in the marketplace of Juchipila, Zacatecas. Mexico. LANNER; B94, D95{PL}, I83M{PL}, N84, O93, *P63*

Pinus monophylla - *Single leaf piñon* {S} Seeds are eaten raw or roasted, or ground and made into pancakes. They are the starchiest of the piñons and have the lowest protein value. Southwestern North America. GIBBONS 1979, LANNER; B74{PL}, B94, C9M, D95{PL}, F85, G43M{PL}, G60{PL}, I83M{PL}, I98M, K22{PL}, K38, K47T, O93, P38, P49, etc.

Pinus parryana → *Pinus x quadrifolia*

Pinus pinea - *Italian stone pine, Pignolia nut* {S} The seeds are eaten raw, roasted and salted, or used in sweetmeats, cakes, puddings, stuffings, *pesto* sauce, *macaroon* cookies, soups, stuffed grape leaves, etc. Romanian cooks grind entire young pinecones and use them to flavor game sauces. Mediterranean region, cultivated. ANGIER, BIANCHINI, ROOT 1980b; C9M, D37{PL}, D95{PL}, D96, *E66*{PL}, F85, I83M{PL}, K47T, K63G, L91M, *N71M*, N84, O53M, *P17M*, R47, etc.

Pinus x quadrifolia - *Parry piñon* {PL} Apparently a natural hybrid. The oily seeds are an important food among the Indians of Baja California. They contain 11% protein, 37% fat, and 44% carbohydrate. Southwestern North America. LANNER, UPHOF; B94{S}, D95, I83M

Pinus roxburghii - *Chir pine* {S} The seeds are sometimes eaten. A sweet manna that exudes from the bark and twigs is used as food. Himalayan region. DONKIN, TANAKA; C9M, C56M{PL}, F80, *H71*, I83M{PL}, *J86*{PL}, K38, *K46*{PL}, O93, P5, *P17M*, Q12, Q18, Q40, Q46, etc.

Pinus sabiniana - *Digger pine* {S} Large, oily seeds are eaten raw or roasted. The soft center of green cones can be roasted and eaten. Leaves are used as a tea substitute. Southwestern North America. CLARKE, JAYNES; A2{PL}, B94, C9M, *C73*{PL}, F80, G60{PL}, *G66*, I83M{PL}, I98M, K38, *N71M*, N93M, O93, P5, *P17M*, etc.

Pinus strobus - *White pine* {PL} The fresh needles are brewed into an aromatic tea rich in vitamins A and C. An acceptable candy is made by boiling the tender new shoots in syrup. The firm, unexpanded male cones can be boiled, or stewed with meat. North America. FERNALD, GIBBONS 1966b, PETERSON, L.; B9M, B32, C11M, D45, D95, E33M, E47, *G9M*, H49, I4, J16, J47, J70{S}, K38{S}, M76, N7T, O53M{S}, *Q32*{S}, etc.

Pinus torreyana - *Torrey pine* {S} The large seeds are eaten raw or roasted. Southwestern North America. MENNINGER, UPHOF; B74{PL}, B94, C9M, C56M{PL}, D95{PL}, F80, G60{PL}, *H71*, I83M{PL}, I98M, K38, *K46*{PL}, K47T, *K48*, O93, *P63*, R47, etc.

Pinus wallichiana - *Indian blue pine* {S} A manna-like substance that exudes from the leaves and twigs is eaten or employed in adulterating honey. The seeds are sometimes eaten. Himalayan region. DONKIN, TANAKA; B94, E6{PL}, E87{PL}, F85, H49{PL}, I83M{PL}, K38, *M51M*{PL}, N0{PL}, *N71M*, O53M, *P17M*, Q12, Q18, Q40, etc.

Pseudotsuga menziesii - *Douglas fir* {PL} A refreshing tea, high in vitamin C, is made from the young leaves and twigs. Young, tender tips impart a subtle, woodsy flavor to foods in which they are cooked. They can be used for dipping into marinades, basting barbecued meats or fowl, or infusing broths. The trunks exude a sweet manna-like substance. Western North America. BRYAN [Re], CLARKE, DONKIN, KIRK; A80M, B9M, *B60*, C9M{S}, C11M, D45, E15{S}, E47, H49, I4, I15{S}, J47, J70{S}, K38{S}, *M51M*, etc.

Pseudotsuga taxifolia → *Pseudotsuga menziesii*

Tsuga canadensis - *Eastern hemlock* {PL} The young tips are used to make a tea and are also ingredients of *root beer* and *spruce beer*. The leaves and twigs yield *spruce oil*, used commercially to flavor chewing gum, ice cream, soft drinks, and candy. Inner bark is used as an emergency food. Eastern North America. FERNALD, HEDRICK 1919, MORTON 1976; B9M, *B99M*, C9M{S}, *D32*, D45, D95, E33M, E47, *G9M*, H49, I4, J16, J47, K38, K47T{S}, M76, N7T, etc.

Tsuga heterophylla - *Western hemlock* {S} Young twigs are boiled with honey or molasses to produce *spruce beer*. Also a source of *spruce oil*, used as a flavoring in the food industry. The inner bark is made into cakes or bread. Western North America. MORTON 1976, YANOVSKY; A2, A80M{PL}, C9M, D95{PL}, E15, I47, I99, *J75M*{PL}, K38, K63G, *K75*, N0{PL}, *N71M*, *P63*

Tsuga mertensiana - *Mountain hemlock* {S} The fresh needles are used as a tea substitute. Inner bark is used as an emergency food. Western North America. HELLER, KIRK; *C33*{PL}, D95{PL}, E63{PL}, E87{PL}, *G66*, I15, I47, I99, *J75M*{PL}, K38, K47T, K63G, *K75*, *N71M*

PIPERACEAE

Heckeria peltata → *Pothomorphe peltata*

Macropiper excelsum → *Piper excelsum*

Piper aduncum - *Wild pepper, Higuillo* {PL} The peppery fruits are used to season food. When black and ripe, they are said to be very sweet. Leaves are sometimes eaten as a potherb. Tropical America. DUKE, VON REIS; E48

Piper auritum - *Hoja de Santa María, Acuyo, Makulan* {PL} The leaves, having the flavor and aroma of sarsaparilla, are used for seasoning tamales, wild game such as armadillo, freshwater snails, soups, and many other dishes. In Honduras, young leaves are sometimes cooked and eaten as greens. The natives of Panama trap a river fish using the leaves as bait. After feeding on it regularly, the flesh of the fish takes on the flavor of the leaf. Recommended for aquaculture applications. Central America. ALTSCHUL, DUKE, HUTSON [Cul], JOLY, MORTON 1976, WILLIAMS, L.; E48, F93G

Piper betle - *Betel leaf* {PL} Aromatic leaves are chewed with betelnuts (Areca catechu). For this purpose, they are smeared with lime and cutch and used as a wrapping for slices of the nuts. Various spices, such as cinnamon, cloves, cardamom, nutmeg, and tamarind may be added to the mixture which is used as a stimulant. Malaysia to Micronesia. BROUK, MACMILLAN, MENNINGER, UPHOF; G96, H51M, N84{S}

Piper cubeba - *Cubeb, Tailed pepper* {S} Dried unripe fruits, called *cubeb berries*, are used as a seasoning, having a strong, spicy odor and an aromatic, bitter, sharp flavor. Forms one of the ingredients of *ras el hanout*, legendary spice mixture of Morocco. Source of an oleoresin that enters into pickles, meat sauces, bitters and tobacco. Malaya, cultivated. MORTON 1976, ROOT 1980b, UPHOF, WOLFERT; F85

Piper excelsum - *Kawakawa, New Zealand pepper-tree* {S} In Polynesia the flower-clusters are eaten raw. Fruits are good to eat when fully ripe. New Zealand and Oceania. COLENSO, LOVELOCK; A79M, J82, N84, O93

Piper guineense - *Ashanti pepper, Benin pepper* {S} The fresh or dried fruit, milder than that of P. nigrum, is used for flavoring soups, rice and other foods. Leaves are also added to soups. Ash from the plants forms a substitute for salt. West Tropical Africa, cultivated. DALZIEL, KUNKEL, MORTON 1976, UPHOF; N84

Piper longum - *Indian long pepper, Jaborandi pepper* {S} Dried, unripe berries are used as a condiment in curries and pickles, or to adulterate black pepper. One of the ingredients of the Moroccan spice mixture *ras el hanout*. India to the Philippines, cultivated. HEDRICK 1919, MORTON 1976, WOLFERT; F85

Piper methysticum - *Kava pepper* {PL} Roots and stems are the source of a stimulating alkaloidal beverage called *kawa* or *ava*, widely consumed in some Polynesian Islands. They are also used as a masticatory. Pacific Islands, cultivated. HEDRICK 1919, MACMILLAN, MASSAL, TANAKA, UPHOF; I59G{PR}, M82

CULTIVARS

Black: (Black Kava) Stems and veins are deep purple to black in color. Has several times the potency of commoner forms. Leaves of this strain appear to be as potent as the roots of other types. A pre-conquest Hawaiian cultivar, still secretly cultivated in some areas. I59G

Piper nigrum - *Black pepper* {S} The pungent fruits, called *peppercorns*, are dried, ground and widely used as a seasoning. Milder-flavored *white pepper* is obtained from fruits whose outer coverings have been removed. Unripe, green peppercorns are pickled in vinegar and used as a relish. The seeds are the source of an oil used to flavor sausages, pickles, canned foods, and beverages. Tropical Asia, cultivated. MACMILLAN, MORTON 1976, OCHSE, SCHERY, UPHOF; A79M, A94M{PR}, E48, F85, M53{PL}, N84, O42, O93, R47, R59

Piper ornatum - *Celebes pepper* {PL} Said to be used as a condiment. Indonesia. KUNKEL; E48

Piper sanctum - *Hierba santa, Acueyo* {PL} The cooks in Vera Cruz wrap their fish in the large, cordate, sassafras-flavored leaves. In other parts of Mexico they are used for flavoring soups. Central America. UPHOF; M82

Piper sylvaticum - *Mountain long-pepper* {PL} In India, the fruiting spikes, both green and ripe, are used as seasonings in curries and pickles. Southern Asia. HEDRICK 1919, WATT; E48

Piper umbellatum* → *Pothomorphe umbellata

Pothomorphe peltata - *Lizard's tail pepper, Gedebong* {PL} Young leaves are boiled or steamed and eaten with rice. They are also used as a wrapping for fish that are seasoned and roasted in hot ashes. The sweetish, ripe fruits are considered a delicacy by children. Brazil. OCHSE; E48

Pothomorphe subpeltata* → *Pothomorphe umbellata

Pothomorphe umbellata - *Segumbar urat, Boombo* {S} Young leaves are eaten raw or steamed and served as a side-dish with rice. They are also used for wrapping other foods. In the Philippines, the leaves and young inflorescences are cooked with fish. The sweetish ripe fruits are eaten as a delicacy. Bark is also used as a condiment. Paleotropics. BURKILL, DALZIEL, KUNKEL, OCHSE; N84

PISTACIACEAE

Pistacia atlantica - *Mt. Atlas pistache, Butum* {S} The turpentine-flavored fruits, called *gadum*, are eaten raw. An excellent edible oil is produced in the Middle East from the very small, crushed nuts. Also used as a rootstock and as a pollen source for P. vera. Canary Islands, North Africa. BAILEY, C., ROSENGARTEN, UPHOF, WHITEHOUSE; C9M, D75, D75{PL}, D81{PO}, *G66*, N84, O93, P5, *Q15G*, S95

Pistacia chinensis - *Chinese pistache, Huang-lien-mu* {S} Young shoots and leaves are eaten as a vegetable. The nuts are roasted and eaten or employed in confectionery. China, cultivated. TANAKA; A79M, C9M, *E66*{PL}, F70{PL}, *G66*, H4{PL}, I28{PL}, *I61*, *I62*{PL}, K38, K47T, N33{PL}, N37M{PL}, O53M, P5, *Q32*, etc.

Pistacia chinensis ssp. integerrima - *Chahar tanknush* {S} The fruit is used to impart flavor to milk. Southwest Asia. TANAKA; N84, O46, Q40

Pistacia integerrima* → *Pistacia chinensis ssp. integerrima

Pistacia khinjuk - *Habul-khazra* {S} Seed kernels are used to impart flavor to milk. Southwest Asia. TANAKA; **U80, W63M**

Pistacia lentiscus - *Lentisk, Lentisk pistache* {PL} A sweet, licorice-flavored resin, *mastic*, derived form the bark of the trunk, is chewed as a breath sweetener. It is also used to flavor a liqueur (*masticha*), *rahat lokum* (*Turkish delight*), puddings, almond paste, cookies, cakes, and candies. Seed kernels are the source of an edible oil, known as *shina oil of Cyprus*. Canary Islands, Mediterranean region. HEDRICK 1919, MALLOS [Re], UPHOF, VON WELANETZ, WHITEHOUSE; L50M{PR}, N84, *Q15G*{S}, R59M, S95{S}

Pistacia mutica - *Turk terebinth pistache* {S} The trunk is the source of a resin, known as *Bombay mastic*, used for chewing in some parts of Iran and Iraq. Seeds are sometimes eaten or pressed for their edible oil. Southwest Asia. JAYNES, UPHOF; *G66*, S36M

Pistacia terebinthus - *Terebinth pistache, Cyprus turpentine tree* {S} The sweet, greenish seed kernels are eaten or pressed for their edible oil. Immature fruits, along with their stems, are preserved in vinegar and salt. Known as *atsjaar*, they are used as a relish to accompany wines served during dinner. Young leaves are cooked and used as a vegetable. Resin from the trunk is used in Iran as a chewing gum. Mediterranean region. HEDRICK 1919, KUNKEL, ROSENGARTEN, TANAKA, WHITEHOUSE; D75, D75{PL}, *H71*, K47T, N84, O93, S95

Pistacia texana - *Texas pistache* {PL} The small nuts, similar to the commercial pistachios, have been eaten locally. Texas. KROCHMAL; *K46*

Pistacia vera - *Pistachio* {S} Nuts are eaten raw, roasted and salted, or used in confectionery, ice creams, cakes, cookies, pies, etc. They also yield an edible oil but due to the high price of the nuts it is not produced commercially. In Iran, the fruits are made into a flavorful marmalade. Eastern Mediterranean to Southwest Asia, cultivated. JAYNES [Cu, Pro], MENNINGER, ROSENGARTEN [Cul, Re],

UPHOF, WHITEHOUSE; C56M{PL}, D95{PL}, *G66*, H4{PL}, I28{PL}, I99, K47T, N84, P5, S95

CULTIVARS {GR}

Kerman: Female. Nut above average in size; shells split well, are easily opened by hand; kernel size above average, of high quality; readily shaken or knocked from tree when ripe. Tree vigorous, upright-spreading; blooms late, produces heavily but biennially. Leading commercial cultivar in the United States. Originated in Chico, California from seeds imported from Iran. BROOKS 1972; A88M, B93M, D75, I83M, *L47, N20*

Peters: Male. Good producer of pollen; its blossoming coincides with early blossoming cultivars, as well as the later blossoming Kerman. In some years it may be slightly early for full coverage of Kerman. Has a tendency to be a loppy, week grower, especially when propagated on P. vera roots. Originated in Fresno, California by A.B. Peters. BROOKS 1972, JAYNES; A88M, B93M, D75, D81{PO}, I83M, *L47, N20*

Sfax: Female. Small nuts of very good quality; percentage of split nuts high; produced in dense clusters like grapes, easily harvested. Ripens very early, late August to early September at Chico, California. Relatively low chilling requirement, about half that of Kerman. Pollinated by Peters. Originated in Sfax, Tunisia. JAYNES; U8{SC}

PISTIACEAE

Pistia stratiotes - *Water lettuce* {PL} The leaves are sometimes added to soups but should be parboiled first to remove the acrid calcium oxalate crystals. Ash of the burned plants is used as a substitute for salt. Tropics. BURKILL, DUKE, TANAKA, WATT; E48, H30, H82, I90M, K85M, M15, M73, M73M, N3M, N84{S}

PITTOSPORACEAE

Billardiera longiflora - *Blue appleberry* {S} The oblong, violet-blue berries of this evergreen, climbing shrub have an agreeable taste and may be eaten out of hand, puréed, or added to fruit salads. Australia. HENDRICKSON, JOHNS, SIMMONS 1972 [Cu]; D62, L91M, N84, O53M, O93, R15M, R33M, S65M

CULTIVARS

White: (Fructo Albo) A cultivar that produces white fruit. SIMMONS 1972; D62

PLANTAGINACEAE

Plantago coronopus - *Buck's-horn plantain, Minutina, Capuchin's beard, Herba Stella* {S} Young leaves may be used in tossed salads. Blanch in boiling water for a few seconds to make them more tender before use. In Italy, they are one of the ingredients of *misticanze*, a mixture of wild and cultivated salad greens that originated in the Marche region. Eurasia. BIANCHINI, LARKCOM 1984, VILMORIN [Cu]; D62, I99, K66, N84, O48, P83M, S55

Plantago juncoides* → *Plantago maritima ssp. juncoides

Plantago lanceolata - *Rib-grass, Ribwort, Lamb's tongue* {S} The young leaves are occasionally eaten. However, they are rather bitter and tedious to prepare as their fibrous strands must be removed before use. Seeds are said to be used like sago. Eurasia, naturalized in North America. FOX, F., LAUNERT, UPHOF; A2, D58, J82, K47T, *N71M*, N84, O48, *Q24*

Plantago major - *Common plantain, Greater plantain* {S} Although fibrous, the leaves are sometimes puréed, used in salads, or as a potherb. It is best to select the leaf blades only, discarding the leaf stalks. Dipped in batter and fried over low heat for about half an hour they are said to resemble potato chips. For use in salads, blanched leaves are recommended. Dried leaves make an acceptable tea. The seeds are eaten parched or ground into meal. Roots are also edible. Northern temperate region. ANGIER, CLARKE [Re], FERNALD, FOX, F., GIBBONS 1979, HARRINGTON, H., KIRK, ZENNIE [Nu]; A2, C11, D58, D62, E61{PL}, F42, F85, J67M, *N71M*, N84, O48, O53M, P1G, R47, S55, etc.

Plantago maritima - *Seaside plantain, Sea plantain* {S} Leaves are occasionally eaten in salads, cooked like spinach, boiled in broths, or pickled like samphire. In Alaska, they are canned for winter use. Northern temperate region. HEDRICK 1919, HELLER, UPHOF; N84, O48

Plantago maritima ssp. juncoides - *Seaside plantain, Goose-tongue* {S} The tender leaves can be dressed with oil and vinegar and eaten as a tasty salad or combined with other salad ingredients, the natural sea-salts contained in the plant giving them a pleasant flavor. Older leaves may be snapped like green beans, boiled, and served with butter. North America. FERNALD, GIBBONS 1964, PETERSON, L.; **Z88**

Plantago media - *Hoary plantain* {S} The sweet inflorescences are sucked by children. Eurasia. KUNKEL; D62, *N71M*, N84, O48, O53M

Plantago ovata - *Blond psyllium* {S} The mucilage contained in the seed coat is used as a stabilizer in ice cream and chocolate manufacture. Sprouted seeds are eaten in salads, soups, stews, etc. Mediterranean region, North Africa, Southwest Asia. TANAKA; E31{PR}, I99 (also see Sprouting Seeds, page 485)

Plantago psyllium - *Psyllium seed, Fleaseed, Fleawort* {S} Sprouted seeds are eaten raw in salads. Due to their mucilaginous qualities they are grown on clay or other porous materials. Eurasia. A2, F85, J82, K49T, N84, O48 (also see Sprouting Seeds, page 485)

PLATANACEAE

Platanus occidentalis - *American sycamore, Plane tree* {PL} The sweet sap has been used in the preparation of syrup and sugar. North America. FERNALD, GIBBONS 1962; C9M{S}, D45, *G66*{S}, H4, H49, *I62*, *J25*, K18, K38{S}, K47T{S}, *L5M*{S}, *M69M*, M76, *N71M*{S}, N93M{S}, etc.

POACEAE (*GRAMINAE*)

Agropyron intermedium* → *Thinopyron intermedium

Agropyron trichophorum* → *Thinopyron intermedium var. trichophorum

X Agrotriticum sp. (Agropyron elongatum x Triticum durum) - *Perennial grain* {S} Seeds are ground into flour and used in baking. Food researchers at the Rodale Press Food Center, in a scientific comparison of the grains, found that perennial grain muffins and yeast rolls were preferred over the same products made with wheat flour. Protein, carbohydrate, and fiber levels were found to be similar to those of conventional wheat flour. ZAHRADNIK.

CULTIVARS

W-21: A warm-climate perennial; winter-kills in northern climates; persists for about 3 years under ideal conditions. Grows to a height of 2 to 4 feet and produces a very stiff, sturdy, spring-like stalk. Seed does not shatter, but is held firmly in its erect seed head, which has the disadvantage of being tight. Susceptible to ergot and smut. One of the highest-yielding perennial grains, producing as much as 25 bushels per acre. The kernels resemble a small winter wheat. Planted like winter wheat in northern regions; can be spring planted and will produce grain the first year in Texas, Florida and some Pacific Coast regions. ZAHRADNIK; G26

Anthoxanthum odoratum - *Sweet vernal-grass, Grass tea* {PL} When crushed or when drying, the leaves give off a sweet, pleasant fragrance and can be used as a substitute for tea. Northern temperate region. CRIBB, FERNALD, GIBBONS 1979; C13M{S}, C43M,

C67M, E61, G84, H3M, J66, J82{S}, K47T{S}, K85, M82, *N71M*{S}, O48{S}, O53M{S}, *Q24*{S}, S55{S}, etc.

Avena abyssinica - *Abyssinian oat* {S} The grain is edible. In Ethiopia, it is harvested and threshed together with barley. East African highlands. TANAKA, ZEVEN; **Y75**

Avena byzantina - *Indian oat, Red oat* {S} Grains are used for food. Mediterranean region, cultivated. BROUK, SCHERY, TANAKA, ZEVEN; **Y17M, Y75, Z98**

Avena nuda - *Naked oat, Hulless oat* {S} Occasionally cultivated as a cereal. The hull is incompletely attached to the grain, yielding a naked seed easily upon threshing. Nevertheless, this species is not much cultivated, primarily because of its inferior yield. It is ideal for small-scale farmers and backyard growers. Cultivated. SCHERY, UPHOF, ZEVEN; N84

CULTIVARS

Freedom: This is a tall cultivar for early spring planting and late summer harvest. A result of five years of selection and seed increases by the research and production staff of Johnny's Selected Seeds. When harvested and threshed, the oat kernels are essentially free of the tough, inedible hulls of common oats. Seeding rate: 96 pounds per acre or 2 to 3 pounds per square foot. G6

Terra: 90 days. Long grain type. Relatively short straw. Should be planted in spring. Very productive for a hulless oat. Considered to be the best of the naked oats in home-garden trials in Maine. E63T

Tibor: 100 days. Large blonde kernels, approximately 5 percent remain covered. Plants grow to 42 to 45 inches tall. Golden tan stalks and leaves. Resistant to smut and to lodging. Recently released by Agriculture Canada Research Station, Ottawa. **T76**

Torch River: 100 days. Attractive, loose hulled plant with tall straw. Useful for human consumption by simple threshing and winnowing. An old cultivar of Canadian origin. G47

Avena orientalis - *Hungarian oat, Turkish oat, Tartarian oat* {S} Occasionally cultivated as a cereal, especially in Southeast Europe. Cultivated. HEDRICK 1919, UPHOF; **W92**

Avena sativa - *Oat* {S} Seeds are made into flour, oatmeal, rolled oats, bran, *groats*, breakfast foods, *sourdough bread, tempeh*, etc. In Belgium, they are used for *white beer*. Darbyshire oat cakes and *barley bannocks*, popular in Scotland, are made from oat or barley flour. The ancient Greeks had a dessert called *plakous*, a cake of oat flour, cheese and honey. Roasted seeds can be used in mock coffees, and in France are employed as a substitute for vanilla. *Sowans* are the soured fermented inner shellings of the grain. Sprouted seeds are used in salads, dressings, and baked goods or dried and made into *sun granola*. Cultivated. LOGSDON 1977 [Cu, Re], RITTER [Re], ROOT 1980a, SCHERY, SHURTLEFF 1979, UPHOF; B49, C9M, D47M, G47M, G71, O48 (also see Sprouting Seeds, page 485)

CULTIVARS

Cayuse: 85 days. Sown in early spring as soon as the soil is workable, 4 pounds per 1,000 square feet. Grows 34 inches tall. *E53*, K49M

Porter: Used as a cover crop and/or grain crop in the North. Use as a quick growing spring-summer green manure crop, or to some extent, as a winter cover crop. Sow at 3 to 4 pounds per 1,000 square feet in early spring for grain, anytime for cover. G6

Probstier: Tall, heavy-yielding oat, grows 35 to 45 inches tall. Very thick brown stalk and leaves. Tan seed. Good yields. Susceptible to smut and rust. Heirloom grown in Minnesota as early as 1866. **T76**

Bromus breviaristatus - *Narrow-leaved brome* {S} Seeds have been used for *pinole*. Has potential as a perennial grain crop, yielding two to three crops a year, as long as plants are kept fertilized and watered. Western North America. G9, J73

Bromus carinatus - *California brome* {S} Seeds are eaten by the Indians of California. Potential perennial grain crop able to survive summer droughts without irrigation. Western North America. YANOVSKY; J73

Bromus mango - *Mango* {S} Was grown as a biennial cereal by the Araucano Indians of Chile until at least the middle of the 19th century. The grains were toasted and ground into flour and used to make an unleavened bread called *cougue* or a *chicha* drink. Grows on infertile acid soils. Thought to be extinct, this species was recently re-discovered. Southern Chile and Argentina. ZEVEN; **W36M**

Coix lacryma-jobi - *Job's tears, Adlay* {S} The hulled grains can be parched, boiled like rice, or milled into flour for making a type of bread. They are also utilized in soups, porridge, drinks, or pastries. In India, the Nagas use the grain for the brewing of a beer called *zhu* or *dzu*. Parched seeds are used as a tea in Japan. Southeastern Asia, cultivated. ARORA, MACMILLAN, SCHERY, TANAKA; A2, C11, C81M, C92, D29{PL}, D62, E81M, F21{PL}, F80, I39, K22{PL}, K85{PL}, L42, L91M, O53M, etc.

Coix lacryma-jobi 'Ma-Yuen' - *Hato-mugi, Japanese barley* {S} Seeds are used as a cereal or brewed into an alcoholic beverage. Roasted seeds are made into a coffee-like beverage. Widely used in macrobiotic cuisine and diets. Unlike Job's tears, the fruits are soft-shelled and easily threshed. ARORA, TANAKA; E56{PR}, E66T{PR}, H91{PR}, *K74*{PR}, **U87, X79M, Y27M**

Cymbopogon citratus - *Lemongrass* {PL} Basal portions of the leafy shoot are chopped and used for flavoring fish, sauces and curries. Outer leaves may be tied in a loop and cooked with food to impart flavor, but are removed before serving. The heart of the young shoots is eaten as a vegetable with rice. A refreshing tea can be brewed from the leaves and served either hot or cold. Lemon grass is substituted for yogurt in the preparation of *nistisemos trahanas* (fasting trahanas), a fermented milk and cereal food. This type of trahanas is used during religious holidays in Greece and Turkey, when it would be sacrilegious to consume animal milks. Cultivated. HERKLOTS, MORTON 1976, OCHSE, SCHNEIDER [Cul, Re], SHURTLEFF 1979, STEINKRAUS; B28, C9, C43M, C81M, D29, F21, G96, H3M, H40, J66, K22, K85, L90G{PR}, M51{PR}, M53, N19M, etc.

Cymbopogon martinii - *Rosha grass* {S} Source of *palmarosa oil*, an essential oil obtained by steam distillation and used to flavor ice cream, gelatin desserts, chewing gum, and bakery products. Tropical Asia. TANAKA; Q46

Cymbopogon nardus - *Citronella grass* {S} Leaves are used for flavoring soups, in cooking fish, and in preparing curries. They are also employed as a tea. Source of *geraniol, citral*, and *citronellal*, essential oils utilized as flavorings for food and drinks. Among them, citral is used to imitate strawberry, lemon, apple, and vanilla flavor. Tropical Asia. TANAKA, UPHOF; A79M, C43M{PL}, F85, H49, N84, O42

Digitaria exilis - *Fonio, Fundi, Acha* {S} The white grain is used as a cereal in parts of Africa, especially by the Hausas of central Nigeria. It is ground to a flour or paste and used for making *couscous* or a gruel eaten with melted butter. Yields are poor but the seed is highly nutritious and palatable. Tropical Africa, cultivated. DALZIEL, HARLAN, SCHERY, UPHOF, ZEVEN; **U37M**

Digitaria iburua - *Black fonio, Hungry rice, Iburu* {S} Cultivated as a cereal by the Hausas of Nigeria and the Lambas of Togo. Used in the preparation of a couscous known locally as *wusu-wusu*, and a beer called *tchapalo*. Often grown between rows of sorghum or pearl millet, and frequently as a mixture with D. exilis. West Tropical Africa. DALZIEL, HARLAN, UPHOF, ZEVEN; **U37M**

Distichlis palmeri - *Wild-wheat, Palmer's saltgrass, Trigo gentil, Nyipa* {PR} The grain may be cooked as a cereal, roasted, or used in muffins and stuffings. When sautéed, it has a nut-like flavor akin to sunflower seeds or pistachios and goes well on ice cream or in salads. It is high in bran and fiber, the fiber content being three times that of wheat. At one time thought extinct, the cultivated form was rediscovered and developed by Dr. Nicholas Yensen of Tucson, Arizona. The plant grows in saline soils but remarkably, grain grown even in full-strength sea water is not salty. Presently wild wheat is mostly sold locally in Arizona through gourmet outlets and at special events. Improved cultivars are patented and not available as seed stock at this time. North America. NIETHAMMER [Re], YENSEN 1987, YENSEN 1988; I16

Echinochloa colonum - *Sawa millet, Jungle rice* {S} Young plants and shoots are eaten raw with rice. The seeds are eaten as a cereal. In the Central African Republic, they are fermented to make beer. Tropics, cultivated. BURKILL, DALZIEL, DE WET, OCHSE, WATT; N84

Echinochloa crusgalli - *Barnyard grass, Cockspur grass* {S} Dried or parched seeds are ground into flour for use in cakes, porridge, and puddings. In Japan, they are used for making macaroni and dumplings. The young plants, stem tips, and the heart of the young culms are eaten raw or steamed. Roasted seeds are used as a substitute for coffee. Northern temperate region. BURKILL, FERNALD, HARRINGTON, H., KIRK, KUNKEL, OCHSE, UPHOF, WATT; D58, E83T, G26, G47M, N11, *N71M*

Echinochloa crusgalli var. frumentacea → *Echinochloa frumentacea*

Echinochloa frumentacea - *Japanese millet, Sanwa millet* {S} The grain is boiled like rice, made into gruel or porridge, or, in India, boiled in milk. The chief merit of the grain is its rapid yield, a crop sometimes being matured within six weeks of sowing. Eastern Asia, cultivated. BROWN, W., MACMILLAN, TANAKA, WATT; D58, N84

Echinochloa stagnina - *Burgu, Dul* {S} A sugar is extracted from the stems and utilized for making sweetmeats and confectionery. The Mohammedans in West Africa prepare a liquor from it. Tropical Africa. DALZIEL, TANAKA, UPHOF; N84

Eleusine coracana - *Ragi, Finger millet* {S} Grains are boiled and eaten as a cereal or porridge, ground into flour for use in cakes, breads, and puddings, or made into a beer-like alcoholic beverage called *marwa*. In India, the flour is boiled in diluted buttermilk and kept overnight for use the next morning. Other fermented foods made from the grain include *ambali*, *kaffir beer*, *busaa*, and *munkoyo*. The leaves are also edible. Tropical Asia, cultivated. BHANDARI, FOX, F., HEDRICK 1919, MACMILLAN, MARTIN 1975, STEINKRAUS, UPHOF, WILKES; F80, K47T, N84

CULTIVARS

Candlestick: (Candlestick Millet) Heads are borne on tall stalks and are shaped like candlesticks. Plants tiller heavily. This millet is grown on 50 million acres in India and Africa, where an almost unlimited number of delicious recipes have been developed. G47

Dragon's Claw: (Dragon's Claw Millet) 130 days. Grows to 3 feet tall. Curved, ornamental seed heads. Seeds smaller than common millet. Stalks stiff, resistant to lodging. Difficult to thresh. Trouble free; good yields. Seeds highly resistant to storage pests. Important crop for natural agriculture enthusiasts. G47, I99, K49T

Eleusine indica - *Wire grass, Goose grass* {S} In Indonesia, the young, tender plants are often gathered and eaten, raw or steamed, as a side-dish with rice. The seeds can be parched and ground into a meal for use in cakes and gruels. Also used for porridge and alcoholic beverages. Tropics, naturalized in North America. DUKE, GIBBONS 1979, KIRK, OCHSE, TANAKA; K47T, N84

Elymus arenarius → *Leymus arenarius*

Elymus canadensis - *Canada wild-rye* {S} Seeds were an important source of food for the Paiute Indians of the Southwestern United States. North America. DOEBLEY, YANOVSKY; *B29M*, *E66M*, F80, *F96*, G47M, J39M, J39M{PL}, J41M, J41M{PL}, J43, K62, *L95*{PL}, *Q24*

Elymus triticoides - *Wild rye, Squaw grass* {S} Seeds were parched and ground into a fine meal, called *pinole*, and consumed by the Indians as porridge or in cakes and drinks. The hairs on the grain must be singed off before it is used as food. Southwestern North America. KIRK, MEDSGER, YANOVSKY; *E66M*, *F96*

Eragrostis abyssinica → *Eragrostis tef*

Eragrostis tef - *Teff* {S} Seeds are used in the preparation of *enjera*, a fermented, pancake-like bread that is consumed as a staple in Ethiopia. The prepared bread is spongy, soft, thin, and sour-tasting. It is generally eaten with a meat, vegetable, or legume stew called *wot*. Teff is also combined with other grains in the making of *talla*, an Ethiopian home-processed beer with a smoky flavor and a tan to dark brown color. Ethiopia, cultivated. MESFIN [Pre, Re], STEINKRAUS, STEWART; C61M, D62, K47T, *K74*{PR}, M63M{PR}, N84, *O1*, O48, O53M, O93

CULTIVARS

Brown Seeded: 120 days. Very small, highly nutritious seeds, about 13% protein. Somewhat richer and more heartier-tasting than White Seeded. Makes a chocolate-brown *enjera*. Also has a slightly higher calcium content. Short plant with very small heads. Heavy yielding. E56{PR}, H31{PR}, H91{PR}, J73

W2-III: Dark green, leafy plant. Semi-open, slightly drooping, dark purple panicle, emerges from foliage. Excellent for arrangements, as it can be cut and dried without loss of color. Selected for ornament but it can also be used for grain, although yields will be lower than those of Brown Seeded or White Seeded. H31{OR}

W2-IV: Fine leaf-blades, somewhat darker than W3-I, 18 to 20 inches in length. Very showy, semi-open, heavily drooping red panicle that emerges from foliage. Can be cut and dried without loss of color. Selected for its ornamental qualities but it can also be used for grain, although the yield will be lower. H31{OR}

W3-I: Slender, light pure-green foliage, 18 to 20 inches in length. Panicle an erect, compact, white spike that emerges from foilage and extends to about 32 inches. Can be cut and dried without loss of color. Selected by Wayne Carlson for ornament but can also be used for grain, although yields will be lower. H31{OR}

W3-IV: Dark green foliage with red highlights, to 25 inches in length. Strong stem. Very compact, erect, 20 inch red panicle; emerges on stem well above the leaves. Can be cut and dried without loss of color. Selected for ornament but can also be used for grain, although yields will be lower. H31{OR}

White Seeded: (Ivory) 120 days. Very small seeds, about 13% protein. Slightly lighter in flavor than Brown Seeded. Should be sown densely as it is a poor weed competitor until fully grown. Also susceptible to lodging. Heavy yielding. The most common cultivar grown. A2, E56{PR}, H31{PR}, H91{PR}

Euchlaena mexicana → *Zea mexicana*

Glyceria fluitans - *Polish manna, Floating manna-grass* {S} The seeds were considered a delicacy in certain parts of Europe and were an article of commerce there well into this century. Flour from the seeds is said to make a bread little inferior to wheat bread. It is also used for thickening soups, gruels and puddings, imparting a slightly sweet, delicate flavor. The sweetish-tasting seeds are also used as a masticatory. Northern temperate region. CROWHURST 1972,

DONKIN, FERNALD, HEDRICK 1919; **V73, V73M, W59M, X35M, X36, X79M, Y10, Y17M, Y43M, Z24**

Hierochloe odorata - *Vanilla grass, Sweet grass, Russian buffalo-grass, Zubrovka* {PL} The leaves have a strong, vanilla-like fragrance and yield an essential oil esteemed in France for flavoring candy, soft drinks, and tobacco. In Poland, one or more blades are put in a bottle of vodka for flavoring. Also said to be used as a coloring agent. Northern temperate region. MORTON 1976, TANAKA; C43M, C61M, E83Z, F35M, G47M{S}, G89, J39M, J42, J42{S}, K2, K2{S}, M82, N29{PR}

Hordeum bulbosum - *Abu suwaif* {S} Grains are used for food. Bulbous roots are chewed or occasionally eaten. Currently being tested as a perennial grain crop in the United States. Mediterranean region to Southwest Asia. TANAKA; **U63, V73M, V89, W3M, W59M, W92, X8, X33, Y10, Y89M, Z24, Z57, Z98**

Hordeum jubatum - *Foxtail barley, Squirrel-tail grass* {S} Seeds are eaten as a cereal or parched and made into a coffee-like beverage. North America. KUNKEL, YANOVSKY; C9M, C61M, D62, *E53M*, E61, E61{PL}, *E91G, F96*, G47M, K47T, L91M, O48, O53M, O93, *Q52*, etc.

Hordeum trifurcatum - *Egyptian barley* {S} Grains are the source of flour used in breads and cakes. North Africa to Asia Minor. UPHOF; **W92, Z98**

Hordeum vulgare - *Barley* {S} The grain is manufactured into bread flour, pearled barley for soup, breakfast cereals, and is the principal grain used for brewing beer. Also fermented into *tempeh, miso* and *enjera*. Roasted seeds are an ingredient of grain coffees. The pressed juice of young seedlings is used as a beverage by natural foods enthusiasts. In powdered form it is marketed as *greenmagma* or *barleygreen*. Protein extracted from the leaves has been recommended as a food supplement. Sprouted seeds are eaten in salads and breads. In Morocco, the immature grains are used for preparing a special type of couscous known as *azenbu*. Source of a natural sweetener called *bakugato* in Japan and sold in the West as *malt sugar, barley jelly sugar*, or *maltose*. *Gofio* is an ancient food of the Canary Islands prepared from parched grains that are ground into flour and kneaded with water into a paste. Cultivated. FAIRCHILD 1930, LOGSDON 1977 [Cu, Re], PIRIE, RITTER [Re], SHURTLEFF 1975, SHURTLEFF 1976, STEINKRAUS, TANAKA, UPHOF, WOLFERT; B49, C9M, C61M, D62, G71, H91{PR}, I43T{PR}, O48 (also see Sprouting Seeds, page 485)

CULTIVARS

Black Alberta: 85 days. Plants grow to 25 inches tall. Two inch head; black seed and awns. Good yields. Grown for spring crops. **T76**

Hordeum vulgare Coeleste Group - *Hulless barley, Hadaka-mugi* {S} One of the most popular varieties in the Far East where the grain is eaten with rice or parched and made into a cooling drink. The grain is often pressed to make it boil more readily. Also an essential ingredient in *miso* manufacture. TANAKA, ZEVEN; G47, I20{PR}

CULTIVARS

Easy-Thresh Hulless: 100 days. Very productive, awned, 2-row type. Long heads of large, plump grains. Very easy to thresh. Makes excellent malt. Has succeeded in home-garden trials in Texas. Grows 24 to 36 inches tall. Planted in spring. **T76, U33**

Ethiopian: A 6-row, bearded barley with bluish kernels. Midseason in maturity. Threshes clean like wheat and rye, yielding a ready to use whole grain. Sow in spring as early as the ground can be worked. E63T

Eureka: A 6-row, bearded barley with glossy, golden-tan kernels. Midseason in maturity. Good seed yields. Will tolerate wetter conditions than Ethiopian. E63T

Excelsior: Large head; long, rough awn; 6-rowed. Purple seeds. Hard to thresh. Makes superior pilaf. Vigorous grower, 36 to 40 inches tall. Somewhat susceptible to lodging. Has done well in home-garden trials in Maine. **T76, U33**

Jet: 75 days. Two-rowed, rough awned barley with a 3 1/2 inch head. Seeds black. Plants grow to 30 inches tall with good yields. Resistant to powdery mildew. Grown for spring crops. Originally from Ethiopia. **T76**

Purple Hulless: 80 days. Rough awned, 4-row barley with a 3 inch head. Purple tinged seed. Plants grow to 30 inches tall with good yields. Hard to thresh. Sown in spring. **T76**

Ranando: 85 days. Rough awned, 6-row barley for spring planting. Medium late in maturity. Good yields. Easy to thresh. Moderately susceptible to lodging. Originally from South Korea. **T76, U33**

Sangatsuga: Small-seeded, hulless, 6-row barley. Kernels are finer-grained or more "ricey" than other cultivars. Excellent fall growth habit, should be tried as a fall-planted overwinter crop in warm winter areas. Inconsistent when planted in spring. Originally from Japan. **T76, U33**

Sheba: 78 days. Dark seeds that thresh out cleanly; 6-rowed. Very upright, relatively short plant. Moderate to heavy yields. Has resisted lodging better than other cultivars in home garden trials. **T76**

Tibetan Hulless: 100 days. Awned, 6-row, spring barley with small dark grains. Three foot tall plant with strong straw, does not lodge easily. Moderate, dependable yields. Hard to thresh by hand. Originally from Tibet. **T76, U33**

Hordeum zeocriton - *Sprat barley* {S} Grains are used for food. Central Asia. HEDRICK 1919; **X79M**

Leymus arenarius - *Sea lyme-grass, Strand wheat* {S} The whole grain, when cooked like rice, is delicious with wild game or other meats, and is very good served with sugar and cream as a breakfast cereal. Strand wheat flour, mixed half-and-half with wheat flour, adds a rich flavor to pancakes, biscuits and muffins. The protein content of the grain rivals that of red beans and salmon. Viking settlers of Iceland cultivated the grain until the turn of this century. Northern temperate region. FERNALD, GIBBONS 1964, GRIFFIN; C9M, D62, D95{PL}, E30{PL}, I63M{PL}, J24{PL}, J37M{PL}, K47T, *L22*{PL}, N84, O48, *Q24*

Leymus racemosus - *Volga wild-rye* {S} Grains are used for food in some parts of the Soviet Union, especially in times of drought. The young underground shoots are sweet and tender and can be eaten raw. Currently being evaluated as a perennial grain crop in the United States. Southeastern Europe. BURRITT, KOMAROV; N84

Milium effusum - *English millet-grass* {S} Seeds are used for making bread. The aromatic leaves have been employed for flavoring tobacco. Northern temperate region. KUNKEL, VON REIS; B28{PL}, E83Z{PL}, *N71M*, O48

Oryza barthii - *African perennial rice* {S} The grain is eaten in some parts of Africa where it is considered to have a good flavor. Occasionally collected and sold in local markets. Grows in water, often as a weed in rice fields. Tropical Africa. DALZIEL, UPHOF, ZEVEN; N84

Oryza longistaminata - *African wild rice* {S} Cultivated as a grain crop in Equatorial Africa. Tropical Africa. UPHOF; N84

Oryza sativa - *Rice* {S} The grain is eaten boiled or steamed. It is also made into cakes, pastries, puddings, starch, *risotto*, etc. *Poha* is flattened grains of rice that puff up when fried; used in India for making *cheewra* or *chiwra*, a granola-like product. Rice bran, when mixed with flour, is suitable for cookies, cakes, muffins, and pancakes. In Japan, it is widely used for pickling vegetables. Also the source of an edible oil. *Chinese black vinegar* is a very dark-colored vinegar made from rice. Sprouted seeds are eaten in salads. Some fermented foods made from the grain include *amazake*, *apem*, *hopper*, *idli*, *dhokla*, *dosa*, *miso*, *sake*, *red rice*, and *puto*. Young seedlings can be used as a vegetable. Tropical Asia, cultivated. DUKE, JAFFREY, LOGSDON 1977 [Cu, Re], SHURTLEFF 1979, STEINKRAUS, TANAKA, UPHOF; A88T{PR}, C27G{PR}, D58, F74{PR}, H91{PR}, K47T, N84, O48 (also see Sprouting Seeds, page 485)

CULTIVARS

Golden Rose: Medium-sized grain. Bred for whole grain brown rice flour. E63T

M-101: (Upland Rice M-101) 120 days. Plants average 3 feet tall and produce good yields (5 lbs./100 sq. ft.). Easy to grow, requires less water than corn, has shown no insect or disease problems. California-type, medium grain rice of the same quality as commercial brown rice. Grows from Albany, New York south to Florida. Requires dehusking prior to cooking. Dehusking equipment for small-scale growers is being investigated. L7M

Oryza sativa Glutinosa Group - *Glutinous rice, Sweet rice, Mochi-gome, No mi* {S} A distinct class of rice with glutinous kernels that bind together when cooked, imparting a unique chewy consistency. The grain is usually steamed, pounded and made into *mochi* cakes, pastries and sweetmeats. It is also ground to flour (*shiratamako*) and processed into dumplings called *dango*, or used for puffed rice. Glutinous rice is the preferred rice for manufacturing the fermented products *mirin*, *tapuy*, *lao chao*, *tapeh ketan* and *tapai*. HAWKES [Re], PORTERFIELD, SHURTLEFF 1975, SHURTLEFF 1979, STEINKRAUS, TANAKA.

CULTIVARS

Calmochi 101: Short grain "sweet" rice, used for making sticky *mochi* rice cakes. Short stature plants. E63T

Oryzopsis hymenoides - *Indian rice-grass, Indian millet* {S} The rather large, nutritious seeds have a pleasing taste and are used as a source of meal for making gruel and cakes, or to thicken soups. Sometimes the ground seeds were mixed with cornmeal and made into dumplings. When ripe, the seeds fall readily from the plant and are easily harvested. Presently being tested as a perennial grain for sandy soils in arid regions. Western North America. CULLY, DOEBLEY, HARRINGTON, H., KINDSCHER, MEDSGER; *B29M*, C4, C9M, D58, D82, *E66M*, F44, F80, G59M, *H64T*, I47, I98M, J25M, K15, K62, N7, N84, etc.

Panicum colonum* → *Echinochloa colonum

Panicum crusgalli* → *Echinochloa crusgalli

Panicum miliaceum - *Proso millet* {S} Seeds are eaten boiled like rice, or ground into flour for use in breads, pasta and dumplings or fermented into *tempeh* and *miso*. To enhance their nutty flavor they are commonly browned in a skillet before being used in casseroles, stews, soufflés, and stuffings. Popular with those who follow a natural foods diet because its high alkaline content counteracts acids and makes it more easily digested. Sprouted seeds are eaten in salads, soups, and breads. Southern Asia, cultivated. LOGSDON 1977 [Cu, Re], SCHERY, SHURTLEFF 1979, TANAKA; B49, C4, C61M, D58, E24, E83T, E97, G26, G47, K5M, K71, N84 (also see Sprouting Seeds, page 485)

CULTIVARS

Dossen Ukrainian Black: One hundred year old family heirloom brought from the Ukraine by the ancestors of Barry Dossenko. Open-pollinated strain further improved by selection. Unique black hulls. E21G, E21G{PR}

Red: (Red Proso) Loose heads of red seeds. Planted in June and harvested mid to late August. K49M

White: (White Proso) Looser heads than Red. Grows 30 inches tall. Planted 6 inches apart. K49M, *M25*

Panicum obtusum - *Vine mesquite* {S} Seeds were ground with cornmeal and consumed as food by the Hopi Indians. Southwestern North America. UPHOF; *H64T*

Panicum palmifolium* → *Setaria palmifolia

Panicum sonorum - *Sonoran panic-grass, Sauwi* {S} The grain is ground and used by the Warihio Indians of northwestern Mexico in basic cereal foods such as *tortillas*, *tamales*, and *atole*. The flour is seasoned with salt and sugar, and mixed with milk to make a nourishing drink. Cultivated on a small scale. Southwestern North America. NABHAN 1984b.

CULTIVARS

Warihio Indian: Small, golden-seeded millet type; contains lysine. Plant by broadcasting during warm rainy season. Fast growing. Rediscovered in 1976 in a very remote area of Sonora's eastern border with Chihuahua. Thought to have been extinct until then. I16

Paspalum commersonii - *Bastard millet, Ditch millet* {S} The grain is ground into meal and eaten. It is harvested with hill rice and mixed with it for food. Tropical Africa. DALZIEL; N84

Paspalum scrobiculatum - *Kodo millet* {S} The grain is cooked and used like rice. In India, it is substituted for rice in the preparation of *dhokla*, *dosa* and *idli*, acid-leavened fermented cakes. Tropical Asia, cultivated. FOX, F., MACMILLAN, STEINKRAUS; **X89**

Paspalum scrobiculatum var. commersonii → *Paspalum commersonii*

Pennisetum americanum - *Pearl millet, Spiked millet* {S} Seeds are eaten like rice, ground into flour which is used in breads and cakes, or employed in the manufacture of numerous alcoholic beverages. In Ghana, the flour is made into a stiff porridge called *tô* and a thin, fermented porridge or paste, locally known as *koko*. It is also mixed with other grains in making the fermented products *dosa*, *enjera* and *uji*. A deep-fried pancake, *marsa*, is also prepared there from the leavened batter of pearl millet flour. Ghanian children often eat the sweet raw grains after threshing. Cultivated. FOX, F., LOGSDON 1977, MACMILLAN, MENNINGER, RAO, STEINKRAUS, TANAKA; D33, D58, G26, K49T

Pennisetum glaucum* → *Pennisetum americanum

Pennisetum typhoides* → *Pennisetum americanum

Phragmites australis - *Common reed-grass, Wild broomcorn* {S} The young shoots are eaten like bamboo sprouts or pickled. Dried stems were made into a marshmallow-like confection by North American Indians. In Japan, the young leaves are dried, ground, and mixed with cereal flour to make dumplings. The partly unfolded leaves can be eaten as a potherb. A sugary gum that exudes from the stem is rolled into balls and eaten as a sweet. The rhizomes are sometimes cooked like potatoes. Although difficult to remove from its hull, the grain is said to be very nutritious. Cosmopolitan. FERNALD, KIRK, MEDSGER, TANAKA; B28{PL}, C64M, D11T{PL}, D58{PL}, *F96*, G26{PL}, J7{PL}, J43, K47T, M16{PL}, N11{PL}, N84, O48, *Q24*, S7M, etc.

Phragmites communis* → *Phragmites australis

Saccharum edule - *Sugar cane inflorescence, Lowland pitpit* {PL} The inflorescences, which are abnormal and remain enclosed within the leaf-sheaths, are eaten raw, steamed, roasted, fried, added to soups or cut into pieces and cooked with meat and stuffed fowl. When properly prepared, it might be used as a substitute for cauliflower. Tropical Asia. HERKLOTS, MASSAL, MAY, R. [Nu, Re], OCHSE; **U41**

Saccharum officinarum - *Sugar cane* {PL} Stems are the source of cane sugar, cane syrup, *molasses*, *rum*, etc. Sugar cane juice is consumed raw as a beverage or fermented into various alcoholic beverages and spirits. The core of fresh stems is often chewed for refreshment, and in Vietnam is used as a tasty skewer for grilling seasoned pastes of fresh shrimp. Unrefined or natural sugar is available in Japan as dark brown cakes known as *kuro-zato*, and in Mexico in the form of cone-shaped loaves called *piloncillo*. In the United States, products such as *brown sugar* are merely mixtures of white sugar and molasses. *Aguardiente* is raw sugar-alcohol, sweetened and usually strongly flavored with anise or other herbs. In the Philippines, a popular and expensive vinegar called *iloco* is prepared from sugar-cane wine. Cultivated. COST 1988 [Cul], MACMILLAN, ORTIZ 1967, SCHERY, SHURTLEFF 1977, STEINKRAUS, UPHOF; C11G{PR}, C56M, E83Z, G13T{PR}, N84{S}, P38

CULTIVARS

Black: Vigorous, productive plants, 6 to 8 feet tall. Stems are thick, firm, purple-black in color, and very sweet. Good for chewing and juicing. Can be grown in a large container in a greenhouse or sun room. M82, N84{S}, P38

Saccharum spontaneum - *Wild sugar-cane, Thatch grass* {S} The heart of the young shoot is eaten, either raw or cooked, as a side-dish with rice. Very young inflorescences, still enclosed within the leaf-sheaths, can be eaten raw, steamed, or roasted, having a sweet taste. Children chew the peeled rhizomes as a substitute for sugar-cane. Ash from burned plants is used as a substitute for salt. Tropics. OCHSE, ZEVEN; Q46

Secale cereale - *Rye* {S} Seeds are an important source of flour used in various breads, including *pumpernickel*, *knackerbröd*, *spisbröd*, *hiivaleipa*, and *limpa*. Rye flour is an essential substrate of the leaven used in making *sourdough bread*. A unique beverage called *sahti* is produced by the home-brewers of Finland. It is made with a mix of barley and rye malts to which hops and juniper berries are added. *Kwass* is an alcoholic drink of Russia prepared from rye malt and rye flower. Roasted grains are used as a substitute for coffee. Sprouted seeds are used in salads and breads. Cultivated. HESSELTINE, JACKSON, M., LOGSDON 1977 [Cu, Re], LONDON [Re], RITTER [Re], SCHERY, STEINKRAUS, UPHOF; B49, D47M, D58, *E66M*, G71, O48 (also see Sprouting Seeds, page 485)

CULTIVARS

Tetra-Petkus: A tetraploid rye developed from the German cultivar Petkus, which was selected from Pirnaer and Probsteier in the 1880's. Long, bright straw; bearded. Very vigorous; tall growing, height 6 feet. Large kernels with good bread-making quality. Ready to combine in the middle of August in Ontario. Good yields, up to 60 bushels per acre. E63T, I99, L87

Secale kuprijanovi → ***Secale montanum***

Secale montanum - *Mountain rye* {S} The grain is made into flour. Mediterranean region to Southwest Asia. TANAKA, ZEVEN; *F96*

Setaria glauca - *Cattail millet* {S} Seeds are eaten in Africa and India. Eurasia, Africa. TANAKA, WATT; L91M, N84, O48, *Q52*

Setaria italica - *Foxtail millet, German millet, Italian millet* {S} The seeds are cooked like rice, parched, added to soups and sauces, or made into porridge, cakes, puddings, or dumplings. In Korea, they are used in the preparation of *yakju* and *takju*, traditional alcoholic beverages. Also made into a syrup. Eurasia, cultivated. FERNALD, LOGSDON 1977, MACMILLAN, SCHERY, STEINKRAUS, TANAKA; C4, D58, E61, E83T, G26, I99, *K1M*, K47T, K71, *M25*, M95M, N84, O48

CULTIVARS

Celestial: Lengthy, robust seedheads. Originally from China. G47

Golden Temple: 120 days. Very productive plant. Heavy seedheads; lodges in rich soil. Seed is used as porridge, flour, and as a main dish, like rice. Third World staple. D87

Golden Thumb: 120 days. Attractive, drought tolerant plant, 3 1/2 feet tall. Golden-hued ears, 5 inches long, spirally embellished with miniature "thumbs". Excellent flavor, nutty, sweet and light. Requires hulling for use. K49T

White French: 45-90 days. Very fast growing with a low water requirement. Adapts to a wide range of soils. Grows to 3 feet tall. P1G, R47

White Wonder: 85 days. Grows 4 feet tall. Lengthy, robust, 8 inch heads. White grain. Heavy yielding, easy to thresh. Superior to all non-white grains. Does well under poor, dry conditions but takes longer to mature. North American cultivar. G47, I99

Setaria palmifolia - *Palm grass, Highland pitpit, Luluwan kebo* {S} Seeds are boiled or roasted and used as a substitute for rice. The heart of the young shoots, called *hoomboot* in Indonesia, is eaten raw, steamed, or cooked with rice. Very young plants are eaten whole, usually raw, as a side-dish with rice. In New Guinea, improved horticultural forms are grown. Southeast Asia. BROWN, W., MASSAL, MAY, R. [Nu, Re], OCHSE, TANAKA; A79M, C9M, C56M{PL}, *E53M*, F85, N84, O93, S7M

Setaria viridis - *Green foxtail* {S} Seeds are used like millet, either boiled, roasted, or ground into flour. Also said to be used as a substitute for coffee. Widespread, weedy. KUNKEL, TANAKA; D58, N84, *Q52*

Sorghum bicolor - *Sorghum, Indian millet, Milo* {S} The seeds are eaten as a cereal, ground into flour, or used for the preparation of various fermented foods and beverages, including *kisra*, *kaffir beer*, *pito*, *urwaga*, and *ogi baba*. Some types are grown for their bitter grains that are used to flavor sorghum beer. Sorghum malt can be toasted and then extracted with water, yielding an attractive unfermented beverage with a malted, chocolate-type flavor. A ready-to-eat breakfast cereal made from sorghum has been developed in the United States and given the name *Captain Milo*. In Guatemala, the popped grains are made into a confection called *alborotos*. Sprouted seeds are eaten. Tropical Africa. FOX, F., LU, SAUER, STEINKRAUS, ZEVEN; D58, F80, N84

CULTIVARS

Black African: 120 days. White grained cultivar used for porridge, gruel and *chappaties*. Sweet and light flavor, good for summertime eating. Drought tolerant plant, 8 1/2 feet tall, bears seeds in a loose panicle. Grains are easily freed from enclosing glumes. May need protection from birds. K49T

Black Kaffir: 120 days. A seed and feed flour grain. Grows 6 1/2 to 8 feet tall. Tolerates drought. Similar to Black African but with a tighter panicle. I99, K49T

Dwarf Grain: Thick seedheads. Large seeds. Grows only 3 feet tall. I99

Gooseneck Brown Durra: 120 days. Reddish-brown grain of a kind used for feed or brewed into native beers. Drought tolerant plant, 6 1/2 feet tall. Stout, conical seedheads held on recurved necks, like geese, hence the name. Not molested by birds. K49T

Norghum: 120 days. Plants grow 3 to 6 feet tall. Seed ears medium-tight; seeds reddish. Needs warmth and a long growing season. Edible grain sorghum. **T76**

Red Kaffir: 120 days. Dark-grained sorghum used for feed or brewed into native beers. Drought tolerant plant, 7 feet tall. Bears seed in a loosely held, upright ear, 8 to 10 inches long. K49T

Tepehuan Popping: Slender plant with many tillers; white-seeded. May be popped and used like popcorn. Plant in early July in low desert areas. Not drought resistant. Collected from Nabogame, an isolated northern Tepehuan village in southern Chihuahua, Mexico. I16, L7M

White Pearl: 130 days. A rare cultivar with plump, pure white seeds. This is the type of grain sorghum preferred for human food. No bitter, toxic tannins like the grain sorghums grown in the United States for feed purposes. Grown in nearly every state in India, where the grain is made into unlimited delicious foods. G47

Sorghum bicolor Saccharatum Group - *Sweet sorghum, Cane sorghum, Sorgo, Imphee* {S} The stems are chewed for their sweet juice which is also made into *sorghum syrup*, *sorghum molasses*, and sugar. The grain is ground into flour for use in breads and pancakes. Stems are also said to be used as a culinary vegetable. HEMMERLY, LOGSDON 1977 [Cu, Pre], MACMILLAN, TANAKA; H64{PR}, J44, K10, K49M{PR}

CULTIVARS

Amber: 120 days. Drought tolerant plant, 8 1/2 to 10 feet tall. Gently drooping panicle with amber colored grains. Juicy stalks are used for manufacturing *sorghum syrup*. K49T

Apache Red: 120 days. Drought tolerant plant, 8 feet tall. Red seedheads that attract birds. The stalk is chewed like candy when seeds have ripened (turned red). Also used for *sorghum molasses*. From the San Carlos Reservation, Arizona. Adapted to grassland/scrub areas. I16, K49T

Ho-K: Stems are sweet and juicy and can be chewed like candy. The juice may also be extracted and boiled down to a syrup that is delicious on pancakes or waffles. Easy to grow. Tops of stalks are used in dried arrangements. I91, L7M

Honey Drip: 90 days. Grows 8 to 10 feet tall. Makes very good molasses of a light color depending on type of soil. Produces excellent syrup that is easy to cook. Heirloom cultivar from a mountain farmer in Kentucky. **T76, U33**

Kansas Orange: Very leafy, juicy sweet stalk, grows 8 to 10 feet tall. Average size, cylindrical head with reddish-yellow seed. Mid to late season maturity. Makes excellent forage and is also used for molasses. *K1M*

Mennonite: 90-100 days. Very thick stalks, grow 7 to 8 feet tall and resist lodging. Large heads of grain; tight, orange-hulled seed heads. Does not produce too many suckers. Makes a light-colored syrup of good flavor. Seeds may be ground to make flour, especially for pancakes. An old heirloom from a Mennonite who used to have a sorghum mill near Jamesport, Missouri. K49M, L7M

O'odham: (Papago) (S. bicolor x S. halepense) Once commonly grown for *sorghum molasses*. The stalks can be chewed. Perennial. Adapted to the low hot desert, where it is planted in spring or with the summer rains. I16

Onavas Red: Very sweet and juicy. Red seeded. Stalks produce numerous tillers. Planted during the summer rains in the low desert. I16

Rox Orange: 100 days. Produces a mid-stout stalk that is sweet, juicy and leafy and grows 6 to 8 feet tall with few tillers. Rounded, yellow-brown seeds with bright red hulls. Light-colored syrup type; makes very flavorful syrup. Yields well. An old heirloom, developed at the Wisconsin Agricultural Experiment Station. *K1M*

Sugar Drip: 90 days. Dual-purpose type, grown for both forage and syrup. The stalk is leafy, stout and slender and very juicy and sweet; grows 8 to 10 feet tall. Best adapted to warm, well drained sandy loam. Good flavor; excellent for syrup. Withstands light frost. Once widely grown commercially in the Southern States. A56, F12, *K1M*, K71

Texas Black Amber: An Heirloom from Waco, Texas. Produces plump black seeds. Molasses type. Adapted to grassland/scrub areas where it is planted in early July under irrigated conditions. I16

White African: 118 days. Very vigorous plant; grows 10 to 12 feet tall. Large-sized, thick stalks; long-jointed; very sweet, medium juicy to juicy. White seed with a black hull. Very old heirloom cultivar. Makes excellent dark-colored syrup. K49M

Sorghum saccharatum* → *Sorghum bicolor

Sorghum vulgare* → *Sorghum bicolor

Sporobolus airoides - *Alkali sacaton* {S} The seeds are parched, ground, and eaten dry or made into mush. Southwestern North America. DOEBLEY, YANOVSKY; *B29M*, C4, *E53*, *E66M*, F79M, *F96*, *H64T*, I47, J25M, K62, *M25*

Sporobolus cryptandrus - *Sand dropseed* {S} Seeds are parched, ground, mixed with water or milk, and made into mush or biscuits. They can also be added to breads, muffins, and cereals. The tiny seeds have the advantage of being easily freed from their husks. North America. CROWHURST 1972, FERNALD, KINDSCHER, KIRK, YANOVSKY; *B29M*, C4, *E53*, *E66M*, F79M, *F96*, G47M, *H64T*, I47, J25M, J43, K62, *M25*, N7

Thinopyron intermedium - *Intermediate wheatgrass* {S} The seeds are eaten as a cereal, or ground into flour and used to make crepes, muffins, rolls, etc. Tests at the Rodale Research Center indicate that intermediate wheatgrass, along with pubescent wheatgrass are the best candidates among the perennial grasses tested for development into perennial grains, based on culinary evaluations. Adapted to areas with 15 inches or more of annual rainfall. Western North America. WAGONER; *B29M*, C4, *E66M*, *F96*, *H64T*, I47, N29M

CULTIVARS

Oahe: Produces seeds that thresh free when the appropriate seed cleaning equipment is used. Better adapted to areas of higher rainfall than Luna and other cultivars of pubescent wheatgrass. Has an endosperm recovery rate of 50%. Oahe whole grain flower does not compare as favorably to wheat flour as does flour made from Luna pubescent wheatgrass. Developed by James Ross at the Brookings South Dakota Agricultural Experiment Station. C4, *E53*, *F96*, I99M, *J64*, K62

Thinopyron intermedium var. trichophorum - *Pubescent wheatgrass* {S} Seeds are eaten as a cereal or porridge, and are also ground into flour for making breads, cakes, pancakes, etc. In culinary tests at the Rodale Press Food Center, muffins made with 100% pubescent wheatgrass flour had a pleasant, sweet and nutty flavor. More drought tolerant than intermediate wheatgrass, growing in areas with 8 to 15 inches of annual precipitation. Western North America. WAGONER; *B29M*, *E66M*, *F96*, I47

CULTIVARS

Luna: Produces 160 pounds, or about 3 bushels of seed per acre. In milling, the endosperm recovery rate is 65% as compared to 70% for wheat, indicating that Luna should be used for whole grain flour rather than fractionated into endosperm flour, germ and bran. Luna whole grain flour compares favorably to that of a high quality dough forming wheat. Developed by the Los Lunas Soil Conservation Service Plant Material Center in New Mexico. C4, *E53*, F79M, *F96*, I99M, *J64*, K62, N29M

Tripsacum dactyloides - *Eastern gama grass, Buffalo grass* {PL} Grains are used for food. Popped kernels are almost indistinguishable from those of Strawberry popcorn. The seed of gama grass consists of 27% protein and it is nearly twice as high in the amino acid methionine as corn. This high protein percentage, three times higher than corn and twice as high as wheat, allows breeders, who are working to develop gama grass as a perennial grain crop, to sacrifice protein content in their effort to achieve greater yields. North America. HEDRICK 1919, JACKSON, W., KINDSCHER; F73, G47M{S}, H70M

X Triticosecale sp. (Triticum spp. x Secale cereale) - *Triticale* {S} Artificial hybrid, the first man-made grain. The grains are ground into flour for bread, pancakes, cookies, muffins, etc. Being low in gluten, it is usually mixed with that of wheat for bread-making. Sprouted seeds can be used like those of wheat and rye. Generally, the hybrids have a higher protein and amino acid content than wheat and the plants are more winter-hardy. But yields have been low in some areas and lodging has been a fairly serious fault. Triticale grain is larger than wheat, but less abundant on the spike. LOGSDON 1977, SCHERY; E31{PR}, E59Z, I20{PR}, I58{PR}, J44, K62, N32, O48 (also see Sprouting Seeds, page 485)

CULTIVARS

7-1: 100-105 days. Spring triticale. Large, plump seeds with excellent milling and baking qualities; seed test weight high, approximately 52 pounds. Short, stocky plant, height about 4 feet compared to the standard of 5 to 6 feet. H7M

Florico: 100-105 days. Spring triticale. Seeds large and plump, not shriveled; test weight high, about 52 pounds compared to the standard of 48 pounds; milling and baking qualities superior. Short, sturdy plant, grows to about 4 feet tall. H7M

Oac Wintri: Plants grow to 50 inches and are resistant to powdery mildew and leaf rust. Large kernels. Susceptible to preharvest sprouting and lodging. Good winter survival. Originally from the University of Guelph, Ontario, Canada. **T76**

Springfest: Spring triticale. Ripens late, about 100 to 105 days after planting. Large, plump kernels; milling and baking qualities excellent; seed test weight high, approximately 52 pounds. Short, sturdy plant, height about 4 feet. H7M

Triticum x aestivum - *Wheat, Bread wheat* {PR} Grains are ground into flour for use in bread, pasta, cakes, biscuits, pies, crackers, dumplings and numerous other fermented and unfermented products. *Chappati flour*, also called *ata*, is generally made from low-gluten wheat and is used for making many kinds of Indian breads. The grain is sometimes eaten as a cereal like rice, or made into bran flakes, shredded wheat, and other breakfast foods. The popped kernels are sometimes marketed as *wheat nuts*. *Bulghur* wheat, popular in the Middle East for *tabouli*, is wheat that has been parboiled, dried, and then cracked. *Fereek* or *fireek* are husked grains of immature whole wheat. The shelled or peeled grain, called *kamh makshour* or *grano*, is used in Middle Eastern and Italian cuisines. *Kishk* is made from a fermented bulghur and yogurt mixture. *Jalebi* is a fermented wheat/yogurt product from India. *Lambic beer* and *weisse beer* are made from wheat. *Amydoun*, wheat flour that has been steeped, drained, and dried in the sun, is used in the preparation of sweet pottages made with violets and other flowers. The sprouted seeds are used for making *essene bread*. Young seedlings, known as *wheatgrass*, are juiced and consumed as a chlorophyll-rich beverage. Roasted grains are used as coffee. *Panocha*, sprouted wheat flour, is considered nutritionally superior. Wheat gluten, known as *minchin* or *fu*, is a high-protein food widely eaten in Far Eastern countries. *Seitan* is wheat gluten that has been marinated in soy sauce and seasoned. Cultivated. JAFFREY, JACKSON, M., SHURTLEFF 1975, STEINKRAUS, TANAKA, UPHOF, VON WELANETZ; A7M, A52M, A88T, B49{S}, C11G, D47M{S}, D62{S}, E56, E66T, G13T, G71{S}, H19M, H91, I16, L50M, L97G, L99, N84{S}, O48{S}, etc. (also see Sprouting Seeds, page 485)

CULTIVARS {S}

Baart: White spring wheat which is very drought tolerant and high in protein. Grown as a winter wheat in California. Originally from South Africa. Was grown widely grown in the United States until the 1950's when it was replaced by shorter-stemmed cultivars for machine harvest. E63T

Early Triumph: 260 days. A tall, high quality, hard red winter wheat, tolerant of most wheat diseases of the Central United States. Grows 36 to 40 inches tall and is a heavy straw producer, which subjects it to lodging on high nitrate soils. Yields 40 bushels per acre on good soil with no chemical fertilizer. A week earlier to ripen than Turkey in Salina, Kansas test plots. E63T

Golden 50: Hard red winter wheat. Beardless, medium-length straw. A local Kansas farmer-miller rates this as "the best tasting wheat, with real wheat flavor". E63T

Kota: A bearded hard spring wheat, high in protein. May be a natural cross between durum and wild wheatgrass. E63T

Logan: Soft red winter wheat. Beardless, medium to long straw. Should perform better in the more humid, higher rainfall Eastern United States than the hard red wheats offered by The Grain Exchange/Garden Grains. Excellent for bread and ideal for crackers, pancakes, pastries and cookies. E63T

Marquis: 90 days. Early hard red spring wheat. Especially suited to forest soils of the Northeast. Easy to hand-thresh. Good milling and baking qualities. Susceptible to leaf and stem rust. Developed from Red Fife and Hard Red Calcutta by C.E. Saunders of the Canada Department of Agriculture, Ottawa, in 1908. E63T

Perennial: (Perennial Wheat) Novelty plant with good productivity and grain flavor. For fall planting. Genetically programmed to lie dormant under winter snow blanket until spring. Some of the plants will live on to produce grain in successive years. G47

Polk: A hard red, spring bread wheat. Not as high-yielding as winter wheat, but planted and harvested during the same growing season. Polk is a high protein, high gluten, medium-height spring wheat with superior bread baking quality. Sow in early spring as soon as ground can be prepared. E63T, G6

Red Fife: Awnless hard red spring wheat. Mother of the North American spring wheat industry. Most popular Canadian hard red spring wheat in the 19th Century. **T76**

Reward: 78 days. Awnless hard red spring wheat, descended from Marquis. Short, fat kernels of good quality. Easy to hand-thresh. Early maturing cultivar tolerant of acid soils. Released in 1928. **T76**, U33

Roughrider: A hard red, winter bread wheat, higher yielding than spring wheat. Roughrider is awned (bearded), medium height, and winter hardy. Developed in North Dakota. Sow August 25 to September 10 in climate similar to Maine, later further south. Grain matures July to Early August. G6

Turkey Red: Hard red winter wheat. Excellent bread making quality and flavor. Tall and bearded. Fair producer under drought conditions. An old cultivar, originally brought to Kansas about 1870 by Mennonite families emigrating from the Ukraine. Parent strain of contemporary bread wheat. E63T, K49T

White Sonoran: Beardless type used to breed Green Revolution wheat. Very drought adapted. Lodges if over-watered. Once grown by the Tohono O'odham Indians, but now endangered. It was their traditional *tortilla* wheat. I16

Triticum baeoticum - *Wild einkorn wheat, Thaoudar wheat* {S} Seeds are occasionally eaten. Southeastern Europe to Iran. BROUK, KUNKEL, ZEVEN; **X79M, Y14M, Y75, Y99, Z98**

Triticum carthlicum - *Persian wheat* {S} Cultivated as a grain crop in the Turkish-Caucasian region up to 2100 meters elevation.

Southwestern Asia, cultivated. UPHOF, ZEVEN; **X8, X36, X79M, Y14M, Y75, Z98**

Triticum compactum - *Club wheat* {S} The grain is made into flour for use in bread, crackers, starchy breakfast food, etc. Southwest Asia, cultivated. SCHERY, UPHOF, ZEVEN; **V84M, X8, X36, Y75**

CULTIVARS

Pima: A beardless soft white wheat grown by the Pima Indians at least as early as 1920. Unusual compact head. Excellent for flour *tortillas*. E63T

Triticum dicoccoides - *Wild emmer* {S} The grain is edible. Southwest Asia. SCHERY, TANAKA; **V84M, Y14M, Y75, Z98**

Triticum dicoccon - *Emmer, German wheat* {S} The grain is ground into flour, made into breakfast foods, etc. Emmer is the oldest cultivated wheat. Its culture is declining, however it is still cultivated in some mountainous areas of Europe. Eurasia, cultivated. SCHERY, ZEVEN; **V50, V84, W92, X8, X33, X36, X79M, Y14M, Y17M, Y29, Y75, Z98**

Triticum durum - *Durum wheat, Macaroni wheat* {PR} The grain is hard, semi-translucent, and especially rich in gluten. Source of *semolina*, used for making pasta, spaghetti, noodles, certain breads, and *couscous* a staple food of North Africa. In Iran and Iraq, the grain is eaten in the form of a local porridge. Durum wheat is preferred for making *trahanas*, a fermented food made from crushed wheat and fermented sheep milk. *Beghrir* is a pale yellow yeast-semolina pancake from Morocco that is cooked only on one side. It is reminiscent of a honey-comb with numerous small holes. Mediterranean region, Eurasia, cultivated. SCHERY, STEINKRAUS, TANAKA, UPHOF, WOLFERT [Pre, Re]; A3, A7M, C42M, H19M, I20, I58, L50M, O48{S}, O53M{S}, O93{S}, S55{S}

Triticum macha - *Macha wheat, Makha wheat* {S} Cultivated for its grain in Soviet Georgia and other parts of Southern Russia. Western Asia. UPHOF, ZEVEN; **X8, X79M, Y14M, Z98**

Triticum monococcum - *Einkorn, Stone Age wheat, One-grained wheat* {S} The grain is edible. Supposed to be the most primitive wheat. Occasionally grown in Germany, Switzerland, and Italy. Europe, cultivated. HEDRICK 1919, UPHOF, ZEVEN; B49, C61M, D87, E81M

Triticum orientale* → *Triticum turanicum

Triticum persicum* → *Triticum carthlicum

Triticum polonicum - *Polish wheat, Astrakan wheat* {S} The large grains are ground into flour which is suitable for making macaroni. Not suitable for bread making. Can be grown very successfully under garden conditions. Eurasia, cultivated. SCHERY, UPHOF, ZEVEN; G47

CULTIVARS

Kamut: Very large kernels, 2 to 3 times the size of modern wheats. Contains significantly higher levels of protein and slightly higher levels of lipids and minerals. Reportedly less allergenic but this has not been substantiated by controlled studies. Produces whole wheat pasta, flour, sprout bread and puffed wheat of superior flavor. Also makes excellent wheatgrass. Thought to have originated in the fertile crescent. Introduced into Montana around 1950. E56{PR}, *H78M*{PR}, *K74*{PR}, *L14M*{PR}, L24{SP}

Triticum spelta - *Spelt, Speltz, Dinkel wheat* {S} The reddish grains are used for flour. Still grown in some areas of Germany where the naked grains are often harvested prematurely. They are then parched and added to soups as *gruenkern*. This product is available at specialty stores in New York and other large cities. Spelt pasta, recently introduced to the natural foods trade, has a delicious nutty flavor. Europe, cultivated. LOGSDON 1977, LOVELOCK, UPHOF, ZEVEN; D62, E31{PR}, F85, G47, H67M{PR}, I97{PR}, J51T{PR}, K47T, L91M, N84, O48, O93, *Q52*, S55

CULTIVARS

Champ: An awnless, brown chaffed cultivar that outyields common spelt by an average of 23.2%. Also contains 1% to 1.57% higher protein. Slightly taller and has considerably improved straw strength. Has very good resistance to leaf rust but is only moderately resistant to powdery mildew. Developed by Howard Lafever at the Ohio Agriculture Research and Development Center. The first public cultivar released in recent decades. *J80*, K10

Triticum sphaerococcum - *Shot wheat, Indian dwarf wheat* {S} Grown as a grain crop in Punjab and Central Provinces of India. Southern Asia, cultivated. UPHOF, ZEVEN; **X79M, Y14M, Y75, Z98**

Triticum timopheevi - *Sanduri, Tschalta sanduri* {S} An ancient grain crop cultivated in Soviet Georgia. Western Asia, cultivated. UPHOF, ZEVEN; **X8, X36, X79M, Y14M, Y29, Y75, Z98**

Triticum turanicum - *Khurasan wheat* {S} The grains are used for flour. Southwest Asia. SCHERY, UPHOF, ZEVEN; **T76, Y75, Z98**

Triticum turgidum - *Rivet wheat, Poulard wheat, English wheat* {S} The grain is made into flour which is used in making macaroni, spaghetti, vermicelli, etc. Cultivated. SCHERY, UPHOF, ZEVEN; F85

Triticum vavilovi - *Vavilov wheat* {S} Grains are used for food in Armenia. Western Asia. BROUK, ZEVEN; **Y75, Z98**

Triticum zhukofskyi - *Zanduri wheat* {S} Cultivated as a grain crop in western Soviet Georgia. Southwest Asia. ZEVEN; **Y75, Z98**

Uniola paniculata - *Sea oats, Beach grass* {PL} The seeds may be cooked and eaten as a cereal. Said to be of very good flavor. North America. MORTON 1977; *F73, J25*

Vetiveria zizanioides - *Vetiver, Khus-khus, Botha grass* {PL} Roots are the source of a volatile essential oil used in India for flavoring sherbets and fruit drinks. In the food industry, it is added to canned asparagus to enhance the flavor. Tropical Asia, cultivated. MORTON 1976, UPHOF; C81M, E5M, E81M{S}, F37T, F85{S}, H40, J82{S}, K22, K85, M82, N19M, Q46{S}

Zea diploperennis - *Diploid perennial teosinte* {S} The seeds are sometimes eaten. A wild relative of maize discovered near El Durazno, Jalisco, Mexico. Crosses with maize to produce fertile hybrids. Mexico. ZEVEN; F80, I16

Zea mays - *Corn, Maize, Indian corn* {PR} The immature seeds are eaten raw, boiled or roasted, in *succotash*, etc.. When cooked and dried they are called *chicos* and are used in stews or chili. Dried seeds are parched and ground into meal for use in breads, cakes and *polenta*, or treated with lye and made into *hominy* and *masa* for use in *tortillas*, *tacos*, *tamales*, *enchiladas*, *atole* and *pinole*. Also made into numerous fermented foods and beverages, including *chicha*, *pozol*, *kenkey*, *koko* and *tesguino*. Corn oil is used in salads and cooking. Roasted seeds are used for coffee. Corn starch is used in confectionery and noodles. Young immature ears are boiled as a vegetable or made into tortillas. The pollen is used as an ingredient of soups. Fresh, succulent silks are chopped fine and mixed with masa in making tortillas. Young tassels are boiled and eaten. The pith of the stems is chewed like sugar cane or is sometimes made into syrup. Sprouted seeds are used in uncooked breads and cereals. Hypertrophies, produced by the corn smut fungus, are consumed. Southern America, cultivated. DUKE, STEINKRAUS, TANAKA, UPHOF, WEATHERWAX, WILL; C57, C64, E68M, G13T, I16, N29 (for cultivars see Corn, page 304, also see Sprouting Seeds, page 485)

Zea mays ssp. mexicana* → *Zea mexicana

Zea mays 'Ceratina' - *Wax corn* {S} Low plants with erect leaves. Grains with waxy endosperm. Probably originated as a mutation in Eastern Asia. Cultivated in China, Manchuria, Burma, and the Philippine Islands. UPHOF; **Y75, Z98**

CULTIVARS

Philippine White Wax: An improved type from the Philippines. Has a chewy texture. D33

Zea mexicana - *Teosinte, Annual teosinte, Maíz café* {S} Young shoots are boiled and eaten. Whole mature seeds can be eaten by first soaking them in water until soft enough to chew. Dried kernels can be popped like popcorn. The young spikes can be eaten before the seeds have matured. In Honduras, the seeds are roasted and mixed with coffee or used as a substitute for coffee. The wild ancestor of maize. Mexico. ALTSCHUL, BEADLE, TANAKA, WILLIAMS, L., ZEVEN; F80, J73

CULTIVARS

Day Neutral: A strain that is not sensitive to day length and will flower and mature seed in northern areas. Developed by George Beadle and Walton Galinat. C7M

Northern Tepehuan Maizillo: Nabogame race. The most distinctive annual teosinte. Grows to 6 feet tall. Prolific. Probably will not flower until after the autumn equinox so may require a greenhouse or frost protection. Produces a good crop in Tucson and the California central valley with minimum protection. From southern Chihuahua. F80, I16

Zizania aquatica - *Wild rice, Indian rice* {PL} The long, black, delicious grain is eaten as an expensive, gourmet cereal. It is commonly cooked with mushrooms and served with game or fowl. Wild rice can also be ground into meal and used for baking in breads, muffins, cakes, and in thickening soups. With recent plantings in California coming into production it is now more readily available and at a lower price. However, some still prefer the flavor of grains harvested from wild stands. North America, cultivated. ANGIER [Re], CREASY 1982 [Cu], FERNALD, GIBBONS 1962, HAWKES [Re], LOGSDON 1977 [Re], TURNER 1979 [Pre, Re]; C64M, D58{S}, D74M{PR}, *F73*, G26{PR}, G26{S}, G47M{S}, H30, K34, K52{PR}, M15, N11, N11{PR}, N11{S}

Zizania latifolia - *Manchurian wild rice, Water grass* {PL} The swollen, infected base of the culms, parasitized by the smut fungus Ustilago esculenta, is eaten by the Chinese as a vegetable, known as *gau sun*, *cane shoots*, *wild-rice stem* and *sticky shoot*. It is parboiled, then sautéed with meats and other vegetables and has a nutty flavor reminiscent of coconut. Seeds are used like rice. The very young inflorescence is cooked and eaten as a vegetable. Eastern Asia, cultivated. DAHLEN [Pre, Cul], FERNALD, HERKLOTS, TANAKA, TERRELL; B28

CULTIVARS {S}

Su Zhou: An early cultivar with tender flesh. *O54*

Zizaniopsis miliacea - *Water millet, Southern wild rice* {PL} The vigorous new tips of the white rhizomes are cut in short pieces, cooked until tender, and served with butter. Southern North America. FERNALD, GIBBONS 1979; *F73*

PODOCARPACEAE

Dacrycarpus dacrydioides - *Kahikatea* {S} The sweet fruits are eaten or used as a masticatory. New Zealand. COLENSO, FULLER, HEDRICK 1919, UPHOF; *N73*{PL}, N84, O93, S43M

Dacrydium cupressinum - *Rimu, Red pine* {S} A resinous substance from the young branches was used by Captain Cook to make an alcoholic beverage resembling spruce-beer. Fleshy fruits are eaten. New Zealand. COLENSO, FULLER [Re], HEDRICK 1919, TANAKA; N84, O93

Dacrydium franklinii* → *Lagarostrobus franklinii

Decussocarpus falcatus - *Outeniqua yellow-wood* {S} The fruits are eaten. Southern Africa. FOX, F.; F85, N84

Decussocarpus nagi - *Nagi* {PL} Young leaves are occasionally parboiled and eaten. Japan. TANAKA; C56M, *E66*, H4, N84{S}

Lagarostrobus franklinii - *Huon pine* {S} Source of an essential oil recommended for the manufacture of vanillin, which is used as a flavoring in ice cream, confectionery, beverages, etc. Tasmania. TANAKA, UPHOF; B94, *P63*, P86{PL}

Podocarpus dacrydioides* → *Dacrycarpus dacrydioides

Podocarpus elatus - *Brown pine, Australian plum, Illawarra plum* {S} The large, fleshy fruit-stalk, resembling a purple-black grape with a waxy bloom, is mucilaginous and resinous in flavor. It is eaten raw or made into jam or jelly. Australia. CRIBB; M7M{PL}, *N79M*, N84, O84, P1G, P5, *P17M*, P38, *Q25*, *Q32*, R15M, R33M, S92

Podocarpus falcatus* → *Decussocarpus falcatus

Podocarpus macrophyllus - *Japanese yew* {S} Fruits are eaten by children in Japan. In Florida, where this tree has been introduced as a hedge plant, they are eaten out of hand or in pies and cakes. Japan, China. TANAKA; C9M, D95{PL}, H4{PL}, *I61*, K47T, N84, *R28*

Podocarpus nagi* → *Decussocarpus nagi

Podocarpus spicatus - *Matai, Black pine* {S} The watery sap was drunk or used in the preparation of a beer-like beverage. Other authors report the young shoots being made into a beverage resembling spruce-beer. Fruits are sweet and edible. New Zealand. COLENSO, FULLER, HEDRICK 1919; N84, O93

Podocarpus totara - *Totara, Mahogany pine* {PL} Fruits are eaten. New Zealand. COLENSO, HEDRICK 1919; L2, *N73*, N84{S}, O93{S}

PODOPHYLLACEAE

Achlys triphylla - *Vanilla leaf, Sweet after death* {PL} A non-commercial volume of a vanilla substitute has been extracted from the leaves. Pacific Coast of North America. E63M

Podophyllum emodi - *Himalayan may-apple* {S} The fruits are eaten. Roots and leaves are considered poisonous, although some authors report the young leaves as being edible. Himalayan region. HEDRICK 1919, TANAKA, WATT; D62, F80, L91M, N84, O35G{PL}, O53M, Q40, R53M

Podophyllum peltatum - *May apple, American mandrake, Wild lemon* {PL} Ripe fruits have a peculiar, agreeable flavor and are eaten raw, cooked, or made into jams, jellies, marmalades, pies, and refreshing beverages. In the South, the juice of the fruit is mixed with Madeira and sugar. Unripe fruits are cathartic. Eastern North America. ANGIER [Re], BURR [Cu, Pro], FERNALD, GIBBONS 1962 [Re], MEDSGER, TURNER 1979 [Re]; B0, B33M, C9, C43M, C56, C81M, D75T, E33M, *G28*, H63, I22, I44, J48, N8, N9M, N9M{S}, etc.

POLYGALACEAE

Carpolobia lutea - {S} The fruits are reportedly very sweet-tasting. Leaves are also eaten. West Tropical Africa. INGLETT, MARTIN 1975; N84

POLYGONACEAE

Antigonon leptopus - *Coralvine, Mountain rose, Bellisima* {S} Tubers are cooked and eaten. Said to have a nut-like flavor. In

Thailand, the flowers are often used as a cooked vegetable. Tropical America. DUKE, PONGPANGAN, UPHOF, WILLIAMS, L.; A79M, C9M, D62, E7M, F85, G25M, G96{PL}, H4, H4{PL}, J27{PL}, N84, O53M, Q12, R33M, S91M, etc.

Atraphaxis spinosa - *Shir-khecht shrub* {S} Source of a yellowish-white manna-like substance eaten as food or used in making sweetmeats. Southwest Asia. DONKIN; **W3M, W92**

Bistorta bistortoides* → *Polygonum bistortoides

Bistorta vivipara* → *Polygonum viviparum

Coccoloba caracasana - *Papaturro, Papaturro blanco* {S} The juicy, white fruits have an acidulous flavor and are often eaten. Northern South America. WILLIAMS, L.; **T73M**

Coccoloba diversifolia - *Pigeon plum, Dove plum* {PL} Fruits are dark-purple, juicy, acid to subacid, and are eaten raw or made into jelly or wine. If held for a few days, they do not spoil readily but lose their astringency and dehydrate somewhat. Sold in local markets of Nassau, Bahamas. Florida, Caribbean region. KENNARD, MORTON 1977; D87G

Coccoloba floridana* → *Coccoloba diversifolia

Coccoloba uvifera - *Sea grape* {S} The fruits are reddish-purple or occasionally off-white, juicy and subacid. They may be eaten out of hand or used for juice, jams, drinks, and syrup. Sea grape jelly has an attractive musky flavor and a distinctive, light lavender color. A potent wine of good flavor can also be made from the fruits. Florida, Caribbean region, cultivated. CREASY 1982, KENNARD, MORTON 1977, RICHARDSON [Pre, Re], STURROCK; A79M, B62, D87G{PL}, E29, E29{PL}, E29{PR}, *E53M*, F85, *J25*{PL}, *L5M*, L91M, N84, O53M, O93, Q41, etc.

Emex spinosa - {S} Leaves are consumed like spinach. Roots are eaten raw or cooked. Mediterranean region. KUNKEL, MARTIN 1975; F85

Fagopyrum cymosum - *Perennial buckwheat, Shakuchiri-soba* {S} The leaves are boiled or steamed and served like spinach. Seeds are also eaten or ground into flour. Central Asia. HEDRICK 1919, TANAKA, WATT; F80, N84, Q40

Fagopyrum esculentum - *Buckwheat, Soba* {S} Hulled kernels, or *groats*, are used in breakfast cereals, *kasha*, and *polenta taragna*. Buckwheat flour is made into pancakes, noodles, and breads or used for thickening soups and gravies. Young seedlings, called *buckwheat lettuce*, are eaten in salads and are widely available in natural foods stores. Beer may be brewed from the grain, and by distillation it yields an excellent spirit. Leaves can be used like spinach. Southwest Asia. BIANCHINI, BROUK, GRIEVE, KULVINSKAS, LOGSDON 1977 [Cu, Pre], UPHOF; A25, A56, B49, C85M, D65, E24, F24, G6, G26, H33, H54, I26, J20, J25M, J34, J44, J97M, K71, L89, N39, etc. (also see Sprouting Seeds, page 485)

CULTIVARS

Giant American: Produces the largest seed of any buckwheat cultivar. Also has the heaviest seed per 100 seed weight. Medium-tall plant, height about 4 feet. Blooms in 30 days. Yields comparable to those of Mancan. Lodging rating of 4.3 on a scale of 1 erect to 9 flat equals that of Mancan. *E23T*

Mancan: An improved type that yields a nutritious grain in 80 days. Medium-tall plant with medium-sized, dark green leaves and white flowers. Approximately 1 plant per 1,000 bears pink flowers. Blooms in 30 days. Yields average to above average crops. Developed by the Agriculture Canada Research Station in Morden, Manitoba. L7M, *L39M*

New Type: A heavy cropper and less liable to blight than other sorts. The kernels are larger and the straw is stouter and heavier. G71

Spanky: An improved type that makes excellent flapjacks. Planted late to mature in the fall, less than one pound per 1,000 square feet. Ripens in 2 to 3 months. K49M

Fagopyrum tataricum - *Tartarian buckwheat, Duck wheat, Dattan-soba* {S} Seeds are eaten or ground into a flour used in various foods. They also yield an edible oil. The leaves are used as a vegetable. Central Asia. FERNALD, HEDRICK 1919, KUNKEL, TANAKA, WATT; D58, E83T, F80, G26, N11

CULTIVARS

Madawaska: (Madawaska Buckwheat) More cold hardy and drought resistant than regular buckwheat. Local cultivar from the upper St. John's Valley, Maine. I99

Oxyria digyna - *Mountain sorrel* {S} The fleshy, succulent leaves have a pleasing acid taste, and may be used raw in sandwiches and mixed salads, as a potherb with peppery cresses, or in thick soups and purées. Eskimos allow it to ferment into a "sauerkraut" that is stored for winter use. Northern and Alpine regions. ANGIER [Re], CLARKE [Cul], FERNALD, HARRINGTON, H., HEDRICK 1919, HELLER, MEDSGER; D62, K47T, N84

Persicaria hydropiper - *Smartweed, Water pepper, Yanagi-tade* {S} Young leaves and stems are roasted and eaten as a vegetable, or made into an acid, peppery condiment. In Japan, the young seedlings are a common market product and are used to garnish many dishes. *Tade-su* is a mixture of the leaves, boiled rice, and vinegar. Eurasia. CRIBB, TANAKA, YASHIRODA; **V50, V73, V73M, V87, X79M, Y10, Y29**

Persicaria hydropiper 'Fastigiatum' - *Hosoba-tade, Water pepper* {S} The small, red cotyledons have a sharp, acrid flavor and are used as a condiment or as a garnish for traditional Japanese raw fish (*sashimi*). TANAKA, UPHOF; *S70*

Persicaria vulgaris - *Lady's thumb, Heartweed, Redleg, Haru-tade* {S} Young shoots and leaves are eaten in salads, stir-fried, or cooked briefly in boiling water and served with butter or vinegar. Eurasia, naturalized in North America. CROWHURST 1972, LARKCOM 1984, MEDSGER, TANAKA; D58, D62, F80, *N71M*, N84

Polygonum aviculare - *Knotgrass, Michi-yanagi* {S} The seeds are eaten or ground into flour for use in pancakes, cookies, and *pinole*. Young leaves and plants are eaten as potherbs. Leaves are also used as a substitute for tea. Eurasia, naturalized in North America. FERNALD, KIRK, KUNKEL, TANAKA; D58, J82, *N71M*, N84

Polygonum bistorta - *Bistort, Snakeweed, Pink plumes, Easter ledges* {S} Young leaves and shoots are an excellent substitute for spinach. In Northern England, they are used in the preparation of a Lenten pudding called *Easter ledger* pudding or *Easter herb* pudding. Rhizomes are roasted, boiled, mixed with seal oil or added to stews. Northern temperate region. GRIEVE [Re], HEDRICK 1919, HELLER, LAUNERT, MABEY [Re]; D62, G82M{PL}, N71M, N84, O48, O53M, P95M{PL}, *Q24*, R53M{PL}, S7M, S55

Polygonum bistortoides - *American bistort* {S} The young leaves have a pleasantly tart taste and can be used as a potherb. Starchy roots are eaten raw, boiled or baked, or added to soups and stews. North America. HARRINGTON, H., YANOVSKY; A2

Polygonum cuspidatum* → *Reynoutria japonica

Polygonum equisetiforme - *Gudhabah* {S} The plants are used as a condiment for tea. Mediterranean region. BAILEY, C.; **W59M**

Polygonum hydropiper* → *Persicaria hydropiper

Polygonum maximowiczii → *Persicaria hydropiper*

Polygonum odoratum - *Rau răm, Vietnamese coriander* {PL} Young leaves have an aroma somewhat reminiscent of coriander and a hot, peppery, but refreshing flavor. They may be used in raw or cooked fish, meat, rice, or vegetable dishes. One of the ingredients of *du'a cân*, a pickled dish resembling sauerkraut. Only the young, green leaves are used as the older, redder leaves have too hot a flavor. Southeast Asia. BOND [Cul, Re], HEDRICK 1919, HUTSON [Cul], KEUBEL [Cu], PAINTER [Re], UPHOF; C43M, D62{S}, G84, J82, M82

Polygonum persicaria → *Persicaria vulgaris*

Polygonum punctatum - *Dotted smartweed* {S} The young shoots are cooked and used as a vegetable. Leaves are used as a seasoning. Parched seeds are eaten as a cereal. North America. MORTON 1963; G47M

Polygonum sachalinense → *Reynoutria sachalinensis*

Polygonum viviparum - *Alpine bistort, Serpent grass* {S} The tuber-like rootstocks are sweet, nutty, and wholesome. They may be eaten raw or boiled, but are best roasted. Young leaves are eaten as a potherb. Circumpolar. FERNALD, HARRINGTON, H., KIRK; D62, N84, O53M, S7M

Reynoutria japonica - *Japanese knotweed* {S} Young shoots are boiled or steamed and eaten like asparagus with butter or sauce, or chilled and served with salad dressing. They have a somewhat acid flavor and can be used like rhubarb in pies, fruit soups, aspic salads, sweet sauces, jams, puddings, chutneys, or wines. Rhizomes are sometimes eaten. Eastern Asia, naturalized in North America. ANGIER, CROWHURST 1972 [Re], FERNALD, GIBBONS 1962 [Pre, Re]; B28{PL}, D37{PL}, F85, J7{PL}, N84, S7M

Reynoutria sachalinensis - *Giant knotweed, Sachaline* {PL} Young shoots and tips are eaten raw in salads, parboiled and served like asparagus, or used in soups. "Rhubarb" sauce, made from the peeled young stems, is of superior quality, with a hint of lemon-flavor. The fruit is eaten, or stored in fish oil for later use. Eastern Asia, naturalized in North America. FERNALD, KIRK, TANAKA; M16

Rheum australe - *Himalayan rhubarb* {S} Leafstalks are eaten raw, cooked, preserved in salt, made into preserves, or dried and stored for future use. They are said to have an apple-like flavor. Young shoots that have been blanched as they emerge from the soil are white, crisp, and free from fiber. Himalayan region. HEDRICK 1919, TANAKA, WATT; F80, I63M{PL}, L66{PL}, N84, O53M, *Q24*, Q40, S7M

Rheum emodi → *Rheum australe*

Rheum nobile - *Sikkim rhubarb* {S} Leafstalks, called *chuka* by the people of Sikkim, are pleasantly acid and are eaten both raw and boiled. Himalayan region. HEDRICK 1919, WATT; N84

Rheum palmatum - *Chinese rhubarb* {S} The leafstalks are sometimes eaten or made into wine and preserves. Mongolia. HEDRICK 1919, TANAKA; J82, K47T, L66{PL}, L91M, N84, S7M

CULTIVARS {PL}

Bowles Crimson: Large, palmately lobed leaves, dark red when young. Flowers large, panicles deep red. P86

Rheum rhabarbarum - *Rhubarb* {S} Leafstalks are pleasantly acid and are stewed or baked in the manner of a fruit and used in pies, cakes, tarts, puddings, sauces, jellies, jams, ice cream, etc. The juice strained from stewed rhubarb can add color and flavor to a fruit punch. Some connoisseurs claim that the juice pressed from hardened old stalks yields a delicious wine rivalled only by champagne. The young inflorescences resemble cauliflower and may be deep fried, or boiled and served "au gratin" with cream sauce. Cultivated. BRYAN [Pre, Re], CARCIONE, GRIEVE, HALPIN [Cul], HILL, JOHNS [Re], VILMORIN [Cu]; D62, F35M{PL}, I99, N84, *Q24* (for cultivars see Rhubarb, page 469)

Rheum tataricum - *Tartarian rhubarb* {S} The leafstalks and unexpanded flower clusters are eaten. Central Asia. HEDRICK 1919; **V73, W3M, X33, Z24**

Rumex acetosa - *Garden sorrel, Broad-leaved sorrel* {PL} The pleasantly acid leaves are eaten raw in salads, as a potherb, pureéd, or used in soups, omelettes, sauces, etc. In France, sorrel is put into ragouts and fricasées, and is the chief constituent of *soupe aux herbes*. They also stuff shad with purée of sorrel, whose oxalic acid softens, and somewhat dissolves the numerous bones. Flowers are eaten as a vegetable or used for garnishing. The juice of the leaves is used to curdle milk. Seeds can be ground and made into bread. Eurasia, cultivated. BRYAN [Cul, Re], GRIEVE, HALPIN, LARKCOM 1984, LEGGATT [Re], MABEY, MORTON 1976, ROOT 1980a, SCHNEIDER [Cul, Re], VILMORIN [Cu]; C3, C3{S}, C9, C43M, E5M{PR}, F24{S}, F44{S}, G6{S}, H46{S}, J85T{PR}, K22, K66{S}, L7M{S}, M46, N19M, *N40*{PR}, N45, etc.

CULTIVARS {S}

Belleville: (De Belleville) Large, pale green leaves, 3 inches long, slightly blistered; petioles lightly tinged with red. A small French cultivar that is hardy, fast growing, and well-proven to be productive under almost any conditions. C53, F33, G68

Blonde de Lyon: (Mammoth Lyon) Large, thick, broad leaves, much rounder than other types; somewhat blistered. Pale green color. Tender and mild flavor. More resistant to bolting than Belleville; often grown in warmer climates. Named after the city of Lyon, France. C92, E7M, E83T, E99, I77, J82, J82{PL}, K49M

Gourmet Brand Verte: Produces large rosettes of tangy foliage. Cold tolerant and ideal for very early spring and very late fall crops. Excellent in salads or an early spring cream of sorrel soup. *E91G*

Larghe Foglie Bionde: Large, pale green leaves. Delicious in salads. Will last for 3 to 4 years before requiring division. Usually harvested by stripping off the outer leaves; not adaptable to cut-and-come-again techniques. Q11M

Low Oxalic Acid: A highly refined selection, bred for low oxalic acid content. The flavor is only slightly sour. L89

Nobel: A new cultivar of sorrel. Leaves are larger, broader and more succulent than other cultivars. J82

Pallagi Nagylevelü: An improved form developed in eastern Europe. N84

Rumex acetosella - *Sheep sorrel* {S} The sour leaves are commonly chewed to quench the thirst. Small amounts of the tender leaves may also be used in purées, soups, mixed salads, drinks, sandwiches, pies, or as an unusual garnish and seasoning for seafood, rice, and potatoes. The roots are also said to be edible. Northern temperate region. CLARKE [Re], FERNALD, GIBBONS 1966a [Re], HARRINGTON, H., TANAKA; D58, F85, L86, *N71M*, N84, O48

Rumex alpinus - *Alpine dock, Monk's rhubarb, Pyrenean sorrel* {S} Young heart-shaped leaves are eaten raw in salads or cooked as a potherb. Also employed as a preservative of unsalted butter during summer months. Eurasia. BURR, MABEY, UPHOF, VILMORIN; D62, K47T, N84

Rumex arifolius - *Maiden sorrel* {S} The young leaves are eaten raw in salads, cooked as a potherb, or added to soups and omelettes. In Norway, they are eaten with milk or mixed with meal and baked. Europe. HEDRICK 1919, ROOT 1980a, VILMORIN; **Y14M, Z24**

Rumex crispus - *Curled dock, Yellow dock* {S} The young, tender leaves, rich in vitamins A and C, are eaten raw in salads, cooked as a potherb, or added to soups. When cooked in a cream sauce, the protein in milk combines with the tannin in dock and removes the astringency that some people find objectionable. The seeds are ground into a meal or flour that can be used in pancakes. Eurasia, naturalized in North America. ANGIER, GIBBONS 1966b, HARRINGTON, H., MEDSGER; C11, D58, D62, E5T, F37T{PL}, F85, I99, J82, K20, N84

Rumex hydrolapathum - *Great water dock, Wild rhubarb* {S} Young leaves are used as a vegetable. Northern temperate region. BROWN, W., HEDRICK 1919, TANAKA; N84

Rumex hymenosepalus - *Canaigre* {S} The crisp, tart leafstalks are excellent eaten in pies like rhubarb. The leaves are eaten, but are cooked in several changes of water to remove the bitter tannin. Seeds are sometimes used in mush. Southwestern North America. CLARKE [Re], KIRK, MEDSGER, UPHOF; F85, I98M

Rumex japonicus - *Gishigishi, Dock, So-ri-jeng-i* {S} Leaves are eaten as a boiled vegetable, put in soups, or dried for later use. Seeds are eaten mixed with rice or ground into flour for making dumplings. Japan. TANAKA; **Y76**

Rumex montanus → *Rumex arifolius*

Rumex obtusifolius - *Broad-leaved dock, Bitter dock* {S} The young leaves can be eaten as a potherb, puréed, or used in soups. When boiling the leaves, the water should be changed once or twice to take away the strong taste. Older leaves usually become bitter. Northern temperate region. FERNALD, MEDSGER; N84

Rumex patientia - *Patience dock, Spinach dock* {S} Leaves are boiled or steamed and eaten like spinach or made into a delicious purée. Their flavor is milder than that of garden sorrel. They should be harvested when young and tender and a fourth part of common sorrel mixed with them. It has the advantage of producing leaves earlier in the season than any other kind. Southern Europe, naturalized in North America. BURR [Cu], FERNALD, LARKCOM 1984, MEDSGER, VILMORIN; N84, O48

Rumex sagittatus - *Surengan, Soorèngan* {S} The sour leaves are cooked and eaten as a spinach. In Java, they are used as a substitute for tamarind in the preparation of savory stews. Indonesia. FOX, F., OCHSE; F85, N84, R41, R77M

Rumex sanguineus - *Bloodwort, Red-veined dock* {S} Young leaves are used as a substitute for spinach. Ornamental in appearance but with coarse-textured leaves. For use in salads, soften by blanching in boiling water for a few seconds. Northern temperate region. HEDRICK 1919, LARKCOM 1984; N84, O48, O53M

Rumex scutatus - *French sorrel, Buckler-leaved sorrel* {PL} The leaves are extremely acid and are used primarily as a flavoring. They are preferred by many gourmets because they add more zest to mixed salads, sauces, and the much-esteemed cream of sorrel soup. Eurasia. GRIEVE, HALPIN, MORTON 1976, VILMORIN; E61, I39, J82, L56, L86{S}, N84{S}, O48{S}, P92, R53M, R53M{S}, S55{S}

Rumex vesicarius - *Bladder dock, Chooka, Katta palak* {S} Acid leaves are eaten raw or cooked. Cultivated as a vegetable in parts of Indonesia and occasionally sold in local markets. Macaronesia to Southwest Asia. BURKILL, OCHSE, UPHOF; E83T

Rumex sp. - *German spinach* {S} Salad green with long, wide, blistered leaves. The tart, distinctive flavor of the leaves is best enjoyed raw in salads, but is also good added to cream sauces for fish or eaten slightly steamed with butter. F80

PONTEDERIACEAE

Pontederia cordata - *Pickerel-weed* {PL} The seeds are eaten raw, boiled like rice, or dried and ground into flour for making bread. Raw seeds have a very acceptable nutty flavor and texture. When slightly parched in an oven they are said to be excellent. Young leaves are cooked as a potherb or chopped and added to tossed green salads, soups, and stews. North America, Tropical America. CROWHURST 1972, DUKE, FERNALD, GIBBONS 1979, MORTON 1977; C49, D75T, G26, G85, H4, H82, I44, *J25*, J37M, K25, M72, M73, M73M, N3M, N11, etc.

PORTULACACEAE

Anacampseros albissima - {S} Used in the preparation of a beer like beverage. Southern Africa. FOX, F.; H52, I33, N69, N84, Q41, S44, T25M

Anacampseros papyracea - {S} Used in the preparation of an alcoholic beverage. Southern Africa. FOX, F.; C27M, G94{PL}, H52, I33, N69, N84, Q41, S44, T25M

Claytonia caroliniana - *Broad-leaved spring beauty* {PL} The tender leaves and stems, when steamed for a short time, make an excellent potherb. They are mild in flavor and are best mixed with stronger tasting greens like sheep sorrel or violets. Corms can be cooked and eaten like potatoes. Eastern North America. FERNALD, GIBBONS 1979, MEDSGER; B0, C9, E63M, N7T

Claytonia megarrhiza - *Alpine spring beauty* {PL} Young leaves and flowering tops are eaten raw in salads or cooked as a potherb. They are succulent, juicy and mild in flavor. The long, thick, fleshy roots are peeled and then boiled or baked. Western North America. GIBBONS 1973, HARRINGTON, H.; C40, G82M, J93T{S}, L13{S}

Claytonia perfoliata → *Montia perfoliata*

Claytonia sibirica → *Montia sibirica*

Claytonia virginica - *Spring beauty, Fairy spuds* {PL} Starchy bulbs are eaten boiled, fried, mashed, in salads, soups, and stews, or cooked with peas like new potatoes. They are said to have somewhat the flavor of chestnuts. Young leaves and stems are eaten raw in salads or steamed and served as greens. Eastern North America. ANGIER, CROWHURST 1972, FERNALD, GIBBONS 1962, KINDSCHER, MEDSGER; C9, C49, D62, D75T, E33M, E63M, *F51*, *G28*, H49, I44, L46, M37M, N9M, N9M{S}, N45, etc.

Lewisia rediviva - *Bitter-root* {PL} The roots are peeled to remove the bitter rind, cut into pieces, boiled for about twenty minutes, and served with butter. During the cooking process the roots become soft and swollen and exude a pink, mucilaginous substance. Dried roots were sometimes stored for a year or two before eating, when they became less bitter. Flathead Indians mixed them with berries, added them to meat or bone marrow, used them to thicken gravies, or in more modern times, ate them with milk or cream and sugar. Western North America. GIBBONS 1979, HARRINGTON, H. [Pre], HART, KIRK, MEDSGER; C40, G82M, H98, I47{S}, I63M, K47M{S}, K79, K98{S}, M35M

Montia fontana - *Water blinks, Water chickweed* {S} Leaves are eaten in salads in North America, and in some mountainous areas of France. Temperate regions. LOVELOCK, TANAKA; **V52, Z88**

Montia perfoliata - *Miner's lettuce, Winter purslane, Cuban spinach* {S} The young, succulent leaves, stems, and flowers are excellent eaten in a tossed green salad. Older leaves can be used as a potherb. For salads, they are often grown as seedling crops using the cut-and-come-again technique. Roots are edible raw and when boiled are said to have the flavor of chestnuts. North America, cultivated. ANGIER [Re], CLARKE, HARRINGTON, H., KIRK, LARKCOM 1984 [Cu], NIETHAMMER, VILMORIN; A2, B49, C53, G59M, I98M, J73, *N71M*, N84, O48, O53M, P83M, *R23*, R53M, S55

Montia sibirica - *Siberian purslane* {S} Leaves can be added raw to mixed salads or they can be cooked for a short time in a small amount of water and served as a green vegetable. North America to Eastern Asia. HEDRICK 1919, HELLER; F85, *Q24*, Q76{PL}

Portulaca oleracea - *Purslane, Pusley, Verdolaga* {S} Succulent leaves and stems are eaten raw in salads, pickled, stir-fried, sautéed, added to capers or olives, or used in casseroles, stews, omelettes, sandwiches, fritters, etc. Their mucilaginous texture makes them a good substitute for okra in gumbo and other creole dishes. To preserve the plant for winter use put it into salt and dry white wine. The seeds are ground for use in gruels, cakes, breads, and pancakes. Sprouted seeds are eaten in salads. Ash of the burnt plant is used as a substitute for salt. Eurasia, cultivated. ANGIER [Re], CRIBB, FERNALD, FOX, F., GIBBONS 1962 [Re], HALPIN [Cul], LAUNERT, MORTON 1977, VILMORIN [Cu]; B49, C11, C53, C85M, F24, F80, G51, G68, G71, I39, I99, L89, *N71M*, O48, O53M, P83M, Q41, etc.

CULTIVARS

Golden: (Goldgelber, Pourpier Doré) Large leaves and stalks with a pale green or yellowish cast that contrasts well with the red stems. Much more upright than regular green cultivated purslane. Grown and used in the same manner. When cooked, the leaves do not differ very much in color from those of the green purslane. VILMORIN; C53, E83T, J7, J82, K2, N84, O48, *R23*, S55

Multi-Branch: Bushy plant, 12 inches tall and 12 or more inches wide. Produces numerous branches that grow out at an angle, and bend down to the ground somewhat under their own weight. Light to dark green leaves. Grayish-green, pink or yellowish-green stems with good texture and flavor. E83T

Portulaca pilosa - *Shaggy purslane, Ke-tsume-kusa* {S} Said to be used as a vegetable. Tropical America. TANAKA; K47T, N84, Q41, R15M

Portulacaria afra - *Elephant grass* {PL} The pleasantly acid leaves are sometimes used to give a tart flavor to a mixed salad. Southern Africa. FOX, F., TATE; B85, E48, F31M, G18, M33G

Talinum crassifolium* → *Talinum triangulare

Talinum cuneifolium* → *Talinum portulacifolium

Talinum paniculatum - *Carurú, Fameflower* {S} The leaves and stems are blanched and used in green salads, cooked in soups, or eaten like purslane. Tropical America. HEDRICK 1919, VON REIS; C13M, C27M, E7M, F85, H52, K47T, L50{PL}, N84, Q41, S44

Talinum patens* → *Talinum paniculatum

Talinum portulacifolium - *Aby, Ndele, Muiki* {S} Leaves are cultivated in some parts of Africa as a spinach. Tropical Africa, Tropical Asia. UPHOF; K47T, N84

Talinum triangulare - *Surinam purslane, Surinam spinach, Water leaf* {S} Young leaves and tender stems, having a slightly sour taste, are chopped and added to salads, parboiled, steamed, sautéed, or used in egusi soup. When cooked they can be excessively soft and mucilaginous, so overcooking should be avoided. Tropical America, naturalized in Florida. HAWKES [Cul], HERKLOTS, MARTIN 1975 [Cu], MORTON 1977, OOMEN, VAN EPENHUIJSEN; D62, K47T

PRIMULACEAE

Lysimachia clethroides - *Gooseneck loosestrife, Oka-tora-no-o* {PL} Leaves are eaten as a vegetable or used as a condiment. Fruits and flowers are also said to be edible. Eastern Asia. KUNKEL, TANAKA, UPHOF; B9M, B28, B30, C2, C9, C32, D95, F57M, G55, H63, I77M, J48, J78, *L95*, M98, etc.

Lysimachia nummularia - *Moneywort* {PL} Leaves and flowers are occasionally used as a tea. Europe. UPHOF; B97M, C43M, F35M, F39M, *G89M*, I22, I63M, I87, I90M, J7, M16, *M65M*, M73M, N9M, N9M{S}, etc.

Primula denticulata - *Indian primrose* {PL} Flowers are eaten in salads. Himalayan region. TANAKA; C40, D62{S}, D95, E63M, I39{S}, J48, J78, K47T{S}, L66, L91M{S}, M98, O53M{S}, *Q24*{S}, Q40{S}

Primula veris - *Cowslip* {S} Flowers are used in salads, conserves, pickles, as a garnish, or fermented into the liquor called cowslip wine. They were also made into a vinegar that was drunk with soda water rather than being used as a condiment. Leaves are eaten raw in salads or used as a substitute for tea. Northern temperate region. GRIEVE, LARKCOM 1984, LEGGATT [Re], MABEY, MACNICOL [Re], MICHAEL, UPHOF; C40{PL}, D62, E33, I39, J48{PL}, J67M, K47T, K53, L66{PL}, L91M, M77M{PL}, N45{PL}, *N71M*, N84, O53M, etc.

Primula vulgaris - *English primrose* {S} The flowers are eaten raw in salads, as a cooked vegetable, or used in conserves, custards, tarts, or confections. Leaves are added to salads, eaten as a potherb, or mixed with other herbs as a stuffing for meat and poultry. Both leaves and flowers can be made into syrup or tea. Europe, cultivated. BRYAN [Re], GRIEVE, HEDRICK 1919, LEGGATT [Re], MACNICOL [Re]; D62, E7M, E33, F24, L55{PL}, L91M, N84, O48, O53M, O89, *Q24*, S7M, S45M

PROTEACEAE

Banksia marginata - *Australian honeysuckle* {S} The flower is filled with a sweet nectar, which may be sucked directly or washed out with water to form a refreshing beverage. Australia. CRIBB, TANAKA; K81M, M7M{PL}, *N79M*, N84, O93, P5, *P17M*, *Q25*, *Q32*, R15M, R33M, R41, R60, R77M, S92, etc.

Brabejum stellatifolium - *Hottentot's almond* {S} Seeds are steeped in water to remove the bitter, mildly poisonous principles, then boiled, roasted and used as a substitute for coffee. South Africa. FOX, F., HEDRICK 1919, MENNINGER; N84

Gevuina avellana - *Chilean hazel, Avellano* {S} The pleasant tasting nuts are eaten raw, having a flavor similar to the European hazelnut. In Chile, they are roasted and sold in small paper bags like peanuts. As a natural food, they contain 12.5% proteins, 49.5% oil, and 24.1% carbohydrates. Chile. MENNINGER, ROSENGARTEN, VALENZUELA; D95{PL}, N84, R47

Grevillea juncifolia - *Tarrakirra* {S} The blossoms may contain appreciable quantities of nectar which can be sipped directly, or mixed with water to make a sweet drink. Australia. O'CONNELL; K81M, N84, R15M, R33M, T7

Grevillea robusta - *Silky oak* {S} One of the richest sources of nectar, it produces masses of golden flowers, each one containing a drop of nectar in its deep throat. This can be sucked directly, shaken into a bowl, or washed out in a small quantity of water. Australia. CRIBB; A79M, C9M, C56M, C92, F85, *I61*, K38, K81M, *L5M*, L91M, O53M, O84, P5, R15M, R33M, etc.

Hakea suberea - *Untjiya* {S} The flowers may yield considerable amounts of sweet nectar that can be sipped with a straw, or mixed with water to form a sweet beverage. Australia. O'CONNELL; K81M, N84, R15M, R33M, T7

Hicksbeachia pinnatifida - *Australian rosenut, Red nut* {S} Nuts are eaten, the flavor being rather agreeable. The bright red husk of the nut resembles a rose hip, hence the name rosenut. In addition to bearing an edible nut, the tree has considerable ornamental value, with its large unusual leaves and bright fruit. Australia. CRIBB, MENNINGER, THIES; *N79M*, N84, *P17M*, P38

Lambertia formosa - *Honeyflower, Mountain devil* {S} The flowers yield copious amounts of sweet nectar. Australia. DONKIN; *N79M*, N84, P5, *P17M*, R15M, R33M

Macadamia integrifolia - *Macadamia nut* {S} The sweet, delicious nuts are eaten raw, roasted, fried, coated with chocolate or carob, used in fancy pastries, candies, ice cream, nut butters, cookies, cakes, and pies. They also yield an edible oil. Sometimes called the smooth-shelled macadamia. Australia, cultivated. CRIBB, JAYNES [Cu], MENNINGER, ROSENGARTEN [Re]; C9M, E29, E29{PL}, E29{PR}, F68{PL}, F85, *H71*, J65{PR}, M20{PL}, N84, O93, *P17M*, P38, *Q25* (for cultivars see Macadamia, page 380)

Macadamia tetraphylla - *Macadamia nut* {S} Nuts are eaten raw, roasted and salted, fried in coconut oil, used in ice cream, nut butters, confectionery, bread, salads, sauces, cakes, biscuits, soups, and milk shakes. Kernels are generally higher in sugar content and lower in oil than those of M. integrifolia, and therefore sweeter. Sometimes called the rough-shelled macadamia, although there are intermediate forms. Australia, cultivated. HASTINGS [Re], JAYNES; F85, H12{PR}, *N79M*, N84, *P17M*, P38, *Q32*, *Q49M* (for cultivars see Macadamia, page 380)

Macadamia x sp. (M. integrifolia x M. tetraphylla) - *Macadamia nut* Natural and artificial hybrids. The nuts are eaten. In subtropical areas, these hybrids appear to be better producers of quality nutmeats than either of the two parent species. (for cultivars see Macadamia, page 380)

Protea cynaroides - *Boer honey-pot, King protea* {S} The sweet nectar of the flowers is consumed directly. South Africa. SCHERY; A79M, C56M{PL}, *E53M*, F85, I83M{PL}, K81M, N84, O53M, O93, P5, P18, *Q32*, R41, R47, R60, R77M, S44, etc.

Protea mellifera → *Protea repens*

Protea repens - *Honey flower, Sugar bush* {S} The nectar of the flowers is consumed directly or made into a delicious syrup, known as *suikerbos stroop*. South Africa. FOX, F., UPHOF; A79M, C56M{PL}, *E53M*, K81M, N84, O53M, O93, P5, P18, *Q32*, R41, R60, R77M, S44, S95, etc.

Telopea speciosissima - *Waratah* {S} The flowers produce copious quantities of nectar that may be sipped directly or used for making a sweet beverage. Australia. CRIBB, DONKIN; K81M, *N79M*, O33, O53M, P5, *P17M*, P18, *Q32*, R15M, R33M, R60, S92

PSILOTACEAE

Psilotum nudum → *Psilotum triquetrum*

Psilotum triquetrum - *Whisk fern, Moa* {PL} The whole plant is made into a tea. Tropics. TANAKA; E48

PTERIDACEAE

Pteris ensiformis - *Sword brake, Hoko-shida* {S} In Indonesia, the young uncurling fronds are steamed and eaten as a side-dish with rice, mixed with other vegetables, or put in stews. Tropical Asia. OCHSE; N84, O93

PUNICACEAE

Punica granatum - *Pomegranate* {S} The refreshing, subacid fruits are eaten out of hand, or used in fruit salads, tossed salads, and desserts. Pomegranate juice can be used in soups, sauces, jellies, ices, or made into a sweet syrup called *grenadine* that flavors drinks, ice cream, cakes, baked apples, etc. The dried seeds, *anardana*, are used as a seasoning in dal, fried *samosa* (pastries), stuffings, and chutneys. Boiled leaves are said to be eaten. Eastern Mediterranean to Southwest Asia. JOHNS [Cul], MORTON 1987a, POPENOE, W. 1920 [Cu, Pro], SCHNEIDER [Cul, Re], TANAKA, UPHOF, VON WELANETZ; A88T{PR}, D77M{PL}, E29, E29{PL}, E29{PR}, H4{PL}, N84, N93M, O53M, O89, P5, *P17M*, Q12, *Q32*

CULTIVARS {GR}

Balegal: Large, roundish fruit, 3 inches in diameter; somewhat larger than Fleshman; skin pale pink, lighter in color than Fleshman; flesh slightly darker than Fleshman, very sweet. Originated in San Diego, California. Selected by Paul H. Thomson. D57{OR}

Cloud: Medium-sized fruit with a green-red color. The juice is sweet and white. From the University of California, Davis pomegranate collection. F43M

Crab: Large fruits have red juice that is sour but with a rich flavor. A heavy bearing tree. From the University of California, Davis pomegranate collection. F43M

Daru: (Dalim, Daran) Small, globular fruit, 2 to 3 inches in diameter; rind yellowish-green, tinged with red; aril deep red to pinkish-white, high in acid. Traditionally sun dried to form the expensive spice *anardana*, used as a souring agent in a large number of preparations. Bush spreading, very hardy, will grow even on very poor and shallow soils. Native to the western Himalayas. **W98M{S}**

Early Wonderful: New distinct cultivar. Large, deep-red, thin-skinned, delicious fruit; ripens about 2 weeks earlier than Wonderful. Medium-sized bush with large, orange-red fertile flowers; blooms late; very productive. *I68*

Fleshman: Large, roundish fruit, about 3 inches in diameter; pink outside and in; very sweet in flavor; seeds relatively soft; quality very good. Originated in Fallbrook, California. Selected by Paul H. Thomson, co-founder of the California Rare Fruit Growers. D57, G17, I83M

Granada: Bud mutation of Wonderful. Fruit resembles Wonderful, but displays a red crown while in the green stage, darker red in color and less tart, ripens one month earlier than Wonderful; flowers also deeper red. Tree identical to Wonderful. Originated in Lindsay, California. Introduced in 1966. BROOKS 1972; *C54*, F11

Home: The fruit is variable yellow-red in color, with light pink juice that is sweet and of rich flavor. Some bitterness. From the University of California, Davis pomegranate collection. F43M

King: Medium to large fruit, somewhat smaller than Balegal and Fleshman; skin darker pink to red; flavor very sweet; has a tendency to split. Bush somewhat of a shy bearer. Originated in Fallbrook, California by Sam King. D57{OR}

Malcolm's Extra Sweet: Very large fruit with sweet, flavorsome juice. Best quality for fresh eating is reached around Thanksgiving. Highly productive, ornamental tree. Adapted to Southeastern growing conditions. The original tree was grown from a seed on a Georgia plantation over 100 years ago. F43M

Muscat Red: (Muskat) Small to medium-sized fruit; rind thin to fairly thick; pulp fleshy, juicy, medium-sweet; seeds soft to medium-hard. Tree a moderately prolific bearer. Originated in India. MORTON 1987a; R0

Muscat White: (Muskat) Large fruit; rind creamy-white tinged with pink, thin; pulp sweet; seeds medium-hard. Tree bears well. Originated in India, where it is desirable for commercial planting in Delhi. MORTON 1987a; R0

Phil's Sweet: Medium to large, roundish fruits; weight 8 to 12 ounces; skin yellowish-green to slightly pink; flesh red with a high sugar content balancing the slight acid overtones; seed carpel sections thin with much pulp, seeds soft. Tree very productive. Originated in Escondido, California by Phil Arena. D57

Plantation Sweet: Original tree, believed to be over 100 years old, was found growing wild on a Georgia plantation by Dr. Silas Harmon of the Coastal Plains Experiment Station, Tifton, Georgia. Highly productive; documented to have survived 0^0 F. without freezing to the ground. Maximum flavor peak of fruit is reached for fresh eating around Thanksgiving. M31M

Sweet: Fruit is lighter in color than Wonderful, remains slightly greenish with a red blush when ripe; pink juice; flavor much sweeter than other cultivars. Excellent in fruit punch. Tree highly ornamental, bears at an early age, productive. *C54, L47*

Utah Sweet: Very sweet, good quality fruit; pink skin and pulp; seeds notably softer than those of Wonderful and other standard cultivars. Attractive pinkish-orange flowers. I83M

Wonderful: Large, deep purple-red fruit; rind medium thick, tough; flesh deep crimson in color, juicy, and of a delicious vinous flavor; seeds not very hard. Better for juicing than for eating out of hand. Plant is vigorous and productive. Leading commercial variety in California. Originated in Florida. First propagated in California in 1896. B93M, E4, F19M, F93, G96, H4, I49M, I83M, I91, *L47*, L99M, M16, M77, N33

Punica granatum 'Nana' - *Dwarf pomegranate* {S} Fruits are edible. The plant is a dense shrub to three feet tall, nearly evergreen in mild winters. Blooms when a foot tall or less. Flowers are orange-red, single, and are followed by small, red fruits. Excellent garden or container plant. Also good for bonsai. TANAKA; A79M, F80, F85, G25M, G96{PL}, H4{PL}, H51M{PL}, I49M{PL}, *I61*, J82{PL}, N37M{PL}, O53M, P5, *P17M*, *Q32*, etc.

PYROLACEAE

Chimaphila maculata - *Spotted wintergreen* {PL} Leaves are nibbled for their refreshing qualities. In Mexico, they are used as a catalyst in the manufacture of *tesguino*, an alcoholic beverage prepared by fermentation of germinated maize. North America, Mexico. FERNALD, STEINKRAUS; A25M, B0, C81M, E33M, F80{S}, K47T{S}

Chimaphila umbellata - *Pipsissewa, Prince's pine* {S} Leaves are nibbled, brewed into a tea, or used as an ingredient of *root beer*. An extract of the leaves is used to flavor candy and soft drinks. In Mexico, the Tepehuano use the herb in the preparation of *navaitai*, an alcoholic beverage made from sprouted maize. North America, Eastern Asia. CROWHURST 1972, FERNALD, GIBBONS 1979, HALL [Re], KIRK, MORTON 1976, STEINKRAUS; A25M{PL}, C49{PL}, D75T{PL}, F85, I44, I47, J78, K47T, N84, O53M

Orthilia secunda - *Herba pirolae* {S} Leaves are occasionally used as a tea. Eurasia. HUTCHINSON; **V52, V84, Y18**

RANUNCULACEAE

Cimicifuga foetida* → *Cimicifuga simplex

Cimicifuga simplex - *Sarashina-shôma* {S} Young leaves are boiled and eaten. The fragrant root is used as a spice. Eastern Asia. TANAKA, VON REIS; D62, M92{PL}, N63M, N84, S7M

Clematis apiifolia - *Botanzuru* {PL} Young leaves are boiled and used as a vegetable. Roasted ones are used as a substitute for tea. Eastern Asia. TANAKA; B96, D62{S}, M77M

Clematis maximowicziana - *Sweet autumn clematis, Senin-sô* {S} Young leaves, after parboiling, are eaten boiled or oil-roasted. Young buds are similarly used or pickled in vinegar. Flowers are also eaten. Eastern Asia. TANAKA; C9{PL}, C92, D62, E7, E97{PL}, *G89M*{PL}, I91{PL}, K47T, L91M, M77{PL}, M77M{PL}, O53M, *Q24*, R78

Clematis paniculata* → *Clematis maximowicziana

Coptis groenlandica* → *Coptis trifolia

Coptis trifolia - *Goldthread, Canker-root, Mitsuba-ôren* {PL} The plant is said to be eaten, or it can be mixed with sassafras-root bark and Irish moss, and brewed into a kind of herbal root beer. The goldthread contributes a bitter flavor and yellow color to the beverage. Northern Asia, North America. GIBBONS 1966b [Re], TANAKA; A25M, C49, D62{S}, D75T, E63M, I31{S}, I44, I87, K47T{S}, N45, N84{S}

Ranunculus bulbosus - *Bulbous crowfoot* {S} The young flowers are pickled. Bulbs are eaten after thorough boiling or drying. Caution is recommended as this plant has a strongly acrid juice that can cause blistering. Northern temperate region. FERNALD, GIBBONS 1979, KIRK; B61M, *N71M*, N84, O48

Ranunculus ficaria - *Pilewort, Lesser celandine* {S} Young leaves are eaten raw in salads and sandwiches or cooked as a potherb. The bleached stems are cooked and eaten. Both the bulbils which form in the leaf axils and the roots can be cooked and served with meat. Flower buds make a good substitute for capers. Eurasia. LAUNERT [Re], UPHOF; D62, N84, P92{PL}, *P95M*{PL}

RESEDACEAE

Reseda odorata - *Mignonette* {S} The flowers are occasionally floated into a bowl of wine. Mignonette flavored salt is used frequently in Turkish cooking, especially with veal and lamb dishes. North Africa, cultivated. BURKILL, MACNICOL; C3, E7M, E89M, E99, F24, I39, I91, J83M, K53, M13M, M46, N19M{PL}, O53M, O89, S55, etc.

RHAMNACEAE

Berchemia discolor - *Munye, Brown ivory* {S} Ripe fruits are sweetish and are eaten fresh, dried or fermented into an alcoholic drink. The pulp is sometimes mixed with millet meal to form a cake which is baked or steamed. Tropical Africa to Arabia. FOX, F., UPHOF; N84

Berchemia racemosa - *Kuma-yanagi* {S} Ripe fruits are eaten. Leaves are eaten as a vegetable or used as a tea substitute. Eastern Asia. TANAKA; **T41M, Z25M**

Ceanothus americanus - *New Jersey tea, Red root* {S} The leaves are gathered while the plant is in full bloom, dried in the shade, and used as a tea substitute. It has an agreeable taste, somewhat resembling that of *Bohea tea*. Does not contain caffeine. North America. ANGIER, FERNALD, GIBBONS 1962, KINDSCHER, MARCIN; D95{PL}, E81M, G47M, H63{PL}, J40, J40{PL}, J41M, J41M{PL}, J42, J48{PL}, J67M, J82, M82{PL}, O48, *Q24*, S55, etc.

Ceanothus cuneatus - *Wild lilac, Snowbrush* {S} The leaves and flowers make excellent tea when steeped in boiling water for about five minutes. Western North America. KIRK; B94, *C73*{PL}, D95{PL}, G60{PL}, I47, I98M, K15, N84, O93, *Q32*

Ceanothus fendleri - *Fendler ceanothus* {PL} Leaves are used as a substitute for tea. The fruits are used for food in New Mexico. Western North America. HARRINGTON, H., YANOVSKY; I63M

Ceanothus ovatus - *Smaller red-root* {S} Young leaves and flowers are steeped in boiling water for about five minutes. The resulting liquid is yellowish in color and tastes similar to Oriental tea, but is considered milder and sweeter. North America. FERNALD, HARRINGTON, H.; J39M

Ceanothus sanguineus - *Oregon tea-tree* {S} A tea is made from the leaves. Western North America. TANAKA; B94, *C33*{PL}, D95{PL}, E15, *E66M*, *G66*, *G66*{PL}, I15, I47, J26{PL}, K38, N84, P5, *Q32*

Ceanothus velutinus - *Sticky laurel, Tobacco brush* {S} The leaves can be used as a substitute for tea. Western North America. HARRINGTON, H.; B94, D95{PL}, E15, *G66*, *G66*{PL}, I15, I47, I63M{PL}, J26{PL}, P5

Colubrina elliptica - *Smooth snakebark, Nakedwood* {PL} In Puerto Rico and the Virgin Islands, the bark is steeped in water to make a cooling drink called *mabi champan*. Sold by street vendors and at soft drink counters. The bark is sold in native markets. Florida, Caribbean region. MORTON 1977; D87G

Colubrina ferruginosa - *Snakebark* {S} The bark is steeped in water to make a cooling drink called *mabi champan*, sold at local soft drink counters in Puerto Rico and the Virgin Islands. Florida, Caribbean region. MORTON 1977; **X94**

Colubrina reclinata* → *Colubrina elliptica

Colubrina texensis - *Hog plum, Coma* {S} Tart fruits are crushed in a mortar and steeped in water to make a cooling drink. Southwestern North America. LATORRE 1977b; B83M

Condalia obovata - *Purple-haw, Blue wood, Capul* {S} The sweet, black fruits are eaten raw or used to make a good jelly. Southwestern North America. MEDSGER, UPHOF; B83M

Gouania domingensis* → *Gouania lupuloides

Gouania lupuloides - *Chewstick, Toothbrush tree* {S} In Jamaica, the aromatic, somewhat bitter stems have been used as a substitute for hops in beer-making. Caribbean region. MORTON 1977; **Z25M**

Gouania polygama - *Limpia dientes* {S} The foliage was once used in Jamaica as a substitute for hops in brewing beer. Tropical America. WILLIAMS, L.; **Y2**

Hovenia dulcis - *Japanese raisin-tree, Kenpo-nashi, Kuai-tsao* {S} The fleshy, thickened fruit-stalks, when dried, have the sweet flavor and texture of raisins and can be used similarly. In China, they are eaten to annul the effects of wine. A sweet extract of the seeds, boughs, and young leaves was used as a substitute for honey. Eastern Asia. CHANG, K., UPHOF, WILSON, E.; B96{PL}, E7M, E87{PL}, G17{PL}, *G66*, H49, I49M{PL}, I83M{PL}, J61M{PL}, K38, K47T, K67{PL}, N93M, O53M, P38, etc.

Krugiodendron ferreum - *Leadwood, Black ironwood* {PL} Ripe fruits are black, juicy, and have a sweet, agreeable flavor. They are usually eaten raw. Florida, West Indies. MORTON 1977; D87G, *J25*

Paliurus spina-christii* → *Ziziphus spina-christii

Phyllogeiton discolor* → *Berchemia discolor

Reynosia latifolia* → *Reynosia septentrionalis

Reynosia septentrionalis - *Darling plum, Red ironwood* {PL} Fruits are dark purple, thin-skinned, with very sweet, agreeable flesh said to resemble blueberries. They are eaten raw or cooked. Florida, West Indies. MEDSGER, MORTON 1977; D87G, *J25*

Rhamnus crocea - *Red berry* {S} The fruits are eaten raw and are excellent mixed with meat. They impart a red color to the mixture, and it has been reported that they will temporarily tinge one's skin red, if eaten in quantity. Southwestern North America. HEDRICK 1919, KIRK; C9M, G60{PL}, I98M, L13

Rhamnus davuricus - *Dahurian buckthorn* {PL} Young leaves are used as a substitute for tea, parboiled and cooked, or fried and eaten. Eastern Asia. TANAKA; M35M

Rhamnus prinoides - *Mofifi buckthorn, Geisho* {S} In Ethiopia, the bark is used as a substitute for hops in the preparation of *talla*, a home-processed beer with a smoky flavor and a tan to dark brown color, and *tej*, a yellow, sweet, effervescent honey wine or *mead*. The roots are used in soup. Fruits are sometimes eaten. Drier Tropical Africa. FOX, F., STEINKRAUS, VON REIS; F85, *G66*, N84, R41, R77M

Rhamnus purshianus - *Cascara buckthorn* {S} The fruits are sometimes eaten. An extract of the bark, with the bitterness removed, is a common flavoring for soft drinks, baked goods, and ice cream. North America. MORTON 1976; A2, A80M{PL}, A91{PL}, B94, C11, E59T{PL}, F85, I47, I99, *J75M*{PL}, N0{PL}, *P63*

Sageretia theezans - *Sweet plum, Kuro-ige* {PL} The fruit is edible. Leaves are used as a tea substitute in Tonkin. They are often mixed with the leaves of Cleistocalyx operculatus. Tropical Asia. UPHOF; E48, F70, N13

Ziziphus abyssinica - *Catchthorn* {S} Pulp of the fruit is pleasant and thirst-quenching and is eaten fresh or mixed with water to make a good drink. In Nyasaland, it is used for making a potent alcoholic beverage called *kachaso*. Drier Tropical Africa. FOX, F., UPHOF; N84

Ziziphus joazeiro - *Joazeiro* {S} Fruits are sometimes consumed by the natives. May have potential as a rootstock for other species because of its non-suckering habit. Brazil. UPHOF; **X88M**

Ziziphus jujuba - *Jujube, Chinese date, Tsao* {S} The ripe fruits are eaten fresh, dried like dates, boiled with millet and rice, stewed, baked, pickled, glacéed, or used as a coffee substitute. They are also used in puddings, cakes, breads, jellies, soups, sweetmeats, etc. In Korea, jujube flour is used in the preparation of *kochujang*, a fermented hot pepper-soybean paste that resembles miso. Cultivated. CHANG, W. [Re], COST 1988 [Cul], JOHNS, POPENOE, W. 1920 [Cu, Pro], STEINKRAUS, TANAKA; C9M, C27G{PR}, C56M{PL}, F80, H4{PL}, I99, K49T, N84, N93M, O53M, P5, *P17M*, *Q32*, Q40, Q46, R47, etc.

CULTIVARS {GR}

Chico: Fruit large; round, with a somewhat flattened blossom end; resembles a crabapple in appearance; most smaller fruits are seedless. Flesh very crisp, with a slightly acid flavor that gives it a character all its own. Tree is more thorny than other cultivars; does not do well in cool, coastal areas. STEBBINS; H53M{SC}

Lang: (Melting) Small, oblong to pear-shaped fruit; skin mahogany red; flesh melting, sweet; begins to ripen near the end of the ripening period for Li; must fully ripen to the mahogany red color before picking. Tree very large, more upright than Li; bears profusely at an early age; Discovered in China by Frank N. Meyer. Introduced in 1924. BROOKS 1972; *C54*, D37, E4, H53M{SC}, I83M, L99M, M31M

Leon Burk Bellflower: Fruits are large, sweet enough to eat out of hand, much more juicy than other cultivars. Tree is a heavy, reliable bearer, self-fruitful in some areas. Original tree is from Tifton County, Georgia, on the rural home of Mr. and Mrs. Jimmy Bellflower. H53M{SC}

Li: Fruit very large, up to 2 inches long; round to ovoid; skin mahogany brown; primarily for eating fresh; ripens in late August; unlike the Lang, it will ripen if picked at the yellow-green stage. Tree more branched and spreading than Lang; reaches a height of 15 to 20 feet after 20 years. Discovered in China by Frank N. Meyer.

Introduced in 1924. BROOKS 1972; A88M, *C54*, D37, E4, H53M{SC}, I83M, L99M, M31M

Sherwood: Large to very large fruit, 1 1/2 to 2 inches long or more; flesh of excellent quality, notably dense in texture. Tree with relatively small thorns, extremely productive. Originated near Shreveport, Louisiana. Introduced by J.S. Akin. H53M{SC}, K67

Shui Men: Medium-sized, elongated fruit. Good only when fresh, does not dry well. Originated in China. Brought into the United States in 1914 by Frank N. Meyer. Introduced in 1924. BROOKS 1972; H53M{SC}

Silverhill: (Silverhill Long) Long, narrow fruit, 1 1/2 to 2 inches in length; skin reddish-brown; flesh sweet, of very good flavor; ripens in midseason. Quality excellent either fresh or dried. Similar to Silverhill Round. F43M, G75, H53M{SC}

Silverhill Round: Plum shaped fruit, about 1 1/2 inches in diameter. When ripe it is a light mahogany color with a sweet, date-like white flesh. Very high sugar content in the hard-ripe stage; has the flavor of a prune when soft-ripe or shriveled. Ripens in September. G17, H53M{SC}

So: Round, medium-sized fruit; skin brown-red; flesh sweet. Tree very gnarled with a zigzag type growth habit. Originated in China. Introduced into the United States in 1914 by Frank N. Meyer. Never released, but has been used in research studies. BROOKS 1972; H53M{SC}

Yu: (Tigertooth) Large, narrow, elongated fruit; tapered toward the blossom end; skin reddish-brown; flesh sweet, firm; keeping quality rather good. Tree tall; main branches with few side branches; leaves large. Originated in China. Introduced into the United States in 1913 by Frank N. Meyer. G17, H53M{SC}

Ziziphus mauritiana - *Indian jujube* {S} The fruits are eaten fresh, dried like raisins, boiled with rice, powdered and made into a meal, or used in jellies, preserves, sauces and beverages. In Venezuela, a jujube liqueur is made and sold as *crema de ponsigne*. Dried fruits are mixed with salt and tamarind pulp to make a condiment. Young leaves are cooked and eaten in Indonesia. Drier Africa to Southern Asia. DUKE, MARTIN 1975, MORTON 1987a [Cu, Pro], STURROCK; F85, N84, P38, Q12, S29

Ziziphus mucronata - *Buffalo thorn, Cape thorn* {S} The fruit is sweetish and mealy when ripe and is eaten fresh, dried, or made into bread, porridge, or a refreshing beverage. Roasted seeds are used as substitute for coffee. Drier Tropical Africa. FOX, F., HEDRICK 1919; F80, K63G, N84, O53M, O93, P5, *P17M*, P38, R41, R77M, S44

Ziziphus oenoplia - *Wine jujube, Anor* {S} Fruits are small, black, acid in flavor and are eaten when ripe. Southern Asia, Australia. ALTSCHUL, CRIBB, WATT; F85, N84

Ziziphus parryi - *California abrojo, Parry jujube, Crucillo* {S} The dry, mealy fruits are eaten or ground into meal for making *atole*. Southwestern North America. WICKSON, YANOVSKY; B94

Ziziphus sativa* → *Ziziphus jujuba

Ziziphus spina-christii - *Christ's thorn* {S} Mealy fruits have a pleasant, subacid taste, somewhat resembling dried apples. They are eaten both fresh and dried. Northern Africa to Southwest Asia. HEDRICK 1919, UPHOF; *G66*, *J0*, K47T, *N79M*, N84, O53M, O93, P5, *P17M*, P38, *P63*, *Q15G*, S95

Ziziphus vulgaris* → *Ziziphus jujuba

RHIZOPHORACEAE

Carallia brachiata - *Carallia wood, Kierpa* {S} An infusion of the leaves is used as a tea. Fruits are eaten or used as a masticatory. Tropics. KUNKEL, TANAKA, UPHOF; F85

Rhizophora mangle - *American red mangrove* {PL} Dried leaves make a most agreeable substitute for tea. Moderation is recommended due to its tannin content, or milk should be added to bind the tannin. The roots, starchy fruits, and the inner portion of the green sprout, or hypocotyl, have been used as emergency foods. Tropical American coasts, West Africa. DUKE, MORTON 1977, TANAKA; A79M{S}, D87G, *F73*, F85{S}, *J25*, M69, N84{S}

ROSACEAE

Acaena anserinifolia* → *Acaena sanguisorbae

Acaena sanguisorbae - *New Zealand bur, Bidi-bidi* {S} The leaves are used as a substitute for tea. Australia, New Zealand. HEDRICK 1919; D62, F85, N84, S43M

Agrimonia eupatoria - *Agrimony* {S} Flowers, leaves, and stems are harvested when the plant is in bloom and brewed into a refreshing tea. Both the fresh and dried herb are used, and the tea can be consumed either hot or cold. Europe. GRIEVE, MACNICOL, MARCIN, PAINTER; C11, C67M{PL}, E61, E61{PL}, F24, H3M{PL}, I39, J67M, K85{PL}, M82{PL}, N45{PL}, *N71M*, O53M, S55

CULTIVARS

Sweet-Scented: Hardy perennial to 3 feet with narrow pinnate leaves. Bright yellow five-petaled flowers in slender, dense spikes. The whole plant is sweet-scented and the flowers have a spicy, apricot-like fragrance. For this reason it is popular in France for making tea. *N71M*

Agrimonia odorata* → *Agrimonia eupatoria

Agrimonia procera* → *Agrimonia eupatoria

Alchemilla vulgaris* → *Alchemilla xanthochlora

Alchemilla xanthochlora - *Lady's mantle* {PL} In Northern England, the leaves are mixed with those of Polygonum bistorta and Persicaria vulgaris in the preparation of a Lenten pudding called *Easter ledger* pudding or *Easter herb* pudding. Europe. MABEY; C67M, C81M, E30, E61, F31T, F35M, F88, G96, H3M, J82, K22, K85, *L95*, N45, *N71M*{S}, etc.

Amelanchier alnifolia - *Saskatoon, Western service berry* {PL} The sweet, blueberry-like fruits are eaten fresh, dried like raisins, stewed, or used in jams, puddings, jellies, pancakes, muffins and pies. American Indians pounded the fruits into cakes which were dried for future use, and also employed the fruit in making *pemmican*. Western North America. HARRINGTON, H., KINDSCHER, MEDSGER, SIMMONS 1972, TURNER 1979 [Re]; A16, A91, *C33*, D95, *G21M*, I15{S}, I47{S}, J25M, J25M{S}, J61M, *J75M*, K63G{S}, K64, M35M, N84{S}, etc.

CULTIVARS {GR}

Altaglow: A white-fruited form of saskatoon. Ornamental, pyramidal shrub, grows to about 15 feet tall. Introduced by the Horticultural Research Centre, Brooks, Alberta, Canada, about 1935. N24M

Beaverlodge: Large, juicy fruit with excellent flavor. H85

Forestburg: Large fruit, about 1/2 inch in diameter, produced on very tight clusters. Mild flavor. Originated in Forestburg, Alberta, Canada by the Beaverlodge Research Station. Introduced in 1963. BROOKS 1972; G75, N24M

Gypsy: Large, juicy fruit of fine flavor. H85

Honeywood: Large, dark-purple fruit with an excellent pleasant flavor; abundantly produced in heavy clusters, up to 15 berries in a cluster. Bushes grow to about 6 1/2 feet in height and will eventually develop into many-stemmed clumps. Bears at an early age. Selected from wild seedlings by A.J. Porter. Introduced by Honeywood Nursery in 1973. Very popular cultivar in Canada. RONALD; A65, B47, F67, G1T, G54, H85, N24M

Idaho Giant: Seedling trees grown from seed that was selected for large size. Recommended for trial plantings intended for home use and local marketing. A91{PL}

Moonlake: Yields large fruits but is a sporadic bearer. White blossoms; beautiful red foliage in autumn. Selected and introduced by George Krahn, Lakeshore Nurseries, Saskatoon, Saskatchewan in 1974. G54

Northline: Large, sweet, good quality fruits. Shrub to 5 feet high. Suckers rather freely. Selected near Beaverlodge, Alberta, Canada. Introduced in 1960 by J.A. Wallace. G75, N26, N26{PR}

Pembina: Fruit is large, sweet, full-flavored; borne on long clusters. Bush upright, slightly spreading, grows 8 to 10 feet high; very vigorous and productive. Does not sucker freely. Developed by Beaverlodge Research Station, Beaverlodge, Alberta, Canada. Introduced in 1952. BROOKS 1972, RONALD; A12, B47, N24M, N26, N26{PR}

Regent: Semi-dwarf shrub; height 4 to 6 feet, 4 foot spread. White flowers in late April followed by an abundant crop of purple-black fruits which ripen in early summer. Excellent for jams and jellies. Autumn foliage in shades of yellow and red. Selected both for berry production and ornament by J. Candrian, Regent, North Dakota. *A74*, C9, *C47*, D65, F43M, *G4*, G67, H42, I49M, I60, *K31*, K64, L70, N37M

Smoky: Fruit large, round; flesh very sweet and juicy, full-flavored; fruit size 1/2 to 5/8 inch. Bush spreading, reaching 6 to 8 feet; reliable and very heavy bearing, single bushes have yielded 88 pounds of fruit in government research trials. Produces suckers freely. Leading commercial cultivar in Canada. Originated in Beaverlodge, Alberta, by W.T. Macoun, Canada Department of Agriculture. Introduced in 1956. BROOKS 1972; A12, A65, A91, B47, F67, G1T, G54, G75, G87, H42, H85, K64, L79, N24M, N26, N26{PR}, etc.

Success: Fruits are up to 1/2 inch in diameter and are very good for eating out-of-hand. Bushy-shrub growing 6 1/2 to 8 feet high; suckers freely. Grown primarily in the eastern Great Plains states. Introduced by H.E. Van Deman of Kansas about 1878, and said to have been grown in Illinois from seeds obtained in Pennsylvania. A91{PL}, D37{CF}, K81

Thiessen: Very productive, with fruits up to 1/2 inch in diameter. Similar to Honeywood in most respects. Tree roundish in form. It differs in its mature height, and may reach 16 feet with age. Selected from wild seedlings and introduced in 1976 by George Krahn, Lakeshore Nurseries, Saskatoon, Saskatchewan. A12, B47, F67, G54

Timm: Large, blueberry-shaped fruit; very sweet and flavorsome; ripens early. Medium-sized tree, produces fruit in its second year. Large showy clusters of white flowers. Ornamental fall colors of yellow, red and maroon. Introduced by the Plant Material Center, Bismark, North Dakota. A91{PL}

Amelanchier arborea - *Downy serviceberry* {PL} The sweet fruits are eaten. North America. TURNER 1979; E32M, *G21M*, K38{S}, K63G{S}

Amelanchier asiatica - *Korean juneberry* {PL} The bluish-black berries are eaten, being of good quality. Eastern Asia. SIMMONS 1972, TANAKA; *P63*{S}, P86

Amelanchier bartramiana - *Bartrum shadblow* {S} Fruits are oval or pear-shaped rather than round like most juneberries. They are sweet and juicy and can be added to muffin and pancake mixes and to fruit sauces. Also dried and stored for future use. North America. CROWHURST 1972, MEDSGER; **U4, V34, Z25M**

Amelanchier canadensis - *Juneberry, Serviceberry* {PL} The sweet fruits are eaten out-of-hand and are also stewed, dried, preserved, added to pancakes and muffins, or made into pies, sauces, jams, jellies and cakes. Dried fruits are used like raisins or currants in puddings and muffins. When thoroughly cooked in puddings or pies, the seeds impart an almond-like flavor to the finished product. North America. ANGIER [Re], FERNALD, FREITUS [Re], GIBBONS 1962 [Re], MEDSGER, SIMMONS 1972; B9M, B32, *C47*, D45, D65, G23, G41, *G66*{S}, I77M, J7, K38{S}, *M69M*, M76, M92, O53M{S}, etc.

CULTIVARS {GR}

Prince William: Large, multi-stemmed shrub; height 10 feet, spreads to 6 feet; large white flowers; orange to red fall foliage color; fruits heavily. Fruit 3/8 inch to 1/2 inch in diameter; purplish-blue; quality good. Selected at Madison, Wisconsin. Introduced by Tom Watson. *K31*, *K37M*

Amelanchier cusickii - *Cusick's serviceberry* {S} Fruits are eaten. Has value in breeding work due to its long clusters, large fruits and large flowers. Western North America. DARROW, YANOVSKY; **Z25M**

Amelanchier denticulata - *Membrillo* {PL} The ripe fruits are eaten fresh and also make excellent jelly. Southwestern North America to Central America. WILLIAMS, L.; F85{S}, N51

Amelanchier florida - *Northwestern serviceberry, Pacific serviceberry* {S} The small, round fruits are eaten raw or used in pies, muffins, and puddings. In Alaska, they are dried and substituted for raisins or currants. Western North America. GIBBONS 1962, HELLER, SIMMONS 1972; **U7M, V34, Y29**

Amelanchier x grandiflora (A. canadensis x A. laevis) - *Apple serviceberry* {PL} Natural hybrid. The sweet fruits are eaten fresh, dried, in pies and other desserts, canned, frozen, or made into wine. North America. LOGSDON 1981; A50, B32, D37, F39M, *K89*, N37M, *R28*{S}

CULTIVARS {GR}

Ballerina: Large shrub or small trees, will reach 15 feet in height. Covered with large white flowers in spring, followed by a crop of red fruits which are very tasty. Named and described by H.J. van de Laar of Holland. F43M, N36

Princess Diana: Small, gracefully spreading tree; yellowish flower buds, opening to white; outstanding, brilliant red fall foliage, colors early and lasts until late in the season. Fruit 3/8 inch in diameter; purplish-blue; edible. Selected at Elm Grove, Wisconsin. Introduced by Tom Watson. *K31*, *K37M*

Amelanchier laevis - *Allegheny shadblow* {PL} The sweet, purplish-black fruits are eaten fresh, dried, or made into jams, sauces, and pies. Eastern North America. HENDRICKSON, LOGSDON 1981, YANOVSKY; *A74*, B9M, C9, *C47*, C58, D95, E33M, G89, *G89M*, J7, *K89*, M77, M92, N84{S}, O93{S}, *P63*{S}, etc.

Amelanchier lamarckii → *Amelanchier x grandiflora*

Amelanchier obovalis - *Southern juneberry* {S} The reddish-purple fruit is very good eaten out-of-hand or in pies, jellies, or blender drinks. Southeastern North America. BULLARD; N84

CULTIVARS {GR}

<u>**Jennybelle:**</u> Fruit reddish-purple when ripe, up to 1/2 inch in diameter; ripens from late May to mid-June; flavor sweet, even when fruit is red and not fully ripe. Small bush, seldom over 10 to 12 feet tall. Produces few suckers, making it easy to manage. Blooms late; comes into bearing at an early age; vigorous and productive. Resistant to drought, frost, and hot temperatures. D37, K67

Amelanchier ovalis - *European juneberry, Snowy mespilus* {S} Berries are red at first, turn black with a purplish bloom when ripe, and are about the size of a black currant. Not particularly palatable but can be used for jam or wine making. Europe. SIMMONS 1972; D62, *G66*, *G66*{PL}, K47T, N84, N93M, P49, S7M

Amelanchier x spicata (A. canadensis x A. stolonifera) - {S} Natural hybrid. The sweet, juicy fruits are eaten. North America. KUNKEL, SIMMONS 1972; K63G, *N71M*, N84

Amelanchier stolonifera - *Quebec berry, Dwarf juneberry* {PL} The sweet, juicy, purplish-black fruit is often used to make jelly. Eastern North America. HENDRICKSON, SIMMONS 1972; D30, D95, *H90*, *K89*, O67{S}, *P63*{S}

Amelanchier utahensis - *Utah serviceberry* {S} Fruits are eaten raw, stewed, dried or used in pancakes, jams, jellies, and wine. Dried fruits are added to soups and stews. Western North America. KIRK; **U7M, Z57**

Amelanchier vulgaris → ***Amelanchier ovalis***

X Amelasorbus jackii (Amelanchier florida x Sorbus scopulina) - {S} Natural hybrid. Juneberry x mountain ash. The fruits are edible but are not very palatable. North America. BEAN, KRÜSSMANN, REHDER; **T41M**

Amygdalus besseriana - *Dwarf almond, Russian almond* {PL} Seeds are the source of an oil being similar but inferior to *bitter almond oil*. Also produces a *bitter almond water*. The fruit is eaten in Siberia. Used as a frost-resistant rootstock for A. communis. Eurasia. UPHOF, ZEVEN; B15M, *C33*, D95, F67, G1T, *G66*, *G66*{S}, K38{S}, K64, *K89*, M35M, N0, N26, N84{S}

Amygdalus bucharica - *Bukhara almond* {S} In breeding, this almond relative may form a source of sweet pits, of high oil content and of good kernel to shell ratio. Central Asia. ZEVEN; *G66*, S36M

Amygdalus communis - *Almond* {S} Seeds are eaten raw, salted, roasted, sprouted, or used in cakes, confectionery and pastry. They can also be blended with water to form *almond milk*, made into *almond butter* or pressed for their edible oil. The tender kernels of young almonds, picked before they are mature, are a traditional delicacy in the Middle East. Almond meal is used in *macaroons* and cakes. Southwest Asia, cultivated. GRIEVE, JAYNES [Cu, Pro], MENNINGER, ROSENGARTEN [Re], UPHOF; D81{PO}, D81M{PO}, *N71M*, N84, N93M, *P63*, Q12, S95 (for cultivars see Almond, page 227)

Amygdalus communis 'Amara' - *Bitter almond* {S} Kernels are the source of *bitter almond oil*, which is detoxified and used as a flavoring for *maraschino cherries*, ice cream, baked goods, extracts, *amaretto* liqueurs, and *orgeat*, a syrup used in beverages. Blanched, crushed kernels are added to peach, cherry, or apricot preserves. GRIEVE, MORTON 1976, VON WELANETZ; *G66*, K38, N84, S95

Amygdalus davidiana - *David peach, Chinese wild peach* {S} The kernels are used in China to flavor confectionery and some special dishes, but they contain prussic acid. Fruits are also edible. Used as a disease resistant, low-chill rootstock. China. BROOKS 1972, GESSERT, TANAKA; *G66*, K38, K47T, N84, P38, *P63* (for cultivars see Peach, page 417 and Rootstocks, page 470)

Amygdalus mira - *Smoothpit peach* {S} Fruits are of the typical freestone peach-type, but have small, ovoid and smooth stones. They are consumed by the natives. China. UPHOF; **Y89M**

Amygdalus nana → ***Amygdalus besseriana***

Amygdalus persica - *Peach, T'ao* {S} The fruit is eaten fresh, dried, canned, processed into jam and juice, in cakes, ice cream and pies, pickled, as peach butter, preserved in brandy, etc. Flowers are eaten in salads, used as a garnish, or brewed into tea. When distilled, they furnish a white liquor, which imparts a flavor resembling the kernels of the fruit. An infusion of the leaves in white brandy, sweetened with barley sugar, is said to make a fine cordial, similar to *noyau*. Eastern Asia, cultivated. GRIEVE, MACNICOL [Re], TANAKA, UPHOF; D81{PO}, D81M{PO}, *G66*, K38, K47T, *N71M*, N84, N93M, O53M, Q12, S95 (for cultivars see Peach, page 417 and Rootstocks, page 470)

Amygdalus persica Compressa Group - *Flat peach, Ping-tzu-t'ao* Fruits are eaten fresh or processed. TANAKA, UPHOF; (for cultivars see Peach, page 417)

Amygdalus persica Nucipersica Group - *Nectarine, Yu-t'ao* {PR} The fruits are eaten out-of-hand, dried, preserved, as a topping for ice cream and cake, canned, brandied, processed into jams, marmalades, pies, fruit leather, added to fruit salads, etc. CARCIONE, CREASY 1982, SIMMONS 1972 [Cu]; <u>H26M</u> (for cultivars see Nectarine, page 396)

Amygdalus persica x Prunus besseyi - *Peche* {GR} Artificial hybrid. Peach x western sand cherry. Combines the late flowering habit of sand cherry with the fruit qualities of the peach.

CULTIVARS

<u>**Windmill Point:**</u> Sweet, juicy fruit with little or no astringency. Very tasty fresh or cooked. Shows promise as a late flowering type that escapes spring frosts. N24M

Aphanes arvensis - *Parsley piert* {S} Young plants are pickled or eaten in salads. Europe. KUNKEL, MABEY; **Y10, Y17M**

Armeniaca brigantina - *Briançon apricot, Alpine plum* {S} The kernels are the source of *huille des marmottes*, an oil used in France in lieu of olive oil. Fruits are occasionally eaten. Europe. HEDRICK 1919, TANAKA; **Y5M, Y89M**

Armeniaca x dasycarpa - *Black apricot, Purple apricot, Susincocco* {S} The plum-like fruits are purple-black in color and have soft, juicy flesh that is subacid to acid. They are eaten fresh, and may also be used in marmalades. Probably a natural hybrid, Armeniaca vulgaris x Prunus cerasifera. Cultivated. SIMMONS 1972, ZEVEN; **T41M**

Armeniaca mandshurica - *Manchurian apricot* {PL} The fruits are small, juicy, subacid to sweet, and can be eaten fresh, stewed, dried, or made into preserves. Northeastern Asia. TANAKA; A65, A91, *B52*, B73M, C63, D76, E32M, E97, G53M, *G66*, H42, H85, I78, K63G{S}, *K89*, L27M, L70, *N19*, P49{S}, S36M{S}, etc.

CULTIVARS {GR}

<u>**Manchu:**</u> Large, round-oblong fruit; skin burnt-orange with blush; flesh orange, slightly dry and acid; cooking quality good, only fair for dessert; ripens in early August. Tree large, vigorous, spreading; very hardy; self-fruitful, bears heavy crops regularly. Seedling of seed brought from northern Manchuria in 1924 by N.E. Hansen, South Dakota Agricultural Experiment Station. Introduced in 1936. ANDERSEN, BROOKS 1972; E97, F91T{SC}

<u>**Manchurian Select:**</u> Hardy ornamental with good quality fruit for jams and preserves. Selected by Jeffries Nurseries of Portage la Prairie, Manitoba, Canada. G1T

<u>**Scout:**</u> Fruit medium to large; flat, oblong-cordate, pointed; skin golden bronze, slightly pubescent; flesh deep yellow, fine, tender;

freestone; quality fair to good as dessert, good canned or for jam; season late July and early August. Tree tall, upright, rounded; moderately vigorous; hardy; productive. Originated in Morden, Manitoba, Canada. ANDERSEN, BROOKS 1972; *D35M*{DW}, E97, *G89M*, *G89M*{DW}, H85, *H90*, L70, M35M{PL}

Sunshine: Large fruit of good quality; resembles Manchu. Tree vigorous; hardy; moderately productive. Open-pollinated seedling selected in 1940. Released by the South Dakota Agricultural Experiment Station in 1950. BROOKS 1972; N24M

Armeniaca mume - *Ume, Japanese apricot* {PL} Fruits are eaten raw, candied, boiled, preserved in sugar, pickled in salt and dried, or made into a liqueur. The pulp is also used in the preparation of *ume-bishio*, a sour jam. Fruits preserved in salt and flavored with red Perilla are known as *umeboshi* or *salt plums* and are popular with those who follow a macrobiotic diet. They are placed in the center of rice balls to give a slightly sour and salty flavor. The fragrant vinegar obtained from the fruit is used for pickling ginger and in salad dressings. In China, the blossoms are used for scenting tea. Young budlings are edible. Japan, cultivated. HEDRICK 1919, SHURTLEFF 1975 [Re], TANAKA, UPHOF; B96, *C54*, D95, E56{PR}, E66T{PR}, E87, F70, *G66*{S}, H91{PR}, K38{S}, K63G{S}, N13, N37M, N84{S}, *P39*{S}, P49{S}, *P63*{S}, etc.

Armeniaca mume 'Microcarpa' - *Ko-ume* {PR} The relatively small fruit is pickled like that of the type. It has its own special flavor, texture and effect. Pickled fruits, known as *ko-umeboshi* or *tiny salt plums*, are sprinkled with sugar and eaten as dessert. Cultivated. TANAKA; E56

Armeniaca sibirica - *Siberian apricot, Môko-anzu* {S} The sour fruits are occasionally eaten. Kernels yield an extract used for flavoring food. Also the source of an edible oil resembling olive oil. Siberia. HEDRICK 1919, TANAKA; *G66*, I60{PL}

Armeniaca vulgaris - *Apricot* {S} Fruits are eaten fresh, dried, stewed, candied, made into paste, used in pastries, pies, cakes, jams, confectionery, preserved in brandy, pickled, etc. Unripe fruits can be used in compotes or bottled in syrup. Source of apricot juice, liqueurs and cordials. Blanched kernels, sometimes called *Chinese almonds*, are eaten raw, roasted, or ground and added to jams, conserves, and the agar-agar based white *almond jelly*. Also the source of an edible oil. Cultivated. COST 1988 [Cul], JOHNS [Cul, Re], TANAKA, UPHOF; A80M{PL}, D81{PO}, D81M{PO}, *G66*, *G66*{PL}, H49, K38, K63G, M63M{PR}, *N71M*, N84, N93M, Q12, Q40, Q46, etc. (for cultivars see Apricot, page 250 and Rootstocks, page 470)

Armeniaca vulgaris 'Ansu' - *Anzu, Ansu apricot* {S} The fruit is eaten like that of the type. Seed kernel oil is used as a substitute for olive oil. The leaves and buds can be eaten. TANAKA; K38, N13{PL}, N84, *P39*, *P63*

Armeniaca vulgaris x Amygdalus persica - *Peachcot* {PL} Artificial hybrid. Apricot x peach. Occasionally cultivated for its edible fruit. Large, yellow-skinned fruits; moderately firm flesh; good flavor which resembles a peach. Tree has the characteristics of the apricot parent. Ripens early to late June. A88M, *C54*, E4

CULTIVARS {GR}

Bill's: Medium-sized, juicy fruits; delicious peach-like flavor with the secondary sweetness of the apricot; ripens in June, 2 weeks earlier than either parent. Excellent for canning, drying or storing. Hardy to Zone 5. A91

Armeniaca vulgaris x Prunus besseyi - *Cherrycot* {GR} Artificial hybrids. Apricot x western sand cherry. Combines the late flowering habit and cold-hardiness of sand cherry with the fruit qualities of the apricot.

CULTIVARS

Yuksa: Western sand cherry x New Large apricot of Europe. Produces an abundance of flowers. Originated in Brookings, South Dakota by N.E. Hansen. Introduced in 1908. HANSEN; F91T{SC}, N24M

Armeniaca vulgaris x Prunus spp. - *Plumcot* {PL} Artificial hybrids. Apricot x various plums. Occasionally cultivated for their edible fruit. UPHOF; A91, *C54*, H65, *I68*

CULTIVARS {GR}

Apex: Apricot x Japanese plum. Large, globular fruit; skin attractive deep pink or light crimson; flesh honey-yellow, firm, rich, aromatic, apricot-like; freestone; ripens about the middle of June. Tree stout, compact, upright growing. Originated in Santa Rosa, California by Luther Burbank. Introduced in 1911. T49M{SC}

Black Pearl: Fruit with dark-blue skin and yellow flesh; freestone; flesh sweet and flavorful. Makes tasty preserves. Ripens in July. Plant with Parfait for heavier fruit set. Does well in locations suitable to apricots. D76, G8

Flavor Delight: (Flavor Delight Aprium) Attractive, 2 inch fruit, resembles an apricot more than Parfait; distinctive flavor and texture, pleasant lingering aftertaste; ripens in early June. Vigorous, upright tree; partly self-fruitful but heaviest crops are produced if cross-pollinized by Royal or Tilton apricots. Requires 600 hours of chilling. Developed by Floyd Zaiger. A88M, I83M, J61M, L1, L33, *N20*

Flavor Queen: (Flavor Queen Pluot) Plum-like yellow fruit with excellent eating qualities; sweet, juicy flesh with an apricot-like aftertaste; ripens in mid-July and can be harvested over a period of several weeks. Needs 500 to 600 hours of chilling. Pollinizer required. Developed by Floyd Zaiger. A88M, I83M, J61M, *N20*

Flavor Supreme: (Flavor Supreme Pluot) Small to medium-sized fruit, 2 1/2 inches in diameter, resembles Satsuma plum; sweet, flavorful red flesh, firm but juicy, resembles Elephant Heart plum; superior to any early plum; ripens in early June in central California. Vigorous, productive tree; needs 500 to 600 hours of chilling. Pollinizer required; pollinate with Flavor Delight or any Japanese plum. Developed by Floyd Zaiger. A88M, I83M, J61M, L33, *N20*

Mesch Mesch Amrah: Red-skinned fruit with yellow flesh. Flavor raspberry-like, sweet to tart, variable from season to season. Thought to be a hybrid of the Japanese plum (P. salicina) and the Mesch Mesch or Musk apricot. Introduced into the United States from Tripoli, Libya. T49M{SC}, U13{SC}

Parfait: (Plum Parfait) Medium-sized fruit, similar to an apricot with red-blushed skin over dark yellow. Flesh is dark yellow marbled with red near the pit, firm, similar to apricot. Very good to excellent flavor, slightly tart. Tree is semi-dwarf, height 10 to 12 feet, spreading; resembles a plum tree in form and is very ornamental. Bears lightly when young. A88M, D76, E97, I83M, L1, *N20*, *O97*

Rutland: Fruit the size of an ordinary apricot with a deep-purple velvety skin. Brilliant red flesh with a strong sub-acid flavor making it suitable for cooking, jellies, and jams. When fully ripe it is an excellent dessert fruit possessing an apricot-plum flavor. Developed by Luther Burbank. Introduced by George C. Roeding in 1907. WICKSON; T49M{SC}

Spring Ruby: Distinctive, purple-leaved plumcot. Furry, red-skinned fruit with orange flesh, of fair quality. Possibly a hybrid of apricot and Prunus cerasifera 'Atropurpurea'. T49M{SC}

Yellow: Medium to large, roundish fruit; skin yellow, smooth; flesh golden-yellow, sweet, juicy; flavor rich and aromatic, apricot-like with plum overtones. Ripens in June. Tree has the characteristics of the plum parent. E4, L99M

Aronia arbutifolia - *Red chokeberry* {PL} Fruits are eaten raw, stewed, or made into jelly. The Indians used them for making *pemmican*, a mixture of fresh fruit, dried meat and melted fat. North

America. HEDRICK 1919, PETERSON, L., YANOVSKY; A34M, B9M, *B15*, C38, D30, D95, *H8*, K38{S}, K47T{S}, K63G{S}, *K89*, M92, N36, *N71M*{S}, N84{S}, P49{S}, R78{S}, etc.

Aronia melanocarpa - *Black chokeberry* {PL} The raw berries have a good flavor but are very astringent, much like choke-cherries. Stewed with sugar or honey they make an acceptable fruit sauce, and are also processed into a very dark, thick, good-flavored jelly. They contain an abundance of pectin and can be added to pectin-deficient fruits to make them jell. North America. FERNALD, GIBBONS 1979; A91, A93M, B15M, D95, *G66*, *G66*{S}, *G89M*, H49, K38{S}, K47T{S}, K63G{S}, *K89*, *M69M*, *N71M*{S}, N84{S}, R78{S}, etc.

CULTIVARS {GR}

Nero: Shiny black fruit; weight about 1.2 grams, whereas fruit of wild specimens usually weigh about 0.6 grams; vitamin C content ranges from 15 to 30 mg. Bears fruit in clusters of 15, the yield per tree being twice that of wild specimens. Also selected for more flavorful fruit. The first commercially available cultivar. Developed in the Soviet Union. F43M

Cercocarpus ledifolius - *Mountain mahogany* {S} The scraped bark makes a flavorful additive to a brew of mormon tea (Ephedra spp.). Western North America. KIRK; B94, C4, D95{PL}, *E66M*, G60{PL}, *G66*, *G66*{PL}, *G89M*{PL}, I47, I63M{PL}, J25M, J25M{PL}, J26{PL}, K47T, N84, etc.

Chaenomeles cathayensis - *Cathay quince* {S} The large, dull-green fruits are not as attractive as those of some Chaenomeles species but make an excellent jelly. They can also be stewed or preserved. China. JOHNS, TANAKA; L91M, O53M

Chaenomeles japonica - *Dwarf Japanese quince, Maule's quince* {S} Fruits are eaten raw, stewed, preserved in brine, baked, or made into jelly. The rich, aromatic juice, as tart as a lemon, is squeezed and used for culinary purposes. Japan, cultivated. HEDRICK 1919, TANAKA; B32{PL}, C9M, *G66*, H49{PL}, K38, K63G, *L47*{PL}, L91M, M76{PL}, *N71M*, N84, N93M, O53M, *P63*, Q40, R78, etc.

Chaenomeles sinensis → *Pseudocydonia sinensis*

Chaenomeles speciosa - *Japanese quince, Flowering quince* {S} The fruits are cooked or parboiled, mashed after having the seeds removed, and then mixed with honey and ginger and made into a beverage. They can also be used for jellies, conserves, or for flavoring apple or other fruit pies. China. SIMMONS 1972 [Cu], TANAKA; *G66*, H4{PL}, K63G, *N71M*, N84, P49, *P63*

CULTIVARS {GR}

Cameo: Low, compact growth; height 3 to 5 feet; very few thorns. Attractive semi-double flowers of soft apricot-pink. Bears edible greenish-yellow fruits with an appealing lemon-like fragrance. Makes fine jelly, jam and preserves. *A74*, B9M, C9, *C47*, D95, E87, F43M, G55, *G89M*, H4, M92, M98, N13

Chaenomeles speciosa var. cathayensis → *Chaenomeles cathayensis*

Cotoneaster nummularia → *Cotoneaster racemiflora*

Cotoneaster racemiflora - *Black-wood* {S} Source of *shir-kist* or *schir-khecht*, a whitish, sweet, manna-like substance used as food in India and Iran. It contains 13% saccharine and 37.5% dextrose. North Africa to Southern Asia. DONKIN, UPHOF; F85, K38, N84, O46, O53M, O93, *P63*, Q40

Cowania mexicana - *Cliffrose, Quinine bush* {S} A refreshing tea can be made by steeping the leaves in hot water for a few minutes. Western North America. KIRK; B94, C4, *E66M*, F79M, G60{PL}, *G66*, *G89M*{PL}, I47, I63M{PL}, J25M, J25M{PL}, O93, P5

Cowania stansburiana → *Cowania mexicana*

X Crataegosorbus miczurinii (Crataegus sanguinea x Sorbus aucuparia) - {S} Artificial hybrid. Hawthorn x mountain ash. Fruits are occasionally eaten, containing up to 300% vitamin P. Developed in 1925 by I.V. Michurin. **X33, Y29**

Crataegus aestivalis - *Mayhaw* {PL} Fruits are eaten raw, pickled, stewed or made into jellies, jams, marmalades, tarts, and preserves. Mayhaw jelly is much prized in some areas of the Southern United States. It has been reported that the juice will keep in the refrigerator for months and still be good for making jelly. Southeastern North America. FREITUS [Re], HEDRICK 1919, LOGSDON 1981, MEDSGER; A80M, B74, D95, H4, *I17M*, K18, N24M, N37M

CULTIVARS {GR}

Big Red: Fruits are bright shiny-red, crabapple-shaped; the largest of any cultivar, with some up to 1 inch in diameter. Tree is a rank grower and it takes a couple of years before it begins to bear regularly. Discovered deep in the Pearl River swamps of southern Mississippi by T.O. Warren, Hattiesburg, Mississippi. F43M, G75, K67

Big "V": (No. 1 Big) Red fruits, about 3/4 inch in diameter. Tree bears heavily; grows with an attractive branching habit. Selected from seedlings growing in the Pearl River swamps of southern Mississippi, by T.O. Warren. Named after the shape of the tree. F43M

Heavy: Fruits are red in color, 1/2 to 3/4 inch in diameter. The heaviest-bearing of any cultivar. Young growth is willowy and twiggy, but matures nicely and stiffens with age. Originated in the Pearl River swamp. Discovered by T.O. Warren. F43M

Mississippi Beauty: Small tree with red fruits ideally suited for making jelly. H4

Super Berry: (Texas Super Berry) Large fruits, as large as Big Red; attractive shellac-red in color. Ripe fruits hang on the tree for a very long time. Earliest blooming of any cultivar. Tree is ornamental both in bloom and with ripe fruit. Selected from seedlings growing in Buna, Texas, by T.O. Warren. F43M, G17, K67

Super Spur: Red fruit, about 3/4 inch in diameter. Spur-type tree has a large, thick, bearing top; has borne 86 commercial gallons of fruit (approximately 3.5 pounds per gallon). Selected from the wild by J.S. Akin of Sibley, Louisiana. F43M, H4, I83M, K67

Yellow: A yellow-fruited cultivar, very ornamental and equal to others in flavor. Appears somewhat less vigorous in growth. F43M

Crataegus azarolus - *Azarole, Mediterranean medlar* {S} The small, apple-like fruits are eaten raw, preserved, or used in jellies, jams, butters, and compotes. In warmer climates the ripe fruit has a fragrant and sugary pulp with a slightly acid flavor, and can be eaten out-of-hand. When grown in more northerly areas, it is more suited for processing into confectionery and jelly as it needs a fairly long after-ripening period. Yellow, red, and white-fruited forms are known. Mediterranean region, Southwest Asia. HEDRICK 1919, JOHNS, SIMMONS 1972 [Cu], UPHOF; K63G, N84, N93M, O53M, O71M{PL}, P5, *P63*

CULTIVARS {GR}

Fruto Blanco: Large, white fruit with a pleasant aromatic flavor. Ripens in September and October. Q24M

Julieta: Small, red fruit with a pleasant aromatic flavor. Ripens in September and October. Q24M

Crataegus crenulata → *Pyracantha crenulata*

Crataegus cuneata - *Nippon hawthorn, Sanzashi* {S} Fruits are eaten raw, dried or made into jam. Also used for brewing wine. Japan, China. TANAKA; F85

Crataegus douglasii - *Black hawthorn* {PL} The sweet, juicy fruits can be eaten fresh, used for jams, sauces, drinks and jellies, or dried and stored for future use. Western North America. KIRK, TURNER 1979 [Re], YANOVSKY; A2{S}, A80M, B94{S}, *C73*, D95, *G89M*, I47{S}, J26, K47T{S}, N84{S}

Crataegus flava - *Summer haw* {PL} The yellowish, somewhat pear-shaped fruits are esteemed for making jellies. Southern North America. UPHOF; N37M

Crataegus laevigata → ***Crataegus oxyacantha***

Crataegus lobulata - {S} Fruits are blue-black, the size of a damson, pear-shaped and said to be as rich in vitamin C as a rosehip. Central Asia. O53M

Crataegus marshalli - *Parsley haw* {PL} The fruits are eaten. Also used as a dwarfing rootstock for C. aestivalis. Southern North America. H4, *I17M*, N37M

Crataegus mexicana → ***Crataegus pubescens***

Crataegus mollis - *Downy hawthorn* {S} Fruits are eaten fresh and are also used for making jellies. North America. MEDSGER; C9M, *G66*, *G89M*{PL}, *H8*{PL}, K38, K47T, K63G, *K89*, L12{PL}, M35M{PL}, M76{PL}, N84, *P63*

Crataegus monogyna - *Maytree, One-seeded hawthorn* {S} Young, tender leaves have a pleasant nutty taste, and are a good addition to a tossed salad. The young buds are used in *spring puddings*. The flowers are mixed with sugar and brandy and made into a liqueur, and are also used in syrups and sweet puddings. Fruits are eaten fresh or used for jellies and wines. Dried leaves are brewed into a tea. Europe, cultivated. LEGGATT, MABEY [Re], MACLENNAN, MICHAEL [Re]; A80M{PL}, C11, *F38*, *G66*, *G66*{PL}, K38, K63G, *N71M*, N84, N93M, O93, P49, *P63*, Q40, *R28*, R78, etc.

Crataegus opaca → ***Crataegus aestivalis***

Crataegus oxyacantha - *English hawthorn* {S} The fruits are eaten raw or fermented into a kind of wine. Young leaves are used as a substitute for tea. The dried fruit pulp can be added to flour. Seeds are used as a coffee substitute. A liqueur is made by mixing the berries with brandy. Southern Europe, cultivated. GRIEVE, HEDRICK 1919, UPHOF; E7M, *G66*, *G66*{PL}, *H8*{PL}, I47, K20, K38, K63G, *N71M*, N84, O93, P49, *P63*, *R28*, R78, etc.

Crataegus pubescens - *Manzanilla, Tejocote* {S} The mealy fruits are eaten in the form of jellies, jams and preserves. For stewing, they are first boiled with wood-ashes to remove the skin, then boiled in hot syrup with red coloring for a short time and hung on nails stuck into poles, much like candied apples. Also used for flavoring rum or carbonated drinks. Mexico. LATORRE 1977a, POPENOE, W. 1920, SIMMONS 1972, WILLIAMS, L.; *G66*, N84, O93, P5

Crataegus punctata - *Dotted hawthorn* {S} Fruits are eaten raw or processed into jellies, sauces, and beverages. North America. TURNER 1979 [Re]; *G66*, K38, N84, O53M, O93, *P63*

Crataegus succulenta - *Succulent hawthorn* {S} The small, bright scarlet fruits have sweet, juicy flesh and are excellent for making jelly. Western Indians pressed the berries into cakes and dried them for winter use. North America. TANAKA, TURNER 1979 [Re]; N84

Crataegus tanacetifolia - *Syrian hawberry* {PL} The fruit is pale-green to yellow touched with red, and has an apple-like aroma and taste that is relished by the Armenians. Asia Minor. HEDRICK 1919, SIMMONS 1972; N84{S}, P86

Cydonia japonica → ***Chaenomeles japonica***

Cydonia oblonga - *Quince* {S} Occasionally used fresh, the aromatic fruits are primarily eaten stewed, preserved with pears, stuffed, or made into pies, marmalades, jams, jellies, fruit leather, candy, and conserves. In Iraq, a drink is made by adding crushed dried seeds to water, simmering for five minutes, and then sweetening to taste. The flowers are edible. Eurasia, cultivated. BIANCHINI, BRYAN [Cu, Cul], JOHNS [Cul], MACNICOL, SCHNEIDER [Pre, Re], SIMMONS 1972, UPHOF, VON WELANETZ; A80M{PL}, D62, *G66*, *G66*{PL}, K47T, M22{PL}, N84, O53M, P49, *P63* (for cultivars see Quince, page 460 and Rootstocks, page 470)

Cydonia sinensis → ***Pseudocydonia sinensis***

Dasiphora fruticosa → ***Potentilla fruticosa***

Docynia delavayi - *Tao-yi* {S} When ripe, the apple-like fruit is eaten. The fresh fruit is also used in ripening persimmons. Fruits of each are arranged in alternate layers in large jars and covered with rice husks, and in ten hours the persimmons are bletted and fit for eating. China. ALTSCHUL, WILSON, E.; **Z25M**

Dryas octopetala - *Mountain avens* {S} Leaves are used as a substitute for tea, called *schweizertee* or *kaisertee* in the European Alpes. Alpine and Arctic regions. UPHOF; D62, E89M, G55{PL}, I39, J7, J67M, J78{PL}, K47T, K79{PL}, L13, L91M, N84, O53M, *Q24*, S7M, etc.

Eriobotrya japonica - *Loquat, Japanese medlar* {PL} The juicy, subacid, refreshing fruits are eaten raw, preserved, stewed, in compotes and fruit salads, dried, made into jelly, pies, sauces, drinks, etc. Loquat pie, if made from fruit which is not fully ripe, is said to have the flavor of cherry pie. Roasted seeds are used as a substitute for coffee. China, cultivated. JOHNS [Cul], MORTON 1987a [Cu], POPENOE, W. 1920 [Cu, Pro], RICHARDSON [Re], SCHNEIDER [Cul, Re], TANAKA, UPHOF; A44M{PR}, A79M{S}, C9M{S}, E29, E29{PR}, H4, H49, I28, I49M, *I61*{S}, J61M, L91M{S}, N37M, *N40*{PR}, N84{S}, O53M{S}, etc. (for cultivars see Loquat, page 380)

Filipendula hexapetala → ***Filipendula vulgaris***

Filipendula ulmaria - *Meadowsweet, Queen-of-the-meadow* {S} The fragrant flowers and leaves are used as a flavoring for herb beers, mead, claret wine, liqueurs, and stewed fruit. Flowers are also made into a syrup which can be used in cooling drinks and fruit salads, or as a topping for ice cream. Young leaves, flowers, and roots are brewed into tea, while the leaves are added to other herb teas as a sweetener. Eurasia. MABEY, MACNICOL [Re], MARCIN, MICHAEL [Re], MORTON 1976, PAINTER [Re]; C11, C13M, F80, G82M{PL}, H3M{PL}, I39, I99, K47T, K53, K85{PL}, M77M{PL}, *N71M*, N84, O53M, S7M, S55, etc.

Filipendula vulgaris - *Dropwort* {PL} Young leaves are used in soups and salads. The tubers have been roasted and eaten in times of food shortage. Eurasia. MABEY, MORTON 1976, UPHOF; B77, B97M, D95, G82M, I63M, J37M, K47T{S}, K53{S}, *L22*, *L95*, *M65M*, M77M, *N71M*{S}, N84{S}, O53M{S}, S7M{S}, etc.

Fragaria americana → ***Fragaria vesca var. americana***

Fragaria x ananassa (F. chiloensis x F. virginiana) - *Garden strawberry, Pineapple strawberry* Artificial hybrid, much cultivated. Fruits are eaten out-of-hand, with cream and sugar, stewed, preserved, used in cakes, pies, ice cream, pastries, made into jam and jelly, fermented into wine, etc. CARCIONE, JOHNS [Cul, Re], TANAKA, UPHOF, VILMORIN [Cu]; (for cultivars see Strawberry, page 503)

Fragaria californica - *California strawberry* {PL} The sweet, aromatic fruits are eaten fresh, dried or preserved. Fresh or dried leaves are used to brew an excellent tea. Western North America. CLARKE, GIBBONS 1962, MEDSGER, YANOVSKY; D95, G60, J73

Fragaria chiloensis - *Beach strawberry* {PL} The large, delicately flavored fruits are eaten raw, stewed, or used in cakes and jams. Leaves can be used for tea. Coastal North and South America. GIBBONS 1979, HEDRICK 1919, HELLER, POPENOE, W. 1924, WICKSON; G60, *J75M*

Fragaria collina* → *Fragaria viridis

Fragaria iinumae - *Nôgo-ichigo* {S} Young plants are eaten in soups or as a potherb. The fruit is also eaten. Eastern Asia. TANAKA; **U7M, V19, X33**

Fragaria moschata - *Musk strawberry, Hautbois strawberry* {PL} The fruit is eaten fresh as a dessert. It is deep violet-red or wine-colored, with white or faintly yellow, or occasionally, somewhat greenish flesh, and with a very strong musky flavor which is something like that of raspberries, or of black currants. Eurasia, cultivated. HEDRICK 1919, SIMMONS 1978, UPHOF, VILMORIN [Cu]; J29

CULTIVARS {GR}

Capron: Small, deep red fruit; flavor very good, aromatic, distinctively musky. Plant medium in size, moderately vigorous; somewhat unproductive due to pollination difficulties. **U7M, U13**

Profumata di Tortona: Small, deep red fruit; flavor very good, aromatic, distinctively musky. Plant large in size, highly vigorous, relatively unproductive. **U7M, U13**

Fragaria ovalis - *Rocky Mountain strawberry* {S} The fruit is eaten fresh, dried, in shortcakes, made into preserves and jams, or used as a flavoring for other preparations. Dried leaves are used for tea. In breeding, it is hybridized with F. x ananassa to convey winter-hardiness, and also for producing everbearing or day-neutral cultivars. Western North America. BROOKS 1972, HARRINGTON, H., ZEVEN; **X33** (for cultivars see Strawberry, page 503)

Fragaria vesca - *Wood strawberry, Fraise des bois* {S} Fruits are eaten fresh with cream, coated with chocolate, as a filling for tarts or made into jam. Young leaves are eaten in salads, and are also parboiled and added to soups. Fresh or dried leaves are used for tea. Northern temperate region, cultivated. KRAFT [Cul, Re], MABEY, MARCIN, MICHAEL [Re], TANAKA; E61{PL}, G15{PL}, G68, *G89M*, I83M{PL}, J82, L86, *N71M*, N84, O48, O53M, R53M, S55

CULTIVARS {GR}

Variegated: (Sow-Teat Strawberry) Deep green leaves, margined with white; white flowers; small, pale-red fruit. E48, G96, H51M, M82

Fragaria vesca var. americana - *American wood strawberry* {PL} The small, light red or pink fruit is eaten fresh, dried or preserved. Leaves are used as a substitute for tea. North America. TANAKA, YANOVSKY; *G89M*

CULTIVARS {GR}

Frost King: Small, spongy, white fruit, mostly bland in flavor. Plant small in size, moderately vigorous; susceptible to leaf spot; suffers from excessive runner production and low yields. **U13**

Snow King: Medium-sized, nearly round fruit; skin and flesh white; flesh very sweet with a wild strawberry flavor. Not attractive to birds due to the color. Mostly a novelty. Originated in Allegan County, Michigan by Burgess Seed & Plant Co. Introduced in 1922. BROOKS 1972; **U13**

Fragaria vesca 'Semperflorens' - *Alpine strawberry* {PL} The fruits are eaten fresh, dried, with sugar and cream, made into jam, mixed with cream for cake fillings, or served with cream cheese. They are also floated in wines and herb punches, such as *Maibowle*. FELL 1982b, HENDRICKSON, PAINTER [Re], SIMMONS 1972 [Cu], VILMORIN [Cu]; A49D, D62{S}, D95, E5M, E5T{S}, E81M{S}, H46{S}, J73{S}, K2, K2{S}, K22, K85, L56, N19M, N84{S}, etc. (for cultivars see Strawberry, page 503)

Fragaria virginiana - *Scarlet strawberry, Virginia strawberry* {PL} Fruits are eaten fresh, preserved, rolled in crepes and pancakes, dried, as a filling for open-faced French tarts, or made into jams and jellies. The leaves make a very pleasant tea. North America. CROWHURST 1972, FERNALD, MEDSGER, TURNER 1979 [Re]; C81M, E33M, G89, J39M, J41M, J41M{S}, J42, J43{S}, *J75M*, L46, N9M, N9M{S}, N37M, N45

Fragaria viridis - *Green strawberry, Hill strawberry* {S} The edible fruits are greenish tinged with red, and have a rich, musky, pineapple-like flavor. They more closely resemble the hautbois strawberry than any other kind. Europe. HEDRICK 1919, TANAKA, VILMORIN; **U7M, X8, X33, Y89M, Z25M, Z98**

Geum canadense - *White avens* {S} Boiled roots are used as a substitute for chocolate. North America. MORTON 1963; B61M, K47T, N84

Geum ciliatum* → *Geum triflorum

Geum rivale - *Purple avens, Water avens, Chocolate root* {S} The fresh or dried reddish-purple rootstock can be used to make a chocolate-like beverage. It is also employed as a flavoring for ale, wine and other liquors. North America. FERNALD, GIBBONS 1979, HARRINGTON, H., HEDRICK 1919, MEDSGER; D62, F85, I31, K47T, N45{PL}, *N71M*, N84, O48, O53M, *Q24*, S7M, S55

Geum triflorum - *Prairie smoke* {S} A decoction of the roots can be used as tea. Western North America. KIRK, YANOVSKY; D95{PL}, G89{PL}, H98{PL}, I37M{PL}, I47, I63M{PL}, J39M, J40, J41M, J41M{PL}, J42, J42{PL}, J43, J48{PL}, K47T, L91M, etc.

Geum urbanum - *Clove root, Herb bennet* {S} The rhizome has the scent of cloves, with a trace of cinnamon and is used as a spice in soups and broths, sauces, mulled cider, apple pie, and stewed fruit. It is combined with orange peel and put into wine. *Augsburg ale* is said to owe its peculiar flavor to the addition of a small bag of clove root in each cask. Northern temperate region. GRIEVE, HEDRICK 1919, MABEY, MICHAEL [Re], PAINTER [Pre, Re], ROOT 1980b [Cu, Cul], UPHOF; A2, C11, C81M{PL}, D62, E61{PL}, F85, H46, J82, *N71M*, O48, O53M, *Q24*, R53M, S7M, S55, etc.

Heteromeles arbutifolia* → *Photinia arbutifolia

Holodiscus discolor - *Ocean spray* {S} The small, dry fruits are eaten raw or cooked. Western North America. KIRK; E15, G59M, G60{PL}, *G66*, I15, I47, J26{PL}, *J75M*{PL}, *N71M*, N84, O93, P49, *P63*, R78

Laurocerasus ilicifolia - *Islay, Holly-leaved cherry* {S} The reddish-yellow fruit is eaten fresh, dried, made into a beverage, or mixed with lemon and sugar to form a sauce. Seed kernels are ground into meal, and after leaching are used in breads, soups and *atole*. Southwestern North America. CLARKE, KIRK [Pre], MEDSGER, YANOVSKY; B92{PL}, B94, C9M, G59M, G60{PL}, *H71*, *I61*, K47T, N84, *P63*

Laurocerasus lyonii - *Catalina Island cherry* {S} Fruits are maroon to black in color, with tough, leathery skin and a very large stone. They can be eaten fresh and are usually of finer flavor than those of L. ilicifolia, some types being comparable to a good sweet cherry cultivar. Southwestern North America. THOMSON 1977; B94, C9M, G60{PL}, *H71*, *I61*, I99, K47T, N84, *P63*

Laurocerasus myrtifolia - *Myrtle-leaved cherry laurel, West Indian cherry* {PL} Seeds have been used for flavoring cherry, plum, and damson wine. West Indies. HEDRICK 1919; D87G, *J25*

Laurocerasus officinalis - *Cherry laurel* {S} Small amounts of the almond-flavored water distilled from the leaves have been used for flavoring puddings, creams, sweetmeats, and custards. Poisonous in large quantities. Eastern Mediterranean region. GRIEVE, HEDRICK 1919, UPHOF; B94, C9{PL}, C76{PL}, D95{PL}, *F53M*{PL}, *I62*{PL}, K63G, *L47*{PL}, N37M{PL}, N84, O53M, P49, *P63*, *R28*, R78, S95, etc.

Malus angustifolia - *Southern crab* {PL} The hard, sour fruits are often used for preserves, pickles, cider, sauces, and jellies. Eastern North America. HEDRICK 1919, MEDSGER, UPHOF; A80M, H4, *I17M*, K18, N37M

Malus baccata - *Siberian crab* {PL} The brilliant red cherry-like fruit makes excellent jelly, and can also be eaten fresh, dried, stewed or preserved. *Verjuice*, a very tart vinegar made from crab apples, is used widely in European cooking. Also used as a cold-hardy rootstock for M. pumila. Eastern Asia, cultivated. MASEFIELD, PROULX, TANAKA, UPHOF, ZEVEN; B53, C9M{S}, *C33*, *C47*, D95, *G66*, *G66*{S}, *H45M*, *H90*, I47{S}, J26, K38{S}, K63G{S}, *N19*, N84{S}, P49{S}, etc. (for cultivars see Apple, page 230)

Malus communis → *Malus silvestris*

Malus coronaria - *Garland crab* {PL} Fruits are hard and sour but are frequently used for making pickles, marmalades, and vinegar. The early settlers collected the crab apples in autumn and buried them until spring when they had lost much of their acidity, and were then made into cider, jelly, or preserves. Eastern North America, cultivated. FERNALD, HEDRICK 1919, MEDSGER, UPHOF; M77M

Malus domestica → *Malus pumila*

Malus fusca - *Oregon crab, Western crab* {S} The fruit is eaten raw or made into jelly, pies, preserves, and applesauce. The residual pulp that remains after making jelly can be sieved, puréed and fermented into cider or it can be added to breads, cakes, and cookies. Also a good source of pectin for jellymaking. Western North America. HELLER, KIRK, TANAKA, TURNER 1979 [Re]; B94, N84, O93, *P63*

Malus hupehensis - *Tea crab, Chinese crab* {PL} In China, the leaves are used for making a palatable, thirst-quenching tea. Much is exported from Shasi. The sour fruit is eaten. Central to Eastern Asia. ALTSCHUL, TANAKA, UPHOF; A69G{SC}, A80M, C9, *G66*{S}, *H8*, *I82*, *K37M*, K38{S}, N84{S}, O53M{S}, *P63*{S}, P86

Malus ioensis - *Prairie crab, Iowa crab* {S} The fruit is eaten raw or made into jelly, preserves, and pickles. American Indians used them for preparing fried crabapples and hot coal-roasted crabapples. North America. FREITUS [Re], YANOVSKY; C9{PL}, *K89*

Malus x micromalus (M. baccata x M. spectabilis) - *Kaido crab* {PL} Probably a garden hybrid. The fruit is eaten. Also used as a rootstock for M. pumila, reportedly being the best dwarfing understock from seed. TANAKA; N84{S}, P86

Malus prunifolia - *Plum-leaf crab, Chinese apple* {S} Fruits are eaten when fresh, and are also preserved in sugar. The tree is highly resistant to frost and drought. Used by I.V. Michurin to breed hybrid cultivars such as Kandil Kitaika, Bellefleur Kitaika, Saffran Peppin, and Saffran Kitaika. Eastern Asia, cultivated. MICHURIN, TANAKA, UPHOF, ZEVEN; A69G{SC}, *G66*, *G66*{PL}, N84, O93, P49, S36M

Malus pumila - *Apple* {S} The fruits are eaten fresh, dried, baked, made into apple butter and apple sauce, candied, in pies and cakes, as juice and cider, fermented into *applejack*, *cidre*, *calvados*, etc. The flowers can be dipped in batter, deep fried and served sprinkled with sugar, or added to fritter batter. Eurasia, cultivated. BRYAN, MACNICOL, PEDERSON, PROULX, TANAKA, UPHOF; D81{PO}, D81M{PO}, *F38*, *G66*{PL}, *H45M*{PL}, H49, K38, K63G, *N19*{PL}, *N71M*, N84, O93, R78 (for cultivars see Apple, page 230 and Rootstocks, page 470)

Malus pumila 'Niedzwetzkyana' - {PL} The edible fruit is purple-red inside and out. TANAKA; J93{SC}, N24M (for cultivars see Apple, page 230)

Malus x robusta (M. baccata x M. prunifolia) - {S} Probably an artificial hybrid. Fruits are edible. Also a vigorous winter-hardy rootstock for M. pumila. Somewhat resistant to fireblight but slightly susceptible to crown rot. REHDER; *G66*, *G66*{PL}

CULTIVARS {GR}

<u>**Red Siberian:**</u> Small, roundish oblate to somewhat oblong fruit; skin smooth, pale yellow striped and blushed with lively red and overspread with blue bloom; flesh subacid, astringent; season September and October. Good for culinary uses. Originated in France. BEACH; P86

<u>**Yellow Siberian:**</u> Medium to large, roundish fruit; skin clear golden yellow; flesh subacid, astringent, good for culinary uses; season September. Tree medium-sized, upright, very hardy; precocious; a reliable bearer, yielding heavy to very heavy crops annually or nearly annually. BEACH; P86

Malus sargentii - *Sargent's crab* {PL} The fruit, large for a crabapple, is eaten. Japan, cultivated. TANAKA; B53, C9M{S}, *C33*, D95, E7M, E47, *F38*{S}, *G66*, *H90*, I77M, K38{S}, K47T{S}, *K77*, *K89*, *N71M*{S}, O53M{S}, R78{S}, etc.

Malus silvestris - *European crab apple, French crab apple, Wild apple* {S} The fruits are mostly tart or sour and are used for making syrup, jelly, apple butter, spiced apples, and wine. They are also roasted and added to *wassail bowl*, a traditional Christmas Eve beverage. *Verjuice* is a very sour vinegar made from crab apples or unripe grapes, which is used in cooking, much like lemon juice. The flowers can be crystallized. Eurasia. MICHAEL [Re], ZEVEN; A80M{PL}, C9M, *G66*, K38, K63G, N84, O93, P49, *P63*, R78, S95

Malus theifera → *Malus hupehensis*

Margyricarpus pinnatus - *Pearl berry, Perlilla, Romerillo* {PL} The fruits are pearl-like, somewhat reminiscent of the mistletoe, and have an agreeable acid flavor. Temperate South America. HEDRICK 1919, VALENZUELA; P86

Margyricarpus setosus → *Margyricarpus pinnatus*

Mespilus germanica - *Medlar* {S} Fruits are eaten, especially after having been exposed to frost and then stored until overripe or "bletted", when they become soft and mellow, and have an agreeable acid flavor somewhat reminiscent of unsweetened apple butter. Fruits that have just begun to ripen make an excellent jelly, orange in color and of a distinctive flavor. Ripe fruits can also be baked or made into jams and jellies. Occasionally used for cider. Eurasia, cultivated. BIANCHINI, JOHNS [Pre, Cul], MABEY, SIMMONS 1972 [Cu], UPHOF; D95{PL}, K38, K47T, M22{PL} *N71M*, N84, N93M, O53M, O93, P49, *P63*, *R28*, R47, R78, S95, etc.

CULTIVARS {GR}

<u>**Breda Giant:**</u> A large fruited cultivar from Holland. F43M

<u>**Dutch:**</u> (Large Dutch) Large, roundish fruits, 2 1/2 inches in diameter with short sepals. Grayish green until ripe, and then russet brown. Ripens in October and is ready by Christmas. Makes a small, spreading, pendulous tree suitable for general cultivation. Heavy cropping. A very old cultivar. SIMMONS 1978; O81

<u>**Large Russian:**</u> One of the largest fruited cultivars. An attractive small tree with very fine foliage. Winner of the Royal Horticultural Society Award of Merit. F43M, R77

<u>**Monstrous:**</u> Very large fruits of good quality. Tree a prolific bearer. O81, S81M

Nottingham: Medium-sized, pear-shaped fruit, 1 inch in diameter with long sepals. Yellow-brown in color, touched with russet; considered the best-flavored medlar. The tree is less vigorous than Dutch, and is suitable for growing as a bush or pyramid. Cropping is very heavy and will produce a good crop when three years old. SIMMONS 1972, SIMMONS 1978; F43M, J61M, L12, O81, P86, R77, S81M

Royal: Medium-sized, round fruits, 1 inch in diameter. They have a good flavor and are pleasantly acid. The tree is a good bearer, very shapely, and makes a good small standard tree. A newer cultivar. SIMMONS 1972, SIMMONS 1978; F43M

Oemleria cerasiformis* → *Osmaronia cerasiformis

Osmaronia cerasiformis - *Osoberry, Indian peach* {S} The fruit is eaten raw or cooked. Western North America. KIRK, YANOVSKY; A2, B94, D95{PL}, F85, N84, O93, *P63*

Padus maximowiczii* → *Prunus maximowiczii

Peraphyllum ramosissimum - *Squaw apple* {S} The fruits are sour when unripe, slightly bitter as they ripen, and when fully ripe are sweetish but with a bitter aftertaste. Fruits that dry on the plants are the sweetest and most desirable. Ripe fruits can be used for jelly or prepared like spiced crab apples. Western North America. GIBBONS 1979, HARRINGTON, H.; B94

Persica davidiana* → *Amygdalus davidiana

Persica mira* → *Amygdalus mira

Photinia arbutifolia - *Tollon, Christmas berry, California holly* {S} The bright red fruits are eaten raw, roasted, steamed or boiled, and are best with a little sugar added. Indians used them dried, ground, and made into mush. They can also be made into cider, in much the same way that manzanita cider is made. Southwestern North America. KIRK, MEDSGER, UPHOF, YANOVSKY; B94, C9M, *C73*{PL}, D95{PL}, G59M, G60{PL}, *H71*, *I61*, I98M, I99, K15, K47T, O53M, O93, *P63*, etc.

CULTIVARS {PL}

Yellow: A yellow fruited form. B92

Potentilla anserina - *Silverweed, Argentine* {PL} The long, crisp roots have a nut-like, somewhat starchy flavor and can be eaten raw, candied, fried, roasted or boiled, and are also added to soups and stews. Leaves are used for tea. Northern temperate region. ANGIER [Re], CROWHURST 1972, FERNALD, GIBBONS 1979, KIRK, KUNKEL, HARRINGTON, H., MABEY; G89, K47T{S}

Potentilla erecta - *Tormentil* {S} Rhizomes are used as a tea. Eurasia. UPHOF; D62, F37T{PL}, J82, *N71M*, N84, O48, P83M, *Q24*, R47, R53M, S55

Potentilla fruticosa - *Bush cinquefoil* {PL} Dried leaves are used as a substitute for tea, called *Kurile tea*. Northern temperate region. FERNALD, HEDRICK 1919, UPHOF; A34M, B9M, B75, E61, G23, J25M, J25M{S}, J41M, J41M{S}, *J75M*, *N71M*{S}, Q40{S}, R78{S}

Potentilla glandulosa - {S} A tea-like beverage is made by boiling the leaves or the whole plant in water. Western North America. YANOVSKY; D62, H4{PL}, I31, O53M

Potentilla palustris - {S} Leaves are used as a substitute for tea. Northern temperate region. KUNKEL; D62, K47T, N84, *Q24*, S7M

Potentilla rupestris - *Rock cinquefoil* {S} The leaves are used as a tea in some parts of Russia and Siberia, called *Siberian tea* or *prairie tea*. Eurasia. HEDRICK 1919, UPHOF; D62, D95{PL}, N84, *Q24*

Potentilla tormentilla* → *Potentilla erecta

Poterium sanguisorba* → *Sanguisorba minor

Prinsepia sinensis - *Cherry prinsepia* {PL} Bright red fruits are edible, having a good flavor. They can be eaten out of hand or made into jellies. Manchuria. TANAKA; F67, *K89*{S}

Prinsepia uniflora - *Suigaku* {S} The juicy, red fruits are eaten. China, Mongolia. ALTSCHUL, TANAKA; S36M

Prinsepia utilis - *Bekar* {S} Fruits are eaten. Seed kernels yield an oil used for cooking. Himalayan region, China. ALTSCHUL, TANAKA, WATT; N84, O46, O53M, Q40, Q46

Prunus alleghaniensis - *Allegheny plum, Porter's plum, American sloe* {S} Ripe fruits are purplish-black, pleasantly acid, and can be eaten fresh or made into jams, jellies, pies, and preserves. North America. CROWHURST 1972, MEDSGER, WAUGH; **T41M**

Prunus americana - *American wild plum* {PL} The pulpy, pleasant-tasting fruits are eaten raw, dried, stewed or processed into preserves, jams, sauces and jellies. Seed kernels can be eaten raw. North America, cultivated. FERNALD, HARRINGTON, H. [Re], KINDSCHER, MEDSGER, UPHOF; A80M, A91, D45, D69, D95, *G66*, G67, H49, I47{S}, J26, K18, K38{S}, K47T{S}, *K89*, *K89*{S}, etc. (for cultivars see Plum, page 446)

Prunus amygdalus* → *Amygdalus communis

Prunus angustifolia - *Chickasaw plum* {PL} Fruits are large, thin-skinned, and have a soft, juicy, sweet pulp that is very good eaten out-of-hand and also makes excellent jellies and preserves. North America, cultivated. CROWHURST 1972, FERNALD, MEDSGER, UPHOF; F91T{SC}, K18 (for cultivars see Plum, page 446)

Prunus angustifolia var. watsonii - *Sand plum, Sand Chickasaw plum, Sandhill plum* {PL} The acid fruits are often used for making pies, sauces, puddings, preserves, and jellies. Western North America. KINDSCHER, MEDSGER, WAUGH; F85{S}, M31M

Prunus armeniaca* → *Armeniaca vulgaris

Prunus armeniaca var. mandshurica* → *Armeniaca mandshurica

Prunus avium - *Sweet cherry, Wild sweet cherry* {S} Fruits are consumed fresh, dried, candied, stewed, in pies, cakes, ice cream, and pastries, made into preserves and jellies, etc. The gum that exudes from the trunk and branches can also be eaten. Eurasia, cultivated. HEDRICK 1919, TANAKA; A80M{PL}, D81{PO}, D81M{PO}, *G66*{PL}, *N71M*, N84, N93M, O53M, P49, *P63*, R78, S95 (for cultivars see Cherry, page 291, and Rootstocks, page 470)

Prunus besseyi - *Western sand cherry, Rocky Mountain cherry* {PL} The sweetish fruits are eaten raw, dried, or cooked. Western North America. MEDSGER, UPHOF, WAUGH, YANOVSKY; A16, C9M{S}, *C33*, D65, D95, E87, G54, G67, J25M, J25M{S}, J26, J61M, K38{S}, L27M, *M69M*, *P63*{S}, etc. (also see Rootstocks, page 470)

CULTIVARS {GR}

Black Beauty: Small, roundish fruit, 3/4 inch in diameter; skin thin, shiny black; flesh firm, juicy, sweet, quality fair to good. Good for canning and eating fresh. Ripens in early August. Bush upright, productive, hardy; height 3 to 4 feet. Originated in Charleswood, Manitoba, Canada by G.F. Chipman. Introduced in 1938. BROOKS 1972; D76, F91T{SC}

Brooks: Very large, roundish-oval fruit, often 1 inch in diameter; skin dark purplish-black, thick, tough; flesh greenish-yellow, firm, juicy, tender, mild for a sand cherry; cans well; ripens during early

August. Bush upright, spreading, vigorous; hardy; productive; makes an ideal low-growing ornamental. BROOKS 1972; F91T{SC}

Golden Boy: Golden-yellow fruits with a delicate, sweet flavor; dessert quality good, makes excellent pies and jams. Can also be canned or used to make a beautiful golden wine. Low growing bush; height 3 to 5 feet. Hardy to Zone 3. D76

Hansen's: Large, reddish-black to purple fruits; very good flavor. Can be used fresh, canned, or preserved. Compact shrub grows 4 to 5 feet tall; ornamental silvery-green leaves; white flowers in the spring. Two or more trees recommended for cross-pollination. Plant 2 to 4 feet apart. Hardy to Zone 3. A91, B15M, *D35M*, D76, E97, G23, G65M, *H8*, H65, I78, L70, N25M, N26

Honeywood: Large fruit, averaging 3/4 to 7/8 inch in diameter; skin dark-purple; quality good for processing. Bush spreading; leaf glossy, dark green, turning coppery bronze in fall; resistant to mildew; requires cross-pollination, with its own seedlings being satisfactory. Also considered to be an ornamental plant. BROOKS 1972; N24M

Sioux: A large sand cherry selected from many thousand seedlings. Not as large as some of the later cultivars but noteworthy for its mild flavor. Originated in Brookings, South Dakota by N.E. Hansen. Introduced in 1902. HANSEN; F91T{SC}

South Dakota Ruby: (Ruby) Medium-sized fruit; skin dark, ruby-red; flesh dark-red, tannic; very suitable for jelly, jam, and sauce. May also be eaten fresh. Bush spreading; height 3 to 5 feet; very productive; ornamental. Hardy to Zone 3. Originated in Brookings, South Dakota by S.A. McCrory, South Dakota Agricultural Experiment Station. Introduced in 1953. BROOKS 1972; D76

Prunus bokhariensis - *Bokhara plum* {S} Fruits are eaten dried, pickled, stewed, or made into preserves. The dried product, called *sour plums* or *aloo bokhara* is sometimes available in Indian and Middle Eastern stores. Cultivated in the Punjab and Kabul, Afghanistan. Himalayan region. JAFFREY, KUNKEL, MACMILLAN; A88T{PR}, **U8**, **Z25M**

CULTIVARS{SC}

Early Large Red #8: A large, red-fruited cultivar from India. **U8**

Prunus brigantina → *Armeniaca brigantina*

Prunus canescens - The fruits are edible. China, Himalayan region. KUNKEL; (for cultivars see Rootstocks, page 470)

Prunus cerasifera - *Myrobalan plum, Cherry plum* {S} The fruits are cherry-like but somewhat larger, thin-skinned, and with flesh that is soft, very juicy, sweet to subacid and pleasantly flavored. They may be eaten fresh or used for pies, tarts and jam. Southwest Asia, cultivated. HEDRICK 1919, SIMMONS 1972 [Cu]; A80M{PL}, D69{PL}, *F38*, K38, M83{PL}, *N71M*, N84, N93M, O53M, P49, *P63*, *R28*, R78, S95 (also see Rootstocks, page 470)

CULTIVARS {SC}

Belciana: Medium-sized, round fruit; skin papery, amber-yellow with a rose tint on the side exposed to the sun; flesh amber-yellow, melting, sweet; stone slightly clinging; ripens early. A wild plum resembling Myrobalan; selected by the Arabs and introduced into France from Algeria in 1878. HEDRICK 1911; **Y83**

De Caradeuc: Medium-sized, globular fruit; skin deep purplish-red with a slight bloom, thin; flesh yellow, soft, juicy, quality only fair; stone clinging; ripens early. Tree a rather large and erect grower; foliage very attractive. Originated near Aiken, South Carolina, between 1850 and 1854. WAUGH; **T49M**

Red: Very small, roundish fruit, about 1 inch in diameter; skin smooth, red; flesh firm, red; flavor good, distinctive; ripens the end of August. Suitable for either dessert or cooking. Tree moderately vigorous; round-headed with slender, upright branches; flowers very early; a poor bearer. SIMMONS 1978; **U8**

Yellow: Very small, round fruit; cherry-like but larger; skin yellow, smooth; flesh yellow, firm, flavor distinctive; quality good for dessert or cooking; ripens the end of August. Tree moderately vigorous, round-headed; productive. Flowers later and is a more regular bearer than Red. SIMMONS 1978; **U8**, **Y83**

Prunus cerasifera 'Atropurpurea' - *Red-leaf plum, Purple-leaf plum* {S} The fruits are eaten. Attractive ornamental trees with reddish-purple leaves. TANAKA; F85, *I23*{PL}, N93M

CULTIVARS {GR}

Allred: Fruit small, up to 1 1/4 inches in diameter; skin and flesh red, quality good, but very high in acidity; makes a delicious jelly. Tree with red leaves and bark; produces well; adapted over a wide area. A colorful ornamental. Originated in Amity, Arkansas by Ross Wolfe of Wolfe Nursery Inc., Stephenville, Texas. Introduced in 1941. BROOKS 1972; *A19*, C37, *C54*, D37{DW}, D76, J93, J93{SC}, L90, M83, M83{DW}, N33

Cocheco: Small to medium-sized, red-blushed fruit; flesh yellow, of high quality for a red leaf plum; resembles Methley. Good fresh or for canning. Tree very disease resistant and hardy; self-sterile, requires a pollinator for fruit production, any Japanese plum being satisfactory. Originated in New Hampshire by Professor E.M. Meader. D37{DW}, N24M

Elsie: Medium to large fruit; skin dark purplish-red; flesh deep dark red, quality excellent, one of the best red leaf plums; resembles Santa Rosa. Tree self-sterile, somewhat of a shy bearer, should be planted with Gerth as a pollinator. Originated in Duarte, California. D57{OR}

Gerth: Medium to large fruit, 1 1/2 inches in diameter; skin dark deep purple; quality very good; resembles Santa Rosa but somewhat smaller; ripens 7 to 14 days before Santa Rosa. Tree self-fertile, has a relatively low chilling requirement. Originated in Vista, California by Otto Gerth. D57{OR}

Hollywood: (P. c. 'Atropurpurea' x P. salicina) Small, red fruit with red flesh; dessert quality good, excellent for jelly and canning; ripens early, with Beauty; hangs well on the tree; resembles Satsuma. Tree very ornamental with early pink blossoms, and red leaves all season. BROOKS 1972; *C54*, D37, *H8*, I49M

Shalom: Small to medium, roundish, deep red fruits; flesh juicy, sweet, dessert quality excellent; resembles Santa Rosa. Ornamental, dwarfish tree with attractive reddish leaves. D57{OR}

Thundercloud: Dark coppery leaves. Flowers light-pink to white. Occasionally sets a good crop of red fruit. Tree grows 20 feet tall by 20 feet wide; somewhat rounded form. B9M, B53, E4, E87, *G30*, *G66*, H49, I9M, *I62*, I77M, *L49*, *M69M*, M76, M83

Prunus cerasoides - *Padam, Wild Himalayan cherry* {S} Fruits are acid and astringent and are only occasionally eaten raw, but are employed for making a well-flavored cherry brandy. The stem is the source of a gum used for adulterating *gum tragacanth*. Himalayan region. HEDRICK 1919, TANAKA, UPHOF, WATT; N84, *P63*, Q40, Q46

Prunus cerasus - *Sour cherry, Pie cherry* {S} The fruits are pleasantly acid and can be eaten out-of-hand or dried. They are widely used for making pies, preserves, cherry cider, puddings, jellies, glacé fruits, and are also canned or preserved in brandy. Also used in the preparation of liqueurs, including *kirschwasser*, *maraschino*, and *ratafia*. Seeds are the source of *cherry kernel oil*, which is used as a salad oil when refined. Leaves are used as a substitute for tea. Eurasia, cultivated. BIANCHINI, SCHNEIDER [Cul, Re], UPHOF;

G66, *G66*{PL}, K63G, O53M, Q40, Q46 (for cultivars see Cherry, page 291)

Prunus cornuta - *Himalayan bird cherry, Jámoi* {S} Fruits are eaten by the natives. Northern India. TANAKA; Q40, Q46

Prunus davidiana* → *Amygdalus davidiana

Prunus dawyckensis - *Dawyck cherry* {S} The sweet fruits are eaten. China. KRÜSSMANN; (for cultivars see Rootstocks, page 470)

Prunus domestica - *European plum* {S} Fruits are consumed fresh, preserved, canned, or made into jam, juice, plum butter, pies, cakes, alcoholic beverages, liqueurs, etc. *Prunella* is a liqueur derived from the fruits, while a distilled product is known as *zwetschenwasser*, *slobovitz* or *slivovica*. The flowers are eaten, used as a garnish for salads and ice cream, or brewed into tea. Eurasia, cultivated. MACNICOL, UPHOF; D81{PO}, D81M{PO}, *G66*, K47T, K63G, P49 (for cultivars see Plum, page 446 and Rootstocks, page 470)

Prunus dulcis* → *Amygdalus communis

Prunus effusa* → *Prunus x gondouinii

Prunus fruticosa - *Dwarf cherry, Mongolian cherry* {PL} The tart fruits are eaten raw or dried, and also make excellent jelly, jams, and pies. Trees have withstood temperatures of -52^0 C. Eurasia. T-ANAKA, ZEVEN; F67, G54, *G66*, *G66*{S}, *G89M*, H42, I60, L27M, M35M, N24M, N26

Prunus glandulosa - *Korean cherry* {PL} Fruits are eaten preserved or pickled. Eastern Asia. TANAKA; *C47*, F85{S}, G23, N84{S}

Prunus x gondouinii (P. avium x P. cerasus) - *Duke cherry, Royal cherry* Garden hybrid. Sweet cherry x sour cherry. The fruits are eaten raw, stewed, preserved, dried, etc. TANAKA; (for cultivars see Cherry, page 291)

Prunus grayana - *Gray's chokecherry* {PL} Salted flower buds and young fruits, having a pungent taste, are consumed in Japan. Eastern Asia. TANAKA, UPHOF; **T41M, U85, U87, V19**

Prunus hortulana - *Hortulan plum, Hog plum* {PL} The fruits are bright red or yellowish-red, juicy, of an agreeable flavor, and are eaten raw or processed into pies, jellies, jams, and preserves. North America, cultivated. FERNALD, MEDSGER, UPHOF, WAUGH; F91T{SC}, *G66* (for cultivars see Plum, page 446)

Prunus ilicifolia* → *Laurocerasus ilicifolia

Prunus incisa - *Fuji cherry* {S} Fruits are eaten. Japan, cultivated. TANAKA; K38, K47T, N84, *P63* (for cultivars see Rootstocks, page 470)

Prunus insititia - *Bullace plum, Damson plum* {S} Fruits are eaten raw or made into preserves and conserves. Eurasia, cultivated. JOHNS [Cul], TANAKA; A80M{PL}, *G66* (for cultivars see Plum, page 446 and Rootstocks, page 470)

Prunus jamasakura - *Yama-zakura* {S} Flowers are pickled in salt and consumed in tea or with rice gruel. Also used as a garnish for bakery goods. The fruit is edible. Eastern Asia. TANAKA; N84

Prunus japonica - *Korean cherry* {S} The red cherry-like fruits have a sweet, agreeable flavor. They are eaten out of hand and also make good pies. Eastern Asia. HEDRICK 1919, TANAKA; D95{PL}, F85, F91T{SC}, N84, P49, *P63*

CULTIVARS

White: A white fruited form. **Y27M**

Prunus lannesiana - *Oshima-zakura* {S} Flowers are preserved in salt and used in tea. Fruits are edible when ripe. Japan. TANAKA; F85

Prunus laurocerasus* → *Laurocerasus officinalis

Prunus lyonii* → *Laurocerasus lyonii

Prunus mahaleb - *Mahaleb cherry, St. Lucie cherry* {S} The leaves, or a decoction obtained therefrom, can be used for flavoring milk. Dried seed kernels, known as *mahlep*, are used in Middle Eastern and Mediterranean cooking to give an intriguing fruit flavor to breads, cookies, confectionery, and sweet pastries. Eurasia, cultivated. MALLOS [Re], TANAKA, VON WELANETZ; A80M{PL}, C9M, D62, E47, *F38*, J66M{PR}, K38, L50M{PR}, *N71M*, N93M, O53M, P49, *R28*, R78, S95, etc. (also see Rootstocks, page 470)

Prunus mandshurica* → *Armeniaca mandshurica

Prunus maritima - *Beach plum* {PL} The fruits are dull-purple, subacid to sweet, and are eaten raw, dried, preserved or used in jams, jellies, pies, sauces, soups, cakes, puddings, etc. They can also be mixed with cider vinegar, cloves, and sugar and made into "beach plum shrub". Eastern North America. ANGIER [Re], GIBBONS 1964 [Re], MEDSGER, MIREL [Cu, Re]; A91, B9M, *B15*, D95, G23, *H8*, H65, K38{S}, K47T{S}, L12, M92, N84{S}, *P63*{S}

CULTIVARS {SC}

Eastham: Large fruit of good flavor. Tree a heavy producer. Seedling discovered in Eastham, Massachusetts by J.M. Batchelor. Introduced in the 1940's. BROOKS 1972; **T41M**

Hancock: Blue-skinned fruit; flesh golden, sweet with little acidity, juicy, flavor excellent for eating fresh; pit small; ripens early. Originated in Fort Hancock, New Jersey by J.M. Batchelor. Introduced in the 1940's. BROOKS 1972; **T41M**

Raribank: Purplish-red fruit of good quality; freestone; ripens during early September at place of origin. Good for jelly or canning. Tree large, vigorous, very resistant to brown rot and Japanese beetle. Originated in New Brunswick, New Jersey by J.H. Clark. Introduced in 1949. BROOKS 1972; **T41M**

Squibnocket: A selection made in Massachusetts for high quality fruit. Also recommended as an ornamental and a soil binder. I60{PL}

Prunus maximowiczii - *Miyama-zakura* {S} Flowers are preserved in salt and stored for future use. The fruit is also edible. Central to Eastern Asia. TANAKA; **T41M, X33, Z25M**

Prunus melanocarpa* → *Prunus virginiana var. melanocarpa

Prunus mexicana - *Mexican plum, Big-tree plum* {PL} The fruit is edible, but of little commercial value. Southwestern North America. TANAKA; H4, *I17M*, I53, N33

Prunus mira* → *Amygdalus mira

Prunus mume* → *Armeniaca mume

Prunus munsoniana - *Wild goose plum* {S} Bright red fruits are eaten, having thin skin and light or dark yellow, juicy, aromatic flesh, often of good dessert quality. Also used in jellies, jams and preserves. North America, cultivated. UPHOF, WAUGH; **T41M** (for cultivars see Plum, page 446 and Rootstocks, page 470)

Prunus myrtifolia* → *Laurocerasus myrtifolia

Prunus nigra - *Canada plum, Canada black plum* {PL} The fruits are eaten raw or stewed, and are also used for making jelly, preserves, pies, sauces, fruit juices, marmalades and plum butter. They can also be dried and used like raisins, or puréed, poured out on wax paper, and dried as fruit leather. North America. MEDSGER, TANAKA, TURNER 1979 [Re], YANOVSKY; G69M, K81 (for cultivars see Plum, page 446)

Prunus padus - *European bird cherry, May day tree* {S} The fruits are occasionally eaten raw but are primarily used for making jam and in the preparation of alcoholic beverages. In Korea, the young leaves are eaten as a boiled vegetable and the flowers are chewed. The bark is used for tea. Eurasia, cultivated. HEDRICK 1919, TANAKA, UPHOF; A65{PL}, *C33*{PL}, G41{PL}, *G66*, *G66*{PL}, *G89M*{PL}, K38, M35M{PL}, M92{PL}, *N71M*, O53M, P49, Q12, R78, S95, etc.

Prunus pensylvanica - *Pin cherry, Bird cherry, Fire cherry* {S} The fruits are usually too sour for eating fresh, but are often made into jellies, syrup, sauces, wines and pies. A gum that exudes from the trunk can be used as a chewing-gum. Eastern North America. ANGIER [Re], FERNALD, GIBBONS 1962, MEDSGER, TURNER 1979 [Re]; F85, *J75M*{PL}, K38, K47T, K63G, *K89*{PL}, N84, *P63*

Prunus persica* → *Amygdalus persica

Prunus pissardii* → *Prunus cerasifera

Prunus pseudocerasus - *Chinese sour cherry, Bastard cherry* {S} Fruits are eaten fresh or preserved, and are also brewed into wine. The flowers are salted and used as a tea. Eastern Asia. TANAKA; U8 (for cultivars see Rootstocks, page 470)

Prunus puddum* → *Prunus cerasoides

Prunus pumila - *Sand cherry* {PL} The ripe fruits have a rich, pleasantly acid, sometimes slightly bitter but palatable flavor and are eaten fresh, dried or preserved. They can also be mixed with sour apple-juice to make a rich jelly. North America. FERNALD, GIBBONS 1979, MEDSGER, TURNER 1979; D95, I60

Prunus pumila var. susquehanae - *Appalachian cherry* {S} The small, purple-black fruits can be quite sweet and juicy and may be eaten fresh or used for pies, jams and fruit sauces. Eastern North America. CROWHURST 1972, GIBBONS 1979; F85

Prunus salicifolia - *Capulin cherry, Capulí* {PL} Ripe fruits are deep purplish-maroon, thin-skinned, and have greenish flesh that is juicy, subacid to sweet, and with a somewhat astringent aftertaste. They are eaten fresh, stewed or made into jams and preserves. In Mexico, they are used as filling for special *tamales*. Very low chilling requirement, adapted to warm winter areas where true cherries are unable to produce. Mexico to Peru. MORTON 1987a, NATIONAL RESEARCH COUNCIL 1989, POPENOE, W. 1924, STEBBINS; C56M, D57, I83M, N84{S}, P38{S}, *Q49M*

CULTIVARS {GR}

Ecuadorian: Very large, round fruit, up to 1 1/2 inches in diameter; light green, sweetish flesh, free of astringency when ripe. Drooping tree, outbears many other cultivars. Originated in Ambato, Ecuador. D57{OR}

Fausto: Fruit large, 3/4 to 1 inch in diameter; flesh green, flavor rich and sweet; ripens late, August to September in Vista, California. Tree upright but drooping, a reliable annual bearer. Has excellent commercial potential. Originated in Ambato, Ecuador by Fausto Perez. D57{OR}

Harriet: Large, flattened globe-shaped fruit, 3/4 to 1 inch in diameter; skin deep purple-black; flesh green, more or less free of astringency, flavor good; seed relatively small. Tree a genetic dwarf, somewhat of a shy bearer which appears to be related to rootstock selection. Seedling of Lomeli. D57{OR}, L6

Huachi Grande: Large to very large, roundish fruits, 1 inch or more in diameter; very mild flavor, lacks the astringency of other capulins; ripens early to midseason. Appears to require high temperatures to develop good flavor. Tree a very heavy producer, tends to over produce in heavy clusters. Originated in Ecuador. D57{OR}, L6

Lomeli: Large, roundish fruit, 1 to 1 1/8 inch in diameter; flesh fairly astringent, flavor good; seeds small. Tree a heavy producer, often yields more than 200 pounds of fruit; bears fruit in clusters. Performs very well in cool coastal locations. Originated in central Mexico. L6

Werner: Small fruit with very good flavor. Tree a light producer, appears to bear better on certain rootstocks; extremely vigorous, can grow 15 feet or more in one year. Originated from seed collected by Wilson Popenoe in Ecuador. Named after Andrew Werner of Santa Cruz, California. L6

Prunus salicina - *Japanese plum* {S} The sweet, juicy fruits are eaten fresh, dried, canned, stewed, made into jams, jellies, fruit leather, puddings, cakes and sauces, or brewed into wine. Eastern Asia, cultivated. CARCIONE, CREASY 1982 [Cu], TANAKA; D81{PO}, D81M{PO}, K38, K63G, N84, *P63* (for cultivars see Plum, page)

Prunus salicina 'Mandshurica' - *Manchurian plum, Ussurian plum* {PL} The fruits are sweet and juicy and can be eaten fresh. They also make excellent jams, preserves, and plum sauce. Also used as a rootstock for European and Japanese plums and their hybrids, being the most cold-hardy understock for this purpose. In breeding, it is a source of good fruit flavor and cold resistance. ZEVEN; A33, A91, D76, E32M, *G66*, H42, K63G{S}, L27M, M35M, N24M, S36M{S}

Prunus salicina x Amygdalus persica - *Plum peach, Peach plum* {PL} Artificial hybrid. Japanese plum x peach. The fruit is reddish-purple with sweet, juicy, golden-yellow flesh and an appealing plum-like flavor. It is eaten fresh or canned. UPHOF; D76, L99M

Prunus serotina - *Wild black cherry, Rum cherry* {PL} Fruits have a slightly bitter but rich, wine-like flavor and are eaten fresh, stewed or made into pies, jellies, sherbet, and *cherry bounce*. Also used for flavoring cider, brandy, rum and liqueurs. The bark is the source of an extract employed by the food industry for flavoring soft drinks, candy, syrups, and baked goods. North America. ANGIER [Re], FERNALD, GIBBONS 1962 [Re], LOGSDON 1981, MEDSGER, MORTON 1976, UPHOF; A80M, A91, *B52*, C11M, D45, D65, D95, *G9M*, H4, I4, K38{S}, K63G{S}, M16, M35M, O53M{S}, etc.

Prunus serotina var. salicifolia* → *Prunus salicifolia

Prunus serrula - *Tibetica cherry, Birch bark cherry* {PL} Fruits are eaten. China. TANAKA; E87, K38{S}, N0, *P63*{S} (for cultivars see Rootstocks, page 470)

Prunus simonii - *Apricot plum, Simon plum* {SC} The edible fruits are variable in quality, some having an agreeable flavor while others are bitter with an almond-like astringency. Widely used in hybridizing, especially in crosses with P. salicina. China, cultivated. UPHOF, WAUGH, ZEVEN; F91T

Prunus sphaerocarpa* → *Laurocerasus myrtifolia

Prunus spinosa - *Sloe, Blackthorn* {S} Ripe fruits are sometimes eaten raw, especially after having been mellowed by frost. They are also made into jellies, syrup, conserves, and *kissel* or used as a flavoring for *sloe gin* and other liqueurs. In France, the unripe fruit is pickled like olives. Leaves are used as an adulterant of tea. The dried fruits can be added to herbal teas. The flowers are edible and may be crystallized or sugared. Eurasia. HEDRICK 1919, LAUNERT, MABEY [Re], MICHAEL [Re], MORTON 1976, TANAKA; F85, *G66*, K67{PL}, M35M{PL}, *N71M*, N84, N93M, O53M, P49, *P63*, *R28*, R78, S7M, S95

CULTIVARS {SC}

Purpurea: A unique form with attractive purple leaves. **U8**

Prunus subcordata - *Sierra plum, Pacific plum, Klamath plum* {PL} The fruits are pleasantly acid and are eaten fresh, dried, or made into delicious preserves, sauces and jellies. The best types have a slight astringency which imparts a distinctive flavor to culinary products made from the fruit. Considered one of the best native fruits of the Pacific Coast region. Western North America, cultivated. HEDRICK 1919, KIRK, MEDSGER, ROBERTS [Cu, Pro], UPHOF, WICKSON; B94{S}, D95, L99M

CULTIVARS {SC}

Kelley's Sierra #2: An improved type apparently selected in northern California for its superior fruit qualities. **U8**

Watkins Sierra #1: One of three Watkins Sierra selections maintained by the USDA National Clonal Germplasm Repository. Selected for improved fruit characteristics. **U8**

Prunus subhirtella - *Rosebud cherry* {S} Flowers are preserved in salt and added to tea. The fruit is eaten. Japan. TANAKA; K38, K63G, N84, P49, *P63*

Prunus susquehanae* → *Prunus pumila var. susquehanae

Prunus tenella* → *Amygdalus besseriana

Prunus tomentosa - *Nanking cherry, Manchu cherry* {PL} Ripe fruits are juicy, subacid to sweet, and are eaten raw or preserved. Unripe fruits are pickled or boiled in honey and served as a delicacy. The buds are cooked and eaten. Eastern Asia, cultivated. HEDRICK 1919, TANAKA, UPHOF; A16, C9M{S}, D65, D95, G16, G67, H42, *H90*, I4, I47{S}, I83M, K38{S}, K64, L79, M16, N26, etc.

CULTIVARS {GR}

Drilea: Round fruit, up to 5/8 inch in diameter; skin bright scarlet, thin, tender; flesh red, firm to melting, tender, sweet, pleasant, quality very good; pit small; season last half of July. Good for dessert, canning, jelly and jam. Bush upright, large, vigorous, dense, spreading; a very heavy annual bearer; tolerant to dry conditions. ANDERSEN, BROOKS 1972; F91T{SC}

Orient: Fruit about 1/2 inch in diameter, flat, depressed; skin bright medium dark-red, attractive, moderately tough; flesh light red, meaty, juicy, pleasantly subacid; stone small, free; quality very good for dessert and jelly; ripens in mid-July. Tree bushy, vigorous; productive, self-fertile, bears second year after planting; ornamental. ANDERSEN, BROOKS 1972; F91T{SC}

Pink Cloud: Hardy, bushy shrub covered with unusual pale pink blossoms in early spring. Bears small, dark red berries, sweeter than the common form. Introduced by Woodland Nurseries. N36

Plumking: An improved type with superior fruit selected by Windmill Point Farm and Nursery. N24M

Red Marble: Improved type with superior fruit. Selected by Windmill Point Farm and Nursery. N24M

Scarlet Gem: Large, attractive, scarlet red fruits of very good quality. Suitable for fresh eating, canning or baking. Bush vigorous, to 8 feet tall; very hardy and productive; begins to bear the next year after planting. N24M

White Ruby: Improved type with superior fruit. Selected by Windmill Point Farm and Nursery. N24M

Prunus umbellata - *Black sloe, Flatwoods plum, Southern sloe* {PL} The fruit is pleasantly acid and is frequently employed for making preserves, jams, and jellies. Southeastern North America. HEDRICK 1919, UPHOF; N37M

Prunus ussuriensis* → *Prunus salicina

Prunus virginiana - *Common chokecherry* {S} The astringent fruits are eaten raw, dried, or processed into jams, jellies, juice, syrup, wine, and pies. Green twigs are stripped of their bark and inserted into roasting meat for flavoring. Nutritious kernels were added to *pemmican*. The bark and twigs are used as a substitute for tea. North America. ANGIER [Re], FERNALD, HEDRICK 1919, KINDSCHER, MEDSGER, TURNER 1979 [Re], YANOVSKY; A16{PL}, A80M{PL}, C9M, *C33*{PL}, I15, I47, J25M, J25M{PL}, J26{PL}, *J75M*{PL}, K47T, K63G, *K89*{PL}, N93M, P49, etc.

CULTIVARS {GR}

Boughen Sweet: Selected for its large, mild fruit, so much milder in flavor than normal that it might be called a sweet or "chokeless" chokecherry. Excellent for jams, jellies and wines. Originated in Valley River, Manitoba by W.J. Boughen, prior to 1923. HANSEN; B47

Boughen's Golden: Attractive ornamental with distinctive yellow fruit. Quite hardy. Flavor of the fruit is similar to the black native chokecherry, but lacks the normal astringency. Originated in Valley River, Manitoba by W.J. Boughen. B47

Centrehill: An improved selection that has tastier and much larger fruit than the wild form. N24M

Chokeless: Selected for superior fruits which are non-astringent to sweet. M35M

Honeywood: Improved selection that has tastier and much larger fruit than wild types. N24M

Maskinonge: Medium-sized, red fruit; sweet and delicious, completely lacking the normal astringency, quality remarkably good. Bush relatively hardy, does not sucker. Possibly of hybrid origin. Originated in the Maskinonge Valley of Quebec. N24M

Mission Red: Identical to the common chokecherry in all traits except for the color of the fruit which is quite unusual and has good ornamental value. It is excellent for winemaking, producing a rich, red-colored wine. F67

Yellow: Identical to the common chokecherry in all traits except for the color of the fruit which is quite unusual and has good ornamental value. It is excellent for winemaking, producing a beautiful, amber-colored wine. F67

Prunus virginiana var. demissa - *Western chokecherry* {S} Fruits are eaten fresh, dried, or made into syrup, jams, jellies, soups, and wine. Indians and early settlers ground the fruits (stones and all) and dried them into cakes which were later soaked in water, mixed with flour and sugar, and used as a sauce. Western North America. CLARKE [Re], KIRK, YANOVSKY; B94, D95{PL}, G60{PL}, *P63*

Prunus virginiana var. melanocarpa - *Rocky Mountain cherry* {S} The fruits are purplish-black when ripe, and are generally larger and less astringent than those of the common or western chokecherries. They can be eaten raw, dried, or processed into jams, jellies, and preserves. Western North America. GIBBONS 1962, MEDSGER, UPHOF, YANOVSKY; B94, *G89M*{PL}, K38, *K89*, N84, *P63*

CULTIVARS {GR}

Schubert: (Red Canadian Cherry, Canada Red Chokecherry) Large, purplish-black fruit; produced in abundance; make excellent jams, jellies or wines. Leaves turn a deep reddish-purple color in late spring and early summer. Mature summer foliage is reddish-purple, fringed with lime-green. Selected from the wild, and introduced by Oscar Will of North Dakota. A65, B15M, *C33*, D65, D95, F67, G41, G54, *G66*, H42, I15{S}, K38{S}, K64, *K89*, L79, N26, etc.

Prunus watsonii* → *Prunus angustifolia var. watsonii

Prunus x sp. (P. besseyi x P. spp.) - *Prairie cherry-plum* Artificial hybrids. Sand cherry x various plums. Fruits are eaten fresh or canned, and are also good for sauces, pies, and preserves. Many people use the juice for wine. Grown primarily in the dry prairie states and provinces of the United States and Canada. CREASY 1982, LOGSDON 1981; (for cultivars see Cherry Plum, page 296)

Prunus x sp. (P. cerasifera x P. salicina) - *Cherry-plum* {GR} Artificial hybrid. Myrobalan plum x Japanese plum. The hybrids are characterized by low-chilling requirements and a later blooming period than Japanese plums. STEBBINS, ZEVEN.

CULTIVARS

Delight: Small, round fruit. Blackish skin with thick, blue-gray bloom. Amber, clingstone flesh. Flavor intermediate between a plum and a cherry - mild, tangy, tart at skin. Midseason harvest. Fruit holds well on tree without loss of quality. Pollinate with Sprite. Low chilling requirement, 300 to 400 hours. Originated by Floyd Zaiger, Modesto, California. STEBBINS; A88M, F19M, I83M, L33, *N20*

Sprite: Small, round fruit. Blackish skin with thick, blue-gray bloom. Juicy, yellow flesh with a sweet, rich flavor. Midseason harvest. Fruit holds well on tree without loss of quality. Semi-dwarf tree; upright; vigorous. Pollinate with Delight. Low chilling requirement, yet cold-hardy. Originated by Floyd Zaiger, Modesto, California. STEBBINS; A88M, F19M, I49M, I83M, L33, *N20*

Prunus x sp. (P. jacquemontii x P. japonica) - *Fall-fruiting bush cherry* {GR} Artificial hybrid. Fruits are eaten fresh, cooked or dried. The hybrids are small bushes, highly disease resistant, and not susceptible to insect problems. The fruits ripen late and are therefore not bothered by birds. They are easily harvested.

CULTIVARS

Jan: Large fruit, similar to a Montmorency sour cherry. Ripe fruits hang on the tree well and if left to become overripe will begin to dry naturally like raisins, enhancing their fresh-eating quality. Bush-like growth habit, to 3 feet high; hardy; productive. Flowers profusely in the spring; ornamental. Pollinate with Joy. Developed by Professor E.M. Meader of New Hampshire. D37

Joy: Large fruit, similar to Jan; ripens in late summer and fall. Suitable for fresh use and pies. Vigorous, ornamental bush, 3 to 4 feet tall; cross-pollinates with Jan; hardy to -30^{0} F. Highly resistant to powdery mildew, Japanese beetles and cherry worms. Developed over a period of 25 years by Professor E.M. Meader. D37

Prunus sp. - *Texas cherry* {PL} Semi-sweet fruit; 3/8 to 1/2 inch in diameter; native to the Abeline, Texas area. K67

Pseudocydonia sinensis - *Chinese quince, Oriental quince* {PL} The fruit is eaten as a sweetmeat, candied, preserved in syrup, or made into a liqueur. Its jùice is mixed with ginger and used as a beverage. China, cultivated. SIMMONS 1972, TANAKA; B96, D30, D95, E6, F85{S}, H4, N37M, N84{S}, *P39*{S}

CULTIVARS {GR}

Chino: Large, fragrant, greenish-white fruit with few seeds. Ripens in October. Adapted to all areas of the South, except Florida. Must be planted with another cultivar for fruit to set. M31M

Dragon Eye: Yellow, medium-sized, hard fruit suitable for pickling. Ripens in October. Must be planted with another cultivar for fruit to set. M31M

Pyracantha coccinea - *Firethorn* {S} Berries are used for making jellies, sauces, and marmalades. Eurasia, cultivated. BRYAN [Cul, Re], CLARKE [Re], ZEVEN; C9M, D62, F80, K38, K63G, N84, N93M, O53M, O93, P5, P49, *P63*, *R28*, R78

Pyracantha crenulata - *Cha-kou-tzu* {S} Leaves are manufactured into a tea-like beverage. Eurasia. TANAKA; N84, O93, *P63*, *Q32*, Q40

X Pyronia veitchii (Cydonia oblonga x Pyrus communis) - {S} Garden hybrid. Quince x pear. The fruit is edible. KRÜSSMANN, TANAKA; **T41M, U30M**

Pyrus angustifolia* → *Malus angustifolia

Pyrus arbutifolia* → *Aronia arbutifolia

Pyrus betulifolia - *Birch-leaved pear, Yeh-li, Manshû-mame-nashi* {S} The flowers, leaves, and fruits are all edible. Also used as a rootstock. China. HEDRICK 1919, ZEVEN; *G66*, *G66*{PL}, *H45M*{PL}, I49M{PL}, K38, K63G, L99M{PL}, *N19*{PL}, *N71M*, N84, O93, P49, S95

Pyrus calleryana - *Callery pear, Mame-nashi* {S} Fruits are eaten after having been exposed to frost. Also widely used as a rootstock. China. ALTSCHUL, TANAKA, ZEVEN; *B52*, C9M, *E66*{PL}, *F51*{PL}, *G66*, *G66*{PL}, H4, H4{PL}, *H45M*{PL}, K38, K47T, *M69M*{PL}, *N19*{PL}, *N71M*, O93, etc.

Pyrus communis - *Pear* {S} Fruits are eaten fresh, dried, preserved in brandy, baked, served with cheese, spiced, made into sweet pickles, marmalades and pies, canned, etc. Some types are used for making pear cider or *perry*. The core is processed into vinegar. Cultivated. CARCIONE, JOHNS [Cul], TANAKA, UPHOF; C9M, D69{PL}, D81{PO}, D81M{PO}, *F38*, *H45M*{PL}, H49, I49M{PL}, K63G, *N71M*, N93M, O93, P49, R78, S95, etc. (for cultivars see Pear, page 426 and Rootstocks, page 470)

Pyrus coronaria* → *Malus coronaria

Pyrus decora* → *Sorbus decora

Pyrus fusca* → *Malus fusca

Pyrus ioensis* → *Malus ioensis

Pyrus japonica* → *Chaenomeles japonica

Pyrus x lecontei (P. communis x P. pyrifolia) - *Southern-cross pear* Artificial hybrid. Common pear x Asian pear. The fruit is occasionally eaten fresh, but is primarily cooked. Hybrids generally have greater resistance to fireblight than either parent, but the quality of the fruit is poorer. REHDER; (for cultivars see Pear, page 426)

Pyrus nivalis - *Snow pear* {PL} The fruit is brewed into cider or *perry*. Eurasia. TANAKA; P86

Pyrus pashia - *Indian wild pear, Himalayan pear* {S} Fruits are eaten when in an overripe state, much like the medlar (Mespilus germanica). Temperate Southern Asia. ALTSCHUL, HEDRICK 1919, TANAKA, WATT; F80, F85, *G66*, N84, O46, O53M, Q40, Q46

Pyrus pyrifolia - *Asian pear, Nashi, Apple pear, Salad pear* {S} The fruits are firm, crisp and juicy when ripe and are eaten out-of-hand, in fruit and vegetable salads, poached, baked, or sautéed. In Asia, they are canned, or processed into fruit nectar and preserves. *Southeastern Asia. GRIGGS, SCHNEIDER [Re], TANAKA; G66, K38, N84, O93, P39, P49* *(for cultivars see Asian Pear, page 252)*

Pyrus ussuriensis - *Chinese pear, Chinese white pear, Harbin pear* {PL} Fruits are eaten fresh. Also used as a rootstock. Eastern Asia. TANAKA; A80M, C58, G1T, *G66*, G67, *G89M*, *H45M*, H85, K38{S}, K47T{S}, M35M, *N19*, N84{S}, O93{S}, P49{S}, etc. (for cultivars see Pear, page 426 and Asian Pear, page 252)

Rosa acicularis - *Prickly rose* {S} The vitamin-rich fruits are eaten raw in salads, sandwich fillings and desserts, made into purées and syrups, or dried and used in soups and teas. Seeds contain high concentrations of vitamin E, and can be ground and used in baking or cooking as a vitamin supplement. Subarctic regions. HELLER, TURNER 1979 [Pre, Re]; A76, *J75M*{PL}

Rosa arkansana - *Low prairie rose* {S} Fruits are rich in vitamin C and are eaten raw, stewed, dried, or used for jellies and syrups. The young shoots can be peeled and eaten. Flowers, roots, fruits, stems, bark and petals are all used for tea. North America. KINDSCHER, TURNER 1979 [Pre, Re]; E7M, F80, I31, J41M, J41M{PL}, *J75M*{PL}

Rosa blanda - *Labrador rose, Meadow rose* {S} Fruits are eaten raw, cooked, or dried and used for tea. The flowers can be processed into *rose water*, cakes, candies, desserts and *rose-petal nectar*, vinegar and honey. Eastern North America. TURNER 1979 [Pre, Re]; F85, J12{PL}, P49

Rosa canina - *Dog rose, Brier rose* {S} The fruits, or *rose hips*, are made into jams, syrup, soups, wine, liqueurs and jellies. Leaves are used as a substitute for tea. The flowers are eaten in salads, and are also candied, preserved, crystallized, added to vinegar, honey, brandy, etc. Eurasia. HEDRICK 1919, LAUNERT, MABEY; D62, F40{PL}, F80, *G66*, *G66*{PL}, I47, J82, K38, *N71M*, N93M, O48, O53M, O93, R78, S55, etc.

Rosa carolina - *Pasture rose* {PL} The fruits are processed into syrup and jam. Flower petals can be eaten in tossed green salads, or made into jelly and wine. Eastern North America. CROWHURST 1972 [Re]; A51M, D95, F40, F71, *G66*{S}, H6, H61M{S}, I60, J12, J39M, J43{S}, K63G{S}, *N71M*{S}, N84{S}, O93{S}, P49{S}, etc.

Rosa centifolia - *Cabbage rose* {PL} Flowers are used for flavoring and scenting tea, wine, vinegar, and honey. The buds can be pickled in white vinegar and sugar, or ground up with sugar to make a conserve. Petals are preserved in syrup, or placed under the crust of cherry pies before baking. China, cultivated. HEDRICK 1919, MORTON 1976, TANAKA; F40, F54, H6, J12

Rosa chinensis - *China rose* {S} Young shoot tips, flower-buds, and opened flowers are parboiled and eaten as potherbs, stir-fried, added to soups, or preserved. China. TANAKA; F54{PL}, *G66*, N84, O93

CULTIVARS {GR}

Cécile Brunner: (Sweetheart Rose) Exquisite, warm pink buds open to small pale-pink double blooms. Delicate fragrance that carries on the air. Vigorous, bushy growth, to 4 feet in mild areas. Rated one of the best-tasting rose cultivars by Mudd's restaurant of San Ramon, California who use the flowers for flavoring honey, confections and sorbets. CREASY 1990; F40, J12, N78

Rosa x damascena - *Damask rose* {PL} Petals are the source of *attar of roses*, *rose absolute*, and *rose water*, used as a flavoring for beverages, candy, ice cream, bakery goods, etc. The young shoots, while still red-colored, are eaten raw or steamed, as a side-dish with rice. Leaves are used as a seasoning. MORTON 1976, OCHSE, TANAKA, UPHOF; F40, F54, J12, N84{S}, P49{S}

Rosa eglanteria* → *Rosa rubiginosa

Rosa gallica - *French rose, Apothecary rose, Rose de Provence* {PL} Flower petals are crystallized or preserved in syrup, and are also dried and used to impart flavor and fragrance to teas, beverages, cakes, honey and liqueurs. Europe, cultivated. FOX, H., MORTON 1976, TANAKA; E84, F40, F54, H6, J12

Rosa gigantea - *Manipur wild tea-rose, Giant rose of the Himalayas* {GR} The large yellow fruit, as large as a small apple, is eaten and sometimes sold in the markets of India. Himalayan region. TANAKA.

CULTIVARS

Belle Portugaise: (Belle of Portugal) Hybrid. Very long, pointed buds open to flesh-pink blossoms, 4 or 5 inches in diameter with long petals. Nicely fragrant, with long cutting stems. Rated one of the best-tasting rose cultivars by Mudd's restaurant of San Ramon, California who use the flowers for flavoring honey, confections and sorbets. Originated by Monsieur Cayeux in the Botanic Garden of Lisbon. CREASY 1990, FAIRCHILD 1930; K4, N78

Rosa macrophylla - *Bhâunra kujoi* {S} The fruit is eaten, and is said to become very sweet when black and overripe. Himalayan region. TANAKA, WATT; D95{PL}, F80, J12{PL}, N78{PL}, N84, O46, O53M, Q40, Q46

Rosa moschata - *Musk rose* {S} Young shoots are eaten, either raw or cooked, as a side-dish with rice. Flowers are consumed fresh or cooked. Cultivated. OCHSE; F40{PL}, F85, J12{PL}, N84, O53M, Q40, Q46

CULTIVARS {GR}

Belinda: Lightly fragrant, bright pink, semi-double flowers; 1 inch in diameter. Has little or no fragrance in filtered light, a light, sweet odor when grown in full sun. Rated one of the best-tasting rose cultivars by Mudd's restaurant of San Ramon, California who use the flowers for flavoring honey, confections and sorbets. CREASY 1990; K4

Rosa moyesii - *Moyes rose* {S} The fruits are eaten fresh, preserved, purèed, made into jams, syrups, soups, etc. Dried fruits can be ground to a powder and added to drinks, waffles, and pancakes. Fruits are very rich in vitamin C, having 1058-1130 milligrams per 100 grams and may be used as a food supplement. Western China. KUNKEL, NOBBS; E84{PL}, F71{PL}, *G66*, H6{PL}, K4{PL}, K47T, K63G, L91M, *N71M*, N78{PL}, N84, O93, P49, R78

Rosa multiflora - *Multiflora rose* {S} Young leaves and budlings are parboiled and eaten. The fruits are eaten raw, or processed into syrup, jam, jelly, and wine. Eastern Asia, naturalized in North America. CROWHURST 1972 [Re], TANAKA; B61M, C9M, *C33*{PL}, D62, *G66*, *G66*{PL}, J32{PL}, K38, K47T, *M69M*{PL}, *N71M*, O53M, O93, *P39*, R78, etc.

Rosa nutkana - *Nutka rose* {PL} The fruit is juicy, pleasantly acid and is a good source of vitamin C. It is dried, powdered and added to tea. The juicy, young shoots can be peeled and eaten in the spring, when still tender. Northwestern North America. HEDRICK 1919, NORTON, TURNER 1979; A2{S}, A76{S}, *C33*, F71, F85{S}, *G66*, I15{S}, I47{S}, I60, J12, J26, *J75M*, K47M{S}, K47T{S}, N78, N84{S}, etc.

Rosa odorata* → *Rosa gigantea

Rosa pimpinellifolia - *Burnet rose, Scotch rose* {S} The small, purple-black fruits are eaten fresh, being unusually sweet and pleasant-tasting. Eurasia, cultivated. GESSERT, HEDRICK 1919; F80, *G66*, K47T, K63G, N78{PL}, N84, O48, O53M, O93, P49, *R28*, R78, S7M

Rosa pisocarpa - *Mortar rose* {PL} Fruits are used for tea, and are also made into jams and jellies. North America. ALDERMAN 1975, KUNKEL; D95, F40

Rosa pomifera* → *Rosa villosa

Rosa rubiginosa - *Eglantine, Sweet briar* {PL} The hips are used for making jelly. In the Middle East, a mixture of the flower petals and honey, called *gulangabin*, is used in confectionery. Sprigs are added to mead as a flavoring. Eurasia, naturalized in North America. JOHNSTON, J., MEDSGER, UPHOF; A80M, B9M, D62{S}, E7M{S}, E84, F45, F54, F80{S}, *G66*, H6, K4, K38{S}, K47T{S}, *N71M*{S}, O53M{S}, S55{S}, etc.

Rosa rugosa - *Rugose rose* {PL} Fruits are eaten fresh, stewed, purèed, or made into jelly, jam, soup, and wine. The flowers are nibbled, prepared as a salad, candied or used for jam, tea and syrup.

Unripe fruits can be peeled, cooked and eaten. The young shoots are boiled or steamed and served as a potherb. Eastern Asia, cultivated. FERNALD, GIBBONS 1966b [Re], HARRINGTON, H.; C9M{S}, C13M{S}, *C47*, D37, F40, F45, *F51*, F54, G23, G67, H6, I60, J16, K4, K38{S}, O53M{S}, etc.

Rosa spinosissima → ***Rosa pimpinellifolia***

Rosa villosa - *Apple rose* {PL} The leaves are used as a substitute for tea, called *Deutscher tee*. Fruits are large, up to an inch in diameter, have a pleasant, acid pulp and are eaten fresh or processed into preserves, wines, puddings, sauces, sweetmeats, and beverages. Eurasia. HEDRICK 1919, JOHNS [Cul, Re], SIMMONS 1972 [Cu], UPHOF; D37, D69, E61, E84, F45, F71, *G66*, *G89M*, L70, N84{S}, S7M{S}

CULTIVARS {GR}

Wolly Dod's: (Double Apple Rose, Duplex) Fruit crimson-colored, ranging in size from 3/4 inch to 1 1/4 inches in diameter, sometimes larger; flavor good. Can be used fresh, dried or candied. Semi-double, clear rosy-purple flowers; heavily-scented, sweetly-fragrant. L7M, N78

Rosa virginiana - *Virginia rose* {S} The buds are eaten by the Chippewa Indians. Eastern North America. YANOVSKY; B9M{PL}, D95{PL}, F40{PL}, F45{PL}, *G66*, *G66*{PL}, H6{PL}, K47T, K63G, *N71M*, N78{PL}, N84, O53M, P49, R78, etc.

Rosa woodsii - *Wood's rose* {S} Fruits are eaten raw, puréed, made into syrup and jelly, or dried for use in soups and teas. North America. TURNER 1979 [Re]; *C33*{PL}, D95{PL}, E15, F71{PL}, *G66*{PL}, I15, I47, J25M, J25M{PL}, J26{PL}, *J75M*{PL}, K38, K47T, K63G, L75, etc.

Rubus albescens → ***Rubus niveus***

Rubus allegheniensis - *Allegheny blackberry* {S} Berries have a pleasant, somewhat spicy flavor and are eaten fresh, or made into jams, preserves and compote. The young shoots can be used in salads. Eastern North America. BRACKETT, CROWHURST 1972, MEDSGER, UPHOF; N84

Rubus arcticus - *Arctic bramble, Arctic raspberry, Alaska berry, Plumboy, Nagoonberry* {PL} The fruit is reddish to dark-purple, very sweet, juicy, highly flavored, and has a pineapple-like aroma. It is delicious when eaten out-of-hand, and can also be employed for making cakes, jams, and sherbet. Leaves are used as a tea in some parts of Norway. Circumpolar. HEDRICK 1919, HELLER, TURNER 1979 [Re], UPHOF; H42, K47T{S}, S30, S69{S} (for cultivars see Raspberry, page 465)

Rubus argutus - *Tall blackberry, Highbush blackberry* {S} The fruits vary in size and quality, but generally have rather large and juicy drupelets. They are eaten fresh or cooked. North America. CROWHURST 1972, MEDSGER; N84

Rubus caesius - *European dewberry* {S} Fruits are consumed raw, used for making jellies and preserves, or brewed into wine. Leaves are used as a substitute for tea. Eurasia, cultivated. HEDRICK 1919, MABEY, TANAKA, UPHOF; N84

Rubus calycinoides - *Hime-fuyu-ichigo* {PL} The fruit is edible. Taiwan. TANAKA; B30, D95, E48, F85{S}, J37M, K22, K85

CULTIVARS {GR}

Emerald Carpet: Orange berries resembling small raspberries that ripen in July. Ornamental, evergreen groundcover grows only a few inches tall in sun or partial shade, and somewhat taller in full shade. Leaves turn an attractive coppery color in the autumn. Evergreen in British Columbia, in colder climates it may lose its leaves. Thornless. Developed at the University of British Columbia. E87, J61M, *M65M*

Rubus canadensis - *American dewberry, Canadian blackberry* {S} Fruits are sweet, juicy, richly-flavored and may be eaten raw, served with cream or made into pies, jams, wine and preserves. North America. CROWHURST 1972, HEDRICK 1919, HENDRICKSON; **U7M**

Rubus chamaemorus - *Cloudberry, Baked-apple berry* {PL} The berries are consumed raw, stewed, preserved, served with cream and sugar or processed into tarts, confections, jellies, vinegar, wine and liqueurs. In Lapland, the berries are preserved by burying them in the snow. Fresh-frozen berries are sometimes available in New York and other large cities. Northern temperate region. FERNALD, HEDRICK 1919, HELLER, HENDRICKSON, MEDSGER, SIMMONS 1972 [Cu], TURNER 1979 [Re]; K79

Rubus crataegifolius - *Kuma-ichigo* {S} Fruits are large, transparent, scarlet, and have a sweet agreeable flavor. They are eaten fresh or brewed into wine. China. HEDRICK 1919, TANAKA, UPHOF; **U7M**, **Z25M**

CULTIVARS {SC}

Jinju Jengal: A cultivar selected in Korea after a study of wild material collected from farms and hilly areas. Notable for its high yield and relatively large (2 grams) firm fruit. JENNINGS; **U7M**

Rubus deliciosus - *Rocky Mountain flowering raspberry, Boulder raspberry* {PL} The fruit is eaten, but in spite of its specific epithet, is not highly valued. Western North America. HARRINGTON, H.; D95, *G89M*, P86

Rubus ellipticus - *Yellow Himalayan raspberry, Golden evergreen raspberry* {S} The fruit has a good raspberry-like flavor, and is eaten fresh or used for making preserves. India, Himalayan region. SIMMONS 1972, UPHOF, WATT; F80, N84, O53M, Q40

Rubus flagellaris - *Northern dewberry, Field dewberry* {S} Fruits are eaten raw, and are also used in pies, jams, jellies, sauces, fruit juices and wines. Dried leaves make a fine tea. The young shoots are peeled and eaten raw. Eastern North America, cultivated. CROWHURST 1972, HENDRICKSON, KINDSCHER, MEDSGER, SIMMONS 1972, UPHOF; **U7M** (for cultivars see Blackberry, page 267)

Rubus fraxinifolius - *Palanau* {S} The fruits are large, red, juicy, sweetish and can be consumed fresh or mixed with ice or milk. New Guinea to the Philippines. RIFAI, TANAKA; F85

Rubus fruticosus - *European blackberry, Bramble* {S} Fruits are consumed fresh, brewed into wine, made into jam, fruit juice, pies, vinegar, syrup, blackberry liqueur, junket, used for coloring wine, etc. Young leaves are used as a substitute for tea. Eurasia, cultivated. HEDRICK 1919, MABEY, MICHAEL [Re], UPHOF; *N71M*, N84, P49, R78

Rubus glaucus - *Andes black raspberry, Mora de castilla* {S} The fruit is light-red to dark-purple, and when fully ripe has a rich, aromatic, pleasantly subacid raspberry-like flavor. It is excellent when eaten with sugar and cream, and is also used to prepare a sweet conserve or syrup, called *jarope de mora*, from which a *refresco* is made. Central America to Ecuador. KENNARD, NATIONAL RESEARCH COUNCIL 1989, POPENOE, W. 1924, WILLIAMS, L.; **U7M**

Rubus hillii → ***Rubus moluccanus***

Rubus hirsutus - *Kusa-ichigo* {S} Fruits are eaten fresh, or made into jam, jelly, fruit juice and wine. Eastern Asia. TANAKA; N84

Rubus ichangensis - {PL} Small, red fruit of good flavor. Eaten in some parts of China. Eastern Asia. TANAKA, UPHOF, WILSON, E.; O35G

Rubus idaeus - *European red raspberry* {S} The fruit is eaten raw, dried, or preserved, and is also processed into jam, pastries, compote, syrup, raspberry liqueur, vinegar, wine, brandy, etc. Dried leaves are used as a substitute for tea. Northern temperate region. JOHNS [Cul], MABEY, MICHAEL [Re], TANAKA, UPHOF; I47, *J75M*{PL}, N84 (for cultivars see Raspberry, page 465)

Rubus illecebrosus - *Strawberry-raspberry, Baloon berry* {PL} The bright-red berries are sour, bitter and unpalatable if eaten out-of-hand. When cooked, they have a pleasant flavor, reminiscent of a mixture of strawberries and raspberries, and can be used for syrup, pies or jam. Eastern Asia. HENDRICKSON, SIMMONS 1972 [Cu]; S30

Rubus laciniatus - *Oregon evergreen blackberry, Cut-leaved blackberry* {S} Fruits are large, sweet, juicy, jet-black when ripe, and are eaten out-of-hand or used for jellies, jams and pies. Naturalized in Western North America. HEDRICK 1919, HENDRICKSON, SIMMONS 1972; I47, K47T, N84

Rubus lasiocarpus* → *Rubus niveus

Rubus leucodermis - *White-bark raspberry, Western raspberry* {S} The pleasant-flavored fruit is eaten fresh, dried or made into jams and sauces. A refreshing tea can be made from the leaves, which are high in vitamin C. Young, tender shoots are eaten. Western North America. CLARKE [Re], HEDRICK 1919, MEDSGER, YANOVSKY; A2, I47, J26{PL}, K47T, N84

Rubus microphyllus - *Mayberry* {S} Leaves are used as a substitute for tea. The large, yellow fruit is eaten. Eastern Asia. TANAKA, UPHOF; **U7M, V19**

Rubus moluccanus - *Ceylon blackberry* {S} The fruit is eaten fresh or made into jams. Southeast Asia to Australia. BROWN, W., BURKILL, TANAKA, WATT; P38

CULTIVARS {GR}

<u>Keri:</u> (Keriberry) Large black fruit; flavor mild, blackberry-like but lacks the distinctive flavor of the wild blackberry. Plant evergreen; strongly armed, thick-stemmed; very vigorous, plant 5 feet apart with 12 to 15 feet between rows. Leaves bright green, rough, ivy-shaped. Fruiting stems are grey-green, darkening with age to almost black. K67

Rubus morifolius* → *Rubus crataegifolius

Rubus x neglectus (R. occidentalis x R. strigosus) - *Purple raspberry* {PR} Natural and artificial hybrids. Black raspberry x red raspberry. Fruits are eaten fresh, preserved, made into jams and jellies, etc. MEDSGER, UPHOF, ZEVEN; <u>M97M</u> (for cultivars see Raspberry, page 465)

Rubus niveus - *Ceylon raspberry, Hill raspberry, Pilai* {GR} The fruit is purple-black when ripe, juicy, and of a sweet, rich black-raspberry flavor. It is eaten raw, served with sugar and cream or ice cream, and is also made into tarts, pies, jellies and jams. Southern Asia. HEDRICK 1919, KENNARD, MACMILLAN, MORTON 1987a [Cu], STURROCK.

CULTIVARS

<u>Mysore:</u> (Mysore Raspberry) Black fruit, covered with soft hairs; flavor mild, slightly sweet, good; seeds small; similar to western native black raspberry; main crop ripens March to May in Florida. Bush evergreen; canes vigorous, growing 10 to 15 feet per season; adapted only in subtropical regions. Very suitable for home gardens. Originated in India as a seedling selection. Introduced into the U.S. in 1948. BROOKS 1972; J36

Rubus occidentalis - *Black raspberry, Blackcap* {PR} Fruits are eaten fresh, dried, in jams, jellies, pies, sherbet and ice cream, canned, served with sugar and cream, preserved, made into vinegar, etc. Young shoots are eaten like rhubarb. The leaves and the bark of the root are used for making a tea-like beverage. North America. MEDSGER, TANAKA, YANOVSKY; <u>A38M</u>, <u>M97M</u> (for cultivars see Raspberry, page 465)

Rubus odoratus - *Rose-flowering raspberry* {PL} The somewhat tart and dry fruits are consumed raw, and are also made into pies, jams, and jellies. North America. CROWHURST 1972, GIBBONS 1979, MEDSGER; C36, E33M, I31{S}, M16, N7T, N9M, N9M{S}

Rubus palmatus* → *Rubus microphyllus

Rubus parviflorus - *Thimble berry* {S} Berries are eaten fresh, or dried and stored for later use. Tender, young shoots are peeled, and consumed raw or boiled. Both the berries and shoots are good sources of vitamin C. North America. CLARKE, FERNALD, HELLER, MEDSGER, NORTON, YANOVSKY; A2, <u>A38M</u>{PR}, A91{PL}, D95{PL}, E15, I47, J26{PL}, *J75M*{PL}, K47T, N84

Rubus parvifolius - *Japanese raspberry* {S} The juicy fruits are eaten raw, made into jam, and brewed into wine. Eastern Asia, Australia, cultivated. CRIBB, HEDRICK 1919, TANAKA; **U7M, V19, V34, X33, Y76** (for cultivars see Raspberry, page 465)

Rubus pedatus - *Trailing wild raspberry* {S} The fruits are juicy and flavorful and are eaten fresh, dried or made into jam. Makes an excellent jelly. Northwestern North America, Eastern Asia. HEDRICK 1919, HELLER, NORTON, TURNER 1979; **U7M**

Rubus phoenicolasius - *Japanese wineberry, Wine raspberry* {PL} The fruit is cherry-red, soft, very juicy, mildly sweet and can be eaten fresh, made into jams and jellies or brewed into wine. Japan, naturalized in North America. GIBBONS 1962, HENDRICKSON, JOHNS, SIMMONS 1972 [Cu], TANAKA, UPHOF; B19, B61M{S}, B75, C63, D95, H42, *H93M*, *J2M*, J61M, M16, N24M, N63M{S}

CULTIVARS {GR}

<u>Bella di Tokyo:</u> Small, tasteful red fruits. Q11M

Rubus procerus - *Himalaya berry* {S} Large, black, thimble-shaped fruits that are eaten raw, dried, or used for cakes, pies, drinks, etc. Temperate Asia, naturalized in North America. CLARKE, HENDRICKSON, ZEVEN; A2

Rubus procumbens* → *Rubus flagellaris

Rubus reflexus - *Sze-poh-lat* {S} The flower is edible. China. VON REIS; **Z25M**

Rubus rosaefolius - *Mauritius raspberry, Bramble of the Cape* {S} Fruits are eaten raw, stewed with sugar, served with coconut cream, or made into jam. The leaves are also edible. Tropical Asia, cultivated. CRIBB, GIBBONS 1967, KENNARD, MARTIN 1975, TANAKA; F80, F85, N84

Rubus rubrisetus - Fruits are eaten. North America. TANAKA; (for cultivars see Blackberry, page 267)

Rubus rugosus* → *Rubus moluccanus

Rubus saxatilis - *Roebuck berry, Stone bramble* {S} Acid fruits are eaten raw, with sugar, or fermented into an alcoholic beverage. Arctic and temperate regions. HEDRICK 1919; K47T, N84, S7M

Rubus shankii - *Shank's blackberry* {S} The large fruits are eaten, being of excellent quality with small, soft seeds. Central America. KENNARD; **U7M**

Rubus spectabilis - *Salmon berry* {S} Fruits are consumed raw, dried or made into tarts. They are juicy and of very good flavor. Indians often ate the berries with half-dried salmon eggs, hence the common name. Young shoots are peeled and eaten raw, roasted, or cooked like asparagus and served with hollandaise sauce. The leaves are used as a tea substitute. Northwestern North America. CLARKE,

GIBBONS 1979, HEDRICK 1919, HELLER, TURNER 1979, YANOVSKY; A2, A15M{PR}, D95{PL}, E15, *J75M*{PL}, K47T, N84

Rubus strigosus - *American red raspberry* The fruit is eaten raw, preserved, made into jams, pies, and syrups, used in sherbets, ice cream, compote, pastries, confectionery, fermented into wine, etc. Young shoots are peeled and eaten raw, or cooked like asparagus. A substitute for tea can be made from the leaves or twigs. North America, cultivated. GIBBONS 1962 [Re], HARRINGTON, H., MEDSGER, TANAKA, TURNER 1979 [Re], UPHOF, YANOVSKY; (for cultivars see Raspberry, page 465)

Rubus trivialis - *Southern dewberry* {S} The berries are large, black and well-flavored and are eaten raw, or used for jams and preserves. Southern North America. HEDRICK 1919, MEDSGER, SIMMONS 1972, UPHOF; **U7M** (for cultivars see Blackberry, page 267)

Rubus ursinus - *Pacific dewberry, California dewberry* {S} Fruits are consumed fresh or dried, and are also made into pies, sauces, jellies and cakes. The half-ripe berries can be soaked in water to make a pleasant drink. Fresh or dried leaves are used for tea. Young shoots are boiled and eaten. Western North America. CLARKE [Re], TURNER 1979 [Re]; A2, I47, I99, J26{PL} (for cultivars see Blackberry, page 267)

Rubus vitifolius - *Pacific blackberry* {PL} The sweet, black fruits have a pleasant flavor and are eaten fresh or used for jellies and preserves. Indians dried them for future use, and pounded the fresh fruit to form cakes and *pemmican*. One of the parents of the Loganberry and Luther Burbank's Primus berry. Western North America. CLARKE [Re], SIMMONS 1972, WICKSON; *C73*

Sanguisorba canadensis - *American great burnet* {S} The leaves are boiled, washed with water to remove the bitterness, and eaten with salt and miso. North America. ALTSCHUL; C9{PL}, F85, G47M, J39M{PL}, K47T, N84

Sanguisorba minor - *Salad burnet* {PL} The leaves, having the taste of cucumber, are eaten in salads, used as a garnish, or added to soups, cooling drinks and *claret cups*. Chopped leaves are often mixed with butter, cottage cheese and cream cheese. Dried leaves can be steeped for tea, and are also added to vinegar. Young seedlings are boiled and eaten. Eurasia, naturalized in North America. FERNALD, HALPIN [Cu, Cul], MARCIN, MEDSGER, MICHAEL [Re], MORTON 1976, TANAKA, VILMORIN [Cu]; C3, C3{S}, C9, C16{S}, C67M, F21, F24{S}, F31T, G84, H46{S}, I47{S}, I77M, K22, N19M

Sanguisorba officinalis - *Garden burnet, Great burnet* {S} Young leaves and flower-buds are consumed in salads, and are also parboiled and eaten fried, oil-roasted, added to soups, or preserved in salt. Leaves are also used as a tea substitute and are added to herb beers. The seeds are used in the preparation of vinegar. Young shoots are mixed with other greens and used as a potherb. Northern temperate region. GRIEVE, MACNICOL, MORTON 1976, TANAKA; D62, F80, M82{PL}, N63M, *N71M*, N84, O48, O53M

X Sorbopyrus auricularis (Sorbus aria x Pyrus communis) - *Bollwiller pear* {S} Artificial hybrid. White-beam x pear. Fruits are eaten. BEAN, REHDER, TANAKA; **X36**

X Sorbopyrus sp. (Sorbus sp. x Pyrus communis) - {GR} Artificial hybrid. Mountain ash x pear. The fruit is eaten.

CULTIVARS

Shipova: Medium-sized, round, yellow fruit with firm deliciously flavored flesh. Productive and scab resistant. Blooms in mid-April and ripens in August. Apparently quite hardy. Originally from Yugoslavia. I49M

Sorbus americana - *American mountain ash* {S} Fruits are processed into jams, jellies, beverages, wines and marmalades. When mellowed by frost, they become palatable and may be eaten raw. Eastern North America. FERNALD, GIBBONS 1979, MEDSGER, TURNER 1979; B9M{PL}, B61M, C58{PL}, E33M{PL}, *F38*, *G4*{PL}, *G66*, K38, K47T, L91M, N84, O93, P49, *P63*

Sorbus aria - *Whitebeam, Chess apple* {S} The fruit is made into brandy, jellies, conserves and vinegar. When ripe, it is brown and speckled with red spots, and can be eaten raw after being "bletted", like the medlar. Eurasia. MABEY, SIMMONS 1972, UPHOF; *C33*{PL}, D95{PL}, K38, L91M, *N71M*, N84, N93M, O53M, P49, *P63*, *R28*, R78, S95

Sorbus aucuparia - *European mountain ash, Rowan tree* {PL} Fruits are processed into preserves, jellies, compotes, wine, bitters, liqueurs, *perry*, syrups, added to soups, etc. Also used as a substitute for coffee. Leaves and flowers are used to adulterate tea. Eurasia, cultivated. GRIEVE, LAUNERT [Pre], MABEY, MICHAEL [Re], TANAKA, UPHOF; A80M, *C33*, D45, E15{S}, E47, E47{S}, G16, G23, G67, I4, K38{S}, *L49*, M35M, N93M{S}, O53M{S}, etc.

Sorbus aucuparia 'Edulis' - *Rowanberry* {PL} The fruits are preserved, and can also be used for jams, jellies, ketchups, sweetmeats, liqueurs, or wine making. JOHNS [Re], SIMMONS 1972 [Cu], TANAKA; F43M, P86

Sorbus aucuparia 'Moravica' - *Mährische eberesche* {S} The fruits are high in vitamin C and make delicious jellies and preserves. They are larger and sweeter than the type. An improved strain, discovered in Czechoslovakia in 1810. ZEVEN; **V73**

Sorbus aucuparia 'Rossica' - *Russian mountain ash* {PL} The large orange fruits are eaten, being sweeter than the type and an important source of vitamin C. Trees are immune to fire blight. Cultivated in the U.S.S.R. since before 1810. TANAKA, ZEVEN; A65, B47, G1T, *G4*, G41, J7

Sorbus decora - *Showy mountain ash* {PL} Fruits are eaten stewed with sugar or made into jelly. North America. PETERSON, L.; *A74*, G1T, *G4*, I15{S}, J7, *K89*, M35M

Sorbus domestica - *Service tree, Sorb apple* {S} The fruit is eaten fresh after it has been exposed to frost, or when overripe and "bletted", like the medlar (Mespilus germanica). Also fermented into wine. In France, it is used for making *perry* or is dried like prunes. Apple-shaped and pear-shaped forms are known. Eurasia, cultivated. BIANCHINI, SIMMONS 1972, UPHOF; K38, K47T, K63G, *N71M*, N84, N93M, O53M, O93, P49, *P63*, P86{PL}, *R28*, R78, S95

Sorbus edulis* → *Sorbus aucuparia

Sorbus latifolia - *French hales, Fontainbleu service tree* {S} The fruit is russet-yellow with conspicuous black dots, and has been sold and eaten in Devon, England. Europe. MABEY, SIMMONS 1972; D95{PL}, K63G, *N71M*, N84, P49, S69

CULTIVARS {GR}

Devoniensis: Was grown for its fruits 50 years ago in Devon, but had been lost since then until recently. Fruits were sold as *sweets* in the "old days". Attractive copper-colored foliage. Tree grows to about 40 feet. F43M, N84{S}

Sorbus scopulina - *Western mountain ash* {S} Fruits are eaten raw, cooked, or dried and are also made into pies, jams, jellies, marmalades and a bitter-sweet wine. Western North America. KIRK, MEDSGER; A2, *C33*{PL}, D95{PL}, G1T{PL}, *G66*, *G66*{PL}, I15, I47, J26{PL}, K38, K47T, M35M{PL}, N84, O93, *P63*, etc.

Sorbus sitchensis - *Sitka mountain ash* {S} The fruits are primarily used in the preparation of jellies, marmalades, jams, wines and liquors. They can also be placed in the top of the jar, as a flavoring, when canning blueberries. Western North America. TURNER 1979 [Re]; D95{PL}, E15, I47, J26{PL}, K47T, N84

Sorbus torminalis - *Checker tree, Chequers* {S} When ripe, the fruit is brown, checkered or speckled with lighter-colored spots, and has soft, fairly sweet flesh that is rich in vitamin C. It can be eaten like the medlar, and is also processed into jellies, conserves, wine, brandy and vinegar. Eurasia. MABEY, SIMMONS 1972 [Cu], UPHOF; K38, K47T, *N71M*, N84, N93M, O93, P49, *P63*, P86{PL}, *R28*, R78, S95

Spiraea beauverdiana - *Alaska spiraea* {S} Leaves are used as a substitute for tea. Northeast Asia to Alaska. KUNKEL; **V34**

Spiraea blumei - {S} Leaves are made into a tea, called *tsui-lan-cha*. Eastern Asia. TANAKA; **T41M, X33, Z25M**

Spiraea chinensis - {S} Leaves are processed into a tea, called *tsui-lan-cha*. China. TANAKA; **T41M, W3M**

Spiraea x pyramidata - *Pyramid spiraea* {S} A tea-like beverage can be made by boiling the stems, leaves, and flowers. Western North America. YANOVSKY; C82, K47T

RUBIACEAE

Asperula odorata* → *Galium odoratum

Borojoa patinoi - *Borojo* {S} The fruit is eaten fresh or used for *refrescos* and sherbets. Popular in parts of Colombia and Panama where it is sold in local markets. Northwestern South America. DUKE, PEREZ-ARBELAEZ, SCHERY; **T73M, W12**

Burchellia bubalina - *Wild pomegranate* {S} The flowers are sucked for their rich nectar. Southern Africa. PALMER; F80, N84, O53M, O93, P5, R41, R77M

Casasia clusiifolia - *Seven-year apple* {PL} When fully ripe the fruit is soft, wrinkled, and prune-like, with black, jelly-like pulp somewhat licorice flavored. It is eaten by making a hole in one end of the fruit and sucking the pulp out. Florida, West Indies. MORTON 1977; D87G, *J25*

Catesbaea spinosa - *Lilythorn* {S} The edible fruit is yellow, pulpy, and of an agreeable flavor. West Indies. HEDRICK 1919; F85

Cinchona succirubra - *Red cinchona* {S} One of the sources of *cinchona bark*, an extract which is used to flavor bitters, alcoholic beverages, soft drinks, condiments, baked goods, and ice cream. Ecuador. MORTON 1976; **T70**

Coffea arabica - *Coffee, Arabian coffee* {S} Roasted seeds are the source of a stimulating beverage. It is served hot, cold, fortified, spiced, with milk or cream, etc. Coffee extract is used for flavoring ice cream, candies, pastries, soft drinks, yogurt, and liqueurs. The red fruits are chewed for their stimulating properties. The leaves, which contain more caffeine than the fruits, are used as a tea substitute. Eastern Africa, cultivated. DAVIDS [Re], GRIEVE, HEDRICK 1919, TANAKA, UPHOF, WRIGLEY; A79M, C9M, D29{PL}, E29, E29{PL}, *E53M*, G96{PL}, I83M{PL}, L9M, N84, O93, P5, *P17M*, P38, R33M, etc.

CULTIVARS

Caturra: More compact, with larger dark-green leaves, and more cold hardy than the species. A precocious bearer and high yielder, thus of great economic importance. Easy to harvest. Tends to overbear. Used as a parent in many current breeding programs. A mutant that probably originated in Minas Gerais, Brazil. WRIGLEY; *E53M*, N84, *Q52*{PL}

Kona: Leaves shiny, 3 to 6 inches long; flowers white, fragrant, when in bloom they make a fine display massed in clusters along the branches. Makes a good houseplant and is a good candidate for bonsai. The berries make a very richly flavored, fairly acid, and overwhelmingly aromatic beverage. Originated in Kona, Hawaii. D57{PL}, H49, M19, M20, N84, O93

Mundo Novo: Vigorous, very productive plant, widely adapted to different soil types. One of the most popular cultivars in Latin America. Considered a natural cross between Sumatra coffee and the Bourbon Vermelho cultivar. Developed in Urupes County, formerly Mundo Novo, in Sao Paulo, Brazil. WRIGLEY; *Q93*{PL}

Nana: Leaves dark, glossy green, wavy-edged; flowers white, fragrant, borne in clusters. Makes a good house plant. This is a dwarf form, particularly useful for pot culture. N84, *O1*, O53M, *Q52*{PL}

Yellow: A yellow-fruited form. Collected in Hawaii. F85

Coffea canephora - *Robusta coffee, Quillow coffee* {S} Roasted seeds are brewed into an alkaloidal beverage. Mostly used in inexpensive blends and instant coffees. Has the highest caffeine content of the Coffea species. The fully formed but unripe berries are boiled whole with herbs, dried in the sun, and used as a masticatory. Tropical Africa, cultivated. TANAKA, WRIGLEY, ZEVEN; E29, E29{PL}, F85

Coffea liberica - *Liberian coffee* {S} Roasted seeds are the source of Liberian or *Liberica coffee*, considered inferior to Arabian, Robusta and Sierra Leone coffees. Adapted to warmer and moister climates than C. arabica. West Tropical Africa, cultivated. MACMILLAN, UPHOF, ZEVEN; F85

Coffea racemosa - *Inhambane coffee* {PL} The roasted seeds are used as coffee. Southern Africa. UPHOF; E29, E29{S}

Coffea robusta* → *Coffea canephora

Coffea stenophylla - *Sierra Leone coffee, Highland coffee* {S} The roasted beans produce coffee of superior quality, claimed to be equal to that of Mocha. Occasionally cultivated in preference to Liberian coffee. West Tropical Africa. DALZIEL, MACMILLAN, TANAKA; N84, P38

Galium aparine - *Cleavers, Goose-grass* {S} Young leaves and stems are steamed and eaten as a vegetable or used in soups, stews, and *Lenten pottage*. Seeds are dried, roasted slightly, and used as a very good substitute for coffee. Dried leaves are used as a tea. Eurasia, naturalized in North America. FERNALD, GIBBONS 1966b, MABEY, MICHAEL; A2, D58, D62, H3M{PL}, J82, *N71M*, N84, O48

Galium odoratum - *Sweet woodruf* {PL} The coumarin-scented herb is used for flavoring fruit cups, cooling drinks, beers, liqueurs, and spiced wines, especially *Maibowle* or *Maywine*. Dried leaves are used as a tea substitute. The sweet-scented flowers are eaten or used for garnishing. Eurasia, cultivated. LEGGATT [Re], MACNICOL, MARCIN, MORTON 1976, PAINTER [Re], UPHOF, VILMORIN [Cu]; B77, C3, C9, C13M{S}, C67M, F21, G84, H40, H46{S}, J78, K22, L66, *M65M*, N19M, N84{S}, etc.

Galium verum - *Yellow bedstraw, Lady's bedstraw, Cheese rennet* {PL} Leaves and flowers contain an enzyme used to curdle milk for cheese and junket. Stems and leaves yield a yellow dye that was used to color *Cheshire* cheese and butter. The flowering tops are used in the preparation of a refreshing, acid beverage. Eurasia, naturalized in North America. FERNALD, GRIEVE, HEDRICK 1919, MABEY, MORTON 1976; C9, C11{S}, C13M{S}, C43M, C67M, E5M, F15M, F24{S}, G84, K22, M53, N19M, N84{S}, O53M{S}

Gardenia augusta* → *Gardenia jasminoides

Gardenia jasminoides - *Cape jasmine* {PL} The fragrant flowers are used to scent *jasmine tea*. They are also eaten raw as a delicacy, pickled, or preserved in honey, when they are called *mi-ts'ai*. Fruits are eaten or used as a yellow coloring for other foods. Southern China, cultivated. ALTSCHUL, BROUK, TANAKA; B32, C56M, D95, F80{S}, F85{S}, G25M{S}, G96, H4, I83M, K18, L91M{S}, O93{S}, *P17M*{S}, *Q32*{S}

Genipa americana - *Genipa, Marmalade box* {S} The fruits, like the medlar, sorbe, and Indian wild pear, are edible only when soft and overripe, when the flavor then resembles dried apples or quinces. They are mostly used in lemonade-like drinks, jellies, sherbets, ice cream, preserves, syrups, soft drinks, liqueurs, or are pickled with vinegar and onions. Tropical America. DUKE, MORTON 1987a, POPENOE, W. 1920 [Cu]; **T73M, X88M, X94, Y2**

Guettarda speciosa - *Angelica* {S} The edible fruit is sweet and savory. Brazil. TANAKA; **Z25M**

Heinsia benguelensis → ***Leptactina benguelensis***

Ixora coccinea - *Pitkuli* {S} Ripe fruits are edible. The flowers are used as a condiment. Tropical Asia, cultivated. ALTSCHUL, BURKILL; F85, G96{PL}, H4{PL}, *L5M*, N84, O93, *Q32*

Kraussia floribunda - *Wild cornel* {S} The small, black fruits are sweet and edible. Southern Africa. FOX, F.; N84, R41

Leptactina benguelensis - *Mulangu, Ngobole ngoshai* {S} Fruits are edible, having a very strong sweet scent. The flowers are sucked for their sweet nectar. Southern Africa. ALTSCHUL, VON REIS; F85, N84

Mitchella repens - *Partridge berry, Squaw vine* {PL} The pleasant, slightly aromatic fruits are sometimes eaten out of hand. North America. FERNALD, GIBBONS 1979, MEDSGER, SIMMONS 1972 [Cu]; A25M, B51{S}, C9, C73M, C76, D62, D75T, E33M, *F51*, F57M, I44, J78, M77M, N7T, N9M, N11, N37, etc.

Morinda citrifolia - *Indian mulberry* {S} Unripe fruits are used in sambals and curries. Ripe fruits are made into a beverage with sugar or syrup. Young leaves, containing 4.5 to 6% protein, are eaten raw, steamed, or as a wrapping in fish dishes. Seeds of some forms are roasted and eaten. Tropical Asia, cultivated. DUKE, OCHSE, TANAKA; F85, O93

Paederia foetida - *Kasembukan* {S} Leaves are eaten raw as a side-dish with rice, grated coconut and chili peppers. Minced leaves are steamed and eaten, added to soups, or mixed with various vegetables and spices, wrapped in a banana leaf, and cooked over a fire. The offensive smell disappears when the vegetable is cooked. Tropical Asia. HEDRICK 1919, OCHSE; F85

Paederia scandens - *Hekuso-kazura* {S} The sweet stem juice is sucked in Taiwan. Eastern Asia. TANAKA; F85

Posoqueria latifolia - *Monkey apple, Fruta de mono* {S} The juicy, yellow fruits are edible. Tropical South America. ALTSCHUL, DUKE; F85, O53M

Posoqueria longiflora - *Kamadani* {S} The fruits, resembling small yellow guavas, are eaten. Eastern South America. PEREZ-ARBELAEZ; F85

Psychotria nervosa - *Wild coffee* {PL} The seeds are used as a substitute for coffee. Pulp of the fruit is edible. Florida. D87G, *J25*, *L5M*{S}

Randia echinocarpa - *Kakwara, Papache* {S} The chopped, ground, and boiled bark is used as a catalyst in the preparation of *tesguino*, an indigenous alcoholic beverage. Edible fruits are much appreciated by the natives. Mexico. ALTSCHUL, STEINKRAUS; F85

Randia formosa - *Raspberry bush, Blackberry-jam fruit, Genipapo do campo* {PL} The sweet fruits are yellow outside, black inside, and are said to taste like molasses or blackberry jam. They are eaten fresh or used in beverages. Tropical America. MARTIN 1987, TANAKA, VON REIS; E29, E29{PR}, E29{S}, F68, F85{S}

Rothmannia globosa - *Bell gardenia* {S} The round fruits have a rather soft and corky shell and flat seeds embedded in an edible pulp. Southern Africa. FOX, F.; F80, N84, *P17M*, R41, R77M

Tapiphyllum parvifolium - *Mountain medlar* {S} The dark brown fruit splits easily into segments like those of an orange and has the flavor of Vangueria spp. It is eaten raw or dried for future use. Southern Africa. FOX, F., TANAKA; N84, R41, R77M

Tocoyena formosa → ***Randia formosa***

Vangueria edulis → ***Vangueria madagascariensis***

Vangueria esculenta - *Chirinda medlar* {S} The bright yellow fruits are edible. Tropical Africa. FOX, F., UPHOF; N84, O53M, O93

Vangueria infausta - *False medlar* {S} The fruits are eaten raw, dried for later use, or used to flavor puddings and porridges. They have an acid, somewhat sweetish-sour flavor. In Transvaal a brandy is distilled from the fruits. Seed kernels are eaten. Tropical Africa. FOX, F.; N84, S29

Vangueria madagascariensis - *Voavanga of Madagascar, Spanish tamarind* {S} The fruits are sweet, subacid, yellowish-green when ripe, with the taste of unripe apples. They may be eaten raw or stewed. If eaten when overripe, like the medlar, the flavor is suggestive of the tamarind. Tropical Africa, Madagascar. KENNARD, MACMILLAN; P5

Vangueriopsis lanciflora - *Wild medlar* {S} The yellow fruits are consumed by the natives. They are reported as being either tasteless or exceptionally well-flavored. Central to Southern Africa. FOX, F., UPHOF; N84

RUSCACEAE

Ruscus aculeatus - *Butcher's broom* {S} The pungent, somewhat bitter, young shoots are cooked and eaten like asparagus. Seeds are used as a substitute for coffee. Eurasia, cultivated. BIANCHINI, TANAKA; K47T, N84, N93M, O48, O53M, R53M{PL}

RUTACEAE

Adenandra fragrans - *Breath of heaven* {S} The strongly aromatic leaves are used as a substitute for tea. Southern Africa. UPHOF; O53M

Aegle marmelos - *Bael fruit, Bengal quince* {S} Ripe fruits are orange, hard-shelled, with an aromatic, pleasant-flavored pulp. They are eaten out of hand, pickled, or used in marmalades, jams, jellies, confectionery, and drinks. The young leaves and shoots are eaten as a vegetable or used as a condiment. An infusion of the flowers forms a refreshing beverage. Twigs serve as chewsticks. Southeast Asia. BURKILL, MORTON 1987a, REUTHER, SIMMONS 1972, STURROCK, UPHOF, WATT; A79M, E29, E29{PL}, E29{PR}, F85, N84, P5, Q12, Q18, Q46

Agathosma betulina → ***Barosma betulina***

Agathosma crenulata → ***Barosma crenulata***

Atalantia buxifolia → ***Severinia buxifolia***

Barosma betulina - *Round-leaf buchu* {S} The strongly aromatic leaves are used in the preparation of a brandy that forms the base of highly popular cocktails in Tunisia. An extract of the leaves is one of the ingredients of a South African herbal wine. Also the source of an essential oil with a camphor-peppermint odor, used by American food manufacturers to flavor candy, ice cream, baked goods, and condiments. Southern Africa. MORTON 1976; N84, R41, R77M

Barosma crenulata - *Oval buchu* {S} Aromatic leaves are used like those of A. betulina for flavoring Tunisian brandy, South African herbal wine, and American processed foods. Southern Africa. MORTON 1976; N84, P5, R41, R60, R77M

Boronia megastigma - *Brown boronia* {S} The fragrant flowers are the source of an essential oil having an aroma of cinnamon and tobacco. Sold as *boronia absolute*, it is employed in food manufacturing to create a black currant flavor and to enrich other fruit flavors in beverages, ice creams, candy, and baked goods. Australia. MORTON 1976; F80, L91M, N84, O33, O53M, O93, P5, *Q25*, *Q32*, R15M, R33M, R47, S92, T7

Casimiroa edulis - *White sapote, Matasano* {S} The fruits are yellow or green when ripe, soft, usually thin-skinned, and have a melting, custard-like pulp with a very sweet flavor. They are best eaten out of hand but can also be dried, frozen, served with cream and sugar, or used in ice cream, milk shakes, and salads. The seeds are reported to be toxic if eaten raw. Other authors state that they may be roasted and eaten like nuts. Central America, cultivated. MORTON 1987a, POPENOE, W. 1920 [Cu, Pro], RICHARDSON [Re], SCHNEIDER [Cul, Re], SIMMONS 1972, STURROCK, THOMSON 1973; A44M{PR}, A79M, *B59*{PR}, C56M{PL}, E29, E29{PL}, E29{PR}, F85, J83T{PR}, *N40*{PR}, N84, O93, P38, Q46 (for cultivars see White Sapote, page 533)

Casimiroa tetrameria - *Wooly-leaf white sapote, Yellow sapote* {S} The ripe fruits have a firm, golden-yellow pulp with a sweet, spicy flavor. They can be eaten out of hand, baked in pies, chilled and served in fruit salads, or made into a butter similar to apple butter. When dried, the fruit retains its color and flavor very well and has a nice chewy texture. Mexico. KENNARD, MOWRY, RAMSAY, STURROCK, UPHOF; N84, P38

CULTIVARS {GR}

Mac's Golden: (Max Golden) Large round fruit, weight 6 to 7 ounces; flesh dark yellow. Excellent, aromatic, mango-like flavor. Tends to have few seeds. Superior to fruits of other cultivars of this species. Originated in Carlsbad, California, by Charles W. Ramsay. Named after Charles McBride. Introduced about 1932. BROOKS 1972; *Q93*

X Citrofortunella mitis (Citrus reticulata x Fortunella sp.) - *Calamondin, Panama orange, Golden lime* {S} Natural hybrid. Very acid fruits are pickled, preserved, or used in drinks, tea, marmalades, sauces, chutneys, jellies and for flavoring the Philippine soy sauce known as *toyo mansi*. Whole fruits, fried in coconut oil with various seasonings, are eaten with curry. The preserved peel is used for flavoring other foods. Philippines, cultivated. JOHNS [Cul], MORTON 1987a [Cu], REUTHER, RICHARDSON [Pre, Re], UPHOF; A79M, E3M{DW}, F68{PL}, F85, G17{PL}, *G49*{PL}, G96{DW}, I83M{PL}, J61M{DW}, *J73M*, N18, N18{SC}, N84, P5

CULTIVARS {GR}

Variegated: Small, spherical fruit; rind striped when immature, orange to orange-red when ripe, thin, smooth, edible; flesh orange, tender, juicy, very acid; seeds few, small; holds on the tree nearly year-round. Tree moderately vigorous, upright, slightly smaller than the standard calamondin; highly productive; very cold-hardy. Foliage variegated with green and creamy white, attractive. E48, F68, *G49*, I83M, N18{SC}

X Citrofortunella sp. (Citrus aurantifolia x Fortunella spp.) - *Limequat* {S} Artificial hybrids. The pleasantly acid fruits are used as a substitute for limes in ades and for flavoring. Limequat hybrids are much more cold hardy than their lime parent. Grown on a small scale in California for the specialty foods market. RAY, REUTHER, STURROCK, UPHOF; *D23M*, N18

CULTIVARS {GR}

Eustis: (C. aurantifolia x F. japonica) Mexican lime x round kumquat. Medium-sized, nearly oval fruit; rind light yellow, very sweet, smooth, thin; flesh light greenish, tender, juicy, in 6 to 9 segments, of fine quality; nearly everbearing but main crop borne in late fall and winter. Tree prolific, hardy, with numerous small thorns; resistant to withertip. BROOKS 1972; E3M{DW}, *G49*, I83M

Lakeland: (C. aurantifolia x F. japonica) Mexican lime x round kumquat. Fruit similar in shape to Eustis, but larger; rind deep yellow, smooth, thin; flesh juicy, of fine quality, with few seeds. Tree nearly thornless, hardy, resistant to withertip. Originated in Eustis, Florida by Walter T. Swingle. BROOKS 1972; R77

Tavares: (C. aurantifolia x F. margarita) Mexican lime x oval kumquat. Medium-sized, obovate to oval fruit; rind pale orange-yellow, smooth, thin, tender, edible; flesh buff-yellow, in 7 to 8 segments, juicy, acid. Tree vigorous with short spines and pink flower buds. MORTON 1987a; *G49*

X Citrofortunella sp. (Citrus x junos x Poncirus trifoliata) - *Yusvange* {SC} Artificial hybrid. Yuzu x trifoliate orange. Cold hardy citrus with fruits that are considered more palatable than either parent, and also other hybrids with one-half trifoliate orange in their parentage. The pulp is mildly sour with a lemon-like flavor and can be used in lemonade, lemon pies, marmalade, on fish or eaten out of hand. Hybridized in 1964 by J.R. Brown. CHAPMAN; **U13**

X Citrofortunella sp. (Citrus reticulata x Fortunella x crassifolia) - *Orangequat* {GR} Artificial hybrid. The fruits may be eaten like a kumquat or used in marmalades. RAY.

CULTIVARS

Nippon: Satsuma mandarin x Meiwa kumquat. Fruit red-orange, small (but larger than the kumquat), broadly oval to obovate; rind sweet, relatively thick and spongy; pulp juicy, slightly acid. Matures early but holds well on tree for several months. Tree slow growing, medium-small, spreading. RAY, REUTHER; G17, *G49*

X Citroncirus webberi (Poncirus trifoliata x Citrus sinensis) - *Citrange* {GR} Artificial hybrid. Trifoliate orange x sweet orange. The acid fruits can be used for drinks and marmalades. Generally the hybrids combine the cold hardiness and bitterness of the trifoliate orange with the larger, more orange-like fruits of the sweet orange. Most cultivars are used as rootstocks. REUTHER, UPHOF; (also see Rootstocks, page 470)

CULTIVARS

Morton: Medium-sized fruit, 3 to 3½ inches in diameter; fragrant, very juicy flesh, nearly seedless. Said to be the best of the citranges for culinary use. Valued for ade and mixed drinks. Also good for pies, jams and marmalade. Ornamental tree; particularly adapted to Texas soils and climate. Much hardier than Satsuma; observed in Texas at 12^{0} F. with 90% defoliation. Also used as a rootstock, although it has limited commercial value. I74, K67, N18{S}

Rusk: Trifoliate orange x Ruby blood orange. Fruit rather small, oblate to spherical, color deep orange with reddish flush. Rind thin; segments about 10. Flesh orange-yellow, very juicy; flavor sprightly acid and only slightly bitter. Tree vigorous, tall-growing, productive, and hardy. An attractive ornamental whose juicy fruit approaches edibility more closely than most citranges. MORTON 1987a, REUTHER; N18{S}

X Citroncirus sp. (Poncirus trifoliata x Citrus limon) - *Citremon* Artificial hybrid. Trifoliate orange x lemon. The fruits are edible. Primarily used as a rootstock. (for sources see Rootstocks, page 470)

X Citroncirus sp. (Poncirus trifoliata x Citrus x paradisi) - *Citrumelo* Artificial hybrid. Trifoliate orange x grapefruit. Fruits are occasionally eaten. Mostly used as a rootstock. I74; (for cultivars see Rootstocks, page 470)

Citropsis daweana - *Mozambique cherry-orange* {S} The fruits are edible. Also a potential rootstock for other Citrus fruits. Southern Africa. FOX, F.; N84

Citrus x amblycarpa - *Djeruk limau* {S} In Indonesia, the extremely fragrant juice of the young or half-ripe fruits is used as a condiment. It is also added to rice flour in the preparation of *ragi* yeast cakes. The leaves are mixed with meat dishes to give them a pleasant taste. Also used as a rootstock. Cultivated. HESSELTINE, OCHSE, ROM; N18

Citrus aurantifolia - *Lime* {S} The acid fruits are cut in half and used as a garnish, pickled, preserved in syrup, made into jam, jelly, and marmalade, or juiced. Lime juice is used in ades, alcoholic drinks, sauces, made into syrup, or employed for flavoring fish, meats, beverages, confectionery, etc. Dried limes are widely used in Persian cuisine. In the Philippines, the chopped peel is made into a sweetmeat with milk and coconut. The minced leaves are sometimes eaten together with roasted meat in Indonesia. Tropical Asia, cultivated. JOHNS [Cul], MORTON 1987a [Cu], OCHSE, REUTHER, SIMMONS 1972, STURROCK, UPHOF; F85, N84, Q12

CULTIVARS {GR}

Bearss: Fruit size similar to a small lemon. Rind thin, shiny, pale yellow at maturity. Flesh pale, greenish yellow, very juicy; mild, acid lime flavor. Does not require much heat to reach ripeness. Tree vigorous, roundheaded; some thorns but less than Mexican lime. The most valuable lime for Western gardeners. Similar if not identical to Tahiti lime. RAY; *A71*, B93M{DW}, *D23M*, E3M{DW}, *F53M*, F68, *G49*, I83M, J61M{DW}, *L47*, *M61M*, *M61M*{DW}, N18{SC}

La Valette: Compact growing lemon x lime hybrid with medium-sized fruit of good acidity. A prolific cropper and easy to grow. R77

Mexican: (Mexican Lime, Key Lime, West Indian Lime) Fruit very small, round, obovate, or short-elliptical. Rind very thin; surface smooth, leathery, tightly adherent; color greenish-yellow at maturity. Flesh color greenish yellow; fine grained, tender, juicy; highly acid with a distinctive aroma. Moderately seedy. Tree medium in vigor and size, spreading and bushy, densely armed with spines. Sometimes called the *bartender's lime*. REUTHER; *D23M*, E3M{DW}, E31M, E48, F68, *G49*, G96{DW}, H4, I83M, J22, *M61M*, *M61M*{DW}, N18{S}, N18{SC}

Tahiti: (Persian Lime, Tahitian Lime) Medium-small fruit; oval, oblong, or short-elliptical. Seeds rare or lacking. Rind thin; surface smooth, tightly adherent; color pale lemon-yellow at maturity. Flesh pale greenish-yellow; tender, juicy, very acid and with true lime flavor. Tree vigorous, broad-spreading, drooping, medium to medium-large. B73M{DW}, F68, G96{DW}, I78{DW}, J22

Thornless Key: (Newell's Thornless Key) Small to medium-sized fruit; skin smooth; flesh seedless, flavor similar to Mexican; resembles Mexican or Key lime. Tree more frost resistant than Mexican, thornless, everbearing. Originated in Orlando, Florida. Introduced in 1945. BROOKS 1972; F68

Thornless Mexican: Medium to small, thin-skinned fruit; seedless. Tree thornless and everbearing. Bud mutation of a Mexican thorny lime. Originated in Weslaco, Texas. Introduced in 1930. BROOKS 1972; I83M

Citrus aurantium - *Sour orange, Seville orange, Daidai* {S} In Mexico the fresh fruits are cut in half and served with salt and hot chili paste. The juice is used in ade, for flavoring fish, or fermented to make wine. Considered the best orange for making marmalade. The dried peel is used in *bouquet garni*. An essential oil derived from the dried peel of immature fruits flavors *grand marnier*, *cointreau*, and *curaçao* liqueurs. Immature fruits are pickled in salt or vinegar or fried in coconut oil. The flowers are used for scenting tea. Southeast Asia, cultivated. MORTON 1987a [Cu, Cul], REUTHER, TANAKA, UPHOF, VON WELANETZ; I83M{PL}, *J73M*, N18, N84, Q12 (also see Rootstocks, page 470)

CULTIVARS {GR}

Bouquet: (Bouquet de Fleurs) Small, somewhat flattened fruit; rind deep-orange, moderately pebbled and well colored, medium-thick, loosely adherent; flesh juicy, sour, seeds few. Small tree with a spreading top consisting of thornless branchlets. A heavy flowering, ornamental cultivar especially suited for use as a hedge plant. I83M

Chinotto: Small, oblate to round fruit, with more or less rough rind surface, and an orange to deep orange color. Small tree with thornless branchlets. Growth habit more or less dense and compact. Grown primarily as an ornamental, although the fruits are also prized and used for candying, preserving, pickling, or crystallizing whole. RAY, REUTHER, TANAKA, UPHOF; G17, G96{DW}, I83M, S59

Nanshô-daidai: Medium-large, obovate fruit; broadly necked and narrowly collared; seedy. Rind medium-thick but easily peeled; somewhat pebbled; color lemon-yellow. Flesh color dull yellow; juicy, acid flavor with bitter aftertaste. Tree vigorous, upright-spreading, and very thorny. Cold hardy. Nanshô is the name of a town in Taiwan, where this fruit was discovered. REUTHER, TANAKA; I74, K67, N18{S}

Citrus x bergamia - *Bergamot* {GR} The peel is the source of a strongly pungent and agreeably aromatic essential oil used as a flavoring for hard candy, baked goods, chewing gum and desserts. The highly acid fruit juice is occasionally used as a vinegar or lime juice substitute. In Morocco, the flowers are preferred for making *orange flower water*. Cultivated. MORTON 1976, REUTHER, TANAKA, UPHOF, WOLFERT.

CULTIVARS

Castagnaro: Round to obovate fruit, frequently with a short neck, sometimes slightly ribbed. Rind surface commonly rougher and the oil somewhat less aromatic than Femminello. The tree is more vigorous and upright and attains larger size than Femminello, but is somewhat less fruitful. REUTHER; *O4*

Femminello: Nearly spherical fruit with smooth rind. Oil somewhat more aromatic than that of Castagnaro, and hence preferred. Apparently a superior selection of Castagnaro, Femminello is considered to be the best bergamot cultivar. The tree is somewhat less vigorous and smaller than Castagnaro, but earlier and more regular in bearing. REUTHER; *O4*

Citrus x depressa - *Shîkwashâ, Hirami lemon* The pulp of the fruit is sweetish, high in pectin, and rather poor-flavored. Mostly used as a rootstock. Cultivated. REUTHER, TANAKA; (for sources see Rootstocks, page 470)

Citrus grandis - *Pummelo, Shaddock, Pompelmousse* {S} Fruits are large, thick-skinned, resembling a grapefruit but with firmer, non-bitter flesh and less juice. Excellent to eat out-of-hand, the pummelo can also be added to fruit salads, preserved, or made into juice, jams, and marmalades. The candied peel is similar to that made from citron and is called *conserve de chadec* in Martinique. *Forbidden fruit*, a liqueur, is partly derived from pummelo which is infused in fine brandy. Southeast Asia, cultivated. MARTIN 1977 [Cu, Pro], MORTON 1987a, REUTHER, SCHNEIDER [Pre, Cul], UPHOF; *B59*{PR}, F68{PL}, F85, *N40*{PR}, N84, O93, Q12

CULTIVARS {GR}

Chandler: Fruit similar to a large grapefruit, globose to oblate; rind medium-thick, light yellow, mostly smooth; core solid, segments 14 to 16; membranes medium thick, seedy. Flesh pink, firm but tender, moderately juicy; juice pleasing but weakly aromatic, medium in soluble solids and acids. Ripe fruit is first harvested in December but lasts until March. Tree vigorous, spreading, with few thorns. *A71*, *D23M*, *G49*, I83M, J22, N18{SC}

Choy: (Choy Pompelmousse) Round fruit, somewhat flattened on the stem end; skin yellow, thin; flesh pale yellow, melting, juicy, subacid with a sweet grapefruit-like flavor; dessert quality excellent; seedless; ripens in winter-spring. Spreading tree with large, glossy, dark green foliage; large, very fragrant blossoms; grows and bears best in hot climates. Brought to Hawaii from Tahiti. J22

Hirado: (Hirado Buntan) Large, oblate fruit, slightly depressed at both ends; seedy; color bright yellow when mature; rind medium-thick, tightly adherent; flesh light greenish-yellow, tender and moderately juicy; flavor a pleasant blend of sugar and acid with a trace of bitterness. Ripens medium-early, keeps well. Tree unusually cold tolerant. Originated in Nagasaki Prefecture, Japan. Introduced in 1910. MORTON 1987a, REUTHER; G17

Reinking: Large fruit; rind smooth, yellow, moderately adherent for a pummelo. Flesh pale yellow, firm but tender, moderately juicy, seedy; good sugar-acid flavor. Fruit tends to fall after maturity. Tree vigorous, with denser foliage than Chandler. Originated in Indio, California. *D23M*, I83M, N18{SC}

Webber: The fruit is large, pink-fleshed, of good quality, and early maturing. This cultivar was collected as a cutting in 1925 by H.J. Webber in Java and introduced to the United States. Grown at David Fairchild's home, the Kampong, in Coconut Grove, Florida, the cultivar was named in honor of Webber by Fairchild. I83M

Citrus hystrix - *Kaffir lime, Ichang lime, Makrut, Djeruk purut* {PL} The fresh or dried leaves impart a pleasant citrus flavor when added to soups and curries. In Indonesia, fresh leaves are often pounded into a jelly and mixed with hot chili pastes. They also flavor an Indonesian soy sauce known as *kecap*. The rind is candied, or dried and used in curry pastes. The lemon-scented fruits are eaten with fish or made into drinks. Philippines. COOK, CRAWFORD [Re], OCHSE, SHURTLEFF 1979, STEINKRAUS, TANAKA, UPHOF; A45{PR}, C94{PR}, I83M, L90G{PR}, S54M

Citrus ichangensis - *Ichang papeda* {GR} The juicy, acid fruits are sometimes eaten. China. TANAKA.

CULTIVARS

Ichang Lemon: (Hsiang-Yüan, Shangyuan) Large, broadly obovate fruit; peel thick, lemon yellow when ripe, very fragrant. Pulp very acid, but with a strong, aromatic aftertaste. Tree erect, much branched with lower branches short. Very resistant to winter cold. The fruit has been used to make lemon pie; some who have made pies from the juice prefer them to regular lemon pies. Probably C. ichangensis x C. grandis. REUTHER, TANAKA; I74, I83M

Sudachi: Small, orange fruit; flesh light orange, seedy, with a tart mandarin-like flavor. Ripens early and should be picked soon after, as they tend to dehydrate in warm climates. The juice of the fruit is used in Japan to add a pleasantly sour taste and aroma to Japanese-style dishes, as lemons are in Western cookery. Possibly an *ichandarin*, C. ichangensis x C. reticulata. REUTHER, TANAKA; I74

Yuko: Large, well-shaped fruit; skin orange; flesh mild, with a mandarin-like flavor. Membrane sections tougher than those of mandarins, but easily peeled. Ripens with Yuzu, holds well on the tree. Used as a substitute for Yuzu. Said to be the least hardy of the C. ichangensis hybrids. Possibly an *ichandarin*, C. ichangensis x C. reticulata. TANAKA; I74

Citrus x jambhiri - *Rough lemon, Jambhiri orange, Mazoe lemon, Citronelle* Natural hybrid. Perhaps C. limon x C. medica. The fruit is occasionally used as a substitute for lemon, for which purpose it is not very suitable due to its scant pulp and moderate flavor and aroma. MORTON 1987a, REUTHER, TANAKA; (for cultivars see Rootstocks, page 470)

Citrus x junos - *Yuzu* {S} Possibly an *ichandarin*, C. ichangensis x C. reticulata. The grated or slivered rind and the juice are used for their distinctive, refreshing fragrance and flavor in Japanese-style dishes, among which soy sauces, miso toppings, soups, and *chiri-nabé*. Occasionally added to *kinugoshi tofu* before solidification. Juice of the fruit is processed into a distinctive citrus-flavored vinegar. The young, dark-green fruit is comparable to citron or lime, the mature yellow fruit to a lemon. A fairly expensive citrus fruit in Japan. Also used as a cold-hardy rootstock. REUTHER, SHURTLEFF 1975 [Re], SHURTLEFF 1976 [Re], TANAKA; E56{PR}, I74, N18

CULTIVARS {PL}

Xian-Zheng: Open-pollinated seedlings of a Chinese cultivar selected in Nanjing for hardiness and fruit quality. B96{CF}

Xie-Zheng: Open-pollinated seedlings of a Chinese cultivar selected in Nanjing for hardiness and fruit quality. B96{CF}

Citrus latifolia → Citrus aurantifolia

Citrus x latipes - *Khasi papeda, Hampur arong* {GR} A large, grapefruit-like fruit having seedy white flesh with a very acid, spicy flavor. It is eaten fresh or processed. May be picked while still green, but after reaching full size and juice content, and held two to three months in cold storage. Very cold-hardy tree. REUTHER, TANAKA; I74

Citrus x limetta - *Limetta, Lumia* {S} The fruit has acid to acidless flesh, the acid cultivars being used as a substitute for lemon. REUTHER, TANAKA; F85

CULTIVARS {GR}

Mediterranean Sweet: (Limetta Romana, Limoncello) Medium-sized, flattened fruit with a prominent nipple; rind thin, light yellowish-orange, adherent; flesh pale yellow, juicy, acidless, insipidly sweet; segments about 11. Tree large, vigorous, upright-spreading; highly productive. Blooms somewhat throughout the year but mainly in spring. REUTHER; *O4*

Citrus x limettioides - *Sweet lime, Lima* {S} The fruit is eaten raw, cooked or preserved. It is very much appreciated in Central America, where it is made into a popular soft drink called *Lim-Jay*. MORTON 1987a, REUTHER, TANAKA, WILLIAMS, L.; N84 (also see Rootstocks, page 470)

CULTIVARS {GR}

Palestine: (Indian) Fruit medium in size, subglobose to oblong or short-elliptic, sometimes faintly ribbed. Seeds few. Rind thin to very thin; surface smooth to very smooth; tightly adherent; color greenish to orange yellow at maturity. Flesh straw-yellow, tender, very juicy; flavor insipid because of lack of acid, and with a slightly bitter aftertaste. REUTHER; *G49*{DW}, I83M, *J73M*{S}, N18{SC}

Citrus limon - *Lemon* {S} The acid fruits and their juice are commonly used in ades, tea, ice cream, sauces, salad dressings, marinades, etc. The peel is grated and used as a seasoning or candied in syrup. Also the source of an essential oil, *cedro oil*, used commercially in beverages, pastries, candies, and *liqueur d'or*. Dried leaves are sometimes mixed with tea leaves for flavoring. Preserved lemons are one of the indispensable ingredients of Moroccan cooking. The flowers are eaten in ice cream, fritters, jams and *lemon flower butter*. Tropical Asia, cultivated. JOHNS [Cul], MACNICOL [Re], MORTON 1987a [Cu], REUTHER, TANAKA, UPHOF, WOLFERT [Pre, Re]; F85, N84 (for cultivars see Lemon, page 371)

Citrus x limonia - *Mandarin lime, Lemandarin* {S} Natural hybrids. Probably C. limon x C. reticulata. The juice of the fruit is used to add a sour taste to foods. MORTON 1987a, REUTHER, TANAKA; N84 (also see Rootstocks, page 470)

CULTIVARS {GR}

Otaheite: (Otaheite Orange, Otaheite Rangpur) Fruit oblate to spherical, furrowed and rounded or slightly necked at the base. Peel orange with small oil glands; thin; pulp orange, juicy, slightly lime-like in aroma and flavor but bland with scarcely any acidity; seedless, or with 3 to 6 small, abortive seeds. Tree dwarf, spreading, thornless.

Considered to be a non-acid form of Rangpur. MORTON 1987a; B73M{DW}, E97{DW}, G96{DW}, I78{DW}

Rangpur: (Rangpur Lime, Canton Lemon) Small to medium-sized fruit, resembles a mandarin orange. Rind yellowish to reddish-orange, thin and moderately loose. Flesh orange, tender, juicy, strongly acid. Seeds fairly numerous. Fruits hold on tree for a long period. Makes excellent marmalade. Also said to be good for pink limeade. Tree usually vigorous and productive; comparatively few and small thorns; cold hardy. REUTHER, STURROCK; *D23M*, E3M{DW}, *F53M*, *G49*, I83M, *J73M*{S}

Citrus x macrophylla - *Alemow, Colo* Possibly C. limon x C. grandis. The strongly acid fruits are sometimes eaten. REUTHER, TANAKA; (for sources see Rootstocks, page 470)

Citrus madurensis* → *X Citrofortunella mitis

Citrus maxima* → *Citrus grandis

Citrus medica - *Citron* {S} Cultivated primarily for the thick rind of the fruit which is sliced and added to salads, or candied and used in fruit-cakes, cannoli, puddings, confectionery, sweet rolls, etc. It is also made into the liqueurs *kitrinos* and *cédratine*. Candied citron can be mixed with nuts to form a stuffing for dates and figs. The juice of some improved cultivars can be utilized in beverages and desserts. Tropical Asia, cultivated. BIANCHINI, HESSELTINE, JOHNS [Cul], MORTON 1987a [Cu], RAY, REUTHER, VON WELANETZ; F68{PL}, F85, N18{SC}, N84, Q46

CULTIVARS {GR}

Corsican: Large, ellipsoid fruit; rind very thick and fleshy, lemon-yellow, rather rough and bumpy; flesh crisp and solid, lacking in juice, seedy; flavor sweet, without acid. Tree small, open and spreading, moderately thorny. Said to the best and most important citron in Corsica. REUTHER; T73M{SC}

Diamante: Large, long-oval to ellipsoid fruit, broadly nippled at the apex; rind smooth, very thick and fleshy, lemon-yellow at maturity; flesh crisp, lacking in juice, but acid, like lemon; seedy. Tree small, open and spreading, moderately thorny. The principal cultivar of Italy. REUTHER; *O4*

Earle: Large, ellipsoid to oblong fruit; rind smooth, very thick and fleshy, light orange-yellow; flesh white or very light yellow, sour; seeds numerous, 60 to 70; season more or less throughout the year; closely resembles Diamante. Tree small, spreading, open, thorny. Originated in Herradura, Cuba by F.S. Earle. Introduced into California in 1914. REUTHER; I83M

Etrog: Fruit medium-small, ellipsoid or lemon shaped; seedy. Lemon yellow at maturity. Rind thick and fleshy; surface slightly ribbed, somewhat rough and bumpy. Flesh crisp and firm, low in juice content; flavor acid. Tree smaller and less vigorous than most citrons. The official citron used in the Jewish Feast of the Tabernacles ritual. The entire fruit is eaten. MORTON 1987a, REUTHER; *D23M*, *G49*, I83M, N18{SC}

Etrog Variegated: Very rare variegated form. Large new leaves emerge a lustrous red-pink streaked rose, then harden to leathery green with brilliant butter-yellow variegation. The fruit is also striped. E48

Fingered: (Buddha's Hand, Buddha's Fingers, Bushukan) The fruit is corrugated, wholly or partly split into a number of finger-like sections. Usually pulp is lacking, or if present is very scanty; seedless or with loose seeds. It is highly fragrant and is used in China and Japan for perfuming rooms and clothing and as an offering on temple altars. Also candied or made into sweetmeats. MORTON 1987a, REUTHER, TANAKA; *D23M*, E48, I83M, J22, N18{SC}

Citrus meyeri* → *Citrus limon

Citrus mitis* → *X Citrofortunella mitis

Citrus myrtifolia* → *Citrus aurantium

Citrus x natsudaidai - *Natsu-mikan, Japanese summer-grapefruit* {GR} Natural hybrid. Possibly C. grandis x C. reticulata. The fruit is eaten fresh or in salads. In Japan, its juice is mixed with that of mandarin, diluted with sweetened and flavored water, and made into ades. Also canned or bottled. The pulp is sometimes canned in syrup or made into candies. Peel is made into marmalade, jam, or candies. REUTHER, TANAKA; *Q93*

Citrus x nobilis (C. reticulata x C. sinensis) - *Tangor* {S} Natural and artificial hybrids. Mandarin x sweet orange. The fruit is usually eaten out-of-hand. MORTON 1987a; F85

CULTIVARS {GR}

King: (King Mandarin, King of Siam) Fruit large, oblate to depressed globose. Rind thick, moderately adherent but peelable. Deep yellowish-orange to orange at maturity. Segments 12 to 14, readily separable. Flesh deep orange, tender, moderately juicy; flavor rich, of very fine quality. Seeds few to many. Late to very late in maturity and stores well on the tree. Tree moderately vigorous, upright and open in growth habit. F68, J22

Mency: Medium-small, slightly oblate, necked fruit; rind reddish-orange, peels readily; flesh sprightly, acid, seedy; ripens early. Sensitive to sunburn and does not hold well on the tree, but good for home use. Mediterranean Sweet orange x Dancy tangerine. Originated by H.B. Frost. REUTHER; N18{S}

Murcott: (Honey Murcott) Medium-sized, oblate to subglobose fruit. Rind thin, rather tightly adherent and not readily peelable; color yellowish-orange at maturity. Segments 11 to 12, moderately adherent. Flesh orange, tender, very juicy; flavor very rich and sprightly. Seeds small, few to numerous. Medium-late in maturity. Tree medium in vigor and size, upright growing. REUTHER; C57M{PR}, E99G{PR}, F68, I76M{PR}, I83M, N18{SC}

Ortanique: Large, very broadly obovoid to slightly oblate fruit. Rind thin, leathery, rather tightly adherent but peelable; color bright yellowish-orange at maturity. Segments 10 to 12. Flesh orange, juicy; distinctive rich, acid-sweet flavor. Late midseason in maturity and holds well on the tree. Tree moderately vigorous, medium-large, spreading and drooping, almost thornless. I83M, J83T{PR}, N18{SC}, *O97*

Temple: (Temple Orange, Royal Mandarin) Medium-large, very broadly obovate to slightly subglobose fruit. Rind deep reddish-orange, medium-thick, moderately adherent but readily peelable. Segments 10 to 12. Flesh orange, tender, juicy; flavor rich and spicy. Medium-late in maturity. Tree of medium vigor, spreading and bushy, somewhat thorny. More cold-sensitive than any of the mandarins or oranges. C57M{PR}, E99G{PR}, F68, *G49*, I76M{PR}, I83M, J22, N18{SC}

Umatilla: Medium-large, broadly ovate fruit; rind medium-thick, reddish-orange, moderately adherent; flesh orange, tender, very juicy, flavor rich but acid, of fine quality; ripens medium-late. Tree slow growing, spreading, productive; resembles Satsuma. Ruby orange x Satsuma mandarin. Grown as a specialty fruit for gift-boxes in Florida. MORTON 1987a, REUTHER; T73M{SC}

Citrus x paradisi (C. sinensis x C. grandis) - *Grapefruit* {S} Natural hybrid. Sweet orange x pummelo. Fruits are widely eaten out of hand as a breakfast fruit, used in fruit salads, or made into juice. An elegant dessert can be prepared by adding honey or brown sugar, butter, and some sherry or rum to grapefruit halves and broiling until browned. Grapefruit juice can be made into excellent vinegar or fermented into wine. The peel is candied and its essential oil is employed in soft-drink flavoring. Grapefruit seed oil, when bleached and refined is used as a culinary oil. CARCIONE, JOHNS [Cul],

MORTON 1987a [Cu], REUTHER, UPHOF; F85 (for cultivars see Grapefruit, page 349)

Citrus x pennivesiculata - *Gajanimma, Carabao lime* {S} The pleasantly acid juice can be used as a condiment. Also used as a tristeza resistant rootstock. ROM, TANAKA; N18

Citrus pyriformis* → *Citrus limon

Citrus reticulata - *Mandarin, Tangerine, Satsuma* {S} The fruits are eaten out of hand, juiced, preserved in syrup, added to salads, or used in confectionery, gelatins, puddings, cakes, liqueurs, etc. When dried, the peel has a sweet, spicy flavor and is used as a condiment and to cut the odors of certain dishes. Mandarin peel oil is employed commercially in flavoring hard candy, ice cream, chewing gum, and bakery goods. Southeast Asia, cultivated. CHANG, W. [Re], JOHNS, MORTON 1987a, REUTHER, UPHOF; C27G{PR}, F85, N18 (for cultivars see Mandarin, page 381, and Rootstocks, page 470)

Citrus sinensis - *Sweet orange* {S} Fruits are eaten fresh, juiced, added to fruit salads, or made into wine. Orange juice is canned or bottled, or used in sherbets, ice cream, jellies, confectioneries, cocktails, etc. The peel is candied, used for flavoring, or processed into marmalade. Flowers are eaten as a vegetable or made into tea. Cultivated. JOHNS [Cul], MACNICOL [Re], MORTON 1987a [Cu, Pro], REUTHER, TANAKA; F85, *J73M*, N18, N84, O93 (for cultivars see Orange, page 407 and Rootstocks, page 470)

Citrus sudachi* → *Citrus ichangensis

Citrus x sunki - *Sunki, Suenkat* The fruit has a strong, spicy rind with a distinctive aroma, and acid flesh. Mostly used as a rootstock. REUTHER, TANAKA; (for sources see Rootstocks, page 470)

Citrus taiwanica* → *Citrus aurantium

Citrus trifoliata* → *Poncirus trifoliata

Citrus yuko* → *Citrus ichangensis

Citrus x sp. (C. x paradisi x C. grandis) - *Pummelit* {GR} Artificial hybrid. Grapefruit x pummelo. Fruits are eaten as a breakfast or salad fruit. The result of a breeding program at the University of California, Riverside in which an essentially acidless pummelo, which imparts low acidity to its progeny, was crossed with a seedy, white tetraploid grapefruit. SOOST 1980.

CULTIVARS

Melogold: (Melogold Grapefruit) Fruit resembles white-fleshed grapefruit cultivars but is more pummelo-like than Oroblanco; larger than Marsh grapefruit and Oroblanco. Exterior rind color is slow to develop but is comparable to Marsh late in the season; thickness is equal to Marsh, thinner than Oroblanco. Flesh tender and juicy, seperating well from the membranes; juicier than Oroblanco; flavor more like a pummelo. SOOST 1986; *A71*, I83M, *M61M*, N18{SC}

Oroblanco: (Oroblanco Grapefruit) Fruit size and shape similar to Marsh grapefruit. Peel color is paler than Marsh; peel thickness is greater. Exterior color is not well developed in fruit harvested in November at Lindcove, California. Flesh is slightly paler with a larger hollow core; tender and juicy, seperating well from segment membranes. Lacks the bitterness of grapefruit, particularly grapefruits grown in cooler areas. Recommended for indoor citrus growers. SOOST 1980; *A71*, *D23M*, D37{DW}, *G49*, I83M, J22, N18{SC}, *N40*{PR}

Citrus x sp. (C. x paradisi x C. sinensis) - *Orangelo* {GR} Natural hybrid. Grapefruit x sweet orange. The fruit is cut in half and eaten with a spoon like a grapefruit, peeled and the sections eaten individually, or they can be squeezed for their juice. Sections can be canned in syrup and the rind can be candied successfully. MORTON 1987a, REUTHER.

CULTIVARS

Chironja: Fruit round to pear-shaped, necked, equal to grapefruit in size; peel a brilliant yellow, slightly adherent, easy to remove; the inner peel non-bitter. Pulp yellow-orange, with 9 to 13 segments having tender walls and much juice; the mild flavor reminiscent of both orange and grapefruit, hardly bitter or acid even when immature. Seed count averages 11, with some fruits having as few as 2. Tree productive. Discovered in Puerto Rico in 1956. MORTON 1987a, REUTHER; I83M, J22

Citrus x sp. (C. x paradisi x C. reticulata) - *Tangelo* {GR} Natural and artificial hybrids. Grapefruit or pummelo x mandarin. The fruits are generally highly colored, aromatic, distinctively and richly flavored, with thin, smooth, and only moderately loose rinds. Most of them are eaten out of hand. On the whole, they comprise the most important group of interspecific hybrids in the genus Citrus. REUTHER.

CULTIVARS

Allspice: Fruit medium-small, slightly oblate to globose; color orange-yellow; seedy. Rind thin, slightly pebbled, and rather adherent. Flesh tender and juicy; rich, tart, spicy flavor and aroma. Midseason in maturity and loses quality if left on the tree much past maturity. Tree and foliage mandarin-like in appearance. I83M

Cocktail: (Cocktail Grapefruit) Tangelo x sweet orange. Medium-sized, rather seedy fruit; deep yellow-orange flesh; very sweet flavor, similar to a grapefruit but with orange overtones. Easy to peel. Produces good-sized fruit even along coastal areas of southern California. I83M

Minneola: (Honeybell) Large, oblate to obovate fruit; neck usually fairly prominent; seeds comparatively few. Rind deep reddish-orange, medium-thin, smooth, moderately adherent. Segments 10 to 12. Flesh orange, tender, juicy, aromatic; flavor rich and tart. Medium late in maturity. Tree vigorous and productive. Cross-pollination recommended. REUTHER; *A71*, *D23M*, D37{DW}, E3M{DW}, E99G{PR}, F68, *G49*, I76M{PR}, I83M, J22, *M61M*, *M61M*{DW}, N18{SC}

Orlando: Fruit medium-large, broadly oblate to subglobose; without neck; seedy. Rind orange, thin, slightly pebbled, fairly adherent. Segments numerous, 12 to 14. Flesh orange, tender, very juicy; flavor mildly sweet. Season of maturity late. Tree somewhat more cold resistant than Minneola. Cross-pollination recommended. REUTHER; *D13*, E31M, G17, I76M{PR}, I83M, N18{S}, N18{SC}

Pearl: Medium-small, slightly oblate fruit. Rind yellow, comparatively smooth, thin and tightly adherent. Flesh firm but tender, juicy, sweet, aroma unique; flavor pleasantly sweet; seedy. Medium-early in maturity and loses quality if left on the tree past maturity. Resembles the grapefruit parent more than the mandarin. Tree vigorous, spreading, drooping; somewhat alternate bearing. N18{SC}

Sampson: Fruit medium-sized, globose to slightly obovate; often somewhat necked; color orange-yellow; seedy. Rind smooth, thin, relatively adherent. Flesh dull-orange, juicy, somewhat acid; flavor with distinctive bitterish tang. More like the grapefruit parent than the mandarin. Late-midseason maturity. Tree vigorous, spreading. E3M{DW}

Seminole: Medium-large, broadly-oblate fruit; color deep reddish-orange; seedy. Rind somewhat pebbled, thin, moderately adherent, though peelable. Flesh rich orange, tender, juicy; flavor sprightly and acid. Resembles Minneola in appearance, but peels easier and matures later. Tree vigorous and productive; self-fruitful. *O97*, *Q93*

Ugli: (Ugly Fruit) Fruit broadly obovoid, usually with a short, strongly furrowed neck; seeds few. Rind dull yellowish-orange, medium-thick, leathery, moderately rough and bumpy, loosely adherent. Segments about 12. Flesh orange, tender, very juicy; flavor rich and subacid. Maturity season late. Originated as a chance seedling in Jamaica around 1917. The grated rind makes a particularly pungent flavoring. MORTON 1987a, REUTHER, SCHNEIDER [Cul, Re]; F68, J22, *O97*, R77

Wekiwa: (Lavender Gem) Fruit medium-small, spherical to obovate or pear-shaped; rind medium-thick, fairly adherent, pale yellow; flesh tender, juicy, flavor sweet and mildly acid; ripens early. Under favorable conditions the rind is blushed with pink and the flesh is amber pink. Very popular specialty market fruit. Considered the finest flavored citrus fruit by many. Duncan grapefruit x Sampson tangelo. REUTHER; G44M{PR}, I83M, *N40*{PR}

Clausena domesticum → Clausena lansium

Clausena excavata - *Pink lime-berry* {S} The sweetish, ripe fruit is edible. Young leaves and flowers are aromatic and are added to curries, or used for flavoring other foods. Indonesia. BURKILL, PONGPANGAN, TANAKA; F85

Clausena lansium - *Wampee, Wampi* {PL} The aromatic, grape-like fruits are eaten fresh, preserved, dried, or made into jams, pies, and refreshing drinks. Flavor varies from sweet, subacid, to sour. The more acid forms are used in making jelly when fully grown but unripe, and fruit drinks when fully ripe. Leaves are put into curries. In Southeast Asia, a carbonated beverage resembling champagne is made by fermenting the fruit with sugar and straining off the juice. China, cultivated. MORTON 1987a, RAY, REUTHER, STURROCK, TANAKA; C56M, E29, E29{PR}, E29{S}, F68, I83M, N84{S}, P38{S}, Q46{S}, *Q93*

Correa alba - *Cape Barren tea* {PL} The leaves were once used as a tea substitute, particularly by sealers on Islands in Bass Strait. Australia. CRIBB; *F53M*

Dictamnus albus - *Fraxinella, Gas plant* {S} An infusion of the dried leaves forms a refreshing, aromatic tea. Mediterranean region to Eastern Asia. MARCIN, MORTON 1976, UPHOF; B9M{PL}, D95{PL}, E5M{PL}, E7M, G16, I39, K63G, *N71M*, O93

CULTIVARS

Pink: (Roseus) Deep pink flowers. Tea made from this form will be less lemony but has an added taste of almond and vanilla. MARCIN; B77, C9, C13M, C92, E5M{PL}, F80, H63{PL}, K38, K85{PL}, L66{PL}, L91M, N93M, O53M, *Q24*, S7M, etc.

White: (Alba) Showy white flowers. Tea made from this form has a lemony fragrance and taste. MARCIN; B77, C9, C13M, D62, E89M, F80, H63{PL}, J91{PL}, K38, K85{PL}, L66{PL}, L91M, O53M, *Q24*, S7M, etc.

Euodia daniellii - *Chôsen-goshuyu* {S} A cooking oil is extracted from the fruit. China-Korea. TANAKA; A50{PL}, A80M{PL}, B96{PL}, E7M, K38, K47T, K63G, M92{PL}, N37M{PL}, *N71M*, N84, O53M, O93, *R28*, S95, etc.

Evodia daniellii → Euodia daniellii

Fagara rhetsa - *Indian pepper* {S} The bark has a lime-pepper flavor and is added to foods as seasoning or cooked in syrup with spices and made into a relish. In South Vietnam, the leaves are used like hops in making rice beer. The unripe fruit has the flavor of orange peel and is used as a spice. Ripe seeds taste like lemon, with a burning after-sensation, and are used as a substitute for pepper. Indonesia. MORTON 1976; **Z25M**

Feronia elephantum → Feronia limonia

Feronia limonia - *Elephant apple, Wood apple* {S} The orange-sized, woody fruit has an aromatic, sour-sweet, somewhat mealy pulp that is eaten raw or made into jellies, preserves, chutneys, and sherbets. The jelly is purple and much like that made from black currants. In Sri Lanka, a popular drink is made by mixing wood apple pulp with coconut milk and jaggery. Young leaves can be eaten raw. Southern Asia, cultivated. MACMILLAN [Re], MORTON 1987a, REUTHER; F85, N84

Fortunella x crassifolia - *Meiwa kumquat, Large round kumquat* {GR} The fruit is round, relatively large, with a tender, sweet rind and relatively sweet or subacid juice. It is considered the best of the kumquats for eating out-of-hand, rind and all. In China, a sweetmeat called *chin-chü-ping* is made by preserving the fruit in sugar. Japan-China, cultivated. MORTON 1987a, RAY, REUTHER, SCHNEIDER [Cul, Re], STURROCK, TANAKA; C56M, *D23M*, F68, F85{S}, G17, *G49*, G96{DW}, I83M, K67

Fortunella hindsii - *Hong Kong wild kumquat, Formosan kumquat* {GR} The small, brilliantly colored fruits are used for making sweetmeats and candy. Although small, the Chinese are said to prize these fruits and to preserve them in honey for use as a spicy flavoring. In the western world, the very thorny shrub is grown only as an ornamental potted plant. Eastern Asia. MORTON 1987a, REUTHER; F85{S}, G96{DW}, M82

Fortunella japonica - *Marumi kumquat, Round kumquat* {GR} Fruits are made into jams, jellies, and preserves. The peel is golden-yellow, smooth, thinner and somewhat sweeter than that of the oval kumquat. The tree is less vigorous, somewhat thorny, and considerably more cold-tolerant. Japan, cultivated. MORTON 1987a, REUTHER, SIMMONS 1972; N18{SC}, N84{S}, *O4*, P38{S}, S59

Fortunella margarita - *Nagami kumquat, Oval kumquat* {GR} The fruits are eaten fresh, preserved in syrup, pickled in vinegar, used as a garnish, or made into marmalades, jams, sauces, and jellies. For eating out-of-hand rind and all, first squeeze and massage the fruit to combine the flavors. After ripening, the fruit gradually loses water content, becomes richer in flavor, and is then at its best for making preserves. Japan-China, cultivated. CARCIONE, JOHNS [Cul], REUTHER, RICHARDSON [Re], SCHNEIDER [Cul, Re], SIMMONS 1972, STURROCK; *A71*, C56M, *D23M*, E3M{DW}, E31M, F68, F85{S}, G17, *G49*, G96{DW}, I83M, J22, J61M{DW}, *M61M*, N18{SC}, N84{S}, O93{S}, etc.

Fortunella spp. x (Citrus sinensis x Poncirus trifoliata) - *Citrangequat* {GR} Artificial hybrid. Kumquat x citrange. The hybrids combine the cold-hardiness of the kumquat and trifoliate orange, being generally more cold-resistant than the citrange, calamondin, and kumquat. REUTHER.

CULTIVARS

Macciaroli: Similar to Sinton, but the fruit is more acid and the tree has a greater tendency towards trifoliation. It is probably the preferred ornamental because its showy flower clusters bloom almost year-round and have a gardenia-like fragrance. A cultivar most commonly grown in Arizona and Texas. RAY; I83M

Thomasville: Nagami kumquat x Willits citrange. Small, globose to oval fruit, averaging 1 1/2 inches in diameter; rind thin, yellow to orange-yellow. Pulp juicy, pleasantly acid when immature, sweetish at maturity; color light green to amber; segments 7 or 8; seeds 0 to 12, averaging 6, small. Good for eating out-of-hand when mature; also excellent for ade or marmalade. Season October to December but juicy and suitable for ade from July to October. Reliably cold tolerant to 10° F. BROOKS 1972, MORTON 1987a; I74, K67

Glycosmis pentaphylla - *Jamaica mandarin orange* {S} The ripe fruit is eaten. Tropical Asia. HEDRICK 1919, WATT; F85, N84, P38, Q46

Limonia acidissima → Feronia limonia

Microcitrus australasica - *Australian finger lime* {PL} Ripe fruits are said to be refreshingly sour when eaten out of hand. They can also be made into a pleasant-flavored marmalade which has a distinctive perfume and is also ornamental, the sliced rings of fruit looking like miniature cartwheels. Use a recipe for lemon marmalade but reduce the amount of water added by about a quarter as the finger limes have less pectin. Australia. CRIBB; I74, I83M

Murraya exotica* → *Murraya paniculata

Murraya koenigii - *Curry leaf* {S} The pungent, aromatic leaves are a common ingredient in curries, chutneys, stews, etc. They are first fried in oil until crisp, at the start of preparing a curry. The leaves retain their flavor and aroma even after drying. When powdered in a grinder or blender the dried leaves can be used in marinades or sprinkled on vegetables or yogurt. Peppery fruits are edible. India. BURKILL, JOSEPH, MACMILLAN, MORTON 1976, REUTHER, SOLOMON, VON WELANETZ; A79M, A88T{PR}, C94{PR}, F85, I83M{PL}, J22{PL}, N84, O42, P38, Q46

Murraya paniculata - *Jasmine orange, Orange jessamine* {S} The leaves are used to flavor curries. Fragrant flowers are used for scenting tea. The red fruit is also edible. Southern Asia. BROUK, HEDRICK 1919, TANAKA; A79M, C9M, C56M{PL}, E7M, E48{PL}, F85, G25M, G96{PL}, *I61*, I83M{PL}, *J25*{PL}, J27{PL}, *L5M*, O42, O53M, P5, *Q32*, etc.

Poncirus trifoliata - *Trifoliate orange* The rind of the fruit can be candied. In China, the bitter fruits are used for seasoning. When first picked the fruit gives very little juice when pressed but after being kept for two weeks they yield about twenty percent juice. A drink can be made from the diluted juice. Young leaves are occasionally boiled and eaten. China. SIMMONS 1972 [Cu], TANAKA; (for cultivars see Rootstocks, page 470)

Ptelea trifoliata - *Hop tree, Wafer-ash* {S} The bitter fruits are sometimes used as a substitute for hops in making beer. A decoction of them added to yeast is said to make it rise more rapidly. Eastern North America. FERNALD, HEDRICK 1919; D95{PL}, I53{PL}, I60{PL}, K38, K47T, K63G, *K89*{PL}, L91M, O53M, O93, P49, *P63*, *R28*, R78, S95, etc.

Ruta chalepensis - *Egyptian rue* {PL} Leaves are used as a condiment. Mediterranean region. ENGLER; M82, N84{S}

Ruta graveolens - *Rue, Herb-of-Grace* {PL} The strongly aromatic leaves are minced and used sparingly in salads, ragouts, vinegars, sandwiches, and vegetable juices. They can also be pickled, brewed into tea, or used for seasoning cheese and chicken. In North Africa, the seeds are employed in the preparation of a palm wine, known as *laqmí*. Mediterranean region, cultivated. GRIEVE, HEDRICK 1919, LATHROP, MACNICOL, MORTON 1976, POPENOE, P., ROOT 1980b [Cul], TANAKA; C3, C3{S}, C13M{S}, C67M, F21, G84, H46{S}, I77M, J66, K22, N19M, N45, N84{S}, O53M{S}

Ruta montana - *Mountain rue* {S} Said to be used as a condiment. Southeastern Europe. ENGLER; N84

Severinia buxifolia - *Chinese box-orange* {S} In China, the plant is esteemed for its leaves, which are used in the preparation of yeast cakes. For this reason it is called *tsau'ping lak* in Cantonese, meaning *wine cake thorn*. Southeast Asia. REUTHER, TANAKA; F85, *L5M*, N84, P38

Skimmia laureola - *Ner, Chamlani* {S} The strongly aromatic leaves are eaten in curries or used for flavoring other foods. Himalayan region. ATAL, TANAKA, WATT; F80, F85, N84, O46, O53M, P86{PL}, Q40

Toddalia asiatica - *Sarukake-mikan* {S} Leaves and the acid, orange fruits are eaten. Also used as a flavoring for other foods. China. ALTSCHUL, FOX, F., TANAKA; N84

Triphasia aurantiola* → *Triphasia trifolia

Triphasia trifolia - *Lime berry, Limon de China* {S} The aromatic, juicy, somewhat mucilaginous fruits are eaten raw, stewed, pickled, or made into jams and preserves. Tropical Asia, cultivated. HEDRICK 1919, KENNARD, TANAKA; E29, E29{PL}, E29{PR}, F85, *L5M*, Q46

Zanthoxylum alatum* → *Zanthoxylum armatum

Zanthoxylum armatum - *Winged prickly ash* {S} Young leaves are used as a condiment. The seeds, known as *Chinese pepper*, are widely employed as a seasoning in China and India. Tropical Asia. BURKILL, MORTON 1976, WATT; F85, N84, O53M, Q12, Q40

Zanthoxylum piperitum - *Sanshô, Japanese pepper* {PL} The dried fruit hulls are ground and used for flavoring soups, buckwheat noodles, and rice dishes. They are often heated to bring out their full aroma, and then combined with salt to make a table seasoning. The whole seeds, called *sansho-no-mi*, are simmered with shoyu and mirin to make *tsukudani*. *Kinome*, the young shoots, are used as a garnish for broiled fish, and lend flavor to soups, salads, and miso. Flowers and immature fruits are pickled or preserved in soy sauce. Japan-China, cultivated. COST 1988 [Cul], MORTON 1976, SHURTLEFF 1975 [Re], SHURTLEFF 1976 [Re], VON WELANETZ [Pre], YASHIRODA; D95, G20M{PR}, N49M{PR}, N84{S}, *P39*{S}, P86

Zanthoxylum planispinum - *Fuyu-sanshô* {S} Young leaves are eaten. The peel of the fruit is used as a spice. Eastern Asia. TANAKA; O67

Zanthoxylum rhetsa* → *Fagara rhetsa

Zanthoxylum simulans - *Szechwan pepper, Chinese pepper, Hua-chiao* {PL} The fruit is dried and used as a condiment, either whole or ground to a powder. It is stronger and more pungent than black pepper. Popular for making seasoned peanut oil, used for stir-fried dishes and for dressing Chinese salads. Dried whole fruits, called *Szechwan peppercorns*, are available in Chinese and specialty stores. China. CHANG, W. [Re], COST 1988 [Cul, Re], TANAKA; C27G{PR}, N37M, N84{S}

SALICACEAE

Populus tremuloides - *Quaking aspen* {PL} The sap of the tree is potable. Inner bark is also used as food. North America. YANOVSKY; C33, C38, D95, E87, *G66*, *G66*{S}, *G89M*, H49, *H90*, I15{S}, I47{S}, J26, *J75M*, *K89*

Salix babylonica - *Weeping willow* {PL} Young leaves, shoots, and flower buds are parboiled and eaten. Older leaves are used to adulterate tea. Also the source of a manna-like substance. Cultivated. DONKIN, TANAKA; *B41*, *B52*, D95, *F51*, H4, *M69M*, M76

Salix caprea - *French pussy-willow* {PL} Source of an edible manna. Europe, cultivated. DONKIN; B9M, B53, B67, C9, D95, E47, *G66*, I77M, J7, K22, *K89*, M92

Salix daphnoides - *Arctic willow* {PL} The young, tender shoots and catkins are eaten fresh or in seal oil by the Eskimos of Alaska. Young leaves are especially rich in vitamin C. Growing tips of the underground rhizomes can be peeled and eaten, raw or cooked. The inner bark is eaten raw. Northern Europe. GIBBONS 1979, HELLER, UPHOF; P86

Salix fragilis - *Crack willow* {S} The leaves and young branches yield a saccharine exudation used as food. Eurasia. DONKIN, HEDRICK 1919; P86

Salix gracilistyla - *Japanese pussy willow, Neko-yanagi* {PL} Young leaves and flowers are parboiled and eaten as a vegetable. Leaves are used as a substitute for tea. Eurasia. TANAKA; K22, P86

Salix pulchra* → *Salix daphnoides

SALICORNIACEAE

Arthrocnemum glaucum - *Glasswort* {S} The plant is used in some parts of Greece in a garlic porridge. Mediterranean region. UPHOF; **Y10**

Arthrocnemum macrostachyum → *Arthrocnemum glaucum*

Salicornia europaea - *Saltwort, Glasswort, Marsh samphire, Pickle weed, Sea bean, Pousse-pierre* {S} Young, salty stems and leaves are eaten raw in salads, cooked as a potherb, pickled, added to soups, or used as a garnish. For pickles, the tender stems and branches are first boiled in their own salted-water before being put in spiced oil or vinegar. The protein-rich seeds are eaten, and can be refined into a high-quality edible oil similar to safflower oil. Northern temperate region. ANGIER, FERNALD, GIBBONS 1964, LAUNERT, MABEY [Cul, Pre], MICHAEL [Re], NIETHAMMER, SCHNEIDER [Re], TANAKA; C11T{PR}, *N40*{PR}, N84, O48

SALSOLACEAE

Salsola kali - *Russian thistle, Tumbleweed* {S} Young shoots are eaten raw in salads, put in soups, or boiled and eaten like spinach. They make an excellent vegetable when served with butter, vinegar or lemon juice, bacon strips or hard-boiled egg slices, or a cream sauce. Because of their mild flavor they can be mixed with stronger flavored greens such as mustard. Northern temperate region. CLARKE [Re], GIBBONS 1979, HARRINGTON, H., NIETHAMMER [Re]; C4, D58

Salsola soda - *Barilla plant* {S} Young leaves and stems are boiled and eaten as a vegetable. Mediterranean region to Southwest Asia. LOVELOCK, UPHOF; **V84, W92, Y10**

Sarcobatus vermiculatus - *Greasewood* {S} The tender young twigs can be cut into short pieces, boiled until tender, then served with butter or cream sauce. Seeds are occasionally consumed. Southwestern North America. KIRK, MEDSGER, UPHOF, YANOVSKY; F85

SALVADORACEAE

Salvadora persica - *Mustard tree* {S} Young shoots and leaves are eaten in salads or prepared into a sauce. The aromatic fruits are eaten fresh, dried like currants, made into a drink, or used as a substitute for mustard seeds. A vegetable salt, called *kegr*, is derived from the ash of the plant. A fat obtained from the seeds is used as a substitute for vegetable butters in chocolate manufacture. Tropical Africa and Asia. DALZIEL, HEDRICK 1919, MENNINGER, TANAKA, UPHOF, WATT; **U94M, Z69M**

SAMBUCACEAE

Sambucus australis - *Seco* {S} Fruits are made into preserves. In Argentina they are commonly used for making wine. Chile, Argentina. ALTSCHUL, UPHOF; **U71M**

Sambucus caerulea → *Sambucus glauca*

Sambucus canadensis - *American elder, Canadian elderberry* {PL} Purple fruits are edible, being high in vitamin C. Usually used in pies, jellies, jams, preserves, drinks, sauces, chutneys, fruit soups, pancakes, muffins, or fermented into wine. Unripe fruits and unexpanded flowers are pickled like capers. The flowers are dipped in batter and made into fritters, added to pancakes and muffins to lighten them and provide a distinct flavor, or made into *elder blow* wine. Dried flowers are used for tea. North America, cultivated. ANGIER, FERNALD, GIBBONS 1962 [Re], MEDSGER; B9M, C81M, E61, F80{S}, G89{S}, H49, I37M, I99{S}, K63G{S}, *K89*, *M69M*, N9M, N9M{S}, N84{S}, P49{S}, etc.

CULTIVARS {GR}

Adams: Since the distinctions between Adams #1 and Adams #2 are somewhat minor, they are not always propagated as such and are merely sold as Adams. For general descriptions see Adams #1 and Adams #2. *A74*, A91, B73M, *C47*, *D35M*, E3, H49, J32, L27M, N24M

Adams #1: Fruit clusters and berries exceptionally large, berries somewhat larger than Adams #2. Plant vigorous, productive; only partially self-fruitful, cross-pollination required. Selected from wild bushes. Originated in Union Springs, New York by William W. Adams. Introduced in 1926. BROOKS 1972; C63, G16, H65, *J63M*

Adams #2: Fruit cluster exceptionally large, berries somewhat smaller than Adams #1. Plant strong, vigorous; only partially self-fruitful, cross-pollination required; somewhat more productive than Adams #1. Originated in Union Springs, New York, by William W. Adams. Introduced in 1926. BROOKS 1972; B75, *J63M*

Ebony King: Waxy, black fruit with high quality crimson juice. Delicate flavor and aroma. Excellent for wine, jelly and pies. Very productive tree, may produce 25 pounds of fruit annually; evergreen during the winter, retaining leaves at temperatures as low as 15° F. Adapted to Southeastern growing conditions. Discovered in Georgia. M31M

Hidden Springs: Fruits ripen evenly in the cluster, making them much easier to sort. Hardy to Zone 5. A local selection by Hidden Springs Nursery. The original tree grew 14 feet tall by the site of an old log home. F43M

Johns: Fruit clusters and berries large; ripens earlier than Adams. Plant extremely vigorous; only partially self-fruitful, cross pollination is recommended. Originated by the Nova Scotia Experiment Station. B73M, B75, C58, C63, E3, H49, H65, J32, J61M, *J63M*, L27M, N24M

Kent: Fruit size and quality equal to Adams but ripens 7 to 10 days earlier. Plant vigorous, productive. Open pollinated seedling of Adams. Introduced in 1947 by E.L. Eaton, Canada Department of Agriculture. BROOKS 1972; C58

Nova: Fruit large, matures early and uniformly in the cluster; sweeter than Victoria and Kent which it resembles. Plant suckers easily; readily propagated by dormant cuttings of one-year old canes. Open-pollinated seedling of Adams #2. Introduced in 1959 at Kentville, Nova Scotia. BROOKS 1972; A91, *C47*, C58, *D35M*, D69, G16, G23, G71, I36, J7, L33, N24M

Scotia: Fruit large, ripens early and uniformly in the cluster; sweeter than Kent and Victoria which it resembles. Plant suckers easily; readily propagated by dormant cuttings of one-year old canes. Open-pollinated seedling of Adams #2. Introduced in 1959 by the Canada Department of Agriculture, Kentville, Nova Scotia. C58

Tarheel: Very vigorous tree, will produce growth up to 6 feet the first year and will often fill with berries the first season, as late as October in colder areas. Berries have a flavor that is subtle and delicate, yet tangy. M31M

Victoria: Fruit size and quality equal to Adams but ripens 3 to 6 days earlier. Plant moderately vigorous, productive, readily propagated by dormant cuttings. Open-pollinated seedling of Adams #2. Introduced in 1957 by E.L. Eaton, Canada Department of Agriculture Research Station, Kentville, Nova Scotia. BROOKS 1972; C58

York: Fruit cluster heavy; berry large, larger than any named cultivar; in a four year test averaged only 9.9% soluble solids, about 3% less than Johns, Scotia and Victoria; ripens after Adams #1 and Adams #2. Plant very large, more productive than Adams #1 and Adams #2. Introduced in 1964 by the New York State Experiment

Station, Geneva, New York. A91, *C47*, C58, *D35M*, D69, G23, *G89M*, H49, I36, J33, J61M, *J63M*, L27M, L33, N24M, etc.

Sambucus chinensis → *Sambucus javanica*

Sambucus glauca - *Blueberry elder, Blue elderberry* {S} The fruits are sometimes eaten raw but they are usually dried before being used in jellies, juices, wines, pies, fruit sauces, sherbets, soups, relishes, etc. Flower clusters are made into fritters or pickles, while the individual flowers can be separated and used in pancakes, muffins, syrups, or vinegars. A tea is brewed from the dried flowers. Western North America. BRYAN [Cul, Re], GIBBONS 1979, HARRINGTON, H., KIRK; A2, A91{PL}, *C73*{PL}, D95{PL}, E15, *E66M*, G59M{PL}, *G66*, I15, I47, J26{PL}, *J75M*{PL}, K47T, K63G, M35M{PL}, N84, etc.

Sambucus javanica - *Chinese elderberry, Chieh-ku-ts'ao, Thuôc moi* {S} Fruits are preserved, used in confectionery, or made into a beverage. Stems, leaves and roots are parboiled and eaten. Tropical Asia. TANAKA, UPHOF; F85

Sambucus melanocarpa - *Black elderberry* {PL} The fruits are used in sauces, pies, muffins, wines, or made into juice. Elderberry juice can be used as a beverage, mixed with other fruit juices and sweetened to taste, or made into syrup and jelly. In making jelly, if the juice is mixed half and half with the juice of crabapples or unripe grapes, additional pectin is not needed. Western North America. TURNER 1979 [Re]; I15{S}, J26

Sambucus mexicana - *Mexican elder* {PL} Dried fruits are used in pies, jellies, wines, syrups, etc. Flower clusters are dipped in batter, fried, and sprinkled with sugar. Individual flowers can be shaken from the stems to add flavor and vitamins to pancakes, muffins, and cakes. Southwestern North America. CLARKE [Re], UPHOF; *C73*, G60

Sambucus nigra - *European elder, Black elder* {S} The fruits are used in wines, chutneys, ketchups, preserves, jams, pies, juices, or made into *pontack sauce*. In Portugal, they are employed for coloring inexpensive port wine. The juice, mixed with equal parts of honey, is used as a spread. Dried flowers are brewed into a sweet tea. Flowers are made into sparkling wines, drinks, fritters, or are added to salads. Shake the blossoms over a salad at the last moment, without washing them, or the fragrance will be lost. Leaves are used to impart green color to oils and fats. Eurasia, cultivated. GRIEVE [Re], HEDRICK 1919, LARKCOM 1984, LAUNERT, MABEY [Re], MACNICOL, MARCIN, TANAKA; A91{PL}, C11, C38{PL}, D62, F80, *G66*, K20, K38, *N71M*, N93M, O93, P49, *P63*, *R28*, R53M, R78, S95, etc.

Sambucus pubens - *American red elder* {S} The bitter fruits are eaten raw or cooked. They were a common food of the coastal Indians of British Columbia. A tea-like beverage is prepared from the roots. North America. TURNER 1979, YANOVSKY; *A74*{PL}, F85, K63G, N84

Sambucus pubens f. xanthocarpa - *Golden elderberry* {S} The golden-yellow fruits are edible. North America. SIMMONS 1972; **U7M**

Sambucus racemosa - *European red elder* {S} Mature fruits, after the seeds have been removed, are a good source of vitamin C and can be used in beverages, wines, and jellies. Eurasia. HELLER, LAUNERT, TANAKA; C9M, E15, *E66M*, *G66*, *G66*{PL}, I15, I47, *J75M*{PL}, K38, K47T, K64{PL}, N9M, N93M, O53M, O93, P49, etc.

Sambucus racemosa var. melanocarpa → *Sambucus melanocarpa*

Sambucus sieboldiana - *Niwatoko* {PL} Young leaves and buds are boiled and eaten as a vegetable or used as a substitute for tea. Japan, Korea. TANAKA; **U85**, **V45M**{S}

SANTALACEAE

Eucarya acuminata - *Quandong, Native peach* {S} When fully ripe, the thin, acid flesh of the fruit is eaten raw, used as a pie filling, or made into prized jams, jellies, and chutneys. It is rich in vitamin C. The flavor is said to improve when the fruits are dried and stored. Seed kernels, having 60% oil content and 25% protein, are roasted and eaten. Australia. CRIBB, MENNINGER, ROSENGARTEN; *N79M*, N84, O33, P5, *P17M*, P38, *Q25*, R15M, R33M, R47, S92, T7

Eucarya spicata - *Australian sandalwood* {S} The edible seeds are somewhat larger than the quandong and are enclosed in a hard shell that is somewhat thinner. They are highly regarded both for flavor and ease of extraction. Australia. MENNINGER; *N79M*, N84, O33, P5, *P17M*, P38, R15M, R33M, S92, T7

Leptomeria acida - *Currant bush* {S} The acid fruits are sometimes eaten raw, otherwise they are said to make uncommonly fine jellies and preserves. Australia. CRIBB, UPHOF; N84

Santalum acuminatum → *Eucarya acuminata*

Santalum album - *White sandalwood* {S} Bark is sometimes chewed instead of betel nuts. The essential oil, distilled from the heartwood and roots, is used as a flavoring in chewing gum, bakery products, ice cream, and candy. Tropical Asia. MORTON 1976, SCHERY, TANAKA; F85, N84, O93, P5, *P17M*, Q12, Q18, Q46

Santalum lanceolatum - *Lanceleaf sandalwood, Bush plum* {S} The edible fruits are deep blue or blue-black when ripe, smaller than Eucarya acuminata, and with sweetish flesh that is of a very agreeable taste. Australia. CRIBB; N84, R15M

Santalum spicatum → *Eucarya spicata*

SAPINDACEAE

Blighia sapida - *Akee, Vegetable brain* {S} Ripe, fleshy arils are eaten raw, fried in butter, curried, or used in filled pastries, soups, stews, soufflés and omelettes. In Jamaica, they are traditionally boiled with salted codfish, onions, and tomatoes. The underripe or overripe aril and the seeds are toxic. Flowers are used in the preparation of an aromatic water. Tropical Africa, cultivated. HAWKES [Re], IRVINE 1952, JOHNS [Cul], MORTON 1987a, POPENOE, W. 1920, RICHARDSON [Re]; A79M, E29, E29{PL}, E29{PR}, F68{PL}, F85, J36{PL}, N84

Blighia welwitschii - *Ankyewobiri* {S} The fragrant leaves are used for flavoring soup. Tropical Africa. IRVINE 1960; N84

Cubilia blancoi - *Kubili* {S} Nutritious seeds are eaten boiled or roasted, being of excellent quality. Contains 5.2% protein, 1.92% fat, 23.13% starch, and 18.83% other carbohydrates. The leaves are used as a vegetable. Indonesia-Philippines. CORONEL, MENNINGER, UPHOF; **X62**

Dimocarpus longan - *Longan* {S} The aril of the fruit is whitish, translucent, somewhat sweet but not as aromatic or flavorsome as the lychee. It is eaten out of hand, dried, preserved in syrup, cooked in sweet and sour dishes, or made into a liqueur. The black, smoky dried fruits are used in slow-cooked soups, or are made into a refreshing beverage. China, cultivated. CHANG, W. [Cul], GROFF, MORTON 1987a, POPENOE, W. 1920 [Cu, Pro], SCHNEIDER [Cul, Re], STURROCK; *B59*{PR}, C27G{PR}, C56M{PL}, E29, E29{PL}, E29{PR}, F85, N84, P38, *Q93*{PL}

CULTIVARS {GR}

Chompoo: (Pink Flesh) High quality fruit with a faint pink tinge in the flesh. It is not canned because of this coloration, pure white flesh being preferred. Matures mid July to early August. Originated in Thailand. *Q93*

Dang: (Red Stem) Heavy bearing cultivar with fair quality fruit but is not particularly crisp. Matures mid July to early August. Originated in Thailand. *Q93*

Haew: (Water Chestnut) A good canning cultivar, but it has a pronounced alternate bearing habit. Matures mid August to early September. Popular in the markets of Thailand where it originated. *Q93*

Isau: Small, round fruit, about 1 inch in diameter; medium-green, thin, brittle shell covered with small protuberances, easily opened; translucent flesh, about 1/4 inch thick, very sweet and juicy with a musky or melon-like flavor reminiscent of a very sweet watermelon. Tolerates light frost and flooding; requires wind protection. O19, O19{S}

Kakus: Delicious longan-like fruit, similar in appearance to Isau but with a yellow or yellow-brown pebbly shell, sometimes slightly larger. The sweet, musky flesh is somewhat less juicy than Isau but has a more distinctive, smokey flavor, somewhat melon-like. Tolerates light frost and flooding. Large, attractive foliage. O19, O19{S}

Kohala: Large to very large fruit; skin brownish; flesh aromatic, sweet and spicy, quality very good to excellent; seed small. Tree produces fairly good crops in mid-summer. The number one commercial cultivar in Florida and Australia. Introduced into Florida from Hawaii by William F. Whitman in 1954. MORTON 1987a, WHITMAN; D57, F68, I83M, *Q93*

Diploglottis australis → *Diploglottis cunninghamii*

Diploglottis cunninghamii - *Native tamarind* {S} The orange-red arils of the fruits are sweet, sub-acid, pleasantly flavored, and are eaten as preserves. Australia. UPHOF; N84, P38

Dodonaea viscosa - *Switch-sorrel, Native hops* {S} The bitter fruits are used as a substitute for hops in making yeast and beer. Leaves are chewed as a stimulant. Seeds are also edible. Tropics, Subtropics. CRIBB, FOX, F., TANAKA; C9M, F79M, F80, *G66*, *J25*{PL}, N84, O93, P5, *Q15G*, *Q32*, R15M, R33M, S29, S92, T7, etc.

Euphoria longan → *Dimocarpus longan*

Lecaniodiscus cupanioides - {S} The sweet pulp of the fruit is eaten. Fragrant flowers are used in some parts of Africa for the preparation of an aromatic water. Tropical Africa. DALZIEL, INGLETT, UPHOF; N84

Litchi chinensis - *Lychee, Litchi* {S} Fleshy arils are sweet, juicy, sub-acid, and have a delicious flavor somewhat reminiscent of Muscat grapes. They are eaten fresh, dried, spiced, pickled, canned in syrup, used in jams, sauces, fruit salads, ice cream, sherbets, or made into wine. The dried fruits, called *lychee nuts*, are eaten, especially at New Year celebrations. Dried tea leaves are soaked in lychee juice, dried again in the sun, then made into a fragrant tea which releases the lychee flavor. China, cultivated. CHANG, W. [Cul], GROFF, MORTON 1987a [Cu], POPENOE, W. 1920 [Cu, Pro], RICHARDSON [Re], ROSENGARTEN, SCHNEIDER [Cul, Re]; *B59*{PR}, C27G{PR}, C56M{PL}, E29, E29{PL}, E29{PR}, F85, *L33M*{PR}, L54{PR}, N84, O93, P38, Q12, Q46

CULTIVARS {GR}

Bengal: Large, round to heart-shaped fruit, borne in clusters of 8 to 30; skin deep pink; flesh firm, rose-scented, flavor excellent; does not leek juice when peeled; seed pointed, fully developed in most fruits, smaller in proportion to flesh than those of Brewster; ripens in June. Tree large, very vigorous, more spreading than Brewster; adapted to alkaline soils. Introduced into Florida in 1929 from a seedling received from Calcutta, India. BROOKS 1972, MORTON 1987a; *Q93*

Brewster: Medium to large, conical or wedge-shaped fruit, borne in clusters of 6 to 20; skin bright red, spiny; flesh soft, more acid than Kwai Mi, seeds often fully formed and large; ripens in June and July. Tree large, vigorous with wide, strong, reinforced branch crotches; leaflets flat, tapering to a sharp point. Originated in Florida. MORTON 1987a; F68, I83M, *Q93*

Groff: Small, heart-shaped fruit, borne in clusters of 20 to 40; skin dull red; has a higher proportion of flesh to seed than other clones growing in Hawaii; ripens August to September. Tree upright; bears in Hawaii where other cultivars fail due to poor flower initiation. Probably a seedling of Haak Yip. Originated at the Poamoho Branch Station, Hawaii Agricultural Experiment Station, Honolulu. Introduced in 1952. BROOKS 1972; J22

Haak Yip: (Haak Ip, Black Leaf) Fruit broad-shouldered, small to medium in size, borne in clusters of 15 to 25; skin medium-red, sometimes with green tinges, soft and thin; flesh is occasionally pinkish, crisp and sweet; ripens in June and July. Tree slow growing, compact; branches fragile, spreading; leaves dark green, long, slightly curled, pointed. Considered one of the best of the Chinese "water" lychees. GROFF, MORTON 1987a; *Q93*

Heung Lai: (Hsiang Li, Fragrant Lychee) Fruit small; skin deep red in color, very rough and with many prickles; flesh very fragrant and delicious and is said to be even better than Kwai Mi, seed very small; prone to splitting; ripens late. Tree upright, with leaves that tend to grow upward. Originated in China. GROFF; *Q93*

Kaimana: Large, nearly heart-shaped fruit; skin deep red, attractive; flesh whitish, translucent, juicy, sweet, of a delicious subacid flavor; round, medium-sized, glossy brown seed; ripens May to July; resembles Kwai Mi but twice as large. One of the best flavored lychees, with no musky aftertaste. Vigorous, spreading tree with long, drooping leaves and branches; bears heavy crops regularly. Released by the University of Hawaii in 1982. MORTON 1987a; J22

Kate Sessions: Medium to large fruit, similar if not identical to Brewster. Reliable producer at place of origin, setting medium to heavy crops every other year. Original tree planted in La Mesa, California by noted horticulturist Kate Sessions, in the 1920's. I83M

Kwai Mi: (Cinnamon Flavor) Small, somewhat heart-shaped fruit, borne in clusters of 15 to 30; skin very rough, red tinged with green on the shoulders; flavor very sweet and fragrant, seeds very small and dry; ripens May to June. The Chinese consider this fruit to be light, or like lean meat in comparison to the No Mai Chee, which is said to be heavy or fatty. For this reason they say Kwai Mi can be eaten in greater quantity. Large, spreading tree with brittle branches. Originated in China. GROFF; J22

Nam Tao Sing: (Rogers No Mai Chi, Salathiel) Large, rounded to ellipsoid fruit, borne in clusters of 10 to 25; skin bright red, brittle; flesh solid and crisp, sweet, fragrant, dry and clean, quality excellent; seeds often small and shriveled. Tree slow growing, spreading. One of the best cultivars for drying. This is a late maturing cultivar of No Mai Chi. *Q93*

Seong Sue Wai: (Gee Kee) Small, rounded fruit; skin slightly rough with many dark spots, red; flesh sweet, lacking in aroma, easily separated from the seed, seeds mostly small; quality medium to good. Leaflets small, long, oval in shape. *Q93*

Tai Tso: (Ta-Tsao, Large Crop, Mauritius) Medium-sized, somewhat egg-shaped fruit, borne in clusters of 15 to 30; skin rough, bright red with many small dots; flesh firm, crisp, sweet, faintly streaked with yellow near the large seed; ripens May to June. Some of the juice leaks when the fruit is opened. Tree vigorous, spreading; a consistent bearer; cold-sensitive; susceptible to limb breakage. Originated in China. GROFF; F68, I83M, *Q93*

Wai Chee: (Wai Chi, Sweet Cliff) Small, round fruit, borne in clusters of 4 to 8; skin yellow overlaid with pinkish-red, medium smooth, with few dots or markings; flesh somewhat watery, seeds large, quality good; ripens very late. Tree compact, upright, slow growing; a regular bearer but susceptible to wind damage; recommended for Florida; needs a cooler climate than that of coastal north Queensland. Originated in China. MORTON 1987a; F68, I83M, *Q93*

Melicoccus bijugatus - *Mamoncillo, Spanish lime, Genipa* {S} Pulp of fruits is juicy, aromatic, somewhat sweet, with a pleasant acid flavor. Usually eaten out of hand, or used in pies, jams, jellies, marmalades, and cooling drinks. The starchy seeds are roasted and eaten as a substitute for cassava. Fresh fruits are sometimes available at ethnic markets. Tropical America, cultivated. DUKE, HEDRICK 1919, MENNINGER, MORTON 1987a [Cu, Pro], POPENOE, W. 1920; E29, E29{PL}, E29{PR}, F85, J36{PL}, N84

CULTIVARS {SC}

Key West: Large green fruit, 1 1/2 inches in diameter, 14 fruit to the pound; borne in bunches like grapes. Quality excellent with a delicious, slightly acid/sweet flavor. Introduced from Key West, Florida by William F. Whitman. WHITMAN; **T73M**

Montgomery: (No. 4) Large fruit with 51.5% pulp, of good flavor; sometimes 18% of fruit has 2 seeds. Tree bears heavily in most years. Originated in Coral Gables, Florida. First evaluated in 1976 by Dr. Carl Campbell of the University of Florida. MORTON 1987a; **T73M**

Newcomb: (No. 3) Good sized fruits with 48.2% pulp, of good flavor. Tree bears heavily in most years. Originated in Key West, Florida by R.G. Newcomb. First evaluated in 1976 by Dr. Carl Campbell of the University of Florida. MORTON 1987a; **U27T**

Queen: (No. 2) Large fruit with 55.6% pulp, only fair in flavor. Tree moderately vigorous. Originated in Key West, Florida by William F. Whitman. First evaluated in 1976 by Dr. Carl Campbell of the University of Florida. MORTON 1987a; **T73M**

Nephelium lappaceum - *Rambutan* {S} The sweet, juicy, translucent flesh of the fruits is excellent eaten out of hand. Or it can be stewed, preserved, used in jams, jellies, and compotes, or canned in light syrup, either as whole fruits or stuffed with pineapple. The seeds are roasted and eaten. They also yield an edible oil. Malaysia, cultivated. ALMEYDA 1979, GARNER [Pro], KUNKEL, MORTON 1987a [Cu, Pro], POPENOE, W. 1920; F85, J22{PL}, N84, O93, R59

CULTIVARS {GR}

Jit Lee: (Deli) Leading commercial cultivar in Singapore. Originally from Indonesia. *Q93*

R 134: Large fruit with firm flesh. Early season cultivar, coming into bearing earlier than others. Originated in Malaysia. *Q93*

R 156: (Muar Gading) Unique yellow fruited cultivar. Originated in Malaysia. *Q93*

Nephelium litchi* → *Litchi chinensis

Nephelium mutabile - *Pulasan* {S} The delicious flesh of the fruits is less juicy than that of the rambutan, sweeter, and of less sprightly flavor. It is eaten raw or used in jams and compotes. Boiled or roasted seeds are used in the preparation of a cocoa-like beverage. They also yield a cooking oil. Malaysia to the Philippines, cultivated. KUNKEL, MORTON 1987a, POPENOE, W. 1920; F85, R59

CULTIVARS {GR}

Meritam: Fruit resembles a rambutan, but is hairless, being instead covered with small protuberances; softer, juicier and more subacid than a rambutan. The skin is either red or green. Vigorous tree, resembles a rambutan; produces fruit in clusters; requires a tropical environment. O19, O19{S}

Nephelium sp. - *Sibau* {S} Sibau is a small, dark red, rambutan-like fruit with a pleasant subacid flavor. The tree has large pinnate leaves, a more upright habit than the rambutan, and is ornamental. Grows well in North Queensland, Australia. Borneo. O19, O19{PL}

Pappea capensis - *Jacket plum, Wild plum* {S} The fruits have pleasant tasting red flesh and are eaten raw, made into beverages and jellies, or fermented into vinegar. Seeds are the source of an edible oil. Southern Africa. FOX, F., HEDRICK 1919; **Y78**

Paullinia cupana - *Guaraná* {S} Roasted, pounded seeds are pressed into a paste which is manufactured into carbonated beverages and a stimulating tea, containing 4.88% caffeine. The sweetened paste, called *Brazilian chocolate*, is used in soft drinks, candy, and for flavoring liqueurs. Guaraná soda is sometimes available in specialty stores that sell Latin American foods. Tropical South America, cultivated. MENNINGER, MORTON 1976, SCHERY, UPHOF; **X79**

Paullinia pinnata - *Apgi, Barbasco* {S} The aril and the sweet, powdery pulp of the fruit are sometimes eaten. Flowers are also edible. Leaves are consumed in the Congo. The roots are used as chewsticks. Tropical America. CORREA, DALZIEL, DUKE, IRVINE 1960, MARTIN 1975; N84

Paullinia sorbilis* → *Paullinia cupana

Pometia pinnata - *Fijian longan* {S} The pulp of the fruit is semi-transparent, white, juicy, and sweet. It is usually eaten out of hand. Oily seeds are eaten after roasting or boiling. Malaysia to Pacific Islands. MENNINGER, TANAKA, WESTER; F85, N84

CULTIVARS

Whitman: Produces 2 1/2 inch diameter fruit hanging in clusters like grapes. Quality of fruit fair. Tree everbearing. WHITMAN; **U27T**

Schleichera oleosa - *Malay lacktree, Koosambi* {S} Young leaves and shoots are eaten raw, in soups, or steamed and served with rice or fish. Unripe fruits are pickled, ripe ones are eaten raw. The seeds are the source of *macassar oil*, sometimes used for culinary purposes. Southern Asia. OCHSE, TANAKA, UPHOF, WATT; F85, Q46

Schleichera trijuga* → *Schleichera oleosa

Talisia olivaeformis - *Yellow genip, Cotopriz, Tinalujo* {S} The fruit is the size and shape of an olive, green or yellow on the outside, with orange-red pulp of somewhat acid but agreeable flavor. It is eaten out of hand or used for jellies. Tropical America. HEDRICK 1919, MARTIN 1987, WILLIAMS, L.; F85

Xanthoceras sorbifolium - *Shiny-leaf yellowhorn* {PL} Flowers and leaves are used for food. The nut is enclosed in a shell similar to a chestnut, is the size of a pea, and is quite sweet. Northern China. HEDRICK 1919; B74, D95, E7M{S}, *G66*{S}, I60, N84{S}, P86

SAPOTACEAE

Achras sapota* → *Manilkara zapota

Argania sideroxylon* → *Argania spinosa

Argania spinosa - *Argan tree, Morocco iron-wood* {S} Seed kernels are the source of a yellow oil served with bread, roasted barley (*sesometa*), or other foods, and also used in cooking like olive oil. Has somewhat the flavor of peanut oil. In Morocco, argan oil is mixed with almond paste and honey to make a delicious almond butter known as *amalou*, or kneaded with grilled wheat germ and honey to form a breakfast gruel called *zematar*. Contains 80% unsaturated fatty acids. North Africa. MORTON 1987b [Nu, Pro], UPHOF, WOLFERT [Cul, Re]; F85

Bassia latifolia* → *Madhuca indica

Bassia longifolia* → *Madhuca longifolia

Bequaertiodendron magalismontanum - *Stemberry* {S} The small, red fruits are fleshy and are sometimes eaten raw. They are also used for making jellies, syrups and drinks. Tropical Africa. KUNKEL; N84, R41

Butyrospermum paradoxum ssp. parkii - *Shea butter tree* {S} Seeds are the source of *shea butter* or *galam butter*, eaten by the natives. Also used as a cooking fat and oil, as a substitute for cacao butter, or for manufacturing margarine. Pulp of the fruit is sometimes eaten. Tropical Africa. DALZIEL, MENNINGER, UPHOF; N84

Butyrospermum parkii* → *Butyrospermum paradoxum ssp. parkii

Calocarpum mammosum* → *Pouteria sapota

Calocarpum sapota* → *Pouteria sapota

Calocarpum viride* → *Pouteria viride

Chrysophyllum albidum - *White star apple* {S} The fruits have a pleasant, sweet-acid flavor and are often sold in local markets. Tropical Africa. DALZIEL, IRVINE 1960; F85

Chrysophyllum cainito - *Star apple, Caimito* {S} The sweet fruits are eaten fresh, parboiled, made into preserves, or eaten as a mixture called *matrimony*, which is prepared by scooping out the inside pulp and adding it to a glass of sour orange juice. When cut transversely, the interior section of the fruit presents a star-like appearance, hence the common name. An emulsion of the slightly bitter seed kernels is used to make imitation *milk-of-almonds*, or nougats and other confections. West Indies, cultivated. GARNER [Pro], JOHNS [Pre], MORTON 1987a [Cu], POPENOE, W. 1920, RICHARDSON [Re], STURROCK; A79M, E29, E29{PL}, E29{PR}, F68{PL}, F85, J22{PL}, N84, P38, *Q93*{PL}, R59, S54M{PL}

CULTIVARS {GR}

Grimal: An improved purple-fruited cultivar that originated in the Florida Keys. *Q93*

Haitian: Fruit purple, well-formed, of high quality; ripens from late January to the end of June. Tree heavy yielding. In Florida, grafted and air-layered trees have borne well even prior to reaching 10 feet in height; seedlings have performed poorly. Grown commercially in Australia. Discovered in Port-au-Prince, Haiti by William F. Whitman. Introduced in 1953. MORTON 1987a, WHITMAN; *Q93*

Philippine Gold: (Manila Gold) Unique greenish-gold cultivar that is popular in the Philippines, where it originated. *Q93*

River Green: An improved green-fruited cultivar that originated in Australia. *Q93*

Weeping: Fruit tennis ball size, purple, of very good quality. Originated as a seedling of Haitian. Distinguished by its weeping or drooping habit. WHITMAN; *Q93*

Chrysophyllum lacourtianum - *Bambu* {S} The red, apple-shaped fruit is highly esteemed by the natives who poke a hole in one end and suck out the juicy, sticky, sweet to subacid sap. Sold in local markets. Tropical Africa. **X44**

Chrysophyllum oliviforme - *Satinleaf, Caimitillo, Olive plum* {S} The lavender pulp of the small, dark-purple fruit is sweet, melting, has a good flavor, and can be used to make an excellent jelly. West Indies. KENNARD, MORTON 1977, STURROCK; D87G{PL}, F85, *J25*{PL}, N84, P38

Dumoria heckelii* → *Tieghemella heckelii

Lucuma nervosa* → *Pouteria campechiana

Lucuma obovata* → *Pouteria lucuma

Madhuca indica - *Butter tree, Mahwa, Mowra, Illipe nut* {S} The fleshy flowers are rich in nectar and are dried and consumed, either raw or cooked. They are also used directly as a sweetener, as a source of sugar, and are fermented into an alcoholic beverage. Both the ripe and unripe fruit is eaten. An edible oil is expressed from the seed which is used as a substitute for *ghee*. India. BURKILL, HEDRICK 1919, MACMILLAN, MACNICOL, MENNINGER, TANAKA, WATT; Q46

Madhuca latifolia* → *Madhuca indica

Madhuca leerii* → *Payena leerii

Madhuca longifolia - *Indian butter tree, Mee* {S} Seeds are the source of *illipe butter*, used in margarine and chocolate, and to adulterate *ghee*. The fleshy edible flowers are eaten dried, roasted, or made into jelly, sugar and wine. Leaves are also edible. Southern Asia. HEDRICK 1919, MACMILLAN, MARTIN 1975, TANAKA, UPHOF; F85

Malacantha alnifolia - *Fafaraha, Afraba* {S} The reddish fruits, similar to coffee berries, have sweet, yellow pulp which is very refreshing. West Tropical Africa. IRVINE 1960, KENNARD; N84

Malacantha warnekeana* → *Malacantha alnifolia

Manilkara bidentata - *Balata, Bullet tree* {S} Fruits are edible. The latex is used for *chicle*. Tropical America. KUNKEL, TANAKA; **T71, T73M, Z25M**

Manilkara hexandra - *Khirni* {S} Fruits are eaten fresh or dried. In India, it is commonly used as a rootstock for Manilkara zapota. Southern Asia. BURKILL, GARNER, WATT; N84, P5, P38, Q46

Manilkara kauki - *Sawo maneela, Sawo kecik* {S} The small, reddish-brown fruits are quite sweet when ripe and are eaten raw, cooked or used for making syrup. Southeast Asia to Australia. CRIBB, HEDRICK 1919, RIFAI; **T71**

Manilkara zapota - *Chico sapote, Sapodilla, Naseberry* {S} When fully ripe, the flesh of the fruit is soft, sweet, and delicious with the flavor of pears, cinnamon, and brown sugar together. It is eaten fresh, preserved, dried, in custards, sherbets, ice cream, pies and muffins, or made into syrup, jams, and vinegar. The very young, leafy shoots are eaten raw or steamed. Stems are the source of a gummy latex, *chicle*, used as a base for chewing gum. Tropical America, cultivated. GARNER [Pro], MORTON 1987a [Cu], OCHSE, POPENOE, W. 1920 [Cu, Pro], RICHARDSON [Re], STURROCK, UPHOF; A79M, *B59*{PR}, D57{PL}, E29, E29{PL}, E29{PR}, F68{PL}, I83M{PL}, J22{PL}, *L5M*, L54{PR}, N84, O93, P38, R59, etc.

CULTIVARS {GR}

Brown Sugar: Fruit medium small, 2 to 2½ inches long, nearly round; skin light, scurfy brown; flesh pale brown, fragrant, juicy, very sweet and rich, texture slightly granular, quality very good; handles and keeps well. Tree tall, bushy; bears heavy crops annually. Originated in Homestead, Florida; introduced in 1948. BROOKS 1972, MORTON 1987a; *Q93*

Cricket Ball: Very large fruit with crisp, granular flesh, very sweet but not distinctive in flavor. Originated in India. MORTON 1987a; R0

Modello: Fruit quality good. Tree not a heavy producer. Originated in Florida. **T73M{SC}**

Ponderosa: Large fruit, with individual fruits weighing up to 350 grams. Fruit of most other cultivars weighs 120-200 grams. Originated in the Philippines. *Q93*

Prolific: Round-conical fruit, 2 1/2 to 3 1/2 inches long and broad; skin scurfy, brown, becoming nearly smooth at maturity; flesh light pinkish-tan, mildly fragrant, texture smooth, flavor sweet, quality good. Tree bears early, consistently, and heavily; only moderately susceptible to rust. Originated in Homestead, Florida. Introduced in 1951. BROOKS 1972, MORTON 1987a; **T73M{SC}**

Russell: Large, roundish fruit, 3 to 4 inches in diameter and length; skin scurfy brown with gray patches; flesh pinkish-tan, shading to greenish-tan under the skin, mildly fragrant, texture somewhat granular; flavor rich and sweet. Tree slower to bear and less productive than Prolific. Originated in Islamorada, Florida. Introduced in 1935. BROOKS 1972, MORTON 1987a; **T73M{SC}**

Sawo Manila: (Sao Manila) Fruits mature in 190 days, and ripen 3 to 5 days after picking. Originated in the Philippines. MORTON 1987a; *Q93*

Tikal: Fruit elliptical to conical, much smaller than Prolific; skin light brown; flavor excellent; ripens very early. A promising seedling selection. MORTON 1987a; *Q93*

Mimusops balata → ***Manilkara bidentata***

Mimusops caffra - *Coast red-milkwood, Tinzol* {S} When ripe, the fruits are red to purple and have sweet, starchy pulp and an agreeable flavor. They are eaten raw or made into a beverage. Southeastern Africa. FOX, F., VON REIS; F85, N84

Mimusops elengi - *Spanish cherry* {S} The fruits are yellow when ripe, somewhat sweet, and are eaten raw, preserved, or pickled. Seed kernels yield an edible oil. Tropical Asia, cultivated. BURKILL, HEDRICK 1919, TANAKA, WATT; F85, *L5M*, N84, P5, *P17M*, P38, Q12, Q18, Q46

Mimusops heckelii → ***Tieghemella heckelii***

Mimusops hexandra → ***Manilkara hexandra***

Mimusops kauki → ***Manilkara kauki***

Payena leerii - *Edoloyan* {S} The scant pulp of the fruit is eaten, and is said to have the taste of Manilkara zapota. Malaya. BROWN, W., BURKILL, TANAKA; **Y2**

Pouteria caimito - *Abiu* {S} A bright yellow fruit with flesh that is whitish, translucent, somewhat sweet, and of a jelly-like consistency. When fully ripe, it is eaten out of hand or used in sherbets and ice cream. It goes well in fruit salads, particularly those containing orange slices to provide acidity, which the abiu lacks. Fruit that is not completely ripe may contain a milky latex that sticks to the lips. Tropical South America, cultivated. MARTIN 1978a, MORTON 1987a, POPENOE, W. 1920; J22{PL}, N84, P38, *Q93*{PL}

CULTIVARS {GR}

Gray's No. 1: Medium to large, round fruit of good flavor; contains one or more seeds. Tree prolific. Originated in Australia where it is grown commercially. WHITMAN; *Q93*

Z1: Fruit has the shape of a Lisbon lemon, is marginally better flavored but smaller than Z2 and Z3. Tree a very heavy bearer, 200 hundred fruit were picked from a tree 6 feet in height. Introduced by Joe Zappala, Queensland, Australia. *Q93*

Z2: Fruit elongated, approximately one pound in weight, with excellent flesh to fruit recovery; flavor good. Tree a good producer. Introduced by Joe Zappala, Queensland, Australia. *Q93*

Z3: Round, fairly large fruit; slightly creamy in texture; flavor good. Flesh to seed ratio is good, even though it has more seeds than Z1 and Z2. Tree a good producer. Introduced by Joe Zappala, Queensland, Australia. *Q93*

Z4: An improved type selected by Joe Zappala of Queensland, Australia. *Q93*

Pouteria campechiana - *Canistel, Egg fruit, Yellow sapote* {PL} Pulp of the fruit is yellow to orange, soft and mealy in texture, and resembles in appearance the yolk of a hard-boiled egg. The flavor is very rich and sweet, somewhat like that of a baked sweet potato. Excellent to eat out of hand or it can be used in cakes, pies, custards, puddings, fruit cups, ice cream, and milkshakes (*eggfruit nog*). Tropical America, cultivated. JOHNS [Cul], MARTIN 1978a, MORTON 1987a [Cu, Pro], POPENOE, W. 1920, RICHARDSON [Re], STURROCK; *B59*{PR}, D57, E29, E29{PR}, E29{S}, F68, I83M, N84{S}, P38{S}

CULTIVARS {SC}

Ross: Small to medium-sized fruit. Probably the best tasting of all canistels. May be a hybrid. Introduced into Florida from Costa Rica, by William F. Whitman. WHITMAN; **T73M**

Pouteria lucuma - *Lucmo, Lucuma* {PL} The fruits are similar to the canistel but are more rounded, are green to brownish-green in color, and the sweet pulp is firm even in fully ripened fruit. In Peru, besides being eaten fresh, the ripe fruit is prepared into a meal or flour that can be mixed with wheat flour, cornmeal, or starch and used in the preparation of many drinks and desserts. Lucmo meal adds a strong odor and color to ice creams, sherbets, puddings, punches and milkshakes. Andean South America. MARTIN 1978a [Cu], MORTON 1987a, NATIONAL RESEARCH COUNCIL 1989, POPENOE, W. 1920; I83M, N84{S}, P38{S}, *Q49M*, S97M

CULTIVARS {SC}

A: Medium-sized round to ovate fruit; skin very thin and easily broken, brownish-green; flesh bright yellow, dry, mealy, very sweet. Ripens in midseason, approximately December through February in California. Tree a heavy producer. **T49M**

Montero: Large, round to broadly oval fruit; skin deep brownish-green, heavily marked or overspread with russet; flesh yellow, dry and mealy, very sweet, flavor good. Ripens early, approximately October through December in California. **T49M**

Rosalia: Large, round to oval fruit, pointed or depressed at the apex; skin thin and easily broken, brownish-green; flesh deep yellow, dry, mealy, very sweet, flavor good. Ripens late, approximately April through June in California. **T49M**

Pouteria obovata → *Pouteria lucuma*

Pouteria sapota - *Mamey sapote, Mamey colorado* {PL} When ripe, the pulp of the fruit is firm, rich and sweet, salmon-red to reddish brown in color, and finely granular in texture. It is eaten out of hand, dried, preserved, or used in sherbets, ice cream, drinks, etc. In Cuba, it is added to *guava cheese* and made into a thick jam called *crema de mamey colorado*. Unripe fruits are used as a vegetable. Ground seeds are added to chocolate, made into a confection, or mixed with cornmeal, sugar and cinnamon and prepared as a nutritious beverage called *pozol*. Central America, cultivated. ALMEYDA 1976b [Cu, Pro], DUKE, JOHNS, MORTON 1987a, POPENOE, W. 1920 [Cu], RICHARDSON [Re], STURROCK, UPHOF; *B59*{PR}, D57, E29, E29{PR}, F68, F85{S}, I83M, N84{S}

CULTIVARS {SC}

Copan: Medium-sized fruit; weight 15 to 32 ounces; flesh red, of excellent quality, contains 1 seed; ripens in July and August. Tree medium-sized, spreading. Leaves turn red in December, then become brown and are shed in spring. Originated in Florida from seed received from Cuba in 1938. MORTON 1987a; **T73M**

Magana: Large to very large fruit; weight 26 to 85 ounces; flesh pink, of good to excellent quality, contains 1 seed; ripens in April and May. Tree small and slow-growing, evergreen; may fruit 1 year after planting. Bears very well in Florida, poorly in Puerto Rico. Introduced into Florida from El Salvador in 1961. MORTON 1987a; **T73M**

Mayapan: Fruit slightly above medium in size; weight 18 to 40 ounces; skin very scurfy; flesh red, of good quality though slightly fibrous, contains 1 seed. Tree tall and erect, slow to come into bearing when grafted but then yields well. Originated in Florida from seeds obtained from Isle of Pines, Cuba in 1940. MORTON 1987a; **T73M**

Pantin: Medium-sized fruit; weight 14 to 40 ounces; flesh pink to red, fiberless, of excellent quality, contains 1 seed. Tree tall; slow growing at first, bears little or no fruit for 2 to 3 years, then becomes more vigorous and yields well. Leaves become brown in winter. Originated in Key West, Florida. MORTON 1987a; **T73M**

Tazumal: Medium-sized fruit; weight 14 to 30 ounces; flesh pink, of good quality, contains 1 or 2 seeds. Bears two crops; one in January and February, a second in July and August. Tree medium-sized, vigorous, bears regularly and heavily; usually evergreen. Originated in Homestead, Florida from a seedling tree received from El Salvador in 1949. MORTON 1987a; **T73M**

Pouteria viride - *Green sapote, Injerto* {S} The pulp of the fruit is pale reddish-brown, melting, sweet, and somewhat juicy. The flavor is similar to that of P. sapote, but more delicate, and the flesh is finer and smoother in texture. It is eaten out of hand or used to make preserves. The latex is used as a base for chewing gum. Central America. KENNARD, MORTON 1987a, POPENOE, W. 1920; E29{PL}, E29{PR}, F85, N84, P38

Sideroxylon dulcificum* → *Synsepalum dulcificum

Synsepalum dulcificum - *Miracle fruit, Miraculous berry* {S} Although the ripe fruit is not sweet to the taste, it has the ability to cause sour foods to seem sweet when eaten or drunk immediately afterwards. This taste-modifying property will cause lemons, limes, grapefruits, rhubarb, and vinegar to taste very pleasantly sweet. Ice cream and other sweet foods become cloyingly sweet. The West African natives use the fruit to sweeten sour palm wine, *pito* (beer), and *kenkey* (fermented maize bread). West Tropical Africa. HEDRICK 1919, INGLETT, KENNARD, UPHOF; A79M, E29, E29{PL}, E29{PR}, F68{PL}, F85, N84, P38

CULTIVARS

Hirsutus: A form with hairy leaves introduced into Florida from Africa some years ago. Small, oval, red fruits; larger than those of the common smooth-leaved type. WHITMAN; **U27T**

Tieghemella heckelii - *Baco nut* {S} Seed kernels are the source of an edible fat called *baku butter* or *dumori butter*, used for cooking and in margarine. West Tropical Africa. DALZIEL, MENNINGER, UPHOF; N84

SAURURACEAE

Houttuynia cordata - *Giâp cá* {PL} The strongly aromatic leaves are eaten in salads, soups, fish stews, or with boiled, fertilized duck eggs, which are not eaten until three days before they hatch. Roots and fruits are also edible. Himalayas to Japan. ALTSCHUL, BOND, KEUBEL, TANAKA, UPHOF; G96, H30, H51M, K22, K47T{S}, K63, K85, M77M, M82

SAXIFRAGACEAE

Astilbe thunbergii - *Toriashi-shôma* {PL} Young plants are cooked and eaten. Leaves are used as a substitute for tea. Japan. TANAKA; M77M, N63M{S}

Bergenia crassifolia - *Badan* {S} The leaves are used as a substitute for tea, called *Tschager tea*. Northeast Asia. HEDRICK 1919, UPHOF; G55{PL}, K47T

Chrysosplenium alternifolium - *Golden saxifrage* {S} Leaves are eaten in salads in some parts of Europe. Eurasia. HEDRICK 1919; **V34, X36, Y10, Y29**

Chrysosplenium oppositifolium - *Cresson de roches, Golden saxifrage* {PL} In the Vosges mountains, the leaves are eaten in salads and soups. Eurasia. HEDRICK 1919, LARKCOM 1984, MABEY; *P95M*

Peltiphyllum peltatum - *Indian rhubarb, Umbrella plant* {S} The thick, fleshy leafstalks are peeled and eaten raw, cooked like asparagus, or added to salads and stews. Pacific Coast of North America. KIRK, MEDSGER; G82M{PL}, H30{PL}, I31, K47T, L91M, M37M{PL}, M77{PL}, N84, O53M, *Q24*, S3M, S7M

Saxifraga crassifolia* → *Bergenia crassifolia

Saxifraga pensylvanica - *Swamp saxifrage* {S} Young, tender, unrolling leaves can be used in salads, eaten as a potherb, or briefly cooked in bacon fat. Eastern North America. FERNALD, GIBBONS 1979, PETERSON, L.; D62, G47M, I31, I63M{PL}, J43, K47T, N84, *Q24*

Saxifraga stolonifera - *Strawberry saxifrage, Yuki-no-shita* {PL} In Japan, the leaves are relished when fried or after being parboiled, in salads. The flower scapes are said to be tasty when salted. China, Japan. TANAKA, YASHIRODA; C36, D62{S}, G96, H4, H51M, H79M, K22, M16, N42, N84{S}

SCHISANDRACEAE

Schisandra chinensis - *Chôsen-gomishi* {S} Young leaves are boiled and eaten as a vegetable. The fruit is eaten fresh or dried. In the Soviet Union, a paste made from the fruit is mixed with Actinidia arguta fruit to counteract the insufficient acidity of the latter, which is used for fillings in the confectionery industry. Eastern Asia. SHISKIN, TANAKA; H4{PL}, K47T, N84, O53M, O93, P49, *R28*

Schisandra repanda - *Matsubusa* {S} The fruits are eaten raw, preserved, or used for tea. Eastern Asia. TANAKA; **V19**

SCROPHULARIACEAE

Bacopa monnieria - *Water hyssop, Rau dâng* {PL} The herb is eaten in salads and soups, as a cooked vegetable, or pickled. Occasionally available in ethnic markets. Tropics. BOND, HEDRICK 1919; *F73*, F85{S}, *J25*

Capraria biflora - *West India tea, Jamaica tea, Te de Santa Maria* {S} An infusion of the dried leaves and flowers is said to be a very agreeable substitute for tea. Central America, West Indies. ALTSCHUL, HEDRICK 1919, TANAKA; **Y2**

Castilleja linariaefolia - *Wyoming paintbrush* {S} The flowers may be eaten raw, being the best tasting of the genus. Western North America. KIRK; *E66M*, F66, F95, I98M, L75

Halleria lucida - *Umbinza, Wild fuchsia* {S} When ripe, the fruits are purple, extremely sweet although slightly astringent, and can be eaten out of hand or added to a fruit salad to give it an exotic look. The flowers are sucked for their sweet nectar. Southern Africa. FOX, F., SIMMONS 1972 [Cu]; N84, P38, R41, R77M

Herpestis monnieria* → *Bacopa monnieria

Limnophila aromatica - *Swamp leaf, Rau om, Keukeuhan* {PL} The leafy stems are eaten raw or cooked, as a side-dish with rice. They have a distinct aroma and flavor and are an essential ingredient in several sweet and sour Vietnamese dishes, including a soup made with tamarind and cantaloupe. Occasionally found at ethnic markets in North America. Southern Asia to Australia. BOND, BURKILL, OCHSE, TANAKA; J82

Limnophila indica - *Ambuli water-plant* {S} The plant is eaten as an aromatic potherb. Southern Asia. TANAKA; F85

Mimulus guttatus - *Yellow monkey-flower* {S} Very young leaves have a slightly bitter flavor and are eaten raw in salads, with a light dressing. Western North America. KIRK, NIETHAMMER, YANOVSKY; I98M, *Q24*

Mimulus langsdorfii* → *Mimulus guttatus

Paulownia tomentosa - *Kiri, Tung* {S} The flowers are eaten with miso. Leaves are parboiled and used as an emergency food. China, cultivated. TANAKA; B61M, C9M, C56M{PL}, E7M, F80, H4, H4{PL}, I4{PL}, K38, K47T, K63G, N84, O53M, O89, R47, etc.

Penstemon confertus - *Yellow penstemon* {S} A tea-like beverage is made by boiling the dried leaves and stems. Western North America. YANOVSKY; K47T

Penstemon confertus var. caeruleo-purpureus* → *Penstemon procerus

Penstemon procerus - *Small-flowered penstemon* {S} Dried leaves and stems are made into a tea-like beverage. Western North America. YANOVSKY; F80, G82M{PL}, I47, K47T, K98, L13, *Q24*

Scoparia dulcis - *Sweet broom* {S} Used as a substitute for tea in the Philippines. In some parts of the West Indies branches are placed in drinking wells to give the water a cool taste. Tropical America. ALTSCHUL, HEDRICK 1919, UPHOF; F85, N84

Verbascum thapsus - *Mullein* {S} An aromatic, slightly bitter tea is made from the dried leaves by steeping them in boiling water for five to ten minutes. A sweeter tea can be brewed by using the fresh or dried flowers. Eurasia, naturalized in North America. CROWHURST 1973, MARCIN, PETERSON, L.; C13M, D29{PL}, F21{PL}, F35M{PL}, H3M{PL}, H61M, I11M, I11M{PL}, K49T, N9M, N9M{PL}, *N71M*, N84, O53M

Veronica anagallis-aquatica - *Water speedwell, Brooklime* {S} Stem tips and young leaves are eaten raw in salads, in bread and butter sandwiches, or cooked as a potherb. When used in salads, their delicate taste and aroma should be enhanced with a light dressing of lemon juice, rather than vinegar. Northern temperate region. BIANCHINI, FERNALD, GIBBONS 1979; D62

Veronica beccabunga - *European brooklime* {S} Young shoots and leaves are mixed with water cress or other strong flavored greens and eaten in tossed salads. When finely chopped they can be combined with chives and added to bread and butter sandwiches. Eurasia. LAUNERT, MICHAEL [Pre, Re]; D62, K47T, N84, O53M, *Q24*, R53M{PL}

Veronica chamaedrys - *Bird's-eye speedwell* {S} The leaves are used as a substitute for tea. Northern temperate region. FERNALD; D62, J24{PL}, *N71M*, N84, O48, S55

Veronica officinalis - *Speedwell* {S} A bitter, tangy tea is made from the fresh flowering herb or dried leaves. Europe. FERNALD, HEDRICK 1919, MARCIN; C81M{PL}, E5M{PL}, E61{PL}, N45{PL}, *N71M*, N84, O48, O53M, *Q24*, S7M

Veronicastrum sibiricum - *Siberia-kugai-sô* {S} Young stems and leaves are eaten raw, oil-roasted, put in soups, or used as a potherb. Flower spikes are eaten as a potherb. Eastern Asia. TANAKA; D62

SIMAROUBACEAE

Picrasma quassioides - *Nigaki* {PL} Small red fruits are eaten. Young buds are used to make a tea. A bitter element, *quassin*, is extracted from this tree and used as a hops substitute in brewing beer. Temperate Southern Asia. TANAKA; P86

Quassia amara - *Quassia, Bitterwood* {S} The bitter bark and wood are substituted for hops in manufacturing beer. An extract is used to flavor spirits, soft drinks, and baked goods. Tropical America. MORTON 1976, WILLIAMS, L.; F85, N84, P28

Simarouba amara* → *Quassia amara

Simarouba glauca - *Paradise tree* {PL} Ripe fruits are eaten raw. The seed kernels yield an oil used in cooking or in the manufacture of margarine. Florida, Caribbean region. DUKE, MORTON 1977, WILLIAMS, L.; D87G, F85{S}, *J25*, N84{S}

SIMMONDSIACEAE

Simmondsia californica* → *Simmondsia chinensis

Simmondsia chinensis - *Jojoba, Pignut, Goatnut* {S} Seeds are eaten raw, parched, or roasted and served with melted butter and salt. The ground seeds are boiled and made into a coffee-like beverage. In Mexico, there is a variation of this which is said to taste like chocolate. They mix the roasted, ground nuts with the yolk of a hard-boiled egg and boil this in water with milk, sugar, and a vanilla bean. California. CLARKE [Re], KIRK, NIETHAMMER [Re], ROSENGARTEN; A2, A79M, C9M, C27M, F24, G45, G45{PL}, G84{PL}, I83M{PL}, J25M, J73, L13, N84, O53M, R47, etc.

SINOPTERIDACEAE

Cheilanthes fragrans - {S} Said to be used as a substitute for tea. Mediterranean region. KUNKEL; Z25M

Pellaea mucronata - *Tea fern, Bird's foot fern* {PL} The dried fronds may be steeped in hot water for fifteen to twenty minutes to produce a fragrant and flavorful tea. Western North America. KIRK; G60

SMILACACEAE

Smilax aspera - *Red-berried rough-bindweed* {S} The young shoots are eaten as a vegetable. Eurasia. TANAKA; N84

Smilax china - *China root, Ma-chia* {S} Young shoots and leaves are eaten as a boiled vegetable or potherb. The fruit is eaten to quench the thirst. Leaves are used as a substitute for tea. Roots are also edible. Eastern Asia. TANAKA; F85

Smilax herbacea - *Carrion flower, Jacob's ladder* {PL} The young, tender shoots, when cooked and served like asparagus, make a delicate and palatable vegetable. When ripe, the blue-black fruits are eaten raw, puréed, or made into jellies and sauces. The fruit sauce is excellent to baste wild meats, and it adds zest and flavor. North America. FERNALD, FREITUS [Re], GIBBONS 1979, HARRINGTON, H.; D75T, F85{S}

Smilax officinalis - *Jamaica sarsaparilla* {S} The dried roots are a source of *sarsaparilla*, used for flavoring soft drinks. Due to their bitter taste, they are normally used as a mixture with other spices, very rarely alone. Central America. BROUK, TANAKA; Z25M

Smilax rotundifolia - *Horse-brier, Greenbrier* {S} Tender, young shoots and unrolling leaves are eaten raw in salads, boiled and served cold with French dressing, steamed like asparagus, or pickled in vinegar. The dried roots are the source of a reddish flour used in soups, breads, cakes, puddings, jellies, and sweet drinks. A beer resembling *root beer* or *sarsaparilla* can also be prepared from the roots. North America. FERNALD, GIBBONS 1966a, GIBBONS 1966b; F85

SOLANACEAE

Capsicum annuum - *Chili pepper, Bell pepper, Cayenne, Pimento, Paprika* {PR} Fruits are eaten raw in salads, fried, stuffed (*chilis rellenos*), roasted, dried, preserved, cooked as a vegetable, pickled in vinegar, made into sauce, or used as a condiment. *La-chiao chiang* or *la-chiang* is fermented, salted red peppers used in China like tabasco sauce. The leaves, having 4 to 6% protein, are eaten steamed as a potherb, oil-roasted, or used in soups and stews. They are thrown into *locro*, a popular Andean soup prepared from potatoes, avocado, and various spices. The powder from the dried, ground fruits of some cultivars is added to food as a coloring. Tropical America, cultivated. ANDREWS [Re], CARCIONE, DUKE, FELL 1982b, HARRINGTON, G. [Cul], HEISER 1969, HERKLOTS, SHURTLEFF 1976, TANAKA, VILMORIN [Cu]; *N40* (for cultivars see Pepper, page 436)

Capsicum annuum var. aviculare - *Bird pepper, Bird's-eye pepper* {S} The small, extremely pungent fruits are used as a condiment, both fresh and dried. They are popular for making jelly and sauce, to which they impart a very special flavor. Leaves can be used as a potherb. Southern North America, Tropical America. ALCORN, ANDREWS [Re], D'ARCY, HEISER 1969, HERKLOTS; A21, I16{PR}

CULTIVARS

Diente Perro Tepín: (Dog's Tooth Tepín) Tiny, very hot fruits. Collected in Mexico. I99

Gordo Pequín: (Broad Pequín) An improved selection of the Pequín with broader fruit. J4

Pequín: (Chili Piquín, Chiltepiquín) 150 days. Oval fruit, 1/2 inch long; green when immature turning purple where pods are exposed to the sun, red when ripe. Plant robust, upright, 4 feet tall and 3 feet wide. Fresh pods are hotter than the dried. Much used for seasoning in the Southwest, either fresh or dried. E15M{PR}, F93G{PL}, G13T{PR}, I16, I63T{PR}, J4, J25M, J73, K49M{PR}, M81T

Tarahumara Indian: Wild perennial collected at the old mining town of La Bufa in Batopilas Canyon, Chihuahua, Mexico. Attractive container plant for cooler climates. Potentially resistant to one or more viruses. I16

Tepín: (Chili Tepín, Chiltepin) 150 days. Round fruit, 3/8 inch across; green when immature turning purple on the parts exposed to the sun, red when ripe. Plant small, spreading, frail-looking; 2 feet tall, 18 inches wide. Dried pods are hotter than the fresh. Available in stores that sell Mexican and Southwestern foods. Good in pots. C13M, C43M, I63T{PR}, J4, J73{PR}, M81T

Texas: Fruit slightly elongated in shape. Collected at Wimberly, Texas on the Edwards Plateau, west of Austin. Attractive container plant for cooler climates. Perennial in warmer climates. I16

Tohono O'odham Indian: (Papago) Pointed fruit from the Baboquivari Mountain in southern Arizona. Slow growing plants that should be started indoors to improve the chance of getting fruit the first year. Freezes back in winter. Perennial in warm climates. I16

Warihio Indian: Wild bird pepper collected at Conejos near Alamos, Sonora, Mexico. Starting plants inside is recommended as these are slow growing plants and this will improve the chance of obtaining fruit the first year. Perennial in warmer climates. I16

Capsicum annuum var. glabriusculum* → *Capsicum annuum var. aviculare

Capsicum annuum x Lycopersicon lycopersicum - *Topepo, Tomato pepper* {S} Artificial hybrids. Sweet pepper by tomato. The fruits are generally eaten in salads. OAKLEY.

CULTIVARS

Top Boy: (F_1) Red fruit, resembles a Marmande tomato but with thick walls. The seed core is very small and the taste resembles a very sweet and juicy pepper. Very productive plant. Ripens earlier than Top Girl. S55

Top Girl: (F_1) Gold-yellow fruit, the size and shape of Marmande tomatoes with thick walls. Very small seed core. Has the flavor of a very sweet and juicy pepper. Very productive plant. Ideal for growing in a greenhouse or plastic tunnel. S55

Capsicum baccatum var. pendulum - *Peruvian pepper, Uchu* {S} The pungent fruits are used as a seasoning. Most commonly found in the dry state or *cusqueño*, the principal condiment for traditional Peruvian foods such as *cau cau, cuye chacatado* and *ceviche*. Andean South America, cultivated. ANDREWS [Re], HEISER 1969, HERKLOTS.

CULTIVARS

Ají Escabeche: Fruit tapered, to 4 inches long; pumpkin-orange when mature; very hot. Plant large, erect, to 6 feet tall. Originally from Peru. U33

Yellow Peru: (Ají Amarillo, Kellu Uchu) Slender fruits, 2 to 2 1/2 inches long, tapered on both ends; yellow when ripe; very hot but flavorful. Plants bushy, 18 inches tall. A year round supply of hot peppers can be obtained by growing 1 or 2 plants in 5 gallon containers. A rare Peruvian cultivar for the gourmet pepper palate. U33

Capsicum cardenasii - *Ulupica* {S} The fruits are very small, aromatic, and in Bolivia, are said to be better tasting than locoto or ají, though much hotter. There they are ground with tomato to make a popular dish, called *jallpa huayka* in Aymara or *ucha llajfua* in Quechua. The ulupica is also used as a pickle, preserved in oil and vinegar. Although commonly sold in the markets of La Paz, the species was not known to science until 1958. Andean South America. HEISER 1969, HERKLOTS; T61M, T65

Capsicum chinense - *Bonnet pepper, Squash pepper* The extremely pungent fruits are used as a condiment. Apparently this is the species that was used by the Carib Indians of the West Indies for torturing captives and for preparing their *pepper-pot*, a sort of camper's stew in which various ingredients are constantly added so that the pot is never empty. Tropical America, cultivated. ANDREWS [Re], HEISER 1969, HERKLOTS; (for cultivars see Pepper, page 436)

Capsicum frutescens - *Tabasco pepper, Chili pepper* The pungent fruits are pickled, used as a condiment, or made into hot-pepper sauce. The young leaves and tops of the stems are occasionally steamed and eaten as potherbs. Tropical America, cultivated. ANDREWS, HEISER 1969, HERKLOTS, OCHSE; (for cultivars see Pepper, page 436)

Capsicum pubescens - *Apple chili, Rocoto, Locoto* {S} The distinctive thick-fleshed, pungent fruits are used as a vegetable, condiment, or made into sauce. In Peru, the seeds are removed and the pod is filled with cheese or sausage and then baked in the same manner as American stuffed peppers. Andean South America, cultivated. ANDREWS [Re], HEISER 1969, HERKLOTS, WILLIAMS, L.; I99

CULTIVARS

Cuzco: Heavy, squat fruit; thick, sweet, flavorful flesh; extremely hot seed core. Bushy, thick-trunked plant; prolific; perennial in warm climates; tolerant of light frost. An ancient strain from Cuzco, Peru. I59G

Manzano Amarillo: (Yellow Rocoto) Fruits blocky, up to 5 inches long, canary yellow when ripe; seeds black. Similar to bell peppers when young; when they turn light green they are rather hot. When fully ripe they are sweet and crisp, except for the seeds and their attachments which stay hot. Sprawling sub-shrub, will bear for up to 15 years in mild climates. F80

Manzano Rojo: (Red Rocoto) Medium-sized, blocky fruits ripen a deep, glossy red, and are milder and more like a bell pepper in flavor than the Amarillo when the core and inner membranes are removed. Though the flesh is sweeter, the core is hotter than Amarillo, giving quite a range of flavors. As an annual it reaches a height of 3 to 5 feet. F80

Cestrum nocturnum - *Night jessamine* {S} The leaves are cooked in fat, with tortillas. Central America, cultivated. KUNKEL; C9M, D29{PL}, E7M, F80, F85, G20, G96{PL}, H4, H4{PL}, *I61*, J27{PL}, L29{PL}, M82{PL}, O53M, O93, etc.

Cyphomandra betacea - *Tree tomato, Tamarillo* {S} The subacid fruits are eaten out of hand, stewed, grilled, baked, pickled, added to salads, or made into jams, jellies, chutneys, conserves, pies, salsas, preserves and sauces. South America, cultivated. FLETCHER [Cu, Pro], HEISER 1969, KENNARD, MORTON 1987a, POPENOE, W. 1920, SCHNEIDER [Pre, Re], SIMMONS 1972; A79M, C9M, C56M{PL}, E49, F80, G96{PL}, L91M, M1, *N40*{PR}, O53M, O89, O93, P5, *P17M*, S91M, etc.

CULTIVARS

Ecuadorian Orange: Fruit is medium orange in color, the size of a large hen's egg; pulp light orange, creamy in texture, less acid than the Ruby Red. Excellent for eating out of hand and also suited for culinary purposes. J23{OR}, R47

Goldmine: A superior cultivar originating in New Zealand and recently introduced. Very large golden-yellow fruit with golden, highly flavored flesh, less bland than Solid Gold, but not acidic. Has superb eating qualities. *O97*{PL}

Inca Gold: A yellow-fruited cultivar said to be less acid than the red types. When cooked the fruit is said to resemble the apricot in flavor. *Q49M*{PL}

Oratia Red: A large-fruited red cultivar, oval to rounded in shape, and with a sharp acid flavor. Good quality for eating out of hand, and excellent for jams and preserves. *O97*{PL}, *Q49M*{PL}

Rothamer: Unusually large fruit, over 3 ounces; skin bright red; flesh golden-yellow, flavor sweet and exotic; seeds dark red; ripens from December to April. Delicious eaten out of hand. Vigorous and heavy bearing plant. Originated in San Rafael, California. T49M

Ruby Red: Large, brilliant red fruit; pulp dark red, tart and flavorful. Fair for eating out of hand, but very good for culinary use. If allowed to ripen for one to three weeks after picking, they will become less acid. The standard cultivar grown for export in New Zealand. I99, T1M

Solid Gold: Large, oval shaped fruit; skin golden-orange in color; pulp soft, less acidic in flavor than Oratia Red. Very good for eating out of hand, with acceptable culinary qualities. *O97*{PL}

Yellow: Fruits the size and shape of a large plum; skin yellowish-orange; flesh yellow, with a milder flavor than the red types. The yellow form is the oldest in cultivation in New Zealand. N84, O93, P38

Cyphomandra casana - *Casana* {PL} The fruit is smaller than a tamarillo, spindle-shaped, green at first becoming yellow-striped, then full golden-yellow when ripe. The pulp is fragrant, sweet, not unlike a blending of the flavors of a peach and a tomato. Others say the flavor is like passionfruit or a juicy Thompson Seedless grape. It is best eaten in a ripe, fresh state. Ecuador, cultivated. CHILD 1985b, RILEY 1983; O93{S}, *O97*, *Q49M*

Cyphomandra crassifolia - *Mountain tomato* {PL} The fruit is green, the size of a hen's egg, and turns a greenish off-white when ripe. Rather bitter if eaten fresh, when cooked into jam or juice it has an unusual pleasant flavor. Closely related to C. betacea. Andean South America. *Q49M*

Cyphomandra fragrans - *Guava tamarillo* {S} Small, orange fruits with pulp that is vaguely reminiscent of guava, though not very exciting when eaten out of hand. Dried fruits lose their leatheriness and have a pleasant sour taste similar to the dried tamarinds used in Indian cookery. Since its skin is tough, it is under assessment in New Zealand for breeding to improve the shelf life of the tamarillo. South America. CHILD 1985b, RILEY 1983; O93, *Q32*

Iochroma fuchsioides - *Pico pico* {PL} The small red fruits are edible. South America. G20

Jaltomata procumbens - *Jaltomate* {S} Leaves are consumed raw, as a potherb, or cooked with eggs. The sweet black fruits are eagerly sought for food by the Tarahumaras of Mexico, either raw, cooked or dried. Roots are eaten raw, boiled, broiled or with radishes. Sold in local markets. Central America. ALTSCHUL, DAVIS, WILLIAMS, L.; F85

Lycium barbarum - *Duke of Argyle's tea tree* {PL} Leaves are used as a substitute for tea. China. TANAKA; P86

Lycium carolinianum - *Carolina wolfberry, Boxthorn* {PL} The bright red berries are reportedly pleasant eating, having a slightly salty taste. North America. MEDSGER; B83M{S}, *J25*, N37M

Lycium chinense - *Chinese boxthorn, Chinese wolfberry, Gau gei choi* {S} The young, soft leaves, having a peppermint-like flavor, are consumed raw in salads, as a potherb, cooked with rice or pork, or used in soups with duck's eggs. After roasting, the seeds are made into a coffee-like beverage. The fruits have a sweet, licorice-like flavor and are eaten raw, dried, added to soups and braised dishes, or used in the preparation of a liqueur. Dried leaves are used as a tea substitute, sometimes called *Lord Macartney's tea*. Eastern Asia, cultivated. COST 1988 [Cul], DAHLEN [Pre, Re], HAWKES, HERKLOTS [Cu, Re], OCHSE, TANAKA, YASHIRODA; D95{PL}, E83T, F85, I99, L59{PL}, N84

Lycium pallidum - *Pale wolfberry, Rabbit thorn* {S} Fruits are eaten fresh, cooked, or dried for future use. The Indians of the Southwest cooked them into a syrup or sauce which was dried, stored, and later recooked into a soup or sauce. They keep well when dried and ground into a meal. Western North America. HARRINGTON, H., KAVENA [Re], KIRK; L13

Lycopersicon esculentum → *Lycopersicon lycopersicum*

Lycopersicon humboldtii - *Tomato do Amazonas* {S} The fruits are eaten. Although small, they have a fine flavor. South America. HEDRICK 1919; Z23M

Lycopersicon lycopersicum - *Tomato* Ripe fruits are eaten raw, added to salads, stewed, purêed, stuffed, made into sauces, pastes, juice, catsup, or used in soups and stews. Unripe fruits are pickled, fried, roasted, or made into marmalade, pies, and relishes. The dried fruits, called *pumate*, are marinated in olive oil and used in gourmet cooking. Fermented tomato juice is marketed as *Biotta* or *Eden*. Flour, made from dried fruits, may be used to flavor and thicken soups, dips, sauces, breads, pancakes, muffins, puddings, and custards. Tomato seed oil is suitable for culinary purposes. South America, cultivated. FELL 1982b, HEISER 1969, HERKLOTS, HUNTER 1973a, KLEIN [Re], KRAFT [Re], LARKCOM 1984, MILIUS, TANAKA, UPHOF, VILMORIN [Cu]; (for cultivars see Tomato, page 514 and Rootstocks, page 470)

Lycopersicon pimpinellifolium - *Currant tomato, German raisin tomato* {S} The small, grape-like fruits are eaten raw, dried, added to salads and soups, or used as a garnish. They also make excellent pickles. Andean South America. HEDRICK 1919, ORGAN, VILMORIN; F85, J82

CULTIVARS

Broad Ripple Yellow: 60 days. Fruits are bright yellow, cherry-sized, borne in clusters, and very tasty. Non-shattering, fruits hold on the vine until picked. Excellent keeper. U33

Non-Shaterring Gold: 68 days. Globe-shaped fruits, 1/2 inch wide, borne in clusters; golden-yellow skin and flesh; tasty. Prolific yielder; does not drop its fruits when ripe. A49G, I99, M1

Non-Shattering Red: 70 days. Very small, pea-sized fruit; grows in clusters; good flavor. Excellent in salads and for garnishing. Very prolific. Holds on the vine until picked. Resistant to frosts. A49G, I99, M1

Puerto Escondido Red: Small, red fruit, 1/2 to 5/8 inch in diameter; typically produced in clusters of 8; drops when ripe. May be added to salads or frozen and later used in cooking. Vines are long, spreading and vigorous. Wild type from Puerto Escondido, Mexico. L7M

Shaterring Red: 70 days. Very small, pea-sized fruit with excellent flavor; drops from the vine when ripe. Harvested by spreading a cloth under the vine and shaking. Good in salads and as a garnish. U33

Nicotiana tabacum - *Tobacco* {S} Tobacco leaf protein, an odorless, tasteless white powder can be added to cereal grains, vegetables, soft drinks, and other foods. It can be whipped like egg whites, liquified, or gelled, and it can take on the flavor and texture of a variety of foods. It is 99.5% protein and contains no salt, fat or cholesterol. Currently being tested as a low calorie substitute for mayonnaise and whipped cream. South America, cultivated. PIRIE, SHEEN; D62, E97, J73, J82, K20, K47T, L86, O53M, Q41, R47, S55

CULTIVARS

Burley: A striking specimen plant with 18 inch leaves and numerous clusters of rose-pink flowers. The plant is best grown at about 30^0 latitude for commercial production. C43M, C43M{PL}

Burley No. 21: 120 days. All-purpose plug tobacco for chewing or wrapping cigars. This sun-cured white burley is also a favorite for pipes and cigarettes. Produces very large white blooms; grows 4 to 6 feet tall. Start seeds indoors 5 to 6 weeks before transplanting. D76, F19M

Hick's Broadleaf: 120 days. A bright, popular flue-cured tobacco. F19M

Mont Calme Brun: (Havana, Havana Large Leaf) A fine Cuban variety of smoking tobacco. Has a very fresh and smooth flavor. Normally grown for cigars but can also be used for pipes and cigarettes. More tolerant of rich soils. F80, G64, I99, N84

Mont Calme Yellow: Yellow, improved Virginia type. Has a rich flavor of high quality. Grows 8 feet tall, with leaves 3 feet long and 1 foot wide. Very productive. Slightly tolerant of frosts. F80, N84

Muscatelle: An aromatic, dark-leaved smoking tobacco. F80, N84

Scherazi Iranian: Strong-flavored smoking tobacco of premium quality. Early maturing. Grows 4 to 5 feet tall. Pink flowers. A2, I99, K49T

Virginia: Dark leaved Virginian tobacco. Ideal pipe and cigarette tobacco. Grows to 6 feet tall. Best grown in light soils. A2, L91M

Physalis angulata - *Cutleaf ground-cherry* {S} The juicy, subacid fruits are eaten raw, fried, stewed, or made into marmalade by cooking in palm syrup. In Costa Rica, they are sometimes used in the preparation of hot chili sauces. Young leaves are used as a potherb. Tropics. HEDRICK 1919, MORTON 1977, WILLIAMS, L.; N84

Physalis edulis* → *Physalis peruviana

Physalis heterophylla - *Clammy ground-cherry* {S} Ripe fruits are eaten fresh, dried, or made into pies, jams, sauces, syrup, and preserves. Pectin must be added when making jam. Dried fruits are sometimes ground into meal or bread. North America. CROWHURST 1972, HARRINGTON, H., KINDSCHER, PETERSON, L.; D58, F80

Physalis ixocarpa - *Tomatillo, Mexican ground-cherry, Tomate verde* {S} Unripe fruits are widely used in *salsa verde*, a mildly hot chili sauce often served with tacos, enchiladas, tostadas, chilis rellenos, and other Mexican dishes. They are also stewed, fried, baked, or used in dressings, purées, curries, and soups. Ripe fruits are sweeter and can be eaten out of hand, added to salads and sandwiches, or used in pies and preserves. Mexico, cultivated. HALPIN [Cu, Cul], HEISER 1969, HERKLOTS, KENNEDY, D. [Cul], KIRK, MORTON 1987a [Cu], ORGAN, SCHNEIDER [Pre, Re], SIMMONS 1972; A87M, B75, C43M{PL}, C82, C89{PR}, D11M, D62, D87, E24, F71M, J20, J25M, L9M, M46, *N40*{PR}, etc.

CULTIVARS

Large Green: Large fruit, 2 to 3 inches across. The large fruit is easier to de-husk to make quantities of salsa but does not store as well as P. philadelphica. I99, J73, L11

Purple: Medium-sized fruit, 2 inches in diameter. A smaller purple fruit that is preferred by some for its sharper flavor, otherwise about the same as the green tomatillo. A49G, I99, K49M, M1

Purple Husk: Fruit somewhat smaller and harder to husk than the green types, should be used in cooking only when fully mature. The decorative purple husks are outstanding as a culinary garnish, particularly when the husk is separated along its ribs into a flower shape, with the fruit forming the flower center. Recommended for the restaurant trade. M46

Rendidora: Fruits are large, yellow-green when ripe, sweet acidic in flavor, and easy to pick since they are about the size of a golf ball. Plants at first grow upright, but then branches become prostrate when loaded with fruits. Ripens 15 days earlier than others and gives 80% greater yield. Good to eat raw, served sliced along with tomatoes. MORTON 1987a; Q34

Verde Puebla: 85 days. Large-fruited, uniform strain. The golf ball size fruits are harvested green for making salsa. Somewhat sweet and tangy if eaten raw after turning slightly yellow. Will split before becoming fully yellow. D68, D76, E97

Physalis peruviana - *Cape gooseberry, Poha, Peruvian ground-cherry* {S} The subacid fruits are eaten out of hand, dried, preserved, stewed, puréed, added to salads, or made into pies, cakes, sauces, jellies, compote, and jams. Using the husk as a handle, the fruits can be dipped into icing, chocolate, or fondant. The fruits often dry naturally on the plant, making a palatable "raisin" that does not have much sugar but is pleasant to eat. Dried fruits are said to be a substitute for yeast. Tropical America, cultivated. HEISER 1969, HERKLOTS [Cu, Nu], JOHNS [Cul], MORTON 1987a [Cu], RILEY 1983, SCHNEIDER [Pre, Re], SIMMONS 1972, WILDER; E33, E49, F21M{PR}, G67M, I83M{PL}, I99, M1, M16{PL}, O48, O89, O93, *Q49M*{PL}, R77M, S59M, S61, S91M, etc.

CULTIVARS

Giallo Grosso: (Large Golden Italian) The fruit is eaten raw or preserved after ripening to a golden-yellow color. In areas with mild winters the plant will last for several years. I77, Q11M

Giant: Large, golden-orange fruit, approximately 1 inch in diameter; delicious flavor. Vigorous, spreading plants grow 3 to 5 feet tall. Requires a long growing season. I99

Goldenberry: Fruits average 1 inch in diameter, with some reaching 2 inches; pulp is very flavorful and sweet. Dried fruits are used in fruit cakes in place of raisins. Said to be frost resistant; it has resisted light frosts which caused tomatoes and other Physalis species and cultivars to die. In cooler climates, it takes 1 1/2 years from seed to bear well. KRAFT, RILEY 1983; I99, L91M

Physalis philadelphica - *Wild tomatillo, Miltomate, Purple ground-cherry* {S} Fruits are eaten raw, stewed, fried, or made into sauces. In Central America, it is perhaps the most commonly used of the fruits of Physalis in hot chili sauces, or used like tomatoes. Cultivated in Guatemala and perhaps elsewhere for its relatively large fruits. North America, Mexico. VON REIS, WILLIAMS, L.

CULTIVARS

Purple de Milpa: Small, purple-tinted fruits are considered the best-flavored tomatillo. They have a sharper flavor that is preferred by some cooks. The fruits can be stored for months by pulling back the husks and stringing them like garlic. Only found as a semi-domesticated weed in the milpas or slash-and-burn cornfields, and is much sought after. J73, K49T, L7M

Tarahumara: Small fruit used for *salsa verde*. Grows wild in the fields. Self seeding. Prolific in Tucson, where it has escaped from cultivation. Adapted to high and low desert areas. I16

Zuni: Small, sweet fruit, excellent in salsas. Prolific plants; plant in spring in high, cool desert areas. Their culture, by the Zuni Indians, predates the tomato. From northern New Mexico. I16, L7M

Physalis pruinosa* → *Physalis pubescens

Physalis pubescens - *Ground cherry, Husk tomato, Strawberry tomato* {S} The subacid to sweet fruits are eaten out of hand, dried, pickled, stewed, added to salads, or used for pies, preserves, sauces, jams, and ice cream toppings. When dried in sugar, ground cherries make an excellent fruit to use in fruit cakes, some cooks preferring them to citron, figs, or even raisins. North America, Tropical America. ANGIER [Re], GIBBONS 1962 [Re], HALPIN [Cu, Cul], MEDSGER, VILMORIN; B73M, C82, C85M, D65, D82, E83T, G16, G93M, J7, J73, K71, L42, M0, M1

CULTIVARS

Cossack Pineapple: 60 days. Small, yellow fruits, about 1/2 inch in diameter. Excellent flavor reminiscent of a sweet pineapple. Excellent for preserves, hot dessert toppings, salads or mock pineapple yogurt. Short, bushy, spreading plant; height 12 to 18 inches. Originally from Eastern Europe. D87, I99, L7M

Goldie: 75 days. A selected strain with apricot-colored fruits, and a clean, sweet flavor when ripe. Slightly larger than Cossack Pineapple, averaging 3/4 inch in diameter. Plants are profusely branching, prolific, and decorative; interesting in flower beds. Bears until frost. G6, I77, L7M, M1

Improved Yellow: 70 days. Fruits grow inside a thin husk, which must be removed before cooking. When ripe, the husk turns brown and the fruit drops from the plant. The fruits may be used as soon as they are ripe or kept for future use. If left in the husks they will keep for several weeks. D11M

Pineapple Cherry: 75 days. Small, sweet fruit has the flavor of a pineapple. Fruits become sweeter each day after the first frost. Very easy to grow. Does well in poor soil. I99

Strawberry: A very old heirloom cultivar said to have a strawberry-like flavor. M1

Physalis viscosa - *Sticky ground-cherry* {S} The thin-skinned, golden yellow fruit is juicy and has a pleasant, subacid, cherry-like flavor. It is eaten raw or cooked. Tropical America, naturalized in North America. FOX, F., MORTON 1976; **T73M**

Saracha jaltomata* → *Jaltomata procumbens

Solanum aethiopicum - *African scarlet eggplant, Mock tomato, Garden egg* {S} The orange-red fruits are cooked and eaten like eggplant, pickled, or used for flavoring other foods. Young shoots are stripped of their numerous flowers and buds, and then finely cut for use in soups. They have a bitter taste. Sometimes known as the *tomato of the Jews of Constantinople*. These people are the Ladinos expelled to Constantinople from Spain about 1500 AD, and whose ancestors possibly carried this crop with them to Spain when they were expelled from Timbuktu about 1400 AD. Tropical Africa, Tropical Asia. DALZIEL, LESTER, VAN EPENHUIJSEN [Cu]; I99, N84, P38 (for cultivars see Eggplant, page 324)

Solanum alibile* → *Solanum sessiliflorum var. alibile

Solanum anomalum - *Children's tomato* {S} Fruits are eaten as a condiment in soups and sauces. They are also dried, preserved, or fermented into *dawadawa*, which can be used as a flavoring. West Tropical Africa. DALZIEL, UPHOF; F85

Solanum aviculare - *Kangaroo apple, Poro-poro* {S} Fully ripe fruits are eaten raw, boiled, baked, stewed with sugar, or made into jam. They should be harvested after having fallen from the branches, when they lose their unpleasant acidity. Also used as an ornamental and a rootstock. Australia, New Zealand. COLENSO, CRIBB, HEDRICK 1919, UPHOF; B92{PL}, F85, I99, L91M, *N79M*, N84, O93, R15M, R47

Solanum x burbankii - *Wonderberry, Sunberry, Msoba* {S} The small, deep-blue fruits are eaten. Often confused with S. scabrum, which has larger, purple-black fruits. Once sold by Gleckler's Seedsmen of Metamora, Ohio who described it as "an annual domesticated blueberry from South Africa...quite similar to the California Sunberry grown by the great Luther Burbank 50 years ago. In colonial days of Africa farm women used Gsoba for tarts, jams, etc...It appears Gsoba would be adapted also for making fermented beverages". Tropical Africa. HEISER 1969, ZEVEN; **V19**

CULTIVARS

Mrs. B's Non-Bitter: 60 days. Plants grow to 3 feet. Fruits are smaller than Garden Huckleberry, borne in clusters; more intense in flavor. Can be eaten raw, but is better cooked or used in jams and pies. I99, K49M

Solanum caripense - *Tzimbalo, Pepino llorón* {S} The fruits, hardly larger than cherries, are eagerly eaten by the South American people. Their sweetish juice makes them palatable although they have little flesh and numerous seeds. In Colombia, they are made into preserves. Closely related to, and hybridizes with S. muricatum. Andean South America. CORRELL, HEISER 1964, HEISER 1969, PEREZ-ARBELAEZ; **U34**

Solanum centrale - *Desert raisin, Akaytjirra* {S} Fruits are eaten fresh when greenish-brown. Dried, shriveled fruits are reportedly similar to sultanas, and after rubbing in the native red sand are said to taste more like raisins. Australia. O'CONNELL; R47

Solanum demissum - *Papa cimarrona, Papa del monte* {S} Tubers are cooked and eaten. They are frequently added to soups and stews as much for flavoring as for their food value. In Mexico, the fruits are cooked and eaten as a sweet, without the addition of sugar. Fully ripened fruits are said to have the odor of mango, papaya, or wild strawberry. Central America. CORRELL; Y75

Solanum fendleri - *Fendler potato, Wild potato* {S} The small tubers are eaten raw, boiled, baked, or roasted. They are said to be pleasant tasting, somewhat like a boiled chestnut. Southwestern North America. GIBBONS 1979, HEDRICK 1919, KIRK, MEDSGER, YANOVSKY; **T87M**

Solanum ferox - *Terong asam, Ma ûk muak* {S} The fuzzy, orange fruits are cooked and eaten. They are made into a sour-relish, or used in curries. Southeast Asia. BURKILL, HERKLOTS, UPHOF, WATT; F85

Solanum gilo* → *Solanum aethiopicum

Solanum hirsutissimum* → *Solanum pectinatum

Solanum incanum - *Palestine nightshade, Meringam, Ikan* {S} The green, unripe fruits are eaten raw or cut into pieces and added to soups, or the pieces may be dried for later use. In Nigeria, both sweet and bitter types are cultivated. Seeds are used in the Sudan for curdling milk. Leaves are also edible. Tropical Africa, Tropical Asia. DALZIEL, MARTIN 1975, UPHOF, VAN EPENHUIJSEN; F85

Solanum indicum - *Terong pipit puteh* {S} Ripe fruits are eaten in soups and sauces. Unripe fruits are used in curries. Leaves are also edible. Tropical Asia. BURKILL, MACMILLAN, TANAKA, UPHOF; F85, Q46

Solanum integrifolium* → *Solanum aethiopicum

Solanum intrusum* → *Solanum scabrum

Solanum jamesii - *Colorado wild potato* {S} Tubers are eaten raw, baked, or boiled. They can be stored for several months, or they can be sliced, dried, and ground into a flour. The Hopi Indians cook the tubers with a saline clay and also reportedly use them in making yeast. Southwestern North America. CORRELL, HARRINGTON, H. [Pre, Re], YANOVSKY; **Y75**

Solanum laciniatum - *Kangaroo apple* {S} The fruit is edible when fully ripe. Australia. CRIBB; *N79M*, N84, O35G{PL}, O53M

Solanum macrocarpon - *Gboma eggplant* {S} Fruits are eaten as a cooked vegetable or used in soups and sauces. The leaves are steamed and served with rice. Tropical Africa, cultivated. LESTER, OCHSE, OOMEN, TANAKA; **U34, W59M, Z98**

Solanum melanocerasum* → *Solanum scabrum

Solanum melongena - *Eggplant, Aubergine, Brinjal* Fruits are eaten raw, fried, baked, stewed, pickled, grilled, marinated, added to soups, stews, and curries, or used in *caponata, ratatouille, Imam bayeldi*, etc. The leaves are mixed with the rice bran and salt in which daikon roots are pickled. Tropical Asia, cultivated. BIANCHINI, HALPIN [Cu, Cul], HEISER 1969, HERKLOTS, OCHSE, SCHNEIDER [Pre, Re], TANAKA, VILMORIN [Cu]; (for cultivars see Eggplant, page 324)

Solanum muricatum - *Pepino dulce, Melon pear* {S} The sweet, aromatic, refreshing fruits are very good eaten out of hand, having the flavor of a ripe muskmelon with a hint of pear or pineapple. They can also be used in fruit salads, as a garnish, served with prosciutto, or made into sauces, jams, and preserves. Occasionally available in specialty markets. Andean South America, cultivated. HEISER 1969, HERKLOTS, NATIONAL RESEARCH COUNCIL 1989, POPENOE, W. 1924, SCHNEIDER [Cul]; E13G{PR}, *N40*{PR}, N84{S}, P38 (for cultivars see Pepino Dulce, page 435)

Solanum nigrum - *Black nightshade, Morelle* {S} Young shoots and leaves are eaten as potherbs or added to soups. Ripe fruits are eaten stewed or made into pies, jams, preserves, puddings, sauces, pastry, or a spicy relish. They are usually cooked with sugar and lemon juice to make them palatable. The unripe fruits contain solanine and should not be eaten. Cosmopolitan. CRIBB, FERNALD, FOX, F., GIBBONS 1979, HARRINGTON, H. [Re], HEDRICK 1919, MACMILLAN, OCHSE, UPHOF, VAN EPENHUIJSEN [Cu, Pro]; A79M, C43M, F85, *N71M*, N84

Solanum nigrum var. guineense* → *Solanum scabrum

Solanum nigrum var. nodiflorum* → *Solanum nodiflorum

Solanum nodiflorum - *Popolo* {S} The leaves are boiled and used like spinach. In Hawaii, they were cooked in underground ovens and eaten with fish as a substitute for poi. Ripe fruits are eaten, and have a peculiar flavor that is agreeable to some. Fresh or dried leaves were made into a tea. Tropics. ALTSCHUL, CRIBB, DALZIEL, DEGENER, UPHOF; **Y2, Z98**

Solanum paucijugum - *Sacha papa* {S} Edible tubers are the size of a pigeon's egg. Fruits are also consumed. Ecuador. CORRELL; **T87M**

Solanum pectinatum - *Lulita* {S} The juicy fruits may be eaten raw but are best cooked with sugar after their fuzz has been brushed off and perhaps after thin peeling. Pulp is acid but the sugar content is relatively high and the flavor is somewhat aromatic. The fruit has extremely fine juice, almost equal to that of the naranjilla, and is used in the preparation of refreshing beverages. Tropical America. HEISER 1985, HERKLOTS; **U34**

Solanum pseudolulo - *Lulo comun, Lulo de perro* {S} Fruits are used in the preparation of refreshing drinks. The pulp is pale yellow and the quality of the juice is generally inferior to that of the naranjilla. Produces fertile hybrids when crossed with the naranjilla. Colombia. HEISER 1969, HEISER 1985, MORTON 1987a; **U34, Z98**

Solanum quitoense - *Naranjilla, Golden fruit of the Andes* {S} The fruits are bright orange, thick-skinned, and have greenish pulp of a very refreshing, subacid flavor that has been likened to a combination of orange, pineapple and tomato. In Ecuador and Colombia, freshly squeezed naranjilla juice is used to make *sorbete*, a green, foamy drink with an appealing sweet-sour flavor of pineapple and strawberry. The juice is also used for flavoring ice cream and sherbets, or made into jam and jelly. In Panama, it is mixed with sugar cane juice to make an unfermented *chicha*. Andean South America, cultivated. DUKE, HEISER 1985, HERKLOTS, MORTON 1987a [Cu, Pro], NATIONAL RESEARCH COUNCIL 1975a, POPENOE, W. 1924, SCHULTES, STURROCK; D33, E29, E29{PL}, E29{PR}, F80, F85, I99, K49T, N84, O89, O93, *O97*{PL}, *Q49M*{PL}

Solanum scabrum - *Garden huckleberry* {S} The purplish-black fruits, when thoroughly ripe, are eaten raw, stewed, or used in jams, jellies, sauces, pies and preserves. They are usually cooked in baking soda first to remove the bitterness, and then prepared with sugar and lemon juice. In West Africa, the leaves are used as a potherb. Cultivated. CHILD 1985a, FELL 1982b [Cu, Pre], FERNALD, HEISER 1969, MARTIN 1975, MASEFIELD, SIMMONS 1978, TANAKA; B73M, C82, D11M, D65, E97, G16, G68, I99, J7, K49M, L42, M1

CULTIVARS

Schwartzbeeren: (Loneberry) 60-75 days. Plant grows to 2 feet tall, self-seeds. Fruits dark-purple, round, 1/4 inch in diameter, borne in clusters. Heirloom cultivar brought by Volga German immigrants to Kansas and Nebraska in the 1880 to 1920 period. **U33**

Solanum sessiliflorum - *Cocona, Cubiu, Orinoco apple* {S} The ovoid fruits, suggestive of large red or yellow apples, have an acid, pale-cream flesh that is distinctly acid. Although the flavor is agreeable, they are not recommended for eating out of hand. When peeled and used whole for making jams, preserves, pies, and sauces, the product might be compared with that of apricot, pineapple, or gooseberry. An acidulous, thirst-quenching drink can also be prepared form the fruits. In Brazil, the leaves are cooked and eaten. Tropical America, cultivated. HEDRICK 1919, HERKLOTS, MORTON 1987a [Cu, Pro], RILEY 1983, SCHULTES; E29, E29{PL}, E29{PR}, I59G, P38

Solanum sessiliflorum var. alibile - *Cocona uvilla* {S} Cultivated as a dessert fruit and source of a refreshing beverage. The fruits are globose, orange-red, more than twice as large as those of other forms of cocona, and are also less acidulous. Colombia. SCHULTES, ZEVEN; F85

Solanum spirale - *Titakuchi* {S} Fruits are eaten raw or cooked. Leaves are cooked and eaten or used as a condiment. Tropical Asia. TANAKA, UPHOF; **Z25M**

Solanum topiro* → *Solanum sessiliflorum

Solanum torvum - *Pea eggplant, Susumber, Plate brush, Pokak* {S} Young shoots are eaten raw or cooked. In the West Indies, especially Jamaica, the half grown, firm berries are boiled and eaten with fish, yams, akees, or in soups and stews. They have a distinctive, bitter flavor. In tropical Asia, they are eaten raw, cooked and served with rice, or used in stews, curries, and chili sauces such as Thailand's *nam prik*. Tropics. COST 1988 [Cul], HAWKES [Re], HERKLOTS, OCHSE, TANAKA, UPHOF; F85, P38

CULTIVARS

Snake Eye: (Lao Green Grape) 135 days. Tiny, round fruit, no more than 1/2 inch in diameter; light yellow-green at harvest stage; seedy flesh. Used in traditional Laotian cuisine. May be used in any stir-fry dish calling for eggplant. Very tall, thorny plant, height 6 feet; bears fruit in grape-like clusters; resistant to nematodes, flea beetles and cold. K49M, L7M

Solanum tuberosum - *Potato* Tubers are eaten boiled, baked, fried, roasted, mashed, or used in soups, stews, dumplings, pancakes, potato salad, etc. Also used for the manufacture of starch and alcoholic beverages, especially *vodka*. In Scandinavia, the national beverage is *aquavit* made from potato alcohol and flavored with caraway, orange or lemon peel, cardamon, and other spices. In South America, they are made into *chuño*. The water from cooked potatoes is sometimes employed in the preparation of leavens used in *sourdough bread* manufacture. Andean South America, cultivated. CARCIONE, FELL 1982b, HEISER 1969, HERKLOTS, TANAKA, UPHOF, VILMORIN [Cu]; (for cultivars see Potato, page 455)

Solanum uporo - *Cannibal's tomato* {S} Red fruits are used like tomatoes in the preparation of sauces. The leaves are eaten as a potherb. Polynesia. HEDRICK 1919, UPHOF; **V73M**

Solanum verrucosum - *Papa morda* {S} Tubers are eaten. A plant considered to be this species was once cultivated by the peasants in the neighborhood of Geneva, Switzerland. The tubers produced were smaller and later in development than S. tuberosum, of excellent flavor, and had yellow flesh. Mexico. CORRELL, ZEVEN; **Y75**

Solanum vestissimum - *Lulo de la tierra fria, Toranja, Tumo* {S} The juice of the fruits is used in the preparation of refreshing beverages. It has an excellent flavor, but the hairs of the fruit are rather bristly, and so the juice is difficult to extract. Colombia. HEISER 1985; **U34**

Solanum wendlandii - *Kishtan, Ixtan* {PL} Used as a potherb in southern Mexico and Guatemala. Central America. CHILD 1985b; C56M, G20, L29

Solanum xanthocarpum - *Yellow-berried nightshade, Thorny nightshade, Makeuwa praw* {S} The slightly bitter fruits are eaten raw, steamed with dips, or cooked in curries. Eaten green (immature), before the seeds mature and become tough. Leaves are used as a potherb. Widely used in Thai cuisine. Southern Asia to Polynesia. COOK, HEDRICK 1919, MACMILLAN, WATT; F85

Withania somnifera - *Kuthmithi* {S} Seeds are used in the Sudan to coagulate milk. Southern Eurasia, North Africa. UPHOF; C13M, C43M, C43M{PL}, D62, F80, I59G, I99, K47T, N42{PL}, N84

SONNERATIACEAE

Duabanga grandiflora* → *Duabanga sonneratioides

Duabanga sonneratioides - *Nepal-lampetis, Bandorhulla* {S} The very acid fruit is eaten fresh or made into a refreshing drink. Indomalaya. TANAKA; **X88M**

Sonneratia caseolaris - *Perepat, Berembang* {S} Ripe fruits are eaten raw or cooked, having a cheese-like flavor. Young ones are used for flavoring chutney and curries. Also employed for making vinegar. Southeast Asia. BURKILL, TANAKA, UPHOF, WATT; F85, N84

SPHENOCLEACEAE

Sphenoclea zeylanica - *Goonda* {S} The leaves and young leafy tops of the stems are steamed and eaten as a potherb, mixed with grated coconut, or served as a side-dish with rice. They have a slightly bitter but pleasant flavor. Often sold in local markets in Java. Tropical Africa, Tropical Asia. BURKILL, OCHSE, UPHOF; N84

STAPHYLEACEAE

Staphylea pinnata - *European bladder-nut, False pistachio, Nez-coupé* {S} The kernels of the fruit are said to taste like pistachios and are eaten in Germany by children. Southern Europe. HEDRICK 1919, ROOT 1980a; F85, K47T, K63G, N84, N93M, P49, *P63*, R78, S7M

Staphylea trifolia - *American bladder-nut* {S} The seeds are eaten raw or they can be used in place of walnuts in chocolate chip cookies. A cooking oil has been extracted from the seeds. North America. GIBBONS 1979, KROCHMAL; *B68*{PL}, D95{PL}, F85, K47T, K63G, N37M{PL}, N84

STERCULIACEAE

Brachychiton diversifolium - *Australian flame, Kurrajong* {S} Seeds are eaten raw, roasted, or used as a substitute for coffee. The yam-like, tuberous roots were a popular item of food with the Aborigines. Australia. CRIBB; A79M, B62, C27M, C56M{PL}, *I61*, I83M{PL}, I99, K77M{PL}, O33, O84, P5, R15M, R33M, R47, S92, T7, etc.

Brachychiton populneum* → *Brachychiton diversifolium

Cola acuminata - *Cola nut, Kola nut* {PL} When chewed, the caffeine-rich seeds act as a stimulant, retard hunger and fatigue, aid digestion, and increase one's stamina. At first bitter, they modify the sensation of taste so that any food or drink, consumed immediately thereafter, seems sweet. Traditionally, they were an ingredient of a stimulating beverage. An extract, prepared from the dried kernels, is used to flavor carbonated beverages, ice cream, candy, baked goods, and liqueurs. The kernels are white, pink or red. Red ones can be used as a natural food colorant. West Tropical Africa, cultivated. MENNINGER, MORTON 1976, ROSENGARTEN, SCHERY; F85{S}, J22

Cola heterophylla - *Monkey cola* {S} The seeds are eaten or used as a masticatory. The leaves are cooked like spinach. West Tropical Africa. KUNKEL, MENNINGER; **Z25M**

Dombeya rotundifolia - *Wild pear* {S} The fruits are edible. Flowers are cooked and eaten as a side-dish to which pumpkin leaves are sometimes added. Tropical Africa. FOX, F., KUNKEL; A79M, F85, P5, *P17M*, R77M

Guazuma ulmifolia - *West Indian elm, Guasimo* {S} Green fruits are eaten raw, cooked, crushed in water to make a beverage, or used to flavor other foods. The sap is employed to clarify syrup in the manufacture of sugar. Tropical America. DUKE, UPHOF; F85, N84

Heritiera littoralis - *Lookinglass tree* {S} Seeds are eaten with fish. The leaves are used in the preparation of *Onge tea*. Old World Tropics. BHARGAVA, TANAKA; F85, N84

Heritiera macrophylla - *Kai-tau-tsz* {S} Natives eat the skin of the fruit with *ping long*. Tropical Asia. ALTSCHUL; **Z25M**

Hermannia hyssopifolia - *Ag-dae-geneesbossie* {S} The plant is used in making an aromatic tea. Southern Africa. FOX, F.; N84

Hildegardia barteri - *Bronyadua* {S} Seeds are eaten raw or roasted, and are said to resemble peanuts in flavor. Also the source of and edible oil. West Tropical Africa. IRVINE 1960, KUNKEL; F85, N84

Kleinhovia hospita - *Mien-tao-kuo* {S} Leaves and flowers are cooked and eaten. Southeast Asia. BURKILL, HEDRICK 1919, TANAKA; F85, N84

Pterospermum acerifolium - {S} The flowers are edible. Southeast Asia. BURKILL, TANAKA; F85, N84

Pterygota alata - *Buddha's coconut* {S} Seeds are parched and eaten. Southern Asia. TANAKA; A79M, F85, N84, P5, *P17M*, Q12, Q46

Sterculia alata* → *Pterygota alata

Sterculia apetala - *Panama tree* {S} The almond-flavored seeds are eaten raw, roasted, or fried. Roasted and ground seeds are mixed with water to form a beverage or sweetmeat. Fruits are also edible. Tropical America. DUKE, KENNARD, TANAKA, VON REIS, WILLIAMS, L.; F85, N84

Sterculia chicha - *Maranhão nut, Castanha do Pará* {S} Seeds are roasted and eaten or used in lieu of cola nuts. They are said to have the flavor of chocolate or of peanuts. Tropical America. MENNINGER, TANAKA; **X88M**

Sterculia foetida - *Java olive* {S} Seeds are eaten raw, roasted, or fried. They are oily and have a pleasant, cacao-like flavor. If eaten in too large a quantity, they have a purgative effect. The rootstock of the young plant is rich in starch, has a flavor similar to jicama (Pachyrhizus erosus), and can be eaten raw. Leaves are also used for food. Tropics. KENNARD, KUNKEL, MENNINGER, PONGPANGAN; F85, N84, O93

Sterculia lanceolata - {S} Seeds are eaten or used as a seasoning for other foods. Southeast Asia. TANAKA; F85

Sterculia tragacantha - *African tragacanth* {S} Source of a tragacanth-like gum that exudes from the stem, used as an adulterant of *gum arabic* in confectionery. The young leaves are cooked and eaten as a potherb. Tropical Africa. DALZIEL, UPHOF; N84

Sterculia urens - *Gular* {S} Stems are the source of *karaya gum*, used like gum tragacanth in the preparation of sweetmeats and other foods. Seeds are roasted and eaten or used as a substitute for coffee. Tropical Asia. HEDRICK 1919, SCHERY, TANAKA; F85

Sterculia villosa - *Udal, Vakenar* {S} Seeds are eaten after roasting or baking. The bark exudes a gum used as a substitute for gum tragacanth. Roots are also edible. Tropical Asia. BURKILL, TANAKA, WATT; F85

Theobroma bicolor - *Peru cacao* {S} The pulp of the fruit is eaten. Seeds are used like cacao, yielding an inferior chocolate called *Nicaragua chocolate*, but good *cocoa butter*. Tropical America. DUKE, UPHOF, WILLIAMS, L.; **X88M**, **X94**

Theobroma cacao - *Cacao* {S} Fermented seeds, called cacao beans, are the source of *cocoa*, *chocolate*, and *cocoa butter*, widely used in confectionery, milk chocolate, pastries, cakes, ice cream, chocolate milk, etc. Traditionally, cacao was mixed with corn meal and made into various beverages. In Tabasco, ground cacao beans are added to the dough in the preparation of *pozol*, a fermented maize dough. The resulting product is called *chorote*. Pulp of the fruit is sucked as a sweet snack, preserved, crystallized, or made into alcoholic beverages and vinegar. Tropical America, cultivated. DUKE, KENNARD, SCHERY, STEINKRAUS, UPHOF; F85, I83M{PL}, J22{PL}, N84, O93

Theobroma grandiflorum - *Capú-assú* {S} The fleshy pulp of the fruit has a pleasant, subacid, aromatic flavor and is eaten fresh or used in sherbets, *refrescos* and *doces*. Brazil. MARTIN 1987, SCHERY, UPHOF; **X88M**

Theobroma subincanum - *Capuahy* {S} Fruit pulp is eaten or made into sweetmeats. Seeds are the source of an inferior cacao. Brazil. UPHOF; **Z25M**

STILAGINACEAE

Antidesma bunius - *Bignay, Chinese laurel* {S} When fully ripe the fruits are slightly sweet and may be eaten raw. Otherwise they are cooked with fish, used in jellies, preserves, fruit punches, syrup and sauces, or made into wine and brandy. Young leaves are eaten raw or steamed and served with rice. They are also mixed with other foods to give a sour flavor. Southeast Asia. KENNARD, MORTON 1987a [Cu, Pro], OCHSE, RICHARDSON [Pre, Re], UPHOF; F85, H49, J36{PL}, P5

Antidesma dallachyanum - *Herbert River cherry, Currant tree* {S} The fruits, which have a very high vitamin C content, are reddish-purple when ripe, larger and with more flesh than A. bunias, and very acid. They are not usually eaten out of hand, but are said to make a deep-red jelly that is equal to that made from the European red currant. Australia. CRIBB, JOHNS, MORTON 1987a, STURROCK; N84, P38

Antidesma ghaesembilla - *Black currant tree* {S} When fully ripe, the reddish-purple fruits are subacid to somewhat sweet. They are eaten raw, used in jams and jellies, or made into *roodjak* with chilis, fish paste, salt, and sugar. Young shoots are eaten as a vegetable or used like tamarind for giving other foods a sour taste. Malaysia to the Philippines. MORTON 1987a, OCHSE; F85, N84, Q46

Antidesma platyphyllum - *Bignay* {S} The pink fruits are eaten raw or made into syrup, jellies, and wine. Hawaii. KENNARD, STURROCK, UPHOF; **Y2**

STRYCHNACEAE

Strychnos cocculoides - *Monkey orange* {S} Pulp of the fruit is juicy and pleasant to eat, sweeter than S. spinosa and hence more popular. Its juice is used fresh, fermented, or made into a refreshing sour-sweet drink. Occasionally the fruit is picked green and ripened by burying it in sand, where it will keep for several months. Seeds may be poisonous if chewed or swallowed. Tropical Southern Africa. FOX, F.; N84

Strychnos innocua - *Nkwakwa* {S} The slimy, sweet pulp of the fruit is eaten or used for making jams. Tropical Africa. KUNKEL, UPHOF; N84

Strychnos spinosa - *Kaffir orange, Natal orange* {S} Ripe fruits have an agreeable, aromatic flavor. They can be eaten raw or used to make a refreshing beverage. The leaves are eaten with couscous. Seeds are somewhat poisonous. Drier Tropical Africa. DALZIEL, FAIRCHILD 1930, FOX, F., IRVINE 1960; N84

Strychnos unguacha* → *Strychnos innocua

STYRACACEAE

Halesia carolina - *Silver-bell tree, Wild olive* {PL} The ripe fruits are chewed for their acidity. Unripe ones are sometimes made into pickles. Southeastern North America. FERNALD, HEDRICK 1919; A93M, C9M{S}, E6, E7M{S}, E87, H4, H49, K38{S}, K47T{S}, M77, N37M, N93M{S}, R78{S}

Halesia tetraptera* → *Halesia carolina

Styrax benzoin - *Sumatra benzoin* {S} The bark is the source of a resin, called *benzoin* or *ansokukô*, used to flavor chewing gum, baked goods, puddings, soft drinks, candies, and chocolates. Malaya. MORTON 1976, TANAKA; F85

Styrax officinalis - *Storax tree* {S} Stems and branches yield a highly perfumed, balsamic gum occasionally used as a condiment. Southwest Asia. KUNKEL; N84

SYMPLOCACEAE

Palura chinensis* → *Symplocos chinensis

Symplocos chinensis - *Sapphire-berry, Sawa-futagi* {S} The small, sapphire-blue berries are used in jams, jellies, and sauce. Japan, Korea, cultivated. FREITUS [Re], TANAKA; *B68*{PL}, E7M, K63G, N84, O67, O93, *R28*

Symplocos paniculata* → *Symplocos chinensis

Symplocos tinctoria - *Sweet leaf, Horse-sugar* {PL} On hot summer days, the leaves are chewed for their pleasantly sweet, slightly acid flavor that is refreshing and relieves one's thirst. North America. FERNALD, GIBBONS 1979; H4, *I17M*, N84{S}

TACCACEAE

Tacca leontopetaloides - *Polynesian arrowroot* {S} Tubers are sometimes eaten boiled or roasted. A starch extracted from them, called *Tahiti arrowroot* or *Fiji arrowroot*, is used in breads and soups, or it is mixed with papayas, bananas, and pumpkins, flavored with vanilla and lemon and cooked into *poi*. Pacific Islands, cultivated. HERKLOTS, MASSAL, UPHOF; F85, N84

Tacca pinnatifida* → *Tacca leontopetaloides

TAMARICACEAE

Tamarix aphylla - *Athel tamarisk, Khora-gaz* {S} A sweet, manna-like substance that forms on the twigs is used to adulterate cane sugar. The Tuareg eat it with porridge or mix it with water to form a refreshing beverage. North Africa to Southern Asia. DONKIN, HEDRICK 1919; *J0*, N84, *P17M*

Tamarix articulata* → *Tamarix aphylla

Tamarix canariensis - *Tamarisk, Manna plant* {S} The sweet, manna-like substance that exudes from the stems is collected and mixed with flour, sugar or honey, and sweet almonds, formed into cakes, and baked into a kind of sweetmeat. Macaronesia, Mediterranean region. DONKIN, HEDRICK 1919; F85, K38, K47T, L91M, N84, N93M, O53M, O93, P49, *P63*, *Q32*, *R28*, S95

Tamarix gallica* → *Tamarix canariensis

Tamarix ramosissima - {PL} The stems yield an edible manna that is used in confectionery. Southern Eurasia. KUNKEL; C9, D95, K47T{S}

TAXACEAE

Taxus baccata - *English yew* {S} The bark is used as a substitute for tea. Fruits are sometimes eaten, however the seeds are considered poisonous. Eurasia, cultivated. HEDRICK 1919, KUNKEL, TANAKA; C9M, D62, *G66*, K38, K63G, L91M, N84, N93M, O53M, O93, P49, *P63*, Q46, R78

Taxus cuspidata - *Japanese yew* {S} The sweet aril, or fruit pulp, is eaten raw, made into jam, or brewed into wine. Caution is recommended, as the seeds of many species are poisonous. Japan. TANAKA; A79M, B9M{PL}, E97{PL}, *F38*, *G66*, I4{PL}, K38, K63G, M76{PL}, *N71M*, N93M, O53M, O93, P5, *P39*, P49, R78, etc.

Torreya californica - *California nutmeg* {S} Kernels are eaten. They also yield an edible oil. Western North America. TANAKA; B94, G59M, *L47*{PL}, N93M, P49, P86{PL}

Torreya grandis - *Chinese torreya* {S} Seeds are roasted and eaten. China. UPHOF; B94, *G66*, N84

Torreya nucifera - *Kaya, Japanese torreya* {S} Seeds are eaten raw, roasted, or used in confectionery. They have an agreeable, somewhat resinous taste. Also the source of an edible oil used in cooking. Sometimes found in Oriental markets. Japan, cultivated. MENNINGER, UPHOF; B74{PL}, B94, G43M{PL}, N84, *P39*, P49, P86{PL}, R78

TETRAGONIACEAE

Tetragonia decumbens - *Sea spinach* {S} The leaves may be used as a substitute for spinach. Southern Africa. MARTIN 1975; N84, R15M, S92, T7

Tetragonia expansa* → *Tetragonia tetragonoides

Tetragonia implexicoma - *Australian spinach* {S} Leaves are cooked and eaten as a substitute for spinach. Australia and New Zealand. HEDRICK 1919; **Y29M**

Tetragonia tetragonoides - *New Zealand spinach* {S} The young, succulent leaves and stem tips are an excellent hot weather substitute for spinach. They may be eaten raw, steamed, boiled, stir-fried, creamed, served with mushrooms, made into a quiche, prepared au gratin, etc. Australia, New Zealand, cultivated. CLARKE [Re], HALPIN, VILMORIN [Cu]; B78, C44, E24, F19M, F82, G16, G68, H66, J7, J73, K22, L7M, L9M, M13M, T1M, etc.

THEACEAE

Adinandra bockiana - *Wong-pan-ch'a-shue* {PL} The black fruit is edible. Also used as a substitute for tea, although Altschul does not indicate which part of the plant is used. Southern China. ALTSCHUL, VON REIS; N37M

Adinandra milletii* → *Adinandra bockiana

Eurya japonica - *Hisakaki* {S} Leaves are used as a tea substitute or to adulterate China tea. China, Japan. TANAKA; N84

TILIACEAE

Corchorus acutangulus* → *Corchorus aestuans

Corchorus aestuans - *Rumput bayam rusa* {S} The leaves are eaten in salads, as a potherb, or used for vegetable bouillon. Old World Tropics. BURKILL, DALZIEL, HEDRICK 1919, TANAKA; F85, N84

Corchorus capsularis - *Jute* {S} Young leaves and shoots are steamed or boiled and eaten with rice. Leaves are also used as a substitute for tea. Tropics, Subtropics. BURKILL, TANAKA, WATT; F85, N91, O39M

Corchorus olitorius - *Jew's mallow, Bush okra, Melukhiya* {S} Very young leaves are used in salads. Older leaves and shoot tips are an excellent hot weather spinach substitute, being high in protein. A popular soup in Egypt and the Near East is made from finely hashed melukhiya spiced with fried garlic and coriander, and cooked with broth of rabbit, chicken, mutton, or goose. The dried leaves, which are available in Middle Eastern stores, are commonly used to thicken soups and stews, or they can be made into tea. Immature fruits are used in salads or as a potherb. Tropics, Subtropics. DARBY, DUKE, MALLOS [Re], MARTIN 1975, TANAKA, VAN EPENHUIJSEN, VILMORIN [Cu]; D33, E83T, F80, F85, L50M{PR}, N84, O53M, R47

Corchorus tridens - *Ligusha* {S} Leaves and young shoots are boiled and eaten as a vegetable or put into soups. Tropics. FOX, F., TANAKA; N84

Corchorus trilocularis - *Al moulinouquia* {S} Leaves are used as a potherb. In Malawi they are cooked with native potashes, the resulting product being mucilaginous and well liked. Cultivated in some parts of Africa and Arabia. Tropics. FOX, F., HEDRICK 1919, UPHOF, ZEVEN; N84

Grewia asiatica - *Phálsa, Dhamin* {S} The subacid fruits are eaten raw, preserved, as a flavoring for sherbets, made into refreshing drinks, or fermented into an alcoholic beverage. The bark is employed for clarifying sugar. Tropical Asia. HEDRICK 1919, KENNARD, MORTON 1987a [Cu, Pro], TANAKA; F85, N84, P38, Q12

Grewia betulifolia* → *Grewia tenax

Grewia caffra - *Wild raisin* {S} The small yellow fruits, about the size of a pea, are eaten after ripening when they are sweet to chew, even when dry. Southern Africa. FOX, F.; C9M, C56M{PL}, *F53M*{PL}, G96{PL}, N84, R41

Grewia hexamita - *Giant raisin* {S} The thin, fleshy pulp of the reddish fruits is eaten raw. Southeastern Africa. FOX, F.; F85

Grewia occidentalis - *Cross berry* {S} Ripe fruits are purplish and quite pleasant to eat raw. The juice is eaten fresh or fermented into an alcoholic beverage. Southern Africa. FOX, F.; L29{PL}, N84, O53M, O93, R41, R77M

Grewia subinaequalis* → *Grewia asiatica

Grewia tenax - *Chari, Tarakat* {S} The orange-red, acid fruits are eaten, having somewhat the flavor of hazelnuts. North Africa to Arabia. TANAKA, UPHOF, WATT; F85

Tilia americana - *American basswood* {PL} The fragrant flowers are used as a salad vegetable or brewed into a sweet, well-flavored tea. A paste of the ground fruits and flowers is said to resemble chocolate in texture and taste. Young leaves are chewed or added to salads and sandwiches. The sweet sap can be boiled down to sugar and syrup. North America. FERNALD, GIBBONS 1966b, GIBBONS 1979; B9M, C9M{S}, D45, D95, *G66*, *G66*{S}, H4, H49, K38{S}, K47T{S}, K64, *K89*, *M69M*, N93M{S}, O93{S}, etc.

Tilia argentea* → *Tilia tomentosa

Tilia cordata - *Small-leaved linden* {S} Flowers are used as a substitute for tea. Northern Europe. UPHOF; *B52*, E47, G1T{PL}, G41{PL}, *G66*, *G66*{PL}, H49{PL}, I9M{PL}, K38, K47T, *M69M*{PL}, M76{PL}, *N71M*, O53M, P49, *Q32*, etc.

Tilia x europaea (T. cordata x T. platyphyllos) - *Common linden, Lime tree* {S} The cooling, glutinous leaves are eaten raw in salads and sandwiches. Flowers have a honey-like fragrance and make an excellent tea that is popular in France, where it is sold under the name of *tilleul*. They are also used as a vegetable or brewed into wine. The sweet sap is a source of sugar. Also the source of an edible manna. Natural hybrid. Europe. DONKIN, LEGGATT, MABEY, MACNICOL [Re], MARCIN, MICHAEL [Re], TANAKA; O93, *Q32*

Tilia japonica - *Shina-no-ki* {S} Young budlings and flowers are parboiled to remove bitterness and then eaten as greens, put in soups, or used as a tea substitute. The fruit is also edible. Japan. TANAKA; D62, N84

Tilia tomentosa - *Linden, Lime tree* {S} Dried leaves are sometimes used as an adulterant of marjoram. Eurasia. BROUK; B9M{PL}, D95{PL}, *G66*, *G66*{PL}, K38, *N71M*, N84, N93M, O53M, O93, P49, *Q32*, *R28*, R78

TRAPACEAE

Trapa natans - *Water caltrop, Jesuit nut, Water chestnut, Ling-chio* {PL} The sweet seed kernels are eaten raw, roasted, boiled, fried like a vegetable, preserved in honey and sugar, candied, or ground into flour for making bread. They have a very agreeable and delicate flavor, very similar to that of boiled chestnuts. In Italy, they are the main ingredient of a famous *risotto*. Available in the fall at Chinatown markets. Eurasia, naturalized in North America. BIANCHINI [Re], COST 1988 [Pre], DAHLEN [Pre, Cul], FERNALD, HEDRICK 1919, ROSENGARTEN, SIMMONS 1972 [Cu], TANAKA; K34, N84{S}

CULTIVARS {S}

Su Zhou: An improved cultivar with red-colored fruit. *O54*

TRILLIACEAE

Medeola virginiana - *Indian cucumber-root* {PL} The white rhizomes are crisp and tender, with the aroma and taste of cucumbers. They are eaten raw as a nibble, boiled and served with butter, mixed into tossed salads dressed with oil and vinegar, or made into dill pickles. Eastern North America. FERNALD, GIBBONS 1966b, MEDSGER; C49, D62, D75T, E33M, I44, K47T{S}, N7T, N84{S}

Trillium erectum - *Red trillium* {PL} Young, unfolding leaves are an excellent addition to salads, tasting somewhat like raw sunflower seeds. They can also be used as a potherb served with butter or vinegar. Eastern North America. PETERSON, L.; C49, D75T, E33M, H49, I44, J78, K18, K79, L91M{S}, M37M, M77M, N7T, N8, N9M, N9M{S}, N45, N84{S}, etc.

Trillium grandiflorum - *White trillium* {PL} Tender young leaves are recommended as a cooked green vegetable. Eastern North America. UPHOF; B33M, C49, D75T, E33M, G82M, I22, I44, J78, K79, L91M{S}, M37M, M77, N7T, N8, N84{S}, N45, etc.

Trillium sessile - *Toadshade, Sessile trillium* {PL} Before unfolding, the leaves may be added to salads, often tasting vaguely like raw sunflower seeds. Or they can be boiled for ten minutes and served with butter or vinegar. Eastern North America. PETERSON, L.; B0, B77, C9, C56, C73M, E33M, E63M, G37M, G82M, J78, J91, K79, N8, N9M, N9M{S}, etc.

Trillium undulatum - *Painted trillium* {PL} Young, unfolding leaves make a good potherb. Boil in salted water for ten minutes and serve with butter and vinegar. Or they can be added to vegetable soups. Eastern North America. CROWHURST 1972; A34M, C49, D75T, E33M, E63M, G37M, I87, M37M, N7T, N8, N84{S}, O57

TROPAEOLACEAE

Tropaeolum majus - *Nasturtium, Indian cress* {S} The leaves have a tangy, watercress-like flavor and are used in salads, sandwich spreads, vegetable dishes, or are stuffed like grape leaves. Flowers have a similar flavor and use and also make an attractive garnish, or can be added to vinegars. Both the flower buds and young fruits may be used as substitutes for capers. Mature seeds are eaten roasted or make a good pepper substitute. Andean South America, cultivated. HALPIN [Cul], LARKCOM 1984, LEGGATT [Re], MACNICOL,

TANAKA, VILMORIN [Cu]; C9M, E5M{PL}, E7M, E89M, F44, H49, J25M, J73, K53, L56, L89, M46, *N71M*, N84

CULTIVARS

Empress of India: A non-trailing, single cultivar with brilliant vermillion-red flowers and small, neat red leaves which are especially attractive in salads. Grows in cascading clumps, making it an excellent cover-up for bare areas, walkways or borders, as well as containers. K66, Q34, S45M

Gourmet Brand Salad Mixture: Designed to provide a large number of large, open-faced nasturtium flowers. Ideal for salads and garnishes. Provides one of the widest color selections available. *E91G*

Whirlybird: Free-flowering dwarf cultivar, includes seven different colors: cream, tangerine, soft salmon, bright gold, deep mahogany, bright scarlet, and cherry-rose. Two and one-half inch, semi-double blooms, borne well above the compact foliage; spurless, making them easier to clean for culinary purposes. Perfect for baskets or in beds. A13, A16, B75, C44, C53, D11M, E97, F13, F92, G87, H33, I91, K66

Tropaeolum minus - *Dwarf nasturtium* {S} Leaves and flowers are eaten in salads or used for garnishing. Unripe fruits and flower-buds are pickled in vinegar and used for seasoning, like capers. For pickling, this species is preferred, as it flowers more abundantly than T. majus. Peru. HALPIN, HEDRICK 1919, VILMORIN [Cu]; G84{PL}, J82, N84

Tropaeolum tuberosum - *Añu, Ysañu, Mashua* {PL} Tubers may be boiled for ten minutes and eaten as a vegetable or added to stews. When boiled they are watery, rather peppery, and have a pleasant vanilla-like odor. They are also frozen after being boiled, and are then considered a delicacy. Or they are eaten in a half-dried state, after having been exposed to the air for some time. The tender young leaves and flowers are also eaten. Peru, cultivated. HERKLOTS, HODGE 1951, NATIONAL RESEARCH COUNCIL 1989, ORGAN, VILMORIN [Cu]; F35M, *Q49M*

TURNERACEAE

Turnera diffusa - *Damiana* {PL} Dried leaves are often used in Mexico as a substitute for Chinese tea and for flavoring liqueurs. Brazil. UPHOF; M82

Turnera ulmifolia - *Damiana* {PL} Dried leaves are used as a substitute for tea or for flavoring. Tropical America. KUNKEL, PEREZ-ARBELAEZ; M82

TYPHACEAE

Typha angustata → *Typha domingensis*

Typha angustifolia - *Narrow-leaf cattail* {PL} The rootstock is boiled and eaten like potatoes, or macerated and boiled to yield a sweet syrup. It also yields a high-protein flour used to make cattail cookies. The pith near the sprouting new stem is roasted or boiled. Young shoots are boiled and eaten raw. The young flower spikes are eaten raw, cooked, or made into soup. Pollen of male spikes can be used to make bread or porridge. Seeds have been roasted and eaten. Widespread. MORTON 1977; C43M, C49, D43, G26, G85, H82, J7M, K25, *L95*, M39, M72, M73, M73M, N3M, N9M, N9M{S}, *N71M*{S}, etc.

Typha capensis - *Cattail* {S} The tender shoots, rhizomes and male inflorescences are used as food. South Africa. FOX, F., KUNKEL, MARTIN 1975; N84, R77M

Typha domingensis - *Cattail, Tabúa* {S} Rhizomes are the source of a starch. The pollen may baked into a bread. Widespread. TANAKA; K47T, N84

Typha elephantina - *Elephant grass, Hagla, Pun* {S} In Sind, India, a kind of bread called *boor, booree* or *booratoo* is made from the pollen, commonly eaten by the natives. Leaves are also edible. Tropical Asia. HEDRICK 1919, MARTIN 1975, UPHOF; F85

Typha latifolia - *Common cattail* {PL} Young, green flower spikes are boiled and eaten like corn on the cob with plenty of butter, or they may be scraped from the cob and baked in a casserole. The pollen can be mixed with wheat flour in pancake and muffin recipes. The rootstocks yield a flour that can be substituted for half the wheat flour in breads, cookies, biscuits, and muffins. Young, bulb-like sprouts are eaten boiled or made into pickles. Tender, inner heart of the stem, called *Cossack asparagus*, is eaten raw or cooked. Widespread. ANGIER [Re], FERNALD, GIBBONS 1962, HARRINGTON, H. [Re]; C43M, E33M, G26, G85, H82, J7M, J41M, K25, M39, M73, N3M, N9M, N9M{S}, N11, *N71M*{S}, O53M{S}, etc.

Typha laxmannii - *Scented flag* {PL} Rhizomes are the source of a meal which is made into cakes. They are also used as a vegetable. Eurasia. HEDRICK 1919; D62{S}, G85, H30, J7M, K47T{S}, K85M, M15, M72, N84{S}

UAPACACEAE

Uapaca guineensis - *Sugar plum* {S} The fruit is edible, having a flavor reminiscent of the medlar. Tropical Africa. DALZIEL, UPHOF; N84

Uapaca kirkiana - *Wild loquat, Mohobo-hobo* {S} Pulp of the fruit is juicy, honey-like, very tasty, and somewhat reminiscent of pears. It is eaten fresh, brewed into a very pleasant wine, or used for making cakes which are fried and eaten. Juice of the fruit is mixed with sorghum meal to form a thin, orange-flavored porridge called *mutundavaira*. Dried fruits have a toffee-like flavor. One of the most popular wild fruits of Zimbabwe, Zambia, Malawi and Mozambique. Recommended for cultivation. Tropical Africa. FOX, F.; N84

ULMACEAE

Ulmus pumila - *Siberian elm, No-nire* {PL} Fruits are made into sauce and wine. Young leaves and budlings are eaten. The bark is processed into noodles. Eastern Asia. TANAKA; B73M, C9M{S}, *F38*{S}, *F51*, *G66*, *G66*{S}, H49, I78, J7, K38{S}, K63G{S}, M31M, *M69M*, M76, N93M{S}, etc.

URTICACEAE

Debregeasia edulis - *Yanagi-ichigo* {PL} The yellow, globose fruits are pleasantly sweet and are said to resemble strawberries. Harvesting is difficult because the fruit is tender and breaks apart easily. The fruit remains on the bush for several weeks, providing a beautiful contrast to the silvery, ornamental foliage. Japan. RILEY 1982, TANAKA, UPHOF; E48, F85{S}

Pipturus argenteus - *Native mulberry* {S} The true fruits of this coastal tree are small brown structures partly embedded in a soft, translucent white body. This fleshy part is sweet and juicy, and makes excellent eating. Bark and leaves are also used. Australia, New Guinea. CRIBB, POWELL; **Y10**

Urtica dioica - *Stinging nettle* {S} Young leaves make a very palatable and nutritious potherb. They are also puréed, creamed, used in soups, made into a beer, or mixed with leeks, broccoli, and rice to form nettle pudding. The juice of the leaves, or a decoction of the herb, is used as a rennet in preparing cheeses or junkets. Nettles may be blanched and eaten like seakale. Dried leaves are brewed into an herbal tea. Eurasia, naturalized in North America. FERNALD, GIBBONS 1966b [Pre, Re], GRIEVE [Re], HALPIN [Cu, Cul], MARCIN; A2, C11, C43M{PL}, C85M, E61{PL}, F24, F80, G68, H46, J82, J82{PL}, K22, M16{PL}, N45{PL}, *N71M*, etc.

Urtica urens - *Dog nettle* {S} Young shoots, leaves, and stem tops are eaten as potherbs or mixed with meal as a relish. Cosmopolitan. CRIBB, FOX, F., MARTIN 1975, UPHOF; F80, *N71M*, N84

VALERIANACEAE

Centranthus macrosiphon - *Long-spurred valerian* {S} The leaves are similar to corn salad and are use in salads in some countries, especially France. They have a slight bitterness which gives them a more distinct and agreeable flavor. Southern Europe. HEDRICK 1919; **V73M**

Centranthus ruber - *Red valerian, Jupiter's beard* {PL} Young leaves are eaten raw in salads and sandwiches, though they are somewhat bitter used in this way. Otherwise they may be boiled and served with butter as greens. Mediterranean region, cultivated. KUNKEL, MABEY; B49, C9, C11{S}, C13M{S}, D62{S}, D95, F39M, G84, H46{S}, H63, J37M, K53{S}, L66, *L95*, M33G, R53M{S}, etc.

Fedia cornucopiae - *African valerian* {S} The leaves are eaten raw in salads or used as a potherb. Will quickly form rosettes of leaves in hot weather when corn salad is not available. Mediterranean region. HEDRICK 1919, UPHOF, VILMORIN [Cu]; D62, O53M

Patrinia scabiosaefolia - *Ominaeshi* {PL} Young plants, stem tips, and flower buds are eaten steamed, fried, oil-roasted, preserved, in soups, or parboiled and dried for later use. Eastern Asia. TANAKA; F57M, H79M, I37M, K22, M77M

Patrinia villosa - *Otokoeshi* {PL} Young plants and flower buds are eaten as a vegetable, either fried, preserved, or as a potherb. Eastern Asia. TANAKA; M77M, N84{S}

Valeriana ciliata - *Tobacco root* {S} The odoriferous roots are prepared for eating by baking in underground ovens for two days. They are then eaten as a vegetable, used in soups, or made into a bread. North America. FERNALD; J43{CF}

Valeriana officinalis - *Garden heliotrope* {PL} The root extract and essential oil are used to flavor ice cream, baked goods, condiments, soft drinks, beer, and liqueurs. Also used, in moderation, as an herbal tea. Eurasia, cultivated. MARCIN, MORTON 1976; C9, C13M{S}, C67M, F21, F24{S}, F31T, G84, J48, K22, K53{S}, N9M, N9M{S}, N19M, N42, O53M{S}, etc.

Valerianella eriocarpa - *Italian corn salad* {S} The young leaves are used in salads. When grown in rich soil, larger leaves are produced that may be used as a potherb. Does not run to seed as readily as the common corn salad, but is less hardy. Mediterranean region. HEDRICK 1919, VILMORIN [Cu]; E83T

CULTIVARS

Piedmont: (Di Piemonte, Seme Grosso di Olanda) Long, pale green, spoon-shaped leaves. Good heat resistance. B8, C53, Q11M

Valerianella locusta - *Corn salad, Fetticus, Mâche, Nut lettuce* {S} The leaves are very mild in flavor, with a delicate quality that makes them seem to melt in the mouth. Widely used in salads where they compliment strongly flavored greens like cress and dandelion, and crisp root vegetables like carrots and radishes. Also used in potato salad, soups, vegetable purées, omelettes, etc. The flowers and flower-stalks are also eaten. Eurasia, cultivated. HALPIN, LARKCOM 1984, LAUNERT, SCHNEIDER [Re], VILMORIN [Cu]; B49, D11M, D76, E5T, E24, E33, *F72*, F82, H54, J20, K22, K71, L42, L89, *N40*{PR} (for cultivars see Corn Salad, page 314)

Valerianella olitoria* → *Valerianella locusta

VERBENACEAE

Aloysia triphylla - *Lemon verbena* {PL} Young leaves are occasionally eaten as a spinach. Otherwise they are used to impart a lemon flavor to fruit cups, jellies, cold drinks, salads, omelettes, salad dressings, vegetable dishes, etc. Also brewed into a refreshing herbal tea. Temperate South America, cultivated. HUTSON [Re], KUNKEL, LATHROP [Cu], MARCIN, MORTON 1976, ROOT 1980b; C3, C9, C43M, C67M, D29, F21, F31T, G84, G96, H40, J66, K22, M53, N19M

Callicarpa japonica - *Beautyberry, Murasaki-shikibu* {S} The leaves are used as a substitute for tea. Eastern Asia. TANAKA; B96{PL}, K63G, *P63*

Clerodendrum serratum - *Senggunggu* {S} Young, bitter stem tops and inflorescences are eaten raw as a side-dish with rice. Or they are roasted briefly and served with hot pepper sauce. Southeast Asia, Malaysia. OCHSE, TANAKA; F85

Lantana involucrata - *Oregano* {S} Leaves are used as a condiment. Mexico. CALPOUZOS; **W59M, Y2**

Lantana rugosa - *Bird's brandy, Chameleon's berry* {S} Leaves are eaten or used for flavoring other foods. The small purplish-black fruits are sweet and juicy and are eaten fresh or mixed with sour milk. Drier Tropical Africa. FOX, F., MARTIN 1975, TANAKA; **Z77M**

Lantana salvifolia* → *Lantana rugosa

Lippia alba - *Licorice verbena, Anise verbena* {PL} The fresh leaves have an intense anise aroma and are prized for flavoring soup, meats, fish, and for making a pleasant tea. In India, they are used as a vegetable. Tropical America. MORTON 1976, TANAKA; D29, F85{S}, G96, H4, J82, M82

Lippia citriodora* → *Aloysia triphylla

Lippia dulcis* → *Phyla scaberrima

Lippia geminata* → *Lippia alba

Lippia graveolens - *Mexican oregano, Té de pais* {S} The leaves have an intense aroma of oregano and are preferred by many over European oregano. They are used for flavoring fish, sausages, *pozole*, tomato sauces, and many other dishes that require a strong oregano flavor. Dried leaves may be brewed into an herbal tea. Sold in specialty stores that carry Mexican and Southwestern foods. Tropical America. MORTON 1976, UPHOF; C13M, C43M{PL}, D26, D29{PL}, D62, *E91G*, F21{PL}, F24, I16{PR}, J66{PL}, K49M, K52{PR}, L86, M53{PL}, N19M{PL}, etc.

Lippia helleri - *Puerto Rican oregano* {PL} Leaves are used as a condiment. They also yield an essential oil that is used in liqueurs. Puerto Rico. MARTIN 1975, MORTON 1976; E5M, F35M, M82

Lippia javanica - *Fever tree, Wild tea* {S} The aromatic leaves, said to have the odor of mint or vanilla, are used as a condiment or a substitute for tea. Tropical Asia, Southeast Africa. FOX, F.; **Z77M**

Nyctanthes arbor-tristis - *Tree of sadness* {S} Flowers are the source of a saffron-yellow dye used as a colorant for food. Southern Asia. CORREA, UPHOF; F85, *N71M*, N84, O53M, P5, Q46

Phyla alba* → *Lippia alba

Phyla scaberrima - *Aztec sweet-herb, Orozuz, Sweet lippia* {PL} The aromatic leaves are occasionally eaten in salads, or used as a condiment. More often they are chewed for their intensely sweet flavor or used to sweeten teas and other beverages. The licorice-flavored roots are chewed. Central America, Caribbean. KUNKEL, WILLIAMS, L.; C13M{S}, C43M, E48, G96, M15T, M82

Premna odorata - {S} Leaves are eaten as a vegetable or used for flavoring other foods. Southern Asia. KUNKEL, MARTIN 1975; F85

Stachytarpheta cayennensis - *Alacrán* {S} Tips of stems are used for flavoring or as a substitute for tea. Tropical America. KUNKEL, PEREZ-ARBELAEZ; D62

Stachytarpheta indica* → *Stachytarpheta jamaicensis

Stachytarpheta jamaicensis - *Bastard vervain, Blue porterweed* {S} Dried leaves are used as a tea or to adulterate China tea, and have been exported to Europe as *Brazilian tea*. Stem tops are used in Java as a flavoring. In Central America, a foaming, porter-like brew is made from the leaves. Caribbean region. BURKILL, MORTON 1977, TANAKA, UPHOF; N84, O53M

Stachytarpheta mutabilis - {S} Leaves are used as a tea or as an adulterant of China tea. Tropical America. CHITTENDEN; F85, O53M

Verbena hastata - *Blue vervain* {S} Leaves are used as a tea substitute. The pleasantly bitter seeds are roasted, ground into a meal, and used for fried cakes and *pinole*. This meal can be leached to remove some of the bitterness. North America. FERNALD, GIBBONS 1979, KIRK; B51, C13M, C43M, C43M{PL}, E61{PL}, F37T{PL}, G47M, H61M, I37M{PL}, J39M, J41M, J41M{PL}, J82{PL}, O53M

Verbena officinalis - *Vervain, Kuma-tsuzura* {PL} Young leaves are parboiled, seasoned and eaten. Also used as a tea substitute. The flowers are fermented into wine or used as a garnish. In Turkey, salt flavored with vervain flowers is popular. Eurasia. KUNKEL, MACNICOL [Re], TANAKA; A2{S}, C11{S}, C13M{S}, C43M, E5M, F35M, F80{S}, G84, H3M, I39{S}, J82, J82{S}, K85, N45, O53M{S}, etc.

Vitex agnus-castus - *Chaste tree, Monk's pepper* {S} The seeds are used as a substitute for pepper. Leaves are also employed as a spice. Forms one of the ingredients of the legendary Moroccan spice mixture *ras el hanout*. Mediterranean region, cultivated. KUNKEL, UPHOF, WOLFERT; A93M{PL}, B96{PL}, C9{PL}, C9M, C43M{PL}, F85, H4{PL}, *J86*{PL}, K38, L63M, N37M{PL}, N93M, O53M, *P17M*, *R28*, etc.

Vitex cienkowskii* → *Vitex doniana

Vitex doniana - *Black plum, Prune noire* {S} The sweet fruit pulp, having somewhat the flavor of prunes, is eaten fresh, mixed with other fruits or made into sweetmeats. Young leafy shoots are eaten as a potherb. The leaves also furnish a substitute for tea. Tropical Africa. DALZIEL, MARTIN 1987, UPHOF; N84

Vitex negundo - *Wu-chih-kan* {S} Both the roots and the leaves are made into a tea-like beverage. The seeds are occasionally used as a condiment. China. KUNKEL, TANAKA; F85, *G66*, H4{PL}, J82, N84, Q12, Q46, *R28*

VIOLACEAE

Viola adunca - *Western dog violet* {S} The leaves may be boiled as greens or dried and used as tea. Western North America. ALDERMAN 1976; K98, N9M, N9M{PL}

Viola canadensis - *Canada violet* {PL} Young leaves and flower buds are eaten raw in tossed salads. When boiled as potherbs, the leaves and flowers are mild-flavored and are best mixed with other greens of more pronounced taste. The flowers can be candied like rose petals and have been used to give flavor to vinegar. Leaves make a good substitute for tea. North America. HARRINGTON, H.; C49, D75T, E33M, E63M, H49, I15M, I44, J48, K22, K85, M77M, N9M, N9M{S}, N37, N37M, N45, etc.

Viola cucullata* → *Viola sororia

Viola japonica - *Ko-sumire* {S} The roots are cut into pieces and mixed with yam starch to make a mucilaginous soup. Japan, Korea. TANAKA; **Y76**

Viola odorata - *Sweet violet* {S} Young leaves are eaten in salads and soups, or dipped in batter and fried. Flowers are candied, used as garnishes, made into syrup, jellies, and marmalade, or added to gelatins, ices, vinegar, honey, wines, and salad dressings. Leaves and flowers can be used to make a soothing tea. The leaf extract is employed to flavor ice cream, candy, and baked goods. Macaronesia and Eurasia. BRYAN [Cul, Re], LATHROP, LEGGATT [Re], MACNICOL [Re], MORTON 1976; C11, C13M, D29{PL}, E7M, F21{PL}, F24, I22{PL}, K53, M98{PL}, N9M, N9M{PL}, N19M{PL}, N84, O53M

Viola papilionacea - *Blue violet* {PL} The leaves, rich in vitamins A and C, are gathered when young and cooked and served like spinach. They are especially good when mixed with watercress, peppergrass, Barbarea, shepherd's purse, or other members of the mustard family. Flowers are made into jams, jellies, sweetmeats, syrup, and aspic salads. North America. CROWHURST 1972, GIBBONS 1966b [Pre, Re], KINDSCHER, ZENNIE [Nu]; B61M, D62{S}, *F51*, G89, H61M{S}, I11M, J39M, J42, N7T, N9M, N9M{S}, N45

Viola pedata - *Birdfoot violet, Wild okra* {PL} Young leaves can be added to salads, boiled or steamed to make a palatable cooked green, or added to soups as an okra-like thickener. Dried leaves are made into tea. The flowers can be candied. North America. PETERSON, L.; B33M, C9, C49, D75T, E33M, *G28*, H49, H63, I15M, I44, J40, J43{S}, K47T{S}, K63, M77, N9M, etc.

Viola sororia - *Marsh blue violet, Wild okra* {PL} Tender young leaves, stems and flowers can be added to salads or cooked as potherbs. Because of their mucilaginous qualities, the leaves are occasionally used as a thickener for soup. North America. CROWHURST 1972, FERNALD, PETERSON, L.; D62{S}, D75T, I22, I87, N84{S}

Viola tricolor - *Johnny-jump-up, Heartsease* {S} The small, fragrant flowers are eaten in salads or used as an attractive garnish. Eurasia, cultivated. LEGGATT [Re]; A53M, D29{PL}, D62, E5M{PL}, E99, F24, F33, F35M{PL}, F80, H3M{PL}, H46, K53, K66, L91M, M82{PL}, *N71M*, etc.

Viola x wittrockiana - *Pansy* {S} The flowers and leaves, stronger in flavor than other violets, are eaten in salads or used as a garnish. Fresh or dried flowers can be used for tea. BRYAN [Cul, Re], LARKCOM 1984, LEGGATT [Re], MACNICOL [Re]; D62, K49M, N84

CULTIVARS

Gourmet Brand Salad Mixture: Large flowered, early-blooming pansy mixture selected to provide a large number of flowers over the longest harvest season. *E91G*

VITACEAE

Cissus capensis* → *Rhoicissus capensis

Cissus discolor - *Trailing begonia, Bantèng* {PL} Young stem tips and leaves are used for giving dishes an agreeable, sour taste. The leaves can also be eaten raw. Tropical Asia. BURKILL, OCHSE; F85{S}, G96, J23{OR}

Cissus quadrangularis - *Edible-stemmed vine* {PL} Leaves and shoots are used in the preparation of *papadums* and curries. The fruits are edible. Tropical Asia. BURKILL, HEDRICK 1919, TANAKA, WATT; A0M, B85, F85{S}, G18, M33G

Rhoicissus capensis - *Cape wild grape* {S} The purplish-black fruits are used for making jellies, said to be of brilliant color and excellent flavor. Young leaves and shoots are cooked and eaten. Southern Africa. FOX, F., HEDRICK 1919, TANAKA, UPHOF; G96{PL}, N84, O53M

Vitis aestivalis - *Summer grape, Pigeon grape* {S} Fruits are eaten raw or used to make juice, jellies, jams, conserves, pies, and wines. Dried fruits are eaten as snacks or in baked goods. The stems yield a sweet, watery sap that is potable. North America, cultivated. TURNER 1979 [Re]; **T41M, T73M, W3M**

Vitis amurensis - *Amur River grape* {S} The fruits are eaten raw or are manufactured into juice and wine. Leaves are eaten as a boiled vegetable. Withstands temperatures of -40°C., making it a possible source of winter-hardiness for V. vinifera. Eastern Asia, cultivated. TANAKA, UPHOF, ZEVEN; K47T, N84, O53M, *P63*, P86{PL}, *R28*, R78, S36M

Vitis argentifolia - *Blueleaf grape, Blue grape* {S} The edible fruits are sweet and agreeable. Eastern North America. HEDRICK 1919; **T41M**

Vitis berlandieri - *Spanish grape* {S} Fruits are eaten raw or made into wine, being of a rich, pleasant flavor. Also used in breeding and as a rootstock. Southwestern North America. HEDRICK 1919, TANAKA, ZEVEN; **Z25M** (for cultivars see Rootstocks, page 470)

Vitis bicolor* → *Vitis argentifolia

Vitis californica - *California grape* {PL} The juicy fruits are eaten raw, dried, or made into jelly, pies, and wine. Tendrils are eaten raw as a pleasantly sour snack. The boiled leaves are used to wrap other foods. Southwestern North America. CLARKE, HEDRICK 1919, KIRK; *C73*, F80{S}

Vitis candicans - *Mustang grape* {S} Fruits are dark purple or wine colored and have a tough skin. They are mostly used for pies and jellies or brewed into wine. Southwestern North America. MEDSGER; **W3M**

Vitis capensis* → *Rhoicissus capensis

Vitis x champini - {S} Natural hybrid. The very large fruits are edible. Southwestern North America. REHDER, TANAKA; **T41M** (for cultivars see Grape, page 339 and Rootstocks, page 470)

Vitis cinerea - *Sweet winter grape* {S} Fruits are eaten fresh, dried for later use, or made into jams and jellies. Sap of the vine is used as a beverage. North America. MEDSGER, UPHOF, YANOVSKY; **T41M**

Vitis coignetiae - *Crimson glory vine, Yama-budô* {S} The fruits are eaten raw or brewed into wine. Young stems and leaf stalks are boiled and eaten. Japan. TANAKA; K38, N84, *P63*, P86{PL}, *R28*, R78

Vitis coriacea* → *Vitis shuttleworthii

Vitis davidii - *Spiny vitis, P'u-tao-tzu* {PL} Fruits are black, globose, and edible though said to be harsh in flavor. China, cultivated. UPHOF, WILSON, E.; F80{S}, P86

Vitis labrusca - *Fox grape* {S} The fruits have a distinct musky odor and taste. They are eaten raw, dried, preserved, made into juice, jellies, jams, pies, conserves, and syrup, used in beverages, candies, and ice cream, or fermented into wine and vinegar. A jelly is also made from the skins. Leaves have a pleasant acid flavor and are eaten cooked, stuffed, used to wrap other foods, or preserved in salt. Eastern North America. ANGIER [Re], GIBBONS 1962 [Pre, Re], MEDSGER, UPHOF; **T41M** (for cultivars see Grape, page 339)

Vitis monticola - *Sweet mountain grape* {S} The large, thin-skinned fruits are white or amber-colored and have tender, juicy, sweet pulp. Southwestern North America. HEDRICK 1919; **T41M, W3M**

Vitis munsoniana - *Bird grape, Bullace grape* {PL} Fruits are round, nearly black, thin-skinned, acid in flavor, and are eaten fresh when fully ripe. Young leaves and stems may be cooked as greens. The old stems will yield sap for drinking. Southern North America. MEDSGER, MORTON 1977; N37M

Vitis quadrangularis* → *Cissus quadrangularis

Vitis riparia - *River bank grape, Frost grape* {PL} The juicy, somewhat acid fruits are eaten raw or dried. Sap of the vine is used as a beverage. In hybridizing, it can be crossed with V. vinifera to introduce resistance to phylloxera. Also used as a rootstock. Eastern North America. HEDRICK 1919, MEDSGER, YANOVSKY, ZEVEN; C58, F67, F80{S}, *G66*{S}, K64, K81 (for cultivars see Rootstocks, page 470)

Vitis rotundifolia - *Muscadine, Scuppernong* {S} The fruits, which grow in loose clusters, are pleasant to eat raw and are excellent for jellies and pies. They are also made into juice, sauces, syrup, wine, and fruit leathers. The cultivars with black or purple-colored fruits have a flavor that is very much like that of the jaboticaba. Southeastern North America, cultivated. FERNALD, GIBBONS 1979, MEDSGER; B94M{PR}, F85, H4{PL}, I98{PR}, N50{PR}, N84 (for cultivars see Muscadine, page 393)

Vitis rupestris - *Sand grape, Sugar grape, Bush grape* {S} Fruits are bluish-black, very sweet, and are eaten out of hand. Can be crossed with V. vinifera to introduce resistance to phylloxera. Also used as a rootstock. Eastern North America. CROWHURST 1972, HEDRICK 1919, ZEVEN; D62 (for cultivars see Rootstocks, page 470)

Vitis shuttleworthii - *Calloosa grape, Leatherleaf* {S} Ripe fruits are eaten raw or used for jelly making. Young leaves and stems may be cooked as greens. Old stems will yield sap for drinking. Eastern North America. MORTON 1977, STURROCK; **T73M**

Vitis simpsonii - *Currant grape* Fruits are edible. Used in breeding resistant varieties for Florida and other hot areas. Southern North America. STURROCK, TANAKA; (for cultivars see Grape, page 339)

Vitis smalliana* → *Vitis simpsonii

Vitis solonis - The fruits are edible. Also used as a rootstock and in hybridizing. North America. (for cultivars see Rootstocks, page 470)

Vitis vinifera - *European grape* {S} Fruits are eaten raw, dried into raisins, made into wine, juice, jellies, liqueurs, vinegar, etc. *Zibebes* are berries that have dried on the vine. *Dibs* or *pekmez*, evaporated grape juice or grape molasses, is used to sweeten tea. Seeds are used to garnish cheeses or pressed for their oil. Grapeseed oil is the favored oil for cooking meat in *fondue bourguignonne*. *Verjuice*, the juice of unripe grapes, is used to lend tartness to sauces. *Dolmas* are grape leaves stuffed with rice, Zante currants, pignolias and other fillings. The flower clusters are used as a vegetable. Eurasia, cultivated. BRYAN [Re], HAWKES [Re], JAFFREY, MACNICOL, ROOT 1980a, UPHOF, VON WELANETZ; E1{PO}, F85, M41M{PR}, O53M (for cultivars see Grape, page 339 and Rootstocks, page 470)

Vitis vinifera Monopyrena Group - *Corinthian grape, Currant grape* {GR} The fresh fruits, no larger than peas, have a sweet, juicy agreeable flavor, and are eaten fresh or dried. When dried, they are known as *passonilla* and furnish the dried currants of commerce. Also used in the preparation of a sweet and aromatic *passito* wine. BIANCHINI, FAIRCHILD 1945, HEDRICK 1919.

CULTIVARS

Black Corinth: (Staphis, Zante Currant, Champagne Grape) Very small, spherical fruits; skin very thin and tender, reddish-black; flesh very juicy, neutral to spicy in flavor, mostly seedless; ripens early. Vine vigorous, productive if girdled or treated with a growth regulator. Cluster small to medium, well filled to compact. Marketed as Champagne grapes when fresh, as Zante currants after drying. Probably originated in Greece. WINKLER; C8M{PR}, *C60*, *C60*{PR}, E39, E39{SC}, I95, I95{SC}, K96M{PR}, *N40*{PR}, S59

Carina: Small black fruit that matures early. Not as inclined to break-down as is Black Corinth. Dries readily into very small raisins of soft texture with a pleasing tart taste. Should be spur pruned. S59

Hannaman: A sport of Black Corinth that is heavier bearing and later maturing. Small black fruit that matures early. Dries readily into soft, pleasantly tart raisins. Should be spur pruned. S59

White Corinth: Small, round fruit, similar to Black Corinth; skin greenish-white to golden yellow when fully matured; flesh sweet and juicy with a sugar content of 20 to 22%. Good fresh or dried. Vine much more productive than Black Corinth. Cluster size similar to Black Corinth. *C60*, *C60*{PR}

Vitis vulpina* → *Vitis riparia

WINTERACEAE

Drimys aromatica* → *Drimys lanceolata

Drimys lanceolata - *Pepper tree, Mountain pepper* {S} The black, pungent fruits and seeds are used as a substitute for pepper and allspice. Australia. HEDRICK 1919, UPHOF; D95{PL}, E63{PL}, L2{PL}, N84, O53M, *P63*, S65M

Drimys winteri - *Winter's bark, Chachaca, Palo de mambo* {S} The aromatic, pungent bark is powdered and used as a condiment in parts of Mexico and Brazil. Chile-Argentina. HEDRICK 1919, UPHOF; L2{PL}, N84, O53M

ZAMIACEAE

Dioon edule - *Chamal* {PL} Seeds are eaten boiled or roasted. They also yield a starch or flour, called *Mexican arrowroot*, used in *tortillas*. Mexico. BROUK, GRIEVE, HEDRICK 1919, UPHOF; A79M{S}, C9M{S}, C78, D43, F69, *G66*{S}, G91M, I28, I85M{S}, N43M, N51, N84{S}, *P17M*{S}, S44{S}

Encephalartos caffer - *Caffir bread* {PL} The trunk and the female cones are the source of a starch used to make a type of bread. Southern Africa. HEDRICK 1919, UPHOF; C78, D43, N43M

Encephalartos hildebrandtii - *Hottentot bread* {PL} Husks of the seeds are dried and ground to a flour used in the preparation of a porridge, called *ugali* or *chapatii*. Southern Africa. MENNINGER; C78, F69, F85{S}, N43M

Lepidozamia peroffskyana* → *Macrozamia denisonii

Macrozamia denisonii - *Burrawang* {S} Stems are the source of an edible starch. The fleshy outer layer of the seeds is eaten after proper preparation. Australia. CRIBB, TANAKA; C78{PL}, D43{PL}, F85, I28{PL}, I85M{PL}, N43M{PL}, N84, O84, O93, P5, *Q25*, *Q32*, R33M

Zamia floridana - *Coontie* {PL} The roots, when properly prepared, were the source of *Florida arrowroot*. Florida Indians, in making their *sofkee stew*, cooked it with the meat of various wild game and vegetables such as corn, tomatoes, and beans. Southeastern North America. MEDSGER, MORTON 1977; D43, *F73*, G91M, H20, *J25*, *L5M*{S}, N84{S}, O93{S}, R33M{S}

ZINGIBERACEAE

Aframomum angustifolium - *Madagascar cardamom, Wild cardamom* {S} The fruits contain an agreeable acid pulp and are eaten fresh. Dried seeds are used like pepper for seasoning. In the Near East they are added to coffee. Eastern Africa, Madagascar. MORTON 1976, UPHOF; **Z25M**

Aframomum daniellii - *Bastard melegueta, Cameroon cardamom* {S} Seeds are used as a condiment. The fruit pulp is agreeably acid and is eaten for refreshment. Tropical Africa. TANAKA; **U71M**, **Z25M**

Aframomum elliotii - *Alligator cardamom* {S} Seeds are widely used to flavor wine, beer, foods, and *ginger beer*. West Tropical Africa. MENNINGER; F85

Aframomum hanburyi* → *Aframomum daniellii

Aframomum melegueta - *Grains of Paradise, Melegueta pepper, Guinea grains* {S} The aromatic, pungent seeds are used for flavoring wine, beer, cordials, liqueurs, meats, and breads. Mixed with ginger and cinnamon, they flavored the wine known as *hippocras*. American food manufacturers use them in ice cream, candy, and soft drinks. They were an important article of trade in Europe as early as the 13th century. The fruit pulp around the seeds is eaten or chewed as a stimulant. West Tropical Africa, cultivated. LOVELOCK, MENNINGER, MORTON 1976, ROOT 1980b, VON WELANETZ; F85

Alpinia caerulea - *Native ginger* {S} Tender, young tips of the rhizome have a distinct ginger-like flavor and may be eaten. The pleasantly acid pulp that surrounds the seeds is also edible. Australia. CRIBB; L29{PL}, P5, *Q25*

Alpinia galanga - *Greater galangal, Laos* {PL} The slightly pungent rhizomes are employed as a flavoring in curries, soups, meats, and fish, or are mixed with other seasonings. Source of an essential oil used to flavor liqueurs such as *Chartreuse*, *angostura* and other bitters, and soft drinks. Young shoots are steamed and eaten. The flowers and flower-buds are eaten raw, steamed, pickled, added to soups, or mixed with chili paste. Red fruits are edible. Tropical Asia, cultivated. COST 1988 [Cul, Re], CRAWFORD [Re], MORTON 1976, OCHSE, SHURTLEFF 1979, VON REIS; A45{PR}, C56M, C94{PR}, L90G{PR}, N34M, N84{S}, P38

Alpinia officinarum - *Lesser galangal* {S} The reddish-brown rhizomes have a spicy aroma and a pungent taste somewhere between pepper and ginger. They have been used to flavor vinegar and the liqueur called *nastoika*. Leaves are also edible. Southeast Asia. BROUK, BURKILL, GRIEVE, MARTIN 1975, UPHOF; **Z11M**

Alpinia speciosa - *Shell ginger* {S} The stems, leaves, and flowers are boiled and eaten. Tropical Asia, cultivated. ALTSCHUL, BURKILL, TANAKA; C56M{PL}, F85, H4{PL}, J27{PL}, L29{PL}, M19, M20, N34M{PL}, N84, O93, P5, *P17M*, P38, *Q32*

Alpinia zerumbet* → *Alpinia speciosa

Amomum cardamon* → *Elettaria cardamomum

Amomum compactum - *Round cardamom, Kepulaga* {PL} Young, pungent shoots are eaten raw, roasted, or cooked and served with rice. The fruits have a sweet, turpentine aroma and flavor and are used as a spice or chewed to sweeten the breath. Seeds are used in cakes. Malaysia. BURKILL, MORTON 1976, UPHOF; H4, J23{OR}, M31

Amomum kepulaga* → *Amomum compactum

Amomum xanthioides - *Bastard cardamom, Wild Siamese cardamom* {S} Seeds are used in China to flavor liqueurs. They have been exported to India and England as substitutes for true cardamom, although their strong camphor flavor is not as pleasant. Malaya. GRIEVE, MORTON 1976; F85

Boesenbergia pandurata - *Temoo kuntji, Chinese keys* {S} The strong, spicy, swollen rhizomes are consumed in soups, stews and sambals or made into pickles. Both the rhizomes and the hearts of the stems are eaten raw as a side-dish with rice. Young leaves and shoots, along with the rhizomes, are cut finely, mixed with coconut and spices, wrapped in a banana leaf and steamed. Malaysia, Indonesia. OCHSE, TANAKA, UPHOF; A45{PR}, C94{PR}, P38

Curcuma angustifolia - *East Indian arrowroot, Tikhur* {S} Rhizomes are the source of a starch, called *Travancore starch*, which forms a good substitute for West Indian arrowroot. Southern Asia. HEDRICK 1919, UPHOF; J27{PL}, N84, O53M

Curcuma aromatica - *Yellow zedoary, Wild turmeric* {PL} The rhizome is pounded and used in curries as a substitute for turmeric. Southeast Asia. BURKILL, TANAKA; R22

Curcuma domestica* → *Curcuma longa

Curcuma longa - *Turmeric, Indian saffron* {PL} The powdered rhizomes are used as a yellow coloring agent and condiment in curries, prepared mustards, cheeses, butter, gravies, sauces, rice, pickles, etc. Leaves wrapped around fish flavor it during cooking. In Indonesia, the young shoots and rhizome tips are eaten raw. India, cultivated. BOND [Re], COST 1988 [Cul], MORTON 1976, OCHSE, SHURTLEFF 1979, UPHOF; C43M, C56M, H40, I83M, J27, K49T, L62M, M82, N34M, P38

Curcuma mangga - *Temu mangga* {S} Young shoots and the tender, white tips of the rhizomes are eaten raw or boiled. Slices of the young rhizomes are cooked with coconut milk and chili paste. Flower clusters are steamed and eaten with rice or used in stews. Southeast Asia. MORTON 1976, OCHSE; Z25M

Curcuma xanthorrhiza - *Tem lawak* {S} Rhizomes are the source of a starch that is made into porridge or pudding-like delicacies. A sweet drink is made by cooking the dried rhizomes in water and adding sugar. The heart of the stems and the rhizome tips are eaten raw. Inflorescences are cooked and served with rice. Southeast Asia. BURKILL, OCHSE; C94{PR}, Z25M

Curcuma zedoaria - *Zedoary* {PL} The leaves, which resemble lemongrass in flavor, are cooked with fish as seasoning. Dried rhizomes are used as a condiment in liqueurs and bitters. Also the source of a starch that is used like arrowroot. The heart of the young shoots is eaten raw or cooked. Slices of the young rhizomes are added to salads. India, cultivated. BOND [Re], MORTON 1976, OCHSE, TANAKA; J27, N34M

Elettaria cardamomum - *Cardamom, Small cardamom* {PL} Aromatic seeds are used to flavor curry powder, cakes, sausages, drinks, cordials, bitters, gingerbread, pickles, coffee, candies, etc. In India, the seeds are chewed after meals to sweeten the breath. The young shoots are eaten raw, steamed, or roasted. Tropical Asia, cultivated. GRIEVE, MORTON 1976, OCHSE, ROOT 1980b, UPHOF; A1M, C9, C43M, C56M, C81M, E5M, E48, F37T, G96, H40, J82, K22, K85, M31, M53, M82, etc.

CULTIVARS

Malabar: (Small Type) Fruits small, green, changing to pale at maturity; borne in clusters of 2 to 3. Plant short, with leafy shoots 2 to 3 meters tall, rarely exceeding 3 meters. Requires less rainfall, and is drought resistant. Suited to lower elevations; less sensitive to sunlight. ILYAS; Dropped by P12

Mysore: (Large Type) Fruits large, green when ripe, borne in clusters of 5 to 7. Plant robust, with leafy shoots 3 to 4 meters tall, sometimes reaching 5.5 meters. Requires plenty of rainfall, and thrives over a wide range of conditions because of hardiness. Suited to higher elevations; sensitive to sunlight. ILYAS; Dropped by P12

Gastrochilus panduratum* → *Boesenbergia pandurata

Globba marantina - {S} The small bulbils are used as a flavoring material. Tropical Asia. BURKILL, TANAKA; F85, O53M

Hedychium coronarium - *Garland flower, Butterfly ginger* {PL} Young buds and flowers are eaten or used for flavoring. Tropical Asia. KUNKEL, TANAKA; A79M{S}, C36, C56M, E48, F27M, F80{S}, H4, H49, I28, J27, L29, M31, M77, N34M, P38{S}, etc.

Hedychium spicatum - *Shukusha, Kachri* {S} The fruit is cooked with lentils. Southern Asia. TANAKA; F80, F85, N84, O46, O53M, Q40{PL}, R22{PL}

Kaempferia galanga - *Galanga, Kenchur* {PL} Young leaves and tender rhizomes are eaten raw, steamed, or cooked with chili paste into a savory side dish. The rhizomes are also used as a condiment, pickled, or used in the preparation of *beras*, a sweet, spicy beverage. Dried rhizomes are used as a substitute for turmeric in curry powder. Tropical Asia, cultivated. COST 1988 [Cul], MORTON 1976, OCHSE, SHURTLEFF 1979; A45{PR}, C94{PR}, J27, N34M

Kaempferia pandurata* → *Boesenbergia pandurata

Kaempferia rotunda - *Kuntji puti* {PL} The young leaves are eaten raw, steamed, or used in stews. Tubers, which have a hot taste, are also eaten. Tropical Asia. BURKILL, MORTON 1976, OCHSE, UPHOF; F27M, J27, M31, N34M, R22

Nicolaia elatior - *Ondje, Torch ginger* {S} Inflorescences are eaten raw, steamed, roasted, or used in curries. The heart of the stems is cooked and served with rice. Half-ripe fruits are eaten in soups and stews. Ripe fruits are eaten as delicacies or made into sweetmeats. Mature seeds are eaten raw. Malaya, cultivated. BURKILL, OCHSE; A79M, F85, N84, O93

Phaeomeria magnifica* → *Nicolaia elatior

Phaeomeria speciosa* → *Nicolaia elatior

Zingiber amaricans - *Lampuyang pahit* {S} The young flower spikes, deprived of the bracts, can be eaten raw, cooked, or added to stews. Rhizome tips, both the old bitter ones and the non-bitter younger ones, are eaten raw with rice. Malaysia, Indonesia. OCHSE; Z25M

Zingiber officinale - *Ginger* {PL} Rhizomes are widely used to flavor cakes, chutneys, curries, stir-fried dishes, beverages, pastry, candies, pickles, etc. Pickled ginger, known as *amazu- shoga*, is usually eaten with *sushi* dishes. Also used in *ginger ale*, *ginger beer*, wine, brandy, and herbal teas. They are sold dry, powdered, preserved in syrup, or crystallized. Very young rhizomes, known as *stem ginger* or *green ginger*, are peeled and eaten raw in salads, pickled, or cooked in syrup and made into sweetmeats. Young, slightly spicy shoots are eaten as a potherb or purėed and used in sauces and dips. Cultivated. COST 1984 [Re], CUDE, DAHLEN [Cul, Re], HARRINGTON, G. [Cu, Cul], JAFFREY, MARTIN 1975, MORTON 1976, OCHSE, TANAKA, UPHOF; C43M, C56M, C60M, D76, E97, F37T, G17, G20M{PR}, H4, H40, H49, J82

CULTIVARS

Chinese Yellow: Dwarf, bushy plant, only reaching 3 feet in height. Small, narrow rhizomes. Mild, distinctive yellow flesh. More flavorful and more potent medicinally than the standard white type of Hawaii, Florida and Fiji. K49T

Zingiber spectabile - *Golden-shampoo ginger* {PL} Rhizomes are used for flavoring. Malaysia, Indonesia. BURKILL, TANAKA; F85{S}, N34M

Zingiber zerumbet - *Zerumbet, Wild ginger, Pinecone ginger* {PL} In Malaysia, the young leaves and shoots are cooked. The ancient Hawaiians used the leaves to flavor meats that were cooked in underground ovens. Young rhizome tips are eaten raw with rice. Tropical Asia, cultivated. DEGENER, MORTON 1976, OCHSE; H49, J27, L29, M7M, N34M

ZYGOPHYLLACEAE

Guaiacum officinale - *Lignum sanctum, Guajacan negro* {S} Source of a resin used for flavoring cakes and chicle. It is also added to edible oils to prevent acidification. Caribbean region. KUNKEL, TANAKA; A79M, F85, N84

Guaiacum sanctum - *Lignum vitae* {PL} The resin is used to flavor cakes and chicle. Caribbean region. KUNKEL; D87G, *J25*, N84{S}

Larrea divaricata → *Larrea tridentata*

Larrea mexicana → *Larrea tridentata*

Larrea tridentata - *Creosote bush* {S} Flower buds are pickled in vinegar and used like capers. The stems and leaves are used as a substitute for tea. Twigs are chewed to alleviate thirst. A resin, obtained from the leaves and twigs, delays or prevents butter, oils, and fats from becoming rancid. Southwestern North America. CLARKE, KUNKEL, UPHOF; C27M, C98, D29{PL}, *E66M*, F79M, F85, G60{PL}, I98M, *J0*, J25M, J25M{PL}, K15, N84, S44

Nitraria schoberi - *Nitre bush* {S} The edible fruits are olive-like, red or purple, and slightly salty but with a very pleasant flavor. Eastern Mediterranean region to Australia. CRIBB, HEDRICK 1919, UPHOF; F80, *N79M*, *P17M*, R15M, S92

Peganum harmala - *Syrian rue* {S} Seeds are used as a condiment. Mediterranean region. TANAKA; B7, C13M, C43M{PL}, F85, G84{PL}, I59G, J82, J82{PL}, O53M

Zygophyllum fabago - *Bean caper* {S} The flower buds are pickled and used as a substitute for capers. Mediterranean region to Southwest Asia. HEDRICK 1919, TANAKA; V50, V73M, V84, W3M, Y10, Y89M, Z19

ALPHABETICAL LISTING OF FUNGI FAMILIES

AGARICACEAE

Agaricus arvensis - *Horse mushroom* {CU} Fruitbodies are edible, choice. The flesh is thick, firm, white, with a scent reminiscent of almonds or aniseseed, and a delicious flavor. Some are up to one foot across when mature. They may be eaten raw in salads, broiled, sautéed, stuffed, in soups, fritters, sauces, casseroles, etc. CRIBB, FERNALD, GIBBONS 1962 [Re], LAUNERT, MABEY [Cul], MILLER, STEINECK [Cu], UPHOF; D87M, D87M{SR}

Agaricus augustus - *The prince* {CU} The fruitbodies are edible. Flesh is thick, meaty, white, with the odor of anise. The caps are large, up to a foot wide. A choice edible that can be eaten raw and is also excellent stuffed with crabmeat, creamed on toast, or in scrambled eggs or soups. MILLER, STEINECK [Cu]; D87M, D87M{SR}, M87, M87{SN}

Agaricus bisporus - *Button mushroom, Champignon* {SN} Fruitbodies are edible. The common mushroom found in food stores. Widely eaten raw in salads, sautéed, stuffed, marinated, fried, or used in soups, sauces, stews, gravies, etc. Recommended for growing outdoors in garden beds. CARCIONE [Pre], CZARNECKI [Cul, Re], GRIGSON [Cul, Re], KERRIGAN, STAMETS [Cu], STEINECK [Cu], VILMORIN [Cu]; D63, D63{KT}, D75M{KT}, E21{CU}, G31M, G31M{KT}, I49, I49{CU}, J60, M87, M87{CU} (for strains see Button Mushroom, page 278)

Agaricus brunnescens → *Agaricus bisporus*

Agaricus campestris - *Meadow mushroom, Field mushroom* {CU} Fruitbodies are edible, choice. This is the common, delicious Agaricus found on lawns throughout North America. They have thick, firm flesh, either white or tinted reddish brown. Raw, they make a tasty savoury if the stalk is removed and the cap filled with cream cheese. Otherwise they may be used to flavor casseroles and rice dishes, or fried in butter and thickened with a little flour and milk. CRIBB, FERNALD, GRIGSON [Cul, Re], MABEY, MICHAEL [Re], MILLER, STEINECK [Cu]; D87M, D87M{SR}

Agaricus silvaticus - *Sylvan mushroom, Scaly wood mushroom* {CU} Fruitbodies are edible. The flesh is thick, firm, white, slowly bruising reddish brown when young or remaining unchanged. It has a pleasant odor and a mild flavor. To keep the food it is cooked with from turning brown, the dark gills are cut off. MILLER, STEINECK [Cu], TANAKA; D87M, D87M{SR}

Agaricus subrufescens - *Almond mushroom* {SN} The fruitbodies are edible, choice. They are said to have the flavor of sweet almonds. Grows during warmer weather than the button mushroom and is less demanding of growing conditions and substrates. Recommended for growing in vegetable gardens. This variety was popular at the turn of the century and was cultivated commercially on the East Coast. KERRIGAN, TANAKA; D87M{CU}, D87M{SR}, J60, M87, M87{CU}

Lepiota naucina - *Smooth lepiota* {CU} Fruitbodies are edible. The flesh is thick and white. CZARNECKI [Cul], MILLER, TANAKA; D87M, D87M{SR}, E21

Lepiota rachodes - *Shaggy parasol, Scaly lepiota* {CU} Fruitbodies are edible. The flesh is soft and white. Very flavorful when young, especially fried, but somewhat tough when old. The tough stalks are not useable. Faintly aromatic with a mild taste. In gardens it can be cultivated in composting areas. ANONYMOUS 1986 [Re], MABEY, MILLER, STEINECK [Cu], TANAKA; D87M, D87M{SR}, E21

Leucoagaricus naucina → *Lepiota naucina*

AMANITACEAE

Amanita caesarea - *Caesar's mushroom, Royal agaric* {CU} Fruitbodies are edible. The flesh is firm, white, with a pleasant odor and taste. It can be eaten raw as a salad after being marinated in lemon juice for four hours, or it can be stewed or broiled. Considered a delicacy by the ancient Greeks and Romans. BIANCHINI [Cul], UPHOF; D87M, D87M{SR}

ASPERGILLACEAE

Aspergillus oryzae - *Koji mold, Hama-natto mold, Hishio mold* {CU} This mold is also involved in the fermentation of *miso*, *amazake*, *shoyu*, *tamari*, *mirin*, *taosi*, *nuruk*, *chiang-yiu*, *meju*, *inyu*, *yukiwari-natto*, *sake*, *kecap*, *brem*, *yakju*, *ragi tapeh*, *kicap*, *tauco*, *doenjang*, and *kochujang*. HESSELTINE, STEINKRAUS, UPHOF; C7M (also see Starter Cultures, page 496)

Penicillium camembertii - *Camembert cheese mold, White mold* {CU} A mold that takes part in the fermentation of Camembert as well as Brie, Neufchâtel, Gournay fleuri, Pennsylvania Dutch cup, Pont l'Evêque, and St. Maure cheeses. BROUK, KOSIKOWSKI, PEDERSON, UPHOF, USDA; C7M (also see Starter Cultures, page 496)

Penicillium candidum* → *Penicillium camembertii

Penicillium caseicola* → *Penicillium camembertii

Penicillium roqueforti - *Roquefort cheese mold, Blue mold* {CU} The conidia of this mold form the dark green veins in Roquefort as well as Gorgonzola, Stilton, and blue cheeses. BROUK, KOSIKOWSKI, PEDERSON, SCHERY, UPHOF, USDA; B91M, C7M (also see Starter Cultures, page 496)

AURICULARIACEAE

Auricularia auricula - *Kikurage, Wood ear, Jew's ear* {CU} The fruitbodies are thick, gelatinous, and virtually stemless. In China and the Far East they are grown commercially, dried, and used in stews, Japanese-style fish sausages, and soups, especially miso and hot and sour soups, often combined with dried lily buds (Hemerocallis sp.). Although bland and tasteless, they readily absorb the flavors of other foods. COST 1988 [Cul, Re], MABEY, MILLER, OCHSE, SHURTLEFF 1975, TANAKA; D87M, D87M{SR}, M87, M87{SN}

Auricularia polytricha - *Arage-kikurage, Cloud ears* {CU} Fruitbodies are consumed as food. They are usually sold dried and are reconstituted for use in cooking. After soaking, they are chewy, gelatinous, slippery, and have little taste although they take on the flavors of other ingredients. Used in soups, casseroles, stir-fried dishes, and as an ingredient of the Chinese dishes *bahmi* and *kimlo*. CHANG, W. [Re], CRIBB, CZARNECKI [Cul, Re], OCHSE, SCHNEIDER [Re], SOLOMON, UPHOF; E21, G31M{KT}, G31M{SN}, J60{OR}

BOLBITIACEAE

Agrocybe aegerita - *Brown swordbelt* {CU} Fruitbodies are consumed as food. Small to medium-sized, with a yellowish-brown cap. Occasionally cultivated and sold in the markets of the Mediterranean area. In southern Italy, it is cultured on poplar wood. In the ornamental garden it can be cultivated on logs, like other wood-inhabiting species. STEINECK [Cu], UPHOF; E21

BOLETACEAE

Boletus mirabilis - *Admirable boletus* {CU} Fruitbodies are edible, choice. The flesh is firm, lemon-yellow, sometimes reddish when bruised. MILLER; D87M, D87M{SR}

Strobilomyces floccopus - *Pine-cone fungus, Old-man-of-the-woods* {CU} The fruitbodies are edible but their taste is not considered outstanding. MEDSGER, MILLER, TANAKA; D87M, D87M{SR}

Suillus grevillei - *Pine-tree bolete, Larch bolete* {CU} Fruitbodies are edible. The flesh is lemon-yellow and becomes spongy in older specimens. The odor is pleasant, the flavor mild. The surface of the cap is easily peeled away. The stalk should be thoroughly cleaned before cooking. MILLER, STEINECK [Cu], TANAKA; D87M, D87M{SR}

CANTHARELLACEAE

Cantharellus cibarius - *Chanterelle, Golden chanterelle, Girolle* {CU} The fruitbodies are cooked and eaten, preserved in oil, or dried for later use. The flesh is firm, light yellowish, and has a truly delicious flavor. One of the most famous and highly valued mushrooms, they are used in stews, soups, omelettes, grain dishes, sauces, or sautéed in butter or oil. The dried powder, known as *gold dust*, is sprinkled on omelettes, salads, pastas, soups, etc. CZARNECKI [Cul, Re], FERNALD, GIBBONS 1962, GRIGSON [Cul, Re], LAUNERT, MICHAEL [Pre], MILLER, QUAINTANCE, SCHNEIDER [Pre, Re], STEINECK [Cu], UPHOF; C11T{PR}, D87M, D87M{SR}, L99{PR}, M41M{PR}, *N40*{PR}

Craterellus fallax - *Black trumpet-of-death, Horn of plenty* {CU} Fruitbodies are edible, choice. D87M, D87M{SR}

CLAVARIACEAE

Clavaria pyxidata* → *Clavicorona pyxidata

Clavicorona pyxidata - *Crowned coral, Kotoji-hôki-take* {CU} Fruitbodies are edible, good to choice. Tan to pale pinkish fruiting body with multiple slender branches and yellow crownlike tips. Flesh tough, white, mild in flavor. MILLER, TANAKA; C7M

COPRINACEAE

Coprinus cinereus - *Ne-naga-no-hitoyo-take* {CU} Fruitbodies are much esteemed as a delicious food by the natives of different parts of the Malayan Archipelago. TANAKA, UPHOF; C7M

Coprinus comatus - *Shaggy mane* {CU} Fruitbodies are edible, choice. The firm caps have a distinct taste and are excellent baked, cooked with eggs, made into ketchup, or simmered in butter with a rich sauce made of the flavorful, black juice that cooks out of them. They should be prepared for the table as quickly as possible or they will dissolve into a black inky mass. CRIBB, CZARNECKI [Cul, Re], FERNALD, GIBBONS 1962, GRIGSON [Cul, Re], MABEY, MICHAEL [Re], MILLER, STAMETS [Cu], STEINECK [Cu], UPHOF; D87M, D87M{SR}, E21, I49, I49{SN}, J60{SN}, M87, M87{SN}

Coprinus macrorhizus* → *Coprinus cinereus

Coprinus micaceus - *Small inky-cap* {CU} Fruitbodies are consumed as food, having a delicate flavor. It is best to harvest them when young, while the gills are still white to very light gray. When the caps are simmered in butter, a great deal of black, watery juice forms which may be thickened with flour to make a rich creamy sauce. Or they can be baked with milk, a beaten egg, seasonings, and dry bread crumbs to absorb the liquid. FERNALD, MILLER, UPHOF; D87M, D87M{SR}

CRYPTOCOCCACEAE

Brettanomyces bruxellensis - *Lambic beer yeast* {CU} A yeast involved in the fermentation of the *lambic beers* of Belgium, lightly hopped beers made from a mixture of barley malt and unmalted wheat. STEINKRAUS; **U15M**

Brettanomyces lambicus - *Lambic beer yeast* {CU} One of the microorganisms that takes part in the *lambic beer* fermentations. Produces acid and alcohol and also contributes to the special flavor of the beer. PEDERSON, STEINKRAUS; **U15M**

Candida holmii* → *Torulopsis holmii

Mycoderma sp. - *Lactic mycoderma* Microorganism that grows on the surface of certain cheeses while they cure, especially Neufchâtel cheese. PEDERSON; (for sources see Starter Cultures, page 496)

Torulopsis holmii - *Kefir yeast, Sourdough bread yeast* {CU} A lactose-negative yeast that is involved in the production of *kefir grains*, and also *sourdough bread*. STEINKRAUS; **T34** (also see Starter Cultures, page 496)

DEUTEROMYCETES

Geotrichum candidum - *Lactic oidia* {CU} Intermediate between yeasts and molds, these microorganisms are used in the manufacture of several varieties of cheeses. They are also involved in the fermentations of *kanji*, *gari*, *pito*, *torani*, *pozol* and *toddy*. HESSELTINE, STEINKRAUS; C7M (also see Starter Cultures, page 496)

Monilia sitophila* → *Neurospora sitophila

Neurospora sitophila - *Onchom mold* The essential mold involved with the fermentation of *onchom*. Different strains are known to produce different pigmentation, with orange, yellow, pink, and white colors all appearing on the same onchom cake. SHURTLEFF 1979, STEINKRAUS, UPHOF; (for sources see Starter Cultures, page 496)

Oidium lactis - *Lactic oidia* Intermediate between yeasts and molds, this microorganism is used in the manufacture of several varieties of cheese. It also takes part in the fermentation of *poi* and *chicha*. HESSELTINE, STEINKRAUS; (for sources see Starter Cultures, page 496)

Oospora lactis - *Lactic oidia* Intermediate between yeasts and molds. Used along with Oidium lactis and Geotrichum candidum in the manufacture of various cheeses. It is also involved in the fermentation of *piima*. (for sources see Starter Cultures, page 496)

HYDNACEAE

Hericium abietis - *Conifer coral mushroom* {SN} Fruitbodies are edible, choice. An attractive mushroom with cascading white icicle-like spines. Best eaten when young. Usually parboiled, then sautéed in butter, the parboiling helping to prevent the sautéed mushrooms from tasting bitter. J61M

Hericium coralloides - *Bear's head tooth, Fungus icicles* {SN} The fruitbodies are consumed. They have a very distinct, branching form with delicate, long white teeth and a subtle, nut-like flavor. These beautiful mushrooms are best prepared by slowly sautéing in butter and serving with vegetables. Or they can be chopped and added to sauces and gravies. MABEY, MILLER, UPHOF; C11T{PR}, J60{OR}

Hericium erinaceus - *Medusa's head, Lion's head, Pompom blanc* {SN} Fruitbodies are eaten. They are very attractive, with coarse tooth-like spines hanging from the body. Tasty when young, but reportedly turns sour with age. After first being parboiled, they are excellent seasoned with garlic butter. TANAKA; M87, M87{CU}, M87{KT}, *N40*{PR}

MONASCACEAE

Monascus purpureus - *Chinese red rice mold* The essential organism for production of *Chinese red rice*, used as a food coloring and also for flavoring. The best strains produce a dark red, water-soluble pigment that readily mixes with other natural pigments and with food. HESSELTINE, STEINKRAUS, UPHOF; (for sources see Starter Cultures, page 496)

MORCHELLACEAE

Morchella angusticeps - *Black morel* {CU} Fruitbodies are edible, choice. The caps have black ridges. MILLER, TANAKA; A38M{PR}, C11T{PR}, E21, E21{SN}, I49, I49{SN}, J60, M87, M87{SN}

Morchella elata - *Snakehead morel* {CU} Fruitbodies are edible, choice. TANAKA; Dropped by M87

Morchella esculenta - *Morel, Yellow morel* {SN} The fruitbodies are cooked and eaten or dried and stored. The meaty texture and rich flavor of the morel makes it one of the best of all edible fungi. It can be stuffed and baked, sautéed in butter, slow simmered in cream or stock, or combined with light meats, fowl, pasta, rice, potatoes, sauces, etc. Dried morels are said to improve in flavor as they age. BURR, CZARNECKI [Cul, Re], FERNALD, MABEY, MILLER, SCHNEIDER [Pre, Re], STEINECK [Cu], UPHOF; A38M{PR}, C11T{PR}, C27, C27{CU}, E21{CU}, E21{KT}, E32{KT}, E63G{KT}, I49, I49{CU}, J61M, L99{PR}, M41M{PR}, M87, M87{CU}, *N40*{PR}, etc.

MUCORACEAE

Actinomucor elegans - *Sufu mold* {CU} The mold generally used in the commercial manufacture of *sufu*. It is one of the best for the production of *pehtze*, the fresh soybean curd inoculated with the grayish hairlike mycelium of the mold. HESSELTINE, STEINKRAUS; T34 (also see Starter Cultures, page 496)

Rhizopus oligosporus - *Tempeh mold* {CU} Pure cultures of this mold are the best so far discovered for the production of *tempeh* from soybeans and other substrates. It also takes part in the fermentation of *shiro-koji*, *ragi tapeh*, *onchom*, *kecap*, and *tauco*. HESSELTINE, SHURTLEFF 1979, STEINKRAUS; M87 (also see Starter Cultures, page 496)

Rhizopus oryzae - *Tempeh mold* {CU} A mold that takes part in the fermentation of tempeh made from velvet bean (Mucuna pruriens), called *tempeh benguk*. In the production of tempeh from soybeans, it is valued for its long hyphae, which form a highly cohesive mycelium and firm cakes. It is also involved in the production of *onchom*, *ragi tapeh*, *lao-chao*, *brem*, and *tauco*. HESSELTINE, SHURTLEFF 1979, STEINKRAUS; T34

PLUTEACEAE

Volvariella bakerii - *Baker's paddy-straw mushroom* {CU} Fruitbodies are edible. T34

Volvariella volvacea - *Paddy-straw mushroom, Chinese mushroom* {SN} The fruitbodies are cooked and eaten or dried for later use. Considered a delicacy, they are used in soups, sauces, stews, casseroles, omelettes, or steamed or stir-fried dishes. Commonly harvested in the early button stage, when they are most flavorful. Dried and canned products are available in Chinatown markets. CHANG, S. [Cu, Nu], CZARNECKI [Cul, Re], GRIGSON [Cul, Re], HERKLOTS, STAMETS [Cu], STEINKRAUS [Pre], UPHOF; E21{CU}, G2{CU}, I7, J60, M87, M87{CU}

POLYPORACEAE

Ganoderma lucidum - *Ling chih, Reishi, Mannen-take* {SN} Fruitbodies are edible. In Chinatown markets, a commercial mushroom confection is available - a pale, translucent, semi-soft candy made from the boiled extract of ling chih. LINCOFF; E2, E21{CU}, I49, I49{CU}, J60, M87

STRAINS {CU}

Western Biologicals #1: A Japanese strain. M87

Western Biologicals #2: A North American strain. M87

Ganoderma oregonense - *Oregon ling chih* {CU} Fruitbodies are edible. E21

Grifola frondosa - *Hen-of-the-woods, Mai-take* {SN} Fruitbodies are edible, choice. They are large, fleshy, up to two feet broad with many smaller overlapping caps. One of the truly delicious mushrooms, they are cooked in soups and stews or prepared as tempura (dipped in batter and deep fried). Some people have a bad reaction to eating them. CZARNECKI [Cul, Re], KAYE, LEIBENSTEIN [Re], MILLER, TANAKA; E2, E21{CU}, I49, I49{CU}, J60, M87

STRAINS {CU}

Western Biologicals #1: A Japanese strain. M87

Western Biologicals #2: A British Columbian strain. M87

Grifola umbellata - *Zhu ling, Umbrella polypore, Chorei-mai-take* {CU} Fruitbodies are edible. MILLER, TANAKA; E21, I49, I49{SN}

Laetiporus sulphureus - *Sulphur-shelf, Chicken-of-the-woods* {SN} Fruitbodies are eaten when fresh or dried, the edible portion being the trimmed margin of the young caps. The fresh mushroom is bright sulphur-yellow to orange and tends to be tough. It should be cut into very thin slices crosswise and stewed for a half-hour or more, or it can be parboiled, chopped finely and mixed with bread crumbs and a white sauce. FERNALD, GIBBONS 1962, MILLER, UPHOF; C11T{PR}, J61M, M87, M87{CU}

Lentinula edodes* → *Lentinus edodes

Lentinus edodes - *Shii-take* {KT} Fruitbodies are eaten raw in salads, cooked, added to soups, fried, broiled, or oil-roasted. Dried ones are similarly used after soaking in warm water, or shredded and used in soup stocks. An essential ingredient of *sushi* in Western Japan, and also Kwangtung-style Chinese dishes. Also used in omelettes, sauces, gravies, pasta dishes, etc. A tea is brewed from them. CZARNECKI [Cul, Re], MORI [Nu, Re], SCHNEIDER [Pre, Re], SHURTLEFF 1976, STAMETS [Cu], TANAKA, UPHOF; A35T, C11T{PR}, C27, C27{CU}, D63, D75M, E21, E21{SN}, F10, F10{PR}, G31M, G31M{SN}, I7, I7{SN}, J60{SN}, K97{SN}, M87, M87{CU}, etc. (for strains see Shiitake, page 480)

Lentinus lepideus - *Scaly lentinus, Matsu-ôji* {CU} Fruitbodies are edible but the taste is said to be somewhat disagreeable. MILLER, TANAKA; T34

Polyporus frondosus* → *Grifola frondosa

Polyporus sulphureus* → *Laetiporus sulphureus

Polyporus umbellatus* → *Grifola umbellata

Poria cocos - *Tuckahoe, Indian bread* {CU} The fruitbodies, growing on roots of trees, are edible. They are consumed as food or employed for making jelly. TANAKA, UPHOF; T34

SACCHAROMYCETACEAE

Hansenula anomala - *Ragi yeast* {CU} A yeast that is involved in the fermentation of *ragi tapeh*, as well as *arrack*, *kanji*, *torani*, *tapeh ketan*, *tapeh ketella*, *brem*, and *yakju*. HESSELTINE, SHURTLEFF 1979, STEINKRAUS; T34 (also see Starter Cultures, page 496)

Kluyveromyces fragilis* → *Kluyveromyces marxianus

Kluyveromyces marxianus - *Primary yeast, Nutritional yeast* {CU} This yeast is grown on cheese whey to produce food yeast, which is used as a nutritional supplement. It also has a role in the fermentation of *kefir* and *pozol*. KOSIKOWSKI, PEDERSON, STEINKRAUS, UPHOF; T34

Saccharomyces beticus* → *Saccharomyces cerevisiae

Saccharomyces carlsbergensis* → *Saccharomyces cerevisiae

Saccharomyces cerevisiae - *Wine yeast, Beer yeast, Bread yeast* {CU} As well as occurring naturally in many fermented products, pure cultures of this yeast are widely used in the food industry. The numerous products include *sake*, *kustarak*, *champagne*, *sherry*, *pulque*, *ginger beer*, *sourdough bread*, *toddy*, *red rice*, *hopper*, *lebadura*, *whiskey*, *brewer's yeast*, *primary yeast*, *puto*, *ragi tapeh*, *kisra*, *ogi*, *pozol*, *chicha*, *kaffir beer*, *busaa*, *tesguino*, *cocoa*, *tibi*, *chu-chong-tsaw*, and *yakju*. BROUK, HESSELTINE, PEDERSON, SCHERY, STEINKRAUS, UPHOF; B11, B91M, C7M, D81T, E13, M69 (also see Starter Cultures, page 496)

Saccharomyces delbrueckii* → *Torulaspora delbrueckii

Saccharomyces fragilis* → *Kluyveromyces marxianus

Saccharomyces kefir* → *Kluyveromyces marxianus

Torulaspora delbrueckii - *Kefir yeast, Sherry yeast* {CU} A lactose negative-yeast that takes part in the fermentation of *kefir*, as well as *sherry* and *colonche*. BROUK, PEDERSON, STEINKRAUS; T34 (also see Starter Cultures, page 496)

Torulopsis taboadae* → *Torulaspora delbrueckii

STROPHARIACEAE

Hypholoma sublateritium - *Perplexing hypholoma, Brick cap, Chestnut mushroom, Kuri-take* {SN} Fruitbodies are boiled and eaten or cooked in soups. The taste is said to be mild to bitter. They are treated with vinegar before being cooked. MILLER, TANAKA, UPHOF; D87M{CU}, D87M{SR}, E2, M87, M87{CU}

Kuehneromyces mutabilis* → *Pholiota mutabilis

Naematoloma sublateritium* → *Hypholoma sublateritium

Pholiota cylindrica* → *Agrocybe aegerita

Pholiota mutabilis - *Changing pholiota* {SN} Fruitbodies are consumed as food. The dark brown caps are small and thin-fleshed but grow in large clusters. It has an agreeable flavor, and is excellent for flavoring soups and stews, to which it gives a rich brown color. Sold in markets, especially in Bavaria. MABEY, UPHOF; M87, M87{CU}

Pholiota nameko - *Nameko* {SN} Fruitbodies are edible, choice, covered with a slippery wet coating. Also called *button mushrooms* in Japan where they are sold fresh or in cans. They are frequently used in miso soups, steamed in a pipkin, or mixed with grated daikon as a topping for chilled tofu. KAYE, SHURTLEFF 1975, STEINECK [Cu], TANAKA, UPHOF; E2, E21{CU}, I49, I49{CU}, M87, M87{CU}

STRAINS

Bansei Shu: Fruiting range 6^0 to 10^0 C. Optimum temperature 8^0 C. E2

Gokuwasei Shu: Fruiting range 8^0 to 15^0 C. Optimum temperature 10^0 C. E2

Wasei Shu: Fruiting range 6^0 to 12^0 C. Optimum temperature 9^0 C. E2

Stropharia rugoso-annulata - *King stropharia, Garden giant, Wine cap* {SN} Fruitbodies are edible, choice. A large, thick-fleshed mushroom with reddish tinged caps and an excellent flavor. Recommended for culture by home growers in outdoor cold frames or garden beds. It commonly occurs in grounds where potatoes have been planted. MILLER, STAMETS [Cu], STEINECK [Cu]; C27, C27{CU}, D87M{CU}, D87M{SR}, E19M{KT}, E21, E21{CU}, E21{KT}, E32, I49, I49{CU}, J60, J61M, M87, M87{CU}, etc.

TRICHOLOMATACEAE

Armillaria mellea* → *Armillariella mellea

Armillariella mellea - *Honey mushroom, Chiodini, Nara-take* {CU} The fruitbodies are edible, choice. They are eaten cooked, pickled or salted. Dried ones may be reconstituted in water, coated with flour, seasoned and fried in oil. MILLER, TANAKA, UPHOF; C7M, C11T{PR}, D87M, D87M{SR}, J66M{PR}, M69

Clitocybe nuda - *Blewits, Murasaki-shimeji, Masked tricholoma* {CU} Fruitbodies are edible, choice. Its striking violet color, firm texture, and good taste give this species high culinary appeal. This mushroom should not be eaten raw, only after cooking or parboiling. Also good for mixing with other mushrooms and for drying. Recommended for home cultivators and natural culture techniques. CZARNECKI [Cul, Re], GRIGSON [Cul, Re], MILLER, STAMETS [Cu], STEINECK [Cu], TANAKA; D87M, D87M{SR}, E21, I49, I49{SN}, J60{SN}, M87, M87{SN}

Flammulina velutipes - *Enoki-take, Velvet stem, Winter mushroom* {SN} The crisp, mild-flavored fruitbody is eaten raw in salads and sandwiches, boiled, sautéed, or used in sukiyaki, one-pot cookery, and as a garnish for clear soups and broths. Cultivated forms, having been grown in darkened environments, are long, thin, and pale white in color. CZARNECKI [Cul, Re], MILLER, SCHNEIDER [Pre, Re], SHURTLEFF 1975, STAMETS [Cu], STEINECK [Cu], TANAKA, UPHOF; D87M{CU}, D87M{SR}, E2, E21{CU}, G2{CU}, G31M, G31M{KT}, I49, I49{CU}, J60, M87, M87{CU}, *N40*{PR}

STRAINS

Hatsuyuki: Fruiting range 4^0 to 13^0 C. Optimum temperature 6^0 to 8^0 C. E2

Maruei: Fruiting range 4^0 to 13^0 C. Optimum temperature 6^0 to 8^0 C. E2

Shibuki: Fruiting range 6^0 to 15^0 C. Optimum temperature 8^0 to 10^0 C. E2

Lepista nuda → *Clitocybe nuda*

Lyophyllum aggregatum → *Lyophyllum decastes*

Lyophyllum decastes - *Hon-shimeji, Japanese honey mushroom, Fried chicken* {SN} Fruitbodies are edible, choice. They are put in soups, or boiled and then eaten with vinegar. In Japan, they are cultured in bottles, producing a bunch of fruiting bodies with tan to grayish-brown caps averaging one inch in diameter. KAYE, MILLER, SHURTLEFF 1975, TANAKA; J60{OR}, M87, M87{CU}, *N40*{PR}

Lyophyllum ulmarium → *Pleurotus ulmarius*

Lyophyllum sp. - *Shimeji, Japanese oyster mushroom, Hira-take* {SN} Fruitbodies are edible, choice. Young caps are black to elegant gray in color, becoming light brown as they mature. The stems have a more chewy texture than other oyster mushrooms. Very young clusters are sometimes harvested before the caps expand for use in gourmet Japanese cooking. Best suited for spring, summer and fall home cultivation. KAYE; E2, E21{CU}, I7

STRAINS

Bansie Shu: Fruiting range 5^0 to 15^0 C. Optimum temperature 8^0 to 12^0 C. E2

Chusei Shu: Fruiting range 8^0 to 15^0 C. Optimum temperature 10^0 to 13^0 C. E2

Wasei Shu: Fruiting range 10^0 to 18^0 C. Optimum temperature 12^0 to 15^0 C. E2

Marasmius oreades - *Fairy ring, Fall mousseron* {CU} Fruitbodies are edible, choice. Although slightly leathery in texture they have a very good flavor that enhances soups, sauces, gravies and vegetable dishes. Can be picked over a comparatively long period. Also dried for winter use. Common in lawns, meadows and other grassy areas where they form circles or rings that expand in size each year. May be grown in gardens or in strips of grass between rows of dwarf fruit trees. Occasionally sold in markets. FERNALD, GIBBONS 1962, LAUNERT, MICHAEL [Pre, Cul], MILLER, STEINECK [Cu], UPHOF; C11T{PR}, D87M, D87M{SR}

Pleurocybella porrigens - *Angel wings, Sugi-hira-take* {CU} Fruitbodies are edible. Some authors list these as being nonpoisonous, others as edible and choice. MILLER, TANAKA; I49

Pleurotus columbinus* → *Pleurotus ostreatus

Pleurotus cornucopiae - *Golden oyster, Savory oyster, Hime-hira-take* {SN} Fruitbodies are edible, choice. They are small to medium, lemon yellow in color, and are highly aromatic. Has slightly thinner flesh than other pleurotes and is therefore more delicate. Can be grown in gardens on short logs or long, prostrate tree trunks. The bright color will enliven parts of an ornamental garden lying in partial shade. STEINECK [Cu], TANAKA; E21{CU}, E21{KT}, E32{KT}, I7, I49, I49{CU}, J60, M87, M87{CU}

Pleurotus cystidiosus - {SN} Fruitbodies are edible. J60{OR}

Pleurotus eryngii - *King oyster, Cardarella* {SN} Fruitbodies are edible, choice. They are medium to large with a light, reddish-brown cap and a tan stem. A robust fleshy mushroom with a sweet flavor and a meaty texture. Native of the southern European steppes and sub-tropical areas of North Africa. UPHOF; E21{CU}, G2, G2{CU}, I49, I49{CU}, J60, M87, M87{CU}

Pleurotus ostreatus - *Oyster mushroom, Tree oyster, Hira-take* {SN} The young, tender fruitbodies are stewed, sautéed in butter, prepared as tempura, used in soups, sauces, polenta, and casseroles, or sometimes dried or preserved in oil for later use. In Italy, they are served with salt cod, pork loins, or sausages. One of the most dependable mushrooms for home cultivation. Has the strongest flavor of the cultivated pleurotes. BIANCHINI, CZARNECKI [Cul, Re], FERNALD, MILLER, SCHNEIDER [Pre, Re], STAMETS [Cu], STEINECK [Cu], STEINKRAUS [Cu], TANAKA; C11T{PR}, C27, C27{CU}, D63, D63{KT}, D75M{KT}, E21, E21{CU}, E21{KT}, F64M{KT}, G31M, G31M{KT}, I7, I49, I49{CU}, J60, K97, M87, M87{KT}, etc.

STRAINS {CU}

#690: Produces grey to grayish-blue mushrooms depending on the cropping condition. A temperature of 78 to 82^0 F. is optimal for fast growth during spawn run. Relative humidity should be 90 to 100%. Duration of spawn run is 10 to 14 days or when the substrate is completely colonized by white mycelium. Cropping lasts for 7 to 10 days with a 10 to 14 day waiting period before the next break. G55M{SN}

Blue Capped: (Blue Oyster) A strain with bluish-gray caps. Produces 1 to 1 1/2 pounds of mushrooms over a period of 6 to 8 weeks in flushes of 2 to 3 weeks apart. Requires a room temperature of 60 to 75^0 F. and strong indirect light. E21, M87

Florida: (Florida Oyster) Cap whitish to gray to pale yellow brown. Flesh thin and white. This strains preference for warmer temperatures recommends it for cultivation during the late spring through early fall. Original strain is from wild specimens first cultivated in 1958 by S.S. Block of Gainesville, Florida. STAMETS; D87M, D87M{SR}, E21, I49, I49{SN}, M87

Sporeless 3200: Produces high quality fruiting bodies and high yields. Mushrooms are of the classical oyster shape with a brownish-gray color. Addresses the allergy problems associated with spores and prevents ecological risk as it is not necessary to filter the air. Can be cultivated on a wide range of straws and agricultural by-products. *A41*{SN}

Sporeless 3210: Produces high quality fruiting bodies and high yields. Mushrooms are trumpet shaped and are gray in color. Addresses the allergy problems associated with spores and prevents ecological risk as it is not necessary to filter the air. Can be cultivated on a wide range of straws and agricultural by-products. *A41*{SN}

Western Biologicals #3: A sporeless strain. M87

Western Biologicals #4: A low temperature strain. M87

Western Biologicals #5: A native British Columbia strain. M87

Pleurotus porrigens → *Pleurocybella porrigens*

Pleurotus sajor-caju - *Phoenix oyster, Indian oyster* {SN} Fruitbodies are edible, choice. Medium to large with a white stem and dark brown cap. A sub-tropical, heat-loving species from the Himalayan foothills. Requires little or no heat shock for fruiting. C11T{PR}, D63{KT}, D75M, E19M{KT}, E21{CU}, G2, G2{CU}, I49, I49{CU}, J60, M87, M87{CU}

STRAINS

#161: Produces light brown to grayish-brown mushrooms depending on the cropping condition. A temperature of 78 to 82^0 F. is optimal for fast growth during spawn run. Relative humidity should be 90 to 100%. Duration of spawn run is 10 to 14 days or when the substrate is completely colonized by white mycelium. Cropping lasts for 7 to 10 days with a 10 to 14 day waiting period before the next break. G55M

Fresh Delight: Heavy producer of mushrooms with a unique, delightful flavor and soft texture. Caps variable in size, 1 to 6 inches in diameter. Thick cluster will produce smaller caps. May be grown year round, but fall and spring weather are most favorable. I7, I7{KT}

Western Biologicals #2: A Dutch strain. M87{CU}

Pleurotus ulmarius - *Elm mushroom, Buna-shimeji, Shiro-tamogi-take* {SN} Fruitbodies are edible. The flesh is firm, hard, tough, white throughout. The odor is pleasant and yeast-like, the taste mild. If the older caps are used only the tender parts should be cooked, though the very young ones can be used entire. FERNALD, GIBBONS 1962, MILLER, STEINECK [Cu], TANAKA; E2

Tricholoma conglobatum → *Lyophyllum decastes*

TUBERACEAE

Tuber gibbosum - *Oregon white truffle* {KT} Underground fruitbodies are edible, very choice. James Beard rated them equal to the Italian white truffle. In preparing them for cooking, they need only be brush-cleaned, and slivered, grated, or crushed. Use them in patés, omelettes, as an insert under the skin of cooking turkey or chicken, or to flavor rice, barley, bulghur, eggs in the shell, sour cream, cheeses, butter, sausage, wine, and brandy. They are harvested commercially in the Pacific Northwest and marketed throughout North America. ANONYMOUS 1987 [Pre, Re], CZARNECKI [Cul, Re]; C11T{PR}, I76, I76{PR}, M99M{PR}

Tuber melanosporum - *Perigord truffle, Black truffle* {KT} Underground fruitbodies are edible, very choice. While the Piedmont truffle is very good raw, the black truffle is best cooked. For example, in *tartufi alla nursina* in which the truffles are finely sliced in layers with cheese and butter, seasoned with basil, nutmeg, oregano, and bay leaves, and then baked. They are widely used to flavor patés, eggs, butter, sauces, pastas, etc. Sometimes sold in jars of arborio rice to which they impart flavor. Truffles can be canned, frozen, or preserved in cognac or armagnac. BIANCHINI, CZARNECKI [Cul, Re], GRIGSON [Cul, Re], PICART [Cu, Re], ROOT 1980b [Cul], UPHOF; A11M, C11T{PR}, H19M{PR}, L99{PR}, M41M{PR}

USTILAGINACEAE

Ustilago maydis - *Corn smut, Huitlacoche* {CU} Fruitbodies are cooked and eaten as a delicacy or dried for later use. Their texture and flavor are unique. In Mexico, they are sold in markets and are widely eaten in omelettes, soups, stews, and vegetable dishes. Some Mexican gardeners encourage the smut by scratching the base of a plant, and pile soil against the scratch so that the fungus spores infect the plant's tissues. They are harvested while still light in color and succulent. FELL 1982b, UPHOF, WEATHERWAX, WILSON, G., YANOVSKY; **T34**

ALPHABETICAL LISTING OF ALGAE FAMILIES

OOCYSTACEAE

Chlorella pyrenoidosa - {CU} Unicellular micro-algae that is used as a food supplement. Contains up to 55% protein with all the essential amino acids. Also has a very high level of chlorophyll, up to 6%. Other vitamins and minerals supplied include vitamins A, B_1, B_2, B_{12}, niacin, calcium, iron, and zinc. Usually added to other foods, including breads, pastas, juices, soups and salad dressings. HILLS, C. 1978, RICHMOND, A. [Cu], TANAKA; C7M, I43T{PR}

STRAINS

Thermophilic: A high temperature strain. C7M

Chlorella vulgaris - {CU} Single-celled microplankton which is rich in protein and is used as a food supplement. Like C. pyrenoidosa, it has a very thin cell wall that makes it more digestible than other species. Very widely distributed over almost all the area on earth. HILLS, C. 1978, RICHMOND, A. [Cu]; C7M

SCENEDESMACEAE

Scenedesmus obliquus - {CU} Unicellular green algae related to Chlorella. Has thin, very soft cell walls making it easily digested. Recommended as a food supplement, similar to Chlorella and Spirulina. Very widely distributed over almost all the area on earth. HILLS, C. 1978, RICHMOND, A. [Cu]; **T34, W34**

ALPHABETICAL LISTING OF BACTERIA FAMILIES

ACETOBACTERACEAE

Acetobacter aceti - *Vinegar bacteria* {CU} Microorganism responsible for the conversion of alcohol into acetic acid, which is the principal compound of vinegar. BROUK, UPHOF; B91M, C7M, D81T, M69 (also see Starter Cultures, page 496)

Acetobacter aceti ssp. xylinum - *Tea fungus bacteria* {CU} The principal microorganism involved in the fermentation of *tea fungus*. Also synthesizes cellulose in the production of the film that forms during the Philippine *nata* fermentation. STEINKRAUS; **T34, U15M** (also see Starter Cultures, page 496)

Acetobacter xylinum → *Acetobacter aceti ssp. xylinum*

BACILLACEAE

Bacillus subtilis - *Natto bacteria* {CU} A microorganism involved in the fermentation of cooked soybeans into *natto*. During the process the proteins of the beans are broken down to amino acids, making the finished product highly digestible. STEINKRAUS; B11, B91M, C7M, D81T, M69 (also see Starter Cultures, page 496)

BREVIBACTERIACEAE

Bacterium linens → *Brevibacterium linens*

Brevibacterium linens - *Red bacteria* {CU} Short, reddish, rod-like bacteria responsible for the taste and orange color of Limburger, Brick, Fontina, Bel Paese, Tilsit, St. Paulin, Pont l'Evêque, Brie and other cheeses. BROUK, KOSIKOWSKI, PEDERSON, USDA; C7M, M69 (also see Starter Cultures, page 496)

LACTOBACILLACEAE

Lactobacillus acidophilus - *Acidophilus milk bacteria* {CU} A bacteria which converts lactose, or milk sugar, into lactic acid, thus making it more digestible. In the commercial production of *acidophilus* milk, skim or partially defatted milk is used. STEINKRAUS; C7M, D81T, M69 (also see Starter Cultures, page 496)

Lactobacillus brevis - *Kefir bacteria* {CU} The microorganism that produces "kefiran", a polysaccharide gum that holds together the bacteria and yeasts in *kefir grains*, the starter culture used in kefir manufacture. STEINKRAUS; T34 (also see Starter Cultures, page 496)

Lactobacillus bulgaricus - *Yogurt bacteria, Thermophilic cheese bacteria* {CU} A bacteria used in most *yogurt* and some cheese starter cultures. It grows best at temperatures of 110 to 116^0 F., and produces total acids of 2.0 to 4.0%. STEINKRAUS; T34 (also see Starter Cultures, page 496)

Lactobacillus casei - *Mesophilic cheese bacteria* {CU} A good agent for the maturing of cheese due to its action on casein. It can be found on the majority of cheeses allowed to mature. The temperature for optimal growth is 86^0 F. Also takes part in the fermentation of *koumiss, kefir, kishk, laban, dahi* and bread. HESSELTINE, MALLOS [Re], STEINKRAUS, UPHOF; B91M, C7M, K1T, M69 (also see Starter Cultures, page 496)

Lactobacillus helveticus - *Thermophilic cheese bacteria* {CU} Used with Streptococcus thermophilus to form a lactic cheese culture that grows best at high temperatures, from 110 to 115^0 F. It also takes part in the fermentation of *dahi* and *busaa*. KOSIKOWSKI, PEDERSON, STEINKRAUS; T34 (also see Starter Cultures, page 496)

Lactobacillus plantarum - *Pickle bacteria* {CU} A lactic-acid producing bacteria that plays a major role in all vegetable fermentations, producing high acidity, often yielding three to four times as much D-lacic acid as species of Leuconostoc. BROUK, PEDERSON, STEINKRAUS, UPHOF; T34 (also see Starter Cultures, page 496)

Lactobacillus sanfrancisco - *San Francisco sourdough-bread bacteria* {CU} A microorganism that has been isolated from sourdough, or *sauerteig bread* of the San Francisco area, and which is responsible for the characteristic sour flavor. STEINKRAUS; T34 (also see Starter Cultures, page 496)

MICROCOCCACEAE

Micrococcus sp. - *Sausage bacteria* A microorganism used with Pediococci and Lactobacilli in the manufacture of dry and semi-dry sausages. PEDERSON; (for sources see Starter Cultures, page 496)

NOSTOCACEAE

Aphanizomenon flos-aquae - *Super blue-green algae* {PR} Freshwater micro-algae consumed as an energizing food supplement. Usually sprinkled on other foods as a condiment, or mixed with juice as a drink. Contains significant levels of protein, chlorophyll, vitamin B_{12}, beta carotene and trace minerals. More assimilable than spirulina or chlorella. Harvested from the mineral-rich waters of Upper Klamath Lake, Oregon, freeze-dried, and marketed in powder, capsule or liquid form. E56

Nostoc commune - *Star jelly, Fairies' butter, Fat choy, Ishi-kurage* {CU} A freshwater blue-green algae that is consumed raw, dried, stir-fried, sautéed with oysters, in sweet dessert soups, or with sugared vinegar. It is also made into a jelly which is then eaten or used as a thickener for other foods. ARASAKI, BROUK, BURKILL, CRIBB, JOHNSTON, H., MADLENER [Nu, Re], TANAKA; C27G{PR}, U15M, W34

Nostoc ellipsosporum - *Fat choy* {CU} Freshwater blue-green algae eaten in a similar manner to N. commune. BROUK; W34

OSCILLATORIACEAE

Arthrospira platensis* → *Spirulina platensis

Spirulina platensis - *Spirulina, Tecuitlatl* A blue-green algae found in saline, usually alkaline, waters. The crude protein in spirulina can reach as high as 72%, which is highly digestible. It also has a high content of vitamins and minerals, including vitamins A, B_2, B_{12}, E, H, and K, calcium, iron, and niacin. Dried into cakes, it was eaten with *mole* by the Aztecs. Near Lake Chad, similar flat greenish cakes called *dihé* or *douhé* are made into a nourishing soup or a thick gravy which is used as a seasoning on millet balls. The powdered form is used as a food supplement in drinks, wafers, protein powders and *pastalina*, a soy-whole-wheat-spirulina noodle. BEASLEY [Re], HILLS, C. 1978, HILLS, C. 1979, JOHNSTON, H., NATIONAL RESEARCH COUNCIL 1975a, RICHMOND, A. [Cu, Re]; (for sources see Starter Cultures, page 496)

PROPIONIBACTERIACEAE

Propionibacterium freudenreichii ssp. shermanii - *Swiss-cheese bacteria, Propionic cheese bacteria* {CU} The bacteria that produces propionic acid, which is responsible for the characteristic flavor and eye formation of Swiss and Gruyere cheeses. BROUK, UPHOF, USDA; M69 (also see Starter Cultures, page 496)

STREPTOCOCCACEAE

Leuconostoc citrovorum* → *Leuconostoc cremoris

Leuconostoc cremoris - *Aromatic lactic bacteria* {CU} Used in combination with Streptococcus species to form a lactic starter culture. Also involved in the fermentation of *ripened-cream butter*, wine and *piima*. KOSIKOWSKI, PEDERSON, STEINKRAUS; T34 (also see Starter Cultures, page 496)

Pediococcus sp. - *Sausage bacteria* A bacteria used with Micrococci and Lactobacilli in the manufacture of dry and semi-dry sausages. PEDERSON; (for sources see Starter Cultures, page 496)

Streptococcus cremoris - *Viili bacteria, Mesophilic cheese bacteria, Aromatic lactic bacteria* {CU} A bacteria involved in the *viili* fermentation and the fermentation of certain cheeses. It has a temperature range of 72^0 C., and produces 0.9 to 1.0% total acids. STEINKRAUS; T34 (also see Starter Cultures, page 496)

Streptococcus diacetilactis - *Mesophilic cheese bacteria, Aromatic lactic bacteria* {CU} Used in the manufacture of sour cream, butter and various cheeses. It also takes part in the fermentation of *dahi*. KOSIKOWSKI, PEDERSON, STEINKRAUS; T34 (also see Starter Cultures, page 496)

Streptococcus lactis - *Mesophilic cheese bacteria, Aromatic lactic bacteria* {CU} A lactic acid bacteria used in the manufacture of sour cream, butter, buttermilk and certain cheeses. It is also involved in the fermentation of *hakko tofu, poi, ogi, mahewu, dahi, laban* and *jalebi*. BROUK, KOSIKOWSKI, PEDERSON, STEINKRAUS, UPHOF; C7M, D81T, M69 (also see Starter Cultures, page 496)

Streptococcus thermophilus - *Yogurt bacteria, Thermophilic cheese bacteria* {CU} One of the principal bacteria in *yogurt* and cheese starter cultures. It grows best at temperatures of 110 to 112^0 F., and produces total acids of 0.9 to 1.1%. STEINKRAUS; T34 (also see Starter Cultures, page 496)

CULTIVAR LISTINGS

ALMOND {GR}

AMYGDALUS COMMUNIS

All-in-One: The best cultivar for edible landscaping, having showy white flowers that bloom late. Semi-dwarf tree is vigorous, medium upright, self fertile and a heavy bearer. Nonpareil-type, soft shelled nuts with a very good, sweet flavor; quality good to excellent. Shell is well sealed; harvest season is late. STEBBINS; A88M, B93M, *C54*, *D23M*, E4, *I68*, I83M, L33, *L47*, *N20*

Butte: Mission x Nonpareil. Nut medium to small, averaging 16 per ounce; shell soft to hard, thick, solid, well-sealed; cracks out about 52% of kernel; kernel medium to small, plump, smooth, few doubles, quality good, pellicle thin; harvested just after Nonpareil. Blooms late; pollinizes with Nonpareil, Mission and Ruby. Tree vigorous; produces well; grows well on almond and peach rootstocks. BROOKS 1972; *B71M*, B74, *D18*, E4, *K73M*

Carmel: Bud-sport of Nonpareil. Nut small, thick, light colored; kernel comprises 60% of nut, averaging 24 per ounce; lighter color than Nonpareil; quality and flavor good. Harvest 3 weeks later than Nonpareil, 1 week earlier than Mission. Early and regular producer of good quality nuts. Tree medium; bears regularly and in clusters. Pollinizes with Nonpareil and Mission. BROOKS 1972; *A9*, *B71M*, *D18*, E4, *K73M*, *L47*

Davey: Medium-sized nut; shell soft, smooth, thin, well-sealed; kernel attractive, with good texture and flavor, pellicle light brown, blanching quality good; doubles few; ripens early, about with Nonpareil. Tree vigorous, upright; blooms with Nonpareil and can be used as a pollinator for it; tends to come into bearing a year later than other cultivars. BROOKS 1972; E1{SC}

Dehn: Hard-shelled nut with a large, plump kernel that has an attractive brown color; resembles Northland and I.X.L. Heavy bearing tree that is relatively cold hardy; requires pollinization. Open-pollinated seedling of Northland; discovered in 1945. Originated in Ogden, Utah by Emil Dehn. Introduced in 1952. BROOKS 1972; M39M

Fritz: Small, ovate nut with a solid, thick, hard to semi-soft shell. Kernel medium to small, smooth and of good quality. Pollinizes with Nonpareil, Mission, and Ruby. Harvested late, with Mission. Originated in Modesto, California by Burchell Nursery. Introduced in 1970. JAYNES; *B71M*, *D18*, *K73M*

Garden Prince:[1] Medium-sized kernel is a sweet Nonpareil-type; well sealed with a soft shell. Self-fruitful, does not need a pollinizer. Tree a genetic dwarf, approximately 8 to 10 feet tall at maturity; productive; good for container planting. Blooms early, with Nonpareil but may be easily protected by covering with a tarp. STEBBINS; A88M, *C54*, F11, *I68*, I83M, L1, L33, *L47*, *N20*

Hall's Hardy: (Hall, Ridenhower) Parentage unknown, but has the characteristics of a hybrid between an almond and a peach. It's main value is as an ornamental with showy pink blossoms and shiny green leaves. The tree is hardy and the self-fertile flowers bloom relatively late. The kernel is slightly bitter. Originated in Coffeyville, Kansas by a Mr. Hall. B75, C63, D76, F19M, F93, J61M, K28, L30, L97, L99M, *M69M*, M76, N24M

I.X.L.: Nuts large with, as a rule, single kernels; shell soft, smooth, thin, not always well-sealed; hulls easily, no machine being needed, nor is any bleaching necessary; flavor very good; ripens in midseason. Tree a sturdy, rather upright grower, with large leaves; pollinates with Ne Plus Ultra. Largely discarded for shy bearing, but desirable in some areas. WICKSON; F91T{SC}

Jordanolo: Large, elliptical nut; shell thin, soft, smooth, attractive light yellow, shelling out about 60%; kernel large, rather plump, quality high, blanches very well; hulls easily; resembles Jordan. Tree upright, vigorous; bears early and heavily; blooms early, usually with or sometimes before Ne Plus Ultra. BROOKS 1972; D81{PO}, E1{SC}, *I68*

Kapareil:[3] Shell thin, being a papershell type, similar to Nonpareil; kernels small, averaging 30 or more per ounce, suitable for the candy-bar trade, rated as good as Nonpareil in eating quality; matures about 1 week before Nonpareil. Tree resembles Nonpareil in size and shape; productive; blooms with Nonpareil; cross-compatible with Nonpareil, Mission and Davey. BROOKS 1972; E1{SC}

Largueta: Large, long, juicy sweet kernel; averages 25 to 27% of total weight of nut. Recommended for cold areas because of the structure of the branches, which partially protect the flowers from frost. Drought and disease resistant. From an area of Spain that has been an almond growing center for centuries. Q24M

Merced:[3] Medium sized nut; shell paper thin, well-sealed, lighter in color than Nonpareil; small, broad kernel, averages 58 to 63% of nut; ripens with Nonpareil. Tree medium-sized, vigorous, upright; blooms with Nonpareil; very prolific; cross-compatible with Nonpareil. Mission x Nonpareil. BROOKS 1972; *A9*, *B71M*, *D18*

Mission:[2] (Texas) Round, hard-shelled nut with a slightly bitter flavor preferred by some; shelling percentage 40 to 45. Resistant to navel orange worm and bird damage. Good for late frost areas as it blooms late; also harvested late, late September or October. Pollinizes with Nonpareil, Ne Plus Ultra, and Carmel. Chilling requirement 284 to 310 hours. The second most important cultivar in California. JAYNES, RUCK; *A9*, A88M, B23M{PR}, *B41*, *B71M*, B74, B93M, C37, *D18*, *I68*, *K73M*, *L47*, *N20*

Ne Plus Ultra:[2] Large, flat nut with a soft shell; rather poor quality kernel with relatively large number of doubles; shelling percent 55 to 60. Early blooming and thus subject to frost damage in most areas. Blooms about a week ahead of Nonpareil, for which it is a common pollinizer. Chilling requirements are relatively low. Nuts drop readily. JAYNES; *A9*, B23M{PR}, *B71M*, B93M, *D18*, D81{PO}, E4, *I68*, *K73M*, *L47*, M39M, *N20*

Nonpareil:[3] The most important almond cultivar in the United States, accounting for over half the commercial production. Smooth, uniform, attractive kernel with paper-thin shell and sweet flavor; light brown in color; shelling percentage 60 to 70. Blooms moderately early, but tends to be somewhat resistant to frost in the early bud stages. Susceptible to noninfectious bud-failure, worm damage, and bird damage. JAYNES; *A9*, A88M, B23M{PR}, *B71M*, C37, *D18*, E4, *G14*, *I68*, I99{S}, *K73M*, *L47*, L99M, M39M, *N20*, etc.

Padre: Kernel plump, broad, averages 25 to 30 per ounce, resembles Mission; shell hard, resists worm damage, represents 45 to 50% of nut; matures moderately late but before Mission. Tree upright, resembles Mission; a productive and consistent bearer; blooms with Mission. Originated in Davis, California by Dale E. Kester. Introduced in 1983. *A9, B71M, D18, K73M*

Peerless:[2] Regular and heavy bearer of a very large nut with a hard shell; shelling percentage 30 to 40. Kernel quality is moderately good. Early blooming and thus susceptible to late frost. Pollinizes with Ne Plus Ultra and Nonpareil. Nuts ripen just after Nonpareil but drop so easily that they are often harvested early. Low chilling requirements. Marketed primarily as an in shell nut during Christmas time. JAYNES; B23M{PR}, *B71M*, *D18*, I99{S}, *K73M*

Price: (Price Cluster) Consistently high yielder of soft-shelled nuts with a high quality sweet kernel; kernel averages 26 per ounce. The nuts are borne along the branches in clusters; resembles Nonpareil in shape but more plump; some double kernels. Tree very heavy bearing; midseason bloomer. Pollinizes with Mission, Nonpareil, and Ne Plus Ultra. BROOKS 1972; A88M, *B71M*, *C54*, *D18*, *K73M*, *N20*

Ruby: Regular, heavy producer of good quality nuts. The shell is thicker, harder, and better sealed than Nonpareil; kernel averages 53% of nut, 28 kernels per ounce. Tree blooms late, 2 to 3 days after Mission; production high; bears regularly. Harvesting period coincides with Mission. BROOKS 1972; *A9, B71M, D18, K73M*

Thompson:[3] Nut small with a soft to paper-thin shell, well-sealed. Plump, white kernel with a mildly bitter flavor, quality good; kernel averages 60% of nut. Productive, early bearing tree, bears consistently; very vigorous; blooms late, usually with Mission. Pollinizes with Mission, and All-In-One. Originated in Clovis, California by L.M. Thompson. Introduced in 1957. BROOKS 1972; *A9, B71M, K73M*

Titan: Seedlings will produce sweet, intermediate flavored and bitter kernels. Also used as a parent to produce almond x peach hybrids. Selections from these hybrids are then used as rootstocks for superior almond cultivars. Trees grafted to these rootstocks are very vigorous, have a deep, well-anchored root system, and are well adapted to poorer soils and where calcareous conditions exist. JAYNES; E62{PR}, E62{S}, F91T{SC}

Vesta:[3] Shell soft, easily cracked; suture closed and tight making the kernels less subject to worm damage than Nonpareil; kernel very similar to Nonpareil, but larger, flavor good; ripens 10 to 14 days after Nonpareil. Tree very vigorous; consistently productive; blooms with Nonpareil, which it pollinates. BROOKS 1972; *A19*, F91T{SC}

AMARANTH {S}

AMARANTHUS SPP.

GRAIN AMARANTH

Mostly A. cruentus and A. hypochondriacus. The former is the most adaptable of all grain amaranth species, and it flowers under a wider range of daylengths than the others. A. hypochondriacus is later maturing which limits its usefulness in more northern areas, however it is the most robust and highest yielding of the grain types.

1011: (R1011) 110 days. Considered to be one of the best and most uniform Mexican grain types. Large golden seeds. Late season maturity. Medium-tall plants with green flower heads that turn pink as they mature. Stout stalks resist lodging. Very similar to 1041. Developed at the Rodale Research Center, Kutztown, Pennsylvania. C25M, E59Z

1023: (R101) (A. hypochondriacus) 150 days. Very bushy, green plant with no predominant seed head; grows up to 8 feet tall; quite resistant to lodging. Produces large, high quality white seeds. Has shown excellent seedling vigor. Matures very late. Should be planted at high densities to discourage bushiness. Developed at the Rodale Research Center, Kutztown, Pennsylvania. C25M

1024: (R103) (A. hypochondriacus) Very bushy, green plant with thick, succulent stalks; quite resistant to lodging. Has small seed heads borne across the top of the plant. Produces high quality gold seeds. Matures very late. Should be planted at high densities to discourage bushiness. Developed at the Rodale Research Center. C25M

1041: (R149) (A. cruentus) Uniform, high-yielding, green plant; height 5 to 6 feet; mostly single-stemmed when planted at recommended densities. Predominantly white-seeded. Medium length growing season. Somewhat resistant to Lygus infestations. The most commonly grown cultivar in the United States. Developed at the Rodale Research Center. C25M

Alegria: (A. cruentus) Produces blonde seed typically used for the traditional confection *alegria*, which is made with popped seed and molasses in central Mexico. I16

All Red: Reddish plants that grow to 7 feet tall; large red seedheads; white seed. Will produce two crops if cut. Can also be used as a potherb. Originated at the Rodale Research Center. K49M

Burgundy: (A. hypochondriacus) 105 days. A widely adapted cultivar. Has yielded well on the Olympic Peninsula of Washington and the windswept plains of north central Kansas. Striking purplish-red foliage, stalks, and seedheads; productive, heavy seedheads; small, creamy white/beige seeds. Height 5 to 7 feet. Young leaves can also be used for greens. A2, D87, E63T, I77, I99, K49T, L11, L79M

Chihuahuan Ornamental: (A. cruentus) From the heart of the Chihuahuan desert, where it is called Sangre de Castilla (the Blood of Noble Spain). The black seed is edible. Can also be used as a potherb. Planted with the summer rains in the low desert. I16

Dreadicus: (A. hypochondriacus) Large, green, tightly packed, matted seedheads resembling dreadlocks; full of golden seed. Tall, long-season plants growing 8 to 10 feet; high yields. Originally from the Mexican highlands. Very good flavor. I99

Golden Giant: (A. cruentus) 120 days. Large orange-golden seedheads on 6 to 8 foot plants; no side branching; green leaves, but golden brown veins, stalks, and flowers. Large seeds are mixed light and dark golden. Early and heavy bearing. Can yield up to a pound per plant. Easily gathered and threshed, but susceptible to lodging. Ornamental. B49, F80, I99, K49T

Golden Grain: (A. hypochondriacus) Very early maturing strain with golden-yellow to orange foliage and seedheads. Uniform, short plants; height to 4 1/2 feet. Easier for mechanical harvest, but less productive than Burgundy. Midseason in maturity. The grain can be added to most bread recipes for a delightfully crunchy texture. A2, A49G, I77, J25M, L7M, L11, L79M

Guarijio Indian: (A. hybridus x A. hypochondriacus) White-seeded grain type commonly used for *tamales*, *pinole*, or popping. From the

Rio Mayo in Sonora, Mexico. Planted in spring or with the summer rains in the low desert. I16

Headdress: 120 days. Short plants, 3 to 4 feet tall; thick heads of grain, some brightly-colored yellow-green. Colorful leaves. Light golden seeds. G47

Intense Purple: (A. hypochondriacus) Tall strain of Burgundy; height 7 to 8 feet. Attractive plants vary from thoroughly reddish-purple to various levels of purple-green variegation on leaves and stems. White seeded. I99, K49M

K112: (A. cruentus) Rodale selection from a cross of a Mexican grain type and an African grain type. Slightly shorter plant than Mexican types, with a more branched habit. Both seed heads and leaves are red. Produces mostly white seed. Matures earlier than Mexican grain types. Has shown some resistance to the tarnished plant bug (Lygus lineolaris). C25M, E59Z

K343: (A. hybridus x A. hypochondriacus) 117 days. Productive grain producer developed at the Rodale Research Center. One of the highest yielding lines in yield trials in Kansas, Nebraska and Minnesota. Grows 5 to 6 feet tall with red flower heads and yellow seed. Has superior resistance to lodging, especially after a frost. Widely grown by a small group of commercial growers. C25M

K432: (A. hybridus x A. hypochondriacus) 95 days. First semi-dwarf grain amaranth from the Rodale Research Center. One of the earliest and best yielding cultivars. Grows 3 to 5 feet tall with large pale pink flower heads and leaves that are purple-blotched when young. Light tan seeds, of good quality for cooking and baking. Easier to combine than taller types. G6

Manna: (A. hypochondriacus) 120 days. Grains resemble sesame seeds and can be used in a similar manner. Also used for milling into flour or as a cooked cereal. Grows taller than corn with very heavy seedheads. K49M

Mayo Indian: (A. cruentus) A black-seeded cultivar from Sonora, Mexico. Seeds are used for esquite (parched), *pinole* and *atole*. The leaves are used as quelítes (greens). Planted in spring or with the summer rains in the low desert. I16

Mountain Pima Green: (A. cruentus) The blonde seeds are ground for *pinole* and the leaves are used for spinach. From the Sonora/Chihuahua border in Mexico. Planted in spring or with the summer rains in the low hot desert. I16

MT-3: 100 days. Early, white-seeded cultivar. Light-green plant, averaging 2 1/2 to 3 feet in height. Good yields. Very uniform. Developed at Montana State University. E24

Multicolor: (A. cruentus) Seedheads vary in color from red to yellow to green. The foliage is also multi-colored - green, red, yellow, white, and mixtures thereof. Slightly later maturing than A. hypochondriacus; yields are usually greater. Variable in height, 4 to 6 feet. A2, L79M

Nepalese: (A. cruentus) 150 days. High-yielding, fairly late-maturing strain, height 6 to 8 feet. Attractive reddish-pink seedheads. Leaves are also red. Apparently prefers higher elevations but has been grown successfully at low elevations in the West Coast and South. A2, I77, I99, K49T, L79M

New Mexico: (A. hypochondriacus) Beautiful pink and white inflorescences that yield golden seed. From a dooryard garden near Rinconada, New Mexico. Planted in spring or with the summer rains in the low hot desert. I16

Piuri: (A. hypochondriacus) Vigorous, green plants; height 4 to 5 feet, prone to lodging. Good yields. Ripens in mid-season. Of South American origin. L79M

Popping: (A. cruentus) 110 days. High-yielding red and tan seed head; breaks off easily in the wind. White-seeded. May be popped in a frying pan or wok at high heat, no oil needed. As with corn, popping is an interesting alternative to grinding or whole-grain cooking. A2

Prima x Nepal: (A. hybridus x A. hypochondriacus) Large, densely-spiked red head; very good yields. Prone to lodging. Early in maturity. Stable cross. Introduced by the Rodale Research Center, Kutztown, Pennsylvania. I99

R1017: Medium-tall plants with mixed green and purple leaves and flowers. Medium-sized seeds, 98% golden. Midseason maturity. Developed at the Rodale Research Center, Kutztown, Pennsylvania. E59Z

R158: (A. cruentus) 93 days. A predominately white-seeded, early maturing, refined grain amaranth with red leaves and stems. Vigorous growing plant that lodges easily; an excellent producer. Medium-sized seeds high in lysine. Sow 1/8 inch deep in rows 24 inches apart, thinned to 3 to 4 inches apart. Harvest, thresh, and winnow after frost. Used for flour, popping, or sprouting. Developed at the Rodale Research Center, Kutztown, Pennsylvania. L7M

Re-Selected R158: (A. cruentus) 95 days. Striking plant with red stalks, leaves, and seed heads; height 4 to 7 feet, depending on seeding rate and soil conditions. Almost 100% white seeded. Early maturity. Re-selected, uniform strain, rated by growers and researchers as the most uniform and refined grain amaranth. The top performer in numerous independent growing and cooking tests. Good popped, milled, sprouted or cooked whole as a cereal. F80, G6

Rodale Multiflora: (A. cruentus) 95 days. Green plant with seedheads that vary in color from red, yellow and green to egg-white; height 5 to 6 feet. Produces an abundance of white seeds. Medium to long season. Recommended for its uniformity, shortness, and yield for machine or hand harvest. I99, K49T, L79M

San Martin: 100 days. Medium-tall plants with mixed green and purple leaves and flowers. Midseason in maturity. Medium-sized seeds are pure golden. Very good yields. E24, E59Z

LEAF AMARANTH

Champa Natia Sag: (Chaulai, Chowlai Bhaji) Dwarf bushy plants. Very sweet leaves and shoots are used in curries. Sown from February to August in India. R50, S59M, S93M

Hartman's Giant: (A. tricolor) Large, vigorous plants, 6 to 8 feet tall; an attractive purple color. Seeds are also purple. Suitable for cereal or for greens and salads. I99

Hijau: Brilliant lime-green, round leaves. Vigorous, upright plants. A fine rare salad cultivar. Can also be boiled or steamed and eaten like spinach. I99

Lal Sag: Bushy plants growing to a height of 2 to 3 feet. In India, sown from February to May and again from September to December. S59M, S93M

Lotus's Purple: Vigorous, upright, thick-topped plants; height 5 feet. Dark, purple seeds. Can be used both as a cereal and as a potherb or for salads. I99

Merah: 80 days. Very attractive bi-colored, heart-shaped, crinkled, dark-green leaves with red veins, resembles a coleus. Slightly sweet, walnut-like flavor makes an attractive addition to salads. Or its large leaves, 5 inches long and 6 inches wide, can be used for wrapping, like grape leaves. Excellent for the edible landscape. I99, J73

Pinang: 80 days. Light-green leaves, 6 to 8 inches long and 3 to 4 inches wide have a mild, sweetish flavor. Appropriate for use in salads, or they can be cooked like spinach. Plants grow 12 to 18 inches tall. J73

Purple Giant: (A. tricolor) Very fast growing, the first cutting ready 3 weeks from seedling emergence. Attractive purple foliage. Black seeds. E59Z

Puteh: (Besar) 80 days. Light green, spade-shaped leaves, 5 to 6 inches long and 5 inches wide with a mild flavor. Good for salads, or they can be cooked like spinach. Plants grow 12 to 18 inches tall. J73

Quintonil: Red stems and maroon tint to leaves. Black seed. The mountain Zapotecs customarily do not plant any green vegetables, but make abundant use of this wild amaranth as a potherb. It is allowed to reseed itself each year in the milpas (cornfields). From 6500 feet altitude; tolerates much rain and cool temperatures. F80

Red Leaf: (A. tricolor) 40-60 days. Small, lightly fuzzy, oval-heart shaped green leaves are overlaid with burgundy red (coleus-like). Multi-stalked plant, 12 to 18 inches tall. Slightly sweet with a unique tangy flavor. Heat tolerant; plant thinly in warm 70^{0} F. soil. A flavorful, colorful salad and cooking green. D55, E59Z, G6, G93M, Q34

Red Stripe: (A. tricolor) 28 days. Large oval leaves patterned with deep red. Height about 18 inches. Easily grown; heat tolerant. Sow in late spring or summer. Good stir-fried with peppers and onions. A favorite vegetable in China, Japan and Africa. F80, F85, K49M, L59, *L79G*

Tampala: (Fordhook Spinach) (A. tricolor) 70 days. Heat-resistant spinach substitute, ready 6 to 8 weeks after sowing; produces all summer. Young, tender leaves cook quickly; also good raw in salads. Stems can be harvested when 4 or 5 inches long and cooked like asparagus. Artichoke-like flavor. B73M, B75, J7, J34, K49M

Tiger Leaf: (Tiger Eye) Broad, medium green leaves with a distinct red blotch in the center. Grows to 3 feet tall and is extremely branching, producing many side shoots. Very productive, easily giving a number of cuttings. E83T, F85

White Round Leaf: (A. tricolor) 50 days. Large, light-green, rounded leaves on bushy plants to 18 inches tall. Easily grown; stands heat well. Sow in late spring through the end of summer. Tender, succulent leaves and young stems are cooked like spinach or added to salads. F80, F85, L59

APPLE {GR}

MALUS PUMILA **MALUS BACCATA**

CIDER APPLES

Included here are "true" hard cider apples, mostly grown in England, France, Spain and Quebec. They are characterized by high acid and tannin levels which make them unfit for table fruit, but give ciders distinctive flavors and body.

Alford: (Sweet Alford) Sweet type. Medium-sized, conical fruit; skin waxy yellow often blushed with pink; flesh white, juicy, sweet and non-astringent. Harvested in October; milling period up to 3 weeks. Yields a pure sweet cider of good quality. Large, slightly spreading tree with forked twigs due to tip bearing. Originated in England. F91T{SC}, H90M{SC}, I36{OR}, Q30{SC}

Amer Gautier: Medium-sized, russet gray fruit; juice bitter-acid, high in sugar and tannin; produces an excellent cider; ripens late. Tree vigorous and productive; very hardy; very late in blossoming. One of the principal cider apples of Picardy, France. I36{OR}

Amère de Berthecourt: Small, yellowish-green fruit, washed with carmine on the sunny side; juice moderately colored, slightly bitter, perfumed, rich in sugar and tannin; quality excellent. Harvest date October 25 at Geneva, New York. Tree very productive, very healthy and vigorous, often drooping under weight of the fruits. Very common in Normandy and Brittany. I36{OR}, M22

Blanc Mollet: Bittersweet type. Small to medium, pale yellow fruits; flesh white; juice well colored, highly perfumed, of good flavor; contains enough sugar and tannin to produce a good keeping cider; quality very good; ripens early, late September to early October. Tree vigorous, hardy; very productive. Originated in Pays d'Auge, France. I36{OR}

Breakwell's Seedling: Bittersharp type. Small to medium-sized, roundish fruit; skin yellow blushed with dark red; flesh white, soft and juicy, mildly sharp, sometimes slightly astringent. Harvested late September to early October; milling period less than 3 weeks, the fruit rotting rapidly. Yields a medium bittersharp, rather thin and light cider of only average quality. Tree medium-sized, spreading, a good pollinator. Originated near Monmouth, England. WILLIAMS, R.; F91T{SC}

Brown Snout: Bittersweet type. Small, conical fruit; skin yellowish-green; flesh white, soft, dry, sweet with slight astringency. Harvested in November; milling period more than 3 weeks. Produces a mild to medium bittersweet cider of average quality. Tree medium-sized, very subject to splitting at the crotches, a good pollinator. Originated in Herefordshire, England. WILLIAMS, R.; I36{OR}

Brown's Apple: Sharp type. Flattened fruit. Harvested in October. Tree medium-sized, slightly spreading. H90M{SC}, I36{OR}, M22

Bulmer's Norman: Bittersweet type. Medium to large fruit high in sugar and tannin; ripens in mid-October, ready for milling up to 3 weeks after harvest. Yields a pleasant cider of characteristic flavor and aroma. Rated as "medium bittersweet", between "mild" and "full". Useful for blending purposes. Tree large and vigorous, spreading; cropping heavy but usually biennial; resistant to fire blight. Useless as a pollinator. WILLIAMS, R.; F91T{SC}, H90M{SC}, I36{OR}, M22

Cap of Liberty: Sharp type. Small to medium-sized fruit; skin pale yellow blushed with crimson; flesh moderately juicy, high in acid, sugar and tannin, aroma poor; ferments slowly. Harvest date September 20 at Geneva, New York. Yields a full-bodied cider of high quality for blending. Tree moderately vigorous, rather sprawling; cropping irregular, but heavy on healthy trees. Very susceptible to scab and canker. Originated in Somerset, England. I36{OR}

Chisel Jersey:[1] Bittersweet type. Small to medium-sized, conical fruit; juice well colored, low in acidity, high in tannin, sugar content good. Harvested late October to mid-November; milling period more than 3 weeks. Yields a cider of marked astringency, usually of full body and good flavor and aroma. Tree medium-sized, vigorous, spreading; consistently high yielding. Originated in Somerset, England. WILLIAMS, R.; F91T{SC}, H90M{SC}, I36{OR}, M22

Cimitière: Bittersweet type. Medium-sized, flat to conical fruits; skin greenish-yellow splashed with crimson; flesh sweet with a dash of bitterness, juice highly colored, fairly well perfumed; keeps and ships very well. Useful for blending with cultivars of little color and mucilage. Harvest date October 10 at Geneva, New York. Tree very vigorous and hardy, exceedingly productive. Originated in Blangy, France. I36{OR}

Court Royal: Sweet type. Large, yellow to greenish-yellow fruit; flesh white, slightly crisp, sweet not astringent. Harvested in November, ready for milling up to 3 weeks after harvest. Yields a pure sweet cider. Sometimes susceptible to scab and brown rot. Tree large, spreading; slow to come into bearing, then yields fairly good crops biennially; useless as a pollinator. WILLIAMS, R.; I36{OR}, M22

Crimson King: Sharp type. Medium to large, conical fruit; skin greenish-yellow blushed with vivid crimson; flesh white, slightly crisp, juicy, acidic, non-astringent. Harvested in mid November; milling period more than 3 weeks. Cider medium sharp, light and fruity, of average to good quality. Tree large, spreading; fairly productive; useless as a pollinator. Originated in Somerset, England. WILLIAMS, R.; I36{OR}

Dabinett: Bittersweet type. Medium to large, roundish fruit; skin green, blushed with dull red; juice low in acid, tannin medium, sugar content fair; fermentation moderate. Produces a very high quality, soft, full-bodied cider. Harvest date September 25 at Geneva, New York. Tree small, spreading; precocious; a regular and heavy bearer; blooms late; pollinates with Michelin. Originated in Somerset, England. WILLIAMS, R.; I36{OR}, J61M, L12, M22

De Boutteville: Bittersweet type. Medium-sized fruit; skin yellowish-red washed with crimson; flesh sweet, well proportioned with sugar and tannin, of alcoholic richness; juice highly colored, very perfumed, of high flavor; quality excellent; ripens in December. Tree vigorous, semi-vertical; hardy; moderately productive. I36{OR}

Dymock Red: Sharp type. Small to medium fruit; skin entirely covered with dark mahogany red; flesh soft and tender, slightly sweet with a pleasant acidity; sugar content average, fermentation slow. Yields a high-grade cider that is medium sharp with some astringency. Can be harvested in late September, but will hang on the tree until November. Tree vigorous, upright, productive. Very susceptible to canker and scab. I36{OR}

Foxwhelp: Sharp type. Small to medium fruit; skin yellow streaked with bright red; juice golden, of high specific gravity, aroma and flavor very characteristic; sugar content high, fermentation moderate. Produces a cider of high-vintage quality, containing the correct balance of sugar, acid and tannin. Harvest date October 1 at Geneva, New York. Tree vigorous and productive. Most famous of the older English cider apples. B27M, B27M{SC}, B72M, C27T{SC}, E84{OR}, G65M, I36{OR}, L1, L12, M22

Fréquin Rouge: Bittersweet type. Small to below medium fruit; skin yellow, highly blushed with red; juice very well colored, intensely perfumed, of high flavor; rich in tannin, acidity sufficient; ripens in November, keeps well. Makes an excellent cider of good color. Tree moderately vigorous, upright, very productive. Old French cultivar of unknown origin. I36{OR}

Fréquin Tardif: (Tardive de la Sarthe) Bittersweet type. Medium to large fruit; skin greenish-yellow striped with red; juice abundant, well colored, perfumed, high in acidity and tannin; ripens in December, keeps well and ships very well. Highly esteemed in France for blending with cultivars of low tannin. Tree hardy, very vigorous and productive, blossoms very late. I36{OR}, M22

Grosse Launette: Medium to large, roundish fruits; skin greenish-yellow, dotted with russet gray near the stem; juice moderately colored, of good flavor, very bitter and astringent, well perfumed, notably rich in sugar and tannin. Good for blending. Tree vigorous and productive, semi-vertical, excessively fertile. Originated in Bretagne, France. I36{OR}, M22

Harry Masters' Jersey: Bittersweet type. Small to medium-sized, conical fruit; skin greenish-yellow blushed with dark red; flesh white, dry, sweet and astringent. Harvested in early November; milling period more than 3 weeks. Cider medium to full bittersweet, of very good quality. Tree medium-sized, semi-spreading; bears good crops biennially; pollinates with Yarlington Mill. Originated in Somerset, England. WILLIAMS, R.; H90M{SC}, I36{OR}, M22

Hughes' Crab: (Hewe's Virginia Crab) Fruit small, about 1 1/2 inches in diameter, nearly round; skin dull red, dotted with white specks, obscurely streaked with greenish-yellow; flesh fibrous, with an acid, rough, astringent flavor; when ground, runs clear and limpid from the press, and ferments very slowly. Often mixed with rich, pulpy apples, to which it imparts a good deal of its fine quality. BETTS, PROULX; B72M, D37, J93, J93{SC}

Kingston Black: Bittersharp type. Medium-sized, conical fruit; skin deep purplish-crimson over yellow-orange ground color; juice moderately sweet, aromatic, pleasantly acidic with an astringent aftertaste. Harvest date September 15 at Geneva, New York. Produces a full-bodied, distinctive cider of "vintage" quality without blending. Tree medium-sized, spreading, fairly productive. Difficult to grow. Susceptible to scab and canker. WILLIAMS, R.; B27M, B27M{SC}, B72M, E84{OR}, G65M, I36{OR}, J61M, L1, L12, M22, M23M{SC}

Major: Bittersweet type. Medium-sized, greenish fruit; juice low in acidity, tannin content medium, high in sugar for an early cultivar; ripens in late September and early October. Produces cider that is among the best of the bittersweets of its season. Tree fairly vigorous, spreading, bears well biennially. Highly esteemed in Devon, England. WILLIAMS, R.; I36{OR}

Maréchal: Bittersweet type. Large, elongate-conical fruit; skin greenish-yellow, striped with red; flesh creamy white, firm and juicy; juice perfumed, well colored, very bitter and astringent but rich. Good for blending. Harvest date October 5 at Geneva, New York. Tree very vigorous and productive; blooms late. I36{OR}

Marin Oufroy: (Ameret) Medium-sized fruit; sweet to slightly bitter; produces an excellent, very clear cider. Ripens in midseason, about October 1 at Geneva, New York. Tree very vigorous and productive, hardy; succeeds even in poor soil. Originated in the Bessin region of France. I36{OR}

Médaille d'Or: Bittersweet type. Small to medium-sized, conical fruit; skin golden-yellow, with grayish-brown russeting. Juice very high in sugar, density and tannin; highly perfumed, strongly astringent and bitter, below average in color. Harvest date September 25 at Geneva, New York; milling period more than 3 weeks. Cider full bittersweet, often alcoholic and fruity, of good quality. Tree small and spreading, hardy, excessively productive. Originated in Normandy, France. WILLIAMS, R.; B72M, I36{OR}, L12, M22

Mettais: Bittersweet type. Medium-sized, flat to globular fruit; skin golden yellow, 75% washed and splashed with bright crimson. Juice highly colored, perfumed, produces a cider of the same red color as the fruit. Tree vigorous, upright; hardy; very productive. Raised from seed by M. Mettais at Amfreville-la-Campagne, France. I36{OR}

Michelin: Bittersweet type. Small to medium-sized fruit; skin yellowish-green to yellow when ripe; juice highly colored, perfumed, of good flavor; high in tannin, acid and sugar. Harvested late October to early November, stores and ships well. Produces a medium bittersweet cider similar to that of Bulmer's Norman. Tree compact, vigorous, upright; hardy; precocious and very productive; somewhat susceptible to mildew. Originated in Yvetot, France. First fruited in 1872. WILLIAMS, R.; I36{OR}, J61M, M22

Néhou: Bittersweet type. Small to medium-sized, conical fruit; skin waxy, butter-yellow, very distinctive; flesh white, soft, easily bruised, juicy, sweet and astringent. Harvest date September 10 at Geneva, New York; ready for pressing up to 3 weeks after harvest. Cider full bittersweet, astringent, fruity, full-bodied, good to excellent in quality.

Tree medium-sized, semi-spreading, yields well. Originated in France. WILLIAMS, R.; I36{OR}, L1

Northwood: Sweet type. Medium-sized, flattened-conical fruit; skin yellowish-green blushed with dark red; flesh white, slightly crisp and juicy, sweet, lacking astringency. Harvested the first half of November; milling period more than 3 weeks. Cider sweet, soft, fruity, neutral, of good quality. Tree medium to large, productive. Originated in Devon, England. WILLIAMS, R.; M22

Porter's Perfection: Bittersharp type. Small to medium-sized, conical fruit; skin greenish-yellow blushed with dark red; flesh white, crisp, juicy, sharp with no astringency. Harvested in late November; milling period more than 3 weeks. Cider medium bittersharp, of average to good quality. Tree large, vigorous, spreading, heavy yielding. Originated in Somerset, England. WILLIAMS, R.; A55{ES}, H90M{SC}, I36{OR}, L1, L1{ES}

Reine des Hâtives: Bittersweet type. Small to medium-sized, somewhat conical fruit; skin greenish-yellow washed with carmine pink; flesh mild, fairly tender, sugary, highly perfumed, of very agreeable flavor; juice not abundant, fairly colored, slightly bitter. Harvested late September to early October. Tree vigorous, upright; blossoms early; very productive. Originated in Yvetot, France. First fruited in 1872. M22{OR}

Reine des Pommes: Bittersweet type. Medium to large fruit; skin greenish-yellow, strongly tinted with deep red; juice sugary, well colored, perfumed, very high in density and tannin, low in acidity. Makes a bitter, full-bodied cider of character. Excellent for blending. Harvest date September 25 at Geneva, New York; keeps well. Tree very vigorous, upright, extremely productive. Originated in Bretagne, France. H90M{SC}, I36{OR}

Stoke Red: Bittersharp type. Small to medium-sized fruit; skin yellow flushed with red; juice high in tannin and density, acidity moderate, sugar content above average; bitter astringency prominent in after taste. Harvested in late November, ready for milling over a period of more than 3 weeks. Produces a fruity cider of "vintage" quality without blending. Tree medium-sized, spreading, fairly vigorous; precocious; bears heavy crops. Originated in Somerset, England. WILLIAMS, R.; I36{OR}, M22

Sweet Coppin: Sweet type. Medium to large, conical fruit; flesh white, soft and sweet with no astringency. Harvested late October to mid-November, ready for milling over a period of more than 3 weeks. Yields a pure sweet cider, or occasionally mildly bittersweet. Tree large, semi-spreading; precocious, bears very good crops biennially. Originated in Devon, England. WILLIAMS, R.; H90M{SC}, I36{OR}, M22

Tremlett's Bitter: Bittersweet type. Medium-sized, conical fruit; skin yellow blushed with red; flesh white, sweet and astringent. Harvest date September 25 at Geneva, New York; ready for milling up to 3 weeks after harvesting. Yields a full bittersweet cider with hard and bitter tannin. Tree medium-sized, spreading; precocious, bears very good crops biennially. Originated in Devon, England. WILLIAMS, R.; I36{OR}, L1, L12, M22

Yarlington Mill: Bittersweet type. Medium to large, conical fruits; juice low in acid, sugary, tannin content medium. Produces a medium bittersweet cider of good body, aroma and flavor. Harvest date October 10 at Geneva, New York; ready for pressing over a period of more than 3 weeks after harvesting. Tree medium-sized, semi-spreading; precocious, bears excellent and regular crops. A superior all-round cultivar. Originated in Somerset, England. WILLIAMS, R.; C27T{SC}, E84{OR}, G65M, I36{OR}, L1

COOKING APPLES

Although the dividing line between cooking and dessert apples is not always sharply defined and there is much overlapping, tart, sharp or sour apples are usually best cooked. Cooking apples which have a high acid content usually become fluffy or frothy when cooked.

SUMMER HARVESTING

Arthur Turner: Large, round to conical fruit; skin light green blushed with orange-red, attractive; flesh yellowish-white, coarse, rather dry, pleasantly acid; ripens early, hangs well on the tree and also keeps well. Requires a longer cooking time than other cultivars, bakes well. Tree upright, of moderate to vigorous growth; bears abundant crops regularly; fairly resistant to scab. Originated in Berkshire, England. Introduced in 1915. SANDERS, SIMMONS 1978; M22

Cauley: Extremely large fruit, 3 inches or more in diameter, often weighing as much as a pound; skin green with faint red stripes; flesh yellow, crisp, juicy; season early July to the end of August; resembles Yellow Newtown. Excellent for culinary and jelly use. Tree a heavy bearer, averaging 26 bushels per tree. Introduced by the Mississippi Agricultural Experiment Station. BROOKS 1972; E29M

Duchess of Oldenburg: (Duchess) Large, roundish fruit; skin pale greenish-yellow, prominently striped and mottled with bright red and crimson; flesh tinged with yellow, firm, crisp, juicy, sprightly subacid, aromatic; too acid for dessert, good to very good for culinary purposes. Tree medium-sized, upright-spreading becoming roundish. Known in Russia in the 1700's. BEACH; A91, A91{SC}, B72M, C58, E84, F53, G16, G16{DW}, G65M, G67, G69M, H65, L1, L12, L27M, M22, etc.

Emneth Early: Medium-sized, conical fruit; skin pale yellow, slightly blushed with red; flesh white, tends to soften quickly, cooks to a froth; ripens very early, during July and August. Tree moderately vigorous, precocious, heavy bearing. Originated in England in 1899. SIMMONS 1978; M22, N24M

Gravenstein: Fruit medium-large, oblate to roundish; skin greenish-yellow, blushed with light and dark red; flesh yellowish, firm, crisp, juicy, sprightly subacid, aromatic; dessert quality very good, excellent for cooking; ripens unevenly. Tree large, vigorous; productive; requires a pollinator. A very old European apple of uncertain origin. BEACH; A39, A55{ES}, B67, B83, D69, E70M{PR}, E84, F11, G79M{DW}, H65, J6{PR}, J61M, L1, L1{ES}, *L47*, L99M, M31T{ES}, etc.

Grenadier: Large, flattened globe-shaped fruit; skin pale green, tinged with yellow; flesh white, crisp, acid, cooks to a froth, good for baking; season mid-August to October. Tree moderately vigorous, a regular and heavy bearer; resistant to scab and canker. Of unknown origin, first recorded about 1860. SIMMONS 1978; M22, P86, Q30{SC}

Hall's Pink:[5] Medium to large, roundish fruit; skin bright red; flesh tinged with red, juicier than Gravenstein; resembles Gravenstein but ripens about 2 weeks earlier. Makes pink applesauce. Tree apparently disease resistant. Originated in Merville, British Columbia, Canada. Introduced in 1980. M22

Keswick Codlin: Medium to large, roundish heart-shaped fruit; skin pale yellow, slightly blushed on the side exposed to the sun; flesh nearly white, tender, very juicy, brisk subacid, very good for culinary use, too acid for dessert unless very ripe. Makes a delicious soft apple purée. Tree medium to large, moderately vigorous. Originated in northern England, about 1790. BEACH, SIMMONS 1978; B72M, E84{OR}, L12, M23M{SC}

Red Astrachan: Medium to large, roundish fruit; skin yellow or greenish, overspread with light and dark red; flesh white, often strongly tinged with red, crisp, tender, juicy, brisk subacid, aromatic; sometimes slightly astringent; quality good for dessert, excellent for cooking. Tree vigorous, upright-spreading; grows well in hot areas.

Originated in Russia. BEACH; A55{ES}, C58, D69, E4, E84, G65M, G67, G79M{DW}, G92, H65, I99M, I99M{DW}, L1, L1{ES}, L27M, L99M, M23M{SC}, etc.

White Astrachan: Fruit medium to large, roundish to roundish oblate; skin waxen yellow or whitish, with faint streaks of red, covered with dusky bloom; flesh white, fine-grained, crisp, tender, perfumed, acid; good for culinary use; season August and September. Tree vigorous; productive; does well in hot areas. Originated in Russia about 1748. BEACH; L1

FALL HARVESTING

Alexander: Large, uniform, roundish-conic fruit; skin greenish or pale yellow, blushed with bright red; flesh nearly white, firm, coarse, moderately crisp, tender, juicy, mildly subacid; dessert quality fair to good, very good for cooking. Tree vigorous, upright-spreading; hardy; moderately productive. Introduced into England from Russia in 1817. BEACH; A91, A91{SC}, B72M, C58, E84, L27M, M22

Bramley's Seedling: (Bramley) Fruit large; flattened, irregular; skin greenish-yellow, slightly blushed red; flesh yellowish-white, firm, coarse, juicy, acid. Excellent for stewing and baking; best for dumplings and canning. Tree very large and vigorous; productive. Most popular cooking apple in Great Britain. SANDERS, SIMMONS 1978; A39, A91, A91{SC}, B27M, B27M{SC}, B72M, E84{OR}, G79M{DW}, J61M, L1, L12, M22, M23M{SC}, N24M

Cellini: Medium-sized, round to slightly flattened fruit; skin pale yellowish-green, blushed and streaked with brownish-red; flesh white, tender, sub-acid, with an unusual resinous flavor liked by some; ripens October to November. Tree stocky, very productive. Originated in England. Introduced in 1828. SIMMONS 1978; M22

George Neal: Large, flat-round fruit; skin green changing to whitish-yellow, often slightly blushed red, thin and smooth; flesh greenish-white, crisp, juicy, coarse; flavor excellent, sweet yet somewhat acid; cooks yellow and remains in intact slices; ripens in midseason. Tree of moderate growth, bears freely and regularly. Originated in Kent, England. Introduced in 1923. SANDERS, SIMMONS 1978; M22

Gloria Mundi: Fruit large to very large, roundish; skin greenish-yellow, sometimes with a faint bronze blush; flesh slightly tinged with greenish-yellow, coarse, moderately crisp, rather tender, juicy, mildly subacid; quality fair for dessert, good for culinary purposes or exhibition. Known in New York, New Jersey and Pennsylvania prior to 1804. BEACH; E84

Golden Noble:[1] Fruit medium to large, round-conical; skin golden-yellow, slightly speckled with grey and brown; flesh creamy-white, slightly soft, juicy, fairly fine-textured; ideal for baking, cooks to a golden rich-flavored froth. Exceeds most other edible apples in vitamin C. Tree small, compact; precocious; bears heavily and regularly. Discovered at Downham, Norfolk, England. Introduced in 1820. SANDERS, SIMMONS 1978; A91, B72M, L12, M22

Howgate Wonder: Very large, round-conical fruit; skin greenish-yellow, blushed and striped with orange-brown or red; flesh creamy-white, firm, fine-textured, fairly acid; excellent for culinary use, becoming dirty yellow and cooking to a froth. Tree vigorous; a heavy and regular cropper. Raised in the Isle of Wight about 1915. SANDERS, SIMMONS 1978; M22, N24M, P86, Q30{SC}

Maidenblush: Medium to large, oblate fruit; skin pale waxen yellow, blushed with crimson, very attractive; flesh white, fine-textured, tender, very juicy, subacid; quality good, especially for culinary purposes. Tree medium-sized, vigorous, spreading. Named by Samuel Allinson of Burlington, New Jersey; first described in 1817. BEACH; A91, A91{SC}, B27M{SC}, B72M, C27T{SC}, D69, E84{OR}, G65M, H65, L1, L12, L27M, M22, M83, N24M, etc.

Milwaukee: Fruit rather large; distinctly oblate, sides often unequal; skin pale yellow or whitish, more or less blushed with red; flesh whitish tinged with yellow, firm, somewhat coarse, crisp, very tender, very juicy, sprightly, brisk subacid; dessert quality fair to good, well-suited for culinary use. Tree moderately vigorous, upright. BEACH; C58, L27M, N24M

Patten Greening: Medium to large, oblate fruit; skin clear pale greenish-yellow, sometimes blushed; flesh tinged with yellow, somewhat coarse, tender, juicy, sprightly subacid; quality good, especially for culinary purposes. Tree moderately vigorous, spreading; very cold hardy; productive. Originated in Charles City, Iowa by C.G. Patten, from seed planted in 1869. BEACH; C27T{SC}, C58

Peasgood Nonesuch: Fruit large to very large; round, slightly flattened; skin golden yellow, blushed and striped with bright crimson; flesh yellowish, soft, very juicy, subacid; cooks to a froth, also very good for baking. Tree moderately vigorous, spreading; fairly productive. Raised by a Mrs. Peasgood at Stamford, Lincolnshire, England from a seed planted in a pot about 1858. SANDERS, SIMMONS 1978; M22, Q30{SC}

Pound Sweet: (Pumpkin Sweet) Large to very large, globular fruit; skin clear yellow, marbled with greenish-yellow; flesh tinged with yellow, medium in texture, firmness and juiciness, decidedly sweet with a peculiar flavor; good for culinary use, especially esteemed for baking or stewing with quinces. Tree vigorous, upright-spreading. Originated in Manchester, Connecticut, prior to 1834. BEACH; A91, A91{SC}, B27M{SC}, B53, B72M, C27T{SC}, C58, G65M, H65, J67{SC}, J93{SC}, L12, L27M

Reverend W. Wilks: Fruit very large; round-conical to conical; skin pale yellowish-green, thinly striped with red; flesh creamy-white, soft, juicy, only slightly acid, cooks to a pale yellow froth. Tree small, compact; prolific, but tends to be biennial, bears fruit on short spurs; disease resistant. Originated in England. Introduced in 1908. SANDERS, SIMMONS 1978; M22, N24M, Q30{SC}

Rhode Island Greening: Medium to large, roundish or slightly conical fruit; skin yellowish pale-green; flesh yellowish, firm, crisp, tender, juicy, rich, sprightly subacid, peculiarly flavored; quality very good for dessert, excellent for culinary purposes. Tree vigorous, spreading; moderately productive. Probably originated in Newport, Rhode Island in the 17th century. BEACH; A53{PR}, A91, A91{SC}, D69, E84, G41, G65M, G79M{DW}, G92, H65, I36, L1, L1{PR}, L12, *M59M*, etc.

Rome Beauty: Medium to large, roundish fruit; skin yellow or greenish, mottled with bright red; flesh nearly white, very firm, crisp, juicy, slightly aromatic, mildly subacid, fairly good for dessert, excellent for baking; keeps and ships well. Tree medium-sized, moderately vigorous; productive. Originated in Lawrence County, Ohio prior to 1848. BEACH; A91, A91{SC}, B72M, *C54*, D76, D81{PO}, D81M{PO}, E84, *F5*, G65M, G72{DW}, *I68*, L1, M31T{ES}, *M69M*, etc.

Tolman Sweet: Medium-sized, nearly globular fruit; skin pale clear-yellow; flesh white, firm, moderately juicy, decidedly sweet; dessert quality good to very good, highly esteemed for pickling, boiling and baking. Tree moderately vigorous, very spreading; long-lived; very hardy. BEACH; A53{PR}, A91, A91{SC}, B27M{SC}, B72M, E84{OR}, G41, G65M, G79M{DW}, H65, I36, L1, L12, L27M, M23M{SC}, N24M, etc.

Warner's King: Fruit large to very large; flat-round to slightly conical; skin yellow, slightly blushed with pinkish-brown; flesh greenish-white, firm, coarse, crisp, juicy, very acid; excellent for culinary use, cooking to a very fine froth. Tree very vigorous and productive. Known since the end of the 1700's in Great Britain. SANDERS, SIMMONS 1978; O81, Q30{SC}

WINTER HARVESTING

Bismark: Large to very large, round-conic fruit; skin pale yellow, prominently blushed and striped with dark-crimson; flesh white, crisp, juicy, subacid, cooks to a greenish-yellow froth. Tree moderately vigorous, spreading; hardy; productive. Probably originated at the old German settlement in Hobart, Tasmania, about 1870. SANDERS, SIMMONS 1978; M22, Q30{SC}

Crawley Beauty:[4] Medium to large, flat-round fruit; skin bright yellow-green blushed with brownish-red, with broken stripes of darker red; flesh greenish-white, firm, not very juicy, tart; flavor fairly good for dessert, improves when cooked; season December to March. Tree vigorous, spreading; resistant to most diseases; blooms late, about the latest flowering of all recorded apple cultivars. Originated in Crawley, England about 1870. SANDERS, SIMMONS 1978; M22, S81M

Crimson Gold: Small to medium-sized fruit; skin red, covered with a dusky bloom. When quartered or sliced and then boiled, the flesh remains solid and takes on a golden yellow color, stained red on the edges by the skin; the result is a product resembling canned peaches; flavor excellent. Developed by Albert F. Etter of Ettersburg, California. Selected for its outstanding quality for canning. E84

Edward VII: (King Edward) Medium to large, roundish fruit; skin pale yellowish-green, faintly blushed with brownish-red; flesh creamy white, very firm but tender, rather coarse, juicy, acid, cooks to a somewhat red, translucent purée. Tree vigorous, upright; moderately productive; slow to come into bearing. Originated in Worcester, England. Introduced in 1908. SANDERS, SIMMONS 1978; B72M, C27T{SC}, G65M, J93{SC}, L12, M22, M23M{SC}

French Crab: (Easter Pippin, Apple John, Two Year Apple) Fruit medium-sized, round to conical; skin yellowish-green, often blushed with dull brownish-red; flesh greenish-white, very firm, crisp, acid, very astringent; good for culinary use; will keep up to 2 years. Tree vigorous, productive. Of French origin; brought to England in 1700. SIMMONS 1978; O81

Lane's Prince Albert: Medium to large, round-conical fruit; skin greenish-yellow, slightly blushed with orange or red; flesh greenish-white, fine-textured, firm, juicy, acid; excellent for culinary use, remaining fairly intact on cooking. Tree small, weeping, of weak growth; suitable for small gardens. Originated in England. Introduced about 1850. SANDERS, SIMMONS 1978; N24M, P86, Q30{SC}

Monarch: Large, roundish fruit; skin pale yellow, blushed and striped with deep-red, attractive; flesh white, soft, acid, good for culinary use. Excellent for grilling. Ripens in November and December, will keep until April with careful storage. Tree vigorous, productive, tends toward biennial bearing; resistant to scab. SIMMONS 1978; M22, N24M, Q30{SC}

Newton Wonder: Fruit large to very large, flat-round; skin bright yellow, blushed brownish-red to very bright red; flesh yellowish, firm, crisp, juicy, acid, slightly astringent; excellent for culinary use, cooking to a yellow froth; ripens in November; keeps in natural storage until April. Tree vigorous, somewhat spreading; productive. Raised at Melbourne, Derbyshire, England, about 1887. SANDERS, SIMMONS 1978; Q30{SC}

White Melrose: An unusual seedless cooking apple. Smooth yellow skin, becomes waxy with age. Excellent for culinary purposes, cooking to a froth. Season early October to November; keeps until February when it will be palatable for dessert. Tree dome-shaped. O81

CRAB APPLES

Apples which are two inches or less in diameter are generally considered crab apples. They vary in flavor, taste and use. Some are suitable for jelly, others for canning and freezing, and still others as small dessert apples. Crossing crab apples and standard apples has produced useful hybrids called *applecrabs*, especially in the prairie provinces of Canada. They are large crab apples that taste like dessert apples.

COOKING

Almata:[5] Fruit large, 2 1/2 inches in diameter, round to conical; skin solid brilliant red; flesh bright red throughout, juicy, pleasantly subacid, suitable for sauce, jelly and pickling; season early winter. Tree very hardy; susceptible to scab; ornamental, with reddish leaves and blossom. Originated in Brookings, South Dakota by N.E. Hansen. Introduced in 1942. BROOKS 1972; A91, B27M{SC}, J67{SC}, L12, L27M, M22, N24M

Callaway: Medium-sized, red fruit; very pleasing flavor, good for jelly; ripens in September. Vigorous, productive tree; pink flowers. B9M, F93, H4, *I82*, *K76*, *M69M*

Cranberry:[5] Fruit small; long, conic pointed; skin dark red; flesh red, crisp, acid; excellent quality for jelly; ripens in early September. Tree vigorous, upright when young; productive; hardy; flowers red; useful as an ornamental. Redflesh x Dolgo. Originated in Wyndmere, North Dakota. BROOKS 1972; A34

Dartmouth: Medium to large, oblate fruit; skin pale yellow, almost entirely overlaid with bright red; flesh yellowish, tinged with red near the skin, fine-grained, juicy, mildly subacid, flavor and quality good. Tree moderately vigorous, upright-spreading; comes into bearing rather early, yields full crops in alternate years. Originated in New Hampshire prior to 1883. BEACH; A69G{SC}, *G66*

Dolgo: Fruit large, 1 to 1 1/2 inches in diameter, long-conical; skin brilliant crimson; flesh very juicy, sprightly, somewhat acid, good for dessert when fully ripe, very good for culinary use. Jells easily, producing a rich, ruby-red jelly of beautiful color and excellent flavor. Tree vigorous, upright-spreading; prolific; hardy. Introduced from Russia by N.E. Hansen of South Dakota, in 1897. A55{ES}, B4, E29M, *E45*, F19M, G69M, G92, *I62*, K64, L1, L1{ES}, L12, L79, M31T{ES}, M35M, *M69M*, etc.

Florence: Medium-sized, oblate fruit; skin yellowish-white, mostly overspread with brilliant pinkish-red; flesh tinged with yellow, coarse, crisp, rather tender, juicy, very brisk subacid, somewhat astringent; quality good for jelly or pickling; season late August and early September. Tree moderately vigorous; precocious; very prolific. Originated in Excelsior, Minnesota by Peter M. Gideon, prior to 1886. BEACH; N33

Geneva: (Geneva Red) (M. pumila 'Niedzwetzkyana') Large attractive fruit; eating quality fair; excellent for jelly. Tree hardy; resistant to apple scab. Originated in Ottawa, Ontario, Canada by Canada Department of Agriculture Research Station. Introduced in 1930. BROOKS 1972; M22, N24M

Hyslop: Medium to large, roundish-ovate fruit; skin clear pale yellow, prominently blushed with dark red; flesh yellow, very firm, at first juicy but eventually becoming dry and mealy, subacid, astringent, good for culinary purposes; season late September and October. Tree vigorous, upright-spreading; a reliable cropper; bears fruit in clusters; very hardy. Origin unknown; first raised sometime prior to 1869. BEACH; B27M{SC}, B72M, *C54*, C58, G69M, *I68*, M22{OR}, M92

John Downie: Medium to large, oval fruit; 1 1/4 inches long, 1 inch in diameter; skin orange-yellow, blushed with scarlet, attractive; makes excellent jelly and preserves. Tree very productive; highly ornamental. Originated in Lichfield, England. Introduced into the

United States in 1927. BROOKS 1972; A69G{SC}, M22, O81, P86, Q30, Q30{SC}, S81M

Ralph Shay: Fruit about 1 1/4 inches in diameter; brilliant red; makes excellent jelly; retains its color longer than others; never drops. Tree vigorous, sturdy; with unusually dark-green, disease resistant foliage. Introduced by Simpson Nursery Company, Vincennes, Indiana. Wolf River x Zumi Calocarpa. Named for Dr. Ralph Shay, formerly in charge of the fruit breeding program at Purdue University. D95, E87, J93{SC}, *K77*

Redflesh:[5] Large oblong fruit, 2 inches long; skin deep red; flesh red, makes a clear red jelly, also good for whole preserves. Tree spreading; blooms late; bears biennially; ornamental, with copper colored leaves and red flowers. Originated in Brookings, South Dakota by N.E. Hansen, South Dakota Agricultural Experiment Station. Introduced in 1928. BROOKS 1972; C58, *H34*, J61M

Redflesh Winter:[5] Fruit round; skin solid red; flesh red, very firm, moderately juicy, pleasantly subacid; excellent for sauce and jelly. Tree ornamental, with dark-colored leaves and abundant purple flowers. Originated in Brookings, South Dakota by N.E. Hansen, South Dakota Agricultural Experiment Station. Introduced in 1946. BROOKS 1972; A91, N24M

Transcendent: Fruit medium to large; roundish-oval, flattened at the ends; skin clear bright yellow with bright red cheek, covered with delicate white bloom; flesh yellow, crisp, juicy, somewhat astringent, subacid, very good for culinary uses; season late August to mid-September. Tree large, very spreading; hardy; bears heavily and annually. Known prior to 1844. BEACH; A88M, B72M, B93M, *C54*, G92, *I68*, J67{SC}, *K76*, L1, M31M, M39M

Whitney: Large, roundish fruit; skin light yellow, largely shaded and striped with red; flesh yellowish, crisp, juicy, mildly subacid or nearly sweet, with slight crabapple flavor; good for dessert when fully ripe, very good for culinary use; season late August and early September. Tree vigorous, upright; precocious; very productive. Originated in Franklin Grove, Illinois by A.R. Whitney, prior to 1869. BEACH; *A74*, B27M, B72M, D65, D76, F53, *G4*, G16, G16{DW}, H65, *I82*{DW}, J32, J93{SC}, L1, L30, L70, L97, M31T{ES}, M39M, etc.

Young America: (Young) Fruit large, one of the largest of the edible crabs; skin bright red; flesh pleasantly acid, flavor distinctive; quality good for dessert, excellent for culinary use. Jelly made from the fruit is clear, beautiful red and of very good flavor; season mid-September. Tree very vigorous and hardy; productive; ornamental. Introduced by the New York Agricultural Experiment Station in 1925. G65M, I36, J93{SC}

DESSERT

Astrachan Crab: Small, flavorful fruit; skin yellow, blushed with red; ripens early. Tree hardy to -50^0 F. with occasional winter injury; produces an abundance of flowers. Open pollinated seedling of Red Astrachan. Introduced by St. Lawrence Nurseries. L27M

Centennial: Fruit oval, 1 1/2 to 2 inches in diameter; skin orange-yellow, fully striped with bright scarlet red; flesh yellow, tender, crisp, juicy; flavor mildly acid, pleasant; dessert quality very good, also good for canned sauce and jelly; ripens in early midseason. Tree vigorous; hardy; very productive; tends toward biennial bearing. BROOKS 1972; *A74*, B4, B72M, J61M, L12, L70, M35M

Chestnut: Applecrab. Fruit large; skin reddish-yellow, russet; flesh yellow, sweet, flavor pleasant, distinctive; dessert quality good, also very good for cooking; ripens in midseason. Tree vigorous; productive; hardy; resistant to cedar rust; a good pollinator. Originated in Excelsior, Minnesota. Introduced in 1946. BROOKS 1972; *A74*, B4, B72M, D65, D69, *G4*, *G38M*, G67, H85, J7, L27M, L70, M35M, N24M

Dawn: Applecrab. Small fruit, 1 1/4 to 1 3/4 inches in diameter; skin well covered with light crimson; flesh white, mildly acid, quality good for dessert and cooking; ripens 10 days before Rescue. Excellent for jam and jelly. Tree productive, extremely hardy. Developed at the University of Saskatchewan. Introduced in 1959. BROOKS 1972; K64

Humboldt: (Jumbo Transcendent) Fruit very large, twice as large as Transcendent; conical; skin cream and pink, glossy, transparent; flesh cream-colored, tinted pink near the skin, firm, juicy, quality very good; ripens in late fall, hangs on the tree long after ripening; resembles Transcendent. Tree ornamental, producing masses of large, fragrant, pink-tinted blossoms. Originated in Ettersburg, California by Albert F. Etter. Introduced in 1944. BROOKS 1972; E84, M22

Kerr: Applecrab. Large, oval fruit, about twice the size of Dolgo; skin bright red; flesh yellow, flecked with dark red, firm, crisp, juicy; flavor sweet, sprightly acid; dessert quality good when mellow, makes good preserves and excellent jelly; season mid-September, keeps well until February. Tree vigorous, very hardy and productive. Originated in Morden, Manitoba. BROOKS 1972; A33, A65, B47, F67, G1T, G54, *G66*, H42, H85, K64, K81, L27M, M22, M35M, N24M, N26, etc.

Renown: Applecrab. Small to medium-sized fruit, 1 1/4 to 1 1/2 inches in diameter; skin yellow splashed with dull red; flesh white, flavor pleasing, excellent for dessert purposes; ripens in early September, stores well. Tree moderately hardy. Originated in Indian Head, Saskatchewan, Canada. Introduced in 1936. RONALD; B47, H85

Rescue: Applecrab. Large, round-ovate fruit, 1 1/2 inches or more in diameter; skin greenish-yellow, washed and striped red; flesh yellowish-white, firm, flavor sweet, subacid, pleasant; season late August; quality good. Tree medium tall, rounded; very hardy; adapted to northern areas. Originated in Scott, Saskatchewan, Canada. Introduced in 1933. BROOKS 1972; A16, A65, B47, C58, G1T, G54, G69M, H42, H85, K64, K81, L79, M22, N24M, N26, etc.

Rosthern 18: Medium to large fruit, up to 1 3/4 inches in diameter; skin greenish-yellow with red stripes; flesh white, pleasant to eat out of hand; ripens in mid-September; keeps well in cold storage. Tree vigorous, hardy, moderately productive. Originated in Rosthern, Saskatchewan, Canada. Introduced in 1936. BROOKS 1972; A91, B47

Rosybrook: Applecrab. Large fruit, about 2 inches in diameter; skin yellowish-green, covered with bright red; flesh cream-colored, quality good for dessert, superior for freezing and canning; stores until December. Tree very precocious and prolific; hardy. Trail x Rescue. Developed at Brooks, Alberta, Canada. F67, G54

Shafer: Applecrab. Medium to large fruit, 1 1/2 to 2 1/4 inches in diameter; skin yellow, blushed with red; flesh yellow, tender, slightly coarse, sweet and pleasant for fresh eating; quality good; ripens in early September. Rescue x Trail. Originated in Poplar Point, Manitoba, Canada. RONALD; B47, G1T, H85, K64

Trail: Applecrab. Fruit large, about 1 1/2 inches in diameter; skin yellow, splashed and striped with orange-red; flesh yellow, dessert and processing qualities good. Tree hardy, productive. Northern Queen x Rideau. Originated in Ottawa, Ontario, Canada by Canada Department of Agriculture Research Station. Introduced in the 1920's. BROOKS 1972; A65, B47, G1T, H85, K64, M35M

Wickson: Small, oblong fruit, 1 to 2 inches in diameter; skin brilliant red; flesh sweet (up to 25% sugar), with abundant, high-flavored juice; suitable for dessert as well as for pickling, jam and jelly, excellent for cider. Tree vigorous; very prolific, produces fruit on 1 year old branches. Originated in Ettersburg, California by Albert F. Etter. Introduced in 1944. BROOKS 1972; B72M, C27T{SC}, E84, L12

DESSERT APPLES

SUMMER HARVESTING

Adina:[2] Large, round-conic fruit; skin red to purple-red with an occasional overlaying stripe; flesh creamy white, firm, juicy; flavor sweet with a distinctive hint of cinnamon; ripens in mid-June. Tree vigorous and precocious. Low chilling requirement, only 350 hours. Originated in Australia. *I68*, L33, L33{DW}

Anna:[2] Large, conical fruit; skin red-cheeked; flesh subacid to sweet, flavor mild; season June and July, sometimes with a second crop in the fall. Tree vigorous; annually productive; requires a pollinator, such as Ein Shemer or Dorsett Golden. Low chilling requirement. Originated in Doar Na Shomron, Israel by Abba Stein. Introduced into the United States in 1965. BROOKS 1972; A44M{PR}, A55{ES}, A82, C75M, *E45*, E70M{PR}, F19M, F93, G17, *G49*, I83M, *K73M*, L1, L1{ES}, L33, *L47*, L90, M1M{PR}, M31M{PR}, *M69M*, etc.

Anoka: (Champion Supreme) Large, conical fruit; skin yellow, heavily striped and overlaid with red; flesh mild, subacid; dessert quality poor, suitable for culinary use; ripens early. Tree very hardy; productive; bears at a very young age, often the first or second year after planting. Originated in Brookings, South Dakota by N.E. Hansen. Introduced in 1920. BROOKS 1972; C27T{SC}, D76, E97, *G4*, G65M, L27M, L70

Apple Babe:[3] Medium-sized, conical fruit; skin red, russet-free, waxy, attractive; flesh crisp, sweet, juicy, very flavorful; ripens about 6 weeks before Garden Delicious; resembles Red Delicious. Tree a genetic dwarf, growing only 8 to 10 feet tall when mature; heavy bearing; pollinized by Garden Delicious. Chilling requirement 700 hours. Originated in Modesto, California by Floyd Zaiger. A88M, E87, G23, *N20*

Beacon: Fruit very large; skin solid red, covering almost the entire surface, tough; flesh juicy, mildly acid; quality good, superior to Maidenblush, Duchess and Wealthy; matures about August 1, 10 to 14 days before Wealthy. Tree productive; resistant to fire blight and scab; quite susceptible to cedar rust. BROOKS 1972; *A74*, *A74*{DW}, A91, A91{SC}, B4, B15M, B27M{SC}, D65, *G4*, G67, *I82*{DW}, L27M, L70

Benoni: Small to medium, roundish to conic fruit; skin orange-yellow, partly covered with lively red, striped with deep carmine; flesh yellow, firm, crisp, fine-grained, tender, juicy, pleasantly subacid; quality good to very good; season August and early September. Tree large, vigorous; yields fair to good crops biennially. Originated in Dedham, Massachusetts, where the original tree was still standing in 1848. BEACH; B27M{SC}, B72M, C27T{SC}, E84{OR}, G92, J93{SC}, L12, M23M{SC}

Beverly Hills:[2] Small to medium-sized, roundish fruit; skin pale yellow with red stripes, splashed with red; flesh white, tender, juicy, somewhat tart; suitable for dessert or cooking; ripens early; resembles McIntosh. Tree medium-sized, vigorous. Low chilling requirement. Originated in Los Angeles, California. Introduced in 1945. BROOKS 1972; *C54*{ES}, *F53M*, G65M, *I68*, I83M, *K73M*, *L47*

Carroll: Medium-large fruit; skin light-green, completely striped with red; dessert quality very good, also suitable for cooking; season late August to early September, keeps well into December. Tree semi-dwarf, growing 8 to 10 feet tall and spreading to 15; hardy; moderately productive. Originated in Morden, Manitoba, Canada. BROOKS 1972; A65, G1T, H85, K64, L12, L27M, M35M, N24M

Cole's Quince: Large, yellow, ribbed fruit; flesh when first ripe firm, juicy, pleasantly acid, excellent for cooking, when very mellow remarkably tender, of a mild, rich, high quince flavor and aroma; ripens in August. An old Maine apple; first described in "Cole's American Fruit Book" published in 1849. A91, B72M, J67{SC}, L12

Dayton:[4] (Coop 23) A new disease resistant apple from the University of Illinois. Medium-sized, roundish fruit; skin cherry red; flesh crisp, juicy, flavor spicy and mildly tart; season late August to early September. Tree vigorous, bears annually. Appears to have good resistance to all major apple diseases. Much more rust-resistant than Prima. D37, J61M, J93

Devonshire Quarrendon: Small to medium, flat-round fruit; skin yellowish-green, heavily blushed with dark-crimson; flesh greenish-white, crisp, firm, very juicy, with a distinctive vinous flavor; season August to September. Tree moderately vigorous, upright-spreading; susceptible to scab. Very old English apple, mentioned in the "Compleat Planter and Cyderist" published in 1690. SANDERS, SIMMONS 1978; B72M, L12, M22

Discovery: Medium-small, flat-round fruit; skin pale greenish-yellow, prominently blushed with brilliant crimson-red; flesh creamy-white tinged with pink, firm, juicy, crisp, fine-textured; flavor good for a summer apple; season mid-August. Tree moderately vigorous, upright-spreading; very productive. Popular commercial cultivar in England. SANDERS, SIMMONS 1978; A69G{SC}, A91, A91{SC}, B72M, C34, *H34*, J61M, L97, M22

Dorsett Golden:[2] Medium to large, round-conic fruit; skin golden yellow, sometimes blushed with light-red on the side exposed to the sun; flesh firm, crisp, juicy, sweet; quality good; ripens early. Tree self-fruitful; excellent pollinizer for Anna. Extremely low chilling requirement, less than 100 hours. Originated in Nassau, New Providence Islands, Bahamas. Introduced in 1964. BROOKS 1972; A55{ES}, A82, C75M, C75M{DW}, *E45*, F19M, F93, G17, I83M, L1, L1{ES}, L33, *L47*, L90, M31M{PR}, *M69M*, etc.

Early Dawn:[2] Medium-sized fruit, about 1/2 pound; skin yellow, blushed with red, attractive; flesh crisp, juicy, aromatic, subacid; suitable for dessert or cooking; ripens in August. Tree vigorous; disease resistant; grows well in hot inland climates as well as under coastal conditions. Low chilling requirement, 250 hours or less. Originated in Ontario, California by L.D. Claypool. *I68*, I83M

Early Harvest: Fruit medium to large; oblate to nearly round; skin clear pale waxen yellow, thin, tender; flesh white, crisp, tender, juicy, at first briskly subacid but eventually becoming milder; suitable for dessert or culinary use; season late July and August. Tree medium-sized, moderately vigorous and productive. Of unknown origin; listed by McMahon in 1806. BEACH; A82, A91, A91{SC}, B72M, C27T{SC}, E84{OR}, *G15M*{DW}, I9M, J32{DW}, J33, J67{SC}, L1{OR}, L12, L27M, M23M{SC}, etc.

Early Joe: Small to medium, oblate-conic fruit; skin pale greenish-yellow, striped and blushed with dull dark-red; flesh tinged with yellow, crisp, very tender, very juicy, mildly subacid; flavor and desert quality excellent; season August and September. Tree moderately vigorous, dwarfish. Originated with Northern Spy in the orchard of Heman Chapin, East Bloomfield, New York. BEACH; A91, A91{SC}, B27M, B27M{SC}, B72M, J67{SC}, L12, M23M{SC}

Early Strawberry: Medium-sized, roundish fruit; skin waxy, entirely red or yellow nearly covered with a rich dark red; flesh whitish-yellow often with streaks of red, crisp, tender, juicy, subacid, aromatic, sprightly; quality very good for dessert or culinary use; season August. Tree hardy; precocious; productive. Originated in New York prior to 1838. BEACH; E84{OR}, J67{SC}, L12, M23M{SC}

Ein Shemer:[2] Fruit medium-sized, conical to roundish; skin greenish-yellow; flesh crisp, melting, tender, moderately juicy, subacid; quality good; season June and July. Tree medium-sized; very precocious; productive; good pollinizer for Anna. Very low chilling requirement. Originated in Doar Na Shomron, Israel. Introduced in 1963. BROOKS 1972; *A9*, A85M, C75M, C75M{DW}, *E45*, E99M, F19M, *G49*, I74, I83M, L33, L90, M31M, M31M{PR}, *M69M*, etc.

Elah:[2] Medium-sized fruit; skin bright canary yellow, 30% covered with a pink blush; flesh crisp, juicy, pleasantly aromatic; season mid-June to late July. Best when eaten slightly before fully ripe, as they tend to become mealy. Tree upright, semi-spreading; very precocious and prolific. Low chilling requirement. Originated in Rehovot, Israel by Chanan Oppenheimer. G17

Garden Delicious:[3] Small to medium-sized, conical fruit; skin yellow-green to golden-yellow, free of striping, lightly blushed with pink in warmer climates, bright red in colder areas; flesh sweet, crisp, flavorful; quality very good; ripens about 2 weeks after Golden Delicious. Tree a genetic dwarf; mature height 6 to 8 feet; slow growing; bears heavily and annually. Ideal for small gardens. Developed by Floyd Zaiger. A88M, B75, *C54*, E4, E87, F19M, G23, *I68*, *L47*, *N20*

Golden Sweet: Medium to large, roundish fruit; skin waxy, clear pale yellow when mature; flesh yellowish-white, firm, fine-grained, moderately tender, juicy, rich, very sweet, aromatic; quality good to very good; season mid-August to late September. Tree large, vigorous, roundish spreading; yields moderate to heavy crops biennially. An old Connecticut cultivar. BEACH; A91, A91{SC}, B27M, B27M{SC}, B72M, C27T{SC}, G99, J93{SC}, L12

Heyer 12: Medium-small fruit, 2 1/2 inches in diameter; skin greenish-yellow; flesh juicy, moderately coarse, acid; quality good for dessert or cooking; season mid-August to September. Tree extremely hardy; productive; late blooming. Valuable as an early apple for northern climates. BROOKS 1972; A16, A65, *A74*, B47, F67, G1T, G54, *G66*, H85, K64, K81, L27M, L70, L79, N26, etc.

Honey Sweet: (Honey Cider) Medium-sized, round-flat fruit; skin light green, blushed with light pink, light russeting; flesh crisp, juicy, sweet, translucent, aromatic; dessert quality good; season early August. Originally used as a blending apple to sweeten early apple cider. Tree upright-spreading; precocious; disease resistant. Rediscovered at an abandoned homesite in the Shenandoah Valley of Virginia. A39, B27M{SC}, B72M, D37, E84{OR}, G65M, G92, L7M, M23M{SC}

Horse: (Yellow Horse, Haas) Medium to large, oblate fruit; skin yellow, nearly covered with deep bright-red; flesh white, firm, somewhat tough, sprightly subacid, slightly astringent; quality poor to fair or sometimes nearly good; season October to early winter. Tree precocious; very thrifty; hardy; productive. Originated on the grounds of Gabriel Cerré, St. Louis, Missouri, prior to 1870. BEACH; B27M{SC}, B72M, E84{OR}, E99M, F19M, F93, G8, G13, G65M, *K76*, M23M, M23M{SC}

Iowa Beauty: A high quality apple good for either dessert or culinary use. Yellow and red skin. Very juicy flesh with a sweet tang; the core becomes pink sugar when overripe. Hardy to about -50° F. Ripens early. Introduced by G.C. Patten. L27M

Irish Peach: Small to medium, flat-round fruit; skin pale yellow, streaked and mottled with light and dark red; flesh greenish-white tinged red, soft, slightly aromatic, fairly juicy, with a rich vinous flavor; quality very good; season early July. Tree moderately vigorous, spreading; an irregular bearer. Of Irish origin; introduced into England in 1820. SANDERS, SIMMONS 1978; B27M, B27M{SC}, B72M, C27T{SC}, E84{OR}, L12, L27M, M22, M23M{SC}, N24M

Jerseymac: Medium to large, conical fruit; skin yellow, blushed with red; flesh yellow-white, medium firm, slightly acid; quality good; ripens early; ships well; resembles McIntosh. Tree vigorous, upright-spreading; precocious; bears heavily and annually; blooms with Gravenstein which it pollinizes. A5, A39, A91, B53, F53, G41, G65M, G99, J93{SC}, K84M{PR}, L12, M23M{SC}, M39M, M92, N33, etc.

July Tart: Fruit large for an early apple; skin light green shading to light yellow when fully ripe; flesh fine-grained, tender, extremely aromatic; dessert quality very good, excellent for frying and freezing; ripens before Gravenstein. Tree large, vigorous; apparently tolerant to scab and fire blight. Local apple from the mountains of Kentucky. C27T{SC}, E84{OR}, J93, J93{SC}, M22, M23M{SC}

Liveland Raspberry: (Lowland Raspberry) Fruit medium to large; skin clear waxen-white, striped, shaded and marbled with light crimson; flesh white, often stained with red, fine-grained, very tender, mildly subacid to sweet; dessert quality good, also makes a fine sauce; ripens in August, with Yellow Transparent. Tree medium-sized; tends toward biennial bearing. Originated in Russia prior to 1883. BEACH; A91, A91{SC}, B27M, B27M{SC}, B72M, E84, L27M

Lodi: Medium-sized, round-conical fruit; skin greenish-yellow, thick; flesh firm, crisp, flavor rich, sprightly; suitable for dessert and culinary use; ripens early, later than Yellow Transparent; resembles Yellow Transparent, keeps longer and does not become mealy and soften at center as quickly. Tree large; tends to bear biennially. BROOKS 1972; A5, B73M{DW}, *E45*, F19M, F53, G16, G16{DW}, G23, G41, G67, J83, J83{DW}, L97, L99M, M31T{ES}, etc.

Lord's Seedling: Medium to large, roundish fruit; skin yellow, more or less russet; flesh very aromatic, of excellent flavor; season late August. Tree a heavy and regular bearer. Originated at Linden, New York by James S. Lord about 1892. A91, B72M, C27T{SC}, E84{OR}, J93{SC}, L12, M23M{SC}

Lubsk Queen: Medium to large, nearly round fruit; skin very smooth, polished and wax-like, brilliant white, more or less covered with solid light rosy-red, very attractive; flesh snow white, firm, juicy, subacid; quality good; season August and September; keeps well for an early apple. Tree moderately vigorous, upright-spreading; very hardy and productive. Imported from Russia by the USDA in 1870. BEACH; A91, B72M, C27T{SC}, E84{OR}, G92, L12, M22

Lyman's Large Summer: Fruit large to very large; skin greenish to pale yellow, smooth; flesh breaking, tender, crisp, juicy, with a pure clean flavor, blending sweet and subacid; suitable for dessert or cooking; season early August. Tree hardy; a tip bearer. Of American origin; first described in 1844. A91, A91{SC}, C27T{SC}, G92, J93{SC}, L12, M22, N24M

Maayan:[2] Round, medium-sized fruit; skin yellow, 50% covered with dark-red, attractive; flesh yellow, juicy, firm, aromatic, flavor sprightly. Ripens from early June to late July, keeps and ships well. Tree vigorous, compact; can be induced to bear in its third year; tends to overproduce. Pollinates with Elah and Michal. Low chilling requirement. Originated in Rehovot, Israel by Chanan Oppenheimer. Introduced in 1967. BROOKS 1972; G17, J93{SC}

Mantet: Medium-sized, roundish fruit; skin heavily washed and striped bright red; flesh fine-grained, tender, juicy, aromatic, sweet, very pleasant; dessert quality excellent; season early to late August. Tree upright; very hardy; productive. Originated in Morden, Manitoba, Canada. Introduced in 1929. BROOKS 1972; *A74*, A91, A91{SC}, B4, B27M, B27M{SC}, C27T{SC}, D65, J93, J93{SC}, L27M, L70, M23M{SC}, N24M

Michal:[2] Medium-sized, roundish fruit; skin light golden-yellow, streaked with light red and orange; flesh juicy, firm, subacid, with good aroma and texture; flavor resembles Jonathan. Ripens mid-June to late July; keeps at room temperature at least 2 weeks, becoming sweeter. Tree precocious, bearing in the third year; very productive. Low chilling requirement Originated in Rehovot, Israel by Chanan Oppenheimer. BROOKS 1972; G17, I83M

Mollie's Delicious: Large to very large, slightly conical fruit; skin light yellow, highly blushed with red, very attractive; flesh crisp, juicy, sprightly, aromatic; quality very good; ripens 3 weeks before Golden Delicious. Tree vigorous, semi-spreading; productive. Originated in New Brunswick, New Jersey. Introduced in 1966. BROOKS 1972; A53{PR}, A85M, C75M{DW}, E29M, *E45*, F19M, F53, F93, G65M, G99, J93, J93{SC}, L90, M23M{SC}, M39M, N33, etc.

Oriole: Fruit large to very large; roundish, oblate; skin yellow-orange, striped and splashed red; flesh tender, fine-grained, juicy, aromatic, subacid; quality excellent for cooking or dessert; ripens early; similar to Duchess of Oldenburg in form and appearance. Tree medium tall, rounded; productive; very susceptible to mildew. BROOKS 1972; A91, A91{SC}, B15M, C27T{SC}, G67, J67{SC}, J93{SC}, L27M, L70, N24M

Ozark Gold: Medium to large fruit; skin smooth, golden-yellow blushed with bright red; flesh fine-grained, crisp, juicy, sweet, aromatic; quality above average for its season and locale; ripens about 3 weeks earlier than Golden Delicious, which it resembles. Tree vigorous, spreading; very hardy; disease resistant. Released in 1971 by the Missouri Experiment Station. A34, A53{PR}, B72M, C27T{SC}, G8, G65M, J93, J93{SC}, *K73M*, L12, M22, M23M{SC}

Parentene: Large, blocky fruit the shape of a well grown Gravenstein; skin light green, turning bright red on the side exposed to the sun; zestful flavor; ripens several weeks earlier than Gravenstein. Thought to be a cross of Gravenstein and Transparent. Local selection from Waldron Island, Washington. A91, A91{SC}, J67{SC}

Pink Transparent:[5] A pink-fleshed sport of Yellow Transparent. Medium-sized, round to conical fruit; skin clear yellow, thin and tender, bruises easily; flesh pink, very tender, tart, good for cooking or dessert; ripens early, has a very short shelf life. Tree vigorous, upright, productive. M22

Primate: Medium to large, roundish-conic fruit; skin pale yellow, often blushed but not striped; flesh whitish, crisp, very tender, juicy, subacid, aromatic, sprightly; quality very good to best; season August and September. Tree medium-large, moderately vigorous, upright-spreading; reliably productive. Originated in Onondaga County, New York, about 1840. BEACH; A91, A91{SC}, B27M, B27M{SC}, B72M, C27T{SC}, E84{OR}, L12, M23M{SC}

Quinte: Fruit medium-sized, round to slightly conic; skin attractive yellow, heavily blushed with red; flesh cream-colored, very tender; very suitable for dessert purposes, being equal to Melba and superior to Crimson Beauty; ripens 7 to 10 days before Melba; ships very well. Tree annually bears good crops; as hardy as McIntosh. BROOKS 1972; A5, A69G{SC}, A91, A91{SC}, C27T{SC}, G41, L27M, N24M

Red Hackworth: Fruit smaller, firmer, and more solid red than Hackworth; flesh nearly white; quality good when fully ripe; ripens in August. Well adapted to the climate and soils of the Tennessee Valley to the Alabama Coastal Plain and east Texas. A good understock in northern Alabama. BROOKS 1972; G13

Red June: (Carolina Red June) Fruit small to medium-sized; skin pale yellow or greenish, nearly overspread with deep purplish-red; flesh white, fine-grained, tender, juicy, briskly subacid; quality good to very good; season late July. Tree moderately vigorous, spreading; a reliable and heavy bearer. An old apple said to have originated in North Carolina. BEACH; A82, A91, A91{SC}, B72M, D76, E84, E99M, F19M, G13, J67{SC}, *K76*, L1, L12, M23M{SC}, M83, etc.

Redfree:[4] Medium-sized, roundish fruit; skin bright glossy red, waxy, attractive; flesh light-colored, crisp, juicy, flavor excellent; ripens 6 weeks before Red Delicious, can be held in storage for up to 2 months. Tree bears annually. Immune to scab and cedar rust. Moderately resistant to fire blight and mildew. C58, F53, J61M, J93

Reverend Morgan:[2] Seedling of Granny Smith that originated in the Houston, Texas area. Skin green, blushed with pinkish red. Excellent flavor and texture. Ripens in August, keeps well. Tree self-fruitful, disease resistant; requires 400 to 500 hours of chilling. Recommended for trial in California and other warm winter areas. G65M, J93{SC}

St. Francis: Medium-sized fruit; skin apple-green, blushed with pink; flesh very crisp, sweet, spicy; ripens very early, 1 week before Yellow Transparent. Ripens unevenly over a 2 week period; does not store. Tree medium-sized; sturdy; with showy white flowers. Selected as a wildling in St. Francis, Maine. C27T{SC}

Starr: Fruit very large to large; oblate to roundish oblate; skin yellowish-green; flesh tinged with yellow, very tender, crisp, very juicy, sprightly subacid, aromatic; quality very good; season August and September. Tree moderately vigorous, upright-spreading, productive. Originated in Woodbury, New Jersey, sometime prior to 1865. BEACH; L12

Summer Pearmain: Medium-sized, round-conic fruit; skin greenish-yellow, more or less covered with dull purplish-red, marbled, splashed and striped with brighter red; flesh yellowish, very fin-grained, tender, almost melting, juicy, aromatic, crisp; flavor mild, rich, excellent; season August and September. Tree large, productive. An old American cultivar; first described in 1817. BEACH; B72M, C27T{SC}, J67{SC}, L1{OR}, L12, M23M{SC}, N24M

Summer Rambo: Large to very large, oblate fruit; skin yellowish-green, striped and mottled with lively pinkish-red; flesh yellowish-green, firm, coarse, tender, very juicy, mildly subacid, somewhat aromatic; quality good; season August and September. Tree vigorous, upright-spreading; precocious. Originated in France in the 16th century. BEACH; A5, B27M{SC}, B53, B72M, C27T{SC}, E84, *H34*, H65, J67{SC}, L12, M22{OR}

Summer Red: Medium-large, oblong fruit; skin highly colored with a bright, solid blush; flesh cream-colored, firm, crisp, juicy, flavor very good when fully ripe; ripens 3 to 4 weeks before McIntosh; matures evenly on the tree. Tree vigorous, spreading; blooms relatively early; bears early and fairly regularly. A88M, B27M{SC}, B67, B67{DW}, C34, C41M, *G14*, *H34*, J61M, J67{SC}, J93{SC}, L97, L99M, M22, M23M{SC}, M39M, N24M, etc.

Summer Rose: Small to medium, roundish fruit; skin very pale yellow, distinctly striped and splashed with bright red and carmine on the exposed cheek; flesh white, fine-grained, crisp, very tender, sprightly, juicy, subacid, agreeable but not rich; suitable for either dessert or culinary use; season July and August. Tree hardy, precocious, productive. Originated in New Jersey prior to 1806. BEACH; A91, B27M, B27M{SC}, B72M, E84{OR}, L1, L12, *N20*

Sweet Bough: (August Sweet) Medium to large, roundish-conic fruit; skin pale greenish-yellow; flesh white, moderately firm and crisp, very tender, juicy, decidedly sweet, slightly aromatic; quality good to very good; season August and early September. Tree moderately vigorous, upright-spreading; productive. Of unknown origin; first described in 1817. BEACH; A91, A91{SC}, B72M, C27T{SC}, D69, H65, J93{SC}, L1{OR}, L12, N24M

Tetofsky: Small to medium, oblate or roundish fruit; skin waxy, greenish-yellow, more or less striped and splashed with attractive bright red; flesh white, firm, crisp, tender, juicy, sprightly, slightly aromatic, subacid; quality fair to good; season late July to early September. Tree small to medium, very upright; very hardy; precocious. Of Russian origin; imported into the United States about 1835. BEACH; G67, L27M

Tropical Beauty:[2] Medium to large, roundish fruit; skin rich carmine red; flesh white, fairly crisp, juicy, with a smooth mild flavor; dessert quality very good; ripens early; resembles Rome Beauty. Tree small to medium; self-fruitful; bears at an early age; low chilling requirement. Adapted to tropical and sub-tropical climates. Originated in Maidstone, South Africa about 1930. BROOKS 1972; *I68*, I83M

Tydeman's Red: (Tydeman's Early Worcester) Medium to large, roundish fruit; skin solid bright red, attractive; flesh yellowish-white, soft, rather coarse, juicy, sweet; quality very good; ripens early, 3 weeks before McIntosh. Tree vigorous, very spreading; productive. Originated in Maidstone, Kent, England. Introduced in 1945. BROOKS 1972; A5, A91, B53, B67, B67{DW}, G41, *G66*, *H34*, I76M{PR}, J61M, J67{SC}, L12, L27M, M23M{SC}, N46, etc.

Valmore:[2] Large, conical fruit; skin yellow, striped with red, waxy; flesh yellowish-white, texture fine, juicy, subacid, aromatic; suitable for dessert and cooking; ripens early with White Astrachan; resembles Stayman Winesap. Tree vigorous, upright, productive; somewhat resistant to delayed foliation. Low chilling requirement. Originated in Visalia, California. BROOKS 1972; I83M

Vista Bella: Medium-sized, roundish fruit; skin blushed with bright red; flesh creamy-white, very firm for an early summer apple, juicy, subacid, flavor and quality good; ripens in early August, with Yellow Transparent. Tree very vigorous; yields heavy crops annually. Originated in New Brunswick, New Jersey. Introduced in 1974. A5, A91, A91{SC}, B27M{SC}, C27T{SC}, F53, G41, G69M, J7, J93, J93{SC}, L12, M22, M23M{SC}, M92, N24M, etc.

William's Pride:[4] (Coop 21) A new disease resistant apple named for Purdue apple breeder E.B. Williams. Medium to large, slightly conic fruit; skin red to dark red; flavor mildly acid, rich, slightly spicy; quality excellent; ripens late July to early August. Can be stored for about one month in common refrigeration. In warmer regions of Zone 6 and south, watercore can be a problem in early production years. D37, F53, J61M, J93

Yellow Transparent: Medium-sized, roundish fruit; skin thin, tender, waxy, clear yellow; flesh white, moderately firm, fine-grained, crisp, tender, juicy, sprightly subacid; quality good to very good; season late July and August. Tree large, upright, moderately vigorous. Imported from Russia by the USDA in 1870. BEACH; A91, A91{SC}, B73M, C58, D69, E84, G41, G79M{DW}, H65, J16, L27M, L97, M31T{ES}, M39M, M76, N26, etc.

FALL HARVESTING

Akane: (Prime Red, Tokyo Rose) Small to medium-sized, flat-round fruit; skin bright solid red; flesh white, firm, crisp, juicy, slightly coarse, flavor slightly acid; quality excellent; ripens in midseason; does not store well but holds well on the tree. Tree semi-dwarf, moderately vigorous; precocious. Originated in Tohoku, Japan. Introduced in 1970. STEBBINS; *A9*, A39, A53{PR}, A91, A91{SC}, B67{DW}, B83, C41M, F53, *G38M*, G99, J6{PR}, J61M, J93{SC}, *K73M*, L97, M39M, etc.

Blenheim: (Blenheim Orange) Medium to large, flat-round fruit; skin yellow, striped and blushed with orange-red; flesh creamy-white, firm but tender, crisp, subacid, with a characteristic nutty flavor, sometimes dry; quality very good for dessert or culinary uses. Tree vigorous, spreading; slow to come into bearing. Discovered about 1740 near Blenheim, England. SANDERS, SIMMONS 1978; B72M, E84{OR}, G41, J93{SC}, L12, M22, N24M

Blue Pearmain: Large, roundish fruit; skin blushed with red, splashed and striped with deep purplish-carmine overspread with an abundant blue bloom, very attractive; flesh yellowish, rather coarse, moderately juicy, mildly subacid, decidedly and agreeably aromatic; quality good; ripens in October. Tree large, moderately vigorous, spreading. An American apple of uncertain origin; first recorded in 1833. BEACH; A91, A91{SC}, B27M{SC}, B72M, C58, E84{OR}, L12, L27M, M22, N24M

Blushing Golden: Medium-sized, round-conic fruit; skin waxy, golden yellow, 50% covered with a light red blush, very attractive; flesh very firm, juicy, subacid, quality very good, rated A plus in customer taste tests of Applesource; ripens 2 weeks after Golden Delicious, which it resembles; ripens in October and November; keeps very well; Tree vigorous, spreading; productive; spur-bearing. Introduced in 1968. BROOKS 1972; A53{PR}, C27T{SC}, K84M{PR}, L33, L33{DW}

Bonum: (Magnum Bonum) Medium to large, oblate fruit; skin yellow, blushed and striped with crimson and dark red; flesh white, often stained next to the skin, firm but tender, juicy, aromatic, mildly subacid; dessert quality very good; season September to November. Tree moderately vigorous, upright-spreading. Originated in Davidson County, North Carolina prior to 1856. BEACH; B27M{SC}

Bottle Greening: Medium to large, round-conic fruit; skin grass-green, thinly blushed with dull pinkish-crimson; flesh nearly white, very tender, very juicy, peculiarly aromatic, pleasantly subacid; quality good to very good; season October to March. Tree moderately vigorous; hardy; productive. Originated on a farm on the dividing line of New York and Vermont, prior to 1866. BEACH; A91, A91{SC}, C58

Breakey: Medium-sized, round-oblate fruit; skin yellow-green, striped and blushed with red and scarlet; flesh white, fine-textured, melting, juicy, flavor mild, spicy; dessert quality very good, also good for sauce or pies; ripens in early September. Tree vigorous, upright-spreading; very hardy. Originated in Morden, Manitoba, Canada. Introduced in 1935. BROOKS 1972; A91, B4, M35M, N24M

Champlain: Medium to large, roundish-conical fruit; skin pale yellow, often with a light crimson blush; flesh white, fine-grained, very tender, juicy, sprightly, subacid; dessert quality good to very good, excellent for culinary use; season late August to October. Tree vigorous, upright-spreading; hardy; reliably productive. Of unknown American origin; first described in 1853. BEACH; A91, A91{SC}, B72M, L12

Chehalis: Medium-sized, conical fruit; skin greenish-yellow, blushed with pink on the side exposed to the sun; flesh cream-colored, medium-fine, crisp, breaking, moderately juicy; flavor pleasantly mild, subacid; ripens 3 to 4 weeks before Golden Delicious, which it resembles. Resistant to scab. Tree upright-spreading, moderately vigorous and productive. BROOKS 1972; B27M{SC}, B67, C27T{SC}, *G14*, *H34*, I49M, J6{PR}, J61M, L99M, M23M{SC}, M39M

Chenango Strawberry: Medium to large, oblong-conic fruit; translucent yellowish-white skin, highly blushed with attractive pinkish-red; flesh white, moderately firm, tender, juicy, mildly subacid, very aromatic; desert quality excellent, also good for culinary use; ripens in September. Tree vigorous, upright-spreading. Originated in Chenango County, New York prior to 1854. BEACH; A91, A91{SC}, B27M{SC}, B72M, C27T{SC}, E84{OR}, G65M, G79M{DW}, G99, H65, J67{SC}, L12, L27M, M22, M23M{SC}, N24M, etc.

Cinnamon Spice: Medium-small fruit; skin predominantly wine-red, slightly blushed with yellow; flesh very rich and sweet, with a sharp cinnamon-like flavor which lingers for some time; ripens late October. Discovered in an old orchard in the Bolinas-Olema Valley of northern California. Introduced by Living Tree Center. G92, K84M{PR}

Collet: Fruit medium-sized; oblate to conic oblate; skin attractive, 80% medium red; flesh white, firm, crisp, texture moderately fine; dessert quality fair to good, excellent as sauce or pie. Tree medium to tall, very hardy, annually productive. Originated in Notre Dame de Lourdes, Manitoba, Canada. BROOKS 1972; A65, B47, G1T, H42, H85, K64, L12, M35M, N24M

Cooke's Seedling: Medium to large fruit; skin pale yellow, striped with red; flesh white, crisp, with a sharp acid flavor; ripens in late September; excellent keeping qualities. Originated in northern California as a seedling raised by David Cook from the seed of the Juneating apple. WICKSON; G92

Cortland: Fruit large; roundish-oblate, uniformly ribbed; skin attractive red, darkly and obscurely striped; flesh white, slow to discolor on exposure to air, fine-grained, crisp, tender, juicy, subacid; quality good; season November to February; resembles McIntosh. Tree vigorous, spreading; precocious; annually productive; very hardy; prolific. BROOKS 1972; A5, A53{PR}, A82, B83, C95{PR}, D69, F42M{PR}, F53, G16, G16{DW}, G23, G41, G79M{DW}, H65, I76M{PR}, J16, M39M, etc.

Cox's Orange Pippin: Fruit medium-sized; round-conical; skin clear yellow, blushed with orange-red, striped with brownish-crimson; flesh cream-colored, fine-textured, fairly firm and crisp, juicy, rich, flavor excellent; season October to December. Tree moderately vigorous, upright-spreading; bears fruit on short spurs. Considered the finest flavored apple in Great Britain, but not as highly esteemed elsewhere. SANDERS, SIMMONS 1978; A53{PR}, A55{ES}, A91, A91{SC}, E84{OR}, F11, G41, G79M{DW}, G92, H65, I49M, J61M, L1, L1{ES}, L99M, etc.

Crimson Beauty: (Scarlet Pippin) Very attractive apple of the Fameuse group. Medium-sized, roundish fruit; skin red-striped; flesh white, firm, crisp, tender, melting, juicy, mildly subacid with a pleasant but not high flavor; season fall and early winter. Tree vigorous, upright; very productive. Originated about 1860 at Lynn, Ontario. BEACH; L27M, M39M

Dakota: Large, round-oblate fruit; skin yellow, blushed with an attractive deep red; flesh creamy-yellow, crisp, juicy, firm, fine-grained, sprightly subacid; excellent for dessert and culinary uses; ripens in mid-September; keeps in common storage for several weeks. Tree vigorous, spreading; productive; hardy. Originated in Mandan, North Dakota. Introduced in 1965. BROOKS 1972; L70, M35M

Detroit Red: Large, roundish-oblate fruit; skin dark crimson, largely striped and splashed with purplish-carmine eventually becoming almost black; flesh white, rather coarse, tender, juicy, mildly subacid, very aromatic; quality good to very good; season the end of September to December. Tree medium to large; moderately vigorous and productive. Supposedly brought into the Detroit area by early French settlers. BEACH; B27M{SC}, E84{OR}, G8{CF}, G92, M23M{SC}

Dr. Mathews: Fruit large; skin dull red, striped with darker red; flesh creamy-white, crisp, juicy, fine-grained, with a mild but sprightly aromatic flavor; quality excellent; ripens in September. An obscure 19th century Indiana cultivar. Was for many years grown in the orchards of the Indiana State Agricultural Station and is still a local favorite wherever known. A53{PR}, A91, A91{SC}, B72M, J93{SC}, L12

Egremont Russet: Medium-sized, flat-round fruit; skin golden-yellow, blushed with brownish-orange, with attractive russeting; flesh creamy-colored tinged with yellow, crisp and firm, fairly juicy, sweet, aromatic, with a rich nutty flavor; season October to November. Tree upright, compact; hardy; bears heavily and annually. Considered one of the best dessert apples in Great Britain. Origin unknown; first recorded about 1880. SANDERS, SIMMONS 1978; B27M{SC}, B72M, C27T{SC}, G92, J93{SC}, L12, L27M, M22, N24M

Ellison's Orange: Fruit medium-sized, round, slightly conical; skin golden yellow, blushed brownish-red with stripes of brownish-crimson; flesh creamy-white, tender, crisp, juicy, with a very rich, distinctive, anise-like flavor; season September and October. Tree precocious; spur-bearing; bears moderate crops biennially. Originated in England. Introduced about 1911. SANDERS, SIMMONS 1978; B27M, B27M{SC}, B72M, G65M, J93{SC}, L12, M22

Empire: Medium-sized, roundish fruit; skin dark red, distinctly striped, waxy, very attractive; flesh cream-colored, crisp, juicy, subacid to semi-sweet, aromatic; dessert quality excellent; ripens 2 weeks after McIntosh; stores well. Tree large, vigorous, upright-spreading; annually productive. McIntosh x Red Delicious. BROOKS 1972; A5, A34, A39, A53{PR}, B83, *C47*, E18M{PR}, F53, G79M{DW}, H65, L33, M22, M39M, *M59M*

Etter's Gold: Fruit medium to large; round, slightly ribbed; skin clear golden yellow, glossy; flesh light yellow, crisp, mildly subacid, sprightly; dessert quality excellent, also good for pies; ripens in October; keeps well; resembles Wagener. Tree very productive; bears annually; produces spurs readily. Wagener x Transcendent crab. Originated in Ettersburg, California by Albert F. Etter. Introduced in 1944. BROOKS 1972; B72M, E84, J93{SC}

Fall Pippin: Large to very large, roundish fruit; skin clear yellow, sometimes faintly blushed; flesh whitish, moderately firm, tender, very juicy, agreeably subacid, somewhat aromatic, rich; quality very good for dessert or culinary uses; season late September to January. Tree large, vigorous; hardy. Of unknown origin; listed by McMahon in 1806. BEACH; B72M, E84{OR}, H65, M23M{SC}

Fallawater: (Tulpehocken) Large to very large, globular fruit; skin yellow, prominently blushed with deep pinkish-red; flesh tinged with yellow or green, firm, coarse, crisp, juicy, subacid to mildly sweet; quality good or nearly so; season November. Tree large, vigorous, upright; productive. Originated in Bucks county, Pennsylvania, sometime prior to 1845. BEACH; B27M{SC}, B72M, C27T{SC}, G92, L12

Fameuse: (Snow Apple) Small to medium, roundish fruit; skin light bright red, very attractive; flesh white, sometimes streaked or stained with red, very tender, juicy, subacid becoming mildly subacid or sweetish, aromatic; dessert quality very good to excellent; ripens in October. Tree vigorous, upright-spreading; hardy; reliably productive. Probably originated in Canada in the early 18th century. BEACH; A53{PR}, A55{ES}, B53, B72M, C58, D69, E84, G16{DW}, G69M, G79M{DW}, H65, J67{SC}, L1, L1{ES}, L27M, etc.

Franklin: Medium to large, conical fruit; skin nearly covered with red, attractive; flesh white, tender, crisp, aromatic, flavor mild; dessert quality high; season late fall and early winter. Tree very susceptible to scab. McIntosh x Delicious. Originated in Wooster, Ohio by the Ohio Agricultural Experiment Station. Introduced in 1937. BROOKS 1972; A53{PR}, L12

Freedom:[4] Large, oblate fruit; skin yellow, blushed and striped with red, attractive; flesh cream-colored, medium-coarse, crisp, tender, juicy, sprightly subacid; quality good for desert, sauce and juice; ripens in early October. Tree vigorous, spreading; precocious; very productive; spur-bearing. Highly resistant to scab; resistant to cedar rust, fire blight and powdery mildew. Originated in Geneva, New York by Robert C. Lamb. Introduced in 1983. A39, C58, D76, F53, G23, H65, I36, J61M, L27M, M22, N24M

Freyberg: Small to medium-sized, round fruit; skin golden yellow, blushed with mahogany red; flesh yellow, fine-grained, firm, crisp, juicy, sweet, quality excellent; ripens shortly after Cox's Orange Pippin; stores well. Tree small, upright, vigorous; spur-bearing;

productive. Connoisseur cultivar for home gardens. Originated in New Zealand by J.H. Kidd. BROOKS 1972; B72M, C27T{SC}, E84{OR}, J61M, J67{SC}, J93, L12, M23M{SC}, N24M

Fuji: Medium to large, round-conical fruit; skin golden-brown, blushed with dull red; flesh creamy-white, very crisp, extremely juicy, very sweet; quality excellent; susceptible to water core; ships and stores well. Popular specialty market apple. Tree slow to come into bearing; requires a long season. Ralls Janet x Delicious. Originated in Aomori, Japan by the Tohoku Horticultural Research Station. BROOKS 1972; *A9*, A53{PR}, E4, F11, F15{PR}, *G38M*, G65M, G99, H49{DW}, H69{PR}, H81M, J93{SC}, *K73M*, L1, L99M, M23M{SC}, etc.

Gala: Medium-sized, oblong-conical fruit; skin bright yellow, heavily striped with bright orange-red, glossy; flesh yellow, fine-textured, firm, crisp, very sweet and juicy; dessert quality very good; ripens with Cox's Orange Pippin; keeps well. Tree vigorous; precocious; annually bears heavy crops; produces spurs freely. Originated in Greytown, Wairarapa, New Zealand. BROOKS 1972; A53{PR}, A88M, C89{PR}, E4, E70M{PR}, E97, *I68*, K84M{PR}, M22, M39M, N24M

Golden Delicious: (Yellow Delicious) Medium-sized fruit, long and tapering; skin pale yellow, occasionally blushed with pink; flesh yellowish-white, crisp, juicy, sweet and aromatic; ripens midseason to late, does not store well. Originated in Clay County, West Virginia about 1890. SIMMONS 1978; A34, A82, *C47*, C58, *D35M*{ES}, F93, G53M, G72, G99, I9M, J32, J33, J69{DW}, K84M{PR}, L30, <u>L97G</u>{PR}, M31T{ES}, M76, M76{DW}, etc.

Goodland: Medium to large, roundish-oblate fruit; skin creamy yellow, splashed and streaked with an attractive bright red; flesh crisp, juicy, tender, sweetly subacid, aromatic; quality excellent for dessert or sauce; season mid-September to mid-January. Tree medium tall; very hardy; annually productive. Originated in Morden, Manitoba, Canada. Introduced in 1955. BROOKS 1972; A65, A91, B47, G1T, H42, H85, K64, K81, L27M, M35M, N24M

Gordon: Medium to large, nearly globe-shaped fruit; skin green, blushed and striped with red; flesh near white, crisp, juicy, firm; quality good for dessert or cooking; ripens in midseason. Tree vigorous, upright; productive; bears regularly; self-fruitful. Prolonged season of flowering and fruiting. Low chilling requirement, about 400 hours. STEBBINS; *D23M*, *G49*, *I68*, I83M, *K46*, *L47*, M39M

Grimes Golden: Medium to large, roundish-conical fruit; clear deep yellow skin with pale yellow or russet dots; flesh yellow, very firm, tender, crisp, moderately juicy, subacid, rich, aromatic, sprightly; quality excellent; season October and November; does not keep well. Tree moderately vigorous, upright-spreading; productive. Originated in West Virginia prior to 1804. BEACH; A5, A53{PR}, A91, A91{SC}, C63, D76, E84, G79M{DW}, G99, H65, I76M{PR}, J93{SC}, L1, L33, M22, M76, etc.

Haralson: Medium to large, roundish-conic fruit; skin yellow, striped or nearly covered with an attractive red; flesh white, firm, moderately tender, fine-grained, juicy, mild, pleasant, subacid; suitable for dessert or cooking; stores well. Tree vigorous, upright; hardy; productive; resistant to fire blight. Grown commercially in Minnesota. BROOKS 1972; A53{PR}, A91, A91{SC}, D65, D65{DW}, D76{DW}, G16, G16{DW}, G67, G69M, *H90*, K64, L12, L27M, L70, L79, etc.

Harold's Large: (Pink-Skinned Maiden Blush) Large, attractive, high quality fruit; skin bright yellow, blushed with intense red; flesh yellow, rich, highly aromatic. Vigorous, precocious tree, often laden with fruit at 2 years of age. Originated with Harold Reep of Mendocino County, California. G92, K84M{PR}

Hawaii: Fruit medium-sized; oblong angular; skin waxy, light golden-yellow; flesh yellow, firm, juicy, pleasantly aromatic, with a strong pineapple-like flavor; ripens in early October; keeps well; resembles Golden Delicious. Tree vigorous, upright; bears fruit on small spurs; biennial, requiring heavy thinning in high-yielding years. Originated in Sebastopol, California. BROOKS 1972; A39, A53{PR}, B27M, B27M{SC}, B72M, C27T{SC}, *H34*, J93{SC}, L12, M22, M23M{SC}

Herring's Pippin: Large, round-conical fruit; skin pale greenish-yellow, almost completely covered with red blush; flesh creamy-white, soft, juicy, slightly coarse, aromatic, with a spicy flavor; suitable for both dessert and cooking; season early October. Tree moderately vigorous, upright-spreading; adapted to cold, heavy soils. Originated in England about 1908. SANDERS, SIMMONS 1978; G92, M22

Hibernal: Fruit large; irregular, oblate to roundish-conical; skin greenish-yellow, blushed with red; flesh yellowish, crisp, tender, juicy, acid, somewhat astringent; dessert quality fair, fine for cooking, said to be good for drying; season September to November. Tree vigorous, very spreading; very productive; extremely hardy. Of Russian origin; introduced into the United States prior to 1880. BEACH; A91, A91{SC}, C41M, L27M

Holiday: Medium-sized, flat-round fruit; skin yellow, overspread with deep bright-red; flesh white, crisp, tender, juicy, aromatic; flavor rich, slightly tart; quality very good; ripens in October, keeps well in cold storage; resembles Macoun. Tree moderately vigorous, upright; somewhat difficult to prune. Macoun x Jonathan. A53{PR}, B27M{SC}, B72M, C27T{SC}, L12, M23M{SC}

Holstein: Fruit medium-large; oblong-conical to round-conical; skin golden-yellow, blushed and striped with red; flesh creamy yellow, firm, juicy, sweet, aromatic, somewhat similar to Cox's Orange Pippin; quality excellent. Tree vigorous, spreading; produces spurs readily; requires pollination. Raised in Schleswig-Holstein, Germany about 1918. SANDERS, SIMMONS 1978; B27M, B27M{SC}, B72M, C27T{SC}, E84{OR}, J93{SC}, L12, M22, M23M, M23M{SC}

Honeygold: Medium to large, round-conic fruit; skin yellow, blushed with bronze; flesh yellow, crisp, juicy, sweet; dessert quality excellent, equal to Golden Delicious but keeps better; ripens October 1. Tree medium-sized, moderately vigorous; hardy. Golden Delicious x Haralson. Recommended where Golden Delicious is marginal. BROOKS 1972; A53{PR}, A91, A91{SC}, B27M{SC}, C58, D65, D65{DW}, F53, G16, *G66*, *G89M*, *H90*{DW}, J7, L27M, L70{DW}, M23M{SC}, N24M, etc.

Hubbardston Nonesuch: Medium to large, roundish-ovate fruit; skin yellow or greenish, blushed and mottled with bright red; flesh whitish slightly tinged with yellow, tender, juicy, aromatic, rich, at first sprightly but becoming mildly subacid mingled with sweet; quality excellent; season October to January. Tree vigorous; precocious; bears heavy crops annually. Originated in Hubbardston, Massachusetts prior to 1832. BEACH; A53{PR}, B27M, B27M{SC}, B72M, C27T{SC}, E84{OR}, J67{SC}, L1, L12, N24M

Itzstedter Apfel: (Prunterkroger) Fruit roundish-oblate; skin smooth, tender, yellow blushed with pink; flavor distinctive, somewhat tart but still sweet, with a hint of almond; ripens in October, keeps moderately well into January. Tends toward biennial bearing. Originated in Itstedt, in northern Germany, and probably dates from the late 19th century. Introduced by Living Tree Center. G92

James Grieve: Medium to large, round-conical fruit; greenish-yellow skin, blushed and striped with brownish-red; flesh creamy-white, firm and crisp, fine-textured, very juicy, flavor excellent; ripens in September; does not keep well. Tree vigorous, upright; readily forms short fruiting spurs; annually produces heavy crops.

Originated in Scotland; first recorded in 1893. SANDERS, SIMMONS 1978; A91, A91{SC}, B53, B72M, L12, M22, N24M

Jefferis: Fruit small to medium, roundish oblate; skin pale yellow, blushed and splashed with red; flesh yellowish-white, firm, crisp, tender, very juicy, mildly subacid; quality very good; season September to January. Tree medium-sized, moderately vigorous; hardy; productive. Originated with Isaac Jefferis, Newlin township, Pennsylvania prior to 1848. BEACH; A39, A91, A91{SC}, B72M, E84{OR}, G65M, J93{SC}, L12, M22

Jenner Sweet: Medium-sized fruit; skin yellow, blushed and striped with red; flavor fine, mildly sweet, typically Fameuse; ripens in mid-autumn; resembles Fameuse. Tree extremely hardy. Open-pollinated seedling of Fameuse; discovered in 1924. Introduced in 1964 by Fred L. Ashworth, Heuvelton, New York. BROOKS 1972; L27M

Jonalicious: (Daniels) Large, round fruit; skin thick and tough, yellow blushed a bright, nearly solid red; flesh tinged with yellow, juicy, firm but tender, aroma distinct; flavor rich, slightly less tart than Jonathan, rated A plus in customer taste tests of Applesource; ripens just after Jonathan which it resembles, keeps better. Tree vigorous, upright, hardy and productive. Originated in Abilene, Texas by Anna Morris Daniels. BROOKS 1972; A39, A53{PR}, L33

Jonamac: Medium-sized, roundish fruit; skin greenish-yellow, prominently blushed with dark red; flesh firm, crisp, juicy, somewhat tart, aromatic; quality very good; ripens a few days before McIntosh, which it resembles; does not keep well. Tree medium-sized, moderately vigorous; productive. Jonathan x McIntosh. A5, A34, A53{PR}, A91, A91{SC}, B67, B67{DW}, C41M, F53, G23, J6{PR}, J93, J93{SC}, *K73M*, L12, M23M{SC}, *M59M*, etc.

Jonathan: (Philip Rick) Small to medium, roundish-conic fruit; skin pale bright yellow overlaid with lively red, striped with carmine; flesh whitish, firm but tender, crisp, juicy, very aromatic, sprightly subacid; quality excellent for dessert and culinary uses; season November to January. Tree small to medium, moderately vigorous. Originated on the farm of Philip Rick, Woodstock, New York prior to 1826. BEACH; A53{PR}, A91, A91{SC}, B75, D76, D76{DW}, D81{PO}, D81M{PO}, E70M{PR}, G79M{DW}, J83, J83{DW}, L1, *L47*, L99M, M31T{ES}, *M69M*, etc.

Kandil Sinap: A novelty cultivar from Turkey. Fruit medium-sized; very tall, narrow, cylindrical; creamy-yellow, porcelain-like skin, washed with a brilliant red blush; flesh crisp, juicy, fine-grained, of excellent flavor; ripens in early October. Tree small, narrow pyramidal; a heavy and regular bearer. A53{PR}, B27M, B27M{SC}, B72M, C27T{SC}, E84{OR}, L12, M22, M23M{SC}, N24M

Kerry Pippin: Small, roundish fruit; skin glossy yellow, sometimes striped on the side exposed to the sun; flesh very firm, crisp, crunchy, with a fine, rich spicy flavor; quality excellent. An old Irish apple, first noted in 1802 in a survey of the Royal Dublin Society of County Kilkenny. J93{SC}, L12, M23M{SC}

Kidd's Orange Red: Medium to large, conical fruit; skin dull yellowish-green, blushed with orange-scarlet, with red stripes and russet patches; flesh light cream, firm but tender, crisp, juicy, sweet, aromatic; quality very good; ripens in October; stores well. Tree vigorous, upright; very productive; resistant to scab; best suited to warm climates. Originated in New Zealand in 1924. SANDERS, SIMMONS 1978; A91, A91{SC}, B27M, B27M{SC}, B72M, G65M, J93, J93{SC}, L12, M22, M23M, M23M{SC}, N24M

King: (Tompkins King) Fruit large to very large; roundish to somewhat oblate; skin yellow, mottled and striped with deep red and bright carmine; flesh yellowish, rather coarse, crisp, tender, aromatic, juicy, subacid; quality excellent for dessert or cooking; season mid-October. Tree vigorous, spreading; hardy; productive. Originated in Washington, New Jersey prior to 1804. BEACH; B67{DW}, D69, E84, *G14*, G92, H65, J67{SC}, J93{SC}, L1, L12, L97, L99M, M22, M31T{ES}

Laxton's Fortune: (Fortune) Fruit medium-sized; round, slightly conical; skin pale yellowish-green, blushed and striped bright red; flesh creamy-white, firm but tender, rather coarse-textured, sweet, flavor rich; quality good; ripens in September. Tree small, compact; precocious; productive; inclined to biennial bearing. Originated in England in 1904. SANDERS, SIMMONS 1978; G92, J93{SC}, L12, M22, M23M{SC}

Lemon: Small fruit; skin attractive yellow, speckled; flesh firm, very sweet, with a delicious lemon-like flavor. Ripens in October, keeps well. Originated in the Constance Lake area of Germany. M22, N24M

Liberty:[4] Medium-sized, oblate fruit; skin yellow, highly blushed with bright red, attractive; flesh yellowish, slightly coarse, crisp, juicy, sprightly; dessert quality good; ripens just after McIntosh. Tree vigorous, spreading; very productive. Highly resistant to scab, resistant to mildew, cedar rust and fire blight. A39, A53{PR}, A55{ES}, A91, A91{SC}, C58, D76{DW}, E84, F53, G16, G23, G65M, G99, H65, J61M, L1, L1{ES}, L33, etc.

Macoun: Small to medium, flat-round fruit; skin pale yellow, almost completely blushed bright red, with very dark red stripes; flesh white, crisp, firm, sweet, aromatic, flavor rich; dessert quality high; ripens 1 month after McIntosh. Tree vigorous, upright; productive. One of the best of the McIntosh type apples. A5, A55{ES}, F42M{PR}, F53, G16, G16{DW}, G23, G41, G79M{DW}, G99, H65, L1, L1{ES}, L12, *M59M*, etc.

Makepeace: Flattened spherical fruit; skin green with an attractive pink blush on the exposed side when mature; flesh nearly white, crisp, juicy, sweet; dessert quality very good, also very good for cooking if picked slightly immature; keeps well at room temperature for 3 to 4 weeks. Tree bears heavily and at an early age; requires about 450 hours of chilling. Well suited to the warm winters of southern California. Originated in Rancho Santa Fe, California. D57{OR}

Mandan: Fruit medium to large; round conic to oblong conic; skin greenish-yellow overspread with orange-red, with dark red splotches; flesh yellowish, firm, crisp, very juicy, mildly subacid; dessert quality excellent, good for culinary uses; ripens early to mid-September. Tree vigorous, spreading; annually productive; hardy; resistant to fire blight. Originated in Mandan, North Dakota. BROOKS 1972; L27M, L70, M35M

McIntosh: Medium-sized, nearly round fruit; skin yellow with a bright red blush; flesh white, sweet, tender, moderately soft and juicy; ripens in midseason. Tree vigorous, productive, hardy. Originated in Ontario, Canada. STEBBINS; A55{ES}, A82, C58, D76, E4, *E45*, E97, F19M, G53M, G69M, G72{DW}, H49, J32, J32{DW}, J69{DW}, L1, L1{ES}, M31T{ES}, etc.

Melrose: Fruit medium to large; flat-round to conical; skin yellowish-green, blushed and streaked with dark brownish-red, very attractive; flesh creamy-white, firm, crisp, juicy, slightly acid, rich; dessert and culinary quality excellent; ripens in October and November. Tree moderately vigorous, upright-spreading; precocious; very productive. BROOKS 1972; A5, A39, A53{PR}, A91, A91{SC}, B67{DW}, C34{PR}, C41M, *G38M*, I76M{PR}, J6{PR}, J61M, J93, L97, L99M, M31T{ES}, M39M, etc.

Monroe: Medium to large, roundish-conic fruit; skin nearly solid red, excellent in appearance; flesh yellow, firm, crisp, juicy, subacid; dessert quality good. Excellent for pies, sauce and baking. Tree vigorous, upright-spreading; bears heavy crops annually; susceptible to powdery mildew. Originated in Geneva, New York by U.P. Hedrick. BROOKS 1972; B72M, C27T{SC}

Mother: Medium to large, roundish-oval fruit; skin golden yellow, nearly covered with bright deep-red; flesh creamy-yellow, tender, juicy, very mildly subacid, aromatic, with a rich distinctive flavor; quality excellent; season late September to January. Tree upright-spreading, moderately vigorous and productive. Originated in Bolton, Massachusetts prior to 1844. BEACH; A39, A91, A91{SC}, B27M, B72M, C27T{SC}, E84{OR}, G92, J93{SC}, L1, L12, M22, N24M

Muster: Small, flat-round fruit; striking orange-red or pink skin with prominent brown or grey spots; flesh pure-white, coarse but crisp, very sweet; quality excellent; ripens in early September. An old American cultivar of unknown origin; first described in 1869. L12, M23M{SC}

Norda: Medium-sized fruit; skin green to yellow, overlaid with red; quality and flavor good; suitable for dessert or cooking, also dries well with very little discoloration of the clear white flesh; ripens in late September; keeps well. Tree very hardy. Developed at the Beaverlodge Research Station, Alberta, Canada. B47, F67, N24M

Nova Easygrow:[4] Large, oblate fruit; skin greenish-yellow, 80% covered with red stripes, moderately attractive; flesh white, crisp, juicy, medium-fine in texture; flavor sweet and sprightly; quality good. Tree moderately vigorous and productive; blooms one day after McIntosh. Strongly resistant to scab; resistant to powdery mildew, cedar rust, and fire blight. A39, C27T{SC}, C58, E91M, F53, I36, J93{SC}, M22, N24M

Ohio Nonpareil: Medium to large, roundish-oblate fruit; skin yellow, overspread with bright red, mottled and striped with carmine; flesh tinged with yellow, crisp, tender, juicy, agreeably subacid, aromatic; quality good to very good; season October and November. Tree medium-sized, spreading, moderately vigorous; hardy. Originated near Massillon, Ohio; first described in 1848. BEACH; A91, A91{SC}, H49, L12

Opalescent: Large to very large, roundish-conic fruit; skin glossy, takes a brilliant polish, bright pale yellow overspread with dark red, very attractive; flesh distinctly tinged with yellow, firm, somewhat coarse, juicy, mildly subacid, aromatic; quality good to very good; season November to February. Tree vigorous, roundish. Originated in Barry County, Michigan; introduced about 1899. BEACH; A91, A91{SC}, B27M{SC}, B72M, C27T{SC}, E84{OR}, H65, K83M, L12

Orenco: Medium to large, roundish fruit; skin nearly solid bright red, attractive; flesh white, tender, juicy, crisp, sweet, mild but piquant; dessert quality high; ripens in mid-September. Tree moderately vigorous, upright-spreading; unproductive; resistant to scab. Introduced by the Oregon Nursery Company of Orenco, Oregon in 1920. BROOKS 1972; A91, A91{SC}, B72M, E84{OR}, J93{SC}, L1, L12, M22, M23M{SC}

Orleans Reinette: (Orleans) Medium to large, flat-round fruit; skin dull golden-yellow blushed with dull orange, covered with patches of grey-brown russet; flesh yellow, very crisp, very juicy, sweet, with a distinct rich nutty flavor; ripens in September and October. Tree vigorous, upright-spreading; hardy; prolific; spur-bearing. Probably of French origin; first described in 1776. SANDERS, SIMMONS 1978; A39, J93{SC}, L12, M22, M23M{SC}

Ortley: Fruit medium to large; oblong-conic, flattened at the base; skin waxy, whitish-yellow to rich yellow; flesh whitish tinged with yellow, crisp, tender, juicy, sprightly subacid; quality very good; season October to February. Tree medium to large, upright, moderately vigorous. Originated in New Jersey, prior to 1817. BEACH; A53{PR}, A91, A91{SC}, B27M{SC}, B72M, L1{OR}, L12

Palouse: Fruit large; oblong-conic, ribbed or scalloped; bright yellow skin, blushed with crimson, splashed and dotted with darker red; flesh yellowish, crisp, tender, juicy, subacid, very aromatic; quality very good; season October. Tree very productive. Originated in Whitman County, Washington, from seed brought from Illinois in 1879. BEACH; A91, A91{SC}, C27T{SC}, J93{SC}, L12

Patterson: Small to medium, slightly oblate fruit; skin greenish-yellow, blushed with red; flesh very mildly subacid, flavor and quality excellent; ripens in midseason; keeps well. Tree extremely hardy. Originated in Saskatoon, Saskatchewan, Canada. Introduced in 1960 for home gardens. BROOKS 1972; B47, F67, G54, M35M

Pettingill:[2] Large, round fruit; skin green overlaid with deep-red; flesh nearly white, firm, crisp, moderately acid; suitable for dessert, good for baking, cooking and sauces; ripens early September to mid-October; keeps and ships well. Tree large, upright, vigorous; very productive; a regular bearer. Low chilling requirement. Originated in Seal Beach, California. BROOKS 1972; *C54*, I83M

Pink Lady:[5] Medium-sized, round-conical fruit; skin yellow overlaid with carmine; flesh pink, fading towards the core, very juicy, medium sweet, aromatic, flavor very good; ripens early to mid-October, does not keep well. Tree small, moderately vigorous, spreading; very productive, requires thinning. Pink Pearl x King of the Pippins. Originated in Rockton, Ontario, Canada by Frederic Janson. B72M, M22, N24M

Pink Pearl:[5] Medium-sized, roundish-oblong fruit; skin transparent, glowing pink from the flesh beneath, extremely aromatic when broken; flesh bright pink, crisp, juicy, rich and sweet; dessert quality very good, also makes a colorful sauce or pie filling; ripens in September. Originated in Ettersburg, California by Albert F. Etter. Introduced in 1944. BROOKS 1972; A53{PR}, A55{ES}, A91, B27M, B53, B72M, *C54*, E84, F11, G92, I99M{DW}, J93{SC}, L1, L1{ES}, L12, M23M, M23M{SC}, N24M, etc.

Pink Pearmain:[5] Fruit larger than Pink Pearl; distinctly shaped; skin red-striped when mature; flesh deeper pink than Pink Pearl, more tart, with the distinctive aromatic flavor that characterizes pink-fleshed apples; ripens in late September, about a month after Pink Pearl. Probably a creation of Albert F. Etter; found growing in an old orchard; named and introduced by Greenmantle Nursery. E84

Pitmaston Pineapple: Small, broadly conical fruit; skin golden-yellow, almost covered with a fine fawn russet; flesh yellowish, crisp, very juicy, sweet, subacid, rich, with somewhat of a pineapple-like flavor; ripens in September and October. Tree small, upright, very suitable for small gardens; productive. Originated in England about 1785. SIMMONS 1978; A53{PR}, B27M{SC}, B72M, C27T{SC}, E84{OR}, J93{SC}, L1, L12

Pomme Royal: (Garden Royale, Dyer) Medium to large, roundish fruit; skin clear pale yellow, more or less flecked with thin russet; flesh yellowish-white, fine-grained, very crisp, tender, aromatic, sprightly, mildly subacid, highly flavored; quality excellent; season September and October. Tree yields good crops biennially. Origin uncertain; known in cultivation during the Revolutionary War. BEACH; A91, A91{SC}, B72M, D37, L12

Porter: Medium to large, conical fruit; skin clear bright yellow, with a faint red blush; flesh yellow, crisp, tender, juicy, subacid, agreeably aromatic, sprightly; quality good to very good for dessert or culinary uses; season September to November. Tree medium to large, vigorous; hardy; precocious; productive. Originated about 1800 with Rev. Samuel Porter, Sherburne, Massachusetts. BEACH; A91, A91{SC}, B72M, E84{OR}, J93{SC}, L12

Prima:[4] Medium to large, round fruit; skin bright yellow, 60% covered with dark red blush; flesh white, juicy, mild, subacid; quality good; ripens 10 days ahead of McIntosh. Tree moderately vigorous, spreading; bears annually when properly thinned. Both fruit and foliage are immune to scab and resistant to fire blight, cedar rust, and mildew. A53{PR}, C27T{SC}, C58, F53, H49{DW}, J61M, J93{SC}, L33, M22, M23M{SC}, N24M

Priscilla:[4] Medium-sized, slightly conical fruit; skin yellow, 65% covered with bright red blush; flesh white to slightly greenish, crisp, coarse, mildly subacid; quality good; ripens with Jonathan. Tree moderately vigorous, spreading. Immune to scab. Resistant to fire blight, powdery mildew, and cedar rust. Good pollinator for Prima. A53{PR}, C27T{SC}, C58, F53, J93, L12, M23M{SC}, N24M

Red Delicious: Fruit medium-sized, long and tapering; skin striped, or solid red with yellowing; flesh white, juicy, sweet; ripens in midseason. Tree large, upright and spreading; very susceptible to scab. Most widely grown apple in the world. Originated in Iowa. STEBBINS; A82, *C47*, *D35M*{ES}, E4, *E45*, F93, G53M, G72, G99, H33, I9M, J32, J32{DW}, J33, J69{DW}, K84M{PR}, L30, M31T{ES}, etc.

Ribston Pippin: Medium-large, round-conical fruit; skin greenish-yellow, blushed and striped with brownish-orange and red; flesh yellow, very firm, crisp, fine-grained, richly sweet, very aromatic; quality excellent; season September and October. Tree vigorous, spreading; bears fruit on short spurs. Originated in England from seed brought from France in about 1688; parent of Cox's Orange Pippin. SANDERS, SIMMONS 1978; A91, A91{SC}, B27M{SC}, B72M, C27T{SC}, E84{OR}, G65M, G79M{DW}, J93{SC}, L1, L12, M22, N24M

Royal Gala: Medium-sized, conic to round fruit; skin solid orange-red, brighter overall red than Gala; flesh yellow-white, firm, juicy, fine-textured; flavor sweet, slightly tart; ripens with Gala, hangs well on the tree. Vigorous, compact tree; prolific, tends to overbear; pollinates Red Delicious and Granny Smith. A53{PR}, F15{PR}, I83M, *K73M*, L33, L33{DW}, M39M, N33

Sekai Ichi: Very large fruit, up to 2 pounds if properly thinned; skin pale pink to darker red; flesh crisp, breaking, juicy, very sweet, mild; quality excellent. One of the highest priced apples in Japan where for the family dessert, a single apple is generally served on a plate in the center of the table from which slices are dispensed. B72M, C27T{SC}, L12{CF}, M23M{SC}

Sierra Beauty: Large, blocky fruit; skin greenish-yellow, striped and blushed with red, attractive; flesh juicy, very crisp, sprightly, tart; dessert quality very good; ripens September to October, keeps very well. An old California cultivar; still grown commercially in Boonville. A53{PR}, A88M, *C54*, E84{OR}, F11, G92, J93{SC}, L1, L1{PR}, L99M, *N20*

Signe Tillisch: Large, flat-round fruit; skin light green or creamy yellow, blushed with pink or orange, waxy; flesh crisp, breaking, juicy, with a fine vinous flavor; quality excellent for dessert or cooking; ripens the first 2 weeks of September. Originated in Denmark; first described in 1889. Considered one of the best dessert apples in Sweden. B72M, L12, M23M{SC}, N24M

Sir Prize:[4] Large, greenish-yellow fruit; skin very thin and tender, bruises easily; flavor slightly acidic; quality good; resembles Golden Delicious. Tree strong, vigorous, hardy; immune to scab; resistant to mildew and cedar rust. Good home garden cultivar, but too tender for commercial markets. A53{PR}, C58, J93{SC}

Skinner's Seedling: (Santa Clara King) Large to very large, oblate fruit; skin rich lemon-yellow, faintly striped with bright red; flesh yellowish-white, very tender, juicy, sprightly, mildly subacid, very aromatic; quality excellent for dessert or sauce; season September and October. Tree vigorous, productive. Originated with Judge H.C. Skinner of San Jose, California, prior to 1870. WICKSON; E84, G92, L1, M23M{SC}

Smokehouse: Fruit above medium to large, roundish-oblate; skin yellow, mottled and striped with bright-red; flesh slightly tinged with yellow, crisp, firm, very juicy, mildly subacid, delicately aromatic, with an agreeable but not high flavor; quality good; season October to February or March. Tree vigorous; hardy; rather precocious; productive. Originated in Lancaster County, Pennsylvania prior to 1837. BEACH; A5, A53{PR}, A91, A91{SC}, B27M{SC}, B53, B53{DW}, B72M, E84{OR}, H65, I76M{PR}, L1, L12, L27M, M23M{SC}, N24M, etc.

Somerset of Maine: Fruit large; skin bright yellow, covered with splashes and stripes of brilliant red; flesh often attractively stained with red, tender, juicy, agreeably subacid; should not be allowed to get over-ripe on the tree. Tree very vigorous, upright-spreading. Originated in Mercer, Maine; first recorded in 1849. A91, A91{SC}, B72M, L12, M23M{SC}

Sops of Wine: Medium to large, roundish fruit; skin greenish-yellow, almost entirely overspread with purplish-red; flesh yellowish often stained with pink, soft, juicy, aromatic, mild, pleasant, subacid; quality good; season August to October. Tree vigorous, precocious. A very ancient English apple; described by Ray in 1688. BEACH; A91, A91{SC}, B27M{SC}, B53, B72M, E84{OR}, H65, J67{SC}, L1, L12

Spartan: Fruit medium-sized, flat-round to roundish-conical; skin solid mahogany red; flesh white, very firm, crisp, juicy, fairly sweet, quality and texture very good, fully equal to McIntosh; ripens 2 to 3 weeks later than McIntosh. Tree upright-spreading; bears heavy crops annually. McIntosh x Yellow Newtown Pippin. BROOKS 1972; A5, A53{PR}, B83, C58, E70M{PR}, F53, G41, *G66*, G69M, G99, I76M{PR}, J6{PR}, J61M, L12, L27M, L97, M31T{ES}, M39M, etc.

Spencer: Medium to large, oblong fruit; skin greenish-yellow, largely blushed with bright scarlet, attractive; flesh creamy-white, crisp, firm, juicy, subacid; quality extremely high; matures about 3 weeks later than McIntosh. Tree vigorous, upright, spreading; very hardy; slow to come into bearing but then high yielding. Originated in Summerland, British Columbia, Canada. BROOKS 1972; C27T{SC}, L12, L27M, M23M{SC}, M92, N24M

Spigold: Large to very large, oblong-conical fruit; skin golden yellow, highly blushed and striped with red, very attractive; flesh creamy-white, very firm and crisp, fine-grained, melting, sweet, sprightly; dessert quality exceptionally high; ripens through October. Tree very vigorous; productive; requires a pollinator. Red Spy x Golden Delicious. A34, A53{PR}, D69, E84, G41, G99, H65, J67{SC}, J93, J93{SC}, *K73M*, L1, L12, M23M, M23M{SC}, etc.

Splendour: Medium-large, roundish fruit; skin yellow, blushed with pinkish-red; flesh yellow, crisp, firm, juicy, very sweet, flavor mild but distinctive; ripens in early September; keeps extremely well for a fall apple. Tree vigorous, spreading; productive. Originated in New Zealand, where it is a commercial export apple. A53{PR}, A69G{SC}, B72M, C27T{SC}, E84, G65M, J93, J93{SC}, L1, M23M, M23M{SC}

St. Edmund's Pippin: (St. Edmund's Russet) Fruit small to medium; flat-round to round conical; skin golden-yellow, heavily covered with fine grayish-golden russet; flesh creamy-white, fairly firm, tender, juicy; flavor very rich and quite sweet but with a nice balance of acidity; season late September to early October. Tree upright-spreading, hardy. Raised about 1870 at Bury St. Edmund's, England. SANDERS, SIMMONS 1978; B72M, C27T{SC}, E84{OR}, J93{SC}, L1{OR}, L12, L27M, M22, M23M{SC}, N24M

Stearns: Very large, roundish-conical fruit; skin yellow, striped with red; flesh crisp, melting, tender, with a rich pure apple flavor; quality excellent for dessert or cooking; ripens in early September. Originated in North Syracuse, New York prior to 1900. B27M, B72M, J93{SC}, L12, M23M, M23M{SC}

Sweet Sixteen: Medium to large, roundish-conical fruit; skin red-striped; flesh cream-colored, firm, crisp, juicy, subacid, aromatic, with a pleasant anise-like flavor; ripens just after McIntosh; keeps well. Tree cold hardy; precocious; blooms late; annually productive; resistant to scab and fire blight. Released by the Minnesota Agricultural Experiment Station. A53{PR}, A91, A91{SC}, B72M, C27T{SC}, D65, D65{DW}, F53, *G4*, *G66*, G67, *H90*{DW}, J93, J93{SC}, L27M, L70, L70{DW}, M23M{SC}, N24M, etc.

Tangowine: Fruit medium-sized; round to slightly elongated; skin dark red over yellow; flesh smooth, medium tender, moderately juicy, pleasantly subacid; quality good; ripens about with McIntosh, keeps well in common storage. Some resistance to scab. Tree large, vigorous, spreading; hardy; produces spurs freely. Originated in Petitcodiac, New Brunswick, Canada. BROOKS 1972; C58

Thornberry:[5] Small, finely formed fruit; translucent yellow skin; flesh raspberry-pink, sprightly, refreshing, with a unique berry-like flavor, not as sweet as Pink Pearl; ripens 2 months later than Pink Pearl; hangs well on the tree. Originated by Albert F. Etter. E84

Twenty Ounce: (Cayuga Redstreak) Very large, roundish to round-conic fruit; skin yellow, washed and splashed with bright red; flesh whitish, coarse, moderately tender, juicy, subacid; suitable for dessert or culinary use; season late September to early Winter. Tree moderately vigorous, upright; precocious; productive. Of uncertain American origin; first recorded about 1844. BEACH; A91, A91{SC}, B72M, C27T{SC}, E84, H65, I36, J67{SC}, L1, L12, M22, *M59M*, N24M

Wagener: Medium to large, oblate fruit; skin glossy, clear pale yellow, striped and mottled with bright pinkish-red; flesh whitish slightly tinged with yellow, fine-grained, crisp, juicy, subacid, aromatic, sprightly; quality excellent; season October or November. Tree small to medium. Originated in Penn Yan, New York from seed planted in 1791. BEACH; A53{PR}, A91, A91{SC}, B27M, B72M, E84, G67, G92, H65, J67{SC}, J93{SC}, L1, L1{PR}, L12, M22, N24M, etc.

Washington Strawberry: Medium to large, globular fruit; skin greenish or yellow, prominently splashed and striped with bright carmen; flesh whitish tinged with yellow, firm, crisp, very juicy, pleasantly subacid, sprightly; quality good to very good; season September or October. Tree vigorous, spreading; hardy; precocious; reliably productive. Originated in Washington County, New York prior to 1849. BEACH; A91, A91{SC}

Wealthy: Medium to large, roundish-conic fruit; skin pale yellow or greenish, blushed and striped with red; flesh whitish sometimes stained with red, crisp, tender, very juicy, agreeably subacid, sprightly, somewhat aromatic; quality good to very good for dessert or culinary uses; season October to January. Tree small to medium, moderately vigorous; very hardy. Originated in Excelsior, Minnesota prior to 1869. BEACH; A91{SC}, B72M, D65, D65{DW}, D69, E84, G16, G65M, G92, H65, *H90*{DW}, I97{PR}, J67{SC}, L1, L27M, M31T{ES}, M39M, etc.

Westfield Seek-No-Further: Medium-sized, roundish-conical fruit; deep yellow skin, overspread with bright pinkish-red, striped with deep carmine; flesh slightly tinged with pale yellow, crisp, tender, juicy, mildly subacid, rich, peculiarly aromatic, sprightly; dessert quality excellent. Tree medium to large, vigorous, spreading; very hardy. Originated in Westfield, Massachusetts prior to 1845. BEACH; A91, A91{SC}, B27M{SC}, B53, B72M, C27T{SC}, C58, D69, E84{OR}, G65M, H65, L1, L12, L27M, M23M{SC}, N24M, etc.

Winesap: Medium-sized, round to oblong fruit; skin yellow heavily striped with red; flesh yellow, firm, coarse, juicy; flavor sprightly, slightly acid; ripens midseason to late, keeps well. Good for dessert or canning. Tree vigorous, slow to come into bearing. First described in 1817. SIMMONS 1978, STEBBINS; A82{DW}, A85M, E4, *E45*, E84, F11, *G66*, G72{DW}, G79M{DW}, J69{DW}, L1{OR}, L90, M22, M31T{ES}, M76{DW}, etc.

Wolf River: Fruit large to very large; broad and flat at the base, often somewhat irregular; skin pale bright yellow, blushed with bright deep-red; flesh slightly tinged with yellow, moderately coarse, tender, juicy, subacid; dessert quality fair to good; season September to December. Tree large, moderately vigorous, very spreading; very hardy. Originated near Wolf River, Wisconsin prior to 1875. BEACH; A91, A91{SC}, C58, D69, E84{OR}, E97, F53, G16, G16{DW}, H65, J32, J67{SC}, L1{OR}, L27M, L70, etc.

WINTER HARVESTING

Adam's Pearmain: (Norfolk Pippin) Fruit medium-sized; conical to long-conical; skin pale golden-yellow, prominently blushed with dull crimson-red, attractive; flesh creamy-white, crisp, juicy, aromatic; quality excellent; season November to March. Tree moderately vigorous, wide-spreading; partially tip-bearing; tends toward biennial bearing. Of English origin. Introduced in 1826. SANDERS, SIMMONS 1978; B72M, C27T{SC}, E84{OR}, G92, L12, M22, M23M{SC}, N24M

Arkansas Black: Medium-sized, nearly round fruit; skin covered with bright red, deepening to purplish-red on the exposed side; flesh yellow, very firm, crisp, moderately juicy, sprightly subacid, quality very good; season December to April or later. Tree moderately vigorous, upright-spreading; unproductive. Originated in Benton County, Arkansas, and bore its first fruit about 1870. BEACH; A39, A53{PR}, A82, C75M, C75M{DW}, E4, E84, F11, F93, G99, J93, J93{SC}, K84M{PR}, L1, L1{PR}, *L47*, L99M, M23M{SC}, etc.

Ashmead's Kernel: Medium-sized, flat-round fruit; skin pale greenish-yellow, prominently covered with cinnamon-brown russet; flesh yellowish-white, firm, crisp, juicy, highly aromatic, subacid; dessert quality excellent; season December to February. Tree moderately vigorous, upright-spreading; bears irregularly. Raised about 1720 by a Dr. Ashmead of Gloucester, England. SANDERS, SIMMONS 1978; A53{PR}, A91, A91{SC}, B72M, C34, G65M, G92, I49M, J61M, J93, J93{SC}, L1, L12, L27M, M23M{SC}, etc.

Baldwin: Large, roundish-conic fruit; skin light yellow, blushed and mottled with bright red; flesh yellowish, very firm, crisp, juicy, agreeably subacid, sprightly; quality very good for dessert and culinary uses; season November to March or April. Tree large, very vigorous, upright-spreading; very productive. Originated near Lowell, Massachusetts, about 1740. BEACH; A53{PR}, A91, A91{SC}, B53, B72M, *D35M*, D74M{PR}, E84, G65M, G79M{DW}, G92, H65, I36, L1, L1{PR}, L12, M23M{SC}, M92, etc.

Belle de Boskoop: Medium to large, roundish-oval fruit; skin golden yellow, mottled, dotted and striped with bright red; flesh creamy yellow, aromatic, firm, coarse, rather dry; good for dessert, excellent for cooking; season December to April. Tree vigorous, upright-spreading; spur-bearing; productive. Originated in Boskoop, Holland about 1856. SANDERS, SIMMONS 1978; A69G{SC}, E84{OR}, G92, J61M, J93{SC}, L12, M22, M23M{SC}, N24M

Ben Davis: Medium to large, roundish-conic fruit; skin waxy, clear yellow blushed with bright red, striped and splashed with bright dark-carmine; flesh whitish, moderately coarse, not very crisp, somewhat aromatic, juicy, mildly subacid; quality good; season January to June. Tree vigorous, upright; hardy; precocious; annually bears heavy crops. An American apple of unknown origin; first recorded in 1857. BEACH; A53{PR}, B27M{SC}, B72M, C27T{SC}, G99, J67{SC}, L12, M23M{SC}

Black Ben Davis: (Gano) Medium to large, roundish-ovate fruit; skin almost completely overspread with brilliant red, becoming dark purplish-red on the exposed cheek; flesh whitish, somewhat coarse, moderately juicy, mildly subacid; quality good; season January to April or May. Tree vigorous, upright, spreading. Said to have originated about 1800 on the farm of M. Black in Washington County, Arkansas. BEACH; B72M

Black Gilliflower: (Sheepnose) Medium to large, long-ovate fruit; skin striped or mostly covered with red, deepening to dark purplish-red or almost black; flesh whitish, firm, rather coarse, moderately juicy eventually becoming dry, mildly subacid, rich, peculiarly aromatic; good for dessert and specialty markets; season November to January or February. Tree large, moderately vigorous, upright-spreading. An American apple of uncertain origin; known in Connecticut as early as the latter part of the 18th century. BEACH; A53{PR}, A91, A91{SC}, B27M{SC}, B53, B72M, C27T{SC}, E84{OR}, G79M{DW}, H65, J67{SC}, L1, L12, M22, M23M{SC}, etc.

Blacktwig: (Paragon) Medium-sized, roundish fruit; skin yellowish, largely covered with dull deep-red; flesh greenish, slightly coarse, juicy, mildly subacid, somewhat aromatic; quality good to very good; season January to May. Tree moderately vigorous, roundish. Originated near Fayetteville, Tennessee, from a seed planted about 1830. Once very popular in the South. BEACH; B72M, G65M, L1, L1{PR}, L12

Braeburn: Medium to large, oval fruit; skin glossy, covered with short stripes of dark crimson, 75% overlaid with dark scarlet blush; flesh pale cream, firm, crisp, very juicy, mildly sweet; quality excellent; ripens very late, keeps well in storage. Tree moderately vigorous, spreading; precocious; productive, with a slight tendency toward biennial bearing. Originated in Nelson, New Zealand. Introduced in 1952. BROOKS 1972; A5, A39, B27M{SC}, B72M, B83, F15{PR}, *G38M*, J93, J93{SC}, M23M, M23M{SC}, M39M

Bullock: (American Golden Russet) Small to medium, roundish-conic fruit; skin attractive, pale yellow, more or less overspread and splashed with thin russet; flesh slightly tinged with yellow, crisp, very tender, juicy, with an agreeable rich, spicy, mildly subacid flavor; quality excellent for dessert or cider; season October to January. Tree vigorous, upright. Originated in Burlington County, New Jersey prior to 1817. BEACH; L27M, M22

Calville Blanc d'Hiver: (White Winter Calville) Fruit medium to large; flat-round, with uneven ribs terminating in unequal ridges at the base; skin pale green with white dots, turning golden yellow in storage; flesh tender, sweet, juicy, aromatic, with a delicate spicy flavor; very high in vitamin C. Tree weak-growing; bears irregularly; requires a warm, sunny location. The classic dessert apple of France; first recorded in 1627; still served for dessert in the finest Paris restaurants. A53{PR}, A55{ES}, E84{OR}, G65M, G79M{DW}, G92, H65, I36, I49M, J93, J93{SC}, L1, L1{ES}, L99M, M22, etc.

Canada Red: (Red Canada) Medium to large, roundish fruit; skin largely overspread with a deep red blush, indistinctly striped with darker red; flesh whitish, crisp, juicy, aromatic, rich, agreeably subacid but becoming too mild toward the end of the season; quality very good; season November to March. Tree moderately vigorous, upright. Probably originated in New England prior to 1822. BEACH; B72M, E84{OR}, L12, M23M{SC}

Canada Reinette: Medium to large, roundish-conic fruit; skin yellow, sometimes blushed, marked with dots or patches of russet; flesh tinged with yellow, firm, moderately tender, coarse, not crisp, juicy, subacid; quality very good; season early winter to March or April. Tree moderately vigorous, spreading. Origin unknown; recorded in France as early as 1771. BEACH; A91, A91{SC}, B72M, G79M{DW}

Claygate Pearmain: Medium-large, oblong-conical fruit; skin dull yellowish-green, slightly covered with grayed-orange blush and light-gray russet; flesh whitish tinged slightly green, crisp, juicy, aromatic, with a rich almost nutty flavor; season December to March. Small, compact tree; very suitable for a small garden; vigorous, upright-spreading; very productive. Originated in Claygate, Surrey, England. Introduced about 1823. SANDERS, SIMMONS 1978; B72M, J93{SC}, L12

Connell Red: (Connell Fireside) Large, slightly conic fruit; skin dark-red, smooth, glossy; flesh creamy white, juicy, firm, tender, crisp, mildly acid; quality high; ships and stores well until April and May. Tree very hardy; very productive. Bud mutation of Fireside. Originated in Dunn County, Wisconsin. BROOKS 1972; A53{PR}, *A74*, *A74*{DW}, D65, D65{DW}, F53, *G4*, G67, I97{PR}, J32, J83{DW}, L27M, L70, L70{DW}, N24M, etc.

Cornish Gilliflower: Fruit medium-large; oblong to oblong-conical; skin deep yellow-green, blushed and streaked dull-red; flesh pale yellow, very firm, very juicy, with a clove-like perfume, flavor sweet and rich; quality excellent; season December to May. Tree moderately vigorous, very spreading; a tip-bearer. Discovered in a cottage garden near Truro, England about 1800. SANDERS, SIMMONS 1978; A91, A91{SC}, B72M, E84{OR}, J93{SC}, L12, M22, M23M{SC}

Court Pendu Plat: (Wise Apple) Fruit medium-sized; round, very flattened at base and apex; skin greenish-yellow, covered with orange-red blush and slight russet; flesh creamy-white, very firm, fairly juicy, aromatic; flavor rich, with a good balance of acid and sugar; season December to April. Tree small, weak-growing, upright-spreading; productive; blooms late. An ancient apple; widely planted in Tudor times. SANDERS, SIMMONS 1978; B72M, C27T{SC}, E84{OR}, F43M, G92, J93{SC}, L12, M22, M23M{SC}

Criterion: Medium to large, long conical fruit, resembles Red Delicious; skin light greenish-yellow, often blushed with rose, very attractive; flesh firm, mild in flavor, quality very good; ripens in October, stores very well. Tree vigorous and productive. A chance seedling found near Parker, Washington in 1968. A53{PR}, A69G{SC}, C27T{SC}, H65, L30, N24M

D'Arcy Spice: Medium-sized, oblong fruit; skin pale greenish-yellow, covered with fine gray russet; flesh white tinged with green, firm, juicy, richly aromatic, with a sweet yet acid, spicy flavor; quality very good; in season from November to April. Requires a hot, dry summer to develop a spicy flavor. Tree of weak and slow growth, moderately productive, tends toward biennial bearing. Originated in England. Introduced about 1850. SANDERS, SIMMONS 1978; M22

Esopus Spitzenberg: Medium to large, roundish-ovate fruit; skin predominantly covered by bright red, attractive; flesh tinged with yellow, crisp, juicy, aromatic, sprightly subacid; quality excellent; season November to February. Tree moderately vigorous, spreading; moderately productive. Originated at Esopus, New York in the late 18th century. Thomas Jefferson's favorite apple. BEACH; A53{PR}, A55{ES}, D37, E84, F11, G79M{DW}, H65, J93{SC}, K84M{PR}, L1, L1{ES}, L1{PR}, L7M, L30, L99M, M31T{ES}, M39M, etc.

Fireside: Large, conical fruit; skin medium-red, lightly striped with darker red; flesh yellowish, medium coarse, moderately tender and juicy, mildly subacid; dessert quality very good; season of use November to April; resembles Red Delicious. Tree vigorous; hardy; resistant to cedar rust. BROOKS 1972; *A74*, A91, A91{SC}, B72M, D65, D65{DW}, E97, F53, *G4*, G65M, G67, *I82*{DW}, J32, L12, L27M, L70, N24M, etc.

Gilpin: (Carthouse) Small to medium, roundish-oblong fruit; skin very smooth and attractive, richly streaked with deep red and yellow; flesh yellow, firm, juicy and rich, becoming tender and sprightly in the spring. Highly regarded for cider in the 1800's. Tree vigorous, spreading, very hardy and productive. B72M, C27T{SC}, L12

Golden Harvey: Small, irregularly round fruit; skin russet yellow with a red cheek, rather rough; flesh yellow, very fine-grained, with a spicy, rich subacid flavor; ripens late. Excellent for dessert or cider. The skin is well known for brandy making. Tree of slender growth, bears well. Originated in Herefordshire, England, likely in the 1600's. B72M

Golden Nugget: (Golden Nugget Spur) Small, broadly-conical fruit; skin predominantly yellow, streaked and splashed with bright orange, sometimes netted and spotted with russet; flesh fine-grained, crisp, very sweet and rich, quality excellent; keeps well. Tree moderately vigorous. Golden Russet x Cox's Orange Pippin. Originated in Kentville, Nova Scotia, Canada. BROOKS 1972; A91, A91{SC}, B72M, C58, D76, G72, J93{SC}, L12, N24M

Golden Russet: Medium-sized, roundish fruit; usually almost entirely covered with yellow or golden russet; flesh yellowish, moderately crisp, tender, juicy, rich, agreeably subacid, quality excellent for dessert, culinary use and cider; season December to April or later. Tree vigorous, spreading; hardy; productive. Very old cultivar of unknown origin. BEACH; A53{PR}, A91, A91{SC}, C58, E84{OR}, F53, G23, G41, G65M, G67, G79M{DW}, G92, G99, H65, J67{SC}, J93{SC}, L1, L27M, etc.

Granny Smith: Medium-sized, roundish fruit; skin grass-green, with conspicuous whitish or pinkish dots; flesh white tinged green, firm, crisp, juicy, tart; suitable for dessert, cooking and sauces; season January to April; keeps well, becoming sweeter in storage. Tree vigorous, upright-spreading; spur-bearing; requires a long season. Originated in New South Wales, Australia prior to 1868. SANDERS, SIMMONS 1978; A53{PR}, A55{ES}, C63, C75M, C75M{DW}, C89{PR}, E4, E70M{PR}, G23, I83M, J83, J83{DW}, L1{ES}, L30, M31T{ES}, M39M, N33, etc.

Green Sweet: Medium-sized, roundish fruit; skin grass-green to greenish-yellow, sometimes blushed with brownish-red; flesh greenish-white, tender, fine-grained, juicy, very sweet; quality very good for dessert and culinary uses; remains crisp, brittle and juicy till spring. Tree medium-sized, vigorous, upright; very productive. An old American cultivar of uncertain origin; first recorded in 1838. BEACH; C58

Hadlock Reinette: Fruit medium-sized; skin blushed bronze-orange, resembling Cox's Orange Pippin; flesh firm, fine-grained, moderately subacid, quality good for dessert or cider; keeps late in cold storage; resembles Golden Russet. Tree very hardy. Originated in Hammond, New York. Introduced in 1964 by Fred L. Ashworth, Heuvelton, New York. BROOKS 1972; L27M

Hudson's Golden Gem: Large to very large, conical fruit; skin covered with dull-yellow russet, very attractive; stem very long; flesh juicy, crisp, subacid, excellent for dessert; hangs on the tree a long time; ripens in late October. Tree vigorous, spreading; productive; bears annually. Originated in Oregon by A.D. Hudson. Introduced in 1931. BROOKS 1972; A53{PR}, A91, A91{SC}, B27M, B27M{SC}, B72M, E84{OR}, G92, G99, J61M, J93, J93{SC}, L1, L12, M22, M23M{SC}, N24M, etc.

Hunt Russet: Medium-sized, roundish-oblate fruit; skin golden russet, with patches of smooth bright red on the cheek; flesh whitish tinged with yellow, tender, juicy, subacid, sprightly becoming mild; quality excellent; season January to April or later. Tree moderately vigorous, upright-spreading; moderately productive. Probably originated in New England in the latter part of the 17th century. BEACH; B27M{SC}, B72M, C27T{SC}, L12

Hyde King: Large to very large, globular fruit; skin glossy, pale green or yellow, thinly blushed with red; flesh whitish, very firm and crisp, rather coarse, juicy, mildly subacid, somewhat aromatic; quality good for dessert and culinary uses; season December to April or May. Tree vigorous; annually productive. Originated prior to 1892. BEACH; E84, L12, M23M{SC}

Idared: Medium to large, roundish fruit; skin nearly solid red over yellow, attractive; flesh white, crisp, fine-grained, juicy, mild, aromatic; excellent dessert and cooking quality; keeps exceptionally well, with flavor improving in storage. Tree vigorous, upright; very productive; somewhat susceptible to fireblight. Jonathan x Wagener. BROOKS 1972; A5, A53{PR}, A91, A91{SC}, B83, C34{PR}, C58, C63, E18M{PR}, F53, G23, *G38M*, J67{SC}, J83T{PR}, J93{SC}, L97, M39M, etc.

Jonagold: Large, roundish-oblong fruit; skin yellow, highly blushed and striped with red, attractive; flesh cream-colored, firm, slightly coarse, crisp, juicy, subacid; quality excellent for dessert or cooking, rated A plus in customer taste tests of Applesource; ripens with Golden Delicious; keeps well in storage up to 6 months. Tree vigorous, spreading; productive; spur-bearing. BROOKS 1972; A5, A53{PR}, B83, C34{PR}, D37, E18M{PR}, F53, G99, H65, J6{PR}, J61M, J93{SC}, L30, M31T{ES}, M39M, etc.

Keepsake: Medium-sized, often irregular fruit; skin predominantly red; flesh light yellow, very crisp, juicy, with a semi-tart, strongly aromatic flavor. Very hard when picked in mid-October, but mellows with age and attains its peak eating quality between December and February. Stores through April. Tree resists fire blight and cedar rust. A53{PR}, *A74*, *A74*{DW}, A91, A91{SC}, C27T{SC}, D65, E84{OR}, F53, *G4*, G67, J67{SC}, L27M, N24M

King David: Small to medium, round fruit; skin medium pale green, overspread with deep dark-red, very attractive; flesh yellow, firm, crisp, juicy, sprightly, briskly subacid; quality very good for dessert, pies and cider; ripens in early November, keeps very well. Tree vigorous; hardy; precocious; productive. Probably Jonathan x Arkansas Black. Found in a fence row in Washington County, Arkansas in 1893. A39, A53{PR}, A91, A91{SC}, B27M{SC}, B72M, E84{OR}, G65M, G92, G99, L1, L12, N33

King of the Pippins: Medium-sized, oblong-conical fruit; skin yellow blushed with brownish-orange, smooth; flesh pale yellow, firm, dry, highly aromatic; flavor very rich, distinctive, vinous, somewhat almond-like; quality excellent; in season November to March. Tree moderately vigorous, upright, very productive. Susceptible to canker. Originated in England. Introduced in 1899. SANDERS, SIMMONS 1978; M22

Knobbed Russet: Unusual looking English apple. Green and yellow, sometimes streaked with scarlet on the side exposed to the sun; surface uneven, overlaid with rough grey and black russet, with welts and knobs worthy of its name. Crisp, rich, sugary, highly flavored flesh of excellent quality. First brought to notice in 1819 in Sussex. B72M, C27T{SC}, E84{OR}, L12, M22

Lady: (Christmas Apple, Pomme d'Api) Small to very small, oblate fruit; skin glossy, clear pale yellow, with a sharply outlined deep red blush, very attractive; flesh white, crisp, juicy, pleasantly aromatic, mildly subacid becoming nearly sweet; quality good to very good; season December to May. Widely used for decorations, especially for Christmas wreaths. Originated in France prior to 1628. BEACH; A53{PR}, A55{ES}, B27M{SC}, B53, B72M, E84, G79M{DW}, G92, H65, I36, L1, L1{ES}, L1{PR}, L12, M22, N24M, etc.

Lady Sweet: (Ladies Sweeting) Medium to large, roundish-conic fruit; skin greenish-yellow, overspread with bright red splashed with carmine; flesh whitish, crisp, tender, juicy, decidedly sweet, with a distinct and pleasant aroma; quality excellent for dessert or culinary uses; season November to April or May. Tree moderately vigorous, upright; precocious; annually yields heavy crops. Originated near Newburg, New York prior to 1845. BEACH; A53{PR}, B72M, C27T{SC}, L12

Limbertwig: (Old Limbertwig) Medium-sized, roundish fruit; skin greenish-yellow, largely blushed with deep red, attractive; flesh yellowish, hard, moderately fine-grained, not very crisp, juicy, aromatic, subacid; quality good; season January to March or April. Tree very productive. An old southern apple. BEACH; B27M{SC}, E84{OR}, G99, L12, M22, M23M{SC}

Malinda: Fruit medium to large; sharply conical, somewhat angular and ribbed; skin rich yellow, blushed with dull red; flesh yellowish-white, firm, juicy, very mildly subacid with a sweet after-taste; quality fair; season late winter. Tree very hardy; comes into bearing late. Originated in Orange County, Vermont; introduced into Minnesota about 1860. BEACH; G67

Mammoth Black Twig: (Arkansaw, Arkansas) Medium to large, roundish fruit; skin yellow, largely overspread with dull deep-red, obscurely striped with darker red; flesh tinged with yellow, very firm, crisp, moderately juicy, subacid; quality good; season December to May. Tree large, vigorous, upright-spreading. Originated near Rhea Mills, Arkansas, from seed planted about 1833. BEACH; A39, A53{PR}, A88M, B27M{SC}, B72M, G13, G99, J93{SC}, M23M{SC}

Margil: Small to medium-sized fruit; flat-round to conical; skin greenish-yellow to yellow, highly blushed and streaked with deep-red; flesh creamy-white, firm, rather dry, sweet, rich, aromatic; ripens in January, will keep hard and crisp well into May. Tree very small and weak-growing, well suited to small gardens. An old English cultivar, known prior to 1750. SANDERS, SIMMONS 1978; B72M, G92, J93{SC}, L12, M22, M23M{SC}, N24M

Mutsu: (Crispin) Medium to large, oblong fruit; skin golden yellow, blushed with orange on the exposed cheek; flesh creamy-white, firm, coarse but crisp, juicy, mildly subacid; dessert quality excellent, rated A plus in customer taste tests of Applesource, also good for culinary use; season late October to early April. Tree large, spreading, very vigorous; annually produces heavy crops. BROOKS 1972; A53{PR}, A55{ES}, B83, E4, E18M{PR}, E84, G23, G99, *K73M*, L1{ES}, L97, M31T{ES}, M39M, *M59M*

Norfolk Royal: Large, round to short conical fruit; skin glossy, pale yellow but almost completely blushed scarlet; flesh white with some red staining, crisp, juicy, sweet, flavor distinctive; ripens late, keeps in natural storage until February. Tree fairly vigorous, very productive. Originated in Norfolk, England. SIMMONS 1978; B72M

Northern Spy: Large, roundish-conical fruit; skin thin, tender, pale yellow highly blushed with pinkish-red; flesh yellowish, very tender, crisp, very juicy, sprightly, aromatic, subacid; quality excellent for dessert or culinary uses; season November to March or April. Tree large, vigorous, upright; very hardy; blooms very late. Originated in East Bloomfield, New York about 1800. BEACH; A5, A53{PR}, C63, C95{PR}, E18M{PR}, E84, F42M{PR}, F53, *G38M*, G92, H65, J16, J93{SC}, L97, L99M, M31T{ES}, etc.

Northwestern Greening: Medium to large, roundish fruit; skin somewhat waxy, clear pale yellow or greenish; flesh tinged with yellow, moderately crisp and firm, juicy, slightly aromatic, mildly subacid; quality good for dessert or cooking; keeps fairly well. Tree vigorous, upright; hardy; yields good crops biennially. Originated in Waupaca County, Wisconsin. Introduced in 1872. BEACH; A5, *A74*, B4, B27M, B53, C58, D65, E97, F53, *G4*, G16, G16{DW}, G67, J32, L27M, L70, N24M, etc.

Paradise Sweet: (Winter Sweet Paradise) Large, roundish-oblate fruit; skin dull-green, blushed with brownish-red; flesh fine-grained, juicy, sweet but sprightly; season early to mid-winter. Tree vigorous, upright; productive, but slow to come into bearing. Probably originated in Pennsylvania, prior to 1845. BEACH; B27M, B53, B72M, M23M{SC}

Peck's Pleasant: Medium to large, oblate fruit; skin bright waxen yellow, blushed with orange-red; flesh yellowish, crisp, juicy, pleasantly subacid, aromatic; quality very good; season October to March. Tree moderately vigorous, upright-spreading; moderately productive. Originated in Rhode Island prior to 1832. BEACH; A91, A91{SC}, B72M, C27T{SC}, H65, L12

Prairie Spy: Large, roundish fruit; skin yellow, blushed with attractive red; flesh creamy-white, crisp, juicy, subacid; dessert and culinary quality high; keeps until spring, with flavor developing and improving while in storage; resembles Northern Spy. Tree vigorous; very hardy; annually productive, but slow to bear; somewhat resistant to scab and cedar rust. BROOKS 1972; A91, A91{SC}, C27T{SC}, D65, E97, F53, *G4*, G16, G16{DW}, G67, J32, J67{SC}, J93{SC}, L27M, L70, N24M, etc.

Ralls Janet: (Ralls, Genet) Medium to large, roundish-oblate fruit; skin yellow or greenish, blushed and mottled with pinkish-red; flesh whitish, firm, crisp, juicy, subacid to sweet, aromatic, pleasant; dessert quality very good; keeps well; season December to May. Tree moderately vigorous, upright-spreading; productive; blooms late. Originated in Virginia prior to 1831. BEACH; A91, A91{SC}, B27M{SC}, B72M, C27T{SC}, E84, G65M, M23M{SC}

Raven: Small to medium-sized fruit; skin of ripe fruit in full sun dark burgundy, almost black; flesh about 50% watercore, yielding a good volume of bright red juice which has excellent flavor and balance and does not turn brown. Also makes very good dried fruit, cider, and a fine wine. Local selection from Waldron Island, Washington. J67{SC}

Reinette Ananas: (Ananas Reinette) Medium-sized, tallish round fruit; skin lemon-yellow blushed with brownish-red; flesh yellowish-white, firm, fairly soft, sweet, juicy, aromatic, with a sub-acid slightly pineapple-like flavor; ripens very late, keeps well. Tree very small and upright, suitable for small gardens, fairly productive. First recorded in 1821. SIMMONS 1978; M22, N24M

Reinette Simirenko: Fruit medium to large, sometimes obscurely ribbed; skin waxy, yellowish-green, usually blushed with pale pink on the side exposed to the sun; flesh tender, very juicy, vinous, subacid, with a very pleasant spicy after-taste; ripens in December and keeps well into spring. Tree moderately vigorous, pyramidal; precocious; high yielding. Originated in the Ukraine in the 19th century; first described in France in 1895. A53{PR}, B27M{SC}, B72M, C27T{SC}, G92, J93{SC}, M22, M23M{SC}, N24M

Ross Nonpareil: (French Pippin) Fruit small to medium; flat-round to short conical; skin pale yellow, blushed and streaked with deep-orange and red, almost covered with russet; flesh creamy-white, crisp, sweet, aromatic, with a pronounced anise-like flavor; season December to February. Tree moderately vigorous, upright; productive. Originated in Ireland; introduced into England in 1819. SANDERS, SIMMONS 1978; B72M, E84{OR}, L12

Roxbury Russet: Medium-large, oblate fruit; skin largely covered with greenish to yellowish-brown russet; flesh tinged with yellow, firm, somewhat coarse, juicy, sprightly subacid; dessert quality good to very good, excellent for juice and cider; season December to May. Tree large, vigorous, roundish-spreading; productive, but tends toward biennial bearing. Originated in Roxbury, Massachusetts, early in the 17th century. BEACH; A39, A53{PR}, A91, A91{SC}, B27M{SC}, B72M, E84{OR}, G65M, G79M{DW}, I36, J67{SC}, J93{SC}, L1, L12, M22, M23M{SC}, N24M, etc.

Royal Limbertwig: Large, round to somewhat conical fruit; skin red, with greenish-yellow stripes and white dots; flesh firm and crisp, aromatic, juicy; ripens late, keeps well. A good all purpose apple. Apple butter made from this cultivar will have an intense aroma when taken from the container. B72M, G65M

Salome: Medium-sized, roundish-oblate fruit; skin pale yellow blushed with pinkish-red, obscurely striped with carmen; flesh tinged with yellow, firm, crisp, juicy, sprightly, subacid; quality good to very good; season November to March. Tree large, vigorous, upright; very hardy; precocious. Originated in Ottawa, Illinois about 1853. BEACH; J93{SC}, L12

Sandow: Medium to large, round-oblate fruit; skin yellow overspread with dull scarlet; flesh yellowish, juicy, tender, crisp, slightly subacid, aromatic; quality very high; season mid-winter to later. Tree very upright; slightly more hardy than Northern Spy; susceptible to fireblight. Open-pollinated seedling of Northern Spy. Originated in Ottawa, Ontario, Canada. BROOKS 1972; C27T{SC}, C58, L27M, N24M

Stark: Medium to large, roundish fruit; skin yellow, blushed and mottled with red; flesh yellowish, very firm, juicy, sprightly, mildly subacid; dessert quality good, very good for baking and drying; season January to June. Originated in Ohio prior to 1867. Tree large, vigorous, upright-spreading; hardy; reliably productive. BEACH; B72M, C27T{SC}, E84, N24M

Stayman Winesap: Medium to large, roundish-conic fruit; skin greenish-yellow, highly blushed with dull-red; flesh slightly greenish, very firm, juicy, aromatic, sprightly, pleasantly subacid; quality very good; season December to May. Tree moderately vigorous, spreading; precocious; annually bears heavy crops. Originated in Leavenworth, Kansas from seed of Winesap planted in 1866. BEACH; A53{PR}, A55{ES}, A82, A91, A91{SC}, E18M{PR}, *E45*, F19M, F93, *G28*, G65M, I76M{PR}, J83T{PR}, L1, L1{ES}, L1{PR}, M31T{ES}, *M69M*, etc.

Stone: (Stone Pippin) Medium to large, roundish fruit; skin pale yellow blushed with dark red, overspread with bluish bloom; flesh nearly white tinged with yellow, somewhat coarse, juicy, mildly subacid becoming nearly sweet; quality good to very good. Tree very hardy and productive. Brought from Bethel, Vermont into Potsdam, New York about 1836 by a Mr. Stone. BEACH; B72M, L27M, M23M{SC}, N24M

Sturmer Pippin: Medium-sized, round-conical fruit; skin greenish-yellow blushed with brown; flesh yellow, very firm, crisp, juicy, rich sub-acid; quality excellent; ripens in November, at its best the following May. Requires a warm summer to ripen properly. Tree moderately vigorous, compact, productive. Originated in Suffolk, England, about 1827. SANDERS, SIMMONS 1978; M22

Surprise:[5] Small, clear green fruit; juicy, sprightly, creamy red flesh; ripens late, during October in central Virginia. Was used in the breeding program of Albert F. Etter, and is one of the parents of his well-known cultivar Pink Pearl. First recorded in England in 1831. B27M, B27M{SC}, B72M, C27T{SC}, L12, M23M{SC}

Swaar: Medium to large, roundish-oblate fruit; skin yellow covered with dots and flecks of russet, often blushed with bronze; flesh yellowish, very firm, crisp, juicy, mildly subacid, aromatic, flavor rich; dessert quality excellent; season November to March or April. Moderately vigorous, spreading tree. Originated in New York prior to 1804. BEACH; A53{PR}, B27M{SC}, B72M, E84, L1, L12, M22, M23M{SC}

Tydeman's Late Orange: Fruit medium-sized, roundish to slightly conical; skin greenish-yellow, blushed with dull brownish-purple, covered with patches of brownish-grey russet; flesh creamy yellow, firm, crisp, sweet, subacid, aromatic, rich; quality excellent; season December to April. Tree vigorous, upright-spreading; productive. Originated at the East Malling Research Station. SANDERS, SIMMONS 1978; A91, A91{SC}, B27M{SC}, B72M, E84{OR}, G92, L1{OR}, L12, M22

Vandevere: (Newtown Spitzenberg, Honey Grindstone) Medium-sized, roundish-oblate fruit; skin deep yellow, blushed and mottled with dull red, striped with carmine; flesh yellowish, crisp, tender, juicy, mildly subacid mingled with sweet, rich, aromatic; quality very good for dessert and cider; keeps until February or March. Tree vigorous, spreading. Originated in Newtown, Long Island, New York prior to 1817. BEACH; B72M, E84

Virginia Gold: Medium-sized fruit; skin smooth, waxy, clear bright yellow blushed with pink; flesh creamy-white, crisp, juicy, mildly subacid; dessert quality very good, also excellent for sauce and pies; ripens very late, does not reach maximum quality and flavor unless held in cold storage until late January. Tree productive; tends toward biennial bearing. Newtown Pippin x Golden Delicious. A5, B27M, B27M{SC}, B72M, E84{OR}, F53, G65M, L12, M76

Waltana: Medium to large fruit; skin greenish-yellow, striped with red; flesh crisp, firm, juicy, subacid; quality excellent for dessert and all culinary purposes, including cider; ripens late October into November, stores until spring; hangs well on the tree. Tree vigorous; annually productive; requires a long growing season. Originated in Ettersburg, California by Albert F. Etter. B72M, *C54*, E84, L1{OR}, L12, M23M{SC}

White Pearmain: (White Winter Pearmain) Medium to large, roundish-ovate fruit; skin slightly waxen, pale yellow lightly blushed with brownish-red; flesh slightly tinged with yellow, crisp, tender, juicy, mildly subacid, sprightly, very pleasantly aromatic; quality very good; season December to March. Tree vigorous, spreading. Originated in the Midwest prior to 1849. BEACH; A53{PR}, A55{ES}, A91, A91{SC}, B72M, B93M, E84, G92, L1, L1{ES}, L1{PR}, L12, M23M{SC}

Willow Twig: (Willow) Medium to large, roundish-conic fruit; skin pale yellowish-green, mottled and blushed with red; flesh yellowish or greenish, very firm, coarse, crisp, juicy, sprightly, slightly aromatic; quality fair to good; season of use January to May. Tree large, vigorous, upright spreading; precocious; annually productive. An American apple of uncertain origin; first recorded in 1848. BEACH; B72M, G65M

Winter Banana: Medium to large, roundish-conic fruit; skin waxy, bright pale yellow blushed with dark pinkish-red, very attractive; flesh whitish tinged with pale yellow, tender, juicy, mildly subacid, distinctly aromatic; dessert quality good, too mild for culinary use; season mid-November to April. Tree medium-sized, vigorous, spreading; precocious; very productive. Originated in Adamsboro, Indiana about 1876. BEACH; A53{PR}, A91, A91{SC}, D81M{PO}, E84, *G14*, G65M, G92, H65, I83M, L1, L1{PR}, L12, L97, M31T{ES}, etc.

Wyken Pippin: Fruit small; flattish round to slightly conical; skin greenish yellow to yellow with an orange-red flush, dotted with russet; flesh cream-colored, firm, crisp, sweet, slightly aromatic, flavor good; season December to March. Tree small, compact, upright; hardy; very productive. An old English cultivar. G92, M23M{SC}

Yates: Small fruit with bright-red, dotted skin; flesh creamy-white tinged with red, very firm, juicy, spicy, aromatic, tart; ripens late, keeps well in regular storage. Popular in the South for dessert, cider making and table decorations. Tree vigorous; very productive; semi-spur-bearing; a good pollinator. Originated in Georgia in 1813. B72M, *E45*, E84{OR}, E99M, *F5*, F19M, F93, G8, G13, G65M, G99, *K76*, M31M

Yellow Bellflower: (Bishop's Pippin) Medium to large, roundish-oblong fruit; skin pale lemon-yellow, often blushed with brownish-red on the exposed side; flesh tinged with pale yellow, crisp, tender, juicy, aromatic; excellent for pie and sauce, dessert quality very good after being held in storage for a few months. Tree very vigorous, upright spreading; hardy; fairly productive. Originated in Burlington

County, New Jersey prior to 1806. BEACH; A53{PR}, A55{ES}, B27M{SC}, B72M, *C54*, C58, E84, G65M, G92, J67{SC}, L1, L1{ES}, L1{PR}, L12, M22, M23M{SC}, etc.

Yellow Newtown Pippin: (Newton Pippin, Albemarle Pippin) Medium to large, roundish-oblate fruit; skin bright yellow, often blushed with pink; flesh yellowish, firm, crisp, tender, juicy, aromatic, subacid to tart; quality good for dessert and culinary uses; season February to May; keeps well. Tree large, vigorous, upright-spreading. Originated in Newtown, Long Island, New York early in the 18th century. George Washington's favorite apple. BEACH; A53{PR}, A55{ES}, E4, E84, F11, G65M, G99, H65, *K73M*, L1, L1{ES}, L1{PR}, L7M, L99M, M31T{ES}, M39M, M76, etc.

York Imperial: (York) Medium-sized, roundish-oblate fruit; skin yellow blushed with pinkish-red, indistinctly striped with carmine; flesh yellowish, crisp, moderately juicy, sprightly becoming mildly subacid or nearly sweet; quality good to very good; season January to April or May. Tree vigorous, upright-spreading; annually productive. Originated in York, Pennsylvania early in the 19th century. BEACH; A91, A91{SC}, B27M{SC}, B53, B72M, E18M{PR}, E84{OR}, G65M, G99, H65, I76M{PR}, J83T{PR}

APRICOT {GR}

ARMENIACA VULGARIS

ORANGE-FLESHED

Alfred: Medium-sized fruit, 1 3/8 inches in diameter, roundish; skin bright orange, sometimes with a pinkish-red blush; flesh orange, moderately juicy, medium firm, fine-grained; flavor excellent, sweet and rich; freestone; ripens early. Tree moderately vigorous; hardy; a consistent producer; blooms early but has some resistance to late frost injury; self-fruitful. I36, L12, N24M

Aprigold:[1] The first genetic dwarf apricot. Grows to only 6 feet tall at maturity. Highly colored, flavorsome fruit of good quality; ripens early. Excellent tub or container plant for the home garden. *O97*

Autumn Royal: Medium to large, somewhat flattened fruit; skin golden-orange, with a slight orange blush; flesh yellow, firm, juicy, slightly acid; ripens in late summer, being the only really late apricot known; may pitburn in hottest summers. Tree large; vigorous; produces regularly. Bud mutation of Royal with the same quality. STEBBINS; *C54*, E4, F11, G92, I83M, L99M

Chinese: (Mormon, Chinese Golden) Fruit small to medium; skin golden-orange, with a red blush, smooth in texture; flesh sweet, juicy, firm, quality fair; ripens unevenly. Tree medium-sized, spreading; hardy; precocious and heavy bearing; blooms late. Good selection for high elevation or late-frost areas. E4, *G14*, *H34*, *H90*, *I68*, L30, *L47*, L99M, M39M, M39M{DW}, M92, *N20*

Curtis: Medium-sized, round fruit; skin rich golden with a bright blush, attractive; flesh medium firm, flavor excellent when fully ripe; ripens about July 27 at South Haven, Michigan; inclined to drop when mature. Tree tall, open, slow growing. Originated in Charlotte, Michigan. BROOKS 1972; B53, K83M, L12

Davanna: A very large, attractive apricot; orange-skinned with a reddish blush and yellow flesh that is very sweet and of the highest quality. Of unknown origin; discovered by a Mr. W.E. Dancy growing in the Arkansas backyard of his daughter, Anna. Hardy and a good cropper in the Chicago area climate. L12{CF}

Deatrick: Fruit large, averages 1 3/4 inches in diameter when a heavy crop is borne, round; skin golden, slightly blushed. Tree vigorous and productive; upright; hardy, setting crops under eastern climatic conditions; tends to be bushy. Originated in Franklin County, Pennsylvania. BROOKS 1972; A5, B53, K83M

Early Golden: Small to medium, roundish oval fruit; skin smooth, pale orange blushed with carmine; flesh yellow-orange, moderately juicy and sweet, of good flavor; freestone; ripens in early August. Tree vigorous; productive; hardy. Origin unknown. WICKSON; A82, D76, F19M, G23, G23{DW}, G72, H49, H49{DW}, H65, I9M, K28, K28{DW}, *L47*, L90, *M69M*, etc.

Farmingdale: Fruit medium-sized, 1 1/2 inches in diameter, roundish; skin orange-yellow with a red blush; flesh orange, moderately juicy, flavor very good; freestone; ripens early. Tree very vigorous; productive; hardy. Originated in Geneva, New York by Robert C. Lamb. Introduced in 1965. BROOKS 1972; C75M, L12

Flora Gold: Small to medium-sized fruit with yellow skin; flesh of very good quality; ripens midseason to late. Tree relatively small but a heavy, consistent cropper; resistant to temperature fluctuations during bloom. Originated in Modesto, California by Floyd Zaiger. A88M, I83M, *N20*

Garden Annie:[1] Fruit medium to large; skin gold to yellow-gold; flesh orange, juicy, firm; semi-freestone. Tree a genetic dwarf, grows 7 to 8 feet tall; self-fruitful; bears a good crop in its 3rd year; lower chilling requirement than Royal. *C54*, E4, *I68*, *L47*, *O97*

Glengarrie: Medium-sized fruit with attractive color and good flavor. Ripens very early, before Newcastle. Tree vigorous, heavy bearing. Suitable for hot climates. *Q93*

Gold Kist:[2] Medium to large fruit; skin yellow with a red blush, has slight tendency to crack; colors 2 to 4 weeks before ripening; flesh orange, firm, flavor mild; quality very good; freestone; ripens early, or 4 to 5 weeks before Royal. Tree large, upright; vigorous; a regular and heavy bearer. Low chilling requirement; highly recommended for warm winter areas. BROOKS 1972, STEBBINS; *D23M*, *I68*, I83M, L33, *N20*

Goldcot: Fruit medium to large, nearly round; skin moderately thick, tough, golden colored; flesh medium-orange, firm, sprightly flavored; shipping quality good; ripens late. For fresh use and home processing. Tree exceptionally strong; very hardy; recommended for areas with a cold, humid climate. BROOKS 1972; A5, B53, B75, D69, D76, D76{DW}, E97, E97{DW}, F53, G16, G41, L12, L33{DW}, N24M

Golden Amber: Fruit large, uniform, symmetrical; skin light orange; flesh yellow, firm, melting, slightly acid; quality excellent; ripens mid-June to mid-July; resists pitburn well. Tree large, upright; hardy; productive; has extended period of bloom, resulting in less loss due to frost injury. A88M, E4, I83M, L1

Goldenglo:[1] Medium-sized fruit; skin golden, blushed with red; flavor mildly sweet; quality high. Tree a genetic dwarf, growing only 4 to 6 feet tall; bears the second year after planting; ornamental. Ideal tub or container plant for the home garden, terrace, balcony, conservatory or sun room. L33, *O97*

Harcot:[3] Medium to large, ovate fruit; skin orange with a slight red blush, attractive; flesh orange, firm, smooth, usually freestone; flavor and texture very good; ripens very early. Sweet, edible kernels. Tree cold hardy; vigorous and productive with good resistance to perennial canker, bacterial spot and brown rot. A88M, *D35M*, E91M, F53, G23, G41, I36, J7, K83M, *N20*, N24M

Hardy Iowa: Small to medium-sized fruit; skin light yellow, thin; flesh firm, very sweet, well-flavored; clingstone; ripens in late midseason, later than Superb which it resembles. Tree very hardy; a prolific annual bearer; blooms later than most cultivars, thus escaping many late frosts. Good for home gardens. BROOKS 1972; D76

Harogem: Fruit small to medium; skin glossy, orange with a bright-red blush, exceptionally attractive and highly colored; flesh orange, very firm, flavor and texture good; freestone; ripens mid to late season; keeps very well at room temperature and in cold storage. Tree cold hardy; consistently productive. Resistant to perennial canker and brown rot. A5, F53, G41, I36, M22, N24M

Hemskirke: Fairly large, conical fruit, somewhat flattened; skin pale yellow with red patches; flesh golden yellow, fine-grained, very sweet and rich; stone medium-sized; kernel bitter; ripens in early August. A hardy tree of stocky growth; fairly productive. SIMMONS 1978; F91T{SC}

Henderson: Fruit large, roundish; skin yellow, with a crimson blush; flesh yellow, thick, slightly fibrous, sweet; semi-clingstone; ripens in late August. Quality good fresh; very good for sauce, canning and jelly. Tree strong; vigorous; very hardy. Originated in Geneva, New York by George W. Henderson. Introduced in 1935. BROOKS 1972; D76, *K60*

Hungarian Rose: Medium to large, sheep-nosed fruit; skin bright yellow, attractive; flesh orange; flavor sweet; excellent to eat fresh, can or dry; ripens mid-July in Zone 6; susceptible to sunburn. Tree self-fruitful, relatively productive. Well known, dependable cultivar. Originated in Hungary. L33

Imola Royal: (Precoce d'Imola) A highly productive cultivar, the fruits of which are large, oval, orange-yellow tinged with red, and with firm, sweet, fragrant flesh. BIANCHINI; O71M

Katy:[2] Large, uniform fruit, slightly flattened on the sides; skin yellow-orange, blushed with red on the side exposed to the sun; flesh deep yellow, firm, freestone; ripens early. Tree strong; vigorous; upright; withstands varying temperatures during blooming season without dropping blossoms. Low chilling requirement. STEBBINS; *B71M*, *D23M*, *I68*, L33, *N20*, *O97*

Large Early Montgamet: Large, roundish fruit; skin yellow-orange mottled with red; flesh juicy, sweet and rich; quality very good. Tree vigorous, moderately productive, blooms late. High chilling requirement. An early ripening sport from the old French cultivar Montgamet, known as early as 1765. **T49M{SC}**

Lisa:[3] Dual purpose apricot. Very large, oval fruit; skin orange, blushed with red; flesh dark orange, juicy, melting, freestone; ripens from mid-July to early August; kernel free of bitterness, tasting much like an almond, high percentage of double kernels, easily removed from the shell, stores well. Tree compact, vigorous; hardy; very ornamental. H65

Luizet: Medium to large, roundish fruit; skin bright yellow, with a carmine flush and darker dots; flesh deep yellow, firm, rich and sweet; ripens in late July. Vigorous, hardy tree; produces fairly good crops. First raised in France, about 1838. SIMMONS 1978; O71M

Mah Wot: Large to very large fruit; flesh orange, very juicy, sweet, not as richly flavored as Ram Roc; similar to Ram Roc but more productive. Along with Ram Roc, considered one of the finest-flavored of all apricots. Introduced into the United States from Iran. **T49M{SC}**

Mesch-Mesch: (Mish-Mish, Musk) Small, round, rather flattened fruit; skin lemon yellow with an orange-yellow blush; flesh transparent, orange, very sweet and rich, musky; ripens during the end of July. Tree moderately vigorous; productive. Of Arabic origin. Has frequently been raised from seed, consequently there are many forms bearing this name. SIMMONS 1978; S95{S}

Moongold: Fruit medium-sized, oblate; skin orange, rather tough; flesh orange-yellow, medium juicy, sweet to slightly subacid, very pleasant, quality very good; fine for dessert and processing; freestone; ripens in late July, before Sungold. Tree vigorous; spreading; intended for the Minnesota climate; self-unfruitful, but pollinated by Sungold. BROOKS 1972; *A74*{DW}, C63, D65, D69, E97, *G89M*, H65, *H90*, J32, L70, M92

Moorpark: Large, round, sometimes slightly flattened fruit; skin maize-yellow with brownish-red flush and darker spots; flesh yellow-orange, firm, juicy, sweet, rich; stone large, free; quality excellent; sometimes one side of the fruit ripens before the other. Long considered the standard of excellence among apricots. Originated in England. Introduced about 1760. SIMMONS 1978; A82, B73M, B73M{DW}, C63, C75M, E4, F19M, G23, G23{DW}, G72, H65, J83, *K73M*, L97, N33, etc.

Morden 604: Fruit large; skin golden-yellow; flesh thick, deep orange, moderately firm, of very fine texture; flavor sweet, pleasing; excellent as dessert, preserves or jam; ripens mid-August. Tree upright, spreading, rounded; vigorous; hardy. Originated in Morden, Manitoba, Canada. BROOKS 1972; G69M, H85, K64

Newcastle: (Early Newcastle) Small to medium-sized fruit; round, with spherical pit; skin lemon yellow; flesh coarse and soft in texture, flavor good; ripens early. Tree large and vigorous; a regular and heavy bearer; needs relatively little winter chill; very subject to brown rot and bacterial gummosis. Originated in Newcastle, California. Introduced in 1881. STEBBINS, WICKSON; *C54*, *I68*, *Q93*

Nugget: Large, roundish fruit; skin well colored, reddish yellow on the side directly exposed to the sun; flesh yellow, flavor good, freestone; resembles Royal but much larger, more highly colored, and ripens earlier. Tree large, vigorous; a regular and heavy producer. BROOKS 1972; *A19*

Pêche de Nancy: (Peach Apricot) Very large, round fruit; skin pinkish-orange with a deep red blush; flesh deep yellow, soft, juicy, very rich, flavor good; ripens the end of August. Tree vigorous, fairly productive. Recommended for small gardens because it takes heavy pruning better than others. Thought to be the parent of Moorpark. SIMMONS 1978; **T49M{SC}**

Perfection: Fruit large, oval, blocky; skin pebbled, light yellow-orange, not blushed; flesh bright orange, firm, quality fair; ripens about 1 week after Wenatchee. Tree vigorous; hardy; blooms early; self-unfruitful. Preferred for commercial plantings in Washington state. Parent of many modern cultivars. BROOKS 1972; A91, B53{DW}, B67, B67{DW}, B83, B93M, C41M, E99M, F53, *G14*{DW}, *H34*, *L47*, M39M, M39M{DW}, N46, etc.

Precious:[3] Orange fruit with soft, sweet and very juicy flesh. The kernel has a sweet almond-like flavor. Largely self-fruitful, its seedlings appear to be close to the parent in fruiting characteristics. Original tree is estimated to be over 100 years old. Still produces excellent crops despite very cold winters, late frosts, and spring temperature fluctuations that would kill most apricot trees. N24M

Puget Gold: (Copeland) Medium-sized, roundish ovate fruit; skin clear yellow blushed with red-orange; flesh deep yellow-orange, firm, sweet; quality good; ripens in early August. Tree moderate to low in vigor, spreading; said to be a natural semi-dwarf. Sets and sizes fruit in cool, frosty spring weather where most other cultivars fail. Discovered in Anacortes, Washington by Jean Copeland. Introduced by Washington State University. I49M, J61M, L99M

Ram Roc: Large to very large fruit; flesh orange, exceedingly juicy, with a very rich flavor resembling that of Moorpark, of excellent quality. Rated one of the finest-flavored of all apricots. Tree relatively unproductive. Introduced into California from Iran in the 1960's. **T49M{SC}**

Reliable:[3] Fruit orange, blushed with red; texture dry and firm, maintaining firmness on the tree for about 10 days after attaining full color; dessert quality fair; ships well; not suitable for canning. Kernel sweet and edible. Tree upright-spreading, vigorous; hardy; bears regularly and heavily. BROOKS 1972; E91M{OR}

Riland: Large, flat-oval fruit; skin light yellowish with a bright, deep red blush over one-half or more; flesh slightly coarse, firm, melting; flavor rich, plum-like, somewhat acid; freestone; keeps well; ripens early, and tends to ripen from pit out. Young trees have vigorous growth and an upright form. BROOKS 1972, STEBBINS; B83, C41M, M39M, N46

Rival: Very large, oval fruit; skin light orange, blushed on the exposed side; flesh deep orange, very firm, low in acid, flavor mild; good for canning but skin turns brown; ripens early to midseason. Tree very vigorous, leggy; productive; requires an early-blooming pollinizer; more resistant to cold than Wenatchee. STEBBINS; B83, C41M, D81{PO}, F53, *H34*, M39M, N46

Royal: (Blenheim) Medium to large, oval fruit; skin pale yellow, dotted purplish-red on the side exposed to the sun; flesh yellow-orange, firm, very juicy, delicately aromatic; stone round, free; kernel bitter; ripens early to mid-season. Tree very productive; low chilling requirement. Principal commercial cultivar in the United States. *A9*, A88M, C37, C41M, *D23M*, E4, *G49*, H26M{PR}, I83M, *K73M*, L1, *L47*, L97G{PR}, M39M, N33, N46, etc.

Skaha: Large to very large, oval fruit; skin well colored with a reddish cheek; flesh orange, meaty, flavor very good when fully ripe; ripens in midseason; resembles Perfection but of better quality. Originated at the Summerland Experiment Station, British Columbia, Canada. A69G{SC}, C41M, F91T{SC}

Sundrop: Fruit medium-sized, roundish to slightly oval; skin bright-orange with a slight red blush, attractive; flesh orange, medium firm, juicy, smooth, flavor sweet and mild; semi-freestone; ripens about 2 days before Alfred. Tree productive; a reliable bearer, bearing heavily in clusters. A69G{SC}, F91T{SC}, I36

Sungold: Round to slightly elongated fruit; sin medium thin, tender, gold with an orange blush; flesh clear orange, tender, medium juicy; flavor very mild and sweet, quality very good; fine for dessert and processing; freestone; ripens in early August. Tree vigorous; exceptionally hardy; self-unfruitful but pollinated by Moongold. BROOKS 1972; *A74*{DW}, D65, D69, E97, *G89M*, H65, *H90*, J32, L70, M92

Sweet Pit:[3] Sweet-kernel type, also called *alpricots*. Fruit large, 2 1/4 to 2 1/2 inches; skin deep-orange; flesh sweet; preferred for jam, drying and roadside markets. Kernel 1/2 to 3/4 inch long, quite sweet, easy to shell, long lasting. Tree self-fertile; winter hardy to Zone 5; can be maintained at 15 feet tall. Still grown commercially in British Columbia at the northern limits of apricot culture. A91{PL}, D76, E97, G53M, J61M

Sweetheart:[3] Produces both fruit and sweet, almond-like kernels. Medium-sized, freestone fruit; juicy and firm, with a sweet, sprightly flavor; quality good for fresh eating, also very good for canning and drying; ripens mid-July in Zone 6. Tree hardy; productive; grows 15 to 20 feet tall; usually bears fruit in its third year. L33, L33{DW}

Tilton: Fruit large to very large, symmetrical; skin orange; flesh yellow-orange, fair flavor when eaten fresh; freestone; ripens evenly, and 7 to 10 days later than Royal; widely used for drying. Tree vigorous; prolific and regular bearer; high chilling requirement. *A9*, A88M, B67, B67{DW}, B83, C41M, D81{PO}, E4, *K73M*, L30, L33, *L47*, L97, L99M, M39M, M39M{DW}, etc.

V510915:[3] Medium to large, oval fruit, cracks if weather is wet; quality and flavor excellent; ripens a week later than Sundrop. Kernel plump and sweet. Tree a consistent producer; hardy. One of the best of the *alpricots*. Sibling of V60031. E91M, E91M{OR}

V60031:[3] Dual purpose apricot. Produces both a fine quality fruit and an excellent nut. Medium-sized nut with a very good flavor, fills well. Tree hardy and productive. Seedling of Reliable. E91M, E91M{OR}

Victoria: (Wilson Delicious) Fruit large; skin red; flesh firm, golden orange, flavor good; ripens in early July in Zone 6. Tree productive; hardy; blooms late. Originated in Hannibal, Missouri by H.J. Jenner. Introduced in 1948. BROOKS 1972; L33, L33{DW}

Wenatchee: (Wenatchee Moorpark) Fruit large, oval, flattened; skin and flesh orange-yellow; suffers from uneven halves and uneven ripening; texture and quality fair; ripens mid-season. Tree a heavy, annual bearer; adapted to Northwest climate conditions. Originated in Wenatchee, Washington. A69G{SC}, A88M, B67, B67{DW}, B83, *G14*, *G14*{DW}, *H34*, M39M, *N20*

Westcot: Medium to large, roundish fruit; skin yellow-orange with a reddish blush; flesh orange, fine-textured, juicy, freestone. Dessert quality very good, especially for a hardy apricot; also holds its shape after cooking. Tree vigorous and productive, has great bud hardiness. Originated in Morden, Manitoba, Canada. Introduced in 1982. A16, G1T, H85, L70, N24M

WHITE-FLESHED

Afghanistan: Medium-sized fruit; skin whitish with a red blush, very smooth; flesh white, rich, juicy, very sweet, too soft and tender for commercial use; flavor and quality excellent; one of the best dessert cultivars. Originated in Summerland, British Columbia, Canada form seeds brought from Teheran, Iran in 1957. L12{CF}

Hunza:[3] White-fleshed apricot from the Hunza region of Pakistan that also has sweet, edible kernels. F43M

Moniqui: Fruit very large, about twice the size of others; skin light cream blushed with bronze-red, velvety, very attractive; flesh juicy, tender, sweet, very low in acid, becomes mushy when fully ripe; quality good fresh or for preserves; ripens in June. Tree large, vigorous; reported to succeed in many different climatic regions of Spain. Requires 800 to 900 hours of chilling. RUCK; L12, O71M

Suphkany: Small, glossy fruit; flesh soft, very sweet. Introduced into the United States from Asia. T49M{SC}

Turkish White: Small fruit; flesh white, very sweet but balanced by some acidity, flavor excellent. Susceptible to shot hole fungus and sunburn. Tree relatively unproductive. Introduced into the United States from Iran in the 1960's. T49M{SC}

ASIAN PEAR {GR}

PYRUS PYRIFOLIA PYRUS USSURIENSIS

RED-SKINNED

Huhoot Li: Medium-sized, roundish fruit; skin highly blushed with red over a yellow ground color, smooth; flesh firm, crisp, juicy; ripens in early October. Tree cold-hardy, productive. *G37*{OR}

Nangon Li: Small to medium-sized, roundish fruit; skin light-green, blushed with red, smooth; flesh firm, crisp, juicy; ripens in early October. Tree cold-hardy, productive. *G37*{OR}

Tarusa Crimson: (Tamared) An attractive Asian pear with a pronounced red or orange blush. Ripens later than other cultivars to spread the season. Crisp when first ripe, it eventually develops a smoother texture, more like a European pear. Vigorous tree with attractive, red-hued leaves when young. Excellent commercial potential and a fine garden fruit tree. L1

YELLOW/BROWN-SKINNED

A-Ri-Rang: (Don Bae, Korean Giant) Very large round fruit, average weight over 1 pound; skin dark brown, russet; flesh very juicy, crisp, sweet, sugar content 14.5%, flavor excellent; ripens late; can be stored in non-refrigerated air cooler into late March. Tree upright-spreading; precocious; productive. A91, A91{SC}, B74, *G37*{OR}, H81M, J61M, J93, J93{SC}

Chojuro: Medium-sized fruit; skin greenish-brown to brown, russet; flesh white, mildly sweet, somewhat bland, core somewhat sour, aroma and flavor distinctive; texture firm, crisp, somewhat coarse and pulpy, some stone cells; quality good; ripens in midseason. Tree medium-sized, spreading; vigorous; very productive; requires a pollinator for best production. Introduced about 1895. GRIGGS; B67, E84, E99M, F11, *G37*, H81M, I49M, I83M, J61M, K67, L1, L12, L30, *L47*, L90, L97, L99M, etc.

Daisui Li: Large to very large fruit, weight 12 to 16 ounces; skin medium green to light green, smooth; flesh white, firm, somewhat coarse, crisp, tender, juicy, subacid to sweet, aroma distinct; ripens the first 3 weeks of September; good shipping and keeping qualities. Tree medium to large, moderately vigorous; a regular and productive bearer; blooms early, usually in the third week of March. Kikusui x Tsu Li. Originated at Davis, California by Ben Iwakiri. *K73M*

Doitsu: Small, variably shaped fruit; skin coarse, tough, predominantly light brown; flesh white, sweet, mild; texture firm, crisp, juicy, pulpy, coarse and slightly granular; quality fair; ripens in mid to late August. Tree small to medium, open, spreading; moderately productive. GRIGGS; F91T{SC}

Hosui: Medium to large, round fruit; skin greenish-brown, russet, medium tough; flesh white to off-white, firm and crisp, fine-textured, very sweet and juicy, quality excellent; ripens in July and August, harvested through November. Tree medium-sized, spreading, very vigorous; productive, requires cross-pollination. Developed in Japan. Introduced in 1972. A5, A88M, B67, B83, D34M{PR}, E4, E87, E99M, F11, *G37*, H81M, I83M, J61M, K67, *K73M*, L1, *L47*, L99M, *N40*{PR}, etc.

Ichiban Nashi: Small to medium-sized fruit; skin light yellow, russet; flesh yellowish-white, soft, juicy, sweet, tender and crisp, quality good; ripens extremely early, late June to early July, harvested through August. Tree moderately vigorous; productive, bears on spurs; pollinated by Chojuro, Kosui, Hosui and Nijisseiki. E4

Ishiiwase: Medium to large fruit; skin greenish-brown to yellowish-brown, russet; flesh white with a faint yellow cast, juicy, faintly sweet; core sour; texture firm, relatively tough, crisp, juicy, relatively few stone cells, quality fair to good; ripens early; resembles Chojuro. Tree large, very vigorous; moderately productive; tends to drop fruit when temperatures are hot. GRIGGS; A88M, B67, E87, E99M, *I68*, I83M, *N20*

Jang Shim Lon: (Muk Gul) Very large, roundish fruit; skin greenish-bronze, russet; flesh dense, crisp, juicy, of mild sweet flavor; ripens in mid-September at place of origin. Similar if not identical with A-Ri-Rang. Originated near the town of Muk Gul in southern Korea. J93{SC}

Japanese Golden Russet: (Taihe) Medium-sized, attractive fruit; skin dark brown, russet; flesh juicy and sweet; ripens in late September. Among the favorites at the Oregon State University test orchards. *G37*{OR}, L12

Kikusui: Medium to large fruit; skin yellowish-green, thick and tough, slightly bitter; flesh white, sweet, mild, with a trace of tartness, aroma faint but distinct; texture firm, tender, crisp, juicy; quality good to very good; ripens in midseason. Tree vigorous, spreading; very productive. Originated in Tokyo, Japan. Introduced in 1927. GRIGGS; A88M, B67, *C54*, E4, E87, F11, *G37*{OR}, H81M, I49M, *I68*, J93{SC}, *K73M*, *L47*, M92, *N20*, etc.

Kosui: Small to medium-sized fruit; skin light green to golden-bronze, partially russet; flesh white, crisp and tender, very juicy, exceptionally sweet, flavor mellow, quality excellent; ripens in early August, harvested through September. Tree vigorous; moderately productive. Recognized in Japan as the highest quality commercial cultivar. B74, B83, E4, *G37*{OR}, *I68*, J61M, J93, J93{SC}, *O97*

Niitaka: Fruit very large; skin brown to golden-bronze, with brown russeting, attractive; flesh white tinted with yellow, coarse, crisp and juicy, somewhat mild but sweetens with storage, quality good; ripens in early October, keeps for several months. Tree very upright, somewhat weak growing; highly productive; not a good pollinator. B74, B67, C34, D34M{PR}, E87, E99M, *G37*{OR}, I49M, *I68*, I83M, J61M

Nijisseiki: (Twentieth Century, Er Shi Shinge) Fruit round to oblong; skin greenish-yellow, thin, tender, smooth; flesh white, sweet, mild, refreshing, slightly tart; core slightly sour; texture firm, tender, crisp, very juicy, somewhat coarse and pulpy; ripens in midseason. Tree moderately vigorous; productive. Most widely grown Asian pear worldwide. Introduced in 1898. GRIGGS; A5, E4, E84, *G37*, *G49*, H81M, I49M, I83M, K67, *K73M*, L1, L30, L99M, M39M, N33, *N40*{PR}, etc.

Okusankichi: (Bansankichi, Nihon Nashi) Medium to large, turbinate fruit; skin tannish-green to tan, tough, relatively thick, russet, somewhat bitter; flesh dull white, mildly tart, refreshing, flavor improves in storage; texture firm, crisp, juicy, relatively few stone cells; quality fair to good; ripens late; stores very well. Tree relatively large, spreading; very vigorous and productive. GRIGGS; *C54*, E87, F43M, *G37*{OR}, H81M, *I68*

Olympic: Large, Korean pear, 3/4 pound or more in weight; skin brown-green, russet; flesh very juicy, somewhat coarse, of very good flavor, sugar content 13 to 15%; season mid-September to early October in the Sacramento Valley, excellent storage life. Tree cold hardy; blossoms with Nijisseiki, Hosui and Bartlett. E4

Seigyoku: Large, oblong fruit; skin light greenish-yellow, usually free of russet, attractive; flesh white, sweet, mild, slightly tart; texture firm, tender, crisp, juicy, somewhat coarse and pulpy, relatively few stone cells; quality very good; ripens early. Tree moderately vigorous; very productive. Seedling of Nijisseiki x Chojuro. GRIGGS; A91, A91{SC}, B67, E87, *G37*{OR}, I49M, J61M, J93{SC}, *L47*, L99M, N24M

Seuri: Fruit large to very large, round to oval; skin greenish-brown, with partial yellow-orange russeting; flesh pure-white, crisp and juicy, fine-grained, aromatic, with a distinctive flavor, quality good; ripens in mid-September, harvested through October. Well liked in taste tests. Tree very vigorous, extremely strong; heavy bearing; blooms early. E87, E99M, *G37*, I49M, J61M, J93, J93{SC}, L99M

Shin Li: Medium to large, round-oblate fruit; skin light green to yellowish-green when ripe; flesh white, firm but tender, fine-grained, crisp, sweet and juicy, quality excellent; ripens with Daisui Li; good keeping and shipping characteristics. Tree medium to large, vigorous; productive; blooms early, with Daisui Li, with less thinning needed. Kikusui x Tsu Li. Originated at Davis, California by Ben Iwakiri. E4, *K73M*

Shinko: Medium to large, oval fruit; skin golden-bronze, russet, thick; flesh white, crisp and juicy, very sweet, flavor rich and distinct; ripens in September, stores until March or April; retains its rich flavor through storage. Rated by Sunset magazine as the best tasting in their test kitchens. Tree precocious; bears very heavy crops regularly; chilling requirement 500 hours. A88M, B67, B74, *C54*, D34M{PR}, E4, E87, F11, I49M, *I68*, I83M, J61M, J93, J93{SC}, *K73M*, L1, L99M, *N20*, etc.

Shinseiho: Fruit very large for an Asian pear; skin light yellow-green; flesh slightly tart-sweet; ripens in the fall. Pollinate with Bartlett or any other Asian pear. A91, A91{SC}, *G37*{OR}, H90M{SC}, J93{SC}, N24M

Shinseiki: (New Century) Fruit medium to large, round to oblong; skin yellow, thick, smooth; flesh white, sweet, mild; texture firm, tender, crisp, juicy, stone cells more numerous than in Nijisseiki fruit; quality good to excellent; ripens early. Tree moderately vigorous, spreading; productive. Seedling of Nijisseiki x Chojuro. Introduced in 1945. GRIGGS; A5, B67, E4, E84, F11, *G37*, *G49*, H81M, I49M, I83M, *K73M*, L1, L99M, M39M, N33, *N40*{PR}, etc.

Shinsui: Small to medium-sized fruit; rounded, somewhat flattened; skin green with brown to orange-brown russet; flesh white, crisp but tender, very sweet and juicy, moderate number of stone cells; quality excellent for its season. Tree an excellent pollinator. Recognized in Japan as the highest quality early maturing cultivar. Constitutes 30% of new plantings in Japan's major nashi growing district. E4, *I68*, J61M, J93{SC}, *O97*

Singo: Very large fruit, average weight up to 1 pound; skin yellowish-tan, attractive; flesh white, tender, juicy; ripens in mid-season, from late September to the first week in October. Tree vigorous, has a tendency to grow very upright; productive; good pollinator for A-Ri-Rang. In order to produce large fruit thinning is required. H81M, J93{SC}

Tsu Li: Ovate to pyriform fruit; skin light green to yellowish-green, slightly bitter; flesh white with a faint tint of yellow, sweet, refreshingly mild, aroma distinct, tender, crisp, juicy, somewhat coarse and pulpy. Tree large, upright, vigorous; requires cross-pollination for best results. An old and famous cultivar in the Shantung Province of northeastern China. GRIGGS; A88M, B67, *C54*, E4, E87, *G37*, *I68*, I83M, K67, L12, L99M, *N20*

Ya Li: Medium to large, pear-shaped fruit; skin light greenish-yellow, smooth; flesh white, mildly sweet, slight trace of tartness, aroma distinctly fragrant; texture tender, crisp, juicy, slightly pulpy and coarse, relatively few stone cells. Tree large, upright; vigorous; requires cross-pollination. An old cultivar, commonly cultivated in northeastern China. GRIGGS; A88M, B67, *C54*, E4, E87, E99M, *G14*, *G37*{OR}, I49M, *I68*, I83M, J61M, J93{SC}, K67, *N20*, *N40*{PR}, etc.

Yakumo: Small to medium-sized fruit; round to oval, with a very short neck; skin bright yellow, smooth, glossy, unblemished; flesh white, fine-grained, crisp, very juicy, sweet; flavor very good, with a subtle melon-like aftertaste; ripens very early, will keep for months in cold storage. A91, B67, E87, I49M, *I68*, J61M, L12, *N20*

Yoinashi: Large fruit; skin yellow to yellow-orange, russet, medium thick; flesh white tinged with yellow, juicy, sweet, fine-grained, tender and crisp, quality excellent; ripens in August and September, harvested through January. Tree moderately vigorous to vigorous, fairly productive; pollinated by Hosui, Ichiban Nashi and Ya Li. E4

Yongi: Large fruit; skin brown to golden brown, with large lenticels; flesh white to off-white, firm, crisp, sweet, of good flavor, quality good to very good; ripens in August, harvested through December. Tree medium to large, fairly vigorous, upright-spreading; pollinated by Nijisseiki, Shinseiki and Chojuro. E4

ASPARAGUS {PL}

ASPARAGUS OFFICINALIS

Brock Imperial: Vigorous hybrid, produces up to 30% larger crops than standard strains. Plump, bright green stalks with tight tips; very tender and fiber-free. Rust resistant and heat tolerant. Matures a week earlier than most, and harvest lasts up to 2 months or more longer. Equally good for fresh eating, canning and freezing. E97, *O53*{S}, Q11M{S}

Conover's Colossal: An very old cultivar, still unsurpassed for quality and earliness, being ready before most other types. Strong grower, producing thick, fleshy stalks. Has the advantage that male seedlings, which are better producers than females, are stockier and denser and more easily selected when planting out. Originated with Abraham Van Siclen of Long Island, New York. Introduced about 1873. B49{S}, N84{S}, O39M{S}, O53M{S}, P83M{S}, *R23*{S}

Early Giant Argenteuil: (D'Argenteuil Hâtive) An old traditional French cultivar, obtained by selection from seedlings of the Giant Dutch Purple. The shoots are notably thicker than those of the parent plant, the head is slightly pointed, and the scales with which it is covered are very closely set, overlapping each other. VILMORIN; B8{S}, G68{S}

Franklin: Large, thick, very solid stalks; perfectly uniform in shape and size. Suitable for both green and white asparagus, but more commonly used as white asparagus. Very precocious and productive. P59M{S}, P69{S}

Glen Smith: Strong, consistent yielder. Spears are approximately 2 inches longer than Viking. Can be brought into production relatively quickly and is recommended for replanting as it shows reasonable tolerance to allotropic conditions. Originated in Sunnyside, Washington by Glen Smith. *A69M*{S}, C85M{S}

Greenwich:[1] All-male hybrid that produces large, uniform spears. Vigorous plant resists all types of stress, including diseases. Tolerant of fusarium. Has proven well adapted to certain sites in New Jersey and Michigan as well as areas in the Midwest and Atlantic seaboard where there is a lighter sandier soil. Developed by Professor J. Howard Ellison of Rutgers University. *A1*{S}, I50, I50{S}, L5T

Jersey Centennial: First hybrid introduced by the New Jersey asparagus breeding program. Large, tender bright-green spears with good quality and excellent appearance. Vigorous and highly productive plants, well adapted to the Northeast. Good rust resistance; increased tolerance to fusarium. Developed by Professor J. Howard Ellison of Rutgers University. Introduced in 1978. A14, F89, G16, G23, I50, I50{S}, J7{S}, J20, J58, L5T, L33

Jersey Giant:[1] All-male type, producing only male plants which are more vigorous and productive than female plants. Since their are no female plants to produce seed, it also eliminates volunteer seedlings in the asparagus bed. Heavy producer of large, attractive, high quality spears with purple bracts and tight purple tips. Yields have consistently surpassed the Washington strains by greater than 300% in tests across the country. Fusarium and rust tolerant. Developed by Professor J. Howard Ellison of Rutgers University. *A1*{S}, A13{S}, B49M, C44, *D35M*, *F63*{S}, *F72*{S}, G16{S}, I50, I50{S}, J61M, K10{S}, L5T

Jersey Prince:[1] All-male hybrid recently released by Rutgers University. Has many of the same fine characteristics as Jersey Giant including high yields, fusarium tolerance and rust resistance. Yield trials have shown it to be well adapted and highly productive in Michigan and Washington. Also productive in Illinois on sites where soils are heavier and contain more clay. I50, I50{S}, L5T

Jumbo: A remarkable new asparagus that is genetically polyploid, which means the plant naturally produces much larger shoots, often double the size of normal strains. It can be relied on to produce tender and succulent stems and significantly larger spears. L91M{S}

Lucullus:[1] All-male type with yields comparable to those produced by Jersey Giant. Very vigorous and disease resistant; can produce up to 1 pound per year per established plant. 100% male plants assures continuous yield and uniformity over the years. F1, G64{S}, N84{S}, *R23*{S}, S55{S}

Martha Washington: Large, crisp, uniform shoots produced in great abundance; tips firm, tightly folded and tender; harvest period extends for up to two months. Excellent for fresh use, canning and freezing. Rust resistant and tolerant to fusarium. A82, E3, F13{S}, *G28*, *G83M*{S}, H42, I91, I91{S}, J7, L65M, *M69M*, S61{S}

Mary Washington: Long, straight shoots, very thick and heavy; color rich dark green, slightly tinged purple at the tightly folded tips. Uniform, heavy yields. Holds a tight bud longer than most. Somewhat rust resistant. Standard fresh market and home garden cultivar. C44{S}, C63, E24, E24{S}, *F72*{S}, G16, G16{S}, H16, H94{S}, J69, J73{S}, M46{S}

Paradise: A sport of Mary Washington, introduced in California in the mid 1930's. Precocious and quick growing. Produces long, thick, very tender stalks with an unusually mild flavor. Retains its color when canned or frozen. Rust resistant and very heavy bearing. Most satisfactory for the small yard. L30

Precoce d'Argenteuil: (Early Argenteuil) Highly esteemed by European gourmets for its large, white stalks and attractive rose-colored scales. I77{S}, Q11M{S}

Roberts: (Mary Washington Roberts Strain) Very large, rich green spears; tender with a low fiber content; holds quality a long time, never becoming stringy or woody. Heavy yielding, vigorous, resistant to rust. Popular with home gardeners and commercial canners. A24, B58, E97, M37M

Ruhm von Braunschweig: (Glory of Braunschweig) Widely used in Austria and Germany for the production of white shoots. Medium early harvests. High yielding. N81{S}, P9{S}

Supermale:[1] All male type; does not produce volunteer seedlings to compete with parent stock. Tender green spears, 3/4 inch in diameter and larger. Early and extremely vigorous. Resistant to rust, root/crown rot and fusarium. Outyields other cultivars. H65

SYN 4-56: Synthetic form of Jersey Giant, derived from one seed parent and two pollen parents. Similar in most ways, including overall productiveness and vigor, but will produce a few female plants and consequent seedlings. Early, vigorous; very productive, producing large, attractive green spears with purple bracts. Tolerant of rust and fusarium. Seed is approximately 70% male, 30% female. A13, A14, *C84*, G64, G71, H33, H33{S}, I50, I50{S}

U.C. 72: Large, dark green spears with fairly compact, purple-tinged heads. Highly productive and tolerant to fusarium wilt and rust. Mary Washington type developed by the University of California, Davis. Highly recommended for home gardeners in California. *A1*{S}, B75M{S}, *C54*, E4, *G13M*, G71M{S}, G93M{S}, *H61*{S}, *L59G*{S}, M29{S}, N16{S}

U.C. 157: Deep green, smooth, cylindrical spears with tight tips and scales; uniform in color and size. Vigorous plants come into production early; have a tendency to produce 3 to 5 spears at one time. Some resistance to fusarium root rot. Widely adapted to California and the major asparagus growing areas. *A1*{S}, A87M{S}, B75M{S}, *C84*, *D74*{S}, G51{S}, G93M, G93M{S}, J34, J34{S}, L33, *L59G*{S}, M29{S}

Viking: (Vineland No. 35) An improved strain of Mary Washington. Vigorous growing plants with heavier stalks and a greater tendency to resist rust. Large spears and tight heads. Recommended for home garden or market. Developed in Vineland, Ontario, Canada. A69M{S}, C85M, D11M{S}, D27{S}, G64{S}, I67M{S}, J7{S}, J82, K20{S}, L42{S}, M13M{S}

Viking KB3: An improved, rust-tolerant Mary Washington type selected for fusarium tolerance and taller, more uniform spears. Much hardier in sub-zero and hot desert climates than all-male, F_1 and F_2 hybrid cultivars. Also shows tolerance to fusarium. C63, *C84*, G44, H16, L42{S}

Waltham: (Waltham Washington) The result of 20 years of breeding by the Waltham, Massachusetts Field Station. Will produce approximately 25% more asparagus than ordinary cultivars. Large, tender spears, uniform in both size and color; heads tighter than most. Buds hold tightly longer, providing an extended harvest period. Bred for increased rust resistance. C63, D76, E97

AVOCADO {GR}

PERSEA AMERICANA

GUATEMALAN

The Guatemalan avocados are primarily winter and spring ripening. Skin varies from thin to very thick and is granular or gritty. The flesh is rich in flavor and relatively high in oil content. Grown in both Florida and California.

Anaheim: Large oval to elliptical fruit, weight 18 to 32 ounces; skin green, glossy, rough, thick; flesh of fair to good flavor, up to 22% oil, but inferior to Fuerte, Hass, and Nabal; seed medium to small. Tree slender, erect, tall; resistant to adverse weather, but cold-sensitive; bears regularly and prolifically, up to 220 pounds annually. Season June to August. MORTON 1987a, ROUNDS; *G49*

Edranol: Medium-sized, pyriform fruit, weight 10 to 12 ounces; skin green, thick, russets badly in interior areas; flavor excellent, quality high, oil content 22.5%; seed small; ripens from February to July at Vista. Tree vigorous, bears heavily, adapted to coastal areas of California. Originated in Vista, California. Introduced in 1932. BROOKS 1972, ROUNDS; S97M

Gwen:[1] Small to medium-sized, ovoid fruit, weight 7 to 12 ounces; skin medium dark-green, medium thick; flavor excellent, nutty, similar to Hass but richer; oil content 18%. Season very long, February to October. Tree small to medium, upright; produces consistently heavy crops; more cold-hardy than Hass. Introduced by the University of California, Riverside. C56M, *D23M*, I83M, L6, *M61M*

Linda: Round to oblong fruit; weight 16 to 48 ounces; skin purple, smooth, medium thick; flavor excellent, oil content 12%; seed small; season May to October. Shipping quality good. Introduced in 1914 by E.E. Knight at Yorba Linda, California from Antigua, Guatemala. ROUNDS; J22

Nabal: Medium to large, nearly round fruit; weight 16 to 24 ounces; skin dark-green, nearly smooth, thick, granular; flesh yellow, green near skin, of high quality; oil content 10 to 15%; seed small, tight. Season June to September in California; January and February in

Florida. Tree strongly alternate-bearing. BROOKS 1972, MORTON 1987a; *B58M*{SC}, C56M, I83M

Pinkerton: Fruit of early crop roundish; late crop fruit pear-shaped with a neck; of medium size, 8 to 14 ounces; skin green, medium-leathery, pliable; flesh thick, up to 10% more than in Hass or Fuerte; smooth-textured, of good flavor, high in oil; of good quality but inferior to Hass and Fuerte; tends to darken in the latter part of the season; seed small. First crop, October or November; second crop, December or January. MORTON 1987a; *B58M*, *B58M*{SC}, C56M, *D23M*, *G49*, I83M, L6

Queen:[2] Very large, pyriform fruit, weight 20 to 30 ounces; skin rough, medium-thick, color dull-purple; flavor fine; oil content 13.5%; seed small. Season July to August. Shipping quality good. Introduced to California in 1914 by E.E. Knight of Yorba Linda, from near Antigua, Guatemala. ROUNDS; I83M

Reed: Medium to large, round fruit, 8 to 18 ounces; skin green, slightly rough, medium thick, pliable, peels easily; flesh cream-colored, smooth, buttery, firm, with a rich, faintly nutty flavor; oil content 18 to 20%; doesn't darken when cut; quality excellent; seed small to medium, tight. Season July to October in California. May remain on the tree for a relatively long time after reaching maturity. BROOKS 1972, MORTON 1987a; *B58M*, *B58M*{SC}, C56M, *D23M*, *G49*, I76M{PR}, I83M

Tonnage: Fruit pear-shaped, medium-large, 16 to 24 ounces; skin dark-green, rough, thick; flesh pale yellow, green near skin, rich in flavor, oil content 8 to 15%; seed medium, fairly tight. Season from mid-October through November in Florida. Tree erect, fairly slender, requiring less distance between trees. BROOKS 1972, MORTON 1987a; J36

Whitsell:[1] Medium-sized, pyriform fruit, weight 10 to 12 ounces; skin very dark-green, thick and rough; flavor very good, rich and spicy, oil content 18%; quality very high. Season February to August, hangs well on the tree. Tree compact, semi-dwarf, mature height 12 feet; precocious and high yielding; of average hardiness. Introduced by the University of California, Riverside. C56M, *D23M*, *G49*, I83M

Wurtz:[1] (Little Cado) Fruit pear-shaped, small to medium, 8 to 12 ounces; skin green, medium thick; quality good, oil content 18%; seed large. Season May to September in California. Tree small and slow-growing, mature height 8 to 12 feet; distinctive weeping growth habit; bears moderately but regularly. Suited for planters, containers, patios, and greenhouse use. Originated in Encinitas, California by Roy Wurtz. Introduced in 1948. BROOKS 1972, MORTON 1987a; *D23M*, *G49*, I76M{PR}, *Q93*

GUATEMALAN X MEXICAN

Bacon: Ovoid fruit, weight 7 to 12 ounces; skin green, thin, smooth; flesh an unusually pale yellow-green; oil content high; flavor good; keeping quality good. Matures November to March in southern California. Tree upright, slender; consistent, a heavy producer; frost tolerance excellent. BROOKS 1972; *B58M*{SC}, B93M, C56M, *D23M*, *G49*, I76M{PR}, I83M, *M61M*

Ettinger: Medium-sized, pyriform fruit; skin bright green, slightly rough, peeling quality excellent; flesh clear light yellow, free of fiber, soft, melting, ripens uniformly, quality excellent; seed large, loose in cavity; ripens early, slightly before Fuerte in Riverside, California. Tree vigorous, very prolific. Seedling of Fuerte. Originated in Kefar Malal, Israel. BROOKS 1972; *B58M*{SC}

Fuerte: Pear-shaped fruit; small to medium or a little larger, 8 to 16 ounces; skin green, slightly rough, thin, not adherent to flesh; flesh green near skin, oil content 12 to 17%; flavor excellent, buttery; seed medium to large. Vigorous, spreading tree with decidedly alternate year bearing habit. Fruit season November to June in California. Natural hybrid originated at Atlixco, Mexico, elevation 6150 feet. Introduced into California in 1911. MORTON 1987a, ROUNDS; *B58M*, *B58M*{SC}, B93M, C56M, *D23M*, *G49*, I83M, *M61M*, *Q93*

Hass:[2] Fruit pear-shaped to ovoid; size medium, 10 ounces; flesh creamy, flavor excellent, no fiber, oil content 18 to 25%; skin leathery, rough, dark-purple to black when ripe, thick; seed small, tight in cavity; keeping qualities excellent; good shipper; ripens in summer. Tree heavy bearing; starts bearing the second year. Leading commercial cultivar in California. BROOKS 1972, MORTON 1987a; *B58M*, *B58M*{SC}, B93M, C56M, *D23M*, E70M{PR}, *G49*, I83M, L6, *M61M*, *Q93*

Jim: (Jim Bacon) Small to medium-sized, pyriform to long-necked fruit; weight 8 to 10 ounces; skin green, medium thick; oil content 14%, quality and flavor very good; seed medium-sized, tight; ripens September to January, ships well. Tree vigorous, semi-upright; a precocious and regular bearer; slightly more frost resistant than Bacon. Seedling of Bacon. Originated in Buena Park, California by Jim Bacon. *B58M*, *B58M*{SC}, *G49*, L6

Lula: Fruit pear-shaped, sometimes with a neck, medium-large; skin almost smooth; flesh pale to greenish-yellow, oil content 12 to 16%; seed large, tight. Season medium-late (mid-November and December). Tree tall; bears early and heavily; cold-resistant, successful in central and southern Florida where it was formerly the leading commercial cultivar. MORTON 1987a; F68, J36, *N53M*

Rincon: Fruit pear-shaped, small to medium, 6 to 10 ounces; skin green fairly thin, smooth, leathery, peels well; flesh buttery, contains 15 to 26.5% oil; fibers in flesh near base turn black when fruit is cut; seed of medium size. Season January to April in California. Tree medium to small; weak growing; a consistent and heavy bearer. BROOKS 1972, MORTON 1987a; S59, S97M

Sharwil: Medium-sized fruit, weight 7 to 13 ounces; resembles Fuerte in shape but a little more oval; skin green, rather rough, fairly thin; flesh rich in flavor, of excellent quality; 15 to 26% oil content; seed small. Tree bears regularly but not heavily. Represents 18 to 20% of all avocados grown in New South Wales and Queensland, Australia. BROOKS 1972, MORTON 1987a; J22, *Q93*, S59

Winter Mexican: Oblong to pyriform fruit, weight 12 to 18 ounces; skin thick, leathery, dark green; seed medium, tight in cavity; season December and January. Tree very vigorous, bears heavily and regularly; very hardy; resistant to scab; susceptible to anthracnose. Originated in Palm Beach, Florida. BROOKS 1972; *N53M*

GUATEMALAN X WEST INDIAN

Most of these hybrids were developed in Florida, where they represent more than half of the more than 20 major and minor commercial cultivars grown there at this time. MORTON 1987a.

Booth 7: Fruit round-obovate, of medium size, 10 to 20 ounces; skin green, glossy, thick, slightly pebbled, brittle; flesh contains 7 to 14% oil; seed of medium size, tight. Season late (December to mid-January). Tree bears prolifically; class "B" for pollination purposes. Originated in Homestead, Florida by William Booth. Introduced in 1935. BROOKS 1972, MORTON 1987a; J36

Booth 8: Fruit oblong-obovate, of medium size, 14 to 18 ounces; skin dull green, rough, fairly thick, brittle; flesh contains 6 to 12% oil; seed medium-large, tight. Season late (November to mid-December). Tree a very prolific bearer; class "B" for pollination purposes. Originated in Homestead, Florida by William Booth. Introduced in 1935. BROOKS 1972, MORTON 1987a; J36, S97M

Choquette: Large, oval fruit, weight 30 to 40 ounces; skin glossy, smooth, dark-green, slightly leathery; flesh thick, yellow, of very good quality, oil content 13%; seed medium, tight. Season January to March. Tree bears heavily in alternate years. Resistant to common avocado diseases. Recommended for home plantings in Florida. BROOKS 1972, MORTON 1987a; F68, J36, *N53M*

Hall: Large, pear-shaped fruit; skin bright-green, attractive, smooth, fairly thick; flesh deep-yellow, oil content 12 to 16%; seed medium-large, tight. Resembles Monroe in being excellent for the limited fancy-fruit market. Season November and December. Tree an alternate but heavy bearer; cold-hardy; subject to scab. Originated in Miami, Florida by Willis Hall. BROOKS 1972, MORTON 1987a; F68, J36

Kahaluu: Fruit obovate to pyriform; weight 12 to 18 ounces; skin smooth, green; flesh rich, oil content high, quality excellent; seed small, tight in cavity; ripens November to January; resembles Fuerte. Tree large, upright, vigorous; bears annually, but only moderately. Originated in Kahaluu, North Kona, Hawaii. BROOKS 1972; J22

Monroe: Large fruit, weight 26 to 36 ounces; skin dark-green, glossy, attractive; flesh yellow, slightly green near skin, fiberless, oil content 10 to 30%; flavor nutty; season December and January. Tree a heavy bearer; class "B" for pollination purposes. Originated in Homestead, Florida by J.J.L. Phillips. Introduced in 1937. BROOKS 1972; F68, J36, *N53M*

MEXICAN

Mexican avocados have thin, tender skin that clings to the flesh. The flesh has a high oil content, up to 30%. Leaves have a pronounced anise-like scent. The tree is more cold-resistant than those of the other races or hybrids, thriving near Puebla, Mexico, at 500 feet above sea level. MORTON 1987a.

Brogdon:[2] Fruit somewhat pear-shaped, weight 7 to 20 ounces; skin purple, very thin; susceptible to handling; flesh yellow, buttery; ripens late July-August. Tree small to medium; vigor moderate; productivity low; very hardy; susceptible to anthracnose. Recommended for Central Florida. Originated in Winter Haven, Florida by Tom W. Brogdon. Introduced in 1951. BROOKS 1972; F68, *N53M*

Mexicola:[2] Fruit very small, spherical to pyriform, weight 3 to 5 ounces; skin black, thin, smooth; flesh of excellent flavor; seed large. Season August to October. Bears early and regularly; very heat and cold-resistant. Much used as a parent in California breeding programs. Originated about 1910 at Pasadena, California; fist propagated in 1912. MORTON 1987a, ROUNDS; *B58M*{S}, *B58M*{SC}, C56M, *D23M*, G17, I28, I49M, I83M, L6

Puebla:[2] Small to medium, obovoid fruit, weight 8 to 10 ounces; skin smooth, glossy, deep maroon-purple; flesh buttery in texture, of a rich nutty flavor, quality very good; seed medium to large, tight in the cavity; season December to February in southern California. Tree vigorous and hardy. Introduced in 1911 from Atlixco, Mexico. POPENOE, W. 1920; T49M{SC}

Stewart:[2] Medium-sized, pyriform fruit; skin slightly rough, a rich dark purple at maturity; flesh clear, bright, light yellow shading to green toward the skin, firm but melting, of excellent quality; ripens from early October to mid-December. Oil content about 8% by Oct 1 to about 16% in mid-November. Tree spreading, strong and vigorous, bears well. BROOKS 1972; *B58M*, *B58M*{SC}

Susan: Small, ovoid fruit, average weight 5 1/2 ounces; skin green, thin, smooth; flesh yellow, buttery, oil content up to 17%; flavor very good, nutty; season September to mid-November; resembles Fuerte. Tree frost resistant; productive. Originated in Baldwin Park, California. *B58M*{SC}, *L47*

Zutano: Fruit pyriform, medium-small, 8 to 12 ounces; skin very thin, light green, russets in inland areas, leathery; oil content medium, 15 to 22%; flavor fair to good; seed medium. Season October to February in southern California. Tree a consistent producer; hardier than Fuerte and Hass; vigorous, upright grower. Originated in Fallbrook, California by W.L. Ruitt. Introduced in 1941. BROOKS 1972; *B58M*{SC}, B93M, C56M, *D23M*, *G49*, I83M, *L47*, *M61M*

WEST INDIAN

West Indian avocados are generally summer and fall ripening. They have leathery, pliable, non-granular skin, and the flesh is low in oil. The leaves are not aromatic. Grown in Florida, the West Indies, Bahamas, Bermuda and the tropics of the Old World. Not grown in California.

Peterson: Fruit obovoid, medium in size, weight 14 to 20 ounces; skin green, smooth, glossy; flavor good, oil content 4 to 7%. Season September through November. Originated in Homestead, Florida by Peter Peterson. Introduced about 1930. BROOKS 1972; J36

Pollock: Oblong to pear-shaped fruit; very large, up to 5 pounds; skin green, smooth, glossy; flesh firm, smooth and fine in texture, deep yellow changing to yellowish-green close to the skin, contains 3 to 5% oil; seed large, frequently loose in cavity. Season early, July to August or October. Shy-bearing. Fruit too large but of superior quality. Originated in Miami before 1896 on the property of H.S. Pollock. MORTON 1987a, POPENOE, W. 1920, ROUNDS; F68, J36, *L33M*{PR}, *N53M*

Russell: Large fruit, weight 24 to 36 ounces; pear-shaped at apex with long neck giving it a total length up to 13 inches; skin green, smooth, glossy, thin, leathery; flesh yellow, of excellent quality; seed small; cavity low in the broad end of the fruit, often a solid neck of flesh 5 to 6 inches long. Season August and September. J36, *N53M*

Simmonds: Fruit large, oblong-oval to pyriform; skin smooth, light-green; flesh of good flavor, oil content 3 to 6%; seed of medium size, usually tight. Season mid-July to mid-September. Tree bears more regularly than Pollock but is less vigorous; sometimes sheds many of its fruits. MORTON 1987a; F68, J36, *L33M*{PR}, *N53M*

Waldin: Fruit oblong to oval, medium to large; skin smooth; flesh pale to greenish-yellow, of good flavor, oil content 5 to 10%; seed medium to large, tight. Season fairly late (mid-September through October). Tree tends to overbear and die back; is hardy. Has been a leading commercial cultivar in central and southern Florida. MORTON 1987a, POPENOE, W. 1920; J36

OTHERS

Fujikawa: Large, oval-pyriform fruit; green skin; green, smooth, melting flesh with high oil content, excellent flavor; small seed; ripens in spring. Vigorous, canopy shaped tree; highly productive. Local Hawaiian selection. J22

Marcus Pumpkin: Notable for its extremely large fruit, often the size of a muskmelon. Relatively low oil content. Small-seeded. Ripens late, in October in Florida. F68, J36, *N53M*

Ota: Large, round-pyriform fruit; green skin; smooth, green flesh with a high oil content; small seed. Vigorous, upright tree; bears in fall and winter. Local Hawaiian selection. J22

Yamagata: Large, oval-pyriform fruit with a curved neck; skin green, thick, gritty; flesh green, smooth, flavor nutty; seed medium sized; ripens over a long season, from March through July. Vigorous, upright tree with dark green foliage; bears heavily. Local Hawaiian selection. J22

BABY VEGETABLES

See Beet, Bok Choy, Carrot, Cauliflower, Corn, Corn Salad, Eggplant, Kidney Bean, Leek, Lettuce, Mustard, Okra, Onion, Pumpkin, Squash and Turnip

BAMBOO

See Bambusaceae in the Botanical listings.

BANANA {PL}

MUSA X PARADISIACA MUSA TROGLODYTARUM

DESSERT BANANAS

Included here are the sweet bananas which are primarily eaten out-of-hand and in various desserts, and also cultivars such as Iholena that are of dessert quality when fully ripe and are also very good cooked.

Brazilian: (Hawaiian Apple) Plants vigorous, sturdy, productive, semi-hardy; mature height 15 to 25 feet; able to stand wind slightly better than other tall cultivars. Medium bunches of small fruit, 4 to 6 inches long; skin medium-thick, yellow; flesh white or cream-colored with a pleasing, slightly acid apple-like flavor. Hardy in dry areas; tolerant to Panama wilt. Has a longer shelf-life compared to other cultivars. Introduced into Hawaii from Java about 1855. POPE; A79M, C56M, D57, E31M, *G77M*, I83M, J81G, J81G{PR}, N84

Carolina King: Shows great promise in extending the range of banana growing in the coastal areas and parts of the Upper South. Dwarf. M31M

Cocos: (Highgate) A dwarf form of Bluefields whose mature height of 10 to 15 feet makes it more windproof and easier to site in a sheltered spot. Bunch size and fruit quality are similar to Bluefields but the individual bananas are shorter, only 5 to 7 inches long. Ornamental plant with contrasting black and ivory coloration of the trunk. J81G

Colorado Blanco:[3] Vigorous plant, 20 to 25 feet tall; bunches 45 to 60 pounds in weight. Plump fruits, 5 to 7 inches long; flesh cream colored, firm, of a distinctive flavor. Resembles Jamaican Red and Green Red in growth habit, fruit characteristics and quality, but the color of the fruit skin is yellow. Productive as well as ornamental. Introduced into Hawaii from Puerto Rico in 1904. POPE; J81G

Double:[2] (Doubling) Fruit similar in size and sweetness to Dwarf Cavendish. Dichotomous fruiting head. Second generation may produce 2 to 4 heads of fruit simultaneously and can total over 100 pounds; first generation will be "normal". Plant resembles a Dwarf Cavendish; 4 to 8 feet tall; fairly wind resistant, but should be planted in a protected place. A79M, E31M, N84

Dwarf Brazilian:[2] (Santa Catarina Prata) Flavor, fruit and shelf life identical to Brazilian. Mature height 10 to 15 feet. Produces bunches of 25 to 50 pounds, 5 to 7 hands per bunch; 5 to 6 inch long fruit. Resistant to Panama wilt. J81G

Dwarf Cavendish:[2] (Dwarf Chinese) Very sturdy plant, 6 to 8 feet tall with broad leaves on short, stout petioles; hardy and wind resistant; a reliable producer. Bunches weigh 40 to 90 pounds. Fruit of medium size, 6 to 8 inches long, of good quality, but thin-skinned and must be handled and shipped with care. Pulp cream-colored, rich and sweet. Found growing in southern China by early travelers to the Orient. MORTON 1987a, POPE; A79M, C56M, D57, D76, E3, E31M, G17, *G77M*, H4, I78, I83M, J81G, M31, M31M, M49M, etc.

Dwarf Jamaican Red:[1 2] Dwarf form of the Jamaican Red whose mature height is only 7 to 8 feet, one-third the height of the standard cultivar. More easily protected from wind, more easily harvested, and quicker to bear. A79M, C56M, E31M, *G77M*, I83M, J22, J81G, L9M, N84

Enano Gigante:[2] (Mexican Dwarf) High-quality, sweet fruit of large size under ideal conditions. Semi-dwarf habit, shorter than Valery; heavy producer. Tender, often needing support when bearing; subject to cigar end rot in cold wet weather. Widely planted as a commercial banana in Mexico and Central America. C56M, *D23M*, D57, I83M, J81G, L29{OR}, M82

Giant Cavendish: Plant reaches 10 to 16 feet; the pseudostem is splashed with dark-brown, the bunch is long and cylindrical, and the fruits are larger than those of Dwarf Cavendish and not as delicate. Produces very large bunches of fruit of excellent quality. MORTON 1987a; A79M, E31M, *G77M*, N84

Golden Aromatic: Medium-sized plant, grows 10 to 12 feet tall. Produces bunches that weigh 30 to 40 pounds, with 4 to 5 hands per bunch. Medium-sized fruit, 6 to 9 inches long; skin golden-yellow; flesh very sweet and aromatic, resembles Gros Michel. Has good shelf life. E31M

Golden Beauty: (I.C. 2) Vigorous plant, 15 to 25 feet tall; bears small to medium bunches of short 4 to 6 inch, golden-skinned bananas that ripen and ship well. Resistant to Panama disease and very resistant to sigatoka. Bred at the Imperial College of Tropical Agriculture in Trinidad in 1928 by crossing the Gros Michel with a wild banana. MORTON 1987a, SIMMONDS 1966; J81G

Golden Pillow: A moderately vigorous plant similar in appearance to Manzano but more slender in all its parts and more pink coloration in the leaf sheaths. Bunches take longer to appear and ripen. The fruit is short, fat, thin-skinned, very sweet and the flavor and texture are somewhat better than Manzano. Mature height is 12 to 16 feet; first harvest 18 to 24 months after planting. A79M, E31M, *G77M*, J81G, L29{OR}, N84

Grande Nain:[2] Plant sturdy, semi-hardy; mature height 5 to 7 feet; vigorous; productive, bunches of fruit commonly weighing over 100 pounds. Currently on of the most important commercial clones in the world. Developed in Central America. A79M, E31M, *G77M*, H4, I83M, N84

Green Red:[1 3] Strong, vigorous plant; mature height 20 to 25 feet; trunk 14 to 18 inches thick at the base; variegated green and red. Produces medium bunches weighing 30 to 50 pounds, 4 to 7 hands per bunch. Stout fruits, 5 to 7 inches long; skin thick, brilliant dark purplish red and gold on ripening; pulp firm, aromatic, cream-colored, of good flavor. Comes into bearing at 20 to 30 months, bears on a one year cycle thereafter. Bud mutation of Jamaican Red. POPE; J81G

Gros Michel: (Bluefields) Very tall, vigorous plant; mature height 25 to 30 feet. Bears fruit in long bunches, weighing 60 to 100 pounds. Needs high temperatures and humidity to ripen its fruit. Large, slightly curved fruit, 7 to 9 inches long; flesh firm, consistency and flavor excellent. Was formerly the leading commercial cultivar in Central America, Latin America and the Caribbean, but has been phased out because of its great susceptibility to Panama disease. Originated in Martinique, West Indies. MORTON 1987a, POPE; A79M, E31M, *G77M*, J81G, N84

Haa Haa:[2 3] Plant low-growing, resembles the Dwarf Cavendish in size with a 6 1/2 to 7 foot trunk; new leaves have burgundy overtones. Fruit medium sized, plump in the middle, tapering towards the ends; yellow-skinned; orange-fleshed. The fruit can be eaten raw or cooked, and when fried is similar in taste to apple fritters. A79M, E31M, *G77M*, J81G, J81G{PR}, L9M, L29{OR}, N84

Hua Moa:[3] Tall Hawaiian cultivar which likes protected locations in filtered light with ample moisture; height 16 to 18 feet. Produces small to medium bunches of very plump, roundish fruits with golden-yellow skin and pinkish-yellow flesh. Flavor sweet and delicious. May be eaten fresh or cooked. Very good when sliced green and fried in hot oil like French-fried potatoes. Also good eaten ripe or baked with cinnamon and brown sugar as a dessert. A79M, E31M, *G77M*, L29{OR}, N84

Ice Cream: (Blue Java) Somewhat leaning trunks, 10 to 15 feet tall; leaf midrib light pink. Flower stalk may be several feet long, but the bunch has only 7 to 9 hands; bunch weight 40 to 60 pounds. Stout, straight fruit, 5 to 7 inches long and up to 2 1/2 inches in diameter, 4 or 5 angled; skin bluish with a silvery bloom when young, pale-yellow when ripe; flesh white, sweetish, eaten raw or cooked. MORTON 1987a, POPE; A79M, C56M, D57, E31M, I83M, J81G, J81G{PR}, L29{OR}, N84

Improved Grande Nain:[2] (Super Dwarf) Plant grows only 5 to 7 feet tall, making it ideal for indoor or container growing. Bunches can weigh up to 150 pounds. The fruit is sweet, delicious and full-sized. Now being grown by the largest banana producer in Central America. E31M

Jamaican Red:[1 3] (Cuban Red) Large plant, 20 to 25 feet tall; takes 18 months from planting to harvest; highly resistant to disease. The pseudostem, petiole, midrib, and fruit peel are all purplish-red, but the latter turns to orange-yellow when the fruit is fully ripe. Fruit of medium size, with thick peel, and light orange-colored pulp that is very aromatic and has a strong distinct flavor when fully ripe. MORTON 1987a; A44M{PR}, A79M, E13G{PR}, E31M, *G77M*, I83M, J81G, J81G{PR}, *N40*{PR}, N84

Kauai Red:[1 3] Large plant, 15 to 20 feet tall. Similar to Maroon but larger. Long, reddish-maroon fruits turn orange when ripe; flesh orange-colored, rich and sweet. Originated in Hawaii. D57{OR}

Kru:[1 3] Attractive, red-trunked plant; mature height 10 to 12 feet; moderate wind tolerance. Red fruits with orange pulp; highly esteemed flavor. Resembles Jamaican Red in appearance and fruit but is more precocious and the flavor is superior. Originally from New Guinea. A79M, E31M, *G77M*, I83M, N84

Lacatan: (Pisang Masak Hijau, Bungulan, Hamakua) Plant rapid growing, tall and slender; height 15 to 25 feet; prone to wind injury, especially when bearing fruit. Produces large bunches weighing 50 to 100 pounds, 6 to 9 hands per bunch. High-quality fruit, 6 to 8 inches long; skin greenish-yellow when ripe. Flavor similar to Cavendish. Poor keeping quality, but good tolerance of Panama wilt. A79M, E31M, *G77M*, J81G, N84

Lady Finger: (Ney Poovan) Plant 20 to 25 feet tall at maturity; has a slender trunk but a heavy root system that fortifies it against strong winds. The bunch consists of 10 to 14 hands, each with 15 to 20 fingers; weight 40 to 65 pounds. Short fruits, 4 to 5 inches long; skin thin, light-yellow; flesh firm, whitish, sweet and extremely rich and agreeable. Resistant to drought, Panama disease and black weevil but subject to sigatoka. MORTON 1987a, POPE; G17, I83M, J81G, J81G{PR}

Mahoe: Vigorous, upright plant, height 16 to 20 feet. Bunches medium to large, of 9 or more hands, the larger with 12 to 18 fingers. Fruits 3 to 5 angled, 4 to 5 inches long and 1 to 1 1/2 inches in diameter, weight 3 to 5 ounces; skin bright yellow, easily removed; pulp light salmon yellow, firm; flavor mild, subacid to sweet, delicious. A favorite in some parts of Hawaii. POPE; A79M, E31M, N84

Manzano: (Apple, Silk) Trunks reclining, 10 to 12 feet tall, only medium in vigor. Produces bunches of 25 to 45 pounds. Plump, slightly curved fruits, 4 to 6 inches long; skin rich, clear yellow; pulp firm, astringent when unripe but pleasantly subacid when fully ripe, apple-scented, drier than most other bananas, of excellent quality. The most popular dessert banana in the tropics. MORTON 1987a; A44M{PR}, A79M, C56M, D57, E31M, G44M{PR}, *G77M*, J81G, J81G{PR}, *L33M*{PR}, N84

Maroon:[1 3] Medium tall plants with slightly red midribs; height 10 to 12 feet. Similar to Kauai Red but smaller. Fruits maroon, turning yellowish-orange when ripe; flesh orange, soft, rich and filling. Originated in Hawaii. D57{OR}

Misi Luki: Bears large bunches of flavorful fruit, 4 to 5 inches long, 1 1/4 to 1 1/2 inches in diameter. First harvest can be expected 15 to 18 months after setting out. Originally from the highlands of Samoa. Has grown well in the warmer areas of New Zealand. *Q49M*

Mysore: Plant large and vigorous, mature height 25 feet; immune to Panama disease and nearly so to sigatoka; very hardy and drought-tolerant. Bears large, compact bunches weighing 50 to 60 pounds, 8 to 10 hands per bunch. Medium-sized, plump, attractive fruit; about 6 inches long; skin thin, bright-yellow; flesh moist, pale yellow, slightly subacid in flavor. The most important banana type of India, constituting 70% of the total crop. MORTON 1987a; A79M, E31M, *G77M*, J81G, L29{OR}, N84

Niño: (Sucrier, Honey) Slender plant, less vigorous than most other cultivars; height 10 to 15 feet; fair wind tolerance. Ornamental, with long narrow leaves and an unusual shade of green and black coloration in the trunk and leaf sheathes. Produces small to moderate sized bunches of small, 4 to 5 inch long fruits that are thin-skinned and very sweet. Best grown in partial shade or morning sun. A79M, E31M, *G77M*, J81G, N84

Oriana:[1 2] Red-skinned fruit, 5 inches long; very sweet white flesh, seeded. Only grows 2 1/2 to 5 feet tall. Discovered growing in very dense jungle under low light conditions. Ideal for indoor culture. E31M

Philippines Lacatan: Medium-tall plant, mature height 15 to 20 feet. Produces moderately large bunches weighing 40 to 60 pounds, with 6 to 8 hands per bunch. Well-shaped, firm fruits, 5 to 7 inches long, of excellent flavor and quality. Susceptible to Panama wilt. Highly esteemed in the Philippines. J81G

Pisang Raja:[2 3] Large, solid green plant with bluish overtones, growing 8 to 10 feet tall; tolerates wind and cold very well. Bears medium to large bunches of medium-length fruit, oval on one end; thick-skinned; orange flesh, very sweet and firm; quality very good. A79M, E31M, *G77M*, J81G, N84

Rajapuri:[2] A vigorous dessert cultivar from India which withstands wind, cold, and adverse conditions. Produces small to medium bunches of sweet, fine flavored fruit. Mature height 8 to 10 feet. One of the favorite bananas of India. A79M, E31M, *G77M*, I83M, J81G, N84

Red Iholena:[3] Very rapid growing plant; mature height 10 to 12 feet; attractively colored with red and ivory on the trunk and reddish-purple undersides of the leaves; moderate wind tolerance. Bunches of yellow-skinned, horn-shaped fruits are borne on brilliant red stalks. Fruit pink-fleshed; flavor very good. A favorite Hawaiian cultivar eaten fresh or cooked. A79M, E31M, *G77M*, I83M, J81G, J81G{PR}, N84

Sabino Dwarf:[2] Plant grows only 4 to 6 feet tall in containers, but has very tasty fruit; very good for growing indoors or on a patio. E31M

Tuu Gia: Thin, green trunk, to 12 feet tall. Long fruits, similar to Bluefields in shape but with a unique, slightly curled tendency. Originated in Viet Nam. D57{OR}

Ty Ty Gold: Found growing at an old southern plantation house fifty years ago. Produces fruit about every other year. Tasty, yellow fruit; ripens around Thanksgiving. M31M, M31M{PR}

Valery: Plant semi-dwarf in stature, mature height 10 to 15 feet; wind and cold resistant. Produces large bunches weighing 60 to 90 pounds, with 8 to 10 hands per bunch. High quality fruit, 7 to 10 inches long. Compared with other clones in cooking trials, it has low ratings because cooking hardens the flesh and gives it a waxy texture. Widely planted as a commercial banana in the tropics. MORTON 1987a; A79M, E31M, *G77M*, I83M, J81G, N84

White Iholena:[3] Stout, vigorous, hardy plant, with a predominant ivory hue on the trunk and pink coloration on the underside of new leaves. Maximum height 10 to 15 feet; moderate wind resistance. Bunches rather small. Fruit 5 1/2 to 6 inches long; pulp firm, light salmon-pink, flavor subacid. Eaten cooked, or raw when fully mature. The skin turns bright yellow several days before the fruits are ready to harvest, therefore they should be left on the bunch until they are soft. POPE; A79M, D57, E31M, *G77M*, J81G, J81G{PR}, N84

Williams: Relatively sturdy plant, 9 to 12 feet high; has considerable red pigmentation; resists Panama disease. Bunch large, heavy, 60 to 90 pounds; 9 to 14 hands per bunch. Fruit larger and more attractive than parent, 7 to 9 inches long, of good quality and flavor; ripens about with Cavendish, which it resembles. Bud mutation of Cavendish. Originated in Coffs Harbor, New South Wales, Australia. Introduced into Hawaii in 1954. BROOKS 1972; A79M, E31M, *G77M*, I83M, J81G, N84

Zanmoreno:[2] Very similar to the Dwarf Cavendish except its maximum height is only 5 to 6 feet. Plant is slower growing, slower to flower, and has a smaller bunch than Dwarf Cavendish, but fruit quality is excellent. Recommended where space is limited or for container culture, indoors or out. J81G

COOKING BANANAS

Included here are the true *plantains*, which are starchy and almost exclusively used as a cooked vegetable, either green, semi-ripe or ripe, and cultivars that can be eaten both cooked and raw but are more often cooked. HAWKES [Re], SCHNEIDER [Cul, Re]. *N40*{PR}

Aeae: (Koae) Tall, vigorous plant, mature height 15 to 20 feet. Very ornamental, the trunk, leaves and fruit are variegated white, gray, and green. Bunches large, heavy. Fruit oblong, 6 to 7 inches long, 3 or 4 angled; pulp coarse, firm, yellow, of fairly good flavor. Primarily used as a cooking banana, though it may be eaten fresh. POPE; F69, J81G

African Rhino Horn: Slender, somewhat fragile plant, 10 to 12 feet tall, needs protection from the wind. Only a few very large fruit (up to 2 feet long and 3 pounds each) are produced which may be cooked green as a vegetable or eaten ripe. Attractive red coloration on the trunk and in the leaf. A79M, E31M, *G77M*, I83M, J81G, N84

Cardaba:[3] Large triangular fruit with a bright, waxy yellow skin. Flesh is pale salmon-orange and when fully ripe is sweet and flavorful with a refreshing tartness. Eaten both raw, and cooked as a starchy vegetable or as a sweet dessert. Fairly good source of vitamin A. Originated in the Philippines. J81G, J81G{PR}

Dwarf Orinoco:[2] Similar to the standard Orinoco in vigor, hardiness and fruit quality but its mature height is only 6 to 7 feet. Bunches are large, reaching 40 to 50 pounds. Can be eaten fresh or cooked. A useful plant where space is limited and easier maintenance is desired. A79M, E31M{CF}, J81G, N84

Eleele:[3] A distinctive Hawaiian cultivar with almost black trunk sheathes, petioles, and midribs. The plants are 20 to 25 feet tall and produce large bunches averaging 60 to 80 pounds in weight. Plump, well-filled fruit; skin thick and tough, clear yellow at maturity; pulp firm, orange colored, of good flavor. A highly prized cooking banana. POPE; J81G

Fehi:[3] (Fe'i) (M. troglodytarum) Vigorous, upright plant, often reaching 36 feet tall; sensitive to cold. Fruit stalk upright growing even when carrying bunches that can weigh 50 pounds. Short, stocky fruit; skin thick, orange to copper-colored when ripe; pulp very firm, orange-yellow, turns a greenish-yellow when cooked. Very good when boiled, baked or roasted. Also known for causing the urine to turn a chartreuse color. POPE; A79M, E31M, *G77M*, J81G, N84

French Horn: Plant 10 to 12 feet tall, rather slender; mostly green with its leaves outlined in red; fair wind resistance. Produces bananas up to 12 inches long which are primarily eaten boiled, fried, baked or broiled but can be eaten raw when thoroughly ripe. A79M, E31M, *G77M*, J81G, N84

Giant Plantain: Rather slender plant; grows to a height of 12 to 14 feet; not very wind tolerant but grows well in protected areas. Produces large fruit usually eaten cooked rather than fresh. The standard plantain of commerce. A79M, E31M, H4, N84

Kaualau: Sturdy, vigorous plant, mature height about 16 feet. Bunches large, 60 to 125 pounds in weight. Straight, plump fruits, 6 to 8 inches long; skin medium thick and tough, rich waxy yellow; flesh light yellow, fine-textured. A Hawaiian cooking banana of excellent quality. The Hawaiian name means "rain on the leaf". POPE; J81G, J81G{PR}

Maia Maoli: Tall, erect, attractive plant; mature height 18 to 22 feet. Produces heavy, well-packed bunches weighing 60 to 90 pounds. Long, round fruits, well-filled at both ends, often weighing 10 to 14 ounces; skin thick and tough, bright waxy yellow at full ripeness; pulp yellow, firm; core distinct; flavor good. Excellent when serves as a cooked vegetable; may also be eaten raw. The favorite cooking banana in the local Hawaiian markets. POPE; J81G

Manaiula:[3] Large, vigorous plant, 18 to 20 feet tall; attractive, with red coloration in the new growth and suckers and the underside of leaves and midribs washed in pink. Produces medium-sized bunches weighing 50 to 75 pounds. Slightly curved, 4 to 5 angled fruit, 6 to 8 inches long; skin thick and tough, waxy yellow when ripe; pulp orange, coarse, firm; core distinct. An excellent Hawaiian cooking banana. POPE; J81G

Orinoco: (Bluggoe, Burro, Better's Select) Medium-tall, sturdy plant, height 12 to 16 feet; very vigorous and particularly hardy. The bunch consists of only a few hands of very thick, three-angled fruits about 6 inches long. Flesh has a salmon tint, is edible raw when fully ripe but is much better cooked, either as a starchy vegetable or dessert sweetmeat, depending on the degree of ripeness when used. MORTON 1987a; A79M, C56M, D57, E31M, *G77M*, J81G, L29{OR}, *N40*{PR}, N84

Orinoco Victoria: Very cold-hardy; easily survived the winter of 1983 in the southern United States. Produces medium-sized bunches of large thick-skinned fruit of good flavor. Can be eaten fresh or cooked. The trunk is thick and strong; reaching 14 to 16 feet. Rapid growing. E31M

Popoulo:[3] Slender plant, 14 feet tall at maturity; prefers a protected location in filtered light with ample moisture. Bunches medium-sized, compact. Short, thick, blunt-ended fruit; 7 inches long and 1 3/4 inches in diameter; skin yellow, medium to thin; pulp firm, light salmon-pink; flavor pleasing, subacid, apple-like. May be eaten fresh or cooked. Well liked Hawaiian cultivar whose name translates to "ball-shaped like a breadfruit". POPE; J81G, J81G{PR}

Puerto Rican Dwarf:[2] Attractive plant with distinctive bronze-salmon coloring in the trunk and leaf sheathes; growing about 7 to 9 feet tall. Produces a small bunch with 3 to 12 fruit of very large size which are delicious cooked. Normally the plant does not require staking and it can produce bunches with individual fruits weighing up to a pound. A79M, E31M, *G77M*, J81G, L9M, N84

Saba: (Sabah) Short, flavorful fruit produced on compact heads; similar to Orinoco. Cold tolerant plant, grows 15 to 18 feet tall. Originated in the Philippines. E31M

BASIL {S}

OCIMUM SPP.

African Blue: (O. kilimandscharicum x O. basilicum) Attractive plant has dark-green leaves with purple veining; flowers and flower-spikes also purple. Height 2 to 3 feet. The whole plant has a sweet camphor-like scent. Hybrid of O. kilimandscharicum and O. basilicum 'Purpurascens' (purple-leaved basil). C43M{PL}

Ball Basil:[1] (Compact Green Bush, Fin Vert Compact) Small, compact plant with a great number of stems and leaves, causing the plant to have the appearance of a round mass or ball. Top leaves are bronze; appealing clove-like scent. Very well suited for growing in pots and ornamental vases. VILMORIN; I91, K22, M82{PL}, N42{PL}

Burgundy Beauty:[4] A striking lettuce leaf basil with attractive maroon foliage; fragrant. Plants grow to 2 feet tall. I39

Cinnamon: Attractive, stocky plants with a warm, spicy, cinnamon-like aroma and flavor with a hint of cloves. Purplish, concave venation on the leaves and dark, rose-colored blooms. Vigorous plants; hardier than other basils. Makes a fine jelly and chutney and is good in fruit salads, sweet-and-sour dishes, rib and chicken marinades, or other dishes where a sweet, spicy flavor is desired. HAMPSTEAD [Re]; B75, C11, C13M, C53, C81M, G51, G84{PL}, J20, K22, K66, *M35*{PL}, M53{PL}, N19M{PL}

Cuban: Medium-sized leaves with good basil flavor and fragrance. Grows to a height of 24 to 30 inches, forming a strong, compact bush. Appears to withstand light frost. M82{PL}

Dark Opal:[4] Attractive, dark-purple leaves with bronze overtones; height 12 to 18 inches; pale lavender-white flowers. Scent and taste are more subtle and delicate than sweet basil. Good for making basil vinegar to which it readily imparts its rich purple color - add a few sprigs of sweet basil to intensify the flavor. Developed at the University of Connecticut in the late 1950's. HAMPSTEAD [Cul, Re], HUTSON [Re]; C3{PL}, C11, C13M, C53, C81M, E5M{PR}, E99, F21{PL}, F24, G84{PL}, I39, J20, K22, K66, *M35*{PL}, N19M{PL}, *N40*{PR}, etc.

Dwarf Italian:[1] Small, compact plant, height 8 to 10 inches; develops into an attractive mound. Deep green, medium-length leaves with a strong pungent scent and good flavor. Excellent for culinary use. M82{PL}

Genovese: (Genova Profumatissima, Perfume Basil) Shiny, bright-green, slightly wrinkled leaves with symmetrical veins often purple in color. Height 18 inches. Intensely strong, almost perfumed aroma and flavor. Very popular for culinary use, especially in tomato salads and *pesto* sauces; combines well with garlic. Very productive; branches vigorously, and can thus be harvested in abundance over a very long season. Widely grown under glass in Italy, this strain is suited for both fresh use and drying. HAMPSTEAD; C53, D92{PL}, E5M{PL}, E81M, *E91G*, F24, G6, I99, J73, K49T, K49Z, K66, L86, Q34, S55, etc.

Greek Bush:[1] (Fine Leaved Miniature) Attractive bushy plant, height 6 to 9 inches; compact, umbrella-shaped form; leaves 1/4 to 1/2 inch long. Extremely strong sweet basil scent; good for all culinary usage. Typically grown in Greek homes and restaurants in pots and window boxes. Excellent for border edgings. J67M, K66, N19M{PL}, P83M, S55

Green Bouquet:[1] Round, bushy plants have miniature, full-flavored leaves 1/4 to 3/4 inch long; use fresh or dried like other basils. Compact plants are perfect for pots, edging, borders, or indoors year-round on a sunny windowsill. Height 10 to 12 inches. *A74*{PL}, B75, D11M, *E53M*, *E91G*, L91M, *M43M*, Q34

Green Bush:[1] (Dwarf, Fin Vert, Fine Green, French, Miniature) Attractive, compact plant; trim and ball-shaped, attaining as much as 2 feet in width. Bright green leaves, only 1/4 to 1/2 inch in length; numerous small clusters of rosy-white flowers. Strong aromatic odor and flavor, similar to that of common sweet basil. Particularly well suited for growing as an ornamental in pots. HAMPSTEAD [Cul, Re], VILMORIN; C11, C13M, C53, C67M{PL}, E5M{PL}, E81M, E99, F24, I39, J20, J82, M53{PL}, M82{PL}, N45{PL}

Green Goddess: Compact plant, grows in a 12 inch, almost round sphere; fragrant, dark-green, oval leaves, 1 1/2 inches by 1/2 inch; very slow to flower so it remains an attractive, spicy mound all season long. Ideal for container growing and indoor pots. *E91G*, G82

Green Ruffles: Fragrant, ornamental leaves are rich green, serrated and crinkled. Height 24 inches. Slightly more subtle flavor, but much larger leaves than common sweet basil. Fine for all culinary uses. Attractive companion to Purple Ruffles. A1M{PL}, B75, C13M, C53, C67M{PL}, C81M, D11M, E81M, *F72*, G51, G84{PL}, H3M{PL}, H40{PL}, L42, *M35*{PL}, etc.

Large Leaf Purple:[4] Plants grow to 3 feet tall; have quite large, intensely purple leaves with a fine, sweet fragrance. Selected from an F_1 hybrid between Lettuce Leaf and Dark Opal. Developed by Peace Seeds. I99, K49T

Lemon:[2] Attractive, spreading, gray-green plants with rather small, thin, pointed leaves and a distinct lemon-like aroma and flavor. Height 12 to 18 inches. Resents transplanting; direct seed where it is to be grown. Good in potpourris, herbal teas, cold drinks and for seasoning poultry and fish. HAMPSTEAD [Cul, Re], HUTSON [Re]; B75, C11, C13M, C53, C67M{PL}, C81M, E5M{PR}, E61, E99, F24, G84{PL}, I39, J20, K22, K66, *M35*{PL}, N19M{PL}, etc.

Lettuce Leaved: Very large medium-green leaves, 3 to 5 inches in length and 4 or more inches in diameter, crimped and undulating. Similar scent to that of common sweet basil but the flavor is not as strong. Low growing, thick-set habit. One of the most vigorous and prolific basils and thus recommended for making *pesto* sauce. Also good as a finger food wrapper. HAMPSTEAD [Cul, Re]; B78, C3, C3{PL}, C13M, C67M{PL}, D29{PL}, *E91G*, F24, I39, J73, K22, L42, L56, M53{PL}, N19M{PL}, etc.

Licorice:[3] (Anise, Oriental, Thai, Horapa) Stems, leaf veins and flower bracts are deep-purple while the flower-stalks are a pale violet. Vigorous plants; height 2 to 3 feet. Very strong licorice or anise-like aroma and flavor. Makes a nice addition to fruit salads and poultry.

Also widely used in Southeast Asian cuisine. COST 1988 [Cul], HAMPSTEAD, HUTSON [Re]; A2, A97{PL}, C11, C13M, C43M, C53, D55, G6, G84{PL}, H3M{PL}, J20, K66, M53{PL}, M82{PL}, N19M{PL}, etc.

Mammoth: Very large, lettuce leaf type, nearly the size of a human hand; ideal for drying, stuffing, or making *pesto* sauce. The leaves are large enough to use for wrapping chicken or fish before grilling. Dries well, and does not get bitter after long cooking. C53, G84{PL}, H3M{PL}, I77, J82

Mexican: Leaves dark-green, glossy, thick; upper stems purple-tinted. Strong, spicy cinnamon-like scent and flavor. Dried, the fragrance keeps for many months. Excellent for tea. Tall, vigorous, bushy growth habit; height 2 to 3 feet. Similar to Cinnamon basil but somewhat coarser. Will grow year round if taken indoors for the winter. C43M, G96, J20, J73, K49T

Mrs. Burns Lemon:[2] A pure strain that has been grown for 60 years in southeastern New Mexico. Many people consider this cultivar far superior to the more common sweet basil. Readily self seeds. Fine for all culinary uses, especially soups, roasts, and fried chicken. Flowers tend to be pink rather than white. C43M, I16, <u>I16</u>{PR}

Napoletano: (Italian) Very large, rounded, deeply crinkled leaves; light green in color; luxuriant. Height 18 inches. Very sweet fragrance and distinctive, mellow, rich flavor is only slightly inferior to that of common sweet basil, with less deterioration after flowering. Especially good for making *pesto* sauce. The cultivar most commonly grown in the Naples region. B97{PL}, C13M, C43M, E5T, F93G{PL}, I91, J73, K2, K66, N42{PL}, O48

Nine Level Tower: 45 days. Oriental type that is relatively richer in flavor than Western basils. When about 8 inches high, the tips should be pinched back to promote side branches and leaves. Very popular in Taiwan and Vietnam where, fresh or dried, it is used to add flavor and fragrance to soups and other foods. D55

Persian Anise:[3] Large plant with purplish foliage. Very aromatic anise-like fragrance and flavor. Excellent for culinary purposes. G96{PL}, J73

Picollo: (Picollo Fino Verde Compatto) Small, light green leaves have intense sweet basil aroma and flavor but the plant has more closely placed leaves and proportionately less stem. Height 2 1/2 feet. Reputed to be the true, authentic *pesto* basil. Particularly favored for this purpose, because unlike common sweet basil it retains its flavor after flowering. HAMPSTEAD [Cul, Re]; C11, C13M, C43M, D62, E5M{PL}, E5T, F24, G84{PL}, H40{PL}, I39, J73, J82, K2, K66, L86, Q34, etc.

Portuguese: Long, drooping, light-green leaves with a spicy aroma and strong flavor. Stems and flower bracts are an attractive purplish color. Excellent for culinary use. Upright, somewhat willowy growth habit; height about 12 inches. M82{PL}

Puerto Rican: Large, distinctly lobed leaves, light-green in color and with a fragrance that is sweet and pungent. Excellent for culinary use. Well formed, dense, bushy growth habit; height approximately 24 inches. M82{PL}

Purple Ruffles:[4] Large, heavily ruffled and fringed purple-black leaves; pinkish purple flowers; larger and showier than Dark Opal. Height 18 to 24 inches. Flavorful, colorful leaves are especially fine for herb vinegars and for garnishing; strongly aromatic when crushed. Germination and early growth tend to be slower than other basils; start indoors for best results. HUTSON [Re]; B75, C9{PL}, C13M, C53, C67M{PL}, D11M, E81M, G51, H3M{PL}, I39, I91, J20, K22, L42, L91M, etc.

Red Ball:[3] (Thyrsiflora) Plants grow 15 to 18 inches tall, and 20 inches in diameter. Leaves are green at the base of the plant but may be purple near the flowers. Inflorescence is in the form of a thyrsus; showy, with lavender or lavender and white flowers and deep purple flower-stalks, bracts, and calyces. The very fragrant aroma is sweet and anise-like. Used in Thai cuisine. An excellent ornamental as well as culinary cultivar. DARRAH, HAMPSTEAD; E5M{PL}, N19M{PL}

Silver Fox: Tall, small-leaved basil; height 2 feet. Light green leaves, edged with a silvery border. A14, E5M{PL}

Spice: (O. basilicum x O. canum) Slender, spreading, bushy plant; 2 to 2 1/2 feet high; leaves dark-green; inflorescence dark-purple. Has a very pleasant, strong, spicy fragrance suggestive of O. sanctum, and is one of the best basils for tea. Easily grown and thrives with little care. It breeds true and self sows as far north as Connecticut. Probably a natural hybrid. DARRAH; I99, J82, M15T{PL}, O48, S55

Spicy Globe:[1] Attractive, bushy, small-leaved cultivar forming a tight mound that retains its shape all season without pinching; height 10 inches, 12 to 18 inches across. Strong aroma; good for all culinary uses. Recommended for pot culture, and as edging for borders and beds. Produces clouds of tiny white flowers in late summer. A1M{PL}, C9{PL}, C16, C67M{PL}, C81M, E81M, *F72*, G51, G84{PL}, H3M{PL}, H40{PL}, I91, K22, K49M, *M35*{PL}, M53{PL}, N19M{PL}, etc.

Sweet Fine: Taller version of bush basil. Compact growth habit; reaches a height of 16 inches. Smaller leaves than common sweet basil but with a similar flavor. D29{PL}, E81M, F15M{PL}, J82, M15T{PL}, M82{PL}

BEET {S}

BETA VULGARIS CRASSA GROUP

GARDEN BEETS

<u>ORANGE-SKINNED</u>

Burpee's Golden: (Golden) 55 days. Attractive, bright golden-orange roots, develop rapidly; best when eaten small, but retain their sweet flavor and do not become fibrous when larger. Will not bleed like red beets. Excellent in salads, gourmet borscht, or pickled. Tops are very good boiled as greens. Sow seeds thickly, as germination rate is lower than other beets. A16, B75, C53, C85M, D82, E24, E49, F19M, F44, *F72*, G16, G44M{PR}, H42, H94, J7, K66, *N40*{PR}, etc.

<u>RED-SKINNED</u>

Hybrid

Red Ace: 55 days. Very early Detroit Short Top type with extremely smooth skin and even, deep red color throughout. Smooth, medium size crown with short, erect tops nearly free of red pigment. Very high sugar content throughout the root and leaf. Bolt and heat resistant and tolerant to cercospora leaf spot. A13, *A69M*, A87M, D11M, D76, F19M, F82, H42, H94, I91, J7, J20, K73, L97

Warrior: 57 days. Highly uniform, globe-shaped, unusually smooth root; tender, smooth-textured, well colored flesh. Includes sugar beet material in its breeding, therefore it is sweeter than other cultivars. Develops very quickly, yet holds its quality even as it grows larger. Good for bunching or processing. Introduced in 1979 by Joseph Harris Seed Co. F13

Open-Pollinated

Always Tender: 75 days. Long season or winter keeper beet. Unsuitable for summer use but in winter storage will remain sweet and tender until late spring. Extra large roots appear rough but have a delicious red interior flesh. M49

Avonearly: A round, fast-growing, early beet; highly resistant to bolting. Suitable for "multi-sowing". Bred in Warwickshire, England. P83M

Badger:[3] 50 days. A gourmet "baby beet", only 1 inch in diameter; the perfect size for appetizers, pickling or canning whole. Dark blood-red roots are tender and flavorful. Rapid-growing, but remains smooth. Small size and tops makes it ideal for planting in limited areas and double rows about 8 inches apart. B13, D11M, I67M

Boltardy: 58 days. Smooth, deep-red roots with very good internal color. Highly resistant to bolting, the solid flesh staying ringless and tender even when grown to a large size; also stands early cold periods especially well. Ample tops make good "greens". Can be sown from early spring into fall. K66, O53M, P83M, *R23*, S61, *S75M*

Bulls Blood:[1] A very old cultivar which is grown especially for its extremely attractive reddish-purple leaves. Best picked when young. S55

Cheltenham Green Top: Long, medium-sized, tapering roots with broad shoulders and dark-red flesh. Bronze-green leaves with red-tinged stems. Very long roots have the advantage of searching for water in dry summers, especially on sandy soils. Hardy; lift with care in late autumn and store. Introduced in 1905. P83M, *R23*, S61, *S75M*

Chioggia: (Dolce di Chioggia, Peppermint Beet, Candy Cane Beet) Attractive rosy-pink skin. White flesh with bright-pink alternating concentric rings. Smooth, medium height tops are solid green with red-shaded stems. Most attractive grated raw but tastier cooked. Becoming well-known in U.S. specialty markets. An old traditional Italian cultivar. B8, D87, G6, H49, I77, K49M, K66, L7M, *N40*{PR}, P83M, Q34, S55

Crapaudine: (Rough Skinned) One of the oldest cultivars, distinguished by the peculiar appearance of the skin, which is black and resembles the skin of a black winter radish. Root rather long, almost entirely buried in the soil; flesh very red, sugary and firm. Leaves almost entirely green, with red stalks. VILMORIN; S95M

Crimson Globe: Medium-sized, globe shaped, 3 inch diameter roots; deep crimson, slightly zoned. Excellent flavor and tenderness; good in salads. Grows quickly for early use. Good keeper; can be sown late for autumn and winter use. An old, well-established favorite. B49

Crosby's Egyptian:[4] (Early Crosby Egyptian, Crosby's Extra Early Egyptian) 55 days. Deep-red, smooth, turnip-shaped root; dark-red internal color, with slight zonation; rapid growing. Tall, erect tops are bright glossy-green; very flavorful; excellent for markets where beets are sold in bunches. Ideal for forcing for early market. Introduced in 1880. *A69M*, C92, D76, E38, G68, G79, H94, K49M, K71, L7M, *L59G*, M46, M95, M95M, N39, N52, etc.

Cylindra:[2] (Tendersweet Cylindra) 60 days. A unique, long cylindrical beet that will give 3 to 4 times the number of uniform slices as a round beet. Smooth, dark-red roots, up to 8 inches long and 1 3/4 inches in diameter, grow almost entirely underground. Will grow over a long season, maintaining its sweet, tender flavor. B73M, B75, B75M, C44, C85M, D11M, D82, E38, F19M, *F72*, F82, G16, H42, H94, L97, N39, etc.

Detroit Dark Red: 58 days. Smooth, globe-shaped, dark-red root; small tap root; interior color blood-red, with indistinct zonation. Tops are 13 to 15 inches tall; glossy dark-green tinged with maroon. Standard all-purpose cultivar. Introduced in 1892. A16, B73M, B75M, E24, F19M, F82, G51, H66, H94, J14{PL}, K73, L7M, L97, M49, M95, N16, etc.

Dwergina:[3] 58 days. Improved short-topped beet in the Detroit Dark Red class. Distinguished by its intense color, tender, dense and smooth texture and sweet flavor. Round, very smooth-skinned beets; completely free from zonation; grows slowly at maturity, staying relatively small. Recommended for "baby beets" as well as growing on to normal size. C53, F44, G6, I77, K50, O53M, S55

Early Blood Turnip-Rooted: (Early Dark Blood Turnip) 55 days. Root smooth, flattened and symmetrical; about 4 inches in depth and diameter; skin deep purplish-red; flesh deep blood-red, sometimes circled and rayed with paler red, remarkably sweet and tender. Adapted for summer or winter use. Known prior to 1863. BURR; *G1M*, G57M, G67M, M95M

Early Red Ball: 48 days. Popular, first early, round beet from direct seeding, outdoors. Perfectly round, medium-sized roots have deep crimson interiors and bright red exteriors. Tops are short. Highly recommended to truck farmers and roadside stands. L42

Early Wonder:[4] (Greentop) 55 days. Semi-globe shaped, smooth-skinned, uniform roots; about 3 inches in diameter; skin dark red; flesh deep red, with lighter zones. Medium-tall, bright glossy-green tops grow quickly and are excellent for bunching and beet greens. A16, B73M, B78, C44, D82, F19M, G51, G68, H66, H94, M13M, M46, M95, N16, N39, etc.

Early Wonder Staysgreen:[4] (Staysgreen) 50 days. A favorite where beets are grown primarily for their greens. These are sold bunched, with large vigorous tops attached to young beets. Extra tall, bright glossy-green, tender, red-veined tops; stay green in cool weather longer than other Early Wonder strains. Smooth, flattened globe-shaped root. E57, G6, H54, *H61*

Flat Egyptian: (Early Flat Egyptian, Egyptian Turnip-Rooted, Noir Plate d'Egypte) Root rounded and flattened, growing almost entirely above ground; becoming irregular as it increases in size; skin very smooth, violet or slate red; flesh deep purple-red. Excellent for forcing for early market. Roots are somewhat flatter when transplanted from indoors to out. Introduced before 1885. VILMORIN; C85M, F33, I67M, P83M

Formanova:[2] (Cylindra Improved, Cook's Delight) 50 days. Unique, cylindrical-shaped root; 6 to 8 inches long and 2 1/2 inches in diameter. Flesh is dark red, tender and flavorful. Especially useful for slicing, the slices being very uniform in size, resulting in little waste. Also very popular for home pickling or freezing. A16, A56, B49, C53, D27, E57, F1, F92, G6, I39, I84, J7, J58, L42, M49, etc.

Forono:[2] 60 days. A long, tankard-shaped beet which grows as much above as below ground. Smooth, ruby-red roots cook quickly and have a high sugar content. Tops are quite short. Suitable for winter storage. Developed especially for canning, the unusual shape making it perfect for uniform slices. E97, G64, L89, P83M, *R23*

Gladiator: 48 days. Early processing type which holds its shape when crowded. Round, smooth beet; small tap root; interior color dark-red, with very little zonation; fine-grained flesh. Medium-green, 13 inch tops. Harvest when golf-ball sized for best flavor. The commercial favorite for canning. E97, G64, J7

Green Top Bunching:[4] 55 days. Attractive, heavy, bright glossy-green tops maintain their appearance well during adverse cooler weather; medium length is ideal for bunching; excellent flavor. Uniform, slightly-flattened, smooth-skinned roots; flesh is sweet, tender and fine-grained. Good all-purpose cultivar. C92, *F63*, F92, G79, G93M, *H61*, K50, K71, K73, L7M, L42, *L59G*, N52

Half Long Red:[2] Smooth, deep-red roots; about 6 to 7 inches long and 1 1/2 to 2 inches in diameter. Recommended for home use. M13M

Little Ball:[3] 45 days. Specially selected for gourmet "baby beets", if closely spaced Little Ball will produce uniform, smooth-skinned, globular roots about the size of a silver dollar. The flesh is sweet flavored whether used fresh or for pickling. Retains its deep-red interior color even after cooking. A16, B75, C85M, F90, G51, H42, I77, I91, J20, J83M, K66, L89, L97, M29, M49, etc.

Little Egypt: 34 days. Extremely early cultivar, maturing 5 weeks from transplanting. Sown indoors March 1st for transplanting outdoors around April 15th. Transplanting changes the shape of the root from flat to perfectly round. Short tops. Deep red interior color. Has a tendency to split when overmature. L42

Little Mini Ball:[3] 54 days. One of the first true "baby beets". Roots are about the size of a silver dollar at maturity; round, not globe-shaped. Used for whole pak pickled beets. Short tops are good for greens. H95, L42

Lutz Green Leaf: 70 days. Very popular for using fresh in summer; roots also hold well for picking into fall and for winter storage. Glossy green, elongated tops with pink midrib have excellent eating quality. Top-shaped roots are rich purplish-red, with dark red flesh shading to lighter zones. Sweet and tender used small or large; even large roots are quick-cooking. A13, D11M, E24, E57, F44, F82, G51, G57M, G71, G71M, I84, J20, K71, L7M, M95, etc.

MacGregor's Favorite:[1] (Dracena Beet) 60 days. An old Scottish heirloom that is very ornamental with a profusion of narrow, spear-shaped leaves that are a striking blood-red with a metallic sheen. Deep-red, elongated, 3 inch roots have a fine flavor. The slender leaves interplant attractively with flowers, borders and beds. C53, E24, I39, I77, L91M, P69, *R23*

Miniature:[3] 52 days. Very small, round beet that can be used as a gourmet "baby beet". At maturity it does not become larger than 2 to 3 inches in diameter, remaining perfectly round. Short tops. Also used for pickling and canning whole. J7

Mobile:[5] 55 days. Unlike most beet seeds, which are actually clusters of seeds forming a fruit, Mobile's seed is "mono-germ", producing only one plant per seed. This built in singling results in more uniform size. Medium tall tops, with smooth, round to slightly top-shaped roots free from zonation. D11M, G6

Mono Germ:[5] 45 days. Produces one sprout per seed instead of several. This provides a more uniform stand of beets without costly thinning. Compares in size, shape, top and interior qualities with the Detroit types. Approximately 375,000 seeds per pound, providing more sprouts than ordinary types that average 240,000 per pound. G64, L42

Monodet:[5] 45 days. A mono-germ type producing only one sprout per seed, thereby reducing the need for thinning. Well-rounded flavorful roots for use in summer and autumn. Tops make excellent "greens" for cooking. S61, *S75M*

Monopoly:[5] 60 days. Mono-germ type, bred to produce only one sprout per fruit. Elongated, globe-shaped root with a fine texture and sweet taste; holds well in the garden without getting pithy or tough. Derived from Boltardy, having the same high quality and resistance to bolting. K66, L91M

Norton:[2] An early cylindrical beet with good bolting resistance and an attractive deep red color. Strong, upright tops. Highly recommended for slicing. K50

Ruby Queen: 60 days. Round, smooth, globe-shaped, deep blood-red root; deep red interiors are free from zonation under normal conditions; very uniform; tender, sweet flesh. Tops are short, bright green, narrow-leaved and turn red in cool weather. Leading canning cultivar in the Northeast. All America Selections winner in 1957. A16, B75M, C44, F1, F19M, G16, G71, *H61*, H95, J7, J58, K73, L7M, M13M, M46, N16, etc.

Spinel:[3] 60 days. Small, Detroit-type "baby beet" bred for the critical gourmet trade of the expensive restaurants of Europe. Smooth, globe-shaped root; bright-red internal color. Can be harvested as a baby beet after 40 to 45 days, but can stand in the field much longer without getting over mature. Often used for whole pack canning. I39, L91M, *R11M*

Sweetheart: 58 days. Round to top-shaped roots are not smooth or uniform, but make up for it in flavor; solid red flesh that's uniform throughout. Sugar beet in the parentage makes this cultivar extra-sweet. Tops are of medium height, tinged with red. For fresh use, canning and storage. Developed by Professor E.M. Meader at the University of New Hampshire. Introduced in 1958. D82, G6, L7M

Winter Keeper: (Long Season) 78 days. Produces a very large, rather rough, almost mangel-like beet with deep red interior. Remains sweet and tender even when very mature. Large green tops can be harvested separately for "greens". Mature beets are easily stored in a bushel of moist sand for winter consumption. C44, D76, E97, F13, F24M, G82, J25M, J58, K49M, L42, L89

WHITE-SKINNED

Albina Vereduna: (Snowhite) 55 days. Large, globe-shaped root; white inside and out. Has a high sugar content and a rich flavor. Unusually thick and durable skins make for excellent storage in the ground during fall and winter. Curled, wavy leaves make tasty "greens". C53, I77, L89, L91M

Albino White: 50 days. A novel "non-bleeding" beet with pure-white, fairly smooth, globe-shaped roots that are sweet and mild-flavored. Makes unusual sliced and pickled beets. Plain green tops may be used as "greens". I97T, K49M, L42, Q34

MANGELS

Large, swollen-rooted beets generally used as animal feed due to their coarseness although some types are suitable for the table when young. Almost certainly originated by crossing a form of garden beet with a leaf beet.

Colossal Long Red: 100 days. Roots frequently grow 2 feet long, about half growing above the surface; weighing up to 15 pounds each. Skin is bright rich-red. Flesh is white, tinted with rose. Relished by livestock, particularly milk cows. K71

Jaune d'Eckendorf: 110 days. Very large, round, yellow, sweet forage beet. Keeps all winter if properly stored. Best planted in late spring for fall harvesting. A good food supplement for rabbits, goats and chickens. Will yield up to 50 tons an acre. For the table, boil and then add butter and chopped chives. I39, Q24M

Mammoth Long Red: (Long Red) 110 days. Roots extremely large, tapering; grow half above ground, half below; weigh up to 30 pounds each; skin light-red; flesh white, tinged with rose. Very productive; will yield from 30 to 40 tons per acre on well-prepared land. Good livestock fodder; also good for table use. A25, A69M, A87M, D65, E97, F80, G16, G57M, G79, G87, H49, I64, J7, K73, M13M, etc.

Yellow Intermediate: (Giant Yellow Intermediate) Large half-long roots, grayish-green above ground, orange below; solid white flesh. Easy to pull and top. Yields well under varied conditions. One of the most widely grown of all mangels. I67M, I99, M13M, M49

SUGAR BEETS

Relatively highly bred types, mostly bred for sucrose extraction commercially. Generally lacking in pigmentation, they have a high root sugar content. Occasionally grown for home sugar extraction or as a home garden vegetable which can be used in soups and stews. Grated sugar beet is said to bring out the true flavor of accompanying vegetables when added to vegetable dishes. BIANCHINI, CLARKE, ORGAN [Cul].

HYBRID

High Sugar: A new hybrid sugar beet with outstanding productiveness. Ideal for normal uses of sugar beets, particularly valuable for stock feeding. A16

OPEN-POLLINATED

Giant Western: 80 days. Grown for sugar making or stock feeding. Roots are medium large; 10 to 12 inches long, 4 inches wide at the shoulder; yellow-fleshed; weigh 2 to 3 pounds each. High sugar content. Will take on the color of red beets when canned with them; will also add sweetness. Yields 20 to 40 tons per acre. Can be used for fall or spring harvest. D76, E97, *I59M*, I64, K71, K73

Giant White: 110 days. A special selection with very large, smooth, firm roots; usually growing about two-thirds above ground when matured. Light-green above ground, white below. Heavy yielding. Long keeping. Combines best qualities of mangels and sugar beets. A69M, D11M, M13M

Half Sugar Rose: 100 days. A cross between a mangel and a sugar beet. Oval-shaped root; green above the ground, white below; flesh white and sweet. Keeps well. Heavy yielding. Mature roots supply food of high nutrient value for feeding purposes. D27, M13M

Half Sugar White: 120 days. Large attractive roots; skin white, green at the crown; flesh white, very sweet. Very rich in food value. Can be harvested easily and is a good keeper. J7

Klein Wanzleben: Long, tapering roots with large shoulders. White skin and flesh. Ideal for sugar manufacture, containing the highest percentage of sugar of any sugar beet. Two large roots can produce 1 cup of sugar and 1/2 cup of blackstrap molasses; 100 tons of roots have yielded as much as 18 tons of sugar. Also used as feed for sheep, but is too sweet for cattle. J7, J82

White Forage: The crisp root is fine for the table when young. Produces an abundance of bright glossy leaves. Flowering stalks can be removed to encourage perennial "greens" production. F42

BLACK WALNUT {GR}

JUGLANS NIGRA

Baum #25: Nut size medium; shell thin, average weight 28.8 grams; kernel averages 6.06 grams, does not fill well; flavor good; ripens in midseason. Tree vigorous; a biennial bearer; subject to anthracnose. Originated in Carlisle, Kentucky by Cullie Baughn. Introduced in 1938. BROOKS 1972; E41M{SC}

Beck: Medium-sized nut, averaging about 37 per pound; shell thinner than average; kernel cracks out nearly 100% in quarters and halves; flavor superior to most cultivars; ripens early. Tree vigorous, symmetrical; produces heavy crops regularly; disease resistant. Won first prize in Michigan nut contest in 1932. BROOKS 1972; I25M{SC}

Bicentennial: Nut size medium to large; flavor good; kernel filling good; cracking quality equal to Thomas. Tree vigorous, a precocious bearer; very hardy. Originated in Huevelton, New York. E91M, E91M{OR}, K16{OR}

Bowser: (Boser) Nut size medium, averaging 30 to 35 per pound; shell very thin, cracking qualities excellent; kernel averages 37% of weight of whole nut; flavor very good. Tree noted for rapid growth. Originated in Xenia, Ohio by John Mitchell Davidson and Homer G. Bowser. Introduced in 1958. BROOKS 1972; E41M{SC}, E62{PR}, E62{SC}, I40{OR}, K16{PL}

Burton: Nut of average size; shell thick, hard to crack, although kernels crack out well; kernel plump, broad, sweet, pellicle light to medium brown. Tree tall. Originated in Hartford, Kentucky by Herbert Burton. Introduced in 1931. BROOKS 1972; I40{OR}

Clermont: Nut 1 1/4 inch long; apex slightly pointed; shell extremely thin, about 1/16 inch thick; kernel creamy white, plump, flavor excellent; cracks out about 40%. Tree produces heavy crops. Resistant to anthracnose. Originated in Clermont County, Ohio by Albert M. Kirtnes. Discovered in 1912, growing along the Ohio River. Introduced in 1959. BROOKS 1972; E91M, E91M{OR}, I40

Cornell: Cracking quality good. Believed to be a seedling of Thomas, which it resembles; ripens earlier. Moderately productive. Originated in Ithaca, New York by W.C. Muenscher. Introduced in 1949. BROOKS 1972; K16{PL}

Deming's Purple:[1] Purple leaves, flowers and husks distinguish this ornamental cultivar, which also has a purple spot on the nutmeat. I25M{SC}

Emma Kay: Has a thin shell, and cracks out a very high percentage of kernels; 30 nuts per pound. Bears heavily in southern Ontario, but in heavy crop years not all the nuts fill well. Nut flavor is reputed to be excellent but the cultivar has not yet been extensively tested. The tree has a spreading crown. Originated in Illinois. JAYNES; E41M{SC}, E62{PL}, E62{PR}, E62{SC}, E91M, E91M{OR}, I40, K16{PL}

Evans: Exceptionally large, well-filled nuts. Will come very close to true from seed as it is an isolated tree. Appears to be a Thomas seedling. A91{PL}

Farrington: Very large nut; shape distinctive; shell somewhat thick, but cracks well; kernel light-colored, flavor mild, fills well. Tree bears early, regularly and heavily. Anthracnose resistant. Originated in Fayette County, Kentucky by O.M. Farrington. Introduced in 1959. BROOKS 1972; E41M{SC}, I25M{SC}, I40

Fonthill: Medium-sized nut; kernel filling very good; good flavor. Tree vigorous, upright; hardy; heavy-bearing; selected for its good qualities as a timber tree. E91M{OR}, E91M{PL}, N24M

Hare: Very large nut; 20 nuts per pound. Large kernel; good cracking quality, with a high percentage of kernel crack-out. Tree blooms late; yields well. Originated in Rushville, Schuyler County, Illinois by F.M. Hare. Introduced in 1930. BROOKS 1972; I25M{SC}, I40

Harney: Nut shell thin, excellent cracking quality; high kernel percentage. Survival rate in all plantings has been below average. Originated in Cynthiana, Harrison County, Kentucky by Cullie Baughn, U.S.D.A. Soil Conservation Service. Introduced in 1939. BROOKS 1972, JAYNES; I40{OR}

Krause: Nut averages about 23 per pound; cracks well; kernel averages about 27% of total weight; quality very good; ripens rather late, first of October. Tree very hardy; very vigorous; produces a great deal of pollen which is shed early. Originated on the farm of Russell Krause, Toddville, Linn County, Iowa. Introduced in 1940. BROOKS 1972; I25M{SC}, K16{OR}

Lamb: (Lamb's Curly) Fairly large nut; quality better than average. Tree a rapid grower; primarily of use for veneer because of curly-grained wood, but in the majority of sites where grafts have been tested, the curly grain has not been observed. Originated in Ada, Michigan by George N. Lamb of the Walnut Manufacturers Association of Chicago. Introduced about 1935. BROOKS 1972; I40{OR}, I60{PL}

Minnesota Native: Self-pollinated seedlings of the hardiest black walnut tested by St. Lawrence Nurseries, Potsdam, New York. The mother tree ripens nuts 2 to 3 weeks before any other black walnut in this area. Nuts are small, but the tree is exceedingly precocious and timber-type. Its seedlings are uniformly vigorous and fast-growing. L27M{PL}

Mintle: Small nut, averaging somewhat less than 10 grams; kernel content about 24% of nut; cracking quality good. It is reputed to have the best flavor of all black walnuts and the ability to store at room temperature for two years without becoming rancid. Survives exceptionally well in plantings. Originated in Glenwood, Iowa by J.R. Mintle. Introduced in 1931. BROOKS 1972, JAYNES; E41M{SC}

Myers: (Elmer Myers) A standard cultivar noted for its very thin shell and good cracking qualities. It has exceptional total-kernel and first-crack kernel percentages and a high recovery of quarters. Resistant to anthracnose. Best adapted to southern growing conditions; at more northern locations kernels tend to be shriveled and bearing is often erratic. Originated in Bellefontaine, Ohio by Elmer R. Myers. Introduced about 1930. BROOKS 1972, JAYNES; E41M{SC}, E62{PL}, E62{PR}, E62{S}, E62{SC}, E91M, E91M{OR}, I25M{SC}, I40, N15, N24M

Northwestern: Produces small nuts that are pollinated by Well Tree. The seedlings from these nuts are very hardy and uniform growers. L27M{PL}

Ogden: Large nut, averages 20.7 grams per nut; cracking quality very good; kernel averages 26.6% of nut; pellicle easily removed. Tree bears well in Arkansas and Oklahoma. Originated in Bedford, Kentucky by Joe Ogden. Introduced in 1928. BROOKS 1972; E41M{SC}, I25M{SC}

Ohio: Well known for its fine cracking qualities. It is moderately resistant to anthracnose, but highly susceptible to husk maggot. Biennial bearer. Discovered in Ohio in 1915. JAYNES; E41M{SC}, E62{S}, I25M{SC}, K16{PL}, N15

Patterson: Yields large nuts that are pollinated by Minnesota Native. Its seedlings are hardy and grow vigorously, showing a straight, timber-type growth habit. K16{OR}, L27M{PL}

Putney: (Green) Exceptionally large nut with good cracking qualities, fills well in short season areas. Produces seedlings that are vigorous and show an excellent timber-type growth habit. Parent tree is probably the largest and oldest black walnut tree growing in northern New York. L27M{PL}

Ridgeway: (Rabbit Ridge) This two-time Kentucky State Fair winner has a very large nut, cracks well, shows anthracnose resistance, and bears heavily. Discovered by Henry Converse. Originated in Illinois. Introduced in 1984. I40

Schreiber: Large nut; very high total kernel percentage; of good quality. Tree bears very well. Originated in New Albany, Indiana by R.H. Schreiber. Introduced in 1941. BROOKS 1972; I40{OR}

Snyder: Cracking quality good. Considered one of the best black walnuts in New York state, but does not fill well in Pennsylvania. Tree vigorous, productive. Originated in Newfield, New York by C.H. Snyder. BROOKS 1972; N24M

Sol: Long, oval, medium to large nut; shell fairly thin; kernel light colored, highly flavored, cracks out 26%; fills and cracks out better than Thomas in area of origin. Tree vigorous; bears heavy crops annually; somewhat resistant to anthracnose as it holds its leaves better than other cultivars. Originated in Greene County, Indiana. BROOKS 1972; K16

Sparrow: Medium to large nut; 27 per pound; hull very thin, hulling readily; shell rather thin, cracking quality good; kernel sweet, rich; quality very good, as good as, or better than Thomas. Ripens about with Snyder and 2 weeks before Thomas. Tree retains foliage well into fall, later than most other cultivars; hardy. Very resistant to anthracnose. Originated in Lomax, Illinois by Harry C. Sparrow. Introduced in 1935. BROOKS 1972; B99{CF}, E41M{SC}, I25M{SC}, I40{OR}, K16{OR}

Stabler: Cracks exceptionally well. Some of the nuts develop with a single lobe. The fruits are very susceptible to husk maggot. Originated in Maryland. JAYNES; I25M{SC}, I40

Stambaugh: A large-kerneled cultivar that bears at an early age. It is susceptible to anthracnose leaf spot infection. Won first prize among 1229 entries in 1926 contest sponsored by the Northern Nut Growers Association. Originated in Browning, Illinois by H.V. Stambaugh. Introduced in 1928. BROOKS 1972; E41M{SC}, G75

Ten Eyck: Nut small; shell fairly thin. Tree blooms late; productive. Originated in Rahway, New Jersey by E.M. Ten Eyck. Introduced in 1921. I40{OR}

Thomas: Large nuts; 30% kernel; cracks well; high-quality kernels with a good flavor. Bears heavily and at an early age. One of the most popular and widely planted cultivars. However, it is considered a poor selection for the Midwest, where the most frequent criticism is that the nuts do nut fill well, especially on trees more than 5 years old. Susceptible to anthracnose which can cause early defoliation and poor nut development. Discovered in Pennsylvania in 1881. JAYNES; C11M{PL}, E4, E41M{SC}, E97, E91M, E91M{OR}, F19M, H65, I25M{SC}, I40, J33{PL}, L33, M76, M83, N15, etc.

Thomas Myers: A selection of Leander Hay, produced by crossing Thomas and Elmer Myers. Probably the same as the Hay cultivar. A very large nut, 20 per pound, with 30% kernel; cracks out easily; medium shell thickness. Bears early, annually, and heavily. Originated in Missouri in 1980. I40

Vandersloot: Very large nut, 23 per pound; good cracking qualities. Nut kernel fills poorly; larger but thicker shell than Thomas; excellent flavor. Tree protogynous flowering. Superceded now by other and better cultivars but still preferred by some growers. Largest black walnut in the 1926 Northern Nut Growers Association contest. Originated in York County, Pennsylvania by C.E. Vandersloot. Introduced in 1927. BROOKS 1972; E41M{SC}, I40

Victoria: Nuts average 21 per pound; kernel equals 24.3% of nut; matures medium late; resembles Thomas. Does not compare in cracking quality with other thinner shelled cultivars. Tree bears young; crops well; vigorous. Resistant to leaf spot. Originated in Marion County, Kentucky by W.G. Tatum. Introduced in 1945. BROOKS 1972; E41M{SC}

Well Tree: A precocious grower which produces large nuts when pollinated by Weschcke or when self-pollinated. The seedlings from these nuts are vigorous and hardy. L27M{PL}

Weschcke: Nut elongated, pointed at both ends; shell thin, cracks easily; kernel sweet, mild, bright, plump; keeps well up to 2 or 3 years without rancidity; ripens in mid-October. Tree vigorous, large, hardy. Originated in River Falls, Wisconsin by Carl Weschcke. Introduced in 1953. BROOKS 1972; E91M, E91M{OR}, L27M{PL}, N24M

Wiard: Nut medium to small; roundish, slightly obovate, uniform; shell fairly thin, cracks well; kernel plump, rich, sweet, quality good; hull thick, heavy. Tree very slow coming into bearing; a shy bearer. Originated in Ypsilanti, Michigan by Everett W. Wiard. Introduced in 1934. BROOKS 1972; K16{PL}

BLACKBERRY {GR}

RUBUS SPP.

UPRIGHT BLACKBERRIES

The type most often grown in northern areas, they grow very tall and upright with long, vicious thorns. Generally easier to care for than trailing blackberries, the canes being self-supporting.

Bedford Giant: Very large, round fruit; skin black, glossy; flesh very juicy, sweet, flavor good; not as seedy as most blackberries; very good for canning and freezing; ripens very early. Very vigorous plant, with stems often 10 feet in length; very productive, the berries being borne in prolific clusters. Thought to have been selected from a Veitchberry seedling. SIMMONS 1978; U7M

Black Satin:[2] Very large, oblong fruit; skin dull black at full maturity; flesh firm, juicy, sweet; quality good; ripens mid-season, mid to late-July. Bush heavy yielding; non-suckering; highly resistant to septoria leaf spot and anthracnose, and moderately resistant to mildew; self-fruitful, but more productive when planted with Dirksen; canes semi-erect. A82, A88M, B43M, B58, C63, F11, F16, F19M, F93, H16, *J2M*, J83, K67, *M65M*, M76, etc.

Brazos: Fruit very large, with size being maintained longer during harvest than Lawton; attractive; flesh fairly firm, somewhat tart; quality good for fresh market; ripens early, earlier than Lawton. Bush vigorous; productive; resistant to stem and leaf diseases; canes erect. Lawton x Nessberry. Originated in College Station, Texas by J.B. Storey. Introduced in 1959. BROOKS 1972; A82, B10, B19, C37, *C54*, C63, D79, E29M, F19M, F68, H4, *K76*, M31M, M83, N33

Brison: Fruit similar to Brazos, but more attractive and with smaller seeds; the flesh is firmer and somewhat sweeter. Recommended for home gardens and pick your own operations. Bush slightly more upright; adapted to the Waco, Texas and south central Texas region. Originated in College Station, Texas by H.H. Bowen, Texas Agricultural Experiment Station. Introduced in 1979. M83, N33

Cherokee: Medium-large fruit; skin black, glossy; flesh firm, sweet; quality good; good for processing; ripens late July. Bush very vigorous and productive; canes very erect in growth habit; moderately thorny. The erect habit results in fruit being borne higher from the ground and more accessible to machine harvest. Developed at the Arkansas Agricultural Experiment Station. A14, B10, B43M, *C54*, C63, F19M, H16, I83M, *J2M*, J83, K17, *M81M*

Chester:[2] Fruit large; skin black; flavor very good; quality high, does not soften, leak or lose color on hot sunny days; ripens after Black Satin. Bush productive, yields about twice as much as most thorned types; very resistant to caneblight. Considered one of the more winter-hardy thornless blackberries; has been grown successfully in Michigan and upstate New York with winter protection. A39, B43M, B58, B75, C21, *C47*, D37, F16, H16, I50, J61M, J69, K17, K67, L33, etc.

Cheyenne: Fruit large, up to 1 inch long; quality excellent; ripens mid-season. Bush productive; canes very erect growing. Excellent for machine harvesting, for processing, pick-your-own operations and home gardens. Developed at the Arkansas Agricultural Experiment Station. B10, B43M, *C54*, *D25M*, D79, F93, I83M, *J2M*, *K1*, L60, M31M, *M81M*

Choctaw: Medium-sized, short conic fruit with an attractive glossy black finish; similar in firmness to Shawnee but slightly less firm than Cheyenne; excellent flavor; significantly small seed size. Ripens very early and tends to be more concentrated in ripening than other cultivars. Very vigorous and prolific plant; very erect growth habit. Developed by Dr. J.N. Moore of the University of Arkansas. A14, C15M, D43M, F16, K17, L60

Comanche: Very large, attractive fruit; skin black, glossy; flesh very firm; quality good to excellent; makes a good frozen or canned pack; also excellent for pies and jams; ripens after Brazos. Canes vigorous, very upright growing; productive; moderately thorny. Developed at the Arkansas Agricultural Experiment Station. A14, A82, B10, D79, *J2M*

Darrow: Large fruit, 1 inch long and 3/4 inch wide; skin black, glossy; flesh firm, mildly subacid, quality good; ripens early or about with Eldorado, continuing over a long period. Bush vigorous; reliable and heavy bearer. Originated in Geneva, New York by George L. Slate. Introduced in 1958. BROOKS 1972; *A74*, A82, B73M, B99, C63, D69, D76, E3, F19M, G23, G71, H16, H65, J69, K71, L33, M76, etc.

Dirksen:[2] (Dirksen Thornless) Large fruit; skin black, glossy; flavor sweet; ripens in early July, or a week sooner than Black Satin. Bush very vigorous; heavy yielding; cold-hardy; resistant to leaf spot, mildew and anthracnose; canes thornless. More cold-hardy than Black Satin, which it resembles. One of the hardiest thornless blackberries. A14, A56, B10, C21, *C47*, *C54*, C63, D76, E4, F19M, M31M

Ebony King: Fruit as large as Eldorado, which it resembles; skin black, glossy; flavor sweet, tangy, pure; ripens early. Bush upright; hardy, having withstood temperatures of 22 degrees below zero; resistant to orange rust; bears annually. Introduced about 1940 by Krieger's Wholesale Nursery, Bridgman, Michigan. BROOKS 1972; B10, B19, C63, E97, *J63M*, N24M

Eldorado: Large, roundish to slightly elongated fruit; skin jet black; flesh firm, juicy; flavor rich, sweet; quality good to very good; ripens early midseason, ripening period long. Bush tall, upright-spreading; hardy and productive; seldom attacked by orange rust. Originated about 1880 near the village of Eldorado, Ohio. HEDRICK 1925; B10, G13, *H90*

Flordagrand: (R. trivialis x) Large, oblong fruit; skin shiny black; flesh somewhat tart, softer than strawberries, juice very red; aroma delightful; very acceptable for pies, preserves and jellies; ripens very early. Bush vigorous; evergreen; canes long, somewhat trailing; adapted to hot, humid summers; winter chilling requirement very short. Originated in Gainesville, Florida. BROOKS 1972; *K76*

Hull:[2] Fruit very large; skin black, glossy when ripe; flesh firm, sweet; quality high, does not soften, leak or lose color on hot sunny days; ripens somewhat later than Black Satin. Bush vigorous; very productive, yields of 19,842 pounds per acre have been reported; slightly more winter hardy than Black Satin. Recommended for home gardens and pick-your-own operations. A24, B19, B43M, B58, B75, *C47*, C63, D37, F19M, F93, H42, I50, *J2M*, J69, *M81M*, etc.

Humble: Small, purple-black fruits with a sweet flavor. Vigorous, erect plant, not a heavy producer. The only major cultivar resistant to double blossom, a serious disease of southern erect blackberries. An older cultivar still popular in parts of the South. MCEACHERN; M83

Illini Hardy: (Illini Winter Hardy) Large, black fruit; flavor sweet, quality good; resembles Darrow. Vigorous, thorny plant; very hardy, has been tested at temperatures as low as -24° F. Should allow blackberries to be grown farther north than previously possible. New introduction from the University of Illinois. H33, I36, L60

Lawton: Large, slightly elongated fruit; skin jet black but becoming bronzed when over-ripe; core large, rather hard; flesh soft, juicy; flavor acid at first, becoming sweet only at full maturity, rich; quality very good; ripens late midseason. Bush tall, upright-spreading; vigorous; productive. Originated prior to 1854. HEDRICK 1925; B10, B19, B43M, C37, C63, H16, *J2M*, M83

Navaho:[2] The first erect-growing thornless blackberry. Short-conic fruit, comparable in size to that of Cheyenne; bright glossy black in color; firmer flesh than Cheyenne and Shawnee; sweeter flavor and smaller seed size than other thornless cultivars. Ripens about 15 days after Cheyenne. Developed by Dr. J.N. Moore of the University of Arkansas. A14, C15M, D43M, F16, K17, L37M, L60

Oklawaha: (R. trivialis x) Fruit about 1 1/8 inches long by 1/2 inch in diameter, somewhat blunt; skin black, turning reddish if exposed to sun after picking; juice deep red, aroma delicate and delightful; ripens 2 to 5 days before Flordagrand, which it resembles. Bush vigorous; canes trailing; semi-evergreen to evergreen; largely self-fruitful. Originated in Gainesville, Florida. BROOKS 1972; U7M

Perron Thornless:[2] Very large fruit; quality excellent; ripens from mid-July to late October. excellent for pick-your-own, home gardens and roadside markets. Very vigorous, suckerless plant; thornless. Developed by W.H. Perron & Co. of Quebec, Canada. Selected for its hardiness. *C47*, I91, J7

Pink Crystal:[1] Medium-sized, attractive pink fruit, nearly transparent when ripe; very delicate, sweet flavor; ripens in late spring. Erect bush; requires another blackberry cultivar for pollination. Originated in Hartford, Michigan by Dean Foster Nurseries. Introduced in 1977. U7M

Rosborough: Fruit very large; flavor sweeter than Brazos which it resembles; quality good; ripens early, average ripening date mid-May; ripens over a long period, approximately 25 days. Bush heavy yielding; withstands moderately dry weather; canes erect. Originated in College Station, Texas by H.H. Bowen, Texas Agricultural Experiment Station. Introduced in 1979. B10, B43M, C37, D79, F19M, F93, *J2M*, L33, M31M, M83, N33

Scottish: Vigorous, cold hardy plant. Yields large crops of medium low acid berries that ripen in late June. Valued because of their unusual flavor and the exceptionally large amount of berries produced by each plant. Originally brought from Scotland in 1907. Has proven reliable under local Tennessee conditions. B10

Shawnee: Fruit very large, attractive; skin black, glossy; flesh firm, very sweet and juicy; ripens later and over a longer period of time than other Arkansas blackberry cultivars. Canes very upright growing. Bush vigorous; disease resistant; productive; in production tests, Shawnee produced 13,391 pounds per acre, compared to 5,598 pounds for Cheyenne. Developed at the Arkansas Agricultural Experiment Station. A14, B10, B43M, C15M, F93, G17, H16, I83M, J58, *K1*, K17, L37M, L60, M31M

Silvan: Large, maroon-black fruit; mild very sweet flavor; excellent fresh or for processing; ripens very early. Vigorous, productive plant; shows excellent tolerance to heavy soils, wind and drought; also very disease resistant. Selected in Victoria, Australia from a progeny raised from a cross made in Oregon between Marion and a Boysen hybrid. JENNINGS; B43M, C15M, I49M, K17, *M81M*

Smoothstem:[2] Fruit large, blunt conic; skin jet black, firm; flavor good; matures about August 1, or a month later than Eldorado. Bush winter hardy at Beltsville and southward; productive; non-suckering; canes thornless, semi-upright, 8 to 10 feet long. Recommended for local market and home gardens. Originated in Beltsville, Maryland. Introduced in 1966. BROOKS 1972; B10, B73M, B99, *C47*, E3, F19M, G53M, I78, M83

Snyder: Small, hemispherical fruit; skin black, quickly becoming reddish black or brownish black; flesh juicy, firm, sweet, rather poorly flavored; quality good only when well grown and well colored; ripens late midseason. Bush tall, upright; vigorous; unusually hardy. Does particularly well on poor, light soils. Originated in Laporte, Indiana by Henry Snyder. Discovered in 1851. HEDRICK 1925; D76

Thornfree:[2] Fruit medium-large, blunt conic; skin glossy black; flavor good, tart; adheres firmly; ripens 3 weeks later than Eldorado. Bush winter hardy at Corvallis, Oregon and Beltsville, Maryland; very productive in fertile soils; canes thornless, semi-upright, 7 to 8 feet long. Originated in Beltsville, Maryland. Introduced in 1966. BROOKS 1972; A82, B43M, *C47*, C63, F16, F19M, G23, H33, H49, H65, *H90*, *J2M*, K71, L33, M39M, M76, etc.

Thornless Evergreen:[2] Fruit large, 1 1/2 inches long; skin black; flesh very firm and sweet; seeds large; quality fair; excellent for pies, jellies and jams. Bush very vigorous and productive; disease resistant; must be propagated from tip layering to preserve thornless trait; canes semi-trailing. Grown commercially in Oregon. STEBBINS; A82, B10, B67, *C54*, E4, *J63M*, K17, L30, *M65M*, *M81M*

Waldo Thornless:[2] Produces high yields of highly-flavored berries that are easy to pick. Unlike some other thornless cultivars, Waldo remains thornless, even from the suckers. Originated in Corvallis, Oregon at the Oregon Agricultural Experiment Station. Named after Dr. George F. Waldo, who developed the Marionberry. C15M, I49M, J61M, K17

White:[3] Small to medium-sized fruit, pure creamy-white when ripe; drupelets large, pearl-like; sweet, delicate, blackberry-like flavor; quality very good. Too soft for commercial production. Bush tall, very vigorous and productive; spring-bearing. Requires another cultivar for pollination. N45M{OR}

Womack: Fruit similar to Brazos, but more attractive and with smaller seeds; the flesh is firmer and somewhat sweeter. Recommended for home gardens and pick your own operations. Bush slightly more upright; adapted to the Waco, Texas and north Texas region. Originated in College Station, Texas by H.H. Bowen, Texas Agricultural Experiment Station. Introduced in 1979. C37, M83, N33

BLACKBERRY-RASPBERRY HYBRIDS

Included here are direct crosses between species of blackberry and raspberry as well as progeny of such crosses. They are characterized by a distinct flavor that combines the best qualities of both parents.

Boysen: (Boysenberry) Fruit very large, 1 1/4 inches or more long; skin dark red to purplish-black; flesh rather soft; aroma distinct; flavor very fine but not as sweet as Young, suggestive of raspberries; ripens 1 week before Young. Bush trailing, more vigorous than Young, high yielding. Originated in Napa, California by Rudolf Boysen. Introduced in 1935 by Walter Knott, Knott's Berry Farm, Buena Park, California. BROOKS 1972; A82, A88M, B43M, C12{PR}, C63, E4, E31{PR}, F11, H49, *J2M*, J61M, K17, K28, L97, M39M, *M65M*, *M81M*, etc.

Logan: (Loganberry) Large fruit, up to 1 1/4 inches long; skin dark-red to dusty maroon, covered with dark hairs that dull its color; flesh firm, very juicy; flavor tart unless fully ripe; excellent for canning and pies. Bush trailing; very vigorous; needs trellis support. Originated in Santa Cruz, California by Judge J.H. Logan. Introduced in 1880. SIMMONS 1978, STEBBINS; B19, B67, C63, E4, E97, I49M, J61M, K17

Marion: (Marionberry) Medium to large fruit; skin bright black; flesh medium firm; quality high with excellent flavor; ripens with Boysen. Excellent for local markets, canning, pies, jams, etc. Bush trailing; a vigorous grower; very productive, has higher yields for a longer period than Boysen; adapted to western Oregon and western Washington. Chehalem x Olallie. Originated in Corvallis, Oregon by George F. Waldo. Introduced in 1956. BROOKS 1972; B67, C12{PR}, C15M, I49M, I99{S}, J61M, K12M{PR}, K17, L30, L97, M39M, M63M{PR}, *M81M*

Nectar: (Nectarberry) Very large fruit; dark red to purplish black; drupelets large, 9 around the core instead of 10 or usually 11 as in Boysen; flesh juicy, somewhat acid, flavor pleasant, seed very small; ripens from late July to late August. Bush trailing; production and habit almost if not identical with Boysen. Thought by many to be a chimera of Boysen, which it resembles. BROOKS 1972, SIMMONS 1978; *C54*, M31M

Ness: (Nessberry) (R. rubrisetus x R. strigosus) Fruit larger than Logan; skin deep-red to blood-red, turning brown when overripe, glossy; drupelets large; flavor of raspberry, high acidity; keeping quality good. Bush very vigorous; growth habit like raspberry; canes up to 15 feet in length. Originated in College Station, Texas by H. Ness. Introduced in 1921. BROOKS 1972; H4

Olallie: (Olallie Berry) Large fruit, slightly longer and more slender than Boysen; skin black, glossy, attractive; flesh firm; flavor good but peak quality reached only at full maturity; excellent for processing. Bush very vigorous; canes trailing; very susceptible to orange rust when grown in a warm climate; winter-chilling requirements shorter than for Boysen. Logan x Young. BROOKS 1972; A88M, C15M, *C54*, E4, F11, I83M, K17, *L47*, *M81M*

Sun: (Sunberry) (R. ursinus x R. idaeus) Similar to Tayberry, but fruits are slightly smaller and are produced much more abundantly. Fruits are also darker colored and sweeter than Tayberry. Originated at the East Malling Research Station. Hybrid cross between a wild blackberry and a red raspberry. JENNINGS; H42, K64

Tay: (Tayberry) Fruit large, long conical in shape; 50% larger than Logan, with a brighter and less downy appearance; skin deep purple when fully ripe; flavor sweet, strong; quality excellent; suitable for fresh market, frozen fruit, jam or wine. Bush similar to Boysen and Young in growth habit; produces fruit on short, strong laterals, making it easy to pick. Originated at the Scottish Horticultural Research Institute. Introduced in 1979. JENNINGS; B43M, B67, C63, D11M, D76, E33, F97, G87, H42, J61M, K17, L30, L33, L97, M31M, *M81M*, etc.

Thornless Boysen:[2] Similar to Boysen but fruit is smaller; bush is less productive. Originated in El Monte, California by D.L. Duffin. Introduced in 1938. Bud mutation of Boysen; discovered in 1936. BROOKS 1972, STEBBINS; B73M, C63, E3, F19M, G23, G72, *H90*, *J2M*, K71, L30, M39M, *M65M*, M76, N33

Thornless Logan:[2] Medium-large, lavender-red fruit, does not darken while ripening; fine hairs dull its color; flesh soft, tart, high in acidity. Excellent for pies, juice, canning, and wine making. Ripens earlier, produces over a longer period, and is more prolific than standard Logan. Plants are more vigorous and canes are stronger. Introduced about 1935. B67, C15M, *C54*, L30, L97, *M81M*

Thornless Nectar: Large, non-glossy fruit; color reddish-black; flesh soft, very juicy, subacid, with a characteristic fragrance; good for canning, freezing and eating fresh. Mutation of Nectar with productive, thornless plants that are much easier to pick. M31M

Thornless Young:[2] Large, dark-red fruit. Similar to Boysen, but is shiny and less acid in taste. Bears 10 days earlier than Boysen, but is about 20% less productive. Good for canning and freezing. Bush vigorous; productive; canes trailing, thornless. *C54*, E4, F19M, M83

Veitch: (Veitchberry) Fruit very large, round oblong; skin purplish-black; flesh juicy; flavor excellent; ripens very early, August until September. Bush vigorous; productive; canes strong, semi-erect. Originated by the famous Veitch nurseries of England. Hybrid cross of a hedgerow blackberry and November Abundance raspberry. SIMMONS 1978; R83

Young: (Youngberry) Fruit very large, roundish, appearance outstanding; skin deep wine-colored, glossy; flavor very sweet, excellent for frozen pack and jam; ripens mid-season. Bush trailing; high-yielding; productive; very vigorous; adapted to east Texas and southern Arkansas. Phenomenal berry x Austin Mayes dewberry. Originated in Morgan City, Louisiana by B.M. Young. Introduced in 1926. BROOKS 1972; B10, B43M, *C54*, C63, *J2M*, M31M, *M81M*

DEWBERRIES

Sometimes called trailing blackberries, they are more tender as a rule than upright types and are generally winter-killed when grown in the North. More difficult to care for with weak canes that must be tied to poles or trellises.

Austin:[2] (Austin Mayes, Austin Thornless) Said to be a seedling of Mayes and similar to that cultivar, but thornless; ripens early to mid-season. Originated about 1918 with J. Parker, Tecumseh, Oklahoma. Introduced in 1924 by J.M. Parker & Son Nursery Company, Fayetteville, Arkansas. HEDRICK 1925; A82, B10, B19, B43M, *C54*, *J2M*, M31M, M83, N33

Carolina: Fruit of good quality, both fresh and processed; resembles Lucretia. Bush dewberry type; thorny; more vigorous, more productive, and more resistant to septoria leaf spot than Lucretia. Austin x Lucretia. Originated in Raleigh, North Carolina. BROOKS 1972; U7M

Gardena:[2] Large, glossy jet black fruit; delicious sweet flavor; ripens very early, about 2 weeks ahead of other types. Thrifty growing plant, easy to pick; practically disease free. Canes nearly thornless, although occasionally a plant will revert and produce thorny canes. B10, H33, *J63M*

Lucretia: (R. flagellaris) Medium to large fruit; skin jet black; drupelets large; core soft; flesh juicy, firm; flavor pleasantly sprightly when fully ripe, otherwise rather tart, rich; quality very good; ripens early. Bush vigorous; trailing; very productive; almost immune to orange rust; susceptible to anthracnose. Originated before 1875. HEDRICK 1925; B10, B19, C63, D76, E97, *J2M*, *J63M*, M31M

Thornless:[2] Large fruit is good in pies, jams and jellies; also makes excellent wine; easy to pick and handle due to its thornless quality. Bush hardy; thrifty; widely adapted. C63

BLUEBERRY {GR}

VACCINIUM ASHEI VACCINIUM CORYMBOSUM

HIGHBUSH

Generally grown in northern areas with 1,000 or more hours of temperatures below 45^0 F. every year. Considered to be superior in flavor to rabbiteye blueberries, however they require more pruning. Southern types are being developed that combine the high quality fruit of the northern highbush with the low chilling requirements of rabbiteyes. Mostly V. corymbosum.

NORTHERN

Atlantic: Fruit cluster loose; berry large, oblate; skin blue, attractive; flesh firm, aroma slight, flavor good, dessert quality medium; resistant to cracking; ripens late, just before Jersey. Bush vigorous, open spreading; very productive; subject to bacterial dieback in Oregon and Washington. BROOKS 1972; H65, M92

Berkeley: Fruit cluster loose; berry medium-large, about 70 per cup, oblate; skin very light blue, very attractive; flesh firm, aroma slight, slightly subacid; dessert quality medium; not subject to cracking; stores well; scar very good; ripens in late midseason, about a week after Stanley and a week before Jersey. Bush medium productive, yields approximately 5 pounds of fruit; height 5 to 6 feet. BROOKS 1972; *A40*, *A64*, B75, C63, C93, *D25M*, *D60*, E4, F11, F16, G23, G72, I73M, J69

Blue Chip: Fruit cluster loose; berry large, averaging 65 per cup; skin light blue; quality very good; scar small to none; ripens in mid-June at Castle Haynes, North Carolina. Bush upright, never spreading; height 4 to 5 feet; a reliable bearer, yields up to 20 pounds of fruit at maturity; disease resistant. F16

Bluecrop: Large, medium loose cluster; berries large, about 65 per cup; skin very light-blue; flesh very firm, subacid, flavor good, dessert quality good, moderately aromatic; resistant to cracking; scar small; ripens early-midseason, about 4 days before Berkeley. Bush upright-spreading, height 4 to 6 feet; vigorous; a consistent producer of 10 to 20 pounds of fruit. BROOKS 1972; A24, *A40*, *A64*, B25, B58, C63, C93, *D60*, E4, F16, G23, H16, I73M, J69, *M3*{SC}, M39M, etc.

Bluehaven: Very large, round fruit, 60 per cup; skin light blue; flesh very firm, flavor and quality excellent; picking scar very small and dry; ripens about July 15 at South Haven, Michigan; holds quality well on bush; can be picked over a 4 to 6 week period. Bush vigorous and hardy; an inconsistent producer, yielding between 5 and 20 pounds of fruit; widely adapted; height approximately 4 feet. BROOKS 1972; C93, F16, F48

Bluejay: Medium-large fruit, about 76 per cup, spherical; skin light blue; flesh firm; mild pleasant flavor, only slightly tart; small, dry scar; will not drop, crack or bleed; ripens early-midseason, 3 to 4 days before Bluecrop. Bush upright, only slightly spreading, height 5 to 7 feet; extremely vigorous; yields 10 to 20 pounds of fruit. *A40*, *A64*, B43M, C93, *D60*, D76, E4, F16, F48, H65, I73M, J69, *M3*, *M3*{SC}, *M81M*, etc.

Blueray: Small, tight cluster; berry very large, about 60 per cup; skin medium light-blue; flesh firm, aromatic, flavor fine; non-cracking; scar medium; ripens in midseason, with Ivanhoe and Rancocas; resembles Dixi. Bush upright, height 4 to 6 feet; very productive, yields 10 to 20 pounds of fruit at maturity. BROOKS 1972; A39, *A64*, B25, B58, B73M, C63, C93, *D25M*, *D60*, E47, F16, G16, H16, J69, J83, M39M, etc.

Bluetta: Medium-sized fruit, about 71 per cup; skin blue-black; flesh firm, has more flavor than Weymouth; ripens early, with Weymouth. Bush short, compact-spreading; height 3 to 5 feet; vigor medium; consistently productive, yields 10 to 20 pounds of fruit; more resistant to spring frosts than Weymouth. BROOKS 1972; A18, *A40*, *A64*, B25, B53, C63, C93, D37, *D60*, F16, F48, G71, H16, H49, H88, M98, etc.

Burlington: Medium tight cluster; berry medium-small, 75 per cup; skin blue; flesh firm, aroma slight; dessert quality very good; small scar; resistant to cracking; matures late, lasting 1 week after Rubel. Bush vigorous, upright spreading; height 5 to 7 feet; an inconsistent producer in colder climates, yielding between 5 and 10 pounds of fruit. BROOKS 1972; A18, E47, F16, F48

Collins: Medium-sized, tight cluster; berry medium-sized, about 70 per cup; skin light blue; flesh very firm, highly flavored, sweet to mildly subacid; resistant to cracking; does not drop; ripens early, midway between Earliblue and Bluecrop. Bush erect, slightly spreading, height 4 to 6 feet; yields between 10 and 15 pounds of fruit. BROOKS 1972; *A40*, *A64*, C63, C93, *D60*, F16, F48, G79M, H88, I73M, *J63M*, J69, L99M

Coville: Fruit cluster loose; berry large, about 65 per cup; flesh firm, flavor tart until ripe, aromatic; dessert quality good; little or no picking scar; resistant to cracking; does not drop; ripens late, 30 days after Earliblue. Bush upright, height 4 to 6 feet; vigorous; productive, yields 5 to 8 pounds of fruit. BROOKS 1972; *A40*, B58, B73M, *C47*, C63, *D25M*, D69, F16, G79M, H49, J16, *J63M*, J69, *M65M*

Darrow: Medium-sized, attractive cluster; berry large, 57 per cup; skin light blue; flesh firm, aromatic, highly flavored, tart to mildly tart depending on maturity; neither drops nor cracks during wet weather; scar medium; ripens about with Coville, which it resembles. Bush erect; vigorous; consistently productive, more so than Coville. BROOKS 1972; *A40*, C93, *D60*, F16, H88, I49M, J61M

Dixi: Medium tight cluster; berry large, round-oblate; skin blue; flesh firm, aromatic, flavor pronounced; dessert quality very good; susceptible to cracking; scar large, poor; ripens late. Bush vigorous, open-spreading; productive. Introduced in 1936. BROOKS 1972; A18, J61M

Earliblue: Fruit cluster medium, long, loose; berry medium to large, about 65 to 75 per cup, oblate; skin light blue; flesh very firm, subacid, flavor good, moderately aromatic, dessert quality good; resistant to cracking; ripens very early, with or before Weymouth. Bush upright, height 4 to 6 feet; vigorous; yields 8 to 15 pounds of fruit. A24, *A40*, B25, B58, *D60*, E47, F16, G23, H88, I73M, J16, J69, K71, L97, L99M, M76, etc.

Elliott: Small to medium fruit, about 75 per cup; skin light blue; flesh very firm, good mild flavor when fully ripe; small, dry scar; won't crack or drop; ripens very late. Bush very upright, slightly spreading, height 5 to 7 feet; consistently yields 10 to 20 pounds of fruit. BROOKS 1972; A18, A24, *A40*, *A64*, C93, D37, *D60*, F16, F48, H16, H49, H88, I49M, I73M, J61M, *M3*, *M3*{SC}, etc.

Herbert: Fruit clusters loose; berry large, averaging 65 per cup; flesh soft; scar large, will leak, making the fruit an unattractive black color; hangs well on the bush; ripens late, about the same time as Jersey, Rubel, and Dixi, earlier than Coville and later than Berkeley. Bush consistently productive. BROOKS 1972; A18, *A40*, D76, E4, F11, F16, G23, H65, H88, J16, J69, L99M, *M81M*

Ivanhoe: Medium loose cluster; berry large, round-oblate; skin light blue, attractive; flesh firm, highly aromatic, flavor subacid, good to excellent; small scar; resistant to cracking; ripens slightly later than Stanley. Bush erect, vigorous; productive; not reliably hardy north of Maryland and Delaware. H65, *M81M*, M92

Jersey: Fruit cluster very loose, long; berry medium-small, about 110 per cup, round-oblate; skin blue; flesh firm, aroma lacking; dessert quality fair; picking scar small; ripens late, with Rubel; keeps well. Bush upright-spreading, height 5 to 7 feet; vigorous; productive, yields 7 to 10 pounds of fruit. Very widely grown. BROOKS 1972; A24, *A40*, B58, B73M, C63, C93, F16, F19M, G23, G45M, H65, J69, J83, L97, *M65M*, etc.

Lateblue: Medium-sized cluster; berry small, about 94 per cup; skin light blue; small stem scars; flesh firm, highly flavored; smaller and ripens 7 days after Coville. Has the outstanding feature of simultaneously ripening its fruit during high temperatures. Bush erect, vigorous, height 5 to 7 feet; consistently productive, yielding about 9 to 12 pounds of fruit. BROOKS 1972; *A40*, C93, H88

Meader: Medium to large fruit, about 65 per cup; skin medium blue; flesh very firm, of good quality; small, dry scar; ripens in midseason. Bush upright, slightly spreading; height 5 to 7 feet. Recommended for areas where winter temperatures drop below -25^0 F., and heavy snow loads are frequent. Originated in New Hampshire by Professor E.M. Meader. B73M, D65, D76, E97, F16

Murphy: Fruit cluster excellent, loose; berry medium-sized, round to round-oblate; flesh firm, flavor good, slightly aromatic; dessert quality fair; scar fair; ripens early. Bush low, spreading, vigorous; highly resistant to canker; as productive as Weymouth. Originated in Atkinson, North Carolina. BROOKS 1972; G72

North Country:[1] Medium-sized fruit, 1/2 inch in diameter; attractive sky-blue skin; quality good, flavor sweet to mild, reminiscent of wild lowbush blueberries; little or no picking scar; ripens early-midseason. Bush vigorous; half-high, height 18 to 24 inches; yields between 2 and 7 pounds of fruit. Can survive winter temperatures of -30^0 to -35^0 F., but production is maximized when snow protection is adequate. *A74*, C93, *D60*, D65, F16, G1T, I36, I49M, J7, L27M, L30, L70, L79, *M81M*

North Sky:[1] Fruit small; skin an attractive sky blue color; flesh firm, highly flavored; quality very good; stores well with refrigeration; ripens early-midseason. Bush 18 to 24 inches; yields between 1 and 2 pounds of fruit. Classified as a half-high but grows as a low spreading bush. Would make an excellent low border for edible landscaping. Can survive winter temperatures of -35^0 to -40^0 F. *A74*, C93, *D60*, D65, F16, *G4*, H16, H42, H65, I36, I49M, J7, J61M, L27M, L70, *M81M*, etc.

Northblue:[1] Large, attractive dark-blue fruit; flesh firm, quality very good; stores well with refrigeration; ripens early-midseason. Bush vigorous; half-high, height 20 to 30 inches; yields between 3 and 7 pounds of fruit annually. Can survive winter temperatures of -30^0 to -35^0 F. A65, A91, B25, C93, *D60*, D65, D76, E97, F16, G16, H16, J61M, L27M, L30, L70, L79, *M81M*, etc.

Northland: Fruit clusters long, loose; berry medium-sized, about 136 per cup, round; skin medium blue; flesh firm, flavor good, reminiscent of wild blueberries; picking scar small and dry; ripens early-midseason. Bush moderately spreading, height 3 to 4 feet; vigorous; a consistent bearer of 15 to 20 pounds of fruit. BROOKS 1972; A24, *A40*, B25, B75, C63, C93, *D60*, D65, F16, F48, G16, G23, G69M, H65, J69, L27M, etc.

Olympia: Medium-large fruit; skin medium blue, thin; flesh aromatic, flavor very good; resists cracking; does not drop; ripens in midseason. Bush very tall, spreading; vigorous; very productive; adapts well to most types of soil. Originated in Olympia, Washington by Joseph Eberhardt. A18, C34, *D60*, I49M, J61M, L97

Patriot: Fruit cluster tight; berry very large, between 50 and 60 per cup, slightly flat; skin medium blue; flesh firm, flavor very good; small, dry, recessed scar; ripens early. Bush upright-spreading, height 4 to 6 feet; very vigorous; consistently yields 10 to 20 pounds of fruit. *A40*, *A64*, B25, B26, C93, *D60*, D69, D76, F16, F48, G16, H65, H88, I73M, L27M, *M3*, *M81M*, etc.

Pemberton: Very loose cluster; berry medium to large, roundish; skin darker blue than Atlantic and Jersey; flesh firm, aroma slight, dessert quality fair to good; scar poor; season late, just before Jersey and Rubel; difficult to pick; cracks some in wet weather. Bush very productive; extremely vigorous. BROOKS 1972; A18, D76, E47, M92

Rancocas: Fruit cluster tight; berry small, about 130 per cup, oblate; flesh firm, crisp, aroma slight, flavor mildly subacid; large scar; dessert quality fair to good; ships well; ripens early-midseason, after Collins; cracks badly in wet weather. Good for processing. Bush upright-spreading, height 5 to 7 feet; a consistent producer of 10 to 20 pounds of fruit. BROOKS 1972; A18, F16, *G43*, G69M, G72

Rubel: Fruit cluster long; berry small, 132 per cup; skin light blue; flesh firm, flavor very good; medium picking scar; ripens late. Bush upright, height 5 to 7 feet; very vigorous; yields between 8 and 10 pounds of fruit. Originated as a wild seedling in Whitesbog, New Jersey. Selected by Elizabeth C. White in the early 1900's. A18, F16, *G43*, G45M, G72, K28

Scammell: Long, tight cluster; berry medium-sized; ripens in midseason. Bush productive, especially in North Carolina; resistant to canker. Originated in Whitesbog, New Jersey by F.V. Coville. Introduced in 1931. BROOKS 1972; M92

Spartan: Very large fruit, about 60 per cup; skin powdery to dark blue; flesh very firm, quality excellent; medium dry scar; ripens early. Bush upright, height 5 to 7 feet; vigorous; yields between 8 and 10 pounds of fruit. After the first 2 pickings the fruit size drops off considerably. A18, *A40*, *A64*, C93, *D60*, F16, F48, I49M, I73M, J61M, *M3*, *M3*{SC}

Stanley: Medium-sized, loose cluster; berry size medium to small in latter part of season; flesh highly aromatic, firm, dessert quality excellent, flavor very pronounced; scar large; ripens early midseason. Bush vigorous, erect; productive. BROOKS 1972; E47, L97

Tophat:[2] Ornamental, dwarf type cultivar. Height of bush only 20 inches at maturity, with a spherical shape of about 20 inches in diameter. Perfect for growing in a pot on the patio or indoors on a sunny windowsill. Berries medium-sized, bright blue, firm, of good flavor. B73M, C63, D65, E97, F16

Toro: Medium-sized fruit, about 75 per standard cup; skin medium blue; flesh firm, flavor good; quality excellent; small, dry scar; ripens early-midseason. Bush upright, height 5 to 7 feet; very vigorous; a consistent and heavy producer. Released by the New Jersey Experiment Station in 1987. F16

Weymouth: Fruit cluster loose; berry medium to large, round oblate; skin dark blue; flesh soft, aroma lacking; dessert quality usually poor; scar medium; tends to drop; season very early. Bush erect, spreading, low in vigor; very productive. Originated in Weymouth, New Jersey by F.V. Coville. Introduced in 1936. BROOKS 1972; A18, E47, G72, N24M

Wolcott: Fruit cluster loose; berry medium-sized, generally round; flesh firm to slightly soft but firmer than Weymouth, aromatic, flavor good, dessert quality medium; season as early as Weymouth, short; scar small. Bush vigorous, semi-upright; resistant to canker; as productive as Weymouth. Originated in Atkinson, North Carolina. BROOKS 1972; M92

SOUTHERN

Avonblue: Medium to large fruit, about 75 or 80 per cup, very round; skin attractive; flavor mild and acid, quality best of the southern highbush cultivars; ripens May 7 at Gainesville, Florida. Bush somewhat spreading, height 4 to 5 feet; yields 7 to 14 pounds of fruit on well-kept irrigated plantings. D37, F16, F48, G17, I83M

Challenger: Large fruit, about 65 per cup; very attractive with a light blue cast that holds up when packed for fresh market; flesh firm; little or no picking scar; ripens May 1 to 3 at Gainesville, Florida about 4 days later than Sharpblue. Vigorous upright bush, height 6 feet. Used for commercial plantings and to pollinate Sharpblue. Released by the University of Florida in 1989. D37, F16, I83M

Flordablue: Fruit medium to large, about 75 to 80 per standard cup; flesh firm, quality very good; stores well; ripens April 27 at Gainesville, Florida. Bush well-proportioned, height 5 to 6 feet at maturity; yields 8 to 16 pounds of fruit; early blooming and self-fertile. Introduced by the University of Florida in 1984. F16

Georgiagem: Medium-sized fruit, about 80 per cup; flesh firm, flavor pleasant; small, dry scars; ripens early, May 8 at Gainesville, Florida. Bush vigorous, tall and upright, height 5 to 6 feet; moderately productive; self-fruitful. Very good for fresh markets. Introduced in 1986 by the Coastal Plains Experiment Station, Tifton, Georgia. D37, F16, *L85*

O'Neal: Very large, attractive fruit with excellent firmness and little to no picking scar. Quality will not deteriorate under high temperatures. Spreading, well-proportioned bush; height 6 feet; will produce fruit in the South without a pollinator; appears to do well in lighter soils where others fail. Earliest ripening highbush cultivar. F16

Sharpblue: Fruit medium to large, about 75 or 80 per cup; quality fair to good; small scar; ripens April 27 at Gainesville, Florida. Bush fast-growing and very vigorous, height 5 to 6 feet; yields 8 to 16 pounds of fruit. The number one southern highbush planted in Florida. D76, F16, F68, G17, I83M, *N20*

Sunshine Blue: Medium-sized fruit, about 80 per cup; flesh very firm, quality good; ripens May 10 through June 15 at Gainesville, Florida; can be stored. Bush 3 to 4 feet tall and wide; yields between 5 and 10 pounds of fruit; appears to tolerate high pH soils better than all other southern highbush and rabbiteye types. Grows well in pots. D76, F16, I83M

RABBITEYE

Native to the southeastern United States. Requires less chilling, only about 500 hours below 45^0 F. every year. Grows taller than highbush types, ranging from 8 to 20 feet tall. Also not as sensitive to soil acidity and is far more heat and drought resistant. Much more productive than highbush blueberries. (V. ashei)

Aliceblue: Large fruit, about 70 to 75 per cup; flesh firm, aromatic, flavor very sweet, quality good; ripens early. Bush tall and spreading, height 6 to 10 feet; yields between 7 and 14 pounds of fruit. Good for fresh or processed sales. D79M, G17, I83M

Baldwin: Fruit medium-sized, dark blue; flesh firm, flavor good; small, dry scars; ripens over a 6 to 7 week period, beginning the same time as Delight. Recommended for pick-your-own and backyard plantings. Bush vigorous, upright, produces large crops regularly. Originated in Tifton, Georgia. *K1*, *L85*

Beckyblue: Large fruit, about 70 to 75 per cup; flesh firm, very sweet with a mild blueberry flavor; quality excellent; no picking scar; ripens early; stores well. Bush tall and upright, height 6 to 10 feet; yields between 8 and 12 pounds of fruit. One of the leading cultivars in north FLorida. A88M, D79M, F16, G17, I83M, *K1*, *N20*

Bluebelle: Large, dark fruit; flavor very good; ripens over a relatively long period of time. Bush upright, moderately vigorous; productive. An excellent cultivar for pick-your-own operations. A82, D79M, G17, I79, I83M, *K1*, *L85*

Bluegem: Medium to large fruit, about 75 to 80 per cup; flavor tart and mildly acid, quality good; ripens in early-midseason. Bush vigorous, spreading, height 6 to 10 feet; yields 10 to 25 pounds of fruit; susceptible to root rot, should be planted in a well-drained location. Introduced by the University of Florida in 1974. F16, G17

Bonitablue: Fruit large, between 70 and 75 per cup; flesh firm, quality excellent, very sweet, with a mild blueberry flavor; no picking scar; ripens early; stores well. Bush tall and upright, height 6 to 10 feet; yields 8 to 22 pounds of fruit. One of the leading cultivars in northern Florida. A88M, D79M, F16, I83M, *K1*, *N20*

Brightwell: Medium to large fruit, between 75 and 80 per cup; skin light-blue; flesh firm, sweet, quality excellent; little or no picking scar; ripens early to midseason and over a long period. Bush tall and spreading, height 8 to 12 feet; vigorous; consistently yields 8 to 14 pounds of fruit. Good for commercial or home use. D79, D79M, E29M, F16, F93, I79, J57M, *K1*, *L85*

Briteblue: Medium-large fruit, about 75 to 80 per cup; skin light blue; flesh very firm, flavor fair; ripens in midseason, later than Tifblue; handles well for distant marketing. Bush open-headed and spreading; height 8 to 12 feet; vigorous; yields 8 to 12 pounds of fruit. A82, D76, D79M, F16, G17, I83M, J57M, *L85*, M31M, *M69M*, M83

Centurion: Fruit medium to large; darker in color than most rabbiteyes; quality good; ripens midseason to late. Bush upright; easy to manage. D79M, F19M, G17, *K1*

Chaucer: Medium-large fruit, about 75 or 80 per cup; quality fair; has a tendency to tear when picked; ripens early to midseason. Bush tall and spreading, height 8 to 12 feet; vigorous; yields 12 to 25 pounds of fruit. Should be planted in areas of low frost damage. D79M, F16

Choice: Fruit small to medium, about 80 or 90 per cup; skin darker than normal; quality very good but mainly used for the process market; ripens midseason to late. Bush tall and upright with some spreading, height 8 to 12 feet; vigorous; yields 8 to 12 pounds of fruit. D79M, F16, G17, *K1*

Climax: Medium to large fruit, about 75 to 80 per cup; quality good; little or no picking scar; ripens early. Bush tall and spreading, height 6 to 10 feet; yields between 8 and 22 pounds of fruit. Good for fresh market or processing. One of the leading pollinators for other rabbiteyes. A82, D79M, *E66*, F16, F19M, F93, G17, G65M, H4, I79, I83M, J57M, *K1*, *L85*, M76, etc.

Delite: Fruit medium to large, about 75 to 80 per cup, round; skin light blue; flavor excellent, not tart before becoming fully ripe as are other cultivars of rabbiteye blueberries; ripens a few days later than Briteblue. Bush tall and upright, height 6 to 10 feet; yields between 8 and 15 pounds of fruit. BROOKS 1972; A82, D76, D79M, F16, F19M, F93, G17, *G28*, G65M, H4, I79, I83M, J57M, *K1*, *L85*, *M69M*, etc.

Garden Blue: Medium-sized, round fruit; skin light blue; flesh firm, flavor good; scar small, dry; ripens early to midseason. Bush upright; vigorous; consistently high yielding; fruit well distributed on long shoots making picking easy. D79M, G72

Homebell: Medium-large fruit; skin medium dark blue; flesh firm, flavor mild; ripens in midseason. Bush very vigorous and fast growing, productive; easy to propagate. Recommended for home gardens. Selected at Tifton, Georgia. Introduced in 1955. BROOKS 1972; J57M, *K76*

Powder Blue: Fruit large, about 75 to 80 per pound; skin powder blue, attractive, stands out well amongst other blueberries; flesh very firm, subacid, distinct blueberry taste; quality very good; ripens in midseason. Bush tall and upright, height 8 to 12 feet; vigorous; yields 8 to 14 pounds of fruit. Good pollinator and companion producer for Tifblue. D37, D79M, F16, G17, I79

Premier: Medium-large fruit, about 75 to 80 per cup; skin light blue; flavor and quality very good; ripens early to midseason; stores very well. Bush tall and upright, height 6 to 10 feet; vigorous; yields 8 to 16 pounds of fruit. Recommended for home and commercial use. A85M, D79, D79M, *E66*, F16, F19M, G17, I79, *K1*, *L85*

Southland: Medium-sized fruit, about 80 to 90 per cup; skin light blue; flesh firm, flavor good; ripens late midseason, with Tifblue; turns soft if stored too long. Bush tall and upright with some spreading, height 8 to 12 feet; yields 8 to 16 pounds of fruit. Recommended for home and commercial use. A82, D37, D79M, G13, G72, I79, I83M, M83

Tifblue: Medium to large fruit, about 75 to 80 per cup; skin very light blue; flesh firm, flavor very good; scar very dry and small; ripens early to midseason. Bush tall and vigorous; height 8 to 14 feet; yields 8 to 25 pounds of fruit. Quality holds up well until the last berries are harvested. The present standard among rabbiteye blueberries. D37, D76, D79M, *E66*, F16, F19M, F93, *G28*, G65M, H4, I79, I83M, J57M, L33, M31M, *M69M*, M83, etc.

Woodard: Fruit large, about 70 to 75 per half-pint cup; skin light-blue, appearance excellent; flesh firm, flavor mild, slightly more acid than Tifblue, quality very good when fully ripe; stem scar dry; ripens early to midseason; holds up well in shipping. Bush spreading, height 6 to 10 feet; precocious; yields 8 to 16 pounds of fruit. D79M, E29M, *E66*, F16, F19M, F93, G17, *G28*, H4, I79, I83M, J57M, L33, *L85*, *M69M*, M76, M83, etc.

BOK CHOY {S}

BRASSICA RAPA CHINENSIS GROUP

COMMON BOK CHOY

Grown for the broad, white or green leafstalks which are widely used in Chinese cuisine. The smaller green-stalked or "baby bok choy" types are becoming popular in specialty markets.

HYBRID

Joi Choy: 45 days. Hybrid version of Lei Choy, with more uniform growth and maturity and more resistance to bolting. Plants grow 10 to 12 inches tall. Petioles are longer and slimmer than Mei Qing Choy. Extra dark green, glossy leaves provide an attractive contrast to the ivory white stalks. Good cold tolerance. Can produce 20% more marketable plants than Lei Choy. F13, G16, G82, G93M, *H61*, H95, I39, I91, J7, K73, L42, L79, L89, M46, M49, etc.

Mei Qing Choy:[1] 45 days. Green stem or "baby bok choy" type, more tender and flavorful than white stem bok choy, and favored by selective cooks. Flat, pale misty green stems form a thick, heavy base with broad, oval, rich green leaves. Compact, vase-shaped plant about 1/2 to 2/3 the size of Prize Choy. Highly bolt-resistant and uniform. Tolerant of heat and cold. Easy to grow. *A1*, B75, D68, F13, F44, G6, I39, I77, J20, K66, L42, L91M, M29, M46, T1M, etc.

OPEN-POLLINATED

Bin-Hup: 50 days. Leaves dark green, smooth, rounded and open. White leaf-stalks, somewhat similar to Spoon Pak Choy and Tai Sai but less fleshy and more dwarf. Adapted to mid-summer to early fall culture, being harvested in the immature stage. Mature greens are also good for cooking and pickling. Heat resistant, but runs to seeds easily on exposure to cold temperatures. *P39*

Canton Dwarf:[1] 42 days. "Baby choy" type. Semi-compact open plant; produces small to medium-sized heads. Leaves glossy dark green, round in shape, with broad white stalks that are very thick and of excellent quality. Very heat tolerant; adapted to the tropics, subtropics, and summer culture in temperate areas. E59, *E91G*, G27M, G93M, *K16M*

Chinese: (Chinese Bok Choy) 60 days. Thick, round, glossy leaves and wide, pale green, crisp stems. Compact and long-standing; excellent resistance to bolting to seed, bolts only when quite mature, if at all. Has good flavor and hearty, wild plant-like quality. Very easy to grow; may be sown from early spring to late fall. G6, O53M

Chinese Flat Cabbage: (Tah Tsai, Tatsoi, Chinese Savoy) Stout, low-spreading plant producing rosettes 12 to 14 inches across of thick, puckered, dark-green leaves with broad, pale green petioles. Leaves and petioles have a thick, dense texture which makes them well suited for cooking in soups. The plants can survive the winter without protection from severe frosts and can also survive heavy falls of snow. Will grow more upright and go to seed in warmer weather. DAHLEN [Pre, Cul], HERKLOTS; D68, D87, E59Z, F13, F44, G6, I39, I77, K66, L42, L59, M46, R47, S55, *S63M*, *S70*, T1M, etc.

Ching Chiang:[1] (Ching Chiang Cabbage) 40 days. "Baby bok choy" type. Small, compact plants growing only 8 inches tall. Smooth, rounded, very tender leaves on thick, crisp, green petioles. Fast growing; grows very well in mild and hot weather. Tolerant to rain and dampness. D55, *L79G*, *Q39*

Horse Ear: (Ma I Pak Choy) Very thick, long petioles of a pure white color, crisp and succulent. Excellent eaten raw, cut up in salads or stir-fried. Very vigorous plant, will not bolt in the hot weather of summer. Popular in Hong Kong where it is sown from May to September. HERKLOTS; E83T

Hung Chin: (Hung Chin Cabbage) 35 days. Medium-tall, semi-upright plants. Light green leaves. Heat and disease resistant. Can be sown spring through fall, though late plantings may bolt. L59

Kwang Moon: 50 days. A loose, semi-round leaf type with thick, pure-white stalks. Tender and delicious. A warm weather cultivar to grow from spring to autumn. Plants grow rapidly and can be harvested from an early stage. Q34, T1M

Lei Choy: 50 days. A slow-bolting strain developed in Holland, which has become popular in the oriental vegetable markets of California. Each plant bears 10 to 14 erect, medium-thick, round, pure-white stalks, 8 to 10 inches long; topped by broad, dark green leaves. Easy to grow. *A1*, A13, B75, G33, G51, G64, G71, G93M, *H61*, H94, K49M, K66, L7M, L42, L91M, N52, etc.

Osaka Chusei: (Osaka-na) 40 days. Round, smooth, yellowish-green leaves. Similar to Maruba Santo, but of superior quality and yields crops up to 20% larger or more. Used as a potherb, added to soups, or pickled. Has considerable heat and cold resistance. An early selection of Osaka Large Latest. *P39*

Osaka Large Latest: 65 days. Tall plant, about 22 to 24 inches, but often marketed at a smaller size by denser than normal planting. Large, spoon-shaped, dark green, smooth-edged, uncrumpled leaves with a wide, fairly thick leaf-stalk. Very late in running to seed. Considered to be an old combination of bok choy and a non-heading type of Chinese cabbage. E83T, J73, *P39*

Prize Choy: 50 days. Large, tender, dark green, spoon-shaped leaves contrast with thick, rounded, solid white stems which form a celery-like base. Vase-shaped heads are 15 to 18 inches tall, compact, heavy, and very attractive with good quality. Slow-bolting. D68, F44, G6, L9

Ryokusai: (F_1) 52 days. Hybrid form of Chinese Flat Cabbage or Tah Tsai. Forms a small, semi-erect rosette of bright pine-green leaves. More erect, and therefore cleaner than open pollinated strains. Slow bolting. Young leaves add color and flavor to salads. Also tasty in soups or cooked like spinach. *K16M*

Seppaku: (Seppaku Tai Sai) 45 days. Larger form of Tai Sai, with mature plants weighing about 2 pounds each. Medium green, spoon-shaped leaves with long, succulent, pure-white petioles that have a somewhat swollen base. A very hardy type, well suited to growing in a cool greenhouse or frame in late fall or early spring. E83T, Q88

Shanghai: (Green Petiole, Green Stalk, Tsing Kang) 45 days. Small, sturdy, erect plants with tender, flat, light green petioles topped by succulent, light green leaves. Harvest can begin at a very early stage. Grows rapidly and tolerates heat very well. Can be planted from spring to autumn, but is more suited to mid-summer growth. A79M, E24, E59, E83T, *G13M*, G93M, H49, I39, K66, L59, N84

Short Green Petiole: Similar to Chin Chiang, but with shorter and thicker green petioles. Equally good for spring, summer and fall crops. D55

Spoon Pak Choy: (Spoon Cabbage) 55 days. Smooth, dark-green, rather succulent leaves; rounded, and the edges curved inward like porcelain chopsuey spoons; large, white midribs. Large, fleshy leaf-stalks; fatter near the base; white, tender and crisp. Forms a clump so dense it has been confused with pe-tsai. Easily bolts to seed if grown in the fall in north temperate regions. E49, K49M, L59, *P39*

Tai Sai: (Taitsai, Japanese Bok Choy) Upright plant, 12 to 13 inches tall; uniform, spoon-shaped, bright green leaves with long, stocky pure-white stalks, thicker at the base. Widely adapted and disease resistant. Used at any stage of its rather quick growth. Matures in 35 days if sown in August or early September; 65 days if sown in mid-September; 85 days if sown in early October in Japan. F44, J73, N39, *P39*, *S63M*

White Stalked: (Chinese Round) 45 days. Medium-tall, erect plant. Very broad, rounded, light-green leaves with thick, pure-white stalks. Tender and delicious either steamed or stir-fried. Highly regarded for home and restaurant use in southern China. Grows quickly and can be planted spring through fall. L59

FLOWERING BOK CHOY

Also known as *tsoi sum*, *flowering white cabbage* or *mock pak choy*, this type is grown for its thick-stemmed flowering shoots which are cut when the yellow flowers begin to open. The stems are tender enough to cook without peeling. Some forms are called *edible rape* or *yow choy*. DAHLEN [Pre, Cul], HERKLOTS, TANAKA.

<u>HYBRID</u>

Bouquet: 60 days. Vigorous, uniform plant produces numerous side shoots. Harvested for the savoy-type leaves, edible flowers and stalks. Unopened buds should be harvested when stalks are about 6 inches long, then pick side shoots as they form. Also used as a cut flower in the Orient. *A1*, E59, I77, L91M, M29, T1M

<u>OPEN-POLLINATED</u>

40 Day Yow Choy: 40 days. Early cultivar from Hong Kong. Does not produce side shoots. Seeds are sown mid-April to September, the main marketing period being June to September. HERKLOTS; *L79G*

50 Day Yow Choy: 50 days. A fast-growing type; quickly goes to flower. Harvest the plant for vegetable use when bolting. Seeds are sown from September to November in Hong Kong. D55, *L79G*

60 Day Yow Choy: 60 days. Slightly slower in bolting than 50 Day Yow Choy. Equally good in quality and taste. Seeds are sown from October to March in Hong Kong. Seedlings are transplanted after 25 to 30 days, 8 inches apart in well-manured beds. One or two side shoots may be harvested after the central stem has been cut a few leaves from the base. HERKLOTS; D55, *L79G*

80 Day Yow Choy: 80 days. A rare cultivar that is larger and slower in bolting. Grown mainly for the tender and delicious leaves and stems. D55, *L79G*

Hong Kong Yow Choy: (Yu Choy, Oil Vegetable) 45 days. Long, light green petioles are topped by rounded, glossy light green leaves. Tender and delicious with a unique sweet flavor; both the stem and leaves are harvested when the plant begins to flower and used in stir-fried dishes. Grows best in spring and fall. May be sown in summer but has a tendency to bolt to flower prematurely. A79M, E59, H49, N84

Kwan-Hoo Choy: (Kwan-Hoo Chin Tsoi Sum) 50 days. Dark green, narrow leaves with slender, lighter green petioles, few in number; grow alternately on a long, smooth, round stem of green color. Widely grown throughout southern mainland China and the whole South Seas area due to its distinguished resistance to heat as well as abundant rainfall. Sweeter than bok choy. J73, *P39*, R47

Long White Petiole: 45 days. Thick, glossy leaves with crisp white stems. Produces a large number of inflorescences for vegetable use. Plant in early spring or fall, and harvest when beginning to bolt. D55

Porcelain Green: 50 days. Very attractive plant having completely smooth and glossy leaves, petioles and flowering stems; a dark almost glistening lime-green color. The crisp, succulent flowering stems are delicious eaten raw. Can be sown all season long. E83T

Short White Petiole: 45 days. Similar to Long White Petiole, but with a shorter white petiole. Equally good in quality and taste. D55

Tsoi Sum: (Flowering White Cabbage) 55 days. A type of bok choy grown for the sake of its flowering shoots. The long, narrow stems are non-clasping, crisp, and are topped by thick, glossy medium-green leaves. Delicious in stir-fried dishes. Unopened flower buds and flowers are also tasty. HERKLOTS; A79M, C82, E24, E59, F85, G93M, H49, I39, J7, L59, M46, O53M

White Stem: (Pak Kwat Tsoi Sum, White Bone Tsoi Sum) The petioles are light green to greenish-white on the inner surface especially towards the base; the main veins of the leaf tend to be whitish on the upper surface. A summer form but is available to a limited extent in winter. HERKLOTS; J73

BROCCOLI {S}

BRASSICA OLERACEA ITALICA GROUP

GREEN SPROUTING

<u>HYBRID</u>

Cleopatra: 50 days. Very early hybrid with large, round, dark-green, very tight center heads; about 6 inches across and with fine beads. Will produce plentiful side shoots of good size if the center is cut deep along the stem. Good resistance to cool weather and dry spells. All America Selections winner in 1964. D27, E38, G79, G87

Emperor: 58 days. Vigorous, early hybrid producing large, uniform dark-green heads that are well-domed, compact and heavy. Generally free from bracting, open florets and other defects. Long stems facilitate harvest. Highly tolerant to black rot, downy mildew and hollow stem. Good secondary side shoot production. Suited for spring or fall crops. A13, D68, E57, *E91G*, *G1M*, G6, *G13M*, I91, *J74*, K10, K50, K73, L42, M29, M49, N52, etc.

Green Comet: 55 days. Upright, compact, 12 to 16 inch tall plants produce rich blue-green, large tight heads; 6 to 7 inches in diameter, without leaves in the center; weight up to 1 pound. Plentiful side shoot production. Resistant to heat and disease. For both spring and fall crops. All America Selections winner for 1969. A16, C44, C85M,

D11M, D65, *E91G*, F19M, G71, H33{PL}, *H61*, H94, J14{PL}, J34, K71, K73, M46, N39, etc.

Green Valiant: 65 days. Uniform, compact plants, 18 to 20 inches tall produce domed, very dense blue-green heads; 7 to 8 inches in diameter with fine beads and heavy stems. Good production of 3 inch diameter side shoots. Thin-skinned, sweet and tender. Adapted to a wide range of seasons, but does especially well when planted for a fall crop, as it shows good frost resistance. *A1*, A13, A87M, D68, E57, *G1M*, G6, *G13M*, G64, *H61*, *J74*, K73, L42, L89, M29, M49, N16, etc.

Packman: 55 days. Heavy yielder of uniform, light bluish-green domed heads, 7 to 8 inches in diameter, set well above the plant. Holds well in hot weather. Excellent side shoot development over an extended period of time. Now the standard, early hybrid broccoli. A87M, C85M, D11M, D76, D76{PL}, *E91G*, F1, *F72*, F82, G6, G16, G71, H42, *H61*, J20, K73, etc.

Premium Crop: 60 days. Medium-sized plant that produces large, compact heads averaging 8 to 9 inches across; rounded, deep-green in color, solid and thick. Small, tight green buds hold longer than most. Produces side shoots, but somewhat fewer than others due to short stem. Excellent quality and uniformity. Resistant to downy mildew. All America Selections winner in 1975. A25, C44, D11M, *E91G*, E97{PL}, F19M, *F72*, G6, G71, *H61*, H95, J7, J14{PL}, J97M, K73, M49, etc.

<u>**OPEN-POLLINATED**</u>

Atlantic: 55 days. Short, compact fast-growing plant suitable for high-density plantings. Produces medium-large, rounded, compact, solid main heads; averaging 6 1/2 inches in diameter, followed by a good crop of large secondary shoots. Good for fresh market, home gardens and freezing. For spring and fall planting. Introduced in 1960. G71, G93M, H54, L7M, P9

Calabrese: (Green Sprouting Calabrese, Early Green Calabrese) 60 days. Tall, upright plant, 24 to 30 inches tall; produces small, deep blue-green central heads, 3 to 6 inches in diameter; numerous smaller side shoots are produced for several months. Good for fresh market, canning and freezing. Introduced to the United States by Italian gardeners around the turn of the century. A69M, B49, D27, D87, E5T, F24M, F80, G57M, G67M, K49M, K71, L7M, L91M, M95, N16, N39, etc.

Dandy Early: 90 days. Compact, non-spreading plants; 18 inches tall, making for closer spacing in small gardens. Produces medium-sized heads, 6 inches in diameter, weighing around 10 ounces each. Good development of side shoots. Crops at most seasons of the year; sowings can be made at 6 week intervals from spring till late summer. L91M

De Cicco: 60 days. A rich-tasting old Italian cultivar with small main heads projected well above the foliage. Non-uniform in maturity, resulting in a long cutting period. Large yields of side shoots can be encouraged by harvesting the main head when 3 inches in diameter or less. For spring or fall crops. A25, C44, C85M, C92, E24, *E91G*, F44, *F72*, *G1M*, G6, G51, H42, H94, K73, L97, etc.

Easy Cut: 50 days. Compact, dome shaped, dark-green heads average about 1 1/2 pounds. Medium, fine green buds. Heads form well above foliage which simplifies harvesting after main cut. Produces a large number of secondary growth ideal for bunching. Early, sturdy erect plants. *E53M*

Green Goliath: 55 days. Large, tightly-budded, blue-green central heads mature over a 3 week period instead of all at once. Good side shoot production extends normal harvest period. Quality very good, either fresh or frozen. Widely adapted. Bred especially for home gardens, to give early, extended harvests. Introduced in 1981 by Burpee Seed Co. B75, C85M, D11M, E32M{PL}, G71M, H94, J32, J58, K49T, L79

Green Mountain: 85 days. Solid, blue-green, fine-budded heads; main head 5 to 6 inches in diameter; good production of medium-sized lateral heads. Stands a long time before bolting. Recommended for short season areas where nights are cold. Originated in Europe. G68

Italian Green Sprouting: (Calabria) 60 days. Vigorous plants producing heavy yields of large, compact dark-green center heads with tight attractive buds, about 6 inches across. Matures uniformly, the medium-sized lateral heads producing over a long season. Good for home gardens, bunching and freezing. A56, B35M, C76M, E59Z, F92, G79, G87, H66, I39, K73, L14, L42, M13M, N39

Morse's 4638: 90 days. A Waltham type producing large, compact, uniform heads, 24 to 26 inches tall. After the center head is cut, the side branches will make small heads continually, extending the harvest season. M46, N39

Northwest 29: 90 days. A high-yielding cultivar recommended for spring and fall planting in the maritime Pacific Northwest and other short season areas. Produces medium-large, dark blue-green heads with small buds, followed by numerous side shoots. Harvest of central heads is 90 days from a spring sowing, 140 days from a fall sowing. F82

Spartan Early: (Spartan) 52 days. Short, compact, uniform plants with heavy central heads, 6 to 8 inches in diameter, solidly packed with medium-sized, deep green buds on short stems. Moderate side shoot production. Standard open-pollinated early broccoli, developed by the Michigan Agricultural Experiment Station. B78, D82, E97, E97{PL}, F19M{PL}, G79, H33, I65M{PL}, J58, K49M, K71{PL}, L7M, L35{PL}

Umpqua: Introduced by Territorial Seed Company, Umpqua has out-performed all other open-pollinated cultivars in Pacific Northwest trials. Produces less side shoots than Waltham 29, but tends to have darker green buds with larger central heads. Good flavor and better uniformity. Not suitable for commercial growers. D68, L89

Waltham 29: 75 days. Dwarf, compact plants producing medium to large main heads of uniform dark blue-green color, followed by a heavy crop of side shoots late into the fall. Thick stalks of even length facilitate bunching and freezing. Widely adapted to late summer and fall harvesting, as it yields best under cool growing conditions. A13, A25, A69M, B75M, C44, D87, E24, E38, G71, *H61*, K27M, L7M, L97, M13M, M95, etc.

PURPLE/RED

Also called *purple cauliflower* and *purple sprouting broccoli*. Many require a long growing season, being adapted to warm winter areas, with heading occurring early the following spring. Easier to grow than either green sprouting broccoli or white cauliflower. The flavor is richer than that of white cauliflower, but milder than that of green sprouting broccoli. E70M{PR}, J83T{PR}

<u>**HYBRID**</u>

Burgundy Queen: 70 days. Earlier harvests, deeper color and smoother heads than regular strains. Attractive deep-purple heads average 6 1/2 inches in diameter and 19 ounces in weight. Upright plants are heat tolerant. Suitable for freezing. I77, L42

Red: (Red Broccoli) 90 days. Unusual true red broccoli, noted for its firm 5 inch diameter, bright red heads, delicious flavor, hardiness and high production of side shoots. When cooked for several minutes in boiling water, heads turn deep green. D11M

Violet Queen: 70 days. Similar to Burgundy Queen in size and shape. Dark purple heads, not as intense as Burgundy Queen which is a slower growing strain. Turns a lime green color when cooked. Also good raw or frozen. Intermediate between cauliflower and broccoli. Recommended for short season areas where cooler night temperatures arrive in late August and September. *A1*, C53, D68, *E91G*, F13, G6, H42, I77, J7, *J74*, K66, L42, L97, M46, *S75M*, etc.

OPEN-POLLINATED

Early Purple Cape: (Early Purple Sprouting, Purple Sicilian) 220 days. Prolific, frost-hardy, dwarf plants; heads compact, medium-sized, firm but tender, purplish-green becoming green when cooked. Leaves almost entire, mid-rib marked with purple. Excellent, sweet flavor. Should be sown in early April for an early harvest the following March. GRAY; A2, B8, B49, C76M, I39, J73, L91M, P83M, Q34, *R23*, S55, *S75M*

King Robert: (King Purple) 75 days. Large spreading plants require plenty of room. Produce very large central heads, deep-purple in color, turning green when cooked. Excellent quality; delicate, mild flavor. Easy to grow; holds well. Recommended for home gardeners and roadside stands. D11M, E49

Late Purple Sprouting: Large, upright plants, bred for overwintering. Produces numerous small, purple heads of excellent, sweet flavor. A longer-flowering strain of Purple Sprouting; from a spring planting, comes into bearing the following April and May, and continues to produce a large number of shoots until July. B49, S55, *S75M*

Purple Cape: 365 days. Plants grow 12 to 18 inches tall, producing medium to large, rich purple heads, very compact and firm. Excellent, mild flavor. Large, dark green leaves, wavy, almost crimped; good to eat when young. Ready for harvesting February through April. May be closely related or synonymous with Early Purple Cape. Very old cultivar, known before 1818. GRAY; B49, I99, L89, L91M, O53M, P83M, S55, *S75M*

Purple Giant: 80 days. Large, spreading plants produce very large, deep-purple heads on long stalks. Quality excellent; flavor mild; very good in salads. Turns green when cooked; freezes well. Harvested in the fall. Highly recommended for home gardens and roadside stands. A13, *A69M*, G71, K49M, M95

Purple Head: 80-85 days. Large, deep-purple, 8 inch diameter central heads; hold well when mature; non-uniform in maturity; will not produce side shoots when cut. Fine quality; mild broccoli flavor; turns green when cooked. Good for fresh use or freezing; makes an attractive addition to salads. Hardy; pest resistant; easy to grow. A16, B75, C85M, *F72*, G16, J20, M13M

Purple Sprouting: 220 days. Large, 24 to 36 inch tall plants are planted in spring to early summer, and harvested the following March and April after overwintering. Extremely hardy, to 10^0 F. Produces numerous small, purple heads that are tender, very sweet-tasting, and turn green when cooked. Stalks and leaves may be cooked as well. A2, C53, C76M, L89, O53M, S45M

Purple Sprouting Christmas: 210 days. Winter-hardy cultivar that produces very heavy crops of medium-small, purple, juicy, full-flavored heads of excellent quality. Extends the harvesting season; from a July transplanting, will start to bear in January and continue into spring. L91M

WHITE SPROUTING

Two types are known. Early cultivars, belonging to the Italica Group, mature January through March and produce small, greenish-yellow, fine-grained floral shoots on long stalks with wide internodes. The late cultivars, belonging to the Botrytis Group, mature March through May and develop larger, greenish-white or white floral shoots on relatively short stalks, some bearing a close resemblance to small cauliflower heads. GRAY.

Early White Pearl: 60 days. Hardy, strong-leaved plants producing a head with fine white curds on a very tender, thick main stem. Resembles green sprouting broccoli. Very suitable for colder areas as well as warmer ones. Sow April through June for a harvest in October and November. E49, T1M

Early White Sprouting: 220 days. Produces abundant, tender, small white heads over a long period. Frost hardy; can be sown in late spring for a fall harvest, or if sown in fall, plants will stand over winter for a crop early in spring. Small and flavorful heads; delicious raw or cooked. P83M, *R23*, S55

Improved White Sprouting: An excellent cultivar from Suttons Seeds that yields delicious, creamy-white, cauliflower-like shoots. Extremely hardy. Will begin to produce from Christmas onwards, being at its best during the later winter months. GENDERS 1975; S45M, S61

Late White Sprouting: 250 days. Hardy, overwintering broccoli that produces numerous small, creamy-white, cauliflower-like heads. Somewhat later than other types, from a spring to early summer sowing will begin to bear the following March and continue into late spring. L89

White Sprouting: 220 days. Hardy, overwintering broccoli sown in spring to early summer for a harvest the following April. Large plants producing numerous, small, creamy-white, cauliflower-like heads that have a mild, delicate flavor. The leaves and stems can be cooked along with the heads. B49, C53, K49M, L91M, O53M, *S75M*

BRUSSELS SPROUTS {S}

BRASSICA OLERACEA GEMMIFERA GROUP

HYBRID

Captain Marvel: 96 days. Compact growth habit; height 26 inches. Sprouts small, 3/4 inch in diameter; round; extremely hard; well-spaced along the stem. Excellent flavor. Matures early but endures winter weather well for an early type. For harvesting October through December. *A1*, *E91G*, H94, L42, L89, M29

Dolmic: 102 days. Smooth, oval dark-green sprouts of excellent flavor and quality; easy to pick; well-spaced along the stem; good holding ability. Early enough to start hand picking in late August or can be machine harvested from early September to late October. C53, L42, M49, N81, *S75M*

Jade Cross: 95 days. Compact growth habit; height 18 to 24 inches. Sprouts medium-sized, about 1 1/2 inches in diameter; oval; dark blue-green; firm and tightly wrapped. Excellent flavor and quality. Early maturing, uniform and very productive. All America Selections silver medal winner in 1959. Especially recommended for short season areas. A16, B35M, C44, D11M, D76{PL}, E38, E97{PL}, F1, F19M, *F72*, G16, G51, G71, H94, I64, J58, M49, etc.

Lunet: Medium-large, firm sprouts have excellent appearance and very good flavor. Dark green in color; well-spaced; suitable for market or freezing. Consistently high yielding. Cold hardy and long-standing. For harvesting November through December. One of the standards for production and quality in Europe. *A1*, C53, *J74*, L89, *S75M*, T1M

Oliver: 90 days. The standard in extra-early brussels sprouts. The flavorful, medium green, smooth sprouts are very large and mature remarkably early. Excellent quality. A vigorous, easy-to-grow cultivar for diverse climates. For August and September harvests. *A1*, B75, F13, G6, K73, N52, *S75M*

Peer Gynt: 140 days. Compact growth habit; height 3 feet. Dark green, firm, medium-sized sprouts; easily picked; remain tightly closed longer than other types. Produces high quality sprouts from the base of the stem right to the top. Excellent for market or freezing. Heavy cropper. Unusual for a hybrid in that it crops over a long period. For harvesting September to January. L91M, P83M, *R23*, S55, S61

Prince Marvel: 95 days. Uniform, upright plants have long petioles offering good insect control; height 3 feet. The tall stalk produces very uniform, firm, round, smooth, medium-sized sprouts from top to bottom that hold well without rot or cracking. Excellent for fresh market and processing. *A1*, A13, D11M, *E91G*, *F72*, *G13M*, G64, I91, J7, J14{PL}, J34, *J74*, J84, K73, L42, M46, P83M, etc.

Stabolite: 150 days. A particularly strong, dense leaf cover protects the sprouts from the effects of rain and frost and keeps them in excellent condition. The attractive, fine-flavored sprouts can be harvested from late December to April. L89, L91M, *R11M*

Valiant: 110 days. Early to midseason type developed in Holland. Produces heavy yields of tight buds on each tall, vigorous stalk. Sprouts are cylindrical in shape; delicate and rich-flavored; both burst and rot-resistant. Plant in early to mid-summer for abundant fall harvests, extending into winter in mild areas. *A1*, J34, K66, L42, M49

Widgeon: 120 days. A productive, cold-tolerant, late cultivar for mid-fall through winter harvest. Smooth, medium-small, dark green sprouts widely spaced on tall plants. Delicious, particularly after several frosts. Considered in England to be one of the highest quality cultivars. G6

OPEN-POLLINATED

Bedford Fillbasket: 95 days. Strong plants produce heavy crops of very large, solid, dark-green sprouts, tightly packed on the stems. Provides a continuous harvest from early autumn until Christmas. Height 3 1/2 to 4 feet. I99, K49T, L91M, O53M, P83M, S55, S61

Cambridge #1: Tall growing plant; height 4 feet. Produces medium-sized, solid, high quality sprouts from the base of the stem right to the top. Good flavor. Early maturing; for harvesting in October and November. P83M

Cambridge #5: 150 days. Popular winter-hardy cultivar. Very late to mature, the solid sprouts remaining firm until New Year when they should be used, not before. High quality, walnut-sized sprouts. Very heavy yields. Cropping continues until March. Height 4 feet. L91M, P83M, *R23*

Early Dwarf Danish: 95 days. Compact growth habit; in some years the short stature allows for snow to insulate and protect the sprouts against freeze damage. Good yields of large, high quality sprouts with very good flavor. Early maturing; well suited to areas with short growing seasons. A2, E24, F44, R47

Early Half Tall: (Continuity) Plant of compact habit; excellent for windy or exposed gardens. Dark foliage. Large, medium-green sprouts of very high quality are produced from top to bottom of the stalk. Height 2 1/2 feet. Very early; for harvesting in September and October. B49, P83M, *R23*

Green Pearl: 100 days. Maturity about the same as Catskill, later than Jade Cross; more uniform. Sprouts larger; smooth, round, and very solid. J7

Long Island: 95 days. Strong, robust plants of compact growth habit; height 18 to 24 inches. Large, thick and close-jointed stalks. Round, tight, dark-green sprouts; 1 1/2 inches in diameter; tender and succulent. Sprouts cover the stalk and are solid the entire length. Good for local markets, home gardens and freezing. For late fall and winter harvests. D65, G71M, G87, H66, I64, K5M, L14, M95

Long Island Improved: (Long Island Improved Catskill, Catskill) 100 days. Comparatively dwarf growth habit; height about 2 feet. Well-covered with medium green, globe-shaped, firm sprouts, 1 inch to 1 1/2 inches in diameter; maturing over a period of several weeks. Freezes very well. Hardy and productive. At one time the principal commercial sprout in California until hybrids with more uniform ripening came on the market. A2, B75M, B78, C44, C92, D82, F19M, F19M{PL}, F82, *H61*, H94, I65M{PL}, K49M, L7M, L35{PL}, L97, M13M, N16, etc.

Noisette: Small to medium-sized, tight sprouts with a very distinctive nutty flavor. An old French cultivar of gourmet quality. Can be picked over a long period, e.g. from late October to mid-February from a mid-June planting. Height 2 feet. P83M, S55

Roodnerf Early Button: (Early Button) 100 days. High yields of small-sized sprouts of excellent quality. Sprouts keeps well on the stem over a long period of time. Bred specially for its small, even, deep-green sprouts. For best quality harvest when not much larger than a thumbnail. Matures in late December. S59M, S61

Roodnerf Late Supreme: 150 days. Medium-tall, highly productive plants. Dark green, medium-sized buttons of high quality; well-spaced along the length of the tall stalk so the sprouts don't rot. Very cold hardy, late-maturing type. Doesn't produce sprouts until November, and continues for at least 2 months. L89

Roodnerf Seven Hills: (Seven Hills) Produces a heavy crop of small to medium-sized, tight sprouts of fine quality. Very hardy; harvest begins in early December, but plants will stand all winter and can be picked as late as March. Most reliable late standard cultivar. B49, P59M, *R23*

Rubine:[1] (Red) A large, late cultivar with small, tight sprouts of a bright crimson color. Lower yields than green types, but of excellent, gourmet flavor. Said to be less attractive to white cabbage butterflies. For harvesting in December. To preserve the color when cooking, a small amount of vinegar should be added. GENDERS 1975, ORGAN; C53, C85M, D76, E97, F13, G64, I39, I99, J20, *J74*, K49M, M46, O53M, Q34, S55, etc.

Stiekema Vrosa Original: 100 days. Tall growth habit. Medium green sprouts; large, tight and uniform; well-spaced and easy to pick. Early and very heavy cropping. C85M

BUTTERNUT {GR}

JUGLANS CINEREA

Ayers: Medium-sized nut; good kernel percentage; has a 30% higher crackout rate than the average cultivar. Tree vigorous, upright; late blooming. Foliage appears to be resistant to the anthracnose fungus and is moderately susceptible to the eriophyid mite. Originated in Bellevue, Michigan by Corwin Davis. Appears to be worth propagating. I40, K16{OR}

Bountiful: (Stark Bountiful) Nut easily cracked and shelled, borne in clusters of 5 or more; flavor very good, mild; ripens in late August to late September in Zone 6. Tree hardy, heavy bearing, self-pollinating, flower blossoms resist frost. For zones 4 to 7. Originated in Bowling Green, Missouri by William K. Erickson. Introduced in 1982. L33

Buckley: Large nut. Tree a very vigorous grower; appears to have some resistance to the anthracnose fungus but is susceptible to the eriophyid mite. Originated in Iowa. Worthy of propagation. I40

Chamberlain: Nut shell large, medium-thick; kernel plump, without ridges, flavor good; skin medium brown; kernel extraction moderately easy; resembles Love; ripens about September 27 in Heuvelton. Tree extremely hardy; somewhat tolerant of melanconis dieback; susceptible to anthracnose. Introduced in 1967 by Fred L. Ashworth, St. Lawrence Nurseries, Huevelton, New York. BROOKS 1972; A91{PL}, E91M{OR}, N24M

Craxezy: Medium-sized nut; cracks easily, yielding twin halves; kernels average 56% of nut; flavor very good. Tree vigorous; hardy; bears heavily; moderately susceptible to melanconis dieback; somewhat resistant to anthracnose. One of the most widely grown butternuts. Originated in Union City, Michigan by H.P. Burgart. Introduced in 1934. BROOKS 1972; A91{PL}, E91M, E91M{OR}, I40, N15, N24M

Creighton: Medium-sized nut; good cracking qualities, cracks out 50% halves. Tree vigorous; leafs out late and retains its foliage after most others are completely defoliated; foliage normally very clean, occasionally susceptible to eriophyid mite. Originated in Clinton County, Pennsylvania by R.L. Watts. I40, K16{OR}

Fort Wood: Tree very productive and is one of the easiest to graft. Foliage is moderately susceptible to the anthracnose fungus and eriophyid mite. State prize winner in Missouri. Appears to be a good nut but needs testing in other areas. K16{OR}

George Elmer: Tree is vigorous and has a rounded nut, medium in size but has not been fully evaluated. Very good cracking qualities. Foliage is susceptible to anthracnose fungus and eriophyid mite. Needs additional study but appears to be a good cultivar. E91M, E91M{OR}, I40{OR}

Kenworthy: Very large nut with an excellent flavor, fills well. Tree vigorous; very hardy; quite dwarfed in size; appears to be resistant to anthracnose fungus and eriophyid mite. Has characteristics suggesting that it may be a hybrid between butternut and heartnut. Originated in Wisconsin. E41M{SC}, E91M, E91M{OR}, N24M

Kinneyglen: Nut cracks easily as kernel comes free from shell when nut is cracked from one end. Kernel averages 57.5% percent of total weight of nut. Open-pollinated seedling discovered about 1940 in Ithaca, New York by S.H. Graham. Introduced in 1942. BROOKS 1972; Dropped by I60{PL}

Love: Nut averages 44 to 71 per pound, depending on seasonal conditions; kernels crack out well; contains 17 to 19% kernel; kernel short, plump, firm; flavor rich. Tree a strong, vigorous grower; comes into bearing early; short-lived in the Northeast due to susceptibility to "bunch" virus disease. BROOKS 1972; K16{OR}

Van Syckle: Nut very large; kernels crack out in halves; flavor excellent. Tree bears heavily. Originated in Johnstown Township, Barry County, Michigan by the Burgess Seed and Plant Company. Introduced in 1959. BROOKS 1972; I40{OR}

Weschcke: Medium to large nut; kernel light-colored, tender; smooth convolutions of shell allow kernels to drop out freely; hull easily removed. Tree extremely hardy; very productive when grafted on black walnut or butternut, but difficult to graft. Originated in River Falls, Wisconsin by Carl Weschcke. Introduced in 1938. BROOKS 1972; I40

BUTTON MUSHROOM {SN}

AGARICUS BISPORUS

BROWN-SKINNED

81 Brown: Noted for its yield consistency and virus resistance even in adverse growing conditions. Steady production through later breaks. Produces high quality medium to dark brown mushrooms for the fresh market. Higher disease resistance than white strains. During spawn run and casing the compost temperature should never be allowed to rise above 72^0 F. G55M

Bavarian Brown: Grows at temperatures of 55 to 70^0 F. Needs no sunlight, just regular watering. Begins producing in 3 to 5 weeks. Yields up to 10 pounds of mushrooms over a 2 to 3 month period. J85{KT}

Italian: (Cremini, Portobello) Known as *cremini* in the button stage and *portobello* after the caps open fully. Cremini have fawn colored caps, are similar to the white button mushroom but have a much firmer texture and a more intense, nutty flavor. Portobello mushrooms are much larger and heavier, may reach 8 inches in diameter and have very dark chocolate, almost black caps and gills. Popular specialty market items. E21{CU}

Royal Tan: {KT} Unusual, rich beige-colored mushrooms. More robust flavor than common white button mushrooms. Prized by gourmets. Begins to produce in one month; will continue to produce for several more months. D76, E97, J20

WHITE-SKINNED

46 White: Produces high yields of smooth white mushrooms over several breaks. Adapted to a wide range of productive growing conditions. High tolerance to verticillium. Does not require as high a carbon dioxide level as hybrids to control pinning. Bed temperatures should never be allowed to rise above 75^0 F. during spawn run or after. G55M

78 Off-White: Prolific producer of first and second break mushrooms. Quality is maintained for fresh market packs during the third and succeeding breaks. Thick, flaked pellicle; off-white in color with good shelf life. Low CO_2 sizing levels. Off-white strains in general are characterized by their flaked or rough surface. G55M

100 Hybrid Off-White: High yielding strain. Produces a white, well-rounded mushroom with a dense, fleshy cap. Cap may be slightly scaled, depending on climatic conditions. Mushrooms are medium to large and have a relatively long shelf life. Temperature should be in the 78 to 82^0 F. range and should not exceed 88^0 F. at spawning and during spawn run; relative humidity should be 90% or more. Highly suited for prepack, fresh bulk or canning purposes. *L77*

110 Hybrid Off-White: High yielding strain. Produces a white, well-rounded mushroom with a dense, fleshy cap. Cap may be slightly scaled, depending on climatic conditions. Mushrooms are medium to large in size and have a relatively long shelf life. Temperature should be in the 78 to 82^0 F. range and should not exceed 88^0 F. at spawning and during spawn run; relative humidity should be 90% or more. Highly suited for prepack, fresh bulk and canning purposes. *L77*

208 Hybrid White: Produces a mushroom with a well rounded cap and good white coloring. Excellent for fresh market as well as the processed market. High percentage of large mushrooms. Very good shelf life, with a thick veil and good holding ability when stored between 33^0 F. and 35^0 F. *A41*

245 Hybrid White: Produces a mushroom that is deep, white and dense with a well rounded cap. Not generally as large as U-1 Hybrid White, but is capable of producing a high percentage of large mushrooms. Very good shelf life and good keeping qualities when stored between 33° and 35° F. *A41*

344 Cream: A cream strain with a very dense cap. The veil does not open as easily as most strains, allowing better sizing and fewer #2 product. Size can be influenced by temperature of the environment. Prefers a slightly cooler air temperature than most. Cap can become slightly scaled with high air movement. Stipe is normally straight, short and white. *A41*

381 White: High yielding strain. Generates a pure white, densely tissued mushroom which is medium to large and has a relatively long shelf life. Often produces about 3/4 of its total yield on the first two breaks. Temperate should be in the 75 to 85° F. range and should not be higher than 95° F. at spawning and during spawn run; relative humidity should be 90% or more. Well suited for prepack, fresh bulk or canning purposes. *L77*

405 Hybrid White: Good producer of large, smooth high quality mushrooms for fresh or processed markets. Tolerant to higher CO_2 and air temperatures than other strains. Responds well to supplementation at spawning. G55M

501 Hybrid Off-White: Produces high quality mushrooms for the fresh market with off-white hybrid's characteristic superior shelf life. Not as sensitive to scaling as first generation off-white hybrids. Produces good size mix when picking for fresh market. 501 will scale, as do all off-whites or off-white hybrid crosses, if exposed to excessive air velocity or dryness. G55M

643 Hybrid Off-White: Produces high quality off-white mushrooms for the fresh market with generally superior shelf-life. Responds well to warmer bed temperatures and slow shocking. Produces good size mix when picking for fresh market. G55M

U-1 Hybrid White: Produces one of the highest quality, fresh market mushrooms. A true cross between the best white and off-white strains. Deep, white and dense, with well-rounded cap shape. Capable of producing one of the highest percentages of large mushrooms. Long shelf life. Thick veil delays opening. Low sensitivity to bruising. *A41*

U-3 Hybrid White: A prolific hybrid strain with the smooth white skin of its smooth white parent and the compressed, fleshy cap of its rough white parent. Not as large as U-1, but good sizing given its high yielding nature. Good to very good shelf life. Somewhat thickened veil delays opening. *A41*

CABBAGE {S}

BRASSICA OLERACEA CAPITATA GROUP

COMMON GREEN CABBAGE

HYBRID

Apex:[1] 95 days. Round, dark-green head; very dense and firm; weight 3 to 5 pounds. Extra short cores for more useable cabbage and less waste. Sweet juicy flavor, of "gourmet" quality. Holds for weeks without cracking. Small, compact plant suitable for close spacing. Good frost resistance. For fall harvest. Suitable for limited cold storage. G6, N81, *R11M*

Grenadier:[2] 65 days. Relatively open plants with few wrappers. Dense, medium-green heads; weight 2 to 2 1/2 pounds; small cores. Crisp, juicy leaves; sweet, delicate flavor. Very good eaten fresh "out of hand" or thinly sliced in salads. Bred to be crack resistant and to hold for very long periods. Tolerant to thrips and tip-burn. G64, G93M, J20, *J74*, K66, L42

Marathon:[4] 93 days. Deep, globe-shaped heads; deep green interior leaves with veined outer leaves. Very dense internal structure and short cores, resulting in extra head weight at harvest. Retains color well after 6 months of storage. Good tolerance to mildew and pepperspot; not yellows tolerant. One of the most popular storage cultivars in Europe. K73, L42

Minicole:[1] 66 days. Small, round to slightly oval heads; good interior color. Very short core means more cabbage and less waste. Few dark-green outerleaves. Can stand for up to 4 months without slitting. Very compact plant; well-suited to dense plantings or container culture. For late summer and fall harvests. D11M, H42, J7, K50, L91M, M49, N81, P9, P83M, *R23*, S45M, S55, S61, *S75M*

Perfect Action:[1] 77 days. Round, dark-green heads; weight 2 to 4 pounds; densely packed interiors, even near the base. Extra short cores for more useable cabbage and less waste. Delicious sweet, juicy flavor and texture. Compact plant, suitable for close spacing. Yellows resistant; very good resistance to splitting. D68, G6

Perfect Ball:[1] 87 days. Later, somewhat larger version of Perfect Action. Uniform, round, dark blue-green heads; good wrapper leaves. Extra short cores for more useable cabbage and less waste. Sweet, juicy flavor. Can be harvested over a prolonged period without loss of quality. Yellows resistant. For summer or fall crops. D68, G6, I77, *R11M*

Safekeeper:[4] 95 days. Hybrid Green Winter type. Much more tolerant to autumn rains and more winter hardy than Green Winter or Storage Green types. Medium length stems. Heavy frame and wrapper leaves give added head protection from early frosts. Sown from June 25th to July 10th for mid-October harvests. Fair tolerance to black rot; not yellows tolerant. L42

Salarite:[2] 57 days. An extra early, semi-savoy ballhead type. Small heads; weight 2 to 3 pounds. Wrapper leaves dark-green, attractively ruffled; thick, tender, juicy and sweet, almost lettuce-like in taste. Interiors solid; butter-yellow in color. Very compact plant. Recommended for home gardeners or super market sales. A32, C53, I39, L42, L89, N81

Shamrock:[2] (Big Apple) 60-65 days. Large, uniform heads; weight 11 pounds; strong, short stems. Few outer leaves. Very crisp and sweet; excellent for salads. Holds without splitting for at least 2 months. For summer and fall crops. Highly commended by the Royal Horticultural Society in 1982. E38, F19M, G64, L91M, *R11M*, T1M

Stonehead:[1] 67 days. Round, very solid, light-green heads; weight 3 1/2 to 4 pounds. Few outer leaves; very short core. Stands a long time without splitting. Compact plant; produces an abundant crop in a small area. Yellows resistant. For early market, home gardens and shipping. All America Selections winner in 1969. B73M, B75, B75M, C44, D65, E97, F1, F19M{PL}, H33{PL}, H42, I39, I65M{PL}, J14{PL}, J20, J34{PL}, K71{PL}, L42, L91M, M13M, M49, etc.

Superelite:[2] 83 days. Round, solid, dark blue-green head; very fancy, thick, tough wrapper leaves; excellent internal quality with a very sweet flavor. Holds its quality for a long time in the field. Resistant to yellows and tip-burn; tolerant to black speck and black rot. *J74*

OPEN-POLLINATED

April Green:[4] 105 days. Most popular Langedijker type in Holland. An excellent keeper; will retain its green color right through the winter. Short stems. Good internal quality and flavor. Exterior color darker green than most other winter types. Recommended for home gardeners and commercial growers. K49M, L42, M49

Brunswick: 90 days. Compact, flattened, dense heads; 9 inches in diameter; weight 7 to 9 pounds. Few outer leaves. Popular for fresh market and kraut. For late summer and autumn crops. Stores very well. Popular in severe climates where late storage types are difficult to mature. Introduced prior to 1876. *C28*, E24, E49, E59Z, *L59G*, *R23*

Charleston Wakefield: 73 days. Improved form of Early Jersey Wakefield, about a week later in maturing but yielding nearly twice the crop. Dark-green, very solid, conical heads, 6 to 8 inches in diameter; weight 4 to 6 pounds; medium-sized core. Good wrapper leaves. Slow bolting. Popular in the South for over-wintering. *A69M*, C92, *D49*, E38, *F72*, G27M, G57M, H54, H66, J34, K49M, K71, L7M, L14, M46, etc.

Christmas Drumhead: 110 days. Large, flattened, solid heads. Dwarf, compact plant; very hardy, productive and reliable. Can be sown later than most other cultivars, July or August for December and January harvests. Introduced about 1903. L91M, P83M, S61

Copenhagen Market: (Copenhagen, Early Copenhagen Market) 68 days. Uniform, globe-shaped light green heads, firm and solid; 6 inches in diameter, weight 3 to 4 pounds. Good wrapper leaves. Stands for a long time without splitting. Compact, short-stemmed plant; heavy yielding. For early markets and home gardens. A16, B75M, C44, D82, *E91G*, F1, *F72*, G71M, H33{PL}, H42, *H61*, H66, H94, I65M{PL}, L97, M95, N16, etc.

Danish Ballhead: 105 days. Medium-sized, round heads, medium dark green with a gray bloom; extremely firm and solid; weight 7 to 9 pounds. Short stem. Good all-purpose cabbage; very good for kraut. Withstands hot, dry weather. Excellent for storage, keeping its fine qualities until spring. Introduced in 1887. A16, A25, B73M, B75M, C85M, D82, E24, F1, F82, G16, G71, H42, L79, L97, M13M, etc.

Decema:[4] 120 days. One of the leading Dutch winter types, specially developed for storage. Uniform, round-oval head; holds an attractive color even after long term storage. Extremely heavy yielding. K50, *R23*

Delicatesse:[2] 70 days. Round, solid, medium-sized heads; of excellent quality and texture, with no coarse ribs. Wrapper leaves few, small. High sugar content; lacks the typical strong cabbage flavor. Excellent in salads and coleslaw. Matures in late summer. E38, *R23*

Earliana: 60 days. Very early Golden Acre type; quite uniform in size and maturity. Small, deep round heads; 4 1/2 to 5 inches in diameter, weight 2 to 2 1/2 pounds; compact and well-folded. Attractive, medium-green color well into interiors. Ideal size, shape and quality for home gardens. Small plants take less space. A16, B75, C85M, C92, D11M, N52

Early Flat Dutch: 90 days. Large, flattened, solid heads; 6 to 7 inches deep, 11 inches in diameter; weight 6 to 10 pounds; short stems, medium-sized core. Few outer leaves; can be planted closely. Excellent for sauerkraut and storage. Resists heat, therefore popular in the South. Introduced prior to 1875. A56, C76M, E97{PL}, F12, *F72*, G51, *G83M*, H54, *H61*, J34, J34{PL}, J70M{PL}, K73, L7M, L35{PL}, etc.

Early Jersey Wakefield: (Early Wakefield, Jersey Wakefield) 65 days. Medium-sized, conical, pale green heads; often tinged with red on the side exposed to the sun; weight 2 to 3 pounds. Outer leaves glaucous-green. Slow bolting, but cracks easily. Small plants permit close spacing. For home and market gardens, or shipping. Introduced prior to 1865. BURR, VILMORIN; A16, B73M, C44, D82, E24, F19M, *F72*, F82, G6, H66, H94, I65M{PL}, J34{PL}, J70M{PL}, L7M, L35{PL}, L97, M46, N16, etc.

Early Round Dutch: (Round Dutch) 80 days. Large, rounded dark-green heads, 7 to 8 inches in diameter, weight 5 to 7 pounds; very solid; short stems. Few outer leaves. Slow to bolt. Adapted to a wide range of conditions. Popular in the South for kraut. Good for early markets and shipping. A87M, C92, E5T, F19M{PL}, *F72*, *G1M*, H66, I65M{PL}, J97M, K49M, K71, L14, *L85*{PL}, M13M, M95M, etc.

Flower of Spring: (Offenham Flower of Spring) Medium-sized, conical pointed, solid heads; compact and short-stemmed; very good flavor. Ideal for autumn or early spring sowing. Selected from Offenham. Introduced about 1905. Still a very popular home garden cultivar in England. O53M, P83M, *R23*, S61, T1M

Glory of Enkhuizen: 75 days. Large, globe-shaped, deep bluish-green heads, 7 1/2 inches in diameter; weight 5 to 10 pounds; good interior quality and flavor. Wrapper leaves few, wavy. Good for cabbage rolls, early kraut and coleslaw. Keeps well. Good market cultivar. A16, *A75*, *C28*, C85M, C92, D27, E24, E38, E59Z, F1, G67M, G79, K49M, *L59G*, *R11M*, etc.

Golden Acre: (Golden Acre Yellows Resistant) 65 days. Early Copenhagen Market type. Uniform, round grey-green heads; firm and dense; 6 to 7 inches in diameter, weight 4 to 5 pounds; medium-sized core; short stems. Good wrapper leaves. Bolts readily. Keeps 60 days after harvest. Small plants permit close spacing. Yellows resistant. A16, A25, B73M, B75M, D82, E24, F19M, F82, G16, G71, H42, *H61*, H94, L35{PL}, L97, M13M, N16, etc.

Green Winter:[4] Medium-large, round heads, good inner quality; weight 6 to 7 pounds. Stem about 9 inches high. Holds its light green color in storage, making it more appealing than standard late white cabbages. Somewhat later than Danish Ballhead. E38, N52

Greenhead:[4] Medium-large, somewhat flattened heads; firm and solid. Short stem. Retains its light green color in storage. Has a more appealing color than white late cabbages and is preferred by stores and super markets. E38

Greensleaves:[3] 110 days. High quality, loose-heading cabbage that provides tender, fresh, dark leafy greens when little else is available. Sow in late summer for a late winter and early spring harvest. Highly commended by the Royal Horticultural Society in 1987. L91M, *S75M*

Greyhound: 64 days. Similar to Early Jersey Wakefield, but much earlier. Small, conical heads, very dense and solid; weight 2 to 3 pounds. Few outer leaves. Very mild flavor; quality good. For spring and fall sowings; can also be over-wintered. Popular in Europe. B49, K49M, L91M, O53M, *R23*, S45M, S55, S61, *S75M*

Harbinger: Small, uniform, conical pointed heads; firm and solid, of good quality and fine flavor. Not prone to bolting. Few outer leaves. Compact plants, suitable for close spacing; very reliable. Recommended for autumn sowing; matures quickly in spring. Introduced about 1891. P83M, S55, S61

Houston Evergreen:[4] 95 days. Round, solid heads; 7 to 8 inches in diameter, weight 3 to 4 pounds. Few outer leaves. For fresh market, shipping, or winter storage. Retains its apple-green color in storage. Hall-tall type. Used primarily on heavy muck land where other Wintergreen types get a bit too tall. A69M, D27, E38, *F63*

Langedijker Late Decema:[4] (Langedijker Late Winter-Keeper Decema) 95 days. Large, nearly round, very firm head. Retains its light green color in storage. Known for its keeping qualities. Heavy producer. C85M

Lariat:[4] Refined, extra-late, "wintergreen" cabbage for long-term storage. Medium-sized, blue green heads; weight 5 to 8 pounds, with smaller heads produced from closer spacing; dense, well packed interiors. Holds its attractive color for several months in storage. Resistant to black rot, pepperspot and frost. Needs early planting for best crop. G6

Late Flat Dutch: (Large Late Flat Dutch) 105 days. Large, roundish, flattened head; very firm and solid; 12 to 14 inches in diameter; weight 12 to 15 pounds. Outer leaves fairly numerous. Good keeper and shipper. Exceptionally hardy; also resists drought. Introduced prior to 1846. VILMORIN; D82, D87, E97, F24M, *F72*, G71, *G83M*, H42, *H61*, H66, I65M{PL}, K73, L35{PL}, M13M, M95, N39, etc.

Marion Market: (Yellows Resistant Copenhagen) 75 days. Round, solid heads, 6 to 7 inches in diameter; weight 3 1/2 to 4 pounds; crisp and tender; good wrapper leaves. Widely used for fresh market and kraut. Resistant to bolting. Medium to large plants, larger and coarser than Copenhagen Market; yellows tolerant. A56, *B1*, B75M, C92, *F63*, G71, G79, H33, *H61*, I64, J58, K27M, *L59G*, M95M

Marner Allfrüh: 65 days. An open-pollinated German cultivar that has the vigor and uniformity of a hybrid. Small to medium, round, compact head; weight 3 pounds. Stands well without splitting. Numerous tennis-ball sized heads can be harvested if sown May through June. B49, N81, P9, *R23*, S27

Noblesse:[2] 70 days. Uniform, round, dark blue-green heads; very solid and firm; weight 3 to 4 pounds. Sweet, mild, faintly cabbage-like flavor; high sugar content; of fine texture and quality. Excellent for salads and coleslaw. Good tolerance to bolting; stands in the garden a long time without splitting. D11M

Penn State Ballhead: (Penn State Danish Ballhead) 100 days. Well-wrapped, slightly flattened ball-shaped heads, very firm and solid; 7 to 9 inches in diameter; weight 8 pounds. Good for kraut. Very resistant to splitting. Keeps perfectly in storage until late spring. Not yellows tolerant. B13, D11M, E24, E38, *F72*, G57M, G79, H49, J58, K20, M13M

Premium Late Flat Dutch: 100 days. Large, solid head, broad and flat on top; bluish-green, often tinted with red or brown; weight 10 to 15 pounds. Inner leaves creamy white; crisp, tender and flavorful. Outer leaves few, tinged with purple when mature. Good for kraut. Excellent storage cabbage; retains its freshness and flavor till late in the spring. Sure Heading. Introduced prior to 1865. BURR; *A69M*, B35M, B73M, D65, D76, *E91G*, F24M, G67M, H49, H94, K49M, K71, L7M, L97, N16, etc.

Primo: (Golden Acre Primo) 65 days. Small, round, ball-like heads; large, heavy, solid hearts. Few outer leaves. Delicate flavor and tenderness. Grows well in any soil. Good market cultivar and ideal for a small family. Best used for successional sowing from February until mid-July. B49, L91M, *R23*

Quick-Green Storage:[4] 90 days. Tested for several years as an early green storage type in the Montreal area. Excellent in short season areas where it is difficult to mature good-sized heads before heavy frosts. Retains good color until spring in storage, harvested with Penn State Ballhead. L42

Quintal d'Alsace: (D'Alsace) 115 days. A 19th century French heirloom. Large, flattened, compact heads, sometimes slightly tinged with brown on the upper part. Harvested in late fall for winter storage. Long standing, old-fashioned choice for the famed sauerkraut of the Alsace-Lorraine region of France. VILMORIN; B75, G68, Q24M, Q34

Wheeler's Imperial: Solid, conical pointed, dark-green heads; dwarf and compact; mild flavor. Sown in early spring for a crop in April and May, and again in August for a late harvest. An old favorite in England. Introduced about 1884. O53M, P83M, *R23*, S61

Winningstadt: (Early Winningstadt, Winnigstadter) Solid, conical pointed, grey-green heads; compact and well-shaped; short stem. Very good flavor. Does well on any soil. Sown in May for a harvest in October, November and December. Stores well. Of German origin; introduced prior to 1860. BURR, VILMORIN; O53M, P83M, *R23*, S55, S61

Wintergreen:[4] Quick maturing, leafy, loose-headed cabbage. Good dark green color. Suitable for growing as spring greens or "collards" early in the season, or small-hearted cabbage in late spring. Very high in vitamins A and C, calcium and other minerals. Produces a good crop at the first cut. Can be direct sown. Hardy. Selected from Offenham. P83M, *R23*, S55, *S75M*

Wisconsin All Seasons: 95 days. Flattened, globe-shaped heads, very solid and uniform; 7 to 8 inches in diameter; weight 8 to 10 pounds. Blue-green outer leaves, white inner leaves. Excellent for kraut. Yellows resistant. Good for home gardens; well-suited for winter storage. Resistant to bolting, drought and hot weather. B75M, D65, *E53M*, E59Z, G57M, G79, *I59M*, I64, J58, K10, K27M, K71, *L59G*, M46, M95M, etc.

Zwaan Jumbo: (Jumbo) 105 days. Very large heads, average weight 20 to 25 pounds, occasionally reaching 35 pounds; very firm and salad. Crisp, pale green leaves, very good for stuffed cabbage. Resistant to splitting. Keeps well. Yields best in peat or muck soils. D11M, D27, K49M

RED CABBAGE

HYBRID

Ruby Ball:[1] 65 days. Nearly spherical, well-filled, deep purplish-red heads; 6 inches in diameter, weight 4 to 5 pounds; very firm and dense; extremely uniform, short-cored. Excellent wrapper leaves. Good color inside and out. Holds well in the field without splitting. All America Selections winner in 1972. A16, C44, D11M, *E91G*, *F72*, G71, G93M, H33{PL}, *H61*, H95, J14{PL}, J20, J34, L89, M46, N16, S55, etc.

Ruby Perfection: 85 days. Medium-sized, round, bright purple-red heads; 6 inches in diameter, weight 3 to 4 pounds; very uniform, firm and solid. Good wrapper leaves; good color right to the core. Holds well without splitting. Not yellows tolerant. Ships well. Ideal for late summer crops, or fall harvests for medium-term storage. B75, D68, *E91G*, *F72*, G6, G16, G64, *H61*, J7, K10, K50, K73, L42, M29, M46, etc.

OPEN-POLLINATED

Baby Early: 65 days. Firm, round, dark red heads with small inner core; 4 1/2 to 5 inches in diameter; weight 2 to 2 1/4 pounds; sureheading. Holds well in the garden without bursting. Excellent raw or cooked. D11M

Langedijker Red Winter Keeper: 100 days. One of the best red winter keepers. Firm, oblong, dark-red heads. Best planted somewhat earlier than other late reds to obtain maximize size heads. C85M

Lasso Red: 70 days. Small, rounded, very firm heads; attractive bright red color; weight 2 to 4 pounds; very uniform. Few outer leaves. Keeps in the field several weeks without splitting. For salads, cooking and red kraut. Can be stored if sown to mature in autumn. D68, E24, E59Z, F44, G6, J20, K49M

Mammoth Red Rock: (Red Rock) 95 days. Large, flattened, dark purplish-red heads; 8 to 10 inches in diameter, weight 5 to 8 pounds; firm and solid; rich, distinctive flavor. Popular for pickling, boiling and kraut. Sure heading. Stands fairly well without splitting. Excellent for storage. Standard large late red cabbage. *A69M*, B35M, C85M,

D11M, D87, E24, F19M, G71, H66, H94, K71, M13M, N16, N39, etc.

Red Acre: 80 days. Globe-shaped, deep purplish-red heads; 5 1/2 to 6 inches in diameter, weight 2 1/2 to 4 pounds; firm and solid. Good wrapper leaves. Holds well for a long period without splitting. Compact, short-stemmed plant; yellows resistant. For spring and summer harvests. Excellent for storage. A16, A25, B73M, B75M, C44, D82, E57, *F72*, F82, F92, H42, *H61*, H94, I65M{PL}, L7M, L35{PL}, L79, M95, etc.

Red Danish: (Red Danish Ballhead) 95 days. Medium-sized, uniform, very solid heads; round, slightly flattened on top; average weight 4 to 6 pounds; good purple-red color. Widely used for pickling and coleslaw. For fresh market or short term storage. Adapted to late summer and fall crops. Fairly tolerant to yellows. *J74*, J84, K50, L42

Red Drumhead: Round to slightly flattened, deep purplish-red heads; 7 inches in diameter; very solid. Fine, sweet flavor; good raw as well as for cooking and pickling. Holds its color well when pickled. Excellent winter keeper. Medium-sized plant; very hardy. Sow in early spring for an autumn harvest. Introduced about 1867. B49, C85M, L91M, O53M, P83M, S45M, S61

Red Meteor: (Meteor) 75 days. Uniform, deep globe-shaped, dark red heads; 6 to 8 inches in diameter; weight 2 1/2 to 4 pounds; very solid and sweet. Very good wrapper leaves. Darker, more uniform, and more stable red color under mild weather conditions than Red Acre. Excellent field-standing ability and cold weather tolerance. G93M, L42, L89, N52

Red Rodan: 140 days. Large, round, very hard heads; 8 to 10 inches in diameter. Surprisingly tender for a cultivar that can often stand until March without decaying. Very vigorous, making it one of the easiest cabbages to grow. L89

Storage Red (Short Stem): 96 days. Globe-shaped heads; weight 7 pounds. Interior quality excellent for coleslaw. Leaves retain a high percentage of juice when shredded after a few months in storage. Excellent exterior color after 6 months of storage. Heads are fairly easy to strip. Upright, high-yielding plant. L42

Testa di Negro: Excellent late maturing cultivar. Very solid, finely ribbed heads. Cooked for kraut or eaten raw as coleslaw. Sown in summer for a harvest in autumn and winter. Originated in Holland. B8, Q11M

SAVOY CABBAGE

Considered to be the best flavored cabbage. Generally milder than others, with a tasty, buttery yellow interior. Makes excellent shredded cabbage or "coleslaw". Also has ornamental value with its wavy leaf edges and blistered leaf surface.

HYBRID

Savoy Ace: 80 days. Uniform, semiglobe-shaped, dark green heads; weight 3 1/2 to 5 pounds; very firm, with a small to medium-sized core. Finely crinkled leaves; sweet, tender flavor. Holds well without splitting. Vigorous, productive plant; resistant to both heat and frost. Tolerant to fusarium yellows. All America Selections winner in 1977. A13, A87M, B73M, B75, F13, *F72*, G16, G71, G82, H54, *H61*, H95, I64, J7, J14{PL}, J20, etc.

Savoy King:[1] 85 days. Uniform, semi-flat, dark green heads; 9 to 10 inches in diameter, weight 4 to 6 pounds; short core. Good flavor and texture. Stands heat better than other savoy types. Can be harvested 2 to 3 times a year in mild climates. Heads somewhat smaller in the spring; lighter green in warm weather. Yellows resistant. All America Selections winner in 1965. A87M, C85M, C92, D11M, D65, *E91G*, F19M, *F72*, G51, K73, L89, L91M, M29, M49, N39, etc.

OPEN-POLLINATED

Green

Alexander's No. 1: 200 days. Large, uniform, solid, dark-green heads. Heavily crinkled leaves. Matures in January and February and holds longer than any other cultivar, well into spring. One of the best open-pollinated late savoys still on the European market. L89, *R23*

Best of All: (Sutton's Best of All) 90 days. Early Drumhead type. Very large, solid, medium-green heads. Outer leaves coarsely crinkled. Stands a long time without splitting. Does well on all soils. Very cold resistant. Harvested during September and October. Introduced about 1897. B49, L91M, P83M, *R23*, S61

Blue Max: (Aubervilliers) 80 days. Slightly flattened, heavily crinkled heads; weight 3 to 4 pounds; attractive, blue and lime-green coloring; tender texture. Outer leaves appear to be resistant to white cabbage butterflies. E24, F44, G6, I77, K49M

Des Vertus: (Large Drumhead) 75 days. Broad, compact heads, flattened on the top; sometimes slightly tinged with a wine-lees-red color; weight 3 pounds. Deep blue-green, moderately crinkled leaves; mild, sweet flavor. Stands heat very well. Very adaptable; can be planted in spring, summer or fall in mild climates. Introduced prior to 1885. VILMORIN; K66, Q24M

Dwarf Green Curled: Medium-sized, slightly flattened heads; very compact and solid; very short stems. Broad, finely crimped, deep clear-green outer leaves; of excellent flavor after they have been softened and made tender by frost. Very hardy; sown for winter harvests in mild climates. Introduced about 1834. VILMORIN; P83M, S55

Langedijker Winter Keeper Savoy:[4] 80 days. Very firm, light-green heads of excellent storage quality. A good market cultivar. C85M, K49M

Ormskirk Late: (Irish Giant Drumhead) Large dark-green heads; very firm and solid. Coarsely crinkled leaves, of good flavor. Will stand for a long time without splitting. Extremely hardy. Sown in May and June for a December through March harvest. An old favorite in the British Isles. Introduced about 1899. O53M, P83M, S55

Perfection Drumhead: (Perfection Drumhead Vertus Strain) 90 days. Large, nearly round, solid, deep green heads. Very finely curled and crinkled leaves; mild in flavor when touched by frost. Compact, short-stemmed plant. Has the size of the Drumhead, with the curled leaves and fine flavor of the savoy. Excellent keeper. Introduced prior to 1888. C85M, G57M

Savoy Chieftain: (Chieftain Savoy, Chieftain Drumhead Savoy) 90 days. Large, slightly flattened head; 8 to 10 inches in diameter, weight 4 to 6 pounds; very firm and solid. Dark green, densely crinkled leaves; mild in flavor. Stands well without splitting. For late summer and fall harvests. All America Selections winner in 1938. A16, A87M, B35M, C44, D11M, E24, F1, F82, G71, *H61*, H94, K73, L97, M13M, M46, etc.

Winter King: 80 days. Very late, hardy Ormskirk type. Uniform, solid, slightly flattened heads; short stems. Finely crumpled, ribbed, dark-green leaves; of excellent quality. More resistant to frost than other savoys; can be kept over winter in mild areas. C85M, *R23*, S61, *S75M*

Red

January King: 110 days. Semi-savoy type. Solid, flattish, light-green heads; weight 3 to 5 pounds; of excellent quality and flavor. Bluish-green wrapper leaves, tinged with purple in cool weather. Compact, very cold-hardy plants. Sown from May to July; harvested November through January. Will stand without splitting for most of the winter. A2, B49, I39, K49M, L89, L91M, O53M, P83M, Q34, *R23*, S61, *S75M*

Red Verona: 100 days. Small, attractive, purplish-red heads merging into green at the center. Lightly crinkled leaves. Delicious when cooked with apples and a dash of vinegar added to preserve its color. Harvested in the fall. U33

San Michele Italian: 100 days. A large red cabbage. The crinkled leaves are not equivalent to green savoy types, however they are deeply veined and padded. K66

CACTUS

See Cactaceae in the Botanical listings.

CARROT {S}

DAUCUS CAROTA SATIVUS GROUP

BABY CARROTS

Gourmet type carrots, bred to develop flavor and bright color while still young. Many have a unique rounded shape. Usually harvested when 2 to 3 inches long. Very popular specialty market item.

Amstel: 55 days. A popular French strain of Amsterdam which may be used for gourmet "baby carrots". Very smooth roots, 4 inches long by 1 inch in diameter; excellent color; sweet, tender flesh. Particularly good for eating raw. Fairly strong tops. F33, I91, S45M, S61

Amsterdam Forcing: 60 days. Very smooth, slender, cylindrical, stump-rooted type for forcing and harvesting early as "baby carrots". Grows 6 or 7 inches long and 1 inch in diameter when mature. Flesh is reddish-orange, juicy, crisp, very sweet, virtually coreless, of excellent quality. Short pale green foliage allows for dense plantings. A2, C85M, K49M, N52, *R11M*, R47, *S75M*

Baby Nantes: (Nantes a Forcer, Baby Finger Nantes) 55 days. An extra early cultivar for planting in the spring, or in a cold frame in the fall. Smooth, orange-red roots; flesh very sweet and tender, coreless. Ready for use when 2 to 2 1/2 inches long. Lift out with spade or trowel as tops are weak and break off easily. D76, F33, L42, M13M

Baby Orange: 53 days. An improved strain of the popular French cultivar Amstel. Roots are bright orange; 2 1/2 to 3 inches long; less fibrous when processed for frozen foods than Little Finger. Tap roots are more distinctive on muck soils than Baby Nantes types. L42

Baby Spike: 55 days. Miniature Amsterdam type, 3 to 4 inches long and 1/2 inch in diameter; crisp, very sweet, with exceptional internal color. Colors up and becomes sweet at an early age. Unlike true Amsterdams which become oversized if not harvested at maturity, Baby Spike holds its quality well past maturity. *C28*, G82, K10

Caramba: 75 days. Amsterdam forcing type. A favorite of market growers in Belgium and Holland. Bred to winter over under straw without cracking, rotting, or losing its tender, juicy texture or mild flavor. Slim, cylindrical, blunt-tipped, smooth roots. Also ideal for harvesting as "mini carrots" at 3 inches in length. K66, L89

Chantenay Babycan: Ideal for the production of "baby carrots". Seed may be broadcast to provide up to 45 plants per square foot. Develops rapidly. Rich colored, with little core and an excellent flavor. S55

Early French Frame: 67 days. Very smooth, nearly round root, seldom exceeding 2 inches in length or diameter; deep orange-red flesh of good flavor. Quick maturing; ideal for forcing under frames and tunnels, or for early successional sowing outdoors. Performs well in shallow soils. M46, S45M, S55, S61

Early Scarlet Horn: (Dutch Early Scarlet Horn, Early Horn) 68 days. A centuries old cultivar of "baby carrot" for greenhouse forcing and early outdoor use. Root nearly cylindrical, blunt-tipped; 6 inches long, 2 1/2 inches in diameter; skin orange-red; flesh deep orange-yellow, fine-grained, of superior flavor and delicacy. Well-adapted to shallow soils. Introduced prior to 1865. BURR, VILMORIN; A2, B49, F25, P83M, *R23*

Fincor: 55 days. A slower growing version of Minicor for mid-summer plantings when hot weather followed by heavy rains causes sudden extra growth, resulting in oversized carrots. Same high quality as Minicor. L42

Golden Ball: (Golden Ball Parisian) 60 days. Very early Parisienne type. Small, round roots; only 1 1/2 to 2 inches in diameter when harvested for "baby carrots"; golden orange throughout; flavor very sweet, excellent. Performs well in shallow soils. *A75*, F33, G71, J20

Lady Finger: 65 days. A gourmet carrot for cooking and serving whole, or canning and pickling whole. Small, cylindrical, golden-orange root; 3 to 5 inches long, 1/2 inch in diameter; flesh tender and sweet, nearly coreless. Short tops. Withstands close planting and produces abundant crops. D65, G79, G87, I84, I91, J25M, J58, K71, *L59G*

Little Finger: 60 days. Cylindrical, well-stumped root; 4 inches long, 1 inch in diameter; skin very smooth; flesh deep-orange, core very small, very sweet and tender; tops 8 to 10 inches tall. High-density planting recommended. A "baby carrot" suitable for canning, pickling or eating fresh. A16, C44, D11M, F19M, F82, F92, G16, G51, *G83M*, H33, H42, H95, J7, L97, M46, etc.

Mini Express: 55 days. Tiny, gourmet carrot. Slim, cylindrical roots; 5 to 6 inches long when mature; sweet orange flesh, tender, crisp, nearly coreless. Pale green, very short tops. Fine quality for salads, canning, pickling or freezing whole. D11M, *S63M*

Minicor: (Amsterdam Minicor) 55 days. A popular Dutch strain of Amsterdam which is used by large commercial packers of baby carrots. Roots are very slender, cylindrical, blunt-tipped; 6 to 7 inches long when mature; flesh deep orange, tender, sweet, fine-grained, never coarse or woody. Usually harvested when 3 inches long. Does well in most soils. C53, C85M, D68, D76, E24, E97, F24M, F44, G6, G82, J84, K66, L42, M49, Q34, etc.

Orbit: 50 days. A new introduction that is highly tolerant to splitting and yellowing when harvested past maturity, in contrast to Parisienne type carrots. Smooth, round, spherical root; approximately 1 inch in diameter; very sweet; short, dark-green tops, 8 to 10 inches tall. Perfect for the home, market garden or specialty trade. *A69M*, *C28*, D11M, D76, F13, F19M, G51, G87, H33, H95, J7, K73, M46, M95M, N39, etc.

Parisian Rondo: (Parisian Ball, Rondo, Round Paris Market, Parisian Market) A 19th century French heirloom that is still popular. Small, uniform, nearly spherical root; only 1 to 1 1/2 inches in diameter when mature; reddish-orange throughout, of excellent sweet flavor. Ideal for processing whole or as a fresh market specialty item. D27, D62, F82, G64, I77, J83M, K49Z, P83M

Parisienne: (Gourmet Parisienne) 55 days. Small, nearly round, gourmet "baby carrot"; grows to only 1 1/2 inches in diameter when mature; flesh rich orange, sweet and flavorful. Easy to grow in all types of soils. Also used whole for canning and pickling. Should be sown thickly for best results. A16, C85M, K12M{PR}

Parmex: 50 days. Paris Market type; an improvement over the standard Planet. A unique round carrot, 1 to 1 1/2 inches in diameter; matures extra early, sometimes with peas. Develops flavor and bright color while still young and smooth. Perfect for growing in heavy soil. For earliest home canning and freezing, and specialty markets. F44, G6, K50

Planet: 55 days. An improved, more flavorful Parisienne type. Root slightly globe-shaped, somewhat flattened on top, about 1 1/2 inches in diameter; deep orange throughout; holds its quality well. Sturdy green tops. Excellent for hard soils and container growing. Soil should be hilled up to shoulders to prevent "green shoulders". C53, K66, L42, *N40*{PR}

Sucram: 65 days. Amsterdam Forcing type. Specifically bred and developed for the select gourmet restaurant and fancy canning trade of Europe. Smooth, slender, cylindrical roots, 2 1/2 to 3 inches long when mature; flesh orange, sweet, tender, of distinct flavor. Good for canning and freezing. D11M, I39, K49M, K49Z, *R11M*

COMMON CARROTS

HYBRID

Apache:[1] 65 days. Contains the new Super Sweet gene which contributes high sugar and vitamin A contents. Very smooth, dark orange root; grows to 10 inches long; has good early tip fill. Tops reach 18 inches tall; are tolerant to alternaria. *A1*, A87M, G64, K73, L42, *L59G*, N52

A-Plus:[1] 65 days. Developed by Dr. Clinton Peterson, the result of new "consumer preferred" plant breeding that is designed to introduce Super Sweet taste and higher vitamin content into new hybrid carrots. Contains 2 1/2 times the carotene and vitamin A of regular strains. Roots medium length, 8 1/2 inches long, dark orange and rich in flavor. A32, C85M, D11M, D33, G6, G16, G51, H42, H95, J20, K73, L42, L79, M49

Ingot:[1] 68 days. Long Nantes type. Contains the Super Sweet gene and extra vitamin A content. Cylindrical, 9 inch long root, fills to the tip quickly; deep orange color; good flavor. Similar to A Plus but more slender and cylindrical. Strong, medium-tall tops. Has better seed quality and uniformity than A Plus. For home use, storage and the specialty fresh market. *C28*, G6, L42

Orlando Gold:[1] 75 days. Contains approximately 50% more carotene and vitamin A than standard cultivars. Extra long, slender root; slightly tapered, almost to a point; rich reddish-orange interior, of high quality and superior flavor; relatively small core. Roots average 12 inches long on muck soils, 10 inches on sand. Introduced in 1982 by Dr. Clinton Peterson. A13, A69M, A87M, C85M, D27, D76, E97, F82, G27M, G79, *H61*, J20, J34, J84, K73, L42, etc.

Savory:[1] 68 days. Contains 40% more vitamin A than Imperator, which it resembles. Crisp and sweet; received the highest flavor ratings in five years of government tests. Slow to mature but retains its flavor well in the field and can be planted quite densely. Short tops. Developed by Dr. Clinton Peterson. J20

Seminole:[1] 66 days. Smooth, uniform roots average 9 inches in length, are dark orange and contain the new Super Sweet gene for higher sugar and vitamin A content. Strong tops have multiple tolerance to leaf diseases, including alternaria and leaf spot. *A1*, A87M, G64, L42, *L59G*, N52

OPEN-POLLINATED

Autumn King: (Autumn King Improved) 70 days. Large, uniform, cylindrical roots; 10 inches long, blunt tipped; crisp, tender flesh, of good flavor, red-cored. A reliable and heavy cropper. Sow in spring for summer use; late May or June for winter storage. Very hardy; can be stored in the ground for long periods. B49, L91M, O53M, P83M, *R11M*, *R23*, T1M

Belgium White:[3] 75 days. Pure white carrot of very mild flavor; 7 to 8 inches long, 3 inches across at the top, tapered and pointed; nearly coreless. Can be harvested small, but retains its flavor and quality when older. Good for steaming or cooking in casseroles. Vigorous and productive. Not hardy; must be harvested before frost. C76M, I39, K49M

Berlicummer: (Berlicummer Bercoro) 65 days. Improved Nantes type. Long, straight, blunt tipped root; up to 10 inches in length, 1 3/4 inches in diameter; orange throughout; coreless; excellent flavor; does not split or crack. One of the best late cultivars; an excellent keeper. For home gardens or market. *A75*, C85M, J20

Beta III:[1] 80 days. Contains 3 to 4 times the carotene and vitamin A of regular strains. Developed by Dr. Clinton Peterson of the University of Wisconsin and the USDA. Initially bred to help prevent vitamin A deficiency blindness in underdeveloped countries. D33

Blanche à Collet Vert:[3] (White Belgian) Root long and thick, sunk in the ground for two-thirds or three-fourths of its length, white on the underground portion, and green or bronze purple above; flesh white, usually tinged with yellow. Heavy yielding. Primarily used for feeding cattle and horses. Introduced prior to 1885. VILMORIN; S95M

Camberley: An excellent combination of Berlicummer and Danvers types. Uniform, 7 to 9 inch long roots, very deep orange throughout. Will grow in heavy soils and can be left in the ground over winter. Bred for the canning market and the increasing numbers of organic commercial growers. B49

Country Purple: An Indian cultivar that is said to be excellent for making pickles and pudding. S93M

Danvers Half Long: (Danvers) 75 days. Roots 5 to 6 inches long by 1 1/4 to 1 3/4 inches thick when used for bunching, tapering to a short-tapered or slightly rounded end; deep-orange flesh, slightly yellower core. Not adapted to heavy or shallow soils. Standard cultivar. Originated in Danvers, Massachusetts. Introduced in 1871. MAGRUDER 1940; A16, A25, B35M, B78, C85M, D82, E24, F19M, F82, H94, K5M, L7M, L97, M13M, M95, etc.

Flakkee Long Flacoro: (Flakkee Long Red Giant) 65 days. Very large, strong root; stump-rooted and red-cored; up to 24 inches long and 4 inches thick. Excellent for storage. High yielding, improved strain. Good flavor. Also used for stock feeding. C85M

Gold Pak: (Gold Pak 28) 75 days. Imperator type. Smooth, tapered, nearly cylindrical root; 9 inches long, 1 1/4 inches in diameter; rich reddish-orange flesh, nearly coreless, of good quality; stores and ships well. Very short tops. Widely used for bunching and cello packs. Needs a deep loamy soil. All America Selections winner in 1956. A16, A69M, B35M, B75, D65, D76, E97, G79, *H61*, H94, J34, J58, K50, K71, M29, etc.

Herz Zino: (Lange Rote Stumpfe Ohne Herz Zino) 85 days. Has appeared in the Guinness Book of World Records as the world's largest carrot, weighing in at 7 pounds 11 1/2 ounces. Also widely grown for juicing, containing 55% juice per carrot. Average length 8 to 10 inches. For late summer and fall crops. Introduced prior to 1875. L91M

Imperator: 70 days. Long, tapered, deep reddish-orange, coreless root. Extensively used for bunching. Adapted only to deep, well-drained sandy or loamy soils. Needs a long growing season of moderate temperatures to produce long, straight, slender, well-colored roots. Originated as a cross between Nantes and Chantenay. Introduced in 1928. MAGRUDER 1940; A16, C85M, D11M, D65, F82, F92, G51, *G83M*, *H61*, H66, H94, J20, K71, M46, N39, etc.

Indian Long Red:[2] Very long and tapering. Offers more of the true carrot taste than the typical blunt spindly forms, and hence is preferred as a sweeter vegetable compared to American cultivars. E49, R50

James Scarlet Intermediate: (James' Intermediate) 80 days. Heaving yielding main-crop carrot from England. Half-long, perfectly symmetrical, tapered root; skin and flesh well-colored, reddish orange; flesh tender, of very good flavor; resists splitting. Requires a rich light soil. Introduced about 1870. VILMORIN; B49, O53M, P83M, *R23*

Juwarot:[1] (Juwarot Double Vitamin A) 70 days. Contains double the vitamin A content of normal cultivars, or about 249 milligrams per kilogram. Large, deep orange root; very sweet and juicy. Heavy yielding; good for winter storage. In some countries carrot juice is made specifically from this cultivar. L91M

Kinko 4 Inch: 55 days. Chantenay type. Small, conical, stump-rooted carrot; deep reddish-orange inside and out; flesh crisp and sweet; quite resistant to cracking. Achieves color and size early. Recommended as first-early carrots, especially on shallow soils. Should be harvested young for best quality. E24, G6, L7M

Kintoki Early Strain:[2] 120 days. An improved strain of Kintoki Regular, distinguished by early coloring and quick growth. Root deep crimson; 8 to 9 inches long, about 1 1/2 inches wide at the shoulder; indistinctly ringed between the nearly same colored core and the exterior. Holds its quality without becoming pithy or broken. Developed by Fujita Seed Co. E49, *P39*

Kintoki Regular Strain:[2] (Crimson Wonder) 140 days. A unique crimson-fleshed carrot from Japan. Long, tapered root; 10 to 11 1/2 inches in length, 2 to 2 1/4 inches wide at the shoulder which is square; skin deep red, glossy; flesh tender and sweet. Best sown from July to October for winter culture in the Northern Hemisphere. E49, *P39*

Kokubu: (Japanese Long) 150 days. An endemic cultivar popular in the eastern half of Honshu, Japan where arable soil is quite deep. Roots are commonly 2 feet or more long, 1 1/2 to 1 3/4 inches wide at the shoulder, gradually tapering to a pointed tip; of deep orange color. A late cultivar adapted to summer sowing for a winter harvest. E49, K49T, *P39*

Kundulus: 65 days. Small, round root; 1 1/2 to 2 inches in diameter; deep orange skin; good flavor. Ideal for quick successional crops and forcing. Produces well when grown very close together. Suitable for window boxes, flats, frames, heavy or shallow soils. Good for freezing and canning. I91, L91M

Kuroda: (New Kuroda) 70 days. Chantenay type. Smooth, medium-sized roots; about 6 inches long, 2 inches in diameter at the crown; tapered and stump-rooted; very good flavor for a Chantenay. Good for heavy soils. For fall crop only; to avoid bolting, do not plant before mid-June. E24, F44, K49T, *L59G*, *R11M*

Long Orange Improved: (Long Orange) 85 days. Roots 12 inches long, 2 inches thick, tapered to a point. Flesh reddish orange with a core of a lighter shade. Useful for both table and stock feeding. Plant in loose soil, and for table use, harvest before roots reach mature size. An improved strain of a cultivar introduced by Dutch breeders in 1620 and brought to North America by early settlers. F25, G57M, H54, L7M

Long Red Surrey: Root very long, narrowing gradually, 5 or 6 times as long as broad, often 12 to 14 inches in length; has a distinctive yellow core. Requires a rather deep soil, but is unusually productive. The long root makes it more drought-tolerant when grown on sandy soils. Introduced about 1834. VILMORIN; P83M

Manchester Table: Uniformly long, cylindrical root with a blunt end; sweet, crisp, deep-orange flesh; small core. French strain of the Nantes type. Sow in spring and summer. P1G

Nantes Half Long: 65 days. Smooth, well-shaped, perfectly cylindrical root; 6 to 7 inches long, 1 to 1 1/2 inches thick for the whole length; flesh deep orange, fine-grained, tender, sweet, practically coreless, of very high quality. Popular for home garden and local market use. A25, B75, C44, C85M, G57M, G87, H94, L7M, M95

Nugget: 60 days. French forcing type. Solid orange color throughout; good resistance to splitting. The nearly round shape makes them well-suited for adding whole to stews. Especially adapted to stiff clay soils and close cultivation. I39

Oxheart: (Guérande) 75 days. Roots short-conic or heart-shaped, very blunt at the lower end; 5 to 6 inches long, 2 to 2 1/2 inches thick; medium-orange, coarse flesh, yellower core. Rapid growing. Produces well on shallow and heavy soils. Originated in France. Introduced prior to 1884. MAGRUDER 1940, VILMORIN; A2, *A69M*, B35M, C85M, D82, E24, J73, K49M, K49T, L7M

Red Cored Chantenay: (Chantenay Long Supreme) 70 days. Large, smooth root; slightly tapered, stump-rooted; 5 1/2 inches long, 2 1/2 inches in diameter at the shoulder; deep orange flesh and core, of high quality. Good for bunching. Widely used for canning and freezing. High yielding. Grows well in most soil types. Introduced in 1929. MAGRUDER 1940; A16, B35M, C85M, D82, F1, F19M, G16, H42, H66, K49T, K73, L7M, L97, M13M, M49, N16, etc.

Red Muscade: 72 days. An old European heirloom that has been replaced in many areas by the more regular shaped carrots, but is still popular in North Africa. Large, irregular, unattractive root, often grows to a pound or more; flesh highly aromatic, thick-meated, juicy, sweet, of excellent flavor; core often tinged with green. Excellent for juicing. Best planted in late summer or autumn; has a tendency to bolt in hot weather. Dropped by G69

Royal Chantenay: 65 days. Smooth, blunt, cylindrical root, tapers only slightly; 6 to 7 inches long, 2 1/2 inches in diameter; reddish-orange, with uniform interior color; sweet, tender flesh. Used for bunching, market, storage, canning or freezing. Recommended where soils are too heavy or shallow for most other carrots. A13, B75M, C85M, D76, F82, G64, H42, *H61*, H95, I91, J7, K71, L79, L89, M95, etc.

Scarlet Imperial Long: Longest carrot known; a record was set in 1975 by a California gardener, who grew a carrot that measured 38 1/2 inches from crown to root tip. Skin and flesh salmon-orange; flesh crisp, sweet in flavor. Best grown in deep loam soil. E49

Scarlet Keeper: 85 days. A large, late cultivar exclusively for fall harvest and winter storage. Heavy, cylindrical, blunt tipped root; 7 to 8 inches long; dark orange with a large, good-colored core. Heavy yielding. Comes out of winter storage in good condition; never turns bitter. E24, K49T

Scarlet Nantes: (Early Coreless) 65 days. Smooth, cylindrical root; 6 to 7 inches long with very little taper; rich orange-red color throughout; flesh sweet, fine-grained, completely free of any heart or core, of very high quality. Freezes and stores well. Excellent for home gardens and market. *A75*, D87, E24, F19M, F44, G6, G71, *H61*, H95, K71, K73, L97, M13M, M46, N16, etc.

Scarlet Wonder:[2] 110 days. Long, tapering root; 12 to 15 inches in length; attractive deep scarlet color; very sweet and tender. Should be grown for cooking rather than fresh use. Suitable only for summer sowing for a fall to winter harvest. Very distinct. E59, M46, *S63M*

Short 'n Sweet: 65 days. Shorter Goldinhart or Red Cored Chantenay type. Short, thick root; 3 to 4 inches long, 2 inches in diameter at the shoulder; bright orange throughout; flesh rich, sweet, juicy. Excellent for canning and freezing. Does well in both heavy and shallow soil. For early summer and fall crops. B75, D65, G71, H94, N52

St. Valery: (New Red Intermediate) 70 days. Very smooth, very uniform root; 10 to 12 inches long, 2 to 3 inches broad at the shoulder; skin bright reddish-orange, attractive; flesh thick, sweet, tender, with very little core. Tops very short and sparse. Performs best in light, rich, well-prepared soil. May be regarded as the connecting link between the half-long and long types. Introduced prior to 1885. VILMORIN; J73, O53M, P83M, *R23*, S61

Topweight:[1] 80 days. Large, smooth root; 10 to 12 inches long, 3 inches in diameter at the full round shoulder; orange-red; good, sweet flavor. Yields well under adverse growing conditions. Will over-winter in the ground for 6 months without deterioration, cracking or splitting. Extremely high in carotene, vitamin A and vitamin C content. A2, D87, E49, P1G, R47

Touchon: (Nantes Touchon, Nantes Special Long) 65 days. Nantes type, but has more intense coloring and is somewhat longer. Smooth, cylindrical roots; 6 to 7 inches long and 1 to 1 1/2 inches broad; deep orange throughout; flesh tender, crisp, sweet, coreless, of very high quality. Good for bunching and winter storage. Sow in spring or summer. A69M, *A75*, C53, D11M, D65, E38, F1, G68, G79, G87, H42, J7, K71, M49, M95, etc.

White Fodder:[3] A mild tasting carrot very much appreciated in France. Very easy to grow and remains deliciously tender even when very large. A safe carrot to eat for those allergic to carotene. S55

White French:[3] A unique white carrot that is a true table carrot, with gourmet qualities. Practically coreless with a delicious, but very mild flavor. Grows entirely below ground and is hardy, which is a great improvement over earlier white carrots. A vigorous grower and a heavy cropper. B49

CAULIFLOWER {S}

BRASSICA OLERACEA BOTRYTIS GROUP

SUMMER CAULIFLOWER

GREEN

Hybrid

Green Harmony: (Flocoli) 80 days. A new cross of broccoli and cauliflower developed in China. Heads pale green in color; medium sized, up to 1 3/4 pounds; tender, with more flavor than cauliflower. Unlike white cauliflower, it does not need to be blanched. Should not be sown before mid-May. E49, L91M, *Q39*

Open-Pollinated

Alverda: 64 days. Very uniform, medium-sized heads with a bright yellow-green curd color. Excellent taste, raw or cooked. Medium-sized, productive plants; easy to grow, no tying required. For summer and autumn production. Becoming popular in specialty markets in Europe and the United States. G6, S27, *S75M*

Bronzino:[1] Very large, yellowish-green heads with small, compact curds. Excellent flavor. An earlier form of Romanesco for short season areas. Matures a full month or so earlier. Q11M

Chartreuse: (Green Ball) 60 days. Pale lime-green heads, resembling cauliflower; flavor very much like broccoli; texture and quality excellent. Does not require tying or blanching like white cauliflower. Developed in America from Pua-Kea cauliflower crossed with Spartan Early broccoli. *E91G*

Minaret:[1] 75 days. A refined Romanesco type. Unusual spiraled, peaked, pale green heads; 4 to 5 inches in diameter. Vigorous, cauliflower-like plants. For spring and fall crops, and winter harvest in mild areas. G6, S27

Romanesco:[1] 85 days. Unique, compact, spiral-pointed heads with a beautiful pale-green, almost chartreuse color and a delicate, sweet flavor. Individual florets make an exceptional crudite, or the entire head may be cut and used as cauliflower. For spring and fall crops, but flavor is enhanced by cool weather. Grown commercially in northern Italy. A2, B49, B75, C53, D11M, D76, G51, G64, I91, K49M, K66, L91M, *N40*{PR}, S55, etc.

Spiral Point:[1] Hardy plants produce a head that is light olive-green in color, with many spiral pointed curds. An unusual type that is widely grown in Italy. Sometimes listed as a broccoli, this and other Romanesco or spiral-pointed types are actually classified as cauliflowers. E49

Venice:[1] 80 days. A spiral-pointed type form Italy with a very fine taste and texture. Spears can be snapped off individually or all together. H42

WHITE

Hybrid

Candid Charm: 75 days. Large, very heavy, deep dome-shaped heads; 7 to 9 inches across; uniform in maturity; quality excellent, non-ricey, long holding ability without purple cast. Excellent for fresh market. Vigorous, semi-upright plant; very high yielding; large dark-green leaves for good curd protection. Does best in cool areas. *A1*, B71, D68, *G13M*, G82, J14{PL}, *J74*, K10, *K16M*, *L79G*, M29

Early Glacier: 65 days. An early hybrid, developed for spring sowing in cool regions. Deep dome-shaped heads are of excellent quality. Plants are compact and erect, with long leaves that provide good head protection. Vigorous growth, good holding ability and uniform maturity. *A1*, *F63*, K10, *K16M*, M49, N52

Glacier: 75 days. Large, deep dome heads with smooth, compact white curds of very good quality. Strong erect foliage ensures good head protection. Excellent for spring sowing and summer-fall harvest. Matures about 10 days later than Early Glacier. Upright, vigorous, heavy yielding plants. Suited for fresh market or processing use. *A1*, D11M, K10, *K16M*, *L79G*, M49

Snow Crown: 50 days. Extremely early, dependable hybrid that shows unusual seedling vigor. Heads are uniform, medium-sized, domed, and solid with good curd quality whether harvested in summer or fall. Flavor mild and sweet. Good resistance to moderate fall frost (25-32^0 F.). All America Selections winner in 1975. A16, A87M, C44, C85M, E32M{PL}, F19M, *F72*, G6, G71, H42, *H61*, H94, K73, L79, L89, M46, etc.

Snow King: 45 days. Extremely early hybrid that stands heat very well, and shows good resistance to various diseases. Heads pure white, well-rounded; weighing 1 to 2 pounds each; free from leafiness and riceyness; holds quality well. Plants are erect, vigorous, with rather large leaves that protect center head from frost and sun. All

America Selections winner in 1969. A16, C44, C85M, D65, D76, D76{PL}, E97, E97{PL}, *F72*, G16, I64, I91, J20, L91M, M29, N16, etc.

White Sails: 68 days. Late main season, self-wrap hybrid. Extra large, 7 1/2 inch heads are very deep, dome-shaped. Heavy self-wrapping leaves protect curd. Tolerant to heat and internal black speck. Outyields White Fox, White Rock types, 2 to 1. L42

Open-Pollinated

Alert: 55 days. Vigorous, short-stemmed plant of the Early Snowball class, but with deeper heads and finer texture than others of this type. Heads are pure-white, about 3 1/2 pounds each. Upright leaves offer somewhat better curd protection and are easier to tie and trim. When grown from spring transplants it is often earlier than Snow Crown. E24, F44, I91, L42

All The Year Round: 70 days. Large, compact well-protected head; holds without going to seed for a long period even in hot weather. Suitable for sowing at most times of the year, but ideal for autumn sowing or sowing under glass in early spring. Good for freezing. Most popular cultivar in Europe. B49, L91M, O53M, P83M, *R23*, S45M, S55, S61, T1M

Andes: 68 days. Dense, heavy, well-domed heads; not susceptible to riceyness or pinking. Strong, upright foliage and heavy wrapper leaves assures good protection without tying. Suitable for early as well as late sowing, having good tolerance to heat as well as cold conditions. Excellent for freezing. *A1*, D68, F44, G6, G64, *J74*, K73, L42, L91M, M49, N52, S61, *S75M*

Dok Elgon: 65 days. Versatile summer cauliflower that competes well with hybrids for the quality of its heads. Protects itself well with vigorous, upright foliage. Excellent for freezing as each floret of the head forms a miniature cauliflower. Can also be September sown to overwinter for spring planting and a June harvest. B49, L91M, N52, *R23*, *S75M*

Dominant: 75 days. Very large, heavy, extra firm, snow-white heads. Vigorous growth gives excellent curd protection. Does best on fertile land and has an extensive root system that provides some tolerance to long dry periods. Highly recommended for the quality late crop. E24, *F63*, K49M, L42, P83M, *R23*

Early Abundance: 47 days. Heads are extra large, deep, mound-shaped, not easily discolored; crisp, tender, and fine-flavored. Vigorous, wide base, outside wrapper leaves provide excellent coverage. One of the earliest maturing cultivars. H33, L42

Early Snowball: (Extra Early Snowball) 60 days. Uniform, small to medium head, 5 to 6 inches in diameter; smooth, thick and heavy; does not discolor during poor weather. Of dwarf habit, with very short outer leaves, allowing it to be planted close together. Standard main crop Snowball type. Known prior to 1888. A2, B78, F82, F92, H33{PL}, H42, H94, H95, J20, J34, J73, K49M, K71, L7M, L35{PL}, M46, etc.

Early Snowball A: (Super Snowball A) 55 days. Uniform maturing, smooth, pure-white heads; 6 inches across, and weighing 3 to 5 pounds each. Medium-sized plant with good leaf coverage. Fine for greenhouse forcing, frames or outdoor culture. A69M, B75M, F1, *F72*, G27M, G71, *H61*, H66, J14{PL}, M13M, M95

Garant:[2] 82-86 days. Early maturing "mini" cauliflower. Specially selected for direct sowing, it is quick-growing, vigorous, without a heavy foliage canopy and will not mature all at once. Harvested when 1 1/2 to 3 1/2 inches across, the small heads are ideal for freezing. Good for small gardens, the plants can be spaced at a distance of only 6 inches x 6 inches. L91M, S55

Hormade: 60 days. Produces large, extra-firm, deep white heads of excellent quality. May be harvested over a long season. Large-leaved, vigorous plants have good self-wrapping ability. Resistant to mildew, heat and water stress. A13, D11M, K50, P9, *R11M*

Perfection: A fast-growing summer cauliflower still popular with market growers in England, but creamy curded and suffering from competition from whiter kinds. Introduced in 1905. P83M, *R23*, *S75M*

Predominant:[2] 90-94 days. Late maturing "mini" cauliflower. Can be sown later than Garant for heads that mature in September and October. Small heads require no trimming and are ideal for freezing. Sow in succession form June onwards. Developed by the National Vegetable Research Station of Great Britain. L91M, *S75M*

Self-Blanche: 68 days. Snowball type, with smooth, pure white heads, 6 1/2 to 7 1/2 inches in diameter. Under cool growing conditions, has the ability to produce wrapper leaves that will curl around the head protecting it from the sun. Early crops will not self wrap during warm weather. Best grown as a fall crop in cool growing areas. A13, B35M, C85M, D65, D82, E24, F19M, *F72*, G79, H94, H95, K50, K73, M13M, N39, etc.

Snow Pak: 80 days. Large, dome-shaped, heavy heads; curds are uniform, creamy-white, deep, firm and smooth. Clasping inner wrapper leaves make it less necessary to tie the leaves for blanching. Well adapted to dry, arid growing areas. For fresh market and processing. A87M, F1, G79, J84, K10

Snowbaby:[2] Small, perfectly formed heads of good quality. By planting 1 foot apart in all directions, 4 "baby" or "mini" cauliflowers, about 4 inches in diameter, can be harvested in the same space needed for 1 regular cauliflower. Make successive sowings from spring to fall. T1M

Snowball X: (Giant Snowball X) 65 days. Large, solid, pure-white head; matures gradually over a period of days, providing a longer cutting period; sure-heading. Outer leaves are long and strong, giving complete protection. Well adapted for use under a wide range of conditions. Highly recommended for home gardens. A16, B75M, D11M, *E91G*, *F72*, J7, *L59G*, M13M

Snowball Y: 70 days. Vigorous growing, high quality Snowball type for an autumn crop. Large, deep, smooth, heavy white head; 6 inches in diameter; matures uniformly over a long harvest period. Heavy outer foliage provides good protection. Recommended for fresh market and home use. *A69M*, *A75*, *F63*, G64, M13M

Stovepipe: 55 days. Medium to large head, 5 to 6 inches in diameter, free of riceyness in hot weather. Tall, smooth, erect, stovepipe-like leaves protect curd from exposure to the sun. Grows well in summer, holding at temperatures of 90 to 95^0 F.; not tolerant of frost. Developed at Michigan State University. Introduced in 1981. H42, L11, L79

Super Snowball: (Early Super Snowball) 55 days. Large, solid, deep, finely-grained, ivory-white head; 6 to 7 inches in diameter; matures evenly; fine quality, mild delicate flavor. Vigorous, compact plants. Extra early Snowball type, yet unexcelled for the late or main crop. For fresh market or freezing. A25, B35M, D27, D65, D76, D82, E38, *E91G*, H42, H94, I64, L79, M29

Veitch's Autumn Giant: (Autumn Giant) 80 days. Very large, firm, beautiful white head; well-covered by the inner leaves; matures in late autumn. Large, vigorous growing plant, with a longish stem; hardy. Very old cultivar, known before 1885. Still popular in England. VILMORIN; A2, A69M, E38, K20, O53M, *R23*

Veitch's Self-Protecting: 80 days. Large, attractive, well-shaped, firm white heads are thoroughly protected by the incurved leaves until maturity. Vigorous, very hardy. Sow in March for a November and December harvest; may be left until January in a sheltered location. Introduced in 1905. B49, L91M, P83M, *R23*

White Fox: 75 days. Produces large, smooth, 8 inch diameter, creamy-white heads of high quality. Very uniform; harvested over a very short period. Leaves are self-wrapping. Deeper, more refined heads than White Top. For spring or fall planting. *A1*, I77, J20, L42, *R23*, *S75M*

White Rock: 75 days. Deep, firm, dome-shaped white heads; 6 1/2 inches in diameter; beautiful, smooth curds. Outstanding self-wrapping ability, can sometimes be grown without tying under cool conditions. Vigorous, erect, medium-sized plants; widely adapted. For late summer and autumn crops. *A1*, G64, *H61*, *J74*, J84, K10, K66, K73, L42, L89, M29, *S75M*

White Summer: 65 days. Firm, deep, smooth pure-white heads; marketable at 6 inches; very good color and texture; can be harvested over a very short period. Excellent curd protection, although tying may be necessary for larger heads. Widely adapted for a mid-season fall crop. *A1*, A13, *F63*, J7, L42, M29

White Top: 70 days. Heads very white, firm and heavy, of high flavor and quality. Medium-sized plant; vigorous and sturdy with strong root systems better able to handle poorer soils; upright outer leaves. Good curd protection is provided by self-wrapping inner leaves. Standard main season, self-wrapping cultivar. G64, J7, L42, M49

WINTER CAULIFLOWER

Adam's Early White: Very hardy, overwintering type. Sow in April for a harvest the following February and March. Has the original creamy curds and flavor. Very old cultivar, introduced about 1850. P83M

Armado Spring: 210-270 days. A blend of 7 high quality, Walcherin-type cauliflowers for overwintering in moderately severe climates (above 10° F.). They produce fine, salad quality curds late March through early May. Each cultivar is bred to produce a highly concentrated harvest; when sown together at one sowing date this blend will increase the length of harvest. L89

Early March: (St. Valentine's) Medium-large plants produce large, 6 1/2 inch, smooth, white heads of excellent quality. Direct seed August 15 to 31 for a late winter harvest. G71M, G93M

Inca: The best overwintering cultivar for the Puget Sound area. Developed and commercially grown in the Skagit valley region. Produces large, firm, high quality heads weighing 2 pounds. Very good frost tolerance; abundant wrapper leaves. Sow seeds in late July and harvest cauliflower from late March to early May. *C28*, F82, L97, *S75M*

Late Queen: 90 days. Very hardy, reliable, overwintering cultivar producing large, cream-curded, well-protected heads of good quality; ready for harvesting in April and May. A selection of English Winter. Popular market cultivar in England for over a century. L91M, P83M, S61

Leamington: Very reliable, overwintering type ready for harvest in April. Large, firm, well-protected heads of high quality. Good for freezing. A selection of English Winter. Very old English cultivar, one of the oldest still in cultivation. A2, P83M

Newton Seale: 180 days. Frost resistant, winter and early spring cauliflower producing high quality curds. Very large, white heads withstand reasonable frosts in January and February. Sow mid-May onwards for a harvest the following spring. Developed by the National Seed Development Organization of Great Britain. L91M

Nine-Star Perennial:[3] (Nine-Star Perennial Broccoli) Tall-growing perennial, producing numerous, pure-white shoots, resembling tiny cauliflowers. Each plant develops a small head surrounded by 9 or 10 smaller ones every spring and early summer, for 4 to 5 years. Plant out at 3 feet apart. Should be planted against a fence, or in an out of the way part of the garden where it can be left undisturbed. ORGAN [Cu]; I99, L91M, O53M, S45M, S61

Royal Oak: For sowing in spring for a harvest the following May, this is a hardy, well-protected cultivar with beautiful, large, firm, pure-white heads. O53M

Snow's Winter White: 110 days. Should be sown late spring for a harvest beginning in December and lasting through March if continuous sowings are made. Cold tolerant, but not recommended for very cold districts where severe frosts are likely to discolor the curds. Easier to grow than spring cultivars. B49, L91M, P83M

St. George: A very hardy and reliable cultivar with large, firm white heads. For spring sowing and harvesting early in the following April. O53M, *R23*

CELERIAC {S}

APIUM GRAVEOLENS RAPACEUM GROUP

HYBRID

Luna: High yielding hybrid with perfectly shaped roots of extremely good quality, both inside and out. Very smooth roots and no hollow crowns; perfectly white interior. Recommended for fresh market, processing and long term storage. K50, N81

Zwindra: 110 days. A high quality Dutch introduction, Zwindra is preferred by the best European market growers. Smooth, round roots are free of internal discoloration, hollow hearts, or pithiness often associated with older cultivars. Uniformly firm, fine-grained, creamy-white flesh with a rich mellow flavor. High-yielding plants with vigorous, dark green foliage. K66

OPEN-POLLINATED

Alabaster: 120 days. Round, healthy, smooth-skinned, turnip-shaped root; white inside and out; fine-textured flesh; remains white even after being cooked; keeps well. Best used when about 2 to 4 inches in diameter. Heavy yielding. B75, J82, K49M, L97

Arvi: 110 days. A long-leaved cultivar producing heavy, smooth, round to flattened roots with excellent internal color. Fairly free of lateral roots. The white flesh doesn't discolor when cooked. Not susceptible to hollow heart. Very vigorous and heavy yielding. Most commercial celeriac growers in Europe use Arvi for its vigour, uniformity and fine appearance. L89, *R11M*, *S75M*

Balder: Fine, large, smooth-skinned, heavy-yielding cultivar resistant to septoria. O53M

De Rueil: Large, light-colored roots, smooth and clean; neck small, with few side roots; flesh an attractive white color, very tender. Short foliage with green petioles. Introduced by Vilmorin. G68

Diamant: Excellent celeriac for fresh market with nicely sized roots and excellent internal quality. Has no hollow crown and very little off shoots. Stands three-quarters above the ground and is therefore very easy to harvest and clean. K50, N81

Dolvi: 120 days. An outstanding cultivar bred for multiple disease resistance and vigor. Large, nearly round, heavy roots; white interior of fine texture; excellent quality and flavor when cooked or used raw; stores well. I39

Giant Prague: (Prague, Smooth Prague, Large Smooth Prague) 115 days. Root large, almost spherical; evenly shaped; without rootlets, except on the bottom; smooth skin; thick, mild white flesh; stores well for winter use. Best quality is obtained if roots are harvested when 3 to 4 inches in diameter. Standard cultivar, introduced prior to 1885. A16, C44, C85M, D11M, D27, E5T, G16, G51, G67M, G71, G79, J7, J20, J84, K20, etc.

Iram: 105 days. Medium-sized, globe-shaped roots, free of off-shoots; pure-white throughout. Excellent flavor and quality. Early maturing. Stores easily. One of the few cultivars that remains white after cooking. J7

Jose: 110 days. Very large roots are round, attractive and relatively smooth and free of offshoots. Tops produce little foliage. The interiors are very white and flavorful, and resist pithiness and hollow heart. Quality very good. Can be planted closer together than other cultivars. C53, G6, P59M

Marble Ball: 105 days. Uniformly large, smooth, globe-shaped roots; quite free of offshoots; flesh white, thick and solid, nearly free of pith; flavor and quality excellent; stores well for winter use. Best used when 2 inches in diameter. Heavy yielding. *F72*, G93M, P83M, S55

Monarch: 120 days. Very large, smooth, pale-colored roots that wash well; firm white flesh; does not discolor when cut or blanched. Heavy yielding. Scab resistant. C85M, N81, P69, *S75M*

Monostorpalyi: 200-240 days. A special cultivar developed in Hungary, with small to medium sized roots and dark green foliage. J73

Prague Model: 110 days. Larger in size than the old Giant Prague cultivar. Has globe-shaped roots with small rootlets, fewer in number; fine-flavored flesh; keeps well for winter use. Needs a rich soil. K49M

CELERY {S}

APIUM GRAVEOLENS

GREEN CELERY

Bishop: A Tall Utah type adapted to central and south coast areas of California. Large plant, 25 inches in height with compact hearts; thick, smooth, round stalks are 11 to 12 inches in length, longer and more deeply cupped than 52-70 types; excellent dark-green color extends well into the basal region. Tolerant to fusarium yellows in some areas. Introduced in 1982. E57

Florida 683: 90-100 days. Bushy, compact, full-hearted plant, 22 to 26 inches in height; medium-green in color blanching to a rich cream; stems broad, thick, solid, 10 to 11 inches long. Resistant to fusarium yellows and mosaic. Selected from Utah 52-70, for higher rib count and better heart formation. *A1*, A87M, C92, *F63*, G64, G79, *H61*, K73, L42, N16

Fordhook: (Burpee's Fordhook, Emperor, Hauser) 130 days. Stocky, compact plants, 15 to 18 inches in height; stalks are thick, stringless, tender but crisp, juicy; after blanching they are a pure silvery-white with a large, tightly folded, full heart of a delicious nutty flavor. Ideal for fall use and winter storage. B13, B75, *F72*, G57M, I67M, I84, J58, J97M, M95M

Fordhook Giant: 120 days. Short, stocky, dark-green plants, 15 to 18 inches in height; easily blanched to a greenish white with a golden heart. Stalks thick, tender and stringless; flavor very good to excellent. C92, K49M

Giant Pascal: 120-130 days. Large, stocky, dark-green plants, 24 inches in height; hearts are tender, brittle and of good quality; broad, distinctly ribbed, thick, solid stalks, blanch easily to a good creamy-white color; quality very good, flavor nutty. Resistant to blight. Standard green celery for the fall market. A13, A25, B73M, C44, C92, F19M, G79, H94, I99, J32, K27M, K49M, K71, L9, L79, N39, etc.

South Australian White: Best-known and most popular Australian blanching cultivar. Tall and vigorous. Widely adapted in all states. P1G, R47

Summer Pascal: 110 days. Vigorous, compact, dark-green plant, 26 to 28 inches high; resistant to blight. Broad, distinctly ribbed stalks are 24 inches tall, 9 inches to the first joint; they are thick and solid, blanching easily to a creamy white color. Hearts are crisp, tender yet brittle, and have good quality. C92, *E91G*, G79, H54, J58

Summit: 100 days. A much darker green color than other green types; medium ribbed, compact, 10 inch long stalks; tolerant of fusarium yellows. Heavy yielding. Slow bolting. *D74*, I77, L42

Surepak: 100 days. An improved strain of Florida 683. Plants are medium-green, very compact and heavy in growth. Ribs average 10 to 12 inches in length. Good heart formation. L42

Tendercrisp: 90-100 days. A productive Giant Pascal type, more uniform and upright than other cultivars. Grows 23 inches high, with compact, massive heads; stalks are 11 to 12 inches long, smooth, glossy, and dark-green in color; large heart; quality and flavor are excellent. Highly recommended for home gardens. *D74*, D76, E97, J58, L42, P1G

Utah: (Utah Green, Utah Tall Green, Utah Golden Crisp) 90-100 days. Vigorous, stocky, compact plants, 20 to 24 inches tall; medium-broad, full rounded, thick, solid stalks that are tender, crisp and stringless; quality very good, rich, nutty flavor; tightly folded hearts; readily blanches white. Popular home garden cultivar. A16, A69M, C85M, D11M, D27, D82, E38, F92, *G83M*, G87, H95, I99, K5M, K49M, L11, etc.

Utah 52-70: (Tall Utah 52-70) 120 days. Green Pascal strain with an upright, compact growth habit, 25 to 30 inches in height; good heart development; dark-green stalks and foliage; 10 to 11 inches to the first joint of the stalk; stalk thick, smooth, solid, tender and crisp, of excellent quality. Highly resistant to bolting under adverse weather conditions. Recommended for home garden and commercial plantings. A2, C92, F1, *F63*, F82, G16, G27M, *H57M*, I64, J20, M49

Utah 52-70R Improved: A tall green Pascal type, more refined and slightly taller than regular Utah 52-70. Very compact, erect plant, 25 inches high; good heart development with thick, smooth, waxy stalks and attractive dark-green foliage. High yielder; susceptible to bolting. Standard market garden and shipping cultivar throughout the United States. *A1*, A87M, B75, B75M, C92, D68, G71, G93M, *H61*, I91, J84, K73, *L59G*, L89, L97, N52, etc.

Utah Early Green: The stalks are broad, rounded, thick and solid. The plant is stocky, full-hearted and compact; blanches readily. Quality very good. D65

Ventura: 80-100 days. A widely adapted, early, tall Utah type with more upright growth and better developed hearts. Plants average 28

inches in height with long, crisp stalks, 13 inches in length, deep glossy-green in color; retain their crispness. Some resistance to some strains of fusarium yellows. Excellent bolt resistance. *D74*, G6, G64, G79, *H61*, J7, K73, L42

Verde a Canna Piena: Vigorous, upright plant with distinct long, slender stalks. Both leaves and stalks are an attractive deep green color. Very fragrant, of excellent flavor. Resistant to disease. Grown especially for a fall crop. Q11M

SELF-BLANCHING CELERY

More compact in growth habit than green celery, if planted close enough together the plants will blanch themselves but their texture and appearance are improved if light can be partly excluded when they are growing. Of very good quality but most are not quite as aromatic as the green types.

Avonpearl: Early maturing English cultivar. Good clear-white color; not as stringy as some self-blanching types. Reputed to be the very best self-blanching celery with the most resistance to bolting. P83M, S55

Cornell #6-19: 95-100 days. Slightly open plant habit; height 24 to 25 inches. Round, stringless, crisp, extra thick stalks. Combines the good qualities of the Pascal type with the earliness, easy blanching character and color of Golden Self-Blanching. Resistant to fusarium yellows but not blight. Recommended for muck or upland soils in the Northeast. Introduced in 1953. A16, *P39*

Gigante di Castelnuovo Scrivia: Large, tall plant, well formed at the base; easily attains a height of 23 inches; readily blanches to an attractive golden-yellow color. Upright, tightly packed stalks. Fragrant, bright green foliage. Sown in spring for a summer and fall harvest. Q11M

Golden Detroit: (Dwarf Golden Self-Blanching) 85 days. Compact, full-hearted plant; height 18 inches; thick, solid stalks; blanches to a medium yellow color. Petiole length 8 inches. Early, widely adapted cultivar similar to Golden Self-Blanching. *D74*

Golden Plume: 90 days. An early yellow market celery that is also recommended for home gardens, and for selling directly from the field. Produces good sized stalks and full, compact hearts which readily blanch to a clear-yellow color; quality very good. Introduced in 1937. L42

Golden Self-Blanching: 85 days. Compact, full-hearted plants, 20 to 25 inches high; thick, solid yellowish-green stalks, 7 to 8 inches long; blanches readily to a golden-yellow color; quality very good, flavor delicate. An early and widely adapted strain suitable for fresh market and home garden use. A16, B49, B78, C85M, D11M, E24, *E91G*, F19M, *F72*, G16, I64, L89, M13M, M46, N39, etc.

Golden Spartan: 118 days. Compact plants to 18 inches high; thick stalks, 6 inches long; easily blanches to a clear, waxy yellow color. Released by Michigan State University. *L59G*, P59M, P83M

Ivory Tower: Very fleshy, smooth white stems. Much taller than Lathom Self-Blanching. Not as tolerant as Lathom to bolting and is best suited to late summer and autumn cropping. Bred by A.L. Tozer Ltd. S61, *S75M*

Lathom Self-Blanching: Very compact, solid-hearted type, no need to earth up; crisp, stringless, yellow stalks; very good, nutty flavor. Early strong grower; heavy cropper; fairly resistant to bolting. Highly commended by the Royal Horticultural Society. *R23*, *S75M*

Paris Golden: (Yellow Self-Blanching) 115 days. Crisp stalks grow 18 to 20 inches tall, blanch easily to a golden yellow. Both the stem and the heart are delicious, and free from string. B13, I67M

Select Golden Self-Blanching: Medium-sized, stocky, compact plants with rich golden-yellow hearts and yellowish-green outer stalks and leaves. Stalks are broad, heavy, tender but crisp and entirely stringless. D65

Verga d'Oro: An Italian cultivar of great merit. Vigorous, upright plant. Exceptionally wide-based, closely packed stalks; an attractive golden-yellow in color. Suitable for sowing in spring for a harvest in summer and fall. I77, Q11M

TRENCH CELERY

English cultivars that are especially adapted to traditional trench culture. Most are very attractive and flavorsome with long stems that turn white, pink or red when blanched. Hardier than Self-Blanching types, being ready for cutting from early winter onward.

Clayworth Prize Pink: Medium-sized, crisp heads; long standing. A standard market cultivar, the best and hardiest of the pinks. Develops its full flavor after a frost. A favorite Victorian cultivar for trenching the traditional way. Similar to Giant Pink. P83M, S55

Giant Pink: Large, sturdy plants with dark-green leaves; long, thick, pale-pink stalks; solid and crisp; excellent sweet flavor. The stalks will color pink to red, depending upon the time of year (redder in cold weather). In hot areas, plant in fall for a spring crop. Heirloom English cultivar. *R23*, S61

Giant Red: 120 days. Large, compact plants; broad, thick, solid, tender and crisp stems are tinged with dark-red. Turns a delicate pink when blanched, making it an unusual addition to salads; also quite attractive when eaten with a dip. Very hardy and productive; will stand well into the New Year in mild climates. Heirloom, known before 1877. L91M, O53M, *R23*, S61

Giant White: Large, compact heads with crisp, solid stems of very good flavor. Maincrop cultivar; resists frosts well. A large, white celery that has been in cultivation for at least 100 years. O53M, P83M, *R23*

Pink: An English cultivar which blanches fairly easily and quickly. Stalks are an attractive pink color; color remains pink even after cooking. Very hardy, will withstand some late frosts. Excellent for table use or for exhibitions. E49, K49M

Red: 110 days. Old flavorful heirloom; stays red when cooked. Hardier than green types. Abundant yielder of spicy celery seed the following season. K49M, K49T

Red Stalk: Vigorous, stocky, branching plants, 24 inches in height. Heirloom. I99

Solid Red: An English cultivar with attractive stalks, which are deep red at the base, fading to pink and green toward the top, and reddish tinged leaves. If blanched, the stalks will turn a beautiful light pink. Retains its color when cooked. Much milder flavor than green cultivars. Excellent served in salads and soups or on a relish tray. A49G, E49

Solid White: 100 days. Vigorous plants, 16 to 20 inches high; erect leaves; fleshy, solid, tender and crisp stalks; after blanching become yellowish-white in color; quality and flavor very good. Excellent for table use or for exhibitions. Heirloom, known before 1877. B49, S61

CHERIMOYA {GR}

ANNONA CHERIMOLA

Bay Ott: Small to medium-sized, rounded fruit, weight 3/4 to 1 1/4 pounds; skin very smooth, with "thumb prints", lacking any large protuberances; flesh very fine-grained, sweet, somewhat seedy; flavor and quality excellent. Ripens from November to March in California. I83M

Bays: Medium to large, rounded fruit, weight 18 to 24 ounces; skin light yellowish-green, covered with conical protuberances; pulp white, juicy, melting, subacid, quality good; ripens February to April. Tree bushy, spreading; a good bearer; does best in coastal areas, especially near Santa Barbara. Produces without hand pollination in some years. BROOKS 1972; *B58M*, J22, L6

Big Sister: Fruit tends to be large, very smooth, with a large "thumb print" pattern. The flesh is very smooth and fine-flavored. Tree sets good crops without hand pollination. Originated in San Diego, California by James Neitzel. Introduced in 1979. Original seed came from the same fruit as the Sabor cultivar. I83M

Booth: Medium to large, conical fruit; skin with slight to moderately developed protuberances; flesh of very good flavor but seedy; sometimes tends to darken on the outside; ripens November to March, handles well. Tree a heavy bearer; more tolerant of temperature extremes than others. Best commercial cultivar, especially in inland areas. Originated in Hollywood, California. Introduced in 1921 by Armstrong Nurseries. BROOKS 1972; *B58M, D23M*, I83M, L6

Chaffey: Medium-sized, short-conical fruit, about 4 inches long; weight 3/4 to 1 pound; skin smooth, thick, resists bruising; flesh light cream, quality and flavor very good; seed small, 30 to 60 per fruit; season December to March along the coast of California. Tree bears regularly; is somewhat productive without hand pollination. Grows well in both inland and coastal areas. BROOKS 1972; I83M, L6

Deliciosa: Medium to small fruit, long-conical in form; skin thin, slightly downy, covered with long protuberances; fairly seedy; ripens in midseason. Flavor very good inland, poor along the coast. Generally bears well but doesn't ship well. Cold-resistant. MORTON 1987a; *Q93*

El Bumpo: Medium to large, conical fruit; skin with large, rounded protuberances, turns yellow when mature; flesh juicy, not seedy; excellent typical flavor; ripens December to March. Soft, edible skin. Probably a seedling of Whaley. Originated in Villa Park, California by Rudy Haluza. Introduced in 1986. I83M

Honeyhart: Medium-sized, conical fruit, weighing up to 2 pounds; skin smooth, plated, yellowish green; flesh smooth-textured, sweet and juicy; flavor and quality excellent; seeds few; ripens November to March. Produces consistently good crops without hand pollination. Originated in Escondido, California by Orton H. Englehart. Introduced in 1976. I83M

Libby: Fruit rounded-conical; skin fingerprinted, may still be green when mature; falls from tree easily when ripe. Very sweet, strong, typical cherimoya flavor. Very early maturing, late September to early October. Probably a seedling of Spain. Originated in Villa Park, California by Rudy Haluza. Introduced in 1986. I83M

Mariella: Large to very large fruit, may weigh up to 7 pounds; skin yellowish-green, knobby; flavor very good; ripens November to March; resembles White. Tree bears without hand pollination. Originated in San Diego, California from seed brought from Argentina. I83M

McPherson: Moderately large fruit; skin smooth but with some development of tubercles; quality good; midseason to late in maturity. Tree vigorous; quite productive even without hand pollination. Originated in Orange, California. Introduced in 1933. BROOKS 1972; J22

Ott: Heart-shaped fruit, averages 3 inches in diameter, weighs 7 to 12 ounces; smaller than Booth or White; skin green with brownish spots, smooth, tough, medium thick, peels easily; flesh yellow, very fine textured, flavor very pronounced and distinct; high sugar content, up to 26.5%; eating quality excellent; seeds 24 to 36 per fruit; season January through April. BROOKS 1972; I83M

Pierce: Small to medium-sized fruit; skin knobby, light green; flesh very sweet, quality very good; seeds few; ripens January to March, has a longer fruiting season along the coast. Tree large, vigorous; a shy bearer with a tendency toward alternate bearing; does best in inland areas. Some production without hand pollination. *B58M, D23M*, I83M, L6

Reretai: Medium to large fruit; flesh sweet and juicy with a very good pleasant flavor, of high quality. Tree a reliable and heavy producer. One of the leading cultivars in New Zealand. *O97*

Sabor: Fruit of variable size, but generally medium; skin often has nubs or protuberances. Flavor pronounced, excellent. Rated as superior in taste to all others at meetings of the California Rare Fruit Growers. Tree bears well without pollination. Originated in San Diego, California by James Neitzel. Introduced in 1979. I83M

Spain: Small to medium-sized, conical fruit, average weight 1 1/2 pounds; skin dark green, very smooth; flesh creamy white, sweet, free of grit cells near the skin; flavor excellent; seeds relatively few, black, shiny; ripens December to April. Tree hardy; bears well in coastal areas without hand pollination; leaves very large. Introduced into California from Spain. I83M, J22, L6, *Q93*

Villa Park: Small to medium-sized, round fruit; skin with small protuberances; flesh sweet, with a rich pineapple-banana flavor; ripens December to March. I83M

Whaley: Medium to large fruit, short, conical; weight 1 1/2 to 2 pounds; skin light green, surface tuberculate; flavor and quality good, although a membrane tends to develop around the seeds; ripens in midseason and later. Tree somewhat smaller and less vigorous than some other cultivars. Originated in Hollywood, California. Introduced in 1927 by Armstrong Nurseries. BROOKS 1972; J22

White: (Dr. White) Fruit medium to large, short-conical with rounded apex; skin medium-thick, semi-smooth; flavor very good, even after fruit is quite soft; seeds few; ripens December to March. Tree bears well in San Diego County, California, especially near coastal areas. Poor bearer without hand pollination. Originated on the White ranch, Lemon Grove, California. Introduced in 1930. BROOKS 1972; *B58M, D23M*, I83M, L6

CHERRY {GR}

PRUNUS AVIUM
PRUNUS X GONDOUINII
PRUNUS CERASUS

DUKE CHERRIES

Also called *royal cherries* or dual-purpose cherries, these hybrids of sweet and sour cherries have a soft texture and semi-sweet flavor. They are valued for their hardiness in unfavorable climates and for their cooking qualities. (P. x gondouinii)

Belle de Planchoury: Medium to large, roundish-ovoid fruit; skin dark red, moderately glossy; flesh reddish, fairly soft, moderately juicy, acid to sub-acid, juice colored; stone small; dessert quality fair, good for cooking; ripens in midseason. Tree fairly vigorous, upright-spreading, resistant to bacterial canker. GRUBB; N24M

Belle Magnifique: (Belle de Chatenay) Very large, heart-shaped fruit; skin rich crimson, glossy; flesh yellowish, very soft, very acid until almost fully ripe, acid when ripe, with uncolored juice; resistant to splitting; ripens during August but will often hang until well into September. Tree vigorous, upright-spreading; needs to be pruned as a sweet cherry; self-incompatible, Morello recommended as a pollinator. SIMMONS 1978; **U8**{SC}

Brassington: Large, dark red, sprightly subacid fruit; ripens with Early Richmond. Tree productive. A chance seedling found in Oceana County, Michigan, prior to 1913. HEDRICK 1915; F91T{SC}, N24M

Kaiserin Eugenie: (Empress Eugenie) Medium to large, roundish fruit; skin very dark crimson, moderately glossy; flesh dark red, soft, juicy, sub-acid, juice moderately colored; dessert quality fair to good, very good for cooking; ripens in early midseason. Resistant to cracking. Tree moderately vigorous, upright, somewhat susceptible to bacterial canker. GRUBB; N24M

Krasa Severa: (Beauty of the North) Large, roundish-oblate fruit; skin dark red to dark purple; flesh dark red, juice light red-purple; flavor slightly sour, refreshing, pleasant; stone medium, semi-clinging; ripens very late. Fine for home canning. Resembles English Morello more than a Duke cherry. Tree upright, productive; moderately susceptible to leaf spot disease and brown rot fungus. Originated in the Soviet Union by I.V. Michurin. BROOKS 1972, MICHURIN; F91T{SC}

Late Duke: A variant of May Duke, ripening from 2 to 4 weeks later. Large, heart-shaped fruit; skin deep red, glossy; flesh pale yellow, soft, juicy, rich, sprightly subacid; quality very good; juice uncolored; stone large. Tree vigorous, upright-spreading; self-compatible; should be pruned as a sweet cherry. Introduced around 1797. HEDRICK 1915, SIMMONS 1978; M39M

May Duke: Roundish, medium to large fruit; skin dark red to nearly black, glossy; flesh dark red, very soft, sweeter than most Duke cherries; flavor rich; juice pinkish; quality very good when ripe; stone smallish. Tree upright, compact; somewhat susceptible to bacterial canker. Partially self-compatible; English Morello recommended as a pollinator. Probably Originated near Médoc, France around 1688. HEDRICK 1915; J93{SC}, M39M

Regina Ortensia: (Reine Hortense) Large, round fruit; skin tender, bright glossy red slightly blushed with amber; flesh pale yellow, with colorless juice, tender and melting, sprightly subacid, flavor excellent; ripens in midseason; susceptible to brown rot. Tree of medium size, upright-spreading, productive. Originated in France early in the 19th century. HEDRICK 1915; N24M

Royal Duke: Large to very large fruit, roundish heart-shaped; skin dark red, very glossy; flesh faintly reddish, fairly soft, only slightly acid, juicy, quality excellent; ripens in mid-July, holds well into August. Highly esteemed for cooking; also good for dessert. Tree extremely upright, moderately vigorous; partially self-compatible, but English Morello recommended as a pollinator. SIMMONS 1978; J93{SC}

SOUR CHERRIES (P. cerasus)

<u>AMARELLE CHERRIES</u> Also called *amarella* or *Kentish cherries*. Similar in appearance to Morellos, but most have lighter colored, less acid flesh with colorless juice. In France, where they are known as *griottes*, they are used in confectionery in many ways and are highly recommended for *cerises à l'eau-de-vie*.

Carnation: Medium-sized, roundish-oblate fruit; skin tender, medium to dark red, somewhat variegated with white or yellow; flesh yellowish-white, tender and melting, sprightly, quality very good; juice abundant, colorless; stone free, separates very readily from the flesh leaving it unusually bright and clean; ripens in midseason or later. Tree medium-sized, spreading, not very productive. First recorded in 1676. HEDRICK 1915; J93, J93{SC}

Dwarfrich:[1] Medium-sized, roundish fruit; similar in color, flavor and flesh texture to Early Richmond, but may average slightly smaller. Bush a true dwarf, growing only 4 feet high; hardy, blooms late; requires a pollinator, Montmorency and English Morello being recommended. Very suitable for small gardens, where it is productive as well as ornamental. Seedling of Vladimir. Originated in Cheyenne, Wyoming. BROOKS 1972; F91T{SC}

Early Richmond: Medium-sized, roundish fruit; skin thin, rather tough, light red changing to dark red; flesh pale yellow, with light pinkish juice, stringy, tender, melting; flavor pleasant, sprightly; good to very good in quality; stone free, small; ripens early. Tree medium-sized, upright-spreading; very hardy. Similar if not identical to the Kentish Red of England. HEDRICK 1915; A82, B73M, C37, *C54*, D76, E3, *G28*, G72, H49, *H90*, I9M, K28, L90, M76, M83, etc.

Meteor: Large, roundish-oval fruit; skin thin, tender, clear light bright-red, very attractive; flesh light bright-yellow, medium firm, medium juicy; flavor mild, pleasantly acid; quality very good; stone small, long oval, very free; ripens in midseason, 7 to 10 days after North Star. Tree very hardy; bears regularly and annually. Introduced in 1952. BROOKS 1972; D65, E84, F19M, F53, G16, G41, *H90*, I36, J7, J16, J93, J93{SC}, L27M, L70, M35M, etc.

Montmore: (Early Montmore, McLain Montmorency) Bud mutation of Montmorency. Fruit larger than Montmorency, which it resembles, of darker color; sour; ripens in June over a relatively short period. Tree somewhat dwarf, spreading. Originated in Knoxville, Tennessee by Lee McLain. Introduced in 1925. BROOKS 1972; D76, E97

Montmorency: Medium to large, roundish fruit; skin bright red, thin, tender, glossy; flesh pale yellow with a reddish tinge, tender, melting, sprightly, tart, of very good quality; juice abundant, light pink; stone free, small; ripens in midseason. Tree semi-dwarf; very productive. Standard sour cherry in the United States. Originated in the Montmorency Valley, France in the 17th century. HEDRICK 1915; A5, <u>A38M</u>{PR}, A39, B83, C63, C75M, E4, F19M, G23, J83, K28, <u>K52</u>{PR}, *K73M*, L30, L97, M39M, N33, etc.

<u>MORELLO CHERRIES</u> Similar to the Amarelle cherries, but with deep crimson-red flesh and colored juice. The tender, juicy flesh is bittersweet, too acid for most palates when eaten raw, but delicious when cooked or preserved in some way.

Del Nord: (Griotte du Nord) Fairly large, roundish fruit; skin dark purplish red, glossy; flesh red, soft, very juicy, sub-acid, quality good; juice deeply colored; stone free; ripens about the end of August. Tree of weak growth, becomes drooping with age; self-compatible, bears good crops. Continental cooking cherry. SIMMONS 1978; F53, F91T{SC}, P59M

English Morello: Large, roundish heart-shaped fruit; skin thin, tender, very dark red becoming almost black; flesh dark red, tender and melting, sprightly, tart; juice abundant, dark-red; quality good; stone free, small; ripens very late. Excellent for cooking, becoming rich dark wine-colored and pleasantly aromatic. Tree small, with drooping branchlets. Very old cultivar of unknown origin. HEDRICK 1915; A91, *C54*, G41, I36, *I68*, *K73M*, L12, *L47*, N24M

Kansas Sweet: (Hansen Sweet) Medium to large fruit; skin mahogany-red; flesh firm, juicy, somewhat sweet for a sour cherry; resembles English Morello; ripens late June to early July. Tree hardy; productive; fruits satisfactorily in the Great Plains area. Bing or Black Tartarian recommended as pollinators. Originated in Wichita, Kansas by H.J. Hansen. Introduced about 1935. BROOKS 1972; B75, *C54*, D76, *G89M*

Mesabi: Skin quite red; flesh lighter red than skin; sugar content midway between sweet and sour cherries; pit smaller than Meteor; very good for sauce and pie; ripens in mid-July; resembles Meteor. Tree spreading, slow growing; heavy yielding; very hardy; tends to bear when small. Originated in Duluth, Minnesota. BROOKS 1972; *A74*, F91T{SC}, L70, N24M

North Star:[1 2] Fruit roundish heart-shaped, about 3/4 inch in diameter; skin bright red changing to a dark, glistening mahogany red at maturity; flesh dark red, juicy, meaty, tender, flavor pleasantly acid; quality good; stone small, easily removed; ripens very early. Tree a genetic dwarf, grows less than 10 feet tall; self-fruitful; excellent for home gardens. BROOKS 1972; *B52*, B73M, C63, C75M, D69, E84, F53, G23, *G28*, G41, H65, J69, J83, L99M

Schattenmorelle: Medium to large, roundish fruit; skin thin and tender, dark red; flesh deep red, tender and melting, sprightly tart; juice abundant, dark-red; quality very good; ripens very late. Excellent for cooking, becoming a rich dark-wine color and pleasantly aromatic. Tree smaller than Montmorency, hardy. German sport of English Morello. F91T{SC}, H90M{SC}, I36, M22

Suda: Fruit roundish heart-shaped, about 3/4 inch in diameter; skin dark purplish-red; flesh dark red, with dark-colored juice, tender, somewhat meaty, sprightly, astringent, very sour; quality poor; stone free; ripens very late. Tree vigorous; rather unproductive. Originated in the garden of a Captain Suda, Louisiana, Missouri, about 1880. HEDRICK 1915; A91

SWEET CHERRIES (P. avium)

PURPLE-SKINNED

Angela: Large, nearly round fruit; skin dark red; flesh firm, juicy, sweet, of good flavor; resistant to splitting; ripens late, with Lambert. Tree a reliable and heavy bearer; more winter hardy than Bing or Lambert; resistant to western x disease and doubling; inter-fruitful with Bing and Lambert. Introduced in 1974. A5, C34, E84, J61M, J93{SC}, *N20*

Annonay: (D'Annonay) Medium-sized, roundish fruit; skin dark red to black, fairly glossy; flesh pinkish, soft, sweet, juicy, slightly sub-acid; stone clinging. Tree of moderate vigor, tall and round-headed; hardy; bears good crops regularly. Valuable because of its early ripening, the beginning of June. Of French origin. SIMMONS 1978; **U8**{SC}

Bing: Very large, heart-shaped fruit, about 1 inch in diameter; skin medium thick, tough; skin color very dark red, almost black; flesh purplish-red with dark purple juice, rather coarse, firm, very meaty, brittle, sweet; of very good quality; stone semi-free large; ripens midseason or later. Tree vigorous, upright-spreading, productive. Originated in Milwaukee, Oregon by Seth Lewelling in 1875. HEDRICK 1915; A82, B83, C8M{PR}, C63, C75M, E4, E97, F19M, F53, G41, J83, *K73M*, L30, L97G{PR}, L99M, M39M, etc.

Black Eagle: Large, roundish, heart-shaped fruit; skin purplish black, fairly glossy; flesh dark red, firm, not very fibrous, sweet and rich; quality very good; stone fairly small; ripens in early July. Tree spreading, drooping; hardy; productive; very susceptible to bacterial canker. Originated in England. SIMMONS 1978; **U8**{SC}

Black Republican: (Republican) Medium-sized, roundish heart-shaped fruit; skin thin, purplish-black; flesh purplish-red, with dark-colored juice, tender, meaty, crisp; flavor sweet or with slight astringency before fully mature; ripens late. Tree large, spreading; tends to overbear. Originated in Milwaukee, Oregon by Seth Lewelling in the mid 19th century. HEDRICK 1915; B83, *C54*, D81{PO}, F53, *G14*, L99M, M39M

Black Tartarian: Long, heart-shaped fruit, less than 1 inch in diameter; skin thin, deep purplish-black, glossy; flesh purplish-red, with dark colored juice, firm, meaty, crisp; flavor pleasant, mild, sweet; of very good to excellent quality; stone free, small; ripens early. Tree characteristically large and upright. Introduced into England in 1794 from Circassia, Russia. HEDRICK 1915; B73M, B83, *C47*, C63, C75M, D81{PO}, E4, E97, F19M, G23, *G28*, H65, J83, *K73M*, M39M, etc.

Blackheart: Medium-sized fruit, heart-shaped but somewhat pointed; skin dark purplish to black, glossy; flesh very dark red, soft, juice plentiful and colored, sweet; quality good; seldom splits. Tree fairly vigorous, very spreading and drooping; productive; hardy. SIMMONS 1978; J93, J93{SC}

Brooks: Fruit uniformly large, particularly for an early-maturing cultivar; skin dark red; flesh firm and crisp, flavor sweet, rich, well balanced; dessert quality very good; susceptible to cracking; ripens early, about 1 week before Bing. When pitted and sun-dried, makes a large meaty "seedless raisin" that is excellent for snacks and baking. Tree upright, hardy, a very productive and regular bearer. *B71M*, H26M{PR}

Cavalier: Medium to large fruit; skin rich purple-black, glossy; flesh firm, very sweet; quality excellent for an early cultivar; resistant to cracking; similar to Schmidt's Bigarreau, but matures 10 days earlier. Good holding qualities for the fresh market. Tree upright-spreading, moderately vigorous; somewhat slow to come into bearing; very hardy, reportedly to -26^0 F. D69, F53

Compact Stella:[1 2] Large, heart-shaped fruit; skin black; flesh black, medium firm, relatively coarse; ripens mid-June to early July. Tree semi-dwarf, 40 to 60% of standard size, natural spur growth reduces height to under 15 feet at maturity; self-fertile, will also pollinize all other cherries. Sets fruit when young, with heavy, consistent crops. B67, C41M, *C54*, D76, E84, E97, F11, *H34*, L12, L33, L97, M22, N24M

Dandeecher:[2] New self-fertile dessert cherry of exceptional fruiting qualities. Yellow-amber skin, flushed with red, turning deep red as the fruit matures; ripens in midseason. Crisp, juicy flesh of excellent flavor. Tree semi-dwarf, round headed, compact; reliably productive; does not require a pollinator. High commercial potential; ideal for home gardens. *O97*

Early Burlat: (Bigarreau Hâtif de Burlat) Fruit large; skin red to dark purplish-red; flesh sweet, medium firm, more so than Black Tartarian but not as firm as Bing; semi-freestone; ripens early, 4 to 7 days before Black Tartarian; susceptible to cracking after rain. Tree moderately vigorous; resistant to buckskin disease. Good pollinator for Bing and Mona. Originated in Morocco. BROOKS 1972, STEBBINS; *B71M*, *C54*, *D18*, E4, J61M

Early Purple Gean: (Early Purple) Large, heart-shaped fruit; skin thin, tender, purplish-black; of very good quality. ripens very early. Flesh sweet, soft, tender, juicy; of the type the French call Guigne, as contrasted to the hard, crisp-fleshed type known as Bigarreau. Tree large, upright-spreading; vigorous; very productive. Introduced about 1688. HEDRICK 1915; L12

Early Rivers: Large to very large, heart-shaped fruit; skin glossy, dark purplish-red, almost black; flesh deep red, soft, melting; juice abundant, colored; quality very good when ripe; stone small; ripens in mid-June. Very popular commercial cultivar in England. Tree vigorous; tends to grow too tall and weeping. Originated as a seedling of Early Purple Gean by Thomas Rivers, about 1872. SIMMONS 1978; L12, P86

Garden Bing:[1 2] Dark reddish-black fruit, closely resembles the standard Bing; ripens in midseason. Tree highly ornamental; a genetic dwarf, approximately 6 feet tall at maturity with a spread of 4 feet;

self-fertile. Excellent for patio containers, where the height can be kept to 3 feet. STEBBINS; A88M, *C54*, E87, F11, *I68*, *N20*

Giant: Large, very dark-red, glossy fruit; flesh dark blood-red, very juicy, sweet, with a fine rich flavor; ripens in California about June 20th. Tree rapid in growth, with large and heavy foliage. First grown by Luther Burbank in 1900 and regarded by him as one of his best creations. HEDRICK 1915; L12

Gil Peck: Large fruit; skin dark purplish-black; flesh firm, juicy, sweet, richly flavored; may occasionally crack, but less than Royal Ann; resembles Giant in shape and quality; ripens in late midseason. Royal Ann x Giant. Originated in Geneva, New York by Richard Wellington. Introduced in 1936. BROOKS 1972; F91T{SC}

Hardy Giant: (Starking Hardy Giant) Fruit large; skin dark red, attractive; flesh firm, sweet, of high quality; resembles Schmidt's Bigarreau; ripens early to midseason. Tree large, upright-spreading; vigorous; extremely hardy; a reliable and heavy bearer. Good pollinator for other sweet cherries, especially Lambert. BROOKS 1972, STEBBINS; B83, C34, D81{PO}, I49M, J61M, M39M

Hedelfingen: (Hedelfingen Risenkirsche) Medium to large, roundish-oval fruit; skin glossy, deep mahogany red, almost black when ripe; flesh dark red, tender yet firm, aromatic; juice abundant, very red; quality good; ripens in mid-July. Tree tall, vigorous; productive; susceptible to bacterial canker. Originated in Hedelfingen, Germany in the 18th century. A5, A14, B53, C63, E38, E84, F53, G23, G41, H49, I36, J93{SC}, K83M, L33, M39M, etc.

Hudson: Medium to large fruit; skin very dark-red; flesh very firm, sweet, of good quality; resistant to cracking, even under extreme conditions; ripens very late, after Lambert, extending the cherry harvest about 10 days; best in its season. Tree very large; open-spreading; resistant to southwest trunk injury. BROOKS 1972; B53, F53, I36, K83M, N24M

Jubilee: Large heart-shaped fruit, averages 1 inch in diameter or more; skin glossy, red to dark red; flesh red to dark red, fine-textured, moderately juicy, moderately firm to firm; flavor ranges from very sweet and mild to sweet and mildly tart; ripens 6 days before Bing. Tree similar to Bing in growth and appearance; effectively cross-pollinated by Bing, Lambert, Royal Ann, etc. BROOKS 1972; *C54*

Kristin: Large, heart-shaped fruit, about 1 inch in diameter; skin tender, glossy, dark purplish-black; flesh sweet, firm, meaty, juicy; crack-resistant; ripens in mid-July in the Finger Lakes region of New York. Tree productive; very winter-hardy, tested for 12 years in Norway. Recommended for roadside stands or pick-your-own operations. C27T{SC}, D76, E97, F53, H65, I36, J61M, J93, J93{SC}

Lambert: Large, roundish heart-shaped fruit; skin reddish-purple, thin; flesh dark red, with scant dark red juice, meaty, firm, sweet, of pleasant flavor; quality very good; subject to cracking; ripens late. Tree vigorous and productive; resistant to doubling in hot climates; often difficult to train and prune. Originated in Milwaukee, Oregon about 1848. HEDRICK 1915, STEBBINS; B53, B67, B83, C41M, E4, F53, *G66*, *H34*, K83M, L1, L99M, M39M, *N20*, N46

Lyons: (Early Lyons) Large, heart-shaped fruit; skin thin, rather tender, very dark red, attractive; flesh reddish, meaty, sprightly, sweet, of very good quality; stone large, semi-clinging; matures very early. Tree vigorous, upright-spreading; a somewhat shy bearer when young, becoming productive with age. Originated near Lyons, France, about 1822. HEDRICK 1915; F91T{SC}, N24M

Merton Bigarreau: Large, round fruit; skin deep mahogany red; flesh dark red, tender, meaty, flavor extremely rich; ripens in midseason. Tree bears heavily and regularly; vigorous; very spreading; self-unfruitful, being pollinated by Black Tartarian, Black Republican and Van. Highly recommended for the home garden by Mr. J.M.S. Potter, Director of the National Fruit Trials in England. BROOKS 1972; F91T{SC}, L12, N24M

Merton Heart: Very large, heart-shaped fruit; skin dark mahogany to nearly black, fairly glossy; flesh dark red, fairly firm, juicy, sweet, flavor excellent; stone large; ripens just after Early Rivers. Tree very vigorous, at first upright but spreading with age; productive; resistant to bacterial canker and blossom wilt. SIMMONS 1978; F91T{SC}

Mona: Large, symmetrical, heart-shaped fruit; skin glossy red to dark red, tender; flesh red to dark red, tender to moderately firm, juice red; flavor sweet, mild, considered to be superior to Black Tartarian but less tart; ripens with Black Tartarian. Tree vigorous; very productive; pollinated by Bing, Black Tartarian, Black Republican, etc. BROOKS 1972; *C54*, *L47*

Ramon Oliva: Very large, heart-shaped fruit; skin deep cherry-red streaked with lighter red, glossy; flesh light cherry-red, soft, sweet, very juicy, flavor good; stone large, adherent. Tree vigorous, spreading with age; susceptible to bacterial canker. Of French origin, introduced about 1900. SIMMONS 1978; Q24M

Reverchon: (Bigarreau Reverchon) Large to very large, roundish fruit; skin very dark red to black, glossy; flesh dark red, very firm, fine-textured, juicy, of very good quality; ripens midseason or later. Somewhat susceptible to cracking. Tree moderately vigorous, round-headed, susceptible to bacterial canker. GRUBB; Q24M

Sam: Medium to large fruit; skin black; flesh firm, black, of fair to good quality; ripens about 1 week earlier than Bing; highly resistant to cracking. Tree vigorous; very hardy; productive; self-unfruitful. Widely planted as a pollinator for Bing, Lambert and Van. BROOKS 1972; A5, B53, B67, C75M, D69, E84, F53, *G89M*, J61M, L97, L99M, M39M, N46

Schmidt's Bigarreau: (Schmidt) Very large, heart-shaped fruit; skin deep purplish-black; flesh purplish-red, very meaty, crisp, tender but firm, sweet; juice abundant, dark-colored; quality good; ripens in midseason. Tree large, upright-spreading; vigorous; slow to come into bearing. Originated in Germany about 1841. HEDRICK 1915; A5, A14, C63, F53, G79M, H49, H65, J16, K83M, M39M

Seneca: Large, round-cordate fruit; skin purplish-black; flesh soft, juicy, melting, sweet, flavor rich; ripens early, 2 weeks before Black Tartarian; resistant to cracking; stone free. Tree vigorous, productive, resembles Black Tartarian. Originated in Geneva, New York by Richard Wellington. Introduced in 1924. BROOKS 1972; F91T{SC}, N24M

Späte Braun: (Late Brown) Large to very large fruit; skin attractive, glossy, dark-red; crisp, solid, juicy red flesh, of excellent flavor; very resistant to cracking. Superior size and texture. Tree prolific. One of 5 cultivars "outstandingly recommended" for the amateur by the late Dr. Reid M. Brooks, Professor of pomology and cherry specialist at the University of California. L12

Stella:[2] The first good-quality, self-fertile black sweet cherry. Large, heart-shaped fruit, resembles Lambert; skin black, fairly susceptible to cracking in rain; flesh black, medium firm, relatively coarse; ripens with Hedelfingen. Tree upright-spreading; productive; tender to winter cold; self-fertile, also a good pollinator for other sweet cherries. BROOKS 1972; B83, C75M, E4, E84, E97, F53, G41, G79M, H65, *H90*, *K73M*, L30, *L47*, L99M, M39M, etc.

Ulster: Fruit large, resembles Schmidt's Bigarreau; skin very dark red; flesh firm, juicy, sweet, crisp; quality good; highly resistant to cracking; ripens in midseason, a few days before Schmidt's Bigarreau. Good for roadside markets. Tree more productive than Schmidt's

Bigarreau. Originated in Geneva, New York. Introduced in 1964. BROOKS 1972; A5, B53, F53, I36, *K73M*, K83M, M39M

Utah Giant: Large, attractive fruit, often sets in large clusters, does not double; skin purple-black; flesh firm, more flavorful than Bing or Lambert; stone medium-sized, partially freestone. Excellent for canning since it retains its firmness, color and flavor after processing. Tree productive; hardy, but susceptible to spring frosts; resistant to western x disease. Released by Utah State Agricultural Experiment Station in 1981. A88M, *C54*, *H34*, *K73M*, M39M, *N20*

Van: Fruit similar to Bing, but somewhat smaller due to overbearing; skin black, very glossy; flesh slightly firmer and equal to Bing in quality; somewhat resistant to cracking; ripens with Bing. Tree vigorous, upright; hardier than Bing; good pollinator for Bing and Lambert. BROOKS 1972; A5, B83, C63, D81{PO}, E4, E84, F53, G23, G41, *H90*, *K73M*, L30, L33, *L47*, L99M, M39M, etc.

Venus: Large, heart-shaped fruit; skin dark purplish-red, glossy; flesh red to black, of high quality, not as firm as Lambert and therefore less subject to cracking; ripens about 5 days after Black Tartarian. Tree has a slight tendency to overset in heavy-crop years, resulting in reduced fruit size. Originated in Vineland Station, Ontario, Canada. BROOKS 1972; G41, I36, J93{SC}, K83M

Vic: Fruit sweet; quality good; ripens with Windsor but is larger and darker in color; satisfactory for freezing and *maraschino cherries*; superior to Windsor in canning tests; sizes well in heavy-crop years. Tree large; consistently heavy bearing. Released as a replacement for Windsor. BROOKS 1972; F53, K83M

Windsor: Fruit slightly oblong to conical; skin dark-red, almost black when mature; flesh light red, with reddish juice, tender, meaty, crisp; flavor mild and sweet; quality good to very good; stone semi-free; ripens late mid-season. Tree large, upright-spreading; vigorous; very productive. Originated in Windsor, Ontario, Canada around 1881. HEDRICK 1915; B75, C63, F53, G41, G79M, H49, H65, K71, K83M, M22, M76

WHITE-SKINNED

Rainbow Stripe: Very distinctive fruit; white with a narrow blood-red stripe from stem to tip, extending through the flesh; most nearly resembles Lambert. Bud mutation of Lambert; discovered in 1925. Originated in Yakima, Washington. Introduced commercially in 1930. BROOKS 1952; **T49M{SC}**, **U8{SC}**

Vega: Fruit large; skin white with a red blush, smooth, very attractive; flesh white, slightly tart, firm; pit small, easily removed; ripens 5 to 8 days before Royal Ann. Recommended for brining, *maraschino cherries* and canning, too tart for dessert purposes until very ripe. Tree upright; vigorous; hardy; very productive. BROOKS 1972; F53, F91T{SC}, G41

YELLOW-SKINNED

Bada: Large, symmetrical, heart-shaped fruit; skin smooth, glossy, cream colored with a medium to high red blush; flesh cream colored, tender, meaty, moderately juicy; flavor mild, being less tart than Royal Ann; resistant to cracking; ripens 4 days before Royal Ann. Tree precocious; productive to very productive; interfertile with Bing, Royal Ann, Van and Mona. BROOKS 1972; E84, *I54*

Corum: Long heart-shaped fruit; skin yellow with an attractive red blush; flesh white with a yellow tinge, tender, meaty, crisp, flavor mild; ripens about 6 days before Royal Ann; moderately resistant to cracking. Tree fairly vigorous; as hardy as Royal Ann; free of known virus diseases; tolerant to bacterial canker. BROOKS 1972; E84, *G14*, L99M

Elton: (Elton Heart) Large, very pointed, cordate fruit; skin pale golden-yellow with a faint red blush, glossy; flesh pale yellow, very tender, juicy, sweet, flavor very good; stone large; somewhat susceptible to splitting; ripens the first half of July. Tree erect, of fair size, lacking in vigor; bears fairly well but irregularly; susceptible to bacterial canker. Originated in England about 1806. SIMMONS 1978; **U8{SC}**

Emperor Francis: Large, roundish heart-shaped fruit; skin yellowish-white blushed with reddish mahogany, fairly glossy; flesh very pale yellow, firm, sweet, rich; juice uncolored, abundant; quality good; sometimes splits badly. Tree small and compact, suitable for the garden. Introduced prior to 1876. HEDRICK 1915, SIMMONS 1978; A5, B53, F53, G23, *H34*, H49, H65, I36, J61M, J93, J93{SC}, *K73M*, K83M, M39M

Goodman Gold: A clear yellow cherry, possibly the old Yellow Glass or Gold cultivar. Fruit somewhat smaller than Bing; has a refreshing tang lacking in red-skinned types; ripens 2 weeks later than Bing. Excellent for pies and canning. Less bothered by birds due to its yellow color. E84

Governor Wood: Large, roundish heart-shaped fruit; skin yellowish-white with a crimson blush; flesh whitish, with abundant colorless juice, tender, meaty; flavor sweet, mild; quality very good; cracks badly in wet weather; ripens in early midseason. Tree vigorous, upright-spreading; productive. First raised in 1842 by Professor Jared P. Kirtland at Cleveland, Ohio. HEDRICK 1915; A82, E84, *F5*, K28, L12, *M25M*

Rainier: Large, slightly obovate fruit, similar to Bing; skin attractive, yellow, highly blushed with rose-red; flesh very firm, juice colorless, of very high quality; ripens 3 to 7 days before Royal Ann; has exceptional holding ability after harvest. Sold for very high prices at specialty food stores. Tree vigorous; very productive; comes into bearing very early. BROOKS 1972; B53, B67, B83, C34, C41M, D81{PO}, E4, E84, F53, H26M{PR}, H69{PR}, *I54*, J93{SC}, L1, L97, M39M, N46, etc.

Royal Ann: (Napoleon) Long heart-shaped fruit; skin color varying shades of bright red over a yellowish background, distinctly mottled; flesh whitish, with a faint yellow tinge, meaty, tender, crisp, sweet; flavor mild, improving as the season advances; quality good to very good; ripens in midseason. Tree highly susceptible to bacterial canker. Widely used for canning and *maraschino cherries*. A very old cultivar of unknown origin. GRUBB, HEDRICK 1915; B83, C41M, C63, E4, E84, E97, F53, G41, H65, *K73M*, L30, *L47*, L97, M39M, M76, etc.

Saylor: Skin pure, clear bright yellow; flesh crisp, juicy, of exceptional sweetness with a distinctive aftertaste. Ripens late. One of the best pure yellow cultivars. From the late Dr. Reid M. Brooks' collection at Davis, California. Origin unknown. A69G{SC}, L12

Sparkle: Medium to small, attractive fruit; skin with a bright luster; flesh white, firm, flavor sweet and sprightly; fairly resistant to cracking; resembles Royal Ann but rounder and less conical, matures 1 week earlier. Tree vigorous, upright; pollinates Bing, Lambert, Royal Ann and Van. Originated in Summerland, British Columbia by A.J. Mann. BROOKS 1972; A69G{SC}

Stark Gold: Attractive, golden fruit with a unique tangy flavor; resistant to cracking; ripens in mid-June in Zone 6. Tree very hardy, has survived winter temperatures of -30^0 F.; performs well in Zones 5 to 7. Pollinate with any other sweet cherry. L33

Sue: Fruit medium-sized, roundish-conic, resembles Royal Ann in general appearance; skin yellow with an attractive bright red blush; juice colorless; flesh nearly as firm as Royal Ann, exceedingly sweet, rich and vinous; of high quality; highly resistant to cracking; ripens slightly earlier than Royal Ann. Tree bears very heavily; pollinated by

Bing, Lambert, Van and Royal Ann. BROOKS 1972; A69G{SC}, B53, L12, N24M

Yellow Glass: Medium to large, roundish heart-shaped fruit; skin thin, tough, light lemon in color, attractive; flesh firm, yellow, meaty, sweet, with colorless juice; quality good; stone large, round, clinging; ripens in mid-July. Tree large, upright; very hardy; productive. Introduced about 1892. HEDRICK 1915; B75, *D35M*, H33, *H90*

Yellow Spanish: Large, heart-shaped fruit; skin bright amber-yellow with a reddish blush, more attractive than Royal Ann; flesh whitish, with colorless juice, tender, meaty, crisp, aromatic; flavor sweet, very good to best in quality; ripens in midseason. Tree very large and vigorous; productive. One of the oldest known cherries, believed to have been described by Pliny and called Graffion by the early English writers. HEDRICK 1915; J16, L12

CHERRY PLUM {GR}

PRUNUS X SP.

Beta: Slightly oval fruit; skin thin, reddish-blue; flesh greenish, moderately firm, very mildly acid, quality good, freestone; resembles Opata. Open pollinated seedling of Opata. Introduced in 1960 for home gardens. Originated in Saskatoon, Saskatchewan, Canada, by C.F. Patterson. G54

Compass: (P. besseyi x P. hortulana) Small to medium-sized, oval fruit; skin thick, tough, dark purplish-red; flesh yellow, rather firm, cling-stone; flavor somewhat sour, quality fair to good. Eaten fresh or cooked. Very good pollinator for other cultivars. Bush-like growth habit; grows to 8 feet; bears the second year after planting. Originated by H. Knudson, Springfield, Minnesota. Introduced in 1897. WAUGH; *A74*, B4, D65, *G4*, G16, G67, K64, L27M, L70, N24M

Convoy: Small, roundish fruit, somewhat larger than Compass; skin scarlet red, moderately tender; flesh yellowish, tender, juicy, nearly sweet; quality good for dessert or canning; ripens during the end of August. Tree very vigorous, upright, narrow; very hardy and productive; an excellent pollinator for other cherry plums. Introduced in 1941 by Boughen Nurseries. ANDERSEN, BROOKS 1972; B47, F91T{SC}, N24M

Deep Purple: (P. besseyi x P. salicina) Large, oval-conic fruit, 1 1/2 inches long; skin deep purple to black; flesh dark rich purple, firm, meaty, moderately juicy; pit small, nearly free; flavor sweet, pleasant; ripens in mid-August, hangs well on tree for up to 2 weeks. Useful mostly for processing; compares favorably with Sapa for jam; more productive than Sapa. Tree vigorous, develops naturally into a wide-spreading bush; bears heavy crops annually; requires a pollinator, such as Compass. BROOKS 1972; B4, F91T{SC}

Dura: Medium to large, oblong fruit; skin dark green, mottled with purple; flesh maroon-purple, crisp, tender, meaty, sweeter and less clingstone than Sapa; quality very good as dessert or canned; season late August to October. Bush low, spreading; very hardy; productive. Originated in Morden, Manitoba, Canada. BROOKS 1972; B47, K81, N24M

Hiawatha: Fruit fairly large, round; skin thin, mottled purple; flesh medium firm, juicy, fairly sweet, semi-freestone; usually ripens during mid-August. Rated first in its class in taste tests, being very good for culinary uses, especially jam. Bush fairly vigorous, spreading; like Sapa it suffers severe winter injury in some seasons, but makes a good recovery. F91T{SC}, N33

Kappa: Medium to large, spherical fruit; skin bluish-black; flesh dark red, sweet, processing quality excellent; ripens in midseason. Originated in Saskatoon, Saskatchewan, Canada by C.F. Patterson. Released in 1960 for home gardens. Derived from Sapa and Oka. BROOKS 1972; N24M

Manor: Medium-sized, roundish fruit; skin dull, dark reddish-purplish; flesh deep red to dark purple, meaty, tender, juicy, sweet; dessert quality very good, fair for canning; ripens in mid-August. Bush hardier and more upright than Sapa; very productive; particularly adapted to northern prairies. Originated in Morden, Manitoba, Canada. Introduced in 1945. ANDERSEN, BROOKS 1972; A65, B47, G1T, H85, K81, N24M, N26

Mansan: (P. besseyi x P. hortulana) Small, oval fruit; skin dark carmine with a heavy bloom; flesh greenish-yellow, firm, mildly subacid, pleasant; quality good for canning; ripens in early September. Tree resembles Compass but hardier; blooms late; to be productive requires a late-blooming cultivar for cross-pollination. BROOKS 1972; F91T{SC}

Oka: Medium-sized fruit, about 1 inch in diameter; skin tough, thick, deep purplish-red; flesh dark red, juicy, firm, quality good. Season from mid-August to early September. Dries naturally into a sweet prune-like fruit; later can be cooked into an excellent sweet sauce. Tree hardy; dwarf, height 4 to 6 feet; bears well. Plant with Sapa for cross-pollination. Originated in Brookings, South Dakota, by N.E. Hansen. Introduced in 1924. BROOKS 1972, HANSEN; B47, D76, E97, N24M

Opata: (P. besseyi x P. salicina) Medium to large fruit; skin dark reddish-purple with blue bloom, thin; flesh yellowish-greenish, firm, flavor very pleasant; stone very small; ripens in late August. Excellent for eating fresh or for jams, jellies, and pies. Vigorous, bush-like growth habit; hardy; bears heavily. Originated in Brookings, South Dakota. Introduced in 1908. Opata is Sioux for "bouquet". HANSEN, RONALD; A16, B47, G1T, G54, H85, J7, K81, N24M

Red Diamond: Fruit large, averaging up to 1 1/2 inches in diameter, maroon when ripe; flesh firm, ruby-red, smooth-textured, high in sugar; pit small and free-stone. Eaten fresh or preserved. Dwarf bush, maximum height 6 feet; bears second year after transplanting, cross-pollination recommended. Very hardy and disease resistant. *A74*, D65, G16

Red Orna: Small, red fruit; flesh red, juicy, sweet. Bush very hardy; an attractive ornamental with brilliant red foliage, and delicate red-pink blossoms; grows well in a variety of soils although sandier, lighter soils are preferred. Insects sometimes have trouble pollinating the small, delicate flowers. N24M

Sapa: (P. besseyi x P. salicina) Small to medium-sized fruit; skin purple-black with a bluish bloom; flesh dark purple, sweet, juicy, clingstone; excellent for canning and jam; ripens very early. Bush-like, compact growth habit, can be pruned to a small tree. Bears on 1 year old wood. Needs a pollinator for best production, Compass recommended. Hardy and productive. Introduced in 1908. CREASY 1982, HANSEN, RONALD; A65, B47, *C54*, E29M, E97, G1T, *G4*, H85, N24M, N26

Sapalta: Medium-sized fruit; skin red-purple; flesh almost black; similar to Sapa but sweeter and with a tendency toward a freestone condition. Ripens the end of July. Good in pies and preserves. Plant with Compass as a pollinator. Originated in Brooks, Alberta, Canada, by the Canadian Pacific Railway. Introduced in 1941. Probably a seedling of Sapa. *A74*, B4, D65, K64, L27M, L70, N24M

Skinner's Favorite: (P. besseyi x P. salicina) Medium-sized, oblong fruit; skin yellow with a purple-red cheek; flesh greenish-yellow; quality good for dessert, excellent for jam. Tree bushy, upright, averages 5 to 6 feet in height. Originated in Dropmore, Manitoba, Canada. BROOKS 1972; F91T{SC}

St. Anthony: (P. besseyi x P. salicina) Large, round fruit, slightly flattened at the base; skin dull purplish-red, medium thick; flesh dark rich red to very deep purple, fine-grained, very juicy, tender, medium firm, subacid; quality fair to good, especially fine for culinary use; ripens in midseason; resembles Sapa. Tree medium to small, upright-spreading, vigorous; bears early and prolifically; hardy. ANDERSEN, BROOKS 1972; F91T{SC}

Wessex: Good quality fruit; dries like a prune. Bush extremely hardy; highly productive; blooms late, escaping spring frosts. Originated in Moose Range, Saskatchewan, Canada by Percy H. Wright. BROOKS 1972; N24M

Winered: (P. besseyi x P. salicina) Medium-sized, round fruit; flesh dark purple, lacks the astringency of native Americana plums; good cooked and for dessert purposes, resembling Damson when cooked. Tree upright, to 5 feet tall; yields well. Originated in Dropmore, Manitoba, Canada. BROOKS 1972; F91T{SC}

CHESTNUT {GR}

CASTANEA SPP.

AMERICAN HYBRID CHESTNUTS

A group of cultivars that show a combination of the American and Chinese chestnut characteristics. Most have large, sweet, easily peeled nuts, blight resistance, upright tree form, ornamental foliage, and are highly productive. Many were developed by noted plant breeders Dr. Robert Dunstan of Greensboro, North Carolina and Earl Douglass of Red Creek, New York. (C. x sp.)

Alachua: Large, sweet, easy to peel nuts. Vigorous, upright, widely adapted tree; begins to bear in 2 to 4 years. Completely immune to chestnut blight. A mature orchard will produce from 1 to 2 tons per acre. Newly released Dunstan hybrid. Very similar to Carolina. C25

Appalachia: Large, sweet, easy to peel nuts. Large, vigorous, upright tree; begins to bear in 2 to 4 years. Completely immune to chestnut blight. Excellent for orcharding, backyard nut production, and landscaping. Newly released Dunstan hybrid. Very similar to Carolina. C25

Carolina: Large, very sweet, dark glossy chocolate-brown nuts; 24 to 28 per pound. Large, spreading, very productive tree. Completely immune to chestnut blight. Excellent for orcharding, backyard nut production, and landscaping. Good pollinator for Revival. A Dunstan hybrid. C25, F19M, I4, I49M

Carpentar: Large, spreading tree. Heavy production of large, very sweet, dark brown nuts. Completely immune to chestnut blight. Excellent for orcharding, backyard nut production, and landscaping. Named for James Carpentar of Salem, Ohio who sent budwood of a blight resistant American chestnut to noted breeder Dr. Robert Dunstan, in the early 1950's. C25

Douglass: A cross between the Manchurian strain of Chinese chestnut and blight resistant American chestnuts. They show occasional blight resistance, are quite hardy, and are more vigorous than either parent. Most are upright in growth habit. Excellent flavor. Hardy to -28^{0} F. A91{PL}, B99{PL}, E62{PL}, E62{PR}, E62{S}, E91M, E91M{PL}, N24M

Douglass #1: Medium sized nut with very good flavor. Kernels fill well. Good bearing qualities. Hardy. Similar to Douglas #1A. Originated in Red Creek, New York by Earl Douglass. E62{PR}, E62{SC}, E91M, E91M{OR}, I60{PL}

Douglass #1A: Large sized nut with a very good, sweet flavor. Early ripening. Good bearing qualities. Very hardy. Good overall blight resistance but not as much as other cultivars. A selection from open pollinated American and Manchurian crosses. E62{PR}, E62{SC}, E91M, E91M{OR}, I60{PL}

Etter: Chinese selections from American hybrids. Blight resistant. Fast growing. Upright in habit. E62{PL}, E62{PR}, E62{S}

Heritage: Tall, vigorous tree, very straight timber-type bole. Bears light crops of medium-sized, elongated, sweet nuts; 45 per pound. Completely immune to chestnut blight. Recommended for timber production, woodlot, and landscape plantings. A Dunstan hybrid. C25

Revival: Produces heavy, yearly crops of very large and sweet-tasting nuts. Nuts average 24 to 32 nuts per pound, compared to Chinese nuts (40 to 100 per pound) and American nuts (75 to 150 per pound). Pellicles are easily removed. Completely immune to chestnut blight. A Dunstan hybrid. The first chestnut ever to receive a U.S. plant patent. B75, C25, F19M, I4, I49M, L33

Sweet Hart: A cross between Dr. Ray Cather's West Virginia sweet chestnut and the Hawk Chinese blight resistant chestnut. Nuts have the sweet taste and high quality of the American chestnut. Found growing in an orchard in Ohio several years ago, the original tree is 40 years old without any signs of blight. Introduced by Boyd Nursery Co. *B52*{PL}, E97, H49

Willamette: Extremely large (18 to 22 per pound), sweet, easy-to-peel, reddish-brown nuts. Medium-sized, upright spreading tree; bears very heavy crops. Completely immune to chestnut blight. One of the best cultivars for commercial orcharding. A Dunstan hybrid. C25, I49M

CHINESE CHESTNUTS

Valued as a blight-resistant chestnut, the Chinese chestnut is resistant but not immune to the chestnut blight fungus and seedling trees vary in susceptibility. The nuts are generally considered less sweet than American or European chestnuts. Nuts do not store well. Mostly C. mollissima.

Abundance: Nut attractive; cleans well; sweet; larger and more prolific than Honan, which it resembles. Originated in Eagle Creek, Oregon by Carroll D. Bush. Introduced in 1941. BROOKS 1972; B99{PL}

Armstrong: Large nut, averages 30 to 35 per pound; kernel very sweet, of excellent quality. Possibly a hybrid of Chinese chestnut and American chestnut. Tree may show timber type growth. Originated in Kentucky. Introduced in 1980. I40

AU-Cropper: Nut large, averages 35 to 40 per pound. Tree bears early and regularly; 50 to 70 pounds per tree at 10 years of age, over 100 pounds when fully mature; hardy and blight resistant. Originated in Auburn, Alabama by Dr. Joseph Norton. *K76*

AU-Leader: Nut large, averages 35 to 40 per pound; flavor excellent; matures in late summer. Tree productive; hardy and disease resistant. Recommended for Zones 4 through 8. Originated in Auburn, Alabama by Dr. Joseph Norton. *K76*

Campbell #1: Large, sweet nut; falls free of the burr at the same time as Layeroka. Tree hardy; a consistent producer yet does not over produce as Layeroka sometimes does, reducing the nut size. Seedling of Layeroka selected by Doug Campbell of Ontario, Canada. A91, E91M, E91M{OR}

Ching Chow: Originated in Swarthmore, Pennsylvania by J. Russell Smith. Introduced about 1950. Seedlings of the Chinese chestnut, from seed originally brought from Nanking, China. Most trees are blight resistant. BROOKS 1972; J16{PL}

Crane: Nut averages about 32 per pound; shell dark-cherry red, nearly completely smooth; quality excellent; keeps exceptionally well. Tree blooms in midseason, with Nanking; both cultivars will cross-pollinate with one another; slightly protandrous; precocious bearer, producing a crop the second year after planting; blight resistant. Adapted to the middle and southern chestnut growing areas. BROOKS 1972; E41M{SC}, G75, I40{OR}

Eaton: Nut averages 30 to 40 per pound; texture, flavor and sweetness are among the very best; matures 3 to 7 days ahead of most Chinese seedlings and as much as 2 weeks ahead of Nanking, Orrin, and Crane. Tree precocious. Selected for its attractive, glossy foliage and ability to produce annual heavy crops of sweet, high quality nuts. Highly recommended for northern chestnut-growing areas. JAYNES; I25M{SC}, I40

Ford's Sweet: Small, sweet kernel that resembles American chestnut. Tree a heavy bearer; begins bearing in 3 to 4 years. Timber type growth. Good wildlife food. Complex hybrid of American, Japanese and Chinese chestnuts. Originated in Indiana. Introduced in 1980. I40

Gellatly #1: Nut sweet; falls free from the burr; fine spines on the burr are not as "prickly" as most others; ripens early, early to mid-September. Tree productive; hardy in Zone 5. From a population of seedlings selected by J.U. Gellatly. A91{PL}

Gellatly #2: Nut attractive; mainly free of the burr; quality good; ripens several days after Skookum and Gellatly #1. Tree very productive and hardy; tested for over 20 years. One of the better selections from a population of seedlings selected by J.U. Gellatly. Related to Skookum and Gellatly #1. A91{PL}

Henry VIII: Large, glossy, mahogany-colored, attractive nut; kernel yellowish in color; excellent nutty flavor and crunchy texture. Initial tree growth is rapid; then growth slows as the tree becomes a heavy bearer. Originated in Wayne, New Jersey by Henry Hartmann. G3M, G75

Jersey Gem: Nut large, glossy, mahogany-red in color, attractive; kernels rich yellow in color; flavor excellent, texture crunchy; matures the first week of October; 95% of the nuts ripen and drop within a one week period. Tree moderately vigorous; a reliable and heavy bearer; tends to yield large nuts regardless of the crop size. Originated in Wayne, New Jersey by Henry Hartmann. G3M

Kuling: Nut averages 35 to 40 per pound; drops free from burr; matures in midseason; keeping quality very good. Tree medium large; moderately upright; vigorous; shoot growth slightly willowy. Originated in Philema, Georgia by the USDA. Introduced in 1949. BROOKS 1972; **T41M**

Layeroka: Medium to large, attractive nut; falls free from the burr when ripe; kernel sweet; ripens in early October. Tree precocious; a reliable and heavy bearer; resistant to blight; very hardy; produces up to 4 burrs per cluster; erect timber type; male bloom sterile, will not pollinate other chestnuts. Originated in Westbank, British Columbia by J.U. Gellatly. A91, A91{PL}, B74, B74{PL}, B99, C34, E62{PR}, E62{SC}, E91M, I49M, I60{PL}, I74{PL}, J61M, K16{S}, L99M, N24M, etc.

Manoka: Large nut, averaging 1 3/8 inches in diameter; shell dark brown; kernel yellow, well flavored, quality good; husk small, thin. Tree hardy, timber type. Originated in Westbank, British Columbia, Canada by J.U. Gellatly. BROOKS 1972; I74{PL}

Meiling: Nut averages 35 to 40 per pound; drops free from burr; ripens midseason; good keeping quality. Tree vigorous; upright; shoot growth fairly stocky; early and heavy bearing. Originated in Philema, Georgia by the USDA. Introduced in 1949. BROOKS 1972; I40

Myoka: Nut large, averaging 1 3/8 inches in diameter; most fall free from the burr; flavor good; peels well; resembles Manoka; ripens slightly later than Layeroka. Tree large, vigorous; erect timber type; blight resistant; a good pollinator. Originated in Westbank, British Columbia by J.U. Gellatly. Introduced in 1950. BROOKS 1972; A91, B74, B74{PL}, C34, I49M, J61M

Nanking: Nut averages 30 to 43 per pound; shape uniform; dark tan in color; few with split shells; harvest season medium late. Tree vigorous; precocious, grafted trees frequently bearing in their second year; heavy bearer of annual crops, often producing a bushel or more of nuts at 10 years of age; midseason pollination. BROOKS 1972, JAYNES; G75, I40{OR}, I60{PL}

Orrin: Large nut, averages 32 per pound; shell attractive, with a dark-mahogany sheen, smooth but with a slightly hairy tip; middle nut of 3 in a burr uniformly thick and not wedge-shaped; keeping quality excellent; matures before Crane and Nanking. Tree blight resistant; upright; a precocious bearer; blooms slightly later than other cultivars. BROOKS 1972; E41M{SC}, G3M, G75, I40

Skioka: Large nut, averaging 1 5/8 inches in diameter and 35 nuts per pound; shell dark brown; not quite as free of the burr as Layeroka; kernel white, free from indentures, quality high; ripens 7 to 10 days after Layeroka. Tree hardy; produces up to 4 burrs per cluster and up to 3 nuts per burr; blooms late, the latter part of June or early July; timber type. Originated by J.U. Gellatly. BROOKS 1972; A91, A91{PL}, I74{PL}

Skookum: Nut attractive, glossy, of good size; falls free from the burr; kernel of good flavor; ripens early. Tree vigorous and productive; hardy to Zone 5; sheds its leaves early in the winter; erect timber form. Selected from a population of Gellatly seedlings as a superior cultivar. Tested for over 20 years. A91, A91{PL}, B74, B74{PL}, H81M, I49M, J61M

Sleeping Giant: Large, shiny, attractive nut; averages about 40 per pound; burr often slightly conical. Tree somewhat spreading; a consistent, heavy bearer; blight free; hardy; leaves large, wide, buff-colored beneath, very glossy above. Complex hybrid of Chinese, Japanese, and American chestnuts. Originated in New Haven, Connecticut by Arthur H. Graves. Introduced in 1960. BROOKS 1972, JAYNES; A91, A91{PL}, I40{OR}

Wards: Nut averages 45 per pound; kernel yellowish, sweet, of high quality; ripens fairly early, September 15 to 20. Tree intermediate in form between the American and Chinese chestnut, very vigorous. From the same breeding line that produced Sleeping Giant, Clapper and others. Rarely seen and well worth growing. A91, A91{PL}

EUROPEAN CHESTNUTS

Produces large, sweet nuts, the kind most often found in supermarkets. Susceptible to the chestnut blight fungus, but planted trees survive outside the natural range of the American chestnut in the Midwest and western United States where they usually escape infestation. More heat tolerant than other chestnuts. Mostly C. sativa.

Canby Black: Large, spreading tree. Nuts are large and very flavorful and peel easily. The mother tree, in Canby, Oregon annually produces 400 to 450 pounds of nuts. C34

Colossal: Nut very large, with the larger ones averaging 11 per pound; skin rather thick, but easy to peel; drops free from the burr; kernel texture fine, very sweet; dries and stores well; ripens late September and early October. Tree vigorous; bears heavily. Originated in Nevada City, California by C.E. Parsons, Felix Gillet Nursery. Introduced in 1925. BROOKS 1972; B74, B74{PL}, B93M{PL}, E4{PL}, I49M, I83M, I83M{PL}, L1{PL}, L99M, N0

Eurobella: Large, sweet nuts that are easily peeled. Suitable for all purposes. Requires 400 hours of chilling. Pollinate with European seedlings. New selection from an established northern California orchard. Introduced by Dave Wilson Nursery. A88M, *N20*

Marron de Lyon: (Lyon) Large, round, light-colored nut of excellent flavor. Tree bears at an early age. Originated in France and was introduced into California before 1880. P86

Prolific: Large, spreading tree; produces medium to large nuts annually in great abundance. Not blight resistant. Not recommended for blight susceptible areas such as the eastern United States. B74, B74{PL}

Silver Leaf: Nut large, slightly smaller than Colossal; easy to peel; flavor sweet. Tree a consistent and annual bearer. As the crop matures, the underside of the leaves turn an attractive silver-gray. Of French parentage. Dropped by I99M

CHICORY {S}

CICHORIUM INTYBUS

HEADING CHICORY

These form large, conical heads, not unlike a cos lettuce in appearance. The inner leaves are naturally blanched through lack of exposure to light and are therefore sweeter than the outer leaves, though the "sweetness" is only relative. LARKCOM 1984.

Bianca di Milano:[1] A Sugarloaf type chicory. Forms a crisp, dense, elongated head with dark-green outer leaves and a creamy-white heart; nearly self-blanching. Harvested in autumn and winter from a late spring to early summer sowing. Can also be used as a cut-and-come-again crop, being cut when about 2 inches tall. Relatively cold hardy. B8, L86, P83M, S55

Crystal Hat: Long oval heads, similar to cos or romaine lettuce in appearance. High yielding and of easy culture. Can be sown as early as the soil can be prepared and every few weeks until August. Withstands summer heat and fall frosts. Rinsing in warm water removes all traces of bitterness and reveals a sweet, tangy flavor. I39

Dolce Bianca: (Dolce Bianca a Cuore Pieno) 85 days. Large, broad, romaine-like head with a full, crisp, golden heart and an attractive flavor. Similar to Sugarloaf, but with broader heads and a deeper, fuller heart. Very early, being ready for harvest by the end of summer. K66, L91M, Q11M

Greenloaf: (Groenlof) A Sugarhat type chicory. Combines the qualities of endive and witloof. Can be used raw in salads or cooked like endive. Sow May through June for a harvest in the fall. C85M

Poncho: (Pain de Sucre Race Poncho) Large, cylindrical, compact heads; thick, crisp outer leaves; tender inner leaves naturally blanch to a whitish-green color. Exceptionally good flavor. Height 12 to 14 inches. Excellent eaten cooked or in salads, like endive. K66, P59M

Snowflake: (Winter Fare) 75 days. Produces 2 to 3 pound, crisp, tight heads in late autumn and winter from a June or July sowing. Easy to grow, no forcing or blanching needed. Very cold resistant and will keep for a full 3 months. L91M

Sugarhat: (Zuckerhut) 85 days. Elongated oval heads, similar to cos or romaine lettuce; weight 2 pounds. Leaves are tender with a sweet, yet slightly tangy flavor. Sow in early spring, and again every few weeks for continuous greens. Stands summer heat and fall frosts. Stores well in a cool place. G51, Q34

Sugarloaf: (Pan di Zucchero, Pain de Sucre) 90 days. Large, upright, slightly twisted, romaine-like head; 18 to 20 inches tall; self-blanching. Thick, crunchy, medium-green outer leaves; translucent inner leaves that form a crisp, tender heart with a very mild flavor. Normally harvested in autumn and winter. Use in salads, for wrapping meats, or in other vegetable combinations. B8, C53, D11M, G51, H49, J7, J73, P83M, R47, S45M, S55, S61

LOOSE-LEAF CHICORY

CATALOGNA Also known as *asparagus chicory* or *radichetta*. Distinguished by their long, relatively thick leaf stalks, and in some cultivars an enlarged flower stalk. A87M, C44, C92, G51, G64, G71, G93M, I39, I67M, J7, J20, K49M, K73, L42, M13M, M46, etc.

Baxter's Special: 70 days. A San Pasquale type selected for darker green color and better plant uniformity and vigor. For market growers who demand a heavy, attractive, thick-leaved catalogna. *A1*, J84

Dentarella: Produces a crop of thick, succulent flowering stems or *puntarelle*. Similar to Puntarella but with a straighter stem. C53

Foglia Dentellata a Costa Larga Bianca: Long, relatively broad, medium-green leaf blades; deeply and irregularly serrated, the lower parts with long, narrow teeth. Broad, fleshy, pure-white, celery-like leaf stalks. Excellent for winter crops. Q11M

Foglia Liscia: Unusual long and narrow leaves, up to 1 1/2 feet. Leaf blades 3 inches in diameter at their widest point. Resembles celery or Swiss chard with its thick, 3/4 inch wide midrib at the base. J73

Foglia Verde Frastagliata: Long, narrow-bladed, irregularly lobed, medium-green leaves. Long, relatively thin and narrow, greenish-white leaf stalks. Spreads 8 to 10 inches across. Strongly bitter flavor. Used in mixed salads, as a cooked green or in stuffings. B8, Q11M

Galatina: (Di Galatina, Abruzzese) Grown mostly for its thick, twisted flowering shoots or *puntarelle*, which are harvested when young and tender in late winter and early spring. Delicious either raw or cooked. B8, Q11M

Pugliese: Long, narrow, dark green leaves; lobed and indented, with pronounced white midribs. Large, broad leaf-stalks, straight and elongated. Utilized for the leaves and stalks in autumn and winter, and for the twisted, flowering shoots or *puntarelle* in the spring. *O60*

Puntarella: (Puntarelle a Pigna) Grown primarily for the chunky *puntarelle* or flowering shoots which develop in spring and have a much-prized flavor, raw or cooked. The twisted shoots are ready about the same time as asparagus. Young leaves can be used in salads. Grows 12 to 18 inches tall. LARKCOM 1984; C53, K66

San Pasquale: (All Seasons) 70 days. Very early strain of Catalogna chicory. Large, vigorous, very productive plant; up to 22 inches across; quickly forms large, compact rosettes that blanch in the center. Broad, light green, deeply cut, dandelion-like leaves; very thick and meaty, yet tender. Grown for early spring greens. Will occasionally produce flowering shoots. *A1*, A87M, C92, *D12*, G79, G82, H54, *L59G*, M29

Small Rooted: 65 days. Similar to the typical Catalogna, except the plant has slightly notched, light-green leaves, and a small taproot. The young leaves make excellent "greens" and are very desirable for use as a salad. G93M

Special: 55 days. Long, deep-green, slender, deeply cut leaves with white midribs. Can be harvested "baby size" 3 or 4 weeks after transplanting, or left to grow into heavy 18 inch tall bunches. Slow bolting. G6

OTHERS

Barbe de Capucin: (Barba di Capuccino, Barbi, Italian Rooted) Long, deeply-cut, dandelion-like leaves. Very little improved or identical to the wild chicory. Young leaves are shredded and used as "greens". Can also be treated in much the same way as witloof, but must be forced in soil. C53, G51, G68

Biondissima di Trieste:[1] (Di Trieste, Bionda di Triestino, Triestino da Taglio) A green cutting chicory very popular in late summer and fall in northern Italy. The smooth, rounded leaves are harvested when very young and tender, only 3 or 4 inches long. Regrows rapidly. Ideal for mesclun or other salad mixes. If thinned to 6 inches, small heads will form in early winter. LARKCOM 1984; B8, C53, K66, P83M, S55

Grumolo Verde: (Grumolo, Ceriolo, Ceriolo Verde) A rugged chicory from the Piedmont region of Italy; will withstand poor soil conditions and extremely low temperatures. Sow from June to October for a seedling crop. If cutting stops in late summer, very early the next spring the plant will form jade-green, ground-hugging rosettes of perfectly shaped leaves. Rather bitter, but blends well in salad mixes. LARKCOM 1984 [Cu]; B8, C53, F24, I39, I77, K66, P83M, S55

Grumolo Verde Scuro: (Grumolo Dark Green) Semi-heading type, with a compact, upright center. Forms attractive rosettes of deep green, rounded leaves with white ribs and veining. Harvested like lettuce for use in salads. Popular in Italy; not often grown in the United States. F80, *O60*

Improved Wild: Highly distinct cultivar with very broad, light green leaves whose bases are wrapped around each other. Can be sown outside from April to August. Does not produce a large head in the spring but numerous leaves, the inner ones occasionally blanching themselves somewhat. E83T

Selvatico di Campo: Long, deeply cut, dandelion-like leaves; very similar to Barba di Capuccino. Strong bitter taste. Mature plants are usually blanched to develop a milder flavor. Also grown for spring greens or as part of a mesclun mix. C53, Q11M

Spadona:[1] (Spadona da Taglio, Lingua di Cane, Dog's Tongue Chicory) Vigorous growing, cutting type chicory. Smooth, narrow-bladed, pale green leaves; lightly and irregularly toothed; fairly bitter. Best harvested when 4 to 6 inches tall. Extremely cold hardy. Plant in spring or fall. B8, C53, G51

RADICCHIO

Also called *red chicory* or red-leaved chicory. The deep-burgundy forms such as Rossa di Verona are often called radicchio rosso, radicchio being the generic Italian name for chicory. Very popular and expensive specialty market item. Can be substituted for Witloof or endive in most recipes. HAWKES, SCHNEIDER [Pre, Re].

FORCING These cultivars can be forced indoors, in the dark, like Witloof chicory. In extremely cold areas this may be the only means of obtaining a winter crop, as the plants would be killed if left outside.

Early Treviso: Selected from Treviso for more precocious growth. Can be seeded in mid-July, after the days have begun to shorten noticeably, and is therefore less likely to bolt. If heads do not form by Labor Day, it should be cut back to an inch above the crown at the beginning of cool weather. C53

Rossa di Treviso:[2] (Treviso, Red Treviso, Rouge de Trevise) Initially green and bitter during hot weather, it is cut back and its second growth produces attractive bright red, cone-shaped heads with pure-white central ribbing and leaf veins. Roots can be forced to produce pale pink chicons. Slightly less hardy than Rossa di Verona. Historically the first red chicory was a Treviso type, developed in the 16th century. B8, C53, E24, E49, F44, G51, G64, G68, I39, I67M, J73, K49M, L91M, M13M, P83M, etc.

Rossa di Verona: (Verona Red, Rouge de Verone) Produces bright red, very tight heads with prominent white midribs and veins. Very cold hardy. Also suitable for forcing and can be grown as a seedling crop. The best known of all the radicchios, and perhaps the most difficult to grow successfully. Recommended for northern areas. B49, C44, C53, D87, E49, F24, F33, G51, G64, G68, I67M, K66, M13M, M46, P83M, etc.

NON-FORCING Generally not adapted to indoor forcing. Some of the newer types will also form full-sized heads outdoors without cutting back.

Adria: 75 days. An improved Marina or Chioggia type. Small, globe-shaped heads; average 3 to 4 inches across and 7 to 10 ounces at maturity. Deep burgundy-red leaves with bright white midribs and leaf veins. Sharp, nutty flavor and tender-crisp texture. Produces 60% marketable heads. Does not tolerate heat; needs cool fall weather for proper color development. *A1*, A13, H95, L42, M29

Alto: 67 days. A heavy, relatively uniform cultivar with good heat tolerance. Similar to Augusto, with larger heads. Promising for spring, summer and fall crops. Fall frost resistance not adequately tested. G6

Augusto: 70 days. Medium-sized, round, deep burgundy-red head; slightly larger than Giulio. One of the most frost tolerant cultivars. Also has good bolting and heat resistance. Produces 85% fully formed heads from a spring sowing compared to only 30 to 40% for Verona types. Can also be planted mid to late summer for a fall harvest. G6, K50, N81

Castelfranco: (Variegata di Castelfranco) Large, crinkled outer leaves; green blotched with red. Inner leaves loose, marbled red and white. Heads are looser than Verona types, but less likely to bolt. Produces well without cutting back. Developed in the 18th century in the Castelfranco region of northern Italy, probably from strains of Treviso and an escarole. B8, C53, F80, G51, K49M, K66, L86, L91M, M13M, Q34, S55

Cesare: 90-100 days. An early Verona type with a high degree of uniformity. Produces small, medium round heads with deep burgundy leaves and white midribs. Tender-crisp texture and mildly bitter flavor. Should be planted later than Giulio, in July, for harvesting in September and October. G71, K50, K66, N81

Chioggia: (Variegata di Chioggia) A red and white variegated, heading type developed from Castelfranco lines. Forms a tighter head than Castelfranco. Foliage is green in summer, becoming variegated in cold weather. Not suitable for forcing. Plant in late summer for a fall and early winter crop. Grows well in sandy coastal soils. B8, G64, I39, I67M, I77, J73, P83M, S55

Giulio: 80 days. An early strain, selected from the Verona type. Produces very uniform, compact, round heads with attractive burgundy leaves and pure-white midribs. Easier to grow than other radicchios; will form full-sized heads without cutting back. Can be succession planted throughout the summer but performs best when seeded in late spring for a mid-summer harvest. Bolt resistant. C53, D11M, D68, F13, F44, G6, I77, K50, K66

Marina: (Chioggia Race Marina) 100 days. Large, compact, solid, bright-red heads variegated with white; weight 8 to 12 ounces each. Good sharp flavor. Easily grown. Sow May through June for a fall harvest; plants may bolt if sown too early. B75, F33, G93M, T1M

Palla Rossa: An earlier Verona type, suitable for spring planting. Produces dark green outer leaves which protect the red interior head. Pure white midribs. Larger, looser heads than Giulio; paler in color.

Can also be planted anytime during the summer, but protect from intense heat. A good alternative to Rossa di Verona. C53, F24, F80, G64, G68, I77, K66, L86

Palla Rossa Precoce: (Palla Rossa Zorzi Precoce) Semi-compact, solid heart, turning red at maturity. An early strain of Palla Rossa with large heads. Red Verona type. B8, E5T, J7

Ronette: 80 days. Nicely closed or rounded head with an intense red color and white veins. Cool September nights improve the flavor. Produces 55% marketable heads; average weight 8 ounces. L42

Silla: A newer cultivar, adapted for early spring planting under row covers. A high percentage will head up without bolting even during a late spring hot spell. Produces deep red heads the size of tennis balls with pure-white midribs and leaf veins. Small, green outer leaves. Compact growth habit permits very close spacing. C53, I77, K50, N81

Sottomarina: (Variegata di Sottomarina) An unusual and very attractive radicchio. Forms large, loose heads that become red speckled with white when mature. Outer leaves are variegated with green and red. Use individual leaves or entire heads. Plant in early spring or late summer. An old cultivar named after the coastal town just south of Venice. B8, S55

Violette: An attractive cultivar that produces medium-sized, deep red heads with white ribs. The quality is best when sown in summer for an autumn harvest. Excellent, robust flavor. F13

ROOT CHICORY

Chiavari: (Di Chiavari) Grown primarily for its root, although the leaves are also used and have a good flavor. The root is thick-collared, creamy white and uniform. Grows over a long season, from early spring until late fall. To prepare, scrape and boil the root until tender. Slice thinly and serve with vinaigrette, or it can be rolled in bread crumbs, deep fried and served with lemon and parsley. K66

Magdeburg: (Large Rooted Magdeburg, Cicoria Siciliana) 120 days. Large, thick, tapered root; 12 to 14 inches long, 2 inches in diameter below the neck; can be cooked like carrots at about 65 days. Mature roots are dried and employed for the manufacture of *coffee chicory*; also used for forcing like Barbe de Capucin. Erect, undivided leaves can be harvested for "greens" at about 65 days. VILMORIN; A2, C17M{PR}, C44, C85M, D11M, E81M, G93M, H3M{PL}, J73, J82, J82{PR}, K49M, L42, L97, M13M, N81, etc.

Soncino: (Radison) Long, narrow roots with creamy white skin and flesh; rather bitter. May be harvested anytime from autumn until the following spring. Popular in Italy where it is considered very healthful and is cooked and eaten in many ways. B8, Q11M

WITLOOF

Also known as ***Belgian endive***, ***French endive*** or ***chicons***. These are grown for their blanched shoots which develop after the root is forced. They are tender and crisp with a typical bitter, aromatic taste. Popular specialty market item. A16, A69M, B75, C85M, D11M, E7M, G51, G71, H49, J20, J73, K73, M13M, M46{PL}

HYBRID

Bea: A Zoom type, with improved ease of utilization. Produces a high percentage of very fine quality chicons. Recommended for forcing without soil or cover from mid-September to mid-April, in particular for a harvest in November-December and February to April. One of the most popular cultivars in France. J7, *R11M*, S95M

Jaz: Produces well-closed, globular heads of good size and quality. Recommended for forcing from January to April at temperatures of 60 to 65^0 F. Suitable for both traditional culture and growing without soil or cover. P59M

Toner: 130 days. Easy to grow and force, by either the traditional method or without soil and cover. Rather short, firm, well-closed chicons of the highest quality. Tested as being the least fussy cultivar for home production. Very early. May be sown mid-April to mid-May for forcing the end of August to the end of September at temperatures of 68 to 75^0 F. G6, P59M, *R11M*

Zoom: 110 days. Developed in France for forcing without being covered. The roots only need to be placed in a cool, dark place for sprouting to begin. Can be set in soil, moist perlite, or water, using trays or pails. Produces small, thick, firm, well-closed chicons of excellent quality. Approximately 21 days from the start of forcing to harvest. Productive and uniform. ^{0} B75, C53, C85M, F33, G64, K50, N81, P59M, *R11M*, S95M, T1M

OPEN-POLLINATED

Alba: Produces large quantities of thick, attractive chicons. Good for forcing during cold weather; not suitable for warm weather forcing, the maximum temperature being about 62^0 F. Not recommended for forcing outside of soil or without cover. An excellent cultivar for home gardeners. P59M

Flash: An early to midseason cultivar, usually sown mid-May to mid-June and harvested from early September to November. Roots are forced from December to April, at temperatures ranging from 60 to 68^0 F. Flash produces uniform, well-closed chicons. K50, N81, *R11M*

Lubert: A very uniform cultivar that produces well closed chicons. Suitable for both midseason and late forcings. K50

Meilof: A late maturing cultivar, about 2 months later than standard witloof in outdoor forcing. May also be used for late forcing indoors. C85M

Mitado: A new witloof cultivar that is a real breakthrough in growing ease. Sow in the open in May, lift roots in late autumn, provide warmth and moisture for 1 to 3 weeks and you can begin to harvest. Developed in Germany. I39

Robin:[2] Produces shoots that are a reddish-pink color after forcing, the first pink Belgian endive. Very good quality. Has good potential as a specialty market item. Suitable for forcing without soil or cover from October to January. Optimal temperature about 55^0 F. C53, P59M

Spectra: Heavy, firm, well-closed heads; resistant to internal browning. Very high yields of top quality chicons. Can be used for both early and late harvests. Especially well suited for growing in water. *R11M*

Trilof: A special market strain with uniform, 6 inch long heads. For forcing indoors or outside. Previously listed as Productiva in the William Dam catalog. C85M

Witloof Improved: 110 days. An outstanding strain that may be used for commercial forcing in home gardens. Heads are similar in appearance to cos lettuce but much shorter. When forced for winter it produces very uniform heads, about 5 to 6 inches in length. F33, K20, L42

CHINESE CABBAGE {S}

BRASSICA RAPA PEKINENSIS GROUP

HEADING

MICHIHLI TYPE The head is in the form of an upright cylinder, 18 to 24 inches in height with the leaves held erect, not noticeably overlapping at the apex. In China, heads are commonly tied to encourage blanching of the heart.

Hybrid

Green Rocket: 50 days. Vigorous and extremely uniform; 4 to 5 pound heads are 18 inches tall, cylindrical and tightly folded, with deep-green leaves and an appealing white interior. Tolerant to most diseases. Sweet, crisp and tender; perfect in salads and stir-fried dishes. Excellent for spring or fall gardens. D11M, J7, M46, N81, *S63M*

Jade Pagoda: 68 days. Cylindrical heads average 16 inches tall by 6 inches in diameter with medium-green, crisp outer leaves and a creamy yellow heart; weight 6.6 pounds. Upright in habit; suitable for close planting. Vigorous and slow to bolt. Resistant to bacterial soft rot and virus. Michihli type that is earlier in maturity and lower in plant height, with more uniformity. *A1*, A13, F13, G64, G82, H54, *H61*, I91, J7, J14{PL}, J34, J84, *K16M*, K22, K73, L42, M29, etc.

Monument: 75 days. Michihli type. Taller and much later than Jade Pagoda; slower to bolt. Glossy green outer leaves; excellent uniformity. Plants average 17 inches high and 8 inches in diameter with firm, well-folded heads. Leaves and ribs have some tolerance to specking. Heavy yields. Mild flavor. *A1*, I77, K73, L42, M29, N81, *S63M*

Open-Pollinated

Chihli: 75 days. Tall, cylindrical, very solid heads; height up to 22 inches, width 5 inches. Broad, dark-green, well fringed outer leaves with white midribs; quality very good. Popular on the East Coast. Can be trimmed for market, still leaving a long, cylindrical head. Upright growth permits closer planting. A69M, D27, G57M, G67M, K20, K27M, L97

Michihli: 80 days. Tall, cylindrical heads average 18 inches high and 4 inches in width; long and slightly tapering to a point; crisp, tender, and tightly folded. Outer leaves are dark green with white ribs. Very good flavor. Heads blanch well, but do not store for long periods like the hybrid types. Standard commercial cultivar. A87M, B75M, B78, C44, D87, E24, F82, G16, G71M, *H61*, H66, K73, L59, M13M, N16, etc.

Sho-Sai: 86 days. Large, sweet Michihli type with bright green outer leaves, yellow green tops, and white hearts. Best sown in fall or winter. Good for salads, stir-fried dishes and pickling. K66

NAPA TYPE The head is round and compact with the leaves usually overlapping at the apex. Some have a flat top, similar to a drumhead cabbage, others have a more or less pointed head.

Hybrid

Blues: 50 days. An attractive early cultivar with disease resistance. Matures with Nagoda #50, is more vigorous, and has stronger bolt resistance. Firm, well-wrapped heads; good quality. Resists downy mildew, alternaria, soft rot, and some viruses. Sow early spring through July. *A1*, G6, *L79G*, M29, N52, *S63M*

China Doll: 64 days. Large, oval heads, 8 to 9 inches tall; medium green leaves, slightly less ruffled than others; excellent stir-fried or as a delicately flavored coleslaw. Exceptionally tolerant to heat; very slow to bolt to seed. Especially recommended for spring sowing. F13

China Express: 64 days. Medium to large, solid, barrel-shaped heads; average weight 5 pounds; medium light-green leaves. Slow to bolt. Suitable for spring sowing in temperate climates. May also be grown in a greenhouse in northern areas. Earlier, slightly smaller version of China Pride with more tip-burn tolerance. *A1*, *F72*, J84, *K16M*, *L79G*, L89, N52, N81

China King: 80 days. Very large, 7 to 9 pound barrel-shaped heads are well folded and their eating quality is excellent. Bred for the main crop harvest of early autumn; can stand in the field until winter gets fairly severe. Club root resistant. D11M, G64, *L79G*, *S75M*

China Pride: 68 days. Large, blocky barrel-shaped heads, average weight 5 1/2 pounds; bright green leaves. Tolerant to many types of diseases including downy mildew, bacterial soft rot, and tip burn. Semi bolt-resistant. An excellent main crop Napa type for summer and fall production in cool areas. *A1*, I77, K10, *K16M*, L42, *L79G*, M29, N81, S61

Nagoda #50: 50 days. Versatile, early cultivar; tolerant of cool spring weather and summer heat. Medium-sized, 3 to 4 pound heads are of the preferred barrel shape. Leaves pale yellowish-green, very tender and crisp; quality good. Sow April through July. G6

Nerva: 46 days. Remarkable earliness and strong bolt resistance combined. Rectangular, 10 inch well closed heads are very heavy for their size. Densely packed, with thick, juicy leaves preferred for stir-fried dishes and pickling. Sow early spring through May. G6, L89, P69

Tropical Pride: 55 days. Vigorous, uniform grower. Very firm, oval-shaped heads, about 10 inches tall; average weight 3 to 4 pounds; medium green leaves; ideal for salads and sandwiches. Resistant to heat. Grows well during the winter in tropical and sub-tropical areas. *E53M*, E83T, G27M, L59, *L79G*

Two Seasons: (Burpee's Two Seasons) 62 days. Very large, oval heads 10 inches tall by 7 1/2 inches wide. Crisp, tender, tightly crinkled leaves and thick, succulent midribs with a sweet, tangy flavor. Holds up well in warm weather; resists bolting. Especially recommended for spring sowing; equally good for fall. Very resistant to soft rot. Keeps well. B75, D11M, L91M, Q34

Open-Pollinated

Aichi: (Shantung Heading) Medium to large, round heads; weight 10 to 12 pounds; blanch easily. Thick, smooth, light green leaves. Good resistance to bolting. Sow July through August. A popular early cultivar introduced into Japan in 1875 from Shantung Province, China. The Aichi group of cultivars was derived from the Santo type. G33

Chang Puh Extra Early: Distinctive type with crinkled, deep green, very smooth, almost shiny leaves. Does not form a large head, but grows quickly in summer weather and is very attractive with its contrasting dark green leaves and very white midribs. Cultivated extensively in Taiwan for export. E83T

Chihfu: (Chefoo) 65 days. Forms medium-large, oval shaped heads; very crisp and solid; pale green to creamy white interior with darker green outer leaves. Grows 10 to 11 inches high and 6 to 7 inches in diameter; weighs 6 to 7 pounds. Winter hardy, and has good storage and transportation qualities. O53M, *P39*

Kyoto No. 3: (Kaga) 70 days. Very large, globular head; 12 inches high and 8 to 9 inches in diameter; weighs 14 to 16 pounds. Well blanched; crisp and tender; outer leaves medium-green colored. Winter hardy and tolerant of virus diseases. Sow in late summer or early spring. C85M, E49, J73, *P39*

Lettucy Type:[1] 45 days. A tall, open-topped Chinese cabbage resembling a large romaine lettuce. The cylindrical heads reach 11 to 12 inches and about 3 pounds very early, with a ruffly appearance and a creamy yellow blanched interior. Leaves are thin, crisp, and of excellent salad quality. Potential specialty market item. Sow May through late summer. G6

Market Pride: 70 days. The standard Japanese autumn market type with light green, well-crinkled outer leaves and pure white hearts. Heads are cylindrical and weigh about 4 pounds. Sow in July. O53M

Matsushima: 80 days. Very dark green outer leaves enclose a round head of light-colored folded over leaves, shaped more like a European cabbage than a typical Chinese cabbage; weight 5 pounds. Quick growing. Sow late June to early July. E83T

Nozaki Early: Light green, compact, barrel-shaped heads; weight 3 to 4 pounds. One of the earliest and most dependable open-pollinated cultivars, suited to earlier sowing than most. Usually does not make as dense a head as hybrids. Sow mid-June through July. A2, F44, R47

Orient Express: 43 days. Small, solid, oblong heads; 6 inches long, 4 1/2 inches in diameter; average weight 22 ounces; well-blanched leaves with a crisp texture and a pleasant, slightly pungent flavor. Very early and heat resistant; holds extremely well in hot weather. B75

Shantung: 60 days. Early, semi-heading cultivar of spreading habit. Heads weigh 4 to 5 pounds, have dense interior leaves that blanch well, and are upright when mature. Outer leaves are light green, smooth and tender. Sow in summer. L59, O53M, *P39*

Shuho Napa: 80 days. Dark green, rounded head that is mild, tender, and succulent. Each head may reach 7 pounds. Leaves crinkled, few in number. Resistant to viruses, rots and mildew. Moderately bolt resistant. Medium tolerance to cold and drought. For autumn crops. K66

South China Earliest: 45 days. Very tender, compact head; 10 to 11 inches tall and about 4 1/2 inches wide at the upper portion; somewhat pointed at the base; weighs about 14 ounces. creamy white colored overall. Resistant to severe summer heat and well tolerant of stormy weather. Sow July to September. E49, J73, *P39*

NON-HEADING

Chin-Tau: 30 days. Fast growing loose-leaved type similar to Santo and Tokyo Bekana. Very easy to grow. An excellent vegetable for stir-fry cooking. D55

Fong-Sun: 30 days. Quick growing loose-leaved type similar to Santo and Chin-Tau. Very easy to grow. One of the most popular garden vegetables in Taiwan. D55

Green Seoul: 35 days. Tall, upright-growing loose-leaf type with long white ribs. Very slow bolting; can be planted in spring, summer and fall. Disease tolerant. Outer leaves can be harvested after 30 days. When mature, it weighs up to 2 pounds. Used in soup, kimchi and as a raw or cooked green. Very popular for short-term kimchee making. Developed in Korea as a selection from the oldest and most important cultivar Gaeseong. *Q3*

Hiroshimana: 75 days. A popular old cultivar of Hiroshima Prefecture, Japan. Leaves are smooth, very wide and rounded, dark-green in color with bluish-white midribs and nearly parallel veins. Succulent, with a unique mild flavor for which it is highly prized. Mostly used for winter cropping and for pickling. E83T, *P39*

Kireba Santo: Very tall, upright, semi-heading plant. Light green outer leaves, toothed at the edges. Produces blanched inner leaves in a similar manner to Ohgon. Grows best in warm summer weather. Thinnings can be eaten after 3 or 4 weeks. E83T

Maruba Santo: 50 days. Fast growing loose heads of smooth, round, light-green leaves with wide crisp white ribs. Leaf blades are very thin, crisp and tender. Can be picked at any stage giving a continual harvest like Swiss chard. Suitable for planting all year round, being especially adapted to tropical and sub-tropical climates. *P39*, *S70*

Ohgon: 70 days. Upright, semi-heading plant, to 15 inches tall; weight 3 to 4 pounds. Light green outer leaves, slightly ruffled at the edges. Produces blanched inner leaves with a rich yellowish-cream color. Can be sown all season long. E83T

Ohi-Maruha Santoh: A non-heading, loose-leaved type with yellowish green leaves and white ribs. Soft and mild taste. For fresh market. Grows fast and very easily. Q88

Round-Leaved Santo: (Round-Leaved Santung) 50 days. Large, erect, fast-maturing plants are non-heading, cold resistant and very easy to grow. The leaves are broad and smooth, medium-green in color, and have white ribs. Quality is very high, either raw or cooked. Sow in spring or fall. D55, L59, *L79G*, M46, O53M, *S63M*

Santo: (Santoh) 60 days. Smooth, serrated, bright green leaves with white ribs. Grows 14 to 16 inches high. Plant where warmth and plenty of moisture can be provided. Sensitive to hot summer sun; sow in spring or fall in most locations. Very old cultivar, introduced into Japan from Shantung Province, China. I77, J73

Semi-Heading Large Type Santo: 60 days. Tall, semi-heading Santo strain; height 20 to 22 inches. Interior leaves yellow to cream colored; outer leaves waved, serrate, of light-green color with wide white ribs of tender quality. Well adapted to cool culture; seed sown in late summer. J73, *P39*

Serrated-Leaved Santo: (Santoh Frilled) Similar to Round-Leaved Santo except the leaves are attractively fringed or serrated. Mild, somewhat sweet flavor. Very hardy; bolts May 1st from a February planting in mild-winter areas. L89, N84, O53M, P83M, Q34, S55

Shirona: Has a broad leafstalk similar to Swiss Chard, which may be eaten separately from the rest of the leaf. Very tender with a delicate but rich flavor. Fast growing vegetable good for catch cropping. Grown extensively in Japan for greens. J73

Tokyo Bekana: 30 days. Very fast growing, to 12 inches high; tender, yellowish-green leaves with frilled edges; flat, white petioles. Does well when planted spring through fall. Cold resistant. Very popular in Japan and Taiwan. D55, *S70*

COLLARD {S}

BRASSICA OLERACEA ACEPHALA GROUP

HYBRID

Blue Max: 68 days. Deep blue-green leaves; slightly crinkled for a unique appearance; larger, denser and more attractive than conventional collards; very good flavor. Very uniform and disease tolerant; widely adapted. Up to 30% higher yielding than Vates. Suitable for fresh markets, home gardens and processing. Introduced in 1982 by Abbott and Cobb. *A1*, F19M, *H57M*, H94, J34, M29

Heavi-Crop: 65 days. A hybrid Vates type with superior vigor and performance. The large, smooth, medium blue-green leaves are closely spaced on the stem and carry more leaf surface down the petioles. Early, very uniform plants are more disease tolerant and recover faster when cut. Up to 30% higher yielding than Vates. Bolt resistance comparable to Champion. *A1*, F19M, *F72*, M29, *S63M*

Hi-Crop: 68 days. Very uniform, slightly crinkled, blue-green leaves; hold their color better than other types; good texture, even in hot weather; mild, sweet flavor. Vigorous, heavy-yielding, upright plants; height 15 inches; clean growth habit; closely spaced internodes. Highly resistant to bolting. Replacing Vates as the standard collard. *A1*, *F72*, I91, L91M, M46, *S63M*

Top Bunch: 71 days. Tall, semi-erect plant; broad, deep-green, slightly wavy leaves. Highly productive, excellent for both home garden and local market sales. Vigorous, rapid regrowth. Generally earlier, more uniform and less susceptible to bolting than open pollinated types. *A1*, *C28*, *F72*, G27M, *K16M*

OPEN-POLLINATED

Cabbage: 70 days. A heading collard with cabbage-like characteristics. Produces very hard, compact, dark-green heads on short stems; height 24 to 28 inches; light-green midribs and leaf veins. Combines the flavors of collards and cabbage. Hardier than cabbage. Very slow bolting, will stand 3 weeks longer than Georgia. *C28*, F19M, *G1M*

Carolina: 70 days. Extremely uniform, dark-green leaves. Upright plant; height 28 to 32 inches; bolting resistance similar to Georgia; very wind and cold tolerant; resistant to one or more races of downy mildew. Released in 1980 by the South Carolina Coastal Experiment Station in Charleston. B1M, F19M, *F63*, *G1M*, K73

Champion: 78 days. Longer standing Vates type released by the Virginia Truck Experiment Station in 1976. Selected to hold longer in the field without bolting. Somewhat taller than the regular strain, to 34 inches. Uniform, vigorous, blue-green leaves; close internodes; good flavor; high yield potential. Adapted wherever collards are grown. A13, *A75*, A87M, F13, *G1M*, G6, H54, *H61*, I77, J84, K73, L42, L89, M29, M95M, etc.

Florida: 45 days. Mildly pungent, cabbage-like leaves. Vigorous plants will outgrow flea beetle problems early in the year, and resist bolting until the end of the growing season. A fine addition to northern gardens in the summer. E24

Georgia: (Georgia Southern, Southern) 70 days. Large, moderately crumpled, blue-green leaves; grow back well after being harvested; mild, cabbage-like flavor is improved by frost. Vigorous, upright spreading plant; height 4 feet or more; produces well in poor soils and under adverse weather conditions. Popular traditional cultivar, introduced prior to 1885. B35M, D82, F19M, *F72*, F92, G71, G68, *H61*, H66, H94, J34, K73, M95, N16, N39, etc.

Georgia Blue Stem: 60 days. A popular old cultivar. Very tall, attractive, long-stemmed plants with leaves growing on widely separated internodes. The leaves can be harvested continuously as the plant quickly forms new ones. C92, G67M, K49M

Green Glaze: (Greasy) 73 days. A unique heirloom cultivar that many southerners refer to as Greasy Collards. Bears a loose cluster of smooth, slightly crumpled leaves that have a bright green sheen, giving the surface a "greasy" appearance. Upright plant; height 30 to 34 inches; slow bolting; resistant to cabbage worm. *C28*, K71, L7M

Morris Heading: (Morris Improved Heading) 80 days. The outer wrapper leaves close together more tightly than others, forming a large, round, very firm rosette which can be harvested for its tender, succulent growth. Dark-green, slightly crinkled leaves. Slow-bolting plants grow 18 to 24 inches tall. An old favorite with excellent flavor. *A75*, C92, *D12*, *F72*, *G1M*, G27M, H54, H66, J34, K49M, K71, L7M, L14, *L85*{PL}, M95M, etc.

Vates: (Blue Stem) 75 days. Broad, thick, dark-green, coarsely crumpled leaves free of purpling; excellent flavor and quality. Upright spreading, heavy-bearing plants; height 24 to 30 inches; fairly resistant to bolting; winter hardy. Very popular standard cultivar. Developed by the Virginia Truck Experiment Station. A87M, B35M, C44, C85M, F19M{PL}, F82, G71, *H61*, H66, I65M{PL}, J14{PL}, K73, L7M, *L85*{PL}, L97, M13M, N16, N39, etc.

CORN {S}

ZEA MAYS

DENT CORN

The kernels of this type have an indentation or depression on the top of the grain. This occurs when the soft, floury core in the middle part of the endosperm shrinks more than the hard, corneous portion. The most widely grown economic race of corn in the United States, it is milled into the yellow cornmeal of the grocery trade.

<u>BLUE-KERNELED</u>

Blue Clarage: (Ohio Blue Clarage, Blue Claredge) 100 days. Highly uniform, semi-dent corn. Distinctive, medium-sized, solid-blue ears. Higher sugar content than most dent corns; may be used as a table corn in the milk stage. Mills easily; makes a speckled blue and white cornmeal with a sweet, nutty flavor; a white meal may be obtained by sifting out the bran. Developed west of the Appalachian Mountains in the Ohio-West Virginia area between 1830 and 1850. F80, L7M

<u>GREEN-KERNELED</u>

Oaxaca Green: 70 days. Stout ears, 6 inches long, dented with smooth, emerald green kernels. Grown for centuries by the Zapotec Indians of southern Mexico for making green flour tamales. Stalks grow 5 to 6 feet tall. Often grown with squash and beans which twine up the corn stalks. K49T

<u>MULTI-COLORED</u>

Hickory King Composite: 95-110 days. Ears 8 to 10 rowed, cob small; large white and yellow kernels (1 to 5% blue). Excellent for roasting in early stages; also fine for cornmeal and hominy. Contains a range of genetic diversity; selections can be made that are adapted to local regions. C59M

Mayo Batchi: A desert staple of Sonora's Mayo River heartland. Short fat ears, with mixed clear, white and yellow kernels. Red cobs. For *elote*, tamales, tortillas and corn beer. Dry farmed in the low hot desert. In temperate climates, plant in spring when danger of frost is past and the soil is warm. I16

Mexican June: (Blue and White) 110 days. Long, plump ears; 8 to 9 inches long, 2 to 2 1/4 inches in diameter; rows 12 to 16, very crowded around the cob and in the row. Blue and white kernels; mostly white at roasting ear stage. Good for roasting ears. Medium heavy stalks; 7 1/2 to 8 1/2 feet tall; often 2 ears per stalk; resistant to heat and drought. Introduced about 1896. TAPLEY 1934; F12, H66, L7M, M95

<u>RED-KERNELED</u>

Beasley's Red Dent: 105 days. Originally a yellow dent which was selected for red color, but still produces a small percentage of yellow and orange ears. Ears 9 to 12 inches long, containing 16 to 20 rows of red kernels. Stalks average 9 feet tall. Excellent resistance to blight and drought. An heirloom discovered in Whitley County, Indiana. L7M

Bloody Butcher: 120 days. Ears 10 to 12 inches long; 12 to 14 rows per ear; kernels cherry-red striped with darker red. Fine flavor. Very good for flour, cornmeal, or corn-on-the-cob when young. Cobs pink or red. Stalks grow 10 to 12 feet tall; 2 to 6 ears per stalk. An old-time cultivar, grown in the United States since 1845. F80, K49M, K49M{PR}, L7M

Bloody Mary: Ears 9 inches long, with 14 to 16 rows of kernels. Kernels large, broad and deep; red with a cream-white dent. White cobs. Stalks 8 feet tall, with ears borne at about 6 feet; 1 to 2 ears per stalk. Very attractive, both in the field and dried on the ear. E63T

Northwestern Dent: 100 days. Attractive small to medium-sized, tapered ears, 6 to 8 inches in length with 12 to 16 rows of kernels; kernels red with white tips. Sturdy stalks, 5 to 6 feet tall. Rare heirloom from the Midwest. E59Z

WHITE-KERNELED

Boone County White: 120 days. Nearly round ears, 9 1/2 to 11 inches long; 16 to 22 medium spaced rows. Thick, blocky kernels, medium to wide and very deep. Cob white, large and heavy. Good for roasting and hominy. Heavy stalks, 9 1/2 feet tall. Originated in Indiana about 1876. A56, E59Z, J44, K71

Hickory King White: 115 days. Medium-long ears, 7 to 8 inches in length, small cob; kernels very wide, thin and deep. Excellent for hominy, the skin of the kernel being easily removed by soaking. Also good for roasting, grits, cornmeal and flour. Heavy stalks, 7 1/2 to 8 feet tall. Popular in the South. Introduced prior to 1888. BURPEE, TAPLEY 1934; A31M, A56, D76, E97, F19M, *G1M*, G27M, H66, J73, K27M, K49M, K71, *K94*, L7M, L14, M95M, etc.

Ojibway White: Rounded, creamy-white kernels; quality good when fresh, makes excellent flour for cornbread or tortillas when dried and ground. A fine cultivar grown since pre-European times by the Ojibwe people, in what is now called Ontario, Canada. Dropped by F80

Pencil Cob: 100 days. Medium-sized ears; surrounded by a thick, tight shuck; very deep kernels, plump and sweet. Unusual, very slender "pencil-sized" cob. Flavorful roasting ears in 76 days. Stalks grow 5 to 6 feet tall; 2 to 3 ears per stalk. Tolerates dry weather well. H66, L14, N16

Posole: 100 days. Large, plump ears. The traditional cultivar of dry dent corn for making *posole*, one of the finest dishes of Southwest cuisine. The hominy of the Southwest. Vigorous, drought-tolerant plants. J25M

Silver King: (Wisconsin No. 7) 100-110 days. Ears 8 to 9 inches long, with 16 slightly wavy rows. Cob glistening white. Kernels creamy white, very wide, of medium depth and thickness. Good for roasting ears. Popular in the northern part of the Corn Belt. Originated by A.J. Goddard of Ft. Atkinson, Iowa in 1862. *G1M*, K71

Silver Mine: 97-110 days. Ears rounded, tapering at the tip, 11 to 12 inches long. Kernel creamy white, of medium depth and width. Cob small, white. Popular for roasting ears in Florida, Georgia, Alabama and Mississippi. Adapted to a wide range of climates and soils; does well on poor soils. Good resistance to earworm. Originated by J.A. Beagley of Sibley, Illinois, in 1890. G27M, K71, L7M

Tait's White: An heirloom white dent, now rare, originally developed and introduced by Tait Seed Company of Norfolk, Virginia. Produces 1 or 2 ears, 8 to 10 inches long, on 6 foot tall stalks. Traditionally used for roasting ears. Adapted from Virginia southward. L7M

Tennessee Red Cob: Large deep-grained ears, up to 12 inches long, 12 to 16 rows. Red cobs. Good for roasting ears or cornmeal. Tall stalks, to 13 1/2 feet. Famous field corn, very popular in Tennessee and other sections of the upper South. K49M

Trucker's Favorite White: (Trucker's White) 95 days. Ears 8 to 10 inches long, 6 to 6 1/2 inches in diameter with 14 to 18 rows. Kernels large and deep, nearly rectangular in shape, creamy white. Excellent for roasting ears. Stalks 8 to 8 1/2 feet, tall and heavy. Particularly popular in the Cotton Belt and all parts of the South. A56, B71, D76, F19M, *G1M*, G27M, G57M, H66, I91, K5M, K49M, K71, L14, M95M, N16, etc.

White Surecropper: 82 days. Large ears with deep kernels. Excellent for roasting, early feed and milling. *D49*, H66

YELLOW-KERNELED

Hickory King Yellow: 115 days. Medium to long ears, 8 to 9 inches in length, small cob; dark-yellow kernels, very wide, thin and deep. Excellent for hominy, the skin of the kernel being easily removed by soaking. Also very good for roasting, grits, cornmeal and flour. Heavy stalks, 8 to 10 feet tall, often produce 2 ears. *K94*{CF}

Minnesota #13: 112 days. Medium-sized, blocky ears, 8 inches in length. For cornmeal, silage and feed grain. Sturdy plant, 7 to 9 feet tall; resists lodging; yields well. An old-time dent corn that is adapted to most of the North. E59Z

Nothstine Dent: 100 days. Medium-sized ears, 7 to 8 inches long; glossy yellow kernels with white caps. Makes a sweet, flavorful cornmeal for baking and cereal. Single stalks, to 7 feet tall. Not high-yielding but of excellent quality. Successful in short season areas. A northern Michigan heirloom. G6

Reid's Yellow Dent: 110 days. Most popular yellow dent corn in the United States. Ears 9 to 10 inches long, with 16 to 22 closely spaced rows. Kernels very deep and narrow, deep yellow with a lighter cap, often tinged with red. Good for roasting ears, hominy, grits and cornmeal. Tall, heavy stalks. Very productive; widely adapted. Originated by Robert Reid of Illinois in 1847. Prize winner at the 1893 World's Fair. A31M, A56, D76, E59Z, F19M, G57M, I97{PR}, J44, K71, L7M

Trucker's Favorite Yellow: (Trucker's Yellow) 77 days. Yellow strain of Trucker's Favorite White, with a red cob. Ears 8 to 12 inches long, with 12 to 14 rows. Used for a quick early crop or for late planting. Popular throughout the South and Midwest. A56, D87, *G1M*, H66, K71, L14

FLINT CORN

The kernels of flint corn are very hard and as in popcorn, nearly all the starch in the endosperm is corneous. When milled into flour it remains as small granules, not as a powdery mass. Before the development of Corn Belt dent, it was the most widely distributed corn in the Northeastern states.

MULTI-COLORED

Indian Flint: (Squaw) 105 days. A hard flint corn, unsurpassed for grinding into cornmeal. Despite the multi-colored ears, the ground cornmeal shows little or no trace of color. I39

Tarahumara Maiz Caliente: "Hot corn" or summer cultivar. Onaveño Race. Small kernels, mixed white, yellow and salmon. Fast growing. For subtropical and low desert areas. In temperate climates, plant in late May or early June. From the Tarahumara Indians of Mexico. I16

Tarahumara Serape: Red and white striped kernels. Similar to Havasupai Chin Mark flour corn. Planted in early July in desert areas. Irrigated. In temperate areas plant in spring when danger of frost is past and the soil is warm. I16

Tepehuan Maiz Colorado: Medium-sized ears. Long, yellow-striped red kernels with beaks on tips. Red cobs. Planted in early July in desert areas. Irrigated. In temperate areas, plant in spring. From Mexico. I16

PINK/RED-KERNELED

Tarahumara Maiz Color de Rosa: 90 days. Medium-sized pink ears. Has somewhat the texture of flour corn and some pointed kernels. Planted with the summer rains in desert areas. In temperate climates, plant in late May or early June. I16

Tarahumara Sitakame: Small, slender, dark red ears. Very attractive. Red cobs. Planted in early July in desert areas. In temperate climates, sow in spring. Dry farmed. From the Tarahumara Indians of Mexico. I16

YELLOW-KERNELED

Amber Flint: An old cultivar with hard corneous starch inside the kernel and a glass-like amber covering. Makes corn foods of excellent flavor. G47

Garland Flint: 110 days. Very early Northern flint corn. Most ears are bright yellow, the balance solid, deep red; 7 to 8 inches long, 8-rowed. Used for cornmeal. Stalk grows 7 to 8 feet tall. Selected by George Garland, one of the last old-time producers of fine traditional New England corn. G6

Longfellow's: 117 days. The standard 8-row Northern flint. Ears 12 to 16 inches long, well-filled to the extreme end of the cob. Kernels large and broad, rich glossy orange. Makes a sweet cornmeal. Stalks 8 to 10 feet tall; extremely productive, often produces 3 full-sized ears per stalk. BURPEE; G6{CF}

Vermont Yellow: 95-100 days. A very early hard yellow corn of fine lineage. Ears 8 inches long, straight, 8-rowed. Good for corn-meal. Stalk grows 6 to 8 feet tall. Matures well in short season areas. A2

WHITE-KERNELED

Rhode Island White Cap: 115 days. An authentic, 8-rowed white flint corn of the Narragansett Indians. Ears slightly larger than Garland, 6 to 7 inches long. Ivory-white kernels. Used for the famous Rhode Island Jonny Cake meal. Stalks grow 6 to 7 feet tall. Recommended for northern gardeners where seasons permit. Still grown commercially near Little Compton, Rhode Island. E67{PR}, T76, U33

Santo Domingo Pueblo: Last of the Rio Grande flints. Prized for making the best *posole* (corn soup). A long-season corn, should be planted as soon after spring frosts as possible. L79M

FLOUR CORN

Kernels of flour corn have an endosperm that consists entirely of very soft, white, opaque starch. It is easier to grind than flint or dent corn, milling easily to a fine flour. Grown primarily in the Southwest and the Northern Plains. The Southwestern form is very distinct, with small kernels and large cobs.

BLUE/PURPLE-KERNELED

Alamo-Navajo Blue: 90 days. Large, full ears of dark bluish-purple to almost black kernels. Popular for grinding into cornmeal for Southwestern blue corn tortillas and *piki* bread. Can also be picked young and eaten fresh. Very vigorous plant; resistant to drought and disease. Also a good ornamental. J25M

Caspecio Blue: The type of corn grown by the Hispanic farmers around the Española and Embudo valleys of northern New Mexico. Large, dark blue kernels on large ears. Strong stalks. Matures about 2 weeks earlier than Taos Blue. High yielding; almost 3,000 pounds per acre. L79M

Hopi Blue: Popular dark-blue corn that makes a sweet blue cornmeal. Widely grown in the Southwest and used in a variety of traditional foods. Precursors of modern strains have been raised continuously for 800 years on the Hopi Indian mesas of northern Arizona, never under mechanized agriculture. Thrives in sandy soils, without irrigation when necessary. Most widely adapted of Hopi corns for other regions. KAVENA [Re]; A2, C81M, G47, H91{PR}, I16, I77, I99, J73, K49M, K49M{PR}, K49T, L7M, L79M

Hopi Purple: Amethyst in color; makes a rich-tasting flour. An ancient strain, crossed and selected by Indian ancestors, for seasonal stability with uncertain moisture. Stalks have large foliage. L79M

Hopi Turquoise: According to legend, the original cultivar given to the Hopis for their migrations. Pale blue kernels make delicious flour. Very adaptable. A2, I77, L79M

Smoky Blue: 105 days. Ears 7 to 9 inches long, with 12 rows of kernels. Kernels rounded, purple to almost black. Makes delicious corn bread and tortillas. White cobs. Modest but reliable yields, even in dry years. E63T

Taos Blue: A strain recovered from 50 years' storage in Taos Pueblo, New Mexico. Very long ears with 12 to 18 rows of dark-blue, nearly black seed. Grown at high elevations at Taos Pueblo, by traditional methods. Prolific when irrigated. Successfully grown in all 50 states. A2, C76M, E59Z, L7M, L11, L79M

MULTI-COLORED

Hopi Coconino: Red, pink, orange, white and striped kernels on medium to large ears. Grown on the high desert. In temperate areas, plant in spring when danger of frost is passed and the soil has warmed up some. I16

Hopi Supai: (Havasupai Chin Mark) Medium-sized ears, 8 to 9 inches long with 12 rows of kernels; striking yellow-white kernels variegated brown and red. Good for flour or parching. Stalks grow 6 feet tall, yield 2 to 3 ears per stalk. Very adaptable. Also called Calico or Chin Mark in reference to its resemblance to traditional Havasupai facial decorations. K49T, L79M

Mandan Bride: 98 days. An early maturing corn that is ornamental as well as useful. Ears 8 inches long, 8 to 12 rowed; come in a striking array of colors including purple, white, variegated, red, yellow, speckled and some with translucent and rosy effects. Good for corn flour and hominy. Originally from the Mandan Indians of what is now North Dakota. A2, E24, G6, I77

RED/PINK-KERNELED

Hernandez Red: Not a pure strain; has a wide range of color characteristics. Some ears are pure red, others are white, blue or yellow. Good for flour or decorative use. L79M

Hopi Pink: 70 days. Medium-sized ears, 8 inches long with 12 to 14 rows of kernels; pink-capped white kernels, some red and white variations. Often matures earlier than other Hopi flour corns. Bushy plants, 4 to 4 1/2 feet tall. Does consistently best in all drought tolerance tests due in part to a long embryonic taproot. A2, K49T, L79M

WHITE-KERNELED

Concho: White corn with very soft kernels. Traditional staple of Hispanic New Mexicans. Ground for flour or parched for snacks. L79M

Hopi White: (Hopi White Hominy) Large white ears and kernels. Makes a fine flour and good *posole* (corn soup). Sand dune grown in the high desert. In temperate climates, plant in spring when danger of frost is past and the soil is warm. A2, J73, L79M

Mayo Tosabatchi: The soft white flour/meal is used for cookies. Reaches the *elote* stage in 70 to 75 days. Blando de Sonora land race. For low hot desert areas. Planted with the summer rains. In temperate areas, plant in late May or early June. I16

Seneca Round Nose: Very large flour kernels on massive 14 to 18 rowed ears. Long, beautiful silks. Pre-Columbian heirloom from New York State. E59Z

Taos White: Long-eared flour corn form a very traditional New Mexico Pueblo at very high elevation. Small kernels with a pink tinge. Prolific when irrigated. I16, L79M

YELLOW-KERNELED

Hopi Yellow: Medium-sized, straight rowed ears; bright yellow, soft textured kernels. Excellent for tortillas and tamales. Planted in July in the high desert. In temperate areas, plant in spring when danger of frost is past and the soil is warm. A2, L79M

Mandan Yellow: 85 days. Ears 6 to 8 inches long, 8-rowed. Rounded, lemon-yellow kernels with soft, white endosperm. Easy to grind. Stalks grow 4 to 5 feet tall. Not recommended for southern growers. Originally grown by the Mandan Indians of what is now North Dakota. A2, E63T

Papago: 80 days. Small, slender, cream-colored ears. Ground into flour for tamales. Drought tolerant; adapted to the extremely arid homeland of the Papago Indians of southern Arizona. Excellent for harsh, dry sites. In wetter climates, or with irrigation, the plants are larger. J25M

Texas Shoepeg: Long, bright yellow kernels with dented beaks. Short red cobs have up to 26 rows. Sweet at the milk stage. Excellent for meal or boiling. From Cranesfill Gap, Texas. I16

POPCORN

Considered the most primitive of corns, the endosperm of popcorn has starch that is almost entirely the hard, corneous, and translucent type. When heated the kernels burst and the soft, palatable inner endosperm is everted. They can also be used for sprouting. Popcorn flour can be made from unpopped kernels or from popped kernels that have been ground in a blender or food processor. KUSCHE [Pre, Re].

BLACK/BLUE-KERNELED

Black: (Blue) 100 days. Larger ears and kernels than standard popcorn. Deep blue to black kernels that pop snow-white with a tinge of bluish-black at the base. Rich, distinctive flavor. Not as vigorous as yellow or white strains, grown for flavor and visual effect. E15M{PR}, I97T, K12M{PR}, L79M

Black Jewell: A modern, hulless dark-blue popping corn developed in Illinois by Merle Litherland, from seed originally obtained in Germany. Pops snow white with a grayish-blue hue. Very thin hull, shatters when it pops; tender, yet crunchy texture; excellent natural flavor. Patented, no planting seed available at this time. A52M{PR}, B19M{PR}

Schroeder's Black: (Black Tie) Large, bluish-black kernels. Pops into large, snow-white flakes with a bluish tint; excellent, crunchy texture; distinctive, nutty flavor. Gourmet quality. Originated in Buhl, Idaho by Elmer Schroeder. K12M{PR}, K37T, K37T{PR}

BROWN-KERNELED

Brown: Ears 4 to 6 inches long, many rowed. Kernels various shades of brown plus other colors. Mostly brown cobs. Maturity varies. Rare. C59M

Chapalote: *Pinole* maize. Used popped; also toasted and ground into a sweet meal. One of the four most ancient corns. Slender ears; small, brown kernels. A long season corn from Mexico, grown in the low hot desert. In temperate areas, plant in spring when danger of frost is passed and the soil is warm. I16

Chocolate Pop: 135 days. Ears average 6 inches long, with 16 to 18 rows of kernels. Kernels chocolate-colored, in several shades of brown. Bright pink silks. Pops and tastes like a well-flavored yellow popcorn, but the hulls are more tender. Very unusual and attractive. Stalks average 5 1/2 to 6 feet tall; produce 2 ears per stalk under good conditions. Good resistance to drought and earworms. L7M

MULTI-COLORED

Cutie Pops: 100 days. A unique, multi-colored, miniature popcorn. Ears 4 inches long; tiny, rainbow colored kernels. Pops white. Can be used as a "baby" Indian corn for dried bouquets, or harvested for miniature white popcorn. G93M, L42

Pretty Pops: 95 days. An ornamental as well as useful popcorn. Ears 4 to 6 inches long; some uniform in color, some mixed. Brightly colored kernels of red, blue, black, yellow, purple and orange that turn white when popped. Excellent nutty flavor; crunchy, never tough. Stalk grows 6 to 7 feet tall. Productive. G93M, I91

Seneca Mini Indian: 100 days. Attractive, slender ears, 4 to 6 inches long; striking multi-colored kernels in bright red, yellow, brown, black, purple, blue, solid, and variegated. Ornamental as well as excellent for popping. Bears 2 to 3 ears per stalk. Should be planted about 6 inches apart to ensure fully miniature ears. F80

Wenatchee: Ears 6 inches long. Multi-colored, translucent kernels. An old Washington favorite. D87

RED-KERNELED

Hybrid

Robust Red S-100: (Indian Red) Medium-sized, elongated, deep red kernels. Pops into bright white flakes with a hint of red at the center. Has a subtle, nut-like flavor of gourmet quality. A modern hybrid developed from Strawberry popcorn by Jim Iverson of Crookham Co. *C68M*, K12M{PR}

Open-Pollinated

Strawberry: 100 days. Short, conical ear; 2 inches long; resembles a red-ripe strawberry in shape and color. Small, dark-red kernels. Pops white. Primarily used for decorating, but can also be used for popping. Stalk grows 5 feet tall; produces 2 to 4 ears. A13, A25, B73M, B78, C82, D11M, D87, *F72*, G16, G51, G71, K66, K73, L97, M46, *N40*{PR}, etc.

WHITE-KERNELED

Hybrid

Peppy: (Burpee's Peppy Hybrid) 90 days. Small ears; 4 inches long. Deep, pointed, hulless kernels; large and tender when popped.

Excellent popping expansion and flavor. Stalk grows 5 to 6 feet tall; high yielding, 2 or 3 ears per stalk. Does well in short summer areas. B75, *F72*, G51, J32

Pop White: 95 days. Small ears, about 4 inches long. Tender, flavorful, hulless kernels. Good popping quality. High yielding; produces 2 to 4 ears per plant. Early enough for most growing seasons. Recommended for home gardens and fresh market. Standard white popcorn. M29

Snow Puff: 90 days. Small ears; 5 inches long. Small, completely hulless kernels with no hard center. Excellent quality, flavor and tenderness. High popping volume for a white cultivar. Stalks grow 5 to 6 feet tall; produce 3 or more ears per stalk. *B1*, B73M, G79, *I59M*, J58, J97M, K10, K27M, K71, K73

White Cloud: (White Cloud Hulless) 95 days. Small plump ears, about 4 inches long; well-filled. Deep, pointed, thin-skinned kernels. Excellent popping expansion; tender, fluffy and hulless; of excellent flavor and quality. Vigorous, sturdy stalks; high yielding. Does well in northern areas. A13, B75M, D11M, E97, *F72*, G16, H42, H94, H95, J20, K50, K50{PR}, K71, K73, L42, M46, etc.

Open-Pollinated

Bearpaw: 95 days. Heirloom strain from New England. Ears somewhat flattened and "paw" shaped at the silk end, hence the name. Large white kernels. Stalk grows 5 feet tall; often produces 2 ears. Grown commercially in Vermont in the early 1900's. By the 1970's there remained only one farmer in Dummerston, Vermont who maintained the seed. A2, F42M{PR}

Japanese Hulless: (Japanese White Hulless, White Hulless) 100 days. Short ears, about 4 inches long. Small white kernels; irregularly set on the cob. Pops snow-white; very tender, with no hard centers, of excellent quality. Stalk 4 1/2 to 5 feet tall; very productive, 3 to 6 ears per stalk. Very popular, old standard cultivar. *A75*, *B1*, B71, D76, E97, *G13M*, H49, H66, J58, J73, K27M, K49M, K71, L14, *L14M*{PR}, M13M, M46, etc.

Pennsylvania Butter-Flavored: 100 days. An heirloom popcorn maintained by the Pennsylvania Dutch since 1885 or earlier. Ears 5 inches long. Small white kernels; very tender and delicious. Stalk grows 8 feet tall; produces 2 or 3 ears. Very drought resistant; will grow in poor soils. L7M

YELLOW-KERNELED

Hybrid

Creme-Puff: 105 days. Medium-sized ears. Tender, high quality kernels with a delicious flavor. Excellent popping expansion. Stalks grow 8 to 8 1/2 feet tall; high yielding, often produces 2 ears per stalk. B75, F19M, *I59M*, J58, K10, K27M

Iopop 12: 100 days. Large, slender, orange-yellow ears; 7 to 8 inches long. Small, deep and rounded kernels, nearly as free of hulls as Japanese White Hulless. Excellent popping volume. Pops to large, very tender, flavorful flakes. Strong, erect, high yielding plant; widely adapted. *C68M*, D65, F13, G16, G79, H33, K10, *L14M*{PR}

Matinee: 110 days. An early maturing, gourmet yellow popcorn. Ears 7 inches long, with 16 rows of kernels; kernels glossy yellow-orange. Expansion ratio 40 to 1; making for very tender popcorn. Stalk grows 7 feet tall. Matures 1 or 2 weeks earlier than other gourmet types. For home gardens and roadside stands. G6

Purdue 410: 110 days. An improved South American type. Tapered ears, 7 to 8 inches long. Unusually large, plump yellow kernels. Excellent popping expansion; produces large, fluffy, nearly hulless popcorn. Sturdy stalks, 6 feet tall; high yielding. Widely used for commercial popcorn. A56, *A75*, *B1*, B75M, C92, E97, *G13M*, G79, G93M, I39, I64, I91, J58, K71, K73, etc.

Robust 10-84: 98 days. Large ear size. Large yellow kernels, 52 per 10 grams with popping volume of 38 MWVT. Pops into very large flakes that are excellent for candied popcorn. Very vigorous plant with high earring potential. Can tolerate more adverse conditions than most hybrids. Does well in short season areas. K73, L42

Robust 41-10: 98 days. Large ears, 7 to 8 inches long with 14 to 16 rows of kernels; large, medium yellow kernels, 145 per ounce; excellent eating quality. High popping expansion; popped flakes are very large and make excellent candied popcorn. Very high yields, with a tendency toward double earring. A13, J84

South American Yellow: (South American Giant, T.N.T.) 100 days. Hybrid version of South American. Large, well-filled ears. Tender, golden-yellow, flavorful kernels that pop perfectly white. Excellent popping expansion. Very productive. B71, G71, G79

Open-Pollinated

Lady Finger: Short, slender ears, 3 to 5 inches in length. Very small, deep yellow kernels. Pops well, leaving few unpopped. Flakes are tiny, tender and delicate with excellent flavor. Too tender to microwave. Also good in dried arrangements. Short, stocky plants bear multiple ears. Heirloom cultivar grown in the Amish communities of Ohio, Indiana and Iowa. J58, K52{PR}

Queens Golden: 90 days. Long, slim ears; 7 inches long, with 12 to 16 rows of kernels. Pearl-type kernels; broad, smooth, yellow. Stalk grows 7 feet tall. A rare old cultivar. G67M

Reventador: Old-fashioned *pinole* corn with translucent kernels. *Maiz reventador* is a generic term for the small-grained pearl popcorns of western Mexico, where they are preferred over other types for making pinole. Forms of Reventador corn have been grown in Sonora, Mexico for at least 200 years. ANDERSON, E.; I16

South American: (South American Yellow) 105 days. Long, slender, tapered ears; 7 to 8 inches long; 14 to 16 rows of kernels. Medium-sized, golden-yellow kernels. Stalk grows 76 inches high. Resistant to bacterial wilt. A56, *A75*, F12, *G1M*, *G83M*, H66, *I59M*, K5M, K10, K49M, L14, N39

South American Dynamite: (South American Giant) 100 days. Very large ears, 9 inches long. Kernels large, nearly round, orange-yellow. Creamy white when popped, mushroom-shaped, with a buttery flavor. Expansion rate 20 to 30 times volume. High yielding; 2 to 3 ears per stalk. *B1*, *D49*, E97, G67M, H49, H54, K71

Tom Thumb:[2] 85 days. Small ears, 3 to 4 inches long. Small, smooth, golden-yellow kernels. Pops very well. Dwarf stalks, only 3 1/2 feet tall, will not shade other garden vegetables; 1 or 2 ears per pod. Very early; matures well in far northern areas. Refined from a genuine New Hampshire heirloom by Professor E.M. Meader, and Johnny's Selected Seeds. D68, D82, G6, L97

SWEET CORN

Kernels of sweet corn are easily recognized by their wrinkled exterior. Their sweetness is the result of a genetic defect in metabolism which prevents the sugars in the kernel from being completely transformed into starch. They require more favorable growing conditions than other types of corn. Mostly used as corn on the cob, they can also be allowed to mature on the plant, cooked, and used as "dried corn", or the dried seeds can be sprouted.

BI-COLOR

Normal Sugary (F_1) The standard sweet corns, they have moderate but varying degrees of sugar due to one or more of the sugary-1 (su)

genes, depending on the cultivar. They are best used immediately after harvest, as their sugars convert to starch rapidly. Isolation is not required.

Bi-Queen: 92 days. Ears reach 8 to 9 inches long, with 14 to 16 rows of sweet, tender kernels; quality resembles Silver Queen. Attractive dark-green husks and long flag leaves. Plant grows 6 1/2 to 7 feet tall; tolerates Stewart's wilt and northern and southern corn leaf blights. Requires 60° F. soil temperature for germination. Silver Queen x Golden Queen. *A1*, A13, A87M, *F63*, G71, G79, *H61*, *I59M*, J84, J97M, K50, K71, K73, M29, M95M, etc.

Burgundy Delight: 80 days. Ears average 7 to 8 inches long, with 12 to 14 rows of kernels; well-filled to the tip. Good yellow and white kernel pattern. Sweet and tender, even when past its prime. Burgundy stalks and husks. Stalk grows 7 feet tall, often with 2 good ears. Very popular mid-season cultivar. For home gardens, roadside stands and pick-your-own operations. D11M, D68, G6, J7, K50, L42, N39

Butter and Sugar: 75 days. Medium-sized, tightly wrapped ears; 7 to 8 inches long, with 12 to 14 rows. Broad kernels; good yellow and white pattern; very sweet and tender, of good quality and flavor. Snaps easily. Dark green husk. Stalk grows 7 feet tall. Excellent cold tolerance and seedling vigor; good resistance to Stewart's wilt. A13, A25, C44, C92, D65, F13, *F72*, G16, G64, H49, J97M, K50, L42, M29, M95M, N39, etc.

Calypso: 82 days. Large, well-filled ears; 8 to 8 1/2 inches long, with 18 to 20 rows of kernels. Narrow, deep yellow and white kernels with excellent eating quality and fine appearance. Sturdy plant grows 7 to 8 feet tall; produces a high percentage of doubles. Becoming a standard for bi-colors, with quality rivaling Jubilee. *A1*, C44, E57, *F63*, *G13M*, G51, G79, G93M, J84, K73, M29, M95M

Duet: 74 days. Large slender ears, 8 to 9 inches long, with 12 to 14 rows of kernels. Attractive yellow and white kernels; tender and sweet with very good flavor that holds well. Excellent for freezing. Green husks tinged with purple; dark green flag leaves. Plants grow to 6 feet tall. For home gardens and roadside stands. E24, G6

Harmony: 73 days. Medium-large ears, 7 to 7 1/2 inches long, well-filled to the tip with 12 to 14 rows of kernels. Narrow yellow and white kernels; tender and sweet with high quality. Deep green husks with plentiful flag leaves. Strong, upright plants with few tillers; show good seedling vigor. Developed for the second-early season. F13, M49

Honey and Cream: 78 days. Ears 6 1/2 to 7 1/2 inches long, with 12 to 14 rows of kernels. Bright kernels of white and yellow, very sweet and tender, of excellent quality. Long, tight husks provide good protection from earworms. Stalk grows 5 to 6 feet tall. Popular home garden cultivar. A25, A56, B13, B75, D82, E97, *F72*, G57M, H33, H42, H49, J20, N16, O89

Honeymoon: 78 days. Large ears, 7 1/2 to 8 inches long, well-filled with 14 to 16 rows of kernels. Medium-sized, deep, yellow and white kernels; tender and sweet. Butter and Sugar quality on a larger, more attractive ear. Uniform plant height of 6 feet. Excellent germination and seedling vigor. Tolerant to maize dwarf mosaic virus and Stewart's wilt. A13, E57, E97, *F63*, G79, G82, J58, L89

Jazz: 70 days. Ears very large for an early corn, 7 to 8 inches long and 2 inches in diameter; well-filled with 14 to 16 rows of kernels. Attractive yellow and white kernels; sweet and tender. Fresh green husks and good flag leaves. Sturdy plants, 5 to 6 feet tall. Good cold emergence. One of the earliest bi-color corns. D68, F1, G6, L79

Sugar and Gold: 66 days. Medium-sized ears, 6 1/2 inches long; well-filled with 10 to 12 rows of tender, sweet kernels. Good for freezing. Plant grows 4 to 5 feet tall with few tillers; tolerates southern corn leaf blight. Performs well in cooler growing areas. Developed in 1942 by Agway and still popular in New England. A13, A25, D65, D68, D76, E97, G82, N39

Sugary Enhanced (F_1) Also called Everlasting Heritage corns, these contain the sugary enhanced (se) gene which modifies the normal sugary (su) gene. The result is increased tenderness and, to a varying degree, sweetness. Conversion of sugar to starch is slowed. No isolation from "normal" sweet corn is necessary to maintain quality.

D'Artagnan: 64 days. One of the earliest maturing sugary enhanced bi-colors. Ears grow 7 1/2 to 8 inches long, with 14 to 16 rows of kernels. Narrow yellow and white kernels; tender and sweet with good holding ability. Superior quality for an early corn. Tight, dark green husks give good protection. Plant grows 5 to 5 1/2 feet tall. *A1*, B1M, *C68M*, D68, *G13M*, G64, G82, H94, J7, K10, K50

Double Delight: 87 days. Long, slender ears; 8 to 9 inches long, 2 inches in diameter, with 16 to 18 rows of kernels; good tip fill. Medium-sized golden-yellow and white kernels, very sweet and tender, of excellent flavor and quality; texture rich and creamy. Holds its sweetness for 7 to 10 days past maturity. Stalk grows 6 to 6 1/2 feet tall. *A1*, C44, *C68M*, D11M, D76, *F63*, *G13M*, G82, H95, I39, K10, M29, N52

Gold-N-Krystal: (Seneca Gold-N-Krystal) 85 days. Uniform ears, 7 1/2 to 8 inches long, with 16 to 20 rows of kernels. Wide, shallow kernels; tender and very sweet, of high quality. Heterozygous type, 25% of the kernels on each ear being sugary enhanced. Tight husks with good flag leaves. G79, *H61*, J84, *J89M*, K10

Gold-N-Pearl: (Seneca Gold-N-Pearl) 68 days. Medium-sized ears, 7 to 7 1/2 inches long, with 12 to 14 rows of kernels; excellent tip cover. Attractive yellow and white kernels; very sweet, tender and flavorful. Homozygous type, 100% of the kernels on each ear being sugary enhanced. Dark green husks; provides better husk protection than others when stressed. Very good cold soil tolerance. Not tolerant to Stewart's wilt. D11M, F1, F13, *F63*, G64, G79, *H61*, *I59M*, I67M, J84, *J89M*, K73, L42, M29, M49, etc.

Kiss 'n Tell: 78 days. Fine-grained, well filled ears; 7 inches long, with 16 to 18 rows of kernels. Very sweet and tender; holds its gourmet quality over an extended harvest period. Dark green husks protect well. Matures about 2 days after Duet and Harmony. Usually 2 ears per stalk. G6

Medley: 73 days. Large ears, 8 to 8 1/2 inches long, 2 inches in diameter; with 16 to 18 rows of kernels, well-filled to the blunt tip. Attractive white and yellow kernels; tender, very sweet, of high quality and excellent flavor. Good for freezing. Dark green husks with good tip cover. Plant grows 6 to 7 feet tall; resists Stewart's wilt. *G13M*, G71, G82, K10, K73

Peaches & Cream: 68 days. Ears 7 to 7 1/2 inches long, with 14 to 16 rows. Kernels average 80% golden yellow, 20% white; very sweet, tender and flavorful. Remains sweet up to 14 days after maturity. Stalk grows 6 1/2 feet tall, produces 2 ears. Does well in short season areas. A69M, B73M, C85M, C92, D11M, D27, D76, F92, G87, H54, K20, K27M, M13M, M46, M95M, N39, etc.

Sweetie Series (F_1) A unique type that contains both normal sugary genes (su) and shrunken-2 genes (sh_2) genes. Provides some advantages over normal sh_2 types. Requires isolation from other sweet corns.

Sweetie Bi-Color: (Sweetie Bi-Color 76) 76 days. Large, slim ears, 8 1/2 to 9 inches long and 2 inches in diameter; with 16 to 18 rows of kernels. Same eating qualities as other cultivars in the Sweetie series. Dark green husks with excellent flag leaf and tip cover; short white silk. Plant grows 5 to 6 feet tall; has good tolerance to northern leaf blight and rust. *G13M*, K73, L42, *L59G*

Xtra Sweet (F_1) Also called Super Sweet, or Shrunken corn due to the effect of the shrunken-2 gene (sh_2) on the appearance of the dry kernel. Its presence creates greatly heightened sweetness and very slow conversion to starch after harvest. Must be isolated from Normal Sugary or Sugary Enhanced corns, or both types will have tough, starchy kernels.

Candy Store: 80 days. High quality supersweet developed by Harris Seeds. Rated best in taste, appearance, yield and uniformity in a comparison test conducted by Organic Gardening magazine. Very good flavor and aroma; very pronounced sweetness. Good for freezing. Also rated better at the end of one week storage. Grows about 5 feet tall. F13

Honey 'n Pearl: 82 days. Large, well-formed ear, 8 1/2 to 9 inches long; with 16 to 18 straight rows of kernels; excellent tip fill. Deep, glossy yellow and white kernels. Extra sweet and flavorful; rated high in All America taste trials. Excellent holding ability. Sturdy, medium-tall plant. All America Selections winner in 1988. B75, C44, D11M, F13, *F72*, F86, G6, G16, G79, *G83M*, H42, H95, I39, I91, K71, K73, etc.

Ivory 'n Gold: 76 days. Large ear, 8 1/2 inches long, 1 3/4 inches in diameter; with 16 well-ordered rows of kernels; fair tip cover under stress. Especially attractive husked appearance. Bright kernels of ivory white and golden-yellow; extra sweet and tender. Tight, medium green husks provide good earworm protection. Very similar to Honey 'n Pearl. D11M, F86, G79, K10, K73, L42, M46, N52

Starstruck: 80 days. The original bi-color Xtra-Sweet. Ears 8 to 9 inches long, with 14 to 16 rows of yellow and white kernels, with good husked and unhusked appearance. Very sweet and tender. Good for corn-on-the-cob and for freezing. G6

Twice-As-Nice: 78 days. Large ears, about 8 inches long, well-filled to the tip with 14 to 16 rows of kernels. Bright yellow and white kernels; tender, extra sweet. Holds for an exceptionally long period, on or off the stalk. Tight, dark green husks. Plant grows 7 1/2 to 8 inches tall with few tillers; tolerates Stewart's wilt and southern corn leaf blight. A13, *F63*

Open-Pollinated

Double Standard: First open-pollinated bi-color sweet corn. Somewhat variable ears, 7 inches long, with 12 to 14 rows of yellow and white kernels; some ears with yellow kernels only. Better than average flavor and tenderness. Early maturing, with unusually good germination in cool soil. Developed by Johnny's Selected Seeds for northern home gardeners, especially seed saving enthusiasts. G6

BLUE/BLACK-KERNELED

Open-Pollinated

Black Aztec: (Aztec) 75 days. Medium-sized ears, 7 to 8 inches long, with 8 to 10 rows of kernels. Kernels bluish-black when mature. Used as corn-on-the-cob or roasting ears in the white-kernel stage. Ground into a sweet, bluish-black cornmeal when dry. Stalk grows 5 1/2 to 6 feet tall, produces 2 ears. Reportedly grown by the Aztecs 2,000 years ago. A2, C82, E56{PR}, F80, G51, I99, K49T, L11, L79M

Black Mexican: 85 days. Slightly tapered ear, 7 to 8 inches long, with 8 rows. Kernels white at milk stage, changing to bluish-black in the late edible and dry stages; tender, very sweet and flavorful. Medium-tall plant; height 5 1/2 to 6 feet; often bears 2 ears per stalk. Very hardy and weather tolerant. Introduced prior to 1865. TAPLEY 1934; E59Z, G67M, L7M

Hooker's Sweet Indian: 75-100 days. Long, thin ears, 5 to 7 inches in length. Fine flavor in white-kernel stage, either fresh or frozen. Kernels bluish-black when mature. Makes a very sweet cornmeal. Stalk grows 4 to 4 1/2 feet tall, produces 2 to 3 ears. Originally obtained by Ira Hooker, over 50 years ago near Olympia, Washington. L89

Midnight Snack: 81 days. Ears 7 to 7 1/2 inches long, with 14 to 16 rows. Kernels wide; ivory white and sweet at milk stage, bluish-black when dry. Makes an excellent sweet cornmeal. Sturdy plant; height 5 1/2 feet. Developed by Professor E.M. Meader at the University of New Hampshire; selected from Black Aztec. E24{CF}

MULTI-COLORED

Open-Pollinated

Bronze-Orange: 90 days. A combination of the old traditional American Indian cultivars Tarahumara Sweet, Guaymas Orange and Faro Chilean. Yellow, orange and red kernels. Short plants, 3 to 4 feet tall, with 3 to 5 ears per stalk. Bears well under variable conditions. Very rare. F80, I99

Cocopah: Medium-sized ears. Large red, white and blue kernels. Sweet and fast-growing. Originally collected in 1868 and 1869, and saved by three generations of Arizona prospectors. Planted with the summer rains in the low hot desert. I16

Rainbow Inca: 85 days. Rare sweet corn with visually attractive cobs and multicolored seeds. Purple, red, yellow, white and blue kernels, paler in the fresh eating stage. Good as fresh corn, either raw or cooked. Stout, robust stalks, 8 to 10 feet tall. From crosses of a large white flat-seeded Peruvian Indian chokelo cultivar, multicolor Southwest Indian corns, and heirloom sweet corns. K49T

RED-KERNELED

Open-Pollinated

Mandan Red: 74 days. A genetically variable sweet corn from the Mandan Indians of the North Dakota area. Ears 6 inches long, with 8 to 12 rows of kernels. Kernels yellowish-white in the milk stage, turning red as the ear dries. Stalk grows 5 feet tall. L7M

Mandan Red Nueta: 85 days. A rare red "sweet" (kernels shriveled when ripe) corn, for roasting rather than fresh (green) use. Short ears, with 10 rows of kernels. Kernels reddish-brown with yellow at the crown; hard when mature. Matures quickly, but thereafter dries slowly. Very short stalk, 2 1/2 to 4 feet tall. A primitive, low yielding corn. Originated in the 19th century or earlier. A2, E59Z, E63T, I77

Warihio Red: 90-120 days. Slender ears with red kernels. Very unusual. Grown only in summer in low hot desert areas. Sown with the summer rains. In temperate regions, sow in late May or early June. I16

WHITE-KERNELED

Normal Sugary (F_1)

Baby:[1] (Miniature) Tiny finger-like ears; tender and delicately flavored. Best when harvested within 5 days of the appearance of silks. The husked and desilked ear, cob and all, is used in stir-fry dishes, vegetable salads and as pickles. Commonly found canned in Oriental and specialty markets, occasionally available fresh. D55, G68, H49, I39

Baby Asian:[1] Medium-sized plant; bears 2 or 3 ears per stalk if plants are thinned to 12 inches apart. Grown as ordinary corn, but harvested 2 or 3 days before or after silk emergence, usually when 4 inches long and about 1/2 inch in diameter. Lower ears are commonly harvested for "baby corn", while the top ear can be left to mature for corn-on-the-cob. D62, K66

Chalice: 78 days. Earlier Silver Queen type. Large ears, 8 to 9 inches long, with 14 to 16 rows of kernels. Sweet, tender, glossy white kernels with a good rich flavor. Attractive, dark green husks with long flag leaves. For home gardens and fresh market. Plant grows to 7 feet tall. Good cool soil emergence and seedling vigor. *A1*, *F63*, *G1M*, G6, *G13M*, G93M, K10, M29, M95M

Quicksilver: 75 days. Medium-sized ears, 7 to 7 1/2 inches long, filled to the tip with 14 to 16 rows of kernels. Small, tight, pearl-white kernels; tender and sweet with very good flavor. Quality similar to Silver Queen, but matures 2 weeks earlier. Sturdy, erect, high yielding plants. Strong germination and seedling vigor in cold soil. F13, F92, *G1M*

Silver Queen: 88 days. Ears 8 to 9 inches long, with 14 to 16 rows of straight kernels; good tip cover. Kernels snow-white, very sweet and tender. Holds for several days without losing quality. Stalk grows 7 1/2 to 8 feet tall. Widely adapted. Tolerant to bacterial wilt and northern and southern leaf blights. Most popular white sweet corn in the United States. A25, A87M, C44, F19M, *F72*, G6, G71, *H61*, H66, K66, K73, M13M, M46, N39

Silver Treat: 85 days. Ears reach 8 to 8 1/2 inches long, with 16 rows of kernels. Small, deep kernels of excellent eating quality that closely resembles that of Silver Queen. Medium green husks with short flag leaves. Vigorous plants, 7 to 8 feet tall with few tillers; produce a high percentage of 2 marketable ears per stalk. Good seedling vigor in cold soils. Resistant to Stewart's wilt and southern corn leaf blight. A13, *F63*, J97M

Stardust: 70 days. Very attractive ears, 7 to 7 1/2 inches long, with 14 to 16 rows of kernels. Small, pearl-white kernels with a high luster; tender and sweet with excellent eating quality. Dark green, clasping husks. Sturdy plants, 5 to 6 feet tall, with moderate tillering. Resistant to Stewart's wilt and southern corn leaf blight, susceptible to drought. Excellent germination and seedling vigor in cold soils. A13, *F63*, G82, I91, J97M

White Sunglow: 68 days. Medium-sized, moderately tapered ears, 7 to 7 1/2 inches long; well-filled to the tip. Sweet, tender, snow white kernels of excellent quality. Vigorous, productive plants, 8 to 9 feet tall. One of the earliest white corns. Recommended for short season areas, or as a first crop corn in more temperate regions. A16, E97, *F72*, G57M, H54, *I59M*, M46, M95M, N52

Sugary Enhanced (F_1)

Platinum Lady: 80 days. Ears average 7 1/2 to 8 1/2 inches long, with 14 to 16 rows of kernels; good tip fill. Narrow, deep, white kernels; very sweet and tender, good flavor, of high quality. Heterozygous type, 25% of the kernels on each ear being sugary enhanced. Green husks, attractively tipped with burgundy. Ships well. Sturdy plant, to 6 1/2 feet tall. Good tolerance to rust, northern corn leaf blight and drought. Very popular. B35M, B75, B75M, C44, *C68M*, D11M, *F72*, G64, G93M, I39, J7, J20, K10, K71, L42, L97, etc.

Silverado: 79 days. Slightly tapered ears, 7 to 8 inches long, with 16 rows of kernels. Snow-white kernels; very sweet and tender with excellent flavor. Good for freezing. Very good husk appearance. Vigorous plant; height 6 to 7 feet; tolerant to Stewart's wilt. Excellent cold soil germination. F13, *G1M*, G93M

Snow Queen: 87 days. Virtually identical to Kandy Korn, except the color is white. Very uniform ears, 9 to 10 inches long, with 16 to 20 rows of kernels. Snow-white kernels, very sweet and tender, of good flavor. Holds its sweetness for 10 to 14 days after harvest. Good seedling vigor. Stalk grows 7 1/2 to 8 feet tall. A69M, B35M, B73M, D65, D76, E97, G79, I64, J32, K71, M46, M95M

White Knight: (Seneca White Knight) 74 days. Large, well-filled ears; 8 to 8 1/2 inches long, with 14 to 16 rows of kernels. Tender, very sweet kernels that hold their quality longer than other sugary enhanced types. Tight husks with excellent dark green flag leaves. Vigorous plant with one tiller; grows 7 1/2 feet tall; partially resistant to Stewart's wilt. *F63*, G79, *J89M*, K10

White Lightning: 90 days. Slender ears, 8 1/2 inches long, with 16 rows of kernels. Kernels snow-white, very sweet and tender, of excellent quality. Heterozygous type, 25% of the kernels on each ear being sugary enhanced. White silk. Seedling vigor superior to other late white hybrids. Stalk grows 8 to 9 feet tall. Tolerant to maize dwarf mosaic strains A and B. Recommended for home gardens, local markets and shipping. *A1*, B35M, *G13M*, G57M, G79, G82, H33, *H61*, J84, K10, L42, M95M

Xtra Sweet (F_1)

How Sweet It Is: 87 days. Slightly tapered ear, 8 inches long, containing 18 to 22 rows of kernels. Kernels pearl-white; tender, crisp, exceptionally sweet. Excellent holding ability, both on the stalk and in storage. Good for all purposes. Widely adapted plant, to 6 1/2 feet tall; produces 2 ears per stalk. Tolerant to Stewart's wilt. All America Selections winner in 1986. B73M, C44, F19M, F82, G6, G16, G71, H42, *H61*, H95, K10, K73, L97, M46, N16, etc.

Silver Extra Sweet: 85 days. Large ears, 7 1/2 inches long and 2 inches in diameter, well-filled with 18 rows of high quality kernels. Dark green husks with multiple flag leaves. Vigorous, compact plant. New introduction from Illinois Foundation Seeds, bred especially for American consumers. F86, G27M, K10

Open-Pollinated

Adams Early: 70 days. Large, heavy ears, 6 to 7 inches long with 12 to 14 rows of kernels. Large, deep, white kernels that lack the sweetness of true sweet corns; quality good when harvested at the correct stage of maturity. Husks very tightly wrapped, difficult to remove. Vigorous, productive plants; height 5 1/2 to 6 feet; tillers entirely absent. Introduced prior to 1848. BURR, TAPLEY 1934; *G1M*

Buhrow's White Desert: 70 days. Result of a cross between Papago corn and a white corn. Will pollinate at temperatures of 90 to 100^{0} F., when most other corns fail. Very drought tolerant; has been known to bear when deeply watered only 3 times in a season. Ears 6 to 9 inches long. Keeps well. Stalk grows 5 to 9 feet tall. J25M

Country Gentleman: (Shoe Peg) 95 days. Medium-sized, tapered ear, 8 to 9 inches long, with irregularly spaced kernels. Kernels white, deep, very long and narrow; sweet, tender, milky, of good quality. Good fresh, frozen and canned; popular for cream-style corn. Moderately heavy stalk, 7 to 7 1/2 feet tall, often produces 2 ears. Originated in Orange, Connecticut by Frank C. Woodruff. Introduced in 1890. TAPLEY 1934; A2, B49, B78, D76, D87, E97, F19M, G71, H66, J70M, J73, K10, K49M, K71, L7M, etc.

Early Pearl: 84 days. Moderately short, nearly cylindrical ears, 5 to 7 inches long with 10 to 12 rows of kernels. Small, shallow kernels; very sweet and tender, of good quality. Husks loosely wrapped and easily removed. Very productive plant with numerous tillers; height 5 1/2 to 6 1/2 feet. Introduced in 1932 by Charles C. Hart Co. TAPLEY 1934; E59Z, L11

Evergreen Early: 96 days. Very old traditional cultivar, selected for earliness from Stowell's Evergreen. Ears 7 to 8 inches long, with 16 to 18 rows of kernels. Deep, medium-broad white kernels; tender, sweet and rich. Good for home gardens, local markets and canning. Heavy stalk, 8 to 9 feet tall; tillers few. TAPLEY 1934; G57M

Honey Cream:[2] 64 days. Well-filled ears, 6 to 7 inches long, with 10 to 12 rows. Kernels silver-white, tender and sweet, with practically no hull. Excellent for canning, freezing and fresh use. Dwarf stalks, 3 1/2 to 4 1/2 feet tall; can be planted close together making it well-suited to small gardens. F24M, G16, I97T

Luther Hill: 82 days. Stalk grows 5 1/2 feet tall; produces 2 ears, 6 inches long. Excellent flavor; fresh ears sell for $3 per dozen in New Jersey. One of the parents of Silver Queen; used by breeders to impart exceptional flavor to hybrid sweet corn. Can be grown as far north as Ontario. Very weak vigor; not recommended as a main crop corn. Originated in Andover, New Jersey in 1902. L7M

Norfolk Market: (Tait's Norfolk Market) 74 days. Very large ears, 9 to 10 inches long, with 12 to 14 rows of pearly white kernels that have excellent quality. Plant grows 6 to 7 feet tall; usually produces 2 ears. Largely grown by home and market gardeners from Norfolk to Florida. Introduced by Tait Seed Company of Norfolk, Virginia. *G1M*, M95M

Six Shooter: 80 days. Novelty corn. Slender ear, with 10 rows of kernels. Small white kernels; solid, meaty and tender, of good flavor. Excellent for freezing. Dried kernels can be used for hominy and cornmeal. Tall, vigorous plant; produces as many as 6 good ears per stalk. D76, E97, I97T, K71

Stowell's Evergreen: 90 days. Slightly tapered ear, 8 to 9 inches long, with 16 to 18 rows. Kernels silver-white at milk stage, sweet and tender. Retains its fresh quality for an extended time. Ripens over a long period. Popular for home gardens, local markets and canning. Stalk grows 7 1/2 to 8 feet tall, produces 1 or 2 ears. One of the oldest sweet corns still in existence. Originated in Burlington, New Jersey prior to 1848. BURR, TAPLEY 1934; A56, D76, D87, E97, F24M, G57M, G67M, G71, G79, I97T, J73, K10, K27M, K49M, L7M, etc.

YELLOW-KERNELED

Normal Sugary (F_1)

Calumet: 82 days. Long, slender ears, 8 to 10 inches in length; with 12 to 14 rows and well-filled tips. Light yellow kernels with very good flavor. Resistant to ear worms. High yielding plants, average height 7 feet; resistant to heat, drought, bacterial wilt and smut. A favorite of many in the Southwest. A27M, *D49*, F19M, J34, L14, N16

Debut: 73 days. Large, very uniform ears, 8 inches long with 16 to 18 rows of kernels; excellent tip fill. Deep, bright golden-yellow kernels; sweet and tender. Dark green husks with attractive flag leaves. High yielding plants; height 6 1/2 to 7 feet. Shows good seedling vigor. Well suited for fresh market or home garden use. *A69M*, B71, *F63*, *G13M*, G16, G64, G93M, J84, K73, N16, N52

Earlivee: 55 days. Medium-sized ear, 6 1/2 to 7 inches long, with 12 to 14 straight rows; good tip fill. Large, golden-yellow kernels, of good flavor. Medium green husks. Short plant; height 5 feet; produces very few tillers. Very popular early maturing cultivar for the northern United States and Canada. A69M, B13, C44, D65, E24, F44, G6, G64, H94, H95, J7, K50, L42, L97, M49, etc.

Early Sunglow: 63 days. Attractive ears, 6 to 7 inches long, with 12 rows of kernels. Deep, medium-yellow kernels; sweet and tender. Green husks, lightly streaked with purple. Stalk grows 5 to 6 feet tall; often produces 2 ears; tolerant to bacterial wilt. Good seedling vigor in cold weather. A13, B35M, B75, D65, D76, F19M, F82, *G83M*, H49, I91, J34, K71, L97, N16, N39, etc.

Golden Beauty: (Early Giant Golden Bantam) 65 days. Slightly tapered ear, 7 to 8 inches long, with 14 rows of kernels; good tip fill under stress. Kernels of medium width and depth, sweet and tender. Dark green husks. Stalk grows 5 to 6 feet tall; resists wilt. Recommended for home gardens and early markets. All America Selections winner in 1955. A69M, B35M, B73M, B75M, C44, C85M, C92, D65, D76, D82, E97, G79, H42, L42, N39, etc.

Golden Cross Bantam: 85 days. Uniform ears, 7 1/2 to 8 inches long, with 10 to 14 rows. Large, deep, rich yellow kernels of good quality. Excellent for market growers and well adapted to freezing and canning. Sturdy stalk; height 6 feet; very prolific. Highly resistant to bacterial wilt. A13, B73M, B75M, C44, F19M, *F72*, F82, F92, G51, *G83M*, H54, J34, M13M, M46, N16, etc.

Golden Queen: 88 days. Yellow version of Silver Queen. Uniform ears, 7 to 9 inches long, with 14 to 16 rows; excellent tip fill. Golden yellow kernels, very sweet and tender, of high quality. Very dark green husks and flag leaves. Stalk grows 7 to 9 feet tall. Tolerant to northern and southern leaf blights. Especially suited for the South. A13, A87M, F19M, G71, G79, G93M, H54, *H61*, H66, I91, J97M, K50, K71, M95M, N16, etc.

Iochief: 89 days. Ears 9 to 10 inches long, with 14 to 18 rows. Uniform, deep, golden-yellow kernels; good "real corn" flavor. Excellent fresh, frozen or canned. Sturdy stalk; height 6 to 7 feet; produces 2 ears. Drought resistant. All America Selections winner for 1951. Rated highest overall in a reader poll conducted by Organic Gardening magazine. A13, *A75*, B73M, B75M, C92, D65, D76, F19M, G82, *G83M*, *H61*, H66, K71, M13M, N16, etc.

Jubilee: (Golden Jubilee) 83 days. Large ears, 8 to 9 inches long, with 16 to rows. Deep, narrow kernels; sweet, tender, flavorful, of high quality. Holds quality well, both on the stalk and after picking. Excellent fresh or for processing. White inner silk. Strong, sturdy stalks; height 7 to 7 1/2 feet. Extremely popular and very widely adapted. A25, C44, F82, G6, G16, *H61*, H94, H95, J7, K73, L97, M13M, M46, N16, N52, etc.

Merit: 80 days. Large, heavy ears, 8 to 9 inches long; with 16 to 18 rows of kernels and well-filled tips. Kernels bright yellow, deep and narrow, tender and sweet with good flavor. Vigorous, productive, widely adapted plants; height 7 feet. Rapidly becoming the favorite yellow corn in the South. A27M, C92, F19M, G57M, G79, *H61*, H66, I91, J34, J70M, J97M, K50, K71, L14, N16, etc.

Seneca Horizon: 65 days. Large ears, 9 to 10 inches long, with 16 to 18 rows; good tip fill. Bright yellow kernels, tender and sweet. Superior eating quality compared to other early cultivars. Good seedling vigor and cold tolerance. Rapid-growing stalks; height 5 to 5 1/2 feet. Suitable for home garden, roadside and commercial use. Excellent for short-season areas. A16, A25, B75M, C85M, E24, E57, F1, *F72*, G16, *H61*, I64, *J89M*, K73, L79, M49, N16 , etc.

Sugary Enhanced (F_1)

Bodacious: 75 days. Ears average 8 inches in length, with 16 rows of kernels well filled to the tip. Deep, golden-yellow kernels; very sweet and exceptionally tender. Homozygous type, 100% of the kernels on each ear being sugary enhanced. Flavor and tenderness hold well after harvest. Excellent for roadside stands and shipping. *A1*, A13, B1M, B71, *C68M*, *G13M*, G79, G64, G82, G87, H94, J84, K10, K50, L79, N52, etc.

Earliglow: 78 days. Earliest of the Everlasting Heritage series. Uniform ears, 8 inches long, with 12 to 16 rows of kernels. Tender, very sweet yellow kernels. Retains sweetness 10 to 12 after harvest. Unusual pink-tinged silks. Sturdy stalks; height 6 to 7 feet. *A69M*, C85M, D11M, D76, E97, G87, I64, J32, K71, L91M, M46, M95M

Incredible: 85 days. An improved Miracle type, with taller plants and higher yields. Ears average 8 inches in length, with 20 rows of kernels and well-filled tips. Exceptionally tender, very sweet kernels with real corn flavor. Homozygous, 100% of the kernels on each ear being sugary enhanced. Good husk protection and better tip fill than Miracle. Stalks grow 6 1/2 to 7 1/2 feet tall. Has multiple disease resistance. *A1*, *A69M*, *C68M*, *F63*, *G13M*, G64, G82, G93M, J20, J84, K10, M95M, N52

Kandy Korn: 89 days. Very uniform ears, 8 inches long, with 16 to 18 rows. Golden yellow kernels; tender, extremely sweet. Holds sweetness for 10 to 14 days after harvest. Heterozygous type, 25% of the kernels on each ear being sugary enhanced. Excellent for freezing and canning. Attractive purple-striped husks; burgundy red stalks. Height 8 to 9 feet. Very good seedling vigor. Adapted to a wide range of climates. B73M, B75M, D82, E57, F19M, *F72*, F82, G16, *H61*, H66, J7, K66, L97, M46, N16, etc.

Miracle: 84 days. Large well-filled ears, 8 1/2 to 9 1/2 inches long, 16 to 20 rows of kernels. Large, light golden-yellow kernels; very sweet and tender. Retains sweetness up to 2 weeks after reaching maturity. Homozygous type, 100% of the kernels on each ear being sugary enhanced. For home gardens, local markets, shipping and processing. White silks. Height 6 to 6 1/2 feet. Good tolerance to rust. A69M, B35M, B75, C44, *C68M*, D11M, D65, G82, G93M, *H61*, H95, I39, J7, J58, K73, L42, etc.

Sugar Buns: 70 days. Ears 7 to 7 1/2 inches long, with 14 rows of kernels. Relatively narrow, deep, medium-yellow kernels, very sweet and tender. Remains tender for up to 2 weeks in the field. Homozygous type, 100% of the kernels on each ear being sugary enhanced. Tight, dark green husk; good flag leaves. Short, sturdy plant. Recommended for home gardens, roadside stands and short-distance shipping. B35M, B73M, C44, D11M, D65, G6, G82, H42, H94, H95, J84, K50, K73, L42, L89, L97, etc.

Tendertreat: 95 days. Well-filled ears, 9 inches long, with 16 to 18 rows. Light golden-yellow kernels; sweet, tender and flavorful. Long-lasting sweetness allows for a longer harvest period. Suitable for home gardens and local markets. Attractive purple stalks; purple and green husks. Good seedling vigor. Large plants; height 9 to 10 feet. *A1*, B49M, D11M, D76, H33, K10, M29, M46, N52

Sweetie Series (F_1)

Sweetie: (Sweetie 82) 82 days. Slightly tapered, well-filled ears; 7 to 8 inches long, with 14 to 18 rows of kernels. Deep, golden-yellow kernels; crisp, tender, exceptionally sweet. Retains sweetness for a long period, both in the field and when harvested. Has 30% fewer calories than regular corn. Height 6 feet. Excellent for home gardens and local markets. A13, B75M, D65, E97, F19M, G16, G27M, G71, G79, G93M, *H61*, J32, K71, K73, L79, etc.

Sweetie 70: 70 days. Large, cylindrical ears, 9 inches long with 12 to 14 rows of kernels and good tip fill. Deep, golden-yellow kernels; crisp and very sweet. Excellent holding ability. Height 5 to 5 1/2 feet. Good disease resistance. *A1*, *G13M*, I64, K10, K73, L42, *L59G*

Sweetie 76: 76 days. Medium-large, slightly tapered ears, 8 1/2 inches long with 14 rows of kernels well-filled at the tip. Golden-yellow kernels; very sweet and crisp. Height 5 to 5 1/2 feet. Has multiple disease resistance. *A1*, *G13M*, I64, K10, K73, L42, *L59G*

Xtra Sweet (F_1)

Crisp 'n Sweet: (Crisp 'n Sweet 720) 87 days. Large ears, 9 to 9 1/2 inches long, with 18 to 20 rows of yellow kernels. Has twice the sugar content of regular sweet corn. Holds its quality for up to 2 weeks, on or off the stalk. Height 7 feet. Resistant to northern leaf blight; tolerant of Stewart's wilt. *A1*, B35M, B71, B75M, E97, *F63*, *G13M*, G51, G64, *H61*, J84, K10, K27M, K73, M49, N16, N52, etc.

Early Xtra-Sweet: 71 days. Same high quality as Illini Xtra-Sweet, but about 2 weeks earlier. Uniform ears, 7 to 9 inches long, with 12 to 16 rows of kernels. Small golden-yellow kernels, extra sweet and tender. Vigorous plant; height 5 to 6 feet; produces few suckers. All America Selections winner in 1971. A69M, B75, D11M, D65, D76, F19M, *F72*, G16, *G83M*, H49, *I59M*, K10, K27M, K71, K73, L91M, M46, etc.

Florida Staysweet: 84 days. Uniform well-filled ears, 7 to 8 inches long, with 14 to 18 rows of kernels. Refined golden-yellow kernels, tender and extremely sweet. Good husk protection and appearance. Very good seedling germination and vigor. Does well in northern areas. Widely used for commercial shipping and freezing. *A1*, F86, *G1M*, G6, G27M, K71, K73, N16, N52

Frosted Gold: (Xtra-Sweet 82) 72 days. Large, uniform ears, 9 inches long. Narrow, golden-yellow kernels; tender and extra sweet with very good flavor. Long holding ability. Superior husk cover ensures minimum insect damage. Excellent germination and seedling vigor. Developed by Illinois Foundation Seeds as an early maturing companion to Illini Xtra Sweet. D11M, *F63*, F86, G82, G79, H33, H94, I64, M95M

Illini Xtra-Sweet: (Illinichief Xtra-Sweet) 85 days. The original Xtra-Sweet hybrid. Twice as sweet as other hybrids at harvest time, four times as sweet 48 hours later. Large ears, 8 inches long, with 14 to 18 rows. Rich golden-yellow kernels, extra sweet and tender. Excellent fresh, frozen or canned. Height 7 feet. *B1*, B75, C85M, D65, F19M, F86, G51, G82, *G83M*, G93M, H49, *H61*, *I59M*, K10, K73, M46, N16, etc.

Northern Xtra-Sweet: (Northern Supersweet) 67 days. Earliest maturing yellow Xtra-Sweet hybrid. Large ears, 8 to 9 inches long, with 16 rows of extra sweet kernels. Attractive unhusked appearance, with dark green husks and long flag leaves. Good seedling emergence and vigor under cool, wet soil conditions. Short, sturdy plant; height 5 feet. A69M, B13, C85M, D65, D68, F86, G6, G16, G64, G79, H94, I67M, K10, L42, M46, etc.

Sugar Loaf: 83 days. Ears 8 inches long, with 16 rows of kernels. Deep, narrow kernels, very sweet and tender. White silk. Relatively strong seedling vigor. Stalk 6 feet tall, produces 2 ears; few suckers. Resistant to rust; tolerant to northern leaf blight and maize dwarf mosaic. For home gardens, fresh market and processing. *G1M*, *G13M*, G71, G79, G82, G87, G93M, *H61*, K73, *L59G*, L79, M95M, N16

Summer Sweet 7200: (Ssupersweet 7200) 78 days. Large, uniform ears, 8 1/2 inches long with 14 to 16 rows of kernels. Glossy yellow kernels, tender and extra sweet. Excellent fresh or frozen. Attractive green husks with good flag leaves. Plants grow 6 feet tall and have multiple disease resistance. Good germination and seedling vigor. *A1*, E57, J58

Open-Pollinated

Ashworth: 69 days. Selected from a composite of numerous early cultivars. Ears 6 to 7 inches long, well-filled with 12 rows of kernels. Kernels bright-yellow, of excellent flavor. Matures with early hybrids. Stalk grows about 5 feet tall. F42, G6, I39M

Early Golden Bantam: (Extra Early Golden Bantam) 70 days. Very uniform ears, 6 to 7 inches long, with 8 rows. Kernels bright golden-yellow, sweet and flavorful, of very good quality. Short, vigorous high-yielding plants; height 5 to 6 feet. A25, A69M, B13, B78, C85M, D27, F44, G16, H94, I67M, J7, K20

Fisher's Earliest: 60 days. One of the earliest open-pollinated sweet corns. Ears 5 to 6 inches long, with 8 to 12 rows of kernels, thin cob. Golden-yellow kernels, very sweet, tender, flavorful. Good for freezing and canning. Short, vigorous plant; height 5 feet; tolerates frost. Developed by Fisher's Garden Store. D82, F44

Golden Bantam: (Golden Bantam 8 Row) 75 days. Slender ears, 6 to 7 inches long, with 8 uniformly straight rows. Large, broad kernels; sweet, tender, very flavorful. Stalk slender, 5 to 5 1/2 feet tall, often produces 2 ears. Still the most popular open-pollinated yellow sweet corn. Introduced by W. Atlee Burpee Company in 1902. TAPLEY 1934; A16, A25, *A75*, B49, B75M, D11M, E24, G71, H42, H66, K49T, L7M, L97, M95, N16, etc.

Golden Early Market: (Gill's Early Golden Market, Golden Market) 68 days. Slightly tapered ear, 6 to 7 inches long, with 10 to 12 rows. Kernels golden-yellow, moderately deep, of good flavor. Slender stalk, 4 1/2 to 5 feet tall; occasionally produces 2 ears. Originated in Portland, Oregon by Gill Brothers Seed Company. Introduced in 1925. TAPLEY 1934; A16, G57M, G87, H94

Golden Giant: 88 days. Slightly tapered ears, 7 to 8 inches long, with 10 to 14 rows. Kernels rather shallow, deep creamy yellow, rich and flavorful. For home gardens, local markets and canning. Height 6 to 7 feet. Introduced in 1917 by Joseph Breck & Company. TAPLEY 1934; G57M

Golden Midget:[2] 68 days. Tiny ears, about 4 inches long, with 8 rows of kernels. Golden-yellow kernels; sweet, tender, flavorful. Very good fresh; ideal for packing in freezer containers. Dwarf plant; height 2 1/2 to 3 feet; produces 3 to 5 ears per stalk. Well-suited to small gardens. A2, A25, A69M, C85M, E24, F24M, G51, H94, I97T, J20, J73, K49M, K71, L11, L97, etc.

Golden Sunshine: (Sunshine) 68 days. Slightly tapered ear, 7 to 8 inches long, with 10 to 12 rows of kernels. Light yellow kernels, moderately broad and medium deep; tender and sweet. Stalk 5 to 5 1/2 feet tall. Originated by A.F. Yeager of the North Dakota College of Agriculture. Introduced in 1926. TAPLEY 1934; G87, J73

Hawaiian Supersweet #9: 80 days. Bred in Hawaii specifically for warmer climates. Has tighter husks to resist borer entrance and is resistant to corn stripe mosaic. Retains its sweetness for 7 to 10 days after harvest without refrigeration. L9M, L11, M19, M32M

Improved Golden Bantam: (Golden Bantam 12 Row) Medium-sized, slightly tapered ear; 6 to 7 inches long, with 10 to 14 rows. Kernels deep, light yellow; tender and sweet. Stalk slender, 4 1/2 to 5 feet tall, often produces 2 ears; tillers numerous. Introduced in 1922 by the Everett B. Clark Seed Company. TAPLEY 1934; A2, F19M, G57M, G79, I39, I97T, J73, K5M, L89

Montana Bantam: 65 days. An extra early strain of Golden Bantam developed by Fisher's Garden Store. Ears 6 to 7 inches long, with 8 rows of deep golden kernels of very good flavor and quality. D82

CORN SALAD {S}

VALERIANELLA LOCUSTA

A Grosse Graine: (Large-Seeded Round, Ronde à Grosse Graine) 45 days. A strong-growing type, differing from common corn salad in the greater size of the plant, and also of the seed, which is nearly twice as large as other kinds. Large, comparatively narrow, grayish-green leaves; thin and very tender. Early maturing. Widely grown in Europe. Introduced prior to 1865. BURR, VILMORIN; F33, G68, J73

Blonde Shell Leaved: 50 days. Small, green, shell-like leaves. Early, fast-growing, produces a good crop, and is extremely resistant to cold. Very popular in France. I39, K49M

Cavallo: 50 days. Ready to harvest in 40 to 50 days and then keeps on producing a mass of fresh flavored, very deep-green leaves. Has a long harvest period; a late summer sowing will guarantee winter salads as it is very hardy. L91M

Coquille de Louviers:[1] (Scallop of Louviers) 40-45 days. Small, attractive, spoon-shaped, glossy-green leaves. Very fine flavor. An autumn and winter grower; plant in September for harvesting December through March. May be harvested sooner for "baby mache". Unique cupped leaves catch the dressing when fixed up in a salad. *A75*, C53, F24M, F33, J73

Elan:[1] Small, glossy, smooth, very attractive leaves. Small, upright plant habit makes it one of the best choices for "baby mache". Resistant to mildew, making it ideal for fall and winter crops where conditions are cold and wet. C53

Grote Noordhollandse: (Large Seeded Dutch, Large Dutch) 50 days. Large, rounded, lush, dark-green leaves. Very early and productive. Most suited for warm winter areas as it cannot tolerate frost; normally planted no later than mid-August for harvesting in October and November. Will germinate under warmer temperatures than other sorts. An old heirloom European strain. I39, K66, L89, *R11M*

Large Round Leaved: Leaves larger, of a deeper green color, thicker, and more succulent than those of common corn salad. The leaves are most tender, and should be cut for use while young and small. Introduced prior to 1865. BURR; C85M, F44

Ronde Maraichère: (Round-Leaved) An heirloom French cultivar which has very distinct short, oval, almost rounded clear-green leaves. Growth is half-erect, instead of spreading, making harvest easier during wet weather. Productive and of rapid growth. Widely grown by market gardeners around Paris. VILMORIN; G68, K66

Verte à Coeur Plein: (Green Full Heart, Dark Green Full Heart, Cabbaging) 40-45 days. A very distinct type with short, roundish, smooth, half-erect, stiff and intensely green leaves. Forms a compact rosette, the heart of which is full and firm. Very agreeable flavor. Holds its quality well when shipped. Very winter hardy. Introduced prior to 1885. VILMORIN; *A75*, B35M, F33, G82, J73

Verte d'Cambrai:[1] (Green Cambrai) 60 days. Compact plant. Small, round to oval, flat, dark-green leaves; 3 to 4 inches long; tender and mild in flavor. High yielding and pest-resistant. Very cold tolerant; best planted in October and harvested February through March. May be harvested sooner for "baby mache". Standard cultivar in France and Germany. A2, B75, E83T, F44, G64, G68, K66, P83M, Q34, S55

Verte d'Etampes: (D'Etampes) Rosette somewhat more compact and stiff than common corn salad. Leaves extremely dark-green in color; rather narrow, and often undulated or folded back at the edges; veins prominent; much thicker and fleshier than those of other cultivars; maintain their freshness longer than any other kind while being brought to market. Remarkably cold tolerant. Introduced prior to 1885. VILMORIN; C53, F24M, G68

Vit: Most vigorous cultivar for spring and fall crops, as well as for over-wintering. Long, glossy green, tender leaves form a heavy bunch. Delicious, mild, minty flavor. Mildew tolerant. D68, G6, N81

COWPEA {S}

VIGNA UNGUICULATA

Big Boy: 70 days. Very prolific bush type pea, producing green pods borne well above the foliage. Pods 8 to 9 inches long, with 13

to 16 oblong peas per pod; peas cream-colored with a light brown eye. Resistant to wilt and nematodes. Similar to blackeye in taste and appearance but shells much more easily. A27M, F12, F19M, *G1M*, G27M, J34, K71, N16

Big Red Ripper: 60 days. A well-flavored table pea with 10 inch long pods, containing 18 large peas per pod. Pods are easy to see amongst the foliage, and plants are resistant to very hot, dry summers. Use green shelled or dry. L7M

Black Crowder: 63 days. Very prolific, high bush-type plant; bears unusually long, green pods at foliage level. Very flavorful peas have a deep-purple cast at the green shell stage, turning black when mature. Easy to shell. *G1M*, H66, L14, M95M, N16

Blackeye White Crowder: Medium early maturing. Medium to small seed; at maturity white with small, incomplete black eye. Medium short, 6 inch long pods, held even with the foliage. F12, H66, L14, N16

Blue Goose: (Gray Crowder) 80 days. One of the best all-purpose cultivars. Excellent for soil building, hay, or edible peas. Heavy, productive vines; height 3 feet. Long pods, producing well-flavored speckled, purplish-gray peas. *G1M*, G27M, H54, H66, L14, M95M

Bombay:[1] (All Seasons Red-Seeded) Superior to any Indian cultivar. Soft and tasty green fruits, one cubit (18 inches) long, generally with red seeds. Can be sown from January to December, but highest yield is obtained if sown in April and September. N91

Brown Crowder: 65 days. Medium-sized pods; about 8 inches long; dark-gray at green shell stage. Seeds are smooth; "crowded" in the pod, thus becoming flattened and misshapen; brown, with a dark-brown eye when mature. Unique, strong nutty flavor preferred by many in the South. Will do well on thin soil. A56, F12, *G1M*, G27M, *H61*, H66, *I59M*, K10, L14, M95M, N16

Burgundy Purple Hull: Semi-bush type purple hull pea with excellent production, quality and shelling characteristics, Long, slender non-shattering pods; bright red at green shell stage, turning light brown; held well above the foliage; easy to harvest, giving good shell-out over a relatively wide range of maturity. Excellent quality for fresh market, freezing or canning. L89G

Calico Crowder: (Hereford Pea, Polecat Pea) 80 days. One of the more flavorful cowpeas, recommended for southern states and warm coastal areas. The 5 1/2 inch long pods are green at the green shell stage and turn dark tan when dry. Dried peas are buff-colored with maroon splashes, especially around the eye. F19M, H66, J34, K49T, L7M, L14

California Blackeye #5: 65 days. Improved strain of Giant Ramshorn. Very vigorous and heavy yielding. Pods are up to 12 inches long, with plump, cream-colored peas larger than ordinary blackeyes. Tall, bunch-type plant with good root system; resistant to nematodes, wilt and other diseases. Leading *black-eyed pea* in the U.S. HAWKES [Re]; A87M, B75M, F12, F19M, G71, G82, G93M, H33, J34, J84, K10, K73, L9M, L14, N16, etc.

Colossus: 60 days. Extra large brown crowder type. Pods 7 to 9 inches long; straw-colored, with a red tinge. Peas are brown when mature. Tends to produce pods in bunches for easy harvest. Popular home garden pea for canning, freezing and green shell peas. Developed by Dr. W.L. Ogle of Clemson University. F19M, *G1M*, H66, J34, K71, L14, M95M

Crimson: Developed to provide an erect-growing Purple Hull type with the pods held high off the ground at the leaf level. Pods are 6 to 7 inches long. Peas medium-sized, light brown in color with an excellent flavor. True bush-type plant; heavy yielding. H66, M46

Dixie Lee: 60 days. Hardy, heavy-bearing plant produces 8 inch pods, turning from green to light yellow; borne well off the ground; easy to shell. Peas are small to medium-sized, brown, and excellent for home or commercial use. Yields 2 crops a season. Nematode tolerant. F19M, *G1M*, H66, K71, L14, N16

Extra Early Blackeye: 50 days. Bears a heavy crop of fine, long, straight well-filled pods. Popular market cultivar because of its earliness. C92

Hercules: A late season brown crowder type that continues producing for 4 weeks or more, longer than most cultivars. Pods are 8 to 9 inches long, reddish at maturity, bear a heavy crop of large size peas of pronounced flavor. Peas are green fresh, brown when dried. Developed by Dr. W.L. Ogle of Clemson University. I91

Iron and Clay: Mixture of Iron and Clay cultivars, producing a heavy growth of vines used for soil improvement and forage. Small seed. Iron and Clay are considered to be among the types brought from Africa by slaves and slave traders to the United States in the 1700's. B55, *G1M*, G27M, H66, L14

Knuckle Purple Hull: (Knucklehull Purple Hull) 65 days. Large-seeded brown crowder type. Strong, erect bush-type plant. Short, 6 inch pods; purple when mature; relatively easy to shell; late maturing. Seeds are dark-brown when mature. Called "knucklehull" because of the large, plump peas. A27M, B71, F12, *G1M*, G27M, H66, K71, L9M, L14, M95M, N16

Lady: (Lady Finger) 65 days. Very small, tender, well-flavored peas; white in green shell stage, turning cream when mature; freeze well when young, and are good for drying when mature; hold well on the vine when green. Bush-type plant; very prolific; excellent for the home garden. B55, F19M, *G1M*, G27M, N16

Lady Cream: 60 days. A good bunch type with an excellent yield of tiny, white peas. Peas hold on the vine well for long periods when green. Fine for freezing. H66, L14

Magnolia: 65 days. Small-sized, very high-yielding blackeye type of excellent quality. Bush-type plants; pods approximately 7 inches long. Good for canning and freezing. Bred to be resistant to fusarium fungi, root knot nematodes, and tolerant to viruses. F19M

Mississippi Cream: High-yielding plants; tolerant to root-not nematodes and most viruses. Pods are 7 inches long; green to nearly white at green shell stage, straw-colored when dry; peas shell much easier if left overnight after picking. Peas are green turning to light cream when dry. N16

Mississippi Purple: 65-70 days. Mississippi Silver x Knuckle Purple Hull. Large-seeded brown crowder type. Pods are about 7 inches long; light green, turning purple first at the tip and along the suture, at which time they will shell; mature over a short time span. Easy to pick and shell. Resistant to most major cowpea diseases. *G1M*, H66, L14, N16

Mississippi Silver: (Mississippi Silverhull) 85-100 days. Large-seeded brown crowder type. Low, bushy plants produce few runners, are somewhat insect resistant. Pods are 6 to 6 1/2 inches long, slightly curved, silver colored at green shell stage. Peas set early at the top of the vines and shell very easily. Excellent in hot, humid southern climates; also does well in northern areas with longer seasons. F12, F19M, G51, G71, G93M, H33, H66, I91, J34, J84, K73, L7M, L9M, M46, M95, N16, etc.

Pink Eye Purple Hull: 65 days. Semi-vining plant grows 18 to 24 inches tall. Pods are 6 to 7 inches long; are held slightly above the foliage; turn purple at shell stage. Peas are medium-sized, rounded on ends; light-green with a red eye at green shell stage, turn white with maroon eye when dry. Good producer, usually produces 2 crops per season. D76, F12, F19M, G27M, G51, G82, G93M, H66, I64, J84, K71, K73, L14, M29, M46, N16, etc.

Purple Hull 49: 60 days. Actually a cross between a blackeye and a crowder. The hull is purple, and the seeds are larger than most blackeyes. An attractive home or market cultivar; also very good for freezing. Erect, bush-type plant; with favorable weather will produce 2 crops in one season. F19M, G27M, H66, J34, L14

Pusa Barsati:[1] 45 days. Heavy-yielding short plant, does not require support. Produces light-green, cylindrical pods, 10 to 12 inches long, stringless. An improved type, recommended for sowing during the rainy season in India. Pods can be harvested after 45 days. Seeds are boldly striped white and dull red. N91, R0, R50, S59M

Pusa Dofasli:[1] (Two Flashes) Bushy plant producing yellowish-green pods, approximately 7 inches long, in great profusion. Suitable for both the plains and hills. In India, grown as an irrigated crop during the summer and as a rainfed crop during the monsoon. S59M, S93M

Pusa Phalguni:[1] 60 days. High-yielding cultivar, suitable for growing in spring to early summer. Dwarf, bushy plants freely produce dark green pods, 7 to 8 inches long. Pods can be harvested after 60 days. R50, S59M

Queen Anne: (Queen Anne Blackeye) 65 days. Very dependable, heavy yielding blackeye introduced by the Virginia Truck Experiment Station. Plants are compact, 26 inches tall and runnerless. Pods are 7 to 9 inches long, with 8 to 12 seeds per pod. Highly recommended for green shell or dry use, freezing or canning. A13, *G1M*, H54, K10, L7M, M29, M46, M95M

Running Conch: 90 days. Produces 7 inch long pods, containing 12 to 14 peas per pod. Gives a clear pot-liquor when cooked. Non-climbing vine. Harder to shell than modern types, but valuable for its ability to resist curculio and suppress weeds. An heirloom, dating from the late 1800's. The original *conch pea* from which the various cream peas were developed. L7M

Snap Pea:[1] 65 days. A cream-type pea. Produces 10 to 12 inch long pods, containing 12 to 14 peas per pod. Best used like a snap bean when young; if allowed to mature, the shelled peas are similar to Texas Cream 40. When cooked it gives a clear pot-liquor. Vigorous, bush-type plant; very resistant to cowpea scab and cercospora leaf spot, fairly resistant to curculio. G27M, L7M

Speckled Purple Hull: Very heavy yielding, bunch-type plants. Pods are curved and grow to a length of about 7 inches. Peas are oblong, dark-brown in color, with lighter speckles. Excellent fresh, canned or frozen. H66, K71, L14

Susanne: 90 days. Semi-cream type. Produces 12 inch long pods, containing 14 to 16 medium-sized peas per pod. Makes a dark pot-liquor when cooked. Vigorous grower; sets fruit on bushy vines, then climbs and produces on corn stalks or on a trellis. May require protection from curculio during periods of hot, dry weather. Highly recommended for flavor and vigor. An heirloom from Alabama. L7M

Tennessee White Crowder: 65 days. Large, rounded seed; eggshell-white with a protruding, light brown eye; cream-pea-like flavor. Pods light green at green shell stage, dark green at maturity; 6 inches long. Vining type plant usually blooms over a longer period than other types. Very good producer if mature peas are kept picked off. B71, D87, H66, L14, N16

Texas Cream 40: 70 days. Bush type, high-yielding conch usually producing 2 crops a season. Long, cream-colored pods are oval, straight, and closely filled with medium-sized, tender cream-colored peas. Pods form at the top of the bush in hands, making for easy picking. Cross between an extra early blackeye and a midseason cream cultivar. F12, F19M, G27M

Tohono O'odham:[1] (Papago) 80 days. Delicious, delicately flavored pods. Small to medium-sized seeds usually have white eyes with black splotches (Dalmatian dog style), but may be all black. Similar to blackeyes but much more prolific and drought resistant, especially in the Southwest. I16

Vining Purple Hull: Long, smooth-skinned pods; very prolific; tinged a beautiful, dark purple-red color while in the shelling stage; easy to shell. Will yield green peas for a considerable length of time. Very productive and disease resistant. H66

Whippoorwill: 80 days. Very prolific, heavy vining type. Green pods, about 10 inches long; medium maturing. Smooth, speckled buff-brown peas. Will bear peas over a long period of time. A good general purpose old standard Southern pea. F19M, G51, H66, J34, L14, N16

White Acre: 75 days. Large, bush-type plant producing green pods with numerous small, creamy-white seeds. Pods set at the foliage level and are light straw-colored. Matures early and bears for a long period of time. The small seeds are harder to shell, but it is still one of the best-liked peas for home use with excellent fresh eating quality. F19M, G27M, K71

Zipper Cream: 70 days. Medium-green pod, turns a light straw color when dried; has a "zipper" for easy shelling. Peas are creamy-white; very large, especially for a cream type; of very good flavor. Low, bushy, compact plants with high yields. Resistant to curculio, stink bug and weevil damage due to its thick pod walls. B55, D76, F12, F19M, G27M, H66, J34, L14, N16

CUCUMBER {S}

CUCUMIS SATIVUS

PICKLING CUCUMBERS

COMMON

Hybrid

Anka: 50 days. Small, uniform fruit; smooth, tender, bright-green skin; crisp, crunchy flesh, with a fine flavor and no trace of bitterness; extremely small-seeded. Excellent eaten whole, fresh from the garden. Vigorous, heavy-yielding vine, produces fruit in three flushes; resistant to disease. The type of pickling cucumber most favored in Germany. I39

Calypso: 56 days. Uniform, straight, medium dark-green fruit; blocky, slightly tapered at the blossom end; white-spined. High yielding, gynoecious vine; highly disease resistant; adapted to high density planting and machine harvest. For home gardens, local markets and commercial production. Introduced by the North Carolina Agricultural Experiment Station. A25, C92, F13, *F72*, G27M, G64, G79, G82, *H61*, J84, J97M, K73, L42, M29, M49, N16, etc.

County Fair: (County Fair '83) 52 days. Dual-purpose cucumber. Can be used for pickling when small, and for slicing if allowed to grow larger. Sweet, non-bitter flavor; white-spined. Seedless if isolated from other cucumbers. High yielding, all-female vine; sets fruit without pollination; highly disease resistant; excellent trellising qualities. D76, E97, G16, H42, I64, I91, J34, L42

Liberty: 54 days. Blocky, nearly cylindrical, dark-green fruit; black-spined. Excellent for pickling whole; also produces uniform slices for bread and butter pickles. Vigorous, widely adapted vine; tolerant to cool spring weather; produces heavily over an extended period;

resistant to or tolerant of most cucumber diseases. All America Selections winner in 1978. B75, C69, E38, *E53M*, *E91G*, G82, I39, J20, K71, L91M

Saladin: 55 days. Short, bright-green fruit; 4 to 5 inches long, 1 1/2 inches in diameter; flesh crisp, tender, non-bitter; white-spined. Dual-purpose; ideal for pickling and salads. High yielding, gynoecious vine; widely adapted; resistant to cucumber mosaic virus, tolerant of powdery mildew and bacterial wilt; well suited for trellising. All America Selections winner in 1979. D65, H33, H42, H94, *I62*{PL}, I91, J20, K66, K71

Open-Pollinated

Boston Pickling: (Green Prolific) 58 days. Smooth, long oval, dark-green fruit; 6 to 7 inches long, 2 1/4 to 2 1/2 inches in diameter; slightly tapered, blunt-ended; flesh tender, crisp, very white; black-spined. Suitable for either sweet or dill pickles. Early and very prolific. Very popular home garden cultivar. Introduced about 1880. TAPLEY 1937; A2, A25, A56, *A75*, C44, E59Z, *G1M*, G57M, G67M, G79, *G83M*, *I59M*, K49M, L97, N39, etc.

Bush Pickle:[3] 45 days. Slightly tapered, cylindrical, medium-green fruit; 4 to 5 inches long; white-spined. Short-vined plant; only 2 to 3 feet in diameter; highly productive over a concentrated period; tolerant to scab and cucumber mosaic virus. Widely adapted. Ideal for container culture and miniature gardens. Introduced in 1982. D11M, D76, *E91G*, F13, *F72*, G16, G27M, G71, G82, H33, H54, *H61*, H94, I91, J20, L42, L79, etc.

Chicago Pickling: 60 days. Uniform, tapered, medium-green fruit; 5 to 6 inches long, 2 to 2 1/2 inches in diameter; nearly square-ended; black-spined. Especially well adapted for use as dill pickles; good for slicing when young. High yielding, precocious vine. Traditional home garden favorite. Introduced in 1888. TAPLEY 1937; A69M, *A75*, B13, B73M, *D49*, D65, G79, G87, I67M, K5M, K49M, M13M

Double Yield Pickling: 50 days. Retains its dark green color longer than most cultivars. Excellent for gherkins and dills. A high percentage of sets produce two fruits at each leaf joint. Susceptible to black spot and scab. For home gardens and retail markets. L42

Early Cluster: (Early Green Cluster) 55 days. Short, medium plump, light-green fruit; tapered towards the stem end; 5 to 6 inches long, 2 1/4 to 2 1/2 inches in diameter; flesh white, seedy, tender, well-flavored; black-spined. Vigorous, productive vine, often bears fruit in clusters near the root. One of the oldest of all cultivated cucumbers. Introduced prior to 1778. BURR, TAPLEY 1937; *F72*, *G1M*, J34, L7M, *L59G*

Early Russian: 50 days. Very short, oval, medium-green fruit; 3 1/2 to 4 inches long, 1 1/2 to 2 inches in diameter; flesh tender, crisp, well-flavored; black-spined. Highly prolific vine; generally bears fruit in pairs; produces until frost. Does well in northern short-season areas. Similar to Early Cluster. Introduced prior to 1854. BURR, TAPLEY 1937, VILMORIN; A2, A16, A25, A69M, D27, G67M, G87, H42, I99, K20, K49M, K71

Edmonson: 70 days. Uniform, whitish-green fruit; about 4 inches long; flesh crisp, tender and non-bitter, even when past its prime. Best used for pickling; also good for slicing. Very hardy, prolific vine; has good resistance to disease, insects and drought. Family heirloom from Kansas since 1913. K49M, L7M

Hokus: 59 days. Long, non-ridged, bright green fruit; white-spined. Good brining properties; stays solid when pickled. Holds dark color well into the larger sizes. Vigorous vine; resistant to scab, tolerant to cucumber mosaic virus; produces more and earlier female flowers than other open-pollinated types. C85M, P9

Japanese Long Pickling: 60 days. Slender, dark-green fruit; 12 to 18 inches long, 1 1/2 inches in diameter; flesh crisp, very mild and easy to digest; extremely small seeds. Should be harvested when about 12 inches long. Excellent for slicing for salads and bread and butter pickles. Often referred to as a "burpless" cucumber. J83M, L42

Jersey Pickle: 55 days. Straight, medium long fruit; 7 to 8 inches in length, 2 to 2 1/2 inches in diameter; skin deep medium green, tinted yellowish-white at the apex; flesh moderately thick, white; black-spined. Used for dill and ripe, sweet chunk pickles; considered too slender and long for smaller sizes. Heirloom that originated in Burlington County, New Jersey. TAPLEY 1937; G57M

Katsura Giant Pickling: Oblong fruit; 12 1/2 inches long, 4 1/2 inches in diameter; skin light green, turning almost white when fully ripe; flesh white, very thick. Good for pickling. An old favorite. Imported from Japan. E49

Mincu:[3] (Baby Mincu) 50 days. Slightly tapered, short oval, bright green fruit; 3 to 4 inches long, 1 3/4 inches in diameter; firm, crisp, snow-white flesh; white-spined. Compact, short-vined plant, only 2 feet in diameter; highly prolific. Ideal for small gardens and containers. Developed at the Minnesota Agricultural Experiment Station. A16, D27, D65, D82, G87, H42, K71

National Pickle: (National Pickling) 56 days. Short, slender, medium-green fruit; 5 1/2 to 6 inches long, 2 inches in diameter; thick walled; black-spined. Widely adapted, high yielding vine. Traditional home garden favorite. Introduced in 1929 by the National Pickle Packers Association. Selected for adaptability to both small pickles sizes and dills. TAPLEY 1937; A16, *A75*, B35M, C85M, *F60*, *F72*, G16, G68, H42, J58, J73, L97, M13M, M46, N16, etc.

Northern Pickling: 48 days. Medium-long, medium green fruit; slightly tapered towards the blossom end; black-spined. Should be picked frequently when small to maintain acceptable color and fruit shape. Relatively short, space-saving vine; resistant to scab, susceptible to mosaic; reliably high yielding. Adapted to cool northern areas. D68, E24, F44, F42, G6, K49M

Picklebush:[3] 52 days. Short, blocky fruit; 4 1/2 inches long, about 1 1/2 inches in diameter; skin light green, moderately warted; white-spined. Suitable for pickling at any stage, from small sweets to large dills. Very compact vine, grows only 20 to 24 inches long; tolerant to powdery mildew and cucumber mosaic virus. Ideal for gardeners with limited space. B75, G51, Q34

SMR 58: (Wisconsin SMR-58) 56 days. Straight, blocky, medium-green fruit; 6 1/2 inches long, 2 1/2 inches in diameter; black-spined. Good processing qualities. Vigorous, prolific vine; widely adapted; resistant to cucumber mosaic virus and scab. Standard home garden and market cultivar. A87M, B73M, B75M, C85M, *F60*, F82, *G1M*, G16, G51, G71, *H61*, J34, K73, L89, M95, etc.

<u>CORNICHONS</u> Small French pickling cucumbers. Traditionally served with meat pâtes and *terrines* (foods cooked in earthenware containers) because their tart pungency cuts the richness of these fatty dishes. VON WELANETZ.

Hybrid

Parigyno: Small, somewhat blocky, medium green fruit; resembles Vert Petit de Paris. Black spined. Remains firm and highly colored when pickled in vinegar. Vine very vigorous and productive, 100% gynoecious; resistant to cucumber mosaic virus. Introduced by Vilmorin. S95M

Open-Pollinated

De Bourbonne: (Cornichon de Bourbonne) Tiny, spiny cucumbers bred especially for making the whole, very small sour pickles that are served with pâté. Should be harvested at 2 to 2 1/2 inches in length. Soak in brine for a few hours, then pack in jars with mustard seed and a few sprigs of tarragon. Cover with vinegar and they will keep for months in the refrigerator. C53, I39, I77, K49Z

Fin de Meaux: (Fine Meaux) 60 days. Similar to Vert Petit de Paris, but fruits are longer and darker green. Should be picked when 2 inches long and 1/2 inch in diameter for cornichon pickles, or at 4 inches long and 1 1/2 inches in diameter for dills. Bears heavily until frost. G68, K49M

Vert de Massy: 53 days. High quality French cornichon. Distinctive fruits, considerably more slender than American pickling cucumbers. May be picked at "baby" finger size for tiny pickles, or when 4 inches long for pickling whole or sliced. Suitable for salads and snacks, with excellent taste and texture. For home gardens and specialty markets. Tolerant to scab. Black-spined. G6, S95M

Vert Petit de Paris: (Small Green Paris) 60 days. European strain of cucumber cultivated especially for use in making cornichons. Short, green, spiny fruit; should be harvested when about 2 inches long. Vigorous, compact, highly productive vine. An old standard cultivar that is very popular with French gardeners. Introduced prior to 1885. BRENNAN [Re], VILMORIN; *A75*, F33, G68, K49M, Q34, S95M

Witlo: 53 days. Tiny, well-shaped, European-style "mini" cucumbers or cornichons. Traditionally used for making very small, sour pickles. Slightly tapered fruit; firm and crisp. Should be harvested frequently, as they are bred to be picked at no more than 2 inches long. Vigorous, productive vine; resistant to cucumber mosaic virus, scab and powdery mildew. K66

SLICING CUCUMBERS

COMMON

Hybrid

Burpless: 60 days. Hybrid version of Japanese long. Straight, slender, bright-green fruit; 10 to 12 inches long; soft, tender, non-bitter skin, does not require peeling; crisp, mild flesh, very low in acid, easy to digest. Excellent for slicing or pickling. Vigorous, high yielding vine; bears over a long period; resistant to downy and powdery mildews. Should be grown on a trellis, otherwise the fruits may curve. A13, B73M, C44, D76, G71, H42, *H61*, H94, J20, J34, J58, K71, K73, L42, L97, etc.

Euro-American: 48 days. Combines the high quality of European greenhouse types with the vigor and productivity of American vines. Cylindrical, bright green fruit; 10 to 12 inches long; skin thin, spineless, palatable; flesh firm, thick and juicy, sweet, free of astringency; small seed cavity, few seeds. Sets fruit without pollination. Scab resistant. For greenhouse or outdoor culture. *E53M*, H95, I91, J20, L89

Pot Luck:[3] 58 days. Slightly tapered, medium dark-green fruit; 6 1/2 to 7 inches long, 2 1/4 inches in diameter; white-spined. Vigorous, short-vined plant, only 18 inches long; extremely productive; tolerant to cucumber mosaic virus and scab. Ideal for pots, window boxes and limited space gardens. A25, C44, D11M, E38, F19M, *F72*, G71, G79, H42, J7, J83M, L79, M13M, M46, N16, etc.

Salad Bush:[3] 57 days. Smooth, uniform fruit, 8 inches long; skin dark green. True dwarf plant, with a spread of only 24 inches; highly productive. Strongly resistant to powdery and downy mildews, target leaf spot, cucumber mosaic virus and scab. Excellent for patio containers. All America Selections winner in 1988. A56, B13, C44, D11M, F13, *F72*, G27M, G82, G87, H33, H95, I91, J20, J34, J84, M49, etc.

Sweet Slice: 62 days. Straight, cylindrical, dark-green fruit; 10 to 12 inches long, 2 1/2 inches in diameter; thin, tender skin, does not require peeling; crisp, non-bitter, extremely sweet flesh. Vigorous vine; productive over a long season; resistant to or tolerant of most cucumber diseases. A25, B73M, B75M, C85M, E49, F1, F82, G16, G51, *H61*, J7, L79, M46, M49, N16, etc.

Sweet Success: 55 days. Smooth, straight, medium-green fruit; 12 to 14 inches long; tender skin; sweet, crisp, mild flesh; white-spined. Vigorous, productive vine; sets fruit without pollination; has multiple disease resistance. Best grown on stakes or trellises. Suitable for greenhouse or outdoor cultivation. All America Selections winner in 1983. A16, B73M, C44, C85M, D11M, F1, F13, F19M, G16, G71, H42, H94, J7, L79, L97, etc.

Tasty Green: (Burpless Tasty Green) 58 days. Slender, dark-green fruit; 12 to 15 inches long; smooth, tender skin; crisp, mild flesh; white-spined. Best when harvested at 9 inches long and 1 inch in diameter. Vigorous vine; highly productive over a long season; tolerates summer heat; resistant to downy and powdery mildews; requires support for best results. C85M, C92, D11M, F1, F13, G33, G51, I39, L59, L91M, M46, M49, P83M, S55, S61, etc.

Open-Pollinated

Ashley: 65 days. Straight, dark-green fruit, tapered at the stem end; 7 to 8 inches long, 2 1/2 inches in diameter; white-spined. Good for shipping. Vigorous, high yielding vine; widely adapted; resistant to downy and powdery mildews. Developed at the Clemson Truck Experiment Station, Charleston, South Carolina. Introduced in 1955. *A75*, C69, F12, F19M, *F60*, *G1M*, G16, G27M, G51, G71, G79, H66, K71, L14, N16, etc.

Blanc Hâtif:[2] (Early White) Quite elongated, almost cylindrical fruit, nearly three times as long as broad; pale green, turning porcelain white as it ripens. Early maturing, but considerably later than Early Russian. Suitable for outdoor culture or forcing under frames. VILMORIN; **U33**

Bush Crop:[3] 60 days. Straight, medium-green fruit; 6 to 8 inches long; flesh crisp, tender, flavorful. Ideal for slicing and salads. Compact, short-vined plant, only 2 1/2 to 3 feet long; nearly free of runners; very productive. Excellent for containers and small space gardens. D11M, *E53M*, *E91G*, F19M, *F72*, G16, H33, H42, H54, *H61*, J20, K73, L79, *M43M*

Crystal Apple:[1] (White Lemon) 65 days. Similar to Lemon, but distinctly lighter in color. Short oval, creamy white fruit; 3 1/4 inches long, 2 1/2 inches in diameter; flesh crisp but tender, sweet, very flavorful; white-spined. Suitable for either slicing or pickling; also very good for stuffing. Vigorous, highly prolific vine. Originated in Australia prior to 1933. TAPLEY 1937; B49, C76M, D62, E49, F80, I77, K5M, K66, L91M, N50{PR}, P83M, R47, S45M, S55, S61, T1M, etc.

De Bouenil:[1] Medium-sized, white fruits borne on spreading plants. Popular in Europe for larger sized pickles because the white color allows the cook to choose the color the relish will be. Can also be used for whole pickles if harvested young, or for salads after peeling. C53

Early Yellow Dutch: (Gele Tros) Fruit longer and later than that of Early Russian; at first yellowish-green, becoming slightly orange-yellow when quite ripe. Usually only one or two fruit on each plant. Adapted to greenhouse or outdoor culture. Introduced prior to 1885. VILMORIN; C85M

Improved Long Green: (Long Green) 68 days. Straight, warted, medium dark-green fruit; 10 to 12 inches long, 2 1/2 to 3 inches in diameter; flesh tender, crisp, mild. black-spined. Suitable for both slicing and pickling. Vigorous, reliably productive vine. Long-time home garden favorite. Introduced in 1870. TAPLEY 1937; A16, A25, *A69M*, C92, E38, F12, F19M, G67M, *G83M*, H42, H49, H66, J73, K71, M13M, etc.

Lemon:[1] (Apple, True Lemon) 65 days. Short oval, lemon-yellow fruit; 3 to 3 1/2 inches long, 2 to 2 1/2 inches in diameter; flesh very thin, white, with a faint lemon-like flavor in late stages of development; black-spined. Excellent for both slicing and pickling. Vigorous, highly prolific vine. Introduced about 1894. TAPLEY 1937; C44, C53, D11M, D82, E24, *F60*, G16, G51, H94, *I62*{PL}, I67M, K71, L97, M46, M95, *N40*{PR}, etc.

Long Paris White:[2] (Bianco Lungo di Parigi) Long, cylindrical white fruit with firm flesh. The best white cucumber for use in salads. Also excellent for pickling. Vigorous, rapid growing vine. I77, Q11M

Marketer: (Early Green Market) 65 days. Straight, slightly tapered, dark-green fruit; 8 inches long, 2 1/2 inches in diameter; flesh white, solid, tender, very small seed mass; white-spined. Vigorous, productive vine. Popular for home gardens, local markets and shipping. All America Selections winner in 1943. B75M, C85M, C92, E97, *F60*, G57M, G71, G79, G93M, H49, H66, H94, L79, M13M

Marketmore 76: 58 days. Dark-green fruit; 8 to 9 inches long; white-spined. Productive vine; has multiple disease resistance. Contains the uniform dark-green color gene which reduces the number of "yellow bellies" at harvest time. For home gardens and commercial production. Developed by Dr. Munger at Cornell University. B1M, B75M, C44, E24, E57, F19M, *F60*, F82, G16, G71, *H61*, J7, K73, M46, N16, etc.

Perfection: (Perfection King of the Ridge) Cross between a frame and a ridge type, with the best qualities of both. Straight, nearly spineless, dark green fruit; 8 to 10 inches in length; excellent flavor. Vigorous, productive, comparatively hardy vine. Once grown extensively for the seaside salad trade in England. I99, L9, P83M, *R23*

Poinsett: 70 days. Cylindrical, dark green fruit, slightly blockier than Ashley; 7 1/2 inches long, 2 1/2 inches in diameter; white spined. Highly productive vine, especially in the Southeast. Strongly resistant to downy and powdery mildews. Moderately resistant to anthracnose and angular leaf spot. A87M, B75M, *D49*, *F72*, G51, G57M, G71M, G79, H66, *I59M*, J34, K27M

Poona Kheera: (Puna White Khira) Very unusual cultivar from India. Small, smooth, greenish-white fruit, 4 to 5 inches long; flesh very tender, crisp, flavorful. May be eaten at all stages, skin and all. Concentrated fruit set. E49, E83T, K49M, R0, R50, S93M

Precoce Grosso Bianco Crema:[2] (Early Large Creamy-White) Unusual Italian cultivar with attractive, creamy-white fruits, 5 inches long and 2 inches in diameter. No bitterness, with a mild, slightly sweet flavor. J73

Spacemaster:[3] 58 days. Smooth, cylindrical, dark-green fruit; 7 to 8 inches long. Compact, short-vined plant, only 2 feet long; extremely productive; resistant to cucumber mosaic virus and scab; should be picked regularly to avoid misshapen fruit late in the season. Well suited to container culture. A13, A25, C44, C85M, D82, E24, G6, *G83M*, H66, H94, J25M, J34, J58, K71, L7M, M46, etc.

Straight Eight: 60 days. Uniform, straight, deep-green fruit; 8 inches long, 2 to 2 1/2 inches in diameter; well rounded at the ends; white spined. Excellent for slicing; also used for pickling when small. Vigorous, productive vine; susceptible to most cucumber diseases. Popular home garden cultivar. All America Selections winner in 1935. TAPLEY 1937; A16, A25, B73M, C44, C85M, D82, F1, *F60*, *F72*, H66, H94, M13M, M46, M95, N16, etc.

Telegraph: (Rollinson's Telegraph, English Telegraph) 60 days. Smooth, glossy dark-green fruit, tapered to a distinct neck at the stem end; 15 to 18 inches long; thin, palatable skin; flesh solid, crisp, of excellent quality; black-spined. Vigorous, productive vine. Suitable for cold greenhouses, frames and outdoor trellis culture. Traditional English cultivar. Introduced prior to 1885. VILMORIN; A69M, D27, D68, F92, H42, K66, L42, M13M, *R23*

Telegraph Improved: 62 days. Smooth, straight, dark-green fruit, distinctly tapered at the stem end; up to 18 inches long; flesh crisp, tender, mild, flavor excellent, very few seeds. Vigorous, high yielding vine; very reliable. Suitable for greenhouse, polytunnel or outdoor culture. Traditional English cultivar. Introduced about 1897. A2, C85M, E33, G51, L91M, P83M, S45M, S55, S61

Tex Long: 65 days. Slender, slightly tapered, dark green fruit; 8 1/2 to 9 inches in length; good for slicing. Good shipping qualities. High yielding vine; produces well under irrigation or dry land farming. Tolerant to downy and powdery mildew. Moderately resistant to anthracnose and angular leaf spot. *D49*, G27M, N16

White Spine Improved: (Fordhook White Spine) 65 days. Uniform, straight, medium-green fruit; 7 to 8 inches long, 2 1/2 to 3 inches in diameter; tapered at the blossom end; flesh thick, seed mass moderately small; white-spined. Suitable for both slicing and pickling. Very productive. An old time favorite. A25, G57M, G67M, M95M, N39

White Wonder:[2] (Long White) 60 days. Medium oval, cylindrical fruit, rounded at the stem end; ivory-white at all stages of growth; 6 to 7 inches long, 2 1/4 to 2 1/2 inches in diameter; flesh nearly white, crisp, firm, very mild; black-spined. Used primarily for slicing, can also be pickled. Introduced in 1893 by W. Atlee Burpee Company. TAPLEY 1937; B73M, D11M, E24, E49, E97, *F60*, *F72*, G64, I97T, J7, J58, K49M, K71, M46, T1M, etc.

Zeppelin: Extremely large fruit, 10 to 12 pounds or more. Has produced some of the largest cucumbers ever grown, including the world record of 13 pounds 10 3/4 ounces. Can be used when green, or after turning golden yellow. It remains firm and juicy and may be sliced thinly, diced or chopped. L91M

GREENHOUSE Also called *European cucumber*, this is the type seen in stores individually wrapped in plastic. They cannot be grown outdoors as they are seedless and self-pollinating. Their culture is quite demanding, and requires exact feeding schedules to maintain deep green color. They are bitter free and easily digested.

Hybrid

Aurelia: 64 days. Very attractive, semi-glossy, dark-green fruit; 14 or more inches long; shallowly ribbed; seedless, bitter free flesh. Strong, open vine; very prolific, produces a high percentage of first class fruits; resistant to leafspot and gummosis. For heated early spring and late fall greenhouse crops and unheated summer poly tunnels. G6

Carmen: Straight, slightly ribbed, glossy dark-green fruit; 13 1/2 to 15 1/2 inches long; short necked; very good flavor and quality. Excellent shelf life. Very prolific, all-female vine; resistant to scab and leaf spot, tolerant to downy mildew and powdery mildew. For heated and unheated culture in spring, summer and autumn. *F72*, L42, *R11M*

Corona: Dark green, slightly ribbed fruit, 10 to 16 inches long; provides 3 or 4 days longer shelf life. Excellent for slicing. Slim, all-female vine is trimmed to an umbrella fashion; does not produce heavy foliage during the summer. Performs well in hot or cold weather. Strongly resistant to botrytis and mycosphaerella. Developed to withstand consistent cooler, 66° F. night temperatures. F1, *F85G*, L42, P9

Farbio: Medium length, slightly ribbed fruit, 14 to 15 inches long; dark green skin; quality high. Vigorous, all-female vine; requires less pruning than other types; relatively small, dark green leaves. Used for year round crops, but spring and summer production is recommended. *F85G*, L42, P69

Fembaby:[4] Dutch "mini" or "baby" greenhouse cucumber. Smooth, cylindrical, dark-green fruit; 8 to 10 inches long; short necked. All-female vine; sets fruit without pollination; resistant to scab, leaf spot, and plant bitterfree. Less demanding than other greenhouse types; suitable for greenhouse or windowsill culture. The result of 8 years of breeding. L91M, *R11M*

Mimi:[4] High quality Dutch greenhouse cucumber of the "mini" or "baby" type. Smooth, very cylindrical, dark-green fruit; 8 to 10 inches long; very short necked. Ripens early. Vigorous, open vine; produces over a long period; resistant to scab and leaf spot, tolerant to downy and powdery mildews. *R11M*

Petita:[4] 60 days. Easy to grow "mini cuke". Has the high qualities of the extra-long European-style cucumbers, in the popular American size. Slightly ribbed, dark-green fruit; 7 to 8 inches long; tender, glossy skin; crisp, sweet flesh. Vigorous vine; highly productive over a long season; resistant to cucumber mosaic virus, race 1. G6, S61

Sandra: 78 days. Straight, slender, dark-green fruit; 15 to 16 inches long; firm, crisp flesh, seedless and completely bitter free. Gynoecious vine, entirely free of male flowers; moderately heavy foliage cover. Noted for its labor saving short, strong laterals. Suitable for growing in any season. Developed to be an improved Toska 70 by the originator of Toska. C85M, *F72*, *F85G*, G64, J7, L42, L91M, P9

Superator: Medium length, straight fruit, 12 to 15 inches long; smooth dark green skin; excellent color and shape. Good shelf life. High yielding, all-female vine; produces well when night growing temperatures are reduced; easy to prune. Slight tolerance to powdery and downy mildews. Resistant to scab, leaf spot and plant bitterfree. J7, L42, *R11M*, *R23*

Toska 70: Straight, slender, glossy deep-green fruit; slightly spined and ribbed; 14 to 15 inches long. Moderately vigorous, gynoecious vine; produces a small quantity of male flowers that must be removed; consistently high yielding during winter months; resistant to scab and leaf spot. Highly recommended for growers who have had no previous experience with this type of cucumber. C85M, *F72*, L42

<u>MIDDLE EASTERN</u> Also called *beit alpha cucumber*, this type is considered by many to be the most delicious salad cucumber. They are smooth-skinned, crisp, tender, bitter free, nearly spineless and require no peeling. Suitable for greenhouse, poly tunnel, and outdoor crops.

Hybrid

Amira: 62 days. Slightly tapered, bright green fruit; 6 to 6 1/2 inches long, 1 1/2 inches in diameter; tender, spineless, non-bitter skin; crisp, sweet, "burpless" flesh. Should be picked when 4 to 5 inches long for best quality. Excellent for slicing and pickling. Very prolific vine; resistant to cucumber mosaic, tolerant to downy and powdery mildews. B75M, D11M, G87, I39, I91, J20, L79, *M43M*, *R11M*

Delila: Most popular gynoecious hybrid of the Beit Alpha type. Dark green fruit; 6 1/2 to 7 1/2 inches long. Vigorous plant; early, with exceptionally high yields; resistant to cucumber mosaic virus and melon mosaic virus race 1. Suitable for all open field production seasons. Grown extensively in the Middle East. *P75M*, T27M

Hylares: 58 days. Attractive, smooth-skinned, glossy bright green fruit; crisp, juicy, bitter free flesh. Traditionally eaten as a thirst-quenching snack on hot summer days, or sliced into a bowl of fresh yogurt with a hint of garlic and mint. Resistant to watermelon and cucumber mosaic viruses. K66

Jordan: 56 days. Straight, cylindrical, glossy green fruit; 6 1/2 to 7 inches long; smooth, non-bitter skin; crisp, easily digested flesh; quality very high. Excellent for either slicing or pickling. High yielding, all-female vine; resistant to cucumber and melon mosaic viruses. *F60*

Niva: An early gynoecious hybrid, with a vigorous plant, dark green fruits and high yields. Resistant to cucumber mosaic virus, powdery mildew and downy mildew. Suitable for growing in regions with summer as well as winter rains, due to mildew resistance. *P75M*

Saria: 56 days. Straight, cylindrical dark-green fruit; smooth, tender skin, requires no peeling; crisp, tender flesh, very flavorful, completely bitter free, small seed cavity. Best picked when about 4 to 6 inches long. All-female and parthenocarpic, requiring no pollination. Resistant to scab and powdery and downy mildews. G6

Sweet Alphee: 55 days. Extra-dark green Beit Alpha type with a small seed cavity and a nice, bitterfree flavor. Ideal for small scale production because it does not need a separate pollinator. Has an extended picking period but must be picked small, no larger than a pickle. Developed for outdoor and poly tunnel crops. Tolerant to scab and both mildews. A13, G6, *K16M*

Tenderfresh: 56 days. Straight, cylindrical, glossy green fruit; 6 1/2 inches long, 1 1/2 inches in diameter; smooth, non-bitter flesh; crisp, "burpless" flesh, very good flavor and quality. Excellent for home grown pickles at shorter lengths. Very prolific, gynoecious vine; resistant to cucumber mosaic virus. Very similar to Jordan. *F60*

Open-Pollinated

Amira II: 70 days. Intermediate in size between ordinary slicing cucumbers and pickling cucumbers. Thin, very smooth skin, does not require peeling. Very fine flavor. Grows better in cool weather than most Middle Eastern types. L89

Beit Alpha M.R.: 58 days. Straight, cylindrical, glossy medium-green fruit; tapered towards the blossom end; 6 1/2 to 7 inches long, 1 1/2 to 2 inches in diameter; tender skin, with fine black spines; crisp, sweet flesh. Excellent for slicing or pickling. Gynoecious vine, entirely free of male blossoms; widely adapted; resistant to cucumber mosaic virus. A32, B49, *F60*, *R11M*

Muncher: (Burpless Muncher) 59 days. Attractive, smooth, medium-green fruit; 6 1/2 to 7 inches long, 2 inches in diameter; bitter free at all slicing stages. Excellent for slicing; can be pickled at smaller lengths. Vigorous, productive vine; resistant to cucumber mosaic virus. A25, B71, D11M, *F60*, P1G

Samson: Smooth, uniform, dark-green fruit. Vigorous, monoecious plant; resistant to cucumber mosaic virus and melon mosaic virus race 1. *P75M*, T27M

<u>ORIENTAL</u> These cultivars have been developed especially for their crispness. Most are very long and narrow and have numerous, long spines which can be easily brushed off. Some newer types produce straight fruit even if allowed to sprawl on the ground, older types should be trellised or the fruit will curve.

Hybrid

Green King: 70 days. Japanese burpless type. Medium-long fruit, about 12 inches in length, uniformly cylindrical from end to end; very fine flavor. Unlike other oriental types which require a trellis for perfectly straight fruit, it produces mostly straight fruit even if allowed to sprawl on the ground. Vigorous grower under cool conditions. L89

Natsuhikari: (Tokyo Slicer) 35 days. Very smooth, dark-green fruit, 12 inches long and 1 1/2 inches in diameter; very low spined; of excellent quality. Very vigorous plant with numerous side branches, enabling a high yield over a long period. Good for sowing from spring to summer. Suitable for growing without support or trellis. D55, *S70*

Palace King: Slender, dark green fruit; 12 or more inches long, only 1 1/2 to 2 inches in diameter; thick, crisp flesh of fine flavor; white-spined. Provides thin-skinned fruit for salads or in mixed pickles. Vigorous, productive vine, produces over a long season; tolerant to powdery mildew. Needs to be trellised for straight fruit. B75

Palace Pride: Refined Suyo type. Ridged, dark green fruit; 10 to 12 inches long; white-spined; small seed cavity. G33

Silver Star: Slender, black-spined fruit; greenish-white, except at the stem end where it is darker green; firm flesh with excellent palatability. Best harvested when about 8 inches long. Primarily used for kimchee and pickling. Vigorous, high-yielding vine; female-node ratio about 72%. Suited for early spring growing in tunnels or greenhouses. *Q3*

Open-Pollinated

Aodai: (Japanese Climbing) 60 days. Straight, cylindrical, bright-green fruit; 9 to 10 inches long, 2 to 2 1/2 inches in diameter; spineless; very crisp, mild flesh. Vigorous, climbing vine; very hardy, also tolerant to heat; can be grown on poles, trellises, or without support. Main stem should be cut to encourage side-branching. I39, *P39*

China Long: (Chinese Long Green) 70 days. Straight, slender, dark-green fruit; prominently ridged and warted; 15 to 20 inches long, 2 to 2 1/2 inches in diameter; firm, crisp, mild flesh, few seeds. Vigorous, high yielding vine; dependable and widely adapted; resistant to mosaic; requires support, or fruit may curve. Introduced in 1862. TAPLEY 1937; B73M, C44, D11M, D27, E5T, H42, K20, K49M, L42, L91M

Early Ochiai: Slender, dark green fruit; 7 to 8 inches long, 1 1/2 inches in diameter; high black spines; quality excellent. Usually harvested when about 6 inches in length. Well suited for forcing. High yielding in cooler areas. When unstaked, fruits coil into "serpent" form. A2

Heiwa Green Prolific: (Heiwa Prolific) 65 days. Straight, bright-green fruit; 9 to 10 inches long, 2 inches in diameter; "burpless", non-bitter. Insensitive to day-length; prolific even under tropical conditions. Can be grown without support outdoors, or trellised in a cold-frame. Very popular in Japan. I99, *P39*

Kyoto Three Feet: (Kyoto Yard Long) 62 days. Long, slender, light bright-green fruit; 24 to 30 inches in length, 1 1/2 inches in diameter; firm, crisp, mild flesh, small seed mass, confined to the blossom end, very good quality. Good for slicing and pickles. Requires trellising to produce the straightest fruit. For early summer planting. E49, G51, I84, J83M, L59, L91M, P83M, S55

Sanjiaku Kiuri: Straight, slender, light-green fruit; 18 to 24 inches long; thin, smooth skin; crisp, mild flesh, very good flavor. Best quality is obtained when harvested at 18 inches in length or less. Excellent for slicing or pickles. Should be grown with support, otherwise the fruit may curve. G33

Suyo Long: (Soo Yoh) 65 days. Slender, deep-green fruit; 12 to 15 inches long; highly ribbed and spined; crisp, sweet, "burpless" flesh, few seeds, very high quality. Excellent for slicing and bread and butter pickles. Vigorous, productive vine; widely adapted; grows well in hot weather; resistant to powdery mildew; requires staking for best results. B75, D55, D68, E24, E83T, G6, G33, J20, J73, L7M, L11, L59, *L79G*, *P39*, Q34, etc.

Tokiwa: (Tokyo Green) 35 days. Very deep green fruit, 12 inches long and 1 1/2 inches in diameter; low spined. Highly prolific vine; very well suited for growing without support or trellis. For sowing from spring through summer. D55, *S70*

Yamato Extra Long: 65 days. Straight, slender, dark-green fruit; 18 to 24 inches long, 1 1/2 to 2 inches in diameter; smooth skin; firm, crisp, mild flesh, few seeds, very good flavor. Excellent for slicing. Should be trellised for best results. E59, H49, I39

CURRANT {GR}

RIBES SPP.

BLACK CURRANTS (R. nigrum)

Baldwin: Medium to large fruit; skin fairly thick and tough; flesh juicy, subacid, very rich in vitamin C; ripens evenly and hangs well on the bush. Medium-sized bush; suitable for small gardens; susceptible to leaf spot and mildew diseases. Main commercial cultivar in England, where it has been cultivated for over 100 years. SIMMONS 1978; D47, N24M

Ben Lomond: Vigorous, upright bush, free of foliage damaging insects. Flowers almost 3 weeks later than Baldwin but fruits at the same time. One of the highest producing black currants and also one of the least prone to mildew. Developed at the Scottish Horticultural Research Institute. D47, P86

Ben Sarek: Large, black fruit of good quality. Small, compact bush, highly productive. Can be planted at 4 foot x 5 foot spacing, yet bears as heavily as full-sized bushes. Resistant to frost and mildew. Developed at the Scottish Horticultural Research Institute. D47

Black September: A late-ripening cultivar with large, firm fruit that has a mild flavor. Makes excellent jam and jelly. Upright bush. D47, I49M, I74, J61M, N0

Blacksmith: Basal berry large, graduating to a small berry at the end of the strig; skin thin and tender; flesh juicy, subacid, somewhat sweet when fully ripe; ripens in midseason, hangs well on the bush. Bush large to very large, spreading; bears a good crop even on light soil. Very easy to pick. Introduced in 1916. SIMMONS 1978; D47, N24M

Boskoop Giant: (Boskoop) Fruit large to very large, but smaller at the end of the strig; skin thin and tender; flesh juicy, rich, subacid, sweetish when fully ripe; ripens early and fairly evenly; does not hang very well. Bush vigorous; production fair to heavy; usually 1 sprig of berries to a spur; strig long and drooping and easy to pick. Raised at Boskoop, Netherlands, before 1895. HEDRICK 1925, SIMMONS 1978; D37, D47, G54, I74, J61M, L99M, N0

Champion: Fruit small to large, round; skin medium in thickness and toughness; skin color dull black; flesh yellowish, firm, not very juicy; flavor sprightly, becoming nearly sweet; quality good to very good; ripens late and unevenly. Bush large; vigorous; upright-spreading. Originated in England; introduced to the United States prior to 1897. HEDRICK 1925; D47, N0

Climax: Large, black fruit; skin relatively thick; flavor briskly subacid; quality good; ripens in mid-season. Bush vigorous and productive; bunches large. Originated by William Saunders, London, Ontario, Canada about 1887, from a seedling of Naples. HEDRICK 1925; G41, G69M, N24M

Consort: (R. ussuriense x) Medium to large fruit, 1/2 to 3/4 inch in diameter; skin bluish-black; flesh somewhat soft; flavor strong; ripens late July; clusters medium long. Bush resistant to white pine blister rust; self-fruitful, not requiring insect pollination; vigorous and productive; upright. Originated in Ottawa, Ontario, Canada. Introduced in 1952. BROOKS 1972; A91, C34, D37, D47, F11, F43M, H16, H65, J29, J61M, K81, L27M, *M81M*, N0, N24M, N26, N26{PR}, etc.

Coronet: (R. ussuriense x) Medium-sized, black fruit; resembles standard black currant cultivars. Bush immune from rust. Originated in Ottawa, Ontario, Canada by Canada Department of Agriculture Research Station. Introduced in 1948. BROOKS 1972; A91, D47

Crusader: (R. ussuriense x) Fruit large; skin black; resembles standard black currant cultivars; ripens later than Consort. Reported to have poor fruit set when planted alone. Most valuable characteristic of the bush is its immunity from rust. Originated in Ottawa, Ontario, Canada. Introduced in 1948. BROOKS 1972; A91, D37, D47

Green's Black: Medium to medium large fruit; skin thick and fairly tough; flavor subacid. Ripens second early to midseason, being ready for harvest just before Wellington. Bush moderately vigorous, very heavy bearing; benefits from cross-pollination; flowers partly resistant to frost damage. Usually 2 or 3 fairly short strigs to a spur. SIMMONS 1978; D47, J61M

Invigo: Mild-flavored fruit; more enjoyable fresh because of its sweetness. A recently released cultivar developed in Germany. D37, D47

Jet: (Malling Jet) Small fruits borne in long clusters, mostly bland in flavor; matures very late, one of the latest. Bush very prolific; flowers late and thus avoids early frost damage. Ideal for U-Pick operations. Highly regarded in Great Britain where it originated. D47, N0

Laxton's Giant: Very large fruit, excellent for exhibition; skin thin and tender; flesh juicy, somewhat sweet when fully ripe, quality very good; ripens early and fairly evenly. Bush vigorous, spreading, resistant to disease and frost, bears heavily. Usually 1 or 2 strigs to a spur. Strigs fairly long, easily picked. Originated in England. Introduced in 1946. SIMMONS 1978; D47

Mendip Cross: Medium-sized fruit; skin thin and tender; flavor subacid to sweet when fully ripe; ripens early July. Unpopular commercially because it ripens unevenly and the overripe berries soon become squashy. Bush medium-sized; spreading; sensitive to poor drainage conditions. Usually 1 or 2 long strigs to a spur. SIMMONS 1978; D47, N0

Noir de Bourgogne: Fruit medium in size; ripens evenly; flavor similar to Boskoop Giant. Bush very productive; the choice pollinator for Boskoop Giant. D37, D47

Silver Gieter: (Silvergieters Zwarte) Fruit large; skin thick and tough; flesh juicy; flavor subacid; quality very good; ripens in early mid-season. Very tall, vigorous bush; production fairly good; strigs long and easily picked. Originated in the Netherlands. SIMMONS 1978; D47, N0, N24M

Strata: Large, roundish fruit; skin purple-black, glossy, very attractive, resembles that of an eggplant; flavor very sweet for a black currant, quality excellent. Bush vigorous and productive, low-spreading. D47

Wellington XXX: Medium to large fruit; skin thick but tender; flavor subacid, somewhat sweet when fully ripe; ripens early mid-season. Berries do not hang well on the bush and often split. Bush large; very vigorous and productive; spreading; strigs usually 1 or 2 to a spur. Popular commercial cultivar in Kent, England. SIMMONS 1978; A91, C34, D11M, D47, P86

Willoughby: Fruit medium to large; skin black; flesh juicy; quality good; clusters large. Bush highly resistant to mildew and white pine blister rust; self-fruitful; very hardy; productive; more spreading than Consort. Originated in Parkside, Saskatchewan, Canada by Walter Willoughby Sr. Introduced in 1953 by Honeywood Lilies & Nursery. BROOKS 1972; A16, A91, B47, D47, F67, I49M, I74, L99M, N0, N24M, N26, N26{PR}

PINK CURRANTS

Couleur de Chair: (Champagne) Bunches medium in length, loose; berries large, pale pink, rather acid; ripens late. Esteemed in France for making jelly. Bush vigorous, productive. Probably a cross between the common red and the common white currant. Introduced prior to 1778. HEDRICK 1925; **T87{SC}, Y83{SC}**

Gloire de Sablons: Fruit small; skin white, striped with red; flavor acid; quality considered poor; bunches short, small. Bush upright; vigorous; moderately productive. Introduced prior to 1858. HEDRICK 1925; **T87{SC}, U7M{SC}, Y83{SC}**

Rosa Hollandische: Reddish-pink, relatively smooth and glossy fruit; quality fair to good. Vigorous, upright-spreading plant, free of thorns; moderately productive; easy to harvest. Originated in Europe. NCGR; **T87{SC}, Y83{SC}**

Tinka: Medium to large, rose pink fruit; sweet flesh, contains a higher percentage of sugar than that of other pink currants. Recently introduced into the United States from Germany. D47

RED CURRANTS

Cherry: Fruit large, not very uniform, round; skin thin, smooth, tough; skin color bright but dark red; flesh very juicy, firm; flavor pleasant, acid or mildly subacid; quality good; ripens early. Bush medium to large; vigorous; upright when young, becoming more spreading with age. Short strigs make picking difficult. Known prior to 1840. HEDRICK 1925; A91, B47, B67, C63, *D59*, E4, H16, H49, I49M, I74, *M81M*, N0, N24M

Fay's Prolific: (Fay) Large, roundish fruit; skin smooth, thin, tough; skin color dark-red; flesh firm, juicy; flavor subacid, sweetish when fully ripe; ripens early mid-season. Bush upright to slightly spreading; moderately vigorous. Originated in Fredonia, New York by George S. Josselyn. Introduced in 1880. HEDRICK 1925, SIMMONS 1978; C58

Jonkheer van Tets: (Von Tets) Medium to large fruit; deep-red in color; flavor subacid; quality very good; ripens early, late June to early July. Bush fairly upright; very productive; mildew and aphid resistant. Strigs of medium length. Seedling of Fay's Prolific; originated in the Netherlands. SIMMONS 1978; D47, G69M, I74, J61M, L12, N0

Laxton's No. 1: Medium-sized fruit; skin very bright red; flesh juicy, seeds small; ripens in midseason, about the middle of July. Strong vigorous bush, upright to spreading; a heavy and consistent bearer. Berries thickly bunched on strigs of medium length. SIMMONS 1978; C34, D47, P86

Malling Redstart: (Redstart) Medium to large fruit; has a stronger flavor and greater acidity than Red Lake; quality very good; ripens late, about 2 weeks after Red Lake. Bush moderately vigorous and upright, a consistent and heavy bearer. Strigs long, with up to 2 secondary trusses. D47

Perfection: Uniformly large fruits, roundish or slightly oblate; skin smooth, thin but tough; skin color medium to dark red; flesh juicy, tender; flavor sprightly subacid becoming mild when fully ripe; quality very good; ripens early mid-season. Bush large, vigorous; upright-spreading; productive. Originated in Rochester, New York by C.G. Hooker in 1887. HEDRICK 1925; C63, H33, *H90*, N24M

Red Dol: High yielding, good quality fruit. Hangs on the bushes long after it is ripe, when most others drop off. Makes excellent jam, jellies and preserves. Origin unknown; introduced to Windy Ridge Nursery by one of the early Canadian settlers. N26, N26{PR}

Red Lake: Fruit large, borne on long stems; skin tough, bright-red; flesh juicy; seeds fairly large but quality equal to that of Perfection; excellent for jelly; ripens late; clusters long, well filled. Bush upright; vigorous; superior to Perfection. Originated in Excelsior, Minnesota by W.H. Alderman. Introduced in 1933. BROOKS 1972, SIMMONS 1978; A16, B43M, B73M, C63, D11M, G16, G23, G41, G54, G71, H16, K64, K81, L30, *M65M*, etc.

Rubina: Large to very large, bright red fruit. Has a noticeably high sugar content. Bush vigorous and productive. Relatively new cultivar developed in Sweden. D47

Wilder: Medium to large, roundish oblate fruit; skin smooth, thin, tender; skin color dark-red; flesh firm, juicy; flavor pleasantly subacid; quality good; ripens late mid-season to late; hangs on a long time after ripening. Bush large; vigorous; upright to slightly spreading; very productive. Originated in Irvington, Indiana by E.Y. Teas about 1877. HEDRICK 1925; A88M, A91, B47, B67, *C47*, *C54*, C63, *D59*, D76, E97, H16, L97, *M81M*

Wilson's Long Bunch: Medium-sized, roundish fruit; color bright but light red; flesh juicy, of good quality. Ripens late, at the end of July and for some time into August as the berries hang well on the bush. Bush moderately vigorous, semi-erect; bears freely; blooms very late. Strigs long. A useful cultivar for extending the season. Widely grown in England. SIMMONS 1978; **T87**{SC}

WHITE CURRANTS (R. sativum)

Bar-le-Duc a Fruits Blanc: A white currant used in the preparation of the famous seedless currant jelly made only in Bar-le-Duc, France, since 1559. In the preparation of this gourmet delicacy a goose feather is used to gently pick out the currant seeds one by one without damaging the berries. HENDRICKSON; **T87**{SC}

Bianca: Large to very large fruit with an exceptionally high sugar content. Bush vigorous and productive. Relatively new cultivar that originated in Sweden. D47

White Dutch: Medium-sized, milky yellow fruit; flesh juicy, fairly sweet when fully ripe; ripens in midseason, about the second week of July. Bush moderately vigorous, upright to spreading, fairly productive. Strigs of medium length. One of the oldest white currant cultivars. SIMMONS 1978; D47

White Grape: Medium to large, round ovate fruit; skin smooth, thin, tender; color clear translucent yellowish-white; flesh firm, juicy; flavor pleasantly subacid; quality good; ripens mid-season. Bush of medium size and vigor; spreading, sometimes sprawling; productive. Strigs difficult to pick without crushing some berries. HEDRICK 1925, SIMMONS 1978; A16, D47

White Imperial: Medium to large, rounded fruit; skin smooth, thin, tender; color creamy white, a shade darker than White Grape; flesh firm, juicy; flavor pleasantly subacid to rich and sweet; quality very good to best; ripens mid-season. Large, dark-colored seeds show through flesh and skin. Bush above medium in size and vigor; broad, spreading; productive. HEDRICK 1925; A91, D47, H16, I36, J61M, L12, N0, N26, N26{PR}

White Jüterborg: (Weisse aus Jüterborg) (R. petraeum) Medium to small, white fruit of good quality. Bush not a heavy bearer. An old European heritage cultivar that still has merit. D47

White Pearl: Large, pale-yellow fruit; flavor briskly subacid; quality good; bunches large, well filled; ripens mid-season. Bush moderately vigorous; upright-spreading; unproductive. Originated in Brussels, Belgium prior to 1875. HEDRICK 1925; D11M, D47, G69M, H85, J7, L12, N24M

White Versailles: Large, light yellow fruit; juicy sweet flesh; ripens early, about the beginning of July. Bush fairly strong, vigorous, upright; very heavy bearing. Strigs of medium length. SIMMONS 1978; D47, G41, P86

DATE {GR}

PHOENIX DACTYLIFERA

Abbada: Attractive, glossy black fruit with frost-like bloom; 2 inches long, 3/4 of an inch wide; cures to black with a purple glume; flesh not thick, soft, melting. Novelty because of its black appearance in variety packs. Early to midseason ripening. Originated in Brawley, California. I83M

Barhi: (Barhee) Small to medium fruit; amber when ripening, deep golden brown when cured; flesh firm but very tender, very syrupy, rich yet not heavy or cloying; relatively little astringency in khalal stage for fresh consumption; highest sugar content - 82% invert sugar. Late ripening. Moderate damage by rain and humidity. Originated in Iraq. <u>C65</u>{PR}, <u>E67M</u>{PR}, I83M

Dayri: (Dairee, Dairi) Fruit medium to large, oblong to oblong-elliptical; skin red when immature, brown to black when soft and ripe; flesh soft, amber, texture good, semitranslucent; flavor good, with a heavy sweetness. Ripens in midseason; ripens well in high humidity and extreme heat. Apparently best adapted to heavy soils. Originated in Iraq. BROOKS 1972; <u>C65</u>{PR}, I83M

Deglet Noor: (Date of the Light) Medium to large fruit; semi-dry; amber on ripening, deeper brown when cured; flesh deep golden brown, conspicuously translucent; flavor delicate, mild, very sweet, distinctive. Susceptible to rain and high humidity. Late ripening, requires a large amount of heat to mature properly. Originated in the Saharan oasis of Balad al Ahmar more than 375 years ago. <u>C65</u>{PR}, <u>E67M</u>{PR}, I83M

Halawi: (The Sweet) Fruit medium large; translucent bright golden brown; skin thin, tender, adheres closely to the flesh; flesh firm but tender, often more like a soft date than a dry date; flavor sweet and honey-like, but not rich; good keeping qualities. Midseason ripening. Originated in Algeria. POPENOE, P.; <u>C65</u>{PR}, <u>E67M</u>{PR}, I83M

Khadrawi: (The Verdant) Medium to large fruit, oblong to oblong-elliptical; translucent orange-brown to light brown in color; skin firm, medium thick, fairly tough; flesh thick, firm and meaty, translucent orange-brown; flavor rich and extremely pleasant, never cloying the palate, even if eaten in quantity every day. Ripens in midseason. Originated in Iraq. POPENOE, P.; <u>C65</u>{PR}, <u>E67M</u>{PR}, I83M

Khisab: (The Abundant Producer) A fresh fruit date, rarely cured. Medium sized, broadly oval fruit; deep amber when ripe; skin moderately thick, tough, coarsely wrinkled; flesh tender, deep amber, 1/2 inch thick, quality fair. Produces fresh fruit later than all other cultivars. Originated in Oman. I83M

Medjool: Large to very large fruit; amber when ripening, reddish brown when cured; flesh soft, rich and delicious, firmer than Barhi, with high invert sugar; needs thinning for largest size and uniformity. Early ripening. Only slightly damaged by occasional rains and high humidity; susceptible to bayoud (fusarium) disease. Originated in Bou Denib, Morocco. C65{PR}, E1G{PR}, E67M{PR}, I83M, N84{S}, P5{S}

Saidy: Fruit large, broad and blocky; semi-dry; skin amber brown; flavor very sweet, almost cloying, improves with storage; excellent keeping quality, but develops sugar crystals. Early to midseason ripening. Medium to high yields; sensitive to saline soil. Originated in Egypt. I83M

Sayer: Medium to medium large fruit, broadly oblong to oblong-elliptical; skin orange-brown, dark, glossy; flesh slightly fibrous, quality only fair; flavor very sweet, not cloying, not rich or distinctive, improves with storage. Ripens in midseason. One of the most tolerant of salt and other adverse factors. Originated in Iraq, where it is one of the most widely grown dates. MORTON 1987a, POPENOE, P.; I83M

Thoory: (The Bull's Date) Medium to large, oblong fruit; ripens and cures to light grayish-brown to straw color; flesh golden brown, thick, firm and nearly dry but not hard or brittle; flavor sweet, nutty, and delicate; does not deteriorate even if kept for a year or more. Sometimes known as the *bread date*. Late ripening. Bears heavily, with clusters of exceptional size. Originated in Algeria. C65{PR}, I83M

Zahidi: Fruit medium sized; surface smooth, glossy, attractive; skin rather thick; flesh translucent golden-yellow close to the skin, whitish near the seed, soft, meaty and full of syrup; flavor sweet, sugary, and not cloying; can be used either as a dry date or a soft date. Much used in the manufacture of *arrak*. One of the earliest dates to mature. Originated in Iraq. POPENOE, P.; C65{PR}, E67M{PR}, I83M

EGGPLANT {S}

SOLANUM AETHIOPICUM   SOLANUM MELONGENA

GREEN-SKINNED

HYBRID

Liao Qui No. 1: 110 days. Medium-early type. Long, ellipsoid fruit; skin green; flesh white, tender, flavor sweet. Plants shorter than other cultivars; height about 2 feet; resistant to lodging; well suited to dense plantings. *O54*

OPEN-POLLINATED

Applegreen: 62 days. Small to medium-sized, egg-shaped fruit, averaging 4 ounces in weight; light-green skin, does not need peeling; mild, non-acid white flesh. Productive, upright plant, sets fruit under adverse northern conditions. Developed at the New Hampshire A.E.S. in 1964. L7M

Louisiana Green Oval: 90 days. Large, round oval fruit, attains a weight of 2 to 4 pounds; resembles Black Beauty, but larger; glistening, light-green skin; quality excellent, flavor mild; seed cavity confined to the blossom end. Best harvested while skin is still glossy. Sturdy, upright plant; height 2 to 3 feet; holds fruit well off the ground. E49

Louisiana Long Green:[1] (Green Banana) 100 days. Long, well-shaped fruit; 8 inches in length, 3 inches in diameter; skin green with dark-green stripes; quality excellent. Similar to Louisiana Green Oval, except for the longer shape. Very prolific plant; height 3 feet. Highly recommended for roadside markets. A49G, E49, L7M

Thai: (Thai Round Green, Green Tomato) 80 days. Small, round fruits, 1 to 2 inches in diameter; borne in clusters; skin green and white, turning gold on full maturity. May be seedy or even bitter, but provides authentic fruits for Southeast Asian cuisine. Excellent for pickling, stuffing and stir-frying. Tall, bushy plants; height 3 feet; some may have thorns. *B59*{PR}, D55, E59

Thai Green: (Thai Long Green, Elephant Tusk) 90 days. Long, slender, cylindrical fruit; 12 to 14 inches in length, 1 1/2 to 2 inches in diameter; skin light-green, thin, attractive; flesh tender, flavor very mild. Vigorous and prolific plant. Heirloom from Thailand. D55, E59, K49M, L7M, *O53*

Tiger Stripe:[1] (Lao Green Stripe) 120 days. Small, round, very attractive fruit; 2 inches in diameter; skin thick, cream-colored overlain with green "tiger stripes" on the upper half of fruit; seedy flesh with a pleasant flavor. Tall plant, to 3 1/2 or 4 feet, withstands light frost. Heirloom from Laos. L7M

PURPLE/PINK-SKINNED

HYBRID

Baby Bell:[2] 55 days. Jet black fruit, 2 inches deep and 1 1/2 inches wide. Dwarf plant, up to 10 inches tall; ideal for 6 inch pots or containers; produces about 6 fruit. Unusual "baby vegetable" for salad bar trade. L42

Classic: 76 days. Recommended where a longer, slimmer fruit shape is preferred. Rich, glossy purple-black color that holds well after picking. Its tapered shape is uniform in all sizes. Vigorous, erect plant; bears abundantly; stands up to stress better than most. F13, *G1M*, J14{PL}

Dusky: 63 days. Medium-sized, long oval fruit, 8 inches in length and 3 1/2 inches in diameter; glossy, purplish-black skin; firm flesh of quality good; ripens extremely early; packs and ships well. Very uniform color and shape. Upright plant; height 2 to 3 feet; high-yielding; resistant to tobacco mosaic virus. Recommended for commercial growers and home gardeners. A16, A87M, B75M, C44, D65, D82, E32M{PL}, F1, *F72*, G51, G71, H94, J7, J14{PL}, K73, L89, L97, M46, etc.

Gourmet Brand Mini:[2] Produces large quantities of small, dark purple fruit on sturdy plants. Should be harvested when no more than 2 inches wide and 3 to 3 1/2 inches long for best yields and quality. *E91G*

Haguro Hitokuchimaru:[2] 35-40 days. A genetically small eggplant. Highly prolific; produces dozens of very small, oval fruits the size of large pecans. Very dark purple, glossy skin. The calyx and stem are deep purple as well. Good for pickles; suitable for processing. Compact, semi-upright plant; tolerant to heat and dry conditions. K66, *Q28*

Ichiban: 58 days. Hybrid oriental type. Long, slender, cylindrical fruit; 10 inches in length, 2 inches in diameter, slightly tapered towards the blossom end; skin dark purple, glossy; flesh soft, slow to develop seeds, quality and flavor good. Tall, upright plant; height 36 to 40 inches; highly productive. For local markets and home gardens. B75M, *F72*, F82, *G83M*, *H61*, H66, H94, H95, I64, I91, J20, J84, L14, L79, M29, M46, etc.

Lavender Cicle:[1] Spineless, easy to pick fruit; 9 inches long, 1 1/2 inches in diameter; weight about 3 ounces; attractive white skin, heavily striped with light purple; white flesh; green calyx. Strong, spreading, well-branched plants; prolific, producing 2 to 3 fruits per cluster. *E53M*

Little Fingers:[2] 68 days. Very early oriental type used for "baby eggplants". Can be picked when 3 to 7 inches long and 3/4 to 1 1/4 inches in diameter. Long, slim, cylindrical fruit; attractive, glossy, dark-purple skin; quality high; spineless. Vigorous plant; bears fruit in clusters of 5 to 10; continues to produce over a long season. F13, K66

Pink Bride:[1] (Asian Bride) Fruit slender and straight, 7 to 8 1/2 inches long and 2 1/2 inches in diameter; weight 3 to 4 ounces; skin pink-violet with white stripes; green calyx; flesh white, tender, of good quality. Similar to Pinky, but long. Small, compact plant; strong-growing and well-branched; bears 2 to 3 fruit on each cluster. E49, K66, *Q39*

Prelane: Long, cylindrical fruit; skin deep violet-black, glossy, attractive; firm, non-bitter flesh, very slow to form seeds. Convenient shape; can be cut into uniform slices or exactly in half for stuffing; lends itself to a variety of different preparations. Bears heavily throughout the season. Resistant to tobacco mosaic virus and cucumber mosaic virus. I39, K66

Short Tom:[2] 75 days. Small fruit, only 3 to 5 inches long and 1 inch in diameter; shiny black skin, thin and tender; excellent eating quality, can be picked when young or left to grow larger. Vigorous plant; sets fruit prolifically. Bred for extremely early harvest at the sacrifice of fruit size. Suitable for container culture. L89, L91M, N52, P83M, S55

OPEN-POLLINATED

Black Beauty: 80 days. Large, round oval fruit, 4 to 6 inches long; skin purplish-black, smooth, glossy; calyx bright green; good quality and flavor; holds color and quality well after being picked. Medium-tall plant; bears 4 to 6 fruit held well off the ground; widely adapted. Popular with home gardeners and commercial growers. Introduced about 1910. B75M, B78, C44, F19M, G16, *H61*, H66, H94, *I62*{PL}, K73, L7M, L9M, M13M, M46, N16, etc.

Chinese Long: (Chinese Long Sword) 75 days. Unusual long, thin fruit; 10 to 12 inches in length, 1 1/2 to 2 inches in diameter; tapers to a sword-like point; skin purple, thin; flesh white, very tender, of good flavor. Robust, heavy-yielding plant; tolerant to diseases. A49G, D55, E49, E59, *P39*

De Barbentane: 70 days. A French heirloom, has been grown in the south of France since the 19th century. Long, cylindrical fruit; skin purplish-black, glossy; flavor good. Sturdy vigorous plant; not highly productive, but hardy. Traditionally used for *ratatouille*, a stew of eggplant, tomato and green pepper. G68

Early Black Egg: 70 days. Small, pear-shaped, slightly blocky fruit; 5 to 6 inches long; skin purple; flesh unusually tender and flavorful. Bushy, purple-tinted plant; height 2 feet; sets well in cool, short season areas. Should be picked when young for best quality and to encourage continuous fruit setting. E24, L7M, L89

Early Long Purple: 75 days. Long, slender fruit, about 12 inches long and 3 to 4 inches in diameter; skin dark violet; flavor very good; ideal for slicing. Bushy, prolific plant; height 24 to 38 inches. Mediterranean type, similar to Violette Longue. Introduced prior to 1885. VILMORIN; A69M, C44, K49M, K73, M95

Extra Long: Fruits are very long and slender, about 12 inches in length and 1 1/2 inches in diameter. Light purple skin and calyx; tender, white flesh. Upright plant; medium early in maturity. L59, *Q39*

Florida Market: 80 days. Very large, oval fruit, 9 inches long and 6 1/2 inches in diameter; skin dark-purple, smooth, glossy; calyx green; resistant to fruit rot. Vigorous, upright plant; height 30 to 36 inches; holds fruit well off the ground; productive over a long harvesting season. Grown widely in Florida for the fresh market. *A75*, A87M, B75M, F19M, *F72*, *G1M*, G27M, G71, H54, *H61*, H66, K49M, K73

Half Long Purple: Standard, half-long oriental type. Fruit 6 to 7 inches long; skin purplish-black, thin; flesh tender and flavorful, of excellent quality. Good for the home garden; easy to grow. Prolific. B35M

Improved Muktakeshi: Oblong, deep-purple fruit; very thin skin; extremely palatable flesh with very few seeds; quality excellent. An improved strain of a traditional Indian cultivar; developed by Sutton & Sons, India. S59M

Italian Pink Bicolor:[1] 75 days. Large, bell-shaped fruit; skin creamy white overlaid with rose-pink vertical stripes. A popular novelty with the European trade. An open-pollinated cultivar with a percentage of off types. I97T, L42

Japanese Purple Pickling: (Purple Pickling) 75 days. Small plants bear early, producing masses of small fruits. Exceptionally full-flavored; good for frying and cooking, excellent for pickling. I39, K49M

Kurume Long: (Kurume Long Purple) Long, slender fruit; 12 inches in length, 2 inches in diameter; skin purplish-black, attractive, glossy; flavor excellent. Resistant to fusarium wilt. A standard long purple type from Japan. Does well in warm areas. D55, E49, E59, H49, *L79G*

Listada de Gandia:[1] 75 days. Fruit egg-shaped, 5 to 6 inches long; skin very attractive, purple with irregular white stripes; calyx green, somewhat spiny; mild-flavored, snow-white flesh, of fine texture. Compact, productive plant; height 2 feet; somewhat drought tolerant; sets fruit well during high temperatures. C76M, I77, L7M

Morden Midget:[3] 65 days. Very early cultivar that produces full-sized fruit on dwarf plants. Medium-sized, oval fruit; purple skin; good flavor. Small, sturdy plant. Most reliable eggplant for far northern gardens. Developed at the Morden Research Station, Morden, Manitoba, Canada. L7M

New York Improved: 80 days. Very large, obovate fruit; skin deep purple, smooth, free of thorns; flesh white, very firm, contains few seeds, of excellent quality. Bushy, compact plant; height 2 to 3 feet; very productive, produces 3 or 4 fruit. An old favorite for local markets and home gardeners; introduced prior to 1865. BURPEE, BURR, VILMORIN; K49M

Pallida Romanesca:[1] (Pale Roman) Large, broad, oval fruit, sometimes ribbed; skin white blushed with lavender-purple; flesh meaty, mild-flavored. Compact plants. Grown for market in Rome. F80, J73

Pingtung Long Improved: (Taiwan Pingtung Long Improved) Light-purple fruits, 8 to 10 inches long, 1 to 2 inches in diameter. Excellent for slicing and pickling. Plants more upright than some of the other eggplants; very early and very productive, producing up to 20 fruits per plant; resistant to extreme heat and humidity. Improved strain of a traditional Taiwanese cultivar. J73

Pinky: 100 days. Very large, blocky fruit, shape similar to Black Beauty; skin light pink-violet; flavor good, very mild; best when small. Sturdy, semi-bushy plant; height 20 to 24 inches; produces 8 to 10 fruits. A49G, E49

Pusa Purple Cluster: A small-fruited cultivar with fruits of a deep-purple color, borne in clusters of 4 to 6. Tall, purplish plant. O39M, R50, S59M

Pusa Purple Long: 46 days. A greatly improved strain from India. An excellent producer of tender, thick, glossy deep-purple fruits, about 12 inches long. Suitable for summer and autumn seasons. Extra early. N91, R50, *S36*, S59M

Ronde de Valence: (Violetta Tonda) 75 days. Small, truly round fruit; skin dark purple, sometimes tinged with green at the shoulders, even when fully ripe; should be picked when the size of a large naval orange or a small grapefruit. Excellent for stuffing. Not very productive; requires a hot climate. Old, traditional cultivar; named after the city on the Rhone River in France. B8

Rosa Bianco:[1] 75 days. Very attractive, globular fruit; 4 to 6 inches in length; skin colored with shades of true lavender and creamy white; calyx very large compared to other eggplants, often enclosing the fruit for days; flesh meaty, of very good flavor. I77, J83M, K49M, K66

Slim Jim:[2 3] 75 days. Long, slender fruit, 4 to 6 inches in length when mature; skin lavender to purple, colors up while still the size of a peanut. Small, compact plant; ideal for growing in pots; produces fruit in clusters close to the main stem; has ornamental violet foliage. Recommended for market gardeners growing "baby" vegetables for the specialty trade. C53

Taiwan Long: 70 days. Long, slender fruit, about 7 inches in length and 1 1/2 inches in diameter; skin purplish-black, glossy; flesh tender; ripens early; should be picked when young. A continuous and heavy yielder, can produce as many as 45 fruits; disease resistant. L59

Violetta di Firenze:[1] Unusual, attractive fruit; rich lavender, sometimes striped with white; very large, round to oblong, grooved. Very good for stuffing or using as a centerpiece. Very spreading, upright plant. Needs high temperatures to mature a crop; cloches and black plastic recommended in far northern areas. C53, I77, J20, Q34

Violette Longue: (Violetta Lunga) 65 days. An early cultivar, very popular in southern France. Fruit oblong-oval, slightly club-shaped, thickest at the blossom end; 6 to 8 inches in length; skin purplish-black, attractive, smooth; flesh firm, contains few seeds, quality excellent; well-suited to slicing. Produces 8 to 10 fruits per plant. Introduced prior to 1885. VILMORIN; B8, C53

RED/ORANGE-SKINNED (S. aethiopicum)

Small Ruffled Red: (Red Ruffles, Hmong Red) 100 days. Small, deeply creased fruit, 2 inches in diameter; skin orange-red; flesh seedy, bitter. Prized in Southeast Asian cuisines for its bitter flavor. Tall plant, height 3 feet; bears fruit in clusters; resistant to nematodes and light frost. K49M, L7M

Sweet Red: 125 days. Small, very attractive fruit; 1 inch in diameter; skin green with dark-green stripes, turning red with dark-red stripes at maturity; strong but non-bitter flavor. Eaten when small and green. Used in Southeast Asian cuisines. Thornless plant; height 3 feet. K49M

Turkish Orange: (Turkish Italian) 75 days. Small, spherical fruit, 2 1/2 inches in diameter; skin bright orange-red; flesh seedy, with an excellent sweet taste. Usually eaten when green; delicious in Thai curry and *caponata*. Tall, hardy plant; produces abundantly; resistant to flea beetles. Said to have originated in Turkey; now used in parts of Italy. I99, L7M

WHITE-SKINNED

White eggplants are generally firmer, less moist, and hold their shape better than purple types. They are also closer-grained, creamier, and less bitter. The flesh can be more heavily seeded, although the seeds are often less acrid. SCHNEIDER [Cul, Re].

HYBRID

Ghost Buster: 80 days. Attractive, deep oval fruit, about 6 to 7 inches in length; bright white skin; slightly sweet flavor. Broad, vigorous, semi-spreading plant; productive; dense, bright-green foliage provides excellent cover for the fruit and holds them well off the ground. Excellent specialty market item. F13, G93M, I77

OPEN-POLLINATED

Baby White Tiger: 80 days. Bite-sized white fruit, about 1 1/2 inches long and 1 inch in diameter; with numerous, crunchy seeds; not bitter. Should be harvested when seeds are light-colored or transparent; if the seeds are brown, the fruit is over-ripe. K49M

Banaras Giant: 63 days. Large, round fruit, 5 1/2 inches long and 5 inches in diameter; skin greenish-white; flesh white, firm, of excellent quality. Semi-erect, spineless plant, height about 20 inches; produces 5 to 9 fruits. Popular Indian cultivar. R0, S59M

Casper: 70 days. An attractive ivory-white version of Blackjack. Fruit averages 6 inches long, 2 3/4 inches in diameter; snow-white flesh, mild, delicate, mushroom-like flavor; green calyx; ripens early. Medium-sized, prolific plant. I97T, K49M, L42, M95

Chinese White: Oval white fruits with very tender skin and a mild, sweet flavor. Turns golden-yellow at maturity, but should be harvested young, when shiny white. Grows well in containers. F80

Dourga: 65 days. An attractive, ornamental eggplant. Fruit cylindrical, 6 inches long and 2 inches in diameter; skin shiny white; flesh white, flavor sweet and delicate; quality excellent. Vigorous, productive plant. *F72*, I77, I91

Long White Cluster: Oblong, creamy white fruits of very good quality. Strong, vigorous plant; bears fruit in clusters. S59M

Long White Sword: 100 days. Elongated, slender, white-skinned fruit; 6 to 9 inches in length, 2 inches in diameter; flesh very meaty, with very few seeds, flavor mild. K49M, L7M

White Beauty: 70 days. Medium-large, nearly round fruit; 4 to 5 inches long, 5 to 6 inches in diameter; smooth, snow-white skin; flesh white, seedy, very full-flavored, quality best when eaten small. Sturdy, bushy plant; height 3 feet; holds fruit well off the ground. K49M, L7M

White Egg: (Japanese White Egg) 75 days. Small fruit, 1 to 2 inches long; the size and shape of a hen's egg; skin white; quality excellent. Prolific plant; height 3 feet; sets fruit continuously over a long season. E59

White Knight: 70 days. Fruit long oval, cylindrical, rounded on end; 8 inches long, 2 inches in diameter; distinctive, shiny white skin; flesh firm, of very good flavor. Productive, well-adapted plant. For fresh market, roadside stands and home gardeners. *A1*, M29

White Oval: (Bianca Ovale) Medium-sized oval fruit; skin pure-white; flavor extremely mild; should be picked when 3 to 4 inches long and still glossy, before the seeds start to develop and the fruit begins to ripen. Good for growing in tubs and pots as well as in the open ground. C53, E49, I77, L7M

ENDIVE {S}

CICHORIUM ENDIVIA

CURLY-LEAVED

Also called *chicorée frisée*, these are flat, low-growing plants with narrowish curled, fringed or indented leaves. They have a tendency to rot in damp, cold weather but are more tolerant of heat than broad-leaved endive, so are used mainly from late spring to autumn. LARKCOM 1984.

Bianca Riccia da Taglio:[1] Tender, delicious, pale green leaves. Especially adapted to cut-and-come-again techniques. When sown thickly will provide an abundance of greens all year long that are excellent in salads. Regrows quickly. Q11M

Elodie: 70 days. Strong, attractive plants; dense, frilly, green outer leaves; crisp but tender mid-ribs; closely-bunched blanched hearts. Has a crunchy texture and a clean, fresh taste. More heat-tolerant than older sorts and produces over a longer harvest season. The fine-cut lacy leaves combine attractively with lettuce. French introduction. I77, K66

Fine de Louviers: (Fine Curled Louviers, De Louviers) 90 days. Very finely curled, indented, yellow-green foliage; forms a nicely compact but curled heart; thin, white ribs. Grows 10 to 12 inches in height. Rosette almost hemispherical in form; contains a greater number of blanched leaves in proportion to its size than other sorts. Introduced prior to 1885. VILMORIN; F33

Fine Maraichère: Very small, compact endive; grows to only 8 inches in diameter. Very frizzy, decorative leaves. Ideal for individual servings, or for picking when very young to use in mesclun. Not hardy; sow in spring and early summer for summer use. P83M, S55

Frisée de Namur: An exceptional French cultivar which can be sown in January for cutting in May and June. May also be sown in autumn for over-wintering under cover. P83M, S55

Green Curled Ruffec: (De Ruffec, Green Curled, Early Green Curled, Giant Fringed Oyster) 85 days. Very large rosette, often 16 to 18 inches in diameter, resembling Moss Curled but fuller in the center. Midrib very white and thick, very tender and fleshy, nearly and inch in diameter but appearing much broader due to the blanching of a large portion of the leaf blade. Suitable for summer and autumn. Bears cold weather remarkably well. Introduced prior to 1865. VILMORIN; A16, A25, C85M, D11M, F1, F92, G16, G51, G71, *G83M*, H94, J14{PL}, J34, L7M, M13M, M46, etc.

Impériale Frisée: (Imperial Curled) An attractive curled type forming a broad, tall, well-furnished rosette. Resembles Green Curled Ruffec, but has lighter colored leaves that are less finely cut, though the segments are very much curled and folded. Unlike other sorts the midrib is not bare at the bottom of the leaf, but up to 1 3/4 inches broad; they are also pure-white for at least half their length. Introduced prior to 1885. VILMORIN; G64

Large Green Curled White Ribbed: (Large Green Curled) 85 days. Commercial type with attractive, bright-green leaves that are long, well-fringed, curled and have a white mid-rib. Large-framed plant, 14 to 18 inches in diameter. Excellent heart; blanches well. Most popular in the South. Tolerant to black heart. *A1*, B78, M29

Moss Curled: (Green Moss Curled, Early Green Moss Curled) 90 days. Rosette rather small, seldom exceeding 10 or 12 inches in diameter. Leaves clear dark-green, very much cut, curled, and crisped, the whole plant resembling a tuft of moss; mid-ribs narrow and very white. Not very productive, but in demand due to its unique appearance. As it occupies little space, it is very suitable for growing under cloches. Introduced prior to 1885. VILMORIN; B13, B49, I67M, I84, L91M, O53M, S45M

Nina: 42 days. An endive of the French Très Fine Maraichère type. Smaller and earlier than Salad King, with long and smooth but deeply cut, toothed grey-green leaves. Like all cultivars of this type, Nina must be harvested early before showing tipburn or bottom rot. A mild, delicious salad ingredient for specialty markets. G6

President: (Giant Green Curled) 85 days. Very large rosette. Deeply cut and frilled, dark-green leaves resemble Salad Bowl lettuce, but with a nicely blanched, creamy yellow-white core that is particularly tasty and tender. One of the hardiest cultivars, withstanding adverse weather in the fall. G79, J58, K49M, L89

Riccia Pancalieri: (Green Curled Pancalier, Grosse Pancalière, Green Curled Upright) 95 days. Forms a very large rosette with a voluminous heart; very curled and crisped leaves have rose-tinted white midribs. The central leaves stand quite erect so that the plant is blanched naturally, without requiring to be tied up. Sow in rows from March to September; use in summer, autumn and winter. VILMORIN; K49M, P83M, S55

Ricciutissima d'Ingegnoli: A distinct cultivar with very finely divided and curled, tender leaves. Produces a full heart of light yellow color and an especially delicious flavor. May be planted from March to August for continuous harvests over a period of 8 months per year. Q11M

Salad King: 80 days. Vigorous, healthy, heavy-bearing plant. Large, attractive, deep-green, finely cut leaves. Deep, full heart may be easily blanched by gathering and tying the outer leaves. Early maturing; for spring, summer and fall crops. Very slow to bolt and resistant to tipburn and hot weather. Not harmed by light frosts. A13, B75M, C44, C92, F13, F44, G6, *G13M*, G93M, *H61*, K71, K73, L42, *L59G*, M95, etc.

Très Fine Maraichère: 46 days. Long and smooth but deeply cut, toothed grey-green leaves with delicate crisp ribs; well-blanched, creamy hearts. Must be harvested early before showing tipburn or bottom rot. Mild, delicious salad ingredient for specialty markets. Grows well in a variety of soils. I77, K66, S95M

White Curled: (Ever-White, Ever-Blanched, Bianca) Rosette not very dense, 14 to 16 inches in diameter; heart loose and open. Leaves pale yellowish-green, having the appearance of being artificially blanched; frilled or curled on the borders. Midrib yellow, tinged with rose-red. Tender and of good quality when very young, otherwise chiefly valued for its unique appearance. Introduced prior to 1865. BURR, VILMORIN; E38, G51

BROAD-LEAVED

Also called *escarole*, *Batavian endive*, *scarole* and *chicorée scarole*, these are larger and taller than curly-leaved endive with broader leaves, somewhat twisted at the base. They are much hardier and more suitable for autumn, winter and, where they have been overwintered, for early spring crops. They require blanching in hot weather, when at their most bitter. LARKCOM 1984.

Broad-Leaved Batavian: (Full Heart Batavian, Batavian Green) 85 days. Leaves yellowish-green; large and broad; 10 inches long, 5 to 6 inches in diameter at the broadest part; thick and fleshy. Very deep, well-blanched, creamy white heart. Introduced from Java via Holland in 1860. BURR; A25, A69M, B49, C44, D82, E24, F44, F92, G27M, G51, G71, H66, J14{PL}, L97, M13M, M46, etc.

Florida Deep Heart: (Florida Full Heart) 85 days. More upright than Full Heart Batavian; grows 12 to 15 inches tall. Thick, crumpled leaves and dense foliage encourages development of a creamy white heart that is less susceptible to basal rot. Standard broad-leaf type; grown extensively in the South for fresh market and shipping. *A1*, A13, F13, G79, *H61*, K73, L7M, *L59G*, M29

Geante Maraichère: Very large, vigorous growing, hardy endive that develops a blanched heart very early in its growth. The rosette is very full and dense, producing many packed leaves in the center of the plant. Outer leaves broad, wavy, irregularly lobed. Plant June through August. G64, S95M

Giant Samy: (Geante Maraichère Race Samy) 90 days. Large, semi-upright heads of glossy greens leaves highlighted by a yellowish-green heart. Very attractive. Vigorous and resistant to diseases. For autumn and spring production. P59M

Gigante Degli Ortolani: Very large plant, easily growing to 15 or 16 inches in diameter. Succulent outer leaves of an attractive bright-green color. Forms a rose colored heart that blanches to a whitish-yellow in a few days. Sown in summer, harvested in autumn and winter. I77, Q11M

Nuvol: 50 days. Large head with broad, wavy, dark-green leaves. Self-blanching, producing a creamy yellow, well-filled heart that is tender, sweet and less bitter than Full Heart Batavian. Slow-bolting; good for spring planting as well as summer, fall and protected crops. G6, *R11M*

Pink Star: Large, broad green leaves with heavy, well-filled hearts that are self-blanching. The mild, tender, somewhat flowery-flavored hearts are unusually fine. Sow in summer for a fall harvest. I39

Sinco: 85 days. Early maturing, vigorous, healthy plant produces a dense mass of large, folded outer leaves with a closely bunched, well-blanched, creamy yellow heart. Leaves are broad, slightly crinkled and dark-green in color. Good tipburn tolerance. French introduction. K66

Wivol: 80 days. Medium-green heads form a rosette of ruffled leaves whose broad central stems make a blanched heart which is very mild and tasty. Hardy to below 7^0 F. Selected specifically to tolerate rain, cold and general adverse weather. L89, *R11M*

UPRIGHT

A possible link between the curly-leaved and broad-leaved types, these have a distinct upright growth habit instead of the usual flat or rosette form. Most are extremely hardy.

Cartocciata d'Ingegnoli: A splendid cultivar that forms large, upright heads that are naturally self-blanching. The outer leaves wrap themselves around the inner heart in a manner similar to crisphead lettuce. Excellent flavor. Can be sown at any time of the year. Q11M

Cornet d'Anjou: Broad leaved, semi-heading type. Very large leaves, almost as broad as long; cut at the edges into numerous long teeth; midrib fan-shaped. Outer leaves unfold and envelope the younger leaves to form a loose head. Can be blanched to mellow its fine flavor. Named for the shape of the heart which resembles the mouth of a horn, or cornet, and the town where it originated, Anjou, France. For spring or fall crops. C53, G68

Cornet d'Bordeaux: A fine old French cultivar which is very hardy. Upright in growth habit, forming a loose head. Very large outer leaves; cut at the edges into numerous long teeth; fan-shaped midrib. Can provide a constant cut-and-come-again crop through the winter. Performs exceptionally well in cold frame, tunnel, or cloche. Leaves make excellent wrappings for various stuffings. LARKCOM 1984; E83T, G68, J73, Q34, S55

Cornetto della Loire: (Cornet de la Loire) Large, elongated, upright plant; pale green in color; outer leaves quickly envelope the inner ones to form a loose head. For autumn production, it may be sown later than others because it grows very rapidly. Very hardy, suitable for growing until the first frost. E83T, *O60*, P59M

FAVA BEAN {S}

FABA VULGARIS

Aprovecho Select: A selection developed in Oregon with unusually large seeds and sweet flavor; excellent for table use: Vigorous, 3 to 4 foot plants. Hardy to below 20^0 F. Has excelled in trials in the maritime Northwest and on the East Coast. A2, I99

Aquadulce: 85 days. Medium-green pods, 14 to 16 inches long and nearly 2 inches wide; 7 to 8 large, white seeds per pod; suitable for fresh use and freezing. Erect plants, 2 to 2 1/2 feet high; not very stout; sometimes quite green and sometimes slightly tinged with red. Extra hardy for autumn sowing to avoid blackfly, and to grow an early spring crop. Introduced around 1844. *A75*, C92, J20, O89, P83M, *R23*, S61

Aquadulce Claudia: 90 days. Long, 15 inch pods; 1 inch diameter seeds have pale greenish skins. Excellent for use as a dry bean; also makes a very good shelling bean. Sturdy plants, growing 3 to 4 feet tall at full maturity. The primary cultivar for a very early crop; can be sown as early as January in mild-winter areas or in the fall. Reliably hardy to 12^0 F. I77, L89, L91M, *R23*, *S75M*

Arnaud: 55-60 days. Small, slightly curved pods, 3 to 5 inches long. Gourmet quality flavor. Matures over a long period, 5 to 6 weeks, with about one harvest per week. Erect plant with 3 or 4 stalks. An early cultivar, popular in eastern Quebec but adapted to a wide range of climates. G64

Banner:[1] Said to be one of the highest yielding, best-tasting commercial small-seeded field types. The stalks also make excellent silage or green manure. Vigorous, 6 foot plants shade out weeds and grasses. Very tolerant of temporarily waterlogged soils in winter. Hardy to at least 10^0 F. B49, I77, I99, L89

Bell:[1] (Bell Bean, Peanut) Small-seeded field type which are also known as *horse beans* or *tick beans*. Round to oval, reddish-brown seeds can be used as dry beans. Also planted as a cover crop, green manure and for silage. Tolerant of a wide range of soil conditions, including wet areas, acid pH, etc. Plants are somewhat taller than those of the large-seeded cultivars. Best sown from October until February in warm-winter areas. F11, G93M, I99M, L79M

Bonnie Lad: 75 days. Pods 5 to 6 inches long; each pod containing 4 or 5 small, very tasty, light-green beans. Compact, neat, erect plants to 15 inches tall; utilize minimal space. L91M

Broad Windsor: (Broad Windsor Long Pod) 85 days. Glossy green, 6 to 8 inch long pods; pods solitary or in pairs, almost always curved, and usually very broad towards the end; each pod containing 5 to 7 large, oblong-shaped, flat, light-green beans used as shell beans. Very upright, 2 to 3 feet tall plants. A16, A69M, C85M, F92, G57M, G82, *G83M*, H42, K49M, L42

Brunette: 72 days. A small, brown-seeded type bearing upright-growing pods in bunches for heavy yields and easy picking; 4 to 5 inch long, thin-walled pods. Seeds are said to stay in a tasty, edible condition longer than other sorts. Lower growing, 18 to 24 inch plants. Sow in early spring for best results. G64, J7, L91M

Bunyard's Exhibition: 75 days. Pods 12 to 14 inches long, smooth and narrow; produce 7 to 8 large, well-flavored white seeds per pod. Very heavy cropping plants, 24 to 40 inches tall. Recommended for spring sowing. I99, L91M, P83M, *R23*

Castillo Franco: One of the best heirloom cultivars grown by the Spanish farmers in New Mexico. Delicious flavor. Prolific bushes, 3 to 4 feet tall. Appears to take the heat in spring better than most cultivars tested. K49T

Coles Early Prolific: White-flowering, dwarf-growing cultivar with medium sized pods. Seeds are small and tender. T1M

Colossal: 70 days. Exceptionally long, 7 to 10 inch pods are produced in abundance on plants that are about 4 feet tall. Plump beans of excellent flavor. Bears so heavily it is necessary to bank the soil up well around the roots to prevent the plants from falling over. Widely used for exhibition. M49, S61

Egyptian Brown:[1] Extremely hardy, small-seeded field type. Grown by ancient Egyptians for protein. Plants grow to 3 feet tall. R47

Exhibition Longpod: 72 days. Pods 4 1/2 to 6 inches long, contain 5 to 7 large seeds per pod; seeds flat, pale green to cream when ready for use as a shell bean. Excellent for freezing. Strong-stemmed plants, 3 1/2 to 5 feet high. Very productive. Some support may be needed in unprotected areas; best planted in "block" rows because of wind. An old English favorite. A69M, K20, T1M

Express: 71 days. One of the fastest maturing cultivars, and from an early spring sowing will outyield others. Produces up to 34 seven inch long pods per plant. Medium-sized, tender, flavorful seeds. Outstanding for freezing as it does not discolor. Winter hardy. I99, L91M, *R23*, S55, *S75M*

Foul Misri: 77 days. Suitable for a late spring and summer sowing, this bean is heat tolerant and has a good root system. Listed as Foul Muddamma by Bountiful Gardens, foul is actually the Arabic name for fava bean, and *foul medammes* is the proper name for stewed fava beans, popular in Egypt and other Arabic countries. DARBY, MALLOS [Re]; B49, L50M{PR}

Frostproof: (Lima Pea) 80 days. Produces flat, straight pods; 7 inches long and 1 1/2 inches wide; 5 to 7 very large seeds per pod. Good fresh or used as dried beans. Productive, upright plants, 2 1/2 feet high with strong, sturdy stems. Very hardy; has survived -24° F. B73M, D65

Giant Exhibition Long Pod: One of the finest of the Longpod cultivars. Very heavy cropper grown from specially selected pods. Pods of good length and beans of very good flavor. Ideal for exhibition. O53M

Green Windsor: A large-seeded cultivar of excellent flavor. Once used for brown Windsor soup but now a favorite for the freezer. For spring sowing only. Introduced in 1831. Similar to Broad Windsor, except for the color of the seeds, which, even when ripe, remain a deep green color. VILMORIN; P83M, *R23*

Imperial Green Longpod: 84 days. Twenty years of painstaking research have developed a plant capable of continually producing 15 to 20 inch long pods, each pod containing up to 9 large beans. L91M, *S75M*

Ipro: 78 days. Medium-seized seed, about half as large as Windsor, means that a quantity of seeds plants more. Plants grow 3 to 3 1/2 feet tall, with an easy-to-pick horizontal set of 5 1/2 inch long pods averaging 5 beans per pod. Bred for tolerance to top yellow virus and hot weather. Very good flavor when cooked fresh. E24, E59Z, F44, G6

Ite: (Beryl) 75 days. Tiny, pea-sized beans; sweet flavored; a gourmet treat. Can be eaten fresh, uncooked in salads, or lightly steamed or boiled. Plants grow 30 inches tall and have 6 inch long pods. A very heavy-yielding main crop cultivar ripening about 7 to 10 days later than Express. L91M

Johnson's Wonderful: An improved cultivar of the Broad Windsor, introduced prior to 1865. Pods are long and contain 6 or 8 beans, which are similar in size and form to the Windsor. Quality and flavor excellent. Early ripening and heavy yielding. BURR; P83M

Masterpiece: (Masterpiece Green Longpod) 88 days. One of the finest green-seeded broad beans. Plants are 30 to 36 inches tall with 8 inch long pods. Excellent fresh or for deep freezing. Grows well under all conditions, being heavier cropping than the Windsors. Introduced in 1894. Highly commended by the Royal Horticultural Society in 1972. L91M, O53M, P83M, *R23*, S61

Minica: 70 days. Small-seeded, brown cooking type; seeds retain their color when cooked. Plants are rather high and firm, with average tillering; pods are well placed on the stem. Pods erect to horizontal, straight, about 4 inches in length. Very high yielding. *R11M*, *S75M*

Polar: 84 days. Outyields, crops earlier, and is better to eat than Aquadulce Claudia. Medium-sized, white seeds are high in starch, and are said to have a 5% higher digestibility factor than other cultivars. Plants grow to 36 inches tall. Hardy for fall sowing in many northern areas or as soon as soil is workable. I99

Portuguese: 60-70 days. Family heirloom which has been in the Lemstrom family for more than four generations. Still grown in Loule, Portugal. Plants grow up to 2 feet tall and each pod contains 8 or 9 beans. Excellent as a shell bean, and can also be used dry. D87

Red Epicure: For sheer flavor there is no broad bean to equal this. So named because the beans are of an unusual rich chestnut color, and they surprisingly possess much of the flavor of the chestnut when cooked. Cooks to a yellow shade. The plant is hardy and a heavy cropper. GENDERS 1975; U33

Relon: Plants grow 36 inches tall and produce very long, 17 to 22 inch long pods, each pod being well-filled with up to 11 green seeds. It means less shelling for a given number of beans. Holds its green color well making it excellent for exhibitions and for freezing. L91M, S61

Suprifin: 84 days. Medium-sized buff colored beans are carried 4 or 5 to a pod; pods are 5 inches long at maturity. Has true broad bean flavor, and is suitable for eating fresh or for deep freezing. Vigorous 36 inch tall plants are very high yielding even under unfavorable conditions; produce 30% more beans than other cultivars. L91M

Tarahumara Habas: Green to beige seed with black hilum. Added to soups or ground and made into thick tortillas. Summer crop in Sierra Madre Mountains of Mexico. Frost hardy. Prolific in Tucson, Arizona. I16

Tezieriviera White-Seeded: 80-90 days. Very early, valuable cultivar has long pods, with each pod containing 6 large, white seeds. Plant is vigorous and productive, with most of the beans maturing simultaneously over a short period. Recommended for planting in early spring before hot weather arrives. Dropped by G69

Tezieroma: 80-90 days. Very vigorous plant, with production spread over a longer period than Tezieriviera White-Seeded. Pods are extremely large, up to 10 inches long, with each pod containing 7 to 8 beans. Especially recommended for areas with cool summer months. Dropped by G69

The Sutton:[2] 84 days. Six inch long, white-seeded pods; 5 small, tender beans per pod; matures early. The pods can be eaten whole even when quite large. Very hardy plant with a branched, bushy growth habit; reaches a height of only 12 inches and yet crops abundantly; perfect for small and windy gardens. Ideal for extra early sowing under tunnels. Award of Merit winner in 1952. GENDERS 1975; L91M, P83M, *R23*, S55, S59M, S61

Witkiem Major: 84 days. Said to be the earliest broad bean for a spring sowing; can crop as quickly as autumn sown cultivars and gives heavier yields. Strong, vigorous plants grow to 36 inches tall; produce very heavy crops of long, thick, 8 to 10 inch pods with green seeds. Developed in Holland. I91, L91M, P83M, *R23*, *S75M*

FEIJOA {GR}

FEIJOA SELLOWIANA

Apollo: Medium to large, oval fruit; smooth, thin, light-green skin with blue-green surface bloom, subject to bruising and purpling; pulp well-developed, slightly gritty; flavor very pleasant, quality excellent; ripens mid to late-season. Tree upright spreading, to 8 feet tall; vigorous and productive; self-fertile, and will pollinate Gemini. *O97*, R77

Beechwood: Medium-sized, elliptical fruit, weight 4 to 6 ounces; skin relatively smooth, dark green; flavor very good, lacking any disagreeable aftertaste. Tree self-fruitful. Originated in Hollywood, California. I83M

Choiceana: (Choiceana Early) Small to medium-sized, round to oval fruit, 2 to 3 1/2 inches long; skin fairly smooth; flavor and quality good; ripens in midseason. Tree moderately vigorous, spreading; almost always, or no less than 42% self-fertile. Originated in Australia. MORTON 1987a; I49M

Coolidge: Small to medium-sized fruit, 4 or more inches in length and 2 1/2 inches in diameter; form pyriform to oblong or elongated; skin somewhat wrinkled; flavor mild, of indifferent quality. Tree upright and strong growing; a reliable and heavy bearer; 100% self-fertile. The most widely planted cultivar in California. Originated in Australia prior to 1908. MORTON 1987a; A88M, *G49*, I49M, I74, I83M, J61M, L99M, *N20, O97*

David: Medium to large fruit; well-shaped, round to oval; skin of sweet and agreeable flavor; flesh texture reasonably good, flavor good; ripens in mid-season. An excellent dual purpose type, ideal as a fresh fruit or useful for canning. MORTON 1987a; *O97*

Edenvale Improved Coolidge: Large, oblong fruit of very good to excellent flavor and quality; ripens in October. Tree slow growing; self-fertile; precocious and productive; grows best in climates similar to cool, coastal areas of southern California. Originated in Santa Cruz, California by Frank Serpa of Edenvale Nurseries. I49M, L6

Edenvale Late: Medium-sized, oblong fruit of very good to excellent quality and flavor; ripens late, in January, and over a long period of time. Tree slow growing; self-fertile; very productive; grows best in climates similar to cool, coastal areas of southern California. Originated in Santa Cruz, California by Frank Serpa of Edenvale Nurseries. I49M, L6

Edenvale Supreme: Medium-sized, oblong fruit of very good to excellent flavor and quality; ripens in November. Best eaten soon after harvest. Tree slow growing; self-fertile; precocious and productive; grows best in climates similar to cool, coastal areas of southern California. Originated in Santa Cruz, California by Frank Serpa of Edenvale Nurseries. L6

Gemini: Fruit small to medium, egg-shaped; skin very smooth, thin, dark-green with a heavy bloom; flavor and texture excellent; ripens in early autumn, earlier than Apollo. Tree upright-spreading, to 8 feet tall; moderately vigorous; high yielding; partially self-fruitful, but cross-pollination is recommended for best fruit quality. *O97*

Jackson: Medium-sized, oval fruit, 2 1/2 inches in diameter; weight up to 4 ounces; skin thick; flesh white, rather dry, sugar content moderate; flavor very strong but pleasant, somewhat sour near the skin; nearly seedless, with smaller seed cavity and more pulp than most cultivars. Ripens in late November, keeps unusually well. Originated in San Jose, California. I83M

Lickver's Pride: Medium to large fruit, weight 6 to 12 ounces. Quality excellent. Tree self-fruitful. I83M

Mammoth: Large, round to oval fruit, to 8 1/2 ounces, resembles Coolidge; skin somewhat wrinkled, thick; flesh somewhat gritty, quality and flavor very good; matures early to midseason; softer and not as good a shipper as Triumph. Tree of upright habit, to 10 feet tall, strong growing; self-fertile, but bears larger fruit with cross-pollination. Selected in New Zealand from seedlings of the Choiceana cultivar. MORTON 1987a; I83M, L6, *O97, Q49M, Q93*

Moore: Large, flavorsome fruit; ripens in midseason. Very vigorous plant. Recommended for trial plantings in California and other areas. I49M

Nazemetz: Large, pear-shaped fruit, averaging 3 ounces in weight; side walls moderately thin; pulp translucent, sweet; flavor and quality excellent; ripens late October to mid-December. Unlike that of many other cultivars, the pulp of Nazemetz does not darken after being cut or as it ripens, but retains its clear color. Tree self-fertile, but bears most heavily when cross-pollinated. Good pollinator for Trask. Originated in San Diego, California by Alexander Nazemetz. A88M, G17, *G49*, I49M, I74, I83M, J61M, L6, *N20*

Pineapple Gem: Small, round fruit of good to very good quality. Mid to late season ripening. Tree self-fruitful but bears heavier crops if cross-pollinated. Does poorly under cool, coastal conditions. Originated in Azusa, California by Monrovia Nursery. G96, I49M

Robert: Medium-sized, very uniform, oval fruits; flesh very juicy, somewhat gritty; flavor mild; ripens very early, up to two months before Triumph and Mammoth. Tree produces heavily when well established; develops undesirable russet leaves; if not cross-pollinated adequately will produce hollow fruit, which cannot be distinguished externally from well pollinated fruit. Originated in New Zealand. *O97*

Smilax: Small to medium-sized, perfectly round fruits; flesh has high sugar content and extremely fine flavor; clear pulp extends almost out to the skin. Tree short and bushy; self-fertile. Originated in San Marcos, California. D57

Smith: One of the earlier selections being grown in the Pacific Northwest. Produces reliable and abundant crops of medium to large fruit. I49M

Trask: Medium to large, oblong fruit, up to 3 1/2 inches long and weighing 3 to 5 ounces; rough, dark green skin; shells thicker and grittier than Coolidge; flavor and quality good to very good; ripens early. Tree self-fertile, but most productive when cross-pollinated; precocious. Ideal pollinator for Nazemetz. Originated as a bud sport of Coolidge. G17, *G49*, I74, I83M, L6

Triumph: Short, oval, plump fruits, not as pointed as those of Coolidge; medium to large; skin uneven but firm; flesh somewhat gritty but with good seed to pulp ratio; excellent sharp flavor; ripens in midseason. Tree upright, of medium vigor; bears very heavily if pollinated. Good pollinator for Mammoth. Along with Mammoth, one of the two leading cultivars in New Zealand. Selected there from seedlings of the Choiceana cultivar. I83M, L6, N84{S}, O93{S}, *O97, Q49M, Q93*

Unique: Fruit large, oval; skin smooth, light-green with a blue-green surface bloom; pulp very smooth in texture, flavor good; ripens early. Excellent as a fresh dessert fruit and also good for canning. Tree upright spreading, to 8 feet tall; vigorous; self-fruitful and precocious; a regular and heavy bearer. Originated in Inglewood, New Zealand by Dennis Barton. *O97*

FIG {GR}

FICUS CARICA

CAPRIFIGS

With the exception of the Croisic cultivar, caprifigs do not produce edible fruit. They are important, however, as a source of pollen for Smyrna type figs. Three crops are produced by a caprifig tree, the spring or profichi crop, the summer or mammoni crop, and the autumn or mamme crop that overwinters in a dormant state.

Croisic: (Cordelia, Gillette) Fruit of profichi crop medium or above, up to 1 3/4 inches in diameter, pyriform with a distinct neck; ribs prominent, with surface often somewhat corrugated; eye fairly large, with yellowish-green scales; color greenish-yellow; interior white; edible pulp insipid, lacking in sugar; staminate flowers few, generally lacking in pollen. Mammoni crop figs much the same as profichi. Tree vigorous and productive. CONDIT; I74

COMMON FIGS

Common fig cultivars produce fruit parthenocarpically, i.e. without caprification. Generally, they develop and mature both breba and fig crops, brebas being the smaller crop of the two. These are much appreciated as fresh fruit early in the season. The figs, or second crop, are also fine for eating fresh, but of the two, are preferred for drying.

DARK-SKINNED

Beall: Medium to large fruit; skin purplish-black; pulp amber, has a delicate, mildly sweet flavor. Tree moderately vigorous; produces 2 crops for fresh fruit purposes. Excellent in Imperial Valley, San Diego County and Fresno, California. Originated in Santa Clara, California by W.A. Beall. Introduced in 1924. BROOKS 1972; D37, I49M, I74

Black Jack:[1] Large to very large fruit; skin purplish-brown; flesh reddish-amber; flavor sweet. Dwarf, spreading plant; does well in pots. Needs protection during the winter in cold areas. D37

Black Madera: Large, oval fruit; skin purple-black; eye small, closed; flesh deep red, sweet, of excellent flavor. Ripens well on the coast of southern California as well as inland. I83M

Black Mission: (Mission, Franciscana) Breba crop good in most seasons; fruits large; color black; pulp light strawberry; flavor rich. Second-crop figs medium to large; eye small to medium; color black; pulp amber to light strawberry; flavor distinctive, rich; quality excellent, both fresh and dried. Used as a fresh fruit, and can also be dried and canned. Introduced at San Diego, California about 1768 from mission stations in Baja, California. CONDIT; A44M{PR}, A88M, *D23M*, D77M, E4, E84, F11, F19M, F68, H4, I49M, I74, I76M{PR}, I83M, J83T{PR}, L1, *L47*, etc.

Bourjassotte Gris: Brebas few, many not maturing properly. Second-crop figs medium, 1 1/2 to 2 inches in length, pyriform; eye medium, open; skin greenish violet, darker at the apex; pulp strawberry, quality fair to good. Caprified figs with violet-brown external color; pulp blood red; flavor subacid, rather strong. Highly regarded in England, especially for forcing. CONDIT; R77

Brogiotto Nero: (Barnissotte) Brebas rare, above medium to large, pyriform, purplish black; pulp strawberry. Second-crop figs medium to large; turbinate-pyriform; color purplish-black. Meat white; pulp light strawberry; flavor fairly sweet and rich; quality good to excellent, especially in coastal climates. Caprified figs larger, subject to spoilage; pulp dark strawberry to blood red. The same cultivar described by Pliny and other Roman writers as Fico Africano. CONDIT; O71M, R59M

Brown Turkey: (Eastern Brown Turkey, Black Spanish, Italian Everbearing) Medium-sized fruit; skin thin and tough, mahogany-brown tinged purple; eye small to medium, partially closed; seeds few; meat white or amber-white; pulp pink or rosy; flavor rich; quality good. Best eaten fresh; not good for canning or drying. Tree cold hardy, stands cold better than most other cultivars. STEBBINS; B74, C63, D77M, E4, F19M, F68, G17, G23, *G28*, G41, H4, I74, I83M, L1, L99M, etc.

Celeste: (Celestial, Malta) Breba crop small, or mostly none. Second-crop figs small, pyriform; eye medium, partly open, but not readily admitting dried-fruit beetles; color violet-bronze to chocolate-brown; pulp strawberry; flavor sweet and rich; seeds hardly noticeable; quality very good. Figs drop and dry without spoiling. Caprified figs are larger; pronounced violet tint outside and dark strawberry inside; flavor subacid. CONDIT; C63, D37, D77M, F19M, F93, G17, H4, H65, I74, I83M, L90, *M69M*, M76, N33

Early Violet: Brebas none. Second-crop figs small to very small, 1 inch long by 1/4 inches in diameter; shape turbinate to oblate-spherical; ribs prominent; eye large, open; color chocolate-brown; pulp strawberry; seeds small; quality fair to good. Susceptible to spoilage. CONDIT; I74

Flanders: Medium-sized, pyriform fruit with a long, slender neck; skin light tawny with violet longitudinal stripes and scattered white flecks; meat white; pulp light strawberry, has a strong, rich flavor; eye medium, tight. Excellent fresh fruit fig for the home garden. Virtually no splitting. Dried figs dark, commercially unattractive. H4, I74

Hardy Chicago: Medium to small, black fruit; flavor sweet and very rich. Originated near Chicago by a gardener who grew the tree up against his home, where it was protected annually and fruited consistently. One year, the tree was not protected and its top growth died due to cold. Surprisingly, the tree produced an abundant crop from the new growth, without protection. B75, D37

Hunt: Breba crop small; fruit small to medium; skin green; pulp red, somewhat dry, mealy, quality poor. Second-crop fruit small to below medium, elongated, pyriform; skin bronze, dull; flesh amber with some red; flavor rich, sweet, quality fair to good; resembles Celeste. In Georgia, fruit parthenocarpic; in California, fruit incompletely parthenocarpic. Originated in Eatonton, Georgia by B.W. Hunt. Introduced about 1932. BROOKS 1972; H4

Magnolia: (Brunswick) Breba crop generally very small; brebas large; color reddish-brown; pulp amber, with a tinge of pink, texture mealy; flavor flat. Second-crop figs medium, oblique-turbinate; color bronze; pulp amber, tinged with strawberry, hollow at center; seeds small or rudimentary; flavor sweet, fairly rich. Quality good fresh; excellent for preserving; inferior for drying. In Texas, it is grown extensively as a preserving fig. CONDIT; D37, F68, H4, I74, J61M, M83

Negronne: (Bordeaux, Violette de Bordeaux) Breba crop fair to good; purplish-black; meat white tinged with violet; pulp strawberry, rich; quality very good. Second-crop figs small to medium, spherical, or pyriform to obovate; color purplish-black; meat white; pulp strawberry, fairly rich in flavor. Good for home planting as tree is dwarf and prolific in fruit production. CONDIT; I74, J61M

Nero: (Black Ischia) Breba crop fair; fruits medium or above; eye medium, open; color purplish black; meat thin, white with a violet tinge; pulp strawberry; flavor fairly sweet and rich. Second-crop figs small to medium, oblique pyriform to turbinate; surface dull, bloom fairly heavy; color purplish-black; pulp strawberry; quality good. CONDIT; D77M, I49M

Osborn's Prolific: (Archipel, Neveralla) Breba crop good. Figs in hot interior valleys above medium; color bronze, tinged with violet; pulp cottony white, tinged with pink; texture spongy or mealy; flavor somewhat strong; quality fair. Second-crop figs variable in size; eye medium, open; color bronze with violet tinge; pulp amber, almost seedless; flavor insipid; quality poor. In cool. coastal climates, fruit sizes are larger, and figs are of good to excellent quality for fresh consumption. CONDIT; A88M, *C54*, D37, D77M, G17, I49M, *I68*, I74, I83M, J61M, L3, L99M, *N20*

Pasquale: (Vernino) Breba crop none. Second-crop figs small to medium; oblate-spherical to pyriform; eye medium, slightly protruding; skin tough or rubbery in texture; color purplish-black on body, greenish toward the base. Meat thin, white; pulp solid, strawberry in color (darker when caprified); flavor fairly rich; quality good. Season late. CONDIT; C25{CF}, D77M, G17, I49M, I74

Pastilière:[1] Brebas none, or rare. Second crop abundant; fruit medium-sized, turbinate or oblate; skin purplish black, fairly tender; meat white; pulp light strawberry, sweet, quality very good; seed coats not developed, or only partly so. Tree compact, of slow growth, dwarfish. CONDIT; U8{SC}

San Piero: (California Brown Turkey, Old Brown Turkey, Granata) Breba crop fair; figs large; color greenish-purple; meat violet; pulp strawberry; flavor rich; quality good. Second-crop figs medium to large, obovate to oblique-pyriform; eye large, open; color purplish-black; pulp strawberry, center hollow; flavor fairly rich. Quality fair to good when matured on the tree. Consumed fresh; worthless for drying. CONDIT; E84, J61M

Texas Everbearing: (Southern Brown Turkey) Medium to large fruit with purple skin; mild sweet flavor, quality good. Very similar to, if not identical with, Brown Turkey. Tree large, very vigorous and productive. Best in the Southwest, especially in higher elevation areas that have a short growing season. MCEACHERN, STEBBINS; A85M, B75, C37, *C54*, *F5*, F19M, F93, G13, *G28*, G72, H4, *I68*, I74, K28, L90, *M69M*, M83, N33, etc.

LIGHT-SKINNED

Adriatic: (Verdone) Breba crop very small, or none. Second-crop figs in hot, interior valleys are medium, turbinate; eye medium, open; color green to greenish-yellow; meat thin, white; pulp light strawberry, somewhat hollow at the center. Flavor fairly rich, of a characteristic fig type. Quality good, especially for drying. In cool climates figs are large, grass-green outside; blood red inside; quality excellent. CONDIT; B74, I49M, I74

Alma: Medium-sized yellow to tan fruit; meat white, thick; pulp light tan with pink undertones in the center, very succulent and sweet; seed hulls hardly noticeable; quality excellent; eye well-sealed. Ripens in late July and early August. Tree compact and rounded, with glossy leaves that are sparse compared to other cultivars; prolific and cold-hardy, displaying prolonged spring dormancy. Introduced in 1974 by the Texas Agricultural Experiment Station. MCEACHERN; *A19*, D37, D77M, G17, H4, I49M, K67, L90, N33

Armenian: Breba crop fruit very large; hollow, thick-fleshed, very flat, deep yellow in color; flesh amber, mildly sweet, quality good. Second-crop fruit not as large but still has rather good quality. Does well in pots. D37

Brogiotto Bianco: (Barnissotte Blanche) Bears a few brebas in some seasons only; the second crop is very prolific, maturing over a long season. Second-crop figs medium; turbinate, somewhat flattened at the apex; eye large, open, often splitting at maturity; skin rather firm, uniformly yellowish-green, with light bloom; meat white, pulp red. Quality excellent fresh; also good for drying. CONDIT; O71M

Conadria: Fruit flesh very firm; smaller eye, lighter dry color and higher sugar content than Adriatic, which it resembles, also more resistant to fruit spoilage. Tree vigorous, precocious; produces two crops; breba crop good, second crop very good. Widely planted in San Joaquin Valley for production of dried figs and in dooryards fo fresh fruit. Originated in Riverside, California by Ira J. Condit. Introduced in 1955. BROOKS 1972; A88M, *C54*, D37, D77M, E4, F11, F19M, G17, H4, I49M, *I68*, I74, I83M, *L47*, M31M, etc.

Deanna: Fruit oblate; eye medium, tight; skin light-yellow; meat white; pulp amber, sweet, quality good; ripens in mid-season. Yields well. Attractive. No splitting. Developed by Ira J. Condit to replace Calimyrna. U8{SC}

DiRedo: Fruit globose with a short, thick neck; skin light yellowish-green; meat white; pulp amber; eye small, tight. Good Verdone type for drying in hot interior valleys; dries light in color; some splitting in adverse weather. I49M

Drop of Honey: Medium to large, light-colored fruit; flesh yellowish, very sweet, of excellent quality. Has an open eye which fills with a drop of nectar to seal off the opening, protecting it from insect damage. I83M

Excel: Fruit medium to large, ovoid to globose; skin light greenish-yellow; meat white; pulp light amber; slightly higher sugar content, with smaller eye than Kadota; less likely to spoil. Excellent Kadota type for fresh fruit, canning, and drying. Virtually no splitting. Tree a strong, vigorous grower. Developed by Ira J. Condit. D57, G17, H4, I74

Florentine: (Italian Honey) Medium-large, spherical to flattened fruit; color bright yellow to green; eye open; flavor sweet; excellent canned quality. Bears over a long season. Similar to, if not identical with, Kadota. H4, I91

Green Ischia:[1] (Verte) Brebas few, or rarely produced. Second-crop figs small, turbinate, without neck, or pyriform; with prominent, somewhat flattened neck; eye small, fairly well closed; color grass-green; meat white; pulp dark strawberry; quality very good. Season late. CONDIT; *A19*, C25{CF}, D37, D77M, F68, G17, H4, I74

Gulbun: Large, oblate fruit; eye medium, tight; skin light greenish-yellow; meat white; pulp light pink, delicately sweet, quality good; few split; ripens in mid-season. Tree productive; does well in containers. Originated by Ira J. Condit. D37, I49M

Ischia: (White Ischia) Breba crop small or none. Second-crop figs small, turbinate; skin greenish-white, transparent, sometimes tinged by the red flesh below; meat white, thin; pulp strawberry, very sweet, rich; ripens early. Good for homemade preserves and pickles. Tree compact, not hardy. Popular in England for pot culture and for forcing, where three crops is the aim. CONDIT, SIMMONS 1978; R77

Kadota: (Dottato) Breba crop none, or fair. Second-crop figs medium to occasionally large; shape spherical to obovate; eye medium, often sealed with drop of gum; skin rather thick, rubbery in texture; color green to golden yellow; meat white; pulp amber; seeds few, small. Flavor very sweet, but lacking distinctive character; quality excellent, especially for preserving and canning; skin of dried fruit somewhat thick and tough. CONDIT; A88M, B93M, *C54*, D37, D77M, E4, F11, *F53M*, G41, H4, I49M, *I68*, I74, *L47*, *N20*, etc.

L.S.U. Everbearing: Fruit medium to large; skin yellow-green; pulp white to amber, sweet, of high quality. Bears from July through the summer and fall. H4

Mary Lane: (Jelly) Medium-sized, round fruit with a short neck; skin yellowish-white, smooth in texture; pulp amber, fills in well, nearly seedless; good, sweet flavor; ripens summer through fall. Good for fresh fruit and canning. Originated in Escondido, California by John Stevenson. *C54*, D57, G17, I74

Monstrueuse: Breba-crop figs medium to large; skin green, tinged with violet from the underlying meat; pulp dark strawberry, rich and sweet, quality very good. Second-crop figs medium or above, turbinate; skin grass green; pulp very light strawberry, sweet and rich, quality very good. Tree vigorous and productive. Does well in the eastern U.S. Originated in France prior to 1868. CONDIT; **U8{SC}**

Nardine: Attractive, oblate fruit; skin light yellow; meat white; pulp amber, sweet, quality good; eye medium, tight; ripens in midseason. Yields well. Few split. Originated in Riverside, California by Ira J. Condit. Developed as a replacement for Calimyrna. I74

Panachée: (Tiger) Brebas none. Second-crop figs medium; shape pyriform; ribs practically absent; surface glossy with a delicate bloom; eyes medium or above, open; color light yellow with alternate stripes of green, the latter fading out at complete maturity; meat thick, white; pulp strawberry, mealy in texture; quality fair to good. Caprified figs are somewhat larger, with pulp blood-red in color. Fruit splits badly, even when uncaprified. CONDIT; D57, H4, I74, I83M

Peter's Honey: (Rutara) High quality fruit has tender glossy greenish-yellow skin when ripe, and very flavorful dark amber flesh. A warm location with southern exposure is important for ripening this cultivar in the Maritime Northwest. Introduced from Sicily. I49M

Petite Negri: Large, black fruit; sweet, exceedingly rich flavor. Tree dwarfish, hardy, sets 2 crops and usually sets more fruit per plant size than other cultivars. Excellent for pot culture, having produced as many as 65 fruits in a 2 gallon container. Resembles Black Mission but hardier and more productive under cool climate conditions. D37

Tena: Fruit oblate with little or no neck, medium in size; skin light greenish-yellow; meat white; pulp light strawberry in color; flavor excellent; eye medium, but very tight. Ripens in mid-season; highly resistant to splitting under adverse weather conditions. Tree a strong grower with ascending branches. D57, G17, I74

Tennessee Mountain: Medium sized fruit; sugar content high enough for use in drying, fig newtons, or preserves. Very hardy tree; bears heavily. Recommended for outdoor growing in marginal areas. Originated in the mountains of Tennessee. Introduced by Dr. Silas Harmon, former Professor of Horticulture at the Coastal Plains Experiment Station in Tifton, Georgia. M31M

Troiano: (White Mission) Breba crop none. Second-crop figs below medium to small, spherical to turbinate; eye large, open; skin prominently checked crisscross at maturity; color yellow, sometimes faintly tinged with brown on the exposed side; meat white; pulp strawberry; quality fair to good. Caprified specimens larger; color green; pulp dark strawberry; seeds fertile. CONDIT; I74

Ventura: (Verdal) Brebas rare. Second-crop figs medium, turbinate to obovate; eye medium, open; skin green; meat thin, white; pulp strawberry; flavor rich, quality good; ripens late but matures well in cool areas. Caprified figs medium to large; pulp solid, blood red, flavor very strong and rich; considerably better in size, appearance, and quality than uncaprified fruit. Season late. CONDIT; D57, G17

White Everbearing: Small to medium-sized fruit; white to greenish-white skin; very sweet, light amber flesh; excellent quality. Very vigorous tree with large, dark-green leaves; highly productive. *A19*, H4

White Genoa: (Genoa) Breba crop small; fruits large; shape oblique-pyriform; eye medium, open; pulp light strawberry, hollow at center; flavor sweet but not rich; seeds few, small; quality fair. Second-crop figs medium or above, somewhat oblique, turbinate; color greenish-yellow, blemished by circular brown spots at maturity; skin thin, tender, peeling readily; pulp amber, tinged with strawberry; texture gelatinous; flavor mild; quality poor; seeds practically none. Very susceptible to spoilage. CONDIT; B93M, *C54*, *D23M*, *I68*, I74, L1, *N20*

White Marseilles: (Marseilles, Blanche, Lattarula, Lemon) Breba crop fair; figs medium or above; color light green; pulp and meat white; seeds large, conspicuous; quality fair to good. Second-crop figs similar to brebas, except for smaller size; shape spherical to oblate. Flavor fairly rich and sweet; quality fair as a fresh fruit, of light weight and poor quality when dried; susceptible to fruit spoilage. Caprification has little effect upon size and color, either of skin or pulp. CONDIT; B67, D37, G17, H4, I49M, I74, J61M, L3, L99M, N0

Yvonne: Fruit obovoid; skin canary-yellow; eye medium, tight; meat white; pulp light strawberry. Matures early, all figs dropping in a short time; virtually no splitting. Originated in Riverside, California by Ira J. Condit. I74

SAN PEDRO FIGS

Cultivars of this class have characteristics intermediate between the common figs and the Smyrna figs. The breba crop develops, matures, and ripens fruit parthenocarpically on the previous year's wood. Fruit of the second crop, which forms on the current year's wood, requires pollination by the fig wasp in order to develop, or they will shrivel and fall from the tree.

DARK-SKINNED

Dauphine: (Violette Dauphine) Breba crop generally good; fruit large, 2 1/2 inches long; ribs broad; eye large, protruding; skin greenish-violet to violet-purple; meat white; pulp light strawberry, flavor fairly rich; especially good for shipping fresh. Second crop figs similar to brebas, except for smaller size. Cultivated extensively in southern France. CONDIT; R77

Pied de Boeuf: Breba crop fair to good; fruits large, oblique-pyriform with a prominent, often curved neck; skin tender, Hessian brown; meat white tinged with pink; pulp light strawberry, texture rather coarse, quality good. Second-crop caprified figs medium to large, prominently ribbed; skin chocolate brown to mahogany red, tender; pulp dark strawberry, flavor rich and sweet, quality excellent. CONDIT; **T49M{SC}**, **U8{SC}**

Royal Vineyard: (Drap d'Or) Breba crop small; fruits large, pyriform; ribs prominent; color light coppery-bronze, attractive; pulp light strawberry; flavor sweet and rich; seeds few. Eating quality excellent; regarded by French confectioners as one of the best figs for crystallized and glacé fruit. Caprified figs of the second crop medium to large; color reddish-brown to violet-brown; pulp strawberry; flavor rich; quality good. CONDIT; C25{CF}, D37

LIGHT-SKINNED

King: (Desert King) Large, pyriform fruit; skin dark green, thin, smooth; flesh pink, sweet, quality excellent; matures in cool coastal climates as far north as British Columbia, Canada; resembles Genoa. Tree moderately vigorous; breba crop prolific; severe dropping of second crop in inland districts. Originated in Madera, California by Sisto Pedrini. Introduced in 1940. BROOKS 1972; B67, C34, *C54*, D77M, G17, I49M, I74, I83M, J61M, L3, L99M, N0

San Pedro: (San Pedro Miro, White San Pedro) Breba crop good; figs medium to large, turbinate; skin yellowish-green; meat white; pulp amber tinged with strawberry, flavor sweet, fairly rich. Second-crop figs medium to large; skin green to yellowish-green; meat white, thick; pulp strawberry, gelatinous; flavor insipid, flat. CONDIT; *O97*, R77

SMYRNA FIGS

Cultivars in this class set virtually no breba crop. The second crop develops on the current season's growth and reaches full maturity only when the flowers are pollinated by the fig wasp and the ovules develop into fertile seeds; the fertile seeds adding a nutty flavor to the meat and pulp. This class contains some of the finest tasting cultivars.

DARK-SKINNED

Marabout: Large, pyriform fruit, 2 1/4 inches in diameter; neck very prominent; eye large, open; skin purplish-black, shading to light green on the neck; pulp strawberry, rather coarse in texture, flavor rich and sweet; quality very good fresh. Season later than that of Calimyrna, with figs continuing to mature over a long period. Introduced into the United States from Algeria in 1928. CONDIT; U8{SC}

Zidi: Large, pyriform fruit; skin violet-black; pulp dark strawberry, rich and sweet; quality excellent fresh. Resembles Marabout superficially but is self-colored throughout, and 50% larger on the average. Tree vigorous, large and open; leaves often very large. Introduced into the United States from Tunisia in 1950. U8{SC}

LIGHT-SKINNED

Calimyrna: (Sari Lop) Breba crop fair in some seasons. Second crop figs large, up to 2 1/2 inches in diameter; eye large, open; skin golden-yellow to light lemon-yellow; pulp amber to light strawberry, flavor rich and sweet; quality excellent both fresh and dried; seeds numerous. Regarded as the "ne plus ultra" of fig cultivars in California. Has been grown in the Meander Valley of Turkey for several centuries. First planted commercially in California in 1886. CONDIT; I76M{PR}, U8{SC}

Snowden: Breba crop none. Second crop good; figs large, pyriform, ribs fairly prominent; skin lemon yellow, attractive; meat white; pulp amber, flavor rich and sweet; quality excellent, both fresh and dried; inclined to split in unfavorable weather. Tree vigorous and productive. Discovered in 1922 on the place of P.W. Snowden, Modesto, California. CONDIT; U8{SC}

FILBERT {GR}

CORYLUS AVELLANA CORYLUS MAXIMA

Barcelona: Medium-large, round nut; kernel rough, averages about 40% of nut. Tree moderately productive and hardy; highly susceptible to bacterial filbert blight and brown stain. Accounts for approximately 85% of the Pacific Northwest filbert production, supplying the inshell market demand for a round nut with good flavor. Has been the leading cultivar for over 60 years. JAYNES; A88M, B67, B74, B75, E4, E91M, *G14*, G75, *H8*, H49, H65, J15M, L30, L97, M39M, N0, *N20*, etc.

Butler: Nut medium-large, oval; shell thicker than Daviana; kernel smooth, averages 46% of nut. Tree productive, much more so than Daviana; hardy; somewhat resistant to bud mite, but much less susceptible than Daviana. Excellent pollinizer for Barcelona and Ennis. Gradually replacing Daviana as the principal pollinizer in commercial orchards of the Pacific Northwest. A88M, B74, B93M, C34, G75, H49, I49M, J15M, J61M, L97, L99M, N0, *N20*

Cassina: Heavy producer of small, thin-shelled nuts that fall free and at the same time as Barcelona. Kernels crackout at 50% of nut and are very even in size, compared to Barcelona with a 40% crackout and kernels of 5 or more size. Will pollinize Barcelona and Ennis. J15M, N0

Comet: Nut very attractive; shell long, thin; kernel clean, smooth, plump. Tree produces good crops if cross-pollinated. Originated in Westbank, British Columbia by J.U. Gellatly. Introduced in 1928. BROOKS 1972; A91{PL}

Cosford Cob: (Miss Young's) Nut medium-sized, oval with a broad shoulder; shell thin, medium brown in color; flavor sweet, quality high; borne in clusters of 2 or 3. Tree upright, fairly vigorous; hardy; a reliable bearer; produces abundant pollen. Will pollinate other cultivars. One of the best English cobs. G75, O81, R77, R83, S81M

Craig: (C. maxima) Large, oval nut; shell medium; kernel large. Tree produces good crops if cross-pollinated. Open-pollinated seedling of Kentish Cob. Originated in Westbank, British Columbia by J.U. Gellatly. Introduced in 1928. BROOKS 1972; A91{PL}

Daviana: Long, medium-sized nut; shell thin, very susceptible to bird and rodent damage; kernel smooth, averages about 48% of nut. Tree unproductive; moderately hardy; extremely susceptible to eastern filbert blight and bud mite; more finely branched than Barcelona. Main pollinizer for Barcelona. Accounts for approximately 7% of the Oregon filbert crop. B67, B93M, E4, H65, J15M, M39M, N0, *N20*

Du Chilly: (Kentish Cob) (C. maxima) Nut large; long and rather flattened with a well-defined seam; shell moderately thick; flavor and quality excellent; has a tendency to remain in the clinging husk when falling from the tree. Tree spreading; heavy yielding; hardy; produces better in colder climates. Pollinized by Butler, Royal and Daviana. Main cultivar in the United Kingdom; selected in Kent, England in 1830. B67, B93M, G75, J15M, L30, M39M, *N20*

Ennis: Large, round nut; kernel smooth, averages 46 to 48% of nut. Tree productive; moderately hardy; somewhat resistant to bud mite. Has a larger nut and is more productive than the standard cultivar, Barcelona. Has less of a tendency toward biennial bearing. Produces approximately 20% fewer blank nuts. Gradually replacing Barcelona in commercial orchards. A91, B74, C34, I49M, J15M, J61M, L97, L99M, N0, *N20*

Hall's Giant: Nut large, round; kernel smooth, averages 40% of nut. Tree hardy; resistant to bud mite; yields poorly. Late-flowering pollinizer compatible with Barcelona and Ennis. Recommended for planting in small numbers along fence rows or odd spaces to cover late-flowering blossoms of the main crop cultivar. JAYNES; A91, B74, C34, G75, J15M, L99M

Jemtegaard #5: (J-5) Late-flowering pollinizer compatible with Barcelona and Ennis. Produces light crops of medium-sized nuts. Recommended for planting in small numbers along fence rows or odd spaces to cover late-flowering blossoms of the main crop cultivar. JAYNES; J15M

Merveille de Bolvert: Selected for quality of flavor and large-sized, sweet nuts. Will make a suitable pollinator for Nottingham and Waterloo. *O97*

Montebello: Small to medium-sized, round nut, borne in large clusters; ripens a week or so before Ennis. Small tree; the best pollinizer for Tonda Gentile della Langhe. Pollinized by Butler and Jemtegaard #5. An Italian cultivar that outyields Tonda Gentile della Langhe. J15M, N0

Nottingham: (Pearson's Prolific) Nut medium-sized; oval, somewhat flattened; kernels sweet and flavorful; matures early. Tree small; heavy bearing; useful as a pollinator. *O97*, R77

Red Aveline: (Red, Avelinier Rouge) Large, oval, thin-shelled nut; kernel smooth, red-skinned, of a sweet nutty, excellent flavor. Heavy yielding tree with long, claret-red catkins. At one time prized in eastern California as a productive sort of good quality. BAILEY, L. 1947; R77

Royal: Barcelona x Daviana. Nut oval, larger than either parent; shell thin; kernel large, rough, averages 43% of nut; color and markings similar to Daviana; ripens about the same time as Barcelona. Tree hardy; produces early and heavily; sheds pollen medium to early; susceptible to bud mite. Introduced in 1934. BROOKS 1972; B75, B93M, B99{PL}, C82{PL}, E15{S}, H65, J15M

Tonda Gentile della Langhe: Small, round nut; sweeter and more flavorful than standard filbert cultivars; ripens a month before Ennis. Most popular cultivar in Italy; widely grown in the Piedmont region. Bears only a moderate crop due to susceptibility to big bud mite. Nearly male sterile, should not be relied upon as a pollinizer for other cultivars. U7M{SC}

Waterloo: Small, oval-shaped, flattened nuts with excellent, flavorful kernels. One of the most popular cultivars in New Zealand. *O97*

Whiteskin: (White, Alba, Avelinier Blanche) Medium-sized, oval nut; kernel covered with a white skin, quality and oil content high. Can be kept in the husk longer than others due to constricted form of husk. Vigorous, heavy bearing tree, produces fruit in clusters. Regarded in England as one of the best cultivars. Does well in California. BAILEY, L. 1947; R77

GARLIC {PL}

ALLIUM SATIVUM

COMMON GARLIC

Bavarian: The bulbs of this garlic are larger than those of the common white garlic, and keep for a very long time. Selected, fine sound bulbs. C92

California Early: (Early California White, Early California Braiding) The well-known white cultivar most commonly seen in markets. Large, clean, well-filled bulbs; flatter than California Late; 10 to 20 cloves per bulb; skin off-white or tan; exceptionally fine appearance; mild delicate flavor. Easily peeled cloves. Matures in about 7 months, but stores for only 4 to 6 months. A57M{PR}, C96, C96{PR}, E59Z, F11, 199, K49T, L7M

California Giant: Very mild, extremely large bulbs; very thin skin. Use in salads, soups, sauces, seasonings, etc. After harvest, replant small bulbs for a new crop. Available October and November; again January through April. Listed as French Mild in Porter and Sons 1988 catalog. J34

California Late: (California Late White, California White) Firm, strong-flavored bulbs of high quality; skin light pink to deep red or pinkish brown when mature. Ripens June through July, 8 months after planting and as much as 2 to 4 weeks later than California Early. Best keeper of all the white garlics, will last from one harvest to the next. Good for braiding. A57M{PR}, D76, F11, G16, I99M, K71

Carpathian: Originally from the Polish side of the Carpathian Mountains in central Europe. It is common throughout the countries in that region. A garlic with good size and an excellent, pleasantly pungent flavor, fine for all cooking needs. Also makes attractive braids. Keeps well, from 6 to 12 months. C24, C24{PR}

Chet's:[1] Large artichoke type. Averages 5 or 6 bulbs per pound, 15 to 20 cloves per bulb; skin papery white, streaked with purple; medium-sized cloves; relatively mild flavor; keeps very well. Reselected from Italian Purple for over 25 years by master gardener Chet Stevenson of Tonasket, Washington. E59Z, L7M

Chinese: Has a lighter, less dense, more oily and somewhat elusive quality when compared to Salt Spring. Bronze-colored cloves are aromatic when cooked. C82, K17M

Dixon: Very large, purple-striped cultivar mistaken for elephant garlic by some people, but it's more pungent and has typical garlic-shaped cloves. E24

Early Italian Red:[1] (Early Italian) A very early maturing artichoke-type garlic. Fairly large bulbs with good reddish-purple color; not as pungent as Italian Red. Looser cloves that are easy to peel. Best red garlic for braiding. Ripens a couple of weeks earlier than Italian Red. F11, I99, I99M, K49M

Inchelium Red: Very large bulbs; 4 to 5 clove layers with 8 to 22 cloves per bulb. Light purple blotching. Cloves milk white or yellowish, with faint purple at base. Extremely vigorous. Found at Nespelem on Colville Indian Reservation in northern Washington. E59Z

Italian: Excellent pungent flavor, far superior to the garlic sold in most states. The original strain was obtained from a certified organic grower in the state of Washington. Italian is usually considered a generic name for small, strongly flavored garlic. E5T, F82, H40, K13

Italian Red: Large bulbs; very large, easily peeled, red-skinned cloves with a consistent symmetrical shape. Very strong, spicy flavor, preferred by garlic connoisseurs. Excellent keeper. Bulbs for planting are available in 2 sizes: 2 inches or larger and 1 to 2 inches. A57M{PR}, C96, C96{PR}, D2M, G93M, I99, I99M

Italian Silverskin: A rare strain of silverskin garlic that originally came from northern Italy. The long keeping quality and flavor has been preserved. All are hand braided and will stay fresh at room temperature from early November until the end of the next summer. C34{PR}

Lerg: Large, broad, flat cloves, very distinctive. Bulbs average 4 to 8 cloves per bulb with few small cloves. Excellent potential as a commercial cultivar. Originated at Christopher Ranch in Gilroy, California. L7M

Mild French Silverskin: Red blush overlaid with dark thin red lines on yellow-white background. Mostly 4 clove layers and 13 to 16 cloves per bulb. Originally from Texas. E59Z

Nichols Silverskin: A strain of silverskin garlic developed through many years of selection for strong flavor, large size, and easy-peeling qualities. Small, individually wrapped cloves; 2 inch diameter bulbs. Good flavor and keeping qualities. I39

Purple: Bulbs are purple-tinted; better flavored and longer keeping than the common white type. Grown in Chile and only available in May. J73

Purple Artichoke:[1] A large, purple-skinned artichoke garlic. The cloves are arranged first in the usual 8 to 10 clove whirl, and then 3 to 8 cloves are formed to the outside and on top along the central stalk, giving a superficial resemblance to a globe artichoke. The virtue of this type is that one can peel off individual cloves like artichoke bracts without disrupting the whole bulb. Mild flavor, good keeper. I99, K49T

Purple Miranda: Large, purple bulbs; approximately 12 cloves per bulb with few small cloves. Some bulbs may produce a curved stalk and purple topsets, and thus superficially resemble rocambole. Very fast maturing, productive and hardy. L7M

Salt Spring: A strong but sweet purple garlic with no bitterness; adds an earthy richness and depth to cooked foods. Easy to peel. Grown on Salt Spring Island, British Columbia for 15 years. K17M

Silverskin: Attractive, firm, pure-white bulb; medium to large in size, about 10 bulbs per pound; large, reddish-purple cloves. Classic culinary type; excellent, strong distinct flavor. Good keeping qualities. Regarded as one of the finest standard white garlics. A57M{PR}, D2M, D2M{PR}, E5M, F35M, I99, K13, K13{PR}, K22, K49T, L97, M46

Skinless: Has only a thin skin around each clove, with no covering at all around the whole bulb. Also very cold hardy. J29

Susanville: Small to medium-sized bulb; 1 to 2 inches in diameter; weight 1/4 pound; skin thin, white; 19 to 22 cloves per bulb; cloves large, somewhat flattened in shape; keeps very well, one month to six weeks longer than California Late. The flavor is excellent for all culinary uses. Introduced in 1982. E59Z, K13

Tipitilla: Mid-season garlic with high oil content and superior flavor. One of the longest keeping cultivars, often storing until the following harvest. Heirloom. K49T

Yugoslavian: From a strain adapted to Hornby Island, British Columbia, this garlic has a crisp texture and a fresh taste. Large size bulbs. Good keeper. C82, K17M

TOP-SETTING GARLIC

A distinct type that produces bulbs as well as a cluster of bulbils at the top of the stalk. Generally hardier and more productive than common garlic but much more difficult to braid. Some cultivars are becoming popular as gourmet items. (A. sativum Ophioscorodon Group)

De Vivo: Produces very large bulbs that are easily peeled. Has excellent commercial potential for the restaurant trade. One of the largest cultivars of top-setting garlic. Heirloom from Dr. Gilbert McCollum of the USDA. L7M{CF}

Early Red: A rare cultivar with medium sized bulbs. Foliage has a wide stem to leaf angle. Does well in the Mid-Atlantic region. Introduced by Southern Exposure Seed Exchange. L7M

French: Medium to large bulbs with dull-purple blotching. Mostly 8 to 10 cloves per bulb with some doubles. Cloves light-brown to purple blushed. E59Z

German Red: Large, bright-purple bulb; weight 1/4 pound; 8 to 12 cloves per bulb; yellow-fleshed, easy to peel cloves. Recommended for those who will use a lot of garlic quickly or who will preserve the garlic by pureeing, dehydrating or placing the peeled cloves in oil. Also produces large topsets, the size of pine nuts. Optimum vigor, flavor and quality occur when grown where winters are cold. C24, C82, K13, K75M, K75M{PR}, L7M

Himalayan: Produces rough-shaped bulbs (up to 2 1/2 inches) consisting of a core of poorly-defined central cloves surrounded by large cloves, mostly on opposite sides of the bulb. Flavorful and pungent. May produce bulbils lower on the stalk, even at the top of the bulb. Extremely cold hardy, may be grown at elevations above 8,000 feet. Originated in Nepal. L7M

Israeli: Produces large underground cloves, plus smaller bulbils on their above-ground stems. Similar to Russian, but somewhat smaller. Quality very good. C82

Italian Purple: Medium sized bulbs have a biting and pungent flavor. They produce clusters of topsets, much like the Egyptian onion. Topset bulblets may require two seasons to produce a full-sized bulb of garlic with separate cloves. The first year it may produce only a single small round bulb resembling an onion set. When these rounds or the cloves from a bulb are planted, they will produce full-sized bulbs in only one season. C24

Korean: A large, attractive rocambole from Korea. Intermediate in size between the smaller garlics and Elephant garlic. Clear, pungent flavor, tangy but sweet. Excellent for sauces, egg dishes, sautés, soups and stews. Introduced into the United States by Southern Exposure Seed Exchange. K49Z

New Mexican: An old strain of top set garlic from the Embudo valley of northern New Mexico. Develops a stalk with sets on the top. Plant in the fall or early spring for a harvest of full-size bulbs the second summer. L79M

Nichols Top Setting: Produces well-developed, medium sized bulbs that are harvested at the end of the growing season. Easy to peel skin; biting and pungent flavor; keeps well. Also produces several small bulbils at the top of each plant. May be planted in the fall or early spring. I39

Romanian Red: Attractive bulbs lined with bright dark-purple. Mostly 4 to 9 cloves per bulb. From Romania via British Columbia, where it is called *red elephant garlic*. E59Z

Russian: Strong growing plant; produces large underground bulbs, plus smaller bulbils on the above ground stems. Similar to Israeli, but somewhat larger. Quality excellent. Very winter hardy. Originally from Grand Forks, British Columbia. C82

Spanish Roja: (Rojas) Very large gourmet type. Reddish skin; 10 cloves per bulb, smaller bulbils on top stems; pungent flavor, good fresh; skin peels easily; excellent keeper. Winter hardy. Northwest heirloom traceable to the Portland area in the 1930's. A33, A91, C24, C82, C96, C96{PR}, D40M, D40M{PR}, E24, E59Z, F66T{PR}, G19M, I99, L7M

GOOSEBERRY {GR}

RIBES SPP.

AMERICAN GOOSEBERRIES

Generally smaller and less flavorful than European types, American gooseberries are more tolerant of heat and cold and can be grown over a wider area. Many are also more resistant to powdery mildew. The dark-skinned cultivars are considered to be the sweetest. Mostly R. hirtellum.

DARK-SKINNED

Canada 0-273:[1] Fruit medium in size, pear-shaped; skin copper red; flavor very good; quality excellent. Bush relatively thornless; pest resistant; light bearing. Originated in Ottawa, Ontario, Canada at the Central Experiment Farm. L12, N0

Captivator:[1] Medium to large, pear-shaped fruit; skin light red to full red when ripe; flavor very sweet; ripens in late July. Bush vigorous and productive; upright, 4 to 6 feet tall; completely thornless; very winter hardy; resistant to mildew. Originated in Ottawa, Ontario, Canada. Introduced in 1952. BROOKS 1972; C15M, H16, I49M, J7, J61M, L12, *M81M*, N0, N24M

Clark: Very large fruit; skin thick, rather tough; skin color greenish-yellow turning red when mature; flesh color red; flavor mild, sweet; quality fair to good; free of mildew; easy to pick; ripens in late mid-season. Bush moderately vigorous; hardy. Originated in Burlington,

Ontario, Canada by M.C. Smith. Introduced in 1922. BROOKS 1972; D37, J61M, N0, N24M

Glenndale: (R. missouriensis x) Fruit roundish-elliptic; skin smooth, thin; skin color dark reddish-purple; seeds small; quality good; excellent for jam; resistant to mildew. Bush vigorous and productive; erect, up to 8 feet tall; resistant to leaf spot and mildew. Best suited for southern limit of gooseberry growing in the United States. Originated in Little Silver, New Jersey. Introduced in 1932. BROOKS 1972; D37, D47

Houghton: Very small, roundish fruit; skin smooth, thin, dull dark red; flesh greenish, moderately juicy, tender, very sweet, of a pleasant rich flavor; quality very good; ripens in midseason. Bush very large, vigorous; upright, becoming very spreading; productive to very productive; very hardy; widely adapted. Originated in 1833 by Abel Houghton, Lynn, Massachusetts. HEDRICK 1925; H33

Josselyn: (Red Jacket) Fruit medium in size, roundish oval; skin smooth; skin color reddish green, becoming pale red when ripe; flesh rich, juicy, fragrant, sweet; quality very good to excellent; early ripening. Bush large, spreading; vigorous and productive; practically free from mildew. Originated in London, Ontario, Canada. Introduced about 1890. HEDRICK 1925; C58, C63, D37, G69M, G71, N0

Mountain: (Pence's Champion) Medium-sized, oblong fruit; skin smooth, thick; skin color dull brownish-purple; flesh moderately juicy, sweet. Bush tall, upright; vigorous; very disease resistant. Does well in hot weather. Discovered by a colony of Shakers about 1846 growing wild at Lebanon, New York. HEDRICK 1925; D37, D47

Pixwell: (R. missouriensis x) Fruit medium in size; borne in clusters and on long stems away from the thorns which makes for easy picking; skin pale green, becoming pink when ripe, thin; few thorns; good for all culinary purposes. Bush compact; hardy; very productive; widely adapted. Originated in Fargo, North Dakota by A.F. Yeager. Introduced in 1932. BROOKS 1972; A16, B19, B67, B73M, C63, *D59*, G16, G23, H16, H65, K64, L30, L79, *M65M*, N26, N26{PR}, etc.

Poorman: (Early Poorman) Medium to large, roundish oval to somewhat pear-shaped fruit; skin smooth, rather tough; skin color pale silvery-green gradually changing to pinkish-red to almost wine-red when ripe; flesh greenish, juicy, tender, aromatic, very sweet; quality excellent. Bush very large and productive; disease resistant. Originated in Brigham City, Utah by William H. Craighead. Introduced in 1896. HEDRICK 1925; A91, B67, *C47*, D37, D47, *G14*, H16, I36, I49M, J61M, L12, L99M, N0

Sylvia:[1] Fruit round, medium in size, about 1 inch in diameter; skin silvery-green, with a light pinkish-red blush when fully ripe; flesh aromatic; quality excellent, flavor mild, sweet, delicious; ripens in mid-July. Bush spreading; heavy bearing; relatively thornless; disease resistant. Originated by William Saunders, Central Experiment Station, Ottawa, Canada. I74, J61M, L12, N0

Welcome: Medium-large fruit; skin light dull-red, glabrous; flesh pink; quality good, flavor tart; seeds few, small; ripens before Pixwell. Often picked when green for use in pies and preserves. Bush vigorous; productive; relatively free of disease, especially anthracnose; spines sparse, short, weak, missing on older wood. Originated in Excelsior, Minnesota. Introduced in 1957. BROOKS 1972; B19, *C47*, C63, D37, *D59*, D65, D76, E97, *H90*, N24M

<u>LIGHT-SKINNED</u>

Colossal: Very large, oval fruit, 1 1/2 inches in diameter; skin translucent green, refreshingly tart; flesh sweet and mild; ripens in mid-July. Ideal for pies, jams or jellies. Bush vigorous, about 5 feet tall; very winter hardy; heavy bearing; disease resistant. B75, D47, N0

Oregon Champion: (Champion) Medium to large, roundish-oval fruit; skin greenish-yellow; quality good, flavor tart; ripens early; holds its color well. Good for pies, jams and wines. Bush vigorous, 3 to 5 feet tall; productive; resistant to mildew. Originated in Salem, Oregon by O.D. Dickinson, prior to 1880. HEDRICK 1925; A88M, A91, B19, B43M, F11, F19M, *G14*, H16, H49, *J2M*, *J63M*, L12, L97, *M65M*, N0, etc.

EUROPEAN GOOSEBERRIES

Generally considered superior to American gooseberries in both size and flavor. However, they require a more moderate climate with less extremes of both heat and cold. The yellow-skinned types are most highly valued for eating out of hand. Mostly R. grossularia.

<u>DARK-SKINNED</u>

Achilles: Very large, elliptical fruit; skin red; flavor sweet; dessert quality very good; ripens late. An old English cultivar still grown in northern Europe where the small unripe berries are used for compote and jelly and the ripe fruit is used for jam and preserving. Bush spreading. D47, I74, L12, N0, N24M

Crown Bob: Medium to large, oblong fruit; skin somewhat hairy, thin; skin color dark-red; flesh firm, juicy, sweet; quality good; ripens in mid-season. Used for dessert or cooking; also good for canning and jam. Bush large, spreading, pendulous; vigorous and productive; fairly resistant to powdery mildew. Has been grown in England for well over 100 years. HEDRICK 1925, SIMMONS 1978; I74, N0

Fredonia: Fruit very large, roundish oval; skin attractive, thick, tough; skin color dark red; flesh tender, mild, juicy, subacid to sweet; quality very good; keeps and ships well; ripens late. Bush vigorous and productive; upright-spreading; thorny. Originated in Geneva, New York by Richard Wellington. Introduced in 1927. Open-pollinated seedling of an unknown English-type. BROOKS 1972; J61M, N0

Hinnonmaki Red: Large fruit; skin dull-red; flavor very good. Good for pies, jams and jellies. Bush vigorous and productive; spreading; very hardy and disease resistant. Developed at the research station in Hinnonmaki, Finland. A65, C58, G1T, J7, K64, N0, N24M

Lancashire Lad: Large, oblong-oval fruit; claret red, becoming dark red when fully ripe, hairy; flesh juicy, flavor fair; at its best when picked green for cooking, excellent for jam, canning and exhibition. Bush fairly vigorous, upright at first but becoming spreading; has good resistance to American powdery mildew. First recorded about 1824. SIMMONS 1978; R87

Lepaa Red: Medium to large fruit; skin red; rich tart flavor. Excellent for pies and jams. Bush exceptionally vigorous; very hardy; disease and pest resistant. Developed at the research station in Hinnonmaki, Finland near the gardening school of Lepaa. First cultivated in 1950. Widely grown in Europe. A91, D47, I74, J61M, L12

London: Very large, oval fruit; skin smooth, dark red to crimson; flavor good; ripens midseason to late. Bush spreading, but makes few branches; requires a rich soil; flowers mid-period. Production very good. One of the best red exhibition cultivars. SIMMONS 1978; T87{SC}

Red Champagne: Small, roundish fruit; skin somewhat hairy, dark red; flesh sweet, of very good quality. Bush vigorous, resistant to mildew. A very old English cultivar once generally grown in eastern North America. HEDRICK 1925; D47

Warrington: (Red Warrington) Fruit small, roundish-oval; firm; skin has a few hairs; skin color light red when ripe; flavor fair to good for dessert; ripens very late. The best cultivar for jam making;

also good for canning, bottling and freezing. A very old English cultivar which has managed to survive. SIMMONS 1978; R87

Whinham's Industry: Large, oval fruit; skin hairy, light to very dark-red; flesh yellowish-green, juicy, tender; flavor very sweet; ripens mid-season. Very popular all-purpose cultivar; excellent for picking green, for canning, freezing and jam making, and for dessert. Bush vigorous and productive; upright; susceptible to powdery mildew. HEDRICK 1925, SIMMONS 1978; C58, D47, G69M, L12, N0, N24M

LIGHT-SKINNED

Bedford Yellow: Large, roundish-oval, very attractive fruit; skin hairy, golden-yellow streaked with red; flesh sweet, of good flavor; ripens in midseason. Bush fairly weak growing, susceptible to damage by sulphur sprays; highly productive; blooms in mid-period. Introduced by Laxton Bros. in 1922. SIMMONS 1978; T87{SC}

Broom Girl: Large, roundish-oval fruit; skin dark golden-yellow; flavor very good; ripens very early. Good for dessert and exhibition. Bush very vigorous and productive, blooms late. Originated in England. Introduced prior to 1852. At on time a good commercial cultivar. SIMMONS 1978; D47

Careless: Large, oval fruit; skin smooth, transparent; skin color green milky white when ripe; flavor sweet; quality good; ripens early mid-season. Good for jams, bottling, canning, freezing and dessert. Bush upright when young but becoming spreading and somewhat pendulous. Most popular cultivar in England. Known before 1860. SIMMONS 1978; *C47*, D47, I49M, L12, N0, N26, N26{PR}, O81

Catherina: (Catherine) Large to very large oval fruit; skin thick, nearly smooth, bright orange-yellow with a few green marks and a single green stripe; flavor sweet, quality very good; ripens late. Bush moderately vigorous; productive; slightly inclined to mildew. Excellent exhibition cultivar. Originated in England about 1840. HEDRICK 1925; B75, D47, L12, N0, O81, R87

Cousen's Seedling: Medium to large, oval fruit; skin clear pale yellow, slightly hairy; flesh firm, sweet, flavor fairly good; ripens very late. Excellent for dessert, cooking, canning and jam. Bush vigorous, spreading, rather prickly, bears well. Popular due to its lateness and attractive color. SIMMONS 1978; D47

Criterion: Very large, oval, plump fruit; skin smooth, deep yellow mottled with green; quality and flavor very good; ripens midseason to late. Excellent for exhibition. Bush large, upright to spreading. Originated in England. R87

Early Sulphur: Medium-sized, roundish oblong fruit; skin thin, covered with rather long hairs; skin and flesh color pale golden-yellow; flavor sweet, fairly good; ripens very early. One of the best early gooseberries for cooking; also excellent for dessert. Bush large, vigorous and productive; upright to spreading. Raised before 1825. SIMMONS 1978; D47, L12, N0, N24M

Glenton Green: Medium-sized, translucent, pale green berries, 1 inch or more in diameter; quality very good. An old English gooseberry rated as "best flavored" by Bunyard. D47

Green Hansa: Large, green fruit with a good balance of sweetness and tartness; quality very good. Suitable for dessert. Bush vigorous, upright-spreading; easy to propagate by cuttings. Originated in England. D47, N0

Gunner: Very large, round-oval fruit; skin dull olive green, somewhat transparent but hairy; sweet, meaty flesh, mild flavor; excellent for dessert, exhibition or jam making; ripens midseason to late. Bush spreading with long, stout shoots; very productive. SIMMONS 1978; D47, R87

Hinnonmaki Gold: (Hinnonmaki Yellow) Fruit very large to exceedingly large, round or oval; skin smooth, shiny; skin color yellowish-green. A dessert berry of sweet, rich flavor. Bred in Finland from large-berried European cultivars and mildew-resisting American cultivars. Completely hardy, surviving the severest winters in Finland. Widely grown throughout Europe. A65, D47, G69M, I74, J7, J61M, K64, L12, L99M, N0, N24M

Hoenings Earliest: (Honing's Fruheste) Roundish, medium to large fruit; skin hairy, thick, beautiful golden yellow; flesh very tender and juicy with a sweet, mild plum-like flavor; quality very good; ripens in early July. Large, vigorous, productive bush. Originated in Neuss, Germany about 1900. One of the earliest and most attractive of gooseberries. SIMMONS 1978; D47, R87

Howard's Lancer: Fruit medium-sized, roundish to oval; skin smooth, transparent, thin; skin color yellowish-green when ripe; flavor excellent. Useful for dessert or picking green for cooking; also good for jam, canning or freezing. Bush large, vigorous and spreading; susceptible to mildew. SIMMONS 1978; D47, Q30, R87

Invicta: Medium-sized, greenish fruit of excellent quality. Ideal for U-Pick operations. Resistant to mildew. One of the newest releases from the East Malling Research Station. (Resistanta x Whinham's Industry) x Keepsake. D47

Keepsake: Fruit medium to large, oval; skin slightly hairy, thin; skin color whitish-green; flesh greenish, juicy, firm; flavor very good; ripens in mid-season, but one of the earliest when picked green for cooking. Excellent for canning and freezing. Bush vigorous and very productive; spreading and pendulous; susceptible to powdery mildew. HEDRICK 1925, SIMMONS 1978; D47, R87

Langley Gage: Large, roundish oval fruit; skin transparent giving it a silvery appearance; skin color pale yellow; flesh very sweet; flavor exceptionally good. Excellent for dessert. Bush strong growing; upright at first but tending to spread with age. Its tendency to produce berries in the center of the bush makes picking difficult. D47, R87

Leveller: Large, oval fruit; skin slightly downy, almost smooth; skin color yellowish-green; flavor excellent; ripens in mid-season. Most widely grown dessert gooseberry in England; like Cox's Orange Pippin of apples, it is the aristocrat of gooseberries. Bush vigorous and productive; spreading and pendulous. SIMMONS 1978; D47, P86, Q30, R87

Pitmaston Greengage: Small, oval fruit; skin smooth, yellowish-green; excellent dessert flavor; ripens midseason to late, hangs on the bush a long time. Bush fairly vigorous and erect; blooms in early mid-period; bears good crops. SIMMONS 1978; T87{SC}

White Lion: Large, oblong fruit; skin slightly hairy, pale whitish-green; flavor very good; ripens very late. Bush vigorous and spreading; high yielding; blooms late mid-period; grows well on soils on which other cultivars do poorly. An excellent late white dessert gooseberry. Can also be picked green for cooking. SIMMONS 1978; D47

Whitesmith: Roundish oval, medium to large fruit; skin thin, tender, downy; skin color very pale cream with slight green tinge; flesh light green, juicy, firm but tender; excellent sweet flavor; ripens mid-season. Popular for both cooking and dessert purposes. Bush vigorous; upright at first but becoming spreading. First raised about 1824. HEDRICK 1925, SIMMONS 1978; D47, H85, L12, N0, N24M

GRAINS

See Amaranth, Corn, Quinoa and Sprouting Seeds in the Cultivar listings. Also see Poaceae in the Botanical listings, and Seeds in the Index of Usage.

GRAPE {GR}

VITIS SPP.

TABLE GRAPES

AMERICAN These are mostly slipskin grapes, characterized by pulp that readily slides out of the skin. They have soft flesh and a distinctive, "foxy" or musty flavor and aroma. Most have moderately vigorous vines that are trailing instead of upright, and are resistant to many insects and diseases. Generally more cold hardy than Vinifera and French hybrid grapes. Mostly V. labrusca.

Blue-Skinned/Seeded

Alden: Large, oval fruit; skin reddish-black, adherent; flesh firm, juicy, meaty, tender, pleasantly aromatic; quality very good; ripens just after Concord. Vine vigorous, productive, tends to overbear; adapted to a wide range of soils; somewhat susceptible to winter injury. Large, loose clusters. Recommended for home garden and local market use. BROOKS 1972; B53, *E0*, G97M, G97M{SC}, H65, I36, I95, I95{SC}, L12, *M81M*

Alwood: Medium-sized fruit; skin blue-black with heavy waxy bloom, slipskin, not subject to cracking; flesh sweet, moderately foxy, flavor comparable to Worden or Concord; quality good; ripens a few days after Fredonia. Vine moderately vigorous, productive; hardy; tolerant to black rot, anthracnose, downy mildew and powdery mildew. Cluster medium-sized, compact. BROOKS 1972; A39, *E0*, I36, *M81M*

Bailey: Medium to large, roundish fruit; skin purplish-black, covered with a heavy blue bloom; flesh moderately juicy and tender, coarse, vinous, quality good; seeds numerous; ripens as late as Catawba; keeps well. Vine vigorous; productive; injured in severe winters. Cluster large, long, compact. Originated in Denison, Texas by T.V. Munson; first fruited in 1889-90. HEDRICK 1908; N33

Bath: Medium-sized, round oval fruit; skin bluish-black; flesh tender, juicy, sweet, quality fair; ripens the end of September in New York; lacks the foxy flavor of Fredonia, which it resembles. Vine vigorous; very productive, tends to overbear; fairly hardy. Cluster medium-sized, compact. Originated in Geneva, New York. Introduced in 1952. BROOKS 1972; C82, I95, I95{SC}, L12, *M81M*

Beaver: Fruit medium-sized; skin black; flesh firm, tender, juicy, separates easily from seeds, highly flavored; quality high; ripens a week before Moore Early; hangs well without cracking or shattering. Makes an excellent jelly. Vine vigorous, productive, self-fertile. Medium-sized clusters. Originated in Mountain Grove, Missouri. Introduced in 1947. BROOKS 1972; L12

Beta: Small to medium-sized fruit; skin bluish-black, slipskin; flesh juicy, foxy, tart; table quality fair, excellent for juice, jams and jellies; ripens early. Vine extremely hardy; productive, self-fruitful. Cluster fairly large. Originated in Carver, Minnesota prior to 1908. HEDRICK 1908; A65, *A74*, B4, B47, C58, D65, D69, E97, G54, G67, J7, K64, L27M, L70, N24M, N26, etc.

Black Spanish: (Lenoir) Small to medium-sized, roundish fruit; skin dark bluish-purple, nearly black, with lilac bloom, rather thick, tough; flesh slightly juicy, tender, subacid, very rich in coloring matter. Popular for juice, jelly and a dark red wine. Vine vigorous, usually quite productive; semi-hardy; tolerant to drought and Pierce's disease. Probably originated in one of the Carolinas or Georgia some time in the 18th century. HEDRICK 1908; *A19*, *C54*, L37M, N33

Blue Lake: (V. simpsonii x) Skin uniformly blue with a light surface bloom; flesh spicy, slightly tart; ripens from late June to late July at Leesburg, Florida. Suitable for fresh and processed juice, jellies and preserves. Vine self-fruitful; resistant to Pierce's disease. Cluster large, loose. Excellent for home gardens in the Deep South. BROOKS 1972; F19M, *K76*, L33, M31M

Bluestar: Medium-sized fruit; skin blue; flavor mildly foxy, pleasant; ripens between Fredonia and Concord. Ripens more evenly than Fredonia or Concord. Vine tends to over-produce unless properly pruned; more consistently productive than Fredonia. Cluster medium-large, tight, attractive. For roadside-stand sales and home gardens. BROOKS 1972; G97M, G97M{SC}

Buffalo: Medium-sized fruit; skin reddish-black, bloom heavy, tough, slipskin; flesh translucent, moderately juicy, tender, sweet, not aromatic; flavor pleasant, tart, spicy; quality excellent; ripens about 1 week before Concord. Vine vigorous, productive, hardy. Medium-large, well-filled cluster. For home gardens and local markets. BROOKS 1972; B67, *E0*, E97, G97M, G97M{SC}, H65, H88, I36, I95, I95{SC}, J61M, L12, *M81M*, N0

California Concord: (Pierce, Isabella Regia) Fruit very large, oblong; skin black, with a light bloom; flesh tender, very sweet, strongly aromatic; quality good for table use, juice and jelly; keeps fairly well. Vine very vigorous, prolific. Cluster large. Bud-sport of Isabella, originating about 1882 with Mr. J.P. Pierce, of Santa Clara, California. HEDRICK 1908, WICKSON; *C54*

Campbell Early: Medium to large fruit; skin dark purplish-black, bloom heavy, slipskin; flesh juicy, slightly foxy, somewhat vinous, sweet; quality good, improves by hanging on the vines; ripens over a long period; keeps and ships unusually well. Vine vigorous, hardy, productive; canes of average length. Originated in Delaware, Ohio in 1892. HEDRICK 1908; B67, *G14*, G97M, G97M{SC}, I95, I95{SC}, M39M, *M81M*, N0

Carman: Small, roundish fruit; skin dark purplish-black, glossy; flesh yellowish-green, not juicy, vinous, spicy, sweetish near the skin to tart by the seeds; ripens just before Catawba; keeps exceptionally well, both on the vine or in storage. Vine vigorous; lacking in productiveness; hardy. Cluster medium-sized, tapering, compact. Originated in Denison, Texas by T.V. Munson. Introduced in 1892. HEDRICK 1908; M83

Champanel: (V. x champini x V. labrusca) Large, globular fruit; skin black; quality excellent when fully ripe (about 2 weeks after turning blue); ripens with Concord. Makes a dark-blue juice and excellent jelly. Vine very vigorous; tolerant to adverse soil and weather conditions; resistant to Pierce's disease. Clusters large, loose, conical. Adapted to the prairies of the Southwest. Originated in Denison, Texas by T.V. Munson. MCEACHERN; *A19*, *C54*, E39, E39{SC}, N33

Concord: Medium to large, roundish fruit; skin black, slightly adherent, bloom blue, abundant; flesh juicy, foxy, sweet near the skin, somewhat tart near the seeds; quality good; ripens in midseason; keeps from 1 to 2 months. Vine vigorous, productive; hardy; widely adapted. Medium to large clusters. Standard American grape for juice, jelly, etc. Originated in Concord, Massachusetts in 1849. A38M{PR}, B58, B73M, C63, C82, D76, E1M{PR}, G23, *G49*, H16, I76M{PR}, J69, J83, L30, M39M, etc.

Conquistador: Attractive deep purple fruit with a light gray bloom; good foxy flavor; ripens mid to late July; resembles Concord. Excellent table and juice grape, also makes good jelly and a beautiful red wine. Medium-sized, tight clusters. Usually grafted onto a nematode resistant rootstock to insure good vigor and highest yields. Resistant to Pierce's disease. Originated in Leesburg, Florida. Introduced in 1983. *E0*, G17, I41M

Favorite: Probably a seedling of Black Spanish. Medium-sized, black fruit, larger than Black Spanish; less acid, of more pleasing flavor. Makes an attractive dark purple juice. Cluster medium to large, similar to Black Spanish in appearance but more compact. Vine very productive, 6 tons per acre or more in favorable seasons. Originated in Brenham, Texas. Introduced about 1938. BROOKS 1972; N33

Fredonia: Fruit large; skin black, thick, tough; quality good, superior to any other black cultivar of its season; inclined to shatter badly at maturity; ripens early. Vine vigorous, fairly productive; hardy; susceptible to powdery mildew. Cane prune. Cluster medium-sized, compact. BROOKS 1972; A82, *B52*, C63, D65, F19M, F93, G16, *G28*, G41, G71, H65, J16, J33, J69, M76, etc.

Herbert: Medium-sized fruit; skin dull black, adherent, bloom heavy; flesh juicy, tender, slightly foxy, sweet near the skin, quality good to very good; ripens with Concord. Vine vigorous and productive. Medium to large clusters. Originated in Salem, Massachusetts by Edward S. Rogers, prior to 1865. HEDRICK 1908; L12

Isabella: Medium to large, oval fruit; skin deep black with a heavy blue bloom, very tough, adherent; flesh juicy, tender, foxy, sweet to subacid; quality good; ripens with Catawba or earlier; keeps and ships well. Vine moderately vigorous and productive, hardy, susceptible to mildew. Cluster medium to large. Introduced about 1816. The most widely grown American cultivar in other parts of the world. Grown commercially in tropical and sub-tropical regions of Colombia, Brazil and India. HEDRICK 1908, WINKLER; *E0*, E39, E39{SC}

Ives: Medium-sized, oval to roundish fruit; skin jet black, slightly adherent; flesh juicy, foxy, sweet near the skin; ripens with Concord or slightly later. Excellent for jelly; also makes a good claret wine. Vine, vigorous, hardy, very productive. Originated in Cincinnati, Ohio by Henry Ives, from a seed planted in 1840. HEDRICK 1908; L12

Kendaia: Medium-sized, spherical fruit; skin bluish-black, slipskin; flesh slightly foxy, moderately acid, flavor distinct, almost muscat-like; somewhat susceptible to cracking; ripens 3 weeks before Concord; fair keeping quality. Vine vigorous, productive, hardy. Cluster medium-sized, conical, well-filled. BROOKS 1972; G97M, G97M{SC}, L12, N0

Lomanto: Medium to large, spherical fruit; skin black, thin but tough; juice claret red; quality excellent; seeds small and few. Vigorous, prolific vine; resistant to rot and mildew; does well on alkaline soils and in hot, dry climates. Nearly extinct cultivar introduced by T.V. Munson in 1902. *A19*, *C54*, I83M, N33

Moore Early: Medium to large, roundish fruit; skin dark purplish-black, adherent, bloom heavy; flesh juicy, fine-grained, slightly foxy, sweet near the skin, somewhat acid at the center; quality fair to good; ripens 2 to 3 weeks earlier than Concord. Vine hardy; moderately productive. Medium-sized, loose clusters. Originated prior to 1871. HEDRICK 1908; J83

New York Muscat: Medium-sized, oval fruit; skin reddish-black, bloom heavy; flesh juicy, richly sweet, with a fine muscat flavor; quality very good; ripens early, with Delaware. Suitable for table use and sweet red wines. Vine moderately vigorous and productive; may suffer winter injury below -15° F. Cluster medium-sized, loose to well-filled. BROOKS 1972; *E0*, E39, E39{SC}, G97M, G97M{SC}, I36, L12, N24M

Niabell: Uniformly very large, spherical fruit; skin jet black; ripens in midseason. Suitable for table use, fresh juice, and semi-sweet wines. Vine vigorous, canes long; productive; tolerant to cold and powdery mildew; grows and fruits well even in shade. Short, conical, well-filled clusters. Spur or cane prune. BROOKS 1972; *C54*

Norris: Large, ellipsoidal fruit; skin deep purple; dessert quality good; ripens in late July at place of origin. Vine vigorous and productive; resistant to Pierce's disease and downy mildew; requires a pollinator. Cluster moderately large. Originated in Leesburg, Florida. BROOKS 1972; N33

Price: Medium-sized, bluish-black fruit; pure, sweet flavor lacking any of the American foxiness; ripens 3 weeks before Concord. Very good for table use and juice. Vine vigorous, productive. Relatively small, medium compact clusters. One of the best cultivars for extra cool areas of the Pacific Northwest because of its ability to ripen early, even in cool weather. *E0*, G97M, G97M{SC}, *M81M*

Schuyler: Fruit medium-sized; skin bluish-black, tough, astringent; flesh soft, juicy, has much of the flavor of a vinifera grape; ripens 3 to 4 weeks before Concord. Excellent for table use, fresh juice, or light red wine. Vine, moderately vigorous; productive; fairly hardy and disease resistant. Cluster large, well-filled. BROOKS 1972; B67, C82, G97M, G97M{SC}, H65, I95, I95{SC}, J61M, L97, *M81M*

Sheridan: Large, round fruit; skin tough, black with a fine light-blue bloom; flesh firm, sweet, delicately flavored; quality very good; ripens late, about 1 week after Concord. Vine moderately vigorous, productive, hardy. Cluster large, compact. Originated in Geneva, New York by S.A. Beach. Introduced in 1921. BROOKS 1972; *E0*, H65, I36, I95, I95{SC}, L12

St. Croix: Medium-sized fruit; skin blue; flesh very juicy, flavor neutral, sugar usually 18 to 20 Brix, acid .80 to .90; ripens early, about 6 weeks before Concord. Makes an excellent, almost neutral vinifera-type red wine. Vine productive; hardy to about -40° F. without protection, less in windy areas. Clusters medium-sized. Originated in Osceola, Wisconsin by Elmer Swenson. *A74*, D69, *E0*, G53, G97M, G97M{SC}, L70, N24M

Steuben: Medium-sized fruit; skin bluish-black, slightly tough; flesh high in sugar, non-foxy, flavor rich and vinous; table quality very good; ripens with Concord, keeps well. Makes an aromatic white wine. Vine vigorous, very productive; hardy; tolerant to downy mildew and black rot. Cluster medium-sized, compact. BROOKS 1972; B39, *E0*, F1, G23, G79M, G87, G97M, G97M{SC}, H33, H49, H65, I36, I95, I95{SC}, L12, M76, *M81M*, etc.

Valiant: Small, dark-purple, slipskin fruit; flesh sweet, mildly foxy; quality very good for its class; ripens 1 month before Concord. Vine vigorous; extremely hardy, to -50° F.; very precocious, often bearing the same year it is planted; self-fruitful. Small, tight clusters. Developed by Dr. Ron Peterson of the University of South Dakota. A65, B4, C58, D76, *E0*, E97, G54, G67, G97M, G97M{SC}, H33, H42, H85, *H90*, K64, L27M, L70, L79, N26, etc.

Van Buren: Medium-sized fruit; skin jet black; flesh juicy, sweet, foxy; table quality good; quality of unfermented juice not equal to Concord; ripens very early; keeps poorly. Vine fairly vigorous, moderately productive; hardy; susceptible to downy mildew. Small to medium, well-filled cluster. Recommended as an early maturing Concord type. BROOKS 1972; B67, *E0*, G97M, G97M{SC}, H65, I95, I95{SC}, *M81M*, N0

Worden: Large, roundish to oval fruit; skin dark purplish-black, glossy, covered with a heavy blue bloom; flesh juicy, slightly foxy, sweet, mild; quality good to very good; ripens 1 or 2 weeks earlier than Concord; does not keep well. Vine vigorous, productive; very hardy. Introduced about 1867. Clusters large, compact. HEDRICK 1908; *A74*, *E0*, H65, L27M, L30, L70, *M81M*, N24M

Blue-Skinned/Seedless

Concord Seedless: Bud-sport of Concord released by the New York Agricultural Experiment Station. Similar color to its parent; smaller clusters and fruit; sweeter flavor; ripens about 1 week earlier. Excellent for pies. Occasional seed vestiges present. Vine vigorous and productive with age. B73M, B75, C63, D76, *E0*, E3, G97M, G97M{SC}, H49, H65, I91, J58, L12, *M65M*, M76, etc.

Glenora: Small to medium-sized fruit; skin blue-black, thin; flesh firm but tender, juicy, sweet, somewhat foxy, entirely seedless; quality very good for table use; ripens 2 to 3 weeks before Concord. Vine vigorous, moderately productive; hardy; resistant to mildew. Clusters loose. Released by the New York Agricultural Experiment Station. A14, *B52*, C63, F19M, *G14*, G23, G97M, G97M{SC}, H49, H65, I49M, I95, I95{SC}, *J63M*, L33, *M81M*, N0, etc.

Mars: Medium to large, round fruit; skin blue, slipskin; flavor rich and sweet, slightly foxy, somewhat resembling that of Campbell Early; ripens about 2 1/2 weeks before Concord; handles and ships well. Vine vigorous, productive; resistant to black rot, anthracnose, powdery and downy mildews. Clusters medium-sized, compact. Originated in Clarksville, Arkansas by Dr. James N. Moore. A39, B22, B43M, B73M, D65, *E0*, F61M, F93, G97M, G97M{SC}, H88, I78, I95, I95{SC}, K67, L33, N33, etc.

Royal Seedless: Seedless Concord type, with somewhat smaller fruit. Fine flavor. Sweeter and more aromatic than Concord. Ripens in August. Very good for table use. Vine vigorous, very productive; more hardy than Concord. Originated in Mankata, Minnesota by Frank M. Schwab. Introduced in 1956. BROOKS 1972; J33

Venus: Fruit large; skin blue-black, attractive, resists cracking; flesh sweet, flavor somewhat reminiscent of muscat; ripens 3 to 4 weeks before Concord. Occasional seed vestiges present. Vine productive, very vigorous; buds out early. Clusters large, compact. Developed at the University of Arkansas by Dr. James N. Moore. *A19*, B22, B43M, C63, *E0*, E83M, F61M, F93, G23, G53M, G97M, G97M{SC}, H16, J61M, L33, L90, N33, etc.

Green-Skinned/Seeded

Diamond: (White Diamond, Moore's Diamond) Medium-sized, roundish fruit; skin greenish-yellow, tough, adherent; flesh juicy, tender, somewhat melting, slightly aromatic, sprightly, sweet, quality very good; ripens slightly before Niagara, keeps well. Makes excellent white grape juice. Vine moderately vigorous, hardy, productive. Clusters medium-sized, compact. Introduced about 1885. HEDRICK 1908; *E0*, G97M, G97M{SC}, H65, I95, I95{SC}, L12, *M81M*

Dutchess: Fruit medium-sized, roundish to oval; skin pale yellowish-green, tough, adherent; flesh juicy, tender, vinous, sweet, of pleasant flavor; quality high; ripens in midseason; keeps and ships well. Vine moderately vigorous and productive, often not hardy. Cluster medium to large, relatively compact. Introduced about 1880. HEDRICK 1908; *E0*, L12

Edelweiss: Medium-sized, greenish-yellow, slipskin fruit; flesh tender, very juicy, sweet, slightly foxy; quality good for table use, juice and wine; ripens with or just after Himrod. Vine vigorous, productive; disease resistant; hardy to about -30° F. without protection. Cluster large. Introduced by the University of Minnesota. *A74*, D65, D76, *E0*, E97, G16, G53, G97M, G97M{SC}, I36, L27M, L70, N24M

Eona: Small to medium fruit; skin white; flesh very sweet, lacks the tartness of purple types; table quality fair, suitable for wine; ripens mid to late September. Vine productive; very hardy; self-pollinating. Clusters loose. Originated in Brookings, South Dakota by N.E. Hansen. Introduced in 1925. BROOKS 1972; C58, N24M

Golden Muscat: Large, round-oval fruit; skin golden-yellow; flesh very juicy, soft, sweet, aromatic, slight muscat flavor; quality excellent; ripens 2 weeks later than Concord. Vine vigorous, productive; not as hardy as Concord; susceptible to powdery mildew and bunch rot. Cluster large, well-filled; subject to cluster spoilage. BROOKS 1972; A88M, B73M, *C54*, *E0*, E3, E4, G97M, G97M{SC}, H49, H65, I36, I83M, I95, I95{SC}, J83, L12, *M81M*, etc.

Green Mountain: (Winchell) Small to medium-sized, roundish fruit; skin light green, covered with a thin white bloom, adherent; flesh juicy, tender, sweet, very good to best in quality; ripens very early, keeps and ships well for an early grape. Vine vigorous, hardy, very productive. Clusters large, moderately compact. Introduced in 1888. HEDRICK 1908; L12

Kay Gray: Medium to large fruit; skin greenish-yellow; flesh firm, slightly foxy, very mild, sugar usually near 20 Brix, acid .70 to .90; ripens about with Edelweiss. Good for table use, juice and wine. Vine productive; disease resistant; hardy to -40° F. unprotected. Cluster small, compact. Originated in Osceola, Wisconsin by Elmer Swenson. *A74*, D69, *E0*, G53, G67, G97M, G97M{SC}, I36, J7, L27M, L70

LaCrosse: Medium-sized, greenish-white fruit; flesh juicy, sweet, flavor neutral; ripens shortly after St. Croix and Kay Gray. Sugar content usually 18 to 19 Brix, acid 1.10 to as low as .90. Mainly a wine grape but pleasant to eat. Good disease resistance. Clusters medium-sized, moderately compact. Originated in Osceola, Wisconsin by Elmer Swenson. G53, G97M, G97M{SC}, L70

Lake Emerald: (V. simpsonii x) Medium to large fruit; skin emerald green to light-golden, fairly tough; flesh soft, sweet, uniquely fragrant, agreeably flavored; juice aromatic, sweet, well-flavored, light-colored; ripens during July at Leesburg, Florida. Primarily for home gardens and local markets in the Deep South. Vine high yielding; tolerant to Pierce's disease. BROOKS 1972; F19M, M31M, N33

Niagara: (White Concord) Medium to large, slightly oval fruit; skin yellowish-green; flesh juicy, foxy, sweet, of good quality; ripens with Concord, keeps fairly well. Vine vigorous; very productive; resistant to powdery mildew. Standard green grape for home gardens and market. Introduced about 1882 by the Niagara Grape Company. HEDRICK 1908; B58, B73M, C63, *D59*, E1M{PR}, G23, G41, G71, J33, J69, J83, L12, L30, *M65M*, N0, etc.

Ontario: Small to medium-sized, greenish-yellow fruit; flesh juicy, tender, very aromatic, rich, slightly foxy; quality very good; ripens 4 weeks before Concord, holds well on the vine. Vine moderately vigorous; productive. Clusters large, loose, single-shouldered. Originated in Geneva, New York. Introduced in 1908. G97M, G97M{SC}, H65, I95, I95{SC}, L12

Seneca: Small to medium-sized, oval fruit; skin thin, tender, yellowish-green becoming a translucent golden; flesh firm, tender, juicy, very sweet, melting, flavor rich, aromatic; quality very good to best; ripens with Ontario, hangs well on the vine. Vine vigorous, productive; hardy; susceptible to powdery mildew; requires long cane pruning. Cluster medium-sized, loose. BROOKS 1972; E39, E39{SC}, G97M, G97M{SC}, H65, I36, I95, I95{SC}, L12

St. Pepin: Medium-sized, greenish-white fruit; flavor fruity, slightly reminiscent of muscat; ripens with LaCrosse. Makes an excellent German-style white wine, and an outstanding non-foxy white juice. Vine female; blooms with LaCrosse which makes a good pollinator for it. Large, loosely formed clusters. Originated in Osceola, Wisconsin by Elmer Swenson. G53, G97M, G97M{SC}, L70

Stover: Medium-large, ellipsoidal fruit; skin translucent light green to golden at maturity; sugar content averages 17 to 18%; flavor mild, free from excessive sweetness or tartness; quality good for table use; ripens in late June or early July. Vine self-fertile; tolerant to Pierce's disease and downy mildew. Cluster medium-sized. Originated in Leesburg, Florida. BROOKS 1972; *E0*, F19M, I41M, *K76*, L33, M31M

Suwanee: High quality light green fruit; excellent flavor much like Thompson Seedless, but with a hint of muscat; resembles Golden Muscat. Also makes a very good wine. Ripens late June to early July. Very vigorous vine; satisfactory on most soils without grafting; resistant to Pierce's disease. Large, compact clusters. Originated in Leesburg, Florida by John A. Mortensen. Introduced in 1983. *E0*, G17, I41M, *K76*

Green-Skinned/Seedless

Himrod: Small, oval fruit; skin greenish-yellow, translucent; flesh tender, juicy, melting, vinous, quality good; small soft seeds; ripens 1 week before Fredonia. Vine vigorous, not productive, fairly hardy. Cluster large, very long, poorly filled. Ontario x Thompson Seedless, the same parentage as Interlaken, Romulus and Lakemont. BROOKS 1972; B58, C63, C82, *D59*, E39, E39{SC}, F19M, G23, G71, G97M, G97M{SC}, J33, L30, *M65M*, N33, etc.

Interlaken: Fruit small; skin greenish-white, adherent; flesh crisp, sweet, entirely seedless, quality excellent; resembles Thompson Seedless but has a flavor reminiscent of Ontario; ripens early. Vine moderately vigorous, productive; semi-hardy; requires long-cane pruning. Cluster medium-sized, loose, tapering. BROOKS 1972; B73M, C63, *D59*, E39, E39{SC}, F19M, G23, G71, G97M, G97M{SC}, L30, L97, M39M, *M65M*

Lakemont: Medium-sized fruit; skin greenish-yellow; flesh crisp, tender, juicy, very sweet; quality very good for table use, makes excellent raisins; ripens 3 weeks after Himrod, keeps very well in cold storage. Vine moderately vigorous; hardy; very productive, tends to overbear; disease resistant. Clusters large, well-filled to compact. A14, *B52*, B67, B73M, *C47*, C63, D65, E83M, G23, G97M, G97M{SC}, H49, H65, I95, I95{SC}, J69, L33, *M81M*, etc.

Orlando Seedless: Medium-sized, round fruit; skin light golden-green, attractive; flesh firm, crisp, very sweet; flavor pleasant, vinous; ripens in early July. Excellent for table use and juice. Vine moderately vigorous, productive; resistant to powdery and downy mildew. Long, tapered, loose clusters. The first seedless grape with resistance to Pierce's disease. Introduced in 1985 by the University of Florida. *E0*, G17, L37M, N33

Remaily: Medium to large fruit; skin greenish-white, adherent; flesh crisp, tender, juicy, sweet, entirely seedless; quality very good for table use; ripens in late midseason. Vine vigorous; more cold-hardy than most seedless grapes; very productive, should be cluster thinned. Clusters large, moderately compact. B39, B53, B75, *E0*, E83M, I36, I95, I95{SC}, L33, *M81M*, N24M

Romulus: Small to medium-sized, roundish fruit; skin greenish-yellow; flesh melting, juicy, vinous, quality good, seedless; resembles Thompson Seedless; ripens with Concord. Vine very vigorous and productive, fairly hardy. Cane prune. Cluster large, shouldered, compact. Originated in Geneva, New York. Introduced in 1952. BROOKS 1972; B39, *B52*, *C54*, C63, *E0*, H49, I36, I95, I95{SC}, L12

Red-Skinned/Seeded

Agawam: Large, roundish fruit; skin purplish-red, thick, tough, adherent; flesh firm, foxy, rich, sweet, aromatic, quality good; ripens soon after Concord, keeps until mid-winter. Vine vigorous, moderately productive; hardy; self-fertile; susceptible to mildew. Clusters medium to large, moderately compact. Introduced about 1861. HEDRICK 1908; G41, G69M, M76

Brilliant: Medium-sized, roundish fruit; skin attractive bright-red, covered with abundant lilac bloom; flesh pale green, juicy, slightly stringy, fine-grained, sweetish at skin but tart near the seeds; quality very good; ripens with Delaware; keeps very well. Vine vigorous; hardy; moderately productive. Cluster large, cylindrical, medium to compact. Originated in Denison, Texas by T.V. Munson. Introduced in 1887. HEDRICK 1908; *C54*, L12, N33

Caco: (Red Caco) Fruit medium to large, roundish; skin light red, thick, attractive; flesh juicy, tender, vinous, rich and sweet; quality good; ripens 7 to 10 days after Concord. Vine moderately vigorous; hardy; very productive. Cane prune. Clusters large, conical, moderately compact. C63, D76, *E0*, G13, G71, H33, H88, *J63M*, J83, L30, *M65M*, M76, *M81M*, M92

Captivator: Fruit large; skin orange-red, with a lilac bloom; flesh very sweet, slightly foxy, flavor excellent; ripens with or just after Himrod, 2 weeks before Concord. Vine vigorous, very hardy. Cluster small, moderately compact. Originated in Denison, Texas by T.V. Munson. *E0*, G97M, G97M{SC}, H49, L12

Catawba: Medium-sized, oval to roundish fruit; skin reddish-purple, adherent; flesh juicy, vinous, often sprightly with some foxiness, sweet and rich; quality very good; ripens late, keeps until March or later. Vine vigorous, hardy, productive. Clusters large, moderately compact. A standard for over 150 years. Origin unknown. Introduced about 1823. BROOKS 1972; A82, B10, B53, B58, B73M, C63, *D59*, *E0*, E3, E39, E39{SC}, *G28*, H65, J69

Daytona: Round, medium to large fruits; skin pale pink covered with a frosty white bloom, thin, attractive; flesh firm, sweet and juicy; dessert quality excellent; ripens early to mid August; resembles Tokay. Rampant growing vines produce large, loose clusters. Resistant to Pierce's disease and downy mildew. Introduced by the University of Florida in 1983. F19M, G17, *K76*

Delaware: Small to medium-sized, roundish fruit; skin light red, thin, adherent; flesh juicy, tender, aromatic, vinous, sprightly and refreshing, sweet, quality excellent; ripens a few days earlier than Concord, keeps well. Vine fairly vigorous and productive, hardy. Clusters small to medium-sized, compact. Was the standard of excellence for American grapes after its introduction about 1851 in Delaware, Ohio. HEDRICK 1908; *C47*, C82, *E0*, E1M{PR}, G13, G71, G79M, *G89M*, G97M, G97M{SC}, H65, H88, J7, J16, J83, L12, M76, etc.

Swenson Red: Medium to large fruit; skin dark-red, non-slipskin; flesh firm, meaty, juicy, sweet, non-foxy; table quality excellent, also makes a good white wine; ripens a month or more before Concord, keeps well in cold storage. Vine productive, hardy to about -30^0 F. without protection. Clusters distinctively shaped. Originated in Osceola, Wisconsin by Elmer Swenson. *A74*, D37, D65, D69, *E0*, E97, *G4*, G16, G53, G97M, G97M{SC}, I36, J61M, L27M, L70, N24M, etc.

Urbana: Medium-sized, round to oval fruit; skin red, thick and tough; flesh firm, crisp, only moderately juicy, seeds large; flavor rich and distinct; ripens late; resembles Catawba. Vine subject to mildew. Originated in Geneva, New York by S.A. Beach. Introduced in 1912. BROOKS 1972; I95, I95{SC}

Vinered: Fruit slightly larger than Catawba; skin tender, an attractive red when well matured; flesh with slightly higher sugar and lower acid content than Catawba. Flavor pleasant, vinous. Dessert quality high. Ripens shortly before Catawba. Vine vigorous; productive, up to 6 or 7 tons per acre. Cluster large to very large, moderately compact. Originated in Vineland, Ontario, Canada. BROOKS 1972; I95, I95{SC}

Yates: Fruit spherical, to 3/4 inch in diameter; skin medium dark-red, very tough, slipskin; flesh meaty, juicy, melting, sweet, flavor very good; excellent keeping qualities; ripens late, 1 week after Concord. Vine vigorous, hardy, productive. Cluster medium-sized, conical, compact. BROOKS 1972; I95, I95{SC}, L12

Red-Skinned/Seedless

Bronx Seedless: Small, oval fruit; skin red, cracks easily during wet weather; flesh soft, juicy, mild in flavor, quality good; ripens 1 week before Concord. Vine vigorous, fairly hardy; productive; susceptible to anthracnose and downy mildew. Cluster large, long conical, loose. Originated in Geneva, New York. Introduced in 1937. BROOKS 1972; G97M, G97M{SC}, I95, I95{SC}

Canadice: Small to medium-sized fruit; skin bright red, thin; flesh soft, rich, vinous, sweet, of very good quality; ripens about 1 week after Himrod, holds well on the vine. Vine moderately vigorous; hardy; very productive, tends to overbear if not pruned; fairly resistant to black rot. Clusters large, well-filled, attractive. B58, B73M, B75, C63, D69, F19M, G23, G97M, G97M{SC}, H16, H65, J69, L30, L33, L97, etc.

Einset: Medium-sized, ovoid fruit; skin bright red with a light, waxy bloom, resistant to cracking; flesh crisp, firm, juicy, flavor non-foxy, quality excellent; ripens early, stores well. Vine productive, extremely hardy for a seedless grape; resistant to botrytis, susceptible to powdery mildew. Cluster medium-small. Introduced by the New York State Agricultural Experiment Station. *C47*, *E0*, I36, I91, I95, I95{SC}, J61M, L33

Reliance: Medium-sized, round fruit; skin pinkish-red; flesh firm, tender, melting, sweet; quality excellent for table use; ripens about 2 1/2 weeks before Concord; stores and ships well. Vine vigorous, productive; widely adapted; very hardy, to about -23° F; susceptible to black rot. Clusters large, compact. Developed by Dr. James N. Moore at the University of Arkansas. B22, B43M, B73M, D65, *E0*, E97, F61M, F93, G16, G23, G97M, G97M{SC}, H16, H65, J58, J61M, L33, N33, etc.

Saturn: Large, oblong fruit; skin bright red, deeper red than Reliance, adherent; flesh firm, very crisp, sweet; vinifera in character; ripens in early September in Zone 6. Fruit quality and appearance are maintained well in storage. Vine moderately vigorous and hardy; precocious, may tend to overbear when young. Clusters medium-sized, compact. Introduced in 1987 by the University of Arkansas. B22, B43M, *E0*, F16, I36, J61M, L33, L37M, N33

Suffolk Red: Fruit large, round; skin bright red, attractive; flesh crisp, meaty, juicy, non-foxy, vinous, entirely seedless, quality excellent; ripens early, 2 to 3 weeks before Concord. Vine very vigorous, fairly hardy; productive; disease resistant. Cluster medium to large, long, loose. Introduced in 1972. *B52*, B53, *C47*, C63, G23, G41, G79M, G97M, G97M{SC}, H65, H88, I49M, L30, L97, *M65M*, etc.

Vanessa: Medium-sized, oval fruit; skin deep red, adherent, very attractive; flesh crisp, firm, juicy, very sweet and aromatic; superior flavor reminiscent of Seneca; dessert quality excellent; ripens early, 7 to 10 days after Himrod. Vine vigorous, moderately hardy and productive. Clusters medium-sized, loose to well filled. Originated in Vineland, Ontario, Canada. Introduced in 1984. B22, B53, *E0*, G97M, G97M{SC}, I36, I95, I95{SC}, J61M, L12, N24M

FRENCH HYBRID Developed by French breeders to combine the wine quality of Vinifera grapes and the durability of American grapes. They have the necessary disease resistance, winter hardiness and the ability to meet adverse conditions while still yielding good red and white table wines. Most were bred as wine grapes but some have excellent dessert qualities.

Blue-Skinned/Seeded

Dattier de Conzieu: (Landot 2832) Large to very large, pale blue fruits with a neutral flavor. Excellent for dessert; also makes delicious jellies and fresh juice. Vine somewhat particular about growing conditions, but worthy of trial. B39

Green-Skinned/Seeded

Dattier de St. Vallier: (Seyve-Villard 20-365) Large, elongated fruit; skin greenish-yellow, thin; flesh tender, meaty, sweet, flavor neutral, dessert quality very good; subject to rot. Vine vigorous, very productive, buds out late; highly tolerant to downy mildew. Must not be allowed to overbear or quality will be indifferent. Cluster large, short conic, loose. BROOKS 1972; B39

Verdelet: (Seibel 9110) Medium-sized, oval fruit; skin golden-yellow often tinged with pink, very attractive, tender, adherent; flesh firm and crisp, flavor neutral but pleasing. Vine moderately vigorous, productive when short cane-pruned. Cluster medium-sized, cylindrical, well filled to compact. An excellent table grape. Also produces an above average wine with a delicate aroma, good balance, and attractive flavor. BROOKS 1972, WAGNER; B39, *C54*, *E0*, E38, G79M, L90, M83, N33

VINIFERA These produce the choicest dessert grapes, characterized by non-slip skin, firm flesh and a relatively mild flavor. Most premium wines are also made from Vinifera grapes. Less hardy than American or French Hybrid grapes, they require a long, warm, drier growing season. More susceptible to insect pests and diseases. The vines are more vigorous and upright growing. (V. vinifera)

Blue-Skinned/Seeded

Black Hamburg: Medium to large, roundish to slightly oval fruit; skin dark purplish-red or purplish-black, bloom heavy; flesh juicy, sweet, of fair flavor and quality; ripens in midseason. Vine of good to moderate vigor. Cluster medium-sized, compact. Of German or Italian origin. Introduced into England in 1720. SIMMONS 1978; N84{S}, R77

Blackrose: Fruit large; skin jet black with a light grayish bloom, tender, very attractive; flesh sweet, juicy, more flavorful than Ribier; quality high; ripens in early midseason. Vine vigorous, productive. Spur or cane prune. Cluster large, conical, well-filled but not usually compact unless girdled. Originated in Fresno, California. Introduced in 1951. BROOKS 1972; E39, E39{SC}

Carolina Blackrose: Large, oval fruit; skin black; flesh firm, dessert quality excellent; resembles Blackrose. Vine vigorous; canes large, robust, somewhat upright; resistant to mildew and phylloxera; somewhat susceptible to black rot. Should be pruned close to prevent over-bearing. Cluster large, heavily shouldered. Originated in Greensboro, North Carolina by Robert T. Dunstan. BROOKS 1972; N33

Exotic: Medium-large, spherical fruit; skin black, splits badly in some localities; flesh firm, crisp, quality good; ripens in midseason, about 10 days later than Cardinal. Vine vigorous and productive; should be spur pruned. Cluster very large, long, well-filled. Originated in Fresno, California. BROOKS 1972; I95, I95{SC}, *J31M*

Gros Colman: Large to very large, round fruit; skin blackish-blue with a delicate bloom, thick but tender, attractive; flesh moderately firm, juicy, sweet, flavor good; ripens very late, keeps well on the vine. Vine vigorous and productive, prefers rather heavy soils. Cluster large, cylindrical, well-filled. SIMMONS 1978, WICKSON; R77

Mrs. Prince's Black Muscat: A very good late cultivar that will ripen in a cool greenhouse. With care will keep until February. Large bunches which hang well. An easy to grow but superb grape. R77

Muscat Hamburg: Large, roundish-oval fruit; skin black, covered with a heavy bloom; flesh sweet; excellent for dessert, also makes a good red wine; ripens in midseason. Vine moderately vigorous; productive. Cluster medium-long, loose, does not require thinning. One of the best black muscat-flavored grapes. SIMMONS 1978; E39, E39{SC}, I95, I95{SC}, *L1M*, *L1M*{SC}

Purple Cornichon: (Olivette Noir) Fruit large, long, with a distinctive more or less curved shape; skin thick, dark-purple with a light bloom, attractive; flesh firm, sweet, of good quality; ripens late, ships exceptionally well. Vine a vigorous grower, spur pruned. Cluster very large, loose, on long stems. WICKSON; S59

Ribier: (Alphonse Lavallée) Large to very large, round fruit; skin nearly black, moderately tough; flesh juicy, sweet, flavor mild, mildly astringent; ripens in early midseason; holds well on the vine. Vine moderately vigorous; very productive. Spur prune. Cluster medium-sized, short-conical, loose. Widely used as a shipping grape in California. B93M, *C54*, E4, E39, E39{SC}, E70M{PR}, F15{PR}, I95, I95{SC}, K96M{PR}, *L47*, *N20*

Tressot Panache:[1] Distinctive cultivar with skin that is mottled or blotched with purple and white. Dessert quality only average, of value mostly as a novelty. An old classic French grape. Probably a chimera of the wine-grape cultivar Tressot Negra. U8{SC}

Blue-Skinned/Seedless

Beauty Seedless: Small to medium-sized, ovoid fruit; skin bluish-black, waxy; flesh firm, tender, flavor spicy; quality good at full maturity; ripens very early, with Perlette. Vine very vigorous; very productive as spur-pruned cordon. Cluster large, conical, heavily shouldered. Originated in Davis, California by H.P. Olmo. The first black seedless cultivar produced by breeding. BROOKS 1972; E39, E39{SC}, G97M, G97M{SC}, I95, I95{SC}, *L1M*, *L1M*{SC}

Black Monukka: Medium-sized, elongated fruit; skin reddish-purple, thin and tender; flesh yellow, crisp, sweet and juicy; ripens in early midseason. Excellent for dessert and raisins, also used for juice and wine. Requires less heat to ripen than Thompson Seedless. Spur or cane prune. Cluster large, very long, loose to well filled. One of the hardiest vinifera grapes. A44M{PR}, A88M, B67, *C54*, *D59*, E4, E39, E39{SC}, F11, F97M{PR}, *G49*, I76M{PR}, *L47*, L99M, M39M, N0, *N20*, N33, etc.

Green-Skinned/Seeded

Calmeria: Fruit large, ovoid-elongated; skin greenish-white, tough; flesh white, meaty, sugar content medium, acidity low. Vine moderately vigorous; very productive. Cluster large, well-filled. A very late maturing cultivar; well adapted for cold storage. Originated in Fresno, California. Introduced in 1950. BROOKS 1972; I95, I95{SC}, *L47*

Cannon Hall Muscat: Fruit medium to large, round to slightly oval; skin thick and firm, pale amber with a heavy bloom; flesh firm, with a strong muscat flavor, quality very good; ripens midseason to late. Vine vigorous, an irregular bearer, spur pruned. Cluster very large, tapering, cylindrical. SIMMONS 1978; R77, S59

Chaouch: An early fruitful cultivar with juicy, sweet, perfumed berries. The favorite grape of the Sultan of Turkey in the 19th century. R77

Chasselas d'Or: Small to medium, round fruit; skin pale amber with a golden tinge, tawny-gold when fully ripe, firm but tender; flesh very juicy, sweet, of pleasant flavor, at first crisp but becoming soft with full maturity. Vine moderately vigorous, bears well. Cluster medium to above medium, long and cylindrical. A famous French dessert grape of the 16th century. SIMMONS 1978, WICKSON; I95, I95{SC}

Ciotat: (Parsley Leaved) Small, round fruit; skin thin, very pale green; flesh firm, sweet; ripens early. Vine vigorous, very productive; of ornamental value because of its parsley-shaped leaves. Cluster small and long, berries loose in the cluster. Known in France since the beginning of the last century. SIMMONS 1978; R77

Early Muscat: Medium-sized, uniform fruit; skin dull yellow; flesh white, firm, meaty, with a distinct muscat flavor; seeds small; ripens very early, just after Perlette and Pearl de Casaba; ships well. Quality excellent for dessert and raisins, also makes a sweet, varietal muscat wine. Vine moderately vigorous; very productive; should be girdled to increase berry size. Cluster large, loose, pyramidal. Originated in Davis, California by H.P. Olmo. BROOKS 1972; G97M, G97M{SC}, L99M

Foster's Seedling: Medium-sized, roundish-oval fruit; skin pale greenish-white; flesh soft, sweet, of good flavor, quality excellent; ripens very early. Vine moderately vigorous, heavy bearing; very suitable for forcing in a greenhouse. Cluster fairly long. Originated about 1835. SIMMONS 1978; R77

Gold: Large, oval fruit; skin tender, with a golden sheen; flesh firm, meaty, with a light but distinct muscat flavor; quality excellent for table use, also used for the production of a light muscat wine; seeds few, small; ripens in early August. Vine moderately vigorous; very productive; canes short. Cluster medium-sized, short, conical, well-filled. Originated in Davis, California by H.P. Olmo. Introduced in 1958. BROOKS 1972; G97M, G97M{SC}, *L1M*, *L1M*{SC}

Italia: (Italian Muscat) Very large fruit; skin golden-yellow, tender; flesh juicy, with a mild muscat flavor; dessert quality excellent, also used for wine; ripens in midseason. Vine moderately vigorous; very productive. Spur prune. Cluster large, loose, conical. Bicane x Muscat Hamburg. Originated in Rome, Italy by A. Pirovano, Institute of Fruit Culture. BROOKS 1972; B93M, *C54*, E4, E39, E39{SC}, I76M{PR}, *L47*

July Muscat: Medium-sized, subovoid fruit; skin whitish-yellow, resistant to weather; flesh greenish-yellow, firm, with a strong muscat flavor; ripens in late July, ships well. Vine vigorous; moderately productive. Cluster loose. Originated in Davis, California by H.P. Olmo. Introduced in 1958. BROOKS 1972; E39, E39{SC}

Lady Finger: Large, slender, very elongated fruit; skin bright green to greenish-white, sometimes blushed with pink, thin, easily bruised; flesh firm, tender, low in acid, with a mild, neutral flavor; ripens in midseason. Vine very vigorous and productive. Spur or cane prune. Cluster conical, compact. *C54*, E4, I83M, I99{S}, *N20*

Madeleine Angevine: Medium-sized, oblong fruit; skin yellowish-green to golden, transparent, rather thick; flesh sweet and juicy, non-muscat in flavor; ripens very early. Vine moderately vigorous, heavy yielding. Cluster medium, compact, shouldered. Suitable for table use, juice and wine. C34, J61M

Monte Senario: Reportedly blessed by Christ when he stayed at the home of a poor farmer in Jerusalem, and brought to Italy by the Crusaders. A start was taken to the Sanctuary of Our Sorrowful Mother in Portland, Oregon in 1933. Vines are offered free in return for a donation to the Sanctuary, which is in need of repairs and updating of buildings. G97M, G97M{SC}

Muscat of Alexandria: (Muscat) Large, oblong fruit; skin light-yellow, tinged with copper when well ripened, transparent, covered with white bloom; flesh very sweet, strongly aromatic, with a decidedly musky flavor; ripens in late midseason; excellent for dessert, also used for raisins and aromatic, somewhat spicy wines. Vine vigorous; moderately productive. Spur or cane prune. Cluster very long, loose, heavily shouldered. Of North African origin; first recorded in 1584. A88M, B93M, *C54*, E4, E39, E39{SC}, H26M{PR}, I83M, *L47*, *N20*

Olivette Blanche: (Lady Finger) Long, slender fruit, broader than Rish Baba; skin darker green than Rish Baba, sometimes tinged with pink, easily bruised; flesh firm and tender, neutral in flavor, quality very good for table use or raisins; ripens in late midseason. Vine very vigorous and productive if cane pruned. Cluster very large, irregular conical, well filled. WINKLER; B93M, *L47*

Pearl of Casaba: (Perle de Czaba) Small to medium-sized, round fruit; skin light golden-yellow, thin, adherent; flesh crisp, meaty, sweet, aromatic, with a light but distinct muscat flavor, contains a single small seed; ripens very early. Vine moderately vigorous; fairly productive; hardy in Michigan. Spur prune. Cluster medium-sized. Originated in Hungary. G97M, G97M{SC}

Queen of the Vineyard: (Scolokertek Kiralynoje) Medium to large, oval fruit; skin greenish-yellow; flesh crisp, meaty, with a delicate muscat-like flavor; ripens with Delight. Originated in Hungary. Widely used for breeding at Davis, California; one of the parents of Perlette, Delight, July Muscat, Gold, Early Muscat and Beauty Seedless. G97M, G97M{SC}

Rish Baba: (Lady Finger) Long, slender fruit, sometimes slightly curved; skin pale greenish-white to light yellow, tender, easily bruised; flesh firm but tender, very low in acid, neutral in flavor; ripens in early midseason. Vine vigorous, moderately productive when cane pruned. Cluster small-medium, long cylindrical, very loose. Originated in Persia. WINKLER; E39, E39{SC}, *L1M*, *L1M*{SC}

Syrian: Large berries of reasonable flavor. Needs heat to mature properly. Ripens late; keeps well. Notable for its ability to produce very large bunches, some over 20 pounds. R77

White Malaga: Large, oval fruit; skin yellowish-green, covered with a white bloom, moderately tough; flesh sweet and tender, quality good for table use, also used for raisins; ripens August into September. Vine a strong grower, very productive. Spur or cane prune. Cluster very large, loose shouldered, long. Grown in southern California in situations where the muscat does not do well. WICKSON; B93M, *C54*, *L47*

Green-Skinned/Seedless

Delight: Medium-sized, oval fruit; skin dark greenish-yellow, thick, resists bruising; flesh firm, crisp, flavor distinct, slightly muscat-like, sometimes astringent; ripens early, just after Perlette; very good for table and raisin use; resembles Thompson's Seedless. Vine moderately vigorous; very fruitful when spur pruned. Cluster large, conical, well-filled to compact. A91, *C54*, *D59*, E39, E39{SC}, G97M, G97M{SC}, I95, I95{SC}, *L1M*, *L1M*{SC}, N0

Emerald Seedless: Medium-large, obovoid fruit; skin greenish-yellow, tender; flesh moderately firm, light green, seedless; ripens in midseason, 2 weeks before Thompson Seedless. Recommended for fancy raisins and as a table grape. Vine vigorous, moderately productive. Cluster large, conical, loose to well-filled. BROOKS 1972; I95, I95{SC}

Fiesta: Medium-sized, oval fruit; skin greenish-white; flesh firm, juicy, sweet, quality very good for dessert or raisins; ripens 1 to 2 weeks before Concord. Vine vigorous and productive. Cluster large. Appears less prone to bunch rot than some vinifera cultivars in rainy Pacific Northwest fall weather. A91, *D59*, E39, E39{SC}, G97M, G97M{SC}, I95, I95{SC}, L37M

Perlette: Medium-sized, spherical fruit; skin white to yellowish, translucent, thin, very tender; flesh translucent, crisp, juicy, flavor mild but distinctive, low in sugar and acidity; ripens very early, 1 month before Thompson Seedless. Vine vigorous; more fruitful than Thompson's Seedless; requires less heat than most vinifera grapes. Spur or cane prune. Cluster large, compact to very compact, requires heavy thinning. A88M, *B41*, B67, *C54*, E4, E39, E39{SC}, E70M{PR}, F11, *G49*, I76M{PR}, I83M, I95, I95{SC}, *J31M*, *L47*, *N20*, etc.

Thompson Seedless: (Sultanina) Small to medium, elongated fruit; skin greenish-white to golden-yellow, thin; flesh crisp, juicy, flavor sweet but mild; ripens early to midseason. Vine very vigorous and productive; does best in hot areas. Cane prune. Cluster large to very large, well-filled. Most popular grape for table use and raisins in California. World's leading raisin grape. Named after W. Thompson of Yuba City, who introduced it into California in 1878. WICKSON; A88M, *D59*, E4, E39, E39{SC}, F93, I95, I95{SC}, *L1M*, *L1M*{SC}, L37M, *L47*, L99M, M83, N33, etc.

Thomuscat: (Seedless Muscat) Somewhat small fruit, mostly seedless, with a muscat-like flavor when fully ripe. Vine low in vigor; sets irregularly; tends to over produce. Cluster rather loose, not uniform. Primarily for home gardens. Muscat of Alexandria x Thompson Seedless. Originated in Fresno, California. Introduced in 1949. BROOKS 1972; E39, E39{SC}

Red-Skinned/Seeded

Cardinal: Fruit large; spherical to oblate, often lobed or creased; skin dark red to reddish-black, thin; flesh greenish, firm, crisp, with a slight muscat flavor; seeds few; ripens very early. Vine very vigorous to rampant; very productive; requires heavy flower cluster removal to increase cluster size. Spur or short cane prune. Cluster medium-sized, short conical, well-filled. Flame Tokay x Ribier. BROOKS 1972; B93M, *C54*, E39, E39{SC}, I95, I95{SC}, *L1M*, *L1M*{SC}, *L47*

Emperor: Large, oval fruit; skin light red to reddish-purple, thick, tough; flesh very firm and crisp, meaty; ripens late; quality good for table use and raisins; ships and stores extremely well. Vine a strong, vigorous grower; very productive; does well in hot interior areas of California. Spur or cane prune. Cluster very large, long-conical, loose. Leading red table grape in California. B93M, *C54*, E39, E39{SC}, I95, I95{SC}, *L47*

Queen: Large, uniform, ellipsoidal fruits; skin dark red; flesh firm at maturity, but not as firm as Flame Tokay, sugar and acid content medium; ripens in midseason, just after Red Malaga, stores and ships well. Vine moderately vigorous, fruitful when spur pruned. Cluster large, loosely winged. BROOKS 1972; I95, I95{SC}

Red Malaga: (Molinera) Large, oval fruits; skin pink to reddish-purple with blue bloom, tender; flesh very crisp and firm, flavor neutral; ripens in early midseason, just before White Malaga; good shipping and keeping qualities. Vine vigorous, well suited for growing on an arbor. Spur or cane prune. Cluster very large, irregular, loose to well filled. WINKLER; B93M, E39, E39{SC}

Tokay: (Flame Tokay) Large to very large, oblong fruit; skin brilliant red to dark red, covered with fine lilac bloom; flesh crisp, juicy, sweet, with a distinctive wine-like flavor; dessert quality good, also used for wine; ripens in late midseason; keeps and ships well. Vine vigorous; grows best where summer nights are cool. Spur or cane prune. Cluster very large, moderately compact, shouldered. One of the leading commercial grapes in California. B93M, *C54*, E4, *L1M*, *L1M*{SC}, *L47*, *N20*

Red-Skinned/Seedless

Flame Seedless: (Red Flame) Small to medium-sized, round fruit; skin light pinkish-red, attractive; flesh firm, crisp, meaty, very sweet; excellent for table use and raisins; ripens early, before Thompson Seedless; hangs well on the vine without loss of quality. Vine very vigorous; very productive. Spur or cane prune. Cluster medium-sized, conical, loose. A88M, *D59*, E4, E39{SC}, E70M{PR}, F11, F19M, F93, G97M{SC}, I76M{PR}, I83M, *L1M*, *L1M*{SC}, L33, L37M, *L47*, L99M, N33, etc.

Ruby Seedless: (King's Ruby) Medium-sized, ovoid fruit; skin reddish-black to dark red, tender; flesh firm, crisp, meaty, sweet; quality excellent for table use or raisins; ripens in late midseason; stores well. Vine very vigorous; very productive. Spur or cane prune. Cluster very large, conical, well-filled, shouldered. Originated in Davis, California by H.P. Olmo. BROOKS 1972; A52M{PR}, A88M, *B41*, *C54*, E4, E39, E39{SC}, G97M, G97M{SC}, I95, I95{SC}, J21M{PR}, *J31M*, *L1M*, *L1M*{SC}, *L47*, *N20*, etc.

WINE GRAPES

AMERICAN

Red-Wine Grapes

Cynthiana: Small, roundish, purplish-black fruit; ripens in late midseason. Vine vigorous and rampant in growth, of less than average productivity. Cluster small to medium. Yields wine that has intense color, and a distinct, agreeable, non-foxy aroma. Can acquire bouquet with aging. Until the appearance of the French hybrids, was considered perhaps the best of the American red-wine hybrids. WAGNER; *E0*

Norton: (Norton's Virginia, Norton's Seedling) Similar if not identical with Cynthiana. Sugar content of fruit above 20%, but is coupled with excessive acidity, so the must requires dilution. Originated in Virginia but achieved its greatest popularity along the banks of the Missouri River, where at one time there was a substantial winemaking industry around the town of Hermann. WAGNER; *E0*

White-Wine Grapes

Blanc du Bois: Round, light green, slipskin fruit; flesh juicy, with a slight muscat flavor. Vigorous, semi-erect vine; resistant to Pierce's disease and downy mildew, tolerant of root-knot nematodes. Cluster moderately compact. Makes a spicy white wine of very good quality. Maintains its fruity quality and delicate sugar/acid balance through fermentation and into the bottle. Released by the University of Florida in 1987. *E0*, G17, *K76*, L37M, N33

Cayuga White: (GW-3) Medium-sized, greenish-white fruit; ripens with Concord. Vine large, vigorous, very productive, moderately hardy; somewhat susceptible to wind damage. Resistant to mildew and bunch rot. Cluster large, compact. Produces an excellent light, fruity wine that resembles White Riesling. Originated in Geneva, New York. Introduced in 1972. B39, *E0*, G97M, G97M{SC}, H65, I36

Elvira: Medium-sized, round, yellowish-green fruit; susceptible to cracking; ripens with Concord, does not keep well. Vine vigorous and productive, hardy, somewhat resistant to diseases. Cluster small to medium, cylindrical, compact. Produces a light wine with a sharp aroma and a slightly foxy flavor. Originated in Morrison, Missouri by Jacob Rommel. Introduced in 1874. HEDRICK 1908, WAGNER; *E0*, *G4*, G41, J7

Horizon: Fruit greenish-white; ripens in late September at Geneva, New York. Vine vigorous, very productive, hardy; responds favorably to grafting. Produces a neutral wine that is fruity, clean, and tart with good body and balance. Lacks any of the flavors associated with native grape cultivars. Introduced in 1983 by the New York State Agricultural Experiment Station. *E0*, I36

Melody: Fruit greenish-white; ripens in early October at Geneva, New York. Vine vigorous, productive, moderately hardy; apparently resistance to powdery mildew and botrytis. Yields an excellent Vinifera-type wine of neutral fruitiness, slightly floral, with good body and balance. Introduced in 1985 by the New York State Agricultural Experiment Station. *E0*, I36

Missouri Riesling: Medium-sized, roundish to oval, yellowish-green fruit; ripens slightly before Catawba, does not keep nor ship well. Vine moderately vigorous and productive, usually hardy. Cluster medium-sized, sometimes cylindrical, well filled to compact. Yields a highly aromatic white wine of fair quality. Originated by Nicholas Grein about 1870. HEDRICK 1908, WAGNER; G97M{SC}

FRENCH HYBRID

Red-Wine Grapes

Baco Noir: (Baco 1) Small, round fruit; skin jet black; flesh soft; ripens early. Vine rampant, resistant to downy mildew, somewhat susceptible to powdery mildew; useful for arbor type plantings. Cluster very small, cylindrical, compact. Produces wine that is highly colored, heavy, bitter and herbaceous in character, requiring long aging to improve. Originated in Bélus, Landes, France by Francois Baco. BROOKS 1972; B39, B75, *E0*, F19M, F43M, G97M, G97M{SC}, H49, H65, I36, L12

Chambourcin: (Joannes Seyve 26-205) Medium-sized, nearly black fruit; ripens in mid-October at Geneva, New York. Vine medium in vigor, moderately hardy, practically disease free; productive when short cane-pruned. Cluster large. Yields a wine without pronounced aroma but with the "sève" or body that many of the hybrid wines lack. Popular in France, especially in the Loire Valley and the Touraine. WAGNER; B39, *E0*, I36

Chancellor: (Seibel 7053) Roundish, jet black fruit; flesh very firm, not juicy; ripens 2 weeks before Concord. Vine moderately vigorous and productive, upright; susceptible to downy and powdery mildews. Cluster medium-sized, cylindrical, fairly compact. Produces very agreeable dark red wines of good body. In France, on of the most popular of all hybrids. Originated in Aubenas, Ardeche, France by Albert Seibel. BROOKS 1972; B39, *E0*, G79M, I36

Chelois: (Seibel 10878) Small, round, firm black fruit; ripens medium early, a week before Concord; may crack in some years. Vine moderately vigorous and productive, susceptible to winter damage and fungal diseases, buds out late. Cluster medium-sized, elongate, compact. Makes a fruity, dry red wine somewhat reminiscent of Burgundy. Best when produced in a hearty style and aged 3 or 4 years. BROOKS 1972; B39, *E0*

De Chaunac: (Seibel 9549) Medium-sized, bluish-black fruit; ripens with Concord. Vine vigorous, productive, hardier and more resistant to disease than many other French hybrids. Cluster medium to large, somewhat loose. Yields pleasant, fruity, well-balanced red wines with good tannin and color. One of the most widely planted French hybrids in New York state. BROOKS 1972; B39, *E0*, G41, H65, I36, J7, N24M

Leon Millot: (Millot, Kuhlmann 194-2) Small, bluish-black fruit; ripens very early, about 1 week before Maréchal Foch. Vine somewhat more vigorous and productive than Maréchal Foch; does well even in the climate of Minnesota. Cane pruning. Produces a wine similar to Maréchal Foch, but deeper in color. Will develop a Burgundy-like bouquet with bottle aging. WAGNER; B39, C34, *E0*, G97M, G97M{SC}, I36, I49M, J61M

Maréchal Foch: (Foch, Kuhlmann 188-2) Very small, bluish-black fruit; ripens very early. Vine very vigorous, not very productive; disease resistant; best adapted to difficult areas with short growing seasons. Cluster small, cylindrical, loose. Produces deep-violet, hearty, Burgundy type wines without blending. Originated in Colmar, Alsace, France by Eugene Kuhlmann. BROOKS 1972; B10, B39, B75, *E0*, F43M, G97M, G97M{SC}, H65, I36, J7, L12, M92, N24M

Villard Noir: (Seyve Villard 18-315) Small to medium, bluish-black fruit; ripens late. Vine moderately vigorous, very productive when spur pruned. Produces a very good heavy-bodied wine that is deep-colored and somewhat astringent. Also excellent for blending. The most widely grown red-wine hybrid in southern France. Well adapted in North America in all but short-season areas. WAGNER; B39, *E0*, I36

Rosé-Wine Grapes

Cascade: (Seibel 13053) Medium-sized, black fruit; ripens very early, with or before Maréchal Foch. Vine vigorous, hardy; very productive; adapted to moist areas with short growing seasons; susceptible to downy mildew. Cluster small. Wine low in color, makes a fine rosé or "blush" wine, blends well with other red French Hybrids. BROOKS 1972; B39, B75, *E0*, N33

Seyve Villard 52-47: Light blue fruit; ripens early. Vine very vigorous, productive when short cane-pruned; hardy and disease resistant. Cluster large, compact. Produces a light-bodied red wine of good quality and a still better rosé. Also used for blending. Fermented free of the skins, the free-run juice makes a delightful *vin gris*. WAGNER; B39

White-Wine Grapes

Aurore: (Aurora, Seibel 5279) Small to medium, spherical fruit; skin golden to light pink; pulp soft and juicy, very good for dessert and juice; ripens very early. Vine vigorous and productive, hardy, subject to black rot. Cluster long, loose to well filled. Makes a light, delicate wine with a neutral to foxy flavor. Often used as a base for champagne. The leading wine grape in New York state. BROOKS 1972; B39, B75, *C47*, F19M, G41, G79M, G97M{SC}, H49, H65, I36, I49M, J7, L12, L37M, M76, M92, N24M, etc.

Joannès Seyve 23-416: Small, very oval fruit; skin pale pink; flesh pulpy, has a good sugar/acid balance; ripens in early midseason. Vine vigorous, moderately hardy, resistant to downy mildew. Cluster large, narrow, loose. Produces a delicately aromatic wine. Considered one of the best of its series. Recommended throughout the Northeast and Middle West. GALET; B39

Rayon d'Or: (Seibel 4986) Round, dull golden fruit; spoils quickly at maturity. Vine moderately vigorous, hardy; a very reliable producer; tolerant to downy mildew and black rot. Cluster medium-sized, cylindrical, compact. Produces a highly aromatic wine with a berry-like flavor, but without the bitterness of many similar hybrids. Also used with some success in the production of sparkling wines. BROOKS 1972; B39, *E0*

Seyval Blanc: (Seyve-Villard 5-276) Small, round, golden-yellow fruit; ripens early to midseason; subject to spoilage. Vine moderately vigorous, hardy; highly productive; fairly resistant to downy mildew. Cluster small, cylindrical, compact. Makes a light, fruity, aromatic wine of superior quality. Widely cultivated in France and the United States. Originated in Saint Vallier, Drôme, France by Seyve-Villard. BROOKS 1972; B39, *E0*, G79M, H65, I36

Vidal Blanc: (Vidal 256) Medium-sized, roundish, greenish-white fruit; ripens in midseason, shortly after Concord. Vine very vigorous, productive when spur- or short cane-pruned, moderately hardy; resistant to mildew. Cluster large to very large, compact. Yields a high quality, clean, neutral wine with good aroma. Originated in the Cognac region of France. WAGNER; B39, *E0*, I36, N33

Vignoles: (Ravat 51) Fruit greenish-white; ripens in early midseason, with or before Concord; prone to cracking. Vine vigorous and hardy, only moderately productive when cane-pruned. Cluster small; very tight, quite susceptible to botrytis. Produces a clean, crisp wine with a touch of tartness, recalling *petit chablis*. Also suitable for champagne. WAGNER; B39, *E0*, I36

Villard Blanc: (Seyve-Villard 12-375) Medium-sized, golden yellow, meaty fruit; matures in late midseason. Vine very vigorous and productive; tolerant to phylloxera, resistant to powdery and downy mildews; does best in areas with a relatively long growing season. Cluster large, loose, compact. Makes a light bodied, fruity, highly aromatic wine of good quality. The most widely planted white hybrid in France. BROOKS 1972; B39, D37, *E0*, F19M, G79M, I36, N33

VINIFERA

Red-Wine Grapes

Alicante Bouschet: Medium-sized, round fruit; skin brilliant-black; juice dark red; ripens in September and October. Vine moderately vigorous, semi-erect, productive. Cluster medium to large, well filled to compact. Used in blends of standard red table and port wines because of its color. Popular with home winemakers. E1{SC}

Barbera: Medium-sized, long oval fruit; black with abundant color in the skin; high in acid content; ripens in September and October. Vine vigorous and productive. Cluster medium-sized, well filled but not excessively compact. Used to produce quality red table wines that are full bodied, high in acid and tannin, and deeply colored when young. Originated in the Piedmont region of Italy. B93M, E39, E39{SC}, L37M

Cabernet Franc: Small, round, blue-black, juicy fruit; ripens in midseason. Vine vigorous, fairly productive, usually long-cane pruned. Cluster small, cylindrical-conical, loose. Susceptible to downy and powdery mildews. Produces very aromatic red wines which have the aroma of raspberry in Touraine and of violet in Chinon and Bordeaux, and are softer and more subtle than the wines of Cabernet Sauvignon. Originally from Bordeaux, France. GALET; *D59*, E39, E39{SC}, *L1M*, *L1M*{SC}, L37M, *N5*

Cabernet Sauvignon: Small, black, very seedy fruit; flavor pronounced and characteristic; ripens in late midseason. Vine very vigorous and productive when cane pruned. Cluster small to medium, loose to well filled. Yields a wine of pronounced varietal flavor, good acidity, good color and excellent balance. Has produced some of the most expensive and highly sought-after red wines of California. WINKLER; A88M, B67, *C54*, D76, E4, E39, E39{SC}, *G14*, I36, I95, I95{SC}, *L1M*, *L1M*{SC}, L37M, L99M, *N20*, etc.

Carignane: Medium-sized, oval, black fruit; ripens in September and October. Vine vigorous, highly productive. Cluster fairly large, well filled to compact. Yields standard, well-balanced red table wines. An important fresh shipping cultivar for home winemaking. Of Spanish origin, but has been grown for centuries in the south of France. B93M, E39, E39{SC}, I95, I95{SC}, *L1M*, *L1M*{SC}

Gamay Beaujolais: Small to medium, short-oval, black fruits. Vine more vigorous and productive than Pinot Noir. Cluster small-medium, conical, compact. Produces either a light or medium-bodied red wine of excellent quality. A clone of Pinot Noir, apparently introduced into California from the Beaujolais region of France. WINKLER; *D59*, E39, E39{SC}, I36, *N5*

Malbec: Fruit moderately acid; ripens early. Vine vigorous, only moderately productive in California, not troubled by disease. Traditionally blended with Cabernet Sauvignon, primarily to soften it and reduce the time required for aging. An ancient French cultivar that is perhaps more widely distributed in France than any other cultivar capable of producing superior wine. WAGNER; *L1M*, *L1M*{SC}

Merlot: Medium-sized, round, bluish-black fruits. Vine fairly productive with head-training and either long spur- or cane-pruning. Cluster medium-large, long conical, loose to compact. Yields wines of fine bouquet that are softer, more supple in texture, and age more rapidly than those of Cabernet Sauvignon. Next in importance to

Cabernet Sauvignon in the Bordeaux region of France. WINKLER; *D59, E0,* E39, E39{SC}, I95, I95{SC}, *J31M, L1M, L1M*{SC}, L37M, *N5*

Mission: Medium-sized, round to oblate fruit; skin brownish-red to reddish-black; flesh firm but juicy, flavor neutral; ripens in late midseason. Vine vigorous, very productive. Cluster large, loose to well filled. Used to produce average or better quality sweet dessert wines, including *angelica* and sherry. Introduced into California during the later part of the 18th century by the Jesuit missionaries. E1{SC}

Napa Gamay: (Gamay) Medium-sized, round fruit; skin thick and tough; ripens in late midseason. Vine vigorous, very productive when head-trained and spur-pruned. Cluster large-medium, conical, well filled. Yields simple but fruity red wines. Also produces fruity rosés of bright pink to slightly orange color. WINKLER; E39, E39{SC}, I95, I95{SC}, J7

Nebbiolo: Fruit high in acid; ripens late; tends to lack color in California, especially in the hotter districts. Vine moderately vigorous, requires short cane or long spur pruning for reliable crops. Yields the very best wines of the Piedmont district of Italy, including the famous dry wines *barolo* and *gattinara*. WAGNER; *L1M, L1M*{SC}

Petite Sirah: Medium-sized, oval fruit; skin black covered with a light silvery bloom; flesh juicy, neutral in flavor; ripens in early midseason. Vine moderately vigorous and productive. Cluster medium-sized, compact. Used for standard red table wines because of its good, stable color. Also used for blended Burgundies. Introduced into California from the Rhône Valley of southern France. E39, E39{SC}, *L1M, L1M*{SC}, L37M

Pinot Noir: Small to medium, oval, black fruits; ripens very early, sunburns badly in warmer districts. Vine moderately vigorous and of low productivity in California. Cluster small, cylindrical, well filled. Recognized as one of the outstanding red wine cultivars of the world, it produces the fine Burgundy wines of France. WINKLER; A91, B67, *D59, E0, G14,* I36, I49M, I95, I95{SC}, *J31M, L1M, L1M*{SC}, L99M, M39M, *N5*, etc.

Ruby Cabernet: Medium-sized, black, juicy fruit; ripens in September and October. Vine vigorous, more productive than Cabernet Sauvignon, more adapted to regions too hot for best quality of Cabernet Sauvignon. Cluster medium-sized, loose to well filled. Produces table wine of high quality, similar to Cabernet Sauvignon but of more intense color and earlier maturation. Carignane x Cabernet Sauvignon. Originated in Davis, California by H.P. Olmo. Introduced in 1948. BROOKS 1972; B93M, E39, E39{SC}

Tinta Madeira: Medium-sized, long-oval jet black fruit; thick but tender skin; ripens in August and September. Vine moderately vigorous and productive. Cluster medium-large, well filled to compact. Used in premium port wine production because of its rich flavor and deep color. Principally grown in the Madeira Islands of Portugal. E39, E39{SC}

Zinfandel: Medium-large, round, reddish-black to black fruit; ripens in September and October. Vine moderately vigorous and productive. Cluster medium-large, well filled to very compact. Widely used in red table wine blends and for full-bodied, intensely flavored varietal wines. An important fresh shipping grape for home wine making. Apparently introduced into California from Hungary about 1860. A88M, B93M, *C54, D59,* E4, E39, E39{SC}, I95, I95{SC}, *J31M, L1M, L1M*{SC}, L37M, *L47, N20*, etc.

Rosé-Wine Grapes

Grenache: Small to medium, round, reddish-purple to black fruit; ripens in September and October. Vine very vigorous and productive. Cluster large, fairly compact. Used for blending in generic rosé wines where it contributes a sweet, somewhat strawberry-like aroma. In France, it yields the famous rosé wine, *Tavel*. Popular with home winemakers. A Spanish cultivar that is grown extensively in southern France and in Spain. B93M, E39, E39{SC}, L37M

Grignolino: Small to medium, oval, reddish-brown fruits. Vine moderately vigorous and productive when head-trained and spur-pruned. Cluster medium-sized, long conical, well filled to compact. Normally produces an orange-pink wine that is distinctly different from most rosé wines. Originated in the Piedmont district of Italy. WINKLER; S59

White-Wine Grapes

Burger: Medium to large, round fruit; skin waxy-yellow, easily broken; flesh soft, very juicy, flavor lacking; ripens late September to early October. Vine moderately vigorous, hardy, very productive. Cluster large, long. Produces a light, neutral wine of fair quality, which is primarily used in blending. Once the most widely planted white Vinifera in California. E39, E39{SC}

Chardonnay: (Pinot Chardonnay) Small, round fruit with an almost ideal balance of sugar and acid. Vine vigorous, moderately productive when cane- and spur-pruned. Cluster small, cylindrical, loose to well filled. Produces some of the best dry white wines of California, having a highly characteristic bouquet and a delicious "stony" flavor. Also yields the famous white Burgundy wines of France. WAGNER, WINKLER; A88M, A91, *C54,* D76, E4, E39, E39{SC}, *G14,* I36, I49M, I95, I95{SC}, *L1M, L1M*{SC}, M76, *N20*, etc.

Chenin Blanc: Medium-sized, oval fruit; skin greenish-yellow, tough; flesh juicy; ripens late August to mid-September. Vine vigorous, very productive. Cluster medium to large, compact. Used to produce quality white table wines. Can also be used in sparkling wine production, in blending, and for sweet table wines. A leading cultivar of the middle Loire region of France. A88M, A91, B93M, *D59,* E4, E39, E39{SC}, I95, I95{SC}, *J31M, L1M, L1M*{SC}, *N20,* N33

French Colombard: (Colombard) Medium-sized, yellowish-green fruit; neutral in flavor and high in acid; ripens in September. Vine very vigorous and productive. Cluster medium-large, well filled. Widely used in California for blending and as the base for some inexpensive champagnes. An important cultivar in the Cognac region of France where it is used in the production of brandy. A88M, B93M, *C54,* E39, E39{SC}, I95, I95{SC}, *J31M, L1M, L1M*{SC}, L37M, *N20*

Gewürztraminer: Small, oval fruits; skin tough, pink to bluish-brown; flesh firm, with a characteristic spicy flavor. Vine moderately vigorous, produces well with cane-pruning. Cluster small, cylindrical, compact. Produces slightly sweet to very sweet wines with a pronounced, spicy, aromatic flavor. Has been grown in Germany for several centuries. WINKLER; A91, B67, *D59, E0,* E39, E39{SC}, *G14,* I36, I95, I95{SC}, *L1M, L1M*{SC}, L99M, *N5*

Gray Riesling: Medium-sized, dull reddish-tan, very firm fruit; ripens in August and September. Vine strong, vigorous, moderately productive. Cluster small to medium, conical, compact. Produces a dry, medium-acid varietal wine with a light fruity flavor. Sometimes blended with Sylvaner or Chenin Blanc to uplift its character. Grown in the Arbois region of France where it is known as Chauché Gris. A91, E39, E39{SC}

Müller Thurgau: Medium-sized, oval fruit; skin green to grayish; pulp firm, fleshy, aromatic; ripens very early. Yields wine rated between Riesling and Sylvaner. Vine vigorous, productive, blooms late. Cluster medium to large. Susceptible to powdery mildew and botrytis. Said to be a cross between Riesling and Sylvaner obtained in 1891 in Switzerland. Grown in cool, northerly regions including

Alsace, Germany, England and the Pacific Northwest. GALET; *D59*, *G14*, I95, I95{SC}

Muscat Blanc: (Muscato di Canelli) Medium-sized, yellowish fruit with a pronounced yet delicate muscat flavor; ripens in August and September. Vine moderately vigorous and productive. Cluster medium-sized, well filled to compact. An important cultivar in southern France where it is renowned in the production of French *muscatels*, and in northern Italy, to produce the *Asti Spumante* wines. *D59*, E39, E39{SC}, I95, I95{SC}, *L1M*, *L1M*{SC}

Orange Muscat: Medium-sized, oblate to round, firm, orange fruits. Vine moderately vigorous and productive. Cluster medium-sized, short conical, compact. Yields wines that are rich in muscat aroma, but not as delicate and rich as those of Muscat Blanc. Originated in Italy where it is known as Muscato Fior d'Arancio. WINKLER; *D59*, E39, E39{SC}

Palomino: (Golden Chasselas) Medium-small, oblate fruit; skin greenish-yellow, somewhat tough; pulp firm, juicy and sweet; ripens late August to early September. Vine moderately vigorous and productive. Cluster large, loose, irregular in shape. The principal sherry grape of Jerez, Spain. In California, it is also important for sherry production, and for blending in champagne or for white table wine. E39, E39{SC}, I95, I95{SC},

Pinot Blanc: Small, round fruits. Vine below average in vigor; moderately productive, fruits well with head-training and short cane-pruning. Cluster small to small-medium, long conical, compact. Produces wines that are distinct in aroma and flavor, smooth, and of good balance, though prone to darken. Grown rather extensively in France. WINKLER; I95, I95{SC}

Sauvignon Blanc: Small, oval to round fruit; skin moderately thin; flavor strong and distinct; ripens in August and September. Vine extremely vigorous, relatively productive. Cluster small, well filled to compact. Used for high quality, varietal dry white wines or natural sweet wines. In the proper blend with Sémillon it is considered to be superior to the wine of either cultivar used alone. WINKLER; A91, *D59*, E39, E39{SC}, *J31M*, *L1M*, *L1M*{SC}, L37M, *N5*, N33

Sémillon: Medium-sized, round fruit; skin yellow, fairly thin; flesh soft, tender, juicy; ripens in August. Vine moderately vigorous, semi-erect, productive. Cluster medium-large, conical. Produces a dry, white, medium-bodied table wine with a fig-like perfume. The most important cultivar in the famous Sauternes district of southwestern France. A91, *D59*, E39, E39{SC}, I95, I95{SC}, *L1M*, *L1M*{SC}, L37M

Sylvaner: Medium-sized, round, bluish to yellow-green fruit. Vine medium in vigor, moderately productive, very susceptible to powdery mildew. Cluster small, cylindrical, compact. Yields wines that possess a delicate, lightly spicy, distinct character. Best known as the source of the Stein wines of Franconia, Germany. WINKLER; E39, E39{SC}, I95, I95{SC}

White Riesling: (Riesling, Johannisberg Riesling) Small to medium-sized, spherical fruit; skin greenish-yellow, speckled with russet dots; flesh juicy, sprightly, somewhat aromatic in flavor. Vine moderately vigorous and productive. Cluster small, cylindrical, well filled. Produces bone dry to very sweet wines with a strong varietal flavor and bouquet. Yields the famous white wines of the Rhine and Moselle valleys of Germany. WINKLER; A91, B67, *D59*, E39, E39{SC}, I36, I49M, I95, I95{SC}, J7, *L1M*, *L1M*{SC}, L37M, M39M, M76, *N5*, etc.

GRAPEFRUIT {GR}

CITRUS X PARADISI

PINK-FLESHED

Foster: Medium-large, roundish fruit; skin moderately thick, pale to light yellow, blushed with pink under favorable conditions; flesh tender, juicy, seedy, flavor good; flesh color chamois, but under favorable conditions pink. Medium early in maturity. Tree large, vigorous, productive. The first pigmented grapefruit cultivar of record in Florida. REUTHER; R77

Ray Ruby: Branch sport of Red Blush first propagated in Texas and introduced into Florida in the 1970's. The peel is redder than that of Ruby Red and the pulp is red though not as intense as Star Ruby throughout the season. MORTON 1987a; E31M

Red Blush: (Ruby Red, Ruby Blush) Fruit similar to Thompson in all respects except for much deeper pigmentation in the flesh (but not in the juice); crimson blush on the rind, especially at points of contact between fruit. Holds on tree as well as Marsh or Thompson but with some fading of flesh color. Bud mutation of Thompson discovered in McAllen, Texas. Introduced in 1934. REUTHER; *A71*, B73M{DW}, C89{PR}, E3M{DW}, E31M, E97{DW}, *F53M*, F68, G17, H69{PR}, I83M, J21M{PR}, J22, *L47*, *M61M*, N18{SC}, etc.

Rio Red: The newest cultivar developed. Darker color than Ray Ruby. Very good quality. Ripens November to May. *A71*, E31M, I83M, *M61M*

Shambar: Fruit seedless; rind and flesh pink; resembles Red Blush. Considered by some to be superior to Marsh in juiciness, flavor, and long storage life. Tree similar to Marsh and Red Blush. Bud mutation of Marsh. Originated in Corona, California. Discovered in 1936. N18{SC}

Smooth Seville: Hybrid. Parentage unknown. Medium-large, somewhat flattened fruit; color reddish-orange at maturity. Rind medium-thick, surface very smooth. Flesh reddish-orange, coarse-textured, juicy; flavor pleasantly subacid with a trace of bitterness. Has a lower heat requirement for maturity than the grapefruit and hence ripens earlier and serves as a satisfactory substitute. Tree vigorous, large, and prolific. REUTHER; S59

Star Ruby: Fruit with a yellow peel, distinctly red-blushed; intensely red pulp and juice, 3 times more colorful than Ruby Red. Though the color decreases with maturity, it is maintained throughout the season. The pulp is smooth and firmer than that of Ruby Red and has a bit more sugar and acid. Seedless or no more than 9 seeds. A branch mutation of the Foster cultivar discovered in San Benito, Texas in the 1930's. Only introduced into cultivation in 1971. MORTON 1987a; *A71*, *D23M*, F68, *G49*, I83M, N18{SC}

Thompson: (Pink Marsh) Medium-sized, oblate to spherical fruit; seeds few or none; pale to light yellow at maturity. Rind medium-thin, tough, surface very smooth. Flesh light to deep-buff more or less flushed with pink, tender and juicy; juice colorless; flavor good, similar to Marsh. Holds on tree unusually well, but with considerable fading of color. Midseason in maturity. Tree vigorous, large, and productive. F68, S59

WHITE-FLESHED

Duncan: Large, round or slightly obovate fruit. Color pale to very light yellow. Rind medium-thick, surface smooth and even. Flesh buff to chamois-colored, tender, very juicy; flavor pronounced and excellent. Medium-early in maturity. Tree vigorous, large, very productive. At one time the leading cultivar in Florida and Texas. Introduced in 1892. F68, G17

Golden Special: Fruit of good size, thin skinned, pale yellow; comparatively seedless with a juicy tangy flavor. Once established the plants become heavy bearing, but like most grapefruit cultivars can develop biennial bearing tendencies. A New Zealand selection much grown in the home garden and also used extensively for commercial production. *O97*, R77

Isle of Pines: (Triumph) Medium-small, roundish fruit, somewhat flattened at both ends; rind medium-thick, pale to light yellow; flesh tender and very juicy, very seedy. Flavor lacking in bitterness, suggestive of the orange, exceptionally good. Ripens early to midseason. Tree less vigorous than most grapefruits but productive. The first named grapefruit, originating in Tampa, Florida and introduced in 1884. MORTON 1987a, REUTHER; F68

Marsh: (Marsh Seedless, White Marsh) Medium-sized, oblate to spherical fruit. Color pale to light yellow at maturity. Rind medium-thin, tough, surface very smooth and even. Flesh buff-colored, tender, very juicy; flavor good but not so pronounced as in some seedy varieties. Holds unusually well on the tree. Tree vigorous, spreading, large, and productive. The leading grapefruit cultivar worldwide. REUTHER; *D23M*, E3M{DW}, E99G{PR}, *F53M*, F68, *G49*, *M61M*, *M61M*{DW}, N18{SC}

Wheeny: (Wheeny Grapefruit) Hybrid. Parentage unknown. Fruit large, oblate or broadly obovate to globose; color pale to light yellow. Rind medium-thin, with moderately rugose surface. Flesh straw-colored, coarse-textured but very juicy. Flavor good but acid, virtually indistinguishable from some grapefruits. Medium early in maturity. Tree vigorous with tendency to alternation in bearing. Ripens in climates too cool for any of the true grapefruits. REUTHER; *Q93*, S59

GUAVA {PL}

PSIDIUM GUAJAVA

PINK/RED-FLESHED

Beaumont: Medium to large, roundish fruit; weight 8 ounces; flesh pink, moderately thick, mildly acid; seedy. Excellent for processing. Somewhat susceptible to fruit rots. Tree vigorous, wide spreading, very productive. Selected from a seedling population derived from fruits found in Halemanu, Oahu, Hawaii. *D23M*, D57{PL}, J22, N84{S}, P5{S}

Hong Kong Pink: Medium to large, roundish fruit; weight 6 to 8 ounces; flesh pinkish-red, very thick, smooth-textured; flavor subacid to sweet, very pleasant; seeds few. Tree spreading, high yielding. Selected at Poamoho Experimental Farm, Oahu, Hawaii from seeds obtained from a clone grown in Hong Kong. D57{PL}

Mardi Red:[1] Medium-sized fruit, 2 to 4 inches in diameter; skin yellow, highly blushed with red; flesh deep red, of excellent flavor, seed cavity small. Tree an attractive ornamental with wine red leaves and pink flowers. Originated in Mardi, Malaysia. I83M{PL}

Maroon:[1] Small to medium-sized fruits; skin purple-green; flesh magenta, flavor deliciously sweet with a subacid tang. Tree upright; very ornamental with distinct, purple-green leaves. Originated in Java. D57{PL}

Red Indian: Medium-large, roundish fruit, of strong odor; skin yellow, often with pink blush; flesh medium thick, red, sweet, quality good; ascorbic acid content averages 195 mg. per 100 grams fresh fruit; total sugars average 7 to 10%; seeds numerous but small. Good for eating out of hand. Originated in Dade County, Florida by Fred Lenz. Introduced in 1946. BROOKS 1952, MORTON 1987a; I83M

Ruby X: Small, roundish fruit; skin greenish-yellow; flesh dark pinkish-orange, flavor delicious, sweet; seed cavity 33% of pulp. Tree bushy, low growing, with vigorous branches drooping outward. Hybrid of the Florida cultivars Ruby and Supreme. D57{PL}

Salvador Bahia: Medium to large, oblong fruits; skin bright yellow; flesh subacid, an attractive pinkish-orange in color; seed cavity 33% of pulp. Tree with a distinct low drooping canopy. Originated in Brazil. D57{PL}

Uma: Small to medium-sized fruit, 2 to 3 inches in diameter; flesh deep pink, of excellent flavor; good pulp to seed ratio. I83M

WHITE-FLESHED

Allahabadi: Large, white-fleshed fruit of good quality; cavity small; seeds few, medium-sized, fairly hard. Considered one of the best eating dessert guavas of India. MORTON 1987a; Q12{S}

BKK Apple:[2] Large, roundish fruit, 5 to 6 inches in diameter; skin bright green; flesh white, subacid, of very good quality. Usually eaten when firm-ripe, like an apple. A new seedless hybrid from Thailand. S54M{PL}

Giant Bangkok: Fruit large to extremely large, up to 1 pound or more, rounded with slight elongation at the stem end; skin light greenish, rough textured; flesh greenish-white, firm, reminiscent of an apple in texture, pleasantly sweet; seed cavity very small. Tree dwarfish, bears when 4 feet tall. Originated in Thailand. D57{PL}

Krom Toon Khao: Medium to large fruit; weight 3 to 8 ounces; smooth, greenish-yellow skin; flesh whitish, flavor mildly sweet, refreshing; seed cavity 25% of pulp. Can be eaten when still firm. Tree very small; bears fruit in clusters; begins producing when 4 feet tall and up. Originally from Thailand by way of Vietnam. D57{PL}

Lucknow 49: Medium to large fruit; weight 8 ounces; flesh cream-white, thick, sweet, relatively smooth-textured; flavor sweet, slightly musky; seeds relatively few. Dessert quality excellent but tends to develop a mushy flavor when fully ripe. High in pectin and therefore desirable for jelly; halves are good for canning. Tree spreading, productive. Ruby x Supreme. Originated in India. MORTON 1987a; R0

Mexican Cream: Small to medium-small, roundish fruits; skin light yellow, slightly blushed with red; flesh creamy white, thick, very sweet, fine-textured, excellent for dessert; seed cavity small, with relatively soft seeds. Tree upright, productive. Originated in Mexico. D57{PL}

Pear: (Pear Guava) Pear-shaped fruits with creamy white flesh. At one time this form was designated as a separate species along with the round form, which is sometimes known as Apple Guava. POPENOE, W. 1920; *D23M*{PL}, F80{S}, N84{S}, O53M{S}, O93{S}, *Q25*{S}, *Q32*{S}

Redland: Fruit very large, pyriform, lacking in musky guava odor; flesh white with relatively few seeds, flavor mild. Ascorbic acid content low. Tree a heavy cropper, susceptible to red algae spot. Developed at the University of Florida Agricultural Research Center, Homestead. Introduced in 1941. BROOKS 1972, MORTON 1987a; F68

Sweet White Indonesian: Large, round fruit, 4 inches or more in diameter; thin, pale yellow skin; thick, white, melting flesh of a sweet, delicious flavor. Edible seeds in cavity surrounded by juicy pulp. Vigorous, fast growing tree; bears several times a year. J22

White Indian: Small to medium-sized, roundish fruit, 2 1/2 to 3 inches in diameter; flesh thick, white, moderately seedy. Excellent, sprightly flavor. Tree somewhat of a shy bearer. Originated in Florida. I83M

White Seedless:[2] An improved selection from Florida with seedless, white flesh of good quality. F68

YELLOW-FLESHED

Detwiler: Medium to large, roundish fruit, about 3 inches in diameter; skin greenish-yellow, moderately thick; flesh yellowish to salmon, medium firm, relatively sweet, of pleasant flavor, quality very good. Tree a very heavy bearer. Originated in Riverside, California in the early 1900's. Selected by H.J. Webber. I83M

HEARTNUT {GR}

JUGLANS AILANTIFOLIA VAR. CORDIFORMIS

Bates: Medium-sized nut; kernel percentage and flavor very good; matures early. Tree vigorous; hardy; bears well. An older standard cultivar. Originated in Lancaster, Pennsylvania by J.F. Jones. E62{PR}, E62{S}, E91M{OR}, E91M{PL}, K16{OR}, N24M

Brock: Nut large; shell perfect; kernel percentage and flavor very good. Tree moderately hardy; heavy bearing. One of the best recent introductions. Originated in Pennsylvania by Garnet Coble. E91M, E91M{OR}, N24M

Callander: Medium-sized nut; kernel averages 31% of nut; cracks out well; flavor very rich; matures early. Tree hardy; bears heavily; protandrous. Original tree noted for producing a large number of heartnut-butternut hybrids (buartnuts) among its seedlings. Originated in Westbank, British Columbia, Canada by J.U. Gellatly. JAYNES; A91{PL}, B74{PL}, E91M, E91M{OR}, N24M

Caloka: Small to medium-sized nut, averages 76 per pound; kernel averages 36% of nut. Originated in Westbank, British Columbia, Canada by J.U. Gellatly. A91{PL}

Canoka: Nut large, averages 50 to 76 per pound; kernel averages 26% of nut. Tree an annual, heavy bearer; requires a relatively long growing season to mature kernels properly. One or two weeks later in vegetating than other cultivars, and thus able to escape spring freeze damage which often seriously shortens the crop of other cultivars. Originated in Westbank, British Columbia, Canada by J.U. Gellatly. JAYNES; D72, I40

Etter: Large nut; cracks out readily; kernel percentage and flavor very good; cracks out very well. Tree exceptionally hardy; productive. Produces high quality seedlings for breeding and selection. Originated in Lemasters, Pennsylvania by Fayette Etter. E62{PL}, E62{PR}, E62{S}, E91M, E91M{OR}, K16, N24M

Fodermaier: Nut quite large, averages 55 per pound; cracks well; kernel of good quality, averages 37% of nut; fine flavor. Tree vigorous; hardy; has withstood temperatures of -20^{0} F. and below. Originated in Dover Plains, New York by John J. Fodermaier. Introduced about 1942. BROOKS 1972; D72, E91M{OR}, E91M{PL}, I40{OR}, N24M

Frank: Medium-sized nut; cracks well. Tree later vegetating than other cultivars with the exception of Canoka. Originated in Kentucky in 1980. I40

Marvel: Nut medium to large; cracks well; quality good; resembles Wright. Tree somewhat hardier than Fodermaier; will pollinate Wright and is pollinated by that cultivar; bears well. Fodermaier x Wright. Originated in Wassaic, Duchess County, New York by Gilbert L. Smith. Introduced in 1948. BROOKS 1972; I40, K16

Rhodes: Medium to large nut; shell thin; kernel percentage very good; cracks easily; flavor and quality excellent. Tree moderately hardy; bears heavily; flowers late, probably self-fruitful. Originated in Covington, Tennessee by George Rhodes. Introduced in the 1940's. E41M{SC}, E91M, E91M{OR}, E91M{PL}, I40

Rival: Medium-sized nut; quality and flavor good; cracks well when dried; resembles Wright. Tree somewhat hardier than Fodermaier; will pollinate Wright and is pollinated by that cultivar; bears well. Fodermaier x Wright. Originated in Wassaic, Duchess County, New York by Gilbert L. Smith. Introduced in 1950. BROOKS 1972; E41M{SC}

Schubert: Nut relatively large; cracks out well; flavor excellent. Tree bears heavily. A select seedling of Rhodes. Originated in Millstadt, Illinois by Kenneth Schubert. Introduced in the 1960's. E41M{SC}

Wright: Medium to large nut; flavor pleasant; very free cracking; flavor resembles butternut. Tree heavy bearing; not resistant to broom disease; very hardy; will pollinate Fodermaier, Marvel and Rival. Originated in Westfield, New York by P.D. Wright and R.P. Wright. Introduced in the 1930's. BROOKS 1972; E91M, E91M{OR}, I40

HERBS

See Basil, Mint, Parsley and Thyme in the Cultivar listings. Also see the Botanical listings, especially Apiaceae, Asteraceae, Geraniaceae and Lamiaceae, and Flavorings, Tea Substitutes, Rennets and other appropriate headings in the Index of Usage.

HICAN {GR}

CARYA X NUSSBAUMERI **CARYA X SP.**

Burlington: (C. x nussbaumeri) Large nut, averaging 55 nuts per pound; quality good; ripens early. Tree productive; comes into bearing slowly. Originated in Des Moines County, Iowa. Introduced in 1940 by Benton and Smith Nut Tree Nursery, Millerton, New York. BROOKS 1972; D72, I40{OR}

Burton: (C. x sp.) Medium-sized nut; shell thin; cracking quality excellent, high kernel percentage; flavor excellent; early maturing. Tree productive; self-pollinating; comes into bearing in 5 to 7 years. Does well in the Midwest, South and Northwest, but not the North-east. Originated in Kentucky. JAYNES; D72, E41M{SC}, E91M{PL}, I40

Country Club: (C. x sp.) Medium-sized nut. Tree a very heavy producer. Originated in Indiana. Introduced in 1980. Original tree grows 100 feet from the Hartmann hican. I40

Des Moines: (C. x nussbaumeri) Moderate producer of fertile nuts, resembling Burlington. Tree grows satisfactorily in southern Illinois. Originated in Burlington, Iowa, near the Des Moines River. Introduced in 1924. BROOKS 1972; I40

Gerardi: Nut large, matures earlier than most northern pecans; more productive than McCallister, less than Burlington which is smaller but earlier. Good flavor and cracking quality. In order to produce a plump meat, good culture and protection from shuckworm and curculio are necessary. Tree protogynous, apparently pollinated by various hickories and McCallister hican. Introduced in 1931. E41M{SC}

Hartmann: (C. x sp.) Medium-sized, thin-shelled nut. Tree a good producer; has red-tinted buds. Originated in Indiana. Introduced in 1980. I40

Henke: (C. x sp.) Nut small; kernel of high quality, fills shell well; ripens early. Good flavor and cracking quality. Tree small; bears precociously and well. Originated in southern Iowa by a Mr. Henke. Introduced in 1932. BROOKS 1972; A91{PL}, D72, E41M{SC}, I40, I60{PL}

Hershey: (C. x sp.) Medium-sized nut; borne in clusters of two and four; fills shell well. Kernel of high quality. Originated in Pennsylvania. Introduced in 1980. I40

Jackson: (C. x sp.) Medium-sized nut; kernel quite tasty. With pollen tree should set heavy crops. Originated in Kentucky. Introduced in 1985. I40

James: Nut large, averages 36 per pound; shell thin, cracking quality very good, 52%; kernel flavorful, of high quality; ripens in late September in Zone 6; keeping quality similar to pecan. Tree hardy; productive; self-pollinating; disease resistant; comes into bearing in 5 to 6 years. For Zones 6 to 8 and warmer areas of Zone 5. Originated in Brunswick, Missouri by George James. I74, L33

McCallister: (C. x nussbaumeri) Very large nuts, seldom well-filled. Vigorous tree; needs an early pollen source. I40

Underwood: (Jay Underwood) (C. x nussbaumeri) Nut large; shell thin; kernel plump, with a fine flavor. Tree protogynous; ornamental. Originated in Fort Scott, Kansas by Jay S. Underwood. Introduced in 1956 by Louis Gerardi Nursery. Native seedling; named by J.C. McDaniel, Illinois Agricultural Experiment Station. BROOKS 1972; I40

HICKORY {GR}

CARYA LACINIOSA | CARYA OVATA

SHAGBARK HICKORIES

Except for the bitternut, this is the hardiest of the hickory species, its range extending from southern Quebec through southern Ontario to Minnesota, south to Florida and Texas. The shagbark fruit is distinguished from the shellbark in that the latter has much larger fruits, 1 3/4 to 2 1/2 inches long. JAYNES. (C. ovata)

Abundance: Shellbark x shagbark hybrid. Nut resembles a shagbark hickory; size medium to large, 7 grams; kernel white, cracks out readily; kernel averages 36% of nut; shell thin. Tree bears annually; topworked trees often bear second year after grafting. Originated in Franklin County, Pennsylvania by Fayette Etter. Introduced in 1947. BROOKS 1972; I40

Bridgewater: Very large nut, to 8.5 grams; kernel averages 46.6% of nut. Susceptible to scab in the South. Recommended by the late Carl Weschcke for the far north, where it also serves as a pollinator for the Weschcke hickory. Originated in Connecticut. I40

Cedar Rapids: Large nut, to 6.9 grams; matures early. Tree bears very well. A good northern cultivar; susceptible to scab in the South. Originated in Iowa. I40

Davis: Medium-sized nut; kernel plump, bright, quality high; cracking quality excellent; ripens at point of origin a little later than Fox; resembles Wilcox. Tree vigorous. Originated in Duchess County, New York by Gilbert L. Smith. Introduced in 1934. Won first prize in the New York and New England Nut Contest of 1934. BROOKS 1972; I40{OR}

Felger: Superior in nut qualities, with kernels averaging 30% of nut. Not precocious, nor heavy bearing. Originated in Smithfield, Ohio by Emmet Yoder. I40

Fox: Kernel light in color, of fine flavor; large percentage crack out whole; ripens early. Tree bears consistently. Originated in Fonda, New York by Roland Fox. Introduced in the late 1930's. First prize winner in the Northern Nutgrowers Association contest of 1934. BROOKS 1972; B99{PL}, I40{OR}

Grainger: Large nut; shell thin; kernel averages high percentage of nut; cracks well. Tree vigorous. Originated on the farm of J.N. Stapleton, Washburn, Grainger County, Tennessee by the Tennessee Valley Authority. Introduced in 1935. BROOKS 1972; E91M, G75, I40{OR}

J. Yoder No. 1: (Yoder) Regular producer of very large (8.5 grams), thin-shelled nuts that crack out whole halves. Flavor and kernel filling very good. Tree precocious, hardy, bears heavy crops. Originated in Smithfield, Ohio by Emmet Yoder. E62, E62{PR}, E62{SC}, E91M, E91M{OR}, G75, I40, N15

Neilson: Large nut with good flavor and good kernel filling; matures early. Tree hardy; precocious; bears very heavily. E62, E62{PR}, E62{SC}, E91M, E91M{OR}, E91M{PL}, I40{OR}, N24M

Porter: Nut large; shell thin; yields high percentage of kernel (46.7%); cracking quality excellent. Originated in Mackeyville, Clinton County, Pennsylvania, on the farm of Ralph R. Porter. Introduced in 1960. BROOKS 1972; B99{PL}, G75, I40{OR}, N15

Sauber: Shellbark x shagbark hybrid, with a nut resembling a large shagbark. A productive cultivar with medium shell thickness and good cracking qualities. Originated in northern Ohio by Paul Sauber. I40

Silvis 303: Large, round nut, to 8 grams; shell thin; kernel averages 45% of nut; quality good. Tree self-pollinating and a good producer. Originated in West Richfield, Ohio by Ray Silvis. I40, N15

Stratford: Shell thin, smooth, nearly white; cracks easily, resembling bitternut hickory; kernel hard, quite smooth, keeps very well; quality high, no bitter taste; oil content quite high, typically shagbark hickory. Tree productive; buds, flaking bark, and leaves typically shagbark hickory. Originated in Stratford, Iowa. Introduced about 1926. BROOKS 1972; I60{PL}

Weschcke: Nut papershell; kernel full and rich, cracking out in entire halves; matures September 1 to 15. Tree grafts well on wild bitternut hickory; produces consistently. Originated in Fayette, Iowa by Carl Weschcke. Introduced in 1936. BROOKS 1972; E41M{SC}, E62, E62{PL}, E62{PR}, E62{S}, E62{SC}, E91M, E91M{OR}, I40, N24M{PL}

Wilcox: Medium-sized nut, to 4.9 grams; flavor good; cracking quality excellent, cracks out in whole halves; kernel averages 41% of nut; keeps well. Tree one of the best producers; bears early; protogynous. Originated in Geneva, Ohio by C.F. Walker, H.L. Jacobs, and W.R. Fickes. Introduced about 1936. BROOKS 1972; E41M{SC}, E62, E62{PR}, E62{SC}, E91M{OR}, G75, I40, N15

Wilmoth: Produces high quality, thin-shelled nuts. Kernel large, light-colored, flavorful. A consistent winner at the Kentucky State Fair. Originated in Glendale, Kentucky by Leslie Wilmoth. Introduced in 1978. I40

Wurth: Large, thin-shelled nut, pointed at one end; cracks out whole halves. A strong vegetative grower, with scab resistance. Original tree produces 2 to 3 bushels of nuts annually. Originated in Paduceh, Kentucky on the farm of Hillary and Vincent Wurth. Introduced in 1978. I40

SHELLBARK HICKORIES

Characterized by a shaggy trunk with even coarser plates than those of the shagbark hickory. It typically grows in lowlands and river bottoms as contrasted with the shagbark hickory which grows on upland soil for the most part. JAYNES. (C. laciniosa)

Bradley: Large nut; kernel large, never tight in shell; cracking quality excellent; shell thickness medium. Tree bears annually; bears precociously after grafting; requires good soil. Originated in Franklin County, Pennsylvania by Fayette Etter. Introduced in 1932. BROOKS 1972; I40

Dewey Moore: Moderate producer of thin-shelled nuts with 33% kernel. Originated in southern Ohio by A.M. Cox. Introduced in 1987. I40

Fayette: Nut large; shell thin, being one of the thinnest of all cultivars; kernels crack out well, flavor good. Tree bears annually. Originated in Franklin County, Pennsylvania by Fayette Etter. Introduced in 1932. Open-pollinated seedling of a native shellbark hickory. BROOKS 1972; B99{PL}, E91M, I40{OR}

Henry: Very large nut; flavor and kernel filling very good. Tree hardy and productive. A vigorous growing far northern selection. B99{PL}, E91M, E91M{OR}, G75, I40{OR}, N24M, N24M{PL}

Hoffeditz: Medium-sized nut, shape not always uniform; kernel of good flavor; cracking quality good. Tree bears annually. Originated in Fayette County, Pennsylvania by Fayette Etter. Introduced in 1930. BROOKS 1972; B99

Keystone: Large nut. The best cracking shellbark ever found by Etter, as kernel always falls from shell. Tree bears annually. Originated in Franklin County, Pennsylvania by Fayette Etter. Introduced in 1955. BROOKS 1972; G75, I40

Lindauer: Very heavy producer of large nuts which crack out whole halves. Medium shell thickness. Tree reported to be precocious and resistant to weevils. Foliage healthy. Originated in Illinois. I40

Nieman: Heavy producer of very large nuts. Shell fairly thick; nut cracks well. Good producer as far north as Iowa. Originated in Illinois. I40

Stephens: An old cultivar that produces very large nuts. Ripens late. Originated in Kansas. I40, I60{PL}

KALE {S}

BRASSICA OLERACEA ACEPHALA GROUP

CULINARY KALES

<u>HYBRID</u>

Blue Armor: 47-57 days. Outstanding hybrid Vates type. Attractive, very deep blue-green leaves are extremely curled and fringed; wide petiole spacing makes harvesting easier. Vigorous, strong-growing, uniform plants have high yield potential. May be suitable for wintering over. *A1*, M29

Blue Knight: 45-55 days. Hybrid Vates type. Earlier, stronger, more uniform and higher yielding. Deep blue-green, firm, curly leaves have less tendency to yellow and hold up well when cut. Uniform, strong grower; yields 7 to 8 inch plants in just 45 days; larger plants in 55 days will outyield open-pollinated types by 50%. Suited to spring or fall planting. *A1*, H94, J7, M29

Winterbor: 60 days. A hybrid Vates type, with thicker well-curled, dark bluish-green leaves. Plants are taller and more vigorous than Vates, growing to 2 or 3 feet, with much greater yield and better cold hardiness. Also yields a much higher percentage of well-curled and ruffled leaves, is slower bolting and more uniform. Excellent for market, shipping or processing. A87M, B71, *C28*, F19M, G6, H54, *H61*, I77, I91, K50, L89, N52

<u>OPEN-POLLINATED</u>

Cottager's:[1] Ribs and leaf veins tinted with pink and purple. Excellent flavor; also produces an abundance of delicious broccoli-like sprouts in the spring. Vigorous, prolific, 3 foot tall plant; long-standing; very hardy. Good for flower arrangements. Introduced prior to 1877. L91M, P83M, S55, S61

Daubenton: (Perennial Daubenton) Distinct, primitive type with an almost woody and branching stem which continues to grow for 4 or 5 years, only some of the branches flowering every year, while the rest continue to grow and produce leaves. Produces delicious green shoots during the winter. VILMORIN; O20

Dwarf Green Curled: (Dwarf Curled Scotch, Dwarf Curlies, Bloomsdale Kale) 55 days. Dwarf, low-growing plant; 12 to 18 inches tall with a spread of 24 to 28 inches. Densely curled, yellow-green leaves; tender and delicate, especially after having been exposed to frost. Very cold hardy. Well suited to light soils and unsheltered sights. Heavy yields in both spring and autumn. Introduced prior to 1865. BURR; A25, B49, B73M, C85M, C92, D27, E38, F92, G51, G57M, G87, K20, K27M, L42, N39, etc.

Flanders:[1 2] (Flanders Purple Borecole, Chou Caulet de Flandre) A large cattle-feeding kale. Similar to, but somewhat smaller than the Walking Stick kale. Also distinguished by the violet-red color of its leaves and stems. Extremely cold hardy. VILMORIN; **Y75, Z98**

Greenpeace:[1] A rare Russian kale from the Greenpeace Experimental Farm in British Columbia. Has purple stems and highly variegated purple and green leaves. An unusual and attractive plant which grows 2 1/2 feet tall. Has survived a winter low temperature of -20° F. L7M

Harvester: 68 days. Very deeply curled leaves; hold their color without yellowing after a heavy frost. Short-stemmed, spreading plant; height 15 inches. Dwarf growth habit protects the stem from heavy frost and keeps plants healthy well into cold fall weather and snow. Hardier than Konserva but not as high yielding. E24

Konserva: 60 days. Broad dark-green foliage; at first medium-curled, becoming well-curled with the onset of cool fall weather. Tall, very high-yielding plant; grows to 24 or 30 inches. Very cold hardy. First class Danish strain. D68, E24, F44, G6, I77, L7M

Lacinato: (Black Cabbage, Cavolo Nero) 100 days. A rather primitive, open kale with very dark green, serrated leaves, 2 to 3 inches wide and 10 inches long. Height 2 feet. Useful for culinary purposes as well as being ornamental. Extremely winter hardy, freezing temperatures tenderize it and bring out its full flavor (a cross between sweet cabbage and kale). Popular in Tuscany and central Italy, where it is used in soups and stews. BIANCHINI; K66

Large-Leaved Jersey:[2] (Sarthe Cow Cabbage, De la Sarthe) Resembles Walking Stick, but is usually not as tall. Remarkable for its very large leaves, often more than 3 feet long and 12 to 14 inches broad. Succeeds best in rich soil in a temperate climate, as it is not perfectly hardy. VILMORIN; **Z98**

Maris Kestrel:[2] A forage kale that resembles Marrow Stem. Shorter and thicker in the stem and less prone to lodging. Very uniform plants with high dry matter and good palatability which insures almost complete utilization of the stem when grazed. B13, M49, N81, *R23*

Marrow Stem:[2] Tall, unbranched, very stout and thick stem; grows 5 feet or more high, 3 to 4 inches in diameter at its thickest part; swollen in the upper two-thirds of its length and filled with a sort of marrow or tender flesh. Thought to be the progenitor of kohlrabi, the flesh is preferred by some for its milder flavor. Should be cut when 2 or 3 inches in diameter. BURR, VILMORIN; C85M, E83T, I99, K49M, M49, *R23*

Mosbacher: (Mosbach Winter Kale) Resembles a cross between the Tall Green Curled kale and Portuguese cabbage. The leaves especially resemble the latter, with very stout stalks, midribs and veins; pale, almost yellowish-green in color. Stem of medium height, 2 to 2 1/3 feet tall; the leaves growing in tiers along its length and bent upwards, not downwards, from their middle. Useful as a table vegetable, and also has merit as an ornamental. VILMORIN; **Z98**

Palm Tree: (Palm Tree Cabbage) Stem straight, or slightly curved; height 6 1/2 feet or more; bears a cluster of leaves at the top. Leaves entire, 2 to 2 1/2 feet long, 3 to 4 inches broad; of a dark, almost blackish, green color; finely crimped like those of Savoy cabbage; spread outward as they grow giving the plant a very elegant, palm-like appearance. Flavor excellent when picked young. Similar to Lacinato. VILMORIN; J73

Pentland Brig: 75 days. Medium-sized plant; 18 to 24 inches tall, 24 inches across. Produces tender, finely curled leaves from early winter through April, then broccoli-like spring sprouts. Good flavor. Very hardy and productive. Excellent for home gardens. Bred in Scotland; a cross between Thousand Headed and a curled-leaf type. B49, S55

Ragged Jack:[1] An old-fashioned ornamental kale. Short, often branching stem. Long, irregularly cut oak-like leaves, variously colored with purple and blue-green. Productive, but unlike most kales, it will not withstand very low temperatures. Introduced prior to 1885. LARKCOM 1984, VILMORIN; K17M, K49M

Russian Red:[1] (Canadian Broccoli) 60 days. Lightly crinkled, oak-like leaves with an unusual purple venation. Flavor and texture very good before a frost. Height 2 1/2 to 3 feet. Not as winter hardy as Konserva. Called Canadian broccoli in reference to its early spring flower buds. Attractive specialty item. A2, D87, E24, F80, G92, I39, I77, I99, K49T, K66, L9, R47

Spurt: 65 days. Dwarf, low-growing plant; height 12 to 15 inches. Produces tender, deep-green, curled leaves in abundance. Crisp, tender stems snap readily for easy harvesting; upright growing, holding the leaves well away from the soil. L91M

Tall Green Curled: (Tall Green Scotch, Tall Scotch Curled) Stem stout and straight, 2 to 3 feet tall. Leaves rather narrow, 16 to 20 inches in length; clear-green; deeply curled and frilled; very tender and flavorsome after having been exposed to the action of frost. Very hardy. Tall form of Dwarf Green Curled; introduced prior to 1865. VILMORIN; C85M, I84, K71, P83M, *R23*, R47, S45M, S61

Thousand Headed:[2] (Branching Borecole) A large forage kale, distinguished from the Walking Stick kale by the numerous side-branches emanating from the main stem. Somewhat shorter, it is generally considered more productive but not as hardy. Originated in western France, prior to 1865. BURR, VILMORIN; A2, I99, L9, P1G, *R23*, S61

Thousandhead Dwarf: A dwarf low-branching strain of Thousand Headed, which develops prolific side shoots earlier and lower on the stem. Exceptionally hardy. Harvest the tender young shoots as they are produced during winter and early spring. S55

Vates: (Dwarf Blue Curled Scotch, Blue Curled Scotch, Dwarf Blue Vates) 55 days. Low-growing, compact, short-stemmed plants; 15 inches tall, with a spread of 24 inches; slow bolting. Finely curled, bluish-green leaves which resist yellowing. Standard dwarf cultivar. Originated in Virginia Beach, Virginia at the Virginia Truck Experiment Station, hence the name. Introduced in 1950. A13, A87M, D76, E24, F19M, G16, G51, G71, G93M, I91, J14{PL}, K71, K73, L97, M46, etc.

Verdura: 60 days. Westlandse Winter type, widely grown in that area of Holland and relished by the Dutch. Compact, vigorous, highly productive plant. Produces thick, curled, dark blue-green leaves that are very tender and sweet. Provides extended harvests throughout the winter. K66

Walking Stick:[2] (Walking Stick Cabbage, Tree Cabbage, Jersey Kale, Chou Cavalier) Stem straight, stiff and strong, comparatively slender; height 3 to 4 feet the first year, up to 12 feet after 3 years. Leaves oval-rounded, often over 2 1/2 feet long; can be picked when young and stuffed like Greek dolmas. Also used as forage. In the Channel Islands, the stems are dried and made into walking sticks. PARKER, VILMORIN; C82, E83T, I99, J73, L91M, O53M, Q11M

Westlandse Winter: 60 days. Deeply curled and frilled dark-green leaves; sweet, with only a hint of a cabbage-like flavor. Tall, thick stalks; can reach 24 inches in height. At the growing point the new leaves form an attractive pale-yellow rosette. L89, *R11M*

Winter Red:[1] Dark-green leaves; irregularly cut and lobed like an oak leaf; turn to various hues of red and purple after the fall frosts. Good raw; tender and sweet when cooked. Becomes a rich, dark-green color when cooked. Very disease resistant. Developed by Territorial Seed Company; the result of breeding work to confirm the origin of such kales. L89

ORNAMENTAL KALES

Also called *salad savoy*, these are grown mainly for their ornamental rather than edible qualities although they are quite palatable, especially after having been exposed to frost. Popular with chefs as a garnish or as a salad ingredient, they can also be cooked like regular kale. GESSERT [Cu], HARRINGTON, G. [Cu, Cul], LARKCOM 1984 [Cu, Cul], SCHNEIDER [Cul]; *N40*{PR}

FLOWERING CABBAGE These are the oldest forms of ornamental kales. Most have a more mounded habit than the flowering kales and the leaves are generally rounded not feathery or fringed. B35M, D11M, D27, F1, G27M, G79, G87, *H61*, I64, I67M, J34, J58, K64{PL}, *L85*{PL}, N39, etc.

Hybrid

Color-Up Series: Compact, uniformly mounded plant; grows 10 inches tall, with a spread of 12 inches. Very clear, intense colors. Color and habit hold up through hard winter freezes, continuing into spring. Withstands variable weather well; resists warm spells and sudden frost alike. Available in red, pink and white. I91

Osaka Series: Attractive wavy edged leaves form bright colored central heads extremely early. Far superior to open-pollinated strains. Vigorous, uniform growth habit; height 12 to 14 inches. Outer leaves green. Available in pink, red and white. B75, C44, *E53M*, *E91G*, *F72*, G82, K10, L42, *M43M*

Tokyo Series: Uniform and more heat resistant than other strains. Grows 8 to 10 inches tall, with a spread of 15 inches. Smooth, wavy edged leaves. Available in red, pink and white. *E53M*, *E91G*, *F72*

Open-Pollinated

Miniature: (Miniature Japanese) 65 days. Tiny plants that look like giant roses, with lovely deep red shades on green. Needs cold weather to bring out the color. Makes an attractive, colorful addition to salads. I39

Red on Green: Traditional, open-pollinated type with wavy green outer leaves and red centers. Brightly colored and fairly uniform. C85M, C92

White on Green: Traditional, open-pollinated type with wavy green outer leaves and white centers. Brightly colored and fairly uniform. C85M, C92

FLOWERING KALE Generally characterized by feathery or fringed leaves as opposed to the rounded leaves of the flowering cabbages. The leaves are also thinner which makes them more suitable for culinary purposes. A25, C53, D11M, D76, E24, F82, F92, G71, G84{PL}, J20, J34, L97, M13M, N39

Hybrid

Coral Prince: 65 days. Feathery, deeply serrated green leaves with a creamy white center. Extremely winter hardy. As the plant is exposed to temperatures of 60° F. or less, the center expands until the plant is filled with color, making a striking contrast with the green feathery border. A16, I39, I77, L89, *Q52*

Coral Queen: Very striking appearance of deeply notched, feathery green leaves offsetting a rose-red center. Hybrid vigor and uniformity. Extremely hardy. C85M, *E53M*, I39, I77, L89, *Q52*

Feather Red: Long, deeply serrated and fringed leaves; the inner area solid red and the outer part dark green with red veining. Height 18 inches. Excellent for fall color. F13, M46

Feather White: Long, deeply serrated and fringed leaves; the inner area solid white and the outer part medium-green with white veining. Height 18 inches. Grow with Feather Red for a striking appearance. F13, M46

Nagoya Series: Heavily fringed leaves develop outstanding, brilliant colors with the onset of cool weather. Height 18 inches. Excellent uniformity not found in open-pollinated cultivars. Available in red and white. Excellent for garden, container or mass plantings. B75, *E53M*, *E91G*, F13, *F72*, J7, J58, K10, L42, L79, M13M, *M43M*, M46

Peacock Series: A striking new type of flowering kale. Produces deeply cut, fringed, feathery leaves on compact, robust, frost hardy plants. Height 12 inches. The leaves begin to turn colors from the plants center, with extended colored areas developing "like webs" as the winter advances, enriching their tones. Available in red and white. *E53M*, *E91G*, *F72*, G64, G82, *H57M*, I91, L42, L91M

Open-Pollinated

Miniature: 65 days. Has a brilliant range of colors. Makes a beautiful pot plant for the patio. Delicious eating. I39

Red on Green: Reddish-purple interior leaves with contrasting green edges; rich bluish green outer leaves. Height 15 inches. Planted in late summer, leaves begin to color at lower fall and winter temperatures. B75, C44, C92, F44, G64, G93M, H95, I91, *L85*{PL}

Sekito: Wavy, green loose-leaf heads with carmine rose fringe. Sow in summer. Becomes more colorful with each frost. E49

White on Green: Green, heavily fringed leaves; creamy white centers. Height 15 inches. High temperatures and excessive amounts of fertilizer will affect the speed and degree of coloration of the leaves. B75, C44, F44, G64, G93M, H95, I91, *L85*{PL}

Willy's: A distinctive ornamental, with centers of deep red fringed by curled green. Light frost improves the flavor. Used for adding color to salads or in place of cabbage in soups and stir-fries. Harvest all winter, removing the leaves. J25

Xmas Fringed Red: Similar to Xmas Fringed White, but with purplish-red centers. C85M, L89

Xmas Fringed White: Green outer leaves, ruffled white centers. Sow in summer. Becomes more colorful with each frost. C85M, E49, L89

KIDNEY BEAN {S}

PHASEOLUS VULGARIS

DRY BEANS

Also called *field beans*, these are the principal beans of commerce. They are harvested after the pods have dried and the seeds inside have shrunk. A good dry bean is especially suited for baking, stewing or use in soups.

BLACK-SEEDED

Bush

Black Coco: First pods form early and make fine snap beans; later, fast developing shell beans form; and finally, plump, black, quick-cooking dry beans. Best for *frijoles refritos*. L89

Black Delgado: Bushy plants bearing small black beans. A very ancient cultivar, widely used by the Zapotecs for soups, on tortillas, etc. Withstands considerable cold and drought. Also used to dye the famous black rebozos of Oaxaca. Classic staple of Mexican cuisine. F80

Black Mexican: (Frijol Negro) Small, oval black bean; tender, with a distinctive flavor; good for making a thick, rich, dark soup. Later maturing than pinto. After the pinto, the most popular bean among the Mexican Indians in California. A2, J73, L11

Black Turtle Soup: (Turtle Soup) 90 days. Small, flattened, jet black seeds; 7 or 8 seeds per pod. Widely used for soups, to which they impart a distinctive flavor and a greenish color, somewhat similar to that of the green turtle soup so popular along southern sea coasts. Very old cultivar that originated in northern South America or Chile. HAWKES [Re], HEDRICK 1931; C76M, D76, E59Z, E97, F19M, I91, J20, K49M, K71, L9, L79M, M46

Hopi Black: Adapted to the high semi-desert, where it is planted in the spring. Prolific at oak elevation with irrigation, but dry or run-off farmed by the Hopi. Can also be used as a dye. I16

Midnight Black Turtle Soup: 104 days. An improved, upright growing, black bean strain. Tall bush does not sprawl, keeping pods off the ground for cleaner beans and fewer problems in wet weather. Small black beans, about the size of pea beans. Good for soups, stews and refrying. Developed by Cornell University. B75, E24, G6

Mitla Black: 110 days. Small, slightly flattened black seeds, 3 to 5 per short pod. Excellent for black bean soup. Compact plant; produces short runners but support required; high yielding. Pre-Columbian cultivar from the Mitla Valley of Oaxaca, Mexico. E59Z

Tarahumara Chokame: Small, round, shiny black seed. From the bottom of Batopilas Canyon, Mexico where it is planted in August and harvested in November. Has grown well in Tucson, Arizona and Madison, Wisconsin. I16

BROWN-SEEDED

Bush

Brown Dutch: A traditional golden-brown drying bean from Holland. Floury texture and an excellent flavor. Popular for baking, boiling, soups and stews. Easy to shell. The flat, light green pods can also be used as snap beans. Very productive. *A75*, B49, C85M, P83M, S55

Ireland Creek Annie's: 80 days. Long, oval light-brown seed with white eye; pods 5 inches long, 5 seeds per pod; excellent flavor, makes its own sauce. Easy to shell. Small but prolific plant; highly resistant to mold and mildew. Does well in short season areas. Heirloom from Ireland Creek Farm in British Columbia, Canada. Introduced from England in the 1920's. I99

Marfax: 90 days. Medium-sized, plump round seed; golden-brown color; resembles Swedish Brown. Good for soup. Originally from New England. A2

Swedish Brown: 85 days. Seed medium to small, oblong-oval, plump; color light brown, marked with darker brown; small white eye; 4 to 5 seeds per pod; nutty flavor. Very hardy; well adapted to northern climates but will grow well in most areas. Brought by Swedish immigrants settling in the upper Mississippi Valley. Still popular in parts of northern Michigan, Wisconsin and Minnesota. HEDRICK 1931; A2, A7M{PR}, A57M{PR}, D68, D87, E24, E59Z, E97, J66M{PR}, M46

GREEN-SEEDED

Bush

Hutterite Soup: 100 days. Round, very plump, light-green seed; very distinctive, resembles an English rugby ball; two small, dark half-circles around the hilum. Excellent for soup, dissolving into a creamy white delicacy. Early maturing. Compact, true bush-type plant; productive; easy to grow. I99, K49T

MOTTLED

Bush

Agate Pinto: 92 days. Medium-sized, broad oval, buff-mottled seeds; spicy flavor. Relatively short cooking time. Bush-type plant, without the sprawling habit of other pinto strains. Resistant to bean rust and common bean mosaic virus. Developed by Rogers Brothers Seed Company. Introduced in 1982. G6, K17M

Anasazi: (Anasazi-Analog) 90-95 days. Strain of Jacob's cattle, identified as one of the few cultivated crops grown by the ancient Anasazi cliff dwellers. White seed, prominently mottled and splashed with maroon. Excellent baked, having a sweet flavor and meaty texture. In Navajo, the word anasazi translates as "the ancient ones". Recently rediscovered by the natural foods industry. C8M{PR}, C76M, D26M{PR}, H91{PR}, I16, I16{PR}, J25M, K49Z, L7M, L79M, M63M{PR}

Appaloosa: 90-110 days. Attractive sibling of the Anasazi bean. White with maroon-and-black mottling, like the rump of an appaloosa. Bush-type plant with short runners that do not require staking, but will climb a fence or cornstalk. From Velarde, in northern New Mexico. J25M

Boleta: (Bolita, New Mexico Bolitas) 100 days. A treasured staple of the Hispanics of northern New Mexico. Pale yellow-green to light brown, veined seed, with squared ends. Very productive low bush; short runners that do not need staking. Originally grown in the highlands of Spain, and said to be the progenitor of the pinto bean. E56{PR}, I16, J25M, L79M

Canadian Wild Goose: 95 days. Small, attractive seed; dark bluish-grey, speckled with grayish-white; orange ring around the eye; small, thin, parchment-like pods. Strong, moderately productive plant; twining growth habit. I99

Jacob's Cattle: (Trout) 85 days. Heirloom New England bean of unknown origin, but very similar to the Anasazi bean. Kidney-shaped seed; white, with deep maroon mottling and speckles; uniquely attractive. Excellent for baking; also good as a green shell bean. Does well in short season areas of the United States and Canada. A2, A25, D68, D87, E24, F24M, G6, I99, J73, K17M, K49M, K49M{PR}, L79M, M46, M49, etc.

Jacob's Cattle Gasless: 90 days. Jacob's Cattle x Black Turtle. Developed by Sumner and Radcliffe B. Pike of Lubec, Maine at the University of New Hampshire, in the 1950's. Coloring identical to Jacob's Cattle. Scientific tests indicate that it causes less than half the flatulence of other beans. Used primarily as a baking bean. U33

Kenearly: 95 days. A baking bean selection made at the Kentville Research Station, Nova Scotia, from the well-known Yellow Eye. Excellent flavor and quality. Good yields. Early maturity; well adapted to most areas of Atlantic Canada and New England. F1, M49

Maine Yellow Eye: (Old-Fashioned Yellow Eye) 92 days. Medium-sized, oval, plump seed; white, blotched with a yellow-gold "eye" near the hilum. Excellent for baking and stewing. Widely grown in Maine and Vermont where it is claimed that it bakes much better and has a better flavor than other strains of yellow eye. HEDRICK 1931; A7M{PR}, D68, G6, L79M, M46

Peregion: 80 days. Highly-regarded Scotia type. Small, slightly oblong seed; tan, with black stripes and speckles; very attractive. Can also be used as a snap bean when very young. Compact, bush-type plant; very prolific. Originated in eastern Oregon. A2

Pinto: 85 days. Medium-sized, broad oval seed; pinkish buff, blotched with medium dark-brown; 5 to 6 seeds per pod; rich, spicy flavor. Essential for Mexican and Southwestern cuisine, especially chile con carne. Vine semi-trailing, spreading. Primarily grown in dry western climates. B73M, D76, F19M, G51, G71, G79, H66, I91, J34, K71, M46, M95, N16

Soldier: (Johnson Bean) 85 days. Attractive New England heirloom. Long, slender, kidney-shaped seed; white, with a reddish-brown "soldier" pattern near the hilum; soft texture, fine flavor; 6 seeds per pod. Very popular for baking and stewing. Hardy, high-yielding plant, 18 inches tall; drought resistant. Does well in cool areas. HEDRICK 1931; A25, D68, E24, E97, F42M{PR}, G6, J73, K49M, L14, L89, M46, M49

Pole

Box: 90 days. Striking purple-on-white cultivar from England. Medium-sized, nearly round seed, distinctively marked with sharply defined color areas of reddish-purple and off white; flat light-green pod with dark green sutures, 4 inches long, 3/4 inch in diameter. Vigorous, highly productive vine. A2

PINK-SEEDED

Bush

Pink: 85 days. Medium-sized seed, light salmon pink with a white hilum; long, narrow pod, 4 inches in length; 4 to 5 seeds per pod. Ideal chili or soup bean, holding its shape well when cooked. Also good as a green shell bean at 60 days. Highly productive. Widely grown in California, the Southwest and in Mexico. Probably originated with the Spanish conquistadors. HEDRICK 1931; M46

Santa Maria Pinquito: 90 days. Very small, square-shaped, pink bean that is low in starch and does not break up when cooked. Only grown commercially on the mesas above Santa Maria, California. Primary ingredient of the Santa Maria style barbecue, which is also unique to this area. According to Pappy's Restaurant of Santa Maria, they are traditionally simmered for 1 1/2 hours with bacon, onion, garlic and chili salsa. I39, I99, J73, K17M, *N40*{PR}

RED-SEEDED

Bush

Charlevoix Dark Red Kidney: 102 days. Very large, attractive seeds, mature at least a week before common dark red types. Provides a tasty, thick broth in soups, stews and chilis. Excellent in summer bean salads. Resistant to anthracnose. **U33**

Montezuma Red: 95 days. A strain of red bean that was being grown by Indians when Cortez arrived in Mexico. Identical beans have been found in pre-historic tombs, estimated to be more than 3,000 years old. Small maroon seed. Excellent for baking and chili. Tolerates a wide range of soils and growing conditions. I39, K17M

Red Kidney: (Chilian) 95 days. Medium to large seeds, long and broad; color ranges from pinkish crimson and reddish brown to a deep mahogany; pod 5 to 6 inches long; 4 to 5 seeds per pod. Widely used in Mexican dishes, bean salads, baked, etc. Large, runnerless plant, 14 to 16 inches tall. HEDRICK 1931; A25, B78, C44, C85M, D82, E24, F19M, *F72*, G71, H66, J7, K17M, M46, N39

Red Mexican: 85 days. Medium-sized, reddish-purple seed; medium green pods. Good baking bean; does not become mushy when cooked. Small plant, to 14 inches tall, with early runners. Grown and prized as a dry-land crop in California since 1855. Originated with the Indians of northern Mexico. HEDRICK 1931; E59Z, M46

Red Peanut: 65 days. Small, red seed; pod 4 inches long, green, turning red at maturity. Used both as a green shell bean and as a dry bean. True bush-type plant, 14 inches tall; very prolific; does well in dry weather. Quick maturing; plant often for a continuous yield. M46

Redkloud: (Redkloud Kidney) 80 days. Heavy yielder of light red seeds. Matures one to two weeks earlier than other red kidney strains, allowing it to be grown as far north as Nova Scotia. Tolerant to halo blight. Resistant to two strains of common bean mosaic and the alpha race of anthracnose. Developed at Cornell University. A13, D68

WHITE-SEEDED

Bush

Great Northern: 85 days. Similar to Navy, but enlarged and rather lengthened; pods 3 to 4 inches long; excellent flavor. Also used as a green shell bean at 65 days. Hardier, earlier, more productive than Navy. Originated with the Mandan Indians of North Dakota. Seed of it has been found in mounds known to be centuries old. HEDRICK 1931; B73M, B75, C92, D11M, D65, D76, E24, E97, F19M, G16, J34, J97M, K49M, K71, M46, etc.

Michelite: 85 days. An improved Navy type resistant to blight. Small, roundish, pearly white seeds. Excellent for pork and beans. Uniform and high yielding, ripens early and evenly. Pods are carried well off the ground for easy harvesting. Developed at Michigan State University. A56, J7

Navy: (Navy Pea, Boston Pea, White Navy) 100 days. Small, oval white seed, quite plump to somewhat flattened; short narrow pods; 6 to 7 seeds per pod. Popular for baking and stewing. Dwarf plant, 14 to 16 inches tall. Principal field bean in the United States; used extensively for the commercial canned baked bean. HAWKES [Re], HEDRICK 1931; *A75*, C44, D11M, D76, E24, E97, G71, G79, I64, K10, K27M, K71, M46, N39

Sanilac: 90 days. Highly improved strain of Navy, resistant to mosaic and bacterial wilt. Heavy yields of glossy white beans. Pods set high on the bush for easy harvesting, and prevent discoloration caused by contact with the ground. Developed by the Michigan Agricultural Experiment Station. *I59M*, J58

Seafarer: (Seafarer Navy) 92 days. Earliest strain of Navy pea beans. Small, nearly round, shiny white seed; good texture and flavor. Excellent for baking and making bean soup; also good as a green shell bean. Vigorous, highly productive plant; tolerant to halo blight, mosaic, and anthracnose. A16, G57M

Walcherse: (Walcherse White, Ruckle) 95 days. Large, round white seed, much larger than Navy beans; outstanding flavor. Excellent for baking and soups. Very prolific. Popular on Salt Spring Island, British Columbia, where it has become known as Ruckle Bean. C85M, K17M

White Kidney: (Cannellini) 100 days. Large, white, kidney shaped seeds; fairly plump to somewhat flattened. Excellent for baking and in dishes where the color of red kidneys is undesirable. Vigorous, spreading plants; height 18 to 24 inches; very productive. Beans of the white kidney type appeared in U.S. catalogs as early as 1822. HAWKES [Re], HEDRICK 1931; C94M{PR}, G57M, G82, H19M{PR}, I67M, J66M{PR}, L50M{PR}

White Marrow: (White Marrowfat) 100 days. Rather short, plump-ovate white seeds, larger than Navy; flat, straight pods, 5 inches long or more; 5 or 6 seeds per pod. Excellent for baking and soups. Large, very spreading plant, with many long, trailing runners. HEDRICK 1931; G57M, L42

YELLOW-SEEDED

Bush

Adventist: 80 days. Small, attractive, amber-colored seed; short pods; 3 to 5 seeds per pod; ripens over a long period of time. Excellent for baking or stewing. Small, compact plant with short runners; does not require support; heavy bearing. Originally from the mountains of northern Idaho. I99, K49M, K49M{PR}

Lemon Yellow: Light yellow beans with an excellent "real" bean flavor. For dry use in all bean dishes. A European favorite. C85M

Sinaloa Azufrado: A bright yellow, tasty staple from irrigated farms in Sinaloa, Mexico. Makes excellent *frijoles refritos*. Adapted to low hot desert areas, where it is planted in early July. In temperate regions, plant in spring when danger of frost is passed and the soil has warmed up some. I16, I16{PR}

Sonoran Canario: Large, yellow-tan, kidney-shaped bean; quick cooking. Grown with irrigation in winter in frost-free, low hot desert areas. Good potential as a winter crop in Yuma, Arizona and San Diego, California. Originally from Mexico. I16

Squaw Yellow: 60 days. Small, golden yellow seed, about the size of the Navy bean. Good for soup. Pods are not used for snap beans. Very early maturing. Short, high-yielding plant. Does well in short season areas. D82, E24

Sulphur: (Brimstone) Small to medium-sized, very plump seed; cream to light sulphur yellow in color, with a faint green to brown eye-ring; pods 4 to 4 1/2 inches long; 5 seeds per pod. Distinctive flavor when baked. Also good as a snap bean. Spreading plant, 12 to 15 inches tall; very few or no runners. Popular in high elevation areas of North Carolina, Virginia and Tennessee. E24, G57M, G67M, *I59M*, J73, K49M, L7M, M95M

Tarahumara Azufrado: Yellow, beige or ocher seed. Tasty staple from the bottom and rim of Copper Canyon, Chihuahua, Mexico. Makes excellent refried beans. Adapted to low hot desert areas, where it is planted in early July. I16, I16{PR}

POPPING BEANS

Also known as *nuñas* and *popbeans*, from Ecuador to northern Bolivia where they are native, they have hard-shelled seeds which are popped in a hot skillet like popcorn, rather than being boiled in hot water. The resulting product is soft and tastes somewhat like roasted peanuts. Traditionally served at main meals as a side dish, or eaten as a snack. Their culture appears limited to cool mountain climates with short daylengths. NATIONAL RESEARCH COUNCIL 1989; D33

SHELL BEANS

Also called *shelly beans*, these are superior when harvested in the green, immature state when the seeds have swollen and the shell has passed the tender, fleshy state, to the point of being thin and rubbery.

COMMON

Bush

Bert Goodwin's: 75 days. New Hampshire heirloom. Large, attractive, mottled-brown seed; pods 7 inches long. Exceptionally rich flavor; excellent with butter or cream; also freezes well. Best shelled when the pod softens and begins to lighten in color. Large, vigorous bush, with some half-runners. J20

Buttergreen: 45 days. Grown for its green shell beans which have a distinctive flavor and mature 2 to 3 weeks earlier than limas. Can also be eaten young as a snap bean. Good for short season areas where other shell beans or limas can't mature. Small, spreading plant. Resistant to common bean mosaic virus. B75, *G1M*, G93M, L7M, M95M

Limelight: 60 days. Small, flat white seeds; 6 seeds per pod. Excellent for shelling when greenish-white, resembling baby lima beans. Broad, flat, Italian-style pods may be picked for snap beans when 3 to 4 inches long. Also used as a dry shell bean. Short, compact, very hardy plant. Developed by Canada Agricultural Research Station, Lethbridge, Alberta. A2, *A75*, D11M, G6, L91M

Low's Champion: (Dwarf Red Cranberry) 65 days. Medium to large, plump, broad-oval seed; dark reddish-maroon when dry; excellent for shelling when green, also used as a dry shell bean; 4 to 5 seeds per pod. Broad, flat pod; very tender and fleshy; good as a snap bean when young. Introduced in 1884. Still popular in New England. HEDRICK 1931; A25, G6

Pole

Lazy Wife: 80 days. Small, very plump seed; ivory-white when mature, marked with a distinct, grayish, vein-like pattern; 5 to 7 seeds per pod. Broad, slender pod, 5 1/2 to 6 inches long; stringless. Quality below average as a snap bean; excellent for shelling. Probably brought to Bucks County, Pennsylvania by German immigrants, prior to 1810. HEDRICK 1931; L7M

Ohio Pole: 85 days. Large, dark-maroon seeds, frosted with white on one end. Used as a shell bean, either in the green shell or dry shell stage. A good producer, yielding 6 to 8 beans per pod. Heirloom. L7M

FLAGEOLETS Gourmet French shell beans, generally considered superior to other shell beans although their production is much lower. Indispensable for *cassoulet* dishes. C3M{PR}, C94M{PR}, J66M{PR}

Bush

Canadian Wonder: (Flageolet Red) Broad, flat pod; 5 to 6 inches long; 5 to 6 seeds per pod. Large, flattened, dark-red seeds. Should be harvested when extremely young for snap bean use. Also used as a dry shelling bean. Popular in England, Australia and New Zealand. Similar to Flageolet Rouge. Originated in Canada, sometime prior to 1873. HEDRICK 1931; *A75*, B49, P83M, *R23*

Cheverbel: Semi-round pods; 5 to 6 seeds per pod. Long, flat, lime-green seeds; of excellent flavor. Best used as a green shell bean. Also used as a snap bean, and as an early ripening dry shell bean for winter use. Dwarf plant, to 15 inches high. L91M

Chevrier: (Chevrier Vert, Flageolet Green) Distinguished from other flageolet types by the intense green color that extends to all parts of the plant. The seeds have a very pronounced green tinge, which is maintained after cooking, and is not merely confined to the surface, but extends through the interior of the seed. Originated about 1878 at Bretigny, France. HEDRICK 1931, VILMORIN; *A75*, C53, F33, G68, J73, K49M, M46, S61

Flageolet Rouge: Straight or slightly kidney-shaped seed; 3/4 inches long, 1/4 inch broad, about 1/4 inch thick; wine-lees red in color; highly prized as a green shell bean in France. Long, straight pods; very good as snap beans. Vigorous plant, about 18 inches tall; hardy and very productive. HEDRICK 1931, VILMORIN; G68

Flambeau: 76 days. Long, slender pods; well-filled with 8 to 10 beans; easily shelled. Small, vivid mint-green beans; tender but firm; of excellent flavor, reminiscent of fresh limas. Excellent frozen. Of gourmet quality, yet surprisingly easy to grow. G6, I77

Flaveol: 85 days. Improved green flageolet type, developed from Chevrier. Small, mint-green seeds; tender and delicately flavored. Recommended for use as a green or dry shelling bean. Can also be used as a snap bean when young. Vigorous, highly productive plant. B75, F44

Masterpiece: (Flageolet Yellow) 55 days. Slender pods, 6 to 7 inches long, almost wholly stringless; fleshy and tender. Large, long-reniform, yellow-buff seeds. Excellent as a green shelling bean or dried for use in soups. Can also be used as a *filet bean* when young. Introduced as a novelty in 1910 by Sutton and Sons. HEDRICK 1931; *A75*, L91M, *R23*, R50, S61

Suma: (Vert Suma) 65 days. Pale jade green, kidney shaped seed, tender and delicious; retains its color when cooked. Can be used green shelled or dried. Excellent sautéed in butter with a sprig of thyme. Requires warm temperatures for germination. Vigorous, very productive plant. Resistant to bean mosaic virus. P59M

Tricolor Mix: A mixture of the three available colors, a deep red, a light lima-like green, and a yellow which actually tends to a light brown shade. J20

Vernel: 60 days. Improved green flageolet type developed by Vilmorin of France. Long, well-filled pods; up to 6 small green seeds per pod; quality excellent. Can be used for green shell and dried beans. Very productive plant; resistant to anthracnose and mosaic. Introduced in 1976. G64, S95M

HALF RUNNERS Intermediate between pole beans and dwarf beans, with short runners. Most are dual purpose types that can be used as snap beans when young and as dry or shell beans when older. Popular in the South.

Mountaineer Half Runner: (Old Dutch Half Runner) 60 days. Round, light-green pod, 4 to 5 inches long; tender and flavorful; becomes stringy as it matures. Small, oval white seeds. Also good as a dry shell bean for baking. High-yielding plant, with 3 foot runners that require no staking; resistant to common bean mosaic virus. Popular home garden cultivar. *A75*, F19M, F24M, *G1M*, G57M, G82, H54, *I59M*, I91, K10, K73, M95M

Parker Half Runner: 52 days. Plump, oval, stringless pod; 5 inches long, 3/8 inch in diameter; tender and flavorful; matures over an extended harvest period. Seeds are excellent for baking, freezing and canning. Harvest snap beans in 52 days, dry shell beans in 90 days. Vigorous, bushy plant with medium length runners. G79

Pink Half Runner: (Peanut) 60 days. Dual purpose bean, can be used as a snap bean when young and later for green and dry shelled beans. Bright red pods, 4 1/2 long when mature. Seeds have a pink color. G57M

Spartan Half Runner: (Striped Half Runner) 60 days. Slender, light green pods, 5 inches long and 3/8 inch wide; stringy when mature. Small tan seeds, striped with brownish-black. Popular as snap beans in the early stage and as shell beans later. Vigorous, bushy plant with medium-long runners. Often planted among corn. G57M, *I59M*

State Half Runner: (State White Half Runner) 60 days. A strain of White Half Runner. Slightly longer and larger pod and larger seed than regular White Half Runner. Oval, slightly curved pod, 5 to 6 inches long; not stringless, but of excellent quality. Vigorous plant, with 3-foot runners that do not require staking. Resistant to common bean mosaic virus and nematodes. *A75*, F19M, *G1M*, G57M, *I59M*, K10, *L59G*

White Half Runner: (Mississippi Skip Bean) 60 days. Very popular in the South as a snap bean or a green or dry shelling bean. White-seeded. Round, medium light-green pods, 4 to 5 inches long; stringless if picked young. Vigorous, bushy plant, with short 3-foot runners; resists heat and drought. Not recommended for northern climates. *A75*, B75, D76, *F72*, G27M, G57M, G79, H49, H66, J34, J58, J84, K27M, K71, L14, *L59G*, M46, M95M, N16, etc.

<u>HORTICULTURAL</u> Also called *cranberry beans* or *October beans*, these cultivars are characterized by pods that are brilliantly splashed with carmine or red in the green shell stage, and by large white or buff-colored seeds more or less splashed and streaked with dark red. <u>A7M</u>{PR}, <u>A52M</u>{PR}, <u>J66M</u>{PR}

Bush

Coco Rubico: Large, very attractive pods, strongly striped and splashed with carmine. Each pod contains 6 large seeds, striped with dark red. Suitable for use as both a green shell and dry bean. Resistant to bean mosaic virus. Introduced in 1976 by Vilmorin of France. S95M

Dwarf Horticultural: (Dwarf Cranberry, Dwarf Wren's Egg) 60 days. Medium to large seed; pinkish-buff, streaked with bright red. Broad, plump pod; white, splashed with carmine in the green shell stage. Primarily used as a green shell bean, being preferred for *succotash* in many areas. Also used as a snap and dry shell bean. Of unknown origin; grown in the United States for over 150 years. HEDRICK 1931; A2, A56, B75, C85M, D82, F24M, *F72*, G79, *H61*, J20, J58, J97M, K71, L14, L97, etc.

French Horticultural: (French's Dwarf Horticultural) 65 days. Plumb, red-speckled seed. Excellent as a green or dry shell bean; freezes and cans well. Flat, round pod; 6 to 7 inches long; turning greenish-yellow, heavily splashed or speckled with bright red; easy to shell. Vigorous plant; with semi-runners; hardy; disease resistant. Selected from Dwarf Horticultural. HEDRICK 1931; A13, A25, B71, C44, D11M, F13, F24M, *F63*, G79, *I59M*, J84, K10, K50, L42, M46, N39, etc.

Scarlet Beauty Elite: (Scarlet Beauty Elite 7 Pod) 70 days. Pods 7 inches long, produced in bunches of 7 per branch. Elongated seeds with attractive shades of purplish-brown and beige. Excellent cooking qualities as a shell bean, also used dried. Superior flavor and productivity compared to Jacob's Cattle. Developed by Professor E.M. Meader. J20

Speckled Bays: (Speckled Bale) 100 days. Plump, broad-oval seed; cream-colored, speckled with red. Good as a green or dry shell bean; very tender, cooks quickly. Prolific and hardy. Local Pacific Northwest heirloom. A2, L89

Taylor's Dwarf Horticultural: (Shelley Bean, Taylor Horticultural Improved) 62 days. Large, oval seed; buff-colored, splashed with red. Excellent for shelling; often used in *succotash*. Thick, flat, oval pod; 5 inches long; light green, turning cream-colored splashed with red at maturity; stringy and fibrous. Semi-running plant, 14 to 18 inches tall. A87M, E97, F19M, G6, H49, H54, H66, H94, J84, K10, K49M, K50, K73, L7M, N16, etc.

Tongue of Fire: (Tierra del Fuego, Horto) 70 days. Large, round seed; buff-colored, splashed with reddish-purple; pods 6 to 7 inches long, ivory-tan, streaked with red. Green shelled beans have excellent flavor and texture, either fresh, frozen or canned. Bicolor lavender flowers. Originally from Tierra del Fuego, Argentina, at the southern tip of South America. A2, *A75*, D87, G6, I77, K17M, K49M

Vermont Cranberry: 60 days. Very popular heirloom bean from New England. Medium-sized, oval-shaped seed; cranberry-colored, mottled and striped with maroon; pod 5 inches long, streaked with red; 5 to 6 seeds per pod; sweet, succulent flavor; easy to shell. High-yielding plant; hardy; disease and drought resistant. Introduced prior to 1876. A2, D87, F24M, J73, M46, N39

Pole

Cranberry Pole: Largest podded and seeded horticultural type. Light buff-colored seed, splashed with dark red; deep orange eye ring. Thick, oval pod, 6 to 7 inches long; dark-green, turning yellowish-green tinged with purple at maturity. G93M

King Horticultural: (Worcester Horticultural, Mammoth Podded Horticultural) Largest-podded and largest-seeded of the horticultural beans, also the most attractively colored and most showy in pod. Long, plump seeds, colored like those of Wren's Egg. Excellent for shelling. Pods 6 to 7 inches long, 7 seeds per pod. Originated near Worcester, Massachusetts. Introduced in 1894. HEDRICK 1931; A25, *I59M*, K10, K49M, M95M, N52

Lingua di Fuoco: Large, straight to slightly curved, roundish pods; 1/2 inch in diameter, 4 1/2 to 5 inches long; striped and splashed with bright red. Seeds salmon colored, striped with white. Fresh beans may be harvested in about 80 days, dry beans after 125 days. Q11M

Red Speckled Fall: 105 days. Large, elongated, plump seeds; light buff, abundantly splashed and streaked with dark-red; excellent flavor. Green shell beans are eaten fresh or canned, however best used as dry shell beans which cook up to make a delicious brown gravy. Drought and heat resistant. Doss family heirloom from Adams County, Ohio. L7M

Stregonta: (Sciabola Rossa) 130 days. Long, slightly curved pods, prominently striped and splashed with bright red; containing large bright red, marbled seeds. Vigorous, highly productive vine. Highly esteemed in Italy for fresh market and home garden use. Q11M

Vermont Cranberry Pole: 60 days. Nearly identical to Vermont Cranberry, except for the climbing habit. Widely adapted plant; produces an abundant supply of tender, flavorful beans. Recommended as a green shelling bean; also very good as a dry baking bean. Very popular in Vermont. A2, M46

Wren's Egg: (Speckled Cranberry, London Horticultural, Bird's Egg) 75 days. Large, broad-oval, very plump seed; light buff, streaked with dark red. Very mealy and flavorful as a green shell bean; also good for baking and stewing when dry. Flat, carmine-streaked pod; of fair quality as a snap bean. Introduced into the United States from England, about 1825. BURR, HEDRICK 1931; E59Z, K49M, K71, M46

SNAP BEANS

Also called *string beans*, although most modern cultivars are stringless or nearly so. Grown for the pods which are cooked when young or at the stage of maturity when they can rightly be called string beans.

GREEN-PODDED

Bush

Baccicia: 52 days. Italian style snap bean. Semi-flat pod; 6 1/2 inches long, 3/8 inch in diameter; tender, stringless, flavor distinct. Seed dull-red, speckled with white. Good for fresh home garden use; not recommended for freezing. Height 18 to 21 inches. G51, G93M

Black Valentine: (Stringless Black Valentine) 50 days. Slender, nearly straight, light-green pod; 5 to 6 1/2 inches long; distinctive flavor. Glossy, jet black seeds. Good for shipping; not recommended for canning. Also used as a dry shell bean for soup. Very hardy plant; height 12 to 14 inches. Introduced in 1897. HEDRICK 1931; A2, *A75*, E59Z, F24M, *G1M*, G57M, G71, H66, J25M, K49M, K49T, L7M, L14, L79M, M46, M95, etc.

Blue Lake Bush: 55 days. Round, slightly curved, dark-green pod; 5 1/2 to 6 1/2 inches long; excellent texture and flavor. Seed white, slow to develop. Especially good for freezing. Popular with commercial canners and packers. Vigorous, upright plant; highly productive over a long period; sets well under adverse weather conditions. A16, A25, B49, B75M, C44, C92, D82, E24, F82, H94, K5M, L59, L97, M13M, M46, etc.

Bountiful: 50 days. Broad, medium-round, yellowish-green pod; 6 to 7 inches long; stringless, brittle, fine-textured, of excellent quality. Good for shipping. Dull straw-yellow seeds. High yielding, dwarf plant; height 15 to 18 inches. Introduced in 1898 by Peter Henderson & Company. HEDRICK 1931; A25, *A69M*, B73M, C44, G57M, G71, H54, H66, J20, J34, K27M, K49M, K71, M46, N16, etc.

Brezobel Stringless: 57 days. French-style slicing bean. Long, broad, flat pod; 6 to 9 inches long, 1 inch in diameter; entirely stringless. White-seeded. Should be picked when young, at about 3/4 inch wide; if picked too late they will be fibrous inside. High yielding plant; disease resistant. Sow only in warm soil; very sensitive to weather changes. C85M

Bulgarian:[5] 50-60 days. Long, flat pod; 6 to 8 inches in length; green, with light violet spots; stringless, of very good flavor. Seed light brown, mottled with violet. For fresh market use. Suitable for early spring, summer and early autumn planting. T27M

Commodore: (Bush Kentucky Wonder) 60 days. Very similar to Kentucky Wonder, but requires no staking. Nearly round, stringless, dark-green pods; 7 to 8 inches long; brittle, meaty, flavorful. Good for canning and freezing. Brilliant, carmine-colored seeds. Upright, high-yielding plant. All America Selections Winner in 1938. A27M, D11M, D76, F19M, F24M, G57M, G79, H66, J58, K27M, K49M, K71, L14, N16

Contender: (Early Contender) 50 days. Oval, slightly curved, medium-green pod; 6 to 7 inches long; tender and stringless. Seed buff-colored, mottled with brown. Matures over a short period of time; ideal for canning and freezing. Vigorous, erect plant; tolerant to hot weather, mosaic and mildew. A87M, B35M, B49, B75M, E38, F19M, F82, G71, H42, *H61*, H66, J7, K73, L7M, N16, etc.

Cyrus: 50 days. Gourmet French style bean that is easy to grow. Very long, slim pod; straight and rounded; excellent flavor and quality. No slicing or preparation required, therefore no loss of flavor. Seed tan, mottled with dark brown. Highly prolific plant; height 16 to 18 inches. K49T, L9, L91M

Daisy:[1] 55 days. "Cascade" or "teepee" type. Medium-green, round pod, 6 to 7 inches long; almost completely stringless; very meaty and flavorful. White-seeded. Seeds develop slowly for an extra-long harvest season. Vigorous, high yielding plant; sets pods well above the foliage for easy picking; resistant to common bean mosaic virus. B73M, D65, D76, E3, E97, G57M, G68, G79, J58, K71

Dandy:[3] 54 days. Gourmet French type "mini bean". Round, slender, straight medium dark-green pod; only 4 inches long; stringless, very tender and flavorful. Small white seed, slow to develop. Erect, compact plant; high yielding; resistant to anthracnose and bean mosaic viruses. Introduced in 1982 by Rogers Brothers Seed Company. A16, *A69M*, B71, C92, D11M, F1, *G13M*, I39, L79, M29

Derby:[2] 57 days. Slender, attractive green pods, up to 7 inches long. Retains good flavor and texture at maximum pod length due to slow seed development. Very upright, bushy plants, height 14 to 20 inches; resistant to common bean mosaic virus. Pods slip easily from stems without the pedicels, making picking easier. All America Selections winner for 1990. B75, D11M, I39, I91, K10, L42, M29, M49, N52

Deuil Fin Precoce: (Petit Gris) An old European favorite. Steel-grey-green pod, of very fine flavor. Seed buff-colored, mottled with purple. Compact, bush-type plant; very high yielding. Ideal for growing under frames, poly tunnels or cloches. B49

Dutch Stringless Green Pod: 50 days. The original Dutch Dubbele Witte zonder draad, a double podded type. Short, green pods; excellent "real" bean flavor. White-seeded. Should only be planted in warm soil during warm weather as it is very sensitive to changes in weather. High yielding, but smaller pods. C85M

Earliserve: 45 days. Very early Blue Lake type. Straight, slender, dark-green pods; 4 inches long. Should be picked often for best quality. Ideal for French style beans. Sturdy, upright plant, height 18 inches. Tolerant to common bean mosaic virus. Recommended for home gardens, fresh markets and pick-your-own operations. B75M, D11M, E97, F44, I64, K10, L42, M95M

E-Z Pick:[2] 55 days. Round, straight, dark-green pods; 6 to 6 1/2 inches long. Very good flavor and texture, fresh, frozen or canned. Unique growth habit, with most of the crop set on top of the plant, on stiff upright stems. Pods hang freely, stay straight, and are easily separated from the plant. Tolerant to common bean mosaic virus. B73M, D65, E97, G6, G27M, I91, L42, N52

Frenchie:[3] (Frenchy) 43 days. Gourmet European "mini bean"; much milder and sweeter than American types. Slender, round dark-green pod; only 3 3/4 inches long; unusually crisp and tender. Small, white seed. Compact, highly productive plant, to 12 inches high; tolerant to common bean mosaic. Featured as a special dish in 4 Star Hotels. G82, L42

Green Ruler: 52 days. High quality bush Romano type. Thick, flat, medium-green pods; 5 to 6 inches long; very meaty, slow to develop any toughness or fiber; distinctive "beany" flavor. Can also be used as a green shell bean. Freezes and cans well. Upright plant, 18 inches tall, highly productive. Resistant to common bean mosaic viruses. Developed by Shigemi Honma of Michigan State University. Introduced in 1977. A13, *F63*, G82, L91M, *S63M*

Green Teepee:[1] 52 days. Straight, round, medium-green pods; 5 to 6 inches long; of very good flavor. "Cascade" or "teepee" type, with pods that are carried well above the foliage, making harvesting easy and providing protection from dirt. H42

Greencrop: 50 days. Broad, flattened, medium-green pod; 6 to 8 inches long; tender and stringless; holds up well on the vine; matures over a short harvest season. White-seeded. Vigorous, upright plant. Bred for northern areas; does not perform well in heat or drought. All America Selections winner in 1957. A87M, B75, C85M, D11M, E24, *F72*, G51, G93M, H66, J34, K49M, K73, L42, M46, N16, etc.

Harvester: Medium-green, round, straight pod; 5 to 6 inches long; white-seeded. Excellent for canning and shipping. Tall, upright plant; high yielding; suitable for mechanical harvesting; resistant to common bean mosaic and the New York 15 strain of bean virus. A69M, *A75*, B75M, C85M, D11M, F92, G27M, G57M, G79, *H61*, K10, M13M, N16, P83M

Harvester Teepee:[1] 51 days. Round, slender, medium-green pods; 8 inches long; of high quality and very good flavor. Produces over a long period. "Teepee" or "cascade bean", with a unique growth habit that facilitates ease of picking and provides protection from dirt. *A75*, J20

Jumbo: 55 days. Bush Romano type. Very large, flattened, dark-green pod; strong, rich, beany flavor; of gourmet quality. Best picked when 6 to 7 inches long, but still stringless at 10 inches or longer. Excellent for freezing. Vigorous plant; tends to lodge with the weight of the pods. Romano x Kentucky Wonder. C44, D11M, D76, E97, F42, G6, G71M, G82, I91, J20, J34, K49T, L91M, M46, N16, etc.

Mini Green:[3] 52 days. Gourmet "mini" or "baby bean". Produces slender, dark-green beans, only 4 inches long; very tender and flavorful; requires no snapping. Excellent fresh, frozen, canned or pickled. For longest harvests and best quality, pods should be picked just as they mature. I91

Montana Green: 50 days. Medium-sized, round, medium-green pod; 6 to 7 inches long; crisp, tender, entirely stringless. Light-buff seeds. Good for freezing and canning. Highly productive. Developed in Montana. Does well in short season areas. D82, F44

Provider: 50 days. Straight, round, medium-green pods; 5 to 6 inches long; tender, low in fiber, slow to wilt. Vigorous, productive plant, bears a concentrated set. Resistant to common mosaic virus and the N.Y. 15 stain; tolerant of powdery mildew. Germinates well in cool spring soils. Standard early market cultivar. D27, E24, F13, F44, G6, G79, H54, *H61*, H66, J20, J84, J97M, K27M, K73, L9M, M49, etc.

Radar: 50 days. Gourmet multi-podded type. Round, very slender, medium-green pod; 6 to 7 inches long; tender, flavorful, entirely stringless. Can be picked at 4 inches in length and cooked without slicing, or left to mature, when it still remains tender. Does not ship well. Height 12 to 15 inches. *A75*, F33

Regal Salad:[4] 52 days. Unique salad bean, without the slightly fuzzy texture present in most beans. Curved pod, 5 to 6 inches long, an unusual bronze in color; excellent flavor raw, superior when cooked. Erect, productive plant. Developed by Professor Elwyn Meader. J20

Remus:[1] 45 days. Produces clusters of pods well above the foliage, making harvesting easy and providing protection from dirt. Long, straight, round pods; up to 10 inches in length; fiberless, tender and flavorful. Vigorous plant, 18 to 20 inches tall; resistant to common bean mosaic virus. I91, L91M

Roma: (Romano) 59 days. Broad, flat, straight medium-green pod; 5 to 5 1/2 inches long; stringless, fleshy, strong distinctive flavor; holds its quality well on the vine. White-seeded. Excellent for French-style sliced beans. Upright plant; productive over a long season; tolerant to bean rust. A25, B35M, D11M, D76, F19M, *F72*, H66, H95, I67M, J7, J58, L97, M13M, M49, N39, etc.

Roma II: 59 days. Bush Romano type; more uniform and higher yielding than other cultivars. Broad, flat, very straight pod; 5 inches long, 3/4 inch in diameter; same distinctive flavor as the traditional pole Romano; holds it quality well. Upright plant, with a concentrated pod set; tolerant to common bean mosaic and several races of bean rust. Introduced in 1979. A16, B75, C44, F1, G16, G71, G93M, *H61*, J34, K66, K71, K73, L79, M29, N16, etc.

Romanette: 60 days. Bush Romano strain with straighter pods than most Romano types. Broad, flat, medium-green pods, 5 to 6 inches long; crisp and tender with a rich, distinctive flavor. Sturdy, upright plant, 16 to 18 inches tall. Resistant to common bean mosaic viruses. A69M, C92, G79, H33, I64

Slenderette: 53 days. Slender, straight, glossy dark-green pod; 5 inches long; stringless, tender and flavorful. Small white seed; slow to develop. Vigorous plant, to 20 inches tall; highly productive over a long period; resistant to common bean mosaic, pod mottle, and curly top virus. *A69M*, D11M, E97, G87, H33, H95, I64, I67M, I84, J25M, K10, M46, M95M, N39

Spartan Arrow: 52 days. Straight, slender, medium-green pods; 5 1/2 to 6 1/2 inches long; meaty, tender, stringless. Excellent for freezing and French style beans. Vigorous, upright plant, height 22 to 24 inches; produces a heavy, concentrated set. Resistant to common bean mosaic virus and the N.Y. 15 strain. Developed at Michigan State University. *A1*, D76, *F63*, *G13M*, *H61*, H66, H94, J84, K73, L14

Stringless Green Pod: (Burpee's Stringless Green Pod) 50 days. Broad, slightly curved, medium dark-green pod; 5 to 6 inches long; fleshy, very brittle, of excellent flavor and quality. Light coffee-brown seed. High yielding plant; height 12 to 15 inches. Introduced in 1894 as the first entirely stringless green podded bean. HEDRICK 1931; A16, A25, B73M, D65, *F72*, F92, H42, H66, H94, J34, K71, L59, M46, N16, N39, etc.

Tendercrop: 55 days. Round, medium-green, stringless pod; 5 to 6 inches long. Seed purple, mottled with tan, slow to develop. For fresh use, canning and freezing. Adapted to mechanical harvesting; also good for home gardens. Upright plant, 18 to 21 inches tall; yields up to 5 tons per acre; resistant to powdery mildew and bean mosaic virus. *A69M*, B73M, C44, D76, E57, F82, G51, H42, I91, J97M, K10, K71, L79M, M46, N16, etc.

Tendergreen: Round, slightly curved, dark-green pod; 4 1/2 to 6 1/2 inches long; stringless, fleshy, tender, brittle, fine-textured, of excellent quality. Seeds brownish-purple, mottled with buff. Good home garden cultivar. Very erect, compact plant, 14 to 18 inches tall; highly productive over a short season; resistant to bean mosaic virus. Introduced in 1922. HEDRICK 1931; A16, A25, A69M, B49, C44, C92, D76, F19M, F92, G71, *H61*, H66, J20, J34, J58, L97, etc.

Tennessee Green Pod: 50 days. Broad, fairly plump, medium dark-green pod; 5 1/2 to 7 inches long; very good flavor. Should be harvested early as mature pods tend to become coarse and fibrous. Medium brown seed. Very dwarf plant, rarely over 1 foot tall. Introduced to the trade in 1904, but grown in the South for many years prior to this date. HEDRICK 1931; A27M, F19M, *G1M*, G27M, G57M, G82, H66, *I59M*, K27M, L14, M46, M95M

The Prince: 55 days. Broad, flat, straight medium-green pod; 6 1/2 inches long; fleshy, very flavorful, stringless if picked young. Seed buff-colored, mottled with reddish-brown. Excellent for freezing. Vigorous, heavy yielding plant. Very popular in England. Highly commended by the Royal Horticultural Society in 1982. Introduced by Sutton and Sons in 1927. HEDRICK 1931; B49, L91M, O53M, *R23*, S59M, S61

Top Crop: 52 days. Round, straight, light medium-green pod; 6 to 7 inches long; stringless, meaty, tender. Seed buff-colored, mottled with brown, develops rapidly. Excellent for canning and freezing. High yielding plant; resistant to powdery mildew and bean mosaic virus. Developed for home garden use. All America Selections winner in 1950. A16, B73M, B75M, C85M, D82, F19M, F44, G16, H42, *H61*, H94, J58, K73, M46, M95, N16, etc.

Pole

Alabama No. 1: (Alabama No. 1 Purple Pod) Thick, oval pod; silver-green, tinged with purple; up to 7 inches long; of excellent flavor, stringless when young. Black-seeded. Vigorous vine; resistant to nematodes. Well suited to growing among corn, having good shade tolerance. Introduced about 1938. F19M, L7M

Blauhilde: A stringless blue pole bean with long, round fleshy pods, 9 inches in length. Higher yielding and healthier than other blue pole types. Turns green when cooked. C85M, N81

Blue Lake Pole: 65 days. Straight, round, dark-green pod; 5 1/2 to 6 inches long, 3/8 inch in diameter; stringless, tender, fleshy, fiberless, distinct flavor. Excellent for canning and freezing. Strong climbing vine; height 5 to 6 feet; heavy yielding over a long period. Widely grown in the Pacific Northwest. A25, A87M, C44, C85M, D11M, D82, E24, E38, F82, H66, H94, L79, L89, M46, M49, etc.

Blue Lake Stringless: 65 days. Round, slightly curved pods, 6 inches long; tender, fleshy, entirely stringless and fiberless; notable fresh, sweet, "beany" flavor. Excellent for fresh eating, canning or freezing. High yielding vine; height 5 to 6 feet; bears continuously throughout the summer. A69M, D27, F80, *G1M*, K5M, M95M

Caseknife: 60 days. One of the oldest cultivars in America, the name Caseknife, and its many strains or synonyms having been noted in the literature since 1820. Slender, flattened, straight, medium-green pod; 7 1/2 to 9 inches long; stringless when young. White-seeded. Strong climbing plant; height 4 t 4 1/2 feet tall; productive over a relatively long period. HEDRICK 1931; G6

Champagne: 60 days. Slender, flat green pod; 8 inches long; stringless until quite large, of high quality. Large white seed; 8 seeds per pod. Also used as a green or dry shell bean. Vigorous, unusually productive vine; height 10 feet. Heirloom. G6

Cherokee Trail of Tears:[5] 85-95 days. Cultivated by the Cherokee Nation, and taken with them over the Trail of Tears when forcibly removed from their lands by the United States Army in the 1800's. Pods 6 to 7 inches long; dark-green striped with purple, turning red when mature. Black-seeded. Also used as a green or dry shell bean. Very productive vine; requires strong support; attractive light-purple flower. D87

Garrafal Oro: (Spanish Gigantic Romano) 65 days. Broad, flattened, light medium-green pod; 9 inches long; juicy, thick-walled, excellent distinct flavor. Pale reddish-brown seed. For home gardens or market. Short vine, rarely exceeding 4 feet; needs less support than other pole types; highly prolific. *A75*, F42, I77, L91M, Q24M, S61

Genuine Cornfield: (Scotia) 75 days. Round, plump, straight pod; 6 to 7 inches long; medium dark-green, shaded with purple-brown at later stages; quite stringy, fleshy, fairly brittle, of very fine texture. Seed buff-colored, mottled with pinkish-brown. Large, vigorous vine; good climbing habit, to 4 1/2 feet tall. Traditionally grown among corn plants. Introduced in 1892 by Joseph Harris Company. HEDRICK 1931; B71, D76, F19M, *G1M*, G79, H66, *I59M*, I99, J73, K27M, K49M, L7M, L14, M46, M95M, etc.

Green Anellino: Unusual, crescent shaped pods; 1/4 to 1/2 inch in diameter, 3 1/2 to 4 1/2 inches long; rounded in form, fleshy, free of strings, rich Romano-like flavor. First harvests in about 85 days. Italian heirloom, much in demand by American chefs due to its flavor and unique shape. C53, Q11M

Jeminez:[5] (Idaho Wonder) 66 days. Long, broad, straight flat-oval pod; 8 to 10 inches in length; light-green, with numerous purple-red stripes and splashes; stringless of high quality; resembles Oregon Giant. Seed buff-colored, striped with brown. Vigorous vine; productive over an extended period. Potential specialty market item. *A75*, D82, G6

Kentucky Mountain Greasy: A long time favorite in the mountains of Kentucky and Tennessee, due to its distinctive flavor. B71

Kentucky Wonder: (Old Homestead, Texas Pole) 70 days. Broad, curved, wrinkled light silver-green pod; 7 to 9 inches long; brittle, tender, slightly stringy, of very good quality and flavor. Buff-brown seed. Medium-sized plant; height 4 1/2 feet; productive over a relatively short period. Most popular pole bean in the United States. Introduced prior to 1864. HEDRICK 1931; A16, B73M, B75M, B78, C44, E24, *H61*, H66, H94, K73, L7M, L9M, M13M, M46

Large Early Greasy: 65 days. Pods grow 4 to 6 inches long, are flattened when young, and have medium strings. Makes a high quality snap bean when picked small. The name "greasy" refers to the lack of plant hairs on the pods. An heirloom from the mountain area of Mars Hill, North Carolina. Has been grown for generations as a drought resistant, cornfield bean. Not a pure strain. U33

Logan Giant: West Virginia heirloom; also a local favorite in southwest Virginia, North Carolina and Tennessee. Pods 5 to 6 inches long; stringless when young. Large, slightly flattened seed, brown with cream frosting on one end, usually 6 per pod. Best used as a dry shell bean. Height 15 inches. L7M

McCaslan: 65 days. Flat, irregularly curved, dark-green pod; 7 to 8 inches long; fleshy, fairly brittle and tender, somewhat stringy, of very good flavor. White seeded. Also used as a green or dry shell bean. Highly productive over a long season. Popular in the South. Originated with the McCaslan family of Georgia. Introduced in 1912 by Hastings Seed Company. HEDRICK 1931; B71, F19M, *F63*, *G1M*, G79, H66, *I59M*, J73, K10, K27M, K71, L7M, M95M

Missouri Wonder: 65 days. Round, plump, slightly curved, medium-green pod; 5 1/2 to 6 inches long; medium-fine in texture, stringless when quite young. Seed mottled tan, striped with brown. Also used as a shell bean. Large, vigorous vine; very reliable yields. Good for planting among corn. Introduced about 1931. HEDRICK 1931; B71, G67M, *I59M*, K10, K27M, K71, M46

Morse's Pole No. 191: 63 days. High-yielding, white-seeded Kentucky Wonder type, resistant to certain strains of rust. Oval, straight dark-green pod; 8 to 9 inches long; stringless at marketable stage. For home gardens or market. *D74*, G27M, H66

Neckarkonigin: 65-70 days. An improved Phenomeen type from Germany. Very long, slender, firm green pod; to 9 inches in length; very fleshy, of excellent flavor, stringless. White-seeded. Can also be used for French-style slicing. C85M, N81, P9

Oregon Giant:[5] (Paul Bunyon) 75 days. Large, broad pod; curved in an S-shape; 8 1/2 to 9 1/2 inches long; light waxy-green, strikingly marked with brownish-purple; meaty, flavorful, stringless when young. Also used as a shell bean. Vigorous climber; highly productive. Very popular in the Pacific Northwest. E24{CF}, F82, F92, H94, I99, J20

Phenomeen: (Phenomenon, Phénomène) 68 days. Extra long, flat-round, nearly straight medium-green pod; 7 1/2 to 9 1/2 inches in length; very fleshy, of excellent flavor, more or less stringy when old, but not fibrous. White-seeded. Originated in Germany about 1905; introduced into the United States in 1913. HEDRICK 1931; C85M, P59M

Poamoho: 66 days. Resistant to nematodes and rust. Well adapted to tropical conditions. Developed by the University of Hawaii's College of Tropical Agriculture. L9M, M19, M32M

Princesse Race Pévir: 60 days. French mangetout type; similar to Cristal. Slightly curved, sub-cylindrical pod; 4 to 6 inches long; green, turning yellow when ripe; free of string or fiber, of excellent flavor. White-seeded. Also used as a shell bean. Moderately vigorous, high yielding plant; height 6 to 6 1/2 feet. F33, P59M

Rattlesnake:[5] 75 days. Round, firm pod; 7 inches long; dark-green, streaked with purple; rich, full-flavored, stringless when small to medium-sized. Seeds light-buff, splashed with brown. Strong climbing vine, to 10 feet tall; very productive; tolerant to heat and drought. *A75*, H66, L7M, L14, *L59G*, M95

Red Speckled Cutshort: (Cutshort) 75 days. Short, very plump pods, 3 to 4 inches long; abruptly rounded to truncate on the end; brittle, fairly fleshy, slightly stringy, flavor excellent. Small, flattened seeds; gray, dotted and splashed with purple crimson; very crowded in the pod. Popular in the South. Known as early as 1835 under the name Corn Bean. HEDRICK 1931; U33

Rentegevers: 75 days. Flat, slender green pod; 6 to 8 inches long; stringless, of excellent flavor. Highly productive over a relatively long period. Originally from the Netherlands. Rentegevers means "interest givers" in Dutch. D87

Romano: (Romano Italian Pole) 65 days. Broad, flat, thick medium-green pod; 5 1/2 to 6 inches long; stringless but slightly fibrous, meaty, rich distinctive flavor; excellent for canning and freezing. Seed buff-colored, with a white eye. Also used as a green shell bean. For home gardens and fresh market. Weak climber. *A69M*, B73M, C44, C85M, D65, F19M, G51, G71, J7, J34, K10, K71, M13M, M46, M95, etc.

Ruth Bible: 52 days. Small pods, about 3 1/2 inches long. Brownish-tan seeds. Best picked when tender and small, as larger pods may have slight strings. Vigorous, trailing vine; bears heavily. A good cornfield bean that does very well in drought. Family heirloom from Kentucky, where it has been grown since at least 1832. I99, L7M

Selma Zebrina:[5] 58 days. Successor to Selma Zebra, with earlier maturity and higher yields. Matures as early as a bush bean, grows only to a height of 6 feet. Light green pod, striped and splashed with purple; stringless, tender, fleshy, highly aromatic and flavorful. Turns green when cooked. Excellent fresh, dried or frozen. I91

Sultans Emerald Moon: (Sultan's Emerald Crescent) During the last century of the Ottoman Empire, strains of pole beans were developed whose pods mimicked the Crescent, the royal symbol of the Sultans. Thought to have been lost, they were recently re-discovered in the kitchen garden of a wealthy tobacco merchant in Izmir, Turkey. Delicious, subtle flavor. Vigorous and disease resistant. D62, K49M

Turkey Craw: Southeastern heirloom from Virginia, North Carolina and Tennessee. According to folklore, it was first cultivated by a hunter who removed a bean from the craw of a turkey he shot, hence the name. Pod grows 3 1/2 to 4 inches long and clings to the vine. Stringless, of excellent fresh quality; also good for drying ("leather britches on a shuck"). Often used as a cornfield bean. L7M

GREEN-PODDED FILET Called *haricot verts* in France, *filet beans* are special green-podded beans bred so that the seeds develop more slowly than in regular beans. Therefore the pods have exceptional flavor and texture; since the flavor, which researchers believe comes from the seed, has time to develop without affecting texture. *N40*{PR}

Bush

Aiguille Vert: 49-57 days. Round, slender, medium dark-green pod; 7 to 8 inches long; meaty, excellent flavor, stringless when young. Best harvested immature, as gourmet "filet" beans. Yellow-buff seed. For home gardens or market. G68

Alpental: 46 days. Uniform, straight, slightly flattened pod; of pleasant flavor, but not as pronounced as other "filet" beans. Matures early and can be harvested over a period of 5 weeks. Vigorous, upright, disease-resistant plant. *A75*, J20

Aramis:[5] 70 days. Uniform, round, very slender pods; 5 to 6 inches long; medium-green, slightly streaked with purple. Excellent flavor and texture, both raw and cooked. Rated highest in flavor in a taste test conducted by Organic Gardening magazine. Vigorous, erect, high-yielding plant; adapted to mechanical harvesting; resistant to mosaic and anthracnose. C85M

Bahalores: 58 days. Round, very slender, medium dark-green pod; 5 1/2 to 6 1/2 inches long; tender, fleshy, extremely flavorful, stringless when immature. Small, white seeds. Best harvested when 4 to 5 inches in length. Resistant to haloblight, anthracnose and bean common mosaic virus 1 & 2. *A75*, D68, J20, K49M

Camile: 55 days. Very straight, slender, medium to dark-green pod; 5 to 7 inches long; tender and flavorful. Black seeded. High yielding plant; can produce up to 12 ounces of beans per square foot of growing space, nearly twice as much as the standard cultivars Fin de Bagnols and Triomphe de Farcy. Resistant to common bean mosaic. Developed in Holland. C53, G64, *R11M*

Delinel: 54 days. An improved strain of Fin de Bagnols. Very slender, straight, medium dark-green pod; 7 to 8 inches long; stringless, tender and flavorful; holds well on the vine. Small-seeded. Best picked when 1/3 inch in diameter or less. Black-seeded. Good fresh canned or frozen. Vigorous, erect, highly productive plant; resistant to common bean mosaic and anthracnose. *D74*, *F72*, J73, M46, M49

Fin de Bagnols: 55 days. Traditional French "filet" bean. Round, straight, very slender, medium dark-green pod; 7 to 8 inches long, 3/8 inch in diameter; tender, sweet, delicate "beany" flavor. Buff-red mottled seed. High yielding plant; resistant to black root. Bagnols is not far from Paris, and it appears that this bean was a specialty of that region during the 19th century. C53, F33, G68, *R11M*

Finaud: A true "filet" bean that is no more difficult to grow than common snap beans. Very slim, straight pods, 6 to 8 inches long. Holds well on the plant without loss of quality. Produces over 75% beans that rated grade A in taste and texture, compared to only 15 to 25% for the standard cultivars Fin de Bagnols and Triomphe de Farcy, even when picked every 3 days. Developed in Holland. C53, K49Z

La Belle:[3] 50 days. "Mini" or "baby" filet bean. Straight, very slender pods; only 3 to 4 1/2 inches long and 1/4 inch in diameter when mature; tender and juicy, of excellent flavor. Should be harvested every other day. Sturdy, compact plant, height 2 to 2 1/2 feet; bears heavily. The current favorites in upscale Continental markets. K66

Marbel:[5] 54 days. New filet bean from France. Very straight, slender, round pod; 7 inches long, 1/4 inch in diameter; dark-green, prominently streaked with violet; very attractive and flavorful. Seed tan, streaked with dark purple. Compact, upright plant; continuous flowering habit allows for 4 or 5 additional harvests; resistant to common mosaic and anthracnose. G6, I77, S95M

Morgane: 54 days. Extra-long, smooth, solid medium-green pod; length 7 to 7 1/2 inches; slightly more slender than Marbel; very good flavor, excellent quality. Brown-seeded. Semi-concentrated harvest. Resistant to common mosaic and anthracnose. Very promising for commercial production. G6, P59M

Nerina: Filet-mangetout type, bred for both "filet" and whole bean use. Slender, glossy dark-green pod; 4 1/2 to 5 inches long; excellent flavor and quality. Should be harvested daily, before they reach 1 inch in diameter. Uniform pod set; high on the plant. D11M

Regalfin:[5] Excellent French cultivar. Very long and straight, round, narrow, filet type pods; attractively marbled with violet; of fine quality. Violet-striped seeds. High yielding, produces numerous pods in clusters. Introduced by Vilmorin. G68

Royalnel: Medium early, filet type. Pods exceptionally long, up to 8 inches in length, perfectly round, very slender; flesh meaty, of excellent quality. Black seeded. High yielding plant; resistant to anthracnose and bean mosaic virus; not subject to lodging. May be sown over a long season. G68, K66, S95M

Triomphe de Farcy:[5] 55 days. Traditional standard in France. Round, slender, straight pod; 5 to 6 inches long, 1/4 inch in diameter; rich bright-green, faintly striped with purplish-blue; tender, extremely flavorful, of excellent quality. Seed dark-brown, mottled with purple. Highly productive plant; resistant to black root. B75, C53, C85M, F33, G6, G68, Q34, *R11M*

Vernandon: 55 days. Filet-mangetout type, a cross between a "filet" bean and a conventional snap bean. Round, pencil-thin, straight deep-green pod; 6 inches long; brittle, tender and flavorful. Should be harvested every 2 to 3 days, when pods are less than 1/4 inch in diameter. Vigorous, high yielding plant; resistant to common bean mosaic and anthracnose. B75, I77, K66

Pole

Fortex: 60 days. Round, extra-long, dark green pod; up to 11 inches in length or more; firm-textured, very flavorful, completely stringless at all stages. Walnut brown seed. May be picked when 7 inches long for extra-fine grade "filet" beans. For home fresh use and freezing, and premium markets. Early and very productive. G6

<u>PURPLE-PODDED</u> Sometimes referred to as *magic beans*, purple-podded beans have excellent flavor and turn dark green when cooked. The plants are especially resistant to cool weather conditions early in the growing season. *N40*{PR}

Bush

Purple Knight: Round, rich dark-purple pod, tender and stringless. Turns dark green when cooked. Excellent raw as an attractive enhancement for salads and vegetable trays. Does well in colder soils. T1M

Purple Queen: 52 days. Round, straight, very evenly colored pod; dark purple, fairly glossy; 6 to 7 inches long; stringless, very flavorful. Seed light brown, shaded with purple. Turns dark green when cooked. Very productive plant; dark purple leaves and flowers; tolerant to bean common mosaic virus and cold soil conditions. *A75*, B35M, D11M, G64, I77

Purple Rouge: (Purple Duke) Unique Bush Blue Lake type with purple pods. Very good quality and flavor. *A75*

Purple Teepee:[1] 51 days. Round, slightly curved, smooth, dark purple pod; 5 to 6 inches long; stringless, tender and flavorful. Light brown seed. Turns an attractive deep forest-green when cooked. Good fresh, canned or frozen. Compact, high yielding plant; bears pods well above the foliage; resistant to mosaic and white and gray molds. *A75*, F19M, G71, I91, J20, L91M

Royal Burgundy: 55 days. Round, slightly curved, dark-purple pod; 5 to 6 inches long; stringless, tender, very rich flavored. Buff-colored seed. Turns bright green after 2 minutes of boiling, providing a built-in blanching indicator for home freezing. Vigorous, upright plant; height 18 to 20 inches. Developed at the University of New Hampshire. A16, C44, C53, C85M, C92, D82, *F72*, G16, H42, H94, K66, L89, L97, M46, N39, etc.

Royalty: 55 days. Round, variably curved, bright-purple pod; 5 inches long; stringless, tender, brittle; quality good, both fresh and frozen. Buff-colored seed. Can be used raw to add color to salads; turns green when cooked. Purple-tinged, purple-flowered plant; produces short runners that do not require staking; germinates in cold, wet soil; resists bean beetles. Developed by Professor E.M. Meader at the University of New Hampshire. A25, B73M, D11M, D65, E24, G6, H66, I77, K71, K73, L7M, L9M, L79, N16

Sequoia: Bush Romano type. Attractive deep purple pods, with typical Romano flavor and meatiness. Purple color makes harvesting easier. A visual as well as a culinary prize. *A75*, C53, I77

Pole

Blue Coco: 55 days. Bluish-purple pods; 6 inches long; 7 seeds per pod. Retains its crisp texture when pickled; excellent for dill beans. Light-cocoa-colored seed. Very productive plant; produces well under high temperature conditions. Very early. K49M

Dow Purple Pod: 85 days. Flat, deep-purple pod; 7 to 8 inches long; good "beany" flavor. Tan, kidney-shaped seeds; 5 seeds per pod. Vigorous, productive vine, requires strong support; purple-tinged leaves, purple stems and flowers. Heirloom. I99, K49T

Louisiana Purple Pod: 67 days. Attractive southern heirloom. Rounded, bright deep-purple pod; 7 to 7 1/2 inches long; stringless when young, very flavorful. Small, light to medium brown seeds. Very productive plant, with bright purple stems and flowers; tolerant to heat and drought. Does well in the North. H66, K49Z, L7M, L14

Purple Peacock: 68 days. Round, reddish-purple pod; tender, stringless, of very good quality. Turns an attractive dark-green after 2 minutes of cooking. Can also be used as a shell bean. Extremely productive vine; purple leaves and flowers. Makes an attractive, quick-growing summer screen. *A75*, B35M, I39, J20

Trionfo Violetto: Large, straight pods; 1/2 inch in diameter, 9 to 10 inches long; an attractive, deep purple color; excellent flavor, free of strings. Turns bright green when cooked. Straw colored seeds. Vigorous, disease resistant, highly productive vines; widely adapted. Good for small gardens. C53, P83M, Q11M

Viola Cornetti: A traditional purple-podded climbing bean from Italy. Produces abundant crops of tender, stringless violet-colored pods, of excellent flavor and quality. Turns green when cooked. S55

Violet Podded Stringless: 67 days. Round, violet-purple pod; 7 inches long; highly refined, tender, stringless pods. Light brown seed. Retains its flavor and high quality even after it becomes very long. High yielding plant; occasionally sets pods that are not completely purple. Germinates well in cool soil; flowers early; tolerant to cool weather. L89

WAX-PODDED

Bush

Beurre de Rocquencourt: (Golden Rocky) 55 days. Very attractive traditional French cultivar. Round-oval, slender, straight, dark golden-yellow pod; 5 to 6 inches long; stringless, fleshy, flavorful. Black-seeded. Excellent for home gardens and local markets. Upright, very prolific plant; resistant to cold and wet growing conditions early in the season. *A75*, C53, C85M, D68, F33, H42, J20, L89

Brittle Wax: (Round Pod Kidney Wax, Burpee's Brittle Wax) 55 days. Round, plump, slightly curved, light golden-yellow pod; 6 to 7 inches long; stringless, brittle, fleshy, fiberless, of excellent quality. Seed chalky white with a black-eye, slow to develop. Used as a cut bean and for canning whole. Height 14 to 16 inches. Introduced in 1900 as Round Pod Kidney Wax. HEDRICK 1931; A69M, *A75*, B13, B75, D27, D65, *F72*, G57M, G64, G79, G87, I67M, J32, L97

Cherokee Wax: 50 days. Thick, oval, straight, golden-yellow pod; 6 to 7 inches long; entirely stringless at all stages, tender, flavorful. Black-seeded. Good shipper. Vigorous, productive plant; produces well during adverse weather conditions; resistant to mosaic virus. All America Selections winner in 1948. *A69M*, B35M, B73M, B75M, C44, D65, D76, F19M, G71, *H61*, I64, K71, L42, M13M, M95, etc.

Dragon Langerie:[5] (Dragon Tongue, Horticultural Wax Bean) 57 days. Long, flat pod; light-yellow, striped with purple, turning red when mature; 7 to 8 inches long; stringless, very flavorful. Light purple-brown seeds, striped with blue. Excellent for French-style sliced beans at the purple-striped stage. Stripes disappear during blanching, indicating freezer readiness. Also good for shelling when the pod turns red. High yielding. *A75*, C53, E24, J20, J73, K49M, M46, *N40*{PR}

Earliwax: (Earlywax Golden Yellow) 50 days. Round, straight, golden-yellow pod; 5 to 6 inches long; stringless, tender, fleshy, very flavorful; retains its high quality long after picking. White-seeded. Excellent for canning and freezing. High yielding plant; resistant to bean common mosaic virus. Popular with market gardeners and truck farmers. *A75*, E97, F44, G64, G79, *I59M*, J97M, M46

Eastern Butterwax: 55 days. Slightly curved, plump, round-oval, golden-yellow pod; 6 1/2 to 7 1/2 inches long; stringless, fleshy, brittle, tender, very flavorful. Black-seeded. Excellent for canning and freezing. Compact, high yielding plant; height 14 to 16 inches. B35M, D11M, E97, F1, I64, I67M, J7, M49

Gold Crop: 52 days. Round, slender, straight, deep golden-yellow pod; 6 to 6 1/2 inches in diameter; stringless, fiberless, of excellent quality and flavor. White seeded. Tolerant to mosaic and curly top viruses, and to blossom drop in hot weather. All America Selections winner in 1974. Developed by the USDA and Washington State University. A25, B75, D11M, D65, E57, F19M, *F72*, G16, G51, H49, H94, H95, J32, K71, L42, etc.

Golden Wax: (Stringless Golden Wax) 50 days. Straight, narrow, oval to flat, golden-yellow pod; 5 to 5 1/2 inches long; stringless, very brittle, of very good flavor and quality. Seed white, with a brownish-purple eye. Good fresh, canned or frozen. Compact, productive plant; height 10 to 14 inches. Popular home garden cultivar. A16, B13, B73M, D76, D82, E38, F92, G71, H42, I67M, L14, N16

Honey Gold: 40 days. Round, unusually straight, deep honey-gold pod; 5 1/2 inches in length. White-seeded. Dwarf, bushy plant, 12 to 14 inches high; very tolerant to common bean mosaic; produces up to 24 pods. Bears extremely early, when fresh produce prices are high. L42

Ice: (Crystal Wax, Crystal White Wax) 59 days. Unique white-podded heirloom. Round, slightly curved, plump pod; whitish or grayish-green in color; 3 1/2 to 4 inches long; stringy, brittle, tender, of good quality. Small, white seeds. Good for canning when very young. Also used as a dry shell bean for baking. Highly productive. Introduced prior to 1883. HEDRICK 1931; D87, I99

Kinghorn Wax: (Resistant Kinghorn Wax) 53 days. Round, nearly straight, bright golden-yellow pod; 6 inches long, 3/8 inch in diameter; stringless, tender, flavorful. White-seeded. Good for processing, canning and freezing. Vigorous, highly prolific plant; height 19 to 22 inches; resistant to bean mosaic virus. A69M, A87M, B13, C44, C85M, D11M, E97, G64, G79, G93M, H33, H42, H95, I67M, K49M, etc.

Lazer: 55 days. Long, slender, very straight pods; 6 inches long; color bright-yellow; fleshy, tender, of high quality. Very slow seed development allows pods to be left on the plant longer without loss of quality. Vigorous, highly productive plant. Resistant to common mosaic virus and the N.Y. 15 strain. Good seed emergence. Introduced in 1982. F13, M49

Mini Yellow:[3] 52 days. Gourmet "mini" or "baby bean". Produces slender yellow pods, only 4 inches long; very tender and flavorful; requires no snapping. Excellent fresh, frozen, canned or pickled. For longest harvests and best quality, pods should be picked just as they mature. I91

Mont d'Or: (Golden Butter) 57 days. Slightly curved, flat, pale yellow pod; 5 to 6 inches long; entirely stringless when young, fleshy, tender, very flavorful, of excellent quality. Black-seeded. High yielding plant, 12 to 16 inches tall; resistant to mosaic and anthracnose. Originated in France prior to 1885. VILMORIN; B49, P83M, *R23*, S55

Pencil Pod: (Pencil Pod Black Wax) 55 days. Round, narrow, curved, clear yellow pod; 6 to 7 inches long; stringless, very brittle, fiberless, of excellent flavor and quality. Black-seeded. Vigorous, productive, widely adapted plant; height 12 to 15 inches. Very popular traditional cultivar. Introduced in 1900. HEDRICK 1931; A16, A25, C85M, D11M, D65, E24, F1, F92, G57M, G79, L7M, L97, M13M, M46, N39, etc.

Roc d'Or: (Rocdor) 55 days. Gourmet French type. Rounded, very slender, straight, bright golden-yellow pod; 6 1/2 to 7 inches long, 1/3 inch in diameter; stringless, of superior texture and flavor. Black-seeded. Excellent fresh, frozen or canned. Upright, highly productive plant; resistant to anthracnose and mosaic virus; tolerant to cool, wet conditions. B75, *D74*, G6, G64, I77, J73, K66, L42, M46

Roma Gold: 55 days. Yellow-podded Roma type. Long, flat, golden-yellow pod; stringless, fleshy, tender, of excellent flavor; retains its quality and flavor even when large and plump. Upright, bush-type plant; easy to pick; very productive over a long season. L79

Slenderwax: 56 days. Uniform, straight, medium-round pods; 5 inches long; stringless, fiberless, of very good flavor. Contains the "instant wax" gene, which turns the pod from green to golden-yellow very early in its development. White-seeded. High yielding plant; height 20 inches; resistant to mosaic, tolerant to heat and white mold. Released by Cornell University. *A1*, D11M, D76, F90, G87, H33, J7, M29, M46, N39, N52

Sungold: 55 days. Straight, round, bright yellow pods; 5 to 6 inches long; tender, rich in flavor, stringless, quality excellent. Attains good color early. White seeds that develop slowly. Upright, compact plant; height 18 to 20 inches. Resistant to common bean mosaic and the N.Y. 15 strain. A69M, *A75*, D27, F13, G82, I64, I67M, K71, L42, *L59G*, M13M

Topnotch Golden Wax: 50 days. Straight, semi-round to flattened pods, 5 1/2 inches in length; pale yellow in color; very meaty, brittle, with a rich buttery flavor; stringless. White-seeded. Compact, productive plant; very disease resistant. Improved strain of Golden Wax. A69M, *A75*, B35M, C44, *D49*, D65, E97, F1, G57M, G79, H54, J58, K20, K27M, M13M, M95M, etc.

Pole

Burpee Golden: 60 days. Broad, flat, butter-yellow pod; 5 1/2 to 6 1/2 inches long, 1 inch in diameter; stringless, tender, fiberless; quality excellent at all stages of growth. Initial growth habit is similar to a bush bean, with very early pod set, then runners form and continue to be productive. B75

Burro d'Ingegnoli: (A Cornetto Largo Giallo Burro d'Ingegnoli) Large, slightly curved, flat pods; 1/2 to 1 inch in diameter, 7 to 8 inches long; golden-yellow in color; stringless. First harvests in about 78 days. Q11M

Kentucky Wonder Wax: (Kentucky Wonder Yellow Wax) 68 days. Slightly curved, round-oval, light-yellow pod; 7 to 9 inches long; stringless when young, very brittle and fleshy, fiberless, of good quality and flavor. Brown-seeded. Also used as a green shell bean. Very popular traditional cultivar. Introduced in 1901. HEDRICK 1931; A25, A69M, B35M, B73M, C44, D11M, D76, E97, G16, I64, K71, L42, L79, L89, M46, etc.

Marvel of Venice: (Wonder of Venice, Merveille de Venise, Meraviglia di Venezia) 70 days. An old traditional Italian cultivar. Yellow Romano type. Broad, flattened, medium-yellow pod; 7 to 7 1/2 inches long; brittle flesh, excellent distinct flavor. Black-seeded. Can also be used as a green shell bean. Moderately productive plant; resistant to mosaic virus. *A75*, B8, I77, P83M, S55

Neckargold: 75 days. Similar to Neckarkonigin green-podded pole bean. Very long, round, crease-backed, deep butter-yellow pod; 7 to 8 inches in length; stringless, of excellent quality. White-seeded. Should be harvested when young. Vigorous, high yielding vine; height 8 feet; somewhat heat tolerant. C85M, N81

Paille d'Or: (Gold Straw) 68 days. Long, round, golden-yellow pods; stringless, of excellent quality. Higher yielding than Kentucky Wonder Wax. J7

Sultans Golden Moon: (Sultan's Golden Crescent) Similar to Sultans Emerald Moon. Developed during the last century of the Ottoman Empire. Pods mimic the Crescent, the royal symbol of the Sultans. Thought to have been lost; recently re-discovered in the kitchen garden of a wealthy tobacco merchant in Izmir, Turkey. Delicious, subtle flavor. Vigorous and disease resistant. D62, K49M

Yellow Anellino: (Yellow Gancetto) Unique, crescent shaped, bright pale-yellow pods; 1/4 to 1/2 inch in diameter, 3 1/2 to 4 1/2 inches long; rounded in form, fleshy, free of strings, rich in flavor. First harvests in about 80 days. Italian heirloom, becoming popular with American chefs. C53, Q11M

KIWI {GR}

ACTINIDIA SPP.

FUZZY KIWIS

The common kiwi, introduced into cultivation by Alexander Allison of New Zealand prior to 1910 and now marketed worldwide. Unlike the hardy kiwis, the skin must be peeled before consumption. Keeps extremely well, up to four months in cool storage. (A. deliciosa)

FEMALE

Abbott: Small to medium-sized, oblong fruit; skin brownish, with especially dense, long, coarse hairs; flesh light-green, flavor good; ripens in early May, keeps well. Resembles Allison. Vine vigorous and productive; precocious; early flowering; produces small fruit unless thinned. Medium chilling requirement. Originated in New Zealand. Introduced in the 1930's. MORTON 1987a, SALE; H53M{SC}, *O97*, S59

Allison: Fruit oblong, slightly broader than Abbott; of medium size, with densely hairy, brownish-skin; flesh light-green, of good flavor; ripens in early May; keeps well. Vine very vigorous, prolific; blooms later than Abbott. Formerly very popular but has lost ground to Hayward. Originated in New Zealand. Introduced in the early 1930's. MORTON 1987a; H53M{SC}

Bruno: Fruit large; elongated cylindrical, broadest at apex; skin darker brown than other cultivars with dense, short, bristly hairs; flesh light-green, of good flavor; ripens in early May. Vine vigorous and productive, blooms with or slightly after Allison. Preferred by some processors because a large number of even slices can be obtained from each long fruit. Relatively low chilling requirement. Also used as a rootstock. MORTON 1987a, SALE; H53M{SC}, N84{S}, O93{S}, *O97*, *P17M*{S}, *Q32*{S}, R33M{S}, S59

Chico Hayward: (Chico) Large, broad oval fruit; skin pale greenish-brown with fine, silky hairs; quality excellent; ripens late. Similar, if not identical to Hayward. Vine bears moderate crops, doesn't require as much thinning as others. Tends to produce some odd-shaped fruit. High chilling requirement. Preferred commercial cultivar in California. Originated in Chico, California by R.L. Smith, Chico Plant Introduction Station. D34M{PR}, E74{PR}, H4, I83M, N6

Dexter: Fruit similar to Hayward, only slightly more elongated; skin hairs stiff and generally come off readily during commercial packing operations. Relatively low chilling requirement; adapted to warm-winter areas. Originated in Queensland, Australia by John Dexter as a seedling of Hayward. H53M{SC}

Elmwood: Extra large fruit, many up to 9 1/2 ounces each as compared to those of Hayward which average 3 to 3 1/2 ounces each; somewhat cylindrical with a very slight narrowing at the midpoint. Vine precocious, usually bears the first year after being grafted; produces few doubles or fans; wood an unusual off-white color. H53M{SC}

Gracie: Fruit elongated, tapers distinctly towards the stem end; similar to Bruno, but with more width and substance. A selection made by Auckland, New Zealand nurseryman John Gracie. SALE; H53M{SC}, *O97*

Hayward: Very large fruit; broad oval, with slightly flattened sides; skin light greenish-brown with dense, fine, silky hairs; flesh light-green, of superior flavor; ripens in early May; keeps better than any other current cultivar. Vine moderately vigorous and productive; blooms very late. Standard commercial cultivar in New Zealand, California, Italy and other areas. MORTON 1987a, SALE; A88M, B93M, F11, F19M, G17, H4, H53M{SC}, I49M, I83M, L6, L82, L99M, O93{S}, *O97*, R33M{S}, etc.

Koryoku: (Japan-86) An excellent new cultivar developed in Japan. The fruit is reportedly better tasting and larger than any cultivar presently marketed. It also ripens 10 days before Hayward. H53M{SC}

Kramer: Large, Hayward type fruit; more solid in the shoulders; of excellent quality. Vine prolific; produces few doubles or fans.

Originated in Te Puke, New Zealand by John Kramer as a selection of Hayward. H53M{SC}

Monty: Fruit small to medium-sized; oblong, tapering slightly at the stem end; skin brownish with dense hairs; flesh light-green, of indifferent quality; ripens in early May. Vine highly vigorous and productive; has a tendency to overcrop, which can adversely affect fruit size; very late blooming. Medium chilling requirement. Originated in New Zealand. Introduced about 1957. MORTON 1987a, SALE; H4, H53M{SC}

Saanichton 12: Grown on Vancouver Island, British Columbia, Canada for over 13 years. The fruit is large and sweet and the plant has not been injured by winter temperatures that have damaged other cultivars. Recommended for the backyard grower and small orchardist. Also being tested by the Saanichton Agriculture Canada Research Station for commercial production and as breeding material. C34, I49M, J61M

Tewi:[1] (Tenerife Kiwi) Medium-sized, oblong fruit, similar to Hayward but somewhat smaller; flesh brilliant green, of good flavor. Vine moderately vigorous; precocious; prolific, produces up to 80 pounds of fruit under ideal conditions; has a very low chilling requirement; blooms very early. Originated in the Canary Islands as a seedling of Hayward. Introduced into the United States in 1980 by Horace Whittaker of Carpenteria, California. H53M{SC}, I83M, L6

Vincent:[1] Medium-sized fruit; resembles Abbott and Allison; flesh sweet, flavor very good. Vine very prolific, sometimes to the point of negatively affecting fruit size. Very low chilling requirement, 200 hours or less compared with the 600 or more needed by most cultivars. Suited to warm winter areas. Originated in Yorba Linda, California by Judge Raymond Vincent. *D23M*, H53M{SC}, I83M, L6, L29

Yellow Mountains: A strain from the Yellow Mountains of China that has relatively small fruit of excellent eating quality. Being tested in North Carolina; has the potential for fruiting more successfully in cooler climates than standard cultivars of kiwi. B96{PL}

MALE

California: The male most commonly used in California for pollinating the Hayward cultivar. Pollinates up to 8 females. Originated in Chico, California. C34, *C54*, F19M

Chico: Bloom dates coincide with those of Monty, Hayward and Chico Hayward, making it an excellent pollinator for these cultivars. *B58M*, *D23M*, F11, H4, L6

Early CC: Several early selections which might show promise for the warmest winter sites such as southern Florida. The early budding of these strains makes them susceptible to any spring frost. H53M{SC}

M Series: Including clones M51, M52 and M56. Selected flowering clones of an established long-flowering ability and high pollen potential suitable for the pollination of female cultivars available at the present time. Particularly useful for pollinating Hayward. For optimum results under various climatic conditions, a small number of all three M Series clones should be planted. H53M{SC}, *O97*

Male: (All Purpose) Non-fruiting, all purpose male used as a pollinator for female vines. Generally, one male plant is recommended for every 8 female vines. Can also be used as a pollinator for A. arguta hardy kiwis. A88M, H4, I49M, L29, N0, *O97*

Matua:[1] Long-flowering type, flowers prolifically over a long period. Along with other long-flowering types, Matua is generally regarded as the best pollinator for all commercial cultivars, including Hayward. Flowers produced in groups of 1 to 5, usually 3; peduncles short-haired. Low chilling requirement, 100 hours or less. MORTON 1987a, SALE; G17, H53M{SC}, I83M, L6, *O97*, S59

Tomuri: Late-flowering type, with a relatively small number of flowers that bloom late in the season. Flowers in groups of 1 to 7, usually 5; peduncles long-haired. Originally selected as a pollinator for Hayward. The standard late season pollinizer. Low chilling requirement, 100 hours or less. MORTON 1987a, SALE; B93M, H53M{SC}, I83M, J61M, *O97*, S59

SELF-FERTILE

Blake: Fruit relatively small, tends to taper near the blossom end; ripens to a 6.5 brix 6 to 8 weeks before Hayward thus substantially extending the fresh kiwifruit season for the backyard grower. Vine precocious, can produce a crop in as little as one year after being grafted; blooms very early, but is reliably pollinated by Matua; reportedly self-fertile; prolific. Originated in the San Francisco Bay area. F16, H53M{SC}, I49M, I83M, J61M

HARDY KIWIS

Small fruited kiwis that have the advantage of growing in areas too cold for the common kiwi. The fruit is smooth-skinned and can be eaten out of hand like a grape, without any peeling. It is also much sweeter than the common kiwi but does not keep nearly as long in storage.

ARGUTA This is the Actinidia species most commonly called the hardy kiwi. It is winter hardy to Zone 4 if the vine is properly hardened off. However it has a bad habit of leafing out much too early in the spring and the whole plant is sensitive to spring frosts. This early breaking dormancy problem seems to exist in Zones 4 through 7. (A. arguta)

Female

74-8: Short, elliptical fruit, above average in size; flesh firm, sweet, of very good flavor. Vine productive; hardy and adaptable. One of the best of the 74 series originating at the Chico Plant Introduction Station. D37, I46, M16

74-49: Large, flat fruits, as short as they are wide; skin smooth; flesh aromatic with a distinctive sweet flavor; ripens in mid-season. Vine vigorous; a reliable and heavy bearer. Originated in Chico, California. Selected for productivity and high fruit quality. D37, I49M, M16

74-55: Medium to large, round, smooth fruits; flavor sweet; ripens somewhat before 74-49. Vine vigorous and productive. Originated at Chico, California. D37, F16, I46, M16

74-62: Exceptionally long, cylindrical fruits with very smooth, clear-green skin. One of the 74 series selected at the now defunct Chico, California Plant Introduction Station. Recommended for its vigor, productivity and flavor. I46

Ananasnaya: (Michurin Ananasnaya, Michurin's Pineapple, Anna) Medium-sized, oval fruit, 1 1/2 inches long and 1 inch in diameter; skin dark green, smooth; flesh light-green, juicy, sweet, has a distinct pineapple-like aroma and flavor. Vine very hardy, will tolerate temperatures of -30^0 F.; a reliable bearer, often produces fruit in bunches similar to grapes. Believed to be a hybrid of A. arguta and A. kolomikta. Developed by the noted Soviet plant breeder I.V. Michurin. MICHURIN; A50, B73M, B74, C34, D37, E87, F16, F43M, I46, I49M, I74, I83M, K67, M16, N0, *N20*, etc.

Dumbarton Oaks: Originally from an old planting found in a garden in the Georgetown area of Washington, D.C. Has been growing there since 1940. The fruit is sweet and above average in size. I46

Geneva #1: Small to medium-sized fruit, about 1 inch long, similar to Meader Female; ripens late. Originally from the New York Experiment Station in Geneva, New York. H53M{SC}

Geneva #2: Small to medium fruit, about 1 inch long, similar to Geneva #1; ripens late. Good cold tolerance. Originated in Geneva, New York by George Slate. H53M{SC}, M16

Geneva HH 1: Medium-sized, smooth skinned fruit with excellent flavor. Vigorous vine appears to be very hardy. Should be pollinated with Male 1971. Tested at the Geneva, New York Experiment Station. F16

Geneva HH 2: Vigorous vine that is very hardy. Should be pollinated with Male 1971. Tested at the Geneva, New York Experiment Station. F16

Langer: (Hood River) Bears medium-sized fruit of fine quality. Original tree is from an old homestead high in the Cascade mountains. Has endured summer drought, deep snow, severe cold and wind, and other adverse conditions. I49M, I83M

Meader Female: Medium-sized fruit; sweet and flavorsome; ripens at the end of August in New Hampshire. Hardy to -25^0 F. Introduced by Professor E.M. Meader of Rochester, New Hampshire after 20 years of selection and testing. Selected for productivity and high fruit quality. D37, D69, H53M{SC}, I46, I49M

Michigan State: (MSU) Medium to large, ribbed fruit, 1 1/2 inches long and 1 inch in diameter; flavor excellent when ripe, good even when not fully ripe. Vine vigorous; perfect flowered; reported to be partially self-fertile, but produces best when planted with a male. Originally from Michigan State University. Possibly a hybrid between A. arguta and A. kolomikta. I46, M16

Male

1971: Used as a pollinator for the Geneva selections. F16

74-32: One of the males selected at Chico, California to pollinate females in the 74 series. Similar to 74-8; possibly a seedling of common origin. H53M{SC}

74-46: Male used to pollinate females in the 74 series. Selected for its exceptionally large number of flowers, an advantage for males because it extends the flowering season. Originated at Chico, California. F16

74-52: An early flowering male used as one of the pollinators in the 74 series. Selected by Dan Milbocker of the Hampton Roads Agricultural Experiment Station from 40 seedlings obtained at the Chico Plant Introduction Station. H53M{SC}

Male: Non-fruiting, all purpose male used a pollinator for female vines. One male can pollinate up to 8 females. Will also pollinate Hayward and other fuzzy female kiwis. A88M, C34, *C47*, D95, F43M, I46, I49M, J61M, K67, N0, *N20*

Meader Male: A good pollinator for Ananasnaya. Has withstood temperatures of -28^0 F. Selected by Professor E.M. Meader. E87, M16

Pacific: Male arguta with a long flowering period. Good pollinator for female argutas. I83M

Self-Fertile

119-40-B: Self-fertile cultivar originally from the Arnold Arboretum. Vigorous grower with large, waxy leaves. Will pollinate other cultivars of A. arguta. H53M{SC}

Issai: Fruit long, up to 1 3/4 inches; sweet, of very good flavor, quality high; seedless when not pollinated. Vine short and compact; bears fruit without a male pollinator, often the first year after grafting, however planting with a male will increase yields. Ideal for the gardener with limited space. Originated in Japan. A91, B75, *C47*, D11M, D37, D76, E87, E97, F16, H53M{SC}, I46, I49M, I74, J61M, K67, L33, M16, etc.

<u>KOLOMIKTA</u> Also called *arctic beauty kiwi*, this species is reportedly hardier than A. arguta, to Zone 3. It is also a striking ornamental, the growing tip and young leaves being covered with magenta hairs and the leaves of the adult male plant variegated with red, white and green. Growing to only 10 feet it is easier to protect in very cold climates and may be suitable for indoor culture. (A. kolomikta)

Female

142-38: Fruit small, rectangular, ribbed. Very flavorsome when eaten dried like a fig or grape. Variegated foliage. H53M{SC}

Arnold Arboretum: (A/O) Small to medium-sized fruit of fine quality; very sweet; ripens early. Originally from the Arnold Arboretum in Massachusetts. I49M

Aromatnaya: Fruit medium-sized; sugar content 20% when ripe, medium high vitamin C content; ripens early to mid-August. Vine productive. I49M

Krupnopladnaya: (Krupnaya Michurinskaya, Large Fruited, Michurin's Large) Fruit very large, smooth-skinned; sugar content 14% when ripe, high in vitamin C; flavor excellent. Vine moderately vigorous, very productive; ornamental; cold hardy to -35^0 F. Originated in Leningrad, U.S.S.R. by I.V. Michurin. D37, E87, I49M

Matovaya: Small to medium-sized fruit; sugar content 16% when ripe, very high in vitamin C; ripens very early. I49M

Nahodka: Fruit medium to large; sugar content 15 1/2% when ripe, medium high in vitamin C; ripens in mid-August. I49M

Oluyhckos: Selected in the Soviet Union for the high quality of its fruit. H53M{SC}

Pautske: Reportedly a large, high-quality fruit. Vine very vigorous. Originated in Lithuania by plant breeder V. Pautske. I49M

Pavlovskaya: Fruit large; sugar content 15% when ripe, medium high in vitamin C; ripens early to mid-August. Vine very productive. I49M

Pozdnaya: (Leningrad Late) Medium to large fruit, of a pleasant flavor; ripens mid to late September. Bears very abundant crops. Originated in the East Siberian taiga. Introduced by I.V. Michurin. Selected for fruit size and taste. H53M{SC}

Rannaya: (Leningrad Early) Fruit of pleasant flavor, ripens in the middle of August. Vine produces abundantly; pollinates Urozhainaya, Pozdnaya and Oluyhckos. Originated in the East Siberian taiga. Introduced by I.V. Michurin. MICHURIN; H53M{SC}

Sentyabraskaya: Medium to large fruit; sugar content 18% when ripe, medium high in vitamin C; ripens in mid-August. Vine productive. I49M

Urozhainaya: (High-Yielding) Medium to large fruit with an excellent sweet flavor; contains 18 1/2% sugar when ripe; also high in vitamin C. Ripens early, beginning in the middle of August. Vine bears a very abundant and regular annual crop. Originated in the East Siberian taiga. Selected for fruit size and early fruiting by I.V. Michurin. MICHURIN; I49M

Male

All Purpose: Non-fruiting, all purpose male used a pollinator for female vines. Pollinates up to 8 female vines. Also a fine ornamental with striking pink, white and green variegated leaves. B74, C34, E87, H65, I49M, J61M

OTHERS

Red Princess:[2] (A. arguta var. cordifolia x A. melanandra) Unique red-fleshed kiwi. Small, oval fruit; thin, palatable red skin; relatively sweet red flesh. Vine moderately vigorous; productive; resembles A. arguta var. cordifolia. Originated in New Zealand by K.J. Nobbs. D37

KOHLRABI {S}

BRASSICA OLERACEA GONGYLODES GROUP

HYBRID

Grand Duke: 48 days. Smooth, uniform, round bulbs; can grow to 4 inches in diameter without becoming woody. Vigorous, upright plants withstand cold soils, light frost, adverse weather conditions and are tolerant to black rot. Good vigor and uniformity. Late in bolting. Will produce a larger crop in less space than Early White Vienna. All America Selections winner in 1979. A87M, C44, D11M, D65, F13, F19M, *F72*, G16, G64, G71, *H61*, H94, J14{PL}, J20, J34, K73, etc.

Kolpak: 38 days. An excellent white hybrid noted for its earliness, uniformity and sweet flavor. Tender flesh does not become pithy or fibrous. Fine-stemmed foliage; flattened-globe shape. Best harvested when 2 to 3 inches in diameter. F90, G6, K50

Purple Danube: 46 days. Smooth, refined round bulbs with fine-stemmed foliage. Superior tenderness and freedom from fiber. Excellent quality. Good uniformity in plant habit, bulb shape and maturity. More vigorous and easier to grow than Early Purple Vienna with deeper and more attractive color. G6{CF}, G64, I77, J7, *K16M*

Winner: 60 days. Vigorous plants produce large, perfectly uniform, semi-globular pale green bulbs with few leaves and mild, tender, sweet flesh. Excellent quality and yields. Remains tender until reaching a diameter of at least 3 inches. Resists becoming woody for many months after maturity in the fall. H95, L89, *S63M*

OPEN-POLLINATED

Blue Danish: 50 days. An improved selection. Tender, fine-textured, reddish-purple bulbs. Bluish leaves. One of the earliest, most refined blue kohlrabies available. L7M

Capri: 45 days. A promising early kohlrabi from Europe. Round, smooth purple-skinned bulbs with few but vigorous leaves. Very tender and crisp with a mild flavor. Highly bolt resistant. For growing year round in the greenhouse and outdoors. G6

Early Purple Vienna: 60 days. Globe-shaped bulbs with a purplish-red color and attractive greenish-white interior flesh. Leaves are smooth and few in number. Similar to Early White Vienna except for the color of the skin. Standard purple-skinned cultivar. Known prior to 1865. BURR; A16, A87M, C44, C85M, E24, E38, F1, F82, G16, G71, H94, L7M, M13M, M49, N39, etc.

Early White Vienna: 55 days. An early dwarf cultivar with short tops and glossy, white to very pale green, medium-sized bulbs. Crisp, tender, succulent white flesh with a mild turnip-like taste. Should be harvested at about 2 1/2 inches in diameter for best quality. Standard white-skinned cultivar. Known prior to 1865. BURR; A16, B75M, B78, C44, D82, E24, G16, G93M, *H61*, H66, H94, J7, K73, L7M, M13M, etc.

Fekara: Attractive, slightly flattened white-skinned bulbs. Uniform and compact in habit. For best quality use when 2 to 3 inches in diameter. A quick maturing white cultivar for outdoors or polytunnels. P83M, S61

Giganté:[1] (Gigant Winter) 130 days. Very large root, typically grows 8 to 10 inches in diameter; average weight 15 to 20 pounds, yet it remains fine-grained and is of good quality throughout. Can be used fresh or cooked at any size, from small to large. Traditionally used for sauerkraut in central Europe. Resistant to root maggots. Excellent for winter storage. Selected from a Czechoslovakian family heirloom by Professor E.M. Meader. I39, L7M

King of the Market: Produces very large, greenish bulbs of good quality. Long leaves. Though slightly late in maturing, it is a very heavy bearer. R0, R50, S59M, S93M

Lauko: 60 days. Although it does well in spring it is highly recommended for autumn cropping. Has a unique internal structure, and in cool autumn weather it becomes woody more slowly than other types. Purple skin and delicate, fine-textured flesh. Sweet, rich flavor. Very cold hardy. G64, L89

Peking: 55 days. Medium-sized bulbs with pale green skin. Pure white flesh of fine quality. Medium in maturity. L59

Prague Early Forcing: 44 days. Very early Prague type, good for hothouse or greenhouse forcing as well as planting outdoors. High quality for market or table use. Short leaves. Uniform in size. Both the bulb as well as the leaves are exceptionally tender and highly flavored. K49M

Purple Delicacy: 70 days. Purple globe-shaped bulb; slow to bolt. Later and larger than Early White Vienna. Medium large plant habit. For growing in summer to early autumn. M46

Purple Speck: (Blauer Speck) 65 days. An extra large, high quality cultivar from Germany. Slightly flattened, bluish-purple bulbs; 2 3/4 to 4 inches in diameter; weight approximately 8 ounces; surprisingly little fiber inside. Large plants with strong foliage. For summer and fall culture. C85M, D11M, P9

Rapid: 45 Days. High quality early kohlrabi. Plants grow 15 to 18 inches tall and produce reddish-purple bulbs, 3 inches in diameter, with smooth, crisp, sweet white flesh. Attractive raw, for dips and salads, or cooked like turnips. I91

Superschmelz: Very large, round, green bulb; 6 to 10 inches in diameter; up to 10 pounds, yet is long-standing, remaining tender and not becoming "woody". Excellent mild, sweet flavor fresh; fair frozen. Better tasting than other very large cultivars such as Purple Speck. P9

LEEK {S}

ALLIUM AMPELOPRASUM PORRUM GROUP

Alaska: (Winter Giant Alaska) 125 days. A very hardy leek for overwintering or winter storage. Thick, solid, pure-white shafts, 8 to 10 inches long. Broad, dark blue-green foliage. Very tender, sweet flavor. Tolerant to disease, bolting and sub-freezing temperatures. C85M, D11M, L42, N52, *R23*

American Flag: 130 days. Large, thick stalks; 7 to 9 inches long, 1 to 2 inches in diameter, blanching to a clear white; leaves medium blue-green. Fine, mild flavor. Strong grower; 15 to 18 inches tall; very hardy and cold resistant. Standard local market and home garden cultivar. A69M, A87M, B73M, C92, D65, F1, F80, F82, F92, G16, G71, G79, H33, H54, M95, etc.

Blue Solaise: (Bleu de Solaise) 140 days. A 19th century French heirloom with 4 to 6 inch long stems and tops that turn almost violet with cold autumn temperatures. Attractive as well as flavorsome. Very hardy and cold resistant. C53, G68, I77

Bulgarian: 120 days. A selection for long white stems and fine flavor. Shaft is about 12 inches long. Recommended for dehydration owing to its high dry matter content. *P75M*

Carentan: (De Carentan, Carentan Winter) 95 days. Long, thick, tender, creamy-white stalks, 2 inches in diameter, topped by deep blue-green foliage. Mild flavor, delicate enough to be enjoyed raw in salads and garnishes. Vigorous; fast-growing; very productive and adaptable. For fall and winter use. *A75*, C85M, H42

Carina: Large, cold-hardy, late fall and winter leek, developed especially for longer stalks. Rather narrow, semi-erect leaves of an attractive blue-green color. Long, tender, non-bulbous stalks of high quality. Matures in autumn and will stand in the ground through winter. Heavy yielding and tolerant of black spot and virus. *A1*, A13, K66, L42, M29

Conqueror: Medium-length, straight, thick stalks; clean blue-green tops that withstand cold; delicate onion-like flavor. Very hardy, one of the best for winter storage or for holding in the garden banked up with earth. J14{PL}

Durabel: Non-bulbous stalks; five inches long to the first joint. Has a much milder flavor and is more tender than other winter-hardy cultivars, which are bred to endure harsh weather. Slow-growing and vigorous; exceptionally late-bolting, remaining in good condition in the garden until late April. L89

Electra: 145 days. Long, thick white stalks of fine quality. Can be harvested early, yet is one of the best for fall and winter crops. Will also store nearly all winter. Fast-growing, cold resistant, dependable and very adaptable. Of French origin. F13, N52

Elephant: (Elefant) 85 days. A large, vigorous, fairly early cultivar with extra thick, smooth, medium length stalks without bulbous ends. Recommended for late summer and fall harvest, or may be stored for winter use. Of French origin. *A75*, C85M, E5T, G64, K49M

Gennevilliers: (Gennevilliers Splendid) A strain of an old French cultivar selected for its long, relatively slender shaft which grows to 10 inches and is free of bulbing. Attractive, upright, dark blue-green foliage. Recommended for mild climates, where it may be left in the ground for winter use if temperatures remain above 30^0 F. G68, I77, *R23*, S55, *S75M*

Giant Carentan: (Monstrueux de Carentan) 140 days. Stem short, very thick, seldom exceeding 6 to 8 inches in length, with a diameter of 3 inches or more in well-grown plants, and occasionally even larger. Leaves very dark bluish-green. Very hardy, suitable for fall and winter crops. An old traditional French cultivar, known prior to 1885. VILMORIN; A2, F33, M13M, P83M, R47, S55

Kilima: 80 days. Rapid-growing early leek with medium blue-green foliage. Long, straight 10 to 12 inch stems of good thickness; free from bulbing. Mild onion-like flavor; well suited for use in salads. Excellent for summer and fall use. No winter hardiness and not suitable for storing. C85M, D11M, J7, J84, N52, *R23*

King Richard: 75 days. High-yielding summer and fall cultivar. Upright, medium green leaves. Long white stems; will reach one foot or more to the first leaf under optimal conditions. Mild flavor. Not hardy enough for overwintering, but will stand heavy frosts of 32^0 F. to 20^0 F. without losing its healthy appearance. C53, D68, D82, E24, F42, F44, G6, I99, J20, K10, K49T, *R23*, S55

Large American Flag: (Broad London) 120 days. Stems 7 to 10 inches long, 1 to 1 1/2 inches in diameter, blanching to a clear white. Hardy, vigorous plant; 15 to 18 inches tall with medium bluish-green, semi-upright leaves. Standard shipping, fresh market and home garden cultivar. A16, *A75*, B35M, B75, B75M, D11M, *F72*, G51, G93M, H49, H94, K71, K73, L79, N39, etc.

Long d'Hiver de Paris: (Long Winter) Long, slender white stalks; about 12 inches long and 1 inch in diameter. Pale gray-green leaves, longer and narrower than those of other types. Withstands the winter well, and is particularly suited for planting in late autumn. An old French cultivar, popular with market gardeners for bunching. Known prior to 1885. VILMORIN; G68

Long de Mézières: (De Mézières Race Danube) Long, white stalks, of good quality. Semi-late in maturity. Very resistant to frost; recommended for harvesting in autumn and winter. Introduced by Vilmorin. G68, S95M

Musselburgh: (Scotch Flag, Giant Musselburgh) 130 days. Large, thick white stem, 8 1/2 to 9 inches long and 2 inches in diameter. Broad, tall, medium-green leaves, spreading in a fan-like manner. Vigorous and very hardy. Popular, widely-adapted local market and home garden cultivar. Originally selected near Edinburgh, Scotland. Introduced in 1834. A2, *A69M*, B13, B49, C92, E57, F19M, G27M, *H61*, I39, J84, K20, L97, M49

Nebraska: 90 days. A fall-winter harvest leek with and attractive appearance and high yields. Thick 10 inch long, smooth, firm white stems with little or no bulbing. Dark blue-green leaves. Good resistance to frost and disease for late fall-winter harvests, and overwintering in moderate climates. G6

Schnittporree:[1] (Cutting Leek) 55 days. Grown for the leaves and young stems which are cut and used like chives or scallions. Good dark green color. Usually harvested in autumn and winter. N81

Splendid: 95 days. Extra long, slim, non-bulbous, 10 inch shafts, blanching to a pure-white; more tender than winter-hardy cultivars. Medium-green foliage. Vigorous and rapid-growing, making good size before autumn. Heavy yielding and somewhat tolerant of frost. Excellent for dehydration. L42, L89

St. Victor: A traditional French cultivar which is very decorative as well as being of excellent quality and flavor. Deep blue-green foliage has a purplish tinge which deepens to violet in cold weather. Very hardy and productive. P83M, S55

The Lyon: (Prizetaker) 135 days. Very long, thick, tender pure-white stems, free from any coarseness. Grows to a large size, yet retains its mild flavor. Very cold hardy. An old, widely adapted English cultivar introduced around 1886. L91M, P83M, *R23*, S61

Titan: 70 days. Extra long early type, of uniform, vigorous growth. Medium-thick white stems; 6 to 8 inches long, 1 3/4 to 2 inches in diameter with a slightly bulbous base. Recommended for summer and early fall harvests. Not cold hardy. B75, *F72*, K10, K49M, K49Z, L42, P83M

Unique: 100 days. Combines outstanding length of 7 to 8 inches with unusual 2 inch thickness. Leaves are dark blue-green. Tolerates extreme cold. Stores very well. K49M, L42

Varna:[2] 70 days. Slender, extra-tall summer leek with upright, light-green leaves. Can reach 18 inches in length to the first leaf. Developed in Europe for processing, Varna has possibilities in U.S. specialty markets bunched like onions for "baby" leeks. May be grown with transplants or by direct seeding at higher than normal densities. G6, I39, N52

Winter Giant: (Winterreuzen, Giant Winter) Very cold hardy, overwintering type. Tall, vigorous plant with long, thick white stems and dark-green leaves. Good flavor. Matures October to January. Excellent for overwintering, after which it will produce over a long period in early spring. Introduced around 1905. K49M, P83M, *R23*, *S75M*

LEMON {GR}

CITRUS LIMON

Eureka: Fruit medium-small, elliptical to oblong, commonly with a short neck. Seeds usually few to none. Color yellow at maturity. Rind medium-thick, tightly adherent. Flesh greenish-yellow, fine-grained, tender, juicy; flavor highly acid. Crop well distributed throughout the year, but mainly in late winter, spring, and early summer. Tree medium in vigor and size, spreading and open, virtually thornless. REUTHER; B93M, B93M{DW}, *D23M*, E3M{DW}, E31M, *F53M*, *G49*, I83M, *L47*, *M61M*, *M61M*{DW}, N18{SC}

Femminello Ovale: (Femminello Comune) Medium-sized, short elliptical fruit; rind medium-thick, yellow, tightly adherent; flesh tender, juicy, very highly acid. Crop well distributed throughout the year but mostly in late winter and spring. Tree of medium vigor and size, nearly thornless, highly productive. Especially responsive to the forcing or "verdelli" treatment of culture. REUTHER; *O4*

Femminello Sfusato: (Femminello Siracusano) Medium-sized, elliptical to oblong fruit; rind medium-thick, tightly adherent, yellow; flesh firm, juicy, highly acid. Crop well distributed throughout the year but mostly in late winter and spring. Tree very vigorous and productive. Due to its pronounced everbearing, everblooming habit it responds very well to the forcing or "verdelli" treatment so distinctive of Sicilian lemon culture. REUTHER; *O4*

Gloria Gold: A true sweet lemon, much superior to the insipid limettas. Acidless flesh with a distinctive sweet flavor. Tree a heavy producer throughout the year. I83M

Improved Meyer: Medium-sized, juicy fruit; slightly sweet when mature, of excellent flavor; holds well on the tree. Tree small to medium, moderately vigorous, spreading; nearly thornless. Hardy, productive; nearly everblooming but with many fruit in mid-winter. Good for hedges and containers. A virus-free selection of Meyer lemon recently developed and introduced by the University of California. *D23M*, D37{DW}, E3M{DW}, *F53M*, *G49*, *I62*, I83M, J61M{DW}, *M61M*, *M61M*{DW}, N18{SC}

Interdonato: (Speciale) Large, oblong fruit; rind thin, very smooth and glossy, yellow at maturity; flesh greenish-yellow, crisp and juicy, seeds very few; flavor highly acid with slight bitterness. Crop produced mainly in fall and early winter. Tee vigorous, usually thornless. Resistant to mal secco disease. Does not respond well to forcing treatment and hence grown primarily for early fruit. Probably a lemon-citron hybrid. REUTHER; *O4*

Lemonade: (Lemonade Fruit) Hybrid. Lemon-shaped fruits of medium size. Pale lemon-yellow skin of medium thickness, peels easily. Flesh lemon-like in texture and appearance; very juicy with a mild, grapefruit-like flavor. Excellent for eating fresh from the tree or juiced as a tangy fruit drink. Tree productive, ornamental. *O97*, R77, S59

Lisbon: Medium-sized, elliptical to oblong fruit. Seed content usually few to none. Rind medium-thick, tightly adherent. Flesh pale greenish-yellow, fine-grained, tender, juicy; flavor very acid. Crop comes mainly in winter and early spring. Tree vigorous, upright-spreading, large, thorny. In California, the cultivar most resistant to adverse conditions such as frost, heat, wind, and neglect. REUTHER; B93M, *D13*, E3M{DW}, J22, N18{SC}, S59

Lunario: (Amalfitano, Quatre Saisons) Distinctive, long elliptical fruit; rind medium-thin, smooth; flesh greenish-yellow, not very juicy, only moderately acid, seedy. Tree of medium vigor and size, strongly overbearing, thornless. Very responsive to forcing but the "verdelli" fruit is smaller in size, and the following winter crop is markedly reduced in size. REUTHER; *O4*, R77

Meyer: (Meyer Lemon) Fruit medium in size, oblong to short elliptical, sometimes faintly ribbed. Rind thin, soft; surface very smooth; tightly adherent; color yellowish-orange to orange. Flesh light orange-yellow, tender, very juicy; lemon-flavored and mildly acid. Moderately seedy. Crop distributed somewhat throughout the year but mainly in winter. Tree small to medium, spreading, nearly thornless, hardy and productive. A very good marmalade fruit when ripe. The flowers have a pleasant lemon taste. Probably a hybrid. REUTHER, STURROCK; B93M{DW}, E31M, F68, G17, G96{DW}, H4, I76M{PR}, J22, K67, *L47*

Monachello: Fruit medium-small, elliptical but tapering at both ends; rind thin and smooth, yellow at maturity; flesh tender, somewhat lacking in juice, acid content lower than most; seeds few or none. Crop well distributed throughout the year but mostly in winter and spring. Tree slow growing, nearly thornless, moderately productive. Well adapted to forcing but with a markedly reduced winter crop. REUTHER; *O4*

Pink Lemonade:[1] Medium-sized fruit; rind striped when immature, solid yellow when ripe; flesh pinkish, juicy, tart. Attractive tri-colored foliage, with two shades of green and white variegation. I83M

Ponderosa: (Ponderosa Lemon, American Wonder, Wonder) Probably C. limon x C. medica. Very large, obovoid fruit; color lemon-yellow; seedy. Rind medium-thick and fleshy; surface smooth, but slightly bumpy and indistinctly ribbed. Flesh pale green, juicy, flavor acid. Fruits mature throughout the year. Tree small, round-topped, productive. Grown mainly as a novelty and ornamental, although the fruit can be used as a lemon substitute. REUTHER; B73M{DW}, *D23M*, E3M{DW}, E31M, E97{DW}, F68, *G49*, G96{DW}, H4, I76M{PR}, I78{DW}, I83M, K22, K85{DW}

Sungold:[2] (Sungold Variegated) Medium-sized, oblong fruit; skin moderately thick, striped with green and yellow when immature, turning solid yellow when ripe; flesh yellow, tender, juicy, very acid; seeds relatively few; resembles Eureka. In season March to September, holds well on the tree. Attractive tri-colored foliage, two shades of green splashed with yellow-gold variegation; new growth burgundy red. E48, *G49*, I83M, *M61M*{DW}

Villa Franca: Fruit medium to large, oval in shape; rind slightly rough in texture, medium-thick, yellow when ripe. Flesh very juicy, greenish-yellow, tangy and acid in flavor; few or no seeds. Tree medium-sized, lightly branched and open in character, generally thornless. Beers in midseason or continuously over a long period. *O97*, *Q93*

LETTUCE {S}

LACTUCA SATIVA

HEADING LETTUCE

BATAVIAN Very distinct French lettuces, hard to classify by American standards. Very crisp, like Romaine or Iceberg types, but sweet and juicy and without bitterness. The plants are at first open, like looseleaf lettuce, becoming more compact and heavy until the heads are densely packed at full maturity.

Green/Yellow

Batavia Crival: New Batavian type. Medium green leaves, crisp and savory. Well filled heads. Suitable for both outdoor culture or under plastic tunnels. P59M

Batavian Loura: (Blond Batavian, White Silesian) Heads very large, but not very firm, roundish or slightly flattened; mature plant 12 to 14 inches in diameter. Outer leaves curled, undulated and broadly toothed at the edges, pale green slightly tinged with red on the margins. VILMORIN; I99, J73, L9

Bogata: 55 days. Very even heads; very crisp, glossy green leaves, slightly fringed on the edges. Black seeds. Can be harvested young as looseleaf lettuce or allowed to mature to form tight juicy "crispheads". For spring planting only. An old French market cultivar; preferred by the French restaurant trade because of superb taste and appearance. D87

Curled German Batavian: (Batavian Alema, Batavia Frisée Allemande) Head large, softish, roundish or slightly flattened, very pale green; mature plant 11 or 12 inches in diameter. Young leaves broad and short, scalloped and undulated at the edges, slightly yellowish green. VILMORIN; J73

Dorée de Printemps: A French Batavian lettuce that produces a full, light green head with tender leaves. Similar to Red Grenoble, but without the red tinges. Can be planted in both spring and fall. P59M, *R11M*

Jana: Large, uniform heads, firm and compact; brilliant green leaves with toothed edges, crisp but tender, of excellent flavor. Very early and productive. Somewhat susceptible to tipburn. Suitable for forcing under glass or plastic tunnels, or for an outdoor crop in May and June. Highly recommended new cultivar from Vilmorin of France. S95M

Kristia: 60 days. Attractive new French Batavian lettuce. Combines the crunchy texture of heading lettuce with the beauty and flavor of looseleaf types. Large, crisp, glossy medium-green leaves with a particularly fine juicy flavor. Good heat tolerance. Suitable for spring, summer or fall crops. K66

Victoria: 52 days. An all-green Canasta type lettuce. Forms a heavy, upright, open head of crisp leaves with a rich, deep green color. Quality excellent; crisp, juicy and notably sweet. Has a long harvest period and ability to produce in hot weather without bolting or bottom rot. Suitable for spring through fall crops. Recommended for the home garden and for specialty and quality conscious markets. F90, G6

Red/Brown

Antina: 55 days. Glossy, medium-green leaves tinged with blush-red along the edges; very crisp and juicy. Can be harvested as a young looseleaf or allowed to mature to form a large head. Holds its quality well during variable weather conditions. Favorite of specialty growers for fine gourmet markets. A first-quality example of the classic Batavian type so widely used in France. I77, K66

Batavia à Bord Rouge: 59 days. Very attractive French lettuce. Large rosettes of crumpled, dark-green leaves, uniformly tinged with deep-red along the edges; flavor initially seems bitter but mellows to a nut-like fineness. Stands for about 45 days without bolting. *A75*, G68, J20

Canasta: 50 days. An attractive French lettuce with shiny, puckered, bright green, red tinged leaves. As Canasta matures, the outer leaves form a whirl around a tall oval head with a cream-colored crisp heart. Tipburn, bottom rot, and bolt resistant. For spring, summer or fall crops. D68, G6, I77, I99, L7M, L89

Cybelle: Large heads with bright light green, ruffled leaves, slightly tinged with red at the edges; of good flavor. Best planted during spring and fall; will begin to fade with the onset of summer heat. Slow to bolt, especially if planted close together. I77, K66

Gloire du Dauphine: Similar to Red Grenoble. Bright green head with tinges of red. A good choice for fall and spring plantings in cool areas. *O60*

Maravilla de Verano: (Vonny) 62 days. Medium early, compact Batavia type. Crisp, deeply indented, undulated reddish-green outer leaves; firm, compact hearts. Very slow bolting. Very good market grower selection for spring and early summer cropping methods. Can also be used as a cutting lettuce after the first harvest. J20, K49Z, *R11M*

Red Grenoble: (Grenobloise Rouge) A very hardy, red-tinted Batavian. The color of the glossy leaves ranges from light green to magenta, and can vary from plant to plant. Does equally well in warm and cold weather; exceptionally resistant to cold, and is also slow to bolt during summer heat. Excellent flavor. *A75*, C53, G64, J20, K49M, K66, *R11M*

Rossia: Somewhat spreading, semi-open, massive growth habit. Medium green leaves, blotched with red. Widely adapted and versatile, can be sown any time during spring, summer and fall. Resistant to lettuce mosaic virus and necrosis. *O60*

Salvina: Moderately compact growth habit; outer leaves abundant, frilled on the margins. Leaves medium green, slightly tinged with shades of red on the tips, often blistered. Suitable for growing in spring and autumn. *O60*

BUTTERHEAD/BIBB Characterized by small, round heads with loosely packed leaves that are soft and tender with a buttery texture and flavor, and a delicate, cream-colored blanched heart. The type of lettuce most prized in Europe. Almost as easy to grow as looseleaf lettuce, and much less demanding than crispheads.

Green/Yellow

Akcel:[1 2] French forcing lettuce; bred especially for growing in greenhouses, tunnels and frames in the early spring. Deep-green, compact, heavy heads. Early; should perform well for the early "baby" lettuce market. C53

Australian Yellow: Very early Butterhead lettuce, resembles loose leaf Simpson types when young. Eventually forms a loose head. Tender, wrinkled yellow leaves. Suitable for growing during any season. K49M

Ben Shemen: 70 days. Large, compact head, weighing 1 to 1 1/4 pounds; medium dark-green, sweet, crispy leaves. Suitable for long distance shipping. Bred for resistance to heat and bolting. Good for late spring planting and southern gardeners. E49, *P75M*

Bibb: (Limestone) 60 days. A distinct butterhead type of fine table quality. Small heads with delicately flavored inner leaves that are blanched yellowish-green. Outer leaves smooth, thick, tender, deep-green tinged with brown. Should be planted early, as it bolts in hot weather. Used for greenhouse production, early local market and home gardens. A25, A87M, B35M, B73M, C53, D11M, F1, G71, *G83M*, H66, I91, J34, K71, N16

Big Boston: 70 days. Large Butterhead type. Solid, tightly folded heads, up to 12 inches in diameter; broad, wavy edged, bright green outer leaves slightly tinged with reddish brown; brittle, tender, buttery heart, blanching to a rich creamy yellow. Stands a great deal of cold without injury. Good for shipping and forcing. Introduced prior to 1894. A25, *A75*, C44, D11M, *D12*, *E53M*, F24M, F44, G57M, G71, I67M, J34

Butter King: 70 days. Improved White Boston type; selected for maturity, uniformity, disease resistance, slowness to bolt and tipburn resistance. Height 7 inches; large, loose head, 5 1/2 inches in diameter; weight 3/4 of a pound. Outstanding eating qualities; does not become bitter. Vigorous even in hot weather. All America Selections winner in 1966. D27, M13M

Buttercrunch: 67 days. A highly refined, long standing Bibb type lettuce developed at Cornell University. Medium-sized, dark green heads; smooth, soft, tender leaves; creamy yellow hearts. Plants reach 12 inches tall when mature; are slow bolting and heat resistant. All America Selections winner in 1963. Very popular for home gardens and local markets. A16, B73M, B75M, B78, C44, C53, E24, E57, G6, G16, *H61*, H94, *I62*{PL}, K73, L7M, M46, etc.

Dark Green Boston: 75 days. Improved White Boston type with deep dark-green leaves. Larger and more solid head than other Boston types; smooth, thick, tender outer leaves; creamy yellow heart; excellent texture and flavor. Resistant to tipburn. Very popular with both home gardeners and commercial growers. *A75*, C92, *E91G*, G27M, G51, G79, G82, G93M, H54, *H61*, J7, J84, K71, K73, M29, etc.

Delta:[1] English forcing lettuce; bred especially for growing in greenhouses, tunnels and frames in early spring. Medium-sized, pale green heads; quick growing. For cold or slightly heated culture. C53

Diamante:[1 2] Greenhouse Bibb or outdoor "mini" lettuce. Bred to grow vigorously with lower light and cooler temperatures than outdoor types. Large, dense, dark-green heads are produced even under cold conditions. Performs well under floating row covers, slitted row covers, poly tunnels, and greenhouses. In warmer weather outdoors, will rapidly form attractive miniature heads, ideal for individual salads. For winter production, being sown October through January and harvested February into April. G6, *R23*

Green Mignonette: (Manoa) 65 days. Small, round heads; deep-green, frilled leaves; firm heart, blanches almost white, very crisp, tender and sweet. Slow to bolt; very heat resistant; does well in warm, semi-tropical areas where other lettuces are not successful. Widely grown in the Manoa area of Hawaii. *A75*, C76M, D82, G68, I39, K49M, K66, *L59G*, P1G, R47

Grosse Blonde Paresseuse: (White Stone, Nonpareil) Mature head large and tall, flattened on the top; very light pale green, almost the color of butter or wax; outer leaves large, very much rounded, slightly crimped, not as pale-colored as the head; quality excellent. Mature plant about 12 inches in diameter. Resistant to bolting. Introduced prior to 1885. VILMORIN; *A75*, F33, G68, S95M

Kagraner Summer: (Orfeo Kagraner Summer) 60 days. French butterhead developed especially for summer crops. Mid-size, medium green heads; rather thick-leaved, with a somewhat open, firm heart. Very slow to bolt or tipburn. Good quality during the toughest season for butterhead lettuce production. *A1*, A16, *A75*, C85M, *D12*, E97, F24M, F33, F44, G6, G68, I77, J20, J25M, J82, K49M, etc.

Kinemontepas: Medium to large heads; grayish-green leaves, of excellent quality and flavor. Black-seeded. Very slow bolting; quality is maintained even under hot and dry conditions. A standard summer lettuce in France. *A75*, C53, G68, L7M

Kloek:[1] A tender green lettuce with large, solid heads. Excellent for cold or slightly heated greenhouses and one of the finest forcing cultivars for spring cutting. Sown from November onwards, it should be ready to harvest in early spring. P83M

Kwiek:[1] Large, quick-growing butterhead. For winter cropping in a cold or unheated greenhouse or poly tunnel. Sow late August for a harvest in November and December. Can also be sown in October. A2, L91M, P83M, S61

Magnet:[1] One of the best forcing butterheads. Produces a large yet tender, pale green head that grows quickly but withstands the early summer heat. Resistant to adverse conditions. C53

May Queen: (Reine de Mai, Regina di Maggio) 60 days. Quick-maturing butterhead for earliest spring sowings outdoors. Medium-sized, pale green heads tinged with reddish brown; creamy yellow hearts blushed with rouge-pink. Also good for growing in cold frames and greenhouses, and fall or late winter sowing in mild winter areas. Nineteenth century heirloom. *A75*, B8, C85M, G68, J73, S61

Mescher: (Schweitzer's Mescher Bibb) 50 days. Dates back to the 1700's. Introduced to the United States from Austria in the early 1900's and maintained as a Schweitzer family heirloom. Forms small, tight, crisp heads of green leaves ringed with red. Excellent appearance and flavor. Best grown in cool weather; has survived temperatures of 28^0 F. A2, E59Z, F42, L7M

Morgana:[1 2] Greenhouse or outdoor "mini" lettuce. Produces heavy, thick-leaved, dark-green heads; very easy to harvest and trim. For spring, fall and winter crops; sowing August through May, harvesting September through June. Outdoors, Morgana makes compact, beautifully formed, well-folded heads for perfect "baby butter" lettuce. G6

Ostinata:[1] 60 days. High quality Boston type with exceptionally long shelf life. Heavy, very attractive head. Compact plant allows for close spacing, yet still yields well. Stands high temperatures in mid summer as well as short day conditions. Excellent resistance to bolting and tipburn. Can be grown under glass, tunnels, in soil or in the open. Responds well to hydroponic culture. *F72*, *F85G*, G64, L42

Perella Green: A very small, open-leaf Butterhead type of good flavor and attractive appearance. Quick-growing; cold-tolerant; usually sown broadcast. Good for fall, spring and early summer plantings. Also suitable for growing in a cool greenhouse. A favorite of Joy Larkcom, author of "The Salad Garden". I77, K66, P83M, Q34, S55

Salina:[1 2] 60 days. Greenhouse or outdoor "mini" lettuce from Holland. Medium small, compact, dark-green heads; mild, non-bitter flavor. Best sown January through August for spring, summer and fall harvest. Resistant to bolting, tipburn and four strains of bremia. Germinates at 64 to 68^0 F. Responds well to hydroponic culture. *F72*, *F85G*, G6, *R23*, S27

Summer Bibb: (Summer Baby Bibb) 62 days. Improved Bibb strain. Small to medium heads, more compact than Bibb; creamy white hearts; thick, tender, medium-green leaves. Slow to bolt, 2 to 3 weeks later than regular Bibb; can be grown all summer. Grows well on upland or muck soils. Also recommended for hotbed and greenhouse use. *A1*, F13, F19M, *F63*, *F72*, G79, G82, G93M, *H61*, J58, J84, K66, K73, M29, N52

Tennis Ball: 70 days. Small to medium-sized head, very solid if grown in cool weather, often loose and open if grown during the summer months; outer leaves deep dark-green, slightly curled, broadly blistered; inner heart white and tender. Resistant to bolting. Extremely hardy. One of the oldest lettuces on record. BURR, VILMORIN; F25, F42, L90M

Tom Thumb:[2] 65 days. A "baby" butterhead well suited for smaller home gardens and window boxes. Very small, solid compact heads, about the size of an apple; light to medium green, crumpled leaves; tender, sweet and of very good flavor. Ideal for serving whole as an individual salad. Introduced prior to 1885. VILMORIN; A16, *A75*, B35M, C44, *D12*, D68, F1, F19M, *F72*, G71, H42, K66, L7M, L79, L97, M46, etc.

Unrivalled: (Attractive) A hardy, quick-growing early cultivar. Compact 6 ounce heads; medium-sized, firm, golden-yellow hearts; few outside leaves; superb flavor. Slow to bolt; very hardy. Sow outdoors in spring and summer. Can also be sown in autumn to heart in the spring in milder climates. Introduced around 1905. B49, O53M, P83M, S61

Val d'Orge: Large, vigorous, very attractive fall butterhead with pale translucent green coloring and a soft, buttery texture. Less frost hardy than others in its class, but fine for an early fall crop. G68, I99

Red/Brown

Babylon: 55 days. Heat resistant red butterhead type lettuce. Thick, well-folded, red tinged leaves are crisp and tender; relatively loose hearts. Very showy. K66, M46

Bon Jardinier: (Du Bon Jardinier) 55-60 days. Attractive medium to large, smooth, undulated heads; thick, medium green leaves lightly tinged with red. Very vigorous and productive. Harvested in summer and autumn. Recommended for home gardens and fresh market; also ships well. *A75*, G68, *L59G*, S95M

Bruna di Germania: (Brown German) Small, reddish-brown French lettuce for overwintering in mild climates. However, it does better with some protection, i.e. a cold frame or poly tunnel. Large, firm flavorful hearts; grows to 8 inches. Noted for its vigorous spring growth. F42, P83M, S55

Brune d'Hiver: (Brown Winter) Compact, rather thick-set plant; head medium-sized, green, overlaid with brownish-red; outer leaves coarsely crimped, much wrinkled; the whole plant seldom exceeds 7 or 8 inches in diameter. Quality excellent. Very hardy; well-adapted to winter culture; bolts readily in hot weather. Introduced prior to 1865. BURR, VILMORIN; A2, C53, I77, K49Z, K66, L7M

Crisp as Ice: (Hartford Bronzehead) 70 days. One of the best hot weather garden cultivars. Compact, medium-sized head; thick, crumpled deep-green leaves with a dark bronze cast; butter-yellow hearts; of fine quality and flavor. C44, G79, I67M, J58

Merveille des Quatre Saisons: (Marvel of Four Seasons, Meraviglia Delle Quattro Stagioni, Red Besson) 65 days. Head roundish, slightly flattened on top; forms very quickly and stays firm for a long time, even in very hot weather. Leaves short, almost round, the edges turned up in a kind of spoon-shape; tinged all over with brownish-red. Can be grown nearly all year round, but does best in spring and summer. Introduced prior to 1885. VILMORIN; *A75*, B8, B75, C53, E24, F33, F42, G68, G92, J20, J73, K49M, K66, M95, P83M, S55, etc.

Perella Red: One of the hardiest winter lettuces grown in the mountainous region of northern Italy. Has survived a temperature of 4^0 F. Very small, compact plant; forms a small heart or rosette. Decorative red strain of Perella Green. Sow in spring or autumn; harvest whole plant or use cut-and-come-again method. F44, I77, K66, P83M, S55

Pirat: (Brauner Trotzkopf) 55 days. Medium-green, gently crinkled leaves, overlaid with a soft brick red. Medium large, well folded, tender hearts blanch to a creamy yellow. Reliable and well adapted to growing throughout the season, even the middle of the summer. Similar to Merveille des Quatre Saisons, but more uniform, bolt resistant and compact. B75, C53, D68, E59Z, F42, F80, G6, I39, I99, K49T, L7M, L9, Q34

Red Boston: 68 days. Medium frame Boston type with rose-red tinged leaves and medium green hearts. Popular novelty lettuce for hydroponic or outdoor growers for the salad bar trade. G64, L42, N52

Red Riding Hood: A red Boston type, similar to Merveille des Quatre Saisons but with better color and bolt resistance. Very large, attractive red heads; best harvested when 8 to 12 ounces. Stands heat and drought well. C53

Rougette du Midi:[2] Small French lettuce with glossy, bronze-red leaves. Very crisp and flavorful. Spring and summer sowings produce a small, unhearted "baby" lettuce very quickly but they are equally quick to run to flower. Also suitable for autumn sowings to overwinter under cloches, or outdoors in mild climates. Attractive enough for the ornamental garden. C53, K66, P83M, S55, S95M

Sangria 58 days. Medium-sized, uniform heads with large, well-folded hearts of pale yellow leaves; average weight 16 ounces. Outer leaves smooth, somewhat wavy, very thick, medium dark-green prominently tinted with a warm, rosy red color. Excellent flavor. Grows well in spring, fall and winter. Good resistant to bolting and tipburn. Tolerant to downy mildew. G6, K66

Yugoslavian Red: 58 days. Heirloom from a peasant family in Marburg, Yugoslavia. Introduced by Southern Exposure Seed Exchange in 1987. Red heads, 10 inches in diameter. The leaves are succulent and have good flavor and color. L7M

CRISPHEAD The most popular form of lettuce in the United States, the Iceberg lettuces being typical. Characterized by solid heads of tightly-wrapped, very crisp leaves. They take about ten days longer than butterheads to mature but stand up to hot weather better without bolting. Considered to have more flavor than butterhead types.

Green/Yellow

All-the-Year-Round: 65 days. Round, compact, very solid head; of a very pale, almost whitish, green color; outer leaves short, roundish, finely crimped and slightly undulated. Tender and crisp, of fine quality. Hardy and very productive; grows well in almost any soil. Suitable for successional sowings any time of year. Introduced prior to 1885. VILMORIN; A2, *A75*, *D12*, D65, K49M, *L59G*, L91M, O53M, P83M, S61

Anuenue: 50 days. Resembles a small iceberg lettuce, only much more heat resistant and easier to grow. Large, well-packed heart; bright glossy green outer leaves, thick, crisp, mild and juicy. Spring, summer and fall crop. Developed by the University of Hawaii. Anuenue means rainbow in Hawaiian. G6, L7M, L9M, L89, M19, M32M

Avoncrisp: 70 days. Similar in appearance to Great Lakes but smaller and 7 to 10 days earlier. Crisp, brittle hearts, of good quality. Slow to bolt. Has some resistance to downy mildew, tipburn, root aphids and grey mold. Sow in summer for a fall harvest. Also ideal for a cut-and-come-again crop. L91M, P83M

Avondefiance: Medium to large, dark green heads; solid, tender hearts; semi-crisp texture. Highly resistant to mildew, making it useful for summer sowing (June through early August). Also highly resistant to root aphids, tipburn and bolting. Does well in warm climates. B49, F42, S61

Chou de Naples: (Couve de Napoles, Neapolitan) Head large, depressed, sometimes almost flat, very pale whitish green; mature plant 12 to 14 inches in diameter. Outer leaves dark green, spreading on the ground, very much curled and undulated at the edges. Keeps the head exceptionally well. One of the original "iceberg" types, and still considered one of the finest heading lettuces in Europe. VILMORIN; I77, J73

Great Lakes: 80 days. A sure heading summer lettuce of the iceberg type. Medium large heads; solid even before they attain full size; dark-green fringed leaves, fold completely over the head. Widely adapted; cold hardy; resistant to tipburn and bolting. Fine for the home garden and excellent for shipping. All America Selections winner in 1944. A16, A25, C44, E38, *F72*, F82, G51, H66, H94, *I62*{PL}, I64, J14{PL}, K71, L97, M95, N39, etc.

Hanson: (Improved Hanson) 75 days. Very large, yellow-green heads; creamy white hearts; texture crisp and tender, flavor sweet. Relatively tolerant to heat and tipburn. Widely adapted to different growing regions. Unsuited for overwintering or forcing. Introduced prior to 1885. A16, *A75*, *D12*, E59Z, K49M, L7M, *L59G*, M95M

Iceberg: 85 days. Quite different from the shipping cultivar New York, which is commonly called Iceberg by produce shippers and green grocers. Large compact, crumpled heads, white inside, crisp and sweet; wavy, fringed light green leaves tinged with brown at the edges. Well-suited to home gardens and local markets; will not stand long distance shipping. A16, A25, B35M, B73M, C53, C85M, F19M, G68, G71, H66, H94, K27M, M13M, M46, N39, etc.

Imperial Winter: 90 days. Very hardy lettuce. One of the largest and best cultivars for sowing in the open in autumn. Very large hearts; medium green leaves; of fine quality. Not recommended for spring or summer sowing, as it will bolt to seed. I99

Ithaca: 75 days. Large, firm heads; well wrapped for good protection; attractive, dark-green, ruffled leaves. High yielding; dependable and uniform-heading. Resistant to heat, bolting, tip burn, and brown rib. Most widely grown lettuce in the Northeast and Mid Atlantic states. A13, A56, C53, E24, E38, F13, F44, G57M, G71M, G82, J58, J84, J97M, K50, K73, etc.

Marmer:[1] 75 days. Large, very firm head with a solid heart and few outer leaves. Bred especially for growing under glass and plastic. Fast growing, with a well closed base. Can be planted densely. Sown from mid August to February for harvesting November to May. L91M, *R23*, S55, S61

Mission: 75 days. An early, heat tolerant iceberg type for hot humid climates. Dense, tight heads, 6 to 8 inches in diameter, crisp and sweet; long, thick outer leaves protect the heads. Matures in early summer, about 7 days earlier than Great Lakes. Excellent for home garden and local market use. Introduced in 1979. *F72*, I91, J34

Montello: 75 days. Iceberg type, widely used for shipping. Large, dark-green heads; crisp, bright green leaves. Highly tolerant to heat, splitting, tipburn, rib blight and corky root rot. Vigorous, widely adapted; does well in the North, South and West. Released by the Wisconsin Agricultural Experiment Station. *A1*, *A75*, *F63*, *F85G*, G16, G64, I64, J58, K73, L9M, *L59G*, M29

New York: (New York Iceberg, Wonderful) 80 days. Large, very dark-green heads; often weighing 3 to 4 pounds, nearly as solid as cabbage; crisp, tender, greenish-white hearts; of good quality. Forms good-sized heads even in hot weather. Introduced prior to 1888. F92, *G83M*, G87, H42, K49M

New York #12: 75 days. Earlier, sure-heading strain of New York. Very large, solid globular heads, up to 12 inches in diameter, often weighing 3 pounds; crisp, yellow heart, buttery flavor; outer leaves medium-green, slightly curled at the edges and formed tightly around the head. Does well in well-drained soil, but is unsuitable for low lying muck lands. Popular with home and market gardeners. A16, *A69M*, *A75*, D11M, *D12*, D27, E38, I67M, K71, M13M

Reine des Glaces: (Ice Queen, Regina dei Ghiaccia, Frisée de Beauregard) 62 days. An unusual crisphead type with very deeply cut, pointed, almost lacy leaves similar to the Cornet endives. Deep-green, crisp heads; small heart; slow bolting. Very attractive. For spring and summer sowings. Introduced prior to 1885. VILMORIN; *A75*, B8, C53, E59Z, G68, I77, I99, K49M, K66, P83M, S55

Trocadero: Distinct, light green heads, tinged with red on the upper part; forms quickly and keeps its shape well; dull green leaves, margined with red. Very good for summer culture, but may be equally well grown in winter or spring. Well adapted for both field culture and the kitchen garden. Introduced prior to 1885. VILMORIN; Q24M

Valdor: 65 days. An excellent winter lettuce, larger and more compact than Imperial Winter. Attractive, solid-green heads; few outer leaves. Used mostly in greenhouses, but can be sown in the open for an early spring cutting. Very cold hardy; good resistance to grey mold. B49, *R23*, S61

Webb's Wonderful: 75 days. Large, solid crisp hearts, of excellent quality; outer leaves dark-green and well curled; distinctive flavor. Stands well in hot weather; recommended for southern gardens. Extremely popular home garden cultivar in Europe. B49, E33, L91M, O53M, P83M, *R23*, S61, T1M

Windermere: Early, compact Great Lakes type. Crisp heads of excellent flavor. Quick to mature, and slow to run to seed. Sow in succession early spring to mid-summer outdoors; also in fall in cold frames for use the following spring. Award of Merit winner, Royal Horticultural Society, 1984. P83M, *R23*, S61

Winter Marvel: Large heads; clear pale-green, smooth, slightly wavy leaves; of fine quality and flavor. Very winter hardy, to 18° F. without protection. Can be sown in fall for an early spring harvest in many areas. Good for home and market gardens. An old European heirloom. A2, C53, D87, J73

Red/Brown

Continuity: 70 days. Extra early crisphead type. Compact, solid, crisp hearts; thick dark-green outside leaves, distinctly tinged with reddish-brown; of excellent flavor; very long standing. Suitable only for spring and summer sowing. Does well on dry, light soils. B49, C53, D68, E97, I39, I99, K49T, L89, P83M, Q34, S61

Pablo: 82 days. Medium to large, very uniform heads; outer leaves deep reddish-brown, slightly toothed; hearts well with crisp, blanched centers. Very reliable. L91M

Rosa: 75 days. Distinctive and colorful Iceberg type. Medium-sized, firm heads, 6 inches in diameter; attractive red in color; crisp and sweet. Resistant to tipburn. For home gardens and local markets. I77, I91, K66, N81

Rosy: 60-75 days. A small iceberg type, similar in form to Ithaca, but with attractive red to burgundy coloring. Tolerant of adverse conditions and slow to bolt. Highly recommended for market gardens. C53

ROMAINE Also known as *cos lettuce*, this type has long, broad, upright leaves that form heads. The leaves are tender and green on the upper portions, and thick, crisp, and juicy near the base. They take longer to mature than other types, but stand hot and dry conditions well without going to seed. Prized for their distinctive flavor, especially in a *Caesar salad*.

Green/Yellow

Balloon: (Ballon) Large, very vigorous plant; large, broad, roundish head, slightly flattened at the top, full and firm; outer leaves not as crimped as Paris White Cos, but greener and more rounded at the ends. Seldom runs to seed. Hardier than Paris White Cos; very suitable for autumn sowing. Introduced prior to 1885. VILMORIN; C53, F33, K49M, P83M

Craquante d'Avignon: (Craquerelle du Midi) An open hearted, semi-romaine type that is especially suited to warm climates, the firm heads being harvested into early June in Florida. Deep green leaves; crisp and crunchy. Resistant to cold and also slow to bolt, making it an ideal choice for the home gardener. Can be planted January through August. C53, I99

Little Gem:[2] (Sugar Cos) 70 days. Intermediate in shape between a cos and a heading lettuce. Small to medium-sized, erect plant; very dark green outer leaves. Forms a very compact creamy-yellow heart, with no waste. Brittle, crisp, very sweet, superb flavor. For spring and summer sowing. Also good for forcing. B49, B75, C53, E59Z, F42, I99, K49Z, K66, L7M, *L59G*, L89, L91M, P83M, *R23*, S55, S61, etc.

Lobjoit's Green Cos: 65 days. Large, compact, firm hearts, closely self-folded. Tall, upright outer leaves, to 12 inches, dark-green in color. Crisp and sweet, of excellent quality. Very bolt resistant. Can be sown for successional sowing throughout the summer, or in mild climates, in the autumn for early spring cutting. B49, E33, F44, I99, *R23*, S61, *S75M*

Paris Green Cos: 66 days. Compact, elongated head, pointed or slightly blunt; outer leaves erect, comparatively narrow, dark green; midribs very white; sweet and crisp. Blanches well without having to be tied. For spring, summer or autumn sowing; also good for forcing. Introduced prior to 1865. BURR, VILMORIN; J73

Paris White Cos: (Blonde Maraîchère) 70 days. Long, cylindrical head; outer leaves large and luxuriant, of a light-green color, slightly crinkled; inner leaves very pale-green, always folded, midrib white and very prominent. Less hardy and a few days later than Paris Green Cos. Very widely adapted. Introduced prior to 1865. BURR, VILMORIN; A69M, B35M, B75, C85M, D11M, D65, D76, E97, F24M, *F72*, H49, I99, J20, L91M, M13M, etc.

Parris Island Cos: Very uniform, tall, cylindrical plants; thick, slightly crinkled, dark grayish-green outer leaves; pale green to creamy white hearts. Heads exceptionally well. Medium slow bolting. Mosaic tolerant. Developed for coastal regions of the Southeast, but widely adapted and used for shipping, local markets and home gardens. A16, *A75*, C44, E24, E57, F82, G6, G64, *H61*, K73, L97, M46, M49, M95, N16, etc.

Romance: 50 days. Large uniform heads, up to 1 pound each. Upright, very smooth dark-green leaves, pale blonde at the center; crisp, sweet, tender. Fast growing. Slow to bolt. Resistant to mosaic virus and mildew. Award of Merit winner, Royal Horticultural Society, 1982. K66, L91M

St. Blaise:[1] A special Romaine type, adapted to early spring planting under row covers. Also does well in outdoor plantings right through the summer. Small, upright, light bright-green heads with few outer leaves. Very heat tolerant. Ideal for intensive gardens. Potential specialty market item. C53

Sucrine: Semi-romaine type with a more or less upright growth habit. Slightly loose head; thick, medium-length green leaves. Crisp, sweet, of excellent flavor. Resistant to cold; sow in fall and winter. Very popular among European home gardeners and market growers and has found ready acceptance in many California specialty restaurants. *A75*, E83T, G68, I77, I99

Valmaine: (Valmaine Savoy) 70 days. Large self-folding type for spring and summer use. Slightly taller and more open-headed than Parris Island Cos and able to stand more adverse weather. Mildly crinkled, dark green leaves, 10 to 12 inches long, of very good flavor. Resistant to downy mildew. Heat tolerant. A87M, B49, B75M, C85M, *E91G*, *F72*, G16, G64, I91, K49M, K73, L42, L89, L91M, M46, etc.

Vaux's Self Folding: The first self-folding cos lettuce. Compact, erect growth habit; self-folding medium-sized, firm heart. Broad, dark-green outer leaves protect the heart. Very popular with market growers for spring and autumn sowing. Introduced around 1873. P83M

Winter Density: 65 days. Distinct type, somewhat intermediate in form between a cos and a heading lettuce. Produces large, compact, very solid hearts; outer leaves very dark-green. Crisp, sweet, of excellent flavor. Slow to bolt and also tolerates light frost. Widely used for autumn sowing. A2, *A75*, B49, C53, *D12*, D68, E24, G6, I99, K49M, K66, O53M, P83M, *R23*, S61, *S75M*, etc.

Yedikule: (Iedukule) Originated in Turkey. Does best if planted in autumn, but is very heat resistant, not bolting or becoming bitter. Performed better than all heat resistant American cultivars in field-trials at the University of California, Davis. J73

Red/Brown

Bath Brown: Leaves of young plant deeply toothed, tinged with red on the edges and veins. Head nearly pointed, pale-green, slightly tinged with dull brown; outer leaves finely toothed on the edges, tinged on all parts exposed to the sun with pale brown on a grayish-green ground. Very hardy; does well under summer or autumn culture. Usually tied up to increase production of tender blanched leaves. VILMORIN; O20

Brown Golding: 70 days. Medium-sized heads; small, red tinged leaves. Very sweet and crunchy. Develops best color in cooler weather. In a test conducted by the Henry Doubleday Research Association it was found to contain 3 times the vitamin C of typical summer lettuces. I99, L9

Majestic Red: 60 days. Compact, very erect plant; medium-sized, tall cylindrical head; distinct, medium dark red color; crisp and sweet with excellent flavor. Adds a unique color to salads. For home gardens and fresh market; also ships well. Shows good resistance to heat and drought. Developed by Sunseeds. D11M, F13, G93M, K10, *L59G*

Red Leprechaun:[2] (Little Leprechaun) Savoy red romaine type, resembling Little Gem. Slightly larger, growing 8 to 12 inches tall, with mature heads that may weigh one pound or more; blanched hearts cream colored, overspread with pale pink. Succulent, puckered leaves, burgundy colored on exposed surfaces. Should be harvested at the three-quarter pound stage. C53, G57M, K49T

Rosalita: 62 days. Medium-large, upright plants; heads average 14 to 16 ounces in weight with a semi-firm heart of creamy yellow leaves. Outer leaves an attractive burgundy color, fading to an emerald green at the base, crisp, sweet and juicy. Not tolerant of hot weather, recommended for spring or fall culture only. Resistant to frost and tipburn. Widely adapted. Developed by Rob Johnston Jr. B75, G6, I91

Rouge d'Hiver: (Red Winter) Young plant deeply tinged with brownish-red; head tall, long, entirely green, with the exception of a brownish-red tinge on the top; outer leaves long, round, deeply colored with reddish brown. Heads well without being tied. Hardy; productive; remarkably slow in running to seed. Introduced prior to 1885. VILMORIN; C53, D68, D87, E59Z, F42, I77, I99, K49M, K49T, K49Z, K66, S55

Rubens Dwarf: 58 days. Semi-dwarf type. Very full, 12-inch heads of open upright leaves. Outer leaves an attractive and unusual deep clear cranberry-red that contrasts with the lime-green hearts. Crisp, juicy, full sweet flavor. Colors are most intense in cool spring and fall weather. I77, K66

LOOSELEAF LETTUCE

GREEN/YELLOW

Baby Oak:[2] 40 days. A new 1/2 to 2/3 size strain of regular Oakleaf, maturing a week sooner. An appealing new cultivar for mini-gardens, greenhouse production, and specialty salad growers. G6

Biondo a Foglie Lisce:[3] 25 days. Quick growing cutting lettuce. Smooth, tender leaves. Broadcast the seed thinly and cut when 2 inches high, or about a month after seeding. Can be cut several times over a long season. C53, S55

Black Seeded Simpson: 45 days. Large, upright plant; broad, crumpled, light green leaves, slightly frilled at the margins. Very tolerant of hot weather. Produces a high quality crop under a wide range of conditions. Longtime home garden and local market favorite. Introduced prior to 1888. B73M, B75M, B78, C44, C53, E24, E57, *F72*, G6, G16, *H61*, H94, L7M, M49, M46, etc.

De Cortar:[3] Never forms a head, but compensates by producing and abundance of leaves which grow again after being cut, thus producing a large supply of lettuce in a limited space. Resembles Oakleaf. Best sown in early spring or autumn. J73

Deer Tongue: (Matchless) 55 days. Loose, upright, medium-sized heads; light-green leaves, distinctively pointed; creamy heart; tender, sweet, of very good quality and flavor. Heat resistant; slow to bolt. Sow in spring through early summer. An old heirloom cultivar that is excellent for home gardens. C53, D87, E24, E59Z, F42, J58, K49T, L7M

Early Curled Simpson: (Early Curled Silesian, Silica Curled) A very old cultivar that is still popular. Large, pale yellowish-green leaves, very much undulated at the margins, curled and rumpled; crisp, sweet and flavorful. Produces a cluster of leaves in the center. White seed. Slow to bolt in hot weather. Introduced prior to 1885. VILMORIN; A56, *D12*, D76, F24M, G51, G71, H33, *L59G*, N39

Feuille de Chene:[3] (Curly Oakleaf, Ricciolina di Quercia) Used almost exclusively as a cutting lettuce. Light green, deeply indented and curled leaves; mild and tender. Easy to grow and harvest; cut entire plant when about 2 inches high, leave to resprout. Slow bolting and heat resistant; sow in succession from early spring into autumn. Will form a loose head at maturity if thinned. B8, C53, P83M, S55

Grand Rapids: 50 days. Large, upright, compact plants form an attractive cluster of broad, fringed and curled light-green leaves. Of high quality; crisp, tender, sweet, flavorful. Resistant to bolting and rot. Very popular for greenhouse forcing and early outdoor culture. A16, B35M, C85M, D11M, E38, *E91G*, F1, *F72*, G16, H42, *H61*, H94, J7, M13M, N39, etc.

Green Ice: (Burpee's Green Ice) 45 days. A fast maturing cultivar that produces large thick bunches of dark glossy green leaves, heavily blistered with wavy, fringed leaf margins. Very crisp texture, tender and mild, of excellent quality. Exceptionally uniform. One of the slowest cultivars to bolt, so it can be used longer. A25, B75, C44, D11M, D68, *F72*, G16, G71, G87, H33, H42, H94, I77, I91, J58, etc.

Lingue de Canarino: Pale green leaves resemble round oak leaves and form a tight bunch. Very mild and flavorful in the spring; retains its high quality right through the summer; very resistant to bolting. Attractive shape and color. Italian name means canary tongues or canary-colored tongues, which suggests the shape and color. D68, J20

Lollo Biondo:[3] (Lollo Green) A popular cutting lettuce; vigorous enough to resprout from a cut stem without loss of leaf quality. Bright yellow-green, very ruffled leaves. Cut leaf by leaf rather than using entire head. Decorative as well as useful. Sow in spring or fall. C53, I77, K66, P83M, Q34, S55

No-Bolt Nimes: Extremely thick leaves with very thick, crisp midribs. Similar to Sucrine, but the leaves are not held upright, they more or less sprawl. Has much less tendency to bolt in hot weather than do many other lettuces. May be sown all season long. Originated in southern France. E83T

Oakleaf: 45 days. Forms a compact rosette of thin, tender, light green oakleaf-shaped leaves. Excellent quality; does not become bitter with age. Stands heat well and resists bolting. Popular old-fashioned lettuce that has been rediscovered as a gourmet specialty. A25, B73M, B78, C85M, D11M, D82, E24, F33, G6, G71, H94, K73, L9M, L89, M95, etc.

Salad Bowl: 50 days. Large, attractive rosette. Long, medium-green, deeply notched and curled leaves; crisp, tender, sweet. Very slow to bolt; resists heat and tipburn well. High quality home garden cultivar, sometimes used for roadside stands and local markets. All America Selections winner for 1952. A16, A25, B49, B78, C44, C53, D82, E24, F19M, G6, G16, H66, J7, L97, M46, etc.

Slobolt: (Harris' Slobolt) 48 days. Similar to Grand Rapids in appearance, but holds 2 to 3 weeks longer without bolting. Light-green, crumpled and frilled leaves; crisp, mild sweet flavor. Remains dwarf and compact even in hot weather; keeps its high quality over a long period. For greenhouse growing as well as outdoors. *A1*, C44, D11M, D65, D76, F13, F19M, *F63*, G64, G79, *H61*, J84, K73, L7M, L42, L89, etc.

Tango: 45 days. Uniform, attractive plants form tight, erect rosettes. Deeply cut and curled leaves; resemble endive in appearance; darker green than most cultivars; tender, tangy, vitamin rich. Cut young during warm weather as it is not very heat tolerant and will run to seed. B75, C53, K66

RED/BROWN

Biscia Rossa:[3] Very attractive, smooth-leaved, red tinged cutting lettuce from Italy. Will give several cuttings when grown as a cut-and-come-again crop, or may be allowed to reach maturity. B8, P83M, S55

Bronze Arrow: (Bronze Arrowhead) Very attractive California heirloom. Large, oakleaf-shaped leaves tipped with reddish-brown. Mild flavor. Long-standing - will stay fresh and flavorful at market-able size for about 3 weeks in hot weather without going to seed. Can be sown year-round in mild climates, September sowings lasting into May. B49, E59Z, F42, L7M

Chadwick's Rodan: 58 days. A European heritage cultivar selected by Alan Chadwick. Medium-sized leaf lettuce that forms a loose head. Upright, paddle-shaped leaves tinged with bronze. Heat resistant. Attractive as well as flavorful. Heads produce very little seed. B49, L7M

Cocarde: 46 days. A "giant red Oakleaf" type. Large, heavy, upright heads; delicate, lobed, dark-green leaves with a rusty red overlay; large yellow-blanched heart. Sow in spring, summer or fall. An unusual French lettuce of very good quality. C53, G6

Flame: 46 days. Attractive lettuce with a distinctly bright red color that is prevalent throughout the leaves and stems. Broad, frilled leaves that hold their color well. Resistant to bolting. Selected from Prizehead. F13, I77, K66

French Red: 46 days. Red-maroon lettuce resembling Black Seeded Simpson in size, plant habit, and leaf appearance. Has a crisp texture and good flavor with a hint of sweetness. Bolts readily and is thus best for cool season areas and northern gardens. L7M

Garnet: 48 days. An improved Prizehead type. Has more red coloration and holds a nicer bunch without over-sizing or folding at the heart. Ruffled, bright green leaves, prominently tinged with red at the tips and where exposed. Crisp and non-bitter. *D74*, G6

Lollo Rosso:[3] (Lollo Red) 52 days. Very attractive red strain of Lollo Biondo; especially well suited to garnishing. Small, circular rosette formed of heavily-frilled, medium green leaves tipped with a strong, warm red. Mild flavor. Very heat tolerant. Used as a cut-and-come-again lettuce, or left to head up for a single serving. For spring or fall sowings. C53, D68, E5T, E33, G6, H42, H49, I77, I99, K49T, K66, L89, M46, O53M, P83M, Q34, S55, etc.

Prizehead: 50 days. Large, upright plant; broad, crumpled, slightly frilled leaves; outer leaves moderately tinged with reddish brown, inner leaves medium green; attractive. Crisp, sweet and tender. Medium slow bolting. Resistant to mosaic virus. Very popular home garden and local market cultivar. A16, A25, D82, E24, E57, F1, G16, H42, *H61*, H66, H95, J7, K73, M13M, M46, etc.

Red Fire: 45 days. Large, intense red leaves; crinkled and frilled at the edges, crisp and tender. Very uniform and productive. Easy to grow; withstands heat as well as cold. Very decorative. M46

Red Oak Leaf: 50 days. Deeply indented leaves, green shaded with hues of burgundy, maroon, crimson or cranberry, depending on climate and conditions. Deepest red colors are obtained when grown in full sun. Sweet and delicate in texture. Resistant to heat and bolting; also grows well in cool weather. Popular with market growers who serve the gourmet restaurant trade. Selected from Red Salad Bowl. I77, I99, K66, Q34

Red Sails: 45 days. Attractive, compact, fringed heads have a bright green background heavily overlaid with deep burgundy red. Mild, non-bitter flavor. Slow bolting. Has 6 times more vitamin A and 3 times more vitamin C than other lettuces. Deep red color intensifies as the lettuce matures. All America Selections winner in 1985. A25, B75M, C53, D87, E57, F19M, G6, G16, *H61*, H95, *I62*{PL}, J7, K73, L7M, L9M, L97, etc.

Red Salad Bowl: 46 days. A wine red strain of Salad Bowl. Radiant burgundy red, deeply lobed leaves form a full rosette; leaf shape resembles Oak Leaf lettuce. Mild, non-bitter flavor. Slow to bolt; holds its quality for a long time. Color is most spectacular during cool weather but grows well in spring, summer and fall. A69M, B75, C53, D76, E24, F44, G6, H49, J20, K27M, K71, M49, M46, P83M, S55, etc.

Rossa d'Amerique:[3] Pale green leaves tipped with a sparkling rose-red. Primarily used as a cutting lettuce when 4 to 6 inches tall, but will form a loose head if thinned. Imported from Italy, where this type of lettuce is known as lattughino da taglio. C53

Rossa di Trento:[3] A broad, crinkled, red-tipped cutting lettuce imported from Milan, Italy. Can be grown nearly year round in mild climates. This type of lettuce is called lattughino da taglio in Italy. C53

Ruby: Bright green, heavily crinkled and frilled leaves, prominently shaded with intense red. Crisp, sweet, succulent. Heat resistant; will stand for a long period of time without bolting to seed. Very decorative. All America Selections winner in 1958. A16, A87M, C44, C85M, E38, F82, G16, G68, G71, *H61*, H94, I67M, K73, M95, N16, etc.

Selma Lollo: 45 days. Uniform, bushy heads, about 12 inches in diameter. Dark pink, very frilled leaf edges contrast attractively with the soft-green base. Excellent flavor. Very decorative. I91

LIMA BEAN {S}

PHASEOLUS LUNATUS

BUSH LIMA BEANS

Burpee Improved: (Burpee's Improved Bush) 75 days. Medium dark green pods, long, broad and moderately thick; 3 to 5 1/2 inches long, produced in clusters; 4 to 5 seeds per pod; seeds large, fairly plump; seed color pale creamy white. Medium to large, erect plant. Introduced in 1907. HEDRICK 1931; A25, B75, B75M, C92, D65, G16, G71, H49, H66, J58, J97M, K71, L42, M13M, M46, etc.

Dixie Speckled Butterpea:[1] 76 days. Slightly curved, oval pods, 3 to 3 1/2 inches long; 3 to 4 seeds per pod; seed small, nearly round; seed color red, speckled with dark carmine. Similar to Dixie White Butterpea except for seed color, and more productive under hot, dry conditions. Good for home and market gardens, either fresh or when dried. F19M, *G1M*, G27M, G71, G82, G93M, H66, I91, J84, K71, L14, *L59G*, M46, N16

Dixie White Butterpea: 70-75 days. Pods medium-sized, broad, oval, 3 1/2 inches long; seeds small, pea-shaped; seed color white; quality very good, tender, has a rich meaty flavor. Strong, vigorous plant; productive; produces well under hot weather conditions. Recommended for home and market gardens. F19M, *G1M*, G27M, H66, I91, J34, K10, K71, L14, *L59G*, M95M

Early Giant: 65 days. Large pods, 5 to 6 inches long; 4 to 5 flat, oval seeds per pod; quality very good, tender, rich and butter-flavored; a good freezer. Rugged, upright plant; height about 18 inches; will bear from July until frost. K71

Eastland: 75 days. Medium-sized pods, 3 to 4 inches long; 3 small, semi-flat seeds per pod; seed color greenish-white; quality excellent. Strong upright plants have excellent yield potential. Resistant to downy mildew races A, B, C and D. Does well in short season areas, the seeds having good tolerance to cold soil. B75M, F13, I91, L42

Fordhook: 75 days. Broad, plump pods, 3 to 4 1/2 inches long, produced in clusters; 3 to 4 large, plump seeds per pod, packed closely together for easy shelling; seed color pale creamy white with a tinge of green; quality excellent, tender and buttery. Decidedly upright, erect plant; productive. Introduced in 1907. HEDRICK 1931; B75, C85M, G57M, H66, I67M, K71, L14, M95M, N39

Fordhook 242: 75 days. Uniformly curved pods, 3 to 4 inches long; 3 to 4 thick, plump seeds per pod; seed color greenish tinged with cream. Higher yielding, more heat tolerant and easier to shell than regular Fordhook. All America Selections winner in 1945. A25, A87M, B73M, B75M, C44, E38, F19M, *F72*, G16, G51, G71, *H61*, J58, K73, N16, etc.

Geneva: 85 days. A baby bush lima with cool soil tolerance; germinates in soil 10^0 cooler than limas usually require, adding about 2 weeks to the growing season. The fresh, shelled beans are light green, flavorful and good for freezing. D68, G6

Giant Improved: 75 days. Slightly curved pods, 5 to 6 inches long; 4 to 5 large beans per pod; easy to shell; quality high; tender, rich and buttery flavor. Vigorous, erect plant; bears until frost. H33

Henderson: 60 to 70 days. Pods dark green; short, broad and slender, 3 to 3 1/2 inches long; 3 to 4 small seeds per pod; seed color pale creamy white; quality good to excellent. Small plant, 12 inches or less; very early; productive over a long period. Introduced about 1883. HEDRICK 1931; A16, A25, A87M, B35M, B73M, F19M, F92, G51, *H61*, H66, H94, J58, M46, M95, N16, N39, etc.

Hopi Beige:[1] (Hopi Tan) Beige and black mottled bean with variations. Good dried or shelled fresh. Medium bush. Adapted to southwestern dryland culture. Formerly Hopi White, a misnomer. K49T, L79M

Hopi Yellow:[1] (Hopi Orange) Beautiful yellow-orange and black mottled bean. Good dried or shelled fresh. Medium bush, 3 feet tall. Adapted to southwestern dryland culture. A2, K49T, L79M

Jackson Wonder:[1 2] (Calico) 65 days. Pods dark-green, broad and slender, 3 inches long; 3 to 4 small seeds per pod; seed color light buff, mottled purplish-black. Upright, spreading plant, 12 to 18 inches tall. Resembles Henderson, but more heat and drought tolerant. Very young pods may be used as a snap bean. Popular in the South for home and market gardens. Introduced in 1888. HEDRICK 1931; A87M, B71, E97, F12, F19M, G93M, H66, I91, J34, J73, K10, K71, K73, L7M, M46, M95M, N16, etc.

Nemagreen: 68 days. A good quality home garden lima with very good resistance to nematodes. Medium-sized pods, 3 inches long; small, flat, pale-green seeds. Good when cooked, frozen or dried. F19M, *G1M*, J34

Pima Beige: Light beige beans can be plain or mottled with black. Prolific plant, will outproduce teparies if water is adequate. I16

Red Calico:[1] Beautiful family heirloom from South Carolina. Medium-small seeds, bright dark-red splashed with black streaks and speckles, very attractive. Plants are drought and heat resistant. Probably a sport of the Red Calico pole lima. L7M

Thorogreen: (Early Thorogreen, Allgreen, Cangreen, Green-Seeded Henderson) 65 days. Pods are 3 inches long and are set high off the ground for easy picking; 3 to 4 small, bright-green seeds per pod. Excellent for canning and freezing. Vigorous, upright plant, to 18 inches tall; bears continuously till frost. Similar to Henderson except seeds are greener. B35M, D11M, D65, D76, E97, F19M, G16, G71, H54, H66, I39, K50, K71, K73, M46, etc.

POLE LIMA BEANS

Black: 80 days. Small to medium-sized beans are dark-violet at green shell stage, black when dry; 4 to 6 beans per pod; easy to shell; flavor very good. Very tall plant; prolific, produces until frost; drought resistant. U33

Black-Eyed Butterbean: 90 days. Medium sized limas of good quality; white with a black eye; quality good. Dries well on the vine, with the black eye developing upon drying. Fairly productive 6 to 8 foot tall plant; likes heat. I99

Burpee's Best: 92 days. Large, straight pods, 4 to 4 3/4 inches long; 3 to 5 large, plump, tender "potato" type seeds per pod. Excellent fresh or frozen. Strong climber may grow 10 to 12 feet tall. Combines the best features of Fordhook bush, with higher yields. B75

Christmas:[1] (Large Speckled Calico) 85-90 days. Broad, flat pods, 5 to 6 inches long; 3 very large, very flat seeds per pod; seed color buff with deep crimson blotches; seed turns to a pink-brown color when cooked and the blotches disappear. Excellent fresh, canned or frozen. Grows 7 to 9 feet tall; yields heavily. D76, F12, F19M, G82, G93M, H66, I39, I91, J34, J84, K49M, K71, L7M, M46, N16, etc.

Cliff Dweller:[1] 90 days. Small, cream-colored seed edged in black, occasionally with a touch of dark wine-red; 3 seeds per pod. Very vigorous and productive plant, up to 10 feet tall; tolerates heat and drought well. Seeds should be picked continuously as they mature. Heirloom. K49M

Dr. Martin: 90 days. Produces very large seeds, with an average weight of 2.3 grams; 3 to 4 seeds per pod; quality and flavor very good. Vigorous plant, 8 to 10 feet tall; very productive - average yield 19.5 pounds of shelled beans per 25-foot row. A rare heirloom. D71, I97T

Dreer's Improved: (Challenger) 90 days. Medium-green pods; very broad and quite plump; 3 to 4 medium large, smooth, plump, "potato" type seeds per pod; seed color dull white with a greenish tinge; flavor tender, sweet and meaty. Excellent for both home and market gardens. Very productive plant, grows 12 feet tall. Introduced in 1875. HEDRICK 1931; U33

Florida Butter:[1] (Florida Speckled Butter) 90 days. Medium dark-green pods, fairly broad and quite slender, 3 inches long; 3 small seeds per pod; seed color light buff, blotched and irregularly spotted with reddish-brown. Vigorous plant, 5 to 8 feet tall; a large yielder over a comparatively long bearing season. Most suitable for the southern states. HEDRICK 1931; A56, A87M, F12, F19M, G27M, G51, G79, G93M, H66, J34, K27M, K71, L14, M46, N16, etc.

Flossie Powell's:[1] 100 days. Medium-sized seed, somewhat plump; light-tan colored with reddish streaks; 2 to 3 seeds per pod. Grows to 8 feet tall; a good producer, yielding well under hot and dry conditions. Very compact leaf growth, would grow well in small spaces with sun. Heirloom. I99

Indian Red Pole: Medium-sized, dull red to dull maroon-red seeds. Heat and drought resistant, yielding prolific crops under adverse conditions. Reported to be of Native American origin. L7M

King of the Garden: 88 days. Medium green pods, broad; quite slender, 6 inches long; 4 to 6 seeds per pod; seeds large, flat; seed color cream-white to very pale green; quality excellent. Vigorous plant, grows 8 to 10 feet tall; heavily productive over a moderately long season. Introduced by Frank S. Platt in 1883. HEDRICK 1931; A13, C44, D76, F13, F19M, *F72*, G16, G51, G71, H66, I91, K71, L7M, M46, N39, etc.

Lineburger: 90 days. Large pods; large seeds, average weight 2.1 grams; 3 to 4 seeds per pod; seed color white; flavor very good. Excellent seed germination. Grows 10 feet tall or more; productive; drought resistant. Similar to Dr. Martin but with narrower pods, slightly smaller seeds, and less production. U33

Prizetaker: 90 days. Pods 6 inches or more long, 1 1/2 inches wide, borne in clusters; easy to harvest; 3 to 5 very large seeds per pod. Quality and flavor excellent both fresh and frozen. Good for home or market gardens. Also recommended for exhibiting at county fairs. B75, *F72*, G57M, G71, G71M, H54, M95M

Sieva: (Carolina) 78 days. Small, slightly curved pods, 3 to 3 1/2 inches long; 3 to 4 small, flat, smooth seeds per pod; seed color medium green when shelled, dull white when dried. Vines productive; reliable; precocious. Excellent for home and market gardens, either fresh, shelled or dried. B73M, B75, D76, F19M, *F72*, G27M, G93M, H54, H66, J73, K5M, K71, L14, M95M, N16, etc.

Willow-Leaved: (Willow Leaf) 65 days. Ornamental plant with dark glossy green leaves and long, narrow, willow-like leaflets. Pods very dark green, short, 3 inches long; 3 or 4 seeds per pod; seed color chalky white; quality fair to good, best when grown in southern states. Introduced in 1891. HEDRICK 1931; H66, L7M, L14

TROPICAL LIMA BEANS

Also known as *Madagascar beans*, these unselected, viny type limas are well adapted to the lowland tropics, especially the highly leached, infertile soils of the more humid regions. Some little-known cultivars have given extraordinarily high yields in tropical rainforest regions. NATIONAL RESEARCH COUNCIL 1979; P1G

LOQUAT {GR}

ERIOBOTRYA JAPONICA

ORANGE-FLESHED

Big Jim: Large, roundish to oblong fruit, 1 1/4 to 1 1/2 inches in diameter; skin pale orange-yellow, medium-thick, easy to peel; flesh orange-yellow, very sweet but with some acidity, of excellent flavor; ripens midseason, March to April. Tree vigorous, upright, highly productive. Originated in San Diego, California by Jim Neitzel. L6

Early Red: Medium-large, pear shaped fruit, borne in compact clusters; skin orange-red with white dots, tough, acid; flesh orange, very juicy, sweet, of fair to excellent flavor; seeds usually 2 or 3. Ripens very early, late January or early February in California. Originated by C.P. Taft in 1909. MORTON 1987a; S97M

Gold Nugget: (Thales, Placentia) Large, round to oblong-obovate fruit; surface yellow-orange to orange in color; skin not thick, tender; flesh orange-colored, firm and meaty, juicy; flavor sweet, somewhat reminiscent of apricot; quality good. Seeds 4 to 5, the seed cavity not large. Ripens late. Fruits borne only a few to a cluster; keep and ship well. Tree vigorous, upright, self-fertile. *D23M*, D57, *G49*, I74, I83M, J22, L6

Mogi: Small, elliptical fruit, weight 40-50 grams; skin light yellow; flesh relatively sweet; ripens in early spring. Tree cold-sensitive; self-fertile. Constitutes 60% of the Japanese crop of loquats. Easier to peel than Tanaka, matures earlier, but is more susceptible to bruising and to cold injury. Selected from numerous seedlings planted at Mogi, Japan. Named in 1925. MORTON 1987a; I83M

Mrs. Cooksey: Large fruit, up to 1 1/2 inches long and 1 inch in diameter; yellow flesh of very good flavor. I83M

Strawberry: Medium-sized fruit with yellow flesh. Named for the strawberry-like flavor detected by some tasters. However, according to others it does not have this flavor. I83M

Tanaka: Fruit very large, usually obovoid; weight 2 to 3 ounces; skin orange-yellow, attractive; flesh firm, rich orange, aromatic, slightly acidic to sweet, of excellent flavor; seeds 2 to 4; ripens very late, the beginning of May in California. Keeps unusually long, if left for a week it wrinkles and dries but does not rot. Tree vigorous and productive. Originated in Japan in the late 1800's. Named after Dr. Yoshio Tanaka. MORTON 1987a; Q24M, S97M

Wolfe: Fruit obovoid to slightly pyriform; skin yellow, relatively thick; flesh juicy, firm, flavor excellent; seeds usually 1 to 3; ripens in winter and early spring, several days later than Advance; suitable for all purposes, but excellent for cooking. Tree to 25 feet tall; blooms during fall and early winter. Originated in Homestead, Florida by Carl W. Campbell. BROOKS 1972; J22

WHITE-FLESHED

Advance: Medium to large, pear-shaped to elliptic-round fruit; deep yellow in color; borne in large, compact clusters. Skin downy, thick and tough; flesh whitish, translucent, melting and very juicy; flavor subacid, very pleasant; quality good; ripens in midseason. Seeds commonly 4 or 5, the seed cavity not large. Tree a natural dwarf; height 5 feet; highly resistant to pear blight. Self-infertile, pollinate with Gold Nugget; a good pollinator for other cultivars. MORTON 1987a, POPENOE, W. 1920; *G49*, I74, I83M, J22, L6

Benlehr: Fruit oval to oblong; size medium, 1 1/2 to 1 3/4 inches long; skin thin, peels very well; flesh white and juicy, flavor sweet; quality excellent. Seeds 3 or 4. Originated as a seedling on the property of Reverend Charles E. Benlehr of Encinitas, California and is the best of the great many seedlings he grew beginning in 1941. I83M

Champagne: Fruit medium to large, oval to pyriform; fruit cluster large, loose. Surface deep yellow in color with a grayish bloom; skin thick, tough, somewhat astringent; flesh whitish, translucent, melting and very juicy; flavor mildly subacid, sprightly and pleasant; quality very good. Ripens late. Seeds 3 or 4, the seed cavity not large. Perishable; good for preserving. Tree self-infertile, prolific. MORTON 1987a; *G49*, I74, I83M, *Q93*

Herd's Mammoth: Fruit large, long and slightly tapering at the stem end; yellow to orange with white to cream-colored flesh. Good quality. Ripens earlier than Victory. Subject to black spot. MORTON 1987a; S59

Victory: (Chatsworth Victory) Large, oval fruit; skin yellow to orange, becoming amber on the side exposed to the sun; flesh white to cream-colored, juicy and sweet. Ripens in midseason to occasionally early. The most popular cultivar in West Australia. MORTON 1987a; S59

Vista White: Small to medium-sized, roundish fruit with blunt calyx end; skin light yellow; flesh pure white, very high in sugar content; ripens 1 to 3 weeks later than Gold Nugget. Excellent for dessert. D57{OR}

MACADAMIA {GR}

MACADAMIA INTEGRIFOLIA
MACADAMIA TETRAPHYLLA
MACADAMIA X SP.

Beaumont: (Dr. Beaumont) (M. x sp.) Round, medium to large nut, 65 to 80 per pound; shell medium-thick; kernel 40% of nut, with a high percentage of grade A kernels; texture and flavor very good. Tree upright; ornamental; new leaves reddish; flowers bright pink, borne on long racemes. Nuts drop over a long period. Recommended for home gardens. Originated in Australia. Introduced in 1965 by the California Macadamia Society. Discovered by Dr. J.H. Beaumont. BROOKS 1972; C56M, *D23M*, *G49*, I83M, J65, J65{PR}, *O97*

Burdick: (M. tetraphylla) Large nut, averaging 40 nuts per pound; shell thin, about 1/16 inch thick, well-filled; kernel averages about 34% of total nut weight, quality good; matures in October. Tree bears annually. A good choice for certain problem climatic areas. Also used as a rootstock. Originated in Encinitas, California. BROOKS 1972, JAYNES; J65{OR}, J65{PR}

Cate: (M. tetraphylla) Nuts medium to large; shell moderately thick; kernels 40% of nut, cream colored, crisp in texture, flavor good to very good; ripens in late October and November, continuing over a period of 6 to 8 weeks. Tree precocious, moderately hardy, shows no alternate bearing tendencies. The most widely adapted cultivar for commercial use in California. Originated on the property of William R. Cate, Malibu, California. C56M, *D23M*, *G49*, H12{PR}, I83M, J65{PR}

Dorado: (M. integrifolia) Medium-sized, uniform nuts, 7/8 to 1 inch in diameter; kernel averages 35% of nut, oil content 75%. Tree medium-tall, upright, attractive; begins to bear after 5 years; self-harvesting; cold resistant. Very productive, often yielding 65 or more pounds of nuts per year. Originated in Hawaii. Introduced by Rancho Nuez Nursery. J65{OR}

Elimbah: (M. tetraphylla) Medium to large nut; shell medium brown, rough, thick; kernel averages about 40% of nut, quality high, flavor excellent; ripens late, harvested over a 6 to 8 month period. Tree vigorous, upright; bears well, especially in interior areas of California. Originated in Caboolture, Queensland, Australia. BROOKS 1972, JAYNES; J65{OR}, J65{PR}

Fenton: (M. tetraphylla) Large nut of excellent quality. Has a distinct hairline fissure in the shell, making it easier to crack than most other cultivars. Ripens over a 3 month period. I83M

James: (M. integrifolia) Medium-sized, uniform nuts, about 1 inch in diameter; kernel averages 40 to 42% of nut, flavor very good, oil content 75%. Tree very tall, columnar; precocious, often producing after 2 or 3 years; self-harvesting. Yields more per acre than any other California cultivar, 60 or more pounds per tree when mature. Originated in La Habra Heights, California. J65

Keaau: (M. integrifolia) Medium-sized nut, averaging about 80 nuts per pound; shell smooth, medium brown, thin; kernel 42 to 46% of nut, color light cream; quality very good; season August to November. Tree moderately vigorous, upright; very productive. Originated in Lawai Valley, Kalaheo, Kauai, Hawaii. BROOKS 1972; J65{OR}, J65{PR}

Keauhou: (M. integrifolia) Medium to large nut, averaging about 54 nuts per pound; shell very slightly pebbled, medium-thick; kernel 37 to 40% of nut, quality tends to vary in different locations. Harvest season relatively short, with most of the crop maturing within about 3 months. Tree vigorous, yields well, extremely resistant to anthracnose. Originated in Kona, Hawaii by W.B. Storey. BROOKS 1972, JAYNES; J65{OR}, J65{PR}

Nutty Glen: (M. x sp.) Medium to large nut, pointed at one end, borne singly or in pairs; kernel recovery 42.6%, good flavor, quality high. Tree upright, quite dense, precocious and high yielding. Performs well in areas with cooler climates. Apparently a natural hybrid that originated in Australia. *O97*

Renown: (D4) (M. x sp.) Medium to large, light-brown nuts, borne singly or in twos or threes; kernel recovery 34.2%, excellent flavor and texture. Tree upright, open, tending to multiple stems; yields well. Like Nutty Glen, it will perform well under cooler climatic conditions. Has not performed well in California. An Australian selection that is apparently a natural hybrid. *O97*

Stephenson: (M. tetraphylla) Nut round, of high quality. Thin shells often split upon drying, allowing entry of fungi. Tree large, open, vigorous, a good producer. Originated in Queensland, Australia. Introduced in 1961. Fairly widely distributed in California. BROOKS 1972; *G49*

Vista: (M. x sp.) Small to medium-sized nut, 3/4 to 7/8 inch in diameter; kernel averages 46% of weight of nut, flavor excellent, oil content 75%. Shell very thin, can be cracked in an ordinary hand cracker. Tree medium-sized, pyramidal; begins to bear after 3 years; self-harvesting; flowers pink. Recommended for both home garden and commercial plantings. Originated in Rancho Santa Fe, California by Cliff Tanner. J65

Waimanalo: (M. integrifolia) Large nuts, occasionally with twin halves; shell relatively thick; kernel 38 1/2% of nut, flavor good, oil content 75%. Tree medium-sized, pyramidal; productive, begins to bear after 5 years; produces nuts in large clusters; resistant to frost and disease. Grows well in cooler climates, particularly near the ocean; also yields good crops inland. Originated at the Hawaiian Agricultural Experiment Station, Waimanalo, Hawaii. J65

MANDARIN {GR}

CITRUS RETICULATA

SATSUMAS

A distinctive type considered to have originated in Japan sometime prior to 1600 A.D. Highly important there where it is called Unshû mikan. The most cold-tolerant of the commercially important citrus fruits, mature dormant trees having survived minimum temperatures of 15 to 18^{0} F. without serious injury. Some cultivars also ripen earlier than any of the oranges or other mandarins. REUTHER; I76M{PR}

Changsha:[1] Small to medium-sized fruit; skin brilliant orange-red, very loose, easily peeled; flesh juicy, sweet but somewhat insipid, segments easily separated, seedy; matures early; resembles Satsuma. Tree highly cold resistance, 10 year old seedlings having survived a temperature of 4^{0} F. in Arlington, Texas. Bearing trees will produce crops of fruit after 7^{0} F. temperatures even though the leaves may fall. MORTON 1987a; G17, I74, K67

Dobashi-Beni Unshu: Satsuma type, distinctive only because of its deep orange-red color. Fruit of good quality, ripening in late November or early December. Tree of medium vigor. Originated as a limb sport of Owari in the orchard of K. Dobashi in Shizuoka Prefecture, Japan and was noted about 1940. REUTHER; *A71*, N18{SC}

Kimbrough: Satsuma type, somewhat more cold hardy than Owari; holds better on the tree. Very good quality. Developed at Louisiana State University. H4

Miyagawa: (Miyagawa Wase) Fruit large for a satsuma, moderately oblate; rind thin, smooth; juice abundant, sugars and acid well-blended, quality excellent; seedless. Matures early and stores well for Wase Unshû. Tree more vigorous than most old Wase clones; productive. Named and introduced by Dr. Tyôzaburô Tanaka in 1923. REUTHER; *O4*

Okitsu: (Okitsu Wase) Fruit somewhat more oblate than Miyagawa, but averages higher in sugar content and matures a week or so earlier. Tree also more vigorous. An early (Wase) type, and since satsumas are characterized by early fruit maturity, the Wase cultivars are very early ripening, in late September and October. REUTHER; *A71*, N18{SC}

Owari: (Owari Satsuma) Fruit oblate to rounded or becoming pear-shaped with age, of medium size. Rind orange, slightly rough, thin, tough, easily separable. Pulp orange, tender and melting; of rich, subacid flavor; segments 10 to 12, loosely separable; nearly seedless, sometimes 1 to 4 seeds. Of ancient and unknown Japanese origin. MORTON 1987a, REUTHER; *A71*, D37{DW}, E3M{DW}, *G49*, H4, I74{DW}, I83M, *M61M*, N18{SC}

Silverhill: (Silverhill Owari) Medium-sized fruit, slightly more oblate than most; rind relatively thin and smooth; seedless. Juice abundant; high in sugars and low in acid, hence very sweet; quality excellent;

stores well. Season of maturity early. Tree very vigorous for a satsuma; markedly cold-resistant. REUTHER; *O97*, R77

OTHERS

Beauty of Glen: (Beauty of Glen Retreat) Medium-sized, oblate fruit; rind thin, firm but easily removed, orange-red at maturity; segments 9 to 13, easily separated; flesh orange-colored, tender, juicy, sprightly flavored; moderately seedy. Midseason in maturity. Originated about 1888 near Brisbane, Australia. Highly popular in Queensland. *Q93*

Choa Chou Tien Chieh Kat: Small, somewhat oblate fruit; rind light orange, thin, easily peeled; flesh light orange, juicy, very aromatic; flavor delicate but sprightly, distinct; moderately seedy. Tree vigorous, upright; very productive, bears in 3 to 5 years from seed; cold hardy, having survived 7^{0} F. in Texas. One of the earliest of the Kat group of mandarins. D37

Clementine: (Algerian) Medium-small to medium fruit, round to elliptical; peel deep orange-red, smooth, glossy, thick, loose but scarcely puffy; pulp deep orange-red with 8 to 12 segments; juicy and of fine quality and flavor; 3 to 6 seeds of medium size; season early but long, extending into the summer. Most important early-ripening mandarin of the Mediterranean basin. MORTON 1987a, RAY, REUTHER, SCHNEIDER [Cul, Re]; *A71*, B93M{DW}, *D13*, *D23M*, E3M{DW}, E31M, *F53M*, *G49*, I83M, *M61M*, *M61M*{DW}, N18{SC}

Dancy: Oblate to pear-shaped fruit, of medium-size; peel deep orange-red to red, smooth, thin, leathery, tough; pulp dark-orange with 10 to 14 segments, of fine quality, richly flavored; 6 to 20 small seeds. Leading tangerine in the U.S., mainly grown in Florida, secondarily in California, and to a small extent, Arizona. MORTON 1987a; B73M{DW}, *D23M*, D65{DW}, E3M{DW}, E97{DW}, *F53M*, F68, *G49*, G96{DW}, H49{DW}, I83M, J22, *L47*, N18{S}, N18{SC}, etc.

Ellendale: Medium-large to large fruit, oblate to subglobose; rind orange-red, medium-thin, relatively adherent though peelable at maturity; flesh bright orange, very juicy; flavor rich and pleasantly subacid; moderately seedy. Late midseason in maturity. Originated about 1878 at Burrum, Queensland, Australia. REUTHER; *Q93*, S59

Emperor: Large, oblate fruit; rind medium-thin, firm but fairly loosely adherent, yellowish-orange to pale orange. Segments 9 to 10, readily separable. Flesh light orange, tender and juicy, flavor pleasant; seeds moderately numerous. Very old Australian cultivar, similar to Ponkan of China and Oneco of Florida. *Q93*, S59

Encore: Fairly large, oblate fruit; rind yellow-orange with darker orange spots, thin, nearly smooth, peels easily; flesh deep orange, juicy; flavor rich and sprightly; seeds numerous; unusually late ripening and late holding on tree. Tree upright, spreading; somewhat alternate bearing. RAY, REUTHER; I83M, *O97*

Fairchild: Medium-sized, oblate fruit; rind dark orange, smooth, peels freely; flesh orange-colored, firm yet tender, juicy; flavor rich and sweet; retains good quality through December; seeds 20 to 30. Best suited as fresh fruit. Tree heat tolerant; adapted especially to Coachella and Imperial Valleys of California. BROOKS 1972; *A71*, I76M{PR}, N18{SC}

Fortune: Medium to large, oblate fruit; peel attractive, orange to reddish-orange, moderately adherent; flesh orange, juicy, firm but tender; flavor sprightly, subacid, pleasing; seeds numerous. Late in maturity and fruit holds well on tree with little loss of quality. REUTHER; E31M, N18{SC}, *O4*

Fremont: Fruit medium in size, oblate in form; rind medium-thick, of moderate adherence but easily peelable, bright reddish-orange. Flesh deep orange, tender and juicy; flavor rich and sprightly. Seeds moderately numerous. Early ripening, but fruit retains quality well past maturity. E3M{DW}, I74{DW}, I76M{PR}, N18{SC}

Honey: Small, oblate fruit; rind light yellowish-orange, faintly pebbled, peels readily; pulp deep orange, flavor exceptionally rich and sweet; seedy; ripens early. Tree vigorous; tends strongly to alternate bearing. Sometimes confused with the Murcott tangor of Florida. RAY, REUTHER; *G49*, I83M, J22, N18{SC}

Imperial: (Early Imperial) Medium-small to medium fruit; rind very thin, leathery, smooth and glossy, yellowish to pale orange at maturity. Segments 9 to 11, easily separable. Flavor pleasantly subacid with an attractive aroma. Comparatively few seeds. Originated about 1890 at Emu Plains, Australia. REUTHER; *Q93*, S59

Kara: Fruit large, up to 3 inches in diameter; skin deep orange, somewhat wrinkled and bumpy; rind thin, peels easily and cleanly, rather tough; pulp deep, rich yellowish-orange, tender, very juicy with a unique aroma, sugar high; flavor rich, excellent, tart until fully mature; ripens very late; not tolerant of cold winters. BROOKS 1972; *D23M*, E3M{DW}, *G49*, I83M, *M61M*, N18{S}, N18{SC}

Kinnow: Large fruit, up to 3 inches in diameter; skin yellow-orange; rind thin, smooth, peels poorly, rather tough; pulp with 9 to 12 segments, separating fairly easily, deep yellowish-orange, moderately tender, very juicy with a unique and very pleasant aroma, sugar very high; flavor very rich, excellent. BROOKS 1972; *D23M*, E3M{DW}, *G49*, I74{DW}, I76M{PR}, I83M, *M61M*{DW}, N18{SC}

Lee: Medium-sized, round fruit, resembles a tangelo. Rind thin, leathery, moderately adherent but readily peelable; color deep yellowish-orange at maturity. Flesh orange; segments 9 to 10, readily separable; tender and melting; juice abundant; flavor rich and sweet. Medium-early in maturity. Clementine mandarin x Orlando tangelo. REUTHER; *A71*, F68, I83M, N18{SC}

Mediterranean: (Willowleaf) Fruit of medium size, oblate to rounded; peel orange, smooth, glossy, thin; pulp orange, with 10 to 12 segments; very juicy, of sweet rich flavor; seeds 15 to 20; matures early. Tree small to medium; reproduces true from seed; produces best fruit in hot, dry climates. MORTON 1987a, RAY; N18{S}, N18{SC}

Nova: Medium-large, oblate to subglobose fruit; rind thin, leathery, moderately adherent but easily peelable, deep yellowish-orange at maturity; segments about 11, easily separable; flesh deep orange, firm, juicy, flavor more pleasant and sweeter than Orlando. Seeds numerous in mixed plantings. Ripens early, reaching its prime in November in Florida. Clementine mandarin x Orlando tangelo. BROOKS 1972; E99G{PR}, N18{SC}, *O4*

Oneco: A form of the famous and highly reputed Ponkan mandarin of South China and Taiwan. Oneco differs, however, in that the fruit is rougher and seedier, ripens somewhat later and retains its quality on the tree much better, although the rind puffs rather badly. Pulp orange-yellow; of rich, sweet flavor. Grown primarily as a home and gift-box fruit. MORTON 1987a, REUTHER; F68

Osceola: Medium-sized, medium oblate fruit; rind moderately adherent but easily peelable, color deep orange to almost coral-red at maturity; flesh deep orange, juicy, flavor rich and distinctive; segments 10 to 11, easily separable; seeds numerous; medium early in maturity. Tree virtually thornless, more upright than Clementine. Clementine mandarin x Orlando tangelo. REUTHER; N18{SC}

Page: Fruit of medium size, broadly oblate to subglobose. Rind medium-thin, leathery, moderately adherent but easily peelable, reddish-orange at maturity. Flesh deep orange, with about 10 segments; tender and juicy; flavor rich and sweet. Seeds moderately numerous. Early in maturity. Clementine mandarin x Minneola tangelo. REUTHER; F68, G17, I83M, N18{SC}

Pixie: Small to medium-sized fruit, variable in shape; rind yellow-orange, peels easily without dripping of juice; flesh medium orange; flavor mild and pleasant; essentially seedless, regardless of exposure to other pollen sources; matures late. Tree somewhat alternate bearing; not successfully grown in the hot dessert. BROOKS 1972; *G49*, I83M, N18{SC}

Ponkan: Fruit large for a mandarin, globose to moderately oblate; rind medium-thick, fairly loosely adherent, orange; flesh orange, tender and melting, juicy; flavor mild, pleasant, aromatic; segments about 10; seeds few; ripens in early midseason. Tree vigorous; distinctive in appearance due to pronounced upright growth habit. One of the most tropical mandarins, the fruit attaining maximum size and quality under such conditions. REUTHER; I83M, N18{S}, N18{SC}

Red Imperial: Similar to Imperial with the exception of the color, which is deep orange-red to scarlet. S59

Robinson: Medium-large oblate fruit; rind thin, tough and leathery, moderately adherent but easily peelable; color deep yellowish-orange at maturity. Flesh deep orange, with 12 to 14 segments; juicy, flavor rich and sweet; seeds moderately numerous; matures early. Tree very vigorous; bears regularly. Clementine mandarin x Orlando tangelo. REUTHER; E99G{PR}, F68

Sunburst: Medium-sized, oblate fruit; rind orange to scarlet; pulp in 11 to 15 segments, with abundant colorful juice; seeds 10 to 20 according to degree of pollination. Matures in a favorable season (mid-November to mid-December). Tree vigorous; thornless; early-bearing; self-infertile, needs cross-pollination for good fruit set. MORTON 1987a; F68, N18{SC}

Wilking: Fruit large, up to 3 1/8 inches in diameter; skin deep yellowish-orange; rind thin to medium, peels fairly well; flesh rich yellow-orange, with 9 to 13 easily separating segments, firm, moderately tender, very juicy; aroma of juice unique; sugar content high; flavor rich and very good, being very sweet late in the season. E3M{DW}, I74{DW}

MANGO {GR}

MANGIFERA INDICA

Aloha: Medium-sized, oval to somewhat square fruit; averages 1 pound in weight and 4 inches in length; skin 3/4 red and 1/4 dusky-yellow, moderately thick; flesh orange, nearly fiberless, juicy, rich and tangy; seed makes up 9% of total weight; ripens in December and January. Tree spreading; an alternate bearer, but usually has some fruit in off years; susceptible to anthracnose. Originated in San Diego, California by Jerry H. Staedeli. Introduced in 1975. I83M

Alphonse: Medium-sized, oblong-ovate fruit; skin yellowish-green to bright yellow blushed scarlet; flesh orange, free from fiber, flavor very rich, quality excellent; seed monoembryonic. Tree broad and spreading, not heavy bearing. Supposedly named for Alphonse d'Albuquerque, one of the early governors of the Portuguese possessions in India. POPENOE, W. 1920; R0

Brooks: Fruit quality fair; not particularly attractive, but late in season (August to October). Tree weak-growing; heavy-bearing. Open-pollinated seedling of Sandersha. Originated in Miami, Florida by the Charles Deering Estate. Introduced in 1924. BROOKS 1972; J22, *Q93*

Carrie: Medium-sized fruit, to 4 inches long, averaging 12 ounces in weight; skin greenish-yellow; flesh very juicy, very rich, aromatic, fiberless, quality excellent; ripens June to July. Tree semi-dwarf, with dense crown. Susceptible to anthracnose. Considered to be one of the best of all mango cultivars for home gardens. Originated in Delray Beach, Florida by Lawrence Zill. Introduced about 1949. BROOKS 1972; F68, J36, *N53M*

Earlygold: Medium-sized fruit, to 12 ounces; skin yellow with an orange-red blush; flesh juicy, sweet, fiberless, quality very good; matures in May and June, being one of the earliest cultivars. Tree upright, moderately vigorous. Resistant to anthracnose. Originated in Pine Island, Lee County, Florida by Frank Adams. Introduced in 1954. BROOKS 1972; *Q93*

Edgehill: Small to medium-sized, oblong fruit; average weight 12 ounces, individual fruits to 1 1/2 pounds; skin dark-green, with a rose blush on the side exposed to the sun, tough, does not peel well; flesh orange in color, sweet and fiberless except for a few short fibers on the ventral suture of the seed. Quality very good to excellent. Seed size medium. Bearing season Thanksgiving to end of April some years. Tree upright, productive, susceptible to anthracnose. Originated in Vista, California. Introduced in 1970. I83M

Edward: Large fruit; skin yellow, with a bright red blush where exposed to the sun; flesh firm, fiberless, juicy, rich, melting, smooth; flavor excellent; high in food value; seed small; ripens June to July. Tree semi-dwarf, spreading, low yielding. Relatively resistant to anthracnose. Considered to be one of the best of all mango cultivars for home gardens. Originated in Coconut Grove, Florida by Edward Simmons. Introduced about 1942. BROOKS 1972; F68, I83M, *N53M*

Fairchild: Medium-sized fruit, average weight about 3/4 pound; skin bright yellow; flesh golden yellow, entirely free from fiber, flavor delicious; seed small, polyembryonic; ripens in July. Tree spreading, bears lightly. Highly resistant to anthracnose. Originated in Balboa Heights, Canal Zone from seeds introduced from Saigon by David Fairchild. J22

Florigon: (Florida Saigon) Medium-sized fruit, to 5 inches and 1 pound; skin deep yellow; flesh fiberless, juicy, sweet, rich, quality excellent; season May and June. Tree small, upright, vigorous; moderately resistant to anthracnose. Probably an open-pollinated seedling of Saigon. Originated in Ft. Lauderdale, Florida by John Kaiser. Introduced about 1947. BROOKS 1972; *Q93*

Glenn: Fruit oval to somewhat oblong; medium to large; skin yellow with an orange-red blush, smooth, thin, tough; separates easily from flesh, many yellow and white dots. Flesh deep-yellow, fiberless, firm, juicy, rich, aromatic, spicy, quality excellent; aroma strong but pleasant, suggesting pineapple; monoembryonic. Season June and July, about 7-10 days before Haden. Originated in Miami, Florida by Roscoe E. Glenn. Introduced about 1950. BROOKS 1972; F68, I83M, *N53M*, *Q93*

Haden: Fruit oval to ovate, plump; size large to very large, length 4 to 5 1/2 inches, weight up to 24 ounces. Surface smooth, light to deep apricot-yellow in color, overspread with crimson-scarlet; skin very thick and tough; flesh yellowish-orange, firm, very juicy, fibrous only close to the seed, and of a rich, moderately piquant flavor; quality good. Season July and August. Originated at Coconut Grove, Florida, as a seedling of Mulgoba. First propagated in 1910. POPENOE, W. 1920; D57, F68, J36, J22, *N53M*, *Q93*

Irwin: Medium-sized, oblong-ovate fruit; skin orange to pink with extensive bright-red blush and small white lenticels; flesh yellow, almost fiberless, with a mild sweet flavor; quality good to very good;

ships well; seed small; season June and July. Tree semi-dwarf, bears heavy crops of fruit in clusters; susceptible to anthracnose. Originated in Miami, Florida by F.D. Irwin. Introduced in 1946. BROOKS 1972, MORTON 1987a; I83M, J36, *Q93*, S97M

Julie: Fruit somewhat flattened on one side, of medium size, greenish-yellow with slight pink blush; fiber very slight; flavor sweet, creamy, excellent; ripens August to September. Tree somewhat dwarf, has 30% to 50% hermaphrodite flowers; bears well and regularly. Adaptable to humid environments and resistant to disease. Fruit is resistant to the fruit fly. Introduced to Florida from Trinidad but has long been popular in Jamaica. The main mango exported from the West Indies to Europe. Originated in Mauritius. MORTON 1987a; F68, I83M, *N53M*

Keitt: Medium to large, rounded-oval to ovate fruit; skin bright-yellow with light-pink blush and lavender bloom, surface smooth, thick, fairly tough, not separating easily from flesh; flesh deep yellow, fairly firm but tender, melting, juicy, some fiber near the seed; flavor rich and sweet, quality very good; monoembryonic; season August and September. Moderately resistant to anthracnose. Considered to be an excellent late-maturing mango cultivar. Originated in Homestead, Florida by Mrs. J.N. Keitt. Introduced about 1946. BROOKS 1972, MORTON 1987a; D57, F68, I83M, J22, *L33M*{PR}, L54{PR}, *N53M*, *Q93*

Kensington Pride: Fruit distinctly beaked when immature, medium-large; skin bright orange-yellow with a red-pink blush overlying areas exposed to the sun. Flesh orange, thick, nearly fiberless, juicy, aromatic, of rich flavor. Polyembryonic. The fruits ship well but the tree is not a dependable nor heavy bearer. The leading commercial cultivar in drier areas of Queensland, Australia. In humid regions it is anthracnose-prone and requires spraying. MORTON 1987a; *Q93*

Kent: Large, thick, ovate fruit; skin greenish-yellow with a dark-red blush and gray bloom; many small yellow lenticels; flesh fiberless, juicy, sweet; very good to excellent; seed small; season July and August and often into September. Tree of erect, slender habit; of moderate size; precocious; bears very well; susceptible to anthracnose. Fruit ships well, but for the market, needs ethylene treatment to enrich color. Originated in Miami, Florida by Leith D. Kent. Introduced in 1944. BROOKS 1972, MORTON 1987a; D57, F68, *L33M*{PR}, L54{PR}, *N53M*, *Q93*

Manila: (Filipino) Small to medium-sized, long pointed fruits; weight 8 to 10 ounces; skin bright yellow-orange, smooth, thin and tender; flesh golden, juicy, non-fibrous, sweet, quality very good; seed small, polyembryonic; ripens October to December. Can be eaten when slightly green. Tree bushy, bears regularly, susceptible to anthracnose. D57, *N53M*, S97M

Mulgoba: Medium-sized, oblong-ovate fruit; skin deep yellow to apricot-yellow, sometimes overspread with scarlet, thick and tough; flesh bright orange-yellow, very juice, free of fiber, of a rich piquant flavor, quality excellent; seed monoembryonic. Season July to September in Florida. The name Mulgoba is taken from that of a native Indian dish, and means "makes the mouth water". POPENOE, W. 1920; R0

Nam Dok Mai: Fruit greenish-yellow with a slight pink blush; average weight 375 grams; fiber slight. flesh orange, firm; flavor sweet, juicy, excellent; quality good. Seed polyembryonic. Susceptible to anthracnose; resistant to black spot; suffers from powdery mildew. Bears regularly in cooler climates, in late mid-season. Originated in Thailand. J36, *N53M*, *Q93*

Ok-Rong: (Oakrong, Dented Breast) Saigon type mango. It is thought to have the highest sugar content of any Florida grown mango. Ok means breast in Thai. Rong means dented, or depression, because the ventral part of the fruit has a Rong or depressed line running along that part of the fruit. Introduced into Florida from Thailand in 1957, by William F. Whitman. J36

Ono: Small, ovate fruit, weight 5 to 8 ounces; skin yellow, tinged with pink on side exposed to the sun; flesh yellow, juicy, melting, fiberless; flavor rich and spicy; ripens in July. Tree upright, susceptible to anthracnose. Primarily for home gardens. Originated in Makiki Heights, Honolulu, Hawaii by R.W. Smith. Introduced in 1958. BROOKS 1972; *Q93*

Pairi: (Pirie) Small to medium-sized, ovate fruit, weight 7 to 10 ounces; skin moderately thick, yellow-green, suffused scarlet around the base; flesh bright yellow-orange, firm but juicy, free of fiber, of pronounced and pleasant aroma and sweet, rich, spicy flavor; quality excellent. Season in south Florida July and August. Tree spreading, bears lightly, susceptible to anthracnose. POPENOE, W. 1920; D57{OR}, R0

Palmer: Large, elongated oval fruit; weight 1 1/4 pounds; skin brightly colored with purple and red; flesh apricot-colored, smooth, nearly fiberless, very sweet; quality good; less aromatic than some; good storage characteristics; ripens July to August. Tree produces well most years; very upright in growth; susceptible to anthracnose. Originated in Miami, Florida by Charles I. Brooks. Introduced in 1946. BROOKS 1972; I83M, J36

Piña: (Pineapple) Medium-sized, roundish fruit; weight 8 ounces; skin light yellow to orange; flesh yellow, slightly fibrous but juicy and sweet, has a distinct pineapple-like flavor; seed polyembryonic; ripens November to December. Tree upright, susceptible to anthracnose. Originated in Mexico. D57

Reliable: Medium-sized, oblong fruit, averages 1 pound in weight; skin tough, lemon-yellow with a deep-red blush on the side exposed to the sun; flesh orange, nearly fiberless; flavor good; slight pleasant aroma; seed small, 9% of fruit; matures November through December. Tree dome-shaped, susceptible to anthracnose. Originated in San Diego, California by Jerry H. Staedeli. Introduced in 1971. I83M{CF}

Sensation: Medium-sized, oval fruit, weight about 12 ounces; skin bright yellow with a dark plum-red blush, thin, adherent; flesh pale yellow, firm, slightly sweet with a distinctive mild flavor, fibers scanty, quality good; season August and September; seed monoembryonic. Tree vigorous, upright; produces heavy crops but tends toward alternate bearing; susceptible to anthracnose. Originated in North Miami, Florida. Introduced in 1949. BROOKS 1972, MORTON 1987a; *Q93*

Southern Blush: Medium to large oblong fruit, weight 1 to 2 pounds; skin yellow, blushed with red; flesh nearly fiberless, sweet and juicy, of good flavor; ripens in midseason, July in Florida. Tree exceptionally vigorous. F68, *N53M*

Surprise: Small to medium-sized, oblong fruit, averages 1 pound in weight; skin yellow-green with bright orange-red blush on side exposed to the sun, thin; flesh yellow-orange, fiberless, juicy, sweet and rich; seed small, 6% of fruit; ripens in November and December. Tree upright, an alternate bearer, susceptible to anthracnose. Originated in San Diego, California by Jerry H. Staedeli. Introduced in 1975. I83M

T-1: Medium to large fruit; skin greenish-yellow blushed with red; flesh sweet, very good to excellent in flavor, absolutely fiberless; seed small; ripens December to January. Tree upright, rounded; bears moderately good crops; susceptible to anthracnose. Quality good, its only drawback being lack of attractive skin color. I83M

Tommy Atkins: Medium to large, oblong-oval fruit; weight 16 to 25 ounces; skin thick, orange-yellow, with a bright to dark-red blush and purplish bloom; flesh medium to dark-yellow, firm, juicy, with medium fiber, of fair to good quality. Harvest season June and July; ships very well, shelf life of 2 weeks. Moderately resistant to anthracnose. Tree vigorous, upright. Originated by Thomas N. Atkins of Ft. Lauderdale, Florida. Introduced in 1948. BROOKS 1972, MORTON 1987a; F68, *L33M*{PR}, *N53M*

Ultimate: Medium to medium-large, roundish fruit; very sweet flesh with little to no fiber; excellent quality. Originated in Spring Valley, California by Peggy Winters. I83M

Valencia Pride: Medium to large, roundish to ovate fruit, weight 1 to 2 pounds; skin yellow-red; flesh sweet, juicy, slightly fibrous, of good flavor; ripens in midseason, July in Florida, ships very well. Tree only moderately vigorous. F68, *N53M*

Van Dyke: Medium-sized fruit, average weight 280 grams; skin yellow-orange with bright red blush, attractive; fiber moderate. Flavor good, sweet, slightly turpentine; quality variable in some areas. Can be significantly affected by "jelly seed". Seed monoembryonic. Ripens July to August. High resistance to anthracnose and black spot. Cropping regular. Originated in Florida. *N53M*{OR}

Winters: (20222) Small to medium-sized, elongated fruit; skin smooth, free of blemishes, attractively colored red and yellow; flesh yellow-orange, fiberless, flavor sweet, very good to excellent; seed small, polyembryonic; ripens October to November. Matures early but with inconsistent yields. Has the ability to ripen all of its fruits off the tree, evenly and completely once they are mature. Originated in Miami, Florida but has proven well adapted to southern California. I83M

Zillate: Fruit greenish-yellow with orange-red purple blush; average weight 625 grams; fiber slight. Flavor sweet-acid, slightly turpentine; quality good. Seed monoembryonic. Susceptible to anthracnose and black spot. Cropping regular, late. Originated in Florida. J22, *Q93*

MELON {S}

CUCUMIS MELO

CANTALOUPE MELONS

The true cantaloupe melons, considered by many to be the finest flavored of all melons. Usually with a hard rind and a rough, warty, or scaly surface, but not netted. Generally they do not "slip" from the vine, and must be cut when ripe. Rarely grown commercially in the United States. Also called *rock melons*.

HYBRID

Chaca: (Early Chaca) 67 days. Exceptionally early Charantais type. Round fruit, 4 inches in diameter, weight 2 to 2 1/2 pounds; rind thin, grayish-green, lightly netted. Firm, deep-orange flesh; very sweet and flavorful; small seed cavity. Does well in cool or short season areas. A16, J20, K10

Charmel: 78 days. Smooth, grey-green fruit; weight 2 to 3 pounds. Aromatic deep-orange flesh, very sweet and rich, small seed cavity. Traditionally served with prosciutto. Very vigorous and productive. Good crack resistance. Tolerant to fusarium wilt and powdery mildew. K10, K66

Flyer: 68 days. One of the earliest Charantais type melons. Grape-fruit-sized fruit; weight 2 pounds; pale-orange tinted skin, rather than the typical grey-green; medium netting, attractive dark green sutures (indented stripes). Thick, sweet, deep orange flesh. Very productive. Ripens most of its crop as picking begins on the later cultivars. D68, G6

Savor: 78 days. Medium-sized, faintly ribbed fruit; weight 1 1/2 to 2 1/2 pounds; smooth grey-green rind, dark-green sutures. Very sweet and aromatic deep-orange flesh, of excellent quality. High yielding. Tolerant to fusarium wilt and powdery mildew. G6, I39

Sweetheart: 70 days. A gourmet charantais melon, specially developed for the North and short season areas. Round-oval fruit, 4 to 5 inches in diameter; smooth, pale grey-green rind. Salmon-red flesh, very sweet and aromatic. Must be harvested at full maturity. Does well in frames or under cloches. Used extensively in England and France. A69M, D11M, P83M, *R23*, S55, S61

OPEN-POLLINATED

Cantalun: Early Charantais type. Medium-sized, roundish fruits; skin gray-green, smooth, thin, slightly ribbed; flesh salmon, very sweet and fragrant, seed cavity small. Vine very productive; bears fruit in clusters; resistant to fusarium wilt race 0. Suitable for outdoor culture or under plastic tunnels. G68, S95M

Charantais: 85 days. The true cantaloupe melon of France, legendary in Provence. Medium-sized, globe-shaped fruit; 3 1/2 inches in diameter; weight 2 1/2 to 3 pounds; smooth, furrowed, grey-green rind. Aromatic, thick, deep-orange flesh; extremely sweet and flavorful. Excellent as a dessert filled with a sweet wine such as Barsac, Marsala, Port or Madeira. B49, C53, F33, *F60*, H42, H49, I39, K49M, *L59G*, S45M, S61

Noir de Carmes: (Des Carmes, Early Black Rock) Fruit nearly spherical, but slightly flattened at the ends; 6 to 7 inches in diameter, weight 2 1/2 to 3 1/2 pounds; ribs clearly but not very deeply marked. Rind smooth, very dark green, almost black turning orange when ripe. Flesh orange, thick, sweet, perfumed, of excellent quality. Introduced prior to 1885. VILMORIN; G68

Santon: Small, roundish fruit; skin grey-green striped with darker green, smooth; flesh salmon, sweet and juicy, of excellent quality. Matures early. Resistant to fusarium wilt and cucumber mosaic virus. Suitable for both outdoor and greenhouse culture. P59M

Vedrantais: 92 days. Excellent charantais melon from France. Globe-shaped fruit; weight 1 to 1 1/2 pounds; rind smooth, light grayish-green, slightly ribbed. Aromatic deep-orange flesh, very sweet and flavorful. Will not slip when ripe; best grown on a trellis or in a greenhouse. Tolerant to fusarium wilt race 1. G68, S95M

MUSKMELONS

Also called *netted melons* or *nutmeg melons*, these are the principal commercial melons grown in the United States. They are not cantaloupes as they are so often erroneously called. The surface is more or less strongly netted. Most are ripe when the stem begins to sperate or "slip" from the fruit.

GREEN-FLESHED

Hybrid

Arava: (Hybrid 820) Galia type, with slightly larger fruit and heavier netting. Round, slightly flattened fruit; weight 2 1/2 to 3 pounds; rind yellow, netted. Flesh light green, sweet and aromatic; small seed cavity. Very early, concentrated yield. Resistant to powdery mildew race 1. Suitable for early production in tunnels and in the open field. Especially adapted to hot climates. *P75M*, T27M

Galia: (Gaylia) 65 days. An Ogen type melon, but larger and more vigorous than others of this type. Round fruit; weight 2 to 2 1/2 pounds; rind yellow, heavily netted; flesh light green, very sweet and aromatic; small seed cavity. Resistant to powdery mildew. Suitable for growing in frames, greenhouses or in the open field. Recommended for home gardens and local markets. K66, L91M, *P75M*, T27M

Inbar: Hybrid Galia type. Round fruit; rind netted, yellow in color; flesh light-green, very sweet and aromatic. Small seed cavity. Matures about a week earlier than Galia. Resistant to fusarium races 0 and 1. T27M

Rocky Sweet: 85 days. Medium-sized, round fruit; weight 3 to 4 pounds; moderately netted, with light sutures; rind dark green, turning yellow, then yellow-orange when ripe. Thick, lime-green flesh; tender, sweet and delicious, without a musky flavor. Stems will "slip" when very ripe. Ships well. Vines very vigorous and prolific. A32, E97, F19M, *F60*, *F63*, G6, G16, G57M, G71, G79, H33, H95, I91, L14, M29, N16, etc.

Open-Pollinated

Boule d'Or: (Golden Perfection, Honey Ball) 120 days. Spherical to slightly oblong fruit; 5 1/2 inches in diameter, weight 2 to 3 pounds. Rind strong and tough, loosely netted; golden-yellow when ripe. Flesh pale green, rather thick, very sweet and agreeably perfumed. Stores well. Introduced prior to 1885. TAPLEY 1937, VILMORIN; Dropped by G69

Extra Early Hackensack: (Early Hackensack) Medium-sized, oblate fruit; skin golden-yellow, mottled profusely with green; flesh light green blending into yellowish green near the cavity, very fibrous, sweet and very highly flavored, mildly aromatic; quality fair to good. Originated in Hackensack, New Jersey about 1884. TAPLEY 1937; K49M

Gold-Lined Rocky Ford: 95 days. Small, nearly round fruit, 5 1/4 inches in diameter; rind smooth, non-ribbed, densely covered with a hard gray netting. Flesh thick, deep green, with an attractive lining of pink or gold at the center. B71

Green Fleshed Cavaillon: Oblong fruit; 6 to 7 inches in diameter, 9 to 10 inches in length; weight 3 pounds; skin smooth, dark-green, thinly and loosely netted when ripe. Flesh pale green, rather firm but very juicy, sweet, and perfumed in warm climates. Introduced prior to 1885. VILMORIN; G68

Green Nutmeg: (Early Green Flesh Nutmeg, Nutmeg) 63 days. Slightly oval fruit; heavily netted, shallowly ribbed; 3 1/2 inches in diameter, weight 2 to 3 pounds. Flesh light green with a salmon center, aromatic, very sweet and sprightly. Best harvested at half slip. G16, I99, K49M, L7M

Haogen: (Ogen, Israel) 80 days. Round fruit; 5 to 6 inches in diameter, weight 3 pounds; smooth green rinds, slightly tinged yellow when ripe; wide green sutures. Pale greenish-white flesh, tinted salmon around the small seed cavity; thick, tender, juicy, very sweet and rich. Vigorous, prolific vines. A2, D87, G71M, G93M, I99, K49M, L9, L11, L91M, N16, O89, S45M, S61

Jenny Lind: 75 days. Small, oblate fruit, flattened at both ends; often with a small knob on the blossom end; 5 to 6 inches in diameter, weight 1 1/2 to 2 pounds. Skin dull brownish-orange, profusely mottled with green. Flesh light green, soft and juicy, very sweet, mildly flavored and lacking in aroma. At one time a popular home garden and local market cultivar. Introduced about 1846. TAPLEY 1937; A2, *A75*, B35M, E59Z, G71, I97T, I99, J20, K49M, L7M, L91M

Noy Israel: Famous Israeli cultivar, similar to Haogen. Globe-shaped fruit; weight about 2 1/2 pounds; rind orange, with green ribs. Flesh green, very sweet and aromatic. Matures in midseason. Suitable for shipping. Resistant to powdery mildew. T27M

Rocky Ford: (Eden Gem, Netted Gem, Nutmeg) 91 days. Nearly round fruit; 4 to 5 inches in diameter, weight 2 to 2 1/2 pounds; heavily netted, slightly ribbed. Flesh green with a narrow gold border near the cavity; very sweet and sprightly. Well-known and popular home garden and short distance shipping cultivar. Introduced about 1885. TAPLEY 1937; B75M, C92, D76, F12, F19M, *F60*, H66, I39, J34, K71, L7M, M95, N16, N39, etc.

Spanish: 140 days. Large, dark-green, netted fruit; weight 8 to 12 pounds. Sweet green-gold flesh. Very sweet even when harvested as immature fruits. Excellent keeper, up to 4 months if kept cool and dry. Vines produce 4 to 5 melons each. J25M

SALMON-FLESHED

Hybrid

Ambrosia: 86 days. Medium-sized, very uniform, nearly round fruit; 6 inches in diameter, weight 4 1/2 to 5 pounds; heavily netted, not ribbed. Flesh salmon, juicy, extremely thick and firm right down to the rind; very sweet, with a unique distinctive flavor. Seed cavity small, with seeds in a tight mass. Vines prolific; resistant to powdery and downy mildew. B75, *E53M*, F19M, *F72*, *G1M*, G51, G71, G79, G93M, I91, J7, J34, J58, K73, M29, M95M, etc.

Burpee Hybrid: 82 days. Round to slightly oval fruit; heavily netted, distinctly ribbed; 6 inches in diameter, weight 4 to 4 1/2 pounds. Flesh deep-orange, thick, firm, juicy, sweet and flavorful, of excellent quality. High-yielding vine; produces very well in northern areas. Popular with home gardeners and market farmers. B75, C85M, *E91G*, *F72*, G71, G79, H54, *H61*, J58, J97M, K50, K73, L42, M13M, N39, etc.

Pancha: 80 days. Hybrid between a Charantais melon and an American muskmelon. Fruit netted, with slight green ribs; 6 inches in diameter, weight about 2 pounds. Solid, deep-orange flesh, very aromatic; flavor very sweet and intense. Vine vigorous; resistant to powdery mildew and fusarium wilt. D68, K66

Tangiers: 78 days. A French hybrid of North African parentage. Small, round fruit, 6 inches in diameter; skin pale lime-green. Flesh deep-orange; has the best flavor characteristics of both honeydew and cantaloupe. Strong, vigorous vine; resistant to powdery mildew and fusarium wilt. Does well in areas usually too cool or marginal for growing honeydew or other exotic melons. K66

Open-Pollinated

Banana: 90 days. Long, cylindrical, tapered fruit; 15 to 18 inches in length, 4 to 4 1/2 inches in diameter; weight 3 1/2 to 4 pounds; netting very sparse, ribs prominent; skin creamy yellow when ripe. Flesh salmon orange to orange, juicy, very sweet, mildly aromatic. Introduced prior to 1883. TAPLEY 1937; A31M, B73M, C92, D76, E97, F19M, *F60*, G16, G51, H66, J34, K49M, K71, L79M, M46, N16, etc.

Bender's Surprise: 90 days. Very large, short oval fruit; 8 inches in diameter, weight 6 to 8 pounds; netted and ribbed; skin grayish-green, turning creamy yellow at maturity. Thick orange flesh, very juicy and sweet, highly flavored, aroma mild and pleasant. Flavor is best 5 to 6 days after harvest. Originated in Albany, New York by Charles Bender. Introduced in 1900. TAPLEY 1937; G79, K49M, L7M

Blenheim Orange: Medium-sized, short-oval fruit; skin thin, finely netted. Thick, very succulent, scarlet flesh; very highly perfumed, of fine flavor. High yielding and extremely reliable. Traditionally grown in greenhouses in England. First raised in 1881 in the gardens of Blenheim Palace. VILMORIN; P83M, *R23*, S61

Chimayo: Hispanic heirloom. Collected in New Mexico and grown out by Judy Goettert and Bob Sullivan in Sells, Arizona. Oval-shaped fruit with sweet orange flesh. In temperate areas, plant in spring when danger of frost is past and the soil has warmed up some. I16

Delicious 51: (Golden Delicious 51) 83 days. Nearly round fruit, 6 inches in diameter, weight 3 to 4 pounds; skin yellow when ripe, with medium to sparse netting and distinct sutures. Thick, firm, orange flesh, of excellent quality. Resistant to fusarium wilt. Excellent for home gardens and nearby markets. A13, A16, A25, A69M, *A75*, B35M, B75M, C85M, D76, E24, G71, J7, K10, L7M, L42, etc.

Early Hanover: (Extra Early Hanover) 80 days. Globe-shaped, slightly flattened fruit; 6 inches in diameter, weight 3 to 3 1/2 pounds; rind light green with slight netting, ribbing shallow, but definite. Sweet, juicy, salmon-orange flesh. Grows well under adverse conditions. Good for home gardens. A2

Emerald Gem: 97 days. Small, nearly round fruit; 5 to 5 1/2 inches in diameter, weight 2 1/2 to 3 pounds; netting sparse, ribs distinct. Skin emerald green, turning yellow when ripe. Thick, rich salmon flesh, sweet and spicy. Suitable for home gardens and local markets. Originated in Benzie County, Michigan by William G. Vorhees. Introduced in 1886 by W. Atlee Burpee Company. TAPLEY 1937; K49M

Far North: 65 days. Hearts of Gold type. Globe-shaped fruit, 4 to 5 inches in diameter; rind sparsely netted, turns yellow when ripe. Flesh deep-salmon to orange, very firm and sweet. Small, compact vine. Successful in areas throughout Canada, where other cultivars fail to mature. A16, D11M, D27, E49, H42, H94, K20, M46

Giant Perfection: 95 days. Extra large, round fruit; 8 to 10 inches in diameter, weight 14 to 15 pounds; heavily netted, distinctly ribbed. Firm, rich, deep-orange flesh; sweet and flavorful; large seed cavity. Selected from the old Perfection cultivar. Productive and reliable. D76, E97, *F60*, K49M, K71

Golden Champlain: 85 days. Moderately small, globular fruit, 5 to 6 inches in diameter; weight 3 to 4 pounds; skin yellowish-brown, profusely mottled with green; flesh pale orange, medium thick, slightly fibrous, moderately soft and juicy; flavor sweet, medium; quality moderately good. Introduced in 1923. TAPLEY 1937; E59Z

Golden Gopher: (Pop-Open Melon) Unusual heirloom from the 1930's. Golden yellow, round-oval fruit; netted on the stem end but free of netting on the blossom end, except for a "belly button" at the tip; flesh intense orange, aromatic, fine-textured, sweet to the rind; flavor not as complex and full-bodied as other melons. Resistant to fusarium, bacterial wilt, and drought. Known as Pop-Open melon because the fruits have a tendency to split when fully ripe. K49M, L7M

Hearts of Gold: (Hoodoo) 90 days. Nearly round fruit, 5 1/2 to 6 inches in diameter, weight 3 to 4 pounds; rind dark green with fine gray netting, distinctly ribbed. Firm salmon flesh, sweet, somewhat sprightly, quality very good. Popular with home gardeners and local markets. Originated in Benton Harbor, Michigan by Roland Morrill. Patented in 1914. TAPLEY 1937; A69M, B75M, C92, E24, *F60*, G51, *G83M*, G93M, H49, H66, K71, K73, M95, M95M, N39, etc.

Honey Rock: (Sugar Rock) Globular fruit, 6 inches in diameter, weight 2 1/2 to 3 1/2 pounds; rind very strong, grayish-green turning yellow at maturity; netting abundant, coarsely interlaced, ribs obscure. Medium-thick, deep-salmon flesh; juicy, sweet, slightly coarse in texture. Good for home gardens. Introduced in 1925. TAPLEY 1937; *A75*, B73M, C85M, D76, E97, F19M, *F60*, *G1M*, G79, H49, H66, *I59M*, J58, J84, K71, M13M, M95M, etc.

Honeybush:[1] 82 days. Oval to roundish fruit; average weight 2 1/2 to 3 pounds; very small seed cavity; flesh thick, bright salmon, firm and juicy, ripens right down to the thin rind. Bush-type vine, grows only 5 to 7 feet in diameter; bears 3 to 6 full-sized melons over an extended period. Ideal for smaller gardens or where space is limited. Tolerant to fusarium wilt. B75, G51, J32

Iroquois: 87 days. Nearly round fruit; 6 1/2 inches in diameter, weight 4 to 6 pounds; grayish-green rind, well netted, with prominent ribbing. Thick, sweet deep-orange flesh; of excellent quality and fine texture. Excellent for short distance shipping. Resistant to fusarium wilt. Standard main crop cultivar for northern areas. C44, C92, D65, D76, E97, G16, H49, *H61*, J7, K71, L42, L89, M13M, N16, N39, etc.

Itsy Bitsy Sweetheart:[1] 70 days. Small, round, heavily netted fruit; 4 inches in diameter, weight 2 1/2 pounds, ideal for individual servings; golden rind. Sweet, thick orange flesh. Dwarf, compact vine, only 3 feet long; perfect for smaller gardens. Very productive and easy to grow. E97, *G13M*, K71, *L59G*

Jake's Indian: Round fruit; weight 2 to 3 pounds; soft rind; nearly smooth, mottled skin. Sweet light-orange flesh. Also known as Barn Snake. L79M

Kansas: An heirloom muskmelon with excellent flavor. Ridged, oval-shaped fruit, moderately netted; weight about 4 pounds. Orange flesh; ripens close to the rind. Vigorous, hardy vine; particularly resistant to sap beetles which destroy fruit of other cultivars. L7M

Medium Persian: 110 days. Large, nearly round fruit; 7 to 9 inches in diameter, weight 7 to 8 pounds; rind dark-green, uniformly and finely netted, not ribbed. Thick deep-orange flesh, sweet and distinctly flavored. Needs a long, warm growing season. I39, K49M, *L59G*

Minnesota Midget:[1] 65 days. Small, globe-shaped fruit; 3 1/2 to 4 inches in diameter; rind deeply lobed, with sparse netting. Thick, golden-yellow flesh, sweet right to the rind; small seed cavity. Dwarf vine, grows only 3 feet long; resistant to fusarium wilt. Ideal for small gardens. Released by the University of Wisconsin. B73M, D65, E24, E97, *F60*, *G83M*, H33, H94, I64, J20, K10, K49M, L91M

Montana Gold: 60 days. One of the earliest maturing muskmelons. Developed by Fisher's Garden Store of Belgrade, Montana to ripen in areas with very short growing seasons. Round, netted fruit; sweet and flavorful. Fruit starts to set with the first blossoms. D82

Musketeer:[1] (Bush Musketeer) 90 days. An improved bush-type melon. Round, heavily netted fruit, 5 1/2 to 6 inches in diameter; weight 2 to 3 pounds. Sweet, fragrant, light-orange flesh; firm and tender. Short-vined plant, spreads only 2 1/2 to 3 feet; sets 4 to 6 fruits. Ideal for small gardens and container culture. Introduced in 1982. A56, C44, D11M, D76, *E91G*, E97, *F72*, G64, H33, H42, H54, I91, J20, L42, L91M, etc.

Old Time Tennessee: 100 days. Large, elliptical fruit, 12 to 16 inches long; weight 12 pounds; rind deeply creased. Sweet, very fragrant, salmon flesh. Flavor excellent, but must be picked exactly at peak ripeness. Will not keep. D87, F24M, H66, K49M, L7M, L14, N16

Pennsweet: 65 days. Small to medium-sized, slightly ribbed, oval fruit, 6 inches long; weight 1 1/2 to 2 pounds; well-netted rind; flesh salmon, thick, juicy and sweet, of high quality, seed cavity very small. Perfect for individual servings. For home garden and local market use. All America Selections winner in 1955. A2

Persian: (Small Persian) 110 days. Nearly round fruit; 6 to 7 inches in diameter, weight 6 to 7 pounds. Rind dark-green, turning yellow-orange when ripe; uniformly covered with a fine netting, no ribbing. Flesh very thick, bright-orange; sweet, with a distinctly pleasant flavor and aroma. Excellent shipping qualities. Adapted to areas of long, warm growing seasons. TAPLEY 1937; E59Z, G51, G93M, J34, K5M

Schoon's Hardshell: (Illinois Hardshell) 90 days. Large, oval fruit; 8 to 9 inches in diameter, weight 5 to 7 pounds; rind heavy, hard, deeply ribbed, with coarse yellow netting. Flesh salmon pink, thick and solid, spicy with a good musky flavor. Resistant to growth cracking. Excellent for home gardens and shipping. *A1*, *A75*, B75M, C92, *F60*, *G1M*, G71, G79, *H61*, J84, K73, M29, N16

Sierra Gold: (Sierra Gold Early Shipper) 85 days. Slightly oval fruit; 6 inches in diameter, weight 3 1/2 pounds; rind yellow-green, slightly netted, almost no rib. Flesh salmon; thick, firm, sweet, of very good flavor. Good for home gardens and commercial use. Resistant to powdery mildew. *A1*, A87M, C92, *F60*, G71M, K27M, *L59G*, N16

Speer: 90 days. Large, elongated fruit; weight 3 to 6 pounds; rind grayish-green, moderately netted. Flesh yellow-orange, sweet. Good for home gardens and local markets. Long popular in the maritime Northwest. Known prior to 1929. Origin unknown, but possibly a hybrid of the Banana muskmelon. TAPLEY 1937; A2

Sweet Granite: 70 days. Oblong, lightly netted fruit; weight 2 1/2 to 3 1/2 pounds. Does well in difficult, cool weather areas. Sweet bright-orange flesh. Flavor and texture remain good if vines stay healthy and fruit is picked promptly at maturity. Moderately vigorous vine; tolerant to fusarium wilt. Developed by Professor E.M. Meader at the University of New Hampshire. A2, A25, D68, E24, E59Z, F42, G6, J25M, K49M

Tang Thai: Medium-sized, cylindrical, dense fruit; rind slightly pubescent when young, medium-green with lighter green stripes, reminiscent of a watermelon; flesh salmon, orange near the seed cavity, slightly sweet; has a strong distinctive aroma when ripe. Easy to grow but not suitable for trellising; grown during the rainy season in the tropics. Young fruits are canned, older ones are used for making refreshing desserts. Occasionally available in ethnic markets. *O53*

Tiger: (Orange Ananas) 75 days. Medium-sized, oval, slightly flattened fruit; greenish-white skin, flecked with yellow-orange. Very sweet orange-red flesh. Does well in a cold frame. C85M

Tip Top: 90 days. Large, globular, moderately ribbed fruit; 6 1/2 inches long; weight 5 to 6 pounds; skin pale yellowish-cream, netting moderately abundant; flesh orange, moderately thick, rather coarse, juicy, sweet; quality very good. Does well in northern areas. Introduced in 1892 by Livingston Seed Co. TAPLEY 1937; F24M

Turkey: 90 days. Long-oval fruit, 12 to 16 inches in length; slightly netted rind, light green sutures; weight 15 to 18 pounds. Thick, firm, flavorful salmon flesh. Keeps better than Old Time Tennessee. For home gardens and local markets. An old cultivar. L7M

Weeks North Carolina Giant: 85 days. Extremely large fruit, average weight 20 to 25 pounds when grown on proper soil in a normal season. Sweet, juicy flesh. Produced the world's largest melon of 39 pounds in 1977. Developed by Edward E. Weeks of Greenville, North Carolina. B73M

WHITE-FLESHED

Hybrid

Marble White: 90 days. Smooth, pure white, globe-shaped fruit; weight 2 to 2 1/2 pounds. Light creamy-white flesh; very sweet, sugar content 16% or more; texture crisp and crunchy. Vigorous vine, sets 2 to 3 fruit; withstands heat and drought well; tolerant to powdery mildew. Highly recommended for the West Coast. I77, M46

Open-Pollinated

Ananas: (Sharlyn) 105 days. Oval-shaped fruit, 6 inches in diameter, weight 4 1/2 to 6 1/2 pounds; rind thin, yellow-orange at maturity; uniformly netted, no ribs or sutures. Flesh white, with gold lining and seed cavity; juicy, very sweet and perfumed. Vigorous vine; tolerant to powdery mildew and crown blight. Long popular overseas. A44M{PR}, *A75*, C76M, E70M{PR}, *F60*, G64, G93M, I76M{PR}, J34, K49M, K66, L11, *L59G*, N16, N52, etc.

Cob Melon: 85 days. Medium to large, globe-shaped fruit; skin soft, mottled with light and dark green, ribbed. Slightly grainy, creamy white flesh; very sweet and melting. Unique, cob-like seed cavity that is easily removed. Large, productive vines. Popular for over a century in old-fashioned home gardens throughout the West. E49, J34

Early Silver Line: 76 days. A unique oriental melon of elongated shape. Small, oval fruit; yellow skin lined with silver sutures, so thin it can be peeled like an apple. Crisp, white flesh; very sweet and fragrant. B75

Ein Dor: Ananas type. Short-oval fruit; weight 2 1/2 to 4 1/2 pounds; rind light-orange, with fine netting. Flesh creamy white, very sweet and aromatic. Resistant to powdery mildew race 1. *P75M*, T27M

Golden Crispy:[2] (F_1) 75 days. Small, very uniform, oval fruit; 4 to 5 inches long, weight 10 to 12 ounces; skin smooth, bright golden-yellow. Flesh white, very sweet and aromatic. Rind extremely thin, edible. Whole fruit can be eaten like an apple, no peeling necessary. Vine prolific, often sets more than 10 fruits; resistant to heat. D11M, E49, E59, G64, M46, *S63M*

Golden Rich:[2] (F_1) Smooth, deep yellow fruit, resistant to cracking; medium thick white flesh, crisp and sweet. Thin, edible rind. Very early. Strong, vigorous growing plant; very productive; resistant to hot and humid weather. *S70*

Hero of Lockinge: Medium-sized, roundish fruit; skin bright yellow, slightly netted; flesh white, very tender, melting, rich, of excellent quality. Traditionally grown in cool greenhouses or frames in England. Introduced about 1884. VILMORIN; *R23*, S61

Honey Gold #9:[2] 85 days. Small, egg-shaped fruit; weight about 10 ounces; rind golden-yellow, smooth, very thin, edible. Sweet, tender white flesh. Can be eaten like a pear, crisp rind, flesh and all. Ideal for trellising. I39

Honey Gold Sweet:[2] (F_1) 90 days. Small, elongated-oval fruit; weight about 10 ounces; skin golden-yellow, smooth and glossy. Flesh white, crisp, sweet and very aromatic. Rind extremely thin, edible. A good keeper. L59

Israeli: (Old Original Israeli) 90-95 days. Ananas type. Large, oval fruit; weight 4 to 5 pounds; rind yellow-orange when mature, netting sparse, no ribs or sutures. Flesh white, with a gold seed cavity; very sweet and aromatic. Vigorous, productive vines. F24M, L14, N16

Yokneam 54: (Ananas Improved) Fruit oval; weight 4 1/2 to 5 1/2 pounds; skin orange-colored, netted. Flesh white, juicy, sweet and very aromatic. Suitable for spring production without irrigation or with auxiliary irrigation. T27M

Yuki Large: Unique, attractive melon from Japan. Small, distinctly ribbed fruit; weight 8 ounces; skin pure-white. Thick white flesh, very sweet and aromatic. E49

WINTER MELONS

Late ripening melons that can be stored longer than other types, some into the winter months. Generally lacking in the musky odor of the muskmelons. Most require a very long growing season. Some prefer a period of cool weather to ripen properly.

CASABA MELONS Usually with rough skins, whereas the Honeydew types are smooth-skinned. The name is derived from the town Kassabah near Smyrna (now Izmir), Turkey

Golden Beauty: 110 days. Long-oval fruit, 7 inches in diameter, weight 7 to 8 pounds; rind very hard, wrinkled, a rich golden color when ripe. Thick white flesh; juicy, sweet, spicy, without aroma; small seed cavity. Excellent for shipping and storage. Needs a long, warm, dry climate. Resistant to crown blight. TAPLEY 1937; A87M, B75M, *F60*, G51, G93M, H49, *H61*, J34, J73, K5M, K10, K49M, *L59G*, M46, N52, etc.

O'odham Kuri Basho: Casaba type fruit. A favorite of Tohono O'odham (Papago) and Pima farmers. Vines produce abundant crops. Adapted to low hot desert areas. In temperate areas, plant in spring when danger of frost is past. I16

Santa Claus: (Christmas Melon) 110 days. Long-oval fruit; 12 inches long, 6 inches in diameter; weight 8 to 9 pounds; rind very hard, wrinkled, golden-yellow with dark green mottling. Thick, white to pale green flesh; juicy, sweet, spicy. Excellent for shipping and storage. Resistant to crown blight. Best adapted to long, warm, dry growing regions. *F60*, G93M, *L59G*, N52

Santo Domingo: 120 days. Santo Domingo Pueblo strain. Large, round, basketball-size fruit. Sweet flesh, varied orange and white. From the New Mexico Pueblo near Santa Fe. Adapted to the high semi-desert. Sown in spring after danger of frost. L79M{CF}

Sunglo: 110 days. A unique casaba type melon with salmon-colored flesh instead of the usual white. Oval fruit, 8 inches long and 7 inches in diameter; weight 6 to 7 pounds; rind pale yellow with green stripes or flecks. Resistant to crown blight. For home gardens, shipping and specialty markets. G93M

Sungold: 85 days. Medium-sized, nearly round fruit, weight 5 to 7 pounds; attractive, golden-yellow skin; thick rind, distinctly ribbed, slightly wrinkled at the stem end. Flesh greenish-white, juicy, very sweet, of excellent quality; keeps well. Short vines; can be planted on closer spacing. Ripens successfully in northern areas. Developed at the University of New Hampshire by Professor E.M. Meader. L7M, L89

Tam Mayan Sweet: Large, round fruit; rind hard, slightly wrinkled, ivory-white at maturity. Thick white flesh, very mild, of good flavor; seed cavity small and dry. Will not slip unless overly ripe. Highly resistant to downy mildew; immune to known races of powdery mildew. G93M, *L59G*, L89G

<u>HONEYDEW MELONS</u> Usually with smooth skins, as opposed to the Casaba types which have rough skins. The original Honeydew melon was named in 1915 and is believed to be identical to the French cultivar, White Antibes.

Hybrid

Earli-Dew: (Early Honeydew) 80 days. Nearly round fruit; 5 to 6 inches in diameter, weight 2 1/2 to 3 pounds; rind smooth, green-gold at full maturity. Thick, rich lime-green flesh; very sweet and tender. Will slip when ripe. Excellent for home gardens. Well suited to most northern areas. Vigorous, productive vine; resistant to fusarium wilt. A87M, B73M, C44, C85M, F13, F19M, *F72*, G16, G71, *H61*, H95, J7, K73, L79, M46, N16, etc.

Honey Drip: 85 days. Large, globe-shaped fruit; weight 2 1/2 to 3 pounds; smooth, creamy white rind. Flesh green, turning cream-colored when fully ripe; aromatic, very thick and juicy, unusually sweet and flavorful; sugar content 14% or more. Imported from Japan. A16, D11M, I91

Morning Dew: 96 days. Very large, oblong fruit; average weight 10 to 12 pounds; flesh green, thick, very sweet. Vigorous vine; tolerant to fusarium wilt race 1, and powdery and downy mildews. Should be started indoors in northern areas. F13

Venus: 88 days. Medium-sized, oval fruit, about 5 1/2 inches in diameter; rind medium-thick, light golden-yellow, slightly netted. Flesh bright green, extremely thick and juicy, sweet and aromatic. Slips easily from the stem when ripe; harvest at full slip. Stores and ships very well. Vines produce heavy crops. B75, D11M, *F72*, N52

Open-Pollinated

Golden Honeymoon: (Gold Rind Honeymoon, Gold Rind Honeydew) 95 days. Uniform, nearly round fruit; 6 1/2 inches in diameter, weight 5 1/2 pounds; rind smooth, creamy white turning an attractive golden color when ripe. Thick, emerald-green flesh; juicy, sweet and spicy. Resistant to sunburn. Ships and stores well. A2, B75M, *F60*, H33, L11, L79M, N16

Green Fleshed: (Honeydew) 110 days. Round-oval fruit, 7 inches in diameter, weight 6 pounds; rind smooth, hard, creamy white when ripe. Flesh emerald green; very sweet and juicy, with a distinct, spicy flavor; medium-sized seed cavity. Excellent for shipping. Resistant to crown blight. Adapted to long season areas. A69M, *A75*, A87M, B75M, F13, F19M, *F60*, G51, G93M, H66, I39, J73, K49M, K71, M95, N39, etc.

Honeyloupe: (U.C. Honeyloupe) 92 days. Short-oval fruit; 5 to 6 1/2 inches in diameter, weight 3 to 5 pounds; rind creamy white, tinted with pale salmon at maturity. Thick, sweet, salmon-orange flesh; distinct flavor; small seed cavity. Slips from vine when ripe. Resistant to verticillium wilt and crown blight; tolerant to sulphur. Honeydew-cantaloupecross; developed at the University of California, Davis. *A75*, *F60*, *I59M*, K5M, L42, N16, N52

Oliver's Pearl Cluster:[1] 110 days. The first bush Honeydew, ideal for the home garden where space is limited. Short-vined plant, only 2 feet across. Round fruit, 4 to 5 inches in diameter; smooth, creamy white rind. Sweet green flesh, of exceptional flavor. K49M

Orange Fleshed: 110 days. Nearly round fruit, 6 inches in diameter, weight 5 to 6 pounds; rind smooth, creamy white when ripe. Thick, sweet, light-orange flesh; flavor intermediate between Honeydew and Crenshaw; small seed cavity. Excellent for market and shipping. Resistant to crown blight. *A1*, *A75*, A87M, B75M, *F60*, G51, G93M, K5M, K10, *L59G*

Tam Dew: 100 days. Medium-large, oval fruit; 6 inches in diameter, weight 5 to 6 1/2 pounds; rind smooth, creamy white at maturity. Thick, light-green flesh; sweet and juicy; small seed cavity. Resistant to downy and powdery mildews. N16, N52

Tam Dew Improved: 95 days. Round fruit; 6 1/2 inches in diameter, weight 5 to 5 1/2 pounds; rind smooth, creamy white, sometimes with a yellow spot where exposed to the sun. Flesh green, lighter towards the seed cavity, which is small; high sugar content. Resistant to downy mildew and races 1 and 2 of powdery mildew. *A1*, A87M, F12, F19M, *F60*, *G13M*, K5M, *L59G*

<u>OTHERS</u>

Hybrid

Early Crenshaw: (Burpee Early Hybrid Crenshaw) 90 days. Large oval fruit, slightly pointed at the stem end; weight 14 pounds; smooth dark-green skin, yellowish-green when ripe. Thick, firm, salmon-pink flesh; juicy, sweet and flavorful. Early enough to ripen in northern areas. Vigorous, prolific vine. *A1*, B75, *F72*, G71, G79, H49, H95, J7, M29, M95M

Gold King: 90 days. Hybrid Yellow Canary type that can be grown in northern areas. Large, oval fruit; weight about 4 pounds; attractive, very thick yellow rind. Sweet, nearly white flesh. Can be stored for several weeks without refrigeration. J20

Honeyshaw: 85 days. Very early hybrid Crenshaw type. Oval-shaped fruit, tapering slightly towards the stem end; 7 to 8 inches in diameter, weight 8 to 9 pounds; rind mottled green, turning yellow at maturity. Thick, tender, pastel pink to orange flesh; sweet and juicy, with a distinctive aromatic flavor. Will ripen in short season areas. A13, D11M, F19M, *F63*, G27M, G79, G82, G93M, I39, I64, I67M, I77, K10, M46

Open-Pollinated

Amarelo Auro de Valencia: Medium-sized fruit turning gold-yellow when ripe. Flesh pale green with a savory sweet flavor. J73

Crenshaw: 110 days. Oval-shaped fruit, slightly tapered towards the stem end; 6 to 6 1/2 inches in diameter, weight 5 to 7 pounds; rind rough, dark green turning mottled yellow when ripe. Thick salmon-pink flesh; very tender and juicy, sweet, of a rich distinctive flavor. Requires a long, warm season. B75M, C92, E49, E70M{PR}, E97, *F60*, G51, G71M, *G83M*, G93M, *H61*, *I62*{PL}, J84, K5M, K49M, K71, M95, etc.

Crenshaw Blanco: (White Crenshaw) 110 days. An improvement on the original Crenshaw. Large, oval fruit, weight about 5 pounds; rind corrugated, becomes creamy white when ripe; flesh salmon-pink, very sweet. Excellent for long distance shipping, specialty markets and home gardens. A87M, G93M

Escondido Gold: Large, elongated fruit; 6 inches in diameter, weight 8 to 10 pounds; skin smooth, light yellow-gold, with streaks of orange or light green. Flesh yellowish-orange; tender, juicy, very sweet and flavorful; of excellent quality. Resistant to drought. Originated in Escondido, California by Stanley Grabinski. The result of 16 years of breeding. A2, A32, G92, L11

Indian Cream: (Cobra Melon) An unusual type, with drier flesh than common melons. Has a very distinct flavor and aroma. Splits when ripe. Usually served sweetened with honey or ice cream. P1G, R47

Jharbezeh Mashadi: Native to northern Persia. Considered by some to be the original form of melon. Oblong-shaped fruit, 18 inches long, 8 inches in diameter; skin mottled green and yellow, becoming split when ripe. Very sweet, honeydew-like white flesh with a crispness similar to watermelon. So sweet it has to be eaten in small amounts. Dropped by J73

Napoletano a Buccia Gialla: Small to medium-sized, oval fruit; skin yellow; flesh whitish, sugary, of excellent flavor. Harvested the end of August, ready for eating the end of September into winter. Keeps and ships very well. Becomes sweeter and more melting as it ripens in storage. Q11M

Napoletano a Buccia Verde: Small to medium-sized, oval fruit; skin green, slightly ribbed, resists bruising; flesh whitish, sugary, savory. Harvested in August, stores well into the winter always becoming sweeter and juicier. Ships very well. Q11M

Pinyonet de Valencia: (Pele de Sapo, Pinonet Piel de Sapo, Toad Skin) 105 days. Oval-shaped, 8 inch long fruit; skin mottled with green and yellow, reminiscent of a frog's skin; netting and sutures absent; flesh white, very sweet, flavor very agreeable. Ripens very early for a winter melon. J73, *L59G*, Q11M

Stutz Supreme: 90 days. Heirloom melon, developed over a 20 year period by Joe Stutz of Chico, California. Large, round fruit, weight 5 to 10 pounds; skin beige, non-netted. Delicious orange flesh. Won't slip when ripe. Ripens midseason; bears well until frost. Requires heat to develop full flavor. A2

Tam Canary: Round-oval fruit; rind hard, slightly wrinkled; skin color light-green, turning yellow-orange at maturity. Flesh white, crisp, flavorful; with a small, dry seed cavity. Will not separate or slip from the vine; should be harvested when yellow. Highly resistant to downy mildew; immune to known races of powdery mildew. A87M, L89G

Valencia: (Valencia Rocket Melon) 110 days. Oval-shaped fruit, with pointed ends; 6 inches in diameter, weight 5 to 6 1/2 pounds. Rind very dark green, appearing black from a distance, very hard, wrinkled and bumpy. Thick, crisp flesh; white with an orange seed cavity lining, very sweet. May be stored for 4 months while retaining high sugar content. Adapted to arid, long season areas. E97, G92, J73

Verte de Treste: Origin unknown. Apparently brought to Toulon in southern France by American soldiers landing from North Africa in 1944, hence its market name, l'Americain. Football-shaped fruit, with dark green skin and sweet pale green flesh, slightly tinged with orange around the seed cavity. Excellent keeper. Dropped by G69

Yellow Canary: (Jaune des Canaries) 110 days. Elongated fruit, 5 1/2 inches in diameter, weight 4 to 6 pounds; rind smooth but slightly wrinkled, bright yellow. Flesh white, with an orange cavity lining at maturity; 2 inches thick; crisp, sweet and aromatic. Requires a long growing season to mature properly. Long popular in the Mediterranean area. *A75*, B75M, D87, *F60*, G93M, H49, *H61*, I99, K66, *L59G*, N16, N52

MINT {PL}

MENTHA SPP.

Black Mitcham: Dark green foliage on purple stems. Makes a soothing, fragrant tea. Grown from disease resistant Black Mitcham stock. I39

Blackstem Peppermint: (Black Peppermint) Tall, upright growth habit. Thick stems of bronze-purple blended with green. Dark green leaves tinged with purple. Reddish-purple flower clusters. Excellent strong peppermint flavor and aroma. High oil content. A49D, C43M, F31T, F35M, F52, G96, J66, M15T

Blue Balsam: (Blue Balsam Tea Mint) Shiny, dark-green leaves with a purplish tint. Height 2 to 3 feet. Has an excellent aroma and flavor, more pungent than peppermint, with a hint of pennyroyal. Excellent for tea. Prefers a shaded location. A49D, C9, C43M, C67M, E5M, E61, F37T, H40, J66, K22, K85, *M35*, M53, M82, N19M, N42, etc.

Candy: (Candy Peppermint) Strong sweet scent, reminiscent of Pep-O-Mint Lifesavers. Reddish stems. Said to be a cross between peppermint and spearmint. A1M, C9, C43M, C81M, D29, E5M, L56

Chocolate Peppermint: (Chocolate Mint) Dark green leaves and stems. Height 12 to 18 inches. Has an attractive peppermint odor and flavor with a rich, aromatic chocolate overtone. Reminiscent of a chocolate peppermint patty. Very good for fruit desserts and ices. A97, C9, C67M, D29, F88, G96, H4, I39, J37M, J66, K22, M53, N42

Curly Peppermint: (M. x piperita) Attractive, very curly-leaved form of peppermint. C9, C81M

Curly Spearmint: (Curly-Leafed Spearmint, Curly Mint) Stems long and weak, to 2 feet high; hairy; sprawls in late summer. Broad, dull, crinkled leaves with a heavily veined undersurface. Pale purple flower spikes. Scent and flavor similar to spearmint but stronger. Also a stronger grower. A49D, C43M, C81M, E61, F15M, F24{S}, J66, L7M{S}, L56, N42

Doublemint: Combines the qualities of both spearmint and peppermint in one plant. When first tasted, there is a definite flavor of spearmint followed by an aftertaste of peppermint. Interesting and flavorful. Height 2 feet. Hardy in Zones 4 to 9. C43M, F93G, N42

Emerald 'n' Gold: (Green and Gold, Variegated Spearmint) (M. spicata) An unusual form of spearmint with dark-green and golden-yellow variegations forming on the leaves in cool spring weather. Same flavor and aroma as spearmint. Height 2 feet. Plant in sun or semi-shade. A1M, B9M, C9, C43M, C67M, C81M, E5M, F93G, H49, K22, L56, L57, M82, N42

Grapefruit: Strong, upright growth habit. Good form; less scraggly than many mints. Large, light grayish-green, ruffled leaves tinged with purple in juvenile stage. Has a spearmint scent and flavor with a strong, distinct grapefruit-like overtone. Height 12 to 18 inches. Rust resistant. Can be used for tea, jellies and potpourri. Developed by the University of Oregon. A97, C43M, C67M, C81M, E61, F37T, H3M, H40, H51M, J66, J82, K22, K85, L56, M53, M82, etc.

Jerusalem: Attractive plant with long leaves tinged with bronze. Has a slight spearmint flavor and aroma. Height 2 feet. Introduced into the United States from the Middle East. Its hardiness is unknown at this time. N42

Julep: Narrow, light green, deeply veined leaves similar to spearmint. Height 2 to 3 feet. Excellent in mint vinegars, fruit salads and iced tea. A14, E5M, F37T

Kentucky Colonel: (Improved Spearmint) (M. x cordifolia) Vigorous, 30 inch tall plant with large, broad leaves. Has a delightful, extra pungent, fruity spearmint flavor and aroma. The Kentucky Derby classic; great for mint juleps. One of the best flavored of all the spearmints. A hybrid of spearmint and applemint. Plant in sun or semi-shade. A1M, A49D, C9, C43M, C67M, C81M, F15M, F31T, G84, G96, H4, J66, J82, L56, M15T, N42, etc.

Lavender: Similar to Orange mint, but when steeped or dried, has distinct overtones of lavender. Smooth, oval grey-green leaves. The stems, veins, and undersides of the leaves are a dark-purple color. Lilac flower clusters. Plant in sun or semi-shade. Originated by Dot Montgillion of Smoke Camp Crafts in West Virginia. A1M, C81M, D92, I39, *M35*, M53

Lebanese: (Lebanese Mint) Compact leaves and dark stems. Fresh, sharp peppermint flavor and fragrance. A1M, E5M, E5M{PR}, F37T, M53

Menthol: (M. spicata) A seed-propagated cultivar commonly sold as peppermint or spearmint. The flavor and odor is pungent, not sweet like the true root-propagated strains. Useful for tea, especially for medicinal purposes. D11M{S}, E99{S}, J82{S}

Mint the Best: Narrow, dark green foliage with an excellent crisp spearmint aroma and flavor. Very popular spearmint type. Excellent for tea, mint juleps and jellies. Vigorous plant; height 2 to 3 feet. A1M, E5M, F21, G96, H3M, H40, L86, M15T

Mintucha: Sicilian culinary herb combining the flavor of oregano and mint. Delicious sprinkled over freshly sliced or quartered tomatoes with a dash of olive oil. Adds unique flavor to many Mediterranean dishes. E5T{S}

Moroccan: An extremely fragrant strain of spearmint grown in Morocco for the making of mint tea. Add a drop of honey, if you wish, for one of the most refreshing herbal teas. Height 2 feet. F35M, H3M, R53M, S55

Narrow-Leaved Spearmint: (M. spicata) Similar to spearmint, but leaves are narrow and tinged purple. Same flavor and aroma as spearmint. An heirloom cultivar, carried by settlers form place to place. Height 12 to 24 inches. K22, K85

Red Raripila: (Raripila Mint, Pea Mint) Round, dull green leaves with unusual reddish veins; stems also reddish. Fruity scent; good flavor. Fine for use in salads, especially good with peas. Height 20 inches. LARKCOM 1984; P92, R53M

Spiral Spearmint: (M. spicata) The opposite leaves curve in opposite directions giving an unusual spiral effect when viewed from above. C43M

Variegated Peppermint: (M. x piperita) Attractive leaves touched with patches and stripes of white. Strong peppermint flavor. Ornamental as well as good for culinary usage. F31T, M15T, M82

Willamette Peppermint: (M. x piperita) Grown commercially in the Willamette Valley of Oregon for the production of peppermint oil. I99

MULBERRY {GR}

MORUS ALBA
MORUS RUBRA
MORUS NIGRA

Bachuus Noir: Sweet, black fruit with a distinctive flavor; best when eaten directly from the tree or made into pies; ripens early, after strawberry season ends. No spraying or pruning is necessary. M31M

Beaman: (Beaman White) (M. alba x M. rubra) Light pink fruit of good size; 1 1/4 inches long, 3/8 inch in diameter; sweet, with no tartness. Original tree has a sound, 4 inch diameter trunk, unusual for a mulberry tree. Appears to be resistant to popcorn disease, which is troublesome in some areas especially to hybrids between M. alba and M. rubra. M16

Beautiful Day:[1] (M. alba) Fruit medium to large; pure-white in color; flesh sweet; very good for eating fresh, excellent for drying. Imported white mulberries that are dried like raisins are sold in many food stores and are one of the better dried fruits. Tree medium-sized, spreading; very productive; requires little care and no spraying. Original tree from Maryland. D37

Black Giant: Large, glossy black fruit; sweet, juicy flesh, with a zestful balance of sweet and sour. Vigorous tree, often grows 6 feet per year. Yields of 40 gallons per tree have been reported. M31M

Boysenberry Black: The mother tree of this cultivar was discovered at an old homestead in Wakulla County, Florida. It is well over 100 years old and bears abundant crops of very large, seedless black mulberries. The flavor is distinct, somewhat reminiscent of boysenberry, sweet and rich with just the right amount of tartness. Makes excellent jams. Ripens early to late May. G17

Chelsea: (M. nigra) Long, dark mulberry-red fruit of fine flavor. Excellent eaten fresh, in pies and preserves or made into wine or "mulberry gin". Will fruit within 2 to 3 years. Originated in England. R77

Collier: (M. alba x M. rubra) Medium-sized, purplish-black fruit, 1 1/8 inches long and 3/8 inch in diameter; flavor sweet, with just a trace of tartness, quality very good, on a par with Illinois Everbearing. Ripens over a long period. Tree of medium size, spreading, relatively hardy, very productive. M16

Cooke: (M. rubra) Large, elongated fruit, 1 1/2 to 2 inches long and 3/8 inch in diameter; skin red-black; has a good combination of sweetness and some tartness. Tree hardy, susceptible to fungal dieback. Originated in Reidsville, North Carolina by Donna Cooke. Shows promise as a widely recommended cultivar. K67

Downing: (M. alba) Fruit medium-sized; 1 1/8 inches long, 1/2 inch in diameter; pink; sweet, with no tartness. Tree wide-spreading; hardy and productive; appears to be mostly M. alba. This is not the cultivar which has been widely sold under the name Downing in the past. C63, E91M, M16

Florida Giant: Long, narrow fruit, 2 to 2 1/2 inches in length; light purple in color; mild flavor. Tall, vigorous tree, to 50 feet or more. Large, heart-shaped leaves, 12 inches wide. D57{OR}

Hunza Seedless:[1] (M. alba) Medium-sized, pure white, seedless fruits. Usually dried and stored by the people of Hunza who use the fruits as a staple part of their diet. Imported Hunza Seedless mulberries sell for $4.25 per 8 ounce package in health food stores. Selected by Dr. Thompson of the USDA on a six month plant collecting expedition to Pakistan. D37, M63M{PR}

Hybrid Black: (M. alba x M. rubra) Large, slightly curved black fruit; 1 1/2 inches long, 1/2 inch in diameter; flavor sweet, quality good to excellent. Tree compact, shrub-like, bears heavy crops. E41M{SC}

Illinois Everbearing: (M. alba x M. rubra) Fruit large and very long, average 12 per ounce; skin black; nearly seedless; flavor good to very good, very sweet, considered best by many; matures over a long season. Tree extremely hardy; very productive; young grafts extremely vigorous. Originated in White County, Illinois on the bottom-lands of the Wabash River. Introduced in 1958. BROOKS 1972; B74, D37, E41M{SC}, E91M, F43M, F68, J61M, K16, K67, L7M, L99M, M16, N0, N24M, N33, etc.

Kaester: (M. nigra) Large, elongated fruit, 1 1/2 inches long and 1/2 inch in diameter; deep purple or black when ripe; juice bright red; flavor very sweet, with good balance between sweetness and acidity. Tree bears heavily, is easily propagated from cuttings. Originated in Los Angeles, California. Introduced in 1971 by Nelson Westree. **T49M**{SC}

Pakistan: Fruit extremely large; 2 1/2 to 3 1/2 inches long and 3/8 inch in diameter; ruby-red in color when ripe; flesh firmer than that of most named cultivars; sweet with a fine balance of flavors, quality excellent. Tree spreading with large heart-shaped leaves. Recommended for the deep South and mild winter areas such as southern California. Originated in Islamabad, Pakistan. D37

Paradise:[2] Medium-sized, lavender fruit, 1 1/8 inches long and 3/8 inch in diameter; flesh exceptionally sweet, seeds few; good fresh and out-of-hand, also dries well. Tree dwarf, 7 feet tall and 6 feet wide at maturity; attractive, with heart-shaped leaves; perfect for gardeners with limited space. D37

Riviera: Elongated, deep purple-black fruits; 1 to 1 1/2 inches in length, 1/2 inch in diameter; flesh slightly juicy and very sweet, dessert quality very good; ripens over a long period, from April to June. Originated in Vista, California. D57{OR}

Rupp's: (Rupp's Romanian) Fruit exceptionally large for a hardy cultivar; 1 3/4 inches long, 3/4 inch in diameter; resembles a plum more than a mulberry; opaque black, mild and sweet. Tree large when mature, should be trained by pruning for easier picking; hardy to -15^0 F. Original tree from Carlisle, Pennsylvania; a seedling of a tree brought from Romania to the United States in the 1940's by an immigrant. D37

Russian: (Tatarica) (M. alba) {PL} Fruit reddish-black; of good quality when completely ripe. Tree bushy; to 35 feet tall; very hardy and drought resistant; widely planted for windbreaks, wildlife food and chicken forage; wood hard and durable. Introduced into Europe from China about 1500 years ago. A82, A91, B9M, *G28*, *G66*{S}, H33, H49, I49M, J33, K38{S}, *K89*, L99M, *M69M*, P38{S}

Scott's Jumbo: Medium to large, blocky, light purple fruit, about 1 1/4 inches long; flavor sweet, good, somewhat lacking in tartness. Ripens over a period of 2 to 3 weeks. Medium-sized, spreading tree; bears heavily. Originated in Kansas by Les Scott. M16

Shangri La: Large black fruit of good quality. Tree with very large, heart-shaped leaves; early bearing. Good for the deep South, but may be cultivated in other areas; has fruited well 6 of 8 years in Maryland. Original tree from Naples, Florida. D37

Stearns: Small to medium-sized, dark black fruit, 3/4 to 1 3/8 inches long and 1/2 inch in diameter; good flavor. Original tree in central New York state bears fruit from early July until hard frost (around the end of September), and still has green fruit when frost hits. Good for home gardeners because it ripens over a long period. M16

Sullivan: (M. nigra) Medium to very large, dark purple-black fruit of excellent quality. Has a strong tendency to double crop in areas with long growing seasons. I83M

Sweet Lavender: Small to medium, elongated fruit, about 1 inch in length; skin light pink to lavender; flesh very sweet, without tartness, quality good fresh, excellent when dried; ripens in mid-summer. Will dry on the tree and can be easily shaken onto a tarp. Tree very hardy. B74

Tehama:[1] (Giant White) (M. alba) Very large, plump fruit, 2 3/4 inches in length and 1/2 inch wide; very sweet, succulent, melting flesh. Attractive, large-leaved tree; hardiness undetermined, but probably adapted in Zones 7, 8, and 9. Originated in Tehama County, California. D37

Thompson: (M. nigra) Medium-sized, light purplish fruit of fair to good quality. Vigorous, very productive tree. I83M

Tiger Red: Berries large and very long, up to 1 1/2 inches; raspberry-red in color; seedless. Flavor excellent, rich, reminiscent of real raspberry. Ripens late May to mid June. G17

Weeping: Medium-sized, black fruit; sweet and pleasant. Tree umbrella-shaped, weeps to the ground; semi-dwarf; about 12 feet tall, 12 to 14 feet wide when mature; long-lived; highly productive; very ornamental. Original tree from northwest of Baltimore, Maryland. D37

Wellington: Fruit medium-sized, 1 1/4 inches long, 3/8 inch in diameter; form long, slender and cylindrical; skin reddish-black; flesh soft, of good flavor; ripens over a period of several weeks. Tree a heavy producer. Originated in Geneva, New York on the property of noted fruit breeder Richard Wellington. May be the old cultivar New American, which was also sold many years ago as Downing. D95, E41M{SC}, I36, J61M, L99M, M16, N0

White:[1] Small to medium-sized, pure white fruit. Flavor very sweet, with no tartness, however not as sweet as Illinois Everbearing. Like other pure white types it is valued because it does not stain and for its excellent qualities when dried. Tree medium-sized, spreading, productive. E41M{SC}, M16

MUSCADINE {GR}

VITIS ROTUNDIFOLIA

PISTILLATE MUSCADINES

Pistillate, or female muscadines bear fruit but are self-sterile unless pollinated by a self-fertile cultivar. For best production, female cultivars should be planted within fifty feet of a pollinating cultivar. The source of pollen will not affect the color, shape or flavor of the grape.

BLACK/PURPLE-SKINNED

Black Beauty: Large fruit, 1 1/4 inches in diameter; skin black, edible; clusters large; quality very good, sugar content 24.5%; ripens mid to late-season. Vine very vigorous. One of the best black muscadines ever developed. F93, K67

Black Fry: Large fruit, up to 1 1/4 inches in diameter; skin black; quality excellent, comparable with Fry; sugar content 20%; ripens uniformly, early to mid-season. Vine very productive; disease resistant. Clusters large. F93

Creek: Medium to small fruit; skin reddish-purple, very thin; clusters large; quality excellent but very high in acid. Has the thinnest skin of all cultivars and is regarded as the best for wine. Considered very good by those who like flavor with a tart sweetness. Ripens very late; not recommended for northernmost areas. Originated in Experiment, Georgia. Introduced in 1938. I79

Dulcet: Medium-sized fruit; skin medium, reddish-purple; quality excellent; very persistent, hangs on vines well after fruit is full-ripe; ripens mid-season. Clusters medium. One of the best cultivars for eating fresh. Recommended for home vineyards. Originated in Experiment, Georgia by J.G. Woodruff, Georgia Agricultural Experiment Station. Introduced in 1928. BROOKS 1972; I79

Farrer: Large fruit; skin black; quality excellent, 23% sugar content; ripens early. Vine vigorous; very high yielding. Clusters large. Some years up to one-half of crop is seedless. F93

Hunt: Medium to large fruit; skin medium, dull black, with abundant pigment prized by manufacturers of wine and frozen pulp; quality excellent; ripens early. Very even in ripening, unusual in muscadine grapes. Clusters large. One of the best all-purpose cultivars; excellent for wine, unfermented juice, jelly and hull preserves. BROOKS 1972; B45M, B73M, E3, E29M, E83M, F93, G13, G72, I79, K28, L90, M31M, *M69M*

Jumbo: Large fruit, largest of any muscadine cultivar so far introduced; skin black; quality good; ripens mid-season to late. The fruit ripens irregularly over several weeks making it an excellent cultivar for home use. Vine productive, disease resistant. Clusters large. B45M, D77M, E29M, F19M, F93, G17, H4, I79, L90, M31M, M76, N33

Loomis: Large fruit; skin medium, burgundy colored; quality excellent, taste panels have rated Loomis the best of all cultivars for fresh eating. Ripens mid-September to October 1st. Vine very vigorous; consistently productive; very disease resistant; winter hardy. Clusters medium to large. Recommended for the fresh fruit market. I79

Pride: Very large fruit; skin medium to thick, purplish-black; quality good; ripens mid-season, and over a 3 to 4 week period. Vine vigorous, winter hardy; production heavy; disease resistance medium to good. Clusters medium to large. Recommended for home use. B45M, I79

Sugargate: Fruit very large; skin dark; flavor excellent, sugar in individual berries up to 21%. Vine very vigorous; production very good. Clusters large. Fruit ripens earliest of all cultivars. Very good for home and commercial use, and fresh fruit sales. Not recommended for Gulf Coast use. F93

Thomas: Small fruit; skin thin, reddish-black; quality excellent; ripens mid-season. Vine vigorous. Clusters medium, compact. One of the best cultivars for making unfermented juice, because of its distinctive flavor. I79

BRONZE-SKINNED

Darlene: (Darling) Fruit 1 1/4 inches in diameter, consistently large throughout vine; not erratic in size like Fry or Farrer; quality excellent, pulp melting, sugar content 24%. F93

Fry: Very large fruit, up to 1 3/8 inches in diameter; skin bronze; quality very good before fully ripe, sugar content high; ripens mid-season. Vines moderately vigorous; production good; susceptible to black rot. Clusters very large. Very highly recommended for home use, local sales, and commercial plantings. B45M, B73M, B75, D77M, E3, E29M, E83M, F19M, F93, G13, G17, H4, I79, *K76*, M31M, etc.

Higgins: Fruit very large; skin pink to reddish-bronze, moderately thick yet tender, edible; quality good when fully ripe; ripens mid to late-season. Vine moderately vigorous; production heavy to over-productive. Clusters large, compact. Very good for commercial or roadside sales. B45M, B73M, D77M, E3, E29M, E83M, F19M, F93, G17, H4, I79, L90, M31M, *M69M*, M76, etc.

Scuppernong: Medium to large fruit; skin medium to thin, bronze; flesh sweet, with an excellent and distinctive flavor; quality excellent; ripens early. Vines vigorous; production good. Clusters medium. Best known and most widely grown muscadine grape; the oldest cultivar but still one of the best. B45M, B75, D76, D77M, E29M, F19M, F93, G65M, G72, I79, I98{PR}, K28, K67, L33, L90, M31M, M76, etc.

Sugar Pop: Large fruit, approximately 1 1/4 inches in diameter; skin bronze; sugar content 21%. Pops open when you eat it. Very vigorous and productive, high production being an outstanding characteristic. F93

Summit: Large fruit; skin medium (thinnest of any large-fruited cultivar), bronze; quality very good; ripens mid-season. Vine vigorous; very productive. One of the best bronze cultivars for home and commercial use. B45M, E29M, F19M, F93, I79

Sweet Jenny: Very large fruit, up to 1 1/2 inches in diameter; skin bronze; quality very good, sugar content 24%; ripens early to mid-season. Vine vigorous; very productive; disease resistant. Clusters high. F93

Topsail: Large, round fruit; skin medium to thick, greenish-bronze; quality excellent; high sugar content, low in acid; ripens mid-season. Vine very vigorous; foliage abundant and disease resistant; persistence good. Clusters medium to small, contain 3 to 5 berries. A good cultivar for home vineyards. BROOKS 1972; *M69M*

Watergate: Large fruit; skin bronze; pulp juicy, melting; flavor excellent; ripens early to mid-season. Vine very vigorous; production good. Recommended highly for home and commercial planting. F93

Yuga: Medium-sized fruit; skin pink to reddish-bronze, thin; quality excellent, flavor sweet; ripens very late. Fruit hangs on the vine well after full-ripe, often until frost. Clusters large. Not recommended for the northernmost areas or commercial plantings. BROOKS 1972; I79

RED-SKINNED

Rosa: Large fruit, up to 1 1/8 inches in diameter; skin pinkish-red; quality good; ripens mid to late season. Very sweet, rated excellent by taste panels. Vine very vigorous. Best of the red grapes. Very good for home use and pick-your-own. F93{OR}

SELF-FERTILE MUSCADINES

Perfect-flowered, or self-fertile muscadines produce both fruit and pollen. They will pollinate themselves as well as pistillate plants. The pollen of individual self-fertile cultivars is more viable on any other cultivar than on its own blooms, therefore it is better to plant more than one cultivar of self-fertile muscadine grape in large plantings.

BLACK/PURPLE-SKINNED

Albemarle: Medium to large fruit; skin blue-black, medium, smooth; flesh sweet, flavor very good; ripens about mid-season. Vine vigorous; very productive; resistant to leaf diseases. Clusters medium. Recommended for home use where a single vine is desired. BROOKS 1972; B45M, I79

Bountiful: Fruit medium to small; skin purplish-black, glossy; quality high, has a rich vinous flavor; ripens late, tends to shatter when fully ripe. Excellent for fresh eating and also good for culinary use. Vine very vigorous; productive; disease resistance good. U8{SC}

Cowart: Fruit very large, one of the largest self-fertile cultivars; skin black; quality good, best of any of the large-fruited cultivars; ripens medium early. Vine vigorous; productive; disease resistance good. Clusters very large. Originated in Experiment, Georgia by B.O. Fry. BROOKS 1972; B45M, D77M, E29M, *E66*, F19M, F93, H4, I79, L33, L90, M31M

Ison: Large fruit, up to 1 1/8 inches in diameter; skin black; quality good, sugar content 20%; ripens uniformly, early to mid-season. Vine very productive; disease resistant. Clusters large. F93

Magoon: Medium to small, round fruit; skin dull reddish-black, heavy; flavor sprightly, aromatic; quality excellent; ripens early to mid-season. Vine vigorous; productive. Clusters medium. Widely adapted to all muscadine growing areas. BROOKS 1972; B45M, F19M, *M69M*

Nesbitt: Large fruit, up to 1 1/8 inches in diameter; skin black; quality very good; ripens over a period of 4 or 5 weeks beginning in early September. Vine vigor medium; production very good. Clusters medium to large. Recommended for pick-your-own, dooryard plantings and fresh fruit sales. Released by North Carolina State University. E83M, F93, G17, I79

Noble: Medium-sized fruit; skin medium, black; quality good; ripens early to mid-season. Vine vigor medium; very productive; persistence good; disease resistance good, except for powdery mildew. Clusters large. Excellent for making a red table wine. B45M, B73M, E3, E83M, F19M, F93, G17, I79, L90, M31M, M76

Regale: Medium-sized fruit; skin black; quality good, high acid taste; ripens late mid-season. Vine vigorous; production good; winter hardy. Clusters medium. Recommended for red wine, juice or jelly. B45M, F19M, I79

Southland: Fruit medium to large; skin purplish-black, non-glossy; quality excellent, flavor very sweet; ripens mid-season. Vine vigorous; disease resistant; persistence good. Recommended for home use and commercial plantings. Originated in Meridian, Mississippi. BROOKS 1972; B45M, D76, E29M, F19M, F93, I79, *K76*, M31M

BRONZE-SKINNED

Carlos: Small fruit, 1/2 inch in diameter; skin medium, bronze, attractive; flavor pleasing, similar to Scuppernong; ripens mid-season. Vine vigorous; very productive; hardy. Cluster intermediate. One of the best bronze muscadines for wine making. Originated in Raleigh, North Carolina. BROOKS 1972; B45M, B73M, E3, E29M, *E66*, E83M, F19M, F93, H4, I79, *K76*, L90, M31M, M76

Chowan: Large fruit; skin medium, light brown to bronze, appearance attractive; flesh subacid, aromatic, flavor good; ripens in early mid-season, about 1 week before Scuppernong, which it resembles. Vine vigorous; very productive. Clusters large. Suitable for home use. BROOKS 1972; B45M, I79, L90

Delight: Fruit large, up to 1 1/8 inches in diameter; skin bronze; quality high, sugar content 23%; ripens in mid-season. Vine very productive. Clusters large. F93

Dixie: Medium-sized fruit; skin bronze; quality excellent; ripens in mid-season. Vine vigorous; highly resistant to disease; very productive. Recommended for home and commercial and fresh fruit sales. E83M, F19M, F93, *K76*, M31M

Dixieland: Fruit large, one of the largest self-fertile cultivars; skin bronze; flavor excellent; ripens medium-early. Similar to Fry in flavor, color and size. Vine vigorous; productive. Recommended for home and commercial planting. F93

Doreen: Medium to large fruit; skin bronze; quality good to excellent; ripens late mid-season. Makes excellent light golden wine. Vine vigorous; winter hardy; production very heavy. Clusters medium to large. Recommended for pick-your-own operations. E83M, F93, I79

Granny Val: Large fruit, up to 1 1/8 inches in diameter; skin bronze; quality very good; ripens in mid-season. Vine productive, with extra high yields; disease resistant. Clusters extra large. F93

Janebell: Large fruit, up to 1 1/8 inches in diameter; skin bronze; quality good, sugar content 22%; ripens mid to late-season. Vine very productive; disease resistant. Clusters large. F93

Pineapple: Fruit large, 1 1/8 inches in diameter; skin bronze; quality good, has the flavor of pineapples. Vine very vigorous and productive; disease resistant. Clusters large. F93

Senoia: Medium-sized fruit; skin pinkish-bronze; quality high, sugar content 20 to 22%; ripens evenly in mid-season. Produces an excellent light red wine. Vine vigorous and productive; disease resistant. Clusters large. F93

Sterling: Large fruit; skin yellow bronze; quality good, similar to Scuppernong; ripens late mid-season. Vine moderately vigorous; productive; winter hardy; disease resistance good. Clusters medium. Recommended for fresh fruit sales, pick-your-own and wine making. E83M, I79

Triumph: Fruit large, one of the largest of the bronze self-fertile cultivars; skin greenish-bronze, thin; quality good. Vine productive; winter hardy; an excellent pollinator. Recommended for home or commercial use. B45M, E83M, F19M, F93, G65M, I79

Welder: Medium-sized fruit; skin bronze; quality excellent; ripens early to mid-season. Makes an excellent wine grape. Vine vigorous; productive. Proven to be the best cultivar for partial shade. Recommended for home and commercial planting, both for wine and fresh fruit sales. B45M, F19M, F93, G17

GREEN-SKINNED

Dearing: Medium to small fruit; skin translucent green, thin; quality excellent, flesh crisper than most other muscadine cultivars, flavor sweet; ripens in late mid-season. Vine productive. Clusters medium. BROOKS 1972; I79, *K76, M69M*

Pamlico: Medium to large fruit; skin medium, light green, appearance attractive; quality excellent; ripens in mid-season, about 1 week before Dearing. Vine vigorous; productive. Clusters medium to large. Good for home use. BROOKS 1972; Dropped by I79

RED-SKINNED

Dixie Red: Large fruit, similar to Cowart in size; skin light red; quality very good, sugar content 18 to 19%; ripens in mid-season. Vine vigorous; high yielding. Clusters very large, containing 12 to 30 berries. Very highly recommended for home and commercial planting. F93

Fry Seedless:[1] Medium-sized, red fruit, similar in color to Redgate; sugar content 20%. Vigorous vine; self-fertile, yet needs to be pollinated by another self-fertile cultivar; tolerant to disease. Erratic yields. F93{CF}

Redgate: Medium-sized fruit; skin light to dark red; quality very good; ripens late to mid-season; does not shatter. Uniform ripening of clusters, very attractive when displayed in baskets. Clusters very large, up to 40 berries per cluster. Recommended highly for home and commercial planting, and fresh fruit sales. F93

WHITE-SKINNED

Magnolia: Large fruit; skin white, smooth, attractive in appearance; quality excellent; ripens in late mid-season, about 1 week later than Scuppernong. Excellent for wine making. Vine vigorous; very productive. Clusters medium to large. Good for commercial and home use. BROOKS 1972; B45M, E29M, E83M, F19M, F93, G17, I79, N33

Roanoke: Medium-sized fruit; skin medium-thick, white with a golden yellow tint; quality very good; ripens in early mid-season, about 1 week before Scuppernong. Vine vigorous; very productive. Clusters medium to large. Good for commercial and home use. BROOKS 1972; B45M, I79

MUSHROOMS

See Button Mushroom and Shiitake in the Cultivar listings. Also see Alphabetical Listing of Fungi Families in the Botanical listings.

MUSTARD {S}

BRASSICA JUNCEA SINAPIS ALBA

MUSTARD GREENS

ORIENTAL Cultivated since the earliest times in China where it is called *Gai choi*, and in India where it is called *Lai*. In China especially, numerous cultivars have been selected for various purposes, such as pickling, drying, preserving in salt, and stir-frying. (B. juncea)

Aka Taka-na:[2] (Aka Chirimen, Red Broad-Leaf Mustard) Large, wavy, dark purplish-red leaves on a green base; wide, somewhat thick, pale green to white ribs; pungent flavor. Eaten fresh, cooked or pickled. Tolerant of cold; also very slow to bolt. G20M{PR}, G33

Ao Taka-na: (Ao Chirimen, Green Broad-Leaf Mustard) Broad, bright green leaves with very succulent, crunchy, white midribs. Pungent leaves become pleasantly spicy when cooked. Midribs are excellent raw in salads or cooked. Grows about 12 inches tall. For summer and early fall sowing. E83T, G33

Chao Chow: 60 days. Sem-heading type, similar to Wrapped Heart. Dark green leaves with thick stems. Very popular for pickling in China and Southern Asian countries. D55

Dai Gai Choi: (Broad-Leaf Mustard, Big-Stem Mustard) 65 days. Large, quick-growing leaves; broadly obovate or oval; more or less hairy when young; about 12 inches long. Broad, thick petioles. Widely grown in south China as an autumn crop. The swollen flowering stems of some cultivars, known as *tsoi sum*, are used, peeled, in the preparation of pickles. HERKLOTS; A79M, D55, E59, E83T, H49, N84

Green-in-Snow: (Red-in-Snow, Hsueh Li Hung, Shia-Li-Hon, Snow Cabbage, Serifon) 50 days. Small plant with pale green leaves. Used in stir-fry dishes, especially those containing lima beans or bamboo shoots. The pickled form is used as a delicious seasoning for fried rice or meat dishes. Can withstand temperatures of 20^0 F. and will make abundant growth in cold frames during the winter. The Chinese name translates as snow inside red, or luxuriant in the snow. CHANG, W. [Re], COST 1988 [Cul], HERKLOTS, VON WELANETZ; C27G{PR}, C85M, D55, E59, F42, I39, I77, J82, K49M, L42, L59, L89, L91M, N84, P83M, S55, S61, *S63M*, etc.

Ha Karashi-na: (Loose Leaf Indian Mustard) Dark green, radish-shaped leaves; quite sweet at first taste, becoming very pungent. More bolt resistant than some, but should be grown in the cool weather of spring or fall. Often used in combination with ginger in soups. G33

Horned: Semi-heading plant with bright green frilled leaves. Each stem flares into a horn, opening the plant into a leafy bush. In cooking, used as a stir-fried vegetable, pickling, or for surrounding meat dishes. Grow in warm weather but not during times of intense heat. Easy to grow. *S63M*

Miike Giant:[2] (Miike Purple Giant) 80 days. Very large, broad, undulate, coarsely crinkled leaves with very striking purple veins and thick mid-ribs. The flavor, though strong and pungent, also has a powerful sweetness to it. Can be sown in early spring, or late summer for autumn and winter use. Very cold hardy. E49, *K16M*, L89, *S63M, S70*

Miike Purple-Tinged:[2] 80 days. Widely spreading plant, about 18 inches tall. Leaves thick and heavily crumpled; green in color, tinged with purplish-red at the edge; mid-ribs very wide, not stringy. Central leaves are apt to head loosely. Very slow bolting, and therefore well adapted to summer growing. Derived from a cross of Szechwan Ts'ing Ts'oi and Osaka Purple-Leaved. C53, *P39*

Nan Foon Non-Heading: (Nam Fong, Nam Fong Loose Leaf) 45 days. Upright, vigorous, fast-growing plant. White leaf-stalks, which are an important part of this vegetable, are white and fleshy, straight, 1 1/2 inches at the widest point. Leaves are dark green in color; not large; thin, but a little coarser than South China Heading. G93M, I39, J73, *P39, S63M*

Osaka Purple-Leaved:[2] 80 days. Spreading plant, 12 to 14 inches tall; comparatively early; stands well until late in the spring. Leaves very large, 20 to 26 inches in length; round, undulated, slightly serrate; tinged purplish-red overall when young, darkening gradually towards maturity. Ribs wide and white. Mild flavor for light cooking and salads. C53, E49, G6, I99, J73, K49M, K49T, *P39*

Peacock Tail: 40 days. Small, fast-growing mustard with tender and delicious leaves. Excellent for stir-fry and pickling. Height 12 inches. D55

Red Giant:[1 2] (Red-Leaved Giant, Giant Red) 90 days. Attractive, large, dark-red, crinkled leaves with light green undersides and white mid-ribs. Harvest at 6 inch "baby" size for salads, or allow to grow to mature height of 16 to 18 inches for steaming or stir-frying. Older stems are very good pickled. Plant in early spring or late summer. Winter hardy and slow to bolt. A2, B75, D87, G6, I77, K66, M46, Q34, *S63M*

Sarepta: (Mooi Ts'oi) A cultivar with very prominently lyrate-lobed basal leaves. The main shoot is very expensive. It is preserved in salt and sold dry, not damp or wet, and then costs about $6 a pound. The leaves and upper part of the stem may be salted and are sold very cheaply. Grown in Hong Kong as a winter crop. HERKLOTS. X36

South China Heading: (Chinese Heading) 60 days. Broad, compact, non-spreading plant; grows to 14 inches tall and weighs about 14 ounces at full maturity. Leaf-stalks white, roundish, very fleshy and crooked, crisp and tender. Leaves broad, undulated, light green, tender and of excellent quality. Becomes tinged with purplish-red when exposed to cold temperatures. G33, J73, *P39*

Swatow: (Leaf Heading, Chiu Chow Dai Gai Choi) 43 days. Large, light-green leaves; succulent, tender and sweet. Forms a solid, tight head in cold fall weather; may not head in hot summer weather. The solid heart is disproportionately small and is a very expensive vegetable in Hong Kong. It can be eaten fresh, or it may be salted or made into sour-salt mustard (*haam suen choi*). DAHLEN [Cul, Re], HERKLOTS; L59, Q34

Swollen-Stemmed: (Pressed Mustard, Cha Choy) 45 days. The peculiar feature of this cultivar is the swollen stem with 7 to 9 protuberances or bulges representing enlarged rudimentary lower petioles. A cool, moist climate is required for this stem development. In Hong Kong, the swollen stems are preserved in salt and pressed in tubs so that much of the liquid inside the stem is squeezed out. HERKLOTS; *E91G, G13M, K16M*, L42, L59

Turnip-Rooted: (Tai Tau Choy) A very distinct form grown for the fleshy, tuberous roots which are similar to white turnips in appearance, texture and flavor. The swollen root-tubers are sliced and preserved in salt or pickled. Cultivated as a winter vegetable near Hong Kong. BAILEY, L. 1894, HERKLOTS, TANAKA, UPHOF; E83T{OR}

Wrapped Heart: (Bau Sin, Paau Sum) 60 days. Large, 16 inch tall plant which develops a heart in cool weather. Leaves dark green; petiole thick and glabrous, the veins nearly white on the inner surface of the blade protected from the light. The whole plant is preserved in salt and vinegar. Also good for frying. The heart is not as hard and compact as that of the Swatow mustard and is not eaten fresh. HERKLOTS; D55, E49, K49T, *Q39, S70*

AMERICAN Newer cultivars developed in the United States where they are very popular in the southern states. Traditionally steamed or boiled as "greens", or stewed with pork and eaten with cornbread to sop up the "pot likker". The curled and frilled types are commonly referred to as *mustard lettuce* in Auckland, New Zealand. (B. juncea)

Florida Broadleaf: 50 days. Vigorous, semi-upright plant with a spread of 16 to 22 inches. Smooth, deep green, broad-oval, thick leaves, slightly serrated and with a distinctive flattened, pale green midrib. Moderately slow-bolting. Popular in the South for local markets, processing and home gardens. A56, A87M, B75M, C44, E38, F19M, *F72*, G51, G68, G93M, H66, J34, K73, M46, N16, etc.

Fordhook Fancy: (Burpee's Fordhook Fancy) 40 days. Deeply curled and fringed, dark-green leaves that curve backward like ostrich plumes. Will stand for a long time without bolting. The feathery leaves make an attractive addition to salads, and have a pleasantly mild flavor when cooked. HALPIN; B75, C92, *D12*, G57M, K49M

Green Wave: (Green Wave Long Standing) 50 days. Large, upright plant; large, broad, medium dark-green leaves with curled and ruffled edges. Similar to Southern Giant Curled, but slower growing and bolting, with more finely frilled leaves, slightly darker in color, and more upright in growth habit. A13, C44, C92, E24, E57, E97, F44, G6, G51, G93M, J20, K73, L42, L89, N39, etc.

Old Fashion: (Old Fashion Ragged Edge, Hen Peck) 40 days. An old favorite which produces long, ruffled leaves that make very fine salad greens. Easy to grow and very hardy. Can be planted in spring or fall. Adapted to cut-and-come-again techniques. Fine quality accounts for its long lasting popularity. *D12, G1M*, G67M, L7M, M95M

Slo-Bolt: 40-45 days. Broad, upright plant; medium dark green leaves with slightly serrated margins and cream-colored midribs. Selected for slow bolting and improved processing color. Produces a darker canned product than Southern Giant Curled. *A1*, A27M, *C28*, J84

Southern Giant Curled: (Giant Southern Curled Longstanding) 45 days. Large, upright plant with a spread of 18 to 24 inches. Large, bright green, long-oval leaves with a crumpled, heavily curled and fringed margin. Slow to bolt. Very popular in the South for greens. Attractive for bunching. A87M, B35M, B75M, F19M, *F72*, G16, G71, H66, H94, J97M, K73, L7M, L97, M13M, M95, N16, etc.

MUSTARD SEED

Burgonde: (B. juncea) 85 days. Small brown seed used for the many different hot brown, stone-ground, and French mustards. Burgonde is the standard cultivar for this usage. Seeds average 9900 per ounce. May also be used as a green manure. C43M, G6, J20, N84, Q34, S55

French Brown: (B. juncea) 60-70 days. An old French cultivar that makes a sharp mustard which is brown in color. The leaves can also be used as greens. D87

Tilney: (S. alba) 95 days. Large yellow seed used in American hotdog mustards and in the English and German yellow mustards or white mustards. Seeds average 4500 per ounce. Tilney is the leading yellow cultivar, developed by the famous mustard producer, Colman Foods Ltd. of Norwich, England. C43M, G6, Q34, R47

NECTARINE {GR}

AMYGDALUS PERSICA NUCIPERSICA GROUP

WHITE-FLESHED

Elruge: Medium-sized, round to oval fruit; skin pale greenish-white, blushed with dark purplish-red; flesh greenish-white, red near the stone, very soft, aromatic, quality high; stone free; ripens the end of August. Tree very hardy; productive. Grown in many parts of the world. SIMMONS 1978; R77

Garden Supreme:[2] Large fruit with white flesh, tinged red; freestone; ripens mid-August. Tree a genetic dwarf; maximum height 5 to 6 feet. E4, *I68*

Gold Mine:[1] Medium-large fruit; skin white with a red blush; flesh white, juicy, flavor very good to excellent; freestone; ripens late mid-season. Tree vigorous and productive. Low chilling requirement. Originated in New Zealand. STEBBINS; A88M, *B41*, B93M, B93M{DW}, *D23M*, E4, *G14, G14*{DW}, *G49, L47*, M92

Heavenly White: Fruit large; skin creamy white, with beautiful dark-red blush; flesh firm, very sweet, aromatic; flavor excellent; freestone; ripens late July to August. Self-fertile. One of the best white-fleshed nectarines. Originated in Modesto, California by Floyd Zaiger. A88M, F11, *N20*

John Rivers: Fruit medium to large; skin white with a crimson blush; flesh greenish-white, tender and juicy, semi-freestone; ripens early. Tree medium-sized; vigorous; ornamental when in bloom. Severely affected by insufficient winter chilling. Originated in England. STEBBINS; *C54*, F91T{SC}, *L47*

Karla Rose: Medium-sized, roundish fruit; skin predominantly an attractive red, with some white blotches; flesh white, juicy, very sweet, flavor and quality excellent; freestone; ripens late-May to mid-June. Tree moderately vigorous and productive; requires 700 hours of chilling. C75M, E99M, F61M, F93

Lafayette: Fruit averages 2 1/4 inches in diameter; skin nearly solid bright red with a smooth finish, very attractive; flesh white with attractive pink near pit, firmness above average, texture good; flavor mild; quality good; freestone; ripens 10 days before Elberta peach. Originated in Blacksburg, Virginia. Introduced in 1967. BROOKS 1972; M76

Lord Napier: Large, oval fruit; skin pale yellow, practically covered by a crimson and brownish flush; flesh very pale green, slightly subacid, tender, melting and juicy; flavor good; stone long-oval, free. Tree a regular and heavy bearer. Raised from Early Albert by Rivers and introduced in 1869. SIMMONS 1978, WICKSON; O81, R77

Morton: Medium-sized fruit, about 2 inches in diameter, spherical; skin thick, white, about 80% red blushed; flesh greenish-white, juicy, melting; semi-clingstone; quality very good; ripens in early mid-season; often escapes brown rot infection. Tree vigorous; hardy; flower showy, self-fertile. Originated in Geneva, New York by H.O. Bennett and R.C. Lamb. Introduced in 1965. BROOKS 1972; L12

Red Chief: Fruit about 2 inches in diameter and length, nearly round with halves tending to be unequal; skin bright red with an attractive finish; flesh white, moderately firm; flavor mild; quality good; freestone; resistant to brown rot. Originated in Blacksburg, Virginia. Introduced in 1952. BROOKS 1972; *E45*, E99M, F93, G13, *H34*, H49{DW}, J83, J83{DW}

Rose: (White Rose) Large, freestone fruit with excellent flavor; resembles John Rivers, but is larger, firmer and has more attractive red skin; ripens during John Rivers season. Tree moderately vigorous; a heavier and more regular producer than John Rivers. Also has a lower chilling requirement. Good backyard cultivar. Originated in Le Grand, California by F.W. Anderson. BROOKS 1972; *B71M*

Silver Lode:[1] Medium-sized fruit; skin creamy yellow, about 75% red-blushed with numerous red dots; flesh white, juicy, fine-grained, sweet; freestone; ripens early to midseason, and over a long period. Tree vigorous; chilling requirement low. Originated in Ontario, California by Herbert C. Swim, Armstrong Nurseries. Introduced in 1951. BROOKS 1972, STEBBINS; *C54*, *I68*, *L47*

Stanwick: Fruit medium-large, roundish oval, slightly heart-shaped at base; skin pale, greenish-white, shaded into deep, rich violet in the sun; flesh white, tender, juicy; semi-freestone; flavor good; ripens late. Tree tends to drop fruit before fully ripe. Originated in England from seed brought from Syria. STEBBINS, WICKSON; *C54*, *G14*{DW}, *I68*

Stribling White Free: Large fruit; skin white, blushed with red; flesh white, juicy, sweet, texture creamy; freestone; ripens early, mid-July to mid-August. Tree vigorous and productive. Medium chilling requirement. Good home orchard tree. STEBBINS; *L47*

Tiger: Medium-sized, uniform fruit; skin pale colored, blushed with red; flesh white, aromatic, juicy, melting; dessert quality excellent. Chilling requirement 600 hours or lower. L1

Violette Hative: Round, slightly tapered fruit; skin pale greenish yellow with a dark crimson blush; flesh nearly white, red near the stone, very soft, sweet, quality very good; stone free; ripens the end of August. Tree vigorous, fairly hardy, productive. A very old French nectarine, known in 1659. SIMMONS 1978; T49M{SC}

YELLOW-FLESHED

Armking: Large fruit, 2 1/4 to 2 1/2 inches in diameter; skin olive-green with an attractive reddish blush; flesh yellow, firm, aroma pronounced, semi-freestone. Tree medium-sized; vigorous; flower non-showy, dark pink. Originated in Wasco, California. Introduced in 1969. BROOKS 1972; *A9*, C75M, I83M

Cherokee: Fruit about 2 1/4 inches in diameter; ovate, symmetrical; skin highly colored with a fine finish; flesh yellow, texture noticeably stringy, flavor rich and above average quality, semi-freestone; ripens 13 days before Lexington. Tree moderately vigorous; productive; has an above average tolerance to brown rot and spring frost. BROOKS 1972; C63, *E45*, E99M, G13

Desert Dawn:[1] Small to medium-sized fruit; skin solid red; flesh yellow, firm, juicy, sweet and aromatic, semi-freestone; flavor rich, distinctive; quality high; ripens early, mid to late May. Tree medium-sized; heavy bearing; requires heavy thinning. Low chilling requirement. Originated in Modesto, California by Floyd Zaiger. STEBBINS; *D23M*, F19M, I83M, *N20*

Double Delight: Attractive dark-red fruit; flesh yellow, flavor rich and sweet, freestone; quality very high; ripens mid-season, about with Heavenly White. Showy pink double blossoms. Originated in Modesto, California by Floyd Zaiger. A88M, F11, *N20*

Durbin: Medium to large fruit; flesh yellow, firm but melting, flavor good, texture medium, semi-freestone; matures early, ripening ahead of Redhaven peach. Tree disease resistant; widely adapted. A82, C75M, E29M, E99M, F19M, F61M, F93

Early Rivers: Large, round, somewhat flattened fruit; skin greenish-yellow, almost covered with a scarlet flush and darker stripes; flesh pale yellow, without red near the stone, very soft, juicy, flavor excellent; stone free; ripens early. Tree hardy; productive. Introduced in 1893. SIMMONS 1978; P86

Erliscarlet: Large fruit; skin golden yellow, with 80% scarlet red blush; flesh yellow, firm. Tree vigorous and productive. Originated in Kearneysville, West Virginia by the USDA-Appalachian Fruit Research Station. Introduced in 1985. A5, C75M, E99M, F61M

Fairlane: Large, oval fruit; skin yellow with a red blush; flesh yellow, firm, smooth textured, flavorful, clingstone; ripens late August to early September. Tree vigorous and productive; flowers large and showy; medium chilling requirement. Originated in Fresno, California. *A9*, *B71M*, *L47*

Fantasia: Large, ovate fruit; skin bright yellow with one-third to two-thirds covered with a bright-red blush, more highly colored than Le Grand; flesh yellow, firm, texture smooth, quality good, freestone; ripens immediately after Flavortop; shipping quality good. Very good for drying. Tree vigorous; productive; self-fertile. Introduced in 1969. BROOKS 1972; A5, *A9*, A88M, B53, B67, B83, C41M, C75M, E4, E99M, F53, I99M{DW}, *K73M*, L1, L99M, etc.

Firebright: Medium to large, ovate fruit; skin golden, blushed with bright cherry-red, highly attractive; flesh yellow, firm, smooth textured, flavor excellent, semi-freestone; ripens early, just after Redhaven peach. Tree moderately vigorous and productive; only medium hardy; has good resistance to bacterial spot. Fruit should be thinned early for optimum size. A5, *A9*, *B71M*, B83, *C54*, *L47*

Flamekist: Large, ovate fruit; skin attractive yellow, blushed with red; flesh yellow, firm, textures smooth, quality excellent; clingstone; ripens 3 weeks after Elberta; ships well. Tree productive; flower large, self-fertile; moderately low chilling requirement. Recommended for areas of low rainfall. BROOKS 1972; *A9*, *B71M*, *N20*

Flavortop: Large, ovate fruit; skin mostly red, with an attractive yellow-spotted undercolor; flesh golden-yellow streaked with red, firm, texture smooth, quality excellent, freestone; shipping quality good; ripens just after Independence. Very good for drying. Tree vigorous; productive; self-fertile. BROOKS 1972; A5, *A9*, B53, *B71M*, B83, E4, E99M, F53, F61M, *G14*{DW}, *H90*{DW}, K83M, M39M, N46

Garden Beauty:[1 2] Fruit large, to 3 inches in diameter when properly thinned; skin yellow with a bright-red blush; flesh yellow, flavorful, clingstone; ripens late, in early September. Tree a genetic dwarf, grows only 5 to 6 feet tall; highly ornamental, with showy dark-pink double blossoms. Low chilling requirement. STEBBINS; E87, H65, *I68*, *N20*, N24M

Garden Delight:[1 2] Large fruit, to 3 inches in diameter; skin yellow with a bright red blush; flesh yellow, melting, rich and flavorful, freestone; ripens late, in mid-August. Tree a genetic dwarf, grows only 5 to 6 feet high; self-fertile; has unusually dense foliage and showy pink blossoms. Low chilling requirement. STEBBINS; A88M, E4, F11, F19M, G23, *I68*, *N20*

Garden State: Large, round oval fruit; skin with greenish-yellow ground color, almost completely covered with red; flesh yellow, firm, juicy, freestone; ripens in late August. Tree vigorous; medium-spreading; flowers large, showy, light pink, self-fertile. Originated in New Brunswick, New Jersey by M.A. Blake. Introduced in 1934. BROOKS 1972; A82, G41, G72, H49, H49{DW}, J33, K28, K28{DW}, *M25M*, *M69M*, M83, N46

Gold: (Gialla di Padova) Fruit large; skin and flesh clear yellow; flavor good. Originated in Padova, Italy. Introduced into the United States in 1926. Renamed Gold in 1932. BROOKS 1972; B53, O71M

Golden Prolific:[2] Large fruit, averaging 2 1/2 inches in diameter; skin yellow, partially mottled orange-red; flesh yellow, red next to the pit, soft; flavor subacid to mild; eating quality fair to good; freestone; ripens evenly in mid to late August. Tree dwarf, average height 6 to 8 feet. First dwarf nectarine to be named and introduced. BROOKS 1972; *C54*, F11

Gulf Pride:[1] (Stark Gulf Pride) Medium-sized fruit, 2 to 2 1/2 inches in diameter; skin covered with 50% red blush; flesh yellow, very firm, flavor excellent; ripens in early May, has good handling and shipping qualities. Very low chilling requirement, about 150 hours. Originated in Modesto, California by Floyd Zaiger. Introduced in 1983. I83M, L33

Hardired: Average sized fruit, 2 1/4 inches in diameter; skin yellow, with 90% brilliant red blush; flesh yellow, medium-firm, texture and flavor good, freestone; ripens uniformly. Tree very hardy, hardiness comparable to Reliance peach; tolerant to brown rot and bacterial spot; self-pollinating. Originated in Harrow, Ontario, Canada. A14, D69, D76, D76{DW}, F53, G23, G41, H49, J7

Harko: Fruit medium, averages 2 1/2 inches in diameter; skin yellow with 90% bright-red blush; flesh yellow, medium-firm, melting; flavor and texture good; almost freestone; uniform ripening, ripens mid-August, or 4 days after Redhaven peach. Tree medium-sized; spreading; hardy; somewhat resistant to brown rot and bacterial spot; self-fruitful. F53, I49M, J61M

Hunter: Large fruit; flesh yellow, juicy, sweet, tender, free to semi-freestone; quality very good; ripens in midseason. Tree mildews badly. Originated in Geneva, New York by U.P. Hedrick. Introduced for trial in 1924. BROOKS 1972; G79M{DW}

Independence: Medium-sized, ovate fruit; skin brilliant cherry-red, attractive; flesh yellow, firm, of good texture and flavor, freestone; suitable for long-distance shipments; ripens early, in late June or early July. Tree productive; moderately vigorous; self-fruitful. BROOKS 1972; *A9*, *B71M*, B93M, E4, I36, *I54*, *I68*, *L47*, L99M, M39M, M39M{DW}, *N20*

June Glo: Medium to large fruit; skin yellow with a red blush; flesh yellow, firm, flavor and aroma excellent, freestone. Tree blooms late, but ripens in June, up to 4 weeks before Fantasia. Excellent tree and bud cold tolerance; good for late frost areas; some resistance to bacterial spot. Originated in Modesto, California by Floyd Zaiger. A88M, *B71M*, F11, F53, J61M, *N20*

Le Grand: (Pot of Gold) Very large fruit; skin yellow with a bright-red blush; flesh yellow, firm, rubbery, clingstone; flavor delicate, semi-acid; ripens late; holds well on the tree. Tree large, spreading; productive; flowers large, showy, pink. Originated in Le Grand, California by F.W. Anderson. Introduced in 1942. BROOKS 1972, STEBBINS; *A9*, *B41*, E4, *I68*, *L47*

Lexington: Medium-sized fruit; skin deep yellow overlaid with medium red; flesh deep yellow, medium firm, texture medium, quality good, freestone. Tree extremely vigorous; has considerable ability to escape brown rot and blossom-season frost; flower showy. Originated in Blacksburg, Virginia. Introduced in 1957. BROOKS 1972; E99M, *F5*, M76

Mericrest: Medium-sized fruit; skin solid dark-red; flesh golden-yellow, flavor excellent, freestone; ripens in Glohaven peach season, or early August in Zone 6. Tree very hardy, withstands winter temperatures of -20^{0} F; resistant to brown rot and bacterial leaf spot; self-fruitful. Originated by E.M. Meader of New Hampshire. A88M, B53, D76{DW}, E97, F53, G53M, H65, H65{DW}, K71, L33, L33{DW}, *N20*

Necta Zee:[2] Large, attractive fruit; skin dark red; flesh yellow, firm, flavorful, clingstone; ripens early to mid-June in central California, 1 month before Nectar Babe. Tree strong, vigorous; a genetic dwarf, growing only 6 feet tall; self-fruitful; needs approximately 500 chilling hours. Developed by Floyd Zaiger. A88M, E87, *I68*, *N20*

Nectar Babe:[2] Skin bright-red; flesh yellow, sweet, rich and flavorful, freestone; ripens in mid-summer, one month earlier than Garden Delight. Tree a genetic dwarf; requires another peach or nectarine for pollinization; produces heavy crops when pollinized with Honey Babe peach. A88M, B75, E4, E87, F11, I49M, *I68*, J61M, L33, L99M, *N20*

Panamint:[1] Medium to large fruit; skin bright red; flesh yellow, freestone; ripens during third week of July. Tree vigorous; productive; has a very short chilling requirement, being adapted to southern California growing conditions. Originated in Ontario, California by Herbert C. Swim, Armstrong Nurseries. Introduced in 1952. BROOKS 1972; *C54*, *D23M*, *G49*, *I68*, I83M, L1, *N20*

Pineapple: Fruit round, fairly large, slightly tapering; skin yellow green but almost covered with bright crimson; flesh golden yellow, faintly red near stone, very soft; flavor distinctive and good; stone small, free. One of the best yellow-fleshed peaches. Raised by Rivers from Pitmaston Orange and introduced before 1870. SIMMONS 1978; O81, R77

Pioneer: Medium-sized fruit; skin red, thin; flesh yellow, streaked with red, especially near the pit; flavor very rich and distinctive; freestone; ripens with Gold Mine. Suitable primarily for home planting and local markets. Tree productive; flowers large, pink, very showy. Originated in Ontario, California by Herbert C. Swim. BROOKS 1972; *C54*

Pocahontas: Fruit medium large, 2 1/8 inches in diameter; ovate; skin highly colored; flesh yellow, slightly stringy, quality good, semi-freestone; ripens 19 days before Lexington. Tree vigorous; productive; resistant to brown rot and spring frosts. Originated in Blacksburg, Virginia. Introduced in 1965. BROOKS 1972; C63, *E45*, E99M, L90

Red Gold: Large to medium fruit; form symmetrical, globose; skin smooth, yellow, overspread with red, medium to thick; flesh yellow, streaked with red near pit, firm, meaty, flavor subacid, eating quality good to best; freestone; ripens evenly, immediately after Sun Grand. BROOKS 1972; A5, A82, B83, C41M, C75M, F19M, F53, F61M, *H90*, *I54*, *K73M*, L33, M39M

Red Sunset:[2] Large fruit with highly colored red skin; flesh yellow, juicy, firm-textured, flavor excellent; freestone; ripens in mid-June. Tree a genetic dwarf, growing only 5 feet tall; highly productive; self-fertile; requires 600 hours of chilling. *C54*, F11

Southern Belle:[1 2] Fruit large; skin yellow overspread with red; flesh yellow, freestone; ripens in early August. Tree a genetic dwarf, growing only 5 feet tall at maturity; very productive; blooms very early. Low chilling requirement, approximately 300 hours at or below 45^0 F. Originated in Le Grand, California by F.W. Anderson. Introduced in 1975. *C54*, *D23M*, I83M

Sun Glo: Large fruit, 3 inches in diameter; skin golden yellow, with 75% red blush; flesh yellow, juicy, firm, quality very good; ripens in midseason, or early August in Zone 6. Tree hardy; productive; thrives in Zones 5 to 8. A5, B83, C75M, E4, E99M, F53, F61M, *H34*, *K73M*, K83M, L33, L33{DW}, L90

Sun Grand: Fruit large, about 2 1/2 inches in diameter; skin yellow with a red blush; flesh yellow, firm, freestone; ripens after John Rivers, about July 5th. Tree large, spreading; productive; flowers large. Very good for drying. Originated in Merced, California by F.W. Anderson. Introduced in 1950. BROOKS 1972; *A9*, B93M, *C54*, E4

Sungem: Medium to large, round fruit; skin yellow, 90 to 100% blushed with deep ruby red; flesh bright yellow, firm, melting, very sweet; semi-freestone; ripens extremely early, early to mid-May. Tree vigorous, semi-spreading; self-fruitful, productive; extremely disease resistant; flowers large, showy, fragrant. Released by the University of Florida. C75M, E99M, F61M, G17

Sunred:[1] Small to medium-sized, round fruit; skin bright red over 90 to 100% of surface; flesh yellow, firm, dessert quality excellent, semi-freestone when fully ripe; ripens early to mid-May in central Florida. Tree requires about 300 hours of winter chilling at or below 45^0 F. to break dormancy. BROOKS 1972, RUCK; *A9*, *A19*, *C54*, *F5*, F19M, I83M, *K76*, *K76*{DW}, M31M

Surecrop: Large, roundish fruit; skin attractive bright red over a yellowish-white undercolor; flesh yellow, firm but tender, juicy, sweet and flavorful, freestone; quality good; ripens mid-August. Tree vigorous; productive; self-pollinating. *A19*, A82, B75, D76, G23, G72, G79M{DW}, *H90*, K28, K28{DW}, L90, *M25M*, M83, M92

OKRA {S}

ABELMOSCHUS ESCULENTUS

GREEN-SKINNED

HYBRID

Annie Oakley: 45 days. Medium-green, slender, five-angled pods; 7 to 9 inches long; spineless; remain tender as they grow to a large size. Earlier than open-pollinated types. Compact, uniform, heavy-yielding plants; height 3 to 4 feet; can be planted at high densities. Excellent for local markets, home gardens and processing. Does well in the North. B75, B75M, D76, E97, F13, F19M, *F72*, G6, G71, H54, J20, J34, K73, M95M, N16, S55, etc.

OPEN-POLLINATED

Annual Wonder: A distinct cultivar, worthy of cultivation all the year round. Greenish-white, smooth, pointed pods; meaty and tender. S93M

Blondy: (White Blondy) 48 days. A short-season okra for Northern gardeners; has performed well in trials as far north as Canada. Spineless, ribbed pods; attractive creamy-lime in color; best picked when about 3 inches long; crisp and firm, yet tender and not stringy. Short, compact plant; only 3 feet tall yet very productive. All America Selections winner for 1986. D11M, D76, E97, F19M, *F72*, G27M, G79, H33, H49, I77, J34, K71, M29, M95, M95M, etc.

Cajun Jewell: Tender pods, up to 6 inches long; excellent flavor. Dwarf, spineless plant, 2 to 4 feet tall; produces early and continues to bear all season if pods are kept cut. A local favorite in Cajun country since the 1950's. L7M

Cajun Queen: 50 days. An early, productive, very hardy okra. Bright, spineless, tapered pods; 5 inches long, and with 6 well-defined ridges. Intense flavor and rich color; won't fade into the background in soups and stews. Height 3 to 4 feet. For processing, home garden and fresh market. B75M, D76, *G13M*, K5M, *L59G*

Candelabra: (Park's Candelabra) 55 days. The first base-branching okra, with 4 to 6 bearing spikes per plant. Requires less space; produces higher yields of thick, tender, flavorful pods per square foot. Open habit makes for easier picking. For best branching habit, thin to 20 inches apart. Developed by an avid garden hobbyist, Mr. L.S. Jennings of Newberry, South Carolina. I91

Clemson Spineless: 55 days. An abundant producer of rich-green, slightly ribbed, straight, pointed, spineless pods; 6 to 7 inches long; of high quality; best picked when 2 1/2 to 3 inches long. Height 4 feet. Standard cultivar for processing, fresh market, and home garden use. All America Selections winner in 1939. Developed by the South Carolina Experiment Station. A87M, B73M, B75M, C44, F19M, G93M, *H61*, H66, K73, L7M, L9M, M13M, M46, M95, N16, etc.

Dwarf Green Long Pod: (Prolific Long Pod Green) 55 days. Sturdy, compact, well-branched, productive plants; height 2 1/2 to 3 feet; easier to pick than tall types. Dark-green, moderately ridged pods; slightly more slender and longer than Clemson Spineless; 7 to 8 inches in length; spineless; of excellent quality. For best flavor, harvest when 1 to 2 inches long. A25, A69M, B73M, C44, D65, D76, F12, G71, G93M, H66, J7, J34, K73, M95, N16, etc.

Emerald: (Emerald Green Velvet) 55 days. A round-podded cultivar popular for processing. High quality dark-green pods are smooth, spineless, slender and thick-walled; 8 to 9 inches long; can be snapped like green beans. Extra length and perfectly round slices are valued for canning and freezing, but best flavor is obtained if pods are picked when 2 to 4 inches long. Vigorous, thrifty plants. Height 5 feet. *A1*, A87M, C92, *D49*, D76, F12, F19M, *F63*, G71, G79, G93M, *H61*, H66, J34, K50, M29, N16, etc.

Evertender: 50 days. Slightly ridged, medium-green pods; average 5 to 7 inches in length when mature. Quality very good; stays tender much longer than others. Medium-sized, unbranched plants; height 4

to 5 feet; have a tendency to lodge. Easy to harvest and has good tolerance to disease and drought. Imported from India. E49, L7M

Flower Bed: 60 days. Medium to large pod, up to 7 inches long; tender and non mucilaginous with excellent flavor. Compact, very prolific plant; height 4 to 5 feet; branches without pruning. Well adapted to small gardens but reaches maximum production when given more room. Developed by James T. Hopper. F68M

Gold Coast: 75 days. Vigorous producer of smooth (nearly unfluted), light-green pods. Small, bushy plant with an open growth habit, height 4 to 5 feet. Highly drought-tolerant and heat-resistant. Sometimes called "the lost okra of New Orleans". Introduced in 1960 by the Louisiana A.E.S. L7M

Lee: (Dwarf Lee) 50 days. Bright-green, firm, tender, spineless pods; 6 to 7 inches long. Compact, bushy plant; height 3 feet; of open habit which makes harvesting easier; shorter stems permit closer planting in limited-space gardens. Dependable producer of uniform pods over a long season. Developed at the University of Arkansas. A27M, D76, F19M, *G1M*, I91, J34, N16

Little Egypt: 60 days. Thin, slightly curved pods, 8 1/2 inches long when dried; medium-spined; lime-green in color. Flavor moderately strong compared to Ever Tender and Clemson Spineless; recommended for those who like a full-flavored okra. Heavily branched, medium-spined plants; height 3 to 4 feet. Drought resistant; high-yielding; low sensitivity to pod harvest and day length. L7M

Louisiana Green Velvet: (Louisiana Velvet) 60 days. Medium-green, slender, round, smooth pods; 6 to 7 inches long; spineless and very tender; retain their color when processed. Well-adapted to canning. Large, vigorous, branching, heavy-yielding plant; height 6 feet; produces all season. Very similar to Emerald. A87M, *D49*, D76, D87, F12, F19M, H66, I77, L9M, L14, N16

Pentagreen: 55 days. An early and high-yielding cultivar from Japan. Medium-green, five-angled, upright, slightly spiny pod; 6 inches long. For best quality, harvest when about 3 inches long. Sturdy, compact plant; 18 to 30 inches tall. Very productive, even in areas usually too cool for okra. C85M, *K16M*, L79

Perkins Mammoth: (Perkins Mammoth Long Pod) 55 days. Pods long and slender, straight, slightly grooved, intensely green in color; length 6 to 8 inches; diameter 1 1/8 inches; fleshy and tender over a long period. Excellent for canning. Strong growing, highly-productive plant; height 4 to 5 feet. D11M, *G1M*, G57M, H54, H66, K49M, K71, L14, L42, M95M, N16, N39

Star of David: 60 days. An Israeli cultivar with a distinctive flavor; recommended for okra lovers who would like to try something different. Short, blunt pods; about 5 inches long and 2 inches in diameter; with 8 to 9 deep grooves. Unbranched stalks grow 8 to 10 feet tall. Highly productive throughout the season. K49T, L7M

Warihio Nescafe: Seeds are roasted, ground and used as a substitute for coffee. Young pods are edible. The very large, mature pods are good for dried arrangements. Attractive yellow flowers with red throats. I16

White Velvet: (Creole) 60 days. Very large, round, velvety smooth pods; greenish-white in color; long and tapering; not prickly to the touch; stay tender longer than other types. Excellent for frying. Height 3 to 5 feet. A standard, traditional cultivar. Introduced prior to 1894. B71, C92, F19M, G67M, H66, K49M, L14

RED-SKINNED

Burgundy:[1] 60 days. Deep-red "baby" pods (2-3 inches long) make very attractive menu additions; older pods remain tender even at 8 inches in length; keep their red color when cooked. Attractive, deep-red stems and branches; red-veined green leaves. High yielding. Ornamental as well as tasty. All America Selections winner for 1988. B75, C44, D11M, D76, E97, *F72*, G6, G27M, G71, H33, H49, I91, J34, L9M, M29, M46, M95M, etc.

Red: 60 days. Tasty pods are rich scarlet; 6 to 7 inches long; hold their color when fresh, but turn green once cooked. Recommended for fresh market, home gardens and processing. Vigorous, medium-sized plants; 3 to 3 1/2 feet tall. Leaves, stems and pods have a reddish tinge. Pods are also ideal for dried arrangements. A21, C92, D76, H66, I99, K5M, K49M, L7M, L14, M95

Red Velvet: 60 days. Long, slender, slightly ribbed, deep-red pods; will retain their color as long as they remain fresh but turn green when cooked; add raw to salads for best use of bright color. Cut when very small before ribs become stringy. Tall, red stalks; height 4 to 5 feet; red-tinged foliage. An old cultivar. F19M, G82, I77, K49T, K71

Red Wonder: Long, red pods, with 7 distinct ridges; longer than other red strains; remain tender until almost mature. Upright plant; height 4 to 5 feet; very ornamental. Excellent quality combined with an attractive appearance. E49, F85, R50

UGA Red: Attractive, reddish plants are semi-dwarf and produce abundant crops of scarlet pods that turn green when cooked. Combines high-yielding ability and ornamental value. A new introduction from the University of Georgia Agricultural Experiment Station. A32

ONION {S}

ALLIUM CEPA — **ALLIUM FISTULOSUM**
ALLIUM X PROLIFERUM

BUNCHING ONIONS

Also called *Welsh onions, green onions, salad onions, spring onions* and *scallions*. Grown for the green tops and the long, usually white stalks or slightly swollen base. Mostly A. fistulosum.

RED-STALKED

Benizome: A unique cultivar with dark violet stalks. The violet color develops well under low temperature conditions. Usually produces 3 to 4 stalks. Useful raw or cooked. I77, *Q28*

Get Set Red: Forms large bulbs the second year; continues dividing. K49M

Red Beard: 60 days. Attractive, red-colored stalk, 12 inches long; crisp, mild and flavorful. Best quality is obtained when harvested just as the bulbs begin to swell. Delicious brushed with oil and grilled over charcoal until soft and sweet. Vigorous plant; height 2 1/2 feet. Bright coloration develops in cool weather; should be planted in late summer for a fall harvest. D11M, K66, L59, *S70*

Red Bunching: (Red Welsh Bunching) Red non-bulbing onion. Grows in clusters of 3 to 4 stalks. Stalk 10 to 12 inches long, bright-red over nearly the entire length, free of bulbing. Mild flavor; good in soups, stews and salads. Very hardy and prolific. Usually grown as an annual. E5T, K85{PL}, M46, Q34

Red Welsh: (Early Red, Ciboule Commune Rouge) 65-70 days. An old form of perennial bunching onion, similar to the true wild Welsh onion. Grows in clusters of 2 to 3 stalks, each stalk 12 to 14 inches long; coppery-red in color. Light green leaves. Strong flavor; use leaves and small bulbs. Can be maintained from season to season by division. Very hardy. C53, N84, O48, P83M, R53M{PL}, S55

Santa Clause: 56 days. Very fine Ishikura type with rose-red stalks. Can be harvested as "spring onions" 6 to 8 weeks after sowing; remains tender and flavorful for 2 to 3 weeks afterwards. Excellent lightly grilled until soft and sweet. Unique color improves with earthing up and intensifies with the onset of cold weather. L91M

SMALL BUNCH Distinct type with very long, narrow, chive-like leaves and a very short white base. Mild flavor.

Fuyuyo: Very slender green bunching onion. Excellent for eating raw or cooking, with a mildly pungent flavor. Suitable for growing in fall and winter. *S70*

Natsuyo: Slender green, chive-like bunching onion with a very short white base. Excellent for eating raw or cooking, with a mildly pungent flavor. Good for shipping. Resistant to disease, especially downy mildew. Suitable for spring and summer sowing. *S70*

WHITE-STALKED

Beltsville Bunching: (A. cepa x A. fistulosum) 65 days. Long, smooth white stalk with a slight swelling, resists bulbing; crisp, very mild and flavorful. Widely adapted; produces well where others may fail. Will stand hot, dry weather better than most cultivars; also very hardy. Resistant to pink root, smut and thrips. Released by the USDA. *A1*, *D12*, *F72*, G79, K49M, K73, L42, M29, M49, N52

Evergreen White Bunching: (Evergreen Hardy Long White, Nebuka) 65 days. Long, slender stalk; 4 to 9 inches to the first leaf; little or no bulbing; tender and mildly pungent. Resistant to thrips, smut and pink root. Extremely winter hardy. Sow in spring or fall. Can also be treated as a perennial by dividing the clumps the second summer to produce a new crop. C85M, D11M, D55, D82, F19M, F44, F82, G6, G16, K71, L59, *L59G*, L79, N16, N39, etc.

He-Shi-Ko: 65 days. Semi-splitting type; produces clusters of stalks when not planted too closely. Long, silver-white stalk, 8 to 10 inches to the first leaf; tender and mildly pungent. Tolerant to both heat and cold; can be over-wintered for an early spring crop. Resistant to pink root, smut and thrips. A16, A69M, C44, *D12*, D65, D76, E59, E97, *G13M*, G64, *G83M*, J7, J20, K73, K85{PL}, M13M, M46, etc.

Hikari: Grows in clusters of approximately 6 stalks. Strong, erect, dark-green foliage. Both leaves and stems are tender, mild and flavorful. Resistant to bulbing. For summer and fall harvests. Can also be sown in the fall for over-wintering. N84, P83M, *R23*, S55, *S75M*

Ishikura: (Ishikura Long White) 65 days. Single stalk type. Thick, cylindrical, non-bulbing stalk; up to 12 inches long to the first leaf, tender and mildly pungent. Tall, upright, pale blue-green leaves; resist breaking. Good shipping qualities. Winter-hardy plant; grows 18 to 24 inches tall. *A75*, E49, K49M, K49T, L42, L91M, N52, S61, *S63M*

Kincho: (Kincho III) 75 days. Single stalk type, similar to Tokyo Long White. Long, slender, pure-white stalks with much better uniformity than Ishikura. For late summer and fall harvests, or for over-wintering. Winter hardy in southern Ontario, New York, Ohio and New Jersey. F13, H54, L42, N52

Kujo Multistalk: (Kujo Green Multistalk) 70 days. Grows in clusters of 3 to 4 stalks. Slender white stalk, 6 inches long to the first leaf. Both leaves and stalks are very tender and flavorful. Height of plant 20 to 24 inches. Can be sown spring through late summer or treated as a perennial. F90, K49M, Q34

Kujyo Regular Strain: 120 days. Grows in clusters of 3 to 4 stalks. Stalks 3/4 inch in diameter at the widest point; soft yet seldom fall over in severe cold temperatures. Very hardy and adapted to over-winter culture, sown in summer or fall. Used widely in the western half of Japan. J73, *P39*

Kuronobori: 60 days. Single stalk type. Slender white stalk, 16 inches long; mildly pungent and flavorful. Dark green leaves; 14 inches long. Suitable for planting at any time of the year. Very popular in Japan and China. D55

Multi-Stalk 5: Grows in clusters of 5 to 6 stalks. White stalks; about 6 inches long. Slender leaves. Both leaves and stalks are extremely tender and tasty. Height of plant 20 to 25 inches. Sow in spring or summer. Can be left in the field during winter. O53M

Multi-Stalk 9: (Iwatsuki) 80 days. Grows in clusters of 8 to 10 stalks. White stalks; 7 inches long. Leaves green, about 12 inches long; moderately thick, soft and sweet. Suitable for sowing at any time of the year. E83T, L59

Shimonita: An autumn and winter cropping cultivar with a unique stalk. Shorter and thicker compared with other bunching onions. Also one of the best tasting bunching onions. For highest quality and yield from an autumn sowing, a planting distance of about 2 1/2 inches within the row is recommended. *Q28*

Supreme Long White: 70 days. Single stalk type. Long, white stalk, up to 14 inches in length. For summer or winter harvests. Very vigorous plant; does well in hot weather; also cold resistant. T1M

Tokyo Bunching: 110 days. Resembles Evergreen White Bunching, but has more upright, stiffer tops and grows with single stems. Little or no bulbing, especially in the fall. For summer and fall harvests; not recommended for over-wintering. *A1*, M29

Tokyo Long White: 68 days. Single stalk type. Long, slender white stalk; 14 to 18 inches long, 3/4 to 1 1/2 inches in diameter; little or no bulb; tender and mildly pungent. Upright, stiff, dark blue-green leaves; about 6 inches long. Excellent for fall and summer bunching; not winter-hardy. Resistant to pink root, smut and thrips. *A75*, B35M, D11M, *D12*, *G13M*, G64, *H61*, H95, J84, *K16M*, K73, L42, L59, O53M

Tokyo Natsuguro: Dark green leaves with long white stalks. Similar to Kuronobori. A long time favorite cultivar in Japan. D55

Tsukuba: (Tsukuba Long White) Single stalk type. Long, thick stalk, 18 to 22 inches to the first leaf; pure-white when blanched; tender and mild; very little splitting. Very dark-green leaves, 7 to 8 per stalk. Heat resistant. Very high yielding. Sow in mid-spring for summer use. K66

White Javelot: 70 days. Beltsville Bunching type. Of better appearance, with longer white stalks and less tendency to bulb. Resistant to hot weather and cold. Finer tops. J7

White Knight: Long white stalks, with relatively little bulbing. Erect, medium tall, medium dark-green tops. Good tolerance to some strains of pink root. A refined and widely adapted cultivar. G93M, N52

White Spear: 85 days. Short white stalks, 4 to 5 inches long; very slow to bulb even in hot, dry weather. Tall, upright, blue-green leaves; weather tolerant, stand up well to stress and heat without falling. Very vigorous and reliable. Resistant to pink root. *A1*, *A75*, *D74*, G6, G71M, G82, *H61*, J84, K73, N52

Yakko Summer: 100 days. A specialty in Osaka, Japan. Leaves slender but numerous. Stands heat better than other cultivars without falling over. Good for late spring sowing. J73, *P39*

LARGE BULBING ONIONS

Some types of bulbing onions are grown for fresh use, others for storage. They are grown from seed or from *onion sets*, which are small, specially grown bulbs. Raising them from sets is easier than from seed, especially in areas with short summers or where spring sowing conditions are likely to be difficult. Sets mature earlier and largely avoid the problem of onion fly, however only a few cultivars are available as sets. LARKCOM 1984. (A. cepa)

RED/PURPLE-SKINNED

Hybrid

Carmen: 118 days. Long-day type. Large, blocky globe-shaped bulb, up to 4 inches in diameter; skin an attractive deep carmine-red; firm interior with uniform, concentric rings that slice nicely; quality very high. Dark red exterior color extends to center of the bulb when cured, showing well on each internal ring. Stores well if sown by mid April. D27, G82, I91, L42, *L59G*, L91M, *M43M*

Red Granex: 165 days. Short-day type. Large, flattened globe-shaped bulb; skin thin, dark red; flesh red, firm, mild. Stores moderately well. Some tolerance to bolting and doubling under good growing conditions. Protect from strong sunlight to prevent bleaching. Resistant to pink root. Standard short-day red onion in the Granex class. *A1*, A87M, G93M, *L59G*

Open-Pollinated

Benny's Red: (Bennies Red) 112 days. Long-day type. An improved Southport Red Globe. Medium to large, deep globe-shaped bulbs; attractive bright red skin; soft, moderately pungent, pink to white flesh. Not for long-term storage. Standard commercial red onion; also good for home gardens. *A1*, A13, B75M, F13, *H61*, K10, K73, L42, *L59G*, L89, M29, M95, N52

Burgundy: (Red Hamburger, Red Burgundy) 120 days. Short-day type. Large, flattened globe-shaped bulb, 3 to 4 inches in diameter; glossy, dark red skin; flesh white, with red ringing; very sweet and fine-textured. Ideal for slicing. Not a good keeper. Resistant to pink root. A56{PL}, A87M, B73M{PL}, C92, D11M, D65, E97, *F72*, H42, H66, I39, I65M{PL}, J14{PL}, J34{PL}, K49M, L9M, N16, etc.

Early Red Burger: 172 days. Intermediate-day type. Medium-large, thick-flat bulb; skin deep dark-red; flesh white with light-red ringing, soft, mildly pungent. Developed as an early fresh market cultivar with good color. Highly non-bolting with good tolerance to pink root. Widely adapted. G93M

Italian Blood Red Bottle:[1] 120 days. Large, spindle-shaped, blood-red bulb. Has a spicy, tangy flavor. Ideal shape for slicing. Can be used in salads or for cooking. Often employed in center-piece arrangements. I39

Red Ball of Karachi: Medium-large bulb, flat but rather deep; skin deep purplish-red; characteristically free from bolting tendencies. Keeps very well in storage. Excellent for sets and mature bulbs. Standard late cultivar of good keeping quality. Sown September to November in Bangladesh. O39M

Red Bermuda: 95 days. Short-day type, similar to Yellow Bermuda and Crystal Wax except for its red color. Medium to large, semi-flat bulb, about 3 inches in diameter; thin red skin; crisp, very mild, pinkish flesh. Excellent in salads and sandwiches. Does not keep well. G57M

Red Brunswick: (Braunschweiger, Rouge de Brunswick) 105 days. Small, very flat bulb, seldom exceeding 2 1/2 inches in diameter; skin intense violet-red, verging on black; flesh white, hard and firm, juicy, mildly pungent. Stores extremely well. Introduced prior to 1865. BURR, VILMORIN; *A75*, D24{ST}, S27, S45M, S61

Red Creole: (Red Creole C-5, Creole C-5) 110 days. Short-day type. Small to medium-sized, thick-flat bulb; skin reddish-buff; flesh reddish-purple, fine-grained, solid, very pungent and flavorful. Stores moderately well. Grows well under hot, humid conditions. *D12*, *D74*, F19M, G27M, G93M, *I59M*, K5M, K49M, *L59G*, M95

Red Giant: 115 days. Long-day type. Large, spherical globe-shaped bulb; thick, reddish-brown skin; light red flesh, with a very mild flavor for an onion that stores well; excellent quality. Keeps extremely well due to its tough skin. *E91G*, K49M

Red Grano: 90 days. Short-day type. Medium to large, top-shaped bulb; red skin; soft, mild flesh. Will store well for 2 to 3 months. Resistant to pink root rot. *A1*, A87M, K5M, *L59G*, *L85*{PL}

Red Torpedo:[1] (Italian Red Torpedo) 100 days. Intermediate-day type. Large, spindle-shaped bulb, often weighs 1 pound or more; skin thin, dry, light purplish-red; flesh very light-red, soft, sweet, mildly pungent. Ideal shape for slicing. Stores moderately well. For home gardens and local markets. Highly productive and non-bolting. Good tolerance to pink root. D11M, D76, E97, *G83M*, G93M, G93M{PL}, *I62*{PL}, I99, I99M{PL}, K49M, *L59G*, L79, *N40*{PR}, Q34

Red Wethersfield:[5] (Large Red Wethersfield) 105 days. Long-day type. Large, comparatively flat bulb, 5 inches in diameter; skin deep purplish-red; flesh medium-firm, pungent, purplish-white. Widely used for the production of red onion sets. Widely adapted. Keeps fairly well. Introduced prior to 1865. BURR, VILMORIN; A16, A25, A69M, *A75*, C44, C63{ST}, *F72*, F92, G93M, J7, J20{ST}, K27M, K71, M13M, N39, N39{ST}, etc.

Rouge de Florence:[1] (Red Florence) Very long, spindle-shaped root, about 6 inches long; bronze pink-red in color. Very mild and sweet. Attractive red color blends well with the pale green stem. Ideal shape for salads and pickling. Relatively insensitive to daylength; may be sown in spring or fall. C53, G68

Ruby: 105 days. Long-day type. An attractive, refined selection of Southport Red Globe. Medium to large, deep globe-shaped bulb; thick, deep red skin; pink, firm, pungent flesh. Tight, relatively heavy, well-retained scales. Well suited to prolonged storage when properly cured. G79, G93M

Southport Red Globe: 110 days. Long-day type. Medium to large, globe-shaped bulb; thick, glossy, purple-red skin; flesh firm, strongly pungent, white tinged with pink. Heavy, deep red scales are well retained during handling and storage. Well-adapted to northern areas. Standard hard red market and storage onion. A13, B49, C85M, *D12*, D65, E57, E97, F92, G16, G93M, H94, J7, J14{PL}, J20, L97, N39, etc.

Stockton Early Red: 180 days. Intermediate-day type. Large, thick-flat bulb; skin thin, dark red; flesh white with light-red ringing, mildly pungent. Short storage period. Very productive and vigorous. Highly non-bolting; tolerant to pink root. Well adapted to central California. G93M, G93M{PL}, *H61*, I99M{PL}, L89

Sweet Flat Red: Similar to Red Hamburger. Large, flat bulb, 3 to 4 inches in diameter; skin red; flesh white, with light-red ringing. Very mild, as mild as Bermudas but better adapted to the Midwest. Excellent for summer salads and hamburgers. Does not store well. G16{PL}

WHITE-SKINNED

Hybrid

White Granex: 170 days. Short-day type. Large, thick-flat bulb; white skin; fairly firm, mild white flesh. Resistant to pink root. Standard white Granex type, very widely grown and popular in onion-producing areas of the South. Released by the USDA and the Texas Agricultural Experiment Station. *A1*, A87M, F12, G27M, H66, J34, J34{PL}, *L59G*, L89M{PL}, *M43M*, N16

White Keeper: 106 days. White Sweet Spanish type. Uniform, globe-shaped bulbs, 3 inches tall, 3 1/2 inches wide; average weight 12 ounces; pure white throughout and resistant to greening on both interior and exterior. Centers are firm, generally multiple but not dividing in any way. Excellent storage capabilities, particularly for a sweet white onion. Tolerant to various strains of pink root. Introduced in 1980. *C68M*, J20

Open-Pollinated

Fresno White: 194 days. Intermediate-day type. Large, thick-flat to flattened globe; thin white skin; soft, white, moderately pungent flesh. For fresh market use; does not store well. Highly productive and non-bolting with good tolerance to pink root. Well adapted to the Central Valley of California. G51, G93M, G93M{PL}

New Mexico White Grano: 185 days. Short-day type. Large, flattened globe-shaped bulb; thin white skin; soft, mildly pungent white flesh. Short storage period. Resistant to pink root. Well adapted to Texas, Arizona and New Mexico. *A1*, A87M, G93M, L9M, *L59G*

Odorless Plain Leaf:[2] Excellent salad onion. Flesh is creamy white, very mild in flavor. Keeps fairly well. Used for early crops. P1G

Ringmaster:[3] (White Sweet Spanish Ringmaster) 115 days. Long-day type. Selected for a high percentage of single centers, ideal for onion rings. Very large, globe-shaped bulb; glossy white skin; medium firm, mildly pungent white flesh. Stores moderately well. Produces a high percentage of jumbo size bulbs. Resistant to pink root. *A75*, D11M, *D12*, G79, G87, H42, *H61*, K5M, K49M, K73, *L59G*

Southport White Globe:[4] 65-120 days. Long-day type. Medium-sized, globe-shaped bulb; thin pure-white skin; very firm, close-grained, pungent white flesh. Stores very well if cured properly. Good for home gardens. Standard storage cultivar in long-day regions; also used for green bunching onions in the spring. C92, *F72*, G16, G71, G93M, *H61*, I64, J7, J20, K49M, K71, K73, M13M, N39, N52, etc.

White Bermuda: 90 days. Short-day type. Medium-large, semi-flat bulb, 2 1/2 to 3 1/2 inches in diameter; thin white skin; very mild, crisp, waxy white flesh. Excellent in salads and sandwiches. Not a good keeper. Widely adapted in southern areas. C63{ST}, D65, G79, *G83M*, H33, H33{PL}, H49, H54, K10, K27M, K27M{PL}, K49M, L89M{PL}, M46, N16, etc.

White Ebenezer:[5] Long-day type. Medium to large, flattened bulb; white skin; firm, mild, clear white flesh. Good keeping qualities. Used for mature onions or small pickling onions; also widely grown for the production of white onion sets. *A75*, *D12*, *G1M*, G57M, G64, I91{ST}, J20{ST}, J84, *L59G*, M95M

White Lisbon:[4] (White Lisbon Bunching) 60-110 days. Bulb round, more or less flattened, 3 to 4 inches in diameter when well grown; skin smooth, thin, clear and white; flesh mild, moderately firm. Widely grown as an early bunching onion. Does not keep well. Introduced prior to 1865. BURR, VILMORIN; A69M, *A75*, B35M, B49, C85M, D65, F92, G79, *H61*, K66, K73, L9M, L42, L89, T1M, etc.

White Sweet Spanish:[4] 75-120 days. Long-day type. Large, globe-shaped bulb; skin white, medium-thick, glossy; flesh white, moderately firm, mildly pungent. Stores fairly well. Also used as a green bunching onion. Standard late white cultivar for long-day regions. A56{PL}, B73M{PL}, C85M, D82, E57, F19M, *F72*, G51, G71, H66, H94, I65M{PL}, J34{PL}, K71, L79, L97, M95, N16, etc.

White Sweet Spanish Bunching:[4] 70 days. Special strain used for bunching or stripping. Uniform, long white stems; slender blue-green tops. Very mild and sweet. Slow to form bulbs, but will reach 5 1/2 inches in diameter if planted as a spanish onion. Harvested from early spring until fall. B75M, *F63*, G82, H42, I64, K73, L97, M95

White Sweet Spanish Jumbo: (White Sweet Spanish Utah Jumbo) 125 days. Long-day type. Very large, globe to deep globe-shaped bulb; white skin; moderately firm, mildly pungent white flesh. Keeps fairly well. High yielding; produces a high percentage of jumbos. Tolerant to thrips. B35M, *E91G*, E97, *F63*, G64, G93M, *I59M*, J14{PL}, L89

<u>YELLOW/BROWN-SKINNED</u>

Hybrid

Keepsweet II: 115 days. Long-day type. Combines the qualities of Sweet Spanish onions and hard, storage types. Large, uniform, globe-shaped bulbs; skin tan-yellow to brown, glossy, well retained; flesh firm, mild. Keeps very well. Very high yielding; does well on marginal muck soil. *A1*

Maui:[6] Short-day Yellow Granex type hybrid. When grown on the slopes of Haleakala volcano on the island of Maui, the volcanic soil and cool climate produce a delicious onion that is high in sugar and moisture and low in bite. SCHNEIDER [Cul, Re]; F85M{PR}, G51, L11, M19, M20, *N40*{PR}

Ring King:[3] 120 days. Short-day type. An early maturing Yellow Spanish type developed for the onion ring trade, but also suitable for fresh market. Large globe-shaped bulb; medium dark-brown skin; firm, moderately pungent white flesh. Keeps moderately well. A87M

Ringmaker:[3] 115 days. Long-day type. Early maturing hybrid with full Spanish parentage. Uniform, very large round bulbs; 3 to 4 inches in diameter; yellow skin; mild flesh. Produces a high percentage of single centers, ideal for onion rings. Excellent storage qualities. *A1*, G6, L42

Spartan Sleeper: 110 days. Long-day type. Medium-sized, globe-shaped bulb; tough light-brown skin, well-retained scales; very firm, pungent, creamy white flesh. Exceptional storage qualities; will keep for 12 to 18 months with a minimum of sprouting if harvested, cured, and stored properly. Released by Michigan State University. *A1*, D11M, E97, K10

Sweet Sandwich: 110 days. Long-day type. Large, slightly top-shaped bulb; light-brown skin; tender, light-yellow flesh. Moderately pungent at harvest, mellowing considerably and becoming sweet after about 2 months in storage. Will keep until April or May. High yielding; tolerant of drought. Developed by Clinton Peterson of the University of Wisconsin. A13, B35M, B75M, C53, D11M, *E91G*, F13, F19M, G6, G16, G64, H42, H95, J7, J14{PL}, K73, L79, etc.

Vidalia:[6] (Vidalia Sweet, Vidalia Granex) Short-day, Yellow Granex type. Large, slightly flattened globes with rounded shoulders; yellow skin; crisp, firm white flesh, extremely sweet and mild; large-ringed. Excellent for onion sandwiches, pickles and onion relish. Resists bolting. Widely grown near Vidalia, Georgia where it is claimed to be "the sweetest onion in the world". SCHNEIDER [Cul, Re], THOMPSON, P. [Re]; A24M{PL}, <u>A24M</u>{PR}, A56{PL}, D76, D76{PL}, E97{PL}, F19M{PR}, *F72*, F80, H49, I65M{PL}, J34, J34{PL}, <u>J49</u>{PR}, K71{PL}, L35{PL}, *L85*{PL}, etc.

Yellow Granex: 165 days. Short-day type. Large, thick flat-shaped bulb; skin light yellow, thin; flesh yellowish-white, moderately firm, very mild and sweet. Keeps fairly well. Resistant to bolting when grown where adapted. Tolerant to pink root. Very widely grown and popular in onion-growing areas of the South. *A1*, A87M, B71, B75, *D12*, F12, F19M{PL}, *F72*, G93M, H66, J34, J34{PL}, L14{PL}, *L59G*, L89M{PL}, *M43M*, etc.

Open-Pollinated

Ailsa Craig: 110 days. Sweet Spanish type from England where it is a traditional exhibition onion. Very large, globe-shaped bulb, weight 2 pounds or more; rich, golden straw-colored skin; firm, sweet mild flesh. Good keeping qualities. For spring or early fall sowing. Introduced about 1899. B49, D11M, E33, G6, L91M, O53M, P83M, *R23*, S45M, S61

Australian Brown:[5] 100 days. Long-day type. Medium-sized, flattened globe-shaped bulb; skin very thick, dark reddish-brown; flesh straw-yellow, firm, extremely pungent. Keeps for a very long time. Popular and more widely adapted for growing "sets". Does best in the coastal districts of central California. *A75*

Bedfordshire Champion: Medium to large, globe-shaped bulb; light-brown skin; firm, mildly pungent white flesh. Excellent storage qualities; keeps well into winter. Consistently heavy yields. Very susceptible to downy mildew. An old traditional English cultivar, still very popular. Introduced prior to 1885. VILMORIN; B49, E33, O53M, P83M, *R23*, S61

Bomo: Long-day type. Medium to large, flattened globe-shaped to oval bulbs; skin brownish-yellow, distinctly striped with reddish-brown; moderately pungent; of high quality. Stores well. Heavy yielding. Originated in Sweden. P69

Early Yellow Globe: 100 days. Long-day type. Medium-sized, globe-shaped bulb; light bronze skin; moderately firm, mildly pungent white flesh. Good shipping and storage qualities. Widely adapted; but particularly well suited to the Northwest and upper Midwest. Introduced in 1980 by Joseph Harris. A13, A16, *A75*, C44, C85M, D11M, D65, E24, E57, F82, G16, J20, K71, M13M, M46, etc.

Giant Zittau: Large, flattened globe-shaped bulb, 4 to 5 inches in diameter; skin attractive, very smooth, almost silky, pale salmon-colored; small neck. Also used for medium-sized pickled onions. Keeps exceptionally well. Highly productive. Suitable for spring or autumn sowing. Introduced prior to 1885. VILMORIN; B49, *S75M*

Golden Ball: 105 days. Unique onion set, adapted to late planting; avoids problems that early sets face, such as premature running to seed, split bulbs and frost damage. Can be planting from mid to very late spring. Produces a very attractive onion with very solid flesh and a rich onion flavor. Excellent for slicing. Keeps well. L91M{ST}

Golden Globe:[5] Long-day type. Medium-sized, oblong globe-shaped bulb; deep golden-yellow skin; firm, mildly pungent flesh. Widely used for the production of yellow onion sets. Can also be harvested as early green onions. Moderately good keeper. A69M, *A75*, *D12*, J20{ST}, J84

Golden Mosque:[5] 105 days. Excellent for producing yellow onion sets. Combines the non-sprouting features of Stuttgarter with the earliness of Ebenezer. Mature onions are almost round. First year sets are elliptical in shape. L42

Imai Early Yellow: Early maturing selection from Senshyu Semi-Globe. Thick, flattened globe-shaped bulb, weighing about 10 ounces; skin pale yellow, thin; flesh firm, pure-white, mildly pungent; quality excellent. Adapted to overwinter culture in mild climates. Bridges the gap between the stored onions from the previous year's crop, and the current crop, not yet ready for use. *R23*, *S63M*, *S70*

James Long Keeping: (James Keeping) Small to medium-sized, pear-shaped bulb, seldom over 2 inches in length; skin coppery red; very fine neck. Excellent storage qualities. Still popular in England, with both home gardeners and commercial growers. Introduced about 1834. VILMORIN; P83M, *R23*, S55

Kelsae Sweet Giant: 110 days. Long-day type. Extremely large, top-shaped bulb, average weight 4 to 5 pounds; dense, solid, very mild flesh; unique sweet flavor. Matures easily in northeastern United States and Canada on sandy soils by mid-September. Excellent for storage. Produced the World Record onion of 7 pounds 7 ounces. J20, L42, L91M, S27

Marushino Yellow: Short-day type. An extra early cultivar that produces bulbs even under short day or lower temperature conditions. Medium-sized, flattened-globe with lemon-yellow skin. Resistant to splitting and bolting. Can be harvested in the middle of March in warmer regions. *Q28*

New Mexico Yellow Grano: 167 days. Short-day type used for early markets. Medium to large, top-shaped bulb; thin, light yellow skin; medium-firm, mild flesh. Short storage period. Resistant to pink root; somewhat tolerant to thrips. For autumn, winter or very early spring plantings in southern areas. *A1*, A2, A87M, K5M, *L59G*, N16

No Tears:[2] 90-95 days. An "odorless" onion developed for those who like the texture and crisp juiciness of onions but dislike the strong lingering aroma and flavor. The aromatic oils have been virtually eliminated. Light, very mild flavor. L91M

Oakey: Large, flat bulb, up to 5 pounds; skin light brown; flesh firm, very pungent and flavorful. Excellent with bread and "real ale". Keeps up to 9 months. Very popular for exhibitions. Heavy yielding. Rare English cultivar, grown in Soham, Cambridgeshire since the 1880's. P83M, S55

Odorless Lime:[2] 90 days. Medium to large, flattened globe-shaped bulb; light straw-colored skin; snow-white flesh. Bright lime-green tops. Entirely odorless and non-irritating. Eliminates tearing and "onion breath". Matures in midseason. E97

Owa Slicer:[1] 100 days. Long, spindle-shaped bulb; skin pale golden-brown; flesh crisp, white, mild and flavorful. Perfect for slicing; produces exactly 10 2-inch slices per bulb. Excellent keeper; stores well into March. Imported from Denmark. E97, K49M

Pukekohe Longkeeper: (M & R Pukekohe Longkeeper) 200 days. Intermediate-day type. Medium to large, globe-shaped bulb; skin amber to golden-brown; flesh white, firm, pungent. Very productive and extremely long keeping. Originated in New Zealand. P1G, T1M

Ringer:[3] (Ringer Grano) 168 days. Short-day type. Large, top-shaped bulb; yellow-brown skin; soft, mild, sweet flesh; very thick rings. Produces a high percentage of single centers, making it ideal for onion rings. Excellent in salads and sandwiches. Also good for fresh market use. High yielding. Resistant to pink root. *A1*, A87M, *L59G*

Senshyu Semi-Globe: (Senshyu Yellow) Heavy yielding Japanese cultivar bred for over-wintering in mild climates. Medium to large, flattened globe-shaped bulb; deep straw-colored skin; firm, mildly pungent flesh. Excellent keeping qualities. Sown late summer to autumn; ready for harvesting mid-June to July. P83M, *R23*, S61, *S63M*, *S75M*

Sturon:[5] Long-day type. Medium-sized, flattened globe-shaped bulb with a thin neck; skin yellowish-brown, moderately thick; flesh firm, juicy, pungent; quality very good. Keeps extremely well. High yielding Stuttgarter type, widely grown in Europe for sets. *R23*, S27

Stuttgarter:[5] (Yellow Stuttgarter, Stuttgarter Riesen) {ST} Long-day type. Medium-sized, flattened globe-shaped bulb; skin light yellow-brown, glossy; flesh firm, white, mildly pungent. Keeps very well. Primarily used for the production of sets. Sets hold very well in storage without sprouting; will not produce seed-stalks when set out in unfavorable weather. *A75*{S}, B73M, C44, C44{S}, C63, C85M, E24, F13, G16, G64{S}, G82, H83, J20, M46, M49, N39, etc.

Sweet Winter: 340 days. Over-wintering onion developed to withstand bolting in sub-zero northern climates. Produces a Stuttgarter shaped set onion from a late summer planting. Matures by the end of June the following spring. Large, thick-flat bulb; skin light yellow; flesh mild and sweet, 50% sweeter than regular set onions. Short storage period. Introduced in 1980. I91, L42, *L59G*, L89

Texas Early Grano: (Texas Early Grano 502) 175 days. Short-day type. Large, uniform, top-shaped bulbs; skin thin, dry, straw-yellow; flesh white, soft, mild and sweet, thick-ringed. Short storage period. Good resistance to bolting and splitting. Tolerant to pink root. Widely used in southern Texas as an early shipper. *A1*, *A75*, A87M, *D12*, *D49*, F19M, *G1M*, G27M, G71M, G93M, J34, J34{PL}, K49M, *L59G*, N52, etc.

Texas Supersweet:[6] (Texas Grano 1015Y) 175 days. Short-day type. Yellow Grano strain, with improved tolerance to pink root. Large, globe-shaped bulb, weight about 1 pound; yellow skin; mild, very sweet flesh. Better storage and handling qualities than other grano types. High yielding. Released by Texas A & M University. Winner of the raw onion category of the National Sweet Onion Challenge. *A1*, A87M, *D49*, H33{PL}, H42{PL}, I65M{PL}, J21M{PR}, J34, J34{PL}, L89G, L89M{PL}, N16

Turbo:[5] 85-100 days. Long-day type. Developed in Holland for sets. Compared to the previous Dutch standard Sturon, Turbo is higher yielding and keeps longer. Produces large, globe-shaped bulbs with deep amber skin and very good flavor. Highly resistant to running to seed, even under conditions of stress. L91M{ST}

Walla Walla Sweet:[6] 110 days. Large, flattened globe-shaped bulb; light brown skin; white, ultra-mild flesh. Considered one of the sweetest onions, along with Granex, Vidalia and Maui. Not for storage. Brought to Walla Walla, Washington from Corsica at the turn of the century by Peter Pieri, a member of the French army once stationed on the island. SCHNEIDER [Cul, Re]; A69M, B35M, B75{PL}, C53, D82, F82, F92, G6, *G83M*, G93M, H94, H95, I99M{PL}, J20, K71{PL}, L97, M62{PR}, etc.

Yellow Bermuda: 100 days. Short-day type. Medium-sized, flattened bulb; skin thin, loose, light straw colored; flesh nearly white, juicy, very mild and sweet. A popular market type grown primarily as a winter crop in the South; also good for home gardens. Highly resistant to pink root. B73M{PL}, C92, D65{PL}, *F72*, G57M, G79, I84, J34, K10, K27M, K27M{PL}, L89M{PL}, N39

Yellow Dutch: {ST} Excellent onion sets from Holland. Produces green onions soon after planting, or if left in the ground will grow into large mature onions for winter storage. Very good texture and flavor. A16, B13, D27, F1, H42

Yellow Ebenezer:[5] 105 days. Long-day type. Medium-sized, slightly flattened bulb; skin brownish-yellow; flesh off-white, very firm, mildly pungent. Highly productive. Good keeping qualities. Widely used for the production of yellow onion sets. Introduced about 1900 from Japan. *A75*, *D12*, E38, E97{ST}, *G1M*, G71{ST}, I39, I91{ST}, J84, K71, L7M, *L59G*, M95M, N39

Yellow Globe Danvers:[5] 110 days. Long-day type. Medium-large, globe-shaped bulb; copper-yellow skin; firm, moderately pungent, clear white flesh; small neck. Excellent keeping qualities. High yielding; also grown for sets. Popular home garden and market cultivar. Introduced prior to 1865. BURR; A25, C92, D11M, D27, E59Z, G57M, G79, G87, H42, H54, H54{ST}, *I59M*, J97M{ST}, K20, M13M, etc.

Yellow Rock:[5] 100 days. Flattened globe-shaped bulb; attractive bronze-yellow skin. Excellent keeping qualities. High yielding. Used extensively for the production of yellow onion sets. Developed by Martin Rispens and Son. J84

Yellow Sweet Spanish: 110 days. Long-day type. Large, globe-shaped bulb, weight often 1 pound or more; skin dark brownish-yellow; flesh medium-firm, pure-white, mild and sweet with a good flavor; small neck. Moderately good keeper. Popular home garden cultivar. A25, B35M, B78, C44, C85M{ST}, D11M, D82, F19M, *F72*, G71, H66, H94, I65M{PL}, J34{PL}, L97, M95, N16, etc.

Yellow Sweet Spanish Utah: (Utah Sweet Spanish, Yellow Valencia Sweet) 115 days. Long-day type. Large, globe to deep globe-shaped bulb; skin dark yellowish-brown; flesh white, moderately firm, mildly pungent; medium small neck. Keeps fairly well if properly cured. Resistant to mildew; somewhat tolerant to thrips. A13, A16, A69M, B75M, C85M, D27, F1, G51, G79, *H61*, H95, K73, M13M, M46

MULTIPLIER ONIONS {ST}

Hardy perennial onions that produce a cluster of bulbs at ground level from a single planted bulb. The larger bulbs are saved for eating, and the medium and small sized bulbs are stored and replanted. They can be grown in pots for forcing *green onions* during the winter. Some types are in demand as gourmet items. A. cepa Aggregatum Group unless otherwise noted.

<u>POTATO ONIONS</u> Also called *hill onions*, *pregnant onions*, *nest onions*, and *mother onions*. Potato onions enjoyed widespread popularity before the turn of the century, and are still a local favorite in some areas of Virginia. When a small bulb (3/4 inch) is planted, it will usually produce one or two larger bulbs. When a large bulb (3 to 4 inches) is planted, it will produce approximately 10 to 12 small bulbs per cluster.

Potato Onion: (Multiplier Onion) Each large bulb divides underground to form 8 to 12 smaller ones; when planted, these produce 1 or 2 large bulbs. Can also be left in the ground for mild cooking onions later in the season. Slightly more pungent than standard onions. A16, B13, D11M, D27, G64, G87, H42, J7, K13, K49M, M13M

Red Potato Onion: Similar to the Yellow Potato Onion in size and flavor, except the bulbs are characterized by a pale pink (not red) flesh. Also hardier and a better keeper. Bronze-red bulb scales; slight vertical ridges. Growing conditions may affect color development of bulbs. Family heirloom from central Virginia. G19M, L7M

White Potato Onion: (White Multiplier Onion) Grows much like other potato onions but produces smaller bulbs, only 1/2 to 1 inch in diameter. Divides underground to form clusters of up to 15 onions. Used for green bunching onions in the spring and fall, or bulbs are prepared as pearl onions. Stores well all winter. Flavor becomes stronger with hot weather. Popular winter onion in the South; also does well in the North. G19M, L7M

Yellow Potato Onion: (Yellow Multiplier Onion) Divides underground to produce clusters of up to 15 onions. Medium-sized bulbs, 3 to 4 inches in diameter depending on growing conditions. Flavorful, yet not strong. Keeps well for 8 to 12 months. Resistant to drought and pink root. Widely adapted; hardy. An heirloom strain dating from 1886. C85M, D65, G19M, L7M

<u>SHALLOTS</u> Mostly compact, medium-sized bulbs with a mild, distinct flavor. Some cultivars are especially valued in gourmet cooking and are very good pickled. Also used for *scallions*. Planted and harvested in essentially the same manner as potato onions. They mature rapidly and will keep longer than bulbing onions, often remaining sound until the following summer.

Bavarian Brown: (Brown) A rare shallot from Bavaria. Bulbs average 1 1/2 inches in diameter, up to 2 1/2 inches when well grown; medium-brown bulb scales; mildly pungent, flavorful, yellow flesh. Excellent keeping qualities. Used for flavoring, and for green tops or scallions. J71, K13

Drittler White: (Nest Onion) Family heirloom brought to the United States by German pioneers who settled in north central Arkansas, on Colony Mountain. The term nest onion originated with these settlers. Maintained by the Drittler family since 1885. Bulbs are variable in size. Widely adapted north to south, and especially well-suited to south Florida and Texas. L7M

Dutch Yellow: (Yellow) Bulbs average 1 1/2 inches in diameter, 2 inches when well grown; yellow-brown bulb scales; yellow to cream-colored flesh. Keeps very well. High yielding; each bulb will grow into a cluster of 8 to 12 shallots. Widely adapted, but only recommended for spring planting from Virginia northward. D2M, D24, E5T, G19M, G87, I99, J82, K13, L7M, L91M

French Red: (Red) Reddish-pink bulb scales; pale purple-pink flesh; mild, distinctive flavor. Prolific; each bulb multiplies to produce up to 30 additional bulbs. Widely adapted, but does not keep as well as other shallots. Valued in gourmet cooking. D2M, E5T, F11, G19M, I99M, J63, J71, K13, K49T, L7M

Frog's Leg: (Pear, Brittany, Chicken's Leg) Large, elongated bulb, resembles a bull frog's legs; dark orange-brown skin; purple-white flesh. One of the mildest shallots, with an excellent sweet flavor. Large size and elongated shape makes them easier to peel and dice. Very productive; each bulb produces up to 15 shallots. G19M, G68, J71, K13

Giant Red: Bright reddish-brown skin; mild, spicy flavor. Excellent raw in salads. Stores well; rarely if ever bolts. Highly productive; each bulb multiplies to produce 10 to 20 additional bulbs. Starts to "sprout" earlier than yellow types. L91M

Grey: In France, grey shallots are considered the best of all shallots and bring premium prices. Large elongated bulb, about four inches long; bulb scales fairly firm, dull grayish brown; purple-white flesh; strong, distinctive flavor. Does not store well. Prolific; each bulb will multiply to produce 20 additional bulbs. G19M, G68, *J63*, K13

Hative de Niort: Large, flask-shaped bulbs with fine deep-brown skin and reddish flesh; produced in clusters of 3 to 4 shallots. Recognized in Europe as the outstanding exhibition shallot. Also excellent for pickling. O20, S61

Odetta's White: Pure-white bulbs, about 7/8 inch in diameter. Delicate flavor. Can be used as a source of scallions, green tops, and pearl onions. Bulbs are especially good pickled. Keeps well, though the bulbs tend to dry out more readily than others. Rare heirloom, carefully tended by a family for three generations. L7M

Prince de Bretagne: Good-sized bulbs, some 3 ounces or more; light reddish-brown skin; white flesh with a purple tinge. Should be planted in spring only. An old reselected grower's strain from Brittany, France. **U33**

Sanders' White: Large bulbs, up to 1 3/4 inches in diameter when well grown; pure white, mildly pungent and sweet. Used for fresh green onions, soups, stews and salads. One of the largest of the white shallots. Excellent keeper. Pre-1900 family heirloom of Thelma Sanders of northern Missouri. L7M

Shallot: (French Shallot) Each bulb divides during the growing season to form a cluster of 6 or more shallots. Can also be harvested for green onions early in the season. Dark orange-brown skin with a pink cast; purple-white flesh; delicate garlic-like flavor. Widely used for flavoring soups, salad dressings, omelettes, etc. Stores well; hardy. B73M, B75, C11, C81M, D29, E5M, F1, F19M, F33{PR}, F35M, F35M{PR}, G6, G16, H3M, J7, J20, J34, K85, etc.

Thai Red: Small to medium-sized bulb; reddish bulb scales; very good mild flavor, not as strong as Tohono O'odham I'Itoi's; resembles French Red. Easy to grow. Collected in the mountains of Thailand. **U26**

Tohono O'odham I'Itoi's: From the Boboquivari Mountains of southern Arizona where the O'odham Papago deity I'Itoi is said to reside. Probably an early introduction from the Old World. Strong, distinct flavor. Produces offshoot scallions most of the year, even when other onions go dormant. Adapted to both high and low desert areas. I16

TOPSET ONIONS Commonly known as *Egyptian onions*, these produce several small bulbs below ground level as well as clusters of tiny aerial bulbils at the top of the flower stalk. The bulbs are strong flavored but the leaves are relished in salads through much of the year and provide a dependable source of *green onions* even in cold climates. The bulbils are sometimes used for flavoring in pickling recipes. (A. x proliferum)

Catawissa: (Catawissa Onion) Very hardy cultivar of Canadian origin, distinguished by its vigorous growth and the rapidity with which the bulbils commence to grow without being detached from the top of the stem. The bulbils divide into tiers, the second set of bulbils producing green shoots, leaves or barren stems to bring the height of the plant to over 2 1/2 feet. VILMORIN [Cu]; G19M

McCullar's White Topset: An heirloom from Mississippi. Similar to the highly esteemed and well known cultivar Pran, from Kashmir and Pakistan, but white-fleshed instead of yellow. Produces a number of 1-inch or larger white bulbs below ground level, plus pea-sized bulbils at the top of the flower stalk. Larger bulbs are used for eating; topsets for replanting. Used primarily as a source of greens when other onions are dormant. H3M{PL}, L7M

Moritz Egyptian: Heirloom from Missouri, grown by several families in a one block area since 1940. Similar to the typical Egyptian onion, but the bulbs are a deeper color (red-purple) and topsets are slightly larger than most strains. An unusual strain that will sometimes produce sets in the middle of the stalk. L7M

Norris Egyptian: An heirloom Egyptian onion which is less pungent and more productive than other strains. Introduced in 1989 by Southern Exposure Seed Exchange. L7M

PEARL ONIONS

Also called *pickling onions*, *boilers*, and *mini* or *baby onions*, these are bulbing onions that are planted thickly and harvested when very small. They are especially suitable for pickling because they don't develop papery outer skins. Most will grow in poorer, drier and less fertile soil than the larger bulbing onions. HAWKES [Re], LARKCOM 1984. (A. cepa)

RED/PURPLE-SKINNED

Purplette: 60 days. The first red-purple skinned mini onion. Glossy, rich burgundy color, turning pastel pink when cooked or pickled. An attractive specialty item either topped or bunched. Can be harvested at golf ball size or very young as "baby onions" with purple pearl ends. Matures early and holds well. F44, G6, H49, I77, K49M, P83M, Q34, S55

WHITE-SKINNED

Aviv: 62 days. Small, flattened globe-shaped bulb; skin thin, delicate, silver-white; flesh mild, flavor very good. Very well suited for pickling. When planted at a suitable depth and density, no thinning is required. Very quick to mature. Sow in spring to early summer. Developed by Hazera Seeds. K66, *P75M*, *R11M*, S61

Barletta: (White Barletta, Early White Pearl, St. Jans) 70 days. High quality cocktail onion from Europe. Small, nearly round bulb, slightly flattened at top and bottom; silky-white in color; flesh crisp and mild, of fine quality. Very uniform in size and shape. Excellent for pickling. A16, A69M, C85M, *D12*, D27, E49, G68, I77, J7, K66, L42, M49, S55

Crystal Wax: (Crystal Wax Bermuda) 95 days. Very attractive White Bermuda strain. Flattened globe-shaped bulb; skin white, thin and waxy; flesh white, coarse, crisp and juicy; very mild flavor. Widely used for bunching and pickling when young. Not a good keeper. Resistant to pink root. A69M, A87M, B75, C92, D76, G64, *H61*, H66, I65M{PL}, J14{PL}, J34, J34{PL}, K49M, K71, K73, L89, etc.

Marzatica: Small, pure white bulbs. Not as quick maturing as Barletta but the bulbs are somewhat larger. Should be sown thickly from August to October for continuous harvests beginning in early winter. Q11M

Paris Cocktail: 85 days. Clear waxy white appearance. Used for fancy pickles, spicy hors d'oeuvres and gourmet dishes. Sow thickly in drills from April to July. No thinning required. D11M

Paris Silverskin: (Early Paris Silverskin, Blanc Hâtif de Paris) Medium-sized, flattened bulb, 2 to 3 inches in diameter; silver-white skin; firm, flavorful white flesh; small neck. Widely used for pickling. Introduced prior to 1885. VILMORIN; E5T, P83M, S45M, S61

Pompeii Perla Prima: 65 days. Similar to the Barletta type but smaller. Typical, flattened globe-shaped bulb; pure-white skin; mild flavor. Widely used for the cocktail onion trade. L42

Quicksilver: 55 days. Very early maturing, high quality, summer "mini onion". Skinless, round white bulb, grows to ping pong ball size; extra thin necks, even in the "pearl" stage. Attractive either fresh, canned or frozen. Harvest by the bunch when needed - "pearl onions" throughout pea picking season, "boilers" later in the summer. D68, F44

Silver Queen: 80 days. Small, round bulbs; skin clear white with a waxy appearance so necessary for pickling. Early maturing. Standard cultivar used by the large canning companies for pickling. D27

Snow Drop: Small white bulb, globe-shaped when young; has excellent pickling qualities. Should be planted thickly and harvested when still small. Resistant to pink root. Improved European type. D27

White Pearl: 75 days. An improved rounder version of the popular standard cultivar Silver Queen. Round, clear white bulbs, slightly waxy in appearance. Attractive European strain that meets the highest demands of the cocktail onion trade. Slightly earlier than Silver Queen or White Queen. L42

White Portugal: (Silverskin, American Silverskin) 100 days. Excellent multi-purpose cultivar. May be used for green or bunching onions when young, "pearl onions" when bulbs form, sets, or mature bulbs. Mature bulbs large, thick-flat; skin clear silver-white; flesh firm, fine-grained, flavorful, mild and sweet. Good storage qualities. Introduced prior to 1865. BURR; A16, *A69M*, C44, C85M, D11M, D76, E38, *F72*, F92, G51, H42, *H61*, K71, L97, M13M, etc.

White Queen: 80 days. An early, fast-maturing white pickling onion. Skin clear white, waxy in appearance; flesh sweet and tender. Standard cultivar used by the large canning companies for pickling. *A69M*

Wonder of Pompeii: 100 days. Small, flattened globe-shaped bulb; silver-white skin; of good quality. Excellent for pickling. Also used whole in soups and stews. Should be sown thickly to produce small, uniform bulbs. I39, K49M

YELLOW/BROWN-SKINNED

New Brown Pickling: Globe-shaped bulb with very attractive deep golden skin. Sown thickly to produce pickling size onions. *R23*

ORANGE {GR}

CITRUS SINENSIS

BLOOD ORANGES

Blood oranges are called the connoisseur's or gourmet's citrus. Their flavor is distinctive and refreshing. It is often described as a rich orange flavor with overtones of raspberries or strawberries. The fruit is a bit hard to peel but excellent for juicing. The juice can be used in mixed drinks or as a base for sauces. Fruit sections can be added to fruit salads, used as a garnish, or made into marmalade. RAY, SCHNEIDER [Re]; A44M{PR}, J83T{PR}, *N40*{PR}

Doblefina: (Oval Sangre) Fruit medium-small to small, oval to oblong; rind difficult to peel, yellowish orange blushed with rose-colored flecks; flesh firm and moderately juicy, with a distinctive fragrance and a mild, pleasant flavor; virtually seedless; ripens late; hangs poorly but ships and stores unusually well. REUTHER; N18{SC}

Maltaise Sanguine: (Malta Blood, Portugaise) Medium-sized, oblong fruit; rind peels easily, external blood coloration well developed under favorable conditions; flesh tender, melting, very juicy, with good blood coloration under favorable conditions; seeds few to none. Flavor and aroma excellent. Late midseason in maturity. REUTHER; R77

Moro: Fruit medium to medium-large, subglobose, round, or obovoid; seeds few or none; rind medium-thick, moderately adherent, and somewhat pebbled. Orange-colored at maturity with light pink blush or red streaks at advanced maturity. Flesh deeply pigmented (almost violet-red), juicy, flavor pleasant. Very early in maturity, but holds well on the tree and stores and ships well. A distinctive aroma develops with advanced maturity. REUTHER; *A71*, B93M{DW}, *D23M*, D37{DW}, E3M{DW}, *G49*, I74{DW}, I83M, J22, J61M{DW}, N18{SC}

Ruby: Medium-sized, globose to slightly oblong fruit; rind medium-thick, well-colored, with reddish flush under favorable conditions; flesh orange, streaked (rather than flecked) with red under favorable conditions, tender and juicy; flavor rich; seeds relatively few. Midseason in maturity. Tree moderately vigorous, compact, medium-large, productive. N18{SC}

Sanguinelli: Fruit similar to Doblefina, but larger, seedier, and often asymmetrical; blood coloration of both rind and flesh much more intense and constant. External red pigmentation rarely equalled by other blood oranges and excelled by none, making the fruit most attractive. Holds on the tree well; also stores and ships well. Tree small to medium, spineless; foliage light-green; productive. REUTHER; *G49*, I83M

Sanguinello: (Sanguinello Commune) Medium-sized, obovoid to oblong fruit; rind medium-thick, moderately tough and adherent, orange-colored at maturity washed with red; flesh rather deeply red pigmented at maturity (more so and earlier than rind), juicy, pleasantly flavored; seeds few or none. Midseason in maturity. Stores and ships moderately well. REUTHER; B93M{DW}, E3M{DW}

Sanguinello Moscato: (Paterno) Medium-large fruit of variable shape; rind orange, strongly blushed with red at the apex, moderately adherent; flesh well-colored, very juicy, aromatic, flavor excellent; seeds few or none; ripens in midseason. Holds well on the tree and ships well. One of the most highly reputed blood oranges. The principal cultivar in the Mount Etna region of Sicily. REUTHER; *O4*

Tarocco: Medium-large to large fruit, variable in form from broadly obovate to globose; rind medium to medium-thick, moderately tightly adherent, yellowish-orange blushed with red at maturity; flesh somewhat firm but juicy, usually well pigmented; flavor rich and sprightly; few or no seeds. Midseason in maturity. Loses quality if left on tree much past maturity and drops badly, but stores and ships well. REUTHER; B93M{DW}, *G49*, I83M, *M61M*, *M61M*{DW}, N18{SC}

COMMON ORANGES

VALENCIAS

Campbell: Fruit indistinguishable from Valencia, but the tree is consistently more vigorous, thornier, larger, broad-topped, and slower to come into bearing than Valencia. The fruit is slightly lower in juice content in coastal regions and has a greater tendency to regreen in interior districts. A nucellar budline. Originated in the Early Campbell orchard, Santa Ana, California. Introduced in 1942. BROOKS 1972, REUTHER; *A71*, N18{SC}

Cutter: Fruit large, slightly more round than standard cultivars. Tree initially free of recognized virus diseases; exceptionally vigorous; slightly slower coming into bearing than standard cultivars. A nucellar seedling. Originated in Riverside, California by H.S. Fawcett, California Citrus Experiment Station. Introduced in 1952. BROOKS 1972; *A71*, N18{SC}

Frost Valencia: Fruit typical Valencia, but has greater vigor and better yield than its seed parent. Tree initially free of psorosis virus carried by seed parent tree. Nucellar seedling of Valencia. Originated in Riverside, California by H.B. Frost, California Citrus Experiment Station. Introduced in 1952. BROOKS 1972; N18{SC}

Olinda: Large fruit; skin thin; flesh sweet, quality good. Valencia type but matures slightly earlier than standard cultivars. Tree vigorous, productive; free of recognized virus diseases. Originated in Olinda, Orange County, California, in the garden of Ollie Smith. Introduced in 1957. BROOKS 1972; *A71*, N18{SC}

Seedless Valencia: A bud variation of Valencia that differs from it in that the fruit is more oblong or oval in form, less seedy (occasionally one or two seeds), and matures earlier (late midseason). Tree vigorous and upright with large leaves that tend to be bunched, giving it a distinctive appearance, and strongly alternate-bearing. Said to have been discovered in the orchard of W. Eathers at North Richmond, New South Wales, Australia, between 1920 and 1925. REUTHER; E3M{DW}, I83M

Valencia: Medium-large, oblong to spherical fruit; seeds few or none. Well-colored at maturity, but regreens thereafter under certain conditions. Rind medium-thick, tough, and leathery. Juice abundant and flavor good but commonly somewhat acid. Fruit holds exceptionally well on tree with little deterioration in quality and ships and stores well. Excellent for processing. Latest maturing of all commercial cultivars. Tree vigorous, prolific, but with alternate-bearing tendency. Very wide range of adaptation. REUTHER; *D23M*, D34M{PR}, E3M{DW}, E31M, *F53M*, F68, *G49*, G96{DW}, I83M, J22, J22{DW}, *L47*, *M61M*

Variegated Valencia:[1] New selection with attractive, tri-colored foliage and fruit. Leaves are 2 shades of green and yellow. The fruit is striped yellowish-orange and green when immature, coloring to a solid orange when ripe. Season of fruiting and flavor are the same as those of standard Valencia. I83M

OTHERS

Belladonna: Medium-large fruit, oblong to oval; rind deep orange at maturity, tightly adherent; flesh moderately juicy, flavor pleasant; quality excellent; ripens in early midseason, but holds well on the tree for several months. Stores and ships well. An old Italian cultivar of unknown origin. REUTHER; *O4*

Cadenera: Medium-sized, globose to slightly oval fruit; rind medium-thin, moderately well-colored; flesh very juicy, flavor and aroma excellent; seeds few or none. Medium-early in maturity. Holds well on th tree and retains its quality. The principal common orange of Spain. REUTHER; C29M{SC}

Calabrese: (Ovale) Medium-large, oval fruit; rind very tightly adherent, well-colored at maturity but regreens if held on the tree long thereafter; flesh juicy and well-flavored at maturity; quality excellent; ripens late. Holds especially well on the tree. Stores and ships well. Tree slow growing; sensitive to cold, heat and desert winds. The principal common orange of Italy. REUTHER; *O4*

Diller: (Arizona Sweet) Small to medium, oblong to ellipsoid fruit; rind medium thick, bright orange; flesh well-colored, juicy, flavor good; seeds comparatively few; ripens early. Tree moderately vigorous; productive under desert conditions; above average in cold tolerance. Originated near Phoenix, Arizona. Introduced about 1920. REUTHER; *D13*

Hamlin: Medium-small, globose to slightly oblate fruit; rind thin, well-colored at maturity; flesh well-colored, tender, juicy, lacking in acid; flavor sweet; seeds very few or none. One of the earliest to mature. Tree moderately vigorous, medium-large, productive, more cold-tolerant than most. Discovered in 1879 near Glenwood, Florida, in a grove later owned by A.G. Hamlin. MORTON 1987a, REUTHER; E31M, F68, I76M{PR}, N18{SC}

Joppa: Medium-sized, globose to slightly oblong fruit; rind medium-thin, well-colored under favorable conditions; flesh light orange, medium-tender, juicy; flavor rich; seeds comparatively few. Midseason in maturity. Originated in 1877 from seed imported from Joppa, Palestine by A.B. Chapman of San Gabriel, California. REUTHER; *Q93*

Marrs: Medium-large, round to slightly oblate fruit; rind medium-thick, well-colored under favorable conditions; flesh well-colored, juicy, lacking in acid; flavor sweet; moderately seedy (depending on pollination). Holds well on tree with little loss in quality. Originated in Donna, Texas by O.F. Marrs. Introduced in 1940. REUTHER; E31M, F97G{PR}, N18{SC}

Mediterranean Sweet: (Maltaise Ovale) Medium-sized, spherical to oval fruit; rind medium-thick, pale in color at maturity with some tendency to regreen, peels readily; flesh pale-colored, moderately juicy; flavor mild; seeds relatively few. Medium-late in maturity. Tree vigorous, large, spreading, drooping; distinctive in appearance. REUTHER; S59

Pineapple: Medium-sized, spherical to slightly obovate fruit; rind highly colored, especially after cold spells; flesh light orange, tender, juicy; flavor rich though sweet; pineapple-scented; moderately seedy. Midseason in maturity. Does not hold on tree as well as some, but is excellent for processing. If the crop is allowed to remain too long on the tree, it may induce alternate-bearing. MORTON 1987a, REUTHER; F68, F97G{PR}, I76M{PR}, N18{SC}

Prata: (Silver) Medium-large spherical fruit; distinctive pale yellow in color; flesh juicy, of rich flavor, very seedy. An old cultivar of very limited importance in Spain and Portugal, found elsewhere only in collections. REUTHER; R77

Salustiana: Medium-large, subglobose to spherical fruit; rind medium-thick, unusually well-colored at maturity; flesh melting, juicy;

flavor rich and sweet; virtually seedless. Early in maturity; said to hold especially well on tree without much loss of quality. Originated near Enova, Valencia, Spain. Introduced about 1950. REUTHER; N18{SC}, *O4*

Shamouti: (Jaffa) Medium-large to large, oval to ellipsoid fruit; rind thick, tough, leathery, well-colored under favorable conditions; flesh light orange, firm, tender, juicy, fragrant, pleasantly sweet-flavored; seedless or nearly so. Fruit peels and segments separate readily. Ships and stores unusually well but does not process well. Originated some time prior to 1844 in an orchard near Jaffa, Israel. REUTHER; E3M{DW}, I83M, J22, J22{DW}, N18{SC}

Trovita: Fruit medium-small, navel structure usually absent or rudimentary; flesh somewhat more tender and juicy than Washington navel, which it resembles, pleasantly flavored; usually has 2 to 6 seeds. Tree vigorous, upright growing; productive, but with a tendency to alternate bearing. Thought to be a seedling of Washington navel. Originated in Riverside, California by Howard B. Frost. Introduced in 1935. BROOKS 1972, REUTHER; E3M{DW}, *G49*, I83M, J22, N18{SC}

NAVEL ORANGES

Atwood: Fruit deep orange-red, of a more intense color than that of Washington, which it resembles; matures earlier, remaining firm very late in the season. Stores on the tree especially well without appreciable loss of quality. Bud mutation of Washington navel. Originated in Lemon Cove, California by Frank Atwood. Introduced in 1945. BROOKS 1972, REUTHER; *A71*, N18{SC}

Cluster Navel: Medium-sized fruit, similar to Valencia but more variable - large, small, and mini-fruit may occur in the same cluster. Flesh sweet, tender and juicy. Matures in January and maintains good eating quality as late as September. Compared to the standard Washington navel, the trees are genetically dwarfed, more dense and compact. Originated as a sport on a Washington navel tree at the Citrus Research Center of the University of California at Riverside. It appeared as a single cluster of 21 oranges resembling a bunch of grapes. N18{SC}

Earli Beck: Very early, high quality Valencia with deep color and high production tendencies. Characterized by early color break, which later turns deep orange in color (Minneola type). Holds, gasses, packs, and ships well. Offers excellent opportunity for higher returns in the early market. *A71*

Fisher: Very early maturing, but rind color break is not early. High sugar/acid ratio early in the season fits well in early districts. Quality good. Good production and fruit size and holds well on the tree. Most common cultivar planted in Kern County, California. *A71*, I83M, N18{SC}

Frost Washington: The first, and one of the most important nucellar budlines of Washington navel. Widely planted in California, Arizona and Morocco. Originated at the University of California Citrus Research Center, Riverside by H.B. Frost. REUTHER; N18{SC}

Gillette: Large, spherical fruit; navel well developed but not prominent; seedless. Well-colored. Flesh color, texture, and flavor similar to Washington. Very early in maturity (about 10 days earlier than Washington) and holds well on the tree. Bud mutation of Washington navel; discovered about 1940. Originated in Hemet, California by A.F. Gillette. REUTHER; C29M{SC}

Lane Late: Late maturing introduction from Australia. Fruit quality, size, and production are good. Holds on the tree as late as June. Offers good opportunity for higher returns in late marketing season for navels. *A71*, N18{SC}, S59

Leng: Fruit medium-small to medium in size, globose; navel uniformly small though well developed; seedless. Color bright orange. Flesh well-colored, juicy, texture medium, flavor only fair. Very early in maturity (a week or 10 days earlier than Washington), but holds fruit well on tree without loss of quality. Originated as a limb sport of Washington at Irymple, New South Wales, Australia. REUTHER; N18{SC}, S59

Newhall: Oblong to ellipsoid fruit, slightly smaller than Washington; color reddish-orange, deeper than Washington; flavor excellent; ripens earlier than Washington. Tree somewhat less vigorous than Washington. Originated as a limb sport near Duarte, California. REUTHER; N18{SC}, *O4*

Robertson: Fruit virtually indistinguishable from Washington except for medium-large size, slightly lower quality, and earlier maturity, which is usually 10 days to 2 weeks. Tree precocious in bearing habit, but somewhat lacking in vigor on sweet and sour orange rootstock. Bud mutation of Washington navel; discovered in 1925. Originated in Redlands, California by Roy Robertson. Introduced in 1936. BROOKS 1972, REUTHER; B93M, *D23M*, E3M{DW}, *G49*, I83M, *L47*, *M61M*, *M61M*{DW}, N18{SC}

Skaggs Bonanza: Fruit resembles Washington, but colors and matures about 2 weeks earlier. Tree precocious; very productive; has a smaller, more dense growth habit than Washington. Budline apparently free of psorosis, exocortis, stubborn, and cachexia. Bud mutation of Washington navel. Originated in Strathmore, California by Everett Skaggs. Introduced in 1964. BROOKS 1972, RAY; I83M, N18{SC}

Summernavel: Large, roundish fruit, 3 to 3 1/4 inches in diameter; rind smooth to slightly pebbled, separates easily from flesh; 8 to 12 segments, juicy, seedless; ripens later than its parent which it resembles. Holds on tree especially well with little loss in internal quality. Bud mutation of Washington; discovered about 1934. Originated in Riverside, California by John Albert Workman. Introduced in 1942. BROOKS 1972, REUTHER; E3M{DW}, *G49*, I83M

Thomson: (Thomson Improved) Medium-large, globose fruit; less well-colored than Washington; flesh firm, well-colored, moderately juicy, flavor good. Ripens very early, 10 days sooner than Washington; holds on the tree poorly. Tree less vigorous and more compact than Washington. Originated as a limb sport of Washington in Duarte, California. Introduced about 1891. REUTHER; *A71*, N18{SC}

Washington: Large, spherical to obovoid or ellipsoid fruit; navel medium to large and sometimes protruding; rind medium-thick, somewhat tender, easily removed, especially well-colored (deep orange); flesh deep orange, of firm texture, moderately juicy; flavor rich; seedless. Fruit holds on tree well but processes poorly. Originated, perhaps as a mutant, in Bahia, Brazil, before 1820. The most popular orange in the world for eating out-of-hand. MORTON 1987a, REUTHER; *A71*, B23M{PR}, B93M, *D23M*, D37{DW}, E3M{DW}, *F53M*, *G49*, G96{DW}, I83M, J22, J61M{DW}, *L47*, *M61M*, N18{SC}, etc.

SUGAR ORANGES

Also known as *acidless oranges*, the sugar oranges have a very low acid content and are insipidly sweet. They correspond to the sweet lemons, limettas and sweet limes. Because of the extremely low acidity of the flesh, they attain edibility early, as soon as the juice content is moderately well developed. REUTHER.

Vainiglia: (Vaniglia Biondo Apireno, Maltese) Medium-small to medium fruit, subglobose to spherical; rind medium thick, well-colored at maturity; seedy. Juicy and sweet flavored but lacking in acid and with slight bitterness, though eating quality generally improves with age. Tree vigorous, medium-sized, very productive. A very old Italian cultivar. REUTHER; *O4*

PALMS

See Arecaceae in the Botanical listings.

PAPAYA {S}

CARICA PAPAYA

CO-1: Medium-sized fruit, weight 3.3 to 5.5 pounds; flesh yellow, sweet, of good quality for eating fresh. Developed at the Tamil Nadu Agricultural University. Plant dioecious; dwarf; first fruits are borne 3 feet from the ground. MORTON 1987a; Q45M, R0, R50

Coorg Honey Dew: Long to oval fruit, average weight 4.4 to 7.7 pounds; flesh firm, yellow, very sweet; cavity large, has fewer seeds than Honey Dew; keeps well. Low-bearing, prolific plant; produces no male plants, female and bisexual plants occurring in equal proportions. A selection from Honey Dew originated at the Chethalli Station of the Indian Institute of Horticultural Research. MORTON 1987a; N84, S59M

Honey Dew: Large, oval-shaped fruit; sweet, yellow-orange, solid flesh. One of the most popular cultivars in India. P5, *Q32*, Q45M, R0, R50, S59M, S93M

Know-You No. 1: (F_1) Large, oblong-elongated fruit; weight 3 1/2 to 6 1/2 pounds; yellow skin and flesh; sweet and flavorful with 12% Brix; ripens early. Thick, sturdy plant; early and heavy yielding; tolerant to papaya ring spot virus. *Q39*

Mexican Red: A rose-fleshed papaya that is lighter in flavor than Mexican Yellow. Medium to very large fruit. Generally not as sweet as Hawaiian types. E31M, L9M

Mexican Yellow: A very sweet and flavorful, yellow-fleshed papaya. Medium to large fruit, can grow up to 10 pounds. Generally not as sweet as Hawaiian types. E31M, L9M

Ranchi: Very large, oblong fruits; deep orange-red inside and out; solid flesh; excellent sweet flavor. Compact, Solo type plant; commences to bear fruit when 3 1/2 to 5 feet high. N84, N91, O93, R0, R50, S59M, S93M

Simla: Dwarf plants produce abundant crops of round-oval fruits. Skin yellowish-blue at full slip, turning paler yellow at table maturity. Flesh firm, thick and juicy, deep-orange in color. Suitable for long-distance commercial shipping as well as home gardens. O39M

Solo: Fruit round and shallowly furrowed in female plants; pear-shaped in bisexual plants; weighs 1.1 to 2.2 pounds; skin orange-yellow when fully ripe; flesh golden-orange, very sweet, of excellent quality. Produces no male plants, only bisexual and female in a 2 to 1 ratio. Introduced into Hawaii from Barbados in 1911. Named Solo in 1919. MORTON 1987a; C56M{PL}, F80, F85, I83M{PL}, L6{PL}, L9M, N84, O53M, O93

Sunrise: (Sunrise Solo, Strawberry) Pear-shaped fruit with a slight neck; averages 22 to 26 ounces depending on location; skin smooth; flesh firm, reddish-orange, sweet, sugar content high; quality and flavor similar to Solo; seed cavity not as deeply indented as other Solo strains, making seed removal easier. Plant precocious, maturing fruit about 9 months after transplanting, at a height of about 3 feet. BROOKS 1972; D33, E31M, L9M, M19, M32M, N84

Sunset: (Sunset Solo) Solo type. Small to medium-sized, pyriform fruit; orange-red skin and flesh. Very sweet. Dwarf, high yielding plant. Originated at the University of Hawaii. E31M, M19, M32M, N84

Tainung No. 1: (F_1) Oblong to nearly round fruit; weight about 2 1/2 pounds; fragrant, red flesh with 11 to 12% Brix; ripens medium early. Vigorous, medium dwarf, prolific plant; easy to grow. Good for shipping. Developed at the Fengshan Tropical Horticultural Experiment Station. *Q39*

Tainung No. 2: (F_1) Large, nearly round to oblong fruit with a pointed blossom end; weight about 2 1/2 pounds; tender, orange-red flesh with good flavor and 13 to 14% Brix; ripens early. Suitable for local markets. Medium dwarf plant. Developed at the Fengshan Tropical Horticultural Experiment Station. *Q39*

Tainung No. 3: (F_1) Nearly round to oblong fruit; larger than Tainung No. 1; weight 2 1/2 to 3 pounds; sweet, yellow-orange flesh of good quality; 11 to 12% Brix; ripens early. Plants are dwarf but vigorous. Developed at the Fengshan Tropical Horticultural Experiment Station. *Q39*

Venezuelan: Fruit orange when ripe; weight 3 pounds. Bisexual herb; grows about 15 feet tall; produces approximately 20 fruits per season. Originally form Venezuela, now grown in Florida. Dropped by F80

Verma's Marvel: Larger and longer than other types. Oblong-shaped fruits are sweet and of pleasing aroma. Very delicious and savory. S93M

Vista Solo: Medium to very large fruit depending on climate; 5 inches wide, up to 18 inches long; skin yellow; flesh orange to yellow-orange. Hardy, compact Solo type producing high quality fruit. Needs fairly hot weather to develop sweetness. Self-fertile. Originated in Vista, California by Ralph Corwin. J23{OR}

Waimanalo: (Waimanalo Solo) Fruit round with a short neck, average weight 16 to 39 ounces; skin smooth and glossy; cavity star-shaped; flesh thick, firm, orange-yellow in color; flavor and quality high; keeps well. Recommended for fresh market and processing. Fruits of female plants are rough in appearance. Average height to the first flower is 32 inches. D33, L9M, L91M, M19, M32M

Washington: Medium to large, oval fruit; excellent, sweet flavor. Heavy yielding. Has dark-red petioles and yellow flowers. Popular in Bombay. MORTON 1987a; N84, O93, *Q32*, Q45M, R0, R50, S59M, S93M

X-77: (Kaymia) Solo type. Small to medium-sized fruit; distinct, blocky shape, very short neck; deep yellow orange skin and flesh; firm, juicy, very sweet flesh. Dwarf, high-yielding plant. Fairly new release from the University of Hawaii. E31M

PARSLEY {S}

PETROSELINUM CRISPUM

LEAF PARSLEY

Afro: 80 days. Tightly-curled, frilly, rich dark-green leaves; held upright on long, strong stems which helps to eliminate soil splash. Very sweet flavor for a curled parsley. Will not become grey or moldy when the weather gets cold. Royal Horticultural Society Award of Merit winner for 1984. Moss Curled selection, developed to be vigorous and productive. K66, L91M

Banquet: 75 days. Attractive, deep-green leaves; finely and tightly-curled; strong, erect stems. Rich green color is particularly fine when grown in cooler seasons. Produces well throughout the season. Good cold weather tolerance for wintering over. Ideal for garnishing and flavoring. Developed in Denmark. *E91G*, F13, H95

Bravour: 75 days. Large, closely-packed, very finely-curled, dark green leaves; long stems. Heavy heads provide excellent yields. Good cold weather tolerance. A leading European cultivar that is a real improvement over older sorts. C53, L42, *R11M*, *S75M*

Champion Moss Curled: 80 days. Deep green leaves, finely cut and curled; almost entirely free from plain leaves; produced in abundance. Compact, vigorous growth habit; to 15 inches tall. Excellent for growing under glass. Very popular with home gardeners. Introduced in 1894. C92, D11M, E97, G64, I64, I67M, J34, K27M, K71, L42, L97, O53M

Clivi: 65 days. Intensely fragrant, finely-indented, crisply-curled leaves. Has the distinction of being the only cultivar whose base leaves do not turn yellow. Rapid growth invites continuous cutting all summer long. Very dwarf, compact and prolific; ideal as a pot plant. L91M

Curlina: 72 days. An early, dwarf, triple-curled strain. Extremely finely-curled, compact leaves; keep their dark green color in hot weather. Globe-shaped, 6 1/2 inch tall plants on very stiff, short stems. An excellent mini parsley for balcony planters or pots. L42

Dark Green Curled: 80 days. A French Perfection type with finely cut and tightly curled dark-green leaves. Rigid, upright stems. Recovery is rapid, offering multiple harvests throughout the summer and fall. Well adapted for summer crops because the foliage does not "yellow out", even under hot, humid growing conditions. Suitable for over-wintering. A13

Dark Green Winter: (New Dark Green) 75 days. Dark emerald-green, curled leaves on very dwarf, compact plants. Will stand the winter better than most other cultivars. L91M, *R23*

Darki: 75 days. Leaves very dark-green, closely placed, heavy and intensely curled. Excellent cold weather tolerance. Holds its fine qualities longer than other types when cut. Vigorous and widely adapted. Gold Medal European strain. D11M, L42

Decora: (Decora Triple Curled) 90 days. Large, well-curled, heavy, dark green leaves; remain curled in hot weather; more resistant to wilting after being cut than others. Compact, vigorous plants with thick stems. Best suited for growing in warm climates as hot weather does not slow growth. C44, G51, G93M, J82, *K16M*, K73

Evergreen: 75 days. Large, dense, dark-green foliage; rather coarsely cut but closely curled. Very uniform. Vigorous, compact plants; tolerant to extremes of hot or cold; definitely more frost resistant than other cultivars. Recommended for both market and home gardens; for dehydrating, flavoring and garnishing. All America Selections winner in 1940. B75M, *C28*, G93M

Exotica: A selection of Moss Curled developed for winter harvesting in mild winter areas. Dark green, well-curled leaves with long stems. Strong, compact plants with good uniformity. Fresh leaves are continuously produced even under cool weather conditions. J82, *K16M*, Q34

Forest Green: 75 days. A special combination double and triple-curled market cultivar. Dark-green leaves. Long, stiff, upright stems help keep the crop clean and bunch easily. Holds its fresh appearance and deep color over a long season without bleaching or browning. Better flavor than most curled types. Good regrowth ability. Popular among Eastern market growers. A13, *A69M*, D11M, F13, G6, G51, G79, H54, *H61*, I39, K73, L7M, M13M, M46, M49, etc.

Greek: A flat-leaved type, originally from the monastery region of Mt. Athos in northern Greece. Probably a very old cultivar. F42

Green Velvet: 80 days. Fully curled, rich deep-green, attractive leaves. Medium-long, strong stalks. Piquant flavor. A top quality parsley for both market and pre-packing. Introduced by Hurst Seedsmen. L91M

Moss Curled: (Triple Curled, Dark Moss Curled) 80 days. Dark green leaves, extremely finely-cut and deeply-curled, resembling tufts of moss. Vigorous, compact plants; 7 to 10 inches tall. Very decorative; especially useful for garnishing. Standard curled-leaf strain. Productive and widely adapted. B75M, C44, C85M, D82, E24, *F72*, F82, F92, G16, H42, *H61*, H66, *I62*{PL}, M46, N16, etc.

Neapolitan: (Gigante d'Italia, Giant Catalogna, Catalogno, Celery-Leaved, Prezzemolo di Spagna) 90 days. Large, flat leaves that are extremely spicy and flavorful; produced in abundance. Very large leaf-stalks, thick and stout in proportion to their length. Large, bushy, vigorous plants; to 3 feet tall. Prized by Italian cooks for all types of seasoning. Can be grown just like common parsley, or the stalks may be blanched and used like celery. BURR, VILMORIN; C53, G51, G84{PL}, I39, I77, J67M, K49M, K66, Q11M, S55

Plain Leaved: (Italian Dark Green, Single Leaf, Flat Leaf, Celery Leaf, Common Single, French) 75 days. Flat, glossy, deeply-cut, dark-green leaves on long stems. Vigorous, erect plant. Excellent, strong, aromatic flavor; preferred by many over that of the curled types. Standard strain for flavoring. Introduced prior to 1806. B75M, C43M{PL}, C44, D82, E24, F24, *F72*, G6, *H61*, K22, K49T, K66, K73, L7M

Sherwood: 75 days. Relatively coarse, double to triple-curled leaves; rich dark-green appearance. Vigorous, very uniform plants; 10 to 12 inches tall. Stays brighter green than European strains in extreme heat and even after multiple harvests. Excellent for local markets and home gardens. An earlier, brighter green version of Darki for early summer and early fall cutting. *A1*, A13, A87M, *F63*, *G13M*, G64, G79, *H61*, J7, J84, K10, K73, L42

Supercurled: 75 days. Highly curled selection, with very dark green color. Retains brighter color after drying better than standard cultivars. Comes back well after cutting. *F72*

Unicurl: 73 days. A breeding breakthrough. The finely-curled, dark green leaves curl in instead of out. Foliage readily shakes free of dust and dirt, making it easier to clean than any other strain. The only parsley with a tolerance to fall rust. L42

HAMBURG PARSLEY

Grown for the thick, parsnip-like roots as well as the flavorful tops. Those which have been subjected to frost usually have a higher sugar content than those harvested during the summer months. Very popular in some parts of Europe, especially Germany. (P. crispum Radicosum Group)

Berliner Halblange: (Berlin Half Long) 140 days. Medium-sized, uniform roots of excellent quality. Originated in Germany. Introduced in 1908. N81, P9

Early Sugar: 78 days. Small, wedge-shaped roots resemble Chantenay carrots and are high in sugar content. Used on heavy soils where parsnips become misshapen. L42

Extralange Starke Oberlaaer: 180 days. A high quality German root parsley with exceptionally long, sturdy roots. Later maturing than some other cultivars. N81

Felhosszu: 180-200 days. Developed in Hungary, where much work has been done to develop different selections of Hamburg parsley. A half-long root which can be stored for long periods. J73

Gamma: Semi-long, tapered, thick roots; smooth, white skin. Medium early maturity. Resistant to disease. Used in the same manner as celeriac. P59M

Korai Cukor: 140-150 days. Early forcing type with short, broad-shouldered roots. Developed in Hungary. J73

Kurze Dicke: (Short & Thick) 120 days. Short, strong, German root parsley adapted to dry areas. N81

Short Sugar: 95 days. An improved cultivar of Hamburg parsley grown for its flavorful root. Short, thick white root; 4 inches in length. Easier to grow, earlier, and sweeter than older cultivars. Stores easily, like carrots and can winter over like parsnips. A very good soup ingredient, especially to give winter soups a fresh flavor. Tops are flavorful. G6, I77

Toso: 95 days. Specially bred for edible roots. Similar in flavor to parsnips, but shorter and better adapted to heavy soils. The roots are about 1 1/2 inches in diameter and 6 to 7 inches long. L89

PARSNIP {S}

PASTINACA SATIVA

HYBRID

Gladiator: 100-105 days. World's first hybrid parsnip. Bred to be more vigorous and consequently a little larger than Cobham Improved Marrow, while retaining the refined shape, smooth white skin, and canker resistance. "True" sweet parsnip flavor. Early maturing. Consistent high quality. Excellent for sowings under adverse conditions because of extra seedling vigor. L91M, *S75M*

OPEN-POLLINATED

All American: (All America) 110 days. Smooth, slender white roots, quite free of rootlets; broad and thick at the shoulders, tapering to a length of 12 inches or more; hollow crowned; very sugary, tender, fine-grained white flesh, small core; attains thickness comparatively early. Excellent keeper; will store well for months. Similar to Hollow Crown, but earlier. A13, A69M, B35M, C44, C92, D76, D82, E97, F13, *F72*, I39, J7, N39

Avonresister: 100 days. Small, conical, round-shouldered roots; more uniform in size and shape than other cultivars; easy to dig. Has the most resistance to canker at the root tops. Uses less space; thin plants to only 3 inches apart. Suitable for pre-packing. Bred at the National Vegetable Research Station, Wellesbourne, England. L91M, P83M, *R23*

Cobham Improved Marrow: 120 days. Half-long, tapered, smooth white roots with a very high sugar content. Outstanding flavor and appearance. Selected for its smooth white skin, refined shape, and resistance to canker. Award of Merit winner in Royal Horticultural Society trials. G6, I77, N52, *S75M*

Fullback: (Short Thick) 95 days. An early cultivar that does well on shallow soils. Short, thick roots; 6 inches long, 3 inches in diameter at the shoulder; smooth, white skin; tender, sweet flesh; very good flavor and quality. Easy to dig. A16, A69M, B75M, H42, *L59G*

Guernsey: (Long de Guernesey) 95 days. Long, tapered roots; relatively flat crown; fine, very clean, creamy-white skin; quality very good. Excellent flavor, particularly after a frost or even after over-wintering in the ground. J20

Harris Model: 120 days. Well-shaped, moderately tapered root; 12 inches long, 2 1/2 inches in diameter; almost no hollow crown; skin whiter than others; very tender, sweet, fine-grained white flesh, medium-sized core. Refined and attractive in appearance. The preferred cultivar for packaging because of its uniform shape and freedom from side roots. A13, A16, A87M, D11M, E24, E57, F1, F44, F82, G6, G16, *H61*, H95, L89, M49, etc.

Hollow Crown: (Long Jersey, Hollow-Crowned Guernsey) 125 days. Long, smooth, tapered roots; up to 18 inches long and 4 inches in diameter at the shoulder. The crown is short, and sunk into the shoulder, so as to form a hollow ring around the insertion of the leaf-stalks. Good for general cultivation; does not require as deep a soil as the Common or Guernsey parsnip. Introduced prior to 1852. BURR; A16, A25, B35M, B78, F19M, F92, G51, *H61*, H94, K5M, L7M, M13M, M46, N39

Improved Hollow Crown: 110 days. Moderately tapered root, with very few side roots; 10 to 12 inches long, 3 inches in diameter at the shoulder; hollow crowned; smooth, white skin; tender, fine-grained white flesh, small core. Stores well. Selected for whiter skin color and slightly longer roots. Standard cultivar for home gardeners. B13, D11M, F1, G71, G79, H42, H54, I67M, J58, L42

Improved Stump Rooted: 95 days. Short, thick, attractive roots; 5 to 8 inches long, 3 inches in diameter at the shoulder; smooth, white skin; tender, very fine-grained, sweet flesh; quality very good. Easy to dig, especially in heavy soils. Early maturing. G16

Offenham: 100 days. An early cultivar adapted to a wide range of soil conditions, but most useful on thin, shallow soils. Half-long roots with broad, thick shoulders and tender, sweet flesh of good flavor and quality. Good for freezing. Very heavy yielding. B49, *R23*

Tender and True: 100 days. Long, uniform, heavily-tapered roots; at least 3 inches in diameter at the shoulder; smooth, white skin; fine-grained flesh, of excellent quality, tender and very sweet; very little core. Good resistance to canker. Does especially well on deep soils. Excellent for both home garden use and exhibition. Named after a popular song. Introduced in 1897. B49, L91M, P83M, *R23*, S45M, S55, S61

The Student: (Sutton's Student) 95 days. Thick, tapering root; varying in length from 15 to 30 inches, depending on soil and culture; hollow crowned, 3 inches in diameter. The flavor is peculiarly sweet, mild and pleasant, perhaps the best of any parsnip. Thrives in dry summers on sandy soils. Originally selected from the wild parsnip by Professor Buckman of the Royal Agricultural College at Cirencester, England. Introduced in the 1860's. BURR; N81, O39M, P83M, *R23*

White Gem: 120 days. A much improved Offenham type bred for increased resistance to canker. Medium-length, wedge-shaped roots with broad, rounded shoulders; very uniform; smooth, exceptionally white skin; of good quality and very sweet flavor. Early maturing and heavy cropping. Good for all soil types, especially clay; very easy to lift. Ideal for home gardens. D11M, N81, P83M, *R11M*, *R23*, S27, S55, S61

White Model: 115 days. Medium length, perfectly straight roots; 6 1/2 to 8 inches long, 2 to 2 1/2 inches in diameter at the shoulder; hollow crowned and with very few side roots; smooth, pure-white skin; tender, sweet, fine-grained white flesh. Well adapted to muck land. D65, J20, J84, K73

PEA {S}

PISUM SATIVUM

GARDEN PEAS

COMMON

Large-Seeded

Alaska: (Earliest of All) 55 days. Smooth, round light-green pods, 2 to 2 1/2 inches long; 5 to 7 peas per pod; smooth, round light green to whitish-green peas, quality fair to good fresh. Light-green vines, to 30 inches tall; heavy bearing; wilt resistant. Popular with home gardeners; the standard among canners. Also used as a dry pea and for sprouting. Introduced prior to 1880. HEDRICK 1928; B73M, B75M, F19M, F82, G6, G57M, *G83M*, H66, H94, J7, J20, L24{SP}, M13M, M46, N16, etc.

American Wonder: 60 days. Short, plump, medium green pods, about 3 inches long; well-filled with 5 to 7 peas per pod; medium green, roundish, sweet peas of very good quality. Stout, dwarfish plant, 10 to 15 inches tall; high yielding. Introduced in 1878. At one time probably the most widely known American pea. HEDRICK 1928; B13, G57M, I67M

Blue Bantam: 64 days. Broad, moderately plump pods, about 3 1/2 inches long; 6 to 8 peas per pod; large deep blue-green peas, sweet, of very good quality. Short, stout vines, 15 to 18 inches tall; very productive. Introduced by Burpee Seed Company in 1902. HEDRICK 1928; A25, D11M, G57M, *G83M*, I39, *I59M*, I64, M95M

Blue Pod:[1] Unique bluish-purple pods. Very sweet peas. Can be used fresh, dried or as an edible-podded pea when young. Long vines; require support. K49M

Burpeeana Early: 63 days. Pods straight, slightly curved at the tip, about 3 inches long; tightly filled with 8 to 10 medium to large, sweet tender peas of excellent quality. Retain color and flavor when quick-frozen. Short, vigorous vines; 18 to 24 inches tall; prolific. B75, G57M, M95M

Curly:[3] 56 days. An improved Novella or semi-leafless type. Short vines produce a dense, interwoven network of tendrils. Can be planted only 10 inches apart and yields are 3 times those of regular peas in the same area. Bears 5 to 6 pods per plant; pods are 3 1/2 inches long; 8 to 10 peas per pod. Somewhat tolerant to pea leaf roll virus. L42

Daisy: Broad, straight, paired pods, about 4 1/2 inches long; 8 to 10 seeds per pod; large, smooth, light-green peas, of excellent quality but slightly thick-skinned. Seeds moderately wrinkled. Vine grows 1 1/2 to 2 feet tall; bears heavily. Introduced in 1892. HEDRICK 1928; P83M

Early Frosty: 64 days. An improved Little Marvel type with twice the yield. Blunt-ended pods, 3 1/2 to 4 inches long; 7 or 8 peas per pod; very uniform, dark green peas, sweet, of very good quality. Excellent for freezing. Vigorous vine, to 28 inches tall; resistant to wilt; produces numerous double pods. A13, A25, B78, C44, D11M, F1, G57M, *G83M*, H42, H94, H95, J7, J97M, K71, N39, etc.

Early Onward: 62 days. Blunt-nosed, deep green pods, about 3 inches long; well-filled with 6 medium green peas, of excellent sweet flavor. Vigorous, compact vine, 2 to 2 1/2 feet tall; very prolific. For spring sowings. Introduced in 1908. Still one of the most popular cultivars in England. O53M, P83M, *R23*, S27, S61, *S75M*

Early Patio:[2] (Patio, Midget) 57 days. True dwarf-type plant, grows only 8 inches tall, yet holds the pods well off the ground; wind resistant. Well suited for growing in garden borders, flower boxes and pots. Produces 2 or more 2 inch long pods at each node. Can be sown thicker to produce more pods per row. D11M, *G83M*, L79

Feltham First: 58 days. Large pointed pods, about 4 inches long; well-filled with sweet, deep-green peas. Excellent for freezing. Vigorous vine, grows 18 inches tall; bears heavy crops; very hardy. Suitable for spring and autumn sowing, or growing under cloches. Popular with market growers in England. B49, L91M, *R23*, S61, *S75M*

Freezonian: 63 days. Blunt-ended, dark green pods, 3 1/2 inches long; 7 to 8 large, well-flavored peas per pod. Dark green vines, to 30 inches tall; resistant to wilt. Excellent for home gardens and quick-freezing. All America Selections winner in 1948. A13, A25, B73M, B75M, C92, D65, F13, G71, *G83M*, H49, H94, J58, K71, L97, M95M, etc.

Gradus: 60 days. Large, pointed, dark-green pods, about 4 inches long; 5 to 8 very sweet peas per pod, of fine quality. Vigorous vines, 4 to 4 1/2 feet tall; moderately heavy bearing. Originated in England about 1890. HEDRICK 1928; P83M, *R23*, S61

Green Arrow: 65 days. Long pointed pods, average 4 to 4 1/2 inches in length; set in pairs near the top of the plant for easy picking; 8 to 11 small, sweet, bright green peas per pod. Vines grow 28 inches tall; resist downy mildew and wilt; can be grown with or without a trellis; are high yielding. Very popular maincrop cultivar. A16, C44, D82, E24, E57, F19M, F82, G6, G16, H66, H94, K73, L97, M46, M49, etc.

Hundredfold: (Laxtonian) 64 days. Broad, straight dark-green pods, about 4 1/2 inches long; 8 or 9 peas per pod; large dark-green peas, tender and sweet. Vigorous, dwarf vines, to 18 inches tall; never need staking. Withstands heat and adverse weather conditions well. A16, C92, E97, G57M, K71, L97, M95

Hurst Beagle: 55 days. One of the earliest wrinkle-seeded peas. Blunt-ended pods, 3 to 3 1/2 inches long; 7 or 8 peas to the pod; excellent sweet flavor. Good for freezing. Vine grows 18 inches high; produces heavily; resists wilt and mosaic viruses. For spring or fall sowings. L91M, *S75M*

Hurst Green Shaft: (Greenshaft) 70 days. Large, pointed pods, 4 to 4 1/2 inches long; 9 to 10 peas per pod; very sweet, of excellent flavor. Very good for freezing. Wrinkled seed. Vine grows 2 1/2 feet tall; produces double pods, all at the top for easy picking; resists downy mildew and fusarium wilt; bears heavily. L91M, O53M, P83M, *R23*, S55, S61, *S75M*

Kelvedon Wonder: (Kelvedon) 65 days. Medium sized, dark-green pointed pods, to 3 inches long; well-filled with medium green, very sweet peas. Excellent for quick-freezing. Dwarf vine, to 18 inches tall; heavy yielding; resistant to mildew. For early spring and successive sowings. Very popular in England. B49, L91M, O53M, P83M, *R23*, S27, S61, *S75M*

Knight: 60 days. Large, broad pods, 3 1/2 to 4 inches long; 9 to 10 peas per pod; medium-sized, bright green, flavorful peas. Vigorous, large-leaved vine, 24 inches tall; bears a single and double set of pods; resists mosaic viruses, powdery mildew and wilt. One of the earliest large-podded peas. For home gardens and local markets. *A69M*, F1, F13, *G1M*, G6, *G13M*, G64, G71, H54, *H61*, J7, J84, J97M, K73, L79, M49, M95M, etc.

Lacy Lady:[3] 60 days. Semi-leafless type. Produces strong tendrils that intertwine and act as a self-support system to hold pods above the soil. Well-filled, 2 1/2 inch long pods are produced in pairs at the top of the plant for easy picking. Fewer leaves allows for greater air movement and more light, reducing the chances of disease and insect infestation. Can be used fresh, canned or frozen. A69M, B73M, D11M, D65, D76, F92, I64, I67M, J58, M46, M95M, N39

Laxton's Progress #9: 60 days. Broad, moderately curved pods, about 4 inches long; 7 to 9 peas per pod; large, oval, dark-green peas, of very sweet flavor. Vigorous, compact vines, 14 to 16 inches tall; resistant to wilt; productive, with mostly single pod set. Standard early market and home garden cultivar. A16, A25, C85M, E57, F1, *F72*, G16, G71, *H61*, J7, K73, L97, M13M, M46, N16, N52, etc.

Lincoln: (Homesteader) 67 days. Medium-sized pointed pods, about 3 1/2 inches long; well-filled with 8 or 9 medium-green, small succulent peas. Excellent for freezing. Compact vine, to 28 inches tall; produces well in hot weather; resistant to wilt. Long time favorite of home gardeners. A16, A25, B75M, C44, C53, C85M, D65, D82, E24, E38, F92, H42, H95, M13M, M46, etc.

Little Marvel: 65 days. Blunt-ended, straight pods, about 3 inches long; 7 or 8 peas per pod; medium-sized, dark green peas, of exceptional quality. Dwarf vine, to 18 inches tall; resistant to wilt; high yielding. An old standard cultivar, popular with home gardeners. Introduced in 1908. HEDRICK 1928; A16, A25, B73M, B75M, F19M, F82, *H61*, H94, J7, K73, L7M, L97, M13M, M46, N16, etc.

Maestro: 60 days. Slender, attractive pod, 3 1/2 to 4 inches long; bears well over an extended picking period; 8 to 10 large, dark-green peas per pod. Vigorous vine, 24 to 36 inches tall; can be grown with or without support; produces a high number of double pods; resists mosaic viruses, powdery mildew and common wilt. B75, D11M, D76, D82, E24, F44, G6, G16, G79, H33, H42, H94, I64, J58, K71, L89, etc.

Novella:[3] (Bikini) 65 days. Semi-leafless or "affilia" type. Produces a profusion of tendrils which interlock and support each other in row spacings of 12 inches or less, forming a "hedge" for easy picking. Sweet, tender peas hold well over a long harvest period; freeze well. Tendrils are tender and fiberless; can be steamed or boiled. Bushy vines; productive, with mostly double pod set; resistant to wilt. A13, A25, D11M, F1, F82, F92, G16, H42, H95, J7, J34, K71, M13M, N39

Olympia: (Early Olympia) 62 days. Improved Progress #9 type. Large pods, averaging 4 to 4 1/2 inches in length, containing approximately 9 peas per pod. Excellent flavor and tenderness. Vine reaches 16 to 18 inches tall, with very vigorous early growth; produces a high percentage of double pods; does not require trellising. Highly disease resistant. A13, A16, B73M, D11M, D65, *F63*, F82, *I59M*, K10, K50, L42

Onward: 70 days. Blunt-nosed, dark green pods, about 3 inches long; 8 or 9 large, very sweet peas per pod. Wrinkle-seeded. Vigorous, short-jointed, dark green vine; height 2 feet; extremely productive, producing pods in pairs; resists wilt. Excellent for successional sowing. The most popular cultivar in the United Kingdom. L91M, O53M, *R23*, S27, S61, *S75M*

Patriot: 65 days. Large, compact pods, 4 inches long; tightly packed with 8 to 10 peas. Dark green, medium-sized peas; tender but firm, with an excellent sweet flavor; retain their texture and flavor after freezing. Medium-sized, double-podded vines, 20 to 22 inches tall; high yielding even under stressful growing conditions. D68, F90, H95, K71, L42, M95M

Perfection: (Perfection Dark Green, Dark Skin Perfection) 65 days. Medium-sized, dark green pods, about 3 1/2 inches long; 7 to 9 bright green peas per pod, sweet and tender. Vine grows 30 inches tall; benefits from staking; tolerant of heat and drought; can be planted late in the season. B35M, E97, *G13M*, I64, *L59G*, L89

Purple Podded:[1] Ornamental, purple colored pods containing well-flavored green peas. Grows approximately 5 feet tall. Should be planted from March through May. S61

Sparkle: 55 days. Blunt medium-green pods, 3 inches long; well-filled with medium-sized, tender, sweet peas. Good for fresh use or processing. Vine grows 18 to 24 inches tall; requires no support; sets a concentrated crop. Resistant to wilt. Standard early, short-vined cultivar for freezing. A25, C44, D65, D76, F1, F13, *F63*, F92, G6, G71, H54, J58, J97M, K50, L89, M49, etc.

Sweet Parsley:[4] (Parsley) 68 days. Unique dual-purpose pea. Both the peas and leafy tendrils are sweet and tender. Strong lateral branches carry the peas at the top for easy picking. Leafy tendrils are high in nutrition and resemble curled parsley; can be used fresh or dried; ideal as a garnish for salads or adding flavor to soups or stews; also good stir-fried. I99, L79

Tall Telephone: (Alderman) 75 days. Broad, curved, dark-green pods, 4 to 5 inches long; 8 to 10 peas per pod; very large, bright dark-green peas, tender and sweet, of excellent quality. Large, heavy, dark green vines, 5 to 6 feet tall. Popular for growing on trellises. Introduced about 1878. HEDRICK 1928; A25, B49, C44, D11M, E24, E38, F1, F82, G71, H66, H94, J7, L97, M46, M49, etc.

The Pilot: 60 days. Large, deep-green pointed pods, 2 1/2 to 4 inches long; 4 to 6 large medium-green peas per pod; quality very good. Also good for drying. Extremely hardy vine; grows 3 1/2 to 4 feet tall. Well suited to spring or autumn sowing. Originated in England prior to 1903. HEDRICK 1928; B49, P83M, *R23*, S61

Thomas Laxton: 60 days. Blunt, dark-green pods, about 3 1/2 inches long; 7 or 8 peas per pod; very large, medium-green peas, sweet and tender. Excellent for canning and freezing. Vine grows 2 1/2 to 3 feet tall; yields heavily; resists wilt. Introduced in 1898. HEDRICK 1928; A25, D68, D76, D87, E24, F19M, H66, H94, J20, J34, K10, K71, M13M, M46, M49, N16, etc.

Tom Thumb:[2] 58 days. Smooth-seeded heirloom pea. True dwarf-type plant, grows 6 to 8 inches tall. Traditionally planted between rows of other crops, otherwise rows are spaced 10 inches apart. Very productive in relation to the size of the vines. Excellent drought and cold tolerance. Introduced prior to 1880. L7M

Triple Treat: 65 days. Dark green pods, 3 to 3 1/2 inches long; containing 7 to 9 tender, flavorful peas per pod. Excellent for fresh use, freezing or canning. High yielding vine, to 30 inches tall; produces triple pods when grown in fertile soil. Very disease resistant. I84, J58, J97M

Twiggy:[3] 70 days. Semi-leafless type. Sends out a profusion of strong tendrils that cling together to provide support for the 24 inch vines. Eliminates the need for support and shades out weeds. Heavy yields of 3 1/2 inch long pods; 3 to 4 pods per node. Medium-sized peas of very sweet flavor. Good for home gardens and freezing. J20

Wando: 70 days. Straight, dark-green pods, about 3 inches long; 7 to 9 medium-sized, dark green peas per pod. Vine grows 24 to 30 inches tall; pollinates well under cold as well as warm growing conditions. Resistant to heat; can be planted later in the season than most cultivars. A25, B73M, C44, E24, F19M, *F72*, G16, G71, H42, H94, L7M, M13M, M95, N16, N39, etc.

Willet Wonder: 70 days. Smooth-seeded pea with better cold tolerance than most other peas. Bushier and shorter than Alaska, and similar to Thomas Laxton in disease resistance. Grown primarily in the Deep South for fresh peas. Also freezes well. L7M

World Record: 60 days. Broad, plump, round to oval pods, 3 1/2 to 5 inches long; 5 to 7 peas per pod; peas round to slightly indented, oval, light green in color, of excellent quality. Slender, productive plant, height 2 1/4 to 2 1/2 feet. Originated by Sutton and Sons before 1907. HEDRICK 1928; A25, F80

Small-Seeded Known as *petit pois* in France, these are considered the finest flavored of all peas. They are bred never to grow very large. Very sweet and delicate, it is best to harvest them no more than an hour before cooking. The traditional French method is to cook them in their pods and then shell them. Not as productive as other peas. KRAFT [Cul, Re]

Frizette: 65 days. Small, dark green pods, about 3 inches long; 2 pods per node; 6 or 7 tiny, tender, extremely sweet peas per pod. For best quality and flavor, harvest when peas are fully formed but very small. Especially bred for fall planting; withstands cold weather well. Tall vine; requires staking. I77

Frostiroy: 55 days. Petit pois or *baby pea* type. Double podded for easy picking. Tiny, very sweet peas, 8 or 9 per pod. Medium-sized vines, to 2 1/2 feet tall; resistant to fusarium wilt and top yellows. C85M

Petit Pois: 58 days. True small-seeded French pea widely used in gourmet dishes. Small pods, about 2 inches long; well-filled with sweet, tender peas of excellent quality. Retains color and flavor when frozen or canned. Very prolific vine; height 20 inches; very hardy; produces double pods. D11M, M46

Petit Provencal: (Meteor) 60 days. Petit pois type from France; one of the best for early production. Small, curved, pointed pods; 7 or 8 very sweet peas to the pod. Should be harvested when young for the best quality. Small, compact vine, 16 to 18 inches tall; should be trellised. Very hardy; can be sown from fall through winter in mild climates. B75, C53, J83M, *R23*, S55, S61

Precovil: 60 days. Large, medium-green pods, 2 1/2 inches long; very small peas, tender and sweet. Bush-type vine, 18 to 24 inches tall; very early and productive; requires support; resistant to wilt and top yellows. Does well in hot summer areas as well as short season areas. I77, K66, S95M

Proval: An improved Petit Provencal. One of the best of the early dwarf peas. Vine grows to 16 inches tall; produces abundantly. Good for field or cold frame production. F33, P59M

Serpette: (Serpette Guilloteaux) Very large, attractive, light green pods; resemble a curved pruning knife in form; each pod contains 10 to 12 small, sweet peas. Smooth seeded type. Ripens in midseason. Tall, upright vine; highly productive. G68, P59M, S95M

Triplet: 64 days. New Petit Pois type. Pods average 2 1/2 to 3 inches long, with 8 peas per pod. Up to 50% triple podded and 3 to 4 sieve size. Excellent honey-like flavor. Recommended for freezing or fresh market. Tolerant to mildew. L42

Waverex: Small, straight, blunt-ended pods; 7 or 8 very small, very sweet, tender peas per pod. Excellent raw, cooked or frozen. For best quality pick when only 1/6 inch in diameter. Semi-climbing vine, 18 inches tall; requires staking; produces a heavy crop; grows well in any cool climate. Developed in Germany for the European market. B49, L91M, S55, S61

<u>EDIBLE-PODDED</u>

Sugar Peas Also called *snow peas* or *Chinese peas*, these lack the parchment-like inner lining of common garden peas. They can be eaten whole and remain sweet and tender until quite large. Widely used in oriental cuisine, especially stir-fried dishes.

Bamby: French cultivar, developed from the original Carouby de Maussane. Has the advantage of being dwarf and an early bearer. Pod remains tender even after peas have formed; requires stringing. Dropped by G69

Caroubel: Developed from Carouby de Maussane. In Maussane, France it makes up part of the traditional *jardinete de printemps* stew, made of lamb and the first spring vegetables, including edible-podded peas. Late producer. Vigorous vine; requires staking; well-adapted to warmer climates. Dropped by G69

Carouby de Maussane: (Roi de Carouby) 65 days. Thin, flat pods, distinctively shaped; 5 inches long, up to 1 inch wide; very sweet and tender. Should be harvested when the peas are barely visible. Vigorous vines; height 3 to 5 feet. Very attractive purple flowers, suitable for ornamental as well as culinary plantings. Originated near Avignon, France in the village of Maussane. C53, G68, P83M, *R23*, S55

Dwarf Gray Sugar: 65 days. Broad, slightly curved, light-green pod; 3 inches long, 1/2 inch in diameter; sweet and tender. Can also be used as a shell pea when past the edible-pod stage. Slender, determinate vines; height 26 to 30 inches; heat and cold tolerant; resists wilt. Standard mid-season cultivar. A16, A87M, C44, C85M, D11M, D65, D82, E38, F19M, G79, J34, K71, L59, M46, M95, etc.

Dwarf Sweet Green: Small flat pods, 2 1/2 to 3 inches long; very sweet and tender. Dwarf vine, grows 1 1/2 to 2 feet tall; extremely prolific. P83M, *R23*, S55

Dwarf White Sugar: 50 days. Thick, succulent pods, 2 to 2 1/2 inches long; sweet, tender and stringless. Retains high quality even if picked over-mature. Vine grows 30 inches tall; remains vigorous and productive longer if pods are picked when peas are one-third to one-half developed. A13, *A69M*, D27, D68, *F63*, G57M, H33, I84, K20, L89

Golden Sweet:[5] 75 days. Unusual yellow-podded sugar pea from India. Large lemon-yellow pods, 3 inches long, set in pairs; tender, sweet, mild in flavor, of very good quality. Easy to pick as their bright yellow color stands out among the green foliage. Vigorous vine, 3 1/2 to 4 feet tall; drought resistant; high-yielding; has attractive bi-color purple flowers. Potential specialty market item. I99

Mammoth Melting Sugar: 75 days. Thick, succulent light-green pods; 4 to 4 1/2 inches long, 3/4 inch wide. Distinct, sweet flavor. Uniform, productive vine; height 4 to 5 feet; requires support; resistant to wilt; hardy and vigorous. Bears over a long period, making it ideal for home gardens. *A69M*, B75, C44, C92, E38, *F72*, G51, G93M, H42, H66, J73, K10, K71, K73, M46, etc.

Norli: 55 days. Thin, succulent pods, 2 1/2 inches long; very sweet and flavorful. Excellent for freezing. Dwarf, white-flowered vine, grows only 18 inches tall; high yielding. Very early maturing; ideal for small-space gardens. C85M, E59Z, K66

Oregon Sugar Pod: 65 days. Smooth, light green pod; 4 inches long, 3/4 inch in diameter; mild flavor, good for freezing. Vigorous, hardy vine; height 24 to 30 inches; widely adapted; very productive over a long period; sets double pods. Resistant to viruses and fusarium wilt. A16, B35M, F44, *F72*, F82, G33, G51, G71, H94, L59, L97, M13M, M49, M95, N39, etc.

Osaya Endo: Oriental cultivar with large tender pods. Climbing, white-flowered vine. G33

Rembrandt: 95 days. Large, broad pod, 4 to 5 inches long; has a sweeter-than-usual flavor when picked on the immature side. Slow seed and string development; becomes sweeter without getting tough. Indeterminate vine; requires a 4 foot trellis for support; begins producing early and continues for a long period of time. I77, L89

Small Pod: Oriental cultivar with sweet and tender pods. Red-flowering, dwarf vine; requires no support. G33

Snowbird: 58 days. Very early maturing cultivar. Heavy yields of 3-inch pods, usually borne in double or triple clusters. Dwarf, erect plant, 16 to 18 inches tall; needs no support; widely adapted. Resembles Dwarf White Sugar. Ideal for short season areas or where space is limited. Also good for fall crops. Introduced in 1978. B75

Snowflake: 65 days. Short-vined type with extra-large pods. Large, dark-green flat pods; 4 inches long, 1 inch in diameter; remain straight. Vine grows 2 to 3 feet tall; resists powdery mildew. May be grown with or without support. *F63*, G6, *G13M*, G64, G71, G79, H42, J7, J25M, K10, M95M, Q34

Snap Peas A distinct type that produces both thick, crisp, succulent pods and a row of sweet, full-sized peas. When the pod is bent it will snap like a fresh snap bean pod. Pods and peas can be eaten together, or the peas can be shelled out and used alone. Developed by Calvin Lamborn of Gallatin Valley Seed Co. A prototype was described by Vilmorin and called *butter pea*. FELL 1982b, SCHNEIDER [Cul, Re], VILMORIN; A38M{PR}, *N40*{PR}

Bush Snapper: 58 days. A space-saving cultivar which can be grown without support; height 23 to 25 inches. Produces a large crop of pods, 3 3/4 to 4 inches long. Resistant to powdery mildew. B75

Early Snap: 62 days. Thick, fleshy pods, 3 to 3 1/4 inches long. Eating quality and yields comparable to Sugar Snap, but matures 10 to 14 days earlier. Compact vine, 18 to 22 inches tall; requires little or no trellising; resists bean yellow mosaic. Suitable for fresh market and U-pick operations. Released by the New York Agricultural Experiment Station. A13, D65, E57, F13, G79

Honey Pod: 70 days. Medium-green, round pod, 3 inches long; thick-walled, very crisp and sweet, nearly stringless; 6 pods per plant; 5 to 7 sweet, tender peas per pod. Uniform in shape and appearance. Compact vine, 20 to 28 inches tall, requires support; very prolific, produces 2 pods per node. Resistant to fusarium race 1. Introduced in 1983. *A69M*, D11M, *G13M*, L79

Maxie: 65 days. Thick, slender pod, 4 inches long; meaty, juicy, sweet and tender. Vigorous vine, 4 to 5 feet tall, requires support; bears a heavy crop early; resists powdery mildew. G71M

Snapie: 62 days. Dwarf Sugar Snap type, ripening 10 to 14 days earlier. Compact vine, about 20 inches tall; resistant to bean yellow mosaic. Suitable for fresh market and U-pick operations. J7

Snappy: 63 days. Thick, fleshy pods, 4 to 4 3/4 inches long; 8 or 9 peas per pod. Matures 7 to 10 days earlier than Sugar Snap. Vigorous, productive vine, up to 6 feet tall; requires strong support; resists powdery mildew. B75, S59M

Sugar Ann: 56 days. Round, bright green pods, 2 1/2 inches long; crisp and sweet. Very good for freezing. Dwarf vine, 16 to 24 inches tall; does not require support; widely adapted; prolific. Ideal for limited-space gardens. All America Selections winner in 1984. B73M, C44, C85M, D82, E24, F19M, *F72*, G6, G16, G71, H94, K73, L7M, M46, M49, etc.

Sugar Bon: 60 days. Round, slightly curved pod; 2 1/2 to 3 inches long; crisp, tender, sweet. Large, medium-green peas, 6 or 7 to a pod. Compact vine, only 18 to 24 inches tall; requires no support; very productive; heat tolerant; resistant to powdery mildew. A25, B75, D76, F12, *F72*, *G13M*, G93M, I91, J34, J83M, L14, L59, M29, N16

Sugar Daddy: 75 days. The first snap pea with stringless pods. Attractive, dark-green pods, 2 1/2 to 3 inches long; slender and stringless; borne in pairs at each fruiting node; will not split during freezing or cooking. Medium-green peas, 6 or 7 per pod. Dwarf vine, 24 to 30 inches tall; resistant to powdery mildew and pea leafroll. A16, B75, C44, D76, E97, G16, G71, *G83M*, H95, I91, J34, K71, L42, M46, etc.

Sugar Mel: (Super Sugar Mel) 68 days. Thick, round pods, up to 4 inches long or more; borne in pairs; 7 or 8 peas per pod. Vigorous vine, 3 to 4 feet tall, requires support; resistant to powdery mildew; high yielding. Rated highest in yield and eating quality of 7 cultivars tested by Organic Gardening magazine. B75M, C53, D82, F13, G71M, H42, H66, I91, J20, J34, K66, L7M, L14, M13M, M95M, etc.

Sugar Pop: 60 days. Stringless snap pea with early yield, up to 2 weeks earlier than Sugar Daddy or Sugar Snap. Round, thick pods, 2 1/2 to 3 inches long; crisp and sweet. Excellent for freezing. Dwarf vine, only 18 inches tall; needs little support; can be planted closer for higher yields; resists powdery mildew and pea leafroll. I91

Sugar Rae: 70 days. Round, dark green pods, 3 to 3 1/2 inches long; borne in pairs; crisp and sweet. Produces 7 or 8 sweet peas per pod. Vigorous dwarf vine, 2 1/2 feet tall; resistant to powdery mildew. Unique in that the plants "stool" at the base, producing up to 5 vines per plant. All vines blossom and bear pods over a long harvest period. B49, D68, F19M, *G13M*, *I59M*

Sugar Snap: 70 days. Round, plump, slightly curved pod; 2 1/2 to 3 1/2 inches long; crisp, sweet, juicy; requires stringing. Medium-green peas, 6 or 7 per pod. Freezes well, but not recommended for canning. Vigorous vine, 6 feet or more tall; needs strong support; resistant to wilt; productive over a long season. All America Selections winner in 1979. B75M, B78, C44, E24, E57, *F72*, G6, G16, *H61*, H66, K73, L7M, L59, M1M{PR}, M13M, M49, etc.

Sweet Snap: 65 days. Medium-green pods, 2 to 3 inches long; crisp and tender; free of fiber. Good for cooking and freezing, not recommended for canning. Semi-climbing vine, 34 inches tall; requires support; high yielding; tolerant to powdery mildew and bean yellow mosaic. A56, A69M, C92, G79, G87, H49, *I59M*, I64, K20, M46, M95M, N39

FIELD PEAS

Also called *soup pea*, *dry pea*, *gray pea* and *dun pea*, this type is grown almost exclusively for the dried seeds which are used in soups and stews or other cooked dishes, and are also sprouted. (also see Sprouting Seeds, page 485)

Austrian Winter: Small, grayish-brown seeds. Very good as a dry soup pea, keeping its firm texture when cooked. Also good for sprouting. Widely sold as a green manure seed. B55, E24, *E53*, E59Z, F11, F12, *G1M*, I99M, J34, J44, J99G, L89, *M25*, M95M

Blue Pod Capucijners: 85 days. Bluish-purple pod, 3 to 4 inches long. Large, grayish-brown seed; makes its own rich, dark-brown gravy. Semi-climbing vine, to 4 feet tall, requires support; has attractive purplish-red flowers. Originally developed by Capuchin monks in France or Holland in the 17th century. C85M, D87, I77, *R11M*

Carlin: Short pods; dark colored, semi-shriveled peas. Has a distinctive flavor. Seeds are soaked for 24 hours and are then at their best when sprinkled with brown sugar and cooked slowly. Tall growing vine, to 6 or 7 feet; needs support; resists rust and mildew; has purple, sweet-scented flowers. GENDERS 1975; U33

Early May: 55 days. Round, yellow seeds; can also be used as an early shelling pea. Strong, quick-growing vine, to 3 feet tall; succeeds in adverse weather. C85M

Holland Brown: Heirloom dry bean, brought from Holland by the first settlers of the Gallatin Valley, Montana. Not for shelling green.

Leave to ripen on the vines and then thresh. Cook and serve like dry beans. Very good producer. D82

Holland Capucijners: (Grey Pea) 85 days. A traditional dry pea, unique to the farm communities of northern Holland. The name Capucijner is derived from the peas markings, said to resemble the ancient cowls of Capuchin friars. Large, wrinkled brown-grey peas are cooked whole and make their own rich brown gravy. Also eaten fresh, although not particularly sweet. Ornamental vines, profusely covered with violet-red and pink flowers. A45{PR}, C94{PR}, G6, I77

Progreta Marrowfat: Developed especially for the production of dried peas for soup or *mushy peas*. Vine grows 2 1/2 feet tall. Not suitable where pea moth is a problem. P83M

Raisin Capucijners: 65 days. Large, flat seeds, mottled with brown and buff; excellent flavor, makes delicious and distinctive pea soup. Can also be used as a green shell pea. Dwarf vine, 24 inches tall; high yielding. C85M, I99

Round Green: 55 days. Round green peas; used primarily for pea soup. Can also be used as an extra-early shelling pea, but is not as sweet as wrinkled-seeded types. Vine grows to 2 feet tall. C85M

PEA SHOOTS

Also called *seedling pea, hoh laan tau* or *dau miu*, these are grown for their young shoots which are used in noodle or chow mein dishes. Plants are grown prostrate on the ground. They are not allowed to develop pods and the flowers are removed as they appear forcing the sweet pea flavor into the leaves and tender stems. Harvested when 4 to 5 inches tall. Sold in bunches in the markets of Hong Kong and Taiwan. Very popular in Shanghai. COST 1988 [Cul], DAHLEN [Cul, Re], HERKLOTS; L59, *L79G, Q28*

PEACH {GR}

AMYGDALUS DAVIDIANA AMYGDALUS PERSICA

CLINGSTONE PEACHES

Most clingstone peaches are more suitable for canning and processing than other types because the firm flesh retains its shape, the juice remains clearer and the color of the flesh remains brighter. Generally more disease resistant than freestones.

RED-FLESHED

Indian Blood: (Indian Cling, Red Indian, Blood Cling) Irregularly shaped, somewhat compressed fruit; skin dull greenish-white, mottled with pink and dark red; flesh red, lighter colored near the stone, juicy, coarse, stringy; quality fair; ripens very late. Widely used for pickling and preserving. Tree large, vigorous; hardy; unproductive. Low chilling requirement. Introduced prior to 1871. HEDRICK 1917; A82, A82{DW}, C75M, D76, *E45*, E97, E99M, F61M, F93, G65M, J33, L12, L90, L99M, M83, N33, N50{PR}, etc.

Strawberry Cling: Fruit medium to large; skin creamy white, blushed with red; flesh white, marbled with strawberry-red, firm, juicy, richly flavored; ripens late. Excellent for home canning. Tree vigorous; spreading; susceptible to insects and disease. Medium chilling requirement. B93M, *C54, L47*

WHITE-FLESHED

Arctic Supreme: Large, round white fruit; flesh firm, perfect for slicing, clingstone; flavor sweet, tangy, excellent for dessert; ripens in late July. Tree self-fruitful; requires approximately 700 hours of chilling. Originated in Modesto, California by Floyd Zaiger. *N20*

Chinese Cling: (Shanghai) Small to medium-sized, round-oval fruit; skin tough, adherent, creamy-white blushed on one side with lively red; flesh white, tender, juicy, aromatic; flavor excellent, being finely balanced between sweetness and sourness, with a distinct, pleasant taste of almond; ripens late. Tree rather weak in growth, upright-spreading, not very hardy, moderately productive. Introduced into England from Shanghai, China by Robert Fortune, in 1844. HEDRICK 1917; F91T{SC}

Mayflower: Medium to large fruit; oval, pointed at the apex; skin greenish-white with a dark red blush; flesh greenish-white, juicy, tender, subacid; quality fair; ripens very early. Tree productive; relatively resistant to leaf curl. Originated prior to 1909. HEDRICK 1917; E84, J33

White Heath: (White English, Heath Cling) Medium to large, round-oval fruit; skin creamy white blushed with red; flesh white, juicy, firm but tender, sweet or somewhat sprightly vinous-flavored; very good in quality; ripens 6 days after Elberta. Susceptible to brown rot. Popular for home canning. Tree vigorous; upright-spreading; hardy; unproductive. Medium chilling requirement. Origin unknown; first raised prior to the Revolutionary War. HEDRICK 1917; *C54*, G13, *L47, N20*

YELLOW-FLESHED

Chilow: Medium-sized, oblong-oval fruit; skin thin, tender, lemon-yellow with a faint, dull blush near the cavity; flesh yellow, tinged at the pit, coarse, meaty, juicy, flavor and fragrance excellent; ripens in midseason. Tree vigorous, moderately productive. Requires 650 hours of chilling. Thought to be a yellow-fleshed seedling of Chinese Cling. HEDRICK 1917; *A19*

Corona: Fruit large, up to 3 1/3 inches in diameter, nearly round; skin golden-yellow, blushed or streaked with red; flesh yellow, red next to the pit, fine-grained, firm; flavor very good; ripens late. Commercial canning clingstone. Tree vigorous, productive. BROOKS 1972; *A9, B71M*, E4, *K73M*

Dixired: Medium-sized, round fruit; skin bright red, attractive; flesh yellow, medium-firm, clingstone; ripens early, about 10 to 12 days before Redhaven, 5 to 6 weeks after Elberta. Quality good for very early shipping and local markets. Tree moderately vigorous; blooms late; tolerant to leaf curl. BROOKS 1972; *A19*, A82, B53, C75M, E29M, E99M, *F5*, F61M, F93, G13, G72{DW}, I9M, *M25M*, M39M, M83, N33, etc.

EarliGrande:[1] Medium to large fruit; skin yellow, 25 to 75% blushed with red; flesh yellow, slightly red next to the pit, firm, of good flavor; clingstone; ripens very early, 55 days before Elberta. Tree very vigorous. Low chilling requirement, 250 hours or less. Particularly well adapted to the south Texas area. *A9, A19*, A88M, *C54*, C75M, E99M, F61M, *I68*, I83M, *L47*, N33

Empress:[3] Medium-sized fruit, about 2 1/4 inches in diameter; skin yellow, blushed with bright red, attractive; flesh yellow, firm, juicy, melting, subacid to mild, of very good flavor; clingstone; ripens evenly, about 3 weeks before Golden Glory; resembles Golden Glory and Rio Oso Gem. Tree genetically dwarf; mature height only 5 to 8 feet; self-fruitful, productive; ornamental. BROOKS 1972; *C54*, C75M, E99M, F11, F61M

Everts: Fruit medium to large; skin yellow, with a medium blush, very attractive; flesh clear yellow, with a pink pit; flavor outstanding when canned; ripens with Halford. Tree productive. Commercial canning clingstone. Named for Major W.S. Everts, for many years manager, California Cling Peach Advisory Board. BROOKS 1972; *A9*

Flordaking:[1] Medium to large fruit, 2 to 2 1/2 inches in diameter; skin yellow, blushed with red; flesh firm, sweet, golden-yellow, clingstone; ripens very early, 57 days before Elberta. Chilling requirement low, 450 hours. Adapted to the warmer areas of the Deep South. Introduced by the University of Florida. A85M, C75M, *E45*, E99M, F19M, F61M, F93, G17, *I68*, *K76*, M31M, *M69M*{DW}, *N20*, N33

Halford: Large, uniform fruit; skin yellow; flesh yellow, nonmelting, clingstone; canning quality excellent; ripens late. Tree a heavy producer. Medium chilling requirement. Traditional commercial canning cultivar in California. Also widely used as a seedling rootstock. Originated in Modesto, California by John Halford. Introduced in 1921. BROOKS 1972; *A9*, *B71M*, B93M, *C54*, *D18*, *K73M*, *L47*, *N20*

Kakamas: Medium-sized, rounded fruit; skin yellow; flesh deep orange-yellow to pit, very firm, fine-textured, flavor distinctive; stone small, cling; ripens late. Excellent for canning. Tree vigorous, very resistant to delayed foliation, a regular and heavy bearer. A leading commercial cultivar in South Africa. Originated in Kakamas, Orange River, South Africa. BROOKS 1972; **U30M{SC}**

Katrina: Large, oval fruit, weight up to 1 pound; skin yellow without blush; flesh yellow, smooth, clingstone, juicy, of good flavor; ripens in November, keeps on the tree to mid-December. Quality especially good for a late ripening peach. Tree vigorous; nearly evergreen, retaining leaves until March when there is a partial drop. Originated in San Jose, California on the property of Joe Massidda. **T49M{SC}**

Klamt: Medium to large fruit; skin yellow, with a medium blush; flesh clear yellow; pit brown; flavor superior when canned; maintains its high quality well. Tree consistently sets good crops. Originated in Davis, California. Introduced in 1964. BROOKS 1972; *A9*, *B71M*, *K73M*

Lemon Cling: Fruit large; oval, resembling a lemon; apex terminating in a large nipple; skin deep yellow, brownish-red where exposed; flesh firm, deep lemon-yellow with red at the stone, juicy, sprightly, vinous, with an agreeable acidity; quality very good when perfectly ripe; ripens in September. Excellent for home canning. Tree vigorous; highly productive; bears regularly. Dates back to before the Revolutionary War. HEDRICK 1917; **T49M{SC}**, **U8{SC}**

Loadel: Uniformly large fruit; flesh clear yellow, firm, with a small pit; ripens in mid-July. Tree vigorous and productive. One of the most widely planted early-ripening commercial clingstones. Originated in Yuba City, California. Introduced about 1950. BROOKS 1972; *A9*, *B71M*, *D18*, *K73M*

Orange Cling: Fruit large, round; skin clear golden-orange, blushed with red; flesh dark golden-yellow, very firm, juicy, with a vinous flavor; clingstone; ripens midseason to late. Very popular for home canning. Tree vigorous and productive. Medium chilling requirement. Originated prior to 1832. HEDRICK 1917; *C54*, *L47*

Tuskena: (Tuscan Cling) Very large fruit; flesh firm but melting, acidic until fully ripe when it has a good flavor; ripens very early, with Early Crawford. Suitable for both dessert and canning. Possibly a clingstone version of the Crawford type. At one time valued as an early shipping peach. Originated in Mississippi prior to 1873. WICKSON; **T49M{SC}**, **U8{SC}**

FLAT PEACHES

A very distinct type with fruit that is very compressed and oblate. Most have holes in the flesh below the pit. Also called *ping-tzu-t'ao*, *pen-tao* or *saucer peach*. Generally, they have low chilling requirements. (A. persica Compressa Group)

Australian Saucer: Small to medium-sized, vertically compressed fruit; skin white, blushed with red on the exposed side; flesh white, cloyingly sweet offset by a pronounced bitter almond flavor; ripens late June to early July. Tree blooms very early, nearly evergreen in mild climates. Relatively low chilling requirement, approximately 300 to 400 hours. Good in warm winter areas, especially hot interior parts of California. **T49M{SC}**

Peento: Flattened, saucer-shaped fruit; skin creamy yellow, mottled and delicately pencilled with red; flesh white, stained red at the stone, juicy, stringy, tender and melting, sweet, mild, with a slight bitter almond-like flavor; quality very good; clingstone; ripens early. Susceptible to blossom end decay. Tree vigorous, open-topped. Adapted to Florida and the warmest parts of the Gulf States. Introduced prior to 1877. HEDRICK 1917; G8

Stark Saturn: Fruit vertically compressed and oblate; skin creamy yellow, highly blushed with red; flesh white, melting, tender, mild and very sweet; freestone; ripens approximately with Redhaven. Unlike most flat peaches, it has a small, tight scar and flesh covering the pit rather than holes in the flesh below the pit. Tree large, vigorous; very productive; resistant to bacterial spot. Considered the best of the flat peaches. L33

FREESTONE PEACHES

RED-FLESHED

Indian Free: (Indian Blood Freestone, Blood Free) Similar to Indian Blood, but freestone. Medium-sized fruit; skin greenish-white, overspread with splashes and stripes of dark red; flesh blood-red throughout, juicy, course, tough and meaty; quality fair; ripens very late. Tree vigorous, hardy. Introduced prior to 1869. HEDRICK 1917; A88M, B93M, *C54*, E4, F11, *I68*, L1, *L47*, *N20*

Strawberry Free: Medium-sized fruit; skin white, blushed with pink; flesh white marbled with strawberry-red, firm, very sweet and rich, of excellent flavor; freestone; ripens early. Tree vigorous, spreading. Relatively low chilling requirement. Very popular in parts of California. A88M, B93M, *C54*, F11, *I68*, L1, *N20*

WHITE-FLESHED

Amsden: (Amsden June) Medium-sized, nearly round fruit; skin greenish-white, blushed with dark red on the side exposed to the sun; flesh yellowish-white, very soft, flavor good; stone large, partially clinging until fully ripe; ripens early. Tree moderately vigorous; bears regularly; hardy. Introduced about 1868. SIMMONS 1978; Q24M, R77

Babcock:[1] Small to medium-sized fruit; skin light pink, blushed with light and deep red, attractive; flesh nearly pure-white, red near pit, tender, very juicy, mild, very sweet; quality good; pit small, free; ripens 2 weeks before Elberta. Tree medium to large; vigorous, spreading; very productive. Low chilling requirement, less than 200 hours. BROOKS 1972, RUCK; A88M, *D23M*, E4, F11, *F53M*, *H34*, *I68*, I83M, *L47*, *N20*

Belle Imperiale: Large, round fruit; skin yellowish, blushed with carmine and purplish-red on the exposed side; flesh yellowish-white, slightly red near the stone, soft, juicy, quality good; stone medium-sized, free. Tree vigorous to moderate in growth; bears heavily. Originated in France. SIMMONS 1978; P59M

Belle of Georgia: Large, roundish-oval fruit; skin creamy white, blushed with red, very attractive; flesh white, tinged with red at the pit, juicy, stringy, tender, sweet and mild, quality good; stone semi-free to free; matures in midseason. Tree large, vigorous; hardy; very productive. Originated in Marshallville, Georgia from seed planted in 1870. HEDRICK 1917; A39, A82, *B52*, C63, C75M, F19M, F53, G23, G79M{DW}, I9M, J69{DW}, L33, N33

Carolina Belle: New release from North Carolina State University. Developed to fill the need for a firm, white-fleshed peach intended for local markets. Fruit 2 1/2 to 3 inches in diameter; ripens about 10 days after Redhaven. Requires approximately 750 chilling hours. C75M, E99M, F61M, N33

Champion: Small to medium-sized fruit; skin creamy white, blushed with light and dark red; flesh white, tinged red at the stone, very juicy, exceedingly tender, sweet, of excellent flavor; stone semi-free to free; matures in early midseason. Tree large, vigorous; very productive. Originated in Nokomis, Illinois by I.G. Hubbard. Introduced in 1890. HEDRICK 1917; D76, F53, H49, H65, I9M, J33, K28, K28{DW}, *K60*, L12, *M25M*

Charles Ingouf: Large flattish-round fruit; skin yellowish-green, blushed with dark red or purplish red on the side exposed to the sun; flesh greenish-white, juicy, sweet, slightly subacid; stone partially clinging. Tree strong and vigorous; slow to come into bearing but then yields well. SIMMONS 1978; P59M

Cumberland: Medium to large, oval-pointed fruit; skin greenish-white, overspread with dull red, fuzzy; flesh white, red at the pit, soft, melting, texture coarse; semi-freestone; ripens 3 weeks before Elberta, hangs well on the tree. Tree vigorous; moderately productive; resistant to bacterial spot; flower large, showy, light pink. Chilling requirement 850 hours. BROOKS 1972; F91T{SC}

Early White Giant: (Stark Early White Giant) Fruit very large; skin white, highly blushed with bright red, attractive; flesh white, juicy, sweet, flavorful; ripens in early July. Tree vigorous and productive; tolerant to bacterial spot. Adapted to Zones 5 through 8. L33, L33{DW}

Eden: Large, roundish fruit; skin creamy white, 60% overspread with red; flesh thick, firm, juicy, sweet and rich; oxidizes slowly for a white-fleshed peach; freestone; ripens in midseason. Good for canning as well as fresh eating. Tree vigorous, very productive, as hardy as Redhaven. Introduced in 1972. I36

El Dulce:[1] Medium-sized fruit, weight about 5 ounces; skin light pink to red; flesh white, rather dry, very sweet; seed small; ripens 7 days later than Babcock. Excellent for eating out of hand, drying or canning. Tree vigorous, spreading, has a low chilling requirement. Seedling of Babcock. Originated in Escondido, California by Orton Englehart. **T49M{SC}**

Erly-Red-Fre: Fruit large, round; skin attractive red, thick; flesh white, greenish near pit, firm, melting; pit small, mostly freestone; ripens 5 to 6 weeks before Elberta. Tree vigorous; hardy; moderately productive. High chilling requirement. BROOKS 1972; A5, B53, D37

Flordahome: (A. davidiana x) Medium to large, oval fruit; skin yellowish-white, 50% blushed with red; flesh white, soft, of fair quality; ripens early. Tree ornamental, flower about 2 inches in diameter; fairly resistant to root-knot nematode. Relatively low chilling requirement, about 400 hours. BROOKS 1972; F19M, *K76*

Flory:[3] Small, white fruit; flesh tender, aromatic, freestone; flavor bland; cans well; ripens in late July. Tree a genetic dwarf, growing only 3 to 5 feet tall at maturity; very large, showy, double red blossoms. Requires approximately 400 hours of chilling. Primarily a home garden ornamental. Originated in Modesto, California by C.R. Flory. Introduced in 1945. *I68*

Four Star:[1] (4-Star Daily News) Medium-sized fruit, 2 1/2 inches in diameter; skin color high; flesh white, quality high, freestone; ripens middle of June. Tree vigorous; flowers large, 2 inches in diameter, double, light pink, abundant. Low chilling requirement. *C54*

George IV: Small to medium-sized fruit; skin creamy white, blushed with pink; flesh whitish, deeply tinged with red near the pit, juicy, stringy, tender, mild, pleasantly flavored; quality good; stone semi-free to free; matures in midseason. Tree large, vigorous; hardy; unproductive. Originated about 1821, in the garden of a Mr. Gill, Broad Street, New York City. HEDRICK 1917; L12

Giant Babcock:[1] Fruit large; skin predominantly red; flesh ivory yellow, streaked outwardly from the stone with shades of red; freestone; resembles Babcock but larger; matures about 12 to 14 days after Babcock. Tree medium to large; vigorous; productive; flowers large, more colorful than Babcock. Low chilling requirement. BROOKS 1972; *N20*

Greensboro: Medium-sized, oblong-oval fruit; skin rather tough, creamy-white blushed with red, pubescence heavy; flesh white, very juicy, tender and melting, mild, sweet, sprightly, freestone when fully ripe; ripens early, keeps and ships well. Tree very large, spreading, very productive, widely adapted. Originated in Greensboro, North Carolina by W.G. Balsey, about 1891. HEDRICK 1917; F91T{SC}

Hiley: Medium to large, roundish-conic fruit; skin thin, tough, greenish-yellow with a dull blush, more or less mottled; flesh creamy-white, stained red at the pit, stringy, firm but tender, sprightly, with a distinct, pleasant flavor; quality very good; ripens early to mid-season. Tree medium in size, lacking in vigor, upright-spreading, very productive. Originated in Marshallville, Georgia about 1886. HEDRICK 1917; F91T{SC}

Honey Dew Hale:[2] Large, roundish fruit; skin white with a pink blush; flesh white, marbled with yellow, with a thin yellow segment from the pit through to the skin along the suture; freestone; ships well. Tree medium in vigor, open, spreading. Bud mutation of J.H. Hale. Originated in New Cumberland, Pennsylvania. Introduced in 1949. BROOKS 1972; **T49M{SC}**, **U8{SC}**

J.M. Mack: Fruit medium to large; round, one-half bulging, unequal; skin cream-colored, lightly streaked and mottled with pink, attractive, smooth, pubescence very short; flesh pure creamy-white right to the stone, firm but very tender, very juicy, with a distinctive aroma and flavor, quality very good; stone free, extremely small; ripens a few days after Champion. Origin unknown, but believed to be Australian. Introduced into the United States in 1926. BROOKS 1972; L12

La White: Large, very attractive fruit; skin white, blushed with rose-pink and red; flesh white flecked throughout with rosy red, juicy, very sweet, low in acid, flavor excellent; freestone; cans well; ripens mid to late June, about 27 days before Elberta. Tree vigorous and productive; requires 650 hours of chilling. Originated in Calhoun, Louisiana. A85M, C75M, E99M, F61M, G17

Lola Queen: Fruit medium-sized; skin pale greenish-white, blushed with pink and red, attractive; flesh white, very juicy, tender and melting, sweet, sprightly; quality very good; stone free; ripens a few days after Champion. Originated in Fayetteville, Arkansas by Professor J.R. Cooper, from a cross made in 1920 of Lola and an old North Carolina peach called Wine. L12

Nectar: Fruit large to very large; round-ovate, apex pointed; skin blushed pink to red; flesh white tinged with red, juicy, soft-melting, sweet, aromatic, of very good quality; pit medium-sized, free, with some split pits; ripens 3 weeks before Elberta; susceptible to brown rot. Tree vigorous; flower non-showy. Considered to be an open pollinated seedling of Stanwick nectarine. BROOKS 1972; A88M, B93M, *C54*, C75M, E4, E99M, F61M, K12M{PR}, *L47*, *N20*

Oldmixon Free: Medium-sized fruit; skin creamy white blushed with red, pubescence coarse, thick; flesh white, deeply tinted with red near the pit, juicy, stringy, tender and melting, sweet and sprightly, quality very good; stone free or nearly free; matures late. Tree very large, vigorous; hardy; rather unproductive. Introduced prior to 1817. HEDRICK 1917; L12

Paradise: Fruit large; skin reddish-white; flesh white, with some red at the pit, has a distinctive flavor and aroma; quality very good; ripens in midseason. Excellent for freezing. Tree bears well. Originated in Paradise, California by J.E. Fisher. Introduced about 1946. HEDRICK 1917; E4

Peregrine: Medium to large, round fruit; skin bright crimson, nearly as smooth as a nectarine; flesh white, firm, melting, very juicy, flavor excellent; ripens in early August. Originated by Thomas Rivers as a seedling of Spencer nectarine. Introduced in 1906. Still a popular commercial cultivar in England. SIMMONS 1978; F91T{SC}, L12, P86, Q30{SC}, R77

Polly: Fruit small to medium-sized; skin white, blushed with red; flesh white, juicy, aromatic, of high quality; ripens in midseason; resembles Champion. Tree very cold-hardy. Well adapted for home orchards in Iowa. Originated in Glenwood, Iowa by S.A. Beach. Introduced in 1934. BROOKS 1972; *C54*, D76, D76{DW}, E97, E97{DW}, H33, *H90*, *H90*{DW}, L12

Raritan Rose: Medium to large, round fruit; skin attractive red; flesh white streaked with red, fine-textured, soft, melting, watery; quality good; freestone; ripens 4 weeks before Elberta. Tree vigorous, spreading; hardy; productive; tolerant to bacteriosis. High chilling requirement. A5, B53, E99M, F53, K83M

Red Ceylon:[1] Medium-sized, oval fruit with a protruding knob at the apex; skin greenish, blushed with deep-red when ripe; flesh white, a rich strawberry-red near the pit, tender, juicy; flavor excellent, sweet-acid with a hint of bitter-almond; seed free, relatively small; ripens in April and May. Tree dwarf, slender; requires no more than 50 hours of chilling. Introduced into Florida in the late 1880's. MORTON 1987a; T73M{SC}

Redrose: Large, round fruit; skin bright red on a white background, attractive, pubescence medium; flesh creamy white, red at pit, melting, moderately firm, fine-textured, of good quality; ripens 2 weeks before Elberta. Tree vigorous; very productive; self-fruitful. BROOKS 1972; A5

Snow Flame: Large, roundish fruit; skin deep dark-red; flesh white, firm, of excellent flavor; good for fresh eating and canning; ripens early to mid-June, ships well. Tree strong, vigorous, very productive. Requires approximately 900 chilling hours. Recently introduced cultivar. *B71M*, *I68*

Springtime: Small to medium-sized fruit, globose with a distinct point; skin yellow, highly blushed with red, pubescence short and abundant; flesh white, tender, soft and juicy; semi-freestone; ripens early. Flowers small to medium, pink, non-showy. Moderately low chilling requirement. Originated in Ontario, California. Introduced in 1953. BROOKS 1972; *C54*, E4

Stump-the-World: (Stump, Stump-of-the-World) Medium-sized fruit; skin creamy white, blushed, mottled and splashed with red; flesh white, strongly stained with red near the pit, juicy, tender and melting, sweet, richly flavored, aromatic; quality very good; ripens late. Tree vigorous and productive. Originated in New Jersey prior to 1840. HEDRICK 1917; L12

Sugar Lady: New white-fleshed freestone, already a favorite at fruit stands. Skin cream-colored with an attractive, dark red blush. Very firm flesh, sweet and rich, slightly tangy. Ripens in early July. Tree self-fruitful; needs approximately 700 hours of chilling. Originated in Modesto, California by Floyd Zaiger. I49M, *N20*

White Hale: Fruit large; round, uniform, slightly pointed; skin greenish-white to cream, overspread with red, fairly attractive, hairs short; flesh white, red around the pit, firm, melting, juicy; quality good; ripens with J.H. Hale. Tree vigorous, upright; very productive; self-fruitful. Originated in New Brunswick, New Jersey by M.A. Blake. Introduced in 1932. BROOKS 1972; A5, B53, C75M, E99M, F53, F61M, *K60*, K83M

Wildrose: Medium to large, round-ovate fruit; skin yellow-green, prominently mottled with dull red, pubescence light; flesh white, red at pit, firm, melting, quality good; pit small, free; ripens 3 weeks before Elberta. Tree vigorous; moderately productive; self-fruitful. Chilling requirement 750 hours at or below 45° F. BROOKS 1972; B53, C75M, F61M

YELLOW-FLESHED

Admiral Dewey: Small to medium-sized, round-oblate fruit; skin thin and tender, adherent, deep orange-yellow blushed with dark red; flesh yellow, juicy, stringy, tender and melting, sweet but sprightly, very good in quality; stone semi-free to free; ripens early. Tree large, vigorous, upright-spreading, hardy, very productive. Originated in Vineyard, Georgia in the latter part of the 19th century. HEDRICK 1917; F91T{SC}

August Etter: Medium-sized fruit; skin yellow; flesh yellow, somewhat fibrous, of good flavor; ripens in late August. Good fresh and for jam; excellent for freezing; not recommended for canning. Tree resistant to leaf curl. Originated in Mendocino County, California by August Etter. E84

August Pride:[1] Large, round fruit; skin yellow, blushed with red, tart; flesh yellow, fine-grained, sweet, aromatic, richly flavored, of very good quality; ripens in midseason, 3 to 4 weeks after Mid Pride. Tree vigorous, upright; productive; blooms early; low chilling requirement, 300 hours or less. Adapted to most mild-winter areas of California. Developed by Floyd Zaiger. I83M, *N20*

Biscoe: Medium-sized, round fruit; skin deep yellow, 50 to 75% covered with a bright red blush, attractive; flesh yellow, firm, melting, fine-textured, of good flavor; ripens about with Redhaven. Tree moderately vigorous; hardy; productive; very resistant to bacterial spot. A5, B53, C75M, E99M, F53, F61M, K83M

Blake: (M.A. Blake) Large, round fruit; skin an attractive red, pubescence slight; flesh yellow, red near the pit, firm-melting, quality good, sometimes too acid, freestone; freezing quality good; excellent for home canning; ripens 1 week before Elberta; resembles J.H. Hale. Tree vigorous; productive; susceptible to bacteriosis. BROOKS 1972; A5, B53, B83, C75M, E99M, F53, F61M, K83M

Bonita:[1] Medium to large fruit; skin light yellow with a deep red blush, attractive; flesh yellow, dark pink near the pit, somewhat fibrous, firm, sweet to subacid, quality good; freestone; ripens in midseason. Tree vigorous, upright; productive. Low chilling requirement. Originated in Riverside, California. Introduced in 1943. BROOKS 1972; A88M, *C54*, *G49*, *I68*, *N20*

Canadian Harmony: Large, round fruit, 2 3/4 to 3 inches in diameter; skin yellow, 80% covered with a red blush, pubescence scant; flesh yellow, slightly red at pit, firm but melting, quality good; ripens 2 weeks before Elberta. Tree very vigorous; hardy; moderately tolerant to bacterial leaf and fruit spot. Recommended for southwestern Ontario. BROOKS 1972; A5, B83, F53, *G14*, *G14*{DW}, G23, G23{DW}, G41, *H34*, *I54*, K83M, M39M

Candor: Uniformly round fruit; skin rich-yellow, 75% covered with a bright red blush, very attractive; flesh yellow, texture very fine, flavor unusually good, highly resistant to browning; semi-freestone; ripens just before Dixired. Tree moderately vigorous; self-fruitful; foliage somewhat resistant to bacterial spot. BROOKS 1972; A5, C75M, E99M, F53, F61M, K83M

Cresthaven: Medium to large, nearly round fruit; skin bright red over gold, very attractive; flesh clear yellow, firm, very resistant to browning; satisfactory for home canning, freezes unusually well; easily pitted by mechanical means; ripens about 1 week before Elberta. Tree vigorous; productive; self-fruitful; above average in hardiness. BROOKS 1972; A5, B53, B83, C75M, E99M, F53, F61M, *G14*, *G14*{DW}, G41, *H34*, *K73M*, K83M, M39M

Delight: Fruit large, up to 3 1/2 inches in diameter; skin well blushed, attractive; flesh yellow, firm, of very good flavor; freestone; ripens about 10 days before Elberta; resembles Rio Oso Gem. Quality very good fresh, frozen or canned. Introduced in 1960 by Fowler Nursery. BROOKS 1972; E4

Desertgold:[1] Medium-sized, round fruit; skin yellow blushed with red, attractive; flesh yellow, moderately firm, semi-clingstone; quality good; ripens early midseason. Tree moderately vigorous; productive; self-fertile. Low chilling requirement, 350 to 400 hours. Recommended for warm winter areas. BROOKS 1972, RUCK; *A9*, *C54*, *I68*, I83M, L33, L33{DW}, *L47*, *N20*

Earlired: Medium-sized, round fruit; skin yellow, 85% covered with a bright red blush, pubescence very light; flesh yellow, firm but melting, medium in texture, of good flavor; clingstone when firm ripe, semi-cling at the soft ripe stage; ripens 19 days before Redhaven. Tree vigorous and productive; requires heavy early thinning for best size. A5, B53, C75M, F61M, G41, *H34*

Early Crawford: Medium-sized fruit; round-oval, bulged near the apex, with unequal halves; skin golden-yellow blushed with dark red, attractive, pubescence thick; flesh deep yellow, rayed with red near the pit, juicy, tender, sprightly, highly flavored, quality very good; ripens in early midseason. Tree large, vigorous; often unproductive. Originated in Middletown, New Jersey by William Crawford, early in the 19th century. HEDRICK 1917; E84, L12

Elberta: Fruit large; skin orange-yellow blushed with red, pubescence thick and coarse; flesh yellow stained with red near the pit, juicy, stringy, firm but tender, sweet to subacid, quality good; resistant to browning; matures in midseason. Tree large, vigorous; very productive; widely adapted to soil and climate. Originated in Marshallville, Georgia from a seed planted in 1870. HEDRICK 1917; B73M, B73M{DW}, B83, C63, C75M, *E45*, G23, G23{DW}, I9M, J69{DW}, J83, J83{DW}, M39M, N33

Emery: Medium-sized, round fruit; skin dull yellow, 50% covered with a red blush; flesh yellow, with less red pigment than Redskin, firm, melting, fine-grained, less juicy than Elberta, flavor excellent; fully freestone; ripens 5 to 7 days later than Elberta. Tree vigorous, productive; resistant to bacterial spot; flower large, showy, self-fertile. BROOKS 1972; A5

Encore: (Stark Encore) Medium to large fruit; skin yellow, blushed with red; flesh yellow, firm, juicy, sweet and flavorful; ripens very late. Good fresh or for canning. Tree productive; resistant to blossom-season frost; very tolerant to bacterial leaf spot. Adapted to Zones 5 through 8. L33

Fairtime: Large, round fruit; skin yellow, 20 to 25% covered by a bright red blush; flesh yellow, with considerable red near the pit, firm but melting, texture smooth, flavor good; suitable for fresh market and freezing; ripens 7 days after Summerset. Tree vigorous and productive; self-fertile. BROOKS 1972; *A9*, *B71M*, C75M, E99M, F61M, *L47*, *N20*

Fay Elberta: Fruit large; skin yellow blushed with red, attractive; flesh yellow, firm but melting, sweet, fine-grained, of very good flavor; ripens midseason to late; resembles Elberta, but more colorful. Excellent for eating fresh, canning, or freezing. Tree productive, requires heavy thinning; flowers pink, showy. Medium chilling requirement. *A9*, A88M, *B71M*, B93M, *C54*, C75M, E4, E99M, F61M, *I68*, *K73M*, L1, *L47*, *N20*

Flavorcrest: Medium to large, round fruit; skin yellow, 80% covered with a red blush; flesh yellow, very firm, smooth-textured, flavor rich, quality excellent; stone semi-cling to free; ripens early to midseason. Tree moderately vigorous; productive. Medium chilling requirement. Released by the USDA. A5, *A9*, *B71M*, B83, *C54*, C75M, E99M, F53, F61M, *H34*, *L47*

Flordagrande:[1] Fruit medium-sized but large for its season; skin bright yellow, 60% blushed with red; flesh yellow, firm, freestone; ripens 103 days from bloom. Tree hardy; tolerant to bacterial spot; flower large, showy, self-fertile. Exceptionally low chilling requirement, only 50 hours. Originated in Gainesville, Florida. Introduced in 1984. *B71M*, E99M, F61M

Flordaprince:[1] Medium-large, round fruit; skin yellow, blushed and striped with red; flesh yellow, firm, quality good; clingstone to semi-free; ripens 7 to 10 days earlier than Desert Gold. Tree very vigorous and productive; more tolerant of desert heat than Desert Gold. Very low chilling requirement, only 150 hours. Widely planted as an early commercial peach in southern California and Arizona. *A9*, *B71M*, *C54*, C75M, *D23M*, E99M, F61M, *I68*, I83M, *K76*, *N20*

Fortyniner: (Merrill 49'er) Fruit large; skin yellow, blushed with bright red, very attractive; flesh yellow, firm, quality excellent; ripens 1 week before J.H. Hale and Elberta; resembles J.H. Hale. Tree vigorous; productive; susceptible to bacterial spot. Medium-high chilling requirement. Originated in Red Bluff, California by Grant Merrill. BROOKS 1972; A69G{SC}, *C54*, E4, *L47*, L99M, *N20*

Frost: Medium to large fruit; skin fuzzy, green-shouldered; flesh pale yellow, soft, sweet, juicy, mostly freestone; quality good for dessert and drying, fair for canning; ripens in mid-August. Tree self-fertile; bears very heavily, must be thinned for best results. Strongly resistant to leaf curl, though not immune. Discovered in Washington by Herb Frost. B67, C34, I49M, J61M, L97, M39M, *N20*

Garden Gold:[3] Fruit large, up to 3 inches in diameter; skin yellow, slightly blushed with red; flesh yellow, red near the pit, soft, melting, of good flavor; ripens 2 to 3 weeks after Elberta. Tree genetically dwarf; mature height only 5 to 6 feet; productive; blooms a week later than other miniature peaches and nectarines; self-fruitful; ornamental. A88M, E87, H65, *I68*, *N20*

Garden Sun:[3] Large full-sized fruit; skin yellow-orange, blushed with red; flesh yellow, sweet, mild, low in acid; freestone; ripens 1 week after Elberta. Tree a genetic dwarf, growing only 4 to 6 feet tall; self-fruitful; flowers large, showy. Needs approximately 500 hours of chilling. Ideal for container growing. Originated in Modesto, California by Floyd Zaiger. F19M, G23, L33, *N20*

Garnet Beauty: Medium to large, oval fruit; skin yellow, overlaid with bright red; flesh yellow, streaked with red, firm, melting, flavor excellent; semi-freestone; ripens 8 to 10 days earlier than Redhaven; hangs on tree well until over-ripe. Tree vigorous and productive; slightly susceptible to bacterial spot. BROOKS 1972; A5, B53, C41M, C63, C75M, E99M, F53, F61M, G41, *K60*, K83M, M39M

Glohaven: Large, nearly round fruit; skin mostly red over deep yellow, attractive, pubescence light; flesh clear yellow, nearly free of red at pit, firm, very resistant to browning; freestone; easily pitted by mechanical means; ships unusually well; cans and freezes well; ripens about 2 weeks before Elberta. Tree vigorous and productive; self-fruitful. BROOKS 1972; A5, B83, C41M, C63, C75M, E99M, F53, F61M, *K60*, *K73M*, M39M, M83

Gold Dust: Small to medium-sized fruit; skin yellow, mottled and streaked with red, smooth; flesh yellow, firm, fine-grained, non-acid but flavorful, of excellent quality; ripens 14 days earlier than Redhaven. Tree large, vigorous; hardy; productive. Relatively low chilling requirement. BROOKS 1972; *C54*, *I68*, *L47*, *N20*

Golden Gem:[3] Fruit large; skin yellow, blushed with red; flesh yellow, red near the pit, very firm, fine-grained, of excellent flavor; ripens early; resembles Rio Oso Gem. Tree genetically dwarf, spreading; mature height only 5 to 6 feet; ornamental. E4, *I68*, *L47*

Golden Glory:[3] Large fruit, averaging 2 3/8 inches in diameter; skin yellow, partially mottled with orange-red; flesh yellow, red next to the stone, soft, melting, subacid to mild, quality fair to good; ripens late. Tree genetically dwarf, spreading; mature height 6 to 8 feet; vigorous and productive; self-fruitful; ornamental. BROOKS 1972; *C54*, F11

Golden Jubilee: Fruit medium to large; oval to oblong, flattened; skin mottled bright red over 1/3 of surface; flesh yellow, red at pit, firm, melting, texture coarse, of very good quality; ripens 3 weeks before Elberta; drops early from tree. Tree sets heavily but is self-thinning. BROOKS 1972; A82, *B52*, C63, G23, G23{DW}, *G28*, G45M, G72{DW}, G79M{DW}, H49, H65, I9M, J69{DW}, M76

Halehaven: Medium to large, round fruit; skin dark red over most of surface, very sweet; flesh yellow, red at pit, firm, melting, quality excellent, freestone; ripens 2 weeks before Elberta. Tree vigorous and productive. Excellent home garden cultivar. BROOKS 1972, STEBBINS; A82, A88M, B73M, C37, G23, G23{DW}, *G28*, H65, I9M, J16, J69{DW}, J83, J83{DW}, L90, N33, etc.

Halloween: Large fruit; flesh yellow, firm, freestone; ripens extremely late, about 70 days after Elberta or about October 10 at place of origin. Tree medium-sized, moderately vigorous, productive. Originated in Red Bluff, California by Grant Merrill. Introduced in 1954. BROOKS 1972; *A9*, A88M, *C54*, I83M

Harbelle: Round fruit, 2 3/4 inches in diameter; skin yellow, 60% covered with a bright red blush, pubescence short; flesh yellow, melting, firm, quality good, freestone; ripens early. Tree small, moderately vigorous; hardy; tolerant to bacterial spot. Originated in Harrow, Ontario, Canada. BROOKS 1972; A69G{SC}, B53, E99M, F53, G41, I36, *K60*

Harbrite: Fruit ovate, 2 1/2 inches in diameter; skin yellow, 80% covered with a brilliant red blush, attractive; flesh yellow, tinged red at the pit, firm, melting, quality good, freestone; ripens 4 weeks before Elberta. Tree hardy; exceptionally productive; highly tolerant to bacterial spot. Recommended for southwestern Ontario. BROOKS 1972; A5, A69G{SC}, C75M, E99M, F53, G41, I36, K83M, M39M

Harken: Fruit large; skin yellow, about 80% covered with a dark red blush, attractive; flesh yellow, medium firm, juicy, fine-textured, sweet and rich; quality good; very resistant to browning; ripens just after Redhaven. Good for canning and freezing. Tree moderately vigorous; productive; moderately hardy; resistant to bacterial spot. A69G{SC}, B53, B83, C34, E99M, F61M, *H34*, I36, I49M, J61M, K83M

Honey Babe:[3] Fruit large, up to 3 inches in diameter; skin yellow, blushed with deep red, attractive; flesh yellow-orange flecked with bright red, firm, sweet and flavorful, highly aromatic, of excellent quality; ripens just before Redhaven. Tree genetically dwarf; productive; ornamental. Chilling requirement 500 to 600 hours. Developed by Floyd Zaiger. A88M, B75, E4, E87, F11, F19M, G23, I49M, *I68*, J61M, L99M, *N20*

J.H. Hale: Very large, round fruit; skin lemon-yellow blushed with dark red, pubescence light; flesh yellow, red at pit, juicy, fine-grained, sweet or somewhat sprightly, of good quality; matures in midseason. Tree vigorous and productive. Originated in South Glastonbury, Connecticut by J.H. Hale. Introduced in 1912. HEDRICK 1917; A5, A82, *B52*, B83, C63, C75M, *G28*, *G28*{DW}, I9M, L90, M39M, M39M{DW}

Jefferson: Fruit large; skin bright red; flesh yellow, very firm, fine-textured, of good flavor; fully freestone; ripens 3 days after Elberta; resembles J.H. Hale. Cans and freezes well. Tree vigorous; reliably productive; buds and flowers tolerant to blossoming-season frost. BROOKS 1972; C75M, E99M, F61M, F93, I36, *K60*, M76, M83, N33

Jerseyqueen: Large, oval fruit; skin yellow blushed with bright red, attractive; flesh yellow, firm, mild but flavorful, of excellent dessert quality; ripens about with Elberta; resembles Blake. Tree vigorous, moderately productive; flower large, showy; buds tender, subject to winter kill. BROOKS 1972; A5, B53, C75M, E99M, F61M, K83M, L12

July Elberta: (Burbank July Elberta) Medium-sized, round fruit; skin greenish-yellow, blushed and streaked with dull red, pubescence heavy and dense; flesh yellow, only slightly red at pit, firm, melting, of very good quality; pit small, free; ripens about 2 weeks before Elberta. Tree vigorous; highly fruitful; susceptible to bacteriosis. Originated in Sebastopol, California by Luther Burbank. Introduced in 1930. BROOKS 1972; B93M, B93M{DW}, F11, *G14*, *G14*{DW}, L33, L33{DW}, *L47*

June Gold: Fruit very large; skin highly colored red; flesh yellow, firm, semi-freestone; ripens early, 15 to 20 days before Redhaven; J.H. Hale type. Suitable for shipping. Tree very productive; flowers showy. Relatively low chilling requirement, 650 hours at or below 45^0 F. Ideal for South Texas planting. BROOKS 1972; *A19*, A85M, *C54*, C75M, E99M, F19M, F61M, *G15M*, *K76*, L90, *M69M*, *M69M*{DW}, N33

Kalamazoo: Medium-sized, roundish-oval fruit; skin thin, tough, greenish-yellow becoming yellow; flesh light yellow, stained with red near the pit, juicy, tender, sweet, mild in flavor, of high quality for either dessert or culinary purposes; stone free or nearly so; ripens late. Tree large, spreading, vigorous, very productive. Originated in Kalamazoo, Michigan about 1869. HEDRICK 1917; F91T{SC}

La Feliciana: Medium to large fruit, 2 1/2 to 2 3/4 inches in diameter; skin yellow, blushed with red; flesh yellow, juicy, sweet, of high quality; ripens in late June or early July. Good fresh or frozen. Tree highly productive; disease resistant. Chilling requirement 550 hours at or below 45^0 F. Excellent home garden cultivar for the lower South. A85M, *C54*, C75M, E99M, F19M, F61M, *K76*, *N20*, N33

La Premier: Fruit large, up to 2 3/4 inches in diameter; round, with unequal halves; skin yellow, highly blushed with red, very attractive; flesh clear yellow, firm, fine-grained, quality very good; cans and freezes very well; ripens about 12 days before Elberta. Tree vigorous; very productive; resistant to bacteriosis and brown rot. Originated in Calhoun, Louisiana. BROOKS 1972; C75M, E99M, F61M

Late Alamar: Fruit large, up to 3 1/2 inches in diameter; skin yellow, highly blushed with red, attractive; flesh yellow, very firm, of very good flavor; ripens in mid-September. Very good for dessert, canning or freezing. Requires a long growing season. E4

Late Crawford: Medium to large fruit; roundish-oval, with unequal halves; skin deep yellow, blushed and splashed with light and dark red; flesh yellow, red at the pit, juicy, firm but tender, sweet but sprightly, richly flavored, quality excellent; ripens late. Tree large, vigorous; not very productive; comes into bearing late. Originated in Middletown, New Jersey by William Crawford, early in the 19th century. HEDRICK 1917; L12

Loring: Fruit large; round to ovate; skin yellow, highly blushed with red, very attractive; flesh yellow, red at pit, firm, melting, of medium texture, quality very good; ripens 10 days before Elberta. Tree very vigorous; productive; tolerant to bacteriosis. Originated in Mountain Grove, Missouri. Introduced in 1946. BROOKS 1972; A5, A82, B83, C37, C75M, *E45*, F53, F61M, F93, H49{DW}, L90, M76, N33

Lovell: Uniformly large, almost perfectly round fruit; skin yellow with a slight blush; flesh fine-grained, firm, solid, clear yellow to the pit; freestone. Superior for canning and shipping; also dries well. Tree high yielding, produces vigorous rootstocks for grafting. Originated in Winters, California by G.W. Thissell. Named in 1882. WICKSON; *G66*, H49, *K73M*, L1

Madison: Medium to large fruit; skin bright orange-yellow, blushed with bright red, very attractive; flesh orange-yellow, bright red next to pit, exceedingly firm, fine-textured, flavor mild and rich, quality very good; ripens 7 days before Elberta. Tree moderately vigorous; very tolerant to blossom-season frost; self-fruitful. Adapted to mountainous areas of Virginia. BROOKS 1972; A5, A39, A91, C75M, E99M, F53, G16{DW}, G23, G23{DW}, G41, I36, *K60*, L33, L33{DW}, M39M, M76, etc.

McKay: Medium to large fruit; skin yellow, blushed with deep dark-red, attractive; flesh yellow-orange, flavorful, of high quality, freestone; resembles Rochester; ripens in late August. Tree very cold-hardy. Originated in Waterloo, Wisconsin by the McKay Nursery Company. Introduced in 1945. BROOKS 1972; L12, N24M

Merrill Beauty: Large, round fruit; skin highly colored; flesh yellow, flavor very good, freestone; tends to ripen on one side; ripens 5 weeks before Elberta, 1 week before Redhaven; resembles J.H. Hale. Tree large, vigorous; a reliable and heavy bearer; self-fertile. Originated in Red Bluff, California by Grant Merrill. Introduced in 1947. BROOKS 1972; L12

Mid Pride:[1] Medium to large fruit; skin yellow, blushed with red; flesh yellow, firm, sweet, very flavorful, quality excellent; ripens in midseason. Good fresh or for canning. Tree very vigorous and productive; blooms early; low chilling requirement, less than 300 hours. Adapted to most mild-winter areas of California. Developed by Floyd Zaiger. *D23M*, I83M, L1, *N20*

Monroe: Fruit large, 2 1/2 to 3 inches in diameter; skin rich orange-yellow, with 60% bright medium-red blush, attractive; flesh orange-yellow, pinkish-red near the pit, firm, smooth, flavor mild, quality very good for its season; ripens about 11 days after Elberta. Tree very vigorous; moderately productive; self-fruitful. BROOKS 1972; B83, C75M, E29M, E32M, E99M, F61M, M76, N33

Muir: Large to very large fruit; flesh clear yellow, dense, rich and sweet; stone small, perfectly free. Good for canning and shipping; peculiarly adapted to drying because of exceptional sweetness and density of flesh. Once the standard dried peach of California. Tree vigorous and productive if grown on rich soil. Originated as a chance seedling on the place of John Muir, near Silveyville, California, about 1880. WICKSON; F91T{SC}, H26M{PR}, L97G{PR}

Norman: Round, medium to large fruit, skin medium yellow, prominently blushed with dark red; flesh deep yellow, slightly tinged with red, very firm, fine-textured, melting, flavor good when ripe; very resistant to browning; ripens 3 to 5 earlier than Ranger. Tree productive; moderately resistant to bacterial spot. BROOKS 1972; A5, C75M, E99M, F61M, K83M

O'Henry: Medium to large fruit, 2 1/2 to 3 inches in diameter; skin brightly colored, pubescence short; flesh yellow streaked with red, very firm, quality good, freestone; ships well; ripens about with Rio Oso Gem. Tree moderately vigorous; productive; flower pink, large, showy. Originated in Red Bluff, California. BROOKS 1972; *A9*, *B71M*, B83, *C54*, C75M, E4, F61M, *K73M*, L1, *L47*, *N20*

Parade: Fruit large, averaging 2 5/8 inches in diameter or more; skin bright yellow, blushed with red; flesh yellow, light red near pit, moderately juicy, firm, flavor mild, subacid, vinous, non-browning; quality good; mostly freestone; ripens very late, 30 days after J.H. Hale. Tree medium-sized, productive; self-fruitful. BROOKS 1972; *A9*, *B71M*, C75M, E99M, F61M, K83M

Peacot: Fruit of good size if thinned early; skin nearly glabrous; flesh yellow, very juicy, somewhat fibrous, rich in flavor; resembles a nectarine. Tree very productive, has a relatively low chilling requirement. Accidental cross of a seedling peach and an experimental nectarine, discovered at Armstrong Nurseries. **T49M{SC}**

Pekin: Medium-sized fruit; skin light yellow, 75 to 85% covered with a bright red blush, pubescence short; flesh yellow, melting, flavor pleasant, more resistant to browning than Redhaven; freestone when soft-ripe; ripens 2 to 3 days earlier than Redhaven. Tree vigorous and productive; self-fruitful; highly resistant to bacterial spot. BROOKS 1972; F91T{SC}

Phil Adrian: Small to medium-sized, roundish fruit; skin golden-yellow blushed with red; flesh juicy, melting, highly perfumed, with a distinctive, intense flavor reminiscent of that of St. John; resembles the Crawford group of peaches. Tree productive. Excellent for home gardens. At one time evaluated as a commercial drying peach. Originated with Phil Adrian, near Escalon, California. **T49M{SC}**

Pix Zee:[3] Fruit orange blushed with red, attractive; flesh firm, yellow, flavor very good, freestone when fully ripe; ripens very early, 3 weeks before Honey Babe. Tree a genetic dwarf, growing only 5 to 7 feet tall; self-fruitful. Needs approximately 500 hours of chilling. Ripens in short season areas where others fail. Originated in Modesto, California by Floyd Zaiger. A88M, E87, *I68*, *N20*

Ranger: Medium to large, nearly round fruit; skin greenish-yellow to yellow, mottled and striped with red; flesh yellow, red at pit, medium firm, melting, medium textured, flavor good; ripens 3 to 4 weeks before Elberta. Tree productive, moderately vigorous; self-fruitful; resistant to bacterial spot. BROOKS 1972; A88M, C37, *C54*, C75M, *E45*, E99M, F61M, F93, G13, *I68*, *L47*, L90, *M69M*, M83, M92, *N20*, N33, etc.

Redhaven: Medium-sized, round fruit; skin yellow, overlaid with red to deep red, attractive; flesh yellow, red at pit, very firm, melting, quality good; non-browning; pit large, usually free when ripe; ripens early, 30 days before Elberta. Tree vigorous; hardy; highly productive, nearly always requiring thinning; self-fruitful. Most widely planted cultivar in the United States. BROOKS 1972; B73M, B83, C63, C75M, F19M, G23, G23{DW}, *K73M*, L97, M39M, N33

Redskin: Medium to large, nearly round fruit; skin deep red over yellow, attractive; flesh yellow, red at pit, melting, of fine flavor, quality somewhat better than Elberta, non-browning; ripens with or slightly ahead of Elberta. Tree vigorous; very productive; self-fruitful; resistant to bacteriosis. BROOKS 1972; A5, A82, B83, C63, C75M, F19M, F93, *G28*, G41, G79M{DW}, M39M, N33

Reliance: Medium-sized, round fruit; skin yellow, splashed with dull red; flesh bright yellow, moderately firm, slightly stringy, of good flavor; ripens evenly, about with Golden Jubilee. Tree productive; extremely winter-hardy. Originated in Durham, New Hampshire by E.M. Meader. Introduced in 1964. BROOKS 1972; A88M, C63, C75M, D69, F19M, F53, G16{DW}, G23, G23{DW}, G41, G53M, H33, H42, H65, L30, M39M, N24M, etc.

Rio Oso Gem: Fruit large, averaging 2 3/4 to 3 3/4 inches in diameter; round to slightly elongated; skin bright red, very attractive; flesh yellow, firm, fine-grained, melting, of good quality; ripens 1 week after Elberta, about 2 weeks after J.H. Hale which it resembles. Tree productive; self-fruitful; susceptible to bacterial spot. BROOKS 1972; A5, *B71M*, B75, C75M, E4, E29M, *E45*, E99M, F61M, I99M{DW}, L1, *L47*, M39M, M76, M83, etc.

Rochester: Medium to large fruit; skin orange-yellow, blushed with deep dark-red; flesh yellow, stained with red near the pit, very juicy, tender and melting, sweet, highly flavored, very good in quality; matures in early midseason. Tree large, vigorous; productive.

Originated near Rochester, New York. Introduced in 1912. HEDRICK 1917; H65, P86

Salway: (Salwey) Large, roundish-oblate fruit; skin downy, creamy yellow blushed with crimson, attractive; flesh deep yellow, stained with red at the pit, juicy, vinous, rich and sweet; freestone; ripens very late. Of good dessert quality; excellent for canning, preserving and evaporating. Tree vigorous, hardy, very productive. Originated in England about 1844. HEDRICK 1917, WICKSON; F91T{SC}

Sam Houston: Medium to large fruit; skin red, attractive; flesh yellow, fine-grained, firm, low in acid, flavor mild; pit unusually small, freestone; ripens with Sunhigh. Tree productive, requires heavy thinning; susceptible to bacterial spot. Relatively low chilling requirement. Originated in College Station, Texas. BROOKS 1972; *A19*, A85M, C37, *C54*, C75M, *E45*, E99M, *G15M*{DW}, *K76*, L90, *M69M*, M83, N33

Slappey: Medium-sized, roundish to conic fruit; skin golden-yellow blushed with red and crimson, extremely thin, pubescence slight; flesh yellow, somewhat mealy, sweet, flavor distinctive, quality good; ripens just before Champion. Popular for home canning. Tree productive. Origin unknown. Introduced prior to 1903. HEDRICK 1917; B53, F91T{SC}, L12, M39M

Southern Flame:[3] Large, yellow fruit overspread with red; flesh yellow, firm, crisp, melting, aromatic; dessert quality very good; freestone; ripens in late July. Tree a genetic dwarf, growing only 5 feet high; blooms early. Requires approximately 400 hours of chilling. Recommended for coastal plantings and other low chill areas. *C54*, F11

Southern Rose:[1 3] Large, yellow fruit blushed with red; flesh yellow, firm, freestone; dessert quality good; ripens late, in early August. Compares favorably with commercial peaches. Tree a genetic dwarf, with mature height only 5 feet; blooms early. Relatively low chilling requirement, approximately 300 hours. *C54*, *D23M*, I83M

Southern Sweet:[3] Medium-sized fruit; skin yellow, slightly blushed with red, attractive; flesh yellow, flavorful; freestone; ripens early to mid-June. Tree genetically dwarf; mature height 4 to 5 feet; productive. Chilling requirement about 500 hours at or below 45^0 F. Originated in Le Grand, California by F.W. Anderson. Introduced in 1975. *C54*

Southland: Medium to large, round fruit; skin yellow, blushed and striped with red, attractive; flesh yellow, red near the pit, firm, melting, non-browning, quality very good to excellent; ripens 18 days before Elberta; resembles Halehaven. Tree vigorous; quite susceptible to bacteriosis; flower large, showy, self-fruitful. BROOKS 1972; C75M, E99M, F61M

St. John: Medium to large, round-oblate fruit; skin thick and tough, orange-yellow blushed with deep, dark red; flesh yellow, very juicy, tender, melting, sweet and rich, sprightly, very good in quality; ripens in early midseason. Tree medium to large, vigorous, upright-spreading, unproductive. Reproduces itself from seed. Originated in the South prior to 1869. HEDRICK 1917; F91T{SC}

Summergold: Medium to large, round fruit; skin yellow, 60% covered with a bright red blush, attractive; flesh yellow, firm but melting, of fine texture, flavor good; freestone; ripens with Loring. Excellent for processing. Tree moderately vigorous; somewhat resistant to bacterial spot; self-fertile. BROOKS 1972; C75M, E99M, F61M

Summerset: Large, round fruit; skin yellow, 25 to 30% blushed with bright red, attractive, pubescence light; flesh yellow, firm but melting, of good texture and flavor; quality high; freestone; ripens 5 to 6 weeks after Rio Oso Gem. Good for canning and freezing. Tree vigorous and productive. BROOKS 1972; *A9*, A88M, *B71M*, B93M, *C54*, L1, *L47*, *N20*

Suncrest: Large, round fruit; skin yellow, two-thirds covered with bright red, attractive; flesh yellow, firm but melting, texture and flavor very good; ripens about 10 before Elberta; suitable for distant shipping. Tree vigorous and productive; self-fruitful; susceptible to bacterial spot disease. Highly rated at fruit tastings. BROOKS 1972; A5, B53, *B71M*, B83, E4, E99M, F53, *G14*{DW}, *H34*, *I54*, *K73M*, M39M

Sunhigh: Fruit medium to large; oval to round, ribbed, apex pointed; skin very attractive, golden-yellow, blushed with bright red, pubescence very short and soft; flesh yellow, flecked with red, fine-textured, flavor very good to excellent, very resistant to browning; freestone when fully ripe; ripens 10 days before Redhaven. Tree vigorous and productive; self-fertile. BROOKS 1972; A5, B53, C75M, E99M, F53, F61M, J16, *K60*, K83M, L12, M76

Suwanee: Large, round fruit; skin yellow, about 80% covered with a red blush, attractive; flesh yellow, firm, melting, texture medium fine, flavor good; freestone; ripens with Golden Jubilee. Tree moderately vigorous; productive; self-fruitful. Chilling requirement 650 hours. Originated in Fort Valley, Georgia. BROOKS 1972; A85M, C75M, E29M, *E45*, E99M, F19M, F61M, F93, *G15M*, G17, *K76*, *K76*{DW}, M31M

Topaz: Large, round fruit; skin 100% red over a bright yellow background, attractive, pubescence light; flesh yellow, very firm, fine-textured, of high quality, non-browning; ripens 20 days before Elberta. Tree vigorous, upright; resistant to bacterial spot; tender to winter cold. Chilling requirement 850 hours at or below 45^0 F. C75M, E99M, F53, F61M, *K60*, *K73M*, K83M, M39M

Triogem: Fruit medium to large; round to oval; skin yellow, overlaid with dull red, attractive; flesh yellow, streaked with red, firm, melting, of high quality; stone large, free; ripens slowly and early, 19 days before Elberta; ships well. Tree vigorous, upright; self-fruitful; sets good crops, requires thinning. BROOKS 1972; A5, A69G{SC}, B53, K83M

Valigold:[1] Very large fruit; skin yellow blushed with red; flesh golden-yellow, firm, subacid, flavor very good; freestone; ripens with July Elberta; resembles July Elberta, but skin more highly colored. Tree vigorous; very productive; bears regularly. Low chilling requirement. Originated in Ontario, California by Herbert C. Swim, Armstrong Nurseries. BROOKS 1972; *A19*

Ventura:[1] Small, oblate fruit; skin yellow, blushed with wine-red, attractive; flesh yellow, firmer than Babcock, subacid, quality fairly good, freestone; ripens midseason, or in early July in southern California. Tree vigorous, upright; productive. Low chilling requirement, less than Babcock. BROOKS 1972; B93M, *C54*, *F53M*, *I68*, *L47*

Veteran: Medium to large, round-oblate fruit; skin yellow splashed with red, attractive; flesh yellow, melting, soft, quality good, low in tannin; semi-freestone to freestone; matures 8 to 10 days before Elberta. Tree vigorous; highly productive; self-fruitful. Originated in Vineland Station, Ontario, Canada. Introduced in 1928. BROOKS 1972; A69G{SC}, B67, B83, F11, *G14*, *G14*{DW}, *H34*, I49M, L99M, M39M, N33

Washington: Fruit large; skin an attractive red; flesh yellow, firm, quality above average; freestone; ripens about 3 weeks before Elberta; superior to Elberta for canning and freezing; resembles Sunhigh. Tree vigorous and productive; somewhat resistant to bacteriosis; flowers showy. Originated in Blacksburg, Virginia. BROOKS 1972; E99M, J33, *K60*, K83M, M76

HONEY PEACHES

A unique class of peaches from southern China with oval, long-pointed, white-fleshed fruit. Regarded by many as the finest flavored of all peaches, they have a very sweet honey-like flavor offset by a hint of bitter almond. The fruit has a tendency to drop prematurely. Relatively low chilling requirements.

Eagle Beak: Small, oblong fruit with a pronounced beak; skin greenish-white blushed with carmine; flesh greenish-white, very juicy, low in acid, exceedingly sweet with a slight bitter almond-like flavor; freestone; ripens the last of July in Zone 7. Tree an annual and heavy bearer. **T49M{SC}, U8{SC}**

Luttichau: Medium-sized, oval fruit; skin white blushed with pink; flesh white, honey-sweet; ripens in mid-June. Tree blooms late, withstanding late frost damage without serious crop loss. Chilling requirement approximately 750 hours. Does well in mild areas. *A19*

Melba: (Improved Pallas) Large fruit; skin pale yellow, blushed with red; flesh white, juicy, honey-sweet; stone small, free; ripens over a long period, early June to mid-July. Tree bears regularly; stands low freezing weather during blooming season. Originated in San Antonio, Texas. Renamed Melba since parentage is unknown and Improved Pallas was misleading. BROOKS 1972; *A19, C54,* N33

Pallas: Small to medium-sized, oval fruit; skin thick and tough, pale white or greenish-white, occasionally blushed with bright red; flesh white, aromatic, very juicy, tender and melting, honey-sweet, rich in flavor, of excellent quality; freestone; ripens in early midseason. Tree medium in vigor, upright-spreading; a regular, heavy bearer. Chilling requirement approximately 750 hours. Originated in Augusta, Georgia in 1878. HEDRICK 1917; *A19*

PEANUT {S}

ARACHIS HYPOGAEA

Carwile's Virginia: 140 days. Pods contain 2 to 4 seeds per pod. Plants have average disease resistance but excellent resistance to drought. Best planted in hills, 3 seeds per hill, 8 to 10 inches apart in hills 2 to 3 feet apart. Family heirloom from southwest Virginia. Grown by Frank Carwile for over 75 years. L7M

Early Spanish: 105 days. Small, sweet kernels of fine quality and flavor. Small, solid, well-filled pods; 2 to 3 kernels per pod. Upright, compact, heavy yielding plants. Easy to grow and very early maturing. Can be grown reliably as far north as Canada. B73M, C81M, D65, E97, G16, H42, L42

Florigiant: 130 days. High-yielding runner type developed in Florida. Medium to large kernels; light red skins. Matures early to mid-season. Very susceptible to leafspot disease; has some resistance to pod breakdown. Plant only on light to medium soils, as heavy soil sticks to pods. Especially recommended for the lower South. F19M, L9M

Florunner: 135 days. Leading commercial runner type, popular in the extreme Southeast. Selected for high percentage of sound mature seed, flavor, quality and yield. Prostrate growth habit with the sequential branching pattern typical of runner and Virginia types. Sixty percent of runner type peanuts are used for peanut butter, and runners account for 72% of the total U.S. production. Released by the Florida Agricultural Experiment Station in 1969. G27M, L89G

Garoy: A cultivar developed in Canada, Garoy is 7 to 10 days earlier than older types and is also much more productive. Each pod contains 3 good-sized kernels. G64, J7

Improved Spanish: 115 days. Early bearing bunch type. The earliest maturing cultivar that produces large kernels. Red-skinned kernels, 1 or 2 per pod. Superior in sweetness and flavor, and also heavier yielding than regular Spanish. For highest yields plant 6 inches apart in 18 inch wide rows. C92, L14

Improved Virginia: 120 days. A productive, large-podded Virginia type. Large, rich-flavored kernels; 1 to 2 kernels per pod. Bush type plant; grows only 18 inches tall which makes cultivation and harvesting easier. Hardy; does well in the North. D76

Jumbo: (Mammoth Jumbo) 125 days. Extra-large, sweet kernels; 2 to 3 kernels per pod; shells easily. Heavy yielding and early maturing. With ordinary growing conditions will produce a crop as far north as Wisconsin. Easy to grow and harvest. G71, H33, J34

Langley: 120 days. Runner type, released by the Texas Agricultural Station in 1986. Selected for its early maturity and high yield potential. In comparison with the commercial standard Florunner, Langley matures about 2 weeks earlier; yields are comparable; seedling vigor is much better, and shelling and processing qualities are equivalent. L89G

Spanish: 110 days. Small, sweet, reddish-brown kernel; 2 to 3 kernels per well-filled pod. Compact, upright growth habit. Rapid-growing and heavy bearing; will produce nuts in northern areas if grown in light, sandy soil with a southern exposure. Spanish type peanuts are used for peanut candies, peanut butter and peanut oil, account for 11% of total U.S. production, and are primarily grown in Oklahoma and Texas. B75, D76, F19M, H49, I77, I91, K71, L9M

Starr: (Starr Spanish) 110-115 days. Pods and seeds are larger than those of the small Spanish types. Pods are thick and therefore percentage of kernels is generally low. Shelling tests have shown that Starr generally yields fewer split kernels than other commercial cultivars. Spanish type developed at the West Cross Timbers Experiment Station, Stephensville, Texas. Introduced in 1961. J34, L89G

Tennessee Red: (Tennessee Red Valencia) 120 days. Small, red-skinned kernels; 3 to 4 kernels per pod; flavor very sweet and mild. Upright plant, to 2 feet high; produces high yielding, easily harvested underground clusters. Will grow as far north as New York if planted by the end of May. A56, C92, I91, J73, L14

Valencia: (Valencia Early Spanish) 115 days. Small, high-quality kernels; very rich and sweet; 3 or more kernels per well-filled pod. Large, productive plants; adapted to a wide range of soils. Valencia type peanuts are in demand for roasting in the shell, account for only 1% of the total U.S. production, and are grown primarily in New Mexico. B13, D11M, D27, F19M, G27M, I67M, L9M, M13M

Virginia: (Virginia Bunch, Early Bunch) 120 days. Large, tan-skinned kernels of high quality; 1 to 2 kernels per pod; matures about a week earlier than Virginia Jumbo. Upright growth habit. Commercially, Virginia type peanuts account for most of the roasted, salted, and inshell or "ball park" peanuts, about 16% of the total U.S. production, and are grown mostly in Virginia and the Carolinas. E97

Virginia Jumbo: (Mammoth Virginia) 120 days. A special, select strain of the Virginia type. Extra large, rich-flavored kernels; 1 or 2 kernels per pod; produces fewer imperfect pods than most other cultivars. Runner type; vines grow 18 inches tall with a spread of 3 1/2 feet. Dependable and productive; well adapted to the North. *B1*, B75, G57M, G79, G93M, I64, I91, J58, K71

PEAR {GR}

PYRUS COMMUNIS
PYRUS USSURIENSIS
PYRUS X LECONTEI

EUROPEAN PEARS

COOKING While most dessert pears can be used for culinary purposes, they need to be picked before they are fully ripe and cooked very slowly in syrup. True culinary pears are hardy and prolific and the fruits possess long-keeping qualities. They are not acid but are hard and generally lacking in flavor and juice.

Green/Yellow-Skinned

Belle Angevine: (Pound, Uvedale's St. Germain) Large to very large, handsomely-shaped fruit, often 3 pounds in weight; skin brilliant in color, very attractive; ripens very late. Dessert quality poor, only fair for cooking. Originated prior to 1867. HEDRICK 1921; L12, M22

Bellisime d'Hiver: Large, oval fruit; skin pale yellow with red flush and conspicuous dots; flesh white and soft; keeps well from November to April. One of the best cooking pears; considered superior to Catillac although it does not turn the same dark red when stewed. A French pear of unknown parentage, known since the 17th century. SIMMONS 1978; Y83{SC}

Catillac: Very large, roundish fruit; skin dull green to yellow, blushed with brownish-red; flesh hard, rough, white, turning deep-red when cooked; ripens very late; will keep until spring. Usually considered to be the best culinary pear. Tree spreading, vigorous; productive; very hardy. A very old French pear, first described in 1665. HEDRICK 1921, SIMMONS 1978; N24M, P1, Q30{SC}

Vicar of Winkfield: (Viker) Fruit very large; oblong-pyriform, with a long, tapering neck; skin pale green, shading to pale yellow; flesh pale yellow, firm, dry, more or less astringent, with a sprightly muskiness; quality inferior for dessert, but excellent for all culinary purposes; ripens very late; keeps well. Tree large, vigorous, very productive. Discovered in France in 1760. HEDRICK 1921, SIMMONS 1978; E84, L12

Red-Skinned

Belle Picarde: Large to very large fruit; skin orange-red, often speckled on the side exposed to the sun; flesh white, melting, very sugary; juice rather abundant, sweet and of a pleasant flavor; ripens very late, and must be carefully ripened off the tree. Good for dessert, but highly recommended for cooking, turning a light pink color. Originated in the village of Charmes, Aisne, France in the middle of the 19th century. HEDRICK 1921; L12

DESSERT

Green/Yellow-Skinned

Abbé Fétel: (Abate) Fruit large to very large, more or less elongated; skin rather thin, pale yellowish-green, bright red on the side exposed to the sun; flesh whitish, melting, very juicy, sugary, aromatic, of excellent quality; ripens late. Originated in France prior to 1889. HEDRICK 1921; L12, O71M

Amiré Joannet: Small, pyriform, slightly obtuse fruit; skin smooth, pale greenish-yellow turning a deep waxen-yellow, washed with pale rose; flesh white, tender, juicy, sugary, perfumed with musk, very agreeable. In some parts of France it ripens about St. John's Day, the 24th of June, hence the name. An ancient pear first recorded in 1660. HEDRICK 1921; L1

Atlantic Queen: Very large fruit, up to 1 1/2 pounds; skin yellow-green; flesh fine-grained, melting, very juicy, sweet, very aromatic; ripens in September. Tree highly prolific; resistant to fireblight; grows well under adverse conditions, including poor soils and close proximity to the seashore. G79M, G79M{DW}, J93{SC}

Aurora: Large, pyriform fruit; skin bright yellow, slightly russet, very attractive; flesh melting, smooth, juicy, sweet, aromatic, of high dessert quality; ripens with or just after Bartlett; keeps well in cold storage until December. Very well suited for the home garden and fresh fruit market. Tree vigorous, spreading; productive. BROOKS 1972; A69G{SC}, I36, J93{SC}, L12, N24M

Bartlett: (Williams' Bon Chrétien) Medium to large fruit; skin pale green, turning to golden-yellow; flesh white, fine-grained, juicy, sweet, slightly subacid with a strong musky flavor; ripens early; keeps for only 2 to 3 weeks in natural storage. Tree moderately vigorous, spreading; very productive. Leading cultivar in the United States. Originated in England about 1770. HEDRICK 1921, SIMMONS 1978; B83, B93M, C63, C75M, E4, G16, G16{DW}, G23, G23{DW}, J69{DW}, J83, L30, L97G{PR}, M31T{ES}, M39M, M39M{DW}, etc.

Beierschmitt: Medium to large, oval-pyriform fruit; skin thin and tender, greenish-yellow to clear pale yellow when ripened, with slight russet; flesh firm, tender, free of stone cells, very juicy, highly aromatic, non-browning when cut; quality excellent; matures in midseason, and ripens well on the tree. Tree somewhat resistant to fireblight. Originated in Fairbanks, Iowa. Introduced in 1927. BROOKS 1972; E84, J93{SC}, N24M

Belle Lucrative: (Fondante d'Automne) Medium-sized, round-conical fruit; skin dull greenish-yellow; flesh tinged with yellow, firm, fine-grained, crisp, buttery, juicy, sweet, quality very good; ripens in midseason. Should be picked when still green; will ripen in 7 to 14 days. Tree vigorous; hardy; productive. Originated in Belgium about 1827. HEDRICK 1921; G79M{DW}, L12

Bergamotte d'Esperen: Medium-sized, round to conical fruit; skin greenish-yellow with dark russet patches; flesh pale yellow, very smooth, of soft texture, pleasantly aromatic, quality excellent; ready for use during December, keeps well until March. Tree upright-spreading, bears well in the right climate, self-fertile. Not suitable for wet or cold areas. Originated in Belgium about 1830. SIMMONS 1978; M31T{ES}, Q30{SC}

Bergamotte d'Pentacote: (Easter Beurré) Medium-sized, pyriform fruit; skin thick and tough, yellow often with a dull brownish-red blush; flesh tinged with yellow, very aromatic, melting, juicy, sweet, with a rich pleasant flavor; quality very good; in season late December to February. Tree medium in size, vigorous, upright-spreading. Grows well only in comparatively warm climates and on light, warm, limy soils. Originated at Louvain, Belgium, about 1823. HEDRICK 1921; U7M{SC}

Beurré Clairgeau: Large, roundish-pyriform fruit; skin yellow, blushed with bright red; flesh white, quite granular, tender and melting, very juicy, sweet, aromatic, with a rich, vinous flavor; quality good; ripens late. Tree vigorous, unusually upright; hardy; reliably productive. Originated in Nantes, France, about 1830. HEDRICK 1921; E84, G79M{DW}, M22, N24M

Beurré Diel: Large, oval-pyriform fruit; skin lemon-yellow, with a faint pinkish-red blush, russet; flesh yellowish-white, firm, melting, very juicy, sweet, rich and aromatic; quality very good; ripens late. Tree spreading, vigorous; hardy; productive. Discovered near Brussels, Belgium in 1805. HEDRICK 1921, SIMMONS 1978; U7M{SC}

Beurré Giffard: Medium-sized fruit; skin dull greenish-yellow, blushed with pinkish-red; flesh tinged with yellow, granular at the center, melting, very juicy, vinous, highly aromatic; quality very good; ripens early. Tree spreading, vigorous; hardy; productive. Discovered in France in 1825. HEDRICK 1921; G41, L1, L12, N24M

Beurré Hardy: (Hardy) Fruit large, obtuse-pyriform, with a rather long neck; skin dull greenish-yellow, with heavy bronze russet; flesh granular, melting, buttery, very juicy, sweet, richly aromatic and somewhat vinous; quality very good to excellent; ripens in midseason. Tree upright, very vigorous. Originated in France, about 1820. HEDRICK 1921; A69G{SC}, J93{SC}, L1, M22, N24M

Beurré Superfin: Medium-sized, round to conical fruit; skin yellow, netted and streaked with light russet; flesh pale yellow, granular, melting, buttery, very juicy, sweet yet with a rich, brisk, vinous flavor, aromatic; quality very good; ripens in October. Tree moderately vigorous and productive. Originated in Angers, France from seed planted in 1837. HEDRICK 1921; J93{SC}, L12

Bosc: (Beurré Bosc) Fruit large; very long, with a tapering neck; skin dark yellow, russet; flesh yellowish-white, tender, juicy, sweet, with a rich, aromatic flavor; quality very good to excellent; ripens late. Tree large, upright; vigorous; very susceptible to fireblight. Originated in Belgium from seed planted in 1807. HEDRICK 1921; A5, B83, C63, E4, E84, G23, G79M{DW}, H65, *K73M*, L1, L97, L99M, M39M

Butirra Precoce Morettini: (Early Morettini) Medium to large fruit; skin greenish-yellow blushed with red, smooth; flesh white, juicy, flavor excellent; ripens 2 to 3 weeks before Bartlett; drops readily as it approaches maturity. Tree very vigorous; self-compatible; susceptible to fireblight. Originated in Firenze, Italy by Alessandro Morettini. J61M, L12, N24M

Chapin: Small to medium-sized, round-oval fruit; skin greenish-yellow, with considerable russet; flesh juicy, melting, richly aromatic, very sweet, of high quality; ripens with Clapp's Favorite; resembles Seckel, but larger. Tree vase-shaped, moderately vigorous; productive. Originated in Geneva, New York by U.P. Hedrick. Introduced in 1945. BROOKS 1972; L12, M22

Clapp's Favorite: Medium to large fruit; skin pale lemon-yellow, mottled with bright red; flesh tinged with yellow, granular at the center, very juicy, melting, sweet, rich; quality very good; ripens in August and September. Tree large, upright; very productive. Originated in Dorchester, Massachusetts by Thaddeus Clapp, prior to 1860. HEDRICK 1921; A5, C63, D69, G16, G16{DW}, G23, G23{DW}, G41, H65, I76M{PR}, J16, J69{DW}, L97, *M69M*

Colette: Medium to large fruit; skin golden-yellow, blushed with pink; flesh firm, melting, juicy, aromatic, sweet, of fine flavor; ripens in August and September, and over a long period of time; resembles Bartlett. Tree spreading; hardy; blooms over a long period of time. Originated in Freeport, Illinois. Introduced in 1953. BROOKS 1972; D76, H65, J67{SC}, J93{SC}, N24M

Comice: (Doyenné du Comice) Fruit large; oval-pyriform, with unequal sides; skin greenish-yellow, blushed with red, russet; flesh tinged strongly with yellow, melting, tender, buttery, very juicy, sweet and vinous, aromatic; quality excellent; ripens late. Tree upright, vigorous; usually productive. Widely used for gift packs. Originated in Angers, France in 1849. HEDRICK 1921; B83, B93M, E4, E84, H69{PR}, J21M{PR}, J61M, *K73M*, L1, L33{DW}, *L47*, L97, L99M, M31T{ES}, M39M, etc.

Conference: Medium to large fruit; calabash-shaped; skin greenish-yellow, with some golden-brown russet; flesh creamy white with a slight salmon-pink tinge, melting, very juicy, sweet, flavor pleasant; ripens in October and November. Tree moderately vigorous; very productive. Leading commercial cultivar in England. Originated there in 1894. HEDRICK 1921, SIMMONS 1978; A69G{SC}, L1, M22, N24M, O71M, P86

D'Anjou: (Beurré D'Anjou) Fruit large, elongated-oval; skin light green at harvest, cream to green after ripening; flesh yellowish-white, firm, but slightly granular, tender, very juicy, with a rich, aromatic flavor; ripens late. Tree large, vigorous; slow to come into bearing. Standard market cultivar for fall and winter. An old French pear of unknown origin. HEDRICK 1921; A5, B83, *D35M*{ES}, E4, F11, G41, H65, *K73M*, L30, *L47*, L97, L99M, M31T{ES}, M39M, M39M{DW}, etc.

Dana Hovey: Small to medium-sized fruit; skin golden-yellow, covered with a thin russet; flesh tinged with yellow, melting, juicy, sweet, highly perfumed, of excellent quality; ripens late. Tree large, upright-spreading; vigorous; productive. Originated in Roxbury, Massachusetts by Francis Dana. Introduced about 1854. HEDRICK 1921; L1, L12

David: (P. ussuriensis x) Medium-sized fruit; 2 3/4 inches long, 2 1/4 inches in diameter under non-irrigated field conditions; skin thin; flesh quality good, not breaking down quickly. Tree extremely hardy. Originated in Saskatoon, Saskatchewan, Canada by C.F. Patterson. Introduced in 1960 for home gardens. K64, L70 M35M, N24M

Des Urbanistes: (Urbaniste) Fruit medium-sized, roundish-pyriform; skin pale yellow, often with a faint russet-red blush; flesh tinged with yellow, granular especially around the core, tender and melting, buttery, juicy, sweet, pleasantly aromatic; quality very good; ripens late. Tree vigorous; productive with age. Originated in the gardens of the religious order of Urbanistes, Mechlin, Belgium about 1783. HEDRICK 1921; L12

Docteur Jules Guyot: (Jules Guyot) Medium to medium small fruit, oval-pyriform in shape; skin somewhat rough, pale yellow with a faint blush and russet dots or patches; flesh white, fine-grained, flavor fair, slightly musky; ripens just before Bartlett, which it resembles. Tree upright, becoming slightly spreading; very productive but tends to be biennial. Originated in France in 1870. SIMMONS 1978; L1

Doyenné d'Eté: (Doyenné de Juillet) Small, conical fruit, 1 1/2 inches long; skin pale yellow, blushed with brownish-red, thin and smooth; flesh white, fine-grained, sweet, very juicy; flavor very good for an early pear; ripens in late July and early August. Tree small, weak growing; a heavy and regular bearer. Good pollinators are Conference, Beurré Hardy and Bartlett. First raised about 1700 by Capuchin monks, at Mons, Belgium. SIMMONS 1978; J61M, N24M

Doyenné Gris: Medium to large, globular fruit; skin yellow-ocher, nearly covered with cinnamon-colored russet, smooth, unblemished; flesh white, tender, melting, very buttery, rich and delicious; of excellent quality; ripens in October. Originated in the garden of the Chartreaux Monastery at Paris around 1750. HEDRICK 1921; L12

Duchesse d'Angoulême: Large to very large fruit; skin dull yellow, russet; flesh white, firm becoming somewhat melting and quite tender when fully mature, juicy, sweet, richly flavored; quality good to very good; ripens late. Tree upright, vigorous; hardy; productive. Originated near Angers, France, early in the 19th century. HEDRICK 1921; G79M{DW}, L1

Dumont: Medium to large, obtuse pyriform fruit; skin attractive yellow, slightly blushed; flesh firm, juicy, flavor rich and sweet; quality very good; ripens late, stores until the end of December. Tree productive; tends toward alternate bearing when older; moderately susceptible to fire blight. An old European cultivar that has not been widely tested in America. I36

Flemish Beauty: Large, roundish fruit; skin clear yellow, blushed with red; flesh yellowish-white, firm, becoming melting and tender, juicy, sweet, aromatic, with a slightly musky flavor; quality very good; ripens in midseason. Tree spreading, vigorous; hardy; productive. Originated near Alost, East Flanders, Belgium, about the beginning of the 19th century. HEDRICK 1921; A33, A91, B67{DW}, C58, *G14*{DW}, G41, *G66*, G69M, H49, J7, L1, L12, L27M, M22, M31T{ES}, M39M, N24M, etc.

Forelle: (Trout Pear) Small to medium, shortened pyriform fruit; skin greenish-yellow, with a brilliant red blush and many conspicuous dots; flesh white, fine-grained, with a delicate sweet flavor; ripens late, November to January. Tree vigorous, spreading; moderately productive. Commonly exported from Europe, and popular in specialty markets. Known since 1670. SIMMONS 1978; L1

Glou Morceau: Medium to large, oval-pyriform fruit; skin greenish-yellow, smooth; flesh white, very smooth in texture, with an excellent very sweet flavor. In season December to January, but ripens in succession over a long period, a number of pickings being recommended. Tree spreading, of moderate to vigorous growth, bears good crops regularly. Originated in the 18th century. SIMMONS 1978; F91T{SC}

Golden Spice: Fruit small; skin clear yellow, blushed with red; flesh light yellow, juicy, aromatic, flavor pleasant, tart, spicy; ripens in midseason; resembles Seckel in size, but not as sweet. Excellent for canning. Tree very hardy; productive; a good parent for further breeding. Originated in Excelsior, Minnesota. BROOKS 1972; C58, G1T, H85, J7, L27M, M22, N24M

Gorham: Fruit large; skin bright yellow, slightly russet; flesh juicy, melting, sweet and vinous, of excellent quality; ripens 10 days later than Bartlett, which it resembles; keeps 6 to 8 weeks longer than Bartlett. Tree upright, dense; vigorous and productive. Originated in Geneva, New York by Richard Wellington. Introduced in 1923. BROOKS 1972; B53, I36, L12, N24M

Harrow Delight: Medium-sized, pyriform fruit; skin yellow blushed with red, attractive; flesh very smooth, free of stone cells, juicy, flavor and quality very good; ripens 2 weeks before Bartlett. Tree hardy; very resistant to fireblight. Released by the Harrow Research Station, Harrow, Ontario, Canada. A39, A91, C27T{SC}, E84, F53, I36, J61M, J93, J93{SC}, L33, M22, N24M

Highland: Large, pyriform fruit; skin smooth, greenish-yellow covered with a thin russet; flesh melting, juicy, sweet, richly flavored; ripens late, keeps well in refrigerated storage until January. Develops better quality if stored about a month before ripening. Tree moderately vigorous; productive; as susceptible to fireblight as Bartlett. Bartlett x Comice. A69G{SC}, C34, I36, I49M, J61M, J93{SC}, L12, N24M

Jeanne d'Arc: Medium-sized, pyriform fruit; skin lemon-yellow when properly ripe, fairly smooth; flesh white, smooth although a little coarse around the core, very juicy, sweet sub-acid, flavor strong and slightly perfumed; should be picked as late as possible, keeps well in natural storage. Tree upright, rather weak, resistant to scab; a precocious and regular bearer. An old French pear. SIMMONS 1978; P59M

John: (P. ussuriensis x) Medium to large fruit; 3 inches long, 2 1/2 inches in diameter under non-irrigated field conditions; skin thin, yellowing well before flesh becomes soft; quality good; ripens in late September. Tree hardy. Originated in Saskatoon, Saskatchewan, Canada by C.F. Patterson. Introduced in 1960 for home gardens. BROOKS 1972; B47, G54, G69M, H85, J7, K64, M35M, N24M

Joséphine de Malines: Small to medium, short conical fruit; skin pale green shading to pale yellow; flesh pinkish at the center when fully mature, very smooth, sweet, perfumed; should be picked as late as possible, preferably the second half of November. At its best for eating during February. Tree moderately vigorous, somewhat weeping; bears heavy crops regularly. One of the best-keeping late pears for a small garden. SIMMONS 1978; M22

June Sugar: Fruit of excellent quality; ripens very early, the end of June in Georgia. Good to eat out of hand or for canning. Tree resistant to fire blight; blooms relatively late; somewhat slow to come into bearing. An heirloom cultivar from Georgia. E84, G65M

Luscious: Small to medium-sized fruit; skin bright yellow blushed with red; flesh firm, very juicy, sweet and flavorful, of very good quality; ripens in early midseason. Not recommended for canning. Tree vigorous; very hardy; productive; resistant, but not immune to fireblight; ornamental. Released by South Dakota State University. A91, B15M, D65, D69, F53, G16, G16{DW}, *G66*, G67, *G89M*, *H90*, J7, J32, J83{DW}, L27M, M35M, N24M, etc.

Madeleine: (Citron des Carmes) Small, roundish-pyriform fruit; skin thin, very tender, dull green, occasionally with a faint brownish blush; flesh slightly tinged yellow, granular at the center, tender and melting, very juicy, sweet, vinous; quality good to very good; ripens in early August. Tree large, vigorous, upright; tender to cold; productive but short-lived. Of ancient and somewhat uncertain origin. HEDRICK 1915; L12

Magness: Medium-sized, oval fruit; skin greenish-yellow, lightly covered with russet; flesh soft, very juicy, almost free of grit cells, sweet, highly perfumed; of very good quality; ripens a week later than Bartlett. Tree very vigorous and spreading; very resistant to fireblight. BROOKS 1972; A5, A39, A82, A91, C27T{SC}, E84, E99M, F43M, J93, J93{SC}, K83M, L1, L12, M22, M76, N24M, etc.

Marguérite Marillat: Fruit large, pyriform-turbinate; skin golden-yellow, blushed with brilliant red, slightly russet; flesh yellowish-white, semi-fine, extremely juicy, aromatic, slightly musky, very rich; ripens in September. Tree very upright, highly productive. Originated near Lyons, France in 1874. HEDRICK 1921, SIMMONS 1978; G79M{DW}, M22

Mericourt: Fruit medium-sized; short-pyriform; skin greenish-yellow, occasionally blushed with dark red; flesh creamy white, buttery, nearly free of stone cells, very juicy; flavor sweet, sprightly subacid; quality excellent; ripens in early midseason. Tree vigorous; hardy; tolerant to fireblight and leaf spot. BROOKS 1972; J93{SC}, L12

Merton Pride: Large, conical to pyriform fruit; skin golden yellow, almost covered with brown russet; flesh creamy, fine-grained, flavor excellent; ripens during the second half of September. Tree moderately vigorous; not very productive; requires two other cultivars for good fruit set. SIMMONS 1978; N24M

Moonglow: Medium to large fruit; skin yellow, blushed with red; flesh white, rather soft, moderately juicy, nearly free of grit cells, flavor mild, subacid; quality good; ripens about 7 days earlier than Bartlett. Tree very upright; vigorous; fruits heavily at an early age; very resistant to fireblight. BROOKS 1972; A82, A82{DW}, A88M, C63, C75M, D69, F19M, F93, G8, *G28*, H65, L33, L90, M22, N33, etc.

Olia: (P. ussuriensis x) Fruit medium to large; pyriform to oval; skin light green to creamy green, with a faint blush; flesh white to creamy, moderately sweet and aromatic, quality low; ripens in midseason. Tree vigorous; productive; very hardy; resistant to fireblight. Originated in Habarovsk, Maritime Province, U.S.S.R. BROOKS 1972; B47, N24M

Olivier de Serres: Medium-sized, round fruit; skin deep olive with patches of fawn, rough; flesh white, fairly smooth, sweet and juicy, flavor good, musky; in season February to April. Tree small, rather weak growing, an irregular bearer. Does best in the long summers of southern France and Italy. First fruited in 1861. SIMMONS 1978; Y83{SC}

Orcas: Fruit large; skin yellow, blushed with carmine, very attractive; flavorful; good for canning, drying or eating fresh; ripens in midseason. Tree vigorous, spreading, open; a consistently heavy producer; resistant to scab. A regional favorite; discovered by Joe Long on Orcas Island, Washington. C34, I49M, J61M

Packham's Triumph:[2] Medium to large, conical-pyriform fruit; skin thin, lemon-yellow when ripe, russet, sometimes with an orange blush; flesh fine-grained, very juicy, melting, flavor particularly rich and pleasing; ripens about 30 days after Bartlett. Tree upright, moderately vigorous; reliably productive. Chilling requirement relatively low, 250 to 500 hours. Originated in Molong, New South Wales, Australia. Introduced at the turn of the century. BROOKS 1972, RUCK; A69G{SC}, J93{SC}, L1, M22, P86

Parker: Fruit medium to large; pyriform, rounded; skin yellow, blushed with red; flesh whitish, juicy, sweet, of pleasant flavor; quality good; ripens in late September. Tree upright, vigorous; fairly hardy; susceptible to fireblight. Originated in Excelsior, Minnesota. Introduced in 1934. BROOKS 1972; *A74*, D65, *G66*, *H90*{DW}, J32, L70

Passe Crassane: Large, round-oval fruit; skin dull pale green, somewhat russet, yellow on the exposed side; flesh white, smooth, very juicy, aromatic, sweet, agreeably sprightly; quality very good; ripens in winter. Very popular in specialty stores. Tree compact and bushy; moderately vigorous and productive. Originated in Rouen, France, in 1855. HEDRICK 1921, SIMMONS 1978; L12, O71M

Patten: Medium to large fruit; skin yellow; flesh tender and juicy, of excellent quality fresh, fair when canned. Should be picked 7 to 10 before its ripening season on the tree, and allowed to ripen normally. Tree among the hardiest of large-fruited cultivars; moderately resistant to blight. Good for home orchards and local markets. Introduced in 1922. BROOKS 1972; *A74*, C58, D65, *G66*, G67, L27M, L70

Précoce de Trévoux: Fruit medium-sized, pyriform-truncate; skin fine and tender, vivid yellow, very finely dotted with green and washed and streaked with carmine on the exposed side; flesh white, fine, melting, juicy, aromatic, sweet and rich; quality good to very good; ripens in August. Originated in France about 1862. HEDRICK 1921; U7M{SC}

Rescue: Large to very large, elongated-pyriform fruit; skin yellow, striped and blushed with bright orange and red, very attractive; flesh juicy, smooth, buttery, mild and sweet, of excellent quality; ripens slightly later than Aurora. Good for canning due to its small core. Tree upright, vigorous. Discovered in Canada by Knox Nomura of Sumner, Washington. J61M, L12

Rotkottig Frau Ostergotland:[1] Small, pyriform fruit with red-streaked flesh of fair quality. Grown mostly as a novelty but may have potential in breeding a red-fleshed pear of good quality. Introduced into the United States form Sweden in 1964. U7M{SC}

Rousselet de Rheims: Small to medium-sized, oval-turbinate fruit; skin greenish-yellow, blushed with reddish-brown; flesh white, fine or semi-fine, almost melting, not very juicy, highly perfumed, rich in sugar; flavor spicy or musky, causing it to be called Spice or Musk pear in colonial America; ripens in September. Very good for candying. Of very ancient, unknown origin, a favorite of Louis XIV of France. HEDRICK 1921; L12

Sanguinole:[1] Small to below medium, variably shaped fruit; skin rather thick and tough, green dotted with gray and red, russet, sometimes blushed with carmine on the exposed side; flesh transparent, red, juicy, sweet, acidulous, more or less musky, agreeable; ripens in August and September, decomposes rapidly. Known in Germany in 1500. HEDRICK 1921; U7M{SC}

Santa Claus: (Fin du Dixneuvième Siècle) Very large, round-conical fruit; skin dull brown-red, practically covered with russet; flesh creamy white, melting, flavor excellent; ripens during Christmas and New Year. Tree upright, vigorous; moderately productive. Originated in France. HEDRICK 1921, SIMMONS 1978; L12

Seckel: Small, round-oval fruit; skin yellowish-brown, marked with russet-red; flesh white, melting, buttery, very juicy, sweet, with a very rich, aromatic, spicy flavor; quality very good to excellent; ripens in October. Tree upright; hardy; productive. Originated near Philadelphia, Pennsylvania by Dutch Jacob, early in the 19th century. HEDRICK 1921; A5, B83, B93M, D69, E84, F19M, G23, G23{DW}, G79M{DW}, H65, J16, J69{DW}, L1, L99M, M39M, etc.

Sheldon: Medium to large fruit; uniform and symmetrical; skin dull greenish-yellow, with a brownish-red blush; flesh whitish, somewhat granular, tender and melting, very juicy, sweet and vinous; quality very good to excellent. ripens in October. Tree large, vigorous; hardy; moderately productive. Originated in Huron, New York, about 1815. HEDRICK 1921; G79M{DW}, J93{SC}, L12, N24M

Sierra: Large, long-pyriform fruit; skin yellowish green when ripe, thin, very tender; flesh very fine and smooth, juicy, very sweet, quality excellent; ripens with Anjou, keeps until February at 31^{0} F. Tree large, vigorous, spreading; hardier than Bartlett. Recommended for home gardens or commercial plantings. Originated in Summerland, British Columbia. BROOKS 1972; A69G{SC}, N24M

Stacey: Fruit small but very sweet; ripens in early September. Tree vigorous; very hardy. Discovered near Staceyville, Maine by Clarke Nattress. Original tree is 108 inches in circumference 4 feet above the ground; at least 250 years old. L27M

Sucrée de Montluçon: Fruit medium-sized, oval-conic, uneven; skin lemon-yellow; flesh palest yellow, transparent, extremely juicy, buttery, lightly acidulous, aromatic, of excellent flavor; ripens in October. Fruit grows in clusters if not thinned. Discovered at Montluçon, France, about 1812, by M. Rochet. HEDRICK 1921; L12

Summercrisp: Medium-sized, pyriform fruit; skin green with prominent red lenticels and a red blush; flesh crisp and juicy with a sweet, mild flavor. Should be refrigerated immediately after harvest while the flesh is still firm. Should not be allowed to ripen on or off the tree as grit cells and browning of the flesh around the seeds then reduce quality. Not suitable for canning. Released by the University of Minnesota in 1986. *A74*, *G4*, *G66*, G67, L27M, L70

Swedish Red:[1] (Swedish Red-Flesh) Small, pear-shaped fruit; skin yellow when ripe; flesh pinkish-red at the core and a section between the skin and core, slightly dry, free of grittiness; flavor pleasant, perfumed; ripens in late July. Valued for the color of its flesh, earliness and hardiness. N24M

Triomphe de Vienne: Medium to large, oval-pyriform fruit; skin greenish-yellow, often blushed with red; flesh white, melting, juicy; flavor rich, sweet, spicy, very good; ripens in midseason. Tree vigorous; hardy; reliably productive. Originated in Vienne, France, in 1864. HEDRICK 1921, SIMMONS 1978; U7M{SC}

Tyson: (Summer Seckel) Medium-sized fruit; round-pyriform, with unequal sides; skin deep yellow, usually blushed; flesh tinged with yellow, tender and melting, very juicy, sweet, aromatic, quality very good; ripens early. Tree very large; vigorous; hardy; productive. Originated in Jenkintown, Pennsylvania about 1794. HEDRICK 1921; A91, D69, G65M, N24M

Ure: Small to medium-sized, oval-conical fruit; skin greenish-yellow; flesh sweet, very juicy, aromatic; of good quality; ripens in mid-September. Excellent for canning. Tree relatively small, finely branched; very hardy; ornamental. Released by the Morden Research Station, Morden, Manitoba, Canada. A33, A65, *A74*, B47, C58, F67, G1T, G54, G69M, H42, H85, K64, L70, L79, N24M, etc.

Verbeln Red:[1] Large, pyriform fruit; skin light green turning yellow when ripe, nearly translucent showing the pigmented flesh; flesh streaked with red; texture poor; quality fair. Ripens later than other red-fleshed pears. Local cultivar from Eastern Europe. U7M{SC}

Vermont Beauty: Medium-sized fruit; skin pale lemon-yellow, blushed with brilliant scarlet, fading at the sides into pinkish-red dots; flesh tinged with yellow, tender and melting, very juicy, with a rich, vinous flavor; quality very good; ripens a week later than Seckel. Tree vigorous and productive. Originated in Grande Isle, Vermont, in the late 19th century. HEDRICK 1921; J93{SC}, L12, N24M

Warren: Medium to large fruit; size and shape variable; skin dull green, with an occasional red blush, slightly russet; flesh melting, juicy, sweet, flavor and quality very good; stores very well. Tree very resistant to fire blight, even under conditions of extreme heat and humidity; widely adapted, hardy in Michigan. Discovered by T.O. Warren, Hattiesburg, Mississippi. A39, D37, F43M, G8, G92, J93, J93{SC}, K67

White Doyenné: Medium-sized fruit; skin pale yellow, with a bright-red blush on the exposed side; flesh yellowish-white, granular, melting when fully ripe, juicy, sweet, with a rich, aromatic flavor; quality very good; matures in early October. Tree large, upright; vigorous; hardy; very productive. Of ancient and unknown origin. HEDRICK 1921; L1

Winter Bartlett: Fruit large; skin yellow, splashed with russet and often blushed on the exposed cheek with bright red; flesh yellowish-white, fine-grained, tender, juicy, sweet, pleasant-flavored; quality good to very good; ripens very late. Excellent quality when canned. Tree large, vigorous; hardy; productive. Originated in Eugene, Oregon, prior to 1880. HEDRICK 1921; E84, *G14*{DW}, M31T{ES}

Winter Nélis: (Bon de Malines) Fruit small to medium-sized, round-conical; skin dull greenish-yellow, almost covered with thin dark-brown russet; flesh yellowish-white, smooth, very juicy, sweet, richly flavored, aromatic; quality very good; ripens very late; stores well. Tree spreading; hardy; productive. Originated by Jean Charles Nélis, Mechlin, Belgium, early in the 19th century. HEDRICK 1921; A88M, B93M, *C54*, *C54*{ES}, E84, G79M{DW}, L12, *L47*, L99M, M22, M31T{ES}, *N20*, N24M

Red-Skinned

Cascade: Large, obovate-pyriform fruit; skin 60 to 90% blushed with bright red, smooth, thin; flesh white, smooth-textured, very juicy, melting, sweet; quality excellent; harvested at the end of the Bartlett season, stores well. Tree vigorous, upright, a heavy and regular bearer. Red Bartlett x Comice. Developed at the Southern Oregon Experiment Station, Medford, Oregon. Introduced in 1987. L99M

Red Bartlett: (Max-Red Bartlett) Bud mutation of Bartlett. Skin dark cranberry red, changing to an attractive bright red after picking; flesh finer grained and higher in sugar than Bartlett; ripens with Bartlett. Shoots and leaves reddish. Produces some limbs that revert back to regular Bartlett; these must be pruned to maintain the red strain. BROOKS 1972; A5, B53, B67{DW}, B83, B93M{DW}, C89{PR}, *G14*{DW}, H33, *H34*, H65, *K73M*, K83M, L1, L30, N46, etc.

Red Clapp's Favorite: (Crimson Red, Kalle, Super Red) Medium to large fruit; round-bodied, with a short, slender neck; skin bright red; flesh white, medium-firm, fine-grained, flavor very good; ripens with Clapp's Favorite. Tree vigorous; precocious, very productive; susceptible to fireblight. Cross-pollinate with D'Anjou, Bartlett and Bosc. A69G{SC}, B83, C41M, *C54*, E4, F53, *H34*, *I68*, J93{SC}, *K73M*, M39M, N24M

Red Comice: Bud mutation of Comice discovered in Medford, Oregon. Skin an attractive red; flavor and texture similar to Comice. Tree similar to Comice, but not as vigorous; foliage tinged with red in the spring and autumn; ornamental. E4, J61M

Red D'Anjou: Bud mutation of D'Anjou. Skin deep red, turning brighter red after ripening; texture and flavor comparable to D'Anjou. Ripens in midseason; keeps well in storage. Tree similar to D'Anjou, but not as vigorous; bark and veins reddish. Produces some limbs that revert back to regular Bartlett; these must be pruned to maintain the red strain. B83, C41M, D76, E4, E97, F15{PR}, *H34*, H65, *K73M*, L99M, M39M, N46

Reimer Red: Medium-sized, short pyriform fruit, resembles Red Bartlett more than Comice; skin yellowish-green prominently blushed with red, more so on the side exposed to the sun; flesh aromatic, buttery, melting. Tree a shy bearer. Red Bartlett x Comice. Originated in Oregon. L1

Rogue Red: Fruit similar in shape to Comice; skin 60 to 80% covered with a red blush; flesh quality excellent; ripens in winter. Tree unusually upright, vigorous; moderately but reliably productive; moderately susceptible to fireblight. BROOKS 1972; A69G{SC}, J93{SC}, M22

Rosi Red: (Rosired Bartlett) Fruit large, obtuse-pyriform; skin thin, tender, maroon-red when mature, dots smaller than on Max-Red Bartlett; flesh white, juicy, fine-grained, melting, buttery; flavor very good, aromatic, mild; dessert and canning quality good. Tree vigorous, upright; hardy; bears regularly and heavily. BROOKS 1972; U7M{SC}

Sensation: (Red Sensation, Sensation Red Bartlett) Large, ovate-pyriform fruit; skin yellow, 80 to 95% covered with a dark red blush; flesh creamy white, melting, tender, moderately juicy, sweet, quality good; ripens in early midseason. Tree medium-sized, upright; somewhat less vigorous than Bartlett. Originated in Australia. BROOKS 1972; A88M, B83, C41M, *C54*, E4, F11, *G37*, *H34*, H49{DW}, *H90*{DW}, *K73M*, *L47*, L99M, M39M

Ubileen: Large, Bartlett-size, pyriform fruit; skin prominently blushed with attractive red; flesh sweet, buttery, flavor very good; ripens early. Best picked firm in early to mid July, as it ripens in 1 week or less. Appears to be very disease resistant. Originated in Bulgaria. I49M

SOUTHERN-CROSS PEARS

The fruit is crisp-fleshed like that of the Asian pear and is ready to eat when picked, requiring no further ripening and will remain edible for several days to several months. Some cultivars will improve in quality when stored in a cool, dark place. They can be stewed for pies, canning or eating as-is, and are also used for preserves, marmalade and relish. Southern style canned pears and pear preserves have a unique chewy, crunchy texture. Sometimes simply called hybrid pears, they are primarily grown in the southern United States. (P. x lecontei)

Ayres: Small to medium-sized fruit; skin golden-russet with an attractive rose tint; flesh juicy, sweet, nearly free of grit cells; good for eating fresh, average for canning; ripens in mid-August. Tree relatively resistant to fireblight. Requires 700 hours of chilling. Garber x D'Anjou. Originated in Knoxville, Tennessee. Introduced in 1954.

BROOKS 1972, MCEACHERN; A82, A88M, *B52*, C75M, E99M, F19M, J93{SC}, M31M, *N20*, N33

Baldwin:[2] Medium to large, oblong fruit; skin light green lightly overlaid with russet; flesh semi-firm, quality good fresh, excellent for canning; ripens in September and October. Tree blooms early; fairly resistant to fireblight; susceptible to early leafspot, resistant to late leafspot. Low chilling requirement. A85M, E29M, F19M, G17, I83M, *K76*, M31M, *M69M*

Douglas: Fruit large, obovate-pyriform; skin pale yellow, heavily russet; flesh tinged with yellow, firm but tender, granular, very juicy, sweet yet with an invigorating flavor; quality good; matures in October. Tree upright, moderately vigorous; very productive. Originated in Lawrence, Kansas about 1897. HEDRICK 1921; *A19*, *C54*, E97, *H8*, M83

Fan Stil:[2] Medium-sized fruit; skin yellow, blushed with red; flesh white, crisp, juicy; ripens in midseason. Tree upright, vigorous; resists fireblight and damage from extreme temperatures. Low chilling requirement. Originated in Texas. A88M, *C54*, I83M

Flordahome:[2] Large fruit; skin green, thin, tender; flesh white, juicy, melting, sweet, flavor mild; ripens mid to late July, stores well. Good fresh; excellent for canning, holding its snow white color for months. Very productive. Low chilling requirement, 150 hours or less. Released by the University of Florida. *C54*, E99M, G17, *I68*, I83M, *K76*, M31M, M31M{PR}

Garber: Large, roundish-oblong fruit; skin pale yellow, often blushed with brownish-red; flesh white, granular, crisp but tender, juicy, neither sweet nor sour, but with a peculiar, pleasant flavor; dessert quality fair, excellent for canning or preserves; ripens in September and October. Tree vigorous, upright-spreading; productive with age; moderately resistant to fireblight. Originated in Columbia, Pennsylvania, sometime prior to 1880. HEDRICK 1921, MCEACHERN; *A19*, C37, *C54*, L90, M83, N33

Hood:[2] Large, golden yellow fruit; flesh creamy white, crisp, juicy, sweet, very good for fresh eating; ripens late July to mid August. Tree vigorous; resistant to blight; an excellent pollinator for Flordahome. Low chilling requirement, 150 hours or less. A88M, *C54*, *E45*, G17, I83M, J93{SC}, *K76*, M31M, *M69M*

Kieffer: Medium to large fruit; skin yellow, blushed with dull red, russet; flesh yellowish-white, very granular and coarse, crisp, juicy, not sweet, often astringent; quality poor; ripens late. Excellent for cooking and canning. Tree upright, vigorous; resistant to fireblight; very widely adapted. Originated near Philadelphia, Pennsylvania, in 1863. HEDRICK 1921; A82, A82{DW}, *B52*, B73M, B73M{DW}, C63, C75M, D77M, F19M, F93, *G28*, I9M, *L47*, M31M{PR}, M83{DW}, N33, etc.

Le Conte:[2] Large, roundish-oval fruit; skin pale yellow, occasionally marked with russet; flesh white, firm but tender, juicy, sweet, strong-flavored; dessert quality good, excellent for preserves; ripens in September and October. Tree upright, vigorous; very productive; a regular bearer; somewhat susceptible to fireblight. Low chilling requirement, 100 to 250 hours. Originated about 1850. HEDRICK 1921, RUCK; *A19*, C37, *C54*, C75M, *E45*, *K76*, L90, M31M, M83, M83{DW}, N33

Maxine: (Starking Delicious, Century Yellow) Medium to large fruit; skin greenish-yellow, attractive; flesh white, medium-firm, moderately granular, subacid, juicy, strong-flavored; quality above average for a hybrid, good fresh, excellent canned; ripens late. Tree vigorous and productive, resistant to fireblight. A39, A91, C27T{SC}, C75M, *D35M*{DW}, D69, E97, G8, G65M{DW}, J93{SC}, L12, N24M, N33

Monterrey:[2] Fruit quite large, round to pyriform; skin yellow; flesh soft, smooth, nearly free of grit cells, quality very good for fresh market and canning; ripens in late August; stores well. Tree vigorous; very resistant to fireblight. Low chilling requirement, recommended for mild winter areas. Originated in Monterrey, Nuevo Leon, Mexico. Introduced in 1952 by Aldridge Nursery. BROOKS 1972; *A19*, A88M, *C54*, I83M, N24M

Orient: (The Orient) Large, nearly round fruit; skin yellow, russet; flesh firm, juicy, slightly sweet, lacking in flavor; good for canning; ripens in mid-August. Tree upright-spreading, vigorous; reliably productive; very resistant to fireblight. Relatively low chilling requirement. Recommended for Tennessee and southward. BROOKS 1972; A82, C63, C75M, *D35M*{DW}, D77M, *E45*, F19M, F93, *G28*, G65M, I9M, J33, L90, M31M{PR}, *M69M*, M76, M83, N33, etc.

Pineapple:[2] Fruit large to very large; pyriform; skin yellow, heavily russet; flesh crisp, flavor somewhat reminiscent of pineapple; good fresh, excellent for canning; ripens in August. Tree vigorous; productive; blooms early; moderately resistant to fireblight, susceptible to early and late leafspot. Low chilling requirement, 100 to 250 hours. RUCK; *A19*, A85M, *C54*, C75M, *E45*, E97, F19M, *G15M*, *K76*, L90, M31M

PERRY PEARS

Comparable to cider apples, perry pears are recognized by the bitterness or astringency which comes from tannin in their juice. The juice of perry pears will ferment to produce alcohol about twenty-four hours after it is expressed. Much more difficult to make than cider, but produces a more delicately flavored drink. LUCKWILL, SIMMONS 1978.

Barland: Round to turbinate fruit; skin green or yellow, slightly russet. Harvested in late September to early October; ready for milling up to 3 days after harvesting. Makes a high acid, medium to high tannin perry, astringent, fruity and of average to good quality. Tree large, spreading. An old cultivar, well known in the 17th century. LUCKWILL; **U7M{SC}**

Barnet: Turbinate to elliptical fruit; skin green or yellowish-green, blushed with orange-red, russet. Harvested in October, easily shaken; ready for milling 1 to 3 weeks after harvesting. Makes a low acid, low tannin perry, pleasant and light, and of average quality. Tree medium to large, shows some tendency to biennial bearing. LUCKWILL; **U7M{SC}**

Blakeney Red: Fruit pyriform or turbinate; skin yellow with a heavy red blush, sometimes streaked, some russeting. Harvested in late September to early October; ready for milling up to 7 days after harvest. Makes a medium acid, medium tannin perry of pleasant average quality when milled at the correct stage of maturity. Tree erect, spreading with age; bears regularly and heavily. LUCKWILL, SIMMONS 1978; **U7M{SC}**

Brandy: Fruit turbinate; skin green to greenish-yellow, blushed with bright red. Harvested in October; ready for milling up to 4 weeks after harvest. Makes a medium acid, low tannin perry of bland aromatic character, rather dark in color and of average quality. Tree small to medium, spreading; bears heavily but biennially. LUCKWILL, SIMMONS 1978; **U7M{SC}**

Butt: (Norton Butt) Turbinate to pyriform fruit; skin greenish-yellow to yellow, slightly russet. Harvested the first half of November; ready for milling 4 to 10 weeks after harvesting. Makes a medium to high acid, medium to high tannin perry, astringent and often fruity, of average to good quality. Tree medium to large, spreading; produces heavily, but often biennially. Widely planted in England. LUCKWILL, SIMMONS 1978; **U7M{SC}**

Gelbmostler: Medium to fairly large, globular fruit; skin greenish-yellow changing to light yellow, often slightly blushed and speckled with russet; flesh yellowish-white, coarse, juicy, very astringent; ripens in September, quickly becomes overripe. Grown in Austria and northern Switzerland for perry or pear wine. HEDRICK 1921; U7M{SC}

Gin: Broad turbinate to oblate fruit; skin green, usually blushed with orange. Harvested the end of October; ready for milling 3 to 5 weeks after harvest. Makes a medium acid, medium tannin perry of average to good quality. Valuable for its long keeping qualities. Tree medium-sized; bears heavily, but often biennially; highly resistant to scab and canker. LUCKWILL, SIMMONS 1978; U7M{SC}

Hendre Huffcap: Elliptical, often irregular fruit; skin green, yellowish-green or yellow slightly blushed with orange. Harvested the first half of October, easily shaken from the tree; ready for milling up to 2 weeks after harvesting. Makes a low to medium acid, low tannin perry, pleasant and light, and always of good quality. Tree large, upright; bears heavy crops annually, the branches sometimes breaking under the weight of the crops. LUCKWILL; U7M{SC}

Normännische Ciderbirne: Very small, turbinate fruit; skin greenish-yellow covered with cinnamon-russet and ashy-gray dots; flesh yellowish-white, rather dry, sweet but with some sprightliness; ripens in September. Excellent for making perry and for distillation. Found growing wild in Normandy and Upper Austria. HEDRICK 1921; U7M{SC}

Red Pear: (Black Horse) Turbinate fruit; skin yellow or greenish-yellow, almost completely blushed with red. Harvested in October; ready for milling up to 3 weeks after harvest. Tree medium-sized, upright; bears heavily but often biennially; widely adapted. Popular for over 400 years and still widely grown in Herfordshire and Worcestershire, the two principal perry growing counties of England. LUCKWILL; U7M{SC}

Taynton Squash: Oblate or turbinate fruit; skin greenish-yellow, sometimes slightly blushed. Harvested the second half of September; ready for milling up to 2 days after harvesting. Makes a medium acid, medium tannin perry of average quality. Tree medium to large, upright; bears heavily but usually biennially. A very old cultivar. LUCKWILL; U7M{SC}

Thorn: Pyriform, sometimes turbinate fruit; skin yellow, russet. Harvested the second half of September; ready for milling up to 1 week after harvesting. Makes a medium acid, low tannin perry of average to very good quality. Tree small, upright; bears heavily. A very old cultivar, once widely planted for dessert and culinary purposes, for which it is now considered too astringent. LUCKWILL; U7M{SC}

Yellow Huffcap: Fruit elliptical; skin green, yellow or yellowish-black, somewhat russet. Harvested the first half of October; ready for milling up to 1 week after harvesting. Makes a medium to high acid, low tannin perry, fruity, well flavored and consistently of good to excellent quality. Tree large, spreading; bears heavily, but often biennially. Widely planted cultivar of high repute. LUCKWILL, SIMMONS 1978; U7M{SC}

PECAN {GR}

CARYA ILLINOENSIS

EASTERN PECANS

Adapted to the humid southeastern states from Louisiana to Florida. Less susceptible to scab and various foliage diseases than are cultivars of western origin. They also generally grow well in the western pecan growing area. JAYNES.

Caddo: Nut small, football-shaped, with points projecting from base and apex; 60 to 70 nuts per pound; shell dark; kernel 58% of nut, attractive, quality good, flavor excellent; adapted to mechanical shelling; matures in midseason. Tree precocious; very productive; protandrous type, needing other cultivars for good pollination. BROOKS 1972; C37, M83, N33

Candy: Medium-sized nut, about 65 per pound; kernel averages 50% of weight of nut; matures early in the season, in September. Tree attractive; a consistently heavy bearer, comes into production after 6 or 7 years; highly resistant to scab; protandrous type, needing other cultivars for good pollination. A85M, *K76*, L90

Cape Fear: Nut resembles Stuart in size and shape but is superior in cracking quality; kernel does not break when shell is cracked; averages 52 to 62 nuts per pound; kernel percentage high, quality excellent including a light color. Tree very vigorous; precocious and heavy bearing; protandrous. Good pollinator for Wichita. BROOKS 1972; A85M, C37, E29M, *I99T*, *I99T*{PL}, *K76*, L33, L90, M31M, *M69M*

Chickasaw: Small to medium-sized nut, averages 55 to 75 per pound; kernel 52 to 58% of nut, of good quality; matures early. Tree vigorous; very precocious and prolific; resistant to scab; protogynous; has good lateral branching. Good all-purpose cultivar, especially recommended for high-density plantings in the Southeast. F19M, *K76*

Choctaw: Nut size similar to that of Success, but of more symmetrical shape; averages 45 per pound; shell unusually thin, being similar to Schley; kernel averages 60% or more of nut, releases well from shell, color bright, oil content high, flavor rich; cracks out very well; matures in midseason. Fine for marketing in shell. Tree vigorous, precocious and heavy bearing; protogynous. BROOKS 1972, JAYNES; A85M, B93M, C37, *C54*, F19M, G88, I83M, *I99T*, *I99T*{PL}, *K76*, *L47*, L90, M83, N33

Desirable: Nut larger than Stuart, averaging 45 to 50 per pound; kernel percentage about 52%; kernel meaty, quality very good; matures in midseason. Tree blooms early; highly resistant to scab; comes into bearing early; a very prolific and consistent bearer; protandrous. Popular in the Southeast. BROOKS 1972; A85M, C75M, E29M, *E45*, F19M, F93, G72, G88, *I99T*, *I99T*{PL}, K28, L90, M31M, M31M{PR}, *M69M*, M83, N33, etc.

Elliot: Nut small, base rounded, apex pointed; 55 to 70 nuts per pound; kernel plump, smooth, straw-colored, of excellent flavor and quality; shell medium thick, very good for cracking purposes; matures in midseason. Tree highly resistant to scab; a shy but consistent bearer; comes into bearing late; protogynous. Introduced about 1925. BROOKS 1972; A85M, E29M, *E45*, F93, *K76*, L90, M31M, M31M{PR}

Forkert: Large nut, about 45 to 50 per pound; kernel averages 60% of nut; matures in late October. Tree precocious, productive; protogynous, sheds pollen after pistillate flowers are receptive. Recommended for new orchard plantings and coastal plantings. An older cultivar which is becoming more popular due to its scab resistance. A85M, C37, *K76*, N33

Gloria Grande: Very large nut, about 35 to 45 per pound; kernel averages 48% of nut, richer in flavor than Stewart; matures late, in October and November; resembles Stuart. Tree productive, comes into bearing after 8 or 9 years; resistant to scab; protogynous, a good pollinator for Stuart. Good home garden cultivar. Originated in Orangeburg, South Carolina. BROOKS 1972; A85M, *K76*

GraKing: Nut large, about 35 per pound, resembles Mahan; attractive; kernel separates easily from shell, averages about 55% of nut; matures early. Tree productive; resistant to scab; protogynous. Originated in Arlington, Texas by O.S. Gray. Introduced in 1959. BROOKS 1972; N33

Hastings: Nut resembles Stuart, but has a thinner shell; cracks easily; quality of kernel good; fills well; matures October 1. Tree medium-sized; hardy; vigorous and productive; tolerant to scab; protogynous. Plant with Desirable for Pollination. BROOKS 1972; F19M, *K76*

Jackson: Very large nut, about 35 per pound; kernel well-filled, averaging 52% of nut; quality high; matures late, in October and November. Tree an early but shy bearer; highly tolerant to scab; protogynous, sheds pollen after pistillate flowers are receptive. A good cultivar for home gardens. A85M, E29M, F19M, *K76*

Kernodle: Large, long nut with a blunt base, similar to Stuart; shell very thin; kernels lighter in color than most other cultivars; quality very good, flavor somewhat like that of a Persian walnut, cracks out easily; ripens late. Tree productive; resistant to scab. Originated in Camp Hill, Alabama. BROOKS 1972; *K76*

Kiowa: Medium to large nut; shape and appearance similar to Desirable; averages 40 to 50 nuts per pound; shell medium soft; kernel 55 to 60% of nut, quality very good; matures late. Tree very precocious and prolific; protogynous. Good for high density plantings. Pollinate with Cherokee. JAYNES; A85M, B93M, C37, *D23M*, E4, E29M, F19M, G88, *I99T*, *I99T*{PL}, *K76*, L90, M83, N33

Mahan: Very large, long nut; 35 to 50 nuts per pound; shell thin; tends toward poor filling on older trees; kernel averages 50 to 57% of nut, flavor rich; resembles Schley but about 60% larger; matures late. Tree vigorous and prolific; early bearing; protogynous; susceptible to scab. Introduced in 1927. BROOKS 1972; C37, *C54*, C75M, D76, *E45*, E97, G13, G88, *K76*, *L47*, L90, *M69M*, M76, M83, *N20*, etc.

Mahan-Stuart: Very large nut, about 32 or 33 per pound; shell thinner than Stuart but thicker than Mahan; quality very good; resembles Stuart in shape but is somewhat longer; matures 10 days before Stuart. Tree vigorous, precocious, blooms 1 week earlier than Stuart. Mahan x Stuart. Originated in Monticello, Florida. BROOKS 1972; *K76*

Mohawk: Nut large, similar to Mahan, averages 35 per pound; shell thin, very attractive; kernel may exceed 60% of weight of entire nut, separates easily from shell; quality high; matures early. Tree vigorous; prolific and moderately precocious; susceptible to scab; protogynous. BROOKS 1972, JAYNES; C37, *C54*, *D23M*, E4, G88, I40, I83M, J21M{PR}, *K76*, L33, L90, M83, *N20*, N33

Moreland: Nut large, averaging 45 per pound; shell very thin; kernel high in oil content, very rich in flavor, fills out well; quality high; has good keeping qualities; similar to Stuart in size and shape. Tree upright; disease resistant; considered one of the few self-pollinating cultivars. Rated one of the top six cultivars for north and central Florida by the University of Florida. G17

Owens: Large, somewhat flat nut, about 45 per pound; shell medium thick, grayish, attractive; kernel averages 46 to 48% of nut, fills well, cracks out readily, practically all halves. Tree stout; moderately productive; tolerant to insects and diseases prevalent in delta areas of Mississippi and Arkansas; highly resistant to scab; blooms 10 days earlier than Stuart. Originated in Cuban Island, Mississippi. BROOKS 1972; A85M, *K76*

Pawnee: Nut large, 45 to 55 per pound; kernel 55 to 62% of nut, of excellent quality; matures very early, as early as September 15 at Brownwood. Tree precocious; vigorous and heavy yielding; protandrous, pollen shedding pattern similar to Cheyenne. Recommended for areas of the traditional pecan belt with shorter growing seasons. Originated in Brownwood, Texas. Introduced in 1984. A85M, C37, *C54*, E4, F19M, F93, G88, I40, *I99T*, *I99T*{PL}, *K76*, L90, N33

Podsednik: Extremely large nut, as little as 22 to a pound; kernel well filled, of good color; matures with Mahan. Tree has strong structure and large leaves; appears to be scab resistant; sheds pollen slightly ahead of pistil receptivity. Recommended for trial plantings. N33

Schley: Medium-sized nut, averages 50 to 65 per pound; shell very thin, fills well; kernel 55 to 60% of nut, of fine flavor, cracks well; matures in midseason. Tree vigorous; slow to come into bearing; a shy bearer in many areas; susceptible to scab; protogynous. Seedling of Stuart. JAYNES; *K76*, L33, L90, M83

Shoshoni: Medium to large nut, averages 40 to 60 per pound; kernel 52 to 58% of nut; matures in midseason. Suitable for commercial shelling. Tree very vigorous, upright growing; highly precocious and prolific; resistant to scab; protogynous, sheds pollen after pistillate flowers are receptive. Suited to high density plantings. C37, *C54*, F19M, G88, I40, *K76*, L90, N33

Stuart: Nut medium-sized, averages 40 to 55 per pound; kernel 44 to 50 percent of nut, quality good; matures in midseason. Tree slow to come into bearing, but continues to yield acceptable crops for up to 45 years; moderately productive; susceptible to diseases; protogynous. Widely adapted to climate and soils. Formerly the standard cultivar in the Southeast. JAYNES; A82, *B52*, C75M, D76, *E45*, E97, F19M, F93, G72, H49, J47M{PR}, K28, L33, L90, M31M{PR}, *M69M*, M76, etc.

Success: Large attractive nut, averages 40 to 55 per pound; shell soft, filling often erratic and poor; kernel 49 to 54% of nut, smooth, plump, creamy, of excellent flavor; matures in midseason, almost 10 days later than Stuart. Tree vigorous; precocious and prolific; susceptible to diseases; protandrous; partially self-fruitful. An old stand-by. *C54*, E4, G88, L90, M83

Sumner: Medium to large nut with excellent kernel quality; matures in midseason. Tree precocious; relatively consistent and heavy yielding; disease resistant; protogynous. Good for high density plantings. A85M, E29M, *K76*, L90, M31M, M31M{PR}

FAR NORTHERN PECANS

Recent discoveries of native pecan groves near the Green Island-Dubuque, Iowa area have shown that pecans can ripen in areas much farther north than previously known. Selections from these trees and from other far northern pecan areas are being tested as far north as Ontario, Canada.

Canton: An extra large, thin-shelled pecan that deserves trial in the commercial zones of Missouri and Kansas. It is proving to be a good producer of early maturing nuts. D72, I25M{SC}

Carlson #3: Selected by R.D. Campbell for trial in Canada because of its early maturity. Nut size and quality are similar to others selected in the New Boston area. Grafts flower in their third or fourth year. D72, I25M{SC}

Devore: Nut small, averages 120 to the pound; white kernels, exceptionally well-flavored, reminiscent of shagbark hickory. Tree a consistent producer; early maturing in central Iowa; should be tried farther north. Also selected by the USDA for breeding in Brownwood, Texas. D72, E62{SC}, I25M{SC}, I40{OR}

Fisher: Nut medium-sized, cracks well; flavor good. Tree produces well at original location and in the Scranton, Pennsylvania area; protandrous. Originated in New Memphis, Illinois by Jacob Fisher. Introduced in 1938. E91M, I40

Fritz: Medium-sized nut; matures early. Tree a strong grower; produces well but comes into bearing very late; protogynous, may be very useful as a late pollen source. At one time considered the most northern native selection, along with Witte. Originated in New Boston, Illinois by Kenneth Fritz. JAYNES; D72

Gibson: Medium-sized nut with good cracking qualities; flavor very good; fills well in the far northern pecan growing region. Tree precocious, two year grafts often bear nuts; a consistent and heavy producer; protandrous. Originated in New Boston, Illinois. D72, E91M, E91M{OR}, I25M{SC}, I40

Green Island: Selections from trees growing at the Green Island-Dubuque area of Iowa. Only trees that have had crops in the past and also show some other merit with regard to nut size, production or early maturity are grafted. These trees are the most northerly adapted native pecans in the world. There are none hardier. D72, E62{SC}, I25M{SC}

Lucas: Nut small to medium, averages 100 to 120 nuts per pound; kernel oily, of fine flavor; cracks and fills well in the far northern pecan growing areas. Tree precocious; hardy; heavy yielding; protogynous. Originated in Ohio in 1965. B99{PL}, D72, E91M{OR}, I25M{SC}, I40

Mullahy: The largest pecan of Iowa origin yet found; cracks out in perfects halves and is of excellent quality. Tree shows some evidence of hickory hybridization; starts bearing early; flowers early, with the native hickory. Hardy to at least -30^{0} F. Early reports indicate ripening in New York, Michigan and Ontario. D72, I25M{SC}, I60{PL}

Rock: One of the largest nuts selected in the upper Mid West. A consistent producer of good quality nuts. The year it was discovered, mature fallen nuts were gathered the first week of October. In comparison, 75 miles to the south nuts of Colby and Major were frozen green on the tree. D72

Voiles #2: A Northern Nutgrowers Association selection used for extending the range of the pecan. Found in central Illinois, it ripens its nuts in late September and early October. Completely hardy in Michigan, with no winter damage at temperatures of -20^{0} F. Ripens in New York and Ontario most years. K16{PL}

Witte: Nut somewhat larger than Indiana, 60 to 70 nuts per pound; blocky, of good shape; kernel 44 to 50% of nut; matures early. One of the best cultivars from this latitude, at one time considered the most northern pecan area, until the more recent discoveries. Tree starts bearing very late; protandrous. Originated in Burlington, Iowa by John H. Witte. Introduced about 1925. BROOKS 1972; D72, I25M{SC}

NORTHERN PECANS

These mature their nuts in a shorter growing season than eastern or western cultivars. Their earlier maturity exposes nuts to greater damage from squirrels, birds, and insects in more southern latitudes than that of Tennessee. The traditional northern pecan growing area includes Oklahoma, Kansas, Missouri, Iowa, Illinois, Indiana, Kentucky and Tennessee.

Chief: Nut large, about 45 per pound; shell medium thin; kernel plump, quality good to excellent; matures with Greenriver. Resembles Greenriver but is much larger. Tree very vigorous; protandrous, with very late pistillate flowering. Originated in Ridgway, Illinois. BROOKS 1972; I40{OR}

Colby: Medium-sized, long oval nut, 55 to 65 per pound; shell thickness medium; kernel averages 45 to 50% of nut, cracks out poorly, flavor good; matures in a 160 day growing season. Tree vigorous and productive; resistant to leaf fungi; retains its foliage late in the fall; protogynous; a heavy pollen producer. Originated in Fayette County, Illinois. D76, E41M{SC}, F19M, I25M{SC}, I40, I74, *K76*, L33, M76

Giles: Nut fairly large, 55 to 65 per pound; shell thin, cracking quality fair; kernel averages 48 to 50% of nut, quality very good; matures late. Tree precocious; regularly productive near the latitude of origin, not as reliable northward; protogynous. Used as a rootstock in some areas. Originated in Chetopa, Kansas. Introduced in 1930. BROOKS 1972, JAYNES; E41M{SC}, E89, I40{OR}, I74

Greenriver: Medium to large nut, 50 to 70 per pound; shell thin; kernel 53 to 54% of nut, plump, quality very good; matures late. Tree large, a prolific and regular bearer; protogynous. Susceptible to frost in central Illinois and occasionally in Kentucky. Later than other northern cultivars but produces good quality nuts where the season is long enough. Originated in Henderson County, Kentucky. E41M{SC}, I40, M76

Hirschi: Nut large, averaging about 56 per pound; cracking percentage 50 to 55%; shell thin, fills well; kernel of high quality. Tree considered to be self-fertile, but will normally produce larger crops when planted with Peruque and Giles. Recommended for all parts of Zone 6 except the extreme northern areas. Original tree discovered at Rich Hill, Missouri about 1940. E89, I25M{SC}, I40{OR}, I74

Hodge: Nut large, one of the finest flavored of all pecans; kernel tender, probably not adapted to commercial cracking. Tree not productive at Urbana, Illinois. Useful only as a late protogynous pollen source, and for breeding purposes. One of the first northern pecans to attract attention. Originated in York, Illinois. Discovered about 1890. BROOKS 1972; I40{OR}

Indiana: Small to medium-sized nut, averages about 77 per pound; quality good; matures in midseason. Tree productive; apparently self-fertile; produces pollen at the proper time to pollinate Major and Peruque. Originated in Indiana. I40

Kentucky: Nut small to medium, averages about 83 per pound; quality good; matures medium-late. Tree productive; apparently self-fertile. Originated in Kentucky. I40

Major: Small to medium-sized, roundish nut, 60 to 80 per pound; shell thin; kernel 42 to 50% of nut, plump and sweet; matures in midseason. Unacceptable for commercial cracking. Tree bears well; protandrous. Pistillate flowers develop over a long period and require pollen from late pollen producers such as Colby, Posey and Greenriver to set a full crop. The standard non-commercial northern cultivar. BROOKS 1972, JAYNES; D76, E41M{SC}, F19M, I25M{SC}, I40, *K76*, L33, M76

Patrick: Small, irregular nut, averages 115 per pound; shell thin, an excellent sheller, yielding about 60% kernel; kernel elongated, light-colored, plump, smooth; flavor good; ripens about midseason. Tree produces well; bears biennially; apparently resistant to pecan scab. Originated in Rogers County, Oklahoma. BROOKS 1972; E41M{SC}

Peruque: Nut small to medium, 60 to 80 per pound; papershell; kernel 55 to 63% of nut, flavor and quality excellent; matures in midseason. Tree vigorous; precocious and prolific; protandrous; bears a heavy crop annually. Thin shell makes it vulnerable to predators in some areas. Originated in St. Charles, Missouri. Introduced in 1955. BROOKS 1972, JAYNES; E41M{SC}, E89{CF}, G75{CF}, I25M{SC}, I40, I74

Posey: Medium-sized nut, about 72 per pound; cracking quality very good; kernel of high quality, flavor very good; matures medium-early. Tree sturdy, symmetrical; protogynous; a good pollen producer. Needs high fertility and adequate cross-pollination to bear well. Originated in Indiana. E41M{SC}, I25M{SC}, I40

Starking Hardy Giant: Large nut, up to 1 1/2 inches in diameter; shell thin; kernel halves oblong with a short point, plump, golden-yellow, flavor distinct, quality good; matures early, the last week of September. Tree medium-sized, vigorous; moderately productive, bears better crops if pollinated with Colby; hardy. Originated in Brunswick, Missouri by George James. BROOKS 1972; I25M{SC}, I74, *K76*, L33

WESTERN PECANS

Cultivars that are suited to the central and western part of Texas and other areas of the Southwest and West where the climate is relatively dry. They are usually very susceptible to scab and various foliage diseases that attack the pecan. Generally not recommended for planting in the eastern pecan growing areas. JAYNES.

Apache: Large, blocky nut, 40 to 60 per pound; shell thin, cracking quality good; kernel smooth, bright, deteriorates slowly in storage, averages 60% of nut; quality high; matures in midseason. Tree vigorous and productive; subject to scab under humid conditions; protogynous. Good seedling rootstock. BROOKS 1972, JAYNES; C37, N33

Burkett: Nut medium to large, round and wide; shell thin; kernel plump, up to 55% of nut, has an excellent, rich flavor; matures in midseason. Tree a regular and heavy producer; protogynous. Does well on high ground in East Texas. Choctaw recommended as a pollinator. Very popular in western areas. Originated in Clyde, Texas. *C54*, G88, *L47*, L90, M83, N33

Cherokee: Medium-sized nut, 50 to 60 per pound; semi-soft shell, cracks well; kernels 55 to 60% of nut, of high quality, color slightly too dark; matures early. Tree vigorous; extremely precocious and productive; protandrous. Well suited for temporary tree or high density plantings. *C54*, G88, M83

Cheyenne: Medium-sized nut, 55 to 60 per pound; shell attractive; kernel 57 to 61% of nut, loose in shell, brightly colored; flavor excellent; matures in midseason. Well adapted to mechanical shelling. Good for high density plantings. Tree very precocious and productive; protandrous, therefore needing a protogynous type for good pollination. BROOKS 1972; A85M, C37, *C54*, E29M, F19M, F93, G88, I83M, *I99T*, *I99T*{PL}, L33, *L47*, L90, M83, *N20*, N33, etc.

Comanche: Large nut, similar in size and form to Burkett, which it resembles. Kernel brightly colored, free of the dark flecks characteristic of Burkett. Tree vigorous; moderately productive; more disease resistant than Burkett when grown under similar climatic conditions. Originated in Brownwood, Texas by L.D. Romberg. Introduced in 1955. Designed to replace Burkett. BROOKS 1972; C37, *C54*, N33

Grabohls: Medium to large nut, about 45 to 55 per pound; shell thin; kernel averages 55 to 60% of nut; matures in midseason. Tree very precocious and prolific; protogynous, sheds pollen after pistillate flowers are receptive. Good for high density plantings. Seedling of Mahan. *C54*

Maramec: Nut large, 40 to 50 per pound; oblong, blocky; shell thin; kernel averages 58 to 59% of nut, of high quality; matures in midseason. Tree large, spreading; vigorous and very productive; hardy; tolerant to pecan scab; has superior foliage until fall. Originated in Maramec, Oklahoma. BROOKS 1972; N33

Shawnee: Medium-sized, slightly elongated nut, about 50 per pound; shell thin, light brown with relatively few dark stripes; kernel averages 60% of nut, smooth, bright in color, flavor excellent, cracks out well; keeping quality very good. Suitable for both in-shell and shelling trade. Tree vigorous; precocious and very productive; protogynous. Originated in Brownwood, Texas. BROOKS 1972; *C54*, L90, M83

Sioux: Nut small, 60 to 80 per pound; shell thin, cracks well; kernel averages 60% of nut, smooth; quality, flavor and appearance excellent, color bright; oil content high, does not deteriorate rapidly in storage; matures in midseason. Tree vigorous; moderately precocious, productive; protogynous. Does well in the Southeast with a good fungicide spray program. BROOKS 1972; C37, *C54*, L90, M83, N33

Tejas: Small to medium-sized nut, averages 50 to 75 nuts per pound; has superior shelling qualities; kernel 50 to 56% of nut; matures in midseason. Tree extremely vigorous; moderately precocious, very prolific; protogynous; holds its green foliage late in the season. C37, G88, I83M, *I99T*, *I99T*{PL}, L90, M83, *N20*, N33

Western: (Western Schley) Medium-sized nut, 45 to 65 to the pound; shell thin; kernel 54 to 59% of nut, of high quality, flavor rich; matures midseason to late. Tree vigorous; precocious and very prolific; protandrous; tolerant of zinc deficiency. The standard shelling cultivar in the western irrigated pecan areas. JAYNES; A88M, B93M, C37, *C54*, E4, G88, I83M, *I99T*, *I99T*{PL}, *L47*, L90, M83, *N20*, N33

Wichita: Nut medium-sized, averaging about 60 per pound; unusually attractive because of neat, purplish-black stripes and splotches on a clear brown shell; kernel 60% of nut, well-filled, of excellent quality; matures about with Western. Tree moderately upright, vigorous; early and heavy bearing; protogynous. BROOKS 1972; A88M, B93M, C37, *C54*, G88, I83M, *I99T*, *I99T*{PL}, *K76*, *L47*, L90, M83, *N20*, N33

PEPINO DULCE {GR}

SOLANUM MURICATUM

Colossal: Very large fruit; mostly cream-colored with light markings of purple; very juicy and sweet, free of soapiness; of good melon-like flavor, especially when vine-ripened. Self-fertile, but yields larger fruit when cross-pollinated. I83M, J23{OR}

Ecuadorian Gold: A market cultivar in South America that produces good crops of pear-like fruits over a long growing season. The fruit has an attractive color, is well-marked, and holds well on the plant. Self-fertile, but should be thinned for better fruit size. J23{OR}

El Camino: Medium to large, egg-shaped fruit with regular purple stripes. Sometimes produces off-flavored fruits identifiable by their brownish-green color. One of two leading commercial cultivars in New Zealand. Released there in 1982 by the Department of Scientific and Industrial Research, from material collected in Chile. I49M

Miski Prolific: Fruit creamy white with a faint salmon glow, lightly striped with purple; flesh deep salmon; flavor rich, sweet and aromatic, with no bitter aftertaste; seeds few or none; matures early. Strong growing plant; bears well without cross pollination. Originated in San Jose, California by Nancy Garrison, as a seedling of the New Zealand cultivar Miski. I83M, J23{OR}

New Yorker: Medium to large, oval fruit, apex pointed; skin smooth, golden yellow when mature, prominently striped with deep purple; flesh firm, juicy, yellow-orange; flavor sweet, virtually free of soapiness; seeds few; keeps for several weeks. Upright growth habit; sets fruit well without cross pollination. Introduced into California by Vincent Rizzo of New York state, from material obtained in Chile. I83M

Rio Bamba: Medium-sized fruit, strongly striped with purple; flavor excellent. Vining growth habit; makes an excellent climber or a hanging basket plant. Dark-green leaves with reddish-purple veins;

purple stems; flowers darker than normal, making an excellent display. Originated in Vista, California by Patrick J. Worley. Named after the city in Ecuador where the original plant was collected. G20, I83M, J23{OR}, L29

Ryburn: An English cultivar, from the best seedling plant so far discovered in Great Britain. It has proved self-fertile and more productive than the majority of seedlings. S30

Temptation: Large, high quality fruit. Introduced by the Nurserymen's Association of Western Australia. D57, I83M

Toma: Medium-sized, oval fruit; 4 inches long, 3 inches in diameter; apex pointed, shoulder well-rounded; skin smooth, cream-colored when ripe, prominently striped with dark purple; pulp firm, light-cream in color, very juicy; flavor sweet and refreshing, with no hint of soapiness; seeds usually present; keeping quality excellent. An important export cultivar in Chile; introduced into New Zealand in 1979, released there in 1983. D57, I49M, I83M, *Q49M*

Vista: Medium-sized fruits have good flavor and aroma. Upright, fairly compact plant of great vigor; self-fertile and heavy yielding; bright green, 3 inch long leaves. Originated in Vista, California by Patrick J. Worley. A cross of Rio Bamba and a seedling from South America. G20, I83M, J23{OR}, L29

PEPPER {S}

CAPSICUM ANNUUM
CAPSICUM FRUTESCENS
CAPSICUM CHINENSE

SWEET PEPPERS

BELL-SHAPED

Hybrid

Chocolate Bell:[6] 75 days. Large, blocky, deep bell-shaped fruit; 4 1/2 inches long; about twice the size of Sweet Chocolate; turns tan, to dark brown, to red when mature. Ripens 10 days later than Sweet Chocolate. Very rare seed imported from Holland. L42

Dutch Chocolate:[6] (Brupa) Retains taste and shelf life of a green bell pepper long after its thick outer walls have turned an attractive brown. Prized by the gourmet trade for its novelty. *A75*, H49, I77

Gold Crest:[1] 62 days. Medium-sized, blocky, 3 to 4-lobed fruit, 2 to 4 inches long; glossy dark-green, ripening to a rich golden-yellow; remarkably sweet tasting, especially at yellow-ripe stage. High quality, either green or yellow. Highly resistant to fruit rot, spot, and russeting. Heavy fruit set; early maturity. G6, I77

Golden Bell:[1] 70 days. Medium-large, blocky, 3 to 4-lobed fruit; light green, turning bright gold at maturity; thick-walled, very sweet. Vigorous, upright plant, 21 inches tall; provides good cover. Adapted mainly for home garden use. Rated first for productivity in a test conducted by Organic Gardening magazine. *A1*, A16, D27, *E91G*, F13, *F72*, H54, *H61*, J7, J20, J34, L89, M46, N16, N39, P83M, etc.

Golden Pepper:[1] (P-324) Medium-sized, blocky, 3 to 4-lobed fruit; dark green, ripening to golden yellow; of very good quality. Ripens in mid-season. Strong, vigorous plant with good fruit cover. Does well in cool maritime climates. L97

Golden Summer:[1] 70 days. Large, blocky, 3 to 4-lobed fruit; pale lime-green, ripening to a rich golden yellow; thick-walled, juicy, sweet. Rated highest for overall flavor in a test conducted by Organic Gardening magazine. Does not ripen yellow in short season areas. Upright plant, 24 to 28 inches tall; resistant to tobacco mosaic virus. Good fruit set; wide adaptability. B49M{PL}, B75, C53, D11M, D76, E97, F19M, *F63*, G6, *G13M*, G51, G64, I91, J34, K73, M0, *M43M*, etc.

Honeybelle: 74 days. Very large, slightly elongated, 3 or 4-lobed fruit; ripens from green to a golden yellow. Vigorous, upright plant; high yielding; resistant to tobacco mosaic virus. Recommended for home gardeners as well as commercial growers. F13

Luteus:[1] 68 days. Large, blocky, mostly 4-lobed fruit; thick-walled; uniform in size. Can be harvested green or after maturing to a golden-yellow. Quick growing, with a notably high yield. Resistant to tobacco mosaic virus. S61

Midal:[2] An oval "white pepper". White when ripe and red at full maturity. Tapered, medium thick wall. Open sturdy growth; very prolific. *A75*, I77

Midnight Beauty:[7] Large, blocky, mostly 4-lobed fruit; thick-walled; glossy deep purple, maturing to a deep red. Adds color to summer salads. Ripens very early. S45M

Oriole:[4] 74 days. Large, blocky fruit, 4 3/4 inches long; mostly 4-lobed; thick walled. May be harvested when dark green or after ripening to a tangerine-orange. Plants are somewhat tolerant of tobacco mosaic virus. L42

Orobelle:[1] 72 days. Medium large, thick-walled, 3 to 4-lobed fruit, 4 1/2 inches long; dark green, ripening to yellow-gold; very sweet. High quality, either green or yellow. Strong, vigorous plant, provides excellent fruit coverage; resistant to tobacco mosaic and potato Y virus; high yielding. *A1*, G6, G71, G93M, *H61*, I91, J84, K10, K73, M0

Purple Belle:[7] 68 days. Blocky, 4-lobed fruit, 4 1/2 inches square; green, ripening to purple, then blood red at full maturity. Bushy, compact plant, keeps the fruit well protected from the sun; resists tobacco mosaic virus. Very popular specialty market item. *A1*, A21, B75, *F72*, G51, G93M, I77, I91, L42, M0, M29, N52, T1M

Quadrato d'Oro:[1] 63 days. Large, blocky fruit, 3 to 4 inches long; glossy green, ripening to a rich golden-yellow; thick-walled, aromatic, juicy, sweet. Rated highest for sweetness in a test conducted by Organic Gardening magazine. Vigorous plant with good leaf coverage; productive; disease resistant. Developed in Holland for Italian and French market gardeners. K66

Scarlet Goliath: Large, blocky, mainly 4-lobed fruit; 4 3/4 inches by 4 3/4 inches; weight about 3/4 pound; smooth, dark black-green skin turns to glistening bright red when ripe; thick flesh. Excellent for fresh market and processing. Short, sturdy plant; early bearing and productive. *E53M*

Open-Pollinated

Albino:[2 3] (Albino Bullnose) Medium-sized fruit; stays white a long time before finally turning red; medium thick-walled, sweet. A colorful and tasty addition to salads. Dwarf bush; disease resistant; may be grown outdoors in far northern regions or in flower pots. E49, J4

Ariane:[4] 70 days. Large, blocky, medium-green fruit ripens to a uniform vibrant-orange, the first true orange in a bell pepper. Heavy and solid, with thick, crunchy flesh. Sweet and flavorful in green or orange stages. Vigorous plants; resistant to tobacco mosaic virus type-O. Developed to honor the House of Orange, the Royal family of Holland. I39, I77, K66

Bull Nose: (Large Bell) 65 days. Medium-sized, blunt-ended fruit; 3 inches long, 2 3/4 inches in diameter; deep green, ripening to scarlet red; thick-walled flesh, mild in flavor except for the ribs which are quite pungent. An old traditional cultivar. A2, G57M, G67M, J4, M95M, R0

California Wonder: 75 days. Large, blocky, 3 to 4-lobed fruit; smooth and glossy; dark green, ripening to bright crimson; thick-walled, up to 3/8 inch; tender, juicy, sweet, without a trace of pungency. Vigorous, upright plant; provides good cover. The archetypical bell pepper; introduced in 1928. A25, B35M, B73M, B73M{PL}, B75M, D11M, E97{PL}, F19M, *F72*, G71, H33{PL}, H66, H94, L97, M13M, M46, N16, etc.

Carnosissimo di Cuneo: Large, oval-pointed fruit, mostly 3 to 4-lobed; skin clear bright-yellow, attractive; flesh sweet, very bulky and exceptionally thick-walled. The principal market grower's pepper in the Piedmont region of northern Italy. Named after the market town of Cuneo. I77, K66, Q11M

Emerald Giant: 74 days. Large, blocky, mostly 4-lobed fruit; 4 1/2 inches long, 3 3/4 inches in diameter; dark green turning red at maturity; thick-walled. Strong, upright plant, 26 to 28 inches tall; productive over a long period; resistant to tobacco mosaic virus. Excellent for fresh market, shipping and home garden use. A69M, B75M, C92, *E91G*, G79, G93M, H54, *H61*, H66, J4, J14{PL}, J84, L14, L79, L97, etc.

Golden Calwonder: 72 days. Smooth, blocky, mostly 4-lobed fruit; 3 3/4 inches long, 3 1/2 inches in diameter; medium-green, turning golden-yellow at maturity; thick-walled, sweet, mild. Strong, upright plant, 22 to 26 inches tall; sets fruit continuously. Popular for fresh market and home garden use. A13, A56, *F72*, G64, G79, G93M, H49, H94, H95, I64, J4, J14{PL}, J97M, K71, M13M, M95M, etc.

Golden Summit: 65 days. A family heirloom, developed over a 200 year span of intensive Yugoslavian market gardening. Attractive golden-green fruit, ripening to a bright gold, turning bright deep red at full maturity; 3 or 4 lobes; very thick-walled, crisp, juicy, sweet. Begins to bear early in the season, even if nights are cool. *E91G*, F24M

Hungarian Yellow Stuffing: 70 days. Very large, 4-lobed fruit; yellow when ripe, turning deep red at full maturity; sweet and mild, without a trace of pungency. Perfect for stuffing. Vigorous, productive plant, with excellent foliage cover that protects the fruit. D11M

Jupiter: 72 days. Very large, extremely blocky, 4-lobed fruit; 4 inches deep, 4 inches wide; green, turning bright red when ripe; thick-walled. Vigorous, high yielding, widely adapted plant; with a dense canopy of leaves that provides protection from sunburn; resistant to tobacco mosaic virus. One of the best open-pollinated cultivars. A87M, E57, *E91G*, F13, *G1M*, *G13M*, H54, *H61*, J4, J34, J58, K73, M0, M29

Keystone Resistant Giant: 75 days. Large, blocky, mostly 4-lobed fruit; 4 1/2 inches long, 3 3/4 inches in diameter; attractive dark green, turning dark red when ripe; thick-walled, sweet and mild. High yielding plant; resistant to tobacco mosaic virus; has heavy foliage that reduces susceptibility to sunscald. A56, C92, D76, E5T, *E91G*, F12, G79, G82, H66, J4, J14{PL}, J34, J84, K27M, L7M, L14, L89, etc.

King of the North: 65 days. Very large, blocky, 3 to 4-lobed fruit; 6 inches long, up to 4 inches in diameter; green, turning bright red when mature; medium thick-walled, crisp, sweet and mild. Large, somewhat spreading plant; resistant to tobacco mosaic virus. Performs well in short summer areas. D68, *E91G*, E97, E97{PL}

Lorelei:[7] Stocky, 4-lobed fruit; ripens to a glossy deep purple on the exterior, with crisp green interior flesh. Has the flavor of a green bell pepper. Especially attractive when served with green, red and yellow peppers. Medium early. High yielding. K66

Merrimack Wonder: 60 days. Medium-sized, blocky, 3 to 4-lobed fruit; 3 1/2 inches square; dark green, ripening to deep red; medium thick flesh, sweet and mild. Developed to set fruit in short summer areas. Also widely adapted as an early cultivar. Introduced in 1942 by the University of New Hampshire. H94, L7M

Midway: 70 days. Improved Staddon's Select type. Large, blocky, 3 to 4-lobed fruit; 4 1/2 inches deep, 4 1/2 inches wide; bright green, turning red when mature; thick-walled, very sweet, mild in flavor. Tolerant to tobacco mosaic virus. Recommended for northern areas and greenhouse production. Popular early main season cultivar. B73M, B73M{PL}, C44, *E53M*, *E91G*, *F72*, G79, I64, J4, J84, K73, L7M, L42

Miniature Yellow: 75 days. Very small, "baby" bell pepper, 1 to 2 inches long and 1 to 1 1/2 inches in diameter. Attractive shape and color. Adds a nice yellow color to salads, or it can be stuffed for hors d'oeuvres or pickled. Prolific, disease resistant plant, produces abundantly and early. K49M, L7M

Permagreen:[5] 70 days. Large, blocky fruit; retains its deep green color when fully mature, does not turn red; sweet and flavorful flesh. Very early. Adapted to the northern United States and Canada. Developed by Professor E.M. Meader of New Hampshire. Introduced in 1965. D65, K49M, L7M

Purple Beauty:[7] 70 days. Medium-sized, 4-lobed fruit, 4 inches square; dark purple; thick-walled. Compact, high yielding plant; provides good fruit protection. Sets well not only in the crown but also as limb set. Developed from the hybrid Purple Bell. C92, D11M, D76, *E53M*, E97, *F63*, *G13M*, G27M, G82, H42, I39, J4, L42, M0

Quadrati d'Asti Giallo:[1] (Asti Square Yellow) Gourmet yellow-ripening Italian pepper. Large, blocky 3 to 4-lobed fruit; ripens to a bright golden-yellow; thick-walled, crisp, juicy, sweet with a hint of spiciness. Excellent for roasting, frying, salads, stuffing or pickling. Vigorous, high-yielding plant; does best in warmer climates. Q34

Ruby King: 75 days. Medium to large, blocky, mostly 3-lobed fruit; 4 to 5 inches long, 3 1/2 inches in diameter; dark green, ripening to a glossy ruby red; thick-walled, crisp, very sweet and mild. Turns red early. Vigorous, productive plant. Very old traditional cultivar. K49M, S93M

Staddon's Select: 70 days. Large, blocky, 3 to 4-lobed fruit, somewhat uneven in shape; glossy green, turning red when ripe; medium thick, crisp and sweet. Tall, bushy plant; high yielding even under hot, dry conditions; resistant to tobacco mosaic virus. Does well in northern areas. A13, D68, E24, E57, *E91G*, F44, *H61*, J25M, K49M, K50, L42, L89, M49

Sweet Chocolate:[6] 65 days. Medium-small, tapered, blunt-nosed fruit; dark glossy green, ripening to a rich chocolate brown; medium-thick walls, sweet and flavorful. The flesh below the skin is an attractive brick red, cooked or raw. Prolific plant; tolerant of cool nights. Developed by E.M. Meader at the University of New Hampshire. C53, E32M{PL}, E59Z, F44, G6, I77, J4, J20, K49M, L7M

Tree: Very large plant, grows 4 to 5 feet tall. One plant produces enough for an average family. Typical sweet bell-shaped fruit, only the plant bears until late fall. Makes a good patio plant. D77M

Violetta:[7] Blocky fruit; deep purple when immature, turning a lustrous red upon full maturity. Turns from purple to green when cooked. Attractive as well as flavorful. Medium-sized, high yielding plant; bears fruit on short joints. Originated in Holland. C53, *F85G*, G64, I77, I99

World Beater: (Chinese Giant) 73 days. Very large, blocky, long-tapered fruit; 6 inches long, 4 1/2 inches in diameter; rich green, turning to cherry red at maturity; moderately thick-walled, sweet and mild. Keeps in prime condition for a long time. Ideal for stuffing. Very productive; yields as many as 32 fruits per plant. C92, E49, J4, K71, L7M, N39, R0, S45M, S61

Yolo Wonder: 75 days. Blocky, 3 to 4-lobed fruit, similar to California Wonder but somewhat longer; attractive green, ripening to red; thick-walled, firm. Bushy plant; gives good protection from sunscald and hail; tolerant of adverse weather conditions; highly resistant to tobacco mosaic virus. A21, A56, A69M, B49, E97, *F72*, G57M, G68, *H61*, I84, J4, J34, K71, N39

PIMENTOS Thick-walled, usually heart-shaped or flattened fruits used for salads, stuffing, roasting, pickling or canning. Some forms are known as *squash peppers* or *cheese peppers*. Many of the sweetest peppers belong to this class.

Canada Cheese: A miniature red pimento which is about the size of a very large cherry pepper. Slightly flattened fruit, resembles Sunnybrook pimento but only 1/3 the size; 2 inches in diameter, 1 1/4 inches deep; green, ripening to red. Does not crack like cherry peppers. Excellent for pickling. J4, L42

Choco:[6] 75 days. Medium-sized, tomato-shaped fruit; glossy dark green, ripening to chocolate brown; thick-walled, very mild and sweet. Good for stuffing and salads. Hardy, productive plant; 2 to 3 feet tall. Does well in northern areas. E49, I99, J4, M0

Gambo: 90 days. Flattened globe-shaped, mostly 4-lobed fruit; 2 1/2 inches deep, 4 inches in diameter; glossy, rich deep-red; crisp flesh, very juicy and sweet. Excellent for stuffing and pickling. Should be harvested when fully red-ripe. Vigorous, medium-tall plant. E49, J4, K49M, *P75M*, T27M

Large Red: 65 days. Very large, tomato-shaped, multi-lobed fruit; 3 inches long, up to 5 1/2 inches in diameter; green, ripening to blood red; extra thick-walled, juicy, very mild and sweet. Ideal for pickling, salads, or as a colorful garnish. Plant grows 22 inches tall; bears fruit upright for easy picking. D11M

Pimento: (Pimento, Red Pimento) 75 days. Medium-sized, uniform, heart-shaped fruit; 3 1/2 inches deep, 2 1/2 inches wide at the top; dark green, ripening to deep bright-red; thick-walled, juicy, very sweet; small seed cavity. Widely used for stuffing, pickling and canning. Vigorous, productive plant. A2, B73M, C44, F12, *F72*, G51, G71M, H49, H66, I39, *I62*{PL}, J4, J34, K71, L97, etc.

Pimento Grande: Medium-sized, heart-shaped fruit; about 3 inches long, 2 1/2 inches in diameter; dark green, ripening to reddish-orange; thick-walled, of fine sweet flavor. Used in cooking; or may be picked red, roasted and peeled, and canned. F71M

Pimento L: 80 days. Large, heart-shaped fruit; 4 1/2 inches long, 3 1/2 inches in diameter; dark green, turning bright red at maturity; very thick-walled, sweet and mild. Widely used for canning. Vigorous, upright plant; height 18 to 24 inches; provides good cover; resists tobacco mosaic virus. *A1*, F19M, G27M, G79, G93M, J4, J84, K66, K73, M0, N16

Pimento Perfection: 75 days. Very smooth, heart-shaped fruit; 3 inches long, 2 1/2 inches in diameter; green, ripening to bright crimson red; flesh unusually thick, very sweet and juicy. Should be harvested when uniformly red. Excellent for stuffing and canning. Upright plant, to 30 inches tall; resistant to tobacco mosaic virus. A56, C76M, C92, D11M, *E91G*, G67M, *H57M*, J4, K10, L7M, *M43M*, M95M

Pimento Select: 72 days. Smooth, heart-shaped fruit; 3 1/2 inches long, 2 1/2 inches in diameter; deep green, ripening to brilliant red; thick-walled, very sweet and mild. Excellent for canning, freezing and pickling. Upright plant; height 33 inches; makes a concentrated set. D76, E97, *G1M*, G82, *I59M*, I91, J4

Red Heart: Large, thick heart-shaped fruits. Voted the best tasting sweet pepper among 25 cultivars grown by Peace Seeds in 1987 and 1988. I99

Sunnybrook: (Sweet Cheese, Burpee's Sunnybrook) 72 days. Tomato-shaped fruit; 2 inches deep, 3 inches in diameter; deep green, ripening to scarlet red; thick, very mild flesh. Excellent for stuffing. Tall, very productive plant. *E91G*, *H61*, J4, L42, M13M

Super Red Pimento: 70 days. Squash or flat-shaped type. An earlier, larger version of the standard pimento. Very large fruit, 5 3/4 inches wide, 3 1/4 inches deep; green, ripening to red; extra thick flesh, sweet and mild. Resistant to tobacco mosaic virus. I77, J4, L42, M0

Yellow Cheese: 73 days. Large, squash-shaped fruit, averages 25% larger than Sunnybrook pimento; green, ripening to yellow, then to orange-yellow at full maturity; thick-walled, sweet and mild. Contrasts well with red or green cheese types in baskets or relish. I77, I99, J4, K49M, L42

OTHERS

Hybrid

Gypsy: 65 days. Wedge-shaped, slightly curved fruit, 3 to 4 inches long; yellow, ripening to orange-red; medium thin walls, crisp and tender, sweet at full maturity; of excellent flavor and quality. Vigorous, spreading plant; height 12 to 20 inches; widely adapted; tolerant of tobacco mosaic virus. All America Selections winner in 1981. B73M, C44, C85M, D65{PL}, D82, F19M, *F72*, G16, G71, *H61*, J7, J58, K73, M0, M46, M49, etc.

Key Largo: 65-68 days. Very large, high quality Cubanelle type. Tapered, slightly curved fruit; 6 to 7 inches long; ripens from a yellow-green to bright orange. Ideal for frying or fresh use with a pleasant sweet flavor. Very high yielding. Excellent for home gardens. F13

Long Green Buddha: 70 days. Long, rather conical fruit; pungent with the seeds intact, has a strong green pepper taste when the seeds are removed. Valuable for its economical size and interesting shape. Compact, bushy plant; height 2 feet; produces 12 to 20 fruit over a long period. J20, *S70*

Twist Green: Small, slender, irregularly curved and wrinkled fruit; 2 1/2 to 3 inches long; thin, medium green skin. For home gardens or fresh market. Upright, slightly spreading plant, about 2 feet tall; high yielding over a long period; sets well under low temperature conditions. Suitable for indoor culture. J4, *Q3*

Open-Pollinated

Aconcagua: 70 days. Large Cubanelle type that can weigh up to 12 ounces. Long, tapered fruit; 2 1/2 to 3 inches wide, 10 to 11 inches in length; medium thick-walled, juicy, medium-sweet. Best harvested when light green. Tall, vigorous plant; sets well early and late. Named after Mt. Aconcagua in Argentina. E49, J4, K49M, K49T, M0

Corno di Toro Red: (Red Bull's Horn) 68 days. Long, tapered fruit, 8 to 10 inches long; color deep vivid red when ripe; similar to Corno di Toro Yellow but narrower and not as curved. Excellent eaten fresh or roasted, peeled, and then marinated. Vigorous, branching plant, bears heavily. C53, F80, I99, J4, J7, J66M, K66, Q34

Corno di Toro Yellow: (Yellow Bull's Horn) 68 days. Fruit about 8 inches long, 1 1/2 inches in diameter at the shoulder; tapered to a curved point, resembling the horn of a bull; ripens to a deep golden-yellow. Has a spicy flavor, neither hot nor very sweet. A traditional favorite in Italy. C53, F80, K66, *L59G*, Q34

Cubanelle: (Cuban) 65 days. Very popular frying pepper. Fruit long, tapering to a blunt end, 2 to 3-lobed; 2 1/2 inches in diameter, 5 to 6 inches in length; yellow-green, turning red-orange when ripe; medium thick-walled, waxy, of spicy flavor. Medium-tall, heavy yielding plant; sets fruit continuously. Introduced in 1958, probably from Italy. ANDREWS [Re]; A21, B1M, B75M, C44, E24, E49, *E91G*, F71M, *F72*, G71, *H61*, I76M{PR}, J14{PL}, J73, L89, M0, N16, etc.

Fehérözön:[2] Short, conical fruit, 3 1/2 to 4 1/2 inches long; borne in clusters; thin-walled; skin smooth, wax-yellow ("white"); flesh sweet. Popular for *letcho*, stuffed paprika, different kinds of pickles and deep-frozen paprika. Used for mid-season and late spring forcing and in outdoor growing for the early market. Resistant to tobacco mosaic virus. Originated in Hungary. SOMOS; J73

Fushimi Long Green: Long, thin fruit; 5 to 6 inches in length, only 1/2 inch wide; glossy, bright-green skin, wrinkled at maturity; thin-walled; sweet mild flavor. Can be sliced in cross-section for tiny rings. Tall, vigorous plant; very prolific. An old traditional Japanese cultivar. E59, J4, J73, *S63M*

Giant Szegedi: 70 days. Hungarian long, tapered yellow bell type. Extra large, top-shaped pendant fruit; 3 1/2 inches wide, 6 inches deep; changes color very uniformly, from pale green-yellow to butter-yellow, to orange-red at full maturity; very thick and sweet flesh. Tolerant to verticillium wilt. I77, J4, L42

Giant Yellow Banana: 60 days. A unique, large, Sweet Banana type from Hungary. Extra long, pendant fruit, to 7 inches long; thicker flesh, sweet flavor. Taller plant, to 26 inches; very prolific, hybrid-like yields; very easy to pick; purple-stemmed. J4, L42

Italia: 55 days. Long Italian Sweet type, similar to Corno di Toro. Long, slightly curved fruit; 2 1/2 inches wide, 8 inches in length; green, ripening to a dark crimson red; sweet, with a full pepper flavor that expresses itself well in sauces and fried preparations. Early and easy to grow. G6, J4, J20

Italian Sweet: (Long John) 65 days. Thin-skinned fruit; 6 to 7 inches long, 2 inches wide at the shoulder, tapering to a blunt point; dark green, turning red at maturity; medium-thick flesh, has a sweet mild flavor when fully ripe. Excellent for frying. Widely adapted throughout the Northeast. A13, B73M, C92, *E91G*, F71M, G51, G79, G93M, I77, I99, J4, J34, L7M, L89

Lipstick: 53 days. Heavy, cone-shaped fruit; about 5 inches long, tapering to a blunt point; attractive dark-green, ripening to a glossy rich red; thick-walled, juicy, flavorful. Good for salads, cooking and roasting. Dependably early, heavy yields, even in cool summer areas. G6, I77

Lombardo: Long, thin fruit, slightly wrinkled at the stem end, tapered to a point; approximately 4 to 4 1/2 inches in length; pale green in color; sweet flesh. Excellent for preserving in olive oil or brine. Very productive plant, grows 2 to 2 1/2 feet tall. Widely used in Italy for fresh market and by the commercial canning industry. Q11M

Marconi: Traditional long red and yellow sweet peppers from Italy. Tri-lobed fruit, slightly curved towards the lower end; up to 12 inches long, 3 inches across at the shoulder. Excellent for salads and frying, both green and when mature. Large plant. Mixed packet. C53

Nardello: (Jimmy Nardello) 75 days. Heirloom Italian frying pepper. Slender, tapered fruit; 1 inch wide, 7 to 8 inches long; green, turning red when ripe; thin-walled, extremely sweet. Excellent for frying or eating raw. Medium-tall, heavy yielding plant; disease resistant. I99, J4

Papri Mild: Long, slender fruit; 6 inches in length, 1 1/2 inches in diameter; deep green, ripening to bright dark red; thick-walled, high in flavor but mild in pungency. Can be dried in the sun or a dehydrator, and powdered for kitchen use. J34

Paradicsomalakú Sarga Szentesi: Small, flattened globe-shaped fruit, about 2 inches across and 1 inch deep; resembles a small pumpkin; green-yellow turning golden-yellow when ripe. Sweet, pleasant flavor. Imported from Hungary. Ask for it by name !. J73

Paradicsomalakú Zöld Szentesi: Small to medium-sized, flattened globe-shaped fruit, 2 inches in diameter; 3-4 ribbed; weight 2 1/2 to 3 1/2 ounces; medium thick-walled; dark green turning red when ripe. Sweet, pleasant flavor. Always picked at full maturity for the home fresh market and for processing. Processed into different kinds of purées, pastes, marinades, dehydrated produce and juice. SOMOS; J73

Peperoncini: 70 days. Tapered, usually wrinkled fruit; 2 1/2 to 3 1/2 inches long, 1 1/2 inches in diameter; green, turning red when ripe; thin-walled, sweet. Excellent for pickling green - harvest when 2 to 3 inches long. Large, upright plant; height 26 to 36 inches. ANDREWS [Re]; A21, D76, E97, F24, F71M, G51, G64, I39, I77, J4, J34, K49M, K66, L42

Red Cherry: (Cherry Sweet) Round, slightly tapered fruit; 1 inch deep, 1 1/2 inches in diameter; dark green, turning red at maturity; medium thin walls. Popular for pickling at either green or mature red stage. Medium-sized, bushy plant; height 18 to 20 inches; sets fruit continuously. A87M, B35M, B75M, E49, *E91G*, F71M, G71, G82, *H61*, H66, *I62*{PL}, J7, L7M, L89, M0, N39, etc.

Romanian White Gypsy:[2] Exotic heirloom from Romania bearing sweet peppers of a cream-white color, several inches long. I59G

Shishitou: Small, irregularly curved and wrinkled fruit; 2 1/2 to 3 inches long, about 1 inch across; thin, pale green skin; crisp and mild flavored. Suitable for tempura. Vigorous, productive, semi-upright plant with short internodes; widely adapted; early and heat resistant. For home gardens and fresh market. J4, *Q28*, *S70*

Sigaretta: Long, narrow fruit, slightly wrinkled at the stem end, tapered to a point; approximately 4 to 4 1/2 inches in length. Sweet, green flesh. One of the best cultivars for pickling in vinegar. B8, J73, Q11M

Slim Pim: Slim green fruit, about 4 inches long, turns red when mature. Best eaten when very young and tender. May be cooked whole in Chinese dishes or stews. Vigorous plants produce early and abundantly. Of Japanese origin. *G13M*, S55

Super Shepherd: 68 days. Very popular Italian Sweet type. Tapered, irregularly curved fruit; 7 1/2 inches long, 2 1/2 inches wide at the shoulder; dark red; unusually thick flesh, sweet and juicy, has a distinct flavor. Perfect length and flesh thickness for processing or frying. G79, J4, L42, M13M

Super Sweet Cherry: 75 days. Dark-green, easy to pick fruit by early July. Large, 1 3/4 inch, dark cherry-red fruit by mid-August. Used for pickling or processing. Exceptionally heavy early yields. Good crack tolerance. Resistant to tobacco mosaic virus. J4, L42

Sweet Banana: (Hungarian Yellow Sweet Wax) 70 days. Long, cylindrical fruit, tapering to a point; 1 1/2 inches in diameter, 6 inches long; waxy yellow, turning red when ripe; medium thick-walled, sweet and mild. Compact, sturdy plant; height 18 to 22 inches; produces an abundance of fruit over a long period. All-purpose cultivar for shipping, processing and fresh market. All America Selections winner in 1941. ANDREWS [Re]; A16, B78, C44, F19M, *F72*, F82, G71, *H61*, H66, *I62*{PL}, J7, L7M, L9M, M13M, M46, N16, etc.

Sweet Pickle:[3] 65 days. Dwarf plant, 12 to 15 inches tall; produces dense clusters of two inch oval fruits - yellow, orange, red and purple, all on the plant at the same time. Ideal as an ornamental bedding plant. Thick-walled fruit, sweet and flavorful, especially in the orange and red stages. Excellent pickled. I77, I91, J4, K49M, L7M

Sweet Plum: A novel cultivar from India. Small, nearly round fruit; 1 inch to 1 1/4 inches in diameter. Excellent for pickling. Prolific bearer. S59M

Tequila Sunrise:[3] 75 days. An ornamental pepper that also has sweet fruit. Tapered fruit; 4 to 5 inches long, 1 inch wide, borne upright; medium green, ripening to a golden-orange. Best used when green. Dwarf, compact plant; 12 to 14 inches tall, 12 inches wide; prolific and widely adapted. Ideal for ornamental borders, window boxes or pots. Introduced in 1979. J4, K49M, L7M, M81T

Zapotec Paprika:[7] Tapered fruit, to 3 inches long; purplish-black, ripening to dull reddish-orange; excellent mild, musky flavor; thin-walled so it dries well. Very productive plant, to 24 inches tall. Fruit ripens well when plant is hung indoors in short summer areas. I99

HOT PEPPERS

MEXICAN/SOUTHWESTERN

Anaheim: Long, tapered, pointed fruit; 7 to 8 inches long, 1 to 1 1/2 inches wide; light green, turning crimson red when ripe; medium thick-walled, mild to moderately hot. Very popular for stuffing when red-ripe. Vigorous, upright plant; height 28 to 30 inches. Widely grown in California and the Southwest. Originated near Anaheim, California in 1903. ANDREWS [Pre, Re], SCHNEIDER [Cul, Re]; C89{PR}, E24, F13, *F72*, G51, G71M, H66, H94, *I62*{PL}, J73, K66, K71, L9M, L89, M46, M95, N16, *N40*{PR}, etc.

Ancho: (Poblano, Mulato) Large, conical fruit; up to 5 1/4 inches long, 3 3/4 inches wide; deep dark-green, turning red at full maturity and reddish-brown when dry; mildly pungent to hot. Widely used for *chilis rellenos*. Plant grows 2 to 3 feet tall; requires a warm climate. Known as Poblano when fresh. Probably the most popular chili in Mexico. ANDREWS [Pre, Re], SCHNEIDER [Cul, Re]; A21, B75, C94M{PR}, F71M, F80, G67M, I39, I63T{PR}, I99, J4, J20, J25M, J66M{PR}, J73, K66, L79M, etc.

Cascabel: Mexican cherry type. Small, oblate fruit; 3/4 inch long, 1 inch in diameter; dark green, turning deep red at maturity and reddish-brown when dry; medium-thin walls; moderately pungent, spicy flavor. Very popular for drying. Medium-large plant, to 3 feet tall. Spanish name means "jingle" or "sleigh bells", referring to the rattle the pods make when dried. ANDREWS [Re], LATORRE 1977a [Re]; I63T{PR}, **U26**

Cascabella: (Cascabelle) 75 days. Small, heart-shaped fruit; 1 1/2 inches long, 3/4 inch in diameter; light yellow, turning deep orange-red at maturity; medium-thick walls, mildly pungent flavor. Widely used when in the yellow state by commercial packers for hot pickled chilis. Medium-large plant, to 3 feet tall. Developed by the Clarence Brown Seed Co. of Fresno, California. ANDREWS; A87M, I77, J66M, K66, N52

Catarina: Small, conical fruit, 3/4 to 1 inch long and 1/4 to 3/8 inch in diameter; skin green, turns red when ripe and translucent when dry; very pungent. Used interchangeably with Cascabel in the dry form, when green it is used in sauces as one would use Serrano. Popular in Mexico and along the Texas border. ANDREWS [Re]; **U26**

Chimayo: 95 days. Legendary chili, developed by the Hispanic residents of Chimayo, New Mexico. Long, slightly curved, blunt-ended fruit; 5 to 6 inches in length; mild when green, quite hot when red. Used for making the *chili ristras* found all over the Southwest. Plant grows 24 to 30 inches tall. J4, J25M, L79M

Coban: Small, conical fruit, 3/4 inch long and 1/2 inch wide; red when ripe; quite hot but flavorful. Traditionally preserved by being smoke dried like the chipotle chile. Planted in spring in the low hot desert. In temperate areas, sow in spring when the soil has warmed up some. From Guatemala, where it is sold in local markets. I16, I63T{PR}

Colorado: Anaheim type chili from New Mexico. Large, tapered, slightly pointed fruit; green, ripening to dark red. Used fresh (roasted and peeled) or dried and powdered. Excellent for *chilis rellenos*. F71M

De Arbol: (Tree Chile) 75 days. Tapered, pointed fruit; 2 1/2 inches long, 3/8 inch wide; light green, turning bright red when ripe; very thin-walled, very hot, although the hotness does not seem to irritate the stomach. Upright plant; 3 to 4 feet tall, 18 inches across; very productive; perennial in warm climates. ANDREWS [Re]; I16, I63T{PR}, J4, J73, K49T, L79M, M81T, *N40*{PR}

De Comida: Glossy red fruit, 4 to 6 inches long; rather hot. Traditionally used in making *mole*, a popular pre-Columbian sauce made from chilis, unsweetened chocolate, onions, tomatoes, cinnamon, etc. Fruit dries well for storage. From the state of Oaxaca, Mexico. F80, J73

Dr. Greenleaf Tabasco: (C. frutescens) 120 days. A virus resistant tabasco pepper developed at the University of Auburn. Produces a heavy crop of very pungent red pods; excellent for hot pepper sauce. Especially adapted to the South. Also an excellent ornamental. F19M

Española Improved: 70 days. A special short-season chili which will turn red and become hot even in cool, northern climates. Long, tapered, medium-sized fruit; dark-green, turning red when ripe; thin-walled; extremely hot; resembles Sandia. Can be used for fresh green chile or dry red products. Developed from a cross of Sandia and an Española Valley native type chili. Released in 1983 by the New Mexico State Agricultural Experiment Station. J25M, K5M, K49T

Guajillo: 58 days. Large, tapered fruit; 4 1/2 to 5 1/2 inches long, 1 to 1/4 inches in diameter; green, turning translucent red when ripe; thin-walled, quite hot. Good for drying. Grows 3 feet tall, 1 1/2 feet wide. Very popular in parts of Mexico, where it is nicknamed Chili Travieso or "naughty chili" due to its fierce bite. ANDREWS [Re]; I63T{PR}, J4, J73

Guero de Guanajuato: Conical fruit, 3 to 4 inches long and 1 to 1 1/4 inches wide, tapering to a point; yellow, turning orange, then red when completely mature; sweet flesh, moderately hot seed walls. Classic yellow hot pepper of Mexico used for pale yellow, regional sauces. Especially popular in the state of Guanajuato. Collected in a local market. **U26**

Habañero: (C. chinense) Square to heart-shaped fruit, often wrinkled; 1 1/2 to 2 inches long; light-green, turning orange at maturity. Has an unusual flavor and scent when ripe. Excellent for sauce. Reportedly the hottest pepper in the world. Requires a long, hot growing season. Spanish name means "of Havana" or "from Havana". ANDREWS [Re]; A21, *E53M*, *G13M*, I39, I63T, I63T{PR}, J4, J25M, J34, J73, J73{PR}, K49T, K66, M81T, M95, etc.

Jalapeño: 75 days. Sausage-shaped fruit, tapering to a blunt end; about 3 inches long, 1 to 1 1/2 inches in diameter; glossy deep-green, turning bright red when ripe; medium-thick walls, very pungent. Very common and popular cultivar; widely used in Mexican and Southwestern cuisine. ANDREWS [Pre, Re], SCHNEIDER [Cul, Re]; B35M, B75M, C44, D82, E49, F71M, G71M, *H61*, H66, H94, *I62*{PL}, I63T{PR}, L7M, M95, N39, etc.

Louisiana Hot: Elongated, tapered fruit, about 4 inches long; green, turning red when mature; very hot. Bears fruit early and prolifically. Heirloom cultivar preserved by the Arledge family of Louisiana. F80, I99, J4, K49T

Mexican Negro: 55 days. Unusual, sausage-shaped fruit; blunt-ended, 3 to 4-lobed, ridged along the length; dark green, changing to dark reddish-brown or black when ripe; thin-walled, with small bumps on the skin; mildly hot. Used for sauces, etc. Also excellent for drying. Grows 3 feet tall, 2 feet across, of fairly easy culture. A89, I16, J4, J73

Mirasol: (New Mexico Chili Improved, Mexican Improved) Fruit 5 inches long, 1 1/4 inches in diameter at the shoulder, tapering to a point; green, turning red at maturity; thick-walled, moderately hot; resembles Guajillo. Good for canning, freezing or drying. Imparts a yellow color to foods that are cooked with it. Borne mostly upright on 27 inch tall plants. Spanish name means "looking at the sun". The original form is a pre-Columbian cultivar. ANDREWS; B75M, I16, I63T{PR}, J4, J25M

New Mexico: Anaheim type, mainly grown along the Rio Grande River, especially around the town of Hatch, New Mexico. Tapered fruit; 4 1/2 to 6 inches long, about 1 1/2 inches in diameter; green, turning red when ripe; mildly hot, but flavorful. Popular for drying. Also used for *chilis rellenos* when green. High yielding plant; 30 inches tall, 15 inches across. J4, J73

Numex Big Jim: (Big Jim) 80 days. Large to very large fruit; 7 to 9 inches long, 2 inches wide at the shoulder, tapering to a blunt end; medium-green, turning red when ripe; thick-walled, medium hot. Used fresh (roasted and dried), dried and powdered, or canned. High yielding plant; provides good leaf coverage. A89, B75M, E97, F71M, *H61*, J4, J25M, J34, J83M, K5M, L91M, M95

Pasilla: Long, slender fruit; 6 to 7 inches in length, 3/4 to 1 inch wide; dark green, turning red, then brownish-black at full maturity; flesh mild, seeds and veins quite hot. Has a distinctive rich, smokey flavor with a hint of chocolate, making it essential for *mole* sauces. Called Chilaca when fresh. ANDREWS [Re], LATORRE 1977a [Re]; C94M{PR}, F71M, I63T{PR}, J66M{PR}, *N40*{PR}

Pico de Gallo: Small, narrow fruit; 3 inches long, tapering to a curved point; very hot. Very prolific, narrow-leaved plant; perennial in warm climates or where protected. From Sonora, Mexico. Spanish name means "rooster's beak". I16, J4

Sandia: 77 days. Tapered, flat, pointed fruit; 7 to 8 inches long, 1 1/2 to 2 inches wide; dark green, turning bright red at maturity; medium-thick walls, very hot when red-ripe. Can be used green or red, fresh or dried. Mainly roasted when green, peeled and frozen. Upright plant, 28 to 30 inches tall. A89, B75M, J25M, J73, K5M, M95

Santa Fe Grande: 75 days. A large Floral Gem type developed to have smoother fruit without "dimpling". Conical, blunt-ended fruit; 3 1/2 inches long, 1 1/2 inches wide at the shoulder; turns yellow at market stage, ripens to orange-red at full maturity. For fresh market, canning and pickling. Vigorous, upright plant; height 25 inches; resistant to tobacco mosaic virus. SCHNEIDER [Cul, Re]; A21, A87M, B75M, *E91G*, E97, F71M, G93M, *H61*, I77, J4, J25M, J73, K5M, K49T, *L59G*, M95, N16, etc.

Santo Domingo Pueblo: Heart-shaped fruit, 3 to 4 inches long, 1 inch in diameter; very hot, but not without a fruity flavor. Used fresh or dried. Similar to Chimayo but pointed. Treasured by the Native Americans of the Santo Domingo Pueblo of New Mexico. J73, L79M

Serrano: 80 days. Slender, cylindrical fruit; 2 1/4 inches long, 1/2 inch in diameter, tapering to a blunt point; medium dark-green, ripening to bright red; medium-thin walls, extremely pungent. Used for fresh market, pickling and sauce. Vigorous, highly productive plant; height 30 to 36 inches. Very popular in Mexico and the Southwest. ANDREWS [Pre, Re], SCHNEIDER [Cul, Re]; A87M, F19M, F71M, *G13M*, *H61*, H66, *I62*{PL}, J4, J25M, J34, J73, K66, K73, N16

Tabasco: (C. frutescens) Small, slender fruit, about 1 inch long; borne upright; yellow-green, turning scarlet when ripe; extremely hot. Used to make the famous Louisiana hot sauce. First raised by Edward McIlhenny at Avery Island, Louisiana from seeds brought from the state of Tabasco, Mexico by an American soldier returning from the Mexican War of 1846-48. ANDREWS [Re], HEISER 1969; G68, J4, J34, J73, K71, M0, M81T

Tabiché: 85 days. Tapered, pointed fruit; 5 inches long, 7/8 inch in diameter; glossy dark green, turning red when mature; smooth, thin-walled, crisp, very hot. Most often used while still green. Good for drying. Grows 2 feet tall, 18 inches wide. From the Zapotec Indians of the state of Oaxaca, Mexico. F80, J4

Tusté: Small, strawberry-sized fruit. Usually picked green, and ground and mixed with tomatoes for sauce. Very hot. Zapotec Indian cultivar from Oaxaca, Mexico. Grown in the cool climate of 7,500 feet elevation. Should do well anywhere in the United States. J4, M81T

OTHERS

Hybrid

Mexi Belle: 70 days. Unique hot pepper with a bell-pepper shape. Medium-sized, 3 to 4-lobed fruit; 4 inches square; medium-green, turning red when ripe; medium-thick walls, mildly hot flesh, pungent ribs. Hotness can be controlled by the amount of interior ribs left on during preparation. Compact plant; tolerant to tobacco mosaic virus. All America Selections winner in 1988. B75, C44, F19M, G6, G71, H42, *H61*, I39, I91, J7, J14{PL}, J34, K10, L79, M0, M46, etc.

Super Cayenne: 70 days. Attractive, slightly curved pods, 3 to 4 inches long; red when ripe; good fiery flavor. Excellent fresh or dried. Compact, spreading plant, height 2 feet; very prolific, bears 3 to 4 dozen peppers per plant; ornamental in appearance. Does well in containers. All America Selections winner for 1990. B75, D11M, I39, K10, M0, M29

Super Chili: 70 days. First hybrid chili pepper. Small, elongated. cylindrical fruit; 2 to 2 1/2 inches long, 1/2 inch wide; pale-green, turning red when ripe; thin-walled, very hot. Harvest at green or mature red stage. Upright, spreading, semi-compact plant; extremely prolific; bears fruit upright; ornamental. All America Selections winner in 1988. B75, C44, F19M, *F72*, G6, G79, H33, I39, I91, J4, J7, J14{PL}, J34, K66, L79, M0, M46, etc.

Open-Pollinated

African Bird: Long, slender fruit, 2 to 3 inches long about 1/2 inch in diameter; medium green, turning bright red when ripe; excellent, spicy hot flavor; resembles De Arbol. Very thin walls, making it ideal for drying, dries quickly. Tall, upright plant; height 5 feet, 18 inches across; very prolific. Widely grown in eastern Africa for commercial cayenne. C94M{PR}, L11

Almapaprika:[2] Small, round or somewhat flattened fruit; 1 inch tall; weight 1 1/2 to 2 ounces; extraordinarily thick-fleshed; skin smooth, ivory-white turning red when mature; pungent. Fruit cavity small. Processed into pickles. The most widely-grown hot pepper in Hungary. SOMOS; J4, J73

Berberé: 90-100 days. Smooth, tapered fruit; 6 inches long, 3/4 inch in diameter; turns bright red when ripe; fiery hot. Very tall, highly productive plant. From Ethiopia, where *berberé* is a generic term for a curry-like paste made of paprika, chilis, and spices. MESFIN [Re], VON WELANETZ; D87, I99

Datil: (C. chinense) Small, slightly undulated fruit, 1 1/2 to 2 inches long and 1/2 inch in diameter; smooth, waxy skin, green turning dark orange when ripe; relatively thin-walled, dries well; extremely hot but with a nice, full flavor, heat units 100,000 to 120,000. Tall, bushy plant, grows to 3 or 4 feet; moderately productive. Popular for relish, jelly and thick, catsup-like pepper sauces. A local favorite in St. Augustine, Florida. Introduced there about 300 years ago by Minorcan settlers. C87{PR}, J4

Eastern Rocket: 65 days. Long, flattened fruit; 2 inches wide at the shoulder, tapering to a blunt point; 4 to 6 inches in length; light yellow-green, changing to a glossy brilliant red when ripe; thick-walled, juicy, medium hot to hot. Good for pickling and salsa. Sets early and prolifically. A13, J4, L89, M49, M81T

Ecuadorian All-Purple Dwarf:[3] Jalapeño-sized fruits; glossy eggplant-purple, turning orange when mature; rather hot. Perennial bush to 2 feet tall; tolerant of cool weather. Stems, leaves and flowers are all purple. Ideal in small pots. Originally from the Upper Pastaza valley of Ecuador. I59G

Elephant's Trunk: Extremely long, tapered fruit, resembles the trunk of an elephant; deep green, changing to dark red; thick-walled, pungent. Good for salads and pickles. Very popular Indian cultivar. R50, S59M, S93M

Floral Gem: Medium-sized, blunt conical fruit, mostly three-lobed; turns a rich red on maturity. Used commercially in the yellow wax state. The pickled product is marketed by Trappey's of Louisiana as *Torrido chili peppers*. Spreading, vine-like plant, highly susceptible to tobacco mosaic virus. Introduced in 1921. ANDREWS; A87M, F71M, G51, J4, L50M{PR}

Fresno Grande: 75 days. Improved Fresno type. Small, conical fruit, tapering to a point; 3 inches long, 1 1/2 inches in diameter; medium green, turning bright red at maturity; medium thick-walled, very pungent. Upright plant; height 20 to 24 inches; sets fruit continuously; resists tobacco mosaic virus. Popular fresh market cultivar. Introduced in 1970. SCHNEIDER [Cul, Re]; F71M, G93M, J34, *N40*{PR}

Githeo Miris: (C. chinense) Mostly undulate, heart-shaped fruit, 2 to 2 1/4 inches long; relatively thin-walled; bright red when mature; extremely hot but with a distinctive flavor characteristic of the species. Good for sauce and drying. Needs a long, hot growing season to ripen properly. Originated in the Maldive Islands. U26

Goat Horn: 70 days. Tapered, cylindrical fruit, often curled and twisted; 5 to 6 inches long, 1/2 to 1 inches wide; deep green, turning cherry red when mature; fiery hot. Good for drying. Short plant; height 18 to 20 inches. E59, J4, L59, *L79G*

Golden Cayenne: Slightly curved, pencil thin, sabre-shaped fruit; 6 inches long; quite smooth with few wrinkles; attractive, golden-yellow color. Very hot, being suitable for East Indian and Thai cuisines. Bushy, upright plant; much more productive than other hot peppers. C13M, L42

Hot Apple: 70 days. Medium-sized, pale butter yellow, tomato-shaped fruit; 2 1/2 inches across, 1 1/2 inches deep; very thick, mild flesh; quite hot at the center core of seeds. Mostly used for pickling and canning; can also be used fresh from the garden. I77, J4, L42

Hot Portugal: 64 days. Large, smooth fruit, tapered to a point; 6 to 7 inches long; green, turning glossy, bright scarlet-red when ripe; thick-walled, fiery hot. Can be used when green, red or dried. Sturdy, high yielding plant. E24{CF}, F13, J4, L42, L89

Hungarian Rainbow Wax: 62 days. Semi-hot, blocky, thick-fleshed fruit, often 3 to 4-lobed. Changes from light yellow through a rainbow of sunset colors to red when fully ripe. Each fruit may have simultaneous hues of yellow, orange and red making striking pickled peppers. Also excellent for relishes, flavoring and salsas. F80, G82

Hungarian Yellow Wax: (Hungarian Long Wax) 70 days. Uniform, slightly tapered fruit; 6 to 7 inches long, 1 1/2 inches in diameter; waxy yellow, turning red at maturity; medium thick-walled, firm, very pungent. Popular for canning and pickling. Strong, upright plant; height 20 to 24 inches; sets fruit continuously. SCHNEIDER [Cul, Re]; A16, B73M, B75M, C44, E24, F71M, G6, *H61*, H66, H94, *I62*{PL}, J14{PL}, K73, L7M, L9M, M13M, M46, etc.

Italian White Wax: Tapered, pointed fruit; 2 to 3 inches long, 1/2 inch in diameter; pale yellow, turning pale red at maturity; moderately thin walls; snappy, mild flavor when picked young, quite pungent if left to mature. Upright plant; height 34 to 40 inches; productive over a long period. Very popular home garden cultivar for pickling. G93M

Large Red Cherry: 75 days. Small, flattened globe-shaped fruit; 1 to 1 1/2 inches in diameter; medium-green, turning dark red when ripe; thick-walled, very hot. Widely used for pickling and canning. Strong, upright plant; height 24 inches; sets fruit continuously over a long harvest period. A13, A16, A87M, B75, C44, *E91G*, E97, *H61*, H94, I39, J4, L42, M0, M13M, etc.

Long Red Cayenne: 70 days. Long, cylindrical fruit, tapered to a point; often curved and twisted; 4 to 5 inches long, 1/2 to 1 inch in diameter; deep green, changing to red when mature; very hot. Widely used fresh, dried, canned and pickled. Large, productive plant. A25, B73M, B75, D11M, D65, E24, *E91G*, H94, J4, J7, J20, L9M, L42, L97, M13M, N39, etc.

Long Slim Cayenne: 72 days. Long, slender fruit, tapered to a point, often wrinkled; 6 to 7 inches long, 1/2 inch wide; dark green, ripening to bright red; highly pungent. Excellent for drying. Vigorous, high-yielding plant; height 20 to 24 inches. Well known and popular cultivar. A87M, C85M, C92, D76, E97, F1, *F72*, *H61*, *I59M*, J4, J34, K71, K73, M0, M46, N16, etc.

Paprika: (Culinary Paprika) 85 days. Short, flattened, 4-lobed fruit; 2 inches long, 4 inches wide; thin-walled, very mild and flavorful. Excellent for drying and powdering. Especially popular in Hungarian cooking. Upright plant, 2 1/2 to 3 feet tall. A2, D76, I39, J4, K49M

Peter Pepper: Appropriately named, penis-shaped fruit; 3 to 4 inches long, 1 to 1 1/2 inches wide; green, turning red when ripe; thin-walled, very pungent. Excellent for pickling when green; also dries well. Large, prolific plant, 20 to 30 inches tall. A21, E49, H66, J4, M81T

Piri-Piri: (Peri-Peri) (C. chinense) Small, extremely hot red pepper from Angola, widely used in Portuguese cooking. Often used for *molho de Piri-Piri* (hot red pepper sauce), or minced and preserved in olive oil. Originated in Brazil. Brought by the Portuguese to Angola, where it became an integral part of the local cuisine. Occasionally found in Indian markets. ANDERSON, J. [Re], VON WELANETZ; M81T

Pricky Nu: 75 days. Small, slender fruit, about 1 1/2 inches long; borne upright; very hot. Very good for drying after turning red. May also be used when green, in the same manner as Jalapeños. Dwarf, ornamental plant, 12 to 18 inches tall; highly productive. F24M, J4

Purple Venezuelan: Very unusual and ornamental pepper with leaves that are dark purple above and green below. Flowers, stems and unripe fruit are also purple. Small, round fruit; 3/8 to 1/2 inch wide; remains purple for some time before changing to green, then bright red when mature; sizzling hot. C43M, M81T

Red Cherry: (Small Red Cherry) 75 days. Small, nearly round fruit; 1 inch long, 1 1/2 inches deep; dark green, turning dark red when mature; medium thick-walled, quite hot. Excellent for pickling and canning. Prolific, upright plant; height 18 to 20 inches. A69M, F71M, G71, G79, *H61*, H66, J34, *L59G*

Red Chili: (Finger Cayenne) (C. frutescens) Slender, conical fruit, borne upright; 2 to 2 1/2 inches long, 1/2 inch in diameter; green, ripening to a brilliant scarlet; exceedingly pungent. Good fresh or dried. Spreading plant, 16 to 20 inches high, 2 feet wide. Requires a long, warm season. Introduced prior to 1865. BURR, VILMORIN; A16, B73M, D76, *F72*, G64, G71, G79, H66, J4, J34, K71, K73, L89, M0, N39, etc.

Rocotillo: (C. chinense) Small, squash-shaped fruit, 1 to 1 1/2 inches in diameter; deep carmine-red when ripe; crisp textured; pungent enough to be interesting, but never caustic. Excellent eaten raw; also makes an attractive garnish. Traditionally used as a condiment with beans or carne asada. Grows well in central Texas but does not attain the size it would in its homeland (Peru). ANDREWS; M81T

Rouge Long: (Long Red, Guinea) Slender, elongated-conical fruit, often curved and twisted; 4 to 5 inches long, 1 inch wide; turns bright red when ripe; mild to very hot, hotness varying from plant to plant. One of the oldest hot peppers in Europe, which has remained essentially unchanged since its introduction in the 1500's by the Spanish. VILMORIN; Dropped by J73

Roumanian: 70 days. Blocky fruit, tapers to a blunt end; 4 inches long, 2 1/2 inches wide; yellow, turning brilliant red when mature; medium thick-walls, sweet flesh, pungent ribs. Used fresh or for canning. Bears continuously until frost. A16, *F63*, F71M, G79, *H61*, I39, I77, J4, J58, J84, M0

Santaka: (Hontaka) 75 days. Very hot red pepper widely used in Japan for traditional dishes and in the spice trade. Slender, tapered fruit; 2 1/2 to 3 inches long, 1/2 to 1 inch wide; green, turning scarlet red when ripe; thin-walled. Small, compact plant; height 15 to 18 inches; sets fruit continuously. Popular in California, where it is called Chili Japones. I63T{PR}, J4, J73, J83M, M81T, *N40*{PR}, *S70*

Scotch Bonnet: (C. chinense) 70 days. Small, roughly bell-shaped fruit, medium thin-walled; very attractive, turns red when ripe; extremely hot but with a distinctive spicy flavor and aroma. Short, compact plant. Popular in Jamaica and other parts of the Caribbean for hot pepper sauce. *B59*{PR}, F27{PR}, J4, L9M

Spur: Small, narrow, slightly curved fruit; 1 to 1 1/2 inches long and 1/2 inch in diameter; green, turning red when ripe, very hot; ripens late. Much used in Oriental cooking. Excellent dried and ground for chili-powder. Grows to 2 feet tall, bears fruit in upright clusters. F80, J4, L59

Sucette de Provence: Hot, thin red pepper specially selected for the climate of countries bordering the Mediterranean basin. Very attractive when threaded and hung to dry. Grows prolifically in hot weather. French name means "Provencal lollipop". Dropped by J4

Suryamukhi: (Surjamukhi, Clustered Suryamukhi) Slender, elongated-conical fruit, borne upright in clusters of 8 to 10; green, turning red when ripe; thick-walled, very hot and flavorful. Produces abundantly for 3 to 4 years; bears throughout the year. One of the best cultivars in India. N91, O39M, R50, S59M, S93M

Szentesi Semi Hot: 60 days. An elite hot Hungarian type. Tapered, pendant fruit; 4 1/2 inches long; lime green, turning an unusual lime yellow, then yellow-orange when mature; medium hot. Sold when lime yellow. For indoor or outdoor production. L42

Taka-No-Tsume: (C. frutescens) 68 days. Old-fashioned Japanese pepper, once widely cultivated in Honshu, Shikoku and Kyushu. Small, flame-shaped fruit; 1 1/2 to 2 inches long, 1/2 inch wide; upright growing in dense clusters at the ends of branches; deep dark-green, turning red at maturity; extremely hot. Dried fruits are powdered or added to pickled scallions. TANAKA; F71M, G20M{PR}, J4, *L79G*

Thai Hot:[3] Tiny, cone-shaped fruit, 3/4 to 1 inch long; green, turning red when mature; extremely hot. Dwarf, compact, mound-shaped plant; 8 inches tall, spreading to 18 inches; highly prolific. Ideal ornamental for patio containers or hanging baskets. C13M, C92, E59, F93G{PL}, G51, G84{PL}, I99, J4, J20, J66M, K49T, K66, M81T, Q34

Tiny Samoa: Extremely small fruit, only 1/8 inch thick and 1/2 inch long; green, turning red when ripe; very hot; Attractive plant with rich green foliage; produces hundreds of fruits. Makes an excellent house plant. E49

Yatsubusa: (C. frutescens) 80 days. Small, tapered fruit, 3 to 3 1/2 inches long; turns red when mature; thin-walled, fiery hot. Productive plant; height 20 inches. Fruits are more easily harvested than those of Santaka. Once widely cultivated in Shizuoka Prefecture Japan and used in the spice trade, now on the verge of extinction. TANAKA; I39, I99, J4, J73

Yellow Squash: (C. chinense) 95 days. Flattened fruit, slightly scallop-edged, resembles a patty pan squash; 2 to 3 inches wide, 1 to 1 1/2 inches deep; medium green, ripening to a golden-yellow; very hot. Extremely productive plant; height 24 inches; requires a long growing season. A21, H66, J4, J34, M81T

PERSIMMON {GR}

DIOSPYROS KAKI **DIOSPYROS VIRGINIANA**

AMERICAN PERSIMMONS

Small-fruited cultivars of the species D. virginiana, which is native to the Eastern United States from the Everglades of Florida, north to southern Connecticut, west to Kansas and south to eastern Texas. Their culture has been extended to southernmost Canada and to the drier western states. All are astringent until fully ripe.

Craggs: Large, somewhat acorn shaped fruit; skin yellowish, often red-blushed, attractive; flesh translucent, light yellow, texture and flavor excellent; seeds few; ripens in midseason, about Sept. 30 in Caseyville, Illinois. Tree sturdy; leaves glossy. Originated in Harrisburg, Illinois by a Mr. Craggs. Introduced in 1949. BROOKS 1972; I40

Dooley: Medium-sized, yellow fruit with a bright apricot-like flavor; ripens in early October. Quickly dries to a date-like fruit. Grows well near the northern limits of persimmon culture. E62

Early Golden: Large fruit, up to 2 inches in diameter; skin orange; flesh orange, mild, dessert quality excellent; ripens mid to late October. Tree will bear fruit if planted alone, but better results are obtained if planted with a pollinator. Probably the most widely planted cultivar in the United States. Selected from the wild in Alton, Illinois about 1880. A91{PL}, E41M{SC}, E62{OR}, E62{PL}, I40, I49M, I60{PL}, J61M{PL}

Ennis: Medium large fruit; flesh rather firm, seedless, quality good; ripens early. Has more fibrous material than high quality seeded cultivars, so that 1 gallon of raw fruit from it will yield no more strained pulp than 1 gallon of fruit from John Rick. Originated in

Bedford, Indiana by Ray G. Ennis. Introduced in 1955. BROOKS 1972, GRIFFITH; I40

Florence: Medium-sized fruit of high quality, resembles Early Golden; flavor excellent; seeds small, giving it a very high flesh/seed ratio; ripens early. Tree occasionally bears a modicum of staminate flowers. Has potential as a parent in breeding. Originated as a seedling of Killen. E41M{SC}

Garretson: Fruit slightly smaller and more spherical than Early Golden; flesh a rich clear orange, very tender, highly flavored; ripens during September and early October, about 10 days ahead of Early Golden; moderately seeded, seeds small. Tree very hardy and productive; nearly identical with Early Golden. Originated in Adams County, Pennsylvania. Introduced about 1921. BROOKS 1972; E41M{SC}, G75{CF}, I40

Gehron: Fruit medium-sized; skin bright orange-red; flesh sweet, nearly 100% seedless; ripens in late November and can hang on the tree until Christmas or early January. Tree with red-colored leaves; highly ornamental. Recommended for the deep south and Texas. Originated near De Ridder, Louisiana by Clyde Gehron. GRIFFITH; H4

Geneva Red: Medium to large fruit, blushed with red on the side exposed to the sun; has a bright apricot-like flavor; ripens in early October. Grows well near the northern limits of persimmon culture. E62

John Rick: Fruit one of the largest and firmest among September maturing American persimmons; flesh a beautiful red, quality excellent; resembles Florence but larger; the small deeply inset calyx minimizes skin punctures. Tree precocious; requires pollination by a 90 chromosome male cultivar, such as William. Originated in Urbana, Illinois by J.C. McDaniel. Introduced in 1963. BROOKS 1972; A91{PL}, B74, E62{OR}, E62{PL}, I40, I60{PL}, J61M

Killen: Fruit slightly larger, firmer and better flavored than Early Golden, which it resembles; ripens slightly later than Early Golden. Tree occasionally bears staminate-flowering branchlets; needs a 90 chromosome pollinator for reliable fruiting. A promising parent in breeding. Originated in Felton, Delaware by Joseph Killen. Introduced about 1930. BROOKS 1972; I40, I60{PL}, K16{PL}, N15

Lena: (Mitchellena) Small to medium-sized, rather flat fruit; skin very tender, orange, attractive; flesh a beautiful red color, soft, of excellent flavor; ripens early and over a long period of time. Culinary qualities very good; frozen pulp maintains its flavor well for a period of one year. Winner of a first prize in the Mitchell, Indiana persimmon festival. E41M{SC}

Meader: Medium-sized fruit; skin orange; flesh sweet, seedless if not pollinated; ripens in early October. Tree very hardy and productive; self-fertile, early bearing; good for cooler areas. Originated near Rochester, New Hampshire by E. M. Meader. Seedling of Garretson. B74, B74{PL}, E41M{SC}, E62{OR}, E62{PL}, G3M, I40, I49M

Miller: Large, roundish-oblate fruit; skin tough, skin reddish-yellow, translucent; flesh sweet, of good quality, seeds rather numerous. Originated in Jackson County, Missouri, where it ripens in September. BAILEY, L. 1947; G75{CF}

Morris Burton: Perhaps the best tasting American persimmon. Small to medium-sized fruit; skin very tender; flesh red, soft when tree-ripe, exceptionally high in sugar; not as early cropping as some. Tree somewhat slow to come into bearing, but then productive. Worth using as a breeding parent. Originated near Mitchell, Indiana by Morris Burton. GRIFFITH; E62{OR}, E62{PL}, G75{CF}, I40

Penland: (Pennland's Seedless) Fruit nearly seedless, varying with the abundance of compatible pollen from native male trees. Quality varies with location, but less sugary than many others. Trees have been killed by temperatures of -20^0 F. Originated near Penland, North Carolina. Introduced about 1937. BROOKS 1972, GRIFFITH; E62{OR}

Pipher: Medium to large, pale yellow fruit; has a bright apricot-like flavor; quality good; ripens in late October. Grows best from Ohio southward. E62{OR}, E62{PL}

Ruby: Small to medium-sized, roundish oblate fruit; skin yellowish-red, shading to deep-red, tender; flesh sweet, of very good quality, seeds few. Tree vigorous and heavy bearing; plant with a seedling for best results. Originated in Cartersburg, Indiana, where it ripens during September and for some time later. BAILEY, L. 1947; D37, I49M

Runkwist: Rather large, seedy fruit of relatively good quality. Once mistakenly thought to be self-pollinating. E41M{SC}, I40

Sweet Lent: Small, attractive fruit, 1 1/2 to 2 inches in diameter; flavor rich and sweet, fine for eating fresh; ripens very late, in December, holds well into March. Dries naturally on the tree, turning to a rich date-like confection. Tree spreading, productive. First discovered on an Ash Wednesday, hence the name. B75, D37

Szukis: Medium-sized, orange fruit; has a bright apricot-like flavor; ripens in late September. Tree hardy, productive; produces male and female flowers, but best grown with a pollinator. E62, E91M

Wabash: High quality, fragrant, early persimmon with parthenocarpic tendencies. Fruit rather small; flavor distinctive and aromatic; flesh redder than any in the Early Golden family; seeds small when present. Leaves color red before falling. Originated in Pinkstaff, Illinois; hardy in Urbana, Illinois, where earliest fruits are ripe in mid-August. GRIFFITH; I40

William: (Williams Male) Produces some small fruits in some years. Mostly grown as a pollinator for other American persimmons. Blooms profusely over an extended period; mostly staminate, but with a few perfect ones producing scattered mediocre fruits. Tree a good rootstock; sturdy, spreading; produces many suckers. Originated in Urbana, Illinois by J.C. McDaniel. Introduced in 1952. BROOKS 1972; E41M{SC}

Yates: Very large, yellow fruit, up to 2 1/8 inches in diameter; fine apricot-like flavor; excellent quality; seedless if grown without a pollinator; ripens very early, in mid-August in southern Indiana. Tree a prolific bearer. Winner of the first prize at the Mitchell, Indiana persimmon festival in 1983. D37, E62, I40, N15

ORIENTAL PERSIMMONS

Large-fruited persimmons whose culture is generally limited to subtropical and warm-temperate regions. A few cultivars are dependably hardy as far north as Pennsylvania. There are two types: astringent and non-astringent, the latter being preferred for eating out of hand. One group of cultivars bears fruit with light- colored flesh when seedless, but after pollination and seed formation, the flesh is dark-colored. (D. kaki)

ASTRINGENT Fruit of astringent types must be fully ripe before eating or they will pucker the mouth. The existence of astringency is closely related to some cultural techniques, especially seed formation. Adapted to cooler areas than non-astringent types. In hot regions they show good coloring and high sweetness but poor texture, and deep black spots develop.

Eureka: Medium to large, oblate fruit, puckered at the calyx; skin bright orange-red; flesh astringent until fully ripe, of good quality; sometimes seedless; ripens late, or in November in Florida; hangs on tree until soft and ripe. Tree small, vigorous; drought and frost resistant; precocious and heavy bearing. One of the most satisfactory cultivars for Florida and Texas. MCEACHERN, MORTON 1987a; *A19*, C37, F93, I74, L33, L90, M31M, M76, M83, N33

Gailey: Fruit small, roundish to conical with a rounded apex; skin dull-red, pebbled; flesh dark, firm, juicy, of fair flavor. Tree small to medium; bears many male flowers regularly and is an excellent cultivar to plant for cross-pollination; has very attractive autumn foliage and ornamental value. MORTON 1987a, POPENOE, W. 1920; C25, *O97*, *Q93*

Great Wall: (Atoma) Small to medium-sized fruit, 2 to 2 1/2 inches in diameter; flat, four-sided; skin orange, with fine black stripes extending around the calyx; flesh yellow, dry, very sweet, astringent; ripens in mid-autumn. Tree relatively slow growing, upright; heavy, but biennial bearing; very cold-hardy; recommended for colder regions; also does well in Florida. MORTON 1987a, SHANKS; B75, C25, D37, G17

Guiombo: Very large, conical fruit, weighing up to 16 ounces; skin thin; flavor excellent. Tree very productive; one of the best cultivars for Florida, but is a biennial bearer when young. Perhaps the same as Korean. MORTON 1987a; C25, G17

Hachiya: Large, oblong-conical fruit, up to 4 inches long; skin glossy, deep orange-red; flesh dark-yellow with occasional black streaks; astringent until fully ripe and soft, then fairly sweet and rich. Seedless or with a few seeds. Ripens midseason to late. Much used in Japan for drying. Tree vigorous, upright-spreading; prolific in California, a scanty bearer in the southeastern United States. MORTON 1987a; C25, E4, F11, F19M, G17, *G49*, H26M{PR}, I49M, I83M, I99{S}, J61M, L1, *L47*, L99M, M77, *N40*{PR}, etc.

Hiratanenashi: Fruit medium-large, oblate, somewhat four-sided; skin bright-orange, thick; flesh astringent, sweet, quality high when fully ripe; seedless; keeps only a short time after curing. Mostly used for drying. Tree medium-large, spreading; has a high annual bearing tendency. An old and popular cultivar in Japan. MORTON 1987a; C25, D37, *O97*

Honan Red: Small, roundish oblate fruit, weight 2 to 4 ounces; thin skin; skin and flesh ripen to a distinct bright orange-red; very sweet and rich. Excellent for fresh eating or drying. Ripens midseason to late, the fruit hanging well on the tree. Tall, upright, moderately vigorous tree; bears good crops. C25{OR}, D57{OR}

Kyungsun-Ban-Si: Fruit medium in size, oblate; 2 1/2 to 3 inches in diameter; flesh orange, sweet and juicy, of high quality; color ripe in early October; keeps well. Vigorous, upright tree with showy dark-green leaves. Has a very low tendency to parthenocarpy, producing more fruit when planted with a pollinator, such as Yamagaki. SHANKS; C25, D37

Okugosho: Medium-sized, round fruit, to 190 grams; skin orange to deep-red; flesh sweet, of good texture, flavor good; suffers from inconsistent astringency loss; ripens in early September. Tree medium-sized, vigorous, spreading; differentiates male flowers, making it suitable as a pollinator. An older cultivar. C25

Peiping: Rounded, medium-sized fruit, averages about 140 grams in weight; skin strong orange; flesh yellow-orange, very astringent until soft unless some artificial treatment is given, quality fair to good; seed content low. Tree relatively slow growing; at maturity somewhat spreading; leaves have essentially no fall coloration. Originated in Round Hill, Virginia by J. Russell Smith. Introduced about 1940. BROOKS 1972, SHANKS; C25

Saijo: Small, elongated fruit; skin dull-yellow when mature; flavor sweet, excellent, ranked among the best by gourmets; seedless; stores well. Mature fruits are attractive when dried, especially if they are treated with sulfur dioxide before dehydration to prevent browning. Tree medium in height; bears consistently; cold hardy to -10^0 F. Japanese name translates as "the very best one". C25, D37, F19M, G17, I49M

San Pedro: Deep orange, oblate fruit of very good flavor; quality excellent; ripens early. Tree small, precocious; has performed well in Maryland. D37

Sheng: Fruit medium to large, 3 to 4 inches in diameter; ribbed, puckered at the calyx; skin yellow-orange; flesh astringent, of high quality; ripens in October, loses astringency uniformly; dries well. Tree open, wide spreading, medium in vigor; irregularly branched; bears annually and more productively when planted with a pollinator, such as Yamagaki. SHANKS; C25, D37, G17

Smith's Best:[1] (Giboshi) Small to medium-sized fruit, 2 1/2 inches in diameter; flesh of seedless fruit yellow, astringent, seeded fruit will be dark-fleshed or "chocolate" colored when soft ripe, without astringency even when hard; color ripe in early October, or 2 weeks earlier than Tecumseh. Compact, densely branched, small tree; heavy bearing. Found at J. Russell Smith's farm in Round Hill, Virginia. SHANKS; D37

Tamopan: Large, somewhat four-sided fruit, broad-oblate; indented around the middle or closer to the base; 3 to 5 inches wide; skin thick, orange-red; flesh light orange, usually astringent until fully ripe, then sweet and rich; of medium quality; seedless or nearly so. Ripens late in Florida; midseason in California. In some parts of China and Japan said to be non-astringent. MORTON 1987a, POPENOE, W. 1920; *A19*, *C54*, E4, F19M, *I68*, I74, L1, L90, M31M, M83, N33

Tanenashi: Medium-sized, round-conical fruit, 3 1/3 inches long and 3 3/8 inches wide; skin light-yellow or orange, turning orange-red, thick; flesh yellow, astringent until soft, then sweet; seedless; ripens early. Tree vigorous, rounded, prolific. Leading cultivar in the southeastern United States. In California, tends to bear in alternate years. MORTON 1987a, POPENOE, W. 1920; A85M, B75, C25, E29M, F19M, F93, G17, *I68*, I74, L33, L90, M31M, M76, M83, N33, etc.

Tecumseh: Small to medium size fruit, 2 to 2 1/2 inches in diameter; flesh yellow, of high quality, seedless; color ripe in early October. Vigorous, densely branched, upright tree; a reliable bearer; very fruitful when planted alone; has good fall color. High tendency to parthenocarpy. May over-produce without pollination, resulting in small fruit size. SHANKS; D37

Yamato Hyakume:[1] Fruit large, elongated, conical; skin orange-red, attractive, streaked black at fruit top; flesh has little tannin when seed content is low, turns chocolate brown with pollination; tends to growth-ring cracking; ripens the end of October; suitable for drying. Tree upright; medium in vigor; bears heavily. MORTON 1987a; C25, G17

NON-ASTRINGENT Fruit of most non-astringent types may be eaten when they are firm-ripe, much like apples. However, many develop a richer flavor if they are allowed to soften somewhat. Adapted to warmer regions than astringent cultivars. In cool areas, this type does not fully mature, they show low sweetness and are poorly colored.

Chocolate:[1] Small to medium-sized, oblong-conical fruit; skin reddish-orange; flesh brown-streaked when cross-pollinated, must be fully soft-ripe before eating; ripens late October to early November. Tree large; vigorous; produces many male blossoms. Recommended as a pollinator for pollination variant cultivars such as Hyakume and Zenji Maru, which require seed formation for the flesh to turn brown. A88M, *C54*, E4, E87, *I68*, L1, *L47*, *N20*, N33

Dai Dai Maru:[1] Fruit of medium size, has a broadly rounded apex; skin orange-red, glossy with a slight bloom; flesh dark, not edible until fully cured; seedless unless cross-pollinated. Tree semi-erect; bears good crops regularly. MORTON 1987a; C25{OR}, *Q93*

Fuyu: (Fuyugaki) Medium-large, oblate fruit, faintly four-sided; 2 inches long, 2 3/4 inches wide; skin deep-orange; flesh light-orange, sweet, mild, non-astringent, even when unripe; seeds few or none. Keeps well; also an excellent packer and shipper. Tree vigorous, spreading, productive. Most popular non-astringent cultivar in Japan and the United States. MORTON 1987a; C25, D34M{PR}, E4, E29M, E87, F11, F19M, F93, F97M{PR}, G17, *G49*, I83M, J61M, L1, *L47*, L90, etc.

Hana Fuyu: (Giant Fuyu) Large, roundish-oblate fruit; skin reddish-orange, attractive, when fully ripe has one of the deepest red colors of any persimmon; flesh quality good, sweeter than Fuyu, non-astringent even when not ripe; usually seedless; ripens in late October. Tree somewhat dwarf; bears regularly but sets a light crop in some seasons; prone to premature shedding of fruit. BROOKS 1972, MORTON 1987a; A88M, C25, *C54*, E4, F19M, G17, *I68*, I83M, *N20*

Hanagosho: Fruit large, flat, four-sided; skin orange; flesh of good texture; flavor and quality excellent; ripens mid to late November; slow in losing astringency in some areas. Tree vigorous, upright; not high yielding; deficient in male flowers. MORTON 1987a; C25, G17

Hyakume:[1] Fruit large, up to 3 inches long; roundish oblong to roundish oblate; skin buff-yellow to light-orange, marked with rings and veins near the apex; flesh dark cinnamon when seeded, juicy, of firm texture, non-melting; flavor spicy, very good. Non-astringent even while the fruit is still hard. Ripens in midseason; stores and ships well. MORTON 1987a; E4, *I68*

Ichikikei Jiro: Medium-large, flat fruit; skin orange; flesh non-astringent even when not ripe, flavor very good; ripens in early midseason. Tree not vigorous, dwarf in habit, height 10 to 15 feet; recommended where space is limited; tolerant to anthracnose. To ensure good fruit production, plant with a suitable pollinator such as Gailey. MORTON 1987a; C25, *O97*

Izu: Medium-sized fruit, around 180 grams; skin burnt-orange, has virtually no brown lumps; flesh soft, with a good amount of syrup, of fine texture; flavor very good; ripens early, from the end of September to mid-October, almost a month earlier than others; keeps well for an early cultivar. Tree somewhat dwarf; bears only female flowers; sets good crops. C25, K67

Jiro: Fruit large, to 250 grams; resembles Fuyu, but more truncated and squarish in cross-section; skin orange-red; flavor and quality excellent; ripens late October and early November, ships well. Tree slightly upright; self-pollinating; tolerant to anthracnose. Second most popular non-astringent cultivar in Japan. C25, *C54*, I49M, K67, L99M

Maekawajiro: Medium-sized, rounded fruit, smoother and less indented than Jiro; rich orange in color; sweet and of good quality; ripens in mid-season, or about with Ichikikei Jiro. Tree slightly upright; must be planted with a suitable pollinator to ensure good fruit yield. Bud mutation of Jiro. *O97*

Maru:[1] Small to medium-sized fruit, rounded at the apex; skin brilliant orange-red, attractive; flesh dark cinnamon, juicy, sweet and rich; quality excellent. Stores and ships especially well. Pollination variant type, after pollination the flesh is dark colored and seeded. Tree vigorous and productive. Generally considered a group name. MORTON 1987a; *I68*

Matsumoto Wase Fuyu: Fruit of medium size, to 180 grams; skin glossy, orange; texture and quality very good; ripens mid to late October, 2 weeks earlier than Fuyu. Tree vigorous, spreading; produces heavy crops if planted with a suitable pollinator. Bud mutation of Fuyu. *O97*

Shogatsu: Medium-sized, flattened fruit; flesh non-astringent, sweet, of fair quality; ripens mid to late November. Tree medium-sized, rounded, spreading; moderately productive; bears an abundance of male flowers, making it a good pollinator. C25

Suruga: Large fruit, weight about 250 grams; skin orange-red; flesh dense, very sweet, sugar content 17.5%, juice moderately thick, quality excellent; non-astringent; seeds few; ripens in November, keeps well. Tree almost free from biennial bearing; recommended for warmer climates. One of the most promising new cultivars, produced by a cross of Hanagosho x Okugosho. C25, K67

Yamagaki:[1] Small, top-shaped fruit without the flavor and sweetness of Smith's Best. A good pollinator for Smith's best and other cultivars. Tree has proven reliably winter hardy; bears both staminate and pistillate fruit and will always produce seeded, non-astringent fruit with dark flesh. The most cold-hardy oriental persimmon with male flowers. D37

PLUM {GR}

PRUNUS SPP.

AMERICAN PLUMS

Included here are hardy, native American plums and their hybrids, which are generally crosses with the Japanese plum (P. salicina). The natives are the hardiest, some tolerating temperatures of -50^{0} F.

GREEN/YELLOW-SKINNED

Dandy: (P. nigra) Medium-sized fruit, about 1 1/4 inches long; skin yellow, blushed with red; quality very good; ripens early. For eating fresh or for culinary use. Tree a prolific bearer. Originated in Valley River, Manitoba, Canada by W.J. Boughen, Boughen Nurseries. Introduced in 1923. BROOKS 1972; B47, G54, N24M

South Dakota: (P. americana) Medium-sized, oval fruit; skin yellow, blushed with bright medium red; flesh yellow, tender, meaty, very sweet; quality very good; freestone; ripens in September. Good for eating fresh or processing. Tree productive; very hardy; self-sterile; an excellent pollinizer for American-Japanese hybrid cultivars. Also an excellent parent for breeding hardy, freestone plums. ANDERSEN, BROOKS 1972; E97, F53

RED/PURPLE-SKINNED

Acme: (P. nigra x) Medium-sized, spherical fruit, up to 2 inches long under non-irrigated field conditions; skin dark red; flesh yellow, dessert quality excellent; ripens in early September. Tree hardy. Originated in Saskatoon, Saskatchewan, Canada by C.F. Patterson. Introduced in 1960 for home gardens. BROOKS 1972; B47, C58, N24M

Aitken: (P. nigra) Medium to large, oval fruit; skin dark red, thin; flesh yellow, flavor moderately rich and sweet, quality good; stone large, clinging; ripens early to midseason. Tree vigorous and productive. Found wild in Aitken County, Minnesota by D.C. Hazelton. Introduced in 1896. WAUGH; U8{SC}

Assiniboine: (P. nigra) Medium-sized, round fruit; skin yellow with a bright red blush and light bloom, thin, astringent; flesh yellow, soft, very juicy, moderately sweet; quality good; ripens in mid-August. Tree upright, vigorous, productive. Widely used in breeding for winter hardiness. Named in 1908. ANDERSEN; A69G{SC}, F91T{SC}, N24M

Bounty: (P. nigra) Medium to large, dark red fruit; flesh orange-yellow, tender, juicy, sweet; quality fair for dessert, good for canning; ripens in late August. Tree upright, spreading; very hardy; productive; suitable for northern conditions. Originated in Morden, Manitoba, Canada. Introduced in 1939. BROOKS 1972; B47, C58

Dropmore: (Dropmore Blue) (P. nigra) Medium to large fruit, 1 1/4 inches in diameter, 1 1/2 inches long; skin purplish-red with a bluish bloom; flesh yellow, sweet, meaty; suitable for dessert and preserves; ripens in mid-September. Tree vigorous; hardy; productive. Originated in Dropmore, Manitoba, Canada. Introduced in 1941. BROOKS 1972; G67, N24M

Elite: (P. nigra x) Large, spherical fruit; skin dark red; flesh yellow, juicy, of very good quality; ripens late, in early September; resembles Acme and Prairie. Tree vase-shaped, low spreading, hardy. Originated in Saskatoon, Saskatchewan, Canada. Introduced in 1960 for home gardens. BROOKS 1972; B47

Grenville: (P. nigra x) Large fruit, 2 inches long; skin red mottled with yellow; flesh golden yellow, dessert quality excellent; ripens in late August; resembles Burbank. Tree very hardy. Originated in Ottawa, Ontario, Canada. Introduced in 1941. BROOKS 1972; A65, B47, C58, G1T, G69M, H85, K64, N24M

Miner: (P. hortulana) Medium to small, round-oblong fruit; skin dull red with a bluish bloom and many yellow dots, thick; flesh yellow, quality fair to good; stone medium large, clinging. One of the oldest native plums known. Originated in Knox County, Tennessee by William Dodd, an officer under General Jackson. WAUGH; **U8{SC}**

Monitor: (P. americana x) Medium to large, roundish ovate fruit; skin thick, dull bronze-red, with very conspicuous russet dots, bloom light; flesh yellow, tender, very juicy, firm, sweet, quality good; clingstone; cracks in rainy weather; ripens in late midseason. Tree vigorous, upright, spreading; very hardy; productive. BROOKS 1972; B75, *G89M*, *H90*

Norther: (P. nigra) Small to medium-sized, oval fruit; skin thin, tender, bright red with light gray bloom; flesh yellowish, juicy, sweet; pleasant as a dessert fruit, fair for cooking; ripens very early. Tree moderately spreading; strong, sturdy; hardy; annually productive; suited to northern prairies. Originated in Morden, Manitoba, Canada. BROOKS 1972; B47, N24M

Patterson's Pride: (P. nigra x) Large fruit, up to 1 3/4 inches in diameter under non-irrigated conditions; skin deep red; flesh orange-yellow, quality excellent for dessert and processing; keeps well in ordinary storage; ripens in mid-September. Tree low-growing; yields well; hardy. Originated in Saskatoon, Saskatchewan by C.F. Patterson. BROOKS 1972; C58, G54, N24M

Pembina: (P. nigra x) Large, round-ovate fruit, tapered to a point; skin red, thick, with a heavy bluish bloom; flesh light yellow, juicy, sweetish; quality good for dessert, only fair for canning; ripens in late August. Originated in Brookings, South Dakota by N.E. Hansen. Introduced in 1923. BROOKS 1972; A65, *A74*, B4, B47, G1T, G54, G69M, H42, H85, K64, K81, L79, N24M

Prairie: (P. nigra x) Large fruit, up to 2 inches long and 1 3/4 inches in diameter under non-irrigated orchard conditions; skin dark red; flesh yellow, dessert quality good; somewhat freestone; ripens in early September; resembles Acme. Tree medium-sized, moderately spreading; hardy. Originated in Saskatoon, Saskatchewan, Canada by C.F. Patterson. BROOKS 1972; B47, G54, K64

Salsberry:[3] Small to medium-sized fruit, 1 1/4 to 1 1/2 inches in diameter; skin maroon to dull reddish; flesh dark maroon, excellent for dessert, also makes superior jam; ripens very early, mid-May to mid-June. Tree a genetic dwarf, mature height only 8 feet; apparently self-fertile, seting heavy crops annually. Very low chilling requirement. Originated in Vista, California. THOMSON 1983; **T49M{SC}**

Supreme: (P. nigra x) Large fruit, up to 2 inches long under non-irrigated field conditions; skin blushed; flesh yellow, dessert quality excellent; ripens in late August. Tree medium upright, slightly spreading; moderately vigorous; free of winter injury at Saskatoon. Originated in Saskatoon, Saskatchewan, Canada by C.F. Patterson. Introduced in 1960 for home gardens. BROOKS 1972; M35M, N24M

Surprise: (P. americana x) Medium to large, roundish-oval fruit; skin bright red with medium bloom, moderately tough, slightly acid; flesh pale yellow, smooth, firm, melting, moderately juicy; flavor rich; quality good; stone oval, clinging. Tree vigorous, productive. Originated in Sleepy Eye, Minnesota by Martin Penning. Named in 1882. ANDERSEN, WAUGH; N24M

Wayland: (P. hortulana) Medium to large, spherical fruit; skin bright cherry red, with numerous white dots and a thin white bloom, thick and firm; flesh firm, meaty, yellow, quality good; stone semi-clinging. Tree vigorous and productive. Originated in a plum thicket in the garden of Professor H.B. Wayland, Cadiz, Kentucky. First propagated in 1876. WAUGH; **U8{SC}**

Weaver: (P. americana) Large, oval fruit with unequal halves; skin thick, orange heavily overlaid with red, bloom bluish; flesh firm, yellow, moderately juicy, quality good; stone large, half-free; season medium late. Tree a strong, upright grower; moderately productive. Found wild near Palo, Iowa by a Mr. Weaver. Introduced in 1875. ANDERSEN, WAUGH; F91T{SC}

Whitaker: (P. munsoniana) Medium to large, roundish fruit; skin thin but firm, yellow-orange with a bluish bloom; flesh yellow, moderately firm, slightly stringy, juicy, flavor sweet and good; stone small, clinging; ripens early. Tree moderately vigorous, upright, hardy, moderately productive. Originated under cultivation with J.T. Whitaker of Texas, prior to 1900. ANDERSEN, WAUGH; F91T{SC}

Wolf: (P. americana) Medium to large, oval fruit; skin thick, tough, crimson over orange, bloom bluish; flesh yellow, quality fair to good, somewhat too acid for culinary use; stone medium large, perfectly free. Tree productive; bears annually; widely adapted. Originated on the farm of D.B. Wolf, Wapello county, Iowa, about 1852. WAUGH; F91T{SC}

EUROPEAN PLUMS

Generally smaller than Japanese plums. They also have more solid flesh, are best when completely ripe, and have a greater range of flavors. They are suitable for dessert or cooking or for both. Most have a high chilling requirement, are late blooming and quite hardy. European plums pollinate only other European plums. Mostly P. domestica.

COMMON

Green/Yellow-Skinned

Alabaster: Very attractive, nearly round fruit; skin clear pale-yellow, entirely covered with a heavy white bloom; flesh firm, meaty but melting, juicy, very sweet and flavorful, quality excellent; ripens in mid-August, 1 to 2 weeks before Pearl. Tree a regular and heavy cropper. Originated by Southmeadow Fruit Gardens, Lakeside, Michigan. Received the highest rating in a four year taste-panel testing. J93{SC}, L12

Coe's Golden Drop: Fruit medium to large; oval, with a prominent neck at the stem end; skin straw-yellow; flesh golden yellow, firm, very juicy, very sweet, flavor apricot-like; stone free; ripens very late. Has been described as the Cox's Orange Pippin or Doyenné du

Comice of the plum world. First raised by Jervaise Coe, at Bury St. Edmund's, Suffolk, England about 1809. HEDRICK 1911, SIMMONS 1978; M22, Q30{SC}

Golden Nectar: Fruit very large; skin golden-amber, thin, tender; flesh amber, flavor excellent; stone very small; ripens evenly; matures in late July, has good keeping qualities. Good fresh or dried. Tree self-fertile. Promising, relatively new cultivar. A88M, F11

Laxton's Delicious: Roundish-oblong fruit; skin deep yellow blushed with red, with lavender-blue bloom and white dots; flesh yellowish, very sweet, very juicy; stone small, clinging; ripens in mid-September, will keep for several weeks after being picked. Tree vigorous, hardy; bears well if properly pollinated. Coe's Golden Drop x Pond's Seedling. SIMMONS 1978; U8{SC}

Pearl: Medium-sized, roundish-oval fruit, with unequal halves; skin golden-yellow, speckled with red dots; flesh deep yellow, juicy, firm but tender, very sweet, aromatic, with a pleasant, mild flavor; quality very good to best; clingstone. Tree vigorous, hardy, unproductive. Originated in Santa Rosa, California by Luther Burbank in 1898. HEDRICK 1911; J93, J93{SC}, L12

Reine Claude de Bavay: Medium to large, round to oblong fruit; skin pale green yellow with numerous white dots; flesh deep yellow, juicy, with a rich gage-like flavor; ripens the end of September, will hang on the tree for several weeks. Tree moderately vigorous, compact, very suitable for small gardens. Introduced about 1843 by Major Esperen, one of Napoleon's cavalry officers. SIMMONS 1978; U8{SC}

Warwickshire Drooper: Medium to large, oval fruit; skin pale yellow, spotted and speckled with brownish-red, bloom light; flesh yellowish, firm, flavor fair to good. Good for preserving, the canned product having excellent appearance and a bright clear-golden color. Tree large, vigorous; very hardy; self-compatible. SIMMONS 1978; O81, Q30{SC}

Yellow Egg: Medium to large, long-oval fruit; skin golden-yellow, covered with thick bloom; flesh golden-yellow, rather juicy, firm, moderately sweet, quality good; stone semi-free or free; ripens late, season short. Very good for canning. Tree large, vigorous; very productive; hardy. Introduced prior to 1676. HEDRICK 1911; B67, B67{DW}, E84, *H34*, H65, J61M, M39M

Red/Purple-Skinned

Belle de Louvain:[1] Cooking plum. Large to very large, long-oval fruit; skin dull purplish-red, covered with delicate bloom; flesh yellow, soft, not very juicy, becoming dark and richly flavored when stewed; stone partially free; ripens in midseason. Makes a fairly good jam. Tree vigorous; partially self-fertile; a biennial bearer. Originated at Louvain, Belgium about 1840. HEDRICK 1911, SIMMONS 1978; O81, Q30{SC}

Black Prince:[1] Small to medium-sized, round to slightly conical fruit; skin bluish-black with light blue bloom; flesh yellowish-green, with a very acid, slight damson-like flavor; stone clinging; ripens with Czar, should only be picked when fully ripe. Excellent for cooking, tarts and canning. Tree open-spreading; partially self-compatible but flowers susceptible to frost damage; bears regular and heavy crops. Very resistant to silver leaf disease. SIMMONS 1978; U8{SC}

Czar:[1] Popular English cooking plum. Medium-sized, roundish oval fruit; skin reddish purple, almost black when ripe; flesh yellowish-green, tender, rather mealy but cooks well and produces a rich red juice, flavor pleasantly acid; ripens very early. First fruited in 1874 and named for the Czar of Russia who visited England during the same year. HEDRICK 1911, SIMMONS 1978; P86, Q30{SC}

De Montfort: Small to medium, roundish-oval fruit; skin dark-purple, with russet dots; flesh green, juicy, sweet, rich; quality good; freestone; ripens during a 3 week period in July. Tree vigorous, spreading; productive; very hardy. Originated in Montfortin, France prior to 1846. HEDRICK 1911; I36, J93, J93{SC}, N24M

Early Laxton: Small to medium-sized fruit; skin pinkish-orange, washed and dotted with rose and violet; flesh golden, juicy, sweet, flavor good; freestone; ripens in mid-July; bruises easily. Good for dessert; excellent for cooking and canning. Tree small; partially self-fertile; highly productive; tends to shed its fruit before properly ripe. Originated in England in 1916. SIMMONS 1978; L12

Early Orleans:[1] (Monsieur Hâtif) Cooking plum. Medium-sized, roundish-oval fruit; skin dark reddish-purple, covered with thick bloom; flesh lemon-yellow, juicy, coarse, firm, sweet, mild but pleasant, with deep red juice when cooked; quality very good; stone free; ripens early, season short. Tree small, vigorous, upright- spreading; hardy; productive. An old French cultivar that has been known for about three centuries. HEDRICK 1911, SIMMONS 1978; P59M, Q30{SC}

Empress: Large to very large, oval fruit; skin purplish-blue; flesh yellow, firm but tender, fine-textured, sweet, quality good; ripens late, about 1 week before President; similar to President. Good for shipping. Tree strong, vigorous, upright; productive; blooms late. B83, C41M, D69, F53, *H34*, K83M, M22, M39M, N46

Kirke's Blue: (Kirke's) Large, round fruit; dark purplish-red, with heavy blue bloom; flesh greenish-yellow, juicy, flavor very good; stone large, free; season mid-September. Tree dwarfish but spreading, making a bush-like tree with many fruiting spurs. Very suitable for small gardens; self-incompatible, pollinated by Czar. Originated in Great Britain. Introduced about 1830. SIMMONS 1978; M22, P86, Q30{SC}

Mount Royal: Medium-sized, roundish fruit; skin dark purple; flesh greenish-yellow, juicy, firm, sweet; quality good; clingstone; ripens in midseason. Tree moderately vigorous; very hardy; self-fruitful, a heavy annual producer. Originated in Outremont, Quebec, Canada by W.W. Dunlop. Introduced prior to 1903. HEDRICK 1911; *A74*, *A74*{DW}, D65, E97, F53, G16{DW}, G41, *G66*, G69M, J7, J93, J93{SC}, L70

Opal: Medium-sized, oval fruit; skin yellow, almost completely covered with purplish-black flush; flesh pale gold, partly transparent, fairly firm, flavor good; stone almost free; ripens in mid-August. Tree moderately vigorous; self-fertile; a regular bearer. Originated in Alnarp, Sweden. Introduced in 1948. SIMMONS 1978; A69G{SC}, D69, F53, L12, N24M

Peach: Medium-large, roundish fruit; skin dark purplish-red, covered with thin bloom; flesh golden-yellow, moderately juicy, firm, subacid, mild; quality good; stone free; ripens early. Excellent for canning. Tree large, very vigorous, spreading; hardy; moderately productive. HEDRICK 1911; B67, B67{DW}, C41M, *G14*, *G14*{DW}, *G66*, *H34*, I49M, J93, J93{SC}, L97, M22, N24M, N46

Pond's Seedling:[1] (Pond) Cooking plum. Medium to large, roundish-oval fruit; skin rose-crimson, with slight bluish bloom; flesh golden-yellow, rather dry, fibrous, firm, mild, flavor fair but good when stewed; freestone; ripens late, season short. Tree vigorous, upright-spreading; partially self-compatible. Originated in England prior to 1831. HEDRICK 1911, SIMMONS 1978; O81, Q30{SC}

President: Large, oval fruit; skin deep purple, almost black, covered with heavy bloom; flesh yellow, dry, with a rich, sweet flavor, good when stewed; freestone; ripens late. Tree very upright, compact; productive; requires a pollinator. Raised by Thomas Rivers of Sawbridgeworth, England. First fruited in 1894. HEDRICK 1911,

SIMMONS 1978; *A9*, B53, B83, B93M, C41M, F53, *G14*, *H34*, K83M, *L47*, M39M, N24M, N46

Purple Pershore:[1] Cooking plum. Medium-sized, oval fruit; skin purple, with a very heavy bloom; flesh yellow, firm, dry, flavor poor but cooks well; stone clinging; ripens in late August. Very suitable for jam and canning. Tree vigorous, upright; self-compatible; cropping heavy but irregular. SIMMONS 1978; O81, Q30{SC}

Ruth Gerstetter: Fruit medium-sized; skin thick and tough; flesh green-yellow, rather firm, subacid, freestone; ripens early, the end of July in Sweden. Tree upright, moderately vigorous; not hardy; unproductive; susceptible to bacterial canker. Originated in Besigheim, Württumberg, by Adolf Gerstetter. Introduced in 1932. BROOKS 1972; O71M

Sannois: Medium to large, roundish-oblate fruit; skin reddish-purple; flesh dark coppery-yellow, juicy, rather coarse, very fibrous, tough, firm, very sweet and flavorful; quality very good; clingstone; ripens very late. Tree small, vigorous, upright-spreading. Originated in Sannois, France prior to 1901. HEDRICK 1911; J93, J93{SC}, L12

Seneca: Large, attractive fruit; skin reddish-blue, resists cracking; flesh yellow, very firm, sweet; freestone; ripens in midseason. Good for eating fresh or canning. Tree upright, moderately vigorous; requires a pollinizer; bears regularly. Introduced in 1972 by the New York State Agricultural Experiment Station. C34, I36, I49M, J61M, J93, J93{SC}, N24M

Victoria: Large, oval fruit; skin pale red, mottled with bright red on the side exposed to the sun; flesh greenish-yellow, firm, fairly sweet, juicy, flavor fair; stone large, free; ripens in midseason. Usually considered the best of all canned plums for it is then tender and juicy, with an attractive pinkish-red color and an almond flavor. Makes a jam of good color and quality. Very popular in Great Britain. HEDRICK 1911, SIMMONS 1978; M22, N24M, P86, Q30{SC}

Yakima: Very large, somewhat oblong fruit; skin bright mahogany red over yellow with heavy bloom, attractive; flesh clear golden-yellow, tender, sweet, moderately juicy, very firm; quality very good; freestone; ripens in late August. Tree vigorous, upright; a very shy bearer unless pollinated with other European plums. Originated in Bingen, Washington. Introduced about 1925. ANDERSEN, BROOKS 1972; A69G{SC}, B83, *G66*, N24M

BULLACES Similar to damsons, but whereas the damsons are oval and purple in color the bullaces are generally round and may be white as well as black. They are useful as late cooking plums. The fruit is usually left on the tree until late fall, until frost has softened its acidity. (P. insititia)

Black:[1] Cooking plum. Small, oval fruit, necked at the stem end; skin purplish-black, covered with a thick bloom; flesh greenish-yellow, juicy, firm, sour or agreeably tart late in the season; stone small, clinging; ripens late. To be at its best for cooking it should be left on the tree until touched by the first frosts. Tree upright or slightly spreading; extremely productive. One of the oldest cultivated plums. HEDRICK 1911, SIMMONS 1978; Q30, Q30{SC}

Langley:[1] Cooking plum, resembles a damson more than the Bullace. Medium-sized, nearly oval fruit; skin blue-black, covered with a slight bloom; flesh greenish, firm, acid, sweet; ripens in October and November. Tree vigorous, upright; self-compatible; prolific. Farleigh damson x Early Orleans. First raised about 1902. SIMMONS 1978; **U8{SC}**, **Y83{SC}**

Shepherd's:[1] Fruit small, good-sized for a bullace; roundish-oval; skin greenish-yellow; flesh firm, juicy, tart; ripens in late October. Useful as a late cooking plum. Tree moderately vigorous, upright; prolific. Of unknown origin. SIMMONS 1978; **Y83{SC}**

White: (Gold) Small, roundish fruit; skin deep amber yellow, with thick white bloom; flesh deep golden yellow, firm, juicy, coarse, fibrous, sour to slightly sweet; stone clinging; ripens late. Tree upright-spreading, moderately vigorous; productive. Very old cultivar of unknown origin. HEDRICK 1911, SIMMONS 1978; Q30, Q30{SC}

DAMSONS Similar to bullaces but generally more oval in shape, with less bloom, ripening at least six weeks sooner and with an entirely different richer and sweeter flavor. They are too astringent to be eaten raw, but are excellent for cooking and preserving. (P. insititia)

Bradley's King: Large, roundish fruit; skin dark purplish-red, with light bloom which gives it a bluish appearance; flesh greenish-yellow, rather dry, somewhat sweet, lacks the true damson tartness; stone free; ripens mid to late September. Tree vigorous, upright; very hardy; productive. One of the largest damsons. Originated in Nottinghamshire, England. SIMMONS 1978; **U8{SC}**, **Y83{SC}**

Briceland: Fruit small; skin dark bluish-purple with a heavy bloom; flesh yellow, spicy, somewhat astringent; pleasant to eat when fully ripe, best used for canning. Makes an excellent rich purple jam when cooked with its skin. Tree semi-dwarfish, upright; well-adapted to conditions near Briceland, California where it was discovered. E84

Damson: (Blue Damson) Small, oval fruit; skin bluish-black, with a heavy bloom; flesh firm, greenish-yellow, juicy, tart; freestone; ripens in midseason. Excellent for jam and jelly. Tree upright-spreading; productive. Brought to Italy from Damascus at least a century before the Christian era, hence the name. HEDRICK 1911; A38M{PR}, A82, *B52*, B73M{DW}, *E45*, F61M, *G28*, G41, G72{DW}, I9M, J83, J83{DW}, K28, L33, *L47*, *M69M*, N50{PR}, etc.

Farleigh:[1] (Crittenden) Small, roundish-oval fruit; skin purplish-black, covered with a very thick bloom; flesh greenish-yellow, firm but tender, sour, sprightly, very rich when cooked but not as rich as Shropshire; stone clinging; ripens early for a damson. Tree exceptionally prolific, with fruit borne in clusters. HEDRICK 1911, SIMMONS 1978; M22, O81, P1, Q30, Q30{SC}, S81M

French Damson: Fruit medium-sized, but the largest of the damsons; roundish; skin dull black, overspread with thick bloom; flesh greenish, juicy, tender, sweet, pleasant and sprightly; quality very good; stone large, variable in adhesion; ripens late. Tree large, vigorous, spreading; hardy; bears abundantly and annually. HEDRICK 1911; I36

Godshill: Small fruit that is quite sweet for a damson. Tree very prolific. Originated at Deacons Nursery, Godshill, Isle of Wight. O81

Krikon: Small, oval fruit; skin blue with a heavy bloom, moderately tough; flesh yellow, rather dry, very crisp, clingstone; quality fair for dessert, very good cooked; ripens in late August. Tree vigorous, upright-spreading; hardy; productive; susceptible to leaf spot. Originated in Sweden. ANDERSEN; F91T{SC}, N24M

Majestic: Fruit large; skin purple with a heavy bloom; freestone; ripens early. Introduced in 1907 by Stone and Wellington of Toronto, Ontario, Canada. HEDRICK 1911; F91T{SC}

Merryweather: Large, round-oval fruit; skin thick, blue-black, covered with light bloom; flesh greenish-yellow, firm, juicy, has a fair damson-like flavor; quality good; stone medium-sized, clinging. Excellent for preserving. Tree vigorous, spreading; self-compatible; prolific. Originated in Nottinghamshire, England about 1909. HEDRICK 1911, SIMMONS 1978; O81, P1, P86, Q30, Q30{SC}, S81M

Shropshire:[1] (Prune) Fruit fairly large for a damson, oval to oblong; skin blue-black, with a dense bloom; flesh golden-yellow, juicy, firm, sugary, astringent, dessert quality good when fully ripe or after a frost, flavor very rich when cooked; stone clinging; ripens late, season long. Excellent for cooking, preserving, bottling and canning. Tree large, vigorous, productive. Originated in England, sometime in the 17th century. HEDRICK 1911, SIMMONS 1978; F53, G79M{DW}, M22, M76

GAGES There is less certainty of the origin of this type than of any other kind of plum and it may well be a distinct species. In Great Britain the gage is considered to possess the best flavor of all plums and has often been crossed with other cultivars. The hybrids usually have the color and flavor of the gage but most are larger, i.e. Cambridge Gage, Laxton Gage. SIMMONS 1978.

Cambridge Gage: Small to medium-sized, round fruit; skin greenish-yellow; flesh greenish-yellow, firm, juicy, with a true gage flavor; ripens in late August. Excellent for dessert, cooking, preserving and canning. Tree vigorous; requires a pollinator; incompatible with Green Gage; not a heavy producer, but consistent. Seedling of Green Gage. SIMMONS 1978; F91T{SC}, L12, P86

Count Althann's Gage: Large, flattened globe-shaped fruit; skin dark purplish-red, with numerous golden-yellow dots, and a thick bluish bloom; flesh light golden-yellow, firm but tender, sweet, mild, pleasant; quality excellent; stone semi-clinging; ripens in midseason. Tree upright-spreading; productive; requires a pollinator. Originated in Hungary prior to 1869. HEDRICK 1911, SIMMONS 1978; J93{SC}, L12

Denniston's Superb: Medium-large, round-oval fruit; skin greenish-yellow, blushed with red; flesh yellowish-green, transparent, firm, fairly juicy, with a rich, vinous flavor; quality very good; stone practically free. Tree vigorous, upright-spreading; a reliable and heavy bearer. Originated in Albany, New York by Isaac Denniston, about 1835. HEDRICK 1911, SIMMONS 1978; P86, Q30{SC}

Early Transparent Gage: Small to medium, roundish fruit; skin pale apricot yellow with white bloom and crimson dots, so thin that it shows the stone; flesh golden yellow, transparent, juicy, very sweet; flavor rich, distinctive when properly ripe; stone small, free. Subject to splitting. A connoisseur's fruit of the highest quality, usually considered the best early gage. SIMMONS 1978; O81

General Hand: Fruit large, one of the largest of the gages; roundish-truncate; skin yellow, covered with thin bloom; flesh golden-yellow, juicy, somewhat fibrous, firm, sweet, with a pleasant, mild flavor; quality very good; stone semi-free or free; ripens in midseason. Tree large, vigorous, spreading; hardy; productive. First fruited in 1790 on the place of General Hand, near Lancaster, Pennsylvania. HEDRICK 1911; L12

Golden Transparent Gage: Large, oblong fruit; skin golden yellow, dotted with red, transparent, showing the stone; flesh transparent, firm, juicy, very sweet, rich, with true high gage flavor; quality excellent; ripens late. Tree small, self-compatible, productive. Originated in England by Thomas Rivers, about 1894. HEDRICK 1911, SIMMONS 1978; L12

Green Gage: (Reine Claude) Small to medium, roundish-oval fruit; skin yellowish green, covered with light bloom; flesh greenish-yellow, very juicy, firm but tender, sweet, mild, flavor rich and aromatic; stone partially clinging; ripens in midseason. Tree moderately vigorous; hardy; productive. The standard in quality for plums since 1699. HEDRICK 1911, SIMMONS 1978; C63, E4, E84, G23, G79M{DW}, H65, *H90*, I36, I83M, L1, *L47*, L97, L99M, M39M, M76, etc.

Imperial Gage: Small, round-oval fruit; skin dull greenish-yellow, covered with thick bloom; flesh golden-yellow, juicy, firm but tender, very sweet, mild; quality very good; stone nearly free; ripens in mid-September. Tree large, vigorous, upright-spreading; hardy; very productive. Originated in Flushing, Long Island, New York from seed planted in 1790. HEDRICK 1911; L12

Jefferson: Medium-sized, roundish-oval fruit; skin greenish-yellow, covered with a thin white bloom; flesh deep yellow, juicy, firm but tender, sweet, mild, pleasant, quality very good; stone semi-free; ripens in midseason. Tree medium to large, vigorous, spreading; productive; hardy. Originated in Albany, New York about 1825. HEDRICK 1911; L12

Laxton's Gage: Medium-sized, round fruit, larger than Green Gage; skin clear yellow; flesh greenish-yellow, fairly soft, juicy, has an excellent gage-like flavor; quality good for dessert, not suitable for canning; ripens the end of August. Tree vigorous, upright to spreading; self-compatible; productive. Originated in England. Introduced in 1919. SIMMONS 1978; I36

Reine Claude d'Oullins: (Oullins Golden Gage) Medium-sized, roundish-oval fruit, with unequal halves; skin light yellow, covered with a light bloom; flesh greenish-yellow, somewhat dry, firm, sweet, not high in flavor; quality good; stone semi-free; ripens early, season short. Tree large, vigorous, spreading; hardy; productive. Originated in France prior to 1866. HEDRICK 1911; I36, L12, P86

Reine Claude Violette: (Purple Gage) Small to medium-sized, roundish fruit; skin light purple covered with golden dots, bloom slight; flesh greenish, transparent, firm for a gage, sweet and rich, juicy, excellent for dessert; stone small, free; ripens late August to early September. Tree upright, vigorous, fairly productive. SIMMONS 1978; U8{SC}

MIRABELLES Little known in this country but highly esteemed in France for the unique apricot-like preserve that can be made from them. They are also used commercially for the manufacture of a spirit. The flavor of most is greatly improved by cooking. SIMMONS 1978.

American Mirabelle: Small, flask-shaped fruit; skin golden-yellow; flesh yellow, sweet, flavor very good, good for dessert and culinary purposes; ripens early; resembles Mirabelle in color but much larger. Originated in Geneva, New York by Richard Wellington. Introduced in 1925. BROOKS 1972; U13{SC}

Mirabelle: Small, roundish-oval fruit, slightly necked; skin light golden-yellow, overspread with thick bloom; flesh light yellow, not very juicy, firm but tender, sweet, mild but pleasant; quality very good; stone free; ripens in midseason. Tree small, round and open-topped, hardy. One of the favorite plums in France where it is in great demand for canning, preserves, compotes, tarts and prunes. HEDRICK 1911; J61M, M22

Mirabelle de Metz: Small, round fruit; skin pale golden-yellow with many red dots, covered with a slight bloom; flesh yellow, transparent, soft, sweet, flavor excellent; stone small, free; ripens in August. Suitable for dessert; also makes delicious conserves. Tree small, round-headed; productive. Very old French cultivar. SIMMONS 1978; U8{SC}, Y83{SC}

Mirabelle de Nancy: (Drap d'Or) Small, roundish-oval fruit; skin golden-yellow, covered with a thin bloom; flesh light golden-yellow, moderately juicy, coarse, firm but tender, sweet, mild; quality excellent; stone free; ripens in midseason. Tree small, upright-spreading; hardy; productive. A very old French cultivar of uncertain origin. HEDRICK 1911, SIMMONS 1978; N24M

Mirabelle d'Octobre: (Late Mirabelle) Small, roundish-oval fruit; skin greenish-yellow, often with a light blush on the side exposed to the sun, covered with thin bloom; flesh yellow, very juicy, aromatic, sweet; quality good; stone semi-free; ripens late. Tree moderately large and vigorous, very hardy, productive. HEDRICK 1911; Y83{SC}

Mirabelle Herrenhäusen: (Mirabelle Double de Herrenhäusen) Small to medium-sized fruit; skin yellow, mottled with red; flesh yellow, sweet, quality good; ripens late, following Mirabelle de Nancy. Tree vigorous, very productive. Originated in Germany prior to 1881. HEDRICK 1911; F91T{SC}

Mirabelle von Flotow: (Mirabelle de Flotow) Fruit small, spherical; skin yellow, dotted with red on the side exposed to the sun; flesh yellow, tender, soft, sweet, with a very pleasant apricot-like flavor; ripens early. Tree vigorous, very productive. Originated in Germany prior to 1873. HEDRICK 1911; N24M

PRUNES Plums that have a high content of sugars and solids, which enables them to be dried without fermenting at the pit. The best cultivars have a small, smooth pit and a rich flavor that survives drying. As fresh fruit they are generally sweeter than other plums.

Bluebell: Fruit large, more so than Stanley; oval; skin blue; flesh firm, yellow, flavor good, sweet; freestone; ripens in mid-September, shortly after Stanley, which it resembles. Tree vigorous, upright, holds fruit through a long harvest period. Originated in Mountain Grove, Missouri. BROOKS 1972; F53, N24M

Bluefre: Large, oval fruit; skin blue; flesh greenish-yellow, firm, thick, sweet, flavor good; freestone; ripens in late August, about 1 week after Stanley; resembles President. Retains its color well when processed. Tree vigorous; precocious, very productive; extremely hardy; holds fruit in good condition for about 30 days after normal harvest time. BROOKS 1972; A5, A69G{SC}, B83, G41, K83M, N24M

Brooks: (Brooks Italian, Lafayette) Large, oval fruit, averages 50% larger than Italian; skin blue; flesh greenish-yellow, very firm, slightly tart, moderately juicy, sweeter than Italian; keeps and ships well; fair canning quality, good drying quality; ripens 1 week earlier than Italian. Tree bears annually. BROOKS 1972; B67, B67{DW}, *G14*, *G14*{DW}, I49M, I76M{PR}, K83M, L97, L99M, N46

Early Italian: (Richards Early Italian) Large fruit, slightly larger than Italian; skin purplish-black; flesh yellow, firm, sweeter than Italian; ripens 10 to 14 weeks before Italian, which it resembles; ships well. Tree less vigorous and weaker than Italian. An excellent commercial cultivar. BROOKS 1972; B67, B67{DW}, B83, C41M, G41, *H34*, I36, *I68*, M39M, M39M{DW}, N24M, N46

Early Italian (Goodman Strain): Medium-sized fruit; skin dark purple, covered with bluish bloom; flesh yellow, juicy, sweet; flavor rich, but not as good as Italian; ripens more than 1 month before Italian. Suitable for dessert, canning or drying. Selected by Ram Fishman of Greenmantle Nursery. E84

French Improved: Medium-sized, oval fruit; skin red to dark-purple, tender; flesh fine-textured, tender, very sweet and rich; ripens August to September. Suitable for dessert, drying, or canning. Tree self-fertile. The leading prune in California. A88M, *B71M*, B93M{DW}, *C54*, F11, *I68*, *L47*, *N20*

German: Small, oval fruit; skin purplish-black, with thick bloom; flesh yellowish-green, firm, sweetish, mild, of pleasant flavor; quality good to very good; stone free; ripens late, ripening period very long. Excellent for all culinary purposes, especially canning; cures into a small but very good, tart, meaty, freestone, elastic prune. Tree medium to large; vigorous; hardy; very productive. HEDRICK 1911; G41

Gerrans: (Gerrans Early French) Bud mutation of Prune d'Agen; sugar content higher than its parent; ripens about 7 to 10 days before Prune d'Agen, which it resembles. Originated in Meridian, California by Lon Gerrans. Introduced in 1962 by Sierra Gold Nursery. BROOKS 1972; *K73M*

Giant Prune: (Burbank's Giant Prune) Large, long oval fruit; skin purplish-red with numerous russet dots; flesh light golden-yellow, coarse, firm, rather sweet, mild, flavor fairly good when cooked; stone clinging; ripens in midseason. Tree moderately vigorous; precocious; bears heavily and annually. Originated in Santa Rosa, California by Luther Burbank. Introduced in 1893. HEDRICK 1911, SIMMONS 1978; O81, Q30{SC}

Imperial Epineuse: (Imperial) Fruit large, slightly obovate; skin purplish red, darker on the side exposed to the sun; flesh greenish-yellow, tender, sweet, rich, of agreeable flavor; quality excellent; stone clinging; ripens late. Tree large, vigorous, spreading, fairly productive. Originated as a chance seedling in the great prune growing district of France, about 1870. HEDRICK 1911; F11, G79M, H26M{PR}, L1, L12

Iroquois: Medium-sized, oval fruit; skin deep blue, attractive; flesh greenish-yellow, firm, subacid, quality fair to good, freestone; ripens 1 week before Stanley; often processed for baby food. Tree medium-sized, upright, spreading; very productive; self-fruitful. BROOKS 1972; G41, I36, N24M

Italian: (Fellenberg) Fruit medium to large, long-oval; skin purplish-black, covered with very thick bloom; flesh yellow, very firm, dry, sweet, aromatic when fully ripe; stone partially free; quality very good to best; ripens late, season short. Excellent for preserving and drying. Tree vigorous, spreading; precocious; a regular and heavy bearer. One of the most widely grown of all plums. HEDRICK 1911, SIMMONS 1978; B67{DW}, B83, E4, E84, F53, G23, G41, G79M{DW}, H65, *H90*, L30, L97, L99M, M39M, M39M{DW}, etc.

Middelburg: Large, oval fruit; skin light to deep purplish-red, covered with thick bloom; flesh light yellow, rather juicy, sprightly when first mature, becoming sweetish, strongly aromatic, pleasant flavored; quality very good; stone semi-free; ripens very late. Tree vigorous, medium-sized; hardy; productive. Originated in Middleburg, New York, sometime prior to 1886. HEDRICK 1911; J93{SC}, L12

Moyer: (Moyer Perfecto) Fruit large, averaging 1 1/2 inches in diameter, ovate; skin thick, blue, bloom heavy and whitish; flesh yellow, firm, juicy, somewhat coarse, quality good, semi-clingstone; ripens about 7 to 10 days after Italian. Excellent for drying. Tree vigorous, self-fruitful. Originated in Roseburg, Oregon by C.E. Moyer. Introduced about 1927. BROOKS 1972; *B71M*, E84, F97M{PR}, H26M{PR}, M63M{PR}

Prune d'Agen: (French, French Petit) Medium small, long oval fruit; skin violet-purple, covered with thin bloom; flesh greenish-yellow, tender, sweet, aromatic; quality very good to best; stone semi-free; ripens late. Excellent for dessert and drying. Tree medium-sized, upright-spreading; hardy; very productive. Of ancient origin; brought to France from Turkey or Persia by Benedictine monks on their return from the Crusades. HEDRICK 1911; B67, B67{DW}, B93M, C94M{PR}, E4, E84, H26M{PR}, J93, *K73M*, L12, L97G{PR}

Silver Prune: Large, oval fruit; skin light yellow; flesh yellowish, firm, juicy, sweet and rich. Dries to a beautiful golden color. Seedling of Coe's Golden Drop, which it resembles, but is much more productive. Originated in Oregon by W.H. Prettyman. WICKSON; H26M{PR}, T49M{SC}

Stanley: Medium to large, oval fruit; skin deep purplish-blue; flesh greenish-yellow, juicy, firm but tender, sweet; stone free; ripens late. Tree large, vigorous, spreading; self-fertile, precocious, bears heavily and annually. Most popular prune cultivar in the United States. Originated in Geneva, New York by Richard Wellington. Introduced in 1926. BROOKS 1972; B73M, B73M{DW}, B83, C63, C75M, G16, G23, G23{DW}, J69{DW}, J83, J83{DW}, K28, M39M, N33

Sugar: Small, oval fruit; skin dark reddish-purple, covered with thick bloom, very tender; flesh golden-yellow, juicy, tender, sweet, mild; quality very good; stone free; ripens early. Excellent fresh; good for drying and canning. Tree moderately vigorous, spreading; hardy; self-fertile, productive. Originated in Santa Rosa, California by Luther Burbank. Introduced in 1899. HEDRICK 1911; A88M, B93M, *C54*, E4, F11, *L47*, *N20*{DW}

Valor:[3] Medium-large fruit; skin dark purple, speckled, attractive; flesh greenish-gold, firm, semi-freestone; quality excellent; ripens with Italian or just ahead of it. Recommended as a fresh fruit cultivar. Tree vigorous and productive; foliage dark. Low chilling requirement. Originated in Vineland Station, Ontario, Canada. F53, I36, N24M

Victor Large: (Victor Large French) Fruit large, larger than Prune d'Agen which it resembles; ripens August 15th to September 15th. Tree medium-sized, moderately vigorous, spreading; hardy; very productive, sets more regularly than Prune d'Agen; tolerant to mites. Introduced in 1970 by Sierra Gold Nurseries. BROOKS 1972; *K73M*

Weatherspoon: Large fruit; skin moderately thick, tough; flesh firm, sweet, aromatic; ripens a week ahead of Italian which it resembles; has good shipping qualities. Tree somewhat thorny; not hardy; blooms heavily but production is not high; requires pollination by other Italian type cultivars. BROOKS 1972; *H34*

JAPANESE PLUMS

With few exceptions, the fruit is larger than that of European plums. It is also juicier, with a pleasant blend of acid and sugar. Most Japanese plums are used for fresh fruit only. They cane be kept longer than European plums and are better shippers. They bloom early and are thus susceptible to spring frosts. Some do well in mild-winter climates. Japanese plums cross-pollinate readily and also pollinate American plums. Mostly P. salicina.

GREEN/YELLOW-SKINNED

Byron Gold: Large, round fruit, 2 inches or more in diameter; skin bright yellow; flesh golden yellow, aromatic, crisp, sweet, quality excellent; ripens late June to early July, keeps very well. Tree vigorous, precocious, productive. Resistant to the bacterial and fungal diseases common to the southeastern United States. C75M, E99M, F61M, G17, M31M

Early Golden: Medium-sized, round fruit; skin golden, blushed with red; flesh golden, firm, smooth, quality good; stone small, free; ripens 10 to 14 days before Shiro. Tree vigorous; productive; self-unfruitful, sets well with pollen from myrobalan; blooms very early; tends to bear biennially. Widely planted in Ontario, Canada. BROOKS 1972; A69G{SC}, F53, G41, *G66*, N24M

Ember: Medium to large, oblong fruit; skin yellow, blushed with red, bloom medium; flesh yellow, firm, fine-grained, tender, juicy, sweet; quality high for dessert or culinary purposes; stone clinging; ripens in early September; keeps well for 2 to 3 weeks after ripening. Tree low, spreading; vigorous; hardy. Originated in Excelsior, Minnesota. BROOKS 1972; A69G{SC}, L33

Great Yellow:[3] Large, roundish fruit; skin thin, clear yellow; flesh clear yellow, fine-textured, with a mild subacid flavor; ripens early. Tree moderately vigorous, hardy. Relatively low chilling requirement. Originated in Sebastopol, California by Luther Burbank. Introduced in 1931 by Stark Brothers Nursery. BROOKS 1972, RUCK; T49M{SC}

Green Egg: A sour plum, craved by some people who appreciate acid fruits sprinkled with a little salt. Enthusiasts frequently prefer this plum to the older cultivar, Green Gage. The spicy flavor is refreshing to those who like to cleanse the palate after a heavy meal. Adapted to Southeastern growing conditions. M31M

Homesteader: (Profanoff) Medium-sized fruit, 1 1/4 inches in diameter; skin yellow-green, overlaid with orange, thin; flesh freestone, of excellent quality; ripens early; resembles Green Gage. Tree hardy, productive; pollinates with Ptitsin #5. Originated in the Soviet Union. C58, G54

Howard Miracle: Medium to large fruit; skin yellow, heavily blushed with red at maturity, thin, tough; flesh yellow, firm, juicy; flavor distinctive, somewhat suggestive of pineapple; freestone; ripens midseason to late; ships well. Tree very vigorous; requires cross-pollination, Wickson and Santa Rosa recommended. Originated in Montebello, California. BROOKS 1972; A88M, B67, B67{DW}, *C54*, E4, F11, *I68*, L1

Inca: Oval, handsomely shaped fruit; skin golden-yellow tinged with crimson, bloom lavender; flesh pale orange, juicy, firm, sweet and flavorful; ripens in midseason. Originated in Santa Rosa, California by Luther Burbank. Introduced in 1919. Highly rated by members of the California Rare Fruit Growers. T49M{SC}

Ivanovka: Roundish fruit, 1 1/2 inches in diameter; skin greenish-yellow, mostly covered with dull bluish-red, overlaid with medium bloom; flesh greenish-yellow to pink, somewhat stringy, very juicy, sweet, sprightly; quality very good for dessert and canning; clingstone; season late August. Tree vigorous, upright-spreading; hardy; productive. Originated in Manchuria. ANDERSEN, BROOKS 1972; B47, F91T{SC}

Kelsey: Large, heart-shaped fruit; skin yellow, tinged and splashed with red, with attractive bloom; flesh yellow, juicy, firm and meaty, rich, pleasant, aromatic; quality good to very good; stone clinging unless well ripened; ripens very late; keeps and ships unusually well. Tree vigorous, upright; productive; an early and regular bearer; tender to cold. Introduced into the United States from Japan in 1870. HEDRICK 1911; *A9*, *B71M*, *C54*, E4, I83M, J93{SC}, *N20*

La Crescent: (Crescent, Golden Minnesota) (P. americana x) Small, oval fruit; skin thin, tender, easily removed, yellow, sometimes faintly blushed; flesh yellow, juicy, very tender, melting, sweet, aromatic, suggestive of apricots, dessert quality good; stone small, free; ripens early. Tree large, extremely vigorous; moderately productive; hardy. BROOKS 1972; *A74*, C58, D69, *G4*, G41, *G66*, G67, J7, J32, L27M, L70

Ptitsin #5: Medium to small, round fruit; skin yellow, covered with a moderately heavy bloom; flesh yellow, smooth, very juicy and aromatic, flavor excellent; freestone; ripens early; resembles Ptitsin #9. Tree vigorous; hardy. Originated in Manchuria. Introduced into Canada in 1939. BROOKS 1972; A16, B47, C58, G54, G69M, H85, M35M

Ptitsin #9: Medium-sized, nearly round fruit; skin green, becoming greenish-yellow when mature; flesh light greenish, firm, meaty, freestone; flavor very sweet, mild, pleasant, somewhat reminiscent of Green Gage; ripens in mid-August. Tree small, rounded, spreading; hardy; productive; adapted to prairie conditions. BROOKS 1972; B47, L27M, M35M

Shiro: Medium-sized, roundish fruit; skin yellow, covered with thin bloom; flesh light yellow, semi-transparent, very juicy, somewhat melting, sweet, mild, lacks character in flavor; quality good; stone clinging; ripens very early. Tree large, vigorous, upright-spreading; tender to cold; productive. Originated by Luther Burbank. introduced about 1897. HEDRICK 1911; A5, B53, B67{DW}, B83, C63, E4, F19M, F53, G23, G41, H65, I76M{PR}, I83M, J16, L33, M39M, etc.

Wickson: Large to very large, heart-shaped fruit; skin yellow, blushed with dark red; flesh amber-yellow, juicy, coarse, somewhat fibrous, firm, sweet, pleasant but not high in flavor; quality good; stone clinging; ripens in midseason; keeps and ships well. Tree vigorous, upright; tender to cold; an uncertain bearer. Originated by Luther Burbank. First described in 1892. HEDRICK 1911; *A9*, *A19*, A88M, B53, B53{DW}, B93M, *C54*, D81{PO}, E4, I83M, K83M, L1, *N20*, N33

RED/PURPLE-SKINNED

Abundance: Small to medium-sized, roundish-ovate fruit; skin dark red, covered with thin bloom; flesh yellow, very juicy, tender and melting, sweet, pleasantly aromatic; quality good; stone clinging; ripens early, season short. Tree large, vigorous, very productive. Imported from Japan by Luther Burbank. Introduced in 1888. HEDRICK 1911; A69G{SC}, B75, *E45*, F53, G13, *G28*, G79M{DW}, J93{SC}, *M69M*, M76, M76{DW}

Beauty: Medium to large, heart-shaped fruit; skin bright red; flesh amber, tinged with red, flavor good fresh or cooked; ripens early; keeps well. Tree vigorous; productive; partially self-fruitful. Relatively low chilling requirement. Originated in Santa Rosa, California by Luther Burbank. Introduced in 1911. RUCK; C34, *C54*, *G14*, *G14*{DW}, I49M, *I68*, I83M, J61M, *N20*, N24M

Bruce: (Bruce's Early) (P. angustifolia x) Fruit medium to large, about 1 1/2 inches in diameter; skin wine-red; flesh deep red, soft, sweet, quality fair; matures very early, being its primary outstanding fruit characteristic. Used primarily for jelly. Tree bears heavily, often produces the first year; requires a pollinator, usually Methley. Originated in Donley County, Texas by A.L. Bruce. Introduced about 1921. BROOKS 1972, MCEACHERN; A82, A85M, C75M, *E45*, E99M, F19M, F61M, G13, G17, *G28*, L90, M31M, *M69M*, M83, M83{DW}, N33, etc.

Burbank: Medium to large, roundish-conic fruit; skin dark red, covered with thick bloom; flesh deep yellow, juicy, tender, firm, sweet, aromatic; quality good; stone clinging; ripens early, season long. Tree large, vigorous; very productive; unusually hardy for a Japanese cultivar. Raised from a seed sentto Luther Burbank by a Japanese agent in 1883. HEDRICK 1911; A82, *B52*, C63, F19M, F53, G23, G23{DW}, *G28*, G41, G79M{DW}, I9M, K28, L30, *M69M*, M76, M76{DW}, etc.

Duarte:[2] Medium to large, heart-shaped fruit; skin deep-red with silver markings; flesh blood red, firm, juicy, flavor good, tart when cooked; quality very good; ripens in midseason; keeps well. Good fresh or canned. Tree vigorous; cold hardy; self-fruitful; a good pollinator for other cultivars, especially Santa Rosa. Originated by Luther Burbank. Introduced in 1900. A69G{SC}, *G66*, K83M, M39M, M39M{DW}

Eldorado: Large, oblong fruit; skin dark red; flesh amber, somewhat dry, clingstone; ripens early, stores well. Good for canning. Tree very upright; requires a pollinator; pollinated by Beauty, Laroda and Wickson. Originated in Sebastopol, California by Luther Burbank. Introduced in 1904. *A9*, *B71M*, B93M, I76M{PR}, K83M

Elephant Heart:[2] High quality "blood plum" (blood red flesh and red juice). Medium to large, heart-shaped fruit; skin thick, dark brownish-purple; flesh blood red, sweet and rich, extremely juicy, juice red; flavor and quality excellent; freestone; ripens late. Tree vigorous; hardy; prolific; self-unfruitful. Originated in Sebastopol, California by Luther Burbank. Introduced in 1929 by Stark Brothers Nurseries. BROOKS 1972; A88M, *C54*, E4, E99M, F11, F53, *G14*{DW}, *I68*, I83M, J93, J93{SC}, L1, L12, *L47*, L99M, M39M, *N20*{DW}, etc.

Explorer: (P. angustifolia x) Medium to large fruit; skin bright purplish-black, covered by a heavy, waxy bloom; flesh deep amber, juicy, sweet, flavor very good, quality high; ripens during the first 10 days in Byron. Tree moderately vigorous, upright-spreading; requires a pollinator; disease resistant. Adapted to all areas of the Southeast. Originated in Byron, Georgia. Introduced in 1981. C75M, E99M, F61M, M31M

Formosa: (Wickson Challenge) Large, oval fruit; skin yellow with a pale bloom until nearly ripe, turning to a clear rich red; flesh pale yellow, unusually firm, sweet and rich, with a slight apricot-like flavor, nearly freestone; ripens in mid-August. Tree vigorous; very productive; susceptible to bacterial leaf spot. Originated by Luther Burbank. Introduced in 1907. SIMMONS 1978, WICKSON; J93, J93{SC}, K83M

Friar: Large, oblate fruit; skin black when fully mature, resists cracking; flesh amber, firm, softens slowly after harvest, quality good; stone small, free; ripens in midseason, several days later than Nubiana. Tree upright; very vigorous and productive; requires a pollinator. BROOKS 1972; *A9*, *B71M*, B83, B93M, C41M, *C54*, E4, *G66*, *H34*, *K73M*, K83M, *L47*, M39M, *N20*

Frontier: Large, round-ovate fruit; skin blue-black, more attractive than other red-fleshed cultivars; flesh red, not as dark as Mariposa, firm, freestone, flavor good, similar to Mariposa; ripens 10 to 14 days after Santa Rosa; softens slowly after picking. Tree vigorous; productive; requires a pollinizer, Santa Rosa and Redheart being effective. BROOKS 1972; *A9*, A69G{SC}, C75M, F61M, K83M

Gaviota: Very large, oval fruit; skin dark red over yellow ground color; flesh yellow, aromatic, juicy, firm, sweet, with a sparkling rich flavor; quality very good; stone extremely small; ripens in midseason. Tree vigorous, productive, blooms late. Originated by Luther Burbank, about 1900. HEDRICK 1911; **T49M{SC}, U8{SC}**

Hanska: Medium-sized, roundish-oblate fruit; skin bright red with a heavy blue bloom; flesh firm, yellow, aromatic, of good quality; stone very small, semi-free. Develops a strong apricot flavor when cooked. Tree very vigorous, three-year old trees attaining a height of 12 feet; hardy. Originated in Brookings, South Dakota by N.E. Hansen. Introduced in 1908. Hanska is the Sioux word for "tall". HANSEN, HEDRICK 1911; *B52*, *G15M*, *G15M*{DW}, J93{SC}

Kahinta: Medium to large, roundish to slightly oval, very heavy fruit; skin dark red, thin, free of acerbity; flesh yellow, firm, sweet, of excellent quality, freestone. Originated in Brookings, South Dakota by N.E. Hansen. Introduced in 1912. Kahinta is the Sioux Indian name for "sweep". HANSEN; G67, J93{SC}, N24M

Lantz:[1] Fruit round, uniform in size and form, about 1 to 1 1/2 inches in diameter; skin dark blue; flesh amber, tender, juicy, makes excellent sauce; clingstone; hangs well on tree; quite resistant to brown rot. Originated in Ames, Iowa by H.L. Lantz. Pollen parent selected by Luther Burbank. BROOKS 1972; F91T{SC}

Laroda: Large, nearly round fruit; skin deep reddish-purple; flesh light amber, light red near the skin, firm, sweet, mildly aromatic, quality good; ripens in midseason; ships very well. Tree vigorous, upright; produces numerous medium-sized spurs and buds; self-unfruitful, being pollinated by Santa Rosa. BROOKS 1972; *A9*, *B71M*, C41M, *K73M*, K83M, L12{CF}, *L47*

Mariposa:[2] (Improved Satsuma) Large, round to heart-shaped fruit; skin maroon, thick, sweet; flesh blood red, firm, tender, juicy, sweet, freestone; sweeter than Satsuma which it resembles; ripens in midseason, holds on the tree 2 to 3 weeks after ripening. Tree medium to large, vigorous, upright. Originated in Pasadena, California. BROOKS 1972; *A9*, *A19*, A88M, E29M, G17, *H34*, I83M, *K73M*, *L47*, *N20*, N46

Methley:[3] Small to medium, round fruit; skin purple, blushed with red; flesh red, soft, very juicy, sweet, flavor distinct; quality good;

ripens early. Tree vigorous, upright; hardy; self-fruitful; productive; a good pollinizer, especially for Shiro. Low chilling requirement, 200 to 250 hours or less. Originated in South Africa. A5, A82, C75M, F19M, F53, F93, *G28*, I9M, I83M, K28, *M69M*, M76, N33

Morris: Medium to large fruit; skin reddish to purplish-black; flesh reddish-purple through to the seed, firm, crisp, flavor good; ripens early, about a week later than Methley. Tree may require a pollinator; slightly resistant to brown rot; very susceptible to black knot. Requires 800 hours of chilling. Originated at Texas A & M University by Dr. J. Benton Storey. MCEACHERN; A39, *C54*, C75M, E29M, *E45*, E99M, F61M, F93, J93{SC}, L90, M31M, M83, N33

Nubiana: Large, flattened fruit; skin deep reddish-blue; flesh light amber, very firm, meaty, moderately sweet, quality fair, turns red when cooked; ripens very slowly, in midseason, after Laroda and before President; ships well; resembles Eldorado. Tree very vigorous, medium upright; highly productive; self-fruitful. BROOKS 1972; *A9*, A88M, B93M, *C54*, L12{CF}, *N20*{DW}

Ozark Premier: Fruit extremely large, round to slightly heart-shaped; skin bright red, tough; flesh yellow, firm, fine-grained, juice tart, flavor good; stone small, clinging; ripens midseason to late, with Burbank, which it resembles. Good fresh or canned. Tree vigorous; hardy; productive; self-unfruitful; fairly resistant to bacterial spot. BROOKS 1972; A5, C63, C75M, F19M, F53, F61M, F93, G41, G65M, J16, L33, L90, *M69M*, N33

Pipestone: Large fruit; skin deep red with a golden blush, thin, tough but peeling easily; flesh golden-yellow, somewhat stringy, sweet, juicy, quality excellent; ripens early. For home gardens and commercial use. Tree vigorous; very cold hardy; reliably productive; requires cross pollination. BROOKS 1972; *A74*, A91, B4, C58, D65, F53, *G4*, G16, *G66*, J93{SC}, L27M, L70, M35M, N24M

Red Ace: (Burbank Red Ace) Medium-sized, round-oval fruit; skin crimson to dull red, bloom pale blue; flesh light-crimson, sweet, delicious, quality excellent; semi-freestone to freestone; resembles Elephant Heart. Tree spreading, very productive, hardy; ripens in mid-August. Originated in Sebastopol, California by Luther Burbank. Introduced in 1929 by Stark Brothers Nurseries. BROOKS 1972; K83M, L33

Red June: Medium-sized, roundish fruit; skin garnet red, covered with thin bloom; flesh light yellow, fibrous, somewhat meaty, sweet, peculiarly aromatic; quality good; stone clinging; ripens early. Tree large, vigorous, upright-spreading; hardy; productive. Introduced in 1893 by Stark Brothers Nurseries. HEDRICK 1911; A82, *E45*, G13, *G28*, G72{DW}, K28, K28{DW}, *M25M*, *M69M*

Redheart:[2] Fruit medium to large; slightly oval to heart-shaped; skin medium to darkish-red, covered with moderately heavy bloom; flesh blood red, sweet, mild, aroma pronounced, firm-melting, meaty, nearly crisp, fine-grained; quality excellent; stone nearly free; ripens early. Tree upright-spreading, very vigorous and productive; self-unfruitful. BROOKS 1972; A69G{SC}, B53, F53, K83M, L33, L33{DW}, N24M

Robusto: (P. angustifolia x) Medium to large fruit; skin solid bright-red; flesh red, juicy, sweet, quality good; stone clinging; ripens approximately 1 week later than Bruce. Tree extremely vigorous and productive; precocious; requires a pollinator; disease resistant. Adapted to most areas of the Southeast. Originated in Byron, Georgia. Introduced in 1982. C75M, E99M, F61M, G17, M31M

Roysum: Medium-large, oblong fruit; skin reddish-blue, adherent; flesh light yellow, firm, slightly acid, juicy, of high quality, freestone; ripens evenly, very late, 2 months after Late Santa Rosa, in early October; keeps very well; resembles Late Santa Rosa. Tree vigorous, spreading, self-fruitful. Originated in Tulare, California. BROOKS 1972; *A9*

San Jose Blood:[2] Very flavorful "blood plum" resembling Elephant Heart. Recommended by members of the California Rare Fruit Growers. Discovered at U.C. Deciduous Field Station, San Jose, California. **T49M{SC}**

Santa Rosa: Large, roundish fruit; skin dark purplish-crimson with russet dots, covered with thin bloom; flesh reddish near the skin, shading to amber near the center, firm, juicy, slightly tart; quality good; ripens early; keeps and ships well. Tree large, vigorous, upright; hardy; productive; widely adapted. Originated in Santa Rosa, California by Luther Burbank. Introduced in 1907. HEDRICK 1911; B83, C63, C75M, D34M{PR}, E4, G23, G23{DW}, *G49*, I83M, J83, J83{DW}, K28, L30, M39M, M39M{DW}, etc.

Satsuma:[2] Small to medium, roundish fruit; skin dark red, covered with thin bloom; flesh blood red, juicy, tender, firm, sweet, flavor very good; stone semi-clinging; ripens in midseason. Tree vigorous, upright-spreading; hardy; productive. Originated by Luther Burbank. Introduced in 1889. HEDRICK 1911; E4, F11, F19M, *G49*, I83M, J61M, *K73M*, L1, L30, L97, L99M, M39M, M39M{DW}

Sierra: Medium-sized, roundish fruit; skin dark purplish-crimson, dotted with russet; flesh yellow, firm, juicy, sweet; semi-freestone; has good eating and keeping qualities; ripens late June to late July. Tree vigorous, fairly self-fruitful at place of origin. Originated in Ontario, California by Herbert C. Swim, Armstrong Nurseries. BROOKS 1972; D57{OR}

Simka: Large, oblong to cone-shaped fruit; skin dark purplish-red; flesh yellowish-white, very firm, sweet; freestone at full maturity; ripens in midseason; keeps well on the tree; resembles Nubiana. Tree medium-sized, vigorous; bears heavily and annually; partially self-thinning. Originated in Fowler, California. BROOKS 1972; *A9*, *B71M*, B83, C41M, M39M

Six Weeks: (Early Six Weeks) Fruit large, oblong; skin yellow, tinged with red, bright cherry-red when over-ripe; quality average; ripens early. Tree vigorous, upright, rapid in growth. Splits badly on both fruit and tree trunk. Named and introduced by J.S. Kerr of Texas, about 1901. HEDRICK 1911; C75M, E99M, F61M

Superior: Large, heart-shaped fruit; skin dark-red with russet dots, covered with heavy attractive bloom; flesh yellow, firm, juicy, flavor sprightly, slightly acid near skin, dessert quality superior; clingstone; ripens in late midseason. Tree vigorous, precocious, prolific. BROOKS 1972; *A74*, C58, *D35M*, D76, D76{DW}, E97, E97{DW}, G23, *G66*, G67, *G89M*, H65, *H90*, J69{DW}, J93{SC}, N24M, etc.

Tecumseh: Medium-sized, round-ovate fruit; skin bright red, covered with bluish bloom; flesh yellow, firm, juicy, subacid; quality good; stone clinging; ripens in mid-August. Tree vigorous; very hardy; reliably productive. Originated in Brookings, South Dakota by N.E. Hansen. Introduced about 1923. BROOKS 1972; A65, B47, C58, E97, G67, H85, N24M

Toka: (P. americana x) Medium to large fruit, tapered to a point; skin orange-red, with a blue bloom; flesh greenish-yellow, very firm, aromatic, with a sweet, rich flavor. Tree moderately vigorous, spreading; very hardy; an excellent pollinator for Japanese and Japanese hybrid plums. Introduced in 1911 by the South Dakota Agricultural Experiment Station. A14, *A74*, B4, *D35M*, D65, D69, F53, *G4*, G16, *G66*, G67, G69M, *H90*, J7, J93{SC}, L27M, L70, N24M, etc.

Underwood: Large, heart-shaped fruit; skin dull red, satin like, astringent; flesh golden-yellow, juicy, melting, tender, slightly stringy, sweet, quality good; stone small, semi-clinging; ripens early, extends over a long season. Tree vigorous; bears regularly and heavily; very hardy; requires a pollinator. BROOKS 1972; A33, *A74*, A91, B4,

D65, D69, D76, E97, G41, *G66*, G67, G69M, J7, J32, J93{SC}, L27M, L33, L70, N24M, etc.

Wade: Large, oblate fruit, 1 3/4 inches in diameter; skin deep red; flesh yellow streaked with red, very juicy, tender, sweet; ripens late May to mid-June. Vigorous, upright tree; precocious; requires a pollinator. Relatively low chilling requirement. E99M, F61M, G8, G17, J93{SC}

Waneta: Fruit large to very large; skin reddish-purple; flesh deep yellow, firm but tender, juicy, sweet; quality good; clingstone; ripens in midseason. Good fresh or for processing. Tree extremely hardy; bears heavily and annually. Originated in Brookings, South Dakota by N.E. Hansen. Introduced in 1913. *A74*, A91, B4, *C54*, D65, D69, D76, E97, *G66*, G67, *G89M*, J93{SC}, L27M, L70

Weeping Santa Rosa:[3] Large, slightly oblate fruit; skin purplish-red with numerous, small yellow dots, covered with blue-gray bloom; flesh pale golden-yellow, juicy, firm, flavor mild, quality good; semi-freestone; ripens in midseason. Tree ornamental, with long slender limbs which bow downward toward the ground; very vigorous and productive. Low chilling requirement, 150 hours or less. BROOKS 1972; A88M, I49M, I83M, J61M, L1, *N20*{DW}

POTATO {PL}

SOLANUM TUBEROSUM

BLUE/PURPLE-SKINNED

All Blue: 80 days. Medium-sized oval tuber; very deep-blue skin; flesh an attractive lavender blue throughout, very moist; slightly smoky flavor; matures in midseason. Good boiled or baked. An exceptionally good keeper. Heavy yielding. C15M, H58M, H58M{PR}, J20, J99G, K49M, K49M{PR}

Blue Mac: 90 days. Medium to large tubers; bluish-purple skin with white flesh; matures very late. Excellent as a microwave baker, boiled or fried. Very vigorous and high yielding. Excellent for home gardens. Wart resistant. Released in Newfoundland in 1979. A95, J99G

Blue Victor: 90 days. Large, blocky, roundish tuber with medium deep eyes; skin lavender with occasional white areas; flesh white, of good flavor and texture; keeps very well. Vigorous, hardy plant, high yielding. An heirloom that is still popular in parts of the potato belt. J99G

Brigus: 80 days. A new, high-yielding release from Newfoundland. Uniform, round tubers; bluish-purple skin; creamy yellow flesh; shallow eyes; matures in midseason. Excellent boiled or baked. Wart and late blight resistant. Shows promise as a very interesting home garden and market type. A95, D11M, J99G

Caribe: 65 days. Very large uniform tuber, with shallow eyes; form round to oblong; bluish-purple skin; tender, creamy white flesh; matures very early. Heavy yielding and reliable. Wide adaptability across the United States and Canada. Was once widely grown in New England for export to the Caribbean, hence the name. A95, E59Z, G64, H42, J20, J99G, K66

Heidzel Blue: 80 days. Oblong, sometimes irregularly shaped tuber with shallow eyes; thick dark-blue skin; white flesh of good flavor; a good keeper. Very good for baking. Extremely vigorous plant with high, dark-green foliage. J99G

Improved Purple Peruvian:[3] A strain of Purple Peruvian, carefully selected for more uniform color. Makes a unique and attractive potato and egg salad. Versatile. Highly productive. Plant in April; harvest mid to late September. I39

Longlac: A unique bluish-purple type. Very attractive long tubers, with shallow eyes; matures in midseason. Good for baking and French fries. A95

Purple Chief: 80 days. Medium to large, oval-shaped tuber; deep purple skin; white flesh; excellent cooking qualities; matures in midseason, keeps well. Equally good cooked in any way. Good yields. An interesting home garden type. Has been grown in Atlantic Canada for many years. A95, J99G

Purple Peruvian:[3] Purple fingerling potato introduced from South America in the 1970's. Long, narrow, dark violet tuber; weight 1/2 to 3/4 pound when mature; flesh purple throughout, of fine texture; matures medium late. One of the main cultivars used in the Altiplano of Peru and Bolivia for making *chuño*. Excellent storage qualities, will keep until June. Attractive, purple-tinged foliage. High yields. A2, E59Z, I99, J99G, K49T

Purple Viking: 80 days. Unique, dark purple skin with pink-red splashes; very white flesh of smooth texture; matures in midseason; keeps very well. Excellent boiled. Good yields of large tubers. Interesting item for fresh markets and gourmet sales. J99G

Scotia Blue: An extremely early and high yielding, elongated potato. Medium purplish-blue skin. Creamy white flesh with a blue aureole slightly below the surface of the skin. Rather dry and excellent for baking. J20

PINK/RED-SKINNED

Bison: 65 days. Uniform, round, medium-sized tuber; smooth, shallow eyes; bright-red skin; pale yellow flesh. Excellent for baking. Cooks up flaky and full of flavor with minimum shrinkage while retaining a smooth, firm texture. A reliable and heavy bearer. Developed in North Dakota. Bred for resistance to late blight and scab. J99G

Blossom: Oblong, somewhat flattened tubers with tapered ends; striking pink skin; delicate light-pink flesh. Good for baking. Heat resistant plant; produces large, very attractive pink flower blossoms. Ornamental as well as useful. K49M

Chieftain: 90 days. Tuber round to oblong, with shallow to medium eyes; attractive red skin; white flesh. Medium-sized, spreading plant; more productive than Norland; moderately resistant to scab and has field resistance to late blight. Canada's leading market red. Released by the Iowa Agricultural Experiment Station in 1968. A95, G64, G93M, J99G, N39

Desiree: 80 days. Very high-yielding English maincrop potato. Tuber oblong, with shallow eyes; skin pinkish-red; deep golden-yellow flesh, of very fine flavor. Excellent cooking qualities; rarely discolors. Produces well from seed, but matures somewhat later and up to 50% of the tubers may have white skin. Highly susceptible to scab. Drought resistant. G6, H58M, H58M{PR}, J14, J99G, J99G{PR}, L91M{S}

Early Rose: 80 days. An old standard, released in Vermont in 1867. Tuber oblong, rather flattened, with medium deep eyes; skin pink, slightly tinged with salmon; white flesh, sometimes streaked with pink; matures early to midseason. Does not keep well. Vigorous and high yielding. VILMORIN; A95, E59Z, J99G

Garnet Chili: 90 days. Tuber large, roundish or oblong with medium deep, rounded eyes; skin thick, purplish-red or garnet-colored; flesh nearly white, dry and mealy when cooked, of very good flavor. Vigorous and productive plant. Originated in Utica, New York in 1853. BURR; J99G

La Rouge: 85 days. Tubers very uniform in size and shape, with deep apical eyes; attractive red skin; matures in midseason; has excellent keeping qualities. Medium-sized, spreading plant; has some resistance to common scab. Released by the Louisiana Agricultural Experiment Station in 1962. H83, I91

Levitts Pink: 80 days. Medium-sized, oval tuber; attractive rose-pink skin; pinkish-red flesh with good flavor and texture. One of the few red-fleshed potatoes, has excellent potential for the gourmet and specialty market trade. J99G

McNeilly: (McNeilly Everbearing) Large, red-skinned tuber; tender light-yellow flesh of very good flavor. Best baked right in the skin. An excellent keeper. Vigorous plant; continues to yield new potatoes well into fall; has foliage that stays green all season. D76

Norwegian:[3] Medium-long, slender tubers with rose to pink skin, yellow flesh and a slightly sweet flavor. Exceptional quality when roasted, also an excellent salad type. A good keeper. Produces numerous medium-sized "fingers". J99G

Pink Pearl: 90 days. Long oval tuber with attractive pink skin and shallow eyes; white flesh, of good flavor and cooking qualities. Matures very late, keeps well. Large, vigorous plant. Wart and blight resistant. Shows promise as an excellent home garden cultivar. A95, H42, J99G

Red Dale: 65 days. Large, round, very uniform tubers; attractive red skin; white flesh; good storage qualities. Excellent for boiling and baking. Will have good market characteristics when planted closely. Very prolific. Resistant to scab and wilt. J99G, N34{PR}

Red Erik: 65 days. Red tubers, with shallow eyes. Excellent baked, steamed or boiled. Heavy yielder, 13% more than Norland; tends to produce "lunkers", so should be planted closely. Tolerates wet soil; has immunity gene for late blight, low resistance to verticillium wilt, medium resistance to scab. Released in Minnesota in 1983; named after Viking explorer Erik the Red. J99G

Red Gold: 80 days. Medium-sized tubers; light red, netted skin; delicate yellow flesh. Excellent boiled, steamed or fried; flavor very good. Matures in midseason. High yielding under most conditions. Appears to have resistance to diseases. A95, J99G

Red LaSoda: 80 days. Tuber round to oblong, with medium deep eyes; very smooth, bright red skin; white flesh; matures in midseason. Ideal for boiling, with no darkening after cooking. Medium-sized, upright plant; somewhat resistant to mosaic, susceptible to common scab; tends to produce misshapen tubers under adverse conditions. Released by the Louisiana Agricultural Experiment Station in 1948. A95, H83, J99G

Red Norland: (Norland) 65 days. Tuber oblong, regular in size and shape, with shallow eyes; skin red, very smooth; flesh white; matures very early. Ideal for boiling, with no darkening of skin. Medium-large, spreading plant; moderately resistant to scab. Introduced by the North Dakota Agricultural Station in 1957. A16, A95, B73M, D65, D76, D82, E97, G16, G71M, H42, H54, H83, J99G, L97, N21M, etc.

Red Pontiac: (Pontiac) 80 days. Tuber round to oblong, with medium-deep eyes; smooth to sometimes netted, intense red skin; matures midseason to late. Ideal for boiling, with only slight darkening after cooking. Also very good fresh from the garden. Large, high-yielding plant; very susceptible to scab; drought tolerant. Very popular with commercial growers and home gardeners. A95, B73M, B75, C63, D65, D76, E97, F19M, G71, H42, H58M{PR}, H83, I99M, J70M, J99G, K71, etc.

Rideau: 80 days. Medium to large tubers; very bright-red skin with crisp, snow-white flesh. Matures in midseason. Has shown resistance to scab and verticillium wilt. A fine market potato; excellent boiled or steamed. High yields of uniform tubers. A95, D11M, J99G

Rose Finn Apple:[3] Fingerling type. Medium-sized, slender tuber; skin rose-buff; flesh deep yellow blushed with red, firm, waxy, of excellent flavor; matures late. Produces numerous, well-clustered "fingers". E59Z, J99G

Rose Gold: 80 days. Very attractive, bright rose skin; waxy, golden-yellow flesh of excellent flavor; matures in midseason. A good all-purpose cultivar, but low starch content makes it a quick boiler, frier and baker. Resistant to scab. Introduced by the University of Guelph. A95, D11M, E59Z, J99G

Ruby Crescent:[3] Large fingerling type, 3 inches long, 1 1/2 inches in diameter; mature tubers weigh 3/4 pound each. Attractive, rose-colored skin; waxy, yellow flesh of very fine flavor, holds together well when cooked. Excellent for boiling, baking or frying. Vigorous vines that yield heavy crops. Good specialty market item. E59Z, I99, J99G, K49M, K49M{PR}, K49T, K66

Sangre: 65 days. Medium to large, very uniform, slightly elongated tuber; weight 4 to 10 ounces; shallow eyes; dark-red skin; white flesh; matures early. Becoming popular with the restaurant trade, being dug early for abundant "small reds" that are boiled and served whole, with the skin on. E24, I99M{OR}, J99G, K49T

Tobique: 80 days. Tuber oblong-flattened, with very shallow eyes; smooth, golden tan skin with pink splashes. Good potato flavor. Excellent boiled, steamed or baked. Makes an attractive specialty market product. A95, J99G

Urgenta: 80 days. Tuber medium-sized, long oval; attractive, smooth, orange-pink skin; pale yellow flesh of excellent flavor; matures in midseason. Good for boiling and baking, the flesh having a fluffy texture when baked. Very productive. Resistant to potato wart and drought. An old standard in Europe since 1953. A95, D11M, E59Z, J99G, K49M

Yellow Rose: 80 days. Pinkish skin with yellow flesh of firm texture; very good flavor; ripens in midseason. Excellent steamed, superb for potato salads. Prolific yielder. E70M{PR}, I76M{PR}, J99G

RUSSET-SKINNED

Acadia Russet: 80 days. Very large, smooth, lightly netted tuber; rich white flesh of fine flavor; matures medium-late. Excellent for boiling or baking. Very vigorous, upright plant; high yielding. More consistent than Russet Burbank. Released in New Brunswick in 1981. A95, B75, J99G

Butte: 90 days. An Idaho favorite. Very large, flat oblong, heavily russet tuber; shallow eyes; white flesh; matures late. Excellent flavor; one of the best for baking. Very good keeper. Compared to Russet Burbank, Butte produces up to 7% more yield, 20% more No. 1 potatoes, 58% more vitamin C and 20% more protein. D76, E97, I99, J99G, N34{PR}

Nooksack: 90 days. Large to very large, uniform, oblong tubers; weight 16 to 18 ounces; fine heavy russet; dry white flesh, excellent when baked; matures late. Stores well and shipping quality is excellent. Vigorous, heavy yielding, broad-leaved plant; well adapted; has good disease resistance. E24, J99G

Norgold Russet: 65 days. Tuber oblong to long, with very well distributed shallow eyes; uniform, heavily netted skin; white flesh. Good for baking, boiling or French fries, with no darkening after cooking. Consistent, high-yielding plant; resistant to scab. Popular with home gardeners. Released by the North Dakota Agricultural Experiment Station in 1964. A95, B73M, C63, D65, D76, *E53*, E97, G71M, I99M{OR}, J99G, N21M

Norkotah Russet: 65 days. Uniform, long-flattened tubers, with shallow eyes; matures early to midseason; stores well. Excellent eating qualities baked, steamed, boiled, French fried, chipped or scalloped. Best fresh from the garden. Heavy yields. Developed in North Dakota by Dr. Robert Johnson, breeder of Bison. E59Z, G16, J99G

Russet Burbank: (Netted Gem) 80 days. Long, cylindrical or slightly flattened tuber; well-distributed, shallow eyes; russet and heavily netted skin. Good for every purpose, but ideal for baking and French fries, with only slight discoloration after cooking. Most widely grown potato in the United States. Original strain selected by Luther Burbank in 1873 from seedlings of Early Rose. A16, A95, C63, D27, D76, D82, E24, G87, H42, H58M, H58M{PR}, H83, I91, I99M, J99G, L89, L97, etc.

Sierra: 65 days. Heavily netted russet type. Tuber long to oblong, medium to large, uniform; has excellent eating qualities; matures early; stores very well. Resistant to scab and hollow heart. Vines show good vigor. Released in Canada. J99G

WHITE/TAN-SKINNED

Arran Pilot: (Salt Water) 80 days. Large, kidney-shaped tuber; white skin; firm, white flesh of outstanding flavor. One of the earliest potatoes to mature. Heavy yielding; resistant to scab and frost, susceptible to blight. Introduced in Great Britain for the 1930-31 season. Named for Arran Island, off the coast of Scotland. J99G

Atlantic: 80 days. Tuber oval to round, with medium shallow eyes; skin white with light to heavy scaly netting; dry white flesh, very mealy for boiling and baking; matures in midseason. Medium large, upright plants; tolerant to scab and verticillium wilt. Yielding ability similar to Kennebec. Introduced in 1976. H83, J99G

Candy Stripe:[1] 80 days. Medium-sized, oval tuber; skin white, striped or blotched with red; white flesh of good flavor and quality. Good baked, boiled or fried. High yielding and disease resistant. Potential gourmet and specialty market item. Originated in Tomales, California. J99G

Cherokee: 90 days. Tuber short elliptical, frequently flattened on one side toward the stem end; medium shallow eyes; very white skin and flesh. Good for boiling and baking. Stores well, retaining flavor for a long period. High resistance to scab and late blight. Adapted to clay and muck soils. Introduced in 1954. A95, D11M, J99G

Chippewa: 90 days. Tuber oval-flattened, with shallow eyes; skin smooth, white; stores exceptionally well. Ideal for boiling, with no darkening after cooking. Medium-sized plant with lilac blossoms; high yielding; tends to produce small tubers under dry conditions; very susceptible to scab. Introduced in 1933 by the USDA. G71, J99G

Early Ohio: 65 days. An old traditional cultivar introduce prior to 1885. Grown in the Red River Valley by most of the early settlers until 1920 when the Irish Cobbler was introduced, yet still grown and favored by many Mid Westerners. Round to oblong tubers; smooth, pinkish-tan skin; deep eyes; matures early. Excellent baker, with a real down home potato flavor. A95, E59Z, J99G

Explorer:[2] {S} 120 days. The first "true potato seed" available to home gardeners. Grown like tomatoes or peppers. Small to medium-sized tuber; thin skin; creamy white flesh. Relatively uniform. Average length 2 inches after 90 days, up to 6 inches at maturity. Will not carry tuber-borne diseases into clean soil. Introduced by Pan-American Seed Company in 1982. A16, E38, F19M, F92, G27M, G64, H42, H94

Green Mountain: 90 days. An old favorite New England cultivar. Tuber brick-shaped, with moderately deep eyes; skin white, sometimes netted; matures late. Excellent culinary qualities, but flesh generally darkens after cooking. Large, heavy yielding plant; subject to misshapen tubers under poor growing conditions. Recommended for light soils where the growing season is cool. Originated by O.H. Alexander of Charlotte, Vermont, in 1878. A95, E59Z, G64, G71, H83, J20, J99G, K49M

Homestead:[2] (F_1) The first hybrid potato from seed. Produces 2 to 4 times the yield of Explorer. Very rapid-growing, with potatoes reaching 4 inches in just 90 days from setting out of plants. Avoids the tuber-borne diseases and cold weather tilling associated with conventional potato culture. Uniform, healthy plants. I91{S}

Hudson: 90 days. Large, spherical tuber with shallow eyes; skin light tan; flesh white. Large plant, emerges quickly after planting; competes well with weeds; greater yielding than Katahdin, but more susceptible to wilt and pink eye. Released by Cornell University in 1972. Very popular in the Northeast. J99G, N39

Indian Pit: 90 days. Small to medium-sized, round tuber; skin smooth, tan splashed with pinkish-red around the deep eyes; white, highly waxy flesh of very good flavor, remains firm when cooked. Well suited to slow simmering, campfire soups and stews. Vigorous, very productive plants. J99G

Irish Cobbler: (Cobbler) 65 days. Medium to large, round to oblong tuber; medium deep eyes; smooth, white skin; white flesh; matures early. May be baked, but is best boiled; darkens after cooking. Consistent, heavy yields; grows well in heavy soils. Somewhat resistant to storage rot. An old standard that is widely adapted. B71, E38, E59Z, E97, G71, H54, H58M{PR}, H83, I99M{OR}, J99G

Jemseg: 65 days. Smooth, round tuber; tan skin; white flesh. Good baking and boiling quality. Considered by many as the earliest maturing cultivar, being harvested in July. Moderate resistance to scab. Grows well in hot, dry weather. Should be planted close together as it tends to "lunker". A95, D11M, J99G

Katahdin: Tuber flattened-spherical, with shallow eyes; skin white, smooth; maintains shape well even under poor growing conditions; matures in midseason. Ideal for boiling, with slight darkening after cooking. Medium-sized plant; not exceptionally high yielding, but very dependable; susceptible to scab. Shallow tuber set can lead to considerable sunburn. Introduced by the USDA in 1932. A95, G71, H54, H83

Kennebec: 80 days. Tuber elliptical to oblong, with shallow eyes; skin and flesh white; matures midseason to late. Good for boiling, baking and French fries; usually cooks white. Very large plant; high yielding; susceptible to scab; subject to sunburn under adverse conditions. Introduced in 1948 by the USDA. A95, B75, C63, D65, D76, E38, E97, F19M, G16, G71, H42, H83, J70M, J99G, K71, L97, N34{PR}, etc.

Norchip: Tuber round to oblong, slightly irregular with deep apical eyes; skin white, smooth; matures early. Medium-large, upright plant; has resistance to flea beetle; moderately resistant to scab. Widely used for commercial potato chips. Introduced in 1969 by the North Dakota Agricultural Experiment Station. C63, G87

Onaway: 65 days. Tuber elongated, with medium deep eyes; skin and flesh white; matures early. Tubers become rough when enlarged. Medium to large, upright plant; high yielding for an early cultivar; somewhat resistant to common scab. Released by the Michigan Agricultural Experiment Station in 1961. A95, J99G

Rosa: Medium-sized, round tuber; smooth, thin bright-white skin, splashed with pink around the eyes; matures in midseason. Keeps well after proper curing. Medium-sized plant; resistant to leaf roll, wilt, early blight and race A of the golden nematode. Hybrid of subspecies andigenum and tuberosum. Released by Cornell University in 1980. E97

Sebago: 80 days. Tuber deep oval to elongated, with shallow eyes; smooth, white skin; matures late. Good for boiling and baking, with no darkening after cooking. Large, upright plant; yields well; widely adapted to soil and climate; somewhat resistant to scab. Introduced in 1938 by the USDA. C63, E38, G64, J99G

Shepody: 90 days. Very long, uniform all-white tubers; shallow eyes; matures late. Heavy yielding. Resistant to verticillium wilt, fusarium wilt, rhizoctonia and net necrosis. Canada's leading French fry cultivar. Also good for baking and boiling. A95, D11M, G64, H83, J99G

Superior: 65 days. Tubers uniform in size and shape; skin white, slightly netted; matures medium early. Excellent market potato. Also a good winter keeper. Medium-sized, upright plant; has good resistance to scab. Tolerates varied spring planting soil and weather conditions. Released by the Wisconsin Agricultural Experiment Station in 1961. D65, G16, G64, G71, H54, H83, J99G, N39

White Elephant: Tuber oblong, of exceptional size, very long, flattened; skin white variegated with pink, especially towards the end remote from the point of attachment; flesh white, of excellent quality; matures late, keeps well. Extremely vigorous plant, high yielding. Introduced prior to 1885. BURPEE, VILMORIN; J99G{OR}

White Rose: (Long White) Large, long, elliptical-flattened tuber; numerous, medium deep pink eyes; smooth, white skin; white flesh; matures early. Ideal for boiling and salads, with generally no darkening after cooking. Does not store well. Very good producer of uniform tubers. One of the most popular commercial market potatoes. A95, E59Z, G93M, J99G, L97, *N40*{PR}

YELLOW-SKINNED

Anna Cheeka's Ozette:[3] Oblong tuber, 2 to 8 inches in length with an unusual number of eyes; thin, yellow skin; yellowish, very tasty flesh. Prolific. Historical heirloom, said to have been brought from Peru in the late 1700's by Spanish explorers and traded with the Makah/Ozette Indian tribe of Washington's Olympic peninsula. J99G

Augsburg Gold: 80 days. Large, round to oblong tuber; golden-yellow skin and flesh; excellent buttery flavor; matures in midseason. Ideal for mashed potatoes. Superior yields. Very promising as a gourmet market potato. J99G

Austrian Crescent:[3] Small to medium, thin, crescent-shaped tubers; up to 10 inches long and weighing 4 to 8 ounces; smooth yellowish skin; light-yellow flesh, moist and dense; matures early. Excellent for potato salad, remaining firm and waxy after boiling. Does not keep well. Heavy bearing. J99G

Bintje: (Yellow Finnish Bintje) 90 days. Small to medium-sized round tubers, with shallow eyes; yellow-brown skin; yellow, fine-textured, waxy flesh; matures late; keeps well. Excellent baked or boiled. High yields; up to 20 or 25 tubers per plant. The most widely grown yellow-fleshed cultivar in the world. Originated in Holland. Introduced about 1911. A95, D27, E59Z, I39, I76M{PR}, J99G, J99G{PR}, K49M, K49M{PR}

Carole: 110 days. Large, uniform, round to oblong tubers; shallow eyes; smooth, shiny, golden-yellow skin; firm, moist, light yellow flesh; very good buttery flavor; excellent storage qualities. Vigorous, heavy yielding plants; somewhat susceptible to scab. J20, J99G

Delta Gold: 80 days. Medium to large, round tuber; light-yellow skin; yellow flesh; matures medium-late. Unlike most yellow-fleshed cultivars, it has a dry, fluffy flesh that is better baked than boiled or fried. Sprouts early in storage. High yielding for a yellow-fleshed type, but about 1/3 less productive than Kennebec. H83, J99G

Fingerling:[3] Light yellow-fleshed salad potato brought to the United States by early German settlers. Long, finger-shaped tuber; 2 to 4 inches in length, 1 inch in diameter; yellow skin; moist, waxy yellow flesh; unique, delicious flavor; matures early. Should be boiled with the jackets on and cut up for salads. Also good fried. G16

German Butterball: 90 days. Large, uniform, round to oblong tubers with shallow eyes; smooth, attractive golden-yellow skin; intense golden-yellow flesh of exceptional flavor and quality. Excellent for boiling and steaming. Dwarf plant with high yields. J99G

German Yellow:[3] (German Fingerling) Medium to large fingerling type. Smooth, golden-yellow skin; rich yellow flesh with a firm, sweet potato-like texture and a unique flavor; very good keeper. Excellent in salads. Extremely prolific. Good specialty market item. A2, E24, J99G

Lady Finger:[3] Long, thin fingerling potato; up to 10 inches long, 1 inch in diameter. Bright yellow skin; light yellow flesh. Medium vigor and yields. J20

Russian Banana:[3] Small to medium-sized tuber; yellow skin; slightly yellow flesh with a waxy texture, very firm when boiled; good potato taste. Matures very late. Heavy yields. Has shown excellent field resistance to disease. Developed in the Baltic region of the U.S.S.R. Very popular across Canada as a market potato. A95, J99G

Saginaw Gold: 80 days. Medium-sized, uniform, roundish tubers; skin very smooth, tan-yellow; pale yellow flesh of excellent texture and flavor; matures in midseason. Very good for boiling, baking and French fries. High resistance to virus and hollow heart. A joint release by the United States and Canada. A95, J99G

Warba's Pink Eye: 65 days. Uniform, oval tuber; skin golden, splashed with pink in and around the pronounced eyes. Excellent steamed, baked, boiled or fried. Keeps well. Resistant to scab. Unique type that shows good promise as a specialty market potato. J99G

Yellow Finn: (Yellow Finnish) 90 days. Large, uniform, oval to round tubers; yellow-brown, lightly russet skin; smooth yellow flesh, more brilliant than others; matures late. Moist, smooth texture with an almost sweet flavor, especially when boiled. Very popular European cultivar, becoming well-known in North American specialty markets. A2, A44M{PR}, G27M, H58M, H58M{PR}, I39, I76M{PR}, I99, I99M, J83T{PR}, J99G, J99G{PR}, K49M, K66, L89, L97, *N40*{PR}, etc.

Yukon Gold: 65 days. Large rounded tuber, with shallow pink eyes; attractive, light yellow-brown skin; rich yellow flesh, of very fine flavor and texture; matures medium-early. Unique for a yellow-fleshed cultivar in that it has good size and also keeps well. Excellent in storage. Medium-large, uniform yields. Released in Canada in 1980. A2, A95, B75, D11M, D27, D74M{PR}, E31{PR}, E59Z, G44M{PR}, G64, H42, H83, J99G, J99G{PR}, K49M, N34, N34{PR}, *N40*{PR}, etc.

PUMPKIN {S}

CUCURBITA PEPO

HYBRID

Autumn Gold: 100 days. Medium-sized fruit, weight 10 to 15 pounds; round to rectangular in shape, nicely ribbed; has good handles; skin rich-orange when mature; flesh deep-orange, firm and meaty, suitable for pies. Contains the "precocious yellow" gene, so even the young fruits are deep yellow and there are no green pumpkins at harvest. Vigorous vine produces 3 or more fruit. All America Selections winner in 1987. B75M, C44, C85M, F19M, *F72*, G6, G16, G71, H95, J7, K73, L79, L97, M46, M49, etc.

Funny Face:[1] 100 days. An early, highly uniform and productive cultivar with short-vine plants, perfect for gardeners with limited space. Deep globe-shaped fruit with flattened ends, 12 inches in diameter; weight 10 to 15 pounds; skin smooth, bright-orange; flesh orange-yellow, thick, coarse, somewhat stringy. Excellent for canning and jack o'lanterns. A16, C92, D76, *F72*, G71, G79, G93M, *H61*, I64, J34, K50, K73, M13M, M49, N16, etc.

Prizewinner: 120 days. Exceptionally large, uniform, roundish fruit; skin bright reddish-orange, smooth and glossy; ribs shallow; blossom scar small; orange flesh of good flavor. Vigorous vine, 30 to 40 feet in length. Largest "true" pumpkin, easily reaching 200 pounds in weight. Easily grown without special care. B75

Spirit:[1] 95 days. Leading hybrid pumpkin for the Halloween trade. Uniform, round fruit; 12 inches in diameter, weight 10 to 15 pounds; moderately ribbed; skin bright orange; flesh thick and meaty, suitable for pies and custards. Early maturing, but keeps well until Halloween. Short-vine plant with only a 5 foot spread, yet it produces a heavy crop of fruit. All America Selections winner for 1977. A13, A16, B73M, D11M, E38, F19M, G16, G71, *H61*, H94, I64, J7, J34, K73, L89, etc.

Trick-or-Treat:[1 2] 105 days. Hulless, "naked" seeded or "eat all" type. Round, very uniform fruit, 6 to 10 inches in diameter; weight 10 to 12 pounds; lightly ribbed; skin light orange; flesh thick, orange, suitable for pies and canning. High-protein seeds are good either raw or roasted. Also good for carving at Halloween. Short-vine plants, 5 to 6 feet long; suited for small gardens. *A1*, B73M, *F63*, *F72*, *G1M*, *G13M*, G16, G71, J20, K10, K73, M29, M95M, N52

OPEN-POLLINATED

Baby Pam: 100 days. Very uniform fruit; 5 inches tall, 5 1/2 inches in diameter; long, tightly secured "handles"; smooth, deep-orange skin; deep-orange flesh, suitable for pies. Also used for painting and for decoration. Vigorous, 10 to 12 foot vines produce a dozen or more fruits each. A13, B35M, D11M, D68, E97, F13, *F63*, *G13M*, G93M, *H61*, K10, K73, M95M, N52

Bushkin:[1 3] 95 days. Bush type triple-purpose pumpkin, fine for pies, carving and seed snacks. Bright golden-orange fruit; weight 8 to 10 pounds; thick, light-yellow flesh of good flavor; keeps well. Medium-large edible seeds have a slight husk. Short-vine plants spread only 5 to 6 feet, produce 1 to 3 fruits each; ideal for small gardens. B75, D11M

Cinderella:[1] 95 days. Uniform, globe-shaped fruit; 10 inches in diameter; smooth, bright orange skin; sweet yellow-orange flesh. Doesn't keep quite as well as vine types. Bush-type vine; needs only 6 square feet of growing space. *S75M*

Connecticut Field: (Yellow Field) 110 days. Fruit moderately large; 10 to 14 inches in diameter, 10 to 18 inches tall; weight 18 to 25 pounds; form variable, globular to long oval, narrowly ribbed; skin bright yellow-orange; flesh thick, coarse, somewhat granular; slight flavor and sweetness; quality poor. Mostly used for canning and jack o'lanterns. Origin unknown, although it was probably grown by American Indians. TAPLEY 1937; A16, B75M, B78, C44, E24, *F72*, G6, G16, *H61*, H66, J7, K73, L7M, M13M, M49, etc.

Ghost Rider: 115 days. Uniform, deep round fruits, average weight 15 to 30 pounds; exterior dark-orange, hard, ridged; flesh yellow-orange to orange, depending on maturity. Unique, long dark-green to black handle. Ideal for processing and jack o'lanterns. H33, H54, J84, K10, K73, L42, N52

Half Moon: Tall, uniform Connecticut Field type with a longer and better attached "handle". Fruit large, 12 to 14 inches in diameter; weight 15 to 20 pounds; deep-globe-shaped, with medium ribbing; skin medium-orange; flesh pale orange, thick, coarse and sweet. Excellent home garden cultivar. *A1*, D11M, *G13M*, G51, G79, J84, K73, L79, M29

Jack-Be-Little:[3] 95 days. Attractive "mini pumpkin". Flattened, deeply ribbed, orange fruit; only 2 to 3 inches in diameter, approximately 2 inches tall, and weighing 2 to 6 ounces. Although very sweet-fleshed for cooking they are most appealing in fall table decorations and for crafts. A good specialty item for farmstands and the florist trade. Vigorous vine; produces 8 to 10 fruits that will keep up to 8 months. B73M, F19M, *F60*, *F72*, F82, G6, G16, G71, *H61*, J7, K73, L9M, L97, M46, N16, etc.

Jack-o'-Lantern: (Halloween) 95 days. Medium-sized fruit; 8 to 12 inches tall, 8 inches in diameter; about the size of a man's head; weight 10 pounds; irregular in shape, from round to quite oblong, slightly ribbed; skin bright yellow-orange; flesh medium-thick, deep yellow, fine-grained, suitable for pies. Very popular for Halloween decorations. A16, B75M, C44, D82, *F60*, *F72*, F82, G79, *H61*, H66, H94, K5M, L97, M46, N16, etc.

Mini Jack:[2 3] 105 days. Round, uniform, bright-orange fruit; only 3 to 6 inches in diameter and weighing but 2 to 3 pounds. Grown primarily for its seeds which are nearly hulless or "naked", and are delicious either raw or roasted. Also good for decorating. Earlier than other small pumpkins. Compact vines produce an abundance of fruit. *F72*, *G1M*, *G13M*, G51, G57M, G93M, J84, K5M, K73, *L59G*, L89, N52

Munchkin:[3] 100 days. High-yielding, attractive "mini pumpkin". Fruit 3 to 4 inches in diameter; flattened with a bright orange, scalloped skin; weight 1/4 pound; flesh orange-yellow, meaty, holds its firmness over a long period; has good sweet pumpkin flavor. Ideal for baking as individual servings; or for stuffing with soup, cranberry sauce, etc. Also used for decorations and carving. Heavy-yielding vines. C61M, E5T, F13, G51, G93M, K66, S55

Northern Bush:[1] 90 days. Bush type pumpkin, developed by Fisher's Garden store form a cross of Cheyenne Bush and Orange Winter Luxury. Fruit averages 6 to 8 pounds, with some occasionally reaching 15 pounds; skin rich-orange; flesh thick, fine-grained, of a rich golden-yellow color. D82

Pankow's Field: 110 days. Large, smooth fruit, deep round to tall in shape; weight 18 to 22 pounds; has good color; resembles Connecticut Field. Excellent for jack o'lanterns. Unusually thick and strong stem, much less apt to break in handling than standard pumpkins. Heavy yields. Introduced in 1981 by Joseph Harris Co. F13, K10, M49

Small Sugar: (New England Pie, Early Small Sugar, Sugar Pie) 100 days. Fruit very small; 8 to 9 inches in diameter, 5 to 6 inches deep; weight 5 to 6 pounds; more or less distinctly ribbed; skin reddish-orange, thick and hard; flesh moderately thick, yellow-orange, fine-grained, sweet and well-flavored. The standard pie pumpkin, introduced prior to 1865. BURR, TAPLEY 1937; A16, B75M, C44, *F60*, *F72*, G6, *H61*, H66, H94, J58, J73, K73, L7M, M13M, M49, etc.

Spookie: 100 days. An improved Small Sugar type with more uniformity, resulting in a higher percentage of marketable fruits. Fruit small to medium, 6 to 7 inches in diameter; weight 5 to 6 pounds;

skin bright-orange, smooth and hard; flesh orange-yellow, thick, fine-grained and sweet; excellent for pies. *G1M*, *H61*, K10, K66, L79, N52

Sugar Baby: (Honey Pumpkin) 95 days. Heirloom pie pumpkin from Minnesota. Fruit averages 8 inches in diameter and 3 1/2 inches deep; skin dark orange, distinctly ribbed; flesh orange, very sweet and dry, makes pies of fine quality. Vines long; prolific; disease resistant, resists mildew better than other cultivars. Introduced in the 1880's. L7M

Sweetie Pie:[3] 110 days. Ornamental "mini pumpkin". Flat, blocky, deeply ribbed fruits; 3 inches in diameter, 1 3/4 inches deep; weight 5 ounces; has old-fashioned pumpkin flavor. Grown from stock seed imported from China, where it is considered a delicacy. Ideal for Halloween and Thanksgiving table decorations. C53, I97T, L42

Triple Treat:[2] 110 days. Triple-purpose, "no waste" pumpkin. Uniformly round fruit, 7 to 9 inches in diameter; weight 6 to 8 pounds, a good size for Halloween carving; bright orange skin; thick, deep orange, medium-fine-grained flesh is excellent for pies and puddings; keeps well for several months in a moderately cool place. Hulless seeds make a delicious high-protein snack, either raw or roasted. B75, D11M, D68, G51, H49, J7, J25M, J58, S55

Winter Luxury: (Luxury Pie, Winter Queen) 105 days. Moderately small fruit; 9 to 10 inches in diameter, 6 to 7 inches deep; weight 7 to 8 pounds; shape nearly globular, narrowly ribbed; skin yellow-orange, uniformly and finely laced with a light gray cork-like netting; flesh pale-orange, moderately thick, slightly juicy, tender and somewhat sweet; quality high. Keeps exceptionally well for winter use. Introduced in 1893 by Johnson & Stokes of Philadelphia. TAPLEY 1937; G16, K49M, L7M

QUINCE {GR}

CYDONIA OBLONGA

Bereczcki: (Vranja) Very large, pear-shaped fruit, golden yellow in color; quality very good; tender when cooked. Tree very vigorous; heavy yielding; comes into bearing early. A very old Serbian cultivar named after Bereczcki, an eminent pomologist. SIMMONS 1978; O81, Q24M, Q30, Q30{SC}, R77, S81M

Champion: Fruit very large, up to 24 ounces, intermediate in shape between an apple and a pear; skin greenish-yellow; flesh yellow, almost as tender as that of an apple, and only slightly astringent; ripens in midseason; keeps very well. Tree vigorous; very productive; bears at an early age. Will often not mature its fruit in regions with a short growing season. MEECH, WICKSON; D76, E97, F43M

Cooke's Jumbo: (Jumbo) Large to very large, pear-shaped fruits, 6 to 8 inches in diameter; yellowish-green skin; white flesh; ripens in September and October. Good for cooking and jelly. Introduced by L.E. Cooke Co. *C54*, I83M, M31M, M92, N24M

Gamboa: Fruit pear-shaped, 5 inches long; skin light, bright yellow; flesh yellowish-white, turning a dark purple-red when cooked; flavor sweeter than most types. Small, very dense tree; ornamental. Originated in Portugal. G92

Meech's Prolific: Large, pear-shaped fruit, up to 18 ounces; skin very fine-textured, bright yellow; exceedingly fragrant; of excellent flavor; ripens 2 weeks earlier than Champion. Tree slow growing; heavy and regular bearing, often commencing to bear when only 3 years old. Originated in Connecticut prior to 1883. MEECH, SIMMONS 1978; O81, Q30, Q30{SC}, S81M

Orange: (Apple) Fruit large to very large, nearly round in shape; skin bright golden-yellow in color; flesh very tender, orange-yellow when raw, turning red when cooked. Quality very good in regions with cool summers, inferior where summer temperatures are high. Leading quince cultivar in the United States. *C54*, D69, E84, G23{DW}, H49{DW}, H65, I36, *I68*, I83M, J61M, M31M, M92

Perfume: Large to very large fruits, up to 1 1/2 pounds each; form oval to slightly rectangular; skin waxy, a glossy bright yellow; very fragrant; flesh tart but flavorful. Tree with attractive pink blossoms. D57{OR}

Pineapple: Fruit similar to Orange, but smoother and more globular in shape. Skin golden-yellow; flesh white and extremely tender, low in astringency, with a slight pineapple-like flavor. Originated in Santa Rosa, California by Luther Burbank. Introduced in 1899. One of the leading commercial cultivars in California. WICKSON; A88M, B67, *C54*, D76, E4, E97, F43M, H4, I49M, *I68*, I83M, L1, L99M, M31M, *N20*, N24M, *N40*{PR}, etc.

Portugal: Very large, oblong-oval fruit; skin almost orange when ripe, very woolly; flesh more juicy than other types, turns fine purple or deep crimson when cooked; flavor very good; ripens very early, 10 days before Orange. Tree vigorous; becoming large and spreading; not productive, and slow to come into bearing. Very old cultivar. SIMMONS 1978; F43M, O71M, P86, Q24M

Smyrna: Large, round to oblong fruit; skin lemon yellow; flesh tender, mild, good to very good in quality; ripens with Orange, but keeps much better. Tree a rapid and vigorous grower, with unusually large leaves. Introduced from Smyrna (now Izmir), Turkey by George C. Roeding, Fresno, California in 1897. B93M, *C54*, D69, E4, F43M, H4, I49M, *I68*, I83M, L12, L99M, M31M, *N40*{PR}

Van Deman: Large, oblong to pear-shaped fruit; skin pale orange; flesh pale yellow, moderately coarse, with a pleasant spicy flavor; retains good flavor after cooking; ripens in September. High yielding tree; considered among the hardiest cultivars. A seedling of Portugal pollinated by Orange. Selected by Luther Burbank. Introduced by Stark Brothers around 1891. I49M, J61M

QUINOA {S}

CHENOPODIUM QUINOA

Ajencha: Medium to large, white and red seeds. Well adapted to hot summer days. From the high elevation Quechua Indians of Bolivia. K49T, L79M

Cahuil: Seed medium-sized, light green with some variation. A good producer in Washington state. Suitable for lower elevations. A2

Calancha: Medium-sized, cream-colored seeds. From the high elevation Quechua Indians of Bolivia. L79M

Cochabamba 250: Medium-sized white seed. Very early maturing. Low in saponin. Originated in Bolivia at high elevations between 18^0 and 19^0 latitude. A2

Colorado 407: Improved, high-yielding, early cultivar developed at the University of Colorado. Nutty-flavored, brown seeds. Soaks faster than other cultivars. Short, stocky, uniform plants. L89

Dave: (Linares 407) Medium-sized seed; yellow-brown in color. Ripens in mid-season, or mid to late summer from an April sowing. Height 5 to 6 feet. Very colorful orange and pink seed heads. Very short-season, high-yielding Chilean cultivar, adaptable to high or low elevations. Named for David Cussack, who was instrumental in bringing quinoa into North American agriculture. A2, E59Z, F42, K17M, K49T, L79M

Early Orange #77: Good production of orange seeds. Upright plant, 4 to 5 feet tall. Attractive orange-yellow seedheads. Early season maturity. E59Z

Faro: Small, yellowish-white seed. Height of plant 4 to 6 feet. Foliage light-green. Mid to long-season type, somewhat later than Linares. Originated at sea level. Performs well at lower elevations. Good-yielding, adaptable cultivar from southern Chile. Best yielding of 16 strains tested by Abundant Life Seed Foundation. A2, E24, E59Z, I99, K49T, L79M, L89

Glorieta: Seed small, brown in color. High yielding plant. Originated in Bolivia at high elevations between 18^0 and 19^0 latitude. A2

Isluga Yellow: Medium-sized yellow seed. Attractive golden-yellow or pink seed heads. Early-maturing, high-yielding, somewhat taller cultivar. Has grown consistently well in a variety of Western mountain and coastal sites. A2, K49T

Jank'a: Medium to small, cream-colored seeds. High yielding plant. From the high elevation Quechua Indians of Bolivia. L79M

Linares: Good yields of golden-yellow, medium-sized seed, high in saponin content. Flavor distinct from commercial quinoa. Ripens in mid-season. Height of plant 5 to 6 feet. Has grown consistently well at both maritime and Rocky Mountain planting sites. Originated in Chile at 36^0 south latitude, and at sea level. A2, E24, K49T, P1G, R47

Linares #509: White seeded, mid to late-season type. Similar to Dave, but with larger greenish-yellow seed heads and a month later in maturity. Somewhat adaptable plant, height 6 feet; very high yielding. E59Z, F42

Llico: Medium-sized brownish-white seed. Greenish-white seed heads. Late season maturity. Non-uniform growth habit and yields. Originated in Chile at a low-elevation site between 34^0 and 41^0 latitude. A2

Millahue: Medium-sized, white seed. One of the first strains to mature. Recommended for lower elevations and California valleys with cooler nights. A2

Multi-Hued: Produces flower heads ranging from red through orange and yellow, to purple and mauve. Height of plant 5 to 6 feet. Very productive in northern latitudes. B49, K17M

Pisk'a: Medium-sized, white seeds. From the high elevation Quechua Indians of Bolivia. L79M

Sajama: (Dulce Saj) Large, white-seeded Bolivian cultivar that is essentially free of bitter tasting saponins. Can be eaten as it is harvested, without the excess washing required of other strains. Late-maturing and comparatively low in yield. The first "sweet" quinoa to be offered to American gardeners. Selected in Bolivia in the 1960's. A2

Sea Level: An excellent strain adapted to sea-level conditions. Grown in lowland California with a reported yield of 1/4 pound of grain per plant. Dropped by F80

Temuco: Very palatable, small white seeds. Ripens in midseason. Yellow-green seed heads (with some golden); large roundish leaves. Height of plant 5 to 6 feet; bears abundant crops. One of the best choices for maritime sites in the Pacific Northwest, but has grown well in the southern Rockies also. Originated in southern Chile at 38^0 latitude. A2, B49, E59Z, I99, K49T

Tunari: Whitish-yellow seeds. Yellow seed heads. Height of plant 4 to 6 1/2 feet. Originated in Bolivia. K49T, L79M

Wila: Large red seeds. From high elevation Aymara Indians near Lake Titicaca in Bolivia and Peru. L79M

RADISH {S}

RAPHANUS SATIVUS

EUROPEAN RADISHES

SPRING/SUMMER HARVESTING

Green-Skinned

Martian: 25 days. Medium-long roots; similar to French Breakfast in shape. Lime green shoulders with a white tip; identical interiors. Makes a nice contrast on a relish tray. I97T, L42

Multi-Colored

Bombay Red: An excellent, attractive Indian cultivar. Long, tapered roots, somewhat irregular in shape; the upper half red, the lower half white. Flesh tender and tasty. Medium-tall tops. Matures early. N91, O39M, R50, S93M

D'Avignon:[1] 23 days. One of the longest of the French Breakfast or "gourmet" type radishes, preferred by epicures for their delicate crunch and gentle fire. Smooth, slender root, about 3 inches long, tapered to a point; 66 to 75% red toward the top, white tipped. G6, Q34, S55

Early White-Tipped Scarlet: (Scarlet White-Tipped Turnip) 22 days. Root roundish, grows 1 to 1 1/2 inches in diameter; skin attractive, bright carmine pink on top, very white on the lower fourth part; flesh white, crisp and sweet. Matures rapidly, but quickly becomes hollow in the center; should be pulled as soon as fully grown. Introduced prior to 1859. VILMORIN; A25, A56, B71, E38, F80, G51, G57M, *G83M*, G87, I84, *L59G*

Easter Egg: (F_1) 28 days. Multi-line hybrid that produces white, red, purple, pink and violet colored radishes. Roots have very good flavor and interior quality, remaining firm and crisp a long time without becoming pithy. Tops are medium height, medium green, and are strap-leaved. A16, A69M, A87M, C44, C53, C85M, D27, F19M, F44, *F72*, H42, I67M, I84, I91, L14, *N40*{PR}, etc.

Eighteen Days:[1] (De Dix-Huit Jours) 18 days. A very quick maturing, half-long, French Breakfast type with a rose-carmine shaft and a white tip. Not recommended for mid-summer sowing. C53, F33, G68, S55, S95M

Flamboyant:[1] (Demi-Long Ecarlate à Bout Blanc) 25 days. French Breakfast type. Semi-long, cylindrical, uniform roots; 2 to 3 inches long; skin vermillion red on the upper two-thirds, snow white on the bottom third. Flesh crisp, tender and mild. Harvest when young for best quality. Short tops. Very popular in France. F33, G68, I77, K66, Q34, S95M

Flamivil:[1] 25 days. French breakfast type. Medium-long, cylindrical root; about 90% intense red, with slightly pointed white tip and slender taproot. The French say that Flamivil, touched with a small splash of white on the tip, looks like it was just dipped in milk. G6, G68, I77, K66, S95M

French Breakfast:[1] 25 days. Very attractive market garden radish. Oblong, blunt-ended root; 1 1/2 inches long, 3/4 inch thick; rose-colored on the upper three-fourths, pure-white on the lower part. Flesh crisp, tender, mildly pungent, becomes hollow in the center if not pulled as soon as it is fully formed. Introduced prior to 1885. VILMORIN; A16, A25, B49, C44, D82, D87, G16, G68, G71, H66, H94, J7, L97, M13M, M95, *N40*{PR}, etc.

Lanquiette:[1] French Breakfast type. Medium-long, cylindrical, fleshy root with a slender tap root. Skin 75 to 80% bright red, 20 to 25% white at the slightly pointed tip. Should be harvested promptly at maturity since its fine flavor and texture does not hold in the garden. Suitable for spring and fall culture, and under glass in winter. E5T, Q34

Long Scarlet Amiens: (Rave Ecarlate d'Amiens) 28 days. Unusual summer type of good quality. Long, straight red roots with white tips; 3 1/2 to 4 inches long; crisp and tender. Slower to mature and "go over" than regular cultivars. F33, L91M

Oliva: 25 days. A multi-colored Italian radish that is plumper than the French Breakfast types. Uniform shape; bright crimson with just the edge of the tip bright white; excellent flavor; resistant to pithiness. Best harvested when 1 to 1 1/2 inches long. K66

Pontvil:[1] 24 days. A very attractive French Breakfast-type radish. Unlike others of this type, Pontvil does not become hollow, hot or woody soon after becoming mature. Stays crisp, sweet and firm long after similar cultivars have run to seed. L91M, S95M

Sezanne: 20-30 days. An attractive, round European radish. Lower portion is white, upper part is pale magenta. Makes a nice contrast to the bright red radishes typically grown in the United States. I77, K66

Sparkler: (White Tip Sparkler) 25 days. Round to globe-shaped root; deep scarlet on the upper portion, pure-white on the lower end; crisp white flesh, never becomes hollow at the heart; holds its crispness long after maturing. Medium-tall tops. Popular for fresh market and home gardens. A16, B49, B75M, D82, E24, F19M, *F72*, G16, H66, H94, K73, M13M, M46, M95, N16, etc.

Pink/Red-Skinned

Cerise: 21-25 days. A round, attractive bright red, highly uniform radish that has been selected in France for market growers. Holds well without becoming hollow or pithy. Short tops. Should be used when small, with the stems attached. Introduced by Vilmorin. G68, S95M

Champion: 24 days. Uniform, globe-shaped roots; bright scarlet skin; crisp white flesh, holds for a long period of time without becoming woody or pithy. Sturdy medium-length tops; good for bunching. For spring or fall crops. Thrives in cool weather. All America Selections winner in 1957. A16, B73M, C44, D82, E24, F19M, F82, G16, G71, H94, J7, L79, M13M, M46, N16, etc.

Cherry Belle: 25 days. Smooth, round root, 3/4 inch in diameter; bright cherry-red skin; crisp, firm, tender white flesh; holds its eating quality well as it is very resistant to pithiness. Short tops. Ideal for home use, market and forcing. All America Selections winner in 1949. A16, B73M, B75M, C44, D82, F19M, F82, G16, H66, H94, J7, K73, L7M, M13M, M49, etc.

Comet: 25 days. Globe-shaped to round roots; skin bright scarlet red; flesh white, fine-textured, exceptionally firm and crisp. Short to medium tops, 3 1/2 to 4 inches tall. Excellent for bunching. Remains firm longer than most early globe types. All America Selections winner in 1936. A16, A69M, C92, D11M, D27, F24M, G79, G93M, *H61*, I64, J58, K73, L42, M13M, M49, etc.

Crimson Giant: 27 days. Large, turnip-shaped root; 1 to 1 1/2 inches in diameter, considerably larger than other early types; skin deep crimson; flesh firm but tender, crisp and sweet; remains in perfect condition several days after pulling. Equally desirable for forcing or outdoor planting. A25, *A69M*, B35M, D11M, D65, G71, G93M, H66, H95, J34, K71, L97, M13M, M95, N39, etc.

Early Scarlet Globe: 20 days. Deep globe-shaped roots; bright red skin; pure-white, crisp flesh, of mild delicate flavor. Short bright green tops, excellent for bunching. For greenhouse or frame forcing, as well as muck or mineral soils. Has more heat tolerance than other cultivars. A13, A25, B35M, C85M, C92, D11M, D65, F19M, G71, H94, J25M, J58, K71, N16, N39, etc.

German Giant: (Parat) 29 days. A very large round radish that is a favorite of home gardeners in Germany. Scarlet red skin; crisp, slightly pungent white flesh. Can be harvested small or after reaching the size of a baseball. Will not split or become woody or spongy. Needs to be thinned to 1 inch apart to reach large size. D76, E49, E97, G68, I99, L9, P9, S27

Long Red Italian: 35-45 days. May grow to 12 inches long when planted in loose, sandy soil. Bright crimson skin; succulent, mildly pungent white flesh. Needs 35 to 45 days to reach maturity, but can be can be harvested and used when smaller. I77, K66

Long Scarlet: (Cincinnati) 25 days. Long root, a considerable portion growing above ground; 7 to 8 inches in length, about 3/4 inch in diameter; skin an attractive deep pinkish-red color, becoming paler towards the tapered lower portion; flesh white, transparent, crisp, mild. Very hardy; can be forced as early as February. Introduced prior to 1865. BURR; *A69M*, *D12*, D76, E97, G27M, G57M, H66, K27M, K49M, L14, *N40*{PR}

Pink Beauty: 27 days. Smooth, round root, grows as large as Champion; unique rose-pink skin; crisp snow-white flesh, very mild flavor. Stays solid and crisp for a long period of time, never becoming woody or pithy. Short tops; easy to bunch. Adds variety to salads and relish trays. D76, E49, E97, H33

Rave Rose Longue: (Saumonée, Long Scarlet, Salmon-Colored) 30 days. Root extremely long and slender, often 5 to 6 inches in length and only about 2/5 inch in diameter; tapered to a point; skin smooth, vinous-red; flesh almost transparent, slightly tinged with pink or lilac, tender, crisp, very mild. Introduced prior to 1885. VILMORIN; G68

Scarlet Globe: 24 days. Smooth olive-shaped root, 1 inch in diameter at its widest point; thread-like tap root; bright scarlet skin; white, brittle flesh, very mild and tender; remains crisp over a long period of time. Small to medium tops. For forcing or outdoor culture. F1, G51, G57M, G79, *G83M*, H42, H49, I64, J84, M13M, P83M

Wood's Early Frame: (Wood's Frame) 20-22 days. Roots very elongated-ovoid, 2 2/5 to 2 4/5 inches long, about 4/5 inch broad; attractive carmine skin, paler at the tip; flesh very white, firm, juicy, very crisp; flavor fresh and pleasant, slightly pungent. Stalks and leaf-veins tinged with coppery red. Popular in England for early frame culture. Introduced prior to 1865. BURR, VILMORIN; U33

Purple-Skinned

Plum Purple: (Purple Plum) 27 days. Smooth, globe-shaped roots; unique bright purple skin; crisp, juicy snow-white flesh, mild flavor; never becomes pithy or hot. Short tops; 4 to 5 inches long. Hardy and highly adaptable. Especially attractive in salads and relish trays. *C28*, D11M, F19M, G93M, H42, H49, K66, K73, L11, *N40*{PR}

White-Skinned

Beer Garden: White radish that grows as large as a turnip. In Germany they are traditionally sliced, dipped in sugar or salt, and washed down with beer. G68

Burpee White: (Burpee's Round White, Snowball) 25 days. Young roots nearly round; enlarge in diameter and become flattened as they grow. Pure-white skin and flesh. Best eaten when 3/4 to 1 inch in diameter, but stays tender, mild, and crisp for a long time. Medium-tall tops. A16, B75, D27, G16, G71M, G87, H42, H94, H95, J34, N52

Candela di Ghiacci: (Long White Italian) A long-rooted white Italian radish that grows to 6 inches in length or more. Very uniform shape; crisp white flesh, mildly pungent. I77, K66

Hailstone: (White Globe Hailstone) 26 days. Globe-shaped root, somewhat larger than Scarlet Globe but not as large as Crimson Giant. Pure-white skin; crisp, tender, mild white flesh; earlier and larger than most round cultivars; holds its quality well. Medium-tall tops. A56, A69M, *B1*, B73M, *D12*, D65, D82, E24, *G13M*, I39, I64, K10, K71, *L59G*

Münchner Bier:[2] (München Bier) 67 days. A unique cultivar that produces masses of thick, tender, juicy, stringless pods at the top of 2 foot stems. Can be added whole or chopped to salads, boiled, steamed or stir-fried. In Germany, the long white roots are sliced thinly, salted lightly, and eaten on black bread or with pretzels and washed down with beer. B49, L91M, N81, P9, P83M, S55

Snow Belle: 26 days. Flattened globe-shaped root with a small tap root; skin pure-white, smooth, attractive; crisp, mild white flesh, tangy flavor; stays firm for a long period of time. Medium, dark green tops. Good for home gardens and bunching. B71, *C28*, D11M, E97, *F63*, G64, G82, H33, J34, K27M, K73, L42, L97, M29, M49, M95M, etc.

White Globe: (White Ball, White Pearl) 25 days. One of the best early white radishes. Uniform round roots; smooth, white skin; crisp, mild, glistening white flesh; holds its quality for a long time, never becoming pithy. A87M, C92, D76, E38, H66, L91M

White Icicle: (Lady Finger) 30 days. Long, slender, tapered root; 5 to 6 inches in length, 1/2 inch thick; thin, tender, snow-white skin; crisp, tender white flesh, mild in flavor; never becomes woody or pithy. Very tolerant of hot summer heat. Easy to force and fine for outdoor culture. A16, A25, B73M, C44, F19M, F82, G6, G16, H66, H94, J7, L7M, L97, M13M, N16, *N40*{PR}, etc.

White Transparent Forcing: Long, cylindrical root, 8 to 10 inches in length, tapered at the end; nearly translucent flesh, crisp but tender, almost juicy, refreshing. Best harvested when 4 to 5 inches long. Suitable for forcing under protected cover. May also be sown outdoors from early spring to fall. E83T

White Turnip: Large, flattened globe-shaped root; skin white; flesh white and semi-transparent, firm, of good flavor but very pungent, best picked when young. Large, erect, clear-green leaves. Can also be grown as a fall radish. Introduced about 1834. BURR, VILMORIN; P83M

Yellow-Skinned

French Golden: (Golden) 32 days. Elongated, slightly tapered root; 4 to 5 inches long, about 1 inch in diameter; light-golden skin; very crisp pure-white flesh with a relatively mild, distinctive flavor. An attractive addition to salads. Very resistant to disease and insect problems. I99, J20

Yellow Oval: 50-60 days. Conical or elongated root, 3 to 4 inches in diameter and 6 to 8 inches long, half growing above ground; orange-yellow skin; juicy flesh with a hot, pungent flavor. E83T

WINTER HARVESTING Winter radishes are those that have such compact and firm-fleshed roots that they will keep through a great part of the winter without sprouting or becoming hollow at the center, as spring and summer radishes do when they are stored for any length of time. The black types are traditionally used by cooks of Russian and Jewish heritage. SCHNEIDER [Cul, Re], VILMORIN [Cu].

Black-Skinned

Black Winter Round: 55 days. A large round radish imported from Italy. Smooth, deep black skin; flesh white, solid, crisp, pungent, of fine quality. Should be sown in July and August for fall and winter use. Will keep all winter stored in moist sand. E49

Long Black Spanish: (Noir Gros Long d'Hiver) 60 days. Uniform, cylindrical roots; 7 to 10 inches long, 2 to 3 inches in diameter; skin very black, somewhat wrinkled; flesh pure-white, firm, compact, pungent. Leaves stout, broad, long. Stores well. Can also be used for sprouting. Introduced prior to 1865. VILMORIN; A2, A69M, C92, D11M, *D12*, D76, E38, F33, G67M, G68, H54, I39, I64{SP}, J7, K49M, M13M, O53M, etc.

Poids d'Horloge: Long, cylindrical, club-shaped root; about 8 inches in length; slightly narrower at the neck than at the root end, somewhat reminiscent of Des Vertus Marteau turnip; skin pure black, smooth; flesh crisp and pungent. Sown in July and August for winter use. Keeps extremely well. P59M

Round Black Spanish: (Noir Gros Rond d'Hiver) 55 days. Root roundish, often top-shaped; 3 to 4 inches in diameter, about 3 inches long; skin black, cracked in longitudinal lines; flesh white, very compact and firm, very pungent. Not very late for a winter radish; may be sown up to the end of July. Keeps exceptionally well. Introduced prior to 1865. VILMORIN; A69M, C44, C85M, D27, D65, G16, G64, G68, G71, J7, K71, K73, M13M, M46, M95, N39, etc.

Winterrettich: 55 days. A round, black-skinned winter radish grown in Germany especially for salads. A favorite Bavarian combination includes leaf lettuce, curly endive, cress, sorrel and chervil. Excellent, pungent flavor. Planted in the fall for a late harvest. Stores well without wilting or losing its crisp texture. N81

Purple-Skinned

Violet de Gournay: 65 days. French heirloom. Long, cylindrical root, slightly tapered toward the end; 8 to 10 inches in length, 1 1/2 inches in diameter; dark-violet skin; pungent pure-white flesh. Stores well. Used for grating into salads, pickling and cooking. Sown in August for a fall and winter crop. Introduced prior to 1885. VILMORIN; C53, E83T, G68, I77, P83M, S55

Red-Skinned

Bartender Red Mammoth: 35 days. Long, tapered root, 7 inches in length and 1 inch in diameter; skin deep red; flesh pink, firm, crisp, pungent. Tops grow 8 to 10 inches tall. Heavy yielder under semi-tropical conditions. For home gardens and fresh market. *L59G*

ORIENTAL RADISHES

DAIKON Also called *Japanese radishes*, these are exclusively white-skinned except for a few which become green where the shoulder grows above the soil. They are generally larger, coarser, later to mature, and more unpalatable in leaf texture than Lo Bok. (R. sativus Longipinnatus Group)

Spring/Summer Harvesting

Early 40 Days: (Kaiware 40 days) 38-45 days. A cultivar developed especially for sprouting. Produces spicy sprouts in 2 to 4 days that can be added to salads, stir-fried, etc. Also grown for the white, mild-flavored roots which grow to 12 inches in length and 2 1/2 inches in diameter. Sow in early spring for an early summer harvest of roots. Tolerant to heat and cold. D55, *Q28*, *S63M*, *S70*

Minokunichi Improved: 55 days. Long, cylindrical root, slightly tapered at the end; 20 to 24 inches in length, 2 to 2 1/4 inches in diameter at the widest point; glistening pure white, fine-grained flesh. Developed from hybrids of different strains of Minowase; selected for resistance to virus diseases, and the ability to be sown earlier in the spring. *P39*

Minowase: (Minowase Early, Minowase Dark Green Leaved) 55 days. Very large, tapered root; 20 to 24 inches long, 2 to 2 1/2 inches in diameter; pure-white skin and flesh; juicy, crisp, mildly pungent flavor. Rapid growing and widely adapted. Heat and disease tolerant. Best sown in May for a summer crop. Optimum temperature for growth is 75^0 F. *D12*, D55, E24, E97, *G13M*, G33, J73, L59, L97, M95, S61, *S63M*

Osaka Shijyunichi:[3] 48 days. Long, cylindrical root, slightly tapered at the tip; 10 to 11 inches long, 1 3/4 inches in diameter; attractive, snow-white skin and flesh. Very early maturing. Grows vigorously in hot weather. Leaves light-green, soft, hairless, palatable; superior to those of other cultivars as a leafy green vegetable. E83T, J73, *P39*

Tokinashi: (All Seasons) 85 days. Pure-white, square-shouldered root, tapering uniformly to a sharp tip; 12 to 15 inches long, 2 to 2 1/4 inches in diameter at the top; flesh fine-grained, crisp, very pungent. Slow bolting; tolerant of cold and severe heat; can be sown in any month where the temperature remains above freezing. A2, B75, C44, C92, D11M, G33, G51, G93M, H94, I39, J20, J34, J73, K49T, L59, etc.

Winter Harvesting

Awa Pickling: 80 days. Long, tapered root; about 18 inches long, one-third of which grows above ground; fine-grained white flesh. Especially good for making *takuan* pickles. Sown from late August to early December in Japan. Developed and improved from a descendent of a cross between Miyashige and White Shouldered Miyashige. J73, *P39*

Mikado: Long, pure clear-white root; 13 to 36 inches in length, 2 to 3 inches in diameter; flesh delicate and sweet. A good winter keeper when planted in late summer. E38, I67M

Miyashige: (Green Neck Miyashige) 78 days. Long, cylindrical, stump-rooted radish; 16 to 17 inches long, 2 to 2 1/2 inches in diameter; skin white, green towards the shoulder; flesh white, solid, crisp, pungent. Excellent for pickling and winter storage. Sown from late August to early September in Japan. F44, G6, G33, I39, I99, J73, K22, K49T, *S63M*, *S70*

Miyashige Long White Neck: Pure-white, pointed root; 14 to 16 inches long, 2 1/2 to 3 inches in diameter. Flesh of very fine texture, mild pungency, and excellent quality. Usually sown at the end of summer (August or September) for harvesting from fall to winter (October to December). G93M, *S63M*

Nerima Longest: (Nerima, Nerima Long White) 90 days. Long, cylindrical root, narrow at the shoulder and tapered toward the tip; 28 to 30 inches long, 3 inches in diameter at the widest point in favorable soil conditions. The flesh is less juicy and easy to dry after harvest, yet is firm and tender. Requires deep soil. C85M, D11M, G33, *H61*, J73, N52, *S63M*

Ohkura: (Winter Queen) 78 days. Pure-white root; square at the shoulder, blunt-ended; 14 to 15 inches long, 3 1/2 inches in diameter; pure-white skin and flesh; mild flavor. Has excellent keeping qualities. Tolerant of virus diseases. Sown between August 20th and September 15th in Japan. E83T, G93M, *H61*, J73, *S63M*

Riso: 85 days. Root cylindrical, slightly tapered toward the bluntly pointed tip; 23 to 25 inches long, nearly 2 1/2 inches in diameter toward the neck. Good for cooking as well as for pickling. Sown from late August to early September in Japan. Derived from Nerima Longest and Nerima Akitsumari. G33, *P39*

Sakurajima: (Sakurajima Mammoth, Mammoth White Globe) 150 days. Very large, flattened globe-shaped root; 13 to 13 1/2 inches in diameter; average weight 40 pounds when mature, occasionally reaching 65 pounds at Sakurajima, Japan. The gigantic root development is attained only in areas where a fertile, light soil underlaid with pumice or lapilli is available, and the growing season is longer than 150 days. Rather sweet flesh; good for boiling or pickling. B73M, C92, D11M, D76, E49, *G13M*, I39, I97T, *S63M*, T1M

Shogoin Large Round: (Shogoin Giant) 85 days. Large, globular root; vertical diameter 5 1/2 to 6 inches, horizontal diameter 5 to 5 1/2 inches, about 1/4 growing above ground. Flesh pure-white, firm, crisp, juicy, mildly pungent, excellent for boiling. Sown in mid August and harvested in early November in Japan. E59Z, G33, G93M, I39, J73, *S63M*

Others

Bisai:[3] Widely used in Japan as a cut-and-come-again seedling crop. Cut with knife or scissors when 2 to 3 inches high. Seed should be broadcast in a small patch from spring to autumn. Also produces delicious radish sprouts. S55

LO BOK Also called *Chinese radishes*, these are more variable than daikon both in the color of their skin, and in their size and shape. The leaves are generally hairless and are more palatable. (R. sativus Longipinnatus Group)

Multi-Colored

Aomaru-Koshin: (Tsung Lo Bok, Beijing Red Core, Green Skin & Red Flesh) 55 days. Short, round root; 4 to 5 inches long, 4 inches in diameter; weight 1 pound; skin green above ground, white below; reddish-purple at the core, with rays spreading through the white flesh. Good raw, in salads, or pickled overnight in sweet vinegar. A good keeper, its sweetness increasing during storage. Popular in the Beijing area of China. E83T, F80, L59, Q34

Green Meat: 50-60 days. An unusual radish from mainland China. Oblong in shape, 3 to 4 inches in length when mature; smooth white skin, green near the shoulder; flesh deep lime-green, pungent. Good sliced or grated with the Red Meat radish. D11M, E59, G64, *S63M*

Misato Rose-Fleshed: 65 days. Large, round-oblong root, about 4 inches in diameter; skin white, green over the upper one-third; flesh rose-red with lighter concentric rings; stores well. Should not be used for spring sowing. A colorful addition to salads; also good cooked. Imported from China. D87, *G13M*, H95, I39, M46

Red Meat: 50 to 60 days. An unusual radish from mainland China. Large, turnip-shaped root; 1 to 1 1/4 inches in diameter when mature; smooth, creamy white skin, lightly tinged with purple; flesh red, pungent. Attractive as well as useful. D11M, D62, D76, G64, N52, *S63M*

Shangtung Green Skin: (Green Long) 50 days. Long, slender root, about 10 inches long, 2 inches in diameter; green above ground, white below; weight about 1 pound; flesh green, crisp, juicy and sweet. Can be harvested in fall and stored until the following spring; the longer it is preserved the sweeter it becomes. Good raw, in salads, or pickled. E83T, L59, *L79G*

Tae-Baek: (F_1) 70 days. Short, blunt white roots tinged with green on the upper third; weight about 2 pounds; very firm and uniform.

Highly tolerant to virus, bacterial soft rot and downy mildew. Suitable for kimchi. Best suited to late summer planting. Can be stored for 4 to 5 months in winter. *A1*, M29, *Q3*

Valentine: 25 days. A novelty radish that is used for salads. Round in shape, with green and white skin, and red interiors at maturity. K49M, L42

Wei Xian Qing: 90 days. Long, cylindrical root; 10 to 12 inches in length; skin dark green above ground, creamy white below; flesh green, crisp, juicy; stores well. May be eaten raw; called *fruit turnip* in China. Sown in mid-August in Shandong Province, China. *O54*

Xin Li Mei: (F_1) 90 days. Cylindrical, turnip-shaped root; skin green, white near the lower end; flesh red. May be eaten raw as a fruit or used in salads. Sown in early August in Beijing, China. *O54*

Pink/Red-Skinned

China Rose: (Chinese Red Winter) Root elongated, thicker at the lower extremity than at the neck, blunt at both ends, very closely resembling the Jersey turnip in shape; 4 to 5 inches long, 2 inches in diameter; skin bright rose-colored; flesh white, very firm, pungent. Leaves broad; leaf-stalks bright pink. Also used for sprouting. Introduced prior to 1865. BURR, VILMORIN; A16, *C14*{SP}, E38, G16, G64, G67M, G71, *H61*, H66, J34, K71, K73, L7M, L59, M13M, M46, M95, N39, etc.

Chinese Short Red: Slightly tapered, cylindrical root; 8 inches long, 2 inches in diameter; bright red skin; juicy, pure-white flesh. Excellent for eating raw, mixed in salads. *S70*

Pink Ball: 70 days. Developed by careful selection from imported cultivars from China. Round roots with bright pink skin and pure white flesh; weight 10 to 12 ounces. High starch content and late pithiness makes it suitable for storage. Tolerant to summer heat, sudden low temperature, and virus disease. Dark green foliage with reddish petioles; somewhat spreading growth habit. *Q3*

Red Coat: (F_1) 45 days. Straight root, tapered towards the top; 7 1/2 to 8 inches long, 2 inches in diameter; purple-red skin; red flesh. Suitable for salads. Vigorous, erect plant; tolerant to mosaic virus; good for close planting. Not recommended for growing under cool weather conditions. *Q39*

Shunkyoh Semi-Long: 35 days. Medium-long, slightly tapered root; about 5 inches in length; attractive red skin; very crisp, pungent white flesh. Can be sown in early spring or fall. Imported form mainland China. D87, M46

White-Skinned

Chinese Improved Earliest:[3] 38 days. Uniform, cylindrical root; about 5 inches long, 1 3/4 inches wide in cross section; skin and flesh white; flesh very tender and juicy, mildly pungent. Leaves dark-green, 12 to 13 inches long, unlobed, hairless, tender, well-suited for cooking with the root. Popular in Fukien, China and Taiwan where similar cultivars are called Kana. E83T, J73, *P39*

Chinese White Celestial: (Chinese White Winter, California Mammoth White) 60 days. Long, cylindrical root, thickest at the lower extremity; 6 to 8 inches in length, about 2 1/4 inches in diameter; between 1 and 2 inches grows above ground; skin and flesh pure-white; flesh mild, lacking in pungency. Good for pickling and winter storage. Introduced prior to 1885. VILMORIN; A69M, B75, C92, D65, *F72*, G71, H49, H66, J97M, K22, K49M, K71, L42, M13M, N39, etc.

Ta Mei Hwa: 55 days. Large, oblong, blunt-ended root; 8 inches long, 3 to 4 inches in diameter; can weigh 3 to 4 pounds when mature; white skin and flesh. Very tasty and mild-flavored; excellent when shredded or grated and added to soups. Quite popular in Chinatown markets. D55, E83T, *L79G*

White Rat: (F_1) 45 days. Small, blunt, attractively shaped white roots weigh about 1 3/4 ounces each; highly uniform; very firm and resistant to pithiness; good pungent flavor. Fine, edible tops. Suitable for *chonggak kimchi*. Best for fall planting at close spacing Retains its shape very well even when grown in high elevation areas. *A1*, M29, *Q3*

LEAF RADISHES

These have been bred specifically for use as a leafy vegetable, before the roots have developed. They are characterized by rapid growth of extra long leaves that are completely free of hairs.

HYBRID

4 Season: 25-30 days. Long, smooth, entire leaves, free of hairs; 12 to 14 inches in length at harvest stage. Vigorous and fast growing; harvestable in 30 to 35 days in spring, 25 to 30 days in summer and autumn. Moderately slow bolting. Tolerant of cold and heat; resistant to virus. Suitable for growing in all seasons. *Q3*

Pearl: 30-35 days. Long, smooth, divided leaves, free of hairs; 12 to 14 inches in length at harvest stage. Harvestable in 35 to 40 days in spring, 30 to 35 days in summer and autumn. Extra slow bolting. Tolerant of heat and cold; resistant to virus. Can be grown during any season. *Q3*

RASPBERRY {GR}

RUBUS SPP.

BLACK RASPBERRIES (R. occidentalis)

Allen: Large, attractive fruit; flesh firm, very sweet. Ripens slightly earlier than Bristol and a large portion of the crop may be picked at one time. Excellent for jam. Good all around cultivar but not outstanding in any one characteristic. Bush vigorous and productive; somewhat resistant to mildew. Originated in Geneva, New York by George L. Slate. BROOKS 1972; A14, B53, *C47*, G16, *G43*, H65, J58, K71

Black Hawk: Fruit large, up to 3/4 inch in diameter, nearly round; skin glossy black; flesh firm, with little or no tendency to crumble, sweet to mildly acid; quality excellent fresh, frozen and processed; ripens in late midseason. Bush vigorous; hardy; yields extremely well; does not sucker; somewhat resistant to anthracnose. BROOKS 1972; A56, A82, B58, *C47*, C63, D76, E3, F16, H33, *H90*, *I43*, *J2M*, J69, J83, L21, L33, L70, etc.

Bristol: Large, conical fruit; skin fairly glossy, attractive; flesh firm, sweet, highly flavored, nearly seedless, quality excellent; ripens in midseason over a period of a couple of weeks. Tall, vigorous bush; hardy; highly productive; generally disease resistant but very susceptible to anthracnose. Very widely planted. BROOKS 1972; A14, A24, B4, B19, B53, B58, *C47*, C63, E32M, F16, H16, H65, I50, J58, J69, L33, etc.

Cumberland: Large, conical fruit; skin glossy black; drupelets large, round, with strong coherence so that the berries do not crumble; flesh firm, juicy, sweet and rich; quality very good; ripens in early midseason. Tall, upright-spreading bush; vigorous; highly productive; susceptible to anthracnose. Introduced in 1896 and still one of the leading cultivars. HEDRICK 1925; A82, B43M, B73M, C63, E3, F11, F19M, *G28*, *J2M*, J83, L30, M39M, *M65M*, M76, *M81M*, etc.

Dundee: Large fruit; skin glossy black, attractive; drupelets small; flesh moderately firm, mildly subacid, of very good flavor and quality; ripens in midseason, somewhat later than Bristol. Tall, vigorous bush; hardy; productive; moderately resistant to mosaic, susceptible to powdery mildew. Introduced in 1927. BROOKS 1972; A14, *C47*, G16, G23, I50

Haut: Medium-sized fruit; flesh firm and cohesive, very sweet, quality excellent; ripens over a longer period than other black raspberry cultivars. Vigorous, high-yielding plant; more productive than Bristol; disease resistant. A24, C21, I36, I50

Huron: Large attractive fruit; skin glossy black; quality good; has all around merit rather than any distinguishing characteristics; ripens early to midseason. Bush vigorous, productive, hardy; not seriously susceptible to anthracnose. Originated in Geneva, New York by George L. Slate. BROOKS 1972; *C47*

Jewel: Large fruit; skin glossy black, attractive, slightly woolly; flesh firm, flavorful, of high quality; ripens in early midseason. Bush vigorous and productive; winter hardy; not susceptible to any serious disease, and only slightly susceptible to mildew. Considered an improvement over Bristol. A14, B10, B19, B43M, B58, *C47*, C63, G23, H65, I36, *I43*, I50, J69

John Robertson: Large, plump fruit; flesh medium firm, juicy, quality very good. Bush productive; one of the hardiest black raspberry cultivars, reliable as far north as Canada. Originated in Hot Springs, South Dakota by John Robertson. Introduced about 1935. B19, D76, E97, *I43*

Lowden: Extremely large fruit; skin dull purplish-black when fully ripe; flesh juicy, sweet, of excellent flavor; canning quality especially good; ripens fairly late. Bush upright, quite vigorous; productive; very winter hardy; resistant to anthracnose. Hybrid of Bristol black and Sodus purple. BROOKS 1972; A14, *C47*, F16, G79M, H16, I50, N24M

Mac Black: Medium to large fruit; ripens late. Bush hardy; often bears into August, and will occasionally produce fruit on the tips of new canes in September and October. Ideal for extending the harvest season. H16

Morrison: Large fruit, one of the largest of the black raspberries; skin glossy, attractive; flesh firm, quality fair; ripens late; resembles Cumberland. Bush productive. Popular in New York, Ohio and Pennsylvania. Originated in North Kingsville, Ohio. BROOKS 1972; H33

Munger: Fruit variable in size, averaging medium, roundish to roundish conic; drupelets numerous; skin black with a light bloom; flesh firm, strongly coherent, juicy, mild, sweet, of good quality; ripens in late midseason. Vigorous, upright bush; hardy; only moderately productive; susceptible to mildew. Introduced in 1897. HEDRICK 1925; A91, B67, C15M, *G43*, H16, L97, L99M, *M81M*

New Logan: (Logan) Fruit medium to large, glossy; flesh firm, sweet, of very good quality; ripens early, about a week before Cumberland and over a short period of time, making for easier picking. Holds its firmness all season. Bush very productive; hardy; highly resistant to mosaic, susceptible to anthracnose. A14, C63, D65, *G43*, H16, H42, H49, *J63M*, *M65M*, M92

Plum Farmer: (Farmer) Large fruit; skin black with a slight bloom; flesh firm, of high quality; ripens very quickly, the entire crop can be harvested in 2 to 3 pickings. Bush hardier than most blackcaps; drought resistant; susceptible to anthracnose, but immune to curl virus. Originated in Ohio. **U7M**

Wyoming: Purplish-black fruit of mild flavor. Makes excellent black jelly or black raspberry pies. Bush quite hardy, heavy yielding. Canes grow very tall and strong and do not sucker. Popular in the Canadian prairie provinces. B47

PURPLE RASPBERRIES (R. x neglectus)

Amethyst: Large, glossy fruit of good quality; always visible on the stem. Bush very hardy, productive, and resistant to disease. Good midseason cultivar for the Midwest. Developed in Iowa and tested over a twelve-year period. HENDRICKSON; **U7M**

Brandywine: Large, round conic fruit; skin reddish-purple; flesh firm, coherent, tart but of good quality; ripens late. Excellent for jams and jellies. Bush large, erect, to 10 feet; very vigorous; hardy; outproduces red cultivars by 25%. Recommended for the home gardener and the commercial grower. A82, B58, *C47*, C63, D11M, E97, F16, H16, H33, H49, *I43*, I50, J61M, *M65M*, *M81M*, etc.

Lowden Sweet Purple: Medium-sized fruit; skin reddish-purple. Has so few hard seeds that it could almost be called seedless. Unlike most purple raspberries, the fruit is sweet and full-flavored. H16

Marion: Fruit large; skin purple; flesh moderately juicy, firm, tart, of good quality; ripens late, one week after Sodus. Bush vigorous, productive; resembles a red raspberry in habit. Popular in the Northeast. Originated in Geneva, New York by Richard Wellington. BROOKS 1972; **U7M**

Rex: Large, meaty fruit, of good dessert quality. Also makes good preserves. Bush upright, very vigorous; highly productive and reliable; disease resistant; hardy to -25° F. or below. Excellent all around cultivar, more stable than Royalty and Brandywine. Adapted to north temperate regions. Originated in Graettinger, Iowa by Joseph Gabrielson. Mutation of Potomac. E23G

Royalty: Large to very large fruit; flesh moderately firm, sweet, dessert quality very good; ripens late. Has a strong raspberry aroma that is preserved in processing. Vigorous bush, not as erect as Brandywine; winter-hardy; productive; resistant to raspberry aphid, the vector of mosaic virus. Excellent for home gardens or pick-your-own operations. A24, B19, B58, C63, *C84*, D37, G16, G23, H16, H65, I50, J69, L30, L33, M77, etc.

Sodus: Fruit large to very large; flesh fairly firm, coherent, sprightly, quality good though quite tart; ripens in midseason, shortly after Latham. Bush very vigorous and productive; winter-hardy; resistant to drought; free from mosaic, but susceptible to verticillium wilt. Introduced in 1935. BROOKS 1972; B19, D65, L70

Success: Medium to large fruit; flesh firm, sweet, highly flavored; quality good fresh, excellent for processing; ripens in midseason. Bush erect, grows to 8 feet tall; heavy yielding; winter hardy where temperatures do not go below -20 to -25° F.; resistant to spur blight. Originated in Durham, New Hampshire. BROOKS 1972; A14, *I43*

RED RASPBERRIES

<u>EVERBEARING</u> Also called fall-bearing or primocane-bearing raspberries, since they bear on the current season's growth or "primocane". They can begin fruiting after less than a year in the garden, usually requiring no trellising or trimming. Since all canes are removed annually, diseases and pests that overwinter in them are virtually eliminated, and their is never a worry about winter injury.

Amity: Medium-large fruit; very firm flesh of excellent flavor; quality high; ripens 5 days earlier than Heritage; tends to adhere to receptacle. Good for fresh marketing, shipping and freezing. Vigorous, productive plant; canes nearly smooth, 4 1/2 to 5 feet tall. Resistant to root rot, somewhat resistant to mildew. B67, *C54* *D35M*, E4, H88, *I43*, *M81M*

August Red: Medium to large fruit; skin crimson red; flavor excellent, sugar content high. Compact, erect bush, growing only to about 3 feet; highly productive; bears earlier than other everbearers; produces an early summer crop on old canes and again in mid-September until freezing weather. Good all purpose cultivar. Reliable in northern areas. Developed by Professor E.M. Meader at the University of New Hampshire. *C47*, C63, D76

Autumn Bliss: Large, oval-conical fruit; skin very dark red; flesh firm, with a pleasant mild flavor; ripens very early, 14 days earlier than Heritage; fairly easy to pick. Bush a superior yielder to Heritage; resistant to some aphid-transmitted viruses. Canes fairly erect; may be grown without support. Bridges the gap between the late summer cultivars and the fall-bearing cultivars. Originated in East Malling, England. C15M, *I43*, I49M, K17, *M81M*

Baba:[1] (Bababerry) Very large fruit, up to 1 inch long; flesh very firm; flavor sweet, rich, tangy, reminiscent of wild raspberries; quality good; ripens in June and again in September and October. Bush extremely vigorous, up to 10 feet in height; spiny. Low chilling requirement; does well in hot, dry areas of southern California; also hardy to 0^{0} F. Discovered in the wild near Idyllwild, California by Mrs. Gertrude Millikan. Introduced in 1979. A88M, *C54*, D37, D76, E4, E97, F16, G17, H4, H16, *I43*, I83M

Durham: Medium-sized fruit; flesh firm, of good flavor; excellent for fresh use and processing; fall crop ripens 2 weeks before the fall crop of Indian Summer. Bush extremely hardy; very vigorous and productive; bears a heavy crop in early summer and again in a few weeks on the new canes. Originated in Durham, New Hampshire by A.F. Yeager. BROOKS 1972; B73M, C63, H33, H88, I78

Fallred: Fruit large, larger than most everbearers; skin red, attractive; flavor very good, quality high; ripens early. Upright, vigorous bush; produces fruit continuously on highly productive primocanes until curtailed by frost; suckers freely; cold-hardy to -25^{0} F. Developed by Professor E.M. Meader at the University of New Hampshire. BROOKS 1972; B19, *C47*, C63, D65, E97, G16, G79M, H33, H65, H88, *H90*, J83, K71

Heritage: Medium-sized, conical fruit; skin brilliant red, attractive; flesh very firm, quality excellent; first crop ripens in mid-July, second crop about September 1 at Geneva, New York. Bush tall, grows 5 to 7 feet; very vigorous; hardy; suckers prolifically; sturdy, requiring no support. Excellent for home gardens. BROOKS 1972; B10, C21, C63, *C84*, E4, F16, *G4*, G16, G23, H16, *I43*, J69, J83, L30, M39M, etc.

Indian Summer: Fruit large, conic; skin bright red, glossy; flesh very aromatic, sweet; crumbles frequently. Quality good as an autumn fruiting cultivar; also useful for jam. Bush very productive; vigorous; hardy; escapes mosaic infection; produces a first crop in July and a second from September to the first hard frost. One of the oldest everbearers still in cultivation. BROOKS 1972; A88M, B19, *C54*, C63, E4, E97, G71

Israel: Medium-sized conical fruit; skin deep red; flesh subacid, highly flavored; quality very good. Bush vigorous; disease resistant; produces a heavy spring crop on old canes and again in the fall on the new canes, until frost. D37

Nordic: Medium-sized fruit, firmer than Boyne, with tougher skin; ripens 14 days after Heritage. Bush very productive; extremely hardy; appears to have more resistance to fungal diseases and aphids than Boyne. Bears a fall crop too late for some northern areas. Good summer producer if primocane production is poor. Boyne x Fallred. Originated at the University of Minnesota. A14, *A74*, C21, *I43*, L70

Oregon 1030:[1] Unique, continual-bearing raspberry, producing fruit from May through late November. Medium-sized fruit of very good quality. Bears fruit on new wood of current season's canes. Formal trellising system not required but some support is helpful. No chilling or heat units required for high quality fruit. I83M

Redwing: Fruit slightly larger and somewhat softer than Heritage; dessert quality superior to Fallred; ripens 10 to 14 days earlier than Heritage. Outyields Fallred and Heritage. More heat resistant than Heritage, having performed well as far south as Georgia. Heritage x Fallred. Released by the University of Minnesota. A14, *A74*, B4, C15M, C21, *C47*, G67, I36, *I43*, I50, K17, L70

Ruby: Very large, conical fruit, up to 50% larger than Heritage; skin bright red; flesh firm, flavor slightly milder than Heritage; does not darken like Heritage; holds very well after picking. Not recommended for pick-your-own. Moderately vigorous plant; productive; highly susceptible to phytophthora root rot. Heritage x Titan. A14, I36, *I43*, I50

Scepter: Fruit large; skin medium red; flesh moderately soft, of good flavor; resembles September; ripens 10 days earlier than September. Bush very vigorous; winter-hardy; highly tolerant to fluctuating winter temperature injury. BROOKS 1972; C63, H16, *I43*

September: Medium to large fruit; skin bright red, attractive; flesh firm, coherent, juicy, sweet, of high dessert quality. Summer crop as early as that of Indian Summer, or about 5 days earlier than Newburgh; fall crop matures 2 to 4 weeks before that of Indian Summer. Bush vigorous; a reliable and heavy bearer; hardy. BROOKS 1972; A88M, B19, *C47*, *C54*, C63, E4, E97, G79M, H88, *I43*, *J2M*, *J63M*, M31M, M92

Southland: Medium-sized fruit, symmetrical and cone-shaped; skin light red, does not darken upon maturity; flesh firm, does not crumble; flavor slightly acid with good dessert quality; ripens early, 2 to 3 days after Sunrise, also produces a substantial crop in early or mid-August. Bush moderately vigorous; highly disease resistant. BROOKS 1972; A14, *C47*, D76, F93, H16, L33, M31M

Summit: Medium-sized, conical fruit; skin dark red, slightly darker than Heritage; flesh firm, of excellent flavor; ripens 10 days earlier than Heritage, ships well. Bush considerably less spiny than Heritage; does quite well in heavier soils; resists root rot. Introduced in 1988. C15M, *I43*, J61M, *L18*, *M81M*

<u>SUMMER-BEARING</u> These bear fruit on "floricanes", or primocanes that have overwintered. They are susceptible to insects and diseases that overwinter in them, and also to winter cold damage. Most are limited to northern areas because the floricanes require a period of winter chilling to break dormancy.

Anelma: (R. arcticus x R. idaeus) Large, spherical fruit, about 3/4 inch long; skin highly colored; flesh very firm, very sweet, of good quality; ripens about a week after Boyne, fruits continuously throughout the summer. Bush spreading; very large and vigorous; very hardy. Canes nearly smooth. Originated in Piikkio, Finland. BROOKS 1972; G64, *I43*

Boyne: Medium-sized fruit; skin dark red, tending to become somewhat purplish-red when over-ripe, medium glossy; drupelets medium to small, cohering firmly; flesh tender, juicy, flavor aromatic, sprightly, moderately acid, superior to Latham in flavor but not as sweet as Chief. Especially adapted to home gardens and local markets. Bush moderately vigorous; very productive. BROOKS 1972; A16, B47, C63, D11M, D65, D69, F67, G16, G54, H42, *I43*, I50, K17, K64, K81, L79, etc.

Canby:[2] (Wonder Thornless) Fruit large, almost equalling Willamette; skin light bright red; flesh fairly firm, sweet, flavor mild; ripens in midseason, with Willamette. Bush very hardy; canes tall, straight, virtually thornless; highly productive; very hardy; immune to aphid, resistant to virus; susceptible to heavy soils. BROOKS 1972;

A14, B19, B73M, *C47*, C63, D65, E3, E97, H16, H49, H88, *I43*, L97, L99M, *M81M*, etc.

Chief: Small to medium fruit; skin cherry red; drupelets medium-sized; flesh very firm, juicy, very sweet, flavor and quality good; ripens early. Excellent for freezing. Bush very winter-hardy, vigorous. Originated in Excelsior, Minnesota. Introduced in 1930. BROOKS 1972; A16, B47, K81

Chilliwack: Fruit large to very large; skin bright red, glossy; flesh firm, very sweet, of excellent flavor; quality exceptionally high; ripens over a short season in July; keeps well. Bush very productive; resistant to root rot, thriving on wetter sites where most others fail. Originated in Vancouver, British Columbia, Canada. C15M, *I43*, I49M, J61M, K17, *L18*, *M81M*

Comet: Medium to large, cone-shaped fruit; flesh moderately firm, very sweet, quality good; matures in midseason, 2 to 3 days before Latham. Good for recipes calling for reduced sugar. Bush hardy; productive; tall, stout; canes medium thorny. BROOKS 1972; D11M, G41

Cuthbert: (R. strigosus) Medium to large, conical fruit; skin dull dark red, with a heavy bloom; flesh juicy, moderately firm, aromatic, sweet and rich, of very good quality; ripens late, season long. Bush tall, vigorous, upright-spreading; not very productive; widely adapted to soils and climate; very susceptible to leaf curl and mosaic. Originated in New York City by Thomas Cuthbert, about 1865. Once the most widely grown red raspberry in North America. HEDRICK 1925; **U7M**

Dormanred:[1] (R. parvifolius x) Large, round fruit; skin light red, glossy; flesh very firm, flavor slightly reminiscent of mulberries; ripens very late. Has the habit of blackberries, and must be trellised; produces vines that grow 15 to 20 feet per season. Low chilling requirement; does well in Florida and other southern states; also survives the winter in St. Paul, Minnesota with snow cover. B19, B43M, E29M, F19M, F93, G8, *G28*, H16, *I43*, *J2M*, *K76*, L33, L60, M31M, N33, etc.

English Thornless:[2] A thornless cultivar that also has sweet fruit. Excellent dessert quality with a good balance of flavors. Bush tall, erect, vigorous; resistant to disease; canes completely smooth and thornless. One of the few sweet cultivars with disease resistance. D37

Festival: Medium-sized fruit; skin medium red; flesh very firm, cohesive, flavor fair, of excellent quality; ripens in midseason, about 10 to 14 days after Boyne. Good for fresh market use as well as for processing. Bush vigorous; tolerant to spur blight. Canes short, nearly spineless. C58, F67, G64, *I43*, I50, J7

Fraser: Fruit large; flesh firm, juicy, sweet, flavor mild, quality very good. Bush extremely hardy; productive; somewhat drought resistant; canes short, stout. Originated in Saskatoon, Saskatchewan by C.F. Patterson. Introduced in 1960 for home gardens. BROOKS 1972; F67

Gatineau: Large, cone-shaped fruit; skin dark red; flesh moderately firm, quality fair; ripens very early. Bush very productive; hardy; very susceptible to anthracnose; canes moderately spiny, medium short. Originated in Ottawa, Ontario, Canada. BROOKS 1972; G64, G69M, H88

Haida: Fruit larger than Boyne; skin medium bright red; flesh very firm, sweet; suitable for fresh market and processing; ripens in late-midseason, about 7 to 10 days after Boyne. Bush very productive; slightly less hardy than Boyne; suckers well; canes moderately spiny. A14, H16, *I43*

Hilton: Large to very large, long-conic fruit; skin medium red, darkens quickly, very attractive; flesh moderately firm, thick, quality fair to good; cavity small; clings to plant until fully ripe; ripens in midseason. Bush compact, vigorous; very productive; hardy. BROOKS 1972; *C47*, C63, D76, H88, *J63M*, *M65M*

Killarney: Fruit somewhat larger than Latham; skin bright medium red, very attractive; flesh firm, sweet, flavor sprightly pleasant, excellent for dessert; good frozen or canned; ripens about a week after Boyne, and has a more prolonged harvesting season. Bush very hardy and productive. BROOKS 1972; B47, B75, *D35M*, G64, H88, *I43*, J7, N26

Latham: Fruit large, frequently 1 inch in diameter, roundish; skin bright red, attractive; flesh firm, but often crumbly, moderately juicy, sprightly; season medium to late, ripening over a long period; quality superior for canning and freezing. Bush vigorous and productive; very hardy. Standard cultivar in the East. Introduced in 1920. BROOKS 1972; B58, B73M, C21, C63, F16, F19M, G16, G23, G41, G71, H16, I50, J69, J83, *M65M*, etc.

Madawaska: Medium-large fruit; skin medium dark-red; flesh moderately firm, with some tendency to crumble, quality fair; ripens early. Tends to be acid and dark when canned or frozen. Bush hardy; very winter-hardy; productive; canes moderately spiny. Originated in Ottawa, Ontario, Canada. BROOKS 1972; B73M, E3, G64, H88

Malling Orion: Medium to large fruit, broad conical or roundish, with comparatively few drupelets; skin medium dark-red, slightly dull; flesh fairly firm; ripens in midseason. Good for canning and freezing. Canes vigorous, numerous, semi-erect; resistant to mildew, susceptible to spur blight and botrytis. SIMMONS 1978; C21

Mammoth Red:[2] (Mammoth Red Thornless) Very large fruit, up to 1 inch long, conical; flesh soft, juicy, aromatic, sweet, highly flavorful. Bush very vigorous, up to 8 feet tall; winter-hardy; highly productive; canes thornless. B75, C63, E97, J32, *K89*

Matsqui: Medium-sized fruit; skin bright medium red, attractive, does not darken on picking; flesh firm, flavor mild; excellent for freezing; ripens with Willamette. Bush productive; hardy; tolerant to botrytis rot, free of mosaic. BROOKS 1972; H88, N26

Meeker: Very large fruit; skin bright red; flesh firm, flavor good; very good for freezing and jam. Bush very tall; vigorous; very productive; somewhat resistant to botrytis fruit rot; requires well-drained soil and mild winters. Excellent for home garden and local market use; also ships well. BROOKS 1972; B67, C15M, C21, C34, H88, *I43*, I49M, J61M, K17, *L18*, L97, L99M, *M81M*

Newburgh: Large, attractive fruit; skin bright red; flesh fairly firm; dessert quality fair to good; keeping and shipping quality very good; does not process well; ripens 3 to 4 days before Latham. Bush productive; very resistant to root rot; widely adapted, being grown in the Northeastern states and the Pacific Northwest. BROOKS 1972; B58, C21, *C47*, C63, D11M, E97, F11, G23, G41, G79M, H88, I50, *J2M*, J69, *M65M*, etc.

Nova: Medium to large-sized fruit; skin dark red; flesh firm, of very good flavor, will freeze well; ripens in midseason. Bush vigorous; winter-hardy; productive; exceptional in that it has shown complete immunity to late yellow rust. C58, F1

Prestige: Fruit medium-large; skin bright red; drupelets large, of poor cohesion; flavor tart, pleasant; quality good fresh, excellent for jams; ripens very early. Bush very vigorous and productive; noticeably free of common raspberry diseases and viruses. Developed by Professor E.M. Meader of New Hampshire. Introduced in 1980. *D35M*, *I43*

Reveille: Very large fruit; skin bright red; flesh of excellent quality; ripens early, with Sunrise. Bush upright, vigorous; productive; suckers freely; very winter-hardy; highly resistant to fluctuating winter temperature injury. Recommended for home gardens, roadside sales and pick-your-own operations. BROOKS 1972; A14, *D35M*, H33, *I43*, I50, M98

San Diego:[1] Dual-season raspberry, bearing spring and fall crops on 1 year-old canes and primocanes. Medium-sized fruit of very high quality. Vine needs traditional trellising and pruning. Requires less than 100 hours of chilling. Does very well along the coast or inland. I83M

Sentry: Medium to large fruit; skin medium red; flesh firm, flavor good, of high quality for fresh use and processing; ripens in early-midseason. Bush tall, vigorous; fairly hardy; more tolerant of fluctuating winter temperatures than Boyne. BROOKS 1972; A24, H16, *I43*

Skeena: Fruit medium to large, conical; skin bright red; flesh firm, of good quality; ripens in late June in most areas. Bush high-yielding; one of the hardiest cultivars; requires excellent drainage; resistant to mosaic virus. Sturdy, upright canes are moderately spiny. Originated in Vancouver, British Columbia, Canada. H88, *I43*, K17, L30, *M81M*

Sumner: Medium to large fruit; skin medium red; flesh firm, sweet, flavor intense; fresh, frozen and processing qualities very good; ripens late, 3 to 5 days after Canby and Willamette. Bush vigorous; productive; very hardy; adapted to moderately heavy soils; resists root rot and yellow rust. BROOKS 1972; B67, C63, L97

Sunrise: Fruit large; skin bright red; flesh firm, flavor and quality excellent, does not crumble; matures very early, nearly 2 weeks before Latham and over a long period of time. Bush very hardy; resistant to leaf spot and anthracnose. Originated in Glen Dale, Maryland by George M. Darrow. Introduced in 1939. BROOKS 1972; A82, M76

Taylor: Very large, long-conic fruit; skin bright red, attractive; flesh firm, flavor and quality very high, does not crumble; excellent for freezing; ripens midseason to late, with Latham. Bush vigorous and productive; more subject to mosaic than Newburgh. Well adapted to all northeastern states. Introduced in 1925. BROOKS 1972; *C47*, *D35M*, D69, H65, H88, I36, I50, M98, N24M

Titan: Large to very large, long-conic fruit; skin bright red; flesh moderately firm, dessert quality average to good; ripens early and over a prolonged season. Bush highly productive; winter-hardy to -15^0 F.; resistant to mosaic virus. Canes stout, nearly spineless, require trellising. Suckering is light to medium, resulting in a well-spaced row. A14, B58, *C47*, D76, F16, G23, H65, I36, *I43*, I50, L33

Willamette: Very large, nearly round fruit; skin dark red; flesh very firm, slightly acid, but lacks an intense raspberry flavor; flavor good for canning, fair for freezing; excellent for shipping; ripens in midseason, with Canby. Bush vigorous; very productive. Grown extensively in Oregon and Washington. BROOKS 1972; B67, B99, C15M, C21, *C54*, C63, F11, *I43*, K17, *L18*, L97, L99M, M39M, *M81M*

YELLOW RASPBERRIES

<u>EVERBEARING</u>

Fallgold: Similar to Fallred, except for the color. Large, round fruit; skin golden yellow; flesh juicy, moderately firm, extremely sweet; ripens in late summer, with harvesting continuing into autumn. Bush moderately vigorous; high yielding; very winter-hardy. Good specialty market item. Developed by Professor E.M. Meader. B43M, C21, C63, D37, D65, E32M, F11, F16, F19M, G16, G23, H33, H65, J7, J61M, *K89*, L30, etc.

<u>SUMMER-BEARING</u>

Amber: Large, long-conic fruit; skin amber; flesh tender, sweet, flavor good, quality very good; ripens in midseason. Bush very vigorous; hardy; productive once established. Originated in Geneva, New York by George L. Slate. Introduced in 1950; intended for home use, not considered of commercial value. BROOKS 1972, HENDRICKSON; A14, B73M, *C47*, H88

Black Gold: (R. occidentalis) Unique pure yellow blackcap. Very sweet flavor, sweeter than most blackcaps. Excellent for eating out-of-hand or for making jams and jellies. Ripens 2 weeks earlier than the common wild blackcap. Discovered growing wild in Virginia. Introduced by Edible Landscaping Nursery. D37

Golden Queen: Medium-sized fruit; skin light yellow, sometimes tinged with pink; flesh soft, sweet, delicately flavored, of very high quality. Excellent for home gardens and local markets. Bush hardy; very susceptible to mosaic; foliage tender, easily injured by strong winds. Originated in Berlin, New Jersey in 1882. Said to be a sport of Cuthbert. HEDRICK 1925; B19, C21, C63

Golden West: Fruit thimble-shaped; skin attractive yellow, becoming pink when over-ripe; drupelets medium small, coherent; flesh medium firm, of fine flavor; ripens late. Bush vigorous; very productive; hardy; immune to raspberry aphid, resistant to yellow rust and mildew. BROOKS 1972; C15M, C21{CF}, J61M

Honey Queen: Medium-sized fruit; skin amber; flesh very juicy, flavor mild, sweet, distinct, aromatic; seeds few; makes excellent jam. Bush vigorous; high yielding; very winter-hardy; produces well on natural rainfall amounts. Adapted to Canadian prairie states. Originated in Alberta, Canada by Robert Erskine. F67, K81, L79, M35M, N24M, N26

RHUBARB {PL}

RHEUM RHABARBARUM

Canada Red: (Canadian Red) Long, thick stalks; exterior dark-red from top to bottom; interior strawberry-red; does not lose its color in cooking. Juicy and sweet; needs less sugar. Very tender, never becomes tough or stringy; skin tender, needs no peeling. Highly productive; stalks can be pulled all summer. Developed in Winnipeg, Canada. A14, A16, A91, B53, C63, D65, E32M, F19M, G16, G41, G71, H16, L27M, L79, *M65M*, M76, etc.

Cawood Delight: A Stockbridge rhubarb. The yield is low but the stalks are of very high quality; shiny and a deep maroon-red. Not suitable for forcing. S81M

Cherry Red: Large, well-colored stalks; cherry-red on outside of stalk, greenish inside; very tart, juicy and tender; has a good blend of tartness and sweetness; holds its quality well. Heavy yielding. Suited for mild-winter areas. A88M, *C54*, H16, I91

Chipman's Canada Red: Large, thick stalks; rich cherry-red all the way through to the core; flesh tender, sweet and juicy; does not lose its color in cooking; good texture. Hardy, vigorous grower. Very heavy yielding. Seldom seeds so it must be propagated by root division. *A74*, *D35M*, D76, E97, H33, H88, *H90*, J83

Crimson Cherry: Bright crimson stalks, up to 2 feet long; red through to the core; keeps its color when cooked. Requires no peeling. Full, rich flavor with a good blend of sweetness and tartness. Reliable producer of heavy crops. E4, H42, L97

Crimson Winter: Medium-sized stalks, 12 to 18 inches in length, 3/4 to 1 inch in diameter; pale greenish-crimson, turning a light clear crimson when cooked; of very good quality. Starts to grow vigorously in October and continues to produce stalks until after the common types make their first appearance some 6 months later. In mild climates will produce stalks abundantly at any season. Originated in Santa Rosa, California by Luther Burbank. Introduced in 1900. HOWARD; R47{S}

Flare: Tall, tender, juicy stalks shade from a rich green to deep ruby-red. Good blend of tartness and sweetness. Rated high for overall flavor in taste tests. Needs less sugar. Reliable producer of heavy crops. Very hardy. E97

German Wine: Large, deep-red stalks; thick yet tender; rich in natural sugars; full of the sweetness of a late-harvested wine grape. Winter hardy; vigorous and productive; will produce crops each spring for years. C85M, E33, F1

Glaskin's Perpetual:[1] Greenish stalks of excellent flavor, never become bitter as they mature. Has the lowest oxalic acid content of any rhubarb. Can be pulled the first year from an early spring sowing. The only rhubarb that can be harvested late in the season as the oxalic acid content remains low. B49{S}, O53M{S}, P83M{S}, *R23*{S}, S55{S}

Holstein Blood Red: (Holstein Red) Vigorous in growth, with erect, thick red to green stalks of excellent quality. Easy to grow. Sow when soil is warm (May-June); ready for harvesting the following summer. C85M{S}, I77{S}

Honeyred: An excellent rhubarb which produces rich, red stalks that are free of the usual stringiness of other cultivars. It requires less sugar than other sorts when used for fruit or desserts. Vigorous, extremely productive plants. Developed by Honeywood Lilies & Nursery. F67, F89, G1T

Irish Giant: A green cultivar of culinary quality especially in early spring, but best grown as a curiosity or as an annual hedge. Stalks are the thickness of an adult's arm and can be 5 feet long. F67

MacDonald: (MacDonald's Canadian Red) Large, tender stalks; deep red inside and out; no peeling needed; lends a deep pink hue to sauces and pies. Extremely vigorous and upright-growing; resistant to wilt and root rot. Excellent production for commercial growers and home gardeners. Developed at MacDonald College, Quebec, Canada. B47, B75, C58, D69, *G43*, I50, J20, *J63M*, K81, L27M

Prince Albert: (Mitchell's Royal Albert, Early Albert) Long, thick, bright red stalks, more angular than channeled; of excellent flavor. The best rhubarb for forcing under brown tin baths and old bottomless buckets. Very early; hardy; prolific. Does well from seed, but discard any that run to flower. Introduced in 1872. VILMORIN; P59M{S}, P83M{S}

Stockbridge Arrow: The first of a new generation of rhubarb cultivars. Stiff, upright growth; long, bright-red stalks; thick, tender, and juicy; small, arrow-shaped leaves. A good forcer; commercially or under bottomless dust bins, for they are too big for buckets. S81M

Stockbridge Harbinger: (Harbinger) Long, high-quality, easily pulled stalks. Ideal for early forcing. S81M

Strawberry: (Strawberry Red) Stalks of good size on mature plants; both the interior and exterior rose-red in color. Flavor mild and pleasing. Never becomes tough or stringy. Do not remove the tender skin; it cooks up well with the stalk. J7, L97

Tilden: (Tilden's Canada Red) A strain that has been selected for many years by the Tilden family for its fine red color. Not as upright in growth habit or as tall as the MacDonald strain, but the stalks are thick and attractive. I50

Timperley Early: The earliest cultivar and the most rapid forcer. Can be forced to be ready for Christmas and pulled outdoors even in February in mild climates. Rather thin, bright-red stalks. O81, R83, S81M

Valentine: Attractive, thick, red stalks; 18 to 24 inches long, 1 to 1 1/2 inches in diameter; flesh deep-red, fine-grained, tender, juicy, very sweet; flavor pleasing; holds up well and does not lose its color during cooking; relatively little sugar required. Heavy yielding and precocious. Excellent for home gardeners. Thrives in areas where winters are cold enough to freeze the ground 3 to 4 inches deep. A56, B47, B75, E97, G16, G23, G41, H33, H65, J58, J69, *K89*, L27M, L33, *M65M*, etc.

Victoria: (Giant Victoria, Myatt's Victoria) Leaf-stalks very large, up to 3 inches at their broadest diameter, 2 1/2 to 3 feet long, up to 2 pounds per stalk; greenish, stained with red; skin rather thick; meat green, tender, not quite as sweet as other cultivars. Extremely heavy producer; excellent for commercial purposes. Reliably hardy. Introduced prior to 1852. BURR, VILMORIN; C63, D11M, D11M{S}, E38{S}, F19M, F82{S}, *G28*, G68{S}, G71{S}, J7, M13M{S}, M46{S}, M76, N39{S}, P83M{S}, etc.

ROOTSTOCKS {GR}

VARIOUS GENERA

APPLE ROOTSTOCKS

Alnarp 2: According to Polish information, the most hardy stock available. Produces trees that are standard sized. Vigorous and well anchored; susceptible to woolly aphid. Induces early bearing and productivity in the scion cultivar. Promising understock for use with interstem combinations. Originated in Alnarp, Sweden. Introduced in 1944. BROOKS 1972; F91T{SC}, M4

Antanovka: Produces vigorous, standard size trees. Very resistant to winter injury. Often planted out and grown for several years before topworking; this insures maximum cold hardiness of the tree's framework. Trees on Antanovka are free from suckering. Widely used where winter hardiness is required. Also bears a large, yellow, white-fleshed apple of average quality. Originated in Siberia. *A74*{PL}, A91, D69{PL}, E93{PL}, *G66*{PL}, *G66*{S}, *H45M*, *I82*{PL}, K63G{S}, L1{PL}, L27M, *N19*{PL}, *N71M*{S}, P49{S}, S36M{S}, etc.

Borowinka: Most compatible and vigorous growing of the cold hardy rootstocks. Cold hardiness about equal to Antanovka. Does noticeably better in heavy moisture conditions. Recommended for Zone 3. *G66*{PL}, *G66*{S}, *I82*{PL}, S36M{S}

Budagovski 9: Produces trees that are M.9 to EMLA 26 size and require support or staking. Induces early fruiting and is compatible with most cultivars. Resistant to collar rot, moderately resistant to powdery mildew and apple scab; very resistant to winter frost. Trees on Budagovski 9 have an open growth habit and bear in 2 to 3 years. Recommended as an interstem for colder apple growing regions. I36, *I75*, *I75*{SC}, J93, M4, N24M

Budagovski 118: Produces trees that are 75% the size of those on seedling rootstocks. Resistant to collar rot and apple scab. Extremely winter hardy; has reportedly survived temperatures of -16^0 C. with no root damage. Can be employed as an interstem base on rich soils or as an understock for spur-type cultivars on poor soils. *I75*, *I75*{IN}

Budagovski 490: Scion cultivars on Budagovski 490 are comparable in vigor to those on EMLA 106. Induces early, very heavy production. Moderately resistant to collar rot. Very winter hardy. Trees on

Budagovski 490 are well anchored and do not require staking. Developed by Dr. Budagovski in Michurinsk, U.S.S.R. *I75*

Budagovski 491: Produces trees that are EMLA 27 to M.9 size. Very precocious and induces heavy production. Scion cultivars on Budagovski 491 are well anchored but require support. Susceptible to collar rot. Very winter hardy. Can be used as an interstem as well as a dwarfing rootstock for home gardening. *I75*

EMLA 7: Produces sturdy trees that are approximately twice the size of those on M.9 or 55% the size of trees on seedling rootstocks. Trees on EMLA 7 have good anchorage and exceptional winter hardiness; are less precocious and have a lower crop efficiency than EMLA 9 or EMLA 26. Moderately resistant to collar rot. A91, *H45M*, H49, *I75*, *I82*, J61M, J93, *N19*

EMLA 9: Has a dwarfing influence on all scions worked on it. Induces cropping early in the life of the tree. Considerably more vigorous and productive than M.9. Trees on EMLA 9 show a wide degree of tolerance to soil conditions; require staking throughout their life; resist collar rot. Fruit is larger and ripens earlier in the season, especially during the early years of the tree's life. *I75*, *I75*{SC}, *I82*

EMLA 26: Scions on EMLA 26 produce a tree 40% the size of that on seedling rootstocks. Trees on EMLA 26 require permanent staking on exposed sites; should be planted with the union a few inches above ground level; produce few but very vigorous suckers; are susceptible to collar rot and fire blight. Not as hardy as EMLA 7. Useful for high density plantings. A91, *H45M*, *I75*, *I82*, J61M, *N19*

EMLA 27: Scion cultivars grown on EMLA 27 grow into small, compact, precocious trees, approximately half the size of trees on EMLA 9. Trees on EMLA 27 rarely sucker; yield heavy crops the second year after planting; show some resistance to apple mildew. Fruit is of good quality. Valuable for small gardens or pot culture. *I75*, *I75*{SC}, J61M, J93, M23M

EMLA 106: (East Malling 106) Produces trees that are 65% the size of those on seedling rootstocks. The most widely used rootstock in high latitude countries due to its heavy cropping potential, moderate vigor, freedom from suckering and resistance to woolly aphids. It is more sensitive to soil moisture than most rootstocks. Susceptible to mildew; not resistant to collar rot. *H45M*, *I75*, *I75*{IN}, *I82*, *N19*

EMLA 111: Produces trees that are similar to, but more vigorous than, EMLA 106; approximately 75% of that on seedling rootstocks. Has a well anchored root system and is resistant to woolly aphids and color rot. Susceptible to mildew. Recommended for dry sandy soils in low rainfall areas. An excellent rootstock for spur-type cultivars. *H45M*, *I75*, *I75*{IN}, *I82*, *N19*

M.7: (Malling 7) Produces trees 55 to 65% of those on apple seedling. Has been the backbone of the U.S. fruit industry during the first 50-year introductory period of rootstocks in the United States. Still the most commonly used stock, the most disease tolerant, and the most adaptable to a range of soil types and climates. Has a tendency to sucker from the roots. ROM; E93, *G66*, M4, N0

M.7a: An improved clone of M.7 which was originally reselected free of the economically important viruses. Produces trees approximately 50% the size of those on apple seedling. Tends to sucker from the roots. About 20% of trees on M.7a require staking in their early years. Trees on M.7a bear heavily. E93, *G66*, I49M, M23M, *N19*

M.9: (Malling IX, Jaune de Metz) The most commonly used dwarfing rootstock throughout the world, both for single-union trees and also for interstem trees. Produces trees 25 to 35% the size of those on apple seedling. Promotes earlier growth and fruit maturity, and precocious cropping. Tends to sucker from the roots; is susceptible to fire blight. Trees on M.9 require support. Widely used in high-density plantings. Originated in France in 1879. ROM; A12, E93, *G66*, H49, I36, *I75*, J93, L1, M4, M23M, N0, *N19*

M.9/MM.106: A two piece interstem stock. Unites the anchorage and soil adaptability of the MM.106 base stock with the dwarfing characteristics of the M.9 stempiece. Inherits the collar rot resistance of M.9. Trees on M.9/MM.106 are slightly larger than those on M.26, and do not require support. They should be planted with the top graft union intersecting the soil surface, the point where the collar rot organism normally attacks. E93

M.9/MM.111: An interstem combination, wherein the dwarfing stem piece M.9 is grafted onto MM.111, and grown 1 year in the nursery before the desired cultivar is propagated to it. Produces trees about 40% the size of those on apple seedling. Trees on M.9/MM.111 are well anchored and drought tolerant. Fruit quality is enhanced. The oldest interstem combination in use. A91, E93, I36, J61M, J93, M23M

M.26: (Malling 26) Produces trees 40 to 50% of those on apple seedling. More vigorous and better anchored than M.9 with most cultivars. Tolerant of extended wet soil conditions; susceptible to collar rot and fire blight. The most winter hardy of the Malling rootstocks now used commercially. Trees on M.26 do not require support when planted in a deep, well-drained soil. ROM; A12, E93, *G66*, H49, I36, I49M, *I82*, L99M, M4, M23M, N0

M.27: Has a very dwarfing effect, producing trees only 4 to 6 feet in height. Very precocious and induces heavy fruiting. Trees on M.27 are well suited for growing in a container or a small yard. Requires staking. Not widely used commercially as a single-grafted tree. More commonly used as interstem material for grafting on vigorous clones. I49M, N0

M.27/MM.111: A two piece dwarfing stock wherein the M.27 is grafted to the MM.11 and grown one year prior to propagating the scion cultivar to it. Produces a tree about 30% of standard, freestanding after establishment, and drought tolerant. Somewhat more vigorous than the stempiece clone on its own roots. J93, M23M

Mark: (MAC 9) Produces trees that are approximately the size of EMLA 26. Trees on Mark are early flowering with good fruit set, highly productive, and open in habit resulting in excellent fruit color. One of the first dwarfing rootstocks which is strongly anchored and free standing without support. Resistant to fire blight; tolerant to cold temperatures. Developed by Dr. Robert F. Carlson at Michigan State University. *H45M*, I36, I49M, *I75*, J61M, J93, L1, M23M, *N19*, N24M

MM.106: (Malling-Merton 106) Produces trees that are 60 to 75% the size of those on apple seedling. Very precocious and more vigorous than M.7. Has shown a tendency for collar rot on poorly aerated soil. Trees on MM.106 are well anchored, do not sucker, and are very productive. Excellent for spur-type cultivars and as an interstem base stock. ROM; E93, *G66*, H49, I36, I49M, *I82*, J93, L1, M4, M23M

MM.111: A semi-standard stock that produces trees 90% the size of those on apple seedling. Not precocious, but more productive than apple seedling. Adapted to a wide range of soil and climatic types and has survived well compared to others. Widely used as an interstem stock base. Trees on MM.111 are well anchored and tolerant of drought. E93, I36, J93, L1, M4, M23M, N0

Ottawa 3: Produces dwarf to semi-dwarf trees, between M.9 and M.26 in size; not free standing. Consistently hardier than M.26; better anchored than M.9. Free of burr-knot and suckering. Resistant to crown rot; susceptible to woolly aphids and fire blight. Well suited to high density planting. Has a tendency to make its scion cultivar overcrop, resulting in small fruit if not properly managed. Developed at the Agriculture Canada Research Station, Ottawa, Ontario. A12, *I75*{SC}, M4

P.1: (Poland 1) Produces trees that are approximately the size of EMLA 26. Requires a rich well-drained soil and doesn't do well in wet soils; resistant to crown gall and mildew. Susceptibility to fire blight and woolly apple aphids is comparable to that of M.9. Trees on P.1 require staking and are suitable for high density plantings. Winter hardiness is comparable with EMLA 111. *I75*, *I75*{SC}

P.2: (Poland 2) Produces trees that are M.9 to EMLA 26 size. Widely used in Poland as an interstem because of its exceptional winter-hardiness. Cropping efficiency is similar to M.9. Trees on P.2 display good open growth. Resistant to collar rot, susceptible to scab and mildew. Used for high density trellis plantings with vigorous cultivars. Precocious; crops in the third year. I36, *I75*, *I75*{SC}

P.14: (Poland 14) Produces trees that are approximately EMLA 26 in size or larger. Less vigorous scions on P.14 are free standing but staking is recommended for the more vigorous cultivars. Resistant to apple scab, powdery mildew, collar rot and crown gall. An ideal stock for spur-type cultivars producing semi-dwarf, free-standing trees. Winter hardiness is comparable to EMLA 106. F91T

P.16: (Poland 16) Produces non-suckering trees that are comparable in size to those on M.9. Induces early fruiting, with cropping occurring in the second year. Requires staking. Resistant to apple scab, powdery mildew, and crown gall; susceptible to fire blight. Suitable for rich, well-drained soils. Recommended for the central and southern states. *I75*

P.18: (Poland 18) Produces free-standing trees that are similar in size to those on EMLA 111. Resistant to collar rot, apple scab, powdery mildew, and crown gall. Adapted to poor, light, sandy soils. Cropping efficiency is slightly lower than EMLA 106. Very winter hardy. Trees on P.18 begin to bear in 3 to 4 years. Developed by Dr. S.W. Zagaya at Skierniewice, Poland. *I75*, *I75*{IN}

P.22: (Poland 22) Trees on P.22 are smaller than those on M.9 and are comparable to those on EMLA 27. Resistant to collar rot, canker, apple scab, powdery mildew and crown gall. Has exceptional winter hardiness. Recommended as an interstem which will produce trees that are M.9 size. Induces early fruiting. Has a cropping efficiency like that of M.9, is better anchored and not as brittle. A91, I36, I49M, *I75*, *I75*{SC}, J61M, J93, L1, M23M

Ranetka Purpurea: Cold hardiness greater than Antanovka but less than Malus baccata. More vigorous than Malus baccata; less problems with incompatibility. Withstands tough situations. Recommended for Zones 2 to 3. *G66*{PL}, *G66*{S}, S36M{S}

APRICOT ROOTSTOCKS

Haggith: Produces standard size trees that are cold hardy, consistently productive, self-fertile and disease tolerant. Haggith seedlings are quite uniform in the nursery row. Scion cultivars on Haggith stocks tend to have wider crotch angles and a more spreading growth than those on Alfred. Originated in Harrow, Ontario, Canada by R.E.C. Layne. Introduced in 1974. *G66*{S}, *M89*{S}

AVOCADO ROOTSTOCKS

Borchard: Chlorosis resistant clonal rootstock of the Mexican race. In grower trials, Borchard has shown superior growth under conditions which normally cause lime induced chlorosis. Also has good salt tolerance, but is susceptible to phytophthora root rot. *B58M*

Duke 7: Root rot resistant clonal rootstock of the Mexican race. Has moderate resistance to avocado root rot; also very good cold and salt tolerance. Preferred by most nurserymen because of superior horticultural qualities. The first commercially successful resistant rootstock. Selected from the Duke cultivar, which was discovered by George Zentmyer of the University of California, Riverside. *B58M*

G6: Mexican race. Primarily used as a source of seedling rootstocks, due to its prolific production of seeds. Has field resistance to root rot comparable to that of Duke 7. Transfers resistance better than Duke 7, however, probably no more than 10% of its seedlings will be resistant. Discovered in 1971 on the slopes of the Acatenango volcano in Guatemala. *B58M*

Martin Grande: (G-755) (Persea schiedeana x) Root rot resistant clonal rootstock. More resistant than either G6 or Duke 7. In field tests, Martin Grande has performed equally well as grafted and ungrafted trees. Has also shown good salt tolerance. Reportedly fails in some alkaline soils. Collected in 1975 by Eugenio Schieber, in the marketplace at Coban, Guatemala. Natural hybrid of Persea schiedeana and the Guatemalan race of Persea americana. *B58M*

Parida: Root rot resistant clonal rootstock. Has high resistance to phytophthora root rot, more so than Duke 7 or G6. Bears large crops at a young age. Somewhat less vigorous than other stocks. Of unknown parentage. *B58M*

Topa Topa: Seedling Mexican rootstock that shows a high rate of survival in clay soils as well as resistance to frost. A prolific seed-bearer. Produces vigorous, relatively uniform seedlings. Extremely susceptible to avocado root rot. A traditional rootstock that was used on many of the initial avocado groves in California. Originally selected in 1907 on the Topa Topa ranch in Ojai, California. *B58M*{S}, *B58M*{SC}

Toro Canyon: Root rot resistant clonal rootstock. Has shown high resistance to phytophthora root rot in test plots, more so than Duke 7 or G6. Also shows good salt tolerance. Discovered as a surviving tree in an infested orchard in Carpinteria, California. *B58M*

Walter Hole: Seedling Mexican rootstock that produces a tree of manageable size, good shape, and healthy color throughout the year. More than 250,000 trees on Walter Hole rootstock have been planted in California since 1977. *B58M*{S}

CHERRY ROOTSTOCKS

Colt: (Prunus avium x Prunus pseudocerasus) Produces trees that are 47 to 55% the size of those on Mazzard seedling. More precocious in the first 2 years of bearing than F12/1. Induces heavy fruit production. Trees on Colt have wider crotch angles than those on Mazzard seedling, and are greatly reduced in vigor when grown on heavy soils. Susceptible to winter cold injury. ROM; J61M, N0

EMLA Colt: (Prunus avium x Prunus pseudocerasus) Produces trees that are 70 to 80% the size of those on Mazzard seedling, 60 to 70% of those on F12/1. Compatible with most sweet and sour cherry cultivars. Resistant to bacterial canker, crown gall and cherry replant disease. Trees on EMLA Colt are well-branched with wide angles; yield significantly larger crops of good quality fruit earlier in the life of the tree. *I75*

F12/1: Compatible with all sweet and most sour cherry cultivars. Resistant to canker; susceptible to crown gall. Very prone to root suckering. Trees on F12/1 adapt to a wide range of loam to clay-loam soils, and are more vigorous than those on Mazzard seedling. Often used in Europe to transform bush form morello cherries into more easily manageable tree forms. A12, E93, M4

G.M. 9: (Prunus incisa x Prunus serrula) Scions on G.M. 9 come into bearing very early and show the greatest reduction in vigor of the Belgium cherry selections. Compatible with most sweet and sour cherry cultivars. Suitable for high density commercial plantings of 300 trees per acre. Introduced by the Fruit and Vegetable Research Station, Gembloux, Belgium. *I75*

G.M. 61/1: (Damil) (Prunus dawyckensis) Scions on G.M. 61/1 are approximately 1/3 to 1/2 the size of scions on F12/1. Very precocious and induces early fruiting. Trees on G.M. 61/1 are less bushy and more open, and much more productive than those on F12/1. Suitable for plantings of 150 to 230 trees per acre. Fruit has increased size and improved color. I36, I49M, *I75*, J61M, J93

G.M. 79: (Prunus canescens) Scions on G.M. 79 are 50% the size of those on F12/1 and are slightly more vigorous than those on G.M. 61/1. Compatible with most sweet cherry cultivars. Trees on G.M. 79 have an open growth habit. Suitable for orchard densities of 130 to 200 trees per acre. Fruit size, color, and yield potential are much greater than F12/1 and Mazzard seedling. *I75*

Mahaleb: (Prunus mahaleb) Produces well anchored, standard size trees. Cannot tolerate poor drainage; very drought resistant. Compatible with most sweet and sour cherry cultivars. Moderately resistant to crown gall; resistant to bacterial canker. Trees on Mahaleb may be slightly smaller, come into bearing sooner, and have a heavier set of fruit than those on Mazzard. Especially popular as a stock for sour cherries. A91, E93{PL}, *G66*{PL}, *G66*{S}, *H45M*{PL}, H49, *I82*{PL}, K38{S}, L1, *N19*{PL}

Mazzard: (Prunus avium) Produces well anchored, standard size trees. Many roots are shallow, resulting in injury by deep cultivation and drought. Compatible with most sweet and sour cherry cultivars. Moderately resistant to oak-root fungus; less susceptible than Mahaleb to peach tree borer. Recommended for soils that are too heavy for Mahaleb. A91, E93{PL}, *G66*{PL}, *H45M*{PL}, I36, *I82*{PL}, K38{S}, L1, *N19*{PL}

CITRUS ROOTSTOCKS

CITRANGES

C-32: Recommended for trial because of its resistance to the citrus nematode, Phytophthora species and tristeza virus. Produces vigorous seedling trees, equal in volume to Troyer, but less dense. More productive than C32. Ruby orange x trifoliate orange. Released in 1985 by the Citrus Research Center, University of California, Riverside. N18{S}

C-35: Recommended along with C-32 because of its resistance to the citrus nematode, Phytophthora species and tristeza virus. Slightly smaller than C32, rather open and subject to some low-branch dieback in older trees. Ruby orange x trifoliate orange. Released in 1985 by the Citrus Research Center, University of California, Riverside. *A71*, N18{S}

Carrizo: Trees on Carrizo are among the most vigorous, growing well on a wide range of soils. They are prone to zinc and manganese deficiency, and are less cold tolerant than those on trifoliate orange, sour orange or Cleopatra mandarin. Carrizo is tolerant to the burrowing nematode. In Florida they grow and fruit unusually well in their early years. Fruit quality is often comparable with that produced on Cleopatra and sour orange. ROM; *A71*, *J73M*{S}, N18{S}, S95{S}

Savage: Has seeds that are highly polyembryonic, but usually produces seedless fruit. Trees on Savage have yielded well and withstood freezes in several trials on sandy and loam soils, and may be suitable as rootstocks for close plantings. The yellow, 2 1/2 to 3 inch fruits yield large amounts of fragrant, good quality juice. I74, N18{S}

Troyer: Along with Carrizo, the only commercially important citrange rootstocks. Trees on Troyer are among the most vigorous, growing well on a wide range of soils. Troyer has poor salt tolerance and sensitivity to exocortis and calcareous soils; not affected by xyloporosis. Susceptible to burrowing nematode. Sweet orange trees on Troyer in California are subject to tristeza decline in coastal areas. ROM; I74, J61M, *J73M*{S}, K67, N18{S}, O93{S}, S95{S}

Uvalde: Has seeds that are highly polyembryonic, but usually produces seedless fruit. Trees on Uvalde have yielded well and withstood freezes in several trials on sandy and loam soils, and may be suitable as rootstocks for close plantings. N18{S}

CITRUMELOS

C.P.B. 4475: Trees on C.P.B. are vigorous, productive and cold hardy. Resistant to nematodes and phytophthora root rot. Good for replants in commercial groves. Swingle is the name reserved for seed source trees propagated by budding from the original Swingle tree, while C.P.B. 4475 trees are propagated from seed. ROM; *J73M*{S}, N18{S}

Sacaton: Trees on Sacaton are small and have potential for high-density plantings. May be susceptible to tristeza in some environments. Lemons on Sacaton have performed well in Arizona and California experiments. Sacaton seeds are polyembryonic but produce about 40% zygotic seedlings. Has been evaluated in the United States with inconsistent results. ROM; K67, N18{S}

Swingle: One of the rootstocks that induces as much cold hardiness as sour orange. Swingle is very tolerant to the citrus nematode and root rot. In Texas, Red Blush grapefruit, Orlando tangelo, and Marrs orange yield and fruit quality surpass that of trees on most other stocks. In California, Swingle is compatible with Lisbon lemon and has performed well in grower trials. *A71*, K67

ROUGH LEMONS

Milam: Possibly a rough lemon hybrid. Resistant to the burrowing nematode; susceptible to the citrus nematode. Has evolved essentially as a special-purpose rootstock in Florida, where commercial trees on this stock behave similarly to those on Rough Lemon. However, Milam has performed poorly in calcareous soil in Texas. ROM; *J73M*{S}, N18{S}

Rough Lemon: An excellent rootstock for warm, humid areas with deep, sandy soils. In such an environment trees on Rough Lemon grow rapidly and are long-lived and highly productive, yielding large fruit with a low total soluble solids content. In arid or coastal environments and clay soils, trees on Rough lemon often decline prematurely. They are notably drought tolerant. Orange, grapefruit and lemon cultivars can be used with Rough Lemon. ROM; *J73M*{S}, N84{S}, *P17M*{S}

Soh Jhalia: Rated as moderately resistant to phytophthora root rot in California seedling screening tests. Has performed well in subsequent field tests. Originated in India. ROM; N18{S}

Volkamer Lemon: (Volkameriana) Has many of the same characteristics as Rough Lemon, although trees on this stock are more cold hardy and have often yielded more fruit with slightly higher juice quality than those on Rough Lemon. Apparently tolerant to mal secco, gummosis and foot rot; susceptible to root rot. Appears to be as susceptible to blight and woody gall as Rough Lemon. MORTON 1987a, ROM; *J73M*{S}, N18{S}, S95{S}

TRIFOLIATE ORANGES

Flying Dragon: Trees on Flying Dragon have been consistently small during field trials in California and Florida. Otherwise their performance is essentially the same as for other Trifoliate Orange selections. Grown primarily as a potted plant in Japan where it is called *hiryo*. It has slender, crooked branches armed with large, downward-curved spines. REUTHER, ROM; *A71*, D37, E6, I74, I83M, N18{S}

Rubidoux: Trees on Rubidoux trifoliate orange are 30 to 60% of standard size. Imparts a greater cold-hardiness to the tree. Susceptible to quick decline virus. Used extensively in the past for orange and grapefruit cultivars. Seedling of trifoliate orange, originating in Riverside, California. Introduced about 1920. BROOKS 1972; *A71*, I83M, N18{S}

Trifoliate Orange: Trees budded to Trifoliate orange are cold hardy, standard sized on heavy soils and dwarfed on light soils, and intolerant of calcareous conditions. Tolerant to phytophthora and the citrus nematode. Yields small, high-quality fruit. Excellent for commercial replantings. The primary rootstock in Japan for large satsuma and unshiu plantings. ROM; A79M{S}, B96, C9, D95, E48, G96, H4, *J73M*{S}, K18, K63G{S}, M77M, N37M, O93{S}, P39{S}

OTHERS

Alemow: (Macrophylla) Trees on Alemow are vigorous, precocious, and fruit heavily when young. Resistant to phytophthora. Juice quality is lower than that for trees on virtually any other rootstock. Scion cultivars other than lemon produce fruit of only marginal quality. Trees on Alemow decline from xyloporosis and tristeza. Popular in California as a stock for lemons. ROM; *J73M*{S}, N18{S}, O93{S}

Citremon 1449: Used as a rootstock for limes, lemons, oranges and grapefruits. Trees grafted to Citremon 1449 have good size and vigor and are adapted to a wide range of soil conditions. Has shown good tolerance of crown rot but is susceptible to tristeza. N18{S}

Cleopatra Mandarin: Trees budded to Cleopatra are capable of achieving a large size, but are often slow to bear. Tolerant to tristeza, exocortis, xyloporosis, cold, and calcareous soils. Juice quality is excellent but fruit size is small, particularly with Valencia scions. Cleopatra is an excellent rootstock for mandarin and related cultivars, and Pineapple and Hamlin sweet oranges. ROM; *J73M*{S}, N18{S}

Rangpur Lime: Trees on Rangpur Lime are vigorous and highly productive, particularly as young trees. Sensitive to cold and phytophthora; very tolerant to drought. Fruit is medium to large with low to moderate juice quality. An excellent stock for deep, sandy soils in humid climates, where grapefruit and sweet oranges yield well. ROM; *G49*, I83M, *J73M*{S}, N18{S}

Ridge Pineapple: A sweet orange cultivar that is tolerant to the burrowing nematode. Has also shown good resistance to tristeza, anthracnose, exocortis and cachexia. Trees on Ridge pineapple are long-lived and have excellent fruit quality. Good compatibility with lemons and limes. Originated in Orlovista, Florida. BROOKS 1972, ROM; *J73M*{S}, N18{S}

Shîkwashâ: (Hirami Lemon) Various scions on Shîkwashâ are average or better in vigor and yield, with generally good fruit size and juice quality. Moderately cold and salt tolerant, but has a high level of tolerance to lime-induced chlorosis; also tolerant of phytophthora and the rootstock-related viruses. Shows promise as a rootstock for mandarins. ROM; N18{S}

Sour Orange: Trees on sour orange are moderately vigorous and their size is generally considered as the standard for comparison. Valued as a rootstock for producing fresh market fruit. Fruit from trees on Sour Orange have high total soluble solids, and high vitamin C content. Navel orange juice quality and flavor are improved on Sour Orange stock. The premier citrus rootstock, common throughout the world where tristeza does not preclude its use. ROM; *A71*, *J73M*{S}

Sunki: (Suenkat) Tolerant to tristeza and xyloporosis like Cleopatra but is affected by exocortis, which is unusual for a mandarin-like fruit. Trees on Sunki are highly salt tolerant, moderately cold hardy, and adaptable to calcareous soils. In Florida, has induced greater yield and higher juice quality than Cleopatra. Commonly used as a stock in China and Taiwan. ROM; N18{S}

Sweet Lime: Trees on Sweet Lime are medium to large. Juice quality is generally poor, but has been slightly better in some instances than that recorded for Rough Lemon. Nucellar scions perform best on Sweet Lime. Valued mainly as a rootstock, although it is grown in some countries for fresh consumption. ROM; I83M, *J73M*{S}

Sweet Orange: Most commercial scion cultivars on Sweet Orange are long-lived, and produce crops often equal to or better than those from trees on Sour Orange. Valencia oranges, mandarins, and lemons on Sweet Orange yield well, with good fruit size and juice quality. Trees on Sour Orange are often slow growing, and perform best on sandy loam soils. Susceptible to phytophthora and drought; tolerant to tristeza and exocortis. ROM; *J73M*{S}

GRAPE ROOTSTOCKS

A x R #1: (Ganzin #1) (Vitis vinifera x Vitis rupestris) Produces vigorous grafted vines that bear good yields of high quality fruit. Resistant to phylloxera; susceptible to nematodes. Roots its cuttings quite readily, and buds and grafts easily. Recommended for use with lighter bearing raisin and table cultivars in deep, heavier soils. B39, E39, E39{SC}, I95, I95{SC}, *J31M*, *J31M*{SC}, *L1M*, *L1M*{SC}

Couderc 1613: (1613) (Vitis solonis x) Imparts moderate vigor to its scions. Resistant to the more prevalent strains of root-knot nematodes; moderately resistant to phylloxera. Cuttings of this stock readily root in the nursery and it buds and grafts easily. Does not sucker excessively, but disbudding is recommended before planting. Widely used with wine, raisin and table cultivars in California. B39, E39, E39{SC}, I95, I95{SC}, *J31M*, *J31M*{SC}, *L1M*, *L1M*{SC}

Couderc 3309: (3309) (Vitis riparia x Vitis rupestris) Scion vines on Couderc 3309 are moderately vigorous and bear well. Has relatively poor compatibility with vinifera cultivars. Cuttings of this stock have medium rooting ability in the nursery; are relatively difficult to bench graft. Resistant to phylloxera; very susceptible to nematodes and drought. Widely used in Europe. B39, *E0*, *J31M*, *J31M*{SC}, *L1M*, *L1M*{SC}

Dog Ridge: (Vitis x champini) Imparts great vigor to its scions. Resistant to nematodes; moderately resistant to phylloxera. Cuttings of this stock root with difficulty, however the rootings bud and graft readily. Suckering may be a problem, therefore disbudding the cuttings is recommended. Only recommended for light, less fertile, sandy soils. Gives best results with heavy-bearing wine and raisin cultivars. E39, E39{SC}, I95, I95{SC}, *L1M*, *L1M*{SC}, N33

Freedom: Produces grafted vines that are vigorous and heavy bearing. Has some resistance to phylloxera and is very resistant to root knot nematodes; not tolerant of drought. Cuttings of this stock root moderately well in the nursery, and it buds and grafts fairly easily. E39, E39{SC}, I95, I95{SC}, *J31M*, *J31M*{SC}, *L1M*, *L1M*{SC}, L37M

Harmony: Vines grafted on Harmony have moderate vigor and bear well. Has some resistance to phylloxera and root knot nematodes, but is not immune to either. Cuttings of this stock readily root in the nursery and vineyard, and it buds and grafts readily. Satisfactory for table grapes; especially suited for Thompson Seedless. E39, E39{SC}, I95, I95{SC}, *J31M*, *J31M*{SC}, *L1M*, *L1M*{SC}, L37M

Salt Creek: (Ramsey) (Vitis x champini) Imparts great vigor to its scions. Very resistant to nematodes; moderately resistant to phylloxera. Roots its cuttings with difficulty, but buds and grafts readily. Performs well with wine and raisin cultivars in light sandy soils of low fertility. Has a greater range of use than Dog Ridge. Suckering is less of a problem than with Dog Ridge, however, disbudding is recommended. E39, E39{SC}, I95, I95{SC}, *L1M*, *L1M*{SC}

SO-4: (Oppenheim #4) (Vitis berlandieri x Vitis riparia) Scion vines on SO-4 are vigorous and productive. Has good resistance to phylloxera and nematodes; not tolerant of drought. Medium compatibility with vinifera cultivars. Cuttings of this stock root with some difficulty and it is not easy to bud or graft. Used commercially in German vineyards. *E0*, E39, E39{SC}, I95, I95{SC}, *J31M*, *J31M*{SC}, *L1M*, *L1M*{SC}

St. George: (St. George 15) (Vitis rupestris) Produces quite vigorous grafted vines. Drought tolerant, highly resistant to phylloxera; susceptible to nematodes and oak root fungus. Very compatible with vinifera cultivars. Cuttings of this stock root readily and it is readily budded or grafted. Suckers profusely, therefore careful disbudding is recommended. B39, E39, E39{SC}, I95, I95{SC}, *L1M*, *L1M*{SC}

Teleki 5BB: (5BB, Kaber 5BB) (Vitis riparia x Vitis berlandieri) Produces grafted vines that are very vigorous. High resistance to phylloxera; moderately resistant to cold and nematodes; not tolerant of drought. Cuttings of this stock do not root well, and it is relatively difficult to graft. Very poor compatibility with Vitis vinifera cultivars. ROM; B39, *E0*, I95, I95{SC}, *J31M*, *J31M*{SC}, *L1M*, *L1M*{SC}

PEACH ROOTSTOCKS

Bailey: Cold hardy seedling rootstock that produces a standard size tree. Develops an abundant root system. Adapts to sandy and sandy loam soils. Resistant to root lesion nematodes. Seedlings may vary in their resistance to cold. Originated in Scott County, Iowa by Jacob Friday. Introduced prior to 1909. A69G{PL}, *A74*, *M89*{S}

Chui-Lum-Tao: Relatively new cultivar from northern China, currently being developed in Canada. One of the hardiest rootstocks for peaches, along with Siberian C and Tzim-Pee-Tao. Moderately tolerant to nematodes. Has performed well as an understock for both nectarines and peaches. *M89*{S}

Citation: Peach-plum hybrid. Produces peach and nectarine trees that are approximately 60% of standard; apricots and plums that are 75 to 80% of standard. Induces early dormancy, cold hardiness and early bearing (often the second year). Strong, well-anchored; does not sucker. Tolerant of wet soils; resists root-knot nematodes. Excellent compatibility with all cultivars. Developed by Floyd Zaiger. *H45M*, I36, L1, N0

Halford: Seedling rootstock that produces a standard size tree. Similar to Lovell in performance. Has proved its consistency and adaptability to a wide range of growing conditions. Not resistant to nematodes. Compatible with all commercially grown cultivars. Also used as a rootstock for Japanese plums and Italian prunes in the Northwest. *G66*{S}, I36

Lovell: Produces well-anchored trees of standard size. Prefers well-drained, sandy loam soils; is sensitive to wet soil conditions. Compatible with all peach cultivars. Highly susceptible to peach tree borer and root knot nematodes. One of the most valuable rootstocks in the United States and Canada. Widely planted where nematodes are not a problem. *G66*, *G66*{S}, H49, I36, *I82*{PL}, *K73M*, L1

Nemaguard: (Amygdalus persica x Amygdalus davidiana) Produces well-anchored trees of standard size. Sensitive to wet soil conditions. Very resistant to most economically important root knot nematodes; highly susceptible to peach tree borer. Has an adverse effect on scions with regard to cold hardiness and bacterial canker. Widely used and preferred stock, especially in California and Florida. *G66*{PL}, *G66*{S}, K38{S}, L1, N33{PL}

Nemared: Similar to Nemaguard, but red leaves of Nemared help identify "missed" buds in the nursery row. Has proven resistance to root knot nematodes. Lacks productivity in soils without nematodes when compared with other rootstocks. Susceptible to wet soils and bacterial canker. F53, *G66*{PL}

Siberian C: Produces semi-dwarf trees that are 75% the size of those on standard seedlings. Transfers cold hardiness to scion cultivars. Induces earlier defoliation and hardening off of the scion cultivar. Susceptible to nematodes. Trees on Siberian C are precocious. Fruit matures earlier. Recommended for colder areas. Also used as a stock for apricot. Originated in Harrow, Ontario, Canada. A69G{PL}, A91, *G66*{S}, *M89*{S}

Tzim-Pee-Tao: Relatively new seedling rootstock from northern China, currently being developed in Canada. One of the hardiest rootstocks for peaches, along with Siberian C and Chui-Lum-Tao. Moderately tolerant to nematodes. Has performed well as an understock for both nectarines and peaches. *M89*{S}

PEAR ROOTSTOCKS

EMLA Quince A: Virus-free re-introduction of Quince A selected at the East Malling and Long-Ashton experiment stations in Great Britain. Resistant to pear decline, root aphid and root knot nematodes; susceptible to fire blight. Produces trees that are relatively vigorous and hardy. Moderately tolerant of wet soils. E93

EMLA Quince C: More dwarfing and precocious than Quince A. Produces trees that are similar in size to those on M.9 apple stock. Resistant to pear decline, crown gall, mildew, nematodes and root aphids. Trees on EMLA Quince C are higher yielding and fruit size is greater than cultivars on Quince A; should not be planted in areas of severe cold. *I75*, J93, *N19*

Kirschensaller: Produces well anchored trees that are 90% the size of those on pear seedling. Slightly more vigorous and uniform. Nearly free of root sprouts. Excellent compatibility. Good resistance to pear decline and oak root fungus; tolerant of wet soil conditions; susceptible to fire blight. Trees on Kirschensaller are precocious and heavy yielding. *G66*{PL}, N84{S}, S95{S}

OH x F: (Old Home x Farmingdale) A hybrid of the Old Home and Farmingdale cultivars. Hardy, widely adapted, and resistant to fireblight and pear decline. Compatible with most important cultivars. Selected by F.C. Reimer of Oregon State University more than 75 years ago. *I75*, I95

OH x F 69: (Old Home x Farmingdale 69) Produces well anchored, semi-dwarf trees, 70% of standard; nearly free of root sprouts. Strongly resistant to fire blight, pear decline, bacterial canker and oak root fungus; susceptible to woolly aphids and root lesion nematodes. Good tolerance to winter cold. A12

OH x F 87: (Old Home x Farmingdale 87) Produces well anchored, semi-dwarf trees, 70% of standard; nearly free of root sprouts. Strongly resistant to fire blight, pear decline, bacterial canker and oak root fungus; susceptible to woolly aphids and root lesion nematodes. Good tolerance to winter cold. A12

OH x F 97: (Old Home x Farmingdale 97) Produces a vigorous, full-sized tree, 10% larger than that of seedling pear. Highly resistant to pear decline and fire blight. Somewhat susceptible to winter injury due to its growing vigor late in the season. Does not do well in heavy, clay soils. *H45M*, I36, J93, *N19*

OH x F 333: (Old Home x Farmingdale 333) Produces well anchored trees that are 70% the size of those on pear seedling. Nearly free of root sprouts. Has good compatibility, even with Asian pears. Resistant to pear decline, fire blight and bacterial canker. Trees on OH x F 333 are cold hardy, precocious and very productive. Fruit quality is very good. Selected by Lyle Brooks. *H45M*, I36, J93, L1, *N19*

OH x F 513: (Old Home x Farmingdale 513) Produces trees that can be maintained at about 15 feet tall. Compatible with all pear cultivars, including Asian Pears. Induces heavy early production and is very hardy. Does well on a variety of soils. Resistant to pear decline, fire blight and bacterial canker. Trees on OH x F 513 are nearly free from suckering. A91, I49M, J61M

Old Home: (Pyrus communis) One of the first clonal pear rootstocks used in the United States. Largely discontinued as a stock because of the very low yield efficiency it induces. It also tends to sprout very badly. Produces standard sized trees. Resistant to fire blight and pear decline; susceptible to root aphid and nematodes. Cuttings of this stock root readily. Still widely used as an interstem. A69G{SC}, G65M, M39M, N24M

Provence Quince: (Cydonia oblonga) Produces trees that are 50 to 65% of standard, larger than those on Quince A or Quince C. Characterized by vigor, resistance to drought, and tolerance to alkaline soils. Resistant to pear decline, root aphid, and nematodes; susceptible to fire blight. Trees on Provence Quince are heavy bearing, but not as hardy as pears on seedling rootstock. *G66*, H49, *I82*

Provence Quince (BA 29-C): Produces trees that are from 1/2 to 2/3 the size of standard pear trees. Compatible with Anjou, Comice and Flemish Beauty; other cultivars require an interstem to form a strong union. More winter hardy than Quince A. Resistant to pear decline, crown gall, nematodes and root aphids. Trees on BA 29-C are precocious and very high yielding. *I75*, *N19*

Provence Quince (Le Page Series C): Produces trees that are about 55% the size of standard pear trees. Compatible with Anjou, Comice and Flemish Beauty; other cultivars require an interstem to form a strong union. More winter hardy than Quince A. Resistant to pear decline, crown gall, nematodes and root aphids. Trees on Le Page Series C are precocious and very high yielding. *I75*

Quince A: (Angers Quince A) Selected from Angers quince at the East Malling research station in the 1930's. Produces trees that are about 50% the size of those on pear seedling. Trees on Quince A are generally precocious and productive. Tolerates wet soils better than Provence Quince; susceptible to fire blight. Widely planted in the more northern regions of Europe. *G66*, *I82*, M4, *N19*

PECAN ROOTSTOCKS

Riverside: Produces more good pecans from seed than any other cultivar. A heavy producer and transmits this quality to its offspring. Trees grafted to Riverside are thriftier and quicker bearing. Reportedly the best pecan stock ever found. Recommended by Texas A & M University. Originated by Cockrell's Riverside Nursery. C37{PL}, C37{S}

PLUM ROOTSTOCKS

Besseyi: (Prunus besseyi) Produces mostly dwarf trees that are poorly anchored. Prone to severe suckering. Compatible with most prunes; incompatible with Damson and Victoria plums. Resistant to crown gall. Trees on Besseyi are productive and very cold hardy. Cuttings of this stock are often easy to root. Seedlings vary widely. E93, *G66*{PL}, *H45M*{PL}, H49, *I82*{PL}, *N19*{PL}

Brompton: (Prunus domestica) Produces very large, well anchored trees, nearly free from suckering. Compatible with most European plums; incompatible with some prunes. Resistant to cold temperatures; susceptible to bacterial canker. Adapted to heavy, damp soils. Trees on Brompton are moderately productive. Widely used in Europe. *G66*{PL}, M4

Marianna 2624: (Prunus cerasifera x Prunus munsoniana) Produces tree that are smaller than peach trees. Widely adapted to different soil types and moisture conditions, however will not tolerate extremely heavy soils. Not well anchored in early years. Resistant to oak root rot, root knot nematodes and prune brownline. Induces heavy production. Fruit is slightly earlier ripening. Best of the Marianna selections. ROM; *H45M*, *I75*, L1, *N19*

Marianna 4001: (Prunus cerasifera x Prunus munsoniana) Produces very large, well anchored trees. Moderately prone to suckering. Compatible with most European and Japanese plums. Resistant to drought and bacterial canker. Induces heavy fruit production. Fruit is slightly later ripening. Widely planted in the United States. *I75*, N0

Myrobalan: (Myro Plum) (Prunus cerasifera) Widely adapted to different soil types and moisture conditions, however will not tolerate extremely heavy soils. Compatible with most European and Japanese plums; poor compatibility with Green Gage and Stanley. Trees on Myrobalan are large, have good anchorage and are very productive. Fruit is slightly later ripening. Best worldwide stock, but highly variable from seed. ROM; A91, E93, *G66*{PL}, *G66*{S}, I36, *I82*{PL}, K38{S}, *N19*{PL}

Myrobalan 29C: (Prunus cerasifera) Adapted to a wide range of soil and moisture conditions. Anchorage is not very good in early years. Compatible with most European and Japanese plums. Somewhat resistant to nematodes; susceptible to prune brownline. Trees on Myrobalan 29C are large and high yielding. Fruit is slightly later ripening. Widely used in the United States. ROM; *H45M*, *I75*, J93, N0, *N19*

Myrobalan B: (Prunus cerasifera) Very vigorous stock with strong anchorage; does not sucker. Difficult to root in the nursery. Wide compatibility, especially with European plums; incompatible with Gages and Mirabelles. Recommended for lighter soils, especially in hot climates. Trees on Myrobalan B come into production late, but bear heavily when mature. M4

Pixy: Produces very dwarf trees. Well anchored, but with a small root system. Nearly free from suckering. Compatible with most European and some Japanese plums. Tolerant to bacterial canker; susceptible to drought. Trees on Pixy are precocious and highly productive. Induces earlier bloom and earlier ripening fruit. Fruit may be slightly smaller. I36, I49M, J61M, J93, L1

St. Julien A: (St. Julien, EMLA St. Julien A) (Prunus insititia) Produces semi-dwarf trees, about 10 to 15 feet tall. Somewhat prone to suckering. Tolerates a variety of soils. Compatible with most European plum cultivars. Resistant to low winter temperatures. Trees on St. Julien A are precocious and moderately productive. Not recommended as a stock for Stanley. Also used as a rootstock for peaches and apricots. *G66*{PL}, *G66*{S}, *H45M*, I49M, *I75*, J61M, L1, L99M, M4, N0, *N19*, R78{S}

St. Julien X: (Prunus insititia) Shows potential as a semi-dwarfing stock for Japanese plums and peaches. Roots easily from cuttings and is resistant in the nursery to leaf spot, but is thorny. It is well anchored, but may sucker badly. Compatible with Ozark Premier and Italian prune. Selected in New Zealand from English seed. ROM; I95

TOMATO ROOTSTOCKS

BF Okitsu 101: Developed by the Japanese Government Station. Resistant to bacterial wilt and fusarium wilt. *S70*

KNVF: A tomato rootstock which gives resistance to corky rot, root knot eelworm, and verticillium and fusarium wilts. Used as a rootstock for cultivars which are susceptible to these problems, especially under greenhouse conditions. P83M, S61. T1M

KNVFR: Resistant to corky root, root knot nematode, verticillium and fusarium wilts, and J_3. *S70*

KNVFR Tm Signal: Resistant to tobacco mosaic virus, corky root, root knot nematodes, verticillium wilt, fusarium wilt (Race 1 & 2), J_3, and related to TMV (Tm2a/+) resistant tomato. *S70*

LS-89: Developed by the Japanese Government Station. Resistant to bacterial wilt and fusarium wilt (Race 1). *S70*

WALNUT ROOTSTOCKS

Paradox: (Juglans regia x Juglans hindsii) Trees grafted onto Paradox are more vigorous and have a greater circumference when grown on volcanic hillside soils. Resistant to some forms of root rot and root lesion nematodes; susceptible to the cherry leaf roll virus (black line disease) and crown gall. Seedling vigor and performance very variable. Widely used as a rootstock for Persian walnuts in California. Originated in Santa Rosa, California by Luther Burbank; first described in 1893. *B71M*{PL}, *D18*{PL}

RUNNER BEAN {S}

PHASEOLUS COCCINEUS

BICOLOR-FLOWERING

Painted Lady: (Bicolor) 90 days. Not as long-podded as modern cultivars, but has a very good flavor; pods 9 to 12 inches long. Flowers half red and half white, the keel and wings being pinkish white, and the standard scarlet-red. Seeds dark brown to black, mottled with creamy white. Suitable for both the vegetable and ornamental garden. Originated before 1855. HEDRICK 1931, VILMORIN; I99, K66, L7M, L91M, P83M, *R23*, S55

PINK-FLOWERING

Sunset: Produces medium-length, richly-flavored pods. Has the added attraction of carrying pale pink flowers. Among the earliest maturing cultivars; can be pinched back and grown as bush beans for exceptionally early crops. L91M, S61

RED-FLOWERING

Best of All: (Challenge) Long pods produced in clusters; can be thinned to produce pods up to 18 inches long; the pods being of fine texture, quality, and flavor. Freezes well. Vigorous, reliable, a heavy cropper. This is the old Challenge cultivar (under a different name according to British regulations). B49, S61

Butler: 65 days. Pods stringless all along their length; also fiberless in the thick flesh surrounding the seed itself; pod length averages 12 inches. Juicy pods remain in edible stage longer than other cultivars. Fast, productive grower; sets well in hot weather. Flower clusters ornamental with a very heavy bloom to stem ratio. B49, L91M, S61

Dwarf Bees:[1] Unique dwarf Scarlet Runner type. Does not produce runners, allowing for easy culture without the need for staking. Good quality pods. Attractive, bright scarlet blossoms. *A75*

Enorma: 92 days. Produces extremely long, slender pods, often up to 20 inches long. More highly flavored than Crusader which it replaces. Seeds purple with some black stripes. If picked young, pods can be used whole; as they mature they form tough strings along the edges which should be removed before cooking. Good freezing and exhibition qualities. Very productive. I99, L91M, *R11M*, S61, *S75M*

Goliath: (Prizetaker) 92 days. A very productive cultivar producing very long pods, often up to 20 inches. It has all the qualities of an outstanding bean: fine texture, heavy cropping, reliability and uniformity. Seeds purple with over 50% black splashes. L91M, *R23*, T1M

Gulliver:[1] Smooth, bright green, fleshy pods, 9 to 10 inches long; completely stringless. Early high-yielding plant; does not produce runners, allowing for easy growing without the labor of tying and staking. Attractive, scarlet flowers. An Improved Hammond's Dwarf type. Developed by A.L. Tozer Ltd. L91M, *S75M*

Hammonds Dwarf:[1] (Hammonds Scarlet Runner Bush) 60 days. A true dwarf, non-climbing cultivar; height 16 to 18 inches. Needs no staking providing pods are picked regularly, however the top may need to be pinched out of an occasional plant to stop them running. Pods 7 to 8 inches long; when picked young they make good snap beans, later they can be used as a shell bean. Introduced in 1961. I77, L91M, M46, P83M, *R23*

Kelvedon Marvel: 84 days. Very early, producing long straight pods very freely. Pods 10 to 12 inches long, somewhat rough. Seeds purple with over 50% black splashes. Shorter than the average runner, growing only 4 to 5 feet tall; most productive if unsupported and left to spread horizontally. L91M, P83M, *R23*, *S75M*

King David: 90 days. Long green pods, 11 to 14 inches; very tasty. Black and scarlet seeds. Very attractive, large clusters of bright scarlet flowers which blossom over a long period of time; also attract hummingbirds. B35M, L97

Pickwick:[1] Compact, bushy plants without runners; height about 12 inches. Ideal for small or exposed gardens or for growing under protection. Quite early maturing, with stringless pods that should be picked regularly for continuity of supply. S61

Prizewinner: 93 days. Produces a large crop of rich green pods, which are straight, smooth-skinned, 20 to 24 inches long, stringless when young, and have a rich bean-like flavor. Seeds purple with some black stripes. Good for general garden use; also used along trellises for the flowers, which are brilliantly red. *A75*, F1, I39, O53M, *R23*, S61

Red Knight: 70 days. Long stringless pods, smoother than the rough-textured older strains; ripen early. Can be picked young as snap beans, or left to mature for dry beans. Very heavy cropping, produces pods all summer long. Vines grow 10 to 12 feet and are covered with crimson blossoms. One of the best modern cultivars. K66, P83M, *R23*, S55

Scarlet Emperor: 90 days. One of the longest-podded cultivars, with flat, slightly fuzzy pods of rich, dark-green color, frequently 15 inches long, but nevertheless of fine flavor and texture. Seeds purple with over 50% black splashes. Preferred by many gardeners for its rich, sweet, bean flavor. Vine a heavy producer, with large sprays of attractive red flowers. *A75*, B49, D11M, I77, I99, L89, L91M, P83M, *R23*, S61

Scarlet Runner: 90 days. Dark green pods, moderately brittle, firm-fleshed, somewhat stringy and rather coarse in texture; quality fair. Seeds very large; shining black to violet-black, mottled with deep red; can be used as green shell beans. Flowers scarlet, very large, 20 to 40 on each long flower-stalk. One of the oldest known cultivars, originating before 1750. HEDRICK 1931; A16, A25, D11M, E7M, E24, E38, F92, G71, H42, J7, L7M, L79, M13M, M46, M49, etc.

Streamline: 91 days. One of the longest cultivars, the pods being up to 18 inches long, straight and narrow; borne in large trusses and over a long period. Flavor very good. A good producer, ideal for those who want to exhibit, and who want to pick enough for a meal quickly. Seeds purple with over 50% black splashes. Good for heavy soils. GENDERS 1975; *A75*, L91M, O53M, *R23*, S61, *S75M*

Tarahumara Tecomari: Produces very large purple, lavender, black and mottled beans. Attractive, red flowers. From the Tarahumara Indians of Mexico. I16

Wild: (Wild Scarlet Runner) Small, speckled, northernmost progenitor of domesticated scarlet runner beans. Beautiful red flowers. Very viney plant, blooms late. I16

WHITE-FLOWERING

Czar: (The Czar) A fine old white-flowered cultivar that produces long, tender, mild-flavored pods for eating green. If left to dry it will produce a crop of plump, fine-tasting white "butter beans". One of the cultivars favored for quick freezing. An heirloom cultivar that was almost lost. P83M, S55

Desiree: A white-seeded, white flowering cultivar that produces long, slender, fleshy pods 10 to 12 inches in length. Exceptional flavor and genuinely 100% stringless. As is it is a shy seeder, there is much more juicy, fleshy, edible area. Suitable for freezing. Bears very heavily, especially in dry conditions when 40 pods per plant can be expected; will attain large crops from a small area. B49, L91M, *R23*

Emergo: 88 days. Long-podded type; white-flowered and seeded. Of good quality, but pods must be picked when young. Vigorous plants withstand adverse weather; are heavy-yielding. *A75*, C85M, P83M, *R11M*

Emergo Stringless: 87 days. Produces an abundance of large (8 to 12 inch), tender, and flavorful beans. Well suited to Northern gardens as it may be planted earlier than other beans and thrives in relatively cool conditions. White-flowered and seeded. Vine length can exceed 10 feet. J20

Erecta: Widely grown as a commercial crop as it is generally accepted as being tolerant of the widest range of growing conditions and having the smoothest, most attractive pods (12 to 14 inches long). L91M

Tarahumara Bordal: 120 days. Large white runner bean, reputed to be one of the best tasting. Dry farmed on thin, rocky soils. From Chihuahua, Mexico. I16

White Aztec: (Dwarf White Aztec, Potato Bean) 55 days. Pods usually long, much curved, flat, dark green with a rough surface. Seeds very large, much thickened, very plump; color glossy white. Has a distinct running, spreading habit that forms a dense mass of runners over the ground around the central stem. Flowers numerous, large, white. Supposedly found in a sealed vase in an ancient Anasazi dwelling in New Mexico. HEDRICK 1931; J25M, K49T, L79M

White Dutch: (Oregon Lima) Resembles Scarlet Runner very closely, differing from it in having stems and leaf veins solid green and flowers and seeds pure white. Seeds very large. Pick when 6 inches long for snap beans; for a meatier taste, pick when 12 inches long, or use later as a shell bean or a baking bean. A very old cultivar, listed by American seedsmen as early as 1825. HEDRICK 1931; A2, I99, M46

White Knight: 73 days. Produces heavy crops of long, thick green beans that are absolutely stringless, crunchy and sweet-flavored. They have none of the toughness or fibrous quality of older runner bean types. Pods grow 8 inches long and can be picked young or allowed to size up and then cut into one or two-inch slices. Mature seeds can be used for shelling or dry beans. K66

RUTABAGA {S}

BRASSICA NAPUS NAPOBRASSICA GROUP

Acme: (Garden Purple Top Acme) 90 days. Small, early, purple top globe-type with sweet yellow flesh of very high quality. Uniform size and shape. High yielding. Recommended by the National Institute for Agricultural Botany of Great Britain. B49, O53M, P83M, *R23*, *S75M*

Altasweet: 90 days. Very large, globe-shaped root, 4 to 7 inches in diameter; skin, smooth, very thin, yellow with a purple top; flesh deep-yellow, tender, fine-grained, very sweet and mild; keeps well in the ground all winter. One of the best tasting rutabagas. A cross of Laurentian and Macomber, Altasweet is similar in form and color to Laurentian, but much milder in flavor. A32, I77, J7, L42, L89, N52

American Purple Top: (American Purple Top Yellow, Golden Neckless) 100 days. Large, smooth, globe-shaped root with small neck and tap root; 4 to 6 inches in diameter; skin bright yellow, purple on top; flesh creamy-yellow, fine-grained, sweet, firm, tender and crisp; stores well. Widely used for home gardens, local market and shipping. Traditional North American cultivar; introduced prior to 1888. A25, B75M, D76, D82, D87, E57, F12, G51, *G83M*, J34, K49M, K71, M46, N16, N39, etc.

Best of All: 90 days. Medium-sized, globe-shaped root with a purple top; to 6 inches in diameter when well grown; flesh creamy-yellow, tender and mild; stores well. Very hardy; will stand in the ground all winter in milder climates. A home garden gourmet cultivar from England. Introduced in 1896. L89, *R23*

Canadian Gem: 120 days. Flesh light-yellow, firm, vary fine-grained and sweet; flavor very good. Extremely hardy; a very good winter keeper in storage. Excellent for fall and winter use in the North. A16, K49M

Champion Purple Top: 90 days. Good quality roots that are improved by frost. Rose-colored skin; yellow flesh. Cooks to a pleasing rich color and flavor. Long keeping. Reliable and widely grown. L91M, P1G, *R23*

Fortune: (Fortune Certified) Similar to York in yields, with a wider tolerance to 6 strains of club root and a good tolerance to storage rot. Appearance, size and color similar to Laurentian or York. Good appearance and table quality. Bred at the Canada Research Station at Mount Pearl. E38, L42

Gaze's Special Purple Top: Has proven to be a very high yielder. Superb table quality with a very mild flavor. Very good keeping qualities; stands up in storage better than Laurentian. Should not be planted too early as the roots can become overly large. E38

Gilfeather: (Gilfeather Turnip) 80 days. Top-shaped, creamy white root; unusually mild, delicate, sweet flavor; smooth in texture when cooked. Can be harvested at 2 1/2 inches in diameter, but will grow much larger without becoming pithy or strong-flavored. Smooth, dark-green leaves make excellent kale-like "greens" when young. Vermont heirloom developed by John Gilfeather (1865-1944) of Wardsboro, Vermont. Possibly a hybrid of turnip and rutabaga. D41M, L91M, M46

Improved Long Island: 90 days. Large, spherical root, purplish-red above ground, light yellow below; taproot small. Flesh yellow, fine-grained, firm, crisp, mild and sweet. K50

Improved Purple Top Yellow: (Burpee's Improved Purple Top Yellow) 90 days. Large, slightly oblong, short-necked, purple top yellow type; free of branching and coarseness of neck. Flesh yellow, solid, sweet and rich; keeps well when mature. Hardy and very productive. For table, stock, storage and shipping. Introduced by Burpee in 1883. C44, G57M, M95M

Laurentian: (Laurentian Purple Top, Laurentian Golden) 105 days. Uniform, nearly globe-shaped, almost neckless roots; 5 to 6 inches in diameter; free of branching; skin creamy-yellow, deep purple on top; flesh pale-yellow, texture fine, flavor mild; keeps well. Moderately short tops. Quality very good for table use; also used for storage, shipping and canning. Most popular rutabaga in North America. A16, C85M, D11M, E24, E38, F1, *F72*, G6, G64, H42, *H61*, J7, K73, L79, M13M, etc.

Macomber: (Sweet German) 88 days. Large, round, almost neckless root; 5 to 6 inches in diameter, weighing up to 5 pounds; skin smooth, white with a greenish-purple top; flesh white, fine-grained, crisp, firm, and mild. Will keep in fine condition all winter in storage. G57M

Marian: 76 days. Uniform, globe-shaped, purple-topped root; up to 8 inches in diameter; flesh yellow, of fine flavor, retains its color when cooked; keeps well. Highly resistant to clubroot, mildew, and root cracking. Vigorous, very productive plant; has shorter, wider leaves that allow for closer spacing. Introduced by the Welsh Plant Breeding Station. L89, P83M, *R23*, S55, S61, *S75M*

Pike: 100 days. A purple top rutabaga similar to Laurentian. Flavorful yellow flesh. The larger tops give better protection to the roots from heavy frost. Can be left in the ground a little later in the fall. Storage quality equal to Laurentian. A local Maine favorite. G6

Purple Top Yellow: 90 days. An old, long-cultivated type, from which, most of the improved yellow-fleshed cultivars have originated. Form regularly egg-shaped, smooth, but with a few small roots at its base; neck short; size large, 4 or 5 inches at its largest diameter; skin purple above ground, yellow below; flesh yellow, firm, of good quality, turns orange when cooked. Very hardy; yields abundantly in rich, deep soils. BURR; B75, H49, H94, I39

Superlative: Large, purple-topped root with a short neck; fine-grained flesh. Heavy yielding. Can be left in the ground even after maturity. Sow in summer and autumn. T1M

Wilhelmsburger Gelbe: (Pandur) 85 days. Very early, very cold-hardy, fiberless cultivar with an attractive pink top and an excellent, mild flavor. Good size. Perfect for short season areas. Has the ability to store in a cool place for several months. L91M, N81

Wilhelmsburger Green Top: Green-topped root; flesh pale orange. Of fine table quality but also used for feeding stock. Keeps well. Has extremely high resistance to club root, a reel boon to farmers who are troubled with this disease. Popular in Atlantic Canada. E38, *R23*

York: (York Certified) Similar to Laurentian but has resistance to some strains of club root. Produces smooth, uniform roots with fine quality yellow flesh and excellent storage capabilities. Selected from Laurentian by the Charlottetown Research Station, Prince Edward Island, Canada. E38, F1, G64, L42, M49

SALAD MIXES {S}

VARIOUS GENERA

Popular in France, where they are called *mesclun* (mesclun and melange are both French words that mean mixture or miscellany), these seed mixes are carefully chosen so that the individual components have generally similar growth rates when planted together. The plants chosen for the mix also complement one another when harvested and form an attractive and tasty salad.

Chef's Delight: A formula blend of Leaf, Butterhead and Romaine types in many shades of dark green, red and light green. Makes delightful, multi-colored salads. K10

Cutting Lettuce: A mixture which combines attractive leaves, looseleaf habit and vigorous regrowth after cutting to give the best possible base for salads. Suitable for cut-and-come again or once over harvesting. As a salad base, about 10 feet or so a week will be required. C53

Fedco Mesclun: Contains a mixture of Mizu-na, Brussels Winter chervil, corn salad, Nina endive, sorrel, Giant Red mustard, arugula, and the following lettuces: Rouge d'Hiver, Red Sails, Red Oak Leaf, Salad Bowl, Green Ice and Black Seeded Simpson. D68

Garnish Mix: A mix for small gardens that makes it possible to add a touch of both beauty and taste to soups, dips, and entrees, without having to maintain a bed of garnishes. Contains Bronze fennel, green fennel, Dukat dill, cutting celery, Catalogno flatleaf parsley, and Bravour curly parsley. C53

Mesclun: A mixture of up to 11 different greens, usually including French lettuces, curled endive, arugula, corn salad, spinach, chervil, cress and chicory. Best harvested when very young. Traditionally gathered by pulling up whole plants. Ideal for broadcast seeding in wide-row and raised bed plantings. G68, J66M, Q34

Mesclun Nicoise: A mixture of endive, chicory, dandelion, upland cress and arugula. It requires a little more attention, but is a must for those who like their salads tart. Best crops will be produced during cool weather. C53

Mesclun Provencal: A traditional French mix popular in Provence, which combines chervil, arugula, Feuille de Chene lettuce and Fine Curled Louviers endive in precise proportion for best effect. Good for the home garden or a balcony planter. C53, F33

Mild Mix: A combination of mellow-flavored, heat tolerant greens that will provide a range of rare greens for salad making right through the hot weather. The early growth is dominated by Mizu-na; as the Mizu-na is cut, an understory of succulent, Golden purslane, Red orach, Brussels Winter chervil, and 3 cultivars of nutty mache begin to take their place. Keep the mixture cut and watered. C53

Misticanza: (Misticanze, Saladisi) An Italian mixture of common and lesser known loose-leaved salad plants, including lettuces, chicories, endives, and water cress, blended in precise proportions. As one variety finishes another appears. Ready for use when the leaves are approximately 5 inches long. For an extra spicy flavor, add arugula and upland cress to the mixture. And for even more variety, add purslane and mache. B8, C53, L91M, P83M, S55

Napa Valley Lettuces: A custom formula blend containing Bibb, Little Gem Romaine, green Oakleaf, Rouge d'Hiver, red Romaine, Red Oakleaf and Rosy Crisphead. Plus Elodie endive for extra texture. K66

Nouvelle Cuisine: A mixture of cut-and-come again greens for complementing standard lettuces. Plant and harvest a ready made salad. Good for gardeners with limited space. Long a tradition in fine French cooking, and becoming a popular trend at better restaurants. B49

Overwintering Mix: Contains a mixture of four or more cultivars for delightful spring salads. Should be sown in mid to late September for a harvest early the following spring. F42

Piquant Salad Greens: A custom formula blend containing peppery sharp arugula, tart-sweet nutty Mizu-na, tangy smooth Giant Red mustard and spicy Curly Cress. Contains enough seed to plant a 3-foot-square area 2 or 3 times. K66

Spring Mix: Contains a mixture of more than five cultivars, including looseleaf and butterhead types. Should be sown February through April for a late spring and early summer harvest. F42

Summer Mix: Contains a mixture of five or more cultivars of both looseleaf and butterhead types. Should be sown April through July for a harvest in late summer and fall. F42

Super Gourmet Blend: A blend of five looseleaf types (Slobolt, Buttercrunch, Red Sails, Salad Bowl and Valmaine) in equal quantities. Even as seedlings, their appearance is quite different and they can be easily thinned to equal proportions in the row. L89

Tangy Mix: Combines flavorful and colorful Japanese mustards with the piquancy of Arugula, the clear peppery flavor of Broad Leaved cress, and the tangy beauty of a range of red and green chicories. Good for livening up a salad of milder greens, or served on its own with a creamy dressing. Best adapted to cool weather, but can be kept going into the dog days of summer by frequent planting and prompt, once-over harvest. Shade and water also help. C53

SHIITAKE {SN}

LENTINUS EDODES

COLD WEATHER

These strains require cool or cold temperatures to fruit; with many, fruiting is arrested or aborted at high temperatures. Mushroom quality is very high due to cool fruiting temperatures. Fastest vegetative growth is near 77^0 F., but growth continues at colder temperatures. They have their highest yield after the second year and logs will produce heavily for four or more years.

#855: Greenhouse or outdoor strain. Vigorous mycelium for good growth. Fruits during 3 seasons (October to June), not in summer, with large flushes at one time. Produces especially well during changes in weather - November, December, January and May. Fruiting temperature 41^0 to 68^0 F. A good strain for drying. I3

#858: Greenhouse or outdoor strain. Fast spawn growth, with first flush within 1 year of inoculation. Fruiting initiated at 50^0 to 59^0 F. After a flush rest logs for 20 days before the next soaking. Best flushes result when logs dry out between flushes. Optimum fruiting temperatures 47^0 to 68^0 F. I3

3 Go: Large-capped, thick and firmly fleshed, this strain is excellent for dry market use. Superior *donko* and *koko* will be harvested. Flushing may occur even during the first winter after inoculation, but after the stimulation of a cold wave, all should flush. Rest logs 50 to 60 days. Optimum fruiting temperatures 59^0 to 64^0 F. E2

4055: Can be grown on a variety of media, including natural or sawdust logs and sterilized straw. Generally, cropping air temperatures range from 50^0 F. to 68^0 F. and relative humidities from 90% to 100%. On natural logs, yield varies from 1 to 2 pounds of mushrooms per log per year for a 3 to 5 year period. *A41*

7 Go: Produces large, uniform bright caps for fresh market use. Rapid-colonizer, expect flushing in autumn of the year of inoculation. A long-time-span fruiting strain; flushes recur from early September until spring (about May) with every rain; largest fruitings occur in fall. Cannot be forced and is not suitable for indoor production. E2

Chuba: Good for dry market use in producing *koko* and *koshin*. Very strong strain; vigorous and aggressive in the spawn run. Growth is relatively rapid; first fruiting is fast; production is large. For fresh market use Chuba's concentrated flushing pattern makes it suitable for growing indoors from November to April. Optimum fruiting temperatures 55^0 to 59^0 F. E2

CS-11: Robust, thick-fleshed caps with a heavy white fringe and short, stout stems, often *Donko* grade. Has a spawn run of 16 to 20 months. A rapid colonizer, growing well at low temperatures. Logs can be fruited 3 times each cool season, will continue to fruit for 4 or more years. Optimum fruiting temperatures 45^0 to 60^0 F. I49

CS-16: Robust, dense, thick-fleshed caps with heavy white fringe, often *Donko* grade. A rapid colonizer, with a spawn run of 16 to 20 months. Fruiting can be induced twice with only a 20 to 40 day resting period between times. Logs will produce for 4 or more years. Optimum fruiting temperatures 45^0 to 64^0 F. I49

CS-118: Medium, thick-fleshed cap with dense white fringe retains in-curved margin longer than other strains. An aggressive, rapid colonizer, has a spawn run of 6 to 12 months. Two or three fruitings can be induced in rapid succession. Logs will produce for at least 3 years. Optimum fruiting temperatures 45^0 to 68^0 F. I49

CW-25: Produces a smooth, medium thick-fleshed, flat-capped mushroom with a lacy ornamentation on rim. Time to first fruiting 12 months. Natural outdoor fruiting season early to late spring, and mid to late fall. Indoor fruiting season fall through early summer. Optimum fruiting temperatures 47^0 to 68^0 F. D75M

Early Winter-Spring: Excellent for the dried market and for larger-sized mushrooms. A precocious strain; expect fruiting after the first summer, after inoculation in fully colonized logs. For the fresh market, use from winter to spring in the fruiting room. The caps do not readily turn up. E2

Ohba: Large-sized, very uniform, thick and primely fleshed mushrooms of good-quality. Brightly colored caps. For dried market use, lower temperatures produce the better quality *donko* and *koko*, while higher temperatures and humidity produce the desirable, uniform, superior *koshin*. Rest logs 45 to 50 days. Optimum fruiting temperatures 59^0 to 64^0 F. E2

RA-32-E: Produces a thick-fleshed mushroom that is honey to dark-brown in color with a very fine velvety bloom on caps. Time to first fruiting 18 months. Natural outdoor fruiting season early to late spring, and mid to late fall. Indoor fruiting season late fall and early spring. Optimum fruiting temperatures 45^0 to 70^0 F. Developed by the Forest Products Laboratory in Madison, Wisconsin. D75M

Snowcap: Produces a large, thick, uniform mushroom brushed with a white tufted veil remnant. Good for seasonal outdoor production. Time to first fruiting 12 months. This strain has a long natural fruiting season with most abundant production occurring in spring and fall. Optimum fruiting temperatures 45^0 to 77^0 F. D75M

Three Aromas: Will fruit prolifically from October through June. It can be forced in November, January, and May when forcing other strains is difficult. Will not fruit in July, August, or September. Flushes are large and can be flushed consecutively. Preferred at the dry market for its solidness and quality. E2

Twice Flowering: Produces a medium to thick-fleshed mushroom that is tan pink to pale brown in color with a dry cap. FLushes are large with few straggling pins. Excellent for early and late season production. Time to first fruiting 6 to 12 months. Natural outdoor fruiting season early to mid spring and late fall. Indoor fruiting season early fall to late spring. Optimum fruiting temperatures 41^0 to 65^0 F. D75M

WARM WEATHER

These strains produce good quality mushrooms at high fruiting temperatures. They are well adapted to fruiting in warm, moist areas from the spring until the late fall when periodic rains or irrigation induce fruiting. Maximum growth during the spawn run is near 77° F., but growth is good at higher temperatures.

#512: Outdoor strain. Produces large mushrooms with medium-thick flesh. Begins fruiting 6 to 12 months after inoculation. A good producer. Optimum fruiting temperatures 50° to 77° F. I3

#852: Greenhouse only strain. Fruits faster than any other strain. Has a fast spawn run that prevents the growth of unwanted contaminants. Sensitive to overwatering, the fruiting area should be well ventilated and less humid. Fruits easiest in hot weather. Optimum fruiting temperatures 50° to 86° F. I3

#853: Greenhouse or outdoor strain. Produces the largest mushrooms with the thickest flesh. Highly productive, even old logs produce large mushrooms. Most strains stop growing at 89° to 93° F., but #853 can grow at temperatures up to 95° F., enduring high summer heat. Slowest to fruit but has the longest production life by 20 to 40%. I3

4 Go: Very prolific strain that produces medium to large mushrooms. Requires a longer incubation period. The second summer after inoculation, fruiting can be forced by soaking, shocking, and re-stacking. Logs with a higher moisture content are recommended for this strain and misting may be required during dry spells. Use thinner logs for indoor production. Rest logs 35 to 40 days. E2

CS-24: Robust, thick-fleshed caps with a thick white fringe; stems thick and well proportioned. An aggressive, rapid colonizer, has a spawn run of 8 to 12 months. Fruitings can be forced 2 or 3 times with a 20 to 40 day resting period or fruitings can be evenly spaced throughout the year. Three to four years of production can be expected. Optimum fruiting temperatures 60° to 72° F., with a maximum of 81° F. I49

CS-125: Medium to thick-fleshed mushrooms with a moderate white fringe are produced at high temperatures. Thin to medium stems. An aggressive, rapid colonizer, with a spawn run of 6 to 12 months. Three fruitings in rapid succession can be achieved if logs are rested the remainder of the year. Optimum fruiting temperatures 50° to 68° F., with a maximum of 86° F. Optimum relative humidity low, 60% to 75%. I49

S-1: Popular, easy to grow strain. Fruits best from mid-May through November. Suitable for greenhouse production in winter. Four to six months from inoculation to first harvest. D40

Sleeping Spring: Produces a thick-fleshed, chocolate brown mushroom of high quality for summer fruit. Has a rapid spawn run, with first fruiting occurring in 14 months. Natural outdoor fruiting season summer through mid fall. Indoor fruiting season late fall through early spring. Optimum fruiting temperatures 50° to 77° F. D75M

V-3: A fast spawn run and early, heavy production characterize this strain. Time to first fruiting 6 months. Optimum fruiting temperatures 50° to 80° F. From the 1986-1987 Ohio Shiitake Project. D63, D75M

WW-44: Produces a thick-fleshed mushroom with lacy ornamentation on cap skirt. Has consistently high quality production during its fruiting season. Time to first fruiting 14 months. Natural outdoor fruiting season summer through mid fall. Indoor fruiting season late fall through early spring. Optimum fruiting temperatures 50° to 77° F. D75M

WW-70: Primarily an outdoor strain. Produces a medium-sized and medium-fleshed, bright brown mushroom. Responds particularly well to soaking in summer months. Time to first fruiting 14 months. Natural outdoor fruiting season mid spring through mid fall. Indoor fruiting season late fall through early spring. Optimum fruiting temperatures 50° to 77° F. D75M

WIDE RANGE

These strains produce mushrooms under a wide range of temperatures and are easily induced to fruit by soaking following a dry period. They are particularly well suited to forced fruiting and can be produced year-round under controlled conditions. Under natural conditions they fruit during the late spring and early autumn. Growth during the spawn run is fastest at 77° F. but higher temperatures can be tolerated.

#510: Greenhouse or outdoor strain. Produces large mushrooms with thick flesh. An early strain that is tolerant to cool weather at higher elevations. Has one of the fastest spawn runs, fruiting 4 1/2 to 5 months after inoculation. First flush is initiated by soaking right after spawn run. After a flush rest the logs for 20 days before next soaking. Optimum fruiting temperatures 50° to 75° F. I3

5 Go: Yields firm-fleshed mushrooms of medium size with bright caps, highly regarded at the marketplace. The vitality of this spawn is good, but spawn run may take up to 2 years. If logs are sprayed and moisture is maintained before soaking, quality and uniformity increase. Rest logs 30 to 35 days. Optimum fruiting temperatures 61° to 72° F. E2

6 Go: A long-time-span fruiting strain, fruiting from late September until the following spring (about May), with every rain. Autumn fruitings are large *koshin* and are suited for dry use. Spring fruitings are medium-sized *koshin* and are very uniform, with good quality. Also an excellent strain for fresh market use with solid flesh, thin stems and uniform caps. Cannot be forced and is not suitable for indoor culture. E2

CS-15: Thick caps with heavy white fringe; thick stems in good proportion to cap. An aggressive, rapid colonizer, has a spawn run of 8 to 12 months. Tolerant to low log moisture content. Often produces mushrooms in clumps. Highest yields are achieved if 3 or 4 fruitings are spaced evenly throughout the year. Three or four years of production can be expected. Optimum fruiting temperatures 50° to 64° F., but will tolerate higher temperatures. I49

CS-41: Medium-thick to thick caps with minimal white fringe. An aggressive, rapid colonizer, has a spawn run of 6 to 12 months. Four fruitings can be evenly spaced throughout the year. Three years of intensive fruiting can be expected. Optimum fruiting temperatures 50° to 64° F., with a maximum of 77° F. Optimum relative humidity low, 60% to 75%. I49

Early Flush: Similar to Early Willamette, but produces smaller mushrooms. Ideal size for 4-ounce prepacks. On sawdust substrates, it does not become brown as fast as Early Willamette. I7

Early Willamette: Produces large mushrooms with a thick cap. An early flush may be expected within 6 to 8 months after inoculation of oak logs outdoors. Suitable also for greenhouse or indoor cultivation. Also ideal for sawdust block cultivation. Has a wide temperature range for fruiting, 50° to 75° F. I7

Hayade 5 Go: Compared to existing early fruiting strains, Hayade 5 Go has very uniform fruitbodies. Even when using plugs, logs inoculated in spring may bear fruit by autumn. By next mid-May to early June, expect the first major fruiting, with forced flushing every 30 to 35 days thereafter. Suitable for year-round production indoors. Optimum fruiting temperatures 61° to 72° F. E2

New Lightning: Fruitbody somewhat smaller than New Sun, with flesh that is slightly softer. Due to its higher moisture content, it is recommended that the fruiting room be kept on the dry side, with good air circulation, for the best product. Fruits up to 3 to 5 months earlier than other strains and produces large volumes. Easy to fruit even during the warmer months of summer. E2

New Sun: Large, high-quality mushrooms with solid, thick flesh. Spawn run is very fast and colonization is early. Compared with other strains New Sun produces an earlier harvest with faster returns. Fruits easily when other strains are difficult to fruit, especially after the natural spring and autumn flushes. E2

Ohzora: Has the largest and thickest flesh of all wide-range strains, even with older logs large mushrooms will be produced. High yielding, 20 to 40% more volume from the life of the log can be expected. Usually shiitake stops growing at 89 to 93^0 F., however Ohzora continues to grow, even at temperatures as high as 95^0 F. During hot dry spells, Ohzora is more tolerant of heat than other strains. E2

West Wind: Very fast spawn run and consistency in yield and mushroom quality make this strain ideal for indoor production. Abundant flushing occurs outdoors when forced or spontaneously with rain and temperate change. A very easy strain to fruit. Time to first fruiting 6 months. Natural outdoor fruiting season mid spring through mid fall. Optimum fruiting temperatures 50^0 to 80^0 F. D75M

WR-46: Fast spawn run and relative ease of fruiting characterize this strain, making it an ideal choice for both indoor and outdoor cultivation. Produces thin-fleshed, honey colored mushrooms during the summer and a thick-capped, bright brown mushroom when temperatures are cooler. Time to first fruiting 6 months. Natural outdoor fruiting period mid spring to mid fall. Indoor fruiting year round. Optimum fruiting temperatures 50^0 to 75^0 F. D75M

SOYBEAN {S}

GLYCINE MAX

FIELD SOYBEANS

Used as dried beans for cooking, flour, *soymilk*, *tofu*, *soy sauce*, *miso*, *tempeh*, etc. They require a longer growing season than Vegetable soybeans, and need to ripen and dry before harvest.

BLACK-SKINNED {PR} For use as dried beans, black soybeans are sweeter, tastier and more versatile than the yellow type. Their rich distinctive flavor can be appreciated alone, or in mixed vegetable dishes. In Korea, they are combined with adzuki beans, glutinous rice, sorghum and millet to form *Five-Grain Rice* (*ogopap*). The pods can be left on the plant to dry, for unlike many cultivars, they don't shatter as the plants begin to yellow. COST 1988, HALPIN; D26M, E56, H91, *K74*, *L14M*

Black Jet: 104 days. Early maturing black soybean developed by Johnny's Selected Seeds for short season areas. The 2 foot tall plants are prolific yielders of medium-sized, jet black soybeans. The beans are thin-skinned, with good flavor and cook more quickly than other black types. G6, I99, K17M, K49T

Hokkaido Black: 100 days. Large, black seed. Good for tofu and soymilk; excellent for baked beans, refried beans and chili if pressure cooked. Somewhat susceptible to shattering. Originally from Japan. **T76, U33**

Kuromane: Large black soybean. Popular in Japan because it's more easily digested than yellow soybeans. Yields fresh green shell beans in 95 days, dry beans in 120 days. K49T

Panther: 120 days. A highly regarded full-season black soybean introduced by Johnny's Selected Seeds. Large, dull-black beans with a very sweet, rich flavor, probably the finest of the dry soybean cultivars. Matures mid to late September from an early June planting. High yielding. G6

YELLOW-SKINNED

Chico: 90-100 days. An excellent cultivar for making tofu and for sprouting. Nice, clear white hilum. High in protein. Recommended for planting in all regions except the extreme North. Developed by the University of Minnesota. M46, M46{SP}

Easycook: 125 days. Straw yellow seeds with a brown hilum; 2 to 3 seeds per pod. Oil content 19.3%. Has been found to cook fully as soft as navy beans in less time after a preliminary soaking of 12 hours. Stout, erect plant. Maturity group VI. Introduced from Shandong Province, China in 1894. PIPER; **U56**

Maple Amber: 106 days. Medium-sized yellow beans with brown hilum. Brown pods with brown pubescence. Matures just before Maple Arrow. Requires 2450 heat units. High yielding plant, grows 28 to 32 inches tall. Well adapted to central Quebec. Developed at Agriculture Canada Plant Research Centre, Ottawa. *G50*

Maple Arrow: 113 days. Very popular early yellow soybean developed in Canada. Grows 30 inches tall. Produces large crops of medium-sized pods containing 2 to 3 beans each. Bright yellow, medium-sized beans have a brown hilum. Very high protein content; rich flavor. Good for processed soy products such as tofu and tempeh. Dependable in short season areas. *G50*, I93M, M46

Maple Donovan: 119 days. Outyields many other cultivars and matures early. Has shown tolerance to unfavorable harvest conditions. Protein content similar to that of Maple Arrow. Easy to distinguish in the field by its wrinkled leaf edges. Developed at Agriculture Canada Plant Research Centre, Ottawa. *G50*, I93M

Maple Glen: 116 days. Medium-sized bean with a yellow hilum. Combines early maturity with a significantly higher yield than other early maturing cultivars. Resistant to powdery mildew, has good tolerance to phytophthora root rot, and has better lodging resistance than Maple Arrow. Developed at Agriculture Canada Plant Research Centre, Ottawa. *G50*, I93M

Maple Ridge: An excellent soybean for processing into tofu or soymilk. A good yielder. Developed at Agriculture Canada Plant Research Centre, Ottawa. K17M

VEGETABLE SOYBEANS

Developed to be eaten in the fresh shell stage, green-seeded vegetable soybeans have a delicious, buttery flavor and a firm but tender texture. In Japan, they are cooked in the pod, popped into the mouth as needed, and served along with beer or sushi to form the summer snack called *edemame*. They are better adapted to northern growing conditions than limas, have more protein, and are higher yielding. HALPIN; B73M, E97, G51, H91{PR}, J34, L59

Agate: 90 days. An early maturing heirloom cultivar, originally introduced from Sapporo, Japan in 1929 by P.H. Dorsett and W.J. Morse. Small, attractive beans are dark-brown blending into greenish-tan at the outer edge. Usually used as a vegetable soybean. Small, determinate plant; height 28 inches; daylength neutral. I99, K49T

Butterbeans: 90 days. Sweet, buttery, bright-green beans are delicious cooked fresh and excellent for freezing. A good percentage of pods contain 3 large beans which are relatively easy to shell. Stocky 2 to 2 1/2 foot tall plants; well-branched and resistant to lodging; produce a prolific crop of pods. Widely adapted. Developed by Johnny's Selected Seeds. E24, G6, L7M

Envy: 75 days. A popular, well-established short season type. Reaches its prime picking stage considerably ahead of lima beans. Bright green beans have the delicious flavor characteristic of the green-seeded cultivars. For fresh shelling or drying. Upright, 2 foot tall plants are heavy yielding. Developed by Professor E.M. Meader at the University of New Hampshire. A2, E24, G6{CF}, J20

Extra Early: 70 days. An early, high-yielding cultivar suitable for short season areas such as southern Canada and the northern United States. Relatively recent release. J7

Fiskeby V: 68 days. Exceptionally hardy and early maturing, will produce a crop as far north as southern Canada. Produces mostly 3 small, light-yellow beans per pod. Contains 39 to 40 percent protein and is very low in the antitrypsin factor that interferes with the digestion of uncooked soy protein. Developed over a 40 year period in Sweden by Sven Holmberg. HALPIN; A2, K20, K49M, L42, N84, P83M, S27, S55

Hahto: 130 days. Large, olive-yellow, flattened seeds; hilum black; 2 to 3 seeds per pod. Oil content 17.9%. Excellent as a green shell bean. Dry seeds need no more preparation than the kidney bean as they cook up very readily. Stout, erect, bushy plant. Maturity group VI. Introduced from Wakamatsu, Japan in 1915. PIPER; **U56**

Hakucho Early: 75 days. A very early cultivar from Japan. Pods uniformly large, about 2 1/2 inches long, bright green; 3 to 4 small, yellow-green beans per pod. Can be cooked as green shelled beans or dried like lima beans. Dwarf plant, only 12 to 14 inches tall; produces a densely concentrated pod set. Very reliable, even for short season areas. Not sensitive to short day-length. *A1*, C85M, E59, *K16M*, *P39*, *S63M*

Kanrich: 82 days. Medium to large, yellowish-green beans, 3 beans to a pod; mild in flavor. Suitable as a green shell bean or for drying. High-yielding plant, produces about 50 pods; resistant to shattering. Best suited to the South and to areas as far north as southern Pennsylvania, where it is green-bean ripe in about 82 days. HALPIN; <u>I97</u>{PR}, **U56**

Okuhara Early Green: 70 days. Medium-sized, yellow-green beans, tender and flavorful. White pubescence. White flowers. Early and prolific. Recommended for home gardens and fresh markets. Very popular in Japan. *S63M*

Prize: 85 days. Erect, bushy plants produce large clusters of pods, each pod containing 2 to 4 beans. Large, oval, plump bright-green beans are good for fresh use, canning, or freezing. Mature dried beans are yellow, nearly round; excellent for winter use, suitable for sprouts. Widely adapted; does well as far south as Florida. B75, C92, D68, D76, F19M, G27M, G57M, G71, H33, I39, I77, J97M, <u>*L14M*</u>{PR}, M95M

White Lion: 70 days. Slightly curved, bright-green pods with white pubescence; contain mostly 3 plump beans of good quality. Vigorous plant, height about 30 inches; produces large clusters of pods. Very popular in Japan. Highly recommended both for fresh market and home gardens. E59, *S63M*

SPINACH {S}

SPINACIA OLERACEA

SMOOTH-LEAVED

A distinct type, mostly of Oriental origin, that is considered the best for salad use. The leaves are thin and tender, with long upright petioles that protect then from rain and make for easier harvesting. They have a sweeter flavor and being flat and smooth are easier to clean.

<u>HYBRID</u>

Benton #2: 45 days. Smooth, thick, broad leaves with a long petiole that makes for easy picking. Upright, bushy growth habit. Very versatile and hardy, showing tolerance to downy mildew and virus. Semi-heat tolerant. M46

Fanfare: Upright, smooth, semi-pointed and cut leaf type. Rapid grower, matures early. Tolerant to heat; not late bolting. Can be sown all year round. Widely adapted. Resistant to downy mildew Race-1, anthracnose and damping off. Round-seeded. Q88

G-One: Broad, smooth, thick and round leaves. Slow bolting, ripens medium early. Heavy yielding. Resistant to downy mildew Race-1 and Race-3; tolerant to damping-off and heat. Good for spring, summer and early autumn harvest. Round-seeded. Q88

Joy-One: Widely adapted late bolting cultivar with upright, long-petioled, semi-savoy leaves. Ripens medium early, extra slow bolting. A very heavy yielder. Resistant to downy mildew Race-1 and Race-2. Good for spring and summer harvests. Round-seeded. Q88

Orient: 45 days. A very vigorous cultivar. Leaves are smooth, dark green, upright-growing and have long petioles. Heat tolerant. Resistant to diseases. L59

Popeye: Smooth, broad, dark-green leaves on long petioles. Tall, upright growth habit. Extra early ripening and mildew resistant. Round-seeded. *O53*, *Q28*

Sputnik: Smooth, dark-green leaves; well proportioned between stalks and leaves. Slow bolting for long harvest possibilities. Resistant to physios 1, 2 and 3 of mildew. Recommended for plantings throughout the spinach production season. K50

<u>OPEN-POLLINATED</u>

Grand Light: 30 days. Upright-growing Oriental type spinach. Smooth, dark-green leaves on long petioles. Excellent for salads, soups or stir-fried dishes. A quick and hardy grower. Easy to grow in fall or spring. A long time favorite in Japan. Prickly-seeded. D55

Münsterlander: 55 days. Smooth, arrow-shaped, narrow leaves; thin and tender. A very old German cultivar popular in the Far East where it resembles the endemic cultivars, except it is slower to run to seed and is more or less resistant to hot or cold temperatures. Prickly-seeded. J73, *P39*, R47

Sohshu: (Early Autumn) 40 days. Smooth, dark-green, long-petioled leaves; thin and tender. Tall, upright-growing plant; tolerant of summer heat. One of the most rapid growing of the Oriental cultivars. Best sown between May and October. Planting later than October should be avoided in temperate zones. J73, *P39*

Summer Green: 25-30 days. Thick, dark green, serrated leaves with long erect-growing petioles. A very quick and sturdy grower from mid-summer to mid-winter, under short-day conditions. Sow seed at regular intervals beginning in early summer for a continuous supply. Q34

Tohko: (Tung-Hu) 55 days. Smooth, arrow-shaped leaves with long, medium-green petioles. The long petioles are convenient for harvesting and bunching. Upright plant; has considerable resistance to cold; also grows rapidly in hot weather. Good for interval sowings during the summer and late fall. Prickly seeded. Introduced into Japan from Tsinan, North China. *P39*

Ujo: 45 days. Smooth, medium-green, long-petioled leaves; thin and tender; quality high, with excellent flavor; matures early. Tall, upright-growing plant; resistant to hot weather. Best sown in late summer for a fall and winter crop. Can also be used in early spring. Prickly-seeded. J73

SAVOY-LEAVED

Better suited for cooking and processing than the smooth-leaved types. The leaves are broader and thicker and more bulk is retained after boiling or steaming. They are also much more difficult to clean due to the rough surface of the leaves.

HYBRID

Indian Summer: 39 days. Large, thick, medium-savoy, dark-green leaves have an excellent flavor. Darker green, more crinkled, and longer standing than Melody. Upright growth habit makes for easier harvesting and cleaner leaves. Tolerant to mosaic virus, blight and races 1 and 2 of downy mildew (blue mold). For spring, summer and fall crops. *A1*, C53, D68, G6, G64, *H61*, K49Z

Melody: 40 days. Semi-savoy type producing large, upright plants adapted for both spring and fall production. Leaves are thick, rounded, and deep-green in color. Popular for fresh market, freezing and canning. Bolt resistant. Vigorous plant growth results in higher than usual yields. Good resistance to cucumber mosaic virus, blight and downy mildew. All America Selections winner in 1977. A87M, B73M, C44, C85M, D82, F1, F19M, F44, G16, H42, *H61*, H94, H95, J7, K73, L79, etc.

St. Helens: A smooth-leaved, hardy over-wintering cultivar. May be planted late summer for fall harvest or late fall (September-October) to over-winter for early spring harvest. Has an erect growth habit and is very resistant to mildew. Medium-long standing type suitable for bunching or processing. Resistant to downy mildew. Introduced in 1981. L97, N52

Tyee: 42 days. Dark-green, semi-savoy leaves. Very upright growth habit. Resists bolting under high temperatures and long day conditions. Compared to Indian Summer, Tyee is darker green, even more upright in growth, and stands over a week longer in hot weather. Good for spring, summer and fall crops, and for overwintering. Tolerant to downy mildew races 1 and 3. A13, A87M, B75, B75M, D11M, E57, F19M, F82, G6, *H61*, H94, K71, K73, L89, M49, etc.

OPEN-POLLINATED

America: 43 days. Very thick, well-crinkled, glossy dark green leaves. Taste trials show America to have a milder fresh taste than other cultivars, but superior taste when stir-fried. Grows 6 to 8 inches high, 10 to 12 inches in width. Intermediate in bolt resistance. Can be used in spring or fall, but is not suited for over-wintering. All America Selections winner in 1952. A16, A69M, *A75*, B75M, C44, D11M, E97, F24M, G64, G71, I99, K71, L7M, L42, L97, etc.

Bloomsdale Long Standing: (Bloomsdale Savoy) 43 days. Thick-textured, heavy, dark-green, fully savoy leaves. Uniform, compact plants, dependable and heavy bearing; heat tolerant. Erect plants remain in the rosette stage for a long time without bolting. Recommended for home and market gardens. Also a popular commercial cultivar, being shipped extensively from the extreme South. Introduced in 1925. MAGRUDER 1938; *A75*, B75M, B78, D82, D87, E24, E57, G16, *H61*, H94, K73, L7M, L97, M13M, M46, etc.

Bouquet: 45 days. Leaves resemble Bloomsdale Long Standing, but are more savoy and dark green. Very good flavor. More tolerant of rain, cold and downy mildew than Winter Bloomsdale. Generally stays in good condition a week or two longer than other types. L97

Broad Leaved Prickly: (Standwell Broad Leaved Prickly) 40 days. A large-leaved, very hardy spinach which is extremely long standing. Short, thick stems with broad, deep-green, fleshy leaves that are produced over a long season. Does well in hot weather. Sow between mid-summer and the following early spring. B49, O53M, P83M, *R23*

Cold Resistant Savoy: 45 days. Dark-green, well-crinkled leaves. Good fresh flavor. May be used for late summer or fall harvests, as well as a wintered-over spinach for early spring cutting. Tolerant to heat, cold and blight. Slightly less resistance to bolting than Long Standing Bloomsdale. K49M, L7M, L42

Dixie Market: 38 days. Rounded, glossy dark-green leaves, thick and well crinkled. Upright, compact plant. More productive than other Bloomsdale types. Grown in fall and for winter production in the South. Resistant to downy mildew and mosaic, tolerant to spinach blight. For home gardens, fresh market and processing. D76, G79, *L59G*

Fall Green: (Improved Green Valley) 45 days. Developed by the University of Arkansas for superior disease tolerance. Highly tolerant of white rust, fusarium, anthracnose, blight, and cercospora. Produces deep green, savoy leaves. For fall production. *A1*, A87M, *C28*, J34

Giant Nobel: (Giant Thick Leaf) 45 days. Large, medium-green leaves, notably thick in texture, moderately crinkled. Cooks very tender, and is of excellent flavor. Highly recommended for canning. Vigorous, spreading plant, often 25 inches across; has a quantity of thick, succulent leaves in the center resembling a half developed head of lettuce. Very heavy yielding. Introduced in 1926. MAGRUDER 1938; A56, *A75*, B75M, C92, *D12*, D76, F24M, *G83M*, H66, H94, *I59M*, K10, K49M, K71, L97, etc.

Giant Viroflay: (Monstrueux de Viroflay) 43 days. Very broad, smooth, dark-green leaves; 10 inches long and 8 inches wide at the base. Large, vigorous-growing plants, often measuring 2 to nearly 2 1/2 feet in diameter. Early and quick-growing as a spring-sown crop, susceptible to bolting. When sown in autumn it yields a considerable crop in spring. An old French cultivar. Introduced prior to 1866. VILMORIN; *A75*, *D12*, F33, G68, K66, K71, *L59G*

Giant Winter: (Geant Hiver) 45 days. Large, smooth, semi-savoy, medium-green leaves. A special strain for late summer or fall seeding for a crop in early spring, also for normal seeding. Cold hardy, remains marketable past Christmas in mild-winter areas. A2, C85M, G68, K49M, *S75M*

Green Valley: 45 days. Semi-savoy type with a tendency to bolt when planted in spring. Best suited for an overwinter crop. The first fusarium-resistant cultivar to be released. Also resistant to white rust. Introduced by the University of Arkansas. A27M

King of Denmark: 45-55 days. Very thick, dark-green, arrow-shaped leaves, semi-savoy; of very good quality either raw or cooked. Very hardy and early maturing. A heavy yielder. Resistant to bolting, remaining in good condition 2 to 3 weeks longer than other cultivars before running to seed. Introduced in 1919. MAGRUDER 1938; A25, *A75*, D27, F92, G87, *I59M*, I67M, K20, K49M, L7M, L91M

Low Acid:[1] A round-leaved cultivar with very little oxalic acid content, and hence said to be the sweetest of all spinach leaves. Very high in vitamins A, C, and E. I99, K49T

Medania: (Mediana) 45 days. Smooth, broad, dark-green leaves; semi-savoy. Vigorous, erect plant. Heat and cold tolerant, stands up to chilly springs and hot dry summers. Winters over well. Can be planted in spring, late summer or fall. Especially bred to resist bolting, allowing for a much longer harvest. Resistant to blue mold races 1 and 3. D76, E97, H54, *H61*, L11, N52, P83M, S55, *S75M*

Monatol:[1] Distinctive and valuable type. Low in oxalic acid, which causes loss of calcium in the blood and locks up the iron contained in spinach. Very good flavor. U33

Monnopa:[1] 45 days. Unique spinach, with low oxalic acid (an agent that causes loss of calcium from the blood). Ideal for baby food. The oxalic acid is also related to the bitterness of spinach and so this cultivar is particularly mild-flavored. Light-green, crinkled leaves. Bolt resistant under reasonable conditions and winter hardy. L91M

Norfolk: 45-55 days. Small compact plants with small, well-crinkled leaves. An old Canadian cultivar from the 1880's. Sow seed in late spring or early summer. One of the hardiest spinaches; has the ability to tolerate -30^0 F. temperatures and still not succumb. D87

Northland: 40 days. Thick, very large, bright-green leaves; rounded at the edges; twice as long as they are broad; moderately crinkled. Borne on long, stout stalks, well above the ground, staying clean and free of dirt. Very early and very hardy. Productive. Blight and wilt resistant. Excellent for early spring plantings. F1

Savoy Supreme: 45 days. Dark glossy green, very crinkled leaves with a distinct lustre. Erect, vigorous plants; productive and long standing. Blue mold tolerant. For spring and early summer sowings. Introduced by the University of Wisconsin. Similar to America. A27M, *C28*, H54, K73

Sigmaleaf: (Suttons Sigmaleaf) 45 days. Moderately crinkled, medium-green leaves with an excellent flavor. Vigorous, erect plants. Can be sown in spring or autumn, and stands fit for use over a long period without running to seed. S45M, S61

Victoria: (Victoria Long Standing) An heirloom cultivar from England where it is one of the standard summer spinaches. Forms an abundance of thick, dark-green leaves, and rarely runs to seed. Good for succession plantings. GENDERS 1975; P83M

Virginia Savoy: (Virginia Blight Resistant Savoy) 40 days. Erect-growing plant with medium to long, rather thick petioles that hold the leaf-blades well above the soil. Leaf-blades dark green, oval-shaped, heavily crinkled. Very cold hardy and resistant to blight, recommended for planting in the fall or early winter where blight may be present. Introduced in 1921 by the Virginia Truck Experiment Station. MAGRUDER 1938; *C28*, C44, G79, *I59M*, J97M, K49M, L7M, M95M

Winter Bloomsdale: 45 days. Thick, dark-green, deeply-crinkled leaves. Long standing and slow growing, offering good production well into the season. Good for early summer production and over-wintering. Cold tolerant, takes temperature extremes better than many hybrids. Resistant to blight, cucumber mosaic virus and blue mold. *A1*, A2, A13, *C28*, D68, F44, F82, G79, G82, *H61*, H66, H94, K50, K73, L97, etc.

SPROUTING SEEDS {SP}

VARIOUS GENERA

Aduki Bean: (Chinese Red Bean) 2-4 days. Use jar method and grow out of direct sunlight; 1/2 cup of seed per quart jar. Soaking time 5 to 10 hours; rinse 3 to 5 times per day. Optimum temperature range 65 to 85^0 F. Best harvested when 1/2 to 1 1/2 inches long. Yields between 3 and 4 cups of sprouts per cup of seeds. *C14*, *F91*, *L14M*, L24, L59, M46, O48

Alaska Pea: (for sources see Pea, page 413)

Alfalfa: 4-7 days. The most popular sprouting seed and one of the easiest to grow. Use jar or tray method and grow out of direct sunlight; 2 1/2 tablespoons of seed per quart jar. Soaking time 8 hours; rinse 2 to 3 times per day. Optimum temperature range 60 to 85^0 F. Best harvested when 1 1/2 to 2 inches long. Should be placed near a window to turn green and develop chlorophyll. Excellent for salads, sandwiches and juicing. B73M, C69M, D3, E70M{PR}, F37T, *F91*, F97M, G16, G82, G91, I43T{PR}, I58, J20, J83T, L24, M63M, O48, etc.

Alfalfa (Dormant): Generally less vigorous and lower yielding than either non-dormant or semi-dormant alfalfas. *C14*

Alfalfa (Non-Dormant): Much more vigorous and higher yielding than either dormant or semi-dormant types. Will produce yields approximately 20% greater than those of dormant alfalfas. *C14*

Alfalfa (Semi-Dormant): Intermediate between dormant and non-dormant types. More vigorous than dormant alfalfas, but not as vigorous as totally dormant alfalfas. Yields are generally 15% greater than dormant types. *C14*

Amaranth: 1-2 days. Use jar method; 2 to 4 tablespoons of seeds per quart jar. Soaking time 12 hours; rinse twice daily. Best harvested when 1/4 inch long and 2 days old for use in salads. For use in baked goods seeds that have sprouted for just 24 hours are best. The sprouts have a flavor that is reminiscent of curry and fenugreek and are excellent in Indian-type dishes. COLE; C25M, I51M, *L14M*

Barley: 1-3 days. Use jar or bag method; 1 1/2 cups of seeds per quart jar. Soaking time 6 to 10 hours; rinse 2 to 3 times per day with cool water. Optimum temperature range 68 to 80^0 F. Best harvested when 0 to 1/4 inch long as soon as the first seeds sprout. Viable seed not readily available, hulled seed may be used even if no shoot appears. Freshly harvested seeds are essential for good results. Used in sprout breads and for barleygrass. B73M, D3, F97M, J83T, *L14M*, L24, O48

Buckwheat (Hulled): 5-6 days. Use jar method; 1/4 cup per quart jar. Soaking time 1 to 4 hours; rinse 2 to 3 times per day. Optimum temperature range 65 to 80^0 F. Place the jar in direct sunlight for a few hours to encourage the leaves to open and turn green. As the leaves open the sprouts should be eaten or placed in the refrigerator. Grows very well in combination with alfalfa seeds. G91, *L14M*

Buckwheat (Unhulled): 8-15 days. Use soil or tray method; about 2 1/2 cups for an 11 by 21 inch tray. Soaking time 8 to 14 hours; do not cover seeds with soil. Optimum temperature range 65 to 80^0 F. Mist the sprouting seeds once a day. Best harvested when 4 1/2 to 6 inches tall. Cut the stems about an inch above the soil. Yields succulent seedlings, called *buckwheat lettuce*, that are an excellent substitute for lettuce. B73M, C95, D3, D26M, F97M, G91, I20, K20, *L14M*, L24, O48

Cabbage: 3-5 days. Use jar or tray method and sprout in indirect sunlight; 3 tablespoons per quart jar. Soaking time 4 to 8 hours; rinse 2 to 3 times per day. Optimum temperature range 60 to 85^0 F. Best harvested when 1 to 1 1/2 inches long. "Green" near window during last day for best chlorophyll development. Sprouts have a pleasant taste, fresh and aromatic. Excellent with a steamed potato or in salads and sandwiches. K20

Chia: 5-10 days. Use clay method. Soak equal amounts of seeds and water in an unglazed clay flower pot saucer. Place in water up to 1/2 inch from the rim and cover with a plate. Do not rinse. Or use a decorative chia sprouter or *chia pet* and spread the mucilaginous seeds over the surface. Optimum temperature range 65 to 85^0 F. Best harvested when 1 to 1 1/2 inches long. "Green" near window during last day for best chlorophyll development. The spicy sprouts are good in salads or eaten as a snack. B7, *F91*, L24, *M15M*

Chico Soybean: (for sources see Soybean, page 482)

China Rose Radish: (for sources see Radish, page 461)

Chinese Cabbage: 4-6 days. Use jar or tray method; 3 tablespoons per quart jar. Soak for 3 to 6 hours; rinse 2 to 3 times per day. Optimum temperature range 65 to 85^0 F. Best harvested when 1 to 1

1/2 inches long. "Green" near window during last day for best chlorophyll development. Sprouts have a rich cabbage-like flavor and are excellent in salads. *C14*, *C28*, C69M, F37T, G16, G82, L24

Clover: 4-6 days. Use jar or tray method; 2 tablespoons per quart jar. Soaking time 3 to 6 hours; rinse 2 to 3 times per day. Optimum temperature range 60 to 85^0 F. Best harvested when 1 1/2 to 2 inches long. "Green" near window during last day for best chlorophyll development. Sprouts are sweet and juicy, similar to alfalfa sprouts but larger and more flavorful. (for sources see Trifolium spp., page 97)

Corn: 3-5 days. Use jar or bag method; 1 1/2 cups per quart jar. Soaking time 10 to 14 hours; rinse 2 to 3 times per day. Optimum temperature range 68 to 85^0 F. Harvest when 1/4 to 1/2 inch long. Sprouts have a somewhat strong flavor and chewy texture when eaten raw. Best in soups, casseroles and breads. Usually ground or blended with water before use. L24

Cowpea: (Black Eye Pea) 2-4 days. Use jar method; 3/4 cup of seeds per quart jar. Soaking time 8 to 12 hours; rinse 3 to 4 times per day. Optimum temperature range 68 to 85^0 F. Best harvested when 1/2 to 1 inch long. Can be used in sprout mixtures with lentils and garbanzo beans, forming up to 10% of the mixture. *C14*, *F91*

Cress: 4-5 days. Use clay method. Soak equal amounts of seeds and water in an unglazed clay flower pot saucer. Put in water up to 1/2 inch from the rim and cover with a plate. Do not rinse. Optimum temperature range 50 to 72^0 F. Best harvested when 1 to 1 1/2 inches long. "Green" near window during last day for best chlorophyll development. Sprouts have a spicy flavor and are good in sprout mixtures. One tablespoon of seed yields 3/4 cup of sprouts. F37T, *F91*, O48

Dill: 4-6 days. One of the few herb seeds which sprouts easily without a high percentage of seed spoilage. Fresh seed is essential for satisfactory results. Use jar or bag method and sprout in indirect sunlight; 2 1/2 tablespoons per quart jar. Soaking time 6 to 10 hours; rinse 3 times per day. Sprouts have a very strong taste and are best used in breads, soups or salad dressings. *C14*, *F91*

Dun Pea: (Field Pea) 2-3 days. Use jar or soil method; 2 cups of seed per quart jar. Soaking time 7 to 10 hours; rinse 2 to 3 times per day. Optimum temperature range 50 to 72^0 F. Makes an excellent sprout, crisp and tender. Should be harvested very small, when sprout first begins to form. Sometimes sold as *porridge pea*. *C14*

English Tea Sandwich Mix:[1] Grows bunched together in a thick layer. A crisp, firm mixture perfect for sandwiches. Mild, spicy flavor. Can be used in salads or for garnishing. Low cost, rapid and easily grown. L91M

Fennel: 7-10 days. Use bag or tray method; 2 1/2 tablespoons per quart jar. Fresh seed is essential for good results. Soaking time 6 to 10 hours; rinse 3 times per day. Optimum temperature 75^0 F. Best harvested when 1 to 2 inches long. Relatively strong-flavored sprouts, but milder than dill sprouts. *C14*, *F91*, L24

Fenugreek: 3-6 days. Use jar or tray method; 1/4 cup per quart jar. Soaking time 4 to 8 hours; rinse 2 times per day. Optimum temperature range 65 to 85^0 F. Best harvested when 1 to 2 inches long. "Green" near window during last day for best chlorophyll development. Sprouts have a unique spicy flavor, but become bitter if left to grow too long. Used in sprouting mixtures with alfalfa and clover, or mung beans and lentils. *C14*, *F91*, L24, L91M, O48

Flax: 2-5 days. Use clay method. Soak equal amounts of seeds and water in an unglazed clay flower pot saucer. Put in water up to 1/2 inch from the rim and cover with a plate. Do not rinse. Optimum temperature range 65-80^0 F. Best harvested when 1 to 1 1/2 inches long. "Green" near window during last day for best chlorophyll development. Two day old sprouts are used in drinks; older sprouts have a somewhat bitter flavor. *C14*, E21G, G91, *L14M*, L24, *M15M*

Garbanzo Bean: 2-4 days. Use jar or colander method and sprout in indirect sunlight; 1 cup per quart jar. Soaking time 8 to 12 hours; rinse 3 to 4 times per day. Optimum temperature range 68 to 85^0 F. Best harvested when 1/2 inch long. Usually cooked for about 10 minutes and eaten as a side-dish, or added to soups, stews, casseroles, rice or vegetables. *C14*, *F91*, *L14M*, L24

Garlic: 12-14 days. Use tray method; 2 tablespoons per quart jar. Soaking time 8 hours; rinse 2 times per day. Optimum temperature range 70 to 75^0 F. Best harvested when 2 inches long. "Green" near window during last day for best chlorophyll development. *C14*, L24

Jaba Radish: A rapid-growing radish used for sprouting. Similar to regular radishes, but more crispy. Good in salads, sandwiches, etc. *A75*

Kaiware Daikon: (Sprouting Daikon) A Japanese radish developed specially for sprouting. Grows very quickly. The white stem reaches 8 to 9 inches in length in 7 to 10 days. Crisp and tender with a spicy radish flavor. SCHNEIDER [Cul, Re]; *A75*, *C14*, *C28*, *D12*, G20M{PR}, *N40*{PR}, *S63M*

Kale: 3-6 days. Use jar or tray method and sprout in indirect sunlight; 3 tablespoons per quart jar. Soaking time 4 to 8 hours; rinse 2 to 3 times per day. Optimum temperature range 60 to 85^0 F. Best harvested when 1 to 1 1/2 inches long. "Green" near window during last day for best chlorophyll development. Sprouts have a mild, cabbage-like flavor and are excellent in salads. L24

Kamut Wheat: (for sources see Triticum polonicum, page 160)

Kidney Bean: 2-4 days. Use jar method; 3/4 cup per quart jar. Soaking time 8 to 12 hours; rinse 3 to 4 times per day. Optimum temperature range 68 to 85^0 F. Best harvested when 1/2 to 1 inch long. Generally not eaten raw due to a digestive inhibitor which is reduced, but not completely eliminated by sprouting. Can be steamed, stir-fried, or ground and fermented overnight. B73M, *L14M*

Lentil: 2-5 days. One of the most popular sprouts and also one of the easiest to grow. Use jar or bag method; 3/4 cup of seed per quart jar. Soaking time 5 to 8 hours; rinse 2 to 3 times per day. Optimum temperature range 60 to 85^0 F. Best harvested when 1/4 to 1 inch long. Sprouts have a sweet flavor and are excellent either raw or added to soups, stews or vegetable dishes. B73M, *C14*, E21G, *F91*, J20, *L14M*, L24

Lima Bean: 3-4 days. Use jar or bag method; 1 cup per quart. Soaking time 12 hours; rinse 3 times per day. Optimum temperature range 65 to 75^0 F. Best harvested when sprout first begins to emerge. *C14*

Long Black Spanish Radish: (for sources see Radish, page 461)

Millet: 1-3 days. Use jar or bag method; 1 1/2 cups per quart jar. Soaking time 5 to 7 hours; rinse 2 to 3 times per day. Optimum temperature range 70 to 80^0 F. Best harvested when 0 to 1/8 inch long. Viable seed not readily available, hulled seed may be used even if no shoot appears. Sprouts have a mild, nutty flavor which blends well with most kinds of foods. Also used for dehydrating and juicing. D3, E21G, F97M, G91, *L14M*, L24

Mung Bean: 3-5 days. Use jar or tray method; 1/3 cup per quart jar. Soaking time 5 to 10 hours; rinse 3 to 5 times per day. Optimum temperature range 68 to 85^0 F. Best harvested when 1 to 3 inches long. One of the few sprouts which should be grown in darkness for best results. Straighter sprouts are produced by the tray method, and when the sprouts are disturbed as little as possible in the container.

Unsprouted or "hard" seeds can be an annoyance, and should be eliminated with a mesh frame. CHANG, W. [Re], DAHLEN [Pre, Re], HAWKES [Re]; B13, B73M, *C14*, C44, D65, F37T, *F91*, G57M, G79, G82, G91, H33, J20, L24, L59, etc.

Mustard: 4-6 days. Use jar or tray method; 3 tablespoons per quart jar. Soaking time 4 to 6 hours; rinse 2 to 3 times per day. Optimum temperature range 65 to 85^{0} F. Best harvested when 1 to 1/2 inches long. "Green" near window during last day for best chlorophyll development. Sprouts have a hot, spicy flavor and can be added to sprouting mixes with alfalfa and clover, forming 10 to 15% of the mixture. Dried sprouts are used as a condiment. (for sources see Brassica nigra, page 46 and Sinapis alba, page 53)

Oats: 1-3 days. Use jar or towel method; 1 1/2 cups per quart jar. Soaking time 3 to 5 hours; rinse 1 to 2 times per day with cool water. Best harvested when 0 to 1/4 inch long. Viable seed not readily available, hulled seed may be used even if no shoot appears. Excellent for sprouted grain bread and juicing. Also good in salads, soups and dressings, or dried and made into *sun granola*. D3, F97M, L24

Onion: 12-14 days. Use tray method; 2 tablespoons per quart jar. Soaking time 8 hours; rinse 2 times per day. Optimum temperature range 70 to 75^{0} F. Best harvested when 2 inches long. Should be placed near a window to turn green and develop chlorophyll. *C14*, D62, *F91*, L24

Pea: 2-5 days. Use jar or soil method; 2 cups of seed per quart jar. Soaking time 7 to 10 hours; rinse 2 to 3 times per day. Optimum temperature range 50 to 72^{0} F. Best harvested when 1/4 to 1/2 inch long. Yields between 3 and 4 cups of sprouts. Can be used in sprout mixtures with lentil, wheat, sunflower and buckwheat, forming 25% to 70% of the mixture. Sprouts are very sweet and are excellent raw, as a cooked vegetable or added to soups. Both green and yellow types are available. *C14*, E31{PR}, *F91*, F97M

Peanut: 2-6 days. Use jar or bag method; 1 cup per quart jar. Soaking time 8 to 12 hours; rinse 2 to 3 times per day. Optimum temperature range 68 to 85^{0} F. Best harvested when 1/4 to 3/4 inch long. Can be used in sprout mixtures with garbanzo beans, lentils, soybeans and mung beans, forming 10 to 25% of the mixture. Dry roasted sprouts make a flavorful, easy to digest snack. In India, a delicacy is prepared by seasoning sprouted peanuts with various spices. ROSENGARTEN; L24

Pinto Bean: 3-5 days. Use jar method; 3/4 cup of seed per quart jar. Soaking time 8 to 12 hours; rinse 3 to 4 times per day. Optimum temperature range 68 to 85^{0} F. Best harvested when 1/2 to 1 1/4 inches long. Yields between 3 and 4 cups of sprouts. Generally not eaten raw due to a digestive inhibitor. Can be steamed and mixed with oil or dressing, or fermented by leaving in a warm place overnight. B73M, *L14M*

Popcorn: 2-3 days. Use jar method; 1 1/2 cups per quart jar. Soaking time 10 to 14 hours; rinse 2 to 3 times per day. Optimum temperature range 68 to 85^{0} F. Harvest when 1/4 to 1/2 inch long. Sprouts are somewhat less sweet than those from sweet corn. Best in soups, casseroles and breads. Usually ground or blended with water before use. *L14M*

Psyllium: 4-8 days. Use clay method. Soak equal amounts of seeds and water in an unglazed clay flower pot saucer. Put in water up to 1/2 inch from the rim and cover with a plate. Do not rinse. Optimum temperature range 65 to 80^{0} F. Best harvested when 3/4 to 1 1/2 inches long. "Green" near window during last day for best chlorophyll development. Sprouts have a mild flavor and are eaten in salads or as a snack. L24, *M15M*

Quinoa: 1-4 days. Use jar or bag method; 1/3 cup per quart jar. Soaking time 2 to 4 hours; rinse 2 to 3 times per day. Optimum temperature range 55 to 80^{0} F. Best harvested when 1/4 to 1 1/4 inches long. "Green" near window during last day for best chlorophyll development. After 1 day of sprouting, sprouts have a mild flavor and can be used like sesame or sunflower seeds. At later stages they have a red tint and are very good in salads and sandwiches. Sprouts develop a slightly bitter taste if grown too long. WOOD, R.; I43T, J56, L24

Radish: 4-5 days. Use jar or soil method; 3 tablespoons per quart jar. Soaking time 4 to 8 hours; rinse 2 to 3 times per day. Optimum temperature range 60 to 85^{0} F. Best harvested when 1 to 2 inches long. "Green" near window during last day for best chlorophyll development. Sprouts have a hot, spicy flavor and are very popular in sprout mixtures with alfalfa and clover, forming about 10% of the mixture. Dried sprouts can be used as a condiment. SCHNEIDER [Cul, Re]; B7, *C28*, C69M, F37T, *F91*, F97M, G16, G82, G91, H25, I58, K20, *L14M*, L24, *M15M*, M46, etc.

Red Lentil: Use jar or bag method; 3/4 cup of seed per quart. Soaking time 5 to 8 hours; rinse 2 to 3 times per day. Optimum temperature range 60 to 80^{0} F. Best harvested when 1/4 to 1 inch long. Both hulled and unhulled types are available. Sprouts have a sweet flavor and are excellent either raw or cooked. *C14*, L24

Rice: 1-3 days. Use jar method; 1 1/2 cups of seed per quart jar. Soaking time 12 to 15 hours; rinse 2 to 3 times per day. Best harvested when 0 to 1/8 inch long. Viable seed not readily available, seed may be used even if no shoot appears. Yields between 3 and 4 cups of sprouts. *L14M*

Rye: 2-3 days. Use jar or soil method; 1 cup per quart jar. Soaking time 6 to 10 hours; rinse 2 times per day. Optimum temperature range 50 to 72^{0} F. Best harvested when 1/4 to 1/2 inch long, when the roots are no longer than the seed. Roots become long and fibrous if allowed to continue sprouting. Should be refrigerated if not used immediately. Excellent for sprouted grain *essene bread*. B73M, D3, G91, H67M{PR}, K74M{PR}, *L14M*, L24, O48

Seed Mix:[1] Specially selected sprouting seed mixture. Contains equal parts of alfalfa, mung bean and green lentil. M63M

Sesame: 2-3 days. Use jar method; 2 cups of seed per quart jar. Soaking time 6 to 8 hours; rinse 3 to 4 times per day. Optimum temperature range 60 to 85^{0} F. Best harvested when 1/8 inch long. Sprouts have a mild flavor after 1 day of sprouting. Can be used in sprout mixtures with sunflower and almond, forming 10 to 20% of the mixture. *L14M*

Snowbean: 3-4 days. First introduced by Thompson and Morgan in 1983 as Sweet Lupin Sprouts, the name was later changed to the current Snowbean Sprouts. It is said to have a particularly desirable sweet, nutty flavor, and to be much more wholesome or substantial compared with other sprouts. L91M

Soybean: 3-4 days. Use jar or colander method; 3/4 cup per quart jar. Soaking time 4 to 8 hours; rinse 3 to 4 times per day. Optimum temperature range 65 to 85^{0} F. Harvest when 1 1/2 to 2 inches long. Best results are obtained with sprouters that have holes in the bottom, so the sprouts are never agitated during rinsing. Generally not eaten raw due to digestive inhibitors, which are not completely destroyed during sprouting. Usually boiled for 10 to 15 minutes with salt and oil and eaten with rice or millet. DAHLEN [Pre, Re], PIPER [Cu, Re]; *C14*, E21G, *F91*, G91, K20, L24, L59, O48

Sunflower (Hulled): 1-3 days. Use jar or bag method; 1 cup per quart jar. Soaking time 2 to 4 hours; rinse 2 times per day. Optimum temperature range 60 to 80^{0} F. Unsprouted seeds should be removed after the second day as they will rot and may spoil the whole batch. Best harvested when 0 to 1 inch long. Excellent in salads, blended fruit drinks, salad dressings, or as an addition to sprouted wheat breads. Also used for making sprouted *seed cheese*. *F91*, *L14M*, L24

Sunflower (Unhulled): 8-15 days. Use soil or tray method. Soak 10 to 14 hours. Optimum temperature range 60 to 80° F. Best harvested when 3 1/2 to 6 inches long. Can be grown in any sunny window. Harvest by cutting 1 inch from the soil, or by pulling the entire plant from the soil. Succulent seedlings, called *sunflower lettuce*, have a rich flavor and are an excellent substitute for lettuce. Also used for juicing, as a snack, for drying, or as a garnish. Contains chlorophyll and many vitamins, minerals and enzymes. C69M, D3, D26M, E70M{PR}, *F91*, *L14M*, L24, O48

Triticale: 2-3 days. Use jar or soil method; 1 cup of seeds per quart jar. Soaking time 6 to 10 hours; rinse with cool water 2 to 3 times per day. Optimum temperature range 60 to 80° F. Best harvested when 1/4 to 1/2 inch long, when roots are no longer than the seed. Excellent for sprouted grain bread. Also good in salads and soups. L24

Turnip: 3-5 days. Use jar or soil method; 3 tablespoons of seed per quart jar. Soaking time 4 to 8 hours; rinse 2 to 3 times per day. Optimum temperature range 65 to 85° F. Best harvested when 1 to 1 1/2 inches long. "Green" near window during last day for best chlorophyll development. Yields between 3 and 4 cups of sprouts. Has an excellent cabbage-like flavor and is eaten in salads. C69M, L24, M46

Vetch: (Vicia sp.) 2-4 days. Use jar method; 3/4 cup of seed per quart jar. Soaking time 5 to 8 hours; rinse 2 to 3 times per day. Optimum temperature range 60 to 85° F. Best harvested when 1/4 to 1 inch long. Sprouts have a sweet flavor similar to lentil sprouts and are very good either raw or cooked. I58

Wheat: 2-3 days. Use jar or soil method; 1 cup per quart jar. Soaking time 6 to 10 hours; rinse 2 times per day. Optimum temperature range 55 to 80° F. Best harvested when 1/4 to 1/2 inch long. Excellent for making sweet, rich, moist sprouted wheat or *essene bread*, which is not baked, merely dried in the sun or a low oven. Also used for *wheatgrass*, harvested after 7 to 10 days, at 5 to 6 inches tall, which is primarily used for juicing. B73M, *C14*, C95, D3, E21G, F97M, G16, G82, G91, <u>K74M</u>{PR}, *L14M*, L24, <u>L24</u>{PR}, O48

SQUASH {S}

CUCURBITA MAXIMA	CUCURBITA MIXTA
CUCURBITA MOSCHATA	CUCURBITA PEPO

SUMMER SQUASH

These are usually harvested when about half-grown, before the seeds have become hard. They can be eaten raw or cooked, but are generally not canned or frozen. Some cultivars, such as Jersey Golden Acorn, can be harvested as summer squash when small or used as winter squash if left to mature. C. pepo unless otherwise noted.

<u>SCALLOP SQUASH</u>

Hybrid

Peter Pan: 50 days. Uniform, well-scalloped fruit, 2 1/2 to 3 inches in diameter at harvest size; small blossom end scar; tender, light green skin; pale green flesh, meaty, of excellent quality. Vigorous, bush-like vine; very productive, produces over a long period; widely adapted. All America Selections winner in 1982. A16, B75, C85M, D65, F13, F19M, G93M, H94, H95, I39, I91, J7, J34, K73, N16, etc.

Scallopini: 52 days. Deep scalloped-shaped fruit, with medium fluting, 2 1/2 to 3 inches in diameter at harvest size; skin dark green; flesh pale green, meaty, sweet and nut-like, reminiscent of zucchini. Compact vines; extremely productive over a long season. Excellent for home gardens and local markets. All America Selections winner in 1977. A87M, B73M, C92, D82, F12, G51, G93M, H94, I39, J20, J34, L42, L89, *N40*{PR}, N52, etc.

Sunburst:[1] 52 days. First hybrid yellow scallop squash. Deep scallop-shaped fruit, with medium fluting; skin soft, bright deep-yellow, with a dark green "sunburst" pattern; tender, creamy white flesh, flavor delicate and buttery. Very attractive when picked as "baby squash", with the blossom still attached. Compact vine; spreads to 2 1/2 feet. All America Selections winner in 1985. C44, C53, E70M{PR}, *E91G*, F19M, G6, G16, G51, H42, H94, I39, J7, J34, K66, K73, L89, *N40*{PR}, etc.

Open-Pollinated

Benning's Green Tint: 55 days. Scallop-shaped fruit; 2 to 2 1/2 inches deep, 3 to 4 inches in diameter at harvest size; skin pale green; flesh pale green, thick, tender, fine-textured. Medium-sized bush; semi-open; very productive over a long period. Popular for home gardens, fresh market and shipping. B35M, D76, E24, E97, F44, *G13M*, G51, G71M, G93M, J73, L89, N52

White Bush: (Early White Bush, White Patty Pan) 55 days. Deep scallop-shaped fruit; 2 1/2 to 3 inches deep, 5 to 7 inches in diameter; skin pale green, nearly white when ripe; flesh milky white, tender, succulent. Compact, bush-like vine; very productive. Very popular home garden cultivar. Of ancient and unknown origin. BURR, TAPLEY 1937; A87M, B75, C92, E38, G71M, H66, I39, J34, K49M, K71, L7M, M13M, M95, N16, N39, etc.

Wood's Earliest Prolific: 50 days. Slightly scalloped fruit; 2 to 2 1/2 inches deep, 3 to 3 3/4 inches in diameter; skin heavily and uniformly tinted with pale green, pale greenish-white when mature. Bush-like vine; very productive, will produce fruits throughout the season when continuously harvested. Introduced in 1899 by T.W. Woods & Sons, Richmond, Virginia. TAPLEY 1937; I99, K49M, L7M

Yellow Bush: (Golden Bush, Early Yellow Bush, Yellow Custard) 60 days. Deeply scalloped fruit; 3 inches deep, about 5 inches in diameter at harvest size; skin deep yellow, irregularly mottled with pale yellow; flesh yellowish-white, firm, fine-grained, flavorful. Bush-like plant, spreading to about 3 feet; very productive. Introduced prior to 1860. BURR, TAPLEY 1937; A69M, *F60*, G64, G71M, G79, I76M{PR}, I99, J34, K49M, K71, L7M, S45M, S61

<u>ZUCCHINI</u>

Hybrid

Arlesa:[1] 48 days. High quality French *courgette* type. Cylindrical fruit; skin glossy green, flecked with lighter green, thin; flesh firm, very flavorful; stays firm and fresh in storage. Best picked at "baby" size, but stays tender when larger. Vigorous, highly prolific plant. Upright bearing habit and relatively spineless leaves and stems makes for easy harvesting. B75, I77, K66

Beiruti: (Amcobellow) Smooth, white fruit; 4 inches long, 1 1/4 to 1 3/4 inches in diameter. Suitable for stuffing. Vigorous vine; 14 to 20 inches long; has a very high concentration of female flowers. First harvest after 40 to 45 days when sown in spring, after 35 to 40 days in autumn. T27M

Butterblossom:[2] 45 days. Developed to produce more prolific yields of extra large, firm golden-yellow male blossoms over a longer season. In Europe the male blossoms, which do not bear fruit, are sold as *squash bouquets* and used for stuffing. Female blossoms will produce fruit if not removed, and are most often sold attached to tiny zucchinis, the size of a little finger. BRENNAN [Cul, Re], SCHNEIDER [Cul, Re]; C53, D11M, F1, F13, F33, *F72*, G64,

G71, *H61*, I39, I91, J7, *J89M*, L7M, L42, L79, M13M, M46, M49, etc.

Cousa: (Lebanese Zucchini, Egyptian White Zucchini) 51 days. Short, cylindrical fruit, 3 to 5 inches long; skin pale greenish-white when young, turning buff colored when ripe; flesh fine-textured, of excellent quality, flavor unique. Easy to find and pick. Widely used in Lebanese and Middle Eastern cuisine. Vigorous, compact, bushy vine; very high yielding. MALLOS [Re]; C81M, E83T, I77, L42

El Dorado: 52 days. Cylindrical, slightly tapered fruits; attractive deep orange-yellow skin; excellent flavor; very quick-maturing. Should be harvested early and often as *courgettes*. Vigorous, strong-growing, bush-type vine; highly productive. E32M, F13

Florina: 50 days. Developed especially for harvesting when only 4 to 6 inches long. Flowers stay attached to the fruit for a long period, making it an ideal crop for specialty growers. Excellent for "gourmet" type cooking. Compact, bush-like vine. C53

Ghada: 48 days. Cylindrical fruit, slightly tapered at the stem end, 5 to 6 inches in length at harvest size; skin light greenish-yellow, very smooth; flavor excellent. Fairly compact, very productive plant. Very early. A standard cultivar in the Middle East where it is popular for stuffing. K73

Gold Rush: 52 days. Uniform, straight fruit, 7 to 8 inches long; skin deep golden-yellow, glossy, with contrasting rich green stems; flesh creamy white, flavorful. Vigorous, open, single-stemmed plant; highly productive; easy to pick. Excellent for home gardens and specialty markets. All America Selections winner in 1980. A16, B75M, C44, C53, D11M, E32M{PL}, F19M, F82, G6, G71, *H61*, H94, K73, L97, M46, N16, etc.

Golden Rocky:[1] (Rocky Gold) 55 days. Long, straight, cylindrical fruit; skin bright golden-yellow, attractive; flesh flavorful, of excellent quality. Good raw or cooked. Develops full golden color at "baby" stage. Vigorous, compact, bush-type vine; very prolific; of open growth habit, making it easier to find and pick fruit. *F63*, J7, J34{CF}, L89, M49

Gourmet Globe:[1] (Apple Squash) 50 days. Globe-shaped fruit, 3 to 4 inches in diameter; skin dark green, with light green stripes; flesh creamy white, firm but tender, very flavorful. Excellent eaten raw in salads; also good for stuffing and sautéing. Specialty market item when picked young as "baby squash". Upright, open-bush type plant; very prolific. A13, E57, F19M, G51, G93M, H33, H54, I77, I91, K66, L91M, M29, N52

Romano:[2] Developed in Italy especially for its blossom size and durability. Blossoms will stay open from early morning until early afternoon, making it a good choice for stuffed squash blossoms. Wide blossom attachment keeps the blossoms firmly on the fruits during growing and cooking. When the fruit is 2 inches long, the blossom will be about the same size or larger. I77

Sardane:[2] 48 days. The large blossoms are excellent for sautéing, or for stuffing and baking still attached to the young fruit. Long, cylindrical fruit; skin deep dark-green, glossy; flesh firm, solid, flavorful. Bush-type, high yielding vine; relatively free of irritating spines. Can be succession sown for a fall crop in mild-winter climates. K66

Spineless Beauty:[3] 50 days. Unique spineless type, free of leaf or stem spines. Uniform, cylindrical fruit, 7 1/2 to 8 1/2 inches long; skin medium green, very smooth, waxy; flesh crisp, white. Vigorous, medium open plant; sets continuously and produces high yields. Easy to harvest, with minimal fruit damage. *A1*, K10, K66

Spineless Zucchini:[3] 48 days. Unique, spineless plant. Stems are free of the sticky spines that cause annoying scratches and itching, making picking much more pleasant. Fruits are 8 inches long, 1 1/2 inches in diameter, with dark green, attractive skin and succulent, flavorful flesh. Prolific over a long period. G93M, *H61*, I91

Open-Pollinated

Black Zucchini: (Black Beauty) 50 days. Straight, cylindrical fruit, slightly ridged; grows to 9 inches long, but best quality is obtained when picked at 6 inches; skin dark blackish-green, glossy; flesh greenish-white, firm but tender, flavorful; small seed cavity. Semi-upright, prolific plant; has an open growth habit for easy picking. A25, B75M, C44, D82, D87, *F60*, *F72*, *H61*, J73, J97M, K73, L7M, L97, M13M, N16, etc.

Burpee's Fordhook:[2] 57 days. Produced more male blossoms than most other summer squash in trials conducted by Burpee Seed Company. Long, cylindrical fruit; straight to slightly curved; skin smooth, deep blackish-green; flesh creamy white, tender, freezes well; best when 8 to 12 inches long. Vigorous, bush-like plant. All America Selections winner in 1942. B75, G57M, J32, N52

Caserta: 55 days. Cylindrical fruit, slightly tapered towards the stem end, 6 to 8 inches in length; skin grayish-green, streaked and mottled with darker green; flesh creamy white. Bush medium large, vigorous, open; very productive. For home gardens, local markets and shipping. All America Selections winner for 1949. C92, *D12*, *F60*, G51, G93M, I64, J84, K5M, *L59G*, M95, N52

Cocozelle: (Italian Vegetable Marrow, Cocozella di Napoli) 55 days. Long, slender, nearly cylindrical fruit; slightly enlarged at the blossom end; ribbed; skin pale greenish-yellow, prominently striped with very dark green; flesh firm, greenish-white, very flavorful. Best harvested when 6 to 8 inches long. Moderately vigorous, bush-type plant. TAPLEY 1937; A87M, C44, D68, E24, E59Z, F44, G27M, I39, *I59M*, J25M, K27M, L9M, L11, L42, N39, etc.

Costata Romanesca: (Roman Ribbed) Very distinct strain of zucchini with long, fluted or ribbed fruit. Medium green-striped skin, with white flecks. Will grow to 2 feet long and still remain tender. Develops a very long ovary at the blossom stage. Usually picked when less than 8 inches long and fried whole, with the flower. When cut the slices are scalloped on the edges. Very large, vining plant. F80, J73

Dark Green Zucchini: 55 days. Cylindrical fruit, slightly tapered towards the stem end; 6 to 8 inches long at harvest size; very dark green skin; flesh greenish-white, fine-textured, of strong flavor. Popular for home gardens and fresh markets. Medium-large, bush-type plant. A2, A16, A69M, B35M, C85M, E24, F19M, F42, G27M, G51, G71M, G93M, H66, K71, M95, etc.

French White: (French White Bush Zucchini) 50 days. Vigorous white bush zucchini from France. Firm flesh, mild but flavorful; seed cavity small. At its peak of flavor when 3 to 5 inches long. Very popular and versatile. Semi-bush type plant. I39

Golden Zucchini: (Burpee's Golden Zucchini) 55 days. Medium-long, slender, cylindrical fruit; attractive, glossy, bright golden-yellow skin; distinctive flavor. Excellent raw or cooked. Compact, bush-type vine. Developed by W. Atlee Burpee Company, from genetic material supplied by Dr. Oved Shifriss, Rutgers University. B75, *F72*, G51, H42, *I62*{PL}, I76M{PR}, K49M, L91M, P83M, S45M, S61

Grey Zucchini: 50 days. Small to medium-sized fruit; straight when young, becoming slightly tapered toward the blossom end; skin smooth, medium-green, mottled with attractive grey specks, very attractive; high quality flesh, small seed cavity; ships and stores well. Bush-type vine; highly productive over a long period. A87M, *D49*, D76, E24, E97, F12, F44, *F60*, G27M, G51, *H61*, H66, K71, L7M, N16, etc.

Long Cocozelle: (Long Dark Cocozelle) 50 days. Long, narrow, straight fruit; skin smooth, dark green, with light green stripes; flesh greenish-white, firm, very flavorful, of excellent quality. Best harvested when 6 to 10 inches long. Vigorous, bush-type plant. Popular home garden and local market cultivar. C92, *F60*, G71, G79, I84, K71, M13M

Long Green Trailing: (Long Green Striped Vegetable Marrow, Green Striped) 58 days. Nearly cylindrical fruit, slightly tapered towards the base; skin irregularly striped with dark and light green; flesh pale greenish-white. Moderately vigorous, trailing vine, 12 to 15 feet long; best grown on a fence or trellis. An old-fashioned English cultivar. TAPLEY 1937; L91M, P83M, S61

Long White Bush: (White Bush Vegetable Marrow) 55 days. Nearly cylindrical fruit; 10 to 12 inches long, 3 to 3 1/2 inches in diameter; skin creamy white; flesh greenish-white, fine-textured, delicately flavored. Very prolific, bush-type plant. An old English cultivar, introduced into the United States prior to 1824. TAPLEY 1937; A16, A69M, B75, D11M, D27, E38, F1, F92, G87, I67M, L42, M13M, M49, *R23*, S61, etc.

Lubnani: (Lebanese White Bush) 40-50 days. Slightly bulbous fruit, tapered at the stem end; weight 1 to 2 pounds; lime green exterior, cream interior; excellent, sweet flavor. Capable of withstanding variable climatic conditions. Very popular in the Middle East. B49

Ronde de Nice: (Tonda di Nizza) 45 days. Unique, globe-shaped zucchini. Skin very fine and delicate, bruises easily, pale green. Very flavorful, greenish-white flesh. Can be harvested up to 5 inches in diameter without loss of quality or flavor. Sauté whole when 1 inch in diameter. Ideal for stuffing when tennis ball size. Very vigorous, quick-growing plant. For home gardens and specialty growers. C53, I99, K66, L91M, P83M, S55

Round Zucchini: 45 days. Small, globe-shaped fruit, 2 1/2 inches in diameter; with slight ridges; skin grey-green; flesh creamy white, firm but tender, flavorful. Ideal for stuffing. Very productive, bush-type plant. C92, D76, E24, E97, *F60*, G64, G67M, *L59G*

Sakiz: 60 days. Long, cylindrical fruit; skin light green to white. Has a mild flavor, reminiscent of patty pan squash. Best picked when young, but remains tender up to 18 inches long. Large, bush-type plant; spreads to 5 feet across; very productive. Has ornamental leaves, making it suitable for edible landscaping. J73

Small Green Algerian: (Petite Verte d'Algérie) 45-50 days. A semi-early North African strain. Produces short fruits, which are rounder than most other zucchini types. Light green skin, with grey-green spots. Especially flavorsome. Bears over a long period of time. Y14M

Table Dainty: 60 days. English marrow type. Medium-sized, cylindrical fruit; skin striped with dark and pale green; flesh very firm, retains firmness when cooked. Good for stuffing; excellent when fried; also makes good wine and marrow jam; keeps well. Vigorous, trailing vine, 18 to 20 feet long; very productive. Introduced by Suttons & Sons of Reading, England, in 1909. TAPLEY 1937; O53M, *R23*, S55, S61

Tatume: 50 days. Oval to slightly elongated fruit; 7 inches long, 5 inches in diameter at maturity; skin medium to dark green, faintly striped with lighter green; flesh firm, flavorful; keeps well. Very vigorous, trailing vine. Popular in Texas and parts of Mexico. Used to prepare a famous Mexican chicken soup. *A1*, A87M, *D49*, *F60*, F71M, J34, L9M, *L59G*, M95

Tender and True: English marrow type. Nearly round fruit, distinctly flattened at top and bottom; 5 to 6 inches in diameter; skin mottled with light and dark green; flesh firm but tender, flavorful. Best harvested when young. Semi-trailing, moderately vigorous vine. Introduced as a novelty in 1907 by Sutton & Sons, Reading, England. TAPLEY 1937; S59M, S61

Winter Zucchini: 65 days. Long, dark-green fruit; usually picked at 6 to 8 inches long when the skin is glossy. Firmer and sweeter than other zucchinis, but less productive. Large, bush-like plant with large leaves that provide cover for cold protection. Adapted to frost-free, coastal areas of southern California. Should be planted between September 15th and October 15th. Hand pollination may be required in weather too cold for bee activity. Developed by Charles B. Ledgerwood of Carlsbad, California. G71M

OTHERS

Hybrid

Goldbar: 60 days. Hybrid straightneck type for commercial and home garden use. Uniform, cylindrical fruits; 5 to 6 inches long at harvest size; smooth, golden-yellow skin; creamy yellow, smooth textured flesh. Compact, bush-type vine; has an upright, open growth habit for easier harvesting; highly productive over a long season. A87M, C44, F12, *F72*, G79, H33, H54, *H61*, H66, J20, J34, J84, K50, K73, N16, etc.

Multipik: 50 days. Straightneck type fruit, 7 to 8 inches long; skin creamy yellow, glossy; flesh light and sweet with a true squash flavor. Strong, bush-type plant; very productive. Resistant to fruit-greening caused by cucumber mosaic virus. Contains a "precocious yellow gene" which causes increased production of female flowers, resulting in early and continuous bearing. F13, *G1M*, J34, K10, N52

Pic-N-Pic: 50 days. Crookneck type, more attractive than standard Yellow Crookneck strains. Bright golden-yellow fruit with small blossom scars; smooth, unwarted skin and tender flesh. Best when picked small. Heavy yielding plant with an open growth habit; bears over a long period. Fruits are easy to see and harvest from a single stem. B75, Q34

Seneca Prolific: 51 days. Productive straightneck type. Long, cylindrical fruit, tapered towards the stem end; smooth, attractive bright yellow skin; light green stems; firm flesh. Erect, bush-type plant allows closer spacing for maximum yields; has an open growth habit for easier harvesting; highly productive throughout the growing season. A87M, B75M, *F72*, *G1M*, G6, G71, G79, *H61*, J84, *J89M*, K73, L42, M29, M95M, N16, etc.

Sun Drops:[1] 50-55 days. Unique, oval-shaped light yellow fruit with a mild, nutty flavor. Perfect for stuffing. Harvest when immature as "baby squash" with the blossom attached, or when fruit is 3 to 4 inches in diameter. Compact, bush-type plant; suitable for the small garden. All America Selections winner for 1990. GORMAN [Re]; D11M, G93M, I39, K10, *M43M*

Sundance: 52 days. Early hybrid crookneck type. Curved, club-shaped fruit; medium thick neck with a full crook, making for less breakage; very smooth, bright yellow skin; firm, creamy white flesh; small blossom scar. Very compact, bush-like plant; widely adapted. Good for home gardens and commercial production. A16, A87M, B73M, C44, D11M, *F72*, G27M, G82, G93M, *H61*, H66, J7, J20, K73, L42, M29, N16, etc.

Open-Pollinated

Argentina Summer: (C. maxima) Flattened, globe-shaped, ribbed fruit; weight 1 to 2 pounds when mature; skin dark green. Best quality is obtained when harvested at about 3 inches in diameter. K49M

Bianco Friulano: Pale yellow crookneck type. Produces a good crop of unusual looking fruit to pick and use throughout the summer. Delicious flavor and good firm texture. S55

Bicolor Spoon: 86 days. Very attractive, bi-colored fruit. Extremely productive, vining plant; yields of up to 100 fruits per hill are common. K49M

Confederate Gold: 52 days. Yellow crookneck type, earlier and more productive than Yellow Crookneck Improved. Very uniform, medium-sized, curved fruits, 9 inches long; neck with a full to half crook; skin attractive, pale lemon-yellow, medium smooth. Large, vigorous, medium open plants. *D74*, G27M

Early Prolific Straightneck: 50 days. Cylindrical, club-shaped fruit; 5 to 7 inches long at harvest size; skin light yellow, sparsely warted; flesh creamy yellow, firm but tender, succulent. Large, semi-open bush; very productive. Standard straightneck type for home gardens, local markets and shipping. All America Selections winner in 1938. A25, B75M, B78, C44, D82, E57, F19M, G71, *H61*, H66, H95, K73, L7M, M46, N16, etc.

Goldarch Crookneck: 42 days. Butter yellow, crookneck type fruit; more cylindrical, with longer bulk and arched neck. Matures 3 to 5 days earlier than Yellow Crookneck. Due to its uniformity, produces a higher percentage of Grade 1 fruit. Remains acceptable at larger sizes because it has practically no warts. Bush habit. G57M

Royal Knight: 50 days. Unique summer squash in the crookneck class. Bottle-shaped fruit with a slightly crooked neck, resembles Yellow Crookneck in size and shape; skin light green with a slight tint of yellow; excellent flavor. Should be harvested before the fruit turns very dark ebony green. Can be eaten fresh or cooked. Introduced in 1982 by Hollar and Co. G27M

Tromboncino: (Zuccheta Rampicante d'Albenga) (C. moschata) Very long, slender fruit; curved at the stem end, bulbous at the blossom end; skin light yellow-green; flesh very firm, flavor mild, sweet, delicious. Best harvested when 8 to 18 inches long. Very vigorous, vining plant, grows 30 to 40 feet in a season; requires a strong trellis. C53, I77, J20, K66, Q11M

Yellow Crookneck: (Early Golden Summer Crookneck, Dwarf Summer Crookneck) 55 days. Distinct, curved, club-shaped fruit, bulbous at the blossom end; 8 to 9 inches long; skin golden-yellow, warted; flesh pale yellowish-white. Freezes well. Moderately vigorous, bush-like plant; very productive. Popular home garden cultivar. Introduced prior to 1828. BURR, TAPLEY 1937; A25, B78, C44, E24, F19M, *F72*, F82, G6, *H61*, H66, H94, K73, L7M, M95, N16, etc.

Zapallito del Tronco: Round, medium-green fruit, 2 1/2 to 3 1/2 inches in diameter; excellent flavor; keeps and ships extremely well. Bushy, upright plant; provides excellent coverage and makes for easy picking. Very popular in South America as a fresh market and home garden cultivar. B49

WINTER SQUASH

Slower growing than summer squash, most require a long season and grow on long, trailing vines. They have shells that are hard enough to permit them to be stored during the winter. Many are canned for use in pumpkin pies.

<u>ACORN SQUASH</u> (C. pepo)

Hybrid

Cream of the Crop: 82 days. Unique creamy-white skinned acorn squash. Uniform fruits weigh 2 to 3 pounds. Golden-cream colored flesh with a mild, nutty flavor. Very good for baking and stuffing; can also be used as a delicious summer squash when immature. Stores well. Compact, bush-type plant spreads 3 to 4 feet. Yields are comparable to the best acorn types. All America Selections winner for 1990. GORMAN [Re]; D11M, G6, G82, G93M, K10, M29, *M43M*, M49

Open-Pollinated

Bush Table Queen:[4] 85 days. Very similar in color, size, shape and keeping qualities to the regular Table Queen. High quality, orange flesh; cooks dry and sweet. Bush-type vine, spreads to only 3 feet in diameter; sets the same number of fruit per plant as trailing types; widely adapted. A25, B75, B75M, *F60*, F82, G79, H66, H94, K10, M95

Ebony Acorn: (Table Queen Ebony) 100 days. Improved Table Queen type. Uniform, acorn-shaped fruit, prominently ribbed; skin deep green, attractive; flesh thick, deep-orange, fine-textured, dry, sweet. Has good keeping qualities. Vigorous, highly prolific vine. Developed by Dr. Henry Munger, Cornell University. A13, *A75*, B75M, B78, C44, E57, E97, F44, *F60*, G6, G51, G71, K66, K73, L89, etc.

Fordhook Acorn: 85 days. Small fruit, 8 to 10 inches long, 3 1/2 to 4 inches in diameter at the blossom end; shape long pyriform; ribbed widely; skin deep cream-colored, irregularly mottled with deep yellow; flesh thin, fine-textured, firm, rather juicy, fibrous, insipid, quality poor. Moderately vigorous vine, 8 to 10 feet long. Introduced in 1890 by W. Atlee Burpee Company. TAPLEY 1937; K49M

Gill's Golden Pippin: 100 days. Very small, deeply ribbed fruit, 1/2 to 3/4 inch in diameter; weight 1 to 2 pounds; golden-yellow skin, slightly streaked with pale yellow; flesh more orange and drier than most acorns. Vigorous, semi-running vines; highly prolific. Old Native American cultivar. K49M

Jersey Golden Acorn: 50-85 days. Dual-purpose squash. Can be harvested as summer squash when small, or left to mature for winter squash. Skin light yellow, becoming bright golden-orange when ripe; flesh pale golden-yellow, thick, fine-grained, sweet and tender; has a nutty flavor when mature. Contains 3 times more vitamin A than green acorn types. All America Selections winner in 1982. B49, B75M, C44, C53, E24, E70M{PR}, F19M, *F60*, G6, *H61*, H94, K73, L7M, M46, M49, *N40*{PR}, N52, etc.

Royal Acorn: (Royal Table Queen, Mammoth Table Queen) 85 days. Similar to Table Queen, but larger and more prolific. Small fruit; 5 1/2 inches in diameter; weight 2 to 4 pounds; medium dark-green skin, sometimes turning yellow to orange at full maturity; flesh pale orange, medium thick, very tender, dry, sweet, flavorful. A87M, B75M, C92, *F60*, *F63*, G71M, G79, H94, K20, K50, L42, L97, M13M, M29, M46, N16, etc.

Snow White:[4] Well-shaped fruit with smooth, pure-white skin. Bush-type plant; produces and abundance of early maturing fruits. Superior to other white acorn types in spite of the fact that it will occasionally produce plants with green fruits. Primary breeding work done by Glenn Drowns of the Seed Savers Exchange. L89

Swan White: (White Acorn) 90 days. Similar in shape to other acorn squash, but with more pronounced ribbing; weight 2 1/2 pounds. Skin snow-white, turning creamy yellow; flesh pale yellow, smooth; flavor delicate and sweet. High in calcium. Can also be harvested when 3 inches long and used like zucchini. High yielding. Good specialty market item. Developed by Mrs. G. Swan, a customer of Stokes Seeds. I77, J20, L42

Sweetnut Hulless:[4 5] Small acorn-shaped fruit; weight 3 to 4 pounds; skin green; of good eating quality. Also produces hulless seeds. Highly productive, bush-type vine. Developed by E.M. Meader at the University of New Hampshire, in the 1950's. I99

Table King:[4] (Table King Bush) 80 days. Small, ribbed fruit, pointed at the blossom end; 5 inches in diameter; weight 1 to 1 1/2 pounds; skin smooth, dark grayish-green; flesh yellow-orange, thick, tender; flavor excellent, improving in storage. Short-vined plant;

widely adapted. Ideal for small gardens. All America Selections Winner in 1974. *A69M*, D11M, D65, E24, F19M, G71, *G83M*, G93M, *H61*, J7, K71, K73, L79, M46, M49, etc.

Table Queen: (Acorn, Des Moines) 85 days. Small turbinate fruit; 5 to 6 inches long; deeply furrowed; skin deep dark green, changing to dull orange in storage; flesh pale orange, firm, tender, moderately dry, moderately sweet, of good flavor; quality good. Moderately vigorous vine, 12 to 15 feet long. The original acorn squash, introduced in 1913. TAPLEY 1937; A16, A25, B35M, B49, B75M, C85M, E38, F1, *F60*, *F72*, G71, L7M, L97, M13M, N16, etc.

BUTTERCUP SQUASH (C. maxima)

Hybrid

All Season:[4] 90 days. Attractive, oval, bright-orange fruit; weight approximately 3 1/4 pounds; has a delicious nutty flavor typical of Buttercup squash. Excellent for baking and winter storage. Bright yellow immature fruits may be eaten as a summer squash in as little as 65 days. Compact plant, spreads only 3 feet, produces 5 to 8 squash. D11M, E97, G82, K10

Sweet Mama:[4] 100 days. High quality "cupless" Buttercup type. Flattened globe-shaped fruit; weight 2 1/2 pounds; skin deep green, with light green stripes and blotches; flesh very thick, deep yellow, very sweet, has a nutty flavor; stores well. Compact, semi-bush type vine, to 4 feet long; somewhat tolerant to wilt and vine borer. Good for home gardens and specialty markets. All America Selections winner in 1979. SCHNEIDER [Cul, Re]; B75, D11M, D65, F1, *G13M*, G51, G93M, H94, H95, I39, I91, J7, J34, L42, M46, M49, etc.

Open-Pollinated

Burgess Strain: 100 days. Relatively uniform, blocky, turban-shaped fruits with a small blossom end "button"; 8 inches in diameter; weight 3 to 3 1/2 pounds; skin deep green, furrowed with light green stripes; flesh medium-orange, fine-grained, fiberless, rich and sweet. Released by the North Dakota Agricultural Experiment Station. A2, A13, D82, E57, F1, *F60*, G6, *H61*, H95, I39, K71, K73, L42, M13M, M46, M49, etc.

Buttercup: 105 days. Unique turban-shaped fruit, with a distinctive protruding "button" at the blossom end; weight 3 to 4 pounds; skin deep green, flecked and striped with grey; flesh deep orange, texture very fine, sweet, of excellent quality and flavor. Moderately vigorous vine, 10 to 12 feet long. Introduced in 1931 by Oscar H. Will & Company, Bismark, North Dakota. SCHNEIDER [Cul, Re], TAPLEY 1937; A16, A25, B75M, C44, C85M, E24, E38, F19M, F82, H42, H94, J7, L89, L97, N39, etc.

Emerald:[4] (Emerald Bush Buttercup) 80 days. An improved strain of bush buttercup. Uniform, turban-shaped fruit; 4 1/2 inches deep, 6 1/2 inches in diameter; medium dark-green skin; thick, orange-yellow, sweet flesh. Short-vine plant, grows 3 to 4 feet across. Ideal for limited space gardens. D68, F1, *F60*, *G13M*, G16, K73, M49

Golden Bush: 90 days. Bush form of Buttercup, earlier in maturity. Distinctive, golden-orange fruit, 3 to 5 pounds in weight. Not a pure strain, some fruits will be all green. D82

BUTTERNUT SQUASH (C. moschata)

Hybrid

Early Butternut: 80 days. Uniform, blocky fruit, bulbous at the blossom end; 10 to 12 inches long; skin smooth, thin and hard, evenly tan; flesh deep orange, medium dry, fine-textured, of very good flavor and quality. Compact, semi-bush vine. Excellent for home gardens and commercial production. All America Selections winner in 1979. A87M, C85M, D11M, D65, *E91G*, F19M, *F72*, G93M, *H61*, I64, J7, J34, K73, L79, N16, etc.

Zenith: 88 days. Exceptionally uniform fruit, averages 2 1/2 pounds in weight; thick, cylindrical neck; smooth, tan skin; flesh deep orange, fine-textured, sweet, of very high quality. High yielding. For home gardens, local markets and commercial growers. *A1*, A32, C92, D82, *F60*, *G1M*, *G13M*, G82, *H61*, I64, J84, K73, L42, M29, N16, etc.

Open-Pollinated

Butterbush:[4] (Burpee's Butterbush) 75 days. The first bush-type butternut, introduced in 1978. Short, compact vine; only 3 to 4 feet long; bears 4 or 5 fruit. Small, blocky fruit; weight 1 1/2 to 1 3/4 pounds; smooth, tan skin; deep reddish-orange flesh. Excellent storage qualities. Ideal for gardeners with limited space. A16, B75, C85M, D11M, G51, G79, H42, H94, H95, J20, J58, N52

Butternut: 95 days. Bottle-shaped fruit; 8 inches long, 3 to 4 inches in diameter at the blossom end; weight 3 to 5 pounds; skin smooth, buff-colored, thin and hard; flesh bright-orange, firm, fine-grained, dry, sweet, of very good quality; keeps very well. Excellent for baking. A16, A25, B78, *D49*, E38, F82, F92, H49, H94, J7, J34, L97, M95M, N39

Hercules: 95 days. Large, straight, blocky fruit; 12 to 15 inches long, 4 1/2 inches in diameter; weight 4 1/2 to 5 pounds; skin buff-colored, thin and hard; flesh rich orange, firm, dry, fine-textured, sweet, of very good flavor and quality; has a very small seed cavity; keeps very well. Vigorous, highly productive vine. All America Selections winner in 1963. E97, *G13M*, G79, *H61*, *L59G*

Ponca: 90 days. Similar to Waltham butternut, but more uniform in size and shape and slightly smaller. Blocky, cylindrical fruit; 6 to 8 inches long; weight 1 1/2 to 2 1/2 pounds; skin smooth, hard, evenly tan; flesh light orange, fine-textured, sweet, of very good quality; has a small seed cavity; keeps well. Highly productive, compact vine. Developed at the University of Nebraska. *A1*, *A75*, B75M, D68, *F60*, G6, *G13M*, *H61*, J84, K49M, K66, K71, K73, L89, M49, N52, etc.

Puritan: 100 days. Smaller strain of Waltham butternut. Uniform, blocky fruit; 7 inches long, 4 inches in diameter; smooth, cylindrical neck free of crooknecks; weight 2 to 3 pounds; smooth, tan skin; rich orange flesh, dry, of very good flavor. Released by the Massachusetts Agricultural Experiment Station. A13

Waltham: 95 days. Uniform, blocky fruit; 8 to 10 inches long, 4 1/2 to 5 1/2 inches in diameter at the blossom end; weight 3 to 4 pounds; skin light tan to buff, thin and hard; flesh dark-orange, fine-textured, medium dry, sweet, of excellent quality and flavor; has a very small seed cavity; stores well. Very popular. All America Selections winner in 1970. B49, B75M, C44, D87, E57, F19M, G6, G16, *H61*, K73, L7M, M13M, M46, M95, N16, etc.

HUBBARD SQUASH (C. maxima)

Autumn Pride:[4] Bush-type hubbard squash developed by the University of New Hampshire. Compact vine, grows only 4 to 5 feet across. Medium to large, orange fruit; weight 8 to 20 pounds, depending on planting distance; flesh bright orange, thick, does not become watery or stringy like many other Hubbard-type squash. Stores well into the winter. I99, J20

Baby Blue: 90 days. Small, flattened to round fruit, 5 to 6 inches in diameter; weight 5 to 7 pounds; skin grayish-blue, warted; flesh yellow-orange, thick, sweet, dry, flavor very good; stores well. Excellent for baking. Ideal size for the average family. Also popular with market gardeners. Semi-bush type. Blue Hubbard x Buttercup. Developed by Professor E.M. Meader. A2, D65, *F60*, *G13M*, G93M, K10, K71, *N40*{PR}

Blue Hubbard: 110 days. Large, nearly globular fruit, with a neck at both ends; 15 to 18 inches long, 9 to 12 inches in diameter; weight 12 to 15 pounds; skin blue-grey, hard and thick, coarsely warted; flesh bright yellow-orange, thick, dry, fine-textured, very sweet; stores extremely well. Highly productive. Standard winter storage type. Introduced in 1909. TAPLEY 1937; A13, A25, C44, D65, E38, *F60*, F92, G6, G71, H66, K73, L89, M13M, M46, M95, N39, etc.

Chicago Warted: (Green Chicago Warted Hubbard, Warted Green Hubbard) 110 days. Largest of the Green Hubbard types. Nearly globular fruit; pointed at the blossom end, rounded at the stem end; 13 to 15 inches long; weight 12 to 14 pounds; skin deep dark-green, heavily warted, thick, very hard; flesh rich golden-yellow, thick, fine-textured, dry, sweet. Good for shipping and storage. Introduced in 1894. TAPLEY 1937; B75M, C92, *F60*, *G13M*, G16, G67M, G79, G82, G93M, *H61*, J84, K71, K73, M13M, M49, etc.

Golden Hubbard: (Red Hubbard) 100 days. Relatively small fruit; 10 to 12 inches long, 8 to 9 inches in diameter; skin slightly warted, orange to orange-red, striped with tan toward the blossom end, attractive; flesh deep orange-yellow, moderately dry and sweet, firm, of good flavor and quality. Keeps very well. Introduced in 1898. TAPLEY 1937; A13, A16, A25, A69M, E24, E38, *E91G*, *F60*, F92, K50, K71, K73, L42, L97, M13M, etc.

Green Hubbard: (True Hubbard, True Green Hubbard) 110 days. Medium-large fruit; nearly globular, tapered at both ends; 12 to 15 inches long; weight 9 to 12 pounds; skin dull bronze green when mature, thick, very hard, slightly warted; flesh orange-yellow, thick, fine-grained, firm, dry, moderately sweet; keeps very well. Introduced about 1798. BURR, TAPLEY 1937, VILMORIN; A16, A25, D11M, D27, E38, *E91G*, F1, *F60*, F92, G79, H54, K50, K71, L9, L97, M46, etc.

Kitchenette: (Baby Hubbard) 105 days. Small, slightly curved fruit, tapered abruptly to a short constricted neck; 8 to 9 inches long; weight 5 to 7 pounds; skin deep green, moderately warted; flesh deep yellow, very fine, dry, sweet, well flavored. Excellent for baking. Ideal for family use. Developed by Richard Wellington. Introduced in 1919. TAPLEY 1937; K10, L42

Little Gem: 80 days. Miniature Golden Hubbard type. Small, bright-orange fruit; weight 3 to 5 pounds; flesh deep orange, thick, dry, fine-grained, sweet and flavorful. Excellent for pies or baking whole. Good storage capabilities. Vigorous, highly productive vine. E49, G68, M49, S55

<u>KABOCHA SQUASH</u> Japanese squash notable for their superior flavor, rich sweetness and nearly fiberless flesh. When baked or steamed they have a balanced flavor of sweet potato and pumpkin. They are also braised, added to salads or pumpkin *risotto*, deep-fried in tempura batter, or simmered in *oden* stew or *dashi* stock. COST 1988 [Cul], SCHNEIDER [Cul, Re]. (C. maxima, C. moschata)

Hybrid

Golden Debut: 105 days. Unique orange-skinned type with skin that is edible after cooking. Medium-sized, oblate fruit; skin attractive, green, turning bright scarlet orange at maturity, with slightly mottled vertical stripes; flesh yellow, very sweet, moist, less starchy than Home Delite. Excellent boiled or baked; ideal for squash pies. E59, *K16M*, M46, N52

Home Delite: 109 days. Very early type. Medium-small, flattened globe-shaped fruit, smaller than Golden Debut. Skin mottled and striped with light and dark-green. Thick, dry, orange-yellow flesh with a sweet chestnut-like flavor. Produces few lateral shoots, making cultivation and harvest easy. E59, G33, *K16M*, M46, N52

Honey Delite: 95 days. Medium-small, flattened globe-shaped fruit; weight 2 to 4 pounds; skin dark forest-green, striped with moss-green; flesh bright rich-orange, very sweet and flavorful, cooks up dry and flaky; quality excellent; stores well. Good specialty market item. G6, I77, *L79G*

Shin-Tosa: (C. maxima x C. moschata) 100 days. Slightly flattened, globe-shaped fruit with shallow ribbing; rind dark green, waxy, somewhat bumpy; weight 4 to 5 pounds. Used by Japanese and Chinese in rice cakes, or steamed or baked like a sweet potato. Very vigorous, productive plant; resistant to disease and insects; does well under dry or wet conditions. E83T

Tetsukabuto: (C. maxima x C. moschata) Nearly round fruit, 8 inches in diameter; glossy dark green rind, lightly mottled and ribbed; thick, deep orange flesh with a very sweet yam-like flavor; stores very well. High yielding. Good specialty market item. Very popular in Japan. Also used as a disease-resistant rootstock for watermelons, melons and cucumbers. E49, *L79G*, *Q28*, *S63M*, *S70*

<u>SPAGHETTI SQUASH</u> (C. pepo)

Hybrid

Go-Getti: An early spaghetti squash hybrid. The fruits are borne in the center of the semi-bush plants. Their exterior is bicolor - orange and green. When the green fades, the fruit is ripe. The "noodles" are cream in color and mild in flavor, which adapts them to a wide array of recipes. *P75M*

Orangetti: 85 days. An attractive orange spaghetti squash. Small, oblong fruit; 8 inches long, 6 inches in diameter; weight 2 to 2 1/2 pounds; skin golden-orange, smooth; flesh bright orange. Higher in vitamins A and C than other types of spaghetti squash. Semi-bush type plant; bears numerous fruit close to the crown. D11M, D76, *E53M*, *E91G*, E97, *F72*, G79, G82, *H61*, I39, I67M, J20, K10, K73, L79, M46, *N40*{PR}, etc.

Tivoli:[4] 98 days. Unique bush spaghetti squash. Medium-large, oval fruit, 9 1/2 inches long and 6 inches in diamter; rind smooth, pale creamy yellow; flesh seperates into noodle-like strands when cooked. Vigorous, space-saving bush, may have a few short vines. All America Selections winner for 1991. *K16M*

White Fall: Oblong, creamy-white fruit; 9 inches long, 6 inches in diameter; weight 5 1/2 pounds; flesh crisp, tender, creamy-white when fresh, turning yellow after cooking (steaming). Fruits reach maturity 40 days after flowering. May be stored for months. Well adapted to mild, cool climates. *Q39*

Open-Pollinated

Spaghetti Squash: (Vegetable Spaghetti) 100 days. Unique squash with spaghetti-like strands of flesh. Small, oval fruit; 8 to 10 inches long, 6 to 8 inches in diameter; weight 1 1/2 pounds; skin yellow, changing to buff-colored when ripe, smooth; flesh golden-yellow; stores well. Usually boiled or baked whole. Can also be used in breads, muffins, pancakes, puddings, etc. Introduced in 1934 by Sakata Seed Company, Yokohama, Japan. FELL 1982a [Pre, Re], SCHNEIDER [Cul, Re]; A16, E24, E57, *F60*, *F72*, G6, G16, H94, J73, L59, M13M, M46, M49, O53M

<u>OTHERS</u>

Cucurbita maxima

Arikara: 72 days. Small, oval-tapered fruit; 9 to 10 inches long; widely ribbed; weight 6 to 8 pounds; skin pale salmon pink; flesh deep yellow, tender, moderately moist and soft, flavor lacking, faintly sweet; quality poor. Extremely dependable producer under drought conditions. Originated with the Arikara Indians of the Fort Berthold reservation, North Dakota. Named and introduced by Oscar H. Will & Company, Bismark, in 1920. TAPLEY 1937; I99, K49M, L7M

Atlantic Giant: (Dill's Atlantic Giant) 125 days. Developed by Howard Dill of Nova Scotia for producing extremely large fruits, weighing 400 pounds or more. A yearly world record holder since 1979. An all-time world record of 612 pounds was obtained from this cultivar in 1984. Yearly international competition was established in 1983 under the rules of the World Pumpkin Federation. B73M, D6, E49, F1, G16, G71, H42, H95, I81, L79, L97, M46, M49, N16

Blue Kuri: 100 days. Japanese squash derived from Hubbard. Small, globular fruit, weight 4 to 5 pounds; skin blue-green, fairly smooth; flesh yellow-orange, thick, dry, fine-grained, very sweet, of good quality. Heavy yielding vine. Does well in short season areas. For roadside stands and specialty markets. A2, G33, G93M, N52, *S63M*

Boston Marrow: 100 days. Nearly globular fruit, abruptly tapered at the stem end; 12 to 14 inches long, 10 to 11 inches in diameter; widely ribbed; weight 12 to 16 pounds; skin apricot-orange; flesh orange-yellow, moderately fine-grained, tender, fairly sweet and rich, moderately moist; quality fair. Introduced in 1831. BURR, TAPLEY 1937; *A75*, F25, G71, I99, K49M

Chestnut: 105 days. Medium-small, flattened globe-shaped fruit; weight 2 to 4 pounds; skin dark slate-green; flesh deep orange, thick, very sweet and dry. Good for storage, with sweetness increasing during the first few weeks after harvest. Moderate yields. The result of "target breeding" for high sugar and dry matter. G6, K49M

Flat White: (Flat White Boer) 100 days. Very flattened, ridged, white-skinned fruit; sweet, orange-colored flesh; leaves no fiber when passed through a sieve. Makes a pie that is lighter in color. Keeps well. Imported from South Africa. G68

Gold Nugget:[4] (Golden Nugget) 85 days. Small, round to slightly flattened fruit; 5 inches in diameter; weight 1 1/2 to 2 pounds; skin bright orange, hard; flesh yellow-orange, thick, fine-grained, of good quality and flavor; keeps well. Short-vined plant; produces 5 to 8 fruit. All America Selections winner in 1966. SCHNEIDER [Cul, Re]; A16, *A69M*, B1M, B73M, D11M, E70M{PR}, E97, F44, *F60*, G6, H94, K49M, *L59G*, L97, M49, *N40*{PR}, P83M, T1M, etc.

Golden Delicious: 105 days. Small, heart-shaped fruit; 10 to 12 inches long, 8 to 10 inches in diameter; weight 8 to 10 pounds; skin reddish-orange, striped with pinkish-buff; flesh orange-yellow, thick, dry, medium-textured, of good quality. Widely used for commercial canning and freezing. Boston Marrow x Delicious. Introduced in 1926. TAPLEY 1937; *A1*, A25, E57, E97, F13, *F60*, *F63*, *G13M*, G79, G82, K10, K71, L42, M46, N52, etc.

Marina di Chioggia: (Chioggia, Sea Squash) Small, flattened fruit; weight 5 to 7 pounds; skin dark grayish-green, coarsely wrinkled with large protuberances; flesh bright orange, very firm, very mealy. In Italy, the fruit is boiled, baked or purééd, and also used in minestrone soup, and an unusual *risotto*. Unripe fruit can be used in relishes and preserves. Widely grown around Venice. BIANCHINI; I77, J73, Q11M

Mayo Blusher: Large, round to elongated fruit; skin light green to white, blushed with pink when fully ripe; flesh apricot-colored, sweet, excellent for "pumpkin" pie; stores well. Adapted to the low hot desert, where it is planted in early spring. I16

Pink Banana Jumbo: 105 days. Very large, cylindrical fruit, slightly curved towards the stem end; 48 inches long; weight up to 75 pounds; skin grayish-green, turning bright pink at maturity, thin, very hard; flesh light orange, thick, fine-textured, sweet, of high quality. Good for pies or baking. Very popular in California. Usually cut in sections for fresh market or used for processing. B35M, B75M, C76M, C92, D76, E49, F92, G51, G82, G93M, *H61*, H66, H95, I67M, J34, K71, N16, etc.

Queensland Blue: 150 days. Small, drum-shaped fruit; 8 to 9 inches in diameter; weight 6 to 9 pounds; skin blue-grey, hard and thin; flesh deep orange, very fine-textured, firm and solid, dry, moderately sweet, of good flavor; quality very good. An old popular Australian cultivar. Introduced into the United States in 1932. TAPLEY 1937; G93M, I77, K49M, P1G, R47, T1M

Red Kuri: (Orange Hokkaido, Uchiki Kuri, Baby Red Hubbard) 92 days. Nearly globular fruit, tapered at both ends; weight 5 to 8 pounds; skin smooth, bright reddish-orange; flesh yellow-orange, thick, fine-grained, dry, sweet and rich; keeps very well. Good for pies. High yielding. Of Japanese origin. B49, D68, E24, E70M{PR}, G6, G92, G93M, H42, I76M{PR}, I77, J83T{PR}, K49M, L9M, *N40*{PR}, N52, N84, S55, *S63M*, etc.

Rouge Vif d'Etampes: (Bright Red Etampes) 125 days. Medium-large, flattened fruit; 9 to 10 inches deep, 16 to 18 inches in diameter; weight 30 to 35 pounds; prominently ribbed; skin bright orange-red, glossy, attractive; flesh coarse, fibrous, moderately moist and tender, quality fair to poor. Originated in France in the middle of the 19th century. TAPLEY 1937, VILMORIN; C53, G68, I77, I99, K49M, P59M

Sibley: (Pike's Peak) 120 days. Relatively small fruit; oblong-pyriform; 10 to 12 inches long; weight 8 to 10 pounds; skin bluish gray; flesh pale orange, very fine-textured, tender, slightly moist, somewhat sweet, of fair flavor and quality. Probably of American Indian origin. Introduced in 1887. TAPLEY 1937; K49M

Spanish Valencia: Large, flattened fruit, hollowed on both ends; weight 15 to 20 pounds; skin grey-green blotched with pink when ripe, often with a light bloom, very hard; flesh yellowish-orange, thick, extremely sweet. Keeps for an exceptionally long time, up to 2 years. Long, trailing vine; tends to be a shy bearer; requires a long, warm growing season. One of the sweetest of all squashes, reminiscent of a high quality, moist-fleshed sweet potato. L11

Sweet Meat: (Oregon Sweet Meat) 110 days. Large, flattened globe-shaped fruit; weight 10 to 15 pounds; skin thick, very hard, slate gray; flesh golden-yellow, thick, fine-grained, very sweet and rich. Has excellent keeping qualities. Local favorite in the Pacific Northwest. Originated in Portland, Oregon by Gill Brothers Seed Co. A2, A69M, D82, E24, F13, F42, F82, G57M, *G83M*, H95, I39, I77, K10, *L59G*, L89, L97, N52, etc.

Triamble: (Triangle) 135 days. Small, trilocular fruit, arranged in a triangle; 4 to 5 inches deep, 10 to 12 inches in diameter; weight 10 to 15 pounds; deeply furrowed; skin bluish-grey, smooth; flesh pale orange, thick, slightly fibrous and granular, somewhat sweet, of fair flavor and quality. Introduced into the United States from Australia, in 1932. TAPLEY 1937; E49, T1M

Turk's Turban: (Turk's Cap) 115 days. Distinct turban-shaped fruit; 10 to 12 inches in diameter; weight 8 to 10 pounds; skin variously striped with red to green to white and orange; flesh light orange, fine-grained, rather juicy, tender; quality poor. Mostly used for ornament. Introduced at the beginning of the 19th century or earlier. BURR, TAPLEY 1937, VILMORIN; A13, B75, B75M, C92, D11M, E24, E70M{PR}, *F60*, G51, G71, G93M, *H61*, J34, K71, K73, M95, N16, etc.

Umatilla Marblehead: 115 days. Large, uniform, oval fruits, often weighing up to 40 pounds; rind grayish-green, slightly ribbed, free of warts; flesh pale orange, very thick (1 1/2 to 2 1/2 inches), fine-grained, quite sweet; flavor and quality very good; keeps well. Vine vigorous, trailing, highly productive; resistant to curly top virus. An old local favorite in Oregon. N52

Whangaparoa Crown: (Crown) 140 days. Small, drum-shaped fruit; blossom scar with a button, giving a crown-like appearance; weight 10 to 12 pounds; skin grey, hard; flesh deep yellow, very firm and hard, slightly stringy, moderately dry and sweet, quality fair to good. Popular in New Zealand and Australia, where it is used for pies and as a cooked vegetable. Introduced into the United States in 1932. TAPLEY 1937; E49, I99, P1G, T1M

Cucurbita mixta

Apache Giant: 125 days. Large, squat pear-shaped fruit; rind dark-green, variegated with pale lime-green streaks; weight 25 to 40 pounds; flesh cream-yellow, 1 1/2 inches thick. Good for pies and baking. From the San Carlos reservation in Arizona. Adapted to the low hot desert. I16, L79M

Chompa:[5] Medium-sized winter squash, usually eaten when young or grown for its edible seed. Grows well in poor soil. From the Zapotec Indians of Oaxaca, Mexico. F80

Golden Stripe Cushaw: 110 days. Strain of Green Striped Cushaw. Large, pear-shaped fruit; long neck, may be straight or crooked; weight 25 to 30 pounds; attractive golden-yellow skin, striped with white; flesh gold-colored, thick, smooth, sweet; keeps well. J25M

Green Striped Cushaw: Medium-large fruit; pear-shaped, with long, slightly curved neck; 16 to 20 inches long; weight 12 to 16 pounds; skin cream-white, mottled with green; flesh pale yellow, coarse and fibrous, moist, slightly sweet, quality poor. Used for pies and baking or for livestock feed. Very popular home garden cultivar. Introduced prior to 1893. KAVENA [Pre, Re], TAPLEY 1937; A87M, D76, E97, F12, *F60*, G71, *H61*, H66, J34, K49M, K71, L7M, M95, N16

Japanese Pie: 115 days. Crookneck type. Skin mottled with dark and light green; flesh buff-yellow, juicy, slightly fibrous and sweet, quality poor. Mainly used for canning and livestock food. Once grown as a novelty for its seeds, "curiously marked or sculptured in the manner of Chinese letters", hence the name Chinese Alphabet squash or Japanese Alphabet squash. Introduced in 1884. TAPLEY 1937; A87M

Pepinas:[5] Grown for its very large, edible seed. Zapotec cultivar, originally from Morelos, Mexico. Appears to be a form of Chompa. Likes hot weather. F80

Santo Domingo: 90 days. Medium-large, pear-shaped fruit; weight 15 to 20 pounds; skin striped with light and dark green; sweet, pale yellow flesh; stores well when not bruised. Can be used as a summer squash when picked young. The tasty seeds are also edible. Drought tolerant. J25M, L79M

Silver Edged:[5] Grown for the large, tasty spectacular seeds, white with silver edging. Seeds are roasted for *pepitas* or used in *pipian sauce*. A Mesoamerican land race. Adapted to the high semi-desert where it is planted in early spring or with the summer rains. I16

Tamala:[5] (Calabaza de Tamala) Very large fruit in 4 distinct shapes: round bowl with thin neck, flattened bowl with thick neck, long heart-shaped, and flattened globe. Skin buff-colored; flesh bright orange, somewhat juicy. Seeds are edible. Grows best in hot weather. F80

Tarahumara: 75-80 days. Variably shaped fruit, form bottleneck to nearly round; weight 5 to 10 pounds; skin striped white and green, hard, warty; mild, sweet flesh. Good for pies and baking, or steaming. Can also be eaten when young like zucchini. Originated with the Tarahumara Indians of Mexico. J25M

Tennessee Sweet Potato: 105 days. Medium-large, pear-shaped fruit; 12 to 15 inches long; weight 12 to 15 pounds; skin pale yellow, striped with greenish-yellow; flesh light yellow, thick, coarse and granular, dry, fine-grained, sweet, of excellent flavor. Popular in the South. Originated prior to 1883. TAPLEY 1937; K49M

White Cushaw: 120 days. Medium-large, crookneck fruit, 18 to 20 inches long and 8 to 9 inches in diameter; weight 12 to 16 pounds; skin pure white, sometimes with faint green stripes; flesh coarse, rather stringy, moist, moderately tender, quality poor. Resembles Green Striped Cushaw. Introduced in 1891. TAPLEY 1937; L7M

Cucurbita moschata

Cheese: (White Cheesequake, Big Cheese, White Cheese) 110 days. Flattened globe-shaped fruit; 12 to 14 inches in diameter; weight 10 to 14 pounds; skin cream-colored; flesh coarse, fibrous, soft, juicy, distinctly sweet; quality poor. Largely grown for canning and stock feed. Named for its resemblance to the standard cheesebox of the 1800's. Originated prior to 1824. TAPLEY 1937; F25

Chirimen: 135 days. Small, flattened globe-shaped fruit; 8 to 10 inches in diameter; weight 8 to 10 pounds; narrowly ribbed; skin dark-green, turning dull bronze-orange in storage, profusely warted; flesh yellow-orange, thick, coarse, slightly moist, moderately sweet. Of Japanese origin. Introduced into the United States about 1922. TAPLEY 1937; G33, N52, *S63M*

Citrouille Brodee d'Eysines: Large, flattened cheese-box-shaped fruit, with deep ribs; weight up to 25 pounds; rind chocolate brown; flesh thick, very deep reddish-orange. Vigorous, prolific vine. Has done well in the Philadelphia area. Introduced from France by Dr. David Unander, a pumpkin breeder on ECHO's Board of Directors. D33

Futtsu Black: 110 days. Flattened globe-shaped fruit, with deep, high ribs; 4 inches long, 7 inches in diameter; heavily warted; skin dark blackish-green; flesh orange-yellow, fine-grained, sweet and nutty. Old-fashioned Japanese cultivar. Very popular for forcing. J73, *P39*

Golden Cushaw: (Mammoth Golden Cushaw) 120 days. Medium-large, curved fruit, bulbous at the blossom end; 18 to 24 inches long; weight 10 to 14 pounds; widely ribbed; skin deep cream-colored, smooth; flesh pale salmon, coarse and granular, fibrous; quality poor. Used for canning and stock food. Originated prior to 1884. TAPLEY 1937; G57M, K49M

Kentucky Field: 125 days. Similar if not identical to Cheese. Flattened globe-shaped fruit; 12 to 15 inches in diameter; weight 12 to 16 pounds; widely ribbed; skin green, turning cream-colored in storage; flesh dull salmon orange, very coarse and fibrous, juicy, slightly sweet; quality poor. Used for canning and stock feed. TAPLEY 1937; C92, *I59M*, K27M

Kikuza: 140 days. Small, ribbed, drum-shaped fruit; 5 to 6 inches deep, 9 to 10 inches in diameter; weight 5 to 8 pounds; skin dull bronze-orange, warted and wrinkled; flesh yellow-orange, fine-grained, moderately dry, tender, crisp, sweet, rather spicy. Of Japanese origin. Introduced into the United States about 1927. TAPLEY 1937; I39

La Primera Calabaza: Improved cultivar of Calabaza or Cuban squash, a long-time favorite in Central and South America and the Caribbean. Round fruit; skin hard, green when ripe; flesh rich orange, thick, fine-grained, very sweet, moist but not watery. Considered mature when the flesh is yellow just beneath the skin. HAWKES [Re], SCHNEIDER [Cul, Re]; *B59*{PR}, D33, K49M, L9M

Marian Van Atta Calabaza: A cultivar of Calabaza or Cuban squash developed over a 15 year period by world famous southern garden writer, Marian Van Atta. Predominately pumpkin-shaped, 8 to 10 inches in diameter; skin green and yellow striped when young, buff-colored when ripe; flesh deep orange, very sweet and fine-grained. L9M

Mediterranean Giant: 100 days. Butternut-shaped fruit; resembles a short, straight Tahitian squash; weight 8 to 10 pounds; smooth, thin, golden-tan skin; very sweet, golden-orange flesh; keeps very well. Can be harvested as a summer squash when 6 to 8 inches long. Large, vigorous vine; does best on a trellis. Local market favorite in southern California. K10

Musquee' de Provence: A regional squash from southern France. Flattened cheese-box shape, deeply ribbed; skin dark orange, smooth, glossy; flesh of good flavor; keeps well into the New Year when properly stored. Fast disappearing from the marketplaces. I77

Neck Pumpkin: 120 days. Similar to Tahitian squash. Large, curved fruit; 18 to 24 inches in length, 4 to 5 inches in diameter at the neck, 9 inches at the blossom end; skin light brown, smooth and hard; flesh orange, thick, solid, dry, sweet. Excellent for pies. A13, J97M, K10

Papaya Pumpkin: (Papaya Golden, Paw Paw) 90 days. Small, ribbed fruit; round-oval, slightly tapered and flattened on top; weight 2 to 2 1/2 pounds; skin dark-green, mottled with yellow, smooth, thin; flesh deep-yellow, thick, tender, flavor very sweet and nutty; strongly resembles a papaya. Vigorous vine; virus and disease tolerant. Very common in Taiwan. D55, I39, R47

Piena di Napoli: (Neapolitan, Carpet Bag Squash, Bedouin Squash) Large, violin-shaped fruit; 16 to 20 inches long; 5 to 8 inches in diameter at the blossom end; weight 30 to 40 pounds; broadly ribbed; skin dark-green, turning dull yellow when ripe, smooth; flesh yellow-orange, thick, very sweet and fragrant. Very productive. BURR, TAPLEY 1937, VILMORIN; J73, Q11M

Seminole Pumpkin: Small, globular fruit, 6 to 8 inches in diameter; slightly furrowed; skin hard, light buff-colored; flesh orange-red, fine-grained, sweet. Good boiled or steamed, excellent when baked. Stores extremely well, a waxy covering forming over the fruit. Highly productive vine; resistant to insects, drought and heavy tropical rains. Adapted to Deep South growing conditions. Found growing wild in Florida by early explorers and settlers. Now confined to the remote Everglades. ERWIN; D33, L9M

Tahitian: (Melon Squash) 150 days. Large, curved fruit, with bulbous blossom end; weight 15 to 40 pounds; skin buff-colored, smooth and hard; flesh deep orange, very sweet and rich, of good quality raw or cooked; keeps extremely well, becoming sweeter in storage. Vigorous vine; resistant to mildew. Believed to be an old cultivar dropped by the seed companies many years ago. A2, A44M{PR}, B73M, D76, E32M{PL}, E97, J34, K49M, L11, L91M, R47

Cucurbita pepo

Aladin: Small, distinctive fruit, looks remarkably like Turk's Turban, with a green base and yellow, red-striped, three-pointed top. Said to be fine flavored, thick, floury and sweet. F80

Delicata: (Sweet Potato Squash) 95 days. Small, cylindrical, narrowly ribbed fruit; 8 to 10 inches long; weight 2 to 3 pounds; skin light cream-colored, striped with dark green; flesh deep orange-yellow, very fine-grained, dry, sweet and rich, quality good. Good specialty market item. Highly prolific vine, 8 to 10 feet long. Introduced in 1894. SCHNEIDER [Cul, Re], TAPLEY 1937; A2, D76, E24, E70M{PR}, E97, G6, *H61*, I39, I99, J25M, K49M, L42, L79M, L89, M13M, *N40*{PR}, etc.

Eat-All:[4 5] Unique, dual-purpose squash. Small, cylindrical fruit; skin cream-colored, striped with dark green; resembles Delicata. Hulless seeds of high nutritional value (35% protein, 40% oil). Can be cut in half and baked as is, the seeds adding a nut-like flavor to the sweet, dry, golden flesh. Or the seeds may be roasted separately as a confection. Developed by E.M. Meader at the University of New Hampshire. U33

Gem: 70 days. Dual-purpose squash. Grapefruit-sized fruits can be harvested as summer squash, when seed development has just begun, and cooked whole by boiling or steaming until the interior is soft, then served with the top removed and topped with a pat of butter. Also used as a very early winter squash when mature, with rich orange flesh. Semi-bush vine, 6 feet in diameter. J82, L89, R47

Huicha:[5] 90 days. Light green, fragrant fruit; orange flesh; delicate flavor; harvested at 8 inches long or less, when sweet and tender. Also preferred for producing edible seed. Very large vine, to 40 feet long; leaves 2 feet across. Makes an excellent shade against summer heat if grown along the sunny side of a house. An old cultivar grown by the Indians of Mexico. F80, J73

Kuta: (F_1) 48 days. Unique, gourmet squash. Young, light green fruit, under 6 inches in length is eaten raw in salads or with dips, being crisp and smooth with a sweet, nutty flavor. Fruits of intermediate maturity may be used like eggplants. Fully mature fruit turns dark green and is excellent for baking or stuffing like a winter squash. Good keeping qualities. Vigorous, prolific vine. G51, I91, J34

Lady Godiva:[5] (Naked Seeded) 100 days. Grown primarily for the green hulless or "naked" seeds that do not require shelling. Can be eaten raw or roasted. High in protein and oil. The flesh can also be baked, boiled or steamed. Yellow-orange fruit, mottled with green. Highly productive vine; often produces 12 to 15 fruit. A32, C53, C85M{CF}, E49, I99, L11, L42, O53M

Lady Godiva Bush:[4 5] Rare bush form of Lady Godiva. Compact, short-vined plants, can be grown close together. Produces 3 to 4 fruit per plant. Round fruits, weighing 6 to 8 pounds; yield 300 to 400 hulless seeds per fruit. Poor quality flesh. I99

Mt. Pima Vavuli:[5] Medium-sized, roundish fruit with dark green skin and orange flesh. Raised mainly for seed or to be eaten when immature as summer squash. L79M

Sweet Dumpling: (Vegetable Gourd) 100 days. Small, flattened globe-shaped fruit; 4 inches in diameter; deep, high ribs; skin ivory-colored, with dark-green stripes; flesh orange, very sweet and tender. Suitable for stuffing. Requires no curing, keeping 3 to 4 months. Medium length vines. Good specialty market item. BRENNAN [Cul, Re], SCHNEIDER [Cul, Re]; A32, B75, C92, E70M{PR}, E97, G6, *H61*, I99, J7, K66, L42, L97, M46, *N40*{PR}, O53M, P83M, S55, etc.

Yellow Large Paris: (Gros Jaune de Paris, Mammoth Pumpkin) Large, flattened fruit, with well-marked ribs; skin salmon-yellow, slightly cracked or netted when ripe; flesh yellow, thick, fine flavored, sweet; keeps well. Used in France to make pumpkin soup and pies. VILMORIN; G68, P59M

STARTER CULTURES {DR}

BACTERIA
YEASTS
MOLDS

BEER YEASTS

BOTTOM-FERMENTING

American Lager: A strain similar to the type used by many American breweries. Will produce a lager with minimal added flavors, ideal when the cleanest possible flavor is desired. Able to ferment over a wide range of temperatures, making it ideal for summer-style beers as well as traditional lager beers. A99T, E68, N17{LI}

Bavarian Lager: Produces a clean and robust German-style lager beer. Ferments to a full flavored, crisp finish without the soft "bready" flavor of some of the more delicate lager yeasts. Brews an excellent lager beer, even at warm temperatures. A99M, N17{LI}

Continental Lager: Rapid fermenter at 46° F., making it a good choice for fast refrigerator lager beers. H10{LI}

Danish Lager: Used by breweries around the world, Danish Lager will produce a lager with a true continental character. Will add a noticeable character to beer and should be used when a mild European flavor is desired. Should not be used at temperatures exceeding 75° F. N17{LI}

Kitzinger Lager: Very slow starting yeast from Germany. Acts like to a true lager. For best results a yeast starter should be made 24 to 48 hours before brewing. A71M, A99T, C51, E68, F64, G5, G39, G83G, H34M, I55

M.eV. American Lager #010: A true lager yeast when fermented at 54° F. Fermentation is not considered to be reliable below 48° F. The yeast flocculates poorly and is therefore not recommended for single stage fermentation. Has such a beautiful aroma and flavor that the sediment even tastes good. H10{LI}

M.eV. American Lager #070: Received from a homebrewing club that had originally obtained it from a large U.S. brewery. A good fermenter at 50 to 54° F. Should also be good for bock beers (over 7% alcohol) as the major breweries are high gravity brewing. H10{LI}

M.eV. German Lager #001: An excellent choice for making German style beers. A strong fermenter between 44 and 50° F., making refrigerator fermentation possible. Also a good choice for bock beers as it can produce high alcohol (over 7%). A high user of nitrogen; recommended only for all malt beers. If mashing, a good protein temperature rest will give best results. H10{LI}

M.eV. German Lager #037: A popular strain in Germany, this yeast produces a high quality beer with some care. Requires a good amino nitrogen pool (protein temp. rest), good oxygenated wort at pitching, and is inhibited by high traub levels. H10{LI}

M.eV. Lager: Excellent yeast for producing continental style lagers. Optimum fermentation temperature is 50 to 54° F., but slows at 46° F. making refrigerator fermentation still possible. Slants of this yeast give off an aroma reminiscent of roses. H10{LI}

Old Danish Lager: Bottom-fermenting yeast used for steam beers and cool fermentation. G39, J52

Pilsner Lager: A sedimentary lager yeast that will settle down firmly and allow the clear beer to be siphoned off. Used by many commercial breweries. It ferments a little slower than other beer yeasts, but it imparts an excellent flavor to the beer. C51, G40

Red Star Lager: Bottom-fermenting yeast used for brewing at room temperature. Best for steam beers and for cold, lager beer fermentations. Ferments beer to a fruity finish with a slight acidic character. Popular fast starting yeast. Settles out readily to produce a very clear beer. Optimum temperature range 43 to 46° F. A71M, A99M, F63M, F64, F65, G5, G39, G83G, I55, J52, K54, N17

Semplex Lager: A bottom-fermenting lager yeast that is furnished to most American and many foreign breweries. It is of superior quality. K54

Vierka Lager: Cold temperature yeast. For best results use a yeast starter. Developed in cooperation with the brewmasters of world famous German breweries. A superior yeast. A99, C51, F63M, G5, G40, G83G, H34M, I55, K54

William's Dry Lager: Has a cleaner flavor than Red Star Lager, however it will not produce as clean a flavor as liquid lager yeast. Produces a dry, slightly thin beer with vague fruity-citric flavors in the aftertaste. N17

<u>**TOP-FERMENTING**</u>

Altbier: German ale yeast. Good for producing strong well hopped ales at 5% alcohol. Very high attenuation. Fermentation is best around 68° F. H10{LI}

Burton Ale: A true English pale ale yeast. Leaves a soft, almost "bready" flavor in the finished ale. Ideal for use in bitter and pale ale type beers, as its mild flavor allows the flavor of the finest hops and malt to be fully appreciated. Slow to start fermentation. N17{LI}

Doric: (Doric Canadian) Canadian yeast from Lallemand. Works equally well at ale and lager temperatures. For single stage fermentation. Clean, crisp and fast starting. A71M, A99, A99M, F63M, F64, G5, G39, H34M, J52

EDME Ale: A popular English import for those who want an authentic British flavor in their beers. A good clean yeast of excellent quality. A71M, A99, A99M, A99T, E68, F63M, F64, F65, G5, G39, G83G, I55

English Ale High Temperature: High temperature ale yeast. Ferments well with no off flavors between 68° F. and 77° F. The young beer has a sharp bite that mellows rapidly with cold aging. The yeast drops out rapidly when cooled below 61° F. H10{LI}

English Brewery Ale: Ferments to a drier finish than Burton Ale, leaving a more robust, dry flavor in the finished ale. A relatively strong-flavored yeast that imparts a complex dry character, ideal for stronger ales and stouts. N17{LI}

German Alt: A traditional German ale yeast. Produces beer not dissimilar in style from English ales, though different in flavor. Generally has a sweeter, more malty flavor than British ale. Ferments beer to mild, almost sweet flavor, a bit fruity in the aftertaste. N17{LI}

Kitzinger Ale: An excellent West German yeast. Somewhat slow starting. For best results a yeast starter should be made 24 to 48 hours before brewing. A71M, A99M, A99T, C51, E68, F64, G5, G39, G83G, H34M

M.eV. Ale: A popular yeast with pub breweries. Top-fermenting only in shallow vessels. Fermentation is best held at 64° F. Tends to produce high diacetyl levels if initial fermentation temperature exceeds 68° F. H10{LI}

M.eV. American Ale: Obtained from a pub brewery in North America. Although considered an Ale yeast, this strain does not top ferment. Ferment above 64° F. H10{LI}

M.eV. English Ale: A clean fermenter, producing little characteristic flavor or aroma. Good general purpose ale yeast. Ferment at 64 to 68° F. H10{LI}

Munton & Fison Ale: (Muntona) A popular English yeast for those who want a real British flavor in their beers. A good clean British ale yeast. For warmer temperature, single stage fermentation. Occasionally causes a long, drawn-out fermentation. A71M, A99, A99M, A99T, C51, E68, F63M, F64, F65, G5, G83G, I55

Old Danish Ale: General purpose top-fermenting yeast for brewing at room temperature. G39, J52

Red Star Ale: Popular general purpose yeast. Produces excellent ales and stouts with a traditional ale flavor. Maximum fermenting power is achieved at room temperature. Starts easily. Ferments rapidly. Sometimes high in ester production. Can also substitute for bread yeast. A71M, A99M, F63M, F64, F65, G5, G39, G40, G83G, H34M, I55, J52, K54{LI}

Stout: Good choice for making porter or stout. Fermentation slows above 5% alcohol. Ferments well between 64^0 F. and 68^0 F. H10{LI}

Whitbread Ale: Produces a thin-flavored beer, with noticeable fruity and ester-like flavors that become pronounced in the aftertaste, and a clearly defined crisp edge. Settles readily in both the fermenter and the capped bottle. Relatively fast to start fermentation. E68

William's Dry Ale: One of the most active and clean flavored dried English ale yeasts. Ferments beer to a soft, clean finish with a delicate "bready" flavor, without a trace of bacteria or wild yeast off-flavors. Relatively slow to start fermentation. Imported from England. N17

OTHERS

Home Brew: A fast fermenting yeast that will endure warmer temperatures than most beer yeasts. Starts easily, just sprinkle on brew. Each packet is sufficient for making 5 gallons of beer. G40

M.eV. Wheat Beer: A strain obtained from Germany. Does not flocculate well, yet still has been used in bottle conditioned beers. Ferment between 61 and 68^0 F. H10{LI}

Steam Beer: Unique style of beer which is a hybrid between top and bottom fermentation. Ferment between 50^0 F. and 61^0 F. At the higher end of this temperature range, the beer may require lagering at about 39^0 F. to reduce diacetyl. Popular in the San Francisco Bay area. H10{LI}

Superbrau: Needs only 4 days of fermentation and the beer is ready to drink in as little as 10 days of aging. Other yeasts require a 7 day fermentation period and at least 2 weeks of aging in the bottle. Makes a much smoother beer without any hint of "cidery" taste found in some homemade beers. L15

Wheat Beer: (Weisse Beer) Two different yeast strains blended together, for the authentic flavor of wheat beer. The wizenbiers of southern Germany are traditionally made with two yeasts, one strain to provide the spicy clove-like character of wheat beer, the other to temper the first strain, keeping the wheat beer from losing its soft mild flavor and beer character. E68{LI}, N17{LI}

DAIRY CULTURES

Acidophilus Milk: A ferment made with Lactobacillus acidophilus. Although it is thick-textured like yogurt, it is called acidophilus "milk". It is credited by many health authorities to possess unique therapeutic properties in the treatment of intestinal disorders. Makes an excellent base for salad dressing, or it can be used like sour cream on baked potatoes. HUNTER 1973b, STEINKRAUS; C23, F7M, F91M, H28, I39, K1T

Aromatic Lactic: Used in the production of sour cream, fermented buttermilk, cultured butter and fresh cheeses such as cottage cheese, Neufchâtel, etc. It is used in either the preparation of starters or directly in the manufacture of the above products. K1T

Blue Mold: (Penicillium roqueforti) A blue mold used to ripen and give flavor to blue-veined cheeses such as Roquefort, Gorgonzola, Stilton and blue cheeses. Blue molds may be added to milk or mixed with the curd. With certain cheeses such as goat's milk cheese they are sprayed on the surface. I30, K1T

Bulgarian Yogurt: Will produce a thick, creamy yogurt that can be made with either whole milk or skim milk. The culture can be kept going for months. Contains Lactobacillus acidophilus. One-third ounce packet will make up to 1/2 gallon of yogurt. I30

Buttermilk: Produces a thick, delicious culture for the same cheeses as the Mesophilic culture. Also makes a delicious cultured buttermilk for use in cooking pancakes, and sour cream. C23, F7M, I30

Chevre Cheese: A new "direct set" culture that produces a rich, creamy chevre goat cheese from goat milk. Excellent as a fresh cheese spread and on bagels. I30

Creme Fraiche: Will make a rich and creamy dessert that can be sweetened with honey, maple syrup or sugar. Very easy to make. Can be served with fresh fruit such as bananas, strawberries, peaches, etc. The starter culture comes in a kit that also includes a dairy thermometer, recipe booklet and cheesecloth. I30

Direct Set A: A "direct set" or "direct vat" inoculant, which may be added directly to warmed milk during the cheesemaking process, saving considerable time. Recommended for Colby, cheddar, Monterrey Jack, cottage and similar cheeses. C23, H28

Direct Set B: A "direct set" inoculant, in powder form, which may be added directly to warmed milk during the cheesemaking process. Recommended for chevre, Feta, Edam, Havarti and Camembert cheeses. C23

Direct Set C: A "direct set" or "direct vat" inoculant, which may be added directly to warmed milk during cheesemaking, simplifying the process and saving considerable time. Recommended for soft, unripened fresh cheeses. C23

Direct Set D Italian: A "direct set" or "direct vat" inoculant, which may be added directly to warmed milk during the cheesemaking process, saving considerable time. Recommended for Mozzarella, Romano, Provolone and Parmesan cheeses. C23

Direct Set D Swiss: A "direct set" or "direct vat" inoculant, which may be added directly to warmed milk during the cheesemaking process. Recommended for Swiss type cheeses. Each packet will set approximately 20 to 24 gallons of milk. C23

Emmenthaler Cheese: Used for making Emmenthaler cheese and other Swiss type cheeses. The culture is added directly to the milk. I30

Flora Danica: The culture recommended in the book "Goat Cheese Small Scale Production" for making a variety of goat cheeses, including Camembert. I30

Fresh Cheese: Produces Cottage cheeses, Pot Cheese, Neufchâtel, sour cream and other soft cheeses as well as buttermilk. F91M, I30, K1T

Fromage Blanc: Produces Fromage Blanc which is similar to cream cheese with a delightfully rich flavor. It can be used as a dip, a cream cheese substitute, in cooking as a substitute for ricotta, or simply spread on bagels. Available as a "direct set" culture which is added directly to milk, saving considerable time. I30

Goat Cheese: An aromatized culture, composed of adapted lactic bacteria. Will transform goat milk into a velvety and delicious cheese. Also produces fresh chevre, blue, Camembert, Coulommiers, Feta and soft goat cheeses. Can be recultured many times. I30, K1T

Hansen's Acidophilus-Yogurt: Contains a combination of Lactobacillus bulgaricus, Streptococcus thermophilus, and Lactobacillus acidophilus. Makes a fermented milk that has the combined good qualities of Bulgaricus yogurt and Acidophilus milk. F7M, I39

Hansen's Yogurt: Makes yogurt that is custard-like in texture with a nutty, mild, almost sweet flavor. F7M, I39

International Yogurt: Yogurt culture in powdered form. Easy to handle, does not spoil, and requires no refrigeration. Can be used with non-fat or skim milk, homogenized or raw milk. C23, F91M, M63M

Kefir: Reusable culture curds that are composed of yeasts and bacteria living symbiotically. Simple to culture. Add any dairy milk to the "grains", stir, and set aside to incubate at room temperature. Stir daily for 2 to 3 days before straining. Use the kefir as a drink, for baking or for making cheese. The curds that remain after the straining can be used to make another batch of kefir. HUNTER 1973b, STEINKRAUS; C23{FR}, E26{FR}, E40{FR}, F91M, I30{FR}, K1T

Lactic Mycoderma: Along with Lactic Oidia, capable of rapid initial growth on the surface of cheeses with their high acidity and high salt content. Prepares the surface for the subsequent growth of Red Bacteria (Brevibacterium linens). Also synthesizes vitamins. K1T

Lactic Oidia: Used in the manufacture of several varieties of semi-soft and semi-hard cheese to prevent the growth of undesirable molds, metabolize lactic acid on the surface of cheese, and promote the growth of cheese ripening bacteria, particularly Red Bacteria (Brevibacterium linens). K1T

Mesophilic Cheese: Used in the manufacture of the majority of cheeses such as cheddar, Monterrey Jack, Stilton, Edam, Gouda, Muenster, blue, Farmhouse and other hard cheeses. Some strains are used in the preparation of starters, others are added directly to milk and contribute to the maturation and enhancing of cheese flavor. H28, I30, K1T

Mozzarella Cheese: Designed for making Mozzarella with store bought homogenized milk. Produces an excellent meltable Mozzarella cheese. Also comes in a kit that includes starter culture, rennet tablets, citric acid, a dairy thermometer and reusable cheesecloth. I30

Propionic Cheese: (Propionibacterium freudenreichii ssp. shermanii) Produces the characteristic "eyes", aroma and flavor associated with Swiss, Gruyere and Emmenthaler cheeses. Must be used in combination with Thermophilic starter for preparing Swiss type cheeses. Maintains its vitality for a year in a refrigerator and 18 months in a freezer. H28, I30, K1T

Red Bacteria: (Brevibacterium linens) Plays an important part in the maturing and the production of flavor of certain cheeses. The softer the cheeses the more rapidly and intensely are they subject to the action of cheese maturing bacteria which constitute the typical superficial flora of soft, semi-soft and semi-hard cheeses such as Brick, Muenster, Limburger, Oka, Port Salut, Anfrom, Camembert, etc. I30, K1T

Rosell Yogurt: In use since 1932, it has a world-wide reputation. Produces an excellent yogurt in 3 or 4 hours. Only one yogurt culture permits the manufacture of yogurt for one month. Also used for making yogurt cheese. Will conserve its efficacy for 24 months if kept cold in its original envelope. K1T

Sweet Acidophilus: A specially selected sweet strain of Lactobacillus acidophilus. Developed by the North Carolina Dairy Foundation. H28

Thermophilic Cheese: Used in the production of cheese whose cooking necessitates high temperatures, such as Mozzarella, Parmesan, Gruyere, Provolone and Swiss cheeses. Can also be used in the preparation of starters or in the direct seeding of the milk intended to be transformed into cheese. H28, I30, K1T

Viili: A sweet cultured milk product that is simple to use. No special incubators or sterile jars needed. Sets at room temperature after a 24 hour incubation period. Has a mild, not tart flavor and a creamy, honey-like texture. Also works well with soymilk. Each culture is a starter for future generations of viili. Introduced from Finland over 85 years ago. E40{FR}

White Mold: (Penicillium camembertii) A mold used to ripen and flavor Brie, Camembert, Coulommiers, and a variety of French goat cheeses. It develops rapidly and confers a good flavor to cheeses in the course of its maturing. The rapid growth also contributes to the prevention of contaminating molds. I30, K1T

SOURDOUGH CULTURES

Alaskan: An Alaskan type sourdough culture that has been maintained for 21 years. The slow rising of the sourdough culture assists in the breakdown of complex carbohydrates to make breads more digestible and delicious. The tart flavor imparted by this culture gives hotcakes, biscuits and muffins their unique distinction. A15M, E40

Austrian: A starter from the old section of Innsbruck. The bakery carries a sign over the entrance proclaiming 1795 as the year the business opened. The culture is especially adapted to rye flours, rises somewhat slowly and produces one of the more sour doughs. WOOD, E. [Re]; L3M

Bahrain: From Bahrain, thought by many to be the ancient Garden of Eden and a curious mixture of the oldest and the newest. The sourdough culture is from the oldest of the oldest. It rises well and is one of the most sour. WOOD, E. [Re]; L3M

Forty Niner: (San Francisco) Obtained from a relative of Ed Wood, author of "World Sourdoughs from Antiquity" who had received it from a prospector of the California gold rush era. The culture rises quite slowly and produces moderately sour dough of exquisite flavor. WOOD, E. [Re]; L3M

French: From a small bakery on the outskirts of Paris that has been in business for over 150 years. The starter rises very well and the dough has one of the mildest sourdough flavors. Interchangeable with the Austrian culture in recipes. WOOD, E. [Re]; L3M

French Lactic: Used in making those delicious crusty loaves of French sourdough breads that everyone loves to eat. Also makes hotcakes light as a feather, and biscuits that melt in your mouth. I39{FR}

Giza: The bakery where this sourdough was found was almost literally in the shadow of the Sphinx in the town of Giza not far from Cairo. In Cairo there are many modern bakeries. This one, in Giza, dates straight back to antiquity. The dough rises well and is moderately sour. WOOD, E. [Re]; L3M

Oregon Pioneer: The same type of "starter" used by early Oregon pioneers in the 1850's. It was taken to the Alaska Gold Rush of 1898 and became the basis of the legendary sourdough starters of that area. The more you use and renew this "starter" the better it becomes. I39{FR}

Red Sea: From one of the oldest ethnic bakeries in Egypt. Found in the village of Hurghada on the shore of the Red Sea. The bread was actually placed on the village street to rise. One of the fastest cultures to rise and has a mild sourdough flavor. WOOD, E. [Re]; L3M

San Francisco: A special strain of sourdough first introduced to the San Francisco Bay area during gold rush days. Sourdough seems to react superlatively to the cool, salty San Francisco air. Produces a bread that is sour yet almost sweet, hard and crisp yet soft, pungent yet mild. B91T

Saudi Arabian: From the desert bedouin of Saudi Arabia who have survived the modern transformation of that country unchanged. The Saudi sourdough is as desert as its bedouin baker. It rises moderately well and has one of the most distinctive flavors of all sourdough cultures. WOOD, E. [Re]; L3M

Yukon: A Yukon prospector gave this starter to the physician father of a medical school classmate of Ed Wood, author of "World Sourdoughs from Antiquity". It produces moderately sour dough and rises well. WOOD, E. [Re]; L3M

SOYFOOD CULTURES

Barley Koji: (Mugi Koji) Miso koji starter. Will produce regular barley or *mugi miso* in 12 to 18 months, and mellow barley or *amakuchi mugi miso* in 1 to 2 months. Not fortified with yeast and Lactobacillus cultures. Includes enough spores for producing 6 pounds of koji. E40

Brown Rice Koji: All-purpose home fermentation culture suitable for producing rice miso, shoyu, sake, rice vinegar and amazake. It can also be used to make sweet vegetable pickles, a delicacy in Japan. Relatively easy to use. E56, E66T, H91, *K74*

Hama-Natto: A Japanese fermented soybean product made by fermenting whole soybeans with koji mold. During fermentation the beans acquire a dark reddish color, but turn grayish-black after being dried in the sun. Hama-natto beans are smooth and soft and have a pleasant, somewhat salty flavor resembling mellow *hatcho miso* or shoyu, but is sweeter. Usually sprinkled over rice, served as an hors d'oeuvre with green tea or cooked with vegetables as a seasoning. SHURTLEFF 1975, STEINKRAUS; E56{PR}, E66T{PR}

Hishio: A quick vegetable miso, generally prepared by fermenting salt-pickled eggplant and white uri melon with a barley koji, and sometimes soybeans that have been split and dehulled. Has a sweet, savory flavor and a juicy, chunky texture. Very easy to prepare and ready to eat in less than a week. Hishio is similar to *chiang*, the Chinese progenitor of all Japanese miso and shoyu. SHURTLEFF 1976 [Re]; E56, *K74*

Natto: Whole soybeans fermented with bacteria. During the fermentation period, the beans become covered with a viscous, sticky material. The quality of the natto is determined, in part, by the stickiness of the beans. Natto is grayish, has a strong musty flavor, and is used with rice or as a side dish. One of the most digestible sources of protein and vitamin B_{12}. HUNTER 1973a; E56, E66T, G20M{PR}, H91, H91{PR}

Red Koji: (Red Rice Koji) Miso koji starter. Will produce red rice miso or *sendai miso* (fermented soybean paste) in 6 to 12 months, and sweet red miso or *edo miso* in 1 to 1 1/2 months. Fortified with yeast and Lactobacillus cultures. Includes enough spores for producing 6 pounds of koji. E40

Rice Koji: (Cultured Rice) Special order organic rice from Lundberg's Farm in California, polished rice, and koji starter. For amazake and misos. Will make 10 quarts of amazake or 3 to 4 pounds of miso, or some of each. Made fresh in small batches. E40, E66T

Seed Miso: Aged unpasteurized seed miso for miso making. Contributes beneficial organisms to get new misos fermenting vigorously. Once miso has been made, some of it can be saved for seed for future homemade misos. E40

Shoyu Koji: Koji starter. Produces *shoyu* or *soy sauce* (fermented liquid soy seasonings) in 6 to 12 months. Fortified with yeast and Lactobacillus cultures. Includes enough spores for making 2 gallons of shoyu. Has a 6 month shelf life if kept cool and dry. E40

Soybean Koji: (Hatcho Koji) Miso koji starter. Will produce soybean or *hatcho miso* in 18 to 24 months, and wheat-free shoyu or *tamari* in 18 months. Fortified with yeast and Lactobacillus cultures. Includes enough spores for producing 6 pounds of koji or 2 gallons of tamari. Has a 6 month shelf life if kept cool and dry. E40

Sufu: A highly flavored, creamy bean paste made by overgrowing tofu with a mold and fermenting the curd in a salt brine/rice wine mixture. It is soft, pale yellow in color, and has a salty flavor somewhat suggestive of anchovies. Also called *Chinese cheese*, *fermented bean curd*, *tofuru*, *fuyu* and *tosufu*. Available in Chinatown markets. CHANG, W. [Re], COST 1988 [Cul, Re], JAFFREY, SHURTLEFF 1975 [Re]; C27G{PR}, U15M

Sweet White Koji: (Light Koji) Rice koji starter. Will produce sweet white or *shiro miso* in 1 month, light yellow or *shinshu miso* in 6 to 12 months, or *amazake* (sweet fermented rice drink) in 24 hours. Fortified with yeast and Lactobacillus cultures. Includes enough spores for producing 6 pounds of koji. E40, H91{PR}

Tempeh: A fermented soybean cake from Indonesia that is a low cost, cholesterol free, high quality protein food that can be made at home. Homemade tempeh tastes fresher, slices better, has a better aroma, and costs far less than commercial tempeh. One pound of dry soybeans will make 1 1/2 to 1 3/4 pounds of delicious tempeh in 24 hours at 85^0 F. E40, H91, L87G, M87

VINEGAR CULTURES {FR}

Cider: Traditionally produced from apple cider. Can also be made from apple wastes. *Switchel* is a refreshing drink, formerly used by New Englanders during haying season. It consists of cold well water and apple cider vinegar. The drink can be sweetened with molasses and flavored with ginger. HUNTER 1973a [Pre], PROULX [Re]; A71M

Malt: Traditionally produced from beer and ale. Now commonly made with malt extract. Can be pasteurized to improve keeping qualities, but will no longer form a "mother". Malt vinegar is always served in England with fish and chips, and can be sprinkled over cooked greens or used in place of cider vinegar in any recipe. HUNTER 1973a [Pre], VON WELANETZ; A71M, A99, F63M

Red: (Red Wine) Interchangeable with White vinegar in recipes except where the red color would affect a pale sauce. *Rosel* or *russell* is a fermented beet-vinegar used during the Jewish Passover, and to make a Russian-type beet soup. The liquid is clear, bright red, and has a wine-like aroma. HUNTER 1973a, VON WELANETZ; A71M, A99, A99T, E1M{PR}, E68, F63M, K54

White: (White Wine) Similar to Red vinegar. The *mother vinegar* can be used to make additional batches of vinegar. During the Renaissance in France vinegar was flavored with pepper, cloves, roses, fennel, and raspberries. By the 18th century, some 92 varieties of scented vinegars and 55 table flavors were known in France. PROULX; A71M, A99, A99T, E68, F63M

WINE YEASTS

Assmanshäuser: Similar to Pasteur Red in some characteristics, but has a slower fermentation rate and an austere fruitiness rather than "grapiness". Produces wines that are spicy, complex, and of medium body and dark color. Sometimes awkward when young, they achieve balance with barrel aging. Often preferred in Pinot Noir over faster yeasts. N27{LI}

Beerenauslese: Several wineries have had good results with this yeast on grapes infected with botrytis. It intensifies the apricot/honey flavors produced by the mold. The fermentation can usually be arrested by chilling and racking. N27{LI}

California Champagne: Slower to moderately vigorous fermenter, with extremely rapid flocculation. Forms large chunks if left to settle undisturbed. Well-suited for bottle fermented sparkling wines, and for aromatic fruit wines that have trouble settling yeast lees. Produces white wines that have a clean, yeasty quality that reminds the taster of champagne even if the wine is still. A99T, E68, G40, I39, N27

Champagne: Ferments colder and drier than Montrachet. Preferred for flavor in making naturally carbonated soft drinks. A99, A99M, E68, I30, J52, K54

Chanson: A yeast of French origin that is preferred by a number of top Chardonnay producers. Wines produced with Chanson have refined and elegant flavors with a graceful emphasis on varietal fruit. Ferments evenly, has low H_2S production, and flocculates well, making compact lees. N27{LI}

Epernay: A very slow fermenting yeast, best for retaining the freshness of fragile, fruity wines. Originated in France. I55

Epernay II: (Red Star Epernay II) Slower fermenting than Montrachet. An excellent general purpose yeast for still or sparkling wines. Produces less foam than Montrachet. Yields a fine, fruity aroma and excellent flavor. Also good for low acid fruit wines, California grape wines and mead. Derived from an isolate of the original Epernay strain at the Geisenheim Institute in Germany. A71M, A99, A99T, E68, F63M, F64, G5, G40, H34M, I55, J52, N27

Etoile: A liquid yeast for sparkling wine from France. Its main use is as a tirage yeast, but it could also ferment the cuvee. A mixed population yeast that combines qualities of subdued yeastiness with crispness. It flocculates well. N27{LI}

Fermivin: An imported yeast from GB Fermentations that ferments rapidly and vigorously. The fermentation may require chilling, but if well-regulated, Fermivin can make clean, varietal wines. Often used to reinoculate stuck wines because of its vigor. N27

Flor Sherry: Some of the better sherries such as Amontillado owe their unique bouquet and flavor to a particular strain of yeast which sometimes forms a thick film on top of the wine. For the advanced winemaker who would like to duplicate this process. Also popular for making sweet and semi-sweet wines. A99T, C51, G40, K54

Fruit: Good for light-bodied reds and whites where some sweetness is to be left. A slow fermenter, leaving a perfumed aroma and fruity flavor. A good choice for apple and other fruit wines. Although cool fermentation (59^0 F.) provides smoothness, rapid cooling will cause this yeast to drop out. H10{LI}

Lalvin 1116: (Lalvin K1-V1116) For white, red and rosé wines. Due to its "killer factor", high alcohol production and good activity at high temperatures, this is one of the best choices for general wine making. An extremely fast starter. The "killer factor" inhibits the growth of sensitive wild yeasts in the must. A71M, A99, F63M, H34M, I55, J52

Lalvin 1118: (Lalvin EC-1118, Prise de Mousse) A strain that has been isolated from the *grand crus* of the champagne region. Has excellent alcohol resistance and a powerful "killer factor". Ferments well over a wide range of temperatures. Can be used for any type of fermentation. Ideal for stuck fermentations and for both the base wine and bottle fermentation of sparkling wines. A71M, A99, E68, F63M, H34M, I55, J52

Lalvin 1122: (Lalvin 71B-1122) Suitable for aromatic wines such as Nouveaux and for wines made with very tart fruit. An excellent choice for both white and red wines where an especially "fruity" aroma is desired. Also used for concentrates. A71M, A99, F63M, H34M, I55, J52

Lalvin SB-1: Ferments to fortified wine levels when given small doses of sugar via the "spoonfeeding" technique. I55

M.eV. Champagne: A champagne yeast that is also a good general purpose white wine yeast. A good choice if making wine with fresh California juice. H10{LI}

Montrachet: An all purpose yeast. Good for making wine from grapes, berries, fruits and vegetables. Very vigorous fermentation. High resistance to sulphur-dioxide. Performs best at 70 to 80^0 F. Excellent flavor characteristics. Very easy to use, can be added to the must without prior starting. A99, A99M, C51, E68, G39, G40, I39, J52, K54

Neutral Flavor: An all purpose yeast now being used by many major wineries in the United States. Good for making wines from fruit, berries, flowers, vegetables or grapes. Produces a firm sediment, a high alcohol content, and has high flavor characteristics. Needs no prior starting, can be added directly to the juice. Fermentation starts rapidly. G40

Pasteur Champagne: Used for Charmat process sparkling wines, delicately flavored white wines where a minimum of yeast flavor is desired, and for barley wines. Also helpful in starting stuck fermentations. For cool and cold fermentations, 65^0 F. and under (but must be started at 70 to 75^0 F.). Has high alcohol tolerance. A99T, C51, G39, G40

Pasteur Red: (French Red, Bordeaux Red) A fast, strong fermenter that is used for full-bodied red wines made for aging in oak and in the bottle. It can help give character to some less robust red grapes, or those that must be picked before optimum flavor development. Produces very complex wines, with a characteristic Cabernet-style concentration of fruit and good color extraction. N27{LI}

Pasteur White: (French White) Intended mainly for dry, crisp white wines. Provides complexity instead of fruitiness and tends to emphasize acidity, making wines that could be described as austere. Sensitive to sudden chilling, it works best at cool, even temperatures. It can be stopped when sweet. N27{LI}

Red Star Beaujolais: A new yeast intended for carbonic maceration fermentations, or just for any fresh fruity red wine. Adapted to perform well in the presence of normal levels of sulphur dioxide. Ferments strongly but leaves a grapey sort of fruitiness that is appreciated in lighter wines. N27

Red Star Flor Sherry: For dry sherry type wines which require development of a sherry-flor film that is responsible for much of the characteristic flavor. Also used for Port and other strong wines. Has been used in the United States since 1963 for the production of submerged culture sherry. A71M, F63M, F64, G5, G83G, H34M, I55, N27

Red Star Montrachet: A popular all purpose yeast suitable for fermentations of red and full-bodied white wines. A strong fermenter with good ethanol tolerance. Has a tendency to produce hydrogen sulfide (rotten egg smell). Recommended only for experienced winemakers whose grapes are known to be relatively free of sulphur dust at harvest. Can produce variable results, depending on juice composition and winemaking skill. A71M, F63M, F64, F65, G5, H34M, I55, N27

Red Star Pasteur Champagne: Generally used for delicately flavored white wines, where a minimum of yeast flavor is desired, for barley wines and for stuck fermentations. Also used to carbonate soft drinks. A fast, usually complete fermenter that is not suitable for wines requiring slow fermentation. Has very good ethanol tolerance.

From the Institut Pasteur in Paris. Used widely in the U.S. since about 1968. A71M, F63M, F65, G5, I55, N17, N27

Red Star Prise de Mousse: A French yeast that is gaining in popularity and has found a niche in the United States for many white wines and some reds. It ferments evenly and usually goes to completion, and its clean, slightly yeasty aroma does not interfere with varietal character, so it can be used for Chardonnay or as a tirage yeast. N27

Sherry: For dry, sherry type wines which require development of a sherry-flor film for proper flavor. A99, A99M, E68, J52

Steinberg: A favorite among winemakers for Rieslings, other German-style wines and apple wines. Produces a distinctive, flowery, complex combination of scents which are best when the wine is fermented cool. The activity of this cold-tolerant yeast can be slowed greatly by chilling but usually resists stopping completely without additional procedures. N27{LI}

Vierka Assmanshäuser: Produces a light, dry Rhine wine. Approximate alcohol content 7 to 9%. Requires 1 pound, 6 ounces of sugar per gallon. Also used for non-alcoholic red currant wine musts which are consumed as health-drinks, and barberry wine. H34M

Vierka Bernkastler: Produces a light, dry Mosel wine. Approximate alcohol content 6 to 8%. Requires 1 pound, 3 ounces of sugar per gallon. Also used for dandelion, orange, and tomato wines. A99T{LI}, K54{LI}

Vierka Bordeaux: Produces a full bodied, dry wine. Approximate alcohol content 7 to 9%. Requires 1 pound, 6 ounces of sugar per gallon. Also used for non-alcoholic bilberry wine musts which are consumed as health-drinks, and Rowan wine. A99T{LI}, C51, F63M, G40{LI}, H34M, K54{LI}

Vierka Burgundy: Produces a full bodied, dry wine. Approximate alcohol content 9 to 12%. Requires 1 pound, 12 ounces of sugar per gallon. A99T{LI}, C51, F63M, G40{LI}, H34M, K54{LI}

Vierka Champagne: Produces a light, dry wine. Approximate alcohol content 5 to 7%. Requires 1 pound of sugar per gallon. A99T{LI}, G40{LI}, H34M, K54{LI}

Vierka Cold Ferment: (Kaltgärhefe) To be used where there is no chance of maintaining a steady 70° to 75° F. for fermentation. Will ferment thoroughly and without fail at temperatures as low as 42° F. Also used for *Swabian must*, the national drink of Baden-Württemberg, Germany which corresponds to the apple-wine of Frankfurt or the cidre of France. A99T{LI}, C51

Vierka Johannisberg Riesling: Produces a light, dry Rhine wine. Approximate alcohol content 8 to 10%. Requires 1 pound, 11 ounces of sugar per gallon. A99T{LI}, C51, H34M

Vierka Liebfraumilch: Produces a full bodied, medium sweet Rhine wine. Approximate alcohol content 9 to 11%. Requires 1 pound, 12 ounces of sugar per gallon. Also used for non-alcoholic apple wine musts which are consumed as health-drinks, and Oregon grape and quince wines. A99T{LI}, C51, G40{LI}, H34M, K54{LI}

Vierka Madeira: Produces a full bodied, sweet wine. Approximate alcohol content 12 to 15%. Requires 3 pounds, 10 ounces of sugar per gallon. Also used for non-alcoholic strawberry wine musts which are consumed as health-drinks, and Rowan wine. A99T{LI}, C51, G40{LI}, H34M

Vierka Malaga: Produces a full bodied, sweet wine. Approximate alcohol content 12 to 15%. Requires 3 pounds, 5 ounces of sugar per gallon. Also used for non-alcoholic blackberry wine musts which are consumed as health-drinks, and Oregon grape and tomato wines. H34M

Vierka Port: Produces a full bodied, aromatic wine. Approximate alcohol content 12 to 15%. Requires 3 pounds, 5 ounces of sugar per gallon. Also used for non-alcoholic cherry wine musts which are consumed as health-drinks. A99T{LI}, C51, F63M, G5, G40{LI}, H34M, K54{LI}

Vierka Sauternes: Produces a full bodied, sweet wine. Approximate alcohol content 12 to 16%. Requires 3 pounds, 5 ounces of sugar per gallon. Also used for pineapple wine and *Swabian must*. A99T{LI}, C51, F63M, G5, G40{LI}, H34M, K54{LI}

Vierka Sherry: Produces a full bodied, sweet wine. Approximate alcohol content 12 to 15%. Requires 3 pounds, 5 ounces of sugar per gallon. Also used for non-alcoholic gooseberry wine musts which are consumed as health-drinks, and orange and tomato wines. A99T{LI}, C51, G40{LI}, H34M, K54{LI}

Vierka Steinberger: Produces a full bodied, medium Rhine wine. Approximate alcohol content 8 to 10%. Requires 1 pound, 8 ounces of sugar per gallon. Also used for apple wine or cidre. A99T{LI}

Vierka Tokay: Produces a full bodied, aromatic wine with high alcohol content. Approximate alcohol content 14 to 16%. Requires 3 pounds, 10 ounces of sugar per gallon. Also used for fig and rosehip wines, and mock pineapple wine made from carob pods. A99T{LI}, C51, G40{LI}, H34M, K54{LI}

York Creek Zinfandel: Isolated in 1979 from a natural fermentation which reached over 18% alcohol in a Zinfandel must from the renowned York Creek Vineyard in St. Helena, California. Very fast and vigorous, it may help encourage high-sugar fermentations toward dryness. Wines other than Zinfandel tend to exhibit Zinfandel-style flavors, such as a berry-like fruitiness, when fermented with this yeast. N27{LI}

OTHER CULTURES

Baking Yeast: Granular baking yeast. One pound equals 48 small yeast cakes. Remains active for 4 months or longer. Use one level tablespoon for each large loaf. A52M, M63M

Chinese Red Rice: When cultured on rice, will yield grains of an intense red color. The red rice is dried and then used for coloring various foods including pickled vegetables, fish, drinks, pastries, sauces and for manufacturing red wine. It is also added to the brining liquid of red sufu to give it color, thick consistency and a distinctive flavor and aroma. Also known as *ang-kak*, *anka*, *beni-koji* and *aga-koji*. COST 1988 [Cul], HESSELTINE, SHURTLEFF 1979, STEINKRAUS, UPHOF; **U15M**

Ironmaster Country Cider: Comes in a kit that includes yeast and concentrate from the apple orchards of Normandy. Each 2.2 pound can makes 2 gallons of sparkling cider. F63M

Onchom: (Ontjom) Produces an orange-red cake-like product resembling tempeh prepared by fermenting peanut presscake, along with solid waste from tapioca manufacture. Has a soft texture and an attractive appearance along with a meaty flavor. Consumed in Indonesia as a side-dish, either in the form of deep fat-fried slices, in the form of small portions in soups, or served as chips, a snack, or topped with sauce. HESSELTINE, SHURTLEFF 1979 [Cul, Re], STEINKRAUS; **U15M**

Pic-L-Cure: (Lactobacillus plantarum) A pure culture ideal for use in pickle making and other vegetable fermentations, including *sauerkraut*, *kimchi*, *gari*, *kishk*, *pak-sian-dong*, *naw-mai-dong*, and *sourdough bread*. STEINKRAUS; H28

Ragi: (Ragie) Yeasts, bacteria and molds, grown on rice flour and sold in the shape of round, somewhat flattened balls or cakes. Used to saccharify starch in the making of Indonesian fermented delicacies such as *tempeh, ontjom, tapé, arrack, beras, brem* and *peuyeum*. HESSELTINE, OCHSE, STEINKRAUS; A45

Red Star Baker's Yeast: Bulk packed for economy. Fresh dried yeast that has superior leavening power. Comes in a reusable jar for easy refrigerator storage. To buy this much yeast in the usual small package would cost considerably more. C64, C95, D3, I39

Rosellac Sausage: Cultures used in the manufacture of sausages. Their use entails several advantages: rapid lowering of the pH and the keeping in check of putrefying bacteria; the binding of lean and fat pieces; increasing of consistency, uniformity of flavor, texture and appearance; and shortening of production time. K1T

Spirulina Algae: (Spirulina platensis) Can be grown in a large bottle and then transferred to a fish tank, pond, or large-scale culture tank. Grows in alkaline waters, with a pH of 9 to 11 as optimum. Sodium bicarbonate and other carbonates should be present. Fresh spirulina is produced at less cost, and with higher nutritional value than the dried spirulina purchased in powder or tablet form. C7M{FR}, I43T{PR}, *K74*{PR}, L17M{PR}

Tea Fungus: {FR} A fermented beverage with a slightly sour flavor comparable to a light wine or apple cider, but without alcohol. During the fermentation process a thick film forms on the surface of the liquid. Has antibiotic properties and is used in healing diets. Also known as *tea cider, tea beer, teeschwamm, kombucha, wunderpilz, hongo, cajnij, fungus japonicus* and *teekwass*. Consumed widely in Russia, Japan, Poland, Bulgaria, Germany, Manchuria and Indonesia. HESSELTINE, HUNTER 1973a, STEINKRAUS; E40{OR}

STRAWBERRY {GR}

FRAGARIA X ANANASSA FRAGARIA OVALIS
FRAGARIA VESCA 'SEMPERFLORENS'

ALPINE STRAWBERRIES {S}

A distinct form of wood strawberry, characterized by long, pointed fruit that is small but much richer in flavor than the common garden strawberry. They do not produce runners and are therefore ideal for edgings or container culture. Can be grown from seed or division. Their very high pectin content makes them better suited to jam making. (F. vesca 'Semperflorens')

Alexandria: (Baron Solemacher Improved) Large conical fruit, up to 1 inch long; skin bright red; juicy, very aromatic flesh with an excellent sweet flavor. Small, upright plant, 8 to 10 inches tall; exceptionally vigorous; productive; very hardy; disease resistant. Earlier bearing than other types. B30{PL}, B75, C92, E33, F13, *F72*, F80, F92, L91M, N84, *Q24*, S45M, S55, S61

Alpine Yellow:[1] Small, very long-pointed conical fruit, 3/4 to 1 inch long; skin color ranges from pale cream to golden yellow; highly aromatic. Has an intense flavor when ripe, preferred by some over the red-fruited types. The yellow fruit is less attractive to birds. J29{PL}, K66, L91M{PL}, M82{PL}, O53M, Q34

Baron Solemacher: (Baron von Solemacher) Medium-sized conical fruit, up to 1 1/2 inches in length; skin bright red; flesh aromatic, flavor very good when thoroughly ripe. Vigorous, upright plant, about 8 inches tall; highly productive. The first widely available alpine strawberry and a standard in Europe. Very similar to Alexandria. HENDRICKSON, SIMMONS 1978; A16, B49, E99, F33, G6, G87, H51M{PL}, I39, I77, L66{PL}, M92{PL}, N84, S45M, S61

Berry Sweet: Sweet, bright red fruit, about 1 inch long. Runnerless, bush-type plant; height about 8 inches; bears from late spring until frost. Thrives in sun or semi-shade. *H57M*

Charles V: Small but flavorful fruit, produced nearly year round in warm climates. Clumping perennial, 2 feet by 2 feet; spreads by seed or divisions. Can be used as a ground cover or in formal garden plantings. Also makes an attractive container plant. M98

Delices: (Delices des Quatre Saisons) Medium-sized conical fruit, very long and slender; flesh very sweet and fragrant. Vigorous growing plants with no runners; highly productive. G69M{PL}, G84{PL}

Mignonette: Large fruit, up to 1 inch long; red skin. Excellent quality and flavor. Exceptionally prolific; very hardy. Makes an attractive edging or ground cover plant. C9{PL}, I77, I83M{PL}, I91

Mt. Omei:[2] Attractive plant with small shiny leaves and white fruit. Seed of this cultivar originally came from Belgium via China. D95{PL}

Pineapple Crush:[1] Large fruit, up to 1 inch long; light cream-yellow skin. Has an unusual fragrance and flavor reminiscent of strawberry mixed with pineapple. Compact, runnerless plant; bears very early and continuously over a long season. C9{PL}, I77, I83M{PL}, I91

Red Wonder: Selected for the deep red color of the fruit. Everbearing plant that produces no runners. Grows 6 to 10 inches tall. Excellent as a ground cover or in the rock garden. E30{PL}, *L22*{PL}, N84

Ruegen: (Benary, Rugen) Medium to large elongated fruit, somewhat smaller than Alexandria; skin deep crimson; flesh aromatic, with an intense sweet strawberry flavor. Compact, bushy plant, about 10 inches tall; very productive and long bearing. One of the standard cultivars in Europe. C85M, F80, I77, J20, J82, J82{PL}, K49M, N42{PL}, N45{PL}, N84, O53M

Ruegen Improved: Rich red fruit; juicy, sweet and tender, of excellent flavor. Long-bearing strain, will bear continuously from early June through October but is especially abundant in the fall. Somewhat larger and more productive than the standard strain. B75, B75{PL}, C9{PL}, I39, M16{PL}, *M65M*{PL}, M77{PL}, *Q24*

Suprême: An excellent French cultivar. Large, conical, bright red fruit; delightfully fragrant, of high quality. Vigorous, clumping plant; produces fruit in abundance. Introduced by Vilmorin. S95M

Tutti Frutti: Round, intense-red fruits with a delicious flavor. Very dwarf, creeping plant, height 2 inches; high yielding. Dark green, contrasting leaves. Excellent for the rockery. N84

White:[2] Small, white fruit with an excellent mild sweet flavor, not as acid as the red-fruited types. The unique white color makes them less attractive to birds. Small, upright plant, 8 inches tall, spreads to 24 inches across. K49M, K79{PL}

Yellow Wonder:[1] Extremely flavorful, pale yellow fruit with small, tender seeds. Very aromatic. Has a distinct flavor preferred by some over the red-fruited types. Allow to ripen fully before picking. Compact plants grow 10 to 11 inches high. B75{PL}, I83M{PL}, K47T, N84, S61

GARDEN STRAWBERRIES

The familiar, large-fruited strawberries that are generally not as flavorful or as aromatic as alpine strawberries. They also produce runners which must be removed or replanted at some point in the management of the strawberry bed. Mostly F. x ananassa.

EVERBEARING Included here are the older, traditional cultivars and the newer types, sometimes called day neutral strawberries. True day neutral types produce buds, flowers and fruit throughout the growing season, regardless of day length, and to a certain extent, region. In areas with winters normally too cold for strawberries, they can be grown as annuals. They are also well suited to windowsill, hanging basket, cold frame or greenhouse culture.

Chandler: Large, long conic to long flat wedge-shaped fruit; skin red, glossy, attractive; flesh firm, red, well-colored to the center, of very good flavor; ripens somewhat later than Douglas; ships well. Recommended for fresh market and processing. Semi-erect plant; self-pollinating throughout the season; produces numerous runners. Originated in Davis, California. Introduced in 1983. A14, F11, G17, G81{CF}, *I41*, I99M, L55M, *M81M*

Chief Bemidji: Large, rounded wedge-shaped fruit; skin bright red; flesh firm, sweet, solid red throughout; held well above the ground. Plant extremely hardy; vigorous and productive; produces 15 to 20 large runners per plant; does well on poor soil. Survives temperatures of -40^0 F. without protection. Originated in Port Hope Township, Minnesota. BROOKS 1972; C63

Fern: Day neutral type, always has fruit in different stages of development. Medium to large, conic to flat wedge-shaped fruit; skin bright red; flesh very firm, sweet, flavor excellent; ripens early. Semi-erect plant, more spreading than Hecker; self-fertile. Runner production good, comparable to Hecker. Low chilling requirement. Originated in Davis, California. Introduced in 1983. A14, G93M, *I41*, M37M, *M81M*

Fort Laramie: Medium to large fruit; flesh very firm, of excellent flavor; recovers quickly after blight or hailstorms. Yields over a long season. Foliage susceptible to mildew. Excellent in mountain, coastal or other cool-winter areas. Can survive temperatures of -40^0 F. HENDRICKSON, STEBBINS; B73M, C63, D65, D76, E3, E24, F1, G16, H33, H42, I99M, L55M, L70, L79, M37M, *M65M*, N33, etc.

Gem: Fruit small, short wedge-shaped to oblate, irregular; skin deep red, glossy; flesh pale red, tart; dessert quality good. Very productive plant, but doesn't bear much spring fruit; very hardy. Susceptible to leaf spots; resistant to leaf scorch. Originated in Farwell, Michigan by Frank J. Keplinger. Introduced in 1933. BROOKS 1972; A82, G72, K28, M83

Hecker: Day neutral type. Large to very large, bright scarlet fruit of excellent flavor. Good for fresh use, freezing and jam making. Fairly cold hardy for a day neutral strawberry. Well suited to prairie conditions due to its earliness. Produces up to 10 months under favorable conditions. Introduced by the University of California. F11, F67, G1T, H42, *I41*, M37M, *M81M*, N26

Le Sans Rivalle: Medium to large, long-conic fruit; skin medium glossy red; flesh fairly firm, flavor very good. Moderately vigorous plant; productive; likes light or medium soil and succeeds in chalky conditions. One of the older everbearing types. Originated in France about 1937. SIMMONS 1978; U7M

Luscious Treat: A dual purpose day-neutral strawberry that can be grown in hanging baskets or in the garden. Starts bearing very early and continues throughout the summer and fall, on both the crown and runners. Glossy fruit, deep red inside and out. Retains its flavor and quality when frozen. L79

Nisqually: Conical fruit of variable size. Appearance and quality good. Everbearing, flower buds being initiated in both short and long days. Produces a moderate crop in June, becoming more productive July through September. Very productive. Tolerant to mildew. Suitable for home gardens and local markets. Originated in Puyallup, Washington. BROOKS 1972; L30

Ogallala: (F. ovalis x) Medium to large fruit; skin rich, dark red, too tender for good shipping; flesh bright red, firm, tender, sweet, of high quality; processes very well. Bears continuously from late May or early June to early November, except for a 3 week period immediately after the spring crop. Very vigorous, extremely hardy plant. A16, C63, D65, D76, E97, F19M, G1T, H42, J34, J83, K64, K81, L33, *M65M*

Ostara: Small to medium-sized, conical fruit; skin red; flesh medium firm, orange-red, flavor moderate; husks very easily. Vigorous, tall, spreading plant; susceptible to mildew; prolific for an everbearer. Originated in Wageningen, The Netherlands. SIMMONS 1978; D76, E97

Ourown: Medium to large fruit, conic to wedge-shaped; skin medium red, glossy, firm; flesh firm, sweet, of good dessert quality; excellent for freezing. Tall, vigorous, winter hardy plant; produces numerous runners. Very good for growing in hanging baskets. B58

Ozark Beauty: Fruit large, often elongated, long-necked; skin firm, glossy; flesh solid, flavor very mild, sweet; dessert quality very good; good for freezing; ripens late. Vigorous, very productive plant; blooms late; produces numerous runners; widely adapted to climate. BROOKS 1972; A39, A82, B73M, C63, C88, E3, E4, F19M, G16, G71, H65, J33, J83, M37M, *M65M*, etc.

Quinalt: Very large, conical fruit; skin attractive, tender; flesh soft, color and flavor good; excellent for freezing. Produces a moderate crop in June, becoming more productive July through September. Vigorous, compact plant; produces many runners; has excellent disease resistance. Main crop from crown; also produces fruit on rooted runners. STEBBINS; A14, B67, B73M, C63, D65, E3, F11, G81, *G89M*, I99M, J83, M37M, *M65M*, *M81M*

Selva: Day neutral type. Large, conical fruit; skin deep red, attractive; flesh very firm, juicy, flavor very good. Produces fruit during November, December and January in coastal southern California, when fruit is unavailable from the standard short-day cultivars. Vigorous plants are prolific runner makers; will flower and fruit effectively independent of day length. Originated in Davis, California. Introduced in 1983. G81, *I41*, I99M, L55M, *M81M*

Shortcake: Long conical fruit; skin very glossy, attractive; flesh red, well-colored to the center, sweet, of excellent flavor. Yields a primary crop of large berries in June, followed by a second crop 6 to 8 weeks later of good medium-sized berries, larger than most other everbearers. Productive in a wide range of soils and climates. B75

Streamliner: Very large fruit; skin rich red; flesh firm, sweet, of excellent flavor and quality. Good keeper for home use. Hardy plant; a heavy spring cropper; makes runners freely. Originated in Lostine, Oregon by Roy C. Edgmand. Introduced in 1944. BROOKS 1972; C63, E97, J83, *M69M*, M83

Sunburst: Very large fruit; skin bright orange-red; flesh very sweet. Hardy, productive plant; bears continuously form June until freezing weather, with heavy crops in early summer and fall. Also well adapted to humid southern climates. Developed by Burgess Seed and Plant Company. M77

Sweetheart: {S} One of the first open-pollinated strawberries from seed. An excellent novelty everbearing type for containers or home garden use. The fruit is 5 times larger than alpine types, but only medium-sized when compared to other everbearers grown from runners. Will produce from late July till fall from a January sowing. B75, C85M, D11M, D27, E32M{PL}, E38, F19M, *F72*, G64, G87, I91, J7, L42, L66{PL}, L91M, etc.

Tillikum: Day neutral type. Small to medium-sized, conical fruit; skin bright red, glossy, attractive; flesh bright red, fairly firm, has a very good semi-tart flavor. Good shipper and keeper. Very productive plant, significantly outyields Quinalt and Fort Laramie; produces for up to 10 months. Has shown good resistance to fruit rot and aphid-transmitted viruses. Released by Washington State University in 1983. B67, F11, *I41*, L97, L99M, *M81M*

Tribute: Medium to large fruit, irregular to short conic; skin glossy, bright red; flesh medium red to the center, firm, flavor acidic but pleasant when consumed fresh and unsugared. Medium-sized plant; very vigorous; highly resistant to red stele and tolerant to verticillium wilt; ripens a heavy spring crop in midseason. B10, B58, *C47*, C55M, C63, E60, G81, H16, H33, I50, J58, J69, L55M, L70, *M81M*, etc.

Tristar: Medium-sized, symmetrical, short conic fruit; skin glossy, deep red at maturity; flesh solid medium deep red, firm, flavor excellent when eaten fresh and unsugared. Small to medium plant, of moderate vigor; produces a medium number of runners; resistant to red stele and tolerant to verticillium wilt; bears a heavy, very early spring crop. B58, B75, C63, E97, G16, G81, G87, H16, I50, J58, J61M, J69, L33, L55M, L70, etc.

Yolo: Day neutral type. Symmetrical, medium to short conic fruit, occasionally wedge-shaped; quality particularly good. Relatively compact plant; somewhat similar to Fern with slightly more elongated leaflets, darker and less yellow than those of Fern. Resistant to verticillium wilt; fairly resistant to mildew; moderately susceptible to common leaf spot. A14

JUNE-BEARING Also called main crop strawberries, these produce one large crop, beginning early in spring and ending with the onset of hot weather. They are generally considered to be more vigorous, heavier bearing and of better quality than everbearing types.

Early Season

Blakemore: Fruit medium-sized, blunt conic, shoulder broad; skin bright red, very attractive, fairly tough; flesh firm, light red, juicy, acid, high in pectin. Very good flavor and dessert quality, also very good for preserving. Vigorous, productive, disease resistant plant; produces runners freely. Adapted to southern states. A1M, A56, A82, B10, B43M, G72, J33, J83, K28, L55M, *M69M*, M83

Cyclone: Large fruit, slightly necked so that the hull is removed easily; flesh brilliant red, juicy, flavor excellent; freezes well. Good for home gardens and local markets; not firm enough for distant shipping. Vigorous, hardy, high yielding plant; produces numerous runners. BROOKS 1972; E97, J32, J83

Darrow: Medium-large fruit; skin firm, glossy, deep red; flesh very firm, uniformly red throughout; flavor good, not as tart as Surecrop; ripens 3 to 5 days earlier than Surecrop. Very productive plant; produces a moderate number of runners; resistant to 5 races of red stele. Named after noted breeder of small fruits George M. Darrow. A14, *C47*, J58, L55M

Douglas: Fruit large, somewhat larger and more uniform than Tioga one of its parents; skin smooth, glossy, deep red; flesh firm, of excellent flavor, sugar content high. Vigorous, high yielding plant; produces numerous runners. Well-suited to coastal and southern California; also does well in the southern United States and is the most popular commercial cultivar grown in Florida. *C54*, G81, *I41*, I99M, L55M

Earlibelle: Medium-large fruit, averages 62 berries per pound, long-conic; skin bright red, turning deep red at maturity, very glossy; flesh a uniform bright red, firm, flavor tart, good. Very vigorous plant; produces runners so freely, they must be thinned for best fruiting performance. BROOKS 1972; A82, E29M, E60, F19M, G81, L55M, *L85*, M31M

Earliglow: Medium-sized, conical fruit; skin tough, glossy; flesh rich red, firm; dessert quality good, very good for freezing; ripens 2 to 3 days later than Sunrise. Vigorous, widely adapted plant; produces numerous runners; resistant to 5 races of red stele, tolerant to wilt. Excellent for pick-your-own operations. A24, A39, B58, B75, C55M, C63, *C84*, C88, G44, H16, H65, I50, J69, J83, K71, M76, etc.

Empire: Large, uniform fruit; skin color light, bright, very attractive, maintained throughout the season; flesh light; dessert quality very good; ripens 4 to 6 days after Premier. Very productive plant; susceptible to leaf spot. Does well in northern areas. BROOKS 1972; J83

Fairfax: Medium-sized fruit, wedge-shaped to short blunt conic; skin quite bright red, turning dark purplish-red when ripe; flesh deep red, mildly subacid, dessert quality excellent. Doesn't keep well, but is ideal for home gardeners. Considered one of the best tasting strawberries. Especially productive when late-season runners are removed. BROOKS 1972, HENDRICKSON; A24, B58, C55M, H65, H88, J69, M92

Florida Ninety: Fruit large; shape unique, long and tapered; skin bright red; flavor excellent; very well-suited for fresh market; ripens extremely early, in November and December. Very vigorous plant; highly productive, having a short rest period; produces numerous runners; very susceptible to leaf spot and leaf scorch. BROOKS 1972; A82, B10, D77M, L55M, *L85*, M31M, M83

Pocahontas: Large, blunt conic, fairly uniform fruit; skin medium to deep red, glossy, attractive, tough; flesh red, medium firm, very tart; dessert quality good, very good for freezing; ripens early, about 1 week after Blakemore. Vigorous, very productive plant; makes runners freely; susceptible to red stele root rot. BROOKS 1972; A14, A24, B10, C63, E60, J58, J69, L55M{CF}, M76, M83

Premier: (Howard 17) Fruit large, long-conic to wedge-shaped, the largest berries furrowed on each side; skin red, attractive, glossy; flesh firm, well-colored to the center, juicy, pleasantly sprightly; quality good. Hardy, productive plant; disease and frost resistant. Originated in Belchertown, Massachusetts by A.B. Howard. Introduced in 1909. HEDRICK 1925; C63, H49, H88

Senator Dunlap: (Dunlap) Medium to large fruit, round-conic, usually with a distinct neck; skin glossy, attractive light red, quickly changing to a dark red; flesh well-colored to the center, juicy, mild, pleasantly flavored; quality good. An old favorite for gardens and local markets. Originated in Urbana, Illinois. Introduced in 1899. HEDRICK 1925; A14, A56, *C47*, C55M, C63, D76, E97, G16, J32, J33, J83, K71, L33, L55M

Sequoia: Exceptionally large, long conic fruit; skin dark red, tender, smooth, attractive; must be harvested at frequent intervals during hot periods or finish will become dull; flesh soft, requiring extra care in handling and shipping; flavor excellent. Begins to bear in January, hitting peak production in March. Performs like an everbearer in mild climates. Well suited to home gardens and "U-pick" farms. BROOKS 1972, STEBBINS; A88M, *C54*, E4, F11, F19M, G17, G81, G93M, *I41*, I99M, L55M, L99M, *M81M*, N33

Sunrise: Fruit medium-sized, conic, symmetrical; skin light, bright red which does not darken, glossy; flesh light pink, firm, subacid; dessert quality good; ripens early. Very vigorous plant; produces runners freely; resistant to 3 races of red stele and to verticillium wilt. BROOKS 1972; A14, A24, A82, B73M, C55M, C63, C88, H49, H88, J58, J69, J83, K28, L33, L55M, *L85*, etc.

Tioga: Medium to large fruit, long-conic to wedge-shaped; skin medium red, glossy, tough; flesh medium red, exceptionally firm, flavor good, acidity medium high; shipping quality excellent. Vigorous, prolific plant; moderately resistant to diseases; widely adapted to all growing areas of California. BROOKS 1972; A88M, *C54*, E4, *I41*, I99M, J83, L33, L55M, *M81M*

Titan: Very large fruit; skin slightly darker than Earlibelle; flesh firm, of good flavor; ripens with Earlibelle. Very large, vigorous plant; high yielding; produces a moderate number of runners; resistant to leaf spot and leaf scorch. Especially well suited for local market and home garden use in the Midsouth and Midwest. *C47*, E60, G81, L55M

Tufts: Large, flat wedge-shaped fruit; skin attractive, evenly colored red; flesh firm, dessert quality excellent, has a pleasing combination of high sugar, tartness and aroma; handles and ships well. Small to medium-sized, vigorous plant; produces runners freely; self-pollinating; yields well over a long season. L55M

Veestar: Medium-sized fruit, conic, uniform; skin medium red, glossy, smooth, attractive; flesh light to medium red, moderately firm, slightly tart, of excellent flavor; ripens early. Upright, medium-sized plant; of medium vigor. Runner production moderate. Originated in Vineland Station, Ontario, Canada. BROOKS 1972; A14, D11M, F1, G64, G69M, I50, J7

Midseason

Allstar: Very large fruit; skin glossy, tough, bright red; flesh firm, mild, sweet, of good quality; excellent for freezing; ripens with Guardian. Vigorous, productive plant; produces numerous runners; resistant to 5 races of red stele, tolerant to verticillium wilt. Performs well under diverse soil, climatic and cultural conditions. A24, B58, B75, C55M, C63, *C84*, C88, D65, G44, H88, I50, J69, J83, K71, M46, *M65M*, etc.

Cardinal: Exceptionally large fruit; flesh firm, uniformly red throughout, of excellent quality when fresh or processed. High yields. Excellent for pick-your-own operations as well as home gardens. One of the leading cultivars in Oklahoma, Missouri, Arkansas, Tennessee and the Southeast. A24, A39, A82, B58, C55M, C63, C88, D76, F19M, F93, H65, J69, J70M, J83, L33, *L85*, etc.

Catskill: Fruit large, long-conic, slightly irregular; skin glossy, bright crimson, attractive; flesh light red, moderately firm, mildly subacid, dessert quality excellent. Very vigorous and productive plant; produces runners freely; adapted to a wide range of soil types; resistant to verticillium wilt. BROOKS 1972; A14, A24, B58, *C47*, C55M, C63, G71, G81, H65, H88, I50, J58, J69, L55M

Glooscap: Medium to large fruit; skin glossy, red; flavor and quality excellent. Good for freezing or fresh market. Very large, high yielding plant; makes runners freely; does best in cool, wet climates. Originated in Kentville, Nova Scotia, Canada. A14, B99, G1T, G64, *I41*, J7, N24M, N26

Guardian: Large, irregular conic fruit; skin light red, glossy; flesh firm, light red, of good flavor; ripens 4 to 5 days later than Surecrop. Moderately vigorous, productive plant; resistant to 5 races of red stele root rot and verticillium wilt; produces a moderate number of runners. BROOKS 1972; A24, A82, B58, C63, *C84*, C88, F19M, G23, G44, H16, H65, H88, I50, J69, J83, *M65M*, M76, etc.

Holiday: Very large fruit, oblate to round oblate; skin bright red, glossy, very attractive, tough; flesh of superior firmness, light red to the center, juicy, mildly subacid, highly aromatic; quality good; freezes well. Exhibits concentrated ripening. Vigorous, productive plant; makes a good matted row of well-spaced runner plants. A14, C55M, G44{CF}, H65

Honeoye: (NY 1409) Very large, conical fruit; skin bright red, glossy, tough; flesh firm, quality very good. Vigorous, very productive plant; produces numerous runners; very winter hardy. Recommended for more northern states and the Midwest. A24, B58, C55M, C63, *C84*, C88, D65, D76, G16, G23, G44, H65, H88, I50, J20, J69, J83, L55M, etc.

Hood: Large, round conic fruit; skin bright medium red, glossy, attractive; flesh light red, medium firm, pleasantly subacid. Excellent for preserves and jams, satisfactory for local fresh fruit markets. Productive plant, yields of 6 tons per acre have been obtained. Very popular home garden cultivar in the Northwest. Originated in Corvallis, Oregon. BROOKS 1972; B67, C34, *I41*, I49M, *L18*, *M81M*

Jewel: (NY-1324) Fruit large, blunt wedge conic-shaped; skin bright red, glossy, very attractive; flesh red, somewhat firmer than average, has a slightly aromatic flavor reminiscent of Holiday, of very good quality. Excellent for freezing and processing. Hardy plant; not resistant to red stele or wilt. A14, B58, *C47*, *C84*, G44{CF}, I36, *I41*, I50, *M81M*

Kent: Very large fruit; skin dark red; flesh firm, red throughout; quality good, excellent for fresh eating and frozen desserts; easily picked. Vigorous plant; produces runners freely. Well adapted to northern climates and shows excellent winter-hardiness. Released by the Kentville Research Station in Nova Scotia. A14, A24, B58, *C47*, C58, *C84*, G16, G44, G64, H42, I50, J20, J58, K64, *M81M*, N24M, etc.

Lester: Large, very symmetrical fruit; skin uniformly deep red, attractive; flesh firm, of good mild flavor; ripens with Surecrop, between Earliglow and Raritan. Resistant to 5 strains of red stele, susceptible to verticillium wilt. Runners freely to produce a fruiting bed of medium density. A14, A24, B53, B58, B75, *C47*, *C84*, C88, G44, G81{CF}, I50, J58, J69, L55M

Midway: Medium to large fruit of irregular shape; skin uniform deep red, tough, glossy; flesh firm, flavor subacid with good dessert quality; freezes well. Moderately vigorous plant; producers runners freely; resistant to the common race of red stele. BROOKS 1972; A82, B58, B73M, C55M, C63, *C84*, C88, D65, G16, G44, I50, J69, J83, K71, L33, *M65M*, etc.

Northwest: Medium to large fruit, conic to long-conic; skin bright crimson, glossy; flesh light red throughout, firm, subacid, well-flavored when sugared, very good for fresh market and commercial freezing, good for canning. Very productive, vigorous plant; grows best on medium-light, well-drained, irrigated soil; resistant to virus diseases. BROOKS 1972; L97, *M81M*

Porter's Pride: Large fruit of flavor good; sufficiently firm for local market but nor for distant shipping. Hardy, vigorous plant; resistant to mildew; productive under prairie conditions. Originated in Parkside, Saskatchewan, Canada, by A.J. Porter, Honeywood Nursery. BROOKS 1972; F67

Puget Beauty: Large, conic to long-conic fruit; skin light crimson, glossy, exceptionally attractive; flesh light bright red, very sweet, aromatic, highly flavored, of fine dessert quality. Produces excellent aromatic preserves. Large to very large plant; very resistant to powdery mildew. Originated in Puyallup, Washington. BROOKS 1972; L97

Raritan: Large, glossy, bright red fruit; flesh firm, dessert quality very good, color acceptable for fresh market but not for processing. Productive plant; produces runners freely, making a good matted row; susceptible to red stele and wilt. Originated in New Brunswick, New Jersey. BROOKS 1972; A14, B53, B58, *C47*, C63, G44, G71, H88, I50, J58, J69, L55M

Redchief: Medium to large cone-shaped fruit; skin deep red, glossy; flesh firm, subacid; of good dessert quality that is maintained in frozen products; ripens 2 to 3 days later than Surecrop. Moderately vigorous plant; produces runners freely; tolerant to 5 races of red stele.

BROOKS 1972; A24, B58, B75, C63, *C84*, C88, F19M, G44, H16, H65, H88, I50, J20, J69, J83, M46, M76, etc.

Redcoat: Medium to large fruit, maintains good size throughout the harvest season; skin glossy, light red, highly attractive; flesh firm, flavor acceptable, color rather light. Acceptable for freezing, good for jam. Tall, vigorous plant; produces runners freely; fairly resistant to powdery mildew. BROOKS 1972; A14, A65, B58, *C47*, C55M, C63, D11M, F1, G16, G64, G69M, H65, H88, J69

Robinson: Medium to large, conical fruit; skin red, attractive; flesh light red, soft, flavor mild; not adapted to freezing. Being replaces by firmer, better-flavored cultivars. Small, vigorous, very productive plant; makes runners very freely; tolerant to virus diseases; very drought resistant. BROOKS 1972; A56, B10, B73M, C55M, C63, D65, E3, H49, H65, H88, I78, J83, L21, L55M

Royal Sovereign: Large, bluntly conical fruit, with some berries that are wedge-shaped; skin brilliant red; flesh pale, firm, subacid, flavor excellent; ripens in midseason. Vigorous, compact plant; very productive; highly susceptible to disease. An old English cultivar, still frequently grown and held in high esteem. Introduced in 1892. SIMMONS 1978; A1M

Scott: Large to very large fruit, symmetrical conic; skin tough, resists bruising; flesh bright red, firm, flavor mild; ripens with Guardian; freezes well. Highly vigorous plant; productive; produces numerous runners; resistant to 5 races of red stele, tolerant of verticillium wilt. Good for home gardens and roadside markets. A14, A24, B53, B58, *C47*, C63, *C84*, E60, G44, H88, I50, J58, J69, L55M, M46, M76, etc.

Snow White:[2] Small to medium-sized, white to creamy white fruit with a flavor similar to regular garden strawberries. Sends out numerous runners and spreads quickly. Relatively small leaves. M82

Sparkle: (Paymaster) Medium-sized fruit, short blunt conic to oblate; skin rather dark red, glossy, attractive; flesh soft, mildly subacid, quality excellent; good for dessert and freezing. Productive to very productive plant; resistant to powdery mildew and one race of red stele. A long time favorite with home gardeners. BROOKS 1972; A24, B58, B75, C63, D11M, D65, F1, G16, G23, G44, H16, H65, H88, I50, J20, J69, J83, etc.

Strasberry: (Strawberry-Raspberry) A strawberry with a unique flavor. The medium to large fruits have the softer texture and sweet taste and flavor of a raspberry. Should be completely ripe before harvesting. Will bear more fruit if planted in combination with other strawberries. G87, H42

Surecrop: Fruit large, round conic, irregular; skin attractive, glossy, tough, light bright red that becomes a rich red but does not turn dark; flesh light red, firm; flavor tart, good; quality good for dessert. Large, very vigorous plant; produces many runners; drought resistant; resistant to several races of red stele. BROOKS 1972; A24, A39, A82, B58, B73M, C63, *C84*, C88, F19M, G23, G44, H65, H88, I50, J69, J83, *M65M*, etc.

Suwannee: Medium to large fruit of excellent flavor. Maintains high flavor and quality under adverse weather conditions when most other cultivars fail. Rated as the best-flavored strawberry by noted breeder and berry connoisseur the late Professor George L. Slate of the New York State Agricultural Experiment Station. BROOKS 1972, HENDRICKSON; **U7M**

Tangi: Medium-large fruit of excellent flavor, very aromatic. Well suited to the Gulf states. Good plant maker and has good resistance to foliar disease. An old cultivar but well accepted by consumers because of its good flavor. A14

Tennessee Beauty: Large, round-conic to wedge-shaped fruit; skin attractive, glossy, medium to deep red, evenly colored; flesh medium red, whitish toward core, firm, subacid, well-flavored; dessert and shipping quality good; freezes well. Vigorous, medium-tall plant; tolerant to virus diseases. BROOKS 1972; A14, A82, C55M, C63, C88, E29M, E60, F19M, F93, G72, G81, J69, K28, L55M, *L85*, M76, etc.

White Pine:[2] (Weiss Ananas) Small, globose fruit, 3/4 to 1 inch long; relatively thin, glossy white skin; firm white flesh. Moderately productive. Primitive cultivar of historical interest selected at the Max Planck Institute for Plant Breeding. NCGR; **U7M**

Late Season

Apollo: Large, symmetrical fruit; skin glossy, attractive, deep scarlet; flesh sweet, flavor good. Medium-sized plant; produces a moderate number of runners; tolerant to leaf spot, leaf curl and powdery mildew; performs well in matted row or hills. Originated in Willard, North Carolina. BROOKS 1972; A14, *C47*, C88, E60, G81, L55M

Blomidon: Large, uniform fruit; skin glossy, medium red, attractive; flesh firm, of very good flavor; ripens about 9 days after Earliglow. Good for fresh market, shipping and freezing. Heavy yielding plant; vigorous and winter hardy. Does best in northern climates. A14, B58, I36, I50, N26

Bounty: Medium-sized fruit; skin medium red, attractive; flesh firm, of very good flavor; ripens 8 to 10 days after Midway. Vigorous, heavy yielding plant; produces runners freely; winter-hardy; not resistant to soil borne diseases. Does best in cold, northern climates. Introduced in 1977 by the Nova Scotia Research Station in Kentville. A14, C58, G64, I50, J7

Canoga: Fruit large to very large, wedge-conic; skin intense red, attractive, very tough; flesh very firm, of good quality. Good for shipping and freezing. Vigorous, productive plant; makes a good matted row. Introduced by the New York Agricultural Experiment Station in 1979. A14, G23, I50

Delite: Medium to large, conical fruit; skin glossy, bright red; flesh moderately firm, pink, aromatic, of good flavor and dessert quality; ripens 5 to 7 days later than Surecrop. Very vigorous, very productive plant; produces runners freely. Released by Southern Illinois University. A14, A24, B53, B58, *C47*, C55M, C63, C88, E60, G44, G81{CF}, J69, L55M

Fletcher: Medium to large conical fruit; skin medium red, glossy, attractive; flesh red, juicy, center solid, flavor subacid, quality very good. Excellent for freezing, being slightly superior to Sparkle. Ripens about 3 days after Sparkle. Tall, vigorous plant; very productive; produces runners freely; resists mildew. BROOKS 1972; C55M, H65, J69

Jerseybelle: Very large, blunt conic fruit; skin very attractive, glossy, medium red, tough; flesh fairly firm, flavor mild, quality good fresh. White streaks remain at core until fully ripe. Large, vigorous plant; moderately productive; produces fewer runner plants than Sparkle; susceptible to red stele and wilt. BROOKS 1972; A24, B58, *C47*, G71, J69, L55M

Lateglow: Large to very large, symmetrical fruit; skin tough, glossy, deep scarlet; flesh firm, medium red, juicy, sweet, aromatic. Ripens with Delite, slightly later than Allstar and Guardian. Medium-sized, vigorous plant; produces runners freely; very resistant to red stele and wilt; tolerant to leaf diseases. A14, A24, B58, B75, C55M, *C84*, E60, G44, G81{CF}, H16, H88, *I41*, I50, J58

Marlate: Large, round conic fruit, easy to pick; skin bright red; flesh firm and sweet. Tall, vigorous plant; produces a moderate number of runners; resistant to some leaf diseases; susceptible to red stele. Particularly adapted to the northeastern states. *C47*, C63, I50

Trumpeter: Large, rounded conic to heart shaped fruit; skin bright red, attractive; flesh an intense red throughout, very firm, juicy, slightly tart, aromatic, flavor very good; freezing quality superior. Very tall and vigorous plant; hardy; highly resistant to root rot; performs well on several soil types. Originated in Excelsior, Minnesota. BROOKS 1972; B4, E97, G44, J83, L55M, L70

Vesper: Very large fruit, up to 1 1/2 inches in diameter; skin medium tough, glossy, very attractive; flesh light red, moderately firm, mildly subacid, flavor very good; ripens 3 to 5 days after Jerseybelle. Requires more frequent harvesting than some other cultivars because it ripens rapidly. Originated in New Brunswick, New Jersey. BROOKS 1972; A14, A24, B53, B58, *C47*, D65, I50, J58, J69

SUNFLOWER {S}

HELIANTHUS ANNUUS

CONFECTIONERY SUNFLOWERS

Mostly used as a snack food, these have large seeds, approximately five-eights of an inch in length, usually striped, and a relatively thick hull which remains free of the kernel and is easily removed. The oil content is about twenty-seven per cent. They are also used as bird food. ROSENGARTEN.

HYBRID

954: 80 days. An improved sunflower that ripens early, has a sturdy, heavy stalk and produces a good-sized head well-filled with large, heavy seeds. Stalks are 5 to 6 feet tall, and instead of branching, usually have but one good-sized, solidly packed head per stalk. G16

D 131: 68 days. Large flower heads, up to 11 inches across, form plump, edible seeds which make excellent snacks or bird food. Sturdy stalks are shorter than Mammoth; grow 5 to 6 1/2 feet tall. B75

Sun 891: 110 days. A high yielding, confectionery type sunflower, earlier and more resistant to lodging than Mammoth types. Grows to 7 feet tall, with heads that average 8 to 12 inches in diameter. One of the principal cultivars used by the top commercial sunflower growers in America. G6

Sunbred 254: 110 days. An extremely heavy yielder with above-average stalk strength, high oil content, a low hull-to-kernel percentage and tasty seeds. Resistant to rust, downy mildew and verticillium wilt. Blooms in 70 days; takes 110 days to mature. Developed by Northrup King. Tested at the University of Minnesota. E97

OPEN-POLLINATED

Apache Brown Striped: Medium-sized heads with brown-striped seeds. Planted in spring in the low desert (after frost danger has passed), or with the summer rains. Originally from the San Carlos Reservation in Arizona. Does well in Tucson. I16

Arikara: Deep purple, almost black seeds with minor variations. Height of plant 6 to 7 feet. Similar to Mammoth Russian. Originally grown by Arikara tribes of South Dakota. L79M

Arrowhead: 76 days. Variable-sized heads average 5 to 6 inches across and produce narrow seeds. Stalks grow 6 feet tall with few side heads. Recommended for areas where late cultivars will not mature. Also makes good bird food for small and medium-sized birds. Originally from Czechoslovakia. L7M

Black Russian: Small black seeds with thin hulls. Excellent for processing into oil or eating raw or lightly toasted. Also makes good bird food. The leaves make good cattle feed, and the stems have ben used for fiber, papermaking and as firewood. F80, H94

Black Stripe: 70 days. Tall, sturdy plant; smaller in size than Grey Stripe, but produces larger harvests of tasty seeds. E97

Dwarf Russian: 68 days. Sturdy, vigorous, early maturing stalks are shorter than Mammoth Russian, yet seed heads are just as large. Seeds are also large. D82

Giganteus: Tall, sturdy stalks; height 8 to 12 feet; usually produce a single large, attractive golden head, about 12 inches in diameter. Seeds are tasty and nutritious roasted. Fine for edible seed production as well as ornament. Also useful as a background or screen. I91, M29

Grey Stripe: (Giant Grey Stripe, Large Grey Stripe, Mammoth Grey Stripe) 85 days. Tall, sturdy stalks reach a height of 8 to 12 feet. Attractive heads up to 20 inches in diameter filled with an abundance of large, thin-shelled plump seeds high in protein. Delicious as a snack and are also valuable as wild bird or chicken feed. A13, A56, A69M, D76, E97, F12, G16, G82, H33, J20, K49M, M95, N52, R47

Havasupai Striped: Long, narrow seeds. Lodging has been a problem in the low desert. Does not do well in Tucson, Arizona. Originally from the bottom of the Grand Canyon. I16

Hopi Black Dye: (Hopi Dye, Tceqa) The hull of the purple-black seeds is used for dying, but the seed kernel is edible. Can make a variety of dye colors, from blue to red, depending on the mordant used. Grows 6 to 8 feet tall, with 5 to 8 inch diameter flower heads plus smaller side heads. Develops aerial roots for better anchorage. Adapted to cool, high desert regions, but can be grown in other areas. A2, E59Z, I16, J25M, L7M

Large-Seeded Tall: Large heads, produced on tall-growing, 5 to 7 foot stalks. The seed is large, is used extensively for eating and has an excellent flavor. H42

Large Single-Headed: Produces nutritious seeds, high in vitamins D and E. Stalks grow 8 feet tall and produce very large heads, up to 24 inches in diameter. Makes a good trellis for beans. I99

Mammoth: 80 days. Large heads well-filled with thin-shelled, striped seeds that are plump and meaty. Makes a high-protein snack; also a valuable bird food. Tall, 6 to 12 foot plants; heavily productive; will thrive on poor soil. B35M, B75, D11M, F13, F82, G57M, G71M, H95, I39, J34, J58, J97M, K66, N39, etc.

Mammoth Russian: (Large Russian, Russian Giant) 80 days. Medium to large, striped seeds; thin-shelled, meaty, rich in flavor. Stalks average 8 to 12 feet tall and produce a large single head with occasional smaller heads. An old standard cultivar, first offered by American seed companies in the 1880's. A2, A16, C85M, D82, G51, G79, H54, H94, K50, K71, L7M, L79, L79M, L97

Sundak: (Early Sundak) 98 days. An improved, early-maturing, rust-resistant cultivar. Large, black seeds with gray stripes. Stalks grow 5 to 6 feet tall, usually with only one flower head per stalk. Heads average 8 to 12 inches in diameter, depending on spacing. A2, E24, G6, H94, K49M, L7M

Sunspot: 60 days. Dwarf, compact, erect plants; grow only 2 feet tall yet produce large, 10 inch diameter heads. Ideal for small gardens, and a natural for children. Blooms in only 60 days and provides weeks of colorful, attractive flowers, right at bed height. Mature heads yield an abundance of nutritious, tasty seeds. I91

Tarahumara White: All-white seeds. Solid gold flower heads. Excellent producer of large heads in low desert areas, with irrigation. Introduced and adapted over a 30 year period of cultivation. Probably of Canadian Mennonite origin, but obtained by the Tarahumara from Chihuahuan Mennonites. Unusual and rare. I16

OILSEED SUNFLOWERS

Primarily used as a source of oil and high-protein meal, these have small black seeds, about three-eighths of an inch long, with a thin hull which adheres to the kernel, and an oil content of about forty per cent. They are also the type preferred for sprouting. ROSENGARTEN.

HYBRID

7111: Black oilseed type sunflower selected for the Northeast. Heads mature in 95 days. Plants average 48 to 50 inches in height. Recommended planting rate is 3 to 5 pounds per acre. A13

OPEN-POLLINATED

Peredovik: 110 days. A Russian strain grown commercially for the pressing of quality sunflower oil for salads and cooking. The small, black, shelled seeds also make good bird food, and excellent poultry and rabbit food. G26, L7M, L11, N11

Polyheaded: Spectacular plants, grow to 8 feet tall and produce 20 to 40 heads per plant, 4 to 8 inches in diameter. Suitable for sunflower seed oil or for sprouting. I99

Progress: 63 days. A commercial cultivar of black oilseed sunflower introduced by Southern Exposure Seed Exchange. Produces single heads about 6 inches in diameter on stalks ranging from 5 1/2 to 7 feet tall. Seed color and pattern predominantly black with occasional black-grey striped seed. For use as bird food or sunflower seed oil. Excellent resistance to stalk breakage and lodging. L7M

Rostov: 90 days. Early-maturing Russian black-seeded type, originally from the Ukraine. Heads average 12 inches or more in diameter. Height of plant 5 to 8 feet. Can withstand heavy rain and winds. A2, D33, L7M, L79M

SWEET POTATO {PL}

IPOMOEA BATATAS

DRY FLESH

Mostly yellow- or white-fleshed, these are more mealy, starchier, and less sweet than moist flesh types. They are classified as dry flesh if they feel "dry" in the mouth, not by their moisture content. Some do especially well, and are favored in, the Northeast and Middle Atlantic states.

Boniato: (Cuban Sweet Potato) Short, plump, irregularly shaped tuber; reddish skin; white flesh, slightly less sweet and drier in texture than moist orange-fleshed types. When baked the skin becomes crunchy and very tasty. Available at Spanish markets in New York and other large cities. HAWKES [Re], SCHNEIDER [Cul, Re]; *B59*{PR}, L9M{CF}, *N40*{PR}

Mexican Purple: Large to very large roots, up to 5 pounds or more; skin brownish-red; flesh deep purple when cooked, dry but nut-like in flavor. Vigorous, productive vine with purple-tinged leaves. Common in the markets of Tijuana. D57

Okinawiian: Small to medium-sized, elongated roots; skin grayish-white; flesh slightly moist when cooked, changes to a lilac-magenta color; flavor rich and sweet. Somewhat of a shy bearer in California, producing roots spottily and away from the center of the plant. Local favorite in Hawaii. D57

Old Kentucky: 120 days. Large, white-skinned roots; flesh cream-colored when cooked, sweet, fiberless, of excellent flavor; Matures late. Keeps very well but is difficult to dig. Vining type that produces roots away from the center of the plant. Old heirloom cultivar. U33

Sumor: A novelty type, developed by Philip Dukes of the USDA Vegetable Breeding Lab in Charleston, South Carolina. Very smooth, light tan skin; white to yellowish flesh, very low sugar content; flavor almost as bland as an Irish potato. Stores well, with sweetness increasing after extended storage. May be baked, mashed, creamed, fried or consumed in salads. Recommended as a substitute crop in climates too hot for growing Irish potatoes. Sumor is the old English word for summer. U33

White Triumph: (White Yam, Southern Queen, Poplar Root, Choker, White Bunch) An unusual white-skinned, white-fleshed cultivar with very dry and very smooth flesh and a sweet flavor. One of the oldest cultivars in the country. E9M, H49, L35

Yellow Jersey: (Little Stem Jersey) Orange skin; very dry, sweet yellow flesh. Resistant to root-knot nematode. Does well in the Northeast and Middle Atlantic states. Sweet potatoes that bake dry are sometimes called Jersey sweet potatoes after the dry-fleshed Jersey group of cultivars such as Big Stem Jersey and Little Stem Jersey. E70M{PR}

MOIST FLESH

Sometimes erroneously called yams, this type has soft, very sweet, yam-like flesh that is usually dark yellow or orange-red. They are classified as moist flesh if they feel "moist" in the mouth, not by their moisture content. They grow particularly well, and are favored in, the Southern states.

All Gold: (Algolds) 100 days. Golden-orange skin; medium-dry, deep golden yellow flesh; flavor very good, improves in storage. Very early, yet stores particularly well. Resistant to the viral disease known as internal cork, and also stem rot. Heavy yielding, vining type plant. Developed for the South, but does well in the Midwest and other areas. D65, E9M

Bush Porto Rico: (Bunch Porto Rico, Vineless Porto Rico, Red Yam) 110 days. Irregular-shaped roots; smooth, copper-colored skin; deep reddish-orange, sweet flesh. Old time favorite for flavor; excellent for baking. Matures 3 weeks earlier than Running Porto Rico. Semi-upright plant; comparatively short, usually only 4 to 5 feet long. Popular with gardeners who have limited space. B75, D65, D76, E9M, E97, F19M, H33, H49, H65, I91, K71, L35, M46

Centennial: 110 days. Root medium to large; cylindrical to tapered; skin bright orange; flesh sweet, deep-orange, has a fine moist texture and flavor. Matures early; "baby bakers" can be dug in 90 to 100 days from set plants. Long, vining type plant. Widely adapted and productive. Tolerates clay soil better than Jewel. Standard cultivar for local market and home gardens. B75, D76, E9M, E97, F19M, G16, H33, H49, H65, I91, K71, L35, M46

Copperskin: (Copperskin Running Porto Rico) Smooth, copper-colored roots with moist, cream-colored flesh. Vigorous vine, produces numerous runners. An old time favorite in the South. E9M

Excel: A new disease and insect resistant cultivar developed by Philip Dukes of the USDA Vegetable Breeding Lab in Charleston, South Carolina. Has shown better "natural" insect resistance than could be expected with the use of chemical pesticide controls. Higher yielding than Southern Delite. Introduced in 1988. L4

Georgia Jet: (Jet) 90 days. Large, uniform roots; skin dark reddish-purple; flesh moist, deep-orange in color, of excellent flavor. Vining type plant. Very early and heavy yielding; often produces table-size roots in only 75 days. Does well as far north as Canada. Released in 1974 as an early market cultivar for Georgia farmers, it has become very popular with small growers. D76, E97, G16, H33, H49, K71, L35, M46

Jewel: (New Jewel, Golden Jewel) 100 days. Skin bright-copper; flesh deep-orange, of soft texture which makes it bake more quickly; flavor rich, quality high. Holds quality and flavor well in long-term storage, up to 50 weeks. Vining type plants; heavy yielding, up to 6 potatoes per plant. Disease resistant. Accounts for 75% of all commercially produced sweet potatoes. D76, E70M{PR}, E97, G16, H33, H49, I91, J14, J34, K71, L35, M1M{PR}

Nancy Hall: (Yellow Yam) 110 days. Skin light-tan; flesh moist, firm, deep-yellow, juicy, waxy and sweet when baked; keeps well. Resistant to soft rot. The "yellow yam" of the 30's and 40's. Although not attractive in appearance, a favorite of older gardeners because of its excellent flavor. Semi-bush type plant. E9M, H49, L35

Nugget: (Red Nugget) Smooth, slightly blocky roots; cylindrical to tapered. Semi-dry, reddish flesh of excellent quality. Widely adapted. Resistant to internal cork, root-knot nematode, fusarium wilt and brown rot. Somewhat weak on sprout production. E9M

Oklahoma Reds: Attractive, deep dark-red roots with moist, whitish to pale yellow flesh. Vigorous, productive vine; yields 200 to 300 bushels per acre. Has good market appeal. E9M

Red Jewel: 150 days. Good yields of red-skinned, orange-fleshed potatoes. Popular with home gardeners because it is especially easy to grow. One of the red-skinned cultivars preferred by consumers in Georgia over their copper-skinned counterparts. E9M, F19M

Rose Centennial: (Rose, Improved Centennial) A root mutation of the popular Centennial cultivar, it has rose-colored flesh instead of the orange of its parent. Same high yields, quality, adaptability and flavor. E9M

Southern Delite: A new disease and insect resistant cultivar developed by Philip Dukes of the USDA Vegetable Breeding Lab in Charleston, South Carolina. Medium-sized, fusiform tuber; skin rose to dark copper; flesh orange, of very good flavor. Baking properties excellent. Vine vigorous, moderately long. Has shown better "natural" insect and disease resistance than could be expected with the use of chemical pesticide controls. Introduced in 1986. L4

Travis: Fast-maturing, moist-fleshed type that has become famous for its heavy yields. Will produce very large, jumbo potatoes if left in the ground too long. Matures 2 weeks before Jewel. Resistant to soil rot. Released in 1980 by Louisiana State University's Sweet Potato Research Station on Yam Avenue in Chase, Louisiana. L35

Vardaman: 110 days. Skin golden-yellow; flesh deep-orange, of rich flavor. Considered to have the best eating quality of the short-vined types; also has better resistance to fusarium wilt. Bush type plant; ideal for small gardens. Heavy yielding and early maturing. Produces well in many parts of the country and on various soil types. D76, E97, G16, H33, H49, H65, I91, K71, L35, M46

SWISS CHARD {S}

BETA VULGARIS CICLA GROUP

CHARD

Grown for the leaves which can be prepared like spinach, as well as the broad, thick, frequently white stalks which are often prepared separately in the manner of asparagus. The leaves are usually considered too coarse for use in salads unless chopped finely.

Argentata: (Costa Argentata) 55 days. An old Italian heirloom, long selected for its good flavor which is mild, clean and sweet. Attractive, vigorous plant has silver-white crispy midribs and deep green crinkled leaves. Long standing; grows several feet tall; will stand a wide variety of weather conditions. B8, I77, K66

Blonde à Carde Blanche: (Silvery Swiss Chard) 55-60 days. Large, broad, light-green leaves which are very much undulated, half erect, and remarkable for the size of their stalks and midribs, which are often 4 inches broad or more. A light and pale color in the leaves is usually accompanied by a mild flavor, while leaves of a dark-green color always have a strong taste. VILMORIN; F33

Blonde de Lyon: (Blonde à Carde Blanche Race de Lyon) Large, light green leaves with very large white midribs; broad white stalks, tender and mild. Relatively short plant; resistant to heat. Recommended for summer culture. G68, S95M

Burgundy:[2] (Burgundy Crimson) 65 days. Heavily crumpled, deep green leaves with maroon overtones; translucent brilliant crimson stems and leaf veins; very rich flavor. A colorful addition to salads, or the leaves can be cooked like spinach and the stems like asparagus. Plants yield until frost. D11M, D27, *E91G*

Compacta Slow Bolting: Compact, slow-bolting cultivar. Dark-green leaves; medium broad white ribs. Height around 18 inches. T1M

Dark Green White Ribbed: (White Ribbed, White Silver) 60 days. Large, upright plant reaches a height of 20 to 26 inches. Produces large, smooth to slightly crumpled dark-green leaves with broad, white petioles. Very productive and flavorful. A popular and proven standard cultivar. A87M, C92, G71, G93M, *H61*, I64, J84, K73

De Languedoc: Resembles de Nice in appearance, having thick white midribs and curly dark-green leaves. Adapted to a wide range of climatic conditions; productive into spring as well as during fall and winter. Recommended for year-round planting, as it resists bolting. Dropped by G69

De Nice: Selected for late summer planting in the region between, Nice, France and the Italian border. It has very thick, very white midribs and deeply curled leaves. It grows quickly, promoting tender leaves, and is resistant to cold. Also very productive grown in plastic tunnels during winter. It will bolt with the onset of spring. Dropped by G69

Dorat: 60 days. Pale yellow-green, deeply-crinkled leaves are mild and tender. Thick, very wide, pure white, mild-tasting stalks. An improved form of Lucullus, with more uniformity and greater vigor. Danish gourmet seed. F92, G64, I77, J7, L89

Fordhook Giant: (Burpee's Fordhook Giant) 60 days. A tall, vigorous strain, about 2 foot tall and 1 foot wide with broad, very crinkled, thick, fleshy dark-green leaves. Broad, thick, greenish-white stems. Yields continuously from early summer until frost. A16, A25, B78, D82, E24, F19M, G6, G68, H42, *H61*, H94, K73, M13M, M46, M95, N16, etc.

French: 60 days. An improvement over common Swiss chard. The green leaves are very tender and flavorful, growing on large white stalks. Heavy yielding, 18 inch tall plants. Can be sown twice a year in milder climates. I39

French Green: Well-developed white midrib with attractive, rumpled, thick, light-green leaves. Slow to bolt; heavy cropping; has some resistance to both heat and cold. A2, R47

Lucullus: 50 days. Extra large, thick, fleshy, heavily crumpled, yellowish-green leaves. Stalks long, rather rounded, pure white. Vigorous, upright plant, growing about 28 inches high. Yields an enormous amount of greens. Similar to Fordhook Giant except for the lighter colored leaves. A25, B73M, B75M, C44, C85M, F1, F19M, G16, G71, L7M, L79, L97, M46, M49, N39, etc.

Markin Giant: Large, dark-green, almost smooth leaves; narrow but fleshy ribs, often 18 to 20 inches or more broad. Vigorous growing, with rapid re-growth after cutting. Strong resistance to curly top virus. A very desirable and decorative cultivar, excellent for markets. O39M

Paros: 55 days. Very large, upright, dark-green crinkled leaves on thick, succulent white stalks. Developed by the French for its flavor, which is distinctly milder and sweeter than ordinary American cultivars. Young leaves can be used in salads. Grows easily, yielding fine-quality harvests from early summer into winter. K66

Rainbow Chard:[1] 60 days. A beautiful technicolor mixture of ornamental Swiss chards. Individual plants variously produce succulent stems in shades of either red, orange, purple, yellow or white. Tender and tasty in the kitchen and excellent material for flower arrangements. B49, K49T, L91M, O89

Redstem Purpleleaf:[2] Unique type with dark-red stems and distinctive, crumpled purplish leaves. Very attractive as well as useful. I99

Rex Wide Ribbed: 55 days. Vigorous and uniform plants with large, glossy, dark-green, heavily crinkled leaves. Broad, silver-white stalks average 2 inches in width. Withstands both cold and warm temperatures, making it suitable for full season production. J7

Rhubarb Chard:[2] (Burpee's Rhubarb Chard) 55 days. Deep-crimson stalks and leaf veins contrast with heavily crumpled dark-green leaves. The roots turn almost white when boiled and are sweeter than red beets. They can be pickled with caraway seeds, turned into golden beets by adding saffron, or prepared with thickened grape juice for *Harvard beets*. C44, C92, D82, G16, *H61*, H94, J7, J34, K73, L42, M13M, M46, M49, M95

Ruby Red:[2] (Ruby) 60 days. An attractive ornamental chard with crumpled, dark greenish-red leaves. The tender, sweet stalks and midribs are crimson in color, which extends into the leaf veins. Has more of a beet flavor than Fordhook Giant. Keep the outside leaves cropped off to have bright red Ruby chard greens. A13, A16, B1M, D76, E24, E57, F1, G6, G71, I39, J25M, K50, K66, L7M

San Francisco Bay: 60 days. Tender, light green leaves with very small midribs, 9 inches long; delicate stems. Excellent flavor, never tough or bitter. Slow-bolting plant; height 18 inches. Originally from Italy, now grows wild around the margins of the San Francisco Bay. J73

Silver Giant: 60 days. Deeply crumpled, medium-green leaves are rich, fleshy and tender. Large, pearl-white stalks and broad midribs. Heavily productive; heat tolerant. D11M

Swiss Chard of Geneva: 60 days. An excellent cultivar with very large ribs and celery-like stalks. So hardy that it withstands severe winters and is suitable for year round culture. Tops are delicious as greens. Prepare stalks like asparagus. I91

Vulcan:[2] 60 days. An improved Rhubarb chard developed in Switzerland. Uniform bright red stems and leaf veins contrast with dark-green crinkled leaves. Leaves and stems are very sweet, with outstanding Swiss chard flavor. I91

White King: 55 days. A uniform selection from Lucullus, with large thick white ribs and extra dark green heavily crinkled leaves. Very upright plant with stalks that appear almost celery-like. Recommended for the critical grower. L42

LEAF BEETS

Grown primarily for the succulent leaves which make an excellent hot weather substitute for spinach. This is the type preferred for use in salads. Included here are the Japanese types which are somewhat intermediate between the chards and the leaf beets.

Banerjee's Giant: An improved strain of Palang Sag. The plants are very robust growing and produce large fleshy leaves double the size of ordinary strains. Sown from August to October in India. S59M

Cut and Come Again: 60 days. Grown for its pale green, chard-like leaves which can be cut frequently when small and used in salads or as a cooked vegetable. Very easy to grow, providing fresh greens through fall, winter and spring in mild climates. Grows quickly. U33

Erbette: (Verde da Taglio) Grown for its fine tasting, smooth textured greens which are used when young like spinach. Makes a very good cut-and-come-again green. Keep it cut and it will continue to produce all season long. B8, C53, Q11M

Nihon: (Japanese Swiss Chard) Broad, deep-green leaves with narrow, thick, light-green stalks. Resembles smooth round-leaved spinach. Stands heat well. An excellent tender green chard for home gardeners. Intermediate between broad-leaved chard and leaf beet. L59

Palang Sag: (Indian Spinach, Palanki, Palak) An annual herb with a prominent taproot, an erect stem with trowel-shaped leaves at the base and leafy spikes. The leaves are used as a salad and for preparing stew. A common inexpensive vegetable seen in the markets of northern India during the cold weather season. Reselected stock of a small-leaved strain. NAYAR, ZEVEN; R0, S59M

Perpetual: (Perpetual Spinach, Spinach Beet, Cutting Chard) 50 days. Rare, fine old European strain related to Swiss chard. Smaller, smooth, succulent dark-green leaves with small midribs. Drought, frost, and bolt resistant. Early maturing; very productive. Has a long "perpetual" harvest. LARKCOM 1984 [Cu]; B49, B75, C53, D11M, F92, L91M, O53M, P83M, *R23*, S45M, S61, *S75M*

Umaina: Japanese type. Broad, dark-green leaves with narrow, thick greenish-white petioles. Heat resistant; very slow bolting. Excellent for summer harvesting both for fresh market and home gardens. Intermediate between broad-leaved chard and leaf beet. *S63M*

TEPARY BEAN {S}

PHASEOLUS ACUTIFOLIUS

<u>**BLACK-SEEDED**</u>

Black: Selected by Bruce Bailey, longtime member of Native Seeds/Search from white teparies purchased many years ago in a Tucson Mexican market. Similar to a historic Tohono O'odham and Yuma cultivar. Adapted to the low hot desert. Plant with the summer rains. I16

Mitla Black: 80 days. Slightly smaller and rounder than Sonoran teparies. Has the same good flavor and nutrition. Excellent in black bean soup. The small pods can be used as a green bean. Less day-length sensitive and grows better in more extreme northern latitudes than Sonoran types, making two crops possible. From the Mitla Valley, Oaxaca, Mexico. I16, J25M, K49T

BROWN/YELLOW-SEEDED

Golden: Somewhat flattened seed. Very prolific bush bean. Drought tolerant; will grow in very hot, dry conditions. Small plant with green, pointed leaves. Space further apart than other beans in wet or cool climates. Irrigating extends the season and yield. L79M

O'odham Brown: 60-90 days. Once commercially cultivated in the United States by the Gila River Pima near Sacaton, Arizona. Favored for vegetable paté. Adapted to the low hot desert where it is planted with the summer rains. Not recommended for humid regions. Known locally as "S'oam bawi". I16, M95

Paiute Yellow: Ocher colored traditional favorite from the Kaibab Indian Reservation in southern Utah. Grown near the Santa Clara River. Adapted to the high desert where it is planted in June or with the summer rains. One of the most northerly tepary beans. I16

Pima Beige and Brown: Beans are mixed shades of beige, gold and tan. Original collection from Santan, Arizona, on the Gila River Indian Reservation. I16

Pinacate: Tan, slightly mottled seeds. Originally obtained from the most extremely arid agricultural area in Mexico, just south of the U.S. border, in the Sierra El Pinacate Protected Zone. Planted with the summer rains in the low hot desert. I16

Sonoran: 90-110 days. Small, delicious beans with over 30% crude protein. Under native desert conditions they require as little as 70 days to mature. Farther north or with cooler temperatures, they require a longer growing season. Native to the Sonoran Desert, the drought tolerant tepary was domesticated by the Papago Indians. J25M

Sonoran Brown: 85 days. One of the earliest cultivars to mature. Has a delicious flavor when used in soups or as a paté. Drought tolerant plant; very productive in intense heat and dry conditions. From the lower Sonoran Desert region. I99, K49T

Tohono O'odham: A red-brown bean from Menenger's Dam on the reservation near the Mexican border. Adapted to the low hot desert where it is planted with the summer rains. I16

Virus Free Yellow: Ocher colored seeds. Selected by the USDA and grown out in Tucson, Arizona. Do not infect by growing near other teparies, as others may carry bean mosaic virus. Planted with the summer rains in the desert. I16

Yaqui: A beige bean from a traditional Yaqui village on Sonora's coastal plain at approximately 80 foot elevation. Adapted to the low hot desert where it is planted with the summer rains. In colder areas, plant in late May or early June. I16

Mottled

Blue Speckles: 96 days. Medium-sized, plump seeds with excellent flavor. Similar to Golden, but fuller seed with blue speckles on white. From southern Mexico but produces a good crop in southern Arizona near 4300 feet elevation. Also grows well in northern New Mexico. Does not tolerate the heat of the low desert. E59Z, I16, I99, K49T, L79M

Brown Speckles: 96 days. Small, plump, light gray seeds speckled with pale brown. Selected from Blue Speckles. Grows well at High Desert Research Farm in Abiquiu, New Mexico, at 6,500 feet elevation. Introduced in 1981 by Good Seed Co. E59Z, I16

Mitla Speckled: 70-90 days. From the Mitla Valley of Oaxaca, Mexico, these are the same as the Mitla Black except for the color and a slightly different, nutty flavor. J25M

WHITE-SEEDED

Colonia Morelos White: Grown by Mexicans under irrigation in a small desert town originally founded by Mormons and where Geronimo agreed to surrender. Planted with the summer rains in the low hot desert. Dropped by I16

Kickapoo White: A transplanted tribe from Oklahoma adopted this native desert crop for their new southeastern Sonora, Mexico home of Rio Bavispe. Planted with the summer rains in the low hot desert. In colder climates plant in late May or early June. I16

Mayo White: Small, white and green beans. Dry farmed in Sinaloa, Mexico on the lower western flanks of the Sierra Madre Mountains near the El Fuerte River. Planted with the summer rains in the low hot desert. I16{PR}

O'odham White: 90 days. Seeds creamy white rather than the more common brown. The extremely dry composition of the bean requires slightly more cooking time than standard dry beans. Once commercially cultivated in the United States by the Gila River Pima, who grew it near Sacaton, Arizona under hot, arid conditions. M95

Paiute White: From the Kaibab Indian Reservation in southern Utah. Grown near the Santa Clara River. Adapted to the high desert where it is planted in June or with the summer rains. Along with Paiute Yellow, one of the most northerly tepary beans. I16

San Felipe Pueblo: Large, white-seeded beans. A traditional crop that is grown with irrigation along the Rio Grande in northern New Mexico. Adapted to the high semi-desert where it is planted with the summer rains. In temperate areas plant in late May or early June. I16

Ures White: Grown on marginal land as a secondary bean crop in Sonora, Mexico where it is popular in soups. Known locally as "tépari blanco". I16

Virus Free White: White seeds. Selected by the USDA and grown out in Tucson, Arizona. Do not infect by growing near other teparies, as others may carry bean mosaic virus. Planted with the summer rains in the desert. I16

Warihio White: 92 days. Medium-large, somewhat flattened, white seeds. Prolific even in hot, dry weather. Native staple in the Mexican Sonoran regions. K49T

THYME {PL}

THYMUS SPP.

LEMON-SCENTED

Doone Valley: New growth is bright gold mixed with a small amount of deep green, highlighted with red in winter. Deep-green, glossy old growth provides a nice contrast. Fresh lemon scent. A moderately fast growing, prostrate cultivar; height 4 to 6 inches. Lavender flowers. Needs winter protection. A49D, C3, C9, C43M, C67M, C81M, E5M, F57M, G84, H51M, J78, J82, J91, K63, L56, *M35*, M82, etc.

E.B. Anderson: Tight-growing evergreen mounds. New growth is gold with maroon undersides and stems, giving it a striking appearance. Older leaves are dark green with a few golden tints in summer, becoming bright gold in winter. Lilac flowers are long lasting. C9, H79M

Golden Lemon Creeping: (T. x citriodorus) Attractive, glossy, dark-green leaves variegated with gold. Strong, fresh lemon scent and flavor. Height 4 to 6 inches. An excellent ground cover for sunny locations with well drained soil. Lavender flower spikes. Mostly ornamental, but can be used for tea. A1M, A49D, C43M, C67M, E5M, F43, H3M, J78, K2, K22, K85

Golden Lemon Upright: (T. x citriodorus) Gold and green variegated leaves, lemon scented. Similar to Golden Lemon Creeping but with a bushy, upright growth habit. Height 8 to 10 inches. Pink flowers. Same uses as lemon thyme. Excellent color contrast in the garden with brilliant golden leaves. A1M, E5M, E61, F43, F93G, G84, H3M, I39, J78, K22, K85

Golden Lemon Variegated: (T. x citriodorus) Dark-green leaves with striking golden and green variegation. Very strong lemon scent and flavor. Thick bushy plants. Uses and culture are the same as common Lemon thyme. C9

Lemon: (Green Lemon) (T. x citriodorus) Attractive, glossy, dark-green to yellow-green leaves. Strong lemon scent and flavor. Hardy, shrub-like plant; grows 10 to 12 inches high; spreads by layering. Small, pale-lilac flowers. Excellent culinary thyme, especially good for tea. C9, C43M, C67M, D29, E7, E61, F21, F31T, F35M, G84, H40, J66, J85T{PR}, K22, *M35*, N19M, etc.

Silver Lemon: A sport of Golden Lemon thyme. Attractive, grey-green leaves edged with creamy-white. Very strong, lemon-thyme scent and flavor. Extra hardy plant; grows to a height of 8 inches. Its excellent scent and color make it a very desirable addition to gardens. C81M, D29, J66, M82

Silver Queen: Striking silver appearance with grey and cream variegated foliage, turns a distinctive maroon in autumn and winter. Rich lemon scent and flavor. Excellent in chicken soup. Mounding, twiggy, spreading subshrub; height 6 to 8 inches; width 24 inches. A good accent plant. F57M, H79M, I37M, J78, K79

OTHERS

Adamovica: Very hardy, low shrub; height 12 inches. Superior flavor. Profuse, pink flowers. An excellent border plant. Originated in the mountains of Yugoslavia. A49D, J66, K22, K85

Broad Leaf English: (Broad Leaf) Large, broad leaves. Grows to medium height. Yields are greater than from other types. A1M, H40, J66

De Provence: A strain from the south of France with excellent flavor. Best grown as an annual. In short season areas, start indoors 8 to 12 weeks before planting out. C53{S}

Dot Wells Creeping: (T. pulegioides) Shiny green leaves with an excellent thyme-like flavor and aroma. Very hardy plant, grows 6 inches tall. Lavender flowers. A superior culinary herb or ground cover. Discovered in Asheville, North Carolina in an old garden landscaped by the famous Biltmore Estate Gardens. E5M, K22

Dot Wells Upright: An upright, shrubby version of Dot Wells Creeping. Leaves and flowers very much the same. Fast growing plant; height 12 inches; spreads by layers. Hardy cultivar with superior taste. E5M, F43, K22

Down Hill Farm: Similar to the common garden thyme but more dwarf growing. Height 5 inches. Has an excellent flavor and aroma. Hardy in zones 4 to 9. Discovered at and named after a farm in Pennsylvania that grew herbs for Washington, D.C. restaurants. N42

English: (English Winter) (T. vulgaris) Medium-sized, oval, dark-green leaves. Semi-creeping habit; grows 10 to 12 inches high and spreads readily. An excellent culinary thyme, with an intense aroma and flavor. The most popular thyme for seasoning poultry, soups, salads, etc. Hardiest of the culinary thymes. Similar to French thyme. C3, C9, C13M{S}, C43M, C67M, D29, E61, F21, F35M, H51M, J66, K22, N19M, N42, N45, etc.

English Wedgewood: A form of English thyme with attractive green-edged leaves, delicately mottled with chartreuse in the center. Height 5 inches. Excellent culinary type with a strong thyme flavor and scent. M82, N42

French: (Narrow Leaf French, Summer) (T. vulgaris) Trim, upright plants; height 10 to 12 inches. Leaves grayish-green; narrower and more delicate than English thyme. Very good culinary thyme. Considered to have a stronger, sweeter flavor than English thyme, preferred by the French. Produces an abundance of foliage over the entire season, making it ideal for multiple harvests. Pink flowers. Needs some winter protection. C9, C13M{S}, C43M, C67M, C81M, D29, *E91G*, G84, H3M, H40, H51M, I39{S}, J66, K22, *M35*, N19M, N45, etc.

German Winter: Somewhat compact, looser growing form of common thyme. Height 8 inches. Very hardy plant; winters over even in cold, harsh climates. Has the same uses as English thyme. C9, C43M, C67M, C85M{S}, F33{S}, F43, G6{S}, G68{S}, H46{S}, K22, K85, L7M{S}, M82, N19M

Golden King: A bush type thyme with dense bright green and golden foliage with mauve flowers. Has a flavor and scent similar to common thyme. R53M

Miniature English Narrow Leaf: Tiny, narrow, grey-green leaves with an intense aroma and flavor similar to French thyme. Low, compact grower, height 3 to 6 inches. Perfect for bonsai. K22, K85, M82

Orange Balsam: Small, narrow leaves with a distinct, strong, orange-thyme fragrance and flavor. Good for tea and culinary purposes. Excellent in fruit salads and salad dressings. Very good border plant, growing only 6 inches tall. Attractive pale-pink flowers. C9, C43M, C67M, C81M, E5M, E61, F31T, G84, H3M, H51M, J66, K22, K85, M53, M82, N19M, etc.

Oregano: (Italian Oregano Thyme) (T. pulegioides) Large, round, glossy, bright-green leaves have the distinct aroma of Greek oregano. Very good culinary thyme, can be used whenever an oregano-thyme flavor is called for. Upright, shrubby growth habit, height 18 inches. Evergreen. Not reliably hardy. One of the showiest thymes when in bloom. A49D, C9, C43M, C67M, E5M, E59T, F31T, H3M, H51M, I39, J66, K22, K85, L56, M82, N42, etc.

Pennsylvania Dutch Tea: (T. pulegioides) Large, soft, bright-green leaves. Has a unique mild flavor and fragrance. Especially good for tea. Very similar in growth and appearance to Oregano thyme. Height 5 to 7 inches. A49D, C81M, K22, M82, N42

Porlock: Excellent culinary thyme. Dense growth, to 12 inches tall. Dark green foliage. Mauve flowers produced early in the summer. Very winter hardy. Similar to common garden thyme in habit and flavor. K22, P92, R53M

Silver: Tall-growing plant, to 18 inches. Foliage variegated green and white. Lavender flowers. Good culinary type, with a strong thyme scent and flavor. Also makes an attractive rock garden, hanging basket or accent plant. A49D, E7, E59T, E61, F21, F31T, F35M, F37T, H3M, H40, H51M, J66, J82, L57, M53, M82, etc.

Ukrainian: A savory thyme used with meat, vegetables and salads. Has excellent flavor and also makes an attractive ground cover. K81

TOMATO {S}

LYCOPERSICON LYCOPERSICUM

PROCESSING TOMATOES

Tomatoes that are processed or prepared in various ways, including paste tomatoes, canning tomatoes, sauce tomatoes, juicing tomatoes, drying tomatoes, stuffing tomatoes and broiling tomatoes.

RED-SKINNED

Hybrid

Early Pear: 70 days. Small, pear-shaped, bright red fruit; weight 2 to 3 ounces; interior very firm and meaty, rich in flavor; keeps well on the vine. Ideal for canning whole or paste. Vigorous, compact, determinate vine; highly prolific; resistant to verticillium wilt, races 1 & 2. D76, E97, M46

La Roma: 62 days. Hybrid Roma type. Uniform, medium-sized fruits; weight 3 to 4 ounces. Vigorous, compact, determinate vine; very prolific, produced 7 times more fruit than standard Roma in field trials. Resistant to verticillium wilt race 1 and fusarium wilt, races 1 & 2. C44, *I62*{PL}, M0, M1

Milano: Long, pear-shaped, deep red fruit; plump, meaty interior, of rich flavor. Cooks down in half the time required for other tomatoes, while maintaining its flavor. Suitable for sauce, paste, drying, or cooking whole. Ripens very early. Compact, determinate vine; very prolific. K66

Perfect Peel: 65 days. Medium-sized, juicy, bright red fruit. Ideal for home canning or freezing because it's so easy to peel. Also good for slicing. Compact, determinate vine; very productive; widely adapted. Resistant to verticillium wilt race 1 and fusarium wilt race 1. Introduced in 1979. *E91G*, *F72*, H42, M0

The Juice: 65 days. Good fresh from the vine, but developed especially for making juice. Medium to large, round, bright red fruit; weight 7 ounces; rich, sweet, mild flavor; extra juicy. Also good for canning. Compact, determinate vine; high yielding. Deep-green foliage. D11M, D76, J83M, M0

Open-Pollinated

Ailsa Craig: 70 days. Uniform, medium-sized, deep-red fruit; very firm, of excellent flavor. Reliably productive, indeterminate vine. For cold greenhouse or outdoor use. Popular in England, where it is commonly broiled for breakfast. Old traditional cultivar that originated in Scotland. B49, L91M, O53M, P83M, *R23*, S61, *S75M*

Alicante: Medium-large, round fruit, 2 to 2 1/2 inches in diameter; non-greenback; interior fleshy, of good color; quality and flavor excellent. Very popular in England where it is broiled for breakfast. Does not wilt when baked or broiled, emerging firm and full-bodied. Tall, indeterminate vine; somewhat resistant to mildew. For cold greenhouses or outdoors. E33, L91M, P83M, *R23*, S61

Amish Paste: 85 days. Heirloom paste tomato from Wisconsin. Very large, heart-shaped fruit; 2 1/2 inches in diameter, 4 1/2 inches deep; interior very meaty, with very little juice, flavor excellent; seeds few; susceptible to cracking. Excellent for sauce or paste. Prolific. U33

Andino: Red plum-shaped fruit; weight 3 to 4 ounces; ripens in midseason. Prolific, determinate vine. Produced over 60 tons per acre in northern California commercial fields, twice the yield of the most widely planted cultivar. Also recommended for home gardens. M1

Bellestar: 72 days. Large-fruited plum type. Very firm, meaty, bright-red fruit; weight 4 to 6 ounces; uniformly high crimson interiors; resists cracking. Quality high for paste, sauce and juice; also has good flavor for fresh use. Large size facilitates hand harvesting and peeling. Compact, well-protected, determinate vine; suitable for high density plantings. For home gardens and roadside stands. Introduced in 1981. D68, E24, G6, L42, M0, M1

Bigro: Red, blocky pear-shaped fruit; weight 3 ounces; ripens in midseason. Slightly shorter than Roma but earlier, more compact and with thicker flesh. Determinate vine; performs best in warm or hot, humid areas; tolerates fusarium wilt. Concentrated fruit set and ripening. M1

Burgess Stuffing:[2] 78 days. Hollow, flattened bell-shaped, bright red fruit; 3 1/4 inches in diameter, 2 1/2 inches deep; widely ribbed. Thick-walled, with a small, central core and mild flavor. Excellent stuffed with cold salads or filled and baked. Also makes attractive, distinctive slices for salads or green tomato pickles. Large, indeterminate vine. A16, B73M, B73M{PL}, M0

Campbell 1327: 72 days. Large, smooth, flattened globe-shaped fruit; weight 6 ounces; good interior color; resistant to cracking. Vigorous, prolific, semi-determinate vine; provides good fruit protection; sets well under unfavorable conditions. Resistant to fusarium and verticillium wilts. Developed by Campbell Soup Company for canning. B75M, *E91G*, G64, G71, G79, H54, *H61*, J7, J14{PL}, K73, L42, M0, M1, M13M, N16, etc.

Carré: (Quebec 1121) 70 days. Large, square fruit; interior dark crimson, very firm and meaty. Excellent for paste and purée. Bred for bulk harvesting; also good for U-Pick operations. Developed by R. Doucet, Agricultural Research Station, St. Hyacinthe, Quebec. J7

Chico III: 70 days. Small, pear-shaped fruit; 2 1/2 to 3 inches in diameter; weight 2 to 3 ounces; firm, solid interior. Excellent for processing and tomato paste. Vigorous, compact, determinate vine; highly disease resistant; sets fruit well at high temperatures; widely adapted. Suitable for mechanical harvesting. *A75*, A87M, G16, G71, I99, K49T, *L59G*, L89, L97, M1

Crack-Proof: (Burgess Crack Proof) 80 days. Large, scarlet fruit; 3 1/3 inches in diameter, 2 1/2 inches deep; weight 9 ounces. Will not crack under average growing conditions, and practically free from cracking under the most adverse conditions. Thin but tough skin facilitates peeling, making it ideal for canning. Ripens uniformly. Medium-tall vine; provides good protection; bears until frost. U33

Dad's Mug:[2] 85 days. Large, blocky, deep-scarlet fruit; thick-walled; partially hollow, with seed cavities along the sides; very firm, meaty flesh of fine flavor. Good for slicing and paste; excellent for stuffing like a sweet pepper when green. Prolific, indeterminate vine. K49M, M0

Del Oro: 72 days. Medium-sized, thick-walled fruit; interior thick and meaty. Excellent for canning whole, freezing, juice or sauces. Vigorous, prolific, determinate vine; resistant to verticillium, fusarium, nematodes and alternaria stem canker. Has a concentrated set. Used by many famous tomato sauce companies. Also good for home gardens. Developed by Harris seeds. F13, M0, M1

Goliath: 85 days. Extremely large, somewhat rough, light red fruit; very solid interior with few seeds, of fine flavor. Ideal for canning. Very large, tall, indeterminate vine; requires strong support. An old heirloom, first grown in the late 1800's. F24M

Grandma Mary's: 75 days. Very large plum-shaped fruit, weighing 8 to 12 ounces. Thick, very meaty pulp with few seeds, of excellent flavor. Delicious eaten fresh. Ripens well if picked green. Indeterminate vine; grows well under adverse conditions. Scarce heirloom cultivar. U33

Heinz 1350: 75 days. Uniform, slightly flattened fruit; weight 6 ounces; bright red interior and exterior color; resists cracking. Prolific, semi-determinate vine; provides good leaf cover; tolerates verticillium and fusarium wilts. One of the leading commercial canning cultivars; also good for home gardens. A13, B75, *E53M*, *F72*, G71, H49, J14{PL}, K73, L7M, L42, L89, M0, M1, M13M

Heinz 1439: 72 days. Slightly flattened, globe-shaped, non-green-back fruit; weight 6 ounces; very meaty interiors; excellent crack resistance; holds well. Compact, determinate vine; provides good leaf cover; tolerates verticillium and fusarium wilts. Has a concentrated set. Developed by H.J. Heinz Company for catsup, purées and sauce. B75M, D76, F19M, *F63*, G79, *H61*, I64, K50, K71, L42, M1, N16

Liberty Bell:[2] 80 days. Hollow, bell-shaped, rich-red fruit; 3 inches in diameter, weight 4 to 5 ounces; deeply ribbed; thick-walled; small, easily removed central seed core; mild flavor. Excellent for stuffing, either hot or cold. Also makes attractive tomato rings or scoops for dips. Vigorous, indeterminate vine. E49, E83T, M1

Moira: 66 days. Bush beefsteak type. Developed for canning, juice, or whole pak. Uniform, round, dark-red fruit; weight 6 to 7 ounces; excellent blood-red interior color; very good flavor. Almost completely resistant to cracking and blossom-end rot, remaining blemish-free even in adverse weather. Compact, determinate vine. D68, F44, L42, M1

Napoli: 80 days. Italian paste type. Small, bright red, plum-shaped fruit; 3 inches long, 1 inch in diameter; weight 2 ounces; thick-walled; interior firm and meaty. Excellent for canning or paste; also good for fresh use. Compact, determinate vine; produces a concentrated set; resists fusarium and verticillium wilts. C85M, C92, E49, J83M, *L59G*, M0, M1, T1M

New Zealand Pear: 80 days. Very large, rough, pyriform fruit; resembles a Bartlett pear; susceptible to blossom-end rot. Green-shouldered, indoor ripening helps ripen the top. Excellent for sauce and paste. Indeterminate vine; requires staking. E70M{PR}, K49M

Nova: 72 days. Early maturing Roma type. Elongated, pear-shaped fruit; 3 inches long, 1 1/2 inches in diameter; weight about 2 ounces; interior firm and meaty. Compact, determinate vine; high yielding; resistant to verticillium wilt and late blight. Does well in cool northern areas. Developed at the New York Agricultural Experiment Station. A2, E24, E59Z, F44, I39M, K49M, L42, M1, P83M, S55

Polish Paste: Extremely large, flavorful, pear-shaped fruit; 5 1/2 to 6 1/2 inches long; often weighs up to one pound; ripens in late August. Large, indeterminate vine; may produce up to 40 or 50 pounds of fruit annually. Developed by Territorial Seed Co., from genetic material obtained from the Seed Savers Exchange. L89

Principe Borghese:[1] An Italian tomato particularly adapted to sun drying and winter preservation. Small, plum-shaped fruit with flattened sides and a nipple on the blossom end; weight 1 to 2 ounces; interior very meaty, with little juice and few seeds. Determinate vine; bears fruit in clusters. In drier climates, branches can be hung up until the fruit is dry and leathery. BIANCHINI; C53, F42, I99, J20, J73, K49M, K49T, M1

Quinte: 70 days. Attractive, medium-sized fruit; weight 7 ounces; high crimson interior and exterior; flesh thick and firm, juicy, core small. Skin peels off like a peach, without scalding. Makes a good quality juice. Compact, determinate vine; prolific; tolerant to verticillium wilt. Rated highly in the Canadian Hand Pick Tomato Trials. Named after the Bay of Quinte canning district in Ontario. L42, M1

Rocky: 90 days. High quality Italian paste type. Very large, plum-shaped fruit; 4 to 6 inches long, 3 to 4 inches in diameter; weight often 1 pound; interior very meaty, flavor sweet and tangy. Large, indeterminate vine; grows to 7 feet tall when trellised; productive over a long period. Introduced from Italy about 60 years ago. D87

Roma: 75 days. Small, plum-shaped, bright red fruit; 3 inches long, 1 1/2 inches in diameter; thick-walled; interior meaty, with few seeds. Excellent for paste, sauce, canning whole or for adding body to juice. Prolific, compact, determinate vine; disease resistant. Very popular home garden cultivar. A69M, A87M, B73M, <u>C8M</u>{PR}, *D35M*{PL}, F82, J20, K71, L7M, L9M, <u>L97G</u>{PR}, M13M, M46

Roma VF: 75 days. Medium-small, plum-shaped fruit; 2 to 3 inches long, 1 1/2 inches in diameter; weight 2 to 2 1/2 ounces; thick-walled; interior dry, meaty, firm, of good color. Adapted to peeling or whole processing. Excellent for sauces and paste. Vigorous, determinate vine; widely adapted; highly disease resistant. A25, *A75*, B49, B75M, C44, C85M, C92, D65, F19M, *F72*, G51, *H61*, J14{PL}, K73, M0, M1, N16, etc.

Ropreco: Italian paste type. Ripens much earlier than San Marzano. Cooks down to a savory sauce or paste. Determinate vine; prolific, outyielding Roma, Nova and others. Spreads to 4 feet in diameter, making it much more manageable than San Marzano, needs no staking or training. I99, K49T, L9, L89

Royal Chico: 72 days. Large Roma type paste tomato. Bright red, plum-shaped fruit; weight 3 to 3 1/2 ounces; firm, meaty interior. Excellent for sauce, paste or canning. Compact, determinate vine; provides good foliage cover; highly disease resistant. More productive than Roma; produces a heavy initial set, then continues to bear until frost. *E53M*, E97, G79, *H61*, H95, L7M, *L59G*, M0, M1, M29, N52

San Marzano: 80 days. Elongated, flat-sided, blunt-ended fruit; 3 to 3 1/2 inches long, 1 1/2 inches in diameter; of deep-red color; resists cracking; holds and stores well. Interior meaty, mild-flavored, free from juicy pulp. Excellent for canning whole or for purée and paste. Vigorous, indeterminate vine; sets fruit in clusters. Very popular standard type. *A75*, B73M, B78, C53, C85M, E49, F92, G64, *H61*, J34, M0, M1, M95, N39

San Pablo: 75 days. Roma type Italian paste tomato. Small, blocky, plum-shaped fruit; 3 inches long, 2 1/4 inches in diameter; weight 2 ounces. Peels more easily than Roma. Recommended for adding body to juice, by mixing half and half with a canning tomato. Determinate, highly productive vine. Developed by the originator of the Peron tomato. E49, M1

Stone: An old reliable cultivar that is excellent for canning. Bright red, slightly flattened, globe-shaped fruit; weight 5 to 7 ounces; ripens uniformly, keeps well. Flavor somewhat acidic. Vigorous, reliably productive, indeterminate vine; provides good foliar protection for the fruit; resists drought and wilt. Introduced prior to 1913. B73M, L7M, M1

Striped Cavern:[2] Hollow stuffing type. Large, blocky, bell-shaped fruit; weight 8 ounces; widely ribbed; very meaty, of good flavor. Has an easily removed central core. Thick walls stay firm, and will not split or crumble making it ideal for stuffing. Also good for slicing fresh. Ripe fruit can be stored for 4 weeks; semi-ripe fruit even longer. L91M

Stuffing:[2] (Pepper Tomato, Hollow Tomato) 75 days. Hollow, bell-shaped, thick-walled fruit; 3 inches in diameter; small, easily removed central seed core. Excellent stuffed with a cold salad or filled and baked. Large, productive, indeterminate vine. A21, I99, J83M

Super Italian Paste: (Giant Italian Paste) 80 days. Very large, elongated, plum-shaped fruit; 4 to 6 inches long, 2 to 2 1/2 inches in diameter; weight 10 to 12 ounces. Interior firm, very meaty, with very little juice and few seeds, of sweet flavor. Excellent for sauce and paste. Prolific, indeterminate vine. E5T, K49M

Super Roma: 70 days. Improved Roma type. Medium-sized, plum-shaped, thick-walled fruit. Interior juicy, nearly seedless, of very good flavor. Bred for ketchup, tomato juice, or soup making. Compact, determinate, prolific vine; resistant to fusarium and verticillium wilts. L91M

Veepick: 73 days. Large Roma type paste tomato. Elongated, flat-sided, blunt-ended fruit; 3 1/4 inches long, 2 inches in diameter; weight 2 ounces; thick-walled. Has excellent color and flavor. Ripens uniformly; peels easily. Compact, determinate vine; tolerant to fusarium and verticillium wilts. L42, M1

Veeroma: 72 days. An early maturing Roma type. Medium-red, plum-shaped fruit; weight 2 ounces; resists cracking. Excellent for sauce, paste, ketchup or whole pak. Compact, determinate plant; higher yielding than Roma; tolerant to fusarium and verticillium wilts. Adapted to hand or machine harvest. J7, L42, M1

YELLOW/ORANGE-SKINNED

Hybrid

Golden Roma: 65 days. Highly uniform, oval to slightly rectangular fruit; bright golden-yellow inside and out; firm, meaty flesh, sweeter and juicier than typical paste tomatoes; holds well on the plant and also keeps well. Makes an attractive golden sauce with a mild, delicate flavor. Combines well with herbs. Also good for slicing or drying. Compact, determinate plant; very heavy yielding. K66

Open-Pollinated

Yellow Bell: 60 days. Unique yellow paste tomato. Plum-shaped fruit; 3 inches long, 1 1/2 inches in diameter; ripens from green to creamy yellow to yellow; flavor excellent, both rich and sweet. Suitable for salads, and for making paste, juice, preserves and yellow catsup. Indeterminate vine; heavy yielding, produces an average of 5 fruits per cluster, up to a maximum of 12 per cluster. Family heirloom from Tennessee. L7M

Yellow Ruffled:[2] (Ruffled, Yellow Ruffles) 80 days. Unusual yellow stuffing tomato. Hollow, distinctly ridged, lemon-yellow fruit; 2 1/2 inches deep, 3 to 3 1/2 inches in diameter; of excellent flavor. When pulp is scooped out, it makes an attractive container for salads, desserts and other stuffings. Productive, indeterminate vine. A49G, E49, I99, K49M, M0, M1

Yellow Stuffer:[2] (Yellow Stuffing) 76 Days. Yellow, bell-shaped fruit, 3 1/4 inches across, a little less in depth; hollow except for a few small seeds around the core; thick-walled; firm flesh with a nice mild flavor, very little juice. Excellent for baking, holding its shape well. Tall, vigorous, indeterminate vine. GORMAN [Re]; C92, D11M, *E53M*, *F63*, *F72*, G27M, G64, G82, H33, H42, H95, I39, L42, M0, M1, etc.

SALAD TOMATOES

Small-fruited tomatoes, ideal for serving whole in salads. Many are very sweet and may be eaten out of hand like a sweet fruit. The various plum and pear types are important specialty market items and are also popular for pickling and preserving.

PINK-SKINNED

Hybrid

Pink Droplet: 60 days. Small, oval plum-shaped, rose-pink fruit; averages 3/4 ounce in weight; flavor quite sweet. Indeterminate vine; produces an average of 70 fruit; should be staked like Sweet 100 or Sweet Chelsea. Resistant to fusarium and verticillium wilts, nematodes and tobacco mosaic virus. L42

Open-Pollinated

Pink Cherry: Small, round, smooth, rose-pink fruit; only 3/4 inch in diameter; of good flavor. Very attractive. Good for salads and pickling. Highly productive vine; sets fruit in bunches of 5 to 7; produces until frost. Heirloom. A49G, E49, M0, M1

Pink Ping Pong: 80 days. Medium-small, round, rose-pink fruit; 1 1/2 to 2 inches in diameter; has an excellent mild flavor; resists cracking. Good for salads and snacks. Extremely prolific, indeterminate vine; tolerant to drought. Heirloom. U33

Pink Plum: 90 days. Plum-shaped fruit; 1 3/4 inches long, 1 1/4 inches in diameter; pink skin and flesh; very good flavor. Productive, indeterminate vine; hardy and drought resistant. Heirloom from Kansas. U33

Pink Salad: 75 days. Small, oval, pink fruit; 1 1/2 inches long, 1 1/4 inches in diameter; two-celled; of excellent flavor. High yielding, determinate vine. Heirloom from Virginia. Raised for the local restaurant trade for over 30 years. Preserved by one farmer for personal use. U33

Whippersnapper:[5] 52 days. Extra-early cherry tomato. Small, oval, dark-pink fruit; 3/4 to 1 inch in diameter; sweet and flavorful. Compact, determinate, multi-branched vine; of trailing habit, only 12 inches tall; often produces over 100 fruit. Excellent for pots and hanging baskets. Should not be pruned or staked. D68, E24, F44, G6, M1, P83M, S55

RED-SKINNED

Hybrid

Cherry Grande: 65 days. Uniform, round, bright red fruit; 1 1/4 inches in diameter; of good flavor; firm enough for shipping. Vigorous, determinate vine; bears fruit heavily in large clusters; provides good fruit protection; highly disease resistant; widely adapted. For home gardens, local markets or commercial production. *A1*, A87M, *E53M*, *G1M*, *H61*, J7, J84, K73, L42, M0, M1, M29, M46, M49

Small Fry:[5] 65 days. Small, round, bright-red fruit; 1 inch in diameter; interior firm, of excellent flavor. Compact, determinate vine; very productive, bears fruit in clusters of 7 or 8; tolerant to fusarium and verticillium wilts and root not nematodes. Ideal for growing in containers or small gardens. All America Selections winner in 1970. B73M, C44, D11M, *D35M*{PL}, F19M, G16, G71, *H61*, H66, J7, J34, K10, L89, M0, M1, etc.

Sweet 100:[3, 10] 65 days. Small, round, bright red fruit; 1 inch in diameter; extremely sweet. Excellent for eating out-of-hand. Has a higher vitamin C content than most tomatoes. Indeterminate, multi-branched vine; requires staking for best results. Extremely productive; produces dozens of fruit per side branch, hundreds on each plant. A home garden favorite. A16, A25, B49M{PL}, C44, D11M, F19M, G16, *H61*, *I62*{PL}, I67M, J7, J14{PL}, K73, L97, M0, M1, M46, etc.

Sweet Chelsea:[3] (Chelsea) 65 days. Small, round, cherry-red fruit; 1 1/2 inches in diameter; interior thick, very firm, flavor very sweet, low in acid, high in sugar; resists cracking and splitting. Vigorous, determinate vine; produces 15 to 20 fruits per cluster, with 10 or more clusters per plant; extremely drought tolerant and disease resistant.

A1, A87M, C85M, *E53M*, *E91G*, H42, I77, J20, *K16M*, K73, L42, M0, M29, M46, T1M, etc.

Open-Pollinated

Baxter's Bush Cherry: (Baxter's Early Bush Cherry) 72 days. Uniform, round, bright-red fruit; 1 inch in diameter; of good flavor; very crack resistant. Will keep for up to 28 days when refrigerated, even when picked ripe. Excellent for shipping. Compact, determinate vine; grows 3 1/2 to 4 feet tall; highly productive, sets well under adverse temperatures. *A1*, A87M, B75, *F72*, G82, G87, M0

Camp Joy: Small, round, bright-red fruit; 1 to 1 1/2 inches in diameter; delicious, full tomato flavor; ripens early. Large, vigorous, indeterminate vine; highly productive over a long harvest season; should be staked for best results. Developed by a small farming cooperative that sells produce to fine restaurants. F42, K66

Chadwick's Cherry: 90 days. Small, round, red fruit; weight about 1 ounce; interior juicy, with a mature, full-rounded sweetness; quality excellent. Vigorous, indeterminate vine; highly productive. Selected by English horticulturist Alan Chadwick. B49

Cheerio: 55 days. One of the earliest red cherry tomatoes. Medium-large, bright red fruit with a delicious, full tomato flavor. For home gardens and local markets. Compact, branching, determinate vine; yields heavily for about 30 days; tolerates cold and adverse weather conditions. Suitable for stake or ground culture. F24M, G6, L89, M1

Early Cherry: 56 days. Round to oval-shaped, bright-red fruit; 1 1/2 inches in diameter; under 1 ounce in weight; flavor mild and pleasant. Compact, determinate vine; produces heavily for about 30 days. Developed at Cornell University. E57

Florida Basket:[5] 55 days. Slightly larger version of Florida Petite. Small, slightly elongated fruit, 1 to 2 inches in diameter; weight 1 3/4 ounces; of excellent flavor. Very short, determinate vine with a prostrate growing habit. When planted in a hanging basket will drape 4 to 6 inches over the edge. Resistant to gray leafspot. *F72*, G27M, M0, M1

Florida Petite:[5] 50 days. Round, deep red fruit, 1 to 1 1/2 inches in diameter; of pleasant flavor. Small, determinate, productive vine; grows only 8 or 9 inches tall and wide; sets fruit on top. Developed for growing in 4 to 4 1/2 inch pots. Resistant to gray leafspot. Susceptible to white fly and soil borne diseases. *F72*, G27M, M0, M1

Gardener's Delight:[3] (Sugar Lump) 68 days. Small, round, bright-red fruit; 1 to 1 1/2 inches in diameter; weight 1/3 to 1/2 ounce; extremely sweet; resists cracking. Excellent for eating out-of-hand. Indeterminate vine; bears long, grape-like clusters, 6 to 12 fruits per cluster; produces until frost. B49, B75, C53, E24, E33, *F72*, G6, I99, L7M, L91M, M0, M1, O53M, S55

Hardy Tom: Small, sweet fruit, lasts a long time on the vine. Will spread and keep producing until the first frost. Resistant to fruit fly. P1G

Large Red Cherry: 75 days. Deep globe-shaped, bright scarlet fruit; 1 1/4 to 1 1/2 inches in diameter; sweet, mild flavor. Excellent for salads, preserving or eating whole. Vigorous, indeterminate, multi-branched vine; highly productive over a long season; resists alternaria stem canker. Standard cherry type. A87M, B75M, E49, G51, G79, G93M, *H61*, I39, K71, K73, M0, M1, M95, N16, etc.

Loomis Potato Leaf Cherry: 80 days. Medium-small, nearly round, bright-red fruit; 1 1/4 inches deep, 1 inch in diameter; of very good flavor. Large, indeterminate, highly productive vine. Unusual potato-like leaves provide excellent fruit protection. E49

Red Cherry: (Small Red Cherry) 75 days. Small, round, bright-red fruit; 1 inch in diameter; weight less than 1 ounce; of good flavor and quality. Fine for salads or eating whole. Vigorous, indeterminate vine; produces an abundance of fruit over a long harvest period; resists fruitworm and high temperatures. Introduced prior to 1865. BURR; A13, B73M, C44, *D35M*{PL}, *E91G*, F1, G71, H66, J7, J20, J73, L7M, L89, M1, M13M, N39, etc.

Red Peach: Small, round, red fruit, sometimes has a slightly fuzzy skin; 1 1/2 inches in diameter; weight 1 ounce; of good flavor. Ripens in midseason. Indeterminate vine. L42, M1

Red Pear: 75 days. Small, bright red, pear-shaped fruit; 2 inches long, 1 inch in diameter; weight 1 ounce; of mild, pleasant flavor. Excellent for salads, preserves or pickling. Vigorous, indeterminate vine; bears fruit in long clusters; highly productive over a long season. Introduced prior to 1865. BURR [Re]; B73M, C53, D11M, E49, E97, F19M, *F72*, *H61*, I39, J7, K49M, K71, L42, M0, M1, M13M, etc.

Red Plum: 75 days. Small, oval, scarlet fruit; 1 1/2 to 2 inches long, 1 inch in diameter; weight 1 ounce. Interior pink, or rose-red, mild, well-flavored, seeds comparatively few. Excellent for salads, pickling and preserving. Indeterminate vine; highly productive; bears fruit in clusters. Introduced prior to 1865. BURR; B73M, E49, *F72*, *H61*, J7, K49M, K66, K71, L42, M0, M1, M13M

Sub Arctic Cherry:[4, 5] 43 days. Small, round fruit; 1/2 inch in diameter; weight just under 1/2 ounce. Small, compact, trailing vine; high yielding, averages over 300 fruits per plant. Ideal for window boxes and hanging baskets. Very cold tolerant, setting fruit under colder conditions than other types. Released by the Beaverlodge Experiment Station, Alberta, Canada in 1976. L91M

Sugar Lump:[3] (Jung's Sugar Lump) 65 days. Smooth, round, deep-red fruit; 1 1/2 to 2 inches in diameter; very sweet, of good quality and flavor. Excellent for eating out-of-hand. Also good for salads, canning whole or juice. Vigorous, indeterminate vine; bears fruit in clusters of 6 to 12; produces until frost. I91, M1

Sweetie:[3] 65 days. Round, bright-red fruit; 1 to 1 1/2 inches in diameter; unusually sweet and flavorful. Has a high vitamin C content. Excellent for snacking, salads, or low-sugar preserves. Vigorous, indeterminate vine; bears fruit in long clusters of 12 to 20 fruit; widely adapted. Should be staked or trellised for best results. A16, B75M, D11M, D65, D76, F19M, F82, G27M, G87, I39, K49M, L79, L89, M0, M1, M13M, etc.

Tiny Tim:[5] 55 days. Small, round, scarlet-red fruit; 3/4 to 1 inch in diameter; of very good quality and flavor. Excellent for salads and relish trays. Compact, determinate vine; grows only 12 to 15 inches tall, 6 to 12 inches in diameter. Very ornamental, with rugose leaves. Ideal for growing in pots, window boxes and flower beds. A16, A25, B73M, C44, C85M, *D35M*{PL}, *F72*, G16, G71, *H61*, K73, L7M, M1, M13M, M46, etc.

YELLOW/ORANGE-SKINNED

Cherry Gold:[5] 45 days. A golden version of Tiny Tim. Deep golden-yellow fruit; the same size as Tiny Tim, but much better flavored. Very compact, determinate vine; grows only 6 inches tall, 6 inches in diameter. Excellent for window sill gardens, or chain store pot plant sales. Introduced by Stokes Seeds. I99, L42, M1

Gold Nugget: 70 days. Round to slightly oval fruit, 1 to 1 1/4 inches in diameter; rich golden-yellow in color; generally resists cracking. Has a delicious, well-balanced flavor resembling Yellow Plum. Most fruits are seedless. Compact, determinate vine; highly prolific. For home gardens or commercial production. Developed by Dr. James Baggett at Oregon State University. D68, D82, G6, I39, I77, I99, K10, L89, Q34

Golden Pygmy:[5] (Yellow Pygmy) Tiny, marble-sized, golden-yellow fruit with an excellent, slightly acidic flavor. Small, compact vine; grows to only 12 inches tall at maturity. Very prolific, bearing continuously until frost. Excellent for pots, tubs and window boxes. E49, I77, K66

Green Grape: 80 days. Distinctive, small, round, yellowish-green fruit; reminiscent of a large muscat grape; 1 to 1 1/2 inches in diameter. Thin-skinned, sweet, juicy and flavorful. Resists cracking. Compact, prolific vine; bears fruit in large, grape-like clusters. K49M

Sundrop: (Burpee's Sundrop) 76 days. Small, globe-shaped, deep orange fruit; 1 1/2 inches in diameter; thick-walled; firm, meaty flesh, sweet flavor. Resistant to cracking or bursting, holding well on the vine even late in the season. Excellent for snacking or relish trays. Indeterminate vine. B75, G51, I99, M0

Yellow Cherry: 75 days. Small, round, bright-yellow fruit; 1/2 to 1 inch in diameter; of mild, sweet flavor. An excellent garnish or addition to salads and side dishes. Vigorous, indeterminate vine; highly productive over a long season; tolerant to heat and drought. Introduced prior to 1865. BURR; A49G, B73M, E49, E70M{PR}, L42, M0, M1, M13M

Yellow Marble: 75 days. Attractive, marble-sized, bright golden-yellow fruit; very sweet and flavorful. Large, indeterminate vine; highly productive; resistant to disease and drought. K49M

Yellow Peach: Small, round, yellow fruit, sometimes has a slightly fuzzy skin; 1 1/2 inches in diameter; weight 1 ounce; of good flavor. Ripens in midseason. Indeterminate vine. L42, M1

Yellow Pear: 75 days. Small, pear-shaped, waxy clear-yellow fruit; 1 1/2 to 2 inches long, 1 inch in diameter; weight 1 ounce; of mild, sweet flavor. Excellent for salads, preserving and pickling. Large, indeterminate vine; highly prolific, produces fruit in clusters. Introduced prior to 1865. BURR; A25, B73M, C53, C85M, D87, E49, F44, *H61*, *I62*{PL}, J7, J34, L7M, M0, M1, M13M, N16, etc.

Yellow Plum: 75 days. Small, plum-shaped, clear-yellow fruit; 1 1/2 inches long, 1 inch in diameter; weight 1 ounce; of mild, sweet flavor. Excellent for salads, preserves or pickling. Vigorous, indeterminate vine; very productive, bears fruit in clusters until frost. Introduced prior to 1865. BURR; B73M, *D35M*{PL}, E49, E97, *F72*, G71, *H61*, J7, K66, K71, K73, L42, M0, M1, M13M, N39, etc.

SLICING TOMATOES

Mostly medium to large tomatoes, ideal for slicing and eating raw in sandwiches and salads. The very large, meaty, richly flavored beefsteak types are especially popular for this purpose.

PINK-SKINNED

Hybrid

Pink Girl: 76 days. Large, smooth, flattened globe-shaped fruit; an attractive pink color; weight 7 to 8 ounces; has excellent tolerance to cracking. Flesh meaty, juicy, of mild flavor. Indeterminate, widely adapted vine; produces heavily until frost. Resistant to fusarium and verticillium wilts and tobacco mosaic virus. For home gardens, local markets, and roadside stands. B73M, B75, D11M, D76, *E91G*, E97, F13, *F72*, G64, G79, *H61*, J7, L42, M0, M1, etc.

Open-Pollinated

Bradley: 80 days. Medium-sized, deep globe-shaped, pink fruit; weight 6 to 7 ounces; green-shouldered; very juicy, mild and flavorful. Strong, semi-determinate, short stake type vine; resistant to fusarium wilt and alternaria stem canker. For home gardens and local markets. *F72*, *H61*, H66, L14, M1

Brandywine: 74 days. Amish family heirloom dating back to at least 1885. Medium-large, slightly irregular, dark reddish-pink fruit; weight 10 to 12 ounces; susceptible to cracking. Flavor extremely fine, distinctive, of gourmet quality. Excellent for slices, salads and sandwiches. Vigorous, indeterminate vine; moderately productive; has potato-like foliage. F24M, I97T, I99, K49M, L7M, M0, M1

Brimmer: (Pink Brimmer) 82 days. Heirloom from Virginia. Large, flattened globe-shaped, purplish-pink fruit; 4 inches in diameter; weight often 2 1/2 pounds or more when well grown. Flesh very meaty, with few seeds and core, mild, low in acid. Indeterminate vine. Winner of the Grand Prize for size and quality at the Jamestown Exposition, sometime prior to 1910. Introduced about 1905. L7M

Dutchman: 80 days. An heirloom Beefsteak type. Large, flattened globe-shaped, dark-pink fruit; 4 to 5 inches in diameter; weight up to 2 pounds. Flesh very solid, low in acid, flavor excellent, mild and sweet. Large, indeterminate vine; unproductive. Similar to Giant Belgium, but somewhat flatter. E49, M0, M1

Dwarf Champion:[6 8] (Tree) 70 days. Unique "stakeless" or thick-stemmed tomato. Very short, stiff stem, 1 inch in diameter, 18 to 24 inches tall; grows perfectly erect without any support. Dwarf indeterminate habit. Rose-pink fruit; weight 5 ounces; firm and meaty, mild, low in acid. First raised in the gardens of the Count de Fleurieu at the Château de Laye, near Villefranche, France, about 1865. BURR, VILMORIN; K71, L42, M1

German Head: 80 days. Beefsteak type. Large, smooth, well-shaped fruit; an attractive dark-pink in color; weight 10 ounces. Flesh juicy, meaty, of excellent flavor. Large, indeterminate vine. Recommended for roadside markets. Very old cultivar. E49

German Johnson: Heirloom from Virginia and North Carolina. Large, flattened globe-shaped fruit; pink with yellow shoulders; weight 16 to 24 ounces. Flesh very meaty, low in acid, with few seeds, of excellent mild flavor. Good for slicing or canning. Indeterminate vine; very productive; fairly resistant to disease. *F72*, L7M

Giant Belgium: 90 days. Very large, deep oblate, dark pink fruit; 4 inches in diameter; weight 1 1/2 to 2 pounds, occasionally up to 5 pounds; smooth at the blossom end. Flesh extremely meaty, low in acid, flavor very good. Excellent for slicing. Also makes fine cocktail wines. Indeterminate vine. Developed in Ohio. E49, J83M, M0, M1

Giant Tree:[7] (Italian Potato-Leaved) 90 days. Very large, round, smooth, pink fruit; weight 1 to 2 pounds; flesh tender but firm, low in acid, mild flavored, with few seeds. Vigorous, strong-stemmed, indeterminate vine; will grow to 15 feet or more if trellised. Has heavy, thick leaves that provide good protection. Excellent for home gardens. *E91G*, *G1M*, M0, M1

Holmes Mexican: 80 days. Very large, oblate fruit, 4 1/2 inches in diameter; can exceed 3 pounds in weight; thick, subacid flesh, few seeds. Vigorous, indeterminate vine. Above average yields. Developed by Ben Quisenberry. H11

June Pink: (Pink Earliana) 75 days. Medium-sized, somewhat flattened fruit; weight 4 to 5 ounces; exterior very attractive, rose-pink, sometimes with green shoulders; interior solid, of excellent flavor; resistant to cracking. Large, vigorous, indeterminate vine; bears fruit in clusters of 6 to 10, produces over a long period. Introduced about 1900. F80, L7M

MacPink: 60 days. One of the few determinate, pink-fruited tomatoes available. Round, pink fruit; weight 5 ounces; of excellent quality and flavor. Extremely productive and early. Developed at Macdonald College of McGill University. G64, J7, M1

Mission Dyke: 70 days. Large, globe-shaped, medium-pink fruit; 3 1/2 to 4 inches in diameter; weight 8 to 10 ounces; smooth shoulders, perfect blossom ends; very mild flavor, of high quality. Large, indeterminate vine; high yielding; resistant to disease and drought. Withstood all tropical conditions when tested in Puerto Rico. E49, M1

Mortgage Lifter: (Pink Mortgage Lifter) Large, well-shaped, dark-pink fruit; weight up to 1 pound; very meaty, with few seeds. Indeterminate vine. An old cultivar that is still in demand. According to folklore it was named by a farmer who sold a crop of these tomatoes to pay off a farm he was about to lose. E49, M0, M1

Oxheart: 85 days. Large, heart-shaped, rose-pink fruit; weight often 1 1/2 pounds, occasionally up to 2 pounds; flesh solid, meaty, mild, with very few seeds. Vigorous, indeterminate vine; best grown in cages to protect fruit from sunscald. An old-fashioned home garden favorite. B73M, C44, C92, D65, D76, E49, *E91G*, F19M, G68, *H61*, J7, K10, L7M, M0, M1, etc.

Pomme d'Amore: 95 days. Small, pink fruit; 2 to 2 1/2 inches in diameter. Medium-large vine; susceptible to wilt. One of the historical *love apples* of colonial Europe. Carried to Mauritius by one of several European governments who claimed that island as a colony. Saved from extinction by the Research Department of Colonial Williamsburg, Virginia. I99, M1

Ponder Heart: Very large pink tomato from Japan. Semi-globe-shaped fruit with a slightly pointed blossom end; very smooth, without ribbed shoulders. Flesh thick and meaty, non-acid, has a small seed cavity. A cross of Ponderosa and Oxheart. E49, M1

Ponderosa: (Pink Ponderosa, Pink Beefsteak) 90 days. Very large, flattened globe-shaped, deep-pink fruit; weight 12 to 16 ounces, some up to 2 pounds; susceptible to cracking and sunscald. Interior firm, meaty, with very few seeds, of excellent mild flavor. Good sliced, canned or stewed. Vigorous, indeterminate vine; produces continuously until frost. Long-time favorite. Introduced in 1891. C85M, *D35M*{PL}, *E91G*, F13, F19M, *F72*, G71, G82, J34, K71, M0, M1, M13M, M46, N16, etc.

Tappy's Finest: 77 days. West Virginia family heirloom. Large, slightly irregular, deep-pink fruit; 3 to 4 inches in diameter; weight 14 to 16 ounces, sometimes up to 2 pounds. Interior very meaty, with small core and few seeds, of extremely fine flavor. Good for slicing and processing, excellent for juice. Indeterminate vine; unproductive. F42, L7M

Tomboy: 66 days. Large, deep oblate, pink fruit; 3 to 4 inches in diameter; weight 1 pound; flesh bright-red, extremely meaty, with very few seeds, mild, low in acid. Excellent for slicing, canning and catsup. Indeterminate vine; high yielding; resistant to fusarium wilt. A56, H33, M1

Watermelon Beefsteak: 75 days. Very large, deep oblate, dark-pink fruit, somewhat reminiscent of a watermelon; weight up to 2 pounds; flesh purplish-red, extremely meaty, sweet and mild. Indeterminate vine. An heirloom strain that dates back over a century. E49, M0, M1

RED-SKINNED

Hybrid

Altacee:[10] Globe-shaped, deep red fruit; weight 7 ounces; flesh very firm, juicy, deep red in color, flavor excellent; resists cracking. Contains as much vitamin C as oranges of equal size. Sturdy, fast-growing, indeterminate vine; bears early and continues heavy production over a long season; appears to be widely adapted. Superior to other high vitamin C cultivars. A32

Better Bush:[8] 72 days. Large, globe-shaped fruit, 3 to 4 inches in diameter; interior firm, meaty, juicy, high in sugar and flavor. Strong, compact plant, 3 to 3 1/2 feet tall, requires little support. Dwarf indeterminate, continuing to bear until frost. Yields are similar to those of large indeterminate vines. Resistant to verticillium, fusarium and nematodes. Ideal for limited-space gardens and containers. I91

Buffalo:[9] Uniform ripening, smooth, deep oblate, very firm fruit. Mixed sizes in the large to very large category, averaging 9 to 10 ounces. Considered by many to be the tastiest large-fruited cultivar for greenhouse culture. Medium early maturity. Tall, vigorous vine; highly disease resistant. *F72*, G6, G64, L42

Caruso:[9] Large, round, slightly ribbed fruit; weight 7 ounces; faint green shoulder; fair green-ripe flavor. Vigorous, open, indeterminate vine; high yielding; early in production. Very tolerant to heat, continuing to set fruit during the summer months. Also sets and fruits under cooler greenhouse temperatures. Particularly recommended for early heated crops and autumn crops. F1, *F72*, *F85G*, G64, L42

Celebrity: 70 days. Large, deep globe-shaped, smooth, deep red fruit; firm flesh with excellent flavor. Strong determinate vine; provides good cover; adapted to a broad range of conditions. Has multiple disease resistance, including genetic resistance to tobacco mosaic virus. Excellent for home gardens and commercial production. All America Selections winner in 1984. A13, B75M, D11M, F13, G6, G71, G79, G93M, H33{PL}, *H61*, H95, J14{PL}, J34, K73, M0, M13M, etc.

Danny:[9] Greenhouse forcing tomato. Round, smooth, uniform ripening, bright-scarlet fruit; lively, tangy flavor. Weight 2 1/2 to 3 ounces from heated early and late crops, 3 1/2 to 4 ounces from summer and early fall crops. Almost completely resistant to cracking and splitting. Barely affected by cool nights. Tall, vigorous plant; highly productive and disease resistant. Excellent for unheated greenhouses. G6, *R23*

Dombo:[9] (Jumbo) Large, green-shouldered fruit; weight 8 to 12 ounces; very firm and flavorful. Medium late maturity. Strong but short-jointed vine; highly disease resistant. Produces 12 clusters of fruit, versus 8 clusters which is standard for non-hybrid cultivars like Vendor. Recommended for spring, summer, and early fall crops. *F72*, *F85G*, G6, L42, *R23*

Early Cascade: 55 days. Medium-sized, deep globe-shaped fruit; weight 4 to 8 ounces; smooth, deep red exteriors; of excellent flavor. Ideal for salads and sandwiches. Also good for canning and sauce. Tall, indeterminate vine; sets fruit abundantly in clusters of 7 to 9; continues to produce heavily all season. Tolerant to verticillium, fusarium and nematodes. A16, C85M, D65, *E91G*, F19M, *F72*, G27M, G64, G79, G87, H42, L89, M0, M1, M13M, M49, etc.

Floramerica: 70 days. Large, deep globe-shaped, deep red fruit; 3 inches in diameter; weight 6 to 10 ounces; of firm texture and excellent flavor. Strong, determinate vine; widely adapted. Tolerant or resistant to 15 genetic disorders and diseases. Excellent for home gardens. All America Selections winner in 1978. Developed by the University of Florida. A16, A25, B73M, B75M, C44, C85M, F19M, *F72*, G16, G71, *I62*{PL}, J7, K73, M13M, M46, N16, etc.

Heartland:[8] 68 days. Medium to large fruit, 3 to 4 inches in diameter; weight 6 to 8 ounces; of good quality and flavor. Compact, self-supporting plant; height 3 to 4 feet; bears all season. Dark green, wrinkled, heavy foliage. Resistant to verticillium, fusarium and nematodes. One of the first dwarf indeterminate tomatoes. J34, M0

Patio:[5] 70 days. Medium-sized, deep oblate fruit; weight 4 to 5 ounces; exterior smooth, deep red; interior firm and flavorful. Strong, compact, determinate vine; high yielding; tolerant to fusarium wilt. Requires support. Developed for growing in tubs or limited space gardens. A13, *D35M*{PL}, F1, G51, G71, G79, G93M, *H61*, H66, *I62*{PL}, J34, J84, K73, M0, M1, M13M, N39, etc.

Pixie:[5] (Burpee's Pixie) 55 days. Smooth, globe-shaped, bright scarlet fruit; 1 1/2 to 2 inches in diameter; flesh meaty, juicy, very flavorful. Compact, determinate, strong-stemmed vine; only 14 to 18 inches tall. Excellent for pots, window boxes, limited-space gardens and hydroponic culture. Does well in cool northern areas. A16, A25, C85M, D11M, *D35M*{PL}, E32M{PL}, *E91G*, F44, *F72*, I77, J32, L91M, M0, M1, S55, etc.

Open-Pollinated

Abraham Lincoln: (Buckbee's Abraham Lincoln) 87 days. Home garden favorite since 1923. Recently re-bred by Shumway's to further improve purity which had diminished over the years. Large, smooth, dark red fruit; sweet, solid and meaty; ripens all the way through. Excellent for slicing, juice or catsup. Indeterminate vine; produces as many as 9 fruits in a cluster, with a total weight of 7 pounds. Has bronze-green foliage. I99, J83M, K71, M0, M1

Angora: 68 days. Medium-sized, smooth, brilliant red fruit; 2 1/2 inches in diameter; flesh firm, mild-flavored; resists cracking. Moderately vigorous, determinate vine. Stems and leaves are covered with grayish-white pubescence, making it attractive enough for the flower garden. Produces a small percentage of glabrous plants which can be rouged out at the seedling stage. E49, E83T, I99, M1

Beefsteak: (Scarlet Beefsteak, Red Ponderosa) 85 days. Very large, flattened, slightly ribbed, brilliant crimson-scarlet fruit; weight 12 to 16 ounces. Solid, meaty, deep red flesh, nearly seedless, with old-fashioned "real" tomato flavor. Excellent for slicing. Vigorous, indeterminate, productive vine. Popular home garden cultivar. Scarlet sport of Ponderosa. A25, E57, F1, G51, G71, H61, H66, J58, K71, K73, M0, M1, M46, N39

Bonny Best: (John Baer) 75 days. Medium-sized, round to deep globe-shaped, bright red fruit; weight 5 to 8 ounces; solid, meaty flesh, with full tomato flavor. Vigorous, indeterminate vine; adapted to a wide range of growing conditions. Has sparse foliage. Long-time favorite for home gardens and local markets. C85M, D11M, *D35M*{PL}, D87, F24M, F44, G6, *G83M*, H61, J20, J25M, K73, M0, M1, M13M, etc.

Break o'Day: 65 days. Medium-large, globe shaped, orange-red fruit; 2 1/2 to 3 inches in diameter; weight 6 ounces. Flesh solid and meaty, with few seeds, low in acid, of very good flavor. Indeterminate vine; matures early and produces abundantly throughout the season; resistant to wilt. Has sparse foliage. Home garden favorite for over 50 years. M1

Bush Beefsteak: 62 days. Medium-large, flattened globe-shaped, deep red fruit; weight 8 to 12 ounces; solid, meaty, rich red flesh, with very few seeds. Ideal for slicing. Vigorous, compact, determinate vine; highly productive, even under adverse conditions. Excellent for home gardens in northern areas. A16, A69M, C85M, D11M, D27, H42, K20, L42, L79, M0, M1

Cal Ace: 80 days. Large, smooth, deep oblate fruit; weight 8 to 12 ounces; uniform ripening; of good texture and flavor. Strong, determinate, highly productive vine; provides good protection. Resistant to fusarium and verticillium wilts. Used extensively for fresh market and home garden production in California. Especially adapted to arid regions. B75M, *E53M*, G51, G93M, H61, K10, K66, K73, *L59G*, M0, M1, N52

Caro Red:[10] 78 days. Contains about 10 times the pro vitamin A found in standard tomatoes. Smooth, globe-shaped, rich orange-red fruit; 2 1/2 to 3 inches in diameter; weight 4 to 8 ounces. Has a rich, distinctive flavor. Prolific, indeterminate vine. Developed at Purdue University. F42, M1

Cold Set:[4] (Outdoor Seeder) 70 days. Seeds germinate in soil as cold as 50° F., and young seedlings tolerate temperatures as low as 18° F. Performs best in cool to moderate climates, without excessive wetness or humidity. Medium-sized, round, blood red fruit; weight 5 to 6 ounces. Determinate, high yielding vine. Introduced in 1963 by Ontario Agricultural College. A2, D11M, D27, E97, I97T, L7M, L42, M1

Costoluto Fiorentino: Unique Italian heirloom. Medium-sized, deeply ribbed fruit, 3 inches in diameter. Good for slicing and eating raw, with excellent flavor and juiciness. J73

Costoluto Genovese: (Ribbed Genova) 90 days. Medium-sized, flattened, slightly ribbed, scarlet fruit; 2 1/2 to 3 1/2 inches in diameter; of excellent flavor. Indeterminate vine. Does well in hot weather, but will continue to produce when the weather turns cool. An old, unimproved cultivar from northern Italy. J73, K49M, K66

Delicious: (Burpee's Delicious) 77 days. Very large, deep globe-shaped fruit; resists cracking. Mostly over 1 pound in weight, with many 2 to 3 pounds. Produced the world record of 6 pounds 8 ounces. Interiors solid, with small seed cavities, of excellent flavor. Perfect for slicing. Indeterminate vine; moderately productive. B75, C44, E5T, *E91G*, E97, *F72*, G64, G71, G79, H61, J7, J58, K49M, M0, M1, etc.

Dinner Plate: 90 days. Beefsteak type. Very large, heart-shaped fruit; average weight 1 1/2 to 2 pounds; susceptible to cracking at the shoulders. Interior very thick and meaty, richly flavored, nearly seedless. Superior for slicing. Indeterminate vine. Heirloom. K71M, M0

Doublerich:[10] 80 days. High vitamin tomato. Contains 50 to 60 units of vitamin C, compared to 12 to 15 in other tomatoes. Medium-sized, globe-shaped, deep scarlet fruit; weight 4 to 8 ounces. Interior bright red, solid, meaty, juicy, with a small amount of seeds. Excellent for canning and juicing. Vigorous, indeterminate, high yielding vine. I99, K49T, M1

Earliana: 65 days. Medium-sized, flattened globe-shaped, bright scarlet fruit; 3 inches in diameter; weight 4 to 5 ounces; thick-skinned; green-shouldered. Solid flesh of good flavor. Vigorous, indeterminate, open-spreading vine; bears fruit in clusters of 6 to 10. Widely grown for early markets. Also good for home gardens. A2, A25, A69M, B13, D65, F24M, *F72*, F92, G57M, G67M, G83M, I64, K27M, L14, M1, etc.

Earlirouge: 65 days. Medium-sized, slightly oblate fruit; weight 6 1/2 to 7 ounces; easily removed peel; resists cracking. Sweet, flavorful, high-crimson interiors. Good for slicing and canning. Compact, determinate vine; sets fruit well at extremes of temperature. For home gardens, local markets and shipping. Developed in Canada. A2, D68, F44, G6, I39M, J7, J25M, K49Z, L42, M0, M1

Early Hi-Crimson: 65 days. Represents a new race of tomatoes. Has twice as much red color as ordinary tomatoes, especially when ripened in cool weather. Large fruit, 3 to 3 1/2 inches in diameter. Semi-determinate vine. D82

Egg: 80 days. Small, egg-shaped, smooth fruit; 2 inches long; weight 3 ounces; resists cracking; keeps well. Firm, non-acid flesh, of very good flavor. Makes excellent juice. Very uniform in size and shape. Strong, high-yielding, determinate vine. E49

Fireball: 65 days. Medium-sized, flattened globe-shaped, rich red fruit; 2 1/2 to 3 inches in diameter; weight 4 to 5 ounces; resists cracking. Compact, determinate vine; produces a concentrated set. Has sparse foliage, should be caged to protect fruit from sunscald. Widely grown for the early basket trade. A25, A69M, B1M, C85M, E24, F92, I64, I67M, I84, L42, *L59G*, L97, M1, N39

Flora-Dade: 75 days. Medium-sized, round to deep globe-shaped fruit; weight about 7 ounces; smooth and firm; jointless. Very productive, determinate vine; well protected by heavy foliage. Well adapted to humid southern areas. Developed by the University of Florida for calcareous soils and adverse conditions. *A1*, A87M, B75M, *F63*, *F72*, *G13M*, G27M, *H61*, J84, K10, *L59G*, M0, M1, M29

Glacier: 54 days. Small, round fruit; 2 1/2 to 3 inches in diameter; weight 2 to 3 ounces; of excellent sweet flavor; resists cracking. Spreading, determinate vine, to 18 inches tall; produces up to 100 fruit, with 60 not uncommon. Does well in cool northern areas. Also successful as a winter crop in southern Florida. Heirloom from Sweden. D11M, D68, E24, J25M, K71M, N39

Glamour: 75 days. Medium-sized, flattened globe-shaped fruit; weight 6 to 8 ounces; exterior bright red, smooth; interior thick-walled, meaty, mild but flavorful; resistant to cracking. High yielding, indeterminate vine. Standard main crop cultivar used by bedding plant growers. B13, B73M, C85M, C92, *D35M*{PL}, *E91G*, F13, *F72*, G79, *H61*, I64, I67M, K50, K73, L42, M0, M1, M13M, etc.

Harbinger: 60 days. Medium-small, bright red fruit; 2 to 2 1/2 inches in diameter; weight 3 ounces; of very good flavor; thin skin, prone to cracking. Ripens reliably off the plant after cold summers in northern areas. Indeterminate vine; highly productive over a long season. Does well under glass. Traditional English cultivar. Introduced about 1910. B49, E33, P83M, S55, S61, *S75M*

Homestead: 80 days. Medium-large, deep globular fruit; weight about 8 ounces; exterior smooth, dark red; interior firm, meaty, flavorful. Strong, semi-determinate vine, requires no staking. Large leaves provide good fruit protection. Resistant to fusarium wilt. Adapted to areas with hot temperatures and high humidity. A27M, G57M, G68, J34, K71, L9M

Imur Prior Beta: (IPB) 60 days. Small to medium-sized, globe-shaped, dark red fruit; 1 1/2 to 2 inches in diameter; weight 2 to 4 ounces; somewhat tough skin; firm, juicy flesh, very flavorful. Large, indeterminate vine; very prolific. Has potato-like foliage. Popular in short-season areas. Released by Washington State University. A2, F82, H94, K49M

Jersey Devil: Long, tapered, pointed fruit, reminiscent of a very large frying pepper; of rich red color; weight 2 to 6 ounces. Interior very sweet, but with a good full tomato flavor, has few seeds. The very firm, immature green fruit makes an excellent pickle. Very large, indeterminate vine; requires staking or caging. Good for home gardens. A49G, M1

Jersey Giant: Similar to Jersey Devil, but larger, less slender and more irregular in shape; equally smooth and crack-free. Long, tapered fruit; 3 1/2 inches long, 1 1/2 inches in diameter; weight 4 to 12 ounces; of good flavor. Early maturing. Indeterminate vine. M1

Jung's Improved Wayahead: 63 days. One of the earliest maturing tomatoes that also has good size. Smooth, slightly flattened, bright scarlet fruit; 3 to 3 1/2 inches in diameter, 1 1/2 to 2 inches deep; weight 4 to 6 ounces. Firm interior, with a full tomato flavor. Determinate vine; highly productive over a long harvest season. G16, I39M, I99, M1

Landry's Russian: 70 days. Canadian heirloom, brought to the prairie provinces many years ago by Russian immigrants. Uniform, medium-sized, round fruit; 2 1/2 to 3 inches in diameter; weight 1/2 pound. Deliciously sweet, deep red flesh. Indeterminate, consistently productive vine. K71M

Long Keeper:[11] (Burpee's Long Keeper) 78 days. Unique storage tomato. Unblemished ripe or partially ripe fruit, when harvested before frost and stored properly, will stay fresh for 6 to 12 weeks or more without a change in flavor or texture. The skin is light, golden orange-red when ripe. Medium red flesh. Firm fruits hold their shape when canned whole. A25, B73M, B75, C44, C85M, F19M, *F72*, G16, H42, J7, L7M, L79, L89, M0, M1, etc.

Manalucie: 85 days. Medium-large, smooth fruit; weight 6 to 8 ounces; flesh firm, meaty, of very good quality; relatively resistant to cracking. Very slow ripening, must be allowed to fully mature before harvesting. Vigorous, indeterminate vine; productive over a long period; provides good foliage cover for protection against sunscald. Has multiple disease resistance. F19M, *F72*, G27M, *L59G*, M0, M1

Marglobe: 75 days. Medium-large, globe-shaped, very uniform fruit; weight 8 to 10 ounces; thick-walled; solid sweet flesh, with a full tomato flavor. Vigorous, determinate, prolific vine; somewhat resistant to fusarium wilt. Long-time home garden favorite. A25, B73M, *D35M*{PL}, D76, E49, F19M, G68, H49, H61, H66, K71, M0, M1, M95, N16, N39, etc.

Marion: 75 days. Medium to large, deep globe-shaped fruit; weight about 8 ounces; exterior smooth, dark red; interior firm, of good flavor. For both home gardens and fresh market. High yielding, indeterminate vine; well protected by heavy foliage; disease resistant. Adapted to the Middle and Upper South. *F72*, *G1M*, H66, K71, L14, M0, M1, M13M

Marmande: (Marmande VF) 65 days. Medium-large, irregularly shaped, slightly ribbed, scarlet red fruit; weight 6 to 8 ounces; solid, meaty, mild flesh, with excellent full tomato flavor. Vigorous, prolific, semi-determinate vine; sets fruit early and under cool conditions; resists wilt. Developed in France by the Vilmorin Company. Very popular in Europe. A75, B35M, C53, C85M, E5T, F33, G68, I77, K66, *L59G*, S61, S95M

Moneymaker: 75 days. Medium-sized, globular fruit; weight 4 to 6 ounces; exterior intense red when ripe, smooth; quality very high. Prolific, indeterminate vine. Sets well in any weather; especially adapted to humid tropical and sub-tropical areas. Also does well in cool greenhouses. B49, D27, E33, F92, *L59G*, L91M, M1, O53M, *R23*, *S75M*

Nepal: 78 days. Medium to large, globe-shaped, bright red fruit; weight 10 to 12 ounces, occasionally over 1 pound; very meaty and flavorful; resists cracking. Retains its excellent "old-fashioned" flavor during cold weather conditions. Vigorous, indeterminate vine; very prolific. Originated in the Himalayas. F24M, G6, I99, M1

New Yorker: 63 days. Medium-sized, roundish fruit; weight 4 to 6 1/2 ounces; exterior smooth, bright scarlet; interior solid, meaty, of fine flavor. Compact, determinate vine; produces fruit in a concentrated set; resiss verticillium wilt. Does well in cool northern or short season areas. B75, C69, E24, F13, *F63*, G87, K10, K73, L42, M0, M1

Oregon Spring: 60 days. Adapted to areas with cool summer nights, setting parthenocarpic fruit when temperatures fall below 50°F.. When night temperatures increase, fruit will be seeded. Medium-sized fruit; weight 6 to 8 ounces; of excellent quality and flavor. Determinate vine; tolerant to fusarium and verticillium wilts. Developed by Dr. James R. Baggett at Oregon State University. D68, E24, F90, G6, H95, I39, I99, K49Z, L89

Pearson: 80 days. Medium-sized, deep globe-shaped fruit; 2 1/2 to 3 inches in diameter. Has a somewhat acid, "old-fashioned" tomato flavor. May have green shoulders, even when ripe. Very good for slicing; also used for canning. Medium-large, determinate plant; tolerant to semi-arid growing conditions. Has good foliage cover that protects the fruit from sunscald. M1

Peron: (Peron Sprayless) 68 days. Medium-large, deep globe-shaped, bright scarlet fruit; 3 to 3 1/2 inches in diameter; weight 8 ounces; solid flesh, of very good flavor. Strong, indeterminate vine; reliably productive; highly disease resistant. Introduced from South America in 1951 by Gleckler's Seedsmen. E49, E59Z, I99, K49M, L11, M0, M1

Porter: 78 days. Small, round-oval, pinkish-red fruit; weight 1 ounce; solid, meaty flesh, of very good flavor; resists cracking. Large, open, indeterminate vine; produces heavily until frost; grows well in poor soil. Has fair foliage color. Exceptionally heat and drought resistant. Developed by V.O. Porter in 1927 for home gardens and local markets in the Southwest. E59Z, F12, H66, J34, L14, M0, M1, M95, N16

Pusa Ruby: 70 days. Medium-sized, uniformly deep-red fruit; 2 inches in diameter; keeps well. Vigorous, indeterminate, prolific vine; very disease resistant. Can be grown throughout the year in warm climates. Very popular with home and market growers in India. E49, N91, R0, R50, *S36*, S59M

Rocket: 50 days. Small, round, medium-red fruit; 1 1/2 to 2 inches in diameter; weight 1 1/2 to 3 ounces. Has a slightly acid flavor. Compact, determinate vine; extremely prolific, requires staking due to the weight of the crop. Standard early tomato in the northwestern parts of Canada. E24, H42, H94, K71M, M1

Rodade: 77 days. Released by South Africa in 1982, as the first cultivar resistant to bacterial wilt, a serious disease in warm subtropical areas. Also resistant to fusarium and verticillium. Very attractive, smooth, firm fruit; ripens evenly. Similar to Flora-Dade, but produces a higher percentage of first grade fruit and is less prone to catfacing and cracking. M0

Russian Red: 80 days. Medium-small, round, scarlet red fruit; 2 inches in diameter; weight 4 to 8 ounces; of good flavor. Strong, upright, medium-tall, determinate vine with thick, heavy foliage cover. Tolerant of lower temperatures than most tomatoes. E49, M1, T1M

Rutgers: 75 days. Medium-large, bright red fruit; weight 8 to 10 ounces; ripens uniformly. Has a rich, mellow, full-bodied flavor. Quality very good for slicing. Vigorous, indeterminate vine; adapted to a wide range of growing conditions. An excellent all-purpose cultivar. Long-time home garden favorite. Also good for local markets and shipping. B49, C44, *D35M*{PL}, D76, F19M, G51, H61, H66, J14{PL}, J34, K71, K73, M0, M1, M46, N16, N39, etc.

Santiam: 58 days. Medium-sized fruit; weight 4 to 5 ounces; thick-skinned; mild, slightly acid, sweet and juicy, of good quality. Vigorous, determinate vine, to 30 inches tall; high yielding; sets parthenocarpic fruit. Resistant to fusarium and verticillium wilts. Sister strain to Oregon Spring. Matures 1 to 2 weeks earlier, depending on the weather. E24, I39, I99, J34, L89

Scarlet Topper: (Pritchard, Pritchard's Scarlet Topper) 75 days. Medium-large, globe-shaped, brilliant red fruit; 3 to 3 1/2 inches in diameter; thick-walled; flesh meaty, solid, with a small seed core, flavor very good; resists cracking. Strong, compact, determinate vine; very productive; resistant to fusarium wilt. All America Selections winner in 1933. Introduced by the originator of Marglobe and Break o'Day. F24M, K71, L7M, *L59G*, M1

Scotia: 60 days. Medium-sized, deep globe-shaped, deep-red fruit; weight 4 ounces; slightly green-shouldered; firm flesh, of good flavor. Determinate vine; reliably productive; sets well in cool weather. Popular home garden cultivar in maritime Canada. E38, F1, L42, M1, M49

Siberia:[4] (Siberian) 50 days. An experimental cultivar smuggled out of Siberia into Canada by a Russian traveler. Will set fruit at 38^0 F. Small to medium-sized fruit; weight 3 to 4 ounces; of fair flavor. Compact, determinate vine; often produces 40 to 60 fruit. Recommended for cold, short season areas where it is difficult to grow tomatoes. Also successful as a winter crop in southern Florida. A2, A49G, D11M, F44, F82, H42, H94, J25M, J82, K49Z, K71M, L7M, N39

Sioux: 75 days. Medium-sized, smooth, globe-shaped, deep red fruit; weight 4 to 8 ounces; solid, meaty, low-acid flesh, with very few seeds; resists cracking. Quality good for slicing. Strong, indeterminate vine; very prolific, even under unfavorable growing conditions. Has medium heavy foliage. For home gardens and local markets. C92, M1

St. Pierre: Slicing tomato with an excellent subacid flavor and tender, thin skin. Large, smooth, globose fruit; juicy flesh. Produces prolifically under adverse conditions of cool weather, little water and no weeding. Very popular in parts of Europe. J73, Q24M, S95M

Stakeless:[6] 78 days. Unique "stakeless" or thick-stemmed tomato. Thick, upright main stem; 1 inch in diameter, 18 to 24 inches tall when fully mature; does not require staking. Medium-large, round fruit; 3 inches in diameter; weight 6 to 8 ounces; solid, meaty, deep red flesh. Dense, potato-like foliage prevents sunscald. Developed at the University of Delaware. B75M, D76, *E91G*, E97, *H57M*, I99, L42, M0, M1, M29

Starfire: 55 days. Medium-large, deep globe-shaped fruit; 2 1/2 to 3 inches in diameter; weight 6 to 8 ounces; solid, meaty, deep red interior, with few seeds. Compact, determinate, prolific vine; prefers light, sandy soils. Has good foliage cover. Adapted to cool, short-season areas. A69M, C85M, D11M, D27, E24, G87, J7, L42, L79, M1, M13M

Stupice:[8] 50 days. Small to medium-sized, flattened, glossy red fruit; 2 inches in diameter; weight 2 to 4 ounces; sweet, juicy, very flavorful flesh. Compact, productive vine; widely adapted. Dwarf indeterminate in habit. Has potato-like foliage. Does well in short-season areas. Introduced by Abundant Life Seed Foundation in 1977. Originally from Czechoslovakia. A2, D87, F44, I99

Sub-Arctic Maxi:[4] 52 days. The largest and most flavorful of the Sub-Arctic series. Small, round to oblate deep red fruit; 2 1/2 inches in diameter; weight 2 1/2 to 3 ounces. Compact, determinate vine; bears early, heavy yields on vigorous lateral branches after the main stem aborts. Has excellent cold set ability. Developed at the Beaverlodge Experiment Station, Alberta, Canada. A69M, C85M, D27, E24, E38, F1, F82, G6, H94, I67M, I97T, J7, J20, K71M, L7M, L42, M0, M1, etc.

Sub-Arctic Plenty:[4] 50 days. Small, roundish fruit; 1 1/2 to 2 inches in diameter; weight 1 1/2 to 2 ounces; of good flavor. Compact, determinate, upright vine. Has a unique "birds nest" growth habit in which the main stem aborts, followed by fast-growing lateral branches that produce concentrated clusters at the center of the plant. Will set fruit during cold weather conditions. A16, D76, E97, G6, H94, L91M, M1

Super Marmande: 72 days. Medium-large, slightly flattened, somewhat irregular fruit; 3 to 4 inches in diameter; weight 6 to 8 ounces; very meaty and extremely flavorful. Excellent for slicing; sometimes used for stuffing. Compact, semi-determinate vine. Suitable for growing out of doors or in cool greenhouses. B49, I99, L91M, P83M, *R23*, S55, S95M

The Amateur:[5] Small to medium-sized fruit; 2 to 2 1/2 inches in diameter; of sweet flavor and excellent quality; ripens early. Compact, determinate vine; grows only 15 inches tall, requires no support; reliably productive, even during adverse conditions. Ideal for growing under cloches or poly tunnels. Very popular in England. O53M, *R23*, S61

Thessaloniki: 68 days. Smooth, uniform, globe-shaped fruit with perfect blossom ends; 2 1/2 to 3 inches in diameter; weight 4 to 6 ounces. Firm, juicy interiors, mild, of very good flavor. Resistant to cracking and sunscald. Very good keeper. Indeterminate vine; highly disease resistant. Developed in Greece. E49, M1

Tip-Top: 74 days. Nearly round fruit, with a distinctive tip; weight 3 ounces. Ideal for salads; also useful for paste due to the low water content and thick walls. Much sweeter than cherry or small paste types. Determinate, high yielding vine; requires no staking; bears fruit in large clusters. J20

Trip-L-Crop:[7] 85 days. Large, bright red fruit; 4 to 5 inches in diameter; weight up to 1 pound; solid, meaty, mild-flavored flesh, contains very few seeds. Excellent for slicing; also good for canning. Vigorous, indeterminate vine, grows 10 to 15 feet tall when trellised; produces as many as 2 to 3 bushels of fruit. A56, B73M, B73M{PL}, D11M, D76, E32M{PL}, F19M, *F72*, J34, K71, M0, M1

Tropic:[9] 80 days. Medium-large, flattened globe-shaped fruit; weight 8 to 10 ounces; green-shouldered; solid, meaty flesh. Strong, high yielding, indeterminate vine; tolerant to heat and high humidity. Has good foliage cover and multiple disease resistance. Adapted to greenhouse culture and outdoor production in the Deep South. A87M, F12, *F72*, *F85G*, G27M, G51, H61, H66, J34, L7M, *L59G*, M0, M1, P1G

Urbana: (Giant Everbearing) 75 days. Large, smooth, bright glossy red fruit; weight 4 to 8 ounces; ripens uniformly, resists cracking. Solid flesh with few seeds, of very fine flavor. Strong, indeterminate, high yielding vine; adapted to a wide range of soils and climates. Matures early and continues to bear throughout the season. All America Selections winner in 1951. M1

Valiant: 67 days. Large, globe-shaped fruit; weight 12 to 15 ounces; exterior very smooth, dark crimson red; interior very solid and meaty, free from acidity, of very good flavor. Ideal for slicing; also fine for juice and canning. High yielding, indeterminate vine; bears fruit in clusters of 3 to 5; sets well even in hot, dry climates. A25, *A69M*, B73M, C69, C92, G87, M1

Vendor:[9] 75 days. Standard non-hybrid greenhouse tomato. Uniform ripening, medium-large, deep globe-shaped fruit; weight 6 to 8 ounces. Interior ripening genes make Vendor better tasting in the green-ripe stage than European hybrids. Semi-compact plant; tolerant to leaf mold and tobacco mosaic virus. Also used for hydroponic and outdoor culture. D27, E38, F44, F92, G6, G64, I67M, L7M, L42, M1, M13M, M49

Victor: 70 days. Medium-sized, smooth, deep oblate fruit; 2 1/2 to 3 inches in diameter; weight 4 1/2 ounces; firm flesh, of very good flavor and quality. Compact, determinate, highly prolific vine. Good home garden cultivar for cool northern areas. All America Selections winner in 1941. Developed by Dr. Yeager at Michigan State University. M1

Victoria: 75 days. Bright red fruit; weight 5 ounces; very mild tasting. Indeterminate vine needs tall support. Not a heavy producer, but its unique flavor makes it worth growing. First introduced in the 1940's in England. F24M

Walter: 75 days. Medium-sized, deep globe-shaped fruit with good internal color; weight 7 ounces; resists cracking. Determinate vine; adapted to both short stake and field culture. Produces high quality fruit even in warm, humid areas. Has multiple disease resistance. Developed at the Bradenton Experiment Station, Bradenton, Florida. A87M, *F63*, *F72*, *G1M*, G27M, G79, *H61*, H66, L7M, L14, M0, M1, N16

West Virginia 63: 70 days. Uniform, smooth, bright red fruit; weight 6 to 8 ounces; resists cracking. Of excellent quality for slicing. Vigorous, indeterminate, high yielding vine; widely adapted; wilt resistant. Has good foliage cover. An improved strain of an old favorite. Introduced for West Virginia's centennial celebration. B73M, L7M, M1

YELLOW/ORANGE-SKINNED

Hybrid

Golden Boy: 80 days. Large, globe-shaped, deep golden-orange fruit; weight 8 ounces; flesh solid, meaty, low in acid, very mild flavored, with few seeds; quality excellent. Strong, vigorous, indeterminate vine; widely adapted; bears fruit in large clusters over an extended season. C44, D76, *E91G*, *F72*, G16, H61, H95, I91, J7, J20, K71, M0, M1, M46, M95M, N16, etc.

Lemon Boy: 72 days. Medium-sized, deep globe-shaped, lemon yellow fruit; weight 6 to 8 ounces; mild, flavorful, lemon yellow flesh. Vigorous, high yielding, indeterminate vine; widely adapted; resistant to fusarium and verticillium wilts and nematodes. Attractive specialty market item. B75, D11M, D76, E97, F19M, *F72*, G64, G79, I39, I91, I99, J14{PL}, J34, L42, M0, M1, M46, etc.

Mandarin Cross: 75 days. Medium to large, semi globe-shaped fruit; weight about 9 ounces; exterior golden-orange, smooth, attractive; interior thick-walled, solid, very meaty, low in acid, mild but flavorful. Vigorous, indeterminate vine; very productive, setting fruit in clusters of 9 or 10. Resistant to heat. H33, I99, K66, M0, M1, *S63M*

Open-Pollinated

Burgess Colossal Golden: Very large, deep oblate, golden- orange fruit; weight 14 ounces, occasionally up to 2 1/2 pounds; thick, meaty, very mild flesh. Large, spreading, well-branched, indeterminate vine. Has heavy foliage cover that gives adequate fruit protection. M1

Caro Rich:[10] 80 days. An improved version of Caro Red, offering higher yields and better flavor. Contains 10 times the provitamin A as other tomatoes. Medium-sized, slightly flattened, deep golden orange fruit; weight 4 to 6 ounces; low in acid, of good sweet flavor. High yielding, determinate vine. Ripens too late for far northern areas. A32, I97T, I99, K49T, L42, M0, M1

Djena Lee's Golden Girl: 80 days. Family heirloom of Djena Lee since the early 1920's. Won first prize at the Chicago Fair 10 years in a row. Medium-sized, golden-orange fruit; 2 to 2 1/2 inches in diameter; weight 7 to 8 ounces; of excellent sweet but tangy flavor. Indeterminate vine. L7M

Golden Delight: 60 days. Medium-sized, flattened globe-shaped, golden yellow fruit; 2 to 3 inches in diameter; weight 3 to 4 ounces. Very low in acid, but rich in flavor. Compact, determinate, high yielding vine. Developed at South Dakota State University. K49M, M1, M49

Golden Ponderosa: (Yellow Ponderosa) 85 days. Yellow beefsteak type. Large, smooth, flattened globe-shaped, golden- yellow fruit; 4 inches in diameter; weight 12 to 16 ounces. Solid, meaty, mild-flavored flesh. Vigorous, indeterminate vine. G57M, K49M, M1

Golden Ponderosa (Railroad Strain): 78 days. A West Virginia heirloom that was propagated and traded by employees of the C & O Railroad in West Virginia, prior to 1940. Somewhat rough, large-cored, yellow-gold fruit; weight 1 pound or more; mild, subacid flesh. Not very tolerant of foliage diseases. L7M

Golden Queen: 80 days. Smooth, slightly flattened, bright yellow fruit; 2 to 3 inches in diameter; weight 4 to 6 ounces; low in acid, of excellent mild flavor. Prolific, indeterminate vine. One of the few yellow heirlooms still available. The most popular large-fruited yellow cultivar until Jubilee was released. Introduced in 1882. F42, I67M, K49M, L42, M0, M1

Golden Sunrise: 78 days. Round, medium-small, golden yellow fruit; smooth, thin skin; excellent mild flavor. Very prolific, indeterminate vine. Adapted to greenhouse or outdoor culture. Popular English cultivar. L7M, L91M, O53M, P1G, P83M, *R23*, S61

Goldie: 90 days. Very large, slightly flattened, golden-yellow fruit with a smooth blossom end; 4 to 4 1/2 inches in diameter; weight 12 to 16 ounces; low in acid, of excellent mild flavor. Vigorous, highly productive, indeterminate vine. Attractive heirloom, dating back to the early 1800's. D87, E49, M1

Hugh's: 89 days. Very large, beefsteak-type fruit, 4 to 6 inches in diameter; weight 2 pounds or more; skin thin, very light yellow; interior meaty, exceedingly sweet and juicy, with very few seeds. Large, indeterminate vine, requires room and heavy stakes. Heirloom from Madison County, Indiana. L7M

Ida Gold: 55 days. Medium-small, round, bright orange fruit; 1 1/2 to 2 1/2 inches in diameter; weight 2 ounces; flavorful, low in acid. Compact, determinate vine; highly productive over a long season. Developed at the University of Idaho for cold northern areas. D68, F44, G6, H94, K49M, K71M, M1, S55

Jubilee: (Golden Jubilee, Burpee's Orange Jubilee) 75 days. Medium-sized, globular, bright golden-orange fruit; 2 1/2 to 3 1/2 inches in diameter; weight 6 to 7 ounces; thick-walled. Solid, meaty flesh, mild and flavorful. Vigorous, high yielding, indeterminate vine. All America Selections winner in 1943. A25, C85M, D11M, *D35M*{PL}, D65, D87, F19M, *F72*, *I62*{PL}, J34, L97, M0, M1, M13M, M95, N16, etc.

Orange Queen: 65 days. Medium-sized, slightly flattened, bright orange fruit with a small blossom scar; weight 4 to 6 ounces; resists cracking. Solid, very meaty flesh, low in acid, with few seeds, of mild flavor. Determinate vine with heavy foliage cover. Does well in northern areas. L42, M0, M1

Persimmon: 80 days. Very large, deep globe-shaped, golden-orange fruit; 4 to 4 1/2 inches in diameter; weight 16 to 24 ounces, some up to 2 pounds. Solid, meaty flesh, with few seeds, has a strong, distinctive flavor. Susceptible to blossom end rot. Excellent for slicing. Large, indeterminate vine; moderately productive. Heirloom. K49M

Sunray: (Golden Sunray) 80 days. Medium-large, globular, bright golden yellow fruit; 2 1/2 to 3 inches in diameter; weight 7 ounces; thick-walled; resists cracking. Firm, meaty flesh, of excellent mild flavor. Vigorous, indeterminate vine; widely adapted; resists fusarium wilt. For home gardens and local markets. A13, E49, E57, *E91G*, F13, G51, G71, G93M, H61, I99, K50, K73, M0, M1, M46, etc.

Taxi: 64 days. Medium-sized, round to slightly oblate, bright yellow fruit with a small stem scar; smooth and blemish free. Firm, meaty, sweet, flavorful interiors. Compact, determinate vine; does not require staking. Ideal for the specialty market trade. E70M{PR}, G6, H49, I99, M1

Valencia: Round, smooth, bright orange fruit; weight 8 to 10 ounces. Firm, meaty interior, with few seeds, has a full tomato flavor. Vigorous, indeterminate vine; requires staking. Developed by Johnny's Selected Seeds from a Maine family heirloom. G6

Verna Orange: 84 days. Very large, orange, heart-shaped fruit of superb flavor. Among the meatiest and most seedless of tomatoes. Resembles Yellow Oxheart except for the color, slightly ribbed shape, and tendency of seed cavities to be semi-hollow. Indeterminate vine. Indiana heirloom. L7M

Yellow Oxheart: 79 days. Very large, bright yellow, heart-shaped fruit; often weighing close to a pound. Interior meaty, small-cored, sweet; flavor rich, full, distinctive, very well-balanced. Suitable for slicing, salads or processing. Has less than average drought and disease tolerance. Family heirloom that originated in Willis, Virginia about 1915. L7M, M1

Yellow Perfection: 70 days. Medium-small, round, deep golden-yellow fruit; 2 inches in diameter; of excellent mild flavor. Ripens well in cool or hot weather. Vigorous, indeterminate vine; highly prolific, sets fruit in clusters of 4 to 6. Has potato-like foliage. Very popular in England. Introduced by Unwin Seedsmen. I99

OTHERS

Big Rainbow: 102 days. Bicolored beefsteak type. Large to very large fruit, average weight 1 1/2 pounds, some 2 to 2 1/2 pounds. Green near the shoulders, yellow-orange at the midsection, pink to bright red towards the blossom end; when fully ripe gold on the stem end and red on the blossom end. Resists cracking. Indeterminate vine; resistant to alternaria leaf spot; continues to bear until frost. Heirloom from Polk County, Minnesota. L7M

Evergreen: (Emerald Evergreen) 72 days. Medium to large fruit, amber green when ripe. Solid, meaty, emerald green flesh, of sweet mild flavor and very good quality. Excellent for slicing, frying, pickling or conserves. Vigorous, indeterminate vine. A49G, E49, I99, K49M, M0, M1

Garden Peach:[11] 100 days. Excellent storage tomato, will keep 5 to 6 months if harvested before frost. Medium-sized, deep globe-shaped fruit; 2 1/2 to 3 inches in diameter. Yellow-orange skin, blushed with pale-pink, slightly fuzzy, thick. Red flesh, of mild flavor that improves with storage. Ripens slowly. Indeterminate vine; produces abundant clusters of fruit. K49M, M0

Georgia Streak: 91 days. Bicolored beefsteak type similar to Old German. Eye-appealing yellow and red inside and out. Predominantly yellow with a red blush and red core on the blossom end. Especially attractive in salads. Indeterminate vine. Heirloom from Georgia. L7M

Green Zebra: 80 days. Medium-small, uniform, round fruit; greenish-amber, striped with deep-green; 2 inches in diameter. Green flesh, with a mild but pleasing flavor. Indeterminate vine; produces heavily until frost. Very striking. U33

Mammoth German Gold: 95 days. Very large fruit; golden-yellow, blotched with red at the blossom end; weight 1 pound or more; susceptible to cracking. Of very fine mild flavor. Resembles fresh peaches when sliced. Vigorous, indeterminate vine; requires staking. U33

Marvel Striped: 90 days. Large, irregular, heart-shaped fruit with very thin skin; orange and yellow, splashed and striped with red; weight 1 pound. Has an intensely sweet flavor. Prolific, indeterminate vine. Originally from Oaxaca, Mexico. A2, F42, I99, K49T

Old German: 95 days. Large, very attractive fruit; yellow, with a red center visible on the surface and throughout the core; often weighs over a pound; of outstanding flavor. Excellent for slicing. Indeterminate vine; not a heavy producer; does not tolerate drought. Mennonite family heirloom from Virginia. Introduced by Southern Exposure Seed Exchange in 1985. L7M

Pineapple: Unique red and yellow striped tomato that can reach 2 pounds. Has distinctive stripes that color the meaty flesh as well. Very attractive when sliced. Indeterminate vine. E49, M0

Pink Grapefruit: 75 days. Medium-sized, flattened globe-shaped fruit, 2 1/2 to 3 1/2 inches in diameter; weight 4 to 6 ounces. Yellow skin. Blushing pink, firm, juicy flesh, low in acid, of delicious mild flavor. Productive, indeterminate vine. E49, M0, M1

Prudence Purple: (Pruden's Purple) 70 days. Large, flattened, distinctly ribbed, pinkish-purple fruit; 4 inches in diameter, 3 inches deep; weight 1 pound or more; resists cracking. Firm, meaty flesh, mild but flavorful, contains very few seeds. Vigorous, prolific, indeterminate vine with potato-like foliage. Heirloom. J20

Purple Calabash: 75 days. Medium-sized, oblate, highly lobed, dark pinkish-purple fruit; 2 1/2 to 3 1/2 inches in diameter; weight 5 to 6 ounces; thin-skinned. Sweet, juicy, seedy flesh, of fair quality for fresh use, excellent for making vinegar. Susceptible to cracking; stores poorly. Vigorous, productive, indeterminate vine. A49G, E49, F80, I99, K49M, M1

Purple Smudge: 75 days. Medium-small, deep oblate fruit; 2 to 2 1/2 inches in diameter; of good flavor, low in acid. Develops a purple fingerprint-like pattern on the shoulder of green fruit that has been exposed to the sun. The shoulder remains dark when fruit ripens to red. Very productive vine with purple-tinged leaves and stems. U33

Ruby Gold: 95 days. Very large, flattened, slightly ribbed fruit; golden-yellow, streaked with red; weight 14 to 16 ounces; susceptible to cracking. Solid, meaty flesh, marbled with red, of very mild flavor. Vigorous, productive, indeterminate vine. West Virginia heirloom. F42, M1

Tigerella: (Mr. Stripey) 56 days. Medium-small, globular fruit; reddish-orange, striped with golden-yellow when ripe; 1 1/2 to 2 inches in diameter; of very fine flavor. Indeterminate vine; highly productive over a long season. Has good disease resistance. Suitable for greenhouse or outdoor culture. *F72*, L91M, P83M, S55, S61

White Beauty: (Snowball) 80 days. Medium-large, ivory white fruit; weight 8 to 12 ounces. Firm, meaty, paper-white flesh, extremely mild and sweet due to high sugar content, contains few seeds. Excellent for slicing. Very attractive in salads. Moderately productive, indeterminate vine. Possibly known as White Apple before 1920. A49G, B73M, D11M, D76, E49, E97, J83M, K49M, L7M, M0, M1

White Potato Leaf: 80 days. Medium-sized, flat, ruffled fruit; creamy white, sometimes streaked with reddish-pink; 3 1/2 inches in diameter. Solid, meaty, aromatic flesh, with a distinct fruity flavor. Makes excellent white tomato sauce. Productive, indeterminate vine with potato-like foliage. U33

White Princess: 100 days. White beefsteak type. Large, flattened, ribbed, ivory-white fruit; 4 inches in diameter. Solid, meaty flesh, high in sugar, mild but flavorful, contains few seeds. Large, productive, indeterminate vine; requires staking. Has sparse foliage cover. U33

White Wonder: 85 days. Medium-sized, flattened, irregular, creamy white fruit with a large blossom scar; 2 1/2 inches in diameter; weight 4 to 8 ounces; susceptible to cracking. Very firm, sweet, white flesh, has a high sugar content. Excellent for slicing. Prolific, indeterminate vine with heavy foliage cover. Attractive and unusual as well as useful. G16, M1

TURNIP {S}

BRASSICA RAPA RAPIFERA GROUP

ROOT TURNIPS

Grown primarily for their roots, they also produce edible leaves, however these are generally not of the same quality as those of the foliage turnips.

BLACK-SKINNED

Longue de Caluire:[1] 55 days. An elongated French turnip that has black outer skin, making it less prone to insect attack. The white flesh is buttery, smooth and sweet. Also produces tasty *turnip greens*. K49M

GREEN-TOPPED

Green Globe: Medium sized, globe-shaped root; very white below, green above ground; flesh pure-white, firm in texture. Becomes spongy and often decays in autumn or early winter. Tops make very good greens. Vigorous growing, hardy plant; produces very heavy crops. Introduced before 1865. BURR; D47M, S59M, S61

Green Top Stone: Globe-shaped roots, green on top, white on the lower part; flesh firm and tender; flavor good, mild. Keeps well. Very hardy; suitable for September sowing and spring harvesting in mild-winter areas. P83M, *R23*, *S75M*

Gros Longue d'Alsace:[1] (Green Tankard) 60 days. Large, succulent, carrot-shaped roots, half-projecting above ground; 12 to 14 inches long, 3 inches in diameter; green above ground, white below. Flesh white, tender and rather juicy. Grown mainly for feeding cattle, however, if pulled while young and tender it is a very good table vegetable. Very old French cultivar. BURR, VILMORIN; E83T, I39

PURPLE-TOPPED

Auvergne: Top-shaped, purple-topped root, 5 inches in diameter. Good as a cooked vegetable at any size. Very hardy, storage turnip usually grown as a fodder crop in Europe. Often survives winter to produce spring *turnip greens* while other cultivars perish. E83T

De Milan:[2] (De Milan Rouge) 35 days. Small to medium-sized, quite smooth, very flat root; pure white on the underground part, and of a lively violet-red color on the upper part. Leaves entire, erect, very short, few in comparison with the size of the root. Very rapid-growing; well adapted for forcing, even in spring. Can be picked young as "baby turnips". Known prior to 1885. VILMORIN; G68, K66

De Nancy: (Rouge de Nancy) 42 days. An attractive form of the Early Flat Purple-Top turnip, remarkable for its earliness, the regularity of its shape, and the very deep color of the upper part of the root. Globe-shaped with deep-violet necks and creamy white bottoms. Creamy flesh, sweet and mild. Pick when young and tender. Known prior to 1885. K66, S95M

Hinona:[1 3] (Aka-Na) 40 days. Long, tapered root; 7 to 8 inches in length, 3/4 of an inch wide; upper one-third above the soil surface colored purple, underground part pure white. Leaves upright, lobed, reddish-purple. A favorite delicacy in Japan, pickled to remove the harshness and served as a garnish. E83T, *P39*

Milan Early Red Top:[2] A quick-forming white globe, topped with rosy red. Successfully grown as a baby vegetable, and a nice change from the standard purple topped turnips. Q34

Purple Top Milan: (Early Purple Top Milan) 35-40 days. Bulb very flat, of medium size, quite smooth, white with a bright purple top. Leaves few, short and of light color, growing very compact and making an exceedingly small and neat top. The pure white flesh is of choice quality, hard, solid and fine-grained. An excellent keeper; keeps all winter. Introduced prior to 1888. BURPEE; C44, E83T, S61

Purple Top Strap Leaved: 50 days. Bulb medium-sized, very flat, smooth, produced almost entirely above ground; skin above clear bright purple, below pure white; flesh clear white, firm, solid, sugary, mild and well-flavored. Early; hardy; very prolific. Traditionally used for New Year's dinner, served lightly mashed with butter and cream. Introduced before 1865. BURR; F25, G79, H66, *I59M*, K27M, L7M, *L59G*, L97

Purple Top White Globe: (Early Purple Top White Globe) 55 days. Smooth, globular root; bright purplish-red above ground, white below; becoming 5 to 6 inches in diameter. Flesh white, firm, fine grained and tender when young. Tops medium, compact, cut-leaved; can be used for greens. Standard home, market garden, and shipping cultivar. Introduced prior to 1895. A16, B73M, B75M, B78, C44, E24, E57, G6, G16, *H61*, H66, H94, L7M, M13M, M49, etc.

Red Tankard:[1] (Herbst Rube, Navet Rose du Palatinat) Long, cylindrical root; 8 or 9 inches in length, 4 or 5 inches in diameter; weight about 3 pounds; skin purple or violet-tinted red above ground, white below; flesh firm, sugary, well-flavored. Early and productive. Generally considered a field turnip, but may be used for the table when young. BURR, VILMORIN; G68

Red-Top Strap-Leaved American Stone: (Rouge Plat Hâtif à Feuille Entière) Uniform, very flat root; skin reddish-purple where exposed to light, white below the soil; flesh very white, close-grained, sugary. Leaves entire, not lobed at the base. Very suitable for frame culture. Slower to run to seed than most turnips. Introduced prior to 1885. VILMORIN; S95M

Veitch's Red Globe: Round, medium-sized roots; skin white with a red top, similar to a French Breakfast radish; white flesh. Matures quickly so it can be sown as late as July and still store well. Introduced about 1882. P83M, S61

Yellow Purple Top Aberdeen: Root spherical or slightly flattened on the top; 6 inches in diameter; yellow on the underground portion, purple on the part above ground, which is about one-third the length of the root. Flesh pale yellow, rather firm. Leaves tall, stout, dark green. VILMORIN; J7

RED-SKINNED

Beni-Maru: (Aka-Kabu) 55 days. Flat-round root, 2 1/2 inches wide and 1 1/2 inches tall; skin deep crimson; flesh of lighter red color with indistinct red stripes, fine-grained, firm, flavorful. Upright leaves with ribs and veins that are tinged with purplish-red. Winter hardy, making it adapted to fall sowing. Keeps well in the field. *P39*

Ohno Scarlet:[3] 55 days. A pale magenta skin with bright white flesh makes Ohno Scarlet an interesting addition to home gardens and an excellent specialty market item. Cook like beets (without peeling). Delicious pickled, the skin tinting the flesh a pleasant rose color. Tall, dark green, red-veined tops are an extra attraction. G6, I77, K49M

Scarlet Ball:[3] (Round Red) Smooth, semi-globe shaped root with deep scarlet-red skin and white flesh. Attractive red stems and red-veined foliage. When cooked unpeeled the entire turnip is suffused with pink. If sliced and held overnight in pickling brine it will be bright scarlet. An old time Asian favorite. E49, E83T, I39

WHITE-SKINNED

Hybrid

Just Right: 28-60 days. A fast-growing hybrid that will produce tender, glossy greens in 28 days, and a smooth, white, flattened, globe-shaped, 5 to 6 inch diameter root in 60 days. White, tender mild flesh. A dual-purpose turnip for fresh market use in late spring and fall. All America Selections winner in 1960. A56, B73M, C92, E97, F13, F19M, G27M, G79, H33, H66, H95, J34, M29, M95M, N16, etc.

Market Express:[2] 38 days. Small, globe-shaped, pure white roots; smooth skin; sweet flesh. The perfect cultivar for "baby" turnips, bunched like radishes, but keeps its crispness and pleasant texture into the 2 to 3 inch diameter size. Dark green, hairless tops with good flavor. Very early. For specialty and ethnic markets. G6, *K16M*, K66

Tokyo Cross: 35-60 days. Semi-globe, perfect shaped, smooth, sweet crisp roots. Both skin and flesh are pure white. Can be harvested at 2 inches in diameter, but continues growing up to 6 inches, while holding the same excellent quality. Leaves can also be used for greens. Has good disease resistance. For spring and summer sowings. All America Selections winner in 1969. A16, C85M, D11M, D65, D76, F19M, *F72*, G16, G27M, G51, G71, H94, J20, J34, K71, M46, etc.

Open-Pollinated

All Seasons: 28 days. Globe-shaped, white skinned, white fleshed turnip that is ready 4 weeks after sowing regardless of the season when sown. Retains its shape long after the roots are fully formed and stays sweet even during hot and dry weather. K49M

Long Des Vertus Marteau:[1] (Jersey Navet) 55 days. Root white; nearly cylindrical, but swollen at the lower end; 5 or 6 inches long, and about 2 inches broad at the thickest part. Flesh white, very tender and sugary. Like radishes the roots become hollow at the center if allowed to grow too large, and are generally harvested for use when about two-thirds grown. Traditional market garden turnip of Paris. VILMORIN; *C28*, C53, E83T, F33, G68, S95M

Pomeranian: (Large White Globe) 70 days. Smooth, globular root, 3 1/2 to 4 inches in diameter; skin white, glossy; flesh white, tender, close-grained, sweet. Large, dark green leaves. Generally cultivated as a field turnip, but is also sown as a garden cultivar, the roots being of good quality for the table if pulled when about half grown. BURR; G57M

Presto:[3] (Tokyo Market Sagami) 30 days. Very small, smooth, uniform, pure-white turnip that can be harvested when the roots are about 1 inch in diameter and used for pickles. Leaves are suitable for use as greens. Easily grown anytime except during periods of extreme heat or cold. C92, D11M, I39, K49M, O53M, S27

Snowball: 40 days. Bulb small to medium in size, nearly spherical, smooth and uniform, 3 to 4 inches in diameter; skin pure-white. Flesh of the young bulb white, fine-grained, tender and sweet; if overgrown or stored for long, it is liable to become dry and spongy. Rapid growing. Known prior to 1865. BURR; B49, G64, G79, *G83M*, G93M, J7, J73, L91M, O53M, P83M, S45M, S61

Teltow:[1] Root entirely sunk in the ground, conical, about 3 inches long; skin grayish-white. Succeeds very well in light, sandy soil. When cooked it has a peculiar flavor, completely different from other turnips - it is milder and more sugary, and the flesh is almost floury, instead of juicy and melting. The peculiar flavor is in the outer rind, when used it should not be peeled. Used in the preparation of a German delicacy called *teltower rüebchen*, produced by browning young turnips in sugar. BURR, HEDRICK 1919, ORGAN, VILMORIN; U33

Tennoji Serrate-Leaved: 45 days. Uniform, flattened, pure white root; 3 1/2 inches wide; of excellent quality. Grows entirely above the ground like a kohlrabi, being called *floating turnip* in Japan. Leaves upright, serrate, tender. Easy to grow. Mostly cultivated as a winter crop. A specialty of Osaka, Japan. *P39*

Tokyo Market: (White Tokyo, Kanamachi Forcing) 30 days. An improvement over Kanamachi, developed for growing with plastic protection or under glass, for an early spring crop. Roots are very small, about 1 1/4 inches wide and 7/8 inch deep when at their best for early marketing. White skin. Solid, white flesh, crisp and mild-flavored. C92, D82, E49, E83T, G33, *H61*, I39, N52, *P39*

White Egg: 50 days. Medium-large, egg-shaped root with thin white skin; 3 1/2 inches long, 2 1/2 inches in diameter; keeps well. Very solid, fine-grained, clear white flesh, sweet, mild and tender. Makes attractive bunches for early market. Fast-growing. Excellent either as a late or early cultivar. Introduced before 1888. BURPEE; *A69M*, *A75*, C44, *D12*, E38, *G1M*, G27M, G67M, H66, K49M, K71, *L59G*, L97

Yorii Spring: 38 days. Small, slightly flattened pure-white roots. Sweet and crisp when about 1/2 inch in diameter. Also produces an abundance of tasty greens. Very early and slow bolting. Does well in cool, short-season areas. E24, F44

YELLOW-SKINNED

Amber Globe: (Large Yellow Globe) 60 days. Root almost round, or more usually top-shaped; pale yellow with a green neck; flesh yellow, fine-grained, sweet, tender and mild. Leaves entire, long, light-colored. Hardy and keeps well until late in the spring. Introduced before 1888. A13, C44, *D12*, E57, *G1M*, G57M, H54, H66, J34, K49M, M95M

Golden Ball: (Orange Jelly) 55 days. Root perfectly spherical when small, slightly flattened when mature; generally 4 or 5 inches in diameter. Skin very smooth and quite yellow. Flesh yellow, softish, fine flavored but slightly bitter. Highly esteemed in Scotland and northern England. Introduced before 1859. VILMORIN; A2, A16, A69M, B49, C85M, D11M, D27, E38, E59Z, F92, G64, I39, I77, J7, K20, P83M, etc.

FOLIAGE TURNIPS

Also called *turnip greens* and *turnip tops*, these are grown primarily for the leaves which are more succulent than those of other turnips. Some cultivars also produce good quality roots or can be used for *broccoli raab*. The best types have leaves which grow rapidly, and resprout quickly after having been cut. SCHNEIDER [Cul, Re].

HYBRID

All Top: 35 days. Vigorous, erect, fast-growing hybrid Crawford type that is especially good for greens. Produces large, smooth, thick, strap-shaped, dark green leaves of very high quality. Regrows very quickly after being harvested. Bolt resistant. Very fibrous roots are not used. Introduced in 1979 by Abbott and Cobb. *A1*, A87M, *C28*, F19M, I91, J84, *K16M*, M29

Topper: 35 days. Very heavy-yielding Shogoin type. Vigorous, upright tops, 24 to 28 inches tall. Thick, smooth, lobed, broad dark-green leaves. For greens, bunching, processing and fresh market. Resistant to turnip mosaic virus. Tolerant to aphids and downy mildew. *A1*, *C28*, *K16M*, M29

OPEN-POLLINATED

Crawford: 50 days. Developed by the University of Arkansas especially for its fine greens. Has very tasty, strap shaped, dark-green leaves that are downy mildew tolerant. Produces small roots that are seldom used. Recommended for planting throughout the South. *C28*, F19M, *G1M*, H66

Namenia: Used for greens only. Fine deeply-cut, light green leaves of good flavor. Can be eaten raw or cooked like spinach. Very fast grower. If cut young, will readily grow back for later cuttings. Readily self seeds. Harbors cabbage root maggot. U33

Nozawa-Na: (Hakabu-Na) Long, dark-green leaves and petioles. Similar to Tennoji Serrate-Leaved but does not produce a usable root. Used both as a fresh green vegetable and for pickling. Vigorous, erect, fast growing plant; tolerant of heat and cold. TANAKA; G20M{PR}, *S70*

Seven Top: (Southern Prize) Fast-growing, cool-weather crop that is grown primarily for its abundant crop of greens. Grows 20 to 22 inches tall. Produces large, dark-green, very tender leaves. Can also be used for *broccoli raab*. Roots are tough and fibrous and are best used for livestock food. Very popular cultivar in the southern United States where it is used as a winter annual. *A75*, B35M, C44, E38, F19M, *G1M*, G71, G93M, *H61*, H66, K71, K73, L7M, N16, N39, etc.

Shogoin: 30-70 days. Excellent dual-purpose cultivar grown both for tops and large roots. Very large tops with broad, serrated, tender leaves, resistant to aphid damage. Smooth, white, globe-shaped roots grow 5 to 6 inches in diameter and have tender, white flesh. Yields greens in 30 days; roots in 70 days. *A75*, C92, F12, F19M, G51, G68, H66, I39, J34, J73, K71, L89, M46, M95, N16, etc.

Turnip Tops Green: Smooth, green leaves with a distinctive taste. Grown for quick early cooking greens in spring. Cut at 6 inch stage, and they will grow back for later cuttings. Cook like spinach. C85M

UNCLASSIFIED {S}

VARIOUS GENERA

Included here are entries that cannot be placed in the Botanical listings or under a cultivar heading, due to the incomplete nature of the descriptions given in the catalogs.

Gallito del Rio: (Little Rooster of the River) The green pods are roasted in embers and the white, flour-like substance between the immature seeds is eaten. The seeds themselves are not eaten. A large, leguminous vine to 30 or 40 feet, with almost white stems and large, smooth, glossy trifoliate leaves. Rises from a long, thick fleshy root which could probably be overwintered indoors in harsh climates. Fragrant violet-rose flowers look like little roosters. F80

German Greens: 60 days. Dark-green, lightly ribbed, smooth leaves; 8 to 10 inches in diameter. Can be eaten raw or cooked. Grows to a height of 5 feet. Pick leaves early and growth will continue, with yields through fall. Disease, drought and insect resistant. I99

Haitian Greens: Bushy plants with dark-green leaves; likes warm weather; would probably mature in 45 to 60 days from transplants. Later has racemes of tiny white flowers followed by red-orange fruits containing one seed. Dropped by U33

Hualpoy: (Chicken Eye) Large pod, resembles a rounded fava bean pod. Round seed, requires peeling of outer skin before consumption, resembles a garbanzo after being peeled. Used as a green shell bean, cooked in soup with onion and black pepper. Laborious to prepare. Large, perennial vine; probably very day-length sensitive; only bears in October and November. From Veracruz, Mexico. U33

Monk's Beard: Very peculiar vegetable with thread-like leaves, long, skinny and succulent. Cook tender stem tips of leaf, changing water once. Has a pasta-like texture. A delicacy in Italy. U33

Mrs. Hawkin's Spinach: Planted early, and weekly after that, the large plants produce tender leaves, large enough to use as wrappers for cabbage rolls. Originally from Australia, but not New Zealand spinach. Related to wild lamb's quarters. Does well in greenhouses or cold frames. C82

Schwarzwurzein: European black root vegetable grown exactly like parsnips or salsify. According to the supplier, "this is not black salsify". C82

WALNUT {GR}

JUGLANS REGIA

PERSIAN WALNUTS

Included here are cultivars primarily grown in California. They are not tolerant to extremely low winter temperatures. When fully dormant, they will withstand 12^0 to 15^0 F. without serious injury. The French cultivars are somewhat more hardy. JAYNES.

Amigo: Large, round nut; shell poorly sealed in some years; kernel 54% of nut, quality high, 80% having light-colored kernels; matures early to midseason. Tree productive, with many clusters of 4 nuts and 80% of lateral buds producing pistillate flowers. Leafs out 14 days after Payne making it a valuable pollinizer for Hartley and Tehama. BROOKS 1972; *A9, B71M*

Ashley: Large, ovoid nut; shell seal fair but adequate; large, plump, light tan kernel, averages 54% of nut, flavor good, quality high; ripens early; resembles Payne. Tree small; early bearing; extremely heavy yielding, with fruitfulness on lateral buds 90% or more. Leafs out early, 4 days after Payne. Chilling requirement medium. BROOKS 1972; *A9, B71M, K73M*

Carmelo: Open-pollinated seedling of Payne. Very large nut; shell well-filled with a kernel of good quality; ripens about with Payne. Not susceptible to blight or sunburn. Tree precocious; productive; leafs out late. Has a lateral growth habit similar to Payne. An excellent home garden and novelty cultivar. BROOKS 1972; *C54*, E4, *N20*

Chandler: Large nut; kernel 49% of nut, kernel color very good; ripens in midseason, a few days after Hartley. Tree moderately vigorous, semi-upright, similar to Vina in characteristics; leafs out 18 days after Payne. Has high fruitfulness with 80 to 90% of lateral buds being fruitful. Pollinate with Hartley and Franquette. Most promising of introductions released by the University of California breeding program. A88M, *B71M, C54, D18*, E4, F11, *K73M*, L1, *N20*

Chico: Nut round; shell seal fair to good; kernel 49% of nut, quality excellent, 90% having light-colored kernels; matures early to midseason. Tree leafs out 6 days after Payne, with 80% of lateral buds producing pistillate flowers. Sheds pollen late, making it a suitable pollinizer for early leafing cultivars such as Ashley, Serr, and Vina. BROOKS 1972; *A9, B71M, K73M, N20*

Eureka: Large, attractive nut, perfectly sealed; kernel light-colored, of excellent quality. Large, vigorous tree; a good producer but slow to come into bearing. Leafs out in midseason, making it moderately susceptible to spring frost damage. Pollinate with Chico. An old California cultivar, available from nurseries since 1911; now being superseded in commercial plantings by cultivars with better yield and nut quality. JAYNES, STEBBINS, WICKSON; *A9, B71M*, B93M, *C54, D18, K73M, L47, N20*

Franquette: Medium to large nut with a well-sealed thin shell; of very good flavor; resists codling moth. Large tree, suitable as a shade tree; partially self-fruitful but has relatively low yields and lacks lateral-bud fruitfulness. Very late leafing; not susceptible to spring frost damage. Slow to come into bearing, but long-lived. Pollinize with Hartley or Chandler. An old French cultivar. Was the most important commercial cultivar in northern California until 1960. JAYNES, STEBBINS; *A9*, A88M, B67, C34, *C54, D18*, E4, F11, I49M, J61M, L1, *L47*, L97, L99M, *N20*, etc.

Hartley: Large nut with a broad, flat base and pointed tip; shell light-colored, thin, seals fairly well; kernel light-colored, not tight in shell; flavor mild. Tree medium leafing, 2 weeks after Payne; very productive but comes into production slower than cultivars with lateral bud fruitfulness. One of the leading commercial cultivars in California, especially for in-shell nuts. BROOKS 1972, JAYNES; *A9*, A88M, B23M{PR}, *B71M*, B93M, *C54, D18*, E4, *K73M, L47, N20*

Howard: Large nut; kernel 50% of nut; kernel color excellent; ripens in midseason, slightly ahead of Hartley. Leafing date quite late, 14 days after Payne. Tree small to medium, semi-upright, moderately vigorous; smaller than Vina and Chandler. Potentially very productive with 80 to 90% of lateral buds being fruitful. Pollinate with Hartley and Franquette. *B71M*, E4

Mayette: Medium to large, rounded nut, with a broad base on which the nut will sit up; shell fairly thin, white; kernel well-filled, richly flavored. Tree medium-sized, spreading; a good bearer; blooms late; moderately precocious, but tends to be biennial. Originated in France. M83

Payne:[1] Medium to small nut; kernel averages 49% of nut with fair color; matures in midseason. Nuts tend to be borne on the outside of the tree and consequently are susceptible to sunburn. Early leafing and therefore quite susceptible to spring frosts and walnut blight. Leafing date of late March in the Central Valley of California is the standard by which other cultivars are compared. Small to medium tree with heavy production. The first important cultivar in California with lateral-bud fruitfulness. JAYNES, STEBBINS; *A9, B71M, C54, D18, K73M, N20*

Pedro: Large nut; shell heavy, fairly well-sealed; kernel light-colored, 50% of nut; flavor excellent; matures midseason to late. Tree small; consistently produces many catkins and sheds pollen over a long period. Can be used as a pollinizer for most early cultivars such as Ashley, Serr and Vina. Very high summer temperatures can injure shell and kernel quality in hotter districts. Excellent for home plantings. BROOKS 1972; A88M, *N20*

Placentia:[1] Medium-sized nut; smooth, thin, strong shell; light tan meat that fills shell; quality good; ripens in midseason. Tree large; heavy bearing; precocious; partially self-fruitful. Early leafing and therefore susceptible to spring frosts. Low chilling requirements; does best in coastal areas and southern California. STEBBINS; *C54, D23M*, I83M

Scharsch Franquette: Medium-sized, well sealed nut; high percentage of light-colored kernels; ripens late, otherwise resembles Franquette. Tree starts bearing both pistillate and staminate flowers earlier in life than Franquette, with approximately 20% of lateral buds producing pistillate flowers. Otherwise, growth characteristics similar to typical Franquette. BROOKS 1972; *B71M, K73M*

Serr: Nut large, similar to Payne; shell thin, seal fair to good; cracking quality good, 96% having light-colored kernels; matures early to midseason. Highly resistant to sunburn. Tree very vigorous when young, grows rapidly; leafs out 5 days after Payne. Only 50% of lateral buds produce pistillate flowers. Early leafing, with moderate danger of spring frost damage. BROOKS 1972; *A9, B71M*, B93M, *C54, D18*, H26M{PR}, *K73M, N20*

Tehama: Nut similar to Payne; shell seal good, making it suitable for in-shell nuts and cracking; kernel 53% of nut, 70% having light-colored kernels; matures in midseason. Tree very productive, with 80% of lateral buds producing pistillate flowers. Leafs out 18 days after Payne. A pollinizer is desirable to help set heavy crops. BROOKS 1972; *A9, B71M, D18, K73M*

Vina: Nut pointed, somewhat similar in shape to Hartley but with a less flattened base; shell seal good; kernel 49% of nut, of high quality, 70% having light-colored kernels; matures early to midseason. Tree a very productive and consistent bearer, with 80% of lateral buds producing pistillate flowers. Leafs out 8 days after Payne. Tolerant of high summer temperatures. BROOKS 1972; *A9, B71M, D18, K73M*

Waterloo: Large, well-filled nut; of good quality and color; matures 1 week later than Eureka. Tree a good producer; leafs out 2 weeks later than Eureka. One of the parents of Tehama. Originated in Stockton, California. BROOKS 1972; *D18, D18*{PL}

CARPATHIAN WALNUTS

Included here are cultivars originating form seed brought form the Carpathian mountains of Poland by Reverend Paul C. Crath and other cold-hardy cultivars, including those brought by German immigrants to Pennsylvania and other states in the 1700's. When fully dormant, they can withstand temperatures of -30^{0} to -35^{0} F. with only minor injury. JAYNES. (J. regia 'Carpathian')

Ambassador: Very cold-hardy, has withstood extreme cold temperatures in Idaho. Produces high quality, thin-shelled, well-sealed nuts. Easy to harvest. Bears very young, often in the first year, with significant crops in 3 years. Good resistance to blight and codling moth; not drought resistant. Grows best on fertile, deep soils. E87, F11, *N20*

Ashworth: Nut rather small, well-shaped; kernel sweet; ripens early. Tree strong, vigorous; very hardy, withstanding temperatures of -36^{0} F. Seeds germinate well. Originated in Heuvelton, New York by Fred L. Ashworth, St. Lawrence Nurseries. Introduced in 1948. BROOKS 1972; E91M{OR}, E91M{PL}, I40{OR}, N24M

Broadview: Large to medium nut; shell soft, well-sealed; cracking quality good; ripens slightly little before Franquette, beginning in early September; keeps well. Tree very productive, lateral bearing; very hardy. Originated in Westbank, British Columbia, Canada by J.U. Gellatly. Introduced in 1930. Seed brought from the ancestral home of the Utki family in Odessa, Russia. BROOKS 1972; C37, E62{PL}, E62{PR}, E62{S}, E91M, E91M{OR}, E91M{PL}, I40, N15

Cascade: Very heavy bearing Russian x Manregian cross. Nut large; shell thin; kernel averages 56% of nut, cracks to halves, has excellent flavor. Tree spreading; very winter-hardy; early bearing. Chambers recommended as a pollinator. Widely planted in the Pacific Northwest. Rated #1 in 1983 Northern Nut Growers Association evaluations. E91M{OR}, H81M, I40

Chambers: Heavy yielding Manregian stock selection from Oregon. Medium large, high quality nuts. Precocious and vigorous growing; hardy. Leafs out 10 days before Franquette or Spurgeon. Highly regarded cultivar for the Pacific Northwest. B74, C34, I49M, J61M

Chopaka: Parent of Cascade. Quality nearly as good but the tree is hardier. Nuts average 20 per pound. Tree upright in form; hardy; precocious; sets nuts in clusters of up to 6 nuts. Has a tendency toward heavy lateral bearing. A91{PL}, H81M

Colby: Medium-sized nut; shell thin, well-sealed; kernel plump, of good flavor, represents 53% of nut; matures early. Tree hardy and fruitful in central Illinois. Probably best adapted to areas north of the Ohio River. Originated in Urbana, Illinois by A.S. Colby, Illinois Agricultural Experiment Station. Introduced in 1952. BROOKS 1972; E91M, E91M{OR}, I40

Fateley: Nut very large; shell rough; kernel quality good. Tree very hardy; vigorous; bears well. Originated in Franklin, Indiana by Nolan W. Fateley. Introduced in 1956 by J.F. Wilkinson, Indiana Nut Nursery. BROOKS 1972; I40{OR}, N15, N33

Fickes: Round, slightly above average, free husking nut; shell very thin, not well sealed; kernel white, very sweet, represents 51% of nut; ripens early. Tree comes into bearing early; prolific; easy to graft. Originated in Wooster, Ohio by W.R. Fickes. Introduced in 1951. BROOKS 1972; E41M{SC}, I40{OR}

Gratiot: Nut averages 12.4 grams in weight; kernel light colored, averages 50.5% of nut; flavor sweet, oil content 65.2%; ripens in midseason, usually late September. Tree bears annually. Originated in Perrington, Michigan by Lee Somers. Ranked second in the 1959 contest of the Michigan Nut Growers Association. BROOKS 1972; K16

Greenhaven: Nut averages 12.73 grams; kernel color light, flavor sweet, oil content 61%, averages 45.8% of nut; ripens in midseason, usually late in September. Tree a consistent annual bearer. Originated in Perrington, Michigan by Lee Somers at Greenhaven Farm. Introduced in 1962. BROOKS 1972; E91M, E91M{OR}

Hansen: Small to medium-sized, round nut; shell very thin, smooth; flavor mild, sweet, good; kernel 60% of nut. Tree small, essentially dwarf; very productive; self-fruitful; hardy; resistant to disease and husk maggot. Bears young and continues with early ripening crops. Of German origin, it was selected in Ohio. The most widely planted winter-hardy cultivar. BROOKS 1972, JAYNES; A91{PL}, B99{PL}, E41M{SC}, E91M, E91M{OR}, E91M{PL}, I40, I60{PL}, K16, K16{PL}, N15, N24M

Helmle: (Helmle #2) Nut small to medium in size, of good quality. Tree very hardy; very productive; slightly later vegetating than most. A good pollinator for most other Carpathian cultivars. Originated in Breckenridge, Illinois by Herman C. Helmle. Introduced in 1954. BROOKS 1972, JAYNES; E41M{SC}, I40

Henry: Nut medium to large; shell sometimes does not seal well; kernel of very good quality. Tree fairly productive. Open-pollinated seedling of Lake. Originated in Bluffs, Illinois by Royal Oakes. Introduced in 1955. BROOKS 1972; E41M{SC}

Himalaya: Medium to large, slightly oval nut; shell thin; kernel of good quality except when there is a cool summer; ripens in September. Tree upright, slightly spreading; vigorous; productive; not injured by temperatures of -42^{0} F. Originated in Kalispell, Montana. Introduced in 1968 by David A. Lawyer, Lawyer Nursery, Plains, Montana. BROOKS 1972; E91M, E91M{OR}, N24M

Holton: Medium-sized, round nut; well sealed; flavor very good; quality excellent; can be stored for up to 2 years. Hardy, vigorous tree. Broadview x Hansen. Introduced by Elwood Holton, past-president of the Minnesota Nut Growers Association. K16{PL}

Idaho: Very large, sweet, excellent eating nut with good quality. Ripens in late September. Tree vigorous; an early and heavy producer; very hardy, withstands extreme cold. *C54*, E4, I15{S}, *L47, N20*

Kentucky Giant: Nut very large; shell thin; flavor good; matures early. Tree blooms late; comes into bearing early, at about 6 years of age; tolerant of low winter temperatures. Bears heavily when well pollinated. Originated in Jefferson County, Kentucky by H.B. Briggs. Introduced in 1956. BROOKS 1972; I40

Korn: Nut averages 29 to 32 per pound; apex pointed, slightly longer than wide; shell quite thin, cracking quality fair to good; kernel bright, very plump, quite sweet, flavor mild; ripens early. Tree vigorous; bears annually. Originated in Berrien Springs, Michigan. Introduced in 1928. BROOKS 1972; E91M, E91M{OR}, I40

Lake: Nut large; shell thin, easy to crack; kernel 50% of nut; quality very good; ripens in mid-season. Tree hardy, productive, starts bearing at an early age. Originated in Bluffs, Illinois by Royal Oakes.

Introduced about 1954. BROOKS 1972, JAYNES; E41M{SC}, E91M, E91M{OR}, I40, L33

Manregian: Large, round nut; shell thin but rather hard, with a grayish cast; kernel dark in color, of excellent quality. Tree very hardy. Also used as a rootstock. Originated in Chico, California. Introduced in 1954. Seedling of a walnut collected in 1906 in the mountains north of Peiping, China by noted plant explorer Frank N. Meyer. BROOKS 1972; B74{PL}, *G14*, M39M{PL}, N0{PL}

McDermid: Large nut; shell rather thick, smooth, apex pointed; kernel sometimes astringent, in other districts kernel quality very good. Tree a vigorous grower. Usually never bears heavily being susceptible to late spring frosts; but in other locations, it bears well and appears to be hardy. Originated in Ontario, Canada. BROOKS 1972; I40{OR}

McKinster: Nut large; kernel 48% of nut; flavor and quality high. Tree very productive; self-pollinating; well adapted to the climate of Ohio and Michigan. Subject to "June drop". Originated in Columbus, Ohio by Ray McKinster. Introduced in 1952. BROOKS 1972, JAYNES; E41M{SC}, I40{OR}, K16{OR}, N15

Merkel: Medium to large nut, resembles the French cultivar Mayette; shell thin; kernel averages 53% of nut; ripens in mid-September. Tree susceptible to husk maggot. Produces a yearly crop that averages 36 pounds of nuts. Originated in Chelsea, Michigan by Henry Merkel. Introduced in 1964. BROOKS 1972; E41M{SC}

Mesa: New Carpathian type from New Mexico. Large, well-sealed nut, resistant to sunburn; thin shell; plump, light-colored kernels of good flavor; ripens in early October. Self-fruitful tree; blooms late; requires 700 hours of winter chilling. Withstands cold as well as hot, dry climatic conditions. *N20*

Metcalfe: Medium-sized nut, averages 42 to 45 per pound; shell thin, light amber; kernel 53% of nut, white, sweet, of very good quality. Tree very vigorous; hardy to -20^0 F; does not bear well. Originated in Webster, New York by Mrs. Ward H. Metcalfe. Introduced in 1952. BROOKS 1972, JAYNES; E91M, E91M{OR}, I40{OR}

Russian: The Russian walnut came to southern British Columbia, Canada with Russian Doukhobor immigrants. These seedlings are crosses of the Russian parent and large-fruited cultivars from a nut breeder's orchard. Used as a hardy nut producer or as a rootstock. A91{PL}

Schafer: Large nut; shell thin, tightly sealed; kernel percentage high; kernel of very fine quality, oily and rich; matures in a short growing season, in early fall. Tree vigorous; tall, spreading; extremely hardy; bears annually and abundantly. Originated in Yakima, Washington by Wilhelm Schafer. Introduced in 1940. BROOKS 1972; I40{OR}

Somers: Nut medium-sized, averages 11.6 grams; slightly elongated, flattened on both ends; shell attractive, cracks easily; kernel color light, averages 55.6% of nut, oil content averages 64.7%; flavor sweet, pecan-like. Ripens in early September, being noted for its early maturity. Tree a consistent annual bearer; hardy to -34^0 F. BROOKS 1972; I40, K16{OR}

Spurgeon: Large nut; shell very thin, with a good seal; kernel light brown, flavor good; matures late. Tree moderately productive; partially self-fruitful, but production can be improved by planting Franquette as a pollinizer. Late leafing, with no danger of spring frost damage. Originated in Vancouver, Washington by John F. Spurgeon. Introduced about 1920. Considered to be a seedling of Franquette. BROOKS 1972, STEBBINS; C34, I49M, J61M

WATERMELON {S}

CITRULLUS LANATUS

RED-FLESHED

HYBRID

Seeded

Flight Light:[4] 75 days. Short oblong fruit; averages about 6 1/2 pounds in weight. Unusual, attractive golden-yellow rind, thin and tough. Tender, juicy, sweet red flesh. Uniform, early and productive. Ships well. *Q39*

Funbell:[1 4] 65 days. Unusual, extra early "icebox" type. Small, round fruit; weight about 4 1/2 pounds; attractive, light yellow rind with light green stripes; sweet, juicy, pink-red flesh. When the green stripes change from green to yellow the fruit is ripe. Widely adapted to various types of soils. Excellent for home gardens. *Q39*

Garden Baby:[1 2] 70 days. An early, short-vined watermelon with good flavor. Round fruit, 6 to 7 inches in diameter; "icebox" size, averaging 6 to 8 pounds; dark-green rind with faint striping; juicy, crisp, sweet red flesh. Seeds very small. Ripens even earlier than Sugar Baby. Prolific vine, 3 to 4 feet long; good for gardens with limited space. C85M, D65, *E53M*, *E91G*, F19M, G6, G79, G82, H42, J20, J58, K10, L97, *M43M*, M46, etc.

Kily Edible Seeded:[3] (Wanli) 80 days. Grown for its large, plump black seeds. Delicious eaten like squash seed, dried or roasted. Very vigorous plant; bears 5 to 6 globe-shaped fruits, each capable of producing 400 seeds or more. Disease resistant. E49, I99, *Q39*

Red Luck:[3] 80 days. Produces large, plump red seeds for roasting and table use. Round, dark-green fruit contains about 400 seeds. Seed count is about 5,000 seeds per kilo. An early setter and a heavy yielder. Vines and leaves are small which allows for close spacing. *Q39*

Red Shine:[3] 80 days. Round fruit with black rind; weight about 5 1/2 pounds. Large red seeds, good for roasting and table use. Seed count is about 5,000 seeds per kilo. Vigorous, widely adapted vine; tolerant to diseases; suitable for close spacing due to its small leaves. *Q39*

Rugger Ball:[1] An extra small "icebox" type. Oblong fruit, weighing only 2 1/4 to 3 1/4 pounds; green rind with dark-green stripes; very sweet, pinkish-red flesh of fine quality. Very small seeds. Bears as many as 10 fruits per plant. Suitable for home gardens. Does well in areas with a very short growing season. Q88

Sun Torna:[1 4] (Sun, Sun God) 68-70 days. An unusual, yellow-rinded "icebox" watermelon. Round, medium-sized fruit; average weight 6 1/2 to 11 pounds; rind light yellow with darker yellow stripes; flesh red, juicy and sweet. Ripens extremely early. For indoor and outdoor cropping. B1M, I77, *R11M*

Sweet Favorite: 80 days. One of the best oblong watermelons for cool, northern areas. Average fruit weighs about 15 pounds; rind bright green with darker stripes; flesh bright scarlet, sweet, of high quality. Small seeds. Ripens much earlier than other oblong cultivars, just after Sugar Baby. Vigorous vine; tolerant to anthracnose and fusarium. All America Selections winner in 1978. *A1*, B75, C44, C85M, D11M, F19M, G6, *G13M*, G16, G64, H95, I67M, J7, L42, M29, etc.

Seedless

Fummy: 90 days. Triploid or "seedless" type. Round fruit, weighs 12 to 14 pounds; thick, tough rind, green with medium-wide dark green stripes; deep-red, crisp, juicy, sweet flesh. Large, vigorous vine; tolerant to anthracnose and fusarium. Diploid pollinator required for fruit set. For fresh market, home gardens and shipping. *A1*, M29

Jack of Hearts: 80 days. An early maturing "seedless" watermelon. Round oval fruit, weighs 10 to 15 pounds; bright green rind with dark green stripes; bright-red, crisp, very sweet flesh, sugar content 10 to 11%, contains very few immature seed coats. Highly disease resistant. Pollinator needed for fruit to set. Plant 2 hills of seedless cultivar to 1 hill of pollinator for best results. *A1*, A13, A87M, C92, D76, E97, *F63*, G71, G82, H33, *H61*, H95, I39, J34, L42, etc.

King of Hearts: 80-85 days. Blocky, slightly oblong fruit; weight 14 to 18 pounds; thick green rind with medium green stripes; firm, medium-textured, bright red flesh, crisp, sweet and delicious. Vigorous, medium-sized plant gives good foliage cover to the fruit. *A1*, A13, A87M, *F63*, H49, *H61*, J84, K10, K73, N52

Nova: 90 days. High-quality "seedless" watermelon that also keeps well. Round fruit, weighs 15 to 17 pounds; rind thick and tough, withstand shipping well, deep green with darker green stripes. Medium firm, deep rosy-red flesh, juicy, of good flavor, has a consistently high sugar content. Vigorous, productive vine. Pollinator required. *A1*, G82, K10, M29

Queen of Hearts: 80-85 days. Triploid or "seedless" type. Oval-shaped fruit, weighs 12 to 16 pounds; rind light green with dark green stripes, thick, resists bruising; flesh bright red, crisp, very sweet. Suitable for shipping. As with all seedless watermelons, environmental conditions may cause partially seeded fruit. *A1*, A13, A87M, *F63*, *G1M*, *G13M*, *H61*, J58, K10

Redball: 80 days. Triploid or "seedless" type. Round to slightly oval fruit, about 8 1/2 to 9 1/2 inches in diameter; weighs 10 to 12 pounds; rind dark green; flesh bright red, firm, very sweet, seedless except for a few immature seed coats. Vigorous, productive vine. Includes seeds of Crimson Sweet to be used as a pollinator. B75

<u>OPEN-POLLINATED</u>

Allsweet: 95 days. Crimson Sweet type. Oblong fruit, 18 inches long, weighs 25 to 30 pounds; medium-green rind with light-green broken stripes, thin, hard, tough; flesh bright red, firm, sweet. Small seeds. Has a longer shelf life than Crimson Sweet, Charleston Gray or Jubilee. Resistant to fusarium wilt and anthracnose races 1 and 3. A32, A87M, B75M, E97, *F60*, *G1M*, G71, G79, *H61*, J34, J84, *L59G*, L79M, M29, N16, etc.

Black Diamond: (Black Cannonball, Florida Giant) 90 days. Large oval fruit, about 15 inches long, weighs 40 to 50 pounds; rind smooth, tough, glossy, dark gray-green; flesh bright red, crisp, tender, sweet, of excellent quality; grayish-black seed. Popular shipping melon in the South. A87M, B73M, B75M, D65, D76, *F60*, *F72*, G16, *H61*, K71, L79M, M46, M95, N16, N39, etc.

Bush Charleston Gray:[2] 90 days. Similar to Charleston Gray, except for the smaller size of the fruit and vine. Oblong fruit, weighs 10 to 13 pounds; rind gray-green; flesh deep red, fine-textured, sugar content high. Short-vined plant, only 3 to 5 feet across; disease resistant. Ideal for small gardens. *A1*, *F72*, G57M, G79, H33, I64, I91, K10, M29

Calsweet: 90 days. A very popular shipping melon in the Southwest, especially California. Blocky-oblong fruit, about 17 inches long, weighs between 25 and 30 pounds; rind light green with dark green stripes; flesh bright red, sweet. Seeds medium-sized, brown. Resistant to fusarium wilt. *A1*, *F60*, G93M, *H61*, M29, N16, N52

Carolina Cross: Long, light green fruit with darker green stripes; red flesh. Has produced the last 6 world record watermelons. Seed was selected from melons weighing 260, 226, 220, 200, 188, 185, and 181 pounds. These seed melons were chosen for size and shape. Germinates poorly in soil temperatures below 85^{0} F. E43M, I81

Charleston Gray: 85 days. Large cylindrical fruit, 24 inches long, weighs 30 to 35 pounds; rind thin, tough, light greenish-gray; flesh red, crisp, free of fiber, quality excellent. Vigorous, productive vine; resists sunburn, wilt and anthracnose. Standard shipping cultivar for the Mid-Atlantic states. B75M, C92, D76, F19M, *F60*, G51, G71, H66, J34, K5M, K71, L42, M46, N39

Chilian Black Seeded: 90 days. Nearly round fruit, about 10 inches long, weighs 12 to 16 pounds; rind thick, tough, medium green striped with dark green; flesh sparkling red, very sweet, delicious. Seeds large, almost black. Attractive market melon of very fine quality. *L59G*

Cole's Early: (Harris Earliest) 80 days. Broad-oval fruit, 10 1/2 inches long, weighs 15 to 20 pounds; rind thin and tender, dark green with light green stripes; flesh light red, sweet, of good quality. Medium-sized, black seeds. Early home garden and local market cultivar. Popular in the northern United States. A2

Congo: 90 days. Large cylindrical fruit, 27 inches long, weighs 35 to 40 pounds; rind very tough, dark green with darker green stripes; flesh deep red, very firm, medium-grained, has a high sugar content. Seeds white to light tan. Very good shipper, but not immune to bruising. Resistant to anthracnose; susceptible to downy mildew and fusarium wilt. All America Selections winner in 1950. B75M, C92, E97, F19M, *F60*, *F72*, G57M, G79, H54, H66, K49M, K71, L14, N16

Crimson Sweet: 85 days. Fruit round to slightly elongated, 12 inches long, weighs 25 to 30 pounds; rind thick, hard, tough, light green with darker green stripes; flesh bright red, very sweet, of fine texture. Seeds medium-sized, brown. Vine vigorous and productive; widely adapted; resistant to anthracnose and wilt. Excellent for fresh market and home garden use. B49, B73M, B75M, F19M, *F60*, *F72*, F82, G16, G71, *H61*, H66, K73, L7M, L79M, N16, etc.

Dixie Queen: 80 days. Attractive, blocky oval fruit; 13 inches long, weighs 25 to 35 pounds; rind very light green with narrow, dark green stripes; flesh deep red, very sweet, free from fiber, of excellent texture. Seeds white. Vine extremely vigorous and productive; resistant to fusarium wilt. Very popular home garden cultivar. A56, *A69M*, B49M{PL}, C92, D65, F19M, *F60*, G71, G79, H33, H54, H66, J84, K49M, K71, K73, N39, etc.

Early Canada: 75 days. Nearly round fruit, about 10 inches long, weighs 10 to 15 pounds; rind grayish-green with fine green stripes and veining; flesh bright red, sweet, of very fine quality. Seeds small, reddish-brown. Very prolific. Widely grown in the Canadian prairie states. A16, A69M, C85M, D11M, D27, D82, E97, *F60*, G87, I67M, L7M, M13M

Far North: 70 days. An early watermelon developed by Fisher's Garden Store from a cross of Sugar Bush and Peacock. Melons are dark-green, weigh 6 to 8 pounds, have bright red flesh and black seeds. D82

Garrisonian: (Rattlesnake, Georgia Rattlesnake) 90 days. Large, cylindrical fruit, about 22 inches long, weighs 35 to 40 pounds; rind hard, light green with attractive "rattlesnake" markings; flesh bright rose, firm, very sweet, of good quality. White seeds with dark tips. Very uniform in size and appearance. Resistant to sunburn and anthracnose; susceptible to wilt. *D49*, E97, *F60*, *F72*, *G1M*, G57M, *H61*, H66, *I59M*, J84, K49M, K71, L14, M29, N16, etc.

Golden Midget:[1 2 4] (Early Golden Midget) 70 days. A unique, short-vine "icebox" type with golden skin. Small oval fruit, 7 to 8 inches long, weighs 6 to 7 pounds; rind thin and tough, green, turning golden-orange at the peak of ripeness; flesh bright red, crisp, very sweet. Small, dark seeds. Bushy, compact vine; ideal for small gardens or container culture. Developed by Professor E.M. Meader. D11M, H42, H94, K49M, L91M

Jubilee: 90 days. A large, late-maturing shipping type for longer season areas. Fruit oblong, 24 inches long, weighs 25 to 35 pounds; rind light green with dark green stripes, medium-thick; flesh bright red, firm, sweet, quality good. Seeds large, nearly black. Vine less prolific than Charleston Gray; resists anthracnose and wilt. A87M, B75M, D76, F19M, *F60*, *F72*, G71, G93M, H66, J34, J58, K10, K71, K73, N16, etc.

King and Queen:[4] (Winter Queen, Winterkeeper, Christmas Melon) 85 days. Nearly round fruit, about 10 inches long, weighs 15 to 20 pounds; rind yellowish-green with faint green stripes, turns pale yellow when ripe; flesh bright scarlet, sweet, almost as firm as a citron melon. Very prolific. Excellent for storage and shipping, keeping until Christmas if picked when ripe and dipped in wax. B75M, C92, D65, D76, E59Z, E97, *F60*, G16, I39, I64, J73, K49M, K71, L7M, *L59G*, M46, N52, etc.

Kleckley Sweet: (Monte Cristo) 85 days. Oblong fruit, 24 inches long and 12 inches in diameter, weighs 30 to 40 pounds; rind dark bluish-green, glossy, thin; flesh bright red, very crisp and fine-grained, extremely sweet, with a broad stringless heart; quality excellent. Large white seeds. Does not ship well. An older cultivar, very popular with home gardeners. *B1*, C92, *G1M*, H66, J73, K10, K27M, K71, L14, *L59G*, M13M

Klondike: (Klondike Dark Green) 80 days. Oblong blocky fruit, 14 inches long, weighs about 25 pounds; rind tough, hard, fairly thick, light-green with irregular stripes of dark-green; flesh scarlet, juicy, sweet, sugar content very high. Small seeds. Ships well. Heavy yielding. B73M, F92, *G83M*, K27M, N39, N52

Moon and Stars:[5] 100 days. Legendary cultivar, rediscovered in rural Missouri by Kent Whealy of the Seed Savers Exchange. Round to oval fruit, weighs about 40 pounds; rind thin, brittle, slightly ridged, dark green with bright yellow spots resembling the "moon and stars"; flesh bright-red, very sweet and rich. Seeds brown with white tips. Foliage is also speckled. D68, K49M, L7M, L11

Mountain Hoosier: 85 days. An old-fashioned cultivar that was once a local favorite in southern Indiana, Ohio, and northern Kentucky. Slightly oblong fruit, weighs 75 to 80 pounds; rind dark green; flesh deep red, sweet, crisp, of very fine flavor. White seeds with slightly black tips. Extremely productive. K49M, L7M, N16

New Hampshire Midget:[1 2] 70 days. Very early "icebox" type for cool, short season areas. Fruit nearly round, about 6 inches across, weighs 4 to 5 pounds; rind thin, light green with dark green mottling and striping; flesh orange-red, of good flavor but coarse. Seeds black, numerous. All America Selections winner in 1951. A25, D65, F1, *F60*, G79, H42, H94, K49M, K71, K73, M13M, M46, M49, N39

Northern Sweet: (Early Northern Sweet, Fourth of July) 75 days. Nearly round fruit, 9 inches long, weighs between 12 and 15 pounds; rind thin, dark green with light green stripes; flesh scarlet red, crisp, tender, very sweet and fine-grained. Seeds light tan. Very early, often ripens by the Fourth of July. Highly productive. A2, B35M, B73M, D65, E97, *F60*, I64, I67M, I99, K71

Petite Sweet:[1 2] 75 days. Short-vined "icebox" type. Small oval-round fruit, weighs 5 to 10 pounds; rind light green with dark green stripes; flesh orange-red, crisp, very sweet. Seeds small, dark brown. Compact, prolific vine, spreads 5 feet or less. Resistant to fusarium wilt and anthracnose. Does well in northern areas. D65, D76, E97

Red-N-Sweet: Developed with the consumer in mind. Round oblong fruit, weighs 25 to 30 pounds; rind medium green with dark green stripes; brilliant red flesh, crisp and sweet, has a high sugar level. Medium-sized seeds. Good tolerance to fusarium wilt and anthracnose. *A1*, N16

Stone Mountain: 90 days. Blocky nearly round fruit, about 15 inches long, weighs 30 to 35 pounds; rind smooth, thick and tough, medium green with darker green veining; flesh deep red, very sweet, all solid heart, with no white hearts or strings, sweet to the rind. Seeds white, tipped with black, few. Very popular home garden and local market type. B71, C69, C92, F19M, *F60*, *G1M*, G57M, G79, H66, *I59M*, K27M, K49M, K71, L7M, L14, etc.

Strawberry: 85 days. Long, medium-sized fruit; 20 inches in length, 8 inches in diameter; weight 15 to 25 pounds; rind dark green with darker green stripes. Intense red flesh, ripens to within 1/2 inch of the rind, of delicate texture and excellent, sweet, distinctive flavor. Very good disease resistance. Home garden cultivar. L7M

Sugar Baby:[1] (Icebox Midget) 75 days. An excellent "icebox" type with the coarse texture and sweetness of larger watermelons. Round fruit, 6 to 8 inches in diameter; average weight 8 to 10 pounds; rind thick, dark green, almost black when mature; flesh bright red, sweet, of fine texture. Seeds small, dark brown. For local markets and home gardeners. A16, B73M, B78, C44, D87, E24, E57, *F60*, *F72*, G6, H94, I76M{PR}, L7M, M13M, M46, N16, etc.

Super Sweet: 95 days. Medium-sized, round oval fruit; 8 inches long, weighs 10 to 15 pounds; rind, thin, tough, light green with dark green stripes; flesh bright red, extremely sweet. Small, black seeds. Resistant to anthracnose and fusarium wilt. Developed by Dr. Charles V. Hall at Kansas State University from the same breeding line that produced Allsweet and Crimson Sweet. K49M, L79M, R47

Sweet Princess: 90 days. Charleston Gray type with extremely small seeds. Large oblong fruit, weighs about 25 pounds; rind light yellow-green with narrow medium green stripes, smooth, thick and tough; flesh light red, crisp, fine-textured. Seeds tan, unusually small, comparable to tomato seed. Resistant to anthracnose and fusarium wilt. *G1M*, I84, N16

Sweet Treat:[2] (Sweetheart) 85 days. Developed by Burpee for limited space gardens. Nearly round fruit, weighs 9 to 14 pounds; rind light green with distinct darker stripes; flesh scarlet, juicy, sweet, has very little fiber. Seeds medium-sized. Vigorous, bush-type vines, spread only 4 1/2 to 5 feet but bear an average of 2 melons per plant. B75, D11M, K27M

Tom Watson: 90 days. Large, oblong fruit, 10 to 12 inches in diameter; weight 30 to 40 pounds; rind dark green with slight mottling, tough and elastic; flesh dark red, somewhat coarse, firm, juicy, sweet. Ships well, especially for long distances. Also a traditional home garden favorite. *D49*, *F60*, *G1M*, G57M, G67M, G79, H66, *I59M*, K27M, K71, L14, M13M, N16

Werner's Baseball:[1] Medium dark-green, softball-sized fruit; tasty, orange-pink flesh. Natural cross with a wild Nigerian watermelon. Moderately small vines. **U33**

WHITE-FLESHED

Cream of Saskatchewan: 85 days. Nearly round fruit, about 10 inches long, weighs 8 to 10 pounds; rind thin, brittle, pale green with dark green stripes; flesh white to creamy white, sweet, very flavorful, of good quality. Seeds black. Prolific. Does well in northern areas. **U33**

Sugar Lump White: 85 days. Nearly round fruit, weighs 8 to 10 pounds; rind thick, medium green with darker green stripes; flesh white, sweet. Seeds black. Vigorous vine, spreads to 10 feet. Unique, heirloom cultivar. **U33**

YELLOW/ORANGE-FLESHED

HYBRID

Seeded

Gold Baby:[1] Round to oval fruit, weighs 5 to 6 pounds; rind light green with darker green stripes; flesh creamy yellow, very sweet and tender. Sugar content 11% by Brix meter. Easy to grow. Quite uniform and prolific. A16, E49, O89, *S63M*

Yellow Baby:[1] 75 days. Round to oval fruit, about 7 inches in diameter, weighs 8 to 10 pounds; rind thin, tough, light green with darker green stripes; flesh bright yellow, crisp, sweet, quality excellent. Seeds small, few. Has better storage qualities than other "icebox" types. All America Selections winner in 1975. B75, *E91G*, F13, G51, H95, I91, J7, K10, K66, L42, *M43M*

Yellow Doll:[1 2] 65 days. A very early maturing, hybrid "icebox" type with yellow flesh. Round fruit, weighs 5 to 8 pounds; rind thin, medium green with very dark green stripes; flesh yellow, crisp, extra sweet. Seeds small, black. Semi-compact vine. A13, B73M, C85M, D76, F19M, *F72*, G16, G93M, *H61*, J34, K73, L89, M46, N16, N39, etc.

Seedless

Golden Fummy: Round fruit, weighing 15 1/2 to 17 1/2 pounds; glossy green rind, with dark-green stripes; crisp, bright yellow flesh with a high sugar content; seedless. Good for long distance shipping and storage. Very vigorous vine; produces a high percentage of marketable fruit. Q88

Honey Yellow: 65 days. An early, yellow-fleshed seedless watermelon. Round fruit, 6 inches in diameter; rind green with dark green stripes; sweet, crisp, golden yellow flesh, remains firm well past ripeness. Keeps longer than seeded types. Vigorous, high-yielding vine. Seeds of Sugar Baby included as a pollinator. I91

Honeyheart: 80-85 days. Small, round fruit; weight 8 to 11 pounds; rind light gray-green with darker green stripes; flesh bright yellow, crisp, juicy, sweet; seedless. Ripens just after Jack of Hearts. For home gardens and fresh market. *A1*, G82, K10

OPEN-POLLINATED

Black Diamond Yellow Fleshed: 90 days. Exactly like standard Black Diamond except for the color of the flesh. Round to oval fruit, weighs 60 to 70 pounds under favorable conditions; rind thin, tough, glossy, dark grayish-green; flesh yellow, tender and sweet. Seeds grayish-black, rather small. Ships well. I99, K5M, N16

Desert King: 85 days. Round to slightly oblong fruit; rind medium thin, tough, light green; flesh deep yellow, very sweet and tender. Seeds grayish black. Holds on the vine a month or more after ripening without losing quality or becoming sunburned. A good shipper. Very drought tolerant. E97, *H61*, H66, J25M, K5M, K10, L14, L79M, N16

Golden Honey: 85 days. Round to oval fruit, about 12 inches long, weighs 30 pounds; rind brittle, medium green with darker green stripes; flesh bright yellow, crisp, tender, of fine flavor. Seeds large, light tan. Very popular with home gardeners and local market growers. C92, E59Z, *F60*, *G1M*, G51, G57M, G93M, H66, I99, J34, K5M

Hopi Yellow Fleshed: 100 days. Small round fruit, weighs 3 to 4 pounds; exceptionally sweet, crisp, full-flavored yellow flesh. Drought resistant; traditionally dry farmed in sand dunes. Crushed seeds are used to grease the stones on which the traditional Indian *piki* bread is baked. I16, J25M

Huichol Yellow Fleshed: Medium-sized, roundish fruit; extremely hard, greenish rind; moderately sweet, yellow flesh. Stores for a long period. Vigorous, relatively productive vine; extremely drought resistant. Also tolerant of mildew. Collected in Mexico. **U26**

Kaho: 87 days. A very early Chinese cultivar, popular in Shanghai. Oblong fruit, 8 1/2 inches long and 4 1/2 inches in diameter; weight 3 1/4 pounds. Rind very thin; grey-green, faintly striped with darker green. Flesh yellowish-orange, juicy, of fine quality and excellent flavor. Well-adapted to greenhouse culture. J73, *P39*

Moon and Stars Yellow Fleshed:[5] A family heirloom from Georgia. Rare white-seeded, yellow-fleshed cultivar of the Moon and Stars class. Rinds have yellow "moons" with many small yellow "stars". Excellent flavor, though not quite as sweet as the pink-fleshed Moon and Stars. Somewhat tolerant to disease and drought. K49M, L7M

Orangeglo: 85 days. Large, cylindrical fruit, grows up to 50 pounds; rind very thin, light green with darker green stripes; flesh solid, very crisp, sweet and flavorful. Seeds cream-colored with dark rings and tips. Vigorous, productive vine. Very popular with local market growers. N16

Tendergold: (Willhite's Tendergold) 80 days. Large, cylindrical fruit; very uniform in size and shape; weighs 22 to 28 pounds; rind tough, dark green mottled with lighter green; flesh sweet, yellow, becomes more orange and sweeter as it matures. Black seeds. A good shipper for a yellow-fleshed melon. Will last 7 to 20 days longer after ripening than Tendersweet Orange Fleshed. A87M, N16, N52

Tendersweet Orange Fleshed: 90 days. Oblong fruit, 18 inches long, weighs 35 to 40 pounds; rind light green with dark green stripes, medium-thick; flesh orange, very sweet and rich. Seeds medium-sized, off white. Of fine eating quality, but must be harvested promptly when mature. Considered sweeter than Tendersweet Yellow Fleshed. *A1*, A87M, B75M, *D49*, *F60*, *G1M*, G51, G93M, H66, J34, K5M, L14, N16

Tendersweet Yellow Fleshed: 80 days. Oblong fruit, about 18 inches long, weighs up to 30 pounds; dark green rind with light green stripes; flesh yellow, very tender, never stringy, of exceptionally high sugar content. Seeds solid white to cream with black rims and tips. A good shipper. H66, K71, L14, *L59G*

Yellow Crimson: 80 days. Nearly round fruit, very similar to Crimson Sweet in size and appearance; rind light green with darker green stripes; flesh bright yellow, of very good flavor. Seeds black. Ripens somewhat earlier than Crimson Sweet. K49M, N16

WHITE SAPOTE {GR}

CASIMIROA EDULIS

Bravo: Selected as having the best flavor in a blind taste test conducted by the North San Diego County chapter of the California Rare Fruit Growers. Produces over-size, yellow-green fruit in the fall. I83M

Chestnut: Medium to large, roundish fruit; up to 4 inches in diameter and 3/4 of a pound; skin greenish-yellow, thin, slightly bitter; flesh golden-yellow, of fine texture; flavor rich, but does not become overly sweet; quality very good; ripens August to September. Keeps and ships well, and has therefore been used as a commercial cultivar. Tree bears very large crops every other year, up to 3 tons. Originated in Vista, California by Wesley C. Chestnut. L6

Denzler: Small to medium-sized fruit, about 3 inches in diameter; light green skin; very smooth white flesh with a sweet, melting flavor; quality excellent fresh; seeds 2 or 3; ripens October to December, handles and ships well. Skin is peeled off and not eaten. Large, vigorous, upright tree; bears lightly. Selected at Mr. Denzler's farm in upper Kona on the Big Island of Hawaii. J22

Fiesta: Small, roundish fruit; skin thick, green; flesh sweet, flavor good; ripens September to December. Tree reliably productive. I83M

Lemon Gold: Medium to large fruit; weight 4 to 6 ounces; skin attractive, light yellow when mature, resists blemishes. Quality very good, with a pleasant slightly acid flavor. Seeds small, usually 4. Season October to November; ripens on the tree and holds there for several weeks without much deterioration. Develops a good flavor when ripened off the tree. Keeps well. Tree bears good crops annually. I83M, *Q93*

Leroy's: Medium to large, flat-ovate fruit; weight 6 to 8 ounces; skin golden colored on the side exposed to the sun, when ripe; flesh sweet, with a distinct, rich butterscotch-like flavor. Ripens over a long season, from August to Christmas. Originated in Vista, California by Leroy Ross. D57

Louise: Small to medium-sized, roundish fruit; skin yellow; quality high; season January to September but will ripen nearly year round in frost-free areas. Tree bears heavy crops. I83M

Luke: Fruit of uneven shape. Should be picked when the hard green turns to more of a yellowish hue, Needs to be wrinkled and rather soft before it is eaten. Tree rather small, up to 6 meters high, with a slight weeping habit; bears heavy crops. Originated in New Zealand. *Q49M*

McDill: Very large, round to oval fruit, up to 1 1/2 pounds; skin thin, light yellowish-green when ripe; flesh sweet but not cloying, eating quality excellent; usually 1 to 3 large seeds; ripens November to December, does not keep well. Tree vigorous, precocious, prolific. I83M, J22, L6, *Q93*

Ortego: Oval fruit, usually with only 1 relatively small seed; average weight 4 to 5 ounces. Has good eating and keeping qualities. Ripens in late mid-season and continues for about 2 months. Tree compact, somewhat drooping; a regular and heavy bearer. Originated in Escondido, California by Orton H. Englehart. **T49M{SC}**

Pike: Large, rounded or oblate fruit, to 4 inches in diameter and 9 ounces; skin dark green, thin, very fragile, somewhat bitter; flesh white to yellowish, of rich, non-bitter flavor. Usually has 4 rather large seeds. Ripens September to December, keeps fairly well. Tree small, bears regularly and heavily. Has been used as a commercial cultivar. Originated in Santa Barbara, California in the late 1920's. BROOKS 1972; **T49M{SC}**

Reinecke Commercial: Fruit irregular in shape, weighs about 5 ounces; skin an attractive golden-orange when ripe; flavor good. Seeds moderate in number. Has excellent keeping qualities, and even if picked prematurely will soften and become fairly good eating. Tree a relatively poor yielder. Originated in San Diego, California by John M. Reinecke. *Q93*

Suebelle: (Hubbell) Medium to small, roundish fruit, weight 2 to 6 ounces; skin green or yellowish-green, bruises easily; flesh custard-like, melting, of excellent flavor; sugar content 22%; seeds few, rather small; ripens July to April; does not store or ship well. Tree precocious; nearly everbearing within a mile of the coast. Originated in Encinitas, California by Susan Hubbell. Introduced in 1931. BROOKS 1972, MORTON 1987a; *D23M*, D57, I83M, L6

Sunrise: Medium to large, roundish to oblate fruit, weight 6 to 10 ounces; irregular in shape; skin light-green turning yellow when ripe, thin, easily bruised; flesh creamy-white, sweet but not cloying, balanced by a delicate lemon-like flavor, very well-textured; quality excellent; ripens July to October. Tree tall, upright, vigorous; very productive, bears 2 crops some years. Originated in Vista, California. **T49M{SC}**

Vernon: Medium to large, roundish fruit; skin relatively thin, yellow when ripe; flesh very sweet, flavor excellent; ripens November to January, keeps relatively well on the shelf. Tree very productive and dependable, bears over a long period of time. Does well in coastal areas. Originated in Vista, California by Wells W. Miller. I83M, L6

SOURCES

DOMESTIC COMMERCIAL

A0M **Abbey Garden Cacti and Succulents** - 4620 Carpinteria Ave., Carpinteria, CA 93013, (805) 684-5112 or 684-1595. Cactus and succulent plants. CAT $2, R & W, PC/CC, OVER, M.O. $20.

A1 **Abbott & Cobb, Inc.** - P.O. Box 307, Feasterville, PA 19047, 1-800-345-Seed. Vegetable seed breeders and growers. CAT FREE, WHLS, CC, OVER, M.O. $200.

A1M **ABC Herb Nursery and Hobby Shop** - Rt. 1, Box 313, Lecoma, MO 65540, (314) 435-6389. Family business offering herb plants, african violets, dried herbs and crafts. CAT $.25, R & W, PC, M.O. $10.

A2 **Abundant Life Seed Foundation** - P.O. Box 772, Port Townsend, WA 98368, (206) 385-7192. Non-profit, tax exempt organization growing and collecting untreated seeds of non-hybrid vegetables, herbs, wild flowers, trees and shrubs, grains and garden flowers. CAT $1, R & W, PC/CC, OVER.

A3 **Acropolis Food Market** - 1206 Underwood NW, Washington, DC 20012, (202) 829-1414. Gourmet and ethnic foods. Specializes in Greek, Middle Eastern and Ethiopian items. *Sells the following product/s:* trahanas and both green and red zatar. CAT (CALL FOR PRICES), RET, PC.

A5 **Adams County Nursery, Inc.** - P.O. Box 108, Aspers, PA 17304, (717) 677-8105. Produces finished one-year old fruit tree nursery stock, including apples, pears, peaches, plums, nectarines, apricots and cherries. CAT FREE, R & W, PC, OVER.

A7M **Aesop's Kitchen and Cupboard** - 222 E. Market, Indianapolis, IN 46204, (317) 632-0269. Specializes in Greek and Middle Eastern foods. Previously known as Athens Imported Foods. *Sells the following product/s:* dried Yellow Eye, Cranberry and Swedish Brown beans, bulghur wheat, couscous, trahanas, and dried mountain tea. CAT FREE, R & W, PC.

A9 **Agri Sun Nursery** - 6910 E. Clarkson Ave., Selma, CA 93662, (209) 896-7444. Commercial tree nursery growing deciduous nursery stock, including peaches, nectarines, apples, plums and almonds. Prepares and ships budwood. CAT FREE, WHLS, PC, OVER, M.O. 100 TREES.

A11M **Agri-Truffle Texas, Inc.** - P.O. Box 39, Dripping Springs, TX 78620, (512) 858-7729. Supplies oak and hazel nut seedlings that have been inoculated with the Perigord black truffle (Tuber melanosporum). CAT FREE, R & W, PC/OC, M.O. 10 TREES.

A12 **Agriforest Technologies Ltd.** - P.O. Box 178, Kelowna, BC V1Y 7N5, Canada, (604) 860-5815. Tissue culture nursery stock including rootstocks of apple, pear and cherry, saskatoon plants. CAT FREE, R & W, PC, U.S. ONLY.

A13 **Agway Inc.** - 1225 Zeager Rd., Elizabethtown, PA 17022, (717) 367-1075. Farmers cooperative handling a full line of vegetable and flower seeds. CAT FREE, RET, PC/CC.

A14 **Ahrens Nursery & Plant Labs** - R.R. 1, Huntingburg, IN 47542, (812) 683-3055. Fruit trees, small fruits including strawberry, raspberry, blackberry, blueberry, gooseberry and currants, asparagus and rhubarb. Also publishes a separate catalog of herb plants. CAT FREE, R & W, PC/CC, OVER.

A15M **Alaska Wild Berry Products** - 528 E. Pioneer Ave., Homer, AK 99603, (907) 235-8858. Mail order gift boxes, sourdough starter cultures. *Sells the following product/s:* wild salmonberry jelly, wild lingonberry jelly and wild highbush cranberry jelly. CAT FREE, RET, PC/CC, CANADA ONLY.

A16 **Alberta Nurseries and Seeds Ltd.** - Box 20, Bowden, AB T0M 0K0, Canada, (403) 224-3544. Complete listing of early maturing garden seed cultivars for short season or high altitude areas. CAT FREE ($2 IN US), RET, CC, OVER.

A18 **Aldrich Berry Farm & Nursery, Inc.** - 190 Aldrich Rd., Mossyrock, WA 98564, (206) 983-3138. Specializes in highbush blueberry plants. Also sells Christmas trees and conifer seedlings and transplants. CAT FREE, R & W, M.O. $25.

A19 **Aldridge Nursery, Inc.** - Rt. 1, Box 8, Von Ormy, TX 78073, 1-800-531-5580 or 292-5415. Low-chill fruit trees, figs, grape vines, nut trees, shade and ornamental trees, palms, native plants and tropical and foliage plants. CAT FREE, WHLS, M.O. $300.

A21 **Alfrey Seeds** - P.O. Box 415, Knoxville, TN 37901, (615) 524-5965 (no telephone orders). Small, single proprietor company selling seed of rare and hard to find peppers, tomatoes and okra. CAT SASE, RET, PC, OVER.

A24 **Allen Company** - P.O. Box 310, Fruitland, MD 21826-0310, (310) 742-7122. Strawberry plant specialists for over 100 years. Also supplies raspberries, blackberries, blueberries and asparagus. CAT FREE, R & W, PC/CC, M.O. 50 STRAWBERRY PLANTS.

A24M **Allen (H.F.) Onion Co.** - P.O. Box 180, Vidalia, GA 30474, 1-800-444-9540. Specializes in Vidalia onions, for both planting and eating. *Sells the following product/s:* fresh Vidalia onions, pickled Vidalia onions, and Vidalia onion relish. CAT FREE, RET, PC/CC, OVER.

A25 **Allen, Sterling & Lothrop** - 191 U.S. Route No. 1, Falmouth, ME 04105, (207) 781-4142 (no telephone orders). Packet and bulk seed supplier of vegetable, herb and flower seeds. CAT $1 REFUNDABLE, RET, PC/CC.

A25M **Allgrove Farm Inc.** - P.O. Box 459, Wilmington, MA 01887, (508) 658-4869. Specializes in terrarium plants and supplies. CAT FREE, RET, PC, M.O. $15.

A26 **Allium Farms** - Box 296, Powers, OR 97466, (503) 439-3675. Specializes in elephant garlic bulbs for planting and eating. CAT FREE, R & W.

A27M **Alma Farm Supply, Inc.** - P.O. Box E, Alma, AK 72921, (501) 632-3194. Vegetable seeds adapted to the Southwest. CAT FREE, R & W, PC.

A29 **Alpine Gardens & Calico Shop** - 12446 Co. F, Stitzer, WI 53825, (608) 325-3824 (no telephone orders). Sedum, Sempervivum and other alpine plants. CAT $1, R & W, PC, M.O. $15.

A31M **Alston Seed Growers** - P.O. Box 875, Littleton, NC 27850. Specializes in non-hybrid, old fashioned field corn. Also offers melons, tomatoes and squash. CAT $1 REFUNDABLE, R & W, CANADA ONLY.

A32 **Alta Seeds** - P.O. Box 253, Potrero, CA 92063. Offers vegetables found to be best suited for home gardeners throughout the United States and Canada. Emphasis is on better flavor and nutritional value. CAT $2 REFUNDABLE, RET, PC/OC, OVER.

A33 **Altiplaño Nursery** - Box 401, Arlee, MT 59821, (406) 726-3765. Hardy fruit and nut trees, garlic cloves, multi-purpose trees and shrubs. CAT FREE, RET, PC.

A34 **Amberg's Nursery** - 3164 Whitney Road, Stanley, NY 14561, (716) 526-5405. Growers of size controlled apple and pear trees available on a wide range of rootstocks. Also offers a custom-budding service. CAT FREE, R & W.

A34M **Amenity Plant Products** - RD #5, Box 265, Mt. Pleasant, PA 15666, (412) 423-8170. Specializes in seeds and plants of native species, especially those indigenous to the Northeast and North Central United States. CAT $1, R & W, PC/CC, OVER, M.O. $3.

A35 **American Bamboo Co.** - 345 West Second Street, Dayton, OH 45402. Specializes in hardy bamboo. CAT FREE, RET, PC, CANADA ONLY.

A35T **American Forest Foods Corporation** - P.O. Box 2196, Henderson, NC 27536, (919) 438-2674. Manufacturer and distributor of certified shiitake mushroom spawn and other exotic mushroom spawn for fall, winter, spring and summer fruiting. Previously known as Carolina Agro-Tech Corporation. CAT FREE, R & W, PC, OVER.

A36 **American Ginseng Gardens** - P.O. Box 168-D, Flag Pond, TN 37657, (615) 743-3700. Ginseng seeds and roots. CAT $1, RET, PC/OC, OVER.

A38M **American Spoon Foods** - P.O. Box 566, Petoskey, MI 49770-0566, (616) 347-9030. Authentic American foods from the Upper Peninsula of Michigan. *Sells the following product/s:* wild pecan meats, hickory nut meats, butternut meats, black walnut meats, Damson plum preserves, Concord grape butter, dried Montmorency cherries, dried morel mushrooms, wild thimbleberry preserves, pickled snap peas, black raspberry butter, dried wild blueberries and dried cranberries. CAT FREE, RET, PC/CC, OVER, M.O. $10.

American Takii, Inc. - 301 Natividad Rd., Salinas, CA 93906. American subsidiary of Takii & Co., Ltd., Japan, which see.

A39 **Ames' Orchard & Nursery** - 6 East Elm St., Fayetteville, AK 72701, (501) 443-0282. Small family-owned nursery specializing in disease and pest resistant fruit trees and berry plants adapted to the Ozarks. CAT $1 REFUNDABLE, R & W, PC.

A40 **Ammon (A.G.) Nursery** - Rt. 532, P.O. Box 488, Chatsworth, NJ 08019, (609) 726-1370. Commercial grower of highbush blueberry plants. CAT FREE, WHLS, PC, OVER, M.O. 50 PLANTS PER CULTIVAR.

A41 **Amycel, Inc.** - P.O. Box 1260, San Juan Bautista, CA 95045, (408) 623-4586. Large commercial producer cf mushroom spawn. Broad selection of strains from Somycel of France, Darlington of England and Horst of Holland. CAT FREE, WHLS.

A44M **Ann Marie's Produce** - 170 Mace St. E-12, Chula Vista, CA 92011, (619) 425-1557. Fresh fruits and vegetables, natural food items. *Sells the following product/s:* dried Black Mission figs, and Black Monukka raisins. CAT FREE, RET, PC.

A45 **Ann's Dutch Import Co.** - 4357 Tujunga Ave., North Hollywood, CA 91604, (818) 985-5551. Exotic foods from Holland and Indonesia. *Sells the following product/s:* laos powder, temoo kuntji powder, kenchur powder, dried Kaffir lime leaves, dried and canned Holland Capucijners peas, shelled candle nuts, keluwak nuts, peteh beans, dried pandan leaves, and dried Indonesian bay. CAT FREE, R & W, PC/CC, OVER.

A48M **Apacha Cactus** - 3441 Road B, Redwood Valley, CA 95470, (707) 485-7088. Cactus and succulent plants. CAT $.50, R & W, PC.

A49D **Apothecary Rose Shed** - P.O. Box 194, Pattersonville, NY 12137. Herb plants and seeds, old fashioned hard-to-find perennials, everlastings, antique roses, and scented geraniums. CAT FREE, RET, PC, M.O. $5.

A49G **Apothecary Seed Company** - P.O. Box 1324, Battle Ground, WA 98604, (206) 686-3573 (no telephone orders). Small, single proprietor company specializing in rare and unusual non-hybrid vegetables, culinary and medicinal herbs, scented plants and natural pest control plants. CAT FREE, RET, PC.

A50 **Appalachian Gardens** - P.O. Box 82, Waynesboro, PA 17268-0082, (717) 762-4312. Ornamental trees, shrubs and perennials both scarce, unusual and rare and old favorites. CAT FREE, RET, PC/CC.

A51M **Appalachian Wildflower Nursery** - Rt 1, Box 275A, Reedsville, PA 17084, (717) 667-6998 (no telephone orders). Offers plants not usually cultivated. Mid-Appalachian natives, with emphasis on shale barrens and pine barrens. Also natives of central and N.E. Asia. CAT $1, R & W, PC, OVER.

A52M **Apple Valley Market** - 9067 U.S. 31, Berrien Springs, MI 49103, (616) 471-3234. Natural food items. *Sells the following product/s:* Kaffree tea, arrowroot powder, Stevia herbal sweetener, black walnut meats, Ruby raisins, wheat nuts, dried cranberry beans, dried red lentils, Black Jewell popping corn and gandules. CAT FREE, RET, PC/CC.

A53 **Applesource** - Route One, Chapin, IL 62628. Unique service offering a wide selection of apples for tasting, approximately 100 varieties. Home gardeners can sample apples of the different cultivars before deciding which to plant. CAT FREE, RET, PC, CANADA ONLY, M.O. $16.

A53M **Applewood Seed Co.** - 5380 Vivian St., Arvada, CO 80002, (303) 431-6283. Wildflower seeds and seed mixtures, culinary herbs, edible flowers, ornamental grasses, everlastings. CAT FREE, WHLS, M.O. $50.

A55 **Arbor and Espalier Co.** - 201 Buena Vista Avenue East, San Francisco, CA 94117, (415) 626-8880. Specialty company offering a wide selection of espaliered fruit trees, mostly apples and pears, and including heirloom cultivars. CAT FREE, R & W, PC/CC.

A56 **Archias' Seed Co.** - 106 East Main St., Sedalia, MO 65301, (816) 826-1330. Vegetable, herb and flower seeds, farm seed, vegetable plants, perennials, and berry plants. Founded in 1884. CAT FREE, R & W, PC/CC, OVER.

A57M **Arjoy Acres** - HCR Box 1410, Payson, AZ 85541, (602) 474-1224. Organically grown garlic for planting or eating, specialty foods. *Sells the following product/s:* preserved lingonberries and dried Swedish Brown beans. CAT FREE, RET, PC.

A64 **Atlantic Blueberry Co.** - R.D. #3, Box 114, Hammonton, NJ 08037, (609) 561-8600. Commercial grower of highbush blueberry plants. Previously known as Galletta Brothers. CAT FREE, WHLS, PC, OVER, M.O. 50 PLANTS.

A65 **Aubin Nurseries** - P.O. Box 1089, Carman, MB R0G 0J0, Canada, (204) 745-6703. Hardy fruit trees, berry plants, grape vines, ornamental trees and shrubs. CAT FREE, R & W, PC/CC, CANADA ONLY.

A69 **Aztekakti** - P.O. Box 26126, El Paso, TX 79926, (915) 858-1130 (no telephone orders). Cactus and succulent seeds. CAT FREE, R & W, PC/CC, OVER.

A69G **B.C. Certified Budwood Assn.** - Research Station, Summerland, BC V0H 1Z0, Canada, (604) 494-8959. Certified, virus-indexed budwood and scions of apples, apricots, cherries, nectarines, peaches, pears and plums, many developed at the Summerland Research Station. Sells primarily to the nursery trade and tree fruit industry. CAT FREE, R & W, PC, U.S. ONLY, M.O. $10.

A69M **B.C. Pea Growers Ltd./The Garden Centre** - Box 1148, Brooks, AB T0J 0J0, Canada, (403) 362-4255. Bulk suppliers of vegetable and herb seeds. CAT FREE, R & W, PC, OVER.

A70 **B & D Lilies** - 330 P Street, Port Townsend, WA 98368, (206) 385-1738. Hardy, long lasting hybrid lily bulbs and species lilies. CAT $3, R & W, PC/CC, OVER.

A71 **B & Z Nursery, Inc.** - 1850 South Newcomb, Porterville, CA 93257, (209) 781-7438. Citrus trees, seeds, rootstocks and budwood. CAT FREE, WHLS, PC, OVER.

A71M **Bacchus & Barleycorn, Ltd.** - 8725 Johnson Drive, Merriam, KS 66202, (913) 262-4243. Supplies and equipment for the home wine and beer maker. CAT FREE, R & W, PC/CC.

A74 **Bailey Nurseries** - 1325 Bailey Road, Saint Paul, MN 55119, 1-800-876-8898. Hardy northern grown fruit trees, ornamental trees and shrubs, garden perennials, conifers, roses. CAT FREE, WHLS.

A75 **Bakker Bros. of Idaho, Inc.** - P.O. Box 1964, Twin Falls, ID 83303-1964, (208) 733-0015. Vegetable seed growers and marketers worldwide. CAT FREE, WHLS, PC/CC, OVER, M.O. $200.

A76 **Baldwin Seed Co. of Alaska** - P.O. Box 3127, Kenai, AK 99611. Small, single proprietor company specializing in Alaskan wild flower seeds. CAT FREE, RET, PC.

A78 **Bamboo Shoot (A)** - 1462 Darby Street, Sebastopol, CA 95472, (707) 823-0131 (no telephone orders). Large selection of hardy and tropical bamboos, both runners and clumpers. Over 80 varieties. CAT $1, R & W, PC, OVER, M.O. $50.

A79 **Bamboo Sourcery** - 666 Wagnon Road, Sebastopol, CA 95472, (707) 823-5866 (no telephone orders). Small nursery specializing in a wide range of bamboos, over 75 varieties. CAT $1, RET, PC, OVER.

A79M **Banana Tree (The)** - 715 Northampton St., Easton, PA 18042, (215) 253-9589. Wide selection of rare and uncommon tropical seeds and bulbs, banana corms, palms, oriental vegetables, ornamentals. CAT $2, R & W, PC/CC, OVER, M.O. $6.50.

A80M **Barber Nursery** - 23561 Vaughn Rd., Veneta, OR 97487, (503) 935-7701. Seedling trees and shrubs. Previously known as Mountain Mist Nursery. CAT FREE, R & W, PC, OVER, M.O. $15.

A82 **Barnes (Vernon) & Son Nursery** - P.O. Box 250L, McMinnville, TN 37110, (615) 668-8576. Over 250 varieties of fruit and nut trees, shrubs, shade and flowering trees, evergreens, wild flowers and perennials. CAT FREE, R & W, PC/CC.

A83M **Barney's Ginseng Patch** - Rt. 2, Box 43, Montgomery City, MO 63361, (314) 564-2575. Ginseng and goldenseal seed and planting roots. CAT $2, R & W, PC, OVER, M.O. $25.

A85M **Bass Pecan Co.** - P.O. Box 42, Lumberton, MS 39455-0042, (601) 796-2461. Large selection of pecan trees. Also other fruit trees, including apple, pear, persimmon, plum and fig. CAT FREE, R & W, OVER, M.O. $10.

A87M **Baxter (Walter) Seed Co., Inc.** - P.O. Box 8175, Weslaco, TX 78596-3175, (512) 968-3187. Full line of vegetable seeds. CAT FREE, R & W, PC, OVER, M.O. $1.

A88M **Bay Laurel Garden Center** - 2500 El Camino Real, Atascadero, CA 93422, (805) 466-3449. Large selection of fruit and nut trees, berry plants, grape vines, kiwi, perennial vegetables, shade trees, flowering shrubs. CAT FREE, R & W, PC.

A88T **Bazaar of India Imports** - 1810 University Ave., Berkeley, CA 94703, (415) 548-4110. Specializes in Indian foods. *Sells the following product/s:* anardana, aloo bokhara, asafoetida powder, amchoor, sev, kewda water, dried ajwain, masoor dal, dried curry leaves, poha, cheewra, dried Kasuri methi, chappati flour, idli mix, dosa mix, jalebi mix, papads, toor dal, whole urid and urid dal. CAT FREE, RET, PC, M.O. $10.

A89 **Bea's Service** - P.O. Box 8422, Calabasas, CA 91302, (818) 340-6704. Specializes in chili pepper seeds from Mexico. CAT FREE, RET, PC, OVER.

A90 **Beahm Epiphyllum Gardens** - 2686 Paloma Street, Pasadena, CA 91107, (818) 792-6533. Specializes in Epiphyllum, Hoya and Rhipsalis. CAT $1 REFUNDABLE, RET, PC.

A91 **Bear Creek Nursery** - P.O. Box 411, Northport, WA 99157. Extensive selection of fruit and nut trees for northern temperate areas, multi-purpose trees and shrubs, apple scionwood, fruit tree rootstocks for home grafting, edible perennials, berry plants. CAT $.50, R & W, PC, OVER.

A93M **Beaver Creek Nursery** - 7526 Pelleaux Road, Knoxville, TN 37938, (615) 922-3961. Specializes in rare, unusual or uncommon ornamental plants. Many are native to the Southeast. CAT $1, RET, PC, M.O. $20.

A94M **Beaverton Foods Inc.** - P.O. Box 687, Beaverton, OR 97075, (503) 646-8138. Gourmet and specialty horseradish, mustards and sauces. *Sells the following product/s:* prepared horseradish, horseradish powder, horseradish sauce, whipped horseradish, cream horseradish and green peppercorns. CAT FREE, R & W, PC, OVER.

A95 **Becker's Seed Potatoes** - R.R. #1, Trout Creek, ON P0H 2L0, Canada. Small, family operated seed potato farm offering a large selection of hard to find, old and new potato cultivars exclusively for home gardeners and hobbyists. CAT $1 REFUNDABLE, RET, PC, U.S. ONLY.

A97 **Bee Riddle Farm** - Rt. 8, Box 326, Conway, SC 29526, (803) 365-0280. Herb plants, scented geraniums, everlasting and perennial flowers. CAT FREE, RET, PC, M.O. 6 PLANTS.

A99 **Beer and Wine Hobby** - P.O. Box 3104, Wakefield, MA 01880, (617) 665-8442. Complete line of home wine and home beermaking supplies and equipment. CAT FREE, RET, PC/CC, OVER.

A99M **Beer Gear** - P.O. Box 25093, Lansing, MI 48909, 1-800-All-Malt. Complete line of beermaking and winemaking supplies for the homebrewer. CAT FREE, RET, PC/CC.

A99T **Beer & Winemaking Cellar** - P.O. Box 33525, Seattle, WA 98133, (206) 365-7660. Beer and wine making supply company. Previously known as The Cellar. CAT FREE, RET, PC/CC, OVER.

B0 **Beersheba Wildflower Gardens** - P.O. Box 551, Beersheba Springs, TN 37305, (615) 692-3575. Native ferns and wild flowers. CAT FREE, R & W, PC.

B1 **Behm and Hagemann, Inc.** - 3021 West Farmington Road, Peoria, IL 61604, (309) 674-5153. Vegetable seeds. CAT FREE, WHLS, PC, OVER.

B1M **Belché Herb Company** - P.O. Box 1305, Schenectady, NY 12301. Small company specializing in culinary herbs and gourmet vegetables. CAT FREE, RET, PC/OC.

B4 **Bergeson Nursery** - Fertile, MN 56540, (218) 945-6988. Fruit trees, berry plants, perennial vegetables, vines, shade and ornamental trees. CAT FREE, RET, PC.

B7 **Berry Tree (The)** - 15368 Mowersville Rd., Shippensburg, PA 17257, (717) 423-6701. Seeds of exotic herbs and spices, sprouting seeds. Also potpourri and other fragrant herbal products. Previously known as James F. Berry Seeds and Natural Products Supply Co. *Sells the following product/s:* Stevia natural sweetener. CAT $1, R & W, PC/CC, OVER, M.O. $50 WHLS

B8 **Berton Seeds Co., Ltd.** - 151 Toryork Dr., Unit 20, Weston, ON M9L 1X9, Canada, (416) 745-5655. Large selection of vegetable seeds, all of which are imported from Italy. Specializes in chicory. CAT FREE, R & W, PC, U.S. ONLY, M.O. $10.

B9M **Bigelow Nurseries** - P.O. Box 718, Northboro, MA 01532, (508) 845-2143. Perennials, herbs, native ferns and wild flowers, roses, vines, trees and shrubs. CAT FREE, R & W, CC.

B10 **Bill's Berry Farm** - 1500 Dotsonville Rd., Clarksville, TN 37042, (615) 648-4030. Family owned business producing berry plants for the home gardener and commercial grower. CAT FREE, R & W, PC, M.O. $20 WHLS

B11 **Biology Store (The)** - 275 Pauma Place, Escondido, CA 92025, (619) 745-1445. Biological supplies including living cultures of algae, bacteria and fungi. Succeeded College Biological Supply Co. CAT FREE, R & W, PC.

B11T **BioQuest International** - P.O. Box 5752, Santa Barbara, CA 93150-5752, (805) 969-4072. Rare and unusual bulbs from Cape Province, South Africa. CAT $1.25, RET, PC, OVER, M.O. $10.

B13 **Bishop Farm Seeds** - Box 338, Belleville, ON K8N 5A5, Canada, (613) 968-5533. Vegetable and farm seeds, forages, grasses. CAT FREE, R & W, PC/CC, CANADA ONLY.

B15 **Bissett Nursery Co.** - P.O. Box 386, Holtsville, NY 11742, (516) 289-3500. Wholesale distributor of trees and shrubs. CAT FREE, WHLS.

B15M **Bitterroot Nursery** - 521 Eastside Highway, Hamilton, MT 59840, (406) 961-3806. Growers of fruit trees, hardy evergreens, shade and ornamental trees, deciduous shrubs, and conifers suitable for planting in the intermountain region. CAT FREE, R & W, PC, OVER.

B19 **Black Diamond Nursery** - Rt. 2, Box 176, Winslow, AR 72959, (501) 369-4354. Red, yellow, purple and black raspberries, gooseberries and blackberries. CAT FREE, R & W, PC.

B19M **Black Jewell Popcorn Inc.** - R.R. #1, St. Francisville, IL 62460, (618) 948-2303. Specialty food items. *Sells the following product/s:* Black Jewell popping corn. CAT FREE, R & W, PC.

B22 **Blossomberry Nursery** - Rt. 2, Box 28F, Clarksville, AR 72830, (501) 754-6489. Specializes in table grape cultivars adapted primarily to the Eastern United States. CAT FREE, R & W, PC, M.O. $10.

B23M **Blue Heron Farm** - P.O. Box 68, Rumsey, CA 95679, (916) 796-3799. Certified organically grown oranges, walnuts and almonds. CAT FREE, R & W, PC, OVER, M.O. 5 LBS.

B25 **Blue Star Laboratories, Inc.** - Rt. 13, Box 173, Williamstown, NY 13493, (315) 964-2295. Specializes in northern highbush blueberries. CAT FREE, R & W, PC, OVER.

B26 **Blueberry Hill** - R.R. 1, Maynooth, ON K0L 2S0, Canada. Native lowbush and highbush blueberry plants. Offers three grades of lowbush blueberries, being the equivalent of one year, two year and mature plants. CAT FREE, R & W, PC, U.S. ONLY, M.O. 2 PLANTS.

B27M **Bluebird Orchard and Nursery** - 429 E. Randall St., Coopersville, MI 49404, (616) 837-9598. Specializes in antique and choice apple cultivars. Approximately 50 are offered as trees, another 150 are available for custom propagation or as scionwood. CAT FREE, RET, PC.

B28 **Bluemel (Kurt) Inc.** - 2740 Greene Lane, Baldwin, MD 21013-9523, (301) 557-7229. Field grown ornamental grasses and grass-like plants, bamboos, aquatic plants, perennials, groundcovers and ferns. CAT $2, R & W, PC/CC, OVER.

B29M **Bluestem Seed Co.** - Rt. 3, Box 32, Grant City, MO 64456, (816) 786-2224. Specializes in harvesting, conditioning and marketing of native warm-season grass seed. Also sells seed of prairie wild flowers and forbs. CAT FREE, WHLS, PC.

B30 **Bluestone Perennials** - 7211 Middle Ridge Rd., Madison, OH 44057, 1-800-852-5243. Hardy perennials offered as small, started plants. CAT FREE, R & W, PC/CC.

B32 **Bobtown Nursery** - R.R. 1, Box 436-P, Melfa, VA 23410, (804) 787-8484. Large grower of rooted cuttings, seedlings and finished plants of hard to find ornamental trees, shrubs and vines. CAT FREE, R & W, PC/OC, OVER, M.O. $50.

B33M **Boehlke's Woodland Gardens** - W 140 N 10829 Country Aire Rd., Germantown, WI 53022. Specializes in rootstocks of northern herbaceous native plants. Ships only during April and September/October. CAT $.50, RET, PC.

B35M **Bojo's Garden Seed** - P.O. Box 1408, Caldwell, ID 83606, (208) 454-8228. Growers of traditional non-hybrid vegetable seeds intended for the home gardener. Emphasis is on flavor. CAT FREE, R & W, PC, OVER.

B39 **Boordy Nursery (The)** - P.O. Box 38, Riderwood, MD 21139, (301) 823-4624. Specializes in French hybrid wine grapes. CAT FREE, R & W, PC.

B39M **Boothe Hill Tea Co. and Greenhouse** - 23B Boothe Hill Rd., Chapel Hill, NC 27514, (919) 967-4091. Native wild flowers and ferns, herbs, everlastings. All plants organically grown. CAT FREE, WHLS.

B41 **Bordier's Nursery Inc.** - 7231 Irvine Blvd, Irvine, CA 92718, (714) 559-4221. Fruit and nut trees, grape vines, bamboo, ornamental trees and shrubs. CAT FREE, WHLS.

B43M **Boston Mountain Nurseries** - Rt. 2 Box 405-A, Mountainburg, AR 72946. Family-owned and operated nursery specializing in small fruits, including raspberries, blackberries, strawberries, grapes, and blueberries. CAT $.50 PLUS SASE, R & W, PC.

B44 **Botanic Garden Company Inc.** - 9 Wycoff St., Brooklyn, NY 11201, (718) 624-8839. Native wild flower seeds, both individual species and regional mixes for all areas of the United States. CAT $1, R & W, PC, OVER.

B44M **Botanicals** - 219 Concord Road, Wayland, MA 01778, (508) 358-4846. Native wild flowers, garden perennials, ornamental trees and shrubs. CAT FREE, R & W, PC, M.O. $25.

B45M **Bottoms Nursery** - Rt. 1, Box 281, Concord, GA 30206, (404) 495-5661. Specializes in muscadine grape vines. CAT FREE, RET.

B47 **Boughen Nurseries** - P.O. Box 12, Valley River, MB R0L 2B0, Canada, (204) 638-7618. Hardy fruit trees, berry plants, grape vines, ornamental trees and shrubs, garden perennials. Established in 1913. CAT FREE, RET, PC, CANADA ONLY, M.O. $20.

B49 **Bountiful Gardens** - 5798 Ridgewood Road, Willits, CA 95490. Non-profit company offering open-pollinated, untreated seeds of vegetables, herbs, grains, flowers and green manures. CAT FREE, R & W, PC/CC, OVER.

B49M **Bountiful Harvest** - P.O. Box 11295, Des Moines, IA 50340-1295, (515) 244-0920. Vegetable plants and seeds, berry plants. CAT $1, RET, PC/CC.

B51 **Bowman's Hill Wildflower Preserve** - Washington Crossing Historical Pk., P.O. Box 103, Washington Crossing, PA 18977-0103, (215) 862-2924. Seed of wildflowers native to Pennsylvania. CAT $1, RET, PC, OVER.

B52 **Boyd Nursery Co.** - P.O. Box 71, McMinnville, TN 37110, (615) 668-9898 or 668-4747. Fruit and nut trees, grape vines, perennial vegetables, flowering shrubs, shade trees. CAT FREE, WHLS.

B53 **Boyer Nurseries & Orchards, Inc.** - 405 Boyer Nursery Road, Biglerville, PA 17307, (717) 677-8558 or 677-9567. Fruit and nut trees, berry plants, grape vines, perennial vegetables, ornamental trees and shrubs. CAT FREE, R & W, PC.

B55 **Bricker's Organic Farms, Inc.** - 824-K Sandbar Ferry Road, Augusta, GA 30901, (404) 722-0661. Vegetable seeds, green manure seeds. Also organic gardening supplies. CAT FREE, RET, PC/CC.

B58 **Brittingham's Plant Farms** - P.O. Box 2538, Salisbury MD 21801, (301) 749-5153. Specializes in virus-free strawberry plants propagated from foundation stock. Also sells asparagus, raspberries, blackberries, blueberries and grape vines. CAT FREE, R & W, PC/CC, OVER.

B58M **Brokaw Nursery Inc.** - P.O. Box 4818, Saticoy, CA 93004, (805) 647-2262. Specializes in certified avocado trees, seed, budwood and rootstocks. Also sells citrus, kiwi and cherimoya. CAT FREE, WHLS, PC, OVER.

B59 **Brooks (J.R.) & Son** - P.O. Drawer 9, Homestead, FL 33090, (305) 247-3544. Grower, packer and shipper of a large selection of exotic tropical fruits and vegetables. *Sells the following product/s:* water coconut, green papaya, and fresh winged bean pods. CAT FREE, WHLS, OVER, M.O. 100 BOXES OF EACH.

B60 **Brooks Tree Farm** - 9785 Portland Rd. N.E., Salem, OR 97305, (503) 393-6300. Commercial seedling nursery specializing in Christmas trees and grafting understock.

CAT FREE, WHLS, PC, OVER, M.O. $25 OR 100 PLANTS.

B61M **Brown (Joseph) Wild Seeds and Plants** - Star Route, Box 226, Gloucester Point, VA 23062, (804) 642-4602. Seeds and plants of North American natives, garden perennials, hardy African species. Previously known as Mid-Atlantic Wildflowers. CAT $1, R & W, PC, OVER.

B62 **Brudy (John) Exotics** - 3411 Westfield Drive, Brandon, FL 33511, (813) 684-4302. Seeds of exotic tropical trees and shrubs, both ornamental and edible. CAT $2 REFUNDABLE, RET, PC, OVER.

B67 **Buckley Nursery Garden Center** - 646 North River Ave., Buckley, WA 98321, (206) 829-1811 or 829-0734. Wide range of fruit and nut trees, berry plants, grape vines, perennial vegetables, flowering shrubs. CAT FREE, R & W, PC.

B68 **Buddies Nursery** - P.O. Box 14, Birdsboro, PA 19508, (215) 582-2410. Shade trees, conifers, flowering shrubs. CAT FREE, WHLS.

B71 **Bunton Seed Co.** - 939 East Jefferson St., Louisville, KY 40206, (502) 584-0136. Vegetable, herb and flower seeds. CAT $1, R & W, PC/CC.

B71M **Burchell Nursery Inc.** - 4201 McHenry Avenue, Modesto, CA 95356, (209) 529-5685. Large commercial grower of fruit and nut trees. CAT FREE, WHLS.

B72M **Burford Brothers** - Route 1, Monroe, VA 24574, (804) 929-4950. Extensive selection of antique and modern apples, approximately 300 cultivars. CAT $1, RET, PC, M.O. 3 TREES.

B73M **Burgess Seed and Plant Co.** - 905 Four Seasons Road, Bloomington, IL 61701. Vegetable and flower seeds, fruit and nut trees, berry plants, grape vines, perennial vegetables, ornamental trees and shrubs. CAT $1, RET, PC/CC.

B74 **Burnt Ridge Nursery** - 432 Burnt Ridge Rd., Onalaska, WA 98570, (206) 985-2873 (no telephone orders). Specializes in unusual trees, shrubs and vines that produce edible nuts or fruits including chestnuts, walnuts, chinkapin, heartnut, ginkgo, paw paw, hardy kiwi, asian pear, fig, beechnut and persimmon. CAT SASE, R & W, PC, CANADA ONLY.

B75 **Burpee (W. Atlee) & Co.** - 300 Park Avenue, Warminster, PA 18974, 1-800-888-1447. One of the oldest and best known seed companies in the United States. Offers a wide variety of vegetable, herb and flower seeds, fruit and nut trees, berry plants, grape vines, bulbs and roots. CAT FREE, R & W, PC/CC.

B75M **Burrell (D.V.) Seed Growers Co.** - P.O. Box 150, Rocky Ford, CO 81067-0150, (719) 254-3318. Vegetable and flower seed growers specializing in muskmelon, watermelon, pepper, squash and tomato. CAT FREE, R & W, PC, OVER, M.O. $25 WHLS

B77 **Busse Gardens** - Rt. 2, Box 238, Cokato, MN 55321, (612) 286-2654. Specializes in herbaceous perennials with emphasis on Hosta, daylilies, Siberian irises and hard to find selected perennials. CAT $2 DEDUCTIBLE, R & W, PC/CC, M.O. $20 ($25 WHLS).

B77M **Butchart Gardens** - P.O. Box 4010, Station "A", Victoria, BC V8X 3X4, Canada, (604) 652-4422. Offers many popular and old fashioned varieties of flowers. CAT $1 REFUNDABLE, OVER, CC.

B78 **Butterbrooke Farm** - 78 Barry Road, Oxford, CT 06483, (203) 888-2000. Traditional and heirloom, non-hybrid vegetable seeds produced organically and chemically untreated. CAT SASE, R & W, PC, OVER.

B83 **C & O Nursery** - P.O. Box 116, Wenatchee, WA 98807-0116, 1-800-232-2636. One of the oldest and largest fruit tree nurseries in Washington. Established in 1906. CAT FREE, RET, PC, OVER, M.O. $30.

B83M **C.T.P.** - P.O. Box 10162, Corpus Christi, TX 78460-0162, (512) 241-7933 (no telephone orders). Small company that collects and sells seed of native Southwest plants. CAT FREE, R & W, PC/OC, OVER, M.O. $5.

B84 **Cactus By Dodie** - 934 E. Mettler Rd., Lodi, CA 95242, (209) 368-3692. Cactus and succulent plants. CAT FREE, R & W, PC, OVER, M.O. $15.

B85 **Cactus By Mueller** - 10411 Rosedale Hwy., Bakersfield, CA 93312, (805) 589-2674 (no telephone orders). Large selection of rooted cactus and succulent plants. CAT $1 DEDUCTIBLE, RET, PC.

B88 **Cactus Patch (The)** - R.R. 2, Box 159, Radium, KS 67550-9111, (316) 982-4670 (no telephone orders). Small nursery specializing in cold-hardy cactus and Yucca. CAT $25, RET, PC, M.O. $5.

B90 **Cal/West Seeds** - P.O. Box 1428, Woodland, CA 95695. Sprouting and forage seeds. CAT FREE, WHLS, PC, OVER.

B91M **California Biological Supply Co.** - P.O. Box 1736, Vista, CA 92083, (619) 727-8929. Biological supplies including living cultures of algae, bacteria and fungi. CAT FREE, R & W, PC.

B91T **California Cuisine** - P.O. Box 5038, San Jose, CA 95150-5038, 1-800-333-1448. Gourmet foods, San Francisco sourdough starter culture. CAT FREE, RET, PC/CC.

B92 **California Flora Nursery** - P.O. Box 3, Fulton, CA 95439, (707) 528-8813. Specializes in unusual and hard to find perennials, herbs and shrubs from Mediterranean climates including California, South Africa, Mediterranean Europe, Australia and Chile. CAT FREE, WHLS, PC.

B93M **California Nursery Co.** - Niles District, Box 2278, Fremont, CA 94536, (415) 797-3311. Large selection of fruit and nut trees, grape vines, citrus and avocadoes, bamboo. One of the oldest nurseries in California. Established in 1865. CAT FREE, RET, PC, OVER, M.O. $30.

B94 **Callahan Seeds** - 6045 Foley Lane, Central Point, OR 97052, (503) 855-1164. Specializes in tree and shrub seeds of Western North American plants. CAT SASE, R & W, PC, OVER.

B94M **Callaway Gardens Country Store** - Pine Mountain, GA 31822, 1-800-282-8181. Regional specialty foods. *Sells the following product/s:* muscadine sauce, jelly and preserves. CAT FREE, RET, PC/CC, OVER.

B96 **Camellia Forest Nursery** - 125 Carolina Forest Rd., Chapel Hill, NC 27516, (919) 967-5529 (no telephone orders). Small nursery specializing in Camellias and uncommon plants from Japan and China. Also carries kiwi and hardy citrus. CAT $.50, RET, PC, OVER, M.O. $15.

B97 **Camelot Herb Gardens** - 2954 Read Schoolhouse Rd., Coventry, RI 02816, (401) 397-4588. Organically grown herb plants, scented geraniums, dried herbs, spices and botanicals, potpourri and other herbal products. CAT FREE, R & W, PC, M.O. $50.

B97M **Camelot North** - Rt. 2, Box 398, Pequot Lakes, MN 56472. Specializes in perennials hardy in Zone 3. Also trees, shrubs and bedding plants. CAT $1, RET, PC.

B99 **Campberry Farms** - R.R. #1, Niagara-on-the-Lake, ON L0S 1J0, Canada, (416) 262-4927. Small nursery offering trees and corresponding seeds of unusually hardy, specialty fruit, nut and ornamental plants. CAT FREE, R & W, PC, OVER, M.O. $20.

B99M **Canale's Nursery** - P.O. Box 51, Shelocta, PA 15774, (412) 354-2801. Commercial grower of Christmas trees, flowering shrubs and shadetrees. Also known as Bricillo Ventures, Inc. CAT FREE, WHLS, PC/CC, CANADA ONLY, M.O. $25.

C2 **Canyon Creek Nursery** - 3527 Dry Creek Road, Oroville, CA 95965, (916) 533-2166. Small, family operated nursery specializing in uncommon perennials. CAT $1, RET, PC.

C3 **Capriland's Herb Farm** - 534 Silver St., Coventry, CT 06238, (203) 742-7244 (no telephone orders). Large selection of herb seeds and plants, scented geraniums and herbal products. Owned by well-known herbalist and author Adelma Grenier Simmons. CAT SASE, RET, PC, OVER, M.O. $5.

C3M **Cardullo's Gourmet Shop** - 6 Brattle St., Cambridge, MA 02138, (617) 491-8888. Gourmet foods from around the world. *Sells the following product/s:* achiote and dried flageolet beans. CAT (CALL FOR PRICES), RET, PC, OVER.

C4 **Carhart Feed & Seed** - P.O. Box 55, Dove Creek, CO 81324. Grains, legumes, seed of native plants for revegetation and reclamation work. CAT FREE, R & W, PC.

C7M **Carolina Biological Supply Co.** - 2700 York Road, Burlington, NC 27215, 1-800-334-5551. Complete line of biological supplies including live cultures of fungi, algae and blue-green algae. Also plants and seeds. CAT $15.65, R & W, PC/CC, OVER.

C8 **Carolina Exotic Gardens** - Route 5, Box 283-A, Greenville, NC 27834, (919) 758-2600. Growers of carnivorous plants and seeds. CAT $1, R & W, PC/OC, OVER, M.O. $10.

C8M **Carr's Specialty Foods** - P.O. Box 1016, Manchaca, TX 78652, (512) 282-9056. Specialty foods, organically grown foods. *Sells the following product/s:* dried Bing cherries, dried Zante currants, dried Roma tomatoes, dried Anasazi beans and dried red lentils. CAT FREE, RET, PC/CC.

C9 **Carroll Gardens** - P.O. Box 310, Westminster, MD 21157, (301) 848-5422 or 876-7336. Broad selection of rare and unusual herbs, trees and shrubs, vines, roses, evergreens and perennials. CAT $2, R & W, PC/CC, M.O. $20.

C9M **Carter Seeds** - 475 Mar Vista Drive, Vista, CA 92083, (619) 724-5931. Bulk distributor of seed of trees and shrubs, ornamental grasses, herbs, wild flowers, palms and hybrid flowers. CAT FREE, R & W, PC, OVER, M.O. $15.

C11 **Casa Yerba Gardens** - 3459 Days Creek Road, Days Creek, OR 97429, (503) 825-3534. Herb farm nursery offering seeds, bulbs and plants grown organically where possible. Also teas, potpourri and other herbal products. CAT SASE, RET, PC, OVER.

C11G **Casados Farms** - P.O. Box 1269, San Juan Pueblo, NM 87566, (505) 852-2433. Specializes in Southwestern foods. *Sells the following product/s:* panocha flour and piloncillo. CAT FREE, R & W, PC.

C11M **Cascade Forestry Nursery** - Rt. 1, Cascade, IA 52033, (319) 852-3042. Seedlings and transplants of northern grown fruit and nut trees, evergreens, ornamental shrubs, timber trees and windbreaks. CAT FREE, R & W, OVER, M.O. $20.

C11T **Cascade Mushroom Co.** - 1705 NW 14th Ave., Portland, OR 97209, (503) 294-1550. Fresh and dried wild mushrooms, fresh wild produce. *Sells the following product/s:* both fresh and dried mushrooms (all species), fresh, flash-frozen and canned Perigord truffles. CAT FREE, R & W, PC, OVER.

C12 **Cascadian Farm** - P.O. Box 568, Concrete, WA 98237, (206) 853-8175. Organically grown fruit-sweetened and honey-sweetened conserves, pickles, relish, sauerkraut. *Sells the following product/s:* honey-sweetened huckleberry conserves, fruit-sweetened Boysenberry and Marionberry conserves. CAT FREE, R & W, PC, OVER, M.O. 6 JARS.

C13M **Catnip Acres Herb Farm** - 67 Christian St., Oxford, CT 06483, (203) 888-5649. Extensive selection of rare and unusual herb seeds and everlastings, approximately 350 varieties. CAT $2, RET, PC/CC, OVER.

C14 **Caudill Seed Co.** - 1201 Storey Avenue, Louisville, KY 40206, 1-800-626-5357. Large selection of sprouting seeds for commercial sprout growers. Also a small selection of organic sprouting seeds. CAT FREE, WHLS, OVER.

C15M **Cedar Valley Nursery** - 3833 McElfresh Rd. SW, Centralia, WA 98531, (206) 736-7490. Specializes in tissue culture propagation of small fruits, vegetables and ornamentals. Large selection of blackberries and raspberries. CAT FREE, R & W, PC, OVER, M.O. $15.

C16 **Cedarbrook Herb Farm** - 986 Sequim Ave. South, Sequim, WA 98382, (206) 683-7733. Seed of culinary herbs, herbs for tea, everlastings and other flowers for drying, herbal products. CAT FREE, RET, PC.

C17M **Central Grocery Co.** - 923 Decatur St., New Orleans, LA 70116, (504) 523-1620. Italian and Cajun food specialties. *Sells the following product/s:* chicory coffee and filet powder. CAT FREE, RET, PC, OVER, M.O. $20.

C20 **Chambers (V.O.) Nursery** - 26874 Ferguson Road, Junction City, OR 97448, (503) 998-2467 (no telephone orders). Azaleas and Rhododendron. CAT FREE, RET, PC, M.O. $30.

C21 **Champlain Isle Agro Associates** - East Shore, Isle La Motte, VT 05463, (802) 928-3425. Disease indexed raspberry and blackberry plants. CAT FREE, R & W, PC, OVER.

C23 **Cheesemaking Supply Outlet (The)** - RD #3, Walheim Road, Parker, PA 16049, (412) 791-2449. Home cheese-making and dairy supplies, including starter cultures for yogurt, cheese, kefir, buttermilk, acidophilus and sour cream. CAT FREE, RET, PC.

C24 **Chesnok Farm** - 1091 Marshland Rd., Apalachin, NY 13732, (607) 687-6501. Organically grown garlic bulbs for planting or eating. Specializes in Carpathian garlic. *Sells the following product/s:* Carpathian garlic braids. CAT FREE, RET, PC.

C25 **Chestnut Hill Nursery** - Rt. 1, Box 341, Alachua, FL 32615, (904) 462-2820. Specializes in Dunstan hybrid chestnut plants. Also offers fig trees and more than 30 cultivars of oriental persimmons. CAT FREE, R & W, PC, OVER, M.O. 20 TREES WHLS

C25M **Cheyenne Gap Amaranth** - H.C. 1, Box 2, Luray, KS 67649-9743, (913) 698-2457. Specializes in amaranth seed and amaranth foods. Has small amounts of seed of several experimental lines developed at the Rodale Research Center. Previously known as Arris A. Sigle. *Sells the following product/s:* whole seed amaranth and amaranth flour. CAT $2, R & W, PC, OVER, M.O. $1.

C27 **Choice Edibles** - 584 Riverside Park Rd., Carlotta, CA 95528, (707) 768-3135. Produces and sells cultures and spawn for many types of fungi, including morels. Actively involved in research and advanced growing techniques. CAT SASE, R & W, PC, OVER, M.O. $10.

C27G **Chong Imports** - 838 Grant Ave., San Francisco, CA 94108, (415) 982-1433. Specializes in Chinese foods. *Sells the following product/s:* dried red and black watermelon seeds, canned winter melon soup, dried longan, dried jujubes, lychee nuts, lychee tea, cellophane noodles, water chestnut flour, bok choy kan, dried fat choy, one hundred unities, golden needles, canned Red-in-Snow, Szechuan peppercorns, dried mandarin peel, prepared sufu, canned dung sun, Chinese black vinegar and canned ginkgo nuts. CAT (CALL FOR PRICES), R & W, PC/CC.

C27M **Christa's Cactus** - 529 W. Pima, Coolidge, AZ 85228, (602) 723-4185. Seeds of cacti, succulents and exotica. CAT SASE, R & W, PC/OC, OVER.

C27T **Christian Homesteading Movement** - R.D. #2G, Oxford, NY 13830. Scion wood for more than 300 apple cultivars, rootstocks, custom grafting services. CAT SASE, RET, PC, OVER.

C28 **Christianson (Alf) Seed Co.** - P.O. Box 98, Mount Vernon, WA 98273, (206) 336-9727. Commercial grower of vegetable and sprouting seeds. CAT FREE, WHLS, CANADA ONLY, M.O. $150.

C29M **Citrus Research Center and Agr. Exp. Station** - Department of Botany and Plant Sciences, University of California, Riverside, CA 92521. Offers limited quantities of budwood intended for production of nursery increase blocks which can be used by the wholesale nursery industry in California as a source of scions for growing certified nursery stock. Some budwood is available to non-participants in this certification program. CAT FREE, WHLS, M.O. $25.

C30 **Clargreen Gardens Ltd.** - 814 Southdown Road, Mississauga ON, L5J 2Y4, Canada, (416) 822-0992. Specializes in hybrid and species orchids. CAT FREE, R & W, PC/CC, OVER, M.O. $50.

C32 **Clifford's Perennial & Vine** - Route 2, Box 320, East Troy, WI 53120, (414) 642-7156. Small nursery selling bareroot, field-grown, one year old, blooming size perennials and vines. CAT $1, RET, PC, M.O. $15.

C33 **Clifty View Nursery** - Rt. 1, Box 509, Bonners Ferry, ID 83805, (208) 267-7129 or 267-8953. Northern grown, cold hardy seedlings and transplants for timber and reforestation. CAT FREE, WHLS, PC, CANADA ONLY, M.O. 50 TREES.

C34 **Cloud Mountain Farm** - 6906 Goodwin Rd., Everson, WA 98247, (206) 966-5859. Specializes in fruit and nut trees that have been carefully selected to perform well and ripen consistently in the maritime Northwest. Also offers rootstocks for grafting, berry plants, ornamental trees and shrubs, and fresh produce in season. CAT $1, R & W, PC/CC, M.O. $15.

C36 **Coastal Gardens & Nursery** - 4611 Socastee Blvd., Myrtle Beach, SC 29575, (803) 293-2000. Daylilies, hostas, ferns, rare and unusual perennials. CAT FREE, RET, PC/CC, OVER, M.O. $30.

C37 **Cockrell's Riverside Nursery** - Rt. 2, Box 76, Goldthwaite, TX 76844, (915) 938-5575. Fruit and nut trees including pecans, almonds, plums, peaches and pears, berry plants, grape vines. Specializes in seeds and seedlings of the Riverside pecan rootstock. CAT FREE, R & W, PC/CC, M.O. $10.

C38 **Cold Stream Farm** - 2030 Free Soil Rd., Free Soil, MI 49411-9752, (616) 464-5809. Specializes in hybrid poplar. Also sells conifers, deciduous trees and shrubs, fruit and nut trees. CAT FREE, R & W, PC, M.O. $5.

C39M **Collins Gardens** - Box 48, Viola, IA 52350. Stratified ginseng seed, ginseng planting roots, goldenseal plants and seed, comfrey plants. CAT FREE, RET, PC.

C40 **Colorado Alpines, Inc.** - P.O. Box 2708, Avon, CO 81620, (303) 949-6464. Small nursery specializing in alpine plants from the Rocky Mountain region and from other alpine regions around the world. CAT $2, RET, PC, OVER.

C41M **Columbia Basin Nursery** - P.O. Box 458, Quincy, WA 98848, (509) 787-4411 or 787-2436. Apples, pears, peaches, plums, cherries, apricots, and nectarines for the commercial grower or home orchardist. CAT FREE, R & W, PC, OVER.

C42M **Community Mill & Bean** - R.D. #1, Route 89, Savannah, NY 13146, (315) 365-2664. Verified organically grown grains, beans, flours, cereals. *Sells the following product/s:* durum wheat kernels, durum wheat flour. CAT FREE, R & W, PC, OVER, M.O. $10.

C43M **Companion Plants** - 7247 North Coolville Ridge Road, Athens, OH 45701, (614) 592-4643. Extensive collection of rare and unusual herb plants and seeds, over 400 varieties. CAT $2, R & W, PC/CC, OVER (SEEDS ONLY), M.O. $15 PLANTS, $5 SEEDS.

C44 **Comstock, Ferre & Co.** - P.O. Box 125, Wethersfield, CT 06109-0125, 1-800-346-6110. Vegetable, herb and flower seeds for northern gardeners, both older traditional cultivars and newer improved types. Established in 1820. CAT FREE, R & W, PC/CC, OVER, M.O. $15.

C47 **Congdon & Weller Wholesale Nursery, Inc.** - Mileblock Road, North Collins, NY 14111, (716) 337-0171. Fruit trees, berry plants, grape vines, hardy kiwi, ornamental trees and shrubs. CAT FREE, WHLS, M.O. $2500.

C49 **Conley's Garden Center** - 145 Townsend Avenue, Boothbay Harbor, ME 04538, (207) 633-5020. Garden center and florist shop offering plants of herbs, perennials, wild flowers and ferns. CAT $1.50, R & W, PC/CC, CANADA ONLY, M.O. $25.

C51 **Continental Brewing Supply** - P.O. Box 1227, Daytona Beach, FL 32015, (904) 253-2368. Complete line of supplies for home wine and beer makers. CAT FREE, R & W, PC/CC, OVER.

C53 **Cook's Garden (The)** - P.O Box 65, Londonderry, VT 05148, (802) 824-3400. Seeds of gourmet vegetables, culinary herbs and edible flowers for home gardeners and specialty market growers. Specializes in lettuce, salad greens and mesclun. CAT $1, R & W, PC/CC, OVER.

C53M **Cook's Geranium Nursery** - 712 No. Grand, Highway 14 No., Lyons, KS 67554, (316) 257-5033. Grower of all types of geraniums including a large selection of scented leaf geraniums. CAT $1 REFUNDABLE, RET, PC/OC, OVER.

C54 **Cooke (L.E.) Co.** - 26333 Road 140, Visalia, CA 93277, (209) 732-9146. Commercial grower of deciduous fruit and ornamental trees, shrubs, grapevines, and small fruits and vegetables. CAT FREE, WHLS, PC, M.O. 100 TREES EACH CULTIVAR.

C55M **Cooley's Strawberry Nursery** - P.O. Box 472, Augusta, AR 72006, (501) 347-2026. Specializes in strawberry plants. CAT FREE, R & W, PC, M.O. 100 PLANTS.

C56 **Cooper's Garden** - 212 W. Co. Rd. C., Roseville, MN 55113, (612) 484-7878 (no telephone orders). Small nursery selling hardy ornamental plants, iris, daylilies, daffodils and wild flowers. CAT $.25, RET, PC, OVER.

C56M **Copacabana Gardens** - P.O. Box 323, Moraga, CA 94556, (415) 254-2302. Tropical and sub-tropical fruit trees and shrubs, palms, bamboos and bamboo-like grasses, rare and unusual tropical and sub-tropical plants. CAT $2, R & W, PC, M.O. $25.

C57 **Cope's (John F.) Food Products, Inc.** - P.O. Box 419, Rheems, PA 17570-0419. Specializes in gourmet food items made from corn. *Sells the following product/s:* dried sweet corn. CAT FREE, RET, PC.

C57M **Coral Reef Gardens** - P.O. Box 8, Goulds, FL 33170, (305) 245-9222. Fresh citrus and avocadoes, gourmet food products. CAT FREE, RET, PC, OVER.

C58 **Corn Hill Nursery Ltd.** - Rte. 890, R.R. 5, Petitcodiac, NB E0A 2H0, Canada, (506) 756-3635. Historical, scab free and commercial cultivars of apples, small fruits, hardy fruit trees, hardy kiwi, ornamentals, hardy roses. CAT $2, R & W, PC/CC/OC, CANADA ONLY (EXCEPT ROSES), M.O. $20.

C59M **Corns, 4B-40** - Rt. 1, Box 32, Turpin, OK 73950, (405) 778-3615. Non-profit organization dedicated to growing and preserving open-pollinated and heirloom cultivars of corn. Seed is organically grown and untreated. CAT $1 REFUNDABLE, RET, PC, OVER.

C60 **Corrin Produce Inc.** - P.O. Box 48, Reedley, CA 93654, (209) 638-3636. Specializes in corinthian grapes. *Sells the following product/s:* both fresh and dried Black Corinth and White Corinth grapes. CAT FREE, WHLS.

C60M **Counter Culture** - P.O. Box 1106, Hawthorne, FL 32640, (904) 684-3217. Russian comfrey roots, ginger roots. CAT FREE, RET, PC.

C61M **Country Garden (The)** - Rt. 2, Box 455A, Crivitz, WI 54114-9645, (715) 757-2045. Specializes in old-fashioned garden plants for cutflowers. Offers seeds and plants of flowers for cutting fresh and grasses suitable for dried arrangements. CAT $1, R & W, PC/CC.

C63 **Country Heritage Nurseries** - P.O. Box 536, Hartford, MI 49057, (616) 621-2491 or 621-2260. Family owned and operated business offering a complete line of fruit and nut trees, small fruits, grapevines and perennial vegetables. Succeeded Dean Foster Nursery. CAT FREE, R & W, PC/CC, OVER.

C64 **Country Variety Store** - 6263 U.S. Route 68 N., Bellefontaine, OH 43311. Amish specialties, natural foods. Previously known as Amish Country Store. *Sells the following product/s:* dried sweet corn. CAT FREE, RET, PC.

C64M **Country Wetlands Nursery** - P.O. Box 126, Muskego, WI 53150, (414) 679-1268. Seeds and plants of wetlands, prairie and woodland species, including wild rice, cattail and chufa. CAT $1, R & W, PC.

C65 **Covalda Date Co.** - P.O. Box 908, Coachella, CA 92236, (619) 398-3441 or 398-3551. Pioneer organic date growers. Also citrus and pecans. *Sells the following product/s:* dried Barhi, Dayri, Deglet Noor, Halawi, Khadrawi, Medjool, Thoory and Zahidi dates. CAT FREE, R & W, PC/CC, OVER.

C67M **Cricket Hill Herb Farm, Ltd.** - Glen Street, Rowley, MA 01969, (508) 948-2818. Over 300 varieties of common and uncommon herb plants, seeds, herbal products and crafts, dried herbs and teas. CAT $1, RET, PC/CC.

C68M **Crookham Company** - P.O. Box 520, Caldwell, ID 83606-0520, (208) 459-7451. Commercial breeder and grower of vegetable seeds. CAT FREE, WHLS.

C69 **Crosman Seed Corporation** - P.O. Box 110, East Rochester, NY 14445, (716) 586-1928. Vegetable, herb and flower seeds. Publishes a packet seed listing for home gardeners. Established in 1838. CAT FREE, R & W, PC, M.O. $3.

C69M **Cross Seed Co., Inc.** - HC-69, Box 2, Bunker Hill, KS 67626, (913) 483-6163. Organically grown sprouting seeds and grains. Family owned business founded in 1943. Raises most, but not all of the products they sell. CAT FREE, R & W, PC, OVER.

C73 **CRP Native Plants Nursery** - 9619 Old Redwood Highway, Windsor, CA 95492, (707) 838-6641. Specializes in California native plants for revegetation, including trees and shrubs, vines, native perennial grasses. Previously known as Environmental Restoration Nursery. CAT FREE, WHLS.

C73M **Cruickshank's Inc.** - 1015 Mount Pleasant Rd., Toronto, ON M4P 2M1, Canada, (416) 488-8292. Bulbs, seeds, perennial and ornamental plants. CAT $1 REFUNDABLE, RET, PC/CC/OC, U.S. ONLY, M.O. $20.

C75M **Cumberland Valley Nurseries** - P.O. Box 471, McMinnville, TN 37110-0471, (615) 668-4153 or 1-800-492-0022. Specializes in peach, plum and nectarine trees. Also grows apple, pear, apricot, cherry and pecan. CAT FREE, R & W, PC, OVER, M.O. $25.

C76 **Cummins Garden (The)** - 22 Robertsville Rd., Marlboro, NJ 07746, (201) 536-2591. Specializes in dwarf and unusual Rhododendron hybrids and species, dwarf conifers, evergreen and deciduous azaleas and companion plants. CAT $2, RET, PC/CC, M.O. $15.

C76M **Curran (John) Specialty Seed Co.** - 14 Cedar Ave., Manahawkin, NJ 08050. Seed of open-pollinated traditional and heirloom vegetables and culinary herbs, selected for fine flavor and resistance to drought and heat. CAT $1, RET, PC/OC, OVER.

C78 **Cycad Gardens** - 4524 Toland Way, Los Angeles, CA 90041, (213) 255-6651 (no telephone orders). Cycad seedlings. CAT SASE, R & W, PC, M.O. $30.

C81M **Dabney Herbs** - P.O. Box 22061, Louisville, KY 40222, (502) 893-5198. Herb plants and seeds, vegetable seeds, native Midwest trees and shrubs, perennials for shade, and herbal products. Succeeded Rutland of Kentucky. CAT $2, R & W, PC/CC, CANADA ONLY.

C82 **Dacha Barinka** - 26232 Strathcona Road, Chilliwack, BC V2P 3T2, Canada, (604) 792-0957 (no telephone orders). Large selection of garlic and rocambole, herb plants and seeds, grape vines, unusual and oriental vegetables, everlasting flowers, and perennial vegetables. CAT SASE, RET, PC, OVER.

C84 **Daisy Farms** - 91098 60th Street, Decatur, MI 49045, (616) 782-6321 or 782-7131. Commercial grower specializing in certified strawberry plants. Also sells raspberry, asparagus, rhubarb and horseradish. CAT FREE, WHLS, PC, OVER.

C85M **Dam (William) Seeds Ltd.** - P.O. Box 8400, Dundas, ON L9H 6M1, Canada, (416) 628-6641. Vegetable and flower seed supplier dedicated to selling untreated seed. Specializes in European and unusual cultivars. CAT $1, RET, PC/CC, OVER.

C87 **Datil Do-it Hot Sauce** - P.O. Box 4019, St. Augustine, FL 32085-4019, (904) 824-2609. Specialty food items. *Sells the following product/s:* dried Datil peppers, Datil pepper hot sauce, relish and jelly. CAT FREE, RET, PC.

C88 **Daugherty Brothers Nursery** - Rt. 1, Box 396, Judsonia, AR 72081, (501) 729-3901 or 729-3982. Specializes in strawberry plants. CAT FREE, R & W, PC, M.O. 100 PLANTS.

C89 **David (Simon)** - 7117 Inwood at University, Dallas, TX 75209, 1-800-525-4800. Fresh produce, gourmet food items. *Sells the following product/s:* nopales cactus leaves. CAT FREE, RET, PC/CC, OVER.

C89M **Davidson-Wilson Greenhouses** - R.R. 2, Box 168, Crawfordsville, IN 47933-9423, (317) 364-0556. Extensive listing of unusual house plants, African violets, and scented geraniums. CAT FREE, R & W, PC/CC, OVER.

C91 **Davis (Corwin) Nursery** - R.F.D. #1, 20865 Junction Rd., Bellevue, MI 49021, (616) 781-7402. Specializes in pawpaw including seeds, seedlings and grafted cultivars. CAT SASE, RET, PC.

C91T **De Baggio (T.) Herbs by Mail** - 923 N. Ivy Street, Arlington, VA 22201, (703) 243-2498. Specializes in improved cultivars of rosemary and lavender. CAT FREE, RET, PC/CC, M.O. 3 PLANTS.

C92 **De Giorgi Co. Inc.** - 1529 North Saddle Creek Road, Omaha, NE 68104, (402) 554-1520. Vegetable, herb and flowers seeds, garden perennials, ornamental grasses, tree and shrub seed. Established in 1905. CAT $1.25, RET, PC, OVER.

C93 **De Grandchamp's Blueberry Farm Inc.** - 15575 77th Street, South Haven, MI 49090, (616) 637-3915. Specializes in highbush and lowbush blueberry plants. CAT FREE, R & W, PC, OVER.

C94 **De Wildt Imports** - Fox Gap Road, R.D. 3, Bangor, PA 18013, 1-800-338-3433. Extensive selection of Asian food specialties. *Sells the following product/s:* shelled candle nuts, laos powder, temoo kuntji powder, temu lawak powder, kenchur powder, Kaffir lime leaf powder, kecap manis, dried curry leaves, canned Holland Capucijners peas, keluwak nuts, fresh frozen peteh beans, urid dal, dried pandan leaves, and dried Indonesian bay. CAT FREE, RET, PC/CC, OVER, M.O. $12.

C94M **Dean & Deluca** - 560 Broadway, New York, NY 10012, (212) 431-1691. Gourmet and specialty food items. *Sells the following product/s:* African bird pepper powder, dried Ancho and Pasilla peppers, dried Cannellini beans, dried flageolet beans, dried Verte du Puy lentils, dried Prune d'Agen plums, Bar-le-Duc currant preserves, and dried pink peppercorns. CAT $2, RET, PC/CC.

C95 **Deer Valley Farm** - R.D. 1, Guilford, NY 13780, (607) 764-8556. Natural and organically grown foods. *Sells the following product/s:* Kaffree tea and Red Zinger tea. CAT FREE, R & W, PC, M.O. $5.

C96 **Delegeane Garlic Farms** - P.O. Box 2561, Yountville, CA 94599, (707) 944-8019. Good selection of garlics, for both planting and eating. CAT FREE, RET, PC, CANADA ONLY, M.O. $3.

C97M **Department of Natural Resources** - State of Ohio, Division of Forestry, Fountain Square, Columbus, OH 43224, (614) 265-6565. Sells selected seedlings of high-sugar maple trees. CAT FREE, R & W, OHIO ONLY.

C98 **Desert Enterprises** - P.O. Box 23, Morristown, AZ 85342, (602) 388-2448. Seeds of native Southwestern wild flowers, grasses, trees and shrubs, other drought resistant plants. CAT FREE, R & W, PC, M.O. 1 POUND.

C99 **Desert Nursery** - 1301 So. Copper, Deming, NM 88030, (505) 546-6264. Specializes in winter-hardy cacti and succulents. CAT $.25, RET, PC, M.O. $10.

D1M **Desertland Nursery** - 11306 Gateway East, El Paso, TX 79927, (915) 858-1130. Rare Mexican cacti and succulents, Southwest desert natives, other drought tolerant plants. CAT $1, R & W, PC/CC, OVER (SEEDS ONLY).

D2M **Dharma Farms** - 4062 Yale Creek Rd., Jacksonville, OR 97530. Specializes in certified organically grown garlic and shallots. *Sells the following product/s:* Silverskin garlic braids. CAT FREE, RET, PC, M.O. 5 POUNDS.

D3 **Diamond K Enterprises** - R.R. 1, Box 30, St. Charles, MN 55972, (507) 932-4308 or 5433. Organic sprouting seeds and grains, flour, nuts and dried fruit. CAT FREE, R & W, PC/CC, OVER.

D6 **Dill's Garden Giant** - 400 College Rd., Windsor, NS B0N 2T0, Canada, (902) 798-2728. Specializes in Dill's Atlantic Giant squash, producer of the World's Largest Squash since 1979. CAT $1, R & W, PC/OC, OVER.

D11M **Dominion Seed House** - Corner of Hwy. 7 & Maple Ave., Georgetown, ON L7G 4A2, Canada, (416) 877-7802. Vegetable, herb and flower seeds, bulbs, perennial vegetable plants, ornamentals, and berry plants. CAT FREE, RET, PC/CC, CANADA ONLY.

D11T **Donaroma Nursery and Landscape** - P.O. Box 2189, Edgartown, MA 02539, (508) 627-8366. Large selection of hardy perennials, native wild flowers. CAT FREE, R & W, PC/CC, OVER.

D12 **Dorsing Seeds, Inc.** - P.O. Box 2552, Nyssa, OR 97913-0552, (208) 642-9081. Vegetable, herb and flower seeds. CAT FREE, WHLS.

D13 **Dos Rios Citrus Nursery** - 2 West 6th Street, Yuma, AZ 85364, (602) 726-5183. Specializes in citrus adapted to desert areas. Previously known as S & S Nursery. CAT FREE, WHLS.

Dow Seeds Hawaii Ltd. - P.O. Box 30144, Honolulu, HI 96820-0144. American subsidiary of Dow & Co., New Zealand, which see.

D18 **Driver Nursery** - 2737 North Avenue, Modesto, CA 95351, (209) 523-2811. Commercial grower of fruit and nut trees including almonds, cherries, cling peaches, walnuts and seedling walnut rootstocks. CAT FREE, WHLS.

Duncan and Davies - P.O. Box 648, Lynden, WA 98264. American subsidiary of Duncan and Davies Nurseries Ltd., New Zealand, which see.

D23M **Durling Nursery, Inc.** - 40401 De Luz Rd., Fallbrook, CA 92028, (619) 728-9572. Containerized stock of citrus and avocado trees, deciduous nuts, sub-tropical fruits, low-chill deciduous fruits, figs, kiwi, olives and grape vines. CAT FREE, WHLS, PC, M.O. $400.

D24 **Dutch Gardens Inc.** - P.O. Box 200, Adelphia, NJ 07710, (201) 780-2713. Dutch bulbs, shallots, onion sets. CAT $1, RET, PC/CC, M.O. $20.

D25M **Dyke Bros. Nursery** - Rt. 1, Box 251, Vincent, OH 45784, (614) 678-2192. Specializes in blackberry and highbush blueberry plants. CAT FREE, WHLS.

D26 **E & H Products** - 78-260 Darby Road, Bermuda Dunes, CA 92201, (619) 345-0147. Seeds of wild flowers and herbs. CAT $1, RET, PC, CANADA ONLY.

D26M **Eagle Agricultural Products** - 2223 N. College, Fayetteville, AR 72701, (501) 738-2203. Organically grown grain and grain products, sprouting seeds. *Sells the following product/s:* dried Anasazi beans, dried black soybeans, whole grain amaranth. CAT FREE, R & W, PC/CC.

D27 **Early's Farm & Garden Centre** - P.O. Box 3024, Saskatoon, SK S7K 3S9, Canada, (306) 931-1982. Vegetable, herb and flower seed, bulbs and farm seed. CAT $2, R & W, PC/CC, U.S. ONLY.

D29 **Earthstar Herb Gardens** - P.O. Box 1022, Chino Valley, AZ 86323, (602) 636-4910. Small family owned business that propagates and grows herbs organically. CAT $1, RET, PC, OVER.

D30 **Eastern Plant Specialties** - P.O. Box 226, Georgetown, ME 04548, (207) 371-2888. Rare and unusual hardy plants including perennials, shade trees and flowering shrubs. CAT FREE, RET, PC/CC.

D32 **Eccles Nurseries, Inc.** - Drawer Y, Rimersburg, PA 16248-0525, (814) 473-6265 or 473-3550. Evergreen seedlings and transplants. CAT FREE, WHLS, PC/CC.

D33 **Echo** - 17430 Durrance Road, North Fort Myers, FL 33917, (813) 543-3246 (no telephone orders). Non-profit research and education organization specializing in seeds and plants of underexploited but important tropical food crops. CAT $1, RET, PC, OVER.

D34M **Ecology Sound Farms** - 42126 Road 168, Orosi, CA 93647, (209) 528-2276. Organically grown oranges, kiwi, Asian pears, persimmons and plums. CAT FREE, R & W, PC, OVER.

D35 **Edelman (Jack)** - P.O. Box 400737, Brooklyn, NY 11240. Single proprietor company specializing in chayote squash. CAT FREE, RET, PC, OVER, M.O. $5.

D35M **Edgewood Wholesale Nursery** - 35 Portland St., Rochester, NH 03867, (603) 332-7388. Fruit trees, berry plants, grape vines, vegetable and herb plants, ornamental trees and shrubs. CAT FREE, WHLS.

D37 **Edible Landscaping Nursery** - P.O. Box 77, Afton, VA 22920, (804) 361-9134. Extensive list of fruit and nut trees for edible landscaping. Specializes in hardy kiwi but also sells mulberries, figs, gooseberries and currants, berry plants, grapes and persimmons. CAT FREE, R & W, PC, OVER.

D40 **Elix Corporation** - Rt. 1, Box 133-1A, Arvonia, VA 23004, (804) 983-2676. Growers, packers and shippers of fresh and dried Golden Oak brand shiitake mushrooms. Also sells shiitake spawn. CAT FREE, R & W, PC, OVER.

D40G **Elixir Farm Botanicals** - General Delivery, Brixey, MO 65618, (417) 261-2393. Specializes in certified organically grown seeds of medicinal plants native to the Ozarks region. CAT FREE, RET, PC.

D40M **Elk (Bob)** - Rt. 2, Box 280, Twisp, WA 98856, (509) 997-4811. Specializes in organically grown Spanish Roja garlic. *Sells the following product/s:* whole Spanish Roja garlic, Spanish Roja garlic powder. CAT FREE, RET, PC.

D41M **Elysian Hills** - RFD #5, Box 452, Brattleboro, VT 05301, (802) 257-0233 (no telephone orders). Specializes in Gilfeather turnip seed. Owns the trademark for Gilfeather which cannot be used without permission. CAT FREE, R & W, PC, OVER, M.O. 5 LBS. WHLS

D43 **Endangered Species** - P.O. Box 1830, Tustin, CA 92681-1830, (714) 544-9505. Large collection of bamboo, palms, cycads, ornamental grasses, and tropical foliage plants. CAT $5, R & W, PC/CC, OVER, M.O. $25.

D43M **Enoch's Berry Farm** - Rt. 2, Box 227C, Fouke, AR 71837, (501) 653-2806. Specializes in upright blackberry cultivars developed at the University of Arkansas Experiment Station. CAT FREE, R & W, PC, M.O. 10 PLANTS.

D45 **Environmental Collaboration (The)** - P.O. Box 539, Osseo, MN 55369. Seedling and transplant nut trees, hardwoods. CAT FREE, R & W, PC, M.O. 5 TREES EACH SPECIES.

D46 **Environmentals** - Box 730, Cutchogue, NY 11935, (516) 734-6439. Ornamental trees and shrubs, dwarf conifers, Northeastern natives. CAT FREE, R & W, PC.

D47 **Eppler (A.I.) Ltd.** - P.O. Box 16513, Seattle, WA 98116-0513, (206) 932-2211. Extensive selection of currants and gooseberries, the original Bauer jostaberry, improved cultivars of Cornelian cherry. CAT FREE, R & W, PC, OVER.

D47M **Ernst Crownvetch Farms** - R.D. 5, Box 806, Meadville, PA 16335, (814) 425-7276. Grains, legumes, cover crop and forage seeds. CAT FREE, R & W, PC, OVER.

D49 **Esco/Kasch Seeds** - P.O. Box 2350, San Marcos, TX 78667-9990, (512) 353-8972. Vegetables seeds, including regional Southwestern specialties. CAT FREE, WHLS.

D55 **Evergreen Y.H. Enterprises** - P.O. Box 17538, Anaheim, CA 92817. Good selection of oriental vegetable seeds, over 50 varieties. CAT $1, R & W, PC, OVER.

D57 **Exotica Rare Fruit Nursery** - P.O. Box 160, Vista, CA 92083, (619) 724-9093. Wide selection of organic and bio-dynamically grown tropical and sub-tropical fruit trees and nuts, bamboo, exotic tropical flowering shrubs, trees and vines, fragrant plants, palms, tropical herbs, spices and vegetables. CAT SASE, R & W, PC/CC, OVER.

D58 **F & J Seed Service** - P.O. Box 82, Woodstock, IL 60098-0082, (815) 338-4029. Specializes in weed and grass seeds for research purposes. CAT FREE, R & W, PC, OVER.

D59 **Fairacre Nursery** - Rt. 1, Box 1068, Prosser, WA 99350-9788, (509) 786-2974. Certified nursery stock of grapes, currants, gooseberries and asparagus. Succeeded Lewis & White. CAT FREE, WHLS, PC, OVER, M.O. 25 EACH CULTIVAR.

D60 **Fall Creek Farm & Nursery, Inc.** - 39318 Jasper-Lowell Rd., Lowell, OR 97452, (503) 937-2973. Grower and propagator of blueberry plants for commercial fruit growers and wholesale and retail nurseries. Rare and uncommon cultivars, new releases. CAT FREE, WHLS, PC, OVER, M.O. 50 PLANTS.

D61 **Fancy Fronds** - 1911 4th Avenue West, Seattle, WA 98119, (206) 284-5332. Temperate ferns, all raised from spores or vegetatively. Specializes in English Victorian cultivars and xeric ferns. CAT $1 REFUNDABLE, R & W, PC, OVER, M.O. $10.

D62 **Far North Gardens** - 16785 Harrison, Livonia, MI 48154, (313) 522-9040 (no telephone orders). Rare flower seed from around the world, wild flowers, herbs and gourmet vegetables, ferns, perennials, aquatics, trees and shrubs, cacti and succulents. CAT $2 DEDUCTIBLE, RET, PC/OC, OVER.

D63 **Far West Fungi** - P.O. Box 428, South San Francisco, CA 94083, (415) 871-0786 (c.o.d. only). Easy to grow, pre-activated mushroom mini-farms, spawn, mushroom growing supplies. CAT FREE, R & W, PC, CANADA ONLY.

D65 **Farmer Seed & Nursery Co.** - P.O. Box 129, Faribault, MN 55021, (507) 334-1623. Vegetable, herb and flower seed, fruit trees, berry plants, perennial vegetable plants, ornamental trees and shrubs. CAT FREE, RET, PC/CC/OC, OVER.

D68 **Fedco Seeds** - 52 Mayflower Hill Dr., Waterville, ME 04901, (207) 872-9093. Regional seed co-op specializing in vegetable seeds for northern areas such as the Northeast, parts of the Rocky Mountains and the Pacific Northwest. Discourages orders from other areas. Subsidiary of Moose Tubers. CAT FREE, R & W, PC, M.O. $35.

D69 **Fedco Trees** - Box 340, Palermo, ME 04354, (207) 993-2837. Regional co-op nursery specializing in unusual and cold-hardy fruit and nut trees, chosen specifically for Maine's climate. CAT FREE, RET, PC, M.O. $50.

D71 **Fern Hill Farm** - P.O. Box 185, Clarksboro, NJ 08020. Specializes in certified, hand selected, Dr. Martin pole lima bean seeds. Also offers pre-germinated, thiram treated seed for improved stands. CAT SASE, RET, PC, OVER, M.O. $5.

D72 **Fernald's Nursery** - R.R. #2, Monmouth, IL 61462, (309) 734-6994. Seedling and grafted northern adapted nut trees. Specializes in pecans. Also offers a custom grafting service. CAT SASE, R & W, PC.

D74 **Ferry-Morse Seed Co.** - P.O. Box 4938, Modesto, CA 95352-4938, (209) 579-7333. Complete line of vegetable seeds for commercial growers. CAT FREE, WHLS, OVER.

D74M **Fiddler's Green Farm** - R.F.D. 1, Box 656, Belfast, ME 04915, (207) 338-3568. Certified organically grown grains, flours and cereals, potatoes. *Sells the following product/s:* Saskatchewan wild rice and Baldwin apple butter. CAT FREE, RET, PC/CC.

D75 **Fiddyment Farms Inc.** - 5000 Fiddyment Rd., Roseville, CA 95678, (916) 771-0800. Seedling and grafted pistachio trees, pistachio seed, pistachio rootstocks. CAT FREE, R & W, PC, OVER, M.O. $50 SEEDS.

D75M **Field & Forest Products** - N3296 Kozuzek Road, Peshtigo, WI 54157, (715) 582-4997. Mushroom growing kits and spawn, supplies and equipment. Large selection of shiitake strains. CAT FREE, RET, PC/CC, OVER.

D75T **Field (Timothy D.)** - 395 Newington Rd., Newington, NH 03801, (603) 436-0457. Native ferns and wild flowers. Succeeded Francis M. Sinclair. CAT FREE, R & W, PC, M.O. $10.

D76 **Field's (Henry) Seed & Nursery Co.** - 407 Sycamore Street, Shenandoah, IA 51602, (605) 665-9391. Vegetable, herb and flower seed, fruit and nut trees, berry plants, ornamental trees and shrubs, perennial vegetable plants. Established in 1892. CAT FREE, R & W, PC/CC.

D77M **Fig Tree Nursery** - P.O. Box 124, Gulf Hammock, FL 32639, (904) 486-2930 (no telephone orders). Large selection of fig trees. Also muscadine grapes, pears and persimmons. CAT $1, R & W, CC, OVER, M.O. $5.

D79 **Fincastle Nursery & Farms** - Rt. 2, Box 169, Larue, TX 75770, (214) 675-4022. Berry plants, grape vines. CAT FREE, R & W, PC.

D79M **Finch Blueberry Nursery** - P.O. Box 699, Bailey, NC 27807, 1-800-245-4662. Specializes in rabbiteye blueberry plants. CAT FREE, R & W, PC/CC/OC, OVER, M.O. $20.

D81 **Firman Pollen Co., Inc.** - 301 North 1st Ave., Yakima, WA 98902, (509) 452-8063. Fruit and nut tree pollen for controlled pollination, including pollen of individual cultivars of apples, cherries, almonds and pistachios. CAT FREE, R & W, PC.

D81M **FirmYield Pollen Services Inc.** - 2626 Rudkin Road, Yakima, WA 98903, (509) 452-1495. Hand-collected fruit and nut tree pollen for controlled pollination of orchards, including Rome, Jonathan and Winter Banana apple pollen. CAT FREE, R & W, PC.

D81T **Fisher Scientific-EMD** - 4901 LeMoyne St., Chicago, IL 60651, 1-800-621-4769. Complete line of biological supplies, including live cultures of algae, bacteria and fungi. Sells mostly to schools. CAT $25, R & W, PC/CC, OVER.

D82 **Fisher's Garden Store** - P.O. Box 236, Belgrade, MT 59714, (406) 388-6052. Small seed company specializing in short season vegetables and flowers. Breeders and introducers of some unusual cultivars. CAT FREE, RET, PC.

D87 **Floating Mountain Seeds** - P.O. Box 1275, Port Angeles, WA 98362, (206) 457-1888. Small family owned seed company specializing in organically grown heirloom vegetables and flowers. CAT $1.50, RET, PC/CC, OVER.

D87G **Florida Keys Native Nursery, Inc.** - 102 Mohawk Street, Tavernier, FL 33070, (305) 852-5515. Specializes in native plants of the Florida Keys. CAT FREE, R & W, PC, OVER.

D87M **Florida Mycology Research Center** - P.O. Box 8104, Pensacola, FL 32505, (904) 478-3912. One of the largest mushroom spore and live culture banks. Also sells mushroom growing supplies and equipment. CAT $5, R & W, PC, OVER.

D92 **Flowerplace Plant Farm** - P.O. Box 4865, Meridian, MS 39304, (601) 482-5686. Herbs, wild flowers, garden perennials, ornamental grasses. CAT $1, R & W, PC, M.O. $10.

D95 **Forest Farm** - 990 Tetherow Rd., Williams, OR 97544-9599, (503) 846-6963. Extensive selection of affordable containerized starter plants, including, ornamentals, perennials, native plants, wild fruits, fragrant plants, plants for birds and wildlife. CAT $2, RET, PC, CANADA ONLY, M.O. 10 PLANTS.

D96 **Forest Seeds of California** - 1100 Indian Hill Road, Placerville, CA 95667, (916) 621-1551. Forest tree seeds for reforestation, woodlots and ornament. CAT FREE, R & W, PC, Overseas.

E0 **Foster Concord Nurseries, Inc.** - Mileblock Road, North Collins, NY 14111, (716) 337-2485. Large selection of table and wine grapes, over 75 cultivars including American, French hybrid and Vinifera types. CAT FREE, R & W, PC/CC, CANADA ONLY, M.O. $200 WHLS

E1 **Foundation Seed & Plant Materials Service** - University of California, Davis, CA 95616, (916) 752-3590. Certified disease-free propagating material intended for the California wholesale nursery industry. Available to non-commercial users in California on a limited basis as resources allow. CAT FREE, RET, PC, OVER, M.O. $25.

E1G **Four Apostles' Ranch** - P.O. Box 908, Indio, CA 92202, (619) 345-6171 (no telephone orders). Certified organically grown dates. *Sells the following product/s:* dried Medjool dates. CAT FREE, R & W, PC.

E1M **Four Chimneys Farm Winery** - R.D. #1, Hall Road, Himrod-on-Seneca, NY 14842, (607) 243-7502. Organically grown wines, grape juice and wine vinegar. *Sells the following product/s:* Concord, Delaware and Niagara grape juice. CAT FREE, RET, PC.

E2 **Four Seasons Distributors** - P.O. Box 17563, Portland, OR 97217-0563, (503) 286-6458. Specializes in mushroom spawn from some of the most famous spawn companies and suppliers of Asia, including Mr. Tahei Fujimoto of the Yamato Mycological Research Laboratory. CAT $2, R & W, PC, OREGON AND WASHINGTON ONLY.

E3 **Four Seasons Nursery** - 1706 Morrissey Drive, Bloomington, IL 61704. Fruit and nut trees, berry plants, grape vines, ornamental trees and shrubs. CAT FREE, RET, PC/CC.

E3M **Four Winds Growers** - P.O. Box 3538, Fremont, CA 94539, (415) 656-2591. Specializes in grafted, true-dwarf citrus including oranges, mandarins, lemons, limes, grapefruits, tangelos and kumquats. CAT SASE, R & W, PC, OVER.

E4 **Fowler Nurseries** - 525 Fowler Rd., Newcastle, CA 95658, (916) 645-8191. Growers of fruit and nut trees for commercial and home orchardists. Also grows and sells forest seedlings for Christmas trees and timber. CAT FREE, R & W, PC/CC, OVER.

E5M **Fox Hill Farm** - 444 W. Michigan Ave., Box 9, Parma, MI 49269-0009, (517) 531-3179. Herb growers, processors and marketers. Products include herb plants and seeds, specialty vegetables, fresh cut produce, fancy foods, and herbal crafts. CAT $2, R & W, PC/CC, OVER, M.O. $15.

E5T **Fox Hollow Herbs** - P.O. Box 148, McGrann, PA 16236. Organically grown herb and specialty vegetable seeds selected for flavor, tenderness, hardiness and disease resistance. CAT FREE, RET, PC.

E6 **Foxborough Nursery** - 3611 Miller Rd., Street, MD 21154, (301) 836-7023 (no telephone orders). Growers of dwarf and unusual conifers, broadleaf evergreens, and deciduous trees. CAT $1, RET, PC, CANADA ONLY, M.O. $25.

E7 **Fragrant Fields** - 128 Front Street, Dongola IL 62926, 1-800-635-0282. Herb plants and seeds, herbal products and craft items. CAT $1, R & W, PC.

E7M **Fragrant Path (The)** - P.O. Box 328, Fort Calhoun, NE 68023. Seeds of fragrant plants, herbs, prairie flowers, rare and old-fashioned perennials, vines, trees and shrubs. CAT $1, RET, PC, M.O. $5.

E9M **Fred's Plant Farm** - Rt. 1, Box 707, Dresden, TN, 38225-0707, 1-800-243-9377. Specializes in sweet potato plants and chewing tobacco. CAT FREE, R & W, PC.

E11 **French's** - P.O. Box 565, Pittsfield, VT 05762-0562, (802) 746-8148. Specializes in imported bulbs. CAT FREE, RET, PC/CC.

E12 **Freshops** - 36180 Kings Valley Hwy., Philomath, OR 97370, (503) 929-2736. Raw hop flowers and beer yeasts for brewing, hop rhizomes for planting. CAT FREE, R & W, PC/CC, OVER, M.O. 12 OZ.

E13 **Frey Scientific** - 905 Hickory Lane, Mansfield, OH 44905, 1-800-225-3739. Biological supplies including living cultures of algae, bacteria and fungi. CAT FREE, R & W, PC.

E13G **Frieda's by Mail** - P.O. Box 58488, Los Angeles, CA 90058, 1-800-421-9477. Exotic gift baskets of fresh fruits and vegetables from Frieda's Finest, one of the nation's leading marketers and distributors of unusual produce. CAT FREE, RET, PC/CC.

E15 **Frosty Hollow Nursery** - P.O. Box 53, Langley, WA 98260, (206) 221-2332. Seeds of Pacific Northwest and Intermountain species of wildflowers, trees and shrubs. Consultants in restoration of disturbed or damaged land. CAT SASE, R & W, PC, OVER, M.O. $10.

E15M **Fruit Basket (The)** - P.O. Box 4, Velarde, NM 87582, (505) 852-2310 or 852-4638. Specializes in blue corn, chile seeds, and Southwestern and Mexican foodstuffs. *Sells the following product/s:* chile Pequín ristras, chile Pequín wreaths, and Blue popping corn. CAT FREE, R & W, PC/CC, OVER.

E17M **Fruitland Nurseries** - RFD #2, Box 490, Thomson, GA 30824. Specializes in bamboo, both hardy and tropical. CAT FREE, RET, PC.

E18M **Fruitworks** - P.O. Box 334, Chambersburg, PA 17201. Small cottage business offering sampler boxes of apples for tasting. Specializes in unique cultivars from the New York and Pennsylvania areas. CAT FREE, RET, PC.

E19M **Full Moon Mushrooms** - P.O. Box 6138, Olympia, WA 98502, (206) 866-9362. Mushroom growing kits. CAT SASE, R & W, PC/CC, OVER.

E21 **Fungi Perfecti** - P.O. Box 7634, Olympia, WA 98507, (206) 426-9292. State-of-the-art equipment for the cultivation of exotic mushrooms, cultures and spawn, professional advice and consultation, and the latest information on new technologies. CAT $3, R & W, PC/CC, OVER, M.O. $10.

E21G **Future Organics** - P.O. Box 228, Butte, ND 58723, (701) 626-7360. Organically grown seeds and grains. Broker for very large bulk orders. Also custom cleaning, blending, bagging of grains, and hulling of barley and millet. Previously known as Dossen Organic Millet. CAT FREE, R & W, PC, M.O. 25 POUNDS.

E21M **G & G Gardens and Growers** - 6711 Tustin Road, Salinas, CA 93907, (408) 663-6252. Fuchsia starter plants. CAT $1, R & W, PC/CC, M.O. 6 PLANTS.

E23G **Gabrielsen (Joseph)** - Box 311, Graettinger, IA 51342, (712) 859-3955. Small backyard nursery offering plants of Rex purple raspberry. Orders booked in the fall only for spring delivery. CAT FREE, RET, PC, M.O. 6 PLANTS.

E23T **Gainer Seed Farm, Inc.** - 624 W. County Line Road, Urbana, OH 43078, (513) 399-1250. Grains, green manure crops, farm seeds. CAT FREE, WHLS.

E24 **Garden City Seeds** - 1324 Red Crow Road, Victor, MT 59875-9713, (406) 961-4837 (no telephone orders). Non-profit organization specializing in open-pollinated vegetable, flower, herb and farm seeds. Also roots and tubers of perennial vegetables. CAT $2, R & W, PC, OVER.

E26 **Garden Goodies** - P.O. Box 1144, Page, AZ 86040, (602) 645-3155. Live kefir grains for culturing milk. CAT FREE, RET, PC/CC, OVER.

E29 **Garden of Delights** - 2018 Mayo Street, Hollywood, FL 33020, (305) 923-20287. Extensive selection of tropical and sub-tropical fruit and nut trees, seeds and seedlings, fruiting palms, and fresh rare fruit in season. CAT $2, R & W, PC, OVER, M.O. $50.

E29M **Garden of Eden (The)** - P.O. Drawer 1552, Auburn, AL 36830, (205) 826-3336. Fruit and nut trees for the Deep South including low-chill apples, peaches and pears, figs, oriental persimmons, rabbiteye blueberries, muscadines, bunch grapes, pecans. CAT FREE, RET, PC.

E30 **Garden Place** - P.O. Box 388, Mentor, OH 44061-0388, (216) 255-3705. Field grown, bare root perennials, ground covers, herbs and ornamental grasses. CAT $1, RET, PC, CANADA ONLY, M.O. $10.

E31 **Garden Spot Distributors** - 438 White Oak Road, New Holland, PA 17557, 1-800-829-5100. Organically grown natural food items. Exclusive East Coast distributor for Shiloh Farms. *Sells the following product/s:* dried red lentils, whole grain quinoa, quinoa flour, Boysenberry juice, and Yukon Gold potato chips. CAT FREE, R & W, PC/CC.

E31M **Garden World** - 2503 Garfield St., Laredo, TX 78043, (512) 724-3951. Rare and unusual plant material. Specializes in bananas, citrus and tropical fruits. Also organizes seed and plant collecting expeditions. CAT $1, R & W, PC, OVER, M.O. $50 WHLS

E32 **Gardener's Supply** - 128 Intervale Road, Burlington, VT 05401, (802) 863-1700. Home mushroom growing kits, garden supplies. CAT FREE, RET, PC/CC.

E32M **Gardeners' Choice** - P.O. Box 8000, Hartford, MI 49057, (515) 244-2844. Fruit and nut trees, berry plants, grape vines, kiwi, annual vegetable seeds and plants, indoor exotics. CAT FREE, RET, PC/CC.

E33 **Gardenimport Inc.** - P.O. Box 760, Thornhill, ON L3T 4A5, Canada, (416) 731-1950. Vegetable seeds, bulbs, unusual plants. North American agents for Suttons Seeds of Great Britain. CAT $3, R & W, PC/CC, OVER, M.O. $15.

E33M **Gardens of the Blue Ridge** - P.O. Box 10, Pineola, NC 28662, (704) 733-2417. One of the oldest nurseries supplying native wildflowers, trees and shrubs. Established in 1892. CAT $2, R & W, PC, OVER, M.O. $10.

E38 **Gaze Seed Co. Ltd.** - P.O. Box 640, St. John's, NF A1C 5K8, Canada, (709) 722-4590. Vegetable and flower seeds, bulbs, trees and shrubs. Selected for their adaptability to the Newfoundland climate. CAT FREE, R & W, PC/CC, OVER, M.O. $10.

E39 **Ge-No's Nursery** - 8868 Road 28, Madera, CA 93637, (209) 674-4752. California certified vinifera grape vines, both for table and wine. Also supplies resistant grape rootstocks and scion wood. CAT FREE, R & W, CC, OVER, M.O. $50.

E40 **Gem Cultures** - 30301 Sherwood Rd., Fort Bragg, CA 95437, (707) 964-2922 (no telephone orders). Most complete selection of starters for home culturing, including tempeh, misos, shoyu, amazake, sourdough, kefir and viili. CAT FREE, R & W, PC, OVER.

E41M **Gerardi (Louis) Nursery** - 1700 East Highway 50, O'Fallon, IL 62269, (618) 632-4456. Scionwood for a wide selection of nut trees, including pecans, walnuts, chestnuts, hickory nuts, heartnuts and butternuts. Also American persimmons and mulberries. CAT SASE, RET, PC.

E43M **Giant Watermelons** - P.O. Box 141, Hope, AR 71801. Seeds of extra large watermelons and muskmelons. Also sells a growers guide which includes a history of record watermelons grown between 1917 and 1987. CAT FREE, RET, PC, OVER.

E45 **Gill Nursery** - Rt. 1, Box 237AA, Baileyton, AL 35019, (205) 796-5618. Deciduous fruit and nut trees, grape vines, shade trees, flowering shrubs. CAT FREE, WHLS.

E47 **Girard Nurseries** - P.O. Box 428, Geneva, OH 44041, (216) 466-2881. Flowering trees and shrubs, ground covers, vines, perennials, berry plants, nut trees, tree and shrub seed. CAT FREE, R & W, PC/CC, OVER, M.O. $20.

E47M **Gladside Gardens** - 61 Main Street, Northfield, MA 01360, (413) 498-2657. Tender bulbs and perennials. Specializes in gladiolus, dahlias, and canna lilies. CAT $1 REFUNDABLE, R & W, PC, OVER, M.O. $10.

E48 **Glasshouse Works** - P.O. Box 97, Stewart, OH 45778-0097, (614) 662-2142. Large collection of unusual, hard to find tropical and sub-tropical plants, hardy perennials, rare tropical herbs and spices. Specializes in forms with variegated foliage or dwarf habit. CAT FREE, R & W, PC/CC/OC, OVER, M.O. $10.

E49 **Gleckler's Seedsmen** - Metamora, OH 43540. Rare and unusual vegetables, many imported from around the world. Specializes in tomatoes and eggplants. CAT FREE, R & W, PC, OVER, M.O. $2.

E50 **Glendale Enterprises** - Rt. 3, Box 77-P, DeFuniak Springs, FL 32433, (904) 859-2141. Specializes in chufa tubers. CAT $1, R & W, PC, OVER, M.O. $5.

E53 **Globe Seed & Feed Co., Inc.** - P.O. Box 445, Twin Falls, ID 83303-0445, (208) 733-1373. Seed grains, cover crop and green manure seeds, native grasses and forbs, seed potatoes. CAT FREE, R & W, PC.

E53M **Gloeckner (Fred C.) & Co.** - 15 East 26th Street, New York, NY 10010, (212) 481-0920. Seed of vegetables, herbs and flowers, garden perennials, tropical foliage plants, exotic trees and shrubs, ornamental grasses, cacti and succulents, fern spores. CAT FREE, WHLS, PC, OVER.

E56 **Gold Mine Natural Food Co.** - 1947 30th St., San Diego, CA 92102, (619) 234-9711. Full-line of hard to find macrobiotic foods including Ohsawa America products, starter cultures. *Sells the following product/s:* umeboshi plums, ko-umeboshi, cafe du grain, kuzu starch, dried Japanese mugwort, yuzu vinegar, daikon pickles, dried burdock, daikon and lotus roots, brown and ivory teff grains, Kamut wheat flakes, canola oil, hato-mugi grain, dried Black Aztec corn, dried Boleta beans, dried black soybeans, prepared hama-natto, dried wheat gluten, seitan and super blue-green algae. CAT FREE, RET, PC/CC, OVER.

E57 **Golden Acres Farm** - R.R. #2, Box 7430, Fairfield, ME 04937, (207) 453-7771 (no telephone orders). Small, family owned vegetable seed company. Each cultivar is evaluated for flavor, disease resistance, adaptation and yield. CAT $2 REFUNDABLE, RET, PC, M.O. $50 WHLS

E59 **Good Earth Seed Co. (The)** - P.O. Box 5644, Redwood City, CA 94063, (415) 595-2270. Seed of oriental and specialty vegetables, oriental food products. Previously known as Tsang & Ma International. CAT FREE, R & W, PC/CC, OVER.

E59T **Good Hollow Greenhouse & Herbarium** - Route 1, Box 116, Taft, TN 38488, (615) 433-7640. Herb plants, scented geraniums, garden perennials, botanicals, herbal products. CAT $1, RET, PC, CANADA ONLY.

E59Z **Good Seed Co.** - Star Route Box 73A, Oroville (Chesaw), WA 98844, (509) 485-3605. Specializes in untreated heirloom and open-pollinated vegetable seeds. Also herbs, everlastings, hardy trees and shrubs. CAT $2, RET, PC, OVER, M.O. $5.

E60 **Goodson (John M.) Nursery** - Rt. 1, Box 111, Mount Olive, NC 28365, (919) 658-3413. Specializes in strawberry plants. CAT FREE, R & W, PC, M.O. 100 PLANTS.

E61 **Goodwin Creek Gardens** - P.O. Box 83, Williams, OR 97544, (503) 846-7357. Organic growers of herb plants and seeds, nursery propagated native American herbs, an extensive list of seeds for hard to find everlastings. CAT $1 REFUNDABLE, RET, PC/CC, CANADA ONLY (SEEDS).

E62 **Gordon (John H.) Nursery** - 1385 Campbell Blvd., North Tonawanda, NY 14120, (716) 691-9371. Grower of hardy and early ripening nut trees, pawpaw, native American persimmons. Also sells seeds and in-shell nut samples of individual cultivars for tasting before purchasing. CAT FREE, R & W, PC, OVER (SEED ONLY).

E63 **Gossler Farms Nursery** - 1200 Weaver Rd., Springfield, OR 97478-9663, (503) 746-3922. Rare and unusual ornamental trees and shrubs. Specializes in magnolias. CAT $1, R & W, PC.

E63G **Gourmet Mushrooms** - P.O. Box 601, Graton, CA 95444. Specializes in morel mushroom kits for home gardeners. CAT FREE, RET, PC.

E63M **Graham (Russell), Purveyor of Plants** - 4030 Eagle Crest Rd. N.W., Salem, OR 97304, (503) 362-1135. Specialty bulbs, lilies, native wild flowers, ornamental grasses, hardy ferns. CAT $2 DEDUCTIBLE, R & W, PC, CANADA ONLY, M.O. $20.

E63T **Grain Exchange/Garden Grains** - 2440 East Water Well Road, Salina, KS 67401. Offers seed of staple grain crops in quantities suited to garden-scale bread patches, including wheat, rye, hulless oats, hulless barley, corn and amaranth. Many cultivars are rare or heirlooms. CAT FREE, RET, PC.

E66 **Grandview Nursery** - Rt. 4, Box 44, Youngsville, LA 70592, (318) 656-5293. Rabbiteye blueberries, muscadines, ornamental trees and shrubs. CAT FREE, WHLS.

E66M **Granite Seed** - P.O. Box 177, Lehi, UT 84043, (801) 768-4422. Native wild flowers and forbs, reclamation grasses, trees and shrubs, green manures, regional wild flower mixes. Specializes in custom blended seed mixtures. Succeeded Porter-Walton. Previously known as Native Plants Inc. CAT FREE, WHLS, M.O. $50.

E66T **Granum Inc.** - 2901 N.E. Blakeley St., Seattle, WA 98105, (206) 525-0051. Specializes in macrobiotic foods. Also starter cultures for natto and other soyfoods. *Sells the following product/s:* pickled shiso leaves, umeboshi plums, ume plum vinegar and concentrate, daikon pickles, jinenjo soba, kuzu starch, kuzu noodles, hato-mugi grain, hato-mugi vinegar, wasabi powder, dried wheat gluten, seitan, prepared hama-natto, dried burdock, daikon and lotus roots. CAT FREE, R & W, OVER, M.O. $150 WHLS

E67 **Gray's Grist Mill** - P.O. Box 422, Adamsville, RI 02801, (508) 636-6075. Specializes in freshly ground, whole grain food items. *Sells the following product/s:* Johnny Cake meal made from Rhode Island White Cap corn. CAT FREE, RET, PC, M.O. 2 LBS.

E67G **Great Artichoke** - 11241 Merritt St., Castroville, CA 95012, (408) 633-2778. Specializes in Green Globe artichokes, both for planting and eating. *Sells the following product/s:* marinated artichoke hearts and marinated artichoke crowns. CAT FREE, R & W, PC/CC.

E67M **Great Date in the Morning** - P.O. Box 31, Coachella, CA 92236, (619) 398-6171. Organically grown dates. Also known as Jim Dunn Organic Date Co. *Sells the following product/s:* dried Barhi, Deglet Noor, Halawi, Khadrawi, Medjool and Zahidi dates. CAT FREE, R & W, PC.

E68 **Great Fermentations of Marin** - 87 Larkspur St., San Rafael, CA 94901, (415) 459-2520. Home winemaking and home brewing supplies, beer and wine yeasts, vinegar cultures, hop rhizomes. CAT FREE, RET, PC/CC, OVER.

E68M **Great Valley Mills** - 687 Mill Road, Telford, PA 18969, 1-800-366-6268. Gourmet and natural foods, Amish specialties. *Sells the following product/s:* dried whole-kernel corn. CAT FREE, RET, PC/CC.

E70M **Green Earth Inc.** - 2545 Prairie Ave., Evanston, IL 60201, 1-800-322-3662. Organically grown fresh produce, natural food items. *Sells the following product/s:* canola oil and canola mayonnaise. CAT FREE, RET, PC/CC.

E71 **Green Escape (The)** - P.O. Box 1417, Palm Harbor, FL 34682-1417, (813) 784-1132. Wide range of rare and common palm trees including indoor, tropical and cold-hardy, more than 240 species in all. CAT $6 REFUNDABLE, RET, PC/CC, OVER, M.O. $40.

E71M **Green Gold Ginseng Co.** - Route 3, Tompkinsville, KY 42167, (502) 487-6441 (no telephone orders). Ginseng seeds and roots. CAT $5.95, R & W, PC, CANADA ONLY.

E73M **Green Horizons** - 218 Quinlan, Suite 571, Kerrville, TX 78028, (512) 257-5141. Seeds of native wild flowers and grasses, both individual species and regional mixes. CAT $1 PLUS SASE, RET, PC.

E74 **Green Knoll Farm** - P.O. Box 434, Gridley, CA 95948, (916) 846-3431. Organically grown kiwi. CAT FREE, R & W, PC, M.O. 1 TRAY.

E75 **Green Plant Research** - P.O. Box 735, Kaaawa, HI 96730, (808) 237-8672. Specializes in Hoyas and other Asclepiads. CAT $1, RET, PC, OVER, M.O. $25.

E81 **Greenery (The)** - 14450 N.E. 16th Place, Bellevue, WA 98007, (206) 641-1458. Specializes in azaleas and rhododendrons. CAT $2, R & W, PC, OVER, M.O. $25.

E81M **Greenfield Herb Garden** - Depot & Harrison, P.O. Box 437, Shipshewana, IN 46565, (219) 768-7110. Herb plants and seeds, herbal products, crafts. CAT $.50 PLUS SASE, RET, PC/CC.

E82 **Greenhaven Farm Nursery** - 3426 Grenlund Rd., Rt. #1, Perrinton, MI 48871, (517) 682-4162. Seed and seedlings of Carpathian walnuts. CAT FREE, R & W, PC.

E83M **Greenleaf Farm & Nursery** - Rt. 3, Box 398, Wendell, NC 27591, (919) 365-6348. Specializes in muscadines and seedless bunch grapes. CAT FREE, R & W, PC.

E83T **Greenleaf Seeds** - P.O. Box 98, Conway, MA 01341, (413) 628-4750 (no telephone orders). Seeds of unusual edibles, including a large selection of oriental vegetables. CAT FREE, RET, PC.

E83Z **Greenlee Nursery** - 301 E. Franklin Ave., Pomona, CA 91766, (714) 629-9045. Extensive selection of ornamental grasses. CAT FREE, R & W, PC, CANADA ONLY, M.O. $25.

E84 **Greenmantle Nursery** - 3010 Ettersburg Rd., Garberville, CA 95440, (707) 986-7504. Wide range of old-fashioned and rare fruit trees and nuts. Also a large listing of unusual roses. Features cultivars developed by pioneer California hybridizer, Albert Etter. CAT $3, RET, PC.

E87 **Greer Gardens** - 1280 Goodpasture Island Rd., Eugene, OR 97401-1794, (503) 686-8266. Rare and unusual ornamentals, fruit and nut trees, hardy kiwi, genetic dwarfs. Specializes in azaleas and rhododendrons. CAT $2, R & W, PC/CC, OVER.

E89 **Greiner (W.) & Sons Nursery** - Box 70, Mulvane, KS 67110, (316) 777-1035. Specializes in grafted Northern pecans. Also sells pecan nuts for eating of varieties raised locally. CAT FREE, R & W, PC.

E89M **Grianan Gardens** - Postal Box 14492, San Francisco, CA 94114, (415) 626-2156 (no telephone orders). Flower and herb seed, hand packed in sampler and standard sizes. CAT $1 REFUNDABLE, RET, PC, OVER, M.O. $2.50.

E91G **Grimes (G.S.) Seeds Inc.** - 201 West Main St., Smethport, PA 16749, 1-800-241-7333. Seeds and plants of vegetables, herbs and flowers primarily for the bedding plant and nursery industry. Previously known as H.G. German Seeds. CAT $15, WHLS, PC/CC.

E91M **Grimo Nut Nursery** - R.R. #3, Lakeshore Rd., Niagara-on-the-Lake, ON L0S 1J0, Canada, (416) 935-9773. Family business providing a wide range of tested, northern hardy, grafted and seedling nut trees from superior strains and selections. Also sells unusual fruit trees. CAT $1 REFUNDABLE, RET, PC, U.S. ONLY.

E93 **Grootendorst Nurseries** - 15310 Red Arrow Highway, Lakeside, MI 49116, (616) 469-2865 (no telephone orders). East Malling fruit tree understock for budding and grafting. Propagators for Southmeadow Fruit Gardens. CAT FREE, R & W, PC, M.O. 10 OF EACH.

E97 **Gurney Seed & Nursery Co.** - 1224 Page Street, Yankton, SD 57079, (605) 665-1930. One of the oldest and largest seed and nursery companies in the United States. Offers vegetable, herb and flower seed, fruit and nut trees, perennial vegetable plants, berries, trees and shrubs. Established in 1866. CAT FREE, RET, PC/CC/OC.

E99 **Halcyon Gardens, Inc.** - P.O. Box 124, Gibsonia, PA 15044, (412) 443-5544. Rare and unusual herb seeds, wild flower seeds, herbs for cats, herb seed collections, gift-packaged herb growing kits. CAT $1 REFUNDABLE, R & W, PC/CC, CANADA ONLY, M.O. $90 WHLS

E99G **Hale Indian River Groves** - P.O. Box 217, Wabasso, FL 32970-9989, 1-800-289-4253. Fresh fruit including citrus and avocadoes, gourmet food items. CAT $2, RET, PC/CC, CANADA ONLY.

E99M **Haley Nursery Co.** - Rt. 5, Smithville, TN 37166, 1-800-251-1878. Specializes in peaches. Also offers apples, pears, plums, cherries, nectarines, Asian pears and apricots. CAT FREE, R & W, PC, M.O. $25.

F1 **Halifax Seed Co.** - Box 8026, Halifax, NS B3K 5L8, Canada, (902) 454-7456. Vegetable, herb and flower seeds suitable for Atlantic Canada. Established in 1866. CAT $1, R & W, PC/CC, OVER.

F1M **Halinar (Dr. Joseph C.)** - 2334 Crooked Finger Road, Scotts Mills, OR 97375. Small nursery specializing in seeds and plants of Alliums, lilies, and daylilies for the discriminating gardener and hybridizer. CAT $.25, R & W, PC, OVER.

F5 **Hallum (H.G.) Nursery** - Rt. 3, Box 354, McMinnville, TN 37110, (615) 668-8504. Fruit and nut trees, conifers, shade trees, flowering shrubs. CAT FREE, WHLS.

F7M **Hansen's (Chris) Laboratory, Inc.** - 9015 W. Maple Street, Milwaukee, WI 53214-4298, (414) 476-3830. Dairy cultures. CAT SASE, R & W, PC.

F10 **Hardscrabble Enterprises** - Rt. 6, Box 42, Cherry Grove, WV 26804, (304) 567-2727 or (202) 332-0232 (no telephone orders). Shiitake mushroom spawn starter kits. *Sells the following product/s:* dried shiitake mushrooms. CAT $3, R & W, PC.

F11 **Harmony Farm Supply** - P.O. Box 460, Graton, CA 95444, (707) 823-9125. Fruit and nut trees for home gardeners, homesteaders and small farmers. Also sells berry plants, wild flower seeds, perennial vegetable plants, garlic, green manure and cover crop seeds. CAT $2, RET, PC/CC.

F12 **Harpool Seed, Inc.** - P.O. Drawer B, Denton, TX 76202-1647, (817) 387-0541. Wholesale distributor of vegetable and farm seeds. CAT FREE, WHLS, PC, OVER.

F13 **Harris Seeds** - 60 Saginaw Dr., Rochester, NY 14623, (716) 442-0410. Vegetable, herb and flower seeds, garden perennials, wild flowers. CAT FREE, R & W, PC/CC.

F15 **Harry and David** - Dept. 8182, Medford, OR 97501-0712, 1-800-547-3033. Fresh produce in season, gourmet and specialty food items. CAT FREE, RET, PC/CC, OVER.

F15M **Hartman's Herb Farm** - Old Dana Rd., Barre, MA 01005, (508) 355-2015. Herb plants, perennials, everlasting plants, dried flower arrangements, herbal crafts. CAT $2, RET, PC/CC, OVER, M.O. $10.

F16 **Hartmann's Plantation, Inc.** - P.O. Box E, Grand Junction, MI 49056, (904) 468-2087 or 468-2081. Extensive collection of highbush, lowbush, rabbiteye and ornamental blueberry plants. Also raspberries, hardy kiwi, feijoa and other exotic fruiting plants. CAT FREE, R & W, PC/CC, OVER.

F19M **Hastings** - P.O. Box 115535, Atlanta, GA 30310-8535, (404) 755-6580. Vegetable, herb and flower seeds, fruit and nut trees, grape vines, berry plants, perennial vegetables, trees and shrubs. Also Vidalia onions for eating. Established in 1889. CAT FREE, RET, PC/CC.

F21 **Havasu Hills Herb Farm** - 3717 Stoney Oak Road, Coulterville, CA 95311, (209) 878-3102 (no telephone orders). Organically grown herb plants, seeds, herbal products. CAT $1, R & W, PC, M.O. $10.

F21M **Hawaiian Fruit Preserving Co.** - P.O. Box 637, Kalaheo, Kauai, HI 96741-0637, (808) 332-9333. Hawaiian food specialties. *Sells the following product/s:* poha preserves, canned poi, and passionfruit juice. CAT FREE, R & W, PC, OVER.

F22 **Heaths and Heathers** - P.O. Box 850, Elma, WA 98541, (206) 482-3258. Specialists in hardy heaths and heathers. CAT SASE, RET, PC/CC, CANADA ONLY, M.O. $12.

F24 **Heirloom Garden Seeds** - P.O. Box 138, Guerneville, CA 95446, (707) 869-0967 (no telephone orders). Seeds of rare and unusual herbs, flowers, specialty vegetables, wild flowers, ornamental perennials. Previously known as Abracadabra Seed Co. CAT $2.50, R & W, PC, CANADA ONLY, M.O. $25 WHLS

F24M **Heirloom Seeds** - P.O. Box 245, West Elizabeth, PA 15088-0245, (412) 384-7816 (no telephone orders). Small, family run seed business specializing in standard, open-pollinated vegetables and flowers. Some selections date back to the 1700 and 1800's. CAT $1 REFUNDABLE, RET, PC.

F25 **Heirloom Vegetable Garden Project** - Department of Vegetable Crops, Plant Science Building, Cornell University, Ithaca, NY 14853-0327. Heirloom vegetables seeds in both individual packets and collections. CAT $1 PLUS SASE, RET, PC.

F27 **Helen's Tropical Exotics** - 3519 Church Street, Clarkston, GA 30021, (404) 292-7278. Gourmet and specialty foods with a Caribbean flavor. *Sells the following product/s:* Scotch Bonnet pepper hot sauce. CAT FREE, RET, PC/CC.

F27M **Heliconia Haus** - 12691 S.W. 104th St., Miami, FL 33186, (305) 238-0494. Specializes in heliconias and gingers. CAT FREE, R & W, PC, OVER.

F31M **Henrietta's Nursery** - 1345 N. Brawley, Fresno, CA 93722, (209) 275-2166. Cactus and succulent plants, seed mixtures. CAT $1, RET, PC/CC, OVER.

F31T **Herb Barn (The)** - Box 31, Bodines Road, Bodines, PA 17722, (717) 995-9327. Herb plants. Dried flowers upon request. Previously known as Dionysos' Barn. CAT $.50, R & W, PC, M.O. $5.

F33 **Herb Gathering** - 4000 West 126th St., Leawood, KS 66209, (913) 345-0490. Gourmet vegetable seeds imported from France, culinary herb and edible flower seeds, herbal crafts, creation garden seeds. *Sells the following product/s:* whole Tahitian vanilla. CAT $2, R & W, PC/CC, OVER.

F35M **Herbfarm (The)** - 32804 Issaquah-Fall City Rd., Fall City, WA 98024, (206) 784-2222. Over 400 varieties of herb plants and perennials, including many unusual selections, herbal products. Also 150 classes each year on gardening, crafts and cooking with herbs. Previously known as Fall City Herb Farm. *Sells the following product/s:* Walla Walla shallots, California bay leaf wreaths. CAT FREE, RET, PC/CC, OVER.

F37T **Herbs-Liscious** - 1702 S. Sixth St., Marshalltown, IA 50158, (515) 752-4976. Family owned business selling 250 varieties of herb plants, dried herbs and spices, herb craft materials, dried herb bunches and flowers. CAT FREE, R & W, PC, M.O. $10.

F38 **Herbst Tree Seed, Inc.** - 307 Number 9 Road, Fletcher, NC 28732, (704) 628-4709. Tree and shrub seed. CAT FREE, WHLS, OVER.

F39M **Heritage Gardens** - 1 Meadow Ridge Road, Shenandoah, IA 51601-0700, (605) 665-1080. Garden perennials, bulbs, ornamental grasses, ferns, ornamental trees and shrubs. Subsidiary of Henry Field's. CAT FREE, RET, PC/CC.

F40 **Heritage Rose Gardens** - 16831 Mitchell Creek Dr., Fort Bragg, CA 95437, (707) 964-3747. Heritage roses, over 250 kinds, species roses. CAT $1, RET, PC, OVER.

F42 **Heymaqua Seed Service** - 2286 South Face Road, Garberville, CA 95440, (707) 923-2248 (no telephone orders). Small, family run business specializing in heirloom vegetable cultivars, herbs and flowers. All seed is organically grown. CAT SASE, R & W, PC, OVER.

F42M **Hickin's Mountain Mowings** - RFD 1, Black Mountain Road, Brattleboro, VT 05301, (802) 254-2146. Fresh produce, gourmet and specialty food items. *Sells the following product/s:* Bearpaw popping corn, West Indian gherkin dill pickles, both dried and canned Soldier beans. CAT FREE, RET, PC.

F43 **Hidden Springs Herb and Fuchsia Farm** - Rt. 14, Box 159-1A, Cookeville, TN 38501, (615) 268-9354. Herb plants, fuchsias. CAT FREE, RET, PC.

F43M **Hidden Springs Nursery** - Rt. 14, Box 159, Cookeville, TN 38501, (615) 268-9889. Specializes in unusual fruit and nut trees for edible landscaping, including medlar, mayhaw, autumn olive, sea buckthorn, juneberry, nut pines and flowering quince. CAT $.45, RET, PC, OVER, M.O. $10.

F44 **High Altitude Gardens** - P.O. Box 4619, Ketchum, ID 83340, 1-800-874-7333. Regional seed company dedicated to making available seeds of vegetables, herbs, wild flowers and native grasses adapted to short season, high altitude climates around the world. CAT $3, R & W, PC/CC, OVER, M.O. $20 WHLS

F45 **High Country Rosarium** - 1717 Downing at Park Ave., Denver, CO 80218, (303) 832-4026. Specializes in old garden, shrub and species roses for cold mountain climates. CAT $1, RET, PC.

F48 **Highlander Nursery** - P.O. Box 177, Pettigrew, AR 72752, (501) 677-2300. Specializes in highbush blueberry plants. Previously known as Shanti Gardens. CAT FREE, R & W, PC, CANADA ONLY.

F51 **Hillis Nursery Co., Inc.** - Rt. 2, Box 142, McMinnville, TN 37110, (615) 668-4364. Nut trees, native wild flowers and ferns, vines, bulbs, flowering trees and shrubs. CAT FREE, WHLS, PC, OVER, M.O. $100.

F52 **Hilltop Herb Farm** - P.O. Box 325, Romayor, TX 77368, (713) 592-5859. Herb plants and seeds, scented geraniums, specialty food items. CAT FREE, RET, PC/CC, M.O. $20.

F53 **Hilltop Trees/Newark Nurseries Inc.** - P.O. Box 578, C.R. 681, Hartford, MI 49057, 1-800-253-2911. Apple, peach, nectarine, pear, cherry, plum and apricot trees, many certified virus-free. Previously known as Hilltop Orchards & Nurseries. CAT FREE, R & W, PC/CC/OC, OVER, M.O. 5 TREES.

F53M **Hines Nurseries** - P.O. Box 11208, Santa Ana, CA 92711, (714) 559-4444. Deciduous fruit trees, citrus, palms, cacti and succulents, ornamental grasses, flowering trees and shrubs. CAT FREE, WHLS.

F54 **Historical Roses** - 1657 West Jackson St., Painseville, OH 44077, (216) 357-7270 (no telephone orders). Old garden roses, species roses. CAT SASE, RET, PC.

F57M **Holbrook Farm & Nursery** - Rt. 2, Box 223B, Fletcher, NC 28732, (704) 891-7790. Perennials, native ferns and wild flowers, ornamental grasses, trees and shrubs. CAT $2 REFUNDABLE, RET, PC/CC.

F59 **Holland Wildflower Farm** - 290 O'Neal Lane, Elkins, AR 72727, (501) 643-2622. Wild flower plants and seeds, herbs, garden perennials. CAT FREE, RET, PC/CC.

F60 **Hollar & Co., Inc.** - P.O. Box 106, Rocky Ford, CO 81067, (719) 254-7411. Commercial vegetable seed grower specializing in cucumber, melon, squash, gourd, and watermelon. CAT FREE, WHLS, PC, OVER.

F61M **Hollydale Nursery** - P.O. Box 26, Pelham, TN 37366, (615) 467-3600. Growers and sellers of fruit trees, primarily for commercial orchards in the Southeast. Specializes in peaches, plums and nectarines. CAT FREE, R & W, PC, OVER.

F63 **Holmes Seed Co.** - 2125 46th St. N.W., Canton, OH 44709, (216) 492-0123. Complete line of vegetable seeds for commercial growers. CAT FREE, WHLS, CC.

F63M **Home Brew International, Inc.** - 1126 So. Federal Hwy., Suite 182, Fort Lauderdale, FL 33316, (305) 764-1527. Home brewing supplies, wine and beer yeasts, vinegar cultures, sourdough starters. CAT FREE, RET, PC.

F64 **Home Brewery (The)** - 16490 Jurupa Avenue, Fontana, CA 92335, (714) 822-3010. Wine and beer making supplies for the home brewer. CAT FREE, RET, PC.

F64M **Home Grown Mushroom Farms** - 3050 Coast Road, Santa Cruz, CA 95060. Oyster mushroom kits in the form of logs and an environmentally controlled tank that maintains constant humidity and cool air exchange. Mushrooms grow more quickly and mature in about a week. CAT FREE, RET, PC.

F65 **Home Sweet Homebrew** - 2008 Sanson St., Philadelphia, PA 19103, (215) 569-9469. Beer and wine making supplies. CAT FREE, RET, PC/CC.

F66 **Homochitto Outdoors** - P.O. Box 630, Meadville, MS 39653, (601) 384-2165 or 384-5779. Southern wild flower seeds, customized wild flower seed mixtures for Mississippi, Alabama and Louisiana. CAT FREE, RET, PC.

F66T **Honey Grove Farm** - P.O. Box 49, Alsea, OR 97324, (503) 487-7274. Tilth certified garlic, for both planting and eating. CAT FREE, R & W, PC.

F67 **Honeywood Lilies and Nursery** - P.O. Box 63, Parkside, SK S0J 2A0, Canada, (306) 747-3296. Lilies and daylilies, ornamental shrubs, fruit trees, berry plants, hardy perennials, roses, Asiatic bulbs. Dr. A.J. Porter, one of the owners, has developed many cultivars now in common use in the prairie provinces and other northern regions. CAT $2, R & W, PC, OVER, M.O. $30.

F68 **Hopkins Citrus and Rare Fruit Nursery** - 5200 S.W. 160th Ave., Ft. Lauderdale, FL 33331. Citrus and avocado trees, rare tropical and sub-tropical fruits. CAT FREE, R & W, PC/OC, M.O. $50.

F68M **Hopper (James T.)** - P.O. Box 621, Vidor, TX 77662. Sells only Flower Bed okra. CAT FREE, RET, PC.

F69 **Horne (Jerry) Rare Plants** - 10195 S.W. 70th St., Miami, FL 33173, (305) 270-1235 (no telephone orders). Small family business selling rare collectors items, especially bromeliads, aroids, platyceriums and cycads. CAT SASE, RET, PC, OVER, M.O. $10.

F70 **Hortica Gardens** - P.O. Box 308, Placerville, CA 95667, (916) 622-7089. Specialists in nursery stock suitable for bonsai training, patio placement, indoor or outdoor gardens. CAT $.50, RET, PC, CANADA ONLY, M.O. $15.

F71 **Hortico Inc.** - 723 Robson Rd., R.R. #1, Waterdown, ON L0R 2H0, Canada, (416) 689-6984 or 689-3002. Ornamental trees and shrubs, hardy perennials, roses, bog plants, ornamental grasses, ferns. CAT $2, R & W, PC, OVER.

F71M **Horticultural Enterprises** - P.O. Box 810082, Dallas, TX 75381-0082. Large selection of chile pepper seed, other hot peppers, Mexican and Southwestern vegetables. CAT FREE, RET, PC.

F72 **Horticultural Products & Supplies, Inc.** - P.O. Box 35038, Charlotte, NC 28235-5038, (704) 374-0900. Supplier of vegetable, herb and flower seeds to the professional grower. Previously known as Brawley Seed Co. CAT FREE, WHLS, PC/CC, OVER.

F73 **Horticultural Systems, Inc.** - P.O. Box 70, Parrish, FL 34219, (813) 776-1760 or 776-2410. Growers of native plants for beach, saline, wetlands and freshwater habitats. Also design, install and maintain revegetation and erosion control projects. CAT FREE, WHLS.

F74 **House of Spices** - 76-17 Broadway, Jackson Heights, NY 11373, (212) 476-1577. Specializes in Indian and Pakistani foodstuffs. *Sells the following product/s:* <u>dried charoli, dried Kabuli Black chick peas, canned tindora, whole vall, vall dal, whole moth beans, whole urid, urid dal, papads, whole toor, toor dal, canned tinda, kewda water, dried ajwain, amchoor, asafoetida powder, whole masoor, dhokla flour and poha</u>. CAT FREE, R & W, PC.

F75M **Howard (Spencer M.) Orchid Imports** - 11802 Huston St., North Hollywood, CA 91607, (818) 762-8275. Specializes in species orchids from around the world. CAT $.45 PLUS SASE, R & W, PC, OVER, M.O. $25.

F78 **Hsu's Ginseng Enterprises Inc.** - P.O. Box 509, Wausau, WI 54402-0509, 1-800-826-1577. Ginseng seed and planting rootlets, fresh ginseng roots in season. CAT FREE, RET, PC/CC, OVER, M.O. 2 OZ. SEED.

F79M **Hubbs Bros. Seed** - 1522 N. 35th St., Phoenix, AZ 85008, (602) 267-8132. Specializes in seed of plants native to Arizona. CAT FREE, R & W, PC, OVER.

F80 **Hudson (J.L.), Seedsman** - P.O. Box 1058, Redwood City, CA 94064. Specializes in rare and unusual seeds from around the world. Also traditional and heirloom vegetables, herbs, and a special collection of Zapotec Indian seeds from Sierra Madre del Sur, Oaxaca, Mexico. CAT $1, RET, PC, OVER.

F82 **Hume (Ed) Seeds, Inc.** - P.O. Box 1450, Kent, WA 98035, (206) 859-1110 (no telephone orders). Family owned and operated business offering vegetable, herb and flower seeds for cool, short season areas. CAT FREE, R & W, PC/CC, CANADA ONLY.

Hungnong Seed Co. - 768 St. Francis Blvd., Daly City, CA 94015. American subsidiary of Hungnong Seed Co., Ltd., Korea, which see.

F85 **Hurov's Tropical Seeds** - P.O. Box 1596, Chula Vista, CA 92012, (619) 426-0091. Seed of over 6,000 species collected from around the world by H. Ron Hurov and collaborators. Specializes in useful plants including tropical fruits and vegetables, rare herbs and spices, palms. Also ornamental and foliage plants. CAT $1, R & W, PC, OVER.

F85G **Hydro-Gardens, Inc.** - P.O. Box 9707, Colorado Springs, CO 80932, (719) 495-2266 or 495-2267. Specializes in lettuce, cucumber and tomato seeds for greenhouse or hydroponic culture. CAT $4, WHLS, CANADA ONLY, M.O. $25.

F85M **Ili Ili Farms** - P.O. Box 150, Kula, HI 96790, 1-800-535-6284. Hawaiian specialty foods and flowers including Maui onions. CAT FREE, RET, PC/CC, OVER.

F86 **Illinois Foundation Seeds** - P.O. Box 722, Champaign, IL 61824-0722, (217) 485-6260. Specializes in Xtra-Sweet hybrid sweet corn. CAT FREE, R & W, PC, OVER.

F86G **In-Ag-Corp.** - 10925 Valley View Rd., Eden Prairie, MN 55344, (612) 941-4525. Specializes in foods made from sweet lupines. *Sells the following product/s:* <u>sweet lupin pasta</u>. CAT FREE, R & W, PC.

F86M **Inca Brand Inc.** - P.O. Box 741, Tonasket, WA 98855, (509) 486-2484. Specializes in bulk quantities of whole quinoa seed for eating. CAT FREE, R & W.

F88 **Indigo Knoll Perennials** - 16236 Compromise Court, Mt. Airy, MD 21771, (301) 489-5131. Garden perennials, herb plants. CAT FREE, RET, PC.

F89 **Inter-State Nurseries** - P.O. Box 208, Hamburg, IA 51640-0208, 1-800-325-4180. Berry plants, perennial vegetables, roses, garden perennials, flowering shrubs. CAT FREE, RET, PC/CC.

F89M **Intermountain Cactus** - 2344 South Redwood Rd., Salt Lake City, UT 84119, (801) 972-5149. Specializes in hardy cactus. CAT SASE, RET, PC, M.O. $15.

F90 **Intermountain Seeds** - P.O. Box 343, Rexburg, ID 83440, (208) 356-9805. Vegetable, herb and flower seeds adapted to the cool night temperatures and short growing season of the Intermountain region. CAT FREE, RET, PC.

F91 **International Specialty Supply** - 820 E. 20th St., Cookeville, TN 38501, (615) 526-1106 or 1-800-992-0029 (orders only). Seed company and sprout equipment manufacturer. Sells everything to run a professional sprout business, including seed, equipment and packaging. CAT FREE, WHLS, PC, OVER.

F91M **International Yogurt Co.** - 628 North Doheny Drive, Los Angeles, CA 90069. Dairy cultures including yogurt, cheese, acidophilus milk and kefir. CAT FREE, RET, PC.

F91T **Irrigated Agriculture Research & Extension Center** - Washington State University, Rt. 2, Box 2953A, Prosser, WA 99350-0687. Propagation material of virus-tested deciduous fruit tree cultivars of interest to researchers, collectors and the commercial fruit industry. CAT FREE, RET, M.O. $10.

F91Z **Iseli Nursery** - 30590 S.E. Kelso Road, Boring, OR 97009, (503) 663-3822. Ornamental trees and shrubs. CAT FREE, WHLS.

F92 **Island Seed Mail Order** - P.O. Box 4278, Station A, Victoria, BC V8X 3X8, Canada, (604) 384-0345 (no telephone orders). Vegetable, herb and flower seeds. CAT FREE, RET, PC, OVER.

F93 **Ison's Nursery & Vineyards** - Rt. 1, Box 191, Brooks, GA 30205, (404) 599-6970. Large selection of fruit and nut trees for the South, berry plants, bunch grapes. Specializes in muscadines and scuppernongs, offering approximately 40 cultivars. CAT FREE, R & W, PC/OC, OVER.

F93G **It's About Thyme** - P.O. Box 878, Manchaca, TX 78652, (512) 280-1192. Herb plants and seeds including Southwestern natives, scented geraniums, everlastings. CAT FREE, RET, PC, M.O. $15.

F93M **J. Intra-World Grain Products** - 570 F Marine View, Belmont, CA 94002, (415) 637-0449. Organically grown specialty food items. *Sells the following product/s:* cafe du grain. CAT FREE, R & W, PC, OVER.

F94 **J & L Orchids** - 20 Sherwood Rd., Easton, CT 06612, (203) 261-3772. Hybrid and species orchid plants and seedlings. Specializes in miniatures. CAT $1, RET, PC/CC, OVER.

F95 **J'Don Seeds International** - P.O. Box 10998-533, Austin, TX 78766, (512) 343-6360. Wild flower seeds, both individual species and mixes. CAT FREE, R & W, PC/CC.

F96 **Jacklin Seed Co.** - West 5300 Riverbend Ave., Post Falls, ID 83854-9499, 1-800-635-8726. Seed of reclamation and environmental grasses, turf grass seed. CAT FREE, WHLS, OVER.

F97 **Jackson and Perkins Co.** - 1 Rose Lane, Medford, OR 97501-0701, 1-800-292-4769. Fruit trees, berry plants, roses, garden perennials, flowering trees and shrubs. CAT FREE, R & W, PC/CC, CANADA ONLY.

F97G **Jacobson (S.M.) Citrus** - 1505 Doherty, Mission, TX 78572, (512) 585-1712. Organically grown citrus. CAT FREE, RET, PC.

F97M **Jaffe Bros. Natural Foods, Inc.** - P.O. Box 636, Valley Center, CA 92082-0636, (619) 749-1133. A 40-year old family business supplying sprouting seeds, dried fruits, nuts, grains, seeds, dates, beans and other organic foods, mostly in five pound quantities. *Sells the following product/s:* Black Monukka raisins, dried Fuyu persimmons and dried Moyer prunes. CAT FREE, R & W, OVER.

G1M **Jeffreys Seed Co.** - P.O. Box 887, Goldsboro, NC 27530, (919) 734-2985. Vegetable seed including older traditional cultivars, cover crop and green manure seeds. Established in 1888. Subsidiary of Cross Seed Co. CAT FREE, WHLS.

G1T **Jeffries Nurseries Ltd.** - P.O. Box 402, Portage la Prairie, MB R1N 3B7, Canada, (204) 857-5288. Hardy fruit trees, berry plants, grape vines, perennial vegetables, ornamental trees and shrubs. CAT FREE, R & W, PC, U.S. ONLY.

G2 **Jemco Mycotechnology Products Co.** - P.O. Box 633, College Park, MD 20740, (301) 454-3994 (no telephone orders). Mushroom spawn plug for shiitake, oyster and other exotic mushrooms. CAT FREE, R & W, PC, OVER.

G3M **Jersey Chestnut Farm** - 58 Van Duyne Ave., Wayne, NJ 07470-4705, (201) 694-1220. Specializes in budded Chinese chestnut trees and budded American persimmon trees. Also offers pedigree American persimmon seed. CAT FREE, RET, PC, M.O. $30.

G4 **Jewell Nurseries Inc.** - P.O. Box 457, Lake City, MN 55041-0457, (612) 345-3356. Fruit trees, berry plants, grape vines, perennial vegetables, ornamental trees and shrubs. Established in 1868. CAT FREE, WHLS.

G5 **Joe and Sons** - P.O. Box 11276, Cincinnati, OH 45211, (513) 662-2326. Beer and wine making supplies for the home brewer. CAT FREE, RET, PC/CC/OC, OVER.

G6 **Johnny's Selected Seeds** - Foss Hill Road, Albion, ME 04910, (207) 437-9294. Breeders and growers of a wide range of vegetables, culinary herbs, grains, and flowers. Specializes in varieties for cool, short season areas and specialty markets. The quintessential alternative seed company. CAT FREE, RET, PC/CC, OVER.

G8 **Johnson Nursery** - Rt. 5, Box 29-J, Ellijay, GA 30540, (404) 276-3187. Small nursery offering fruits and nuts, shade and ornamental trees. Specializes in antique peach cultivars. CAT $1, R & W, PC/CC, M.O. $12.50.

G9 **Johnson Seeds** - P.O. Box 543, Woodacre, CA 94973. Hand-collected seed of California native grasses suitable for ornamental gardens or naturalizing. Also annual and perennial wild flower seed. CAT $.50, R & W, PC/OC, OVER.

G9M **Johnston Nurseries** - R.D. 1, Box 100, Creekside, PA 15732, (412) 463-8456. Commercial grower of bare root seedlings and transplants of Christmas trees, ornamentals and hardwoods. CAT FREE, WHLS, PC, CANADA ONLY, M.O. 25 OF EACH.

G13 **Joppa Nursery Co.** - P.O. Box 134, Joppa, AL 35087, (205) 586-4471. Fruit and nut trees, berry plants, grape vines, shade trees, flowering shrubs. CAT FREE, RET, PC.

G13M **Jordan Seeds** - 6400 Upper Afton Rd., Woodbury, MN 55125, (612) 738-3422. Complete line of vegetable seeds for commercial growers. CAT FREE, WHLS.

G13T **Josie's Best New Mexican Foods** - P.O. Box 5525, Santa Fe, NM 87501, (505) 983-6520. Specializes in Mexican and Southwest Indian foods. *Sells the following product/s:* whole dried Pequín peppers, crushed dried Pequín peppers, panocha flour, dried sweet corn chicos, and piloncillo. CAT FREE, RET, PC.

G14 **Joyce Farms** - Rt 3, Box 222, Sherwood, OR 97140, (503) 625-6834. Dwarf, semi-dwarf and espaliered fruit trees, grape vines, berry plants, nut trees, conifers, deciduous shrubs, shade and flowering trees. CAT FREE, WHLS, PC, OVER, M.O. 10 OF EACH.

G15 **Joyce's Garden** - 64640 Old Bend Redmond Hwy., Bend, OR 97701, (503) 388-4680. Ultra-hardy perennials, ground covers and herbs. CAT $2, R & W, PC.

G15M **Judkins (H.J.) & Son Nursery** - Rt. 4, Box 190, Smithville, TN 37166, (615) 597-7215. Fruit and nut trees, grape vines, shade trees, flowering shrubs. CAT FREE, WHLS, M.O. 10 OF EACH.

G16 **Jung (J.W.) Seed Co.** - 335 S. High St., Randolph, WI 53957, (414) 326-4100. Vegetable, herb and flower seed, fruit and nut trees, berry plants, grape vines, perennial vegetables, bulbs, trees and shrubs. Established in 1907. CAT FREE, RET, PC/CC.

G17 **Just Fruits Nursery** - Rt. 2, Box 4818, Crawfordville, FL 32327, (904) 926-5644. Complete list of container grown fruits, nuts and berries, both common and exotic, suitable for growing in Zones 8 and 9. Offers numerous cultivars developed at the University of Florida. CAT $2, R & W, PC, M.O. $25.

G18 **K & L Cactus Nursery** - 12712 Stockton Blvd., Galt, CA 95632, (209) 745-4756. Cacti and succulent plants and seed. CAT $2 REFUNDABLE, RET, PC/CC, OVER, M.O. $20.

G19M **Kalmia Farms** - P.O. Box 3881, Charlottesville, VA 22903. Specializes in multiplier onions, shallots, topset onions and garlic. CAT FREE, RET, PC.

G20 **Kartuz Greenhouses** - 1408 Sunset Drive, Vista, CA 92083, (619) 941-3613. Exotic tropical flowering plants, rare fruits and nuts including passionfruit, Babaco papaya, pepino, Malabar chestnut and acerola. CAT $2, R & W, PC/CC, OVER, M.O. $15.

G20M **Katagiri & Co., Inc.** - 224 East 59th St., New York, NY 11022, (212) 755-3566. Specializes in Japanese food items. *Sells the following product/s:* pickled Aka Taka-na, rakkyo-zuke, nara-zuke, pickled Nozawa-Na, amazu-shoga, takuan, konnyaku, shirataki, dried kampyo, dried sanshô, dried Taka-No-Tsume peppers, kinako, and prepared natto. CAT FREE, R & W, PC, OVER.

G21M **Keeling (Forrest) Nursery** - Hwy. 79, Elsberry, MO 63343, 1-800-332-3361. Ornamental trees and shrubs, seedling transplants. CAT FREE, WHLS, M.O. 50 OF EACH.

G23 **Kelly Nurseries** - P.O. Box 800, Dansville, NY 14437-0800, 1-800-325-4180. Fruit and nut trees, berry plants, grape vines, perennial vegetables, general ornamental nursery stock. CAT FREE, RET, PC/CC.

G25M **KEO Entities** - 348 Chelsea Circle, Land O'Lakes, FL 34639, (813) 996-4644 (no telephone orders). Seed of exotic tropical plants. CAT FREE, RET, PC, OVER.

G26 **Kester's Wild Game Food Nurseries, Inc.** - P.O. Box 516, Omro, WI 54963-0516, (414) 685-2929. Specializes in seed, roots and tubers of aquatic plants, grains, and forages for feeding wildlife and developing wildlife habitats. *Sells the following product/s:* whole grain wild rice habitat collected in northern Wisconsin and Minnesota. CAT $2, R & W, PC/CC, CANADA ONLY.

G27M **Kilgore Seed Co.** - 1400 W. 1st St., Sanford, FL 32771, (305) 323-6630. Vegetable, herb and flower seeds suited to Florida and other Gulf Coast states. CAT $1 DEDUCTIBLE, RET, PC/CC, OVER.

G28 **Killian Hill Nursery Co.** - RFD 2, McMinnville, TN 37110, (615) 668-8003. Fruit and nut trees, grape vines, berry plants, perennial vegetables, Tennessee wild flowers, shade and ornamental trees and shrubs. CAT FREE, WHLS, PC.

G30 **King Wholesale Nurseries** - R.D. #14, Greensburg, PA 15601, (412) 834-8930. Commercial growers of shade trees, evergreens, flowering trees and shrubs. CAT FREE, WHLS, PC/CC.

G31M **Kinoko Company Ltd.** - P.O. Box 14551, Oakland, CA 94614. Home mushroom growing kits, spawn, mushroom growing supplies, herbal mushroom teas. CAT FREE, R & W, PC, OVER.

G33 **Kitazawa Seed Co.** - 1748 Laine Ave., Santa Clara, CA 95051-3012, (408) 249-6778 (no telephone orders). Specializes in Japanese vegetable seeds. CAT FREE, R & W, PC, OVER.

G37 **Klein (Joseph) Nursery Co.** - 15215 S.E. Webfoot Rd., Dayton, OR 97114, (503) 868-7556. Specializes in Asian pear trees, both bare root and container grown. CAT FREE, WHLS, PC.

G37M **Kline Nursery Co.** - 17401 S.W. Bryant Rd., Lake Grove, OR 97035, (503) 636-3923. Lilies, hardy ferns, Pacific Northwest native perennials. CAT $2, RET, PC, M.O. $15.

G38M **Knolview Nursery & Farm, Inc.** - 10906 Monitor-Mckee Rd. N.E., Woodburn, OR 97071, (503) 634-2344. Commercial grower of apple, pear and cherry trees. Subsidiary of Oregon Rootstock, Inc. CAT FREE, WHLS, OVER, M.O. 100 OF EACH.

G39 **Koeppl's Master Brewing** - 2311 George, Rolling Meadows, IL 60008, (312) 255-4478. Wine and beer making supplies. CAT FREE, RET, PC/CC/OC.

G40 **Kraus (E.C.)** - P.O. Box 7850, Independence, MO 64053, (816) 254-7448. Complete line of wine and beer making supplies and equipment for the home brewer. CAT FREE, RET, PC/CC.

G41 **Kraus (V.) Nurseries Ltd.** - Carlisle, ON L0R 1H0, Canada, (416) 689-4022. Fruit and nut trees, berry plants, grape vines, perennial vegetables, roses, ornamental trees and shrubs. CAT FREE, R & W, PC/OC, OVER.

G43 **Krieger's Wholesale Nursery Inc.** - P.O. Box 116, Bridgman, MI 49106, (616) 465-5522. Raspberries, blueberries, currants and gooseberries, grapes, rhubarb and asparagus. CAT FREE, WHLS, M.O. $75.

G43M **Kristick (M.A.)** - 155 Mockingbird Rd., Wellsville, PA 17365, (717) 292-2962. Specializes in dwarf and unusual conifers and maples. CAT FREE, RET, PC, OVER.

G44 **Krohne (William) Plant Farms** - Rt #6, Box 586, Dowagiac, MI 49047, (616) 424-3450 or 424-5423. Family owned nursery and farm specializing in strawberry and asparagus plants for gardeners, farmers, u-pick operations and other nurseries. CAT FREE, R & W, PC, M.O. 25 PLANTS.

G44M **Krystal Wharf Farms** - R.D. 2, Box 191A, Mansfield, PA 16933, (717) 549-8194. Organically grown fresh fruits and vegetables, natural food items. CAT FREE, RET, PC.

G45 **KSA Jojoba** - 19025 Parthenia St., Northridge, CA 91324, (818) 701-1534. Specializes in jojoba seeds and plants, and jojoba based products. CAT $.50 PLUS SASE, WHLS TO THE PUBLIC, PC, OVER.

G45M **Kuenecke (Gerhard)** - R.D. 2, Box 136, Montrose, PA 18801. Fruit and nut trees, berry plants, conifers. CAT FREE, R & W, PC.

G47 **Kusa Research Foundation** - P.O. Box 761, Ojai, CA 93023. Specializes in traditional edible seed crops of folk origin, especially rare cereal grains. Emphasis is on crops which can be grown by gardeners and small-scale farmers. CAT $1 DEDUCTIBLE, RET, PC, OVER.

G47M **La Fayette Home Nursery, Inc.** - P.O. Box 1A, La Fayette, IL 61449, (309) 995-3311. Specializes in native grasses, prairie wild flowers, forbs and trees and shrubs for wetland and woodland restorations. CAT $.50, R & W, PC/CC, OVER.

G49 **La Verne Nursery Inc.** - 1001 Nashport St., La Verne, CA 91750, (714) 599-0815. Large selection of avocado and citrus, deciduous and sub-tropical fruit and nut trees, grape vines, grafted ornamentals. CAT FREE, WHLS, OVER, M.O. $200.

G50 **Labon Inc.** - 1350 Newton St., Boucherville, PQ J4B 5H2, Canada, (514) 641-4979. Cereals and legumes, cover crop and green manure seeds, onion and garlic sets, berry plants, grape vines. CAT FREE, WHLS.

G51 **Lagomarsino Seeds Inc.** - 5675-A Power Inn Rd., Sacramento, CA 95824, (916) 381-1024. Vegetable, herb and flower seed, wild flower mixes, field and pasture seed, vegetable plants. CAT FREE, RET, PC.

G52 **Lake Odessa Greenhouse** - 1123 Jordan Lake St., Lake Odessa, MI 48849, (616) 374-8488. Specializes in geranium plants. CAT FREE, R & W, PC/CC.

G53 **Lake Sylvia Vineyard Nursery** - Rt. 1, Box 149, South Haven, MN 55382. Specializes in extra hardy grape vines recently developed in Minnesota and Wisconsin. CAT FREE, RET, PC, M.O. 10 OF EACH.

G53M **Lakeland Nurseries Sales** - P.O. Box 4, Hanover, PA 17333-0004, (717) 637-5555. Unique and unusual items for the small home gardener. CAT FREE, RET, PC/CC.

G54 **Lakeshore Tree Farms Ltd.** - R.R. 3, Saskatoon, SK S7K 3J6, Canada, (306) 382-2077. Growers of extremely hardy fruit and nut trees, berry plants, grape vines, ornamental trees and shrubs. Nursery stock that will survive -50 degrees fahrenheit. CAT $2, R & W, PC/CC/OC, OVER.

G55 **Lamb Nurseries** - E. 101 Sharp Ave., Spokane, WA 99202, (509) 328-7956. Rare and hardy perennials, rock garden plants, vines, flowering trees and shrubs. CAT FREE, R & W, PC, OVER, M.O. $25 WHLS

G55M **Lambert (L.F.) Spawn Co.** - P.O. Box 407, Coatesville, PA 19320, (215) 384-5031. Large supplier of mushroom spawn for commercial mushroom farms. CAT FREE, R & W, OVER.

G57M **Landreth Seed Co.** - P.O. Box 6426, Baltimore, MD 21230, (301) 727-3922. Vegetable, herb and flower seed, including many unique and heirloom vegetable cultivars. America's oldest seed house, established in 1784. CAT $2, R & W, PC, OVER.

G59M **Larner Seeds** - P.O. Box 407, Bolinas, CA 94924, (415) 868-9407. Specializes in seed of California native plants, including wild flowers, grasses, trees and shrubs. Catalog offers a "backyard restoration gardener" approach with edible and useful attributes stressed. CAT $1.50, R & W, PC, OVER.

G60 **Las Pilitas Nursery** - Star Rt. Box 23X, Santa Margarita, CA 93453, (805) 438-5992 (no telephone orders). Plants and seed for an extensive list of California native plants, including wild flowers, perennials, grasses, trees and shrubs. CAT $4, R & W, PC, OVER.

G64 **Laval Seeds, Inc.** - 3505 boul. St.-Martin Quest, Chomedey, Laval, PQ H7T 1A2, Canada, (514) 681-4888 or 331-1248. Vegetable, herb and flower seeds, perennial vegetables, berry plants, roses, bulbs, tree and shrub seed. CAT FREE, R & W, PC/CC, OVER.

G65M **Lawson's Nursery** - Rt.1, Box 472, Ball Ground, GA 30107, (404) 893-2141. Over 100 cultivars of old-fashioned apple trees, cherries, peaches, pears, apricots, plums and pecans. CAT FREE, R & W, PC/CC, OVER.

G66 **Lawyer Nursery Inc.** - 950 Highway 200 West, Plains, MT 59859, (406) 826-3881. Commercial nursery specializing in seedlings, liners and rootstocks for ornamental, forestry, fruit tree and conservation purposes. Also publishes a separate catalog of tree and shrub seed from around the world. CAT FREE, WHLS, PC/CC/OC, OVER, M.O. $100.

G67 **LBG Nursery** - Rt. 5, Box 130, Princeton, MN 55371, (612) 389-4920. Small family nursery specializing in organically grown fruit trees for northern areas. Also offers native shrubs, trees and ornamentals. CAT SASE, R & W, PC.

G67M **Le Champion Heritage Seeds and Plants** - P.O. Box 1602, Freedom, CA 95019-1602, (408) 724-5870. Small company specializing in old-fashioned, home garden vegetable cultivars introduced at least 40 years ago. Also some heirlooms, oriental greens, edible flowers and gourds. CAT $.50, RET, PC.

G68 **Le Jardin du Gourmet** - P.O. Box 75, St. Johnsbury Center, VT 05863. Imported vegetable and flower seed, herb plants and seeds, shallots, garlic, rocambole, leek plants, gourmet food products. CAT $.50, R & W, PC/CC, OVER.

G69M **Le Réveil de la Nature** - R.R. 1, St.-Philibert, PQ, G0M 1X0, Canada, (418) 228-1268. Organically grown fruit and nut trees, grape vines, berry plants, perennial vegetables, ornamental trees and shrubs. CAT $1, R & W, PC/OC, U.S. ONLY, M.O. $50.

G71 **Ledden (Orol) & Sons** - P.O. Box 7, Sewell, NJ 08080-0007, (609) 468-1000. Vegetable, herb and flower seed, perennial vegetables, berry plants, grape vines, farm seed. CAT FREE, R & W, PC/CC.

G71M **Ledgerwood (Charles B.)** - 3862 Carlsbad Blvd., Carlsbad, CA 92008, (619) 729-3282. Specializes in vegetable, herb and flower seed that is adapted to coastal southern California growing conditions. Also sells some of their own introductions, such as Winter Zucchini. CAT $1, RET, PC, M.O. $1.

G72 **Lee's Nursery** - P.O. Box 489, McMinnville, TN 37110. Fruit and nut trees, berry plants, grape vines, hardy kiwi, shade trees, flowering shrubs. CAT $1, R & W, PC.

G75 **Lennilea Farm Nursery** - R.D. #1, Box 683, Alburtis, PA 18011, (215) 845-2077. Grafted nut trees, unusual fruits including American persimmon, pawpaw, jujube, saskatoon, mulberry and mayhaw. CAT SASE, RET, PC, M.O. $10.

G77M **Lessard (W.O.) Nursery** - 19201 S.W. 248th St., Homestead, FL 33031, (305) 247-0397 (no telephone orders). Large selection of banana corms, over 30 cultivars. Previously known as Tropical Spices, etc. CAT $1, WHLS, PC, OVER.

G79 **Letherman's Inc.** - 1221 Tuscarawas St. E., Canton, OH 44707, (216) 452-5704. Vegetable, herb and flower seeds for commercial growers and home gardeners. CAT FREE, R & W, PC/CC.

G79M **Leuthardt (Henry) Nurseries Inc.** - Montauk Highway, P.O. Box 666, East Moriches, NY 11940, (516) 878-1387. Dwarf, semi-dwarf and espalier fruit trees, grape vines, berry plants. Many rare and choice older cultivars. CAT FREE, R & W, PC.

G81 **Lewis Strawberry Nursery Inc.** - P.O. Box 24, Rocky Pt., NC 28457, (919) 675-2394 or 675-9409. Specializes in strawberry plants. CAT FREE, R & W, PC/CC, OVER, M.O. $10.

G82 **Liberty Seed Co.** - P.O. Box 806, New Philadelphia, OH 44663, (216) 364-1611. Complete line of vegetable, herb and flower seeds for home gardeners, market growers and commercial bedding plant operations. CAT FREE, R & W, PC/CC, M.O. $10.

G82M **Life-Form Replicators** - P.O. Box 857, Fowlerville, MI 48836, (517) 223-8750. Rare and unusual perennials and rock garden plants. CAT FREE, R & W, PC.

G83G **Lil' Olde Winemaking Shoppe** - 4S245 Wiltshire Lane, Sugar Grove, IL 60554, (312) 557-2523. Complete selection of homebrewing supplies, wine and beer yeasts. CAT FREE, RET, PC.

G83M **Lilly (Charles H.) Co.** - 7737 N.E. Killingsworth, Portland, OR 97218-4097, (503) 256-4600. Vegetable, herb and flower seeds. CAT FREE, WHLS, OVER, M.O. 5 LBS.

G84 **Lily of the Valley Herb Farm** - 3969 Fox Ave., Minerva, OH 44657, (216) 862-3920. Growers of over 400 varieties of herb plants, scented geraniums, perennial flowers and everlastings. CAT $2, R & W, PC, OVER, M.O. $10.

G85 **Lilypons Water Gardens, Inc.** - P.O. Box 10, Lilypons, MD 21717-0010, (301) 874-5133 or (713) 934-8525. Aquatic plants, including water lilies, lotus, cattail, arrowhead, Chinese water chestnut, watercress and taro. CAT $5, R & W, PC/CC, OVER.

G87 **Lindenberg Seeds Ltd.** - 803 Princess Ave., Brandon, MB R7A 0P5, Canada. Vegetable, herb and flower seeds, perennial vegetables, grape vines, berry plants. CAT FREE, RET, PC/CC, U.S. (SEEDS ONLY).

G88 **Linwood Nurseries** - 3613 West Linwood Ave., Turlock, CA 95380, (209) 634-1836. Grafted pecan trees. Oldest pecan nursery in the West, established in 1915. CAT FREE, R & W, PC, OVER.

G89 **Little Valley Farm** - Route 3, Box 544, Spring Green, WI 53588, (608) 935-3324. Seeds and plants of Midwestern natives including wild flowers, grasses, vines, trees and shrubs. CAT $.25, R & W, PC.

G89M **Little Valley Nurseries** - 13022 E. 136th Ave., Brighton, CO 80601, (303) 659-6708. Fruit trees, wild flowers, garden perennials, conifers, shade trees, flowering shrubs. CAT FREE, WHLS, PC, M.O. $500.

G91 **Living Farms** - Box 50, Tracy, MN 56175, (507) 629-4431. Organic sprouting seeds and grains, grown on farms at least three years removed from the use of herbicides, pesticides and insecticides. CAT FREE, R & W, OVER.

G91M **Living Stones Nursery** - 2936 N. Stone Ave., Tucson, AZ 85705. Specializes in lithops, mesembryanthemums and other unusual succulents. Succeeded Ed Storm Inc. CAT $1.50, R & W, PC, OVER, M.O. $10.

G92 **Living Tree Center** - P.O. Box 10082, Berkeley, CA 94709-5082, (415) 528-4467. Large selection of historic apple trees, over 70 cultivars. Also crab apple, pear, apricot and quince trees, vegetable seeds, organic almonds and almond butter. Previously known as Centre for Community Self Sufficiency. CAT $7, R & W, PC, OVER.

G93M **Lockhart Seeds, Inc.** - P.O. Box 1361, Stockton, CA 95205, (209) 466-4401. Vegetable, herb and flower seed, primarily for farmers and market gardeners. Many specialty cultivars. CAT FREE, R & W, PC/CC, OVER, M.O. $10.

G94 **Loehman's Cacti and Succulents** - P.O. Box 871, Paramount, CA 90723, (714) 846-4328. Cactus and succulent plants. CAT FREE, RET, PC, M.O. $10.

G96 **Logee's Greenhouses** - 55 North St., Danielson, CT 06239, (203) 774-8038. Rare and unusual indoor tropical plants, over 2,000 varieties including citrus, herbs, scented geraniums, cacti and succulents, ferns, and orchids. CAT $3 REFUNDABLE, RET, PC, OVER, M.O. $15.

G97M **Lon's Oregon Grapes** - P.O. Box 7632, Salem, OR 97303. Extensive listing of table grapes, both American and vinifera, adapted to a wide range of climates. Also scion wood and custom grafting services for cultivars not listed in catalog. Private grape breeder using the nursery to pay some of the expenses of his breeding program. CAT SASE, R & W, PC/OC, OVER.

G99 **Long Hungry Creek Nursery** - Box 163, Red Boiling Springs, TN 37150, (615) 699-2784. Small nursery specializing in apple trees, both antique and modern, selected for flavor, disease resistance and late blooming qualities. CAT SASE, R & W, PC/OC, OVER.

H3M **Lost Prairie Herb Farm** - 805 Kienas Rd., Kalispell, MT 59901, (406) 756-7742. Family-run business specializing in organically grown herb plants and seeds for cold, northern areas. Offers over 200 varieties, including scented geraniums, ground covers and everlastings. CAT $2, RET, PC/CC, M.O. 4 PLANTS.

H4 **Louisiana Nursery** - Rt. 7, Box 43, Opelousas, LA 70570, (318) 948-3696 (no telephone orders). Large selection of fruit and nut trees, berry plants, grape vines, bananas, herbs, aquatic plants, bamboo, cacti and succulents, gingers, palms, tree and shrub seed. CAT $3.50, RET, PC, OVER, M.O. $25.

H6 **Lowe's own-root Roses** - 6 Sheffield Rd., Nashua, NH 03062, (603) 888-2214 (no telephone orders). Custom grown own-root roses. CAT $2, RET, PC, OVER.

H7M **Lupin Triticale Enterprises** - P.O. Box 187, Perham, MN 56573, (218) 346-2580. Specializes in sweet lupin and triticale seeds. CAT FREE, R & W, PC, OVER, M.O. $50.

H8 **Lustgarten (Baier) Farms & Nurseries** - Jericho Turnpike (Route 25), Middle Island, NY 11953, (516) 924-3444. Fruit and nut trees, berry plants, grape vines, shade trees, flowering shrubs. CAT $1, WHLS, M.O. $100.

H10 **M. eV. Research** - P.O. Box 123, Waterloo, ON N2J 3Z9, Canada, (519) 742-7227. Yeast cultures for home brewers and micro breweries. Also laboratory and consulting services for micro breweries. CAT FREE, R & W, PC/CC, OVER.

H11 **M. Holmes Quisenberry** - 4626 Glebe Farm Rd., Sarasota, FL 33580. Sells only Holmes Mexican tomato seeds. CAT SASE, RET, PC, M.O. 200 SEEDS.

H12 **Macadamia Land Nursery** - 2562 Mountain View Dr., Escondido, CA 92027, (619) 745-3417. Specializes in Cate macadamias. *Sells the following product/s:* <u>in shell macadamias, both fresh and roasted macadamia nut meats</u>. CAT (CALL FOR PRICES), R & W, PC, OVER.

H16 **Makielski Berry Nursery** - 7130 Platt Rd., Ypsilanti, MI 48197, (313) 434-3673 or 572-0060. Fruit trees, berry plants and perennial vegetables. Specializes in small fruits, including raspberries, blackberries, blueberries, grapes, strawberries, currants and gooseberries. CAT FREE, R & W, PC/CC, OVER, M.O. 5 OF EACH.

H19M **Manganaro Foods** - 488 Ninth Ave., New York, NY 10018, (212) 563-5331. Gourmet imported Italian foods. Established in 1893. *Sells the following product/s:* <u>both fresh and marinated cippolini, semolina, dried Cannellini beans, dried chestnuts, chestnut flour, grano wheat, and chickpea flour</u>. CAT FREE, R & W, PC/CC.

H20 **Mann's (Ann) Exotic Plants** - 9045 Ron-Den Lane, Windermere, FL 32786-9238, (407) 876-2625. Hybrid and species orchids, palms, aroids, bromeliads, tropical foliage plants. CAT $1, R & W, PC, CANADA ONLY, M.O. $20.

H23M **Maplewood Seed Co.** - 311 Maplewood Lane, Roseburg, OR 97470. Maple tree seed for horticulturists, collectors, hobbyists and bonsai specialists. CAT SASE, RET, PC, OVER.

H25 **Marcella's Garden** - P.O. Box 362, Colonial Heights, VA 23834. Herb seeds, herbal products, sprouting seeds. CAT FREE, RET, PC.

H26M **Mariani Orchards** - 1615 Half Road, Morgan Hill, CA 95037, (408) 779-5467. Large selection of rare and common sun-dried fruits and nuts. *Sells the following product/s:* <u>dried Muir peaches, dried Blenheim apricots, Muscat of Alexandria raisins, dried nectarines, dried Moyer, d'Agen, Silver and Imperial prunes, Brooks cherry "raisins", dried Rainier cherries, dried Hachiya persimmons and Serr walnut meats</u>. CAT FREE, R & W, PC/CC.

H28 **Marschall Dairy Products** - P.O. Box 592, Madison, WI 53701, (608) 258-7210. Dairy cultures for both home culturing and commercial scale dairy manufacture. CAT FREE, R & W.

H30 **Maryland Aquatic Nurseries** - 3427 N. Furnace Rd., Jarrettsville, MD 21084, (301) 557-7615. Large selection of aquatic and bog plants. CAT $2, R & W, PC, CANADA ONLY.

H31 **Maskal Forages, Inc.** - 1318 Willow, Caldwell, ID 83605, (208) 454-3330. Specializes in teff, the ancient grain of Ethiopia. *Sells the following product/s:* <u>whole grain teff and teff flour</u>. CAT FREE, R & W, PC, CANADA ONLY, M.O. 2 POUNDS.

H33 **May (Earl) Seed & Nursery** - 208 N. Elm Street, Shenandoah, IA 51603, 1-800-831-4193. Complete line of vegetable, herb and flower seed, fruit and nut trees, berry plants, grape vines, perennial vegetables, ornamental trees and shrubs. CAT FREE, RET, PC/CC.

H34 **May Nursery Co.** - P.O. Box 1312, Yakima, WA 98907, (509) 453-8219. Commercial grower of apples, pears, peaches, plums, apricots, nectarines and cherries. CAT FREE, WHLS, OVER.

H34M **Mayer's Cider Mill, Inc.** - 699 Five Mile Line Road, Webster, NY 14580, (716) 671-1955. Home brewing supplies, beer and wine yeasts. CAT FREE, RET, PC/CC.

H37M **McClure & Zimmerman** - P.O. Box 368, Friesland, WI 53935, (414) 326-4220. Specializes in rare species bulbs. CAT FREE, RET, PC/CC.

H40 **McCrory's Sunny Hill Herb Farm** - Star Rt. 3, Box 844, Eustis, FL 32726, (904) 357-9876. Herbs and scented geraniums, approximately 150 varieties. CAT $.50 REFUNDABLE, R & W, PC/CC.

H42 **McFayden Seeds** - P.O. Box 1800, Brandon, MB, R7A 6N4, Canada, (204) 726-0759. Vegetable, herb and flower seed, fruit and nut trees, berry plants, grape vines, perennial vegetables, ornamental trees and shrubs. Succeeded Robertson-Pike Co. CAT FREE, RET, PC/CC/OC, U.S. ONLY.

H45M **Meadow Lake Nursery Co.** - P.O. Box 1302, McMinnville, OR 97128, (503) 852-7525. Seedling and clonal deciduous fruit rootstocks, ornamental trees and shrubs. CAT FREE, WHLS.

H46 **Meadowbrook Herb Garden** - Rt. 138, Wyoming, RI 02898, (401) 539-7603. Bio-dynamic herb farm offering a large selection of herb seeds, dried herbs and spices, teas, Dr. Hauschka cosmetics and other herbal products. CAT $1, R & W, PC/CC, CANADA ONLY, M.O. $10.

H49 **Mellinger's Inc.** - 2310 W. South Range Rd., North Lima, OH 44452-9731, 1-800-321-7444. Extensive selection of vegetable, wild flower, cover crop and grain seed, fruit and nut trees, berry plants, perennial vegetables, herb plants and seed, ornamentals. CAT FREE, R & W, PC/CC, OVER.

H51M **Merry Gardens** - P.O. Box 595, Camden, ME 04843, (207) 236-9064 (no telephone orders). Herbs, scented geraniums, cacti and succulents, ornamental plants for home and conservatory. CAT $1, RET, PC/OC, CANADA ONLY, M.O. $10.

H52 **Mesa Garden** - P.O. Box 72, Belen, NM 87002, (505) 864-3131. Cactus and succulent plants and seed. CAT $.50, RET, PC/OC, OVER.

H53 **Meta Horticulture Labs** - 635 Town Mountain Road, Pikeville, KY 41501, (606) 432-1516. Large selection of gourd seeds. Also tree and shrub seed, Queen Ann's pocket melon. CAT $1 REFUNDABLE, RET, PC/CC, OVER.

H53M **Meyer (Roger and Shirley)** - 16531 Mt. Shelley Circle, Fountain Valley, CA 92708, (714) 839-0796 (no telephone orders). Scionwood of kiwifruit, approximately 20 cultivars, Actinidia arguta and other hardy kiwi, and jujube. CAT FREE, R & W, PC, OVER, M.O. $10.

H54 **Meyer Seed Co.** - 600 S. Caroline St., Baltimore, MD 21231, (301) 342-4224. Vegetable, herb and flower seeds, berry plants, cover crop and green manure seed. CAT FREE, R & W, PC/CC.

H57M **Michell (Henry F.) Co.** - P.O. Box 160, King of Prussia, PA 19406, 1-800-422-4678. Vegetable, herb and flower seeds for commercial growers. CAT FREE, WHLS, PC, OVER.

H58M **MicroCulture, Inc.** - P.O. Box 3004-222, Corvallis, OR 97339, (503) 754-7771. Specializes in certified seed potatoes, both mini tubers and normal size. Also organically grown specialty potatoes for fresh market packed in 50 pound boxes. CAT FREE, R & W, PC/CC, OVER, M.O. 1 BAG.

H60 **Midwest Cactus Sales** - P.O. Box 163, New Melle, MO 63365, (314) 828-5389 (no telephone orders). Specializes in plants of hardy cactus. CAT $.50, RET, PC, M.O. $5.

H61 **Midwest Seed Growers** - 10559 Lackman Rd., Lenexa, KS 66219, (913) 894-0500. Wholesale distributors of vegetable and flower seed for the market grower trade. CAT FREE, WHLS, PC/CC, OVER, M.O. $15.

H61M **Midwest Wildflowers** - Box 64, Rockton, IL 61072. Specializes in seeds of wild flowers common to the Midwestern United States. CAT $.50, RET, PC, CANADA ONLY, M.O. $2.40.

H63 **Milaeger's Gardens** - 4838 Douglas Ave., Racine, WI 53402-2498, (414) 639-2371. Herb plants, perennial flowers, native woodland and prairie wild flowers, prairie grasses, roses. CAT $1, RET, PC/CC, M.O. $25.

H64 **Miller Farms** - R.R. 2, Box 172-A, Milford, IN 46542. Regional specialty food items. *Sells the following product/s:* sweet sorghum syrup in one gallon jugs. CAT FREE, R & W, PC, M.O. 1 GALLON.

H64T **Miller Grass Seed Co., Inc.** - P.O. Box 886, Hereford, TX 79045, (806) 258-7288. Native warm season grasses, wild flowers, trees and shrubs, cover crops and green manures. CAT FREE, WHLS.

H65 **Miller Nurseries Inc.** - 5060 West Lake Road, Canandaigua, NY 14424, 1-800-828-9630. Wide selection of hardy fruit and nut trees, berry plants, grape vines, hardy kiwi, perennial vegetables, shade trees, flowering shrubs. CAT FREE, R & W, PC/CC.

H66 **Miller-Bowie County Farmers Assn.** - P.O. Box 1110, Texarkana, TX 75504, (214) 794-3631. Large farmers co-op offering a wide range of vegetables seed, including many older traditional cultivars. Previously known as Aurora Gardens and Bunch's Seeds. CAT $.50, RET, PC, OVER, M.O. $2.50.

H67M **Millstream Natural Health Supplies** - 1310-A E. Tallmadge Ave., Akron, OH 44310, (216) 630-2700. Certified organically grown fruits and vegetables, natural food items. *Sells the following product/s:* spelt bread, Essene rye bread. CAT FREE, RET, PC.

H69 **Mission Orchards** - P.O. Box 6947, San Jose, CA 95150-6947, 1-800-33-1448. Fresh produce, gourmet and specialty food items. CAT FREE, RET, PC/CC.

H69T **Missouri Dandy Pantry** - 212 Hammons Dr. East, Stockton, MO 65785, 1-800-872-6879. Specializes in black walnuts and other gourmet food items. *Sells the following product/s:* black walnut kernels, black walnut brittle, chocolate covered black walnuts, black walnut caramel popcorn. CAT FREE, RET, PC/CC, OVER.

H70M **Missouri Wildflowers Nursery** - Rt. 2, Box 373, Jefferson City, MO 65109-9805, (314) 496-3492. Seeds, spores and plants of native wild flowers, forbs, grasses, ferns and shrubs. CAT $1, RET, PC.

H71 **Mistletoe Sales** - P.O. Box 1275, Carpinteria, CA 93013, (805) 684-0436. Extensive seed listing of trees and shrubs, perennial flowers and palms. CAT FREE, WHLS, OVER.

H78M **Montana Flour & Grains** - P.O. Box 808, Big Sandy, MT 59520, (406) 378-3105 or 622-5503. Specializes in certified organically grown Kamut wheat. CAT FREE, WHLS, M.O. 10,000 LBS.

H79M **Montrose Nursery** - P.O. Box 957, Hillsborough, NC 27278, (919) 732-7787. Garden perennials, native wild flowers, herbs. CAT $2, RET, PC.

H80 **Moon Mountain Wildflowers** - P.O. Box 34, Morro Bay, CA 93443, (805) 772-2473. Seeds of North American native wild flowers. Over 60 individual species plus 15 mixtures that are customized for the geographical regions of the U. S., including Alaska. CAT $1, R & W, PC/CC, OVER.

H81M **Moon's Nursery** - P.O. Box 1097, Oroville, WA 98844, (509) 476-3188. Fruit and nut trees including apples, walnuts, chestnuts and hardy kiwi. Specializes in Asian pears. CAT FREE, R & W, PC, M.O. 5 TREES.

H82 **Moore Water Gardens** - P.O. Box 340, Port Stanley, ON N0L 2A0, Canada, (519) 782-4052. Water lilies, lotus and other aquatic plants. CAT FREE, R & W, PC, CANADA ONLY.

H83 **Moose Tubers** - 52 Mayflower Hill Drive, Waterville, ME 04901, (207) 257-3943 (no telephone orders). Specializes in seed potatoes, some organic, all without systemic treatment. Also cover crop seed, onion sets and sunchokes. Discourages orders from outside the Northeast. CAT $.50, R & W, PC, M.O. $25.

H85 **Morden Nurseries Ltd.** - P.O. Box 1270, Morden, MB R0G 1J0, Canada, (204) 822-3311. Extra hardy fruit and nut trees, berry plants, grape vines, flowering shrubs. Specializes in apple crabs and saskatoons. CAT FREE, RET, PC, U.S. ONLY.

H87M **Morse Elephant Garlic** - 2805 Green Acres Lane, Coos Bay, OR 97420, (503) 269-5726. Elephant garlic for planting or eating. CAT FREE, R & W, PC, CANADA ONLY, M.O. 1 LB.

H88 **Morss (Walter K.) & Son** - R.F.D. 2, Boxford, MA 01921, (508) 352-2633. Specializes in small fruits including strawberries, raspberries, blueberries, grapes, currants and gooseberries. CAT FREE, R & W, PC.

H90 **Mount Arbor Nurseries** - P.O. Box 129, Shenandoah, IA 51601, 1-800-831-4125. Fruit and nut trees, berry plants, grape vines, perennial vegetable plants, ornamental trees and shrubs. CAT FREE, WHLS, OVER, M.O. $500.

H90M **Mount Vernon Research and Extension Unit** - Washington State University, 1468 Memorial Highway, Mount Vernon, WA 98273-9788. Sells a limited amount of deciduous fruit tree scionwood intended for the commercial nursery industry, collectors and researchers. CAT FREE, RET.

H91 **Mountain Ark Trading Co.** - 120 South East Ave., Fayetteville, AR 72701, 1-800-643-8909. Extensive collection of organically grown macrobiotic foods, including grains, seeds, beans, nuts, sea vegetables and soyfoods. Also tempeh and natto starter cultures. *Sells the following product/s:* dried Hopi Blue corn, dried Anasazi beans, dried black and vegetable soybeans, whole grain teff, whole grain quinoa, hato-mugi grain, prepared natto, jinenjo soba, umeboshi plums, dried adzuki bean sprouts, greenmagma, amazake, daikon pickles, dried wheat gluten, seitan, rice bran, arrowroot powder, and dried lotus roots. CAT $1, R & W, PC/CC, OVER, M.O. $100 WHLS

H93M **Mountain Ornamental Nursery** - P.O. Box 83, Altamont, TN 37301, (615) 692-3424. Berry plants, wild flowers, shade trees, flowering shrubs, hardy ferns, tree and shrub seed. CAT FREE, WHLS.

H94 **Mountain Seed & Nursery** - P.O. Box 9107, Moscow, ID 83843, (208) 882-8040. Vegetable, herb and flower seed for cold short-season areas. CAT $1 REFUNDABLE, R & W, PC/CC, OVER.

H95 **Mountain Valley Seeds & Nursery** - P.O. Box 3988, Logan, UT 84321, (801) 752-0247. Specializes in vegetable, herb and flower seeds for northern areas. CAT FREE, R & W, PC/CC.

H98 **Mt. Tahoma Nursery** - 28111-112th Avenue East, Graham, WA 98338, (206) 847-9827. Rock garden and woodland plants, native alpines of Washington State. CAT $1, R & W, PC/CC, CANADA ONLY.

I3 **Mushroompeople** - P.O. Box 159, Inverness, CA 94937, (415) 663-8504. Specializes in shiitake mushroom spawn, both sawdust and plug spawn, for the wood-lot farmer and the commercial grower. CAT FREE, R & W, PC/CC, OVER.

I4 **Musser Forests Inc.** - P.O. Box S-89M, Indiana, PA 15710-0340, (412) 465-5685. Evergreen and hardwood seedlings and transplants for nurseries, landscaping, lining out and reforestation. CAT FREE, R & W, PC/CC, OVER, M.O. 10 OF EACH.

I7 **Mycotek** - 7421 Pudding Creek Drive S.E., Salem, OR 97301-9253, (503) 370-7674. Home mushroom growing kits, mushroom spawn, pre-inoculated shiitake sawdust bags for commercial production of fresh shiitake mushrooms. CAT FREE, R & W, PC, CANADA ONLY.

I9M **National Arbor Day Foundation** - 100 Arbor Ave., Nebraska City, NE 68410, (402) 474-5655. Non-profit organization working toward a goal of improved tree planting and tree care throughout America. Offers fruit and nut trees, flowering shrubs, shade and ornamental trees. CAT $2 (FREE WITH $10 MEMBERSHIP), RET, PC/CC.

I11 **Native American Seed** - 2701 Cross Timbers, Flower Mound, TX 75028, (214) 539-0534. Family farm specializing in seeds of Texas native plants, wild flowers and grasses for environmental restoration. CAT $1, R & W, PC/CC.

I11M **Native Gardens** - Rt 1, Box 464, Greenback, TN 37742, (615) 856-3350. Seeds and plants of native ferns, grasses, wild flowers, herbs, perennials, trees and shrubs. All plants are nursery propagated, none are collected from the wild. CAT $1, R & W, PC, M.O. $10.

I15 **Native Seed Foundation** - Star Route, Moyie Springs, ID 83845, (208) 267-7938. Native plants of the Pacific Northwest and southern British Columbia, including fruit and nut trees, conifers, and shrubs. CAT $.25, R & W, PC, OVER.

I15M **Native Seeds, Inc.** - 14590 Triadelphia Mill Rd., Dayton, MD 21036, (301) 596-9818. Wild flower seeds in packets and bulk quantities. Also regional mixes as well as custom mixes. CAT FREE, R & W, PC/CC, OVER.

I16 **Native Seeds/Search** - 2509 N. Campbell Ave. #325, Tucson, AZ 85719, (602) 327-9123 (no telephone orders). Non-profit conservation group working to preserve the wide diversity of crops grown by Native Americans in the Greater Southwest. *Sells the following product/s:* whole grain amaranth, amaranth flour, dried tepary beans, wild wheat grain, dried whole chiltepines, sweet corn chicos, dried Azufrado beans, dried Anasazi beans, panocha flour, and dried Mexican oregano, Mt. Pima wild oregano, Mexican tarragon and Mrs. Burns lemon basil. CAT $1.00, RET, PC, OVER.

I17M **Natives Nurseries** - P.O. Box 2355, Covington, LA 70434, (504) 892-5424. Specializes in trees and shrubs native to the Southeast. CAT FREE, WHLS.

I19 **Natural Gardens** - 4804 Shell Lane, Knoxville, TN 37918, (615) 482-6746. Seeds and plants of wild flowers and garden perennials. Features plants that attract butterflies and birds to the garden. Will not sell plants collected from the wild. CAT $1 REFUNDABLE, RET, PC, CANADA ONLY (SEEDS), M.O. $7.50.

I20 **Natural Way Mills Inc.** - R.R. 2, Box 37, Middle River, MN 56737, (218) 222-3677. Certified organically grown grains, flours and cereals, sprouting seeds. *Sells the following product/s:* whole durum wheat, durum wheat flour, whole triticale, triticale flour, triticale meal and amaranth flour. CAT FREE, R & W, PC, OVER.

I22 **Nature's Garden** - P.O. Box 574, Scio, OR 97374, (503) 649-6772. Native wild flowers, herbs, alpines, rock garden plants, hardy ferns, garden perennials. CAT $1.25 DEDUCTIBLE, R & W, PC, OVER, M.O. $15.

I23 **Nature's Way Wholesale Nursery** - 8905 Edith Blvd. N.E., Albuquerque, NM 87113, (505) 898-9258. Specializes in natives, garden perennials, ground covers and drought tolerant plants. CAT FREE, WHLS.

I25M **Nebraska Nut Growers Association** - P.O. Box 4644, Lincoln, NE 68504, (402) 472-3674. Seed and scionwood distribution program of the non-profit Nebraska Nut Growers Association designed to encourage tree plantings that will produce nuts and small fruit. CAT FREE, RET, PC, OVER, M.O. $10.

I26 **Necessary Trading Co.** - Box 305, New Castle, VA 24127, (703) 864-5103. Specializes in biological pest control and natural soil management products, including green manure seed mixes. CAT $2 REFUNDABLE, R & W, PC/CC, OVER, M.O. $350 WHLS

I28 **Neon Palm Nursery** - 1560 Sebastopol Rd., Santa Rosa, CA 95407, (707) 578-7467. Hardy palms and subtropicals, cacti and succulents, cycads, rare trees and shrubs, conifers, garden perennials, ornamental grasses, ferns. CAT $1, R & W, PC, M.O. $50.

I30 **New England Cheesemaking Supply Co.** - 85 Main St., Ashfield, MA 01330, (413) 628-3808. Home cheese making supplies and dairy products, including starter cultures for yogurt, cheese, kefir, buttermilk and sour cream. CAT $1, R & W, PC/CC, OVER.

I31 **New England Wild Flower Society, Inc.** - Garden in the Woods, Hemenway Rd., Framingham, MA 01701. Non-profit organization established in 1922 to promote the appreciation, knowledge and conservation of native plants. Sells seed collected in the wild and at their botanical garden. CAT $1 PLUS SASE, RET, PC, OVER, M.O. 5 PKTS.

I33 **New Mexico Cactus Research** - P.O. Box 787, Belen, NM 87002, (505) 864-4027 (no telephone orders). Extensive collector's list of cacti and succulent seeds, over 1,000 varieties. Also seed of natives and exotics. CAT SASE, R & W, PC, OVER, M.O. $5.

I36 **New York State Fruit Testing Coop. Assn.** - P.O. Box 462, Geneva, NY 14456, (315) 787-2205. Small growers' cooperative specializing in new and noteworthy hardy fruit tree cultivars recommended for testing by the pomologists at the New York State Agricultural Experiment Station. Also sells scion wood of all cultivars growing at the Experiment Station. CAT FREE, R & W, PC, OVER.

I37M **Niche Gardens** - 1111 Dawson Road, Chapel Hill, NC 27516, (919) 967-0078 (no telephone orders). Specializes in nursery propagated Southeastern natives. Also offers other North American natives, selected garden perennials, ornamental grasses and under used trees and shrubs. CAT $3, RET, PC, OVER, M.O. $15.

I39 **Nichols Garden Nursery Inc.** - 1190 North Pacific Hwy., Albany, OR 97321, (503) 928-9280. Large selection of herb plants and seed, elephant garlic, seeds of oriental, European and specialty vegetables, perennial vegetables, beer and wine making supplies, starter cultures. *Sells the following product/s:* dried Cascade and Willamette hops, dried yerba maté. CAT FREE, R & W, PC/CC, OVER.

I39M **Noel's Garden Seeds** - R.D. #2K, Oxford, NY 13830. Small family business specializing in open-pollinated vegetable seeds for home gardeners in the Northeast. CAT SASE, RET, PC.

I40 **Nolin River Nut Tree Nursery** - 797 Port Wooden Rd., Upton, KY 42784, (502) 369-8551. Extensive listing of grafted nut trees, including pecans, walnuts, heartnuts, butternuts, chestnuts, hicans and hickories. Also native American persimmons. Previously known as Leslie H. Wilmoth Nursery. CAT FREE, R & W, PC.

I41 **Norcal Nursery** - P.O. Box 1012, Red Bluff, CA 96080, (916) 527-6200. Specializes in everbearing and day neutral strawberries and strawberry cultivars suitable for California growing conditions. CAT FREE, WHLS, OVER, M.O. 1500 OF EACH.

I41M **Nordmann (Ben J.) Inc.** - P.O. Box 621, De Land, FL 32721-0621, (904) 734-4712. Specializes in disease resistant bunch grapes adapted to the South. CAT FREE, R & W, PC.

I42 **North Central Comfrey Producers** - P.O. Box 195, Glidden, WI 54527, (715) 264-2083. Specializes in comfrey plants and cuttings, fresh comfrey roots, and dried comfrey products. *Sells the following product/s:* fresh comfrey roots, dried comfrey leaves. CAT FREE, R & W, PC, M.O. $5.

I43 **North Star Gardens** - 19060 Manning Trail N., Marine on St. Croix, MN 55047-9723, (612) 433-5850. Bare root and tissue culture red, black, purple and yellow raspberries, over 30 cultivars. CAT $4, R & W, PC.

I43T **Northbest Natural Products** - P.O. Box 31029, Seattle, WA 98103. Sprouting seeds, natural food items. *Sells the following product/s:* whole grain quinoa, quinoa flour, quinoa pasta, chlorella powder, spirulina powder, spirulina flakes, dried wheatgrass, dehydrated alfalfa sprouts and greenmagma. CAT FREE, R & W, PC.

I44 **Northeastern Ferns & Wildflowers** - Pleasant Street, Newfields, NH 03856, (603) 772-1136. Hardy native orchids, ferns and wild flowers collected from the wild. CAT FREE, R & W, PC/OC, CANADA ONLY.

I45M **Northern Groves Hardy Bamboo** - 3328 S.E. Kelly, Portland, OR 97202, (503) 232-1860. Specializes in hardy bamboos. CAT SASE, R & W, PC.

I46 **Northern Kiwi Nursery** - R.R. #3, Niagara-on-the-Lake, ON L0S 1J0, Canada, (416) 468-5483 or 468-7573.

Specializes in hardy kiwi. CAT FREE, R & W, PC, OVER.

I47 **Northplan Seed Producers** - P.O. Box 9107, Moscow, ID 83843, (208) 882-8040. Native tree, shrub and wild flower seed including grasses and legumes for reclamation, revegetation and landscaping. Subsidiary of Mountain Seed & Nursery. CAT $.50 OR SASE, R & W, PC/CC, OVER.

I49 **Northwest Mycological Consultants** - 702 N.W. 4th St., Corvallis, OR 97330, (503) 753-8198. Spawn and cultures for different strains of shiitake mushrooms, other exotic mushrooms, mushroom growing supplies. Also provides consulting and design to growers. CAT $2 REFUNDABLE, R & W, PC/CC, OVER.

I49M **Northwoods Nursery** - 28696 S. Cramer Rd., Molalla, OR 97038, (503) 651-3737. Specializes in exotic and unusual fruits and nuts, including hardy kiwi, fig, persimmon, pawpaw, cherimoya, feijoa, pepino, heartnut, buartnut and butternut. CAT FREE, R & W, PC/CC, OVER.

I50 **Nourse Farms, Inc.** - Box 485, RFD, South Deerfield, MA 01373, (413) 665-2658. Strawberries, raspberries, blackberries, horseradish, rhubarb and hybrid asparagus. Specializes in tissue culture, virus-free stock. CAT FREE, R & W, PC, OVER.

I51M **Nu-World Amaranth** - P.O. Box 2202, Naperville, IL 60567, (312) 420-7395. Specializes in amaranth seed for planting, sprouting quality amaranth and amaranth foods. *Sells the following product/s:* whole grain amaranth, amaranth flour, amaranth granola cereal, puffed amaranth, and custom bread-making flour blends. CAT FREE, R & W, PC.

I52 **Nuccio's Nurseries** - P.O. Box 6160, Altadena, CA 91003, (818) 794-3383 (no telephone orders). Specializes in camellias and azaleas. CAT FREE, R & W, PC, OVER.

I53 **Nursery at the Dallas Nature Center** - 7575 Wheatland Road, Dallas, TX 75249, (214) 296-2476. Native plants of North Central Texas, especially threatened and rare species, including prairie grasses, wild flowers, trees and shrubs. Offers both seed collected from the wild and organically grown plants. Previously known as Greenhills Environmental Center. CAT FREE, R & W, PC/CC/OC, OVER.

I54 **O & O Nursery** - 6925 Joseph St. SE, Salem, OR 97301, (503) 364-6162. Commercial grower of peaches, cherries, nectarines, Asian pears and blueberries. CAT FREE, WHLS, M.O. 10 OF EACH.

I55 **O'Brien's Cellar Supplies** - P.O. Box 284, Wayne, IL 60184, (312) 289-7169. Home brewing supplies, wine and beer yeasts. CAT FREE, RET, PC/CC.

I57 **Oak Hill Gardens** - P.O. Box 25, Dundee, IL 60118-0025, (312) 428-8500. Specializes in orchids, bromeliads, and unusual tropical house plants. CAT FREE, R & W, PC/CC, OVER.

I58 **Oak Manor Farms, Inc.** - R.R. #1, Tavistock, ON N0B 2R0, Canada, (519) 662-2385. Organic sprouting seeds and mixes, organic grains, beans, flours and cereals. *Sells the following product/s:* durum wheat kernels, durum wheat flour, triticale kernels, and triticale flour. CAT $1, R & W, PC/CC, U.S. ONLY, M.O. $15.

I59G **Of the Jungle** - P.O. Box 1801, Sebastopol, CA 95473. Rare tropical ethnopharmalogical plants, seeds and botanical products including tribal medicines, vegetables, herbs and fruits. Also exotic oils and extracts. *Sells the following product/s:* dried Stevia herb and kava root. CAT $1, RET, PC, OVER.

I59M **Ohio Seed Co. (The)** - P.O. Box 87, West Jefferson, OH 43162, (614) 879-8366. Complete line of vegetable, herb and flower seeds. CAT FREE, WHLS.

I60 **Oikos Tree Crops** - 721 Fletcher, Kalamazoo, MI 49007, (616) 342-6504. Native shrubs and trees selected for disease resistance, especially nut bearing trees including hybrid oaks, pecans, chestnuts, walnuts and filberts. Also minor fruits. CAT FREE, R & W, PC, OVER, M.O. $25.

I61 **Ojai Valley Seeds** - P.O. Box 543, Ojai, CA 93023, (805) 646-7743 (no telephone orders). Seeds of ornamental trees and shrubs, fruits and nuts, palms, and foliage plants. CAT FREE, WHLS, OVER, M.O. $15.

I62 **Oki Nursery Co.** - P.O. Box 7118, Sacramento, CA 95826-0818, (916) 383-5665. Ornamental trees and shrubs, hardy perennials, vegetable plants. CAT FREE, WHLS, M.O. $250.

I63M **Old Farm Nursery** - 5550 Indiana St., Golden, CO 80403, (303) 278-0754. Rare and unusual perennials, Rocky Mountain and Southwest natives, ornamental grasses. CAT $1.50, RET, PC/CC.

I63T **Old Southwest Trading Co.** - P.O. Box 7545, Albuquerque, NM 87194, (505) 831-5144. Specializes in Mexican and Southwestern foods. *Sells the following product/s:* dried whole Ancho, Cascabel, Coban, De Arbol, Guajillo, Habañero, Jalapeño, Mirasol, Pasilla, Pequín, Tepín, and Santaka peppers, powdered De Arbol, Ancho and Pasilla peppers, crushed De Arbol and Pequín peppers, Habañero pepper sauce. CAT FREE, RET, PC/CC, OVER.

I64 **Olds Seed Co.** - P.O. Box 7790, Madison, WI 53707, (608) 249-9291. Vegetable, herb and flower seeds, perennial vegetables, wild flower seed. Established in 1888. CAT $2.50 REFUNDABLE, R & W, PC, OVER.

I65M **Omaha Plant Farms, Inc.** - P.O. Box 787, Omaha, TX 75571. Vegetable plants including cabbage, cauliflower, brussels sprouts, broccoli and collards. Specializes in onion plants. Also known as Brown's Omaha Plant Farms Inc., Jim Brown Plants, and W.G. Farrier Plant Co. CAT FREE, R & W, PC.

I67M **Ontario Seed Co., Ltd.** - P.O. Box 144, Waterloo, ON N2J 3Z9, Canada, (519) 886-0557. Vegetable, herb and flower seeds. CAT FREE, RET, PC/CC.

I68 **Orange County Nursery** - 13249 East Firestone Blvd., Norwalk, CA 90651-5017, (714) 523-7720 or (213) 921-0361. Fruit and nut trees, including many low chill cultivars, shade trees, flowering shrubs. Major suppliers of oriental persimmons and Asian pears. Established in 1888. CAT FREE, WHLS, PC, OVER, M.O. $200.

I73M **Oregon Blueberry Farms** - 8474 Hazelgreen Rd., Silverton, OR 97381, (503) 873-4791. Specializes in highbush blueberries. CAT FREE, R & W, PC, CANADA ONLY, M.O. 50 PLANTS.

I74 **Oregon Exotics Rare Fruit Nursery** - 1065 Messinger Rd., Grants Pass, OR 97527. Rare and unusual, cold hardy sub-tropicals including a large selection of figs. Also hardy citrus, feijoa, passionfruit, loquats and exotic vegetables. Previously known as Black Oak Nursery. CAT FREE, R & W, PC, M.O. $10.

I75 **Oregon Rootstock, Inc.** - 10906 Monitor-Mckee Rd. N.E., Woodburn, OR 97071, (503) 634-2209. Complete line of controlled-size understock for apples, pears, cherries and plums. Also interstems and interstem wood for grafting. CAT FREE, WHLS, PC, OVER, M.O. 100 OF EACH.

I76 **Oregon Truffle Farms** - P.O. Box 1590, Florence, OR 97493-0103, (503) 997-7596. Inoculated Douglas fir seedlings for growing the Oregon white truffle in orchards. Also leads an annual gourmet truffle and mushroom tour of Europe. *Sells the following product/s:* Oregon white truffle paste. CAT FREE, R & W, PC, OVER.

I76M **Organic Foods Express** - 11003 Emack Road, Beltsville, MD 20705, (301) 937-8608. Organically grown fresh produce in season, natural food items. *Sells the following product/s:* Black Monukka raisins, Red Flame raisins, and dried whole Brooks prunes. CAT FREE, RET, PC.

I77 **Ornamental Edibles** - 3622 Weedlin Court, San Jose, CA 95132, (408) 946-7333. Seeds of over 400 varieties of gourmet vegetables and edible flowers for urban landscapes, container gardens and specialty growers. CAT $1, RET, PC.

I77M **Owen Farms** - Route #3, Box #158-A, Ripley, TN 38063, (901) 635-1588. Ornamental trees and shrubs, garden perennials. CAT $1, RET, PC, CANADA ONLY.

I78 **Owen (Richard) Nursery** - 2300 East Lincoln St., Bloomington, IL 61701, (309) 663-9551. Fruit and nut trees, berry plants, grape vines, perennial vegetables, flowering shrubs, garden perennials, indoor exotics. CAT FREE, RET, PC/CC.

I79 **Owen's Vineyard and Nursery** - Highway 85, Gay, GA 30218, (404) 538-6983. Specializes in muscadine and scuppernong grape vines and rabbiteye blueberry plants. CAT FREE, R & W, PC, OVER.

I81 **P & P Seed Co.** - 14050 Gowanda State Road, Collins, NY 14034, (716) 532-5995. Specializes in extra large squash and watermelon cultivars for competition. Publishes a newsletter on extra large vegetables and sponsors the "World Pumpkin Weigh-Off". CAT FREE, R & W, PC/OC, OVER.

I82 **Pacific Coast Nursery Inc.** - 18616 NW Reeder Road, Portland, OR 97231, (503) 224-2277. Dwarf fruit trees, flowering crabapples, clonal and seedling fruit tree rootstocks. CAT FREE, WHLS.

I83M **Pacific Tree Farms** - 4301 Lynwood Drive, Chula Vista, CA 92010, (619) 422-2400. Wide selection of fruits, nuts and berries for both temperate and tropical regions. Also flowering trees and vines, California natives, conifers and rare plants of many types. CAT $1.50, R & W, PC/CC/OC, OVER.

I84 **Page Seed Co.** - P.O. Box 158, Greene, NY 13778, (607) 656-4107. Vegetable, herb and flower seeds. CAT FREE, R & W, PC.

I85 **Palmer (D.) Seed Co.** - 4701 Gila Ridge Road, Yuma, AZ 85365, (602) 344-3365. Specializes in Texas Hill artichokes. CAT (CALL FOR PRICES), WHLS, PC, OVER.

I85M **Palms for Tropical Landscaping** - 6600 S.W. 45th St., Miami, FL 33155, (305) 666-1457. Extensive listing of palms, both seeds and plants. CAT SASE, RET, PC, OVER.

I87 **Panfield Nurseries Inc.** - 322 Southdown Rd., Huntington, NY 11743, (516) 427-0112. Specializes in hardy woodland plants, including wild flowers, bog plants, bulbs and ferns. CAT FREE, R & W, PC.

I89 **Papaya Tree Nursery** - 12422 El Oro Way, Granada Hills, CA 91344, (818) 363-3680. Small, family nursery specializing in unusual tropical and sub-tropical fruits. Ships only Babaco papaya plants at this time. CAT FREE, R & W, PC.

I89M **Paprikas Weiss Importer** - 1546 Second Avenue, New York, NY 10028, (212) 288-6117. Specializes in Hungarian foods and other gourmet and specialty food items. *Sells the following product/s:* candied angelica, dried chestnuts, and whole dried carob pods. CAT $3, R & W, PC/CC, OVER.

I90M **Paradise Water Gardens** - 14 May Street, Whitman, MA 02382, (617) 447-4711. Water lilies, lotus, other aquatic and bog plants. CAT $3, RET, PC/CC, M.O. $15.

I91 **Park (George W.) Seed Co.** - Cokesbury Road, Greenwood, SC 29647-0001, (803) 223-7333. Vegetable, herb and flower seeds, fruit and nut trees, grape vines, berry plants, perennial vegetables, garden perennials, bulbs. Established in 1868. CAT FREE, R & W, PC/CC.

I93M **Parsons Seeds Ltd.** - P.O. Box 280, Beeton, ON L0G 1A0, Canada, (416) 729-2202. Cereals, grains, cover crop and green manure seeds. CAT FREE, R & W.

I94 **Passiflora Wildflower Company** - Rt. 1, Box 190-A, Germantown, NC 27019, (919) 591-5816. Native wild flower seeds and plants, custom meadow mixes. CAT $1, RET, PC, CANADA ONLY.

I95 **Patchwork Nursery/Sunset Vineyard** - Rt. 1, Box 328, Forest Grove, OR 97116, (503) 357-3259. One-year old clonal rootstock liners of pear and plum. Also offers a wide range of table and wine grapes, both American and vinifera, as well as grape rootstocks. CAT FREE, R & W, PC.

I97 **Paul's Grains** - Route 1, Box 76, Laurel, IA 50141, (515) 476-3373. Organically grown grains and grain products, fresh apples. *Sells the following product/s:* dried Reid's Yellow Dent corn, Reid's Yellow Dent cornmeal, corn flour, corn grits and corn bran, dried Kanrich soybeans, spelt flour and spelt cereal. CAT FREE, R & W, PC.

I97T **Paul's Premium Seeds** - P.O. Box 370147, San Diego, CA 92137-0147. Small company specializing in rare, unusual, and heirloom vegetables. CAT FREE, RET, PC, CANADA ONLY.

I98 **Paulk Vineyard** - Rt. 1, Box 40, Wray, GA 31798, 1-800-468-7870. Specializes in fresh muscadines in season and muscadine foods. *Sells the following product/s:* muscadine grape juice, non-alcoholic sparkling muscadine cider, muscadine jelly, preserves and sauce. CAT FREE, RET, PC/CC.

I98M **Payne (Theodore) Foundation, Inc.** - 10459 Tuxford St., Sun Valley, CA 91352, (818) 768-1802. Non-profit organization dedicated to perpetuating the native flora of

California. Offers an extensive seed listing of California native wild flowers, grasses, trees and shrubs, as well as seed mixtures. CAT SASE, R & W.

I99 **Peace Seeds** - 2385 S.E. Thompson St., Corvallis, OR 97333, (503) 752-0421. Extensive collection of useful and diverse plants, including heirloom and high nutrition vegetables, herbs, natives, medicinals and endangered species. Most are organically grown or wildcrafted. CAT $3.50, R & W, PC/OC, OVER.

I99M **Peaceful Valley Farm Supply** - P.O. Box 2209, Grass Valley, CA 95945, (916) 272-4769. Berry plants, garlic, vegetable plants, bulbs, grains, cover crop and wild flower seeds. CAT $2, RET, PC/CC, CANADA ONLY, M.O. $20.

I99T **Pecan Valley Nursery** - P.O. Box 854, Stephenville, TX 76401, (817) 965-5031. Seedling and grafted pecan trees. CAT FREE, WHLS.

J0 **Pecoff Brothers Nursery and Seed Inc.** - Rt. 5, Box 215 R, Escondido, CA 92025, (619) 744-3120. Specializes in native and exotic trees, shrubs and perennials for erosion control and adverse areas. CAT $5, WHLS, OVER.

J2M **Pense Nursery** - Rt. 2, Box 330-A, Mountainburg, AR 72946, (501) 369-2494. Specializes in small fruits including a large selection of blackberries. Also dewberries, raspberries and gooseberries. CAT FREE, WHLS, PC, M.O. 25 PLANTS.

J4 **Pepper Gal (The)** - 10536 119th Ave. North, Largo, FL 34643. Seeds for over 200 cultivars of hot, sweet and ornamental peppers. CAT FREE, RET, PC, CANADA ONLY.

J6 **Perkins Variety Apples** - 816 Sims Rd., Sedro-Woolley, WA 98284, (206) 856-6986. Large selection of apples for tasting. Call first for mail order availability of individual cultivars. CAT FREE, RET, PC.

J7 **Perron (W.H.)** - 515, Labelle Blvd, Chomedey, Laval, PQ H7V 2T3, Canada, (514) 332-2275. Vegetable, herb and flower seeds, fruit and nut trees, berry plants, grape vines, perennial vegetables. Separate catalog offers herb and vegetable plants, ornamental trees, roses, aquatic plants and ornamental grasses. CAT $2, R & W, PC/CC/OC, CANADA ONLY.

J7M **Perry's Water Gardens** - 191 Leatherman Gap Road, Franklin, NC 28734, (704) 524-3264 or 369-5648. Water lilies, lotus, cattail, arrowhead, other aquatic and bog plants. CAT $2, R & W, PC/CC, OVER.

J8 **Peter Pauls Nurseries** - Canandaigua, NY 14424, (716) 394-7397. Specializes in carnivorous plants. CAT FREE, R & W, PC/CC, OVER.

J12 **Pickering Nurseries Inc.** - 670 Kingston Rd., Hwy #2, Pickering, ON L1V 1A6, Canada, (416) 839-2111 (no telephone orders). Extensive list of roses, over 700 cultivars. Specializes in antique roses. CAT $2, RET, PC, U.S. ONLY, M.O. 3 PLANTS.

J14 **Piedmont Plant Co., Inc.** - P.O. Box 424, Albany, GA 31703, (912) 883-7029. Large selection of vegetable plants including cabbage, broccoli, collards, leeks, onions, tomatoes, eggplants and peppers. CAT FREE, RET, PC/CC.

J15M **Pierce & Sons Nurseries, Inc.** - P.O. Box 92, Dundee, OR 97115, (503) 538-2363. Large selection of filbert trees for orchard and backyard planting. Also offers ornamental filberts, including contorta, pendula and red leaf. CAT FREE, R & W, PC, OVER.

J16 **Pikes Peak Nurseries** - R.D. 1, Box 75, Penn Run, PA 15765, (412) 463-7747. Evergreen and hardwood seedlings and transplants, ornamental and flowering trees and shrubs. CAT FREE, R & W, PC/CC, CANADA ONLY, M.O. $10.

J20 **Pinetree Garden Seeds** - R.R. 1, Box 397, New Gloucester, ME 04260, (207) 926-3400. Broad range of vegetables including many open-pollinated and limited space cultivars, gourmet and ethnic vegetables, uncommon flower seeds, sprouting seeds, perennial vegetables, berry plants. CAT FREE, RET, PC/CC, OVER.

J21M **Pittman & Davis, Inc.** - P.O. Box 2227, Harlingen, TX 78551, (512) 423-9327 (fax). Fresh produce and other gourmet food items. Specializes in fresh citrus. CAT FREE, RET, PC.

J22 **Plant It Hawaii** - P.O. Box 388, Kurtistown, HI 96760, (808) 966-6633. Tropical fruit and nut trees, citrus and avocado including local Hawaiian selections. Also tropical herbs and spices such as cinnamon, clove, cocoa, curryleaf, black tea, and kola nut. CAT FREE, R & W, PC, OVER, M.O. 12 TREES.

J23 **Plant Kingdom (The)** - P.O. Box 7273, Lincoln Acres, CA 92047, (619) 267-1991. Rare and exotic tropical plants, including an extensive collection of Passiflora, both flowering and fruiting. Also papaya, tree tomato and pepino. CAT SASE, RET, PC.

J24 **Plantage (The)** - P.O. Box 28, Cutchogue, NY 11935, (516) 734-6832. Herb plants, garden perennials, ornamental grasses. CAT FREE, WHLS.

J25 **Plants for Tomorrow** - 16361 Norris Rd., Loxahatchee. FL 33470-9430, (407) 790-1422 or 790-1440. Trees and shrubs, palms, ground covers, aquatics, beach revegetation plants. Specializes in native and naturalized plants of Florida. Subsidiary of South Florida Seed Supply. CAT FREE, WHLS, M.O. $.50.

J25M **Plants of the Southwest** - 930 Baca St., Santa Fe, NM 87501, (505) 983-1548. Seeds and plants of native Southwestern wild flowers, grasses, trees and shrubs, unusual Southwestern vegetable and herb seed, cover crops. CAT $1, R & W, PC/CC, OVER.

J26 **Plants of the Wild** - P.O. Box 866, Tekoa, WA 99033, (509) 284-2848. Specializes in container grown trees, shrubs and wild flowers native to the Pacific Northwest. Subsidiary of Palouse Seed Co. CAT $1, R & W, PC, OVER.

J27 **Plumeria People (The)** - P.O. Box 820014, Houston, TX 77282-0014, (713) 496-2352. Exotic tropical plants including gingers and hibiscus. Specializes in plumeria. CAT $1, R & W, PC, OVER, M.O. $15.

J29 **Plumtree Nursery** - 387 Springtown Road, New Paltz, NY 12561. Small nursery specializing in gooseberries, currants and musk strawberries. CAT FREE, RET, PC.

J31M **Ponderosa Nurseries Inc.** - 1662 E. Prosperity, Tulare, CA 93274, (209) 686-2874 or 688-6626. Vinifera grape vines both table and wine, certified grape rootstocks. CAT FREE, WHLS.

J32 **Pony Creek Nursery** - Tilleda, WI 54978, (715) 787-3889. Vegetable, herb and flower seeds, fruit and nut trees, berry plants, grape vines, perennial vegetables, shade trees, flowering shrubs. CAT FREE, RET, PC/CC.

J33 **Ponzer Nursery** - H.C.R. 33, Box 18, Rolla, MO 65401, (314) 341-2593. Fruit and nut trees, berry plants, grape vines, perennial vegetables, shade trees, vines, flowering shrubs. CAT FREE, RET.

J34 **Porter & Son, Seedsmen** - P.O. Box 104, Stephenville, TX 76401-0104, (817) 965-5600 (no telephone orders). Vegetable, herb and flowers seeds for the Southwest, annual and perennial vegetable plants. Specializes in tomatoes, peppers, watermelons and muskmelons. CAT FREE, RET, PC, M.O. $2.50.

J36 **Possum Trot Tropical Fruit Nursery** - 14955 S.W. 214th St., Miami, FL 33187, (305) 251-5040. Large selection of mangoes, avocadoes and other tropical fruits and nuts. CAT SASE, R & W, PC, OVER, M.O. $150.

J37M **Powell's Gardens** - Rt. 3, Box 21, Princeton, NC 27569, (919) 936-4421. Daylilies, perennials, herbs, dwarf conifers, ornamental trees and shrubs. CAT $2.50, R & W, PC/OC, OVER.

J39M **Prairie Moon Nursery** - Rt. 3, Box 163, Winona, MN 55987, (507) 452-1362 or 452-5231. Large selection of seeds and nursery propagated plants native to the "driftless" area of Minnesota, Wisconsin, Iowa and Illinois. CAT $1, R & W, PC.

J40 **Prairie Nursery** - P.O. Box 306, Westfield, WI 53964, (608) 296-3679. Seeds and plants of prairie wild flowers and grasses. CAT $2, R & W, PC/CC, OVER (SEED ONLY), M.O. $15.

J41M **Prairie Restoration Inc.** - P.O. Box 327, Princeton, MN 55371, (612) 389-4342. Seeds and plants of prairie wild flowers and grasses for restoring native plant communities. CAT FREE, R & W, PC.

J42 **Prairie Ridge Nursery** - 9738 Overland Rd., Mt. Horeb, WI 53572-2832, (608) 437-5245. Seeds and plants of native wild flowers and grasses. All plants are propagated from seed collected and grown in their nurseries. CAT FREE, R & W, PC, OVER, M.O. $25.

J43 **Prairie Seed Source** - P.O. Box 83, North Lake, WI 53064-0083. Specializes in prairie wild flowers and grasses native to southeastern Wisconsin. CAT $1, RET, PC, OVER.

J44 **Prairie State Commodities** - P.O. Box 6, Trilla, IL 62469, (217) 235-4322. Open-pollinated field corn seed, grains, legumes, cover crop and green manure seeds. Previously known as Stodden Seed Farms. CAT $1, RET, PC.

J47 **Pride (Orlando S.) Nurseries** - 145 Weckerly Rd, Butler, PA 16001, (412) 283-0962. Shade trees, evergreens, flowering shrubs. CAT FREE, RET, PC.

J47M **Primera Pecans** - P.O. Box 1301, Corsicana, TX 75151, 1-800-333-9507. Pecans and other gourmet food items. CAT FREE, RET, PC/CC, OVER.

J48 **Primrose Path (The)** - R.D. 2, Box 110, Scottdale, PA 15683, (412) 887-6756. Choice perennials, woodland and rock garden plants, ferns. CAT $1.50 REFUNDABLE, R & W, PC.

J49 **Prissy's of Vidalia** - P.O. Box 1213, Vidalia, GA 30474, 1-800-673-7372. Regional southern gourmet foods. Specializes in Vidalia onions. *Sells the following product/s:* fresh Vidalia onions, pickled Vidalia onions, Vidalia onion relish and Vidalia onion salt. CAT FREE, R & W, PC/CC, M.O. 2 CASES WHLS

J51M **Pueblo to People** - 1616 Montrose #3700, Houston, TX 77006, 1-800-843-5257. Non-profit organization focusing on cottage industry crafts produced by native women in developing countries of Central America. *Sells the following product/s:* dried cashew apples. CAT FREE, RET, PC/CC, CANADA ONLY.

J51T **Purity Foods, Inc.** - 2871 W. Jolly Road, Okemos, MI 48864-3547, (517) 351-9231. Specialty food items. *Sells the following product/s:* organically grown hulled spelt, spelt flour and spelt pasta. CAT FREE, R & W, PC.

J52 **Purple Foot (The)** - 3167 S. 92nd St., Milwaukee, WI 53227, (414) 327-2130. Wine and beer making supplies for home brewers. CAT FREE, RET, PC.

J53 **Putney Nursery, Inc.** - Putney VT 05346, (802) 387-5577. Seeds of herbs, garden perennials, wild flowers and alpines. Also wild flower meadow seed mixtures. CAT FREE, RET, PC/CC, M.O. $6.

J56 **Quinoa Corporation** - P.O. Box 1039, Torrance, CA 90505, (213) 530-8666. Sprouting quality quinoa, quinoa food items. *Sells the following product/s:* whole grain quinoa, quinoa flour, quinoa pasta. CAT FREE, R & W, PC.

J57M **Rabbiteye Farms Nursery** - Rt. 2, Box 30, Homerville, GA 31634, (912) 487-5504 or 487-2278. Specializes in rabbiteye blueberry plants. CAT FREE, R & W, PC.

J58 **Raber's Greenhouse & Nursery** - Box 212, Route 62, Berlin, OH 44610. Vegetable, herb and flower seeds, berry plants, grape vines, perennial vegetables, shade trees, flowering shrubs. CAT FREE, R & W, PC, CANADA ONLY.

J60 **Rainforest Mushroom Spawn** - Box 1793, Gibsons, BC V0N 1V0, Canada, (604) 886-7799. Mushroom spawn for commercial and hobby growers. CAT $2, RET, PC, OVER.

J61M **Raintree Nursery** - 391 Butts Rd., Morton, WA 98356, (206) 496-6400. Broad selection of fruit and nut trees, berry plants, perennial vegetables, bamboo, mushroom spawn, and windbreak trees. Specializes in flavorful, disease resistant cultivars for organic growers and edible landscapers. CAT FREE, RET, PC/CC, M.O. $10.

J63 **Raleigh Gardens** - 24236 Evergreen Rd., Philomath, OR 97370, (503) 929-5431. Small family farm specializing in elephant garlic, gray shallots and rocambole, for both eating and planting. CAT FREE, WHLS TO THE PUBLIC, PC, OVER, M.O. 5 POUNDS.

J63M **Rambo's (L.J.) Wholesale Nurseries** - 10495 Baldwin Road, Bridgman, MI 49106, (616) 465-6771. Grape vines, raspberries, blackberries and dewberries, strawberries, blueberries, currants and gooseberries, elderberries, perennial vegetables. CAT FREE, WHLS.

J64 **Ramsey Seed Co.** - P.O. Box 352, Manteca, CA 95336, (209) 823-1721. Cover crop and green manure seeds, native grasses. CAT FREE, WHLS.

J65 **Rancho Nuez Nursery** - P.O. Box 666, Fallbrook, CA 92028, (619) 728-6407. Seedling and grafted macadamia nut trees, in shell macadamia nuts, macadamia confections, custom grafting service, husking and cracking services. *Sells the following product/s:* both raw and roasted shelled macadamia nuts, chocolate covered macadamias, macadamia nut brittle. CAT FREE, R & W, PC.

J66 **Rasland Farm** - N.C. 82 at U.S. 13, Godwin, NC 28344, (919) 567-2705. Herb plants, scented geraniums, everlasting flowers, herbal products. CAT $2, R & W, PC, OVER, M.O. $10.

J66M **Ratto (G.B.) International Grocers** - 821 Washington St., Oakland, CA 94607, 1-800-325-3483. International specialty food items, gourmet vegetable seed collections, starter cultures. *Sells the following product/s:* dried Cannellini, Swedish Brown, cranberry and flageolet beans, whole mahlep, pickled caper berries, dried whole Ancho and Pasilla peppers, Ancho chili powder, filet powder, dried Verte du Puy lentils, ground Sicilian sumac, tapioca flour, cassava meal, dried chestnuts, candied angelica, dried honey mushrooms, and Tahitian vanilla. CAT FREE, RET, PC/CC, OVER.

J67 **Raven Island Nursery** - Waldron Island, WA 98297. Large collection of apple cultivars. Will only ship scions and budwood for grafting. CAT $.25, RET, PC, M.O. $5.

J67M **Ravenswood Seeds** - 6525 West Bluemound Road, Milwaukee, WI 53213. Rare imported flowers and herbs. CAT $1.50, RET, PC/CC, OVER.

J68 **Ray's (Steve) Bamboo Gardens** - 909 79th Place South, Birmingham, AL 35206, (205) 833-3052. Specializes in cold-hardy bamboos. CAT $1, RET, PC, M.O. $20.

J69 **Rayner Bros. Inc.** - P.O. Box 1617, Salisbury, MD 21801, (301) 742-1594. Dwarf fruit trees, berry plants, grape vines, perennial vegetables, evergreens. Specializes in strawberries. CAT FREE, RET, PC/CC.

J70 **Recor Tree Seeds** - 9164 Huron, Denver, CO 80221, (303) 428-2267 or 428-9883. Seeds of conifers and maples. CAT SASE, R & W, PC.

J70M **Red River Farms** - Rt. 10, Box 1010, Tyler, TX 75707. Small, family owned farm offering onion and cabbage plants, seed potatoes, strawberries and vegetable seeds. CAT FREE, RET, PC/CC, M.O. $2.50.

J71 **Red's Rhodies** - 15920 S.W. Oberst Lane, Sherwood, OR 97140, (503) 625-6331. Large selection of Vireya rhododendrons. Also publishes a separate list of shallot sets. CAT $.50, R & W, PC, OVER.

J73 **Redwood City Seed Co.** - P.O. Box 361, Redwood City, CA 94064, (415) 325-7333. Seeds of unusual and heirloom vegetables, herbs, useful plants from around the world. Specializes in hot peppers. The original alternative seed company. *Sells the following product/s:* Habañero pepper salsas, and dried Tepín peppers. CAT $1, R & W, PC/OC, OVER.

J73M **Reed Bros. Citrus/Holm Citrus Seeds** - P.O. Box 1863, Dundee, FL 33838-1863, (813) 439-1916. Registered and certified citrus seed. CAT FREE, WHLS TO THE PUBLIC, PC, OVER, M.O. $25.

J74 **Reed's Seeds** - 3334 N.Y.S. Rt. 215, Cortland, NY 13045, (607) 753-9095. Specializes in hybrid cabbage, broccoli, cauliflower and brussels sprouts. CAT FREE, WHLS, OVER.

J75M **Reid, Collins Nurseries Ltd.** - P.O. Box 430, Aldergrove, BC V0X 1A0, Canada, (604) 856-4218. Commercial grower of forest tree seedlings, native trees and shrubs, herbaceous perennials, ferns. CAT FREE, WHLS, PC, OVER.

J77M **Rex Bulb Farms** - P.O. Box 774, Port Townsend, WA 98368, (206) 385-4280. Lily bulbs, dahlia tubers, iris. CAT $1, RET, PC/CC, OVER.

J78 **Rice Creek Gardens** - 11506 Highway 65, Blaine, MN 55434, (612) 754-8090. Rock garden plants, herbs, alpines, wild flowers, rare perennials, ferns, aquatic plants, dwarf conifers, flowering shrubs. CAT $2, R & W, PC, CANADA ONLY, M.O. $35.

J80 **Rice Seed Farms** - 2348 No. 5th St., Freemont, OH 43420, (419) 332-5571. Commercial grower of farm seeds. CAT FREE, WHLS, OVER.

J81G **Richardson's Seaside Banana Garden** - 6823 Santa Barbara Ave., La Conchita, CA 93001, (805) 643-4061. Wide selection of banana corms for planting, including many rarities. Also fresh fruit in season for eating. CAT FREE, RET, PC.

J82 **Richters** - P.O. Box 26, Goodwood, ON L0C 1A0, Canada, (416) 640-6677. Extensive listing of herb plants and seeds, gourmet and ethnic vegetable seed, everlastings, wild flowers, alpine flowers, herbal products. *Sells the following product/s:* dried Magdeburg chicory roots. CAT $2.50, R & W, PC/CC, OVER.

J83 **Rider Nursery** - Rt. 2, Box 90A, Farmington, IA 52626, (319) 878-3313. Fruit and nut trees, berry plants, grape vines, perennial vegetables, ornamental trees and shrubs. CAT FREE, R & W, PC/CC.

J83M **Ripley's Believe It or Not** - 10 Bay Street, Westport, CT 06880-4800, (203) 454-1919. Rare and unusual vegetable seeds, ethnic vegetables. Specializes in extra large varieties. Previously known as Grace's Garden. CAT $1, R & W, PC/CC.

J83T **Rising Sun Organic Produce** - P.O. Box 627, Milesburg, PA 16853, (814) 355-9850. Organically grown and bio-dynamic fresh produce, sprouting seeds, natural food items. CAT FREE, RET, PC.

J84 **Rispens (Martin) and Son, Inc.** - P.O. Box 5, Lansing, IL 60438, (312) 474-0241. Complete line of vegetable seeds. CAT FREE, R & W, PC.

J85 **River Valley Ranch** - P.O. Box 898, New Munster, WI 53152, (414) 539-3555. Specializes in Bavarian Brown mushroom growing kits. CAT FREE, RET, PC.

J85T **Riverview Farm** - Fall City, WA 98024, (206) 391-0393. Fresh-cut, organically grown culinary herbs. CAT (CALL FOR PRICES), R & W, PC, CANADA ONLY, M.O. $100.

J86 **Roadrunner Tree Farm** - P.O. Box 1900, Borrego Springs, CA 92004-1900, (619) 767-3310 or 767-5348. Specializes in drought tolerant trees and ornamentals for the Southwest. CAT FREE, WHLS.

J88 **Robin (Clyde) Seed Co.** - P.O. Box 2366, Castro Valley, CA 94546, (415) 581-3468. Wild flower seeds, wild flower seed mixes. CAT $2, R & W, PC/CC, OVER.

J89M **Robson Seed Farms Corp.** - 1 Seneca Circle, Hall, NY 14463-0270, (716) 526-6396. Breeder of Seneca Brand hybrid vegetables, including sweet corn, squash and cucumber. Also introduced the Butterblossom squash. CAT FREE, WHLS.

J91 **Rocknoll Nursery** - 9210 U.S. 50, Hillsboro, OH 45133-8546, (513) 393-1278. Unusual rock garden plants, garden perennials, native wild flowers and ferns, shade trees, flowering shrubs. CAT $.50, RET, PC/CC, M.O. $25.

J93 **Rocky Meadow Orchard & Nursery** - Rt. 2, Box 1104, New Salisbury, IN 47161-9716, (812) 347-2213. Full line fruit tree nursery specializing in superior flavored cultivars for both the home and commercial orchard. Also supplies rootstocks for grafting and maintains and extensive scion orchard for custom propagation. CAT $.50, R & W, PC.

J93T **Rocky Mountain Rare Plants** - P.O. Box 20483, Denver, CO 80220-0483. Specializes in habitat-collected seed of alpines native to western North America. CAT FREE, RET, PC/CC, OVER.

J97M **Rohrer (P.L) & Bro., Inc.** - P.O. Box 25, Smoketown, PA 17576, (717) 299-2571. Vegetable, herb and flower seeds, grains, green manure and cover crop seeds. CAT FREE, R & W, PC.

J99 **Romney Farms** - 26021 SW 199th Ave., Homestead, FL 33031, (305) 247-7479. Specializes in coconut palms. CAT FREE, R & W, PC.

J99G **Ronniger's Seed Potatoes** - Star Route, Moyie Springs, ID 83845, (208) 267-7938. Small, family-operated farm supplying organic seed potatoes to farmers, gardeners and hobbyists, over 100 cultivars. Also potatoes for eating and cover crop seeds. CAT $1, R & W, PC, CANADA ONLY.

K1 **Rose Creek Plantation** - 2451 Elder Mill Road, Watkinsville, GA 30677, (404) 769-8647. Specializes in highbush blueberries and upright blackberries. CAT FREE, WHLS.

K1M **Rose Seed Co., Inc.** - P.O. Box 6, San Jon, NM 88434, (505) 576-2241. Specializes in sweet sorghums. CAT FREE, WHLS.

K1T **Rosell Institute Inc.** - 8480 boul. St.-Laurent, Montreal, PQ H2P 2M6, Canada, (514) 381-5631. Large selection of dairy cultures for commercial and home production including yogurt, cheese, kefir and acidophilus milk. CAT FREE, R & W, PC, OVER, M.O. $10.

K2 **Rosemary House (The)** - 120 So. Market St., Mechanicsburg, PA 17055, (717) 697-5111. Herb plants and seeds, scented geraniums, herbal products. CAT $2, R & W, PC, OVER, M.O. $50 WHLS

K4 **Roses of Yesterday & Today, Inc.** - 802 Brown's Valley Rd., Watsonville, CA 95076, (408) 724-3537 or 724-2755. Specializes in old, rare and unusual roses. CAT $3, RET, PC/CC, OVER.

K5M **Roswell Seed Co.** - P.O. Box 725, Roswell, NM 88202-0725, (505) 622-7701. Specializes in vegetables and flowers adapted to the Southwestern United States. CAT FREE, RET, PC/CC, M.O. $5.

K10 **Rupp Seeds, Inc.** - 17919 Co. Road. B, Wauseon, OH 43567, (419) 337-1841. Vegetable, herb and flower seeds. CAT FREE, R & W, PC/CC.

K11M **Russ (Jim & Irene)** - HCR 1, Box 6450, Igo, CA 96047, (916) 396-2329. Family nursery specializing in sedums and sempervivums. CAT $.50, R & W, PC, OVER, M.O. $10.

K12M **Rykoff (S.E.) & Co.** - P.O. Box 21467, Los Angeles, CA 90021, (213) 622-4131. Gourmet and specialty food items. *Sells the following product/s:* pickled Parisienne carrots, canned Nectar peaches, Marionberry preserves and Indian Red, Black Tie and Blue popping corns. CAT FREE, RET, PC/CC.

K13 **S & H Organic Acres** - P.O. Box 1531, Watsonville, CA 95077-1531, (408) 983-7226. Large selection of garlic, elephant garlic, shallots, multiplier onions and Egyptian onions. *Sells the following product/s:* loose Elephant garlic cloves, Elephant garlic rounds, Elephant garlic mini-heads, and Silverskin garlic braids. CAT FREE, R & W, PC/CC, OVER, M.O. 30 LBS. WHLS

K15 **S & S Seeds** - P.O. Box 1275, Carpinteria, CA 93013, (805) 684-0436. Seeds of wild flowers, native and naturalized grasses, trees and shrubs, custom revegetation mixes. Subsidiary of Mistletoe Sales. CAT FREE, WHLS, OVER.

K16 **Saginaw Valley Nut Nursery** - 8285 Dixie Hwy., Rte. #5, Birch Run, MI 48415, (517) 652-8552. Small nursery specializing in hardy nut and fruit trees, including walnuts, chestnuts, butternuts, heartnuts, and pawpaws. CAT SASE, RET, PC, OVER, M.O. $5.

K16M **Sakata Seed America, Inc.** - P.O. Box 877, Morgan Hill, CA 95037, (408) 778-7758. Vegetable and flower seeds. CAT FREE, WHLS, OVER.

K17 **Sakuma Brothers Farms, Inc.** - P.O. Box 427, Burlington, WA 98233, (206) 757-6611. Specializes in raspberries and blackberries. CAT FREE, R & W, PC.

K17M **Salt Spring Seeds** - Box 33, Ganges, BC V0S 1E0, Canada, (604) 537-5269 (no telephone orders). Small seed company specializing in organically grown, high-protein vegetables and grains adapted to Canadian climates. Mostly beans, soybeans, garlic and quinoa. CAT FREE, RET, PC, CANADA ONLY.

K18 **Salter Tree Farm** - Rt. 2, Box 1332, Madison, FL 32340, (904) 973-6312. Specializes in Southeastern natives including trees and shrubs, wild flowers, vines and groundcovers. CAT SASE, R & W, PC.

K20 **Sanctuary Seeds/Folklore Herb Co.** - 2388 West 4th, Vancouver, BC V6K 1P1, Canada, (604) 733-4724. Open-pollinated, untreated vegetable and herb seeds, sprouting seeds, botanicals, dried herbs and spices, natural food products. CAT $1, R & W, PC/CC, OVER.

K22 **Sandy Mush Herb Nursery** - Rt. 2, Surrett Cove Rd., Leicester, NC 28748, (704) 683-2014. Extensive listing of herb plants and seeds, scented geraniums, perennial vegetables, ornamental grasses, everlastings. CAT $4, RET, PC/CC, M.O. $20.

K25 **Santa Barbara Water Gardens** - P.O. Box 4353, Santa Barbara, CA 93140, (805) 969-5129. Water lilies, lotus, other aquatic and bog plants. CAT $1, RET, PC, M.O. $30.

K27M **Saunders Seed Co., Inc.** - P.O. Box 98, Tipp City, OH 45371, (513) 667-2313. Vegetable, herb and flower seeds. Specializes in bulk seed at retail prices. CAT FREE, R & W, PC/CC.

K28 **Savage Farms Nurseries** - P.O. Box 125, McMinnville, TN 37110, (615) 668-8902. Fruit and nut trees, berry plants, grape vines, hardy kiwi, shade trees, evergreens, flowering shrubs. CAT FREE, RET, PC.

K31 **Scarff's Nursery Inc.** - 411 N. Dayton-Lakeview Rd., New Carlisle, OH 45344, (513) 845-3821. Ornamental trees and shrubs, conifers, shade trees. CAT FREE, WHLS.

K33M **Scheepers (John), Inc.** - R.D. 6, Phillipsburg Rd., Middletown, NY 10940, (914) 342-1135. Specializes in bulbs and garden perennials. CAT FREE, RET, PC/CC.

K34 **Scherer & Sons** - 104 Waterside Rd., Northport, NY 11768, (516) 261-7432. Large selection of water lilies, lotus and other aquatic and bog plants. CAT FREE, RET, PC/CC.

K37M **Schmidt (J. Frank) & Son Co.** - P.O. Box 189, Boring, OR 97009, (503) 663-4128. Ornamental trees and shrubs, flowering crabapples, conifers. CAT FREE, WHLS.

K37T **Schroeder's Popcorn** - Rt. 1, 3519 North, 1400 East, Buhl, Idaho 83316, (208) 543-4470. Specializes in gourmet popping corn, both for planting and eating. *Sells the following product/s:* Schroeder's Black popping corn. CAT FREE, R & W, PC.

K38 **Schumacher (F.W.) Co., Inc.** - 36 Spring Hill Rd., Sandwich, MA 02563-1023, (508) 888-0659. Broad range of tree and shrub seed for nurserymen and foresters, including a selection of seed for fruit tree understock. CAT FREE, R & W, PC, OVER.

K39M **Sciabica (Nick) & Sons** - P.O. Box 1246, Modesto, CA 95353-1246, (209) 577-5067. Growers and producers of olives and olive products. Specializes in unrefined 100% varietal olive oils. *Sells the following product/s:* Mission, Manzanillo, and Sevillano varietal olive oils. CAT FREE, R & W, PC, M.O. 1 CASE.

K41 **Scott Bros. Nursery Co.** - P.O. Box 581, McMinnville, TN 37110-0581, (615) 473-2954. Specializes in ground covers and native ferns and wild flowers. CAT FREE, WHLS, M.O. 100 OF EACH.

K46 **Seatree Nurseries Inc.** - P.O. Box 92, East Irvine, CA 92650, (714) 651-9601. Ornamental trees and shrubs, palms, eucalyptus, conifers, shade trees. CAT FREE, WHLS.

K47M **Seed Shop (The)** - Tongue River Stage, HC-32, Miles City, MT 59301-9804, (406) 784-2213. Seeds of cacti and succulents. CAT FREE, RET, PC.

K47T **Seed Source (The)** - Rte. 68, Box 301, Tuckasegee, NC 28783. Seed of more than 7,000 unusual plants, including alpines and rock garden plants, bulbs, culinary and medicinal herbs, ornamental grasses, wild flowers, perennials, trees and shrubs. Previously known as Maver Nursery. CAT $4, R & W, PC, OVER, M.O. $25.

K48 **Seedco** - 20253 Elfin Forest Road, Escondido, CA 92029, (619) 471-1464. Seeds of trees and shrubs, palms, eucalyptus, tropical foliage plants. CAT FREE, R & W, OVER.

K49M **Seeds Blüm** - Idaho City Stage, Boise, ID 83706, (208) 343-2202 (no telephone orders). Specializes in heirloom vegetables and flowers, listing over 1,000 varieties. Also gourmet, ethnic and regional specialties, edible flowers, herbs, perennial vegetables, and collections such as butterfly gardens and hummingbird gardens. *Sells the following product/s:* light amber sweet sorghum syrup, dried Adventist and Jacob's Cattle beans, Hopi Blue cornmeal, Bloody Butcher cornmeal, Pequín pepper ristras and wreaths. CAT $3, RET, PC, OVER.

K49T **Seeds of Change** - 621 Old Santa Fe Trail, #10, Santa Fe, NM 87501, (505) 983-8956. Large selection of edible plants. Specializes in traditional open-pollinated vegetable seeds. Also does contract growing of commercial quantities. All seeds are organically grown. CAT FREE, R & W.

K49Z **Seeds West Garden Seeds** - P.O. Box 2817, Taos, NM 87571, (505) 758-7268. Heirloom and gourmet vegetable seeds, culinary herbs, native wild flowers. Selected for their ability to perform well in short season, high elevation areas of the West. CAT $1, RET, PC/CC.

K50 **Seedway, Inc.** - Hall, NY 11463-0250, (716) 526-6391. Vegetable, herb and flower seeds for the home gardener or commercial grower. Distributor for Bejo Seeds of Holland. *Sells the following product/s:* White Cloud (Fabu-Pop) popping corn. CAT FREE, R & W, PC/CC, OVER.

K52 **Select Origins** - Box N, Southampton, NY 11968, (516) 288-1382. Gourmet and specialty foods. *Sells the following product/s:* dried Mexican oregano, Lady Finger popping corn, dried pink peppercorns, Canadian wild rice, cured Picholine olives, and dried Montmorency cherries. CAT FREE, RET, PC/CC.

K53 **Select Seeds** - 81 Stickney Hill Road, Union, CT 06076. Seeds of old-fashioned flowers, both annual and perennial. CAT $1.50, R & W, PC, CANADA ONLY, M.O. $75 WHLS

K54 **Semplex** - 4159 Thomas Ave. North, Minneapolis, MN 55412, (612) 522-0500. Complete selection of home wine and beer making supplies. CAT FREE, RET, PC/CC, OVER.

K57M **Shady Hill Gardens** - 821 Walnut Street, Batavia, IL 60510, (312) 879-5665. Growers and breeders of geraniums, over 1,000 cultivars including many scented geraniums. CAT $2 REFUNDABLE, R & W, PC, M.O. $5.

K60 **Shahan Brothers Nurseries** - P.O. Box 876, Tullahoma, TN 37388, (615) 455-3297. Fruit trees, evergreens, shade and ornamental trees. CAT FREE, WHLS.

K62 **Sharp Bros. Seed Co.** - P.O. Box 140, Healy, KS 67850, (316) 398-2231. Grains, legumes, native prairie grasses, wild flowers and forbs including individual species and mixes. CAT FREE, R & W, PC.

K63 **Sharp Plants Inc.** - Rte. 68, Box 301, Tuckasegee, NC 18783, (704) 298-4751. Garden perennials, herbs, ornamental grasses, flowering shrubs, native ferns and wild flowers. Subsidiary of The Seed Source. CAT FREE, R & W, PC, M.O. $20.

K63G **Sheffield's Seed Co.** - 273 Auburn Road, Route 34, Locke, NY 13092, (315) 497-1058. Tree and shrub seed.

CAT FREE, R & W, PC, OVER, M.O. 2 GRAMS EACH SPECIES.

K63M **Shein's Cactus** - 3360 Drew St., Marina, CA 93933, (408) 384-7765. Cactus and succulent plants grown from seed or cuttings, none collected from the wild. CAT $1, RET, PC, M.O. $15.

K64 **Shelmerdine Nurseries** - 7800 Roblin Boulevard, Headingley, MB R0H 0J0, Canada, (204) 895-7203. Complete line of prairie hardy nursery stock including fruit and nut trees, berry plants, grape vines, perennial vegetables, herbs, shade trees, flowering shrubs. CAT FREE, R & W, PC/CC/OC, OVER.

K66 **Shepherd's Garden Seeds** - 6116 Highway 9, Felton, CA 95018, (203) 482-3638 or (408) 335-5400. Specialty vegetables chosen for flavor and fresh eating quality, baby vegetables, culinary herbs, edible flowers, everlastings, old-fashioned garden flowers. Also publishes a separate bulk list featuring many cultivars formerly offered by Le Marché Seeds International. CAT $1.50, R & W, PC/CC, CANADA ONLY.

K67 **Sherwood's Greenhouses** - P.O. Box 6, Sibley, LA 71073, (318) 377-3653 (no telephone orders). Single proprietor nursery offering unusual fruit trees not commonly found in large nursery listings. CAT SASE, R & W, PC.

K71 **Shumway's (R.H.)** - P.O. Box 1, Graniteville, SC 29829, (803) 663-9771. One of America's oldest mail order seed companies, established in 1870. Specializes in traditional open-pollinated vegetables and flowers. Also fruit and nut trees, berry plants, grape vines, perennial vegetables. CAT $1 REFUNDABLE, R & W, PC/CC, OVER.

K71M **Siberia Seeds** - Box 3000, Olds, AB T0M 1P0, Canada, (403) 556-7333. Small, family-run seed company specializing in open-pollinated, heirloom tomatoes for cold, short season areas. CAT SASE, R & W, PC, OVER.

K73 **Siegers Seed Co.** - 8265 Felch St., Zeeland, MI 49464, (313) 724-3155. Complete line of hybrid and open-pollinated vegetable seeds. CAT FREE, R & W, PC, OVER.

K73M **Sierra Gold Nurseries** - 5320 Garden Highway, Yuba City, CA 95991-9499, (916) 674-1145. Commercial grower of deciduous fruit and nut trees for orchardists and retail nurseries. CAT FREE, WHLS, PC, OVER, M.O. 10 OF EACH.

K74 **Sierra Natural Foods Inc.** - 440 Valley Drive, Brisbane, CA 94005, (415) 468-8800. Ohsawa macrobiotic foods, starter cultures. *Sells the following product/s:* dried black soybeans, wasabi powder, shiso leaf powder, pickled shiso leaves, black sesame seeds, black sesame seed crackers, hato-mugi grain, teff grain, teff flour, wild kuzu root powder, jinenjo soba, spirulina powder, Kamut wheat pasta and dried lotus seeds. CAT $4, WHLS, OVER, M.O. $100.

K74M **Sill House Bakery** - Coxe Farm, Old Lyme, CT 06371, (203) 434-9501. Specializes in organic grain essene bread-products. *Sells the following product/s:* wheat and rye essene breads. CAT FREE, RET, PC.

K75 **Silvaseed Company** - P.O. Box 118, Roy, WA 98580, (206) 843-2246. Specializes in conifer tree seed from the Pacific Northwest. CAT FREE, R & W, PC, OVER, M.O. 1 LB.

K75M **Silver Springs Nursery** - HCR 62, Box 86, Moyie Springs, ID 83845, (208) 267-5753. Specializes in native ground covers. Also organically grown garlic for both eating and planting. *Sells the following product/s:* German Red garlic braids. CAT FREE, R & W, PC.

K76 **Simpson Nurseries** - P.O. Box 160, Monticello, FL 32344, (904) 997-2516. Large selection of fruit and nut trees, berry plants, grape vines, ornamental trees and shrubs. CAT FREE, WHLS.

K77 **Simpson Nursery Co.** - P.O. Box 2065, Vincennes, IN 47591, (812) 882-2441. Flowering crabapples, hawthorn, flowering pears, deciduous holly. CAT FREE, WHLS, PC, OVER.

K77M **Singer's Growing Things** - 17806 Plummer St., Northridge, CA 91325, (818) 993-1903. Specializes in unusual succulent plants other than cactus. CAT $2 DEDUCTIBLE, R & W, PC/CC, OVER, M.O. $15.

K79 **Siskiyou Rare Plant Nursery** - 2825 Cummings Rd., Medford, OR 97501, (503) 772-6846 (no telephone orders). Over 1,000 varieties of hardy, cold climate plants for the rock garden and woodland garden. Specializes in alpines. CAT $2, RET, PC, CANADA ONLY.

K81 **Skinner's Nursery** - Box 220, Roblin, MB R0L 1P0, Canada, (204) 564-2336. Hardy fruit trees, berry plants, herbs, ornamental trees and shrubs. CAT FREE, R & W, PC, U.S. ONLY.

K81M **Skittone (Anthony J.)** - 1415 Eucalyptus Dr., San Francisco, CA 94132-1405, (415) 753-3332. Specializes in unusual flower bulbs for pot culture and for cut flowers, many from South Africa. Also seed of Australian natives. CAT $1, R & W, PC, OVER.

K83M **Slaybaugh Bros. Nursery** - 587 Orchard Lane, Aspers, PA 17304, (717) 677-8342. Dwarf, semi-dwarf and standard fruit trees including apple, peach, nectarine, pear, cheery, plum and apricot. CAT FREE, R & W, PC, M.O. $20.

K84M **Sleepy Hollow Farm** - 44001 Dunlap Road, Miramonte, CA 93641, (209) 336-2444. Organically grown apples sold by the box. CAT SASE, R & W, PC, M.O. 1 BOX.

K85 **Sleepy Hollow Herb Farm** - Jack Black Road, Lancaster, KY 40444, (606) 269-7601. Herb plants and seed, scented geraniums, potpourri and other herbal products. CAT FREE, RET, PC/OC, CANADA ONLY, M.O. $14.

K85M **Slocum Water Gardens** - 1101 Cypress Gardens Blvd., Winter Haven, FL 33880-6099, (813) 293-7151. Water lilies, lotus, Chinese water chestnut, other aquatic and bog plants. CAT $2, R & W, PC, OVER.

K89 **Smith Nursery Co.** - P.O. Box 515, Charles City, IA 50616, (515) 228-3239. Fruit and nut trees, berry plants, grape vines, ornamental trees and shrubs. Also seed of native trees and shrubs. CAT FREE, WHLS, PC, OVER.

K94 **Snapp (J.P.) & Sons** - Rt. 3, Box 68, Limestone, TN 37681, (615) 257-6341. Sells only Yellow and White Hickory King corn seed. CAT FREE, WHLS, PC, OVER.

K96M **Soghomonian (Joe) Inc.** - 8624 S. Chestnut Ave., Fresno, CA 93725, (209) 834-2772. Certified organically grown grapes and raisins. Also known as Three Sisters.

Sells the following product/s: fresh Champagne grapes and dried Zante currants. CAT FREE, R & W, PC.

K97 **Sohn's Oak Forest Mushrooms** - 610 So. Main St., Box 20, Westfield, WI 53964. Spawn of shiitake and oyster mushrooms, mushroom growing supplies. CAT FREE, RET, PC, OVER.

K98 **Solar Green Ltd.** - Rt. 1, Box 115A, Moore, ID 83255, (208) 554-2821. Specializes in habitat collected seed of alpines and perennials native to the Western United States. CAT $1.50 REFUNDABLE, RET, PC.

L1 **Sonoma Antique Apple Nursery** - 4395 Westside Rd., Healdsburg, CA 95448, (707) 433-6420. Antique apples and pears, cider apples, apple cultivars for custom grafting, rootstocks, espaliered apples and pears, other fruit and nut trees. Also offers a tasting box of 12 different apple cultivars. CAT $1, R & W, PC/CC, CANADA ONLY, M.O. 1 TREE.

L1M **Sonoma Grapevines** - 1919 Dennis Lane, Santa Rosa, CA 95403, (707) 542-4801. Specializes in grafted vinifera grape vines, both table and wine. Also offers disease resistant grape rootstocks. CAT FREE, R & W.

L2 **Sonoma Horticultural Nursery** - 3970 Azalea Ave., Sebastopol, CA 95472, (707) 823-6832. Specializes in rhododendrons, azaleas and companion plants. CAT $1.50, R & W, PC/CC, M.O. $30.

L3 **Sorum's Nursery** - Rt. 4, Box 308J, Sherwood, OR 97140, (503) 628-2354. Azaleas and rhododendrons, fig trees. CAT FREE, R & W, PC.

L3M **Sourdoughs International, Inc.** - P.O. Box 1440, Cascade, ID 83611, 1-800-888-9567. Offers eight authentic sourdough cultures discovered in the Middle East, Europe and North America. Each culture has different wild yeast and lactobacilli producing unique flavors and textures of bread. CAT FREE, RET, PC/CC.

L4 **South Carolina Foundation Seeds** - Cherry Road, Clemson University, Clemson, SC 29634-9952. Supplies Foundation quality seeds and propagating material of cultivars developed by plant breeders at Clemson University. CAT FREE, R & W, PC.

L5M **South Florida Seed Supply** - 16361 Norris Rd., Loxahatchee, FL 33470-9430, (407) 790-1422 or 790-1440. Seeds of tropical fruit trees, Florida natives, palms, ornamental trees and shrubs. CAT FREE, WHLS, PC/OC, OVER, M.O. $25.

L5T **South Jersey Nursery** - P.O. Box 838, Elmer, NJ 08318. Specializes in all-male asparagus cultivars developed at Rutgers University. CAT FREE, RET, PC, OVER, M.O. 25 OF EACH.

L6 **South Seas Nursery** - P.O. Box 4974, Ventura, CA 93004, (805) 647-6990. Large selection of tropical and sub-tropical fruit and nut trees, including avocado, feijoa, cherimoya, passionfruit, kiwi, guava, white sapote and Malabar chestnut. Previously known as Trade Winds Nursery. CAT SASE, R & W, PC, OVER.

L7M **Southern Exposure Seed Exchange** - P.O. Box 158, North Garden, VA 22959. Open-pollinated, heirloom, and traditional cultivars of vegetables, flowers and herbs adapted to the Mid-Atlantic and Southern states. Specializes in rare perennial multiplier onions, topset onions and garlic. CAT $3, R & W, PC, OVER.

L9 **Southern Oregon Organics** - 1130 Tetherow Road, Williams, OR 97544, (503) 846-7173. Organically grown vegetable, herb and flower seed available as individual packets or "Garden Spectrum Seed Sets". CAT $1 REFUNDABLE, RET, PC, OVER.

L9M **Southern Seeds** - P.O. Box 2091, Melbourne, FL 32902, 1-800-356-1631. Specializes in open-pollinated vegetables for tropical and subtropical areas. Also offers banana corms, papaya seed and chayote squash fruits for planting. CAT $1, RET, PC, OVER.

L11 **Southern Sun Seeds** - Rt. 6, Box 2097, Escondido, CA 92026. Small family-owned seed company specializing in non-hybrid, untreated vegetable and herb seeds adapted to southern California growing conditions. CAT FREE, RET, PC, M.O. $10.

L12 **Southmeadow Fruit Gardens** - P.O. Box SM, Lakeside, MI 49116, (616) 469-2865 (no telephone orders). Over 500 varieties of choice and unusual fruit trees for the connoisseur and home gardener, including apples, pears, peaches, plums, grapes, cherries, quinces and medlars. CAT FREE, RET, PC, M.O. $14.

L13 **Southwestern Native Seeds** - Box 50503, Tucson, AZ 85703. Seed of native wild flowers, trees, shrubs, cacti and succulents from the deserts, tropics, and mountains of the American West and Mexico. CAT $1, RET, PC, OVER.

L14 **SPB Sales** - P.O. Box 278, Nash, TX 75569, (214) 838-5616. Regional seed company specializing in vegetable and flower seeds for small farmers and gardeners in the South. Also offers a large selection of onion plants. CAT FREE, R & W, PC/CC, OVER, M.O. $5 LBS. WHLS

L14M **Specialty Grain Co.** - 12202 Woodbine, Redford, MI 48239, (313) 535-9222. Certified organically grown grains and legumes, sprouting seeds, natural food items. *Sells the following product/s:* flaked Kamut wheat, Iopop 12 and Japanese Hulless popping corns, dried black and Prize soybeans. CAT FREE, WHLS, OVER.

L15 **Specialty Products International, Ltd.** - P.O. Box 784, Chapel Hill, NC 27514, (919) 929-4277. Specializes in Superbrau brewing yeast and Superbrau beer making kits. CAT FREE, RET, PC/CC, M.O. $15.

L17M **Spirit Mountain Productions** - P.O. Box 654, North San Juan, CA 95960, (916) 265-3907 ext. 654. Specializes in nutrient protected, low heat, spray-dried spirulina algae grown in Hawaii. *Sells the following product/s:* spirulina powder, spirulina tablets. CAT FREE, R & W, PC, M.O. $100 WHLS

L18 **Spooner (Ken M.) Farms** - 9710 SR 162 East, Puyallup, WA 98374, (206) 845-5519. Certified strawberry and raspberry plants. CAT FREE, WHLS, PC, OVER, M.O. 25 PLANTS.

L21 **Spring Hill Nurseries** - P.O. Box 1758, Peoria, IL 61656, (309) 691-4616. Berry plants, garden perennials, ornamental grasses. CAT $2, RET, PC/CC.

L22 **Springbrook Gardens Inc.** - P.O. Box 388, Mentor, OH 44061-0388, (216) 255-3059. Field grown, bareroot herb plants, garden perennials, ferns, ornamental grasses, ground covers. Subsidiary of Garden Place. CAT $1, WHLS, PC, CANADA ONLY, M.O. 12 OF EACH.

L24 **Sprout House (The)** - 40 Railroad St., Great Barrington, MA 01230, (413) 528-5200. Very extensive collection of organic sprouting seeds, more than 35 different types. Also supplies for sprouting including their own unique inventions: the flaxseed sprout bag and the indoor vegetable kit. *Sells the following product/s:* fresh wheatgrass by the pound, and frozen wheatgrass juice. CAT FREE, RET, OVER.

L26 **Squaw Mountain Gardens** - 36212 S.E. Squaw Mtn. Rd., Estacada, OR 97023, (503) 630-5458. Rock garden plants, including a large selection of sedums and sempervivums. CAT FREE, R & W, PC, OVER.

L27M **St. Lawrence Nurseries** - R.D. 5, Potsdam, NY 13676, (315) 265-6739 (no telephone orders). Fruit and nut trees selected for northern climates, to -50 degrees Fahrenheit. Specializes in antique apple trees and edible landscaping plants. CAT FREE, RET, PC, OVER.

L29 **Stallings Nursery** - 910 Encinitas Blvd., Encinitas, CA 92024, (619) 753-3079. Exotic flowering sub-tropical trees, shrubs, vines and perennials, fruit trees, banana plants, bamboos, palms, gingers. CAT $3 REFUNDABLE, RET, PC, OVER, M.O. $30.

L30 **Stanek's Garden Center** - East 2929 27th Ave., Spokane, WA 99223, (509) 535-2939. Fruit and nut trees, berry plants, grape vines, hardy kiwi, perennial vegetables, roses. CAT FREE, RET, PC.

L33 **Stark Brothers Nurseries** - P.O. Box 2171, Louisiana, MO 63353, 1-800-325-4180. Wide range of fruit and nut trees, berry plants, grape vines, kiwi, perennial vegetables, shade trees, flowering shrubs. One of the oldest mail order nurseries in America, established in 1816. CAT FREE, R & W, PC/CC.

L33M **Starr Organic Produce** - P.O. Box 561502, Miami, FL 33256, (305) 262-1242. Wholesale distributors of organically grown tree-ripened fruits and vegetables, including citrus, avocadoes, bananas, mangoes, papayas, lychees and carambolas. *Sells the following product/s:* dried Apple bananas. CAT FREE, WHLS.

L35 **Steele Plant Co.** - Box 191, Gleason, TN 38229, (901) 648-5476 (no telephone orders). Family owned business specializing in sweet potatoes. Also offers plants of onions, cabbage, broccoli, cauliflower and brussels sprouts. CAT $.50, R & W, PC, M.O. 12 PLANTS.

L37M **Stephenville Vineyard & Supply** - P.O. Box 1197, Stephenville, TX 76401, (817) 968-6590. Grapevines, berry plants. CAT FREE, R & W, PC.

L39M **Steyer Seeds** - 6154 N. Co. Rd. 33, Tiffin, OH 44883, (419) 992-4570. Grains, green manure crops, farm seeds. CAT FREE, WHLS.

L41 **Stock Seed Farms** - Rt. #1, Box 112, Murdock, NE 68407, (402) 867-3771. Seed of prairie grasses and wild flowers. CAT FREE, R & W, PC, OVER, M.O. $5.

L42 **Stokes Seeds Inc.** - P.O. Box 548, Buffalo, NY 14240, (416) 688-4300. Growers and breeders of a complete line of vegetable, herb and flower seeds, ornamental grasses, tree seed. Breeding program focuses on sweet corn, tomatoes, peppers and asparagus. United States branch of Stokes Seeds Ltd., Canada, which see. CAT FREE, R & W, PC/CC, OVER.

Stokes Seeds Ltd. - P.O. Box 10, St. Catherines, ON L2R 6R6, Canada.

L46 **Strand Nursery Co.** - Rt. 3, Box 187, Osceola, WI 54020, (715) 294-3779. Hardy dormant fern roots and wild flowers. Established in 1897. CAT $.25, R & W, PC, M.O. 20 ROOTS.

L47 **Stribling's Nurseries, Inc.** - P.O. Box 793, Merced, CA 95341, (209) 722-4106. Deciduous fruit and nut trees, citrus and avocadoes, berry plants, grape vines, shade trees, flowering shrubs. CAT $1.50, WHLS, PC/OC, OVER.

L49 **Stropkey (John G.) & Sons Nurseries, Inc.** - 485 Bowhall Rd., Painesville, OH 44077, (312) 352-9535 or 352-1803. Ornamental shrubs, shade trees, broad leaf evergreens. CAT FREE, WHLS, CC, M.O. $50.

L50 **Succulenta** - P.O. Box 480325, Los Angeles, CA 90048, (213) 933-8676 (no telephone orders). Rare and exotic cactus and succulent plants. CAT $1, R & W, PC.

L50M **Sultan's Delight** - P.O. Box 253, Staten Island, NY 10314, (718) 720-1557. Specializes in Middle Eastern foods. *Sells the following product/s:* dried Cannellini beans, dried melukhiya leaves, semolina, couscous, chick pea flour, dried Foul Misri beans, mastic gum, Torrido chili peppers, zatar, whole mahleb, both whole and ground Sicilian sumac, khishk, dried lupini beans, salep, and bulghur, kamh makshour and fereek wheats. CAT FREE, R & W, PC/CC, M.O. $15.

L54 **Sunburst Tropical Fruit Co.** - 7113 Howard Road, Bokeelia, FL 33922, (813) 283-1200. Offers boxes and gift baskets of fresh tropical fruit in season, including citrus, mangoes, lychees, guavas, sapodillas and sugar apples. Also dried tropical fruits, preserves and chutneys. *Sells the following product/s:* both fresh and dried guavas, dried carambolas, both fresh and dried mangoes and dried bananas. CAT FREE, R & W, PC/CC.

L55 **Sunlight Gardens** - Rt. 1, Box 600-A, Andersonville, TN 37705, (615) 494-8237. Wild flowers and ferns native to Eastern North America, traditional garden perennials. CAT FREE, R & W, PC, M.O. $15.

L55G **Sunny Caribbee Spice Co.** - P.O. Box 3237, St. Thomas, U.S.V.I. 00801, (809) 494-2178. Specialty food items from the Caribbean area. *Sells the following product/s:* nutmeg jam. CAT FREE, RET, PC/CC, OVER.

L55M **Sunny Rows Plant Farm** - Rt. 1, Box 189-C, Currie, NC 28435, (919) 283-5605. Specializes in strawberry plants. CAT FREE, R & W, PC, M.O. 25 OF EACH.

L56 **Sunnybrook Farms** - P.O. Box 6, Chesterland, OH 44026, (216) 729-7232. Herb plants, scented geraniums, garden perennials, cactus, indoor foliage plants. CAT $1, RET, PC/CC, OVER, M.O. $10.

L57 **Sunnypoint Gardens** - 6939 Hwy. 42, Egg Harbor, WI 54209, (414) 868-3646. Family owned business specializing in herb plants, scented geraniums and garden perennials. CAT $1, R & W, PC/CC, M.O. $10.

L59 **Sunrise Enterprises** - P.O. Box 10058, Elmwood, CT 06110-0058, (203) 666-8071 (no telephone orders). One of the largest selections of oriental vegetable seeds in North America. Also plants of unusual vegetables and fragrant flowers, sprouting seeds, flower seeds. CAT $1

REFUNDABLE, R & W, PC, CANADA ONLY, M.O. $5.

L59G **Sunseeds Genetics, Inc.** - P.O. Box 1438, Hollister, CA 95023, (408) 636-9278. Commercial breeders and growers of a full line of vegetable seeds. CAT FREE, WHLS, OVER.

L59M **Sunset Nursery Inc.** - 4007 Elrod Ave., Tampa, FL 33616, (813) 839-7228 or 837-3003. Specializes in bamboo, both hardy and tropical. CAT SASE, R & W, PC/CC, M.O. 1 PLANT.

L60 **Sunshine Farms** - R.R. 1, Box 92, Macon, MS 39341, (601) 726-2264. Blackberry and raspberry plants and root cuttings. Specializes in upright blackberries developed at the Arkansas Agricultural Experiment Station. CAT FREE, R & W, PC, OVER.

L62M **Sunshine State Tropicals** - P.O. Box 1033, Port Richey, FL 34673-1033, (813) 841-9618. Exotic tropical plants. CAT FREE, R & W, PC, CANADA ONLY, M.O. $12.

L63M **Sunstream** - P.O. Box 225, Eighty Four, PA 15330, (412) 222-3330. Beekeeping supplies, including seeds of honey plants. CAT $1 REFUNDABLE, RET, PC, OVER, M.O. $10.

L65M **Superior View Farm** - Rt. 1, Box 199, Bayfield, WI 54814, (715) 779-5404. Hardy field grown herbs, garden perennials, rhubarb and asparagus. CAT FREE, CAT FREE, PC, CANADA ONLY, M.O. $25.

L66 **Surry Gardens** - P.O. Box 145, Rte. 172, Surry, ME 04684, (207) 667-4493. Large variety of garden perennials, herb plants, wild flowers, ornamental grasses. CAT FREE, R & W, PC/CC, M.O. $15.

L67 **Survival Services** - P.O. Box 42152, Los Angeles, CA 90042, (213) 255-9502 (no telephone orders). Specializes in epasote. Also conducts wild food and survival skills outings. *Sells the following product/s:* dried epasote herb, whole carob pods, dried white sage leaves, and dried California bay leaves. CAT FREE, R & W, PC/OC, OVER.

L69 **Swan Island Dahlias** - P.O. Box 800, Canby. OR 97013, (503) 266-7711. Growers and hybridizers of dahlia. *Sells the following product/s:* Dacopa coffee substitute. CAT $2, R & W, PC/CC, OVER, M.O. $10.

L70 **Swedberg Nursery** - Box 418, Battle Lake, MN 56515, (218) 864-5526. Fruit and nut trees, berry plants, grape vines, hardy kiwi, perennial vegetables, shade trees, flowering shrubs, hardy native ferns and wild flowers. CAT FREE, R & W, PC/CC, M.O. $10.

L75 **Swift (Dean) Seed Co.** - P.O. Box B, Jaroso, CO 81138, (719) 672-3739. Specializes in source-identified seed of conifers, shrubs, and wild flowers native to the Western United States. CAT FREE, R & W, PC, M.O. 1 LB OF EACH.

L77 **Sylvan Spawn Laboratory, Inc.** - West Hills Industrial Park, Kittanning, PA 16201. Large commercial supplier of button mushroom spawn. CAT FREE, WHLS.

L79 **T & T Seeds Ltd.** - Box 1710, Winnipeg, MB R3C 3P6, Canada, (204) 956-2777. Vegetable, herb and flower seeds, fruit and nut trees, berry plants, grape vines, shade trees, flowering shrubs. Specializes in varieties for cold, short season areas. CAT $1, RET, PC/CC, U.S. ONLY (SEED).

L79G **Tainong Enterprises Co.** - P.O. Box 1053, Carlsbad, CA 92008, (619) 757-7679. Specializes in oriental vegetable seeds. CAT FREE, WHLS.

L79M **Talavaya Seeds** - P.O. Box 707, Santa Cruz Station, Santa Cruz, NM 87567, (505) 753-5801. Non-profit organization specializing in traditional, open-pollinated vegetable seed of the indigenous peoples of the American Southwest. CAT $1, RET, PC/CC, OVER.

L82 **Tanimoto (Mike) Nursery** - 285 Standish Lane, Gridley, CA 95948, (916) 846-3145. Specializes in Hayward kiwi fruit vines. CAT FREE, R & W, PC.

L85 **Taylor (Lewis) Farms Inc.** - P.O. Box 822, Tifton, GA 31793, (912) 382-4454. Strawberry and rabbiteye blueberry plants, vegetable plants including onion, cabbage, collard, broccoli, cauliflower and flowering kale. CAT FREE, WHLS, PC/OC, OVER.

L86 **Taylor's Herb Gardens Inc.** - 1535 Lone Oak Rd., Vista, CA 92084, (619) 727-3485. Herb plants, scented geraniums, extensive listing of herb seeds. One of the largest herb plant growers in the United States. CAT FREE, R & W, PC, M.O. 6 PLANTS.

L87 **Teepell Seed Company** - R.R. #1, Elgin, ON K0G 1E0, Canada, (613) 359-5254. Seed of Tetra Pektus rye, dent and flint corns. CAT FREE, R & W.

L87G **Tempeh Lab (The)** - P.O. Box 208, 156 Drakes Lane, Summertown, TN 38483-0208, (615) 964-3574. Specializes in tempeh inoculum, including commercial grade tempeh starter and tempeh spore powder and tempeh kits for home culturing. Non-profit project of the Global Village Institute for Appropriate Technology. CAT FREE, R & W, PC, OVER.

L89 **Territorial Seed Co.** - P.O. Box 27, Lorane, OR 97451, (503) 942-9547. Specializes in vegetable cultivars that grow well in cool summers and mild, wet winters. Also sells seed of herbs, flowers, green manures and quinoa. CAT FREE, RET, PC/CC, CANADA ONLY.

L89G **Texas Foundation Seed Service** - Texas Agricultural Experiment St., College Station, TX 77843-2581, (409) 845-4051. Distributors of Foundation quality vegetable and crop seeds developed by the Texas Agricultural Experiment Station plant breeders and other public supported plant breeders. CAT SASE, R & W, PC, OVER.

L89M **Texas Onion Plant Co.** - Box 871, Farmersville, TX 75031. Specializes in Texas sweet onion plants. CAT FREE, R & W, PC.

L90 **Texas Pecan Nursery Inc.** - P.O. Box 306, Chandler, TX 75758, (214) 849-6203. Fruit and nut trees, muscadines, bunch grapes, shade trees, flowering shrubs. Specializes in Eastern and Western pecans. CAT FREE, R & W, PC, $50.

L90G **Thai Grocery** - 5014 N. Broadway, Chicago, IL 60640, (312) 561-5345. Specializes in Thai and Chinese foods. *Sells the following product/s:* both fresh and dried laos, dried kaffir lime leaves, both fresh and dried lemon grass, one hundred unities, lily root flour, fresh coriander root, wet tamarind, tapioca flour, grass jelly and canned yanang leaves. CAT (CALL FOR PRICES), RET, PC.

L90M **Thomas Jefferson Center for Historic Plants** - Monticello, P.O. Box 316, Charlottesville, VA 22902, (804) 295-3060. Collects, preserves and distributes historical vegetable, herb and flower seeds, including many grown by Thomas Jefferson at Monticello. CAT FREE, RET, PC/CC.

L91M **Thompson & Morgan** - P.O. Box 1308, Jackson, NJ 08527, (201) 363-2225. Wide range of vegetable seeds, including gourmet and ethnic specialties, herbs, sprouting seeds, flowers, ornamental grasses, tree and shrub seed. CAT FREE, R & W, PC/CC/OC, OVER.

L95 **Tideland Gardens** - P.O. Box 549, Chestertown, MD 21620, (301) 778-5787. Field grown garden perennials, natives, ornamental grasses, ferns, deciduous shrubs. CAT FREE, WHLS, CC, M.O. $50.

L97 **Tillinghast Seed Co.** - P.O. Box 738, La Connor, WA 98257, (206) 466-3329. Vegetable, herb and flower seed, fruit and nut trees, berry plants, grape vines, perennial vegetables, wild flowers, green manures. CAT FREE, RET, PC/CC/OC, OVER.

L97G **Timber Crest Farms** - 4791 Dry Creek Rd., Healdsburg, CA 95448, (707) 433-8255. Dried fruits and nuts, dried tomato products. *Sells the following product/s:* dried carambolas, dried Roma tomatoes, dried Golden Delicious apples, dried Royal apricots, dried Bartlett pears, dried Muir peaches, dried Bing cherries, dried Prune d'Agen plums and wheat nuts. CAT FREE, R & W, PC/CC, OVER.

L97M **Timbercreek Farm** - P.O. Box 849, Bloomington, IL 61701. Specializes in organically grown eating grade elephant garlic. CAT FREE, RET, PC.

L99 **Todaro Bros.** - 555 Second Ave., New York, NY 10016, (212) 532-0633. Imported and domestic gourmet foods. *Sells the following product/s:* dried morel and chanterelle mushrooms, both fresh and marinated cippolini, dried chestnuts, chestnut flour, chickpea flour and grano wheat. CAT FREE, RET, PC.

L99M **Tolowa Nursery** - P.O. Box 509, Talent, OR 97540, (503) 535-5557. Wide range of common and unusual fruit and nut trees, berry plants, grape vines, hardy kiwi, rootstocks for grafting, ornamental and multi-use trees. CAT SASE, R & W, PC.

M0 **Tomato Growers Supply Co.** - P.O. Box 2237, Fort Myers, FL 33902, (813) 332-4157. Specializes in seed of tomatoes and peppers, including more than 150 cultivars of tomato. CAT FREE, RET, PC/CC.

M1 **Tomato Seed Co., Inc.** - P.O. Box 323, Metuchen, NJ 08840, (201) 548-9036. Small company specializing in seed of tomatoes. Over 300 cultivars, plus related plants such as tomatillo, tree tomato, garden huckleberry and ground cherry. CAT FREE, RET, PC, OVER.

M1M **Totally Organic Farms** - 2404 "F" St., Suite 101, San Diego, CA 92102, (619) 231-9506. Organically grown fresh fruits and vegetables, natural food items. CAT FREE, RET, PC.

M3 **Tower View Nursery** - 70912 CR-388, South Haven, MI 49090, (616) 637-1279. Specializes in certified and virus tested highbush blueberry plants. CAT FREE, WHLS, M.O. 100 OF EACH.

M4 **Traas Nursery Ltd.** - 24355 48th Ave., R.R. 7, Langley, BC V3A 4R1, Canada, (604) 534-2433. Large selection of rootstocks for grafting, including apples, pears, cherries and plums. CAT FREE, R & W, PC/OC, U.S. ONLY.

Traas Nursery Ltd. - P.O. Box 1433, Sumas, WA 98295. United States branch of Traas Nursery Ltd., Canada, which see.

M5M **Tradewinds Bamboo Nursery** - P.O. Box 70, Calpella, CA 95418, (707) 485-0835. Hardy, sub-tropical and tropical bamboo. Focus is on species suitable for edible bamboo shoots, usable cane and ornamental value. Succeeded Panda Products Nursery. CAT SASE, RET, PC, OVER, M.O. $40.

M7M **Trans-Pacific Nursery** - 16065 Oldsville Rd., McMinnville, OR 97128, (503) 472-6215. Rare and unusual perennials, climbers, trees and shrubs from around the world. CAT $2 REFUNDABLE, R & W, PC/CC, OVER, M.O. $10.

M8 **Transplant Nursery** - Parkertown Rd., Lavonia, GA 30553, (404) 356-8947. Native and evergreen azaleas, rhododendrons. CAT FREE, R & W, PC/CC, M.O. $25.

M13M **Tregunno Seeds Ltd.** - 126 Catharine St. North, Hamilton, ON L8R 1J4, Canada, (416) 528-5983 or 528-5984. Vegetable and flower seeds. CAT FREE, R & W, PC, CANADA ONLY.

M15 **Tricker (William) Inc.** - 7125 Tanglewood Dr., Independence, OH 44131, (216) 524-3491. Water lilies, lotus, wild rice, arrowhead, water chestnut, other aquatic and bog plants. Established in 1895. CAT $2 DEDUCTIBLE, R & W, PC/CC, OVER.

M15M **Trinity Herb** - P.O. Box 199, Bodega, CA 94922, (707) 874-3418. Herb and spice company specializing in organically grown and wild harvested herbs. Also carries sprouting seeds. CAT $1, WHLS, PC, M.O. $25.

M15T **Triple Oaks Nursery & Florist** - Delsea Drive, Franklinville, NJ 08322, (609) 694-4272. Herb plants, scented geraniums, dried herbs and spices, herbal crafts and products. CAT SASE, RET, PC.

M16 **Tripple Brook Farm** - 37 Middle Rd., Southampton, MA 01073, (413) 527-4626 (no telephone orders). Wide range of edible and useful plants including hardy kiwi, mulberries, feijoa, herbs, natives, hardy cactus and bamboo. CAT FREE, R & W, PC, OVER.

M19 **Tropical Seeds** - P.O. Box 11122, Honolulu, HI 96828, (808) 395-0524. Seeds of exotic tropical flowering trees, palms, papayas, Maui onions. Also vegetable cultivars developed at the University of Hawaii. Succeeded Aloha Air Flora. CAT $1 REFUNDABLE, R & W, PC, OVER, M.O. $4.50.

M20 **Tropicals Unlimited** - P.O. Box 1261, Kailua, HI 96734, (808) 262-6040. Seeds and plants of exotic tropical foliage plants, flowering trees, tropical fruits and nuts, Kona coffee, Maui onion. CAT $1, R & W, PC.

M22 **Tsolum River Fruit Trees** - Box 68, Merville, BC V0R 2M0, Canada, (604) 337-8004. Organically grown fruit trees including an extensive collection of heirloom apples. Also custom grafting services and scionwood. CAT $3.50, RET, PC, CANADA ONLY.

M23M **Turkey Hollow Nursery** - HCR 3, Box 860, Cumberland, KY 40823, (606) 589-5378. Caters to the small buyer looking for unique or connoisseur apples. Offers a small selection of trees, rootstocks for grafting, scion wood of over 300 cultivars, and tree ripened fruit for gift boxes or sample boxes. CAT FREE, R & W, PC.

M25 **Turner Seed Co.** - Rt. 1, Box 292, Breckenridge, TX 76024, (817) 559-2065. Small grain, native grasses, green manure and cover crop seeds. CAT FREE, WHLS.

M25M **Turner's Bend Nursery** - Rt. 6. Box 175, McMinnville, TN 37110, (615) 668-4543. Fruit and nut trees, grape vines, native wild flowers, shade trees, evergreens, flowering shrubs. CAT FREE, WHLS.

M29 **Twilley (Otis S.) Seed Co., Inc.** - P.O. Box 65, Trevose, PA 19047, (215) 639-8800. Vegetable and flower seeds for the small commercial grower of fresh market vegetables, bedding plants and cut flowers, and for the home gardener. CAT FREE, R & W, PC/CC, OVER.

M31 **Ty Ty Plantation Bulb Co.** - P.O. Box 159, Ty Ty, GA 31795, (912) 382-0404. Rare and common bulbs, garden perennials, hardy native ferns. CAT FREE, R & W, PC/CC, OVER.

M31M **Ty Ty South Orchards** - Corridor Z, Ty Ty, GA 31795, (912) 386-1919 or 382-0404. Broad range of common and unusual fruit and nut trees, muscadines, bunch grapes, berry plants, shade trees, flowering shrubs. Also sells fresh fruit and nuts in season. CAT FREE, R & W, PC, M.O. $15.

M31T **U.S. Espalier Nursery** - 16850 N.E. Leander Dr., Sherwood, OR 97140. Specializes in espalier apple and pear trees. CAT FREE, RET, PC/CC.

M32M **University of Hawaii Seed Program** - Department of Horticulture, 3190 Maile Way, Room 112, Honolulu, HI 96822, (808) 948-7890. Vegetable and fruit cultivars developed at the University of Hawaii for tropical areas, including papayas, kidney beans, tomatoes, sweet corn and lettuce. CAT FREE, R & W, PC, OVER.

M33G **Unusual Plants** - 10065 River Mist Way, Rancho Cordova, CA 95670, (916) 366-7835 (no telephone orders). Specializes in unusual perennials, cacti and succulents, herbs, scented geraniums, and tropical foliage plants. Previously known as Robert B. Hamm. CAT $3, R & W, PC, CANADA ONLY.

M33M **Upper Bank Nurseries** - P.O. Box 486, Media, PA 19063, (215) 566-0679. Specializes in hardy bamboo. CAT SASE, R & W, PC, OVER.

M35 **Valley Creek Nursery** - P.O. Box 364, Three Oaks, MI 49128-0364, (616) 426-3283. Herbs, scented geraniums, ground covers, miniature roses. CAT FREE, WHLS, PC.

M35M **Valley Nursery** - P.O. Box 4845, Helena, MT 59604, (406) 442-8460. Cold hardy plants including fruit and nut trees, berry plants, shade trees, flowering shrubs. CAT $.25, R & W, PC/OC, OVER, M.O. $25.

M37M **Van Bourgondien Bros.** - P.O. Box A, Babylon, NY 11702, 1-800-645-5830. Berry plants, asparagus, garlic and onion sets, garden perennials, bulbs, flowering shrubs. CAT FREE, RET, PC/CC.

M39 **Van Ness Water Gardens** - 2460 North Euclid Ave., Upland, CA 91786-1199, (714) 982-2425. Water lilies, lotus, other aquatic and bog plants. CAT $3, RET, PC/CC, OVER, M.O. $15.

M39M **Van Well Nursery** - P.O. Box 1339, Wenatchee, WA 98801, (509) 663-8189. Large selection of dwarf, semi-dwarf and standard fruit and nut trees, berry plants, grape vines. CAT $1, R & W, PC/CC, OVER.

M41M **Vanilla, Saffron Imports** - 949 Valencia St., San Francisco, CA 94110, (415) 648-8990. Gourmet and specialty food items. *Sells the following product/s:* both fresh and dried golden chantarelle and morel mushrooms, morel powder, grapeseed oil. CAT FREE, R & W, PC.

M42 **Varga's Nursery** - 2631 Pickertown Rd., Warrington, PA 18976, (215) 343-0646. Extensive listing of hardy and tropical ferns. CAT $1, R & W, PC, CANADA ONLY, M.O. $25.

M43M **Vaughn's Seed Co.** - 5300 Katrine Ave., Downers Grove, IL 60515-4095, (708) 969-6300. Vegetable, herb and flower seeds, tropical foliage plants, garden perennials, ferns, cacti and succulents. CAT FREE, WHLS, PC/CC, OVER.

M45M **Veldheer Tulip Gardens, Inc.** - 12755 Quincy St. & U.S. 31, Holland, MI 49424, (616) 399-1900. Specializes in spring and fall bulbs. CAT FREE, R & W, PC/CC, CANADA ONLY.

M46 **Vermont Bean Seed Co.** - Garden Lane, Box 250, Fair Haven, VT 05743-0250, (802) 265-3387. Vegetable, herb and flower seeds, everlastings, sprouting seeds. Specializes in beans and oriental greens. CAT FREE, R & W, PC/CC, OVER.

M47M **Vermont Wildflower Farm** - P.O. Box 5, Rt. 7, Charlotte, VT 05445-0005, (802) 425-3931. Wild flower seed including individual species, regional mixtures and custom mixtures. CAT FREE, R & W, PC/CC, Overseas.

M49 **Vesey's Seeds, Ltd.** - P.O. Box 9000, Calais, ME 04619-6102, (902) 566-1620. Vegetable, herb and flower seeds tested for areas with short growing seasons such as the New England States and the Maritime provinces of Canada. United States branch of Vesey's Seeds Ltd., Canada, which see. CAT FREE, RET, PC/CC, OVER.

Vesey's Seeds Ltd. - York, PE C0A 1P0, Canada.

M49M **Vesutor Ltd.** - P.O. Box 561663, Charlotte, NC 28256, (704) 597-7278. Specializes in micro propagation of exotic plants, including banana and pineapple. CAT FREE, RET, PC/CC.

M51 **Vietnam House** - 242 Farmington Ave., Hartford, CT 06105, (203) 524-0010. Specializes in Vietnamese foodstuffs. *Sells the following product/s:* both fresh and dried lemon grass. CAT FREE, RET, PC, M.O. $10.

M51M **Viewcrest Nurseries, Inc.** - 12713 N.E. 184th St., Battle Ground, WA 98604, (206) 687-5167. Evergreen transplants and seedlings for nurserymen, Christmas tree growers and reforestation. CAT FREE, WHLS, PC, OVER, M.O. 100 OF EACH.

M53 **Village Arbors** - 1804 Saugahatchee Road, Auburn, AL 36830, (205) 826-3490. Herb plants, scented geraniums, flowering perennials, herbal products. CAT FREE, R & W, PC/CC.

M59M **Wafler Nurseries** - 10662 Slaght Rd., Wolcott, NY 14590, (315) 594-2649. Dwarf and semi-dwarf apple trees for the commercial fruit grower. CAT FREE, WHLS, PC, M.O. 30 TREES.

M61 **Walker (Mary) Bulb Co.** - P.O. Box 256, Omega, GA 31775, (912) 386-1919. Specializes in bulbs and garden perennials. CAT FREE, RET, PC/CC.

M61M **Walker-Vice Nursery** - 11050 Mystery Mountain Rd., Valley Center, CA 92082, (619) 749-1615. Specializes in citrus and avocado. CAT FREE, WHLS, OVER.

M62 **Walla Walla Gardener's Association** - 210 N. Eleventh St., Walla Walla, WA 99362, (509) 525-7070 or 525-7071. Fresh produce in season. Specializes in Walla Walla Sweet onions. CAT FREE, R & W, PC/CC.

M63M **Walnut Acres** - Penns Creek, PA 17862, (717) 837-0601. Grower and distributor of organic foods since 1946. Also offers sprouting seeds and starter cultures. *Sells the following product/s:* dried Anasazi beans, whole grain quinoa, canola oil, Hunza apricot kernels, Hunza dried white mulberries, dried Moyer prunes, fruit-sweetened Marionberry conserves, whole grain teff, teff flour, dried adzuki bean sprouts, and sweet lupin pasta. CAT FREE, R & W, PC/CC, OVER, M.O. $250 WHLS

M65M **Walters Gardens, Inc.** - P.O. Box 137, Zeeland, MI 49464, (616) 772-4697. Berry plants, grape vines, perennial vegetables, ornamental grasses, perennial flowering and foliage plants. CAT FREE, WHLS, OVER.

M69 **Ward's Natural Science Establishment** - P.O. Box 92912, Rochester, NY 14692-9012, 1-800-962-2660. Complete selection of biological supplies, including living cultures of algae, fungi and bacteria. Also plants and seeds. Established in 1862. CAT $15, R & W, PC, OVER.

M69M **Warren County Nursery, Inc.** - Rt. 2, Box 204, McMinnville, TN 37110, (615) 668-8941. Fruit and nut trees, berry plants, grape vines, perennial vegetables, shade trees, flowering shrubs, conifers, Tennessee wild flowers. CAT FREE, WHLS, PC, OVER, M.O. 10 OF EACH.

M72 **Water Ways Nursery** - Route 2, Box 247, Lovettsville, VA 22080, (703) 822-9052. Water lilies, cattail, arrowhead, watercress, other aquatic and bog plants. CAT $1, R & W, PC.

M73 **Water Works (The)** - 111 E. Fairmount St., Coopersburg, PA 18036, (282) 4784. Water lilies, lotus, cattail, arrowhead, sweetflag, other aquatic and bog plants. CAT $1, R & W, PC/CC.

M73M **Waterford Gardens** - 74 East Allendale Rd., Saddle River, NJ 07458, (201) 327-0721. Complete selection of water plants and supplies, including water lilies, lotus, Chinese water chestnut, taro, arrowhead, cattail and marsh marigold. CAT $4, R & W, PC/CC, OVER.

M75 **Wavecrest Nursery & Landscaping Co.** - 2509 Lakeshore Dr., Fennville, MI 49408, (616) 543-4175. Specializes in rare and unusual ornamental trees and shrubs. CAT FREE, RET, PC/CC, OVER.

M76 **Waynesboro Nurseries** - P.O. Box 987, Waynesboro, VA 22980, (703) 942-4141. Fruit and nut trees, berry plants, grape vines, perennial vegetables, shade trees, flowering shrubs, conifers. CAT FREE, R & W, PC/CC, M.O. $20.

M77 **Wayside Gardens** - 1 Garden Lane, Hodges, SC 29695-0001, 1-800-845-1124. Fruit trees, berry plants, herbs, bulbs, roses, garden perennials, ornamental trees and shrubs. CAT $1 REFUNDABLE, RET, PC/CC.

M77M **We-Du Nurseries** - Rt. 5, Box 724, Marion, NC 28752, (704) 738-8300 (no telephone orders). Specializes in nursery propagated Southeastern natives, rare and unusual rock garden and woodland plants including oriental counterparts of native wild flowers. CAT $1 REFUNDABLE, RET, PC, OVER, M.O. $10.

M81M **Weeks Berry Nursery** - 6494 Windsor Isle Rd. N., Keizer, OR 97303, (503) 393-8112. Raspberries, blackberries, high bush and half-high blueberries, grape vines, currants and gooseberries, perennial vegetables, hop cuttings. CAT FREE, WHLS, M.O. $100.

M81T **Weeks (Christopher E.) Peppers** - P.O. Box 3207, Kill Devil Hills, NC 27948. Small, single proprietor seed company specializing in hot peppers. CAT FREE, RET, PC.

M82 **Well-Sweep Herb Farm** - 317 Mt. Bethel Rd., Port Murray, NJ 07865, (201) 852-5390 (no telephone orders). Extensive list of herb plants including many rare varieties, scented geraniums, herb seed, garden perennials, dried flowers and other herbal products. CAT $1, R & W, PC, M.O. $5.

M83 **Wells (Bob) Nursery** - P.O. Box 606, Lindale, TX 75771, (214) 882-3550. Fruit and nut trees, berry plants, grape vines, perennial vegetables, roses, shade trees, flowering shrubs. CAT FREE, R & W, PC.

M87 **Western Biologicals** - P.O. Box 283, Aldergrove, BC V0X 1A0, Canada, (604) 228-0986. Extensive selection of exotic mushroom spawn, live cultures, home mushroom growing kits, grower's supplies, laboratory equipment, tissue culture supplies. CAT $2, CAT FREE, PC/CC, OVER, M.O. $5.

M89 **Western Ontario Fruit Testing Assn.** - Research Station, Harrow, ON N0R 1G0, Canada, (519) 738-2251. Rootstock seeds of peach and apricot produced from virus-indexed trees. Also distributes for testing nursery stock selections of apricot, peach, pear and nectarine developed at the Harrow Research Station. CAT FREE, WHLS, PC, OVER, M.O. 100 SEEDS.

M90 **Westgate Gardens Nursery** - 751 Westgate Dr., Eureka, CA 95501, (707) 442-1239. Specializes in azaleas and rhododendrons, rare ornamental trees and shrubs. CAT $4, RET, PC.

M92 **Weston Nurseries** - P.O. Box 186, Hopkinton, MA 01748-0186, (508) 435-3414. Wide range of nursery stock including fruit trees, berry plants, grape vines, shade trees, flowering shrubs, herbaceous perennials and roses. CAT FREE, R & W, PC.

M95 **Westwind Seeds** - 2509 N. Campbell Ave. # 139, Tucson, AZ 85719. Open-pollinated, untreated vegetable, herb and flower seeds. Focus is on cultivars adapted to extremes in climate, including heat and drought. CAT FREE, R & W, PC, M.O. $100 WHLS

M95M **Wetsel Seed Co.** - P.O. Box 791, Harrisonburg, VA 22801-0791. Vegetable, herb and flower seeds, garden perennials, grains, green manure and cover crop seeds, wild flowers. CAT FREE, R & W, PC/CC, OVER.

M97M **Whistling Wings Farm, Inc.** - 427 West St., Biddeford, ME 04005, (207) 282-1146. Specializes in gourmet raspberry foods. *Sells the following product/s:* black raspberry jam and purple raspberry jam. CAT FREE, R & W, PC/CC, OVER.

M98 **White Flower Farm** - Rt. #63, Litchfield, CT 06759-0050, (203) 496-9600. Berry plants, herbs, garden perennials, ornamental shrubs. CAT $1, RET, PC/CC.

M99M **White Truffle Foods Inc.** - 829 7th St., Lake Oswego, OR 97034, (503) 635-6444. Specializes in fresh Oregon white truffles. CAT FREE, R & W, PC.

N0 **Whitman Farms** - 1420 Beaumont N.W., Salem, OR 97304, (503) 363-5020. Fruit and nut trees, berry plants, grape vines, kiwi, rootstocks for grafting, seedling trees and shrubs. Specializes in currants and gooseberries. CAT $.50 PLUS SASE, R & W, PC, M.O. $10.

N1M **Whitney Gardens & Nursery** - P.O. Box F, Brinnon, WA 98320-0080, (206) 796-4411. Species and hybrid azaleas and rhododendron. CAT $2.50, RET, PC/CC, OVER.

N3M **Wicklein's Aquatic Farm & Nursery** - 1820 Cromwell Bridge Road, Baltimore, MD 21234, (301) 823-1335. Water lilies, lotus, Chinese water chestnut, cattail, arrowhead, other aquatic and bog plants. CAT $2, R & W, PC/CC, CANADA ONLY.

N5 **Wiemer (Herman J.) Vineyard, Inc.** - Rt. 14, Box 38, Dundee, NY 14837, (607) 243-7971 or 243-7983. Specializes in grafted vinifera wine grapes. CAT FREE, WHLS, PC/CC, OVER.

N6 **Wil-Ker-Son Kiwifruit Ranch & Nursery** - 661 East Evans Reimer Rd., Gridley, CA 95948, (916) 846-5561. Bare root kiwi nursery stock. CAT FREE, R & W, PC, OVER.

N7 **Wild and Crazy Seed Co.** - P.O. Box 895, Durango, CO 81302. Seeds and seed mixes of native wild flowers and shrubs of the Four Corner States region. CAT FREE, R & W, PC.

N7M **Wild Seed Inc.** - P.O. Box 27751, Tempe, AZ 85285, (602) 968-9751. Wild flower seed, both individual species and mixes adapted to various climatic regions of the Southwest. CAT FREE, RET, PC.

N7T **Wildflower Nursery** - 1680 Highway 25-70, Marshall, NC 28753, (704) 656-2681. Native wild flowers and shrubs. Previously known as Griffey's Nursery. CAT FREE, R & W, PC, OVER.

N8 **Wildflower Source (The)** - P.O. Box 312, Fox Lake, IL 60020, (312) 740-9796 (no telephone orders). Rare and unusual native plants for the connoisseur, including wild flowers, ferns and orchids. CAT $1, R & W, PC, CANADA ONLY.

N9M **Wildginger Woodlands** - P.O. Box 1091, Webster, NY 14580. Native and naturalized plants of the Northeast including wild flowers, ferns, and trees and shrubs. Seeds and spores available by special order only. CAT $1 REFUNDABLE, RET, PC, M.O. $10.

N11 **Wildlife Nurseries** - P.O. Box 2724, Oshkosh, WI 54903-2724, (414) 231-3780. Seeds for wildlife plantings, native grasses and legumes, grains, chufa, arrowhead, wild rice and other aquatic plants. Established in 1896. *Sells the following product/s:* wild harvested Wisconsin wild rice. CAT $1, RET, PC/CC/OC, OVER, M.O. $15.

N11M **Wildseed Incorporated** - P.O. Box 308, Eagle Lake, TX 77434, 1-800-848-0078. Wild flower seed, both individual species and regional mixes suited to all areas of the United States. CAT FREE, R & W, PC/CC, OVER.

N13 **Wildwood Gardens** - 14488 Rock Creek Rd., Chardon, OH 44024, (216) 286-3714. Pre-bonsai plants including deciduous trees and shrubs, dwarf conifers, grasses and ground covers. Also finished bonsai. CAT $1, R & W, PC, M.O. $25.

N15 **Wiley's Nut Grove Nursery** - 2002 Lexington Ave., Mansfield, OH 44907, (419) 756-0697. Seedling and grafted pecans, walnuts, butternuts, chestnuts, filberts, hickory nuts, American persimmons and pawpaws. CAT $.25, R & W, PC.

N16 **Willhite Seed Co.** - P.O. Box 23, Poolville, TX 76076, (817) 599-8656. Seeds of vegetables, herbs and wild flowers. Specializes in muskmelons and watermelons. CAT FREE, R & W, PC/CC, OVER.

N17 **William's Brewing** - P.O. Box 2195, San Leandro, CA 94577, (415) 895-2739. Home brewing supplies, beer yeasts. CAT FREE, RET, PC/CC.

N18 **Willits & Newcomb** - P.O. Box 428, Arvin, CA 93203, (805) 366-7269. Specializes in citrus seed and virus-tested citrus budwood. CAT FREE, R & W, OVER.

N19 **Willow Drive Nursery** - Rt. 1, 348-5 NW, Ephrata, WA 98823, (509) 787-1555. Seedling and clonal fruit tree rootstocks, shade trees, flowering shrubs. CAT FREE, WHLS.

N19M **Willow Oak Flower & Herb Farm** - 8109 Telegraph Rd., Severn, MD 21144, (310) 551-2237. Herb plants, scented geraniums, garden perennials, everlasting flowers, wreaths and other herbal products. CAT $1.50, R & W, PC, M.O. $50 WHLS

N20 **Wilson (Dave) Nursery** - 19701 Lake Road, Hickman, CA 95323, (209) 874-1821. Wide selection of fruit and nut trees, berry plants, grape vines, kiwi and hardy kiwi, shade trees, flowering shrubs. CAT FREE, WHLS.

N21M **Wilton's Organic Certified Potatoes** - P.O. Box 28, Aspen, CO 81612, (303) 925-3433. Certified organically grown Norland and Norgold Russet seed potatoes. CAT FREE, R & W, PC/CC, OVER, M.O. $9.75.

N24M **Windmill Point Farm and Nursery** - 2103 Perrot Blvd., N.D., Ile Perrot, PQ J7V 5V6, Canada, (514) 453-9757. Extensive listings for a broad range of common and unusual fruit and nut trees, berry plants and grape vines, including many rare and unique selections. CAT $2.50, RET, PC.

N25M **Windy Hills Farm** - 1565 East Wilson Rd., Scottville, MI 49454, (616) 757-2373. Nut tree seedlings, hardwoods, ornamental shrubs, trees and shrubs for attracting wildlife. CAT FREE, R & W, PC, CANADA ONLY.

N26 **Windy Ridge Nursery** - P.O. Box 301, Hythe, AB T0H 2C0, Canada, (403) 356-2167. Hardy fruits including apples, strawberries, currants, gooseberries, raspberries and cherry plums. Specializes in saskatoons. Will ship fresh fruit in season by bus throughout western Canada.

CAT FREE, R & W, PC/CC, U.S. ONLY (SASKATOONS), M.O. $100 U.S.

N27 **Wine Lab (The)** - 477 Walnut St., Napa, CA 94559, (707) 224-7903. Large selection of rare wine yeasts, both liquid and dry. CAT $5, R & W, PC/CC, OVER.

N29 **Winter Sun Trading Co.** - 18 East Santa Fe, Flagstaff, AZ 86001, (602) 774-2884. Organically grown, traditionally wildcrafted herbs of the Southwest. *Sells the following product/s:* dried corn pollen, dried sweet grass, dried oregano de la sierra, and dried rosemary mint. CAT $3, RET, PC, M.O. $10.

N29M **Winterfeld Ranch Seed** - P.O. Box 97, Swan Valley, ID 83449, (208) 483-3683. Registered and certified seed of native wild flowers and prairie grasses. CAT FREE, R & W, OVER.

N32 **Wolf River Valley Seeds** - N. 2976 County Hwy. M, White Lake, WI 54491, (715) 882-3100. Specializes in sweet lupin seeds. CAT FREE, R & W, PC.

N33 **Womack's Nursery Co.** - Rt. 1, Box 80, De Leon, TX 76444-9660, (817) 893-6497. Wide range of fruit and nut trees, berry plants, grape vines, ornamental trees and shrubs adapted to Texas and adjoining states. Specializes in pecans. CAT FREE, R & W, PC, M.O. $15.

N34 **Wood Prairie Farm** - R.F.D. 1, Box 164, Bridgewater, ME 04735, (207) 429-9765. Family farm specializing in certified organically grown potatoes for both planting and eating. CAT FREE, RET, PC/CC.

N34M **Wood (Tom) Herbs** - P.O. Box 100, Archer, FL 32618, (904) 495-9168. Specializes in rare and interesting gingers, both edible and ornamental. CAT FREE, RET, PC, M.O. $20.

N36 **Woodland Nurseries** - 2151 Camilla Rd., Mississauga, ON L5A 2K1, Canada, (416) 277-2961. Ornamental trees and shrubs. CAT $4, R & W, PC.

N37 **Woodland Rockery** - 6210 Klam Rd., Otter Lake, MI 48464, (313) 793-4151. Garden perennials, native and naturalized ferns and wild flowers, ornamental grasses. CAT FREE, RET, PC, M.O. $15.

N37M **Woodlanders** - 1128 Colleton Ave., Aiken, SC 29801, (803) 648-7522 (no telephone orders). Large selection of rare and hard-to-find trees and shrubs, vines, palms, garden perennials, and bamboos, both native and exotic species. CAT $.65, RET, PC, OVER, M.O. $15.

N39 **Woodruff & Royce Seed Co.** - RD #2, Box 2751, Whitehall, NY 12887, (518) 499-0628. Vegetable, herb and flower seeds, perennial vegetable plants, seed potatoes. Succeeded Royce Seeds Ltd. CAT $.25, RET, PC/CC, CANADA ONLY.

N40 **World Variety Produce** - P.O. Box 21407, Los Angeles, CA 90021, (213) 588-0151. Over 500 rare and exotic produce items. *Sells the following product/s:* dried jack fruit, dried carambola, shelled coquito nuts, dried De Arbol and Santaka peppers, nopales cactus leaves, dried Hachiya persimmons, cocktail avocados, Strawberry popping corn, sun dried bell peppers, red currants and dried Santa Maria Pinquito beans. CAT FREE, WHLS TO THE PUBLIC, OVER.

N42 **Wrenwood of Berkeley Springs** - Rt. 4, Box 361, Berkeley Springs, WV 25411, (304) 258-3071. Large selection of herbs, garden perennials, scented geraniums, rock garden plants. CAT $1.50, R & W, PC/CC, M.O. $30.

N43 **Wright (Dick)** - 38660 De Luz Road, Fallbrook, CA 92028, (619) 728-2383. Rare and unusual succulents. CAT FREE, WHLS, M.O. $50.

N43M **Wrinkle (Guy) Exotic Plants** - 11610 Addison St., North Hollywood, CA 91601, (818) 766-4820. Rare succulents, orchids, cycads, palms. CAT $1, R & W, PC, OVER, M.O. $15.

N45 **Wyrttun Ward Herbs & Wildflowers** - 18 Beach Street, Middleboro, MA 02346, (508) 866-4087. Herb plants, native and naturalized wild flowers. CAT $1, RET, PC/CC, OVER, M.O. 6 PLANTS.

N45M **Ya-Ka-Ama** - 6215 Eastside Road, Forestville, CA 95436, (707) 887-1541. California natives, large selection of ornamental grasses. Specializes in plants developed by Luther Burbank. CAT FREE, RET, PC.

N46 **Yakima Valley Nursery** - 6461 Powerhouse Rd., Yakima, WA 98908, (509) 966-0410. Dwarf, semi-dwarf and standard fruit trees including apples, pears, peaches, apricots, cherries, nectarines and plums. CAT FREE, R & W.

N49M **Yoshinoya** - 36 Prospect St., Cambridge, MA 02139, (617) 491-8221. Specializes in Japanese foods. *Sells the following product/s:* dried sanshô, dried kampyo, konnyaku, pickled rakkyo, and kinako. CAT (CALL FOR PRICES), RET, PC/CC, M.O. $25.

N50 **Youngbloods of Sapphire** - P.O. Box 100, Sapphire, NC 28774, (704) 966-4466. Regional and specialty food items. *Sells the following product/s:* pickled Crystal Apple cucumbers, watermelon rind pickles, Blue Damson plum preserves, muscadine grape jam, and Red Indian peach jam. CAT FREE, RET, PC.

N51 **Yucca Do Nursery** - P.O. Box 655, Waller, TX 77484, (409) 826-6363 (no telephone orders). Specializes in Texas and Southeastern natives and their Mexican and Asian counterparts, including trees and shrubs, perennials, grasses and palms. CAT $.50 PLUS SASE, RET, PC, M.O. $15.

N52 **Zenner Brothers Seed Co., Inc.** - 1311 S.E. Gideon St., Portland, OR 97202, (503) 231-1019. Vegetable seeds, garlic and onion sets. CAT FREE, R & W, PC.

N53M **Zill Nursery** - 6671 Tara Court, Boynton Beach, FL 33437-9548, (407) 732-3555. Specializes in mango and avocado. CAT (CALL FOR PRICES), WHLS, PC, M.O. 300 TREES.

OVERSEAS COMMERCIAL

N63M **Albiflora, Inc.** - P.O. Box 24, Gyotoku, Ichikawa, Chiba, 272-01, Japan, 0473 58-7627 (no telephone orders). Large selection of seeds of Japanese native plants. CAT 2 IRC, R & W, BANK DRAFT, OVER, M.O. ¥ 5000, ENGL.

N69 **Andreae (Dieter) Kakteenkulturen** - Postfach 3, Heringer Weg, D-6111 Otzberg-Lengfeld. Germany, Seeds and plants of cacti and succulents. CAT FREE, RET, PC, OVER.

N71M **Appel (Conrad) GmbH** - Bismarckstrasse 59, D-6100 Darmstadt, Germany. 6151 852-200. Seeds of trees, shrubs and wildflowers. CAT FREE, WHLS, PC/OC, OVER, ENGL.

N73 **Appleton's Tree Nursery** - Main Road South, Wakefield, Nelson, New Zealand, 054 28309. Grower of deciduous and evergreen, hardy and temperate climate trees and shrubs from seed. Could supply seed to overseas clients where importing of live plants is difficult. CAT FREE, WHLS, BANK DRAFTS, OVER, M.O. 100 PLANTS, ENGL.

N78 **Austin (David) Roses** - Bowling Green Lane, Albrighton, Wolverhampton WV7 3HB, England, U.K., 090 722-3931. English roses, species roses, shrub roses, etc. CAT 75 PENCE, R & W, OVER, M.O. £75 OVER, ENGL.

N79M **Australian Seed Co.** - P.O. Box 67, Hazelbrook, NSW 2779, Australia, (61) 47 586-132. Large selection of tree and shrub seeds, most of which are endemic to Australia. CAT FREE, WHLS, BANK DRAFT, OVER, M.O. $25, ENGL.

N81 **Austrosaat A.G.** - P.O. Box 40, A-1232 Vienna, Austria, 67 45480. Vegetable, herb and flower seeds. CAT FREE, R & W, OVER.

N84 **B & T Associates** - Whitnell House, Fiddington, Bridgwater, Somerset TA5 1JE, England, U.K., (278) 733-209. Extremely large selection of common and exotic seeds, probably the largest of its type in the world, covering well over 25,000 species. Publishes a series of lists in various categories. CAT 2 IRC, R & W, PC/CC, OVER, ENGL.

N91 **Bankim Prosad Ghosh & Co.** - Belur Station Road, Bally-711 201, Howrah District, West Bengal, India, 033 64-2445 or 64-1449 (no telephone orders). Producer and seller of a large variety of vegetable and jute seeds. Also propagates fruit, flower and ornamental plants. Established in 1920. CAT FREE, R & W, LETTER OF CREDIT, OVER, M.O. 1 KILOGRAM, ENGL.

N93M **Barilli & Biagi** - Casella Postale 1645-AD, I-40100 Bologna, Italy, 051 370-542 or 356-997. Seeds of conifer and deciduous trees and shrubs. CAT FREE, R & W, PC/CC/OC, OVER, M.O. 10 LBS, ENGL.

O1 **Benary (Ernst)** - Postfach 1127, 3510 Hann. Munden 1, Germany, 05541 8091. Growers and breeders of annual and perennial flower seeds. CAT FREE, R & W, OVER.

O4 **Bertolami (A.) Nurseries** - S.S. 18, Km. 382, 100, 88040 Lamezia Terme (CZ), Italy, 0968 209-124 (no telephone orders). Largest nursery in the Mediterranean area for citrus and olive plants. Also grows other fruit trees and ornamentals. CAT FREE, R & W, WIRE TRANSFER, OVER.

O19 **Borneo Collection (The)** - P.O. El Arish, QLD 4855, Australia, 70 685-263. Unique collection of tropical fruits and nuts, many collected in Borneo and introduced into Australia for the first time. Will ship seeds anywhere. Plants can be shipped to Hawaii and other tropical countries, not to the United States mainland. CAT FREE, R & W, OVER, ENGL.

O20 **Boyce (J.W.) Seeds** - Bush Pasture, Lower Carter St., Fordham, Ely, Cambs. CB7 5JU, England, U.K., 0638 721-158. Vegetable, herb and flower seeds. CAT FREE, R & W, U.K. ONLY, ENGL.

O33 **Bushland Flora** - P.O. Box 189, Hillarys, WA 6025, Australia. Specializes in seeds of Australian native plants, including trees, shrubs, flowers, fruits and nuts. CAT FREE, R & W, PC/OC, OVER, ENGL.

O35G **Cally Gardens** - Gatehouse of Fleet, Castle Douglas DG7 2DJ, Scotland, U.K. Approximately 500 varieties of new and rare garden plants (including old types), propagated each year from a collection of 2000 plus. CAT £2, RET, STERLING BANK DRAFT, OVER, M.O. £50, ENGL.

O39M **Capital Seed House** - 190, S. Bangla Road, Khulna, Bangladesh, 23772 or 23663. Vegetable and flower seeds, tree and shrub seeds, indoor decorative plants. CAT FREE, R & W, LETTER OF CREDIT, OVER, ENGL.

O42 **Carnivorous & Unusual Seeds** - 3 Normandy Ave., Para Hills, SA 5096, Australia, 08 264-2825. Specializes in carnivorous plants, seeds and tubers. CAT IRC, RET, PC/OC, OVER, ENGL.

O46 **Chadwell Himalayan Seed** - 81 Parlaunt Rd., Slough, Berks., England, SL3 8BE, U.K. Small seed company specializing in hardy Himalayan species suitable for rock gardens, perennial borders and larger gardens. CAT $2, R & W, PC/OC, OVER, ENGL.

O48 **Chambers (John) Wild Flower Seeds** - 15 Westleigh Road, Barton Seagrave, Kettering, Northants NN15, 5AJ,, England, U.K., 0933 681-632. Large selection of seeds for British wild flowers, ornamental and cultivated grasses, everlastings, herbs, agricultural crops, sprouting seeds. CAT FREE, R & W, STERLING DRAFT, IMO, OVER, M.O. £6 OVER, ENGL.

O53 **Chia Tai Company, Ltd.** - 299-301 Songsawad Rd., Bangkok 10100, Thailand, 233 8191-9 (no telephone orders). Seeds of Chinese and tropical vegetables. CAT FREE, WHLS, BANK DRAFT, OVER, M.O. US $500.

O53M **Chiltern Seeds** - Bortree Stile, Ulverston, Cumbria, England LA12 7PB, U.K., 0229 581-137. Mail-order seed company offering a wide variety of seeds of hardy plants, wild flowers, trees and shrubs, cacti, annuals, houseplants, greenhouse exotics, oriental vegetables, traditional English vegetables and herbs. CAT $3, RET, PC/CC/OC, OVER, ENGL.

O54 **China National Seed Corporation** - No. 11 Nong Zhan Guan Nan Li, Beijing, China, 304 652-592 or 657-331 (no telephone orders). State-owned company dealing with seed production and distribution of seeds of cereals, oil crops, vegetables, fruit trees, medicinal crops, flowers and teas. CAT FREE, WHLS, LETTER OF CREDIT, OVER, M.O. 10 KILOGRAMS, ENGL.

O57 **Christian (P & J)** - P.O. Box 468, Wrexham, Clwyd LL11 3DP, North Wales, U.K., 0978 366-399. Specializes in rare and unusual species bulbs, corms, rhizomes and tubers plus alpine and herbaceous subjects in winter. All are raised in cultivation from stocks of known wild sources. CAT £3, R & W, CC/OC, OVER, ENGL.

O60 **Clause Italia S.p.A.** - Strada della Madonnina, 13, 10078 Venaria (Torino), Italy, 011 495564-492816. Vegetable and flower seeds. CAT FREE, WHLS, OVER.

O67 **Cooper (Mrs. Susan)** - Churchfields House, Cradley, Malvern, Worcs. WR13 5LJ, England, U.K., 088 684-223. Temperate tree and shrub seed exchange, payment not usual. Very small scale supplier. CAT SASE, RET, PC, OVER, ENGL.

O71M **Cuciti Vivai** - Villa Barone, Casella Postale 57, 98057 Milazzo (ME), Italy, 090 928-4237 (no overseas telephone orders). Large selection of fruit trees, grape vines, olives and ornamental plants. CAT FREE, R & W, PC/CC, OVER.

O81 **Deacons Nurseries** - Godshill, Isle of Wight PO38 3HW, U.K., 0983 522-243. Very large selection of fruit trees and small fruits, grown from certified stock, grape vines, nut trees, perennial vegetables. CAT FREE, R & W, PC/CC, U.K. ONLY, ENGL.

O84 **Department of Forestry, Queensland** - G.P.O. Box 944, Brisbane, QLD 4001, Australia, 07 234-0104 (no telephone orders). Supplies seed for a wide range of native and exotic trees and shrubs, with many being indigenous to Queensland. Also improved strains of Pinus. CAT FREE, RET, OC, OVER, ENGL.

O89 **Digger's Mail Order** - 105 Latrobe Parade, Dromana, VIC 3936, Australia, 059 87 1877. Supplies a wide range of seeds and bulbs, including Australian natives, old fashioned varieties for cottage gardens, trees and shrubs, herbs, and mini vegetables and space savers. CAT A $2, RET, PC/CC, OVER, ENGL.

O93 **Dow (Peter B.) & Co.** - P.O. Box 696, Gisborne 3800, New Zealand, 079 83408. Bulk seed supplier of most flowers, trees, shrubs and palms. CAT $5.50, R & W, PC/CC, OVER, ENGL.

O97 **Duncan & Davies Nurseries Ltd.** - P.O. Box 340, New Plymouth, New Zealand, 64 67-48789 (no telephone orders). Major New Zealand tree and shrub nursery. Significant young plant exporter to Europe, Asia and North America. Specializes in ornamentals, fruiting plants and New Zealand natives. CAT $10, R & W, BANK DRAFT, OVER, M.O. 1000 PLANTS WHLS, ENGL.

P1 **Eden Nurseries** - Rectory Lane, Old Bolingbroke, Spilsby, Lincs., England, U.K., 07903 582. Small nursery specializing in hardy, unusual and old fashioned fruit trees, including apples, pears, plums, damsons, cherries, quince and medlar. CAT SASE, R & W, PC, U.K. ONLY, ENGL.

P1G **Eden Seeds** - M.S. 316, Gympie 4570, Australia, 071 86-5230. Specializes in traditional, non-hybrid vegetable and herb seeds, preferably from local sources and bio-dynamically or organically grown. Also offers tree and shrub seed. CAT $1, R & W, PC, OVER, ENGL.

P5 **Ellison Horticultural Pty., Ltd.** - P.O. Box 365, Nowra, NSW 2541, Australia, 6144-214255. Bulk seed supplier of Australian natives and exotic tree, shrub and palm seed. CAT FREE, R & W, PC/OC, OVER, M.O. $25, ENGL.

P9 **Erfurter Samenzucht KG** - Weigelt & Co., Postfach 80, D-6229 Walluf 1/Rheingau, Germany, 06123 71066 or 71067. Vegetable and flower seeds. CAT FREE, R & W, OVER.

P17M **Farrar (M.L.) Pty., Ltd.** - P.O. Box 1046, Bomaderry, NSW 2541, Australia, 044 217-966. International seed merchants specializing in seed of trees and shrubs, palms, grasses and forages. CAT $5, WHLS, BANK DRAFT, OVER, M.O. $25, ENGL.

P18 **Feathers Wild Flower Seeds** - P.O. Box 13, Constantia 7848, Republic of South Africa, 021 742-432. Specializes in seed of the indigenous flora of southern Africa, mainly Proteaceae and Ericaceae. CAT FREE, R & W, PC/OC, OVER, M.O. $12, ENGL.

P28 **Florestas Rio Doce S.A.** - Reserva Florestal da CVRD, Avenida Amazonas 491, CEP 30187, Linhares, ES, Brazil, 212-4466. Seeds of tropical trees occurring at the CVRD reserve in Minas Gerais, Brazil. CAT FREE, R & W, OVER.

P38 **Fruit Spirit Botanical Gardens** - Dorroughby, NSW 2480, Australia, 066 895-192 (no telephone orders). Very large collection of useful plants, including tropical and subtropical fruit species and their cultivars, nuts, palms, medicinals and species suitable for agro-forestry. Most seed is personally collected to order. CAT $1, R & W, BANK DRAFT, OVER, M.O. $15, ENGL.

P39 **Fujita Seed Co.** - P.O. Box 211, Osaka C, Osaka 53091, Japan, 06 445-2401 (no telephone orders). Grower and exporter of vegetable seeds, flower seeds and bulbs, grass and legume seeds, and tree and shrub seeds. Publishes separate catalogs or price lists for each class. CAT FREE, WHLS, BANK DRAFT, OVER, M.O. $100, ENGL.

P49 **Geigle (Ch.) Nachf. GmbH** - Herrenberger Strasse 54, D-7270 Nagold, Germany, 07452 3041-43. Tree and shrub seeds. CAT FREE, R & W, BANK DRAFT, OVER, M.O. £6, ENGL.

P59M **Gonthier (MM. Ch.) Fils** - 5240 Wanze, Belgium. Vegetable, herb and flower seeds, fruit trees. CAT FREE, R & W, OVER.

P63 **Greenfingers Treeseeds** - Milner House, 36-38 East Prescot Rd., Liverpool L14 19W, England, U.K., 051 259-5581. Extensive listing of tree and shrub seed. CAT FREE, WHLS, BANK DRAFT, OVER, ENGL.

P67 **Gunson Seeds** - Nature Road, Zesfontein, 7409, Petit, 1512, Republic of South Africa, (011) 965-1711. Pasture, legume and fodder crop seeds. CAT FREE, WHLS, OVER, ENGL.

P68M **Häberli Nursery** - Obst-Und Beerenzentrum AG, CH-9315, Neukirch-Egnach TG, Switzerland, 071 662-454. Specializes in improved jostaberry cultivars. CAT FREE, WHLS, BANK DRAFT, EUROPE ONLY.

P69 **Hammenhögs Fro AB** - Box 111, 270 50 Hammenhög, Sweden, 0414-40475. Vegetable, herb and flower seeds. CAT FREE, R & W, OVER.

P75M **Hazera Seeds Ltd.** - P.O. Box 1565, Haifa 31015, Israel, 04-671173. Growers and breeders of vegetables and field crops. CAT FREE, WHLS, LETTER OF CREDIT, OVER, ENGL.

P83M **Heritage Seeds** - HDRA Sales Limited, Ryton-on-Dunsmore, Coventry CV8 3LG, England, U.K., 0203 303-517 (no telephone orders). Mail order branch of the Henry Doubleday Research Association. All sales go towards research into safe methods of growing. Complete organic gardening catalog offers heirloom English vegetables, oriental vegetables, herbs, green manures, garden flowers and wild flowers. CAT FREE, RET, PC/OC, OVER, ENGL.

P86 **Hillier Nurseries (Winchester) Ltd.** - Ampfield House, Ampfield, Romsey, Hants., SO51 9PA, England, U.K., 44 794-68733. Internationally renowned growers who celebrated their 125th anniversary in 1989. Offers a wide array of deciduous trees and shrubs, conifers, fruit and nut trees, climbers, roses and hardy perennials. CAT FREE, R & W, PC/CC/OC, OVER, ENGL.

P92 **Hollington Nurseries Ltd.** - Woolton Hill, Newbury, Berks. RG15 9XT, England, U.K. Specializes in herb plants and scented plants. CAT £2, R & W, PC/CC, OVER, M.O. £500 EXPORT, ENGL.

P95M **Hoog (Michael H.)** - P.O. Box 3217, NL-2001 De Haarlem, The Netherlands, 023 31-1373. Main suppliers of botanical specialties, flower bulbs and hardy perennials to botanical gardens and institutions overseas. CAT $2.50 REFUNDABLE, WHLS, PC/OC, OVER, M.O. $500, ENGL.

Q3 **Hungnong Seed Co., Ltd.** - Woojin Bldg., 1338-20, Seocho-Dong, Seocho-Ku, Seoul 137-072, Korea, 02 553-0971. Breeders and growers of vegetable seeds. CAT FREE, WHLS, OVER, ENGL.

Q11M **Ingegnoli (Fratelli) S.p.A.** - Corso Buenos Aires, 54, Milano 20124, Italy. Venerable Italian seed house established in 1817. Extensive range of vegetable, herb, flower and forage seeds. Particularly large selection of chicories. Also offers fruit trees and grape vines. CAT FREE, R & W, PC, OVER, M.O. 30.000 LIRA.

Q12 **Inland & Foreign Trading Co., Ltd.** - Block 79A, Indus Road #04-418/420, Singapore 0316, 272-2711 or 278-2193. Harvesters, processors and distributors of legume cover crop, pasture, shrub and tree seeds. CAT FREE, R & W, PC/OC, OVER, ENGL.

Q15G **Israflora** - P.O. Box 502, Kiryat-Bialik 2700, Israel, 04 737-155. Specializes in tree and shrub seed of arid and semi-arid regions in which plants are used for afforestation, conservation, grazing, windbreaks, sand dune stabilization, timber and fuel production. CAT FREE, WHLS, OVER, M.O. $150, ENGL.

Q18 **Jagriti Seeds Suppliers** - 113 Panditwari, P.O. Prem Nagar, Dehra Dun, Uttar Pradesh, India. Wide range of seeds of forest trees, ornamentals, grasses and forages, shrubs, hedges and bamboo. CAT FREE, R & W, BANK DRAFT, OVER, ENGL.

Q24 **Jelitto Staudensamen** - Postfach 560 127, D-2000, Hamburg 56, Germany, 01149 4103-15258 (telefax orders). Large selection of perennial seed, over 2,000 species available in amounts ranging from 10 grams to 1 kilogram. CAT FREE, WHLS, PC, OVER, M.O. $22, ENGL.

Q24M **Jesus Veron y Cia, S.A.** - Apartado 141, Zaragoza, Spain, 88-1007 or 88-2576. Vegetable and flower seeds, fruit and nut trees, grape vines, ornamental trees and shrubs, roses, bulbs, indoor plants and palms. CAT FREE, R & W, OVER.

Q25 **Jodi-Seeds Pty., Ltd.** - P.O. Box 288, Cleveland, QLD 4163, Australia, 07 206-6133. Collectors and distributors of seed of Australian natives, palms, flowers, exotic trees and shrubs. CAT FREE, WHLS, BANK DRAFT, LETTER OF CREDIT, OVER, M.O. $25 OVER, ENGL.

Q28 **Kaneko Seeds Co., Ltd.** - 50-12 Furuichimachi, 1-Chome, Maebashi City, Gunma-Ken 371, Japan, 0272 51-1611. Breeders and growers of vegetable and flower seeds. CAT FREE, WHLS, OVER, ENGL.

Q30 **Keepers Nursery** - 446 Wateringbury Rd., East Malling, Maidstone, Kent ME19 6JJ, England, U.K., 0622 813008. Extensive collection of temperate fruit trees and berry plants. Specializes in older and unusual cultivars. Can supply budwood overseas. CAT SASE, RET, PC, ENGL.

Q32 **Kershaw (H.G.) Pty., Ltd.** - P.O. Box 84, Terrey Hills, NSW 2084, Australia, 02 450-2444. Wholesale seed company handling both native and exotic species. Over 2,200 varieties of rare and popular banksias and eucalyptus, exotic ferns, indoor plants, climbers and protea. CAT $5, WHLS, BANK DRAFT, OVER, M.O. 10 GRAMS, ENGL.

Q34 **King's Herbs Limited** - P.O. Box 19-084, Avondale, Auckland, New Zealand. Seeds of standard and unusual herbs, cottage garden plants, gourmet and oriental vegetables, dried flowers and gourds. CAT $4.50, R & W, PC/OC, OVER, M.O. $7, ENGL.

Q38 **Knize (Karel)** - P.O. Box 10248, Lima 1, Peru. Seeds and plants of cacti and succulents. CAT FREE, R & W, PC/OC, OVER, ENGL.

Q39 **Know-You Seed Co., Ltd.** - 26, Chung Cheng 2nd Rd, Kaohsiung 80244, Taiwan, Republic of China, 07 291-9106. Breeders and growers of vegetable seeds. CAT FREE, WHLS, OVER, ENGL.

Q40 **Kohli (P.) & Co.** - Park Road, Near Neelam Theatre, Srinagar, Kashmir 190009, India, 73061. Seeds of a broad selection of trees, shrubs, climbers, perennials, alpines and bulbs from Kashmir and the western Himalayas. Can also arrange for shipment of seeds and bulbs of Indian origin. Established in 1928. CAT 5 IRC, R & W, PC, OVER, M.O. $30, ENGL.

Q41 **Köhres (Gerhard)** - Wingerstrasse 33, Bahnstrasse 101, D-6106, Erzhausen/Darmstadt, Germany, 06150 7241. Seeds of succulents, palms, cacti and mesembryanthemum. CAT FREE, R & W, PC/OC, OVER.

Q45M **Kumaon Nursery** - Ranikhet Road, Ramnagar, Nainital District, 244 715, India, 39 121. Seeds of vegetables, fruits, ornamental flowering trees and flowers. Also sells papain, pure honey and beeswax. CAT FREE, R & W, BANK DRAFT, OVER, M.O. 2500 RUPEES, ENGL.

Q46 **Kumar International** - Ajitmal 206121, Etawah, Uttar Pradesh, India. Producers, collectors and suppliers of seeds of conifers, ornamental, flowering and forest trees, palms, hedges, shrubs, herbs, bamboos, fodder and grasses, and green manures. CAT FREE, R & W, PC/CC/OC, OVER, M.O. 1 KILOGRAM, ENGL.

Q49M **Landsendt Subtropical Fruits** - 108 Parkers Road, Oratia, Auckland, New Zealand, 09 818-6914. Seeds and nursery stock of rare and commercial subtropical fruit and vegetable crops, many introduced from Andean South America. Also exotic ornamentals and timber trees. CAT NZ $1.50, R & W, PC/OC, OVER, M.O. 100 PLANTS EXPORT, ENGL.

Q52 **Leen de Mos** - P.O. Box 54, 2690 AB's, Gravenzande, The Netherlands, 01748-12031. Suppliers of flower seeds, vegetable seeds and tropical seeds and young plants. CAT FREE, WHLS, PC, OVER, M.O. 1,000 SEEDS.

Q76 **Margery Fish Plant Nursery (The)** - East Lambrook Manor, South Petharton, Somerset TA13 5HL, England, U.K., 0460 40328 (no telephone orders). Unusual cottage garden plants, herbs. CAT 50 PENCE, RET, PC, U.K. ONLY, ENGL.

Q88 **Mikado International Inc.** - 1203 Hoshikuki, Chiba City 280, Japan, 472 65-4847 (no telephone orders). Producers, breeders and suppliers of a wide range of vegetable seeds for processors, commercial growers and gardeners. Subsidiary of Mikado Seed Growers Co., Ltd. CAT FREE, R & W, PC, OVER, ENGL.

Q93 **Mountain Views Nursery** - 45 Pavilion St., Pomona, QLD 4568, Australia, 071 851-375. Large supplier of fully container grown commercial and exotic tropical fruit trees. Over 100,000 in stock. Will ship overseas on request. CAT FREE, WHLS, PC/OC, OVER, ENGL.

R0 **Namdeo Umaji & Co.** - 161-167 Dr. Ambedkar Road, Byculla, Bombay 400 027, India, 872-5674 or 872-2628. Seed growers and merchants handling vegetable and flower seeds, ornamentals, roses, and grafted fruit trees. CAT FREE, R & W, PC/OC, OVER, ENGL.

R11M **Nickerson-Zwaan b.v.** - P.O. Box 19, 2900 AA Barendrecht, The Netherlands, 01806-13277. Breeders and growers of vegetable seeds especially suitable for warm climates. CAT FREE, WHLS, OVER, ENGL.

R15M **Nindethana Seed Service** - R.M.B. 939, Woogenilup, WA 6324, Australia, 61 98-541066. Specialists in Australian native plant seeds. Approximately 2,200 species, many rare and difficult to obtain. CAT $1, R & W, PC/OC, OVER, M.O. $5, ENGL.

R22 **Nurseryman's Haven** - Kalimpong 734301, India, 03552-435. Large supplier of exotic flowering bulbs, shrubs and forest tree seedlings, vegetable and fruit seeds and plants, species and hybrid orchids, and cacti. CAT FREE, R & W, PC, OVER, ENGL.

R23 **Nutting & Sons Overseas Ltd.** - Station Road, Longstanton, Cambridge CB4 5DU, England, U.K., 0954 60332. Bulk supplier of ornamental, herb and vegetable seeds but also covers a wide range of species including trees, shrubs, cacti, unusual and exotic items. CAT FREE, WHLS, BANK DRAFT, OVER, M.O. £30, ENGL.

R28 **Old Farm Nurseries (The)** - P.O. Box 1, 2700 AA Boskoop, The Netherlands, 01727-14442. Tree, shrub, conifer and vine seeds. CAT FREE, WHLS, BANK DRAFT, OVER, ENGL.

R33M **Orriell (D.) Seed Exporters** - 45 Frape Avenue, Mt. Yokine, Perth, WA 6060, Australia, 619 344-2290. Well established Australian seed house exporting to over thirty five countries. Publishes separate lists of cold-hardy Australian eucalypts, palms and cycads, drought resistant trees and shrubs, Australian natives, exotic species for greenhouse and outdoors and bonsai. CAT $3, R & W, PC/OC, OVER, ENGL.

R41 **Parsley's Cape Seeds** - P.O. Box 1375, Somerset West, Cape 7130, Republic of South Africa, 24 51-2630. Collectors, growers and distributors of South African wild flower seed, from annuals to trees. Specialists in Proteaceae, Ericas and Pelargoniums. CAT FREE, R & W, PC/OC, OVER, ENGL.

R47 **Phoenix Seeds** - P.O. Box 9, Stanley, Tasmania 7331, Australia, 004 58-1105. Specializes in non-hybrid seed of useful plants, including vegetables, fruit trees, herbs, native food plants, green manures and cover crops. Proceeds go towards encouraging natural, organic culture. CAT FREE, RET, PC, OVER, ENGL.

R50 **Pocha Seeds Pvt., Ltd.** - Post Box No. 55, Near Sholapur Bazaar, Poona 411 040, India, 671-978 or 671-979 (no telephone orders). One of the oldest seed companies in Asia, established in 1884. General garden supplies, including seeds of vegetables, flowers, trees, grasses, hedges and forages, plants and bulbs. CAT $3, R & W, BANK DRAFT, OVER, M.O. $20, ENGL.

R52 **Potterton & Martin** - The Cottage Nursery, Moortown Road, Nettleton, Caistor, Lincs. LN7 6HX, England, U.K. Small old fashioned nursery producing most of the plants sold. Supplies alpines, dwarf shrubs and conifers, ferns, and dwarf hardy or semi-hardy bulbous plants. CAT $3, R & W, STERLING CHECKS, OVER, ENGL.

R53M **Poyntzfield Herb Nursery** - Black Isle, By Dingwall, Ross-shire, Scotland, U.K. Herb nursery specializing in over 300 varieties of popular, unusual and rare herb plants and seeds. All are grown using organic or biodynamic methods. CAT $2, RET, BANK DRAFT, OVER, M.O. £6, ENGL.

R59 **Pride of Laguna Nursery** - Km. 72, Maharlika Highway, Alaminos, Laguna 4001, Philippines. Single proprietor nursery selling exotic fruit trees and seeds. CAT FREE, R & W, BANK DRAFT, OVER, M.O. 500 SEEDS EACH SPECIES, ENGL.

R59G **Primac Seeds** - P.O. Box 943, Murwillumbah, NSW 2484, Australia, 6166 72-1866. Growers, processors and exporters of a wide range of vegetable, grain, pasture and forage seeds. Previously known as J.H. Williams & Sons Pty., Ltd. CAT FREE, WHLS, OVER, ENGL.

R59M **Primavera Grandi Vivai** - Svincolo Ponte Verdura, Km. 136 S.S. 115, 92016 Ribera (Agrigento), Italy, 09 256-1877 (telefax). Specializes in plants for Mediterranean climates, including fruit trees and ornamental trees and shrubs. CAT FREE, R & W, PC/CC/OC, OVER.

R60 **Protea Seed & Nursery Suppliers** - P.O. Box 98229, Sloane Park 2152, Republic of South Africa, 011 782-5215. Large selection of tree and shrub seed indigenous to South Africa and Australia, especially Proteaceae and Erica. CAT $1, R & W, PC/OC, OVER, M.O. R25, ENGL.

R77 **Reads Nursery** - Hales Hall, Loddon, Norfolk, WR14 6QW, England, U.K., 050846-395. Extensive collection of fruit and nut trees, grape vines, citrus, figs, conservatory plants, climbers and wall shrubs. CAT FREE, R & W, BANK DRAFT, OVER, M.O. £10, ENGL.

R77M **Realexotica** - 1C Church Street, Whitchurch, Hampshire RG28 7AD, England, U.K. Seed distributors specializing in Southern Hemisphere flora. CAT FREE, WHLS, PC, OVER, ENGL.

R78 **Renz (Martin) Nachf. GmbH & Co. KG** - Postfach 102, 7270 Nagold-Emmingen, Germany, 07452 67-277 (telefax). One of the largest European forest tree seed dealers. CAT FREE, R & W, LETTER OF CREDIT, OVER, M.O. 100 GRAMS, ENGL.

R83 **Roger (R.V.) Ltd.** - The Nurseries, Whitby Rd., Pickering, North Yorkshire, YO18 7HG, England, U.K., 0751 72226. A 75 year old plus family company growing over 2,500 varieties of hardy garden trees, fruits and nuts, herbs, shrubs, conifers, heathers, alpines and herbaceous plants. CAT 60 PENCE, R & W, PC/CC, U.K. ONLY, ENGL.

R87 **Rougham Hall Nurseries** - Ipswich Road, Rougham, Bury St. Edmunds, Suffolk IP30 9LZ, England, U.K., 0359 70577 or 70153 (no telephone orders). Specializes in hardy perennials, grasses and gooseberries. Separate catalog of gooseberry plants lists approximately 200 cultivars. CAT 65 PENCE, RET, PC/OC, OVER, ENGL.

R93 **Rust-En-Vrede Nursery** - P.O. Box 231, Constantia 7848, Republic of South Africa, 021 794-1085. Mail order business dealing in bulbs native to South Africa. Also seeds of bulbous plants. CAT FREE, RET, PC/OC, OVER, M.O. R40, ENGL.

S3M **Scholz Samen** - Postfach 13 01 73, D-4800 Bielefeld 13, Germany. Seeds of alpine plants and perennials. CAT FREE, R & W, OVER.

S7G **Seed Export** - P.O. Box 543, Guatemala City, Guatemala, 26125 or 515247. Seeds of tropical forest species, mainly pine seed for industrial reforestation projects in tropical countries. CAT FREE, R & W, LETTER OF CREDIT, OVER, ENGL.

S7M **Seedalp** - Case Postale 282, CH-1217 Meyrin/Geneva 1, Switzerland. Producer and distributor of perennial seeds of alpine plants and horticultural flowers. Succeeded Correvon Ltd. CAT $5 REDEEMABLE, R & W, PC, OVER, M.O. SF30.

S27 **Siemen Oy** - PL 73, 04301 Hyrylä, Finland, 90 257-033. Vegetable, herb and flower seeds. CAT FREE, R & W, OVER.

S29 **Silviculturist** - P.O. Box 95, Lushoto, Tanzania, 32 (no telephone orders). Government organization dealing in forest tree seeds. CAT FREE, R & W, BANK DRAFT, OVER, ENGL.

S30 **Simms (Clive) Nursery** - Woodhurst, Essendine, Stamford, Lincs., PED 4LQ, England, U.K., 0780 55615. Small nursery specializing in plants that will bear edible fruits, especially those which are less well known. CAT FREE, R & W, OVER, ENGL.

S36 **Sodhai Ram & Sons** - Vidyapith Road, Varanasi, Uttar Pradesh 221002, India, 53929. Grower and breeder of vegetable and flower seeds. CAT FREE, R & W, BANK DRAFT, OVER, ENGL.

S36M **Sojuzplodoimport** - 32/34 Smolenskaja Sq., Moscow G-200, U.S.S.R., 244-2258. Tree and shrub seed. Previously known as Export Khleb. CAT FREE, R & W, OVER, ENGL.

S43M **Southern Seeds** - The Vicarage, Sheffield, Canterbury, New Zealand, 0516 38-814 (no telephone orders). Alpine seeds of New Zealand, especially from the Southern Alps. Some species of trees and shrubs are also available. Seeds are collected from the wild. CAT $2, RET, PC/OC, OVER, M.O. $25, ENGL.

S44 **Southwest Seeds** - 200 Spring Road, Kempston, Bedford, MK42 8ND, England, U.K., 0234 58970. Specializes in cactus, succulent, dessert and carnivorous plant seeds, mostly collected in their native habitat. CAT FREE, RET, PC/OC, OVER, ENGL.

S45M **Specialty Seeds** - 24 Jolimont Terrace, Jolimont, VIC 3002, Australia, (03) 65 03448. Vegetables, herbs, British wild flowers, garden flowers. Principal Australian agent for Suttons Seeds. CAT A$4, R & W, PC, OVER, ENGL.

S54M **Suanchareon Nursery L.P.** - 8/6 Krungkasem Rd., Bangkok 10200, Thailand, 02 280-3521. Tropical fruit trees, palm seeds, ornamental plants. CAT FREE, R & W, BANK DRAFT, OVER, ENGL.

S55 **Suffolk Herbs** - Sawyers Farm, Little Cornard, Sudbury, Suffolk CO10 0NY, England, U.K., 0787 227-247 (no telephone orders). Large range of herbs from all over the world, native British wild flowers, unusual, heirloom and oriental vegetables. CAT FREE, R & W, PC/CC, OVER, ENGL.

S59 **Sunraysia Nurseries** - P.O. Box 45, Gol Gol, NSW 2738, Australia, 050 248-502. Australia's largest producer of grape vines, over 80 cultivars. Also specializes in citrus, avocado, olives and other subtropicals. CAT A $5, R & W, CC, OVER, M.O. A $25, ENGL.

S59M **Sutton & Sons (India) Pvt. Ltd.** - P.O. Box 9207, Calcutta 700 071, India, 91 3329-0472 (no telephone orders). Producers and sellers of flower and vegetable seeds. CAT FREE, R & W, BANK DRAFT, OVER, M.O. $10, ENGL.

S61 **Suttons Seeds, Ltd.** - Hele Rd., Torquay,, Devon TQ2 7QJ, England, U.K., 0803 62011. Well known British company founded in 1806. Large selection of vegetables, flowers, herbs and wild flowers. CAT FREE, R & W, BANK DRAFT, OVER (WHLS ONLY), M.O. £5, ENGL.

S63M **Takii & Co., Ltd.** - P.O. Box 7, Kyoto Central 600-91, Japan, 075 365-0123. Breeders and growers of vegetable seed. CAT FREE, WHLS, OVER, ENGL.

S65M **Tasmania Forest Seeds** - Summerleas Farm, Kingston, Tasmania 7050, Australia, 002 29-6387. Specializes in tree and shrub seed of Tasmania. CAT FREE, R & W, BANK DRAFT, OVER, M.O. $5, ENGL.

S69 **Thuya Alpine Nursery** - Glebelands, Hartpury, Glos. GL19 3BW, England, U.K., 548 (no telephone orders). Unusual alpine plants, shrubs and trees. CAT 4 IRC, RET, PC, OVER (SEEDS ONLY), M.O. £4, ENGL.

S70 **Tokita Seed Co., Ltd.** - Nakagawa, Omiya-shi, Saitama-ken 330, Japan, 048 683-3434. Breeders and growers of vegetable seed. CAT FREE, WHLS, OVER, ENGL.

S75M **Tozer (A.L.) Ltd.** - Pyports, Cobham,, Surrey KT11 3EH, England, U.K., 0932 62059 (no telephone orders). Vegetable seed breeders and growers. CAT FREE, WHLS, STERLING CHECK, OVER, ENGL.

S81M **Tweedie (J.) Fruit Trees** - 504 Denby Dale Road West, Calder Grove, Wakefield WF4 3DB, Yorks, England, U.K., 0924 274-630. Fruit tree nursery specializing in a wide range of fruit trees and berry plants, both old and new. CAT SASE, R & W, PC, U.K. ONLY, ENGL.

S91M **Vardi's Nurseries Ltd.** - Mishmar Hashivah 50 297, Israel, 960-4254 or 960-4230. Seeds of unusual vegetables and fruit trees, ornamental plants. CAT FREE, R & W, OVER, ENGL.

S92 **Vaughan's Wildflower Seeds** - P.M.B. 2, Gingin, WA 6503, Australia, 619 575-7551. Seeds of Australian native trees, palms, climbing and indoor plants. CAT FREE, R & W, PC, OVER, ENGL.

S93M **Verma Seed Co., Pvt., Ltd.** - 53 Kasgaran, P.B. No. 67, Bareilly 243 001, Uttar Pradesh, India, 0091 0581-74650. Growers and sellers of vegetable, flower, fruit, grass, forestry, hedge and tree seeds. CAT FREE, R & W, LETTER OF CREDIT, OVER, ENGL.

S95 **Versepuy** - B.P. 10, Le Ridereau-Andard, 49800 Trelaze, France, 41 549-678. Tree, shrub and vine seed. CAT FREE, R & W, OVER, M.O. FF500, ENGL.

S95M **Vilmorin-Andrieux Ets.** - Poste 399, La Menitre', 49520 Beaufort-En-Vallee, France, 41 475-221. Famous French seed house established in 1742. Wide range of seeds of vegetables, herbs, flowers, trees and shrubs, indoor plants and vines. CAT FREE, R & W, OVER.

S97M **Vivero Yautepec** - Apartado Postal 447, Cuernavaca, Mor., Mexico, 91 739-40357. Large selection of tropical and subtropical fruit trees. CAT FREE, R & W, OVER.

T1M **Watkins Seeds Ltd.** - P.O. Box 468, New Plymouth, New Zealand, 067 86-800 (no telephone orders). Vegetable, herb and flower seeds supplied commercially to market growers and nurserymen. Retail packets seeds via mail order and garden centers. CAT NZ $2, R & W, PC/CC/OC, OVER, M.O. NZ $15, ENGL.

T7 **Western Australian Wildflower Society, Inc.** - P.O. Box 64, Nedlands, WA, Australia 6009. Seeds of Western Australian wild flowers. Some collected by voluntary workers. Most purchased through commercial seed suppliers. CAT $.50, RET, PC/OC, OVER, ENGL.

T25M **Young (Roy)** - 23 Westland Chase, West Winch, King's Lynn, Norfolk PE33 0QH, England, U.K., 011 0553-840867 (no telephone orders). Large selection of seeds of cactus and succulent plants from all over the world, approximately 2,000 different types. CAT 2 IRC, R & W, BANK DRAFT, OVER, M.O. £5 OVER, ENGL.

T27M **Zeraim Seed Growers Co., Ltd.** - P.O. Box 103, Gedera 70 700, Israel, 08 591356 or 592760. Seed growers company of the Israel Farmers Federation offering vegetable and field crop cultivars. CAT FREE, R & W, LETTER OF CREDIT, OVER, ENGL.

DOMESTIC NON-COMMERCIAL

T34 **American Type Culture Collection** - 12301 Parklawn Drive, Rockville, MD 20852. Non-profit service institution that has what is believed to be the largest single collection of diverse biological cultures anywhere in the world. The collection includes bacteria, fungi, yeasts and algae. Distribution of cultures is restricted to individuals and organizations with appropriate credentials and laboratory facilities for handling microorganisms and genetic material.

T41M **Arnold Arboretum** - 125 Arborway, Jamaica Plain, MA 02130-2795. Propagating material is available to research scientists, educators, nursery people and specialty-plant collectors. There is a fee to offset costs of providing assistance. Will not supply propagating materials for plants that are available commercially in North America.

T49M **California Rare Fruit Growers** - The Fullerton Arboretum, California State University, Fullerton, CA 92634. Organization dedicated to the introduction and distribution of new fruits, and of superior cultivars of the more established fruits, primarily for home utilization as grown under California conditions. Services include a periodical seed exchange and an annual scion exchange.

T54 **College of Tropical Agriculture** - Kauai Branch Station, University of Hawaii, 7370-A Kuamoo Road, Kapaa, Kauai, HI 96746. Provides limited quantities of propagating material to researchers and other governmental institutions.

T61M **Department of Botany** - Miami University, Oxford, OH 45056.

T63T **Department of Horticulture** - Louisiana State University, 137 Julian C. Miller Hall, Baton Rouge, LA 70803. Attention: William Blackmon.

T65 **Department of Vegetable Crops** - University of California, Davis, CA 95616.

T67M **Division of Agriculture** - ODRD, Kolonia, Ponape State, Trust Territory of the Pacific, Eastern Caroline Islands 96941.

T70 **Edison Winter Home and Botanical Gardens** - 2350 McGregor Boulevard, Fort Myers, FL 33901. Government agency which provides seeds to serious collectors when time and resources permit, as no money has been set aside for this work.

T71 **Fairchild Tropical Garden** - 10901 Old Cutler Road, Miami, FL 33156. Plant material is available to other botanical gardens, universities, members and on a very limited basis, to commercial growers. Only small, representative samples are supplied which are collected by volunteers.

T72M **Florida Department of Agriculture, Division of Forestry** - Miami Coconut Seed Orchard, 13607 Old Cutler Rd., Miami, FL 33158. Provides propagating material free of charge to other scientific institutions.

T73M **Fruit and Spice Park** - 24801 S.W. 187th Ave., Homestead, FL 33031. Unique collection of fruits, spices, nuts and economic plants from around the world. More than 500 varieties on 20 acres, plus a one acre demonstration herb and vegetable garden. Limited quantities of seed and scion wood are available to researchers and collectors.

T76 **Grain Exchange (The)** - 2440 East Water Well Road, Salina, KS 67401. Network of gardeners and farmers working toward preservation of genetic diversity in cereal and other staple seed and related crops. Seeds are offered to members only.

T87 **International Ribes Association** - P.O. Box 130, Booneville, CA 95415-0130. Newly formed society dedicated to the worldwide promotion of currants and gooseberries. Provides propagating material to members on a first come, first served basis.

T87M **Interregional Potato Introduction Station** - USDA-ARS, University of Wisconsin, Peninsula Experiment Station, Sturgeon Bay, WI 54235.

U1 **Mayaguez Tropical Agriculture Research Station** - P.O. Box 70, Mayaguez, PR 00709.

U4 **Montréal Botanical Garden** - Montréal, Canada. Exchanges seeds with other botanical gardens and arboreta only.

U7M **National Clonal Germplasm Repository** - 33447 Peoria Rd., Corvallis, OR 97333. Government agency that distributes limited quantities of plant material for research purposes to national and international scientists free of charge. Reasonable requests from the general public are also honored.

U8 **National Clonal Germplasm Repository** - Department of Pomology, University of California, Davis, CA 95616. Clonal crop germplasm of Vitis, Prunus, Juglans, Pistacia, Olea and Ficus is available to researchers in limited quantities on request.

U13 **North American Fruit Explorers** - R.R. 1, Box 94, Chapin, IL 62628. A network of amateur and professional fruit aficionados devoted to the discovery, cultivation, and appreciation of superior cultivars of fruits and nuts. Seeds and scionwood are available through an exchange page in the quarterly journal.

U14 **North Central Plant Introduction Station** - Iowa State University, Ames, IA 50010.

U15M **Northern Regional Research Center** - 1815 North University St., Peoria, IL 61604. Maintains a large collection of bacteria, yeasts and molds. Cultures are available upon request to researchers and to members of the general public who have laboratory facilities.

U26 **Quail Botanical Gardens** - P.O. Box 5, Encinitas, CA 92024. Government institution that honors all reasonable requests from the general public.

U27T **Rare Fruit Council International** - P.O. Box 561914, Miami, FL 33256. The original society dedicated to the introduction and promotion of tropical fruit. Access is provided by seed and plant exchange programs.

U29M **Rodale Research Center** - P.O. Box 323, Kutztown, PA 19530.

U30M **Saanichton Plant Quarantine Station** - 8801 East Saanich Road, Sidney, BC V8L 1H3, Canada. Distributes limited quantities of virus-tested propagating material of deciduous fruit tree cultivars.

U33 **Seed Savers Exchange** - P.O. Box 70, Decorah, IA 52101. Grassroots genetic preservation project focused on heirloom and endangered vegetables. Seeds are traded between members and non-members.

U34 **Solanaceae Enthusiasts** - 3370 Princeton Court, Santa Clara, CA 95051. Non-profit educational society that provides a forum for practical horticulturists dedicated to developing new and interesting Solanaceae for food crops. Provides seed of rare plants to members at cost.

U37M **Southern Regional Plant Introduction Station** - USDA-ARS, University of Georgia, Experiment, GA 30312.

U41 **Subtropical Horticultural Research Unit** - United States Department of Agriculture, 13601 Old Cutler Road, Miami, FL 33158.

U53M **University of Guelph Arboretum** - Guelph, Canada. Operates on an exchange basis with cooperating institutions and serious collectors.

U53T **University of Kentucky** - College of Agriculture, Department of Agronomy, Lexington, KY 40546. Attention: Michael Collins.

U56 **USDA Northern Soybean Germplasm Collection** - University of Illinois, 1102 South Goodwin Avenue, Urbana, IL 61801. Government institution that honors all reasonable requests for seeds for research purposes.

U63 **Western Regional Plant Introduction Station** - 59 Johnson Hall, Washington State University, Pullman, WA 99164-6402. Government agency that distributes limited quantities of plant material for research purposes to national and international scientists free of charge. Reasonable requests from the general public are also honored.

OVERSEAS NON-COMMERCIAL

U71M **Agricultural Research Organization** - The Volcani Center, Bet Dagan, Israel. Government institution that publishes a list of introductions each year and an exchange of seeds takes place with other research organizations world wide.

U76 **All India Coordinated Project on Rape and Mustard** - Haryana Agricultural University, Hissar 125004, Haryana, India.

U80 **Arab Center for the Studies of Arid Zones and Dry Lands** - P.O. Box 2440, Damascus, Syria.

U85 **Arboretum Waasland** - Kriekelaarstraat 29, B-2770 Nieuwkerken-Waas, Belgium. Publishes an Index Seminum primarily for exchanging seeds with other institutions, secondly for selling to members at cost.

U87 **Aritaki Arboretum** - 2566, Koshigaya, Koshigaya-shi, Saitama-ken 343, Japan.

U93M **Bancos de Germoplasma** - Instituto Columbiano Agropecuaria, A.A. 151123 El Dorado, Bogota, Columbia.

U94M **Baringo Fuel and Fodder Project** - Nakuru, Kenya. Government development project concerned with planting trees that produce a fodder crop for livestock, and can successfully grow in semi-arid areas. Seeds are available for exchange with other institutions only.

V19 **Botanical Garden** - Tôhoku University, Kawauchi, Sendai 980, Japan.

V34 **Botanical Garden** - Latvian Academy of Sciences, Salaspils -1, 229021 Latvia, U.S.S.R. Government institution that honors all reasonable requests from the general public.

V45M **Botanical Garden of the Kirghiz Academy of Sciences** - 50-letia Oktiabria Street, 1a, 720676, G.S.P., Frunze 64, U.S.S.R.

V50 **Botanical Garden of the University** - Illés utca 25, H-1083 Budapest, Hungary. Exchanges seeds with other institutions, serious collectors and commercial interests. Requests that the general public make inquiries through their local institution.

V52 **Botanical Gardens** - University of Oulu, SF-90570, Oulu, Finland. Government institution that honors all reasonable requests from the general public, which it suggests be made through local institutions.

V73 **Botanischer Garten der Karl-Marx Universität** - Linnéstrasse 1, 7010, Leipzig, Germany.

V73M **Botanischer Garten der Martin Luther Universität** - AM Kirchtor 3,, 4020 Halle, Germany.

V83M **Botanischer Garten der Universität** - Am Fasanengarten 2, D-7500 Karlsruhe 1, Germany.

V84 **Botanischer Garten der Universität Bonn** - Meckenheimer Allee 171, D-5300, Bonn 1, Germany. Honors all reasonable requests from the general public.

V84M **Botanischer Garten der Universität Erlangen** - Loschgerstrasse 3, D-8520 Erlangen, Germany.

V85 **Botanischer Garten der Universität Graz** - Holteigasse 6, A-8010 Graz, Österreich, Austria.

V87 **Botanischer Garten und Rhododendron Park** - Bremen, Germany. Encourages an exchange of seeds between other institutions and collectors. Does not want requests from the general public.

V89 **Botanisk Have** - Park-og, Kirkegårdsforvaltningen, Toldbodgade 5, DK 8000, Århus-C, Denmark.

V99 **Cathedra Botanicae Academiae** - Agriculturae Lituanae, 234324 Kaunas, Lithuania, U.S.S.R. Government institution that honors all reasonable requests from the general public.

W3M **Central Republic Botanical Garden** - Ukranian Academy of Sciences, Timiryazevskaya St. 1, 252014 Kiev, Ukraine, U.S.S.R. Government institution that honors all reasonable requests from the general public.

W5 **Central Siberian Botanical Garden** - Zaeltsovsky District, 630090 Novosibirsk, U.S.S.R.

W11 **Centro de Pesquisa Agropecuario do Tropico Umido** - EMBRAPA, C.P. 48, 66.000 Belem, Para, Brazil.

W12 **Centro Experimental Palmira** - Instituto Columbiana Agropecuario, A.A. 233, Palmira Valle, Columbia.

W16 **Centro Nacional de Recursos Geneticos** - EMBRAPA, C.P. 10.2372, 70.770 Brasilia D.F., Brazil.

W20 **Chelsea Physic Garden** - 66 Royal Hospital Road, London SW3 4HS, England, U.K. Private institution that will honor reasonable requests from the general public where possible.

W22 **Chollipo Arboretum** - 344-16, Yonhui-dong, Sodaemun-ku, Seoul 120-113, South Korea. Non-profit, private arboretum exchanging seeds with 120 institutions and individuals worldwide.

W28M **College of Horticulture** - Kerala Agricultural University, Trichur-680 654, Kerala, India.

W34 **Czechoslovak Academy of Sciences** - Institute of Botany, Department of Hydrobotany, Dukelská 145, CS-379 82 Trebon, Czechoslovakia.

W35 **Czechoslovak Academy of Sciences** - Institute of Botany, CS-252 43, Pruhonice, Czechoslovakia.

W35M **Darwin Botanic Garden** - P.O. Box 84, Darwin, NT 5794, Australia. Generally deals only with similar scientific institutions.

W36M **Departamento de Botánica Agrícola** - I.N.T.A., 1712 Castelar, Argentina.

W54 **Department of Plant Science** - Faculty of Natural Resources, Prince of Songkla University, Haadyai, Songkla, Thailand.

W59M **Dipartimento di Scienze Botaniche** - Università degli Studi, Via Archirafi, 38, 90133 Palermo, Sicily, Italy. Honors inquiries from the general public, who should make requests through their local institution.

W63M **Division of Horticultural Research** - CSIRO, Private Bag, Merbein, Victoria 3505, Australia.

W77M **Estacion Experimental** - Instituto Boliviano de Tecnologia Agropecuaria, Casilla 5783, La Paz, Bolivia.

W78M **Estacion Experimental "San Roque"** - CRIA-III, INIPA, Apartado 307, Iquitos, Peru.

W83M **Estacion Experimental "Santa Catalina"** - INIAP, C.P. 340, Quito, Ecuador.

W90 **Faculty of Agriculture** - University of Peradeniya, Peradeniya, Sri Lanka.

W92 **Faculté Mixte de Médicine et de Pharmacie** - Jardin Botanique, 16, boulevard Daviers, 49100 Angers, France.

W98M **Fruit Research Station** - Kandaghat H.P. 173 215, India.

X8 **Gradina Agrobotanica** - Institutu Agronomic "Dr. Petru Groza", Cluj, Romania. Does not honor requests from the general public, only those from research institutions and those storing germplasm.

X10 **Gradina Botanica a Universitatu "Al. I. Cuza"** - Str. Dumbrava Rosie nr. 7-9, 6600 Iasi, Romania.

X14 **Highlands Agricultural Research St.** - Department of Primary Industry, Aiyura, P.O. Box 384, Kainantu, Papua New Guinea. Government institution mandated to carry out sustainable agriculture research. Has a very limited collection of traditional vegetables for exchange.

X30 **Hortus Botanicus Johannesburgensis** - Emmarentia, South Africa. Will exchange material on a reciprocal basis only with bona fide botanical gardens.

X33 **Hortus Botanicus Principalis** - Academiae Scientiarium, Moscow, 127276, U.S.S.R.

X35M **Hortus Botanicus Universitatis Varsoviensis** - Al. Ujazdowskie 4, 00-478 Warsaw, Poland.

X36 **Hortus Botanicus Universitatis Wratislaviensis** - Wroclaw, Poland. Accepts requests from other institutions, serious collectors and commercial interests only.

X38 **Hortus Botanicus Vrije Universiteit** - Van der Boechorststraat 8, 1081 BT, Amsterdam, The Netherlands. Encourages the general public to make requests through their local institution.

X39 **Hortus Centralis** - Cultura Herbarum Medikarum, Facultas Medica, Universitas Purkyniana, Komenskeho nam. 2, CS-662 43 Brno, Czechoslovakia.

X44 **Imeloko Agroforestry Project** - B.P. 1377, Bangui, Central African Republic. Project of the Hope International Development Agency working to promote agroforestry as an alternative to "slash and burn" farming in Africa, and around the world. Honors all requests from the general public.

X47 **Institut Botanic de Barcelona** - Avenida de la Muntanyans s.n., Parc de Montjuïc, Barcelona, 08004, Catalunya, Spain.

X62 **Institute of Plant Breeding** - National Plant Genetic Resources Laboratory, University of the Philippines at Los Baños, 4031 College, Laguna, Philippines. Encourages the general public to make requests through their local institution.

X63 **Institute of Plant Introduction and Genetic Resources** - "K. Malkov", 4122 Sadovo District, Plovdiv, Bulgaria.

X77M **Instituto Nacional de Investigaciones Agrarias** - Jose Abascal 56, Madrid, Spain.

X79 **Instituto Nacional de Pesquisas da Amazonia** - C.P. 478, 69.000 Manaus, Amazonas, Brazil.

X79M **Instytut Hodowli i Aklimatyzacji Roslin** - Ogrod Botaniczny, ul. Jezdziecka 5, 85-687 Bydgoszcz, Poland. Generally exchanges seeds only with other botanical gardens. Suggests that the public make requests through their local institution.

X82 **International Institute of Tropical Agriculture** - P.M.B. 5320, Ibadan, Nigeria.

X88M **Jardim Botanico do Rio de Janeiro** - Rio de Janeiro, Brasil,. Seeds are offered for exchange with other scientific institutions only.

X89 **Jardim e Museu Agrícola Tropical** - Calcada do Galvao, 1400 Lisbon, Portugal.

X94 **Jardin Botanico de Universidad de San Carlos** - Centro de Estudios Conservacionistas, Avenida de La Reforma 0-63, Zona 10, Guatemala.

X98 **Jardin Botanico "Jorge Victor Eller T."** - Universidad Autonoma de Guadalajara, Av. Patria 1201, Guadalajara, Jalisco, C.P. 44110, Mexico. Generally maintains an exchange of seeds with other educational and scientific institutions only.

Y2 **Jardin Botanico Nacional de Cuba** - Ciudad de la Habana, Cuba. Offers a free exchange of seeds to other botanical gardens and scientific institutions. Cannot accept requests from the general public.

Y5M **Jardin Botanique Cantonal** - 14 bis, Avenue de Cour, CH-1007 Lausanne, Switzerland.

Y10 **Jardin Botanique de l'Université de Liège** - Sart-Tilman, B-4000, Liège, Belgium. Furnishing of seeds and spores is gratuitous as a rule, on an exchange basis.

Y14M **Jardin Botanique de la Ville et de l'Université** - Besançon, France. Will exchange seeds with other institutions and serious collectors. Does not accept requests from the general public.

Y17M **Jardin Botanique National de Belgique** - Domaine de Bouchout, B-1860 Meise, Belgium. Honors all requests from other institutions and collectors on an exchange basis.

Y18 **Jardin Botaniques de la Ville de Nice** - 20, traverse des Arboras, F-06200 Nice, France. Encourages reciprocal exchanges between other institutions and collectors. Cannot accept requests from the general public.

Y27M **Kanagawa Prefectural** - Ofuna Botanical Garden, 1018, Okamota, Kamakura-shi, Kanagawa-ken, 247, Japan.

Y29 **Kaunas Botanical Garden** - Botanical Institute of the Lithuanian Academy of Sciences, Botanikos 4, Kaunas 233019, Lithuania, U.S.S.R. Encourages the general public to make requests through their local institution.

Y29M **King's Park & Botanic Garden** - West Perth, W. A., 6005, Australia. Surplus seed is distributed free to botanical gardens which issue seed exchange lists and to scientific institutions which require seed for research purposes. Private collectors and the general public should apply through their local official institutions.

Y42 **Lowlands Agricultural Experiment Station** - Department of Primary Industry, P.O. Box Keravat, Rabaul, Papua New Guinea.

Y43M **Lystigardur Akureyrar** - Public Park and Botanic Garden, Akureyri, Iceland. Honors requests from other institutions, collectors and commercial interests only.

Y49G **Manie Van Der Schijff Botanical Garden** - Department of Botany, University of Pretoria, Pretoria 0002, Republic of South Africa.

Y75 **N.I. Vavilov All-Union Institute of Plant Industry** - 44, Herzen Street, 190000 Leningrad, U.S.S.R. Honors all requests from collectors, institutions and commercial interests on the basis of equivalent exchange. Encourages the general public to make inquiries through their local institution.

Y76 **Nanjing Botanical Garden** - Nanjing, Jiangsu, People's Republic of China.

Y78 **National Botanic Garden** - Harare, Zimbabwe. Exchanges seeds with other institutions, collectors and commercial interests only.

Y81 **National Bureau of Plant Genetic Resources** - Indian Agricultural Research Institute, New Delhi, India 110012.

Y83 **National Fruit Trials** - Brogdale Experimental Horticulture Station, Faversham, Kent ME13 8XZ, England, U.K. Will provide reasonable quantities of material for breeders and other research and official collections overseas free of charge. Cannot normally supply private individuals due to the cost and difficulties over plant health regulations.

Y83M **National Horticultural Research Institute** - Idi-Ishin, PMB 5432, Ibadan, Nigeria.

Y89M **Nikita Botanical Gardens** - Yalta, Crimea 334267, Ukraine, U.S.S.R.

Y99 **Orto Botanico della Universita Pisa** - Via Luca Ghini, 5, 5-56100 Pisa, Italy.

Z3M **Parks and Recreation Division** - Blenheim, New Zealand. Will exchange seeds with other institutions and collectors. Cannot accept requests from commercial interests or the general public.

Z5 **Philippine Root Crop Research and Training Center** - Visayas State College of Agriculture, Baybay, Leyte 7127-A, Philippines.

Z7M **Plant Genetic Resources Laboratory** - Agricultural Research Council, P.O. Box 1031, Islamabad, Pakistan.

Z11M **Plantentuin der Rijksuniversiteit Gent** - Gent, Belgium. Would like to encourage exchanges between serious collectors, other institutions, and commercial interests but does not want requests from the general public.

Z12 **Plew Horticultural Experiment Station** - Chantaburi Province, Thailand.

Z15M **Programa de Investigacion en Cultivos Andinos** - Universidad Nacional de San Cristobal de Huamanga, Ayacucho, Peru.

Z19 **Real Jardín Botánico** - Plaza de Murillo, 2, 28014 Madrid, Spain. Government institution that honors all reasonable requests from the general public.

Z23M **Research Center for Agrobotany** - Institute for Plant Production and Qualification, H-2766 Tápiószele, Hungary. Government gene bank that provides material free of charge on an exchange basis. Suggests that the general public inquire through their local institution.

Z24 **Research Institute of Ecology and Botany** - Hungarian Academy of Sciences Botanical Garden, H-2163 Vácrátót, Hungary. Accepts requests from other institutions and collectors only.

Z25M **Royal Botanic Garden** - Edinburgh, Scotland EH3 5LR, U.K. Honors requests for plant material from its Catalog of Plants to institutions and private individuals with whom they have established plant exchange relationships. Plant material is not available to the general public, nor is material available on a sales basis.

Z37 **Seccion de Alimentos** - Universidad del Valle, Apartado Aereo 25360, Cali, Columbia.

Z53 **Station d'Amelioration des Plantes Maraicheres** - INRA, Domaine Saint-Maurice, 84140 Montfavet-Avignon, France.

Z54 **Station de Botanique et de Pathologie Vegetale** - INRA, Villa Thuret - 62 Bd du Cap, B.P. 2078, 06606, Antibes, France.

Z57 **Stavropol Botanical Garden** - Lenin Street 478, 355027 Stavropol, U.S.S.R.

Z63 **Taiwan Forestry Research Institute** - 53 Nan-Hai Rd., Taipei, Taiwan, Republic of China. Honors all reasonable requests from the general public, who should make inquiries through their local institutions.

Z67M **Technische Universität Dresden** - Wissenschaftsbereich Biologieder Sektion Forstwirtschaft, Plennerstrasse 7, 8223 Tharandt, Germany. Encourages the general public to make requests through their local institution.

Z69M **Tree Seed Program** - Ministry of Energy & Regional Development, P.O. Box 21552, Nairobi, Kenya.

Z72 **Unidad de Recursos Geneticos** - Centro Agronomico Tropical de Investigacion y Ensenanza, P.O. Box 15, Turrialba, Costa Rica.

Z77M **Universidade Eduardo Mondlane** - Departamento de Botânica, Maputo C.P. 257, Mozambique.

Z84 **University of Dublin** - Trinity College Botanic Garden, Dublin, Republic of Ireland. Does not have the resources to supply seed to the general public, however reasonable requests by interested individuals are always met, if possible.

Z88 **University of Uppsala Botanic Garden** - Uppsala, Sweden. Accepts requests on an exchange basis with other institutions, collectors and commercial interests only.

Z91M **Vegetable and Ornamental Crops Research Station** - Ano, Mie 514-23, Japan.

Z98 **Zentralinstitut für Genetik und Kulturpflanzenforschung** - Corrensstrasse 3, 4325 Gatersleben, Germany. Gene bank that preserves germplasm of cultivated plants (land races, obsolete and more recent cultivars) and their wild relatives. Small seed samples are available free of charge to scientific institutions and breeders and on a limited scale to interested private persons.

BIBLIOGRAPHY

Abrams, Leroy, and R.S. Ferris. Illustrated Flora of the Pacific States. 1923-60. Stanford University Press. Stanford, California. Four volumes.

Akamine, Ernest K., et al. Passion Fruit Culture in Hawaii. 1954. University of Hawaii, Agricultural Experiment Station. Circular 345. Honolulu. Reprint, 1979.

Alcorn, Janis B. Huastec Mayan Ethnobotany. 1984. University of Texas Press. Austin.

Alderman, DeForest C. Native Edible Fruits, Nuts, Vegetables, Herbs, Spices, and Grasses of California. II. Small or Bush Fruits. 1975. University of California, Cooperative Extension. Leaflet 2278. Berkeley.

Alderman, DeForest C. Native Edible Fruits, Nuts, Vegetables, Herbs, Spices, and Grasses of California. IV. Herbs, Spices, and Grasses. 1976. University of California, Cooperative Extension. Leaflet 2895. Berkeley.

Aldunate, C., J. Armesto, V. Castro, and C. Villagrán. Ethnobotany of Pre-Altiplanic Community in the Andes of Northern Chile. 1983. *Economic Botany* 37 (1): 120-135.

Almeyda, Narciso, and Franklin W. Martin. Cultivation of Neglected Tropical Fruits With Promise: Part 1. The Mangosteen. 1976a. United States Department of Agriculture. New Orleans.

Almeyda, Narciso, and Franklin W. Martin. Cultivation of Neglected Tropical Fruits With Promise: Part 2. The Mamey Sapote. 1976b. United States Department of Agriculture. New Orleans.

Almeyda, Narciso, and Franklin W. Martin. Cultivation of Neglected Tropical Fruits With Promise: Part 4. The Lanson. 1977. United States Department of Agriculture. New Orleans.

Almeyda, Narciso, Simón E. Malo, and Franklin W. Martin. Cultivation of Neglected Tropical Fruits With Promise: Part 6. The Rambutan. 1979. United States Department of Agriculture. New Orleans.

Almeyda, Narciso, and Franklin W. Martin. Cultivation of Neglected Tropical Fruits With Promise: Part 8. The Pejibaya. 1980. United States Department of Agriculture. New Orleans.

Altschul, Siri von Reis. Drugs and Foods from Little-Known Plants. 1973. Harvard University Press. Cambridge, Massachusetts.

Andersen, E.T., and T.S. Weir. Prunus Hybrids, Selections and Cultivars, at the University of Minnesota Fruit Breeding Farm. 1967. Univ. of Minn. Agr. Exp. Sta. Tech. Bull. 252.

Anderson, Edgar. Pinole. 1945. *The Herbarist* 11. 33-39.

Anderson, Jean. The Food of Portugal. 1986. William Morrow and Co. New York.

Andrews, Jean. Peppers: The Domesticated Capsicums. 1984. University of Texas Press. Austin.

Angier, Bradford. Feasting Free on Wild Edibles. 1972. Stackpole Books. Harrisburg, Pennsylvania.

Anonymous. The Wealth of India. 1950. Council of Scientific and Industrial Research. New Delhi.

Anonymous. Tamu - TexSel. 1972. Texas Agricultural Experimental Station. No. L-1084. College Station.

Anonymous. Wild Mushroom Cookery. 1986. Oregon Mycological Society. Portland.

Anonymous. The Cookbook of North American Truffles. 1987. North American Truffling Society. Corvallis, Oregon.

Anonymous. Tamcot GCNH: A Glandless, Multi-Adversity Resistant Cotton Variety. 1988. Texas Agricultural Experimental Station. No. L-2266. College Station.

Arasaki, Seibin, and Teruko Arasaki. Vegetables from the Sea. 1983. Japan Publications. Tokyo.

Arora, R.K. Job's Tears (Coix lacryma-jobi) - a Minor Food and Fodder Crop of Northeastern India. 1977. *Economic Botany* 31 (3): 358-366.

Atal, C.K., and B.M. Kapur, eds. Cultivation and Utilization of Aromatic Plants. 1982. Regional Research Laboratory. Jammu-Tawi, India.

Badillo, Victor M. Monographia de la Familia Caricaceae. 1971. Universidad Central de Venezuela. Maracay.

Bailey, Clinton, and Avinoam Danin. Bedouin Plant Utilization in Sinai and the Negev. 1981. *Economic Botany* 35 (2): 145-162.

Bailey, L.H. Recent Chinese Vegetables. 1894. Cornell Univ. Agr. Exp. St. Bull. 67. Ithaca.

Bailey, L.H. The Standard Cyclopedia of Horticulture. Revised edition, 1947. Macmillan Co. New York. Three volumes.

Bairacli-Levy de, Juliette. Herbs for the Dairy. 1975. *Organic Gardening* 22 (8): 66-68.

Balick, Michael J., and Stanley N. Gershoff. Nutritional Evaluation of the Jessenia bataua Palm: Source of High Quality Protein and Oil from Tropical America. 1981. *Economic Botany* 35 (3): 261-271.

Beach, S.A. The Apples of New York. 1905. New York Agricultural Experiment Station. Albany. Two volumes.

Beadle, George W. The Ancestry of Corn. 1980. *Scientific American* 242 (1): 112-119.

Bean, W.J., et al. Trees and Shrubs Hardy in the British Isles. Eighth edition, 1970-80. John Murray. London. Four volumes.

Beasley, Sonia. The Spirulina Cookbook. 1981. University of the Trees Press. Boulder Creek, California.

Bedigian, Dorothea, and Jack R. Harlan. Nuba Agriculture and Ethnobotany, with Particular Reference to Sesame and Sorghum. 1983. *Economic Botany* 37 (4): 384-395.

Bennett, F.D., and C. Nozzolillo. How Many Seeds in a Seeded Breadfruit, Artocarpus altilis (Moraceae) ?. 1987. *Economic Botany* 41 (3): 370-374.

Betts, E.M. Thomas Jefferson's Garden Book. 1944. American Philosophical Society. Philadelphia.

Beutel, Mary. Kiwifruit Cook Book. 1982. Kiwi Growers of California. Carmichael, California.

Bhandari, M. M. Famine Foods in the Rajasthan Desert. 1974. *Economic Botany* 28 (1): 73-81.

Bhargava, N. Ethnobotanical Studies of the Tribes of Andaman and Nicobar Islands, India. I. Onge. 1983. *Economic Botany* 37 (1): 110-119.

Bianchini, Francesco, and Francesco Corbetta. The Complete Book of Fruits & Vegetables. 1976. Crown Publishers. New York.

Blackmon, W.J., ed. 1986a. *Apios Tribune* 1 (1).

Blackmon, W.J., and B.D. Reynolds. The Crop Potential of Apios americana - Preliminary Evaluations. 1986b. *HortScience* 21 (6): 1334-1336.

Blankenship, Dianna C., and Betty B. Alford. Cottonseed: The New Staff of Life. 1983. Texas Women's University Press. Denton.

Blount Jr., Floyd. Farkleberries as a Rootstock for Blueberries. 1976. *California Rare Fruit Growers Yearbook* 8. 70-72.

Bocek, Barbara R. Ethnobotany of Costanoan Indians, California, Based on Collections by John P. Harrington. 1984. *Economic Botany* 38 (2): 240-255.

Bond, Robert E. Southeast Asian Herbs and Spices in California. 1988. *Petits Propos Culinaires* 30. 11-33.

Brackett, Babette, and Maryann Lash. The Wild Gourmet. 1975. David R. Godine, Publisher. Boston.

Brand, J.C., et al. The Nutritional Composition of Aboriginal Bushfoods. 1981. *Proceedings of the Nutrition Association of Australia* 6. 170.

Brennan, Georgeanne, Isaac Cronin and Charlotte Glenn. The New American Vegetable Book. 1985. Aris Books. Berkeley, California.

Bretting, P.K. Folk Names and Uses for Martyniaceous Plants. 1984. *Economic Botany* 38 (4): 452-463.

Britton, N.L., and A. Brown. An Illustrated Flora of the Northern United States and Canada. Second edition, 1913. Dover Publications. New York. Reprint, 1970. Three volumes.

Britton, N.L., and J.N. Rose. The Cactaceae. Second edition, 1937. Dover Publications. New York. Reprint, 1963. Four volumes.

Brooks, Reid M., and H.P. Olmo. Register of New Fruit and Nut Varieties 1920-1950. 1952. University of California Press. Berkeley.

Brooks, Reid M., and H.P. Olmo. Register of New Fruit & Nut Varieties. Second edition, 1972. University of California Press. Berkeley.

Brouk, B. Plants Consumed by Man. 1975. Academic Press. London.

Brown, F.B.H. Flora of Southeastern Polynesia - III. Dicotyledons. 1935. Bernice P. Bishop Museum. Bull. 130. Honolulu.

Brown, W.H. Useful Plants of the Philippines. 1954. Bureau of Printing. Manila. Three volumes.

Brucher, H. Tropische Nutzpflanzen. 1977. Springer-Verlag. Berlin and Heidelberg.

Bryan, John E., and Coralie Castle. The Edible Ornamental Garden. 1974. 101 Productions. San Francisco.

Bullard, A.J. Amelanchier obovalis: The Consummate Juneberry for the Southeast. 1987. *Pomona* 20 (3): 17.

Burkill, I.H. A Dictionary of the Economic Products of the Malay Peninsula. 1935. Ministry of Agriculture and Cooperations. Kuala Lumpur. Reprint, 1966.

Burpee Seed Co. Burpee's Farm Annual. 1888. W. Atlee Burpee Co. Philadelphia. Reprint, 1975.

Burr Jr., Fearing. The Field and Garden Vegetables of America. 1865. J.E. Tilton and Co. Boston.

Burritt, Brad. Leymus: A Plant with a History of Human Use. 1986. *The Land Report* 28. 10-12.

Calpouzos, Lucas. Botanical Aspects of Oregano. 1954. *Economic Botany* 8 (3): 222-233.

Carcione, Joe, and Bob Lucas. The Greengrocer. 1972. Chronicle Books. San Francisco.

Cavalcante, Paulo B. Edible Palm Fruits of the Brazilian Amazon. 1977. *Principes* 21. 91-102.

Chang, K.C., ed. Food in Chinese Culture. 1977. Yale University Press. New Haven.

Chang, Shu-Ting. The Chinese Mushroom. 1972. The Chinese University of Hong Kong. Hong Kong.

Chang, W.W., et al. An Encyclopedia of Chinese Food & Cooking. 1970. Crown Publishers. New York.

Chantiles, Vilma Liacouras. The New York Ethnic Food Market Guide & Cookbook. 1984. Dodd, Mead & Co. New York.

Chapman, William B. Hardy Citrus Tests: Yusvange #1. 1975. *Pomona* 8 (2): 75-76.

Chauhan, D.V.S. Vegetable Production in India. Second edition, 1968. Ram Prakash and Sons. Agra, India.

Cheney, Ralph Holt, and Elizabeth Scholtz. Rooibos Tea, A South African Contribution to World Beverages. 1963. *Economic Botany* 17 (3): 186-194.

Child, Alan. Edible Fruits in Solanum L. 1985a. *Solanaceae Enthusiasts Quarterly* 1 (2): 2-16.

Child, Alan. Relatives of the Tamarillo. 1985b. *Solanaceae Enthusiasts Quarterly* 1 (4): 7-16.

Chittenden, F.J., et al. Dictionary of Gardening. Reprint ed., 1965-69. Royal Horticultural Society. Oxford. Four volumes and supplement.

Clarke, Charlotte Bringle. Edible and Useful Plants of California. 1977. University of California Press. Berkeley, California.

Clift, Crafton. Hancornia-Bunchosia. 1981. *Rare Fruit Council International Newsletter* 15. 46.

Coit, J. Eliot. Carob or St. John's Bread. 1951. *Economic Botany* 5 (1): 82-96.

Cole, John N. Amaranth: From the Past for the Future. 1979. Rodale Press. Emmaus, Pennsylvania.

Colenso, William. On The Vegetable Food of the Ancient New Zealanders before Cook's Visit. 1880. *Transactions of the New Zealand Institute* 13. 3-38.

Collins, J.L. The Pineapple. 1960. Leonard Hill. London.

Condit, Ira J. Fig Varieties: A Monograph. 1955. *Hilgardia* 23 (11): 323-538.

Cook, Alan D., ed. Oriental Herbs and Vegetables. 1983. *Plants and Gardens* 39 (2).

Coons, Mary P. Relationships of Amaranthus caudatus. 1982. *Economic Botany* 36 (2): 129-146.

Cornell, Julien. Herbs in Vermouth. 1975. *The Herbarist* 41. 35-36.

Coronel, Roberto E. An Annotated List of Edible Nuts in the Philippines. 1984. *Western Australian Nut & Tree Crop Assn. Yearbook* 9. 48-54.

Correa, M. Pico, et al. Dictionário das Plantas Uteis do Brasil e das Exóticas Cultivadas. 1926-1975. Ministério da Agricultura. Rio de Janeiro. Six volumes.

Correll, Donovan S. The Potato and it's Wild Relatives. 1962. Texas Research Foundation. Renner, Texas.

Cost, Bruce. Ginger East to West. 1984. Aris Books. Berkeley, California.

Cost, Bruce. Bruce Cost's Asian Ingredients. 1988. William Morrow and Company. New York.

Crawford, William, and Kamolmal Pootaraksa. Thai Home Cooking from Kamolmal's Kitchen. 1985. New American Library. New York.

Creasy, Rosalind. The Complete Book of Edible Landscaping. 1982. Sierra Club Books. San Francisco.

Creasy, Rosalind. Edible Flowers. 1990. *Organic Gardening* 37 (2): 47-49.

Cribb, A.B. and J.W. Cribb. Wild Food in Australia. 1974. William Collins Publishers. Sydney.

Croft, James R, and David N. Leach. New Guinea Salt Fern (Asplenium acrobryum complex): Identity, Distribution, and Chemical Composition of its Salt. 1985. *Economic Botany* 39 (2): 139-149.

Crosswhite, Frank S. The Annual Saguaro Harvest and Crop Cycle of the Papago, with Reference to Ecology and Symbolism. 1980. *Desert Plants* 2 (1): 3-61.

Crowhurst, Adrienne. The Weed Cookbook. 1972. Lancer Books. New York.

Crowhurst, Adrienne. The Flower Cookbook. 1973. Lancer Books. New York.

Cude, Kay. For a Lively Spice - Grow Ginger. 1985. *California Rare Fruit Growers Newsletter* 17 (3): 10-15.

Cully, Anne C. Indian Ricegrass (Oryzopsis hymenoides): A Potentially Useful Wild Grass Adapted to Dunal Habitats. *In* Management and Utilization of Arid Land Plants: Symposium Proceedings. 1986. Rocky Mountain Forest and Range Experiment Station. Forest Service. USDA. Fort Collins, Colorado.

Czarnecki, Jack. Joe's Book of Mushroom Cookery. 1986. Atheneum. New York.

D'Arcy, William G., and W. Hardy Eshbaugh. New World Peppers (Capsicum - Solanaceae) North of Columbia: A Resume. 1974. *Baileya* 19 (3): 93-105.

Dahlen, Martha, and Karen Phillipps. A Popular Guide to Chinese Vegetables. 1983. Crown Publishers. New York.

Dalziel, J.M. The Useful Plants of West Tropical Africa. 1937. Crown Agents for the Colonies. London. Three volumes.

Dana, M.C. Cranberry Cultivar List. 1983. *Fruit Varieties Journal* 37 (4): 88-95.

Darby, William J., Paul Ghalioungui, and Louis Grivetti. Food: The Gift of Osiris. 1977. Academic Press. London.

Dark, Sandra. Have You Tried Cucuzzi ?. 1983. *Organic Gardening* 30 (4): 102.

Darrah, Helen H. The Cultivated Basils. 1980. Buckeye Printing Co. Independence, Missouri.

Darrow, George M. Minor Temperate Fruits. *In* Advances in Fruit Breeding, Jules Janick and James N. Moore eds. 1975. Purdue University Press. West Lafayette, Indiana.

Davids, Kenneth. Coffee: A Guide to Buying, Brewing, & Enjoying. Second edition, 1981. 101 Productions. San Francisco.

Davis IV, Tilton, and Robert A. Bye Jr. Ethnobotany and Progressive Domestication of Jaltomata (Solanaceae) in Mexico and Central America. 1982. *Economic Botany* 36 (2): 225-241.

de Peters, Edward J., and Donald L. Bath. Canola Meal Can Replace Cottonseed Meal in Dairy Diets. 1985. *California Agriculture* 39 (7-8): 26-27.

de Sounin, Leonie. Magic in Herbs. 1941. M. Barrows & Company. New York.

de Veaux, Jennie S., and Eugene B. Shultz, Jr. Development of Buffalo Gourd (Cucurbita foetidissima) as a Semiaridland Starch and Oil Crop. 1985. *Economic Botany* 39 (4): 454-472.

de Wet, J.M.J., et al. Domestication of Sawa Millet (Echinochloa colona). 1983. *Economic Botany* 37 (3): 283-291.

Degener, Otto. Plants of Hawaii National Park: Illustrative of Plants and Customs of the South Seas. 1930. Braun-Brumfield, Inc. Ann Arbor, Michigan. Reprint, 1975.

der Haroutunian, Arto. Middle Eastern Cookery. 1982. Century Publishing Company. London.

Dirar, Hamid A. Kawal, Meat Substitute from Fermented Cassia obtusifolia Leaves. 1984. *Economic Botany* 38 (3): 342-349.

Doebley, John F. "Seeds" of Wild Grasses: A Major Food of Southwestern Indians. 1984. *Economic Botany* 38 (1): 52-64.

Domico, Terry. Wild Harvest: Edible Plants of the Pacific Northwest. 1978. Big Country Books. Blaine, Washington.

Donkin, R.A. Manna: An Historical Geography. 1980. Dr. W. Junk bv Publishers. The Hague.

Dore, William G. The Wild Canada Onion. 1970. *The Herbarist* 36. 35-38.

Doutt, Margaret. Ramps. 1970. *The Herbarist* 36. 30-33.

Drysdale, William T. Cherry of the Rio Grande. 1971. *California Rare Fruit Growers Yearbook* 3. 26-38.

Duke, James A. Isthmian Ethnobotanical Dictionary. 1972. Published by the author. Fulton, Maryland.

Durand, Herbert K. Texas Mahonia - A Neglected Economic Plant. 1972. *Economic Botany* 26 (4): 319-325.

Durand, Herbert K. Tropical Blueberries. 1978. *California Rare Fruit Growers Newsletter* 10 (4): 15.

Durand, Herbert K. Blueberries for Everybody. 1979. *Pomona* 12 (2): 100-102.

Dutta, P.K., H.O. Saxena and M. Brahmam. Kewda Perfume Industry in India. 1987. *Economic Botany* 41 (3): 403-410.

Eighme, Lloyd E. Vaccinium in the Wild. 1980. *Pomona* 13 (3): 151-154.

Endt, Annemarie. 101 Ways of Using Paw Paws. 1981. Landsendt Subtropical Fruits. Auckland, New Zealand.

Engler, A., and K. Prantl, et al. Die Natürlichen Pflanzenfamilien. 1889. W. Engelmann. Leipzig.

Erwin, A.T., and E.P. Lana. The Seminole Pumpkin. 1956. *Economic Botany* 10 (1): 33-37.

Essig, Frederick B., and Yun-fa Dong. The Many Uses of Trachycarpus fortunei (Arecaceae) in China. 1987. *Economic Botany* 41 (3): 411-417.

Evelyn, John. Acetaria. 1699. Prospect Books. London. Reprint, 1982.

Fairchild, David. Exploring for Plants. 1930. Macmillan. New York.

Fairchild, David. The World Was My Garden. 1945. Charles Scribners' Sons. New York.

Felger, Richard S., and Mary Beck Moser. Columnar Cacti in Seri Indian Culture. 1974. *The Kiva* 39 (3-4): 257-275.

Felker, Peter. Uses of Tree Legumes in Semiarid Regions. 1981. *Economic Botany* 35 (2): 174-186.

Fell, Derek, and Phyllis Shaudys. The Vegetable Spaghetti Cookbook. 1982a. Pine Row Publications. Washington Crossing, Pennsylvania.

Fell, Derek. Vegetables: How to Select, Grow, and Enjoy. 1982b. HP Books. Tucson, Arizona.

Fernald, Merritt Lyndon, Alfred Charles Kinsey, and Reed C. Rollins. Edible Wild Plants of Eastern North America. Second edition, 1958. Harper & Row. New York.

Fisher, Bonnie. 'Instant Fruit' - It's Hard to Ask More. 1977. *Organic Gardening* 24 (6): 74-75.

Fleisher, Alexander, and Zhenia Fleisher. Identification of Biblical Hyssop and Origin of the Traditional Use of Oregano-group Herbs in the Mediterranean Region. 1988. *Economic Botany* 42 (2): 232-241.

Fletcher, W.A. Growing Tamarillos. 1975. New Zealand Ministry of Agriculture and Fisheries. Bulletin 307. Wellington.

Fox, F.W., M.E. Norwood Young, et al. Food from the Veld. 1982. Delta Books. Johannesburg and Cape Town.

Fox, Helen M. Gardening with Herbs for Flavor and Fragrance. 1933. Dover Publications. New York. Reprint, 1970.

Franke, Wolfgang. Vitamin C in Sea Fennel (Crithmum maritimum) an Edible Wild Plant. 1982. *Economic Botany* 36 (2): 163-165.

Freitus, Joe. Wild Preserves. 1977. Stone Wall Press. Boston.

Frey, Darrell. Ferns in Permaculture Design. 1985. *The International Permaculture Seed Yearbook* 3. 42-43.

Fuller, David. Maori Food and Cookery. 1978. A.H. & A.W. Reed. Wellington, New Zealand.

Gade, Daniel W. Achira, the Edible Canna, Its Cultivation and Use in the Peruvian Andes. 1966. *Economic Botany* 20 (4): 407-415.

Gade, Daniel W. Ethnobotany of Cañihua (Chenopodium pallidicaule), Rustic Seed Crop of the Altiplano. 1970. *Economic Botany* 24 (1): 55-61.

Galet, Pierre. A Practical Ampelography. 1979. Cornell University Press. Ithaca, New York.

Galil, J. An Ancient Technique for Ripening Sycomore Fruit in East-Mediterranean Countries. 1968. *Economic Botany* 22 (2): 178-190.

Garner, R.J., Saeed Ahmed Chaudhri, et al. The Propagation of Tropical Fruit Trees. 1976. Commonwealth Agricultural Bureaux. Slough, England.

Genders, Roy. Vegetables for the Epicure. Revised edition, 1975. Robert Hale & Co. London.

Genders, Roy. Scented Flora of the World. 1977. St. Martin's Press. New York.

Gentry, Alwyn H., and Richard H. Wettach. Fevillea - a New Oil Seed from Amazonian Peru. 1986. *Economic Botany* 40 (2): 177-185.

Gessert, Kate Rogers. The Beautiful Food Garden. 1983. Van Nostrand Reinhold. New York.

Gibbons, Euell. Stalking the Wild Asparagus. 1962. David McKay Co. New York.

Gibbons, Euell. Stalking the Blue-Eyed Scallop. 1964. David McKay Co. New York.

Gibbons, Euell. Stalking the Good Life. 1966a. David McKay Co. New York.

Gibbons, Euell. Stalking the Healthful Herbs. 1966b. David McKay Co. New York.

Gibbons, Euell. Beachcomber's Handbook. 1967. David McKay Co. New York.

Gibbons, Euell. Stalking the Far Away Places. 1973. David McKay Co. New York.

Gibbons, Euell, and Gordon Tucker. Euell Gibbons' Handbook of Edible Wild Plants. 1979. The Donning Co. Virginia Beach, Virginia.

Gladstones, J.S. Lupins as Crop Plants. 1970. *Field Crop Abstracts* 23 (2): 123-148.

Gorman, Marion. Star Stuffers. 1989. *Organic Gardening* 37 (1): 47-48.

Goulart, Frances Sheridan. Cooking with Carob. 1980. Garden Way Publishing. Charlotte, Vermont.

Gray, A.R. Taxonomy and Evolution of Broccoli. 1982. *Economic Botany* 36 (4): 397-410.

Greenwell, Amy B.H. Taro: With Special Reference to its Culture in Hawaii. 1947. *Economic Botany* 1 (3): 276-289.

Grieve, Mrs. M. A Modern Herbal. 1931. Dover Publications. New York. Reprint, 1971. Two volumes.

Griffin, Lisa C., and R.M. Rowlett. A Lost Viking Cereal Grain. 1981. *Journal of Ethnobiology* 1 (2): 200-207.

Griffith, Eugene, and Mary E. Griffith. Persimmons for Everyone. 1982. North American Fruit Explorers. Arcola, Missouri.

Griggs, William H., and Ben T. Iwakiri. Asian Pear Varieties in California. 1977. University of California. Division of Agricultural Sciences. Pub. No. 4068. Berkeley.

Grigson, Jane. The Mushroom Feast. 1975. ALfred A. Knopf. New York.

Groff, George Weidman. The Lychee & Lungan. 1921. Orange Judd Co. New York.

Grubb, Norman H. Cherries. 1949. Crosby Lockwood & Son, Ltd. London.

Hackett, Clive, and Julie Carolane. Edible Horticultural Crops. 1982. Academic Press. North Ryde, Australia.

Hall, Walter, and Nancy Hall. The Wild Palate. 1980. Rodale Press. Emmaus, Pennsylvania.

Halpin, Anne Moyer. Unusual Vegetables. 1978. Rodale Press. Emmaus, Pennsylvania.

Hamilton, Lawrence S., and Dennis H. Murphy. Use and Management of Nipa Palm (Nypa fruticans, Arecaceae): A Review. 1988. *Economic Botany* 42 (2): 206-213.

Hampstead, Marilyn. The Basil Book. 1984. Long Shadow Books. New York.

Hansen, N.E. Plant Introductions (1895-1927). 1927. South Dakota Agr. Exp. Sta. Bull. 224. Brookings.

Hanson, A.A., D.K. Barnes and R.R. Hill, Jr. eds. Alfalfa and Alfalfa Improvement. 1988. American Society of Agronomy. Madison, Wisconsin.

Harlan, J.R., J.M.J. de Wet, and A.B.L. Stemler, eds. Origins of African Plant Domestication. 1976. Mouton Publishers. The Hague.

Harrington, Geri. Grow Your Own Chinese Vegetables. 1978. Macmillan. New York.

Harrington, H.D. Edible Native Plants of the Rocky Mountains. 1967. University of New Mexico Press. Albuquerque.

Harris, Lloyd J. The Book of Garlic. 1974. Panjandrum Press. San Francisco.

Hart, Jeff. Montana: Native Plants & Early Peoples. 1976. Montana Historical Society. Helena.

Hastings, Sunny, and Desiree Taylor. Cooking with Macadamias. 1983. Published by the authors. Maryborough, Australia.

Hawkes, Alex D. A World of Vegetable Cookery. Revised edition, 1986. Simon & Schuster. New York.

Hedrick, U.P., ed. The Grapes of New York. 1908. New York State Agricultural Experiment Station. Albany.

Hedrick, U.P., ed. The Plums of New York. 1911. New York State Agricultural Experiment Station. Albany.

Hedrick, U.P., ed. The Cherries of New York. 1915. New York State Agricultural Experiment Station. Albany.

Hedrick, U.P., ed. The Peaches of New York. 1917. New York State Agricultural Experiment Station. Albany.

Hedrick, U.P., ed. Sturtevant's Edible Plants of the World. 1919. Dover Publications. New York. Reprint, 1972.

Hedrick, U.P., ed. The Pears of New York. 1921. New York State Agricultural Experiment Station. Albany.

Hedrick, U.P., ed. The Small Fruits of New York. 1925. New York State Agricultural Experiment Station. Albany.

Hedrick, U.P., ed. Peas of New York. 1928. New York State Agricultural Experiment Station. Albany.

Hedrick, U.P., ed. Beans of New York. 1931. New York State Agricultural Experiment Station. Albany.

Hegyi, Helen. The Edible Fruited Cacti. 1971. *California Rare Fruit Growers Yearbook* 3. 39-50.

Heiser, Charles B. Origin and Variability of the Pepino (Solanum muricatum): A Preliminary Report. 1964. *Baileya* 12. 151-159.

Heiser, Charles B. Nightshades: The Paradoxical Plants. 1969. W.H. Freeman and Co. San Francisco.

Heiser, Charles B. The Sunflower. 1976. University of Oklahoma Press. Norman.

Heiser, Charles B. The Totora (Scirpus californicus) in Ecuador and Peru. 1978. *Economic Botany* 32 (3): 222-236.

Heiser, Charles B. Ethnobotany of the Naranjilla (Solanum quitoense) and Its Relatives. 1985. *Economic Botany* 39 (1): 4-11.

Heller, Christine A. Wild Edible and Poisonous Plants of Alaska. Revised edition, 1981. University of Alaska, Coop. Ext. Serv. Pub. No. 28.

Hemmerly, Thomas E. Traditional Method of Making Sorghum Molasses. 1983. *Economic Botany* 37 (4): 406-409.

Hendrickson, Robert. The Berry Book. 1981. Doubleday & Co. New York.

Herklots, G.A.C. Vegetables in South-East Asia. 1972. George Allen & Unwin. London.

Hesseltine, C.W. A Millennium of Fungi, Food, and Fermentation. 1965. *Mycologia* 57 (2): 149-197.

Hexamer, F.M. Asparagus. 1918. Orange Judd Co. New York.

Hill, Albert F. The Pie Plant and its Relatives. 1945. *The Herbarist* 11. 21-27.

Hills, Christopher. Food From Sunlight. 1978. University of the Trees Press. Boulder Creek, California.

Hills, Christopher. Rejuvenating the Body through Fasting with Spirulina Plankton. 1979. University of the Trees Press. Boulder Creek, California.

Hills, Lawrence D. Comfrey: Past, Present and Future. 1976. Faber and Faber. London.

Hilty, Ivy E., et al. Nutritive Values of Native Foods of Warm Springs Indians. 1980. Oregon State University Extension Service. Extension Circular 809. Corvallis.

Hitchcock, Susan Tyler. Gather Ye Wild Things. 1980. Harper & Row. New York.

Hodge, W.H. The Edible Arracacha. 1954. *Economic Botany* 8 (3): 195-221.

Hodge, W.H. Three Native Tuber Foods of the High Andes. 1951. *Economic Botany* 5 (2): 185-201.

Hodge, W.H. The South American "Sapote". 1960. *Economic Botany* 14 (3): 203-206.

Hodge, W.H. Wasabi - Native Condiment Plant of Japan. 1974. *Economic Botany* 28 (2): 118-129.

Holloway, H.L.O. Seed Propagation of Dioscoreophyllum cumminsii, Source of an Intense Natural Sweetener. 1977. *Economic Botany* 33 (1): 47-50.

Howard, W.L. Luther Burbank's Plant Contributions. 1945. Cal. Agr. Ex. St. Bull. 691. Berkeley.

Howell, Christopher. First Fruiting Reports. 1984. *Rare Fruit Council International Yearbook*. 45.

Hughes, Phyllis. Pueblo Indian Cookbook. Second edition, 1977. Museum of New Mexico Press. Santa Fe.

Hunter, Beatrice Trum. Fermented Foods and Beverages. 1973a. Keats Publishing Co. New Canaan, Connecticut.

Hunter, Beatrice Trum. Yogurt, Kefir, & Other Milk Cultures. 1973b. Keats Publishing Co. New Canaan, Connecticut.

Hutchinson, John. The Families of Flowering Plants. Third edition, 1973. Oxford University Press. Oxford.

Hutson, Lucinda. The Herb Garden Cookbook. 1987. Texas Monthly Press. Austin.

Ilyas, M. The Spices of India - II. 1978. *Economic Botany* 32 (3): 239-263.

Inglett, G.E., and Joann F. May. Tropical Plants with Unusual Taste Properties. 1968. *Economic Botany* 22 (4): 326-331.

Irvine, F.R. Supplementary and Emergency Food Plants of West Africa. 1952. *Economic Botany* 6 (1): 23-41.

Irvine, F.R. Woody Plants of Ghana. 1961. Oxford University Press. London.

Jackson, Michael. The World Guide to Beer. 1977. Running Press. Philadelphia.

Jackson, Wes. New Roots for Agriculture. 1980. Friends of the Earth. San Francisco.

Jaffrey, Madhur. Madhur Jaffrey's World-of-the-East Vegetarian Cooking. 1982. Alfred A. Knopf. New York.

Jaynes, Richard A., ed. Nut Tree Culture in North America. 1979. The Northern Nut Growers Assn., Inc. Hamden, Connecticut.

Jeffrey, C. A New Combination in Thladiantha (Cucurbitaceae) for a Chinese Medicinal Plant. 1979. *Kew Bulletin* 33 (3): 394.

Jennings, D.L. Raspberries and Blackberries: Their Breeding, Diseases and Growth. 1988. Academic Press. London.

Johns, Leslie, and Violet Stevenson. The Complete Book of Fruit. 1979. Angus and Robertson. London.

Johnston, H.W. The Biological and Economic Importance of Algae, Part 3. Edible Algae of Fresh and Brackish Waters. 1970. *Tuatara* 18, 19. 19-35.

Johnston Jr, James W. The Mead Maker uses Herbs. 1973. *The Herbarist* 39. 42-49.

Joly, Luz Graciela. Feeding and Trapping Fish with Piper auritum. 1981. *Economic Botany* 35 (4): 383-390.

Jones, Dorothy Bovee. The Great Dittany of Crete - Then and Now. 1973. *The Herbarist* 39. 13-18.

Jones, Marge. Baking with Amaranth. 1983. Published by the author. Deerfield, Illinois.

Joseph, Salikutty, and K.V. Peter. Curry Leaf (Murraya koenigii), Perennial, Nutritious, Leafy Vegetable. 1985. *Economic Botany* 39 (1): 68-73.

Kajiura, I. Lesser Known Japanese Fruits. 1980. *Journal of the New Zealand Tree Crops Assn.* 5 (1): 22-29.

Kauffman, C.S., et al. Amaranth Grain Production Guide. 1984. Rodale Press. Emmaus, Pennsylvania.

Kavena, Juanita Tiger. Hopi Cookery. 1980. University of Arizona Press. Tucson.

Kaye, Geraldine C. Japanese Successfully Tame Favorite Wild Mushrooms. 1985. *Mushroom* 3 (3): 36-39.

Kelsey, Harlan P., and William A. Dayton. Standardized Plant Names. Second edition, 1942. J. Horace McFarland Company. Harrisburg, Pennsylvania.

Kennard, William C., and Harold F. Winters. Some Fruits and Nuts for the Tropics. 1960. United States Department of Agriculture. Misc. Pub. No. 801. Washington, D.C.

Kennedy, C.T. And Now, Jostaberry. 1990. *California Rare Fruit Growers Newsletter*. 22 (3): 12-13.

Kennedy, Diana. The Tortilla Book. 1975. Harper & Row. New York.

Kerrigan, Rick. Mushrooms in Your Garden. 1984. *Organic Gardening* 31 (1): 64-67.

Keubel, K.R., and Arthur O. Tucker. Vietnamese Culinary Herbs in the United States. 1988. *Economic Botany* 42 (3): 413-419.

Kindscher, Kelly. Edible Wild Plants of the Prairie. 1987. University Press of Kansas. Lawrence.

Kirk, Donald R. Wild Edible Plants of the Western United States. 1970. Naturegraph Publishers. Healdsburg, California.

Klein, Maggie Blyth. The Feast of the Olive. 1983. Aris Books. Berkeley, California.

Komarov, V.I., ed. Flora of the U.S.S.R., Vol. II. Graminae. 1934. Office of Technical Services, U.S. Department of Commerce. Washington, D.C. English translation, 1963.

Kosikowski, Frank. Cheese and Fermented Milk Foods. Second edition, 1982. Kosikowski and Associates. Brooktondale, New York.

Kraft, Ken, and Pat Kraft. Exotic Vegetables. 1977. Walker and Company. New York.

Krochmal, Arnold, and Connie Krochmal. Uncultivated Nuts of the United States. 1982. United States Department of Agriculture. Agric. Info. Bull. 450. Washington, D.C.

Krüssmann, Gerd. Manual of Cultivated Broad-Leaved Trees and Shrubs. 1986. Timber Press. Portland, Oregon. Three volumes.

Kulvinskas, Viktoras. Nutritional Evaluation of Sprouts and Grasses. 1976. OMango d'Press. Wethersfield, Connecticut.

Kunkel, Gunther. Plants for Human Consumption. 1984. Koeltz Scientific Books. Koenigstein, Germany.

Kusche, Larry. Popcorn. 1977. HP Books. Tucson, Arizona.

Lanner, Ronald M., and Harriette Lanner. The Piñon Pine: A Natural and Cultural History. 1981. University of Nevada Press. Reno.

Larkcom, Joy. Salads the Year Round. 1980. Hamlyn Publishing Group. Feltham, England.

Larkcom, Joy. The Salad Garden. 1984. The Viking Press. New York.

Lathrop, Norma Jean. Herbs: How to Select, Grow, and Enjoy. 1981. HP Books. Tucson.

Latorre, Dolores L. Cooking and Curing with Mexican Herbs. 1977a. Encino Press. Austin, Texas.

Latorre, Dolores L., and Felipe A. Latorre. Plants Used by the Mexican Kickapoo Indians. 1977b. *Economic Botany* 31 (3): 340-357.

Launert, Edmund. Edible & Medicinal Plants of Britain and Northern Europe. 1981. Hamlyn Publishing Group. London.

Leggatt, Jenny. Cooking with Flowers. 1987. Fawcett Columbine. New York.

Leibenstein, Margaret. The Edible Mushroom. 1986. Ballantine Books. New York.

León, Jorge. The "Maca" (Lepidium meyenii) A Little Known Food Plant of Peru. 1964. *Economic Botany* 18 (2): 122-127.

Lester, R.N., et al. Variation Patterns in the African Scarlet Eggplant, Solanum aethiopicum L. *In* Infraspecific Classification of Wild and Cultivated Plants, B.T. Styles (ed.). 1986. Oxford University Press. Oxford.

Lewis, J. The Classification of Cultivars in Relation to Wild Plants. *In* Infraspecific Classification of Wild and Cultivated Plants, B.T. Styles (ed.). 1986. Oxford University Press. Oxford.

Lincoff, Gary. Mushroom Hunting in the Marketplace. 1983. *McIlvainea* 6 (1): 13-15.

Lionnet, Guy. The Double Coconut of the Seychelles. 1976. *West Australian Nutgrowing Society Yearbook* 2. 6-20.

Logsdon, Gene. Small-Scale Grain Raising. 1977. Rodale Press. Emmaus, Pennsylvania.

Logsdon, Gene. Clover Fit to Eat. 1980. *Organic Gardening* 27 (9): 142.

Logsdon, Gene. Organic Orcharding. 1981. Rodale Press. Emmaus, Pennsylvania.

London, Mel. Bread Winners. 1979. Rodale Press. Emmaus, Pennsylvania.

Lovelock, Yann. The Vegetable Book: An Unnatural History. 1973. St. Martin's Press. New York.

Lu, S., and C.E. Walker. Laboratory Preparation of Ready-to-Eat Breakfast Flakes from Grain Sorghum Flour. 1988. *Cereal Chemistry* 65 (4): 377-379.

Luckwill, L.C., and A. Pollard. Perry Pears. 1963. University of Bristol. Bristol, England.

Lusas, E.W., and G.M. Jividen. Characteristics and Uses of Glandless Cottonseed Food Protein Ingredients. 1987. *Journal of the American Oil Chemists Society* 64 (7): 973-986.

Mabey, Richard. Food for Free. 1972. William Collins Sons & Co. London.

MacLennan, Catherine. Wines from the Gardens and Fields of Scotland. 1975. *The Herbarist* 41. 37-40.

MacMillan, H.F. Tropical Planting & Gardening with special reference to Ceylon. 1962. Macmillan & Co. London.

MacNicol, Mary. Flower Cookery. 1967. Fleet Press. New York.

Madlener, Judith Cooper. The Sea Vegetable Book. 1977. Clarkson N. Potter. New York.

Magruder, Roy, et al. Descriptions of Types of Principal American Varieties of Spinach. 1938. United States Department of Agriculture. Misc. Publ. No. 316. Washington, D.C.

Magruder, Roy, et al. Descriptions of Types of Principal American Varieties of Orange-fleshed Carrots. 1940. United States Department of Agriculture. Misc. Publ. No. 361. Washington, D.C.

Mallos, Tess. The Complete Middle East Cookbook. 1979. McGraw-Hill. New York.

Mann, Louis K., and William T. Stearn. Rakkyo or Ch'iao T'ou (Allium chinense) A Little Known Vegetable Crop. 1960. *Economic Botany* 14 (1): 69-83.

Marcin, Marietta M. The Complete Book of Herbal Teas. 1983. Congdon & Weed. New York.

Martin, Franklin W., and Henry Y. Nakasone. The Edible Species of Passiflora. 1970. *Economic Botany* 24 (3): 333-343.

Martin, Franklin W. Tropical Yams and Their Potential: Part 2. Dioscorea bulbifera. 1974. United States Department of Agriculture. Agr. Hand. No. 466. Washington, D.C.

Martin, Franklin W., and Ruth M. Ruberté. Edible Leaves of the Tropics. 1975. Agency for International Development. Mayaguez, Puerto Rico.

Martin, Franklin W., and Eugenio Cabanillas. Leren (Calathea allouia), a Little Known Tuberous Root Crop of the Caribbean. 1976a. *Economic Botany* 30 (3): 249-256.

Martin, Franklin W. Tropical Yams and Their Potential: Part 3. Dioscorea alata. 1976b. United States Department of Agriculture. Agr. Hand. No. 495. Washington, D.C.

Martin, Franklin W., and William C. Cooper. Cultivation of Neglected Tropical Fruits With Promise: Part 3. The Pummelo. 1977. United States Department of Agriculture. New Orleans.

Martin, Franklin W., and Simon E. Malo. Cultivation of Neglected Tropical Fruits With Promise: Part 5. The Canistel and its Relatives. 1978a. United States Department of Agriculture. New Orleans.

Martin, Franklin W., and Lucien Degras. Tropical Yams and Their Potential: Part 5. Dioscorea trifida. 1978b. United States Department of Agriculture. Agr. Hand. No. 522. Washington, D.C.

Martin, Franklin W., and Ruth M. Ruberté. Vegetables for the Hot, Humid Tropics: Part 3. Chaya, Cnidoscolus chayamansa. 1978c. United States Department of Agriculture. New Orleans.

Martin, Franklin W. Vegetables for the Hot, Humid Tropics: Part 4. Sponge and Bottle Gourds, Luffa and Lagenaria. 1979. United States Department of Agriculture. New Orleans.

Martin, Franklin W. Okra, Potential Multiple-Purpose Crop for the Temperate Zones and Tropics. 1982. *Economic Botany* 36 (3): 340-345.

Martin, Franklin W., Carl W. Campbell, and Ruth M. Ruberté. Perennial Edible Fruits of the Tropics: An Inventory. 1987. United States Department of Agriculture, Agr. Hand. No. 642. Washington, D.C.

Masefield, G.B., et al. The Oxford Book of Food Plants. 1969. Oxford University Press. London.

Massal, Emile, and Jacques Barrau. Food Plants of the South Sea Islands. 1956. South Pacific Commission, Tech. Paper No. 94. Noumea, New Caledonia.

Maxwell, Lewis S. Florida Fruit. 1967. Published by the author. Tampa.

May, Peter H., et al. Subsistence Benefits from the Babassu Palm (Orbignya martiana). 1985. *Economic Botany* 39 (2): 113-129.

May, R.J. Kaikai Aniani: A Guide to Bush Foods, Markets and Culinary Arts of Papua New Guinea. 1984. Robert Brown & Associates. Bathurst, Australia.

McCurrach, James C. Palms of the World. 1960. Harper & Brothers. New York.

McEachern, George Ray. Growing Fruits, Berries, & Nuts in the South. 1978. Pacesetter Press. Houston.

McGregor, S.E. Insect Pollination of Cultivated Crop Plants. 1976. United States Department of Agriculture. Washington, D.C.

McKilligan, Rusty. Still More Than You Ever Wanted To Know About Geraniums. International Geranium Society. Hollywood, California.

Medsger, Oliver Perry. Edible Wild Plants. 1939. Macmillan. New York.

Meech, W.W. Quince Culture. 1888. Orange Judd Co. New York.

Menninger, Edwin A. Edible Nuts of the World. 1977. Horticultural Books. Stuart, Florida.

Mesfin, Daniel, J. Exotic Ethiopian Cooking. 1987. Ethiopian Cookbook Enterprises. Falls Church, Virginia.

Mgeni, A.S.M. Bamboo Wine from Oxytenanthera braunii. 1983. *Indian Forester* 109 (5): 306-308.

Michael, Pamela. All Good Things Around Us. 1980. Holt, Rinehart, and Winston. New York.

Michurin, I.V. Selected Works. 1949. Foreign Languages Publishing House. Moscow.

Milius, Susan. Making Flour from Fruits and Vegetables. 1981. *Organic Gardening* 28 (9): 102-110.

Miller Jr., Orson K. Mushrooms of North America. 1978. E.P. Dutton. New York.

Mirel, Elizabeth Post. Plum Crazy: A Book About Beach Plums. 1973. Clarkson N. Potter, Inc. New York.

Mitchell, George F. Home-Grown Tea. 1907. U.S. Dept. of Agr. Farm. Bull. 301. Washington, D.C.

Moldenke, Harold N., and Alma L. Moldenke. Plants of the Bible. 1952. Chronica Botanica. New York.

Morgan, W.T.W. Ethnobotany of the Turkana: Use of Plants by a Pastoral People and their Livestock in Kenya. 1981. *Economic Botany* 35 (1): 96-130.

Mori, Kisaku. Mushrooms as Health Foods. 1974. Japan Publications, Inc. Tokyo.

Morton, Julia F. The Emblic (Phyllanthus emblica L.). 1960. *Economic Botany* 14 (2): 119-128.

Morton, Julia F. Principal Wild Food Plants of the United States Excluding Alaska and Hawaii. 1963. *Economic Botany* 17 (4): 319-330.

Morton, Julia F. Herbs & Spices. 1976. Golden Press. New York.

Morton, Julia F. Wild Plants For Survival in South Florida. Fourth edition, 1977. Fairchild Tropical Garden. Miami.

Morton, Julia F. Rooibos Tea, Aspalathus linearis, a Caffeinless, Low-Tannin Beverage. 1983. *Economic Botany* 37 (2): 164-173.

Morton, Julia F. Indian Almond (Terminalia catappa), Salt-tolerant, Useful, Tropical Tree with "Nut" Worthy of Improvement. 1985. *Economic Botany* 39 (2): 101-112.

Morton, Julia F. Fruits of Warm Climates. 1987a. Published by the author. Miami, Florida.

Morton, Julia F., and Gilbert L. Voss. The Argan Tree (Argania sideroxylon, Sapotaceae), a Desert Source of Edible Oil. 1987b. *Economic Botany* 41 (2): 221-233.

Morton, Julia F. Notes on Distribution, Propagation, and Products of Borassus Palms. 1988. *Economic Botany* 42 (3): 420-441.

Moscoso, Carlos G. The West Indian Cherry - Richest Known Source of Natural Vitamin C. 1956. *Economic Botany* 10 (3): 280-294.

Mowry, Harold, L.R. Troy, and H.S. Wolfe. Miscellaneous Tropical & Sub-tropical Florida Fruits. 1941. University of Florida, Agricultural Extension Service, Bull. 109. Gainesville.

Nabhan, Gary. Mesquite: Another Great American Legume. 1984a. *Organic Gardening* 31 (4): 114-115.

Nabhan, Gary, and J.M.J. de Wet. Panicum sonorum in Sonoran Desert Agriculture. 1984b. *Economic Botany* 38 (1): 65-82.

National Research Council. Underexploited Tropical Plants with Promising Economic Value. 1975a. National Academy of Sciences. Washington, D.C.

National Research Council. The Winged Bean: A High Protein Crop for the Tropics. 1975b. National Academy of Sciences. Washington, D.C.

National Research Council. Making Aquatic Weeds Useful. 1976. National Academy of Sciences. Washington, D.C.

National Research Council. Tropical Legumes: Resources for the Future. 1979. National Academy of Sciences. Washington, D.C.

National Research Council. Amaranth: Modern Prospects for an Ancient Crop. 1984. National Academy Press. Washington, D.C.

National Research Council. Lost Crops of the Incas. 1989. National Academy Press. Washington, D.C.

Natusch, Sheila. Wild Fare for Wilderness Foragers. 1979. William Collins (Publishers) Ltd. Auckland, New Zealand.

Nayar, M.P., and K. Ramamurthy. Beta vulgaris var. orientalis, a Useful Green Vegetable of Northern India. 1977. *Economic Botany* 31 (3): 372-373.

NCGR - National Clonal Germplasm Repository. Descriptors, Plant Evaluation Sheets, Observation Data, etc. 1990. Corvallis, Oregon.

Nearing, Helen, and Scott Nearing. The Maple Sugar Book. 1950. Schocken Books. New York.

Niethammer, Carolyn. The Tumbleweed Gourmet. 1987. University of Arizona Press. Tucson.

Nishi, Sadao. Hakuran: An Interpsecific Hybrid Between Chinese Cabbage and Common Cabbage. *In* Chinese Cabbage, N.S. Talekar and T.D. Griggs (eds.). 1981. Asian Vegetable Research and Development Center. Shanhua, Tainan, Taiwan.

Nixon, R.W., and J.B. Carpenter. Growing Dates in the United States. 1978. USDA Agric. Inf. Bull. 207. Washington, D.C.

Nobbs, K.J. The Rose as a Fruit. 1980. *Pomona* 13 (3): 123-134.

Norton, Helen H. Plant Use of Kaigani Haida Culture: Correction of an Ethnohistorical Oversight. 1981. *Economic Botany* 35 (4): 434-449.

Nyerges, Christopher. Guide to Wild Foods. 1982. Survival News Service. Los Angeles.

O'Connell, James F., Peter K. Latz, and Peggy Barnett. Traditional and Modern Plant Use Among the Alyawara of Central Australia. 1983. *Economic Botany* 37 (1): 80-109.

Oakley, Hugh. The Buying Guide for Fresh Fruits, Vegetables, Herbs and Nuts. 1980. Blue Goose, Inc. Hagerstown, Maryland.

Ochse, J.J. Vegetables of the Dutch East Indies. 1931. A. Asher & Co. Amsterdam. Reprint, 1980.

Okoli, 'Bosa E., and C.M. Mgbeogu. Fluted Pumpkin, Telfairia occidentalis: West African Vegetable Crop. 1983. *Economic Botany* 37 (2): 145-149.

Okoli, 'Bosa E. Wild and Cultivated Cucurbits in Nigeria. 1984. *Economic Botany* 38 (3): 350-357.

Oomen, H.A.P.C., and G.J.H. Grubben. Tropical Leaf Vegetables in Human Nutrition. 1978. Royal Tropical Institute. Amsterdam.

Organ, John. Rare Vegetables for Garden and Table. 1960. Faber and Faber. London.

Ortiz, Elisabeth Lambert. The Complete Book of Mexican Cooking. 1967. M. Evans and Company. New York.

Ortiz, Elisabeth Lambert. The Book of Latin American Cooking. 1979. Alfred A. Knopf. New York.

Painter, Gilian. Cooking With Unusual Herbs. 1983. Published by the author. Auckland, New Zealand.

Palmer, E. and N. Pitman. Trees of South Africa. 1961. A.A. Balkema. Capetown.

Parker, Southcombe, and G. Stevens Cox. The Giant Cabbage of the Channel Islands. Second Edition, 1974. Toucan Press. Guernsey, Channel Islands.

Pederson, Carl S. Microbiology of Food Fermentations. 1971. Avi Publishing Co. Westport, Connecticut.

Perez-Arbelaez, Enrique. Plantas Utiles de Colombia. Fourth edition, 1978. Litografia Arco. Bogota.

Peters, Charles M., and Enrique Pardo-Tejeda. Brosimum alicastrum (Moraceae): Uses and Potential in Mexico. 1982. *Economic Botany* 36 (2): 166-175.

Peterson, Lee. A Field Guide to Edible Wild Plants. 1977. Houghton Mifflin. Boston.

Peterson, Thomas C. The Siberian Pea Shrub. 1982. *Organic Gardening* 29 (2): 118-119.

Picart, Francois. Truffle: The Black Diamond. 1980. Agri-Truffle, Inc. Dripping Springs, Texas.

Piper, Charles, and William Morse. The Soybean. 1923. McGraw-Hill. New York.

Pirie, N.W. Leaf Protein and its By-Products in Human and Animal Nutrition. 1987. Cambridge University Press. Cambridge.

Pongpangan, Somchit, and Suparb Poobrasert. Edible and Poisonous Plants in Thai Forests. Science Society of Thailand.

Pope, W.T. Banana Culture in Hawaii. 1926. Hawaii Agr. Exp. St. Bull. No. 55. Honolulu.

Popenoe, Paul B. Date Growing in the Old World and The New. 1913. West India Gardens. Altadena, California.

Popenoe, Wilson. Manual of Tropical & Subtropical Fruits. 1920. Hafner Press. New York. Reprint, 1974.

Popenoe, Wilson. Economic Fruit-bearing Plants of Ecuador. 1924. *Contributions from the United States National Herbarium* 24 (5): 101-134.

Porterfield Jr., W.M. The Principal Chinese Vegetable Foods and Food Plants of Chinatown Markets. 1951. *Economic Botany* 5 (1): 3-37.

Powell, J.M. Ethnobotany. *In* New Guinea Vegetation, K. Paijmans (ed.). 1976. Elsevier Scientific Publishing Co. Amsterdam.

Prance, G.T., and M. Freitas da Silva. Flora Neotropica. Caryocaraceae. 1973. Hafner Publishing. New York.

Proulx, Annie, and Lew Nichols. Sweet & Hard Cider. 1980. Garden Way Publishing. Charlotte, Vermont.

Quaintance, Cheryl. There's Gold Dust in Those Hills. 1986. *Mushroom* 4 (4): 9-11.

Quin, J.P. Food and Feeding Habits of the Pedi. 1959. Witwatersrand University Press. Johannesburg.

Ramachandran, Kamala, and B. Subramaniam. Scarlet Gourd, Coccinia grandis, Little-Known Tropical Drug Plant. 1983. *Economic Botany* 37 (4): 380-383.

Ramsay, Charles W. The Yellow Sapote. 1973. *California Rare Fruit Growers Yearbook* 5. 21-23.

Rao, S. Appa, Melak H. Mengesha, and D. Sharma. Collection and Evaluation of Pearl Millet (Pennisetum americanum) Germplasm from Ghana. 1985. *Economic Botany* 39 (1): 25-38.

Ray, Richard, and Lance Walheim. Citrus: How to Select, Grow & Enjoy. 1980. HP Books. Tucson, Arizona.

Rehder, Alfred. Manual of Cultivated Trees and Shrubs. Second edition, 1951. Macmillan Co. New York.

Reuther, Walter, H.J. Webber, and L.D. Batchelor. The Citrus Industry, Volume I. Revised edition, 1967. University of California Press. Berkeley.

Reynolds, G.W. The Aloes of Tropical Africa and Madagascar. 1966. The Aloes Book Fund. Mbabane, Swaziland.

Reynolds, P.K. The Banana. 1927. Houghton Mifflin. Boston and New York.

Richardson, Dr. Mabel W. Tropical Fruit Recipes. 1976. Rare Fruit Council International. Miami.

Richmond, Amos. Handbook of Microalgal Mass Culture. 1986. CRC Press. Boca Raton, Florida.

Richmond, Sonya. International Vegetarian Cookery. 1976. Arco Publishing Co. New York.

Rifai, Mien A., and Ischak Lubis. Fruits. 1977. Food and Agriculture Organization of the United Nations. Rome. English edition, 1980.

Riley, John M. The Pitanga. 1971. *California Rare Fruit Growers Yearbook* 3. 14-25.

Riley, John M. Texas Persimmon. 1976. *California Rare Fruit Growers Yearbook* 8. 82-83.

Riley, John M. Two Exotic Suggestions...For the Adventurous. 1982. *California Rare Fruit Growers Newsletter* 14 (4): 5-7.

Riley, John M. Solana: Fruit of the Future. 1983. *California Rare Fruit Growers Yearbook* 15. 47-72.

Ritter, Joe, and Allan Safarik. Mock Java. 1977. General Printers. Surrey, British Columbia.

Roberts, A.N., and L.A. Hammers. The Native Pacific Plum in Oregon. 1951. Oregon Agr. Exp. St. Bull. 502. Corvallis.

Rodale, J.I., ed. How to Grow Vegetables and Fruits by the Organic Method. 1961. Rodale Press. Emmaus, Pennsylvania.

Rohde, Eleanor Sinclair. Vegetable Cultivation and Cookery. 1938. The Medici Society. London.

Rom, Roy C., and Robert F. Carlson. Rootstocks for Fruit Crops. 1987. John Wiley & Sons. New York.

Romanko, R.R. Guide to American Hops. *In* Steiner's Guide to American Hops. 1973. S.S. Steiner, Inc.

Ronald, W.G., and H.J. Temmerman. Tree Fruits for the Prairie Provinces. 1982. Agriculture Canada. Pub. 1672/E. Ottawa.

Root, Waverly. Food. 1980a. Simon & Schuster. New York.

Root, Waverly, ed. Herbs and Spices: The Pursuit of Flavor. 1980b. McGraw-Hill. New York.

Rosengarten Jr., Frederic. The Book of Edible Nuts. 1984. Walker and Company. New York.

Rounds, Marvin B. Check List of Avocado Varieties. 1950. *California Avocado Society Yearbook* 34. 178-205.

Ruck, H.C. Deciduous Fruit Tree Cultivars for Tropical and Sub-Tropical Regions. 1975. Commonwealth Agricultural Bureaux. Farnham Royal, England.

Sacks, Frank M. A Literature Review of Phaseolus angularis - The Adsuki Bean. 1977. *Economic Botany* 31 (1): 9-15.

Sale, P.R. Kiwifruit Culture. 1985. New Zealand Government Printing Office. Wellington.

Sanders, Rosanne. The Apple Book. 1988. Philosophical Library. New York.

Sauer, Jonathan D. The Grain Amaranths and Their Relatives: A Revised Taxonomic and Geographic Survey. 1967. *Ann. Missouri Bot. Gard.* 54 (2): 103-137.

Sawyer, Sharon. A New Way with Squash. 1985. *Organic Gardening* 32 (8): 31-32.

Schery, Robert W. Plants for Man. Second Edition, 1972. Prentice-Hall. Englewood Cliffs, New Jersey.

Schneider, Elizabeth. Uncommon Fruits & Vegetables: A Commonsense Guide. 1986. Harper & Row. New York.

Schultes, Richard Evans, and Rafael Romero-Castañeda. Edible Fruits of Solanum in Columbia. 1962. *Harvard University Botanical Museum Leaflets* 19. 235-286.

Scott, Barbara S. Brussels Sprouts: A Winter Treat. 1984. *Organic Gardening* 31 (4): 40-42.

Shanks, James B. Persimmons: Fruiting and Landscape Trees for Maryland. 1988. Coop. Ext. Serv., Univ. of Maryland, Pub. No. 112-88. College Park.

Sheen, Shuh J., and Vera L. Sheen. Functional Properties of Fraction 1 Protein from Tobacco Leaf. 1985. *Journal of Agricultural and Food Chemistry* 33 (1): 79-83.

Shiskin, B.K., ed. Flora of the U.S.S.R., Volume XV. 1949. Keter Publishing House. Jerusalem. English translation, 1974.

Shurtleff, William and Akiko Aoyagi. The Book of Tofu. 1975. Autumn Press. Brookline, Massachusetts.

Shurtleff, William and Akiko Aoyagi. The Book of Miso. 1976. Autumn Press. Kanagawa-ken, Japan.

Shurtleff, William and Akiko Aoyagi. The Book of Kudzu. 1977. Autumn Press. Brookline, Massachusetts.

Shurtleff, William and Akiko Aoyagi. The Book of Tempeh: Professional Edition. 1979. Harper & Row. New York.

Simmonds, N.W. The Grain Chenopods of the Tropical American Highlands. 1965. *Economic Botany* 19 (3): 223-235.

Simmonds, N.W. Bananas. Second edition, 1966. Longman. London and New York.

Simmons, Alan F. Growing Unusual Fruit. 1972. Walker and Company. New York.

Simmons, Alan F. Simmons' Manual of Fruit. 1978. David & Charles. London.

Sing, Phia. Traditional Recipes of Laos. 1981. Prospect Books. London.

Singh, H.B., and R.K. Arora. Soh-phlong, Moghania vestita A Leguminous Root Crop of India. 1973. *Economic Botany* 27 (3): 332-338.

Singh, R.N. Mango. 1978. Indian Council of Agricultural Research. New Delhi.

Smith, Arlo Hale. The Chestnut. 1976. *California Rare Fruit Growers Yearbook* 8. 15-51.

Smith, Joseph C. Notes on Growing Passifloras in La Mesa. 1979. *California Rare Fruit Growers Yearbook* 11. 56-58.

Soegeng-Reksodihardjo, Wertit. The Species of Durio with Edible Fruits. 1962. *Economic Botany* 16 (4): 270-282.

Solomon, Charmaine. The Complete Asian Cookbook. 1976. McGraw-Hill Book Co. New York.

Somos, András. The Paprika. 1984. Akadémiai Kiadó. Budapest.

Soost, Robert K., and James W. Cameron. Oroblanco: A New Grapefruit Hybrid. 1980. *California Agriculture* 34 (11-12): 16-17.

Soost, Robert K., and James W. Cameron. Melogold, a New Pummelo-Grapefruit Hybrid. 1986. *California Agriculture* 40 (1-2): 30-31.

Stamets, Paul, and J.S. Chilton. The Mushroom Cultivator. 1983. Agarikon Press. Olympia, Washington.

Stebbins, Robert L. and Lance Walheim. Western Fruit, Berries, & Nuts. 1981. HP Books. Tucson, Arizona.

Steineck, Hellmut. Mushrooms in the Garden. English translation, 1984. Mad River Press. Eureka, California.

Steinkraus, Keith H., ed. Handbook of Indigenous Fermented Foods. 1983. Marcel Dekker. New York.

Stewart, Robert B., and Asnake Getachew. Investigations of the Nature of Injera. 1962. *Economic Botany* 16 (2): 127-130.

Stone, Benjamin C. Studies in Malesian Pandanaceae XVII: On the Taxonomy of 'Pandan Wangi', A Pandanus Cultivar With Scented Leaves. 1978. *Economic Botany* 32 (3): 285-293.

Sturrock, David. Fruits for Southern Florida. 1959. Horticultural Books. Stuart, Florida. Reprint, 1980.

Styles, B.T., ed. Infraspecific Classification of Wild & Cultivated Plants. 1986. Clarendon Press. Oxford.

Tanaka, Tyôzaburô. Tanaka's Cyclopedia of Edible Plants of the World. 1976. Keigaku Publishing Co. Tokyo.

Tapley, William T., Walter D. Enzie, and Glen P. Van Eseltine. Sweet Corn of New York. 1934. New York State Agricultural Experiment Station. Albany.

Tapley, William T., Walter D. Enzie, and Glen P. Van Eseltine. The Cucurbits of New York. 1937. New York State Agricultural Experiment Station. Albany.

Tate, Joyce L. Cactus Cookbook. Third edition, 1976. Cactus and Succulent Society of America. Arcadia, California.

Terrell, E.E., and L.R. Batra. Zizania latifolia and Ustilago esculenta, a Grass-Fungus Association. 1982. *Economic Botany* 36 (3): 274-285.

Thies, Noel. Hicksbeachia, A Neglected Native Australian Nut. 1976. *West Australian Nutgrowing Society Yearbook* 2. 46-51.

Thompson, Bruce. Syrup Trees. 1978. Walnut Press. Fountain Hills, Arizona.

Thompson, Pam. The Original Vidalia Onion Cookbook. 1981. Vidalia Chamber of Commerce. Vidalia, Georgia.

Thomson, Paul H. The Carob in California. 1971. *California Rare Fruit Growers Yearbook* 3. 61-102.

Thomson, Paul H. The White Sapote. 1973. *California Rare Fruit Growers Yearbook* 5. 6-20.

Thomson, Paul H. The Pawpaw: Brought up to Date. 1974. *California Rare Fruit Growers Yearbook* 6. 138-180.

Thomson, Paul H. The Carissa in California. 1976. *California Rare Fruit Growers Yearbook* 8. 73-81.

Thomson, Paul H. The Catalina Island Cherry. 1977. *California Rare Fruit Growers Newsletter* 9 (2): 6-7.

Thomson, Paul H., ed. Avocado Grower's Handbook. 1983. Bonsall Publications. Bonsall, California.

Thomson, Paul H., ed. Kiwifruit Handbook. 1988. Bonsall Publications. Bonsall, California.

Turner, Nancy J., and Adam F. Szczawinski. Wild Coffees, Teas and Beverages of Canada. 1978. National Museums of Canada. Ottawa.

Turner, Nancy J., and Adam F. Szczawinski. Edible Wild Fruits and Nuts of Canada. 1979. National Museums of Canada. Ottawa.

Undset, Sigrid. Some Notes Upon the Use of Herbs in Norwegian Households. 1945. *The Herbarist* 11. 9-14.

Uphof, J.C.Th. Dictionary of Economic Plants. Second edition, 1968. Verlag Von J. Cramer. Lehre, Germany.

Usai, Angelino. Acorn Bread and Geophagy in Sardinia. 1969. Editrice Sarda Fratelli Fossataro. Cagliari, Sardinia. Abridged English Translation by Susan Mazzarella, 1980.

USDA. Cheeses of the World. 1972. Dover Publications. New York.

Valenzuela, J., C. Rojas, I. Godoy, and W. Lobos. Native Fruits and Nuts of Chile. 1984. *Western Australian Nut & Tree Crop Assn. Yearbook*. 9. 44-47.

van Epenhuijsen, C.W. Growing Native Vegetables in Nigeria. 1974. Food and Agriculture Organization of the United Nations. Rome.

van Wyk, P. The Marula, Sclerocarya caffra, an African Nut Tree. 1976. *West Australian Nutgrowing Society Yearbook* 2. 53-60.

Varisco, Daniel M. The Qat Factor in North Yemen's Agricultural Development. 1988. *Culture and Agriculture* 34. 11-14.

Vaughan, J.G., A.J. Macleod, and B.M.G. Jones. The Biology and Chemistry of the Cruciferae. 1976. Academic Press. London.

Vilmorin-Andrieux, MM. The Vegetable Garden. English edition, 1885. Jeavons-Leler Press. Palo Alto, California. Reprint, 1976.

von Aderkas, Patrick. Economic History of Ostrich Fern, Matteuccia struthiopteris, The Edible Fiddlehead. 1984. *Economic Botany* 38 (1): 14-23.

von Reis, Siri, and Frank J. Lipp, Jr. New Plant Sources for Drugs and Foods from the New York Botanical Garden Herbarium. 1982. Harvard University Press. Cambridge, Massachusetts.

von Welanetz, Diana, and Paul von Welanetz. The Von Welanetz Guide to Ethnic Ingredients. 1982. J.P. Tarcher, Inc. Los Angeles.

Wagner, Philip M. A Wine-Grower's Guide. 1976. Alfred A. Knopf. New York.

Wagoner, Peggy. Perennial Grain Research at the Rodale Research Center. 1987 Summary. 1988. Rodale Press. Emmaus, Pennsylvania.

Watt, Sir George. A Dictionary of the Economic Products of India. 1889-1896. Superintendent of Printing. Calcutta. Six volumes.

Waugh, F.A. Plums and Plum Culture. 1910. Orange Judd Co. New York.

Weatherwax, Paul. Indian Corn in Old America. 1954. The Macmillan Co. New York.

Wester, P.J. The Food Plants of the Philippines. Third edition, 1924. Dept. of Agr. Nat. Res. Manila.

Whallon, Dorothy, and Robert Whallon. The Herbal Teas of Crete: Thryba. 1977. *The Herbarist* 43. 43-45.

Whistler, Roy L. Industrial Gums from Plants: Guar and Chia. 1982. *Economic Botany* 36 (2): 195-202.

Whitehouse, W.E. The Pistachio Nut - A New Crop for the Western United States. 1957. *Economic Botany* 11 (4): 281-321.

Whitman, William F. Personal communication. 1990. Bal Harbour, Florida.

Whitney, Leo D., F.A.I. Bowers, and M. Takahashi. Taro Varieties in Hawaii. 1939. University of Hawaii. Agr. Exp. St. Bull. No. 84. Honolulu.

Wickson, Edward J. The California Fruits and How to Grow Them. Seventh edition, 1914. Pacific Rural Press. San Francisco.

Wilder, G.P. Fruits of The Hawaiian Islands. Revised edition, 1911. The Hawaiian Gazette Co. Honolulu.

Wilkes, H. Garrison. Interesting Beverages of the Eastern Himalayas. 1968. *Economic Botany* 22 (4): 347-353.

Will, George F., and George E. Hyde. Corn Among the Indians of the Upper Missouri. 1917. University of Nebraska Press. Lincoln. Reprint, 1964.

Williams, Louis O. The Useful Plants of Central America. 1981. *Ceiba* 24 (1-2): 1-342.

Williams, R.R., and R.D. Child. Cider Apples and their Characters. 1960-65. University of Bristol. Long Ashton Res. Sta. Ann. Reports. Bristol, England.

Wilson, E.H. A Naturalist in Western China. 1913. Doubleday, Page & Co. New York.

Wilson, Ellen Gibson. A West African Cookbook. 1971. M. Evans & Co. New York.

Wilson, Gilbert L. Agriculture of The Hidatsa Indians. 1917. J & L Reprint Company. Lincoln, Nebraska. Reprint, 1977.

Wilson, Hugh D. Domesticated Chenopodium of the Ozark Bluff Dwellers. 1981. *Economic Botany* 35 (2): 233-239.

Winkler, A.J., J.A. Cook, and L.A. Lider. General Viticulture. Second edition, 1974. University of California Press. Berkeley.

Winter, Peggy. A Great New Blueberry Plant, The Cactus. 1979. *California Rare Fruit Growers Newsletter* 11 (4): 10-12.

Winters, Harold F. Ceylon Spinach (Basella rubra). 1963. *Economic Botany* 17 (1): 195-199.

Withee, John E. Growing and Cooking Beans. 1980. Yankee, Inc. Dublin, New Hampshire.

Wolf, Ray. Home Soyfood Equipment. 1981. Rodale Press. Emmaus, Pennsylvania.

Wolfert, Paula. Couscous and Other Good Food from Morocco. 1973. Harper & Row. New York.

Wood, Ed. World Sourdoughs from Antiquity. 1989. Sinclair Publishing. Cascade, Idaho.

Wood, Rebecca. Quinoa: The Supergrain. 1989. Japan Publications. Tokyo.

Wrigley, Gorden. Coffee. 1988. Longman. Harlow, Essex.

Yanovsky, Elias. Food Plants of the North American Indians. 1936. United States Department of Agriculture, Misc. Pub. No. 237. Washington, D.C.

Yashiroda, Kan, ed. Handbook on Japanese Herbs and Their Uses. 1968. *Plants & Gardens* 24 (2).

Yensen, Nicholas P. Development of a Rare Halophyte Grain: Prospects For Reclamation of Salt-Ruined Lands. 1987. *Journal of the Washington Academy of Sciences* 77 (4): 209-214.

Yensen, Nicholas P. Plants for Salty Soil. 1988. *Arid Lands Newsletter* 27. 3-10.

Young, Robert A. Flavor Qualities of Some Edible Oriental Bamboos. 1954. *Economic Botany* 8 (4): 377-386.

Young, Robert A., and Joseph R. Haun. Bamboo in The United States: Description, Culture, and Utilization. 1961. United States Department of Agriculture. Agr. Hand. No. 193. Washington, D.C.

Zahradnik, Fred. Nature's No-Till: Perennial Grains May One Day Put the Bread on Our Tables. 1985. *The New Farm* 7 (3): 38-41.

Zennie, Thomas M., and C. Dwayne Ogzewalla. Ascorbic Acid and Vitamin C Content of Edible Wild Plants of Ohio and Kentucky. 1977. *Economic Botany* 31 (1): 76-79.

Zeven, A.C., and J.M.J. de Wet. Dictionary of Cultivated Plants & Their Regions of Diversity. Second edition, 1982. Centre for Agricultural Publishing and Documentation. Wageningen, The Netherlands.

INDICES AND APPENDICES

INDEX OF PRINCIPAL VERNACULAR NAMES

Abiu Pouteria caimito
Abo Annona senegalensis
Abricó do Pará Mammea americana
Abu suwaif Hordeum bulbosum
Aby Talinum portulacifolium
Abyssinian banana Ensete ventricosum
Abyssinian cabbage Brassica carinata
Abyssinian gooseberry Dovyalis abyssinica
Abyssinian mustard Brassica carinata
Abyssinian oat Avena abyssinica
Abyssinian tea Catha edulis
Acaí Euterpe oleracea
Acanthus-leaved thistle Carlina acanthifolia
Acerola Malpighia punicifolia
Acha Digitaria exilis
Achillea noire Achillea atrata
Achira Canna edulis
Achoccha Cyclanthera pedata
Acidophilus milk bacteria Lactobacillus acidophilus
Acinos Acinos arvensis
Acueyo Piper sanctum
Acuyo Piper auritum
Adam and Eve Aplectrum hyemale
Adam's needle Yucca filamentosa
Adder's grass Dactylorhiza maculata
Adlay Coix lacryma-jobi
Admirable boletus Boletus mirabilis
Aduki bean Vigna angularis
Adzuki bean Vigna angularis
Afraba Malacantha alnifolia
African boxwood Myrsine africana
African breadfruit Treculia africana
African cabbage Brassica carinata
African copaida balsam Daniellia oliveri
African horned cucumber Cucumis metuliferus
African linden Mitragyna stipulosa
African mammee apple Mammea africana
African mangosteen Garcinia livingstonei
African oil palm Elaeis guineensis
African perennial rice Oryza barthii
African potato Coleus parviflorus
African scarlet eggplant Solanum aethiopicum
African tragacanth Sterculia tragacantha
African tulip tree Spathodea campanulata
African valerian Fedia cornucopiae
African wild rice Oryza longistaminata
African wormwood Artemisia afra
African yam bean Sphenostylis stenocarpa
Agati Sesbania bispinosa
Agati Sesbania grandiflora
Agricultural mustard Sinapis arvensis
Agrimony Agrimonia eupatoria
Agrito Mahonia swaseyi
Agrito Mahonia trifoliolata
Ag-dae-geneesbossie Hermannia hyssopifolia
Ahuijote Erythrina glauca
Aimbe Rungia klossii
Ainu mulberry Morus alba var. indica
Air potato Dioscorea alata
Air potato Dioscorea bulbifera
Ai-yü-tzu Ficus pumila var. awkeotsang
Ajefowo Celosia trigyna
Ajong Baccaurea angulata
Ajowan Trachyspermum ammi
Ajwain Trachyspermum ammi
Akagi Bischofia javanica
Akar kapajang Hodgsonia macrocarpa
Akar kunyit-kunyit Tiliacora triandra
Akaytjirra Solanum centrale
Aka-mono Gaultheria adenothrix
Akebi Akebia quinata
Akee Blighia sapida
Akita-buki Petasites japonicus var. giganteus
Aki-gumi Elaeagnus umbellata
Aki-no-tamura-sô Salvia japonica
Al moulinouquia Corchorus trilocularis
Alacrán Stachytarpheta cayennensis
Alaska berry Rubus arcticus
Alaska spiraea Spiraea beauverdiana
Alcaparro Cassia tomentosa
Alcapparra Capparis spinosa
Alecost Balsamita major
Alehoof Glechoma hederacea
Alemow Citrus x macrophylla
Alexanders Smyrnium olusatrum
Alexandrian laurel Calophyllum inophyllum
Alfalfa Medicago sativa
Alfilerea Erodium cicutarium
Algaroba Prosopis chilensis
Algerian tea Paronychia argentea
Algerian tea Paronychia capitata
Algerita Mahonia haematocarpa
Alibangbang Bauhinia malabarica
Alicoche Echinocereus conglomeratus
Alkali bulrush Scirpus paludosus
Alkali sacaton Sporobolus airoides
Alkanet Anchusa officinalis
Allegheny blackberry Rubus allegheniensis
Allegheny chinkapin Castanea pumila
Allegheny plum Prunus alleghaniensis
Allegheny shadblow Amelanchier laevis
Allgood Chenopodium bonus-henricus
Alligator apple Annona glabra
Alligator cardamom Aframomum elliotii
Alligator juniper Juniperus pachyphlaea
Allspice Pimenta dioica
All-heal Prunella vulgaris

Aracá Psidium guineense
Araca-boi Eugenia stipitata
Arage-kikurage Auricularia polytricha
Araticú grande Annona montana
Arborescent philodendron Philodendron selloum
Arbre à beurre Caryocar villosum
Archangel red dead-nettle Lamium purpureum
Arctic beauty kiwi Actinidia kolomikta
Arctic bramble Rubus arcticus
Arctic raspberry Rubus arcticus
Arctic willow Salix daphnoides
Areuj kathembang Embelia ribes
Argan tree Argania spinosa
Argentine Potentilla anserina
Argyle apple Eucalyptus cinerea
Arida Tetrapleura tetraptera
Arizona barrel cactus Ferocactus wislizenii
Arizona black walnut Juglans major
Arizona walnut Juglans major
Arjoon sadura Terminalia glabra
Armenian cucumber Cucumis melo Flexuosus Group 'Armenian'
Aromatic lactic bacteria Leuconostoc cremoris
Aromatic lactic bacteria Streptococcus cremoris
Aromatic lactic bacteria Streptococcus diacetilactis
Aromatic lactic bacteria Streptococcus lactis
Arracacha Arracacia xanthorhiza
Arrayan Amyrsia foliosa
Arrayan Mitranthes sartoriana
Arrow arum Peltandra virginica
Arrowhead Sagittaria latifolia
Arrowhead Sagittaria sagittifolia
Arrowleaf balsam-root Balsamorhiza sagittata
Arrowroot Maranta arundinacea
Artichoke Cynara scolymus
Arugula Eruca sativa
Asafoetida Ferula assa-foetida
Asam payo Salacca conferta
Asam susur Hibiscus acetosella
Asatsuki Allium ledebourianum
Asaza Nymphoides peltata
Ash pumpkin Benincasa hispida
Ashanti pepper Piper guineense
Ashok Saraca bijuga
Ashweed Aegopodium podagraria
Ash-leaved maple Negundo aceroides
Asian pear Pyrus pyrifolia
Asiatic ginseng Panax pseudoginseng
Asparagus Asparagus officinalis
Asparagus bean Vigna unguiculata ssp. sesquipedalis
Asparagus lettuce Lactuca sativa Angustana Group
Asparagus pea Tetragonolobus purpureus
Asphodel Asphodeline lutea
Assaí palm Euterpe edulis
Assyrian plum Cordia myxa
Astrakan wheat Triticum polonicum
Ataco Amaranthus quitensis
Atemoya Annona x atemoya
Athel tamarisk Tamarix aphylla
Attoto yam Dioscorea cayenensis
Aubergine Solanum melongena
Aurmá-rana Thalia geniculata
Australian bottle tree Adansonia gregorii
Australian bush-cherry Syzygium paniculatum
Australian cress Spilanthes acmella
Australian finger lime Microcitrus australasica
Australian flame Brachychiton diversifolium
Australian honeysuckle Banksia marginata
Australian passionfruit Passiflora herbertiana
Australian pea Dolichos lignosus
Australian plum Podocarpus elatus
Australian rosenut Hicksbeachia pinnatifida
Australian saltbush Atriplex semibaccata
Australian sandalwood Eucarya spicata
Australian spinach Chenopodium murale
Australian spinach Tetragonia implexicoma
Autumn olive Elaeagnus umbellata
Auvergne lentil Vicia monantha
Avellano Gevuina avellana
Avocado Persea americana
Azarole Crataegus azarolus
Azores bay Laurus azorica
Azores thyme Thymus caespititius
Aztec marigold Tagetes erecta
Aztec sweet-herb Phyla scaberrima
Azuki bean Vigna angularis
Azusa Catalpa ovata
Baba de boi Syagrus comosa
Babadotan lalaki Synedrella nodiflora
Babassú Orbignya martiana
Bacaba de azeite Oenocarpus distichus
Bacaba oil-palm Oenocarpus bacaba
Bachelor's button Centaurea cyanus
Baco nut Tieghemella heckelii
Bacuparí Rheedia brasiliensis
Bacuripari Rheedia macrophylla
Bacury-pary Rheedia macrophylla
Badan Bergenia crassifolia
Bael fruit Aegle marmelos
Bagu Gnetum gnemon
Baimo Fritillaria verticillata
Baked-apple berry Rubus chamaemorus
Bákli Lagerstroemia parviflora
Balata Manilkara bidentata
Baldmoney Meum athamanticum
Balingu shahri Lallemantia iberica
Ballar Dolichos lignosus
Ballhead onion Allium sphaerocephalum
Balm Melissa officinalis
Balm mint Mentha aquatica var. crispa
Balm of Gilead Cedronella canariensis
Baloon berry Rubus illecebrosus
Balsam apple Momordica balsamina
Balsam fir Abies balsamea
Balsam of Peru Myroxylon balsamum var. pereirae
Balsam of Tolu Myroxylon balsamum
Balsam pear Momordica charantia
Balsamic sage Salvia grandiflora
Baltracan Laser trilobum
Balú Erythrina edulis
Bambara groundnut Voandzeia subterranea
Bamboo palm Raphia vinifera
Bambu Chrysophyllum lacourtianum
Bammerwa Elaeagnus umbellata var. parvifolia
Banana Musa x paradisiaca
Banana de Macaco Philodendron bipinnatifidum
Banana passionfruit Passiflora antioquiensis
Banana passionfruit Passiflora mollissima
Banana shrub Michelia figo
Banana yucca Yucca baccata
Bandorhulla Duabanga sonneratioides
Báns Dendrocalamus strictus
Bantèng Cissus discolor
Baobob Adansonia digitata
Baput Dolichos malosanus
Baranga Kydia calycina
Barba de viejo Melocactus ruestii
Barbados cherry Malpighia punicifolia
Barbados gooseberry Pereskia aculeata
Barbasco Paullinia pinnata
Barbed-wire cactus Acanthocereus tetragonus
Barbeen Arabis caucasica
Bard vetch Vicia monantha

Black elder	Sambucus nigra
Black elderberry	Sambucus melanocarpa
Black fonio	Digitaria iburua
Black gram	Vigna mungo
Black gum	Nyssa sylvatica
Black haw	Viburnum prunifolium
Black hawthorn	Crataegus douglasii
Black hickory	Carya illinoensis
Black highbush blueberry	Vaccinium atrococcum
Black hollyhock	Alcea rosea 'Nigra
Black huckleberry	Gaylussacia baccata
Black huckleberry	Vaccinium ovalifolium
Black ironwood	Krugiodendron ferreum
Black locust	Robinia pseudacacia
Black lovage	Smyrnium olusatrum
Black maple	Acer nigrum
Black medic	Medicago lupulina
Black morel	Morchella angusticeps
Black mulberry	Morus nigra
Black mustard	Brassica nigra
Black nightshade	Solanum nigrum
Black pepper	Piper nigrum
Black persimmon	Diospyros texana
Black pine	Podocarpus spicatus
Black plum	Vitex doniana
Black raspberry	Rubus occidentalis
Black rhum palm	Borassus aethiopum
Black sage	Salvia mellifera
Black salsify	Scorzonera hispanica
Black sapote	Diospyros digyna
Black sloe	Prunus umbellata
Black spruce	Picea mariana
Black sugar-maple	Acer nigrum
Black truffle	Tuber melanosporum
Black trumpet-of-death	Craterellus fallax
Blackberry-jam fruit	Randia formosa
Blackcap	Rubus occidentalis
Blackthorn	Prunus spinosa
Black-wood	Cotoneaster racemiflora
Bladder campion	Silene vulgaris
Bladder dock	Rumex vesicarius
Bladder nut	Diospyros whyteana
Bladderpod	Isomeris arborea
Blade apple	Pereskia aculeata
Bledo	Amaranthus hypochondriacus
Bledo extranjero	Chenopodium berlandieri
Blessed thistle	Cnicus benedictus
Blewits	Clitocybe nuda
Blond psyllium	Plantago ovata
Blood leaf	Iresine herbstii
Bloodwort	Rumex sanguineus
Blue appleberry	Billardiera longiflora
Blue camass	Camassia quamash
Blue crown passion-flower	Passiflora caerulea
Blue dicks	Brodiaea pulchella
Blue elderberry	Sambucus glauca
Blue flax	Linum perenne
Blue grape	Myrciaria vexator
Blue grape	Vitis argentifolia
Blue guarri	Euclea crispa
Blue gum	Eucalyptus globulus
Blue lilly pilly	Syzygium coolminianum
Blue lotus of Egypt	Nymphaea caerulea
Blue lotus of India	Nymphaea stellata
Blue lupin	Lupinus angustifolius
Blue mallee	Eucalyptus polybractea
Blue mallow	Malva sylvestris
Blue mold	Penicillium roqueforti
Blue porterweed	Stachytarpheta jamaicensis
Blue quandong	Elaeocarpus grandis
Blue Ridge blueberry	Vaccinium corymbosum var. pallidum
Blue sage	Salvia clevelandii
Blue tangle	Gaylussacia frondosa
Blue vervain	Verbena hastata
Blue violet	Viola papilionacea
Blue water lily	Nymphaea caerulea
Blue wood	Condalia obovata
Bluebeard sage	Salvia viridis
Blueberried honeysuckle	Lonicera caerulea var. edulis
Blueberry elder	Sambucus glauca
Blueleaf grape	Vitis argentifolia
Boa constrictor	Rathbunia alamosensis
Bodmon sok	Phlomis tuberosa
Boer honey-pot	Protea cynaroides
Bog bilberry	Vaccinium uliginosum
Bog myrtle	Myrica gale
Bog rosemary	Andromeda glaucophylla
Bogbean	Menyanthes trifoliata
Bog-rosemary	Chamaedaphne calyculata
Bog-tea	Ledum palustre
Bok choy	Brassica rapa Chinensis Group
Bokhara plum	Prunus bokhariensis
Bok-hop	Lilium brownii
Boldo	Peumus boldus
Bolivian sunroot	Polymnia sonchifolia
Bollwiller pear	X Sorbopyrus auricularis
Bonavista bean	Lablab purpureus
Bonnet D'Eveque	Barringtonia butonica
Bonnet pepper	Capsicum chinense
Boombo	Pothomorphe umbellata
Boowah kontol monjèt	Ficus hirta
Borage	Borago officinalis
Borneo olive	Canarium odontophyllum
Borojo	Borojoa patinoi
Bory bamboo	Phyllostachys nigra f. boryana
Botan	Paeonia suffruticosa
Botanzuru	Clematis apiifolia
Botha grass	Vetiveria zizanioides
Bottle gourd	Lagenaria siceraria
Boulder raspberry	Rubus deliciosus
Bower berry	Actinidia arguta
Box huckleberry	Gaylussacia brachycera
Boxthorn	Lycium carolinianum
Box-elder	Negundo aceroides
Bracken	Pteridium aquilinum
Braganza	Brassica oleracea Tronchuda Group
Bramble	Rubus fruticosus
Bramble of the Cape	Rubus rosaefolius
Brazil cherry	Eugenia dombeyi
Brazil cress	Spilanthes acmella 'Oleracea'
Brazil nut	Bertholletia excelsa
Brazilian cherry	Eugenia uniflora
Brazilian fireweed	Erechtites valerianifolia
Brazilian guava	Psidium guineense
Brazilian mallow	Abutilon megapotamicum
Brazilian pepper	Schinus terebinthifolius
Brazilian pine	Araucaria angustifolia
Bread wheat	Triticum x aestivum
Bread yeast	Saccharomyces cerevisiae
Breadfruit	Artocarpus altilis
Breadnut	Artocarpus altilis 'Seminifera'
Breadseed poppy	Papaver somniferum
Breath of heaven	Adenandra fragrans
Briançon apricot	Armeniaca brigantina
Brick cap	Hypholoma sublateritium
Brier rose	Rosa canina
Brigham Young tea	Ephedra torreyana
Brinjal	Solanum melongena
Bristly sarsaparilla	Aralia hispida
British leek	Allium ampeloprasum var. babingtonii
Broad bean	Faba vulgaris
Broadleaf chives	Allium senescens

Horse gram Macrotyloma uniflorum
Horse mango Mangifera foetida
Horse mushroom Agaricus arvensis
Horse purslane Zaleya pentandra
Horsemint Monarda fistulosa
Horsemint Monarda punctata
Horseradish Armoracia rusticana
Horseradish tree Moringa oleifera
Horsetooth amaranth Amaranthus lividus
Horseweed Conyza canadensis
Horse-brier Smilax rotundifolia
Horse-heal Inula helenium
Horse-mint Mentha longifolia
Horse-sugar Symplocos tinctoria
Hortulan plum Prunus hortulana
Hosoba-kisuge Hemerocallis minor
Hosoba-suikazura Lonicera henryi
Hosoba-tade Persicaria hydropiper 'Fastigiatum'
Hotaru-bukuro Campanula punctata
Hotei-chiku Phyllostachys aurea
Hottentot bread Encephalartos hildebrandtii
Hottentot fig Carpobrotus edulis
Hottentot tea Helichrysum serpyllifolium
Hottentot tobacco Tarchonanthus camphoratus
Hottentot's almond Brabejum stellatifolium
Hound's tongue Cynoglossum officinale
Hô-no-ki Magnolia hypoleuca
Hsiang-ju Elsholtzia ciliata
Hsin-i Magnolia kobus
Hsuan-tso Spondias axillaris
Hsüeh-li Ficus pumila
Huang-lien-mu Pistacia chinensis
Huauzontle Chenopodium nuttaliae
Hua-chiao Zanthoxylum simulans
Hudson Bay currant Ribes hudsonianum
Huisnay Spathiphyllum phryniifolium
Huitlacoche Ustilago maydis
Hulless barley Hordeum vulgare Coeleste Group
Hulless oat Avena nuda
Húng gioi Mentha arvensis ssp. haplocalyx
Hungarian chamomile Chamomilla aurea
Hungarian oat Avena orientalis
Hungry rice Digitaria iburua
Huni Hernandia moerenhoutiana
Huon pine Lagarostrobus franklinii
Husk tomato Physalis pubescens
Hyacinth bean Lablab purpureus
Hyssop Hyssopus officinalis
Ibe Jessenia polycarpa
Ibuki-jakô-sô Thymus quinquecostatum
Iburu Digitaria iburua
Icaco plum Chrysobalanus icaco
Ice plant Mesembryanthemum crystallinum
Ice-cream bean Inga edulis
Ice-cream bean Inga paterno
Ice-cream bean Inga sp.
Ichang lime Citrus hystrix
Ichang papeda Citrus ichangensis
Ichô Ginkgo biloba
Idar Leptadenia hastata
Igikindye Dolichos malosanus
Iglayglih Carrichtera annua
Ikan Solanum incanum
Ilama Annona diversifolia
Illawarra plum Podocarpus elatus
Illinois bundleflower Desmanthus brachylobus
Illipe nut Madhuca indica
Illyrian cotton-thistle Onopordon illyricum
Imbé Garcinia livingstonei
Imbú Spondias tuberosa
Imphee Sorghum bicolor Saccharatum Group
Inca wheat Amaranthus caudatus
Incense tree Canarium schweinfurthii
Inchu Phoenix pusilla
Indian almond Terminalia catappa
Indian barberry Berberis aristata
Indian barberry Berberis lycium
Indian blue pine Pinus wallichiana
Indian bread Poria cocos
Indian breadroot Psoralea esculenta
Indian butter tree Madhuca longifolia
Indian cabbage Stanleya pinnatifida
Indian capers Capparis sepiaria
Indian cassia Cinnamomum tamala
Indian chickweed Mollugo verticillata
Indian corn Zea mays
Indian cress Tropaeolum majus
Indian cucumber-root Medeola virginiana
Indian dill Anethum graveolens 'Sowa'
Indian dwarf wheat Triticum sphaerococcum
Indian fig Opuntia ficus-indica
Indian gamboge tree Garcinia morella
Indian jalap Operculina turpethum
Indian jujube Ziziphus mauritiana
Indian kale Xanthosoma sagittifolium
Indian lettuce Lactuca indica
Indian long pepper Piper longum
Indian mallow Abutilon guineense
Indian millet Oryzopsis hymenoides
Indian millet Sorghum bicolor
Indian mulberry Morinda citrifolia
Indian mulberry Morus alba var. indica
Indian mustard Brassica juncea
Indian oat Avena byzantina
Indian olibanum tree Boswellia serrata
Indian oyster Pleurotus sajor-caju
Indian peach Osmaronia cerasiformis
Indian pennywort Centella asiatica
Indian pepper Fagara rhetsa
Indian pokeberry Phytolacca acinosa
Indian potato Apios americana
Indian primrose Primula denticulata
Indian prune Flacourtia rukam
Indian rhubarb Peltiphyllum peltatum
Indian rice Zizania aquatica
Indian rice-grass Oryzopsis hymenoides
Indian rose chestnut Mesua ferrea
Indian saffron Curcuma longa
Indian sage Pluchea indica
Indian salad Hydrophyllum virginianum
Indian salad Lactuca indica
Indian sarsaparilla Hemidesmus indicus
Indian shot Canna coccinea
Indian snakewood Cecropia peltata
Indian sorrel Hibiscus sabdariffa
Indian spinach Beta vulgaris Cicla Group
Indian strawberry Echinocereus engelmannii
Indian tree hazel Corylus colurna var. jacquemontii
Indian trumpet-flower Oroxylum indicum
Indian turnip Arisaema triphyllum
Indian wild pear Pyrus pashia
Indian wintergreen Gaultheria fragrantissima
Indigo Indigofera tinctoria
Indigo bush Amorpha fruticosa
Indonesian bay Syzygium polyanthum
Indonesian cassia Cinnamomum burmannii
Indo-konnyaku Amorphophallus campanulatus
Ingá mirim Inga marginata
Ingá-assú Inga cinnamomea
Ingá-cipó Inga edulis
Inhambane coffee Coffea racemosa
Injerto Pouteria viride
Inkberry Ilex glabra
Inland roselle Abelmoschus ficulneus

Ki-sasage	Catalpa ovata
Klamath plum	Prunus subcordata
Klontjing	Spondias mangifera
Knob celery	Apium graveolens Rapaceum Group
Knotgrass	Polygonum aviculare
Knotted marjoram	Origanum majorana
Kobushi	Magnolia kobus
Koda tree	Ehretia acuminata
Kodo millet	Paspalum scrobiculatum
Kohlrabi	Brassica oleracea Gongylodes Group
Koji mold	Aspergillus oryzae
Kola nut	Cola acuminata
Komatsu-na	Brassica rapa Perviridis Group
Koma-tsunagi	Indigofera pseudo-tinctoria
Koma-yuri	Lilium amabile
Komo	Amaranthus x sp.
Konini	Fuchsia excorticata
Konivari	Hyptis suaveolens
Koosambi	Schleichera oleosa
Kordofan pea	Clitoria ternatea
Korean angelica	Angelica gigas
Korean cherry	Prunus glandulosa
Korean cherry	Prunus japonica
Korean chestnut	Castanea x sp.
Korean juneberry	Amelanchier asiatica
Korean mint	Agastache rugosa
Korean mulberry	Morus australis
Korean nut pine	Pinus koraiensis
Korila	Cyclanthera pedata
Koropuku	Gaultheria antipoda
Kotoji-hôki-take	Clavicorona pyxidata
Kotukutuku	Fuchsia excorticata
Kozo	Broussonetia kazinoki
Ko-akaza	Chenopodium ficifolium
Ko-sumire	Viola japonica
Ko-ume	Armeniaca mume 'Microcarpa'
Kua tom luet	Stephania hernandifolia
Kuai-tsao	Hovenia dulcis
Kuanga	Vigna luteola
Kubal madu	Willughbeia angustifolia
Kubili	Cubilia blancoi
Kudzu	Pueraria lobata
Kuini	Mangifera odorata
Kukui	Aleurites moluccana
Kuma-ichigo	Rubus crataegifolius
Kuma-tsuzura	Verbena officinalis
Kuma-yanagi	Berchemia racemosa
Kundang	Bouea macrophylla
Kundong	Garcinia sp.
Kuntji puti	Kaempferia rotunda
Kupa	Syzygium polycephalum
Kupu-kupu	Bauhinia tomentosa
Kuranda nut	Elaeocarpus bancroftii
Kuranda quandong	Elaeocarpus bancroftii
Kureel	Capparis decidua
Kuri	Castanea crenata
Kuri	Hypholoma sublateritium
Kurol	Bauhinia variegata
Kuro-chiku	Phyllostachys nigra
Kuro-ige	Sageretia theezans
Kuro-usugo	Vaccinium ovalifolium
Kuro-yona	Pongamia pinnata
Kurrajong	Brachychiton diversifolium
Kurrat-nabati	Allium kurrat
Kusa-ichigo	Rubus hirsutus
Kusa-nemu	Aeschynomene indica
Kutcha bloodwood	Eucalyptus terminalis
Kuth	Saussurea lappa
Kuthmithi	Withania somnifera
Kuwa	Morus alba var. stylosa
Kuwai	Sagittaria sinensis
Kuware-shida	Diplazium esculentum
Kuweni mango	Mangifera odorata
Kuzu	Pueraria lobata
Kuzu-ingen	Pueraria phaseoloides
Kwai-muk	Artocarpus hypargyraeus
Kwei-chu	Phyllostachys makinoi
Kwei-hua	Osmanthus fragrans
Lá deaong	Phrynium capitatum
Lá moi	Stephania hernandifolia
La'i	Cordyline fruticosa
Labdanum	Cistus ladanifer
Labrador rose	Rosa blanda
Labrador tea	Ledum groenlandicum
Lactic mycoderma	Mycoderma sp.
Lactic oidia	Geotrichum candidum
Lactic oidia	Oidium lactis
Lactic oidia	Oospora lactis
Lady's bedstraw	Galium verum
Lady's finger	Abelmoschus esculentus
Lady's leek	Allium cernuum
Lady's mantle	Alchemilla xanthochlora
Lady's smock	Cardamine pratensis
Lady's thumb	Persicaria vulgaris
Lahong	Durio dulcis
Lai	Durio kutejensis
Lakoocha	Artocarpus lakoocha
Lala palm	Hyphaene natalensis
Lal-nati	Amaranthus atropurpureus
Lamb mint	Mentha spicata
Lamb's cress	Cardamine hirsuta
Lamb's quarters	Chenopodium album
Lamb's tongue	Plantago lanceolata
Lambert's filbert	Corylus maxima
Lambic beer yeast	Brettanomyces bruxellensis
Lambic beer yeast	Brettanomyces lambicus
Lampuyang pahit	Zingiber amaricans
Lamwick plant	Phlomis lychnitis
Lanceleaf sage	Salvia reflexa
Lanceleaf sandalwood	Santalum lanceolatum
Landra	Raphanus raphanistrum ssp. landra
Langsat	Lansium domesticum
Lanzone	Lansium domesticum
Laos	Alpinia galanga
Lapland rosebay	Rhododendron lapponicum
Larch bolete	Suillus grevillei
Lard seed	Hodgsonia macrocarpa
Laredo mahonia	Mahonia trifoliolata
Large bitter-cress	Cardamine amara
Large cane	Arundinaria gigantea
Large round kumquat	Fortunella x crassifolia
Large-fruited biscuit-root	Lomatium macrocarpum
Laserwort	Laserpitium latifolium
Late low blueberry	Vaccinium vacillans
Latjira	Achyranthes aspera
Lauki	Cassia leschenaultiana
Lauki	Lagenaria siceraria
Laurel	Laurus nobilis
Laurel	Terminalia tomentosa
Laurel leaf	Syzygium polyanthum
Laurel magnolia	Magnolia virginiana
Laurel negro	Cordia alliodora
Lavandin	Lavandula x intermedia
Lavender cotton	Santolina chamaecyparissus
Lavender sage	Salvia lavandulifolia
Lead tree	Leucaena latisiliqua
Leadplant	Amorpha canescens
Leadwood	Krugiodendron ferreum
Leaf celery	Apium graveolens Secalinum Group
Leatherleaf	Vitis shuttleworthii
Leather-leaf	Chamaedaphne calyculata
Leek	Allium ampeloprasum Porrum Group
Leichtlin's camass	Camassia leichtlinii
Lemandarin	Citrus x limonia

Mad-dog weed	Alisma plantago-aquatica
Mafaffa	Xanthosoma maffafa
Magellan barberry	Berberis buxifolia
Maguey	Agave americana
Maguey ceniso	Agave salmiana
Maguey manso	Agave atrovirens
Mahaleb cherry	Prunus mahaleb
Mahoe	Hibiscus tiliaceus
Mahogany pine	Podocarpus totara
Mährische eberesche	Sorbus aucuparia 'Moravica'
Mahwa	Madhuca indica
Maiden sorrel	Rumex arifolius
Maidenhair fern	Adiantum capillus-veneris
Maidenhair tree	Ginkgo biloba
Maíz café	Zea mexicana
Maize	Zea mays
Mai-take	Grifola frondosa
Majorano mexicano	Salvia ballotaeflora
Makeuwa praw	Solanum xanthocarpum
Makha wheat	Triticum macha
Makrut	Citrus hystrix
Makulan	Piper auritum
Malabar chestnut	Pachira aquatica
Malabar gourd	Cucurbita ficifolia
Malabar spinach	Basella alba
Malagueto chico	Xylopia frutescens
Malanga blanca	Xanthosoma sagittifolium
Malay apple	Syzygium malaccense
Malay lacktree	Schleichera oleosa
Malay licorice	Abrus pulchellus
Malayan mombin	Spondias mangifera
Male bamboo	Dendrocalamus strictus
Male orchis	Orchis mascula
Mamang	Gynandropsis gynandra
Mamão	Jacaratia spinosa
Mamao bravo	Jacaratia spinosa
Mamey colorado	Pouteria sapota
Mamey de Santo Domingo	Mammea americana
Mamey sapote	Pouteria sapota
Mame-nashi	Pyrus calleryana
Mammee apple	Mammea americana
Mamoncillo	Melicoccus bijugatus
Mamorana grande	Pachira insignis
Mança caballo	Echinocactus horizonthalonius
Manchu cherry	Prunus tomentosa
Manchurian apricot	Armeniaca mandshurica
Manchurian gooseberry	Actinidia kolomikta
Manchurian plum	Prunus salicina 'Mandshurica'
Manchurian walnut	Juglans mandschurica
Manchurian wild riçe	Zizania latifolia
Mandarin	Citrus reticulata
Mandarin lime	Citrus x limonia
Mandioca	Manihot esculenta
Mandioca brava	Manihot glaziovii
Mangaba	Hancornia speciosa
Mangabeira	Hancornia speciosa
Mangel wurzel	Beta vulgaris Crassa Group
Mangis hutan	Garcinia hombroniana
Mango	Bromus mango
Mango	Mangifera indica
Mango melon	Cucumis melo Chito Group
Mangosteen	Garcinia mangostana
Maniçoba	Manihot glaziovii
Manila tamarind	Pithecellobium dulce
Manioc	Manihot esculenta
Manipur wild tea-rose	Rosa gigantea
Manketti nut	Ricinodendron heudelotii
Manketti nut	Ricinodendron rautanenii
Mankin-aoi	Hibiscus surattensis
Manmohpan	Terminalia ferdinandiana
Manna ash	Fraxinus ornus
Manna gum	Eucalyptus mannifera
Manna gum	Eucalyptus viminalis
Manna plant	Tamarix canariensis
Mannen-take	Ganoderma lucidum
Mansanilla	Anthemis cotula
Manshû-mame-nashi	Pyrus betulifolia
Manshû-ukogi	Acanthopanax sessiliflorus
Manuka	Leptospermum scoparium
Many-spined opuntia	Opuntia polyacantha
Manzanilla	Crataegus pubescens
Mao gwa	Benincasa hispida 'Chieh-Qwa'
Mao qua	Benincasa hispida 'Chieh-Qwa'
Mao tsoh	Phyllostachys pubescens
Maprang	Bouea macrophylla
Maquis pea	Pisum sativum ssp. elatius
Maracujá grande	Passiflora alata
Maracujá mirim	Passiflora warmingii
Maracujá peroba	Passiflora edulis f. flavicarpa
Marajah palm	Bactris maraja
Marama bean	Tylosema esculentum
Marang	Artocarpus odoratissimus
Maranháo nut	Sterculia chicha
Mararay	Aiphanes caryotifolia
Marbleberry	Ardisia escallonioides
Margarita	Cosmos caudatus
Maricao	Byrsonima spicata
Marmalade box	Genipa americana
Marschall thyme	Thymus pannonicus
Marsh blue violet	Viola sororia
Marsh hog's-fennel	Peucedanum palustre
Marsh mallow	Althaea officinalis
Marsh marigold	Caltha palustris
Marsh samphire	Salicornia europaea
Marsh thistle	Cirsium palustre
Marsh woundwort	Stachys palustris
Martinez piñon	Pinus maximartinezii
Marula	Sclerocarya caffra
Marumi kumquat	Fortunella japonica
Marvel of Peru	Mirabilis jalapa
Maryland dittany	Cunila origanoides
Masaki	Euonymus japonicus
Mashua	Tropaeolum tuberosum
Masked tricholoma	Clitocybe nuda
Masterwort	Angelica atropurpurea
Masterwort	Peucedanum ostruthium
Mastic thyme	Thymus mastichina
Matai	Eleocharis dulcis
Matai	Podocarpus spicatus
Matara tea	Cassia auriculata
Matasano	Casimiroa edulis
Matatabi	Actinidia polygama
Mateba-shii	Lithocarpus edulis
Matsubusa	Schisandra repanda
Mauka	Mirabilis expansa
Maule's quince	Chaenomeles japonica
Mauritius raspberry	Rubus rosaefolius
Mauve	Modiola caroliniana
Maximilian's sunflower	Helianthus maximilianii
May apple	Podophyllum peltatum
May day tree	Prunus padus
Mayagyat	Canarium asperum
Mayan breadnut	Brosimum alicastrum
Mayberry	Rubus microphyllus
Mayflower	Epigaea repens
Mayhaw	Crataegus aestivalis
Maypop	Passiflora incarnata
Mayten tree	Maytenus boaria
Maytree	Crataegus monogyna
May-chang	Litsea cubeba
May-weed	Anthemis cotula
Mazani palm	Nannorrhops ritchieana
Mazoe lemon	Citrus x jambhiri
Ma-chia	Smilax china

Pita	Aechmea magdalenae
Pitahaya	Acanthocereus tetragonus
Pitahaya	Cereus peruvianus
Pitahaya	Hylocereus polyrhizus
Pitahaya	Hylocereus undatus
Pitahaya	Lemaireocereus queretaroensis
Pitahaya agria	Machaerocereus gummosus
Pitahaya de Agosto	Echinocereus conglomeratus
Pitahaya dulce	Marshallocereus thurberi
Pitahaya roja	Hylocereus ocamponis
Pitahayacita	Cleistocactus baumanii
Pitanga	Stenocalyx pitanga
Pitanga da praia	Eugenia uniflora
Pitanga tuba	Phyllocalyx edulis
Pitkuli	Ixora coccinea
Pito	Erythrina berteroana
Pito	Erythrina rubrinervia
Pitomba	Phyllocalyx luschnathianus
Pixirica	Clidemia hirta
Pi-pi-chui	Convallaria keiskei
Plane tree	Platanus occidentalis
Plane-tree maple	Acer pseudoplatanus
Plantain	Musa x paradisiaca
Plate brush	Solanum torvum
Pleas nut	Carya x brownii
Pleurisy root	Asclepias tuberosa
Plum granny	Cucumis melo Dudaim Group
Plum of Martinique	Flacourtia inermis
Plum peach	Prunus salicina x Amygdalus persica
Plumboy	Rubus arcticus
Plumcot	Armeniaca vulgaris x Prunus spp.
Plum-leaf crab	Malus prunifolia
Poet's jasmine	Jasminum officinale
Poha	Physalis peruviana
Poi sag	Basella alba
Poka	Passiflora ligularis
Pokak	Solanum torvum
Poke salad	Phytolacca americana
Pokeberry	Phytolacca americana
Pokeweed	Phytolacca americana
Poleo	Hedeoma drummondii
Polish manna	Glyceria fluitans
Polish wheat	Triticum polonicum
Polynesian arrowroot	Tacca leontopetaloides
Polynesian chestnut	Inocarpus edulis
Pomegranate	Punica granatum
Pomegranate melon	Cucumis melo Dudaim Group
Pomme de liane zombie	Passiflora rubra
Pomo celery	Lomatium utriculatum
Pompelmousse	Citrus grandis
Pompom blanc	Hericium erinaceus
Pond apple	Annona glabra
Popolo	Solanum nodiflorum
Poro-poro	Solanum aviculare
Porter's plum	Prunus alleghaniensis
Portia tree	Thespesia populnea
Portuguese cabbage	Brassica oleracea Tronchuda Group
Posh-té	Annona scleroderma
Possum haw	Viburnum nudum
Pot marigold	Calendula officinalis
Pot marjoram	Origanum onites
Potato	Solanum tuberosum
Potato bean	Apios americana
Potato bean	Pachyrhizus erosus
Potato onion	Allium cepa Aggregatum Group
Potato yam	Dioscorea bulbifera
Potherb mustard	Brassica rapa Japonica Group
Poulard wheat	Triticum turgidum
Pousse-pierre	Salicornia europaea
Prairie cherry-plum	Prunus x sp.
Prairie crab	Malus ioensis
Prairie flax	Linum lewisii
Prairie mallow	Sidalcea neomexicana
Prairie onion	Allium stellatum
Prairie smoke	Geum triflorum
Prairie turnip	Psoralea esculenta
Prescott chervil	Chaerophyllum bulbosum ssp. prescottii
Preserving melon	Citrullus lanatus Citroides Group
Prickly amaranth	Amaranthus spinosus
Prickly chaff flower	Achyranthes aspera
Prickly currant	Ribes lacustre
Prickly gooseberry	Ribes cynosbasti
Prickly lettuce	Lactuca serriola
Prickly pear	Opuntia ficus-indica
Prickly pear	Opuntia pottsii
Prickly pear	Opuntia tenuispina
Prickly rose	Rosa acicularis
Prickly samphire	Echinophora spinosa
Prickly sow-thistle	Sonchus asper
Pride of Barbados	Caesalpinia pulcherrima
Primary yeast	Kluyveromyces marxianus
Primrose malanga	Xanthosoma violaceum
Prince's pine	Chimaphila umbellata
Prince's plume	Stanleya pinnatifida
Pring tjendani	Leleba multiplex
Procumbent yellow wood-sorrel	Oxalis corniculata
Propionic cheese bacteria	Propionibacterium freudenreichii ssp. shermanii
Proso millet	Panicum miliaceum
Prostrate amaranth	Amaranthus graecizans
Protopea	Vigna unguiculata
Provision tree	Pachira aquatica
Prune noire	Vitex doniana
Prussian asparagus	Ornithogalum pyrenaicum
Psyllium seed	Plantago psyllium
Pubescent wheatgrass	Thinopyron intermedium var. trichophorum
Puerto Rican guava	Psidium microphyllum
Puerto Rican oregano	Lippia helleri
Puha tiotio	Sonchus asper
Pulasan	Nephelium mutabile
Pummelit	Citrus x sp.
Pummelo	Citrus grandis
Pumpkin	Cucurbita pepo
Pun	Typha elephantina
Púna	Ehretia acuminata
Punjab rai	Brassica tournefortii
Purple amaranth	Amaranthus lividus
Purple angelica	Angelica atropurpurea
Purple apricot	Armeniaca x dasycarpa
Purple avens	Geum rivale
Purple cauliflower	Brassica oleracea Italica Group
Purple Chinese gooseberry	Actinidia purpurea
Purple coral-pea	Hardenbergia violacea
Purple crowberry	Empetrum atropurpureum
Purple gentian	Gentiana purpurea
Purple granadilla	Passiflora edulis
Purple ground-cherry	Physalis philadelphica
Purple passionfruit	Passiflora edulis
Purple poppy-mallow	Callirhoe involucrata
Purple prairie-clover	Petalostemon purpureum
Purple raspberry	Rubus x neglectus
Purple tephrosia	Tephrosia purpurea
Purple-haw	Condalia obovata
Purple-leaf plum	Prunus cerasifera 'Atropurpurea'
Purple-leaved filbert	Corylus avellana f. fusco-rubra
Purslane	Portulaca oleracea
Pusley	Portulaca oleracea
Puttyroot	Aplectrum hyemale
Pyramid spiraea	Spiraea x pyramidata
Pyrenean sorrel	Rumex alpinus
Quailgrass	Celosia argentea

Soap-tree yucca	Yucca elata
Soba	Fagopyrum esculentum
Society garlic	Tulbaghia violacea
Sodad	Capparis decidua
Soh-phlong	Flemingia vestita
Sok nam	Saraca bijuga
Soko	Celosia argentea
Soksokeun-phul	Scutellaria baicalensis
Soldier orchid	Orchis militaris
Som kop	Hibiscus acetosella
Soncoya	Annona purpurea
Sonoran panic-grass	Panicum sonorum
Soorèngan	Rumex sagittatus
Sopei nut	Klainedoxa gabonensis
Sorb apple	Sorbus domestica
Sorghum	Sorghum bicolor
Sorgo	Sorghum bicolor Saccharatum Group
Sotetsu	Cycas revoluta
Souari nut	Caryocar nuciferum
Souci des Champs	Calendula arvensis
Soup celery	Apium graveolens Secalinum Group
Sour cactus	Coryphantha vivipera var. arizonica
Sour cherry	Prunus cerasus
Sour orange	Citrus aurantium
Sour plum	Ximenia caffra
Sour tupelo	Nyssa ogeche
Sourdough bread yeast	Torulopsis holmii
Soursop	Annona muricata
Sour-grass	Oxalis acetosella
Sour-top blueberry	Vaccinium myrtilloides
South African doum palm	Hyphaene natalensis
South American crowberry	Empetrum rubrum
South American sapote	Quararibea cordata
Southern bayberry	Myrica cerifera
Southern blackhaw	Viburnum rufidulum
Southern California black walnut	Juglans californica
Southern cane	Arundinaria gigantea
Southern crab	Malus angustifolia
Southern cranberry	Vaccinium erythrocarpum
Southern dewberry	Rubus trivialis
Southern hackberry	Celtis laevigata
Southern huauzontle	Chenopodium berlandieri
Southern juneberry	Amelanchier obovalis
Southern pea	Vigna unguiculata
Southern shagbark	Carya carolinae-septentrionalis
Southern sloe	Prunus umbellata
Southern wild rice	Zizaniopsis miliacea
Southernwood	Artemisia abrotanum
Southern-cross pear	Pyrus x lecontei
Sowbane	Chenopodium murale
Soyabean	Glycine max
Soybean	Glycine max
So-ri-jeng-i	Rumex japonicus
Spanish bayonet	Yucca aloifolia
Spanish cherry	Mimusops elengi
Spanish chestnut	Castanea sativa
Spanish dagger	Yucca aloifolia
Spanish dagger	Yucca elephantipes
Spanish dagger	Yucca schidigera
Spanish garlic	Allium sativum Ophioscorodon Group
Spanish grape	Vitis berlandieri
Spanish jasmine	Jasminum officinale 'Grandiflorum'
Spanish licorice	Glycyrrhiza glabra
Spanish lime	Melicoccus bijugatus
Spanish manna	Cistus ladanifer
Spanish marjoram	Thymus mastichina
Spanish mint	Mentha requienii
Spanish needles	Bidens pilosa
Spanish oyster-plant	Scolymus hispanicus
Spanish plum	Spondias purpurea
Spanish radish	Raphanus raphanistrum ssp. maritimus
Spanish sage	Salvia lavandulifolia
Spanish salsify	Scolymus hispanicus
Spanish tamarind	Vangueria madagascariensis
Spanish thyme	Plectranthus amboinicus
Spanish woodbine	Ipomoea digitata
Sparachetti	Brassica rapa Ruvo Group
Sparkleberry	Vaccinium arboreum
Spearmint	Mentha spicata
Spearscale	Atriplex patula
Speedwell	Veronica officinalis
Spelt	Triticum spelta
Speltz	Triticum spelta
Spice bush	Lindera benzoin
Spice tree	Xylopia aethiopica
Spider flower	Cleome viscosa
Spiderherb	Gynandropsis gynandra
Spiderwort	Tradescantia virginiana
Spignel	Athamanta sicula
Spignel	Meum athamanticum
Spike lavender	Lavandula latifolia
Spiked millet	Pennisetum americanum
Spiked rampion	Phyteuma spicatum
Spiked wormwood	Artemisia genipi
Spinach	Spinacia oleracea
Spinach beet	Beta vulgaris Cicla Group
Spinach dock	Rumex patientia
Spindle tree	Euonymus europeus
Spiny bamboo	Bambusa arundinacea
Spiny bitter melon	Momordica cochinchinensis
Spiny calalu	Amaranthus spinosus
Spiny hackberry	Celtis spinosa
Spiny sago palm	Metroxylon rumphii
Spiny vitis	Vitis davidii
Spirulina	Spirulina platensis
Spleen amaranth	Amaranthus hybridus
Spoonwort	Cochlearia officinalis
Spotted cat's-ear	Hypochoeris radicata
Spotted gentian	Gentiana punctata
Spotted golden thistle	Scolymus maculatus
Spotted gum	Eucalyptus maculata
Spotted hawkweed	Hypochoeris maculata
Spotted monarda	Monarda punctata
Spotted touch-me-not	Impatiens capensis
Spotted wintergreen	Chimaphila maculata
Sprat barley	Hordeum zeocriton
Spring beauty	Claytonia virginica
Spring cress	Cardamine oligosperma
Sprouting broccoli	Brassica oleracea Italica Group
Sprouting vetch	Vicia sp.
Squash melon	Praecitrullus fistulosus
Squash pepper	Capsicum chinense
Squashberry	Viburnum edule
Squaw apple	Peraphyllum ramosissimum
Squaw berry	Rhus trilobata
Squaw currant	Ribes cereum
Squaw grass	Elymus triticoides
Squaw huckleberry	Vaccinium stamineum
Squaw mint	Hedeoma pulegioides
Squaw tea	Ephedra nevadensis
Squaw vine	Mitchella repens
Squawroot	Perideridia sp.
Squirrel-tail grass	Hordeum jubatum
St. John's bread	Ceratonia siliqua
St. John's mint	Micromeria bromeii
St. John's wort	Hypericum perforatum
St. Lucie cherry	Prunus mahaleb
St. Thomas tree	Bauhinia tomentosa
Stagbush	Viburnum prunifolium
Staghorn sumac	Rhus typhina
Stanford's manzanita	Arctostaphylos stanfordiana
Star anise	Illicium verum
Star apple	Chrysophyllum cainito

Star cucumber Sicyos angulata
Star gooseberry Cicca acida
Star jelly Nostoc commune
Starfruit Averrhoa carambola
Star-of-Bethlehem Ornithogalum umbellatum
Stemberry Bequaertiodendron magalismontanum
Sticky geranium Geranium viscosissimum
Sticky ground-cherry Physalis viscosa
Sticky laurel Ceanothus velutinus
Stinging nettle Urtica dioica
Stink currant Ribes bracteosum
Stock Matthiola incana
Stone Age wheat Triticum monococcum
Stone bramble Rubus saxatilis
Stone mint Cunila origanoides
Storax tree Styrax officinalis
Stork's-bill Erodium cicutarium
Strand wheat Leymus arenarius
Strawberry blite Chenopodium capitatum
Strawberry cactus Echinocereus enneacanthus
Strawberry jicama Polymnia sonchifolia
Strawberry pear Hylocereus undatus
Strawberry saxifrage Saxifraga stolonifera
Strawberry spinach Chenopodium capitatum
Strawberry tomato Physalis pubescens
Strawberry tree Arbutus andrachne
Strawberry tree Arbutus unedo
Strawberry tree Muntingia calabura
Strawberry-raspberry Rubus illecebrosus
Striped calabash-nutmeg Monodora tenuifolia
Striped maple Acer pensylvanicum
Stubble turnip Brassica rapa Rapifera Group
Subalpine fir Abies lasiocarpa
Succulent hawthorn Crataegus succulenta
Sudji Dracaena angustifolia
Suenkat Citrus x sunki
Sufu mold Actinomucor elegans
Sugar apple Annona squamosa
Sugar beet Beta vulgaris Crassa Group
Sugar bush Protea repens
Sugar bush Rhus ovata
Sugar cane Saccharum officinarum
Sugar cane inflorescence Saccharum edule
Sugar grape Vitis rupestris
Sugar leaf Stevia rebaudiana
Sugar maple Acer saccharum
Sugar palm Arenga pinnata
Sugar pine Pinus lambertiana
Sugar plum Uapaca guineensis
Sugarberry Celtis occidentalis
Sugi-hira-take Pleurocybella porrigens
Suigaku Prinsepia uniflora
Suikazura Lonicera japonica
Sulphur-shelf Laetiporus sulphureus
Sumac Rhus chinensis
Sumatra benzoin Styrax benzoin
Summer grape Vitis aestivalis
Summer haw Crataegus flava
Summer savory Satureja hortensis
Summer squash Cucurbita pepo
Sun hemp Crotalaria ochroleuca
Suna-kôsho Peperomia pellucida
Sunberry Solanum x burbankii
Sunchoke Helianthus tuberosus
Sunflower Helianthus annuus
Sung-lo-cha Syringa microphylla
Sunki Citrus x sunki
Sunset hibiscus Abelmoschus manihot
Super blue-green algae Aphanizomenon flos-aquae
Supplejack Flagellaria indica
Surelle sensitive Biophytum sensitivum
Surengan Rumex sagittatus
Surinam cherry Eugenia uniflora
Surinam purslane Talinum triangulare
Surinam spinach Talinum triangulare
Susincocco Armeniaca x dasycarpa
Susumber Solanum torvum
Suwarnkung Caryota rumphiana
Suzuran Convallaria keiskei
Swamp black currant Ribes lacustre
Swamp cabbage Sabal palmetto
Swamp hickory Carya cordiformis
Swamp leaf Limnophila aromatica
Swamp lily Thalia geniculata
Swamp maple Acer rubrum
Swamp milkweed Asclepias incarnata
Swamp onion Allium validum
Swamp saxifrage Saxifraga pensylvanica
Swamp white oak Quercus bicolor
Sward fruit tree Oroxylum indicum
Swede Brassica napus Napobrassica Group
Swedish coffee Astragalus boeticus
Swedish turnip Brassica napus Napobrassica Group
Sweet acacia Acacia farnesiana
Sweet after death Achlys triphylla
Sweet alyssum Lobularia maritima
Sweet Annie Artemisia annua
Sweet autumn clematis Clematis maximowicziana
Sweet basil Ocimum basilicum
Sweet bay Laurus nobilis
Sweet bay Magnolia virginiana
Sweet birch Betula lenta
Sweet briar Rosa rubiginosa
Sweet broom Scoparia dulcis
Sweet calabash Passiflora maliformis
Sweet cherry Prunus avium
Sweet cicely Myrrhis odorata
Sweet coltsfoot Petasites frigidus
Sweet coltsfoot Petasites japonicus
Sweet coltsfoot Petasites palmatus
Sweet corn-root Calathea allouia
Sweet cup Passiflora laurifolia
Sweet fennel Foeniculum vulgare
Sweet fern Comptonia peregrina
Sweet flag Acorus calamus
Sweet gale Myrica gale
Sweet garcinia Garcinia dulcis
Sweet goldenrod Solidago odora
Sweet granadilla Passiflora ligularis
Sweet grass Hierochloe odorata
Sweet gum Liquidamber styraciflua
Sweet Hottentot-fig Carpobrotus deliciosus
Sweet iris Iris pallida
Sweet lavender Lavandula latifolia
Sweet leaf Symplocos tinctoria
Sweet leaf bush Sauropus androgynus
Sweet lime Citrus x limettioides
Sweet lippia Phyla scaberrima
Sweet locust Gleditsia triacanthos
Sweet lupin Lupinus albus Saccharatus Group
Sweet mace Tagetes lucida
Sweet marigold Tagetes lucida
Sweet marjoram Origanum majorana
Sweet mountain grape Vitis monticola
Sweet myrrh Osmorhiza longistylis
Sweet orange Citrus sinensis
Sweet plum Sageretia theezans
Sweet potato Ipomoea batatas
Sweet prayer-plant Thaumatococcus daniellii
Sweet rice Oryza sativa Glutinosa Group
Sweet root Hedysarum boreale
Sweet shrub Calycanthus floridus
Sweet sorghum Sorghum bicolor Saccharatum Group

INDEX OF VERNACULAR AND OTHER NAMES OCCURRING ELSEWHERE IN THE TEXT

INDEX OF USAGE AND EDIBLE PARTS

Orbignya martiana, Orchis mascula, O. morio, Pandanus tectorius, Panicum sonorum, Parinari capensis, Parkia filicoidea, Passiflora alata, P. antioquiensis, P. caerulea, P. edulis, P. incarnata, P. laurifolia, P. ligularis, P. maliformis, P. manicata, P. mollissima, P. platyloba, P. seemannii, P. tripartita, P. vitifolia, Photinia arbutifolia, Phytelephas macrocarpa, Pithecellobium dulce, Podophyllum peltatum, Polymnia sonchifolia, Pouteria lucuma, P. sapota, Prosopis chilensis, P. juliflora, Prunella vulgaris, Prunus cerasus, Pseudocydonia sinensis, Psoralea glandulosa, Pyrus communis, Raphia farinifera, Rhus aromatica, R. copallina, R. coriaria, R. glabra, R. integrifolia, R. trilobata, R. typhina, Robinia pseudacacia, Rubus glaucus, R. ursinus, Saccharum officinarum, Salvia apiana, S. carduacea, S. columbariae, S. hispanica, S. multicaulis, S. reflexa, S. tiliaefolia, Sambucus melanocarpa, S. racemosa, Schinus molle, Solanum pectinatum, S. pseudolulo, S. quitoense, S. sessiliflorum, S. sessiliflorum var. alibile, S. vestissimum, Sorghum bicolor, Sterculia apetala, Strychnos cocculoides, S. spinosa, Symphytum x uplandicum, Tagetes patula, Tamarix aphylla, Telopea speciosissima, Terminalia glabra, Teucrium polium, Treculia africana, Triticum x aestivum, Vitis amurensis, V. labrusca, V. rotundifolia, V. vinifera.

BULBILS, AERIAL ROOTS - Allium canadense, A. x proliferum, A. sativum, A. ursinum, Dioscorea alata, D. bulbifera, D. japonica, D. oppositifolia, Pandanus tectorius, Ranunculus ficaria.

CALYCES - Abelmoschus esculentus, Bombax buonopozense, Calonyction album, Dillenia indica, Hibiscus sabdariffa, Salmalia malabarica.

CAPERS, CAPER SUBSTITUTES - Allium ursinum, Bauhinia variegata, Bellis perennis, Berberis vulgaris, Boscia albitrunca, Caltha leptosepala, C. palustris, Capparis decidua, C. ovata, C. sepiaria, C. spinosa, Cassia tomentosa, Cercis canadensis, C. occidentalis, C. siliquastrum, Clematis maximowicziana, Genista tinctoria, Larrea tridentata, Levisticum officinale, Muscari botryoides, Piper nigrum, Ranunculus ficaria, Rhus coriaria, Sambucus canadensis, Sarothamnus scoparius, Tropaeolum majus, T. minus, Ulex europaeus, Zygophyllum fabago.

CHOCOLATE SUBSTITUTES - Butyrospermum paradoxum ssp. parkii, Camellia sinensis, Canarium ovatum, Castanea dentata, Ceratonia siliqua, Chenopodium pallidicaule, Cinnamomum japonicum, Geum canadense, G. rivale, Irvingia gabonensis, Nephelium mutabile, Oenocarpus bacaba, Orbignya martiana, Salvadora persica, Sapium sebiferum, Shorea robusta, Simmondsia chinensis, Theobroma bicolor, T. subincanum, Tilia americana.

COCONUT-OIL SCENTS - Ageratum conyzoides, Angiopteris lygodiifolia, Calophyllum inophyllum, Cananga odorata, Hernandia moerenhoutiana, Pandanus tectorius, Sigesbeckia orientalis.

COFFEE SCENTS - Abelmoschus ficulneus, A. moschatus.

COFFEE SUBSTITUTES - Abelmoschus esculentus, A. ficulneus, A. moschatus, Acacia giraffae, A. karroo, Adansonia digitata, Arachis hypogaea, Arctium minus, Asparagus officinalis, Astragalus boeticus, Avena sativa, Balsamorhiza sagittata, Boscia albitrunca, Brabejum stellatifolium, Brachychiton diversifolium, Brosimum alicastrum, Canarium asperum, Canavalia ensiformis, Cassia auriculata, C. bicapsularis, C. floribunda, C. occidentalis, C. tora, Castanea dentata, C. sativa, Ceratonia siliqua, Cicer arietinum, Cichorium intybus, Cocos nucifera, Coffea canephora, C. liberica, C. racemosa, C. stenophylla, Coix lacryma-jobi 'Ma-Yuen', Copernicia prunifera, Cornus mas, Crataegus oxyacantha, Crescentia cujete, Cyperus esculentus, Daucus carota, Diospyros kaki, D. virginiana, D. whyteana, Echinochloa crusgalli, Eriobotrya japonica, Fagus grandifolia, Ficus carica, Galium aparine, Genista tinctoria, Glycine max, Gossypium herbaceum, Gymnocladus dioicus, Helianthus annuus, H. annuus ssp. lenticularis, H. tuberosus, Hibiscus sabdariffa, Hordeum jubatum, H. vulgare, Ilex latifolia, Iris missouriensis, I. setosa, Juniperus communis, J. horizontalis, J. scopulorum, Lathyrus japonicus ssp. maritimus, Leontodon hispidus, Leucaena latisiliqua, Linum usitatissimum, Lupinus albus, L. luteus, Lycium chinense, Mahonia swaseyi, Musa x paradisiaca, Nelumbo nucifera, Parkia biglandulosa, P. biglobosa, Phoenix dactylifera, P. reclinata, Phytelephas macrocarpa, Pisum sativum, Pithecellobium flexicaule, Psophocarpus tetragonolobus, Psychotria nervosa, Quercus robur, Ruscus aculeatus, Sarothamnus scoparius, Scolymus hispanicus, Scorzonera hispanica, Secale cereale, Setaria viridis, Silybum marianum, Simmondsia chinensis, Sium sisarum, Sonchus arvensis, Sorbus aucuparia, Sterculia urens, Symphytum officinale, S. tuberosum, Tamarindus indica, Taraxacum officinale, Tephrosia purpurea, Tetragonolobus purpureus, Trigonella foenum-graecum, Triticum x aestivum, Ugni molinae, Umbellularia californica, Vicia tetrasperma, Vigna angularis, V. unguiculata, Voandzeia subterranea, Zea mays, Z. mexicana, Ziziphus jujuba, Z. mucronata.

EGG WHITE SUBSTITUTES - Althaea officinalis, Malva neglecta, Opuntia pottsii.

FATS - Butyrospermum paradoxum ssp. parkii, Byrsonima crassifolia, Garcinia morella, Irvingia gabonensis, Madhuca longifolia, Mangifera indica, Pentadesma butyracea, Raphia farinifera, Salvadora persica, Sapium sebiferum, Shorea robusta, Terminalia kaernbachii, Theobroma bicolor, T. cacao, Tieghemella heckelii, Virola surinamensis.

FERMENTATION PRODUCT SUBSTRATES - Abelmoschus esculentus, Aleurites moluccana, Allium chinense, Ananas comosus, Apium graveolens Rapaceum Group, Arachis hypogaea, Artocarpus altilis, A. chaplasha, Avena sativa, Bambusa arundinacea, Beta vulgaris Crassa Group, Brassica juncea, B. oleracea Capitata Group, B. rapa Chinensis Group, B. rapa Pekinensis Group, B. rapa Rapifera Group, Cajanus cajan, Camellia sinensis, Canavalia ensiformis, C. gladiata, Capsicum annuum, Carica papaya, Cassia obtusifolia, Ceiba pentandra, Chenopodium quinoa, Cicer arietinum, Citrullus lanatus ssp. colocynthoides, Cocos nucifera, Colocasia esculenta, Cucumis melo Conomon Group, C. sativus, Cycas revoluta, Cyrtosperma chamissonis, Daucus carota Sativus Group, Durio zibethinus, Eleusine coracana, Ensete ventricosum, Eragrostis tef, Eutrema wasabi, Faba vulgaris, Glycine max, Gossypium herbaceum, Gynandropsis gynandra, Helianthus annuus, Hibiscus tiliaceus, Honkenya peploides, Hordeum vulgare, Hordeum vulgare Coeleste Group, Ipomoea batatas, Lablab purpureus, Leucaena latisiliqua, Lupinus angustifolius, Lycopersicon lycopersicum, Manihot esculenta, Mucuna pruriens, Olea europaea, Oryza sativa, O. sativa Glutinosa Group, Oxalis oregana, Oxyria digyna, Pangium edule, Panicum miliaceum, Parkia biglandulosa, P. biglobosa, P. filicoidea, Paspalum scrobiculatum, Pennisetum americanum, Phaseolus lunatus, P. vulgaris, Pisum sativum, Polygonum odoratum, Psophocarpus tetragonolobus, Raphanus sativus Longipinnatus Group, Secale cereale, Sesamum indicum, Sesbania grandiflora, S. sesban, Solanum anomalum, S. tuberosum, Sorghum bicolor, Theobroma cacao, Triticum x aestivum, T. durum, Vigna aconitifolia, V. mungo, V. radiata, V. unguiculata, Zea mays, Zingiber officinale, Ziziphus jujuba. (also see Alcoholic Beverages and Vinegars)

FERMENTATIVES - (see bacteria, molds and yeasts)

FLAVORINGS - Abelmoschus moschatus, Abies balsamea, Abrus pulchellus, Acacia concinna, A. farnesiana, A. leucophloea, A. nilotica, Acanthopanax divaricatus, Achillea atrata, A. decolorans, A. erb-rotta ssp. moschata, A. ligustica, A. millefolium, A. nana, Acinos alpinus, A. arvensis, Acorus calamus, A. gramineus, Adansonia digitata, Adiantum capillus-veneris, Aegle marmelos, Aframomum angustifolium, A. daniellii, A. elliotii, A. melegueta, Agaricus bisporus, Agastache cana, A. foeniculum, A. mexicana, A. neomexicana, A. rugosa, Albizia montana, Aleurites moluccana, Alliaria petiolata, Allium ampeloprasum, A. ampeloprasum Porrum Group, A. cepa, A. cernuum, A. drummondii, A. fistulosum, A. kurrat, A. obliquum, A. odorum, A. oleraceum, A. x proliferum, A. rubellum, A. sativum, A. sativum Ophioscorodon Group, A. schoenoprasum, A. schoenoprasum var. sibiricum, A. scorodoprasum, A. validum, A. wallichii, Aloe macrocarpa, Aloysia triphylla, Alpinia galanga, A. officinarum, Ambrosia maritima, Amelanchier canadensis, Ammi majus, Amomum compactum, A. xanthioides, Amorpha fruticosa, Amygdalus besseriana, A. communis 'Amara', A. davidiana, A. persica, Amyrsia foliosa, Anacardium occidentale, Anacyclus pyrethrum, Anethum graveolens, Angelica archangelica, Annona senegalensis, Anthemis cotula, Anthriscus cerefolium, A. sylvestris, Antidesma bunius, A. ghaesembilla, Apium graveolens, Arabis alpina, Aralia hispida, A. nudicaulis, A. racemosa, Ardisia boissieri, Armeniaca mume, A. sibirica, Armoracia rusticana, Artemisia abrotanum, A. absinthium, A. afra, A. asiatica, A. dracunculus, A. dracunculus 'Sativa', A. frigida, A. genipi, A. glacialis, A. judaica, A. ludoviciana, A. maritima, A. pontica, A. princeps, A. stelleriana, A. umbelliforme, A. vulgaris, Asarum canadense, A. caudatum, Athamanta cretensis, Backhousia citriodora, Balsamita major, Barbarea verna, Barosma betulina, B. crenulata, Bauhinia malabarica, B. tomentosa, Berberis vulgaris, Berlandiera lyrata, Betula alleghaniensis, B. lenta, Bischofia javanica, Bixa orellana, Blighia welwitschii, Borago officinalis, Boronia megastigma, Bouea macrophylla, Brassica juncea, . nigra, B. rapa, Bunium bulbocastanum, Bupleurum rotundifolium, Caesalpinia gilliesii, Calamintha grandiflora, C. nepeta, C. sylvatica, Calathea allouia, Calendula arvensis, C. officinalis, Calycanthus floridus, C. occidentalis, Cananga odorata, Canarium album, C. commune, C. schweinfurthii, Canavalia maritima, Canella winterana, Cannabis sativa, Cantharellus cibarius, Capsella bursa-pastoris, Capsicum annuum, C. annuum var. aviculare, C. baccatum var. pendulum, C. cardenasii, C. chinense, C. frutescens, C. pubescens, Cardamine amara, Cardaria draba, Carica papaya, Carissa edulis, Carum carvi, Carya illinoensis, Ceiba pentandra, Celtis occidentalis, Chaenomeles japonica, C. speciosa, Chamaemelum nobile, Chamomilla aurea, Chenopodium ambrosioides, C. ficifolium, Chimaphila umbellata, Chlorophora excelsa, Chrysanthemum coronarium, Cicca acida, Cimicifuga simplex, Cinchona succirubra, Cinnamomum aromaticum, C. burmannii, C. iners, C. japonicum, C. loureiri, C. obtusifolium, C. tamala, C. zeylanicum, Cissus discolor, Cistus albidus, C. creticus, C. ladanifer, C. salviifolius, C. villosus, X Citrofortunella mitis, Citrullus lanatus ssp. colocynthoides, Citrus x amblycarpa, C. aurantifolia, C. aurantium, C. x bergamia, C. hystrix, C. x jambhiri, C. x junos, C. x latipes, C. x limetta, C. limon, C. x limonia, C. x paradisi, C. x pennivesiculata, C. reticulata, C. sinensis, C. x sunki, Clausena excavata, C. lansium, Cleome monophylla, C. viscosa, Clinopodium vulgare, Cnicus benedictus, Coffea arabica, Cola acuminata, Commiphora myrrha, Comptonia peregrina, Conradina verticillata, Conyza canadensis, Copernicia prunifera, Coptis trifolia, Cordia alliodora, Coriandrum sativum, Cornus mas, Costus afer, Crambe orientalis, Crataegus pubescens, Crithmum maritimum, Crocus sativus, Croton reflexifolius, Cryptotaenia canadensis, C. japonica, Cucumis melo Conomon Group, Cuminum cyminum, Curcuma aromatica, C. longa, C. zedoaria, Cymbopogon citratus, C. martinii, C. nardus, Cyperus longus, Dahlia pinnata, Daniellia oliveri, Daucus carota, D. carota Sativus Group, Dendrobium salaccense, Dentaria diphylla, D. laciniata, Descurainia sophia, Dianthus caryophyllus, Dillenia philippensis, Diospyros kaki, Dovyalis hebecarpa, Dracontomelon dao, Drimys lanceolata, D. winteri, Durio zibethinus, Echinocactus grandis, Elettaria cardamomum, Elsholtzia ciliata, Embelia ribes, E. robusta, Emblica officinalis, Eriodictyon californicum, Eruca sativa, Eryngium foetidum, Eucalyptus globulus, E. leucoxylon, E. polybractea, E. smithii, Euterpe oleracea, Eutrema wasabi, Fagara rhetsa, Ferula assa-foetida, F. foetida, Filipendula ulmaria, Foeniculum vulgare, F. vulgare Azoricum Group, Fortunella hindsii, Fraxinus angustifolia, F. excelsior, Fumaria officinalis, Galinsoga parviflora, Garcinia cochinchinensis, Gaultheria procumbens, Gentiana cruciata, G. lutea, G. pannonica, G. punctata, G. purpurea, Geum rivale, G. urbanum, Glechoma hederacea, Glehnia littoralis, Globba marantina, Glycyrrhiza echinata, G. glabra, G. lepidota, G. missouriensis, Guaiacum officinale, G. sanctum, Guazuma ulmifolia, Gynandropsis gynandra, Gynura sarmentosa, Hamatocactus hamatacanthus, Hedeoma drummondii, H. pulegioides, Hedychium coronarium, Hedyosmum mexicanum, Helichrysum italicum, H. petiolatum, Hemerocallis lilio-asphodelus, Hemidesmus indicus, Heracleum lanatum, H. persicum, H. sphondylium, Hibiscus acetosella, H. surattensis, Horsfieldia irya, Humulus lupulus, Hyptis pectinata, H. suaveolens, Hyssopus officinalis, Iberis amara, Ilex vomitoria, Illicium floridanum, I. verum, Inula helenium, Iris x germanica, I. x germanica 'Florentina', I. pallida, Ixora coccinea, Jasminum humile, J. officinale, J. sambac, Juglans nigra, Juniperus communis, J. rigida, J. scopulorum, Kaempferia galanga, Lannea grandis, Lantana involucrata, L. rugosa, Laser trilobum, Laserpitium latifolium, L. siler, Laurelia sempervirens, L. serrata, Laurocerasus myrtifolia, L. officinalis, Laurus azorica, L. nobilis, Lavandula angustifolia, L. x intermedia, L. latifolia, Lentinus edodes, Leonurus cardiaca, Lepidium campestre, L. latifolium, L. meyenii, L. sativum, L. virginicum, Leptotes bicolor, Levisticum officinale, Ligularia kaempferi, Ligusticum monnieri, Lilium brownii, Limnophila aromatica, Lindera benzoin, L. glauca, Linum lewisii, L. perenne, Lippia alba, L. graveolens, L. helleri, L. javanica, Liquidamber orientalis, L. styraciflua, Litchi chinensis, Litsea cubeba, Lobularia maritima, Ludwigia suffruticosa, Lunaria annua, Lysimachia clethroides, Magnolia denudata, M. grandiflora, M. hypoleuca, M. kobus, M. virginiana, Mangifera caesia, Manihot esculenta, Marrubium vulgare, Medicago laciniata, Megacarpaea polyandra, Melaleuca leucadendron, Melilotus alba, M. altissima, M. officinalis, Melissa officinalis, Mentha aquatica, M. aquatica var. crispa, M. arvensis, M. arvensis f. piperascens, M. arvensis var. villosa, M. x cordifolia, M. x gentilis, M. longifolia, M. x piperita, M. pulegium, M. requienii, M. spicata, M. suaveolens, M. x verticillata, M. x villosa 'Alopecuroides', M. x villosa-nervata, Meum athamanticum, Michelia champaca, Micromeria bromeii, M. juliana, Milium effusum, Mirabilis jalapa, Monarda austromontana, M. citriodora, M. didyma, M. fistulosa, M. fistulosa var. menthaefolia, Monascus purpureus, Monodora myristica, M. tenuifolia, Morchella esculenta, Moringa oleifera, M. ovalifolia, Murraya koenigii, M. paniculata, Myrica cerifera, M. gale, M. pensylvanica, Myristica fragrans, Myroxylon balsamum, M. balsamum var. pereirae, Myrrhis odorata, Myrsine africana, Myrtus communis, Nasturtium officinale, Nelumbo nucifera, Nepeta cataria, Nigella arvensis, N. damascena, N. orientalis, N. sativa, Nothoscordum inodorum, Ocimum basilicum, O. canum, O. gratissimum, O. gratissimum var. viride, O. micranthum, O. sanctum, Ocotea pretiosa, Oenanthe javanica, Olea africana, O. europaea, Oncosperma filamentosum, Onopordon acanthium, Origanum dictamnus, O. majorana, O. x majoricum, O. onites, O. pulchellum, O. syriacum, O. tytthantum, O. vulgare, O. vulgare ssp. hirtum, Osmorhiza claytonii, O. longistylis, Oxalis corniculata, O. tuberosa, Paeonia officinalis, Panax japonica, P. pseudoginseng, Panda oleosa, Pandanus amaryllifolius, P. fascicularis, Papaver orientale, P. rhoeas, Parkia biglandulosa, P. biglobosa, P. filicoidea, P. javanica, P. speciosa, Pastinaca sativa, Paullinia cupana, Pectis papposa, Peganum harmala, Pelargonium crispum, P. exstipulatum, P. fragrans, P. graveolens, P. melissinum, P. nervosum, P. odoratissimum, P. tomentosum, P. torento, Peperomia acuminata, P. maculosa, Perideridia sp., Perilla frutescens, Persea americana, P. borbonia, Persicaria hydropiper, P. hydropiper 'Fastigiatum', Petasites japonicus, Petroselinum crispum, P. crispum Hortense Group, Peucedanum ostruthium, P. palustre, Peumus boldus, Phlomis lychnitis, Pholiota mutabilis, P. nameko, Phrynium capitatum, Phyla scaberrima, Picea glauca, P. mariana, Pimenta dioica, P. racemosa, Pimpinella anisum, P. major, P. saxifraga, Pinus pinea, Piper aduncum, P. auritum, P. cubeba, P. guineense, P. longum, P. nigrum, P. ornatum, P. sanctum, P. sylvaticum, Pistacia chinensis ssp. integerrima, P. khinjuk, P. lentiscus, Platymiscium pinnatum, Plectranthus amboinicus, Pleurotus ostreatus, Pluchea indica, Pogostemon cablin, P. heyneanus, Polianthes tuberosa, Poliomintha incana, P. longiflora, Polygonum odoratum, P. punctatum, Poncirus trifoliata, Portulacaria afra, Pothomorphe umbellata, Premna odorata, Prunus mahaleb, P. serotina, P. spinosa, P. virginiana, Pseudotsuga menziesii, Psoralea esculenta, Pulmonaria saccharata, Punica granatum, Pycnanthemum virginianum, Quassia amara, Raphanus raphanistrum, R. raphanistrum ssp. maritimus, Reseda odorata, Rhamnus purshianus, Rhus coriaria, R. ovata, Ridolfia segetum, Rosa centifolia, R. x damascena, R. gallica,

Rosa rubiginosa, Rosmarinus officinalis, Rumex acetosella, R. sagittatus, R. scutatus, Rungia klossii, Ruta chalepensis, R. graveolens, R. montana, Salacca conferta, Salvadora persica, Salvia apiana, S. clevelandii, S. columbariae, S. fruticosa, S. glutinosa, S. grandiflora, S. indica, S. lanigera, S. lavandulifolia, S. mellifera, S. multicaulis, S. officinalis, S. pomifera, S. pratensis, S. rutilans, S. sclarea, S. triloba, S. verbenaca, S. viridis, Sanguisorba minor, S. officinalis, Santalum album, Santolina chamaecyparissus, Sassafras albidum, Satureja hortensis, S. montana, S. thymbra, S. viminea, Saussurea lappa, Schinus molle, S. terebinthifolius, Scolymus hispanicus, Scoparia dulcis, Scorodoearpus borneensis, Sedum acre, Sesamum indicum, Sicana odorifera, Sinapis alba, S. arvensis, Sison amomum, Sisymbrium altissimum, S. officinale, Skimmia laureola, Smilax herbacea, S. officinalis, Smyrnium olusatrum, Solanum aethiopicum, S. anomalum, S. demissum, S. quitoense, S. spirale, Sonneratia caseolaris, Sorbus sitchensis, Sorghum bicolor, Spirulina platensis, Spondias dulcis, S. mangifera, S. mombin, Stachytarpheta cayennensis, S. jamaicensis, Sterculia lanceolata, Styrax benzoin, S. officinalis, Suaeda maritima, Symphytum officinale, Syzygium aromaticum, S. jambos, S. polyanthum, Tagetes filifolia, T. lucida, T. minuta, T. patula, Tanacetum parthenium, T. vulgare, Tephrosia purpurea, Tetrapleura tetraptera, Teucrium polium, Thlaspi arvense, Thymbra spicata, Thymus broussonetii, T. caespititius, T. capitatus, T. x citriodorus, T. herba-barona, T. mastichina, T. pannonicus, T. praecox ssp. arcticus, T. pulegioides, T. quinquecostatum, T. vulgaris, T. zygis, Tilia tomentosa, Toddalia asiatica, Tordylium apulum, Trachyspermum ammi, Trifolium ornithopodioides, Trigonella arabica, T. caerulea, T. foenum-graecum, Tropaeolum majus, Tsuga canadensis, T. heterophylla, Tuber gibbosum, T. melanosporum, Tulbaghia violacea, Turnera diffusa, T. ulmifolia, Umbellularia californica, Urena lobata, Vaccaria pyramidata, Vaccinium scoparium, Valeriana officinalis, Vangueria infausta, Vanilla planifolia, Verbena officinalis, Vernonia anthelmintica, Vetiveria zizanioides, Viola canadensis, V. odorata, V. sororia, Vitex agnus-castus, V. negundo, Vitis vinifera, Volvariella volvacea, Wedelia biflora, Xylopia aethiopica, X. frutescens, Zanthoxylum armatum, Z. piperitum, Z. planispinum, Z. simulans, Zingiber officinale, Z. spectabile, Z. zerumbet.

FLOWERS - Abelmoschus esculentus, A. manihot, Abutilon guineense, A. megapotamicum, Acacia concinna, A. nilotica, A. oshanessii, A. podalyriaefolia, A. spectabilis, Aegle marmelos, Agapetes variegata, Agave deserti, Albizia julibrissin, Alcea rosea, Allium sativum, A. schoenoprasum, A. tuberosum, Aloe chabaudii, A. greatheadii, A. littoralis, A. macrocarpa, A. zebrina, Alpinia galanga, A. speciosa, Alternanthera sessilis, Althaea officinalis, Amygdalus persica, Anchusa azurea, A. capensis, A. officinalis, Annona senegalensis, Antigonon leptopus, Aquilegia buergeriana, Arabis alpina, Ardisia boissieri, Asarum canadense, Asclepias speciosa, Averrhoa bilimbi, A. carambola, Azadirachta indica, Azalea indica, A. kaempferi, A. oldhamii, Balanites aegyptiaca, Balsamita major, Bauhinia purpurea, B. variegata, Bellis perennis, Beloperone californica, Benincasa hispida, Berberis aristata, Borago officinalis, Boswellia serrata, Brodiaea pulchella, Broussonetia kazinoki, Caesalpinia pulcherrima, Calamintha sylvatica, Calendula arvensis, C. officinalis, Calochortus gunnisonii, C. nuttallii, Caltha leptosepala, C. palustris, C. palustris var. barthei, Calyptronoma dulcis, Camellia japonica, C. sinensis, Campanula punctata, Canavalia maritima, Capparis decidua, Caragana ambigua, Cardamine hirsuta, Carica papaya, Cassia auriculata, C. fistula, C. occidentalis, C. siamea, C. tomentosa, Castilleja linariaefolia, Catalpa ovata, Ceiba pentandra, Celastrus paniculatus, Centaurea cyanus, C. nigra, Cercis canadensis, C. occidentalis, C. siliquastrum, Chimonanthus praecox, Chrysanthemum coronarium, C. indicum, C. x morifolium, Cichorium intybus, Citrus x bergamia, C. limon, C. sinensis, Clematis maximowicziana, Cleome integrifolia, C. monophylla, Commelina communis, Convallaria keiskei, Cordia dichotoma, C. myxa, Crataegus monogyna, Crateva religiosa, Crotalaria glauca, C. longirostrata, C. ochroleuca, Cucurbita foetidissima, C. maxima, C. mixta, C. moschata, C. pepo, Cydonia oblonga, Dahlia pinnata, Dianthus barbatus, D. caryophyllus, D. plumarius, Diphysa robinioides, Dolichandrone rheedii, D. stipulata, Dolichos malosanus, Dombeya rotundifolia, Durio zibethinus, Epigaea repens, Erechtites valerianifolia, Eruca sativa, Erythrina americana, E. berteroana, E. glauca, E. herbacea, E. rubrinervia, Erythronium albidum, E. americanum, Euterpe oleracea, Eutrema wasabi, Feijoa sellowiana, Fernaldia pandurata, Ferocactus acanthodes, F. viridescens, F. wislizenii, Filipendula ulmaria, Fouquieria splendens, Freycinetia banksii, Fritillaria verticillata, Galinsoga parviflora, Galium odoratum, Gardenia jasminoides, Geranium viscosissimum, Gladiolus cruentus, G. dalenii, G. ecklonii, Gliricidia sepium, Gynandropsis gynandra, Hamatocactus hamatacanthus, Hedychium coronarium, Helwingea japonica, Hemerocallis dumortieri, H. fulva, H. fulva 'Kwanso', H. lilio-asphodelus, H. middendorffii, H. middendorffii var. esculenta, H. minor, Hesperoyucca whipplei, Hibiscus cannabinus, H. diversifolius, H. rosa-sinensis, H. schizopetalus, H. syriacus, H. tiliaceus, Hylocereus undatus, Hyssopus officinalis, Indigofera dosua, I. pseudo-tinctoria, I. pulchella, Ixora coccinea, Jasminum officinale, Kleinhovia hospita, Lablab purpureus, Lamium album, L. purpureum, Lavandula angustifolia, Lecaniodiscus cupanioides, Leichhardtia australis, Leonotis nepetaefolia, Leonurus cardiaca, Leptadenia hastata, Lespedeza bicolor, Leucaena latisiliqua, Lilium amabile, L. brownii, L. lancifolium, L. longiflorum, L. sargentiae, Litsea cubeba, Lobularia maritima, Lonicera henryi, L. japonica, Luffa acutangula, L. cylindrica, Lysimachia clethroides, Madhuca indica, M. longifolia, Magnolia denudata, M. grandiflora, M. hypoleuca, M. kobus, Mahonia aquifolium, Malus pumila, M. silvestris, Malva sylvestris, Mangifera indica, Marshallocereus thurberi, Matthiola incana, Medicago polymorpha, Mimosa pudica, Monarda didyma, M. fistulosa, Montia perfoliata, Moringa oleifera, Musa x paradisiaca, Muscari botryoides, M. neglectum, Myrtillocactus geometrizans, Myrtus communis, Narcissus jonquilla, Nauclea latifolia, Nelumbo nucifera, Nuphar luteum, Nymphaea caerulea, N. odorata, N. stellata, Nymphoides indica, N. peltata, Ocimum basilicum, Oenothera biennis, Oncosperma filamentosum, Opuntia basilaris, Ornithogalum umbellatum, Oroxylum indicum, Oxalis deppei, O. stricta, O. violacea, Pachira aquatica, P. insignis, Pachycereus pringlei, Paeonia officinalis, P. suffruticosa, Pandanus tectorius, Papaver rhoeas, Passiflora caerulea, P. incarnata, Patrinia scabiosaefolia, P. villosa, Paullinia pinnata, Paulownia tomentosa, Pelargonium graveolens, Pentaglottis sempervirens, Pergularia daemia, Perilla frutescens, Perovskia atriplicifolia, Petasites frigidus, P. japonicus, P. japonicus var. giganteus, P. palmatus, Phaseolus coccineus, Pithecellobium lobatum, Plumeria rubra, Polianthes tuberosa, Poliomintha incana, Primula denticulata, P. veris, P. vulgaris, Prosopis juliflora, Prunus domestica, P. grayana, P. jamasakura, P. lannesiana, P. maximowiczii, P. padus, P. pseudocerasus, P. spinosa, P. subhirtella, Psophocarpus tetragonolobus, P. tetragonolobus, Pterocarpus indicus, P. marsupium, Pterospermum acerifolium, Pueraria lobata, Pyrus betulifolia, Ranunculus bulbosus, Reseda odorata, Rhododendron arboreum, Ribes cereum, R. nigrum, Robinia neomexicana, R. pseudacacia, Rosa blanda, R. canina, R. carolina, R. centifolia, R. chinensis, R. gallica, R. moschata, R. multiflora, R. rubiginosa, R. rugosa, R. virginiana, Rosmarinus officinalis, Rubus reflexus, Rumex acetosa, Salmalia malabarica, Salvia officinalis, S. sclarea, S. verbenaca, Sambucus canadensis, S. glauca, S. mexicana, S. nigra, Sanguisorba officinalis, Sansevieria gracilis, Saraca bijuga, Sarothamnus scoparius, Sauropus androgynus, Scorzonera hispanica, Sesbania bispinosa, S. grandiflora, S. sesban, Sinapis arvensis, Sisymbrium irio, Sonchus asper, Sophora davidii, S. japonica, Stellaria media, Syringa vulgaris, Syzygium jambos, Syzygium malaccense, Tacazzea apiculata, Tagetes erecta, T. patula, T. tenuifolia, Tamarindus indica, Tanacetum vulgare, Taraxacum albidum, T. officinale, Telosma cordata, Thelesperma gracile, Thespesia populnea, Tilia americana, T. x europaea, T. japonica, Trachycarpus fortunei, Tradescantia virginiana, Tragopogon porrifolius, T. pratensis, Trevesia palmata, Trifolium hybridum, T. pratense, T. repens, Tropaeolum majus, T. minus, T. tuberosum, Tulbaghia alliacea, T. violacea, Tussilago farfara, Valerianella locusta, Vallaris heynei, Veltheimia bracteata, Verbena officinalis, Viola canadensis, V. odorata, V. papilionacea, V. pedata, V. tricolor, V. x wittrockiana, Wisteria floribunda, W. frutescens, W. sinensis, Xanthoceras sorbifolium, Ximenia americana, Yucca aloifolia, Y. baccata, Y. brevifolia, Y. elata, Y. elephantipes, Y. filamentosa, Y. glauca, Y. schidigera, Zanthoxylum piperitum.

FOOD BINDERS, THICKENERS - Abelmoschus esculentus, Adansonia digitata, Brasenia schreberi, Callirhoe involucrata, Carya illinoensis, C. ovata, Castanea sativa, Ceratonia siliqua, Ceratotheca sesamoides, Chamaenerion angustifolium, Citrullus lanatus ssp. colocynthoides, Colocasia

R. flagellaris, R. fraxinifolius, R. fruticosus, R. glaucus, R. hirsutus, R. ichangensis, R. idaeus, R. illecebrosus, R. laciniatus, R. leucodermis, R. microphyllus, R. moluccanus, R. x neglectus, R. niveus, R. occidentalis, R. odoratus, R. parviflorus, R. parvifolius, R. pedatus, R. phoenicolasius, R. procerus, R. rosaefolius, R. rubrisetus, R. saxatilis, R. shankii, R. spectabilis, R. strigosus, R. trivialis, R. ursinus, R. vitifolius, Sabal etonia, S. palmetto, S. texana, Sageretia theezans, Salacca conferta, S. edulis, Salvadora persica, Sambucus australis, S. canadensis, S. glauca, S. javanica, S. melanocarpa, S. mexicana, S. nigra, S. pubens, S. pubens f. xanthocarpa, S. racemosa, Sandoricum koetjape, Santalum lanceolatum, Sarcocephalus xanthoxylon, Satyria warczewiczii, Saurauia nepaulensis, Sauropus androgynus, Schisandra chinensis, S. repanda, Schleichera oleosa, Schotia latifolia, Sclerocarya birrea, S. caffra, Scorodocarpus borneensis, Sechium edule, Serenoa repens, Sesbania bispinosa, S. grandiflora, S. sesban, Shepherdia argentea, S. canadensis, Shorea robusta, Sicana odorifera, Sicyos angulata, Simarouba glauca, Smilacina racemosa, Smilax china, S. herbacea, Solanum aethiopicum, S. anomalum, S. x burbankii, S. caripense, S. centrale, S. demissum, S. ferox, S. incanum, S. indicum, S. laciniatum, S. macrocarpon, S. melongena, S. muricatum, S. nigrum, S. nodiflorum, S. paucijugum, S. pectinatum, S. pseudolulo, S. quitoense, S. scabrum, S. sessiliflorum, S. sessiliflorum var. alibile, S. spirale, S. torvum, S. uporo, S. vestissimum, S. xanthocarpum, Sonneratia caseolaris, X Sorbopyrus auricularis, Sorbus americana, S. aria, S. aucuparia, S. decora, S. domestica, S. latifolia, S. scopulina, S. sitchensis, S. torminalis, Sphenocentrum jollyanum, Spondias axillaris, S. dulcis, S. mangifera, S. mombin, S. purpurea, S. tuberosa, Stauntonia hexaphylla, Stelechocarpus burakol, Stenocalyx pitanga, Stenocereus stellatus, Sterculia apetala, Streblus asper, Streptopus amplexifolius, S. roseus, Strychnos cocculoides, S. innocua, S. spinosa, Styphelia triflora, Syagrus coronata, Symplocos chinensis, Syzygium aqueum, S. aromaticum, S. coolminianum, S. cordatum, S. cumini, S. guineense, S. jambos, S. leuhmanni, S. malaccense, S. moorei, S. paniculatum, S. polycephalum, S. samarangense, Talisia olivaeformis, Tamarindus indica, Tapiphyllum parvifolium, Taxus baccata, T. cuspidata, Terminalia bellarica, T. catappa, T. ferdinandiana, Tetracarpidium conophorum, Tetragonolobus purpureus, Tetrapleura tetraptera, Theobroma bicolor, T. cacao, T. grandiflorum, T. subincanum, Thespesia populnea, Tilia americana, T. japonica, Toddalia asiatica, Toona sinensis, Trichocereus chiloensis, T. spachianus, Trichosanthes cucumerina, T. cucumeroides, T. kirilowii, T. kirilowii var. japonica, Triphasia trifolia, Uapaca guineensis, U. kirkiana, Ugni molinae, Ulmus pumila, Uvaria chamae, Vaccinium angustifolium, V. arboreum, V. arctostaphylos, V. ashei, V. atrococcum, V. bracteatum, V. caesariense, V. calycinum, V. cereum, V. corymbosum, V. corymbosum var. pallidum, V. crassifolium, V. darrowi, V. deliciosum, V. erythrocarpum, V. floribundum, V. lamarckii, V. macrocarpon, V. membranaceum, V. myrsinites, V. myrtilloides, V. myrtillus, V. ovalifolium, V. ovatum, V. oxycoccus, V. padifolium, V. parvifolium, V. praestans, V. reticulo-verosum, V. scoparium, V. sempervirens, V. stamineum, V. uliginosum, V. vacillans, V. vitis-idaea, Vangueria esculenta, V. infausta, V. madagascariensis, Vangueriopsis lanciflora, Viburnum alnifolium, V. cassinoides, V. cotinifolium, V. edule, V. lentago, V. nudum, V. odoratissimum, V. opulus, V. prunifolium, V. rufidulum, V. trilobum, Vigna aconitifolia, V. angularis, V. radiata, V. umbellata, V. unguiculata, V. unguiculata ssp. cylindrica, V. unguiculata ssp. sesquipedalis, Vitex doniana, Vitis aestivalis, V. amurensis, V. argentifolia, V. berlandieri, V. californica, V. candicans, V. x champini, V. cinerea, V. coignetiae, V. davidii, V. labrusca, V. monticola, V. munsoniana, V. riparia, V. rotundifolia, V. rupestris, V. shuttleworthii, V. simpsonii, V. solonis, V. vinifera, V. vinifera Monopyrena Group, Voacanga thouarsii, Voandzeia subterranea, Washingtonia filifera, Willughbeia angustifolia, Ximenia americana, X. caffra, Yucca baccata, Y. elata, Y. filamentosa, Y. glauca, Y. schidigera, Zanthoxylum piperitum, Ziziphus abyssinica, Z. joazeiro, Z. jujuba, Z. mauritiana, Z. mucronata, Z. oenoplia, Z. parryi, Z. spina-christii.

GALLS - Acacia aneura, Azalea indica, A. nudiflora, Salvia pomifera.

GELS - Aloe barbadensis, Amorphophallus rivieri, A. variabilis, Daucus carota Sativus Group, Ficus pumila, F. pumila var. awkeotsang, F. racemosa, Nostoc commune, Stephania hernandifolia.

GUMS - Acacia aneura, A. giraffae, A. karroo, A. nilotica, A. pendula, A. pycnantha, A. senegal, A. tortilis, Anogeissus latifolia, A. leiocarpus, Araucaria angustifolia, Astragalus gummifer, Bauhinia retusa, Boswellia serrata, Ceratonia siliqua, Cistus ladanifer, Cochlospermum religiosum, Copernicia prunifera, Cyamopsis tetragonolobus, Garcinia morella, Lagerstroemia parviflora, Lannea grandis, Larix occidentalis, Penaea mucronata, Phragmites australis, Plantago ovata, Prosopis glandulosa, P. juliflora, P. spicigera, Prunus avium, P. cerasoides, Sterculia tragacantha, S. urens, S. villosa, Tamarindus indica.

HOPS SUBSTITUTES - Acacia myrtifolia, Achillea millefolium, Artemisia abrotanum, A. absinthium, Calluna vulgaris, Daviesia latifolia, Dodonaea viscosa, Fagara rhetsa, Glechoma hederacea, Gouania lupuloides, G. polygama, Humulus lupulus var. cordifolius, Menyanthes trifoliata, Origanum vulgare, Picrasma quassioides, Ptelea trifoliata, Pteridium aquilinum, Quassia amara, Rhamnus prinoides, Sarothamnus scoparius, Teucrium scorodonia.

HYPERTROPHYS - Psophocarpus tetragonolobus, Zea mays, Zizania latifolia.

HYPOCOTYLS - Adansonia digitata, Borassus aethiopum, B. flabellifer, Cocos nucifera, Hyphaene natalensis, H. thebaica, Rhizophora mangle.

INFLORESCENCES - Acer macrophyllum, Amaranthus viridis, Artocarpus altilis, A. heterophyllus, A. lakoocha, Asclepias incarnata, A. speciosa, A. syriaca, A. tuberosa, Barbarea vulgaris, Betula papyrifera, Brassica carinata, B. napus, B. nigra, B. oleracea Acephala Group, B. oleracea Alboglabra Group, B. oleracea Botrytis Group, B. oleracea Italica Group, B. rapa, B. rapa Ruvo Group, Bromelia pinguin, Cakile edentula, C. maritima, Calathea allouia, Cardamine pratensis, Carica papaya, Carludovica palmata, Celosia argentea, Chamaedorea costaricana, C. graminifolia, C. tepejilote, Chenopodium album, C. bonus-henricus, C. ficifolium, C. nuttaliae, Clerodendrum serratum, Cochlearia anglica, C. officinalis, Cocos nucifera, Colocasia esculenta, Copernicia prunifera, Crambe orientalis, Cryptotaenia canadensis, Curcuma mangga, C. xanthorrhiza, Daucus carota, Dioscorea bulbifera, D. oppositifolia, Erythrina americana, E. berteroana, Foeniculum vulgare, Gnetum gnemon, Karatas plumieri, Lathyrus davidii, Levisticum officinale, Limnocharis flava, Musa x paradisiaca, Nannorrhops ritchieana, Nicolaia elatior, Nypa fruticans, Ornithogalum pyrenaicum, Phoenix dactylifera, Piper excelsum, Pluchea indica, Pothomorphe umbellata, Raphanus sativus, R. sativus Longipinnatus Group, Rheum rhabarbarum, R. tataricum, Rhopalostylis sapida, Saccharum edule, S. spontaneum, Salix babylonica, S. daphnoides, S. gracilistyla, Sambucus glauca, S. mexicana, Samuela carnerosana, Sinapis arvensis, Smyrnium olusatrum, Spathiphyllum phryniifolium, Spondias mangifera, Trachycarpus fortunei, Typha angustifolia, T. capensis, T. latifolia, Vitis vinifera, Yucca brevifolia, Zea mays, Z. mexicana, Zizania latifolia, Zizia aurea.

LEAVES, LEAFY SHOOTS - Abelmoschus esculentus, A. manihot, A. moschatus, Abutilon guineense, Acacia concinna, A. farnesiana, A. nilotica, Acanthopanax divaricatus, A. sessiliflorus, A. sieboldianus, Achillea millefolium, Achyranthes aspera, Acrocomia intumescens, A. mexicana, A. sclerocarpa, Actinidia kolomikta, A. polygama, Adansonia digitata, Adenanthera pavonina, Aegle marmelos, Aegopodium podagraria, Aeschynomene indica, Agastache rugosa, Agave americana, A. deserti, A. utahensis, Aglaia odorata, Agrostemma githago, Albizia julibrissin, Alcea rosea, Alchemilla xanthochlora, Alliaria petiolata, Allium akaka, A. ampeloprasum, A. ampeloprasum Porrum Group, A.

Cowania mexicana, Crataegus monogyna, C. oxyacantha, Crocus sativus, Cunila origanoides, Cyclopia subternata, Cymbopogon citratus, C. nardus, Dalea sp., Dictamnus albus, Dioscorea cayenensis, Diospyros virginiana, Dracocephalum moldavica, Dryas octopetala, Dryopteris fragrans, Ehretia microphylla, Elaeodendron orientale, Empetrum nigrum, Ephedra nevadensis, E. torreyana, E. viridis, Epilobium hirsutum, Eriodictyon californicum, Eugenia uniflora, Euphorbia helioscopia, Eurya japonica, Filipendula ulmaria, F. vulgaris, Foeniculum vulgare, Fragaria californica, F. chiloensis, F. ovalis, F. vesca, F. vesca var. americana, F. virginiana, Fraxinus excelsior, Galium aparine, G. odoratum, Gaultheria fragrantissima, G. myrsinites, G. procumbens, Geranium incanum, G. thunbergii, Geum triflorum, Glechoma hederacea, Glycyrrhiza glabra, G. lepidota, Grindelia squarrosa, Gynostemma pentaphyllum, Hardenbergia violacea, Hedeoma drummondii, H. pulegioides, Hedyosmum mexicanum, Helichrysum italicum, H. serpyllifolium, Heliotropium curassavicum, Hemerocallis dumortieri, Heritiera littoralis, Hermannia hyssopifolia, Hibiscus sabdariffa, H. syriacus, H. tiliaceus, Humulus lupulus, Hydrangea aspera, H. macrophylla, Hypericum perforatum, Hyptis suaveolens, Hyssopus officinalis, Ilex cassine, I. glabra, I. latifolia, I. opaca, I. paraguariensis, I. verticillata, I. vomitoria, Jasminum humile, J. officinale, Juglans regia, Juniperus communis, J. horizontalis, J. scopulorum, J. virginiana, Kennedya prostrata, Larrea tridentata, Laurus nobilis, Lavandula angustifolia, Ledum glandulosum, L. groenlandicum, L. palustre, L. palustre var. diversipilosum, Leonurus cardiaca, Leptospermum ericoides, L. flavescens, L. laevigatum, L. liversidgei, L. petersonii, L. pubescens, L. scoparium, Lespedeza bicolor, Levisticum officinale, Lindera benzoin, L. obtusiloba, Linum usitatissimum, Lippia alba, L. graveolens, L. javanica, Lithospermum officinale, Lomatium macrocarpum, L. nudicaule, Lonicera japonica, Ludwigia suffruticosa, Lycium barbarum, L. chinense, Lysimachia nummularia, Magnolia kobus, M. virginiana, Malus hupehensis, Malva neglecta, M. sylvestris, Marrubium vulgare, Matricaria matricarioides, Medicago sativa, Melaleuca genistifolia, M. leucadendron, Melissa officinalis, Mentha aquatica, M. aquatica var. crispa, M. arvensis, M. arvensis var. villosa, M. cervina, M. longifolia, M. x piperita, M. pulegium, M. spicata, M. x villosa 'Alopecuroides', Micromeria bromeii, Monarda austromontana, M. citriodora, M. clinopodia, M. didyma, M. fistulosa, M. punctata, Monardella odoratissima, M. villosa, Morus alba, M. alba var. stylosa, Muntingia calabura, Myrica cerifera, M. gale, Myrrhis odorata, Nepeta cataria, Ocimum gratissimum var. viride, O. kilimandscharicum, O. sanctum, Olea africana, Origanum dictamnus, O. majorana, O. onites, O. vulgare, O. vulgare ssp. hirtum, Orthilia secunda, Osmorhiza longistylis, Paeonia lactiflora, Panax japonica, P. pseudoginseng, P. quinquefolius, Paronychia argentea, P. capitata, P. jamesii, Pelargonium graveolens, Pellaea mucronata, Penstemon confertus, P. procerus, Peperomia pellucida, Persea americana, P. borbonia, Petalostemon candidum, P. purpureum, Petrorhagia prolifera, Petroselinum crispum Hortense Group, Phytolacca rivinoides, Picrasma quassioides, Pimenta dioica, Pimpinella anisum, Pinus edulis, P. sabiniana, P. strobus, Plantago major, Plectranthus amboinicus, Plumeria rubra f. acutifolia, Polygonum aviculare, P. equisetiforme, Potentilla anserina, P. erecta, P. fruticosa, P. glandulosa, P. palustris, P. rupestris, Primula veris, P. vulgaris, Prosopis juliflora, Prunus cerasus, P. domestica, P. lannesiana, P. padus, P. pseudocerasus, P. spinosa, P. subhirtella, P. virginiana, Pseudotsuga menziesii, Psilotum triquetrum, Psoralea glandulosa, Pycnanthemum incanum, P. muticum, P. pilosum, P. virginianum, Pyracantha crenulata, Ratibida columnifera, Rhamnus davuricus, Rhizophora mangle, Rhododendron lapponicum, Rhus aromatica, R. ovata, Ribes nigrum, R. odoratum, Rosa acicularis, R. arkansana, R. blanda, R. canina, R. nutkana, R. pisocarpa, R. rugosa, R. villosa, R. woodsii, Rosmarinus officinalis, Rubus arcticus, R. caesius, R. flagellaris, R. fruticosus, R. idaeus, R. leucodermis, R. microphyllus, R. occidentalis, R. spectabilis, R. strigosus, R. ursinus, Ruta graveolens, Sageretia theezans, Salix babylonica, S. gracilistyla, Salvia ballotaeflora, S. grandiflora, S. lanigera, S. mellifera, S. officinalis, S. pomifera, S. rutilans, S. triloba, Sambucus canadensis, S. glauca, S. nigra, S. pubens, S. sieboldiana, Sanguisorba minor, S. officinalis, Sassafras albidum, Satureja douglasii, S. hortensis, S. montana, S. thymbra, S. viminea, Schisandra repanda, Scoparia dulcis, Scutellaria baicalensis, Sida rhombifolia, Sideritis theezans, Smilax china, Solanum nodiflorum, Solidago canadensis, S. graminifolia, S. missouriensis, S. odora, S. virgaurea, Sophora japonica, Sorbus aucuparia, Spiraea beauverdiana, S. blumei, S. chinensis, S. x pyramidata, Stachys officinalis, Stachytarpheta cayennensis, S. jamaicensis, S. mutabilis, Symphytum officinale, S. x uplandicum, Syringa microphylla, Tabebuia pallida, Tagetes lucida, Talauma ovata, Tanacetum parthenium, T. vulgare, Taraxacum albidum, T. officinale, Tarchonanthus camphoratus, Taxus baccata, Teucrium massiliense, Thelesperma filifolia, T. gracile, Thuja occidentalis, Thymus x citriodorus, T. praecox ssp. arcticus, T. vulgaris, Tilia americana, T. cordata, T. x europaea, T. japonica, Toona sinensis, Trifolium agrarium, T. hybridum, T. incarnatum, T. pratense, T. repens, Trigonella caerulea, T. foenum-graecum, Tsuga canadensis, T. mertensiana, Turnera diffusa, T. ulmifolia, Tussilago farfara, Ugni molinae, Ulex europaeus, Urtica dioica, Vaccinium arctostaphylos, V. myrtilloides, V. myrtillus, V. scoparium, V. vitis-idaea, Valeriana officinalis, Verbascum thapsus, Verbena hastata, V. officinalis, Veronica chamaedrys, V. officinalis, Viburnum cassinoides, V. setigerum, Vicia cracca, V. sativa, Viola adunca, V. canadensis, V. odorata, V. pedata, V. x wittrockiana, Vitex doniana, V. negundo, Wedelia biflora.

VANILLA SUBSTITUTES - Achlys triphylla, Avena sativa, Cymbopogon nardus, Galium odoratum, Hierochloe odorata, Lagarostrobus franklinii, Leptotes bicolor, Melilotus alba, M. officinalis, Melittis melissophyllum, Mondia whytei, Trigonella foenum-graecum, Vanilla pompona, V. tahitensis.

VEGETABLE CURDS - Abelmoschus esculentus, Glycine max, Gossypium hirsutum Nonglanduliferous Group, Lablab purpureus, Lagenaria siceraria, Luffa cylindrica.

VEGETABLE SALTS - Achyranthes aspera, Asplenium nidus, Borassus flabellifer, Capparis decidua, Ceiba pentandra, Cyperus flabelliformis, C. haspan, Eleocharis dulcis, Euterpe oleracea, Heliotropium curassavicum, Heracleum lanatum, Iriartea ventricosa, Musa x paradisiaca, Orbignya martiana, Petasites palmatus, Piper guineense, Pistia stratiotes, Portulaca oleracea, Rhus chinensis, R. javanica, Sabal palmetto, Saccharum spontaneum, Salvadora persica, Tussilago farfara, Voacanga thouarsii, Zaleya pentandra.

VINEGARS - Anacardium occidentale, Ananas comosus, Arenga pinnata, Armeniaca mume, Betula lenta, B. papyrifera, B. populifolia, Borassus flabellifer, Bromelia pinguin, Carissa edulis, Chamaenerion angustifolium, Cicca acida, Cicer arietinum, C. songaricum, Citrus x junos, C. x paradisi, Cocos nucifera, Corypha elata, Dillenia indica, Diospyros virginiana, Malus baccata, M. silvestris, Mangifera indica, Manilkara zapota, Musa x paradisiaca, Nypa fruticans, Oenocarpus distichus, Oryza sativa, Pappea capensis, Primula veris, Pyrus communis, Rubus chamaemorus, R. fruticosus, R. idaeus, Saccharum officinarum, Sonneratia caseolaris, Sorbus aria, S. torminalis, Syzygium cumini, S. guineense, Theobroma cacao, Vitis labrusca, V. vinifera.

YEAST HOSTS, FERMANTATIVE ORGANISM HOSTS - Artemisia annua, Cosmos caudatus, Mestoklema tuberosum, Physalis peruviana, Ptelea trifoliata, Severinia buxifolia, Solanum jamesii, Trichodiadema stellatum.

INDEX OF SPECIES NATIVE TO OR NATURALIZED IN NORTH AMERICA

Abies amabilis, A. balsamea, A. excelsior, A. lasiocarpa, Abronia latifolia, Acacia greggii, Acanthocereus tetragonus, Acer circinatum, A. grandidentatum, A. macrophyllum, A. nigrum, A. pensylvanicum, A. rubrum, A. saccharinum, A. saccharum, A. spicatum, Achlys triphylla, Adiantum capillus-veneris, Aegopodium podagraria, Agastache cana, A. foeniculum, A. neomexicana, A. urticifolia, Agave asperrima, A. atrovirens, A. deserti, A. parryi, A. salmiana, A. utahensis, Alisma plantago-aquatica, Allium canadense, A. cernuum, A. drummondii, A. geyeri, A. schoenoprasum var. sibiricum, A. stellatum, A. tricoccum, A. unifolium, A. validum, A. vineale, Amaranthus graecizans, A. hybridus, A. retroflexus, Ambrosia artemisiifolia, Amelanchier alnifolia, A. arborea, A. bartramiana, A. canadensis, A. cusickii, A. denticulata, A. florida, A. x grandiflora, A. laevis, A. obovalis, A. x spicata, A. stolonifera, A. utahensis, X Amelasorbus jackii, Amorpha canescens, A. fruticosa, Amphicarpaea monoica, Andromeda glaucophylla, Angelica atropurpurea, Annona glabra, Anthoxanthum odoratum, Apios americana, Aplectrum hyemale, Arabis alpina, Aralia hispida, A. nudicaulis, A. racemosa, A. spinosa, Arbutus menziesii, Arctium lappa, A. minus, Arctostaphylos columbiana, A. glauca, A. patula, A. uva-ursi, Ariocarpus fissuratus, Arisaema triphyllum, Armoracia rusticana, Aronia arbutifolia, A. melanocarpa, Artemisia dracunculus, A. frigida, A. ludoviciana, A. vulgaris, Arundinaria gigantea, Asarum canadense, A. caudatum, Asclepias incarnata, A. speciosa, A. syriaca, A. tuberosa, Asimina grandiflora, A. parviflora, A. triloba, Astragalus crassicarpus, Atriplex canescens, A. confertifolia, A. semibaccata, Azalea nudiflora, Balsamorhiza hookeri, B. sagittata, Barbarea vulgaris, Batis maritima, Beloperone californica, Berlandiera lyrata, Betula alleghaniensis, B. lenta, B. nigra, B. papyrifera, B. populifolia, Blephilia ciliata, B. hirsuta, Bourreria ovata, Brassica nigra, Brodiaea douglasii, B. pulchella, Bromus breviaristatus, B. carinatus, Cacalia atriplicifolia, Cakile edentula, Calla palustris, Callirhoe involucrata, Calochortus gunnisonii, C. nuttallii, Calonyction album, Caltha leptosepala, C. palustris, Calycanthus floridus, C. occidentalis, Camassia leichtlinii, C. quamash, Campanula rapunculoides, Canella winterana, Canna flaccida, Capsicum annuum var. aviculare, Cardamine oligosperma, Carnegiea gigantea, Carpobrotus aequilaterus, Carya carolinae-septentrionalis, C. cordiformis, C. floridana, C. glabra, C. illinoensis, C. laciniosa, C. myristiciformis, C. ovata, C. tomentosa, Casasia clusiifolia, Cassia occidentalis, Castanea alnifolia, C. dentata, C. x neglecta, C. ozarkensis, C. pumila, Castilleja linariaefolia, Ceanothus americanus, C. cuneatus, C. fendleri, C. ovatus, C. sanguineus, C. velutinus, Celtis laevigata, C. occidentalis, C. reticulata, C. spinosa, Centaurea nigra, Cercidium floridum, C. microphyllum, Cercis canadensis, C. occidentalis, Cercocarpus ledifolius, Chamaedaphne calyculata, Chamaenerion angustifolium, C. latifolium, Chenopodium album, C. ambrosioides, C. berlandieri, C. botrys, C. capitatum, C. nuttaliae, Chimaphila maculata, C. umbellata, Chiogenes hispidula, Chionanthus virginicus, Chlorogalum pomeridianum, Chrysolepis chrysophylla, C. sempervirens, Cirsium arvense, C. vulgare, Claytonia caroliniana, C. megarrhiza, C. virginica, Cleome integrifolia, Clinopodium vulgare, Clintonia borealis, Coccoloba diversifolia, C. uvifera, Colubrina elliptica, C. ferruginosa, C. texensis, Commelina communis, Comptonia peregrina, Condalia obovata, Conradina verticillata, Conyza canadensis, Coptis trifolia, Cordia boissieri, Coreopsis cardaminifolia, Cornus canadensis, Corylus americana, C. cornuta, C. cornuta var. californica, Coryphantha vivipera var. arizonica, Cowania mexicana, Crataegus aestivalis, C. douglasii, C. flava, C. marshalli, C. mollis, C. punctata, C. succulenta, Cryptotaenia canadensis, Cucumis melo ssp. agrestis, Cucurbita foetidissima, C. x sp., C. x sp., Cunila origanoides, Cylindropuntia fulgida, C. imbricata, Cyperus rotundus, Dasylirion texanum, D. wheeleri, Daucus carota, D. pusillus, Dentaria diphylla, D. laciniata, Descurainia pinnata, D. sophia, Desmanthus brachylobus, Diospyros texana, D. virginiana, Distichlis palmeri, Dryopteris fragrans, Dudleya edulis, Echinocactus horizonthalonius, Echinocereus dasyacanthus, E. engelmannii, E. enneacanthus, E. stramineus, E. triglochidiatus, Echinochloa crusgalli, Ehretia anacua, Elaeagnus commutata, Eleusine indica, Elymus canadensis, E. triticoides, Empetrum atropurpureum, Ephedra nevadensis, E. torreyana, E. viridis, Epigaea repens, Eriodictyon californicum, Erodium cicutarium, E. moschatum, Erythrina herbacea, Erythronium albidum, E. americanum, E. oreganum, Eugenia axillaris, Fagus grandifolia, Ferocactus acanthodes, F. viridescens, F. wislizenii, Forestiera neo-mexicana, Fouquieria splendens, Fragaria californica, F. chiloensis, F. ovalis, F. vesca, F. vesca var. americana, F. virginiana, Fritillaria camtschatcensis, Galinsoga parviflora, Galium aparine, G. verum, Gaultheria myrsinites, G. ovatifolia, G. procumbens, G. shallon, Gaylussacia baccata, G. brachycera, G. dumosa, G. frondosa, G. ursina, Geranium viscosissimum, Geum canadense, G. rivale, G. triflorum, Glechoma hederacea, Gleditsia triacanthos, Glyceria fluitans, Glycyrrhiza lepidota, G. missouriensis, Gossypium hirsutum, Grindelia squarrosa, Gymnocladus dioicus, Halesia carolina, Hamatocactus hamatacanthus, Harrisia aboriginum, H. fragrans, H. simpsonii, Hedeoma drummondii, H. pulegioides, Hedysarum boreale, H. mackenzii, H. occidentale, Helianthus annuus, H. annuus ssp. lenticularis, H. giganteus, H. x laetiflorus, H. maximilianii, H. tuberosus, Hemerocallis fulva, Heracleum lanatum, Hesperoyucca whipplei, Hierochloe odorata, Holodiscus discolor, Honkenya peploides, Hordeum jubatum, Humulus lupulus, Hydrocotyle sibthorpioides, Hydrophyllum canadense, H. virginianum, Ilex cassine, I. glabra, I. opaca, I. verticillata, I. vomitoria, Illicium floridanum, Impatiens capensis, I. pallida, Iris missouriensis, Isomeris arborea, Juglans californica, J. cinerea, J. hindsii, J. major, J. microcarpa, J. nigra, Juniperus horizontalis, J. pachyphlaea, J. scopulorum, J. utahensis, J. virginiana, Krugiodendron ferreum, Lactuca serriola, Lamium amplexicaule, Larix occidentalis, Larrea tridentata, Lathyrus japonicus ssp. maritimus, Laurocerasus ilicifolia, L. lyonii, Ledum glandulosum, L. groenlandicum, Lepidium campestre, L. virginicum, Leucanthemum vulgare, Lewisia rediviva, Leymus arenarius, Ligusticum scoticum, Lilium superbum, Lindera benzoin, Linum lewisii, L. perenne, Liquidamber styraciflua, Lithocarpus densiflora, Lomatium californicum, L. dissectum, L. macrocarpum, L. nudicaule, L. utriculatum, Lonicera japonica, Lophocereus schottii, Lupinus perennis, Lycium carolinianum, L. pallidum, Lycopus uniflorus, Madia sativa, Magnolia grandiflora, M. virginiana, Mahonia aquifolium, M. haematocarpa, M. nervosa, M. repens, M. swaseyi, M. trifoliolata, Malus angustifolia, M. coronaria, M. fusca, M. ioensis, Malva neglecta, M. parviflora, M. sylvestris, M. verticillata, Mammillaria meiacantha, Marrubium vulgare, Marshallocereus thurberi, Matricaria matricarioides, Matteuccia pensylvanica, Medeola virginiana, Medicago lupulina, Mentha aquatica var. crispa, M. arvensis, M. arvensis var. villosa, M. x gentilis, Menyanthes trifoliata, Menziesia ferruginea, Mimulus guttatus, Mitchella repens, Modiola caroliniana, Mollugo verticillata, Monarda citriodora, M. clinopodia, M. didyma, M. fistulosa, M. fistulosa var. menthaefolia, M. punctata, Monardella odoratissima, M. villosa, Montia fontana, M. perfoliata, M. sibirica, Morus rubra, Muscari botryoides, Myrica cerifera, M. gale, M. pensylvanica, Negundo aceroides, Nelumbo lutea, Nuphar advena, N. luteum, Nymphaea odorata, N. tuberosa, Nyssa aquatica, N. ogeche, N. sylvatica, Oenanthe sarmentosa, Oenothera biennis, O. hookeri, Olneya tesota, Onoclea sensibilis, Opuntia basilaris, O. dillenii, O. humifusa, O. linguiformis, O. phaeacantha, O. polyacantha, O. pottsii, O. tenuispina, O. vulgaris, Ornithogalum umbellatum, Oryzopsis hymenoides, Osmanthus americana, Osmaronia cerasiformis, Osmorhiza claytonii, O. longistylis, O. occidentalis, Osmunda cinnamomea, O. claytoniana, Oxalis acetosella, O. oregana, O. stricta, O. violacea, Oxyria digyna, Panax quinquefolius, P. trifolius, Panicum obtusum, P. sonorum, Paronychia jamesii, Passiflora incarnata, Pectis papposa, Pellaea mucronata, Peltandra virginica, Peltiphyllum peltatum, Peniocereus greggii, Penstemon confertus, P. procerus, Peraphyllum ramosissimum, Perideridia sp., Persea borbonia, Persicaria vulgaris, Petalostemon candidum, P. purpureum, Petasites frigidus, P. palmatus, Phaseolus acutifolius, P. acutifolius var. tenuifolius, P. metcalfei, P. polystachyos, Photinia arbutifolia, Physalis heterophylla, P. philadelphica, P. pubescens, P. viscosa, Phytolacca americana, Picea glauca, P. mariana, Pinus cembroides, P. coulteri, P. edulis, P. jeffreyi, P. lambertiana, P. monophylla, P. x quadrifolia, P. sabiniana, P. strobus, P. torreyana, Pistacia texana, Pithecellobium flexicaule, Plantago lanceolata, P. major, P. maritima, P. maritima ssp. juncoides, Platanus occidentalis, Podophyllum peltatum, Poliomintha incana, Polygonatum biflorum, Polygonum aviculare, P. bistorta, P. bistortoides, P. punctatum, Pontederia cordata, Populus tremuloides, Potentilla anserina, P. fruticosa, P. glandulosa, Proboscidea louisianica, P. louisianica ssp. fragrans, P. parviflora, Prosopis chilensis, P. glandulosa, P. pubescens, Prunella vulgaris, Prunus americana, P. angustifolia, P. angustifolia var. watsonii, P. besseyi, P. hortulana, P. maritima, P. mexicana, P. munsoniana, P. nigra, P. pensylvanica, P. pumila, P. pumila var. susquehanae, P. serotina, P. subcordata, P. umbellata, P. virginiana, P. virginiana var. demissa, P. virginiana var. melanocarpa, Pseudotsuga menziesii, Psoralea esculenta,

Ptelea trifoliata, Pycnanthemum incanum, P. muticum, P. pilosum, P. virginianum, Quercus agrifolia, Q. alba, Q. bicolor, Q. garryana, Q. lobata, Q. macrocarpa, Q. muehlenbergii, Q. palustris, Q. prinus, Q. rubra, Ranunculus bulbosus, Raphanus raphanistrum, Ratibida columnifera, Reynosia septentrionalis, Reynoutria japonica, R. sachalinensis, Rhamnus crocea, R. purshianus, Rhexia virginica, Rhodiola rosea, Rhus aromatica, R. copallina, R. glabra, R. integrifolia, R. ovata, R. trilobata, R. typhina, Ribes americanum, R. aureum, R. bracteosum, R. cereum, R. cynosbasti, R. divaricatum, R. hirtellum, R. hudsonianum, R. lacustre, R. missouriensis, R. odoratum, R. triste, Robinia neomexicana, R. pseudacacia, Rorippa islandica, Rosa acicularis, R. arkansana, R. blanda, R. carolina, R. multiflora, R. nutkana, R. pisocarpa, R. rubiginosa, R. virginiana, R. woodsii, Roystonea elata, Rubus allegheniensis, R. argutus, R. canadensis, R. chamaemorus, R. deliciosus, R. flagellaris, R. idaeus, R. laciniatus, R. leucodermis, R. occidentalis, R. odoratus, R. parviflorus, R. pedatus, R. phoenicolasius, R. procerus, R. rubrisetus, R. spectabilis, R. strigosus, R. trivialis, R. ursinus, R. vitifolius, Rumex acetosella, R. crispus, R. hymenosepalus, R. obtusifolius, R. patientia, R. sanguineus, Sabal etonia, S. minor, S. palmetto, S. texana, Sagittaria latifolia, S. rigida, Salicornia europaea, Salsola kali, Salvia apiana, S. ballotaeflora, S. carduacea, S. clevelandii, S. columbariae, S. mellifera, S. reflexa, Sambucus canadensis, S. glauca, S. melanocarpa, S. mexicana, S. pubens, S. pubens f. xanthocarpa, Sanguisorba canadensis, S. minor, Sarcobatus vermiculatus, Sassafras albidum, Satureja douglasii, Saxifraga pensylvanica, Scirpus californicus, S. paludosus, S. validus, Sedum acre, S. rhodanthum, Serenoa repens, Sesuvium portulacastrum, Shepherdia argentea, S. canadensis, Sicyos angulata, Sidalcea neomexicana, Silene vulgaris, Silphium laciniatum, Simarouba glauca, Simmondsia chinensis, Sinapis arvensis, Sisymbrium altissimum, S. officinale, Sium cicutaefolium, Smilacina racemosa, Smilax herbacea, S. rotundifolia, Solanum fendleri, S. jamesii, Solidago canadensis, S. graminifolia, S. missouriensis, S. odora, Sorbus americana, S. decora, S. scopulina, S. sitchensis, Spiraea x pyramidata, Sporobolus airoides, S. cryptandrus, Stachys palustris, Stanleya pinnatifida, Staphylea trifolia, Stellaria media, Streptopus amplexifolius, S. roseus, Symphytum tuberosum, Symplocos tinctoria, Talinum triangulare, Taraxacum officinale, Thelesperma filifolia, T. gracile, Thinopyron intermedium, T. intermedium var. trichophorum, Thlaspi arvense, Thuja occidentalis, Tilia americana, Torreya californica, Tradescantia virginiana, Tragopogon dubius, T. pratensis, Trapa natans, Trillium erectum, T. grandiflorum, T. sessile, T. undulatum, Tripsacum dactyloides, Tsuga canadensis, T. heterophylla, T. mertensiana, Tussilago farfara, Umbellularia californica, Uniola paniculata, Urtica dioica, Uvularia sessilifolia, Vaccinium angustifolium, V. arboreum, V. ashei, V. atrococcum, V. caesariense, V. corymbosum, V. corymbosum var. pallidum, V. crassifolium, V. darrowi, V. deliciosum, V. erythrocarpum, V. lamarckii, V. macrocarpon, V. membranaceum, V. myrsinites, V. myrtilloides, V. ovalifolium, V. ovatum, V. oxycoccus, V. parvifolium, V. scoparium, V. sempervirens, V. stamineum, V. uliginosum, V. vacillans, V. vitis-idaea, Valeriana ciliata, Verbascum thapsus, Verbena hastata, Veronica anagallis-aquatica, V. chamaedrys, Viburnum alnifolium, V. cassinoides, V. edule, V. lentago, V. nudum, V. prunifolium, V. rufidulum, V. trilobum, Viola adunca, V. canadensis, V. papilionacea, V. pedata, V. sororia, Vitis aestivalis, V. argentifolia, V. berlandieri, V. californica, V. candicans, V. x champini, V. cinerea, V. labrusca, V. monticola, V. munsoniana, V. riparia, V. rotundifolia, V. rupestris, V. shuttleworthii, V. simpsonii, V. solonis, Washingtonia filifera, Wisteria frutescens, Yucca aloifolia, Y. baccata, Y. brevifolia, Y. elata, Y. filamentosa, Y. glauca, Y. schidigera, Zamia floridana, Zizania aquatica, Zizaniopsis miliacea, Zizia aurea, Ziziphus parryi.

INDEX OF SPECIES NOT LISTED IN KUNKEL

Abutilon megapotamicum, Acacia myrtifolia, A. oshanessii, A. podalyriaefolia, A. spectabilis, Acer circinatum, A. grandidentatum, A. pensylvanicum, A. spicatum, Achillea atrata, A. decolorans, A. erb-rotta ssp. moschata, A. ligustica, A. nana, Achlys triphylla, Acinos alpinus, Actinidia coriacea, A. melanandra, Aechmea magdalenae, Agastache cana, A. mexicana, Agave tequilana, Ageratum conyzoides, Agrimonia eupatoria, X Agrotriticum sp., Albizia odoratissima, Allium aschersonianum, A. longicuspis, A. x proliferum, Aloe macrocarpa, Alpinia caerulea, Amelanchier denticulata, Amygdalus bucharica, Anacampseros albissima, A. papyracea, Anchusa azurea, Aplectrum hyemale, Arabis caucasica, Aralia hispida, Arctostaphylos stanfordiana, Arenga wightii, Ariocarpus fissuratus, Aronia melanocarpa, Artemisia annua, A. genipi, A. pontica, Artocarpus anisophyllus, Asimina parviflora, Atraphaxis spinosa, Atriplex semibaccata, Austromyrtus dulcis, Baccaurea angulata, Baeckea virgata, Bauhinia carronii, B. hookeri, Beilschmiedia anay, Beloperone californica, Betula papyrifera, Blephilia ciliata, B. hirsuta, Bombax ellipticum, Boronia megastigma, Brodiaea douglasii, Bromus breviaristatus, Buddleia asiatica, Bunchosia argentea, Calamintha grandiflora, C. nepeta, Canarium asperum, Canna flaccida, Cardamine oligosperma, Carica goudotiana, C. x heilbornii, C. parviflora, Carpobrotus deliciosus, Carya x nussbaumeri, Castilleja linariaefolia, Ceanothus cuneatus, Centaurea cyanus, C. nigra, Cercocarpus ledifolius, Chamaedorea costaricana, Chimaphila maculata, Chrysophyllum lacourtianum, Cinchona succirubra, Citrus x amblycarpa, C. x bergamia, C. x jambhiri, C. x latipes, C. x limettioides, C. x macrophylla, C. x pennivesiculata, Conradina verticillata, Convallaria majalis, Cowania mexicana, X Crataegosorbus miczurinii, Crataegus lobulata, C. marshalli, Croton reflexifolius, Cynara humilis, Cyperus longus, Cyphomandra casana, C. crassifolia, Daviesia latifolia, Desmanthus brachylobus, Dianthus barbatus, D. plumarius, Dioscorea opposita, Diphysa robinioides, Diplotaxis muralis, Dracocephalum moldavica, Enchylaena tomentosa, Ephedra viridis, Epidendrum cochleatum, Eriodictyon californicum, Erythrina glauca, Eucalyptus cinerea, E. citriodora, E. eximia, E. foecunda, E. gomphocephala, E. gummifera, E. intermedia, E. leucoxylon, E. maculata, E. pachyphylla, E. papuana, E. polybractea, E. radiata, E. rubida, E. smithii, E. stuartiana, E. tereticornis, Eugenia carissoides, Eulychnia acida, Euonymus europeus, Ferula communis, Fevillea cordifolia, Fragaria ovalis, Fuchsia arborescens, F. cordifolia, Fumaria officinalis, Gaultheria ovatifolia, Gentiana cruciata, G. lutea, G. pannonica, G. punctata, G. purpurea, Geranium viscosissimum, Geum canadense, G. triflorum, Glottiphyllum linguiforme, Glycine tabacina, Glycyrrhiza missouriensis, Gouania polygama, Grevillea juncifolia, G. robusta, Grindelia squarrosa, Hakea suberea, Hardenbergia violacea, Hedyosmum mexicanum, Hedysarum occidentale, Helichrysum italicum, H. petiolatum, Hernandia moerenhoutiana, Hydrocotyle vulgaris, Impatiens pallida, Inga micheliana, Iochroma fuchsioides, Iris pallida, Jasminum odoratissimum, Kennedya prostrata, Khadia acutipetala, Lambertia formosa, Lantana involucrata, Laurocerasus myrtifolia, Lavandula x intermedia, Leichhardtia australis, Lemna minor, Leonotis nepetaefolia, Leonurus cardiaca, Leptactina benguelensis, Leptospermum coriaceum, L. ericoides, L. laevigatum, L. petersonii, Leymus racemosus, Linum perenne, Lippia helleri, Litsea garciae, Lobularia maritima, Lomatium californicum, Lycium carolinianum, Macaranga grandifolia, M. tanarius, Matricaria matricarioides, Melittis melissophyllum, Melocactus ruestii, Mentha cervina, M. x cordifolia, M. requienii, M. x villosa-nervata, Micromeria bromeii, Mimosa pudica, Mitragyna stipulosa, Modiola caroliniana, Monarda clinopodia, M. punctata, Monardella odoratissima, Muscari botryoides, Myoporum deserti, Myrciaria glomerata, M. vexator, Narcissus jonquilla, Neocardenasia herzogiana, Nicotiana tabacum, Nigella orientalis, Ocimum kilimandscharicum, Oenothera hookeri, Onopordon illyricum, Opuntia linguiformis, O. pottsii, O. tenuispina, Oreocereus hendriksenianus, Origanum x majoricum, O. pulchellum, O. tytthantum, Orthilia secunda, Osmorhiza occidentalis, Oxalis oregana, Pandanus fascicularis, Paronychia argentea, P. capitata, Passiflora adenopoda, Pelargonium crispum, P. exstipulatum, P. fragrans, P. graveolens, P. melissinum, P. nervosum, P. odoratissimum, P. tomentosum, P. torento, Penstemon procerus, Pentaglottis sempervirens, Phyllanthus nobilis, Phyllostachys arcana, P. elegans, P. rubromarginata, Picea abies, Pimpinella major, Pinguicula vulgaris, Pinus ayacahuite, P. maximartinezii, P. x quadrifolia, Pistacia texana, Platymiscium pinnatum, Podocarpus elatus, Pogostemon heyneanus, Polygonum punctatum, Protea cynaroides, Psychotria nervosa, Pycnanthemum incanum, P. muticum, P. pilosum, Pyracantha coccinea, Quassia amara,

Quercus x bebbiana, Rheedia longifolia, Rhipsalis cassutha, Romulea bulbocodium, Rubus procerus, R. reflexus, Salix caprea, Salvia ballotaeflora, S. clevelandii, S. glutinosa, S. mellifera, S. rutilans, Santolina chamaecyparissus, Sarcocephalus xanthoxylon, Schinus terebinthifolius, Sedum acre, S. rhodanthum, Sidalcea neomexicana, Sigesbeckia orientalis, Solanum x burbankii, S. centrale, S. demissum, S. paucijugum, S. scabrum, S. verrucosum, S. wendlandii, Solidago graminifolia, Sorbus latifolia, Spiraea x pyramidata, Spondias axillaris, Stachys officinalis, Streptopus roseus, Symphytum tuberosum, Syringa vulgaris, Syzygium coolminianum, S. leuhmanni, S. moorei, Tagetes tenuifolia, Talauma ovata, Telopea speciosissima, Terminalia ferdinandiana, Tetragonia decumbens, Teucrium scorodonia, Thelesperma filifolia, Thinopyron intermedium, Thymbra spicata, Thymus caespititius, T. x citriodorus, T. herba-barona, T. pannonicus, T. pulegioides, Tiliacora triandra, Trachymene glaucifolia, Trichosanthes cucumeroides, Trifolium agrarium, T. hybridum, T. incarnatum, T. ornithopodioides, Trillium erectum, T. sessile, T. undulatum, Triticum zhukofskyi, Vaccinium reticulo-verosum, V. sempervirens, Verbascum thapsus, Viburnum odoratissimum, Vicia grandiflora var. kitaibeliana, Viola papilionacea, V. pedata, V. tricolor, V. x wittrockiana, Vitis solonis, Willughbeia angustifolia, Wisteria frutescens, Zea diploperennis.

INDEX OF FAMILIES AND GENERA

APPENDIX A: ABBREVIATIONS USED

FOR TYPE OF PRODUCT OFFERED

CF - Crop Failure, Sold Out, Temporarily Unavailable
CU - Pure Cultures (Fungi, Algae, Bacteria)
DR - Starter Cultures (Dry)
DW - Dwarf Nursery Stock
ES - Espalier Nursery Stock
FR - Starter Cultures (Fresh)
GR - Grafted, Clonal Nursery Stock
IN - Interstems
KT - Mushroom Kits
LI - Starter Cultures (Liquid)
OR - Available On Request, Special Order, Custom Grafting, etc.
PL - Plants, Seedlings, Bulbs, Divisions, Corms, etc.
PO - Pollen
PR - Produce, Products
S - Seeds, Spores
SC - Scionwood, Cuttings, Benchgrafts
SN - Mushroom Spawn
SP - Sprouting Seeds
SR - Mushroom Spores
ST - Onion Sets

FOR ANNOTATED BIBLIOGRAPHICAL CITATIONS

CU - Culture
CUL - Culinary
NU - Nutrition
PRE - Preparation
PRO - Propagation
RE - Recipes

IN DESCRIPTIONS FOR SOURCES

CAT - Catalog
CC - Credit Cards
ENGL - English Language Catalog
IMO - International Money Order
IRC - International Reply Coupon
M.O. - Minimum Order
OC - Other Currencies
OVER - Overseas
PC - Personal Checks
R & W - Retail and Wholesale
RET - Retail
SASE - Self-Addressed Stamped Envelope
WHLS - Wholesale

APPENDIX B: ENDNOTES USED IN THE CULTIVAR LISTINGS

Almond

1. Genetic dwarf
2. Low-chill
3. Papershell

Apple

1. High vitamin c
2. Low-chill
3. Genetic dwarf
4. Multi-disease resistant
5. Pink-fleshed

Apricot

1. Genetic dwarf
2. Low-chill
3. Sweet-pit

Asparagus

1. All Male

Avocado

1. Dwarf
2. Purple-skinned

Banana

1. Red-skinned
2. Dwarf
3. Orange-fleshed

Basil

1. Dwarf
2. Lemon-scented
3. Anise-scented
4. Purple-leaved

Beet

1. Red-leaved
2. Cylindrical
3. Baby
4. Bunching
5. Mono-germ

Black Walnut

1. Purple

Blackberry

1. Pink
2. Thornless
3. White

Blueberry

1. Half-high
2. Dwarf

Bok Choy

1. Baby

Brussels Sprouts

1. Red

Cabbage

1. Short-cored
2. Salad type
3. Loose-heading
4. Wintergreen

Carrot

1. High vitamin A
2. Red-skinned
3. White-skinned

Cauliflower

1. Spiral-shaped
2. Mini or baby
3. Perennial

Cherry

1. Genetic dwarf
2. Self-fertile

Chicory

1. Cutting
2. Pink chicons

Chinese Cabbage

1. Lettuce-leaved

Corn

1. Baby
2. Dwarf

Corn Salad

1. Baby

Cowpea

1. Edible-podded

Cucumber

1. Round
2. White-skinned
3. Short-vined
4. Mini or baby

Eggplant

1. Striped
2. Mini or baby
3. Dwarf

Endive

1. Cutting

Fava Bean

1. Small-seeded
2. Edible-podded

Fig

1. Genetic dwarf

Garlic

1. Artichoke

Gooseberry

1. Thornless

Grape

1. Mottled

Guava

1. Red-leaved
2. Seedless

Kale

1. Purple-leaved
2. Forage

Kidney Bean

1. Teepee
2. Easy-pick
3. Mini or baby
4. Salad type
5. Striped

Kiwi

1. Low-chill
2. Red-fleshed

Kohlrabi

1. Winter

Leek

1. Cutting
2. Baby

Lemon

1. Pink-fleshed
2. Variegated

Lettuce

1. Greenhouse
2. Mini or baby
3. Cutting

Lima Bean

1. Mottled
2. Edible-podded

Mandarin

1. Cold-hardy

Melon

1. Short-vined
2. Edible-rinded

Mulberry

1. Pure white
2. Genetic dwarf

Muscadine

1. Seedless

Mustard

1. Baby
2. Red-leaved

Nectarine

1. Low-chill
2. Genetic Dwarf

Okra

1. Baby

Onion

1. Spindle-shaped
2. Odorless
3. Ring
4. Also bunching
5. Set
6. Ultra-mild

Orange

1. Variegated

Pea

1. Blue-podded
2. Dwarf
3. Semi-leafless
4. Edible-leaved
5. Yellow-podded

Peach

1. Low-chill
2. Marble-fleshed
3. Genetic Dwarf

Pear

1. Red-fleshed
2. Low-chill

Pepper

1. Yellow-ripening
2. White-skinned
3. Dwarf
4. Orange-ripening
5. Green-ripening
6. Brown-skinned
7. Purple-skinned

Persimmon

1. Dark-fleshed

Plum

1. Cooking
2. Blood
3. Low-chill

Potato

1. Striped
2. True-seed
3. Fingerling

Pumpkin

1. Short-vined
2. Hulless
3. Mini or baby

Radish

1. French Breakfast type
2. Edible-podded
3. Edible-leaved

Raspberry

1. Low-chill
2. Thornless

Rhubarb

1. Low oxalic acid

Runner Bean

1. Dwarf

Spinach

1. Low oxalic acid

Sprouts

1. Mixes

Squash

1. Baby
2. Butterblossom
3. Spineless
4. Short-vined
5. Hulless, edible-seeded

Strawberry

1. Yellow-skinned
2. White-skinned

Swiss Chard

1. Multicolor-stalked
2. Red-stalked

Tomato

1. Drying
2. Stuffing
3. Ultra-sweet
4. Cold-set
5. Dwarf
6. Stakeless
7. Climbing
8. Dwarf indeterminate
9. Greenhouse
10. High-vitamin
11. Storage

Turnip

1. Elongated
2. Baby
3. Pickling

Walnut

1. Low-chill

Watermelon

1. Icebox
2. Short-vined
3. Edible-seeded
4. Yellow-rinded
5. Spotted

Addendum

page 15, before Masumori add: **Kansai:** Vigorous, upright, rapid growing plant. Small leaves with long, uniform leaflets and good coloration. Suitable for growing in both water or open fields, but particularly adapted to water culture. Popular with market growers in Japan. *Q28*, Q88

page 15, before Masumori, add: **Kanto:** Small leaves with a unique fragrance. Suitable for seeding in both spring and autumn. Disease resistant. Q88

page 15, after Masumori, add: **Shirokuki:** Selected, disease resistant cultivar. Also very resistant to bolting. Suitable for winter and spring shipments. *Q28*

page 57, before Burbank's Spineless, add: **Actual:** Upright grower that produces abundant crops of nearly seedless, pale yellow fruit of excellent flavor and quality. Developed by Luther Burbank and introduced in 1911. N45M{SC}

page 57, after Malta, add: **Pyramid:** Strong, upright grower with large, thick, heavy, light-green smooth slabs. Forage type, considered one of the very best for stock and poultry feeding. Can also be cooked for human consumption. Developed by Luther Burbank and introduced in 1909. HOWARD; N45M{SC}

page 196, after Salsola kali, add: **Salsola komarovi** - *Oka-hijiki* {S} The young leaves are used as a potherb, put into soups, or eaten as *ae-mono* (In Japan, mixed foods served with a seasoned dressing are called *ae-mono*). Eastern Asia. SHURTLEFF 1975, TANAKA; *Q28*

page 302, after China Pride, add: **Kokasanto:**[1] 90 days. Large, cylindrical, open-topped head weighing over 9 pounds, resembles romaine lettuce; good head formation; interior blanches to a distinct golden-yellow color. High quality and sweet taste. Excellent for salads or pickling. Resistant to disease and frost. *Q28*

page 337, after Achilles, add: **Black Velvet:** (R. divaricatum x) Small, grape-like fruit, about 5/8 inch in diameter; unique, very attractive, reddish-black to jet-black color. Dessert quality very good. Very vigorous, easy to grow bush. Worcesterberry hybrid that originated in England. D47

page 485, after Amaranth, add: **Aokei Kaiware Daikon:** Sprouting daikon with a bluish stalk and a characteristic hot, spicy flavor. *Q28*

page 487, after Sesame, add: **Shirokei Kaiware Daikon:** Sprouting daikon with a white stalk and a mildly pungent flavor, not as spicy as Aokei Kaiware Daikon. *Q28*

page 499, after Giza, add: **King Arthur:** One half of this starter crossed the prairie in a covered wagon over 70 years ago. The other half was flown to Seattle from Alaska during the world's fair. One was too tart, the other too sweet, but combined they produced an excellent bread. G29

page 548 add: **E14M From the Rainforest** - 8 East 12th St., #5, New York, NY 10003, 1-800-327-8496. Dried tropical fruits and nuts, many collected by native, rainforest peoples. CAT FREE, R & W, PC/CC, OVER.

page 549 add: **E38M Gazin's** - P.O. Box 19221, New Orleans, LA 70179, 1-800-262-6410. Specializes in gourmet cajun and creole foods. *Sells the following product/s:* roasted whole marrons, dried Montmorency cherries, pickled Jerusalem artichokes, coffee chicory, filé powder, freeze-dried green peppercorns, canned flageolets, Picholine olives, walnut oil, and preserved cloudberries. CAT FREE, RET, PC/CC, OVER.

page 550 add: **E68G Great Southwest Cuisine Catalog** - 630 West San Francisco, Santa Fe, NM 87501, 1-800-872-8787. Vegetable seeds, Mexican and Southwestern food specialties. *Sells the following product/s:* Habañero chili salsa, whole dried Habañero chilis, blue corn tortillas, Scotch Bonnet pepper sauce, Scotch Bonnet pepper flakes, dried Boleta beans, blue popping corn, and rocoto chili salsa. CAT $2, RET, PC/CC, OVER.

page 555 add: **G29 King Arthur Flour Baker's Catalogue** - R.R. 2, Box 56, Norwich, VT 05055, 1-800-827-6836. Grains and flours for breadmaking, sourdough starters, baker's yeast. *Sells the following product/s:* amaranth flour, teff flour, triticale kernels and triticale flakes. CAT $2, RET, PC/CC.

page 560 add: **I8 Naka Nursery Inc.** - 40735 Mission Blvd., Fremont, CA 94539, (415) 490-3996. Ornamental trees and shrubs, ground covers, fruit trees. CAT FREE, WHLS, M.O. $35.